opus VINO

opus
VINO

LONDON, NEW YORK, MELBOURNE, MUNICH, AND DELHI

Senior Project Editor Gill Pitts
Senior Project Art Editor Jane Ewart
Senior Editors Emma Rice, David Williams
Senior Art Editor Paul Jackson
Editors Jamie Ambrose, Lara Maiklem, Andrew Roff, Robert Sharman, David Summers
Designers William Hicks, Katherine Raj, Kathryn Wilding
Editorial Assistants Louisa Cornford, Natasha Hodgson, Sam Priddy, Jaime Tenreiro
Cartography Assistant Roxanne Benson-Mackey
Managing Editors Dawn Henderson, Angela Wilkes
Managing Art Editors Marianne Markham, Christine Keilty
Senior Jackets Creative Nicola Powling
US Editors Shannon Beatty, Nichole Morford, Margaret Parrish, Jenny Siklos, Rebecca Warren
Senior Production Editor Jennifer Murray
Senior Production Controller Alice Sykes
Creative Technical Support Adam Brackenbury, Sonia Charbonnier
Index Jane Parker

Cartography Digital Cartography by Tom Coulson and Martin Darlison at Encompass Graphics Ltd., Hove, UK

Photography Commissioned bottle photography by Alex Havret

DK INDIA
Managing Art Editor Romi Chakraborty
Managing Editor Glenda Fernandes
DTP Manager Balwant Singh
Editor Garima Sharma
Designer Shruti Singh Soharia
DTP Designers Neeraj Bhatia, Tarun Sharma

First American edition 2010

Published in the United States by
DK Publishing, 375 Hudson Street, New York, NY 10014

10 11 12 13   10 9 8 7 6 5 4 3 2 1
178711—November 2010

A catalog record for this book is available from the Library of Congress.

ISBN 978 0 7566 6751 1

DK books are available at special discount when purchased in bulk for sales promotions, premiums, fund-raising, or educational use. For details, contact: DK Publishing Special Markets, 375 Hudson Street, New York, NY 10014 or SpecialSales@dk.com

Color reproduction by Colourscan, Singapore
Printed and bound by Leo Paper Products Ltd. in China

DK would like to thank The Wine Society Ltd. for supplying bottles of wine to photograph.
www.thewinesociety.com

Discover more at
www.dk.com

CONTENTS

OPUS VINO AUTHORS

As editor-in-chief of *Opus Vino*, Jim Gordon oversaw this young, dynamic team of writers. He also wrote the North America and California introductions, the Mendocino and Lake section, and the Glossary. Jim's 25-year career in the wine industry includes working as managing editor of *Wine Spectator* for 12 years and helping to set up Wine Country Living TV for NBC. Currently, he is the editor of *Wines and Vines* magazine, based in California. Jim lives in Napa with his wife and children, where he makes wine for himself and his friends.

Sarah Abbott MW
Sarah Abbott wrote the Côte de Beaune section of Burgundy, and the Côte de Nuits panels. It was a bottle of burgundy that got her totally hooked on wine and into the wine trade. In 2008, after more than 10 years working with UK wine importers, she founded Swirl, a wine events company that aims to bring wine alive for the unitiated. Sarah also acts as a consultant for wine importers on marketing and communication, and judges at international competitions. *www.swirl-me.co.uk; Twitter: SarahAbbottMW*

Sarah Ahmed
London-based freelance wine writer Sarah Ahmed contributed to the Loire chapter, one of her favorite wine regions. It is no exaggeration to say that the Loire prompted her career change from law to wine. Bitten by the wine bug when she tasted a Moulin Touchais Coteaux du Layon 1986, she remains the strongest of advocates of Chenin Blanc, dry or sweet. Sarah believes that no other region comes close to replicating the Loire's minerality, intensity, and elegance of expression of its Sauvignon Blanc, Chenin, and Cabernet Franc. *www.thewinedetective.co.uk*

Jane Anson
Jane Anson wrote the Bordeaux (where she is based) and Southwest France chapters. A full-time wine writer, she was shortlisted for the Louis Roederer Wine Feature Writer of the Year 2009. Jane's passion for wine started in South Africa in 1996, when the Cape Winelands (and a Nederburg Syrah) enchanted her and she discovered that wine is a combination of politics, history, and geography as well as a drink to savor. Jane is the Bordeaux correspondent for *Decanter* magazine, and she contributes to the *South China Morning Post* in Hong Kong. *www.newbordeaux.com*

Andrew Barrow
A self-styled gastronome, Andrew Barrow wrote the Alsace section. For more than 15 years, he has worked at the forefront of wine and food on the internet, first via an email newsletter (when such things were cutting edge) then via his top-rated blog Spittoon.biz and Twitter, with stints writing for AOL and *The Guardian* along the way. Andrew is never happy without a glass of wine in hand, Alsatian obviously, as this is simply the best region in France for combining food and wine, although other writers in this book might disagree! *www.spittoon.biz; Twitter: @wine_scribbler*

Tyler Colman
Tyler Colman wrote the Beaujolais section of Burgundy and much of the Loire. He thinks that Chenin Blanc is wildly underrated, whether from the Loire or elsewhere. Tyler teaches wine classes at New York University and is the author of two books, *A Year of Wine* and *Wine Politics*. He has contributed wine articles to the *New York Times*, *Food & Wine*, *Wine & Spirits*, *Forbes*, and *The Guardian* as well as the *Oxford Companion to Wine*. Tyler also writes the agenda-setting blog, *www.drvino.com*.

Laurie Daniel
A journalist for more than 30 years, Laurie Daniel wrote most of the section covering California's Central Coast. She lives in the Santa Cruz Mountains and has written extensively about the Central Coast and its wines for a range of publications. Although Laurie grew up in wine-deprived surroundings in the Midwest, she quickly developed an interest in wine after moving to California. In 1993, she began writing about wine on a regular basis and has contributed to many newspapers, magazines, and websites. Find out what's in her glass at *twitter.com/ldwine*.

Mary Dowey
Mary Dowey, who wrote the Southern Rhône chapter, was a travel and food writer until wine tickled her palate. As a columnist for the *Irish Times*, she traveled the wine world, finding its eccentric characters and exquisite landscapes just as exciting as the wine. Gradually, Mary developed a special interest in the Southern Rhône, providing an excuse to escape gray Dublin for year-round sunshine. Now with a Côtes du Rhône base, Mary writes about the region for various publications including *Decanter*. *www.marydowey.com; www.provencefoodandwine.com*

Mike Dunne
A California native who has spent almost 40 years writing about the state's wine scene, Mike Dunne is the author of the Inland California and Mexico sections. After working as a wine columnist, restaurant critic, and food editor of *The Sacramento Bee*, Mike now divides his time between homes in Northern California and the southern stretches of Baja California in Mexico, exploring the wine regions of both countries and writing about his discoveries. A frequent judge on the wine competition circuit, he writes of his travels at his blog. *http://ayearinwine.blogspot.com*

Sarah Jane Evans MW
Writer and broadcaster Sarah Jane Evans wrote the Spain chapter (except sherry, ironically). While working in Madrid when taking a year off before college, Sarah Jane discovered Spanish wine, and continued to "research" sherry as a student at Cambridge University, where it was served at tutorials. She has been associate editor of the BBC's *Good Food Magazine* and president of the Guild of Food Writers. A Master of Wine, Sarah is also a member of the Gran Orden de Caballeros de Vino. Her books include *Seville* and (her other passion) *Chocolate Unwrapped*. *www.sarahjaneevans.co.uk*

Catherine Fallis
The author of the Mâconnais and Côte Chalonnaise sections, Catherine Fallis, aka the grape goddess®, was introduced to wine while backpacking around Europe. But it was while living in Florence and Paris that she really developed her palate. In 1993, Catherine joined the harvest team at Châteaux Pichon-Baron and Lynch-Bages in Bordeaux. Today, Catherine is an entertaining speaker, author, and educator, and has a particular affinity for southern Burgundy, where great wines at everyday prices abound. *www.planetgrape.com*

Michael Franz
Michael Franz wrote the Northern Rhône chapter. He fell in love with wine as an impoverished student, and studied it by applying to academic conferences located in wine regions and attending them—partially. In addition to contributing to wine magazines, instructing culinary academies, and working as a consultant for 13 restaurants, Michael is editor and managing partner of Wine Review Online. Prior to this, he was the wine columnist for *The Washington Post* for 11 years. He is also Professor of Political Science at Loyola University in Maryland. *www.winereviewonline.com*

Doug Frost MW
The author of the US Heartland and Southern states sections, Doug Frost is one of only three people to have passed both the Master Sommelier and Master of Wine exams. He has written several books, including *Uncorking Wine* and *On Wine*. He also hosts Check Please!, a weekly US TV show, and is the wine and spirits consultant for United Airlines worldwide. *Cheers Magazine* honored Doug as Beverage Innovator of the Year 2009. He runs two wine competitions, the Mid-American Wine Competition and the Jefferson Cup Invitational. *www.dougfrost.com; Twitter: winedogboy*

David Furer
Writer of the Begium, the Netherlands, and Luxembourg and much of the Central and Southeastern Europe sections, David Furer first became interested in the wines of these regions when traveling there as a tourist. While working at an English liquor store he found the best affordable offerings from Romania, Bulgaria, and Hungary. Eighteen months working at German wineries provided insight into the rigors good growers endure. A columnist for the US *Sommelier Journal*, David is an Advanced Sommelier and Certified Wine Educator.

Caroline Gilby MW

Caroline Gilby wrote the Bulgaria, Czech Republic, and Slovakia sections. She fell in love with wine while studying for her PhD in plant sciences, and abandoned a career behind a microscope in favor of wine buying. Her first job as a junior wine buyer took her to Eastern Europe in early the 1990s. The pace of change, distinct cultural differences, and rise of exciting new producers post-communism continues to fascinate Caroline and influence her wine writing. Caroline never looked back, becoming Master of Wine in 1992. *http://carolinegilby.wordpress.com*

Francis Gimblett

A belief that North Africa can produce world class wine is at the heart of Francis Gimblett's career. In 2008, when he began the Wine Adventurer project, Francis set out to discover whether this potential was being realized. He has since visited every major North African producer and concluded that in some quarters, it is. His career path has covered catering, wine broking, winemaking, and teaching, and entertainment and writing. As captured in his website, he has a passion to experience the less encountered. *www.thewineadventurer.com*

Jamie Goode

Jamie Goode wrote the chapters on Australia, New Zealand, and Portugal—three countries he has a particular fondness for. He first visited them under the pretext of attending scientific conferences there. Subsequently, he gave up an unpromising career as a science editor to travel the world drinking wine. Jamie was one of the first wine bloggers, writing as the Wine Anorak. He has a weekly column for UK newspaper *The Sunday Express* and writes for a number of magazines. His books include *The Science of Wine* and *Natural Wine* (publishing in 2011). *www.wineanorak.com*

Lindsay Groves

The author of the Turkey and Lebanon sections, Lindsay Groves has a fondness for the more esoteric wine regions of the world. Originally trained in winemaking and viticulture in Niagara, Canada, Lindsay went on to gain certification as a sommelier followed by the Wine & Spirits Education Trust (WSET) Diploma. With Toronto as a home base, she currently works as a freelance wine journalist writing for a variety of publications both at home and abroad. She is looking forward to beginning studies for the Master of Wine qualification in the near future.

Susan Kostrzewa

The author of the South Africa chapter, Susan Kostrzewa's passion for South Africa and its wines began when visiting Kruger Park and the Cape on a travel writing assignment in 1999. Before relocating to Manhattan in 2005, Susan lived for 10 years in the San Francisco Bay Area, specializing in food, wine, and travel writing. Today, she tastes and rates South African wines for *Wine Enthusiast Magazine*, where she is executive editor. Beyond exotic travel and wine exploration, she is also a devotee of cooking Moroccan and Indian cuisine, snowboarding, and indie music.

JIM GORDON

JANE ANSON

LINDSAY GROVES

SUSAN KOSTRZEWA

SARAH ABBOTT MW

TYLER COLMAN

CATHERINE FALLIS

Peter Liem

Peter Liem wrote the chapter on Champagne. Although American by birth, Peter makes his home quite literally next to the Champenois vineyards in the small, wine-producing village of Dizy, near Epernay. The only professional English-language wine writer currently living in the Champagne region itself, Peter writes for *Wine & Spirits* and *The World of Fine Wine*, as well as writing and publishing ChampagneGuide.net, a comprehensive and original online guide to the wines and wine producers of the region. *www.champagneguide.net*

Jeffrey Lindenmuth

As a full-time writer focusing on wine, spirits, and beer, Jeffery Lindenmuth has traveled the world in search of a good drink. In this book, he explores the wineries of New England, New York, and the Mid-Atlantic states. An avid outdoorsman who spent his youthful summers laboring in fields of strawberries, corn, and turnips in Pennsylvania, Jeffrey is attracted to wine not only for its flavor, but also with agrarian empathy, often emphasizing wine's role as an agricultural product and a part of everyday healthful dining in his contributions to *Cooking Light*, *Men's Health*, and other forums.

Wink Lorch

Wink Lorch wrote the Jura and Savoie chapter, having developed an interest in these fascinating wine regions, which are not far from her home in the French Alps. Wink originally worked in the UK wine trade and in the past 20 years as a wine writer, educator, and editor, based mainly in London. In 2007, with the growing interest in wine tourism, she created the Wine Travel Guides website, focusing on wine regions in Europe. The new freedom of mobile technology allows Wink to participate in social media while skiing or walking in the mountains. *www.winetravelguides.com*

Sarah Marsh MW

Sarah Marsh wrote the Chablis, Meursault, and Côte de Nuits sections of Burgundy. A background in PR and journalism, together with a zest for life and love for beauty, led her to wine, wine writing, and Burgundy in particular. Her online specialist review of the region, the Burgundy Briefing, is read by subscribers all over the world. Sarah became a Master of Wine in 2004: her dissertation, on Pinot Noir in the Côte d'Or, is one of a handful to have been awarded a distinction. Her passions include travel, art, music, and cooking—as her appearance as a BBC Masterchef finalist testifies. *www.sarahmarsh.com*

Jane Masters MW

As a true Francophile, Jane Masters spends a fair amount of her time in Southern France. She wrote the Languedoc, Roussillon, Provence and Corsica, and Vins de Pays chapters. Following her passion for food and wine, Jane set off for France after university, where she trained as a winemaker at the Institute of Enology in Bordeaux and worked in various wineries in France and Corsica. After returning to the UK in 1992, she worked for Marks & Spencer, sourcing wines from around the world.

Jane qualified as a Master of Wine in 1997, and in 2005 she set up her consultancy business, Mastering Wine.

Peter Mitham

Peter Mitham wrote the Canada chapter, drawing on more than a dozen years of tasting experience across Canada and the US. A seasoned business writer, he began writing about the wine industry following a visit to California's Napa Valley in November 1997. He currently lives in Vancouver, British Columbia, where he writes about viticulture and the wine business in the Pacific Northwest and Canada for *Wines and Vines* and other publications. When not filing stories about wine, he covers commercial real estate in Vancouver (and also plays the accordion).

Michael Palij MW

Michael Palij is the author of the Central Italy and South and the Islands chapters. Michael emigrated to the UK from Canada in 1989 and worked as a sales assistant in a wine store. Many bottles and six years later he qualified as a Master of Wine and moved to the Cotswolds as a buyer for a regional wine merchant. Lambrusco was big business in those days and he was promptly dispatched to Italy to secure a better deal. Happily, his company got the price they needed and he fell in love with all things Italian. He now visits Italy 20 times a year. Traveling the backroads deep into southern Italy reminds him of just what an enchanting—and undiscovered—part of the world it is.

Tim Patterson

The author of the northern parts of the Central Coast chapter and Southern California, Tim Patterson loves these areas because they are under the wine radar, overshadowed by the glitz of Napa and Sonoma. Underdog wine regions and glamour-free grapes interest him as both a wine drinker and wine writer, and along with the techie-geeky aspects of actual winemaking, provide endless topics for several trade and consumer publications. Tim makes gallons of wine in his garage every year just to keep himself honest and blogs erratically at *www.blindmuscat.typepad.com*.

Stuart Pigott

Since moving to Berlin in 1993, London-born writer Stuart Pigott's pointed and original journalism has earned him the reputation of being a rebel with a cause. Stuart's writing focuses on the renaissance of the wine industries in the German-speaking countries and the winemaking revolution under way in China and Japan. His writing welds his training in cultural history with his education at Germany's famous Geisenheim wine school and the experience gained through 25 years of exploring wine. He is currently filming a major TV series on German wine for the Bavarian broadcasting authority. *www.stuartpigott.de*

Emma Rice

Emma Rice is the author of the England and Wales section. She first got seriously interested in wine at the age of 17 after tasting Krug 1979 at a dinner attended by many of the UK's wine luminaries, at which she worked as a wine waiter. Her entire working life has revolved around wine: PA to a burgundy merchant, editor of Hugh Johnson's *Pocket Wine Book*, one of the first graduates of the BSc in Viticulture and Oenology at Plumpton College in the UK, and enologist at a Napa Valley winery. Today, Emma works as a winemaker and enologist, as well as running her wine analysis laboratory in Sussex. *www.customcrush.co.uk*

Peter Richards

Peter Richards oversaw the South America chapter, writing the Chile and Argentina sections—countries he finds particularly captivating. It was while Peter lived and worked in Chile that he first became interested in wine, and he has gone on to forge a successful career as a writer and broadcaster, specializing in wine. He writes prodigiously for many publications and has written the odd-off book, including *The Wines of Chile*. Peter recently launched the Winchester Wine School with his wife Susie Barrie MW. In 2010, they were named joint IWSC Communicators of the Year. *www.winchesterwineschool.com*

Eleonora Scholes

With Russian as her mother tongue, Eleonora Scholes has an inside take on wine in the former Soviet Union and she wrote the Russia, Moldova, and Ukraine sections. Having switched from her career in marketing in the early 2000s, Eleonora now works as an independent wine and gastronomy journalist, and is also engaged in business analysis of the Russian wine market. Her articles are published by various media, as well as on her website in both Russian and English. *www.eleonorascholes.ru*.

Lisa Shara Hall

Lisa Shara Hall is very proud of the wines of her home region, the Pacific Northwest, and is the author of that chapter. She pioneered coverage of this area almost 20 years ago and has been writing about it ever since for various publications. Lisa is also the author of *Wines of the Pacific Northwest*. Sherry, especially Manzanilla, is one of her favorite wines (a cold bottle is always in her refrigerator), and she also wrote this section. Lisa is senior editor of *Wine Business Monthly* and is currently studying for the Master of Wine qualification.

Magandeep Singh

India's only professional and qualified wine and food writer and first French-certified Sommelier, and international TV show host, Magandeep Singh divides his time between globetrotting the vineyards and tasting the gastronomic delights of the world and writing about them back at home in India. Magan has worked with the most prestigious establishments in the industry for almost a decade, both in India and abroad. His interests, however, don't stop at food and wine: he constantly looks for new things to tickle his fancy, such as making cocktails, rollerblading, golf, and playing the saxophone.

Tim Teichgraeber

Wine writer and entertainment lawyer Tim Teichgraeber wrote the Napa Valley and Carneros chapters. He began his wine career as a retail salesman while finishing college in Minnesota. A friend coaxed him into writing about wine for a local paper, and he later became the wine columnist for the *Minneapolis Star Tribune*. In 2000, Tim moved west to San Francisco, seeking adventure and a closer connection to American vineyards. He now visits the nearby Napa Valley regularly, and contributes articles to top newspapers and magazines, including the *San Francisco Chronicle* and *Decanter*.

Tara Q. Thomas

The author of the chapters on Greece, Cyprus, and Israel, Tara Q. Thomas is an editor at *Wine & Spirits Magazine* in New York. A former chef who fell in love with Greek wines while working in an Athens kitchen (don't ask), she's since subsidized her obsession with everything Mediterranean by specializing in the region's wines. The author of *The Complete Idiot's Guide to Wine Basics*, she currently lives and works in Brooklyn and is an avid blogger. *www.taraqthomas.com; Twitter: @tqthomas*

Dirceu Vianna "Junior" MW

The author of the Brazil and Uruguay sections, Dirceu Vianna "Junior" is originally from Brazil, where he studied Forest Engineering and Law, before moving to London in 1989. In 2008, Junior became the first South American male Master of Wine and received the Viña Errazuriz Award for excellence in the Business of Wine. Currently wine development director for the Coe Group of companies, he is also a wine educator, technical consultant, freelance writer, and judge in many international wine competitions.

Wolfgang Weber

Wolfgang Weber wrote the Northeast and Northwest Italy and Tuscany chapters and Slovenia. He began his wine career when he helped with the 1997 harvest during a backpacking trip in Chanti Classico. Wolfgang has worked almost exclusively in the wine trade, including two vintages as a cellar rat in the mountains above the Napa Valley. Wolfgang is the former senior editor and Italian wine critic at *Wine & Spirits* in the US. His writing and photography has appeared in *Wine & Spirits*, the *San Francisco Chronicle*, and the *LA Times*. *http://spume.wordpress.com*

Alder Yarrow

San Francisco Magazine calls Alder Yarrow, who wrote the Sonoma and Marin chapter, "the wine world's brightest cyberstar" and his website, Vinography.com, is considered one of the world's leading wine blogs. Started as a personal project to keep track of Alder's notes about food and wine, the award-winning site has since grown a large and devoted international readership. Vinography concentrates on sharing the stories, the people, and the passion behind wine from a decidedly down-to-earth perspective. *www.vinography.com*

PETER LIEM

ALDER YARROW

JEFFREY LINDENMUTH

WOLFGANG WEBER

JANE MASTERS MW

TIM TEICHGRAEBER

PETER MITHAM

Traditional methods, such as the drying of grapes for Vin Santo, are just as important as new techniques.

A NEW LOOK AT THE NEW WORLD OF WINE

During the year in which this ambitious new wine book was created, evidence of the fast-changing pace of the world of winemaking was easy to find. While the classic region of Bordeaux rolled out its top-quality 2009 vintage for a first taste, other wine regions old and new uncorked a profusion of dazzling wines. A perfumed Pinot Noir from the suburban hills of Stuttgart, Germany, a balanced and appetizing Cabernet Franc from Brazil, and a smooth blend of Sémillon and native Assyrtiko grapes from Greece, are just a few examples of the diverse options I tasted.

With so much going on, *Opus Vino* had to be ambitious to cover it all. Some wine books have maps, others have wine reviews, still others explain the terms and techniques of wine. But here in one comprehensive volume we recommend the best wineries in each country and region, introduce their most influential characters, map dozens of vineyard districts, provide visitor information, describe recent vintages, and in an extensive glossary explain label terminology, grape varieties, wine classifications, and much more.

Opus Vino presents a new look at the new world of wine from a new generation of distinguished wine writers. Thirty years ago, it was possible for an individual author to taste and review virtually every fine wine on the international market every year or two. Today, it is impossible for one person to know them all, so *Opus Vino* called on 38 authors with specialties in various wine regions to illuminate this vast new world of wine.

Many of our writers are young, others have a youthful taste for adventure that constantly spurs them on to explore vineyard regions and discover what is driving change in winemaking. Some first learned about wine as bloggers, diverging from careers in high-tech or academia; others are experienced wine-book authors, newspaper and magazine journalists; still others are television broadcasters, Masters of Wine, and a few are winemakers themselves. This crew knows classic wines, but thirsts for new taste experiences, too.

Possibly the most important information our writers present in these pages is which wines to buy. The producers that are featured in this book are the producers that our writers highly recommend—based on their own recent tastings and research. The writers have selected only the top-quality established wineries and the most promising younger wineries by weighing up our exacting criteria, major points of which include:

Top Winery

- Makes wine of very high or outstanding quality
- Has a long track record for quality, relative to its region
- Makes well-known collectible or special occasion wines
- Is a leader in its region in grape-growing and/or winemaking techniques
- Performs particularly well in a special wine category

Rising Star Winery

- Makes wine of very high or outstanding quality
- Shows potential to be tomorrow's classic winery
- Has been innovative in choice of variety, grape-growing, and/or winemaking techniques
- May have a great price/quality ratio

Since wine is a product of the earth, and varies almost as much according to where grapes are grown as to what variety of grapes they are, *Opus Vino* needed to show precisely where on the earth the great vineyards and wineries reside. The book includes specially commissioned maps that outline specific wine-growing districts, or appellations, and locate the recommended producers in each. These details not only help you to picture the origin of the wine you may be drinking, but also to plan an exploration of your own to the vineyard regions of the world.

When you do use *Opus Vino* for travel planning, please remember to contact your target producers in advance to be sure when, where, and if they welcome visitors to the winery or a tasting room.

This book was written by people who drink wine, love wine, and know wine in order to help you enjoy the subject and, more importantly, the beverage, as much as they do. Armed with their knowledge, you can avoid the intimidation of wine buying and wine appreciation and get right to the point, which is enjoyment. Ultimately, only you can decide which wines match your taste, your favorite foods, and your entertaining style—because there are no rights and wrongs in wine choices, only considered opinions.

Our writers have done their jobs well if *Opus Vino* lends you more confidence in wine-buying decisions, helps you develop your own list of favorite wines, assists you in giving wine gifts, and enhances your dining and entertaining experiences with family and friends.

May your next glass always be more enjoyable than your last!

North America's first successful wine may have been made from native Scuppernong grapes by French Huguenot settlers in Florida, around 1563. Efforts to grow European vine varieties were less successful on the new continent, including Thomas Jefferson's well-documented attempt in Virginia about 200 years later.

Early Spanish missionaries had better luck when they colonized the Pacific Coast of Mexico and what is now California. Commercial-scale wine production, however, first prospered in the Ohio River Valley from about 1830 to 1860, when banker Nicholas Longworth of Cincinnati made wine from 2,000 acres (810ha) of vines, mostly the native variety, *Vitis labrusca*.

Winemaking began in earnest in California after the Civil War of the 1860s, and enjoyed its first boom in the 1880s. But then came a series of wine industry disasters: the phylloxera vine-root louse, Prohibition in the United States and Canada, and World War II. American soldiers, who had been stationed in Europe, brought back a taste for imported table wine. Slowly, the more affluent Americans of the 1960s and 1970s began to drink more domestic wines, too.

By the 1990s, vineyards were spreading faster than Starbucks, while thousands of amateurs put on rubber boots to become winemakers. This winemaking mania eventually overtook not only the famous regions, but almost everywhere in between. At the same time, North Americans uncorked a new thirst for wine that went beyond special occasions and caught up with beer for the first time.

Few generalizations apply to the vast landscape of North American wine, yet one could say that the geographic and climatic options, coupled with an apparently limitless entrepreneurial urge, have enabled winemakers here to experiment and create a dynamic winemaking culture that could not have been imagined 50 years ago.

NORTH AMERICA

CALIFORNIA

CANADA

UNITED STATES
OF AMERICA

San Francisco

CALIFORNIA

Los Angeles

PACIFIC
OCEAN

■ California   MEXICO

The same sunshine that backlights the breakers at Malibu Beach also makes California an easy place to produce wine. The Pacific coastal valleys and the interior basin enjoy a long growing season with little or no rainfall and very few clouds to interfere with the ripening of wine grapes. The results, from Temecula in the far south, to Mendocino in the north, are full-flavored wines that seem natural partners with California's bold, ethnically diverse cuisine. Wines from Napa Valley and Sonoma County may lead the field in terms of prestige, but ignoring California's other far-flung vineyards eliminates a host of taste experiences worth savoring. Robust Zinfandel grows in the Gold Rush country; a site near Silicon Valley makes classic Cabernet Sauvignon; and several vineyards now produce wine in—where else?—Malibu.

California's first vineyards were planted by Spanish Catholic missionaries in the 1700s, yet the wine industry of today is only about 50 years old. The grapevine pest, phylloxera, wiped out many of the original vineyards in the late 1800s, and then nationwide Prohibition, from 1920 to 1933, bolted the cellar doors of all but a few dozen wineries. Further hampered by World War II, the wine industry did not begin real growth until the 1960s. Since then, however, wine quality and quantity have both advanced dramatically. Several international-class wine styles have emerged: Pinot Noir and Zinfandel from Sonoma County, Cabernet Sauvignon and Merlot from Napa Valley, Syrah and Pinot Noir from the Central Coast, and Chardonnay from a host of locations.

Not all parts of California were created equal in terms of potential wine quality, however. The state's geography, defined by a flat, central valley flanked by low coastal mountains on the west and the rugged Sierra Nevada on the east, dictates to a large extent where fine wine versus ordinary table wine can be be grown.

While most Californian wine regions are undoubtedly hot on a July afternoon, the coastal valleys and mountains experience daily temperature swings of up to 40°F (22°C), year round, thanks to the chilly currents of the Pacific Ocean that flow down the coast from Alaska. The nighttime lows help the grapes retain their natural acidity while the daily highs add the necessary sugar content. This combination of acidity and sugar allows the development of flavor components for expressive wines that are reminiscent of Anjou pear (in Chardonnay), ripe black cherries (in Cabernet Sauvignon), and wild blackberries (in Zinfandel).

Grapes from the hotter interior areas give mostly soft, straightforward wines for everyday drinking. The word "California" in prominent type on a label usually means that the wine is blended from the less prestigious areas, while specific place names, such as Santa Cruz Mountains or Paso Robles, tend to mean better quality and, therefore, higher prices.

California is a big place. It is the most populous state of the United States with more than 37 million people, has the 10th-largest economy in the world, a landmass three-quarters the size of France, and sophisticated industries in Hollywood and Silicon Valley. Yet it also includes oyster farms on the Marin County coast, goat cheesemakers in Sonoma and lavender farms in Santa Barbara. The scope of wine production varies as widely. Large corporations have taken over production of supermarket wines, while small wineries keep popping up like wild mustard blossoms between the vine rows in winter.

It is difficult to generalize about quality and value. The least expensive wines may be highly processed, but easy to drink. Those in the middle range have the personality of their grape varieties and locations. The very best examples seek price parity with Bordeaux and Burgundy, from where they got much of their inspiration. Yet the very best have earned it. The nostalgic perfume of a 20-year-old Oakville Cabernet or the delicious pairing of a Russian River Chardonnay with cold, cracked Dungeness crab could convince almost anyone.

Buds start to develop on the vines at the Rubicon Estate vineyard in Rutherford, Napa Valley, in early spring.

NAPA VALLEY AND CARNEROS

California

Napa County

For many, Napa Valley is synonymous with California wine. Located one hour's drive north of San Francisco, Napa Valley is home to many of America's iconic wineries and may be the world's most toured wine region. Napa Valley is a viticultural Shangri-la with a range of cool to warm climates in a territory that covers 485,000 acres (196,275ha), making it approximately one-eighth the size of Bordeaux. The vineyards produce California's most expensive and lauded wines, and they do it on the state's most expensive agricultural land, with prime sites reaching stratospheric prices. It is an environment that demands great fortunes, lures great talent, and produces extraordinary and unique wines.

Major grapes

 Reds

Cabernet Sauvignon

Merlot

Petite Sirah

Pinot Noir

Sangiovese

Syrah

Zinfandel

 Whites

Chardonnay

Sauvignon Blanc

Semillon

Vintages

2009
Beautiful crop for all varieties. Late rains caused rot in the last Cabernet Sauvignon. Should be excellent.

2008
Severe spring frosts and fall forest fires made for a challenging vintage.

2007
Near-perfect conditions; effortlessly balanced wines.

2006
Hits and misses. Some rot in Chardonnay and Pinot Noir. Some Cabernets have great structure.

2005
A perfect fall; opulent red wines with supple tannins.

2004
Delicious wines for most varieties with soft tannins that will not need long aging.

Wild grapes grew naturally in Napa Valley long before George Calvert Yount planted the first cultivated vines in 1836, in what is now Yountville. It was not long before Charles Krug established the first commercial winery in the valley in 1861, and the wine industry quickly expanded as other wineries like Schramsberg, Beringer, Inglenook, and, a little later, Beaulieu Vineyard were founded in the years following California's 19th-century gold rush.

The early days of Napa Valley were not without challenges. At the turn of the 20th century, the vine pest phylloxera decimated many vineyards. That menace was followed, in 1920, by Prohibition. A number of wineries survived by making legal sacramental wine, but the industry emerged from Prohibition a shadow of its former self. Georges de Latour, the founder of Beaulieu Vineyard, recruited winemaker André Tchelistcheff from France, and the modern era of Napa Valley began.

In 1965, a new leader emerged: Robert Mondavi left his family's winery (Charles Krug) and founded Robert Mondavi Winery in Oakville. Mondavi would be Napa Valley's champion for the next 40 years, insisting that it could stand with the best wine regions in the world. He also forged several international partnerships, most notably with the Rothschild family of Bordeaux to establish Opus One, and promoted wine as essential to fine living.

Today, Napa Valley is being passed down to the successors of these pioneers and new arrivals, but it now has a well-established identity as a leader in both price and quality in the production of Cabernet Sauvignon that is not likely to waver.

Cabernet Sauvignon is not the only grape that thrives in the diverse climates, exposures, and soils of Napa Valley. Zinfandel was the favorite grape prior to Prohibition, and it continues to excel. Cabernet Franc, Merlot, Petit Verdot, and Tuscan and southern Italian varieties also stand out in the warmer north of the valley, as do Sauvignon Blanc and Semillon. In the cooler south, in Carneros, where morning maritime fog often intrudes from the San Pablo Bay, Pinot Noir and Chardonnay shine, and Merlot and Syrah can be exceptional.

Within the larger Napa Valley AVA (the first to be designated in California, in 1981) there are 15 recognized sub-AVAs: Los Carneros, Oak Knoll District of Napa Valley, Stags Leap District, St. Helena's, Yountville, Oakville, Rutherford, Calistoga, Mount Veeder, Spring Mountain District, Diamond Mountain District, Atlas Peak, Howell Mountain, Chiles Valley District, and Wild Horse Valley.

The terrain of Napa Valley is a product of the collision of the Pacific, the Farallon, and the North American plates, which formed the up-thrust Mayacamas Mountains, separating Napa from Sonoma in the west, and the volcanic Vaca range that borders Napa Valley proper to the east. All of this geological turmoil has endowed Napa Valley with at least 33 distinct soil types, scattered about the region, which imbue wines with complexities of flavor even within single vineyard sites.

Napa Valley wines are the most expensive of North America's wines, and in many cases no expense is spared in producing them. Crop yields are low for Cabernet Sauvignon; the region accounts for approximately 8% of California's vineyard area, but only 4% of its wine volume. Most farming is done by hand, and sustainable winemaking is widely practiced.

Wine-growing, winemaking, and marketing consultants play an important role in a region where there is a steady stream of new arrivals, purchasing wineries with little prior experience, but a deep appreciation of fine wine and the idyllic scenery of Napa Valley.

Acacia Carneros

Founded in 1979, Acacia was one of the most important pioneers of Carneros Chardonnay and Pinot Noir, and still produces very consistent and good-quality wines. The floral, spicy Carneros Pinot Noir is very good value, and the single-vineyard Lone Tree Pinot Noir offers more depth at a higher price. Acacia's strongest suit is Chardonnay. The Carneros bottling is a perennial good-value choice and its Sangiacomo Vineyard Chardonnay, from a site on the Sonoma side of the Carneros region, is especially exotic. The wines are made by Matthew Glynn.

2750 Las Amigas Rd., Napa, CA 94559
www.acaciavineyard.com

Ancien Wines Carneros

Since 1992, chemist-turned-winemaker Ken Bernards, formerly of Domaine Chandon and Truchard, has made Pinot Noir and Chardonnay from his own vineyard in Carneros. Later, he added Pinot Noir bottlings from other regions, like Russian River Valley and Santa Barbara County, as well as a Pinot Gris from the Sangiacomo Vineyard in Carneros. The wines are handmade and quite exceptional. His Carneros Pinot Noir and Chardonnay are particularly good value, thanks in part to his collaboration with veteran viticultural consultant Ann Kraemer.

4047 East 3rd Ave, Napa, CA 94581
www.ancienwines.com

Anderson's Conn Valley Vineyards
St. Helena

The Anderson family have been growing grapes and producing wine in Conn Valley for over 25 years, making them one of the early adopters of this rugged valley just over the Vaca Mountains. Tom Anderson, who helped his father plant the estate vineyards, now manages the estate with his wife Ronene. Chief vintner Mac Sawyer makes estate-grown Cabernet Sauvignons that are often described as Bordeaux-like in their elegance, with hints of cedar and cigar often present. The estate also makes good Sauvignon Blanc, Chardonnay, and Pinot Noir.

680 Rossi Rd., St. Helena, CA 94574
www.connvalleyvineyards.com

Antica Napa Valley Atlas Peak

Antica Napa Valley is Tuscan vintner Piero Antinori's second act in Napa Valley. After planting this estate, formerly known as Atlas Peak, to Sangiovese in the 1980s, Antinori was forced to confront mediocre results and slack demand for Sangiovese in the 1990s. After leasing the vineyard and winery to Atlas Peak for a number of years, and significant replanting of the estate, Antinori reentered the game with a Cabernet and Chardonnay winery in 2004. Both varieties are now proven in this locale, and the new brand is off to a promising start. ★ Rising star

3700 Soda Canyon Rd., Napa, CA 94558
www.anticanapavalley.com

Araujo Estate Diamond Mountain

The Eisele Vineyard has been under continuous grape cultivation since 1881 and was bought by namesakes Barbara and Milton Eisele in 1969. Bart and Daphne Araujo purchased the 38 acre (15ha) vineyard, on a gravelly alluvial fan, in 1990, and updated the facilities.

ACACIA
A PIONEER IN CARNEROS, ACACIA
CHARDONNAY IS GOOD VALUE

ASTRALE E TERRA
CABERNET SAUVIGNON DOMINATES THIS
BORDEAUX-STYLE BLEND

The vineyard and winemaking team includes Michel Rolland, Matt Taylor, and Françoise Peschon. The estate Cabernet Sauvignon is Araujo's pride and joy, but in addition to this, the estate also produces a fine Syrah. Other products from the Biodynamic and organically farmed estate are grappa, olive oil, and honey.

No visitor facilities
www.araujoestatewines.com

Artesa Carneros

The Spanish Cordoníu Group first established this stunning modern winery as Cordoníu Napa to produce sparkling wine, but by 1997 the owners had decided to produce still wines and renamed the winery Artesa. Artesa's estate-bottled Pinot Noir and Chardonnay are boldly flavored, well-made wines. Artesa sources grapes for its Cabernet Sauvignon, Merlot, and other wines from all over the Napa and Sonoma valleys, and could be criticized for being a Jack-of-all-trades, master of none. Some of the small-lot bottlings, like the very good Reserve Tempranillo, are a pleasant surprise.

1345 Henry Rd., Napa, CA 94559
www.artesawinery.com

Astrale e Terra Atlas Peak

Italian for "Heaven and Earth", Astrale e Terra was founded by a partnership led by Paul Johnson in 1997. The estate is off to a pretty good start, with vineyards managed by Doug Hill and wines made by Scott Harvey, formerly of Folie à Deux. Its flagship red is a Bordeaux-style blend called Acturus, and the property also produces estate-grown Cabernet Sauvignon, Merlot, and Syrah, and a Sauvignon Blanc from purchased grapes.

5017 Silverado Trail, Napa, CA 94558
www.astraleeterra.com

Atlas Peak Vineyards Atlas Peak

Piero Antinori founded this brand from his plateau estate atop Atlas Peak, but he later sold it. He retained the vineyards and winery, though, leasing them back to the brand until recently. Today, Atlas Peak is owned by the Ascentia Wine Group. The wines are made at Buena Vista winery by consulting winemaker Nick Goldschmidt, and include one Cabernet Sauvignon-based red wine from each of the Napa Valley Mountain AVAs and a Napa Valley Cabernet Sauvignon. Although the wines are made from purchased grapes, they are excellent.

18000 Old Winery Rd., Sonoma, CA 95476
www.atlaspeak.com

Barnett Vineyards Spring Mountain

For the last few years, Barnett's wines have been extremely good across the board, from its estate-grown Cabernet Sauvignon and Merlot to Pinot Noirs and Chardonnays made from purchased grapes. All are clean, modern, and precise, with great depth of fruit. David Tate, appointed winemaker from the 2007 vintage, brings a good deal of international experience to the 40 acre (16ha) Spring Mountain estate, which has been owned by Fiona and Hal Barnett since 1983. Production has grown to around 60,000 bottles per year. ★ Rising star

4070 Spring Mountain Rd., St. Helena, CA 94574
www.barnettvineyards.com

NAPA VALLEY

Located less than an hour's drive north of San Francisco's Golden Gate, Napa Valley runs roughly south to north, girded by the Mayacamas Mountains on the west and the Vaca Mountains on the east. At the southern base of the valley, the alluvial fan of Los Carneros is cooled by both the Pacific Ocean and San Pablo Bay, suiting it best to Pinot Noir and Chardonnay. Summer daytime temperatures on the valley floor increase incrementally moving north on Highway 29. Oak Knoll and Yountville produce restrained Cabernet Sauvignon and Merlot. Oakville, Rutherford, and Calistoga deliver progressively riper Cabernet Sauvignon, Zinfandel, and more. Napa's most nuanced and ageworthy Cabernets are produced from the rocky hillside and mountain vineyards that ring the valley floor.

ST. SUPÉRY
VIRTÚ
2005 NAPA VALLEY WHITE WINE

PRODUCED AND BOTTLED BY ST. SUPÉRY VINEYARDS & WINERY
RUTHERFORD CALIFORNIA 94573   13.7% ALCOHOL BY VOLUME

FREEMARK ABBEY
2007
SAUVIGNON BLANC
NAPA VALLEY

DUCKHORN VINEYARDS
2005
NAPA VALLEY
CABERNET SAUVIGNON

SPRING MOUNTAIN AND ST. HELENA

- Anderson's Conn Valley Vineyards **39**
- Barnett Vineyards **26**
- Benessere Vineyards **12**
- Beringer Vineyards **29**
- Corison Winery **34**
- Covenant **30**
- Duckhorn Vineyards **19**
- Fantesca **24**
- Flora Springs **48**
- Forman Vineyards **38**
- Freemark Abbey **21**
- Guilliams **25**
- Hall Napa Valley **33**
- Heitz Cellar **35**
- Howell Mountain Vineyards **23**
- Joseph Phelps **37**
- Long Meadow Ranch **32**
- Marston Family **27**
- Newton Vineyard **31**
- Philip Togni Vineyards **23**
- Pride Mountain **23**
- Schweiger **26**
- Seavey **40**
- Snowden **39**
- Spottswoode Estate **30**
- Spring Mountain Vineyards **28**
- St. Clement **23**
- Terra Valentine **23**
- Trinchero Family **20**
- Vineyard 7 & 8 **25**
- Vineyard 29 **22**

RUTHERFORD AND CHILES VALLEY

- Beaulieu Vineyard **56**
- Cakebread Cellars **55**
- Caymus Vineyards **59**
- Chappellet Vineyards **44**
- Continuum Estate **43**
- Del Dotto **49**
- Franciscan Estates **46**
- Frog's Leap Winery **58**
- Grgich Hills Estate **52**
- Hewitt Vineyard **51**
- Honig Vineyard and Winery **57**
- Kuleto Estate **42**
- Mount Veeder Winery **56**
- Piña Napa Valley **60**
- Provenance Vineyards **50**
- Quintessa **45**
- Rubicon Estate **53**
- St. Supéry **54**
- Staglin Family **55**
- Volker Eisele Family **41**
- Whitehall Lane Winery **47**

CALISTOGA AND HOWELL MOUNTAIN

- Bennett Lane **2**
- Burgess Cellars **13**
- CADE **18**
- Chateau Montelena **4**
- Cuvaison Estate Wines **9**
- Dunn Vineyards **16**
- Frank Family Vineyards **11**
- Ladera **15**
- O'Shaughnessy Estate **17**
- Outpost Winery **14**
- Schrader Cellars **5**
- Sterling Vineyards **8**
- Storybook Mountain **1**
- Summers Estate Wines **3**
- Viader Vineyards **13**

DIAMOND MOUNTAIN

- Diamond Creek **6**
- Schramsberg Vineyards/ J. Davies **10**
- Von Strasser Vineyards **7**

MENDOCINO COUNTY
LAKE COUNTY
YOLO COUNTY
SONOMA COUNTY
Windsor
SOLANO COUNTY
NAPA COUNTY
MARIN COUNTY
CONTRA COSTA COUNTY
PACIFIC OCEAN

Napa Valley AVA
Wine regions shown on main map

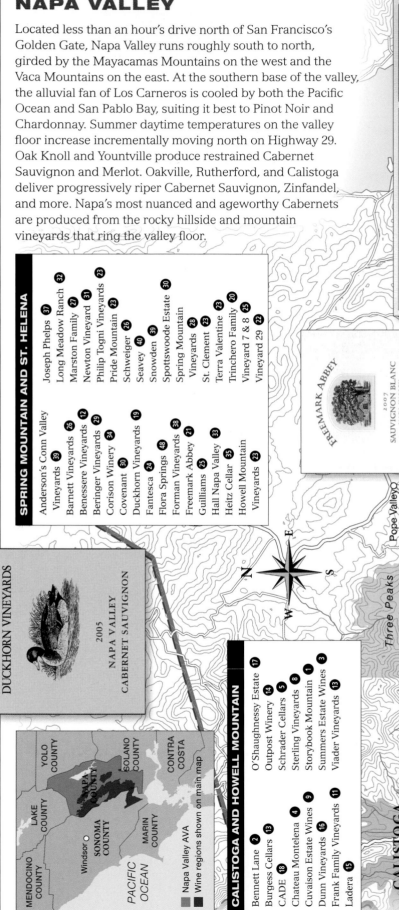

Pope Valley
Angwin
Three Peaks
HOWELL MOUNTAIN
Deer Park
Sanitarium
St Helena
ST HELENA
RUTHERFORD
NAPA COUNTY
Lake Hennessey
Moore Creek
Sage Canyon
Conn Creek
Bell Canyon Reservoir
Mill Creek
Zinfandel
SPRING MOUNTAIN
DIAMOND MOUNTAIN
Calistoga
CALISTOGA
Woodleaf
564m (1850ft)
N A P A

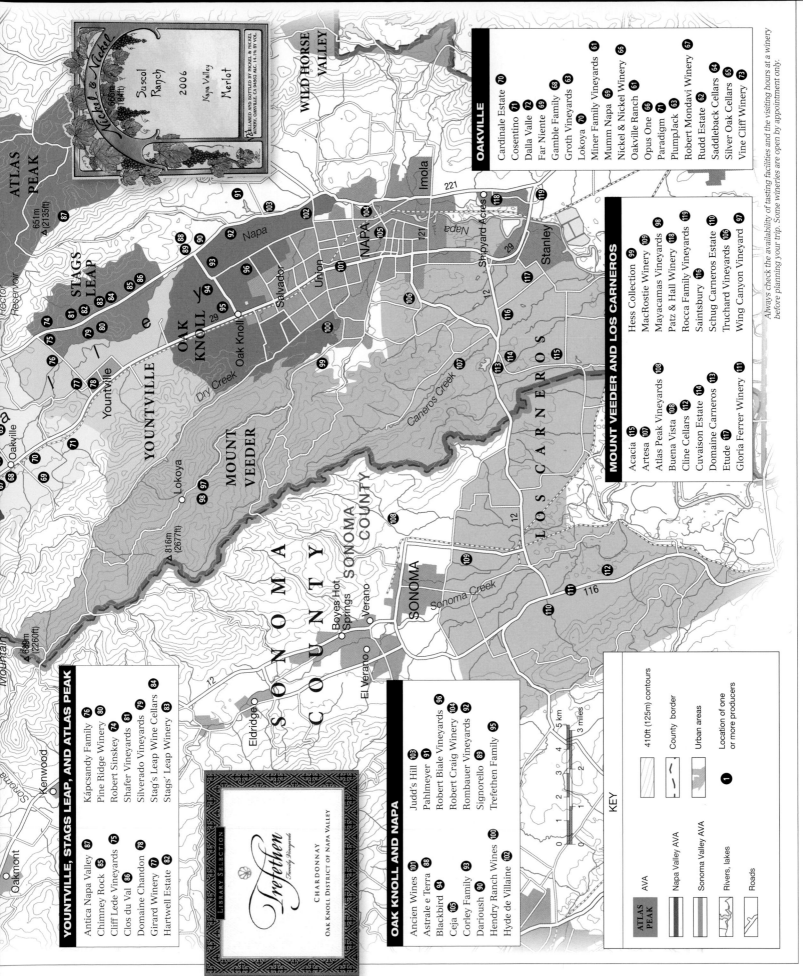

OAKVILLE

Cardinale Estate 70	Miner Family Vineyards 61
Cosentino 71	Mumm Napa 69
Dalla Valle 72	Nickel & Nickel Winery 61
Far Niente 69	Oakville Ranch 66
Gamble Family 68	Opus One 66
Groth Vineyards 63	Paradigm 71
Lokoya 70	PlumpJack 63
	Robert Mondavi Winery 67
	Rudd Estate 62
	Saddleback Cellars 64
	Silver Oak Cellars 65
	Vine Cliff Winery 73

MOUNT VEEDER AND LOS CARNEROS

Acacia 115	Hess Collection 99
Artesa 107	MacRostie Winery 109
Atlas Peak Vineyards 108	Mayacamas Vineyards 98
Buena Vista 108	Patz & Hall Winery 118
Cline Cellars 112	Rocca Family Vineyards 119
Cuvaison Estate 114	Saintsbury 116
Domaine Carneros 113	Schug Carneros Estate 110
Etude 117	Truchard Vineyards 106
Gloria Ferrer Winery 111	Wing Canyon Vineyard 97

Always check the availability of tasting facilities and the visiting hours at a winery before planning your trip. Some wineries are open by appointment only.

YOUNTVILLE, STAGS LEAP, AND ATLAS PEAK

Antica Napa Valley 87	Kápcsandy Family 76
Chimney Rock 85	Pine Ridge Winery 80
Cliff Lede Vineyards 75	Robert Sinskey 74
Clos du Val 86	Shafer Vineyards 81
Domaine Chandon 78	Silverado Vineyards 79
Girard Winery 77	Stag's Leap Wine Cellars 84
Hartwell Estate 82	Stags' Leap Winery 83

OAK KNOLL AND NAPA

Ancien Wines 101	Judd's Hill 103
Astrale e Terra 88	Pahlmeyer 91
Blackbird 94	Robert Biale Vineyards 96
Ceja 105	Robert Craig Winery 104
Corley Family 93	Rombauer Vineyards 92
Darioush 90	Signorello 89
Hendry Ranch Wines 100	Trefethen Family 95
Hyde de Villaine 102	

KEY

ATLAS PEAK	AVA
	Napa Valley AVA
	Sonoma Valley AVA
	Rivers, lakes
	Roads
	410ft (125m) contours
	County border
	Urban areas
1	Location of one or more producers

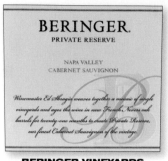

BERINGER VINEYARDS
ONE OF NAPA'S OLDEST WINERIES SAT ON ITS
LAURELS FOR YEARS BUT IS BACK ON FORM

CHATEAU MONTELENA
THIS WINE'S PREDECESSOR BEAT FRANCE'S
BEST AT THE JUDGEMENT OF PARIS IN 1976

Beaulieu Vineyard Oakville

Beaulieu Vineyard, founded by French-born Georges de Latour in 1900, is as historically significant as any in the valley and, under winemaker André Tchelistcheff, it was one of the first Napa wineries to focus on Cabernet Sauvignon as its flagship variety. Eighteen million bottles of every color are made each year under this Diageo-owned label, but quality is uneven and exceptional wines are rare. Its flagship Georges de Latour Private Reserve Cabernet Sauvignon is a fine wine, but no longer a benchmark. However, the winery is reportedly bringing in consultant Michel Rolland to patch things up.

1960 St. Helena Highway, Rutherford, CA 94573
www.bvwines.com

Benessere Vineyards St. Helena

John and Ellen Benish have owned the 42 acre (17ha) Benessere Vineyard since 1994, and have remained committed to making Italian-style wines despite intense commercial pressure to make Cabernet Sauvignon. Chris Dearden has been winemaker and general manager since 1995. Benessere offers a nice alternative to the classic varieties that dominate the valley's tasting rooms, with very good-quality Sangiovese, Pinot Grigio, and recently, a delicious red made from Aglianico, the most noble variety of southern Italy.

1010 Big Tree Rd., St. Helena, CA 94574
www.benesserevineyards.com

Bennett Lane Calistoga

Randy and Lisa Lynch founded Bennett Lane in 2003 and hired winemaker Rob Hunter (formerly of Sterling, Markham, and Robert Keenan) to make their wines. The house-style is unpretentious, fruit-driven, concentrated, and modestly oaked—an approach that has been very successful, especially in the red wines. The Cabernet Sauvignon is good and consistent, as is the Maximus, a blend of Cabernet, Merlot, and Syrah. In addition to the winery, the Lynches field a regional NASCAR team.

3340 Highway 128, Calistoga, CA 94515
www.bennettlane.com

Beringer Vineyards St. Helena

Founded in 1876 by Jacob and Frederick Beringer, Beringer Vineyards is a successful and formidable operation. Having changed hands several times in recent decades, it has held steady with winemaker Ed Sbragia at the helm, and is now part of the Foster's group. At times in the past 20 years, reserve reds and whites were coarsely and heavily oaked, but the current head winemaker, Laurie Hook, has polished the wines and the flagship Private Reserve Cabernet Sauvignon is excellent, blended from sites throughout the valley. Vineyard manager Bob Steinhauer also deserves credit for developing first-class vineyards in the valley over the past 30 years.

2000 Main St, St. Helena, CA 94574
www.beringer.com

Blackbird Oak Knoll District

Blackbird's delicious Merlot, one of the very best in the valley, demonstrates the grape's affinity for the climate and clay alluvial soils of Napa's Oak Knoll District. The vineyard was first planted in 1997 and sold grapes to a number of wineries before the property was purchased in 2003 by Michael Polenske, former CEO of Chase Manhattan Bank, and began to bottle its own estate wine. Polenske also restored an historic stone building dubbed "Ma(i)sonry" in Yountville to serve as a tasting facility for Blackbird and other producers. ★**Rising star**

1330 Oak Knoll Ave, Napa, CA 94558
www.blackbirdvineyards.com

Bond Estates Oakville

Bond Estates is a separate venture by the Harlan Estate team of Bill Harlan, winemaker Bob Levy, and vineyard manager Mary Hall, with Master Sommelier Paul Roberts as director. The concept was to make small amounts of terroir-driven wines from purchased grapes in partnership with six small hillside vineyards around Napa Valley. The wines include single-vineyard wines from Melbury (near Lake Hennessey), Quella (Eastern Vaca Hills), St. Eden Vineyard (north of Oakville), Vecina Vineyard (Oakville, near Harlan), Pluribus Vineyard (Spring Mountain), and a blended second wine called Matriarch. ★**Rising star**

No visitor facilities
www.bondestates.com

Bryant Family Vineyard Napa Valley

Don Bryant's small, 15 acre (6ha) vineyard, located on Pritchard Hill, overlooks Lake Hennessey at an altitude of 1,500ft (460m), bringing the advantage of cooling breezes from the lake. It produces amazingly complex and ageworthy Cabernet Sauvignon. The estate wine was one of the original "cult" Cabernets and carries a price tag to prove it. The original winemaker was Helen Turley, but today the wine is made by Philippe Melka with consultant Michel Rolland.

No visitor facilities
www.bryantwines.com

Buena Vista Carneros

Buena Vista was founded by Hungarian Count Agoston Haraszthy in 1857, making it one of the oldest wineries in California. Though the brand has passed through many hands, the landmark original winery still houses Buena Vista's tasting room. In the hands of successive corporate owners, Buena Vista had become somewhat unfocused, but it has reorganized and downsized, having found a stable home within the Ascentia Wine Group. Winemaker Jeff Stewart crafts reliable, reasonably priced Chardonnay and Pinot Noir, plus a smaller amount of exceptional Syrah from Buena Vista's 700 acre (283ha) Ramal Estate Vineyard.

18000 Old Winery Rd., Sonoma, CA 95476
www.buenavistacarneros.com

Burgess Cellars Howell Mountain

This venerable winery, east of St. Helena, dates back to the 1880s and was purchased by Tom Burgess in 1972. It has been a model of consistency, perhaps never reaching staggering heights, but always delivering concentrated, brambly mountain wines. Winemaker Bill Sorenson has been with Burgess from the beginning. The winery produces Cabernet Sauvignon, Merlot, and Syrah (the terrific Zinfandel has sadly been discontinued) from two sites on Howell Mountain and one in Yountville.

1108 Deer Park Rd., St. Helena, CA 94576
www.burgesscellars.com

CADE Howell Mountain

With its state-of-the-art winery recently opened, the PlumpJack winery offshoot, CADE, looks to be a Howell Mountain producer of some promise. The 21 acre (8.5ha) vineyard is on a 54 acre (22ha) Howell Mountain estate, at an elevation of 2,000ft (610m). San Francisco's Mayor Gavin Newsom, Gordon Getty, and John Conover are investors. To date, there is a small-production, ripe blackberry-flavored Howell Mountain Cabernet Sauvignon and a Napa Valley Cabernet Sauvignon blended from sources such as To Kalon, Dr. Crane, and other premium vineyards. An Estate Cabernet Sauvignon is a new wine recently on the market. ★ Rising star

360 Howell Mountain Rd. South, Angwin, CA 94508
www.cadewinery.com

Cakebread Cellars Rutherford

Cakebread developed a strong reputation through the 1980s and 1990s as a dependable producer of ripe, fleshy Cabernet Sauvignon and generous, oaky Chardonnay. It was founded by photographer Jack Cakebread, who purchased the 22 acre (9ha) estate from family friends in the early 1970s. Today, Cakebread controls 340 acres (138ha) of vines and makes a dozen wines from Napa Valley and elsewhere. The most ageworthy is Cakebread Benchland Select Cabernet Sauvignon.

8300 St. Helena Highway, Rutherford, CA 94573
www.cakebread.com

Cardinale Estate Oakville

Owned by Jess Jackson and Barbara Banke of Jackson Family Estates, Cardinale produces one wine, a superb and expensive Napa Valley Cabernet Sauvignon. The grapes come from Keyes Vineyard at 1,700ft (520m) on Howell Mountain, Veeder Peak Vineyard at 1,500ft (457m) on Mount Veeder, and the legendary To Kalon vineyard on the Oakville Bench. Chris Carpenter has been the winemaker since 2001, with a good run of vintages. The mountain fruit manifests itself in a complex, concentrated wine with stony minerality and firm structure.

7600 St. Helena Highway, Oakville, CA 94562
www.cardinale.com

Caymus Vineyards Rutherford

Charlie Wagner and his son Chuck, who runs Caymus today, founded this estate in 1972. They planted their Rutherford vineyard with cuttings from Nathan Fay's Stags Leap District vineyard and focused on making top-flight Cabernet Sauvignon. Caymus Special Selection has been one of the best since its first vintage in 1975 and is produced in sufficient quantities to be sold overseas as a great example of California's fruit-driven style. The standard Napa Cabernet is also worthy of attention.

8700 Conn Creek Rd., Rutherford, CA 94573
www.caymus.com

Ceja Carneros

The story of the Ceja family is perhaps the most touching of the valley, and proof that hard work can still establish a foothold in this exclusive location. Pablo Ceja emigrated to the US from Mexico and worked for Napa wineries, ultimately establishing a home for his wife Juanita and sons Pedro and Armando, who were encouraged to go to college. Armando studied viticulture at UC Davis. Pedro married the energetic Amelia Morán Fuentes, and later the family pooled their resources to buy 15 acres (6ha) of land in Carneros, establishing Ceja Vineyards. Strong offerings include their cool-climate Carneros Merlot and Chardonnay, and good-value Vino de Casa white blend.

1248 First Street, Napa, CA 94559
www.cejavineyards.com

Chappellet Vineyards Napa Valley

Donna and Molly Chappellet's estate is perched at 1,200ft (366m) atop Pritchard Hill, overlooking Lake Hennessey. The family were instrumental in establishing this area as a great spot for Cabernet Sauvignon. Chappellet Cabernet Sauvignons are not overly ripe, have serious structure, and age well. The Pritchard Hill Cabernet Sauvignon and Signature Cabernet Sauvignon are better than ever and deliver good value. The Mountain Cuvée Bordeaux-style blend and dry Chenin Blanc are also very drinkable wines.

1581 Sage Canyon Rd., St. Helena, CA 94574
www.chappellet.com

Chateau Montelena Calistoga

Chateau Montelena was founded by Alfred Tubbs in the 1880s, but fell into disrepair during Prohibition, before being restored and completely replanted by Jim Barrett and his son Bo (husband of Heidi Peterson Barrett) after they acquired the estate in 1972. Their 1973 Chardonnay triumphed at the 1976 Judgement of Paris and the estate has produced formidable Cabernet Sauvignon, Chardonnay, and Zinfandel ever since. "Montelena" comes from the French pronunciation of Mount St. Helena, at the foot of which the beautiful chateau sits.

1429 Tubbs Lane, Calistoga, CA 94515
www.montelena.com

Chimney Rock Stags Leap District

Chimney Rock was developed by a South African couple, Hack and Stella Wilson, starting in 1980. Doug Fletcher has been the winemaker since 1987 and, in 2000, Terlato Wines International purchased a majority stake in the winery. Based out of a distinctive Cape Dutch-style winery on Silverado Trail, Chimney Rock wines are consistent and somewhat informed by Bordeaux: in particular, the Elevage, a restrained blend of Cabernet Sauvignon, Merlot, and Petit Verdot, and the Elevage Blanc, a plump, rounded blend of Sauvignon Blanc and Sauvignon Gris.

5350 Silverado Trail, Napa, CA 94558
www.chimneyrock.com

Cliff Lede Vineyards Stags Leap District

Canadian construction mogul Cliff Lede purchased the S Anderson estate in 2002 and hit the ground running. He and viticulturist David Abreu converted the sparkling wine estate to red wine production almost overnight, quickly establishing a reputation for Cabernet Sauvignon (including its flagship Poetry bottling), a fine Bordeaux blend, and a supple, floral Sauvignon Blanc. Philippe Melka takes on winemaking duties from 2010. Already a formidable venture, this young estate continues to evolve and improve. Well-heeled visitors may also enjoy the luxury Poetry spa hotel. ★ Rising star

1473 Yountville Cross Rd., Yountville, CA 94599
www.cliffledevineyards.com

ANDRE TCHELISTCHEFF

No winemaker played a greater role in the maturation of the California wine industry than the man known as "The Maestro". Born to an aristocratic family in Moscow in 1901, André Tchelistcheff studied enology, fermentation, and microbiology in France before being lured to California by Georges de Latour. Latour was the French founder of Beaulieu Vineyard, which had emerged from the fog of Prohibition as Napa Valley's most prominent estate. Once in California, Tchelistcheff devoted himself to refining Cabernet Sauvignon and initiated Beaulieu Vineyard's "Georges de Latour Private Reserve", which immediately became one of Napa Valley's iconic wines. Over the years, he trained a legion of California's most prominent contemporary winemakers and mentored such luminaries as Robert Mondavi, earning another nickname: "The Dean of California Winemakers".

DIAMOND CREEK VINEYARDS
A PIONEER OR DIAMOND MOUNTAIN, THIS
ESTATE IS ENJOYING A RENAISSANCE

CLINE CELLARS
A RHONE RANGER, CLINE'S MOURVEDRE IS
EXCEPTIONALLY RICH AND SPICY

Cline Cellars Carneros

Wine-grower Fred Cline's original winery was located near his ancestral home in Contra Costa County, and early success came from exploiting great old-vine Zinfandel and Mourvèdre from that area. In 1991, he bought a 350 acre (142ha) estate in Carneros on the site of an old Spanish mission, and planted several Rhône varieties. Standout wines include the powerful Big Break and Live Oak Zinfandels and the sublime, eucalyptus-scented Small Berry Mourvèdre, one of the best in the state. Cline's inexpensive California Syrah, Cool Climate Syrah from the Sonoma Coast, and Oakley Red deliver great value.

24737 Arnold Drive, Highway 121, Sonoma, CA 95476
www.clinecellars.com

Clos du Val Stags Leap District

Founded in 1972 by businessman John Goelet and continuously managed by French winemaker Bernard Portet, Clos du Val maintains a tradition of producing elegant red and white wines that run a bit leaner and less ripe than those of its neighbors—wines that often show their best at the table. Look for this estate's Stags Leap District Cabernet Sauvignon, Reserve Cabernet Sauvignon, and recently improved Pinot Noir. Clos du Val's most noteworthy white may be its Rubenesque Ariadne, a toasty, barrel-fermented Semillon blended with Sauvignon Blanc.

5330 Silverado Trail, Napa, CA 94558
www.closduval.com

Colgin Vineyards Napa Valley

Vintner and wine auctioneer Ann Colgin makes a series of top-quality small-production red wines with a team consisting of French-born winemaker Allison Tauziet, vineyard manager David Abreu, and consulting enologist Alain Raynaud. The wines are sold only to restaurants and through the winery's mailing list. Notable wines include the Herb Lamb Vineyard Cabernet, made from 14 rows of a small vineyard in the foothills of Howell Mountain, and the IX Estate Bordeaux-style blend made from Colgin's estate overlooking Lake Hennessey.

No visitor facilities
www.colgincellars.com

Continuum Estate Napa Valley

Continuum is the latest venture of Tim, Marcia, and the late Robert Mondavi in the form of a single Cabernet Sauvignon-based blend. Grapes for the inaugural 2005 and 2006 vintages came from the To Kalon vineyard at Robert Mondavi Winery in Oakville but, the current owner of the vineyard, Constellation, cut off the supply of grapes. In 2008, the Mondavis purchased a new estate on Pritchard Hill. Off to a good start, Continuum is still a work in progress. ★ Rising star

1677 Sage Canyon Rd., St. Helena, CA 94574
www.continuumestate.com

Corison Winery St Helena

Cathy Corison's restrained Cabernet Sauvignons have a devoted following, especially among restaurateurs and sommeliers, who appreciate their taut structure and vibrant acidity. Corison, a veteran of Staglin, York Creek, and Long Meadow Ranch, makes two Cabernet Sauvignons from organic benchland vineyards on the Rutherford–St. Helena border, including Kronos Vineyard, one of the oldest in the area. She also makes a tiny amount of Gewurztraminer from Anderson Valley.

987 St. Helena Highway, St. Helena, CA 94574
www.corison.com

Corley Family Oak Knoll District

The Corley family have been growing grapes here for about 35 years, and started their own winery in 1980. Today, they make wines under their own name and the Monticello brand, after their visitor center, which is a replica of former US President Thomas Jefferson's Virginia residence. Corley muddled through the 1990s with very average wines, but things have been improving since Chris Corley took over winemaking duties. The best wines are the Corley Reserve Cabernet Sauvignon, the lively State Lane Cabernet, and the estate-grown Pinot Noir made with Heirloom and Dijon clones. ★ Rising star

4242 Big Ranch Rd., Napa, CA 94558
www.corleyfamilynapavalley.com

Cosentino Yountville

Mitch Cosentino started out in Modesto in 1981, building up a small, respected brand before relocating to Yountville in 1989. He was the first to release a Meritage red Bordeaux-style blend in 1989, and that wine, dubbed The Poet, is still one of his best bottlings. Variety is the spice of Cosentino's winemaking life. Between his Yountville winery and sister wineries in nearby Pope Valley and Lodi, he works with dozens of grape varieties to make wines that are full of California flair.

7415 St. Helena Highway, Napa, CA 94558
www.cosentinowinery.com

Covenant St. Helena

Covenant is the joint venture of Jeff Morgan, a former *Wine Spectator* editor and wine educator, and Leslie Rudd of Rudd Estate and the luxury deli, Dean and DeLuca. The two men saw that there was demand for a better quality Kosher wine from California and set about creating one. Covenant produces two very high quality non-mevushal (unpasteurized) Kosher red wines. The eponymous Covenant Cabernet Sauvignon is the flagship wine, produced from 3 acres (1.2ha) of the Larkmead Vineyard north of St. Helena. The second wine is called "C", and is also a 100% Cabernet Sauvignon. ★ Rising star

930 Crane Ave., St. Helena, CA 94574
www.covenantwines.com

Cuvaison Estate Wines Carneros

Cuvaison was a historic Calistoga estate, first established in 1969. It was bought 10 years later by the Swiss Schmidheiny family along with substantial vineyards in Carneros, and the Brandlin Vineyard on Mount Veeder. The winery is now located in the vineyard at Carneros, but a tasting room and caves are still located in Calistoga. Best known for Pinot Noir and Chardonnay, the Mount Veeder and Brandlin Vineyard Cabernet Sauvignons are good, as are the smaller-production Carneros and Diablo Syrahs. The wines are made by Steve Rogstad, a veteran of both Saintsbury and Spring Mountain Vineyards.

1221 Duhig Rd., Napa, CA 94559
www.cuvaison.com

Dalla Valle Oakville

Now a legendary Napa estate, Dalla Valle was founded in 1986, when Gustav and Naoko Dalla Valle purchased a superb vineyard site on a plateau in the eastern hills of Oakville. Winemaker Heidi Peterson Barrett deserves much credit for taking Dalla Valle's Cabernet Sauvignon and its Maya blend of Cabernets Sauvignon and Franc to cult status. Naoko Dalla Valle and Barrett's successors, Mia Klein, then Michel Rolland, along with Fausto Cisneros, the long-time viticulturist and cellarmaster, also deserve credit for keeping it there. The site itself, rocky and west-facing, produces extremely concentrated, very ripe wines that have great structure.

No visitor facilities
www.dallavallevineyards.com

Darioush Stags Leap District

This estate was founded in the late 1990s by Darioush Khaledi, owner of a chain of grocery shops in Southern California. Its Ancient Persia-inspired architecture strikes a dashing pose in the Stags Leap District. The wines, in particular the Signature Cabernet Sauvignon and Shiraz, are opulent and gaining refinement. ★ Rising star

4240 Silverado Trail, Napa, CA 94558
www.darioush.com

Del Dotto Rutherford

Dave and Yolanda Del Dotto were serious wine collectors who bought a vineyard in St. Helena in 1988. They made some decent Cabernet Sauvignons before hiring consultant Nils Venge in 1997 to improve them further. In 2000, the family opened their caves at another location for comparative barrel tastings, and recently opened a new Venetian-inspired facility on Highway 29 to offer structured, hands-on tasting opportunities for visitors to the valley. Their Napa Valley Cabernet Sauvignon and Giovanni's Reserve Cabernet/Sangiovese are highlights.

1445 St. Helena Highway South, St. Helena, CA 94574
www.deldottovineyards.com

Diamond Creek Vineyards
Diamond Mountain

If there is one winery that brought an elite reputation to Diamond Mountain Cabernet Sauvignon, it was Al Brounstein's Diamond Creek Vineyards. The terroir-driven Gravelly Meadow, Red Rock Terrace, and Volcanic Hill selections were rather stiff, bordering on austere, and demanding age. In the last decade, the wines have become more finely polished, possessing lucid fruit, curt minerality, and firm tannins that will age gracefully. This estate is making better wines than ever before. ★ Rising star

1500 Diamond Mountain Rd., Calistoga, CA 94515
www.diamondcreekvineyards.com

Domaine Carneros Carneros

Although she is not the first strong female figure to lead a sparkling wine house, the winemaker and general manager of Domaine Carneros, Eileen Crane, has certainly left her mark on California sparkling wine. Crane helped to start Gloria Ferrer before she was tapped by Claude Taittinger to head Domaine Carneros in the late 1980s, and she has helmed this estate ever since. In addition to its flagship Le Rêve Blanc de Blancs, there is a fine Brut and some very good still Pinot Noirs. The

DOMAINE CHANDON
FOUNDED BY MOET & CHANDON IN 1973, THIS ESTATE IS A SPARKLING WINE PIONEER

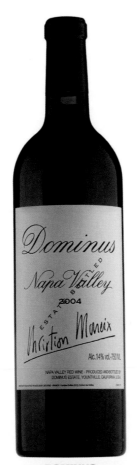

DOMINUS
BORDEAUX'S POWERFUL MOUIEX FAMILY MAKE A POWERFUL NAPA WINE

imposing château-like winery, perhaps a little gaudy when first built, has become a welcoming sight for visitors driving up to Napa from San Francisco.

1240 Duhig Rd., Napa, CA 94559
domainecarneros.com

Domaine Chandon Yountville

Yountville's climate is a little too warm for growing grapes for sparkling wines, so Domaine Chandon uses cooler climate grapes from Carneros, and some Chardonnay from nearby Mount Veeder, to supplement its home estate fruit. Owned by luxury goods group LVMH, this property's early sparklers were plump and sweet—overly so. Lately, the wines seem to have more focus, and the winery's reserve Étoile series has more depth and grace. The winery also makes a very drinkable still Pinot Meunier.

1 California Drive, Yountville, CA 94599
www.chandon.com

Dominus Yountville

The Bordeaux vintner Christian Mouiex invested in Napa Valley's Yountville AVA in 1982. This was rightly seen as a ringing endorsement of Napa Valley's growing stature, but Mouiex was no stranger to California: he had studied enology at the University of California in the late 1960s. Located in the southern part of Napa Valley, Dominus produces only two wines: the eponymous Dominus and its more affordable sibling, Napanook, both Cabernet Sauvignon-driven Bordeaux-style blends, and both very noble wines. Sadly, the estate is not visitor friendly, so the general public are not able to enjoy the striking winery designed by Swiss architects Herzog and de Meuron.

No visitor facilities
www.dominusestate.com

Donum Estate Carneros

The Donum Estate is a 200 acre (81ha) Carneros estate, planted to Pinot Noir and Chardonnay, that was retained by Anne Moller-Racke after she and her ex-husband sold Buena Vista to Allied Domecq in 2001. Consulting winemaker Kenneth Juhasz makes the wines, which are all estate-bottled. Donum's Pinot Noirs and Estate Chardonnay continue to improve, placing this property near the top of the heap of Carneros Pinot Noir producers. Of particular note is Donum's fragrant and supple West Slope Pinot Noir. ★ Rising star

No visitor facilities
www.thedonumestate.com

Duckhorn Vineyards St. Helena

Dan Duckhorn has done one heck of a job running Duckhorn Vineyards since he and wife Margaret founded the label in 1976. It has grown into a substantial concern with spin-off Paraduxx, and has given birth to Goldeneye in Alexander Valley. It did not hurt that when Merlot took off in the 1990s, Duckhorn was already making one of the very best. With New Zealander Bill Nancarrow making the wines since 2007, the Napa Valley Merlot, Estate Grown Merlot, and Howell Mountain Merlot are consistently precise, rich, and structured, as is the Napa Valley Cabernet Sauvignon.

1000 Lodi Lane, St. Helena, CA 94574
www.duckhorn.com

FANTESCA
ANOTHER WINERY IMPROVING UNDER HEIDI
PETERSON BARRETT'S CARE

Dunn Vineyards Howell Mountain

Randy Dunn made wine at Caymus in its formative mid-1970s to mid-1980s period, before staking out a claim on Howell Mountain in the northeast quadrant of the valley. Dunn would become the most important pioneer in Howell Mountain, making complex, sometimes polarizing, Howell Mountain and Napa Valley Cabernet Sauvignons that reflected the rugged terroir of their mountain origins. These wines were built to last—they are often compared to Bordeaux in style—and it is not uncommon to see vertical collections in fine restaurants. At times, Dunn's Cabernets can be as rustic as the setting in which they are grown. In recent years, Randy's son, Michael, has been taking more responsibility in the cellar.

No visitor facilities
www.dunnvineyards.com

Etude Carneros

There are not that many wineries that do Pinot Noir and Cabernet Sauvignon equally well, but under the guidance of founder Tony Soter, this Carneros estate has done just that. Today, the winery is owned by Foster's, and winemaker Jon Priest carries on Soter's Burgundian techniques. There are several single-vineyard wines, but the Heirloom Pinot Noir and Napa Cabernet Sauvignon never disappoint. Etude's stylish Pinot Gris and superb Pinot Noir rosé are also worth the hunt.

1250 Cuttings Wharf Rd., Napa, CA 94558
www.etudewines.com

Fantesca Spring Mountain

Yet another rising star of Spring Mountain, Fantesca is a relative newcomer founded by Best Buy executives Susan and Duane Hoff in 2004, after consultant Cary Gott brought the property to their attention. The initial bottlings were already in barrel when the winery was purchased but, after first hiring Nils and Kirk Venge, and then later Heidi Peterson Barrett, to make the wines, the quality of the Estate Cabernet Sauvignon and Russian River Valley Chardonnay is on the rise. Jim Barbour oversees the vineyard near the base of the mountain. ★ **Rising star**

2920 Spring Mountain Rd., St. Helena, CA 94574
www.fantesca.com

Far Niente Oakville

In 1979, Gil Nickel purchased a run-down vineyard on Highway 29 and set about restoring this 1885 winery. Nickel, with partners Larry Maguire and winemaker Dick Hampson, succeeded in building the brand through the 1980s and 1990s, with bold Cabernet Sauvignon, rich, oaky Chardonnay, and lavish gold labeling. The wines are very good, but have always been a tad expensive. Far Niente's late-harvest Semillon/Sauvignon Blanc, Dolce, is one of the finer dessert wines in Napa.

1350 Acacia Drive, Oakville, CA 94562
www.farniente.com

Flora Springs St. Helena

Flora Springs is a family operation that has already moved into the third generation, having been founded by Jerry and Flora Komes in 1977. The Komes-Garvey family owns several vineyards in the valley, totalling almost 650 acres (263ha), making them very important growers. Longtime assistant winemaker Paul Steinauer was promoted to winemaker in 2008. Flora Springs is best known for Trilogy, a very fine and on-point blend of Cabernet Sauvignon, Cabernet Franc, and Merlot. Its Rutherford Hillside Reserve Cabernet Sauvignon is excellent, and there is also a good Sangiovese.

1978 West Zinfandel Lane, St. Helena, CA 94574
www.florasprings.com

Forman Vineyards St. Helena

After a long stint as winemaker at Sterling Vineyards in the 1970s, proprietor Ric Forman (also a successful consultant) founded Forman Vineyards at the base of Howell Mountain. His aim was to make classic Cabernet Sauvignon and Chardonnay from his original St. Helena vineyards and another estate vineyard on the Rutherford bench. His Cabernet Sauvignon is usually blended with estate-grown Merlot, Cabernet Franc, and Petit Verdot. His Chardonnay is generally made without undergoing malolactic fermentation to preserve its crispness.

1501 Big Rock Rd., St. Helena, CA 94574
www.formanvineyard.net

Franciscan Estates St. Helena

Justin Meyers (Silver Oak) made Franciscan's first Cabernet Sauvignon in 1975. The winery grew steadily through the 1980s and 1990s under the guidance of vintner and owner Augustin Huneeus, who released the winery's first Meritage Bordeaux blend, Magnificat, in 1985. Another notable wine is its Cuvée Sauvage, a wild yeast-fermented Chardonnay first produced in 1987, inspiring a trend that is very much in fashion two decades later. Today, the winery is owned by Constellation and continues to make dependable wines.

1178 Galleron Rd., Highway 29, St. Helena, CA 94574
www.franciscan.com

Frank Family Vineyards Rutherford

Successful television executive Rich Frank and his wife Connie bought the historic Kornell Champagne Cellars winery, originally known as Larkmeade, in Rutherford in 1990. At first they decided to focus on growing, then later started their own label and bought some land in Carneros to supply Chardonnay and sparkling wine grapes. Their Rutherford Reserve Cabernet Sauvignon is excellent and their reasonably priced Napa Valley Cabernet Sauvignon delivers good concentration and value. They also make vintage Brut and Blanc de Noirs sparkling wines.

1091 Larkmead Lane, Calistoga, CA 94515
www.frankfamilyvineyards.com

Freemark Abbey St. Helena

Josephine and John Tychson bought this St. Helena estate in 1886 and began to expand the vineyards. After John's death from tuberculosis, Josephine continued the business. The estate passed through a stream of owners, making some decent wines. Winemaker Ted Edwards became a partner in 1993, and in 2006 Jackson Family Estates acquired the property. Even the 2005 vintage of the Napa Valley Cabernet Sauvignon shows the value of the infusion of capital and leadership that has come with the Jackson purchase. This is one to watch. ★ **Rising star**

3022 St. Helena Highway North, St. Helena, CA 94574
www.freemarkabbey.com

FROG'S LEAP WINERY
SUSTAINABLE FARMING PRACTICES PRODUCE
THIS RELIABLE, GOOD-QUALITY RED

Frog's Leap Winery Rutherford

Frog's Leap vintner John Williams has been an active and articulate advocate of sustainable growing techniques in Napa Valley. His winery, located in an attractive red barn on the flats of central Rutherford, produces very nice Cabernet Sauvignon, Merlot, and Sauvignon Blanc that is clean and easy to drink. His wines deliver good value, and reflect great integrity in farming. Also worth trying is the very good Zinfandel, traditionally blended with Petite Sirah and Carignane for added structure.

8815 Conn Creek Rd., Rutherford, CA 94573
www.frogsleap.com

Gamble Family Vineyards Oakville

Tom Gamble is a Napa Valley native who bought his first vineyard in 1981 and now owns six small vineyards in prime locations throughout the valley. Most of the grapes are sold, but some are retained by winemaker Jim Close, who makes some sturdy, concentrated wines including Paramount, a Bordeaux-style red blend, the Family Home Vineyard Cabernet Sauvignon, and the superb Heart Block Sauvignon Blanc, one of the most delicious (and pricey) Sauvignon Blancs of Napa Valley. ★ **Rising star**

7554 St. Helena Hwy, Oakville, CA 94562
www.gamblefamilyvineyards.com

Girard Winery Napa Valley

Girard was founded 35 years ago, making it practically middle-aged for Napa Valley. Vintner and wine industry professional Pat Roney purchased a majority interest in Girard in 2000, opened a tasting room in Yountville and, with the help of accomplished winemaker Marco DiGiulio, produces a variety of wines with an emphasis on mountain-grown Cabernet Sauvignon. Girard's excellent and ageworthy Diamond Mountain Cabernet, Artistry (a red blend), and Petite Sirah made from 100-year-old vines in Calistoga, are the standouts of the portfolio.

6795 Washington St, Yountville, CA 94599
www.girardwinery.com

Gloria Ferrer Winery Carneros

The Ferrer family, of the Cava cellar Freixenet, have proven their ability with this standout California sparkling wine estate. Their Brut and Blanc de Noirs are probably the best-value sparkling wines in California, and their reserve Royal Cuvée and Carneros Cuvée wines are unquestionably top shelf. The key to this estate's success has been the 20-year collaboration between winemaker Bob Iantosca and winegrower Mike Crumly.

23555 Carneros Highway, Sonoma, CA 95476
www.gloriaferrer.com

Grace Family Oakville

The production of the 3 acre (1.2ha) Grace vineyard would barely warrant a mention except for its extraordinary following. Former stockbroker Dick Grace invested in a small plot of land in Napa Valley and, when Caymus's Chuck Wagner tasted his Cabernet Sauvignon, it became clear that Grace was onto something special. A decade later, those grapes begot a winery and label of their own. The wine is expensive, ageworthy, and sought-after.

No visitor facilities
www.gracefamilyvineyards.com

Grgich Hills Estate Rutherford

Miljenko "Mike" Grgich is a living legend of Napa Valley, and was one of the first inductees to the Vintner's Hall of Fame. Gentle, spry, and still very involved in his winery, he is easy to spot with his trademark beret. Grgich made the 1973 Chateau Montelena Chardonnay that won the 1976 "Judgement of Paris" tasting, before starting his own winery in 1977. Grgich Hills Estate recently became one of the first certified Biodynamic vineyards in Napa Valley and, though never bad, the wines seem to be somewhat improved. Grgich's Zinfandels may be the best wines, but the Cabernets and Chardonnays are also good.

1829 St. Helena Highway, Rutherford, CA 94573
www.grgich.com

Groth Vineyards Oakville

In 1981, Dennis and Judy Groth bought a 121 acre (49ha) vineyard in the heart of Oakville across from the fabled Silver Oak. Groth developed a very loyal following for its supple Cabernet Sauvignons that showcase Oakville's classic black fruit and elegance. Like others in this region, Groth replanted many of its vineyards in the 1990s because of phylloxera, and quality suffered, but the wines are now back on track: Groth's Napa Valley Cabernet is comparatively good value, and the refreshing, clover-scented Sauvignon Blanc is worthwhile.

750 Oakville Cross Rd., Oakville, CA 94562
www.grothwines.com

Guilliams Spring Mountain

John and Shawn Guilliams farm a beautiful amphitheater-shaped vineyard near the top of Spring Mountain. The site had been a vineyard since the 1890s, but was abandoned and had to be cleared and replanted after the couple bought it in the late 1970s. Their winery was first known as La Vielle Montagne before they changed it to Guilliams. Their estate Cabernet Sauvignon is made in a subtle, barely ripe style, with dark fruit and brambly minty notes that works very well in most vintages.

3851 Spring Mountain Rd., St. Helena, CA 94574
707 963 9059

Hall Napa Valley Rutherford

Entrepreneur Craig Hall and his wife Kathryn, the former US ambassador to Austria, whose family have grown grapes in Mendocino for decades, have spent a significant fortune over the past decade establishing themselves as powerhouse Napa Valley Cabernet producers. Their primary winery and caves are located at their Sacrache Vineyard on the Rutherford bench, and they also operate a visitor center in St. Helena. Look for their reasonably priced Hall Napa Valley Cabernet Sauvignon and Kathryn Hall Napa Valley bottling. Also try their pricier Bergfield Vineyard Cabernet from St. Helena and Exzellenz Sacrache Vineyard Cabernet from Rutherford, both very rich, delicious wines. ★ **Rising star**

401 St. Helena Hwy South, St. Helena, CA 94574
www.hallwines.com

Harlan Estate Oakville

Bill Harlan, a property developer and part-owner of the Silverado Country Club, is the proud owner of this 240 acre (97ha) estate and 40 acre (16ha) vineyard in the western Mayacamas hillsides of Oakville. Harlan

AGING NAPA CABERNET SAUVIGNON

Napa Valley produces wines from Cabernet Sauvignon that tend to be riper, fruitier, softer, and slightly more alcoholic than those of Bordeaux. That said, Napa Valley has a broad range of microclimates, exposures, and altitudes that can produce diverse styles of Cabernet Sauvignon, and the influence of the winemaker should not be discounted.

Over the past few decades, winemakers of the Napa Valley have, for the most part, adopted a style that strives for wines to be relatively approachable and well-balanced upon release and that will gain some complexity over a period of 3 to 10 years. In some cases, the wines are capable of aging quite gracefully for decades. The leaner soils of Napa's mountain and benchland vineyards produce structured wines that generally have the best aging potential.

HESS COLLECTION
THE SUMMIT VINEYARD ON MOUNT VEEDER
PRODUCES GREAT MOUNTAIN CABERNET

routinely delivers one of Napa's most coveted Cabernet Sauvignons. Winemaker Bob Levy, with oversight from consultant Michel Rolland, makes only 18,000 bottles per year of the extraordinarily complex and seamless Estate Cabernet and a second wine called The Maiden. Harlan Estate is one of Napa's highly desirable cult Cabernets with a long waiting list of would-be buyers, and collectors are often willing to pay two to three times the release price for each new vintage.

No visitor facilities
www.harlanestate.com

Hartwell Estate Vineyards
Stags Leap District
This small hillside Stags Leap estate was established by Bob Hartwell, an avid wine collector who had worked in the aerospace and plumbing industries, and his wife Blanca. Famed enologist Michel Rolland is their consulting winemaker, working with Hartwell's resident winemaker Benoit Touquette, a veteran of several Bordeaux wineries who has worked with Rolland elsewhere. The sturdy and layered Estate Reserve Cabernet Sauvignon is a benchmark Stags Leap District wine. Their Miste Hill Cabernet is a bit softer and more accessible upon release. ★ Rising star

5795 Silverado Trail, Napa, CA 94558
www.hartwellvineyards.com

Heitz Cellar St. Helena
Joe Heitz worked with André Tchelistcheff at Beaulieu Vineyard before starting his own operation in 1961. He made some of California's greatest early Cabernet Sauvignons in the 1970s, including the legendary, eucalyptus-laced 1974 Heitz Martha's Vineyard, and will also be remembered for the minerally Chardonnays he made at Stony Hill. Today, the estate is run by his son, David, who is also the winemaker. The estate's reputation has faded over the last two decades but the Martha's Vineyard (replanted after 1992) and Trailside Vineyard Cabernet from Rutherford are still great, if a tad pricey.

436 St. Helena Highway, St. Helena, CA 94574
www.heitzcellar.com

Hendry Ranch Wines Napa Valley
George Hendry took over his family's 117 acre (47ha) vineyard, near the base of the Mayacamas range, after his father passed away unexpectedly. He has cared for it his entire life, while designing Cyclotron particle accelerators on the side. The transitional climate where the vineyard is situated allows Hendry to make a good assortment of wines, from Cabernet Sauvignon to Albariño. The real stars of the portfolio are the Block 28 and Block 7 & 22 Zinfandels, which can be absolutely brilliant, combining spicy aromas, blue-black fruit, and great structure.

3104 Redwood Rd., Napa, CA 94558
www.hendrywines.com

Hess Collection Mount Veeder
The Hess Collection is worth a visit for the location on the summit of Mount Veeder and Donald Hess' superb art collection. The winery is one of several owned by the Hess family, and generally produces very good wines, from the Hess Select Chardonnay (great value) to the Estate Cabernet Sauvignon from Mount Veeder, with

occasional lapses. For several years, the vineyards have been undergoing massive replanting, which will likely pay dividends over the next decade.

4411 Redwood Rd., Napa, CA 94558
www.hesscollection.com

Hewitt Vineyard Rutherford
The Hewitt Vineyard is a fine site adjacent to what is now the Rubicon estate on the western Rutherford bench. It was first planted in the 1880s and was bought by William A. Hewitt, the head of Deere & Company (makers of John Deere tractors), who replanted it to Cabernet Sauvignon. The grapes were sold to other wineries until the family decided to reserve some for a single-vineyard wine in 2001. The wine has classic Rutherford dust aromas, bold red and black fruit, and good structure. ★ Rising star

1698 St. Helena Highway, Rutherford, CA 94573
www.hewittvineyard.com

Honig Vineyard and Winery Rutherford
Count on Honig to deliver consistent value in its Napa Valley Cabernet Sauvignon and Sauvignon Blanc. Between the reliable winemaking of Kristen Belair, affable proprietor Michael Honig, and exemplary leadership in sustainable agriculture, Honig has earned a loyal following and an enviable reputation for its Sauvignon Blancs, in particular, the Rutherford Sauvignon. Its best red wine might be the Bartolucci Cabernet from the base of Spring Mountain, but its less expensive Napa Valley Cabernet always over-delivers.

850 Rutherford Rd., Rutherford, CA 94573
www.honigwine.com

Hourglass St. Helena
Located in the St. Helena AVA near Grace Family, Vineyard 29, and Colgin's Tychson Hill Vineyard, Hourglass has made a big early splash with its hard-to-find 100% Cabernet Sauvignon. The wine comes from a tiny 4 acre (1.6ha) hillside vineyard owned by Napa native Jeff Smith and his wife, Carolyn. Smith's father, Ned, had grown Zinfandel there until it was devoured by phylloxera and replanted to Cabernet. The winemaker is Bob Foley, known for his fine work at Pride Mountain, Robert Foley, and Switchback Ridge. ★ Rising star

No visitor facilities
www.hourglasswines.com

Howell Mountain Vineyards
Howell Mountain
Howell Mountain Vineyards was founded in 1988 with the aim of making top-notch Cabernet Sauvignon and Zinfandel from the Beatty Ranch and Black Sears vineyards on Howell Mountain. At 1,800ft (550m), the Beatty Ranch has both Cabernet Sauvignon and Zinfandel planted, while the organically farmed, 2,400ft (732m) elevation Black Sears Vineyard has 20 acres (8ha) of Zinfandel, producing exceptionally concentrated fruit with superb structure. Howell Mountain Vineyards was bought in 2005 by the Chow Family's company, Rutherford Bench LLC. Their winemaker is Dave Phinney from Orin Swift Cellars.

3000 Highway 29, St. Helena, CA 94575
www.howellmountain.com

HEITZ CELLAR
THE LEGENDARY HEITZ MARTHA'S
VINEYARD CABERNET SAUVIGNON

Hundred Acre Napa Valley

Bad boy Napa vintner Jayson Woodbridge makes very small amounts of wine, from the 10 acre (4ha) Kayli Morgan Vineyard and 15 acre (6ha) Howell Mountain Ark Vineyard, under this label, with assistance from prolific consultant Philippe Melka. The wines were lauded by critic Robert Parker. If you are interested in trying them, you will have to join the waiting list, but Woodbridge also makes some very affordable (and intensely concentrated) wines for the brand Layer Cake. ★ Rising star

No visitor facilities
www.hundredacre.com

Hyde de Villaine Carneros

Hyde de Villaine, or HdV for short, is a joint venture of star Carneros grower Larry Hyde and Aubert de Villaine, the general manager of Burgundy's Domaine de la Romanee-Conti, who also happens to be married to Hyde's sister Pamela. HdV's finest wines are the minerally and intense HdV Carneros Chardonnay and slightly less expensive De la Guerra Carneros Chardonnay, both of which are made from vines up to 25 years old. HdV also makes a small amount of Syrah and a cool-climate, restrained Merlot/Cabernet blend called Belle Cousine.

588 Trancas St, Napa, CA 94558
www.hdvwines.com

Joseph Phelps Vineyards St. Helena

Founded in 1972 by Joseph Phelps in Spring Valley, overlooking St. Helena, this winery makes a wide variety of wines, and does almost everything well. With enviable consistency it has been a trailblazer on several fronts. The flagship wine, Insignia, was one of the first Bordeaux-style blends from Napa Valley, and Phelps released its first Syrah in 1974. The Napa Valley Cabernet Sauvignon, the Backus Vineyard Cabernet from Oakville, and Insignia are all magnificent, and the winery makes some of the best Syrah in California from Hyde Vineyard in Carneros. It also owns Freestone, a new Sonoma Coast venture.

200 Taplin Rd., St Helena, CA 94574
www.jpvwines.com

Judd's Hill Napa Valley

Judd's Hill belongs to Art and Bunnie Finkelstein, the founders of Whitehall Lane. After selling Whitehall Lane in 1988, they bought a 14 acre (5.7ha) vineyard in the eastern hills above Lake Hennessey and opened a winery and custom crush facility on Silverado Trail. The winery is named for their son, Judd, who is actively involved in all aspects of the winery when not pursuing his other passion, playing ukulele with his band The Maikai Gents Featuring the Mysterious Miss Mauna Loa. The Cabernet Sauvignon is spicy and aromatic with juicy red fruit.

2332 Silverado Trail, Napa, CA 94558
www.juddshill.com

Kápcsandy Family Winery Yountville

Lou and Roberta Kápcsandy and their son, Louis Jr., purchased Beringer's highly regarded State Lane Vineyard in Yountville in 2000, and replanted it to Cabernet Sauvignon/Merlot/Cabernet Franc with help from Helen Turley and John Wetlaufer. Next, they hired consulting winemaker Denis Malbec, of Bordeaux's Château Latour, and local winemaker Rob Lawson to make the wines, and

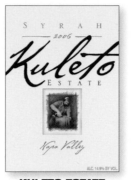

KULETO ESTATE
A REFINED SYRAH FROM LOW-YIELDING VINES IN THE VACA HILLS

HEWITT VINEYARD
A FINE SINGLE-VINEYARD RUTHERFORD CABERNET WITH GREAT STRUCTURE

Pina Vineyard Management to grow the grapes. The resulting red wines are, not surprisingly, pretty spectacular and expensive. They produce an Estate Cabernet Sauvignon, an Estate Cuvée of almost equal proportions of Cabernet and Merlot with a bit of Cabernet Franc, and the Merlot-dominated Roberta's Reserve. ★ Rising star

1001 State Lane, Yountville, CA 94599
www.kapcsandywines.com

Kuleto Estate Napa Valley

Another great winery in the Vaca range with a view of Lake Hennessey, Kuleto Estate was established by restaurateur Pat Kuleto, but in 2009 he sold a majority stake to Foley Wine Estates. The beautifully rugged 800 acre (324ha) ranch has about 80 acres (32ha) of vines, mostly on moderately steep slopes that are naturally low yielding. Winemaker Dave Lattin makes complex, refined Cabernet Sauvignon, Zinfandel, Sangiovese, Syrah, and Pinot Noir with ample fruit and a good backbone of tannin and minerality. There are a few single-block selections produced in small quantities. ★ Rising star

2460 Sage Canyon Rd., St. Helena, CA 94574
www.kuletoestate.com

Ladera Howell Mountain

Ladera's Pat and Anne Stotesberry have established themselves as top-flight mountain Cabernet Sauvignon producers with their Lone Canyon and Howell Mountain gems. Both are artfully made by winemaker Karen Culler and reflect the distinct terroirs of Mount Veeder at the southwestern corner of the valley and Howell Mountain in the northwest. The Napa Valley Cabernet combines fruit from both sources. Ladera's HQ is the refurbished Brun & Chaix Winery, a stone fortress of a winery on Howell Mountain that was originally built in 1886.

150 White Cottage Rd. South, Angwin, CA 94508
www.laderavineyards.com

La Sirena Calistoga

La Sirena is the private label of superstar winemaker Heidi Peterson Barrett, started when she was hired to make a batch of Sangiovese for a client. The client backed out and Barrett started her own brand with the wine. It no longer includes Sangiovese, but does feature a Napa Cabernet Sauvignon blended from a few sources, a Napa Syrah, a single-vineyard Syrah from her own Barrett vineyard, and a dry Muscat Canelli called Moscato Azul. ★ Rising star

No visitor facilities
www.lasirenawine.com

Lewis Cellars Oak Knoll District

Former racing car driver Randy Lewis and his wife Debbie founded Lewis Cellars in 1992. They make a Bordeaux-blend called Cuvée L, three Cabernet Sauvignons, two Syrahs, Merlot, Sauvignon Blanc, and four Chardonnays, mostly from grapes purchased from good vineyards throughout Napa Valley. Lewis's house style, particularly for the reds, is big, dark, and ultra-ripe, but the wines carry their intensity remarkably well. The wines are made by Brian Mox, a veteran of Laird Family Estate and Etude. ★ Rising star

No visitor facilities
www.lewiscellars.com

Mustard flowers between rows of still-dormant Cabernet Sauvignon vines. The plant is used as a cover crop.

OAKVILLE RANCH VINEYARDS
QUALITY CHARDONNAY AND CABERNET
SAUVIGNON FROM ORGANIC GRAPES

LOKOYA
FINE CABERNET SAUVIGNON WINES FROM
THE FOUR MOUNTAIN AVAS

Lokoya Mount Veeder

Lokoya is a Jackson Family Farms winery devoted to exploring the potential of Cabernet Sauvignon from Napa Valley's mountain terroirs—from its home estate on Mount Veeder, to Spring Mountain, Diamond Mountain, and Howell Mountain. The winery is named for the Lokoya tribe of Native Americans who once lived in the area. The four Cabernets have been made by Christopher Carpenter since 2000, and are uniformly excellent, giving a wonderful comparative look at the distinct personalities of Napa's top mountain districts.

7600 St. Helena Highway, Oakville, CA 94562
www.lokoya.com

Long Meadow Ranch Napa Valley

Long Meadow Ranch, run by Ted and Laddie Hall and their son Christopher, produces a lot more than wine. In addition to some very good Cabernet Sauvignon, the Halls produce olive oil, grass-fed Highland beef, eggs, and other produce, on the main 650 acre (263ha) ranch and on a couple of smaller properties. The wines are made from organically grown grapes by the experienced Ashley Heisey. The price of the estate Cabernet Sauvignon has stayed relatively low, and the winery also offers a good-value, unpretentious red blend called Ranch House Red.

738 Main St, St. Helena, CA 94574
www.longmeadowranch.com

MacRostie Winery Carneros

Steve MacRostie made wine for Sonoma's Hacienda Winery for a dozen years before starting his own operation in 1987. He makes impeccably restrained and minerally Carneros Chardonnay from fruit purchased in both Napa County and Sonoma County, and very nice, sometimes exceptional, Syrah and Pinot Noir from his own sustainably farmed Wildcat Vineyard in the southwestern, Sonoma County quadrant of Carneros. His Carneros Pinot Noir from purchased grapes is pretty good, too.

21481 8th St. East 25, Sonoma, CA 95476
www.macrostiewinery.com

Marston Family Vineyards Spring Mountain

This 40 acre (16ha) vineyard dates back to the 1890s and has been owned by the Marston family since 1969. The terraced vineyards rise from 700ft to 1,100ft (213m to 335m) on the south slope of Spring Mountain. In 1992, they were replanted with the help of Bob Steinhauer of Beringer, in exchange for Beringer's 25-year right to most of the grapes. Ten tons of the best grapes are retained by Marston and made into a spectacular Spring Mountain Cabernet with tremendous complexity and structure by winemaker Philippe Melka. ★ **Rising star**

3600 White Sulpher Springs Road, St. Helena, CA 94574
www.marstonfamilyvineyard.com

Mayacamas Vineyards Mount Veeder

Based out of an 1889 stone winery, Mayacamas has been in the hands of Robert and Elinor Travers since 1968, and Bob is still the winemaker. The wines have not changed much over the years, and they were once much appreciated for their austerity and longevity. Mayacamas's bony, hyper-tannic Cabernet Sauvignon is a bit of an anachronism that has failed to keep pace with improved winemaking techniques. The winery's minerally Chardonnay is the best current offering.

1155 Lokoya Rd., Napa, CA 94558
www.mayacamas.com

Merus St. Helena

The husband-and-wife team of Mark Herold and Erika Gottl started Merus in a Napa garage in 1998 and over the next 10 years the 18,000-bottle Cabernet Sauvignon production wine earned rave reviews. In need of capital, the founders sold the winery to William Foley in 2007, but continued working for the brand. Herold was replaced as winemaker by Paul Hobbs a year later. The brand recently moved into a winery in St. Helena, dramatically increasing production capacity for the wine. Foley says he intends to continue the ultra-rich style of the wine.
★ **Rising star**

No visitor facilities
www.meruswines.com

Miner Family Vineyards Oakville

Owned by Dave and Emily Miner, Miner Family Vineyards is located on the eastern bench of Oakville, near the Oakville Ranch estate of Dave's parents. Miner makes a variety of red and white wines using grapes from Napa Valley and elsewhere. There is a good Sangiovese from Mendocino and some great Pinot Noirs from Garys' Vineyard and Rosella's Vineyard in the Santa Lucia Highlands. Quality is very high across the board, but the winery's flagship wines are its Oracle red blend from the Stagecoach Vineyard on Napa's Atlas Peak, the Oakville Cabernet Sauvignon bottling, and its full-flavored and lavishly textured Wild Yeast Chardonnay.

7850 Silverado Trail, Oakville, CA 94562
www.minerwines.com

Mount Veeder Winery Mount Veeder

As a long-time sister winery of Franciscan, Mount Veeder Winery followed Franciscan into the Constellation Brands wine empire. The wines are decent, if slightly rustic, examples of Mount Veeder Cabernet Sauvignon sourced from three vineyards between 1,000ft and 2,000ft (305m and 610m) in elevation. The wines, made by Janet Myers, seem to have lost some of their former luster, or perhaps they have just been out-paced by others in the region. Try the entry-level Mount Veeder Cabernet before moving on to the reserve.

1178 Galleron Road, St. Helena, 94574
www.mtveeder.com

Mumm Napa Rutherford

Why this joint venture between the original partners, Mumm Champagne and Seagram, decided to base itself in Rutherford is a bit of a mystery—the climate is not the best for making sparkling wine. They do own 112 acres (45ha) of vineyards in cooler Carneros, however, and also buy grapes from Anderson Valley in Mendocino County. The resulting wines are solid and continue to improve. The highlight is the DVX reserve *cuvée*, usually released with about 8 years of age, which has great depth and structure.

8445 Silverado Trail, Rutherford, CA 94573
www.mummnapa.com

Newton Vineyard Spring Mountain District

Newton's steep, terraced Spring Mountain vineyards, with varied exposures and soils, produce sturdy, minerally Cabernet Sauvignon, Cabernet Franc, and Merlot, but its unctuous, unfiltered Napa Chardonnay is also a treat. Upgrades in the vineyard, bankrolled by new owner LVMH, should herald even better things to come. Also new since 1997, winemaker Chris Millard is a skilled veteran of Sterling Vineyards, with a knack for making superbly balanced, clean wines. Newton's less expensive range of Red Label wines are good value. ★ Rising star

2555 Madrona Ave., St. Helena, CA 94574
www.newtonvineyard.com

Nickel & Nickel Winery Oakville

Nickel & Nickel, a spin-off winery of Far Niente, is a product of the California single-vineyard wine craze of the 1990s, when it seemed anyone could charge a premium for a wine that was vineyard designated. The Nickel family, with partners Larry Maguire and Dirk Hampson, make 13 single-vineyard Cabernet Sauvignons with triple-digit prices, three Napa Valley Merlots, two Syrahs, and a Sonoma Coast Pinot Noir. The wines are very good, but not the most outstanding value.

8164 St. Helena Highway, Oakville, CA 94562
www.nickelandnickel.com

Oakville Ranch Vineyards Oakville

Located on a high, sloping plateau in the Vaca range, the 350 acre (142ha) Oakville Ranch estate was purchased in 1989 by Mary and the late Bob Miner, a former executive at one of the world's largest software companies, Oracle. The estate has consistently made exceptionally good Cabernet Sauvignon and Chardonnay that offer great comparative value. Today, the wines are made by Ashley Heisey, who also makes Sonoma Coast Syrah under her own Marelle label. The vineyards are overseen by Phil Coturri, an advocate of organic viticulture.

7781 Silverado Trail, Napa, CA 94558
www.oakvilleranch.com

Opus One Oakville

Robert Mondavi and Baron Philippe de Rothschild (proprietor of Château Lafite and Château Mouton in Bordeaux) announced in 1980 that they would come together to produce a benchmark Napa Valley Cabernet Sauvignon. They released their first vintage in 1985, and later built a stunning limestone winery in Oakville, across Highway 29 from the Robert Mondavi Winery. Opus One became the first luxury California wine to be widely sold in Europe and Asia. After Constellation's acquisition of Robert Mondavi Corporation in 2004, Constellation reached an accord that gave the Rothschilds control of vineyard management, marketing, and administration, and quality is improving.

7900 St. Helena Highway, Oakville, CA 94562
www.opusonewinery.com

O'Shaughnessy Estate Winery

Howell Mountain

Another prime vineyard developed with the help of Beringer, in exchange for a longterm grape contract. O'Shaughnessy Estate is a rising star of Howell Mountain that regularly contributes Del Oso Vineyard grapes to Beringer Private Reserve. The winemaker, Sean Capiaux, makes a Howell Mountain Cabernet Sauvignon from the estate vineyards, which is refined, deep, and ageworthy, as well as a smaller-production Mount Veeder Cabernet Sauvignon from a vineyard purchased later by Betty O'Shaughnessy. There is also a tiny amount of exceptional Merlot produced from the Howell Mountain estate. ★ Rising star

Angwin, CA 94508
www.oshaughnessywinery.com

Outpost Winery Howell Mountain

Outpost seems such an appropriate name for this winery, devoted to Zinfandel, Cabernet Sauvignon, Grenache, and Petite Sirah when so many other wineries with this caliber of terroir are focused on Cabernet. Zinfandel and Grenache, like Cabernet, love lean soils, and Outpost has rightfully earned a reputation as a first-rate producer of all three. The wines, made by Thomas Rivers Brown, have a dedicated following and are all superior examples of Howell Mountain's characteristic concentrated fruit and moderately tannic graphite and mineral notes.

2075 Summit Lake Drive, Angwin, CA 94508
www.outpostwines.com

Pahlmeyer Napa Valley

Jayson Pahlmeyer got started with fruit from a friend's family vineyard in Coombsville and, since releasing his first wine in the 1980s, has consistently produced excellent Cabernet Sauvignon-based red wines and luscious Chardonnays. In the early years, he was assisted by winemaker Helen Turley, who was later succeeded by her protégé, Erin Green. Pahlmeyer's wines are naturally fermented with wild yeasts, for added complexity. The excellent Merlot and proprietary red wine are blended from several low-yielding sites, including Waters Ranch on Atlas Peak, developed by David Abreu. The Jayson range of wines delivers good value.

2387 Atlas Peak Road, Napa, CA 94558
www.pahlmeyer.com

Paradigm Oakville

Founded in 1976 by Ren and Marilyn Harris, Oakville's Paradigm is as much known for its fine Merlot and excellent Cabernet Franc as it is for its Cabernet Sauvignon. Remarkably, star winemaking consultant Heidi Peterson Barrett has been the winemaker here since 1991, which shows how early the Harrises were tipped off to her talent. Ren Harris is one of the valley's most successful real estate agents, and everyone knows that real estate agents get all of the good gossip first.

1277 Dwyer Rd., Oakville, CA 94562
www.paradigmwinery.com

Patz & Hall Winery Napa Valley

With land prices spiralling upward, friends Donald and Heather Patz, Anne Moses, and winemaker James Hall, partnered in 1988 to start the Patz & Hall winery without land of its own. Instead, they would source and purchase ultra-premium grapes from some of the best Chardonnay and Pinot Noir vineyards scattered throughout California. The winery operates out of a "salon" located in an unassuming industrial park south of Napa, where visitors with an appointment can taste their outstanding wares,

HEIDI PETERSON BARRETT

Many investors in Napa Valley's vineyards are newcomers to the wine business who made their fortunes elsewhere. The enlistment of a famed vineyard manager and winemaking consultant can bring fast progress and beneficial publicity to a new estate or, in some cases, new life to an old one.

A Napa Valley native, daughter of vigneron Richard Peterson, and married to Bo Barrett (of Chateau Montelena), Heidi Peterson Barrett established herself in the 1990s as Napa Valley's top consulting winemaker after winning superlative reviews as winemaker for Dalla Valle. She earned further accolades for producing other "Cult Cabernets" at Screaming Eagle and Grace Family. In addition to consulting, she makes wine under her own label, La Sirena.

Other prominent consultants in Napa Valley include David Ramey, Philippe Melka, Sarah Gott, Nils and Kurt Venge, and the omnipresent Michel Rolland.

including the Hudson and Zio Tony Ranch Vineyard Chardonnays and Hyde and Alder Springs Vineyard Pinot Noirs. ★ **Rising star**

851 Napa Valley Corporate Way, Suite A, Napa, CA 94558
www.patzhall.com

Philip Togni Vineyards
Spring Mountain District

Philip Togni studied under the enologist Emile Peynaud in Bordeaux before planting his vineyard at the top of Spring Mountain in 1981. The vineyard was replanted in the 1990s because of phylloxera. Togni's long-lived, complex, Château Margaux-inspired Cabernet Sauvignon blended with Merlot, Cabernet Franc, and Petit Verdot has found many fans, including top critics. His straight Cabernet is also very well-received. He also makes a sweet Black Muscat called Ca' Togni.

3780 Spring Mountain Rd., St. Helena, CA 94574
www.philiptognivineyard.com

Piña Napa Valley Rutherford

The Piña family goes back several generations in Napa Valley and have been important growing consultants since John Piña founded John Piña Jr. and Sons in the 1960s. Today, the four Piña brothers, Larry, Davie, Ranndy, and John, own five vineyards in Napa Valley and a winery on the Silverado Trail in Rutherford. Winemaker Anna Monticelli makes three dense, luscious Cabernet Sauvignons, including a great one from the Pina's Buckeye Vineyard on Howell Mountain. ★ **Rising star**

8060 Silverado Trail, Napa, CA, 94558
www.pinanapavalley.com

Pine Ridge Winery Stags Leap District

Pine Ridge, a 250 acre (101ha) estate, was founded in 1978 by former Olympic skier Gary Andrus, who later founded Archery Summit in Oregon. Today, both of these wineries are owned by the Crimson Wine Group. Michael Beaulac, from St. Supéry, was recently appointed as winemaker. The estate is focused on Cabernet Sauvignon and has been a steady performer for decades. Cabernets from several AVAs in the valley are offered as well as a complex Dijon Clones Chardonnay and a very good dry Chenin Blanc.

5901 Silverado Trail, Napa, CA 94558
www.pineridgewinery.com

PlumpJack Oakville

San Francisco's Mayor Gavin Newsom and friends Gordon and Bill Getty have partnered in a few business ventures under the PlumpJack name—including this winery, which produces very high-quality, fruit-driven Cabernet Sauvignon, Syrah, and Chardonnay. They were one of the first Napa wineries to embrace screwcaps for half of their Cabernet bottling. Mayor Newsom has now embraced sobriety, yet the partners have unveiled another new winery on Howell Mountain, called CADE.

620 Oakville Cross Rd., Oakville, CA 94562
www.plumpjackwinery.com

Pride Mountain Vineyards Spring Mountain

This 235 acre (95ha) estate straddles Napa and Sonoma counties at the top of Spring Mountain in the Mayacamas range. The property is owned by Carolyn, Steve, and

Suzanne Pride and emerged as a powerhouse in the 1990s with full-bore, dense wines. The remarkable site continues to produce very fine Cabernet Sauvignon and Merlot—sourced from both sides of the border between Napa and Sonoma, as are the Reserve Cabernet and Claret. The Vintner Select Cabernet Sauvignon is made from Napa grapes only.

4026 Spring Mountain Rd., St. Helena, CA 94574
www.pridewines.com

Provenance Vineyards Rutherford

The relatively young Provenance Vineyards replaced Beaucannon Vineyards near St. Helena. They make good-quality Cabernet Sauvignon, Merlot, and Sauvignon Blanc from Rutherford and Oakville, including renowned viticulturist Andy Beckstoffer's section of To Kalon Vineyard. Winemaker Tom Rinaldi is a valley veteran with experience at Freemark Abbey, Rutherford Hill, and Duckhorn. His wines have a sense of place and a bit of "Rutherford dust" character, but are a touch tame and best for early drinking.

1695 St. Helena Highway South, Rutherford, CA 94573
www.provenancevineyards.com

Quintessa Rutherford

Quintessa is the home estate of Agustin Huneeus, one of the greatest wine businessmen of the last century, and his wife, Valeria. The Chilean-born former CEO of Concha y Toro built the core of what is now the world's largest wine company, Constellation Brands. The beautiful 280 acre (113ha) estate surrounds a lake on rolling hills in the center of the valley. It is planted solely to Bordeaux varieties and winemaker Charles Thomas (formerly of Cardinale and Rudd) makes just one wine, a Bordeaux-style red blend that has always been good but has room for improvement.

1601 Silverado Trail, Rutherford, CA 94573
www.quintessa.com

Richard Partridge St. Helena

Orange County electrical engineer and wine collector Richard Partridge has a small family winery that produces a very nice, refined Napa Cabernet Sauvignon and a small amount of Chardonnay. Winemaker Jeff Fontanella, a Nils Venge disciple, makes the wines from sources that change from year to year. New vineyards are being planted in St. Helena, which could see the operation convert from hobby winery to something more serious.

No visitor facilities
www.richardpartridge.com

Robert Biale Vineyards Oak Knoll District

Bob Biale's ancestors emigrated from northern Italy to Napa Valley and started growing grapes in the 1930s, but the Biales did not bottle their own wine until 1991. In two decades, Bob Biale has earned a deserved reputation as one of the best Zinfandel and Petite Sirah vintners in California. He makes an assortment of wines from very old single-vineyard sites, from his own Aldo's vineyard (named for his father), to other sources in Napa, Sonoma, Lodi, and Contra Costa. His wines are big and dark with ripe fruit flavors, but are also polished and precise.

4038 Big Ranch Rd., Napa, CA
www.robertbialevineyards.com

PATZ & HALL WINERY
MENDOCINO'S ALDER SPRINGS VINEYARD
PROVIDES THE FRUIT FOR THIS FINE PINOT

PINE RIDGE WINERY
A NEW WORLD CHARDONNAY MADE FROM
OLD WORLD BURGUNDIAN CLONES

Robert Craig Winery Howell Mountain

Former Hess Collection general manager Robert Craig is a mountain Cabernet Sauvignon specialist who makes wines from Spring Mountain, Mount Veeder, and Howell Mountain at a small winery on Howell Mountain (the tasting room is located in downtown Napa). The wines are consistent and deliver the sturdy tannins and minerality characteristic of mountain Cabernet produced in lean, low-yielding soils. Craig's Mount Veeder and Howell Mountain wines are his most impressive.

625 Imperial Way, Napa, CA 94559
www.robertcraigwine.com

Robert Foley Vineyards Howell Mountain

Winemaker Robert Foley is a fixture in Napa Valley, having begun his career in 1977. He attained elite status making rich, layered Cabernet Sauvignons at Pride Mountain Vineyards on Spring Mountain and specifically for making great Napa mountain wines with polished tannins. He continues that tradition on Howell Mountain on the east side of the valley with his Howell Mountain Cabernet Sauvignon, Merlot, Claret, Petite Sirah, and Charbono. His first vintage at his home estate was 1998. In his spare time, this esteemed Napa winemaker plays guitar in The Robert Foley Band.

No visitor facilities
www.robertfoleyvineyards.com

Robert Mondavi Winery Oakville

In 2004, the Robert Mondavi Corporation, including Robert Mondavi's iconic Oakville winery, was sold to Constellation Brands in the wake of in-fighting that splintered the Mondavi family. Although the Mondavis are no longer associated with this property, Constellation has done a respectable job of continuing Robert Mondavi's vision of combining wine with the arts and the Mondavi Reserve wines continue to be made by Genevieve Janssens, who has worked at the estate since the late 1970s. The winery has also retained 550 acres (223ha) of the first-rate To Kalon vineyard on the Oakville bench that dates back to the late 1800s. To Kalon supplies both the great Robert Mondavi Reserve Cabernet Sauvignon and the unctuous, exotic Reserve Fumé Blanc, one of the world's great Sauvignon Blancs.

7801 St. Helena Highway, Oakville, CA 94562
www.robertmondaviwinery.com

Robert Sinskey Vineyards
Stags Leap District

The Robert Sinskey winery is based on Silverado Trail in Stags Leap, and the winery makes a very good "SLD" Cabernet Sauvignon. Most of the wines are Pinot Noir and Alsatian varieties from Carneros, where the family first established vineyards. The fruit is 100% organic and/or Biodynamic and the wines emphasize elegance and finesse. A good illustration is the racy, burgundy-inspired Three Amigos Vineyard Pinot Noir from Carneros.

6320 Silverado Trail, Napa, CA 94558
www.robertsinskey.com

Rocca Family Vineyards Yountville

Mary Rocca and her husband, Dr. Eric Grigsby, bought a 21 acre (8.5ha) parcel in Yountville in 1999 and planted it to mostly Cabernet Sauvignon and Syrah. With the help

QUINTESSA
A SINGLE WINE FROM A SINGLE VINEYARD, PRODUCING A CLASSIC BORDEAUX BLEND

PROVENANCE VINEYARDS
THIS CABERNET SAUVIGNON OFFERS A TASTE OF THE FAMED RUTHERFORD DUST

of winemaking guru Celia Welch Masyczek, the Roccas produce a handful of sturdy, concentrated red wines. The Yountville Cabernet and Syrah are their best received wines to date, and their Bad Boy Red, a youthful blend of Cabernet Sauvignon, Cabernet Franc, and Petit Verdot is a good introduction. There should be room for improvement for this young operation. ★ **Rising star**

129 Devlin Rd., Napa, CA 94558
www.roccawines.com

Rombauer Vineyards St. Helena

Koerner Rombauer and his wife, Joan, moved to Napa Valley in 1972 and eventually planted their own vineyard in 1981. The brand grew steadily through the 1980s and 1990s and became well known for producing a decadent, buttery style of Chardonnay that became strongly identified with Napa Valley. Rombauer also produces a series of Cabernet Sauvignons from various AVAs in Napa Valley, a rich Zinfandel from its home estate and a late-harvest botrytised Chardonnay called Joy.

3522 Silverado Trail, St. Helena, CA 94574
www.rombauer.com

Rubicon Estate Oakville

Director Francis Ford Coppola's cinematic achievements draw many international tourists to his family's estate winery, and few leave unsatisfied with the wine. The winery was originally built by sea captain Gustave Niebaum in 1880, and was called Inglenook. It became one of California's great early wineries. The 235 acre (95ha) estate produces some great wines, including the superb flagship Rubicon Cabernet-based blend and the brambly berry-flavored Edizione Pennino Zinfandel. Famed Master Sommelier Larry Stone is the general manager and Scott McLeod is the winemaker.

1991 St. Helena Highway, Rutherford, CA 94573
www.rubiconestate.com

Rudd Estate Oakville

Leslie Rudd, Kansas wine and spirits distributor and chairman of luxury deli chain Dean and DeLuca, must be credited with exceptional taste and uncompromising standards. Given a few more years, his Napa venture will likely be a formidable estate. Located on the eastern side of Oakville, and equipped with state-of-the-art caves and facilities, this young estate's Oakville Estate Red and Estate Grown Cabernet have been very good, if not as thrilling as some of the neighborhood competition. The plump, Bordeaux-style Sauvignon Blanc/Semillon from Mount Veeder is also worthwhile. ★ **Rising star**

500 Oakville Cross Rd., Oakville, CA 94562
www.ruddwines.com

Saddleback Cellars Oakville

Nils Venge made some great Cabernet Sauvignons at Groth in the 1980s and he, and his son Kirk, remain prominent winemaking consultants in the valley. Saddleback is their home estate. Left to their own devices, they make sturdy, ageworthy Cabernet Sauvignon and zesty Chardonnay and Pinot Blanc, as well as a remarkably good Charbono under their own Saddleback label.

7802 Money Rd., Oakville, CA 94562
www.saddlebackcellars.com

SCHRAMSBERG VINEYARDS
A HISTORIC WINERY KNOWN AS A PIONEER OF
SPARKLING WINE IN THE 20TH CENTURY

SILVERADO VINEYARDS
A SILKY-TEXTURED SAUVIGNON BLANC
WITH FRESH CITRUS NOTES

Saintsbury Carneros

Founded by burgundy-lovers David Graves and Richard Ward in 1981, Saintsbury focused on Pinot Noir from the start and quickly made a name for itself and for the Carneros region. With accomplished, longtime winemaker Byron Kosuge running the cellar, the quality of Saintsbury's Pinot Noir and Chardonnay remains very high, from their lightly oaked, entry-level bottling, Garnet, to their single-vineyard wines from the estate's Brown Ranch. They also make a single-vineyard Pinot Noir from Stanly Ranch, the oldest Pinot Noir vineyard in Carneros, planted by Louis Martini in the 1950s.

1500 Los Carneros Ave., Napa, CA 94559
www.saintsbury.com

Scarecrow Rutherford

Proprietor Brett Lopez, a photographer from Los Angeles, named his vineyard "Scarecrow" in homage to his grandfather, Joseph Judson Cohn, the producer of *The Wizard of Oz*. The 24 acre (9.5ha) vineyard on the Rutherford Bench, including a 2 acre (0.8ha) plot of 60-year-old Cabernet Sauvignon vines, was acquired in the same deal that gave Francis Ford Coppola the Rubicon estate. The estate produces just 6,000 bottles of its own Cabernet each year, made by winemaker Celia Welch Masyczek (Staglin, Rocca Family). ★**Rising star**

No visitor facilities
www.scarecrowwine.com

Schrader Cellars Oakville

Fred Schrader and winemaker Thomas Brown make concentrated Cabernet Sauvignons with a no-holds-barred, full-bore style that top critics seem to like. Grapes are sourced from some great sites, such as the Andy Beckstoffer-owned Old Sparky section of To Kalon Vineyard and his George III Vineyard. There are also their own, more value-priced, Double Diamond offerings, the Bomber X Napa Valley Cabernet Sauvignon, and Amber Knolls Vineyard Cabernet from another of Beckstoffer's vineyards in the Red Hills of Lake County. ★**Rising star**

No visitor facilities
www.schradercellars.com

Schramsberg Vineyards/J. Davies
Diamond Mountain

German-born Jacob Schram first established this estate in 1862. After a good run of success, a series of misfortunes, culminating in Prohibition, shuttered the winery. Jack and Jamie Davies bought it in 1965 and set about making California's best traditional-method sparkling wine—and succeeded in doing so. For two decades, their Blanc de Blancs has been a benchmark. Lately, their reserve J. Schram and Brut Rosé have also been superb. The hand-dug caves of the property and historic California flag collection definitely warrant a stop. Today, the winery also makes very fine Cabernet Sauvignon from the base of Diamond Mountain under the J. Davies label.

1400 Schramsberg Rd., Calistoga, CA 94515
www.schramsberg.com

Schug Carneros Estate Carneros

Winemaker Walter Schug and his wife Gertrud emigrated to California from Germany in 1961. Schug would become the founding winemaker of Joseph Phelps Vineyards, where he made California's first Bordeaux-style blend, Insignia. After a decade at Phelps, he set up his own winery in Carneros in 1980 to focus on Pinot Noir and Chardonnay. Schug's Pinot Noir is a bit more tannic, leaner, and spicier than some of his neighbors' wines.

602 Bonneau Rd., Sonoma, CA 95476
www.schugwinery.com

Schweiger Spring Mountain

Fred Schweiger's estate near the top of Spring Mountain has been a slow, steady development. He and his family bought the land in the early 1960s, cleared it and planted vines in the 1970s, then sold grapes to others through the 1980s. In 1994, Schweiger unveiled its own bonded winery and Fred's son Andrew was named winemaker in 1999. Schweiger's Cabernet Sauvignon and Merlot are very dependable wines, full of ripe red fruit with structure.

4015 Spring Mountain Rd., St. Helena, CA 94574
www.schweigervineyards.com

Screaming Eagle Oakville

Jean Phillips' Screaming Eagle Cabernet Sauvignon, made from a tiny block of her 60 acre (24ha) vineyard, skyrocketed to fame in the 1990s, as did its price, reaching $500 a bottle upon release and often much higher as collectors competed for the 6,000-bottle annual production. Made by Heidi Peterson Barrett, the wine received lavish praise from some and condemnation from others, who find its concentrated cassis flavors too sweet or syrupy. In 2006, Phillips sold the ranch and label to businessman Charles Banks and his partner Stanley Kroenke, part-owner of NBA team the Denver Nuggets.

No visitor facilities
www.screamingeagle.com

Seavey Napa Valley

Seavey is located east of the Silverado Trail in Conn Valley. In 1979, Bill and Mary Seavey bought the property, which, in the 1870s, had been home to the Franco-Swiss Farming Co. The Seaveys replanted the vineyard while Bill Seavey continued to practice law in San Francisco. The grapes were sold to Raymond Vineyards until the Seaveys began to bottle their own wine in 1990. Philippe Melka is the winemaker and does a fantastic job with the supple and concentrated Estate Cabernet Sauvignon and second wine, Caravina, also a Cabernet. ★**Rising star**

1310 Conn Valley Rd., St. Helena, CA 94574
www.seaveyvineyard.com

Shafer Vineyards Stags Leap District

Shafer Vineyards was founded by John Shafer in 1972, just as some of the region's other estates were getting started. His bright, affable son, Doug Shafer, has been the estate's winemaker and president since 1994. Shafer's Hillside Select Cabernet Sauvignon, made from a steep vineyard in the Vaca Mountains, is one of California's most refined, consistent, and universally respected wines. The other wines from Shafer's six vineyards in Stags Leap and nearby do not suffer by comparison. All show the meticulous hands-on care of Napa native Elias Fernandez, their vineyard manager and winemaker.

6154 Silverado Trail, Napa, CA 94558
www.shafervineyards.com

Signorello Oak Knoll District

Located on the Silverado Trail just north of Napa, Signorello is a 100 acre (40ha) estate purchased by Ray Signorello Sr. in the mid-1970s. There are about 40 acres (16ha) of vineyards, with a little less than half devoted to Cabernet Sauvignon. Ray Signorello Jr. is the winemaker and does a great job with the optimally ripe Estate Cabernet Sauvignon and Padrone Reserve Cabernet. Their Chardonnays, especially Hope's Cuvée and Vielle Vignes, have great focus and intensity. This estate seems to be very much on the right track. ★ Rising star

4500 Silverado Trail, Napa, CA 94558
www.signorellovineyards.com

Silver Oak Cellars Oakville

Founded in 1972 by Justin Meyer, the former winemaker of Christian Brothers, and Colorado oilman Raymond Duncan, Silver Oak became one of the most successful Cabernet Sauvignon brands of the 1980s. Though the original winery was in Oakville, the earliest Cabernet Sauvignons were from Alexander Valley. Today, Silver Oak makes Cabernet Sauvignon from both Napa and Sonoma valleys. The wines are plump and fruity with soft tannins, and aged primarily in American oak. The brand once had tremendous cachet, but with production up to 840,000 bottles per year, Silver Oak's Cabernets are now fairly easy to find at the supermarket.

915 Oakville Crossroad, Oakville, CA 94562
www.silveroak.com

Silverado Vineyards Stags Leap District

Silverado was founded in the late 1980s by Walt Disney's daughter, Diane, and her husband Ron Miller, a former professional American football player and later CEO of Walt Disney Productions. The Millers now have six vineyards in the Napa Valley. Their Napa Valley Cabernet Sauvignon is relatively easy to find, reasonably priced, and generally offers a winning combination of ripe fruit and good structure. Particularly impressive and ageworthy is their Limited Reserve Cabernet. Also recommended is their Miller Ranch Sauvignon Blanc with ripe melon and citrus flavors.

6121 Silverado Trail, Napa, CA 94558
www.silveradovineyards.com

Snowden St. Helena

Scott and Randy Snowden (brothers, and children of the founders Wayne and Virginia) are primarily growers, farming four vineyards on a long strip of property in the Vaca hills between the Silverado Trail and Conn Valley. Snowden's grapes regularly go into wines from Silver Oak, Frank Family, and Viader. Winemaker Diana Snowden Seysses makes two minerally, black-fruited Cabernet Sauvignons from the estate: The Ranch and a Reserve Cabernet. There is also a voluptuous, partially barrel-fermented Sauvignon Blanc from one of Andy Beckstoffer's vineyards.

360 Taplin Rd., St. Helena, CA 94574
www.snowdenvineyards.com

Spottswoode Estate St Helena

This historic estate dates back to 1882 and was revived by Mary and the late Dr. Jack Novak in 1972. Located near the base of Spring Mountain just northeast of St. Helena,

SCHUG CARNEROS ESTATE
MORE EUROPEAN IN STYLE, THIS PINOT NOIR IS LEANER THAN MOST NAPA OFFERINGS

SHAFER VINEYARDS
A STEEP VINEYARD SITE PRODUCES SHAFER'S MOST REFINED OF CABERNETS

Spottswoode has consistently produced elegant, complex Cabernet Sauvignon, but in the last few years has kicked it up another notch. The Estate Cabernet, made by Jennifer Williams and consultant Rosemary Cakebread, is dazzling. The less expensive Lyndenhurst bottling is excellent and offers good value. The smooth, fleshy Sauvignon Blanc made from purchased grapes is also quite good. ★ Rising star

1902 Madrona Ave., St. Helena, CA 94574
www.spottswoode.com

Spring Mountain Vineyards
Spring Mountain

If you have seen *Falcon Crest*, you might recognize Spring Mountain's Victorian homestead from the opening credits, but this winery is no Hollywood stage set. It consistently produces layered and complex wines from one of the great AVAs of Napa Valley. The Estate Cabernet Sauvignon, the Elivette blend of Cabernet Sauvignon, Merlot, Cabernet Franc, and Petit Verdot, and a decadent, mouth-filling Sauvignon Blanc are outstanding. Like the best Napa mountain reds, these wines warrant cellaring.

2805 Spring Mountain Rd., St. Helena, CA 94574
www.springmountainvineyard.com

St. Clement St. Helena

St. Clement is a small winery, but a real gem in the crown of the Foster's wine group. Despite some ownership and personnel changes, quality has somehow been consistent over the past 15 years, and its flagship "Oroppas" (the name of former Japanese owner, Sapporo, backward), a Cabernet Sauvignon-based blend, is one of the biggest steals in the valley. In Danielle Cyrot the winery has yet another great up-and-comer in the cellar and continues to produce high-quality and stylish wines across the board.

2867 St. Helena Highway, St. Helena, CA 94574
www.stclement.com

St. Supéry Rutherford

St. Supéry is owned by southern French wine producer Robert Skalli and his family. The winery sits on Highway 29 in Rutherford, but its key estate is the Dollarhide Ranch in the Pope Valley, east of Calistoga. This vineyard supplies the grapes for St. Supéry's world-class Dollarhide Ranch Sauvignon Blanc and very good Dollarhide Ranch Cabernet Sauvignon. Other good wines are the Meritage red and white wines, called Virtú and Elu respectively. Longstanding CEO Michaela Rodeno retired recently after tapping Emma Swain to succeed her.

8440 St. Helena Highway, Rutherford, CA 94573
www.stsupery.com

Staglin Family Vineyard Rutherford

This property on the western bench of Rutherford was planted by André Tchelistcheff in 1965 and supplied fruit for Beaulieu's Georges de Latour Private Reserve before it was purchased by Shari and Garen Staglin in 1986. With the help of grower David Abreu, and a succession of top winemaking consultants including Michel Rolland, Staglin emerged in the 1990s as the preeminent Cabernet Sauvignon producer in Rutherford, and one of the best of the valley. Winemaker Fredrik Johansson scored near perfection with the 2006 Estate Cabernet Sauvignon,

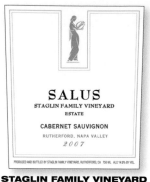

STAGLIN FAMILY VINEYARD
RUTHERFORD'S BENCHMARK CABERNET
FROM THE RUTHERFORD BENCH

raising the bar yet again. Their reserve red wine, Salus, is dependably excellent and do not skip over Staglin's lucid Chardonnnays.

1570 Bella Oaks Lane, Rutherford, CA 94573
www.staglinfamily.com

Stag's Leap Wine Cellars
Stags Leap District
Warren Winiarski's Stag's Leap Wine Cellars emerged from the 1970s as one of California's most recognizable Cabernet Sauvignon labels. It had pulled off a stunning upset of Bordeaux rivals at the famous 1976 Judgment of Paris tasting with its first vintage of 1973 SLV Cabernet made from three-year-old vines. This winery's top Cabernets—Cask 23, Fay Vineyard, and SLV—continue to have a devoted following and have kept pace with the times. They remain excellent examples of classic Stags Leap terroir with deep red fruit, olive, cedar, and anise notes and exceptional overall balance. In 2007, the estate was sold to Chateau Ste Michelle and Piero Antinori.

5766 Silverado Trail, Napa, CA 94558
www.cask23.com

Stags' Leap Winery Stags Leap District
Easily missed from the Silverado Trail and not open to visitors without an appointment, Stags' Leap Winery is tucked into the basalt palisades of the Vaca Mountains, just off the Silverado Trail. The 100-year-old estate was a resort in the 1920s and includes a beautiful and allegedly haunted manor house. The wines are not too shabby either, especially the sturdy The Leap Cabernet Sauvignon, the rightfully renowned Petite Sirah, and the unique and rare estate-bottled Ne Cede Malis red blend.

6150 Silverado Trail, Napa, CA 94558
www.stagsleap.com

Sterling Vineyards Calistoga
One of the powerhouse brands to emerge from California in the 1970s, Sterling was founded by a group of Sterling Paper Company executives including Peter Newton, who would later found Newton Vineyards. The quality of Sterling's wines have not quite kept pace with the rest of the valley, and some of the best wines, like the Three Palms Merlot, come from vineyards owned by others. The winery is a great place to visit, though, with a gondola that carries visitors 300ft (90m) up to a tasting room with towering views over northern Napa Valley.

1111 Dunaweal Lane, Calistoga, CA 94515
www.sterlingvineyards.com

Storybook Mountain Vineyards
Calistoga
Jerry and Ingrid Seps make some of the most unique and inspiring Zinfandels at their property, northwest of Calistoga. From the 1880s to Prohibition, the estate was known as Grimm's Vineyards and Wine Vaults. In 1976, the couple bought the run-down estate and started making the Zinfandels that became their flagship wines, most notably the Mayacamas Range, Estate Reserve, and Eastern Exposures wines. The latter is co-fermented with a small percentage of Viognier in the spirit of Côte-Rôtie.

3835 Highway 128, Calistoga, CA 94515
www.storybookwines.com

STAG'S LEAP WINE CELLARS
BE SURE TO GET THE APOSTROPHE IN THE
RIGHT PLACE—A SINGLE STAG IN THIS CASE

Summers Estate Wines Calistoga
Jim and Beth Summers' first vineyards were in Knights Valley in Sonoma then, in 1996, they bought their current property in Calistoga, replanting 50 acres (30ha) of vines. Vineyard manager and winemaker Ignacio Blancas makes ripe, fruity wines that deliver good value. The best are the estate-grown Reserve Cabernet Sauvignon, Checkmate Bordeaux blend, Knights Valley Merlot, and their La Nude unoaked Chardonnay, sourced from Alexander Valley. They are also the largest producer of Charbono in Napa Valley, making 24,000 bottles.

1171 Tubbs Lane, Calistoga, CA 94515
www.summerswinery.com

Switchback Ridge Calistoga
Switchback Ridge wines are sourced from the family vineyard of John, Joyce, and Kelly Peterson in Calistoga, with the wines made by Bob Foley (Robert Foley, Hourglass, Pride Mountain). Together they produce good, concentrated, and polished Cabernet Sauvignon and Merlot, plus a titanic and layered Petite Sirah that ranks with the best from Napa Valley. The family have owned this estate since 1914 and in 1990 they converted about 20 acres (8ha) of the property to vineyards to make the wines.

No visitor facilities
www.switchbackridge.com

Terra Valentine Spring Mountain
Inventor and engineer Fred Aves built this unique stone winery and villa by hand through the 1960s, infusing it with Greco-Roman imagery and calling the estate Yverdon. As his health declined, so did the estate, until it was bought, restored, and replanted by Angus and Margaret Wurtele. The couple have chosen to work with a young crew, including winemaker Sam Baxter, who is doing a great job with Terra Valentine's Cabernet Sauvignons. Their basic Spring Mountain Cabernet is great value, and the Wurtele and Yverdon bottlings are excellent and improving as the vines mature. ★ **Rising star**

3787 Spring Mountain Rd., St. Helena, CA 94574
www.terravalentine.com

Trefethen Family Vineyards
Oak Knoll District
The Trefethen family owns some 565 acres (230ha) of vineyards in the Oak Knoll District, planted mostly to Chardonnay, Cabernet Sauvignon, and Merlot. Many feel Trefethen has not kept pace with the rest of the valley or its own potential. The cooler climate and restrained style, however, are appreciated by some for their food-friendliness. A 2002 Library Reserve Cabernet tasted in 2009 was excellent, with tremendous complexity, nice black fruit, and great balance. The Chardonnay also seems improved, with pristine green apple and stone fruit flavors unburdened by excessive oak.

1160 Oak Knoll Ave., Spanish Flat, CA 94558
www.trefethen.com

Trinchero Family Estates St. Helena
Sutter Home winery was founded in 1874 and bought by the Trinchero family in 1948. The family struck gold with White Zinfandel rosé in the 1980s and built a strong portfolio of brands, establishing M Trinchero in St. Helena, acquiring Montevina in Amador County, Folie à

Deux, Joel Gott Wines, and Napa Cellars. Each of these labels consistently deliver clean, concentrated wines that are quintessentially Californian, and very good value.

3070 St. Helena Highway North, St. Helena, CA 94574
www.trincherowinery.com

Truchard Vineyards Carneros

Tony and Jo Ann Truchard started in 1974 with 20 acres (8ha) of abandoned prune orchard that they replanted to grape vines. Today, they own a contiguous estate of almost 400 acres (162ha), with 270 acres (110ha) of vines. They sell grapes to over 20 wineries, and built a winery in 1989 to make their own label. The Truchards have found a loyal following for their earthy, bright, and terroir-driven Pinot Noir, Chardonnay, and Cabernet Sauvignon, and a Merlot with barely ripe black cherry, cola, and tea notes.

3234 Old Sonoma Rd., Napa, CA 94559
www.truchardvineyards.com

Viader Vineyards Howell Mountain

Delia Viader's estate is on Howell Mountain, with steep vineyards planted to Bordeaux varieties and Syrah. The Argentina-born Viader raised four children while managing her estate during the 1990s and, today, all four of them are involved in the business. Since 2006, Michel Rolland has served as consultant. The winery produces a Cheval Blanc-inspired blend, a Syrah, and "V", a Petit Verdot-based blend. Viader has also been making single-vineyard wines from other sources under its Dare series.

1120 Deer Park Rd., Deer Park, CA 94576
www.viader.com

Vine Cliff Winery Oakville

Vine Cliff is an often overlooked, small, family winery with steep hillside vineyards on the eastern side of Oakville. It makes three Cabernet Sauvignons: a Napa Valley Cabernet, an Oakville Estate bottling, and the flagship Private Stock 16 Rows Cabernet, all of which are capable of extraordinary depth. Proprietor Rob Sweeney seems to be doing a great job of fine-tuning the estate with help from winemaker Rex Smith and consultant Celia Welch Masyczek, who has worked for Staglin, Hartwell, and Rocca Family. ★ Rising star

7400 Silverado Trail, Napa, CA 94558
www.vinecliff.com

Vineyard 7 & 8 Spring Mountain

Vineyard 7 & 8 is an ambitious estate venture started in 1999 by New Yorkers Launnie and Weezie Steffens. It is managed by their son, Wesley, former cellarmaster at Harlan Estate. The estate released its first wines, the "7" Estate Chardonnay and "8" Cabernet Sauvignon in 2004, both made in a restrained style with good focus and complexity. In 2007, winemaker Luc Morlet, formerly of Peter Michael Winery, joined the team. This is definitely an estate worth keeping an eye on. ★ Rising star

4028 Spring Mountain Rd., St. Helena, CA 94574;
www.vineyard7and8.com

Vineyard 29 St. Helena

Vineyard 29 was founded in 1989, by Theresa Norton and Tom Paine who, with the help of viticulturist David Abreu, planted the vineyard with cuttings from Grace Family. In 2000, Chuck and Anne McMinn purchased the home estate vineyard at the base of Spring Mountain as well as the Aida vineyard a couple of miles to the north. With David Abreu tending the vineyards, and the talented Philippe Melka in the cellar, this winery is on the up. Highlights are the Vineyard 29 Cabernet Sauvignon and Aida Proprietary Red and Zinfandel. ★ Rising star

2929 Highway 29, St. Helena, CA 94574
www.vineyard29.com

Volker Eisele Family Estate Chiles Valley

Volker Eisele is an outstanding Chiles Valley estate that has been owned for 35 years by Volker and Liesel Eisele. The grapes are organically farmed within the rugged confines of Chiles Valley, east from the rest of Napa Valley, and the wines are made by their son, Alexander Eisele, who has a very deft touch with Cabernet Sauvignon. This estate is proving single-handedly that Chiles Valley is capable of making first-class wines. ★ Rising star

3080 Lower Chiles Valley Rd., St. Helena, CA 94574
www.volkereiselefamilyestate.com

Von Strasser Vineyards Diamond Mountain

One of the leading acts on this tough mountain, Von Strasser produces lucid, clean wines with some of the stiff, minerally structure that is inherent in this northwest Napa Valley mountain's terroir. Made by Rudy Von Strasser, the modern range includes the Estate Diamond Mountain Cabernet Sauvignon and several single-vineyard offerings, from Sori Bricco to Rainin and Post. The vineyards face mostly to the east, producing fragrant, focused fruit with clean black and red fruit flavors redolent with minerality. ★ Rising star

1510 Diamond Mountain Rd., Calistoga, CA 94515
www.vonstrasser.com

Whitehall Lane Winery Rutherford

This small- to medium-sized Rutherford winery routinely delivers very nice and reasonably priced wines, especially its Napa Valley and Reserve Napa Valley Cabernet Sauvignons, which are very classic Napa in their style, with plenty of fruit, but also licorice, olive, and mineral notes that make them more elegant than some of the valley's more bombastic offerings. Whitehall Lane has been owned by the Leonardini family since 1993, and the family's home vineyard provides the fruit for the outstanding Leonardini Vineyard Merlot.

1563 St. Helena Highway, St. Helena, CA 94574
www.whitehalllane.com

Wing Canyon Vineyard Mount Veeder

Wing Canyon is a small winery established by Kathy and Bill Jenkins, who purchased a rugged 160 acre (65ha) ranch in 1983. They slowly planted vines and built a small winery, making their first wine in 1991. They grow Cabernet Sauvignon, Merlot, Cabernet Franc, and Chardonnay. There is a lovely Cabernet Sauvignon that is fragrant, elegant, and structured and in many ways typical of Mount Veeder. The Cabernet Franc is produced only in select vintages and their tiny production of lightly oaked Chardonnay is minerally and zesty.

3100 Mount Veeder Rd., Napa, CA 94558
www.wingcanyonvineyard.com

TOURISM IN NAPA VALLEY

Napa Valley's vintners were among the first to open their doors to visitors seeking a taste of the wine country lifestyle. Today, Napa Valley is one of the top tourist attractions in California, attracting direct consumer spending estimated at $1.3 billion per year. In addition to hundreds of full-time public tasting rooms, the valley boasts a number of luxurious spa resorts, from the classic Auberge du Soleil to newcomers like The Carneros Inn. Calistoga is home to new resort Solage, and a number of older hot spring resorts.

Excellent restaurants abound. They include The French Laundry and Bistro Jeanty in Yountville, Terra and Tra Vigne in St. Helena and La Toque in Napa. There are also 10 public and private golf courses in the valley, the most prestigious being Silverado Resort and Meadowood.

Another popular attraction is Daryl Sattui's recently opened medieval-style fortress-cum-winery extravaganza, Castello di Amoroso on Diamond Mountain.

SONOMA AND MARIN

California
Sonoma and Marin Counties

In the world of California wine, Sonoma is the pretty, but shy girl in bad glasses standing behind the class beauty. It is hard to get much attention when the spotlights are perpetually turned on Napa. But what Sonoma lacks in sizzle compared to its famous neighbor, it more than makes up for in soul and sheer diversity. From the sun-drenched Dry Creek Valley to the frigid coastal ridges of the Sonoma Coast, and the cool, bright inclines of Chalk Hill, the slightly rustic, hippie haven of Sonoma County encompasses a vast area of wine-growing potential. Just to the south, Marin County hosts a tiny but growing cadre of vineyards and wineries seeking out even more extreme planting sites.

Major grapes

 Reds

Cabernet Sauvignon

Grenache

Merlot

Pinot Noir

Syrah

Zinfandel

Whites

Chardonnay

Sauvignon Blanc

Viognier

Vintages

2009
A near-ideal vintage, until rains midharvest. Wine quality very much depends on when the grapes were harvested.

2008
Killer frosts in spring, heat spikes later on. Patience was rewarded with good quality.

2007
Very good to excellent for most varieties; low winter rainfall meant smaller yields.

2006
A cool spring led to mixed quality. White grapes fared well, as did the early reds.

2005
A cold and wet spring was a disaster for some Pinot Noir sites; yields were down, but quality was very good.

2004
Smooth and uneventful with an early harvest due to heat spikes. Very concentrated.

Like most of California's wine regions, Sonoma and Marin counties owe their initial wine-growing roots to the Spanish missionaries who planted vines everywhere they settled, to produce their essential sacramental wine. California's commercial wine industry, however, indisputably began in Sonoma, thanks to an enterprising Hungarian immigrant named Agoston Haraszthy who founded Buena Vista winery in 1855.

Sonoma County, by virtue of its size and diverse geography, is best considered not as one wine region but as several. Deeply forested coastal ridges, warm grassland valleys, river bottom floodplains, and rolling mountain foothills all feature in the county's landscape. The county's 13 different American Viticultural Areas (AVAs) are based, in part, on these wildly different microclimates and their underlying geologies.

Despite this diversity, a good deal of Sonoma owes its climate to the presence, or absence, of a single meteorological phenomenon: fog. Especially during the heat of summer, cool ocean air, drawn inland by the warmer valleys, blankets the coast, sneaks through gaps in the coastal range, and winds its way up river valleys to keep temperatures in Sonoma lower by several degrees than in neighboring counties.

The main artery for this natural air-conditioning is the Russian River, which lends its name to Sonoma's central AVA and, thanks to pioneers such as Davis Bynum, Rochioli, and Dehlinger, to stellar Pinot Noirs and Chardonnays. These grape varieties also thrive in the Sonoma Coast AVA overlooking the Pacific, in the Los Carneros AVA, which Sonoma shares with Napa, and in the single foggiest place in the county, the Green Valley of Russian River Valley AVA, whose official boundaries are actually defined by the fog patterns.

Grapes needing more heat, like Cabernet Sauvignon, are grown with great success in the Alexander Valley, Knights Valley, and Sonoma Valley AVAs. Zinfandel, often from treasured vines that can be more than a century old, thrives in Dry Creek Valley along with Grenache, while the steeper areas of the Chalk Hill, Sonoma Mountain, and Rockpile AVAs offer opportunities to grow everything from Viognier to Merlot.

Sonoma's true heart is Burgundian, however, thanks to cult producers such as Kistler, Williams-Selyem, and Marcassin, who sell exquisitely made Chardonnays and Pinot Noirs to mailing list customers who pay whatever they are asked without hesitation. Sonoma's Zinfandels, made by producers like Rafanelli and Limerick Lane, have an equally fanatical following. In the right hands, and more importantly the right site, Sonoma's Cabernet Sauvignons can be profound, as Peter Michael Winery's "Les Pavots" blend has been proving for decades.

Though it hardly registers in volume or size compared to Sonoma, the even foggier and colder Marin County has quietly become a source of excellent Pinot Noir and, in one improbable but remarkable case, Riesling. With just 175 acres (71ha) under vine and only a handful of local wineries, it will be some time before Marin can be considered a truly significant wine region. There are, however, some big names from Sonoma beginning to bottle Pinot Noir from Marin's vineyards, and its future looks bright.

Acorn Winery/Alegria Vineyards
Russian River Valley

Acorn's Alegria Vineyards are interplanted with a number of different varieties, as vineyards were in the early days of California winemaking. The grapes are all harvested, crushed, and fermented together. Much less common today, this practice is known as making a field blend, and is one of the things that make Acorn Winery worth paying attention to. Bill and Betsy Nachbaur run this small operation, just outside Healdsburg, which not only specializes in field blends but also grows varieties uncommon in the area, including Dolcetto and Barbera.

12040 Old Redwood Highway, Healdsburg, CA 95448
www.acornwinery.com

Adobe Road Winery Sonoma Coast

Adobe Road started as a garage project for Kevin and Debra Buckler, eventually becoming more than a hobby with their first commercial vintage in 1999. Funded by Kevin's success in the car-racing business, the winery now offers a broad portfolio of wines made in modest quantities from vineyard sources around Sonoma, as well as Napa County. Wines of note are the Pinot Noir Rosé and the Cabernet Sauvignon from Dry Creek Valley.

1995 S McDowell Blvd., Petaluma, CA 94954
www.adoberoadwines.com

Anaba Sonoma Valley

The recently launched Anaba has attracted a lot of notice with its small portfolio of extremely well-made wines. The range features two classic Rhône blends under the name Coriol, a white wine and a red wine, both of which are excellent. The new incarnation of the old Castle Winery, Anaba's first bottlings have been from fruit purchased elsewhere in Sonoma. The estate vineyards have since been replanted and will begin to feature in the winery's portfolio in the coming years. ★ Rising star

60 Bonneau Rd., Sonoma, CA 95476
www.anabawines.com

Anakota Winery/Verité Knights Valley

Focusing exclusively on Cabernet Sauvignon from Knights Valley AVA, Anakota is one of two projects in Sonoma marking the collaboration between Jess Jackson, of Jackson Family Estates, and French winemaker Pierre Seillan. The winery produces two single-vineyard wines from its estate vineyards, Helena Montana and Helena Dakota. Seillan's other project with Jackson, Verité, shares the winemaking facility, and also focuses on Sonoma with three Bordeaux blends, from mountain fruit. Both labels are made in a spare-no-expense fashion and are impressive examples of what Sonoma is capable of. When it comes to producing world-class red wines, Sonoma can even rival Napa Valley. ★ Rising star

4611 Thomas Rd., Healdsburg, CA 95448
www.anakota.com

Arista Winery Russian River Valley

A newcomer in the Russian River Valley, Arista has quickly asserted itself as a quality producer of vineyard-designated Pinot Noir, all carefully made by winemaker Leslie Cisneros. The winery's estate vineyards are only just coming on stream, so for now, the wines are made from excellent vineyard sources in Sonoma as well as the

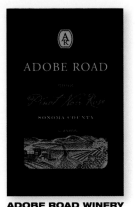

ADOBE ROAD WINERY
CRISP AND DRY WITH REFRESHING FLAVORS
OF CRANBERRY AND WATERMELON

ANAKOTA WINERY
COOLER HILLSIDES YIELD A STRUCTURED,
DENSE WINE WITH BRIGHT FRUIT

Anderson Valley. Look for their Toboni Vineyard and Ferrington Vineyard Pinot Noirs, and do not miss their Gewurztraminer, which can be bought at the winery after a stroll in the stunning Japanese garden. ★ Rising star

7015 Westside Rd., Healdsburg, CA 95448
www.aristawinery.com

Arrowood Vineyards Sonoma Valley

Arrowood Vineyards was started as a side project while founder Dick Arrowood was busy putting Sonoma's Chateau St. Jean on the map, as head winemaker. Arrowood has been one of Sonoma's better-known names for more than two decades. At its height, Arrowood's finest wines were its Chardonnays, but the portfolio has broadened to include big Bordeaux- and Rhône-style red wines. Purchased by the Mondavis in 2000, the winery has changed hands several times since then, but Dick Arrowood still remains at the helm.

14347 Sonoma Highway, Glen Ellen, CA 95442
www.arrowoodvineyards.com

Audelssa Estate Sonoma Valley

With its impressive terraced vineyards on the side of the Mayacamas Mountains, Audelssa Estate focuses mostly on making red wines in the Bordeaux style (though in some vintages they have made a Chardonnay). The winery got its name by combining the names of founder Dan Schaefer's two daughters. In addition to the Bordeaux varieties, the winery has started bottling a Zinfandel, as well as a blend named Tephra, which is an unlikely, but tasty mix of Cabernet Sauvignon, Merlot, Syrah, and Zinfandel.

2992 Cavedale Rd., Glen Ellen, CA 95442
www.audelssa.com

Auteur Russian River Valley

Auteur is one of the more impressive new wine labels to arrive on the scene in the last 10 years. Owning no vineyards, proprietor and winemaker Kenneth Juhasz buys Pinot Noir and Chardonnay grapes on contract from top growers in northern California and Oregon, to craft intense, yet elegant wines. Unmistakably New World in quality, the wines are extremely well made across the portfolio, especially the Sonoma Stage Pinot Noir from the Sonoma Coast AVA, and the Manchester Ridge Pinot Noir from the Mendocino Ridge AVA. ★ Rising star

No visitor facilities
www.auteurwines.com

Baker Lane Sonoma Coast

Started by serial restaurateur Stephen Singer, Baker Lane remains a small, lesser-known wine label making Pinot Noir and Syrah. The wines are made from both purchased grapes and the estate's sustainably farmed vineyards outside of Sebastopol in the Sonoma Coast AVA. The wines are distinctively cool climate, with Old-World styling that appeals to those seeking subtlety rather than sizzle. In addition to the estate bottlings, the winery's Hurst Vineyard wines are also excellent. Production totals a miniscule 18,000 bottles. ★ Rising star

No visitor facilities
www.bakerlanevineyards.com

SONOMA AND MARIN

Marin offers little sign of "wine country" to the visiting traveler, with wineries and vineyards often in separate locations and not geared for visitors. Sonoma, on the other hand, presents almost the opposite problem, with clusters of wineries spread over a wide area, the distance between them often confounding would-be visitors. Among Sonoma's 13 different AVAs, the highest concentration of wineries is found in the Alexander Valley and Dry Creek Valley around the towns of Geyserville and Healdsburg, in the Russian River Valley south of Healdsburg, and in the Sonoma Valley between the towns of Kenwood and Sonoma.

SONOMA MOUNTAIN AND SONOMA VALLEY

Arrowood Vineyards 75	Pride Mountain Vineyards 63
Audelssa Estate 70	Ravenswood 78
Benziger Family Winery 73	Roessler Cellars 79
Bucklin Vineyards 75	Saxon-Brown 79
Chateau St. Jean 65	Sbragia Family Vineyards 74
Deerfield Ranch 66	Sebastiani Winery 79
Gundlach Bundschu Winery 80	Sojourn Cellars 79
Hanzell Vineyards 77	St. Francis Winery 64
Imagery Estate 71	Ty Caton 72
Kenwood Vineyards 65	Valley of the Moon Winery 76

ALEXANDER VALLEY AND KNIGHTS VALLEY

Anakota Winery/Verité 25	Medlock Ames 24
Blue Rock Vineyard 4	Michel-Schlumberger Wine Estate 11
Francis Ford Coppola Winery 10	Peter Michael Winery 27
Hanna Winery 26	J. Rickards Winery 4
Jordan Vineyard 12	Stuhlmuller Vineyards 23
Longboard Vineyards 25	

GREEN VALLEY AND CHALK HILL

Chalk Hill Estate 28	Limerick Lane 29
Dutton Estate 52	Littorai 51
Freeman Winery 49	Marimar Torres 48
Hartford Family Winery 45	Wind Gap Wines 46
Iron Horse Vineyards 47	

DRY CREEK VALLEY

Bella Vineyards 6	Dry Creek Vineyards 17
Ferrari-Carano Vineyards 5	Gallo Family Vineyards 19
Fritz 3	Kokomo Winery 8
Mazzocco Sonoma 14	Nalle Winery 16
Montemaggiore 18	Papapietro Perry 8
Quivira Vineyards 17	A. Rafanelli 17
Rancho Zabaco 15	Ridge Lytton Springs 13
Rued Winery 15	Truett Hurst Vineyards 7
Unti Vineyards 9	

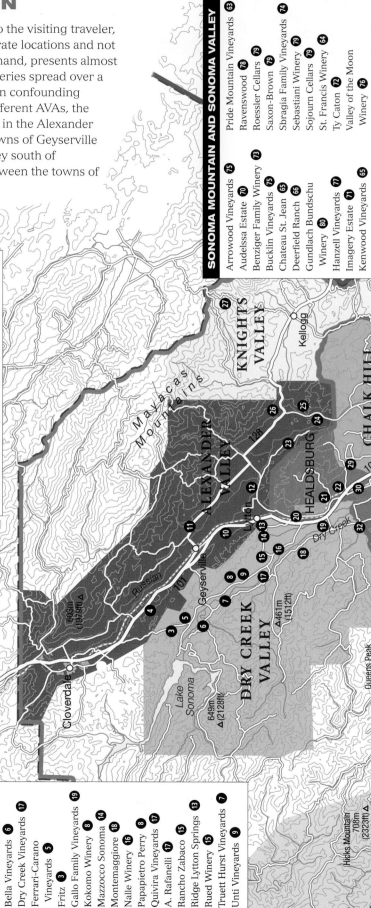

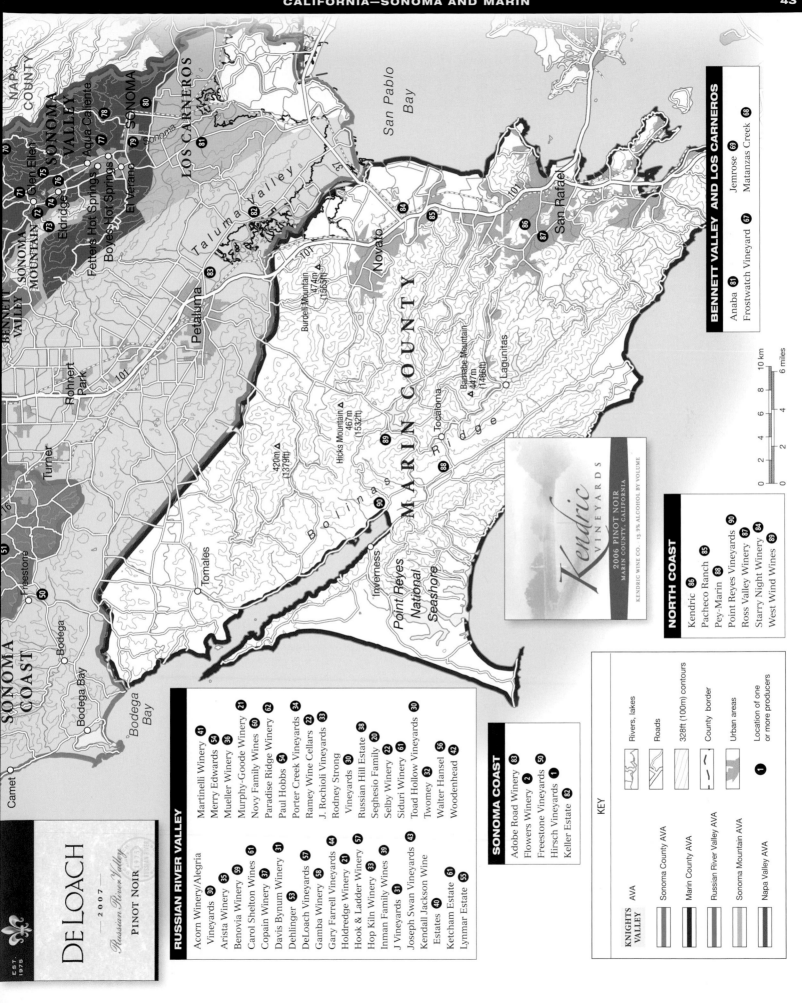

San Pablo Bay

NAPA COUNTY

SONOMA VALLEY

LOS CARNEROS

70
71
72 73 74 75 76 77 78 79 80
SONOMA MOUNTAIN
Glen Ellen
Eldridge
Fetters Hot Springs
Boyes Hot Springs
Agua Caliente
El Verano
Sonoma
81

BENNETT VALLEY

Petaluma
83
82
Taluma Valley
37
101

Burdell Mountain
474m
(1565ft)

Rohnert Park
101
Turner
16

MARIN COUNTY

Novato
84
85
San Rafael
86
87

Barnabe Mountain
447m
(1466ft)
Lagunitas

Hicks Mountain
467m
(1532ft)
89

420m
(1379ft)

88

Bolinas Ridge

90

SONOMA COAST

51
Freestone
50
Camet
Bodega
Bodega Bay
Bodega Bay

Tomales

Tocaloma

Inverness

Point Reyes National Seashore

BENNETT VALLEY AND LOS CARNEROS

Anaba 81
Frostwatch Vineyard 67
Jemrose 69
Matanzas Creek 68

NORTH COAST

Kendric 86
Pacheco Ranch 85
Pey-Marin 88
Point Reyes Vineyards 90
Ross Valley Winery 87
Starry Night Winery 84
West Wind Wines 89

Kendric VINEYARDS
2006 PINOT NOIR
MARIN COUNTY, CALIFORNIA
KENDRIC WINE CO. · 13.9% ALCOHOL BY VOLUME

Scale
0   2   4   6   8   10 km
0   2   4   6 miles

RUSSIAN RIVER VALLEY

Acorn Winery/Alegria Vineyards 30
Arista Winery 35
Benovia Winery 59
Carol Shelton Wines 61
Copain Winery 37
Davis Bynum Winery 31
Dehlinger 53
DeLoach Vineyards 57
Gamba Winery 58
Gary Farrell Vineyards 44
Holdredge Winery 21
Hook & Ladder Winery 57
Hop Kiln Winery 33
Inman Family Wines 39
J Vineyards 31
Joseph Swan Vineyards 43
Kendall Jackson Wine Estates 40
Ketcham Estate 61
Lynmar Estate 55
Martinelli Winery 41
Merry Edwards 54
Mueller Winery 36
Murphy-Goode Winery 21
Novy Family Wines 60
Paradise Ridge Winery 62
Paul Hobbs 54
Porter Creek Vineyards 34
Ramey Wine Cellars 22
J. Rochioli Vineyards 33
Rodney Strong Vineyards 30
Russian Hill Estate 38
Seghesio Family 20
Selby Winery 22
Siduri Winery 61
Toad Hollow Vineyards 30
Twomey 32
Walter Hansel 56
Woodenhead 42

SONOMA COAST

Adobe Road Winery 83
Flowers Winery 2
Freestone Vineyards 50
Hirsch Vineyards 1
Keller Estate 82

KEY

Rivers, lakes
Roads
328ft (100m) contours
County border
Urban areas
1 Location of one or more producers

AVA
Sonoma County AVA
Marin County AVA
Russian River Valley AVA
Sonoma Mountain AVA
Napa Valley AVA

KNIGHTS VALLEY

DE LOACH
EST 1975
Russian River Valley
2007
PINOT NOIR

CAROL SHELTON WINES
A RICH, CHOCOLATEY ZINFANDEL FULL OF
BLACK FRUITS AND WITH A PLEASING ACIDITY

Bella Vineyards　Dry Creek Valley

This family-run winery has made its mark with delicious Zinfandels and Syrahs in the last few years. Scott and Lynn Adams bought their vineyard in 1995 and have slowly been expanding their portfolio of wines as they deepen their own expertise. Winemaker Joe Healy, with the help of consulting winemaker Michael Dashe, has been crafting high-quality wines from their estate, as well as other vineyards owned by their family in Dry Creek Valley and neighboring Alexander Valley. The Adams' Big River Ranch vineyard has become a well-known source for high-quality Zinfandel.

9711 West Dry Creek Rd., Healdsburg, CA 95448
www.bellawinery.com

Benovia Winery　Russian River Valley

Benovia is focused on Pinot Noir from various cool-climate sites around California. It is a relatively new producer (established in 2005) which just happens to have a secret weapon: proprietor Joe Anderson owns the Cohn Vineyard, one of the oldest plantings of Pinot Noir in the Russian River Valley. The winery produces a Pinot Noir from this vineyard as well as several others from the Russian River and Sonoma Coast AVAs, along with a few Chardonnays and a Zinfandel from the Cohn Vineyard.

3339 Hartman Rd., Santa Rosa, CA 95401
www.benoviawinery.com

Benziger Family Winery　Sonoma Valley

Benziger Family Winery defies easy categorization. Their Glen Ellen wines were once ubiquitous on grocery store shelves across America. Glen Ellen, the brand, was sold in 1993, while the winery continued to produce very large quantities of wine for national distribution. Today, Benziger has partially reinvented itself with an intense focus on sustainability. The top tiers of the portfolio, their Estate, Signaterra, Tribute, and de Coelo wines, are hand-crafted from Biodynamically farmed vineyard sites in some of Sonoma County's most extreme microclimates.

1883 London Ranch Rd., Glen Ellen, CA 95442
www.benziger.com

Bjornstad Cellars　Russian River Valley

Greg Bjornstad runs his eponymous winery as a one man operation but, with his experience, it is not hard to understand how he manages to do it so successfully. Bjornstad got his start on the farming side of the business managing vineyards for top producers such as Flowers, Newton, and Joseph Phelps. In 1999, he started the successful Tandem Winery with Greg LaFolette, and then went on to found Bjornstad Cellars, his own label, in 2005. The winery makes several Chardonnays and Pinot Noirs from vineyards in Sonoma County. ★**Rising star**

No visitor facilities
www.bjornstadcellars.com

Blue Rock Vineyard　Alexander Valley

Named for the blue-green serpentine rock that dominates the soil at this small family farm, Blue Rock Vineyard has been making miniscule quantities of high-quality red wine for a decade. Proprietor Kenny Kahn, along with winemaker Nick Goldschmidt, produces about 21,600 bottles of Cabernet Sauvignon and Syrah. The winery,

DAVIS BYNUM WINERY
A FINE BALANCE OF RIPENESS AND ACIDITY
FROM A WARM SPOT IN RUSSIAN RIVER

located next door to Silver Oak, also grows a few rows of Malbec, which have been known to end up in a bottle. Blue Rock's compelling Syrah is an earthy, almost austere wine and the Cabernets have admirable restraint.

24511 Rich Ranch Rd., Cloverdale, CA 95425
www.bluerockvineyard.com

Bucklin Vineyards　Sonoma Valley

Bucklin's Old Hill Ranch is widely accepted as the oldest actively farmed vineyard in Sonoma County; the Zinfandel vines date back to well before the turn of the 20th century. Now owned by Anne and Otto Teller, and operated by their children since 2000, Bucklin produces a very fine, organically farmed Zinfandel from the Old Hill property as well as a Cabernet Sauvignon and wines from grapes purchased from other growers. The portfolio is generally high quality, but the crown jewel is undoubtedly the Old Hill Zinfandel.

8 Old Hill Ranch Rd., Glen Ellen, CA 95442
www.buckzin.com

Carlisle Winery　Russian River Valley

Software engineer-turned-winemaker Mike Officer and his Carlisle Winery represent an early version of the winemaking ventures that are much more common today. Officer began making Zinfandel in his garage in the mid-1990s, and his obsession took over his life. Officially launched in 1998, Carlisle has grown into a successful winery, and Officer left his day job in 2004 to concentrate on winemaking, along with his wife and co-winemaker Jay Maddox. Carlisle is well known for its Zinfandels and red Rhône varietals, including its Petite Sirah.

No visitor facilities
www.carlislewinery.com

Carol Shelton Wines　Russian River Valley

One of the early female pioneers in the largely male-dominated California wine industry, Carol Shelton was studying poetry at University of California, Davis when she stumbled on the winemaking program. In 2000, after 19 years as a winemaker, she started her own label focused exclusively on Zinfandel, and her wines quickly won wide acclaim. Shelton makes around 60,000 bottles of wine annually, spread across several creatively named Zinfandels.

3354-B Coffey Lane, Santa Rosa, CA 95403
www.carolshelton.com

Chalk Hill Estate　Chalk Hill

Chalk Hill, well known for its widely distributed Chardonnay, is the result of the considerable efforts and investment of founder Frederick Furth. He first glimpsed the property from his plane in 1972. Now totalling more than 1,400 acres (567ha), this massive estate makes a large portfolio of wines, including Cabernet Sauvignon, Merlot, Pinot Gris, Sauvignon Blanc, Chardonnay, and, recently, a Syrah. Chalk Hill's top bottlings, including Founder's Block Chardonnay and Furth Bordeaux Blend, are usually excellent. The estate is very hospitality oriented, and is a good bet for an afternoon visit.

10300 Chalk Hill Rd., Healdsburg, CA 95448
www.chalkhill.com

Chasseur Russian River Valley

After finding out that someone had already taken the name "Hunter" for their winery, Bill Hunter decided that the French translation, "Chasseur", sounded better anyway. Since 1994, Hunter has been making exquisite small-production, single-vineyard Pinot Noirs and Chardonnays to growing acclaim. A one-man brand and operation, Chasseur's wines can be hard to find, but they are not hard to like. Elegant and poised, they are beautifully and consistently made. The Chardonnays evoke comparisons with the Old World, and the Pinot Noirs are positively outstanding. Highly recommended.

No visitor facilities
www.chasseurwines.com

Chateau St. Jean Sonoma Valley

Founded in 1973, Chateau St. Jean is part of the old guard of Sonoma, and has grown to produce a very large, and somewhat undistinguished, portfolio of wines. The winery was an early pioneer of vineyard-designated wines, but won its greatest acclaim for its Cabernet Sauvignon-based blend, Cinq Cépages. Now part of the Foster's Wine Estates portfolio, the winery continues to produce a broad range, including the famed Cinq Cépages. Winemaker Margo Van Staavere has been making the wine for more than two decades.

8555 Sonoma Highway, Kenwood, CA 95452
www.chateaustjean.com

Copain Winery Russian River Valley

Copain's co-founder Wells Guthrie left an administrative job at *Wine Spectator* magazine in 1997 to be a harvest intern in France's Northern Rhône Valley. He returned with a passion to make European-style wines in California and has not looked back since. Guthrie, with the help of partner Kevin McQuown, has turned Copain into a celebrated boutique winery known for restrained, elegant wines in the Burgundy and Rhône styles. While the winery owns a tiny patch of vineyard, most wines are made from very fine purchased fruit. In particular, look for the James Berry Vineyard Syrah from Paso Robles.

7800 Eastside Rd., Healdsburg, CA 95448
www.copainwines.com

Corda Marin

Brothers Hank and David Corda opted to close their family's dairy farm in the late 1980s and instead planted 50 acres (20ha) of grapes. The Corda family have been farming in Marin County in one form or another since the late 19th century, so their latest incarnation and success as vintners does not come as a huge surprise. The winery, which is the largest grower in the county, produces a number of different wines from Cabernet Sauvignon, Merlot, Syrah, and Pinot Noir. The Pinot Noir is the best of the portfolio and excellent value.

No visitor facilities
707 781 9310

Davis Bynum Winery Russian River Valley

Davis Bynum is a pioneering winery claiming many firsts, including being the first winery established along Westside Road in the heart of the Russian River Valley. The road now hosts some of the top Pinot Noir producers in the country. Davis Bynum was also the first to produce a single-vineyard Pinot Noir from the Russian River Valley, in 1973. The winery continues to make good Chardonnay and Pinot. In 2007, founder Davis Bynum sold the winery to the Klein family, but remains involved.

11455 Old Redwood Highway, Healdsburg, CA 95448
www.davisbynum.com

Deerfield Ranch Sonoma Valley

The unassuming winery Deerfield Ranch makes wines from over 15 vineyards around northern California—everything from Sangiovese to Zinfandel to Pinot Noir. Winemaker and proprietor Robert Rex also produces his own grapeseed oil. Rex's Pinot Noirs and red blends are his best wines, especially the Pinot Noir from the very old Cohn Vineyard, and the moderately priced Red Rex, an unlikely blend of Cabernet Sauvignon, Merlot, Syrah, Petit Verdot, Sangiovese, Cabernet Franc, and Zinfandel.

10200 Sonoma Highway, Kenwood, CA 95452
www.deerfieldranch.com

Dehlinger Russian River Valley

One of the original boutique wineries in the Russian River Valley, Dehlinger has been producing highly sought-after wines for more than three decades. Established by Tom Dehlinger in 1975, when some areas of the Russian River Valley were still considered dubious territory, the winery has grown in stature far more than it has grown in size. Currently producing only around 84,000 bottles of wine each year, the winery mostly sells its coveted Pinot Noirs, Chardonnays, and Syrahs to restaurants and mailing list customers. The winery also makes a Cabernet Sauvignon and an excellent rosé.

4101 Vine Hill Rd., Sebastopol, CA 95472
www.dehlingerwinery.com

DeLoach Vineyards Russian River Valley

DeLoach Vineyards was established in 1973 by forward-thinking Cecil DeLoach, a retired fireman from San Francisco. The winery grew from its small, early beginnings into one of the better known Sonoma wine brands, with an oversized production and wide national distribution. Since the winery was purchased by French wine magnate Jean-Charles Boisset, in 2003, the wines have increased significantly in quality at the top end of the portfolio. Most of the OFS (Our Finest Selection) wines and the single-vineyard wines are made with great care from Biodynamic, organic, and sustainably farmed vineyards.

1791 Olivet Rd., Santa Rosa, CA 95401
www.deloachvineyards.com

Derbès Russian River Valley

A tiny operation, Derbès winery deserves special attention for its extremely fine Chardonnay and Pinot Noir. Owner and winemaker Cécile Lemerle-Derbès grew up in France and practiced her winemaking craft around the world before moving to California. She worked at a number of California wineries, including a stint at Opus One, before setting up her own label in 2001. Now she crafts exquisite wines in very small quantities from some of the best sources of Pinot Noir and Chardonnay in Sonoma. ★ Rising star

No visitor facilities
www.derbeswines.com

CHARDONNAY HEAVEN

Consisting of 856 acres (346ha) of owned or leased vineyards, the Dutton Ranch is one of the highest-quality sources for Chardonnay in all of California. The ranch, which has been family owned and farmed since 1964, is the continuation of a farming tradition started by Warren Dutton in 1881, when he bought the family's first 200 acre (81ha) farm outside Santa Rosa. After half a century of growing fruit trees and hops, the family switched to growing wine grapes, and their vineyards have produced some of the most celebrated Chardonnays in America. The list of wineries making single-vineyard wines from Dutton Ranch grapes reads like a who's who of top California wineries: Kistler, Cain, Chasseur, Patz & Hall, and Lewis, to name just a few. The latest generation of the family includes brothers Steve and Joe Dutton, who each have their own wineries: Dutton-Goldfield and Dutton Estate.

DRY CREEK VINEYARDS
A RICH, POWERFUL WINE WITH SMOOTH
TANNINS AND DEEP RED FRUIT

FERRARI-CARANO VINEYARDS
A CLASSIC BORDEAUX BLEND THAT
AGES BEAUTIFULLY FOR A DECADE

Dry Creek Vineyards Dry Creek Valley

Some wineries have been around for so long that when they started, naming themselves after the place they made wine was far more about practicality than branding. Family-owned and operated since being founded by David Stare in 1972, the winery has always been the standard bearer for the Dry Creek Valley. And with good reason. The winery manages to produce a vast range of wines of unusually consistent quality. The top bottlings, such as the Beeson Ranch Zinfandel and the Endeavour Cabernet Sauvignon are extremely high quality.

3770 Lambert Bridge Rd., Healdsburg, CA 95448
www.drycreekvineyard.com

DuMOL Russian River Valley

DuMOL founders Kerry Murphy and Michael Verlander have carefully crafted a jewel of a winery focused on making distinctive Chardonnay and Pinot Noir from 25 acres (10ha) of Biodynamically farmed sites on the ridges and hillsides of the Russian River Valley. Winemaker Andy Smith crafts extremely well balanced, ageworthy wines which, at their best, are electrifying. The wines are given simple Irish surnames in keeping with Murphy's heritage. While known for its Burgundian varietals, the winery also produces one or two Syrahs and a Viognier. All the wines are sold exclusively to a mailing list.

No visitor facilities
www.dumol.com

DuNah Estate Russian River Valley

The 44 acre (18ha) DuNah Estate sits just outside the town of Sebastopol in Russian River Valley. The retirement dream of owners Rick and Diane DuNah, the winery's 10 acres (4ha) of sustainably farmed vineyards are planted with Pinot Noir and Chardonnay, which winemaker Greg LaFolette turns into less than 36,000 bottles of wine. In addition to the estate wines, DuNah also produces a Syrah/Sangiovese blend from Mendocino, a very good dry Gewurztraminer, and a Pinot and a Chardonnay made from other Sonoma and Sonoma Coast vineyards.

no visitor facilities
www.dunahwinery.com

Dutton Estate
Green Valley of Russian River Valley

Dutton Ranch, just outside the little town of Graton, grows nearly 1,100 acres (445ha) of wine grapes, most of which are sold to many of California's top wineries. However, some of the grapes go into Dutton Estate, under the supervision of Joe Dutton, who, along with his brother Steve, runs Dutton Ranch today. Joe and winemaker Mat Gustafson make many different small production wines. Keep an eye out for the Dutton Palms Chardonnay and, from the vineyard next door, the Manzana Pinot Noir—both good expressions of the foggy Green Valley AVA.

8757 Green Valley Rd., Sebastopol, CA 95472
www.duttonestate.com

Dutton-Goldfield Winery
Green Valley of Russian River Valley

Dutton-Goldfield Winery, a partnership between winegrower Steve Dutton and winemaker Dan Goldfield, represents the other half of the Dutton Ranch legacy.

Steve co-owns the family ranch with his brother Joe, and uses grapes from the family's vineyards in Dutton-Goldfield's small-production wines. The winery focuses on Chardonnay, Pinot Noir, and Syrah, made from estate fruit as well as select vineyard sites around Sonoma County. The Dutton Ranch Chardonnay is particularly worth seeking out for its balance and classic flavor profile, as is the Sanchietti Vineyard Pinot Noir.

No visitor facilities
www.duttongoldfield.com

Enkidu Winery Sonoma Valley

Winemaker and owner Phillip Staehle spent nearly a decade as a winemaker at Carmenet vineyards in the late 1980s and early 1990s. Enkidu Winery, named after a character in the ancient Epic of Gilgamesh, is Phillip's attempt to get back to his roots, so to speak. Enkidu purchases fruit from growers around Sonoma and Napa. The wines are made in small quantities with great care, and a tendency toward letting the fruit shine without much oak influence. Do not miss the Humbaba red blend, an excellent wine and fantastic value. ★Rising star

No visitor facilities
www.enkiduwines.com

Ferrari-Carano Vineyards Dry Creek Valley

Ferrari-Carano is one of the most visible wineries in Sonoma's Dry Creek Valley. Well known for its beautiful gardens, it is a frequent stop on many tours. Started by Don Carano in 1985, the vineyard now consists of more than 1,400 acres (567ha) and two separate wineries. The best wine of the portfolio is the intense, smooth, red Bordeaux-blend, Trésor. The limited-production Eldorado Noir, a Black Muscat, and Eldorado Gold, from Semillon and Sauvignon Blanc, are also worth seeking out.

8761 Dry Creek Rd., Healdsburg, CA 95448
www.ferrari-carano.com

Flowers Winery Sonoma Coast

When Walt and Joan Flowers first visited this property, they had to hike in to see it. There were no roads, nor were there many people who thought that growing grapes that far out on the Sonoma Coast was really a good idea. But the Flowers proceeded to build what may be the quintessential Sonoma Coast winery. Since 1993, the winery has been making stellar and long-lived Pinot Noirs and Chardonnays with lots of French oak. Try the Moon Select range of wines, from their best vineyards.

28500 Seaview Rd., Cazadero, CA 95421
www.flowerswinery.com

Fort Ross Vineyards Sonoma Coast

Fort Ross Vineyards is a mere mile from the crashing surf of the rugged Pacific Coast, and would be noteworthy for its beautiful Pinot Noirs alone. However, this winery stands out for producing one of the best Pinotages in the world. Owners Lester and Linda Schwartz met while at college in South Africa and, when they decided to start a winery, they planted this South African crossing of Pinot Noir and Cinsault, along with their estate Pinot Noir and Chardonnay. All of their wines are highly recommended.

No visitor facilities
www.fortrossvineyard.com

Francis Ford Coppola Winery
Alexander Valley

Movie director Francis Ford Coppola hardly needs an introduction. A long-time wine-lover, Coppola purchased the historic Inglenook Estate in Napa and built a very successful wine brand. The Coppola empire has since been divided into his eponymous winery in Alexander Valley and Rubicon Estate, which remains in Napa. The Sonoma establishment offers a vast range of wines, but Coppola's Diamond Collection wines stand out for great value and consistent performance.

300 via Archimedes, Geyserville, CA 95441
www.franciscoppolawinery.com

Freeman Winery Sonoma Coast

After successful careers in business and academia respectively, Ken and Akiko Freeman decided to pursue their mutual love of great Pinot Noir. They bought a small winery in 2001 and purchased grapes from small growers in western Sonoma County, slowly growing their winery to its current 65,000-bottle production. The wines, made by Akiko, are delicate, poised, and ageworthy. Her Ryo-Fu Chardonnay is outstanding, and the Akiko's Cuvée Pinot Noir is tremendous. The estate's own vineyards have recently come on stream. ★ **Rising star**

1300 Montgomery Rd., Sebastopol, CA 95472
www.freemanwinery.com

Freestone Vineyards Sonoma Coast

Vintner Joseph Phelps, well known for his eponymous Napa winery, which produces acclaimed Bordeaux-style wines, searched for years to find the right place to build a second winery focused on Burgundy-style wines. In 1999, he found 100 acres (40ha) of vineyards in the Sonoma Coast AVA near the town of Freestone, and Freestone Vineyards was born. Farmed Biodynamically (as are all of Phelps's vineyards), the winery began producing Pinot Noir and Chardonnay in the 2005 vintage. The wines, so far, are showing promise. ★ **Rising star**

12747 El Camino Bodega, Freestone, CA 95472
www.freestonevineyards.com

Fritz Dry Creek Valley

Fritz winery is worth visiting for its architecture and gardens alone. This subterranean winery, with its cascading hillside of herbs, wildflowers, and native plants, also happens to make excellent wines. Founders Jay and Barbara Fritz, with their son Clayton and winemaker Brad Longton, produce a top-notch Zinfandel as well as one of the best Cabernet Sauvignons made in Dry Creek Valley. Wine lovers with a bit of a sweet tooth will want to keep an eye out for their late-harvest Zinfandel.

24691 Dutcher Creek Rd., Cloverdale, CA 95425
www.fritzwinery.com

Frostwatch Vineyard Bennett Valley

The owner of Frostwatch Vineyard, Brett Raven, was a lawyer who bought vineyard land in Sonoma's Bennett Valley, and fell more in love with it than he had expected. After leaving his law practice in 1995, he plunged head first into the wine business, working in cellars by day and taking winemaking classes at night. After working at

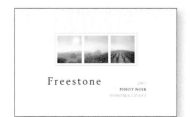

FREESTONE VINEYARDS
A COOL GROWING SEASON WITH SUMMER FOG MEANS BRIGHT, STONY FLAVORS

FREEMAN VINEYARDS
RYO-FU MEANS "COLD WIND" IN JAPANESE, AND MEANS DELICACY IN THIS WINE

several wineries, Raven recently began to make his own wine. He now concentrates fully on Frostwatch, where he makes a range of wines with particularly excellent Merlot and Chardonnay. ★ **Rising star**

5560 Bennett Valley Rd., Santa Rosa, CA 95404
www.frostwatch.com

Gallo Family Vineyards Dry Creek Valley

Gallo Family Vineyards is the current incarnation of one of North America's most successful wine brands. The Gallos are also one of California's two winemaking dynasties (the other being the Mondavis of Napa). Now run by Gina and Matt Gallo, grandchildren of founders Ernest and Julio, the winery continues to produce vast quantities of wines that are sold everywhere. The wines to pay attention to are the single-vineyard and estate wines, especially the Cabernet Sauvignons, which are serious and substantial.

320 Center St., Healdsburg, CA 95448
www.gallosonoma.com

Gamba Winery Russian River Valley

The Gamba family have been farming grapes on this plot of land in the Russian River Valley since Augustino Gamba purchased it in 1947. In 1999, Augustino Jr. and his wife launched the Gamba label, producing small quantities of Zinfandel and Cabernet Sauvignon from the family's organic, dry-farmed (without irrigation) vineyard. The Gamba Zinfandel has become one of the benchmarks for the AVA, and is now highly sought-after, with good reason; this Zinfandel is one of the best in Sonoma.

2912 Woolsey Rd., Windsor, CA 95492
www.gambawinery.com

Gary Farrell Vineyards
Russian River Valley

Gary Farrell can see his career mapped out in the vineyards below his perch on a ridge above the Westside Road. Farrell got his winemaking start in 1978, working for some of the region's pioneers who are his neighbors today. He began his own label in 1982 and, in 2000, he built his own winery and tasting room. Farrell's focus and passion have always been on Pinot Noir, and with current winemaker Susan Reed this continues to be the case.

10701 Westside Rd., Healdsburg, CA 95448
www.garyfarrellwines.com

Gundlach Bundschu Winery
Sonoma Valley

Few wineries in California can boast 150 years of continuous family ownership, but Gundlach Bundschu is one of them. Founded in 1858 by Bavarian immigrant Jacob Gundlach as the Rhinefarm vineyard, it produced renowned wines until Prohibition. Resurrected by the family in 1938, the estate sold its grapes to others until 1970, when it re-opened its doors. After 30 years of growth, the winery decided to make only wines from its estate-grown fruit, and quality seems to be increasing. Recent vintages of the Pinot Noir (low yields, hand-harvested, and aged in French oak) have been excellent.

2000 Denmark St., Sonoma, CA 95476
www.gunbun.com

Halleck Vineyards Russian River Valley

Marketing executive Ross Halleck and his wife Jennifer grow 1 acre (0.4ha) of grapes behind their house, from which they make their top bottling of Pinot Noir in appropriately small quantities. The winery also sources grapes from around Sonoma County. Winemaker Rick Davis and consultant Greg LaFollette manage the annual production. The proceeds of this backyard vineyard have been dedicated to putting the Halleck's three sons through college. The winery's top bottling, the aptly named Three Sons, is excellent. ★ **Rising star**

No visitor facilities
www.halleckvineyard.com

Hanna Winery Russian River Valley

Home winemaking is often a slippery slope to vineyard ownership, as Dr. Elias Hanna can attest. The Syrian-born heart surgeon bought 12 acres (5ha) in the Russian River Valley in 1970, and he and his children dabbled in home winemaking with growing enthusiasm. Today, Hanna owns 600 acres (245ha) of land and farms 250 acres (100ha) of estate vineyards in the Russian River Valley, Alexander Valley, and Sonoma Valley AVAs. The winery's Bordeaux-styled wines are the best efforts, with the Bismark Mountain Cabernet Sauvignon and Russian River Valley Sauvignon Blanc leading the way.

9280 Highway 128, Healdsburg, CA 95448
www.hannawinery.com

Hanzell Vineyards Sonoma Valley

Hanzell is held in great reverence among true California Pinot Noir connoisseurs, for its heritage, the quality of the wines, and the great lengths and expense that are sometimes required to acquire a bottle or two. The estate vineyard, planted in 1953, is the oldest Pinot Noir vineyard in North America, and the single bottling of Pinot is sold only to mailing list customers. The winery produces a range of Chardonnays as well, including the Sebella label, which is more readily available, if no less popular. All the wines, made for 30 years by winemaker Bob Sessions (who recently handed over the reins to Michael McNeil), age beautifully over several decades. Highly recommended.

18596 Lomita Ave., Sonoma, CA 95476
www.hanzell.com

Hartford Family Winery
Green Valley of Russian River Valley

Tucked into a hillside that overlooks rolling vineyards and a forested valley, Hartford Family Winery is but a stone's throw from the Russian River itself. Founded in 1994 under the name Hartford Court, as part of Jess Jackson's vast wine empire, the winery initially focused on making Russian River Valley Pinot Noir and Zinfandel. Over time, Chardonnay has been added to the mix and the winery makes remarkable examples of all three. From the Highwire Zinfandel to the Seascape Chardonnay and the Velvet Sisters Pinot Noir, the wines are excellent.

8075 Martinelli Rd., Forestville, CA 95436
www.hartfordwines.com

Hirsch Vineyards Sonoma Coast

In 1980, David Hirsch planted the first Pinot Noir vineyard in the region that would become known as the Sonoma Coast. Hirsch Vineyards represents an increasingly common phenomenon in California wine. For 20 years, its grapes were sold, and the subsequent wines became some of the most iconic California Pinot Noirs in history. Following the lead of other established grape growers, the Hirsch family started their own winery in 2002 and now make a couple of very good Pinot Noirs and a Chardonnay. This is a winery to watch for obvious reasons. ★ **Rising star**

45075 Bohan-Dillon Rd., Cazadero, CA 95421
www.hirschvineyards.com

Holdredge Winery Russian River Valley

A lawyer by day, winemaker by night, John Holdredge started making wine in 2001, out of a combination of passion and curiosity. Since then the winery has slowly grown to its current production of around 24,000 bottles of mostly Russian River Pinot Noir, with a little Syrah thrown in for good measure. Holdredge's Pinot Noirs are finely detailed and beautifully composed, not to mention very fairly priced. The winery has a tasting room on the square in downtown Healdsburg. ★ **Rising star**

51 Front St., Healdsburg, CA 95448
www.holdredge.com

Hook & Ladder Winery Russian River Valley

After selling one of the most successful wine brands in California history for a very hefty sum, you would think the DeLoach family might rest on their laurels for a bit. But once a winemaking family, always a winemaking family, apparently. The new brand, Hook & Ladder, a nod to Cecil Deloach's career as a fireman, makes good-value wines of decent quality from the family's 375 acres (152ha) of grapes. In particular, look for The Tillerman, a secret blend of white grapes that is quite refreshing.

2027 Olivet Rd., Santa Rosa, CA 95401
www.hookandladderwinery.com

Hop Kiln Winery Russian River Valley

A historic property on Westside Road south of the town of Healdsburg, Hop Kiln Winery takes its name from the huge building that is one of the country's best-preserved examples of a hop kiln. The old kiln now houses the winery's tasting room, and is worth a visit for the lovely architecture. Founded in 1976, the winery became known for its value-priced white and red blends. More recently, the winery has begun producing an ultra-premium Pinot Noir under a new brand called HKG.

6050 Westside Rd., Healdsburg, CA 95448
www.hopkilnwinery.com

Imagery Estate Sonoma Valley

Owned by the Benziger family, Imagery Estate began as a pet project of Joe Benziger, who wanted to experiment with less common grape varieties. After meeting local artist Bob Nugent as the two tried to break up a fistfight on a golf course, Benziger hired Nugent to create a painting for his first label. More than 20 years later, every Imagery Estate wine still bears a unique piece of art curated by Nugent. The estate's Biodynamically farmed vineyard yields excellent Sauvignon Blanc and Cabernet Sauvignon, to name but two.

14335 Highway 12, Glen Ellen, CA 95442
www.imagerywinery.com

Inman Family Wines Russian River Valley

On a break from college, Englishman Simon Inman fell in love with Burgundy while working in cellars in Nuits-St-George. Then, on another trip to California, he fell in love with his wife Kathleen in a winery tasting room, and the two moved to Russian River to pursue their dream of winemaking. Since 2000, the Inmans have farmed their Olivet Grange Vineyard organically to produce small lots of Pinot Noir and Pinot Gris for their own label and for other wineries who purchase their fruit.

5793 Skylane Blvd., Windsor, CA 95492
www.inmanfamilywines.com

Iron Horse Vineyards

Green Valley of Russian River Valley

In 1970, when they bought their 110 acre (46ha) property in the western reaches of Sonoma County, Barry and Audrey Sterling were told by the state's top viticulturalists that they were crazy to think they could grow Chardonnay and Pinot Noir in the foggiest part of the county. But the pair had visited Burgundy, and thought it was worth a try. Today, Iron Horse is one of America's best known and most prestigious family-run wineries. Regularly served at the White House, the winery's sparkling wines are among California's best, and their still wines have made great strides in recent years.

9786 Ross Station Rd., Sebastopol, CA 95472
www.ironhorsevineyards.com

J Vineyards Russian River Valley

Occupying the defunct Piper-Sonoma cellars in Russian River, J Vineyards represents the newest generation of sparkling wine producers in California. Begun by Jane Jordan, daughter of the founder of the well-known Jordan Vineyard in Sonoma's Alexander Valley, J Vineyards makes a large portfolio of still and sparkling wines, all packaged in the winery's modern, label-less bottle (they are engraved instead). Of particular note are the winery's late-disgorged sparkling wines (meaning a longer aging period), which are well worth the effort and cost to obtain.

11447 Old Redwood Highway, Healdsburg, CA 95448
www.jwine.com

Jemrose Bennett Valley

Few wineries in their second commercial vintage have a line-up of wines as strong as Jemrose, a newcomer to the Bennett Valley. But few wineries have Michael Browne of Kosta Browne making the wine and Greg Bjornstad as the viticulturalist. Jemrose represents a retirement dream for marketing executive James Mack, who bought 20 acres (8ha) of hillside vineyards in Bennett Valley. With business partner Keith Jaffee, Mack launched a very small winery (18,000 bottles) focusing on Rhône varieties. The winery's Foggy Hill Grenache and Cardiac Hill Syrah are exceptional, as is the unusual blend of Syrah and Merlot called Gloria's Gem. ★Rising star

6628 Bennett Valley Rd., Santa Rosa, CA 95404
www.jemrosewines.com

Jordan Vineyard Alexander Valley

Very few wineries in Sonoma County are as synonymous with Cabernet Sauvignon as Jordan Vineyard. Founded in 1972 by Tom Jordan, the winery's first vintage was made by the legendary Napa winemaker André Tchelistcheff. The winery produces a single Cabernet Sauvignon and a single Chardonnay each year, which are nothing if not consistent in their quality. This is admirable considering the winery's high production levels. The relatively wide availability of Jordan's wines make them a popular choice wine on lists around the country, and one of the most recognized brands from Sonoma.

1474 Alexander Valley Rd., Healdsburg, CA 95448
www.jordanwinery.com

Joseph Swan Vineyards

Russian River Valley

After a career as an airline pilot, Joseph Swan decided there would be no better way to spend his retirement than growing and making wine. In 1967, he bought a small vineyard near Forestville, which he planted with Chardonnay and Pinot Noir. While waiting for his vines to mature he started making Zinfandels from purchased fruit, to nearly instant acclaim. These days, the winery is known, in particular, for a more rustic style of both Zinfandel and Pinot Noir. The winery's Cuvée de Trois Pinot Noir is one of the greatest-value Pinots in Sonoma.

2916 Laguna Rd., Forestville, CA 95436
www.swanwinery.com

Kalin Cellars Marin

Kalin Cellars winemaker, Terry Leighton, is one of the most unique in California. He believes that among other things, time plays a big role in the making of wine. Which is why, at any given moment, the current release from Kalin Cellars is anywhere from 12 to 16 years older than those from nearly any other winery in the country. The latest vintage to be released is the distinctive 1994 Cuvée LD Sonoma Chardonnay, aged in 50% new French oak for 10 months and bottled in 1995. This is Old World winemaking at its finest; no fining for the reds, no filtration, lots of oxygen, and intriguing flavors.

No visitor facilities
www.kalincellars.com

Kamen Estate Sonoma Valley

Kamen's vineyards are carved out of the rocky hillsides of the Mayacamas Mountains and have a nearly single-minded focus on Cabernet Sauvignon. Founded by Hollywood screenwriter Robert Kamen, who bought 280 acres (113ha) of pristine mountainside (no roads, no water, no power) in 1980, the estate produces a Cabernet Sauvignon and a Syrah, as well as a rosé and a special Cabernet bottling called the Kashmir Cuvée. The vineyards are Biodynamically farmed, some by hand due to their extreme slopes. The wines tend to be big and ripe.

No visitor facilities
www.kamenwines.com

Kanzler Russian River Valley

Buying land in wine country can be a tricky business. If you are not careful you will end up owning a winery. Steve and Lynda Kanzler bought 12 acres (5ha) to build a house, which they did, but when they asked what they should plant on their land, everyone said the same thing: Pinot Noir. In 2004, they began making their own wine with the help of friend and winemaker Greg Stach. Their sought-after Pinot Noirs are sold only to their mailing list.

JAMES D. ZELLERBACH

Planted in 1953 by the visionary James D. Zellerbach, with the singular goal of producing grand cru quality wines that would rival those of Burgundy, Hanzell Vineyards is widely regarded as the oldest Pinot Noir vineyard in America. Zellerbach was a wealthy industrialist who went on to be the US ambassador to Italy. With the help of winemaker Ralph Webb, Zellerbach changed many of the ways in which wine was made in California. Between them, they pioneered the use of temperature-controlled stainless steel fermentation tanks, aging in small French oak barrels, the use of inert gas to reduce oxidation, and the deliberate induction of malolactic fermentation in the barrel. But the true Zellerbach legacy remains the Hanzell Vineyard, now a total of 42 acres (17ha), and the quality of wines that it continues to produce.

KENDALL JACKSON
THIS WINE FROM THE HIGHLAND ESTATES
BRAND STANDS OUT IN THE RANGE

KENWOOD VINEYARDS
WITH SPICY DARK FRUIT, THIS WINE IS
DELICIOUS AND EXCELLENT VALUE

The Sonoma Coast Pinot Noir spends 15 months in 30% new French oak, while the Reserve Pinot spends the same time in 100% new French oak. ★ **Rising star**

No visitor facilities
www.kanzlervineyards.com

Keller Estate Sonoma Coast

The southernmost winery in the Sonoma Coast AVA, Keller Estate sits abreast a hill in the low-lying area known as the Petaluma Gap. This is a channel for fog from the Pacific to the west and San Pablo Bay to the south. Established in 2001 by the Keller family, after a few years of experimental grape-growing, Keller Estate has become well known for its moderately priced, high-quality wines from the La Cruz vineyard, especially the Pinot Noir, Chardonnay, and Syrah. The excellent El Coro Pinot Noir is their top wine. ★ **Rising star**

5875 Lakeville Highway, Petaluma, CA 94954
www.kellerestate.com

Kendall Jackson Wine Estates

Russian River Valley
Founded by lawyer Jess Jackson in 1982, Kendall Jackson Wine Estates has grown to be one of the most successful wine brands in American history, and the 10th largest wine producer in the country. The Jackson wine portfolio includes many other independent wine brands, most of which are much higher quality than the wines produced under the Kendall Jackson name. However, the range of limited-production wines made under the Highland Estates label is excellent and worth seeking out. Look for, in particular, the Trace Ridge Cabernet Sauvignon from Knights Valley and the Camelot Highlands Chardonnay from further south.

5007 Fulton Rd., Santa Rosa, CA 95403
www.kj.com

Kendric Marin

A one-man operation, Kendric is both the idea of owner Stewart Johnson, and the product of his personal labors. Johnson farms the vineyards, harvests the grapes (with a little help), and makes the wines. The winery, named after his father, produces Pinot Noir from a vineyard north of Novato, and a Syrah, grown on a ranch owned by Johnson's mother, in the Shenendoah Valley. Both wines are well made and the Pinot Noir is among the better ones made in Marin. ★ **Rising star**

36 Monterey Ave., San Anselmo, CA 94960
www.kendricvineyards.com

Kenwood Vineyards Sonoma Valley

Some wineries with almost four decades of history and production levels over 3.6 million bottles have grown beyond the point of quality. If you tasted only the entry level wines from Kenwood Vineyards, you might easily dismiss them. However, Kenwood continues to consistently produce an excellent top wine—The Artist Series Cabernet Sauvignon, whose label sports the work of a world-famous artist every year—as well as a top tier of wines from the Jack London Vineyard, which are very good. The winery is part of the Korbel company.

9592 Sonoma Highway, Kenwood, CA 95452
www.kenwoodvineyards.com

Ketcham Estate Russian River Valley

Having retired after selling their respective technology companies, Mark Ketcham and Steve Rigisich like to joke that owning a winery was the result of one too many bottles one night. Presumably Ketcham was sober when he bought 16 acres (6.5ha) in the Russian River Valley, which is the source of most of the fruit used to make the two bottlings of Pinot Noir that Ketcham Estate produces. The wines, which also include a small-production Viognier made from purchased fruit, are made by Michael Browne of Kosta Browne Winery and are sold only to a mailing list.

448 Ignacio Blvd., Novato, CA 94949
www.ketchamestate.com

Kistler Vineyards Russian River Valley

No California Chardonnay is more well-known or sought-after than that of Kistler Vineyards. Founded in 1978, the winery has long been a cult producer of the variety. Vineyard sources include the Durrell Vineyard on the Sonoma Coast, and the Hudson Vineyard in Carneros. Still family-run, the wines are made by Steve Kistler, with help from family friend Mark Bixler. The winery also produces a couple of acclaimed Pinot Noirs, which, along with the Chardonnays, are available only to mailing list customers.

No visitor facilities
www.kistlervineyards.com

Kokomo Winery Dry Creek Valley

Wineries tend to beget winemakers. It is not all that uncommon for cellarhands, working at wineries both big and small, to be given the opportunity, facilities, and encouragement to make a barrel of their own wine during harvest time. On occasion, these little projects are merely the first step toward a successful winery, as was the case with Kokomo Winery. Just five years after he produced his first vintage in 2004, winemaker and owner Erik Miller now runs his own brand. Make sure you do not miss out on his Zinfandels and Grenache rosé. ★ **Rising star**

4791 Dry Creek Rd., Healdsburg, CA 95448
www.kokomowines.com

Kosta Browne Russian River Valley

Few wine producers have rocketed to prominence with quite the fanfare that this small producer of Pinot Noir has received. With a mere five vintages under their belts, founders Dan Kosta and Michael Browne recently sold a 51% stake in their winery for $40 million. This multi-million-dollar valuation was no doubt due, in part, to their 96-point scores in the *Wine Spectator*. Other critics dislike what they describe as wines that are too big and ripe. Regardless, the wines are extremely well made, if difficult to find. Kosta Browne sells primarily to restaurants, rather than retail outlets, and its mailing list of private customers. ★ **Rising star**

No visitor facilities
www.kostabrowne.com

Limerick Lane Russian River Valley

Occupying 30 acres (12ha), and taking its name from the street that leads to the winery entrance, Limerick Lane has been producing top-quality Zinfandel since the owners decided to make some wine of their own instead of selling all their fruit. In 1993, owner Michael Collins built a winery on the property and, in 1997, hired winemaker Ross Battersby, who has been making the wines ever since. Do not miss the lush Collins Vineyard Zinfandel, and try the good-value Collins Estate Reserve wine (a blend of 50% Cabernet Sauvignon, 25% Zinfandel, and 25% Syrah).

1023 Limerick Lane, Healdsburg, CA 95448
www.limericklanewines.com

Littorai Russian River Valley
Littorai's owner was the first American ever to be hired as a winemaker by a Burgundian domaine. Ted Lemon has a track record for making Pinot Noir that is hard to match. He trained in Burgundy and worked for several producers there, before returning to America to found Littorai in 1993. The winery's Chardonnays and Pinot Noirs from the estate vineyard, and wines made from purchased fruit from other top sites in Sonoma and Mendocino counties, are highly sought after for very good reason. The Chardonnays show restrained use of oak and great acidity, while the Pinot Noirs are beautifully expressive.

788 Gold Ridge Rd., Sebastopol, CA 95472
www.littorai.com

Longboard Vineyards Russian River Valley
Longboard's owner, Oded Shakked, thinks surfing and wine have a lot in common, namely, balance and passion. After a brief career as a surfboard maker and beach bum, Israeli-born Shakked trained as a winemaker at University of California, Davis, and worked harvests in Bordeaux and Napa before settling down in Sonoma County to ply his trade. The first commercial vintage for Longboard was 1998, and, since that first harvest, Shakked has been slowly growing a portfolio of about a dozen wines, the best of which are his Syrahs.

5 Fitch St., Healdsburg, CA 95448
www.longboardvineyards.com

Lynmar Estate Russian River Valley
Lynn Fritz purchased the Quail Hill Vineyard in 1980, establishing the Lynmar winery in 1990. The vineyard had been producing Chardonnay and Pinot Noir in the Russian River Valley for at least a decade before his purchase. Lynmar Estate produced its first commercial vintage in 1994 and the winery operated rather quietly until recently, when the quality of the wines improved under the direction of winemaker Hugh Chappelle (previously of Flowers Vineyard and Winery) and consultant Paul Hobbs. The Quail Hill Pinot Noir and Chardonnay are both excellent wines.

3909 Frei Rd., Sebastopol, CA 95472
www.lynmarwinery.com

Mantra Winery Dry Creek Valley
Grape growing has been the Kuimelis family business for about 40 years. Mike and Lorene Kuimelis farm grapes in Sonoma County and were content to continue into their retirement, but their son, Mike Jr., had other plans. In 2000, he launched Mantra Winery with a few hundred cases of Cabernet Sauvignon made in a barrel in the garage. Now producing a few thousand cases

LYNMAR ESTATE
SELECTED BARRELS GO INTO THIS CUVEE TO EXPRESS THE UNIQUE TERROIR OF QUAIL HILL

KISTLER VINEYARDS
KISTLER'S CHARDONNAYS ARE ICONS OF CALIFORNIA WINEMAKING

of wine from their shared facility in Dry Creek Valley, Mantra is a serious commercial operation that makes excellent wines. Their Cabernet Sauvignon and Bordeaux blends merit particular attention, as does their Alexander Valley Zinfandel. ★ Rising star

No visitor facilities
www.mantrawines.com

Marcassin Russian River Valley
Helen Turley is one of California's most sought-after consulting winemakers. Known for producing some of Sonoma's and Napa's most renowned wines, Turley started Marcassin as a small personal project along with her husband John Wetlaufer. The 10 acre (4ha) Marcassin vineyard is on the Sonoma Coast, planted to Pinot Noir and Chardonnay, and the wines are made at Martinelli Vineyard. The label also purchases grapes to make wines from some of Sonoma's other top vineyards. With roughly 30,000 bottles made, and most of the wine sold only to mailing list customers, Marcassin's wines are some of Sonoma's most exclusive and hard-to-find bottlings.

No visitor facilities
707 942 5633

Marimar Torres
Green Valley of the Russian River Valley
The Torres name has several centuries of history in the wine world, thanks to a dynasty of pioneers from Spain. Marimar Torres came to California from Barcelona in 1975 and, by 1986, she had begun planting her own vineyards. The winery makes an effort to display and celebrate its Catalan heritage, from the architecture of the winery to Marimar's cookbooks. The organically and Biodynamically farmed wines are well made, especially the Cristina Pinot Noir and the Acero Chardonnay. The name Acero comes from the Spanish for steel, referring to the fact that this Chardonnay never sees any oak, making its pure fruit flavor stand out.

11400 Graton Rd., Sebastopol, CA 95472
www.marimarestate.com

Martinelli Winery Russian River Valley
It is hard to miss the big red Martinelli Winery barn as you head west on River Road into the heart of the Russian River Valley. Young immigrant Guiseppe Martinelli settled outside of Forestville in 1887. He and his wife worked until they had saved up enough to buy a small plot of land, which has been farmed by Martinellis ever since. With a broad portfolio of wines, some still from that original plot of land, Martinelli is best known for its Zinfandels and Pinot Noirs, made by winemaker Bryan Kvamme with help from the consulting winemaker Helen Turley, whose own vineyards border those of Martinelli.

3360 River Rd., Windsor, CA 95492
www.martinelliwinery.com

Matanzas Creek Winery Bennett Valley
Founded in 1977, in what was at the time an obscure region of Sonoma County known as Bennett Valley, Matanzas Creek Winery is as beautiful as it is pioneering. Surrounded by meticulously maintained gardens of lavender, the winery has been one of Sonoma's most consistent producers since it released its first vintages.

The golden-brown, grass-covered hills above the Gallo Sonoma vineyard are a clue to the California location.

MONTEMAGGIORE
WONDERFULLY BALANCED BETWEEN
BRIGHT FRUIT AND EARTHY SPICE

A pioneer of Sonoma County Pinot Noir, the winery produces a wide range of wines that have recently become more confident in their understated style, thanks to winemaker François Cordesse. The earthy, low-alcohol Cabernet Sauvignon, sourced from Knights Valley vineyards, is especially worth trying.

6097 Bennett Valley Rd., Santa Rosa, CA 95404
www.matanzascreek.com

Mazzocco Sonoma Dry Creek Valley

Diane and Ken Wilson have been buying up vineyards and wineries at a measured pace since the 1980s. Today, they farm a large swathe of vineyards, and own several wineries including Mazzocco Sonoma. While Diane herself is a winemaker, the Wilsons employ Antoine Favero as winemaker and he makes excellent Zinfandels and Chardonnays, among other wines. The grapes are from other Wilson vineyard properties as well as purchased from growers in the region.

1400 Lytton Springs Rd., Healdsburg, CA 95448
www.mazzocco.com

Medlock Ames Alexander Valley

Two friends, Christopher Medlock James and Ames Morison, shared the dream of creating a vineyard and winery. Together they set out in 1998 to make that dream real. After visiting hundreds of potential sites in Northern California, the pair settled on a vineyard in Alexander Valley, and spent nearly a decade creating a distinctive winery with a strong portfolio of wines from organically grown grapes. Originally focused on Merlot, as well as Cabernet Sauvignon, the winery has recently begun making Pinot Noir. The Bell Mountain Merlot remains the star of their offerings. ★ **Rising star**

13414 Chalk Hill Rd., Healdsburg, CA 95448
www.medlockames.com

Merry Edwards Russian River Valley

Merry Edwards was once given the nickname "The Queen of Pinot", and it has stuck, not because she particularly cares for it (she does not), but because she easily qualifies for such an honor. One of the first female graduates from the prestigious University of California, Davis viticulture and enology program, Edwards has been making Pinot Noir in Northern California for more than 30 years. After working as a winemaker for many others, she began her own label in 1997, and has not looked back. Edwards recently built her own winery and tasting room which are now open to the public. Look for the Meredith Estate Pinot Noir, and her Sauvignon Blanc, which is among the highest rated in the country.

2959 Gravenstein Highway North, Sebastopol, CA,
www.merryedwards.com

Michel-Schlumberger Wine Estate
Dry Creek Valley

There are not many wineries in Dry Creek Valley that do not make Zinfandel, but Michel-Schlumberger is one of them. The winery prefers instead to focus, as it has for a long time, on Bordeaux varietals and blends made from cooler hillside vineyards. The estate was founded in 1979 by the Swiss-born Jean-Jacques Michel. Now run by Jacques Schlumberger, who joined Michel as a partner in 1991, the estate continues to produce very nice Cabernet

MANTANZAS CREEK WINERY
THE COOL CLIMES OF BENNETT VALLEY MAKE
FOR A BALANCED, ELEGANT CHARACTER

Sauvignon-based wines and other red wines under the stewardship of winemaker Mike Brunson, who has been with the estate since 1993.

4155 Wine Creek Rd., Healdsburg, CA 95448
www.michelschlumberger.com

Montemaggiore Dry Creek Valley

Named after the small mountain village in Italy where owner Vincent Ciolino's family has been growing grapes and olives for generations, Montemaggiore's first vintages have been remarkably good, and have quickly grabbed the attention of the critics. Producing a portfolio based around Syrah (Ciolino's favorite grape variety), as well as olive oil, the winery has made an early and strong commitment to Biodynamic farming for both crops. The wines are wonderfully complex and rich, from the single-vineyard Syrahs to the Super Tuscan-style blends. This is a producer to watch closely. ★ **Rising star**

2355 West Dry Creek Rd., Healdsburg, CA 95448
www.montemaggiore.com

Mueller Winery Russian River Valley

Robert Mueller began his winemaking career in 1977, and worked for more than 14 years before he had the money to build a winery. After serving as a custom crush facility (contract winemaking) for a couple of years, Mueller finally built up enough capital to begin buying top-quality Pinot Noir grapes from the Russian River Valley, and start making his distinctive and elegant wines. This family-run outfit produces a modest range of wines, the highlights of which are the lovely, ageworthy Pinot Noirs, especially the Emily's Cuvée, aged in French oak barrels (50% of which are new).

6301 Starr Rd., Windsor, CA 95492
www.muellerwine.com

Murphy-Goode Winery Alexander Valley

Murphy-Goode may now be more famous for its viral marketing campaigns than its wines, thanks to a contest it sponsored, in 2009, to hire a resident wine blogger. Part of the Jackson Family Wines portfolio, Murphy-Goode's wines are made by the son of one of the founders. Like many Jackson-owned estates, it operates with a certain degree of autonomy. The original portfolio of Fumé Blanc and Chardonnay has shifted to focus more on red wines from Alexander Valley. Their top wine is the Snake Eyes Zinfandel, blended from the best lots in each vintage.

20 Matheson St., Healdsburg, CA 95448
www.murphygoodewinery.com

Nalle Winery Russian River Valley

For 25 years, Nalle winery has been marching to the beat of a different drum in the Russian River Valley. From alcohol levels consistently lower than many neighbors, to the whimsical cartoons that adorn the well-known Zinfandel bottling, the wines of the Nalle family have never pretended to be anything other than what they are. Their 15,600 bottles of wine, mostly Zinfandel with a little Pinot Noir and Chardonnay, are made by Bob Nalle and his son Andrew, with help from winery dog, Solo.

2383 Dry Creek Rd., Healdsburg, CA 95448
www.nallewinery.com

Novy Family Wines Russian River Valley

After their runaway success with their first Pinot Noir project, Siduri Wines, Adam Lee and Dianna Novy Lee wanted to make Syrah, but that was not part of the Siduri charter. So, with the help of Dianna's family, they started another wine brand, and their Midas touch for winemaking seems to have rubbed off very well. Novy Family Wines produces an incredible array of small- to tiny-production wines made from purchased grapes. From Syrah and Zinfandel, to Viognier and, most recently, a sparkling wine, it is hard to go wrong with any of these wines, but the Syrahs are the real gems.

980 Airway Court, Santa Rosa, CA 95403
www.novyfamilywines.com

Olsen Ogden Wines Russian River Valley

Like many small labels without any estate vineyards, Olsen Ogden was forged out of the dreams of its two founders. John Ogden left the high-tech world disillusioned and searching for something more fulfilling. Winemaker Tim Olsen left some big winery brands to look for an opportunity to start his own. The two met randomly and began a new chapter together. They have recently released their first Pinot Noirs, but the winery's initial focus on Syrah continues to deepen as their wines grow more profound. Look for their Stagecoach Vineyard Syrah, in particular. ★ Rising star

No visitor facilities
www.olsonogdenwines.com

Owl Ridge/Willowbrook Cellars
Russian River Valley

Entrepreneur John Tracy decided to leave Silicon Valley behind for the world of wine in the late 1990s. He bought a piece of property in the Russian River Valley that was already planted to Pinot Noir and Chardonnay. With the help of winemaker Joe Otos, he founded Willowbrook Cellars, and made his wine in rented facilities. Ever the entrepreneur, Tracy decided to open his own winery where many small labels now make their wines. He also started a new project to make Bordeaux-style wines under the Owl Ridge label. Both Willowbrook and Owl Ridge wines are competently made and good value.

No visitor facilities
www.owlridge.com

Pacheco Ranch Marin

Pacheco Ranch has been family-owned since the original land grant of 6,680 acres (2,700ha) was made to Ignacio Pacheco in the middle of the 19th century. The Pacheco Ranch's 5 acres (2ha) of vines were planted in 1970 by Pacheco's descendants. The historic property's carriage house has been converted to a winery. Winemaker Jamie Meves has been making the family's 6,000 bottles of Cabernet Sauvignon since 1979. The estate produces this single wine each year and it is notable for its restrained alcohol levels thanks to the cool Marin climate.

235 Alameda Del Prado Rd., Novato, CA 94949
www.pachecoranchwinery.com

Papapietro Perry Dry Creek Valley

It may be hard to pronounce, but that has not stopped Papapietro Perry from acquiring an avid following for its lush, small-production Pinot Noirs and Zinfandels. Ben Papapietro and Bruce Perry were fellow newspapermen who discovered a mutual love of wine and a shared Italian cultural heritage. After working harvest at a friend's winery, the two started making wine in their garage and, after eight years of toying with the idea, they started their own wine label in 1998. Look for their Peters Vineyard Pinot Noir from the Russian River Valley.

4791 Dry Creek Rd., Healdsburg, CA 95448
www.papapietro-perry.com

Paradise Ridge Winery Russian River Valley

While many wineries in Russian River Valley are close together, Paradise Ridge sits off on its own. The 156 acre (63ha) estate was originally just a secluded retreat for its owners, Walter Byck and Marijke Byck-Hoenselaars, but they suspected it could produce wine. Within a year of buying the property in 1978, they had begun to plant grapes. Little by little the vineyard was built up and the grapes were sold to others, until 1991, when the Paradise Ridge Winery was founded. Winemaker Dan Barwick makes, among other things, a 100% barrel-fermented Nagasawa Vineyard Chardonnay.

4545 Thomas Lake Harris Drive, Santa Rosa, CA 95403
www.prwinery.com

Paul Hobbs Russian River Valley

For true fans of Sonoma County wine, Paul Hobbs rarely needs an introduction. One of the most accomplished and sought-after winemakers in California, Hobbs originally studied to be a medical doctor, but a few classes in botany sidetracked him into viticulture and enology. Hobbs made a name for himself as chief enologist at Napa's Opus One winery, and consulted at many top Napa wineries before starting his own winery in 1991. Hobbs is a master of both Burgundian and Bordeaux varietals, resulting in an impressive portfolio of Pinot Noirs, Chardonnays, Cabernet Sauvignons, and Syrahs, all of which are exceptional.

3355 Gravenstein Highway North, Sebastopol, CA 95472
www.paulhobbs.com

Peay Vineyards Sonoma Coast

Brothers Andy and Nick Peay searched the entire state for an "extreme" site to plant a vineyard, and eventually settled on a windy, cold ridge a stone's throw from the Pacific Ocean on Sonoma's coast. In the grounds of an old fruit orchard they planted Pinot Noir, Syrah, Marsanne, Roussanne, and Viognier and set about making exceptional cool-climate Burgundian and Rhône style wines under the guidance of talented winemaker Vanessa Wong. The entire range of wines is noteworthy, in particular the tiny-production Viognier from 1 acre (0.4ha) of vines. ★ Rising star

No visitor facilities
www.peayvineyards.com

Peter Michael Winery Knights Valley

Superlatives are best avoided in the vast world of wine, but few would be able to argue with the suggestion that Peter Michael Winery may make the best Bordeaux-style wine in Sonoma County. Founded by Sir Peter Michael, entrepreneur and former CEO of Cray UK (the supercomputer company), the winery owns several steep, volcanic hillside vineyards in Knights Valley, which are

SONOMA ZINFANDEL

No single grape has become more uniquely identified with California wine than Zinfandel. While more than one wine region might vie for the right to the title of Zinfandel headquarters, Sonoma County has a compelling case to make for its candidacy. Plantings in Sonoma County can be traced back to at least the 1850s and, while many old vineyards were ripped out during Prohibition, Sonoma's Dry Creek Valley hosts some treasured ancient vines, most notably the vineyard at Bucklin's Old Hill Ranch, which was planted in 1885.

On the back of an international obsession with White Zinfandel (a sweet, blush-style wine), red Zinfandel wines have again become quite popular. Sonoma produces at least two main styles of Zinfandel: a ripe, peppery version from Dry Creek Valley, and a more restrained black fruit offering from certain areas of the Russian River Valley.

QUIVIRA VINEYARDS
EVERYTHING A ROSÉ SHOULD BE—CRISP,
JUICY, AND DRY AS A BONE

farmed with a variety of sustainable, organic, and Biodynamic methods. The Les Pavots vineyard blend of Cabernet Sauvignon, Cabernet Franc, and Merlot is aged for 18 months in 100% French oak. It is always outstanding, as well as hard to find. Most of the wines are only sold to the winery's mailing list customers.

12400 Ida Clayton Rd., Knights Valley, Calistoga, CA 94515
www.petermichaelwinery.com

Pey-Marin Marin
Pey-Marin winery is one of the most established and successful wineries in Marin. Founder Jonathan Pey worked for years in the cellars of Burgundy, Australia, and Napa, while Susan, his wife, continues to be a top restaurant wine buyer. The duo have been growing and making wine under their Pey-Marin and Mount Tamalpais labels for a decade now. Their organically grown grapes scale the steep, foggy hillsides just inland from the Pacific. The cool climate makes an excellent Riesling and their Trois Filles Pinot Noir can hold its own with some of California's best.

10000 Sir Francis Drake Blvd., Olema, CA 94950
www.marinwines.com

Pfendler Vineyards Sonoma County
Pfendler Vineyards was the dream of its founder, entrepreneur Peter Pfendler, who began planting grapes in southern Sonoma County in 1992. Pfendler unfortunately succumbed to cancer before seeing the fruits of his labor go to market. Inaugurated in 2007 by Kimberly Pfendler, in her husband's memory, the winery produces about 12,000 bottles of Pinot Noir and Chardonnay, plus a little bit of rosé from some of Sonoma County's cooler vineyard sites in the Petaluma Gap. The wines are made by consulting winemaker Greg Bjornstad. ★ **Rising star**

No visitor facilities
www.pfendlervineyards.com

Point Reyes Vineyards Marin
One of the earliest wineries to be established in Marin County, Point Reyes Vineyards has been making wine for almost 20 years. It is situated in a little nook along the famous coastal Highway 1. Husband-and-wife team Steve and Sharon Doughty are the third generation of their family to farm in Marin, and together they operate their small vineyard, winery, and guest-house. The winery produces small amounts of Pinot Noir and sparkling wine from the estate vineyard, as well as wines made from grapes purchased around Sonoma County.

12700 Highway 1, Point Reyes Station, CA 94956
www.ptreyesvineyardinn.com

Porter Creek Vineyards
Russian River Valley
Situated next to Porter Creek (which gives the winery its name), this father-and-son operation, founded in 1982, produces some of the most distinctive, but often overlooked, wines in the Russian River Valley. This is a winery completely without pretension. Visitors are welcomed into an ancient shack for a tasting room, and the winery does very little in the way of promotion or marketing. The modest portfolio of Biodynamically made wines is stewarded by Alex Davis, who took over from his

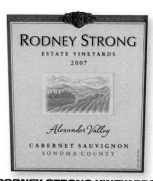

RODNEY STRONG VINEYARDS
OAK AGING FOR 18 MONTHS GIVES THIS WINE
SOFT TANNINS TO BALANCE THE FRUIT

father in the 1997 vintage. Every wine is worth seeking out, but the Chardonnay, Viognier, Pinot Noir, and Carignane are especially tasty. The Viognier is reminiscent of a Condrieu from the Rhône, while the Carignane comes from very old vines in Alexander Valley, giving the wine great depth.

8735 Westside Rd., Healdsburg, CA 95448
www.portercreekvineyards.com

Pride Mountain Vineyards
Situated precisely on the border of Sonoma and Napa counties, at the summit of the Mayacamas Mountains, Pride Mountain Vineyards is a single winery divided by county bureaucracy. Forced to have two separate facilities, one on either side of the county line, Pride's wines are sometimes labelled with Sonoma County, sometimes with Napa, and sometimes with both. A site for winemaking since the 1890s, Pride has been family-run since its founding in the early 1990s, when winemaker Bob Foley helped make its wines famous. Today, the winemaking team is led by Sally Johnson, who produces a nice line-up of wines including the well-regarded Merlot and Cabernet Sauvignon. The Viognier and Sangiovese both come solely from Sonoma.

4026 Spring Mountain Rd., St. Helena, CA 94574
www.pridewines.com

Quivira Vineyards Dry Creek Valley
Founded in 1987, Quivira Vineyards was one of California's earliest pioneers in sustainable agriculture and environmental consciousness. Solar powered, Biodynamically farmed, with weeding by resident goats, Quivira represents a dedication to environmental sustainability that is truly commendable. Thankfully, the wines have also recently become quite good under new ownership and the winemaking talents of Steven Canter. In particular, the winery is one of a select few making Grenache in Dry Creek Valley, and its rendition may well be the best of those. It spends 15 months in oak, 10% of which is new. Keep an eye out for their rosé as well, fermented with wild yeasts and 10% Mourvèdre for a little added spice.

4900 West Dry Creek Rd., Healdsburg, CA 95448
www.quivirawine.com

A. Rafanelli Dry Creek Valley
Few Sonoma County Zinfandels are as difficult to obtain as those made by Rafanelli. The wines are sold only to mailing list customers and winery visitors, and are rarely, if ever, found in retail outlets or restaurants. The Rafanelli family now boasts four generations of grape farming in the Dry Creek Valley, and continues to operate with little fanfare. They employ zero marketing, concentrating instead on consistent production of Zinfandel, Cabernet Sauvignon, and Merlot from their vineyards. Despite their well-deserved reputation for Zinfandel, their Cabernet may be the highest-quality wine they produce.

4685 West Dry Creek Rd., Healdsburg, CA 95448
www.arafanelliwinery.com

Ramey Wine Cellars Russian River Valley
There are wineries that bear the names of their owners for romantic reasons, and there are those that are named after their owners because that name means something

in the world of wine. Ramey Wine Cellars is the eponymous effort of David Ramey, a highly successful winemaker for many top California wineries. In 1997, he struck out on his own to create a new winery dedicated to making small lots of wine the way he wanted to make them. Situated in Healdsburg, where he lives, Ramey Wine Cellars produces Cabernet Sauvignon from top Napa Valley vineyards, along with two distinctive Syrahs from the Sonoma Coast, and Chardonnay from Carneros and Sonoma.

25 Healdsburg Ave., Healdsburg, CA 95448
www.rameywine.com

Rancho Zabaco Winery Dry Creek Valley
Rancho Zabaco is one of the many brands owned by Gallo Family Vineyards, but merits its own mention here both for its special emphasis on Zinfandel, and its great value for money. Rancho Zabaco wines, made by winemaker Eric Cinnamon, are widely available in the US. The winery also produces some much more limited bottlings of Zinfandel, including a few single-vineyard designated wines from some noteworthy sites, including the Monte Rosso vineyard.

3387 Dry Creek Rd., Healdsburg, CA 95448
www.ranchozabaco.com

Ravenswood Sonoma Valley
"No Wimpy Wines" is the motto of the Zinfandel-focused Ravenswood. Founder Joel Peterson has grown this winery over three decades from a small operation into one of the most recognized California wine brands. Zinfandel remains the winery's primary bailiwick, across a large portfolio, from mass-produced wines to their single-vineyard wines that continue to be high-quality renditions of the signature grape. In addition to the Old Hill and Big River Zinfandels, make sure not to miss Icon, the winery's unique and delicious Rhône blend.

18701 Gehricke Rd., Sonoma, CA 95476
www.ravenswood-wine.com

J. Rickards Winery Alexander Valley
Jim and Eliza Rickards have been growing grapes for nearly 30 years in the Alexander Valley. Content to sell their Cabernet Sauvignon to Silver Oak and their Zinfandel to Dry Creek Vineyards, the pair always made a little wine in their garage for drinking with dinner. Under increasing pressure from enthusiastic family and friends, in 2005 they began making wine commercially under the J. Rickards label. Their initial vintages have been outstanding, especially their Zinfandel, which is already one of Alexander Valley's best. ★**Rising star**

24505 Chianti Rd., Cloverdale, CA 95425
www.jrwinery.com

Ridge Lytton Springs Dry Creek Valley
It is hard to figure out what to call the Dry Creek Valley location of the winery based in the Santa Cruz Mountains. Branch office? Second location? Outpost? Sister winery? Run effectively as a separate winery but managed by the same folks and with the same philosophy, Ridge Lytton Springs is simply the place the Ridge Zinfandels have called home for decades. Purchased by Ridge in 1991, after several decades of making wine there, the tasting

ROSS VALLEY WINERY
ARTISTS AND FRIENDS HELP TO MAKE
THIS STRAWBERRY-INFLECTED ROSE

RANCHO ZABACO WINERY
THE GALLO FAMILY'S ZINFANDEL OUTPOST
PRODUCING EXCELLENT-VALUE WINES

room offers the same wines as the Santa Cruz location, including the famous Monte Bello Cabernet Sauvignon and Geyserville Zinfandel.

650 Lytton Springs Rd., Healdsburg, CA 95448
www.ridgewine.com

J. Rochioli Vineyards Russian River Valley
One of the most famous producers and growers of Pinot Noir in California, Rochioli is undeniably one of North America's finest vineyards. The Rochioli family have been farming in the Russian River Valley since the beginning of the 20th century. Winemaker Tom Rochioli is the third generation of his family to make wine from the meticulously kept vineyards that lie on the floodplains off Westside Road, south of Healdsburg. The winery's Rochioli Vineyards label offers appellation-designated Sauvignon Blanc, Pinot Noir, and Chardonnay, while the J. Rochioli label offers the sought-after single-vineyard Chardonnays and Pinot Noirs. The latter are sold exclusively to the mailing list, on which it can take years to secure a spot. Top wines include the River Block, West Block, and Little Hill vineyard Pinot Noirs.

6192 Westside Rd., Healdsburg, CA 95448
www.rochioliwinery.com

Rodney Strong Vineyards
Russian River Valley
After retiring in 1959, professional dancer Rodney Strong began making wine, first at home, and then, after some commercial success, at a winery he built in the Alexander Valley. By the mid-1980s, his wine was found in practically every grocery and liquor store across the US. Rodney Strong still makes large quantities of mostly ordinary wine for the national market, but recently released two expensive, single-vineyard wines, Rockaway and Brothers Ridge, which are a significant step up in quality from the rest of the portfolio.

11455 Old Redwood Highway, Healdsburg, CA 95448
www.rodneystrong.com

Roessler Cellars Russian River Valley
It is no surprise that after 35 years of owning and managing restaurants, Roger Roessler has developed an interest in wine. When some friends, who owned a vineyard, offered him some Pinot Noir grapes in 2000, Roessler Cellars was born. Joined by his brother Richard and winemaker Scott Shapley, Roessler has built a portfolio of small-production Pinot Noirs and Chardonnays from vineyards across Northern California. The wines are extremely high-quality and consistently elegant, especially the Brousseau and Hein Family Vineyard Pinot Noir. The winery planted its own vineyards in 2003 and has recently begun to produce estate-grown wines. ★**Rising star**

380 First St., West Sonoma, CA 95476
www.roesslercellars.com

Ross Valley Winery Marin
Paul Kreider runs the tiny Ross Valley Winery more like a collective than a commercial concern. While his wines are for sale, replete with funky labels created by artist friends, the operation is staffed by volunteers, friends, family, and merrymakers every harvest. Along with red and white wines made from fruit purchased from various

SEBASTIANI WINERY
THE TOP OF THE RANGE WINE FROM THE
UBIQUITOUS SEBASTIANI RANGE OF WINES

growers in Sonoma and Carneros, the winery also produces mead and several other apéritif and digestif concoctions. You can turn up with an empty vessel and have it filled with selected wines—ideal for picnics.

343 San Anselmo Ave., San Anselmo, CA 94960
www.rossvalleywinery.com

Rued Winery Dry Creek Valley
Husband-and-wife team Steve and Sonia Rued started their winery in 2004, after decades of growing grapes to sell to other wineries. The Rued family have a long history of growing grapes in Sonoma County, and continue to farm more than 160 acres (65ha), with a small portion of that fruit ending up in bottles with the family name on them. Both Steve and Sonia were winemakers before they were married, and now they are jointly responsible for each vintage. The two produce several good-quality, reasonably priced wines, including their Zinfandel and Sauvignon Blanc from Dry Creek Valley.

3850 Dry Creek Rd., Healdsburg, CA 95448
www.ruedvineyards.com

Russian Hill Estate
Russian River Valley
While the wine world gets more corporate, Sonoma persists in hosting a large percentage of truly family-run outfits, representing the dreams and life savings of their founders. Russian Hill Estate, founded by Edward Gomez and Ellen Mack is a perfect example of this. Gomez, a retired doctor and perpetual tinkerer, made wine at home for a while before deciding to go all-out and buy the land that makes up Russian Hill Estate in 1997. His nephew, Patrick Melley, makes the wines, which include some very nice single-vineyard Pinot Noirs.

4525 Slusser Rd., Windsor, CA 95492
www.russianhillestate.com

Saxon-Brown Sonoma Valley
Old family vineyards are a treasure trove for many great Sonoma wines. After a 16-year career as a winemaker, notably for Chateau St. Jean, in 1997 Jeff Gaffner decided he was ready to launch his own wines. These are made from the 16 acre (6.5ha) Casa Santinamaria Vineyard which his family have been farming for three generations. From this 100-year-old vineyard, Gaffner makes balanced, ageworthy Zinfandel (actually a field blend of five varieties) and Semillon. The winery also produces Syrah and Pinot Noir from purchased grapes. At only 20,400 bottles total production, the wines are not easy to find, but are worth the effort.

255 West Napa St., Sonoma, CA 95476
www.saxonbrown.com

Sbragia Family Vineyards Dry Creek Valley
It is only a matter of time before any talented winemaker eventually wants his own winery, and the Sbragia Family Vineyards label is another project born of this desire. For winemaker Ed Sbragia, who was head winemaker at Beringer (in Napa Valley) for 24 years, the decision to start his own winery was more than about just having a bottle with his name on it. It was all about continuing his family's wine-growing legacy in Sonoma County. Sbragia's father was a vintner in Dry Creek Valley in the 1960s, and now Sbragia and his son Alex are making

wine together at their newly opened winery. Look out for their Cimarossa Cabernet Sauvignon—from a carefully selected mountain site. ★ Rising star

9990 Dry Creek Rd., Geyserville, CA 95441
www.sbragia.com

Sean Thackrey Marin
Call him the wine wizard of Bolinas. The enigmatic winemaker Sean Thackrey is right at home in this town. Persons unknown keep cutting down the single road sign pointing to the town. Self-taught in winemaking and iconoclastic in his approach, Thackrey nonetheless makes outstanding wines despite quite unconventional methods. Since 1980, he has been making mostly red wines in the open-top fermenters in his backyard, under some eucalyptus trees. His multi-vintage red blend Pleiades is the easiest to find, but tracking down either his Orion blend or Andromeda Pinot Noir is well worth the effort.

No visitor facilities
www.wine-maker.net

Sebastiani Winery Sonoma Valley
Founded in 1904 by Samuele Sebastiani, the Sebastiani Winery has long been a fixture of the historic downtown Sonoma scene, and an icon of Sonoma County winemaking. With a massive production of more than 96 million bottles, Sebastiani's inexpensive wines can be found nearly everywhere in the United States. The upper reaches of the portfolio contain good-quality wines, from the small-production Cherryblock Cabernet Sauvignon to the Carneros Pinot Noir.

389 Fourth St. East, Sonoma, CA 95476
www.sebastiani.com

Seghesio Family Vineyards
Alexander Valley
The story of Seghesio Family Vineyards is the quintessential Sonoma winery history. Started by the young Italian immigrant Edoardo Seghesio in 1895, the same year he planted 56 acres (23ha) of Zinfandel, Seghesio has been run by his descendants ever since. With purchased grapes and high aspirations, the Seghesio brand grew to produce more than 1.5 million bottles in the early 1990s but, in 1993, Ted and Peter Seghesio boldly decided to cut production to what they could produce from their own 100-year-old family vineyard. Apart from the old-vine Zinfandel grown there, the winery also produces a white wine from Arneis.

14730 Grove St., Healdsburg, CA 95448
www.seghesio.com

Selby Winery Russian River Valley
Started by David Selby in 1993 after a lifelong obsession with wine, Selby Winery is now run by his daughter Susie Selby, who took over as owner and winemaker upon his death in 1997. From estate vineyards and purchased fruit, Selby makes about 120,000 bottles of wine each year, spread across small lots of various grape varieties. The Merlot is a perennial favorite and, for those with a sweet tooth, the winery sometimes makes a late-harvest Zinfandel that can be purchased in their tasting room.

215 Center St, Healdsburg, CA 95448
www.selbywinery.com

SELBY WINERY
A RIPE MERLOT THAT DELIVERS FOR ANYONE
WHO LOVES PLUM AND CHOCOLATE

Siduri Winery Russian River Valley

Siduri Winery may not have been the first extremely successful winery that owned no vineyards, but this small label started by husband and wife Adam and Dianna Lee has been the model for countless others in the 15 years since it began. With little more than a few thousand dollars in savings and modest experience as winemakers, the couple sought out small quantities of Pinot Noir from top growers in California and Oregon, which they vinified and bottled under the name of the Babylonian goddess of wine. Every wine they make is highly acclaimed and sought-after for good reason.

980 Airway Court, Santa Rosa, CA 95403
www.siduri.com

Skipstone Ranch Alexander Valley

Entrepreneur and venture capitalist Fahri Diner knows a thing or two about building brands and management teams. His wife Jill Layman knew a stunning piece of property when she saw it, too. Together they launched Skipstone Ranch, a winery and olive oil producer, which they have staffed with some of the industry's top talent. Ulises Valdez manages the vineyards, Phillipe Melka consults with on-site winemaker Andrew Levi, and superstar sommelier Emily Wines consults. The estate's Oliver's Blend red wine is a flashy, high-octane production, but shows great promise. ★ **Rising star**

No visitor facilities
www.skipstoneranch.com

Sojourn Cellars Sonoma Valley

Erich Bradley's official title is winemaker. Craig Haserot's official title is winetaster. These two friends met in Sonoma and decided to forge a partnership based on their mutual love of two grapes that are not often found consorting: Pinot Noir and Cabernet Sauvignon. Purchasing fruit from key growers in Sonoma, Napa, and Mendocino, Bradley makes small lots of completely hand-crafted wines with an incredible attention to detail and an insistence on traditional practices like native yeast fermentations, basket pressing, and the lack of fining or filtration. The results are fantastic. ★ **Rising star**

141 East Napa St., Sonoma, CA 95476
www.sojourncellars.com

Sonoma Coast Vineyards Dry Creek Valley

Like so many of those with long, successful careers in the wine industry, John and Barbara Drady eventually found themselves the owners of vineyards in what they like to refer to as the "extreme" Sonoma Coast. Near the town of Freestone, just a few miles and a few low hills away from the Pacific, the Dradys produce Pinot Noir, Chardonnay, and Sauvignon Blanc with the help of winemaker Anthony Austin. Even from the first vintage in 2002, the wines have distinguished themselves as balanced, delicate, and delicious. ★ **Rising star**

No visitor facilities
www.sonomacoastvineyards.com

Sonoma-Cutrer Vineyards
Russian River Valley

US Air Force pilot Brice Cutrer Jones founded Sonoma-Cutrer after getting his MBA in 1972. In 1981, Jones decided to focus his successful winery entirely on

STARRY NIGHT WINERY
DO NOT LET THE LOCATION FOOL YOU.
THIS IS SERIOUSLY GOOD ZINFANDEL

SKIPSTONE RANCH
RECENTLY RELEASED, THIS INAUGURAL
VINTAGE SHOWS GREAT PROMISE

Chardonnay, which it has done with a vengeance ever since. Brown Forman Corporation purchased the winery in 1999, and by then it had become the top producer of Chardonnay in the country, selling more bottles in fine dining restaurants than any other brand. The winery's ubiquitous Russian River Ranches Chardonnay continues to offer very high quality for the price.

No visitor facilities
www.sonomacutrer.com

St. Francis Winery Sonoma Valley

It is a mark of its success that many believe St. Francis Winery to be one of Sonoma's oldest family wineries. It does have a long history, but one that only goes back to 1971, when owner Joe Martin and his wife Emma purchased a vineyard in Sonoma, and then, 8 years later, built their own winery which they christened St. Francis. Now making north of 3 million bottles of wine, St. Francis has managed to keep quality high for its size. Look for the single-vineyard reds in particular.

100 Pythian Rd., Santa Rosa, CA 95409
www.stfranciswine.com

Starry Night Winery Marin

An amateur winemaking operation in a garage, with an obsession with Zinfandel, has now become a 168,000-bottle winery with the same obsession. Friends Wayne Hansen, Bruce Walker, Mike Miller, and Skip Granger got into winemaking for the fun and fascination of it, but ended up being too good at it to leave their operation at an amateur level. They took winemaking classes, honed their skills and, in 1999, became a commercial winery. Their focus is still on Zinfandel, of which they produce several bottlings in the unromantic setting of an industrial park winery in Novato.

55 Frosty Lane, Novato, CA 94949
www.starrynightwinery.com

Stuhlmuller Vineyards Alexander Valley

Some of the most interesting wineries in Sonoma are run by families that got their start growing grapes for others, before jumping into the business with their own label. Stuhlmuller Vineyards is a great example. The Stuhlmuller family started growing Chardonnay, Cabernet Sauvignon, and Zinfandel in 1982 and, after graduating from college in 1994, the young Fritz Stuhlmuller decided his family should make their own wine. With a winery built in 2000, the estate produces 72,000 bottles of wine under the guidance of winemaker Leo Hansen. The Chardonnay is especially good and is also extraordinarily good value.

4951 West Soda Rock Lane, Healdsburg, CA 95448
www.stuhlmullervineyards.com

Suacci Carciere Russian River Valley

After raising their kids together in the town of Sebastopol, the Suacci and Carciere families knew a lot about each other. So, when the Suacci's planted a tiny 3.5 acre (1.4ha) plot they owned with Pinot Noir, and it turned out to be a really good vineyard, the idea of joining together to make a wine from it was not a daunting proposition. In 2006, John Suacci and Andy Carciere hired the talented young Ryan Zepaltas (who also works for Siduri Winery) to make the label's wines,

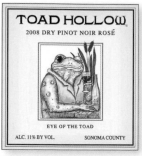

TOAD HOLLOW VINEYARDS

AN EXCELLENT PROVENCAL-STYLE ROSE
NAMED AFTER A CLASSIC ENGLISH BOOK

TERLATO FAMILY VINEYARDS

THIS FINE PINOT IS A SMALL SCALE WINE
FROM A LARGE-SCALE WINE EMPIRE

which include a Chardonnay made from fruit from the highly rated Heintz Vineyard. Both the Pinot Noir and Chardonnay are outstanding. ★ **Rising star**

No visitor facilities
www.suaccicarciere.com

Tandem Wines Russian River Valley

Originally a partnership between two very talented winemakers, Greg La Folette and Greg Bjornstad, the winery continues to be run by La Folette after the pair broke up. One of the top winemakers of Pinot Noir and Chardonnay in California, La Folette continues to make Tandem wines even as he flies around the globe as a consulting winemaker. The winery produces an array of wines, each made in minute quantities from top growers around northern California. Look for the Ritchie Vineyard Chardonnay and the Auction Block Pinot Noir, the latter being blended from the best barrels of the vintage.

No visitor facilities
www.tandemwinery.com

Terlato Family Vineyards
Russian River Valley

The Terlato family was in the wine business for about 50 years before its name appeared on the front of a bottle as opposed to the back. Terlato Wines is now one of the United States' largest and most successful wine empires. Primarily an importer, it also owns several vineyards. Founder and patriarch Anthony Terlato is joined in this latest venture by his sons Bill and John, and winemaker Doug Fletcher, who also makes the wines for several other Terlato Vineyards brands. All the wines are well made, but the Pinot Noirs especially so. ★ **Rising star**

No visitor facilities
www.terlatovineyards.com

Terremoto Marin

The owners of Terremoto, Chris and Karen Gallien, are Midwesterners turned California winemakers. Like many small vintners, they followed their love of wine to its extreme logical conclusion. With some encouragement from winegrowers and winemakers they had befriended in their many trips to Sonoma and Napa, they set up shop in a small industrial park in Novato where they make a few hundred cases of inexpensive wine. Of the four wines they produce, their Syrah is the best. Look for the funky, brightly colored labels.

No visitor facilities
www.terremotocellars.net

Toad Hollow Vineyards Russian River Valley

Toad Hollow's winemaker and owner, the late Todd Williams (who went by the name Dr. Toad), got a little help from his friend Rodney Strong (or The Dancing Badger), and a lot of inspiration from Kenneth Grahame's *The Wind in the Willows* to start this winery. Originally a small project to do something "fun", the winery has grown to a production of millions of bottles. The winery owns 103 acres (42ha) of vineyard and several sub-brands, but continues to make good quality wine. In particular, look out for the Eye of the Toad rosé.

409A Healdsburg Ave., Healdsburg, CA 95448
www.toadhollow.com

Truett Hurst Vineyards Dry Creek Valley

A multi-generational partnership between industry veterans Paul Dolan, Philip Hurst, and his son Heath, Truett Hurst Vineyards (purchased in 2008) has been conceived as a project to fully embody the principles of Biodynamic wine-growing and winemaking. With the help of viticulturalist Mark De Meulanaere and winemaker Virginia Lambrix, the estate farms 26 acres (10.5ha) of vineyards and 5 acres (2ha) of Biodynamic gardens. It is too early to fully evaluate the new efforts, as the winery is still working out the kinks, but this is one to watch.

5610 Dry Creek Rd., Healdsburg, CA 95448
www.truetthurst.com

Twomey Russian River Valley

Few wine lovers have not heard of Silver Oak, the famed Cabernet Sauvignon producer. Twomey is the sister brand to Silver Oak and, instead of Cabernet Sauvignon, it focused on a high-end *cuvée* of Merlot, based in Napa Valley. More recently, Twomey opened a second facility in Sonoma County, taking over the former Roshambo winery with its sleek modern architecture. In conjunction with this move, the winery began to produce Pinot Noir and Sauvignon Blanc. The star of the line-up, however, continues to be the meticulously produced Merlot.

3000 Westside Rd., Healdsburg, CA 95448
www.twomeycellars.com

Ty Caton Sonoma Valley

The Caton family purchased an abandoned turn-of-the-20th-century wine estate in the Sonoma Valley in 1981, thinking that eventually they would restore it. Sometimes though, such plans hibernate until the next generation comes along to put them into action. In 1997, Ty Caton replanted roughly 40 acres (16ha) of the ancient vineyards and, with the help of friend and mentor Peter Mathis of Ravenswood, made his first vintage of wine in 2000. Since then, Caton has continued to make a few thousand cases of wine from his vineyards each year. His unusual Tytanium red blend of Cabernet Sauvignon, Petite Sirah, Syrah, and Malbec is excellent.

8910 Sonoma Highway, Kenwood, CA 95454
www.tycaton.com

Unti Vineyards Dry Creek Valley

While it is little more than a decade old, Unti Vineyards operates with the confidence of a more established winery. The estate was founded by Mick, George, and Linda Unti with a clear vision to produce great Mediterranean-style wines from Dry Creek Valley. The winery's 50 acres (20ha) are planted with a number of grape varieties uncommon to the area, including Montepulciano, Barbera, Picpoul Blanc, and more. From these, the winery crafts excellent wines that are distinctive and built to age. Their rosé, from Grenache and Mourvèdre (the vines are Châteauneuf-du-Pape clones), is one of the best in California, and is released young.

4202 Dry Creek Rd., Healdsburg, CA 95448
www.untivineyards.com

Valdez Family Winery Russian River Valley

The story behind this winery is the story of a man named Ulises Valdez. It is also the story of the American Dream writ large in the wine industry. From his start as an indigent illegal immigrant, and underage field worker pruning grape vines, Ulises Valdez has risen to be the owner of Valdez and Sons Vineyard Management, a 900 acre (364ha), 70-employee company in Sonoma County that farms grapes for some of the country's top winemakers. Now some of those very same winemakers (Jeff Cohn, Paul Hobbs, and Marc Aubert) are making wine for the latest chapter in Ulises's story: Valdez Family Winery. Like Ulises himself, the wines produced are nothing short of stupendous. ★ **Rising star**

No visitor facilities
www.valdezfamilywinery.com

Valley of the Moon Winery Sonoma Valley
Most people have forgotten that Sonoma is a Native American word that roughly translates as "Valley of the Moon". Operated as a winery since 1863, the former Madrone Winery was renamed Valley of the Moon when it was sold to new owners in 1941. It changed hands again in 1997, but retains its name. The winery produces a wide array of reasonably priced, good-quality wines, including their distinctive Cabernet Sauvignon with aromas of mint—it is aged for nearly two years in French and American oak barrels.

777 Madrone Rd., Glen Ellen, CA 95442
www.valleyofthemoonwinery.com

Vergari Wines Russian River Valley
Financial-analyst-turned-winemaker David Vergari worked his way up from the bottom rung of the industry ladder, starting with a degree from University of California, Davis. After a period working as a harvest intern in Spain and Australia, he returned to have a solid career as research enologist, then winemaker, at several California labels, before leaving to start his own. Despite living in southern California, Vergari farms vineyard plots on longterm contracts with excellent growers, and makes small quantities of delicious wine. In particular, his Van der Kamp and DuNah Pinot Noirs are worth buying.

No visitor facilities
www.vergariwines.com

Walter Hansel Russian River Valley
Walter Hansel made a good living as the owner of several car dealerships in Sonoma County in the 1970s. In 1978, he began plowing his savings into vineyard land that accumulated to 65 acres (26ha) over the course of 20 years. Unfortunately, Hansel passed away just as his son Stephen was harvesting the first vintage that would go to make their own wine. Mentored by friends and neighbors including, notably, Tom Rochioli, Stephen has continued to produce excellent, ageworthy Pinot Noirs that are some of the most reasonably priced in the area.

5465 Hall Rd., Santa Rosa, CA 95401
www.walterhanselwinery.com

West Wind Wines Marin
Nurse Cynthia Klock and her doctor husband, John live in the Nicasio Hills and farm a tiny 2 acres (0.8ha) of grapes, but nonetheless manage to make several hundred cases of wine each vintage. How is this possible? Because other wineries donate grapes. West Wind Wines is all about giving. They donate 100% of the profits from the sale of their rudimentary wines (and the olive oil they also make from donated olives) to the Gilead House, a local shelter and charity for homeless mothers with children, who lend a helping hand during harvest.

333 Willow Rd., Nicasio, CA 94946
www.westwindwines.com

Williams Selyem Russian River Valley
Burt Williams and Ed Selyem started their winery in 1981 in a garage over their love of Zinfandel. Owned by the Dyson family since 1998, Williams Selyem still makes a Zinfandel, but the winery became one of California's original cult wineries for its Pinot Noir. Winemaker Bob Cabral makes pale, elegant Pinots from some of the finest vineyards in California, including his famous neighbor Rochioli. Available only to mailing list customers, the top bottlings include Flax, Hirsch, and Vista Verde vineyards.

No visitor facilities
www.williamsselyem.com

Wind Gap Wines Russian River Valley
Wind Gap Wines is the second incarnation of celebrated winemaker Pax Mahle, whose name was affixed to Pax Wine Cellars until recently, when irreconcilable differences split Mahle from his co-owner and majority shareholder. This new brand focuses on small lots of wine made the way that Mahle wants, from meticulous berry selection to wild yeast ferments, to neutral oak aging for his whites, and occasionally even weirder stuff. For example, long skin contact on his Pinot Gris, in an obscure Italian tradition, which produces an aromatic orange-colored wine. ★ **Rising star**

6450 First St., Forestville, CA 95436
www.windgapwines.com

Woodenhead Russian River Valley
Nikolai Stez has long had a thing for fermentation. It started when his Russian immigrant parents taught him how to make "kvas" out of overripe fruit. Once he became old enough to actually drink the stuff, his experiments turned more serious, eventually leading him down the path that would have him working 17 harvests at Williams Selyem winery as an assistant winemaker. Together with his wife Zina Bower, Stez runs their tiny winery entirely by hand, making small lots of outstanding Pinot Noir and Zinfandel from vineyards in both Sonoma and Mendocino counties. ★ **Rising star**

5700 River Rd., Santa Rosa, CA 95401
www.woodenheadwine.com

Zepaltas Wines Russian River Valley
Wisconsin native Ryan Zepaltas literally stumbled into the winemaking business after his dreams of making it big as a skateboarder fizzled out rather quickly. From a begrudging first job as winery grunt, handed to him by a family friend, to cellar rat at famed Siduri Wines, Zepaltas's transformation was as rapid as it was thorough. And just as quickly he has started his own label to an avalanche of early acclaim. Zepaltas Wines currently produces 17 different Pinot Noirs, Syrahs, and Chardonnays in microscopic quantities. All are worth trying if you can find them. ★ **Rising star**

No visitor facilities
www.zepaltaswines.com

GRAND CRU PINOT NOIR

America does not use a cru system to identify vineyard quality as do the French wine regions of Burgundy or Bordeaux, but if it did, few could argue against Rochioli Vineyards receiving Grand Cru status. The Rochioli family have been farming their vineyards on the banks of the Russian River for almost 100 years. Wine produced from their Pinot Noir grapes made several other wineries famous, including, most notably, Williams Selyem, before the family decided to launch their own brand in 1982. Under the guidance of winemaker Tom Rochioli, now the third generation to run the family's farm, the winery produces two tiers of wine. The Rochioli Vineyards wines are regional blends, while the J. Rochioli label is used for their vineyard-designated wines (mostly Pinot Noir) that are sold only to mailing list customers. Rochioli wines are known for their ageworthiness—good vintages can improve over several decades.

MENDOCINO AND LAKE COUNTIES

State of California
Mendocino and Lake wine regions

Mendocino County is a free-thinking region, where Pinot Noir, Italian-style reds, and Alsace-style whites stand out. Vineyards share the rugged, forested terrain with a sparse population of humans. The county's remoteness, it's dearth of paved roads, even its spectacular 120 miles (195km) of Pacific coastline have kept it beyond the reach of most travelers to Northern California since it was first settled in the 1850s. These factors slowed the development of the wine industry in Mendocino and neighboring Lake County, while enabling (or forcing) many of its vineyards and wineries to pursue their own survival strategies in the absence of the ready commercial opportunities enjoyed by wineries closer to civilization.

Major grapes

 Reds

Cabernet Sauvignon

Carignan

Merlot

Petite Sirah

Pinot Noir

Syrah

Tempranillo

Zinfandel

 Whites

Chardonnay

Gewurztraminer

Riesling

Sauvignon Blanc

Vintages

2009
Rain during harvest hurt quality in some Zinfandel and Petite Sirah.

2008
Drought, frost, and wildfires challenged grape growers.

2007
Great for Pinot Noir and most other varieties.

2006
Good for Pinot Noir and Bordeaux-blend reds; very good for Zinfandel.

2005
Very high quality in Anderson Valley in particular.

2004
Sunny, hot weather made rich and powerful wines.

In Mendocino County's warmer inland sections and on the remote ridge tops that rise above the morning fog, Italian immigrants in the early 20th century discovered they could grow the Zinfandel, Petite Sirah, and Carignan that reminded them of home. From the 1960s, urban American exiles found vineyard sites in Anderson Valley, where Riesling and Gewurztraminer made aromatic and refreshing white wines, and Pinot Noir seemed promising.

French company Roederer first proved that Anderson Valley could make world-class sparkling wine. Today, it is not bubbly but Anderson Valley Pinot Noir that is Mendocino's hottest item among wine connoisseurs. It is lighter than most California renderings, but shows more concentration than Oregon Pinot. Think of a seductive Chambolle-Musigny from Burgundy, but with riper fruit flavors.

Cabernet Sauvignon, Merlot, and Sauvignon Blanc rank among the region's most widely planted grape varieties, but a good percentage of these grapes travel south to Sonoma County. To taste distinctive Mendocino wines, drinkers can confidently pick dark-tinted Petite Sirah and raspberry-scented Zinfandel from pioneering winery Parducci, and a rare blend of red varieties that is made only here, called Coro Mendocino.

The seclusion that attracted the free thinkers had positive influences on grape growing here. The Mendocino County Winegrape Commission brags that their county is "America's Greenest Wine Region". Nearly 3,950 acres (1,600ha) of a total 18,000 acres (7,300ha) of wine grapes are certified organic, and another 690 acres (280ha) are either certified, or on their way to becoming, Biodynamic. Many environmental leaders of California wine's are here, including Fetzer Vineyards and its offspring winery, Bonterra.

One of these Fetzer spin-offs, Ceàgo Vinegarden, sprouted in Lake County on the shores of Clear Lake and is one of the few wineries in the world where you can arrive by boat. In the flat areas around the lake, and in the shadow of dramatic Mount Konocti, Sauvignon Blanc and Chardonnay vines have replaced many of the former pear orchards. On the hillsides and high plateaus nearby, Cabernet Sauvignon and Merlot, plus Syrah and Tempranillo, have created ambitious wines that are slowly gaining renown for their powerful fruit flavors and vibrant textures. Newish wineries, including Brassfield, Six Sigma, and Shannon Ridge, plus veteran winemaker Jed Steele of Steele Wines, are bringing attention to Lake County's 8,800 acres (3,560ha) of vineyards and wineries.

Lake resembles Mendocino County, with an absence of trendy restaurants and the oversized egos of other wine regions. Winemakers here march to a different beat. They have found the grapes and wine styles that suit their geography and microclimates, and persist in making excellent wines that go well beyond the chocolate and vanilla of Cabernet and Chardonnay.

Black Kite Cellars Mendocino

A small Pinot Noir producer near Philo in Anderson Valley was inspired by the wines of Burgundy and by a bird—a species of kite native to Mendocino County. The Green family of Black Kite divides its 40 acre (16ha) vineyard into smaller blocks, and then vinifies the grapes from each block separately but using the same method, as is the tradition in Burgundy. Founded in 2003, by the 2007 vintage Black Kite was making at least four different Pinots totaling 900 cases, including an enticing and delicious River Turn Block Pinot. ★ Rising star

No visitor facilities
www.blackkitecellars.com

Bonterra Vineyards Mendocino

Bonterra was the first widely distributed US wine brand to put its money where its principles were by only using organically grown grapes. This spin-off from Fetzer Vineyards is a separate winery on the McNab Ranch in Mendocino County. Long-time winemaker Robert Blue makes very steady, if not flashy wines, including a range of five whites topped by a Reserve Chardonnay, plus Merlot, Syrah, Zinfandel, and Cabernet Sauvignon. An especially rare red blend called The McNab goes one step beyond organic, using Biodynamically grown grapes.

12901 Old River Road, Hopland, CA 95449
www.bonterra.com

Brassfield Estate Lake

Since 1998, Jerry Brassfield and company have pioneered a small viticultural area called High Valley, which measures 3 by 9 miles (4.8 by 14.5km) on the east side of Clear Lake and lies a few hundred feet higher. They converted native oak woodlands and cattle pasture to vineyards, planted 19 grape varieties ranging from Gewurztraminer to Zinfandel, and soon began varietal bottlings of a broad spectrum of wines to ascertain which would perform best in the long run. As the name implies, all of Brassfield Estate's wines are grown, made into wine, and bottled on the property.

10915 High Valley Road, Clearlake Oaks, CA 95423
www.brassfieldestate.com

Breggo Cellars Mendocino

Breggo is a newcomer to Anderson Valley, developed on a 203 acre (82ha) former sheep ranch close to Highway 128 (Breggo means sheep in the local Boontling dialect). Co-founder Douglas Ian Stewart has sold the winery business, but not his 7 acre (3ha) vineyard, to Cliff Lede, who owns a Napa Valley winery of the same name. Stewart intends to remain as an equity partner and continue to guide the winemaking. Breggo makes three Pinot Noir wines, including a Ferrington Vineyard offering that is distinctive and Burgundian in style, plus five different whites, a rosé, and a Syrah. ★ Rising star

11011 Highway 128, Boonville, CA 95415
www.breggo.com

Ceàgo Vinegarden Lake

Few wineries anywhere can match the waterfront ambience of Ceàgo Vinegarden on the shore of Clear Lake in Lake County. Owner Jim Fetzer's idea was to build a showplace in this somewhat scruffy bass fishing destination that would call attention to the 8,000 cases of

BONTERRA ZINFANDEL
BONTERRA HAS BEEN MAKING WINE FROM ORGANICALLY GROWN GRAPES SINCE 1987

BRASSFIELD ESTATE
TROPICAL FRUIT FLAVORS ARE BALANCED BY CRISP ACIDITY IN THIS SAUVIGNON BLANC

"green" wines he makes from his Biodynamic vineyards and winery. Visitors can arrive by car, boat (using the dock on the lake), or air (if one flies a seaplane). The dozen wines offered are made largely from Bordeaux varieties, plus Chardonnay, Syrah, and an old California favorite, Muscat Canelli.

5115 East Highway 20, Nice, CA 95464
www.ceago.com

Drew Family Cellars Mendocino

Drew Family Cellars is proving with its high-quality Pinot Noir and Syrah wines that not every highly rated new winery in California reflects a lifestyle decision by already wealthy owners. Jason Drew studied viticulture and enology in California, went to Australia for a master's degree in enology, and worked for four other California wineries before starting his own with wife Molly in 2003. Their small winery, 3 miles (5km) from the coast, was finished in 2005. Drew's 2007 Pinot Noir from Monument Tree Vineyard is a classic example of the varietal, smelling of baking spices and fresh cherries—very appetizing. ★ Rising star

No visitor facilities
www.drewwines.com

Eaglepoint Ranch Mendocino

When John Scharffenberger sold his share of the sparkling wine business that he founded to French luxury goods firm LVMH in 1995, he kept the 80 acre (32ha) vineyard that his family planted in 1975 on mountain slopes above the Ukiah Valley. (He became a chocolatier as well). Casey Hartlip is his partner at Eaglepoint Ranch, where they sell grapes to other wineries while saving a portion to make an unusual collection of their own wines: a tangy Albariño, a high-scoring Petite Sirah, a varietal Grenache, and a fine example of the region's proprietary wine, Coro Mendocino (which is largely Zinfandel).

5399 Mill Creek, Ukiah, CA 95482
www.eaglepointranch.com

Elke Vineyards Mendocino

It is a rare vintner who started as an apple juice producer. While some fans remember Mary Elke Organic Apple Juice (which is still made in small quantities), the Elke family have owned vineyards for 20 years in Napa and Mendocino. Since 1997, the family have bottled some of their own wine while selling grapes to great California brands such as Roederer Estate and Au Bon Climat. Elke Blue Diamond Pinot Noir from the family's Donnelly Creek Vineyard in Anderson Valley shows lots of body and personality. Value-oriented Pinot, Chardonnay, and a rosé are labeled Mary Elke. ★ Rising star

12351 Highway 128, Boonville, CA 95415
www.elkevineyards.com

Esterlina Vineyards Mendocino

The Mendocino winery of the Sterling family, Esterlina ("sterling" in Spanish), is situated above a hillside vineyard near Philo in Anderson Valley. Esterlina makes a dozen wines from this site, including a lovely Pinot Noir with a lingering finish, and an exciting, off-dry and aromatic Riesling from the tiny Cole Ranch AVA. Esterlina, in fact, owns all the grape vines in the 189 acre (76ha) appellation, which is the nation's smallest.

MENDOCINO AND LAKE COUNTIES

Vineyards in Mendocino County are mostly in the relatively flat, warm interior valley through which the Russian River runs, and which is well suited for full-bodied red wines, Sauvignon Blanc, and, in some spots, Chardonnay. The county itself is an AVA, and is further divided into nine other AVAs with two more pending approval. Anderson Valley is the best known and coolest in climate, favouring Pinot Noir and Alsace grape varieties. Mendocino Ridge is defined not only by length and width but also by elevation—only sites above the fog line are included (the locals refer to it as "islands in the sky"). Lake County includes the large Clear Lake AVA and the smaller Red Hills Lake County and High Valley AVAs.

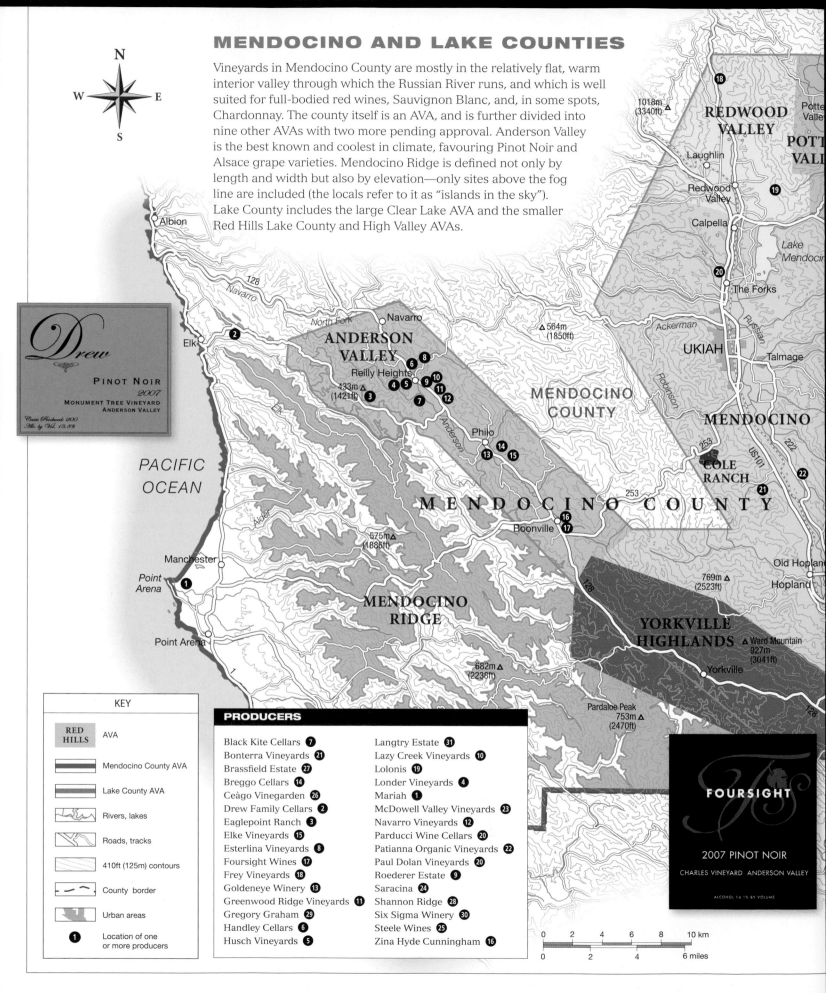

KEY

RED HILLS	AVA
	Mendocino County AVA
	Lake County AVA
	Rivers, lakes
	Roads, tracks
	410ft (125m) contours
	County border
	Urban areas
1	Location of one or more producers

PRODUCERS

Black Kite Cellars	**7**	Langtry Estate	**31**
Bonterra Vineyards	**21**	Lazy Creek Vineyards	**10**
Brassfield Estate	**27**	Lolonis	**19**
Breggo Cellars	**14**	Londer Vineyards	**4**
Ceàgo Vinegarden	**26**	Mariah	**1**
Drew Family Cellars	**2**	McDowell Valley Vineyards	**23**
Eaglepoint Ranch	**3**	Navarro Vineyards	**12**
Elke Vineyards	**15**	Parducci Wine Cellars	**20**
Esterlina Vineyards	**8**	Patianna Organic Vineyards	**22**
Foursight Wines	**17**	Paul Dolan Vineyards	**20**
Frey Vineyards	**18**	Roederer Estate	**9**
Goldeneye Winery	**13**	Saracina	**24**
Greenwood Ridge Vineyards	**11**	Shannon Ridge	**28**
Gregory Graham	**29**	Six Sigma Winery	**30**
Handley Cellars	**6**	Steele Wines	**25**
Husch Vineyards	**5**	Zina Hyde Cunningham	**16**

Drew

PINOT NOIR
2007
MONUMENT TREE VINEYARD
ANDERSON VALLEY

FOURSIGHT

2007 PINOT NOIR

CHARLES VINEYARD ANDERSON VALLEY

ALCOHOL 14.1% BY VOLUME

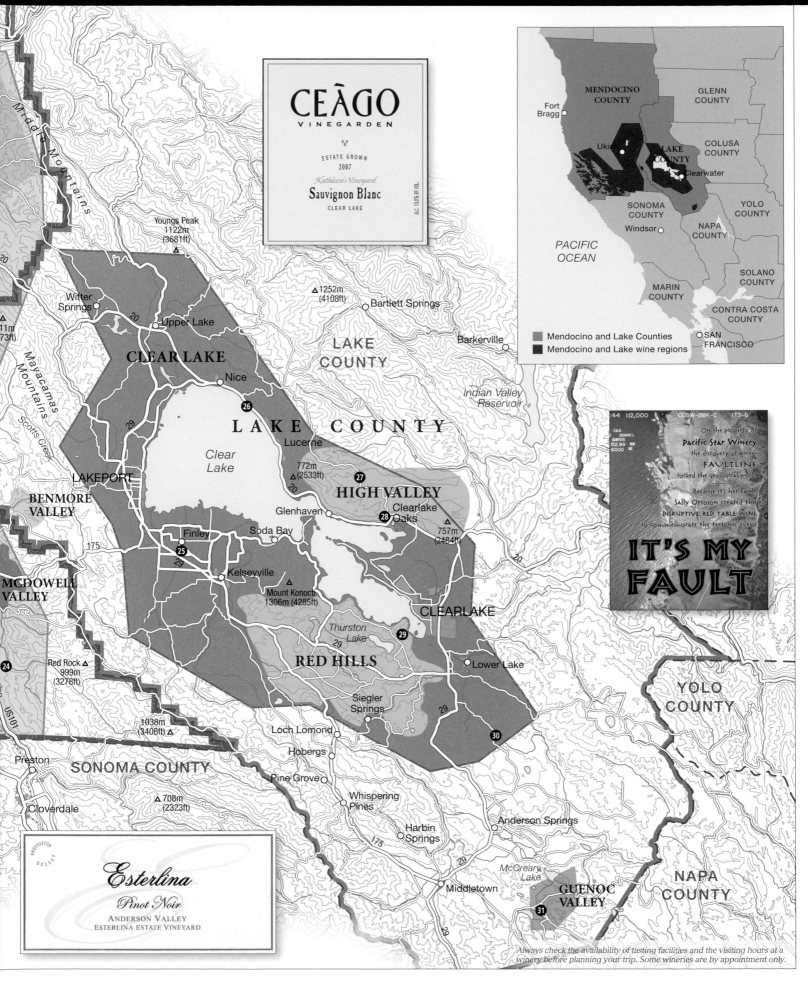

CEÀGO
VINEGARDEN

ESTATE GROWN
2007

Kathleen's Vineyard
Sauvignon Blanc
CLEAR LAKE

ALC. 13.0% BY VOL.

MENDOCINO COUNTY
GLENN COUNTY
Fort Bragg
Ukiah
LAKE COUNTY
COLUSA COUNTY
Clearwater
SONOMA COUNTY
YOLO COUNTY
Windsor
NAPA COUNTY
PACIFIC OCEAN
MARIN COUNTY
SOLANO COUNTY
CONTRA COSTA COUNTY
SAN FRANCISCO

■ Mendocino and Lake Counties
■ Mendocino and Lake wine regions

Middle Mountains

20

1111m (3473ft)

20

24

US101

Mayacamas Mountains

Scotts Creek

Youngs Peak 1122m (3681ft)

Witter Springs

Upper Lake

CLEAR LAKE

Nice

LAKE COUNTY

Bartlett Springs

△1252m (4108ft)

Barkerville

Indian Valley Reservoir

26

LAKE COUNTY

Clear Lake

Lucerne

772m △(2533ft)

20

27

HIGH VALLEY

Clearlake Oaks

28

757m △(2484ft)

20

LAKEPORT

Glenhaven

Soda Bay

Finley

25

29

Kelseyville

BENMORE VALLEY

MCDOWELL VALLEY

Mount Konocti 1306m (4285ft)

CLEARLAKE

Thurston Lake

29

Red Rock △ 999m (3278ft)

RED HILLS

29

Lower Lake

1038m (3406ft)△

Siegler Springs

29

30

Preston

SONOMA COUNTY

△708m (2323ft)

Loch Lomond

Hobergs

Pine Grove

YOLO COUNTY

Cloverdale

175

Whispering Pines

Harbin Springs

Anderson Springs

29

:44 1:2,000   CDBW-BBK-C   173-6
CALIF. RESOURCES SURVEYS 152.95 MM 6000

On the property of
Pacific Star Winery
the discovery of a new
FAULTLINE
rocked the geological world
....
Because it's her Fault,
Sally Ottoson created this
DISRUPTIVE RED TABLE WINE
to commemorate the tectonic event

IT'S MY FAULT

McCreary Lake

GUENOC VALLEY

NAPA COUNTY

Middletown

31

29

PROPRIETOR SELECT

Esterlina
Pinot Noir
ANDERSON VALLEY
ESTERLINA ESTATE VINEYARD

Always check the availability of tasting facilities and the visiting hours at a winery before planning your trip. Some wineries are by appointment only.

FREY VINEYARDS
THE FRESH HOUSE STYLE WILL APPEAL TO
THE MORE ADVENTUROUS PALATES

The family also grow grapes in nearby Alexander Valley and Russian River Valley (northern Sonoma) and the Everett Ridge Winery near Healdsburg. ★ **Rising star**

1200 Holmes Ranch Road, Philo, CA 95466
www.esterlinavineyards.com

Foursight Wines Mendocino
Four members of the Charles family grow the grapes and make the wine at tiny three-year-old Foursight Wines in Anderson Valley. A vineyard came first, growing Pinot Noir, Sauvignon Blanc, and Semillon. Next came Foursight Charles Vineyard Pinot Noir, a structured and firmly acidic wine that forms a nice contrast with the extra ripe style of many California Pinots. Foursight ferments Pinot Noir with native yeast, and makes one version with no new oak barrels. It also crafts a winning Sauvignon Blanc in stainless steel tanks and, all in all, seems to enjoy being different. ★ **Rising star**

14475 Highway 128, Boonville, CA 95466
www.foursightwines.com

Frey Vineyards Mendocino
The Frey family (pronounced fry) operate on a quiet back road in Mendocino County what may be the oldest organic winery in the United States. Their whites, reds, rosés, and dessert wines number 20 different bottlings, all of which are labeled either organic or Biodynamic. While an expanding minority of California wines are made from organically grown grapes, the Frey wines are also processed organically without the use of sulfites or any other synthetic additives. As a result, they exhibit a house style that is aggressively fresh, and does not appeal to everyone at first. But neither does a good Stilton.

14000 Tomki Road, Redwood Valley, CA 95470
www.freywine.com

Goldeneye Winery Mendocino
In a valley where many wineries are promiscuous regarding grape varieties, Goldeneye focuses exclusively on Anderson Valley Pinot Noir. Winemaker Zach Rasmuson bottles two brands: Goldeneye and Migration. The Goldeneye Pinots are more expensive and more heavily oak-flavored. Confluence, Gowan Creek, and The Narrows are all vineyard-designated, while the newest offering, Ten Degrees, is a small-production item selected from the best lots of all the vineyards and is priced accordingly. The Migration Pinots are slightly lighter and more perfumed. Since its founding in 1996 by the owners of Duckhorn Vineyards in Napa Valley, Goldeneye has grown rather quickly, based on the high quality of its Pinot Noirs, its impressive array of owned vineyards, and its casually elegant hospitality center along Highway 128.

9200 Highway 128, Philo, CA 95466
www.goldeneyewinery.com

Greenwood Ridge Vineyards Mendocino
Colorful is a good word to describe Greenwood Ridge Vineyards. It is one of the oldest wineries in Anderson Valley (it was founded in 1980) and is energized by innovations such as solar power and biodiesel-fueled vehicles. Owner Allan Green trained as a graphic artist, and applies his creativity through unusual silk-screened wine labels, an annual wine tasting competition for his

GOLDENEYE WINERY
UNLIKE MOST ANDERSON VALLEY WINERIES,
GOLDENEYE ONLY PRODUCES PINOT NOIR

wine club members, a flock of bright pennants flapping over the tasting room, and a mostly appealing assortment of wines—tasty Zinfandel, Pinot Gris with a rich buttery texture, Pinot Noir that rings true for the region, and luxurious sweet Rieslings.

5501 Highway 128, Philo, CA 95466
www.greenwoodridge.com

Gregory Graham Lake
California wine entrepreneurs consist of two main types. One has made a fortune in another industry first. The other has worked hard as an employee in the wine industry but burned with desire to own a vineyard and winery of their own. Gregory Graham is one of the latter, having toiled at Napa Valley wineries including Rombauer, where he was head winemaker, before he and his wife Marianne bought their current winery site in the Red Hills AVA of Lake County in 2000. The winery was built in 2006. Graham's experience shines through in well-crafted vineyard-designated Zinfandel, Syrah, Grenache, and other wines.

13633 Point Lakeview Road, Lower Lake, CA 95457
www.ggwines.com

Handley Cellars Mendocino
Milla Handley's wines are as unpretentious and laid-back as the rustic-looking farm (which was certified organic in 2005) where she grows and ages them. While many California wineries try hard to be heard, Handley seems confident enough to speak softly and simply deliver flavorful, deftly balanced, easy-to-drink Burgundy and Alsace varietals year after year. Her Gewurztraminer is all honey and rose petals and is appetizingly dry. The Pinot Noir from Holmes Vineyard is superbly balanced and delicious. Her estate-grown Chardonnay shows fine concentration and complexity, but no obvious oak. An estate-grown brut rosé might be the only merely good wine in the line-up.

3151 Highway 128, Philo, CA 95466
www.handleycellars.com

Husch Vineyards Mendocino
Travelers through the remote Anderson Valley have stopped to taste wine and picnic at the pioneering Husch winery since its first harvest in 1971. This popular wine producer now makes 21 different wines (only six of which are widely distributed) including a light, sweet Gewurztraminer, a tangy Sauvignon Blanc grown in the Ukiah Valley, and three Pinot Noirs that capture the vivid cherry flavors and bright texture typical of Anderson Valley. The Oswald family have owned and operated Husch since 1979.

4400 Highway 128, Philo, CA 95466
www.huschvineyards.com

Langtry Estate Lake
The only winery in Lake County's Guenoc Valley makes such a fuss about its founder, Lillie Langtry—a famed Victorian beauty who performed at opera houses and saloons in the Wild West—that one could forget how good its wines (labeled either Langtry or Guenoc) can be. The property covers more than 21,000 acres (8,500ha) of remote land with just 449 acres (182ha) of vines, some of which extend across the county line into Napa. The crisp

Guenoc Sauvignon Blanc Lake County provides great value. The Langtry Estate Petite Sirah is a smooth behemoth. The property is well worth a visit.

21000 Butts Canyon Road, Middletown, CA 95461
www.langtryestate.com

Lazy Creek Vineyards Mendocino

Founded in the early 20th century, Lazy Creek is not only one of the oldest wineries in Mendocino County, it is also one of its most unique. In blind tastings, the Lazy Creek wines stand out not for their extremes but for their restraint. Sloping hillside vineyards, many old vines, and low yields add to the terroir evident in a smoky, apple-tinged dry Gewurztraminer, a distinctive Chardonnay, an aromatic but steely Riesling, and a restrained, tannic Pinot Noir that needs some aging. Hans and Theresia Kobler bought the property from the Parducci family in 1982 and ran it for 26 years. New owners Don and Rhonda Carano of Ferrari-Carano winery in Sonoma County appear to share their predecessors' respect for the individuality of this historic estate.

4741 Highway 128, Philo, CA 95466
www.lazycreekvineyards.com

Lolonis Mendocino

One of the oldest family-owned vineyards in Mendocino County has raised its game in the last decade. With an organic approach to grape-growing in Redwood Valley and a deft touch in the cellar from winemaker Lori Knapp (formerly of St. Francis), Lolonis is a very good brand to rediscover. The luscious, buttery Chardonnay, comfortable Ricetti Vineyard Zinfandel and a full-bodied Merlot, dubbed Petros, are winners. The intense Orpheus Petite Sirah should improve for at least 10 years.

1905 Road D, Redwood Valley, CA 95470
www.lolonis.com

Londer Vineyards Mendocino

Relatively new to Anderson Valley (the first vintage was in 2001), Londer Vineyards quickly found its groove and now reigns as one of the top-quality Pinot Noir properties in the valley as well as an often outstanding producer of Chardonnay and both dry and sweet Gewurztraminer. The premium-priced Paraboll Pinot Noir faced no better contenders in a tasting held for wine writers of 35 Anderson Valley grown Pinots from 2006. The Londer winery lies off the beaten track, but visitors can now sample and buy these rare offerings at a new tasting room in the small town of Boonville, California.

4830 Monte Bloyd Road, Philo, CA 95466
www.londervineyards.com

Mariah Mendocino

Mariah is one of very few wineries in the Mendocino Ridge AVA where the wine-growing land is exclusively on ridge tops above the morning fogs and very near the Pacific Ocean. Founders Dan and Vicki Dooling have lived here since 1979—many miles from the nearest town. They make velvety Zinfandel, and two stand-out Syrahs, both with distinctive floral accents. The Syriah Syrah is more approachable, while the Mariah Syrah is for aging.

Point Arena, CA 95468
www.mariahvineyards.com

McDowell Valley Vineyards Mendocino

With vineyards planted to the Rhône grape variety of Syrah as early as 1919, McDowell Valley Vineyards (established in 1970) was a "Rhône Ranger" long before the term became popular in the 1980s. Today, its fertile vineyard in the sunny, warm growing area of the McDowell Valley AVA, which lies on the southwestern slopes of the Mayacamas Mountains, still grows Syrah along with Grenache and other grapes. The winery takes these grapes and turns them into a variety of wines, ranging from a Syrah rosé to an Aussie-style Shiraz, and from a Coro Mendocino blend based on Zinfandel to a non-vintage port-style dessert wine.

13380 South Highway 101, Hopland, CA 95449
www.mcdowellsyrah.com

Navarro Vineyards Mendocino

Founders Ted Bennett and Deborah Cahn were not quite the first urban émigrés to settle in Mendocino County to make wine, but somehow the couple embody the back-to-the-land, earth-first philosophy that flowered in the region in the 1970s. Today, on a tour of his estate, Ted points out the sheep that trim the weeds in the organic vineyards, a new trellis set-up that shades the grapes a bit more than the ubiquitous vertical-shoot-positioned system, and new drainage culverts that allow spawning salmon to climb streams on the dramatic hillside property. Navarro wines—Riesling, Gewurztraminer, Chardonnay, and Pinot Noir—fit like your favorite blue jeans and won't wear a hole in your pocket.

5601 Highway 128, Philo, CA 95466
www.navarrowine.com

Obsidian Ridge Lake

The owners of Obsidian Ridge Vineyard, the Molnar family, must have a sense of adventure. They bought a winery in California's Carneros district in 1973, when it was mostly pasture land, they invested in a wine barrel cooperage in Hungary (from where the family emigrated) and, in the late 1990s, they planted Cabernet Sauvignon and Syrah in this high-elevation Lake County (now Red Hills) vineyard laced with the sharp, black stones that native Americans used as weapons. While the Carneros Chardonnays and Pinot Noirs (labeled Molnar Family and Kazmer & Blaize) can be superlative, the Red Hills Lake County reds, particularly the full-bodied Cabernet Sauvignon, are catching up quickly. ★ Rising star

Winery and vineyards open by appointment only
www.tricyclewineco.com

Pacific Star Winery Mendocino

One of the few wineries anywhere with a direct view of an ocean, Pacific Star makes an eccentric but high-quality mix of mostly red wines sourced from vineyards around Mendocino County and farther afield. Owner and winemaker Sally Ottoson credits the salt air, and the Pacific surf crashing into a sea cave under her cellar, as the magic touches in her small-scale winemaking efforts. Offerings range from an everyday red varietal blend named It's My Fault (for a seismic fault running under the property) to a sophisticated, layered red Coro Mendocino wine blended from Zinfandel and other varieties.

401 North Main Street, Fort Bragg, CA 95437
www.pacificstarwinery.com

THE FETZER DIASPORA

It is difficult to talk about Mendocino or Lake County wines without the name Fetzer cropping up. Fetzer Vineyards remains the area's largest winery, producing more than a million cases annually, and the Fetzer brand is one of the most common in wine shops and supermarkets across the United States. The Fetzer family no longer owns the namesake winery, having sold it in 1992 for an amount estimated at $100 million to Brown-Forman, a large spirits and wine company based in Kentucky and best known for Jack Daniel's whiskey. Family members have spread out, but mostly not too far. Their money and energies are hard at work throughout the area, growing wine grapes and making wine under vineyard names and wine brands (but not Fetzer, which was excluded in the sale) such as Patianna, Ceàgo, Saracina, Oster, and Dark Horse.

ROEDERER ESTATE
THIS 60/40 BLEND OF PINOT NOIR AND
CHARDONNAY HAS A SALMON-PINK HUE

PARDUCCI WINE CELLARS
THIS VELVETY RED BURSTS WITH RASPBERRY
AND BLACKBERRY FRUIT FLAVORS

Parducci Wine Cellars Mendocino

For much of the 20th century, Parducci stood alone as a Mendocino County winery, selling wine to the public rather than strictly shipping bulk wine to other wineries. Owner John Parducci was the face of Mendocino winemaking, as his company made many varietals, but few so outstanding in their fields as his Petite Sirah. That tradition continues under the ownership of the Thornhill family and under the winemaking leadership of Paul Dolan, the ex-president of Fetzer Vineyards and probably the most vociferous proponent of Biodynamic grape growing in the United States. Today, the Parducci Petite Sirah True Grit is a more robust version than ever.

501 Parducci Road, Ukiah, CA 95482
www.parducci.com

Patianna Organic Vineyards Mendocino

There is something happening at this Fetzer family operation that merits special attention from adventurous wine drinkers. A blind tasting of Patianna's Biodynamically grown Chardonnay and Sauvignon Blanc shows an extra dimension of vitality that may stem from the non-chemical grape-growing practices used in the Mendocino County vineyard. A spicy ginger-citrus flavor animates the outstanding Chardonnay and a savory character distinguishes the memorable Sauvignon Blanc.

13340 Spring Street, Hopland, CA 95449
www.patianna.com

Paul Dolan Vineyards Mendocino

Paul Dolan may be the leading advocate of environmental stewardship in American winemaking. His words carry extra weight because he and his two sons also grow remarkably good wines at their Dark Horse Ranch, perched on a ridge above the Russian River. Dolan manages the Parducci winery in Ukiah but he seems most at home in the organic biosphere of the vineyard. In addition to several very good organically grown wines, a certified Biodynamic blend called Deep Red, made mostly from Syrah, brims with fruit flavors. ★ Rising star

501 Parducci Road, Ukiah, CA 95482
www.pauldolanwine.com

Roederer Estate Mendocino

It seems illogical that Mendocino County, known for its Pinot Noir, Gewurztraminer, and Zinfandel, could also be home to arguably the best sparkling wine producer in the Americas, but it is true. This California outpost of French champagne firm Louis Roederer makes a brilliant range of fizzes. The classy Roederer Estate Brut non-vintage is easily the match of most champagnes that sell for twice the price, and the L'Ermitage vintage-dated *cuvée* is a special occasion sparkling wine with regal bearing. Roederer uses only grapes from its own vineyards, mostly Chardonnay and Pinot Noir, and blends in Reserve wine aged in oak casks—a rare technique even in Champagne.

4501 Highway 128, Philo, CA 95466
www.roedererestate.com

Saracina Mendocino

With little fanfare, this boutique winery and wine cave along Highway 101 has blossomed into a star with successive releases of excellent Mendocino wines since its first offering in 2002. This is not surprising when one considers that Saracina and its second brand, Atrea, were created by veteran vintner John Fetzer and his wife Patricia Rock. Saracina Sauvignon Blanc is vibrant and rich, the Zinfandel is a classic raspberry concoction, and the Petite Sirah is grand, smoky, and gorgeous. Even more exciting is the velvet-textured Atrea Old Soul Red.

11684 South Highway 101, Hopland, CA 95449
www.saracina.com

Shannon Ridge Lake

Founder Clay Shannon, an unabashed Westerner, wears a Stetson and cowboy boots. He rides herd over the second-biggest vineyard operation in Lake County, with 472 acres (191ha) in the High Valley AVA and 250 acres (101ha) in the Red Hills AVA on the other side of the lake. (Beckstoffer Vineyards is number one but does not make its own wine.) Shannon Ridge opened in 2002, and gifted winemaker Marco Giulio produces more polished wines each year, including a flavor-focused Grenache, an assertive Zinfandel, and a fast-selling Syrah-Zinfandel blend called The Wrangler.

12599 East Highway 20, Clearlake Oaks, CA 95423
www.shannonridge.com

Six Sigma Lake

In the Wild West landscape of remote Lake County, vast tracts of land and big dreams still come together to shape the future. Founders Kaj and Else Ahlmann grew up in Denmark, but in 1999, after a career with a General Electric division where Kaj mastered the business discipline called Six Sigma, they bought a 4,300 acre (1,740ha) ranch, dedicated most of it to a permanent conservation easement, and planted vineyards. Of the many good wines, the spicy, full-bodied Tempranillo is the most memorable. ★ Rising star

13372 Spruce Grove Road, Lower Lake, CA 95457
www.sixsigmaranch.com

Steele Wines Lake

After more than 40 years of winemaking, Jed Steele is still expanding his horizons. Steele Wines in Kelseyville, Lake County, makes dozens of varietals and blends using three brands: Steele, Shooting Star, and Writer's Block. Steele grows 15% of his grape supply and buys more from as far north as Washington State and as far south as Santa Barbara, from where the excellent Bien Nacido Vineyard Pinot Noir comes. DuPratt Vineyard Zinfandel grows on 80-year-old vines on the Pacini ranch in Mendocino Ridge.

4350 Thomas Drive, Highway 29, Kelseyville, CA 95451
www.steelewines.com

Zina Hyde Cunningham Mendocino

The winery may be just 10 years old, but the Cunningham family winemaking tradition dates back to 1862, when the founder and namesake made his first vintage in Sonoma County. Cunningham now crafts a laundry list of at least 15 wines, all of them professionally produced, including a handful of real stars, such as an Anderson Valley Pinot Noir that was all harmony and balance at four years. The attractive winery tasting room in charming Boonville is worth a visit.

14077 Highway 128, Boonville, CA 95415
www.zinawinery.com

Several species of oak are native to California, and the trees can often be seen in vineyard areas.

CENTRAL COAST

The Central Coast, as an American Viticultural Area, is so huge that it is practically meaningless. It stretches roughly 250 miles (400km) along California's coast, from the San Francisco Bay Area in the north to Santa Barbara County in the south. It encompasses 4 million acres (1.6 million ha), of which about 100,000 acres (40,500ha) are planted, and parts of 10 counties. An appellation this large has myriad climates and terrains, so just about any grape variety performs well somewhere in the region. Vineyards in places like the rugged Santa Cruz Mountains tend to be tiny; those in the broad Salinas Valley of Monterey County can be vast. Wineries, too, run the gamut from small artisan producers to big, corporate-owned facilities.

Major grapes

 Reds

Cabernet Sauvignon

Pinot Noir

Syrah

Zinfandel

Whites

Chardonnay

Sauvignon Blanc

Vintages

2009

A small crop with heavy rain in mid-October. Good quality in Chardonnay and Pinot Noir, if harvested before the rain.

2008

Spring frosts, summer heat, September rain, and a small crop. Monterey whites and Santa Barbara Syrah and Bordeaux varieties fared well.

2007

Excellent quality nearly everywhere, with good concentration and intensity.

2006

Monterey Chardonnay and Pinot Noir are excellent, as are Santa Barbara's Bordeaux varieties. Elegant wines from Paso Robles. Uneven quality.

2005

A large crop, with uneven quality. Producers who limited yields made excellent wines.

2004

A hot, dry season resulted in ripe wines with elevated alcohol. Most wines are best drunk young.

One thing that all of the Central Coast shares is some degree of maritime influence—fog, wind, and cool nighttime temperatures—all courtesy of the chilly Pacific Ocean.

At the northern end of the Central Coast is the San Francisco Bay AVA, established mostly for marketing purposes. This AVA includes the Livermore Valley, an area 40 miles (64km) east of San Francisco that gained international recognition in the late 1800s. Things have gone up and down since then, but the huge diurnal temperature swings (day to night), and gravelly, rocky soils, give Livermore great natural assets. Nearby, in communities like Berkeley and Alameda on the eastern side of San Francisco Bay, enterprising winemakers produce wines in warehouse space, following the lead of wineries like Rosenblum Cellars and Edmunds St. John.

South of San Francisco, the Santa Cruz Mountains, too, had a heyday in the late 1800s. This rugged, heavily wooded area in the coastal mountains was one of the first American Viticultural Areas to be defined by elevation. Property is expensive because of the area's proximity to Silicon Valley, so the land available for vineyards is limited, and a number of wineries import grapes from other areas.

Monterey County, on the other hand, has plenty of space for planting vines—the county has more than 40,000 acres (16,000ha) of vineyards, the most in the Central Coast. An estimated 70% of the fruit is vinified elsewhere and often goes into blends with a California or Central Coast appellation. Although cool conditions predominate, and Chardonnay and Pinot Noir are the leading varieties, Monterey County's eight smaller appellations have a variety of climates. One of those AVAs, the Santa Lucia Highlands, is gaining prominence for its lush, ripe Pinot Noirs.

Paso Robles, in San Luis Obispo County, is the fastest-growing California AVA, with more than a five-fold increase in wineries in the past decade. Although all of Paso Robles is a relatively warm growing region, the west side, closer to the ocean, is more rugged, rainier, and slightly cooler, while the east side, with its wide-open terrain, lends itself to bigger vineyards. Paso Robles has long been known for Zinfandel and Cabernet Sauvignon, but Rhône varieties are the hot ticket these days. The much cooler Edna Valley and Arroyo Grande Valley occupy the southern end of San Luis Obispo County and are known for Chardonnay and Pinot Noir.

Those two varieties are also what Santa Barbara County has gained a reputation for, although warmer areas further inland ripen Rhône and Bordeaux varieties successfully. The county has a series of transverse valleys that funnel the ocean influences. At the north is the cool Santa Maria Valley AVA; just south of that is the Los Alamos Valley, which does not have appellation status. The long Santa Ynez Valley includes the Sta. Rita Hills AVA in the west and the newly minted Happy Canyon AVA at the warmer, inland end.

A Donkey and Goat Winery
San Francisco Bay
Like many California winemakers, Tracey and Jared Brandt got inspired about wine while living in France; in their case, the connection is more than nostalgia. These wines showcase expressive California fruit, to be sure, but also the traditions of Old World winemaking: modest alcohol levels, bright acidity, wild yeasts, avoidance of new oak, and a general commitment to making "wines for the table, not the cocktail glass." Made in a warehouse, mostly from single, cool-climate vineyards, Syrah is the house specialty, and is intense and very focused. ★ **Rising star**

2323 B Fourth St., Berkeley, CA 94710
www.adonkeyandgoat.com

Alban Vineyards San Luis Obispo County
Alban Vineyards, founded in 1989, was the first US winery devoted exclusively to Rhône varieties. It was also an anomaly in Edna Valley, which at the time was all about Chardonnay. But John Alban had been captivated by a bottle of Condrieu while studying enology, so he planted Viognier, then Roussanne, and finally Grenache, Syrah, and Mourvèdre. Along the way, he has become one of America's leading experts on Rhône varieties. Alban's whites are rich and aromatic; the reds, many named for specific vineyard blocks, are dense and spicy.

No visitor facilities
www.albanvineyards.com

Alma Rosa Winery Santa Barbara County
Richard Sanford is a Santa Barbara County pioneer. He planted the first Pinot Noir vines in what is now the Sta. Rita Hills AVA and established Sanford Winery. He sold his namesake winery, founding Alma Rosa in 2005. He still has two vineyards totaling more than 100 acres (40ha) in the Sta. Rita Hills, and both are certified organic. Alma Rosa produces Pinot Noir, Chardonnay, Pinot Gris, and Pinot Blanc, from both Sanford's vineyards and purchased grapes. Winemaker Christian Roguenant makes wines that are flavorful and impeccably balanced. ★ **Rising star**

7250 Santa Rosa Rd., Buellton, CA 93427
www.almarosawinery.com

Arcadian Winery Santa Barbara County
Joe Davis, who started Arcadian in 1996, is something of an iconoclast. His website says it all: "Challenging the Style of the New World." While his colleagues produce Chardonnays, Pinot Noirs, and Syrahs that are ripe, lush, and fat, he favors a style that is more refined and elegant, with higher natural acidity. The wines can take time to develop, but they also tend to age better than many California examples. Vineyard sources are some of the best on the Central Coast, such as Pisoni, Sleepy Hollow, Clos Pepe, Dierberg, and Stolpman.

4457 Santa Rosa Rd., Lompoc, CA 93436
www.arcadianwinery.com

Au Bon Climat Santa Barbara County
Winemaker Jim Clendenen founded Au Bon Climat in 1982 with partner Adam Tolmach (now of Ojai Vineyard). Pinot Noir and Chardonnay are the focus, made from grapes sourced from some top vineyards, notably Bien Nacido Vineyard and Clendenen's own Le Bon Climat.

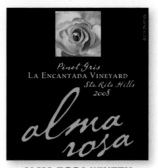

ALMA ROSA WINERY
A SOFT AND ROUNDED PINOT GRIS
WITH GREAT ACIDITY

AU BON CLIMAT
A GOOD-VALUE PINOT FROM BURGUNDIAN
CLONES IN THE BIEN NACIDO VINEYARD

Clendenen makes wines under other labels, such as Bricco Buon Natale and Clendenen Family Vineyards, and he also works with less-common grapes such as Mondeuse and Teroldego. Clendenen has an outsize personality, but his wines are restrained and elegant.

No visitor facilities
www.aubonclimat.com

L'Aventure San Luis Obispo County
Stephan Asseo was educated in Burgundy and worked in Bordeaux, but he chafed against the restrictions of the French appellation system. After searching for more than a year, he found Paso Robles. With a partner, he bought 120 acres (49ha) and started a winery. Asseo makes unconventional blends, including the Estate Cuvée, from Syrah, Cabernet Sauvignon, and Petit Verdot. The wines are ripe and powerful, with generous oak.

2815 Live Oak Rd., Paso Robles, CA 93446
www.aventurewine.com

Baileyana Winery San Luis Obispo County
The Nivens, owners of Paragon Vineyards, are long-time grape growers in the Edna Valley and partners with Diageo in Edna Valley Vineyard. In the early 1990s, family matriarch Catharine Niven wanted to concentrate on a smaller wine project, which became Baileyana. The Nivens planted a new vineyard, Firepeak, and built a modern winery, which is also used as a custom crush facility. The reserve Pinot Noir and Syrah, both designated Grand Firepeak Cuvée, are outstanding. The Nivens have since started a white wine brand called Tangent (the Albariño is excellent); Trenza (Spanish-inspired blends); and a high-end Pinot Noir brand called Cadre.

5828 Orcutt Rd., San Luis Obispo, CA 93401
www.baileyana.com

Bargetto Winery Santa Cruz Mountains
Bargetto Winery was launched the day after the repeal of Prohibition in the US, in 1933. Pinot Grigio is currently the winery's bestseller—when the Bargettos planted it in 1993, there were only 66 acres (27ha) of Pinot Grigio in California. Now, the winery is concentrating more on higher-end wines such as Pinot Noir, Merlot, and a robust red blend of Italian grape varieties called La Vita from their Regan Estate Vineyards. Bargetto also produces popular fruit wines and mead under the Chaucer's label.

3535 North Main St., Soquel, CA 95073
www.bargetto.com

Beckmen Vineyards Santa Barbara County
Beckmen Vineyards was founded in 1994 in the Santa Ynez Valley by Tom Beckmen and his son Steve. They started with 40 acres (16ha) outside Los Olivos, then purchased a 365 acre (148ha) hillside parcel in Ballard Canyon, which they named Purisima Mountain Vineyard. Purisima's location, with elevations ranging from 750ft to 1,250ft (256m to 380m), has proven to be a sweet spot for Rhône grape varieties. Beckmen's Syrahs and Grenaches are ripe without being over the top. There is also a very good, affordably priced blend, Cuvée Le Bec. Purisima Mountain Vineyard is certified organic and Biodynamic.

2670 Ontiveros Rd., Los Olivos, CA 93441
www.beckmenvineyards.com

CENTRAL COAST

The Central Coast AVA stretches roughly 250 miles (400km) along the California coast, starting just south of San Francisco, and encompasses numerous smaller appellations. Wineries and tasting rooms tend to cluster near population centers, while rural parts of Alameda, Monterey, San Luis Obispo, and Santa Barbara counties are home to most of the appellation's vineyards. Temperatures in most vineyard areas are moderated by the influence of the Pacific Ocean's cold waters, but some sites are downright cold, while others are warmer because they are more protected by the mountains that rise up near the coast.

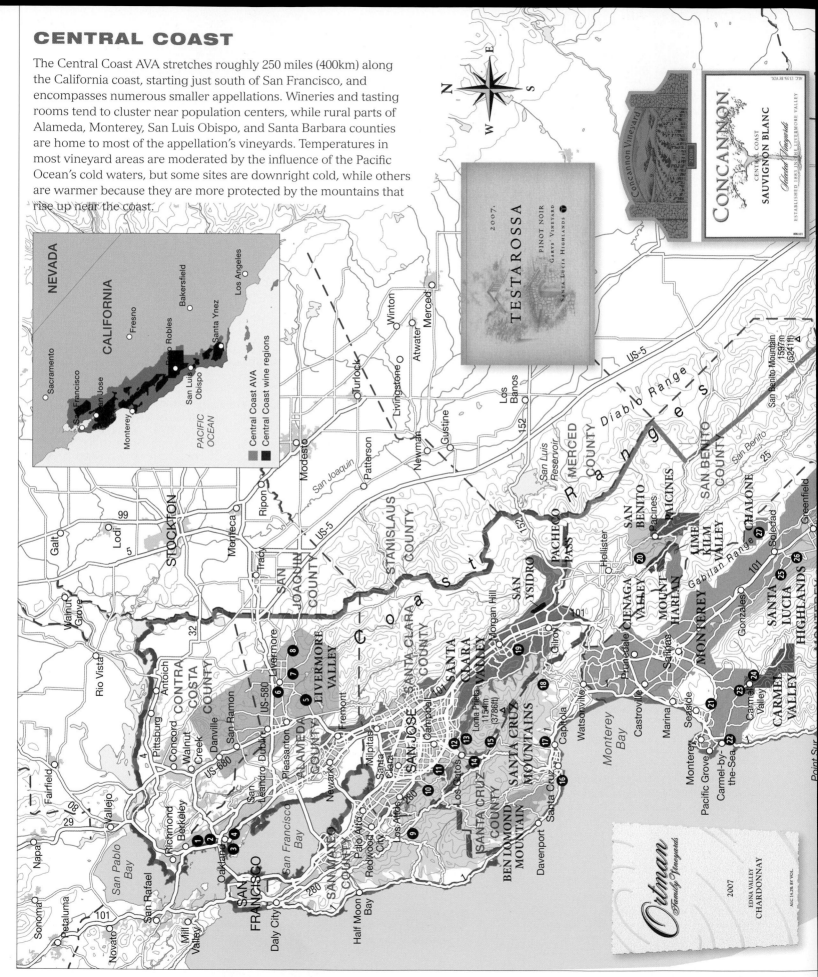

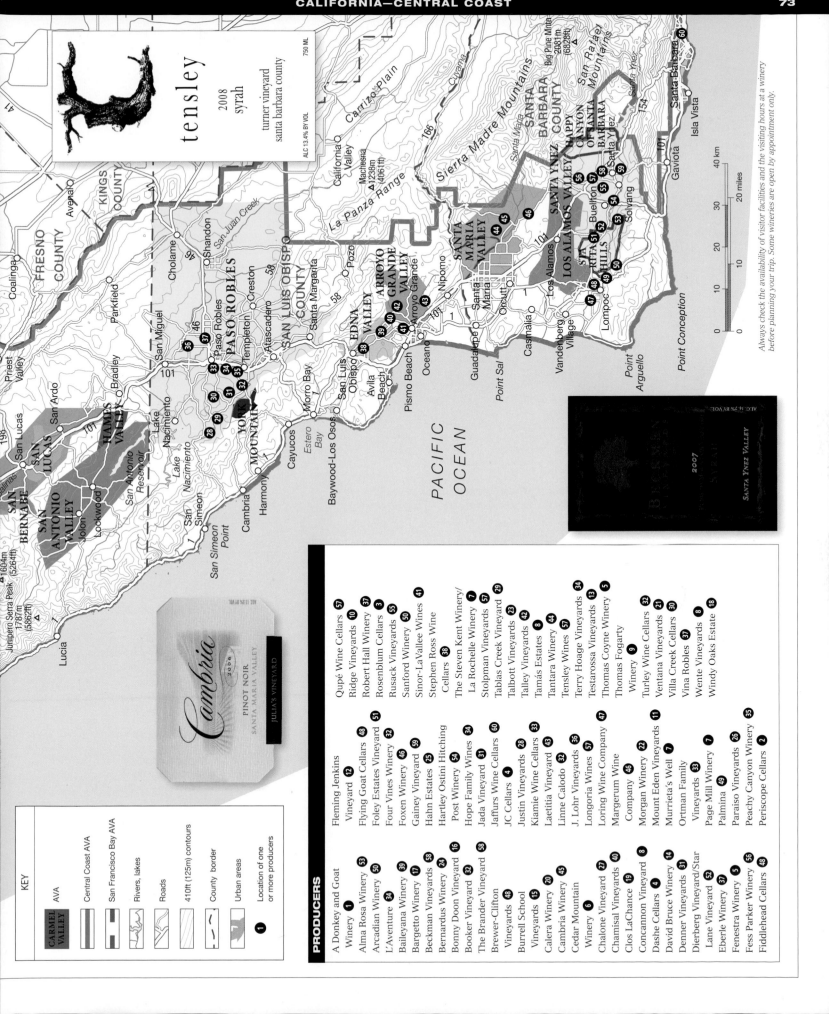

tensley

2008
syrah

turner vineyard
santa barbara county

ALC 13.4% BY VOL 750 ML

Cambria
2006
PINOT NOIR
SANTA MARIA VALLEY
JULIA'S VINEYARD

Always check the availability of visitor facilities and the visiting hours at a winery before planning your trip. Some wineries are open by appointment only.

KEY

CARMEL VALLEY	AVA
	Central Coast AVA
	San Francisco Bay AVA
	Rivers, lakes
	Roads
	410ft (125m) contours
	County border
	Urban areas
①	Location of one or more producers

PRODUCERS

A Donkey and Goat Winery **1**
Alma Rosa Winery **53**
Arcadian Winery **50**
L'Aventure **34**
Baileyana Winery **39**
Bargetto Winery **17**
Beckmen Vineyards **58**
Bernardus Winery **24**
Bonny Doon Vineyard **16**
Booker Vineyard **32**
The Brander Vineyard **58**
Brewer-Clifton Vineyards **48**
Burrell School Vineyards **15**
Calera Winery **20**
Cambria Winery **45**
Cedar Mountain Winery **6**
Chalone Vineyard **27**
Chamisal Vineyards **40**
Clos LaChance **19**
Concannon Vineyard **8**
Dashe Cellars **4**
David Bruce Winery **14**
Denner Vineyards **31**
Dierberg Vineyard/Star Lane Vineyard **52**
Eberle Winery **37**
Fenestra Winery **5**
Fess Parker Winery **56**
Fiddlehead Cellars **48**

Fleming Jenkins Vineyard **12**
Flying Goat Cellars **48**
Foley Estates Vineyard **51**
Four Vines Winery **32**
Foxen Winery **46**
Gainey Vineyard **59**
Hahn Estates **25**
Hartley Ostini Hitching Post Winery **54**
Hope Family Wines **34**
Jada Vineyard **31**
Jaffurs Wine Cellars **60**
JC Cellars **4**
Justin Vineyards **28**
Kiamie Wine Cellars **33**
Laetitia Vineyard **43**
Linne Calodo **32**
J. Lohr Vineyards **36**
Longoria Wines **57**
Loring Wine Company **47**
Margerum Wine Company **46**
Morgan Winery **22**
Mount Eden Vineyards **11**
Murrieta's Well **7**
Ortman Family Vineyards **33**
Page Mill Winery **7**
Palmina **49**
Paraiso Vineyards **26**
Peachy Canyon Winery **35**
Periscope Cellars **2**

Qupé Wine Cellars **57**
Ridge Vineyards **10**
Robert Hall Winery **37**
Rosenblum Cellars **3**
Rusack Vineyards **55**
Sanford Winery **50**
Sinor-LaVallee Wines **41**
Stephen Ross Wine Cellars **38**
The Steven Kent Winery/La Rochelle Winery **7**
Stolpman Vineyards **57**
Tablas Creek Vineyard **29**
Talbott Vineyards **23**
Talley Vineyards **42**
Tamás Estates **8**
Tantara Winery **44**
Tensley Wines **57**
Terry Hoage Vineyards **34**
Testarossa Vineyards **13**
Thomas Coyne Winery **5**
Thomas Fogarty Winery **9**
Turley Wine Cellars **32**
Ventana Vineyards **21**
Villa Creek Cellars **30**
Vina Robles **37**
Wente Vineyards **8**
Windy Oaks Estate **18**

Beckmen Vineyards
2007
SYRAH
SANTA YNEZ VALLEY
ALC 14.7% BY VOL

BONNY DOON VINEYARD
A BLEND THAT VARIES FROM YEAR TO YEAR
BUT ALWAYS PAYS HOMAGE TO THE RHONE

Bernardus Winery Monterey County

Bernardus, the leading producer in the Carmel Valley AVA, is owned by Dutch native Bernardus "Ben" Pon, a former racer who thought the area would be ideal for Bordeaux grape varieties because of its hot days and cold nights. The estate vineyard is the source for Marinus, Bernardus' Bordeaux-style red blend, an elegant wine with a slightly savory quality. The winery also produces a vivid, fruity Sauvignon Blanc, made with grapes from Arroyo Seco. The supple Pinot Noirs from Bien Nacido Vineyard and Rosella's Vineyard are also good bets.

5 West Carmel Valley Rd., Carmel Valley, CA 93924
www.bernardus.com

Bonny Doon Vineyard Santa Cruz Mountains

Randall Grahm wanted to make the great American Pinot Noir when he started Bonny Doon in 1981, but he became more closely associated with the Rhône Ranger movement in California. He also developed a reputation for his witty marketing. More recently, Grahm has downsized his company so he can focus on smaller-production wines and Biodynamic viticulture at his Monterey County vineyard and a new property in San Benito County. Bonny Doon's flagship wine is a lively Rhône-style blend, Le Cigare Volant. Another wine that stands out is the fresh, fragrant Albariño.

328 Ingalls St., Santa Cruz, CA 95060
www.bonnydoonvineyard.com

Booker Vineyard San Luis Obispo County

Eric Jensen started planting his 45 acre (18ha) vineyard on the west side of Paso Robles in 2000. It is a low-vigor site, with a variety of exposures and elevations, calcareous shale soils, and not much water, so yields are very low. At the beginning, Jensen sold his grapes (mostly Rhône reds), but in 2005 he started keeping a little fruit for his own Booker Vineyard label. The wines have the typical Paso Robles ripeness, but they are also remarkably fresh. Jensen achieves this balance through judicious blending of grape varieties. ★ **Rising star**

2640 Anderson Rd., Paso Robles, CA 93446
www.bookerwines.com

The Brander Vineyard Santa Barbara County

Fred Brander is a master of Sauvignon Blanc. He makes several, in a variety of styles. The basic, affordably priced *cuvée* combines tank and barrel fermentation; the Au Naturel is tank-fermented and gets extra skin contact; and the Cuvée Nicolas adds some Semillon and oak aging. There are even vineyard-designated Sauvignon Blancs. One thing you will not find is the gooseberry and tomato stalk, New Zealand-style of Sauvignon Blanc. The winery also produces other wines, including Merlot and Cabernet Sauvignon, but Sauvignon Blanc is the ticket here.

2401 Refugio Rd., Los Olivos, CA 93441
www.brander.com

Brewer-Clifton Vineyards
Santa Barbara County

Greg Brewer and Steve Clifton teamed up in the mid-1990s to produce Chardonnay and Pinot Noir in the cool, windy region that was to become the Sta. Rita Hills AVA. The partners have a range of single-vineyard wines, as well as Sta. Rita Hills blends for both grape varieties.

At Brewer-Clifton, whole-cluster fermentation is standard Pinot practice, whereas it is experimental elsewhere. The Pinots, in particular, are highly sought-after. Brewer is also the winemaker for Melville and his own label, Diatom; Clifton has the Palmina brand.

329 North F St., Lompoc, CA 93436
www.brewerclifton.com

Burrell School Vineyards
Santa Cruz Mountains

The red, one-room Burrell School, which dates back to 1854, is a landmark in the summit area of the Santa Cruz Mountains. It is now home to the winery that bears its name. Owners Dave and Anne Moulton began developing the estate vineyards in 1990 and produced their first wine in 1991. They now make a range of wines from estate and purchased grapes. Fanciful names play on the school theme, like the Honor Roll Merlot, Principal's Choice Pinot Noir, and Valedictorian, a Bordeaux-style red blend.

24060 Summit Rd., Los Gatos, CA 95033
www.burrellschool.com

Calera Winery Monterey County

Calera Winery is actually in neighboring San Benito County, while its vineyard in the Mount Harlan AVA shares an important characteristic with those in Monterey's Chalone appellation: limestone soils. Calera's founder, Josh Jensen, trained in Burgundy and believes that limestone soils are critical to making world-class Chardonnay and Pinot Noir. He found Mount Harlan after scouring maps from the state's bureau of mines. Calera is especially well-known for its superb, expressive Pinots from the estate's six distinct blocks: Selleck, Jensen, Reed, Ryan, de Villiers, and Mills. Other offerings include a well-priced Central Coast Pinot Noir and a very good estate Viognier.

11300 Cienega Rd., Hollister, CA 95023
www.calerawine.com

Cambria Winery Santa Barbara County

The Tepusquet Vineyard was planted in the Santa Maria Valley in the early 1970s. In 1986, it was acquired by Kendall-Jackson's Jess Jackson and his wife, Barbara Banke, and became the estate vineyard for Cambria Winery. Some of the original Tepusquet plantings remain, but much of the vineyard was replanted, with a new focus on Pinot Noir and Chardonnay. The Julia's Vineyard Pinot Noir, with production of more than 500,000 bottles, is consistently good value. Cambria also sells grapes to other small wineries for the Julia's Vineyard Artisan Program.

5475 Chardonnay Lane, Santa Maria, CA 93454
www.cambriawines.com

Cedar Mountain Winery
San Francisco Bay

The Livermore Valley is home to the Lawrence Livermore National Laboratory as well as to vineyards, and a number of the "lab rats" from this advanced research facility have turned themselves into cellar rats in second careers. Earl and Linda Ault are prime examples, both trained in physics, both in love with food and wine, they have been bottling wine from estate-grown and local

CALERA WINERY
NECTARINE, JASMINE, AND HONEYSUCKLE
AROMAS AND A REFRESHING BALANCE

grapes since 1990. Perseverance has landed Cedar Mountain's flagship Cabernet Sauvignon on wine lists around the country, no mean feat for a producer this small.

7000 Tesla Rd., Livermore, CA 94550
www.cedarmountainwinery.com

Chalone Vineyard Monterey County
Chalone is dry and stark—seemingly an inhospitable place to grow grapes. But grapes have been grown in its limestone-rich soils since 1919. The site's modern history dates from the 1960s, when Richard Graff arrived and built a reputation for exceptional Chardonnay. In recent years, the winery has undergone ownership changes (it is now part of drinks giant Diageo) and winemaker changes, so it remains to be seen what direction the wines will take. The Chardonnay has a distinct minerality; Pinot Noir is rich and ripe; Syrah shows promise.

Stonewall Canyon Rd. and Highway 146, Soledad, CA 93960
www.chalonevineyard.com

Chamisal Vineyards San Luis Obispo County
Formerly Domaine Alfred, this property became Chamisal Vineyards after founder Terry Speizer sold the winery in 2008 to Crimson Wine Group. Chamisal is the historic name of the property, which was first planted in 1972, making it one of the Edna Valley's earliest vineyards. The winery gained a reputation for its big, bold Pinot Noirs, and winemaker Fintan du Fresne has continued that style. Pinot and Chardonnay are the focus, with a reserve tier called Califa. There is also a very good Chardonnay that spends no time in oak.

7525 Orcutt Rd., San Luis Obispo, CA 93401
www.chamisalvineyards.com

Clos LaChance Santa Cruz Mountains
Clos LaChance's owners, Bill and Brenda Murphy, began with a tiny plot of Chardonnay in their backyard in the Santa Cruz Mountains. Eventually, they started buying grapes and expanded into commercial production. In the late 1990s, they struck a deal with the developers of a private golf resort in the Santa Clara Valley to plant a vineyard and build a winery. The warmer location gave Clos LaChance the opportunity to branch out into varieties like Syrah and Zinfandel, but Santa Cruz Mountains Chardonnay and Pinot Noir are still significant players in their line-up.

1 Hummingbird Lane, San Martin, CA 95046
www.closlachance.com

Concannon Vineyard San Francisco Bay
Along with its Livermore neighbor Wente, Concannon Vineyard dates to 1883, and its fortunes since then have been like the luck of its Irish founder: up and down. Concannon survived Prohibition by making sacramental wine; it was the first winery to release a single varietal Petite Sirah in 1964; and it spent two decades passing through various corporate hands. It is now experiencing a renaissance with the financial backing of The Wine Group. Petite Sirah is still the specialty, but it is flanked by excellent Rhônes, Sauvignon Blanc, and intriguing small-lot wines. Concannon has always had the best stretch of rocky soil in Livermore; now it has solvency.

4590 Tesla Rd., Livermore, CA 94550
www.concannonvineyard.com

Dashe Cellars San Francisco Bay
Between them, Michael and Anne Dashe have worked at top-tier wineries on three continents, as well as in several prime California wine regions, working alongside several internationally known winemakers. They have been making their own wine since 1996, and the combination of training and learning by osmosis shows. The wines are consistently well made and intensely flavored, but also balanced and nuanced. Zinfandels are a specialty, including the admirably restrained l'Enfant Terrible; the Dry Riesling is a refreshing oasis in a world of Big Reds. ★ **Rising star**

55 4th St., Oakland, CA 94607
www.dashecellars.com

David Bruce Winery Santa Cruz Mountains
David Bruce was among the vintners who led a resurgence of wine production in the Santa Cruz Mountains from the late 1950s to the early 1970s. A dermatologist and home winemaker, Bruce bought 40 acres (16ha) at 2,200ft (750m) elevation in 1961 because he thought it would be ideal for Pinot Noir. Nearly 50 years later, Bruce produces a range of Pinots, from both the estate and from grapes purchased from other appellations. The winery's style of Pinot has become riper in recent years, but the wines still maintain some elegance.

21439 Bear Creek Rd., Los Gatos, CA 95033
www.davidbrucewinery.com

Denner Vineyards San Luis Obispo County
You could say that Ron Denner made his fortune digging ditches: actually, the money came from selling trench-digging machines. That enabled him to buy land in Paso Robles for a vineyard and winery. The vineyard is planted with a wide range of grape varieties, and much of the fruit is sold. The Denner Vineyards label focuses on Rhône varieties and Zinfandel. The whites are luscious yet rich; the reds are ripe, plump, and complex. The flagship wine is a red Rhône blend called—what else? —The Ditch Digger. ★ **Rising star**

5415 Vineyard Dr., Templeton, CA 93465
www.dennervineyards.com

Dierberg Vineyard/ Star Lane Vineyard Santa Barbara County
Jim Dierberg has owned Hermannhof Winery in Missouri since 1974, but Missouri is not the best place to grow vinifera grapes. In 1996, he purchased land in the warm Happy Canyon area and planted Star Lane Vineyard; later the same year, he bought property in the cool Santa Maria Valley for Dierberg Vineyard. He has since added a vineyard in the Sta. Rita Hills. The Dierberg label encompasses Pinot Noir, Chardonnay, and Syrah, with the rich Pinot being the best wine. Star Lane produces Sauvignon Blanc, Merlot, and two rich, ripe, highly extracted Cabernet Sauvignons.

1280 Drum Canyon Rd., Lompoc, CA 93436
www.dierbergvineyard.com

Eberle Winery San Luis Obispo County
When Gary Eberle arrived in Paso Robles in 1973, there were only three wineries. He started the now-defunct Estrella River Winery and became a Syrah pioneer. He was the first California vintner to produce a wine made

GAINEY VINEYARD
A STA. RITA HILLS CHARDONNAY WITH
MINERAL AND TROPICAL FRUIT FLAVORS

FLYING GOAT CELLARS
A FRESH BURST OF RASPBERRY FRUIT IS
COUNTERED BY SPICY COMPLEXITY

from 100% Syrah (released in 1978), and for years he was the only source in the state for Syrah vines (the Estrella clone). In 1983, he opened Eberle Winery, where he has built his reputation for Cabernet Sauvignon and Syrah. There is also a much-awarded Viognier.

3810 Highway 46 East, Paso Robles, CA 93447
www.eberlewinery.com

Edmunds St. John San Francisco Bay
Steve Edmunds and his wife Cornelia St. John have been making noteworthy Rhône-style wines in Berkeley, and various other locations in the East Bay, since 1985, when the Rhône upsurge in California was in its unconventional infancy. Edmunds is a traditionalist, minimalist, terroir-seeking winemaker whose varietal Syrahs and blends, many of which are vineyard-designated, convey a sense of place and steer clear of high-extract, high-oak overlays. Outside the Rhône zone, Edmunds ventures into things like Gamay Noir and Vermentino with delightful results.

No visitor facilities
www.edmundsstjohn.com

Epoch Estate Wines San Luis Obispo County
Epoch Estate established its first vineyard in 2004 on Paso Robles land once owned by Polish pianist and politician Ignacy Jan Paderewski, who grew Zinfandel grapes there. A second vineyard was planted in 2008. The focus is on Rhône grape varieties—Syrah, Mourvèdre, Grenache, Roussanne—as well as Tempranillo. Justin Smith of Saxum is the consulting winemaker, and the early wines reflect his style: ripe, dense, and powerful. One that stands out is Philosophee, a blend that is mostly Grenache and Mourvèdre. The first wines will be released in 2010. A winery to watch. ★ **Rising star**

No visitor facilities
www.epochwines.com

Fenestra Winery San Francisco Bay
Fenestra is the Livermore Valley at its most down to earth. The site goes back to Livermore's glory days in the late 19th century; the winery buildings are one cut above ramshackle. The tasting room is as snobbery-free as they get. Fenestra makes more wines than anyone can count, all of them serviceable and modestly priced, and some definitely worth tracking down—the various Rhône varieties, recent forays into Portuguese Touriga grapes, and the ever-popular, budget-friendly True Red.

83 Vallecitos Rd., Livermore, CA 94550
www.fenestrawinery.com

Fess Parker Winery Santa Barbara County
Baby boomers in the US grew up watching Fess Parker on television in the 1960s as frontiersman Daniel Boone. When his acting career was over, Parker became a real estate developer. In 1987, he bought a Santa Ynez Valley ranch and established his namesake winery and vineyard, a popular stop for tourists. The winery has narrowed its focus to Pinot Noir, Syrah, Chardonnay, and Viognier, most of them made in a lush, ripe style. A non-vintage, mostly Rhône blend, Frontier Red, is good value.

6200 Foxen Canyon Rd., Los Olivos, CA 93441
www.fessparker.com

Fiddlehead Cellars Santa Barbara County
Kathy Joseph focuses on two varieties at Fiddlehead Cellars: Pinot Noir and Sauvignon Blanc. Her Sauvignon Blancs—there are three of them, each made in a different style—are made from Santa Ynez Valley grapes. Joseph is probably better known for her Pinots. Three of them hail from the 100 acre (40ha) estate vineyard in the Sta. Rita Hills, Fiddlestix, which Joseph owns in partnership with Foster's Wine Estates. The *cuvée* called Lollapalooza is lush, dark, and velvety. The line-up also includes an Oregon Pinot Noir and a lively rosé, Pink Fiddle.

1597 East Chestnut Ave., Lompoc, CA 93436
www.fiddleheadcellars.com

Fleming Jenkins Vineyard
Santa Cruz Mountains
Olympic gold medal figure skater Peggy Fleming and her husband, Dr. Greg Jenkins, developed their winemaking passion after they planted a 1 acre (0.4ha) Chardonnay vineyard on their property. At first they sold the grapes, but Jenkins, a retired dermatologist, started taking winemaking classes. Their first commercial vintage was in 2003. Syrahs are among the stars here, including one produced from grapes grown in the Livermore Valley vineyard owned by football hall-of-fame coach and TV broadcaster John Madden. Fleming Jenkins Victories Rosé raises money for breast cancer research and awareness (Fleming is a breast cancer survivor).

45 West Main St., Los Gatos, CA 95030
www.flemingjenkins.com

Flying Goat Cellars Santa Barbara County
Winemaker Norm Yost started Flying Goat in 1999, while he was the winemaker at Foley Estates. Although he makes a little Pinot Gris and rosé sparkling wine, the single-vineyard Pinot Noir, made in small lots, is the focus. All the wines offer ample fruit, yet they display the differences found in the various vineyard sources. The spicy, supple bottling from Dierberg Vineyard in the Santa Maria Valley is particularly appealing; Pinot Noirs from sites in the Sta. Rita Hills have darker, riper flavors.

1520 East Chestnut Court, Lompoc, CA 93436
www.flyinggoatcellars.com

Foley Estates Vineyard
Santa Barbara County
William P. Foley II, chairman of Fidelity National Inc., got started in the wine business with the acquisition of Lincourt Vineyards in the Santa Ynez Valley, then went on to establish Foley Estates in the Sta. Rita Hills. The Foley Pinot Noirs from the Rancho Santa Rosa vineyard are especially good—bright, supple, and spicy. The winemaker is Kris Curran. Foley has been on a buying spree—among his acquisitions is Firestone Vineyard in the Santa Ynez Valley.

6121 East Highway 246, Lompoc, CA 93436
www.foleywines.com

Four Vines Winery San Luis Obispo County
Four Vines was founded in 1996 with the idea of focusing on Zinfandel from four of California's best appellations—hence the name. So far, founder and winemaker Christian Tietje has found only three appellations that suit him: Paso Robles, Sonoma County, and Amador County. He has branched out into Syrah and also has an eclectic

line-up affectionately known as the "freak show," with names like Heretic (Petite Sirah) and Loco (Tempranillo). The wines are bold but, for the most part, balanced. There is also a crisp, unoaked Chardonnay called Naked.

3750 West Highway 46, Templeton, CA 93465
www.fourvines.com

Foxen Winery Santa Barbara County

The "Foxen Boys," Bill Wathen and Dick Doré, have been producing wine together since 1985. Wathen makes the wine; Doré sells it. The winery and estate vineyard are part of the historic Rancho Tinaquaic, which has been in Doré's family since the early 1800s. The partners also source fruit from vineyards around the county: Pinot Noir from Sta. Rita Hills and Santa Maria Valley; Bordeaux and Rhône varieties from Santa Ynez Valley. The Pinots are ripe and lush, the Syrahs rich and concentrated. Also of note is a delicious old-vine Chenin Blanc.

7600 Foxen Canyon Rd., Santa Maria, CA 93454
www.foxenvineyard.com

Gainey Vineyard Santa Barbara County

The Gainey family purchased a 1,800 acre (730ha) ranch in the Santa Ynez Valley in 1962. The ranch is used for cattle, horses, farmland, and, since the early 1980s, wine grapes. The original ranch is in a warmer area, so in the 1990s, the family added a property in the cooler region that became the Sta. Rita Hills AVA. The Limited Selection Pinot Noir stands out; the Chardonnay from the same range is tinged with minerality. Limited Selection Sauvignon Blanc, which spends time in oak, has its fans.

3950 East Highway 246, Santa Ynez, CA 93460
www.gaineyvineyard.com

Hahn Estates Monterey County

Nicky Hahn first made his mark in Monterey wine with the Smith & Hook Cabernet Sauvignon from the Santa Lucia Highlands—an appellation that is really too cool to ripen Cabernet Sauvignon reliably. He later established the Hahn Estates label and expanded his vineyard holdings. Cabernet now comes from Paso Robles, while vineyards in Monterey County focus more on cool-climate varieties. A recent addition to the line-up is the Lucienne label, devoted to single-vineyard Pinot Noir. The Hahn portfolio also includes the less expensive Cycles Gladiator brand.

37700 Foothill Rd., Soledad, CA 93960
www.hahnfamilywines.com

Happy Canyon Vineyard

Santa Barbara County

Happy Canyon Vineyard is part of the Piocho Ranch, owned by the Barrack family. The Barracks are polo enthusiasts and also raise polo ponies on the ranch. The vineyard and winery are focused on Bordeaux varieties, which have proven successful in Happy Canyon. The wines are blends, and some of the proprietary names are linked to polo—Chukker, for example, refers to a period of play in a polo match. The top wine is the aromatic, structured, Cabernet-based Ten-Goal. Doug Margerum is the winemaker. ★ Rising star

No visitor facilities
www.happycanyonvineyard.com

FOUR VINES WINERY
THE BIKER ZINFANDEL HAS A HINT OF
MOURVEDRE FOR AN EXTRA KICK

HAHN ESTATES
A LIGHT STYLE OF PINOT NOIR IDEAL
FOR PICNICS OR JUST ON ITS OWN

Hartley Ostini Hitching Post Winery Santa Barbara County

Chef/restaurateur Frank Ostini and former commercial fisherman Gray Hartley started out making wines for Ostini's Hitching Post, a restaurant in Buellton, but the wines are now in broader distribution. Pinot Noir is the focus, and the winery and restaurant got a huge boost in 2004 when they were featured in the movie *Sideways*. The Pinots are rich but well-balanced, with ample fruit; the flagship is Highliner, a blend of the best barrels. The duo also makes a Syrah and a Cabernet Franc-based blend.

406 East Highway 246, Buellton, CA 93427
www.hitchingpostwines.com

Heart O' The Mountain

Santa Cruz Mountains

Vines were planted at the Heart O' The Mountain estate in the 1880s. The filmmaker Alfred Hitchcock owned the property from 1940 to 1974, entertaining his Hollywood friends here. When Bob and Judy Brassfield acquired the estate in 1978, they decided to re-establish the hillside vineyard and produced their first vintage of Pinot Noir in 2005. The winery does not have much of a track record, but the first two vintages of the plump yet elegant Pinot make this a producer worth watching. ★ Rising star

No visitor facilities
www.heartothemountain.com

Hope Family Wines San Luis Obispo County

The Hope family started as growers in Paso Robles. In the 1980s, they sold Cabernet Sauvignon to Caymus Vineyards for their Liberty School label. The Hopes eventually took over the Liberty School label and also established Treana, which produces a red blend based on Cabernet Sauvignon and Syrah, and a white Rhône-style blend. Austin Hope became the winemaker in 1998 and added a line under his own name that focuses on Rhône varieties. Syrah and Grenache are especially good.

1585 Live Oak Rd., Paso Robles, CA 93446
www.treana.com

Jada Vineyard San Luis Obispo County

When cardiovascular surgeon Jack Messina planted Bordeaux and Rhône varieties on 60 acres (24ha) in Paso Robles, he did not intend to produce his own wine. That changed in 2005, when he hired Scott Hawley to produce wines for the Jada label. The wines have names like Jack of Hearts, a reference to Messina's profession. The style is ripe and powerful, but not over the top. ★ Rising star

5620 Vineyard Drive, Paso Robles, CA 93446
www.jadavineyard.com

Jaffurs Wine Cellars Santa Barbara County

Craig Jaffurs has come a long way from his old career in the aerospace industry. He discovered a passion for Rhône varieties, and those are the only grapes he works with. Although Jaffurs owns no vineyards, the winery sources fruit from some of Santa Barbara's best, including Bien Nacido, Thompson, and Stolpman. The rich, aromatic Syrahs are the stars here. The Jaffurs wines are made away from wine country, in the city of Santa Barbara.

819 East Montecito St., Santa Barbara, CA 93103
www.jaffurswine.com

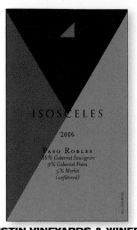

JUSTIN VINEYARDS & WINERY
THIS FLAGSHIP BORDEAUX BLEND HAS
WON INTERNATIONAL RECOGNITION

JC Cellars San Francisco Bay
Jeff Cohn handled a lot of the winemaking chores at Rosenblum Cellars as it climbed to the top of the charts among California Zinfandel producers in the 1990s. Since then, his more focused efforts with his own Oakland-based label have more than demonstrated his skills in the cellar. JC Cellars emphasizes Syrah and other Rhône reds and whites and, naturally, Zinfandel. Most are single-vineyard efforts, done up in high-extract California style but with due respect for terroir. ★ **Rising star**

55 Fourth St., Oakland, CA 94607
www.jccellars.com

Jonata Wines Santa Barbara County
Jonata Wines was founded in 2000 by money manager Charles Banks and developer Stanley Kroenke, who together went on to buy Screaming Eagle in the Napa Valley. (Banks has since left both ventures.) Jonata's first commercial harvest was in 2004. The winery focuses on the red Bordeaux varieties, but its location in the Ballard Canyon area, next to Stolpman Vineyards and Beckmen's Purisima Mountain Vineyard, means Jonata is also a great spot for Syrah—and winemaker Matt Dees makes a luscious one called La Sangre de Jonata. The El Desafio de Jonata Cabernet Sauvignon is dense, ripe, and extracted. ★ **Rising star**

No visitor facilities
jonata.com

Justin Vineyards & Winery
San Luis Obispo County
When Justin Vineyards & Winery was founded in 1981 by banker Justin Baldwin and his wife Deborah, there were fewer than 10 wineries in Paso Robles. The vineyard, which is just 13 miles (21km) from the Pacific Ocean, is planted with mostly red Bordeaux varieties. Cabernet Sauvignon accounts for much of the production, and the flagship wine is an elegant blend of Cabernet, Merlot, and Cabernet Franc called Isosceles. The Syrah/Cabernet blend, Savant, is also very good. The showpiece winery includes a four-room inn and small restaurant.

11680 Chimney Rock Rd., Paso Robles, CA 93446
www.justinwine.com

Kiamie Wine Cellars San Luis Obispo County
Aram Deirmenjian and Greg Johnson, with the help of Steve Glossner, started Kiamie in Paso Robles in 2005. Glossner's contacts, as a Paso Robles veteran, helped Kiamie source fruit from some of the best vineyards. The top wine is Kiamie Kuvée, a red blend that varies from year to year to take advantage of the best grapes the partners can buy. There is also an excellent White Kuvée that has been a blend of Viognier and Roussanne. Glossner's style is rich, yet very fresh and well balanced. ★ **Rising star**

1111 Riverside Ave, Paso Robles, CA 93446
www.kiamiewines.com

Laetitia Vineyard San Luis Obispo County
Laetitia, in the cool Arroyo Grande Valley, began life as Maison Deutz, a sparkling wine project. The venture failed, and a new owner began the transition to still wines. The vineyard, which is within sight of the ocean, is now more than 600 acres (245ha), with almost three-quarters devoted to Pinot Noir. The Laetitia Pinots are ripe, smooth, and spicy. Also good is the cool-climate Syrah. Laetitia still produces fine sparkling wines. The company also owns the Nadia and Barnwood brands.

453 Laetitia Vineyard Drive, Arroyo Grande, CA 93420
www.laetitiawine.com

Lane Tanner Winery Santa Barbara County
At a time when some Pinot Noirs are getting ever-riper and more Syrah-like, Lane Tanner's approach is refreshing. She pursues a more elegant, delicate style. Take her Pinot Noir from Julia's Vineyard in the Santa Maria Valley. Tanner is one of a half-dozen vintners who make wine from that vineyard, and she is always the first to pick. The result is very lively, with more savory nuances. She also makes Syrah—also lively and elegant.

No visitor facilities
www.lanetanner.com

Linne Calodo San Luis Obispo County
Linne Calodo was started in Paso Robles in 1998 by winemakers Matt Trevisan and Justin Smith; the two parted ways, and Smith started Saxum. Trevisan's philosophy is to blend varieties to achieve balance and complexity. The result is wines like Problem Child, a plump, approachable blend of Zinfandel, Syrah, and Mourvèdre, and Sticks and Stones, an aromatic, meaty combination of Grenache, Syrah, and Mourvèdre. The tiny quantities are sold mostly through a mailing list.

3030 Vineyard Drive, Paso Robles, CA 93446
www.linnecalodo.com

J. Lohr Vineyards San Luis Obispo County
Jerry Lohr first planted vines in Monterey County in the early 1970s. In 1988 he purchased land in Paso Robles and now owns more than 3,000 acres (1,215ha) in Monterey, Paso Robles, and Napa Valley. The Paso Robles operation is focused on reds: Bordeaux varieties, Zinfandel, and Syrah. The top wines are the Hilltop Vineyard Cabernet Sauvignon and the Cuvée Series, a collection of three Bordeaux-style blends. The affordable South Ridge Syrah and Seven Oaks Cabernet Sauvignon are excellent value.

6169 Airport Rd., Paso Robles, CA 93446
www.jlohr.com

Longoria Wines Santa Barbara County
Rick Longoria worked for others during the early days of his eponymous winery but, by the late 1990s, he was devoted to the project full-time. Longoria makes a range of wines, but Pinot Noir from various Santa Barbara County vineyards is clearly the focus. Particularly good is the Pinot from the Fe Ciega vineyard. Longoria also works with some Spanish grapes—the Tempranillo is a fine example of that variety. Syrahs are also good, especially the ripe, spicy version from Alisos Vineyard.

2935 Grand Ave., Los Olivos, CA 93441
www.longoriawine.com

Loring Wine Company Santa Barbara County
Brian Loring freely admits that he is obsessed with Pinot Noir. Maybe that is why he makes more than a dozen of them in a typical year. In 1997, while helping out during harvest at Cottonwood Canyon, he ended up working with two barrels of his own Pinot. More than

MORGAN WINERY
FROM THE ONLY ORGANIC VINEYARD IN THE
AVA, THIS PINOT IS AGED IN FRENCH BARRELS

a decade later, he is making his large range of Pinot Noirs in Lompoc, using purchased fruit. Loring's Pinot Noirs are plump and ripe, with lots of fruit. Since the 2004 vintage, he has bottled all the wines under Stelvin screw caps, which are still relatively unusual in California.

1034 West Aviation Drive, Lompoc, CA 93436
www.loringwinecompany.com

Margerum Wine Company
Santa Barbara County
Doug Margerum has been an important figure on the Santa Barbara wine scene for almost 30 years. As proprietor of the Wine Cask restaurant and liquor store (he is back after a few years' hiatus), Margerum was a big backer of Santa Barbara wine and held an annual futures tasting. In 2001, he began making wine of his own. The line-up has grown to encompass a wide range. Whites are crisp and steely; his Sauvignon Blancs are outstanding. The Syrahs are excellent, too. Margerum is also the winemaker for Happy Canyon Vineyards and consults for several other wineries.

5249 Foxen Canyon Rd., Los Olivos, CA 93441
www.margerumwinecompany.com

Mer Soleil Monterey County
The Mer Soleil vineyard—named for the two natural forces that influence the growing conditions, sea (*mer*) and sun (*soleil*)—was developed in 1988 by the Wagner family of Caymus Vineyards in Napa Valley. There are two vineyard sites in the Santa Lucia Highlands, one at the northernmost, cooler end, and another in the warmer south. Charlie Wagner II, a fourth-generation winemaker, produces three wines: a rich, barrel-fermented Chardonnay; an unoaked Chardonnay called Silver that is fresh but complex; and a late-harvest, botrytized Viognier called Late.

No visitor facilities
www.mersoleilvineyard.com

Morgan Winery Monterey County
When Dan Lee started Morgan Winery in 1982, his first wine was a Monterey Chardonnay that quickly won recognition. Lee still produces Chardonnay—several of them, in fact—but these days, the winery is better known for its Pinot Noirs from the Santa Lucia Highlands, including the bottling from his certified-organic estate vineyard, known as Double L. The Morgan style is rich without being over the top, and the wines show great balance. Also noteworthy are the peppery, cool-climate Syrahs and the unoaked Metallico Chardonnay.

204 Crossroads Blvd., Carmel, CA 93923
www.morganwinery.com

Mount Eden Vineyards
Santa Cruz Mountains
The winery currently known as Mount Eden was established in 1942 by Martin Ray, an important figure in Santa Cruz Mountains viticulture who once owned the Paul Masson winery. Ray quarreled with his investors, who banished him and rechristened the estate as Mount Eden in the early 1970s. Winemaker Jeffrey Patterson has been with the winery since 1981. The low-yielding estate vineyard, which climbs from 1,600ft to 2,000ft (490m to 680m), is the source of a distinctive and long-lived

Chardonnay. The estate Cabernet Sauvignon is very good; Pinot Noir is steadily improving. There is a very reasonably priced Chardonnay from Edna Valley grapes.

22020 Mt. Eden Rd., Saratoga, CA 95070
www.mounteden.com

Murrieta's Well San Francisco Bay
Named after a legendary 19th-century California bandit, and located on a property with deep roots in Livermore Valley history, Murrieta's Well started as a partnership between Phil Wente and winemaker Sergio Traverso in 1991. The view is as pretty as any in the valley; the wines can, and do, hold their own with any in the state. The winery has always specialized in Old World Bordeaux-style blends, including a Red and a White Meritage, both reliable and respected. In 2004 came the Zarzuela, a Portuguese/Iberian red blend packed with Douro-like flavors. It all goes to make this bandit's watering hole one of Livermore Valley's gems.

3005 Mines Rd., Livermore, CA 94550
www.murrietaswell.com

The Ojai Vineyard Santa Barbara County
The Ojai Vineyard is actually in Ventura County, but owner-winemaker Adam Tolmach's winery is still a Santa Barbara operation in spirit. Tolmach had co-founded Au Bon Climat with Jim Clendenen, but left to start his own venture, and most of his grapes still come from Santa Barbara County. Tolmach makes more than a dozen wines, in small quantities, including multiple bottlings of Syrah, Pinot Noir, and Chardonnay. The wines are superb: complex, nuanced, lively, and rich without being heavy.

No visitor facilities
www.ojaivineyard.com

Ortman Family Vineyards
San Luis Obispo County
Chuck Ortman has worked or consulted for Napa Valley wineries such as Heitz, Far Niente, and Shafer. In 2003, he retired as the winemaker for Meridian Vineyards, a label he founded and subsequently sold to the Foster's Group. Retirement from the Paso Robles winery gave him more time to devote to his family's label, working with son Matt. Ortman Family specializes in Pinot Noir, including a plump, supple wine from the Fiddlestix Vineyard in the cooler Sta. Rita Hills. There is also an exemplary Edna Valley Chardonnay.

1317 Park St., Paso Robles, CA 93446
www.ortmanvineyards.com

Page Mill Winery San Francisco Bay
Calling Page Mill Winery a rising star is a misnomer, since the label turned out toothsome wines for decades in the Santa Cruz Mountains, before relocating to Livermore Valley in 2004. Since then, second-generation winemaker Dane Stark has demonstrated an aptitude for turning local fruit into first-rate Sauvignon Blanc, Petite Sirah, and Syrah—wines that always show off fruit and varietal character, and often that elusive "something more" that makes a wine drinker pay attention. ★ Rising star

1960 South Livermore Ave., Livermore, CA 94550
www.pagemillwinery.com

RHONES ON THE CENTRAL COAST

Rhône grape varieties such as Syrah, Grenache, and Viognier are now widely planted in California, but San Luis Obispo County has, in many ways, been ground zero. At Estrella River in Paso Robles, Gary Eberle was the first in California to produce a wine made from 100% Syrah (released in 1978). Alban Vineyards, founded in 1989 in the Edna Valley, was the first US winery devoted solely to Rhône varieties, and John Alban has advised countless vintners on planting such grapes. Perhaps most important was the arrival in Paso Robles of Tablas Creek Vineyard, owned by importer Robert Haas and the Perrin family of France's Château de Beaucastel. They propagated cuttings from the Rhône Valley, greatly increasing the variety of available vine material. It is fitting that the Hospice du Rhône, the world's largest celebration of Rhône variety wines, is held every year in Paso Robles.

Monterey County may be home to the "broccoli capital of the world," but grapes are equally important here.

PEACHY CANYON WINERY
THIS GOOD-VALUE PASO ROBLES ZINFANDEL
BLEND IS A GREAT FOOD WINE

Palmina Santa Barbara County

Steve Clifton of Brewer-Clifton started Palmina in 1995 to make food-friendly wines from northern Italian grape varieties grown in Santa Barbara County. Whites range from Arneis to Malvasia Bianca to Pinot Grigio, while reds include Barbera, Dolcetto, and Nebbiolo. Clifton says he is not trying merely to emulate the Italian versions of these grapes, but he is also steering away from the ultra-ripe versions often found in California. The Nebbiolos are some of the finest versions found outside Piedmont. Steve's wife, Chrystal, also makes a little wine under the Botasea label.

1520 East Chestnut Court, Lompoc, CA 93436
www.palminawines.com

Paraiso Vineyards Monterey County

Paraiso Vineyards, planted in 1973 by Rich Smith for some investors, is one of the Santa Lucia Highlands' oldest vineyards. Smith bought the vineyard in 1987 and started producing a little wine the next year under the Paraiso label. Though Smith was a pioneer in the region, he was not farming with an eye to quality until recently. The wines, too, have made dramatic improvements. Pinot Noir and Syrah stand out. There is also a good, fairly dry Riesling. Grapes are sold to a handful of small wineries.

38060 Paraiso Springs Rd., Soledad, CA 93960
www.paraisovineyards.com

Peachy Canyon Winery
San Luis Obispo County

With a load of Zinfandel grapes from Benito Dusi's vineyard, Doug and Nancy Beckett started Peachy Canyon in 1988 in Paso Robles. More than 20 years later, Zinfandel is still the focus at Peachy Canyon, with more than half a dozen separate bottlings. Their son Josh Beckett is now the winemaker. The winery also produces a range of other wines, mostly reds. But the ripe, bold Zinfandels are the best bets here. There is even a fortified wine made from Zinfandel. The Zinfandel called Incredible Red is excellent value.

1480 N. Benthel Rd., Templeton, CA 93465
www.peachycanyon.com

Periscope Cellars San Francisco Bay

Warehouse wineries on shoestring budgets thrive on personality, and Periscope Cellars, housed in a former submarine repair facility, has it in spades. Winemaker Brendan Eliason has eclectic taste in grape varieties (he is a big fan of Petit Verdot), a knack for blending (the Deep Six blend contains six grapes from five appellations), an eye for good-value grape sources (including excellent fruit from Lodi), and a tireless commitment to building a local customer base with one imaginative winery event after another. ★**Rising star**

1410 62nd St., Emeryville, CA 94608
periscopecellars.com

Pisoni Vineyards Monterey County

Gary Pisoni is a larger-than-life figure in the Santa Lucia Highlands. In 1982, he planted 5 acres (2ha) of Pinot Noir on a cattle ranch owned by his family; the vineyard has since grown to 45 acres (18ha), mostly Pinot. Grapes are sold to other top Pinot producers, such as Siduri, Testarossa, and Arcadian, but the family also makes a

QUPE WINE CELLARS
FERMENTED IN OLD OAK BARRELS, THIS WINE
CAN BE AGED FOR 10 YEARS OR DRUNK NOW

voluptuous Pinot of its own under the Pisoni label. The Pisonis are partners in Garys' Vineyard. Pinot Noir, Syrah, Chardonnay, and rosé are made under the Lucia label.

No visitor facilities
www.pisonivineyards.com

Qupé Wine Cellars Santa Barbara County

Bob Lindquist was working at Zaca Mesa Winery when he started making some wine of his own. Since the beginning, he has made Syrah and Chardonnay, wines that continue to be important to his portfolio today. Lindquist now makes several Syrahs, all of them very well balanced with smoky, peppery nuances—unlike the jammy, high-octane Syrahs produced by many of his neighbors. Newer additions include an excellent, minerally Marsanne and a juicy Grenache from Purisima Mountain Vineyard. Lindquist is also involved in wife Louisa's Verdad label, specializing in Spanish varieties.

2963 Grand Ave., Los Olivos, CA 93441
www.qupe.com

Rhys Vineyards Santa Cruz Mountains

Kevin Harvey, a software engineer and venture capitalist, had his Pinot Noir epiphany about 20 years ago. He started studying the variety and ultimately planted a tiny vineyard in his backyard, making the wine in his garage. Harvey thought the Santa Cruz Mountains were a good place to explore the effect of site on the wines and went on to establish five small vineyards. (He has since added one in Anderson Valley.) These outstanding Pinot Noirs display differences, but share an earthy complexity rather than being all about lush fruit. ★**Rising star**

No visitor facilities
www.rhysvineyards.com

Ridge Vineyards Santa Cruz Mountains

Monte Bello ridge in the Santa Cruz Mountains was first planted to grapes in the 1880s. In 1959, a group of engineers bought some of the historic land and called it Ridge Vineyards. Paul Draper, now CEO, joined Ridge as winemaker in 1969. Ridge is well-known for its Zinfandels and has a winery at its Lytton Springs Zinfandel property in Dry Creek Valley, Sonoma. But its flagship is Monte Bello, an elegant, long-lived Bordeaux-style blend from the historic property of the same name in the Santa Cruz Mountains. A small amount of excellent Monte Bello Chardonnay is also produced.

17100 Monte Bello Rd., Cupertino, CA 95014
www.ridgewine.com

Roar Wines Monterey County

Gary Franscioni is one of the most respected grape growers in Monterey's Santa Lucia Highlands. His Rosella's Vineyard (named for his wife) and Garys' Vineyard, which he co-owns and farms with Gary Pisoni, are the sources of some of the finest Pinot Noirs in California. (He recently planted two more vineyards in the area, too.) In 2001, he decided to produce a little wine from his vineyards under the Roar label. The lush, intense wines—Pinot Noir, Syrah, and Chardonnay—are made by Ed Kurtzman in Roar's new winery in San Francisco.

No visitor facilities
www.roarwines.com

Robert Hall Winery San Luis Obispo County

When shopping-center developer Robert Hall retired, he moved to Paso Robles and bought land for a vineyard. But he was not ready to stop building. Before long, he had founded a winery and started construction. While the dominant style in Paso Robles is big and ripe, Robert Hall's winemaker Don Brady takes a more restrained approach, producing well-balanced wines with lower alcohol levels. There is a range of styles, but some of the best wines are made from Rhône grapes, including the blends called Rhône de Robles and Blanc de Robles.

3443 Mill Rd., Paso Robles, CA 93446
www.roberthallwinery.com

Rosenblum Cellars San Francisco Bay

After years as a home winemaker, veterinarian Kent Rosenblum started releasing commercial Zinfandels made with purchased grapes in the East Bay in 1978. The number of regions and vineyards represented grew and grew, and by the mid-1990s, Rosenblum Cellars was the King of the Zinfandel Hill, with more than a dozen highly rated, highly anticipated releases a year, most in a big, bold, brash style. From a former railroad facility in Alameda, Rosenblum produces a range of excellent wines beyond Zinfandel, including Rhônes and Bordeaux varieties, sparkling wines, and dessert wines. The winery has launched the careers of several other winemakers.

2900 Main St., Alameda, CA 94501
www.rosenblumcellars.com

Rusack Vineyards Santa Barbara County

Rusack was established in 1995, but the wines have made dramatic improvement since the arrival, in 2001, of winemakers John and Helen Falcone. Although Pinot Noir is an important part of the portfolio, the Rusack estate vineyard is in a location that is too warm, so fruit is purchased from top vineyards in the Santa Maria Valley and Sta. Rita Hills. The Pinots are juicy, flavorful, and well balanced. There is also a very good Syrah from the estate vineyard and others in the Ballard Canyon area.

1819 Ballard Canyon Rd., Solvang, CA 93463
www.rusack.com

Sanford Winery Santa Barbara County

When Richard Sanford and Michael Benedict planted a vineyard at the western end of the Santa Ynez Valley in 1971, the conventional wisdom was that the area was too cold to ripen grapes. Sanford founded his winery in 1981, and the area, now awash with vines, eventually became known as Sta. Rita Hills. Sanford left in 2005, after the Terlato family acquired a majority interest. It is unclear what direction the wines will take under the new owners and a new winemaker, but recent releases have been good, especially the racy, well-balanced Chardonnay.

5010 Santa Rosa Rd., Lompoc, CA 93436
www.sanfordwinery.com

Saxum Vineyards San Luis Obispo County

Justin Smith was a founder of Linne Calodo in Paso Robles, but he left and, in 2000, started Saxum, where he produces some of Paso Robles' most highly sought-after wines. Smith makes Syrah and Rhône blends, with some of the best wines coming from his family's James Berry Vineyard. The steep site is dominated by calcareous soils—the Bone

ROBERT HALL WINERY
A BLEND OF WHITE RHONE GRAPES WITH QUINCE, NECTARINE, AND HONEY FLAVORS

RIDGE VINEYARDS
THIS BORDEAUX-STYLE RED IS SOMETIMES CALLED "AMERICA'S FIRST GROWTH"

Rock block is rife with fossilized whale bones—and yields are low. The wines are intense and ripe, with a strong minerality and are sold through a mailing list.

No visitor facilities
www.saxumvineyards.com

Sea Smoke Cellars Santa Barbara County

Sea Smoke, with a focus on Pinot Noir, was established in 1999 in the Sta. Rita Hills. The 105 acre (42ha) vineyard is a showpiece: 26 blocks, on south-facing hillsides, planted with 10 clones of Pinot (and a little Chardonnay). The Pinots have the dark color and concentration typical of the area, and they quickly attained cult status. The *cuvée* Botella is the most approachable. The wines labeled Southing, Ten (from all 10 clones), and One Barrel (the best barrel) are bigger and more complex.

No visitor facilities
www.seasmokecellars.com

Sinor-LaVallee Wines
San Luis Obispo County

When Mike Sinor was the winemaker at Domaine Alfred in the Edna Valley, he crafted big, opulent Pinot Noirs, because that was the style the owner wanted. The wines received stellar reviews, but Sinor preferred Pinots that were more traditional and elegant. Now that he has his own label, Sinor (along with wife Cheri LaVallee-Sinor) is pursuing that style. His two best wines are the supple, spicy Pinot from Talley Rincon Vineyard and the more muscular wine from Aubaine Vineyard. ★ **Rising star**

2195 Corbett Canyon Rd., Arroyo Grande, CA 93420
www.sinorlavallee.com

Stephen Ross Wine Cellars
San Luis Obispo County

Steve Dooley's fascination with wine began when he was growing up in Minnesota, where he experimented with making wine from rhubarb and dandelions. After enology school, he spent 10 years at Louis M Martini Winery in the Napa Valley, then seven years as winemaker at Edna Valley Vineyards. He started Stephen Ross (Ross is his middle name) in 1994. Dooley's forte is Pinot Noir; particularly good are the muscular yet elegant bottlings from Aubaine Vineyard and Stone Corral Vineyard. His Chardonnays are well-balanced, as is his peppery Paso Robles Zinfandel.

178 Suburban Rd., San Luis Obispo, CA 93401
www.stephenrosswine.com

The Steven Kent Winery/
La Rochelle Winery San Francisco Bay

This is an offshoot from the collaboration between the Mirassou and Wente families. Steven Kent Winery has aimed—and largely succeeded—at making some of Livermore Valley's most serious Cabernet Sauvignon. The newer La Rochelle range focuses exclusively on Pinot Noir—not from toasty Livermore, but from prime regions around California and Oregon—all served at the winery with matching artisan cheese plates. Kent and La Rochelle are going to snazz up the sometimes sleepy Livermore Valley.

5443 Tesla Rd., Livermore, CA 94550
www.stevenkent.com

TABLAS CREEK VINEYARD
2007 WAS A GREAT YEAR FOR THIS HOMAGE
TO RHONE'S CHATEAU DE BEAUCASTEL

Stolpman Vineyards Santa Barbara County

When Stolpman Vineyards was developed in the early 1990s, in the Ballard Canyon area, the idea was to sell the fruit. But when wines from the vineyard starting winning rave reviews, the Stolpman family decided to produce its own label, starting with the 1997 vintage. Plantings at the vineyard have changed over the years, and the focus now is on Rhône varieties, particularly Syrah. The winery also works with a Tuscan consultant, Alberto Antonini, on a New World style of Sangiovese. Since 2001, Sashi Moorman has been the winemaker.

2434 Alamo Pintado Ave., Los Olivos, CA 93441
www.stolpmanvineyards.com

Tablas Creek Vineyard

San Luis Obispo County

Tablas Creek is a partnership between former wine importer Robert Haas and the Perrin family of Château de Beaucastel in Châteauneuf-du-Pape. The partners bought the Paso Robles property in 1989, after a year-long search, and imported cuttings legally from France for their vineyard, which is certified organic. The arrival of a leading producer from Châteauneuf-du-Pape helped catapult Paso Robles into the spotlight. The cuttings that Tablas Creek imported were eventually supplied to other California vintners, and have become an important source of Rhône vineyard material. The flagship wine is a Mourvèdre-based blend called Esprit de Beaucastel.

9339 Adelaida Rd., Paso Robles, CA 93446
www.tablascreek.com

Talbott Vineyards Monterey County

Talbott Vineyards has long been known for its Chardonnays, both from the winery's Sleepy Hollow Vineyard in the Santa Lucia Highlands and from the Diamond T. Estate above Carmel Valley. Pinot Noir has been more of a work in progress. That is starting to change now that Robb Talbott has hired Dan Karlsen, previously of Chalone Vineyard, as winemaker. He is aiming for a style that is a little riper, with more purity of fruit. Early results have been promising. Talbott also makes wines under the Logan, Case, and Kali Hart labels.

53 West Carmel Valley Rd., Carmel Valley, CA 93924
www.talbottvineyards.com

Talley Vineyards San Luis Obispo County

Three generations of Talleys have farmed the Arroyo Grande Valley. For years, the crop was vegetables, but in 1982, grapes were planted on sloping ground that was not ideal for row crops. The Talleys still grow vegetables, but today they are known among wine lovers for their rich, distinctive Pinot Noirs and Chardonnays from the Rincon and Rosemary Vineyards. Talley also makes wine from its properties in nearby Edna Valley. A second label, Bishop's Peak, produces less-expensive wines such as the Rock Solid Red blend from mostly purchased fruit.

3031 Lopez Drive, Arroyo Grande, CA 93420
www.talleyvineyards.com

Tamás Estates San Francisco Bay

Tamás Estates is one of several Livermore Valley producers developed out of a symbiotic history with Wente Vineyards. This project brought a branch of the winemaking Mirassou family to the area along with winemaker Iván Tamás Fuezy, in 1984. Since then, Tamás Estates has developed into the valley's leading producer of Italian varietal wines, offered up with no pretence, and great value. The line-up includes Pinot Grigio, Barbera, Sangiovese, smaller-lot reserve wines, and of course, Zinfandel, an honorary Italian grape in most of California.

5489 Tesla Rd., Livermore, CA 94550
www.tamasestates.com

Tantara Winery Santa Barbara County

Bill Cates and Jeff Fink started Tantara in 1997. At their winery in the Santa Maria Valley, they focus on Pinot Noir from some of the best-known vineyards on the Central Coast, such as Garys' and Pisoni Vineyards in the Santa Lucia Highlands; Talley-Rincon in Arroyo Grande Valley, and Bien Nacido, Dierberg, and Solomon Hills vineyards in the Santa Maria Valley. (There are also several Chardonnays in the range.) The Pinots are rich and ripe, although they also manage to maintain some elegance.

2900 Rancho Tepusquet Rd., Santa Maria, CA 93454
www.tantarawinery.com

Tensley Wines Santa Barbara County

Joey Tensley started his winery in 1998 to make single-vineyard Syrahs from Santa Barbara County. More than half the production is a ripe, smoky Syrah from Colson Canyon Vineyard; many other bottlings are made in lots of 2,400 bottles or less. The cool-climate Turner Vineyard Syrah is peppery, dense, and bright. A little Grenache was added to the roster in 2006 and a white Rhône blend has also been introduced. Joey's wife, Jennifer, also makes a velvety Pinot Noir under a second label, Lea.

2900 Grand Ave., Los Olivos, CA 93441
www.tensleywines.com

Terry Hoage Vineyards

San Luis Obispo County

Retired professional football player Terry Hoage is not just writing the checks at his Paso Robles winery. He is also making the wines (along with his wife, Jennifer) and even built the small winery himself from recycled wood. From their 17 acres (7ha) of Rhône grape varieties, both red and white, they are crafting a range of blends with proprietary names that reflect both wine and Hoage's football experience. An example is The Pick, which in football, refers to an intercepted pass. The wines are big and ripe yet well balanced.

870 Arbor Rd., Paso Robles, CA 93446
www.terryhoagevineyards.com

Testarossa Vineyards Santa Cruz Mountains

Rob Jensen and his wife Diana were Silicon Valley engineers who started by making a little wine in their garage in the early 1990s. Soon they were producing on a commercial scale, and managed to buy Pinot Noir and Chardonnay from some of California's top vineyards, including Bien Nacido in Santa Barbara and Pisoni, Garys', and Sleepy Hollow in Monterey. Pinot Noir and Chardonnay are the focus today, although Testarossa also makes a little Syrah. The wines are more complex, balanced, and textured under winemaker Bill Brosseau.

300-A College Ave., Los Gatos, CA 95030
www.testarossa.com

TERRY HOAGE VINEYARDS
LAYERS OF RICH BLACK FRUITS AND SPICY
LIQUORICE INTERTWINE IN THIS SYRAH

Thomas Coyne Winery San Francisco Bay

Take a funky, historic property, add a former home winemaker with a science background who loves to tinker, but will not touch email, and you get the Thomas Coyne Winery, one of Livermore's quirkiest and best small producers. Coyne has a way with Merlot, with hand-crafted, well-blended Rhônes, and just about whatever else strikes his small-lot fancy—like the Portuguese varieties he has lately been experimenting with. Down-to-earth artisan winemaking at work, and working well.

51 E Vallecitos Rd., Livermore, CA 94550
thomascoynewinery.com

Thomas Fogarty Winery
Santa Cruz Mountains

Thomas Fogarty, a cardiovascular surgeon and inventor of a device that was the forerunner of the catheter used for angioplasty, got interested in wine when he joined the Stanford University faculty in 1969. He made a little wine at home before founding a winery in 1981. Winemaker Michael Martella has been with the winery since the beginning. Of the range, the Pinot Noir has improved markedly in recent years, and Martella makes several of them. There are some good Santa Cruz Mountains Cabernet Sauvignons and an excellent Monterey Riesling.

19501 Skyline Blvd., Woodside, CA 94062
www.fogartywinery.com

Tondré Wines Monterey County

Tondré Alarid, a vegetable farmer in the Salinas Valley, owned land in the Santa Lucia Highlands. The land was not the best for row crops, but his neighbors were putting in wine grapes, so he and his son Joe started planting Pinot Noir in 1997. The 100 acre (40ha) vineyard is called Tondré Grapefield—a reference to how Tondré planted lettuce and broccoli fields and, now, a grape field. Most of the grapes are sold, but the family and winemaker Tony Craig produce a small amount of spicy, structured Tondré Pinot Noir. ★ **Rising star**

No visitor facilities
www.tondrewines.com

Turley Wine Cellars San Luis Obispo County

Napa Valley-based Turley Wine Cellars joined the Paso Robles wine scene in 2000 with the purchase of the 80-year-old Pesenti Vineyard. The Pesenti wines in those days could be described charitably as rustic, but Larry Turley recognized the potential of the old vineyard. The winery's Pesenti Vineyard Zinfandel is made in the typically huge Turley style. Turley's Paso Robles location is also noteworthy because its tasting room offers customers who are not on Turley's mailing list a chance to taste and buy some of the wines.

2900 Vineyard Drive, Templeton, CA 93465
www.turleywinecellars.com

Ventana Vineyards Monterey County

Doug Meador, who established Ventana Vineyards in the Arroyo Seco area in the 1970s, was considered a viticulture pioneer in Monterey. His grapes went into numerous award-winning wines—many of them made by other wineries. Ventana's own wines were more inconsistent. The winery changed hands in 2006, and the new owners have injected new enthusiasm, and money,

into the operation. The emphasis is on Chardonnay and Pinot Noir (the latter was never a focus under Meador), although the winemaker Reggie Hammond also makes outstanding Pinot Gris, Riesling, and Gewurztraminer.

2999 Monterey-Salinas Highway, Monterey, CA 93940
www.ventanawines.com

Villa Creek Cellars San Luis Obispo County

Through his Paso Robles restaurant, Villa Creek, Cris Cherry got to know a number of the area's vintners. In 2001, they talked him into making some wine, and now Villa Creek Cellars produces about 36,000 bottles a year. The focus is on Rhône grape varieties, mostly reds, and Tempranillo from some of Paso Robles' top vineyards. Many of the wines are blends with proprietary names. Cherry has been tweaking his bold, ripe style to make the wines more elegant and food-friendly.

5995 Peachy Canyon Rd., Paso Robles, CA 93446
www.villacreek.com

Vina Robles San Luis Obispo County

Vina Robles has been flying under the radar since it was founded in Paso Robles in the late 1990s. It is owned by Hans Nef, an engineer from Switzerland who hired Matthias Gubler, another Swiss native, as winemaker. Gubler has at his disposal more than 1,200 acres (486ha) of estate vineyards, though most of the fruit is sold. Among Vina Robles' best wines are Signature, a generous, rich blend based on Petit Verdot, and a dark, dense Petite Sirah. Gubler strives for a style that is fully ripe without being jammy or candied.

3700 Mill Rd., Paso Robles, CA 93446
www.vinarobles.com

Wente Vineyards San Francisco Bay

Founder Karl Wente got in on the ground floor in the Livermore Valley in 1883. Today, the fourth and fifth generations of the Wente family still own and run Livermore's flagship winery. The family was instrumental in pressing for land-use policies that saved Livermore's vineyards from being developed for housing. For years, Wente has been way ahead of the California pack in exporting its wines around the world. In the meantime, the winery puts out a broad range of still and sparkling wines, always reliably varietal and often good value. In recent years, the "Nth Degree" label has pushed the ultra-premium envelope for the region.

5565 Tesla Rd., Livermore, CA 94550
www.wentevineyards.com

Windy Oaks Estate Santa Cruz Mountains

Former management consultants Jim and Judy Schultze planted 3 acres (1.2ha) of Pinot Noir in 1996, on a former apple orchard outside the town of Corralitos. That vineyard has now expanded to 18 acres (7ha) of Pinot Noir and 1 acre (0.4ha) of Chardonnay and, in 2001, the Schultzes built a small winery. Total production is fewer than 35,000 bottles, but there are nine estate-grown Pinot Noirs, differentiated by factors such as clone, vineyard block, and use of wild yeast. The Windy Oaks range of Pinot Noirs is bright, lively, and supple.

550 Hazel Dell Rd., Corralitos, CA 95076
www.windyoaksestate.com

VIRTUAL WINEMAKING INNOVATIONS

The surge in activity on the Central Coast in the 1980s and 1990s brought with it creative new business strategies for grape growing and winemaking. Departing from the traditional model—where a winery would own all its vineyards and winemaking facilities—decentralized arrangements sprang up, allowing passionate winemakers to enter the business without the otherwise vital and massive capitalization.

Bien Nacido Vineyards in Santa Barbara pioneered the practice of custom farming different vineyard blocks, sometimes even rows, for different customers. This meant that small, emerging labels could get quality grapes grown to their specifications. The counterpart in winemaking was custom crush wine production—winery facilities offering the full range of winemaking services and equipment under one roof for multiple wine labels. Custom crush and custom farming have spread across California, providing the infrastructure for the recent explosion of small, new, upscale labels, including some very recognizable names on the Central Coast and elsewhere.

SOUTHERN CALIFORNIA

OREGON
NEVADA
San Francisco
PACIFIC
OCEAN
CALIFORNIA   ARIZONA
Los Angeles

 California
Southern California

Southern California covers a vast landscape, half the size of Italy and much more varied in soil and climate. In the first half of the 19th century, it was California's wine heartland, home to huge vineyard operations and gargantuan wineries shipping wine across the country. Vine diseases and financial speculation brought this golden age to an abrupt end in the mid-19th century, and since then, Southern California—outside of Santa Barbara, considered part of the Central Coast—has labored in the shadow of Napa Valley and the north. But with all that land and millions of wine drinkers, an eclectic wine industry still flourishes, based in improbable places from the suburban housing developments of the Temecula Valley to the Hollywood Hills.

Major grapes

Reds

Barbera

Cabernet Sauvignon

Grenache

Merlot

Syrah

Tempranillo

Zinfandel

Whites

Chardonnay

Marsanne

Pinot Gris

Rousanne

Sauvignon Blanc

Viognier

Vintages

Southern California has vintage differences like anywhere else, but because it is such a sprawling collection of disparate growing areas, generalizations are impossible. In addition, many of the best producers are under the radar of the national wine magazines, which rate vintages elsewhere. The best solution is to taste the wines and decide for yourself.

In terms of sheer volume, Southern California holds its own, with the Central Valley vineyards around Fresno and Madera contributing mightily to the production of mass-market wines. Most of these grapes end up in interchangeable, anonymous bottles. At the other end of the spectrum, Southern California's determined band of fine wine producers has had to wage its own struggle for recognition.

One of the misfortunes that befell the original southern vineyards was Pierce's disease—known then as Anaheim disease after the town where it erupted, now home to Disneyland. Pierce's can kill vines within a year or two, and in the late 1990s, it made a frightening comeback, spread by a new insect carrier, the glassy-winged sharpshooter. The starting point for the new vector of this pestilence was the Temecula Valley, 90 miles (145km) southeast of Los Angeles, an emerging wine region since the 1970s. The initial impact on Temecula's vineyards was devastating, and alarm bells went off throughout the state about the peril the glassy-winged sharpshooter posed.

Rumors of Temecula's demise, however, were greatly exaggerated. Through a combination of advanced research and old-fashioned pest management, government funding, and grower contributions, the threat in Temecula was beaten back to the status of a minor irritant. A statewide inspection program has succeeded in keeping the problem from spreading. In the meantime, the desire for a day out in wine country among the 15 million or so thirsty wine drinkers in the surrounding area (the mega-sprawl stretching from Los Angeles to San Diego to San Bernardino) has helped Temecula's vineyard plantings and winery population to expand.

Further north, in Cucamonga, pockets of Southern California's former glory hang on. Ringed by encroaching warehouses and sub-divisions, a string of old, rustic vineyards, most managed by the Galleano Winery, produce intense, low-yielding Zinfandel and other varieties that even Northern California winemakers covet.

The southern end of the state, in the mountains east of San Diego, is the birthplace of California's oldest wine traditions, which date back to the end of the 18th century with the Mission Fathers who worked their way north, bearing Christianity and vine plantings. Quality in local wineries recently has been uneven, but a new cohort of winemakers appear determined to raise the bar and put California's first wine region back on the map.

Finally, to the west, in the upmarket hills above Los Angeles, the most unlikely winegrowing area of all has proven to be more than a playground for well-heeled Hollywood hobbyists. With good elevation, a cooling ocean influence, and plenty of hillside microclimates to choose from, the best spots have turned out to be serious contenders. Is some vanity involved? This question may be asked equally of investors in Napa Valley or Bordeaux.

Even in the low-glamor southern portion of California, a decent winery is rarely more than an hour away—something that can not be said for other large states and many countries. Southern California's wine scene is more a jumble than a juggernaut—precisely why it is worth knowing.

Callaway Vineyard and Winery
Temecula

When the glassy-winged sharpshooter and Pierce's disease hit Temecula in the mid-1990s, Callaway's vineyards were the hardest hit, leaving scars where vines had been only a year before. The winery, at the time Temecula's largest, decided to shift its primary focus to the Central Coast, and was acquired by a drinks conglomerate. Meanwhile, the old outpost in Temecula, under the Callaway Vineyard and Winery label, is back with a more focused production, and the quality shows. Wines range from Bordeaux reds to Sauvignon Blanc, Pinot Gris, Muscat Canelli, and several dessert wines.

32720 Rancho California Rd., Temecula, CA 92589
www.callawaywinery.com

Galleano Winery Cucamonga
A chapter of California wine history remains alive and well at this complex on the edge of the Cucamonga Valley in Riverside County. The Galleano family have been here since 1927; the properties are listed on the California and National Register of Historic Places. The old, bush vines give low yields and concentrated flavors. Hemmed in by warehouses and developments, Galleano still puts out a line of excellent-value wines, and consistently wins competitions with its fortified wines. One of these, an Angelica, is a delicious bridge to an earlier era. A wine style rather than a brand, it is made from the old-time Mission variety, fortified with grape brandy.

4231 Wineville Ave., Mira Loma, CA 91752
www.galleanowinery.com

Hart Winery Temecula
Many Temecula Valley wineries come with restaurant and resort facilities, but Hart Winery, one of the best, has operated since the late 1970s out of a modest wood-frame building that could be mistaken for a rural general store. Winemaker Joe Hart knows his stuff, and makes an eclectic range of flavorful, balanced wines—including Zinfandel, Syrah, Cabernet Franc, Barbera, Viognier, and a delightful Grenache rosé, all well priced. Conscientious winemaking triumphs over razzle-dazzle.

41300 Avenida Biona, Temecula, CA 92591
www.thehartfamilywinery.com

Moraga Vineyards Los Angeles
Located in Bel Air, in suburban Los Angeles, Moraga Vineyards started out as a horse ranch, which is what you would expect in this genteel area next door to Beverly Hills. Since 1978, the focus has been grapes and wine—in fact, just two wines, the Moraga Red (a Bordeaux blend) and the Moraga White (all Sauvignon Blanc). Both wines are exceptionally well-crafted, giving fresh meaning to an over-used adjective: seamless. The limited-production estate wines have gone from having a small cult following to a large cult following, despite the unlikely location.

650 North Sepulveda Blvd., Bel Air, CA 90049
www.moragavineyards.com

Orfila Vineyards San Diego
San Diego County has a winemaking tradition stretching back to the first Mission plantings, but few modern wineries with reputations beyond their tasting rooms. One exception is Orfila Vineyards in the San Pasqual

HART WINERY
AN UNASSUMING WINERY THAT LETS
THE WINES SPEAK FOR THEMSELVES

ROSENTHAL MALIBU ESTATE
"M" IS FROM A SINGLE-VINEYARD BLOCK AND
AGED IN FRENCH OAK BARRELS FOR 2 YEARS

Valley, founded in 1994 by Argentine Ambassador Alejandro Orfila. The vineyards were first planted to cash-flow Chardonnay, but then replanted, by Napa winemaker Leon Santoro, to better-suited Rhône varieties and Sangiovese. Santoro produced a string of excellent vintages of Syrah, Roussanne, Marsanne, and Viognier. Sadly, he died in 2009, but the quality level remains high.

13455 San Pasqual Rd., Escondido, CA 92025
www.orfila.com

Rosenthal Malibu Estate
Los Angeles

When movie studio owner George Rosenthal planted vines on his Malibu Hills estate in 1987, few people took him seriously. Over the years, other producers sprang up, Malibu-Newton Canyon became an official AVA, and both the Rosenthal wines and reputation have evolved nicely. The wines include a good Chardonnay that is light on its feet, and a Cabernet Sauvignon built for finesse rather than muscle. The 1500ft (500m) elevation is the key to the premium fruit—and it makes for a great view.

100 Wilshire Blvd., Santa Monica, CA 90401
www.rosenthalestatewines.com

San Antonio Winery Los Angeles
Based in urban Los Angeles, San Antonio Winery is a survivor—it has been around since 1917. The winery produced sacramental wine during Prohibition and today, the Riboli family makes wine from grapes grown all over the state, competing at every price point. The Maddalena and San Simeon wines from Monterey and Paso Robles are excellent value; the high-end Riboli Family wines from Napa's Rutherford Bench hold their own; and the homey, bustling winery itself is definitely worth a visit.

737 Lamar St., Los Angeles, CA 90031
www.sanantoniowinery.com

South Coast Winery Temecula
South Coast's winery is part of a full-service lifestyle destination—resort, restaurant, spa, the works. But the wines are more than an afterthought: the winemaking team of Jon McPherson and Javier Flores has twice earned the accolade California Winery of the Year. The modestly priced wines range from Cabernet Sauvignon to Tempranillo, from Riesling to Roussanne, and from still wines to sparkling, most made from Temecula fruit. The lower-end wines deliver clean fruit, the higher-tier Syrahs and Cabernets offer much more. ★Rising star

34843 Rancho California Rd., Temecula, CA 92591
www.wineresort.com

Wilson Creek Winery Temecula
Wilson Creek is a winery in motion—in a good direction. While some past offerings have tended toward the off-dry and generic, under new winemaker Etienne Cowper, a Temecula fine wine pioneer, the label is putting out some excellent bottles. In a broad range of still and sparkling wines, among the most interesting are the Estate Syrah, rich and nicely balanced, and a port-like Petite Sirah dessert wine with more depth of flavor than many similar California efforts. ★Rising star

35960 Rancho California Rd., Temecula, CA 92591
www.wilsoncreekwinery.com

INLAND CALIFORNIA

California
Inland California

It may be the coastal appellations that get the glory: Santa Barbara, Sonoma, and Napa, where wine-themed movies get shot, and where bottles with three-digit price tags originate, but Inland California is where Americans look for their everyday wines, the bottles they brag about when talk turns to bargains. Any idea that this area is all about rustic reds sold in jugs with screwcaps is wide of the mark: in fact, the wines reflect Inland California's tremendous size and range. At its heart are the sprawling San Joaquin and Sacramento valleys; further inland, along the valleys' eastern edge, are the Sierra Foothills. Together, these regions form the historic foundation of the state's commercial wine trade. They were the ones who showed the way.

Major grapes

 Reds

Barbera
Petite Sirah
Sangiovese
Syrah
Zinfandel

 Whites

Chardonnay
Sauvignon Blanc
Viognier

Vintages

2009
Grapes picked early expected to yield balanced wines; those picked later may be less so.

2008
Bad weather reduced yields but the Zinfandel, Sangiovese, Barbera, and Syrah that survived are bright and crisp

2007
Excellent for Zinfandel and Barbera in the foothills.

2006
A torrid July intensified ripe flavors in Zinfandel, Sangiovese, and Syrah

2005
Weather extremes yielded intense Zinfandel, Petite sirah, Barbera, and Syrah, and even some Cabernet Sauvignon.

2004
Zinfandels range from jammy to balanced; Barbera broadly flavored and approachable.

Several of the more prominent contributors to the development of the state's wine trade sprang from Inland California. Brothers Ernest and Julio Gallo founded their pivotal eponymous winery in Modesto. Brothers Robert and Peter Mondavi emerged from Lodi. One of California's early governors, Leland Stanford, owned the largest vineyard in the world at the northern reaches of the Sacramento Valley. The only grocer to be inducted into the state's Vintners Hall of Fame, Darrell Corti, is based in Sacramento. Just to the west of Sacramento is Davis, the site of the University of California's acclaimed Department of Viticulture and Enology.

Today, a wine with the appellation "California" will be almost invariably from the Central Valley, more than 450 miles (720km) long, some 40 miles (64km) wide, its flat, rich soil yielding two-thirds of the state's wine grapes. Within that vast boundary, however, several sub-appellations are rising in stature: Lodi for dense Zinfandels; Madera for knock-off "ports;" Clarksburg for lush Petite Sirah and fruity Chenin Blanc.

The most dynamic and diverse winemaking of Inland California, however, is along the Sierra Foothills, a winding belt of manzanita, poison oak, pine trees—and vineyards—stretching for 120 miles (195km) on granite slopes above the valley floor. This is where gold was discovered in 1848, setting off decades of immigration supported by a complex infrastructure that included the building of railroads, logging of the forests, and the planting of vineyards and building of wineries. In the wake of the Gold Rush, as many as 100 wineries sprang up in and around the mining camps and, for years, more grapes were harvested in the Mother Lode (the historic term for the gold fields) than in Napa Valley and Sonoma County. Then, as the gold ran out, the miners and their supporting players moved away and Prohibition and vine pests moved in. The wineries were abandoned as the vineyards withered.

The turnaround began in the early 1970s, propelled by enthusiastic home winemakers who wanted to go commercial but could not afford land in the pricier coastal appellations. Almost without exception, they capitalized on the grape that has flourished in the Foothills since the Gold Rush, the variety most closely identified with California: Zinfandel. It is perfectly suited to the hot and arid terrain, yielding hefty and brash wines.

But the vintners who rediscovered the region four decades ago were an adventurous lot. They used Zinfandel initially to secure their place in the wine trade, then as the springboard for the exploration and invention that characterizes the Foothills today. Zinfandel still rules, but intense Syrahs, supple Sangioveses, and angular Barberas are gaining the region new respect.

Lithesome Sauvignon Blancs and plump Viogniers are the strongest whites. Unlike the Central Valley further downhill, this is not Chardonnay country. A high peak or a dark glen occasionally yield a good Cabernet Sauvignon, Pinot Grigio, Pinot Noir, or Riesling of surprising clarity and agility. For the most part, however, the Sierra Foothills, also fittingly known as the "cow counties," turn out muscular and bracing reds most at home when served with beef, and more often than not that still means Zinfandel.

Amador Foothill Winery Amador County

The husband-and-wife winemaking team of Ben Zeitman and Katie Quinn quietly release the finest single-vineyard Zinfandels in the Sierra Foothills. The elegance for which these wines are known is also evident in one of the few clear and vigorous Sangioveses to emerge from the Foothills, and in the complex Katie's Cote, an almost 50/50 blend of Syrah and Grenache. The Semillon comes close to these, but others do not quite attain the same level.

2500 Steiner Rd., Plymouth, CA 95669
www.amadorfoothill.com

Boeger Winery El Dorado County

In 1972, Greg and Sue Boeger bought a Gold Rush-era homestead in El Dorado County and began to plant vines. They made the first wine in the county since Prohibition, and since that auspicious start, they have combined a sensitive respect for place with a smart eye for modern marketing. Early on, they ignored conventional wisdom to make one of the more refined Merlots to emerge from the Foothills. Their son, Justin Boeger, is now the winemaker, embracing oak more enthusiastically than his father.

1709 Carson Rd., Placerville, CA 95667
www.boegerwinery.com

Bogle Vineyards Yolo County

Bogles have been farming the rich soil of the Sacramento and San Joaquin River Delta, south of Sacramento, for six generations, but only in 1968 did they start to cultivate vines. That tentative 20 acre (8ha) plot has grown to 1,200 acres (485ha), contributing to the nearly 14.5 million bottles the family makes annually. They have developed an international market largely with a readily accessible Petite Sirah and a juicy Merlot. Their Chardonnay is soft, yet hugely popular, while production of their Pinot Noir and Riesling cannot keep up with demand.

37783 County Rd. 144, Clarksburg, CA 95612
www.boglewinery.com

Bronco Wine Company Stanislaus County

Since 2000, Fred Franzia has compensated for the inconsistency of his flagship varietals, marketed under the brand Charles Shaw, or "Two Buck Chuck," with gumption and bluster. Based at Ceres in the heart of the Central Valley, he controls about 40,000 acres (16,200ha) of vines and sells millions of cases a year under more than 50 brands, some of which—Salmon Creek, ForestVille, Napa Ridge—show occasional brilliance at bargain prices.

6342 Bystrum Rd., Ceres, CA 95307
209 538 3131

Crew Wine Company Yolo County

The husband-and-wife team of John and Lane Giguiere are at it again, making stylish wines at come-hither prices. They did it in the 1980s by creating R.H. Phillips Winery and introducing popular wines such as Toasted Head Chardonnay. After selling Phillips, they returned in 2005 to the Dunnigan Hills, with Crew Wine Co. With steady winemaking, artful marketing, and popular prices, they are replicating their success with Matchbook Tempranillo, Mossback Pinot Noir, and Sawbuck Malbec. ★Rising star

12300 County Rd., Zamora, CA 95698
www.crewwines.com

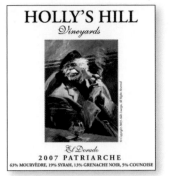

HOLLY'S HILL VINEYARDS
PATRIARCHE IS A TRIBUTE TO THE VARIETALS AND STYLE USED IN CHATEAUNEUF-DU-PAPE

BOGLE VINEYARDS
A REFRESHING RIESLING THAT BALANCES SLIGHT SWEETNESS WITH ACIDITY

Delicato Family Vineyards
San Joaquin County

With cautious intelligence, Delicato Family Vineyards has been expanding production and refining quality since founding father Gaspare Indelicato began to plant vines in the rich San Joaquin Valley at Manteca in 1924. The brand Delicato Family Vineyards is identified today mostly with mass-produced, bargain-priced mainstream varietals, in particular Shiraz. However, the family's third generation now oversees a broad portfolio of specialty brands such as Gnarly Head, Loredona, Irony, and 337, some of which take advantage of Central Valley fruit while others draw from coastal appellations.

12001 South Highway 99, Manteca
www.delicato.com

C.G. Di Arie Winery El Dorado County

As a food scientist, Chaim Gur-Arieh used no end of ingredients and techniques to create modern mealtime wonders. He left that world a decade ago to make wine, embracing the discipline's more traditional and rigid customs. Since then, he and his wife, the artist Elisheva Gur-Arieh, have become widely recognized for combining the Old World's sense of place with the New World's appreciation of forthright fruit flavors. Their portfolio celebrates both the region's history (with Zinfandel, Petite Sirah, and Barbera) and its potential (Tempranillo, Primitivo, and Syrah).

19919 Shenandoah School Rd., Plymouth, CA 95669
www.cgdiarie.com

Ficklin Vineyards Madera County

Just after World War II, Walter Ficklin saw that if he was going to make fine wine in the hot and dry San Joaquin Valley, he would need to cultivate varieties with a history of thriving under those conditions. He chose traditional Portuguese grapes, and focused on making a California version of port. His attention to detail laid the foundation for the state's most consistently faithful emulation. His heirs have veered off into novelties such as hazelnut-flavored ports, but Ficklin's strength remains finely crafted tinta, tawny, and vintage ports.

30246 Ave. 7½, Madera, CA 93637
www.ficklin.com

Holly's Hill Vineyards El Dorado County

Perched high on a ridge in western El Dorado County, Holly's Hill Vineyards is making the broadest and deepest case for the future of Rhône Valley varieties in the Sierra Foothills. This is what the husband-and-wife winemaking team of Carrie Bendick and Josh Bendick do—make wine with such varieties as Mourvèdre, Roussanne, Grenache, and Syrah. Since their first harvest in 2000, their keen stewardship of the vineyards and their commitment to French aesthetics have resulted in definitive varietals and in such masterly blends as Patriarche, inspired by Châteauneuf-du-Pape.

3680 Leisure Lane, Placerville, CA 95667
www.hollyshill.com

Jeff Runquist Wines Amador County

Jeff Runquist harvests grapes from vineyards throughout California, but when he built his own winery in 2008, he chose a site in Amador County. This is where he began

QUADY WINERY
ELYSIUM IS A ROSE-SCENTED DESSERT WINE
MADE FROM THE BLACK MUSCAT GRAPE

MICHAEL-DAVID WINERY
GRAPES FROM SEVEN OF LODI'S FINEST
ZINFANDEL GROWERS, DEVILISHLY COMBINED

his winemaking career in 1980, and it has long been the source of fruit for his more acclaimed releases. Runquist makes luxurious wines in which the expression of fruit and oak is more important than traces of terroir. It is a formula that has made him one of California's more honored winemakers. ★ **Rising star**

10776 Shenandoah Valley Rd., Plymouth, CA 95366
www.jeffrunquistwines.com

Jessie's Grove Winery Lodi
Farming has been going on at the Lodi site of Jessie's Grove Winery since founding father Joseph Spenker began to grow wheat here in 1868. He segued into wine grapes 20 years later. Some of those vines still contribute to the family's wines, most notably its lively, silken, and complex Carignane. Aside from five Zinfandels, each distinct in its own way, the rest of the line-up, in particular Cabernet Sauvignon and Chardonnay, appears to be inspired more by market considerations than terroir.

1973 W Turner Rd., Lodi, CA 95242
www.jessiesgrovewinery.com

Karly Wines Amador County
Former fighter pilot Buck Cobb and his wife, Karly, know something about staying the course. Since establishing their winery in Amador County's Shenandoah Valley in 1978, they have shown each vintage that Sauvignon Blanc is the green grape most at home in the Foothills. Their Zinfandels, in particular the Saddie Upton and Warrior Fires, are all about hardy terroir, while their lip-smacking Mourvèdre, El Alacran, shows they are as committed to the future as they are respectful of the past.

11076 Bell Rd., Plymouth, CA 95669
www.karlywines.com

Lange Twins Winery & Vineyards Lodi
Langes have been farming at Lodi since the 1870s. They started with watermelons, moving into grapes in 1916. In 2003, twin brothers Bradford and Randall established their eponymous winery, which today employs nine members of the family. Their basic line-up of mainstream varietals is respectable, if a bit costly, while their proprietary blends, such as the Bordeaux-inspired, Lodi-designated Midnight Reserve, are capable of delivering Napa Valley composure and complexity at a fraction of the price. ★ **Rising star**

1525 East Jahant Rd., Acampo, CA 95220
www.langetwins.com

Lavender Ridge Vineyard
Calaveras County
Rich Gilpin likes to grow grapes. His wife Siri Gilpin is just as eager about lavender. Together, they combine their passions on a sunny and sloping site west of Angels Camp, in the heart of the old gold fields. They share their bounty—wines from the vineyard, soaps from the lavender—in a tasting room just on the other side of Angels Camp, in the old mining town of Murphys. Rich Gilpin grows only Rhône varieties, and his gutsy yet balanced varietals and blends make a persuasive case that they have a solid future in California.

425 Main St., Murphys, CA 95247
www.lavenderridgevineyard.com

Madroña Vineyards El Dorado County
Since planting Madroña's first vines 3,000ft (900m) up the Sierra Foothills in 1973, the Dick Bush family has been committed to one of the more varied and more consistently reliable wine portfolios in the region. The Bushes have not shunned the region's most established varietal, Zinfandel, but they have had more success with varieties not usually associated with the Foothills, including Cabernet Sauvignon, Gewurztraminer, Cabernet Franc, Chardonnay, and Riesling.

2560 High Hill Rd., Camino, CA 95709
www.madronavineyards.com

McManis Family Vineyards
San Joaquin County
The McManis family have been farming grapes in the northern San Joaquin Valley since 1938, but only in 1997 did members of the fourth generation start to build a winery at Ripon. Since then, their red wines, in particular Cabernet Sauvignon, Petite Sirah, and Syrah, have won converts for their astute mix of exuberant fruit-forward flavors and everyday prices. Aside from a stunning Viognier, their whites have yet to realize equal acclaim.

18700 East River Rd., Ripon, CA 95366
www.mcmanisfamilyvineyards.com

Michael-David Winery Lodi
As a measure of just how deceiving appearances can be, consider brothers Michael and David Phillips. Country boys, they are more at home selling heirloom tomatoes at farmers markets than hobnobbing at black-tie winemaker dinners. But behind their produce stand and pie shop thrives one of the more market-savvy wineries in California's Central Valley. Their sumptuous wines, often marketed under such proprietary names as 7 Deadly Zins and Earthquake, are not for everyone because of their sweetness and weight, but production continues to expand as popularity grows.

4580 West Highway 12, Lodi, CA 95242
www.lodivineyards.com

Miraflores Winery El Dorado County
After a long tenure in Napa Valley, Marco Cappelli packed up his belongings and like a latter-day argonaut headed deep into the Sierra Foothills, not far from where gold was discovered in 1848. He bought a vineyard and began to consult for Mother Lode wineries, but he is most closely identified with Miraflores Winery. There, his Bordeaux blend and Barbera are less impressive than his deep and supple Syrahs, while two of the more stubborn varieties in the area, Pinot Grigio and Muscat Cannelli, yield surprising complexity and length under Capelli's stewardship. ★ **Rising star**

2120 Four Springs Trail, Placerville, CA 95667
www.mirafloreswinery.com

New Clairvaux Vineyard Tehama County
The Trappist monks of the Abbey of New Clairvaux planted their vineyard at Vina, in the far northern reaches of Sacramento Valley. This is precisely where the early California governor Leland Stanford cultivated what was, in 1889, the largest vineyard in the world. The monks are reviving Stanford's failed dream of producing fine table wine. Unlike Stanford, the monks are focused on

hot-weather varieties, with Tempranillo, Petite Sirah, and Albariño showing the most promise early on. Syrah is not showing so much potential. ★ **Rising star**

26240 Seventh St., Vina, CA 96092
www.newclairvauxvineyard.com

Quady Winery Madera County

Perhaps because of his background in pyrotechnics, Andrew Quady lit up the customarily reserved wine industry of California's Central Valley when he switched to winemaking in 1975. Instead of copying the more middling table wines typical of the area, Quady and his wife Laurel jumped into the production of dessert wines, starting with fiery emulations of port based on Zinfandel from Amador County. Their port, which they prefer to call Starboard, remains the backbone of the winery, where they also turn out intrepid dessert wines made with Orange Muscat and Black Muscat.

13181 Rd. 24, Madera, CA 93639
www.quadywinery.com

Scott Harvey Wines Amador County

Scott Harvey combines his upbringing in the Sierra Foothills with his winemaking training in Germany to produce wines that couple the power of Amador County with the classic restraint of Europe. Early on, he foresaw Barbera's current standing as the new darling of the region, producing wines that showcase the varietal's versatility and accessibility. While Harvey is widely respected as the man who has done the most to raise the winemaking profile of the county over the past four decades, his Syrahs have not performed as consistently as his Zinfandels and Barberas.

79 Main St., Sutter Creek, CA 95685
www.scottharveywines.com

Sobon Estate Amador County

Silicon Valley rocket scientist Leon Sobon packed up his young family to move to Amador County's Shenandoah Valley in 1977 to pursue his passion for making port. After first establishing Shenandoah Vineyards in 1989, the Sobons bought the historic D'Agostini Winery nearby, which dates from 1856, renaming it Sobon Estate. Leon Sobon still makes port, but Shenandoah Vineyards today is celebrated largely for its range of husky Zinfandels, while Sobon Estate focuses on concentrated vineyard-designated Zinfandels. Their wines from Rhône varieties are mixed.

14430 Shenandoah Rd., Plymouth, CA 95669
www.sobonwine.com

Terra d'Oro Winery Amador County

Established in 1970 as Montevina Winery, the facility was rechristened Terra d'Oro in late 2008 to recognize its reborn emphasis on wines made with Foothill fruit; *terra d'oro* is Italian for "land of gold." Owned by Trinchero Family Estates of Napa Valley, Terra d'Oro is one of the more corporate operations in the Foothills, producing serviceable Sangiovese, Barbera, and Syrah. It retains its high profile largely on the strength of Zinfandels such as its nuanced Amador County, the layered and balanced Home Vineyard, and the dense and beefy Deaver.

20680 Shenandoah School Rd., Plymouth, CA 95669
www.terradorowinery.com

Terre Rouge Wines Amador County

Former San Francisco Bay Area wine merchant Bill Easton and his wife Jane O'Riordan show that the Sierra Foothills is not a one-trick pony. Zinfandel put the region on the wine map, but Easton, under his Terre Rouge brand, turns out persuasive echoes of the Rhône Valley in such signature releases as his flagship Ascent, a pointed and pensive Syrah, the most expensive wine of the region. He does not ignore Zinfandel, however, and crafts interpretations, under the Easton brand, ranging from a light-style Amador County to a composed late harvest.

10801 Dickson Rd., Plymouth, CA 95669
www.terrerougewines.com

Uvaggio Lodi

Long before the term Cal-Ital was coined to describe California wines made from Italian grape varieties, Jim Moore had faith that Vermentino, Nebbiolo, Barbera, and the like would find a welcome place on the American table. Though Cal-Ital virtually disappeared from the lexicon of California vintners as they learned just how difficult Sangiovese and Nebbiolo are to master, Moore remains a believer. His shrewd Vermentino, Barbera, and Moscato, which are all made with fruit from Lodi, show that lean, sharp, and nimble wines are not the province of Italy alone.

6711 Washington St., Yountville
www.uvaggio.com

Vino Noceto Amador County

With patience, candor, and warmth, Jim and Suzy Gullett exemplify the kind of vintner drawn to the Sierra Foothills since the region's renaissance began in the late 1960s. They were pioneers looking for a novel way for a place to express itself most profoundly through wine. In their case, the grape and wine is Sangiovese. They yearly release eight variations, from a bright, spicy, and long-living Shenandoah Valley to a bracing and astonishingly fruitful grappa.

11011 Shenandoah Rd., Plymouth, CA 95669
www.noceto.com

Yorba Wines Amador County

For more than 20 years, Ann Kraemer has been a highly respected vineyard manager in Napa Valley. But when the opportunity came up to create her own vineyard early this century, she chose the Sierra Foothills for its intriguing mix of soils and exposures. She planted 34 acres (14ha) east of Sutter Creek in Amador County with such rugged, warm-weather varieties as Tempranillo, Zinfandel, and Syrah. Over the past couple of years, she has garnered wide acclaim for the finely structured authority and friendly juiciness of the resulting wines. ★ **Rising star**

No visitor facilities
www.yorbawines.com

BARBERA

In California's Sierra Foothills, Zinfandel is firmly established as the black grape of choice. Sangiovese, Mourvèdre, and Syrah are showing promise, but no black grape is challenging Zinfandel for prominence more than Barbera. While Barbera is far behind Zinfandel in plantings, its stature is rising fast. In two out of three recent years, an Amador County Barbera was named best red wine at the California State Fair. At the Alessandria International Competition in Piedmont, Italy, Barberas from Amador County consistently have won high awards in the foreign wing of the judging.

Barberas from such producers as Terra d'Oro, Sobon Estate, Scott Harvey, Macchia, Karmere, Boeger, Runquist, Latcham and Cooper are not as lithe and tangy as some Italian examples of the varietal, but their customary ripe fruit flavors, generous oak, and warmth and mass make them increasingly popular on both sides of the Atlantic.

PACIFIC NORTHWEST

The rapidly developing wine regions of Oregon and Washington State are often referred to collectively as the Pacific Northwest. And while there are many differences between the two in terms of climate, grape varieties, and wine style, their histories are broadly similar. Wine was made in both states before Prohibition intervened, but, after its repeal in 1933, *Vitis vinifera* was slow to re-establish itself, and the production of quality wine on any scale did not really get going in either state until well into the second half of the 20th century. In Oregon today, wine production follows the Willamette River Valley in the cooler north from just south of Portland, and then widens to include the warmer southern regions of the state. In Washington, 90 percent of the grapes are grown in the arid region east of the Cascade Mountains.

The story of the modern Oregon wine industry really begins in 1961. It was then that Hillcrest Vineyard was established near Roseburg (well south of today's concentration of grape growing) by the late Richard Sommer. Sommer was a refugee from the University of California at Davis, where he had been firmly advised that vinifera grapes could not be grown in Oregon. He was determined to prove his former professors wrong, and he was joined, in 1964, by Charles Coury of the eponymous winery, who planted Alsatian varieties on his estate in Washington County in 1964. Two years later, another Davis refugee, the late David Lett of The Eyrie Vineyards, first planted Pinot Noir vines in the northern end of the Willamette Valley.

The influence of the pioneering Lett (who is now known in Oregon as "Papa Pinot") extends far beyond his role in the early plantings of what would become Oregon's signature red grape variety. It was Lett's 1975 Eyrie Vineyard Pinot Noir that first put Oregon on the map as a fine wine producer in a French-sponsored 1979 tasting of French wines and their New World counterparts. In that tasting, the Eyrie was placed second, and it repeated the trick when Burgundy merchant Robert Drouhin staged a follow-up tasting to confirm the results. Drouhin eloquently endorsed the upset by purchasing land a stone's throw from Lett's in the Dundee Hills.

The Willamette Valley—the largest and most important grape-growing region in Oregon—has since established its reputation as one of the world's best regions for producing Pinot Noir, in a style that sits between the rich, broad California examples and the nervy, racy Burgundian versions. Southern Oregon sees more warmth and less rain and can grow thicker-skinned grapes, such as Cabernet Sauvignon and Tempranillo well.

The story of Washington, meanwhile, is bound up with the formation of two large companies: during the 1960s the AWG (American Wine Growers), which later became known as Chateau Ste Michelle, and Associated Vintners, which became Columbia Winery. Both companies have had a profound influence on the development of the Washington wine industry. The AWG, for example, was responsible for hiring the famed and highly respected Californian consultant André Tchelistcheff to help work out which varieties would work best in the region, while Associated Vintners, originally a group of hobby winemaking academics from the University of Washington, made their own experiments. Intriguingly, Tchelistcheff's nephew, Alex Golitzen, would later achieve fame with his critically acclaimed Quilceda Creek line of wines. Over the years, many of Washington's top winemakers have spent time working at one of the two giants, whose influence continues despite the recent rapid growth in the number of wineries in the state.

The modern-day Washington scene has become known for producing top-quality wines from Merlot, Syrah, and Riesling. But its warm, sunny growing season means it has had success with a number of other varieties, both red and white, and its producers are still shaping the region's identity.

Moisture-laden fog rolls through the Dundee Hills AVA of the Willamette Valley in northern Oregon.

WASHINGTON STATE

State of Washington

Wine regions of Washington

— Area shown at larger scale on pp.96-97

Washington is a state of two distinct halves. Divided perpendicularly by the Cascade Mountains, it is cooler and wetter to the west of this volcanically formed barrier than it is in the lands to its east. Think of rainy Seattle on one side of the mountains. Then think of the desertlike conditions to the east, where the climate is defined by the "rain shadow" effect caused by those mountains. Very little moisture reaches the eastern half of the state, making irrigation essential. But for growers with access to water, the arid climate, combined with the long daylight hours of the growing season at this relatively northern latitude, make these vineyard lands close to ideal for growing wine grapes marked by complex fruit flavors and bright acidity.

Major grapes

 Reds

Cabernet Franc

Cabernet Sauvignon

Merlot

Syrah

 Whites

Chardonnay

Riesling

Semillon

Vintages

2009
A difficult vintage with problems posed by a very hot summer and October frost.

2008
A terrific year. Perfect weather conditions created super wines that will be long-lived.

2007
A strong year for Washington with good wines of all varieties.

2006
A warm summer led to big rich wines of great color and flavor.

2005
A classic Washington vintage with some great wines.

2004
A vintage of good, solid, balanced, and flavorful wines.

It is no surprise, therefore, that the vast majority of Washington State's wine production is drawn from grapes grown in the east of the state. Indeed, the Puget Sound AVA is the only officially recognized wine region on the west side of the Cascades. A mere 1% of the state's wine grapes are grown here, and just a few wineries produce wines from grapes grown in the AVA, generally from cooler-climate varieties such as Madeleine Angevine, Siegerebbe, and Müller-Thurgau.

In stark contrast, the largest, broadest Washington appellation is the Columbia Valley AVA. This enormous AVA sprawls east of the Cascades, covering almost half of the state, and encompassing several smaller AVAs such as Yakima Valley, Red Mountain, Walla Walla Valley, Horse Heaven Hills, Wahluke Slope, Rattlesnake Hills, Columbia Gorge, and Snipes Mountain. Until the Washington wine industry really began to take off in the 1980s and 1990s, this was fruit-farming country, and many wine grape growers still produce cherries, apples, and table grapes. These days, however, the landscape, from the Columbia River in the south to the land north of the Yakima River, is increasingly dotted with vinifera vines.

Although high quality fruit and wines can be found throughout the Columbia Valley AVA, two of the smaller AVAs found within its borders have developed reputations for producing Washington's best wines. The first is the Red Mountain AVA, which is both the smallest—with 700 acres (280ha) in the southeastern corner of the Yakima Valley

AVA—and the warmest growing region in Washington, with more heat accumulation days than elsewhere. Some of the state's best vineyard land is here, with 15 producers and such sought-after vineyards as Klipsun and Ciel de Cheval. On Red Mountain, Merlot sometimes behaves like Cabernet Sauvignon, showing bigger tannins and expression than is usual in a grape that is generally regarded as soft.

The Walla Walla Valley may be the state's most respected region, despite its somewhat remote location in the far southeastern corner bordering (and including) Oregon. Consisting of 1,600 acres (650ha) with a range of elevations, almost all of the 100-plus wineries operating in this two-state AVA are located on the Washington side. An increasing number of wineries have vineyards in the valley—some 1,500 acres (600ha) have been planted, much of them on the Oregon side. Established names such as Leonetti, Woodward Canyon, and L'Ecole No 41 work alongside superstar newcomers like Waters and Gramercy Cellars.

Another notable AVA is the state's newest, Lake Chelan. Located in north-central Washington amid stunning lake-filled natural beauty, it is home to 15 producers who also buy grapes from vineyards in other parts of the Columbia Valley. Finally, the Columbia Gorge AVA straddles both sides of the Columbia River for a stretch of about 500 acres (200ha), with more than 20 producers on either side of the border between Washington and Oregon.

Abeja

Meaning "bee" in Spanish, Abeja is a collaboration between businessman Ken Harrison and his wife Ginger, and long-established winemaker John Abbot and his partner Molly Galt. The wines are made by Abbot (who also looks after the vineyards) in a barn at The Inn of Abeja, a beautiful, upmarket bed and breakfast that makes a great, if expensive, base for visiting the region. Ultimately, production at Abeja will reach 6,000 cases, primarily of Cabernet Sauvignon. The wines so far show lovely elegance and complexity.

2014 Mill Creek Rd., Walla Walla, WA 99362
www.abeja.net

Amavi Cellars

Amavi Cellars is part of the same stable as fellow Walla Walla winery Pepper Bridge; a partnership between Pepper Bridge owner Norm McKibben, winemaker Jean-François Pellet, McKibben's sons, Travis Goff, and Pepper Bridge partners Ray and Diana Goff. It produces lovely, approachable, ageworthy wines, focusing on estate-grown Cabernet Sauvignon and Syrah, plus small amounts of a rich, tasty barrel-fermented Semillon/Sauvignon Blanc, an always sold-out rosé, and a few dessert wines, typically available only in the tasting room.

3796 Pepper Bridge Rd., Walla Walla, WA 99362
www.amavicellars.com

Andrew Will Winery

Named after the son (Will) and nephew (Andrew) of quirky owner, Chris Camarda, Andrew Will Winery began in 1989. In 1994, the Camardas moved to Vashon Island, a short ferry ride from Seattle, and built a winery for their 4,300-case production. They have since planted 36 acres (15ha) of vineyards in Eastern Washington, but they also source fruit from some of the state's best growers. Camarda makes varietal Merlot, Cabernet Sauvignon, Cabernet Franc, Sangiovese, and a number of blends. Whatever the ingredients, the wines are among Washington's best, with expression and depth.

No visitor facilities
www.andrewwill.com

Barnard Griffin

Rob Griffin and Deborah Barnard began making their own wine in 1977, when Griffin came to Washington to work for Preston Winery. Griffin moved on to work for Hogue Cellars and as a consultant to several Washington producers until completion of the Barnard Griffin winery and tasting room in 1996. Barnard Griffin owns no vineyards, but relies on long-term contracts for fruit for wines such as the delicious Reserve Syrah. All the wines are well crafted, with bright acidity and depth of fruit.

878 Tulip Lane, Richland, WA 99352
www.barnardgriffin.com

Betz Family Winery

Bob Betz is one of the few Masters of Wine making wine in the US, and since starting out in 1997, his mantra has been: keep small, keep simple, and keep focused. Production now stands at 3,500 cases—the most Betz says he can manage by himself. Based in Woodinville near Seattle, Betz buys in his fruit from top vineyards. He is best known for his range of high-quality Syrahs, but he

ANDREW WILL WINERY
SORELLA IS A SUPERB BORDEAUX-STYLE
BLEND OF FOUR RED GRAPE VARIETIES

ABEJA
ABEJA BELIEVES CABERNET SAUVIGNON
WILL BE WASHINGTON'S SIGNATURE VARIETY

also produces blends based on Grenache (in a Southern Rhône style), Cabernet Sauvignon, and Merlot. The wines are hard to find, but certainly worth seeking out.

13244 Woodinville Redmond Rd. NE, Redmond, WA 98052
www.betzfamilywinery.com

Bookwalter Winery

Bookwalter Winery has been producing small lots of high-quality wine in the Tri-Cities area since 1983. John Bookwalter, formerly in sales and marketing, has been the main man since 1997, helped by consultant winemakers Zelma Long and, latterly, Claude Gros. There is a range of varietal wines, a number of off-dry whites, and focused, complex proprietary red blends.

894 Tulip Lane, Richland, WA 99352
www.bookwalterwines.com

Buty Winery

Caleb and Nina Buty Foster founded their Walla Walla-based winery in 2000. The grapes are sourced from the state's top vineyards, and from the Fosters' own 10 acre (4ha) organic vineyard in the Milton-Freewater area of Walla Walla, which they converted from an orchard. The Fosters make focused wines packed with flavor, such as a floral Semillon blend, and an earthy, complex Champoux Vineyard Cabernet Sauvignon/Cabernet Franc.

535 East Cessna Ave., Walla Walla, WA 99362
www.butywinery.com

Cadaretta

Named for a ship that once carried the owner's goods to market, Cadaretta is a newish winery in Walla Walla. Currently relying on purchased fruit from across the state, Cadaretta planted its own vineyards in 2008. Standouts are the crisp, unoaked Sauvignon Blanc/Semillon blend and a big, structured Cabernet Sauvignon that is lovely despite abundant oak. ★ **Rising star**

1102 Dell Ave., Walla Walla, WA 99362
www.cadaretta.com

Cadence Winery

Former airplane designer Ben Smith and former lawyer Gaye McNutt own this Woodinville-based winery dedicated to Bordeaux-style blends. Named after the Red Mountain vineyards where the grapes are sourced—such as Ciel du Cheval, Taptiel, Klipsun, and the couple's own Cara Mia—the wines offer deep flavor, but are neither too heavy nor too extracted.

9320 15th Ave., Unit CF, Seattle, WA 98108
www.cadencewinery.com

Cayuse Vineyards

Cayuse's French owner, Christophe Baron, makes some of the most sought-after wine in Washington. His specialty is Syrah, grown on the Oregon side of Walla Walla in rocky soils similar to the *galets* of Châteauneuf-du-Pape, but his six Biodynamic vineyards also have space for Cabernet Franc, Cabernet Sauvignon, Grenache, Merlot, Tempranillo, and Viognier. Yields are very low, resulting in wines of great depth, elegance, and complexity.

No visitor facilities
www.cayusevineyards.com

COLUMBIA VALLEY

The Yakima Valley and Walla Walla Valley AVAs both feature a concentration of Washington State's most important vineyards and wineries. Located between the towns of Benton City and Richland, at the eastern end of the Yakima Valley, Red Mountain is the smallest (4,040 acres/1,635ha) but also arguably the most prestigious Washington AVA. To the south of the Yakima Valley AVA, stretching to the Columbia River, is the Horse Heaven Hills AVA, home to celebrated vineyards such as Alder Ridge, Andrews Horse Heaven, Champoux, and Wallula Gap. Grapes are often transported back west across the Cascade Mountains to wineries in the Seattle area.

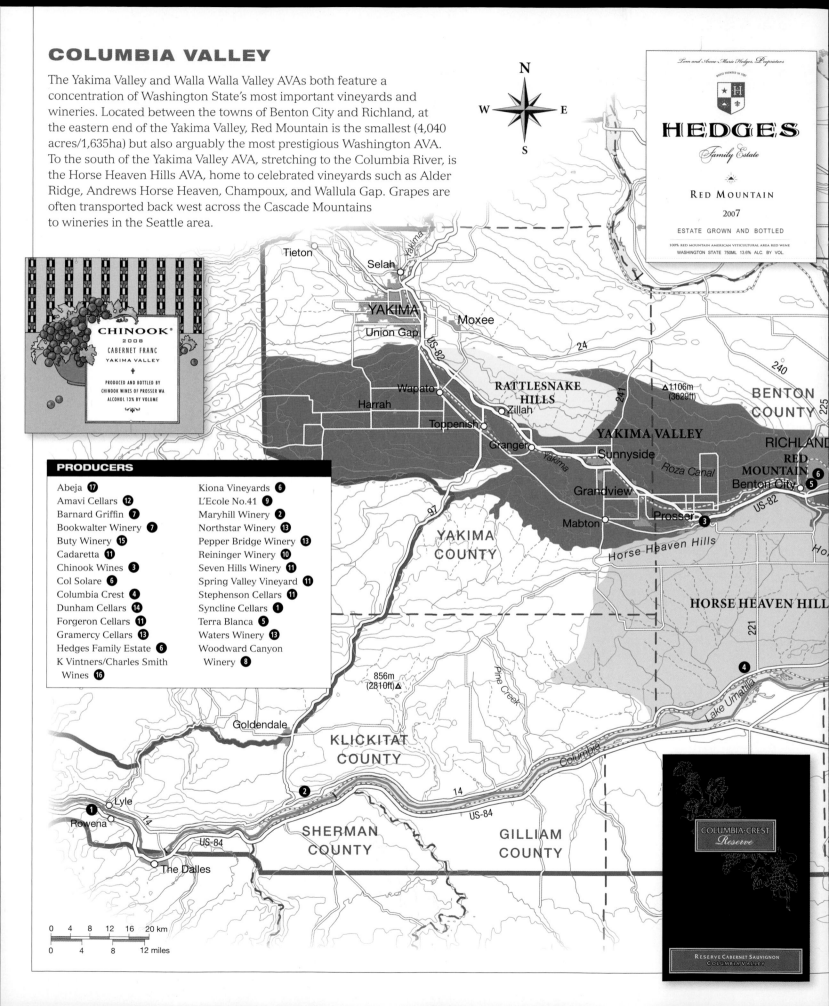

PRODUCERS

Abeja **17**	Kiona Vineyards **6**
Amavi Cellars **12**	L'Ecole No.41 **9**
Barnard Griffin **7**	Maryhill Winery **2**
Bookwalter Winery **7**	Northstar Winery **13**
Buty Winery **15**	Pepper Bridge Winery **13**
Cadaretta **11**	Reininger Winery **10**
Chinook Wines **3**	Seven Hills Winery **11**
Col Solare **6**	Spring Valley Vineyard **11**
Columbia Crest **4**	Stephenson Cellars **11**
Dunham Cellars **14**	Syncline Cellars **1**
Forgeron Cellars **11**	Terra Blanca **5**
Gramercy Cellars **13**	Waters Winery **13**
Hedges Family Estate **6**	Woodward Canyon
K Vintners/Charles Smith	Winery **8**
Wines **16**	

CHINOOK
2008
CABERNET FRANC
YAKIMA VALLEY

PRODUCED AND BOTTLED BY
CHINOOK WINES OF PROSSER WA
ALCOHOL 13% BY VOLUME

Tom and Anne-Marie Hedges, Proprietors

HEDGES
Family Estate

RED MOUNTAIN
2007
ESTATE GROWN AND BOTTLED

100% RED MOUNTAIN AMERICAN VITICULTURAL AREA RED WINE
WASHINGTON STATE 750ML 13.6% ALC. BY VOL.

COLUMBIA·CREST
Reserve

RESERVE CABERNET SAUVIGNON
COLUMBIA VALLEY

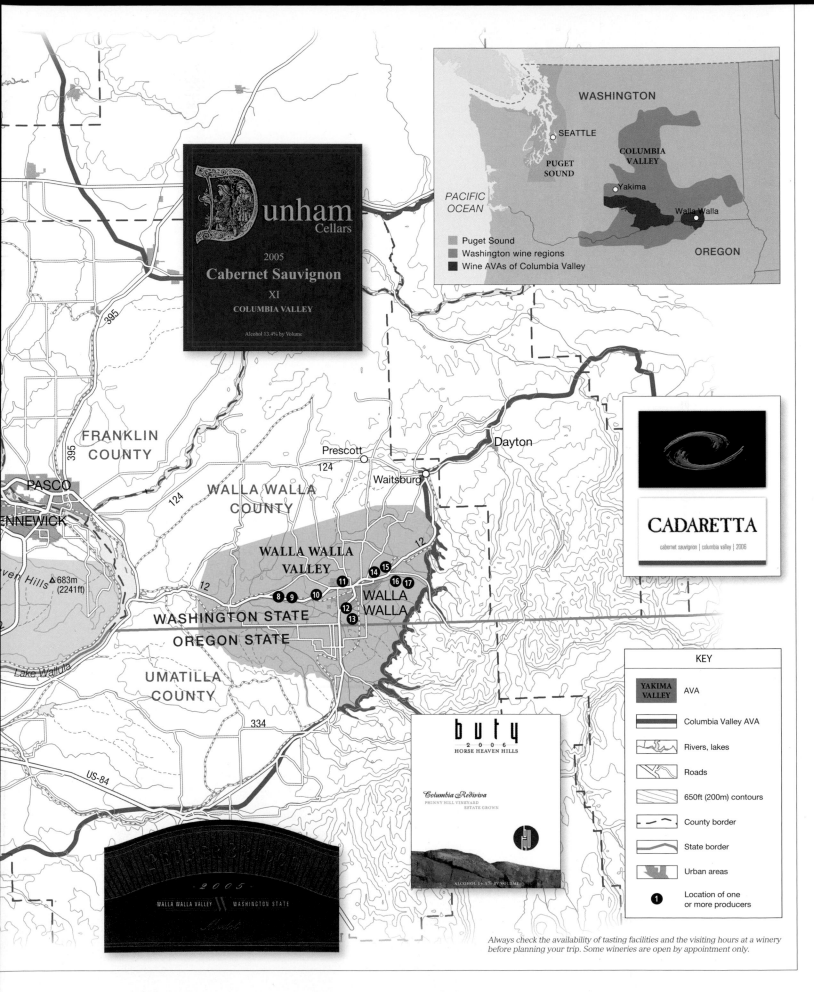

WASHINGTON

SEATTLE

PUGET
SOUND

COLUMBIA
VALLEY

PACIFIC
OCEAN

Yakima

Walla Walla

OREGON

Puget Sound
Washington wine regions
Wine AVAs of Columbia Valley

Dunham
Cellars

2005

Cabernet Sauvignon

XI

COLUMBIA VALLEY

Alcohol 13.4% by Volume

FRANKLIN
COUNTY

PASCO

KENNEWICK

Dayton

Prescott
124

Waitsburg

WALLA WALLA
COUNTY

WALLA WALLA
VALLEY

△683m
(2241ft)

14 15

8 9   10   11

16 17

12
13

WALLA
WALLA

WASHINGTON STATE

OREGON STATE

Lake Wallula

UMATILLA
COUNTY

334

US-84

CADARETTA

cabernet sauvignon | columbia valley | 2006

buty
2006
HORSE HEAVEN HILLS

Columbia Rediviva
PHINNY HILL VINEYARD
ESTATE GROWN

ALCOHOL 14.5% BY VOLUME

KEY

YAKIMA VALLEY	AVA
	Columbia Valley AVA
	Rivers, lakes
	Roads
	650ft (200m) contours
	County border
	State border
	Urban areas
1	Location of one or more producers

Always check the availability of tasting facilities and the visiting hours at a winery before planning your trip. Some wineries are open by appointment only.

K VINTNERS/CHARLES SMITH
THE POWERFUL OLD BONES SYRAH HAS
BEEN A BIG HIT WITH THE CRITICS

Chateau Ste Michelle

Chateau Ste Michelle is Washington State's first, largest, and in many ways most important, winery. It can trace its history back to the Repeal of Prohibition, but today's company began in earnest with the merger of Pommerelle Wine Company and the National Wine Company to form American Wine Growers in 1954. In 1967, American Wine Growers began a new line of wines called "Ste Michelle Vintners" under the direction of the renowned California winemaker André Tchelistcheff, before changing its name to Chateau Ste Michelle on the construction of its Woodinville headquarters in 1976. Ste Michelle now owns more than 3,500 acres (1,420ha) of vines (its Cold Creek vineyard, planted in 1972, is one of the oldest in the state) and it produces around 1 million cases of wine each year. Ste Michelle could make it the region's 800-pound gorilla, so much larger is it than any other producer in the state. But the organization has used its position responsibly, and has promoted Washington wines, and wine in general, almost more than its own brands. Best known for its fine Rieslings, Ste Michelle also produces some high-quality Merlot and Cabernet Sauvignon, and is involved in a number of high-profile joint ventures across the state.

14111 NE 145th St., Woodinville, WA 98072
www.ste-michelle.com

Chinook Wines

In 1983, husband-and-wife team Clay Mackey (ex-Chateau Ste Michelle viticulturist) and Kay Simon (ex-Chateau Ste Michelle winemaker) combined their broad experience and set about the goal of creating top-quality Yakima Valley wines at Chinook Wines. The couple produces Chardonnay, Sauvignon Blanc, Semillon, Merlot, Cabernet Franc, and Cabernet Sauvignon grapes, and their most interesting wines are the fresh and lively Semillon and the delicious, varietally true-to-form Cabernet Franc.

220 W. Wittkopf Loop, Prosser, WA 99350
www.chinookwines.com

Col Solare

A joint venture between Chateau Ste Michelle and the renowned Tuscan producer Marchese Piero Antinori, Col Solare's winery boasts an impressive, and beautiful, site on the top of Red Mountain, with its vineyards fanning out on the slopes below. The Col Solare wine itself is made by a team drawn from both partners in the business, with Marcus Notaro in day-to-day control. It is a seamless blend of Cabernet Sauvignon, Merlot, Cabernet Franc, Petit Verdot, and Syrah that tastes of smooth and rich black fruit and cocoa. A second wine, Shining Hill, is made from grape lots sourced from top vineyard sites throughout the Columbia Valley and declassified lots from Col Solare. This wine sees less time in oak and is for more immediate drinking.

50207 Antinori Rd., Benton City, WA 99320
www.colsolare.com

Columbia Crest

Owned and operated by Chateau Ste Michelle, Columbia Crest released its first wine in 1985, from its own vineyards, planted in 1978. From the beginning, this winery's mission has been to showcase high-quality Washington wine at an affordable price. Given its scale (Columbia Crest produces more than 1 million cases a year), it is perhaps not surprising that quality can occasionally get lost. But prices are certainly low, and both the critically acclaimed Reserve range and Columbia Crest's top wine, Walter Clore Private Reserve, are more than a match for most of the other leading wines produced in the state.

Hwy 221 Columbia Crest Drive, Paterson, WA 99345
www.columbia-crest.com

Columbia Winery

Columbia Winery was one of the first wineries in Washington State and a large one, too, its headquarters located across the street from Chateau Ste Michelle. For years, Columbia was led by the pioneering winemaker, David Lake MW, who graciously championed the brand until his death in late 2009. Lake was the first winemaker to produce Syrah, Cabernet Franc, and Pinot Gris in Washington, and forged the long-term and dedicated relationship with the highly respected Red Willow Vineyard. The wines of the vineyard-designate line, the small lot series, and the wine club-only Stone-Cutters Series are well made and appealing. Columbia is part of Icon Estates, a division of the important American multinational, Constellation Wines.

14030 NE 145th St., Woodinville, WA 98072
www.columbiawinery.com

DeLille Cellars

One of the best producers in Washington State, DeLille Cellars produces Bordeaux blends such as the big, muscular Chaleur Estate and the silkier, softer Harrison Hill, both of which are great when consumed young, but even better with a bit of age. DeLille's Doyenne Syrah is equally fine, a brawnier style than most, but with lovely rich fruit, blanketed in oak. The white—based on a classic Bordeaux blanc—shows a floral richness and a generous hand with oak.

14208 Woodinville-Redmond Rd. NE, Redmond, WA 98052
www.delillecellars.com

Dunham Cellars

Once an assistant winemaker at L'Ecole No. 41, Eric Dunham has been devoting his talents to his own brand since 1997. Dunham's wines are big, oaky, and concentrated, and they are made for the long haul. The wines are produced at the old Walla Walla airport, but future plans include a new production facility located near Lowden on the Dunham family's old farm.

150 E. Boeing Ave., Walla Walla, WA 99362
www.dunhamcellars.com

Eroica

Produced at Chateau Ste Michelle as a joint project with Ernst Loosen of Weingut and Dr. Loosen of the Mosel Valley, Eroica's off-dry Riesling gets lots of praise from the critics for its balance and lovely citrus character, although the acidity is not always sufficient to balance the sugar. The project also makes Single Berry Select, a botrytized dessert wine in the style of a German Trockenbeerenauslese (TBA), and, when weather permits, an Icewine.

14111 NE 145th St., Woodinville, WA 98072
www.eroicawine.com

EROICA
THE LUSCIOUS RIESLING ICEWINE IS MADE
FROM FRUIT FROZEN ON THE VINE

Fielding Hills Winery

A young winery, using vineyards first planted in 1998, Fielding Hills released its first wine in 2002. The Cabernet Sauvignon in particular is lovely, very spicy with a strong dose of meatiness from the Syrah that is blended in—the concentration of flavors is amazing. The Syrah is almost as nice, very gamey and smoky with a healthy dose of oak. Alcohol levels can be high.

1401 Fielding Hills Drive, East Wenatchee, WA 98802
www.fieldinghills.com

Forgeron Cellars

Forgeron's winery/tasting room is located in what used to be a blacksmith's shop, and its name is taken from the French word for the trade, a word that also means "experienced, expert craftsman." It is an appropriate name because winemaker Marie-Eve Gilla certainly crafts lovely, elegant wines, in particular her full-bodied Cabernet Sauvignon, understated Chardonnay, and lively, rich Roussanne, using fruit sourced from 12 contracted vineyards located across the Columbia and Walla Walla valleys.

33 W. Birch St., Walla Walla, WA 99362
www.forgeroncellars.com

Gorman Winery

Another young Woodinville winery, the fast up-and-coming Gorman Winery sources fruit from east of the mountains from top vineyard sites. The wines have fanciful names—The Big Sissy (Chardonnay), The Evil Twin (a blend), Zachary's Ladder (a blend), The Pixie (Syrah), and The Bully (Cabernet Sauvignon)—but they are powerful, focused, and concentrated. Production, at around 1,600 cases, is small.

19501 144th Ave. NE C500, Woodinville, WA 98072
www.gormanwinery.com

Gramercy Cellars

Based in Walla Walla, Gramercy Cellars was started by master sommelier Greg Harrington in 2005 with a focus on Syrah, although Cabernet Sauvignon, Tempranillo, Riesling, and a bit of Willamette Valley (Oregon) Pinot Noir are also produced. The Syrah is stunning: very meaty and elegant, with a silky texture and a long finish—a serious wine. ★ **Rising star**

1825 JB George Rd., Walla Walla, WA 99362
www.gramercycellars.com

Hedges Family Estate

Washington native Tom Hedges began his adventures in the wine industry in 1986, selling American wines to the Taiwanese. He soon set up what was then Hedges Cellars, selling his first wines to the state-run alcohol monopoly in Sweden and other exotic clients before having a crack at the US market. The beginnings of Hedges as a serious estate winery, however, really date to 1991, when Tom and his wife Anne-Marie purchased land on the then largely unknown Red Mountain, establishing their first winery in the process. The Hedges—including Tom's brother, Pete, a brewer by training who now runs the winemaking operation—have since concentrated their efforts on increasingly high-quality, but affordable Cabernet Sauvignon and Merlot. But they also use a number of other varieties, including the Chardonnay,

Marsanne, and Sauvignon Blanc from which they make a distinctive, tasty white blend, CMS, and the trio of port varieties that go into their very small-production, port-style fortified red. Besides the Red Mountain winery, a tasting room in Issaquah, just east of Seattle, serves as a visitor center.

53511 N. Sunset Rd., Benton City, WA 99320
www.hedgesfamilyestate.com

JM Cellars

John and Peggy Bigelow craft wines in Woodinville from top vineyard sites across the Columbia Valley. These include their signature Tre Fanciulli (Cabernet Sauvignon-led) blend, as well as the powerfully elegant Longevity, a rich Merlot-dominated wine. Amazingly, John was a software executive until 2006, when he left technology behind and made winemaking his full-time work.

14404 137th Place NE, Woodinville, WA 98072
www.jmcellars.com

Januik Winery

Former Chateau Ste Michelle head winemaker Mike Januik forged out on his own in 1999 to make focused Chardonnay, Merlot, Syrah, and Cabernet Sauvignon. Januik's Merlot is a particular strength, and the Klipsun Vineyard wine, with its raspberry fruit and firm tannins, is a great expression of what good-quality Merlot should be. Januik also makes wine for Novelty Hill, with whom he shares his Woodinville tasting room and winery.

14710 Woodinville-Redmond Rd. NE, Woodinville,
WA 98072; www.januikwinery.com

K Vintners/Charles Smith Wines

Charles Smith is a colorful character who once managed rock bands in Denmark. His life in wine began when he moved to Walla Walla, where he knew just one person: Syrah king Christophe Baron of Cayuse. Baron gave Smith a small lot of Syrah and the rest is history. Smith learned well and now produces many *cuvées* of his big, dense Syrahs loaded with smoke, olives, spice, and meat. The top wines do not come cheap, but Smith does make some less expensive wines for drinking young.

820 Mill Creek Rd., Walla Walla, WA 99362
www.kvintners.com

Kiona Vineyards

The Williams family behind Kiona Vineyards and Winery planted the first vineyards on what is now known as Red Mountain in 1975. Still family-owned and operated, they produce a wide range of good-quality varietals from their estate vineyards and from purchased fruit. Their best wine is not their most expensive: the Estate Lemberger is fabulous—a spicy black-fruited wine with silky texture, framed with judicious oak.

44612 N. Sunset Rd., Benton City, WA 99320
www.kionawine.com

L'Ecole No. 41

L'Ecole No. 41 takes its name from the schoolhouse it once was. It is owned and run by winemaker Marty Clubb, who fashions stylish wines from top vineyards in the Walla Walla and Columbia valleys. Clubb's top wines are both Cabernet Sauvignon-based blends from Walla

ALLEN SHOUP

Allen Shoup is the partnership champion of Washington. During the 20 years that he was CEO of Chateau Ste Michelle, Shoup brought in Ernst Loosen and Piero Antinori for joint projects with the company that have continued to thrive. But his vision of world-class winemakers coming to Washington to make wine has continued since his departure from the state's largest producer. At his Long Shadows Vintners, based in Walla Walla, Shoup has brought in such international players as Ambrogio and Giovanni Folonari from Tuscany, Michel Rolland from Bordeaux, Armin Diel from Germany, and John Duval from Australia, as well as recruiting US superstars Randy Dunn, Philippe Melka, and Agustin Huneeus. Each winemaker has their own wine, with their own proprietary name—Long Shadows is the name of the project that represents them all. By championing these winemakers, Shoup has kept the spotlight on the quality of Washington. After all, why else would these big names come to Eastern Washington?

L'ECOLE NO. 41
MARTY CLUBB'S COLUMBIA VALLEY
SEMILLON IS AN ACCESSIBLY PRICED HIT

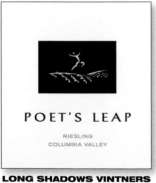

LONG SHADOWS VINTNERS
POET'S LEAP IS MADE BY RENOWNED
GERMAN WINEMAKER ARMIN DIEL

Walla vineyards: The Apogee is full of Christmas spices, tobacco, and black fruit, while The Perigee shows more red fruit and mocha. Clubb also makes a trio of Semillons, of which the Columbia Valley bottling, though the cheapest of the three, is the standout with its pure, crisp, bright, citrus-tinged fruit.

41 Lowden School Rd., Lowden, WA 99360
www.lecole.com

Leonetti Cellar

The wines of cult winery Leonetti Cellar are so highly prized its mailing list is closed. Still, those wines—a Cabernet Sauvignon, a Merlot, and a Sangiovese, plus a Reserve blend—justify the demand. Made from impeccable fruit and using an array of international oak barrels, they are tight and taut at the time of release, and need time to show their best. That is certainly the case with the dense Reserve blend, which is packed with black fruit, smoke, and cedar. Founder Gary Figgins produced his first wines in 1978, making him and his childhood friend Rick Small (of Woodward Canyon) the first to put Walla Walla on the map. Figgins' son, Chris, now runs the operation.

No visitor facilities
www.leonetticellar.com

Long Shadows Vintners

Founded by Washington wine pioneer Allen Shoup (former CEO of Chateau Ste Michelle), Long Shadows Vintners is a collection of ultra-premium wineries operated by acclaimed winemakers from some of the world's major wine regions. Each winemaker is a partner, producing a single Columbia Valley wine that represents the best of its kind, and reflects their signature style. The wines are all world class: expressive and profound, with great depth and clarity.

1604 Frenchtown Rd., Walla Walla, WA 99362
www.longshadows.com

Maryhill Winery

When Craig and Vicki Leuthold established Maryhill Winery in 1999, they chose a plot of land adjacent to where the legendary pioneer Sam Hill had tried to establish an independent farming community some 100 years earlier. The Leutholds' dream involved contracting growers in the lower Columbia Gorge, Yakima Valley, Horse Heaven Hills, and Wahluke Slope, and today they produce 27 wines, using 18 grape varieties. Among the best are the Barbera Reserve (full of spice and depth) and their lovely Zinfandel. The winery attracts a number of visitors for its onsite concerts.

9774 Hwy 14, Goldendale, WA 98620
www.maryhillwinery.com

McCrea Cellars

McCrea Cellars, founded in 1988 by Doug McCrea, was Washington State's first winery entirely dedicated to Syrah and other Rhône varieties. The wines show true varietal character and elegance. As well as the Rhône varieties, McCrea makes an unusual and tasty Picpoul, full of lemony deliciousness and bright acidity.

11515 Eagleview Lane, Rainier, WA 98576
www.mccreacellars.com

Northstar Winery

Owned by Chateau Ste Michelle, Northstar is principally dedicated to Merlot. It makes two *cuvées* based on the variety, one using fruit from the Columbia Valley and one from the Walla Walla Valley, plus a second wine, Stella Maris, that uses declassified fruit from both. The Columbia Valley blend shows deep flavors of cherry and plum; the Walla Walla *cuvée* has more chocolate notes. Northstar also has an impressive new white wine, Stella Blanc, a blend of Semillon with a little Muscadelle that expresses lovely lemony flavor with hints of apple, a slight tropical note, and a bright, crisp finish.

1736 JB George Rd., Walla Walla, WA 99362
www.northstarwinery.com

Pacific Rim Riesling

Celebrated California winemaker Randall Grahm's Riesling project, Pacific Rim, used to be part of Grahm's Bonny Doon empire, but is now an independent winery, with offices in Portland and a winery in the Columbia Valley near the Tri-Cities. It remains obsessed with Riesling, however, and the winery even produces a useful pamphlet on the subject called *Riesling Rules* (available from its website). Among the many Rieslings produced by Pacific Rim are four single-vineyard wines (including the Biodynamic Wallula Vineyard), plus dry, organic, sweet, and dessert wines. All of them are delicious: textbook pure and very expressive. A Chenin Blanc and a Gewurtztraminer are also produced.

8111 Keene Rd., West Richland, WA 99353
rieslingrules.com

Pepper Bridge Winery

The family-owned Pepper Bridge estate produces high-quality Cabernet Sauvignon and Merlot from its Walla Walla Valley vineyards, where there is a commitment to sustainable viticulture. Ray Goff and Norm McKibben are partners and a Swiss ex-pat, Jean-Francois Pellet, is winemaker. McKibben used to be Mr. Washington as chairman of the Washington Wine Commission. He is now Mr. Walla Walla, and is full of knowledge about wine production in the region. The wines show beautifully: the Cabernet Sauvignon offers smooth, dark fruit and spice, and great balance. The Merlot is velvety and full of plush chocolate and red fruit.

1704 JB George Rd., Walla Walla, WA 99362
www.pepperbridge.com

Quilceda Creek Vintners

Quilceda Creek's Alex Golitzan began making wine in his garage, guided by his uncle, the great California winemaker André Tchelistcheff. Golitzen set up Quilceda Creek winery in 1978 and it is now arguably the most important, highest-rated Cabernet Sauvignon producer in Washington. With winemaking now in the hands of Golitzan's son, Paul, the wines, which can be consumed young or after 25–30 years of bottle age, have purity, rich texture, and balance, with the Cabernet Sauvignon showing a floral note and a palate of violets, cassis, plum, and chocolate. This kind of quality comes at a price, however: other than the relatively accessible red blend, the wines are among the most expensive in the state.

No visitor facilities
www.QuilcedaCreek.com

Reininger Winery

In 1997, Chuck and Tracy Reininger realized their dream and started making wine from bought-in grapes in the Walla Walla Valley. In 2000, their project went up a gear when they planted Ash Hollow Vineyard with Merlot, Cabernet Sauvignon, Malbec, and Syrah. By 2003, they had bought another patch of land and converted a series of potato sheds into a new winery. That same year, Tracy's brothers joined the winery with their wives. The Reininger wines remain small-scale, with the focus very much on Walla Walla Valley fruit. The second label, Helix, from the Columbia Valley, has a larger production.

5858 W. Highway 12, Walla Walla, WA 99362
www.reiningerwinery.com

Seia Wine Cellars

Seia Wine Cellars, Rob and Kim Spalding's small Seattle-area operation, crafts high-quality Syrah wines from top vineyards across Washington. The Clifton Hill Syrah is a beauty, full of plush blackberry jam and chocolate notes. The Alder Creek Syrah is very different, with bigger tannins and more restraint. This relatively new property is one to watch as it grows. ★ **Rising star**

No visitor facilities
www.seiawines.com

Seven Hills Winery

After it was founded by Casey and Vicky McClellan in 1988, Seven Hills Winery spent 10 years on the Oregon side of the Walla Walla Valley before moving to downtown Walla Walla. Casey is a fourth-generation Walla Walla farmer who helped his father plant the famed Seven Hills Vineyard, and with Vicky he has made at least two other pioneering moves: bottling Walla Walla's first varietally labeled Malbec and planting its first Tempranillo. The couple also source from Red Mountain for wines such as the Ciel du Cheval Red blend, which has deep red fruit, fresh acidity, and polished tannins.

212 North 3rd Ave., Walla Walla, WA 99362
www.sevenhillswinery.com

Spring Valley Vineyard

Founded by the Derby family, but owned since 2005 by Chateau Ste Michelle, the Spring Valley Vineyard owns 115 acres (47ha) of Merlot, Cabernet Franc, Syrah, Cabernet Sauvignon, Petit Verdot, and Malbec in the Walla Walla Valley. The wines—such as Uriah, Frederick, Nina Lee, Derby, and Muleskinner—take their names from Derby family history, and rate highly for smooth richness, bold fruit flavors, and plush, soft tannins.

1663 Corkrum Rd., Walla Walla, WA 99362
www.springvalleyvineyard.com

Stephenson Cellars

Dave Stephenson opened his 1,200-case winery in Walla Walla in 2001. He produces small quantities of Cabernet Sauvignon, Merlot, Syrah, and Viognier. His Syrahs are lovely wines, all polished red fruits and blueberries, a bit smoky, with long, silky finishes. Stephenson started out as a consultant to wineries, but now focuses mostly on his own production.

15 South Spokane St., Walla Walla, WA 99362
www.stephensoncellars.com

QUILCEDA CREEK
THE CABERNET SAUVIGNON IS QUITE SIMPLY ONE OF THE GREATEST RED WINES IN THE US

SEVEN HILLS WINERY
THE PIONEERING MCLELLANS MAKE BEAUTIFULLY BALANCED WINES

Syncline Cellars

Poppy and James Mantone of Syncline Cellars have a passion for Rhône-style wines. They started their winery in 1999 and immediately started working with vineyards planted with classic varieties from the French region such as Viognier, Grenache, Mourvèdre, Roussanne, Cinsault, Counoise, and Syrah. Their passion is evident in wines such as the 2007 Cuvée Elena, a blend of 70% Grenache, 17% Mourvèdre, with the balance Carignan, Cinsault, and Syrah. This is a great wine, with terrific aromatics of spice, *garrigue*, and red fruit leading to a palate of wonderfully concentrated fruit in a decidedly elegant package.

111 Balch Rd., Lyle, WA 98635
www.synclinewine.com

Terra Blanca

Terra Blanca Winery and Estate Vineyards sits on 300 acres (120ha) of Red Mountain land. The project is the work of owner/winemaker Keith Pilgrim, who is noted for his well-made Cabernet Sauvignon, Syrah, Merlot, and a signature Bordeaux-style blend known as Onyx. The last offers flavors of black fruit and chocolate, with a smooth, stylish texture. Pilgrim also makes a blend based on the Piemontese grape, Nebbiolo. The wine, Pantheon, is lovely, although it must be said its style makes it barely recognizable as Nebbiolo.

34715 N. DeMoss Rd., Benton City, WA 99320
www.terrablanca.com

Waters Winery

Waters Winery's winemaker Jamie Brown is responsible for some very striking Syrahs. He has three single-vineyard wines based on the grape, plus another version sourced from vineyards across the Columbia Valley. Pick of the bunch is the Loess Vineyard Syrah *cuvée*, which is an absolute beauty, full of black cherries, blueberries, anise, and meatiness, plus a bit of spice and gaminess to give it the real Syrah edge. The wine is co-fermented with 3% Viognier, and Brown only makes 190 cases of it each year. Alongside all the Syrah, Brown also makes a Cabernet Sauvignon, a Viognier, and the Merlot-dominated Interlude blend.

1825 JB George Rd., Walla Walla, WA 99362
www.waterswinery.com

Woodward Canyon Winery

One of the earliest of the pioneers in Walla Walla, Rick Small started the now widely respected Woodward Canyon Winery with his wife Darcey Fugman-Small in 1981. Along with their 41 acre (17ha) estate vineyard in the Walla Walla Valley, the Smalls source fruit from a handful of well-established growers, and they also part-own Champoux Vineyard. Woodward Canyon makes a wide range of reds and whites, but the best wine remains their estate wine. Produced on the family's former wheat farm, on which Small focuses like a father dotes on his child, the result is amazing: a seamless blend of four varieties (generally headed by Merlot) sporting black fruit and dark chocolate that develop in the glass, the firm texture and understated character (this is not a fruit bomb) leading to a long and layered finish.

11920 W. Highway 12, Lowden, WA 99360
www.woodwardcanyon.com

OREGON

State of Oregon
Wine regions of Oregon
— Area shown at larger scale on p.103

Oregon is a young wine region, but definable subregions have already emerged. The state now has 16 American Viticultural Areas (AVAs), and they owe their existence as much to tangible geological differences as they do to marketing requirements. Major geological events—such as shifting plates, erupting (basaltic) volcanoes, and flooding from breaking Ice Age dams—gave Oregon's soil the characteristics that have in turn defined the flavor profile of its wines. The Willamette Valley is Oregon's broadest AVA, with six sub-appellations dividing the valley's core into smaller sections. Southern Oregon is one large AVA divided into four smaller areas. But it is the northern Willamette Valley that claims most attention, and primarily for its Pinot Noir.

Major grapes

🍇 Reds
Cabernet Sauvignon
Pinot Noir
Syrah

🍇 Whites
Chardonnay
Gewurtztraminer
Pinot Blanc
Pinot Gris
Riesling

Vintages

2009
An early but potentially high-quality vintage.

2008
A brilliant year that will rank among the top vintages. Great expression and balance with a promise of good longevity.

2007
A cooler, wet vintage that is great for whites and very good for reserve reds. The wines are elegant rather than rich.

2006
A year for big rich wines that can be a bit high in alcohol.

2005
A cooler fall helped produce very fine wines with great definition.

2004
Wild temperature shifts and changes created varietal wines of good quality.

The largest of the northern Willamette Valley's AVAs is Chehalem Mountains. It encompasses more than 30 wineries and 100 vineyards, and has both volcanic and two types of sedimentary soils. These result in a diverse range of flavors, from elegant red fruits to deep, firmly structured black fruits to briary elements. Notable producers here are Ponzi, Adelsheim, and Chehalem.

The much smaller Ribbon Ridge AVA forms a pocket between the Chehalem Mountains and Yamhill-Carlton District AVAs and contains just 20 vineyards and five wineries. The soils are quick-draining, and few producers feel the need to irrigate. The wines show black fruit and wood spices (clove, nutmeg, cinnamon). Some of the top names in the state are based here, including Brick House, Beaux Frères, and Patricia Green.

Yamhill-Carlton District boasts 30 wineries and 60 vineyards. The terroir is mostly comprised of sedimentary soils, on lower slopes. Wines tend to show cocoa, fresh earth, and slightly lower acidity.

The famous Dundee Hills AVA is home to 25 wineries, including the renowned Domaine Drouhin Oregon and The Eyrie Vineyard, as well as the bustling town of Dundee. Considered to be the epicenter of Oregon wine country, the hills are also known as the Red Hills of Dundee because of their red volcanic Jory soils. The wines typically show bright red fruit and a rich body.

The up-and-coming McMinnville AVA lies west and southwest of the town of the same name, and

is home to just 14 wineries and 750 acres (300ha) of vineyard. Recent arrivals such as Maysara have proved there might be good promise in the warmer, drier, and higher-elevation sites of this relatively far-flung area. One sees black fruited and earthy wines with strong tannins and a pronounced acid backbone. They tend to be highly pigmented and tannic from the drier conditions.

The Eola-Amity Hills AVA forms a series of slopes to the west-northwest of Salem and enjoys lower temperatures because of a break in the Coast Range that allows cool maritime breezes to blow through. Wine from here shows a concentrated black-fruited character with high acidity. The 30 wineries in this region include top performers such as Bethel Heights, Cristom, and Evesham Wood.

There is more to Oregon than the Willamette Valley, however. Southern Oregon is an AVA that refers to the large area south of the Willamette Valley, and is very much positioned in opposition to the north. It encompasses the Umpqua Valley and Rogue Valley AVAs. Within the Rogue Valley is the Applegate Valley, a region to keep one's eye on, as it is growing in size and quality.

In the north of the state, along the Columbia River, two AVAs are shared with Washington State: the Columbia Gorge, a higher-elevation and warmer region, and the better-known Walla Walla Valley.

WILLAMETTE VALLEY

With around 12,000 acres (4,900ha) of vineyards, the Willamette Valley is Oregon's largest AVA. It is 150 miles (240km) long, and 60 miles (100km) wide, and spread into six further AVAs. Vineyards are largely found to the west of the Willamette River, on the foothills of the Coast Range of mountains, and at altitudes of up to 1,100ft (340m). Around 30 miles (50km) south of Portland, the Dundee Hills AVA is famed for its striking, red, volcanic Jory soils.

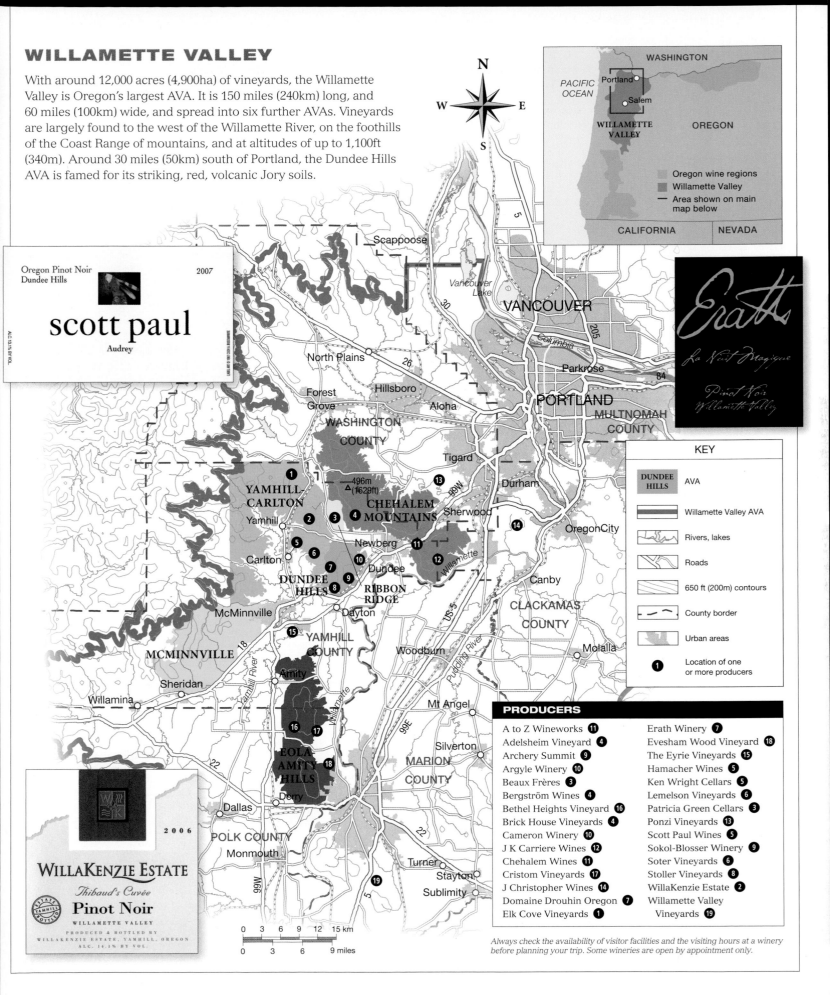

Oregon Pinot Noir
Dundee Hills   2007

scott paul

Audrey

ALC 13.1% BY VOL

2006

WILLAKENZIE ESTATE

Thibaud's Cuvée

Pinot Noir

WILLAMETTE VALLEY

PRODUCED & BOTTLED BY
WILLAKENZIE ESTATE, YAMHILL, OREGON
ALC. 14.1% BY VOL.

KEY

DUNDEE HILLS	AVA
	Willamette Valley AVA
	Rivers, lakes
	Roads
	650 ft (200m) contours
	County border
	Urban areas
1	Location of one or more producers

PRODUCERS

A to Z Wineworks	**11**	Erath Winery	**7**
Adelsheim Vineyard	**4**	Evesham Wood Vineyard	**18**
Archery Summit	**9**	The Eyrie Vineyards	**15**
Argyle Winery	**10**	Hamacher Wines	**5**
Beaux Frères	**3**	Ken Wright Cellars	**5**
Bergström Wines	**4**	Lemelson Vineyards	**6**
Bethel Heights Vineyard	**16**	Patricia Green Cellars	**3**
Brick House Vineyards	**4**	Ponzi Vineyards	**13**
Cameron Winery	**10**	Scott Paul Wines	**5**
J K Carriere Wines	**12**	Sokol-Blosser Winery	**9**
Chehalem Wines	**11**	Soter Vineyards	**6**
Cristom Vineyards	**17**	Stoller Vineyards	**8**
J Christopher Wines	**14**	WillaKenzie Estate	**2**
Domaine Drouhin Oregon	**7**	Willamette Valley Vineyards	**19**
Elk Cove Vineyards	**1**		

Always check the availability of visitor facilities and the visiting hours at a winery before planning your trip. Some wineries are open by appointment only.

A TO Z WINEWORKS
A TO Z LOOKS FOR PURITY AND INTENSITY
IN ITS CLASSIC OREGON PINOT GRIS

ABACELA
THE TEMPRANILLO CUVEE SHOWS ABACELA'S
MASTERY OF THIS SPANISH GRAPE VARIETY

A to Z Wineworks

A to Z Wineworks is a joint venture between winemakers Sam Tannahill (ex-Archery Summit) and his wife Cheryl Francis (ex-Chehalem) with Deb and Bill Hatcher (ex-managing director of Domaine Drouhin Oregon). Having started out as a négociant in 1998, A to Z Wineworks became Oregon's largest winery with the purchase of Rex Hill Vineyards in 2007, and it now sources fruit from vineyards across Oregon. The prices have stayed low, but the quality is always very high. Each of the principals also makes their own wines: Francis Tannahill's Gewurztraminer, white blend, Syrah, and Pinot Noir, and William Hatcher's Pinot Noirs are high-priced beauties made in miniscule quantities.

Dundee, OR 97115
www.atozwineworks.com

Abacela

Earl and Hilda Jones' Abacela in the southern Umpqua Valley is one of the most interesting vineyards in Oregon. Tempranillo is the Jones' signature variety. They planted it in southern Oregon in 1992 after a US-wide search for vineyard land suited to the grape, assisted by their son, Greg Jones (who has since become a leading authority on climate change and its effects on wine). The Tempranillo is certainly the standout, although the Syrah and Malbec also reflect the property's terroir, and prove just how high the quality of wine can be south of the Willamette Valley.

12500 Lookingglass Rd., Roseburg, OR 97471
www.abacela.com

Adelsheim Vineyard

David Adelsheim is the unofficial dean of the Oregon wine industry, helping to craft most of Oregon's major wine laws, and weighing in on all the issues in the state. Adelsheim's original 15 acres (6ha), planted near his house at Quarter Mile Lane in 1992, has grown to 190 acres (77ha), producing 40,000 cases a year. Dave Paige, the winemaker since 2001, produces quality, balanced wines that compete with any in the state. Pinot Noir is the signature, made in a number of different *cuvées*, but there are experiments with Auxerrois, as well as Pinot Blanc, Chardonnay, Pinot Gris, and even a Willamette Valley Syrah. ★ **Rising star**

16800 NE Calkins Lane, Newberg, OR 97132
www.adelsheim.com

Archery Summit

Until its impressive gravity-fed winery was constructed in 1995, Archery Summit's grapes were trucked to the Pine Ridge Winery in the Napa Valley (both wineries were then operated by the late Gary Andrus). They are still siblings, with the same insurance company owner. Huge, concentrated Pinot Noirs are the focus. These are wines that many consider to be Oregon's finest, and perhaps they would be if the oak were a little less prominent. They are certainly expensive, with release prices up to $100 per bottle and more. The vineyards—the Estate, Arcus (the former Archibald Vineyard), and the Red Hills Vineyard (former Fuqua Vineyard)—produce some of the most focused, well-structured fruit in the state.

18599 NE Archery Summit Rd., Dayton, OR 97114
www.archerysummit.com

Argyle Winery

Argyle is Oregon's—and for many, the United States'—top sparkling wine producer, owned by Petaluma Wines of Australia. Winemaker Rollin Soles also crafts very elegant still Pinot Noir and Chardonnay, as well as one of the best dry Rieslings in Oregon (in tiny quantities). Most of the fruit comes from the Dundee Hills, supported by a newer vineyard in the Eola Hills. A good stop on a wine country visit, the winery sits across the street from the area's top dining on Highway 99 in downtown Dundee.

691 Hwy 99W., Dundee, OR 97115
www.argylewinery.com

Beaux Frères

Michael Etzel deserves great credit for spotting the potential in this former pig farm in the northern Willamette Valley. Coming across it while on vacation in 1986, he purchased the property with his brother-in-law (or *beau frère*), the renowned wine critic Robert Parker, and over the next few years, transformed it into a vineyard, its 88 acres (36ha) planted exclusively to Pinot Noir. A third partner, Robert Roy, came on board in 1991, and Beaux Frères winery was created by renovating and developing one of the barns. Over the years, the style has evolved from big and powerful to refined and elegant. Since 2006, the vineyard has been farmed according to Biodynamic principles.

15155 NE North Valley Rd., Newberg, OR 97132
www.beauxfreres.com

Bergström Wines

John and Karen Bergström moved to Dundee from Portland and planted the Bergström Vineyard, a 15 acre (6ha) southeast-facing gentle slope overlooking the Willamette Valley, as a legacy for their children. Son Josh, a Burgundy-trained winemaker, and his four siblings, are all involved with the winery and its three Biodynamic vineyards, which cover 40 acres (16ha) and two appellations in Oregon's Northern Willamette Valley. The winery produces 10,000 cases of ultra-premium Pinot Noir, Chardonnay, and Riesling. In a play on the Dr. Loosen range of German wines, one of the Rieslings is called Dr. B after winery founder Dr. John Bergström.

18215 NE Calkins Lane, Newberg, OR 97132
www.bergstromwines.com

Bethel Heights Vineyard

Brothers Ted and Terry Casteel and their wives Pat Dudley and Marilyn Webb operate the well-regarded Bethel Heights. Most of the couples' children have a role at the winery, too, and Terry's son, Ben, has been making the wines since 2005. Estate wines include the elegant, well-structured Flat Block and South East Block *cuvées*. In 1996, Bethel Heights began purchasing Pinot Noir from vineyards in other AVAs including Freedom Hill Vineyard and Nysa Vineyard. All of the wines consistently show balance, understatement, and complexity.

6060 NW Bethel Heights Rd., Salem, OR 97304
www.bethelheights.com

Brandborg Vineyard

Terry and Sue Brandborg craft lively and elegant wine from their base near Elkton in the Umpqua Valley. Elkton is very different from the rest of the Umpqua, much cooler and wetter with higher elevations in the Coastal Mountains; the vineyards here range from 750–1,200ft (229 to 366 meters) in elevation. When the Brandborgs arrived in the area in 2000 looking for great Pinot Noir sites, they learned that Pinot Noir had been grown there since 1972. Their Pinot Noirs are fresh and improve in quality each year. The Riesling is a beauty, with crisp acidity and a true varietal flavor. This is a brand to watch.

345 First Street, Elkton, OR 97436
www.brandborgwine.com

Brick House Vineyards

Former CBS foreign correspondent Doug Tunnell returned to his native Oregon to plant grapes in 1990. He has since become one of the best producers in Oregon, known for small quantities of earthy, well-structured, polished wines produced from Biodynamic vineyards. Highlights include Tunnell's Gamay, which is treated like Pinot Noir and resembles fine *cru* Beaujolais. Brick House is only open to the public on Thanksgiving and Memorial Day, but on those days, it is worth a visit.

18200 Lewis Rogers Lane, Newberg, OR 97132
www.brickhousewines.com

Cameron Winery

Cameron Winery is all about fine, balanced wines crafted by the quirky Jon Paul, a talented winemaker with experience in Burgundy, California, and New Zealand. Paul only makes a few *cuvées* of Pinot Noir, a Chardonnay, a Pinot Blanc, and The Giuliano blend (named after his son, Julian), but his wines are a hit with the restaurant trade. His newest project is an estate-grown Nebbiolo, which he debuted just before the VinItaly trade fair at a restaurant in Alba, Piemonte. A total of about 4,000 cases is produced.

8200 Northeast Worden Hill Rd., Dundee, OR 97115
www.cameronwines.com

J. K. Carriere Wines

Jim Prosser crafts mostly Pinot Noir and a small quantity of both Chardonnay and a pale rosé called Glass (also from Pinot Noir). Prosser's Pinot Noirs show strong berry character and bright acidity, and always reflect the vineyard where the grapes were grown. Therefore, the Shea bottling from the Yamhill-Carlton area shows more tobacco and floral notes, while the Gemini from the Chehalem mountains shows stronger acidity and more red fruit. All the wines are very elegant and ageworthy.

9995 NE Parrett Mountain Rd., Newberg, OR 97132
www.jkcarriere.com

Chehalem Wines

Harry Peterson-Nedry planted his first Pinot Noir vineyard in Ribbon Ridge in 1980 as a hobby. By 1990, he had founded Chehalem, and winemaking had become a full-time job. Peterson-Nedry makes stellar white wines including two Rieslings, two *cuvées* of Pinot Gris, oaked and unoaked Chardonnay, a Pinot Blanc, and a lovely Grüner Veltliner. He also makes a number of *cuvées* of very ripe-styled, fine Pinot Noir, with his Ridgecrest the top-tier example. Peterson-Nedry's daughter, Wynn, has recently joined her father in the winery.

31190 NE Veritas Lane, Newberg, OR 97132
www.chehalemwines.com

ADELSHEIM VINEYARD
THE COMPLEX ELIZABETH'S RESERVE USES PINOT NOIR FROM EIGHT VINEYARDS

ELK COVE VINEYARDS
THE WILLAMETTE VALLEY PINOT NOIR BALANCES POWER WITH ELEGANCE

J. Christopher Wines

A quirky but solid producer of Pinot Noir from the Dundee Hills, J. Christopher also produces whites (Sauvignon Blanc, Chardonnay, Riesling), a solid rosé made from Grenache, Syrah, and Viognier, and a very good and meaty Syrah from the Columbia Gorge. Winemaker Jay Somers has an understated and elegant style, and his 2007 Pinot Noir—not a particularly strong red vintage in the Willamette Valley—may well have been the wine of the year: very silky and elegant with bright berry fruit.

2636 S.W. Schaeffer Rd., West Linn, OR
www.jchristopherwines.com

Cristom Vineyards

Cristom Vineyards' founder and owner, Paul Gerrie (an engineer by training) and winemaker Steve Doerner (formerly at California's Calera) are both committed to vineyard-driven wines. They farm seven distinct vineyards on 65 acres (26ha) in the Eola-Amity Hills, as well as purchasing fruit from respected vineyards across the valley. The wines have a unique style. Doerner believes in pressing whole clusters of grapes and typically employs about 50% of his vines' capacity in each vintage. This results in highly structured, focused, and elegant wines, from the simple Mt. Jefferson blend, through a host of single-vineyard wines up to the Sommers Reserve Pinot Noir. Alongside Pinot Gris, Chardonnay, and Pinot Noir, Cristom has also championed cool-climate, estate-grown Viognier and Syrah.

6905 Spring Valley Rd. NW, Salem, OR 97304
www.cristomwines.com

Domaine Drouhin Oregon

Burgundian négociant Robert Drouhin was drawn to Oregon when a Pinot Noir from the state (Eyrie Vineyard Pinot Noir) out-performed some of Burgundy's best at a tasting in France in 1979. Drouhin went on to plant a vineyard and build a winery right next door to Eyrie in the Dundee Hills. The entire Drouhin family comes to Oregon for harvest, but it is Robert's daughter, Veronique Drouhin-Boss, who serves as official winemaker for the Oregon operation, visiting the winery three or four times each year. Drouhin-Boss crafts the wines in the same fashion as in Burgundy, with judicious use of oak and a very gentle expression. There is an obvious style that links the French and Oregon wines; finesse and refined elegance rule.

6750 Breyman Orchards Rd., Dayton, OR 97114
www.domainedrouhin.com

Elk Cove Vineyards

Adam Godlee Campbell has succeeded his parents, who founded Elk Cove in 1977, at this Gaston estate. The focus is on ripe, expressive Pinot Noir and well-made, intense Pinot Gris, but that is by no means all that Elk Cove offers. The Pinot Noir rosé, Riesling, Pinot Blanc, white blend, Oregon Syrah, and a very pretty sparkling wine are also worth a look. The vineyards now cover more than 180 acres (73ha) on four sites in the Northern Willamette Valley. The Pinot Noir from the La Bohème Vineyard is Elk Cove's most elegant wine.

27751 NW Olson Rd., Gaston, OR 97119
www.elkcove.com

EVESHAM WOOD VINEYARD
THE BLANC DU PUITS SEC IS DELICIOUSLY
FLORAL AND GREAT VALUE

Erath Winery

Dick Erath was one of the early pioneers in the Willamette Valley in 1972—a winemaking graduate from the University of California at Davis looking to prove the world wrong about producing Pinot Noir so far north. Erath sold up to Chateau Ste Michelle in 2006, bringing Washington's largest producer south into Oregon for the first time. Winemaker Gary Horner crafts delicate, fruit-forward wines at all prices, from the basic supermarket wines for which Erath is best known, to the expressive Dundee Hills single-vineyard wines, Leland and Niederberger, and the top *cuvée*, La Nuit Magique.

9409 NE Worden Hill Rd., Dundee, OR 97115
www.erath.com

Evesham Wood Vineyard

Mary and Russ Raney have developed a cult following for their Evesham Wood wines since they started out in 1986. Located on a lower terrace of the Eola-Amity Hills' eastern slope, their 13 acre (5ha) estate vineyard, Le Puits Sec, was planted in 1986. The soils are primarily basalt-derived volcanic and are very well-drained, yielding aromatic Pinot Noir with great structure and finesse, as well as excellent Chardonnay and Alsace varieties. The winery's Cuvée "J"—an homage to Burgundy's Henri Jayer—is a lovely wine showing finesse and elegance against a perfumed bouquet.

3795 NW Wallace Rd., Salem, OR 97304
www.eveshamwood.com

The Eyrie Vineyards

The late David Lett of Eyrie Vineyards was Oregon's Pinot Noir founding father. Known as Papa Pinot, he first planted cuttings in 1965 in Corvalis while researching a permanent vineyard site. In 1966, he replanted them in the north end of the Willamette Valley, in the Dundee Hills, convinced Burgundian varieties would fare better in Oregon than California. Lett also believed Pinot Gris, Pinot Meunier, Muscat Ottonel, true Pinot Blanc, and Chardonnay would do well in western Oregon. And these are the varieties that The Eyrie Vineyards makes today. Lett's wines were elegant and delicate, pale in color, and totally ageworthy. Fortunately for us, son Jason is carrying on the tradition.

935 NE 10th Ave., McMinnville, OR 97128
www.eyrievineyards.com

Hamacher Wines

Experienced winemaker Eric Hamacher arrived in Oregon, or as he calls it, "Pinot's Promised Land," in the 1990s in pursuit of the perfect Pinot Noir. He now has eight vineyards across the Willamette Valley, at elevations ranging from 250ft (76m) to 825ft (250m), with numerous clones and soil types. But he prefers blends to single-vineyard wines, and the balanced, elegant Hamacher Chardonnay and Pinot Noir suggest he is on to something. The "H" series offers a great-value alternative.

801 N. Scott St., Carlton, OR 97111
www.hamacherwines.com

Ken Wright Cellars

Ken Wright is very much a cult winery, generally selling out its wines before they are even bottled—it was only during the recent economic downturn that the wines made their way into retail for the first time. The eponymous owner is passionate about Pinot Noir and its ability to reflect the Oregonian terroir. He also produces two whites—a Chardonnay from Celilo Vineyard near White Salmon, Washington, and a Pinot Blanc from Freedom Hill Vineyard—and the Tyrus Evan brand, named after his sons, and focusing on warm-climate varieties including Syrah, Cabernet Franc, Malbec, and blends from Oregon and Washington vineyards.

120 N. Pine St., The Depot, Carlton, OR 97111
www.kenwrightcellars.com

King Estate

King Estate is located on 1,000 acres (400ha) of beautiful (and certified organic) land in the southern end of the Willamette Valley near Eugene. It is best known for its basic Pinot Gris, a consistent wine that is blended from grapes grown in vineyards across the state. But it is the Domaine wines—based on estate-grown grapes—that really sing. The Estate Pinot Noir, for example, which is full of red berries and spice and with a very long finish, is particularly lovely. Other options include a series from well-known vineyards such as Croft and Freedom Hill, and the good-value Acrobat range. With its restaurant and visitor center, and its own range of jams, King Estate is a tasty, educational destination.

80854 Territorial Rd., Eugene, OR 97405
www.kingestate.com

Lemelson Vineyards

Eric Lemelson, son of a wealthy inventor, used part of his inheritance to purchase land and set up a winery near Carlton. He bought the land in 1997, and with the help of Eric Hamacher (his first winemaker, now in charge of his own eponymous winery) had a new gravity-fed winery up and running for the stellar 1999 vintage. Anthony King is winemaker now, and he crafts expressive Pinot Noir, Pinot Gris, and Chardonnay from organically certified grapes. The Pinot Noirs show elegant character and great length.

12020 NE Stag Hollow Rd., Carlton, OR 97111
www.lemelsonvineyards.com

Patricia Green Cellars

Patty Green produces a tremendously broad selection of Pinot Noirs from a range of dry-farmed vineyards in some of the better sites in Ribbon Ridge, Dundee Hills, Chehalem Mountains, and the Eola Hills. The wines, like Green herself, are big on personality, and, as well as the Pinot Noirs, include a Chardonnay and a Sauvignon Blanc. They are well-priced, too, and recently Green added a Dollar Bill Sauvignon Blanc, albeit selling at ten times that amount.

15225 NE North Valley Rd., Newberg, OR 97132
www.patriciagreencellars.com

Ponzi Vineyards

Founded in 1970 and one of Oregon's wine pioneers, Ponzi Vineyards is the work of the entrepreneurial, eponymous family who also began Oregon's first microbrewery (since sold) and who run a wine bar and bistro in Dundee. Now in the hands of the second generation of the family, Ponzi owns 120 acres (50ha) of sustainably farmed vineyard in Chehalem Mountains,

LEMELSON VINEYARDS
LEMELSON STRIVES TO MAKE UNIQUE
ORGANIC PINOT NOIR

and winemaker Luisa Ponzi produces alluring Pinot Noir, Pinot Gris, Pinot Blanc, Chardonnay, and Riesling, as well as a Dolcetto and a fabulous, bright Arneis.

14665 S.W. Winery Lane, Beaverton, OR 97007
www.ponziwines.com

Scott Paul Wines
Scott Wright left his job as general manager for Domaine Drouhin Oregon in 2004 to focus on his own wines at Scott Paul full time. Based in downtown Carlton, Wright produces only Pinot Noir and owns no vineyards. Instead he buys fruit from respected low-yielding sources such as Shea, Maresh, Stoller, and Ribbon Ridge vineyards, to make wines that display great finesse and grace. Wright also imports fine burgundies, and visitors to his tasting room will find them served alongside his wines, with the latter far from outclassed.

128 South Pine St., Carlton, OR 97111
www.scottpaul.com

Sokol-Blosser Winery
Bill Blosser and Susan Sokol Blosser planted their first vines in 1971 in the Dundee Hills, and the estate now boasts 87 acres (35ha) of organically farmed grapes. The couple also buy in fruit for their two most popular *cuvées*, both non-vintage blends: Evolution, a blend of 10 white varieties that is perfect with spicy Asian foods; and Meditrina, a juicy, soft, but vibrant blend of Syrah and Pinot Noir. Also impressive are a Pinot Gris and two *cuvées* of Pinot Noir, with the latter duo usually showing mocha, black cherry, and the distinctive Dundee Hills forest-floor earthiness.

5000 NE Sokol Blosser Lane, Dayton, OR 97114
www.sokolblosser.com

Soter Vineyards
Tony Soter earned fame as a high-flying consultant in Napa. Today, the consulting takes a back seat as Soter and his wife Michelle focus their energies on their twin Pinot Noir projects: Etude in California and Soter Vineyards in Oregon. The latter is a hands-on operation producing elegant, silky Pinot Noir, full of brambly black fruit, and bright, flinty sparkling wines. There is also a Cabernet Franc sourced from the California vineyard.

Carlton, OR 97111
www.sotervineyards.com

Stoller Vineyards
Stoller Vineyards' 373 acre (150ha) estate on the southern slopes of the Dundee Hills in Yamhill County, was a turkey farm until the 1980s. Now it is a thriving producer of mainly Pinot Noir, run by the husband-and-wife duo Bill and Cathy Stoller. Today wines are made by Melissa Burr, and her belief in whole-cluster fermentation has brought structure, backbone, and finesse to wines that were once merely soft.

16161 NE McDougall Rd., Dayton, OR 97114
www.stollervineyards.com

Troon Vineyard
Troon Vineyard's winemaker Herb Quady grew up with wine—his father is the celebrated California sweet and fortified wine specialist Andrew Quady—and he has clearly inherited a talent for small-scale winemaking. All the wines Quady makes at Troon are estate grown, and most of them are produced in quantities of less than 300 cases. The delicious Zinfandel and Vermentino show great promise for this reinvigorated winery—varietally correct, structured, and fruity.

1475 Kubli Rd., Grants Pass, OR 97527
www.troonvineyard.com

Valley View Winery
Originally established in the Rogue Valley by pioneer Peter Britt in the 1850s, Valley View's first incarnation ended with Britt's death in 1906. The name was revived in 1972 by the Wisnovsky family for their own vineyard and winery in the Applegate Valley, some 9 miles (14km) from the original site. Today, Valley View sources a wide variety of grapes from the Applegate and Bear Creek Valleys of the Rogue Valley. The Anna Maria wines, which are produced only in the best vintages, are the standouts, with the Tempranillo showing a core of dusty fruit with plum and black cherry flavors.

1000 Upper Applegate Rd., Jacksonville, OR 97530
www.valleyviewwinery.com

WillaKenzie Estate
One of a number of Frenchmen attracted to Oregon to make Pinot Noir, WillaKenzie Estate's Bernard Lacroute started planting the first of his 100 acres (40ha) of vines in Yamhill County in 1992. Since then, Lacroute has added a winery and another vineyard in the Dundee Hills, and today the focus is Pinots Noir, Blanc, and Gris, plus a little Gamay and Pinot Meunier. The winemaking is left to another Frenchman, Thibaud Mandet, and his Cuvée Pinot Noir is a medium-bodied wine, lifted with bright acidity, red fruit and spice notes—a wine that needs food to show off its best.

19143 NE Laughlin Rd., Yamhill, OR 97148
www.willakenzie.com

Willamette Valley Vineyards
Located beside the highway in Salem, Willamette Valley Vineyards is Oregon's only publicly traded wine estate. It is also one of the state's biggest, producing 120,000 cases each year, including brands such as Tualatin Estate and Griffin Creek. The company is looking to build a separate winery in Carlton to serve the Elton Vineyard it now leases in the Eola Hills—the Elton *cuvée* itself has great structure and purity of fruit.

8800 Enchanted Way, Turner, OR 97392
www.willamettevalleyvineyards.com

Wooldridge Creek Winery
Ted and Mary Warrick had been happy to sell the majority of the fruit grown at their Wooldridge Creek Vineyard to other producers, until they met winemaking couple Greg Paneitz and Kara Olmo in 2002. Since then, the two couples have pooled their skills (growing and winemaking) to produce 2,500 cases of quality wine each year. The Cabernet Sauvignon and Zinfandel wines are their best *cuvées*, showing good varietal character and gentle, understated expression.

818 Slagle Creek Rd., Grants Pass, OR 97527
www.wcwinery.com

DAVID LETT
David Lett began it all. He was the first to plant Pinot Noir (and Pinot Gris) in Oregon—and he certainly never let anyone forget it. Lett could be a curmudgeon, but he was a true believer in Oregon and its ability to produce world-class Pinot Noir. He had the courage to produce wines that did not show well in their youth. Like the great Burgundian Pinot Noirs they tried to emulate, Lett's Eyrie wines showed better six to eight years after the vintage—and they aged forever. Lett first put Oregon on the map when his wine came second in a blind tasting in Paris in 1979, which pitted a range of red Burgundies against a handful of New World rivals. Robert Drouhin, the distinguished Burgundian producer, could not believe it and staged a second competition. The Eyrie came second again. Drouhin was so impressed he later bought land and built a winery in Oregon a stone's throw from Lett's vines. Lett produced more Pinot Gris than Pinot Noir, but Pinot Noir was his passion and pride.

Sunlight streaks through a rainstorm passing through the Applegate Valley AVA in southern Oregon

NEW YORK AND NEW ENGLAND

United States of America
New York and New England
Finger Lakes wine region

The frigid winters of New England and New York can prove not merely challenging for classic European *Vitis vinifera* wine grapes—they can be downright deadly. It was the cold-hardy American *Vitis labrusca* vines that formed the basis of the early wine industry in New York, beginning in the 17th century, followed by hybrids of the two species. These vines still dominate the region, and while a lot of that production goes into juice and jam, New York is now the third-largest wine producer in the US. By taking advantage of the moderating effects of the Atlantic and deep lake waters, and by selecting suitable grape varieties and clones, producers are succeeding in producing fine wine on a scale once thought impossible.

Major grapes

🍇 Reds

Cabernet Franc

Cabernet Sauvignon

Merlot

Pinot Noir

🍇 Whites

Chardonnay

Gewurztraminer

Riesling

Sauvignon Blanc

Vintages

2009

Wet and very challenging for reds across the Northeast. Rieslings are still reliable.

2008

Very good for Riesling and Finger Lakes whites. Less consistent on Long Island.

2007

A landmark vintage. Warm, dry weather produced ripe and concentrated reds in the Finger Lakes and The North Fork.

2006

A cool and damp harvest favored the whites and made some reds dilute. A challenging vintage.

New York includes 259 wineries and four major wine-growing regions—Finger Lakes, Hudson River, Long Island, and Lake Erie—with several sub-appellations.

The Finger Lakes region is still widely planted with the labrusca and hybrid grapes that were originally farmed for sale to large wineries such as the Taylor Wine Company (founded in 1891) and Widmer. As Prohibition reared its head, many large wineries floundered or left the region. Not until the Farm Winery Act of 1976, which allowed small growers to become direct sellers of their wine, did the industry rebound. Today, the Finger Lakes boasts more than 100 wineries, many of which balance the tradition of sweet, hybrid wines with a determination to achieve the region's full potential with European varieties.

Gewurztraminer, Chardonnay, and, especially, Riesling achieve irrefutable success in the Finger Lakes. Best of all, prices are surprisingly affordable. A series of glacial lakes, such as Seneca Lake, which, reaches 600ft (180m) deep, are instrumental in moderating winter temperatures, yet red wines remain the Finger Lakes' Holy Grail. Harsh winters can result in severe mortality rates for Merlot, which joins Cabernet Franc and Pinot Noir among the leading reds. There exists a temptation for over-cropping in years when the opportunity presents itself. However, by limiting yields, and forgoing some vintages altogether, quality-oriented wineries such as Damiani and Shalestone are demonstrating the potential of Finger Lakes reds.

The Hudson River Region produces a modest 1,000 tons (900,000kg) of grapes to the Finger Lakes' 40,000 tons (3.6 million kg), but it shows a similar potential for quality. This historic region includes the oldest continuously operating winery in the US, Brotherhood Winery, founded by French Huguenot Jean Jacques in 1837. The Hudson River Valley acts as a conduit, drawing both maritime breezes and city dwellers inland. The most widely planted grape is the hybrid Seyval Blanc.

The latest land-grab in New York occurred on Long Island, where farming now competes with affluent weekenders for a piece of this desirable coastal retreat. New York's fastest-growing wine region, Long Island includes around 50 producers across two smaller American Viticultural Areas (AVAs), The North Fork and The Hamptons, separated by Great Peconic Bay. Louisa Thomas Hargrave established the first winery only in 1973, so Long Island has been fine wine-focused from the start, and is the only New York region where vinifera dominates. Whites include Chardonnay, Riesling, and Sauvignon Blanc, while Merlot, Cabernet Franc, and Cabernet Sauvignon often combine in blends that deserve comparison to Bordeaux. Long Island wines have struggled with their own stigma, namely that they are overpriced. While this may have been true in the past, not only has quality continued to rise, but many wineries have added excellent entry-level wines that have helped shed the region's elitist reputation.

In the New England states, wineries tend to hug the safety of the coast even more closely. Those that reside inland often purchase grapes, or plant cold-resistant hybrids exclusively. Even in Maine, however, quality wine is emerging at the hands of intrepid vintners.

FINGER LAKES

Although the wineries of the Finger Lakes are concentrated around four of the 11 lakes, a thorough tour requires some circuitous travel: Seneca and Cayuga lakes are each nearly 40 miles (65km) long, with wineries on both sides. Owing to these natural formations, wineries share a sense of community with their particular lake. The warmest location on the southeastern shores of Seneca Lake, referred to locally as the Banana Belt, results in the cluster of wineries there.

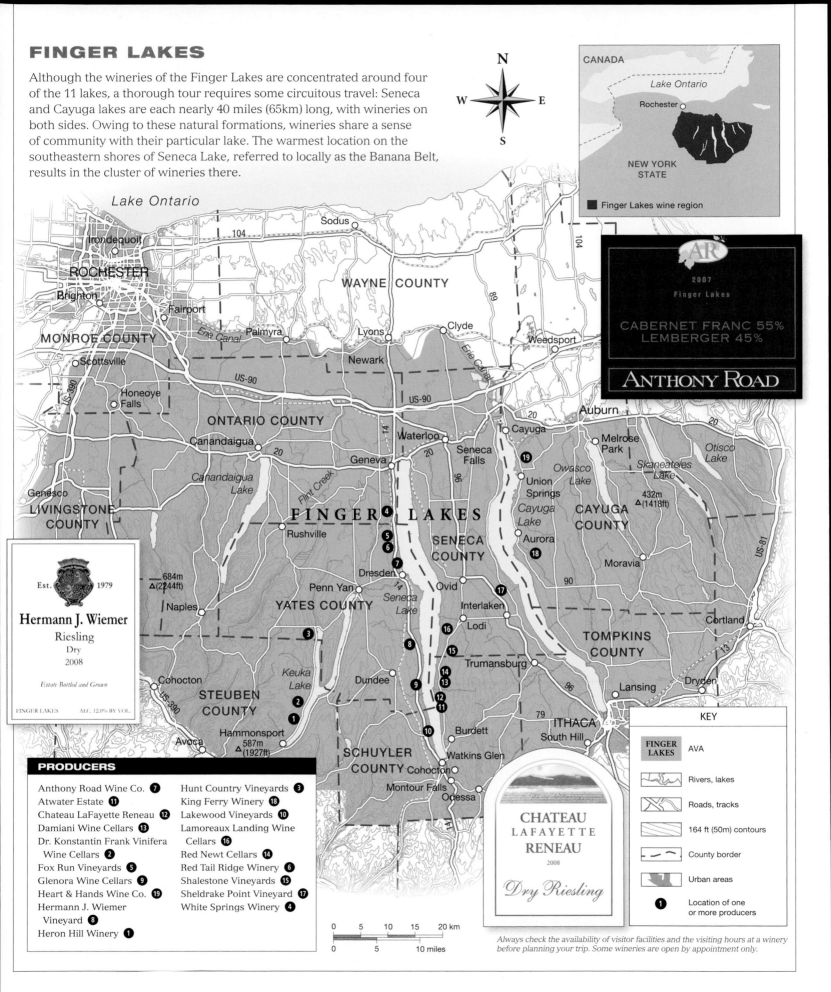

CANADA

Lake Ontario

Rochester

NEW YORK STATE

■ Finger Lakes wine region

2007
Finger Lakes

CABERNET FRANC 55%
LEMBERGER 45%

ANTHONY ROAD

Est. 1979

Hermann J. Wiemer

Riesling
Dry
2008

Estate Bottled and Grown

FINGER LAKES   ALC. 12.0% BY VOL.

CHATEAU
LAFAYETTE
RENEAU
2008

Dry Riesling

PRODUCERS

Anthony Road Wine Co. **7**
Atwater Estate **11**
Chateau LaFayette Reneau **12**
Damiani Wine Cellars **13**
Dr. Konstantin Frank Vinifera
   Wine Cellars **2**
Fox Run Vineyards **5**
Glenora Wine Cellars **9**
Heart & Hands Wine Co. **19**
Hermann J. Wiemer
   Vineyard **8**
Heron Hill Winery **1**

Hunt Country Vineyards **3**
King Ferry Winery **18**
Lakewood Vineyards **10**
Lamoreaux Landing Wine
   Cellars **16**
Red Newt Cellars **14**
Red Tail Ridge Winery **6**
Shalestone Vineyards **15**
Sheldrake Point Vineyard **17**
White Springs Winery **4**

KEY

FINGER LAKES   AVA

Rivers, lakes

Roads, tracks

164 ft (50m) contours

County border

Urban areas

1   Location of one
        or more producers

Always check the availability of visitor facilities and the visiting hours at a winery before planning your trip. Some wineries are open by appointment only.

0   5   10   15   20 km

0   5   10 miles

**DR. KONSTANTIN FRANK
VINIFERA WINE CELLARS**
DR. FRANK'S CHARDONNAY IS
CHARACTERISTICALLY FRESH AND ZESTY

BEDELL CELLARS
THE FRUIT-DRIVEN FIRST CRUSH IS A
BLEND OF MERLOT AND CABERNET FRANC

Anthony Road Wine Company New York

Ann and John Martini began their winemaking life working with hybrid grapes on the west side of Seneca Lake in 1973, before replanting to vinifera (except for a parcel of Vignoles) and opening Anthony Road in 1990. An array of Rieslings, running the gamut from dry to sweet, offer consistently juicy, minerally, and delicious value across the range. Unoaked Chardonnay provides a simple quaffer, but most surprising is the success of the Martini's inky blend of plush and smoky Lemberger with the herbal tea leaf flavors of Cabernet Franc.

1020 Anthony Rd., Penn Yan, NY 14527
www.anthonyroadwine.com

Atwater Estate New York

Ted Marks created Atwater Estate from the mothballed Rolling Vineyards on the southeastern shore of Seneca Lake in 1999. An entrepreneur, Marks brought with him a sophistication that is missing in many Finger Lakes wineries. From the packaging to the reliably delicious Riesling and Gewurztraminer, quality is immediately apparent. Unlike many in the region, winemaker Vincent Aliperti knows how to let a touch of sweetness bring the bright fruit and acid balance of Atwater wines to life.

5055 Route 414, Hector, NY 14841
www.atwatervineyards.com

Bedell Cellars New York

Owned by Michael Lynne, former co-chairman and co-CEO of New Line Cinema, Bedell obviously has big-screen ambitions. With contemporary artist-designed bottle labels, and prices on a par with the best of the West Coast, Bedell sets the bar high at its state-of-the-art winery, completed in 2005. Bedell's winemaking team excels at blending at every level, from the sophisticated, supple, flagship Bordeaux blend, Musée, to the entry-level First Crush line (introduced with the 2008 vintage), and mid-priced, multi-varietal blends called Taste. Founding winemaker Kip Bedell oversees 78 acres (32ha) of vines. Corey Creek wines are made here as well.

36225 Main Rd., Cutchogue, NY 11935
www.bedellcellars.com

Chamard Vineyards Connecticut

Located just 2 miles (3 km) from Long Island Sound, Chamard might be considered a mainland Long Island winery, although it technically resides in the Southeastern New England AVA. The winery, completed in 1988, sits among 20 acres (8ha) of estate vines, with 16 acres (6.5ha) dedicated to Chardonnay, which performs well in both a lush, creamy reserve wine and a crisp and citrussy Stone Cold White, made without oak or malolactic influence. The remainder of Chamard's 6,000-case annual production comes from small parcels of Merlot, Pinot Noir, Cabernet Sauvignon, and Cabernet Franc.

115 Cow Hill Rd., Clinton, CT 06413
www.chamard.com

Channing Daughters New York

The Channing Daughters winery began with Chardonnay plantings on Walter Channing's Bridgehampton farm in 1982. And it could be argued that this grape remains the star for its pleasing minerality and superb balance. With Larry Perrine as partner and CEO since 1996, the winery produces a large selection of small-production whites and rosés, reflecting innovation, excitement, and playfulness. In addition to the region's popular grapes, you will find Tocai Friulano, Muscat Ottonel, and Malvasia used successfully in an ever-expanding array of white blends. One such wine is Clones, which includes 10 clones of Chardonnay and five other white grapes. ★ Rising star

1927 Scuttlehole Rd., Bridgehampton, NY 11932
www.channingdaughters.com

Chateau LaFayette Reneau New York

When Chateau LaFayette Reneau's Dick Reno purchased a dilapidated farm in 1985, making wine was never part of his retirement plan. Finding himself in the ironically named banana belt, the warm pocket of wineries on Seneca Lake's southeastern quadrant, Reno soon replaced plots of native vines with vinifera, mostly Riesling and Chardonnay, which yield excellent wines. The winery's French moniker comes from his grandfather, but Bordeaux is a passion of Reno's—he has the region's only Petit Verdot vines, and winemaker Tim Miller makes cellar-worthy Cabernet Sauvignons in the best vintages.

5081 Route 414, Hector, NY 14841
www.clrwine.com

Damiani Wine Cellars New York

Since their first vintage in 2004, winemaker Lou Damiani and grape grower Phil Davis have quickly made a name for their winery and their 23 acres (9ha) of fruit. Whites include Riesling, and a Chardonnay with great balance of freshness and fine oak. Red wines are clearly their passion, however. Rising above the crowd in terms of character and complexity, the Meritage of Cabernet Sauvignon, Merlot, and Cabernet Franc is full-bodied and well structured, as is an unfined and unfiltered Barrel Select Merlot with its rounded palate and silky tannins. ★ Rising star

5435 Route 414, Hector, NY 14841
www.damianiwinecellars.com

Dr. Konstantin Frank Vinifera Wine Cellars New York

In 1962, the Dr. Konstantin Frank winery on Keuka Lake ignited the vinifera revolution, in the Finger Lakes and throughout the northeast, banishing Concord grapes to the jam jar. Third-generation owner Fred Frank employs a diverse team of international winemakers. In addition to the excellent fleet of minerally Dr. Frank Rieslings and Chardonnays, the winery has a more widely available Salmon Run label. The original stone house includes a separate basement winery, Chateau Frank, dedicated solely to sparkling wine production, including a berry-laden rosé made from Pinot Meunier.

9749 Middle Rd., Hammondsport, NY 14840
www.drfrankwines.com

Fox Run Vineyards New York

With 55 acres (22ha) planted to Chardonnay, Cabernet Franc, Gewurztraminer, Riesling, Merlot, Lemberger, Gamay, Cabernet Sauvignon, and Pinot Noir, Fox Run pushes the envelope for Finger Lakes wines. Run by owner Scott Osborn and winemaker Peter Bell, (formerly of Dr. Konstantin Frank), It is one of only a few vineyards in the region to adopt Vertical Shoot Positioned trellising (VSP), achieving riper wines with rich fruit, while preserving acidity and minerality. The Chardonnay, Riesling, and Pinot Noir seem to benefit in particular, with these reserve wines commanding some of the region's loftiest prices.

670 Route 14, Penn Yan, NY 14527
www.foxrunvineyards.com

Glenora Wine Cellars New York

Known as much for its scenic inn and the thumping disco music in its tasting room as for its wines, Glenora produces a large range of wine styles to the tune of 45,000 cases. Winemaker Steve DiFrancesco, who has worked with Glenora for 20 years, runs the gamut from fruit wines to non-vintage hybrid blends and, of course, vinifera. Riesling tops the quality white wines, while reds are generally clean, easy, and medium-bodied. Newly introduced are a tasty rosé of Pinot Noir, and a Sangiovese, that shows big acidity and good varietal character.

5435 Route 14, Dundee, NY 14837
www.glenora.com

Grapes of Roth New York

While winemaker Roman Roth makes a huge number of different wines in his day job at Wölffer Estate, there is no Riesling in that portfolio. Here, Roth makes a few hundred cases of superb Riesling from East End fruit, that shows incredible purity and elegant aromatics of flowers and spice. Roth began the venture with Merlot in 2001 and currently focuses on just these two wines, sold primarily through his mailing list. ★ Rising star

No visitor facilities
www.thegrapesofroth.com

Heart & Hands Wine Company
New York

Heart & Hands, a tiny gem of a winery, released its first vintage in 2006 and, despite the small production (currently about 1,200 cases) and lack of established estate vineyards, is showing great potential. Tom Higgins is co-owner with his wife Susan, and he credits his Burgundian inclinations and fondness for limestone soils to his experience at California's Calera. Fruit is obtained from top growers, including Hobbit Hollow Farm on Skaneateles Lake, and crushed in one of the region's few basket presses. A spicy Pinot Noir shows hints of cola and British Christmas cake. Estate vineyards will include Pinot Noir and Riesling. ★ Rising star

4162 State Route 90 N., Union Springs, NY 13160
www.heartandhandswine.com

Hermann J. Wiemer Vineyard New York

In pedigree, appearance, and style, the wines of Hermann J. Wiemer Vineyard may be the most authentically Teutonic in the Finger Lakes. Born into a wine family in Bernkastel, Germany, the eponymous founder (who remains a consultant) settled into the Finger Lakes and crafted his first Riesling vintage in 1979. Impressive Rieslings of impeccable balance remain his signature, particularly the succulent, juicy, and off-dry Late Harvest, which is more a literal translation of the German Spätlese style than a dessert wine. The vineyard achieves similar success with elegant Chardonnays and vintage bubblies.

3962 Route 14, Starkey, NY 14837
www.wiemer.com

FOX RUN VINEYARDS
THE 2008 FOX RUN RESERVE RIESLING IS
FULL OF SCINTILLATING ACIDITY

CHANNING DAUGHTERS
CLONES IS A COMPLEX, BARREL-AGED
CHARDONNAY-LED BLEND

Heron Hill Winery New York

Heron Hill Winery, near the southern tip of Keuka Lake, took root when John and Josephine Ingle planted 12,000 vines in 1972. Like many of the larger Finger Lakes wineries, it produces dozens of different wines, ascending through the Classic, Ingle Vineyard, and Reserve ranges. The Rieslings and Chardonnays show good quality across the board, while the reds are simple and enjoyable, with the floral and spicy Reserve Blaufränkisch a highlight. The Gamebird Series blends vinifera and hybrid grapes. Bernard Cannac, formerly of Long Island's Castello di Borghese, is the winemaker.

9301 County Route 76, Hammondsport, NY 14840
www.heronhill.com

Hunt Country Vineyards New York

Hunt Country Vineyards' director of winemaking, Jonathan Hunt, is the sixth generation to work the 170 acre (69ha) Keuka Lake family estate planted by his parents with wine grapes in 1973. The wines have been steadily improving for decades. A non-vintage red blend, Alchemy, combines Finger Lakes Cabernet Franc, Cabernet Sauvignon, and Noiret in a supple, easy-drinking, lightly spicy and smoky bargain. Of the whites, the Pinot Gris is a refreshing surprise, showing generous stone fruits, nice body, and great minerality. The latest innovation comes in an aromatic off-dry hybrid, Valvin Muscat. Most wines are suitable for vegans.

4021 Italy Hill Rd., Branchport, NY 14418
www.huntwines.com

King Ferry Winery New York

Founded by Peter Saltonstall on his former family farm in 1984, King Ferry was the first winery in Cayuga Lake. It produces about 10,000 cases annually, using both Finger Lakes and Long Island fruit. The lean and minerally Rieslings under the label Treleaven are consistently good, but the Chardonnays are the great surprise, ranging from off-dry and unoaked to buttery and creamy. An Icewine made from Vignoles nicely balances sweet tropical fruit with fresh acidity.

658 Lake Rd., King Ferry, NY 13081
www.treleavenwines.com

Lakewood Vineyards New York

With 75 acres (30ha) of vines located in a former orchard on Seneca Lake, Lakewood is a family operation. Founded by dentist Frank Stamp in 1951, it includes a hodgepodge of grapes. The juicy Rieslings with their bright fruit never disappoint, and winemaker Chris Stamp shows innovation by aging and fermenting up to a third of the Chardonnay in New York oak barrels for an extra dash of terroir, achieving an oaky but balanced style. An Icewine, a spritzy Cayuga called Cameo, port, and mead are all boldly creative novelties.

4024 State Route 14, Watkins Glen, NY 14891
www.lakewoodvineyards.com

Lamoreaux Landing Wine Cellars
New York

Lamoureaux's founder, Mark Wagner, has a familiar Finger Lakes tale—a long family history of farming Vitis lambrusca and French-American hybrid grapes before shifting to vinifera and winemaking in the late 1970s.

MACARI VINEYARD

MACARI'S SAUVIGNON BLANC IS BRIMMING
WITH CITRUS FLAVORS AND MINERALITY

With about 100 acres (40ha) currently under vine on the east side of Seneca Lake, Lamoreaux's production favors whites, making three different Rieslings and two Chardonnays, including a reserve that balances lovely citrussy acidity with brioche and honey. Although smaller in production, new red releases, such as the Cabernet Franc-dominated 76 West, also show great potential.

9224 Route 414, Lodi, NY 14860
www.lamoreauxwine.com

Macari Vineyard New York

Macari Vineyard, a 500 acre (202ha) waterfront estate, has been in the Macari family for 50 years, but grapes only arrived on the scene in 1995. Joseph Macari Jr. is faithful to his family's farming heritage, embracing sustainable practices and biodiversity on the 180 acres (70ha) of vines. Macari's wines are affordably priced for the region, and a reliably striking Sauvignon Blanc shows good grassy varietal character reminiscent of New Zealand. Rosé is dry and refreshing, while the non-vintage Sette, a blend of Merlot and Cabernet Franc, is a great-value red.

150 Bergen Ave., Mattituck, NY 11952
www.macariwines.com

Millbrook Vineyards New York

Millbrook's John Dyson is a former New York State commissioner of agriculture. And it is no coincidence that he held the post as the seminal New York Farm Winery Act of 1976 opened the door for hundreds of wineries. Millbrook's 30 acres (12ha) of estate vineyards are primarily focused on Chardonnay, followed by Cabernet Franc, Pinot Noir, and Tocai Friulano. Millbrook sources additional fruit for New York-designate wines (which are larger production and in some cases even better), and an annexed Central Coast vineyard, Vista Verde, supplies California fruit. The Dyson family also owns California's Williams Selyem and Tuscany's Villa Pillo.

26 Wing Rd., Millbrook, NY 12545
www.millbrookwine.com

Newport Vineyards Rhode Island

About half of Newport's 60 acres (24ha) of vines are on the Nunes family farm, which was purchased by the great-grandfather of owners John and Paul Nunes in 1917. Originally dating to 1701, the rock-walled farm is blessed with an island climate, moderated by the Gulf Stream and Narragansett Bay. The wide-ranging portfolio of wines mixes hybrid and vinifera grapes. The most widely sold are the white blend, Great White, and Rochambeau, a simple, fruity Cabernet Sauvignon/Landot Noir blend.

909 E. Main Rd., Middletown, RI 02842
www.newportvineyards.com

Osprey's Dominion New York

Osprey's Dominion is a North Fork winery with 90 acres (36ha) under vine, producing a large array of wines, including sparklers and fortified wines. The Flight Meritage of Merlot, Cabernet Sauvignon, and Cabernet Franc is a perennial winner. However, reasonably priced whites, including an unoaked Chardonnay and a Sauvignon Blanc, are fresh, juicy, and pleasing bargains.

44075 Main Rd., Peconic Long Island, NY 11958
www.ospreysdominion.com

Peconic Bay Winery New York

Established in 1979, Peconic Bay is a pioneering North Fork vineyard, and later winery, that was purchased by Paul and Ursula Lowerres in 1999, following several years of ambitious vineyard acquisitions. The 6,000- to 8,000-case production includes good-value, non-vintage Nautique table wines and only slightly pricier varietal bottlings. The Chardonnay is the most notable, made in a variety of styles such as the rich, yet crisp La Barrique and a stainless steel-fermented version with good fruit and complexity. Veteran Long Island winemaker Gregory Gove previously worked at Hargrave and Pindar.

Cutchogue, NY 11935
www.peconicbaywinery.com

Red Newt Cellars New York

Owned by David and Debra Whiting, Red Newt Cellars' compound on the eastern side of Seneca Lake includes a popular bistro that serves many Finger Lakes wines. The operation has no vineyards, and buys fruit from within about 5 miles (8km) of the winery. The readily available Circle Label Rieslings, with their youthful exuberance and touch of sweetness, are bargains. The single-vineyard Merlot, Cabernet Franc, and Gewurtztraminer are solid, sophisticated efforts, with prices to match.

3675 Tichenor Rd., Hector, NY 14841
www.rednewt.com

Red Tail Ridge Winery New York

Unlike most Finger Lakes estates, which are often reclaimed vineyards, the 34 acre (14ha) Red Tail Ridge estate was carved from virgin wilderness by Mike Schnelle. With the help of his wife, Nancy Irelan, Schnelle planted Riesling, Chardonnay, Pinot Noir, and then northern Italy's Teroldego. The larger-production wines, such as the Rieslings with their balance of sugar and racy acidity, and the Burgundian Pinot Noir, are typically less than 1,000 cases. Several wines number as few as 50 cases. A supple, plummy, peppery Lemberger is sourced from Martini Family Vineyard.

846 State Route 14, Penn Yan, NY 14527
www.redtailridgewinery.com

Sakonnet Vineyards Rhode Island

The pioneering Sakonnet was founded in 1975, and it now produces 30,000 cases annually. It works with vinifera grapes and Vidal Blanc, the latter a versatile mainstay of the property that is transformed into a crisp, zesty white, a barrel-fermented Fumé, and an Icewine. It also co-stars with Gewurtztraminer in the affordable, aromatic, dry Petite white table wine. Blending vinifera with Chancellor similarly succeeds in Rhode Island Red. The Newport series references the maritime location, while fulfilling the need for downright cheap seaside quaffers.

162 West Main Rd., Little Compton, RI 02837
www.sakonnetwine.com

Shalestone Vineyards New York

Amid a sea of generalists juggling dozens of wines, including hybrids and fruit concoctions, Shalestone proudly declares: "Red is all we do," as a warning to the tour-bus throngs. With a mere 6.5 acres (2.6ha) of Cabernet Sauvignon, Merlot, Cabernet Franc, Syrah, and Pinot Noir, Shalestone is one of the Finger Lake's more elusive

SHELDRAKE POINT VINEYARD

SHELDRAKE'S DRY ROSE BLENDS CABERNET
FRANC, GAMAY, AND GEWURTZTRAMINER

wineries. Established by Rob and Kate Thomas in 1995, it continues as a truly small family operation. The Cabernet Franc-based reds achieve ripeness, but reflect the cool climate, proving that sometimes it pays to specialize.

9681 Route 414, Lodi, NY 14860
www.shalestonevineyards.com

Sharpe Hill Connecticut
Sharpe Hill winery and restaurant hangs its hat on the high-production, off-dry white blend, Ballet of Angels. But the dry white wines are far more inspiring. Among the Chardonnays are a Connecticut Vineyard Reserve, an American-designate Chardonnay, and a critically lauded Long Island wine. Other grapes include Melon de Bourgogne and Vignoles, which makes an impressive late-harvest wine. Reds include Cabernet Franc, Carmine, and an easy-drinking St. Croix. ★ **Rising star**

108 Wade Rd., Pomfret, CT 06258
www.sharpehill.com

Shelburne Vineyards Vermont
Founded in 1997 by Ken and Gail Albert, Shelburne is intrepid not just for its dedication to Vermont-grown grapes, but for achieving organic vineyard certification despite the humid summers and frigid winters of the northeast. Cold-hardy varieties of choice include Riesling, Zweigelt, and a host of hybrids, including the latest from Minnesota: Louise Swenson (white) and Marquette (red). Fans of dessert wines will relish Rhapsody, made from the Arctic clone of Riesling. ★ **Rising star**

6308 Shelburne Rd., Shelburne, VT 05482
www.shelburnevineyard.com

Sheldrake Point Vineyard New York
The second vineyard to grace this point of land jutting from the midpoint of the western coast of Cayuga Lake, Sheldrake Point has 43 acres (17ha) producing 8,000 cases annually. Riesling vines are concentrated at the higher elevation; Pinot Noir grows near the dock that welcomes sailing visitors. Gamay was added recently, but it is Sheldrake's affordable whites that shine: juicy Riesling, austere Gewurztraminer, and delightful Pinot Gris.

7448 County Rd. 153, Ovid, NY 14521
www.sheldrakepoint.com

Shinn Estate New York
Shinn Estate was founded by artist Barbara Shinn and chef David Page, who also run the popular Greenwich Village restaurant, Home. Although the estate has only 20 acres (8ha) under vine, it has a number of interesting wines, many showing a chef's penchant for blending, flavor-building, and creativity. Coalescence includes Chardonnay, Sauvignon Blanc, Merlot, and Viognier. Anomaly is a still Blanc de Noir. Reds include the flagship Wild Boar Doe, with black cherry, espresso, and firm tannins, and several other well-made Bordeaux blends.

2000 Oregon Rd., Mattituck, NY 11952
www.shinnestatevineyards.com

Sparkling Pointe New York
Established in 2003 by Cynthia and Tom Rosicki, Sparkling Pointe consists of a modest 10 acres (4ha) of vineyard dedicated exclusively to traditional champagne varieties and the production of sparkling wine. Winemaker Gilles Martin honed his art at California's Roederer Estate Winery and now oversees the production of three *méthode Champenoise* wines. The Topaz Imperial is a standout—a golden-amber rosé with red berry fruit and apple tart. The flagship Brut Séduction rivals true champagne in price and taste. ★ **Rising star**

39750 County Rd. 48, Southold, NY 11971
www.sparklingpointe.com

Stoutridge Vineyard New York
Constructed on the site of a pre-Prohibition era winery established in 1902, Stoutridge's winery is high-tech, gravity-fed, and solar-powered. Owner Stephen Osborn avoids fining, filtering, and acid adjustment to make unique regional wines, including a range of varieties sourced from a single neighboring farm. Several Hudson Valley AVA wines, mostly hybrid blends, are currently being produced. Estate wines will come from three vineyards planted to Riesling, Pinot Blanc, Pinot Noir, Teroldego, Sangiovese, and Refosco. ★ **Rising star**

10 Ann Kaley Lane, Marlboro, NY 12542
www.stoutridge.com

Westport Rivers Vineyard Massachusetts
Add Massachusetts to the list of unlikely places that produce excellent sparkling wine in the US. Westport Rivers, New England's largest winery, was founded by Bob and Carol Russell in 1982 and first planted by their oldest son. It remains a family operation. The 78 acres (32ha) of estate vineyards supply the majority of the fruit, and are dominated by Chardonnay, Pinot Noir, and Pinot Meunier, a classic recipe for their assorted vintage sparklers. The flagship Brut Cuvée RJR, a full-bodied, toasty Pinot Noir assemblage, is the largest-production sparkler. Still wines include Alsatian varietals and a balanced Chardonnay.

417 Hixbridge Rd., Westport, MA
www.westportrivers.com

White Springs Winery New York
In 2003, Carl Fribolin planted vines on his White Springs Farm hoping to prevent erosion. That geological necessity now totals 40 acres (16ha) planted with eight vinifera varieties. White wines of note include Riesling, of course, as well as a fresh herb-tinged Sauvignon Blanc. Even with many vines just coming to maturity, the wines are showing well and they are well priced. The winery is located 5 miles (8km) from the tasting room; both are on the western side of Seneca Lake. ★ **Rising star**

4200 Route 14 South, Geneva, NY 14456
www.whitespringswinery.com

Wölffer Estate New York
The victim of a tragic accident in 2008, Christian Wölffer would be proud of the ongoing efforts at the family winery he founded in 1988 on former potato fields. Fellow German winemaker Roman Roth shows great versatility at the grand 55 acre (22ha) estate, with lively whites, solid yet supple reds, late-harvest, and sparkling wines. The dry rosé (with Chardonnay in the blend) is a benchmark of summertime drinking on Long Island.

139 Sagg Rd., Sagaponack, NY 11962
www.wolffer.com

DR. KONSTANTIN FRANK

Dr. Konstantin Frank (1897–1985) was the unlikely champion of fine wine east of the Mississippi, having directly or indirectly inspired every winemaker in the region. Frank, a native of Ukraine with a PhD in viticulture, arrived with his family in New York in 1951. He secured a position at Cornell University's Geneva Experiment Station, where accepted thinking dictated that only native *Vitis labrusca* and French-American hybrid grapes could endure the cold New York climate. Frank's insistence on the potential of classic European vinifera varieties found little audience at Cornell, but Charles Fournier, a local winemaker who had arrived in the region from France, indulged his ideas. Frank pioneered many grapes in the region (including Riesling and Pinot Noir), became an outspoken critic of hybrids, and opened his Finger Lakes winery in 1962. His tenacity and generous spirit convinced others to follow, and his legacy can be tasted throughout the northeast.

MID-ATLANTIC AND THE SOUTH

Mid-Atlantic and the South

The mid-Atlantic and southern states have a long history of struggle when it comes to European grapes. The Jamestown colony in Virginia had planted *Vitis vinifera* vines by 1609, only to be troubled by American pestilence, which also thwarted Thomas Jefferson at Monticello and William Penn in Pennsylvania. Before the American Revolution, similar efforts were made from New Jersey to Louisiana, mostly in the hope of impressing the Crown. All failed. Hybrid grapes took hold, only to be impeded by the Civil War in the 1860s, and then Prohibition in the 1920s. Only since the 1970s, with new legislation and careful consideration of site and variety, have centuries of perseverance paid off, making this one of the fastest growing quality wine regions in the US.

Major grapes

 Reds

Barbera

Cabernet Franc

Cabernet Sauvignon

Chambourcin

Malbec

Merlot

Petit Verdot

 Whites

Chardonnay

Seyval Blanc

Vidal Blanc

Viognier

Vintages

2009
A soggy year in the southeast, with very uneven wines.

2008
A drought vintage with good wines in the southeast.

2007
Some decent wines despite the severe spring frost.

2006
A drought year. Some of the reds still show character.

2005
A rough year for reds and the whites are all past drinkable.

2004
A few reds are still drinking well from this solid vintage.

Until 1981, New Jersey's industry was hampered by puritanical legislation limiting the number of wineries in the state. Today, there are two exclusive American Viticultural Areas (AVAs): Outer Coastal Plain and Warren Hills. The "Garden State" makes many fruit wines, but the most planted grapes are Cabernet Sauvignon, Cabernet Franc, and Chambourcin (red), and Seyval Blanc, Chardonnay, and Vidal Blanc (white).

Hybrids play an important role in Pennsylvania, which has more than 100 (mostly small) wineries. The state has some exclusive AVAs, but its larger ones are shared with neighboring states: Lake Erie (New York and Ohio), Central Delaware Valley (New Jersey), and Cumberland Valley (Maryland).

Virginia enjoys a diverse range of geographical features suited to wine-growing, including the Blue Ridge and Appalachian mountain ridges and their accompanying valleys, and the coastal plain. There are more than 140 wineries dotted across the state's six AVAs. European varieties dominate, led by Chardonnay, Cabernet Franc, Merlot, Cabernet Sauvignon, and Vidal Blanc. Viognier, Norton, and Petit Manseng show great potential.

Perhaps the single most significant development in Virginia and neighboring Maryland is that wineries are now choosing sites that are suited to wine grape cultivation, rather than simply planting on existing farms and plantations. In Maryland, Cabernet Sauvignon and Chardonnay are the most planted red and white grapes. Malbec, Barbera, Viognier, and Petit Verdot plantings are on the rise.

The Carolinas share some of the coastal advantages of Virginia, although they trail their northern neighbor in size, output, and quality. Only a handful of wineries have consistently crafted good wines; most producers are still moving from hybrid vines to vinifera. Still, the region's winemakers have greatly improved hybrid wines, and delicious off-dry and dessert wines are made, as well as a growing number of dry reds and whites from both hybrids and vinifera.

Georgia, a relative newcomer to modern wine, has hitched its star to vinifera vines. The state's northeastern vineyards, in and around the Chattahoochee National Forest, offer warm temperatures ameliorated by high elevation. Although viticulture was attempted a few centuries ago, disease and pests laid waste to those attempts, just as they did throughout the rest of the East Coast. Today, however, good examples of Viognier, Cabernet Franc, Petit Verdot, Touriga Nacional, Petit Manseng, and many others can be found.

Kentucky and Tennessee are largely dependent upon hybrids, but they are enjoying the fruits of experience and better techniques, and harbor a group of good wineries. Florida and some of the other southeast states are still experimenting with wines made from other fruits, from new hybrids such as Blanc de Bois, and from much maligned, native Muscadine vines such as Scuppernong. The sticky-sweet, dusty-bitter charms of Muscadine wines are not for everyone, but they are worth trying with powerful Asian sweet and sour foods.

Alba Vineyard New Jersey

Located a few miles outside the Delaware River town of Milford, Alba has been repeatedly selected as the best of New Jersey's 30-plus wineries. Saved from bankruptcy in 1998, Alba includes 45 acres (18ha) of estate vineyards that consistently produce juicy, bright Riesling and crisp Chardonnay. The Estate Barrel Reserve Chardonnay, made from Dijon clones of the variety, is toasty and creamy on the palate. Alba also makes an array of regionally popular sweet fruit wines and Dolcina, made with flash-frozen Delaware and Riesling grapes.

269 Route 627, Village of Finesville, Milford, NJ 08848;
www.albavineyard.com

Arrington Vineyards Tennessee

Arrington Vineyards may be owned by country music legend Kix Brooks, but having a famous owner does not mean the winery lacks serious purpose. Indeed, the winery was hatched before Kix came on board, but it was his involvement that allowed winemaker Kip Summers to flesh out his vision. The vineyard is still young, and the vinifera grapevines planted there may yet prove less appropriate then grape choices still to come, but the Syrah is solid and cherry-rich, and the white wines are trim and well-balanced. A dessert wine, Muscat Love, is perfumed and fun.

6211 Patton Rd., Arrington, TN 37014
www.arringtonvineyards.com

Barboursville Vineyards Virginia

Owned by Italy's Zonin family and managed by winemaker Luca Paschina, Barboursville demonstrates its Italian affinity with Sangiovese, Barbera, and a Nebbiolo Reserve. The latter shows good varietal character and is crafted using 60-gallon barriques from a Piemontese cooper. However, it is the Merlot-based, Bordeaux-like Octagon that steals the show with its smoky plum, coffee, and cocoa flavors, loamy earth, and supple tannins. In a final nod to Italy, Malvaxia Passito is a dense and honeyed dessert wine made with air-dried Moscato Ottonel and Vidal.

17655 Winery Rd., Barboursville, VA 22923
www.barboursvillewine.com

Biltmore Estate North Carolina

Biltmore is a remarkable place to visit, even if wine is not your chief interest. Built as an excessive expression of the Vanderbilt family's wealth in 1895, the grounds were designed by Frederick Olmstead; today, the remarkable estate is visited by more than 1 million people each year. Biltmore has been producing wine since 1985 from vineyards established 14 years earlier. The majority of the wines are made from grapes grown elsewhere (often from California) but the estate wines have been improving. The Estate Viognier is soft and aromatic; the Estate Riesling has a similar profile, but is sweeter. All of the sparkling wines are estate bottled; the sparkling Muscat (called Pas de Deux) is floral and vibrant.

1 Approach Rd., Asheville, NC 28803
www.biltmore.com

Black Ankle Vineyards Maryland

First planted in 2003 by Ed Boyce and Sarah O'Herron, Black Ankle has garnered deserved praise beginning with their first vintage in 2006. While not certified, vineyards

BARBOURSVILLE VINEYARDS
THE POWERFUL OCTAGON IS A BORDEAUX
BLEND MADE BY ITALIANS IN VIRGINIA

CHADDSFORD WINERY
A SMOKY RED FROM AN EXCEPTIONAL
VINTAGE FOR PENNSYLVANIA

follow many organic and Biodynamic principles and are densely planted, defying conventional wisdom for the humid climate. Wines are made exclusively from estate fruit. Crumbling Rock, a Cabernet Franc-dominated Bordeaux blend, has received critical acclaim in Maryland for its smooth kirsch and tobacco flavors. Leafstone Syrah is filled with juicy blackberry fruit, laced with aromas of coffee, vanilla, and smoked meat. ★ **Rising star**

14463 Black Ankle Rd., Mt. Airy, MD 21771
www.blackankle.com

Chaddsford Winery Pennsylvania

Founded in 1982 by Eric Miller, whose family founded New York's first farm winery Benmarl Vineyards, Chaddsford includes the 30 acre (12ha) Miller Estate Vineyard, located about 600ft (180m) above sea level in the Brandywine Valley. Wines include light-hearted, off-dry hybrid blends, and lighter-bodied Pinot Noir, Syrah, and Italian varietals, culminating in the Miller Estate wines. Miller Chardonnay is a showpiece in good vintages, achieving a nice balance of richness and lean green apple fruit with lovely chalky minerality. Merican, a Cabernet Sauvignon-based blend produced in select vintages, is rich in both flavor and price for the region.

632 Baltimore Pike, Chadds Ford, PA 19317
www.chaddsford.com

Childress Vineyards North Carolina

Perhaps some readers will be suprised to learn of a winery built by one of the most famous NASCAR racers, but lots of other wealthy and less famous people have done the same and have done it well. Racer Richard Childress began by testing varieties in his own backyard and he has hired wisely as well; winemaker Mark Friszolowski is one of the most respected professionals on the Atlantic Coast. The portfolio includes light, refreshing Pinot Gris; gently floral Viognier; crisp, melon-flavored Sauvignon Blanc; and the dry, distinctive Trio (Pinot Gris, Chardonnay, and Viognier). As yet, the wines are not always exciting, but quality is correct and improving.

1000 Childress Vineyards Rd., Lexington, NC 27295
www.childressvineyards.com

Frogtown Cellars Georgia

With 40 acres (16ha) of grapes planted to 17 grape varieties, the Kritzer family is being smart about the business of starting a winery at Frogtown. The red wines are still improving, though they can compete with others from this part of the country. Audacity (a Cabernet/ Sangiovese blend) is savory and spicy and the Tannat has sinewy power. Among the whites, the off-sweet Vidal Blanc, Cachet, is really fun—cleaner and zippier than many such wines—and the MRV (Marsanne, Roussanne, and Viognier) is proof that these people have a clear vision for where they want the project to go.

700 Ridge Point Drive, Dahlonega, GA 30533
www.frogtownwine.com

Horton Vineyards Virginia

Horton Vineyards' founder, Dennis Horton, considers himself more viticulturist than enologist. And it is that confidence that led him to identify Rhône varieties, specifically Viognier, as suited to Virginia's hot, humid summers. His introduction of Viognier vines in 1990 and

LINDEN VINEYARDS
THE HARDSCRABBLE VINEYARD PRODUCES
WINES THAT DEVELOP WELL WITH AGE

the excellence of the early 1993 vintage put Virginia on the wine map. Horton even makes a sparkling Viognier, aged six years on the lees. Other pioneering varietal contributions include: the revival of the Norton grape in the region; tropical fruit-flavored Petit Manseng; Pinotage with bright berry and acidic backbone; and wines from Marsanne, Mourvèdre, and Touriga Nacional.

6399 Spotswood Trail, Gordonsville, VA 22942
hortonwine.com

Kluge Estate Virginia
Established in 1999 by Patricia Kluge, this estate currently produces about 35,000 cases of wine annually near the Blue Ridge Mountains. Michel Rolland consults on both the icon Kluge Estate New World Red and little sibling Simply Red, both of them medium-bodied Cabernet Sauvignon-dominated blends offering good value and large production. However, Kluge remains best known for the "SP" range of tasty and affordable traditional method sparkling wines, with Laurent Champs of the Vilmart & Cie Champagne house working as consulting winemaker. Chardonnay-based bubblies are delicious—lively, with touches of toast and hazelnut.

100 Grand Cru Drive, Charlottesville, VA 22902
www.klugeestateonline.com

Lakeridge Winery Florida
Florida may epitomize the grapevine's most hostile climate, but native varieties in the Muscadine family are made for such hot and humid conditions. Muscadine wines are the past, present, and, perhaps, the future of Florida's wines. Muscadine wines, even more than the hybrids that populate so many of the vineyards in the southeastern US, smell funny to some people; it is a sticky-sweet smell, like a collision of dried pineapple, flowers, and bad 1960s musk cologne. Maybe that is not fair, but the point is Muscadine wine is distinctive, and Lakeridge's Muscadine wines manage the exotic perfumes while offering a balanced wine of apple and citrus elements.

19239 U.S. Hwy 27, Clermont, FL 34715
www.lakeridgewinery.com

Linden Vineyards Virginia
Linden's owner and winemaker, Jim Law, utilizes fruit from the Virginia Blue Ridge to produce about 5,000 cases annually. The Hardscrabble vineyard, which Law planted in 1983 on the former Hardscrabble farm (and which he tends to personally), produces consistently captivating wines under the vineyard name. The Chardonnay is crisp and lively, with citrus and stone fruit, minerally acidity, and just enough undercurrent of oak to impart a French flair that would make Thomas Jefferson swoon. Hardscrabble Red, a blend of Cabernet Sauvignon, Merlot, Petit Verdot, and Cabernet Franc, is supple with graphite and fennel nuance.

3708 Harrels Corner Rd., Linden, VA 22642
www.lindenvineyards.com

Persimmon Creek Vineyards Georgia
Sonny and Mary-Ann Hardman opened Persimmon Creek in 2000. Since then, they have been extraordinarily savvy at getting their wines in front of smart people in the industry. The quality is still improving—the whites are clean and correct, with just a touch of sweetness to the

Riesling and the Seyval Blanc. The reds need some polish, but the Riesling Eiswein—grown on the estate and picked in December—is sticky-sweet with enough acidity to finish with balance.

81 Vineyard Lane, Clayton, GA 30525
www.persimmoncreekwine.com

Pinnacle Ridge Winery Pennsylvania
Established in Berks County in 1993 by Brad Knapp, Pinnacle Ridge utilizes estate and locally grown fruit to create an array of Pennsylvania Dutch Country wines. Knapp showed great proficiency with sparkling wines early on, but has pulled back to focus more on still wines. Whites include a handful of affordable hybrids and a slightly off-dry unoaked Chardonnay. Traminette displays the rose, lychee, and generous body of its parent, Gewurztraminer. Among the reds, the Pinot Noir has good intensity while the Chambourcin is plush, with floral, liquorice, and spice notes. ★ **Rising star**

407 Old Route 22, Kutztown, PA 19530
www.pinridge.com

Rockhouse Vineyards North Carolina
Lee Griffin and Martha Cassedy knew they wanted to create a North Carolina winery when they purchased the property that became Rockhouse Vineyards in 1989. By 1998, it had evolved from a hobby to a commercial winery based on Merlot, Cabernet Sauvignon, and Chardonnay. It still focuses on Bordeaux grapes, though the climate offers wines that are lighter and more about red than black fruits. The light, charming Viognier is also recommended and, wisely, there is also a nice Chambourcin, from a hybrid well-adapted to the climate.

1525 Turner Rd., Tryon, NC 28782
www.rockhousevineyards.com

Sugarloaf Mountain Vineyard Maryland
Opened in 2006, the state-of-the-art Sugarloaf Mountain Vineyard is a short drive from Washington, D.C. and is planted mostly to red Bordeaux varieties. Cabernet Franc is the signature wine, in an ultra-ripe style with supple tannins, but Cabernet Sauvignon also shows great varietal character with cassis and cedary oak. Three red blends each use all five Bordeaux varieties on site, with the unfined, unfiltered EVOE! the newest addition. The 4,500-case production is rounded out by Chardonnay and a crisp, citrussy Pinot Grigio. ★ **Rising star**

18125 Comus Rd., Dickerson, MD 20842
www.smvwinery.com

Tiger Mountain Vineyards Georgia
In 1995, John Ezzard returned to the mountain where he was born, and planted Tiger Mountain Vineyards. It was foolhardy then, but seems rather prescient now as the 2,000ft (600m) elevation provides more balanced ripening than northeastern Georgia might otherwise offer. John and wife Martha have focused on grapes that raise eyebrows: Norton, Tinta Cão, Tannat, Petite Manseng, Touriga Nacional, and Malbec. All are solid but the Tannat is tough and intriguing, while the Petite Manseng shows a charming mix of honey and citrus.

2592 Old Hwy 441, Tiger, GA 30576
www.tigerwine.com

PERSIMMON CREEK VINEYARDS
PERSIMMON CREEK'S RIESLING
IS CRISP, BALANCED, AND FLORAL

Barboursville Vineyards in Virginia grows predominantly Italian varieties, reflecting the nationality of the owners.

UNITED STATES HEARTLAND

United States Heartland

Outside the established wine regions of the US, most of the vineyards and wineries are relatively recent concerns. And the people behind these nascent companies are all learning as they go. Yes, Ohio's wine industry was established over a century ago, and, yes, Missouri has wineries that date back to the mid-19th century, but the arrival of Prohibition spelled the end of production for those. The producers in many of the states profiled over the following pages are rapidly improving because they have adopted grapes that have only recently been created or discovered. Grapes such as Catawba and Concord may be as old as the United States, but they are not the reason why things have become so interesting in the US Heartland in the past decade or so.

Major grapes

 Reds

Cabernet Sauvignon
Chambourcin
Chancellor
Norton
Syrah

 Whites

Gewurztraminer
Pinot Gris
Riesling
Seyval Blanc
Traminette
Vidal Banc

Vintages

2009
A good vintage in Colorado and Texas, and Missouri fared well, but difficult elsewhere.

2008
Conditions throughout the region were made tricky by Hurricane Ike.

2007
A fantastic vintage in Michigan, good in Idaho, but a killer freeze in the Midwest.

2006
A good vintage for Colorado and Michigan and an excellent one in Idaho.

2005
A very good vintage in Michigan, Texas, Colorado, and the Southwest.

2004
Rain from hurricanes posed problems for most regions.

Instead, grapes such as Vidal Blanc, Vignoles, Traminette, Chambourcin, Chancellor, Edelweiss, Brianna, and many other varieties that nobody has yet heard about (and a few that still do not have names) have offered careful viticulturists and smart winemakers a chance to compete with the Cabernet Sauvignon and Chardonnay producers on the West Coast.

Climatic challenges throughout many of these states have necessitated the development of these new grapes: the famous *Vitis vinifera* vines (the Eurasian varieties such as Cabernet Sauvignon and Chardonnay) die in the harsh winter, wither in the melting sun, or see their grapes turn to goo from rain and rot.

Typically, native American *Vitis labrusca* vines produce grapes that are too tart to make fine or even good wine. But hybridizing vinifera with native American varieties results in sturdy and tasty grapes for winemaking.

Still, disease overwhelms even some hybrid vineyards, especially in Texas and the Southeast. New husbandry techniques might save the day; and other grapes, including some early or even accidental hybrids, might win in the end.

Meanwhile, in pockets by the Great Lakes where climatic extremes are ameliorated by the lakes themselves, white aromatic grapes such as Riesling, Pinot Gris, Pinot Blanc, and Gewurztraminer are not only competing, they are sometimes improving on what has been done with those same grapes in more familiar terrain. Ohio's new Wine Quality Program is actively promoting Ohio-grown wines of consistent quality. Michigan has to be considered one of the top wine-producing states in the country.

Away from the vagaries of the Midwest's weather patterns, the crazy extremes of the Upper Plains, and the soggy South, it increasingly seems that vinifera grapes can survive. From Arizona to Colorado and Idaho, the vineyards are hot and dry, but they are also often free from disease and pests. With irrigation and intelligent grape choices, those states' winemakers have increased quality. By contrast, Idaho still buys most of its produce from Washington State—and why not? There are lots of good grapes grown there. But Idaho vineyard quality has lagged as a result. You have to need good grapes to learn how to grow grapes well.

Colorado winemakers have realized that, though the state may be generally too hot and dry, a healthy dose of irrigation and the cooling effects of high-elevation vineyard sites can give rise to fragrant Rieslings, sappy Syrahs, and some tangy Bordeaux-style whites and reds. Arizona and New Mexico's producers have also fastened onto mountain-top grape growing in order to ameliorate the hot Southwest sun.

Texas does not have such options, but it has a boundless optimism and regional pride that has helped drive the industry. Having said that, those same attitudes now hold the state back. Texans see nothing wrong with planting Chardonnay, Cabernet Sauvignon, and Sauvignon Blanc—grapes that will likely never benefit from its relentless sun. But because the wines sell, they believe they must be good wines. If only it were true. Only a handful of Texas producers are focused on grapes that will probably provide a future foundation: Grenache, Syrah, Mourvèdre, Muscat, and especially two old locals, Black Spanish and Lomanto.

Augusta Winery Missouri

Augusta Winery's Tony Kooyumjian (who also works at Montelle Winery) is arguably Missouri's top winemaker. He does it all here: brilliant Chambourcin, elegant Norton, tangy Vidal Blanc, complex Vignoles, aromatic Traminette, gorgeous Icewine, and rich port.

5601 High St., Augusta, MO 63332
www.augustawinery.com

Becker Vineyards Texas

Success can breed complacency, but not at Becker, which has been more adaptable than most wineries in the great state of Texas. Rather than stick solely to easy-to-sell varieties such as Cabernet Sauvignon and Chardonnay, Becker has had success with Viognier, Grenache (both as a rosé and a big red), Barbera, Malbec, Mourvèdre, Syrah, Carignan, sweet and lively Muscat Canelli Amabile, and a very intriguing, barrel-kissed Chenin Blanc.

464 Becker Farms Rd., Stonewall, TX 78671
www.beckervineyards.com

Black Star Farms Michigan

A tourist destination as much as it is a winery, Black Star Farms boasts a farm, a creamery, a B&B, and a distillery, as well as two other tasting rooms in other locations. The distilled products are first rate, and provide the fortification for cherry, maple, and pear dessert wines, as well as a fascinating Pineau des Charentes-like white dessert wine. The light wines vary from solid to delightful, with the whites (from Pinot Gris, Chardonnay, and Riesling) most reliable. The A Capella Riesling Icewine is outstanding, as sweet and unctuous as you would expect but with enough crispness for balance.

10844 E. Revold Rd., Suttons Bay, MI 49682
www.blackstarfarms.com

Bookcliff Vineyards Colorado

Bookcliff is located in the college town of Boulder, but the vineyards themselves are up in the cool, elevated regions near Palisade on the Western Slope. Owners John Garlich and Ulla Merz make complex, dry reds and powerful sweet wines from Chardonnay, Merlot, Cabernet Sauvignon, Cabernet Franc, Viognier, Riesling, Black Muscat (in the rich Adagio), and Orange Muscat (the aromatic Allegretto).

1501 Lee Hill Rd. 17, Boulder, CO 80304
www.bookcliffvineyards.com

Boulder Creek Winery Colorado

Jackie and Mike Thompson's fan base for Boulder Creek means that virtually all their sales are limited to Boulder, though the grapes are sourced from up on the Western Slope. If you are in Colorado, you should seek out their delicious Syrah (with its blueberry notes), Riesling, Viognier or Chardonnay, or their noble VIP Reserve, a Bordeaux-style red blend. ★ Rising star

6440 Odell Place, Boulder, CO 80301
www.bouldercreekwine.com

Callaghan Winery Arizona

Callaghan Winery succeeds despite its sunny Southwestern location because of elevation: grapes such as Mourvèdre, Petit Verdot, Grenache, Petite Sirah, and especially Tempranillo enjoy a slower ripening cycle

AUGUSTA WINERY
THE HYBRID CHAMBOURCIN
GRAPE CAN PRODUCE VIBRANT WINES

BOOKCLIFF VINEYARDS
MELON AND SPICE FLAVORS
CHARACTERIZE BOOKCLIFF'S VIOGNIER

in the chilly nighttime temperatures found at 4,800ft (1,500m). Owner Kent Callaghan wisely prefers to blend in wines such as: Lisa's Selection (a barrel-fermented mix of Viognier, Riesling, Marsanne, Roussanne, and Malvasia); Caitlin's (a Mourvèdre/Syrah/Zinfandel blend with black cherry and plum notes); Padre's (a restrained mix of Tempranillo, Petit Verdot, Cabernet Sauvignon, and Cabernet Franc); and the exuberant Back Lot (Mourvèdre, Syrah, Zinfandel, and Grenache).

336 Elgin Rd., Elgin, AZ 85611
www.callaghanvineyards.com

Canyon Wind Cellars Colorado

Another winery from the burgeoning scene on Colorado's beautiful Western Slope, Canyon Wind sits on the edge of the Bookcliffs (a folded series of mesas). The eponymous winds provide cooling effects in the summer and a moderating influence when frost arrives. The Christensen family makes well-balanced, cool-climate whites and reds, including sappy, worthy Syrah, Tempranillo, and Petit Verdot. The top wine, IV, set a needlessly high benchmark price for Colorado, though the wine is fascinating.

1500 Argentine St., Georgetown, CO 80444
www.canyonwindcellars.com

Chateau Grand Traverse Michigan

In 1974, it seemed unlikely that Chateau Grand Traverse would thrive—except to founder Ed O'Keefe, who focused upon Riesling from the beginning despite advice to the contrary. Chateau Grand Traverse is still synonymous with Riesling; there are nine in all. The Whole Cluster Riesling and the Lot 49 Riesling show mineral notes, despite doses of sugar. The rest range from dry to syrupy-sweet to powerfully rich Botrytis Riesling and Icewines. There is also excellent Gamay, and the Edelzwicker is a mouthful of Gewurztraminer, Pinot Gris, Pinot Blanc, and Muscat.

12239 Center Rd., Traverse City, Michigan 49686
www.cgtwines.com

Fall Creek Vineyards Texas

Fall Creek's Texan wine pioneers Susan and Ed Auler are not always as adventurous as they could be these days. But they make one of the best wines Texas has yet produced, Meritus. A Bordeaux-style blend dominated by Cabernet Sauvignon, with a little Merlot and Malbec, Meritus has the burly tannins associated with warm-to-hot-climate Texas, but lots of depth, intensity and length. Their white wines are soft and pretty, and the Sauvignon Blanc/Semillon blend, Cascade, is refreshing and layered.

1820 County Rd. 222, Tow, TX 78672
www.fcv.com

Flat Creek Estate Texas

Flat Creek is a little ahead of the pack in Texas Hill country. It makes some surprisingly delightful Sangiovese (punningly named Super Texan), though it is still debatable if the grape will thrive in this unrelievedly sunny clime. Far more promising are the Orange Muscat wines, whether off-dry (Muscato d'Arancia), sweet (Muscato Blanco or Travis Peak Select Burnt Orange), or as Orange Muscat Mistella: fresh grape juice mixed with grape spirit.

24912 Singleton Bend East Rd., Marble Falls, TX 78654
www.flatcreekestate.com

PEND D'OREILLE WINERY
A CABERNET SAUVIGNON-DOMINATED
BORDEAUX BLEND WITH A TOUCH OF SYRAH

KINKEAD RIDGE
THIS BLEND OF VIOGNIER AND ROUSSANNE IS
PRODUCED IN TINY QUANTITIES

Garfield Estates Colorado

Garfield is a new estate, with vineyards purchased in 2000 and a German winemaker (Rainer Thoma) still getting used to the elevation (nearly 5,000ft/1,500m along the Western Slope) and growing conditions. The last few vintages have moved from promise to achievement, however. The lip-smacking Syrah is full of red fruits, the Semillon is fascinatingly mineral, and the Viognier, Sauvignon Blanc, and Muscat Ottonel are full of character.

3572 G Rd., Palisade, CO 81526
www.garfieldestates.com

Gruet Winery New Mexico

The high desert of New Mexico seems the least likely home for world-class sparkling wine, but after a quarter of a century of excellence, the high quality of Gruet wines no longer surprises. The Gruet family skillfully blends Pinot Noir and Chardonnay in a soft and gentle Brut, textured Blanc de Noir and rosé, and two richer luxury *cuvées* under the rubric of the founder, Gilbert Gruet. It is no novelty act: Gruet makes more than 100,000 cases of bubbly as good as any in the country. The four very nice table wines (two each from Pinot Noir and Chardonnay) are not often as impressive as the sparklers.

8400 Pan American Frwy NE, Albuquerque, NM 87113;
www.gruetwinery.com

Hell's Canyon Winery Idaho

Restaurateur-turned-winemaker Steve Robertson of Hell's Canyon is a pioneer in Idaho. His vineyards, just above the Snake River in Treasure Valley, represent the oldest estate wine production in the state. It is as warm as any site in the northwest, but the proximity to the river means air drainage, and the wines are balanced and (sometimes) long lived. Bordeaux varieties and Syrah are standouts: Seven Devils Red (a Bordeaux blend), and the Merlot and Cabernet Sauvignon Reserves are dense and barrel-laden. Deerslayer Syrah and the Syrah Reserve are no less oak-influenced but have more charm and flesh.

18835 Symms Rd., Caldwell, ID 83607
www.hellscanyonwinery.org

Holy-Field Winery Kansas

For Holy-Field's father-and-daughter team, Les and Michelle Meyer, the production of quality wine has been a lonely pursuit until very recently. After all, there are very few other producers in the state of Kansas. Still, their off-dry Vignoles and Late Harvest Vignoles offer peach and even apricot lushness, and their Cynthiana, Chambourcin, and red blends have also been impressive.

18807 158th St., Basehor, KS 66007
www.holyfieldwinery.com

Inwood Estates Texas

Inwood Estates is a work in progress. Its stable includes some of the most interesting wines in Texas, and the Cornelious (100% Tempranillo) is a great indicator that Texas is still exploring which grape varieties offer the best hope for the future. Inwood's portfolio is not huge, but there is also a tangy Palomino/Chardonnay and a dense, earthy Tempranillo/Cabernet Sauvignon. ★**Rising star**

1350 Manufacturing St., Dallas, Texas 75207
www.inwoodwines.com

Jack Rabbit Hill Winery Colorado

High atop a mesa sits Jack Rabbit Hill, a Biodynamic vineyard and winery, and an artisanal distillery. Chickens and sheep graze in pens between the vines, and serious Riesling and Syrah have been produced in the short time since Jack Rabbit began crafting its high-elevation wines. ★**Rising star**

26567 North Rd., Hotchkiss, CO 81419
www.jackrabbithill.com

Kinkead Ridge Ohio

Among the more than 100 wineries in Ohio, Kinkead Ridge has been the most consistent. The Revelation Red and Revelation White blends are among Ohio's most compelling wines. Owner Ron Barrett's experience in Oregon may explain his gentle touch with Cabernet Franc, which has vibrant herb, earth, and red fruits. The floral, honeyed Viognier/Roussanne is delicious, too. ★**Rising star**

904 Hamburg St., Ripley, OH 45167
www.kinkeadridge.com

Koenig Winery Idaho

The Koenig brothers are applauded as much for their dessert wines and distilled spirits as for their table wines. Their Three Vineyard Syrah is layered and persuasive; their Viognier Williamson Vineyard carries the pretty aromas and texture the grape deserves. Koenig's Cuvee Alden Private Reserve (a Cabernet Sauvignon/Merlot/Cabernet Franc blend) is very firm and even austere, but the Bitner Vineyard Chardonnay is tangy and juicy. The top red, Cuvee Amelia Reserve Syrah, powerfully stands up to a long sojourn in new French oak, but the Windridge Vineyard Icewine is something really special. ★**Rising star**

20928 Grape Lane, Caldwell, ID 83607
www.koenigdistillery.com

Left Foot Charley Michigan

Left Foot Charley winemaker Bryan Ulbrich has crafted vinous beauties for others over the years, so it is no surprise that his own label now sets the standard for the state of Michigan, if not the entire US Heartland. Ulbrich's ability with aromatic white grapes has been on display since the winery's foundation in 2004. Riesling, Gewurztraminer, Pinot Blanc, and Pinot Gris all exhibit an exciting purity of fruit that shows those grapes in their most distinct and vibrant expressions.

806 Red Drive, Traverse City, MI 49684
www.leftfootcharley.com

Les Bourgeois Vineyards Missouri

Les Bourgeois offers a panoramic view of the Missouri River and a rapidly improving collection of hybrid wines. Its Norton Premium Claret has gained in balance and depth of late, and the Chardonel is one of the best in the country. Indeed, all the white wines are seductive: LaBelle, Solay, Riverboat White, and especially the Vignoles/Traminette.

14020 W. Highway BB, Rocheport, MO 65279
www.missouriwine.com

L Mawby Wines Michigan

With more than 30 years of sparkling winemaking under his belt, Larry Mawby continues to develop his substantial stable of wines from both vinifera and hybrid grapes. He uses apricot-tinged Vignoles in the appropriately creamy Cremant and the gentle Talismon, Seyval Blanc in the lemony Sandpiper and various blends of those grapes along with Pinot Noir, Chardonnay, Pinot Meunier, and Pinot Gris. At present, the best wines are often those with a jot of hybrid in them; wines such as Conservancy and Jadore also have some additional stuffing from a pleasing amount of residual sugar. The second label, M Lawrence, offers good value.

4519 S. Elm Valley Rd., Suttons Bay, MI 49682
www.lmawby.com

McPherson Cellars Texas

Kim McPherson has wine in his blood: his father, a Texas Tech University professor, was an early proselytizer for Texas wine; his brother has made wine for decades in southern California. McPherson's folksy demeanor belies a dedicated, passionate winemaker behind some of the most interesting wines in the state: weighty Grenache-Syrah Rosé, vibrant Viognier, and the utterly charming Tre Colore (a Carignan/Syrah/Viognier blend). His lively, balanced Grenache-Mourvèdre may be the best wine in the state, and the Sangiovese (first planted by his father in 1996) is low-key and spicy, like its winemaker.

1615 Texas Ave., Lubbock, TX 79401
www.mcphersoncellars.com

Montelle Winery Missouri

As with his work at Augusta, Tony Kooyumjian's efforts at Montelle prove he is one of the stars of Midwestern winemaking. His ability to fashion delicious wines from hybrid grapes may be the best evidence that such grapes have a great future in the marketplace. Montelle offers a wealth of benchmark bottlings: a wonderful Norton (a grape known as Cynthiana in this part of Missouri), and a first-rate, raspberry-lush Chambourcin, as well as delightful port, Seyval Blanc, Vignoles, Chardonel and Icewine, and some excellent red and white blends. Tony also makes a not-to-be-missed Framboise, as well as one of the top eaux-de-vie in the country.

201 Montelle Dr., Augusta, MO 63332
www.montelle.com

Pend d'Oreille Winery Idaho

After more than two decades of growing Idaho wine, Steve and Julie Meyer are still eager to evolve and try new things at Pend d'Oreille. They now have a Sangiovese and a Primitivo to join their stable of crisp and tangy Pinot Gris, rich and toasty Chardonnay, soft and floral Viognier, rich and unctuous Malbec and the usual suspects (but no less worthy) Syrah, Merlot, and Cabernet Sauvignon. They also produce a surprisingly delightful little table blend, Bistro Rouge.

220 Cedar, Sandpoint, ID 83864
www.powine.com

Ravenhurst Winery Ohio

While Ravenhurst makes some tasty table wines, it is the sparkling wines that vault this producer ahead of so many others in Ohio. Perhaps unexpectedly, the winery is not alongside Lake Erie, but lies nestled in a little valley northwest of Columbus, where the extremes of winter are (somewhat) mitigated. Owners Chuck Harris and Nina Busch have an instinctive understanding of the style

MONTELLE WINERY
TONY KOOYUMJIAN MAKES GREAT WINES
FROM THE GRAPE CYNTHIANA, OR NORTON

LES BOURGEOIS VINEYARDS
LES BOURGEOIS CHARDONEL IS FULL OF
APPLE AND PEAR FLAVORS

of sparkling wine most likely to succeed in the American marketplace; they do not push the strong lees character (yeast, cookies, toast) but allow the fruit to shine.

34477 Shertzer Rd., Mount Victory, OH 43340
(937) 354-5151

Ste Chapelle Idaho

That Ste Chapelle does not enjoy wider recognition is the fault of its owners, Ascentia Wine Estates, which has far bigger fish to fry. Wine lovers should skip the pleasant but pedestrian wines at the bottom end in favor of the top wines. The white wines are the primary strength: peachy Riesling and Dry Riesling, and apricot-sweet Gewurztraminer are all crowd pleasers, and Riesling Special Harvest is, well, special. Winemaker Chuck Devlin also makes spectacular, absurdly inexpensive Icewine.

19348 Lowell Rd., Caldwell, ID 83607
www.stechapelle.com

Stone Hill Winery Missouri

With a picturesque home vineyard (planted solely to Norton) and its listed mid-19th-century buildings, Stone Hill is worth a visit. The underground cellars date back to 1847, the beginning of Stone Hill's long pre-eminence among mid-American wineries, though it was halted by Prohibition. The Held family re-opened the winery in 1965 and, under the tutelage of chief winemaker David Johnson, no Missouri winery has greater national visibility than Stone Hill. Johnson continues to oversee great fortified wines: the dense Norton Port and nutty Cream Sherry are world class. And Stone Hill Chardonel (light and tangy), Traminette (floral and crisp), Norton (a powerhouse), Vidal Blanc, Vignoles, and Seyval Blanc are the equal of any in the state.

1110 Stone Hill Hwy, Hermann, MO 65041
www.stonehillwinery.com

Two Lads Winery Michigan

Two Lads Winery's Chris Baldyga grew up among the Michigan vines and spent his youth working in the state's fledgling industry. He has teamed up with South African winemaker Cornell Olivier to quickly outshine most others in the state. They make two superb Pinot Gris (one green-apple tangy, the other peach and apple soft), and elegant Cabernet Francs and Merlots. Their sparkling wine spends five years on the lees and is very complex.

16985 Smokey Hollow Rd., Traverse City, MI 49686
www.2lwinery.com

Wollersheim Winery Wisconsin

The late Bob Wollersheim built a thriving winery in the same spot where Agoston Haraszthy toiled 150 years ago before heading off to help found the California wine industry. Wollersheim's son-in-law, the Beaujolais native Philippe Coquard, is the winemaker both here and at sister winery Cedar Creek, and he makes sleek, clean, and pretty wines from grapes grown both in Wisconsin and other states. The Wisconsin offerings include two from Marechal Foch: Ruby Nouveau (bright and fruity) and Domaine Reserve (spicy redcurrant notes), and a decadent Icewine from St. Pepin grapes.

7876 State Rd. 188, Prairie du Sac, WI 53578
www.wollersheim.com

CANADA

Isaac de Razilly is reputed to have planted the first vines "as they do in Bordeaux" near present-day Lahave, Nova Scotia in the early 1630s. Whether these vines were used for making wine is unknown; however, a company of Capuchin monks at the settlement is known to have made sacramental wine from native grapes. For much of Canada's history, it was not wine, but beer, cider, and spirits that provided strength and cheer for the population, either because settlers could grow the raw materials needed to produce the beverages or because the drinks were stable enough to last the harsh winters. Today, annual wine consumption averages 4 gallons (15 liters) per person, providing a ready market for domestic wineries that have transformed themselves over the past 30 years into rising international stars.

Contemporary winemaking in Canada dates from the 1970s, when governments granted the first winery licences since the end of Prohibition. While some visionaries had experimented with the European vine species *Vitis vinifera*, the majority of plantings were hybrids of *Vitis labrusca* vines, native to North America and hence deemed appropriate to Canada's climate.

The signing of the Canada–US free trade agreement in 1988 led to the wine industry's transformation. Vineyards were replanted with vinifera varieties to yield wines that could compete against wine from California and elsewhere. Growers met the new competition with panache, and began producing palatable wines to boot. The early plantings of the 1960s and 1970s suggested the initial varieties, and today there are approximately 21,000 acres (8,500ha) of vinifera grapes in Canada. Production is split almost evenly between British Columbia and Ontario, with a minor amount in other provinces.

At the same time as the vineyards were being replanted, the industry launched a quality assurance initiative known as the Vintners' Quality Alliance. This sought to set a benchmark for quality and, in the long term, establish a national appellation system similar to those found in other countries. The program has so far been confined to British Columbia and Ontario, where it guarantees that wines are made solely from grapes grown in Canada, and have met the approval of a tasting panel.

Canada's emergence as a wine nation has not been without hurdles. The country is known for Icewine, made from grapes that have been left to freeze on the vine at temperatures of 17.6°F (-8°C) or lower. But such low temperatures have on occasion inflicted significant losses on vineyards in both British Columbia and Ontario.

Moreover, Canada has had to develop identities for wines that producers previously named after similar wines in Europe. In the 1950s, Chateau-Gai drew the ire of France by showcasing a Canadian "champagne"; battles have also been waged over the term "Icewine". These debates were resolved in 2003, and the last remaining terms such as "Canadian sherry" are to be phased out in 2013.

Canada's maturing wine industry is attracting international interest. France's Boisset family and Groupe Taillan have launched joint ventures with Vincor Canada, whose growth attracted the attention of the Constellation Brands drink multinational. Constellation bought Vincor in 2006.

Andrew Peller, formerly known as Andrés Wines, is now the largest Canadian-owned winery. Peller's strategy of buying up small wineries points to the latest trend in Canada's evolving wine industry: the growth of boutique wineries. The economic booms of the late 1990s and mid-2000s saw millions of dollars invested in smaller properties developed as much for the wine as the lifestyle. A sign that the industry was finding its feet, many of the wineries are destined to define winemaking in Canada for a new generation.

Vine leaves turn yellow then red in the fall at Gehringer Brothers Estate in British Columbia's Okanagan Valley.

WEST CANADA

British Columbia's Okanagan Valley has developed rapidly over the past decade, and wineries have played no small part in this. Where once Okanagan was a summer playground of beaches and orchards, it is now one of the prime wine-growing regions in Canada. Spurred on, at least in part, by destination wineries such as Anthony von Mandl's Robert Mondavi-inspired venture near Kelowna, the region has won for itself the title of "Napa North". But British Columbia's wine is not only about Okanagan—wineries also exist in the neighboring (and equally arid) Similkameen Valley, the lush Fraser Valley, and on Vancouver Island. However, with the exception of Similkameen, those regions require grapes from the Okanagan to round out their own production.

Major grapes
 Reds

Barbera

Cabernet Franc

Cabernet Sauvignon

Merlot

Pinot Noir

Syrah (Shiraz)

 Whites

Chardonnay

Gewurztraminer

Pinot Blanc

Pinot Gris

Sauvignon Blanc

Vintages
2009
A short crop benefitted from good fruit set and good growing conditions.

2008
Variable weather but a good vintage with high sugars in the Icewine grapes.

2007
Mostly excellent growing conditions, though cool, favoring white wines.

2006
Stable conditions benefitted both red and white grapes.

2005
Cool weather reduced yields, but helped produce balanced, crisp white wines.

2004
Summer heat favoring red grapes was followed by a cool fall.

Oblate priest Father Charles Pandosy planted the first vineyards at a mission he established in 1859 near Kelowna, with sacramental wine the goal. Commercial winemaking did not begin in earnest until the 1920s, and the oldest winery still in existence, Calona Wines, was established in 1932.

British Columbia's wine industry was founded on hybrid varieties and their preeminence continued until the mid-1970s, when a government-run trial of vinifera varieties supplied by Dr. Helmut Becker of Germany's Geisenheim University showed the potential for widespread plantings of vinifera vines. The same period saw Walter Hainle produce Canada's first commercially released Icewine in 1978 (he had been making it since 1973, however). British Columbia began licensing estate wineries in 1980 and today there are more than 150 grape wineries in the province.

The total area devoted to vines exceeded 10,000 acres (4,000ha) in 2010, a tally some consider too great for a cool-climate region and an industry that is small by international standards. Growers are pushing the limits of arable land with the vines that do exist, and while notions of climate change have prompted some growers to take bets on remote locations, the Okanagan and Similkameen valleys remain the best locales for most producers.

An arid climate moderated by Lake Okanagan—plus an hour more light per day than is experienced in California by virtue of its northerly latitude—provides Okanagan vineyards with temperate growing conditions that allow grapes to mature gradually through a long growing season. The harvest begins as early as late August and the last varieties are typically picked in October.

The northern tip of the Sonoran Desert reaches into the Okanagan at Osoyoos, where the climate is not unlike some parts of Washington State to the south. The country here yields some of the best red wine grapes in Canada. Black Sage Road, between Oliver and Osoyoos and the winery-thick Golden Mile on the opposite side of the valley along Highway 97, are key production areas. Canada's first Zinfandel was produced here, and a number of producers are finding success with Barbera, Malbec, and Pinotage. The equally arid Similkameen Valley is a 30-minute drive to the east.

North of McIntyre Bluff, from Okanagan Falls to Kelowna, is the central Okanagan. The area includes the Naramata Bench, which some believe could emerge as the valley's first sub-appellation. A number of premium wineries have been drawn by its natural beauty, defined by clay bluffs and gentle slopes that allow air drainage and the moderating influences of Lake Okanagan. Grapes from vineyards north of Kelowna produce crisp, aromatic wines.

The damp coastal climate of the Fraser Valley is an obstacle to significant grape production, with white varieties, including Bacchus and Madeleine Sylvaner, leading local plantings.

Without mountains shaping the local climate, Vancouver Island is considerably drier. Wineries here cluster in the Cowichan Valley (the name Cowichan comes from the local Native North American dialect term for "warm land"). Vineyards produce several varieties, including Pinot Noir and Ortega. Many source fruit from the Okanagan, as do wineries on Saturna, Salt Spring, and other islands where viticulture is in its infancy.

OKANAGAN VALLEY

Significant variation in climate and growing conditions exist in the Okanagan Valley. Wineries in the North Okanagan—north of Kelowna—are quintessential cool-climate producers, whose wines often bear floral characters and crisp acidity. South of Kelowna to Penticton, wineries and vineyards yield balanced wines that reflect the moderating influence of Lake Okanagan. The arid country south of Penticton—and more particularly, south of Oliver to the US border —offers some of the best red-grape growing conditions in Canada. The fruit typically yields bold flavors and well-structured wines with excellent aging potential.

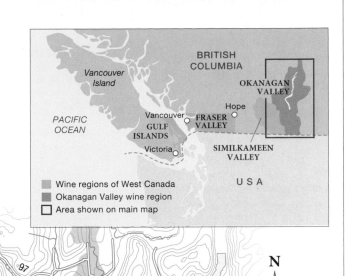

PRODUCERS

Antelope Ridge Estate **18**	Laughing Stock Vineyards **7**
Black Hills Estate **12**	Mission Hill Family Estate **4**
Blasted Church Vineyards **9**	Orofino Vineyards **15**
Blue Mountain Vineyard **10**	Poplar Grove Winery **8**
Burrowing Owl Estate **19**	Quails' Gate Estate **3**
CedarCreek Estate **5**	Road 13 Winery **17**
Church and State Wines **11**	Sandhill Wines **2**
Gehringer Brothers Estate **14**	Sumac Ridge Estate **6**
Gray Monk Estate **1**	Tinhorn Creek Estate **13**
Inniskillin Okanagan **16**	

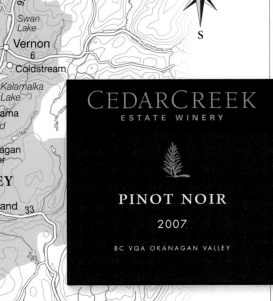

0 4 8 12 16 20 km
0 4 8 12 miles

KEY

OKANAGAN VALLEY	Wine region
	Rivers, lakes
	Roads
	650ft (200m) contours
	International border
	Urban areas
1	Location of one or more producers

Always check the availability of visitor facilities and the visiting hours at a winery before planning your trip. Some wineries are open by appointment only.

BLUE MOUNTAIN VINEYARD
THE PINOT BLANC IS BLENDED FROM OAKED AND UNOAKED LOTS TO GIVE COMPLEXITY

Antelope Ridge Estate Okanagan Valley

Olivier Combret's ageworthy wines came under a new moniker in 2006, shedding the Domaine Combret label for a more contemporary image. The expertise behind the wines is the same, although Combret, a Frenchman, now seeks a New World style that departs from his Old World origins. The exceptional location of his South Okanagan vineyard has attracted others—notably, former Vincor head Donald Triggs—to the same bench overlooking Oliver's so-called Golden Mile. Wines worth investigating include the crisp Unoaked Chardonnay and the rich red Cabernet Sauvignon/Cabernet Franc blend Equilibrium.

32057 Rd 13, Oliver, British Columbia V0H 1T0
www.anteloperidge.com

Averill Creek Vineyard Vancouver Island

Averill Creek was the dream of physician Andy Johnston, who planted its first grapes in 2001. The first vintage occurred three years later, and Johnston's rich examples of Pinot Noir have since won awards at several competitions. The 2006 Pinot Noir is a classic example of his work. It has dark fruit flavors that match the wine's deep ruby hue and a hint of smokiness that derives from aging the wine in a mix of French oak barrels. The 2007 could be even better.

6552 North Rd, Duncan, British Columbia V9L 6K9
www.averillcreek.ca

Black Hills Estate Okanagan Valley

Black Hills' signature red wine, Nota Bene, has long enjoyed a devoted cult following. Indeed, it seems likely that the wine's reputation played a significant part in garnering the investors needed to set the winery on solid financial ground in 2007. Working from a sleek modernist building that eschews the Tuscan or adobe stylings of many surrounding wineries, Black Hills continues to craft wines on the Okanagan's Black Sage Road—and they are well worth the attention they have received. In addition to Nota Bene, Black Hills' Chardonnays show rich flavors now and promise for the future.

30880 Black Sage Rd, Oliver, British Columbia V0H 1T0
www.blackhillswinery.com

Blasted Church Vineyards
Okanagan Valley

Quirky, distinctive labels have helped boost the popularity of the wines of Chris and Evelyn Campbell's Blasted Church. The couple took over the estate in 2002 when it was known as Prpich Hills—the previous, Croatian-born proprietor Dan Prpich's nod to California's famous Grgich Hills Estate. The current name pays tribute to a local church dismantled in the 1920s using dynamite. Merlot is an important element of Blasted Church's production and future ambitions, but it also makes several whites including the popular Hatfield's Fuse, a crisp blend of five white grapes.

378 Parsons Rd, Okanagan Falls, British Columbia V0H 1R0
www.blastedchurch.com

Blue Mountain Vineyard Okanagan Valley

Ian and Jane Mavety have taken Europe as the model for their winemaking at Blue Mountain, producing their first commercial vintage in 1991. Governed by a zeal for perfection and attention to detail, Blue Mountain releases a reserve tier of wines only when it believes there is enough fruit of sufficient caliber to give the range the outstanding quality it deserves. Some critics believe Blue Mountain offers British Columbia's best expression of Pinot Blanc, with a style that does not let the grape outshine itself, but Blue Mountain's Pinot Gris and Pinot Noir also command attention.

2385 Allendale Rd, Okanagan Falls, British Columbia V0H 1R0; www.bluemountainwinery.com

Burrowing Owl Estate Okanagan Valley

Burrowing Owl founder Jim Wyse's joint venture with Calona Wines gave him a partnership with two of the industry's visionaries—the grape grower Dick Cleave and the winemaker Howard Soon. Cleave watched over the vines while Soon defined the style of Calona's sister winery, Sandhill. Wyse, meanwhile, pursued his own vision under the Burrowing Owl label, crafting rich red wines at a landmark facility perched on the bench opposite Oliver. The wines have won significant acclaim, but fall well short of demand. The Cabernet Franc, Syrah, and Bordeaux-style Meritage are all notable.

100 Burrowing Owl Place, Oliver, British Columbia V0H 1T0
www.bovwine.ca

CedarCreek Estate Okanagan Valley

A celebrated producer of Pinot Noir, CedarCreek attracted veteran California and Washington State winemaker Tom DiBello in 2000. Prior to his departure early in 2010, DiBello charted a course for CedarCreek through both fire and economic downturns. The philosophy is simple: grow good grapes, and make good wine. Backed by the vision and business expertise of the Fitzpatrick family (Ross Fitzpatrick is a former Canadian senator, son Gordon ran the family's mining interests before joining CedarCreek), CedarCreek has twice been named Canada's winery of the year at the Canadian Wine Awards.

5445 Lakeshore Rd, Kelowna, British Columbia V1W 4S5
www.cedarcreek.bc.ca

Church and State Wines Vancouver Island

Aspirations expressed in Church and State's ambitious building have only recently started being fulfilled. Kim Pullen bought the winery in 2005, rechristening it with a down-to-earth name that seems somewhat at odds with the many stellar red wines it has been producing. Quintessential, a bold, Bordeaux-style red, has won several major honors for its 2006 vintage. Church and State will launch a second winery under the same name in the Okanagan, the source of its red grapes, in 2010. The original winery will continue to produce wines using grapes from Vancouver Island.

1445 Benvenuto Ave, Brentwood Bay, British Columbia V8M 1J5 / 31120 87th St, Oliver, British Columbia V8M 1J5.
www.churchandstatewines.com

Domaine de Chaberton Fraser Valley

Domaine de Chaberton, just east of Vancouver, is the ideal tourist stop as well as an accomplished producer. The first winery in the Lower Mainland, it benefitted from the expertise of winemaker Dr. Elias Phiniotis. Its Pinot Noir, at ten years old, is characterized by notes of red berries and mellow spices, while its Bacchus blends are

GRAY MONK ESTATE
THE UNOAKED PINOT GRIS IS A FRESH, BUT CONCENTRATED, WINE

young table wines offering fresh flavors. Botrytis-affected Ortega grapes yield a luscious dessert wine. Several white varieties are grown on the winery's 55 acre (22ha) property in Langley, but its red grapes primarily come from the Okanagan. Original owners Claude and Inge Violet sold the property in 2005 and the new owners have since debuted a second label, Canoe.

1064 216 St, Langley, British Columbia V2Z 1R3
www.domainedechaberton.com

Gehringer Brothers Estate
Okanagan Valley

Aromatic whites betray the German origins of Gehringer Brothers Estate, a Southern Okanagan winery that has made its name as a reliable producer of good-value wines across the price spectrum. Consistent quality, enticing varietals, and well-made blends make Gehringer Brothers a standout winery despite the growth in competition in recent years. Owners Walter and Gordon Gehringer exported to the US for a while, but maintain a low profile at home despite a diverse selection of whites (Ehrenfelser, Pinot Auxerrois, a Schönburger-Gewürztraminer blend) and the addition in recent years of Pinot Noir, Merlot, and Cabernet Sauvignon.

13166 326 Ave, Oliver, British Columbia V0H 1T0
250 498 3537

Gray Monk Estate Okanagan Valley

George and Trudy Heiss named first their vineyard, then their winery for the Pinot Gris grape. The cool climate of the North Okanagan gives Gray Monk's wines an attractive balance that makes them ideal for pairing with seafood. A tasting of several vintages of the winery's namesake grape from 1982 onward highlighted the longevity of Gray Monk's wines. But do not overlook the winery's other offerings, which fall into the basic Latitude 50 tier to the premium Odyssey range. In between are a fragrant—and rare—Rotberger rosé, as well as crisp whites with rich mineral and citrus characters.

1055 Camp Rd, Okanagan Centre, British Columbia
V4V 2H4; www.graymonk.com

Inniskillin Okanagan Okanagan Valley

An established producer in British Columbia's Okanagan Valley, with veteran winemaker Sandor Mayer at the helm, Inniskillin Okanagan is among the wineries testing the limits of Okanagan viticulture with a handful of new grape varieties running from Malbec to Zinfandel. Complementing a line of established offerings—like its Ontario namesake, Inniskillin Okanagan makes a rich, stone-fruit flavored Icewine, made here from Riesling grapes—a "Discovery" vineyard produces Malbec, Marsanne, and Pinotage. Its balanced, peppery Malbec is expensive compared to Argentina's most popular offerings, but smooth. The local expression of Pinotage reflects the South Okanagan terroir. ★ **Rising star**

Rd 11 West, Oliver, British Columbia V0H 1T0
www.inniskillin.com

Laughing Stock Vineyards
Okanagan Valley

David and Cynthia Enns named Laughing Stock Vineyards, their Naramata winery, as a play on their former financial industry careers. Fortunately, their wines have not lived up to the second meaning of the moniker. Deep yet balanced reds and rich but refreshing white Bordeaux-style blends are the hallmarks of this boutique winery. Having attracted a following with their Portfolio and Blind Trust blends since the original 2003 vintage (released in 2006), the Enns have set their sights on a small-lot future rooted in an innovative barrel program (the Enns and Road 13's Michael Bartier have a mutual interest here). ★ **Rising star**

1548 Naramata Rd, Penticton, British Columbia V2A 8T7
www.laughingstock.ca

Lotusland Vineyards Fraser Valley

Lotusland has been hitting its stride in recent years as it seeks a local character for its wines, a strategy that extends to planting high-profile Swiss clones developed by the renowned grape breeder Valentin Blattner. Noble grape varieties traditionally have not done well in the temperate Fraser Valley, east of Vancouver, but David Avery, Lotusland's owner and winemaker, is working to change that. One of his most popular wines remains a dry Merlot made from Okanagan-grown grapes produced in accordance with organic standards. ★ **Rising star**

28450 King Rd, Abbotsford, British Columbia V4X 1B1
www.lotuslandvineyards.com

Mission Hill Family Estate Okanagan Valley

Anthony von Mandl's landmark winery overlooking Okanagan Lake is a tribute to the inspiration von Mandl drew from the pioneering California wine producer, Robert Mondavi. The dramatic statement the building makes is matched by a range of wines crafted by longtime head winemaker John Simes, whose 1992 Grand Reserve Barrel Select Chardonnay won the 1994 Avery's Trophy for Best International Chardonnay at the International Wine & Spirit Competition in London. Its top tier wines include Perpetua, a Chardonnay in the tradition of its illustrious forebear (which continues to taste well today). But Mission Hill's great hope is Oculus, a deep Bordeaux-style blend made from South Okanagan fruit and named after one of the winery's many intriguing architectural features.

1730 Mission Hill Rd, West Kelowna, Okanagan Valley,
British Columbia V4T 2E4; www.missionhillwinery.com

Orofino Vineyards Similkameen Valley

Saskatchewan natives John and Virginia Weber came to the Similkameen Valley in 2005, opening a small winery in a building constructed from straw bales. Known more for its fruit stands and organic farms, the arid Similkameen is becoming known for its wines—with its whites showing best. Orofino's Chardonnay (apple-rich with the warmth of oak) and Riesling (a hit of acid balancing the richness) are priced well below the depth of their flavors. The 2006 Chardonnay was aged in Canadian oak. Orofino is also making headway with Merlot and other varieties. ★ **Rising star**

2152 Barcelo Rd, Cawston, British Columbia V0X 1C0
www.orofinovineyards.com

Osoyoos Larose Okanagan Valley

Winemaker Pascal Madevon was enthusiastic about the quality of the first vintage (2001) made at Osoyoos Larose, when the vines were just two years old. Today, he

BC PINOT BLANC

Some grapes are shorthand for a particular region—Grüner Veltliner for Austria, say, or Sauvignon Blanc for New Zealand. In her thesis for her Master of Wine qualification, Vancouver wine educator Barbara Philip examined the potential for Pinot Blanc to become British Columbia's signature grape. The variety had proved a success in the province's early vinifera trials, and it is certainly reliable, despite slipping from ranking among the top five in BC to 10th place in the province's most recent grape census. Many BC winemakers are not convinced, however, arguing that Pinot Blanc lacks glamour. And the lack of champions led Philip to conclude that Pinot Blanc is unlikely to become the region's signature grape. That is not to say she does not enjoy it. "Its peachy-floral notes and crisp acidity take me immediately to the Okanagan," she says. "I have tasted many Pinot Blancs from around the world and think that we make it as well or better than any other region."

SUMAC RIDGE ESTATE
SUMAC RIDGE'S OKANAGAN REDS ARE
DESIGNED WITH FOOD IN MIND

considers each vintage an improvement on the previous one as the vines continue to mature. A joint-venture between Vincor Canada and France's Groupe Taillan, the winery's signature wine, Le Grand Vin, is a Bordeaux-style red rich in ripe cherry flavors and pepper, with a smack of tannin that bodes well for aging. The wine certainly has its admirers, although many critics believe it is somewhat overpriced. Le Grand Vin also has an approachable sibling in Pétales d'Osoyoos, the winery's second-label red, which retails for about half the price of the first-label offering. ★ **Rising star**

No tasting facilities
250 498 4981

Poplar Grove Winery Okanagan Valley
Poplar Grove touts The Legacy, a Bordeaux-style blend of four red grapes, as its signature wine with a cellaring potential of 10 years. But for those who want something sooner, Poplar Grove's rich varietal Cabernet Franc offers steady tannins and a smack of pepper. In 2009, the estate also introduced some affordable white and red blends. Poplar Grove's rise as one of the key wineries along the Naramata Bench is matched by a fine line of artisan cheeses. Partners Tony and Barb Holler joined founders Ian and Gitta Sutherland in 2007 to construct a new winery and develop 110 acres (45ha) of vineyard in the South Okanagan to accommodate growth.

1060 Poplar Grove Rd, Penticton, British Columbia V2A 8T6
www.poplargrove.ca

Quails' Gate Estate Okanagan Valley
A big-league professionalism characterizes the mid-size Quails' Gate Estate. It produces 50,000 cases a year on a property planted by the Stewart family in 1960. The winery began to hit its stride during the 1990s, when the Stewarts eschewed hybrid varieties and focused on premium production. The opening of a rather grand new winery in 2008 capped a multi-year expansion program that testified to the winery's maturity. Quails' Gate's 2007 Pinot Blanc was the sole BC wine served to US President Barack Obama on his first state visit to Canada, while exceptionally fine late harvest and port-style wines round out a portfolio boasting more than a dozen offerings.

3303 Boucherie Rd, Kelowna, British Columbia V1Z 2H3
www.quailsgate.com

Road 13 Winery Okanagan Valley
Mick and Pam Luckhurst bought Road 13 Winery—which was then known as Golden Mile Cellars—in late 2003. It was the beginning of a journey that has seen the couple—and winemaker Michael Bartier—win acclaim across North America, not to mention a seal of approval from the BC lieutenant-governor. Road 13's portfolio includes basic red and white blends, a rich Old Vines Chenin Blanc made from 40-year-old vines (some of the oldest in the Okanagan), and the solid Bordeaux-style 5th Element blend. An extensive barrel program is giving Bartier a knowledge base (not to mention a range of treatments and flavor profiles) from which to continue improving Road 13's production.

13140 Rd 13, Oliver, British Columbia V0H 1T0
road13vineyards.com

Sandhill Wines Okanagan Valley
Pioneering small-lot and single-vineyard wines made from grapes including Cabernet Sauvignon and Sangiovese have established Andrew Peller's Sandhill Wines in the BC wine landscape. Sandhill winemaker, Howard Soon, produces crisp, refreshing whites, especially the Pinot Blanc, Pinot Gris, and Sauvignon Blanc. But those with patience might want to lay down some of Sandhill's small-lot wines from its vineyards on the Black Sage Road. Of particular note is "three", a richly colored and expressive blend of four grapes led by Sangiovese and Barbera, produced in lots of 300 cases.

1125 Richter St, Kelowna, British Columbia V1Y 2K6
www.sandhillwines.ca

Sumac Ridge Estate Okanagan Valley
When Sumac Ridge founder Harry McWatters sold his estate to Vincor for Can$10 million in 2000, two factors were key to the deal. The first was McWatters' visionary talent for developing wines such as Stellar's Jay Brut, BC's best-known sparkling wine. The second was his development of vineyards in the South Okanagan that have yielded premium red grapes for Bordeaux-style blends. The wines improve with age, too; a 2001 Cabernet Sauvignon tasted in 2009 retained the character of the variety with a mature structure—testimony to the quality of the original fruit. A sparkling Chardonnay developed for the 2010 Winter Games in Vancouver is rich with apple and honey character, and may become a regular offering.

17403 Highway 97N, Summerland, British Columbia V0H1Z0; www.sumacridge.com

Tinhorn Creek Estate Okanagan Valley
One of the few BC wineries that distributes outside the province, Tinhorn Creek enjoys increasing demand at home for winemaker Sandra Oldfield's handiwork. Age-worthy yet affordable, Oldfield's Merlot and Cabernet Franc are popular examples of South Okanagan reds from the so-called Golden Mile south of Oliver. Oldfield's white blend, Two Bench, delivers a shifting line-up of grapes for a crisp new experience each year. Tinhorn Creek also produces a Kerner Icewine smacking of stone fruit and honey.

32830 Tinhorn Creek Rd, Oliver, British Columbia V0H 1T0
www.tinhorn.com

Venturi-Schulze Vineyards
Vancouver Island
One side of the Venturi-Schulze operation is its production of conventional wines from Ortega and Pinot Noir grapes in keeping with Vancouver Island's cool maritime climate. The real fascinations for most followers, however, are its balsamic vinegar and its singular dessert wine, Brandenburg No. 3. Tasting either of these is a memorable experience. The vinegar is thick and sharp and the wine a rich amber redolent of honey and caramel. Also notable is Venturi-Schulze's Brut Naturel sparkling wine, an early vintage of which was served to Queen Elizabeth II in 1994. The grapes come exclusively from Vancouver Island vineyards.

4235 Vineyard Rd, Cobble Hill, British Columbia V0R 1L5
www.venturischulze.com

TINHORN CREEK
FULL OF CITRUS NOTES, THE 2BENCH WHITE
IS SUITED TO HARD CHEESES OR SHELLFISH

EAST CANADA

Vinland, the old Norse name for the coast of North America where Greenlanders found grapes and established a small, short-lived colony in the 11th century, seems acutely prescient today. The wild grapes the Greenlanders discovered heralded the potential for winemaking that would inspire later European immigrants such as Johann Schiller, who planted wild vines near Toronto in 1811 and produced wine for his neighbors, ultimately earning recognition as the father of Canada's wine industry. Today, Canada's four original provinces—Ontario, Quebec, Nova Scotia, and New Brunswick—dominate grape winemaking in East Canada, with vineyards located from the shores of the Great Lakes east to the Atlantic, although not Newfoundland.

Canada
— Area shown at larger scale on p.133

Canada's first commercial winery was set up on Pelee Island in Lake Erie in 1866. The use of native grapes and labrusca hybrids dominated vineyards throughout East Canada until the 1980s. Vidal remains key for Ontario Icewine, while L'Acadie Blanc and Maréchal Foch are important varieties in Quebec's Eastern Townships and Atlantic Canada, where Nova Scotia's Annapolis and Gaspereau valleys boast wineries.

A cool, damp climate and frigid winters challenge grape production in Eastern Canada, where diverse, rugged, and ancient geographies limit grape growing to select areas where conditions are favorable. Ontario growers benefit from the moderating effects of Lake Erie and Lake Ontario, but humid summers increase disease pressure. Harvest typically begins in mid-August for hybrid varieties, with vinifera grapes gathered in September and October. Temperatures begin to drop in November, allowing Icewine production by early January.

Quebec, Nova Scotia, and New Brunswick growers have identified grape varieties and practices that help address the short growing season and harsh winters that can see temperatures dip to -22°F (-30°C).

Retreating glaciers left rich, mineral-laden soils around the Great Lakes that favor cultivation of traditional Burgundian varieties such as Chardonnay, Gamay, and, more recently, Pinot Noir. Riesling is also popular, while many growers see merit in Cabernet Franc. Significant replanting of vines in the wake of losses following the severe winters of 2003 and 2005 have allowed growers to experiment with and select new varieties and clones deemed to work best under local conditions.

The variety of soils and localized climatic conditions in Ontario have led to the designation of four primary appellations—Lake Erie North

Shore, Niagara Peninsula, Pelee Island, and Prince Edward County. Niagara includes two regional appellations and 10 sub-appellations defined in 2005 following an extensive technical study, and many wineries are now producing single-vineyard wines from within these areas.

On the other hand, the bulk importing of wine from South America and elsewhere to supplement local production remains a contentious issue, with many producers fearing that the practice—largely at the hands of Ontario's biggest wineries—tarnishes the industry. A common term is "Cellared in Canada," which is used to denote wines made in Canada, but does not necessarily indicate the use of much—or indeed any—Canadian-grown grapes. The term is set to be phased out, as are the tax breaks producers receive for making such wines, and it is hoped that this will encourage a movement toward wines made from Canadian fruit. However, it seems likely that some wineries will continue to use the term "Cellared in Canada" for the next few years, and that the issue of imported wine will persist.

The clamor reflects a growing pride in Ontario wine that points to the industry's maturity. Stratus Vineyards, for example, is backed by Toronto investors with keen business sense, and Niagara is home to most of Canada's celebrity-owned wineries (hockey great Wayne Gretzky and actor Dan Aykroyd produce wine here).

Similarly, the Nova Scotia wine industry did not get started until the early 1980s, but it has since attracted talent such as Bruce Ewert, who formerly worked at British Columbia's Sumac Ridge Estate Winery. Support from the Cold Climate Oenology and Viticulture Institute in St. Catharines, Ontario, promises to give Nova Scotia wineries the expertise needed to make the best of a challenging environment.

Major grapes

Reds
Cabernet Franc
Gamay
Maréchal Foch
Merlot
Pinot Noir

Whites
Chardonnay
L'Acadie Blanc
Ortega
Pinot Gris
Riesling
Vidal

Vintages

2009
The cool growing season boosted acid levels, to the benefit of Icewines.

2008
The cool spring and summer produced good white wines.

2007
Warm, dry weather yielded one of the best red vintages.

2006
Humidity delayed ripening in an otherwise stable growing season.

2005
There was a short crop, but the quality was excellent.

2004
Steady maturation of the grapes was rounded out by autumn heat. A good vintage for Icewine.

INNISKILLIN NIAGARA
INNISKILLIN'S TRAILBLAZING ICEWINES ARE
AMONG THE WORLD'S BEST DESSERT WINES

CHATEAU DES CHARMES
THE BARREL-FERMENTED CHARDONNAY
MUSQUE IS RICH AND BUTTERY

L'Acadie Vineyards Gaspereau Valley

Bruce Ewert, a former winemaker at British Columbia's Sumac Ridge Estate Winery, is applying his ambition to L'Acadie Vineyards, one of the newest wineries in Nova Scotia. Situated in the Gaspereau Valley, L'Acadie uses certified organic grapes from its own vineyard and hopes to eventually achieve organic certification for its winery. Ewert is bringing his West Coast experience to the production of Nova Scotia sparkling wines using traditional methods, producing his first vintage in 2008. L'Acadie Vineyards also produces Eclipse, a red wine made from dried Marechal Foch, Leon Millot, and Luci Kuhlmann grapes with hints of berry and chocolate. ★ Rising star

310 Slayter Rd, Gaspereau, Wolfville, Nova Scotia B4P 2R1
www.lacadievineyards.ca

Cave Spring Cellars Niagara Peninsula

Cave Spring has garnered several awards in recent years for rich white wines rounded out by a period in oak barrels. Opened in 1986 after more than a decade of growing vinifera varieties on the Beamsville Bench, Cave Spring's flagship varieties include Chardonnay and Riesling, but it also offers Pinot Noir, Cabernet Franc, and Gamay wines with the subtle stylings appropriate to the local climate. Rieslings are lush with restrained aromatics that deliver sophistication across several price points.

3836 Main St, Jordan, Ontario L0R 1S0
cavespring.ca

Château des Charmes Niagara Peninsula

Rich, minerally wines are the hallmark of this family-run winery with the guts and grandeur of its owners' Gallic heritage and an innovative spirit. A willingness to embrace new practices has helped make it one of Ontario's premier wineries, and its alert vineyard staff gave it Gamay Droit, a clone all its own. Château des Charmes produces luscious expressions of Chardonnay Musqué (which it pioneered) as well as Riesling, and red wines including Pinot Noir and the Bordeaux-style blend Equuleus (a limited-edition red produced in select years only).

1025 York Rd, Niagara-on-the-Lake, Ontario L0S 1J0
www.chateaudescharmes.com

Closson Chase Vineyards
Prince Edward County

Backed by Deborah Paskus's reputation for producing Chardonnay, Closson Chase opened in 2004 with a vision of producing no more than a few thousand cases annually. Its focus in Prince Edward County is to take the region's cool climate and terroir and produce wines that match the best of Burgundy. The region's limestone soils yield Chardonnay and Pinot Noir grapes that produce distinctive, minerally wines, while Paskus's stylings draw out the fruit. Closson Chase also sources grapes from the Beamsville Bench in the Niagara region. ★ Rising star

629 Closson Rd, Prince Edward County, Ontario K0K 2J0
www.clossonchase.com

Creekside Estate Niagara Peninsula

Creekside is the second winery for partners Peter Jensen and Laura McCain-Jensen, who cut their teeth at Habitant Vineyards (now Blomidon Estate) in Nova Scotia's Annapolis Valley. It regularly wins recognition for its Sauvignon Blanc with hints of tropical fruit, while oak barrels help tame its pioneering plantings of Shiraz, which is made with a dash of Viognier like the Côte Rôtie in the Rhône. Creekside's winemaking team also produces wine for other labels, including Wayne Gretzky Estate Winery and British Columbia Icewine producer Paradise Ranch Wines Corp.

2170 4th Ave, Lincoln, Ontario
www.creeksidewine.com

Fielding Estate Niagara Peninsula

This young winery on the Beamsville Bench won early awards for its Cabernet Sauvignon/Merlot Reserve wine, which could be laid down for up to 10 years. That figure is significant in a cool-climate region where, just a decade ago, a mere six or seven years' aging was believed to be the limit. Current winemaker Richie Roberts has built on the early successes with innovative blends (his Red Conception mixes seven red varieties with a splash of Chardonnay) while the winery's Viognier—with a characteristic hint of tropical fruit—is also attracting a following. ★ Rising star

4020 Locust Lane, Beamsville, Ontario L0R 1B2
www.fieldingwines.com

Henry of Pelham Family Estate
Niagara Peninsula

One of a number of Canadian producers that have introduced sub-labels in recent years, Henry of Pelham enjoys a distinguished history. Its founders, the Speck family, have connections with Pelham Township extending back to 1794. Its wines have a similar dignity, flowing from vines cropped low to produce grapes yielding intense flavors. Accolades arrive regularly for its barrel-chested Baco Noir, not to mention its sparkling wines. Like many other Niagara wineries, it has also found success with Riesling and Chardonnay, which are part of a reserve tier that also includes a Cabernet Sauvignon/Merlot blend and a Pinot Noir.

1469 Pelham Rd, St. Catharines, Ontario L2R 6P7
www.henryofpelham.com

Hillebrand Niagara Peninsula

A destination winery complex points to Hillebrand's success at the hands of winemaker Jean-Laurent Groux, who picked up where predecessor Benoît Huchin left off. Huchin oversaw development of Trius, one of the winery's best-loved brands, while Groux, before his move to Stratus in 2004, diligently sought to improve the quality of the winery's production. This extended from the most affordable tiers to the expensive, single-vineyard Chardonnays and Rieslings that smack of aromatic tropical fruit. These small-lot wines have flourished with the 2005 declaration of Niagara sub-appellations. Dignified, but expressive of their fruit, under current winemaker Darryl Brooker, Hillebrand's wines continue to be reliable expressions of the Niagara terroir.

1249 Niagara Stone Rd, Niagara-on-the-Lake,
Ontario L0S 1J0; www.hillebrand.com

Inniskillin Niagara Niagara Peninsula

Donald Ziraldo and Karl Kaiser opened Inniskillin Niagara in 1975, Ontario's first winery since the end of Prohibition in 1927. Inniskillin, though not the first Ontario producer of Icewine (that honor went to

NIAGARA PENINSULA

Lake Ontario, the Niagara River, and the Niagara Escarpment dominate and demarcate the several subregions of Ontario's Niagara Peninsula. The escarpment gives its name to a regional appellation that runs from Grimsby in the west to St. Catharines, and contains three subregions. The escarpment reflects warmth pushed by breezes off Lake Ontario, and offers shelter from winds that sweep in from the southwest. Vineyards around Niagara-on-the-Lake, also the name of a regional appellation, occupy a flat terrain offering good exposure and soils that have given rise to four distinct subregions.

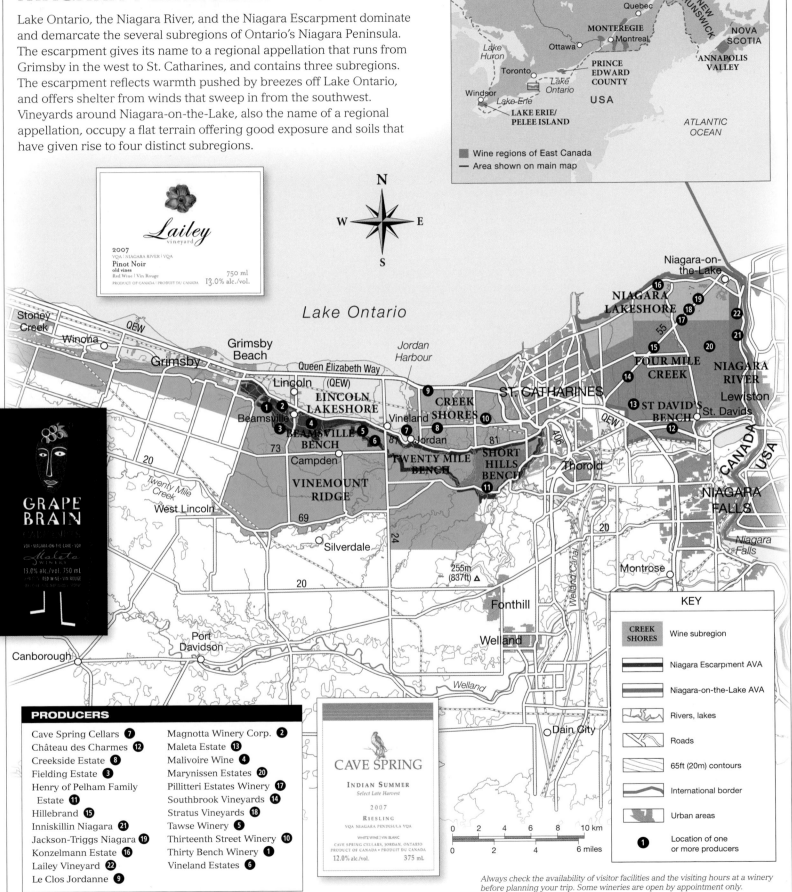

PRODUCERS

Cave Spring Cellars **7**
Château des Charmes **12**
Creekside Estate **8**
Fielding Estate **3**
Henry of Pelham Family Estate **11**
Hillebrand **15**
Inniskillin Niagara **21**
Jackson-Triggs Niagara **19**
Konzelmann Estate **16**
Lailey Vineyard **22**
Le Clos Jordanne **9**

Magnotta Winery Corp. **2**
Maleta Estate **13**
Malivoire Wine **4**
Marynissen Estates **20**
Pillitteri Estates Winery **17**
Southbrook Vineyards **14**
Stratus Vineyards **18**
Tawse Winery **5**
Thirteenth Street Winery **10**
Thirty Bench Winery **1**
Vineland Estates **6**

KEY

CREEK SHORES — Wine subregion
Niagara Escarpment AVA
Niagara-on-the-Lake AVA
Rivers, lakes
Roads
65ft (20m) contours
International border
Urban areas
1 — Location of one or more producers

Wine regions of East Canada
— Area shown on main map

Always check the availability of visitor facilities and the visiting hours at a winery before planning your trip. Some wineries are open by appointment only.

SOUTHBROOK

THE WINES OF THE POETICA SERIES EACH
FEATURE A POEM ON THE LABEL

Hillebrand Estates in 1983), scored the landmark victory for the product at Bordeaux's Vinexpo wine trade fair in 1991 when its 1989 Vidal Icewine took home the show's top award, the Grand Prix d'Honneur. Brought into the Vincor fold in 1995, Inniskillin has steadily expanded its production. Under the direction of current winemaker Bruce Nicholson (formerly of Vincor's Okanagan properties), Inniskillin is producing an evolving line of select-vineyard white wines including the award-winning 2007 Winemaker's Series Two Vineyards Riesling.

1499 Line 3, Niagara-on-the-Lake, Ontario L0S 1J0
www.inniskillin.com

Jackson-Triggs Niagara Niagara Peninsula
Winemaker Marco Piccoli believes in cold-soaking many of his white grapes at crush to better express the Niagara Peninsula's terroir. Barrel-aging is done judiciously, primarily for the Grand Reserve premium wines; the 2007 Grand Reserve Meritage (a white, Bordeaux-style blend) is aged in old barrels, while the 2007 Grand Reserve Chardonnay spent nine months in new French oak, giving it a subtle warmth. Piccoli's reds also show the influence of time in barrel. Jackson-Triggs's Icewines exhibit mandarin orange marmalade flavors, but a distinctive offering is the 2007 Grand Reserve Cabernet Franc Icewine, with its flavors of strawberry, dark chocolate and—as Piccoli points out—a Viennese *sukertorte*.

2145 Regional Rd 55, Niagara-on-the-Lake, Ontario L0S 1J0
www.jacksontriggswinery.com

Jost Vineyards Malagash Peninsula
Jost Vineyards sits on the north shore of Nova Scotia by the warm waters of the Northumberland Strait. Vineyards at the winery, and in the Annapolis and Gaspereau valleys, yield fruit for a representative sampling of Nova Scotia wines. Originally licensed in 1983, the winery opened to the public in 1986. L'Acadie Blanc, Nova Scotia's signature grape, has the mildness of Sauvignon Blanc but expresses itself richly in winemaker Hans Christian Jost's hands. Jost also oversees the production of a range of specialty products including fruit- and maple syrup-based wines.

48 Vintage Lane, Malagash, Nova Scotia B0K 1E0
www.jostwine.com

Konzelmann Estate Niagara Peninsula
The shores of Lake Ontario attracted Stuttgart's Herbert Konzelmann in 1984 because the local climate matched that of France's Alsace. The winery opened in 1986 and now produces more than 30 wines. Strong on fruit but with the distinctive minerality of the soils fringing Lake Ontario, wines such as the Pinot Blanc have garnered international attention. But Konzelmann's Icewines garner the most awards, and bear cellaring. Vidal produces a smooth Icewine, with raisin and dried apricot notes, that avoids the overpowering honeyed tones exhibited by many such wines.

1096 Lakeshore Rd, Niagara-on-the-Lake, Ontario L0S 1J0
www.konzelmann.ca

Lailey Vineyard Niagara Peninsula
Lailey Vineyard has acquired a reputation for its rich Chardonnays, but is also building a portfolio of respectable red wines including Pinot Noir and Cabernets Franc and Sauvignon. Underpinning the winemaking of

LE CLOS JORDANNE

LE CLOS JORDANNE'S CHARDONNAY
REFLECTS NIAGARA'S LAKESIDE TERROIR

Derek Barnett is the viticultural expertise of Donna Lailey, in 1991 the first woman to be named as Ontario's "Grape Queen." She oversees a vineyard established by her father-in-law, William Lailey, in the 1950s that hosts some of the oldest Chardonnay vines on the Niagara Peninsula. The winery launched in 1999 and now produces approximately 7,000 cases annually in an unassuming modernist building adjacent to the family vineyard.

15940 Niagara Parkway, Niagara on the Lake,
Ontario L0S 1J0; www.laileyvineyard.com

Le Clos Jordanne Niagara Peninsula
One of two ventures Vincor Canada has launched with French producers (in this case, the Boisset family), Le Clos Jordanne occupies a former nursery warehouse overlooking Lake Ontario. Despite high aspirations, its inaugural 2003 vintage was small due to cold weather that dramatically reduced yields. A small amount was released in 2006 with the much larger 2004 vintage. Since then, winemaker Thomas Bachelder has produced noteworthy wines including a Pinot Noir bearing a distinct Ontario tang characterized by hints of forest berries and lakeside limestone, and a 2005 Claystone Terrace Chardonnay with a winsome minerality and a touch of oak, which took top honors over wines from France and California in a competition at Montreal in June 2009. ★ **Rising star**

2540 South Service Rd, Jordan Station, Ontario L0R 1S0
www.leclosjordanne.com

Magnotta Winery Corp. Niagara Peninsula
A pioneer of sparkling Icewine, Magnotta has dubbed itself, "The Award Winning Winery," on account of having 3,000 awards to its credit—more than any other winery in Canada. A major producer of Icewine, it is also responsible for the widest selection of wines made in accordance with Ontario's Vintners' Quality Alliance standard—150 products, including the Amarone-style Enotrium, a blend of Merlot, Cabernet Franc, and Cabernet Sauvignon grapes. Chardonnay and Pinot Noir are also specialties, in keeping with the terroir of the Niagara Peninsula where it owns 180 acres (73ha).

4701 Ontario Street, Beamsville, Ontario L0R 1B4
www.magnotta.com

Maleta Estate Niagara Peninsula
Red wines are a strength of Maleta Estate winery in a sea of Riesling and Chardonnay. Its flagship Meritage combines Cabernet Sauvignon, Cabernet Franc, and Merlot grapes grown at its property in the Four Mile Creek sub-appellation below the Niagara Escarpment. Being relatively flat, the vineyards enjoy good sun exposure during the day and gradual cooling at night for steady maturation. Maleta has also won recognition for its sparkling wines and Icewine. With winemaker Arthur Harder, owner Daniel Pambianchi is building on founder Stan Maleta's early successes.

450 Queenston Rd, Niagara-on-the-Lake, Ontario L0S 1J0
www.maletawinery.com

Malivoire Wine Niagara Peninsula
A commitment to environmentally friendly growing practices has not hampered Malivoire's rise. It was during her tenure as winemaker at Malivoire that Ann Sperling was named Ontario Winemaker of the Year on

account of her work with its Chardonnay, Pinot Noir, and Old Vines Foch. Current winemaker Shiraz Mottiar continues to produce rich, well-rounded wines. Barrel aging—and in some cases, fermenting—of the Chardonnays offers the palate a treat like buttery baked pears (with a smack of spice). Small lots keep the wines in demand; ageability keeps them in the cellar.

4260 King St East, Beamsville, Ontario L0R 1B0
www.malivoirewineco.com

Marynissen Estates Niagara Peninsula
Patriarch John Marynissen's death in 2009 marked the end of an era in Ontario winemaking. Marynissen's wines built on a history of Niagara grape-growing dating back to 1953, and he is credited with introducing Cabernet Sauvignon to the Niagara Peninsula, and crafting ageable wines from the variety, too. The 2007 Solstice (an earthy blend of spicy Merlot, Syrah, and Cabernet Sauvignon) was served to the Prince of Wales in 2009, but is tipped to improve until 2018.

1209 Concession 1, Niagara-on-the-Lake, Ontario L0S 1J0
www.marynissen.com

Pillitteri Estates Winery Niagara Peninsula
Canada's largest estate Icewine producer, Pillitteri launched in 1993. Its Icewine production draws on grapes ranging from Vidal, Ontario's traditional Icewine grape, to more recent additions such as Sémillon and—in 2009 —Sauvignon Blanc. The wines express the concentrated flavors of the various varieties from which they are made, along with the distinctive honeyed quality that makes Icewine appealing. Among its notable Icewine vintages, 2004 and 2009 are particularly fine. In addition, Pillitteri also produces table wines from a variety of white and red grapes, including Cabernet Franc.

1696 Niagara Stone Rd, Niagara-on-the-Lake,
Ontario L0S 1J0; www.pillitteri.com

Southbrook Vineyards Niagara Peninsula
Sceptics of fruit wines might easily dismiss Southbrook Vineyards, which began life producing award-winning wine from berries that its farm north of Toronto could not sell. A move to the Niagara Peninsula in 2009 is repositioning it as a contender in the field of grape wineries, however. It attracted winemaker Ann Sperling from Malivoire Wine Co. in 2005, a year after she was named Ontario Winemaker of the Year. Sperling recently launched Poetica, a reserve tier of wines showcasing vintages from 1998 onward. Southbrook's owner, Bill Redelmeier, believes Poetica demonstrates "Niagara's ability to produce ageable wines." ★Rising star

581 Niagara Stone Rd, Niagara-on-the-Lake,
Ontario L0S 1J0; www.southbrook.com

Stratus Vineyards Niagara Peninsula
Stratus's contemporary winery and labels made it one of the hottest new wineries to launch on the Niagara Peninsula in 2004. Having poached winemaker Jean-Laurent Groux from Hillebrand Estates, Stratus has focused on premium blends. Its varietal wines typically fetch lower prices than the flagship Stratus Red and Stratus White blends, the simple names of which conceal the wines' sophistication as much as the modernist winery structure veils the equipment that makes it possible.

Though within sight of the much larger and no less contemporary Jackson-Triggs winery, Stratus has earned a reputation as a small producer seeking elegance rather than attention. ★Rising star

2059 Niagara Stone Rd, Niagara-on-the-Lake,
Ontario L0S 1J0; www.stratuswines.com

Tawse Winery Niagara Peninsula
There is a distinctive New World sweetness in the Rieslings from Tawse Winery, though owner Moray Tawse's inspiration comes from the Old World. Winemaker Deborah Paskus, who established Closson Chase in 2004, laid the foundation for Tawse. It now has France's Pascal Marchand, who oversaw preparations for nearby Le Clos Jordanne, Vincor's joint venture with the Boisset family. Tawse has racked up a number of awards since opening in 2005, including Ontario Winery of the Year. In addition to Riesling, its production includes Cabernet Franc and Pinot Noir.

3955 Cherry Ave, Vineland, Ontario L0R 2C0
www.tawsewinery.ca

Thirteenth Street Winery Niagara Peninsula
When it is over-cropped, Gamay Noir can produce a lighter wine with some mineral character but little complexity. The dark expressions Thirteenth Street produces are somewhat more serious, however (red fruit and earthiness come to mind), and the estate is often described as Canada's best producer of Gamay. Thirteenth Street regularly wins awards for its sparkling wines, which at 3,600 to 4,800 bottles are among its largest production lots. Less than 200 cases are made of most of its wines, so demand regularly outstrips supply.

1776 Fourth Ave, St Catharines, Ontario L2R 6P9
www.13thstreetwinery.com

Thirty Bench Winery Niagara Peninsula
Started in 1993, Thirty Bench was sold to Andrew Peller in 2005. Situated on the Beamsville Bench, it focuses on small-lot wines, mirroring its parent company's efforts with the Sandhill winery in British Columbia. Thirty Bench's Riesling wines are the jewels in a crown that also includes red wines typical of the minerally terroir overlooking Lake Ontario. The delicacy of the single-vineyard Rieslings suggests a capacity to surprise as the wines age.

4281 Mountainview Rd, Beamsville, Ontario L0R 1B0
www.thirtybench.com

Vineland Estates Niagara Peninsula
Allan and Brian Schmidt have close ties to Canada's wine business. The family has been involved in grape-growing for at least three generations now, and Schmidt Senior is now a viticulture consultant whose experience includes setting up Sumac Ridge. The brothers have been making their own name with vineyards on the Niagara Escarpment, where solid acid levels help give verve to Rieslings redolent of apple and pear, and with hints of citrus. The red fruit flavors of Vineland's Cabernet Francs are balanced by crisp aromatics garnered in the cool-climate Niagara region.

3620 Moyer Rd, Vineland, Ontario L0R 2C0
www.vineland.com

DONALD ZIRALDO

Ziraldo Icewine might not have attracted much notice when it debuted in November 2009 had it not been for the people behind it—Donald Ziraldo and Karl Kaiser, founders of Inniskillin Niagara. The pair helped establish Icewine as Ontario's leading wine export, and the new wine reflects both the industry's progress over the past 30 years and the entrepreneurial spirit and commitment to excellence underpinning Ziraldo's career. A founding chair of Ontario's Vintners' Quality Alliance, Ziraldo believes Italy's pride in local products (his parents were from Friuli) is something Canada should emulate. A case in point is Icewine, which people easily associate with a country often envisioned as snow-bound. "We were able to take a very old German tradition—making ice wine as a holiday beverage—and create a Canadian icon primarily because we are 'blessed' with cold winters," he says. The beverage quickly became Canada's signature product, and a premium-tier calling card.

MEXICO

Aside from sun, surf, and sand, nothing comes easily to Mexico, and wine is no exception. While wine grapes have been grown across this tortured land since the 16th century, and while the nation claims the oldest winery in the Americas, Mexico's wine history has been erratic. As a consequence, the nation's wine culture remains small, scattered, and struggling for identity. But that is changing, albeit slowly. Growers are settling into enclaves somewhat secure from the country's tropical heat and humidity. And winemakers are recognizing that their reputation will be built more with Tempranillo, Grenache, and other warm-climate varieties than with such cool-climate strains as Chardonnay and Pinot Noir.

Major grapes

Reds

Cabernet Sauvignon

Grenache

Merlot

Mourvèdre

Nebbiolo

Petite Sirah

Syrah (Shiraz)

Tempranillo

Zinfandel

 Whites

Chardonnay

Viognier

Vintages

2009
A warm, dry winter and mild summer led to austere wines.

2008
The whites are soft, and the Grenache and Nebbiolo are fresh and balanced.

2007
A year for ripe, perfumed Grenache, but the whites are often marred by over-ripeness.

2006
A strong year for Cabernet Sauvignon, with strong, persistent Grenache.

2005
An outstanding year for Cabernet Sauvignon, Chardonnay, and Merlot.

2004
A year for luscious Merlots, complex Rhône varieties, and beefy Nebbiolo.

While vineyards are being developed in such promising mainland regions as the Zacatecas Valley and the Parras Valley, Mexico's wine trade is concentrated largely in and about the Guadalupe Valley at the northern reaches of the parched Baja Peninsula along the country's west coast.

Most historians trace the region's wine heritage to industrious Jesuit friars who established a mission in 1697 at Loreto, far down the east side of the peninsula. But Guadalupe Valley's rise as Mexico's premier appellation did not in fact start until 1905, with the immigration of a group of Russian Molokans, pacifists who fled the mother country rather than fight for the czar.

Though most of the Molokans subsequently moved out of the valley, they left behind vineyards, cellars, and the lessons they had learned about growing wine, to provide the foundation for the area's current wine renaissance.

The Guadalupe Valley's wine trade has developed and diversified more by intuition than plan. Therefore, no one knows how much of the valley is planted to wine grapes, with informed estimates running from 21,000 acres (8,500ha) to 42,000 acres (17,000ha), with most settling on around 30,000 acres (12,000ha). Neither is there a consensus on how many wineries call the valley home—estimates run from 30 to 50.

Where there is universal agreement, however, is in the contention that the Guadalupe Valley and a couple of neighboring areas produce between 80% and 90% of all the wine made in Mexico— a figure that currently stands at a little more than 22 million gallons (1 million hectoliters) a year.

At about 14 miles (7km) long and 5 miles (3km) wide, the Guadalupe Valley is a gently rolling terrain bracketed with abrupt hills. Vineyards benefit by a notch in the coastal range that allows Pacific breezes to cool vineyards. In the early days, grapes were used largely for brandy, and it is only during the past 50 years that the industry has moved more into premium table wines. Consequently, there is still a great deal of experimentation among growers looking to find the most expressive match of variety and site. The Molokans had early success with Grenache, which continues to be seen as one of the area's more promising grapes. Others are Tempranillo, Petite Sirah, and Syrah, though some producers have had surprising, if uneven, success with Cabernet Sauvignon, Chardonnay, Viognier, and Merlot.

While the valley is home to a few corporate producers, most wineries release no more than a couple of thousand cases a year, some just a few hundred. Most welcome visitors graciously, if casually, though reservations are recommended or required, and tasting fees can be high.

Two other cautionary notes: the valley has few formally trained and seasoned winemakers, and wines can be coarse, though the proportion of refined releases is rising. Secondly, several wineries are far back on washboard roads best traversed by the patient driver of a 4x4 vehicle.

Droughts, and the diversion of much of the valley's water, threaten to brake the region's momentum. But if those matters can be resolved, Mexico just might become known for its wine as well as its *cerveza*, tequila, and mezcal.

Adobe Guadalupe Guadalupe Valley

As they search for the best pairing of grape and place, most wineries in the Guadalupe Valley are content to focus largely on the release of individual varietal wines. Confident Adobe Guadalupe, on the other hand, went straight for the complexity of blends. All five of the blends produced here are named after angels, a reflection of the spirituality that prompted Adobe Guadalupe's founders, Donald and Tru Miller, to establish the winery a decade ago. The Miguel is a profound Tempranillo tempered with Grenache and Cabernet Sauvignon, while the Kerubiel is a hearty yet graceful mix of six Rhône Valley varieties. Also well worth looking out for is Adobe Guadalupe's well made Oaxacan mezcal, which goes by the rather apt name of Lucifer. ★ **Rising star**

Parce A-1 S/N, Ruta de Guadalupe, Francisco Zarco, Guadalupe Valley, Municipio de Ensenada, BC
www.adobeguadalupe.com

Casa Madero Parras Valley

Casa Madero can trace its lineage all the way back to 1597 and the founding of a land-grant hacienda with vineyard in the Parras Valley in the state of Coahuila. That gives Madero the right to claim the title of oldest winery in the Americas, although commercial production has not been continuous throughout that time. The Parras Valley's high elevation and fertile soils help yield aromatic and well-rounded wines from Cabernet Sauvignon, Chardonnay, and Shiraz under the Casa Madero and Casa Grande labels. While the rest of the Casa Madero line-up may not be quite as impressive, the appealing pricing is helping to boost sales.

Emilio Carranza Sur 732, Monterrey Parras de la Fuente, Hacienda San Lorenzo, Parras, Coahuila
www.madero.com.mx

Casa de Piedra Guadalupe Valley

In 1997, winemaker Hugo D'Acosta who—had trained in France, Italy, and California—teamed up with his brother, architect Alejandro D'Acosta, to establish Casa de Piedra in the Guadalupe Valley. In the years since then, the brothers have emerged as the valley's enological godfathers, working on a huge variety of projects. As well as the Casa de Piedra project, the brothers have variously spent their time consulting for several other winemakers, founding a winemaking school, and creating a second winery, Paralelo, where the towering poured-adobe walls are inset with the tread of old tractor tires found on the property. Hugo D'Acosta's virtually flawless winemaking is best represented by the racy qualities and citrus flavors of his unoaked Chardonnay at Casa de Piedra. But keep an eye, too, on the Bordeaux-inspired blends that are starting to emerge from Paralelo.

Km 93.5 Mexico Highway 3, San Antonio de las Minas
www.vinoscasadepiedra.com

Monte Xanic Guadalupe Valley

The name Monte Xanic derives from a mix of the Spanish and Cora Indian languages, translating roughly as "the mountain of the flower that blooms after the first rain." But the inspiration for the winemaking philosophy at this Guadalupe Valley winery is strictly French. Since the

VINEDOS MALAGON
VINEDOS MALAGON'S EQUUA IS A BLEND OF GRENACHE AND PETITE SIRAH AGED FOR SEVEN MONTHS IN NEW OAK

CASA MADERO
CASA MADERO'S OAK-AGED CHARDONNAY IS FULL OF TROPICAL FRUIT FLAVORS

winery was established in 1987, winemaker Hans Backhoff and his four partners have consistently shown, in vintage after vintage, that refined Cabernet Sauvignon and Merlot can indeed be made in the desert—and at prices that make them competitive with imported wines. While the Cabernet Sauvignons and Merlots are fleshy and firm, and the Chardonnay is quite startling in its richness, many of the other wines in the extensive Monte Xanic portfolio are sound but somewhat unexciting by comparison.

Calle Principal a Ejido Francisco Zarco, Valle de Guadalupe, Ensenada, BC; www.montexanic.com.mx

Viñedos Malagon Guadalupe Valley

A latter-day hacienda, complete with inn, church, and winery, Viñedos Malagon occupies one of the larger and more historic stretches of land in the Guadalupe Valley. Grenache has been promising to make quality wine in this region for more than a century. And at Viñedos Malagon the variety is finally living up to its potential in such wines as the smooth and spicy Equua Cosecha, and the earthy yet fresh Malagon Family Reserva, where it plays a strong supporting role to Cabernet Sauvignon in the blend. ★ **Rising star**

Calle Sexta 75, Francisco Zarco, Municipio de Ensenada, BC 22750; www.vinedosmalagon.com

Vinisterra Guadalupe Valley

After establishing his vineyard at San Antonio de las Minas in the Guadalupe Valley in 2000, Vinisterra's Guillermo Rodriguez relied heavily on Merlot. However, in the years since then, Vinisterra has evolved in a completely different direction, becoming instead the most promising producer of Tempranillo in the Guadalupe Valley. At the head of the pack of wines produced at Vinisterra is the intense yet friendly Tempranillo bottled under the Macouzet label. A concentrated and balanced blend of Syrah and Mourvèdre is also well worth seeking out. Vinisterra occupies a handsome red-brick building flanked by vineyards populated by fattening chickens. As for the Merlot, it would probably be better off being grafted to the more promising varieties. ★ **Rising star**

Calle Sexta 984-3, Zona Centro, Ensenada, BC 22800
www.vinisterra.com

Vinos LA Cetto Guadalupe Valley

Vinos LA Cetto is Mexico's largest and most progressive winery, producing some 900,000 cases every year. Its position as market leader means it is saddled with the burden of expectation, and also subject to questions about whether a producer of this kind of scale can ever be of notable quality. That latter question is especially pertinent given the winery's youth (it was founded in 1974) and its challenging location (Baja California Norte). However, thanks to the patience, diligence, and adventurous spirit of Camillo Magoni, Cetto's winemaker since its inception, much of the red wine production is indeed notable, particularly the Cabernet Sauvignon, Petite Sirah, Zinfandel, and, as unlikely as it seems, Nebbiolo. Aside from a fresh and lithe Viognier, on the other hand, the whites tend to be one-dimensional and somewhat abrupt in the finish.

Km 73.5 Carretera Tecate El Sauzal, Valle de Guadalupe, BC; www.lacetto.com

Though few recognize it as such, South America is the wine world's most prolific (and, arguably, historic) producer outside Europe.

European vine stock was introduced into South America in the early 1530s, shortly after its arrival in Mexico but long before the likes of South Africa and Oceania. Rooting the vine in South America's rugged expanses was undertaken ostensibly for religious reasons, but also for basic sustenance and entertainment. It was also, more darkly, a way of asserting long-term proprietorial land rights. Nowadays, this colorful, complicated continent is embracing and expressing its cultural roots in ever more confident fashion, and one of the most vivid expressions of this trend is its wines.

Argentina is the world's fifth-largest wine producer, a land of passionate producers and charismatic wines. Traditionally, a thirsty domestic market has accounted for the lion's share of production. Today, a focus on exports has led to huge improvements in quality and the country is starting to deliver on its enormous potential.

Chile may be slender in stature, but it is home to some dizzying geographical diversity and an efficient, market-oriented workforce. It delivers some of the world's best value everyday bottles as well as ever more challenging, terroir-driven wines of depth and elegance.

Brazil is the continent's rising force, a populous and increasingly wealthy nation with a growing taste for, and ambition to produce, wine. Historically a specialist in sparkling wine, regions such as Santa Catarina and São Francisco are now making quality still wines.

Elsewhere in South America, Uruguay is a substantial producer and consumer of wines, with often family-based firms making characterful, fresh-flavored wines. Peru, Venezuela, and Ecuador all make wine, some of it delightful, reinforcing the value and potential of the noble vine in this protean continent.

SOUTH AMERICA

CHILE

Chile is an extraordinary country. This thin slip of a nation clings to the southwest coastline of South America, stretching across 2,670 miles (4,300km) yet averaging a spindly 112 miles (180km) across. Its northern extremities are sun-blasted, desiccated desert; its southern tip disintegrates into icy Antarctic waters. The towering, petrified wall of the Andes forms its eastern border; the chilly, vast Pacific Ocean marks its western edge. In the midst of this natural cacophony can be found an absorbing, diverse nation whose wine industry is in the throes of a profound and exhilarating change. What was once widely considered a safe yet uninspiring producer is fast becoming one of the wine world's hottest properties. And there is more to come.

Major grapes

 Reds

Cabernet Sauvignon

Carmenère

Malbec

Merlot

Pinot Noir

Syrah

 Whites

Chardonnay

Gewurztraminer

Riesling

Sauvignon Blanc

Viognier

Vintages

2009
Good if variable: a hot, dry, high-yielding year.

2008
Moderate to good: warm summer; pleasant wines if less intense than the 2007s.

2007
Outstanding, especially for reds; great balance.

2006
Moderate to good: fresh styles, successful whites.

2005
Very good: long season gave complex wines, best are reds.

2004
Moderate to good: uneven vintage, best are ripe and intense.

Chile's varied geography is the key to its viticultural promise. Once, the majority of wines were produced in the flat, fertile, well-watered heartlands of the Central Valley, with predictably bland results. In the last decade though, ambitious producers have pushed back the country's wine limits at all compass points, searching out challenging terrains to make increasingly individual and rewarding wines. The process remains ongoing but is already proving its worth; helping to redefine the country's vinous output in the minds of wine-lovers the world over from everyday staple to fine wine.

San Antonio, Bío Bío, Elqui, Limarí, Malleco, and Casablanca are all previously little-known regions that have entered the lexicon of fine Chilean wine in recent years, with more certain to follow. What all these areas have in common are forward-thinking, quality-led producers, poorer soils, and cooler conditions than the Central Valley norm—often hillsides and varied exposures—all of which imbues the wines with complexity.

This movement is not restricted to the so-called new regions: traditional areas like Maipo, Aconcagua, Colchagua, and Maule are also busy repositioning themselves. Much of this is the result of painstakingly detailed research into soils, roots, plants, weather, and fruit, which is now having a marked impact on wine quality and diversity.

Commercial success is the real bedrock on which Chile's wine industry has been able to grow, however. In 1990, as the country returned to democracy after a period of military rule, 160,000 acres (65,000ha) of vines yielded 92m gallons (350m liters) of wine, 12% of which was exported. By 2007, the national wine vineyard stood at more than 290,350 acres (117,500ha); by 2008, exports represented 68% of production; by 2009, Chile was making more than 264m gallons (1bn liters) of wine. Indications are that the growth will continue.

Chilean wine has come a long way since the mid-16th century when Spanish conquistadors and missionaries planted the first vines. The historical legacy of this era can be found in traditional areas of Chile where País (Mission) grapes are made into crude *chicha* (a homemade fermented drink).

These days, however, the dominant variety in Chile's vineyards is Cabernet Sauvignon, which accounts for more than a third of the total planted area. Carmenère, the lost variety of Bordeaux which gives that distinctive peppery edge to so-called Chilean "Merlot," is increasingly being fêted in its own right. Chardonnay is coming into its own in areas such as Limarí and Leyda. Syrah, Sauvignon Blanc, and Pinot Noir are some of Chile's most exciting varieties, with increasingly diverse, elegant, and complex styles emerging. Old-vine Carignan and Malbec in the deep south are enjoying a delicious renaissance, while the likes of Riesling, Petit Verdot, and Gewurztraminer are all starting to shine.

Appellation reform, a burgeoning boutique movement, uptake of organic and biodynamic cultivation, steadily increasing vine age, enhanced environmental awareness, a new generation of talented winemakers: all this points to a bright future for Chile's wine industry. Whatever the end result, it promises to be a fascinating journey.

Almaviva Maipo

Arguably Chile's most high-profile joint venture, Almaviva was formed in 1996 by Concha y Toro and the Rothschilds of Bordeaux first growth Mouton. The project was built around a prime section of Concha vineyard on the gravel-loams of Puente Alto. The first vintage was 1996 and since then, much in the periphery has changed—winemakers, management structure (the winery is now effectively independent), plus a new system of underground irrigation). Happily, the wine itself has remained largely untouched: a polished, tight-knit, yet spicy blend of Cabernet Sauvignon, Cabernet Franc, and Carmenère that ages elegantly and is unquestionably one of the country's finest (and priciest) reds.

Avenida Santa Rosa 821, Paradero 45, Puente Alto, Santiago
www.almavivawinery.com

Altaïr Vineyards and Winery Cachapoal

Altaïr first breathed life in 2001 as a joint venture between Château Dassault of Bordeaux and San Pedro, formed around a prime 178 acre (72ha) vineyard in the Cachapoal foothills near Totihue. From 2007, San Pedro took sole charge. The vineyards, at 2,000–2,600ft (600–800m) altitude and mainly planted to Cabernet Sauvignon, make ageworthy, savory wines. Talented winemaker Ana María Cumsille identifies Syrah as a bright prospect but stresses the importance of Cabernet to both wines: Sideral and top wine Altaïr. Eschew the awkward first bottlings (2002) and savor the refined 2003 Sideral and focused, layered 2005 Altaïr. ★ **Rising star**

Avenida Vitacura 4380, Piso 3, Vitacura, Santiago
www.altairwines.com

Amayna (Viña Garcés Silva) San Antonio

The affluent Garcés Silva family originally acquired their 1,730 acre (700ha) estate in coastal Leyda, San Antonio for livestock (one of many business interests). But vines were planted in 1999 and the first commercial release (2003) received critical acclaim. This was largely due to the thrillingly uncompromising nature of the Sauvignon Blanc: an intensely structured, grapefruit-and-fennel scented white that spoke eloquently of its origins. This remains the portfolio stand-out, though the succulent oaked version, fast-improving Chardonnay, and new Syrah are all well worth trying.

Fundo San Andres de Huinca, Camino Rinconada de San Juan, Leyda, San Antonio; www.vgs.cl

Antiyal Maipo

Compost piles, wildlife (including llamas), and good humor abound at the Espinoza family wine operation. Well-known winemaker Alvaro Espinoza, who helped pioneer organic and biodynamic wine in Chile, started his own project in 1998, using grapes from his garden and his parents' farm, and making the 3,000-bottle production in his garage. A decade on, Antiyal has more vineyards, a new winery, another wine (Kuyen), and makes 19,000 bottles. Both organic and biodynamic cultivation methods are practiced. Kuyen is a pleasantly peppery, meaty red while Antiyal has a joyously visceral, spicy appeal all of its own.

Padre Hurtado 68, Paine, Santiago
www.antiyal.com

ANTIYAL
A BOUTIQUE PRODUCER USING BIODYNAMIC AND ORGANIC METHODS

ALMAVIVA
UNQUESTIONABLY ONE OF CHILE'S FINEST—AND PRICIEST—WINES

Aquitania Maipo

The self-styled "four musketeers" behind this project are respected Chilean winemaker Felipe de Solminihac, champagne man Ghislain de Montgolfier, and well known Bordeaux winemakers Paul Pontallier and Bruno Prats. Formed in 1990, this was a pioneering project in its time: the first stand-alone terroir winery in Chile's modern era. Yet the wines never quite lived up to expectations so, in 2001, changes were made, the wines re-branded, and grapes bought in from further afield in Maipo. The reds are now improved: Agapanto has a simple, minty style and Lazuli is structured yet restrained. The steely, rich SoldeSol Chardonnay, grown in southerly Malleco, is superb.

Avenida Consistorial 5090, Peñalolén, Santiago
www.aquitania.cl

Casablanca Casablanca

This coastal producer blazed a trail for cool-climate Chilean Sauvignon Blanc in the mid-1990s, but then lost its direction. Things are now improving under the leadership of energetic winemaker Andrés Caballero and the wines are once more reflecting a sense of risk and adventure. It is with Casablanca fruit that this winery is at its most exciting—try the vivid Sauvignon Blanc and peppery Syrah in the rewarding Nimbus range.

Rodrido de Araya 1431, Macul, Santiago
www.casablancawinery.com

Casa Marin San Antonio

Everything about Casa Marin is a force of nature, from its unique terroir to its fiercely individual wines via its charismatic and charming owner, Mariluz Marín. Set in rolling hills 2½ miles (4km) from the chilly Pacific Ocean, this artisan winery built its name on intense, spicy, and structured Sauvignon Blancs: Laurel has a light, charming style, Cipreses is wilder and more challenging. Pinot Noirs tend to be rich and toasty in style, while the succulent, deftly oaked Sauvignon Gris, vibrant and arresting Riesling, and beautifully meaty Syrah are all wonderful creations. Recently the wines have taken on more restraint and elegance—a good thing provided that the scintillating individuality is preserved at all costs.

Lo Abarca, Valle de San Antonio
www.casamarin.cl

Casas del Bosque Casablanca

The Cuneo family have made the transition from department store owners to successful winery proprietors with remarkable ease. Since its first, largely indifferent bottlings in the 1990s, Casas del Bosque has improved quickly and efficiently, becoming one of Casablanca's stand-out producers. A prime 605 acre (245ha) site in western Casablanca, along with a talented winemaking team, fashion intense Sauvignon Blanc and stylish, savory Syrah. There is excellent value at all levels. Visitor facilities include tours, tastings, a shop, and a restaurant named "Tanino."

Hijuela 2 Ex Fundo, Santa Rosa, Casablanca
www.casasdelbosque.cl

Concha y Toro Maipo

With a winery as historic, influential, and diverse as Concha y Toro, it is difficult to know where to start. Chile's biggest producer is also one of its best, achieving

CHILE

Chile's wine map is inevitably a long, thin affair that delightfully resists all attempts to constrain it within the boundaries of the printed page. Such is Chile's anarchic geography. The country is divided into 13 political regions running north to south, whose boundaries provide the rough framework for the wine regions (or "valleys"). This runs contrary to good wine sense, because in Chile the north-south axis counts far less in climatic terms than the east-west axis, which brings into account the influence of the chilly Pacific Ocean (west) and the vertiginous Andes Mountains (east). Within all regions, there is considerable and ever-increasing vinous diversity.

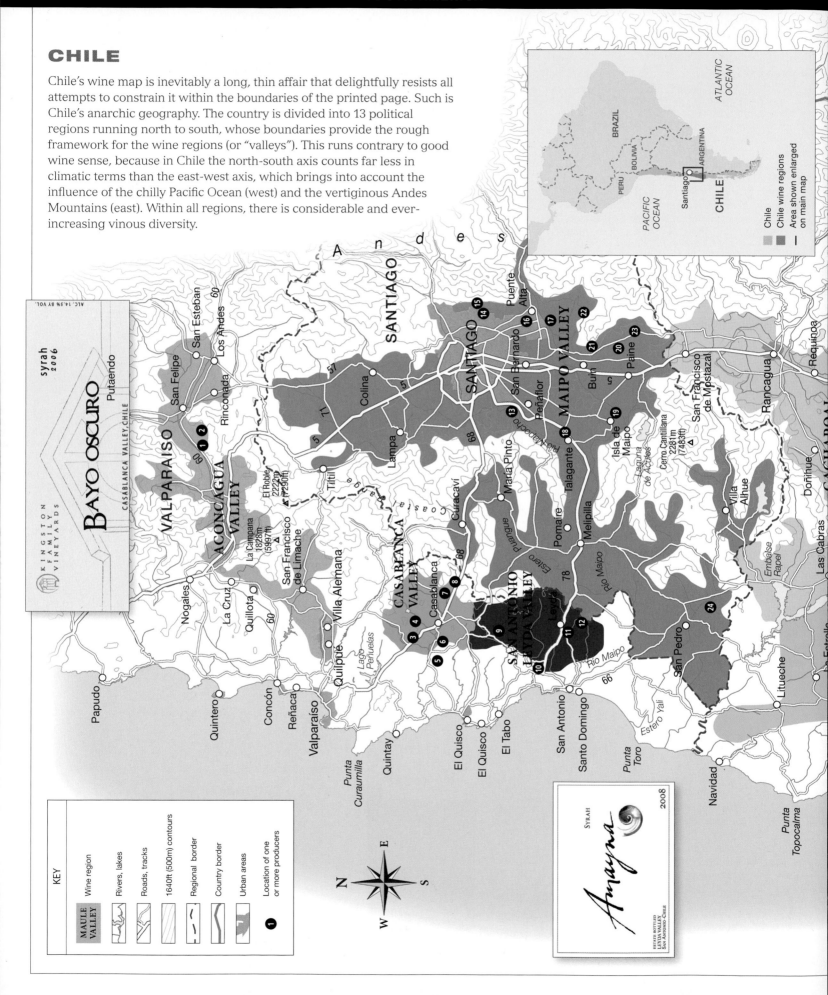

ALC. 14.5% BY VOL.

syrah
2006

KINGSTON
FAMILY
VINEYARDS

BAYO OSCURO

Putaendo

CASABLANCA VALLEY, CHILE

SYRAH

Amayna

2008

ESTATE BOTTLED
LEYDA VALLEY
SAN ANTONIO-CHILE

KEY

MAULE VALLEY   Wine region

Rivers, lakes

Roads, tracks

1640ft (500m) contours

Regional border

Country border

Urban areas

1   Location of one or more producers

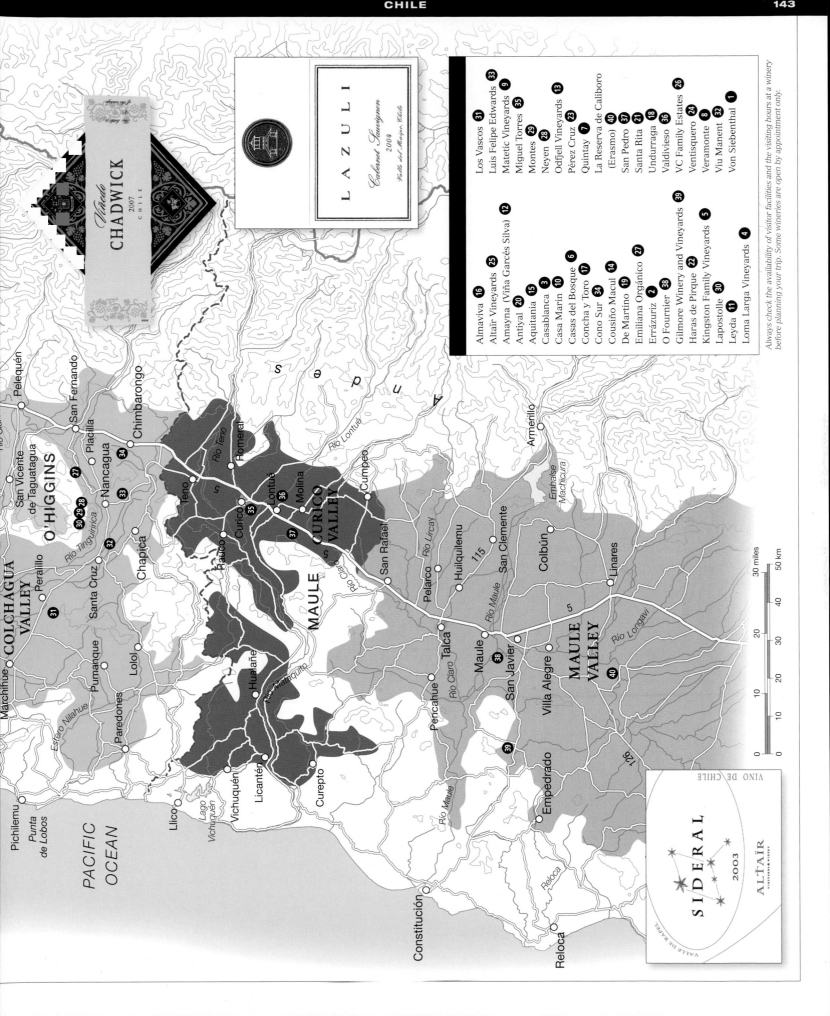

Always check the availability of visitor facilities and the visiting hours at a winery before planning your trip. Some wineries are open by appointment only.

Almaviva 16
Altaïr Vineyards 25
Amayna (Viña Garcés Silva) 12
Antiyal 20
Aquitania 15
Casablanca 3
Casa Marín 10
Casas del Bosque 6
Concha y Toro 17
Cono Sur 34
Cousiño Macul 14
De Martino 19
Emiliana Orgánico 27
Errázuriz 2
O Fournier 38
Gilmore Winery and Vineyards 39
Haras de Pirque 22
Kingston Family Vineyards 5
Lapostolle 30
Leyda 11
Loma Larga Vineyards 4

Los Vascos 31
Luis Felipe Edwards 33
Matetic Vineyards 9
Miguel Torres 35
Montes 29
Neyen 28
Odfjell Vineyards 13
Pérez Cruz 23
Quintay 7
La Reserva de Caliboro (Erasmo) 40
San Pedro 37
Santa Rita 21
Undurraga 18
Valdivieso 36
VC Family Estates 26
Ventisquero 24
Veramonte 8
Viu Manent 32
Von Siebenthal 1

CONO SUR
"SUPER" WINEMAKER ADOLFO HURTADO IS
PARTICULARLY ADEPT WITH WHITES

consistently high quality not just with stand-out icons like Don Melchor and Almaviva but also with excellent value lines Frontera, Casillero del Diablo, and Marqués. New venture Maycas de Limarí is showing outstanding promise with its tangy Chardonnay and spicy Syrah. Marcelo Papa, Enrique Tirado, and Ignacio Recabarren are some of Chile's finest winemakers. Concha's wines have made a lot of friends, not just for itself, but for Chile.

Avenida Virginia Subercaseaux 210, Pirque, Santiago
www.conchaytoro.com

Cono Sur Colchagua

Why is Cono Sur one of Chile's best wineries? Simple: it unites one of the country's top winemakers (Adolfo Hurtado: catchphrase, "super") with excellent vineyards and the solid backing of parent company Concha y Toro. Since its inception in 1993, Cono Sur has blazed trails with environmentally friendly production, branded wine (Isla Negra), screwcaps, and Pinot Noir. On the latter, Hurtado has worked with Burgundian Martin Prieur to introduce complexity and elegance to the wines: top bottling Ocio is outstanding. Hurtado is one of Chile's most accomplished white wine makers, testament to which are the superb 20 Barrels Chardonnay and Sauvignon Blanc. What's more, the best is yet to come.

Chimbarongo, Rapel Valley
www.conosur.com

Cousiño Macul Maipo

This venerable Chilean producer was founded in 1856 by industrialist Matías Cousiño in an area where the conquistadors first planted vines in the 1500s. French vine stock and expertise laid the foundations for many successful years but by the late 1990s, a lack of dynamism and Santiago's urban sprawl threatened the winery's existence. The sixth-generation owners sold much of the vineyard in Macul and set up a new base further south in Buin. The wines are now more modern and fruit-forward, but the best, including Finis Terrae and icon Lota, retain the winery's hallmark structure and sophistication.

Quilin 7100, Penalolen, Santiago
www.cousinomacul.cl

De Martino Maipo

"Reinventing Chile" is an ambitious motto for any winery, but with De Martino, it rings true. The cash flow from an uninspiring but lucrative bulk wine and juice business gives visionary winemaker Marcelo Retamal freedom to roam. And boy does he get around. Retamal has been a prime mover in pushing back the limits of Chilean wine, bringing the concept of terroir to the fore and making ground-breaking wines all over the country. Structured Chardonnay from Limarí, brooding Syrah from Choapa, ferruginous old-vine Malbec and Carignan from Maule: De Martino's Single Vineyard range is a delicious education. Carmenère is also a specialty. But be warned: these are not wines for the faint-hearted.

Manuel Rodríguez 229, Isla de Maipo
www.demartino.cl

Emiliana Orgánico Colchagua

Visiting Emiliana Orgánico's Los Robles estate is not just about tasting wine. You meet the animals. You witness the homeopathic remedies stewing. You bask in the sheer vitality of it all. But when you do taste the wines, you're rarely disappointed: this is an excellent range, from the entry-level Adobe via the reliable Novas up to the expansive Coyam and dense G. This offshoot of parent winery Emiliana (itself a subsidiary of Concha y Toro) has been a great success since it was launched in 1998 and now counts over 2,470 acres (1,000ha) of vineyards managed under organic and biodynamic methods.

Nueva Tajamar 481 Torre Sur. 701, Las Condes, Santiago
www.emiliana.cl

Errázuriz Aconcagua

Resting on laurels is not in this producer's vocabulary. Errázuriz is an historic yet forward-looking producer, one of Chile's finest, pioneering, among other things, organics, biodynamics, joint ventures, light-weighting, wild ferments, Syrah, hillside planting, and coastal Aconcagua. A striking new winery in Panquehue marks another step forward for this high-achieving enterprise. The range is diverse and rewarding. Also part of this perennially impressive stable are the icon projects Viñedo Chadwick (a structured Cabernet Sauvignon from Puente Alto) and Seña, a characterful Bordeaux blend now sourced exclusively from a biodynamically farmed vineyard in central Aconcagua.

Avenida Antofagasta, Panquehue, V Region
www.errazuriz.com

Falernia Elqui

The Elqui Valley is a blustery, pristine part of Chile where hippies, winemakers, and astronomers rub shoulders under clear blue skies. Wine is a newcomer to this scenic northern region, which is traditionally fruit and brandy-producing country. Falernia is the winery that put it on the wine-lover's map, with its daring and beautiful Syrahs, all perfumed florality and meaty, peppery, black olive savoriness. High-altitude Pedro Jimenez and semi-dried Carmenère are further USPs.

Ruta 41, Km 46, Casilla 8 Vicuña, IV Region
www.falernia.com

O Fournier Maule & San Antonio

This is the latest addition to the O Fournier portfolio after Ribera del Duero and Mendoza. José Manuel Ortega spent three years scouring Chile's best terroirs and, in 2007, settled on western Maule for reds and Lo Abarca (San Antonio) for whites. New wineries are planned in both locations but, meanwhile, the wines are already impressive. Urban delivers solid value with crunchy, refreshing reds and zippy whites, while Centauri comprises expressive and intense wines. Top reds are structured and polished. ★ **Rising star**

Camino Constitución, Km 20, San Javier, Talca
www.ofournier.com

Gillmore Winery and Vineyards Maule

Gillmore is all about personality. In the first instance, the careering, prodigious mind of winemaker (and brewer) extraordinaire Andrés Sánchez and the bright talent of his wife, viticulturist Daniella Gillmore. Then there are the wines: made from dry-farmed vines in Loncomilla, coastal Maule, typically with a fresh, almost northern Italian firmness and aging capacity. Cabernets Sauvignon and Franc excel. These are wines with a real sense of

GILLMORE
FRESH AND AGEWORTHY WINES FROM
DRY-FARMED VINES IN COASTAL MAULE

individuality and Chilean character. The impressive onsite accommodation and a menagerie make visitors welcome to this unique spot. ★**Rising star**

Camino a Constitución Km 20, San Javier
www.gillmore.cl

Haras de Pirque Maipo

A striking horseshoe-shaped winery tucked into a hilly amphitheater overlooking a panorama of vines and thoroughbred horse paddocks: such is the impressive scene at Haras de Pirque. Suave father-and-son team Eduardo and Eduardo Matte own and run this winery in the high Pirque subzone of Maipo. All wines are estate grown, the vineyard having been established in 1992. The wines walk a tightrope between leafy under-ripeness and raisined alcoholic excess. Only some succeed; pick of the bunch is Albis, a rich, mint-flecked Cabernet/Carmenère blend made in partnership with Italy's Piero Antinori.

Camino San Vicente, Sector Macul, Pirque, Casilla 247
Correo Pirque; www.harasdepirque.com

Kingston Family Vineyards Casablanca

Michigan-born Carl John Kingston came to Chile in the 1900s searching for gold and bought a 7,410 acre (3,000ha) farm in coastal Casablanca. The estate is now paying handsome returns in fruit and wine: Kingston sells 90% of its grapes and vinifies small amounts of rich Sauvignon Blanc, spicy Pinot Noir and savory Syrah from its rolling 200 acre (80ha) vineyard 9 miles (15km) from the coast. The Syrah steals the show: top wine Bayo Oscuro is dense yet lifted and refined. ★**Rising star**

No visitor facilities
www.kingstonvineyards.com

Lapostolle Colchagua

French ambition meets Chilean reality at Lapostolle, with intriguing results. Owned by the Marnier Lapostolle family, the winery has exclusive Chilean rights to consultant Michel Rolland. The heart of the operation is Apalta (Colchagua), where old, dry-farmed vines and a stunning $10m winery combine to make icon Clos Apalta, a heady, perfumed, expansive red blend. Cuvée Alexandre is a dependable range, its reds showcasing the winery's hallmark clean, ripe-fruited, oak-matured style (the Apalta Merlot performs particularly well). Whites are less successful. All estate vineyards are organically managed, with biodynamic certification pending.

Camino San Fernando a Pichilemu, Km 36, Cunaquito,
Comuna Sta Cruz; www.casalapostolle.com

Leyda San Antonio

The name says it all: this was the original producer in San Antonio's Leyda Valley, founded in 1997 and first planted in 1998 after an 5-mile (8-km) pipeline was installed to ferry the all-important irrigation water from the Maipo River. From the start, the wines have been characterful and elegant, especially in Pinot Noir, Chardonnay, and Sauvignon Blanc. Now Syrah, Sauvignon Gris, and Riesling are also performing well. In 2007, the winery came under new ownership (Luksic/San Pedro) and Pinot-phile winemaker Rafael Urrejola left. One to watch.

Avenida Del Valle 601 of.22, Ciudad Empresarial, Santiago
www.leyda.cl

Litoral (Ventolera) San Antonio

Litoral was established in 2005 as a joint venture between one of Leyda's highest profile wine growers, Vicente Izquierdo, and winemaker Ignacio Recabarren. Since then, Recabarren has distanced himself from the project and the GEO winemaking team assumed control under Alvaro Espinoza from the 2009 vintage. The brand is Ventolera and it excels in Sauvignon Blanc, made in a delightfully taut, mineral-infused style. Gently bittersweet Pinot Noir and buttery Chardonnay are promising. Riesling and Gewurztraminer are new to the range. ★**Rising star**

No visitor facilities
www.geowines.cl

Loma Larga Vineyards Casablanca

Freshness, elegance, and vibrant personality are the hallmarks of this coastal Casablanca producer's wines, all of which come highly recommended. Some 365 acres (148ha) are planted in hillside and piedmont areas, of which 100 acres (40 ha) are used for Loma Larga wines (the rest is sold off). Yields are low and French winemaker Emeric Genevière-Montignac is not afraid to make edgy wines of real personality. Sauvignon Blanc (tangy, layered), Malbec (floral, inky, and savory), and Syrah (delightfully meaty, peppery) all shine here. ★**Rising star**

Avenida Gertrudis Echeñique 348, Depto. A, Las Condes,
Santiago; www.lomalarga.com

Los Vascos Colchagua

Since 1988, this traditional Colchagua winery has been controlled by the Rothschild family of Bordeaux first growth Lafite. It has built up a steady following primarily around its very consistent Cabernet Sauvignon, from the entry level to the silky, refined Le Dix. Innovation is not this winery's strong point but positive signs for the future include new hillside plantings, creditable whites from Casablanca, and the complexity achieved by blending the Grande Réserve with Carmenère, Syrah, and Malbec.

Camino Pumanque Km 5, Peralillo, VI Region
www.vinalosvascos.com

Luis Felipe Edwards Colchagua

The family-owned LFE is a winery in the process of shedding the straightjacket of convention and emerging as a diverse and worthwhile producer. Previously, the estate had made bulk wine and lost many of its valuable old vines in the process. Own brands came in the 1990s, but it was not until the new millennium and an ambitious expansion project that LFE started to come into its own. New land in Leyda was just what the whites needed— the Sauvignon Blanc is excellent—and a grand hillside planting scheme is giving good results in Malbec, Shiraz, and Petite Sirah, helping to put this winery on the up.

Fundo San Jose de Puquillay, Nancagua, VI Region
www.lfewines.com

Matetic Vineyards San Antonio

Having become one of Chile's largest landowners via success in livestock, forestry, and steel, the Matetic family decided to give wine a try in 1999. They used their picturesque, self-contained 22,240 acre (9,000ha) Rosario estate for the purpose. Since then, the winery has made a name for itself producing powerful yet intensely savory and silken Syrahs off decomposed granite hillsides. Top

ALVARO ESPINOZA

Alvaro Espinoza's son has a nickname for him: "Señor Perfecto." It pretty much sums up this multi-award-winning yet thoughtful and humble man who has done much to further the cause of Chilean wine. Espinoza's introduction to wine came courtesy of his father Mario, a winemaker and professor at the Catholic University of Chile. Having gained experience in Chile and abroad, Espinoza helped pioneer the development of organic and biodynamic viticulture in Chile, the former at Carmen and both, subsequently, at Emiliana Orgánico. In 1998 he started up his own wine operation (Antiyal) in his garage at home; his wife Marina was relieved when a new winery was recently completed nearby. Espinoza now consults widely and makes wines through the excellent GEO operation. His wines tend to have a hedonistic, visceral appeal. Very Chilean, full of character, very appealing. Just like the man.

The Andes form the eastern border of the Colchagua Valley region, which lies to the south of Santiago.

NEYEN
THE CARMENERE AND CABERNET
SAUVIGNON GRAPES IN THIS BLEND COME
FROM VINES UP TO 120 YEARS OLD

SAN PEDRO
WINEMAKER MARCO PUYO HAS USHERED IN
A BRIGHT NEW ERA AT THIS BIG PLAYER

line EQ offers maximum intensity; many prefer Coralillo for its restraint. All vineyards are certified organic and the visitor facilities are excellent.

Fundo Rosario, Lagunillas, Casablanca
www.mateticvineyards.com

Miguel Torres Curicó

Noted Spanish producer Miguel Torres first came to Chile in the 1970s looking to expand his family wine operation beyond Catalonia. The subsequent investment helped spur the modernization of the Chilean wine industry and Torres has been quietly innovating ever since, for example with organics, clonal development, new varieties (Tempranillo, Albariño, Mencía), vineyards in slate soils (a homage to Priorat), and wine tourism. Vineyards are spread across Curicó and Maule. The basic lines are sound; picks of this bunch include the late harvest Riesling and ageworthy Manso de Velasco Cabernet Sauvignon.

Panamericana Sur Km 195, Curicó
www.migueltorres.cl

Montes Colchagua

This perennial Chilean favorite has come a long way since it was first founded in Curicó as Discover Wine in 1988. High-flying winemaker Aurelio Montes has overseen an impressive evolution, yet the focus is always on user-friendly premium wines that are satisfying at all levels. Reds from Apalta and Marchihue blend ripeness with appetizing structure, while whites from Leyda and Casablanca offer crisp, well-defined flavors. Folly Syrah is exhilarating in its intensity, Purple Angel a masterclass in Carmenère. New operations in Argentina and California are perpetuating this impressive producer's momentum.

Avenida del Valle, Huechuraba, Santiago
www.monteswines.com

Neyen Colchagua

Neyen is an impressively structured, spicy blend of old-vine Cabernet and Carmenère grown in a scenic self-contained amphitheater in prime Apalta country. The suave, blue-fruited 2005 vintage is the best to date; 2006 was the first made in the new onsite winery. New steep hillside plantings of Carmenère and particularly Syrah look promising, though none has yet been blended into Neyen. Winemaker Patrick Valette and viticulturist Eduardo Silva consult. **★Rising star**

Camino Apalta Km 11, Comuna Santa Cruz, Colchagua, VI Region; www.neyen.cl

Odfjell Vineyards Maipo

Norwegian shipping magnate Dan Odfjell originally came to Chile on business and ended up buying land in the hills west of Santiago. Initially planted to fruit orchards, the estate's transition to vineyard began in 1992. The focus is almost exclusively on red wines, some of which are laudably edgy and individual (most notably the wild, inky Malbec from Curicó and bright, herb-scented Carignan from Maule). The stylish, characterful Orzada wines are excellent, while Aliara is an increasingly interesting cross-regional red blend.

Camino Viejo a Valparaiso 7000, Padre Hurtado, Santiago
www.odfjellvineyards.cl

Pérez Cruz Maipo

The graceful simplicity of the Pérez family's winery in Huelquén is a joy to behold: light, wood, and stone combine in graceful harmony. Originally used for alfalfa, almonds, and cattle, the estate sits on a shallow slope at 1,475ft (450m) altitude and was first planted to vines in 1994. Production is exclusively red and comprises six wines, all of which proudly convey the mint-tinged dark fruit and broad, spicy structure typical of Alto Maipo. Highlights include a fleshy, floral Cot (Malbec) and the impressively peppery, succulent Quelen blend of Petit Verdot, Carmenère, and Cot.

Fundo Liguai de Huelquén, Paine, Maipo Alto
www.perezcruz.com

Quintay Casablanca

This Casablanca-based operation was formed in 2005 when eight partners—mainly grape growers—clubbed together to make one top-end Sauvignon Blanc. Right from the start, both the project and wine had a focus and ambition that boded well. Fruit is sourced from the Casablanca and Leyda appellations. Clava is the less expensive label and includes a fine Chardonnay that is restrained yet complex. Top bottling Quintay contains an elegantly smoky, bittersweet Pinot Noir. Both lines are excellent in Sauvignon Blanc. **★Rising star**

San Sebastián 2871, Office 201, Las Condes, Santiago
www.quintay.com

La Reserva de Caliboro (Erasmo) Maule

The prime mover behind this promising venture is urbane Italian count and vermouth heir Francesco Marone Cinzano. Having settled on the rural wilds of Maule's westerly hills as the place to diversify outside Tuscany, Cinzano linked up with the Manzano family to make one ambitious red blend: Erasmo. Scraggly, struggling dry-farmed vineyards on the banks of the river Perquilauquén yield a rugged, herb- and earth-tinged red made from Cabernets Sauvignon and Franc and Merlot. The best vintages to date are 2003 and 2005. Vin-Santo style Torontel is a delightful house curio. **★Rising star**

Carretera San Antonio, Caliboro Km 5.8, San Javier
www.caliboro.com

San Pedro Curicó

Traditionally one of the big beasts on Chile's wine scene, San Pedro faltered at the start of the 21st century as a result of management upheavals and chasing volume. The sheer rapidity of change in Chile can be astonishing, however, and so it has proved with San Pedro. Bright winemaking spark Marco Puyo has ushered in a new era of elegant, engaging wines with a true sense of origin. Vibrant Sauvignon Blanc and intensely savory Syrah from Elqui sum up this trend brilliantly, as does the new-look Cabo de Hornos, formerly pure Cabernet, now deftly blended with Syrah and Malbec.

Avenida Vitacura 4380, Piso 6, Vitacura, Santiago
www.sanpedro.cl

Santa Rita Maipo

This historic producer continues to evolve. Owner Ricardo Claro died in 2008; the Claro group remains in charge. Australian consultant Brian Croser was hired in

2009. Meanwhile, new vineyards in Colchagua and Limarí are starting to come on stream—the latter already producing dense, savory Syrah. For now, Santa Rita remains an intriguing blend of the traditional and modern. The ageworthy, linear Casa Real icon red falls into the former category; the intense Floresta range the latter. Sister wineries Carmen and Doña Paula continue to perform solidly. Atmospheric visitor facilities in Alto Jahuel include a museum, park, and hotel.

Camino Padre Hurtado 0695, Alto Jahuel/Buin, Maipo
www.santarita.com

Tabalí Limarí

Set amid the dusty expanse and vast skies of the southern Limarí plateau, Tabalí's geography is remote. No doubt this is how the Luksic family wanted it, for this is an estate owned by the powerful clan that controls the San Pedro Tarapacá group, among many other business interests. Tabalí is essentially a joint venture between Guillermo Luksic and San Pedro, and as such is the sister winery to Viña Leyda, formed around plantings first installed in 1993. These vines have yielded excellent Chardonnay and Syrah to date, ripe yet with an engaging freshness and vibrancy that is coastal Limarí's hallmark.

Hacienda Santa Rosa de Tabali Ovalle, Rute Valle del Encanto, Limari Valley; www.tabali.cl

Undurraga Maipo

At the turn of the 20th century, Undurraga was in trouble, the result of feuding owners and overly traditional wines. Ultimately, the Colombian Picciotto family prevailed, ousting the Chilean Undurragas, with whirlwind tycoon José Yuraszeck heading up operations. His inspired first move was to install the talented Rafael Urrejola, ex Viña Leyda, to create a new line, Terroir Hunter (now abbreviated to T.H.). With its superb range of expressive and complex wines, T.H. has rejuvenated Undurraga as a world-class producer. Further reforms are still needed, but things bode well.

Camino Melipilla, Km 34, Santa Ana, Maipo
www.undurraga.cl

Valdivieso Curicó

After developing a taste for French fizz, Alberto Valdivieso established a sparkling wine facility in Santiago in 1879. The business was successful and, in the early 1990s, the company diversified into still wines. The latter now occupies the limelight, with a decent portfolio of wines assembled under the aegis of Kiwi winemaker Brett Jackson. By far the best range is the Single Vineyard, showcasing Jackson's knack for identifying and cultivating individual sites. "Solera Bordeaux blend" Caballo Loco is ageworthy and consistent; Carignan/Mourvèdre/Syrah blend Éclat is challenging and wild.

Luz Pereira 1849, Lontué
www.valdiviesovineyard.com

VC Family Estates Cachapoal

VC (formerly Córpora) is a group of wineries owned by the Ibañez family and comprising Agustinos, Gracia, Porta, and Veranda in Chile and Universo Austral in Argentina. All the wineries have commendably ambitious aims, but wines can be variable. Inevitably, there is overlap in sourcing between the wineries; the best way to find quality

UNDURRAGA
THE T.H. RANGE EXEMPLIFIES UNDURRAGA'S COMMITMENT TO FINDING NEW TERROIRS

TABALI
FRESH, VIBRANT WINES FROM THE REMOTE SOUTHERN LIMARI PLATEAU

is to seek out the best vineyards. The increasingly expansive Bío Bío plantings—a key focus in the group—are delivering attractive Pinot Noir and Chardonnay, while Alto Cachapoal yields dense, savory Syrah.

Avenida Vitacura 4380, Piso 18, Vitacura, Santiago
www.cw.cl

Ventisquero Maipo

Ventisquero is a young winery, founded in 1998, but one that has already achieved success thanks to a talented winemaking team and considerable investment ($60m by 2006) by owning company Agrosuper. Much of this has gone into buying vineyards for self-sufficient production, a risky policy, but one that has benefited the wines. Improvements are still needed, understandably given Ventisquero's rate of initial growth. Stand-outs include the dense, layered Pangea and Vértice reds made in Apalta with ex-Penfolds Grange winemaker John Duval. Vineyard projects in formerly uncharted areas and efforts to reduce carbon emissions also merit praise.

La Estrella Avenida, 401, Office 5P, Punta de Cortés Sector, Rancagua; www.ventisquero.com

Veramonte Casablanca

It is transition time for this ground-breaking Casablanca winery. Run by the Chilean Huneeus family, Veramonte made its name in the 1990s with reliably crisp Sauvignon Blanc. In time, it became clear its elevated position in eastern Casablanca was also suited to some reds, but not all, hence the recent move into Marchihue (Colchagua) to source its top Primus blend. Similar changes include an upgrade of Sauvignon production and a renewed focus on Pinot Noir with consultant Paul Hobbs. Cruz Andina is a new Argentine wine made with Carlos Pulenta.

Ruta 68, Km 66 Casablanca
www.veramonte.com

Viu Manent Colchagua

This traditional Colchagua winery first existed as a jug wine négociant in downtown Santiago in the 1930s. Vineyard ownership did not come until 1966 when the family purchased its current site in Cunaco, where old Cabernet and Malbec vines grew on the flat valley floor. Today, these vines still provide the foundation for Viu's most celebrated wines such as the rugged, ink-and-nutmeg infused Viu 1. Beneficial recent developments include new vineyards in western Colchagua and whites from Casablanca and Leyda.

Santa Cruz, Colchagua
www.viumanent.cl

Von Siebenthal Aconcagua

The impressive first release from this Panquehue newcomer was the 2002 vintage. Things have improved since. Owned by charismatic Swiss lawyer Mauro von Siebenthal with four partners, the focus is exclusively on Aconcagua reds. The house style is bold and broad, yet with an enticing refinement and charm. Carabantes and Parcela #7 are expressive and moreish. Toknar is a vivid, arresting Petit Verdot while new Carmenère-based icon Tatay de Cristóbal 2007 has received rave reviews.

Calle O'Higgins, Panquehue, Aconcagua
www.vinavonsiebenthal.com

ARGENTINA

Size is important in Argentina. The country is vast—sprawling across 1.1 million square miles (2.8 million square kilometers), it is the eighth-largest nation in the world. Its vineyards huddle in the skirts of the highest mountain range outside Asia and yield a crop that is the wine world's fifth largest. Yet within this immensity resides a universe of passionate small producers, varietal diversity, and wines that contrive to blend spell-binding charm with vivid individuality. Until recently, a voracious domestic market slaked its thirst on most of the nation's wine production, but change is afoot. Recent decades have seen investment, improvement, and a renewed desire to compete on the global stage. Has the sleeping giant fully awoken? Only time will tell.

Major grapes

 Reds

Bonarda

Cabernet Franc

Cabernet Sauvignon

Malbec

Merlot

Tempranillo

 Whites

Chardonnay

Sauvignon Blanc

Semillon

Torrontés

Vintages

2009
Moderate to good: hot dry year; ripe, fruit-forward reds.

2008
Very good: not too warm; expressive, concentrated wines.

2007
Good: rainy but few complications; wines have structure and aging potential.

2006
Excellent: intensely aromatic whites, balanced reds.

2005
Moderate to good: coolish year gave decent whites and Malbec.

2004
Moderate to good: warm year, ripe wines.

Altitude and latitude are the keys to understanding Argentine wine. Much of western Argentina is essentially a high-altitude desert; the fierce heat and brutal aridity become more extreme as you move north toward the equator. Much-needed water and respite from the heat come with proximity to the Andes mountains. This is why the north of Argentina boasts some of the world's highest vineyards (at more than 9,840ft/3,000m above sea level). The subtle interplay of altitude and latitude weaves its magic in diverse vinous form all along Argentina's spine.

The beating heart of Argentine wine production is Mendoza. With its 393,000 acres (159,000ha) of vineyards, it accounts for 80% of national wine production. In recent years, traditional quality areas around Luján de Cuyo have been bolstered by exciting new developments in higher altitude locations in the Uco Valley and San Carlos. This trend is fast creating a complex yet thrilling viticultural map, not to mention a host of extrovert, enthralling wines.

In the Patagonian south (Río Negro, Neuquén), the blustery winds and bright skies help create wines that mix solidity with grace. Up north in Salta and Catamarca, the air is thin and the landscape lunar. Here, the wines are as rugged and uncompromising as the surroundings, a testament to the perseverance of their creators. In between the two extremes there is much to discover.

Argentina's signature variety is Malbec. Its classic styles veer between floral-scented, effortless drinkability and brooding intensity—but are always soft, generous, and spicy. The best Cabernet Sauvignon wines fuse great structure and density with elegant texture. Cabernet and Malbec combine to form some of Argentina's finest reds. Varietal diversity is one of Argentina's great strengths and the likes of Cabernet Franc, Syrah, Bonarda, Merlot, and Tempranillo all make excellent reds here, often in blends.

If Malbec has a white equivalent, it is the scented, exotic Torrontés, a specialty of Argentina's northern reaches. Chardonnay, especially when grown at high altitude and vinified sensitively, is proving successful. Although the climate typically does not suit Sauvignon Blanc, in the right hands, this variety is making crisp and concentrated white wines. Both Viognier and Semillon can also shine.

Today, Argentina is a proud and innovative wine producer. It has been through many crises in recent decades, both economic and wine-related, but a combination of social stability, ongoing investment, and the sheer energy of expectation is spurring the country's producers on to increasingly great things.

A new generation of brilliant winemakers is gradually taking the helm, from Mauricio Lorca to Matías Michelini. From the likes of LVMH (Chandon) to Pernod Ricard (Graffigna), Diageo (Navarro Correas), and Sogrape (Flichmann), multinational investment continues to drive development. Ambitious, adventurous wineries continue to push back boundaries (see Viña Alicia's eclectic portfolio for proof). Best of all, the fruits of Argentina's labor are being welcomed by an increasingly diverse and appreciative audience, lured by the appealing tourist facilities or simply the natural verve and charisma of the wines.

Achaval-Ferrer Luján de Cuyo (Perdriel)

One of the leading lights on the Argentine wine scene, Achaval-Ferrer produces some of the country's most sought-after wines. Since its inception in 1998, the project has been owned and run by Argentines Santiago Achaval (president) and Manuel Ferrer, along with Italians Roberto Cipresso (winemaker) and Tiziano Siviero. Old vines in prime sites, extremely low yields, and long oak aging give wines of structure, density, and great finesse. The top three wines all come from single vineyards: graceful Altamira from La Consulta, spicy Mirador from Medrano, and scented Bella Vista from Perdriel.

Calle Cobos 2601, Perdriel (5509), Mendoza
www.achaval-ferrer.com

Alta Vista Luján de Cuyo

The French d'Aulan family, for many years owners of Piper-Heidsieck champagne, first came to Argentina in the 1980s to make sparkling wines. They established Alta Vista in 1996, renovating a beautiful 19th-century winery and focusing on single-vineyard Malbec. Owner Patrick d'Aulan is not afraid to admit they have not always got things right ("too much oak; excessively low yields") but now the focus is on "finding our maturity and equilibrium." Malbecs in the Single Vineyard and Grande Reserve Terroir lines showcase the diversity of Mendoza, with elegant tannins and lifted acidity.

Alzaga 3972, Luján de Cuyo, Mendoza
www.altavistawines.com

Altos Las Hormigas Luján de Cuyo

Altos las Hormigas translates as "ants heights," and appropriately, the Argentine expression "a job for ants" refers to patient, back-breaking labor—a typical scene in this modest winery is busy and chaotic, littered with barrels, half-empty glasses, and lots of gesturing. This Italian-Argentine partnership has evolved steadily since the mid-1990s (though not without the odd hiccup), generally crafting intense, attention-grabbing Malbecs that are also well-grounded and structured. The Reserva Malbec is inky, dense, and elegantly bittersweet. Bonarda is now also a focus. Winemaker Alberto Antonini consults.

9 de Julio, 309-5500 Mendoza
www.altoslashormigas.com

Benegas Luján de Cuyo (Mayor Drummond)

Benegas is a young winery with a long history. Tiburcio Benegas is one of the founding fathers of Mendoza's wine industry and the family owned Trapiche until the 1970s. It was not until 1998 that Federico J. Benegas Lynch launched the family back into front-line winery ownership—a feat accomplished in style. Using fruit from a long-established family vineyard in Maipú (the winery is 3 miles/5 km up the road in Luján), Benegas makes primarily red wines with real personality, concentration, and class. Cabernet Franc, Syrah, and the Meritage blend stand out.

Cruz de Piedra, Maipú, Mendoza
www.bodegabenegas.com

Cabernet de los Andes Fiambalá Valley

The silver-haired, sun-weathered Carlos Arizu is a man with a genial, almost wicked smile. He boasts an impeccable winemaking heritage, but is clearly not one to do things the easy way. His vines grow in one of the most

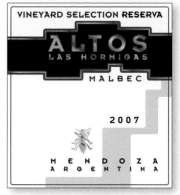

ALTOS LAS HORMIGAS
ATTENTION-GRABBING MALBEC FROM AN
ITALIAN-ARGENTINE PARTNERSHIP

CATENA ZAPATA
THE CATENA ALTA WINES ARE LIMITED-
PRODUCTION SINGLE VARIETALS

desolate, sun-blasted corners of Argentina—the Fiambalá Valley, Catamarca—where the daytime heat is offset by the dizzying altitude (around 16,400ft/1,500m). Organic and biodynamic methods are employed and the best reds show great purity and concentration of fruit. This is a winemaker to watch. ★ Rising star

No visitor facilities
www.tizac-vicien.com

Carinae Viñedos Maipú (Cruz de Piedra)

Frenchman Philippe Subra originally came to Argentina in the late 1990s to work as an electrical engineer. In 2003, he started devoting his energies to a new wine project, which he christened Carinae (after the constellation; Philippe is also an amateur astronomer). The small-scale production is made in a renovated winery in Cruz de Piedra, Maipú. Grapes are sourced from predominantly old vines in the surrounding estate and two further vineyards in Perdriel. Consultant Michel Rolland's team makes the wines, which are a finely wrought blend of concentration and elegance. ★ Rising star

Videla Aranda 2899, Cruz de Piedra, Maipú, Mendoza
www.carinaevinos.com

Carlos Pulenta Wines
Luján de Cuyo (Vistalba)

Carlos Pulenta's Vistalba estate is a world unto itself. The neat adobe-hued complex houses plush guest suites, a top-class restaurant (La Bourgogne) and cavernous, pristine wine cellars featuring concrete tanks designed by Carlos himself. All around are gnarled olive trees, which make vintage estate olive oil, and 124 acres (50ha) of vines, whose fruit makes the polished, intense Vistalba reds. Pulenta also sources fruit from Uco (much of which is used for the lively Tomero ranges) and Torrontés from Cafayate. Progenie is the new sparkling wine, a blend of Pinot Noir and Chardonnay. A word of warning: alcohol levels have been creeping up of late. ★ Rising star

Roque Saenz Pena 3531, Vistalba, Mendoza
www.carlospulentawines.com

Catena Zapata Luján de Cuyo (Agrelo)

Undoubtedly one of Argentina's leading wineries, Catena consistently produces some of the country's most ground-breaking, appealing, and best-value wines. This is the result of decades of hard work in both vineyard and winery, spurred on by father-and-daughter team Nicolás and Laura Catena. Pioneering work into high-altitude viticulture, Malbec clones, and blending has not only given ever more complex and beguiling Catena wines, both white and red, but also set a valuable example for others. Successful spin-offs include Argento and Caro, a joint venture with Château Lafite Rothschild of Bordeaux. The top red blends plus high-altitude Chardonnay and Malbec are outstanding.

J. Cobos, Agrelo, Luján de Cuyo, Mendoza
www.catenawines.com

Chacra Rio Negra

Old-vine Pinot Noir is the focus of this small-production Patagonian winery. Chacra was established in 2004 when urbane vintner Piero Incisa della Rocchetta, of Sassicaia fame, bought an abandoned plot of Pinot Noir vines planted in 1932. Other old vines have followed, as has

ARGENTINA

In Argentina's vineyards, you are never far from a scenic mountain backdrop. The nation's vines shadow the continental spine of the Andes, which provide cooling altitude and meltwater for irrigation. As might be expected of this free-spirited nation, the appellation system is cheerfully Byzantine in its complexity—but do not let this put you off. Terroir-driven winemaking is increasingly important in Argentina, whether it be from San José, San Rafael, or San Juan. Political provinces and departments (Mendoza, Luján de Cuyo) provide the broad-brush boundaries for the wine regions. Beyond this, the wines themselves are proving increasingly lucid and reliable guides to the intricacies of the nation's geography.

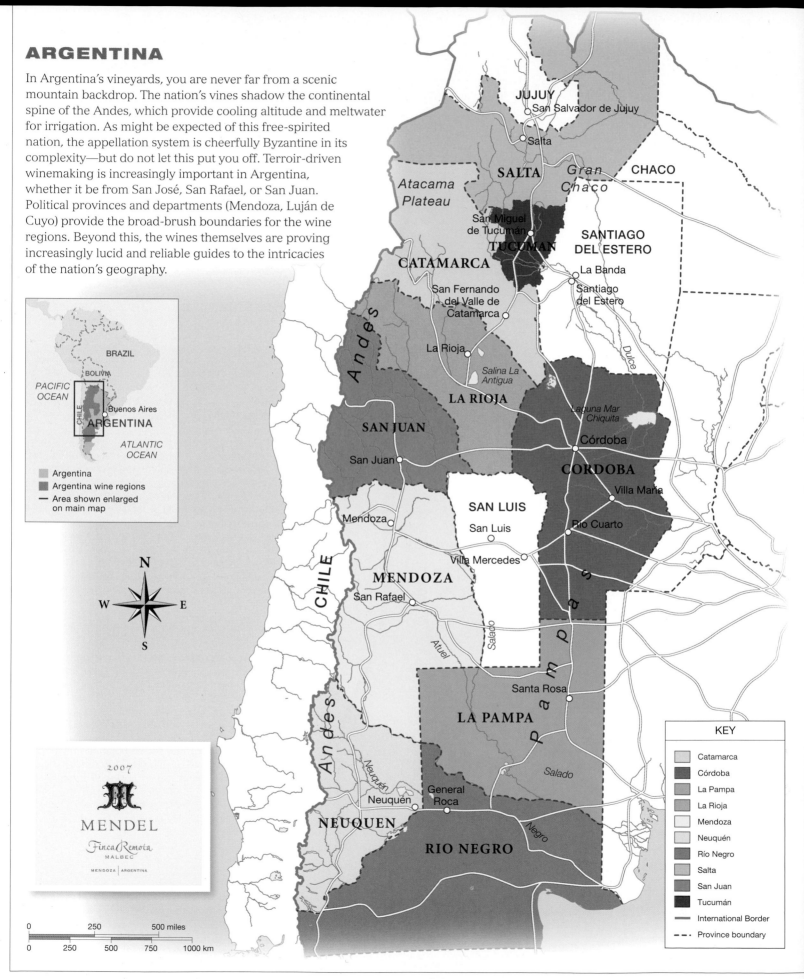

PACIFIC OCEAN
BRAZIL
BOLIVIA
CHILE
ARGENTINA
Buenos Aires
ATLANTIC OCEAN

■ Argentina
■ Argentina wine regions
— Area shown enlarged on main map

N
W   E
S

MENDEL
2007
Finca Remota
MALBEC
MENDOZA | ARGENTINA

0   250   500 miles
0   250   500   750   1000 km

JUJUY
San Salvador de Jujuy
Salta
SALTA
Atacama Plateau
Gran Chaco
CHACO
San Miguel de Tucumán
TUCUMAN
SANTIAGO DEL ESTERO
CATAMARCA
La Banda
Santiago del Estero
San Fernando del Valle de Catamarca
Andes
La Rioja
Salina La Antigua
LA RIOJA
Dulce
Laguna Mar Chiquita
SAN JUAN
Córdoba
San Juan
CORDOBA
Villa María
SAN LUIS
Mendoza
San Luis
Río Cuarto
Villa Mercedes
CHILE
MENDOZA
San Rafael
Atuel
Salado
Pampas
Santa Rosa
LA PAMPA
Salado
Neuquén
General Roca
Neuquén
NEUQUEN
Negro
RIO NEGRO

KEY

■ Catamarca
■ Córdoba
■ La Pampa
■ La Rioja
■ Mendoza
■ Neuquén
■ Río Negro
■ Salta
■ San Juan
■ Tucumán
— International Border
-- Province boundary

MENDOZA

Mendoza is Argentina's vinous center of gravity. This engine-room of national wine production has a long winemaking tradition and an increasingly bright future. Ever-growing diversity and increasingly assured winemaking are at the heart of this. Mendoza's traditional quality heartlands run south from the city (Vistalba, Luján, Perdriel, Agrelo). Farther southwest, the higher-altitude Uco and San Carlos areas are just as exciting. Watch these spaces.

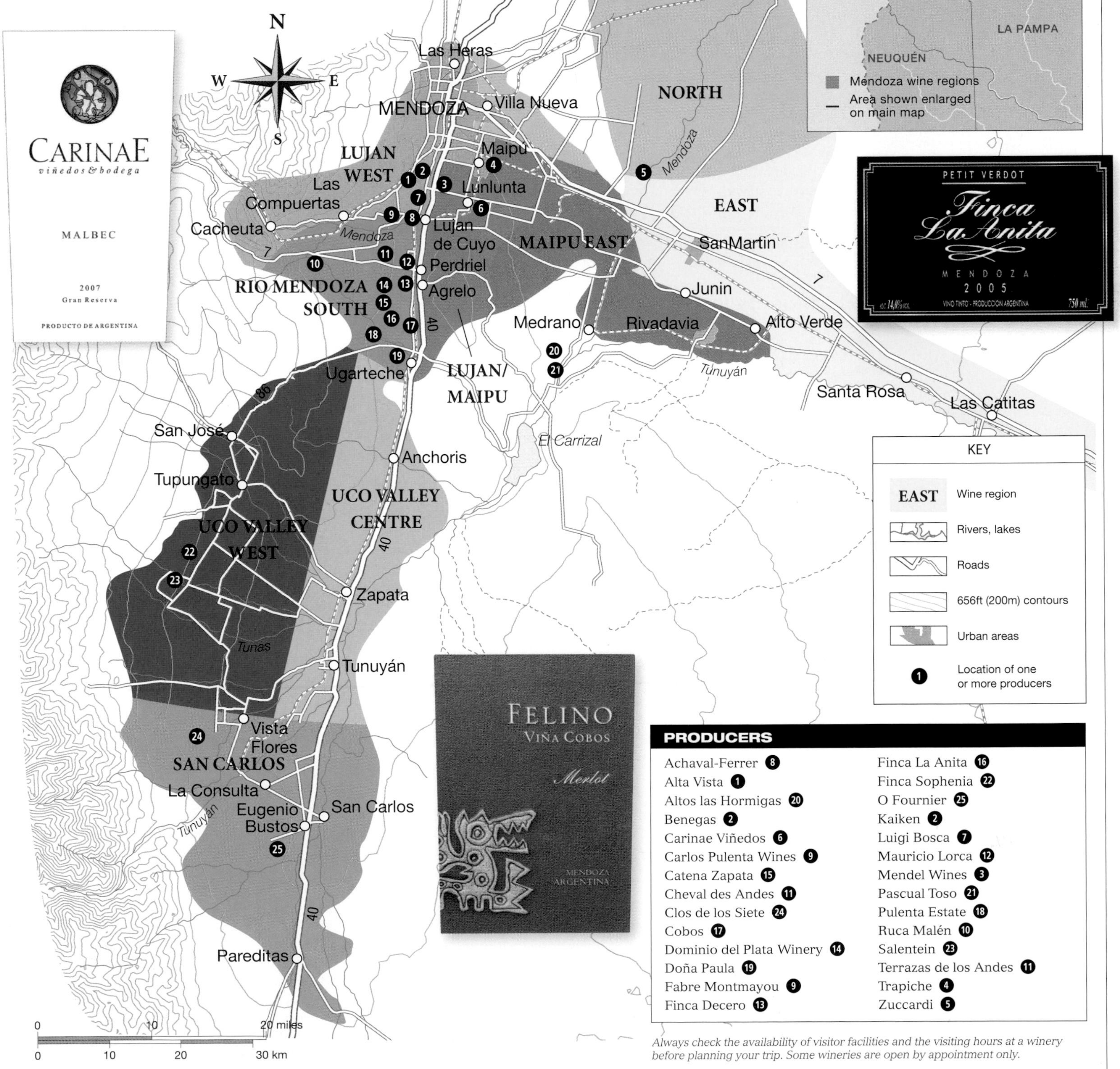

KAIKEN *ultra*

MALBEC
2006 / MENDOZA ARGENTINA

FINCA LA ANITA
PETIT VERDOT
MENDOZA
2005
VINO TINTO · PRODUCCION ARGENTINA   750 mL.

CARINAE
viñedos & bodega

MALBEC

2007
Gran Reserva

PRODUCTO DE ARGENTINA

KEY

EAST	Wine region
	Rivers, lakes
	Roads
	656ft (200m) contours
	Urban areas
❶	Location of one or more producers

FELINO
VIÑA COBOS
Merlot
MENDOZA
ARGENTINA

PRODUCERS

Achaval-Ferrer ❽	Finca La Anita ⓰
Alta Vista ❶	Finca Sophenia ㉒
Altos las Hormigas ⓴	O Fournier ㉕
Benegas ❷	Kaiken ❷
Carinae Viñedos ❻	Luigi Bosca ❼
Carlos Pulenta Wines ❾	Mauricio Lorca ⓬
Catena Zapata ⓯	Mendel Wines ❸
Cheval des Andes ⓫	Pascual Toso ㉑
Clos de los Siete ㉔	Pulenta Estate ⓲
Cobos ⓱	Ruca Malén ❿
Dominio del Plata Winery ⓮	Salentein ㉓
Doña Paula ⓳	Terrazas de los Andes ⓫
Fabre Montmayou ❾	Trapiche ❹
Finca Decero ⓭	Zuccardi ❺

Always check the availability of visitor facilities and the visiting hours at a winery before planning your trip. Some wineries are open by appointment only.

O FOURNIER

A WHIRLWIND OF PASSION AND AMBITION IN SAN CARLOS IN THE UCO VALLEY

LUIGI BOSCA

AN HISTORIC ESTATE PRODUCING MODERN WINES FROM LUJAN DE CUYO AND MAIPU

Danish winemaker Hans Vinding-Diers (of nearby Noemía) and some spectacular, highly individual wines. The floral, layered Treinta y Dos is undoubtedly the star, though all these Pinots are an intriguing blend of classic, ageworthy character with a decidedly Argentine spice, florality, and dynamism. ★ **Rising star**

Avenida Roca 1945, General Roca, Rio Negro 8332
www.bodegachacra.com

Cheval des Andes Luján de Cuyo (Perdriel)

This joint venture between Terrazas de los Andes and St-Emilion A-lister Château Cheval Blanc has made a strong debut. The common link in ownership comes courtesy of Bernard Arnault, head of LVMH (owner of Terrazas) and co-proprietor of Cheval Blanc. Pierre Lurton, winemaker at Cheval Blanc, saw the potential of blending Cabernet Sauvignon with old-vine ungrafted Malbec as well as the virtue of not adopting a didactic Bordelais mentality. Since 1999, the style has evolved and now combines elegance (fine tannin, good structure) with Argentine spice and ripeness.

Thames y Cochabamba, Perdriel, Luján de Cuyo, Mendoza
www.chevaldesandes.com

Clos de los Siete Uco Valley (Vista Flores)

The idea was simple. Globetrotting consultant Michel Rolland persuaded French investors to join him in an ambitious project. Namely, to plant 2,100 acres (850ha) of virgin land in the high-altitude Vista Flores area of Uco, split the property up into seven parts, and allow each partner to make their own wines while contributing a stipulated amount to one joint wine: Clos de los Siete (first vintage 2002). The wine is decent enough, with a ripe, spicy, uncomplicated style. There are currently four wineries: Flechas de los Andes, Monteviejo (Lindaflor), Cuvelier los Andes, and DiamAndes. All wines are notably high in alcohol. This is a project to watch.

Tunuyán, Mendoza
www.dourthe.com

Cobos Luján de Cuyo (Perdriel)

In 1997, Luis Barraud and Andrea Marchiori—newly graduated winemakers and husband and wife—visited California wine country. The result was Cobos, formed in association with renowned Californian winemaker Paul Hobbs. Fast forward a decade and the operation not only has a dramatic, modern winery, but is widely lauded for its show-stopping reds packed full of spicy, fruit-forward flavor. Hobbs' talent for making luxuriant yet structured Cabernet Sauvignon is a feature of all ranges, from the good-value Felino to top-of-the-range Nico. The best wines are sourced from Andrea's father's vineyard in Perdriel.

Costa Flores y Ruta 7, Perdriel, Luján de Cuyo, Mendoza
www.vinacobos.com

Colomé Calchaquí Valley

Colomé is a winery that pushes the limits. Located in the fierce heat, aridity, and isolation of the Calchaquí Valley, the winery lies 7,200ft (2,200m) above sea level, while its highest vineyards grow (astonishingly) at over 10,200ft (3,100m). Despite the adverse conditions, Colomé has been a farm for centuries, and a winery since 1831 (some vines date back to 1854)—making it one of Argentina's oldest wine operations. Swiss businessman Donald Hess

acquired the property in 2001. The Malbec is muscular and brooding, yet with great tannic finesse; Tannat and Torrontés are specialties. A successful hotel and visitor center operate on site.

Ruta Provincial 53 Km 20, Molinos 4419, Provincia de Salta
www.bodegacolome.com

Dominio del Plata Winery
Luján de Cuyo (Agrelo)

Nuclear physics' loss was winemaking's gain when Susanna Balbo chose the latter. This formidable businesswoman and winemaker founded Dominio del Plata in 1999 with viticulturist Pedro Marchevsky after both had worked at Catena for many years. Right from the start, their focus was on precision viticulture, sustainable farming, and skilful winemaking. Initially variable, the wines are now consistently polished and broadly appealing, from the good-value Crios line to the more expensive bottlings BenMarco, Susanna Balbo Signature, and buxom range-topper Nosotros.

Cochabamba 7801, Agrelo (5507), Mendoza
www.dominiodelplata.com

Doña Paula Luján de Cuyo (Ugarteche)

This consistent yet innovative producer is arguably the most promising in the Chilean Claro Group's portfolio. Much of this is down to the restless drive and attention to detail of winemaker Edgardo del Popolo ("Edy" to his friends). Its traditional strengths of zesty Sauvignon Blanc and floral Malbec have been augmented recently by a raft of innovative wines incorporating Tannat, Torrontés, Shiraz, Viognier, and Cabernet Franc. Though many wines remain works in progress, all are well worth a try.

Av. Colón 531, CP 5500, Ciudad, Mendoza
www.donapaula.com.ar

Fabre Montmayou Luján de Cuyo (Vistalba)

First, some clarification on names. The venture was initially established in 1992 by Frenchman Hervé Joyaux Fabre and his business partner Montmayou. The winery in Mendoza was named Domaine Vistalba; a subsidiary operation was set up in Patagonia using the Infinitus brand. Now the Fabre Montmayou brand is the main one, with Phebus as the cheaper line—both brands are made in both locations. Though some of the lesser examples can be variable in quality and the project continues to evolve, in general the wines show admirable finesse and definition.

Roque Saenz Peña, Vistalba, Luján de Cuyo, Mendoza
www.domainevistalba.com

Finca Decero Luján de Cuyo (Agrelo)

Finca Decero is a stylish bright young thing with great potential. Winery and vineyard were built from scratch (the translation of "decero") in Agrelo at 3,400ft (1,050m) altitude. The first vintage release was 2006. The focus is entirely on reds—primarily Malbec, Cabernet Sauvignon, and Petit Verdot—sourced from the Remolinos estate vineyard. The attention to detail (for example, basket pressing all reds) and hands-on approach bodes well, as does the vibrant personality and Old World finesse of the wines. Paul Hobbs consults. ★ **Rising star**

Bajo las Cumbres 9003, Agrelo, Mendoza
www.decero.com

Finca la Anita Luján de Cuyo (Agrelo)

Many New World wineries aim for individuality in their wines; few deliver. Finca la Anita is one of the blessed minority. Set up by brothers Manuel and Antonio Mas in the early 1990s, this winery was conceived in homage to a classic European estate. Though characterful, the extensive white range (all proudly unoaked) is overshadowed by the delightful rusticity and compelling character of the reds. These are rough-edged gems of wines, to lay down and meditate over. Informative, pithy back labels complete the no-nonsense charm of this unique producer.

Calle Cobos, Agrelo, Luján de Cuyo, Mendoza
www.fincalaanita.com

Finca Sophenia Uco Valley (Tupungato)

Sophenia's considerable success in its brief history is due to a combination of well-designed high-altitude vineyards and smart winemaking. Credit for the former goes to founding partner Roberto Luka, for the latter to Matías Michelini. The scenic, fresh-aired estate lies at 3,900ft (1,200m) altitude in the Gualtallarí area of Uco and consistently produces fine Sauvignon Blanc, Merlot, and Malbec. Top range Synthesis is excellent, especially the elegantly rounded red blend, while good value is to be had in the Altosur brand. Freshness and harmony are hallmarks of the best wines. ★ **Rising star**

Ruta 89 Km 12.5, Camino a los Arboles, Tupungato,
Mendoza; www.sophenia.com.ar

O Fournier San Carlos

José Manuel Ortega Gil-Fournier was once a clean-shaven, high-flying banker. Now this bearded, bespectacled human whirlwind is one of Argentina's most passionate and ambitious producers. Fruit is sourced 30% from own vines and 70% from local producers in the high-altitude (3,900ft/1,200m) vineyards around San Carlos, Tempranillo being the largest crush. Wines are consistently excellent. The basic Urban range is reliably sound; B Crux is often commendable (especially the Sauvignon Blanc). The ageworthy, savory charms of A Crux wines are outstanding, while the new O. Fournier Syrah/Malbec blend is brooding and spicy.

Calle Los Indios 5567, La Consulta, Mendoza
www.ofournier.com

Kaiken Luján de Cuyo (Vistalba)

Not content with being massively influential in his home country, Chilean winemaker Aurelio Montes is spreading his global reach, to Argentina and now California. Kaiken was his first step in this adventure, named after the wild geese that fly over the Andes. The wines are very much in the trademark Montes mold: rich and heady, with well-integrated oak and a certain life's-too-short kind of swagger. Malbec and Cabernet Sauvignon are the focus, sourced from sites around Mendoza including Uco. A rosé and the Icon label Malbec are the latest additions. ★ **Rising star**

Roque Saenz Pena 5516, Vistalba, Luján de Cuyo, Mendoza
www.kaikenwines.com

Luigi Bosca Luján de Cuyo (Mayor Drummond)

To call Luigi Bosca a traditional producer would be to render it a disservice. Historic, definitely: this well-known winery is now in its fourth generation of Arizu family ownership (current incumbents being clean-cut brothers Alberto and Gustavo). The wines are deftly made and modern in style, with excellent depth in the range. Six vineyards across Luján de Cuyo and Maipú, under Arizu ownership since the early 1900s, provide the fruit. Wines are characterful at the lower end, often refined and complex at the top, with the Gala blends particularly rewarding.

San Martin 2044, Mayor Drummond, Luján de Cuyo,
Mendoza; www.luigibosca.com.ar

Masi Tupungato Uco Valley (Tupungato)

The Boscaini family has grown wine in Northeast Italy for six generations. More recently, the family has moved into Tuscany and Argentina, the latter operation comprising a high-altitude vineyard in Tupungato and three wines, all excellent. The estate's motto is, "Argentine soul, Venetian style"—and it shows. Passo Blanco is a delightfully scented, mouth-coating blend of Pinot Grigio and Torrontés. For the succulent, layered Passo Doble red, Malbec wine undergoes a second fermentation with slightly dried Corvina grapes. Top red Corbec (semi-dried Corvina with 30% Malbec) is a dense, creamy, cherry-fueled delight.

No visitor facilities
www.masi.it

Mauricio Lorca Luján de Cuyo (Perdriel)

Mauricio Lorca has been described as the winemaking equivalent of Mohammed Ali: a big man with a notable lightness of touch. Already nearing heavyweight status, Lorca is one of the rising stars of the Argentine wine scene. His work at various wineries, including the excellent Eral Bravo, Enrique Foster, and Viña Alicia has been consistently impressive. His new personal venture is based around a low-yielding vineyard at 3,400ft (1,050m) altitude in the Vista Flores area (Uco Valley). The proudly unoaked Gran Opalo red blend is an excellent example of this producer's gift for making wines of vivid character and great harmony. ★ **Rising star**

Brandsen 1039, Perdriel, Luján de Cuyo, Mendoza
www.mauriciolorca.com

Mendel Wines Luján de Cuyo (Mayor Drummond)

Roberto de la Mota is one of Argentina's best-known winemakers, so when he decided to start his own project with the Sielecki family in 2002, it went straight on the map. Not even a serious car accident could dent Roberto's passion; the wines continue to deliver consistently refined, refreshing character with a typically Argentine wildness and intensity. Their old-vine Malbec and Cabernet Sauvignon grow in Perdriel and Mayor Drummond. The dense, spicy Unus is a blend of Malbec with 30% Cabernet from Luján, while Finca Remota is pure Malbec from Uco. ★ **Rising star**

Terrada 1863, Mayor Drummond (5507), Luján de Cuyo,
Mendoza; www.mendel.com.ar

Noemía Rio Negra

Noemía is unique in several ways. It is a Danish-Italian partnership—between winemaker Hans Vinding-Diers and Italian Countess Noemí Marone Cinzano, of the eponymous vermouth family. It uses old-vine fruit from ungrafted Malbec vineyards planted in the 1930s and 1950s and farmed biodynamically in the Patagonian

DIZZY HEIGHTS: ALTITUDE AND ARGENTINE WINE

Argentina has vineyards as high as 9,800ft (3,000m) above sea level (equivalent to a third of the way up Mount Everest). So what does this mean for the wines? "It takes the edge off the desert climate," says Catena winemaker Mariela Molinari. The two key effects relate to temperature and light intensity. Both maximum and minimum temperatures are lower at high altitude. This means that, during the summer, the plants retain better natural acid balance in the fruit. The "hang time," or natural ripening curve, is longer and smoother, so producers can harvest later in the season when the berries have developed more complex flavors. Higher levels of sunlight also seem to give thicker skins and a higher concentration of aromatic, polyphenolic, and other compounds including carotenoids, tannin, and resveratrol, but often without the wines proving astringent. The risks? Frost, hail, and high alcohol. But in Molinari's words: "We are going higher!"

PULENTA ESTATE
CONCENTRATED, COMPLEX GRAN CORTE IS
THE PRODUCT OF IMPECCABLE FACILITIES
AND CONSIDERABLE INVESTMENT

RUCA MALEN
ARGENTINE WINES WITH A DISTINCTLY
FRENCH ACCENT

desert. Top bottling Noemía is explosive and racy, full of caramel, sweet spice, and damson tones. J. Alberto is an impressively grippy and brooding wine, while A. Lisa (made from younger vines) shows excellent floral and peppery lift.

Ruta Prov 7, Km 12, Valle Azul (Rio Negro)
www.bodeganoemia.com

Pascual Toso Maipú (Barrancas)

Founded in the late 19th century, Pascual Toso is one of Argentina's traditional producers. Nearly 90% of total production is sparkling wine. It is only since the beginning of the 21st century that the winery has moved into fine wine production, hiring Californian consultant Paul Hobbs and investing more than $25m. Results have been impressive, with a basic range delivering sound value for money and altogether more concentration and intricacy at the top end. Cabernet Sauvignon and Malbec are house specialties, combining to spectacular effect in the glossy, solid top wine, Magdalena Toso.

Alberdi 808, San Jose 5519, Mendoza
www.bodegastoso.com.ar

Pulenta Estate Luján de Cuyo (Agrelo)

Brothers Hugo and Eduardo Pulenta belong to one of Argentina's historic winemaking families, which until the late 1990s controlled the giant Peñaflor group. Their father Antonio planted what is now their 335 acre (135ha) estate, in Alto Agrelo, in 1991 with a range of varieties; the brothers continued the heritage by founding the winery in 2002. Facilities are impeccable; testament to considerable investment. The wines do not come cheap, but they are impressive. La Flor is the basic line and excels in Pinot Gris and Malbec. The Pulenta Estate range is more concentrated and complex, while Gran Corte is the pick of the stylish Gran range. ★**Rising star**

Gutiérrez 323 (5500), Ciudad, Mendoza
www.pulentaestate.com

Ruca Malén Luján de Cuyo (Agrelo)

Ruca Malén makes Argentine wine with a French accent. Its owners are Jean Pierre Thibaud, former chairman of Bodega Chandon in Argentina, and Burgundian Jacques Louis de Montalembert. Fruit is sourced from Luján de Cuyo and Uco and the wines show a distinct freshness and lift, which makes for a chic house style. The basic Yauquén line exhibits excellent varietal character and everyday charm. Ruca Malén is a step up in concentration, while Kinien betrays deft blending and use of oak. Visits to the winery can incorporate blending games and vertical tastings.

Ruta Nacional Nro 7 Km 1059, Agrelo, Luján de Cuyo,
Mendoza; www.bodegarucamalen.com

Salentein Uco Valley (Tunuyán)

Bodegas Salentein is a complex operation whose nerve center is set in a stunning estate high in Uco's breathless plateau. Dutch capital and Argentine expertise combined to make this venture one of the pioneers of this area in the late 1990s. In its 4,940 acre (2,000ha) estate, there are 1,730 acres (700ha) of vines planted, some as high as 5,600ft (1,700m) altitude. Initially the winery was lauded for its Sauvignon Blanc and Pinot Noir; more recently, the best performers have been scented Malbec and sleek Merlot. Outstanding facilities make for a memorable visit.

Ruta 89, Los Arboles, Tunuya, Mendoza
www.bodegasalentein.com

Terrazas de los Andes
Luján de Cuyo (Perdriel)

Terrazas is the still wine off-shoot of Chandon Argentina; both are owned by multinational luxury goods group LVMH. The core concept behind Terrazas ("terraces") since it began in 1999 has been matching each variety to a specific altitude, which governs ripening sequence and thus, in theory, quality. The wines tend to be appealing rather than exciting, but their consistency is commendable and quality generally high. Malbec, Cabernet Sauvignon, and Chardonnay are strengths.

Thames y Cochabamba, Perdriel, Luján de Cuyo, Mendoza
www.terrazasdelosandes.com

Trapiche Maipú

Trapiche is one of Argentina's largest wine producers and belongs to the mighty Peñaflor group, which also controls Finca las Moras, Santa Ana, and Michel Torino. Trapiche owns some 3,090 acres (1,250ha) of vineyards and sources from 300 producers across Mendoza, with a total production of 35 million bottles. Winemaker Daniel Pi has greatly improved the wines since arriving in 2002. Headline wines are the range-topping Single Vineyard Malbecs—intense, silky, and characterful—but other ranges provide decent value, especially Broquel.

Nueva Mayorga, Coquimbito, Maipú, Mendoza
www.trapiche.com.ar

Val de Flores Uco Valley (Vista Flores)

World-famous winemaking consultant Michel Rolland is seemingly ubiquitous in Argentina. Yet there are only two wines he calls his own: Val de Flores and Yacochuya, the latter a bruising, rugged, uncompromising Malbec grown at more than 6,600ft (2,000m) altitude in Cafayate. Val de Flores was conceived after Rolland regularly drove past a plot of old vines on his way to Clos de los Siete in Vista Flores (Uco Valley). He subsequently bought the 32 acre (13ha) vineyard with 50-year-old Malbec vines along with partner Philippe Schell. This pricey red is sun-baked and feisty with notes of cream, fig, and leather.

No visitor facilities
www.rollandcollection.com

Zuccardi Maipú

It is impossible to resist José Alberto Zuccardi's unique brand of energy, determination, and humility. He has built a mini wine empire in eastern Mendoza, complete with superb visitor facilities including a restaurant, art gallery, and even tours by hot air balloon and classic cars. A relentless drive for innovation has led to vineyards being developed in the Uco Valley and exotic varieties coming on stream (Caladoc and Marselan are excellent in the eclectic Textual range). Organic vineyards, a sparkling Bonarda, even a delicious port-style red: Zuccardi caters for all tastes. The Q range is the portfolio stand-out.

Ruta Provincial 33 Km 7.5, Maipú, Mendoza
www.familiazuccardi.com

BRAZIL

When we think of Brazil, what usually comes to mind are beautiful beaches, carnival, and soccer. Few would associate the country with wine, despite it being one of the 20 largest wine-producing countries in the world, with a history of wine cultivation dating back almost 500 years. When it comes to producing export-quality wines, Brazil is very much in its infancy. Nevertheless, a small group of quality-conscious producers are making wines worthy of international recognition. In South America, Brazilian sparkling wines already enjoy a reputation as an affordable alternative to champagne, and they are steadily gaining ground overseas. And many southern Brazilian producers are banking on Merlot as their flagship grape.

Vines were first introduced to Brazil in 1532 at Capitania of São Vicente, which today is part of the state of São Paulo. The hot, humid region proved unreceptive to grape-growing, but the more benign, cooler climate of Rio Grande do Sul, the southern most state, bordering Argentina and Uruguay, fared much better. Today, Rio Grande do Sul is responsible for more than 90% of total wine production in Brazil, including some of the country's finest wines.

Although vines are planted in the majority of Brazil's 26 states, aside from Rio Grande do Sul, there are two regions of special interest. The first is the up-and-coming São Francisco Valley, which enjoys a tropical climate in the northeast of the country at 8° latitude. The second is Santa Catarina, just to the north of Rio Grande do Sul. Here, high-altitude vineyards (some of them as high as 4,430ft/1,350m) are producing some of Brazil's most exciting wines in a region where temperatures can fall as low as 14°F (-10°C), accompanied by snow.

The Brazilian wine industry really began to gain momentum in the early 1970s. As the country's population reached 90 million, and with consumption and interest in wine increasing, international companies saw Brazil as an attractive market and began investing.

The arrival of these multi-nationals led to considerable improvement in production techniques. Along with introducing new technology into the wineries, foreign investors

such as Martini & Rossi (1973), Moët & Chandon (1973), Seagram (1974), and National Distillers (1974) were responsible for planting large areas of *Vitis vinifera*, including Cabernet Sauvignon, Merlot, Pinot Noir, Chardonnay, and Sauvignon Blanc among many others. Today, Brazil is the third most important wine producer in South America after Chile and Argentina, with approximately 30,000 acres (12,000ha) of vinifera vineyards.

Since the Brazilian government eased import barriers in 1990, local producers have faced increasing competition from several wine-producing regions, notably Chile and Argentina. As a consequence, the Brazilians themselves have been drinking far less of their own country's wines, and Brazilian producers' share of the domestic market has dropped from around two-thirds to a quarter. For this reason, producers are increasingly looking to export markets to sell their wines—and with some success. The top 10 destinations for Brazilian wines at present are the United States, Paraguay, the Netherlands, Japan, Germany, the Czech Republic, Portugal, Russia, the United Kingdom, and Angola.

Part of this success can undoubtedly be ascribed to the novelty factor of Brazilian wines. But there is more to it than that. At their best, Brazilian wines tend to be restrained and elegant, leaning toward a European style with moderate alcohol levels, making them very much in tune with current drinking trends.

Major grapes

Reds

Cabernet Franc

Cabernet Sauvignon

Merlot

Pinot Noir

Touriga Nacional

Whites

Chardonnay

Gewurztraminer

Sauvignon Blanc

Vintages

2009
A challenging, cold vintage of high rainfall and spring frost.

2008
A good vintage with intense sunlight, normal average temperatures, and low rainfall.

2007
Rainfall was below average, but most of it fell in March, affecting late-ripening grape varieties.

2006
A challenging year of drought, hail, and above average rainfall in March.

2005
One of the best modern vintages with very little rain and above average temperatures.

2004
A very good vintage with more sunshine and less rain than usual.

CAVE GEISSE

CHILEAN WINEMAKER MARIO GEISSE IS AN
EXPERT PRODUCER OF SPARKLING WINES

Angheben Encruzilhada do Sul (vineyards)

Angheben is the name of an 11th-century tribe of Celts
from the Austrian-Italian border, but for the past decade,
it has been synonymous with some of Brazil's finest
wines. The reason for this is the eponymous winery
founded in 1999 by renowned professor and enologist,
Idalencio Francisco Angheben. The well-traveled
professor and his son, Eduardo, make wines from the
Encruzilhada do Sul vineyards, which sit on a foundation
of granite rocks and sandy soils. The range is consistent,
featuring a respectable sparkling wine and a Touriga
Nacional with excellent varietal definition.

*RS 444, Km 4, Vinhedos Valley, Bento Gonçalves,
95700-000; www.angheben.com.br*

Boscato Rio das Antas Valley

Boscato is a small family winery combining tradition
and innovation to make intriguing wines. Its vineyards
are situated at 2,600ft (800m) above sea level on rocky
soils in a climate of long, harsh winters and hot summers
with prolonged sunshine. Boscato has won multiple
awards: in 2009 alone it picked up medals at respected
wine shows in Canada, Italy, Germany, and Belgium.
One of the stars of the range is undoubtedly the
Merlot Grande Reserva, which is delicious despite
its somewhat firm texture.

*VRS 314, Km 12,5, Nova Pádua, 95275-000
www.boscato.com.br*

Casa Valduga Vinhedos Valley

The Valduga brothers have transformed their family
business, Casa Valduga, in recent years, investing heavily
both in the vineyard and the winery. The range is large,
but while some of the wines are world class, more work
is required to achieve consistency across the board. Not
surprisingly, given that Valduga has Latin America's
largest sparkling wine cellar, the best wine is a sparkling
—the Casa Valduga Brut 130. The company is also heavily
involved in wine tourism in the beautiful, mountainous
Vinhedos Valley region, where it has a fine restaurant and
a bed and breakfast facility.

*Linha Leopoldina, Vinhedos Valley, Bento Gonçalves,
95700-000; www.casavalduga.com.br*

Cave Geisse Vinhos da Montanha

Situated in the beautiful Serra Gaúcha, Cave Geisse was
founded by Chilean immigrant Mario Geisse, who, when
he arrived in Brazil, was originally destined for a career
making sparkling wine at Chandon of Brazil. However,
Geisse soon realized the area's immense potential for
sparkling wines and headed to the Pinto Bandeira district
of Bento Gonçalves. Most of Cave Geisse's vineyard
plantings consist of the Champagne varieties Pinot Noir
and Chardonnay. The technology employed here also
mirrors the French region, resulting in some of the best
sparkling wines in Brazil.

*Linha Jansen, Distrito de Pinto Bandeira-Bento Gonçalves;
www.cavegeisse.com.br*

Cordilheira de Sant'Ana

Sant'Ana do Livramento

Unlike most wineries in Brazil, Cordilheira de Sant'Ana is
not the continuation of family tradition, but the fruition of
a lifelong dream shared by Gladistão Omizzolo and

Rosana Wagner. The two winemakers, who between
them have more than 60 years' experience in the drinks
industry, founded Cordilheira de Sant'Ana after a long,
extremely detailed search for the perfect vineyard
location. Research on the project started in 1999, but
it was not until 2005 that the winery finally opened
with a production capacity of 160,000 bottles and 114
acres (46ha) of vineyards. The white wines—made from
Chardonnay, Gewurztraminer, and Sauvignon Blanc—
are particularly promising.

*Vila Palomas, Sant'Ana do Livramento, 97573-970
www.cordilheiradesantana.com.br*

Dal Pizzol Faria Lemos

Dal Pizzol is a boutique winery in Faria Lemos, Bento
Gonçalves, producing around 28,000 cases of wine
annually as well as a small production of grape juice.
Grape varieties used here include Cabernet Sauvignon,
Merlot, Cabernet Franc, Pinot Noir, Tannat, Ancellotta,
Chardonnay, Sauvignon Blanc, and Gewuztraminer,
but one of the stars is the Portuguese grape, Touriga
Nacional, which makes an excellent red wine. The
expansive premises takes in a local restaurant (open by
appointment only), attractive lakes, a collection of exotic
plants, and Dal Pizzol's enoteca, which houses a broad
collection of old vintages.

*RST Km 4,8 Faria Lemos, Bento Gonçalves, 95700-000
www.dalpizzol.com.br*

Lidio Carraro Vinhedos Valley

The determined and hard working family behind Lidio
Carraro established their own vineyards in 1998 after
detailed research into the soil and climate of the Vinhedos
Valley. The first wines followed in 2002, announcing the
arrival of a serious boutique producer. The production is
certainly small—just 3,500 bottles for some wines—and
the wines, produced from Merlot, Cabernets Sauvignon
and Franc, Nebbiolo, Malbec, Tannat, and Tempranillo,
are entirely unique. The philosophy is to preserve the
purity of fruit, which means that no oak is used at any
point during the production process. All the same, prices
are exceptionally high by Brazilian standards.

*RS 444 Km 21, Vinhedos Valley, Bento Gonçalves,
95700-000; www.lidiocarraro.com*

Miolo

In 1897, an Italian immigrant, Giuseppe Miolo, purchased
a small plot of land with his life savings. It was from these
humble beginnings that the largest wine producer in
Brazil emerged. Today, the Miolo Wine Group includes
a grand total of six independent projects: Miolo Winery
(Vinhedos Valley), Fortaleza do Seival (Campanha), RAR
(Campos de Cima da Serra), Lovara (Serra Gaucha),
Fazenda Ouro Verde (Sao Francisco Valley), and the
recently acquired Almaden. In total, the company has
2,840 acres (1,150ha) of vineyards, but it is not concerned
only with quantity. With the help of the renowned,
globetrotting French consultant Michel Rolland, Miolo
also produces some of Brazil's best wines—Merlot
Terroir, the Lote 43 Bordeaux blend, and the outstanding,
sparkling Millésime. Old World in style, this trio is
restrained, elegant, and complex.

*RS 444 Km 21, Vinhedos Valley, Bento Gonçalves,
95700-000; www.miolo.com.br*

LIDIO CARRARO

DA'DIVAS IS A BEAUTIFUL, RICH, UNOAKED
VERSION OF CHARDONNAY

Perini Farroupilha

In 1970, Benildo Perini began an ambitious project: to transform his family business from a small-scale producer of wines strictly for the local market into a large corporation making quality wines with broad appeal. He succeeded. Perini now has 227 acres (92ha) of vineyards producing around 4.3 million gallons (16.5 million liters) of wine a year—a figure that inflated considerably following the buy-out of Casa Vinicola de Lantier, the neighboring winery where Perini used to rent winemaking facilities. Based in Garibaldi in the Italian-flavored region of the Trentino Valley, Perini has a very large range, but the best wines are sparkling, most notably a suitably Italianate non-vintage Prosecco.

Santos Anjos, Farroupilha-RS Caixa Postal 83 CEP 95180-000; www.vinicolaperini.com.br

Pizzato Vinhedos Valley

The Pizzato family arrived in Brazil from Venice in 1875, and began their vinous adventures making wine to be used for medicinal purposes in the local hospital. But their status as one of Brazil's top winemaking families really dates back from 1999, when the modern winery was founded. Today, the family has 104 acres (42ha) of vineyards spread over two regions—the Vinhedos Valley and Doutor Fausto—producing a mere 7,000 cases a year. Infectiously enthusiastic and quality-conscious in everything they do, their range includes some sound sparkling wines, and a handful of superb reds made using Merlot as the principal grape variety.

Via dos Parreirais, Vinhedos Valley, Bento Gonçalves, 95700-972; www.pizzato.net

Quinta da Neve São Joaquim

The state of Santa Catarina is renowned for having the coolest climate in Brazil, and is fast developing a reputation for making fine wine thanks to producers such as Quinta da Neve. Established in 1999, the da Neve estate has 15 varieties planted at altitudes above 3,280ft (1,000m), and its philosophy is very much that of the boutique winery. That means small production (around 50,000 bottles a year) but also maximum attention to detail. The acclaimed Portuguese enologist, Anselmo Mendes, is the man behind the wines, which include such well-crafted gems as the excellent Cabernet Sauvignon and a Pinot Noir that is arguably Brazil's finest expression of the variety to date.

Rodovia SJM 270, Km 15, Distrito de Lomba Seca, Sao Joaquim-Santa Catarina; www.acavitis.com.br

Rio Sul Vinibrasil São Francisco Valley

The project of respected Portuguese producer Dão Sul, Rio Sul Vinibrasil started its life in 2002. Its base is a 500 acre (200ha) estate in the half-barren landscape of the São Francisco Valley, up in the northeast of the country at 8° south latitude—a geographical position that has led to the wines being described as "new latitude." Winemaking operations are controlled by a former Portuguese Winemaker of the Year, Carlos Lucas, who draws on Cabernet Sauvignon, Syrah, and Alicante Bouschet, among other varieties, to create the modern, fruit-forward styles of the Rio Sul range.

Fazenda Planaltino-Zona Rural Lagoa Grande-PE CEP 56395-000; www.vinibrasil.com.br

SALTON
SALTON IS ONE OF SEVERAL BRAZILIAN PRODUCERS MAKING A SUCCESS OF MERLOT, AS IN THE POWERFUL DESEJO

MIOLO
MIOLO TERROIR MERLOT SHOWS BRAZIL'S POTENTIAL FOR BORDEAUX-STYLE REDS

Salton Distrito de Tuiuty

Founded in 1910, the multi-award-winning Salton winery has always been respected for its high-quality still wines. But in recent years, it has added another string to its bow, becoming Brazil's largest single producer of sparkling wines. Its finest wines are the Cabernet/Merlot/Tannat blend, Talento, and the 100% Merlot Desejo, while the Salton Volpi range is also consistently good. Sparkling wines worth looking out for include the Volpi Brut (a Chardonnay/Riesling blend), the Moscatel, the Prosecco, and the sparkling rosé, Poética, as well as the Brut Èvidence, which is made in the traditional champagne method using Chardonnay and Pinot Noir.

Rua Mário Salton 300, Distrito de Tuiuty CEP 95700-000, Bento Gonçalves – Rio Grande do Sul; www.salton.com.br

Villa Francioni São Joaquim

The lifelong dream of founder Manoel Dilôr de Freitas, Villa Francioni takes its name from de Freitas's mother, Agripina Francioni. Situated 3,900ft (1,200m) above sea level in a dry and cool environment, Francioni makes some of Brazil's most exciting wines, with attention to detail in the vineyard, strict selection at harvest time, and respect for the terroir. Among the many varieties produced is Petit Verdot, which the winery claims was the last parcel of vines to be harvested in the Southern Hemisphere in 2009. The Chardonnay and Pinot Noir are among Brazil's finest of each variety.

Rodovia SC 438-Km 70, São Joaquim, Santa Catarina, 88600-000; www.villafrancioni.com.br

Villaggio Grando Município de Agua Doce

It was a family friend from an Armagnac-producing family who first gave Villaggio Grando founder Maurício Carlos Gran the idea that Agua Doce was one of the best places in the world for making wine. A Bordeaux enologist later confirmed the potential of the high-altitude (4,430ft/1,350m above sea level) site, and Villaggio was born soon after, in the mid-1990s. The climate is cool, with temperatures as low as 14°F (-10°C) in the winter. But there is plenty of sunshine: during harvest time between March and May, the sun is up from 5:30 a.m. to 8 p.m., resulting in well-structured, ageworthy wines. Chardonnay and Merlot are both good, but it is arguably Sauvignon Blanc that has the greatest potential at this producer.

Rodovia SC-451, Km 56, Agua Doce, 89654-000 www.villaggiogrando.com.br

Vinhos Don Laurindo Vinhedos Valley

Don Laurindo Brandelli's family is certainly not new to wine, having sold grapes and made wines for themselves and their friends ever since Brandelli's grandfather first arrived in Brazil from Verona in Italy in 1887. But the Brandelli family only moved into commercial wine production when Brandelli and his sons first set up Vinhos Don Laurindo in 1991. Quality has risen steadily since then, and the wines have gradually carved out a niche for themselves. The key grape varieties used here are Merlot, Cabernet Sauvignon, and Malbec, but Brandelli's Italian roots can be seen in the use of the indigenous Italian grape, Ancellota.

Estrada do Vinho 8, da Graciema, Vinhedos Valley, 95700-000; www.donlaurindo.com.br

URUGUAY

Despite its small size, Uruguay is South America's fourth-largest wine producing country, with approximately 25,000 acres (10,000ha) of vineyards. The most important region is Canelones, to the north of the capital Montevideo, which is responsible for 60% of all wine production. In terms of its geography and soils, Uruguay resembles Bordeaux's Right Bank. The majority of the soils are a mixture of clay with a high percentage of calcareous soil, and the gently rolling hills provide good natural drainage. Although Cabernet Sauvignon, Sauvignon Blanc, and Chardonnay all play a role, it is the Tannat grape that represents the history of Uruguay and its winemaking tradition and is almost certainly its best-known variety.

Major grapes

Reds

Cabernet Franc

Cabernet Sauvignon

Merlot

Pinot Noir

Syrah

Tannat

 Whites

Chardonnay

Sauvignon Blanc

Semillon

Viognier

Vintages

2009

The whites tend to lack freshness and aroma, the reds are very concentrated and sometimes overly tannic.

2008

In general there were some excellent whites, but the reds were inconsistent.

2007

A challenging vintage due to wind and rain. Late varieties such as Cabernet Sauvignon and Tannat did badly.

2006

An excellent vintage for fresh whites and intense reds.

2005

Warm days and cool nights produced one of the best harvests in Uruguay's history.

2004

A very good year for whites, but the reds are rather light.

Alto de Ballena Sierra de la Ballena

In search of an ideal vineyard location, Paula Pivel and Alvaro Lorenzo found the rocky soils of Sierra de la Ballena ("whale hills") 8 miles (13km) from the ocean, strategically located near Punta del Este where grapes ripen slowly. Today, their vineyards consist of 20 acres (8ha) planted to varieties such as Merlot, Cabernet Franc, Syrah, Viognier, and Tannat. Two premium wines are available, a Merlot and a Tannat/Viognier blend, with the latter being the best wine in the range. A Viognier, a Cabernet Franc/Tannat rosé, and a fortified dessert Cabernet Franc are made in small quantities and offered to visitors at the estate.

Ruta 12, Km. 16.400, Sierra de la Ballena, Maldonado
www.altodelaballena.com

Bodega Bouza Montevideo

Bodega Bouza is a family-run boutique winery convinced that working on a small scale promotes better quality. A total of 54 acres (22ha) is planted, with 32 acres (13ha) in Las Violetas and 22 acres (9ha) in Montevideo, and some 90,000 bottles are produced each year. A total of five grape varieties are blended to produce a number of different wine styles, including Albariño, which the family claims is the first of this variety to be planted in South America. The flagship wines, from good vintages, can be delicious, but require time to mature. Bouza also makes a great example of varietal Tannat that shows what the variety can do in Uruguay. The winery has a restaurant where it is possible to taste and buy limited-edition wines alongside the local cuisine.

Cno. De la Redencion 7658 bis, Montevideo
www.bodegabouza.com

Bodega Castillo Viejo San Jose

With the support of international winemakers, three generations of the Etcheverry family have managed to balance tradition with modern techniques. The Castillo Viejo estate extends over 320 acres (130ha), with a total production of 330,000 gallons (1.5 million liters) of wine. Its modern history dates back to 1986, when the family began converting its vineyards and planting French varieties including Sauvignon Blanc, Chardonnay, Merlot, Tannat, Cabernet Sauvignon, and Cabernet Franc. At the same time, they introduced new equipment, from crushers to bottling facilities. Oak barrels, both French and American, were also introduced and, in 2008, the family started harvesting at night to improve the quality of the

fruit entering the winery. In 2005, the impressive, limited-edition El Preciado, was created. Despite all the changes, in general, the house style remains distinctly traditional with restrained fruit and firm structure.

No visitor facilities
www.castilloviejo.com

Bodega Marichal E Hijo Etchevarría

Bodega Marichal E Hijo's roots go back to the 1910s, when Isabelino Marichal arrived in Uruguay from his native Canary Islands. Marichal initially concentrated on planting vineyards, but by 1938, a winery was set up. Today Marichal, with its 70 years of family winemaking tradition, has developed into one of Uruguay's most important boutique wineries. Situated around 30km (20 miles) from the ocean in the Etchevarría region on mild slopes and calcareous soils, its small size enables the entire crop to be picked by hand, providing an annual production of 200,000 bottles. Varieties include well-made Tannat, Merlot, Cabernet Sauvignon, Cabernet Franc, Pinot Noir, Chardonnay, Semillon, and Sauvignon Blanc.

Ruta 64, Km. 48.500, Etchevarría, Canelones, CP 90000
www.marichalwines.com

Bodegas Ariano Hermanos
Constancia and El Colorado

Ariano Hermanos prides itself on combining Old World tradition with the latest wine technology and highly specialized technicians. The estate produces 330,000 gallons (1.5 million liters) annually and is based on 250 acres (100ha) spread over two regions, Constancia in Paysandu and El Colorado in Canelones. Both regions benefit from benign climates, with Constancia enjoying cool evenings and sunny days, and El Colorado moderated by Atlantic breezes. Ariano is one of Uruguay's most forward-thinking producers, converting its vineyards using French varieties of the highest quality. The work is starting to pay off, if wines such as the excellent Nelson Ariano Tannat the estate's flagship wine —are anything to go by.

Ruta 48, Km. 15, Las Piedras, Canelones, CP 90200
www.arianohermanos.com

Bodegas Carrau Las Violetas

Back in the 1930s, Juan Carrau arrived in Uruguay with a plan to continue with the winemaking tradition of his Catalan family. Carrau's legacy for future generations has been some of Uruguay's oldest plantings of Nebbiolo and Tannat, situated just north of Montevideo in the Las Violetas region, known for its rich clay soils. More recently, additional vineyards have been established 1,000ft (300m) above sea level in the Cerro Chapeu region, providing excellent drainage and grapes with great intensity. The finest wine from the Carrau range is Amat, a 100% Tannat made in honor of family patriarch, Francisco Carrau Amat (1790–1860). Passionate about culture and education, the company dedicates Tuesday as a day for school visits to the winery, so children can begin to understand wine, while drinking grape juice.

Cesar Mayo Gutierrez 2556, Montevideo, CP 12400
www.bodegascarrau.com

De Lucca El Colorado

Reinaldo De Lucca is one of the great characters of Uruguayan wine. "El Tano," as he is known, was one of the pioneers in the reconstruction of the Uruguayan wine industry 20 years ago. His winery is situated 20 miles (30km) from the Atlantic Coast with 125 acres (50ha) spread over El Colorado, Rincón del Colorado, El Colorado Chico and Progreso in the heart of the Canelones region, which is among the most ancient viticultural areas in Uruguay. In terms of style, the red wines of De Lucca are traditional, with elegant fruit underpinned by firm tannic structure.

Ruta 48, Km. 13.100, El Colorado, Canelones
www.deluccawines.com

Establecimiento Juanicó Juanicó

The Deicas family have owned and managed Establecimiento Juanicó since 1979. Throughout that time they have been dedicated to producing the highest quality wines, and they have had a joint venture with Bernard Magrez of Bordeaux's Château Pape Clément since 1999. The estate has more than 620 acres (250ha) of vineyards in Canelones, Uruguay's main wine area, and it is one of Uruguay's most advanced wineries. Capacity is approximately 990,000 gallons (4.5 million liters) using stainless steel, concrete tanks, and both French and American oak barrels for aging. Juanicó aims to achieve the perfect balance between tradition and innovation.

Ruta 5, Km. 37.800, Juanicó, Canelones, 90400
www.juanico.com

Juan Toscanini e Hijos
Canelón Chico and Paso Cuello

Don Juan Toscanini and his wife left Geneva in 1894 to settle in Canelón Chico, 20 miles (30km) north of Montevideo in the Río de la Plata region. They founded their winery in 1908. Today, Toscanini has a total of 460 acres (185ha). High-density plantations, which are hand harvested, have helped cement Toscanini's position as one of Uruguay's most important wineries. Grape varieties include Merlot, Cabernet Sauvignon, Cabernet Franc, Syrah, Tannat, Chardonnay, Sauvignon Blanc, Tebbiano, Semillon, and Gewürztraminer. The range is large, and it is true that work is required to improve consistency. However, a number of wines merit attention, including the Tannat Reserve and TCM, an intriguing blend of Tannat, Cabernet Sauvignon, and Merlot.

Ruta 69, Km. 30, Canelón Chico, Canelones
www.toscaniniwines.com

PIZZORNO
A LONG FAMILY TRADITION GIVEN A MODERN TWIST BY A NEW ZEALAND WINEMAKER

PISANO
THE FRAGRANT TORRONTES IS JUST ONE OF PISANO'S MANY WELL-MADE WINES

Pisano Progreso

Pisano's estate sits on calcereous soil in the heart of the Río de la Plata region. The estate's proximity to the ocean means big differences between day and night temperatures, which in turn makes for much greater flavor intensity in the finished wines. Pisano produces 380,000 bottles each year from small parcels, and the aim is to produce wines with a European profile. The flagship wine here is Arretxea Premium Grand Reserve—a blend of Tannat, Cabernet Sauvignon, and Merlot, that is deeply colored, with intense and complex fruit and tannic backbone. An important player in developing Uruguay's image as a wine producer overseas, Pisano currently has its wines in more than 35 countries.

No visitor facilities
www.pisanowines.com

Pizzorno Canelón Chico

With more than a century of experience, Pizzorno is one of Uruguay's best boutique wineries. It was founded in 1910 by Don Próspero José Pizzorno, and Pizzorno's grandson, Carlos, continues today with the same love and respect for nature and his family's tradition of producing good-quality, quintessentially Uruguayan, handcrafted wines. Vineyards are cultivated and harvested by hand with 50 acres (20ha) located in the Canelón Chico region. The vineyards have been replanted using French varietals and are supported by the New Zealand winemaking consultant, Duncan Killiner. The red wines are very well-made with the Merlot/Tannat blend the standout.

Ruta 32, Km. 23, Canelón Chico, Canelones
www.pizzornowines.com

Viña Varela Zarranz Las Piedras

Twenty years after acquiring the Pons farm in 1965, the second generation of the Varela Zarranz family took charge of the winery. After initial experiments with French stocks, new vineyards were created and healthy clones gradually replaced old-vine stock. Over the past 20 years, the varietal composition of the vineyard has been almost completely transformed, so that there are now 270 acres (110ha) of 80% red and 20% white. There has been some investment in the winery, but historical integrity is maintained in the central building and cellar, which date back to 1892. The best red wines include Tannat Crianza and Teatro Solis Tannat Roble.

Ruta 74, Km. 29, Joaquín Suárez, Canelones, CP 91200
www.varelazarranz.com

Vinos Finos H Stagnari
Nueva Hespérides and La Puebla

Hector Stagnari gained experience studying in Bordeaux and the Rhône Valley in the late 1970s. In 1996, he returned to France to select the clones he wanted to plant in the Nueva Hespérides region. His winery is situated on the banks of the River Uruguay and in close proximity to the River Dayman and the Salto Grande lake, where the temperatures can vary by more than 36°F (20°C) between the day and the evening, greatly benefiting the ripening process. The ideal location, family craftsmanship, and innovative technology have combined to provide Stagnari with intriguing wines such as Daymán Tannat.

Ruta 5, Km. 20, Canelones
www.stagnari.com

Portugal is currently one of the most interesting and diverse wine nations. A relatively small, thin country on the western margins of Europe, it has retained its unique identity in the wine world largely through its range of indigenous grape varieties, which have helped prevent its wines taking an anonymous, international direction.

Until the 1990s, there were two rather separate elements to Portuguese wine. Most visible internationally was the British-dominated port trade, based in Vila Nova de Gaia, over the river from Porto, where the fortified wines from the spectacular Douro Valley were matured and traded. Then there were the less well-regarded table wines, mostly inexpensive quaffers destined to slake the thirst of Portugal's—and former colony Brazil's—workers.

This has all changed. While port is still important, Portugal's table wines have improved beyond recognition in the last 15 years, and in particular the Douro is now producing some world-class red wines from its incredible vineyards. The Alentejo has also emerged as an important wine region, and both Bairrada and Dão have dozens of quality-minded producers making some superb wines, many of which are red. Vinho Verde, in the north, is earning a reputation for serious whites from Alvarinho, and the traditional bulk-producing regions of the Ribatejo and Estremadura—now renamed Tejo and Lisboa—are making some commercially astute wines, too. Other regions include the Setúbal Peninsula (including Terras de Sado) near Lisbon, and the Beira Interior, a northerly extension of the Alentejo running up the east of the country, hemmed in by mountains. Even the hot Algarve in the south is beginning to make respectable wines.

The Portuguese wine scene is quite dynamic, yet many of the wines are under the radar of most wine lovers abroad. But it is well worth making the effort to get to know these ever-improving wines.

PORTUGAL

DOURO

ATLANTIC OCEAN

Braga
Porto
Douro

LISBON

■ Douro wine region

The Douro is not only one of the world's greatest wine regions, it is also one of its most beautiful. It is hard not to be seduced by the scale and wildness of the terrain, with the steep, terraced vineyards rising up from the River Douro and its tributaries. For centuries, the Douro's pre-eminent position in the wine world rested on the quality of its fortified wines, known as port. These were once the only serious wines to be found in the region, but not anymore. Today, an increasing number of high-end table wines are being made. The combination of schistous soils, steep slopes, old vines, and distinctively Portuguese grape varieties, in the right hands, results in some seriously interesting, ageworthy red wines and fast-improving whites.

Major grapes

 Reds

Sousão

Tinta Amarela

Tinta Cão

Tinta Roriz

Touriga Franca

Touriga Nacional

Whites

Gouveio

Rabigato

Viosinho

Vintages

2009
A warm vintage, but many of the wines seem to be turning out very well.

2008
A really good vintage. The wines are looking very promising, with bright, focused fruit and nice acidity.

2007
A superb vintage, with wonderful fruit purity and some richness.

2006
A difficult vintage, with a very hot growing season and some hail problems in certain areas. The average quality is not great.

2005
A good to very good vintage with some classic wines.

2004
A very good-quality vintage with lovely fruit purity. Some superb wines were made.

One of the world's most spectacular wine regions, the Douro boasts more than 96,000 acres (39,000ha) of vineyards. More than its size, however, what makes the region so distinctive is that over 70% of those vineyards are planted at gradients of up to 30%. This is mountain viticulture on a grand scale.

Located inland from the beautiful, bustling old city of Porto, the Douro is now relatively accessible by road, but in the past this region was quite remote. Sheltered by mountains from the influence of the Atlantic, the Douro enjoys a very different climate from Porto, with cold winters and hot, largely dry summers. The soils are also quite special, based on schist (most of the rest of northern Portugal is granitic). This combination of climate and low vigor soils makes this a great place for growing top-quality wine grapes.

There are three subregions within the Douro. Traveling east from Porto, the first encountered is the Baixo Corgo, which is cooler and has higher rainfall than the others. Next is the Cima Corgo, the traditional heart of the region, and responsible for the most elegant, compelling wines. Finally, stretching almost to the Spanish border is the Douro Superior, which is warmer and not all as steeply sloped. This wild country has increasingly been tamed and developed with vineyards.

Port has historically dominated the Douro's production. It is only recently, since around 2000, that a significant number of high-end table wines have been made from these special terroirs. While port is still very important for the region, table wines are currently causing more excitement.

Douro reds are typically a blend of several grape varieties, with Touriga Nacional, Tinta Roriz, Touriga Franca, Tinta Cão, Tinta Amarela, and Sousão the most important. The wines vary in style, but there is frequently a common theme of ripe blackberry, dark cherry, and plum fruit, with fine but firm structure and a distinct minerality. There is usually a pleasant savory twist to the wines, and while most have not been made for all that long, all the signs are that the best wines will develop well when they are given the chance to age for five to ten years in the bottle.

Quality red wine production may be a new phenomenon in the valley, but an even more recent, and no less exciting, development has been the emergence of top Douro whites. While most parts of the Douro are too warm for most white grape varieties, some vineyards higher up the slopes, and facing north, are now turning out some very stylish whites from varieties such as Viosinho, Gouveio, and Rabigato.

Alves de Sousa

Domingos Alves de Sousa, aided by his son Tiago, is now making some first-class Douro table wines. He has five properties (Quinta da Gaivosa, Quinta do Vale da Raposa, Quinta das Caldas, Quinta da Estação, and Quinta da Avaleira) in the Baixo Corgo, which together constitute a sizeable 270 acres (110ha). Initially a grower, Domingos has been making wines since 1991, and they have improved considerably of late. Gaivosa is a traditional, dense, ageworthy red; Abandonado, from very old vines at Raposa, is even better. The dense, sweet, ripe Vinha de Lordelo, from selected bits of Gaivosa, is perhaps the best.

Pousada da Cumieira, Apartado 15, 5030-055 Santa Marta de Penaguião; www.alvesdesousa.com

Aneto

Aneto is a relatively new producer from the Douro, based in Alijó, with Francisco Montenegro of Quinta Nova as the winemaker (it is his own project). The venture started in 2001 based on 17 acres (7ha) of vines, and the first vintage was the 2002 red, with a white added in 2007 from a separate vineyard. The reductive white wine is interesting if a little funky, and the reds are really impressive, with lovely fruit purity. Production of each of the wines is small, up to 6,000 bottles. ★ **Rising star**

Quinta do Paço, 5050-090 Godim, Peso da Régua
www.aneto.com.pt

Azeo

Azeo is the project of winemaker João Brito e Cunha. Previously winemaker at Lavradores de Feitoria, Brito e Cunha now works as a consultant winemaker for a number of producers, including Churchill. He has been developing his own wines since 2002, and his aim is to make gastronomic terroir wines with good acidity. His reds combine the freshness of fruit from the Cima Corgo with the richness of fruit from the warmer Douro Superior. The 2005 is pure and fresh, but with real density. Brito e Cunha is very keen on Viosinho, which he regards as possibly the most promising white variety in the region. Look out for the Ázeo Branco Reserva, with lovely taut minerality and subtle oak influence. ★ **Rising star**

Rua Augusto César, 99, 5000-591 Vila Real
934 041 413

Bago de Touriga

This small producer in the Douro was formed in 1998 by winemaker Luis Soares Duarte and João Roseira of Quinta do Infantado. The idea here is to make expressive, terroir-driven wines from bought-in grapes sourced from a range of old-vine vineyards; wines that score on elegance and not power. The pair work in conjunction with vineyard owners, but don't own any of their own. The wines, under the brands Gouvyas, Montevalle, and Terroso, are really interesting. Look out for the fantastic Gouvyas Reserva 2005. As well as the reds, stylish whites are also made here.

Urb. Vila Paulista, Lote 65, 5000-262 Vila Real
932 66 71 48

Barca-Velha/Quinta da Leda

One of Portugal's legendary red wines, Barca Velha is the top wine from Casa Ferreirinha, and was first made in 1952. For a long time, it was the Douro's only serious table

CONCEITO
CONCEITO WORKS WONDERS WITH THE INTRIGUINGLY NAMED RED GRAPE, BASTARDO

BARCA-VELHA
FOR MANY PEOPLE, BARCA VELHA REMAINS THE DOURO'S, AND PORTUGAL'S, FINEST RED

wine. So far, just 15 vintages have been released, the most recent in 2000, which is only now on the market. Barca Velha was owned by A A Ferreira, but in 1987 the company was acquired by Sogrape, the current owners. It has always been made from grapes from the Douro Superior, and for a long time the core of the wine came from Quinta Vale Meão. These days, the majority of the blend comes from Quinta de Leda, purchased by Ferreira in 1978, where the wine is made. The style is quite old-fashioned, but not rustic, and the wine ages really well (indeed, it demands time in bottle). Also worth looking out for are the second wine, Casa Ferreirinha, and the relatively new Quinta da Leda—both are really impressive.

Quinta da Leda
www.sograpevinhos.eu

CARM

Casa Agrícola Roberodo Madeira, usually abbreviated as CARM, has 153 acres (62ha) of vines in the Douro Superior, from which winemaker Rui Madeira is making stylish, fruit-driven wines. It also makes olive oil, with a further 540 acres (220ha) of olive groves. Six estates are owned by the Madeira family (Quinta do Bispado, Quinta de Calabria, Quinta do Côa, Quinta das Marvalhas, Quinta da Urze, and Quinta das Verdelhas) and they have been organically farmed since 1995, with CARM one of the few in the region to work this way. Pick of the wines are the regular and reserve wines from Quinta do Côa, which show freshness and purity of ripe, dark fruits.

Rua da Calábria, 5150-021 Almendra
www.carm.pt

Casal de Loivos

Casal de Loivos is owned by the Pereira de Sampayo family, high up in the Douro overlooking Pinhão. The wine is made by Cristiano van Zeller and his team at Quinta do Vale D Maria, and shows freshness and definition. It is a cool spot that does better in the warmer years, but which makes elegant wines.

No visitor facilities
www.casadecasaldeloivos.com

Chryseia

A joint venture between the Symington family and Bruno Prats (who used to own Cos d'Estournel in Bordeaux), Chryseia is an ambitious red wine. Sleek, ripe, lush and modern, it has been criticized by some for not having a sense of place; others just love the style. The second wine, PostScriptum, is made in a similar style, and in some lesser vintages is the top wine when no first wine is made. The first vintage was 2000.

5130-111 Ervedosa do Douro, S João da Pesqueira
www.chryseia.com

Conceito

Conceito is a relatively new producer based in the Douro Superior. Young winemaker Rita Ferriera Marques is allowed full license to do her best with the grapes from her mother Carla Ferriera's properties, and the results so far have been very impressive. There are three vineyards, all in the Teja valley. Quinta da Veiga, Quinta do Chão-do-Pereiro (both 50acres/20ha), Quinta do Cabido (57 acres/23ha), and a 25 acre (10ha) vineyard at the top of the valley, where there is some granite used solely for whites.

DOURO

The Porto e Douro region, to give the DOC its proper name, is truly spectacular. As the contour lines on the map indicate, this is mountain viticulture on a grand scale, with the majority of the vineyards planted on steep slopes leading down to the River Douro and its various tributaries. Mountains protect the Douro from the Atlantic weather systems that Porto on the coast is influenced by, and the region experiences a continental climate of cold winters and hot summers. Temperatures increase and rainfall decreases as you follow the Douro toward the Spanish border, with the result that the Douro Superior is the warmest and driest of the three subregions indicated on the map.

2007 **2007**

CÔTTO

DOURO
Denominação de Origem Controlada
Engarrafado
na
Quinta

14,0% alc./vol.   750ml

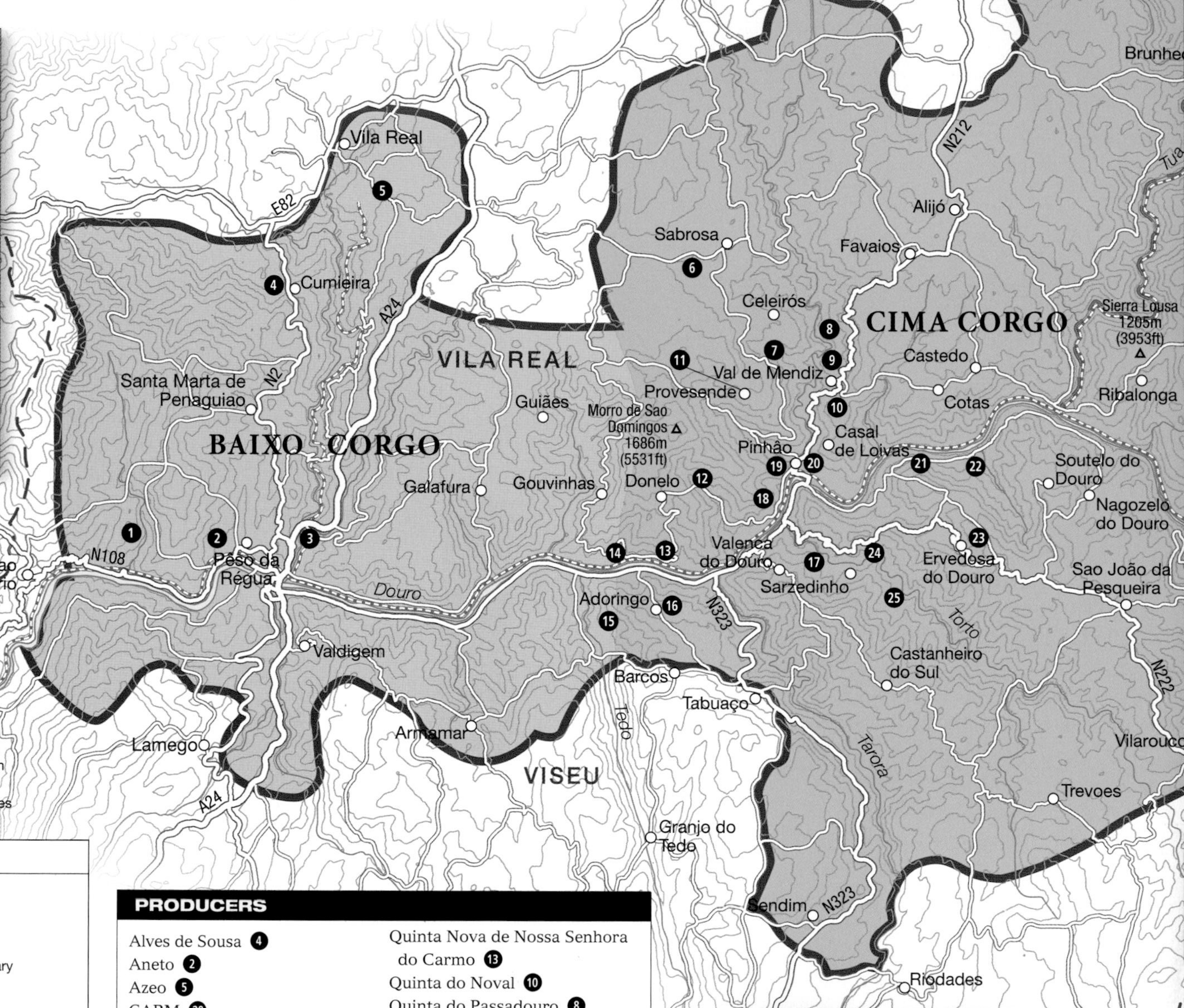

KEY

CIMA CORGO	Subregion
	DOC boundary
	Rivers, lakes
	Roads
	330ft (100m) contours
	Regional boundary
	Country border
	Urban areas
①	Location of one or more producers

PRODUCERS

Alves de Sousa ④
Aneto ②
Azeo ⑤
CARM ㉙
Casal de Loivos ⑲
Chryseia ㉓
Conceito ㉖
Duorum ㉗
Lavradores de Feitoria ⑥
Niepoort ⑮
Poeira ⑪
PV ㉑
Quinta do Côtto ①
Quinta do Crasto ⑭
Quinta do Infantado ⑫
Quinta de Macedos ㉕

Quinta Nova de Nossa Senhora do Carmo ⑬
Quinta do Noval ⑩
Quinta do Passadouro ⑧
Quinta do Portal ⑦
Quinta de Romaneira ⑳
Quinta de Roriz ㉒
Quinta de la Rosa ⑱
Quinta de São José ㉑
Quinta do Tedo ⑯
Quinta do Vale Dona Maria ㉔
Quinta do Vale Meão ㉘
Quinta do Vallado ③
Ramos Pinto ⑰
Wine & Soul/Pintas ⑨

QUINTA DO
PORTAL   RESERVA
DOURO | RED WINE
PRODUCT OF PORTUGAL

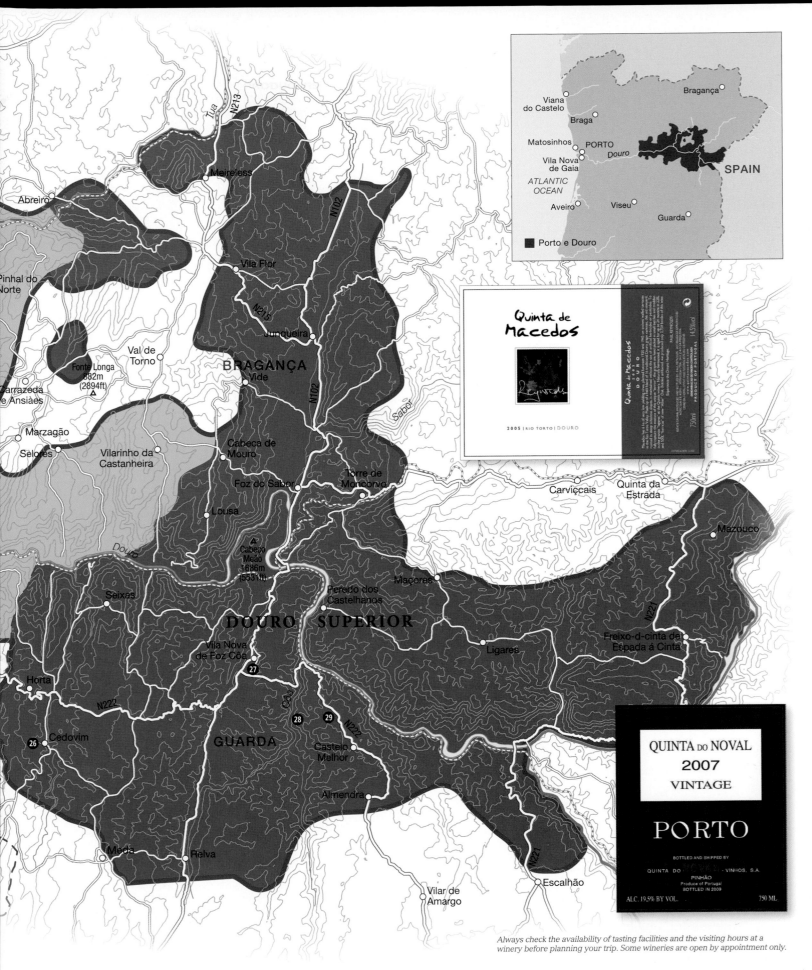

Viana do Castelo
Braga
Bragança
Matosinhos
PORTO
Douro
Vila Nova de Gaia
ATLANTIC OCEAN
Aveiro
Viseu
Guarda
SPAIN

■ Porto e Douro

Abreiro
Meireless
Pinhal do Norte
Vila Flor
N213
Tua
N102
N215
Junqueira
Val de Torno
Fonte Longa 882m (2894ft) △
BRAGANÇA
Vide
N102
Sabor
Carrazeda de Ansiães
Marzagão
Selores
Vilarinho da Castanheira
Cabeça de Mouro
Foz do Sabor
Torre de Moncorvo
Carviçcais
Quinta da Estrada
Lousa
Cabeço Meão 1686m (5531ft) △
Mazouco
Douro
Seixas
Peredo dos Castelhanos
Maçores
DOURO SUPERIOR
Vila Nova de Foz Côa
27
Ligares
N221
Freixo-d-cinta de Espada á Cinta
Horta
N222
Côa
28
29
N222
GUARDA
Cedovim
26
Casteio Melhor
Almendra
N221
Meda
Relva
Vilar de Amargo
Escalhão

Quinta de Macedos
Reynolds
2005 | RIO TORTO | DOURO

QUINTA DO NOVAL
2007
VINTAGE
PORTO
BOTTLED AND SHIPPED BY
QUINTA DO NOVAL - VINHOS, S.A.
PINHÃO
Produce of Portugal
BOTTLED IN 2009
ALC. 19,5% BY VOL.   750 ML

Always check the availability of tasting facilities and the visiting hours at a winery before planning your trip. Some wineries are open by appointment only.

QUINTA DO PASSADOURO
EX-NIEPOORT WINEMAKER JORGE BORGES
HAS HELPED PUT PASSADOURO ON THE MAP

The first wines from the Conceito (which translates as "concept") label were made in 2005; prior to this the grapes were sold to other producers. The Bastardo is unusual and amazing, with its pale color and haunting, leafy, spicy perfume. The Douro white is world-class. The two reds, the Tinto and the Contraste, are both excellent, with lovely freshness and purity.

Largo da Madalena 10, Cedovim 5155-022
www.conceito.com.pt

Duorum

Duorum is latin for "from two." It is a joint project between two of Portugal's best-known enologists, João Portugal Ramos and Jose Maria Soares Franco. Ramos is the king of the Alentejo—a consultant winemaker turned wine-grower whose own estate has grown to be one of the largest private companies in the region. Soares Franco was for 27 years the custodian of Barca Velha, the famous Douro wine that is now part of the Sogrape stable. As well as two famous enologists, the "from two" also refers to the fact that the wine is a blend from two rather different parts of the Douro: the Cima Corgo and Douro Superior, further upriver toward the Spanish border. Currently, the Douro Superior vineyards are rented, but Duorum has also purchased 370 acres (150ha) which are being converted into a spectacular quinta called Castelo Melhor. Three wines are made, beginning with the 2007 vintage. Duorum Colheita is well-priced, fresh, and brightly fruited; the Reserva is a step up in both price and quality, with dark, meaty fruit and some complexity. A cheaper wine, Tons de Dourum, is very attractive and brilliant value. Vintage port is also made. ★ **Rising star**

Estrada 222, 5150-146 Vila Nova de Foz Coa
www.duorum.pt

Lavradores de Feitoria

This is an interesting project, which began in 1999. Eighteen quintas throughout the Douro are involved in a collaborative venture. A central winemaking team makes the wines, and where a particular quinta performs well enough, a wine is made with the name of the quinta on it; otherwise, the grapes are used for blending. The idea is to create brands that have a bigger impact on the marketplace than each of the quintas would alone. The basic red wine, Três Bagos, is good value for the price, and the Três Bagos Grande Escolha is a step up. There's also a lovely Sauvignon Blanc made under the Três Bagos label, from a cooler site in the Douro. The top wines are Quinta da Costa and the superbly elegant Meruge.

Zona Industrial de Sabrosa, Lote 5, apartado 25, Paços, 5060 Sabrosa; www.lavradoresdefeitoria.pt

Niepoort

Since taking the reins of the family business, the talented Dirk Niepoort has transformed this small port house into what is arguably Portugal's most celebrated winery. Beginning with the experimental Robustus in 1990, and continuing with Redoma (since 1991), Batuta (1999), and Charme (2001), Dirk has made world-class wines that have helped demonstrate the potential of the Douro for table wines as well as ports. Along with his red wines, Dirk's whites are profound (Tiara is a fine, Riesling-style wine of purity and freshness; Reserva Branco is Burgundian and ageworthy), and look out also for small-production lots labeled "Projectos," as well as

the relaunch of the incredible Robustus with the 2004 vintage. Niepoort's ports are also in the very top tier, with the vintage being one of the very best in 2003 and 2007 and some serious tawnies and Colheitas. Left-field projects include collaborative wines such as Girosol (a Loureiro from Vinho Verde) and a Palomino Fino table wine from Equipo Navajos. Anything with Niepoort's name on the label is sure to be interesting.

Quinta de Nápoles, Tedo, 5110-543 Santo Adriao
www.niepoort-vinhos.com

Poeira

Poeira, which translates as "dust," is the wine of Jorge Moreira. It hails from his own Quinta de Terra Feita de Cima, which he purchased in 2001. It is a 37 acre (15ha) estate with 22 acres (9ha) of vines, including three of old vines. The talented Moreira is also winemaker at Quinta de la Rosa, and his quest is to make wines of elegance and precision that have good aging potential. First released in 2001, Poeira is acknowledged as one of the most serious of all Douro reds, and is made from a north-facing vineyard, which helps it retain its acidity and structure. Po de Poeira, the second wine, is worth seeking out, as is the focused white Alvarinho. ★ **Rising star**

5060-283 Provesende
www.poeira.pt

PV

PV is a new Douro wine company founded in 2004 by Jorge Borges, José Maria Cálem, and Cristiano Van Zeller. The first wines were made in a leased winery before the move to a refurbished winery in Vilarinho de Cotas for the 2005–2007 vintages. But things took a new direction when PV acquired access to the Cálem family's spectacular Quinta da Foz in 2008, which is also when the first port was made. The main wine is VT. ★ **Rising star**

5085 Pinhão
www.pvwines.com

Quinta do Côtto

One of the pioneering band of quality table wine producers in the Douro, Miguel Champalimaud's Quinta do Côtto is based in the cooler Baixo Corgo (lower Douro). He has 125 acres (50ha) of vines, and the star wine is the dense, complex Grande Escolha, with the berry-ish estate wine not far behind. But also worth seeking out is a white wine called Paço de Teixeró, which is actually made from grapes grown in the Vinho Verde region, although it is more full-bodied and elegant than most. Champalimaud achieved notoriety in Portugal (the home of cork) for being the first producer to switch to screwcaps for some of his wines.

Quinta do Côtto Cidadelhe, 5040-154 Mesão Frio
www.quintadocotto.pt

Quinta do Crasto

In Quinta do Crasto, their estate that juts out above the river, the Roquette family has a jewel of the Douro. Featured in the famous tiles at Pinhão station, the quinta has 320 acres (130ha) of vineyards, including two that make single-vineyard wines in the best years: Ponte and Maria Theresa. The wines are made by Aussie winemaker Dominic Morris, assisted by Manuel Lobo, in a rich, fruit-forward style, and include a well-regarded Reserva,

QUINTA DO CRASTO
THE HIGHLY SUCCESSFUL CRASTO MAKES
VOLUPTUOUS WINES IN A MODERN STYLE

a Touriga Nacional, and a Tinta Roriz. Crasto's success in the USA has helped establish the Douro's international reputation. It has recently planted 250 acres (100ha) in the Douro Superior at Quinta da Cabreira.

Gouvinhas, 5060-063 Sabrosa
www.quintadocrasto.pt

Quinta do Infantado

In 1979, Quinta do Infantado, based near Pinhão in the Cima Corgo, became famous for being the first producer in the modern era to make, bottle, and sell its ports directly from its estate. It is also one of the Douro's leaders in organic viticulture. João Roseira is in charge of production, and as well as making some excellent vintage and late bottled vintage port, he also makes serious table wines from the family's 50 acre (20ha) vineyard.

5085-217 Covas do Douro
254 738 020

Quinta de Macedos

Macedos is a small property in the Rio Torto valley of the Douro, owned by English couple Paul and Philippa Reynolds. They have 17 acres (7ha) of old vines and make only table wines in traditional granite *lagares*. Quinta de Macedos is an intense, sweetly fruited wine with real presence, flirting with being just a little too ripe. Second wine Pinga do Torto is deliciously rich, with dark fruits.

Sarzedinho, 5130-141 Ervedosa do Douro
www.quintamacedos.com

Quinta Nova de Nossa Senhora do Carmo

Quinta Nova de Nossa Senhora do Carmo is beautifully situated, a short way upstream of Quinta do Crasto in the Cima Corgo. It has 210 acres (85ha) of vines, and it is now one of the top table wine producers in the region. The entry-level Pomares white and red are both deliciously fresh. Grainha red and white, the next step up, are impressive. But the stars of the show are pure, unoaked Colheita; aromatic, expressive Reserva; beautifully floral Touriga Nacional; and refined, complex Grande Reserva. An icon wine is in the planning. The ports are good, but more of a work in progress. ★ **Rising star**

Largo da Estação, 5085-034 Pinhão
www.quintanova.com

Quinta do Noval

Historic Quinta do Noval endured a dark period in the 1980s and early 1990s before it was purchased by French insurance company AXA in 1993. In came Brit Christian Seeley, and he turned things around to the point where Noval is now making some of the Douro's best wines and ports. As well as the legendary Nacional port, made from a small, rather ragged-looking plot of ungrafted vines, the vintage port and second label Silval are now all in top form. The Quinta Noval table wine and second wine Cedro do Noval, which have been produced since 2004, are among the best in the Douro. There is also an impressive new varietal Syrah, Labrador. All the wines and ports come from the 320 acres (130ha) of splendidly situated estate vineyards in the Pinhão valley.

Rua do Vale, 5060 Sabrosa
www.quintadonoval.com

Quinta do Passadouro

Passadouro is a beautiful quinta with 50 acres (20ha) of vines in Vale do Mendiz, in the Pinhão Valley. It was purchased by Belgian Dieter Bohrmann in 1991. Until 2003, the wines were made by Dirk Niepoort, and some of the Passadouro grapes were used by Dirk in his Redoma red. Then, when Niepoorts's winemaker, Jorge Borges, quit, he was hired by Bohrmann and the Niepoort connection was severed. Borges has done a good job with the table wines, which show lovely purity and definition. Passadouro Reserva is now one of the Douro's top reds, and the regular Passadouro is also superb. Ports are also made here, and the vintage port is excellent.

Vale de Mendiz, 5085-101 Pinhão
www.quinta-do-passadouro.com

Quinta do Portal

Portal is a mid-sized, family-owned winery in the Douro Valley. Traditionally, they used to make port wines, and all their wines were sold to shippers. From 1991, the family started building the Quinta do Portal project, focusing on both table wines and ports, and buying some new quintas. Portal has five properties in the Pinhão Valley, with over 247 acres (100ha) in all. The first wines were released in 1994. French wine scientist Pascal Chatonnet has been consulting at Portal since the beginning, with winemaking in the hands of Paolo Coutinho. Initially, quality was a bit patchy, but recent vintages have been much better. Reserva and Grande Reserva have been very impressive wines since 2005, and the Portal vintage port and special *cuvée* Portal+ vintage port are deliciously focused, with intense, sweet, pure fruit.

Celeirós do Douro, 5060-909 Sabrosa
www.quintadoportal.com

Quinta de Romaneira

The beautiful Romaneira had fallen into disrepair when it was taken over by a consortium including Christian Seely (of Noval fame) in 2004. The substantial Grade A vineyards were the lure for Seely, and they are being renovated, with 200 acres (81ha) currently in production, and the potential to expand to 494 acres (200ha). The wines so far have been stunningly good: second wine R de Romaneira is a bargain; the Quinta wine is beautifully focused and elegant. The vintage port is also thrilling. As well as wine, there is a small, luxury hotel and a restaurant.

Rua António Manuel Saraiva, 5085 Alijó
www.quintadaromaneira.pt

Quinta de Roriz

Roriz is a historic port quinta. From 1815, it was in the hands of the van Zeller family, but it was bought by the Symington family, who had been part owners with media magnate João van Zeller, in May 2009. Located in the Douro Superior, some 3 miles (5km) upriver from Pinhão, it has 494 acres (200ha), with 104 acres (42ha) of vines, and a new winery completed in 2005. Roriz has been making what are now known as single quinta vintage ports since the 19th century, and the style is rich, intense, and ripe. Impressive table wines are also made in the same style. Second wine Prazo de Roriz is a bargain, offering lovely ripe, pure dark fruits for the price.

Ervedosa do Douro, 5130-113 S João da Pesqueira
www.quintaderoriz.com

UNESCO WORLD HERITAGE SITE

The Douro Valley, a UNESCO World Heritage Site, must be the most spectacular of all wine regions. There are three ways to access it: by rail, road, or river. Trains run from Porto's San Benito station, and are cheap, if a little basic. It takes ages to reach Régua, but from there on, the views from the train track, which runs along the river, are beautiful. An alternative would be to drive to Pinhão, in the heart of the region, and then catch the train up to Poçino, high in the Douro Superior near the Spanish border. The perfect option would then be to take a boat back down to Pinhão and do some quinta-spotting. Driving around the Douro is difficult, slow, and in some cases perilous, but if you want to visit specific quintas, then this is the only option. There are now many places (including several quintas) where you can stay overnight in the region. However you choose to visit, you'll never forget your first sight of the spectacular, steeply terraced Douro vineyards.

Terraced vineyards follow the contours of the hills above Pinhão in the heart of the Douro Valley.

RAMOS PINTO

THE COLLECTION RED IS SAID TO BE INSPIRED
BY THE SENTIMENTS OF THE BELLE EPOQUE

Quinta de la Rosa

This beautiful quinta, just a stone's throw downriver of Pinhão, has been owned by the Berqvist family since 1906. Sophia Berqvist runs things here, assisted by talented winemaker Jorge Moreira. Since Moreira joined the team in time for the 2002 vintage, the quality of the wines and ports made here has risen substantially. Under his guidance, La Rosa has also bought and partially replanted a new vineyard at Quinta das Bandeiras in the Douro Superior, opposite the famed Quinta do Vale Meão, to supplement the 136 acres (55ha) of vines at La Rosa. The estate red is delicious, but things really begin to get serious with the Reserve, made mostly from old vines. Moreira's style is about elegance rather than just power, and this is shown in the wines. The first wine from Bandeiras was a 50/50 joint venture between Moreira and La Rosa called Passagem, and shows lovely purity.

Pinhão 5085-215
www.quintadelarosa.com

Quinta de São José

Quinta de São José is the family property of winemaker João Brito e Cunha, who also makes the wines of Ázeo. It's beautifully situated, in front of Quinta do Romaneira, and has north-facing schistous slopes. The Brito e Cunha family bought it in the late-1990s and began the task of renovating the 50 acre (20ha) quinta, which was in a poor state. João aims for freshness and elegance in his wines, which he achieves here. Look out for the bright, expressive 2005 Tinto and the inexpensive, lightly oaked 2007 Colheita with its fresh, floral perfume.

Ervedosa do Douro, 5130-123
www.quintasjose.com

Quinta do Tedo

California-based barrel salesman Vincent Bouchard and his wife Kay bought the Quinta do Tedo in 1992. On the south bank of the Douro in the Cima Corgo, it has 35 acres (14ha) of vineyards. The first vintage of the impressive, nicely defined red table wine was 2003. The ports are good, too, made in a ripe, sweet style.

5110-548 Santo Adriao, Armamar
www.quintadotedo.com

Quinta do Vale Dona Maria

Cristiano van Zeller's Quinta do Vale Dona Maria has established a reputation for distinctive, elegant Douro reds since it started in 1996. In 2003, a high-end *cuvée*, CV, was added to the range, with more concentration and new oak. Winemaking is in the hands of Sandra Tavares, also of Wine & Soul and her family property Chocapalha, and she takes the fruit from 25 acres (10ha) of old mixed vineyards. A single-quinta port is also made here, but it is the table wines that steal the show.

Ervedosa do Douro 5130-055
www.valedonamaria.com

Quinta do Vale Meão

Vale Meão is a historic quinta that is now established as one of the frontrunners in the Douro table wine revolution. It started life as one of the shrewd acquisitions of the celebrated Dona Antónia Adelaide Ferreira. The quinta has remained in the family and is owned today by Francisco ("Vito") Olazabal, previously president of the

AA Ferreira enterprise, and this is where the grapes went to, forming the bulk of the legendary Barca Velha. In 1998, Olazabal decided to go it alone and use the grapes from his estate to make his own wine, together with his son (also called Francisco, but known as Xito). The estate consists of a sizeable 153 acres (62ha) of vines, with three different soil types, each contributing to the final wine: slate, granite, and alluvial gravel. The first release was the 1999, which was met with great critical acclaim; subsequent releases have been even better, and this is now one of the top wines in Portugal. Second wine Meandro is also superb, and something of a bargain.

5150-501 Vila Nova de Foz Coa
279 762 156

Quinta do Vallado

Vallado, in the Baixo Corgo of the Douro, has been in the Ferreira family since 1818. It was renovated in the 1960s by Jorge Maria Cabral Ferreira, and then, on his death in 1992, the estate was taken over by his brother-in-law, Guilherme Álvares Ribeiro. Ribeiro began producing estate-bottled table wine and port, enlisting his winemaking cousin Xito Olazabal (of Quinta do Vale Meão), nephew Francisco Ferreira (general manager), and Cristiano van Zeller (commercial help). The wines are very good, with the stars being a rich, intense Reserva; a beautifully aromatic Touriga Nacional; and a sturdy, opaque Sousão. Some good, tawny ports are also made.

Vilarinho dos Freires, 5050-364 Peso da Régua
www.wonderfulland.com/vallado/

Ramos Pinto

Ramos Pinto has been an important company in the recent history of the Douro. There are four estates at the heart of the operation: two in the Douro Superior and two in the Cima Corgo, near Pinhão. Of the former, Quinta de Ervamoira was planted in 1974 as a sort of experiment in planting grape varieties in separate plots and in vertical rows, which allowed for mechanization. They tried 12 varieties, and from these selected five, work which was to prove controversial but influential for future plantings in the region. Table wine production began in earnest here in 1990 with the release of the good-value Duas Quintas red. The first Reserva was made in 1991, and has since been made every year apart from 1993, 1996, and 1998, and is a big step up in quality. The Reserva Especial has so far been made in 1995, 1999, and 2000.

Quinta do Bom Retiro
www.ramospinto.pt

Wine & Soul/Pintas

Since their first vintage in 2001, husband-and-wife team Jorge Borges and Sandra Tavares have established Pintas as one of the Douro's top table wines. In 2003, they added a vintage port, and then a second red, Pintas Character, as well as Guru, a white from old vines. All the wines are made under the winery name of Wine & Soul. Pintas itself comes from a single old vineyard in Vale de Mendiz, where their small winery is located, and is also the name of their exuberant dog. The signature style here is refinement and sophistication, rather than the rustic wildness the Douro is sometimes known for. ★Rising star

Av Júlio de Freitas, 6, Vale de Mendiz, 5085-101 Pinhão
936 161 408

QUINTA DE LA ROSA

THE RESERVE IS A SUPERB DEMONSTRATION
OF THE ELEGANT LA ROSA HOUSE STYLE

PORT

The spectacular Douro Valley in northern Portugal is home to an original fortified wine style: port. A sweet wine, made by adding brandy spirit to part-fermented grape juice, port comes in two styles: ruby (fruit-dominated, bottled early) and tawny (complex wines aged for longer in wood). Top vintage ports, which are only made in the best years, are able to develop fabulous complexity over many decades in bottle. The best 20- and 30-year-old tawny ports are also superb, but receive less attention. For many years, the port trade was dominated by the large port houses, many of them with British connections. But in recent years, increasing numbers of Douro quintas (estates) have been making their own ports.

Douro wine region
Location of port lodges in Vila Nova de Gaia

In a class of its own, port is a unique fortified wine style (although it has been imitated elsewhere). It derives its flavor, strength, and sweetness from the process of adding spirit to still-sweet, part-fermented grape must. The origins of port date back to the late 17th century, when war between France and England cut off most of Britain's supply of wine, leading to an increased demand for the wines of Portugal (an English ally). Problems with adulteration and over-production destabilized the industry in the 18th century, leading to price collapses, which were remedied by the Marques de Pombal, who instituted the world's first system of origin control and regional classification of wines in the Douro, in 1757.

For a long time, the port trade has been dominated by the large port houses, based in Vila Nova de Gaia, over the river from Porto. Until 1986, any ports destined for export had to pass through Vila Nova, and this protectionist rule prevented smaller producers from entering the port market. Now, many smaller quintas are also bottling their own ports, as well as making table wines. This has made the whole scene more dynamic.

There are two distinct categories of port: ruby and tawny. Ruby is a slightly confusing term, because it is also used to describe the cheapest ports, but it refers to the fruity style of port, aged for a relatively short time in larger oak vats and bottled while there is still lots of dark fruit.

Tawny ports are aged for much longer, typically in 158.5-gallon (600-litre) barrels known as pipes, and develop a complex cedary, nutty, more raisiny character, with a lighter, orange-brown color.

Of the ruby styles, the best-quality wines are the vintage ports. These are made only in the best years (referred to as "declared" vintages, of which there are typically three a decade), and are bottled after just two years. They are intended for cellaring, and can last 30–50 years. Single quinta vintage ports are made from a single property. Some quintas make them every year; port houses tend to produce them only in non-vintage port years. Late bottled vintage (LBV) ports were introduced in the 1960s and offer some of the qualities of vintage port at much lower prices. The best are labeled "traditional" or "unfiltered." These are bottled after six years in wood and do not need aging. Basic ruby ports that do not fall into this category can be good value, but vary in quality.

Tawny ports are a neglected treasure, and are most commonly a blend of vintages, sold by the average age of the component wines. There are 10, 20, 30, and (less commonly) 40-year-old tawnies, but the best combination of complexity and affordability is usually found with the 20-year-olds. Colheitas, which are popular in Portugal but less commonly seen overseas, are vintage-dated tawnies. White port is also made, but it is usually of relatively little interest.

Major grapes

🍇 Reds

Tinta Amarela

Tinta Barroca

Tinta Cão

Tinta Roriz

Touriga Franca

Touriga Nacional

🍇 Whites

Gouveio

Malvasia Fina

Viosinho

Vintages

2009
A difficult vintage, with hot conditions.

2008
A very good vintage with some attractive ports.

2007
A great year, with a slightly cool growing season but perfect conditions at harvest. The vintage ports are superb.

2006
A difficult, hot vintage.

2005
A very good vintage with some brilliant single-quinta ports.

2004
A very good vintage, resulting in some extremely fruity ports.

2003
A hot, but extremely good vintage for vintage port. Some of the top ports are superb bets for long aging.

FONSECA GUIMARAENS

THE RENOWNED FONSECA VINTAGE PORT IS
FABULOUSLY CONCENTRATED

A A Ferreira

This historic port house was famously developed by Dona
Antónia Adelaide Ferreira. Widowed in her early 30s, she
took charge of the company, which she expanded
considerably. In the 1950s, Ferreira pioneered serious
Douro table wines with the release of the legendary
Barca Velha in 1952. Ferriera was purchased by Sogrape
in 1987. Vineyard holdings include Quinta do Porto,
Quinta do Caedo, Quinta do Seixo, and Quinta da Leda
(now the main source of grapes for Barca Velha). The
Ferreira vintage ports are consistently good.

Rua da Carvalhosa 19/105, Vila Nova de Gaia
223 745 292

Burmester

Dating back to 1750, Burmester is probably best known
for its colheitas—vintage-dated tawny ports. It was
acquired by Amorim in 1999, which then sold Burmester
minus the impressive Quinta Nova estate, which it
retained, to Sogevinus, the current owners in 2005. Douro
table wines are also made under the Burmester label. The
20-year-old tawny and any of the colheitas you can locate
are well worth the effort taken to find them.

Rua Barão Forrester, Vila Nova de Gaia
www.burmesterporto.com

Cálem

Part of the Sogevinus portfolio, Cálem was founded in
1859 with the goal of trading port with Brazil in exchange
for exotic hardwoods, using its own fleet—which is why
the Cálem logo features a large ship. As one of the
Portuguese-owned port quintas, Cálem's main market is
the domestic one. Wines are made in the Douro at São
Martinho da Anta, and then aged in the lodges at Vila
Nova de Gaia. The main grape source is Quinta do
Arnozelo in the Douro Superior, a 500 acre (200ha) estate
with 250 acres (100ha) of vines. When Cálem was sold, its
spectacular Quinta da Foz remained in family hands and
is now the source of table wines and ports under the PV
label. Cálem's vintage ports are very good but probably
not in the same league as the very best from the region.
Colheitas and tawnies are also made here.

Avenida Diogo Leite 344, Vila Nova de Gaia
www.calem.pt

Churchill

Despite its thoroughly traditional-sounding name,
Churchill is the newest of the British-owned port
companies. It was founded in 1981 by Johnny Graham,
whose family once owned Graham, one of the best-
known port houses. Johnny Graham spent the early part
of his career at Cockburn before, in 1981, he formed his
own port company, Churchill Graham (Churchill is his
wife's name), making wines based on the Borges de
Sousa family's vineyards. In 1999, Churchill bought
Quinta da Gricha, a 250 acre (100ha) property next door
to Roriz in the Cima Corgo, and Quinta do Rio in the Rio
Torto valley. Churchill makes some excellent ports and
table wines from these properties, and has recently
added some fruit from the Douro Superior to the blend.
Regular Churchill table wine is excellently priced; Quinta
da Gricha is more expensive, but fantastic.

Rua Da Fonte Nova 5, 4400—156 Vila Nova De Gaia
www.churchills-port.com

CHURCHILL

JOHNNY GRAHAM'S RELATIVELY YOUNG PORT
HOUSE IS ALREADY HIGHLY REGARDED

Cockburn

Now owned by the multinational drinks company Beam
Global, the Cockburn house produces a full roster of
commercial ports. These are now packaged in a
distinctive, square-shouldered bottle, and take their place
alongside impressive vintage and single quinta port.
Quinta dos Canais, in the Douro Superior, is very much
the jewel in Cockburn's crown. This 740 acre (300ha)
estate was purchased by Cockburn in the late 1980s, and
has been redeveloped with new plantings by variety.
Cockburn claims that this estate has the world's largest
planting of the Touriga Nacional grape variety, and it is
the basis of the Cockburn vintage ports and, in non-
vintage years, a single quinta port (labeled Quinta dos
Canais). Miguel Côrte-Real is the respected winemaker
in charge of these wines.

Rua das Coradas, Vila Nova de Gaia
www.cockburns.com

Croft

The Fladgate Partnership (which includes top port houses
Taylor and Fonseca) purchased Croft from drinks giant
Diageo in 2001. Since then, it has been working hard to
improve quality. This should be possible, because Croft
owns one of the Douro's most impressive wine estates,
Quinta da Roêda, a short distance upriver from Pinhão
in the Cima Corgo. Natasha Bridge, enologist wife of
Fladgate CEO Adrian, is in charge of the Croft ports.
It is a historic port house that has been operating under
its current name since 1736, and the ports are currently
very good, but not quite in the premier league. A recent
innovation has been Croft Pink, a rosé port that is
something of an acquired taste.

Largo Joaquim Magalhães 23, Vila Nova de Gaia
www.croftport.com

Delaforce

The Delaforce house can trace its history back to 1868,
when it was founded by George Henry Delaforce. The
Delaforce family sold it in 1968, but remained associated
with the house until 2001, when, as a sister brand to
Croft, it was sold to the Taylor Fladgate Partnership.
Delaforce's single quinta port, Quinta da Corte, is
frequently superb, and its vintage port can be very fine.

Rua Azevedo Magalhães 314, 4430-022 Vila Nova de Gaia
www.delaforce.pt

Dow

One of the leading port houses, Dow is part of the
Symington family's portfolio. Three quintas contribute
to Dow's ports. The most important is Quinta do Bomfim,
which has 120 acres (50ha) of well-situated, south-facing
vineyards, and is located in the heart of the Cima Corgo,
just upstream of Pinhão. Then there are Quinta da
Senhora de Ribiera, with 50 acres (20ha) of vines, and
two quintas privately owned by the Symington family
(Quinta do Santinho and Quinta da Cerdeira, totaling 44
acres/18ha). Dow's is one of the top vintage ports, made
in a slightly drier style than some, with real fruit focus
and firm structure. In the years when it is not made,
single quinta ports from both Bomfim and Senhora de
Ribiera may be released.

Trav Barão de Forrester, Vila Nova de Gaia;
www.dows-port.com

Fonseca Guimaraens

One of the greatest of the port houses, Fonseca has been part of the Taylor Fladgate Partnership since the late 1940s. It was founded in 1822, and by 1840 had become the second-largest shipper of port. The house style is one of richness and complexity. Much of the modern reputation of Fonseca is based on the work of Bruce Guimaraens (who made the vintages from 1960 to 1992) and his son David (winemaker since 1994). The heart of the blend comes from Quinta do Panascal in the Tavora Valley of the Douro, a 188 acre (76ha) property with 109 acres (44ha) of vineyards that was purchased by Fonseca in 1978. Other quintas owned by Fonseca are Quinta de São António and Quinta do Cruzeiro. As well as the thrilling vintage port and excellent Guimaraens and Panascal single quinta bottlings, Fonseca also make an impressive, fruit-driven organic port, Terra Prima. Entry level bottling Bin 27 is great value for money.

Rua Barão de Forrester 404, Vila Nova de Gaia
www.fonseca.pt

Graham

The Graham family entered the port business in 1820, and in 1890 acquired the fabulous Quinta dos Malvedos. But this was sold off during difficult financial times, and then in 1970, the Symingtons acquired Graham, later reuniting it with Malvedos, which they also purchased. It has a deserved reputation as one of the top port houses, consistently making excellent vintage ports in declared years. The house style is one of dense, rich, sweet ports with considerable structure and the ability to age well for 30 or 40 years. When the vintage port is not declared, single quinta Malvedos is usually released, and this is often superb. Tawnies and LBV are less impressive, made in a more commercial style. As well as Malvedos, vineyard sources include Quinta das Lages and Quinta da Vila Velha.

Rua Rei Ramiro 514, Vila Nova de Gaia
www.grahams-port.com

Quinta do Vesuvio

Quinta do Vesuvio, located in the Douro Superior, is one of the great estates of the Douro. The property was developed in its current guise by António Bernardo Ferreira, who purchased it in 1823. António's son inherited the estate; his wife was the famous Dona Antónia, who was widowed shortly after and went on to develop a grand portfolio of Douro properties. The current fame of Vesuvio is down to the Symingtons, who purchased the property in 1989. They have redeveloped it and expanded the vineyard holdings to some 320 acres (130ha). The focus of Vesuvio is vintage port, but a recent addition to the range has been a beautifully expressive Quinta do Vesuvio table wine. Vesuvio is right up there with the top port houses in quality terms: this is one of the great vintage ports of the Douro, even though it is technically only a single quinta port. Top recent vintages are 1991, 2000, 2001, 2003, and 2007.

No visitor facilities
www.quintadovesuvio.com

Sandeman

Since 2002, Sandeman has been owned by Portugal's largest private wine company, Sogrape, which purchased it from beverage giant Seagram, which had been custodian

SANDEMAN
THE SANDEMAN FIGURE WAS PLAYED BY
ORSON WELLES IN A TV ADVERTISEMENT

WARRE
THE WARRE HOUSE STYLE IS RICH BUT
SLIGHTLY DRIER THAN MOST HOUSES

of the brand since 1980. Sandeman is currently a brand used for a range of ports, madeiras, sherries, and brandies, and actually dates back to 1790 when George Sandeman began trading in port and sherry in London. George Sandeman opened his own port lodge in Vila Nova de Gaia in 1811, and today another George Sandeman, the seventh generation of the family to be involved with the business, is at the helm. While the focus is on more commercial wines, some serious products—such as vintage port, Vau Vintage, and 20-year-old tawny port—are also made.

Largo de Miguel Bombarda 3, Vila Nova de Gaia
www.sandeman.eu

Smith Woodhouse

Smith Woodhouse was acquired along with its sister house, Graham, by the Symington family in 1970. The vintage ports here are both very good quality and very reasonably priced, although they are not quite in the same league as the top Symington properties. Look out for the traditional, unfiltered LBV, which is a bit of a bargain.

Travessa Barão de Forrester, Vila Nova de Gaia
www.smithwoodhouse.com

Taylor

One of the top port houses, Taylor has a long history and can boast a string of firsts. It introduced the hugely successful LBV style with the 1965 Taylor's LBV, and was the first to release a single quinta port (1958 Quinta da Vargellas). Vargellas, acquired in 1893, is the heart of the operation, located in the Douro Superior, with its own railroad station. But two quintas in the Cima Corgo, Terra Feita and Junco, are also significant contributors to Taylor's ports. The vintage port is consistently superb, with concentrated dark, brambly fruit, firm structure, and the ability to age for many decades: it is one of the very best of all, and the 2007 is truly great. Single quinta port from Vargellas is released in undeclared years, and can be very good indeed. Small quantities of a thrilling Vargellas Vinha Velha are also made in some years (just five vintages since 1995 have been released).

Rua do Choupelo 250, Vila Nova de Gaia
www.taylor.pt

Warre

William Warre, who was to found a significant family port dynasty, arrived in Portugal from the UK in 1729. But the company that bears the Warre name can trace its history back to 1670, making it the oldest British-owned port house. The Symington family became involved in the late 19th century, and Warre is now part of its impressive roster of port houses (the family bought the last of the Warre family shares in 1961). In addition to four of its own quintas (Cavadinha, Retiro Antigo, Telhada, and Bom Retiro Pequeno), Warre sources grapes from vineyards privately held by various members of the Symington family. Warre's is regularly among the very best of the vintage ports, and the Quinta da Cavadinha single quinta port, made in undeclared years, is also worth looking for.

Travessa Barão de Forrester 85, Vila Nova de Gaia
www.warre.com

BEST OF THE REST OF PORTUGAL

Despite its small size, Portugal is a diverse wine-producing country with several wine regions that each have distinct identities. In the cool, damp far north, there are crisp whites from the Vinho Verde region, while in the hot southern Alentejo big, fruit-dominated red wines are the specialty. Between these two regions are the fruity, commercially astute wines from the regions around Lisbon, while the more northerly Dão and Bairrada regions produce fine reds with distinct personalities. It takes a bit of work to get to know Portugal's regions and unique grape varieties, but these rapidly improving wines certainly repay any effort to make their acquaintance.

Major grapes

 Reds

Alicante Bouschet

Aragonêz (Tinta Roriz)

Baga

Touriga Nacional

Trincadeira

 Whites

Alvarinho (Albariño)

Encruzado

Loureiro

Verdelho

Vintages

It is almost impossible to give vintage generalizations for a range of regions that spread from Portugal's coastal far north to the inland south. In general, however, 2009 was an excellent vintage in almost all areas, while 2008 was unseasonably cool and damp during May and early June, with excellent harvest conditions. 2007 was also a cool vintage, particularly in the Beiras, with whites faring better than reds. By contrast, 2006 was a hot vintage, with high temperatures causing problems, and 2005 was affected by drought in the south, but was otherwise very good.

Portugal's wine scene is dynamic: in the last decade scores of new producers have started to make top-quality wines for the first time, and quality is now higher than it has ever been. It is also diverse, with a range of different climates and soil types from the south to the north of the country. All of this, coupled with Portugal's treasure trove of indigenous grape varieties, makes this country a happy hunting ground for adventurous wine lovers.

Aside from the spectacular Douro region, which is covered earlier in its own section, the Alentejo is the most important wine region. Located in the south of the country, it is a region of wheat fields, cork groves, and vineyards. The hot, sunny climate produces ripe, sweetly fruited red wines that range from cheap and gluggable to structured and intense. Aragonêz, Alicante Bouschet, and Trincadeira are the key varieties in Alentejo. While the whites tend to lag a little behind the reds, they can be delicious, with bright peach and citrus fruit flavors and often a kiss of oak.

At the other extreme, the Vinho Verde region in the northern part of the country (situated above Porto) is emerging as a source of serious, fresh, minerally white wines from the Alvarinho (known in Spain as Albariño) and Loureiro varieties. A red Vinho Verde, made from Vinhão (Sousão), is also produced here. Vinhão is a teinturier (red fleshed) variety, which gives the wines an intense color with fresh acidity, vibrant fruit, and grippy tannins.

The northern third of the country is the Beiras, which consists of three regions. The most significant of these regions is the Dão, which produces elegant, almost Burgundian-styled, reds from Touriga Nacional, Tinta Roriz, Jaén, and Alfrocheiro on sandy/granitic soils. Whites, from varieties such as Encruzado, Bical, and Sercial, can be fresh, bright, and minerally. Bairrada is a region that is dominated by the red grape Baga, which can be tough and tannic, but in the right

hands makes nicely poised, ageworthy reds that bear a resemblance to good Nebbiolo in style, with firm tannins. The emerging region of the Beira Interior, a northward extension of the Alentejo, is hemmed in by the mountains in the east of the country and is showing promise for bright, pure, fruit-driven reds.

Closer to Lisbon there are three regions that are still in transition from bulk production to good quality, highly drinkable yet affordable reds and whites. The Lisboa region (until very recently known as Estremadura) is home to fresh whites and attractive, fruit-driven reds. The Tejo (until recently labeled Ribatejo) also makes appealing, fruit-driven reds. The Setúbal Peninsula, with its sandy soils, is responsible for juicy and fruit-driven reds, crisp whites, and a delicious and ageworthy sweet white called Moscatel de Setúbal. Foreign varieties, such as Syrah and Cabernet Sauvignon, are making some inroads in these regions, but often they are used in blends with Portuguese varieties.

The Portuguese island of Madeira makes some fantastic fortified wines, which were discovered by pure accident. The island is located on an important trade route and supplied wine for passing ships that was fortified with alcohol to survive conditions at sea. It was found that when the wine casks were baked in the tropical heat of a voyage, all sorts of interesting flavors developed. This heating process is replicated in the way madeira is produced today.

There are five key Madeiran grape varieties. The first is Tinta Negra Mole, a red grape that is Madeira's workhorse variety. The four classic grapes—Sercial, Verdelho, Bual, and Malmsey—typically make wines with sweetness that varies in that order (Sercial is quite dry and Malmsey is very sweet). Because madeira is exposed to oxygen and heat through its development, an open bottle will keep in good condition for years.

PORTUGAL

Portugal's wine regions run the length of the country, and also include Madeira. Most northerly is the Vinho Verde region, where the relatively cool, damp climate creates fresh whites. To the south lies the Beiras, which includes Bairrada and Dão. The regions labeled Lisboa and Tejo were, until very recently, known as Estremadura and Ribatejo, respectively. Southern Portugal is dominated by the Alentejo, an important region with a warm climate, specializing in rich, ripe reds.

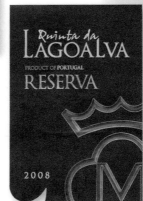

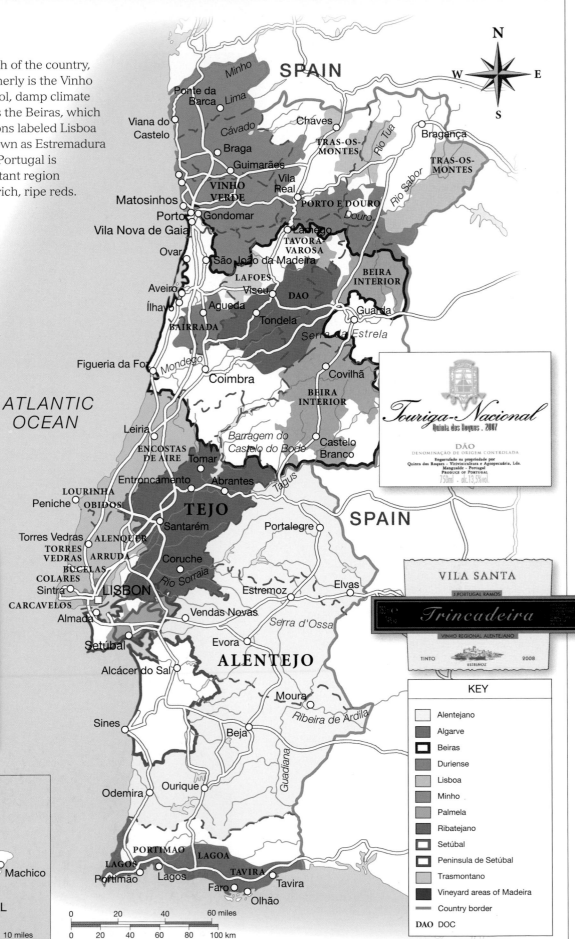

KEY

- Alentejano
- Algarve
- Beiras
- Duriense
- Lisboa
- Minho
- Palmela
- Ribatejano
- Setúbal
- Peninsula de Setúbal
- Trasmontano
- Vineyard areas of Madeira
- Country border

DAO DOC

Afros Vinho Verde

This biodynamic producer is currently making some of the region's best wines from its 49 acre (20ha) property, Quinta do Casal do Paço. They are made from the white Loureiro and red Vinhão (also known as Sousão) grape varieties. The white is precise, pure, and aromatic, with lovely minerality. The red is a striking wine, typical of red Vinho Verdes, being intensely colored, vibrant, fresh, pure, and joyful with wonderfully immediate raspberry, cherry, and plum fruit, backed by high acidity and firm tannins. 2007, 2008, and 2009 are all good vintages; in 2006, the red was also made as a sparkling wine and a sparkling white is made in most vintages. ★**Rising star**

Quinta Casal do Paço, Padreiro (S Salvador), 4970-500 Arcos de Valdevez; www.afros-wine.com

Aliança Vinhos de Portugal Bairrada

A significant producer, with around 988 acres (400ha) of vines, Aliança was founded in 1927 and is based in Bairrada. Until 2007, when the company was purchased by José Berardo of Bacalhôa, it was known as Caves Aliança. As well as a property in Bairrada, Aliança also own wine estates in several other Portuguese regions. Their broad range includes five top wines: the lush, sweet, and powerful Quinta dos Quatro Ventos Reserva from the Douro; the brightly fruited Quinta da Garrida from the Dão; the polished red-berry fruit and oak-influenced Quinta da Terrugem from the Alentejo; and the cherry and black-currant-fruited Quinta das Baceladas from Bairrada.

Rua do Comércio 444, 3781-908 Sangalhos www.alianca.pt

Alvaro Castro Dão

Alvaro Castro is one of Portugal's top winemaking talents. He has two quintas in the Dão: the 35 acre (14ha) de Sães, where the winery is located, and the 74 acre (30ha) da Pellada, in the foothills of the Serra da Estrela. He also has a share of the vineyards that used to be owned by Casa de Passarela. From these he fashions some fantastic expressions of Dão, ranging from the affordable Quinta de Sães, to the lushly fruited yet elegant Quinta da Pellada Reserva. There are also two special, high-end *cuvées*: the rich, forward, and elegant Pape and the denser, more structured Carrocel, both of which are fantastic. Alvaro Castro's whites are also quite serious and include the high-end Primus from Pellada, which is mineralic and ageable. It also makes a structured, ageworthy Dão/Douro blend in conjunction with Dirk Niepoort, called Dado.

Quinta da Pellada, 6270-141 Pinhanços 238 486 133

Anselmo Mendes Vinho Verde

Anselmo Mendes is one of the leading winemakers from the Vinho Verde region in the north of Portugal. He was born in the Monção subregion, which is famous for its Alvarinhos and where he is currently based. Before starting his own production he worked for the CVRVV, the local body that is responsible for Vinho Verde; he also worked for Borges, where he still consults. Mendes made his first wine under his own name in 1998, but, while his own wines have achieved critical acclaim, he still works as a consultant for several well-known

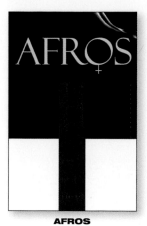

AFROS
OPAQUE, INKY-DARK, AND RED-BLACK IN COLOR, THIS IS A REMARKABLE WINE

SANTA ISIDRO DE PEGOES
A UNIQUE TERROIR HELPS TO CREATE THIS FRESH, STRUCTURED WINE

Portuguese producers. Muros Antigos Alvarinho is a pithy white with some freshness, while the Muros Antigos Loureiro shows a brighter, herby, lively sort of character. Muros de Melgaço Alvarinho is fermented in French oak and shows nice intensity and texture. Anselmo Mendes Alvarinho is his best white wine. It employs some skin maceration, which results in lovely, herby, melony, tangerine and pear fruit.

Travessa Senhor De Matosinhos, 4400-305 Vila Nova de Gaia www.anselmomendes.com

Artwine Bairrada

This is a fusion of two different estates in Bairrada. Artwine has 49 acres (20ha) of vines in the Cantanhede district and makes more modern-style wines under the Blaudus brand—the first of these wines was released in 2003. Quinta de Baixo is more classically Bairrada, making wines in a more traditional style since 1980. Blaudus Touriga Nacional is sweet and lush, with vibrant blackberry and cherry notes. Baixo Garrafeira is an intense, mouthfilling, savory wine that is a blend of Baga and Touriga Nacional. Baixo Clássico is a varietal Baga that has delicious red berry and cherry fruit, with a firm, dense, savory structure and the capacity to age well.

Rua Professor Joaquim Pires Dos Santos, 3060-260 Cordinha Cantanhede; 231 423 180

Bacalhôa Vinhos de Portugal
Setúbal Peninsula

Dating back to 1922, Bacalhôa used to be known as J. P. Vinhos. During the 1980s, it was one of Portugal's more forward-thinking wine companies, making some very fresh, fruity everyday wines, as well as five brands that survive to this day—Quinta da Bacalhôa, Cova de Ursa Branco, Má Partilha, Catarina Branco, and Tinto da Ânfora Tinto—with Australian Peter Bright as the winemaker. Today, Bacalhôa is headquarters to the expanding wine empire of José (Joe) Berardo, one of Portugal's richest men. Berardo also owns Quinta do Carmo in the Alentejo, has a third of the shares in Sogrape's holding company, holds shares in Henriques & Henriques in Madeira, and is a majority shareholder in Aliança. The Bacalhôa portfolio is consistently good, with the standouts being the black-currant-fruited Quinta da Bacalhôa (a varietal Cabernet Sauvignon), the powerful, rich Palácio da Bacalhôa, and a range of sweet Moscatels.

Estrada Nacional 10, Vila Nogueira de Azeitão, 2925-901 Azeitão; www.bacalhoa.com

Barbeito Madeira

This family-owned madeira producer was established in 1946. Its philosophy is to only offer wines that have been aged in the traditional manner (old French oak is used for aging), not artificially heated and with no added caramel or deacidification. This is authentic madeira, and everything Barbeito makes is extremely interesting. One of its main innovations is to bottle "single harvest" wines in 17fl oz (50cl) bottles. This acts as a superb introduction to fine madeira without the high cost of proper vintage wines, which by law must be aged for 20 years in cask and two years in bottle. Look for the excellent Barbeito 10 Years Old wines, the single-harvest Tinta Negra Mole, and, of course, the amazing vintage wines. The Barbeito Malvazia 30 Years Old is incredible, with complex notes of marmalade, herbs, and old wood, with a lovely sweetness.

Estrada da Ribeira Garcia, Parque Empresarial de Câmara de Lobos, 9300-324 Câmara de Lobos
www.vinhosbarbeito.com

H M Borges Madeira
Henrique Menezes Borges formed this company in 1877 and it is still in family hands, with the fourth generation now involved. In addition to cheaper products, which are not of any particular merit, they make a full range of 10 year old and 15 year old wines, and have recently begun to specialize in Colheitas—wines from a single vintage that are not old enough to be proper vintage madeiras.

Rua 31 de Janeiro, No. 83, 9050-011 Funchal
www.hmborges.com

Campolargo Bairrada
Campolargo has two quintas with a total of 420 acres (170ha) of vineyards. In the middle of the largest vineyard, near Anadia, there is an impressive new winery and cellar that were completed in 2004. While the Campolargo family has been involved in wine-growing for many generations, it has only been making its own wines since 2000. The family takes a modern approach, growing lots of international varieties as well as the local specialties. A broad portfolio of well-made wines are produced, including the straight Campolargo, a lush, aromatic varietal Pinot Noir (sometimes with a splash of Baga), the elegant, ripe, pure Termeão (a Touriga Nacional-dominated blend) and the perfumed, softly textured Calda Bordaleza (a Bordeaux blend).

Quinta de S Mateus, 3780-180 S Mateus, S Lourenço do Bairro, Anadia; www.campolargovinhos.com

Cartuxa Alentejo
This winery is owned by Fundaçao Eugénio de Almeida, a charitable foundation formed in 1963 by a wealthy landowner, and has estates around the town of Evora in the Alentejo. The jewels in the crown are the Pêra-Manca red and white, with the red, which is made in a traditional but complex and ageworthy style, being one of Portugal's most sought-after wines. The Catuxa red is also worth looking out for—it has lovely elegance and some nonfruit complexity. In the years when Pêra-Manca is not made, a Cartuxa Reserva is released. New additions to the range from 2005 are the red and white Scala Coeli, which are high-end wines from international varieties.

Estrada da Soeira, 7000-769 Evora
www.cartuxa.pt

Casa de Cello Dão
This impressive producer has quintas in the Dão and Vinho Verde regions of Portugal. Quinta de Cello is located near Amarante and makes white wines from the Arinto, Alvarinho, Chardonnay, Loureiro, Malvazia, and Avesso varieties, under the name Quinta de Sanjoanne. Look for the Sanjoanne Superior, a bold, grassy, minerally white that is a blend of Alvarinho and Malvazia. Quinta da Vegia, in the Dão, has 49 acres (20ha) of vines, from which it makes some impressive wines. Porta Fronha is great value for money, with fresh, dark cherry and blackberry fruit;

BARBEITO
THE 20 YEAR OLD MALVASIA IS RICH AND INTENSE WITH A CARAMEL AND TOFFEE EDGE

CAMPOLARGO
SOME CABERNET SAUVIGNON IS INCLUDED IN THIS PREDOMINANTLY LOCAL-VARIETY BLEND

Quinta da Vegia Reserva is one of the region's best wines. It shows lovely floral aromatics and dark, brooding, complex fruit flavors.

Mancelos, 4605-118 Vila-Meã Amarante
www.casadecello.pt

Casa de Mouraz Dão
Casa de Mouraz is a small, family-owned farm that has been making its own wine since 2000. The nine different plots cover 32 acres (13ha) and are farmed biodynamically. Both the red and the white Dão are brilliant, with vibrant, pure fruit and lovely minerality. The top wine is the Private Selection, with pure, elegant cherry and berry fruits. ★ **Rising star**

Quinta do Outeiro, Mouraz, 3460-330 Tondela
232 822 872

Casa de Saima Bairrada
One of the most traditional Bairrada producers, and one of the best, Casa de Saima believes in the potential of the Baga grape for making complex, ageworthy reds that are often a bit tannic and difficult in their youth. Graca Miranda, the owner and winemaker, farms 49 acres (20ha), split over 12 plots. The top red, Garrafeira, is complex, tannic, and savory, and repays patience. The Regular Tinto, also quite complex and with lovely freshness, is good value. They also make whites and a sparkling wine.

3780-102 Sangalhos
234 743 278

Casal Branco Tejo
Located on the left bank of the River Tagus, in the Tejo region, Casal Branco is a significant estate of 2,718 acres (1,100ha), with 346 acres (140ha) of vineyards. Jose Lobo de Vasconcelos is in charge—his family has been running the estate since 1775. Since he took over in 1986, the vineyards have been reorganized and quality has improved. A new winery was finished in 2004. In addition to value-for-money wines, some high-end reds are made under the Falcoaria and Capucho labels.

2080-362 Benfica do Ribatejo
www.casalbranco.com

Caves São João Bairrada
If you like traditional-styled, ageworthy Portuguese reds at a good price, then look for the wines of Caves São João. This is a family-owned company, founded in 1920 and based in Bairrada. Frei João and Frei João Reserva are both attractive, savory, traditional styled Barraidas with Baga dominating the blend. The Caves São João Reserva is the top wine. A blend of wines from Bairrada and Dão, it shows dense yet smooth cherry and plum fruit with dark spiciness and lots of tannin. These wines age very well.

São João da Azenha, Anadia, 3781-901 Avelãs de Caminho
www.cavessaojoao.pt

Cooperativa Agrícola de Santa Isidro de Pegões Terras de Sado
Known more simply as the Pegões Co-operative, this is one of Portugal's leading co-operatives. It is based in the Terras do Sado region, near Lisbon. Jaime Quenderas is the talented winemaker behind an impressive and

CORTES DE CIMA

THE FLAGSHIP WINE IS MADE FROM SELECTED BATCHES AND BARREL-AGED FOR 12 MONTHS

affordable range of wines. There are 140 growers, 30% of whom farm 90% of the total vineyard area, which is currently 2,900 acres (1,174ha). The co-operative pays 50% more for grapes than the average for the area, which is an incentive for quality. Look for the red and white Colheita Seleccionada wines: the red shows intense, spicy black fruits with nice structure, while the white has bold citrusy fruit with some creamy richness.

Rua Pereira Caldas No. 1, 2985-158 Pegões Velhos
www.cooppegoes.pt

Cortes de Cima Alentejo

Owned by Hans Jorgensen, a Dane, and his Californian wife, Carrie, Cortes de Cima has for some years been one of the most modern and forward-thinking estates in the Alentejo. Based in Vidigueira, it has over 250 acres (100ha) of vines, making a broad portfolio of wines from the inexpensive, highly drinkable Chaminé, through a range of red varieties, up to the top wines—Cortes de Cima Reserva and Incógnito. The latter is its top Syrah, which, when first released, had to hide its identity because growing Syrah at the time was illegal—hence the name. All the wines are ripe and sweetly fruited, but always retain balance and focus.

7960-189 Vidigueira
www.cortesdecima.com

D'Oliveiras Madeira

Although Pereira D'Oliveira is the name of the company, the madeiras it makes are simply labeled D'Oliveiras. This is a producer with history: the current owners, Anibal and Luis D'Oliveira, are grandsons of the founder and their head office is located in a building that dates back to 1619. Their specialties are Colheitas (single harvests) and Reservas (their term for vintage wines), and they are all superb. Colheita Terrantez 1988, from a rare grape variety, is off-dry and tangy, with amazing flavors of herbs and warm spices. Colheita Malvazia 1987 is rich, but expressive, with a lemony freshness that combines nicely with sweet raisiny complexity. Reserva Sercial 1969 is a complex, thrilling wine with notes of old furniture and herbs and amazing length, while Reserva Boal 1968 is sweet and spicy with complex notes of citrus fruit and old casks.

Rua Ferreiros 107, Funchal 9000-082
291 220 784

Dão Sul Dão

Dão Sul, now also known as Global Wines, is a large, dynamic company that is based in the Dão, but makes wines in several regions. It owns three Dão estates (Cabriz, Grilos, and Casa de Santar), two in the Douro, and one each in Estremadura, Bairrada, and the Alentejo. The wines are consistently good, with some real high points. Look out for two Dão whites, the Casa de Santar Reserva and Paço das Cunhas de Santar Vinho do Contador, as well as a bevy of impressive reds—Monte da Cal Vinho de Saturno (Alentejo), Quinta das Tecedeiras Reserva (Douro), Encontro 1 (Bairrada), Quinta de Cabriz Escolha (Dão), Paço das Cunhas de Santar Vinho do Contador (Dão), and CCCC (a high-end pan-Portugal blend).

Quinta das Sarzedas, 3430-909 Carregal do Sal
www.daosul.com

ESPORAO

PEACH, LIME, AND GRAPEFRUIT DEVELOP INTO HONEY AND MELON WITH AGE

Dona Maria Alentejo

Júlio Tassara de Bastos is one of the leading winemakers in Portugal's Alentejo region. In 1992, he sold 50% of the family property, Quinta do Carmo Garrafeiras, to Domaines Barons de Rothschild (Lafite). The winery and office operations were transferred to the Carvalhas estate, where a new winery was built, but Júlio later sold his stake in the winery, and returned to his own operation. While he still owned the house at Quinta do Carmo itself, he was no longer able to use the name, so he started a new operation called Dona Maria. Júlio has 131 acres (53ha) of vineyards, with an emphasis on the same special, old clone of Alicante Bouschet that was at the heart of the classic Quinta do Carmo Garrafeiras. The first grapes from Dona Maria were harvested in 2003, and Júlio is now making some excellent wines that range from an elegant rosé to a dense and structured Reserva. The jewel in the crown is the immense Júlio B. Bastos Alicante Bouschet. ★ **Rising star**

7100-055 Estremoz
www.donamaria.pt

Ermelinda Freitas Terras do Sado

This family estate in the Terras do Sado region was established in 1920 and used to be a bulk wine company. Jaime Quendera started as winemaker here in 1998, and from 2000 the estate started bottling its own wines. From 321 acres (130ha) of vines, Quendera is fashioning some tasty, well priced wines, including a bold and intense Alicante Bouschet; a ripe, darkly fruited Reserva from Castelão, Touriga Nacional, and Syrah; and the Leo d'Honor, which is a fabulously dark and structured old-vine Castelão.

Rua Manuel João Freitas, Fernando Pó—CC1 2501,
2965-621 Aguas de Moura; www.ermelindafreitas.pt

Esporão Alentejo

One of the Alentejo's largest wineries, Esporão is majority-owned by the Roquette family, which is also owner of Quinta do Crasto in the Douro. Located near Reguengos, it has 1,483 acres (600ha) of its own vineyards and two wineries, one for reds and one for whites. It crushes 9,000 tons (9,144 metric tons) of grapes each vintage. Since the first wine was released under this label in 1989, Esporão has been a great ambassador for the wines of Alentejo, with a high profile in export markets. Unsurprisingly for a winery headed up by an Australian winemaker, the talented David Baverstock, Esporão's wines are made in a style that is more New World than Old. The wines display forward fruit as their dominant feature, often assisted by some oak. The Reserva Tinto and Branco are worth looking out for; they are nicely balanced wines that are reasonably priced. From 2007, the single-varietal wines have been upgraded and reduced in volume, from 20,000 bottles a year down to 6,000, which has resulted in a leap in quality. Look for the Touriga Nacional, which shows great intensity and a nice marriage of ripe fruit with oak.

Finagra, Reguengos de Monsaraz
www-en.esporao.com

Filipa Pato Beiras

Filipa Pato is one of the bright young talents of Portuguese winemaking. She is the daughter of Luis Pato, the famous Bairrada producer. Like her father,

Filipa studied chemical engineering, before gaining experience at Château Cantenac Brown in Bordeaux, Finca Flichman in Argentina, and the Margaret River Leeuwin Estate in Australia. Arriving back in Portugal in 2001, Filipa decided to make wines in Beiras. Without any vineyards of her own, she set about establishing her own brand, making wines from rented vineyards in both Bairrada and the neighboring Dão region. Her top wines are the Lokal Silex (from Dão) and Lokal Calcário (from Bairrada). Both are stunningly good, with amazing fruit purity and length. Filipa has also started making wines with her husband, William Wouters, under the label Vinhos Doidos, which translates as "Crazy Wines." Bossa is a party white, and Nossa is a complex wine from the Bical and Encruzado varieties. ★ Rising star

Rua de Santo Andre 39, 3780-502 Ois do Barra
www.filipapato.net

Fita Preta Vinhos Alentejo

This is a modern-thinking producer that makes a rich, dark, seductive estate wine called Preta, and also a more approachable and affordable brand, provocatively named Sexy. It also makes Palpite white and red wines that sit between the two. David Booth, who is originally from England, is the viticulturalist and António Maçanita is the winemaker. They began their venture together in 2004, when they realized they had access to some superb grapes and were able to rent spare winery capacity.

Herdade do Outeiro Da Esquila, Evora
www.fitapreta.com

Gloria Reynolds Alentejo

Based in the slightly cooler, more northerly part of the Alentejo, at Portalegre, Gloria Reynolds is owned by the Reynolds family (another branch of the family owns Herdade do Mouchão), who moved from England to Portugal in the 19th century. Their 101 acres (41ha) of vines are mainly planted with Alicante Bouschet, Trincadeira, and Aragonêz. The wines are named after various members of the Reynolds clan: Carlos Reynolds is a fresh, cherryish red with ripe, supple fruit; Julian Reynolds is sweetly fruited with bright cherry and berry fruits; and Gloria Reynolds is spicy, dense, and earthy, yet also elegant.

Monte Figueira de Cima, 7340, Arronches
www.gloriareynolds.com

Henriques & Henriques Madeira

Dating back to 1850, this is the third-largest madeira producer on the island, and the one with the greatest vineyard holdings. A 1992 expansion program resulted in a new winery and head office. While the company is still owned by the families that became partners during the 1930s and 1940s, José Berardo (of Bacalhôa Vinhos de Portugal) now has a 20% stake in the company. Winemaker Luis Pereira is currently making some exciting wines, of which the pick of the bunch are the bold, nutty 10 year old Verdelho; the fresh, citrusy, and tangy 15 year old Verdelho; the rich, raisiny 15 year old Malmsey; and the thrillingly complex 1998 Single Harvest. The vintage wines are also superb.

Sitio de Belém, 9300-138 Câmara de Lobos
www.henriquesehenriques.pt

Herdarde da Comporta Terras do Sado

Camporta is a 29,650 acre (12,000ha) estate on the Alentejo coast that is currently being developed as a large, integrated tourism project—part of the plan is to include a high-quality winery. The 74 acre (30ha) Herdade da Comporta wines were first made in 2003, and fall into the Terras do Sado region. A richly fruited Antão Vaz and a bright, grapefruity blend of Antão Vaz with Arinto make up the whites. The top red is a blend of Aragonêz and Alicante Bouschet, which offers lovely, lush, intense, pure dark fruit. These are top-quality wines that are made in a ripe, modern style. ★ Rising star

Espaco Comporta, 7580-610 Comporta
www.herdadedacomporta.pt

Herdade dos Grous Alentejo

A new, high-end producer in the warm Beja district of the Alentejo, Herdade de Grous is managed by the well-known consultant winemaker Luís Duarte. In addition to 173 acres (70ha) of vines, the 1,730 acre (700ha) property, which is owned by a German company, also has olive trees, livestock, a restaurant, and a hotel. The wines are superbly focused, with sweet dark fruits. Moon Harvested is an intense, focused, fruit-driven red, with lovely purity of fruit. The Reserva is a touch more intense, with incredible concentration and some oak influence. 23 Barricas has wonderful aromatics and vivid dark fruits—it is incredibly rich yet still balanced. ★ Rising star

Albernôa, 7800-601 Beja
www.herdadedosgrous.com

Herdade do Mouchão Alentejo

Mouchão has been owned by the Reynolds family for over 100 years and is one of the Alentejo's most interesting estates. Most of the property is given over to cork oaks, but there are also 94 acres (38ha) of vineyards that are mainly planted to Alicante Bouschet. The ultra-traditional winery turns out some spectacular wines. Dom Rafael is inexpensive and characterful, but the real fun starts with the Mouchão estate wine, which is densely fruited, structured, and complex, with real potential for development. The top wine is the Mouchão Tonel 3-4, a full-throttle but well-balanced wine that is only made in the best years.

7470-153 Casa Branca
www.mouchaowine.pt

Herdade do Rocim Alentejo

Located between Vidigueira and Cuba in the Lower Alentejo, Herdade do Rocim has 148 acres (60ha) of vines. It was bought by Terralis Ltd. in 2000, and for the last few years has been subject to intense restructuring, with the redevelopment of the vineyards and construction of an architecturally striking new winery. The top wine is Grande Rocim, an Alicante Bouschet-based wine of real intensity and power. The next tier down is the Olho de Mocho red (quite serious, with lovely floral perfume and well defined fresh berry fruits), white (citrusy and minerally, with some grapefuit pith notes), and rosé. These are followed by the more affordable Rocim, which shows sweet, ripe, berryish fruit. The wine tourism project here is well worth visiting.
★ Rising star

Estrada Nacional 387, Apartado 64, 7940-909 Cuba
www.herdadedorocim.com

CORK

Portugal is at the heart of the world's cork industry. Corks are made from the bark of the cork oak, which is harvested every nine years from trees that have reached maturity. The harvested bark is seasoned outdoors before the production process begins. First, the bark is boiled, to soften and clean it. While it is pliable, it is flattened and trimmed. The best pieces of bark are hand-punched to produce top-quality corks; the next grade are machine-punched; and smaller pieces are used to make disks for end pieces for technical corks or granulated and glued together to make agglomerate cork. Cork taint is a familiar problem associated with natural cork. It is caused by small quantities of contaminating TCA (2-4-6-trichloroanisole) that occurs naturally in some cork bark. Efforts to eliminate it have been partially successful, but some wines are still ruined by this musty-smelling taint.

JOSE MARIA DA FONSECA
FRUITY AND BALANCED WITH SOFT TANNINS,
THIS WINE IS PERFECT WITH CHEESE

MALHADINHA NOVA
THIS POWERFUL AND EXPRESSIVE WHITE
IS FRESH, WITH GOOD ACIDITY

Herdade das Soberanas Terras do Sado

Located in the Terras do Sado region, Soberanas is near the coast and benefits from both the warmth of the Alentejo, which lies inland, and the cooling influence of the Atlantic Ocean. The estate is owned by the Ferro Jorge family and has 59 acres (24ha) of vines, most of which were planted in 2002. Paulo Laureano is the consultant winemaker. Soberana is a dense, darkly fruited wine, but the sweetness of the fruit is offset by nice freshness. By contrast, S de Soberanas is a bit of a monster; bold and rich, with great concentration and power, it works surprisingly well. ★ **Rising star**

*Monte Soberana de Baixo, Herdade, 7595-077 Torrão
www.soberanas.com*

João Portugal Ramos Alentejo

João Ramos is one of the success stories of the modern Portuguese wine industry. In a relatively short time, his eponymous winery has grown from a small base to one of the largest in the Alentejo, and with their modern upfront fruit and clear varietal labeling his wines have also been a hit on the export markets. Ramos started his career with Quinta do Carmo in 1985. Although he developed quite a reputation for his consulting work, João was eager to make his own wine. He started acquiring vineyard land in 1990, and in 1997 built his first winery by renovating a building on an old property. It has now been fully renovated and houses the current operation, with two separate wineries. João now has 371 acres (150ha) of his own vineyards and 494 acres (200ha) under contract. The wines are of a uniformly high standard and are very astute commercially. The top wine is Marques de Borba Reserva, which can develop nicely in bottle.

*Vila Santa, 7100-149 Estremoz
www.jportugalramos.com*

José Maria da Fonseca Setúbal Peninsula

Formed in 1934, José Maria da Fonseca is Portugal's oldest family-owned table wine company—the seventh generation of the family is now involved. The company is based in Azeitão, in the Terras do Sado region of the Setúbal Peninsula, and is famous for two of Portugal's historic brands: Periquita (a bright, cherry-fruited red) and Lancers Rosé. The current winemaker is the dynamic Domingos Soares Franco. The family owns around 1,977 acres (800ha) of vines spread across several regions. The top wines include Domini Plus from the Douro, Hexagon from the Terras do Sado, the Private Collection DSF range, José de Sousa from the Alentejo, and the FSF (a blend of Trincadeira, Syrah, and Tannat) from Terras do Sado. It also makes fabulous sweet Moscatels, including the rare Moscatel Roxo (purple Muscat), which is a specialty.

*Quinta da Bassaqueria, 2925-511 Azeitão
www.jmf.pt*

Justino's Madeira

Vinhos Justino Henriques Filhos was formed in 1870, and was a family-run business until 1953, when the French drinks distribution company La Martiniquaise became the majority shareholder. A good slice of Justino's production is sold to France in bulk as cooking madeira, but it has to be denatured by adding salt and pepper first to make this shipment legal. Despite this, Justino's best wines are superb, and the 10 year old wines are particularly impressive. The 10 year old Sercial is pale with lovely lemon and herb aromatics and real complexity. The 10 year old Verdelho has a tangy orange peel character and bags of complexity, with good acidity, and the 10 year old Boal is rich, spicy, herby, and complex, with some whiskeylike notes. Even better is the 10 year old Malvasia, which has sweet and sour lemon and raisin characters, with great concentration and thrilling complexity.

*Parque Industrial da Cancela, 9125-042 Caniço Santa Cruz
291 934 257*

Luis Pato Bairrada

Luis Pato is the best-known producer in the Bairrada region. Although he is widely regarded as the modernizer who brought a struggling region back to life, his wines have a traditional side to them and he is also a champion of the local red grape, Baga. Luis trained as a chemical engineer before taking over his parents' winery in the early 1980s. From the start he experimented by destemming the grapes and using small oak barrels, some of which were new. Since 1999 his wines have not been labeled Bairrada, but by the broader designation of Beiras, because of a conflict with the authorities. Altogether, he has assembled 161 acres (65ha) of vineyards, divided into 20 separate blocks in various terroirs within Bairrada. From these, he makes a range of reds, whites, and sparkling wines. The range is quite complicated, but at its core are four top reds: the Vinhas Velhas, Vinha Pan, Vinha Barrosa, and the remarkable Pé Franco, made from ungrafted vines that Pato recently planted in his Riberinho vineyard. There is also a serious white wine called Vinho Formal. All these wines are worth seeking out.

*Ribeiro da Gândara, 3780-017 Amoreira da Gândara,
Anadia; www.luispato.com*

Malhadinha Nova Alentejo

Malhadinha Nova has only been going since 2003, but this beautiful estate near Beja, in the south of Alentejo, is already recognized as one of the region's best producers. The Soares family, which owns a successful chain of wine stores and a distribution business in the Algarve, purchased it in 1998 and renovated it. Consulting winemaker Luis Duarte is well known in the region, and the estate now has 67 acres (27ha) of vines, as well as a beautiful luxury hotel. Top-quality whites are made from Antão Vaz, Arinto, Roupeiro, and Chardonnay, but it is the focused, intense red wines, made from Touriga Nacional, Syrah, Cabernet Sauvignon, Aragonêz, Alicante Bouschet, and Alfrocheiro that steal the show. They are ripe, but still fresh, with lovely fruit purity. Look for the sweetly fruited, pure Monte da Peceguina red, the intense Malhadinha Tinto, and the small-production, high-end Marias de Malhadinha. ★ **Rising star**

*Albernôa, 7800-601 Beja
www.malhadinhanova.pt*

Paço de Camões Alentejo

A relatively new Alentejo producer, whose first vintage was in 2006 from vineyards planted in 2001 and 2002. The estate has been in the hands of the Reynolds family (which also owns Herdade do Mouchão) for six generations. It is now owned by Claire Pinsent, who inherited it from her father, Victor Reynolds, in 1984.

Zéfyro is the name of the entry-level wines: the Viognier is really attractive, with bright fruit, while the red is fresh and fruit-focused. The top wines are called Canto X: the white, a Viognier, shows lovely ripe, herb-tinged fruit and the red is packed with fresh berry fruit. This is a winery to watch. ★ **Rising star**

Herdade Do Paço De Camões, 7000-000 Evora
266 977 141

Quinta do Ameal Vinho Verde

Pedro Araújo's Ameal is a fairly serious interpretation of Vinho Verde. His focus is on quality, in a region that is more commonly associated with cheap and cheerful glugging whites. Ameal is based in Lima, a subregion of Vinho Verde where the Loureiro grape performs best, and is one of the leading proponents of this variety. The relatively low yields Pedro gets from his vines shows in the added concentration and poise of the wines he produces. Two different wines are made, and both are excellent. The Escolha is fermented and aged for six months in French oak: it is minerally and lemony with some breadth and texture from the oak. The Louriero is matured in stainless steel and shows beautifully fresh lemon and pear fruit, with nice mineral notes.

4990–707 Refóios do Lima, Ponte do Lima
www.quintadoameal.com

Quinta das Bágeiras Bairrada

Màrio Sérgio Alves Nuno is the winemaker and owner of Bágeiras, which he set up in 1990. The vineyard area is 59 acres (24ha), which is quite large for the region, and is split between red and white varieties. The wines are serious and reminiscent of the great Italian reds from Sangiovese and Nebbiolo, with their structure and acidity. Màrio Sérgio makes his Baga wines traditionally with whole bunches in the *lagar* (the open receptacle where fermentation and maceration take place). The wine then goes into large oak vats of 660 gallons (2,500 liters) and larger. The top wine is the Reserva Tinto, which has some Touriga Nacional in the blend and ages beautifully. The white wines are also superb, as are the sparkling wines, which are made in a brut nature style with no dosage.

Fogueira, 3780-523 Sangalhos
www.quintadasbageiras.pt

Quinta do Cardo Beira Interior

Part of the Compania das Quintas group, Quinta do Cardo is one of the top properties in the Beira Interior. It is a substantial estate: there are around 250 acres (100ha) of vines growing at an altitude of 2,300ft (700m), which makes them the highest vineyards in Portugal. Síria is a fresh, bright, lemony white with some pithy bitter notes; the Tinto shows lush, seductive black currant and dark cherry fruit; while the Selecção de Enólogo, a varietal Touriga Nacional, is brooding, seamless, and lush with pure dark fruits.

6440-999 Figueira de Castelo Rodrigo
271 377 131

Quinta do Carmo Alentejo

Originally owned by the Bastos family, Carmo was for a while part of the Domaines Barons de Rothschild (Lafite) empire. José Berardo, of Bacalhôa Vinhos de Portugal, initially became a partner before buying the entire

QUINTA DO CARDO
FRESH AND SUCCULENT, THIS IS A WELL-STRUCTURED AND ELEGANT WINE

property in 2008. It is a large estate of around 2,500 acres (1,000ha), of which 370 acres (150ha) are vineyards that have quite an emphasis on the foreign grape varieties Syrah and Cabernet Sauvignon. The wines are made in a polished, modern, slightly international style.

Herdade das Cavalhas, Gloria, Estremoz
www.lafite.com

Quinta do Carvalinho Bairrada

This 35 acre (14ha) estate near Mealadha in Bairrada grows the international varieties Syrah, Cabernet Sauvignon, and Merlot, as well as the local varieties Baga, Rabo de Ovella, and Bical. The Syrah is primary and intense with lovely fruit and acidity; there is also a beautiful Syrah-based sparkling red wine. The sparkling white Bairrada is also very good. There is also a Tourismo, which is mainly drunk by German tourists.

Largo Dr Henrique Navega No. 1, 3050-580 Ventosa do Bairro; www.quintadocarvalhinho.pt

Quinta do Centro Alentejo

This property is owned by English businessman and wine writer Richard Mayson, in partnership with consulting winemaker Rui Reguinga. He purchased 49 acres (20ha) in Portalegre, in the north of the Alentejo, renovated them, and is now making wine here. So far the only wine released is Pedra Basta, which shows focused dark fruits with nice balance. It is also good value for money.

No visitor facilities
www.richardmayson.com

Quinta de Chocapalha Lisboa

Quinta de Chocapalha is an impressive 111 acre (45ha) estate, located in the Lisboa region (previously known as Estremadura), owned by Alice and Paulo Tavares da Silva. They purchased the property in the 1980s and have made significant investments in the vineyards. In 2000, they began making their own wines, with their daughter Sandra as the winemaker—she also performs winemaking duties at Quinta do Vale Dona Maria in the Douro and Pintas, also in the Douro, which is the winery she owns with her husband, Jorge Borges. Some of the grapes from the Chocapalha vineyards are still sold to other producers. The wines are consistently good, blending together modernity with tradition. Look out for the exuberantly fruity white Fernão Pires, the affordable Tinto (made from Touriga Nacional, Tinta Roriz, Alicante Bouschet, and Castelão), the fresh, leafy Cabernet Sauvignon, and the dense, forward Reserva Tinto (mainly Touriga Nacional, with Tinta Roriz and a dribble of Syrah). ★ **Rising star**

2580-081 Aldela Galega da Merceana, Alenquer
www.wonderfulland.com/chocapalha

Quinta de Covela Minho

A very interesting, biodynamic estate that is located in the Minho on the boundary with the Douro. Unfortunately, Covela's future looks uncertain because of financial difficulties, but it is worth making the effort to seek these wines out if you can. Branco Escolha is tight, fresh, and pithy with citrus fruit to the fore. Colheita Seleccionada Branco is minerally, but has some nutty, toasty notes from barrel fermentation. The Palhete is a halfway house between rosé and red: it is savory, full-bodied, and dry. Tinto Escolha is a deliciously vibrant, dark fruit-dominated

LUIS PATO
FROM VINES THAT ARE MORE THAN 80 YEAR OLD, THIS WINE WILL AGE FOR 15–20 YEARS

QUINTA DOS ROQUES
THE VARIETAL ENCRUZARDO IS FRESH AND
CLEAN WITH PLENTY OF PERSONALITY

blend of Touriga Nacional, Merlot, Cabernet Franc and Syrah, while the Colheita Seleccionada Tinto is a Cabernet Franc/Merlot/Touriga Nacional blend that is aged in oak after a long maceration and shows Bordeaux-like depth.

4640 S Tomé de Covelas
254 882 412

Quinta dos Cozinheiros Beiras

Located just 5 miles (8km) from the Atlantic in the west of the Beiras region, near Figuera da Foz, Cozinheiros is a boutique producer that is responsible for some interesting wines. Poerinho is a red wine from the Baga variety with an appealing, savory, spicy quality. Lagar is nicely aromatic with elegant, spicy red fruits, while the top wine is Utopia, which is aromatic, sweet, spicy, and slightly balsamic. All the reds are slightly old fashioned and have real character. Sadly, Jose Mendonça, the man behind Cozinheiros, was killed in an accident in February 2009.

3090-769 Marinha das Ondas
www.quintadoscozinheiros.com

Quinta dos Currais Beira Interior

José Diogo Tomás, a wine-loving doctor from Lisbon, purchased this property in 1989. It is a 297 acre (120ha) estate in the Beira Interior, with 74 acres (30ha) of vines. The first vintage was in 2001 and the wines are really good. Colheita Seleccionada Branco is a deep-colored white wine with powerful, pithy fruit. Síria is a boldly flavored white with lovely purity of citrus fruit. The regular Tinto is fresh and quite savory, while the Reserva, a blend of Touriga Nacional, Aragonêz, and Castelão, is stylish, concentrated, and lush, with some tannic structure.

Castelo Branco, Capinha 6230-145
www.quintadoscurrais.com

Quinta da Falorca Dão

The name is a little confusing here: Falorca is the vineyard, thus the wine is Quinta da Falorca, but the company name is Quinta Vale das Escadinha, which is where the cellar is. The Figueiredo family has 32 acres (13ha) of vines and from these make some lovely expressions of Dão. Look for T-nac, an unoaked Touriga Nacional with amazingly bright, pure, floral aromatics and taut dark cherry and blackberry fruit. The Quinta da Falorca Garrafeira is even better, with a brooding, sweet, dark-fruit nose and a complex, refined, structured yet elegant palate.

Largo de Camões 15, 2410-127 Leiria
244 821 517

Quinta da Lagoalva de Cima Tejo

A large 13,590 acre (5,500ha) estate in the Tejo region, of which just 111 acres (45ha) are devoted to grape vines. The wines are solidly good, with the highlights being a fresh, almost Burgundian Alfrocheiro with plummy fruit, and a structured, rather dense Syrah. A new winery was built in 2002, and Rui Reguinga acts as consulting winemaker.

2090 Alpiarca
www.lagoalva.pt

Quinta do Monte d'Oiro Lisboa

José Bento dos Santos' estate in the Lisboa (formerly Estremadura) region is famous for its widely acclaimed,

QUINTA DA FALORCA
THIS UNOAKED TOURIGA NACIONAL IS DARK,
PLUMMY, AND SPICY

Syrah-based Monte d'Oiro Reserva, which has a dense, earthy structure under the bright cherry and red berry fruit, with some perfume from the splash of Viognier in the blend. He also makes other interesting wines, including Madrigal (a varietal Viognier), Vinha da Nora (Syrah with a bit of Cinsault), Aurius (a blend of Touriga Nacional, Syrah, and Petit Verdot), and Têmpera (Tempranillo, also known as Tinta Roriz). The very top Syrah, Homenagem a António Carqueijeiro, is only made in the best years, and is intense and quite oaky in its youth.

Freixial de Cima, 2580-404 Ventosa, Alenquer
www.quintadomontedoiro.com

Quinta do Mouro Alentejo

Miguel Louro, a dentist by training, and his son Luis run this overachieving 54 acre (22ha) Alentejo property. The first vintage was in 1994 and Luis Duarte has been consultant winemaker here since 1998. The wines are fantastic. Regular Quinta do Mouro is a special wine and particularly so in good vintages such as 2005, which shows thrilling, dense, sweet, dark fruits, with well-defined structure. Keep your eyes open for the Gold Label, which is only made in the best years and spends 18 months in new French oak. The second label, Zagalos, is a drinkable wine with a serious side.

7100 Estremoz
268 332 259

Quinta de Paços Vinho Verde

Quinta de Paços makes wines from four properties in Vinho Verde, including Quinta de Boavista. Wines are made in two sites, but Paços itself is based near Barcelos, an area where the Loureiro variety dominates. Their Louriero/Arinto blend is superfresh and citrusy, with a long, lemony finish. Morgado do Perdigão is a blend of Alvarinho and Louriero, and adds a subtle nuttiness and some peachy richness to the crisp fruit. Casa do Capitão-mor Alvarinho is bright with a savory lemon pith character, and the Prazo de Cotovia is an inky, bloody, meaty red Vinho Verde.

Rio Côvo Sta-Eulália, Rua Dr Teotónio da Fonseca, 171,
4750-484 Barcelos; www.quintapacos.com

Quinta do Perdigão Dão

Architect José Perdigão is also a small wine producer in the Dão, with 17 acres (7ha) of vines. His soft-textured, cherry-fruited Alfrocheiro is appealing, and the Reserva has lovely, ripe, dark cherry and blackberry fruit, but the star of the show is the beautifully aromatic, floral, dark-fruited Touriga Nacional, which is well worth looking out for.

3500-543 Silgueiros, Viseu
www.quintadoperdigao.com

Quinta dos Roques Dão

Quinta dos Roques, at Abrunhosa do Mato (between Nelas and Mangualade), is a family-owned Dão producer managed by Luís Lourenço, with help from consultant winemaker Rui Reguinga. The vineyards at Dos Roques were replanted from 1978 onward, and in 1990 the first wines were produced bearing the quinta's name. The 100 acres (40ha) of vines are split two-thirds red (Touriga Nacional, Tinta Roriz, Jaén, Alfrocheiro, Tinta Cão, and Rufete) and one-third white (Encruzado, Bical, Malvasia

Fina, and Sercial). In 1997, the family bought out another Dão Quinta, Das Maias, and now owns the majority of this 86 acre (35ha) property, which is located at a higher altitude, in the foothills of the Serra da Estrela. The wines are bottled separately to preserve the different identities of these two estates and the overall quality is high. The reds are modern, dark, and self-assured, but with a degree of elegance. The whites are clean and fresh, but not lacking in personality. Varietal expressions of Jaén, Alfrocheiro, Touriga Nacional, Tinta Cão, and Encruzado are made, as well as blends such as the high-end Reserva and Garrafeira.

Rua da Paz, Abrunhosa do Mato, 3530-050 Cunha Baixa
www.quintaroques.pt

Quinta de Sant'Ana Lisboa

Quinta de Sant'Ana is the family property of James and Ann Frost. James is English and Ann is German; the property was previously owned by her parents, Gustav and Paula von Fürstenberg. The quinta is located in what was until recently known as the Estremadura region, but is now referred to as Lisboa. Wine is a recent development for Quinta de Sant'Ana. In 1999, James sought the advice of viticulturalist David Booth and his enologist colleague António Maçanita, and began planting vines. The first wines were released in 2005 and there are now 28 acres (11.5ha) of vineyards, with woodland, orchards, and paddocks making up the balance of the 109 acre (44ha) estate. The range now includes wonderfully fresh and precise varietal Riesling, Verdelho, Alvarinho, and Sauvignon Blanc, as well as a richer Fernão Pires. Reds include a vibrant, focused, berryish Tinto and the more structured, dense, and beautifully dark-fruited Reserva. A new development is the stunning Pinot Noir, which was first made in the 2009 vintage.

2665-113 Gradil, Concelho de Mafra
www.quintadesantana.com

Quinta do Zambujeiro Alentejo

Zambujeiro is owned by a Swiss wine enthusiast, Emil Strickler, who bought the property in 1998. Three wines are made from 74 acres (30ha) of vines: Monte do Castanheiro, Terra do Zambujeiro, and Zambujeiro. Only around 6,000 bottles of the top wine, Zambujeiro, are made each year from miniscule yields, and it sells for high prices. The wines are made in a very ripe, intense, and lush style, with great concentration and impact. They are certainly impressive, but sometimes flirt with overripeness.

Monte do Zambujeiro, Rio de Moinhos, 7150, Borba
www.zambujeiro.com

Sogrape

Portugal's largest family-owned wine company, Sogrape makes wines across most of Portugal's wine regions and they are invariably very good. Their biggest seller is Mateus Rosé, but other wines in their extensive portfolio are likely to be of more interest. In Vinho Verde, their Gazela is one of the leading brands. It is fresh, bright, a bit spritzy, and inexpensive, and more than 1 million gallons (5 million liters) are made each year. Azevedo, a fresh, lemony white that is very pure, is a step up from Gazela. Pena de Pato is a new brand that includes wines from Dão, Alentejo, and Douro: all of them are very good

examples of their regions, and are excellent bargains. Moving up in price, Callabriga in regular and reserva forms is a brand with wines from the same three regions; look for the super Dão and Douro Reservas, which show good regional typicity. In 1990, Sogrape bought Quinta dos Carvalhais in the Dão, and this is making some of the best wines in the region. It also owns Quinta da Leda in the Douro.

Apartado 3032, 4431-852 Avintes
www.sograpevinhos.eu

Terrenus Alentejo

This is the personal project of winemaker Rui Reguinga, who makes the wines at Quinta do Centro, where he is in partnership with Richard Mayson (their company is called Lusitano Dream). The Terrenus white is made from old-vine Arinto and is bold, intense, and lively. The red shows fresh, bright cherry fruit with subtle sappiness, and is made from old vines in the Serra de São Mamede. Reguinga's style is one that favors freshness and elegance over power.

Travessa do Calvário, No. 26, 2080-174 Almeirim
www.ruireguinga.com

Valle Pradinhos Trás-os-Montes

Located in Trás-os-Montes, the rather remote region north of the Douro, this estate was initially established in 1913 as a family retreat—vines were only planted later. It is currently run by Maria Antónia Mascarenhas and the winemaking is in the capable hands of Rui Cunha, who also makes the wines at Quinta de Covela. There is something a little wild and edgy about these wines, which reflect the wildness of the region they come from. The white is a blend of Riesling, Gewürztraminer, and Malvasia Fina, and is aromatic and crisp. The estate wine is a blend of Touriga Nacional, Cabernet Sauvignon, and Tinta Amarela, and is fresh and plummy, with a savory, spicy streak. The Reserva is mostly Cabernet Sauvignon and shows concentrated sweet black currant fruit, with a tarry edge and some tight structure.

Casal de Valle Pradinhos, 5340-422 Sesulfe, Macedo de Cavaleiros; www.vallepradinhos.pt

THE DIFFERENT FACES OF TOURIGA NACIONAL

Touriga Nacional is the most famous of Portugal's indigenous grape varieties. It is not favored by viticulturalists, however, as it is difficult to grow, very sensitive to weather conditions during flowering, and yields can be variable. But when it is good, it really is very good, making wines with wonderful floral, violety aromas as well as dark cherry and blackberry fruit. It shows different characteristics depending on where it is grown. In the Douro, where it forms the bulk of new plantings, it makes quite rich, dense wines with more blackberry character than cherry—this is largely due to the warm climate and schistous soils. In the Dão, which has granitic soils and a cooler climate, the wines are fresher and more elegant, with dark cherry fruit and accentuated floral notes. In the hot Alentejo, Touriga Nacional is richer, darker, and spicier. Some think that Touriga Nacional, for all its qualities, works best as part of a blend. In the Douro, this is almost certainly the case, and it is probably also true for the Dão. But the commercial lure of making single-variety wines is strong, and so it looks as if we will see more varietal Touriga Nacionals in the years to come.

Grapes have grown in Spain for millennia. Around 3,000 years ago, the Phoenicians are thought to have introduced grapes to Andalucía, in the south—although in those days, the wine made from them was more a simple, vinegar-like commodity than an art form. Nearly six centuries of Roman occupation introduced techniques such as fermentation in stone troughs and smaller amphorae for storage, skills that were quickly adopted by the indigenous Celtic and Iberian tribes. Following the fall of the Roman Empire, the conquering Moors may, as Muslims, have prohibited the consumption of alcohol, but nonetheless encouraged its distillation for use in perfumes and cosmetics.

The return of Christian culture in the Middle Ages brought with it a renewed demand for wine, both within and outside of the Church. Although heavy and either very sweet or *rancio* (literally "rancid": fully oxidized), Spanish wine was soon being exported as far afield as the New World. In the centuries that followed, more refined and lighter styles developed and the industry grew, even in the face of setbacks such as the arrival of the phylloxera vine louse or the Spanish Civil War.

Today, Spain is a vibrant wine nation. At 2.87 million acres (1.16 million ha), it has the largest vineyard area in the world, 97.4% of which is used for wine. Its 73 Denominación de Origen (DO) zones produce red, rosé, and white still wines, as well as sparkling Cava. Yet the excitement in Spain today lies in seeking discoveries outside traditional regions. Its five most widely planted grapes are Airén, Tempranillo, Bobal, Garnacha Tinta, and Monastrell, but there are also abandoned pre-phylloxera vines waiting to be revived. There are Atlantic and Mediterranean influences, and microclimates that stretch from the heights of volcanic mountains to sea level. With these resources, Spain has the opportunity to produce some of the world's greatest wines— and it does. The potential, however, exists to produce many more.

SPAIN

RIOJA

ATLANTIC OCEAN

FRANCE

Bilbao

Barcelona

MADRID

PORT.

SPAIN

Mediterranean Sea

 Rioja wine region

Rioja *is* Spanish wine. For many consumers around the world, there is no other wine from Spain. This erroneous assumption has played to Rioja's advantage for over a century. The region benefited early from sending its exports by rail, so it is no surprise that some of its most historic wineries are clustered around the railway in Haro in the Barrio de l'Estación, or station district. Rioja's winemaking practices established its appeal: the lengthy storage of Tempranillo in American oak casks creates an elegant wine with faint echoes of strawberry fruit, good acidity, and rounded vanilla from the oak. Maturation time in barrel and then in bottle only adds to its attenuated appeal.

Major grapes

 Reds

Garnacha

Graciano

Mazuelo (Cariñena)

Tempranillo

Whites

Garnacha Blanca

Malvasía

Viura (Macabeo)

Vintages

2009
A very promising vintage, especially in Rioja Alta and Rioja Baja.

2008
The wines are fresh, with slightly lower alcohol levels.

2007
The crop was relatively small, and the wines are not exceptional.

2006
Wines are aromatic and fresh, and are maturing early.

2005
Another historic vintage. The pleasure lies in sampling both 2004 and 2005 and arguing about which is better.

2004
Historic vintage, especially following the wet 2002 and the hot 2003.

The name "Rioja" originates from the River Oja: *río* is Spanish for "river," hence *Río-oja*. Given the dominance of the Ebro, it is surprising that such an insignificant river as the Oja should have become so important, but the naming of wine regions has never been straightforward.

It is certainly the River Ebro that links the three different regions of Rioja. Starting from the northwest, the Rioja Alavesa lies north of the Ebro, and produces wines that are ready to drink young. The Rioja Alta, south of the Ebro, is altogether hotter and produces wines suitable for aging. It benefits particularly from the Graciano grape, which brings a definite freshness to its wines. To the east of both zones lie the Rioja Baja, where Garnacha is a main focus: it flourishes in the warmer climate. For a long time, the Rioja Baja was seen as the "poor relation" of the Riojas, producing the lowest-quality wine. However, the return of Alvaro Palacios to his family winery in the region, and the recognition by winemakers internationally that old-vine Garnacha is exceptional, have done much to restore the profile (and prices) of the region.

These three grape varieties—Tempranillo, Graciano, Garnacha (the French Grenache)—make the typical Rioja red blend, alongside Mazuelo (known as Cariñena elsewhere in Spain, and Carignan in France). The cherry-fruited Tempranillo is dominant, making up 75–90% of blends, and 100% in some modern-style wines.

For whites, Viura (or Macabeo) is the main variety, sometimes with an added dash of Malvasía and Garnacha Blanca. Until recently, it produced relatively undistinguished, low-acid, easily oxidized wines, but new winemaking techniques have radically improved and freshened these tired white Riojas.

Rioja was the first Denominación de Origen declared in Spain, in 1926. Like Jerez, the region chose to take the blending route, whether of estate grapes or bought-in material, because this practice allowed the creation of large businesses able to handle the complications of exporting. Only in very recent times have new winemakers entered Rioja and established a tradition of estate-grown, estate-bottled, and single-vineyard wines.

One important influence was Professor Emile Peynaud of Bordeaux University, the most influential enologist of his generation. He was invited to the region by Enrique Forner, who went on to found the Marqués de Cáceres winery. Back in the 1970s, Peynaud showed Forner how to make younger, fresher wines with more fruit and less oak.

On the whole, the changes have been beneficial for wine lovers. Rioja still has an unjust reputation for making wines drowned in old oak, but those days are long gone. To be sure, the flavors of Rioja today are varied, depending on the microclimate, the soil, and the grower. Yet the quality of the fruit and barrel selection have improved immeasurably both whites as well as reds.

Where next for Rioja? Spain's economic woes may have put the breaks on building glossy new wineries. Instead, perhaps we can hope winemakers will continue to pay attention to their vines, and, above all, reduce the high prices for showy wines.

Abel Mendoza

Abel Mendoza is the son and grandson of wine-growers, yet despite his pedigree in Rioja, he can be counted among the region's modernists. He makes wines according to his own choices, and tries to reflect the characteristics of his different vineyards. He began in 1988 by making young wines, but over time he has transformed his production into serious reserve wines. These include Tempranillo and Graciano *grano a grano*, which literally means "grape by grape," referring to the fact that the grapes used to make the wines are hand-selected. His top wine is the Selección Personal. Of particular interest is Mendoza's Malvasía, which he produces alongside his Viura; this particular grape is uncommon as a single-varietal today in the region.

Carretera de Peñacerrada 7, 26338 San Vicente de la Sonsierra, La Rioja; 941 308 010

Amézola de la Mora

A top-quality vineyard with some 245 acres (100ha) of its own vines. Based in the Rioja Alta, the family grows Tempranillo, Graciano, and Mazuelo. Since the tragic death of Iñigo Amézola de la Mora, great-grandson of the founder, in a car accident in 1999, the estate has been run first by his widow, and now his daughters. The fresh Viña Amézola is a value-for-money Crianza with plenty of typicality. Iñigo Amézola, the tribute wine, is made from 100% Tempranillo, has plenty of structure, and will blossom over five to six years.

Paraje Viña Vieja, 26359 Torremontalvo, La Rioja
www.bodegasamezola.net

Artadi

Artadi is the brand name of Cosecheros Alaveses, and it has come to represent one of the leaders in transforming the traditional face of Rioja. Winemaker Juan Carlos Lopez de Lacaille impresses with his scrupulous attention to the wines, which attain consistently good results at all levels. Whether he is working with the bright, carbonic maceration Joven, the Viñas de Gain Reserva, or the serious, old-vine Pagos Viejos, he manages to reveal the pure expression of each vineyard. At the top of the range, Grandes Añadas is only produced in the best years, while the 6 acres (2.4ha) single-vineyard El Pisón is a Reserva made from high-altitude Tempranillo vines that are more than 25 years old. In Navarra, Artazuri (established in 1996) shows promise of the same excellence. In the latest (1999) project, El Sequé, in Alicante, Lopez de Lacaille is proving that he has equal ability with Monastrell, which he blends with some Cabernet Sauvignon, and Syrah. The arrival of Artadi in Alicante has undoubtedly put that region back on the wine map, and reinforces the status of Monastrell as a fashionable grape variety in Spain.

Carretera Logroño, 01300 Laguardia, Alava
www.artadi.com

Baigorri

Before pulling the cork on a Baigorri bottle, visit the website, first making sure the sound is turned up. It may seem a little self-conscious, yet it charmingly represents the designed aspect of the entire project. Baigorri is one of the remarkable new wineries in Rioja, a glass box above ground giving the only clue to the winery that is sunk beneath it. The work of a local architect, the building is as carefully thought out as the wines.

BERONIA
THE NEW RESERVAS FROM THIS IMPROVING
WINERY SHOW GOOD CHERRY FRUIT

AMEZOLA DE LA MORA
MADE FROM TEMPRANILLO IN
AN EXCEPTIONAL VINTAGE

In addition to the seductive, modern reds, try the Blanco Fermentado en Barrica ("Barrel Fermented White"), an award-winning 100% Viura.

Carretera Vitoria-Logroño, Km 61, 01307 Samaniego, Alava
www.bodegasbaigorri.com

Baron de Ley

This winery is relatively new (1985) to Rioja, yet it has an ancient heritage: the estate is situated in a 16th-century Benedictine monastery, proving once again that the Benedictines knew exactly where the best wines came from. Baron de Ley focuses on *reserva* and *gran reserva* wines aged in French and American oak. Check out the 7 Viñas: a very interesting (and very successful) blend of all seven permitted Rioja varietals (five red and two white), including around 50% Tempranillo, with Graciano, Garnacha, Mazuelo, and Viura. Baron de Ley also owns Bodegas Museum in Cigales.

Carretera Mendavia-Lodosa 5, 31897 Mendavia, Navarra
www.barondeley.com

Berberana

Berberana is simply the tip of the iceberg of wineries that form the Arco group. For many consumers, it is the first Rioja brand they meet. Berberana wines offer consistency and value, as well as an appealing introduction to the softness and red fruits of Rioja. Arco's influence is widespread, stretching from Lagunilla, the Marqués de Griñón brand, and Marqués de la Concordia to Hacienda de Susar (Rioja), the Durius wines sourced from along the River Douro, and Marqués de Monistrol (Cava), as well as a range of Italian wineries, including Chianti Classico producer Villa Cafaggio.

No visitor facilities
www.unitedwineries.com

Berceo

Bodegas Berceo is the Rioja producer of the Luis Gurpegui Muga group, which also produces wines in Navarra, Extremadura, and Chile. Most noteworthy of the Rioja wines are the cherry-fruited, minerally Los Dominios de Berceo Prefiloxérico, which comes from old-vine material in the Baños de Ebro district of Rioja Alavesa; and the Dominios de Berceo 36, from a 20 acre (8ha) Tempranillo vineyard planted in 1936—a significant year in the history of Spain, given the outbreak of the country's civil war. All *reservas* and *gran reservas* are aged in French oak.

Calle de las Cuevas, 26200 Haro, La Rioja
www.gurpegui.es

Beronia

Only a few years ago, Beronia would not have rated a place in this guide. The wines, especially the *gran reservas*, were of the old style, faded and lacking in fruit. That was then. Today, this slumbering giant ranks as a rising star because it is being transformed under the ownership of the sherry family González Byass, whose other properties in Spain include Viñas del Vero (Somontano), Vilarnau (Cava), and Finca Constancia (Toledo). With attention to detail in the vineyards and the cellar, the team is making good progress. ★ **Rising star**

Carretera Ollauri-Nájera, Km 1800, 26220 Ollauri, La Rioja
www.beronia.es

RIOJA

Given that Rioja represents 40% of Spain's wine production, it is not surprising that it is about 62 miles (100km) long and 25 miles (40km) wide, covering the valley of the River Ebro. To the north, it is bordered by the Sierra Cantabria, to the south, by the Sierra de la Demanda, and the terroir in between varies greatly. The warm Rioja Alta region in the west has traditionally been regarded as the highest quality, with the slightly cooler Alavesa coming second. With improved viticulture, both regions produce fine wines and are matched also by the hotter, drier, Mediterranean-influenced Rioja Baja, so often the poor relation.

PRODUCERS

Abel Mendoza **7**	Fernández de Piérola **26**	Olarra **23**
Amézola de la Mora **9**	Finca Allende **5**	Ontañon **27**
Artadi **19**	Finca Egomei **30**	Ostatu **13**
Baigorri **18**	Finca Valpiedra **17**	Paisajes y Viñedos **5**
Baron de Ley **28**	Heredad Ugarte **18**	Palacios Remondo **31**
Berceo **3**	Hermanos Peciña **13**	Pujanza **20**
Beronia **4**	Ijalba **24**	Ramón Bilbao **3**
Bilbaínas **3**	Izadi **12**	Remelluri **6**
Bodegas Riojanas **10**	La Rioja Alta **3**	Remírez de Ganuza **13**
Breton **16**	Lan **15**	Roda **3**
Campo Viejo **22**	López de Heredía **3**	Sierra Cantabria **7**
Castillo de Sajazarra **2**	Luis Cañas **12**	Tobia **8**
Contador **11**	Marqués de Cáceres **10**	Valsacro **29**
Contino **21**	Marqués de Riscal **14**	Valserrano **12**
CVNE **3**	Marqués de Vargas **27**	Viña Salceda **14**
Dinastía Vivanco **5**	Miguel Merino **5**	Viñedos del Ternero **1**
El Coto **25**	Montecillo **17**	Ysios **12**
Faustino **25**	Muga **3**	

BODEGAS RIOJANAS, S.A.

CASA FUNDADA EN 1890

RIOJA

DENOMINACIÓN DE ORIGEN CALIFICADA

VIÑA ALBINA®

✯✯✯✯✯

EMBOTELLADO POR

BODEGAS RIOJANAS, S.A.

CENICERO-ESPAÑA
PRODUCTO DE ESPAÑA

75 cl

GRAN RESERVA

BAY OF BISCAY

Santander
Bilbao
Donostia-San
Sebastián
FRANCE

PAÍS VASCO

Vitoria-
Gasteiz
Pamplona

NAVARRA

Burgos
Logroño

LA RIOJA

CASTILLA-LEÓN

ARAGÓN

Zaragoza

■ Rioja wine region

Hacienda Praddolagar
Rioja

Denominación de Origen Calificada

M

Variedades *Tempranillo,*
Garnacha y Mazuelo.

Cosecha *2000*

Botellas producidas *6.000*

Botella nº *744 P10066*

Alcohol *14 % By Vol.*

Elaborado y embotellado por
Bodegas y Viñedos del Marqués de Vargas, S.A.
Logroño - España
Produce of Spain
Contains Sulfites

750 ml e

Marañón
Aguilar

Linares
Sansol

Yécora/
Iekora
Torres
del Rio

N111

Assa
25 26
Oyón
24
Viana

21
22
23
27

LOGROÑO
A68

Villamediana
de Iregua

Murillo
de Río Leza

Alberite

N111
Leza

Ribafrecha

Calvijo

Nalda

Lagunilla
del Jubera

Sierra de la Laguna

Leza

San Román
de Cameros

▲ Atalaya
1518m
(4980ft)

Enciso

NAVARRA

Lazagurría

Sesma

Mendavia

Agoncillo

Ebro

28

Lerín

▲ 506m
(1660ft)

Lodosa

Ega

Andosilla

RIOJA BAJA

Ausejo

El Villar
de Arnedo

San
Adrián

Ebro

Tudelilla

1338m
(4389ft) ▲

Bergasa

Arnedo

Arnedillo

LA RIOJA

Quel

650m
(2132ft) ▲

Autol

Turruncún

Yerga
1101m
(3612ft) ▲

30

CALAHORRA

29

Azagra

Funes

Rincón
de Soto

Aldeanueva
de Ebro

Moncavuelo
504m
(1653ft)

Falces

Peralta

Marcilla

A15

N121

Arguedas

ALFARO
31

E804

A15

N232

414m
(1358ft) ▲

Ebro

Grávalos

Linares

San Pedro
Manrique

Valdemadera

Valdelaville

Cigudosa

Alhama

Magaña

Cintruénigo

Fitero

Cervera del
Rio Alhama

Aguilar del
Río Alhama

Añamaza

ZARAGOZA

N113

Murchante

Cascante

TUDELA

E804

KEY

RIOJA ALTA	Rioja subzone
▬	Cava DO
〰	Rivers, lakes
▱	Roads
▨	165ft (100m) contours
▬ ▬	Province border
▨	Urban areas
❶	Location of one or more producers

0   5   10 km
0   5   10 miles

Always check the availability of tasting facilities and the visiting hours at a winery before planning your trip. Some wineries are open by appointment only.

BODEGAS RIOJANAS
THE OLD MONTE REAL WINES ARE FINE EXAMPLES OF THE ELEGANT, DELICATE RIOJAS

CVNE
VINA REAL TYPICALLY SHOWS BLACKBERRY AND MOCHA TONES WITH FIRM TANNINS

Bilbaínas

One of the old stagers in Rioja's history, Bodegas Bilbaínas was established in 1901 under this name in Haro in the Rioja Alta. It now has a substantial holding of 617 acres (250ha) of vineyards. It remains a producer of the classics, with elegant, vanilla, and cherry-scented *reservas* and *gran reservas*. Viña Pomal, first produced in 1911, has all the delicate characters of mature Rioja, while La Vicalanda has more power and fruit. Since 1997, Bilbaínas has been owned by Cava house Codorníu, which transformed the bodega.

Calle de la Estación 3, 26200 Haro, La Rioja
www.bodegasbilbainas.com

Bodegas Riojanas

A visit to Bodegas Riojanas in Cenicero in the Rioja Alta is a trip back in time. It may not be the oldest bodega here (founded 1890), but it has been careful to preserve antique tools. Riojanas uses American oak, according to Riojan tradition, and had preserved a fascinating library of wines. Being able to taste back through them is a privilege, particularly the delicate, very mature Monte Real Gran Reservas. Today's wines can be variable. Viña Albina is the more modern range. One speciality is a botrytised sweet white wine that has been barrel-fermented and matured.

Carretera de la Estación 1-21, 26350 Cenicero, La Rioja
www.bodegasriojanas.com

Breton Spain

Established in 1985, Breton has substantial holdings of over 247 acres (100ha) of vines across the Rioja Alta. The estates include the largest, Loriñón, Dominio de Conte, and the tiny Pago del Camino, all of which are produced as separate wines. The bodega specializes in quality *crianza* and *reserva* wines. The Loriñón wines, which consist of blends of the local varieties, are typical modern Riojas, while the complex, dense 100% Tempranillo Alba de Bretón and the finely oaked Domino de Conte are particularly good.

Carretera de Fuenmayor, Navarrete, 26370 La Rioja
www.bodegasbreton.com

Campo Viejo

For many consumers worldwide, Campo Viejo *is* Rioja. Although the label may not tell you how to pronounce the region of origin (*ree-OCH-ha*) its classical appearance and the yellow and orange colors make its identity plain. While the entry-level wines lack a real sense of place, do not overlook the Gran Reserva, which is a full-bodied, powerful style with strong oak overtones. Dominio is a Tempranillo/Graciano/Mazuelo blend packed with dense, fleshy fruit, and reflects the modern approach to Rioja: hence its lack of a *reserva* classification.

Camino de Lapuebla 50, 26006 Logroño, La Rioja
www.campoviejo.com

Castillo de Sajazarra

The Castillo de Sajazarra is indeed a real, medieval castle, four-square and turreted, on the top of a hill in northern Rioja at a major historic crossroads. The Sajazarra bodega is a family project. At 1,300–2,300ft (400–700m), the vines are at some of the highest altitudes in the Rioja

Alta, and the wines undoubtedly benefit, with a bright freshness that gaves them age-ability. Digma is a smoky, toasty, modern classic, with black fruits overlaid by licorice and mocha. This is a wine that is built to last, with its full fruit and firm, tannic grip.

Calle del Río, 26212 Sajazarra, La Rioja
www.castillo-de-sajazarra.com

Contador

It is not easy trying to decide whether to list this wine under "C" for Contador, or "B" or "R" for the name of the proprietor/winemaker. In this case Benjamin Romeo's name is just as important as his brands. Romeo has been described as the leading "garage" producer of Spain, for his personality, but especially for his focus on creating the very best wines. Now established in a shiny new winery in San Vicente de la Sonsierra, his wines are made predominantly from Tempranillo, with fine new French oak and plenty of character.

Carretera Baños de Ebro, Km-1, 26338 San Vicente de la Sonsierra; www.bodegacontador.com

Contino

Near Laguardia in the Rioja Alavesa, Contino is a period property with a beautiful, quietly distinguished single vineyard in a region known for its brands. It was Contino that revived the estate concept in Rioja. Thanks to its thoughtful winemaker, Jesus Madrazo, it aims consistently high. While part-owned by CVNE, Contino preserves its very separate identity. The regular Reserva has always been well received, and the arrival of the single-varietal Graciano caused a stir. This quickly won a reputation for itself as a top-quality wine that magically tamed the rare and famously difficult Graciano grape variety. It soon led to a small explosion of Graciano brands throughout Rioja. Viña del Olivo, named after the ancient olive tree that grows in the vineyard, is the top-end Tempranillo blend; it is a modern expression but with the signature refinement of the winemaker.

Finca San Rafael, 01321 Laguardia, Alava
www.cvne.com

CVNE

Pronounced *coo-ne*, the Compania Vinícola del Norte de España dates back to 1879. The original buildings in Haro provide a charming insight into the old days, although there have been many subsequent extensions and changes to them. In recent years, the mainstream Riojas have been of variable quality, but improvements are showing now which started at the top and are slowly working their way downward. Imperial is a Reserva, and CVNE declares Gran Reservas of it in excellent years; the name is said to come from the original bottle size, which was a British Imperial pint: about 17.6 floz (50cl). The icon wine of the winery is Real de Asúa, named after the family. The Viña Real wines are produced in a glamorous circular winery that perches on a hilltop in a dominating position. Circular wineries are always a risk, because the tanks and barrels need to be calculated carefully to fit, yet Viña Real looks to have it just right. The wines are attractive, with generous, broad fruit; the top wine, Pagos de Viña Real, is full of appeal, with a dense palate and savory finish.

Barrio de la Estacíon, 26200 Maro, La Roja
www.cvne.com

Dinastía Vivanco

Briones is buzzing. For such a small town, there is plenty of significant activity. Finca Allende grabs the international headlines; Miguel Merino is more of an insider's favorite; and now the Vivancos have launched a museum for the industry. Usually the words "museum" and "wine" are anathema, but this monument to wine culture is well worth a visit during any trip to the region. The Vivancos have been wine producers in the area for almost a century, and are now creating wines that match the quality of the museum. Of particular interest are the Graciano and the Garnacha.

Carretera Nacional 232, 26330 Briones, La Rioja
www.dinastiavivanco.com

El Coto

Despite being founded as recently as 1970, El Coto has a reassuringly traditional appearance. The style is classical, with plenty of American oak barrels in the cellar to impart the customary ripe, supple texture. In the vineyards, Tempranillo vines dominate, ensuring that the young wines have a crunchy, red-cherry freshness. Coto de Imaz, the Gran Reserva, shows a complex blend of syrupy fruits, old leather, and smoky spices that typifies more mature Riojas. The more modern, more glamorous Barón de Ley was launched by the same owners in 1985.

Camino Viejo de Oyón, 01320 Oyón, Alava
www.elcoto.com

Faustino

Faustino is one of the well-known names of traditional Rioja. It promises creamy, vanilla, American oak, a midweight palate, and cherry fruit in the classical style. It also guarantees memorable antique pastiche packaging for some of its wines, complete with frosted bottles and metallic cages that echo Don Quixote. These days, the bodega also produces modern styles: De Autor Reserva Especial is the top wine in the range. Faustino owns several other brands, including Campillo in Rioja and the new Portia which is based in Ribera del Duero.

Carretera de Logroño, 01320 Oyón-Oion, Alava
www.bodegasfaustino.es

Fernández de Piérola

A relatively new arrival (1996) to the Rioja Alavesa, this family bodega is succeeding by its narrow focus on the vineyard and its low-growing bush vines, which demand labor by hand throughout the season. The altitude and the soils give the wines an elegant minerality. The barrel-fermented Viura has plenty of texture from lees aging. The reds are all 100% Tempranillo, culminating in Vitium, which is made from vines that are 80–100 years or more old, and is aged in French and American oak. The result is deliciously intense, with finely controlled fruit and a persistent finish. ★ Rising star

Carretera de Logroño, 01322 Moreda de Alava, Alava
www.pierola.com

Finca Allende

In the quiet heart of the village of Briones in the Rioja Alta lies the outstanding bodega of Miguel Ángel de Gregorio and his sister, Mercedes. Their focus on specific vineyards and terroir epitomizes the new approach to Rioja and could not be more different from the classical style of blending across vineyards and varietals. Indeed, it is hard to find fault with any of de Gregorio's wines. His fermented white Rioja (a Viura/Malvasía blend) is strikingly good and impresses all those who criticise Viura as boring; his Finca Allende is a well-built, bold 100% Tempranillo. His two top wines are Calvario, which is an expressive, spicy wine from a single vineyard created the same year as Artadi's El Pisón; and Aurus, with 15% Graciano and 25 months in new French oak. Both have the structure and capacity for long aging, and are sold at collectors' prices. De Gregorio's latest project is Finca Coronado Vino de la Tierra de Castilla, which first appeared in 2001. Made from his family's estate, the wine is a blend of Cabernet Sauvignon and five other red varieties.

Plaza Ibarra 1, 26330 Briones
www.finca-allende.com

Finca Egomei

Finca Egomei produces just two wines. Egomei expresses its 14 months in new French oak with fine cedar and savory oak overlaid by rich, dark fruits. Alma, already much garlanded with awards, is mainly Tempranillo with 25% Graciano. Deeply colored, it reveals a sumptuous richness, with opulent black fruits, dark chocolate, and tar, all bound by 18 months in new French oak. The bodega is the top winery in the A&B group (run by four sisters); their other properties include Camilo Castilla (Navarra) and Bodegas Peinado (La Mancha).

Carretera de Corella, 26540 Alfaro
www.bodegasderioja.com

Finca Valpiedra

Finca Valpiedra is the flagship of the Martínez Bujanda family. Now in its fifth generation, the family has vineyards all across Rioja, and supplies a very attractive range of wines. Valdemar and Conde de Valdemar are well-priced, modern Riojas; Inspiración de Valdemar is the "high expression" Rioja: very bold and dense. Finca Valpiedra is a spectacular estate, caught in a bend of the River Ebro, and managed with serious technical analysis of the vineyard and careful handling in the winery. Finca Antigua is the family's property in La Mancha.

Término Montecillo, 26360 Fuenmayor, La Rioja;
www.familiamartinezbujanda.com

Heredad Ugarte

The Ugarte family traces its wine-growing history back to the 1870s. Like so many in the region, the contemporary focus on quality began as recently as the late 1990s. The company's top wines reveal the special kind of concentration that is derived from low-yielding old vines. Martin Cendoya, a key figure in the firm in the 1950s, stands out as the name of a fine Reserva. The fruit, mainly Tempranillo with some Garnacha and a dash of Mazuelo, is dense with cherries, and overlaid with roasted mocha and earthy mushroom tones. The tannins are soft, and there is a fine minerality on the finish.

Carretera Vitoria-Logroño, Km 61, 01309 Laguardia, Alava;
945 282 844; www.heredadugarte.com

WHAT HAPPENED TO THE AMERICAN OAK?

Once upon a time, red Rioja was stored in old oak barrels for a minimum of one year (plus two years in bottle) for a *reserva*, two years (plus three years in bottle) for a *gran reserva*. American oak adds a vanilla aroma to the cherryish Tempranillo fruit. The result is a classic aged Rioja, pale in color, soft in tannins, and a blend of vanilla, leathery, mushroomy sweetness, that is ready to drink. The American oak used to be the tell-tale clue to a Rioja in a blind tasting. By contrast, today's producers, aware of international trends, are macerating grapes longer for deeper color and flavor, using French oak barrels, and releasing the wines soon after bottling. The wine is darker, fruitier, denser, and more tannic—and lacking in the traditional sweetness. French oak provides more elegance; it also costs more. Many producers therefore use a blend of American and French oak to dilute the vanilla without losing it altogether, and to balance the books. Experiments continue with Spanish, Slovenian, and the dominant and rustic Russian oak. Whichever way you look at it, the traditional taste of Rioja is disappearing.

HERMANOS PECINA
CHOBEO IS THE BODEGA'S FLAGSHIP WINE, A RICH, POWERFUL, PURE TEMPRANILLO RIOJA MADE IN THE MODERN STYLE

LOPEZ DE HEREDIA
RIOJA AS IT USED TO BE: WITH MATURE, ELEGANT POWER

Hermanos Peciña

The Peciña brothers (and brother-in-law) run the winery started up by their father, Pedro, in 1992 in the Rioja Alta. The business began as a small venture, but they have now developed a visitor reception facility alongside quality wine production. From 124 acres (50ha) of vines, the Peciñas produce a portfolio of Tempranillo-dominated reds, with just a seasoning of Garnacha and/or Graciano to create wines with vanilla and leather aromas in the classic style of Rioja. Their top-of-the-range wine is Chobeo de Peciña: 100% Tempranillo, full and powerful, with plenty of extraction.

Carretera Vitoria Km 47, San Vicente de la Sonsierra, La Rioja, www.bodegashermanospecina.com

Ijalba

Ijalba earns its place in this selection both for its modern, lively approach to young Rioja, and for its early loyalty to a single varietal of the rare Graciano grape, second only to Jesus Madrazo's outstanding version at Contino. While Ijalba may not be so expert at label design, the philosophy of the business certainly is. It was the first certified organic estate in Rioja, and its vineyards, laid out over poor soils left from open-cast mining, have won awards for the transformation of the landscape. ★ **Rising star**

Carretera de Pamplona, Km 1, 26006 Logroño, La Rioja www.ijalba.com

Izadi

This Rioja Alavesa bodega has been the beneficiary of a boost in the quality stakes, with consultancy from Mariano García, former winemaker of Vega Sicilia. The wines are certainly well-made, expressive Riojas. Owners Grupo Artevino also own Vetus in Toro and Villacreces in Ribera del Duero, and has a majority ownership of a new project from Rioja called Orben. Orben itself is a dense, supple Rioja, and, like Malpuesto, the other wine from the same winery, has quickly won serious critical interest. Artevino is also known for its activities promoting wine tourism.

Herrería Travesía 2, No. 5, 01307 Villabuena de Alava/ Eskuernaga, Alava; www.izadi.com

La Rioja Alta

La Rioja Alta is one of the great names of Rioja, based in the historic station district of Haro, with 890 acres (360ha) of vineyards at its disposal. It is a business that has managed to move very successfully with the times, still managing to make correct, convincing classical Riojas, but now alongside modern, fruit-forward wines. The Gran Reserva 890, with six years in American oak and at least the same again in bottle, was named after the foundation of the company in 1890, and reveals Rioja's classical flavors of sweet fruit blended with elegant oak. The 904 Gran Reserva only gets four years in oak. Viña Ardanza has more apparent fruit, and the same elegance that runs right across the range. Viña Alberdi has just two years in oak. La Rioja Alta owns the Torre de Oña winery, which produces the modern Rioja Baron de Oña. It has also built a new winery in Ribera del Duero, producing Aster wines, and owns an investment in Rías Baixas, where it produces the youthful Albariño Lagar de Cervera.

Avda de Vizcaya 8, 26200 Haro, La Rioja www.riojalta.com

Lan

The quality at Lan, based in Fuenmayor in the Rioja Alta, is steadily improving. The range extends from today's well-priced introductory wines through to powerful, high-expression bottlings. Lan Edición Limitada is a wine that, for once, lives up to the promise of its name, with plenty of select, succulent fruit, and a spicy finish. Like Culmen and Viña Lanciano, it comes from a single vineyard. It is interesting to note that, in addition to "classical" American and "modern" French oaks, Lan has also been experimenting with some Russian oak on both Lanciano and Edicion Limitada.

Paraje Buicio, 26360 Fuenmayor, La Rioja www.bodegaslan.com

López de Heredía

Every visit to Rioja must include a detour to the distinctive red-roofed, historic López de Heredía in Haro, ideally at harvest-time. The central look-out tower (also originally designed as an advertisement for the brand) has the Basque name of *Txori-Toki*, or "bird house." At the bodega, visitors are transported back to the 1880s as they watch grapes arrive stacked in deep, dark, red-painted conical hods. Inside, the huge, unbelievably ancient wooden vats are still in use. You will find no glints of stainless steel here, and undoubtedly there is a touch of Harry Potter about this magical place. The practice of long aging the wines continues, and not just where the reds are concerned. The remarkable Viña Tondonia Gran Reserva Rosado has more than four years in barrel, and an equally impressive Viña Tondonia Gran Reserva white is aged for more than nine years. The latest generation of the family is led by the energetic María-José, who preserves the heritage while carefully adjusting to change. By seemingly standing still, López de Heredía is coming back into fashion again.

Avenida de Vizcaya 3, 26200 Haro, La Rioja www.lopezdeheredia.com

Luis Cañas

Luis Cañas is a shining example of just how successful the transfer of a business from father to son can be. Juan Luis took over the winery in 1989, with the intention of building on the established business. With a new winery in 1994 and subsequent expansion, the Cañas brand now covers not only great-value young wines, but also award-winning special selections. Hiru 3 Racimos is a powerful wine, which shows the weight of French and American oak, but is softened by dense fruit. Amaren is full of cherry and strawberry fruit, with bold vanilla and spice overtones.

Carretera Samaniego 10, 01307 Villabuena, La Rioja www.luiscanas.com

Marqués de Cáceres

Of the triumvirate of famous Riojan marquesses—Cáceres, Murrieta, and Riscal—Cáceres is the youngest (1970) and won its reputation for its new approach to Rioja. The consultant at the outset was the famed professor from Bordeaux, Emile Peynaud, and he introduced a range of what at the time were radical approaches, but which seem only natural now: stainless-steel vats, temperature controls, shorter times in newer, cleaner, French (not American) oak barrels. Gaudium is a contemporary take on this approach, with very pure mocha and spice aromas, and an intense palate that shows beautifully rounded tannin as well as good, rich fruit.

Carretera Logroño, 26350 Cenicero, La Rioja
www.marquesdecaceres.com

Marqués de Murrieta

The great name of Marqués de Murrieta celebrates both the traditional and the new. The former is represented by its magnificently mature Castillo Ygay wines (of Gran Reserva status) and particularly the Reserva Especial; both spend a long time in cask and offer an ideal opportunity to experience great old-style Rioja. The top wine, Dalmau, is a polar opposite, crafted in a much more modern style, yet it still retains the Murrieta elegance. The white Capellania Reserva is one of the most serious interpretations of Viura in Rioja, produced in a boldly oaked style.

Carretera de Logroño-Zaragoza, 26006 Logroño, La Rioja
(Visitor facilities from 2011); www.marquesdemurrieta.com

Marqués de Riscal

Marques de Riscal is another historic Rioja house, one of several in the region bearing an aristocratic name. It enjoyed early winemaking influences from Bordeaux, and still proudly displays its 19th-century awards and decorations on its distinctive period labels. Like many of its competitors in Rioja, it chose to sell off several vineyards in the 20th century; perhaps the circle has turned, as increasing numbers of new wineries decide to focus on the single-estate concept. Today, Riscal is probably more famous worldwide for the glinting titanium roofs of the Frank Gehry-designed hotel next door to the winery in Elciego, a multicolored extravaganza that sets the sky alight. In the winery itself, the quality of the classical Riscal Riojas has been uneven in recent years; however, the newer, modern label Baron de Chirel offers bold and expressive wines in a very different style. Riscal's white wines from Rueda are also worth mentioning, and the company is also successfully producing fresh, crunchy, young Verdejos.

Calle Torrea 1, 01340 Elciego, Alava
www.marquesderiscal.com

Marqués de Vargas

A family business, based in the Rioja Alta, the current marqués has been the driving force behind the improved quality and the focus only on *reservas*. A château-style bodega was constructed, yields were controlled in the vineyard, and Michel Rolland was brought in to advise. Today, the wines are aged with a mix of American, French, and Russian oaks. The result is pure, intense, powerful wine, with fine notes of creamy cedar and vanilla oak. The Privada Reserva is complex, with coffee and truffle tones. The top wine is Hacienda Pradolagar.

Carretera de Zaragoza, Km 6, 26006 Logroño, La Rioja
www.marquesdevargas.com

Miguel Merino

Miguel Merino is a man of great charm and character who knows Rioja better than anyone. That is partly because he made his name as an exporter of Spanish wine. However, he then embarked on the risky proposition of making wine instead, settling in Briones,

MARQUES DE MURRIETA
THE MODERN FACE OF RIOJA, YET DALMAU
STILL SHOWS HALLMARK ELEGANCE

MUGA
A FINE EXPRESSION OF A TEMPRANILLO
IN A VERY GOOD YEAR

and establishing a small business that focuses on hand-picking grapes and scrupulous management of classical wines. The first vintage was 1994, and he has prospered ever since. In particular, the *gran reservas* produced in top vintages show great potential to age.

Carretera de Logroño 16, 26330 Briones, La Rioja
www.miguelmerino.com

Montecillo

There is one reason why Montecillo wines taste as consistent and as classic as they do: the redoubtable María Martínez, who has been the winemaker here for some three decades. She came up the hard way, the rare female in her class, and has learned how to form her own opinions and defend them. This has helped in the changing world of Rioja, where Montecillo remains true to tradition. Martínez buys grapes to ensure top quality and ages the wines longer than is usual. They are great value, and show soft tannins with fresh acidity. The company is owned by Osborne in Jerez.

Calle San Cristobal 34, 26360 Fuenmayor, La Rioja
www.osborne.es

Muga

Muga offers an impressive, confident introduction to the types and styles of Riojan wines. For many, the salmon-colored, pure-fruited Rosado is a benchmark rosé from the region; for others, the Prado Enea is the classic example of a Gran Reserva, with its mature colors and leathery, spicy character. Nevertheless, the Muga family keeps moving with the times, offering Torre Muga, as a different, sumptuous, even velvety take on Tempranillo. Their latest creation is Aro, a tribute to Haro, where they are based, and the result of work with old vines and smaller vats.

Barrio de la Estación, 26200 Haro, La Rioja
www.bodegasmuga.com

Olarra

Olarra was in the first wave of architectural innovation back in the 1970s, when the Y-shaped bodega was contructed. The wines quickly established themselves as pleasing, elegant blends of the classic varietals. Cerro Añón remains the highlight of the range, with the younger Reserva showing more appeal than the older Gran Reserva. Ondarre, the sister winery, was founded just over a decade after Olarra, in order to specialize in a smaller production of *reservas*, such as the Mayor de Ondarre, and barrel-fermented white wines.

Polígono de Cantabria, 26006 Logroño, La Rioja
www.bodegasolarra.es

Ontañon

A visit to the Ontañon bodega in Logroño is designed to have plenty of tourist appeal: the place features a museum of modern art, "flamenco Thursdays," and plenty more besides. While entertaining, these divert attention from the wine, which is consistently good and mainly Tempranillo, showing round, fleshy fruit balanced with young, toasty oak. The top label is the ambitious Colección Mitologia; however, the best at present is the Reserva.

Avenida de Aragón 3, 26006 Logroño, La Rioja
www.ontanon.es

The stunning Ysios bodega, nestled below the Sierra de Cantabria, was designed to blend into the landscape.

VALSERRANO
IN A REGION OF BLENDS, A 100% MAZUELO
RIOJA STANDS OUT IN THE CROWD

RODA
THE PREMIUM "I" IS GENERALLY MADE FROM
VERY OLD, LOW-YIELDING VINES

Ostatu

Ostatu has two reasons to tempt consumers. Based in Samaniego in the Alavesa, it is a family winery—an increasingly rare occurrence. The Saenz de Samaniego family have a long history in the region. Furthermore, they have had the advice of Hubert de Broüard of Château Angélus, with a focus on old vines and lower yields. Typical of this new style is the Reserva, made from 50-year-old vines, fermented in stainless steel, and aged in French oak. The result is a wine that is focused on succulent black fruit balanced by fine cedar, and showing plenty of spice on the finish. Gloria de Ostatu basically is the Reserva on steroids: boldly extracted, with meaty, spicy notes lifting the dense fruit. This one is full of character, and certainly not for the faint-hearted.

Carretera Vitoria 1, 01307 Samaniego, Alava
www.ostatu.com

Paisajes y Viñedos

Paisajes y Viñedos is a company that takes a strictly non-traditional approach to Rioja. The project was started in 1998 by Miguel Angel de Gregorio of Finca Allende and Barcelona-based wine merchant Quim Vila. Its purpose is to select the best grapes from the best terroirs in given vintages. At the outset, the DO did not permit printing the origin of the grapes on the label, and this gave rise to the practice of giving them a name and number instead. The wines are typically made in a vibrant, modern style.

Plaza Ibarra 1, 26330 Briones
941 322 301

Palacios Remondo

Alvaro Palacios has won international fame for his wines in Priorat. In 2000, after his father's death, he also took over the running of the 247 acre (100ha) family estate in the Rioja Baja and proved that he could work the same magic in a different terroir. His father's vineyards were 100% Garnacha; today Tempranillo dominates. The wines reflect the generosity and warmth of the Baja, and as an additional benefit, they are much more accessibly priced than the Priorat treasures. The bargain is the Vendimia: young, lively, juicy, and red-fruited. Top of the range is Propiedad Herencia, a blend of (mainly) Garnacha, Tempranillo, Mazuelo, and Graciano: full of fruit and with plenty of French oak to balance.

Avenida Zaragoza 8, 26540 Alfaro, La Rioja
941 180 207

Pujanza

Coming from a family with a long history in Rioja, it seems almost inevitable that Carlos San Pedro should build a winery of his own. In 1998 he did exactly that, creating a very precise facility that reflects his exacting standards of grape selection and winemaking. From 99 acres (40ha) of vineyards he makes just two wines: Pujanza and Pujanza Norte (first vintage 2002). Pujanza is 100% Tempranillo, aged in French oak: a full-bodied, succulent red. Pujanza Norte is, again, Tempranillo with French oak, from which he has extracted a deep color, and a serious concentration of fruit. ★**Rising star**

Carretera de Elvillar, 01300 Laguardia, Alava
bodegaspujanza.com

Ramón Bilbao

The name Ramón Bilbao has been known in Rioja for almost a century. In 1999, the business was acquired by Diego Zamora, a major beverage company. The investment has widened the Bilbao range, topped by Mirto as the icon label. Both *reservas* and *gran reservas* exhibit the pure, ripe sweetness of American oak influence. The Edición Limitada has the intensity of hand-selected fruit, while Mirto is a dense expression of Tempranillo with toasty French oak and notes of blackberries. Bilbao also owns Mar de Frades (Rías Baixas) and Cruz de Alba (Ribera del Duero).

Avenida Santo Domingo 34, 26200 Haro, La Rioja
www.bodegasramonbilbao.es

Remelluri

Remelluri is one of Spain's more gloriously situated wineries, tucked away in the foothills of the Sierra de Tolono. The combination of poor soils and altitude gives the wines a pure, bright acidity. The fine reds are Tempranillo-dominated. The white is of particular interest, because it still shows signs of the contribution made by the young Telmo Rodríguez when he was working on the family estate. A lush and full-bodied, complex blend of Moscatel, Garnacha Blanca, Sauvignon Blanc, Viognier, Chardonnay, and Roussanne, it reveals his ambition and creativity.

Carretera Rivas de Tereso, 01330 Labastida
www.remelluri.com

Remírez de Ganuza

Fernando Remírez de Ganuza's winery sits in the ancient heart of the town of Samaniego, in the Rioja Alavesa. He is one producer who has transformed the image of the Alavesa, and of modern Rioja with it, despite a relatively narrow range of wines. Erre Punto is a young, fresh, fruity red made by carbonic maceration. Fincas de Ganuza is definitely a step up, and like all the serious reds, is made from Tempranillo with a dash of Graciano, and a fine use of oak. The top wine is Trasnocho.

Calle Constitución 1, 01307 Samaniego, Alava
www.remirezdeganuza.com

Roda

Based in Haro, the most traditional of Rioja towns, Roda, which is a restrained but nevertheless glinting modern winery, is symbolic of the new Spain. The contrast between ancient and modern could not be marked, given its position in the Barrio de l'Estación: the original location for Haro's first wineries close to the railway line, next door to the historic López de Heredía. No expense has been spared, either in winery or vineyard. Extensive search for the best Tempranillo, Graciano, and Garnacha have resulted in sourcing grapes from some 20 different vineyard plots. Scrupulous handling in the carefully designed, gravity-fed winery has created voluptuous, silky, modern wines, with added texture from French oak. Roda II is the entry-level wine, Roda I is the premium offering, and Cirsion (named after the thistle logo of the winery) is the top wine. The name Roda was created from the surnames of owners Mario Rotllant Solá and Carmen Daurella De Aguilera.

Avenida Vizcaya 5, Barrio de la Estación, 26200 Haro,
La Rioja; www.roda.es

Sierra Cantabria

Who can resist a bodega that calls its barrel-fermented and lees-aged white blend Organza? Not, it seems, the critics, who consistently give it exceptional ratings. The same critical acclaim goes to the rest of the Sierra Cantabria wines, a classical Rioja range from *joven* through to *gran reserva*, as well as the Eguren family's other properties. The Egurens are not new to the business; they have been making wine in Rioja since 1870. However, the latest generation has raised the family's profile via expansion to new estates. A fairly recent acquisition (1991), Señorio de San Vicente is based in San Vicente de la Sonsierra, where they have revived the rare local Tempranillo Peludo, so named for its furry skin. At the outstanding Viñedos de Paganos estate, the Egurens are producing single-vineyard wines: the powerful, punchy El Puntido and its counterpart, the elegant, rounded La Nieta. They also own Dominio de Eguren, a classified Vino de la Tierra, in addition to their Toro property Teso la Monja. Rare indeed to find such consistent excellence.

Amorebieta, 3, 26338 San Vicente de la Sonsierra, La Rioja
www.eguren.com

Tobia

The story of Tobia is one of transformation, of family vineyards in the Rioja Alta to highly rated individual wines. Oscar Tobia started out in 1994 and has come to critical success by refitting the cellar, selecting grapes from 40- and 50-year-old vines, stemmings to enhance the succulence and ripeness of the wine, using French oak, and bottling the wine without filtering it. Wines include a barrel-fermented *rosado* and a Graciano, plus the impressive Alma de Tobia: fermented in barrel, with cinnamon spice and fleshy red fruits. ★ **Rising star**

Carretera Nacional 232, Km 438, 26340 San Asensio,
La Rioja; www.bodegastobia.com

Valsacro

The Escudero brothers come from several generations of wine growers. Valsacro is their own ambitious project, based in the poor soils of the Rioja Baja, where they have been planting low-yielding vines to ensure plenty of flavor and expression. Their white is a rich, toasty, American-oaked, creamy, lees-aged Chardonnay/Viura blend. The Valsacro red includes Garnacha from 100-year-old vines in addition to Tempranillo and other local varieties. Dioro is a mouth-filling, ripe red, aged in French oak, with plenty of intensity and extract. ★ **Rising star**

Carretera N-232, 26510 Pradejón, La Rioja
www.valsacro.com

Valserrano

Strictly speaking, Valserrano is Viñedos y Bodegas de la Marquesa, named after the marquesa who was grandmother of the present owner, for Valserrano is still a family business. What makes their wines interesting to fans of Rioja is that they produce single-varietal versions of the local grapes that are usually used for blending: Mazuelo (known as Carignan in France), Garnacha, and Graciano. Their most serious Tempranillo blend is the single-vineyard Finca Monteviejo, which has plenty of tannin, fruit, spice, and oak, plus a warming note of alcohol.

Herrería 76, 01307 Villabuena, Alava
www.valserrano.com

Viña Salceda

Based in Elciego in the heart of the Rioja Alavesa, this is a good example of how Rioja wineries are regularly being turned around and improved by virtue of new ownership. The explanation for the transformation of Salceda can be found in the fact that the Chivite family from the next-door Navarra region acquired the winery in 1998. Investment in the cellar and the vineyards and a new winemaker have had positive results. The Reserva has all the typical aromatics of earthiness, sweet spice and ripe fruit you would expect, along with firm tannins, and a full body.

Carretera de Cenicero, Km 3, 01340 Elciego, Alava
www.vinasalceda.com

Viñedos del Ternero

The Ternero estate is a beautiful and remarkable place. It is also unique as the only Rioja to be made in the Burgos province. The estate dates back to the 9th century, and its farm once supported a now-defunct monastery. In 2003, winemakers Ana Blanco and Carlos González were asked to start a winery, a small enterprise that fits neatly into the old buildings. Ana has close ties with the estate, since she has lived here since she was four days old. The wines reflect their origins: handmade and high-quality. ★ **Rising star**

Miranda de Ebro, 09200 Burgos
www.vinedosdelternero.com

Ysios

Ysios is an enterprise that is perhaps destined to be more famous for the undulating roof of its bodega, designed by Santiago Calatrava, than its wines. Nevertheless, the wines have their own distinction. The winery is set dramatically below the Sierra Cantabria amid 185 acres (75ha) of vines, and concentrates on Tempranillo. Ysios only makes *reservas* and special blends. The latest blend, launched in 2010, is dedicated to Basque artist Eduardo Chillida. The firm is part of the Domecq group, which also includes Campo Viejo and Age in Rioja, Tarsus in Ribera del Duero, and Pazo de Villarei in Rías Baixas.

Camino de la Hoya, 01300 Laguardia, Alava
www.domecqbodegas.com

DAZZLING ARCHITECTURE

The ancient standing stones that punctuate the Riojan landscape point to an equally ancient history. Yet against this backdrop there is an astonishing display of modern architecture. Bodegas require bold solutions if they are not to cover the landscape with anonymous sheds. These radical designs often shock and attract. The undulating roof of Santiago Calatrava's Ysios appears to move in the landscape, as does Frank Gehry's titanium extravaganza over the Marqués de Riscal hotel. Roda's footprint above ground may be relatively unobtrusive, but its gravity-fed winery extends far underground. Next door at López de Heredía, Zaha Hadid's visitors center is a space-age pod in the midst of the ancient winery. At Darien, surfaces project like a rugged stone wall, while at Viña Real, the circular cellar looks like a vast barrel. Rioja is worth a visit for its enterprising architectural solutions, as well as its wine.

NAVARRA

ATLANTIC
OCEAN
FRANCE
Bilbao
Barcelona
MADRID
PORT.   SPAIN
Mediterranean
Sea

■ Navarra wine region

On wine lists and wine shelves, Navarra's position is all too obvious: always second best to its more glamorous neighbor, Rioja. Yet on the ground, Navarra is a place of great enchantment, with a profound sense of its individual place in history. In medieval times, the powerful kingdom of Navarra stretched as far as Barcelona. Buildings from this era remain to charm visitors, and a number of wineries shelter inside these reminders of the past. At the same time, however, Navarra's wine industry is strictly modern—due in part to the fact that it has benefited from more than 30 years of research by its pioneering vine and wine research station, EVENA, which is a leader in Spain.

Major grapes

 Reds

Cabernet Sauvignon

Garnacha Tinta

Graciano

Mazuelo

Merlot

Tempranillo

 Whites

Chardonnay

Garnacha Blanca

Malvasia

Moscatel

Viura

Vintages

2009
Best for varieties with a long ripening season, such as Cabernet.

2008
A cooler vintage, good for rosados and early-ripening varieties such as Tempranillo.

2007
A long, dry, not-too-hot summer played to Navarra's strengths: these wines will age.

2006
Erratic weather, both wet and hot, favored only the best producers.

2005
A great vintage, with lots of charm.

2004
A good vintage, with some great wines.

Tucked in between the Pyrenees and the Ebro, the river that forms the eastern boundary of Rioja, with chilly influences from the Atlantic and the soothing warmth from the Mediterranean, Navarra has plenty of natural resources to give it cheer. The soils are varied, and the hillsides provide varied microclimates as well as different positions toward the sun. Winemakers here are spoiled for choice.

It is these people, the winemakers and the grape-growers, who are an essential aspect of Navarra's terroir. Because it lacks the glamour of Rioja, the province also lacks much of the new money and the big corporations that populate the landscape beyond the Ebro. Yet while Navarra's wineries may, on the whole, be less impressive architecturally, the people who run them more than make up for any lack.

For example, the benchmark family business of the Chivites has invested in the Pago de Arínzano. At Ochoa, Javier Ochoa led EVENA's wine research and was the driving force behind the revival of Moscatel. The result is that, today, Navarra's sweet Moscatels (particularly Chivite's) are the best in Spain. Following in their father's footsteps are the next generation of Ochoas: Adriana and her sister, Beatriz. At Pago de Larrainzar, another pair of siblings, Miguel and Irene Canalejo, are in charge. Navarra is also peopled by ambitious new arrivals such as José María Fraile and Alicia Eyralar at Tandem.

The thread that links them all is the Camino de Santiago, the traditional pilgrim route to the shrine of Saint James at Santiago de Compostela. The travel-weary pilgrims of the old days appreciated the wines, and the same historic route they traveled passes beside or close by wineries and vineyards. Today, modern pilgrims—some of them speeding past on bicycles—are still a regular sight, with their loaded backpacks. The sound of their voices and singing drifts over the fields. They are a reminder that Navarra's modern wine industry, with its shiny stainless-steel tanks, its quantities of new-oak barrels, and its gleaming laboratories, is a place where history is ever present.

If Navarra faces one difficulty, it concerns its loyalty to international grape varieties. The province's closeness to France means that Chardonnay (3% of all plantings and the most widely planted white), Cabernet Sauvignon (15%), and Merlot (13%) are long-established, although Tempranillo still manages to rule the reds here (37%). Nowadays, the trend in Europe is to track down local grape varieties and exclude the international ones, a practice that may ultimately overwhelm or dilute local flavors.

The result of this diversity and wide focus is that Navarra seems to be behind the times, and lackluster in its support of Spain's regular red varieties. Above all, it looks confused. Are its *rosados* as good as they could be? Is Navarra a world leader in Garnacha wines? There are some shining examples. Is Navarra clearly different from Rioja? It should be. Too often, however, it is seen as the cheaper "little brother."

Castillo de Monjardin

Castillo de Monjardin is one of the relative newcomers to the Navarra wine scene. Founded in 1993, its fairly traditional appearance conceals all the right kinds of modern winemaking equipment. Its position on a hillside also enables the careful handling of grapes and wines by gravity flow rather than pumping. With the winery's focus on international varieties, the wines themselves reflect the new Navarra. The most successful are certainly the Chardonnays, which balance a full palate with a lively freshness, and have an added richness from oak.

Viña Rellanada, 31242 Vilamayor de Monjardin
www.monjardin.es

Chivite

The Chivite wines reveal the potential of Navarra's diverse soils. Highlighting the fact that the region succeeds with international varieties, the Chardonnays are very good: the Colección 125, in particular, is outstanding. The entire Colección range, which celebrates the winery's 125th anniversary, is impressive. The family's acquisition, in 1988, of the Señorío de Arínzano estate led to a no-expense-spared integration of historic architecture with a glinting new winery. It has become the first officially recognized Pago, or vineyard-estate, in the north of Spain, and the wine that bears its name is a Tempranillo/Cabernet/Merlot blend produced in 2000 and launched in 2008. It promises to be succulent, complex, and structured.

Ribera 34, 31592 Cintruenigo
www.bodegaschivite.com

Dominio Lasierpe

With 3,200 acres (1,300ha) of vineyards, Dominio Lasierpe is one of the largest vineyard-owners in Navarra. The winery, as is widely the case across Spain, has recently received a complete change of equipment as well as a new approach to its winemaking practices. Lasierpe's young reds are fresh and good value. The Flor de la Sierpe selection is of special interest, and has been designed (according to the winery) for international tastes, with a greater density of fruit and use of oak. Thankfully, the dense fruit of the Old Vine Garnacha ensures the oak has been held in check.

No visitor facilities
www.dominiolasierpe.com

Inurrieta

Founded in 2001, which is very young in winery terms, Inurrieta is nonetheless making good progress. A family business, it owns all 570 acres (230ha) of its vineyards and has created an attractive and cleverly organized range of wines. Norte ("North") is a Cabernet/Merlot blend with a dash of "experimental" (that is, not officially permitted) Petit Verdot—very youthful and spicy, with a savory finish. Altos de Inurrieta, made from Cabernet Sauvignon blended with 25% Graciano, is a powerful combination of cedar and mocha with a balsamic lift. Laderas de Inurrieta is a single-varietal Graciano that is alive with liquorice, velvety violet, and blackberry tones, all nicely wrapped up in rounded tannins. ★**Rising star**

Carretera de Falces-Miranda de Arga Km. 30, 31370 Falces
www.bodegainurrieta.com

SEÑORÍO DE SARRIA
SARRIA'S AROMATIC MOSCATEL IS A GOOD
EXAMPLE OF A CHARMING NAVARRAN WHITE

CHIVITE
THE COLECCION BLEND IS WELL-ROUNDED
AND FULL OF RICH FRUIT FLAVOR

Irache

It is hard to escape history in Navarra, and Irache's vineyards are no different. The demands of the region's royal palaces and the steady flow of pilgrims to Santiago de Compostela have ensured that the vineyards here have been supplying wine since the 12th century. Irache itself was founded in 1891, and its juicy reds and light *rosados* remain popular today. The bodega includes the Prado de Irache estate, which was granted Vino de Pago (single-estate) status. The wine is made mainly from Tempranillo grapes but rounded out by some Cabernet Sauvignon and Merlot. The result is sumptuously aromatic, with notes of oak overlaid by roasted fruit and mocha flavors.

Monasterio de Irache 1, 31240 Ayegui
www.irache.com

Luis Alegre

Luis Alegre founded the winery that bears his name near Laguardia in the late 1960s. New investment some 30 years later has given the business new impetus; there is also a fashionable (and female) wine consultant, and winemaking now takes place in small vats to gain maximum expression of the terroir. Other developments include aging the timber for oak barrels on the premises so that the development of flavors in the wood can be monitored as it matures. The Selección Especial is 95% Tempranillo and reveals plenty of ripe raspberry fruit together with creamy notes, the sweetness restrained by a crunchy freshness and balancing tannin.

Carretera de Navaridas, 01300 Laguardia
www.bodegasluisalegre.com

Malumbres

Few would say that 1940 was a promising year in Spain's history. Yet it was during that year that Vicente Malumbres chose to establish his wine business, and for the next four decades he continued to sell off his wine in bulk, as was typical at the time. In 1987, however, the focus of the business changed to high quality. Today, minimum chemical treatments in the vineyard are partnered by wild-yeast fermentation in the winery, and Vicente's son, Javier, has created wines that are individual and expressive. They are dense and full of texture—and also good value.

Calle Santa Bárbara 15, 31591 Corella
www.malumbres.com

Nekeas

Nekeas has rapidly won a good reputation for itself. It was established in the Nekeas Valley (hence the name) in 1990, by eight families who could see the potential of the site, which lies in the shelter of the Sierra Perdón mountain range. Today, international grape varieties such as Viognier, and "foreigners" such as Malbec, jostle the more traditional Tempranillos and Garnachas. What captures consumers' attention are the top wines. Odaiza is a bold, oaked Chardonnay, while El Chaparral de Vega Sindoa is a typical, lively expression of spicy Garnacha made from old vines. Finally, Izar de Nekeas is a Cabernet/Merlot/Tempranillo blend that has been enriched by the use of French oak.

Calle Las Huertas, 31154 Añorbe
www.nekeas.com

ROSADOS

Until recently, Navarra was famed for its *rosados*, or pink rosé wines. Made from Garnacha, they had refreshing and uncomplicated strawberry fruit. Then the New World's rosés arrived, with vibrant colors, flavors—and marketing. Navarra has had to pull itself together. In the vineyard, yields have been reduced to improve quality. In the winery, *rosados* are not pressed, or blended from whites and reds. Navarra uses the classic *saignée* or "bleeding" method where, after crushing, there is a short maceration (steeping) time, then the liquid is bled off and fermented. New-wave Navarran rosés have bright fruit, with flavors and colors often enlivened by Merlot, Cabernet Sauvignon, and Tempranillo. Packaging and marketing are improving, too. So is Navarra back in the pink? Not yet—but it is moving in the right direction.

Ochoa

The vivacious, good-humored Adriana Ochoa is surely destined to be a leader in the new generation of Navarra winemakers, just as her father, Javier, has been in his. Javier Ochoa's important contribution has been to enological research in the province, and his own wines, of course, have benefited from his wisdom. Best of the wide offering here is the top-end red Reserva. The delicate, sweet Moscatel is also a cut above, while the sparkling Moscato is just a good, fun fizz. A delicious curiosity is verjuice, a version of the medieval vinegar condiment made from unripe grapes.

Alcalde Maillata, No. 2, 31390 Olite
www.bodegasochoa.com

Orvalaiz

Situated at a crossroads on one of the pilgrim routes to Santiago, Orvalaiz encourages weary travelers to ease their journey by calling in and sampling some wine. Visitors will find a co-operative winery that was founded in the 1990s with the intention of featuring international (French) varieties in addition to Tempranillo. Today, the winery is big business, offering a selection of young, fresh reds as well as a Viura-dominated blended white and a Cabernet Sauvignon *rosado*. Most impressive are the Septentrion (or North Star) wines; these are the top selection, aged in French oak.

Ctra. Pamplona-Logroño, Obanos
www.orvalaiz.es

Otazu

All the wines of Otazu show a refreshing acidity that is a direct result of the strong influence of the nearby Atlantic; indeed, Otazu claims to be the most northerly red-wine producer not just in Navarra, but in the whole of Spain. The architecture is impressive, with echoes of France's châteaux alongside a well-proportioned barrel cellar. The freshness of this microclimate lends a balance to the ripe, powerful Chardonnay, and adds a crunchy character to the red blend, Palacio de Otazu. In 2009, Otazu achieved the official recognition of Pago (single-estate) status, alongside Irache.

No visitor facilities
www.otazu.com

Pago de Cirsus

There may be very few signposts to Pago de Cirsus, but there is little chance of getting lost—even (and perhaps especially) at night. The castle tower of this luxurious hotel/winery, owned by filmmaker Iñaki Nuñez, is dramatically illuminated. Despite the name of the winery, it is not one of the handful of Pago-designated properties recognized as single estates by Spain's official regulatory body. Be that as it may, the Tempranillo/Shiraz Selección Opus 11 is still very much an attractive wine, rich with bold oak, fleshy fruit, and a tannic grip. The barrel-fermented Chardonnay and sweet Moscatel are also intense and full-flavored examples that are well worth seeking out.

Avenida de Ribaforada Km. 5, 31523 Ablitas
www.pagodecirsus.com

Pago de Larrainzar

This is a young project, although the Larrainzar family's history in Navarran wine dates back over a century. The new enterprise was started by a Navarran businessman, the great-grandson of the original owner. His children have joined him, and their goal is to make top-quality wines. Hand-picking of Merlot, Cabernet Sauvignon, Tempranillo, and Garnacha, careful selection, vats of different sizes, French-oak barrels… such attention to detail typifies their work. The first vintage released was 2004, and the style so far suggests modern wines full of expression and complexity. ★ **Rising star**

Camino de la Corona, 31240 Ayegui
www.pagodelarrainzar.com

Príncipe de Viana

The first Príncipe de Viana, born in 1423 and heir to the throne of Navarra, was deprived of his rights and forced to flee his kingdom. Fast-forward 560 years to the founding of this winery, and its success, by contrast, has been solid. The winery now owns 1,040 acres (420ha) and contracts the same again, and has become a strong exporter of Navarran wine. Currently, the most successful wines are its young styles, where the pure, cherry Tempranillo fruit is not obscured by oak. A speciality is the Late Harvest Chardonnay, which boasts an alluring gold color and a full-bodied palate with balancing acidity.

Calle Mayor 191, 31521 Murchante
www.principedeviana.com

Señorío de Sarría

Sarría hides away inside an extensive estate in one of the loveliest sites for a winery. Wine has a history here, but it is only recently that the wines have seriously improved. Viñedo No 5, a Garnacha *rosado*, is a fine example of how Navarra *rosado* should be: fruity, but with a savory vinous finish. There is an attractive range of varietal reds; Viñedo No 7 Graciano from bush vines is the best, with its floral aromas, lively citric acidity, and elegant palate. The sweet Moscatel also has plenty of charm and is abundantly aromatic, succulent, and spicy.

Señorío de Sarría, 31100 Puente la Reina,
www.bodegadeSarría.com

Tandem

From the gravity-fed winery, you can view the regular trickle of pilgrims on one of the routes to Santiago de Compostela. Many of today's travelers bicycle, however, so they miss the impressive concrete-and-glass structure as they speed past. In less than a decade, general manager José María Fraile and winemaker Alicia Eyralar have made impressive progress. They focus on Tempranillo, Cabernet Sauvignon, and Merlot, using 20-year-old vines, concrete fermentors, and French oak. Ars Macula is the spicy top wine; Ars Nova, the lighter, cherry-fruited second label. ★ **Rising star**

Carretera Pamplona-Logroño, Km. 35,9, 31292 Lácar
www.tandem.es

Long rows of vines stream away from Villamayor de Monjardín in the Tierra Estella subzone.

CASTILLA Y LEON

Castilla y León wine regions

The region of Castilla y León plays a special part in Spain's history. In 1469, Isabella, heir to the throne of the Kingdom of Castile, married Ferdinand, heir to the throne of the Kingdom of Aragón. The "Catholic monarchs," as they became known, eventually unified the northern part of the country and drove the country's Muslim occupiers southward out of Spain. This history is still very much visible in the beautiful castles and churches that sprawl across Old Castile—not to mention plenty of its wine labels. In all, this is one of those rare regions that offers every style of wine that a wine lover could want (and at every price), made by traditional and new-wave winemakers, in garages and vast, shiny warehouses.

Major grapes

 Reds

Cabernet Sauvignon

Garnacha

Juan García

Merlot

Syrah

Tempranillo (in all its synonyms)

 Whites

Albillo

Sauvignon Blanc

Verdejo

Viura

Vintages

2009
Sunshine with showers before harvest promises healthy fruit and some exceptional wines.

2008
Rains meant it was essential to pick out the best fruit. A good vintage in Rueda.

2007
A difficult year: frost risk in cold vineyards, such as parts of Ribera del Duero. Toro was disappointing, too.

2006
A hot year in many areas, giving warm, structured wines.

2005
Challenging; a risk of green, underripe fruit. A good year for carefully selected grapes.

2004
Good for Ribera del Duero, Toro, and Cigales.

As Spain's largest autonomous region, containing no fewer than nine provinces, Castilla y León offers diversity. There are soils so sandy that the phylloxera vine louse could never settle there, and others that are impossibly stony. The summers can be unbearably hot and the winters equally severe. The result is that it can be difficult to generalize about the typical style of one DO as against another. Without doubt, the region offers the adventurous winemaker a range of opportunities. Vega Sicilia, in Ribera del Duero, is one of Spain's most famous names, yet while it was founded in 1864, the real growth in the region has come more than a century later with a flurry of start-ups since the mid-1990s. Some of these are in established DOs; in addition to Ribera del Duero there are now Cigales, Rueda, and Toro. Others work in the two areas that have only very recently achieved DO status: Arribes and Arlanza. A number of the best or most fascinating wines are entirely outside the DO regulations and qualify as "mere" Vinos de la Tierra de Castilla y León.

Historically, the wines of this region were mainly made from red grapes. The dominant variety is Tempranillo, which carries a myriad of aliases: Tinto Fino, Tinto de País, Tinta de Toro, and so on. In addition, there is Garnacha, and some fascinating local reds, such as Juan García and Prieto Picudo, which are being rescued by pioneers working on the Portuguese border. Increasingly, in the glamorous wineries with substantial investment that cover Ribera del Duero, the international varieties Cabernet Sauvignon, Merlot, and Syrah are found in the blends, and even occasionally Pinot Noir.

For the white varietals, the regional star is Verdejo: green-tinged in color, passion-fruit, and limelike in flavor. Once upon a time it made sherry-style wines but now pneumatic presses and stainless steel in the winery produce wines in Rueda to challenge Sauvignon Blanc. There is Sauvignon Blanc, too, and a fair amount of Viura. Once renowned for making flabby wines and drab white Riojas, Viura is improving with careful handling.

Castilla y León is a land of contrasts, right down to its viticulture and winemakers. The same grower may have vineyards of regular rows of young vines that have trained across canopies and are machine-harvested at night under floodlight, as well as unevenly spread, low-growing old bush vines that can only be picked by hand.

Tracking down these old bush vines and bringing them back to life is central to the work of many of Spain's new generation of winemakers. Castilla y León certainly has an impressive quantity of such material. Typically, the vineyards are patchy, where vines have died, yet these are the vines whose roots reach deep for scant water and survive in the hottest years. Their fruit is powerfully flavored, adding depth and intensity to a blend.

Note that Bierzo, which is within the region's boundary, is included in "Green Spain," where it more naturally sits.

Aalto Ribera del Duero

Mariano García founded Aalto with Javier Zaccagnini, former director of the Ribera del Duero *consejo regulador* (regulatory body) and a group of investors in 1999. In a short time the wine has won international fame. The winery aims to make the best selection of Tinto Fino (Tempranillo) from the region. This approach to blending is the opposite of the vineyard-focused, terroir approach of, for instance, García's former employer, Vega Sicilia. Aalto is made from the best old bush-vine fruit from a selection of vineyards; Aalto PS is the special selection. These and the wines García produces at his family wineries, Mauro (Tudela del Duero) and Maurodos (Toro), and his other consultancies, ensure that he is widely regarded as Spain's leading winemaker.

Paraje Valjeo de Carril, 47360 Quintalla de Arriba
www.aalto.es

Abadía Retuerta

Vino de la Tierra de Castilla y León

Founded in 1996, Abadía Retuerta perches just outside Ribera del Duero DO, but in terms of quality should really be viewed as Ribera. This old abbey grows Tempranillo, but also has Syrah, Cabernet Sauvignon, and Petit Verdot to work with in its blends. Winemaker Angel Anocibar was the first Spaniard to get an enology doctorate at Bordeaux University. The accessibly priced Rívola offers a good expression of the estate; of the top wines, Pago Negralada, 100% Tempranillo, is sumptuously scented with cedar, vanilla, and black fruits, and is equally bold and spicy on the palate.

47340 Sardón del Duero, Valladolid
www.abadía-retuerta.es

Agrícola Castellana Rueda

This co-operative was founded in 1935, not long before the outbreak of the Spanish Civil War, by a group of 30 wine-growers. The winery still has the concrete vats from those early days, although these have been outnumbered by the quantity of stainless steel. Through temperature-controlled fermentation, Agrícola Castellana is successful at making appealingly clean, vibrant Verdejos and Sauvignon Blancs under several brand names, including Cuatro Rayas and Azuzmbre.

Carretera Rodilana, 47491 La Seca, Valladolid
www.cuatrorayas.org

Alonso del Yerro Ribera del Duero

A young business (2002), this reflects many of the new ideas in Ribera del Duero. Javier Alonso and María del Yerro are the founders, and they have taken the trouble to recruit two of the best-known French consultants: Claude Bourguignon, a biodynamic vineyard specialist, and for winemaking, Stéphane Derenoncourt from Bordeaux. The wines show a certain French elegance. Their vineyards, at around 2,645ft (800m), are young but promising. They make two wines, both dense from long post-fermentation maceration. María spends 18 months in oak and has more concentration than Alonso del Yerro, which is a fine blend of cherry fruit, liquorice, cedar, and a fresh mineral tone. Students of pruning will enjoy the excellent animations on the website. ★ Rising star

Finca Santa Marta, Carretera de Rosa a Anguix Km 1,8,
09300 Roa; www.vay.es

ALONSO DEL YERRO
AT 14.5% ALCOHOL BY VOLUME, MARIA IS A
SERIOUSLY DENSE TEMPRANILLO

ALVAREZ Y DIEZ
CRISP AND HERBACEOUS, THIS SPANISH
SAUVIGNON SHOWS GREAT CHARACTER

Alvarez y Díez Rueda

Alvarez y Díez is a good example of the thorough transformation Spain has made in white winemaking. The company, founded in 1941, originally made traditional sherry-style whites in its subterranean cellars, but in 1977, the de Benito family acquired the business and invested in working with the Verdejo grape. The goal of the next generation, Alvaro and Juan, has been to refine and refresh the Verdejo and Viura wines, and develop Sauvignon Blanc, resulting in the very successful Mantel Blanco brand of crisp, grassy wines. Also belonging to the same family is Veracruz, which producers the crisp, exotic Ermita.

Calle Juan Antonio Carmona, 12, Nava del Rey, 47500
Valladolid; www.alvarezydiez.es

Anta Banderas Ribera del Duero

Bodega Anta Natura became Anta Banderas in 2009, when film star Antonio Banderas bought a substantial stake. It looks to be a sound investment. Anta was started 10 years earlier by the Ortega family, who invested in a striking winery of wood and glass. The wines are numbered after their months in oak: a4, a10, a16. The a16 stands out in the line-up with classic aromas of lifted red cherries, toasty oak, and spice giving way to succulent red fruit and fine-textured new oak. This is a wine that needs time to develop. ★ Rising star

Carretera Palencia-Aranda de Duero Km 68, 09443 Villalba
de Duero, Burgos; www.antabodegas.com

Antaño Rueda

Antaño was set up in 1988 by a group of restaurateurs to produce wine for their businesses. The thoroughly restored 16th-century property is now entirely owned by José Luis Ruiz Solaguren, founder of the José Luis tapas bars. The winery has astonishing collections of books, glassware, and paintings and 2 miles (3km) of ancient underground cellars. Antaño produces good, fruity Rueda Verdejos (100% Verdejo) and Ruedas (white blends with a minimum of 50% Verdejo), a Chardonnay, an *espumoso* (sparkling), and juicy Tempranillos.

Calle Arribas 7-9, 47490, Rueda, Valladolid
www.bodegasantano.es.com

Avelina Vegas Rueda

Deep in the Segovian countryside, the huge, brand-new winery of Avelina Vegas stands ready to process serious quantities of grapes. The family business, set up by one of two brothers who have since gone their separate ways in wine, has a well-established red wine brand in Ribera del Duero called Montespina. The Rueda Verdejo Montespina has a crisp freshness and ripe lime and lemon fruit. With this capacity in the winery, they have the potential to develop a good range of brands.

Calle Real de Pino, 36, 40460 Santiuste de San Juan Bautista,
Segovia; www.avelinovegas.com

Belondrade y Lurton Rueda

Belondrade y Lurton is a wine that helped build the profile of Rueda Verdejos. Frenchman Didier Belondrade recognized the region's potential to succeed with Burgundian winemaking. The result, Belondrade y Lurton (originally produced with Jacques Lurton), is 100% Verdejo, fermented and aged for 10 months in

BODEGAS FARINA
COLEGIATA IS MADE FROM 100% TINTA DE
TORO (TEMPRANILLO) GRAPES

French oak. It was one of the first wines to prove that Verdejo had the structure and quality to benefit from oak aging. In 2000, Belondrade moved into a modern winery, where he also makes two Vinos de la Tierra, named after his daughters: Apolonia, made with younger fruit and less oak, and Clarisa, a Tempranillo *rosado*.

Quina San Diego, Camino del Puerto, 47491 La Seca, Valladolid; www.belondradeylurton.com

Bienvenida Toro

The delightfully named Bienvenida ("Welcome") is nevertheless a project with serious intent, run by winemakers with firmly established reputations. César Muñoz, who consults widely in Ribera del Duero and Toro, has come together with Alberto and Eduardo García, sons of Mariano García, whose own projects include Paixar in Bierzo and Los Astrales in Ribera del Duero. The wine is made in concrete fermenting tanks: old technology now very much back in fashion. Using very concentrated low yields, the wine shows dense mocha and black-fruit notes.

C/Las Bodegas, 49810 Toro
0983 403 094

Bodega Gótica Rueda

On a low hill just outside Rueda, María Jesús Díez de la Hoz really does have a Gothic winery, complete with crenellations to the roof and a fine collection of ironwork and religious art inside. She has converted her father's grape-growing business into a winery, and in so doing has won recognition for her Trascampanas Verdejo. This has underlyng tropical-fruit tones, a full body as a result of keeping the wine on its lees, a zesty freshness, and a clean, minerally finish.

María Jesús de la Hoz Monsalve SL, Plaza Mayor 13, 47490 Rueda; www.bodegagotica.com

Bodegas Bohórquez Ribera del Duero

Bohórquez is a relatively new enterprise, founded in 1999. The vineyard land around Pesquera was carefully researched for complementary soil types and aspects, and the first wine was made in 2002 from bought-in grapes. Vintage 2005 (released 2008) contained the first grapes from the estate's own vineyards. The results are promising: the 2005 has deep, ripe, black fruits laced with sweet spices. The character of new oak is apparent but will integrate with time.

Carretera Peñafiel 47315 Pesquera de Duero, Valladolid
www.bodegasbohorquez.com

Bodegas Fariña Toro

Miguel Fariña is the key man behind the creation of the DO of Toro in 1987. His father set up the original winery in 1942, and today the Fariña estate—with a new winery inside the DO boundary—is a very substantial family business with 618 acres (250ha) of vineyards. He makes a young carbonic maceration wine (just like a Beaujolais Nouveau) in addition to serious oak-aged styles. The Gran Colegiata Campus is made with grapes taken from vines that are up to 140 years old, and shows their concentration as well as the typical Toro structure.

Carretera de Moraleja, 49151 Casaseca de las Chanas, Zamora; www.bodegasfarina.com

Bodegas Félix Sanz Rueda

Félix Sanz has over 74 acres (30ha) of vines, from which he makes Rueda DO wines as well as Vino de la Tierra de Castilla y León. Of particular note is his Viña Cimbron label, which offers a Verdejo, a Sauvignon Blanc, a Verdejo/Viura, and a barrel-fermented and aged Verdejo blend. These are fascinating wines for comparison, with similar varietals from the same region and the same winemaker. The unoaked single varietals are generally the most interesting. Sanz also makes Montenegro Tinto in Ribera del Duero, a joint project with winemakers Joan Mila from Penedès and Joan Ayuso, an academic and consultant.

Ronda Aradillas, 47490 Rueda, Valladolid
www.bodegaFélixsanz.es

Bodegas Rodero Ribera del Duero

One of the most important details to note about Bodegas Rodero is that until 1990, this estate used to supply grapes to Vega Sicilia, at which point the owners chose to make their own wines. Their previous history explains the style of their wines today. Theirs are wines in the classical hierarchy: Joven, Crianza, Reserva. The Gran Reserva, with its time spent in French and American oak, is structured for long aging. TSM is the most modern of the wines here, and shows the most immediate appeal, with a fine, tannic finish.

Carretera Boada, 09314 Pedrosa de Duero, Burgos
www.bodegasrodero.com

Bodegas Vizar

Vino de la Tierra de Castilla y León
A shiny new winery stands in the midst of this historic estate, which today produces everything from traditional Tempranillo to the more modern red arrivals to the region, Merlot and Syrah. The modern technology and the commitment to quality is producing very polished wines, bold and expressive with rounded, well-managed tannins. The Syrah shows typical fruit with a light, peppery character, and in the Selección is a Tempranillo/Syrah blend with a Spain-meets-the-Rhône personality. The Syrah is rounded out by the Tempranillo's generous cherry fruit.

Carretera N-122 (Valladolid-Soria) Km 341, 47329 Villabáñez
www.bodegasvizar.es

Carmen Rodríguez Méndez Toro

Carmen Rodríguez Méndez is an excellent example of a family of wine-growers who turned to winemaking in 2003. The production is very small, at around 21,000 bottles, and the focus is on handcrafted wines. The vineyards are situated in separate plots around southeastern Toro, with some very old, pre-phylloxera vines, and they are managed without any artificial pesticides or treatments. Carodorum Issos is the young wine and receives just four months in French oak; Carodorum, meanwhile, has 14 months, while the old-vine Selección Especial spends 18 months in new French oak.

Carretera Salamanca, Km 4350, 49800 Toro
0980 568 005

BELONDRADE Y LURTON
THE GRAPES FOR QUINTA APOLONIA COME
FROM RELATIVELY YOUNG VINES

César Príncipe Cigales

The Príncipe family, like so many in Cigales, used to make *rosados* to sell in bulk. They finally decided to use these grapes to make their own red wine, which they launched in 2000, and showed the potential for the region to make serious reds. Their vineyards are scattered across the DO: small parcels of 50-year-old bush vines as well as recent plantings of a mixture of Tempranillo and Garnacha. The wine benefits from this complexity of age and fruit, as well as from careful selection and modern winemaking.

Carretera Fuensaldana-Mucientes 1 Km, 47194 Fuensaldana
0983 583 242

Cillar de Silos Ribera del Duero

A family-run business, with 119 acres (48ha) of vineyards, Cillar de Silos produces Tempranillo-based *rosados* and reds. The top wine is aged for 16 months in French oak, a process that produces a weighty, structured wine with balsamic, liquorice, and toasty oak influences. The Cillar de Silos Joven is a contrast, with young, crisp-tasting fruit that is ideal for early drinking.

Paraje el Soto, 09370 Quintana del Pidio, Burgos
www.cillardesilos.es

Conde Ribera del Duero

These are wines that come with a pedigree: the owner is Isaac Fernández, nephew of Mariano García, former winemaker of Vega Sicilia. The style is new-generation (winemaking without a grandiose winery), with the focus on grapes (some grapes come from the highest vineyards in the region), long macerations, scrupulous winemaking, and aging in American and French oak. Neo and Neo Punta Essencia are the top wines: very deep and opulent, more intense and rounded than many from Ribera del Duero. ★ Rising star

Carretera Nac'l 122, Km 274,5, 09391 Castrillo de la Vega, Burgos; www.bodegasconde.es

Covitoro Toro

Covitoro shows just what a successful co-operative can achieve when its members set their minds to it. Founded in 1974, well before the DO was formed, it can now draw upon 2,500 acres (1,000ha) of vines, 1,000 acres (400ha) of them more than 50 years old. Both classic and modern expressions of Tinta de Toro are made. Marques de la Villa is a traditional Reserva aged in American oak. Canus Verus has a more glossy, black-fruit appeal, with a firm, tannic grip and shorter French and American oak aging.

Carretera de Tordesilla 13, 49800 Toro
www.covitoro.com

Cuevas Jiménez Ribera del Duero

Driving north up the A1 from Madrid, the Cuevas Jiménez winery stands clearly on the left beyond Aranda del Duero, at the heart of the DO. Iron is the family's original business: hence the symbolic iron "F" on the front of the winery, and the name of the wine, Ferratus (from the Latin for a soldier "armed or clad in iron"). They make Ferratus and Sensaciónes from bush-vine Tempranillo. Boldly oaked, this is one of the new styles of Ribera del Duero.

Carretera de Madrid a Irún, Km 16, 09370 Gumiel de Izán
www.ferratus.es

Dehesa de Los Canónigos
Ribera del Duero

Dehesa de los Cañonigos was one of the great church estates (originally owned by 22 *canónigos*, or canons from the Cathedral of Valladolid), which was appropriated by the state in the mid-19th century. Today, it covers 1,500 acres (600ha), although only 175 acres (70ha) are actually vineyard. The estate produces a range of red wines. The Reserva and Gran Reserva are both Tinto Fino (Tempranillo) with some Cabernet Sauvignon and a dash of (the white) Albillo. The style is classical, and the Gran Reserva in particular reflects its 32 months in oak, with leather and toasty notes.

Carretera Renedo-Pesquera, Km 39, 47315 Pesquera de Duero, Valladolid; www.bodegadehesadeloscanonigos.com

Díaz Bayo Ribera del Duero

The Díaz Bayo go back 10 generations in the region and some of them can remember the pre-phylloxera days, when there was a very different style of wine and winemaking. Their new winery has concrete, stainless-steel, and French oak fermenters, and despite their long history, they are continuing to experiment, producing well-balanced, modern styles. The Díaz Bayo wines, called Nuestro ("Ours"), declare their time in barrel on the label, rather than describing themselves as a less accurate *crianza* or *reserva*. Thus "10 meses" has spent 10 months in oak (*mes* is "month" in Spanish).

Camino de los Anarinos, 09471 Fuentelcésped, Burgos
www.bodegadiazbayo.com

Domaine Bernard Magrez Toro

The fact that the French château owner Bernard Magrez chose Toro as an investment location over Rioja or Ribera del Duero confirms the region's potential. It also once again highlights the appeal of Toro to French winemakers, and the contribution they make in taming the wildness and toughness of the terroir. These wines retain the power of their region but show the Magrez commitment to ripe tannin and the supple fruit that goes with it. Magrez makes Paciencia and Temperancia, and also shares a business with actor Gérard Depardieu, Les Clés du Terroir. In Toro, Depardieu is involved in the winemaking of Spiritus Sancti, while in the Magrez domaine in Priorat, his wine is Sine Nomine; the Magrez wine is called Herència del Padrí.

No visitor facilities
www.bernard-magrez.com

Dominio de Atauta Ribera del Duero

The success of this estate is based on its old bush vines, which somehow managed to escape the phylloxera vine louse when it arrived at the end of the 19th century. Local boy Miguel Sánchez, subsequently top Madrid wine distributor, set about recuperating the abandoned Tinto Fino (Tempranillo) vines with French-born winemaker Bertrand Sourdais. Based at the far east end of Ribera del Duero, a gravity-fed winery and biodynamic management of the vineyard assist in the creation of powerful wines: opaque and supple with an elegant balance. Valdegatiles and Llanos de Almendro are fine examples of the terroir and the investment involved.

Carratera a Morcuera, Atauta, 42345 San Esteban de Gormaz (Soria); www.dominiodeatauta.com

PRIETO PICUDO AND FRIENDS

In a world where Cabernet Sauvignon rules, there is an understandable desire to track down local, indigenous grape varieties—what Spanish viticulturalists call *autochthonous* ("aboriginal"), following the ancient Greek. Currently, north-central and northwest Spain are leading the way. Prieto Picudo is a grape that is native to the province of León, and is found in Tierra de León DO, Vino de Calidad de Valtiendas, and Vino de Valles de Benavente. It grows in tight, conical bunches in unforgiving soils and harsh climates. The wines, even the *rosados*, are deeply colored. Being a thick-skinned variety it has firm tannins, which are relieved by underlying red fruits. By contrast, the Juan García grape is found in the border zone, in Zamora province, and is a thin-skinned grape that is ideally suited for making young wines. Rufete, a favorite in Arribes del Duero DO, is the lightest of all three in terms of color, but can enhance the fruity characters of blends.

EBANO
EBANO 6 SPENDS FOUR MONTHS IN FRENCH
OAK, THEN TWO MONTHS IN BOTTLE

ESTANCIA PIEDRA
THIS RED'S POWERFUL FRUIT IS BALANCED
BY GOOD SOLID TANNINS

Dominio del Bendito Toro

Another successful project run by a French winemaker, this time Antony Terry, who formerly worked at Quinta de la Quietud and set up this small winery near Toro in 2004. He farms Tinta del Toro vines (some 80 years old) organically. Each of his three reds show careful oak management to tame the tannins: Silver has six months in French oak, Gold 12 months. El Titan is as bold as its name suggests, and needs time to integrate. He also makes a tiny quantity of *vin de paille* ("straw wine") from grapes dried on straw to concentrate the sugars. ★**Rising star**

Plaza Santo Domingo 8
0980 693 306

Dominio de Pingus Ribera del Duero

Pingus is one of those rare wines, made in tiny quantities, that almost immediately won global fame on its launch in 1995. Blonde-haired and Danish, Peter (nicknamed "Pingus" to distinguish him from winemaker uncle Peter Vinding-Diers) Sisseck has become as much of a cult as his wines. Managed biodynamically since 2000, the old-vine Tinto Fino (Tempranillo) is pruned to very low yields. In the tiny winery (designed for winemaking, not wine tourism) by the River Duero, the wine is aged in 100% new oak. The result is a bold wine that needs time to mellow. It is rich and fleshy, with an overlay of mocha, shows firm tannins, a bright acidity, and clean minerality to finish. The second wine is Flor de Pingus. The newest project is with local growers to make a very accessible red, (the Greek letter psi). Sisseck also consults at Hacienda Monasterio in Ribera del Duero, Viñas de la Vega del Duero nearby, and Clos d'Agon (Priorat).

Hospital, 47350 Quintanilla de Onésimo, Valladolid
0639 833 854

Dominio de San Antonio Ribera del Duero

A young, small (25 acre/10ha) winery, earning a strong reputation. Attention to detail is apparent throughout. Low-yielding Tempranillo makes three wines: La Soledad, from particularly poor soils; Las Favoritas, an annual blend of the best parcels; and Dominio de San Antonio, from bought-in grapes. Maturation is in a mix of French, American, and Central European oak barrels, of different sizes. ★**Rising star**

Carretera Madrid-Irún, Km 163,5 (Camino de Sinovas), CP 09400 Aranda de Duero; www.dominiodesanantonio.com

Ebano Ribera del Duero

The shiny, ultra-modern winery houses stainless-steel fermenters and French oak barriques for its two wines: Ebano and Ebano 6, both 100% Tempranillo. These are made in a modern style, with ripe, rounded fruit, notes of cooked fruit and vanilla, brisk acidity, and firm tannin. The finish has a clean, minerally character.

Carretera Nac. 122, Km 299,6, pol 1 parcela 32 47318 Castrillo de Duero; www.ebanovinedosybodegas.com

Elias Mora Toro

The "two Victorias," Victoria Pariente and Victoria Benavides, cannot put a foot wrong. Pariente works in Rueda, Benavides in Toro. In Toro vineyards, the climate is dry and continental, the soil stony—ideal for long-lived hardy vines, which are on their own rootstocks (phylloxera did not come this far). Benavides' focus is on the vineyard rather than a glossy winery. The result is wines of exceptional density and power, particularly the Gran Elias Moro, which spends 17 months in French oak.

San Román de Hornija, 47530 Valladolid
www.bodegaseliasmora.com

Emilio Moro Ribera del Duero

The story of Emilio Moro's wines reflects the modern history of Ribera del Duero and the tendency of producers to choose their own style. The winery opened in the late 1980s and now draws on some 173 acres (70ha) of Tinto Fino (Tempranillo). A decade later, in 1998, Emilio Moro stopped ranking the wines by *reserva* or *gran reserva*. Instead, each wine has its own name and character. First came Malleolus, followed by Malleolus de Valderramiro in 2000, made from the oldest vines and aged in American oak; finally top wine Malleolus de Sancho Martín appeared in 2002: complex and powerful.

Valoria, Peñafiel Road, 47315 Pesquera de Duero, Valladolid; www.emiliomoro.com

Ermita del Conde Vino de la Tierra de Castilla y León

All around Ermita the region is alive with history and with traces of previous inhabitants: the Celtiberians, the Romans, medieval buildings. The winery, by contrast, is a mere stripling, having been founded in 2006. It draws on 30 acres (12ha) of Tempranillo, Cabernet Sauvignon, and Merlot to make two reds: Ermita del Conde and Pago del Conde (this is only made in the best years). The grapes go through two sorting tables to select top-quality fruit. They also make a white, Viña Sulpicia, from Albillo, a local white variety. ★**Rising star**

Camino de Torre 1, 09410 Coruña del Conde, Burgos
www.ermitadelconde.com

Estancia Piedra Toro

Estancia Piedra is one of Toro's brightest stars. It was established in 1998, when Scottish-born tax lawyer Grant Stein saw the light and set up a winery. He has some 173 acres (70ha) of Tinta de Toro vines, some planted in 1998, and one block planted in 1927; the latter is used for Paredinas, the top wine. The investment has been substantial and well-managed, showing itself rapidly in modern wine produced with minimum intervention in the grapes. There are no rustic tannins here; instead, there is plenty of pure, dark fruit and new French oak.

Carretera Toro-Salamanca Km 5, 49800 Toro
www.estanciapiedra.com

Félix Callejo Ribera del Duero

A family enterprise, Félix Callejo started in 1989, and now has the next generation working in the enterprise, which has over 250 acres (100ha) in production. The 4 Meses en Barrica has youthful juiciness, while the Crianza and Reserva have more structure and intensity. The Gran Reserva spends 24 months in second-use French oak (so that the oak is not dominant) and the fruit remains lively. Selección Viñedos de la Familia is made from the best fruit, matured for only 15 months in new French oak, to give a riper, denser, more modern take on Tinto Fino.

Avenida del Cid, Km 16,400, E-09441 Sotillo de la Ribera
www.bodegasFélixcallejo.com

Finca Sobreño Toro

Finca Sobreño was created by a group of winemakers from Rioja who recognized the quality of the wine coming out of Toro, and the potential of the Tinta de Toro vines. Their first wine was made in 1998, and the estate now owns 200 acres (80ha) of vineyard and manages another 222 acres (90ha). In a short space of time, Finca Sobreño has become established as a producer of well-made, well-priced, polished modern wines from Tinta de Toro (Tempranillo), with none of the rough edges than are still obvious in many Toro reds.

Carretera N-122, Km 423, Aptdo. 52, 49800 Toro
www.sobreno.com

O Fournier Ribera del Duero

With wineries in Chile and Argentina, the Fournier family name is fulfilling its mission to produce fine wine in Spanish-speaking countries. In Ribera del Duero, its 148 acres (60ha) of stony vineyards are mainly devoted to Tinta del País (Tempranillo). The Urban range, as in Chile and Argentina, is the entry level wine. Next up is Spiga, vibrant with red fruits edged by tarry tannins, and aged for 12 months in French oak, and Alfa Spiga, which has 20 months. Finally, comes O Fournier, the top brand at each winery. This version is very bold, enriched by 18 months in French and American oak.

Finca El Pinar, 09316 Berlangas de Roa, Burgos
www.bodegasofournier.com

François Lurton Toro

François Lurton is carving out quite an empire for himself in Spain. From his new winery he makes wines for the Toro and Rueda DOs as well as Vino de la Tierra de Castilla y León. His most significant Toro is Campo Eliseo, a joint undertaking with Michel Rolland. The wine, which is 100% Tinta de Toro (Tempranillo), is sumptuously rich and dense. The second label is Campo Alegre. The El Albar range, made from grapes grown in Toro, has now become a Vino de La Tierra because of technical details to do with viticulture. These are all very well-balanced, elegant styles. In Rueda, the Hermanos Lurton label makes fresh, crisp Verdejos and Sauvignon Blancs, both of which show strong French influences. De Puta Madre is a fascinating sweet white made from Verdejo.

Camino Magarin, 47529 Villafranca de Duero
www.francoislurton.com

Fuentenarro Ribera del Duero

Fuentenarro and its vines lie at about 2,625ft (800m). The family owns all its own vineyards and makes wine in a very typical, unglamorous family winery, which is more than adequate for making Tempranillo *jovens*, *crianzas*, and *reservas*, and cellaring them in French and American oak. From year to year, the wines are showing improvement, in particular the Vendimia Seleccionada, which is currently displaying the benefits of using only the best fruit.

Calle Constitución 32, 09311 La Horra, Burgos
www.fuentenarro.com

Garciarévalo Rueda

This is a small family business, and it aims for quality, producing a Verdejo blend as well as a series of monovarietal Verdejos. What distinguishes the top

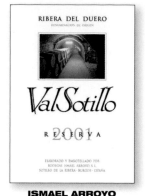

wines here is the work done in the winery with the lees to build flavor and texture—a practice that is increasingly common across Rueda. This is most obvious in the Tres Olmos Lias, which has a complex texture, and a fine, bright acidity to counter the richness.

Plaza de San Juan 4, 47230 Matapozuelos
www.garciavalo.com

Hacienda Monasterio Ribera del Duero

Cult winemaker Peter Sisseck was initially involved here as general manager when the present owners arrived in 1991 before he left to set up at Dominio de Pingus. As a result, Hacienda Monasterio wines gained international attention. Sisseck remains as a consultant, working with winemaker Carlos de la Fuente. In the vineyard Tinto Fino (Tempranillo) grows alongside Cabernet Sauvignon, Merlot, and Malbec. This Bordeaux-oriented blend imparts floral aromas to the wine, as well as black-fruit flavors and a firm structure.

Carrater Pesquera-Valbuena, 47315 Pesquera de Duero (Valladolid); www.haciendamonasterio.com

Hijos de Antonio Barceló Ribera del Duero

The Barceló business is impressive, and its 100 years of slow, then rapid expansion mirrors the history of Spain. Don Antonio Barceló Madueño started in Málaga as one of the early exporters of Spanish wine. Real growth began with Bodegas Peñascal in Castilla y León in 1973, Viña Mayor in Ribera del Duero in 1986, Bodegas Palacio in Rioja in 1999, followed by acquisitions in Toro and Rueda, and now a range of good-value, modern wines. All the company's wines show a subtle understanding of consumer tastes. Typical is the Viña Mayor, a Crianza with a perfumed aroma and a soft, juicy palate. Secreto is the Reserva: more boldly oaked but softened by ripe fruit.

Carretera Valladolid-Soria, Km 325, 6, 47350 Quintanilla de Onésimo, Valladolid; www.habarcelo.es

Hornillos Ballesteros Ribera del Duero

Perhaps not the easiest winery name to pronounce, but it is democratic, representing the names of business partners Miguel Hornillos and Javier Ballesteros. They make a young team, but both have experience, having grown up in families who work in wine. This experience shows itself in their rapid rise in the wine-critic ratings. The main range is called MiBal, made from Tinta del País (Tempranillo). The wines show the result of careful selection in their ripe, rounded character. Perfil is fermented in new oak, then matured in new French oak for 30 months. The result is bold, toasted, and spicy, well-structured, with ripe fruit. ★ **Rising star**

Camino Tenerias 9, 09300 Roa de Duero, Burgos
www.hornillosballesteros.es

Ismael Arroyo Ribera del Duero

Ismael Arroyo is one of the more modest producers of Ribera del Duero's top wines. This even shows itself in the winery buildings above ground, which conceal old cellars and tunnels dug into the hillside. The style of the wines is powerful, all of them made

JUAN MANUEL BURGOS
A VIOLET-COLORED, CONCENTRATED WINE
WITH PLENTY OF SWEET BERRY FRUIT

LOS ASTRALES
WITH CRISP FRUIT AND RIPE TANNINS,
ASTRALES IS VERY ACCESSIBLE

from Tinta del País (Tempranillo). The top-flight wines are the Val Sotillo range, showing expressive mulberry/damson fruit, with a firm, dry finish.

C/ Los Lagares, 71, 09441 Sotillo de la Ribera, Burgos
www.valsotillo.com

Javier Sanz Rueda

Javier Sanz (no relation to the other Sanz family on these pages) describes himself as *viticultor* (grape-grower) and puts that simple job description firmly on his labels. He is quite right to do so, for his wines are a pure expression of the 257 acres (104ha) of vineyard he owns and works. He makes a barrel-fermented Verdejo, but undoubtedly the single-varietal unoaked whites are his most successful. Rey Santo is his young Verdejo/Viura blend.

San Judas 2, 47491 La Seca, Valladolid
www.jsviticultor.com

José Pariente Rueda

The Pariente hillside vineyards promise quality, with cold nights and harsh winters, and above all the pebbly soils. The key figure is the winemaker, Victoria Pariente, who rose to fame as one of the "two Victorias": two gifted winemakers; the other Victoria (Benavides) is at Elias Mora in Toro. Working with the Verdejo planted by her father, José, Pariente makes one supremely fresh white, and another more structured one that spends seven months in French oak. As an interesting contrast, she has now started to make a Sauvignon Blanc from bush vines over 25 years old: among the first planted in Rueda.

Carreterade Rueda Km 2,5, 47491 La Seca, Valladolid
www.josepariente.com

Juan Manuel Burgos Ribera del Duero

Founded in 1999 with 49 acres (20ha) of vineyards in the eastern part of Ribera, this winery is still in its infancy. Burgos makes three wines from Tinto Fino (Tempranillo), all with the name Avan: Nacimiento (a young wine), Concentracion (from a better selection of more concentrated grapes), and Cepas Centenarias (made from pre-phylloxera 100-year-old vines). With small-batch production and precise winemaking, the wines are all supple and bursting with blueberry and blackberry fruit, which is underlined by firm tannin. ★ **Rising star**

Calle de la Aranda, 39, 09471 Fuentelcesped, Burgos
www.byvjuanmanuelburgos.com

La Mejorada Vino de la Tierra de Castilla y León

La Mejorada must surely be one of Spain's lovelier wineries. The building is a former monastery that dates back to the 15th century. The monastery itself was a place of great importance, but it fell into disuse. Its *mudéjar* (Islamic-Spanish) chapel was designated as a National Monument in 1931. The winery was built in what was originally the cloister. There are currently three wines made here: Villalar, which is mainly a Cabernet Sauvignon with 10% Tempranillo; Las Norias, from Tempranillo; and Las Cercas, the top wine. This is made from 60% Tempranillo, 40% Syrah, and spends 36 months in oak

Monasterio de La Mejorada, 47410 Olmedo, Valladolid
www.lamejorada.com

La Setera Arribes del Duero

This is one of Spain's tinier wineries, on the border with Portugal, where the River Duero cuts a steep path through the granite. Sara Groves-Raines, from northern Ireland, and her husband, Patxi Martínez, originally settled here to farm goats and make cheese. Then Telmo Rodríguez and English wine merchant Simon Loftus encouraged them to locate old vines and make wine with the local Juan García grape. They now produce a complex, aromatic Malvasía, and fresh *rosados* and chunky reds from Juan García. They also make a delicious Touriga Nacional, with grapes purchased in Portugal. ★ **Rising star**

Fornillos de Fermoselle, 49232 Zamora
www.lasetera.com

La Soterrana Rueda

La Soterrana is one of the newest wineries in Rueda. The creation of the company by a group of businessmen is yet another sign of the rapidly growing national recognition of the DO as a source of top-quality young white wines. Here they make Verdejo Viura blends as well as single-varietal Verdejo, and a Sauvignon Blanc. The Verdejo shows classic green color highlights and has a brisk, intense acidity. The Sauvignon is more powerful, with a ripe, fruity character.

Carretera Nacional 601, Km 151, 47410 Olmedo, Valladolid
www.bodegaslasoterrana.com

Leda Viñas Viejas
Vinos de la Tierra de Castilla y León

One of a number of interesting new projects populating Castilla y León, along the lines of Abadía Retuerta and Mauro. Winemaker César Muñoz, also of Montebaco in Ribera del Duero, is working with old-vine Tinto Fino that comes from within the Cigales and Ribera del Duero DOs, and making sumptuously dense, structured wines. The first vintage, 1998, was an immediate success, and the wines have continued to gain attention. Más de Leda is the second wine; Sara Soto, a Cigales red, is named after the owner's daughter, who is disabled, and proceeds go to a charity to support her. ★ **Rising star**

Mayor 48, 47320 Tudela de Duero, Valladolid
www.bodegasleda.com

Lezcano-Lacalle Cigales

This relatively small family business with 38 acres (15.5ha) of vineyards at an altitude of 2,625ft (800m) makes wines that are not in the least showy, but illustrate well what Cigales is all about: particularly that it isn't a poor relation of Ribera del Duero. The blends include some Merlot and Cabernet Sauvignon, but the essence is Tinto Fino, which shows fine structure and depth, with cedary, liquorice notes. The Reserva is aged in Missouri oak.

47292 Trigueros del Valle, Valladolid
www.bodegaslezcano.com

Liberalia Enologica Toro

The name "Liberalia" refers to the Roman god Liber, who was a forerunner of Bacchus, the god of wine. This is one hint of winery founder Juan Antonio Fernández's interest in art and culture. Bach and Handel can also be heard in the cellar, to encourage calm and stillness. According to his website—and depending on the wind and his mood—Fernández plays classical music in the vineyard.

There are plans for cultural events, and for a serious wine-tourism project. Beyond all this are the wines themselves, which are powerful, with firm tannins from Tinta de Toro (Tempranillo). There is also a light, sweet white wine, Uno: a Tinta de Toro/Albiño blend.

Camino del Palo, 49800 Toro-Zamora
www.liberalia.es

Los Astrales Ribera del Duero

This is a winery to watch. In 2000, a family of growers named Romero de la Cruz decided to make their own wines. The family's winemaking consultant was a smart choice: the influential Eduardo García (of Leda), son of the equally influential Mariano García (formerly of Vega Sicilia, now of Mauro and other projects). Using old-vine Tinto Fino (Tempranillo) together with some newer plantings, the supple, finely oaked Crianza spends 17 months in French oak, with a little American oak thrown in for good measure. Christina is the name of the top selection: an intense and complex wine, built for cellaring. ★ Rising star

Carretera Olmedillo, Km 7, 09313 Anguix, Burgos
www.astrales.es

Magallanes Ribera del Duero

Winemaker César Muñoz has an excellent pedigree, having worked with a number of top properties in the region, including Leda and Victoria, and currently including Monte Baco, Bohorquez, and Cesar Príncipe. Magallanes is his own project, in which he produces wine from Tinto Fino (Tempranillo) vineyards which, at 3,275ft (998m), are the highest in Ribera del Duero. The grapes undergo a long, slow extraction, and this makes for a powerful, spicy, full-bodied wine that benefits from time in the cellar.

No visitor facilities
www.cesarmunoz.es

Mähler-Besse Toro

The Mähler-Besses made their names in France (Bordeaux, to be exact) as négociants, and by becoming co-owners of Château Palmer in 1938. Their interests spread widely, and in 1980 they started to invest in Spain, having recognized its untapped potential and its usefulness to their international portfolio. Jumilla was the first region of choice, where the Taja brand of Monastrells and Monastrell blends have become well-established. Oro is the company's latest wine project in Toro, where it is made with Tinta de Toro (Tempranillo). The Joven is a young, fresh, fruity red; the Selección sees eight months in oak barriques while the Reserva has 20 months.

49, rue camille Godard, 33000 Bordeaux, France
www.mahler-besse.com

Margón Tierra de León

Tierra de León is one of Spain's newest DOs (2007), and is a good place to discover the Prieto Picudo grape, both as a red wine and in its traditional form as a *rosado*. Margón is a new enterprise by two families who have employed winemaker Raúl Perez, one of Spain's stars: hence the diverse and imaginative range. In addition to the local white Albarín, some of it fermented in Austrian oak, and the Prieto Picudo (fermented in French oak),

there is some Verdejo Icewine, harvested on a snowy day. Sometimes rustic, always interesting: this is one to watch. ★ Rising star

Avenida de Valencia de Don Juan, 24209, Pajares de Los Oteros; www.bodegasmargon.com

Marqués de Velilla Ribera del Duero

Based near La Horra, Marqués de Velilla's extensive winery—a blend of château-type architectural styles—receives fruit from the almost 494 acres (200ha) of its own vineyards. Detailed work on soil structure and water availability to identify separate plots has guided plantings of Tinto del País (Tempranillo), Cabernet Sauvignon, Merlot, and Malbec. The investment has been carried through into the winery, and the wines show ripe fruit with plenty of oak. Top wine Doncel de Mataperras is round and supple with lively acidity and integrated tannins.

Carretera de Sotillo, 09311 La Horra, Burgos
www.marquesdevelilla.com

Matarredonda Toro

Alfonso Sanz is one of the more recent arrivals in Toro (2000), and has quickly made an impression. He owns 153 acres (62ha) of Tinta del Toro, including pre-phylloxera old vines. Warm, sandy soils and a warmer climate make for big wines with ripe alcohol. Juan Rojo is aged for eight months in oak, with a finely balanced palate of fruit and spice; Libranza is more boldly structured; aged for 14 months in oak, it needs time to mature in bottle. ★ Rising star

Carretera Toro-Valdefinjas, Km 2,5, 49800 Toro, Zamora
www.vinolibranza.com

Matarromera Ribera del Duero

Founded in 1988, the Matarromera winery is set on a hillside with views over Valbuena de Duero. The vineyard is planted mainly with Tinto Fino and produces *crianzas* through to *gran reservas*. The American/French oak-aging creates classic Ribera del Duero. The group owns two other wineries in the Ribera Del Duero DO: Emina (the word for a monk's daily ration of wine (9fl oz/250ml), and Renacimiento. At Renacimiento, Rento is a powerful, spicy wine. Of interest at Emina is the 3 Barricas collection: three wines, each made with different oaks (French, Spanish, and American). The Matarromera group has a strong interest in wine tourism, centerd on Emina, whose visitor facilities include a wine interpretation center. Other properties include another Emina winery in Rueda, which makes grassy Verdejos (notably Selección Personal Carlos Moro), and the good-value Valdelosfrailes in Cigales.

Renedo-Pesquera Road, Km 30, 47359 Valbuena de Duero;
www.matarromera.es

Montebaco Ribera del Duero

Located at around 2,789ft (850m), the Monte Baco estate has some of Ribera del Duero's higher vineyards, which lends a freshness to the wines. It was founded in 1982 by grape-growers, and has since been transformed by the construction of a glinting winery. The consultant is the widely traveled César Muñoz, who manages the dense, succulent fruit with care, matching it with French and American oak. The Vendimia Seleccionada shows the

PHYLLOXERA

It is one of the well-known facts of the European wine industry that the phylloxera vine louse devastated vineyards at the end of the 19th century and the beginning of the 20th, as it gnawed its way through vine roots all across Europe. It then traveled with plant material overseas and has continued to wreak havoc all over the world. Less well-known is the fact that some vineyards escaped attack, and a number of these happen to be in Castilla y León. The reason is that the little louse hates sand. Thus, between Valladolid and Zamora, for instance, there are vineyards with vines that predate the arrival of phylloxera. What wine fans find particularly interesting is that these gnarled, blackened bush vines are growing on their own roots, so that they are expressing the character of the soil without the intervention of root material grafted on from another plant.

PALACIO DE BORNOS
COOL FERMENTATION TECHNIQUES MEAN
THIS VERDEJO HAS PLENTY OF FRESH FRUIT

intensity of 60-year-old vines, together with 16 months in barrel and another 22 months in bottle, making an intense and very complex style. Montebaco also makes its own fresh, floral Rueda Verdejo.

47359 Valbuena de Duero, Valladolid
www.bodegasmontebaco.com

Naia Rueda

Only founded in 2002, Naia has moved rapidly beyond "rising star" status to become a permanent feature in the Rueda firmament. There are two clues to its success: the deep gravel soils, and winemaker Eulogia Calleja. Careful selection of the fruit is followed by cold maceration of the grapes in their juice before the fermentation to develop aromas and texture—and the results are evident in the wines. K-Naia has a zesty acidity. Naia shows the richness of the lees aging, together with citrus-fruit freshness. Náiades, the top wine, is made from grapes that grow in mineral-rich soils; since 2007, a reduced oak regime in the winery is allowing the elegant fruit to shine.

Camino San Martín, 47491 La Seca
www.bodegasnaia.com

Numanthia Toro

This is one of the wineries that put Toro on the world map—not just the Spanish one. It was founded by the Eguren family in 1998, whose other stellar properties include Sierra Cantabria, Viñedos de Paganos, and Señorío de San Vicente in Rioja, and was sold to Moët Hennessy in 2008. Numanthia continues to shine: the 100 acres (40ha) of vineyards include some pre-phylloxera vines, while the temperature variation from day to night fosters dense but fresh fruit. Numanthia Termes is the "little brother" of the wine family, but it is in no way the lesser of the two icons here, with a real expression of the winery's style. Numanthia is rich in supple, cooked fruits, fine cedary oak, and chocolate touches. Termanthia is made from tiny yields of the oldest vines to create a layered, intense wine with mineral hints and a plummy complexity.

Calle Real, 49882 Valdefinjas, Zamora
0980 699 147

Ossian Rueda

Ossian lies to the far east of Rueda, very close to Viñedos de Nieve. It started life in 2005 outside the Denominación de Origen, because it did not fit in with the regulations. Ossian organically farms very old, low-growing, pre-phylloxera bush vines in the highest part of the DO. The people behind the business are Javier Zaccagnini, co-founder of Aalto, and grower Ismael Gozalo. Their focus is 100% Verdejo, which they age in French oak barrels of three sizes up to 132 gallons (600 liters). The wines are deeply complex, with herbal, spicy intensity, good minerality, and notable alcohol. ★ Rising star

Calle San Marcos 5, 40447 Nieva, Segovia
www.ossian.es

Otero Vino de Calidad de Valles de Benavente

The Oteros admit that the name of their region is a bit of a mouthful, but they don't see the need to go to all the bureaucratic trouble of changing to a DO with a punchier title. The family started out in winemaking during the first decade of the 20th century, but only now—a century

later—have they become a focus of attention because of their use of the (mainly Spanish) Preito Picudo grape. The Crianza shows bright cherry fruit, and *rosados* from the same grape have a deep color and similar fresh fruit.

Avenida El Ferial 22, 49600 Benavente
www.bodegasotero.es

Pago de los Capellanes Ribera del Duero

"The Land of the Chaplains" recalls the religious ownership of this estate which, up until the 19th century, was church property. The Rodero-Villa family established the winery in 1996, but has rapidly won attention for the quality of its wines. The 272 acres (110ha) of vineyards are made up of Tinto Fino (Tempranillo) with some Cabernet Sauvignon and Merlot. The Tinto Roble wine is a full-flavored youngster made in the house style; the top wines are single-vineyard parcels, El Picón and El Nogal. El Nogal is the bolder and richer of the two.

Camino de la Ampudia, 09314 Pedrosa de Duero, Burgos;
www.pagodeloscapellanes.com

Pago de Carrovejas Ribera del Duero

The classic dish in Segovia is roast suckling pig, and restaurateur José María Ruíz Benito dreamed of making a wine to match it. Founded in 1988, the estate (the name means "the way the sheep walk along") has more than fulfilled his dream, creating wines with a crisp freshness. The vineyards below the picturesque castle of Peñafiel are 75% Tinto Fino (Tempranillo), the rest made up of Cabernet Sauvignon. Three wines are made: a Crianza, a Reserva, and a special selection called Cuesta de Las Liebres, each showing increasing density and power.

Camino de Carraovejas, 47300 Peñafiel, Valladolid
www.pagodecarrovejas.com

Palacio de Bornos Rueda

Antonio Sanz made the Palacio de Bornos label one of the most popular Verdejos around. He started in 1976, well before the Rueda DO was created. Subsequently, he became one of the pioneers in Sauvignon Blanc and sparkling wines. The wines remain fresh and fruity, and the winery is now part of the Taninia group that includes Señorío de Sarría (Navarra), Guelbenzu (Rioja), Toresanas (Toro), and Vallebueno (Ribera del Duero). Sanz's children, Ricardo, Marco, and Alejandra, the sixth generation, now run their own business at Sitios de Bodega.

Carretera Madrid-Coruña Km 170,6, 47490 Rueda,
Valladolid; www.palaciodebornos.com

Páramo de Guzmán Ribera del Duero

The winery was established in 1998, but the name of the brand was well known before that, because Páramo de Guzmán had already won a reputation for unpasteurized ewes-milk cheeses. The project was to make wines that matched the quality of the cheese. The business owns 62 acres (25ha) of vineyards and makes red wines from Tempranillo at each level of oak-aging, using French, American, and Hungarian oaks. The Reserva, with 24 months in oak, has a fine match of mature oak and spicy fruit. The top wine is the Raíz de Guzmán, aged for 23 months in new French oak, then 24 months in bottle

Carretera R-30, 09300 Roa, Burgos
www.paramodeguzman.e.telefonica.net

PAGO DE LOS CAPELLANES
ALL OF THIS ESTATE'S WINES ARE MADE
FROM TEMPRANILLO GRAPES

Pérez Pascuas Ribera del Duero

Three brothers make up the partners in the business, which was one of the early names in Ribera del Duero, before the DO was actually formed. They grow Tinto Fino, with a small amount of Cabernet and Merlot, and mature their wines in a blend of American and French oak. Their wines show a more traditional style with a firm grip of tannin, and the top wines need time to soften.

Carretera Pedrosa de Roa, 09314 Pedrosa de Duero, Burgos
www.vinapedrosa.com

Pesquera Ribera del Duero

Alejandro Fernández is one of the great characters of this DO. A man of determination, he was a former industrialist whose family vineyard lay opposite Vega Sicilia, and was able to draw upon his technical and business experience to achieve global success. His wine was different from his neighbor's—shorter oak aging, for one thing—and Fernández knew how to sell. He has gone on to repeat the experience with Condado de Haza, Dehesa la Granja (Zamora), and El Vínculo (La Mancha).

Calle Real 2, 47315 Pesquera de Duero, Valladolid
www.pesqueraafernandez.com

Protos Ribera del Duero

Visitors landing at Madrid's Barajas Airport may notice the same approach to architecture there as at the Protos winery. Both were designed by the Richard Rogers partnership, and are a sign that Ribera del Duero is keen to keep up with its neighbor, Rioja. Protos' beginnings were humble: it started in 1927 as a co-operative of growers. Today's wines, everything from a young Rosado, to a Gran Reserva, are all Tinto Fino (Tempranillo) in American oak. There is a Crianza that also impresses, with a rich palate lifted by cherry fruit, and a long, fresh, chalky finish. Protos also makes a Verdejo in Rueda.

C/Bodegas Protos, 24-28 E-47300 Peñafiel, Valladolid
www.bodegasprotos.com

Quinola Toro

This is a real *vino de garaje*, or "garage wine," launched in 2006. Jaime Suarez, trained in France and Australia, makes just 6,000 bottles from 90-year-old Tinta de Toro that grows at 2,800ft (850m). The grapes are handled with precision to ensure that the rounded tannins match the deep, sumptuous fruit. A modern take on old vines. ★ **Rising star**

Carretera Nacional 122, Km 412, 47540, Pedrosa del Rey,
Villaesther de Arriba; www.quinola.es

Quinta de la Quietud Toro

Jean-François Hebrard's background as consultant to top French wine estates taught him to recognize a good vineyard. The old bush-vine Tinta de Toro in the arid soils of the estate promised quality, so Hebrard bought the vineyard and moved to Toro from Bordeaux. The result has been rapid success. The good-value Corral de Campanas has the floral appeal of the grape with none of the raisined fruit: a frequent risk with Tinta de Toro. Next up, Quietud is denser, bolder, with more forward oak. Top wine La Mula is the finest selection: a very extracted style.

Camino de Bardales, Apdo de Correos 34, 49800, Toro www.
quintaquietud.com

PESQUERA
THE TINTO PESQUERA IS A SMOOTH, FRUITY, TEMPRANILLO, RICH IN TANNINS

RIBERA DE PELAZAS
SOFT, RIPE, AND JAMMY, THIS RED SPENDS 12 MONTHS IN OAK

Real Sitio de Ventosilla Ribera del Duero

Real means "royal" in Spanish, and the "Royal site of Ventosilla's" connections with royalty go back to the days of Queen Isabella of Castile, who purchased it in 1503. Several kings subsequently stayed here. Today it is a hotel set in an extensive estate of over 7,413 acres (3,000ha), of which 1,236 acres (500ha) are vineyards. The wines are typically made of 95% Tempranillo blended with less than 5% Cabernet Sauvignon and Merlot, then matured in American oak before being given a final polish of three months in French oak. The Gran Reserva has the classic rounded sweetness you would expect of Ribera del Duero wines.

10 Km de Aranda de Duero, Carretera Palencia (C-619),
09443 Gumiel de Mercado, Burgos; www.pradorey.com

Reina de Castilla Rueda

It is remarkable how quickly one can establish a winery if one sets one's mind to it. Reina de Castilla is just such a model. A group of 22 growers, owning a total of 4,717 acres (1,909ha), formed a co-operative in 2006. In the briefest of times they have built a capacious, modern winery that is better-looking than many of the rectangular sheds that pepper the Rueda countryside. Inside they make a small range of modern whites; the Reina De Castilla Verdejo is particularly good, with its white peach and fennel tones and minerally complexity.

Camino de la Moya, 47491, La Seca, Valladolid
www.reinadecastilla.es

Rejadorada Toro

Another of Toro's stars, Rejadorada's (the name means "the golden grille") clue to success is its winemaker, who is also the technical director of the local research station. The Remesal family are determined to focus on small production, and source vines from family and friends. The first vintage was made in 1999, in a small, old palace in the center of Toro. In 2003, a winery was opened outside the city. They make only three wines from Tinta del Toro: Rejadorada, which is a lively expression of the variety with just six months in French and Romanian barrels; Novellum Crianza, with 12 months' aging in a blend of French, American, and Romanian oak; and the bold, well-built Sango, which is made with fruit from vines that are over 80 years old; the wine is then aged for 18 months in French oak.

C/ Rejadorada, 11, 49800 Toro
www.rejadorada.com

Ribera de Pelazas Arribes

Situated right up against the River Duero (aka Douro in Portuguese) on its border with Portugal, the Arribes region is revealing plenty of diversity in the wines that originate from its varied vineyard sites. It is also rescuing and revealing the individual characters of the local grape varieties. Ribera de Pelazas is one of the wineries waving the flag for the Juan García grape. In particular its Gran Abadengo, a Reserva, shows the softer, friendlier appeal of this variety.

Camino de la Ermita, Pereña de la Ribera, 37175 Salamanca
www.bodegasriberadepelazas.com

TABULA

THE BOUTIQUE WINERY'S "5" IS FULL OF RICH, BLACK FRUIT MATCHED BY CREAMY OAK

VEGA SICILIA

THE NAME IN SPAIN. THIS PURE TINTO FINO IS A ROUNDED, RIPE, OAKY RED

Sastre Ribera del Duero

This is a model of a family business that has made the leap from grower to producer with outstanding success. When the Sastres established their own estate in 1992, they made a deliberate choice to go for low yields and top quality. In the vineyard, Jesus Sastre follows biodynamic principles, and his wines reflect this focus in their concentration and structure. They make just 1,500 bottles of top wine Pesus (Tinta del País/Cabernet Sauvignon/Merlot), which undergoes "400% new oak" (four sets of new barrels) over 24 months' aging. As a result, it shows great density and richness, with sweet liquorice, prune, and mocha tones. Regina Vides, 100% Tinta del País, is modern and powerful, with supple fruit. The Crianza is more accessible.

San Pedro, 09311 La Horra
www.vinasastre.com

Shaya Rueda

This tiny bodega, packed to the gills with equipment, is a new joint venture between US importer Jorge Ordoñez and the Gil family of Jumilla. Situated on the eastern edge of Rueda, it draws on pre-phylloxera vines. The hand picked grapes are received into a vibrating container, which moves them without breaking them. There are two wines: the 100% Verdejo, which has an elderflower quality, and the Shaya Habis, barrel-fermented and aged in different sizes and shapes of French oak. The winemaker used to work at Naia, and promises to match (or even overtake) his master there. ★Rising star

40462 Aldeanueva del Codonal, Segovia
www.orowines.com

Sitios de Bodega Rueda

Marco, the manager; Ricardo, the winemaker; Alejandra, marketing and media: three children of Antonio Sanz started their own business in 2005 at Sitios de Bodega. The name comes from the traditional term for the place where a grower could set up shop, and the project derives from their eagerness to develop a new approach to Rueda. They own 124 acres (50ha) of organically managed vineyard and produce popular blend Con Class, the Palacio de Menade range of varietal dry whites, and a sweet late-harvest white. In addition, the team manages an old family winery founded in 1870, Terna (meaning "three"). They make serious whites from old, pre-phylloxera vines, and a structured red from regional grape Prieto Picudo. A name to watch. ★Rising star

Cuatro Calles, 47491 La Seca
www.sitiosdebodega.com

Tábula Ribera del Duero

Toward the western border of Ribera, just sneaking inside the DO, lies the modern winery of Tábula, which has quickly reached high ratings. The wines' modern appeal is based on the quality of the limestone soils, double selection of the grapes, fermentation in oak vats, and aging in mainly French oak. The youngest wine, Damana 5, is direct and juicy with five months in oak, a blend of Tempranillo with 5% Cabernet Sauvignon. Gran Tábula sees 18 months in barrel, and is 100% Tempranillo. The Top wine is the lush, fleshy Clave, with powerful notes of toasted mocha. ★Rising star

Carratera de Valbuena, Km 2, 47359 Olivares de Duero, Valladolid; www.bodegastabula.es

Terrazgo Bodegas de Crianza
Arribes del Duero

A tiny project in the glorious Arribes del Duero nature reserve, three winemaking students set up this winery together. Working with old bush vines of local varieties – the cherry-ish Juan García, the youthful Rufete, and the mouth filling Bruñal—they work in small batches to build a wine with a highly individual personality. Just one wine, Terrazgo, is produced: complex and original it is a blend of the three varieties that is fermented in stainless steel and oak, and matured in French, American, and Hungarian oak. ★Rising star

Portugal 7, 49232 Fornillos de Fermoselle, Zamora
www.terrazgo.com

Val de Vid Rueda

With its vineyards 2,297ft (700m) or more above sea level, Val de Vid can rely on fresh, ripe fruit with good acidity in all but the very hottest years. The company was created in 1996 with a focus on Verdejo. Its Eylo (Verdejo with 35% Viura, 5% Sauvignon Blanc) has a lively freshness. Condesa Eylo has Verdejo's typical mouth-filling richness, while Val de Vid is enriched with time spent on its lees.

Carretera Valladolid Medina Km 25,3, 47239 Serrada
0983 559 414

Valderiz Ribera del Duero

This family business, with 185 acres (75ha) of vineyards, is run by Tomás Esteban and sons Juan and Ricardo. They farm organically, and in 2000 introduced biodynamic management in part of the vineyard. In the winery, the process is also entirely natural, with spontaneous fermentation and no added acid, sugar, tannin, or enzymes. Wines include Valderiz, with creamy, spicy oak and rounded tannins; and top wine Tomás Esteban, with sumptuous, dense fruit and warm alcohol. Both are effectively Reservas made from Tinto Fino (Tempranillo).

Carretera Pedrosa, Km 1, 09300 Roa de Duero, Burgos
www.valderiz.com

Valdubón Ribera del Duero

Valdubón belongs to the Ferrer family, which owns Cava producer Freixenet as well as Morlanda in Priorat and Segura Viudas in Penedès; both are members of their Heredad Collection. The wine style is classic Ribera del Duero: 100% Tempranillo, cherry-fruited and balsamic, with firm tannins and increasing proportions of French as opposed to American oak on the higher-ranked wines.

Antigua Carretera, Nacional 1, Km 151, 09460 Milagros, Burgos; www.valdubon.com

Valduero Ribera del Duero

Most of the Valduero winery hides away in tunnels excavated within a hillside, where 3,500 American oak barrels and a million bottles can sit quietly—the essence of the *reserva* and *gran reserva* styles. The García Viadero family owns 494 acres (200ha) of Tinto Fino (Tempranillo) and from it makes wines with a classical structure, with notes of leather and mocha over the red cherry. The Viadero's other properties include Arbucala in Toro, and Rincón de Navas in Rioja.

Carretera de Aranda, 09440 Gumiel del Mercado, Burgos;
www.bodegasvalduero.com

Vega Sicilia Ribera del Duero

The most famous winery in Spain, Vega Sicilia was founded in 1846 and sat in relative isolation until the Ribera del Duero DO was formed in 1982. The significant influence was Mariano García, who joined as winemaker in 1966 and remained for 30 years, then moved on to his own projects at Aalto, Mauro, and Maurodos. The Alvarez family have owned the winery since 1982, and continued the serious investment. The winery may not match the modern architecture that appears in the region today, but winemaker Xavier Ausás runs a glintingly polished and clean operation, with a scrupulous attention to detail. There are three wines: Reserva Especial, a non-vintage from top years; Único, a Gran Reserva, released after 10 years, superbly mature and elegant, and finely integrated; and Valbuena 5, released after five years. The Alión winery next door was launched in 1991 to make modern reds. Aged in new French oak, these Tinto Finos (Tempranillos) are more muscular wines: an interesting contrast in style. In 1997, the Alvarezes acquired Pintía, in Toro, where they make bold wines with typically firmer tannins.

E-47359 Valbuena de Duero
www.vega-sicilia.com

Villaester Toro

Good-value wines from the Belasco family, which also owns Marco Real and Señorío de Andión in Navarra, Viña del Sopié in Rueda, and Belasco de Baquedano in Argentina. The Taurus Crianza, made from 40- to 50-year-old bush vines, shows bright cherry fruit and soft spices. Top label Villaester undergoes a 30-day maceration after fermentation to extract all possible flavor and structure from the grapes, then a secondary malolactic fermentation in new French oak barrels to craft yet more texture. The result is a bold, powerfully built wine, full of extract.

Villaester de Arriba, 47540 Pedrosa del Rey, Valladolid
www.familiabelasco.com

Viñas del Cénit Tierra del Vino de Zamora

The remarkable thing about vineyards here is the soft sand overlying the red clay. Shoes sink, and it is easy to see why phylloxera never invaded. Viñas del Cénit is a shiny, newish project (2003) making serious modern Tempranillos, with ripe alcohol and bold new oak. It was acquired in 2007 by a subsidiary of agriculture firm Inveravante, which also bought Viña Nora (Rías Baixas) and Naia (Rueda), set up wineries in Rioja and in Tierras de Castilla, and has a 55% stake in Alvaro Domecq (Jerez).

Carretera de Circunvalación, 49708, Villanueva de Campeán
www.bodegascenit.com

Viñas de la Vega del Duero Sardon de Duero

This is a joint project between one of Spain's top winemakers, Peter Sisseck (of Dominio de Pingus), and Jérome Bougnaud. The vineyards lie on the western side of the Ribera del Duero region, and are planted with Tinto Fino, and a selection of Bordeaux varieties. Like Pingus, the vineyard is managed biodynamically and has been since the project began in 2002. The wine, Quinta Sardonia, is bold, dense, forward, and ripe, with a chalky, minerally quality. The wine may be classified Vino de la Tierra, but its quality proves it is far superior. ★ Rising star

Granja Sardón, 47340 Sardón de Duero
0650 498353

Viñedos de Nieva Rueda

The region's oldest vines grow on the eastern edge of Rueda. José María (technical director), and his brother, Juan Miguel Herrero Vedel (director general), run the winery; their treasure is very old Verdejo. Some has been planted as high as 2,789ft (850m) on stony soils, some on its own rootstock. The result is consistently excellent. Los Navales is light and young; Pie Franco reveals the purity and slow-to-blossom intensity of old-vine Verdejo. The Sauvignon Blanc, meanwhile, is bold and green with an elegant palate—one to give New Zealand a surprise.

Camino Real, 40447 Nieva, Segovia
www.vinedosdenieva.com

Vinos Sanz Rueda

One of the oldest wineries in Rueda, dating back to 1870. Today, it makes the most modern young wines on the edge of Rueda town (next door to the Palacio de Bornos winery, where the son of the family went to set up his own business). Exceptional examples are the two wines from the Finca la Colina: a Verdejo and a Sauvignon Blanc. Both show powerful expression and character: products of a fine terroir and careful selection.

Carretera Madrid-Coruña Km 170,5, 47490 Rueda
www.vinossanz.com

Vizcarra-Ramos Ribera del Duero

"Garage" production meets Ribera del Duero in Juan-Carlos Vizcarra-Ramos' boutique operation. Old vines are mixed with some newer plantings, and careful selection and small-batch production yield wines with a succulent intensity and silky tannins. The two top labels are named after Vizcarra-Ramos's daughters, Ines and Celia; both have a small amount of Merlot added to the Tempranillo. ★ Rising star

Finca Chirri, 09317 Mambrilla de Castrejón
www.vizcarra.es

Yllera Rueda

Yllera's Viña Cantosan was launched in the 1970s and was one of the first signs that regional white grape variety Verdejo could make a memorably fresh, aromatic white. Cantosan continues and the range here at Yllera now includes a barrel-fermented version as well as *espumosos*: traditional-method sparkling wines made from 100% Verdejo. Here the Yllera family are now in their sixth generation and winemaking has extended across neighboring DOs Ribera del Duero (Bracamonte), Rioja (Coelus), and Toro (Garcilaso), as well as Vino de la Tierra de Castilla y León (notably the deeply extracted Tempranillo Yllera Dominus).

Carretera Madrid-Coruña Km 173,5, 47490 Rueda
www.grupoyllera.com

TELMO RODRIGUEZ

How to pin down Telmo Rodríguez? An intense, dynamic character, he was one of the first of Spain's flying winemakers. Rodríguez made his name rediscovering the country's treasures and making good-value wines, either under his own brands, or for retailers under theirs. Basque by birth, he brought his family's estate, Remelluri, to international fame before leaving in 1994 to start his own business. In Málaga, he revived Moscatel vines to create the floral, candied Molino Real, which restored Málaga's status. In Rioja, Lanzaga continues to improve. In Toro, (Gago; Pago La Jara) as elsewhere, he has located bush vines and propagated them by layering: burying a branch in the ground to form a root. Rodríguez also works in Ribera del Duero, Cigales, Navarra, Valdeorras (making the excellent Godello, Gaba do Xil), and Castilla y León (Pegaso).

CATALONIA

■ Catalonia and Balearic Islands wine regions

Surely the Catalans have it all: their own living language; a coastline crowded with beaches that also provides access across the Mediterranean; fine ingredients and outstanding gastronomy, including a restaurant, El Bullí, that has been regularly voted the best in the world. The same is true when it comes to wine. Catalonia, or Catalunya as it is called in Catalan (and Cataluña in Spanish), is home to Spain's traditional-method sparkling wine: 95% of the country's Cava is produced in the region. Its modern whites are original, individual wines, and its reds range from popular young labels to stratospherically priced, globally famous names. Then there are the more sumptuous whites and reds, the sweet wines, and the traditional oxidized specialities called *rancio*.

Major grapes

Reds

Cabernet Sauvignon/Franc

Cariñena

Garnacha Tinta

Merlot

Syrah

Tempranillo

Whites

Albariño

Chardonnay

Garnacha Blanca

Macabeo

Xarel-lo (Pansà Blanca)

Vintages

2009
Very promising across the board. Drink rosados ASAP.

2008
A cool vintage kept alcohol down; fruit shines through.

2007
Excellent, but all but the best whites should be drunk soon.

2006
For some, like Conca de Barberà, an excellent, fresh year; for hotter zones, fruit was baked.

2005
A great year in some parts of Catalonia, but Montsant and Priorat were disappointing: some hard wines.

2004
A very good year, with some excellent wines.

The Catalans are rightly proud of their region, but they suffered for this independent spirit during the long period of fascist government that followed the Spanish Civil War. Since the 1970s, though, Catalonia has come bouncing back: in its economy, its architecture, its soccer, the success of the 1992 Olympics in Barcelona, and its wines. Old vineyards have been revitalized, new ones planted, and, particularly since 1990, there has been a flurry of new wineries and new Denominación de Origens (DOs).

The most famous of the latter is Priorat, also known as Priorato in the Castilian- and English-speaking worlds. This mountainous region had spent the latter half of the 20th century on the verge of collapse, following the destruction of vines by the phylloxera vine louse and the postwar desertion of its villages, yet a group of pioneers managed to turn its fortunes around by working the scant soil and creating wines that have won international acclaim—and sky-high prices. Slowly, jobs and tourism have revived the local economies, and the region gained the sought-after, high-quality tier of Denominación de Origen Calificada (DOCa) status—only the second to do so, after Rioja.

From Priorat, enthusiasm spread to neighboring Montsant. Here, they have revived the reputations of Garnacha and Cariñena, which were long criticized as workhorse grapes. Garnacha has now joined the ranks of the serious varietals, with seminars being held around the world for enthusiasts.

Priorat and Montsant are only one part of Catalonia's rebirth. The region's wine industry begins right up against the French Mediterranean border, where the mountains roll down to the sea at Empordà, and there is a burgeoning production of fine-quality reds. Farther south, toward Gerona, the widely scattered DO of Costers del Segre is full of interest, with vineyards growing such unexpected varieties as Albariño and Riesling. In Alella, there is a trend toward white wines, and its nearby neighbor of Pla de Bages has become a good source of reliable, well-priced wines. In the hills behind Barcelona, Miguel Torres has helped put Conca de Barberà on the map by creating exceptional wines from beautiful vineyards near Milmanda Castle and by the *grans muralles* ("great walls") of a Cistercian monastery.

Catalonia abounds in religious history, from the priory that gave its name to Priorat, to the winery of De Muller in Tarragona, which continues to make communion wine. There is also the monastery of Montserrat, which dominates the mountains around Barcelona.

Between Montserrat and the sea lies Penedès, with its remarkable concentration of Cava producers. The Cava houses are monuments to the Catalans' ability to sell their wares.

Finally, the Balearic Islands should not be overlooked as far as winemaking is concerned. Mallorca is the largest, and as a wine producer it is also the most important. Venture inland from the beaches and away from the tourist haunts and you'll come across extensive vineyards. Yet very little wine is exported beyond Spain: with 12 million visitors, Mallorca can easily sell much of its wine on the island. Menorca, Formentera, and Ibiza (Vino de la Tierra de Eivissa) all produce wine, and may one day match Mallorca's success.

Whether on the islands or the mainland, Catalans have retained their famous adaptability. Nowhere is this more evident than in its wines.

4 kilos Vino de la Tierra de Mallorca

Francesc Grimalt, formerly of An Negra, started this project in 2006 with musician and marketing expert Sergio Caballero, who gives the brand its style. The 4 kilos name denotes the very modest initial investment of 4 million pesetas. The wines reveal Grimalt's fascination with the red Callet grape, which is sourced from across the island. The second wine is 12 Volts, named after the expression of energy in a battery, and is a four-varietal blend led by Callet. All wines are modern, deeply extracted, and well-balanced: a rapid result from a skilled winemaker selecting the best fruit. ★ **Rising star**

1a. Volta, Puigverd 168, 07200 Felanitx, Mallorca
www.4kilos.com

Abadal Pla de Bages

It is hard to believe that the DO Pla de Bages is so young (1995), given that a winery like Abadal already presents such a confident, established image. Pla de Bages lies inland from Barcelona, and is host to a growing number of modern winemakers who are more than capable of using French varietals as well as Spanish ones. Of the Abadal whites, the Picapoll is ripe and crisp; of the reds, the Cabernet Franc/Tempranillo will charm lovers of Cabernet Franc's elegant structure. Merlot 5 is a blend of five varietal clones.

Maised D'Avinyó, 08279 Avinyó, Barcelona
www.abadal.net

Acústic Montsant

The Acústic wines are originals, refecting the philosophy of owner Albert Jané Ubeda. He does not want to make wine to fit modern, globalized styles. His white wine, from Garnacha Blanca, Macabeo, and Pansàl, shows zesty acidity and a complex, textured palate. The Acústic red is an almost 50/50 blend of the local red grapes. Brao ("brave") demonstrates how it is possible to make good wine and still keep the prices down.

St Lluis 12, 43777 Els Guiamets, Tarragona
629 472 988

Albet i Noya Penedès

For those who prefer to drink wines from organically grown grapes, Albet i Noya is a blessing. The firm is one of the most reliable and interesting organic producers in the world. It makes a point of the fact that sulfur dioxide levels are kept as low as possible. The brand's appeal is global, too—and not just to consumers who prefer organically grown grapes. The quality of the wines is high throughout the range of Spanish and international varieties, including some scarcer reds such as Caladoc and Arinarnóa. The Cava is also very reliable.

Can Vendrell de la Codina, 08739 Sant Pau d'Ordal, Barcelona; www.albetinoya.com

Alella Vinícola Alella

A walk in Alella Vinícola's vineyards reveals the Mediterranean to the east and Barcelona to the south: a clue to the nature of the business as it now stands. The company started as the Alella co-operative in the first decade of the 20th century, and was a bustling winery serving the city with one popular brand: Marfil ("marble"). As Barcelona encroached, however, the vineyards began to disappear. In 1998, Alella Vinícola

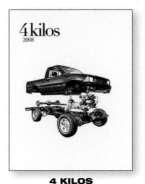

4 KILOS
ISLAND STYLE: THE JAZZ-FUNK LABEL
HERALDS A MODERN, BALANCED WINE

ALBET I NOYA
ORGANIC BY NATURE, WELL-MADE
AND HIGH-QUALITY BY DESIGN

became a private company. The Marfil name continues, now joined by Ivori, a serious white blend that is fermented in French oak. Look for the traditional sweet wines.

Rambla Àngel Guimerà 62, 08328 Alella, Barcelona
www.alellavinicola.com

Alemany i Corrio Penedès

In a region of large producers, the winery of husband-and-wife team Laurent Corrio and Irene Alemany is tiny. Both studied in Burgundy; Corrio is French. From their Merlot, Cabernet Sauvignon, and Cariñena vines they produce just 10,000 bottles. Their first wine, Sot Lefriec, was named after Corrio's grandmother, and shows the density and power to be expected of a "garage" wine, with small production and careful avoidance of oxygen in the winemaking. Pas Curtei is the second label. ★ **Rising star**

Melio 78, Vilafranca del Penedès, 08720 Barcelona
938 172 587

Alvaro Palacios Priorat

Fresh from working in Bordeaux at Château Pétrus, and from a Rioja family, Palacios Remondo, Alvaro Palacios set up his own winery in Priorat in 1989. He applied his knowledge of modern fine winemaking to the old vines with immediate success. With his combination of winemaking skill and force of personality, he has been significant in building the global reputation and high prices of this isolated zone. Palacios talks passionately of his wine's semi-spiritual qualities. Les Terrasses is the most accessibly priced, with sumptuous black fruit, liquorice, spice, and supple tannins. Finca Dofi reveals Priorat's classic minerality, and is a well-priced version of the exceptional top wine, L'Ermita. Both wines are old-vine Garnachas and leaders in the movement to restore the reputation of top-quality Garnacha/Grenache in Spain and France.

Afores, 43737 Gratallops, Tarragona
977 839 195

Àn Negra Vino de La Tierra de Mallorca

This is the star that has spread glamour across the island wines. Established in Felanitx in 1994, it lies within the Pla i Llevant DO but prefers the independence of Vino de La Tierra status. The focus is on local varieties, and every wine is of interest—although prices can be eye-watering. Quíbia immediately attracts: a floral, minerally white blend of Prensal and (red) Callet. An 2 is a young red blend that spends a year in oak; An, 95% Callet, shows dense, aromatic fruit with a ripe, spicy note and a firm grip on the finish from 17 months in French oak. Son Negre, a similar blend, is the special selection of the best Callet.

Avda 3a Volta 18, 07200 Felanitx, Illes Balears
www.annegra.com

Biniagual Binissalem Mallorca

This lovely estate is where George Sand stayed with her lover, Frederic Chopin, in the 19th century. It closed following the economic collapse of the 20th century, but it was purchased in 1967, and has been carefully restored. Wine production began again in 1999, with the same attention to detail. Gran Verán, a Manto Negro/Shiraz blend, is particularly good: the Shiraz adds real weight,

CATALONIA

The traditional day trip for a visitor to Barcelona was to Penedès, to see the great Cava cellars or the extensive Torres visitor center. In recent times, there has been much more for a wine lover with a car to explore. From the fiercely hot coast to the cool hills inland, Catalonia has a diversity of terroirs that produces an equally wide range of wines, from the crisp and sparkling to the sweet and concentrated. A regional highlight has to be Priorat, with its steep, slate vineyards, and the surrounding Montsant. Here, there seems to be a permanent mist resting on these hills, which only adds to their otherworldliness.

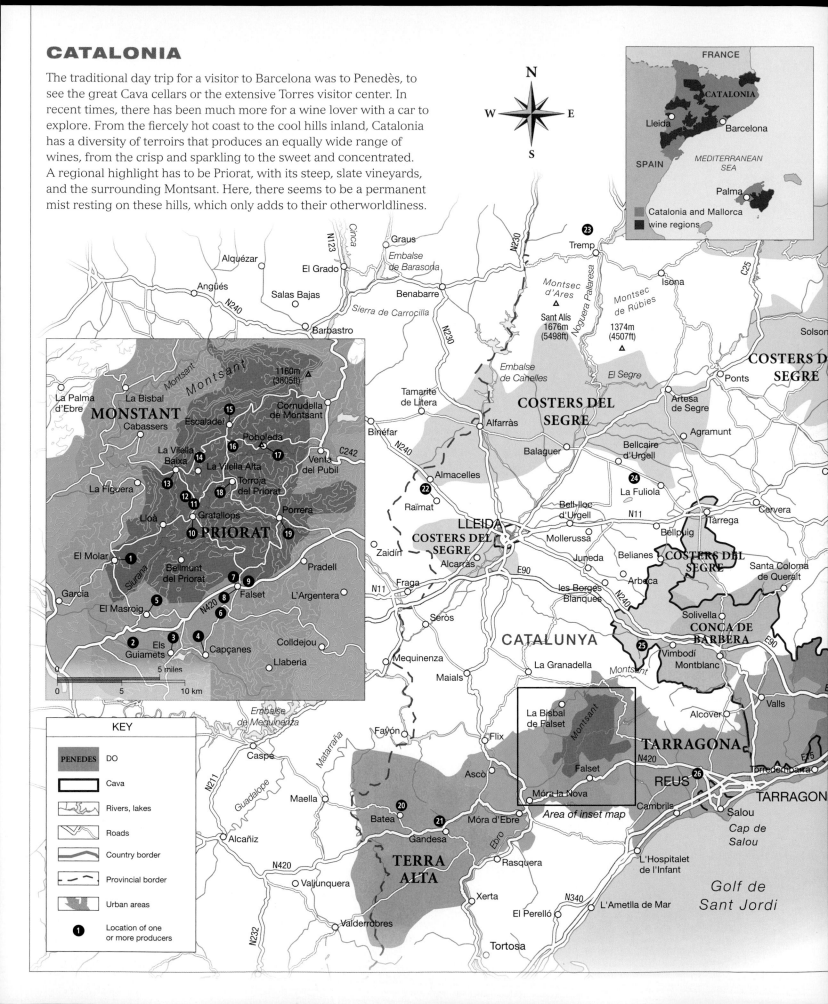

FRANCE
CATALONIA
Lleida
Barcelona
SPAIN
MEDITERRANEAN SEA
Palma

Catalonia and Mallorca
wine regions

KEY

PENEDES	DO
	Cava
	Rivers, lakes
	Roads
	Country border
	Provincial border
	Urban areas
①	Location of one or more producers

MONTSANT
PRIORAT
COSTERS DEL SEGRE
CONCA DE BARBERA
TERRA ALTA
TARRAGONA
CATALUNYA

PRODUCERS

4 Kilos 46	Clos d'Agon 34	Mas Doix 17
Abadal 31	Clos Mogador 10	Mas d'En Gil 5
Acústic 3	Clos I Terrasses 10	Mas Igneus 11
Albet i Noya 30	Combier-Fischer-Gérin	Mas Martinet 10
Alella Vinícola 33	Associés 19	Mas Perinet 16
Alemany i Corrio 29	Costers del Siurana 10	Miquel Gelabert 44
Alvaro Palacios 10	De Muller 26	Miquel Oliver 43
An Negra 47	Domini de la	Morlanda 7
Biniagual 39	Cartoixa 1	Mortitx 37
Binigrau 40	Dominio de Terroir al	Parés Baltà 27
Buil i Giné 12	Limit 18	Portal del Montsant 6
Can Blau 7	Edetària 21	Raimat 22
Can Majoral 41	Etim 8	Ribas 39
Can Rafols dels	Ferrer-Bobet 7	Ripoll Sans 11
Caus 30	Jaume Mesquida 42	Sangenís i Vaqué 19
Castell d'Encus 23	Joan d'Anguera 2	Scala Dei 15
Castell del Remei 24	Joan Sangenís 19	Tomàs Cusiné 25
Castillo Perelada 35	José L Ferrer 38	Toni Gelabert 45
Celler de Capçanes 4	L'Encastell 19	Torres 28
Celler Laurona 7	Macía Batle 36	Vall-Llach 19
Celler del Pont 13	Marqués de Alella 32	Venus La Universal 9
Cims de Porrera 19	Mas Alta 14	Vinos Piñol 20

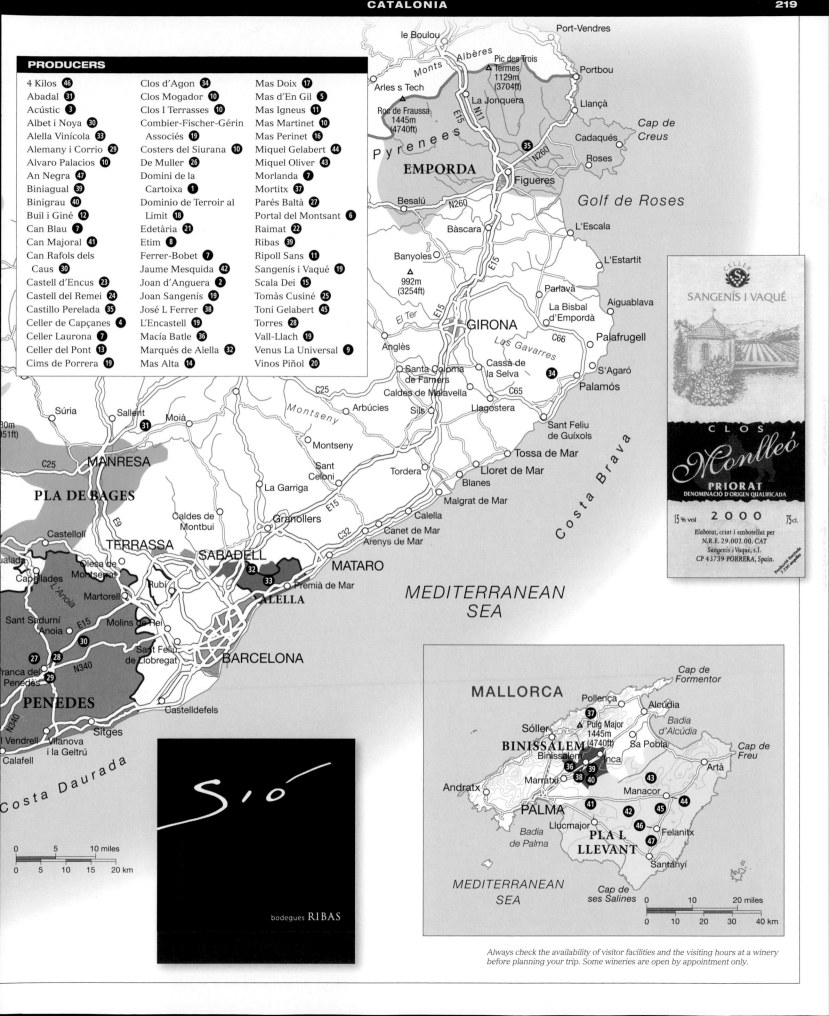

Map labels (Catalonia):

le Boulou · Port-Vendres · Albères · Monts · Pic des Trois · Termes 1129m (3704ft) · Portbou · Arles s Tech · La Jonquera · Llançà · Roc de Fraussa 1445m (4740ft) · Pyrenees · EMPORDA · N260 · Cap de Creus · Cadaqués · Roses · Figueres · Golf de Roses · Besalú · N260 · L'Escala · Bàscara · L'Estartit · Banyoles · 992m (3254ft) · Parlavà · L'Estartit · La Bisbal d'Empordà · Aiguablava · El Ter · GIRONA · Palafrugell · Anglès · Las Gavarres · Cassà de la Selva · S'Agaró · C66 · Palamós · Santa Coloma de Farners · Caldes de Malavella · C65 · C25 · Arbúcies · Sils · Llagostera · Sant Feliu de Guíxols · Montseny · Súria · Sallent · Moià · Montseny · Tossa de Mar · MANRESA · Sant Celoni · Tordera · Lloret de Mar · PLA DE BAGES · La Garriga · Blanes · C25 · Granollers · Malgrat de Mar · Costa Brava · Caldes de Montbui · E15 · Calella · Castellolí · TERRASSA · C32 · Canet de Mar · SABADELL · Arenys de Mar · MATARO · Olesa de Montserrat · MEDITERRANEAN SEA · Capellades · L'Anoia · Rubí · Premià de Mar · Martorell · ALELLA · Sant Sadurní d'Anoia · E15 · Molins de Rei · BARCELONA · Sant Feliu de Llobregat · Franca del Penedès · N340 · PENEDES · Castelldefels · Vilanova i la Geltrú · Sitges · El Vendrell · Vilanova · Calafell · Costa Daurada

Scale: 0 5 10 miles · 0 5 10 15 20 km

Mallorca inset:

MALLORCA · Cap de Formentor · Pollença · Alcudia · Sóller · Puig Major 1445m (4740ft) · Badia d'Alcúdia · BINISSALEM · Sa Pobla · Cap de Freu · Binissalem · Inca · Andratx · Marratxí · Artà · Manacor · PALMA · Badia de Palma · Llucmajor · PLA I LLEVANT · Felanitx · MEDITERRANEAN SEA · Cap de ses Salines · Santanyí

Scale: 0 10 20 miles · 0 10 20 30 40 km

Always check the availability of visitor facilities and the visiting hours at a winery before planning your trip. Some wineries are open by appointment only.

Wine label: CELLER · SANGENÍS I VAQUÉ · CLOS Monlleó · PRIORAT · DENOMINACIÓ D'ORIGEN QUALIFICADA · 15 % vol · 2000 · 75 cl. · Elaborat, criat i embotellat per N.R.E. 29.002.00. CAT Sangenís i Vaqué, s.l. CP 43739 PORRERA, Spain. · Producció limitada 7.330 ampolles

Label: Sió · bodegues RIBAS

CASTELL D'ENCUS
SPANISH RIESLING FINALLY COMES OF AGE
IN EKAM, HELPED BY A LITTLE ALBARINO

the palate is supple and soft, and the finish long. Finca Biniagual Verán also adds Cabernet to this pair, giving complex, powerful eucalyptus and balsamic notes.

Ap de correus 5, 07350 Binissalem, Mallorca
www.bodegabiniagual.com

Binigrau Binissalem Mallorca
A relatively small winery with a good pedigree: brothers Miguel and Mathias Batle are members of the Macia Batle family who set up on their own in 2002. Production is now up to 90,000 bottles. Mathias Batle is very respectful of the environment, and several of his wines are organic, including the Ecològic Rosat (rosé), from Manto Negro and Merlot—a youthful burst of berry fruits and spice. Obac blends the vineyard's five red varietals to make a midweight style that is perfumed, has a citric lift and a firm, dark finish. ★ **Rising star**

Calle de Fiol 33, 07143 Biniali, Mallorca
www.binigrau.es

Buil i Giné Priorat
This is another family with a long history in the region who returned to take up where its predecessors left off. The makers gave their first wine, in 1997, the memorable name Giné Giné, after their grandfather. It shows the minerality of the soil, along with youthful red fruit. The Rosat (*rosado* in Castilian) is a fine example of a rosé wine: the Garnacha/Merlot blend provides a basket of fruit. Joan Giné Giné is their version of the weighty, tannic Priorat style. The family also makes reds in Montsant and Toro, and a crunchy, fresh Verdejo in Rueda.

Carretera Gratallops, Vilella Baixa Km 11,5, 43737
Gratallops, Priorat; www.builgine.com

Can Blau Montsant
Can Blau is a joint project located in the village of Mas Roig between US importer Jorge Ordoñez and the Juan Gil family of El Nido in Jumilla. The winemaker is Australian Sarah Morris, who built her experience at Torbreck in the Barossa Valley. Can Blau is densely colored; its dark berry fruit silky with a firm grip of tannin. Given its 20 months' aging in French oak, it benefits from several years' maturation in bottle. Mas de Can Blau is altogether bolder, more dense, and powerfully oaked. ★ **Rising star**

Carretera de Bellmunt, 43730 Falset, Tarragona
690 818 509

Can Majoral Pla i Llevant
Can Majoral earns its place as a rising star for its sheer adventurousness. The business started in 1979, and now the nephew has taken over from his uncle. He favors organic farming with some biodynamic practices, and has converted to this wholeheartedly, despite the fact that he was a student of technical winemaking in Spain and Australia. Innovations include some experimental plantings of the aromatic white grape Giró, Riesling, and the red Gargollasa, and perhaps less seriously, Pinot Noir. Cabernet/Merlot/Syrah blend San Roig is a dense, smoky, and raisined wine that is well worth trying. ★ **Rising star**

Callejón del Campanar, 07210 Algaida
www.canmajoral.com

Can Rafols dels Caus Penedès
This is a lovely old property, high up in the massif mountains. The isolation enables the avoidance of synthetic chemicals in the vineyard and commercial yeasts in the winery. They have a wide range of French varietals in the vineyards and draw on these successfully in two multivarietal blends: Petit Caus red and white. Other wines of interest include a plummy, meaty, red-colored Rosado, a Riesling, and a Pinot Noir. Aso seek out the barrel-fermented white El Rocallís, made from rarely seen Italian grape variety Incrozio Manzoni.

Masía Can Rafols dels Caus, 08793 Avinyonet del Penedès,
Barcelona; www.canrafolsdelscaus.com

Castell d'Encus Costers del Segre
Costers del Segre is one of the most fragmented DOs in Spain. Castell d'Encus is one of the higher (2,620–3,280ft/800–1,000m), more distant vineyards. The site dates back to the 11th century, and the stone basins where the monks made wine are still visible. Today, it is home to a very promising project run by Raúl Bobet, former chief winemaker at Torres. He wanted a site cool enough to make Riesling (with a little Albariño). The result, Ekam, is impressively zesty and very persistent, with a lightly bitter edge. Taleia is a Sauvignon/Semillon blend, lean and creamy. ★ **Rising star**

Carretera Tremp a Sta. Engracia, Km 5, 25630, Talarn, Lleida
www.encus.org

Castell del Remei Costers del Segre
This estate was always interesting: an extensive, dynamic property influenced by Bordeaux in the late 19th century. Eventually the business faltered, but it was snapped up by the Cusiné family, an important name in the DO. The equipment was entirely renovated and the wines renewed. Oda, the Chardonnay/Macabeo blend, is a classic for the region, with eight months in cask; Gotim Bru (a local name for Tempranillo) is a Cabernet Sauvignon/Merlot/Tempranillo blend, and a Garnacha matured in American oak has a balsamic richness. The Oda red is bolder and more structured. Cérvoles, a related estate, has an impressive array of modern wines. Particularly strong is the complex, barrel-fermented Chardonnay/Macabeo, with its creamy, herbal notes, and the red Estrats, a Cabernet Sauvignon-dominated blend, with an impressively pure minerality.

Finca Castell del Remei, 25333, Penelles, Lleida
www.castelldelremei.com

Castillo Perelada Empordà
There is a crenellated castle at Perelada, which includes not just a winery, but also a chic hotel and spa as well: worth a detour if the beaches are too full. At the *castillo*, the wine is definitely improving, catching up with the quality of the tourist offerings. The Cavas are also becoming fresher and livelier. Among the still wines, promising developments include Ex Ex, which is 100% Monastrell; and Finca Garbet, a 100% Syrah. A specialty is the Garnatxa de l'Empordà, a fortified wine made the traditional way from white and red Garnacha, and aged in a solera system for 12 years.

Plaça del Carme 1, 17491 Perelada, Girona
www.castilloperelada.com

CLOS MOGADOR
RENE BARBIER'S WINES TEND TO BE BOLD
BUT WITH TYPICAL PRIORAT FRESHNESS

Celler de Capçanes Montsant

A strong contender for Spain's best co-op, with a broad range of well-made, great-value wines. Created in 1933, it became a successful quality wine business following a commission from the Jewish community of Barcelona to produce a kosher wine. The result, Flor de Primavera ("spring flower"), is a Cabernet Sauvignon/Garnacha/Cariñena blend, and is excellent. Mas Collet is a good-value introduction to the flavors of Montsant. The top wine is Cabrida, 100% old-vine Garnacha; bold, tough, and dense.

Carrer Llaberia 4, 43776 Capçanes, Tarragona
www.cellercapcanes.com

Celler Laurona Montsant

Laurona started in 1999 as a joint venture between René Barbier of Clos Mogador and Englishman Christopher Cannan, a shipper of top wines since the 1970s at Europvin. Cannan's first investment in winemaking was Clos Figueras in Priorat, on the advice of Barbier. New partners have entered the Laurona business since its early days, but the style remains. Of the two wines, Laurona reflects Montsant's diverse soils, with Garnacha, Cariñena, Syrah, Cabernet Sauvignon, and Merlot. The small-production Selecció de 6 Vinyes is intended to be a modern remake of the traditional Garnacha/Cariñena blend.

Carretera de Bellmunt, 43730 Falset, Tarragona
www.cellerlaurona.com

Celler del Pont Priorat

This producer is the very essence of the new spirit of winemaking in Spain. Created by a group of friends with connections to Priorat, the winery hides behind an anonymous door in La Vilella Baixa. Winemaker Montse Nadal, who also teaches enology at Tarragona University, makes just one wine: Lo Givot. This is an organically grown Garnacha/Cariñena/Cabernet Sauvignon/Syrah blend aged in French oak, with 10% American oak barrels. Blackberries mingle with liquorice and exotic spices, together with the scent of vanilla and cedar from the oak.

Calle del Riu 1, 43374 La Vilella Baixa, Priorat
www.cellerdelpont.com

Cims de Porrera Priorat

Cims means "summit," and describes the position of the vineyards on the slopes around the village of Porrera. These wines are a project at the local co-op under the auspices of one of Priorat's leading winemakers, Sara Pérez, and her brother, Adriá. They show a clear expression of Cariñena, its spicy fruit complemented by lesser amounts of Garnacha and Cabernet Sauvignon. Single-vineyard Finca Pigat and Finca La Tena are both 100% Cariñena: big, bold, dense wines, with the high alcohol typical of the grape variety. The Classic is only made in the best years.

Carretera de Torroja, 43739 Porrera, Tarragona
977 828 233

Clos d'Agon Catalonia

A winery that was bound to catch the critics' eyes. A group of Swiss friends bought top-quality vineyards in the Empordà region of Catalonia, near the coast west of Girona. They recruited Peter Sisseck of Pingus to make the first vintage (he still consults). The white is a classic southern Rhône blend of Roussanne, Viognier, and Marsanne; the two reds draw on Cabernets Sauvignon and Franc, Syrah, Merlot, and Petit Verdot. The result is impressively pure and powerful, with vibrant blue- and blackberry fruit, and cedary, oaky tones. ★**Rising star**

Mas Gil SL, Apt Correus 117, 17251 Calonge, Costa Brava
www.closdagon.com

Clos Mogador Priorat

One of Priorat's great names. René Barbier's colleagues in the Priorat renaissance included Alvaro Palacios, Josep Lluis Pérez (Clos Martinet), and Carles Pastrana (Costers del Siurana). Barbier advises at a number of wineries. The estate is named after a novel, *Les Gens de Mogador*, written by his great aunt, which is about family life near Mont Ventoux. Small, steep, dry-farmed, and very low-yielding vineyards produce concentrated wines from the local grapes, along with Cabernet, Syrah, and—unexpectedly—Pinot Noir. Clos Mogador is very bold and complex, dense with tannin, and with Priorat's keynote freshness. Barbier also owns Clos Nelin, one of the region's most distinguished white wines, and Clos Manyetes, a profoundly complex Cariñena/Garnacha blend.

Camí Manyetes, 43737 Gratallops, Tarragona
closmogador.com

Clos I Terrasses Priorat

There was one woman among the original Priorat pioneers: French-born Daphne Glorian. Her tiny vineyard's bush vines yielded just enough grapes to make a bottle of wine, vinified for her at Clos Mogador. She now has her own property (formerly Alvaro Palacio's). Married to US importer Eric Solomon, the US is where the majority of Glorian's production ends up. Clos Erasmus regularly wins the highest scores, and is a powerful combination of tense minerality, with deep extract, and roasted ripe fruit and exotic spice. Laurel is the second wine.

Valls 24, 43737 Gratallops, Tarragona
977 839 426

Combier-Fischer-Gérin Associés Priorat

This has the air of an old-fashioned joke about three famous winemakers: two Frenchmen from the Rhône (from Châteauneuf-du-Pape and Côte-Rôtie) and a Dutchman from Provence, setting up shop on a hillside in Priorat. Yet this is not a joke—just an opportunity for some great winemaking with varieties they already know well: Garnacha and Syrah. Ríu has just 2% Syrah and is the most accessible of the wines. Trio Infernal 0/3 is the Garnacha-based white, and then the range rises through 1/3 and 2/3. 2/3 is a dark, profound Cariñena, with marked minerality.

Del Pont 9, 43737 Gratallops, Tarragona
977 839 403

Costers del Siurana Priorat

Carles Pastrana was a leader of the pioneers who revived Priorat. He has been handsomely rewarded by old-vine Garnacha and Cariñena and newer plantings of Merlot, Cabernet Sauvignon, and Syrah. Clos de l'Obac is a dense, deeply extracted wine, aged in French oak. (The winery is widely known as Clos de l'Obac, despite its real name of Costers del Siurana.) Miserere is the powerful single-estate top wine. Dolç de l'Obac is a fascinating sweet red made

LLICORELLA

Every technical conversation about wine around the world turns to a conversation about soil. Clay, sand, loam... In Priorat they are onto something special, and they know it. This is a soil you can taste, not just scuff with your shoe. Of volcanic origin, the topsoil is a mix of slate and glinting quartz. Below this lies a brownish mix of particles of slate and quartz. This is the soil they call *llicorella*. Combined with the region's very hot, very dry summers, vines grown on *llicorella* are low-yielding, with concentrated fruit, producing high alcohol levels and a mineral note that is almost salty.
The lack of *llicorella* is what separates Priorat from Montsant in taste—and price—terms.

L'ENCASTELL
DENSE BUT APPROACHABLE, MARGE
IS A MODERN GARNACHA BLEND

JAUME MESQUIDA
FRUIT IS THE WATCHWORD IN THIS FRESH
CABERNET SAUVIGNON/MERLOT BLEND

from Garnacha, Cabernet Sauvignon, and Syrah: it is fully ripe, with round tannins and a mochalike richness.

Camí Manyanetes, Pol. 11, 43737 Gratallops, Tarragona
www.costersdelsiurana.com

De Muller Tarragona
This is one of the great old names of Catalonia, dating back to 1851. It was a different world then, and the company still remains loyal to traditional style, especially sweet wines, wines aged in soleras similar to those in Jerez, and *rancio* wines: aged, oxidized wines based on Garnacha. It is particularly famous for its communion wine. De Muller is a large company, able to offer sparkling wine as well as a full range of still whites and reds, among them a good, modern Cabernet Sauvignon. It also produces wine in Priorat.

Camí Pedra Estela 34, 43205 Reus, Tarragona
www.demuller.es

Domini de la Cartoixa Priorat
As the name suggests, the vineyard land here once belonged to the Carthusian monks of the priory (*priorat*) of Scala Dei, who needed wine for sacramental purposes. The vines are grown organically, and from them the Pérez Dalmau family makes Galena and Clos Galena. Miguel Pérez is an enologist and university professor who is enthusiastic about his wines. Galena is a red blend, aged in French and American oak, full and fleshy with liquorice and balsamic highlights. Clos Galena has a resounding tannic core, but with generous balancing fruit.

Camí de la Solana, 43736 El Molar, Tarragona
www.closgalena.com

Dominio de Terroir al Limit Priorat
It was the powerful impression left by a tasting of Clos Martinet 1994 and Clos Mogador 1994 that prompted one of South Africa's brightest winemakers, Eben Sadie, to book a trip to Priorat. Now, with Dominik Huber from Germany, he works with a number of vineyard parcels producing very small quantities. Innovations in the cellar include concrete egg-shaped fermentors, which they like to use for the easily oxidized Garnacha. Dits del Terra ("Fingers of the Earth") was their first wine, and there are plans for a greater diversity of styles. Dits is strong on tannin and extraction, with plenty of black fruit and a graphite minerality. ★ **Rising star**

Calle de Baixà Font 12, Torroja del Priorat 43737
977 828 057

Edetària Terra Alta
The vines may be old, but this is a young enterprise with plenty of energy, its white grapes echoing the promise of Terra Alta's characterful whites. Here they blend Garnacha Blanca with some Muscat, Macabeo, even "experimental" Viognier, which is not yet formally permitted in the DO. Fermentation and maturation take place in French oak, which adds texture and complexity. Reds are made from an old version of Garnacha—Garnacha Peluda—as well as from a collection of spicy blends. The sweet red Dolç, from Garnacha and Cabernet, has a fleshy, red-fruit appeal. ★ **Rising star**

Finca El Mas, Carretera Gandesa, Vilalba, 43780 Gandesa,
Tarragona; www.edetaria.com

Etim Montsant
Etim's wines are impressively good value for money in a notoriously pricy region. They are made at the co-op in Falset, an ornate building designed in Gaudì style. Etim makes a wide range of wines. Blanco is a good introduction to the potential of Garnacha Blanca; Seleccio Syrah is similar to Rhône reds; and the red Verema Tardana is a lip-smacking example of Montsant's sweet reds.

Calle Miquel Barceló 13, 43730 Falset, Tarragona
977 830 105

Ferrer-Bobet Priorat
Sergí Ferrer-Salat and Raúl Bobet make a powerful partnership. Ferrer-Salat is a successful businessman with a strong interest in wine; Bobet was technical director of Torres for 16 years. Their glass-fronted winery, perched like a flying saucer on top of a hillside, hides a treasure trove of small oak vats. In the vineyard their goal is to work organically. The first vintage was 2005 and headed a poll for the top wine in Spain. The 2006 has a floral purity above the power of the mid-palate. The Selecció Especial has a savory, leathery intensity. ★ **Rising star**

Carretera Falset a Porrera, 43730 Falset, Tarragona
www.ferrerbobet.com

Jaume Mesquida Pla i Llevant
The Jaume Mesquida winery is tucked tightly into the center of the village of Porreres. Brother and sister Bárbara and Jaume are the fourth generation, and they took over in 2004: a young, dynamic pair with ambitions for the business. Jaume's first step has been to convert to biodynamics in the vineyard. Chardonnays are promising; the unoaked version is fresh, with an exotic edge. The Rosat de Rosa is a fruity Cabernet Sauvignon/Merlot blend; and the Cabernets have a distinct purity. ★ **Rising star**

Calle de la Vileta 7, 07260 Porreres, Mallorca
www.jaumemesquida.com

Joan d'Anguera Montsant
This estate is two centuries old, but it qualifies as a rising star because it is now in the hands of a new generation, brothers Joan and Josep. It specializes in Syrah (introduced by their father), and is in conversion to biodynamic production. Garnatxa is a young, bright 100% Garnacha; at the top end of the scale Bugader is 95% Syrah/5% Garnacha. Bold and spicy with firm tannins and warm alcohol, it also has typical black currant Syrah fruit.

C/Major, 43746 Darmós, Tarragona
www.cellersjoandanguera.com

Joan Sangenís Priorat
This family business in Porrera supplied grapes to the local co-op for many years, until Joan Sangenís started the winery in 1995. He has 198 acres (80ha) of vines to draw from, with an average age of 50 years, some more than 100. Self-taught, and an observant, thoughtful winemaker, Sangenís produces two ranges. Cal Pla wines emphasise fruit. Mas d'En Compte are more structured. Particularly interesting is the exotic, fleshy, barrel-fermented Mas d'En Compte, a rare Priorat white from Garnacha Blanca, Picapoll (France's Picpoul), Pansà Blancà, and Macabeo.

Plaza de Esglèsia 6, 43739 Porrera, Spain, Tarragona
977 828 045

José L Ferrer Binissalem Mallorca

José L Ferrer is the largest of Binissalem's wineries, and one of the island's grand old names, founded in 1931. Visitors are welcome, and it is a good place to see how winemaking equipment has developed over time. Ferrer is still changing. It has a new consultant who came from Macía Batle; it is experimenting with barrels (including Russian and Mongolian oak); and its modern Dues blends are having some success (notably the Syrah/Callet). Also look for the sweet Moscatel, Veritas Dolç.

Conquistador 103, Carretera Palma-Alcudia, 07350 Binissalem, Mallorca; www.vinosferrer.com

L'Encastell Priorat

A family business with a history of selling wine to other producers. Carme Figuerola and Raimon Castellví turned it around in 1999, building a new winery, and making two wines from their two small estates. The bulk of production is Marge, a Garnacha blend aged in French oak barrels (that have already been used once) and in American oak. The result is an approachable Priorat, with the typical structure and density. Its big brother is Roquers de Porrera, altogether bolder and more complex. ★ Rising star

Carrer del Castell 13, 43739 Porrera, Tarragona www.roquers.com

Macía Batle Binissalem Mallorca

In a world of health and safety regulations, Macía Batle's open-door policy is welcome. Visitors are encouraged to walk around the winery; as they say, they like to show there are no secrets. Visitors to the island should be sure to sample the *blanc de blancs* sparkling Prensal/Chardonnay. Reds show the potential of Manto Negro, the grape that has to make up at least 50% of any Binissalem red. The Reserva Privada has a fleshy richness, with hints of orange and raisined fruit characteristic of the island.

Camí de Coanegra, 07320 Santa Maria del Cami, Mallorca www.maciabatle.com

Marqués de Alella Alella

One of the most widely recognized names in the Alella DO, mainly due to the backing of its owner, Cava house Parxet. Marqués de Alella specializes in white wines. Single-varietals include a fresh Xarel-lo (aka Pansà Blanca); an oaked, spicy, opulent Chardonnay; and a fruity, floral Viognier. All are fresh, well-balanced styles, with relatively low alcohol levels: a good choice for summer.

08106 Santa Maria de Martorelles, Barcelona www.marquesdealella.com

Mas Alta Priorat

A young project with a great pedigree, run by a team that includes well-known French merchant Michel Tardieu. Formerly called Vinyes Mas Romani, the property, with its 60-to-100-year-old vines, is near Clos Erasmus. Artigas is a Garnacha blend made from younger vines, with cedary notes. La Bassetta is a step up, with more depth and concentration. La Creu Alta shows the power and briskness of Cariñena in its blend, softened by silky tannins, and showing complex notes of truffle, blackberries, and an underlying minerality. ★ Rising star

Carretera T-702, Km 16,8, 43375 Vilella Alta, Tarragona www.bodegasmasalta.com

MAS MARTINET
A WELL-KNOWN NAME IN PRIORAT, WITH WINES MADE FROM LOW-YIELDING VINES

MARQUES DE ALELLA
WHITE WINES ARE A SPECIALITY, ALL OF THEM LIGHT AND REFRESHING

Mas Doix Priorat

The Doix family launched this winery in Poboleda in 1998, although the family's interest in wine-growing dates back to the 19th century. In a very short time, Doix wines have won international attention. The Costers de Vinyes Velles (70- to 100-year-old Garnacha and Carignan) has sumptuous, fleshy, black cherry and blueberry fruit, with cedar and cigar influences from French oak, and a long, expressive finish. The second wine, Salanqués, has bright fruit, with focused, fresh acidity, and fine tannins.

Carrer del Carme 115, 43376 Poboleda www.masdoix.com

Mas d'En Gil Priorat

In a region with a short history, Mas d'En Gil is one of the latest newcomers, established as a sizeable 310 acre (125ha) estate at the turn of the millennium. The Pere Rovira family, wine merchants from Penedès, bought the Masía Barril estate in Bellmunt in southern Priorat and produce not just wine but also olive oil and *agredolç* (sweet vinegar). Most impressive of the range is Coma Blanca, one of Priorat's top whites, reflecting the terroir's minerality, overlaid with exotic fruit and bold, lingering intensity.

43738 Bellmunt del Priorat, Tarragona www.masdengil.com

Mas Igneus Priorat

Mas Igneus is Priorat's leading producer of wines from organically grown grapes. The region is ideal for organics—the lack of rot-causing rain in the summer avoids the need for chemical treatments. The business was originally a joint project begun in 1996 between the Poboleda co-operative and others, including Josep María Albet, best-known for organic wines at Albet i Noya in Penedès. The co-op withdrew, but individual organic growers remain. Costers de Mas Igneus is laden with lush cassis and raspberries, with a firm, minerally finish.

Carretera Falset a La Vilella Baixa, Gratallops, Tarragona www.masigneus.com

Mas Martinet Priorat

Clos, now Mas, Martinet was started by enologist Josep Lluis Pérez, now joined by his children, Sara and Adriá. Sara (married to René Barbier Jr.) is one of the new stars of Priorat and consults for many properties in the region, including Cims de Porrera. The first wine, Clos Martinet, is made from grapes taken from very low-yielding vines (as low as 17.5oz/0.5kg per vine) and is aged with 60% new oak, revealing the typical power of Priorat, but with refinement.

Carreterade Falset a Gratallops, Km 6, 43730 Falset, Tarragona; www.masmartinet.com

Mas Perinet Priorat

Mas Perinet stretches across the boundaries of Priorat and Montsant, which makes for an interesting comparison of the terroirs. In Priorat, Perinet and Perinet+ are multivarietal blends; Perinet+ shows an intensity of roasted coffee and raisined fruit. In Montsant, Clos Maria is a textured, rounded white, made from Garnacha Blanca, Chenin Blanc, Moscatel, and Macabeo. Gotia (Cabernet Sauvignon/Merlot/Garnacha) is briskly modern.

T-702 PK 1,6, 43361 La Morera de Monsant, Priorat www.masperinet.com

The picturesque 11th-century Castillo de Milmanda lies at the heart of the Torres estate in Conca de Barberá.

VALL-LLACH
IDUS IS AN IMPRESSIVE BLEND OF CARIÑENA,
MERLOT, SYRAH, CABERNET, AND GARNACHA

Melis Priorat Priorat
As students at UC Davis, Victor Gallegos and Javier López Botella were introduced to Priorat by José Luis Pérez. Fifteen years later, in 1999, they bought a property outside Torroja del Priorat. Top wine Melis consists of old-vine Garnacha with Cariñena, Syrah, and Cabernet Sauvignon. Second wine Elix has less Garnacha, but has Merlot for breadth. Gallegos draws on his experience with Pinot Noir, gained at Sea Smoke (Santa Barbara, California). Innovations include refrigerated containers at harvest, and a mix of vat and barrel sizes to tame tannins. ★**Rising star**

No visitor facilities
www.melispriorat.com

Miquel Gelabert Pla i Llevant
Gelabert is one of the experts on Mallorcan varietals and his vineyards house plenty of the island's grapes, as well as plenty of international ones, including the white Jumillo, and the red Giró Negre. Early success with his Chardonnay built his reputation. Golos, a local blend of Callet and Manto Negro, is ripe and spicy, and a little hot. His Callet-dominated Gran Vinya Son Caules is a reserve style: floral but with eucalyptus and cedar on the nose. It is vibrant with lively acidity and a firm, tarry finish.

Calle Sales 50, 07500 Manacor, Mallorca
www.vinsmiquelgelabert.com

Miquel Oliver Pla i Llevant
Oliver is a leader in Pla i Llevant and has been a modern business since its foundation in 1912. Current winemaker Pilár Oliver is the fourth generation, and her Merlot, Aia, has won high marks; it is a bold, dense creation, with red currant and meaty aromas, and a complex palate of charcoal and mocha tones. A close second is the structured, roasted Syrah, followed by Ses Ferritges: a blend of Callet, Cabernet, Merlot, and Syrah. This, too, has the power of the previous wines, as well as a savory, toasty intensity.

Calle Font 26, 07520 Petra, Mallorca
www.miqueloliver.com

Morlanda Priorat
Now part of the Freixenet Cava group, Morlanda was founded in the late 1990s as Viticultors del Priorat and is based in Bellmunt, surrounded by hills. The most dominant of these is Morlanda, which lends its name to one of the wines as well as the winery. The intention is to create serious, high-profile wines, such as the super-extracted, boldly flavored, fig-and-spice Prior Terrae. Morlanda itself is powerful, with mocha and toasted coffee aromas, a creamy palate, and a savory, roasted finish.

Partida Palells, Mas Subirà, 43738 Bellmunt de Priorat,
Tarragona; www.morlanda.com

Mortitx Vino de la Tierra de Mallorca
Mortitx is the brainchild of friends who wanted to make good wine and encourage a regional agricultural revival. Cabernet Sauvignon, Syrah, Monastrell, and Malvasía are grown at 1,300ft (400m) in the Tramontane Mountains; they also plan to plant some old local varieties. The first wines were made in 2006. L'U, a blend of the red varietals with 20 months in French oak, is dark, and spicy. ★**Rising star**

CarreteraPollença, Lluc, Km 10,9, 07315 Escorca
www.vinyesmortitx.com

Parés Baltà Penedès
An old family estate, Parés Baltà produces an impressively wide range of still wines, red and white, dry and sweet, and Cavas. Among the most interesting whites are a single-varietal Xarel-lo called Calcari, and a Gewürztraminer called Ginesta. Of the reds, Marta de Balta is a spicy Syrah; Absis, a firmly structured blend of Tempranillo, Merlot, Cabernet Sauvignon, and Syrah; and Hisenda Miret is a fruity Garnacha. The family also owns the Gratavinum winery in Priorat.

Masía Can Balta, 08796 Pacs del Penedès, Barcelona
www.paresbalta.com

Portal del Montsant Montsant
The Portal project in Montsant was launched in 2003, two years after Portal del Priorat. There is one man behind both: architect Alfredo Arribas—with help from winemaker Ricardo Rofes. They were joined in 2007 by Australian winemaker Steve Pannell. In a short time, the result has been a characterful, individual range of wines. Santbru is one of the most interesting Monsant whites: complex, textured, and herbal. The old-vine Cariñena, Santbru Carinyenes Velles, has spicy, roasted notes over ripe, supple fruit.

Carrer de Dalt, 43775 Marçá, Priorat
www.portaldelPriorat.com

Raimat Costers del Segre
The big name in this DO is Raimat, which undoubtedly put Costers del Segre on the map. Manuel Raventós, head of the family that owns Cava house Codorníu, purchased the run-down estate in 1914 and began slowly to improve it. There has been serious investment in choosing the right clones of Tempranillo, and the right vineyard management, and famous consultants from the US and New Zealand have been employed. One recent arrival is the crunchy Viña 24 Albariño: zesty, but with a Mediterranean richness.

Carretera Lleida, 25111 Raimat
www.cervoles.com

Ribas Vino de la Tierra de Mallorca
The Ribas family has been making wine since 1711, yet despite this very old pedigree the family is at the same time very modern. Sara Pérez from Montsant and Priorat consults. The vineyard has some less-usual varietals such as Viognier and Chenin Blanc, and it is reviving the local red, Gargollasa. Ribas de Cabrera is a Pérez project, and blends Manto Negro with international varieties to make a deep, complex wine. Sió Gargollasa reveals a light body with cherry fruit, while Sió is the top wine: a vibrant blend with a savory depth.

Camí de Muntanya 2, 07330 Consell, Mallorca
www.bodeguesribas.com

Ripoll Sans Priorat
Marc Ripoll's wine business may be young, having begun only in 2000, but the vines he uses pack plenty of years of concentration and intensity into their fruit. His winery is based in Gratallops, and the barrels are tucked away in a beautifully restored vaulted cellar. Closa Batllet is a red blend of old-vine Cariñena and Garnacha with younger Cabernet Sauvignon and Syrah, and is

TORRES
POWERFUL AND FRESH, MILMANDA
IS TORRES' TOP CHARDONNAY

aged in French and American oak. The result is a deeply colored and firmly structured wine, and it has won critical acclaim.

Baixada de la Consolació 4, 43737 Gratallops, Tarragona
www.closabatllet.com

Sangenís i Vaqué Priorat
This is the story of a family whose ties with Porrera go back to the 17th century. After the economic collapse of the early 20th century, Pere Sangenís and Conxita Vaqué revived the tradition of winemaking in the old cellar that belonged to Conxita's grandfather. Their wines are typically aged in French and American oak for a year. This shorter aging leads to wines that are more approachable when young, without the weight that distinguishes the blockbusters of the region.

Plaça Catalunya 3, 43739 Porrera, Tarragona
www.sangenisivaque.com

Scala Dei Priorat
The winery of Scala Dei is an integral part of the history of the region of Priorat. It is situated in the village of Scala Dei, beside a ruined 12th-century monastery and under the shadow of "holy mountain" Montsant. In the isolation of the mountains, the monks lived a reflective life, and were famous for making a profoundly dark wine. Major Cava producer Codorníu now has an interest in the property and its 220 acres (90ha) of vineyards, which are mainly Garnacha, with some plantings of Cariñena, Cabernet Sauvignon, and Syrah. The white wine is distinctive, with a round, almost oily richness.

Mitja Galta 32, 43379 Scala Dei, Tarragona
977 827 055

Tomàs Cusiné Costers del Segre
After working at Castell del Remei and Cérvoles, Tomàs Cusiné set out on his own. The first harvest was 2006, so the winery qualifies as a rising star because of its youth, not a lack of experience. The altitude, (700miles/1,126km) gives the wines a definite freshness. Add to this Cusiné's creative approach, with careful blending of parcels, oak barrels, and varietals. Auzells, for instance, is a unique white blend of Macabeo, Sauvignon Blanc, Parellada, Viognier, Chardonnay, Müller-Thurgau, Muscat, Riesling, Albariño, and Roussanne. The reds, too, are modern and individual: a taste of the new Spain. ★**Rising star**

Plaça de Sant Sebastià 13, 25457, El Vilosell, Lleida
www.tomascusine.com

Toni Gelabert Pla i Llevant
Toni Gelabert, Miquel Gelabert's brother, started in wine 30 years ago, and has made a reputation for characterful wines. He has a strong interest in biodynamics, a trend that is growing slowly across the island. His Chardonnay shows a creamy spice-and-nutmeg elegance; his Torre d'es Canonge Blanc is a fascinating blend of the aromatic local Girò (95%) with Viognier. A golden wine, fermented and matured in French oak, it is high in alcohol and has a supple texture. His 100% Syrah has a seductive aroma, and a rich, complex palate.

Camí dels Horts de Llodrà Km 1,3, 07500 Felantix, Manacor
www.vinstonigelabert.com

Torres Catalonia
Miguel A. Torres earns his place in the all-encompassing Catalunya DO because he fought for the flexibility to draw upon grapes outside or across the existing Catalan zones. In this respect (as in so many others), Torres has been the driving force for change. As the world's markets have grown, so has his business. Visitor centers and wine tourism, icon wines, screwcap closures, single-vineyards, almost-disappeared great varieties, de-alcoholized wines… in all of these areas he has been a leader. By adapting his business to climate change, he has also shown the way. If there have been occasions when the wines have been solid rather than exciting, then a new development has refreshed the range. There are a number of modern classics: Viña Esmeralda, the clever and popular Moscatel Gewürztraminer blend; Milmanda, the top Chardonnay; the serious Mas La Plana Cabernet Sauvignon; and Grans Muralles, a fascinating blend of reclaimed local varieties. New developments include Salmos, a wine from Priorat; and Ibéricos, a Rioja. Torres also owns Jean León wines, another pioneer of French grape varieties in Penedès.

M Torres 6, 08720 Villafranca del Penedès, Barcelona
www.torres.es

Vall-Llach Priorat
Porrera was one of the many Priorat hill villages that were dying on their feet before the wine industry brought back jobs to the region. Catalan singer Luis Llach invested in old vineyards in the early 1990s and founded Vall-Llach. The original Garnacha and Cariñena are supplemented by newer Cabernet Sauvignon, Syrah, and Merlot. Embruix ("bewitching" in Catalan) is the most immediately accessible (and accessibly priced) wine, with a refined elegance. Idus spends 18 months in oak, and top wine Vall-Llach is bold, and spicy, with a firm, tannic profile.

Calle de Pont 9, 43739, Porrera, Tarragona
www.vallllach.com

Venus La Universal Montsant
Who else could call her winery by this name than the brilliant, effervescent winemaker Sara Pérez? Pérez, whose father was one of the original founders of the new Priorat, is dedicated to the region and consults widely, including at Dominio do Bibei in Galicia. Her wines from Falset have helped put the young DO of Montsant on the world map. Venus is the boldest, biggest wine, from Syrah and Cariñena. Dido is a lighter style, full of strawberry Garnacha fruit balanced by a mineral purity.

Carretera de Porrera, 43730, Falset, Tarragona
www.venuslauniversal.com

Vinos Piñol Terra Alta
Terra Alta is, as its name suggests, a hilly region. The vines are cooled by sea breezes and the local *cierzo* wind, which assists the freshness of the whites. The DO offers variety, as it permits a number of grape varieties. Piñol's production includes Nuestra Señora del Portal: a fruity Garnacha Blanca blend, which shows mineral and herb notes. The reds benefit from old vines, and have a fresh spiciness. A speciality of the region is sweet wines, so seek out Piñol's sweet offerings, made from Garnacha Blanca and Garnacha Tinta.

Calle de la Algars 7, 43786 Batea, Tarragona
www.vinospinol.com

TORRES

From rags to rags in three generations: this is the risk of family businesses. One wine family that has made it successfully to the fourth generation is Torres. Miguel A. Torres transformed the family company into a global phenomenon. One of the ways he achieved this was by instituting a retirement age (70) and protocols for family members joining the business, after his own disagreements with his father. What, then, of the fifth generation? Will his children be capable—or willing—to keep the brand alive, given the very different economic circumstances in which they now find themselves?

Of Miguel's three children, two are active in the business. Mireia studied chemistry and then winemaking at Montpellier University. She has been technical director since 2004, and the Nerola wines from the Conca de Barberà are hers. Her brother, Miguel Torres, five years her junior, was marketing director in 2005. During his tenure the brand launched new wines from Ribera de Duero (Celeste), Priorat (Salmos), and Rioja (Ibéricos), as well as the nonalcoholic Natureo. He is now executive president of Torres Chile. Not the easiest of inheritances, perhaps, but for now the signs are certainly promising for the new generation.

CAVA

Cava comes from Penedès, right? Actually, not quite. Cava, which is Spanish sparkling wine made according to the traditional method (what the French call the *méthode champenoise*), comes not only from Penedès, but also from the larger region of Catalonia, and even a few zones beyond that. However, for all intents and purposes, when talking about Cava, "the wine produced in the Penedès area" is a reasonable shorthand. Cava has been made commercially since 1872, when Josep Raventós of Codorníu decided to start production. Not everyone was confident that he would attract Spain's champagne-drinkers to Cava, yet he proved the doubters wrong—and many more of the world's consumers have proved him right.

Major grapes

Reds

Garnacha Tinta

Monastrell

Pinot Noir

Trepat

Whites

Chardonnay

Macabeo

Parellada

Xarel-lo (Pansà Blanca)

Vintages

2009
A rollercoaster of a year with heat, rain, and hailstorms, yet it turned out well for the best winemakers.

2008
The rain risked mildew on the fruit, but it became a fresh year, with clean wines.

2007
Another cool year, fostering ideal moderate alcohol, well-structured base wines for Cava production.

2006
Cooler weather led to slower ripening and lower yields, but ultimately fresh, fruity wines.

2005
Better than 2004, but not as good as in other parts of Spain.

2004
Not a particularly good year—drink up.

The name "Cava" probably comes from the Spanish word for an underground cellar—and there are miles of those in San Sadurní d'Anoia, the heart of Cava production. It was not until 1994 that the European Union banned the use of the words "champagne" and *méthode champenoise* beyond the demarcated region of northern France. Fortunately for Spain, "Cava" was already fairly well-recognized. Beyond Catalonia, Cava production was also permitted in parts of Aragón, Navarra, La Rioja, País Vasco, Extremadura, Valencia, and Castilla y León.

Cava producers made a fundamental contribution to the popularization of traditional-method sparkling wines. This was the invention of the equipment to mechanize the riddling process— the gradual turning of the bottle that is necessary in order to tip the dead yeasts into the bottle neck—in French, *remuage*. By putting the bottles into metal cages, large numbers of wines could be processed. Some producers still perform riddling by hand, but around the world (as well as in Champagne), most traditional-method sparkling wine is produced in this way.

Four white grape varieties are permitted in Cava. Xarel-lo (pronounced *sha-REH-lo*), also known as Pansà Blanca in Alella, is a grape that provides weight and structure. There are a few single-varietal Xarel-lo Cavas and still wines that are interesting to try. Macabeo (Rioja's Viura) can provide acidity, when fresh. Parellada gives a creamy aspect. All three need to be handled carefully so that they do not become bland or

overblown: characteristics of cheaper Cavas. Undoubtedly, Chardonnay works well in Cava. However, it is reasonably argued that this international grape, by its clear structure and the way it dominates blends, spoils the authenticity of a Cava. As for the reds, the ripe-fruited Garnacha Tinta, Monastrell (the French Mourvèdre), the pale-colored Trepat (used for *rosados* in Penedès), and Pinot Noir are all permitted. As with Chardonnay, there are several *rosados* from Pinot Noir that work better than anything produced by Trepat or a blend of the Spanish grape varieties.

According to regulations, all Cavas must carry a four-point star on the bottom of the cork. Equally, Cava must spend nine months on its lees, or dead yeast cells; in fact, many Cavas spend much longer than that. A *reserva* spends 18 months minimum, a *gran reserva* 30 months. It is clear that Cava can be a wine of real seriousness. The difficulty for the reputation of the good Cavas is that poor-quality grapes make wines that have flavors somewhere between apple skins and earth, with occasionally more appealing flavors of melon and pear.

A few brands, underpinned by substantial advertising campaigns, have become very popular in Spain and elsewhere. Others are being sold in supermarkets at derisory prices. This is not the way to build a successful industry. For those producers who are making hand-riddled wines with top-quality grapes, it is almost impossible to sell the wines at the prices they deserve. Who, after all, wants to pay champagne prices for wines that are not champagne?

Agustí Torelló

Once seen, never forgotten, Torelló's Kripta comes in a glass bottle shaped like an ancient amphora, a shape that naturally makes you want to hold it like a baby, or lay it carefully on its side. This is not simply clever, gimmicky packaging because the Torelló family's wines are consistently good, with a very clear, pure house style. They are Cava specialists and remain loyal to the classic Cava grape varieties. The wines are generally made to be *brut nature*, "naturally dry," or free from any added sugar (dosage) at the disgorgement stage; the style is usually known as zero dosage in French.

La Serra (Camino de Ribalata), Apartado de Correos 35, 08770 Sant Sadurní d'Anoia; www.agustitorellomata.com

Castellroig

The Sabaté i Coca family has been gaining attention for their Cavas in recent years. They put it down to old vines, careful selection, the use of oak on some wines, and long aging to make the wine more complex without allowing it to become tired. They work with the local Spanish grape varieties. Top of the range is the Sabaté i Coca Reserva Familiar: a Xarel-lo/Chardonnay blend in which the Xarel-lo is fermented in oak before the wine is aged for 36 months to make a lean and powerful Cava.

Carretera Sant Sadurni d'Anoia a Vilafranca del Penedès (c-243a), Km 1, 08739 Subirats; www.castellroig.com

Castell Sant Antoni

The Castell winery is located just outside Sant Sadurní d'Anoia. It works to a clear philosophy of using only free-run juice and no press wine. Just five grape varieties go into Castell Cavas: Xarel-lo, Parellada, Macabeo, and Chardonnay for the whites, and Garnacha and Pinot Noir for reds. A dedicated Cava house, it produces a wide range of wines, all of them of consistently high quality. Castell isn't afraid to give its wines time, either; in addition to the usual *gran reservas*, the Torre de l'Homenatge is aged for approximately 10 years (120 months). The result is a complex wine, full of crystallized fruit flavors and hints of roasted nuts, with a persistent finish.

Passeig del Parc 13, 08770 Sant Sadurní d'Anoia www.castellsantantoni.com

Cellers Carol Vallès

This winery is based in Subirats, a district that is situated between the main Cava centers of Sant Sadurní d'Anoia and Vilafranca del Penedès. They like to make the point that Subirats is a rare part of this highly populated part of Spain where the vineyards have not been overwhelmed by factories and housing. Cellers Carol Vallès began to sell Cava under its own brand in 1996. Its best wines are the brut nature (zero dosage) wines, especially the Parellada i Faura Millennium Reserva. An interesting distinguishing feature is the metal caps that cover the top of the corks, which are illustrated with lovely, miniature paintings of the company's winery or its vineyards.

Corral del Mestre, Can Parellada, 08739 Subirats (Barcelona) www.cellerscarol.com

AGUSTI TORELLO
THE BUTTERY, TOASTY KRIPTA IS GIVEN
A MINIMUM OF FOUR YEARS' BOTTLE-AGE

FREIXENET
A LIVELY, DRY CAVA, WITH CLASSIC NOTES OF
TOAST AND DRIED FRUITS

Codorníu

Without Codorníu, there might have been no Cava—or at least not quite so early. It was Josep Raventós who studied the traditional method of making champagne in 1872 and became determined to make the investment necessary to produce sparkling wine in Spain, initially known in the region as *xampagnet*. The winery, with its modernist architecture by a student of Gaudí, and its extensive underground cellars, is one of the most popular winery visits in Penedès. The wines have been unexciting, but there is a revived focus on quality. The Pinot Noir Rosado and the toasty, crunchy Selección Raventós (50% Chardonnay, 50% Xarel-lo/Macabeo) are very reliable. The name Codorníu? It comes from the heiress, Anna de Codorníu, who married into the Raventós family. The Raimat wineries also belong to the Codorníu group.

Avenida Jaume Codorníu, 08770 Sant Sadurní d'Anoia www.codorniu.es

Freixenet

Pronounced *fresh-eh-nay*, this Cava business epitomizes the entrepreneurial and commercial spirit of the Catalans. Although already wine producers, the Ferrer family only started to make Cava in 1914. They went on to create two famous brands: Carta Nevada in 1941 and Cordon Negro in 1974, and showed how extensive advertising and marketing could build brands. In the process, they also managed to create a global awareness of Cava. The Ferrers went on to establish the Gloria Ferrer winery in California, and made a number of other acquisitions abroad, including Yvon Mau in France and champagne house Henri Abelé . In Penedès, they also own Cava producers Segura Viudas and Castellblanch.

Joan Sala 2, 08770 Sant Sadurní d'Anoia www.freixenet.com

Gramona

A tasting at this winery swiftly changes any misconceptions of Cava as pedestrian. Cousins Jaume and Javier (one the technician, the other the artist) have an extensive experimental vineyard, and make a broad range of wines, sparkling and still. Top of the range are the complex 10-year-old Celler Battle Gran Reserva, with notes of vanilla and white fruits, and the toasty, nutty vintage Cava III Lustros Gran Reserva. Best value is the Gran Cuvee. The innovation shows in the table wines, including the barrel-fermented Xarel-lo, the Gewürztraminer Icewine (by cryoextraction), and the botrytis Sauvignon Blanc.

Calle Industria 36, 08770 Sant Sadurni d'Anoia, Barcelona www.gramona.com

Jané Ventura

The climate in the Jané Ventura vineyards, located in Tarragona province in the *baix*, or lower Penedès region, is Mediterranean, with the sea on one side, the mountains in the distance, and dry, sandy terrain studded with olive trees. The family has made wine here since 1914, although they only entered the Cava business in 1990. Cavas are hand-riddled, and the wines are made from traditional varietals. The fruity Rose is 100% Garnacha. The Brut Nature Vintage Gran Reserva is impressive, and retains good acidity despite its hot origins.

Carretera de Calafell 2, 43700 El Vendrell www.janeventura.com

RAVENTOS I BLANC
MONASTRELL ENLIVENS THE TRADITIONAL
CAVA GRAPES IN THIS NEW RAVENTOS ROSE

PARXET
AFTER AT LEAST 36 MONTHS' BOTTLE-AGE,
THE MARIA CABANE IS FRESH AND FRAGRANT

Juvé y Camps

This family business is one of the grand old names of Sant Sadurní d'Anoia. They have been making wine since 1796, although they were relatively late arrivals to the Cava business, starting up production in 1921. The Juvé y Camps style is traditional and weighty, and the flavors are bold, making for expressive wines that are underpinned by fine acidity, with an elegant rush of bubbles. The focus is on local grapes, with three exceptions: the single-varietal Rosé Pinot Noir, the Milesimé Chardonnay, and the blended Gran Reserva, where Chardonnay is one of four components.

Calle de Sant Venat 1, 08770 Sant Sadurní d'Anoia
www.juveycamps.com

Marqués de Monistrol

Marqués de Monistrol is one of Cava's established names, founded in the late 19th century, and now in the bestselling Cava lists in several countries. In addition to the range of popular Cavas, there is a structured, firm Premium Cuvée Brut Nature, with fresh acidity from the Chardonnay in the blend. The winery is now part of the extensive United Wineries group, which owns a range of high-profile names, including the popular Berberana brand, Vega de la Reina (Rueda), Lagunilla and Marqués de Griñon (Rioja), and Durius (Castilla y León). Under the Marqués de la Concordia name, the firm has launched Haciendas de España, a wine tourism project of hotels and tasting rooms. Also in the same group are Argentinian and Italian properties, led by Villa Cafaggio in Chianti.

No visitor facilities
www.mmonistrol.com

L'Origan

In the center of the Cava town of Sant Sadurní d'Anoia, L'Origan occupies old cellars, built in 1906, most of which are underground. L'Origan itself is a new project, although one using traditional practices. Much of the wine is fermented in oak barrels; here they make a point of blending in previous vintages in the classic technique to develop a richer, more complex palate, and the bottles are riddled by hand. The result is powerful, creamy, leesy wines packed in an untraditional, original bottle.

Avernó 30, 08770 Sant Sadurní d'Anoia
www.lorigancava.com.es

Parés Baltà

The first vines on this estate were planted in 1790, where the winery now stands. Fast-forward nearly two centuries to 1978, when the present family, themselves wine-growers, bought the property. Today, they manage a growing portfolio of wines, including still, sparkling, and sweet, and the two wives of the grandsons are the winemakers. In 2004, Parés Baltà was certified organic, and its owners have their own flock of sheep to assist with the compost. There are two ranges of wines: Micro Cuvées and Classic. The Micro Cuvée Blanca Cusiné, a Pinot Noir/Chardonnay blend, with the Pinot fermented in French oak, is particularly rounded and rich.

Masía Can Baltà, 08796 Pacs del Penedès
www.paresbalta.com

Parxet

A quick drive up the coast from Barcelona is Tiana, and there among the unforgiving granite soils lies the small winery of Parxet. The Raventós Basagoiti family makes still wines here, and also own the Marqués de Alella winery in Alella, Basagoiti in Rioja, and Tionio in Ribera del Duero. Their Cavas are carefully made. The modernist Anniversario is a Pinot Noir/Chardonnay blend that is partly fermented in new Allier oak and aged for a minimum of three years. The more traditionalist María Cabané Extra Brut Gran Reserva is a classic blend with the addition of Xarel-lo.

Mas Parxet, 08391 Tiana (Barcelona)
www.parxet.es

Raventós i Blanc

Directly across the road from the splendid period buildings of Codorníu lies the modern elegance of Raventós i Blanc, built around a 500-year-old oak tree. It was the Raventóses, who founded Codorníu back in 1551, but this family enterprise got underway as recently as 1986. The winery has something of the château about it, surrounded by its vineyards (another 20% of grapes are bought in). The aim of the project is to focus on quality, and the wines show the skill that comes from long experience in the business, particularly the *gran reservas*. In addition to the Cava grape varieties, they also have some Chardonnay, Cabernet Sauvignon, and—less usual in the region—Monastrell.

Placa del Roure, 08700 Sant Sadurní d'Anoia
www.raventosiblanc.com

Recaredo

Established in 1924, Recaredo is definitely a renewed business, with a new generation in charge. Brothers Josep and Toni Mata focus on the terroir, and they follow biodynamic principles in the vineyard, making space for the necessary piles of compost. Once in the winery, they make only single-vintage wines (no non-vintage blends, as is more usual for Cava producers), all the wines are turned by hand (rather than in electronic cages), and they only make brut nature wines. These are savory and serious; a specialty is the 100% Xarel-lo Turo d'en Mota, which shows a vivacious acidity.

Mata Casanovas SA, Tamarit 10, 08770 Sant Sadurní d'Anoia; www.recaredo.es

Sumarroca

Cava is only part of the Sumarroca family business, but it is a wine taken seriously. The Sumarrocas own their vineyards, something that is not common in Cava, and from them they make all types and styles of wines. The most interesting of their Cavas is undoubtedly the Gran Brut Allier. Chardonnay, Xarel-lo, and Parellada are fermented in Allier oak barrels. After the second fermentation in bottle, the wines are left on their lees for two-and-a-half years. The result is structured Cavas, with toasty, savory notes, and the company's distinct finesse.

El Rebato, 08739 Subirats, Barcelona
www.sumarroca.es

Vineyards are terraced to cope with the steep slopes in this hilly part of Penedès within the Cava DO.

GREEN SPAIN

Green Spain wine regions

"Green Spain" takes in the northwest coast of Spain and its related inland regions. The highlight of a visit to the city of Santiago de Compostela is the dramatic cathedral, which for centuries has been a destination for pilgrims to the tomb of Saint James. Yet the Church has not always been the driving force here: before Christianity established itself, the region was populated by Celts, and following them, Romans, and Visigoths, and more. Today, visitors can still encounter isolated pockets in the hills where it seems that the modern world has never arrived. It is the old vineyards in these tucked-away places that the new wave of vine-hunters are tracking down. They recognize in the old vines a concentration and individuality often lacking in so many modern commercial wines.

Major grapes

 Reds

Mencía

Monastrell

Whites

Albariño

Godello

Loreiro

Torrontes

Treixadura

Vintages

2009
A very promising year indeed throughout the region.

2008
Excellent wines in Rías Baixas. Warmer, riper styles in the Chacolí DO.

2007
Mixed outcomes in Rías Baixas. Good vintage in Bierzo, with generally ripe fruit matched by less oak.

2006
An excellent vintage in Bierzo: well-structured wines with potential for aging.

2005
Wines are cool, fresh, and well-balanced, but required careful selection of grapes.

2004
At their best, some very fine Bierzos.

Green Spain is a world unto itself. Given the combination of the ocean and the rain, growth is lush here—which makes it the greenest part of the entire country. The region includes the north Atlantic coastal areas where they make Chacolí (Txakolina in Basque): the naturally spritzy white wine that is poured from a height into a small glass to encourage the froth. It also includes Bierzo, which, in strict political terms, belongs to Castilla y León, but geographically, climatically, and in wine business terms is much more closely tied to Rías Baixas and its satellites.

Thanks to the popularity of the wines of Rías Baixas, it often seems as if Green Spain produces only white wines, and of those, only Albariño. In fact, a surprising number of red wine grapes are grown—and not just in Bierzo. However, the bulk of what Rías Baixas produces is certainly Albariño; the white grape is transformed into wine that has flavors ranging from a citric, herbal freshness to peachy warmth, depending on the year and the winemaker. It is no wonder that this wine became all the rage with seafood in Madrid's smartest restaurants, pushing up demand and prices.

The surrounding Denominación de Origens (DOs)—Ribeiro, Ribeira Sacra, and Monterrei—each offer their own different versions of Albariño and blends. At present, the most interesting of all is the inland region of Valdeorras, where the honeyed Godello is being resuscitated and made into pure, young wines or impressive barrique-aged versions.

One of the most subtle and judicious winemakers in Valdeorras is Rafael Palacios, younger brother of Alvaro, who made his name in Priorat. Alvaro has assisted their nephew, Ricardo Pérez, in establishing a winery in Bierzo called Descendientes de J Palacios (named after the brothers' father, José). Bierzo is blessed with old bush-vine Mencía, which can produce deeply colored, flavorful reds when handled well. If not, then winemakers risk creating reds full of hard tannins and firm acidity—as well as trying to use too much new oak to mask what remains. In recent years, however, the top wineries have managed to overcome these growing pains, and have been producing enjoyable, individual wines. Mencía is undoubtedly the latest fashionable red grape of Spain to be discovered. Another red variety, Monastrell, has also become more established.

One of the other significant names in the region is Raúl Pérez. He is usually called a winemaker, but his work illustrates the character of Green Spain. His role here is more as a viticulturist: seeking out the best sites and the old vines, and breathing new life into the vineyard. After that, any winemaker's role is simply not to interfere too much with the resulting wine. Many of Pérez's wines remain good value, but that is bound to change. Wines with Alvaro Palacios' name attached have already reached the stratosphere in terms of prices.

Yet the majority of the wines being made in Green Spain have yet to be discovered. They are owned mostly by small businesses, which have equally small distribution. For the present, there is plenty of wine to enjoy in this emerald-colored region, but much of it will need to be savored in Spain itself—along with the freshest of fish.

A Tapada Valdeorras

A Tapada is one of the leading names in Valdeorras, and is often more commonly known by the name of the family, Guitián, which is the brand they give to the wines. In 1985, the Guitián siblings replanted 22 acres (9ha) of Godello vines in the land that surrounds their property. They made their first wine in 1991, and it was immediately acclaimed. Sadly, Ramón, who led this project, was killed in a motorcycle accident, but Carmen and Senén have continued the work with the assistance of leading Galician white winemaker José Hidalgo. The barrel-fermented Godello, released in 1996, also gained critical favor.

Finca a Tapada, 32310 Rubía de Valdeorras, Ourense
988 324 197

Adega Eidos Rías Baixas

This winery was founded in 2000 by local grower Manuel Villalustre. He has 20 acres (8ha) of vineyards in 100 small parcels, which he picks by hand from the overhead canopies that are typical of the region and takes to his winery, built in 2003. The wines are well presented, with a clear identity. Eidos is the young, single-varietal Albariño from the granitic soils of the Val do Salnés, with a fine line and a peachy character. Veigas de Padriñán is made from grapes selected from 40- to 70-year-old vines, and shows a greater intensity. Contraaparede is aged for over three years in stainless steel, and is a very good example of just how well Albariño adapts to aging. ★ **Rising star**

Padriñán 65, 36960 Sanxenxo, Pontevedra
www.adegaeidos.com

Adegas Galegas Rías Baixas

Adegas Galegas works with Albariño, but also with local white varieties Treixadura and Loureiro, producing a range of different styles. Most distinctive is the Veigadares, an Albariño blend. This is barrel-fermented in French and American oak and then lees-aged in stainless-steel tanks. This technique produces a controlled exposure of the fruit to oak and oxygen, which allows the wine to develop a creamy texture without excessive oak. Galegas belongs to Grupo Galiciano, as does the Dehesa de Rubiales winery (Castilla y León), and others in Bierzo, Valdeorras, and Montsant.

Meder, 36457 Salvaterra do Miño, Pontevedra
www.adegasgalegas.es

Algueira Ribeira Sacra

Algueira is in a lovely position on the River Sil, with a restaurant that rewards any visitor who makes the journey. Owner Fernando González, formerly a banker, has benefited from the advice of the consultant winemaker Raúl Pérez, whose skill lies in focusing on old vines and implementing careful vineyard management in order to produce the best grapes—which, in turn, produce the best wine. The winery makes both white and red wines. Brandán is the young Godello; Algueira is a Godello blend. The reds are made from the cherry-fruited Mencía grape, and the Merenzao label is full of character: meaty, with jammy fruit and spices.

★ **Rising star**

Doade, 27460, Lugo
www.adegaalgueira.com

ALGUEIRA
PIZARRA IS MADE FROM THE MENCIA GRAPE
AND SPENDS AT LEAST SIX MONTHS IN OAK

ADEGA EIDOS
A HEADY ALBARINO, WITH HINTS OF SMOKE
AND MINERALS ALONGSIDE PEARLIKE FRUIT

Ameztoi Chacolí de Guetaria (Getariako Txakolina)

The Ameztoi family has been making Chacolí de Guetaria wines (one of two Chacolí DOs) for seven generations. Their vineyards, which feature clay and sandy soils, are within sight of San Sebastián by the Atlantic coast, and receive plenty of influences from the sea and the abundant rainfall. The crisp, crunchy, naturally spritzy white is made from the local Hondarribi Zuri grape mixed with 10% Hondarribi Beltza, a local red variety. They also make a rosé version with 50% of each.

20808 Getaria, Gipuzkoa
www.txakoliameztoi.com

Bodega del Abad Bierzo

The name means "The Abbot's Cellar," and the winery is a modern construction, begun in 2003, with all the necessary high-tech equipment. Abad makes both whites and reds from Godello and Mencía. In the eponymous Abad range, the best wines are the Mencías: Carracedo is the top wine and the most individual. More successful is the newer, modern Gotin del Risc collection—the name comes from *gotin,* which means "a small glass of wine drunk with friends," while "Risc" was the name of a local winemaker. These are serious wines: there is a creamy, herbal Godello, aged on its lees, as well as an oaked Mencía called Essencia.

24549 Carracedelo, El Bierzo, León
www.bodegadelabad.com

Castro Ventosa Bierzo

Records suggest that the Pérez family has been making wine near the Roman hill fort of Bergidum Flavium (from which the Bierzo region takes its name) since 1752. The company began bottling under the Castro Ventosa brand in 1989, and now owns 185 acres (75ha) of its own Mencía wines, which makes it the largest owner of the variety in the DO. The current generation of siblings and cousins in charge includes Raúl Pérez, one of Spain's leading winemakers. Castro Ventosa's wines are made and managed by an independent team. Valtuille Cepas Centenarias is the finest expression of the vineyard.

Finca El Barredo, 24530 Valtuille de Abajo, León
www.castroventosa.com

Castrocelta Rías Baixas

A young winery, dating back to just 2006, Castrocelta was formed by some 20 grape-growers and producers in the Val do Salnés zone. Their name draws attention to the Celts, thought to be the original inhabitants of the area. They farm 91 acres (37ha) of Albariño, and their Albariño Castrocelta has a fresh, zesty, expressive palate, with more emphasis placed on the variety's crispness than its peachiness. There is also a Selección, based on the best grapes and aged on its lees, while Heredium is a wine made from their youngest vines.

LG Quintáns, 17 Sisán 36638, Ribadumia
www.castrocelta.com

César Enríquez Diéguez Ribeira Sacra

This is a winery that is better known by the name of its wine—Peza do Rei. Founded in 1992 in A Teixeira, and with a winery built in 1998, César Enríquez Diéguez is

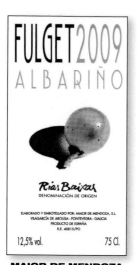

MAIOR DE MENDOZA
SUPPLE, FRUITY ALBARIÑO, WITH
GOOD CONCENTRATION AND DEPTH

DOMINIO DO BIBEI
LALAMA IS AGED FOR 21 MONTHS ON ITS
LEES TO OBTAIN MAXIMUM FLAVOR

developing a reputation for elegance among the top wineries of this reviving DO. Diéguez has been replacing non-native vines with Godello and Mencía. The reds are proving particularly successful, with rich, earthy, floral, and roasted-coffee aromas and flavors, and relatively soft tannins.

Abeleda 32764, A Teixeira (Ourense)
988 203 450

Descendientes de J Palacios Bierzo
The "descendants" in this case are the influential Alvaro Palacios and his nephew, Ricardo Pérez, who began this exceptional project in Corullón in 1999. The wines rapidly became benchmarks for the region and established Bierzo as a DO to watch for its serious winemakers. Just as Palacios talks passionately about the spiritual aspect of Priorat, so Pérez does about the vineyards that were originally established by medieval monks. He farms Mencía biodynamically, across 74 acres (30ha) of bush vines in 200 small plots. Pétalos is the most accessible, lightly oaked of the wines, while Villa de Corullón is more dense, selected from older vines. There are also a number of other very small-production, unfined, unfiltered wines, all of them offering a distinct expression of the slate and quartz terroir.

Avenida Calvo Sotelo 6, 24500 Villafranca del Bierzo, León
987 540 821

Dominio de Tares Bierzo
Dominio de Tares is eager to explain that the scattered nature of the old vines in Bierzo means that the château concept of a winery amid vines does not work—hence its location in an industrial park. Nevertheless, the wine that comes out of the winery is consistently good, making the Dominio one of the top three or four wineries in the Bierzo DO. There are several Mencía reds, notably Tares P3, which is aged in American oak, and the Cepas Viejas ("Old Vines"), aged in a blend of American and French oak. Proving that there is more to Bierzo than red wine, the Dominio de Tares Godello is a rich, barrel-fermented style. Other brands in the group include Lusco, from Rías Baixas, and Dominio Dostares in Castilla y León, where they make Prieto Picudo reds, most notably the juicy Estay and the dense, spicy Cumal.

Los Barredos 4, 24318 San Román de Bembibre, León
www.dominiodetares.com

Dominio do Bibei Ribeira Sacra
With its steep, terraced vineyards and schistous, slate soils, it was perhaps inevitable that Sara Pérez and René Barbier Jr. of Priorat should be drawn to the region of Ribeira Sacra, which has so many similarities to their own vineyards. Javier Dominguez invited them to advise him on his project, and the first results are structured, individual wines. The winery itself is a striking modern proposition set in an historic landscape. They work mainly with Mencía for reds and with Godello and Treixadura for whites. There is not a stainless-steel tank to be seen, however: either oak vats or, for some of the whites, concrete egg-shaped fermenters are used. The reds wines are called Lalama and Lacima; the whites Lapena and Lapola.

Langullo 32781
www.dominiodobibei.com

Emilio Rojo Ribeiro
The luxuriantly moustachioed Emilio Rojo established this winery in 1987. A former telecommunications engineer, he returned to his native Galicia to rediscover the old grape varieties in Ribeiro, which has a long tradition of winemaking. Rojo's achievement has been the revival of the obscure Lado grape. He makes one wine in tiny production: a blend of Treixadura, Loureiro, Lado, Albariño, and Torrontés. With that combination of aromatic grapes, the result is bound to be very floral—and so it proves.

Lugar de Remoiño, 32233 Arnoia, Ourense
988 488 050

Estefanía Bierzo
Founded in 1999 by the Frías family, Bodegas Estefanía draws upon some 99 acres (40ha) of old bush vines scattered in small parcels across steep, hard-to-manage hillsides. The intention was to produce high-quality, single-varietal wines from Mencía, and the owners here are achieving this by keeping the quality of their fruit consistent, and putting enough investment into the winery (including the barrel cellar, which has 80% French-oak barrels made by no fewer than 20 different French coopers). Tilenus is the accessible young red made from Mencía, while Pieros is bolder, the contrast a result of its grapes coming from the oldest vines. The winery also makes Clan in Castilla y León from the local red Prieto Picudo, and Castillo de Úlver organic reds from Tempranillo.

Carretera de Dehesas a Posada del Bierzo, 24390
Ponferrada, León; www.tilenus.es

Fillaboa Rías Baixas
The owners of the estate, the Masaveu family, have had connections with winemaking in Spain since the 14th century, although they subsequently moved into other businesses. They returned to wine with the purchase of Murúa in Rioja and Pagos de Araíz in Navarra, and finally Fillaboa (meaning "the good daughter") in 2000. There are three wines: Albariño Fillaboa, boldly aromatic, with notes of citrus and white flowers; a supple Fermentado en Tino, fermented in 2,000 vats for low-oak effects; and the powerful Selección Finca Monte Alto, which they say is the only single-vineyard estate wine in the DO.

Lugar de Fillaboa, Salvaterra de Miño 36459, Pontevedra
www.bodegasfillaboa.com

Gancedo Bierzo
The owners of Gancedo describe themselves firmly as *viticultores* (grape-growers) who make their own wines. They stress that they have not inherited vineyards, but came into the business as outsiders. They started out seriously in the vineyard in 1998, and did not begin work on building a winery until a decade later. They farm 32 acres (13ha), most of which are 60- to 100-year-old vines, from which they make four wines from Godello and Mencía. Most notable are the Herencia del Capricho, which is fermented Godello in new oak, and the Xestal and Ucedo labels: seriously structured Mencías, designed for further aging in bottle. ★Rising star

Plaza del Parque 9, 24548 Cacabelos, León
987 563 278

Gargalo Monterrei

Just down the hill from the three-star Parador de Verín (Hotel Verín) is the altogether more glamorous winery of local man and fashion designer, Roberto Verino. The winery and its team are as fashionable as the man himself, and the building's internal walls are decorated with fashion photography—a rarity in the typical winery world of concrete and stainless steel. In the vineyards, Verino is trialing a range of the obscure local grapes, both red and white. The red wines show promise here, but for the moment, his mainstream releases are white wines made using the local Godello and Treixadura varieties.

Rua do Castelo 59, Verín, Ourense
www.bodegasgargalo.com

Gerardo Méndez Rías Baixas

This is a tiny winery, set amid typical Galician gray-stone buildings, and tucked away just inland from the Atlantic and its sea mists. Gerardo Méndez and his daughter, Encarna, make a very pure, appley Albariño do Ferreiro from their 12 acres (5ha) of land. Their second wine is the powerful Cepas Vellas ("Old Vines"). The vines certainly deserve this billing. Grown on their own roots, they predate the arrival of the phylloxera vine louse over a century ago. The concentration of the fruit in wines made from these low-yielding vines creates a complex, layered palate with citrus fruit and fine herb flavors.

Galiñanes 10 Lores, 36969 Meaño, Pontevedra
www.bodegasgerardomendez.com

Godeval Valdeorras

Godeval lies at the center of the history of Valdeorras winemaking. The winery itself is located in the beautifully restored 13th-century monastery of Xagoaza, and some of the originators of the 1970s project to revive the Godello grape were also the founders of Godeval. The property was established with 27 acres (11ha) and has now grown very substantially, all the time focusing on significantly lower yields than is usual in the area in order to concentrate the fruit. The first wine was released in the mid-1980s and remains a marker for Godello, with its ripe, round palate. The Cepas Vellas ("Old Vines") is also very good.

Avenida de Galicia 20, 32300 O Barco de Valdeorras,
Ourense; www.godeval.com

Guimaro Ribeira Sacra

This tiny winery has shot to stardom in recent times. The reason for its ascendance has been the appearance on the scene of the highly rated and much-traveled winemaker Raúl Pérez. There are several wines being made here, including Guimaro, which is an unoaked young Mencía red, and El Pecado, the wine responsible for the winery's fame. The question remains whether these labels will be too overextracted and alcoholic, or whether they will come to balance the more delicate character of Mencía. There is plenty of experimentation in progress here, which makes Guimaro a winery to watch. ★ Rising star

Sanmil, 41 Santa Cruz de Brosmos, 27425 Sober, Lugo,
Galicia; 982 152 508

Losada Bierzo

Losado is a new arrival on the Bierzo scene, although its winemaker has previous solid experience at top winery Dominio dos Tares. The estate's vines grow on clay rather than the more common slate soils, but Losada sees this as no hindrance, pointing out that some of the world's best wines are grown on clay. The associates behind the project were eager to make a good impression from the very beginning: their architect designed the wineries for the blue-chip estates of Aalto, Artadi, and Clos d'Agon. Currently, there are two wines: Losada and Altos de Losada, both Mencía-based, and both promising. ★ Rising star

Carretera A Villafranca Le-713, Km 12, 24540 Cacabelos,
León www.losadavinosdefinca.com

Luna Beberide Bierzo

Luna Beberide was one of the earlier arrivals in Bierzo, set up in 1987. The estate's 198 acres (80ha) of vineyards contain Mencía, but also a range of international red and white varieties, including Cabernet Sauvignon, Merlot, Gewürztraminer, and Chardonnay, as well as Petit Manseng and Moscatel (from which they make a sweet wine called Alma de Luna). Nevertheless, it is for the local red variety, Mencía, that the company has attracted the most attention. The Mencía Luna Beberide is a fine example of how the grape makes a young wine, juicy and fresh, with keynote cherry fruit.

Antigua Carretera Madrid-Coruña, Km 402, 24540
Cacabelos, León; www.lunabeberide.es

Maior de Mendoza Rías Baixas

Based in the Val do Salnés area, the Barros family have been growing Albariño since the 1970s. The winery was launched under this name when the DO was created. They make several different styles of Albariño; the most successful is undoubtedly Fulget. This has won recognition for its powerful, fruity character, its complex texture, and a delicate lift of bitterness on the finish.

Rua Xiabre 58, Trabanca-Sardiñeira, Carril, 36600 Vilagarcía
de Arousa; www.maiordemendoza.com

Manuel Formigo Ribeiro

This is a family business, run by Manuel Formigo and his wife and now continuing into the next generation. A shiny winery complete with its own laboratory sits in the old family home inside 200-year-old walls. Here they grow the range of local varietals on hard, stony soils, with vines aged between five and 15 years. This is a company in transition from the traditional to the modern, and the first results look promising. Formigo also makes local reds and a version of *vino tostado*, a Ribeiran artisanal tradition of a sweet wine made from dried grapes.

Cabo de Vila 49, 32448 Beade, Ourense
www.fincateira.com

Martín Códax Rías Baixas

The Martín Códax winery started life in 1985 as a co-operative, and has since developed into a substantial business. The focus is on three wines: Martín Códax is a fine example of Albariño and has become recognized as one of the modern classics. Burgans is made to have

THE CAMINO DE SANTIAGO

Pilgrims have been making the journey to the tomb of Saint James, the patron saint of Spain, at Santiago de Compostela, for a millennium. There are a number of routes, starting variously from France, Spain, and Portugal. In recent years, the pilgrimage has become popular again: some take part for spiritual reasons, others for the personal achievement and the companionship en route. The traditional walkers can be identified by their long walking sticks—and their scallop shells. There is a more recent fashion for cycling, for those who cannot afford quite as much time away from work. Whichever route they take, all pilgrims pass many wineries. The Camino websites are filled with tips about bodegas that offer a warm welcome, and ease the path of the weary pilgrim with a welcome glass of wine.

PALACIO DE FEFINANES
THE BOTTLE MAY BE MOSEL-SHAPED, BUT
THE WINE IS 100% YOUNG, FRESH ALBARINO

a little residual sugar, while Organistrum is fermented in French oak, then aged on its lees in stainless steel to add complexity without dominating the fruit with oak. Codáx also occasionally makes Gallaecia, a late-harvested wine with botrytis influences that give it honeyed, exotic notes.

Burgáns 91, 36633 Vilariño Cambados, Pontevedra
www.martincodax.com

Palacio de Fefiñanes Rías Baixas
Palacio de Fefiñanes is steeped in history. The bodega is set in a remarkable palace that dates from 1647. Although the winemaking is a more recent development, having begun in 1904, it is still the oldest in the region, and remains one of the best. The labels on the bottles echo the estate's history, but the wines inside are perfectly modern. The Albariño has a pure freshness, with notes of lime and fennel. For those who like their Albariño barrel-fermented, 1583 has a smoky, textured appeal. The top wine, Fefiñanes III Año, has a richness from time spent on lees. ★ **Rising star**

Plaza de Fefiñanes, 36630 Cambados, Pontevedra
www.fefinanes.com

Pazo Casanova Ribeiro
Pazo Casanova is one of several newcomers to this reviving DO. It was founded in 2000 by hoteliers from Baiona, and is a family estate with its own 18th-century house. They grow the main local white grape varieties and make two blends dominated by Treixadura: Casanova, a generous, fresh white; and Casanova Maxima, a Treixadura/Godello blend with a herbal, floral profile. ★ **Rising star**

Camino Souto do Río 1, 32990, Santa Cruz de Arrabaldo,
Ourense; www.pazocasanova.com

Pazo Señorans Rías Baixas
Here is a winery that consistently remains one of the best. It is set around a lovely old Galician house, where husband-and-wife team Marisol Bueno and Javier Mareque manage 20 acres (8ha) of vineyards. Marisol learned the business of making and selling the wine, and became president of the local *consejo regulador*, or regulatory council. The proof of her ability lies in the Señorans wines. Pazo Señorans is a supple, rounded Albariño, while the Selección de Añada, the top wine of the vintage, has an elegant peach and rose-petal richness. They also make the typical herbal *aguardientes* (high-alcohol "fire-waters").

Vilanoviña, 36616 Meis, Pontevedra
www.pazodesenorans.com

Peique Bierzo
The Peique family started up business in 1999: a great year for the founding of wineries in Bierzo. They are based in Valtuille de Abajo, near the center of the former gold-mining industry. Three generations now work in the business, which focuses on small production, with expertize backed up now by the academic training of the younger generation. Their wines are Mencías, a young, unoaked Tinto, which shows the character of the varietal; Viñedos Viejos, which has 12 months in a blend of oak barrels; and Selección Familiar, full of succulent fruit with toasty oak.

24530 Valtuille de Abajo, Villafranca del Bierzo, León
www.bodegaspeique.com

Prada a Tope Bierzo
A remarkable mansion (Spain-meets-Swiss chalet) has been vigorously restored by the enthusiastic José Luis Prada, who took on the project in 1984. This is not just a winery; they also produce chestnuts, cherries, figs, and much more besides: plenty of food for passing travelers, plus a hotel. The Prada a Tope Palacio de Canedo isn't just about entertainment, though. It makes Mencías in a range of styles, including a rosado, a young, juicy red that undergoes carbonic maceration, and the serious, oak-aged Prada a Tope.

Calle La Iglesia, 24546 Canedo, El Bierzo, León
www.pradaatope.es

Quinta da Muradella Monterrei
The most exciting new project in Monterrei, and one that highlights the treasures of the Galicia region. Winemaker José Luis Mateo began business in 1991 with 35 acres (14ha), where he has revived a remarkable portfolio of local grape varieties: reds are made from Bastardo, Zamarrica, Brancellao, and Arauxa, while whites include a Doña Blanca and the delightfully named Monstruosa de Monterrei, among others, in addition to the more usual names. In 2000, Mateo started to work with influential winemaker Raúl Pérez, and the wines are full of interest. Alanda is the barrel-fermented Doña Blanca blend, Gorvia the Mencía red, Quinta da Muradella the barrel-fermented Bastardo. ★ **Rising star**

Avenida Luis Espada, 99, 32600 Verín, Ourense
988 411 724

Rafael Palacios Valdeorras
Valdeorras means "Valley of Gold," and Rafael Palacios has been conjuring up some golden wines since he started producing in 2004. Where his older brother (Alvaro) works with tannins and oak with red grapes in Priorat and Rioja, Rafael proves that he is more than satisfied with making white wines; he was behind Palacios Remondo's impressive Placet, a white Rioja. His Louro do Bolo comes from Godello vines grown at 1,969ft (600m), plus a little Treixadura, and shows Palacios' care in grape selection. There is a delicious richness on the palate, although it sees no oak, and delicate citrus-fruit notes alongside remarkable complexity. As Sortes Val do Bibei is its cask-fermented and cask-aged big brother, and reveals a fine depth and texture—a very individual wine. ★ **Rising star**

Avenida Somoza 81, 32350 A Rúa, Ourense
www.rafaelpalacios.com

Raúl Pérez Bierzo
Raúl Pérez was born in Valtuille de Abajo, where his family owns the Castro Ventosa winery. At his own winery in Valtuille, he makes Ultreia San Jacques. This is a silky, sumptuous version of Mencía, showing the generally unexplored potential of this grape variety when fully ripe. The fact that he does not produce a range of wines from here is simply because he spends his time working with growers and winery owners, seeking out the best old-vine material across Spain. Look for Bodegas Margón in Tierras de León, where he advises on the Pricum wines, and Landi & Pérez, where he works in Castilla y León with the other vineyard star, Daniel Gómez Jimenez-Landi.

C/Bulevar Rey, Juan Carlos 1º Rey de España, 11B, 24400
Ponferrada, León; www.raulperezbodegas.es

PAZO SEÑORANS
SELECCION DE ANADA IS 100% ALBARIÑO AND
AGED FOR 34 MONTHS IN STAINLESS STEEL

Regina Viarum Ribeira Sacra

Regina Viarum takes its name from ancient Latin, which refers to the Roman road that once ran through the region. It was founded in 2002 by a group led by the head of Celta de Vigo soccer club. Their investment is in wine tourism as well as wine, so the buildings occupy a splendid position over the River Sil. The winery currently owns 49 acres (20ha) and buys in more grapes in order to make some Godellos alongside the Mencías that are its main focus.

27424 Doade, Sober, Lugo
www.reginaviarum.es

Rosalía de Castro Rías Baixas

This is not a typical wine co-operative. The third-largest in Galicia, it is a wine business with a creative heart, where 60% of the partners are women. The co-op has over 400 members, with 500 acres (202ha) of vineyards in 1,900 small plots, and a modern production capacity of 2 million bottles. The artistic aspect shows in the name they chose when founding their business in 2005: Rosalía de Castro was Galicia's leading Romantic poet of the 19th century, and her style influences the marketing here. Rosalía de Castro is the mainstream young, fresh Albariño. The Paco & Lola brand, with a stylish, youthful design, is nevertheless a serious wine, intensely fruity and expressive.

Xil, Meaño Pontevedra, Galicia
www.Rosalíadecastro.eu

Terras Gauda Rías Baixas

One of Rías Baixas' top wineries, Terras Gauda shows real excellence and originality. Terras Gauda itself is 70% Albariño, and the rest is made up of a blend of Louriero and Caiño Blanco grapes. This is definitely a case where the sum is convincingly better than the (admittedly very good) individual parts. The wine is complex, with highlights of jasmine and orange peel. The Etiqueta Negra label shows good intensity, with the smoky complexity of oak aging. In Bierzo, the same company has established Bodegas Pittacum, which has rapidly earned itself a high reputation for the quality and seriousness of its Mencía-based reds.

Carretera Tui, A Guarda, Km 46, 36760 O Rosal, Pontevedra
www.terrasgauda.com

Txomin Etxaniz Chacolí de Guetaria

The archives of Guetaria mention a Domingo de Etxaniz back in 1649. In more recent times, the winery on this site was involved in the creation of the Chacolí Guetaria DO in 1989. The vineyards lie on a headland above the Atlantic, west of San Sebastián. Here they grow just two grape varieties: Hondarribi Zuri (white) and Hondarribi Beltza (red), and from them make three wines: the classical Txomin Etxaniz Chacolí, which is naturally spritzy; Eugenia, a sparkling wine; and Uydi, a sweet, late-harvest still wine.

No visitor facilities
www.txominetxaniz.com

Val de Sil Valdeorras

The inland DO of Valdeorras has a long history of wine production, and the Prada family are part of that, planting the first vineyards here after the ravages of phylloxera near the end of the 19th century. The

TXOMIN ETXANIZ
CHACOLI SHOULD BE FRESH AND ZINGY, AND TXOMIN ETXANIZ HAS ALL THE RIGHT MOVES

TERRAS GAUDA
GAUDA'S BODEGAS PITTACUM ARM IS PRODUCING REDS OF CHARACTER

distinctive slate soils enhance a mineral aspect in the Val de Sil wines. Godello is the mainstay, producing the rounded young Montenovo; and Valdesil, the complex, minerally, lees-aged flagship wine. Pezas de Portela comes from the prevalent *pezas,* or slate, and is aged in French oak for a broad, textured profile. In Bierzo, two Mencía reds are made: a juicy Valderroa, and the special selection Carballo.

Calle Córgomo, 32348 Vilamartín de Valdeorras, Ourense
www.valdesil.com

Valdamor Rías Baixas

Founded in 1990 by a group of businessmen, the Valdamor winery draws on a blend of young and very old vines from the Val do Salnés area. The Albariño grapes are hand picked, and vinified separately, plot by plot. The result, with the unoaked wine, is a powerful and expressive example: the fruit is lively and there are pleasing floral notes with a firm undertone of acidity—very good value for money. The winery also makes two other wines: a richer style, aged on its lees for 18 months, and a second that is aged in French oak for six to eight months to develop a richer texture.

Calle Valdamor, 8 Xil, 36968 Meaño, Pontevedra
www.valdamor.es

Viña Mein Ribeiro

Viña Mein is a relative newcomer to Ribeiro, since the replanting of its vineyards did not take place until 1998. However, the excellent quality of the wine produced since then has established its reputation firmly and helped to rebuild the profile of Ribeiro within the family of Galician wines. Javier Alén's goal was to replant the local grapes—Treixadura, Godello, Loureiro, Albariño and Albillo—as well as three experimental red varieties from the region. There are two wines: the Viña Mein, and the barrel-fermented version. The former is taut and tense; the latter a little rounder.

Lugar de Meín, 32420 Leiro, Ourense
www.vinamein.com

Vinos Valtuille Bierzo

Marcos García Alba heads this tiny family business. It was not until 2000, however, that he decided to move from more or less private winemaking into investing in the necessary equipment in order to make and sell wines commercially under the label Pago de Valdoneje. He manages the 49 acres (20ha) of vines himself, and is a self-taught winemaker. In 2004, he launched a special selection from the vineyard called Viñas Viejas, which is ripe and roasted with firm tannins, and has a production of just 4,000 bottles. ★ **Rising star**

La Fragua, 24530 Valtuille de Abajo, León
987 562 112

BEST OF THE REST OF SPAIN

Spain is currently the most exciting country in Europe when it comes to wines, and some of these are made outside of the more familiar, classic regions. That is why there is nothing in the least demeaning for the wineries in the following pages to be gathered together into a "rest of Spain" group. Here you will find producers that are among the most exalted in Spain. As Vinos de Pagos, or designated single estates, they have been granted their own DO status—similar to the French Grand Cru. At the other end of the scale are the Vinos de Mesa and Vinos de la Tierra. While these are considered table wines and not in the same classification league, these tiny properties may be run by a single winemaker whose passion is to make true "garage" wines.

Major grapes

 Reds

Bobal

Cabernet Sauvignon

Garnacha

Merlot

Monastrell

Petit Verdot

Syrah

Tempranillo

 Whites

Moscatel in the south and east, elsewhere local and international varieties

Vintages

2009
A very warm year, which may lead to overheated reds in hot central/southern regions.

2008
A cooler year with some uneven ripening. The north promises fresher wines.

2007
A very good year, with good potential for reds for cellaring.

2006
Uneven weather conditions across the growing season meant only the best producers made great wines.

2005
Generous harvests in many regions, but some wines lack complexity.

2004
After the scorching heat of 2003, more balanced wines.

In between these two extremes lie the co-operatives and large private wineries which, historically, were the engines of bulk-wine production. Yet they, too, have transformed their quality from dull and cheap to excellent value-for-money wines full of regional character. There are businesses of every type in this middle ground: family wineries specializing in one grape variety; wine producers from other regions arriving to expand their portfolios; and "new money"—bankers, industrialists, lawyers—entering wine for the first time and building glamorous wineries, strong on lifestyle as well as new oak. The biggest single winery in Spain—in Valdepeñas—is also included here.

Perhaps the most significant transformation has been an improvement in quality throughout the whole spectrum of production and across these varied regions. In the northeast, Campo de Borja, Cariñena, and Calatayud are looking up, making wines that are genuinely good value rather than merely rustic. Further south, the former workhorse regions of La Mancha, Jumilla, Yecla, and Valdepeñas have become hunting grounds for the new generation of winemakers seeking out century-old vines and varietals. Meanwhile, Spain's capital can take pride in its own pioneering producers in the Vinos de Madrid DO, currently on an upward path after a history of making cheap wine for the city's bars. South of Madrid, Méntrida is making its mark, thanks to the attention of committed viticulturists and winemakers.

Many of these parts of Spain focus on red varietals suited to the extremes of heat and cold.

In Andalucía, the glamorous new wineries are all centered around red wines, some made from local varieties, others from internationals such as Cabernet Sauvignon, Syrah, and Petit Verdot. Only in Somontano, practically on the French border, is the climate really fresh enough for success with white wines. Somontano shows evidence of foreign influences in its extensive plantings: everything from Gewürztraminer to Merlot.

For sweet wines, it is necessary to go to the east coast where wines made from Moscatel have a long pedigree. Most exciting of all are the old, sweet wines of the Málaga DO, and the traditional, sweet, oak-aged fondillóns, made from the red Monastrell grape in Alicante.

Monastrell, the Mourvèdre of Spain, is one of the favorites of the new generation of winemakers in the center eager to rediscover and improve on the terroir of the past. It is especially favored by growers in Alicante and Murcia because it can survive on low rainfall and extreme heat.

Bobal is another characterful red grape variety that is prevalent in the Utiel-Requena DO. Difficult to grow, with tough tannins that can be hard to tame, it can make rich, bold reds, and full-flavored *rosados*.

There is still plenty of Tempranillo to be found, especially among the producers of modern, international style wines. In fact, there is plenty of everything and plenty more to come. There are new grapes to be tried and old vines to be revived. The "rest of Spain" is in the process of developing modern classics which, in due course, will deserve individual attention of their own.

SPAIN

The most notable feature in a map of Spain is its mountains. The Pyrenees isolated Spain from the rest of Europe for centuries, and the inland mountains remain a strong influence on the styles of Spain's wines. The other notable influence, visible on any map, is the sea: chilly from the Atlantic, refreshing from the Mediterranean. That is why Txacolí (Txakolina), the Basque country's crunchy white wine, tastes so different from a sweet Moscatel from Alicante. This is also why the new generation of winemakers are busy traveling, talking to the old growers, and tracking down Spain's disappearing varieties.

Bodegas y Viñedos
SANCHEZ MULITERNO
Denominacion de Origen PAGO GUIJOSO

Magnificus

2006

14,5% vol.

75 cl.

qubél
revelación

VINOS DE MADRID
DENOMINACIÓN DE ORIGEN

75 cl. e

Bodega y Viñedos
Gosálbez Orti
POZUELO DEL REY
ESPAÑA
ELABORADO Y EMBOTELLADO
EN LA PROPIEDAD POR

NRE 26/6122-M

Map labels

Bay of Biscay
Ferrol
A Coruña
Gijón
Santander
Santiago de Compostela
RIBEIRA SACRA
Lugo
Oviedo
Bilbao
ARABAKO TXAKOLINA
BIZKAIKO TXAKOLINA
GETARIAKO TXAKOLINA
Donostia-San Sebastián
Cordillera Cantábrica
Vitoria-Gasteiz
Pamplona
FRANCE
Pyrenees
RIBEIRO
Vigo
Ourense
BIERZO
León
Ponferrada
VALDEORRAS
MONTERREI
Burgos
RIOJA
NAVARRA
Logroño
SOMONTANO
EMPORDA COSTA BRAVA
RIAS BAIXAS
Miño
CIGALES
COSTERS DEL SEGRE
Girona
Valladolid
RIBERA DEL DUERO
Zaragoza
Lleida
PLA DE BAGES
ALELLA
Duero
Barcelona
TORO
RUEDA
Sistema Ibérico
CONCA DE BARBERA
PENEDES
Salamanca
Embalse de Almendra
CARINENA
CALATAYUD
TERRA ALTA
Tarragona
TARAGONA
MONTSANT
PRIORAT
Menorca
PORTUGAL
Sistema Central
Guadalajara
Embalse de Alcántara
MADRID
MONDEJAR
MANCHUELA
UTIEL-REQUENA
Castellón de la Plana
Palma
Mallorca
Talavera de la Reina
Getafe
Toledo
RIBERA DEL JUCAR
VALENCIA
Tagus
MENTRIDA
Valencia
Cáceres
Guadiana
LA MANCHA
VALENCIA
Ibiza
Balearic Islands
Ciudad Real
Albacete
Júcar
Badajoz
VALDEPENAS
ALMANSA
RIBERA DEL GUADIANA
Puertollano
JUMILLA
YECLA
ALICANTE
ATLANTIC OCEAN
Sierra Morena
Córdoba
Segura
BULLAS
Alicante
Elche
Jaén
Sistemas Béticos
Murcia
CONDADO DE HUELVA
Seville
Guadalquivir
Cartagena
Huelva
MONTILLA-MORILES
Granada
3481m (11421ft)
Sierra Nevada
MALAGA
Gulf of Cadiz
JEREZ-XERES-SHERRY
Málaga
Cádiz
Marbella
Algeciras
Strait of Gibraltar
Mediterranean Sea

N W E S

0 50 100 miles
0 50 75 150 200 km

UN VINO DE
MANUEL MANZANEQUE

NUESTRO SYRAH 2006

DENOMINACIÓN DE ORIGEN
FINCA ELEZ

Canary Islands inset

Lanzarote
La Palma
Canary Islands
Santa Cruz de Tenerife
Fueteventura
Tenerife
Las Palmas de Gran Canaria
La Gomera
Gran Cananria
ATLANTIC OCEAN
El Hierro

KEY

	Andalucia
	Aragón
	Baleares
	Canarias
	Castilla-la Mancha
	Castilla y León
	Catalunya
	Galicia
	La Rioja
	Madrid and Extremadura
	Navarra
	País Vasco
	Valencia and Murcia
——	International border

TORO DO

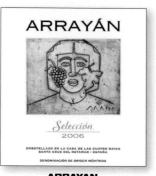

ARRAYAN
SOFT FRUIT FLAVORS MINGLE WITH FIRM
TANNINS IN THIS WELL-BALANCED RED BLEND

Alto Almanzora Valle de Almanzora, Almeria

Of all the new wineries in Spain, this is one of the
newest, especially since it does not sit within a defined
DO. The winery itself is in the village of Lucar, east of
Granada, and is a substantial presence on the hillside.
The huge painting of a pregnant mare on the side of
the building represents a fertility symbol of a people
local to this area in the Palaeolithic era. Opened in
2004, Alto Almanzora has a capacity for no less than
264,000 gallons (1 million liters) of wine. Consultant
winemaker Rafael Palacios has already managed to
make a very successful red blend called Este, which
is good value for money.

Paraje "El Marchalillo", 04887 Lucar, Almería
www.bodegasaltoalmanzora.com

Altolandon Manchuela

One of Manchuela's top producers, showing the
potential for local grape varieties. The fact that
Altolandon is working so successfully with Malbec,
just as Finca Sandoval is with Touriga Nacional,
proves the quality of the terroir in this region
and its potential for the future. Planted at an elevation
of more than 3,281ft (1,000m), Altolandon's vineyards
are as high as the name suggests. This mountain
freshness enables them to make a barrel-fermented
Chardonnay that is unexpectedly lively for one so far
south. The reds are best, whether local Bobal,
Monastrell blends, or more international Cabernet
Sauvignon and Syrah.

Carretera N330, Km. 242, 16330 Landete, Cuenca
www.altolandon.com

Alvarez Nölting Utiel-Requena

This is a young Valencian winery that has only
relatively recently become a part of the Utiel-Requena
DO. It was set up in 1998 by Juanma Alvarez Nölting, a
young winemaker with ambitions to make exceptional
wines. Tragically, he was killed in 2002, but the work
he began has been continued by a number of his
friends and associates. In 2010, the winery relocated
to a new site, which provided greater opportunities
to focus on vinification techniques. The wines are
classic blends—Tempranillo and Cabernet Sauvignon;
Chardonnay and Sauvignon Blanc;—and they are bold
and well structured.

C/Colón 7, 21, 46004 Valencia
www.alvareznolting.com

Arrayán Méntrida

Arrayán (the name is Spanish for "myrtle") is located
to the northeast of Toledo. The winery was set on its
path by two famous names. The first was Australian
viticulturist Richard Smart, who advised in the
planting, in 1999, of 64 acres (26ha) of Cabernet
Sauvignon, Merlot, Syrah, and Petit Verdot. The other
was Miguel Angel de Gregorio, the renowned owner
of Finca Allende in Rioja, who advised in the winery.
In a relatively short space of time, the range of single-
varietal red wines, in addition to a collection of blends,
aged in French oak in the modern style, have made
a promising start. ★ Rising star

Duque de Sevilla 12, 28002 Madrid
www.arrayan.es

Bernabeleva Vinos de Madrid

Bernabeleva—the name means "the bear's forest"—is
one of the Vinos de Madrid DO's young stars within
the important subzone of San Martín de Valdeiglesias.
The land was purchased by the Bulnes family in 1923.
War and other matters intervened, but finally, with the
advice of consultant Raúl Pérez, the project was started
in 2006. The small winery is finely equipped with
concrete and oak fermenters. The focus is on Garnacha,
drawing on 74 acres (30ha) of old vines in granitic soils.
Winemaker Marc Isart has converted production to
biodynamics. The early wines showed a little too much
new oak, but the fruit is powerful, the style modern. He
also works with Albillo, the local white grape variety,
giving it lees aging. ★ Rising star

Carretera Avila-Toledo Km. 81,5, 28680 San Martín de
Valdeiglesias; www.bernabeleva.com

Bodega del Jardín 1851
Vino de la Tierra de Ribeira de Queiles

This is the original estate of the Guelbenzu family
(founded 1851). In 2009, the Guelbenzu brand and most
of its vineyards were sold to Grupo Taninia, of the Caja
de Ahorros de Navarra. However, the Guelbenzu family
retains the original winery and 57 acres (23ha) of the
"garden vineyard," and from this makes Bordeaux-style
reds. 2 Pulso is a blend of Tempranillo, Merlot, and
Cabernet Sauvignon and is delightfully floral and
fragrant, with a bold palate full of red fruit and
liquorice, as well as a firm grip and a long finish.
1 Pulso is a fresh Tempranillo/Garnacha blend.

Calle San Juan 14, 31520 Cascante, Navarra
www.bodegadeljardin.es

Bodegas Almanseñas Almansa

This young estate was set up by a group of local people
assisted by four Spanish winemakers: Esther Nin,
Pep Aguilar, and Patri Morillo (all with experience in
Priorat), and Óscar Priego. They are working with
74 acres (30ha) of Garnacha Tintorera—usually seen
as a workhorse varietal used for its deep color— 49 acres
(20ha) of Monastrell, and 25 acres (10ha) of other red
varieties. The results are very promising. They make four
wines. Of these, Adaras is intended to be the pure
expression of Almansa. One curiosity is their natural
sweet wine, Dulce de Adaras, which is made from
Sauvignon Blanc. ★ Rising star

Carretera Alpera CM 3201, Km. 98, 60, 02640 Almansa,
Albacete; www.ventalavega.com

Bodegas Aragonesas Campo de Borja

This winery was created out of the merger of two
co-operatives, and on this occasion proves that large size
can bring benefits; it is not only small that is beautiful.
It has a dominant presence in the DO: Aragonesas
produces 70% of the wine made from Campo de Borja's
18,286 acres (7,400ha) of vineyards. Garnacha dominates,
and the style of winemaking is aiming at fresh fruit (with
fermentation in stainless-steel tanks) with creamy, sweet
oak from aging in American casks. The old-vine Coto
de Hayas Garnachas are very good, particularly the
Fagus special reserve.

Carretera de Magallón, 50529 Fuendejalón, Zaragoza
www.bodegasaragonesas.com

BERNABELEVA
ALL OF THE VIÑA BONITA WINES COME
FROM A SINGLE SOUTH-FACING VINEYARD

Bodegas Bentomiz DO Málaga/Sierras de Málaga

Bentomiz is a young winery founded in 2003 by a Dutch couple, André Both and Clare Verheij. In restoring the vineyards they owned, they recognized the potential in the Axarquia slate soils above the city of Málaga itself, and in the Moscatel de Alexandria grapes. Today they make four wines under the Ariyanas label: a dry Moscatel called Terruño Pizarroso ("slate terroir"), and two naturally sweet Moscatels, which are golden and floral but also refreshing. In addition, they make a dry red blend from Cabernet Sauvignon, Tempranillo, and the local Romé grape. ★ **Rising star**

Finca Almendro, Pago Cuesta Robano, 29752 Sayalonga, Málaga; www.bodegasbentomiz.com

Bodegas Bernabe Navarro Alicante

This is a young winery committed to reviving the reputation of the DO of Alicante. The estate, Casa Balaguer, which dates back to the 19th century, has varied soils and some old vines that are planted on their own rootstocks. The main grape here is Monastrell, but they also have Tempranillo and Syrah and are experimenting with Graciano, Malbec, and Garnacha Tintorera. In the winery, they are trialling French, American, Spanish, Central European, and Russian oak barrels. This level of research and attention to detail is apparent in the quality of the Casa Balaguer and Beryna wines. ★ **Rising star**

Plaza de la Constitución, 03380 Bigastro, Alicante www.bodegasbernabenavarro.com

Borsao Campo de Borja

Borsao has won a reputation for outstanding value for money in recent years. It is a business that was originally formed in 1958 by a group of growers and makes wine from some of the very oldest vines in the region. The grapes grow in the shadow of the Moncayo Mountain, and the wines gain freshness from the extremes of day and night temperatures. Red wines are the specialty here, in particular Syrah, Tempranillo, and Merlot. Campo de Borja wines have become known for their rustic energy, but Borsao's Tres Picos proves that Garnacha can be seriously polished.

50540 Borja, Zaragoza www.bodegasborsao.com

Canopy Méntrida

The tiny Canopy winery was set up in 2003 by three winemakers who wanted to reverse the poor reputation of Méntrida, which for too long had been focused on the production of bulk wine. The owners located old vineyards of Garnacha, plus some Syrah, and won immediate recognition for the wines they made from them: La Viña Escondida, Tres Patas, and Malpaso— two single varietals and a blend. Today, the business is run by two of the original trio. ★ **Rising star**

Calle Avenida de Barber No. 71, 45004 Toledo www.bodegascanopy.com

Carchelo Jumilla

Carchelo has substantial vineyard holdings of almost 700 acres (283ha). The winery was founded in the early 1980s and is one of the pioneers in the Jumilla DO. Grape varieties planted include Syrah, Cabernet

BODEGAS BENTOMIZ
THE SWEET, FRESH, AND MINERALLY
ARIYANAS DULCE MAKES AN IDEAL APERITIF

CASA CASTILLO
THIS MONASTRELL/CABERNET SAUVIGNON
BLEND IS FOCUSED AND LONG

Sauvignon, and Merlot as well as Monastrell and Tempranillo; unlike many producers in this region, they hold back on strong oak flavors. The young wine, Carchelo, is made mainly from Monastrell and only sees a few months in oak; on the palate, it reveals a supple raspberry character. Altico is a ripe, blackberry-fruited Syrah, with up to six months in oak. Canalizo is an organically farmed Syrah blend.

Casas de la Hoya, 30520 Jumilla, Murcia www.carchelo.com

Casa Castillo Jumilla

The first winery was built on this estate in 1870, but the Nemesio family launched the contemporary business in 1991, and have 430 acres (174ha) of vineyards, mainly Monastrell, but also with Tempranillo, Syrah, and Cabernet Sauvignon, producing a collection of excellent wines. The young Monastrell shows lively expressions typical of the variety; the Valtosca Syrah, which is aged in French oak, is powerful and long. The two top wines are Las Gravas, a Monastrell blend that is fermented in underground stone tanks, and Pie Franco, similarly fermented but made from ungrafted Monastrell vines that were planted in 1941; it shows the low yields and concentration of age.

Carretera Hellín-Jumilla, Km. 15,7, 30520 Jumilla, Murcia www.casacastillo.es

Casa de la Ermita Jumilla

Casa de la Ermita may only be a relatively recent arrival in the Jumilla region, but it has already made a strong impression. The winery is one of a number whose modern approach to winemaking and understanding of making wines for export markets has transformed the reputation of this DO—and of Monastrell itself. The Monasterio de Santa Ana is becoming a standard for the region, with its young cherry fruit. The Petit Verdot Casa de la Ermita is an elegant single-varietal wine, while the sweet wines— one made from Monastrell, one from Viognier—are both worth investigating.

Carretera del Carche, Km. 11,5, 30520 Jumilla, Murcia www.casadelaermita.com

Castaño Yecla

Ramón Castaño launched his business in 1950 at a time when Yecla was still dealing in bulk wine. Since then, he and his children have remained one step ahead, introducing a bottling line, cooling equipment, selection tables—everything a modern winery needs for quality. There is one other distinguishing factor: the 741 acres (300ha) of Monastrell vines owned by the family, which make the distinctive rich, dark, cherry wines, notably the 100% Monastrell Hécula, the Castaño range, plus the more popular Espinal wines. In addition, the Castaños are involved in joint projects with some major customers. Viña al Lado de la Casa, made with Barcelona merchant Quim Vila, is a Garnacha/Cabernet Sauvignon blend that shows juicy fruit and finely managed tannin.

Carretera Fuentealamo 3, 30510 Yecla, Murcia www.bodegascastano.com

Cortijo Los Aguilares
DO Málaga and DO Sierras de Málaga

José Antonio Itarte and his wife, Victoria, found their own piece of the good life in 1999 when they purchased the Cortijo los Aguilares estate near Ronda, with its mixed farming of olives, cereal grains, and pigs. In 2000, after a careful soil study, they added vines to the mix: Cabernet Sauvignon, Merlot, Petit Verdot, and some Pinot Noir. Their top wine at present is Tadeo, which is a Petit Verdot/Syrah blend that shows good potential for the future.

Puente de la Ventilla, Ctra. Ronda A Campillos Km. 5, Apt. Correos 119, 29400 Ronda; www.cortijolosaguilares.com

Dehesa del Carrizal   Vinos de Pago

Set in the province of Ciudad Real, south of Toledo, Dehesa del Carrizal is one of Spain's few Vinos de Pago (single-estate DOs). The altitude, along with cooler winters, makes it best suited to growing international grape varieties. There are more than 49 acres (20ha) planted with Chardonnay, Cabernet Sauvignon, Merlot, and Syrah, and some Tempranillo. The Chardonnay has a reasonably cool elegance, while the Cabernet has firm acidity underlying a full, spicy palate with minty new oak, and a persistent finish. The top wine is the powerful Colección Privada, a blend of Cabernet Sauvignon, Merlot, and Syrah.

Dehesa del Carrizal Country State, Retuerta del Bullaque, Ciudad Real 13194; www.dehesadelcarrizal.com

Dominio de Valdepusa   Vinos de Pago

Carlos Falcó, Marqués de Griñon, has many "firsts" to his name when it comes to wine in Spain. He studied at the University of California–Davis, and brought Cabernet to his 7,413 acre (3,000ha) estate on the boundary of Méntrida. Being outside a Denominación de Origen, he was able to experiment; with different grape varieties, with drip irrigation, and with canopy management—all features that Spain's official wine regulatory bodies originally banned. In the end, of course, he had more than made the case for the estate becoming a Vino de Pago and this has been vindicated by the consistent excellence of the Dominio's wines. Falcó has not stopped at Valdepusa, however. At El Rincon in the Vinos de Madrid DO, he makes a polished Syrah/Garnacha blend.

Finca Casa de Vacas, 45692 Malpica de Tajo, Toledo www.pagosdefamilia.com

El Regajal   Vinos de Madrid

The distinctive feature of this winery, which only produces one wine called Selección Especial, is the butterfly on its label. As it happens, 77 of Iberia's 225 butterfly species live here, at Aranjuez, in one of the lowest parts of the Vinos de Madrid DO—which is why El Regajal's 32 acres (13ha) of vines flourish alongside a major butterfly conservation project. The vineyard is planted with Tempranillo and Cabernet Sauvignon as well as a little Merlot and Syrah. The wine itself shows succulent black-cherry fruit, with dominant new oak when young, and will benefit from cellaring.

28300 Aranjuez, Madrid
913 079 636

DEHESA DEL CARRIZAL
THIS BALANCED SINGLE-ESTATE RED IS FULL OF CHARACTERISTIC BERRY FLAVORS

HUERTA DE ALBALA
AFTER 14 MONTHS IN OAK, THIS IS AN INTENSE, PLUMMY, FIGGY RED WITH SPICY OAK NOTES

Enate   Somontano

From the beginning (1991), Enate has had ambitions to create top-quality wines. The modern glamor of the winery indicates the serious investment involved, and it is also known for its distinctive labels, which incorporate paintings commissioned from contemporary artists. A wide range of wines are produced here—everything from the main international varieties typical of Somontano to Tempranillo. Top of the white range is Chardonnay, particularly the unoaked 234. There is also a juicy *rosado*, and of the reds, the Reserva Especial is exceptional. Enate also owns Viñedos de San Martín in Vinos de Madrid, a fine source of old-vine Garnachas.

Avenida de las Artes 1, 22314 Salas Bajas
www.enate.es

Enrique Mendoza   Alicante

There is no doubt where this particular winery believes quality lies: in the vineyard, which is why the company logo features the words '"Enrique Mendoza, Viticultor [grape-grower]." Mendoza set up the business in the late 1970s, and since then his winery has become known for real quality across a selection of styles. These range from the international Chardonnays and Cabernet Sauvignons, to local grapes such as Moscatel and Monastrell. Top reds are Bordeaux blends such as Peñon de Ifach, and Santa Rosa, which is dominated by Cabernet Sauvignon. The top sweet Moscatel is called Moscatel de la Marina.

Partida El Romeral, 03580 Alfaz del Pi, Alicante
www.bodegasmendoza.com

Ercavio   Vino de la Tierra de Castilla

Ercavio was established in 1988 by a trio of internationally experienced winemaker friends, who called themselves *más que vinos* ("more than wine"). After working in Rioja, they set themselves up as a consultancy in Spain. Their winery is located in Dosbarrios, east of Toledo, where their focus is on Garnacha and Cencibel (aka Tempranillo). Of particular interest is the fact that they have revived an old winery that had traditional *tinajas*, or clay urns. They age their top wine, La Plazuela, in these. Their latest release, La Meseta, is a Tempranillo/Syrah blend that is aged in French oak.

Plazuela de la Iglesia 1, 45311 Dosbarrios, Toledo
www.bodegasercavio.com

Félix Solís   Valdepeñas

This is an estate with an impressive array of statistics. Founded by Félix Solís in 1952, the winery in the Valdepeñas DO presses more grapes than any other in Spain—198,000 tons' worth (180 million kilos), and has 14 bottling lines and capacity for 18 million bottles. The winery in La Mancha can process a further 10.6 million gallons (40 million liters). The flagship wine is the Viña Albali, which, despite the volumes produced, remains consistently good value for money. The gran reservas in the range have traditional Spanish flavors of sweet oak and ripe fruit. Félix Solís also owns the Pagos del Rey brand in Rueda, as well as Viña Bajoz in Toro.

Autovía de Andalucía, Km. 199, 13300 Valdepeñas
www.felixsolis.com

Finca Élez Vinos de Pago

At Finca Élez, one of the few Vinos de Pago (single-estate DOs) in Spain, the climate can be extreme. At 3,281ft (1,000m), temperatures can drop as low as -4°F (-20°C) in the winter. Manuel Manzaneque turned this continental chill to an advantage when he launched his first Chardonnay, avoiding any cloying richness that can sometimes be associated with the grape. His focus is now on Syrah, as well as Cabernet Sauvignon, Tempranillo, and Merlot. With the reds he shows an ability to produce round, ripe tannins. His Syrah has a deep-purple intensity, with aromas of tobacco smoke, red fruit, and violets. The palate is medium-bodied, with a long finish with plenty of fruit.

Carretera Ossa de Montiel, 02610 El Bonillo, Albacete; www.manuelmanzaneque.com

Finca Sandoval Manchuela

Hats off to respected journalist Victor de la Serna for daring to cross the line from critic to creator. In 2000, he established this small wine estate with vineyards at between 2,625–3281ft (800m and 1,000m) and it is now one of Manchuela's top wineries. He makes vibrant, modern wines with the local Monastrell and Bobal, and also Syrah and some Touriga Nacional. Finca Sandoval is mainly Syrah, and is deeply colored with bluish highlights. The wine is aged in French and American oak barrels for 11 months and shows a bright acidity, with notes of mocha and red berries.

16237 Ledaña, Cuenca, Castilla-La Mancha
616 444 805

Gosálbez-Orti Vinos de Madrid

The owners of this business are as interesting as their wines. Carlos used to be a pilot for Iberia airlines who spent his free time reading enology textbooks. His wife, Estrella, was the mayor of the nearby town for over a decade. Neither of them is going to drift into easy retirement. The project began in 1992, and the first harvest took place in 2000. The vines are organically farmed. Their main interest is Tempranillo, with some Cabernet Sauvignon and Syrah to assist in poor years. Top wine is Qûbel Excepción: rich, spicy, and aromatic.

Real 14, Pozuelo del Rey, 28813 Madrid
www.qubel.com

Guelbenzu Vino de la Tierra de Ribera de Queiles

The Guelbenzu wines have a long history. The winery was established in 1851 and showed its wines at the London Universal Exhibition that same year. With bold branding, Guelbenzu rapidly became a memorable example of the seriousness of Navarra's winemakers. The estate was part of the Navarra DO until 2002, when the owners decided to leave in order to gain greater flexibility in winemaking. Evo and Azul are the most accessible wines; Lautus, a Tempranillo blend, is powerful, with roasted mocha notes and brisk tannins. Guelbenzu wines are now entering a new phase. In October 2009, the family sold the majority of their vineyards to Grupo Taninia (owners of Señorío de Sarría (Navarra), Palacio de Bornos (Rueda), Toresanas (Toro), and Vallebueno (Ribera del Duero)). The family is now making wine as Bodega del Jardín 1851.

San Juan 14, 31520 Cascante, Navarra
948 85 00 55

Gutiérrez de la Vega Alicante

Felipe Gutiérrez de la Vega's winery specializes in Moscatel, in all its sumptuous diversity. One of the most well-known examples is Casta Diva Cosecha Miel, which was served at the wedding of the Príncipe de Asturias, the son of the King of Spain. While sweet, it has a floral charm and a citric lift. He also makes the traditional sweet red of the region, fondillón. This is usually produced from Monastrell, which is then fortified and aged, often like sherry. The result is an oxidized, tawny wine with a softening edge of sweetness.

Carretera Quintanes, 03792 Parcent, Alicante
www.castadiva.es

Hispano-Suizas Utiel-Requena

Hispano-Suizas was one of the great names in cars before World War II. It was originally a joint project between Swiss and Spanish partners. The young Hispano-Suizas winery is the same: Swiss-born Marc Grin is now in charge of marketing and exports, and his partners are two Spaniards: technical manager Rafael Navarro and winemaker Pablo Ossorio, who is also the technical director at local winery Murviedro. Their Impromptu label recently won highest ratings in Spain for a Spanish Sauvignon Blanc. They also make Bassus, a Pinot Noir, and blends of the local Bobal with international varietals. A winery to watch. ★ Rising star

Cronista Carreres 9, 7ºL, 46003 Valencia
www.bodegashispanosuizas.com

Huerta de Albalá Vino de la Tierra de Cádiz

Tucked away in the hills behind Arcos de la Frontera, Huerta de Albalá is a real find. It is an entirely new project that was begun by Vicente Taberner, who spent some time searching for a site before finally deciding on this isolated spot, which was once part of a Roman town. No expense has been spared, with a gravity-fed winery, oak fermenting vats, and a modern area for guests. On the estate, 178 acres (72ha) are laid to vines, including the local Tintilla de Rota (Rota is a town on the coast). There is a popular range of wines called Barbazul, as well as the more serious Taberner. Taberner No. 1 is Huerta de Albalá's top wine, a dense expression of Syrah blended with Merlot and Cabernet Sauvignon.

Carretera CA 6105, Km. 4, Apartado de Correos 320, 11630 Arcos de la Frontera, Cádiz; www.huertadealbala.com

Jeromín Vinos de Madrid

Jeromín is one of the largest producers in the Vinos de Madrid DO, with an extensive range of wines. Founded in 1986, it now accounts for over a quarter of DO wine sales. Its whites are made from Malvar, a local grape variety that has an aromatic profile. For the reds, it uses Tempanillo, Syrah, Cabernet Sauvignon, Merlot, and Garnacha in a variety of blends. Among the most popular is Grego (named after winemaker Gregorio Jeromin), a Tempranillo/Syrah/Garnacha blend that boasts a limpid black-cherry note, and a firm, concentrated finish. The top-rated wine is Manu Vino de Autor, a blend of all five red varieties: ripe and supple with minerally notes and rounded tannins.

Carretera San José 8, 28590 Villarejo de Salvanés
www.vinosjeromin.com

A SLICE OF CHEESE AND A GLASS OF WINE

All good wine tastes a little better when partnered by the fine foods of its local region, and nowhere is this more true than in central and southern Spain. Despite the globalization of ingredients, Spain still holds on to its classic flavors. They are bold: garlic, olive oil, sherry vinegar, paprika, ewe- and goat-milk cheeses, lamb and pork, cured ham, spicy sausages—and of course, plenty of seafood. In central Spain, the crunchy, hearty Monastrell meets its match with peppery chorizo sausages. In Madrid, the dense, alcoholic Garnachas of Vinos de Madrid are made for *cocido Madrileño*, the traditional stew of chickpeas with meat and vegetables. In Andalucía, the slivers of juicy *pata negra* cured hams add complexity and richness to the new wave of silky reds made in the modern style. To finish? A fine, sweet Moscatel or Málaga with *turrón de Alicante*: hard almond nougat.

Jiménez-Landi Méntrida

This enterprise, based in a 17th-century family house, was begun in 2004 with 67 acres (27ha) of vineyards in the extreme continental climate of the Méntrida region. The vines are organically farmed, and the main grape variety is Garnacha, which is complemented by other international grapes such as Syrah. Daniel Gómez Jiménez-Landi has won a global reputation for the elegance and expression of his wines, which he ferments in a careful mix of different containers, and ages in different sizes of oak barrel. Sotorrondero is a Syrah-dominated blend; Piélago is 100% Garnacha grown on granite and sand and showing very intense fruit and fine grain; and Fin del Mundo, made from 70-year-old Garnacha vines, displays a savory breadth with bold, punchy tannin. ★ **Rising star**

Avenida de la Solana, No. 45, 45930 Méntrida, Toledo www.jimenezlandi.com

Jorge Ordóñez Málaga and Sierras de Málaga

Jorge Ordóñez certainly gets around. The US-based wine importer knows what his customers want, as his interests in Spain show. His Málaga wines are a particularly striking example of this golden touch. Telmo Rodríguez may have arrived in Málaga first, but Ordóñez has made not one but five excellent wines from Moscatel. He was able to work briefly with Austrian sweet-wine king Alois Kracher before the latter's early death. Ordóñez is a leading partner in the Orowines group, along with the Gil brothers (Miguel and Angel) from Jumilla (and others). They bring together interesting Spanish wineries that are working mainly with indigenous grapes, and several of them employ winemakers from the New World. A number of these wineries are located in fashionable regions such as Calatayud, Bierzo, Rueda, Campo de Borja, and Rías Baixas, and make equally fashionable wines, including Ordóñez's own Wrongo Dongo, a Monastrell from Jumilla.

Carretera Velázquez 31, La Mata, 29700 Velez, Málaga www.jorge-ordonez.es

Juan Gil Jumilla

The Gil Vera family have proved to be one of the major driving forces behind the new image of Jumilla. In 1916, Juan Gil built a winery; today his great-grandchildren are in charge. There have been many changes throughout the last 100 years, but more important has been continuity in the scrupulous attention paid to quality in the vineyard and in the winery. The estate makes a young, juicy Monastrell called 4 meses (*mes* is Spanish for month) and another called 12 meses that is aged, as the name suggests, for 12 months. Then there is La Pedrera, which is made from specially selected grapes grown in high-altitude vineyards. There is also La Pedrera Monastrell/Syrah. The Juan Gil influence does not stop there, however. Orowines is an association that was formed between US-based Spanish wine importer Jorge Ordóñez (see entry above), and the pair are behind some of the most interesting and individual small wineries in Spain. Alto Moncayo, Atalaya, Ateca, Avanthia, La Cana, Shaya, Triton, Volver, Can Blau, Orowines Jumilla—some of the wines from these producers are found today on many of the world's best wine lists. Also in the group is the very highly rated Jumilla winery

LA BASCULA
THE GAUNTLET FEATURES PLENTY OF SWEET CHERRY FRUIT WITH GOOD OAKY TOUCHES

MALAGA VIRGEN
THE MOSCATEL GRAPES THAT MAKE THIS WINE ARE SUN-DRIED ON ESPARTO GRASS

El Nido, a joint project undertaken with Australian winemaker Chris Ringland.

Portillo de la Glorieta 7, Bajo, 30520 Jumilla, Murcia www.juangil.es

La Báscula Yecla

The partners in this undertaking are Englishman Ed Adams MW and Bruce Jack, winemaker and head of Constellation Wines in South Africa. Their mission is to make a range of individual wines from across some of Spain's most individual terroirs. So far that has included an exceptional sweet Moscatel with Gutiérrez de la Vega near Alicante, and red wines in Rioja, Terra Alta, and Jumilla (Turret Fields). Another called the Gauntlet is made with Monastrell grown on ungrafted bush vines, and has a fine perfume and a good tannic grip.

No visitor facilities www.labascula.net

Licinia Vinos de Madrid

Licinia's first vintage was in 2006, and it has already made an impact. The partners include the highly regarded winemaker Olga Fernández and viticultural specialist José Ramón Lissarrague from Madrid's technical university. They make just one wine: a Tempranillo/Syrah/Cabernet blend. The selection is extreme: the grapes are sorted twice, cluster by cluster and berry by berry. The wine is dense in color, and spicy and intense, with well-integrated oak and round tannins on the palate. There is Merlot growing in the vineyard, but so far it has not made it into the blend. ★ **Rising star**

Carretera Carrera del Poniente 10, 28530 Morata de Tajuña, Madrid; www.bodegaslicinia.es

Lobban Wines Calatayud

Lobban Wines is definitely an original. Scottish winemaker Pamela Geddes worked in Australia and Chile before setting up business in Spain. Her first wines were made at Bodegas Castaño in Yecla. In 2007, she opened her own tiny winery, making three wines: a red, and a sparkling red and rosé. El Gordito is a Garnacha/Shiraz/Tempranillo blend showing a bold, expansive character—indicative of Geddes's time in Australia. Another influence from Down Under is the sparkling Shiraz La Pamelita. Initially made with Monastrell from Yecla, the plan is to move on to Calatayud Shiraz.

Carretera Creueta 21, St Jaume Sesoliveres, 08784 Piera www.lapamelita.com

Luzón Jumilla

Luzón was established in 1978. It has over 1,483 acres (600ha) of vineyards, and a substantial investment in a new winery and American and French oak barrels. It produces wines across the price range, from young wines to Vinos del Autor, all of them of reliable quality and individuality. There are varietals from Monastrell, Syrah, and Tempranillo, right up to the Alma de Luzón and Altos de Luzón wines. These top wines, generally from 70% Monastrell with Cabernet Sauvignon and Syrah, spend 22 months in new oak, and are complex, deeply flavored, spicy wines.

Carretera Jumilla-Calasparra Km. 3,1, 30520 Jumilla, Murcia www.bodegasluzon.es

Málaga Virgen Málaga and Sierras de Málaga

Málaga Virgen is one of the great names of Málaga wine which, like many traditional wines, has fallen out of fashion. In working with sumptuously sweet Pedro Ximénez grapes, and also with Moscatel, the family business, now into its fourth generation, is producing classically sweet wines. Given today's changing palates, they have been dabbling in reds. However, Moscatel and the classic Spanish Pedro Ximénez (PX) dessert wine remain their specialty, and both are aged in barriques and clay *tinajas*. Seek out the sumptuous PX Reserva de Familia 30 Años, and the Seco Trasanejo 30 Años.

Finca Vistahermosa, Autovía A-92 Km. 132, 29520 Fuente de Piedra, Málaga; www.bodegasMálagavirgen.com

Marañones Vinos de Madrid

Marañones is a new arrival to the Vinos de Madrid DO, following in the wake of others such as Marc Isart at Bernabeleva and is eager to seek out the best old vineyards. Peña Caballera is one of Marañones' first Garnachas; the fruit is light and fresh, the style is tannic and structured, emphasized by keeping a certain amount of stems from the grape in the vat as the wine ferments. There is also some Syrah in the vineyard, as well as the local white, Albillo. This is made into Picarana, a complex, oaked wine. ★ **Rising star**

Carretera Hilero 7, Nave 9, 28696 Pelayos de Presa, Madrid www.bodegamaranones.com

Murviedro Valencia

Murviedro earns its place in this section by its sheer consistency and popular appeal. It has helped win for the DOs of Utiel-Requena, Alicante, and Valencia a reputation for full-flavored young wines. A number of these are sold under supermarket private labels and all represent good value for money. The most ambitious examples include Expresión from Valencia: a powerful, roasted blend of Monastrell and Garnacha. Then there are Corolilla, made from Bobal, and Cueva de La Culpa, a blend of Bobal and Merlot, both from Utiel-Requena, as well as some sweet Moscatels from Alicante.

Ampliación Polígono El, Romeral, 46340 Requena, Valencia www.murviedro.es

Mustiguillo Vino de la Tierra de Terrerazo

Mustiguillo is a relatively young enterprise that was set up in eastern Valencia; it is effectively part of the Utiel-Requena DO, but prefers to work outside its jurisdiction. This is one of the few producers to take the Bobal grape seriously, and the company is convinced that it can be used to make some top wines—despite the fact that Bobal can be a little rustic and tends to ripen unevenly. Tempranillo, Syrah, and Cabernet Sauvignon are also grown in the vineyards to provide some background support. Mestizaje is the entry-level wine with plenty of oak; Finca Terrerazo shows all the possibilities of Bobal with supple warmth and real intensity; and Quincha Corral is more structured.

★ **Rising star**

Carretera N-330, KM 195, 46300, Las Cuevas de Utiel, Valencia; 962 304 483

PAGO LOS BALANCINES
HUNO IS A ROBUST BLEND OF TEMPRANILLO, CABERNET SAUVIGNON, AND MERLOT

PAGO DE VALLEGARCIA
THIS 100% VIOGNIER IS FULL OF TROPICAL AND STONE-FRUIT FLAVORS

Ortiz Vino de la Tierra de Extremadura

Ortiz is currently a one-wine producer. Its Mirabel label is a confident blend of 70% Tempranillo and the remainder Cabernet Sauvignon. With consultant Anders Vinding-Diers, cousin of Peter Sisseck of Pingus fame, on board, Mirabel is far from ordinary. This is a smoky, peppery wine on the nose, ripening into deep, succulent fruit with a creamy oakiness—a modern take on a traditional region.

Carretera Sevilla 34, 06200, Almendralejo, Badojoz www.bodegasortiz.com

Pago de Vallegarcía
Vino de la Tierra de Castilla

Pago de Vallegarcía is a no-expense-spared property that was established by banker and businessman Alfonso Cortina, who hired Australian viticulturalist Richard Smart to advise him on the layout and management of the vineyard. Cortina has chosen to plant only French varieties in the company's 77 acres (31ha). These include Merlot, Cabernets Franc and Sauvignon, Syrah, and Petit Verdot. The lone white wine made here is Viognier, and it is already among Spain's most highly rated Viogniers. The Syrah is a fine expression of the grape, while Hipperia, a blend of the Bordeaux varietals, is intended to be the flagship wine, but perhaps could do with time to develop its identity.

Finca Vallegarcía, 13194 Retuerta del Bullaque, Ciudad Real www.vallegarcia.com

Pago del Vicario Vino de La Tierra de Castilla

Brothers Antonio and Ignacio Barco launched their ambitious Pago del Vicario company in 2000. Today, there is not only a modern winery, with all the expected equipment, but the company also boasts a comfortable hotel and restaurant. The 321 acres (130ha) of vineyard contain the classic Bordeaux grape varieties as well as Tempranillo and Garnacha Tintorera, and for the whites, the Barcos have planted Chardonnay and Sauvignon Blanc. The most successful of their wines to date are the Agios Tempranillo/Garnacha, and 50-50, a Cabernet Sauvignon/Tempranillo blend. There is also a small production of a sweet Merlot called Dulce. The winemaker is Susana López, who worked with Peter Sisseck of Pingus in Catalonia.

Carretera Cacabelos, Polígono 908, Parcela 155, San Clemente; www.pagodelvicario.com

Pago Los Balancines Ribera del Guadiana

The Ribera del Guadiana DO covers the key growing regions of the far-westerly region of Extremadura. This estate is based in Oliva de Mérida, and its first wines were launched in 2008. Alunado is an impressive, barrel-fermented Chardonnay with a good, tropical-fruit character, while Huno, a Cabernet Sauvignon/Tempranillo/Merlot blend, shows particular promise. Pago Los Balancines subsequently launched Huno Matanegra, which boasts an even more powerful structure than Huno. In the 99 acres (40ha) of vineyards, the owners are also experimenting with Bruñal, Garnacha Tintorera, Petit Verdot, and Graciano. ★ **Rising star**

No visitor facilities www.pagolosbalancines.com

RAMOS-PAUL
A BLEND THAT FEATURES RED FRUIT FLAVORS
WITH HINTS OF CINNAMON

Pagos del Moncayo Campo de Borja

Another of Spain's family businesses, this time run by a father and son, and recently established with the purpose of making a small collection of fine wines. Its vines are mainly 80-year-old Garnacha, although some Syrah is planted as well. In the tiny winery, they make a Garnacha, a Syrah, and a blend. The approach is artisanal: all the grapes are crushed in the traditional way, by foot in large vats. To date, the Garnacha is proving to be the estate's most impressive wine, with powerful, ripe fruit matched by creamy oak. ★ **Rising star**

Carretera Z-372, Km. 1,6, 50580 Vera del Moncayo, Zaragoza; www.pagosdelmoncayo.com

Pirineos Somontano

The promise of the Somontano region has attracted the attention—and subsequent investment—of not one but two sherry houses. While González Byass has purchased the Viñas del Vero estate, the Barbadillo group acquired 76% of the Pirineos co-operative. They bring marketing and winemaking expertise to Pirineos, which dates back to 1964. What distinguishes the Pirineos estate, however, is that it produces wines from the local varieties as well as from international ones. The winemakers are doing extensive work with the red Parraleta and Moristel (Monastrell) grapes. Marboré, which is a blend of these along with Tempranillo, Merlot, and Cabernet Sauvignon, sports a fine, spicy, crunchy character.

Carretera Barbastro-Alquezar Km. 3.5, 22300 Barbastro Huesca; www.bodegapirineos.net

Rafael Cambra Valencia

Rafael Cambra is one of Valencia's stars, proving that this Denominación de Origen has so much more to offer than just oranges and beaches. This is no longer a wine region of clichés, and red wine specialist Cambra shows exactly what can be done. At the Cambra estate, he makes a shiny, modern Cabernet Sauvignon/Cabernet Franc blend, as well as working with Monastrell. He is also in charge of El Angosto, the family estate, where his Viña Los Almendros is a ripe and expressive blend of Syrah, Garnacha Tinta, and Marselan; the latter is a little-known hybrid of Cabernet Sauvignon and Grenache that was created in France in 1961.

Cami de les Naus Artesanais 14, Fontanaras dels Alforins 46635 Valencia; www.rafaelcambra.es

Ramos-Paul Serranía de Ronda

José-Manuel Ramos-Paul and his wife, Pilár, face a serious uphill drive when they come up to the winery from their home in Seville; it is hidden away between Ronda and Grazalema at an elevation of 3,281ft (1,000m). They have taken advantage of their hillside position to create an impressive cellar in the limestone slope, with a château-style winery on top, amid the ruggedly beautiful countryside. In the vineyard they have planted Tempranillo, Cabernet Sauvignon, Syrah, and Merlot, from which they make just one wine. Yet this will definitely be a wine to watch as the vines mature.

29400 Ronda, Málaga
www.ramos-paul.com

PAGOS DEL MONCAYO
THIS CAMPO DE BORJA SPENDS
10 MONTHS IN AMERICAN OAK

Ricardo Benito Vinos de Madrid

This family business was founded in 1940, and it has become well-established as a wine tourism and private party destination. However, the owners are also very serious about their wines, and they have well over 618 acres (250ha) of vineyard from which to make a selection. Ricardo Benito produces a broad selection of styles, but the company gains the most attention for the boldly named Divo Gran Vino de Guarda, made from 100% Tinto Fino. This red regularly wins high ratings for its deep, sumptuous fruit, its well-handled oak, and its rounded tannins.

Carretera Charcones, 28007 Navalcarnero
www.bodegasricardobenito.com

San Alejandro Calatayud

One of Calatayud's most successful co-operatives, San Alejandro was founded in 1962. It currently has 350 members, who together own 2,718 acres (1,100ha) of vineyards located at between 2,461 and 3,609ft (750–1,100m), many of them very old bush vines that grow on stony soils. The co-op has been transformed in the last decade. It now has a young, outward-looking team that is assisted by visiting winemakers from the New World, France, and the UK who are familiar with the tastes of consumers in export markets. They make a wide range of wines; the Baltasar Gracian collection is the best.

Carretera Calatayud, Cariñena, Km. 16,4, 50330 Miedes, Zaragoza; www.san-alejandro.com

Sánchez Muliterno Pago Guijoso

The first vines were planted on the Sánchez Multerno estate in 1985, and the winery itself followed in 1993. Then, in 1995, it was granted Vinos de Pago DO status (single-estate), only the second after Dominio de Valdepusa. The vineyards lie at 3,281ft (1,000m), where *guijos,* or pebbles, lie over sandy loam on the borders of the provinces of Albacete and Ciudad Real. A range of international and experimental grape varieties (including Nero d'Avola, Tannat, and Zinfandel) have been planted. The wines include Vega Guijoso, which is a blend of classic Bordeaux grapes with Tempranillo, and Viña Consolación, a straightforward Bordeaux blend.

Carretera de Ossa de Montiel a El Bonillo, Km. 11, 02610 El Bonillo, Albacete; www.sanchez-muliterno.com

Señorío de Barahonda Yecla

Señorío de Barahonda has, as one of its claims to fame, the reputation of being the oldest winery in Yecla. In history terms, however, this means that it dates back to 1925—well before the establishment of the Denominación de Origen in 1975. The winery now belongs to the Candela family, and their focus with this brand is to produce fine wines from Monastrell grapes. The company also offers a restaurant for visitors. The top Monastrells in the range are Summum, a powerful wine full of toasty oak; El Remate, which features a rounded, ripe palate and mocha notes; and Heredad Candela, with cooked fruit and balsamic notes.

Carretera Pinoso Km. 3, 30510 Yecla, Murcia
barahonda.com

Tagonius Vinos de Madrid

This young winery, which was established in 2000, is now producing modern wines with the backing of substantial investment from the Foxá hotel group. The estate, which lies southeast of Madrid, also produces olive oil, vinegar, and milk. Tagonius makes red wines, and in addition to Tempranillo, they have Cabernet Sauvignon, Merlot, and Syrah available for blends. The fruit is reliably dense and supple, and the wine is matured in new French and American oak barrels from a variety of coopers. Kosher wines are also made under the Tikvah brand.

Carretera Tielmes a Carabaña, Km. 4'400, 28550 Tielmes
www.tagonius.com

Vicente Gandía Utiel-Requena

Vicente Gandía is one of the most historic names in the Utiel-Requena DO, a family business with a winery that was established in 1885. Today, they continue to make the regular favorites of the Valencia region, particularly sweet Moscatels such as Fusta Nova, and the popular Castilla de Liria range. Recent investment has been geared toward producing serious reds, using Syrah and Cabernet Sauvignon in addition to Bobal and Tempranillo, at the Hoya de Cademas estate. The top wine is Generación 1: a bold, Bobal-dominated blend.

Carretera Cheste a Godelleta, 46370 Chiva, Valencia
www.vicentegandia.com

Viñas del Vero Somontano

Viñas del Vero is an archetypal Somontano winery, offering the very wide range of varietals for which the Denominación de Origen has become well known: Gewürztraminer, Chardonnay, Merlot, Pinot Noir, Cabernet Sauvignon, Syrah. Critics might say that this lack of local vines shows a lack of imagination, and that it just goes to show that it is taking time for the Somontano DO to establish an identity for itself. However, at Viñas del Vero, the consistent quality of the wines puts these doubts to rest. Two labels impress. Secastilla is made mainly from a Spanish grape (Garnacha) and is produced from old vines and aged in French oak, with no filtering; the result is a succulent, polished wine. Miranda de Secastilla is the second label. The other serious wine here is Blecua, first made in 2002. Made in its own winery from triple-selected Cabernet Sauvignon, Merlot, and Garnacha, it is fermented in French oak vats, and aged in French barrels for 20 months. It is intended for cellaring for up to 10 years. Viñas del Vero was purchased by González Byass in 2008.

Carretera de Naval Km. 3, 722300 Barbastro
www.vinasdelvero.es

Viñedos Cigarral Santa María

Vino de la Tierra de Castilla

Restaurateur, retailer, cooking-school owner, and more, Adolfo Muñoz created a tiny vineyard and bodega called Viñedos Cigarral on the outskirts of Toledo in 1997. He says it is the only urban vineyard in Spain, putting it alongside vineyards in Paris, Vienna, and Malibu. While output is small, the winemaking is serious. The project is very young and the wines, which are labeled as Pago del Ama, have yet to prove themselves.

Nonetheless, the Syrah and Cabernet Sauvignon both show promise, as ripe, rich, spicy wines made in the modern style.

Carretera Cerro del Emperador, 45001 Toledo
www.cigarralsantamaria.com

Viñedos de Mancuso

Vino de la Tierra de Valdejalon

The Navascués family of Aragón and Carlos San Pedro of Rioja are behind this venture, which was launched in the Jarque de Moncayo with the aim of producing old-vine Garnacha. They are part of the contemporary trend to seek out and revive the abandoned Garnachas of central Spain, and it is a movement which, in this case, is having some very promising results. The winery produces some 10,000 bottles, of which one-third is devoted to the Mancuso label. This is a dense, ripe Garnacha that is aged in French oak for 14 months: mouth-filling and modern. The second wine is Moncaíno de Mancuso, which is made in a younger style and is aged in French and American oak for seven years.

No visitor facilities
www.mancuso.es

Virgen de la Sierra Calatayud

This is Calatayud's oldest winery, established in 1950, and only now gaining due recognition as the region's wine becomes fashionable. Like the majority of the DO's producers, Virgen de la Sierra is a co-operative, and it has the great benefit of its members' holdings of century-old bush vines, which still manage to flourish in dry, stony soils in extremes of temperature. Garnacha dominates for the red wines while Macabeo leads the whites. Capricho is the top wine of the Cruz de Piedra range, and is made from a selection of grapes from the top vines. The wines are aged in French, American, and East European oak. The Albada label focuses on American oak flavors.

Avenida de la Cooperativa 21-23, Villarroya de la Sierra,
50310 Zaragoza; www.bodegavirgendelasierra.com

A TRIP TO THE CANARY ISLANDS

Producers in the Canary Islands built their reputation on "Canary Wine," and it is undoubtedly the case that it is well worth sampling the local sweet wines on a trip to the islands. Try, for instance, the Malvasías of La Palma, the traditional *rancio* wines of El Hierro, and the Humboldt sweet wines of Bodegas Insulares Tenerife in the DO of Tacoronte-Acentejo. The same company's red, the Viña Norte Maceración Carbónica, is produced like a young Beaujolais and makes a very good, juicy red on a summer evening. The soils of the Canaries are volcanic, and visitors can imagine that they are in the vineyards of Santorini, in Greece. As in Santorini, the producers here are developing young whites (from varieties such as Listán, Malvasia, Albillo, and Moscatel) and reds (from Tintilla, Listan Negro, and Negramoll). There is some way to go yet, but the signs so far are promising.

SHERRY

ATLANTIC OCEAN
FRANCE
Barcelona
MADRID
PORT.   SPAIN
Seville   Mediterranean
Sea

■ Jerez-Xérès-Sherry wine region

Sherry, or Jerez, is a triangular region located in southeastern Spain and bordered by the small cities of Jerez de la Frontera, Sanlúcar de Barrameda, and El Puerto de Santa María. The term "sherry" also refers to the classic fortified style of wine originally produced in and around the town of Jerez. Over the centuries, the style has had its ups and downs in terms of popularity. Today, the region boasts 25,000 acres (10,000ha) of vines, with an annual production of about 3 million bottles, which is considerably less than in its heyday during the 1970s. In recent years, however, producers have been trying to shed the "granny drinks this" image. And they have had some success in the UK and US, where sherry sales have begun to grow a little again.

Major grapes

🍇 **Whites**

Muscat (Moscatel)

Palomino

Pedro Ximénez (PX)

Vintages

Sherry's unusual production methods mean vintages, while important for producers, are considerably less so for consumers. Sherry is made using a solera, a system of barrel-aging that incorporates wines from different vintages. Any fortified sherry on the market will therefore be a blend of wines from many different years.

In 1993, Spanish national law established the Denominación de Origen (DO) system, and Jerez was the first official DO in Spain in 1935. Sherry's soils are unique white chalk called *albariza*, a word that derives its origin from the language of the Moors, who once governed the region. *Albariza* soils are porous, but hold water, and are composed of 25 to 40% limestone. With irrigation prohibited, the water-holding properties are essential. The white soils also reflect sunlight on to the grapes.

The fortified sherry can only be made from three authorized grape varieties: Palomino, Pedro Ximénez (PX), and Muscat (Moscatel). Sherry differs from other wines in the way it is treated after fermentation. The fermented wine is first fortified with brandy and then, if it is destined to be a fino style, a yeast called flor is allowed to grow on top. The oloroso style is fortified to a strength where the flor cannot grow, usually about 17 degrees alcohol. The other styles of sherry fall between the two: flor-based manzanilla for wines grown in or near Sanlúcar; then those with more time in the oxidative solera system: amontillado, palo cortado, and cream styles.

Another distinguishing feature of sherry is the solera system. Barrels are never emptied, and they are also not kept full, which means the wines are in contact with more oxygen than is normally the case in wine production. This leads to the nutty, oxidative flavors that mark sherries. The older barrels get topped off by newer ones, in a three- or four-tiered system; sherries are bottled from a blend of ages to create a house or desired style.

The term "VOS" refers to a special bottling of wines from an old solera with an average age of at least 20 years, only applicable to amontillado, oloroso, palo cortado, and PX. "VORS" refers to the same, but at a minimum of 30 years old.

Sherry producers have registered the names Jerez/Xérès/Sherry and will prosecute producers of similar wines from other places using the same name. For that reason, wines from the Montilla-Moriles DO cannot be called sherry, even if they are produced from the same grape varieties (typically Pedro Ximénez but with Palomino represented as well) in the same type of solera style. The Montilla-Moriles wine region is situated in the province of Córdoba and covers 17,300 acres (7,000ha). The term *"generosos"* refers to a range of wines from dry, fresh fino through amontillado to palo cortado and oloroso. The finos have more body than those of Jerez; the amontillados are dry and hazelnutty, with a light mahogany color. The olorosos are dry and deep mahogany in color. The PX wines are almost black in color and richly sweet because of the high sugar content. These are made from the juice of sun-dried PX.

The region's Pedro Ximénez is of increasing importance. These grapes can be sold legally to Jerez (for addition to sweet styles and cream sherrys) and Málaga producers. Experimental plantings in Málaga for table wine production, as yet not permitted in DO wines, signals that Montilla-Moriles may be developing a sub-denomination for young red and white table wines.

Alvear Montilla-Moriles

Alvear is a top producer of Pedro Ximénez-based wines, located outside the official sherry boundaries, near Córdoba, in the Montilla-Moriles DO. All the same style of sherry look-alikes are produced, but using only the PX grape. By drying the grapes, the wines naturally reach an alcohol of 15 degrees, so they do not require fortification and they have distinctive, dried-fruit flavors.

María Auxiliadora 1, 14550 Montilla
www.alvear.eu

Bodegas Tradición Jerez de la Frontera

All sherries produced at Tradición carry the VOS or VORS designation. Only amontillado, oloroso, palo cortado, and PX are made, from barrels Tradición buys from other bodegas. The palo cortado, based on wines from Domecq (now Harveys) and Croft and further aged, is an amazingly complex, elegant wine.

Plaza Cordobeses 3, 11408 Jerez de la Frontera
www.bodegastradicion.com

Bodegas Williams & Humbert
Jerez de la Frontera

Williams & Humbert claims to be the largest bodega in Jerez. It has some 1,600 acres (650ha) in Jerez, and a huge, if somewhat industrial-looking, bodega. The most famous wine here is the Dry Sack Sherry, but the Amontillado VORS and VOS Palo Cortado are both elegant, complex wines well worth seeking out.

Ctra. Nacional IV, Km 641, 11408, Jerez de la Frontera
www.williams-humbert.com

Equipo Navazos Jerez de la Frontera

Equipo Navazos is an intriguing project. It is run by a group of members, headed by Eduardo Ojeda and the part-time wine writer, and full-time criminology professor, Jesús Barquín, among others. They buy barrels (butts) of sherry and Montilla wines from top producers to bottle as their "La Bota de" (the butt of) selections of the finest of all the types of sherry. They are major purists, going for a bit of age and a lot of focused concentration in their chosen wines. The website clearly lists the source of each wine, all with a unique number and all from prestigious bodegas. The team also has a project with Dirk Niepoort, from the Douro Valley in Portugal: the Navazos–Niepoort 2008 is an unfortified palomino fermented in butt, with five months of biological aging under flor. Look for the No. 10, a Manzanilla Passada that offers great depth and purity. ★Rising star

No visitor facilities
www.equiponavazos.com

González Byass Jerez de la Frontera

The most famous product at González Byass is Tío Pepe: a very good, basic fino sherry. But there is far more to this old (established 1835) bodega than just that one wine. The company has vineyards throughout Spain and is a major producer of brandy. And, with some soleras dating back to 1848, it produces some fabulous old sherries such as the intense Oloroso Dulce Matúsalem VORS.

Calle Manuel Maria González 12, 11403 Jerez de la Frontera
www.gonzalezbyass.com

ALVEAR
THE INTENSE ALVEAR AMONTILLADO IS
MADE FROM DRIED PX GRAPES

GONZALEZ BYASS
THE CRISP, DRY TIO PEPE IS A CLASSIC FINO
THAT MAKES A GREAT MATCH FOR TAPAS

Grupo Estevez Jerez de la Frontera

Grupo Estevez comprises five top wineries across the sherry region and 700 vineyards. The best known for quality among the group are La Guita Manzanilla and the pago (single-vineyard) Valdespino. The Valdespino pago was given by the king to a knight in 1430 and registered in the 17th century; it was kept in the family until Grupo Estevez bought it in 1999. All the wines are focused, yet elegant. Inocente is an unusually rich, barrel-fermented fino full of nutty, brioche-like flavors with long length.

Carretera national IV, Km 640, 11408 Jerez de la Frontera
www.grupoestevez.es

Harveys Jerez de la Frontera

Harveys, now owned by the Beam Global drinks multinational, is renowned for one wine: Bristol Cream, a blend of every style of sherry packaged in a Bristol blue glass bottle. But there is quality across the board, including a lovely fino, and some great VORS wines.

Calle Pintor Muñoz Cebrián, 11402 Jerez de la Frontera
www.bodegasharveys.com

Hidalgo Sanlúcar de Barrameda

Founded in 1700, Hidalgo is now in the hands of Hector Hidalgo, the seventh generation to run the bodega. Its home is Sanlúcar, where the flor is different near the sea, river, and marshland that surround the town. It is cooler too, with a moderate climate and no frost. La Guitana is the flagship, a slightly salty, almost racy fino; the Manzanilla Pasado is a longer-aged version, with unbelievable length and verve. The bodega owns more than 495 acres (200ha) of vineyards, which include some 80-year-old vines.

Calle Clavel 29, 11402 Jerez de la Frontera
www.emiliohidalgo.es

Lustau Jerez de la Frontera

Lustau has long championed *almacenistas*, stockholders who buy sherry or must from the farmers and mature it in their own bodegas. *Almacenistas* do not have a license for bottling their own wine, and traditionally their sherries were sent for inclusion in the large commercial blends. But Lustau recognized that they had strong individual merit. Lustau has sought out *almacenistas* who match up to their standards and promoted their brands on an individual basis. The range is broad, and the quality consistent. Almacenista Manzanilla is a salty, fresh wine with good depth of flavor; the Solera Reserva Emilin is an aged Moscatel, full of orange-blossom aromas.

Calle Arcos 53, Apartado Postal 69, 11402 Jerez de la Frontera www.emilio-lustau.com

Sandeman Jerez de la Frontera

Sandeman has been a pioneer in the branding and advertising of its products, with recognizable images familiar to most. The bodega in Jerez is a major visitor center with a museum and a historical tour that is well worth taking. Old butts dating back 170 years are still in use. Look for the Royal Ambrosante PX with its dried-fruit aromas and explosive palate.

Calle Pizarro 10, 11403 Jerez de la Frontera
www.sandeman.eu

It is hard to think of France without a bottle of wine featuring somewhere in the picture. Wine here is part of the cultural as well as physical landscape, even if consumption levels have been falling in recent decades. Wine-growing in France dates back to Roman times, probably starting out around Nîmes and in the Rhône Valley. Today, France regularly competes with Italy for the title of the world's largest wine producer (making around 8 billion bottles per year).

Pick a wine style, and you are going to find it somewhere in France, and once you head up into the quality-focused AC territory, it is likely to be a benchmark for producers of similar wine styles made outside its borders. Even celebrated producers of iconic bottles elsewhere will readily agree that the wines of Bordeaux, Champagne, the Rhône, and Burgundy are worldwide references to the alchemy between man, soil, and grape. And the fact that over 90% of fine wine sold at auction is French proves that this country still holds huge allure.

Today, vines cover 2.16 million acres (872,000ha) of France, and there are around 144,000 different producers, from glamorous châteaux to large co-ops to one-man garage operations, and everything in between. In terms of range and pricing, French wine styles vary from basic Vin de Table to over 400 ACs. The diversity of the landscape helps create these contrasts: from the high-altitude wines of the Jura and Savoie in the Alps to the land-locked continental styles of Alsace and Burgundy, and the oceanic influences in Bordeaux and the Loire Valley to the Mediterranean heat of Corsica and Provence. Add this to the stubbornly French style of winemaking, where reflecting regional differences and the nuances of terroir is prized far more highly than creating consistent styles and easy branding, and you begin to realize why the diversity of French wine is unlikely to recede.

FRANCE

BORDEAUX

Bordeaux wine region

Ask a friend to name a wine region and chances are that the name Bordeaux will make an appearance; the region is so well-known that it can suffer from over-familiarity, even with people who have never opened a bottle. Its name is indelibly linked to some of the world's most iconic and expensive bottles, but suffers from the image of being over-complicated and snobbish. Many drinkers feel they simply do not know enough, or do not want to know enough, to navigate through the 10,000 châteaux that are crammed into this small corner of southwestern France. And yet, despite producing just 1.5% of the world's wine, Bordeaux continues to exert a pull, fascinating not only wealthy collectors and stuffy intellectuals, but winemakers and wine-lovers around the world. Unlocking its secrets is part of the fun.

Bordeaux is France's second-largest AC wine-growing area, with 296,520 acres (120,000ha) of vines, clocking in at just over ten times the size of Alsace and just under five times the size of Burgundy. But it is its location rather than its size that is key to understanding not only the nature of these wines, but their fame. The name Bordeaux itself, *au bord de l'eau* (by the water), is a major clue: the region is close enough to the Atlantic Ocean to give a maritime climate, far enough north on the 45th parallel to allow a long growing season that gives delicacy of flavors, and enough acidity to allow long aging potential. It also allows just enough unpredictability to make hedging your bets a good idea, and so winemakers developed an expertise over the centuries in blending different grape varieties. The complexity and balance that blending gives is key to the success of these wines.

More prosaically, the proximity of the Atlantic meant access to trading routes, thus allowing the wines to gain in stature and renown for almost 2,000 years. The city of Bordeaux is 50 miles (80km) inland, offering a safe harbor that has seen merchants from England, Ireland, the Netherlands, and Germany make it their home in successive waves since the 12th century. Bordeaux became part of the English crown for three centuries, when Eleanor of Aquitaine brought it as a dowry to her marriage to the man who became King Henry II of England. The wine of Bordeaux was, at that time, what we know today as "clairet"—a lighter style of red wine that spends only a short period in contact with the grape skins. Today, 70% of Bordeaux wine is still sold through négociants (merchants), and almost 40% of it is exported.

In terms of modern wine styles, Bordeaux is a primarily red wine region, with red grapes accounting for 89% of the plantings. Merlot takes up around two-thirds (170,840 acres/69,138ha), and Cabernet Sauvignon a little less than one-third (70,045 acres/28,347ha). There are small amounts of Cabernet Franc and Petit Verdot, and even smaller plantings of Carmenère and Malbec.

Of the 11% of production that is white wine, 8% is dry white and 3% sweet. The most prevalent white grape planted is Sémillon, with 19,027 acres (7,700ha) of vines, followed by Sauvignon Blanc at 12,602 acres (5,100ha), then a smattering of Muscadelle and tiny traces of Ugni Blanc, Folle Blanche, Sauvignon Gris, and Colombard.

To get an idea of styles, it helps to bear in mind the concept of terroir. This is discussed a lot in Bordeaux, so much so that it becomes tempting to dismiss it—but it is central to what wines taste like. Translating the concept is hard, but essentially it is a meeting of climate, topography, and soil, with the human hand guiding them all.

Put another way, it explains why Merlot thrives on the Right Bank, with its clay-rich, relatively cool, water-retaining soils. It is an early-ripening variety that does not like to get too hot. On the Left Bank, where gravel predominates, Cabernet Sauvignon works far better, as it needs the heat generated by the sun on the stones to fully ripen up.

There are other contributing factors to wine styles in Bordeaux, for example, the density the vines are planted to in the vineyard. Higher density increases competition between vines for water and nutrients, hopefully improving their quality.

Another clue to the importance of terroir in Bordeaux is the system of *mise en bouteille au château*. This indicates that the grapes come from one vineyard and the wine is bottled at the estate. Most estates have two labels: one for their *grand vin* and another for the lesser wines, but both will be bottled on site. This means that each bottle of wine is necessarily an expression of the specific ground on which it is grown—not only because the Bordelais believe in the concept, but also because the local wine laws insist that they must do so....

The top-ranked Château Ausone lies at the heart of the
St-Emilion appellation on the Right Bank.

THE MEDOC

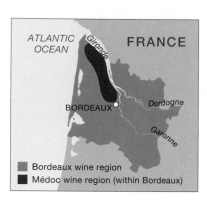

ATLANTIC OCEAN
Gironde
FRANCE
BORDEAUX
Dordogne
Garonne

■ Bordeaux wine region
■ Médoc wine region (within Bordeaux)

The Médoc, despite being home to some of the region's biggest names, is one of Bordeaux's most recent wine-growing areas; having just 500 years under its belt compared to 2,000 in St-Emilion. It is also, in theory—although the Médocains seem to forget this at times—one of its most cosmopolitan areas because it was built and then populated by successive waves of foreigners: the Dutch, the English, the Irish, and now, increasing numbers of Americans and Japanese. The name refers to the overall land on the Left Bank of the River Garonne, but the Médoc is divided into the four "big guns" of Margaux, St-Julien, Pauillac, and St-Estèphe, and four less well-known appellations, which are concentrated on here.

Major grapes
🍇 **Reds**
Cabernet Sauvignon
Merlot
Petit Verdot

Vintages
2009
An excellent year—powerful wines with great potential from near-perfect conditions.

2008
A cool summer caused problems, but fall was dry and sunny. Good wines from those who waited.

2007
A cool summer meant difficulty in ripening. Some good wines, but patchy.

2006
An ideal start to the season, but later rain threatened gray rot. The best producers made quality wine.

2005
Ideal growing conditions gave rich wines that have a long life ahead. Price increases less steep in these appellations.

2004
A classic vintage, with good yields. The wines now offer excellent value for money.

2003
Cabernet Sauvignon fared best in the extreme heat.

2001
An overlooked vintage, boasting many elegant wines.

The regional appellations of Médoc and Haut-Médoc, together with the village appellations of Moulis and Listrac, account for over 65% of the plantings on this thin peninsula between the Atlantic Ocean and the Gironde Estuary. It was this proximity to water that made the region unusable for most agriculture—and habitation—for much of its history. When Dutch engineering expertise drained its marshy interior in the 17th century, the gravel terroir beneath became apparent, and winemaking could begin in earnest. The Médocains have been busy making sought-after wines ever since, although the four top appellations of Margaux, St-Julien, Pauillac, and St-Estèphe—which lie closest to the river and its resulting transport—have stubbornly outshone their neighbors for centuries.

The 1855 classification system used in those better-known appellations does not figure prominently in these less prestigious ACs. Instead, the Cru Bourgeois system takes precedence. Only red grapes are allowed under any of the Médoc appellations, but that is not to say that white grapes are not grown here. You will find small pockets of mainly Sauvignon Blanc and Sémillon vines, but any resulting wines—even from the best estates—will be bottled as AC Bordeaux Blanc.

Cru Artisan wines are staging something of a renaissance, although their overall number remains small (44 at last count). The name refers to purely family-run properties, with an average of 15 acres (6ha) or less, who grow, produce, market, and sell the wines themselves.

Geographically, AC Haut-Médoc is closest to the city of Bordeaux and stretches up (off and on, around the boundaries of village appellations) to St-Estèphe. The AC Médoc heads north toward the mouth of the estuary, and is a sprawling, picturesque (but at times desolate) area with many small estates, interspersed with fishermen's huts whenever the estuary comes into view.

In terms of size, AC Médoc represents 35% of the total vineyard area at 19,130 acres (7,742ha), and over half of the growers in the appellation belong to co-operatives. AC Médoc also differs from the other local appellations in having more Merlot planted than Cabernet Sauvignon. AC Haut-Médoc, in contrast, has 28.5% of the total land with 11,507 acres (4,657ha), but here there is more Cabernet Sauvignon, and the majority of growers are independent, making wines that command a slightly higher price.

Moulis is the smallest appellation of the peninsula at 1,564 acres (633ha), with almost 50% Merlot planted. It has 53 growers, many of whom are small family estates, making wines that are often close to Margaux in style, with supple tannins. The name comes from the *moulins* (windmills) that were once common in this part of the Médoc. They were used to produce flour for bread and reflect the fact that both Moulis and Listrac form the highest parts of the region. It is at Listrac that the Médoc climbs up to 148ft (45m) above sea level, which is as high as things get around here. With 1,651 acres (668ha), Listrac represents 4% of the Médoc vineyard, and makes wines that are similar to its neighbor Moulis, but often with slightly more tannin and structure.

These less-celebrated areas can represent real value for money, and, although the best wines need hunting out, a little patience can lead you to some of the most exciting bottles in Bordeaux.

THE MEDOC

The four ACs of Médoc, Haut-Médoc, Moulis, and Listrac cover a wide geographic area, from the suburbs of Bordeaux city to the south, right up toward the mouth of the Gironde Estuary. Here you can find many well-priced, good-quality châteaux, often family run and with many selling bottles direct from the estate.

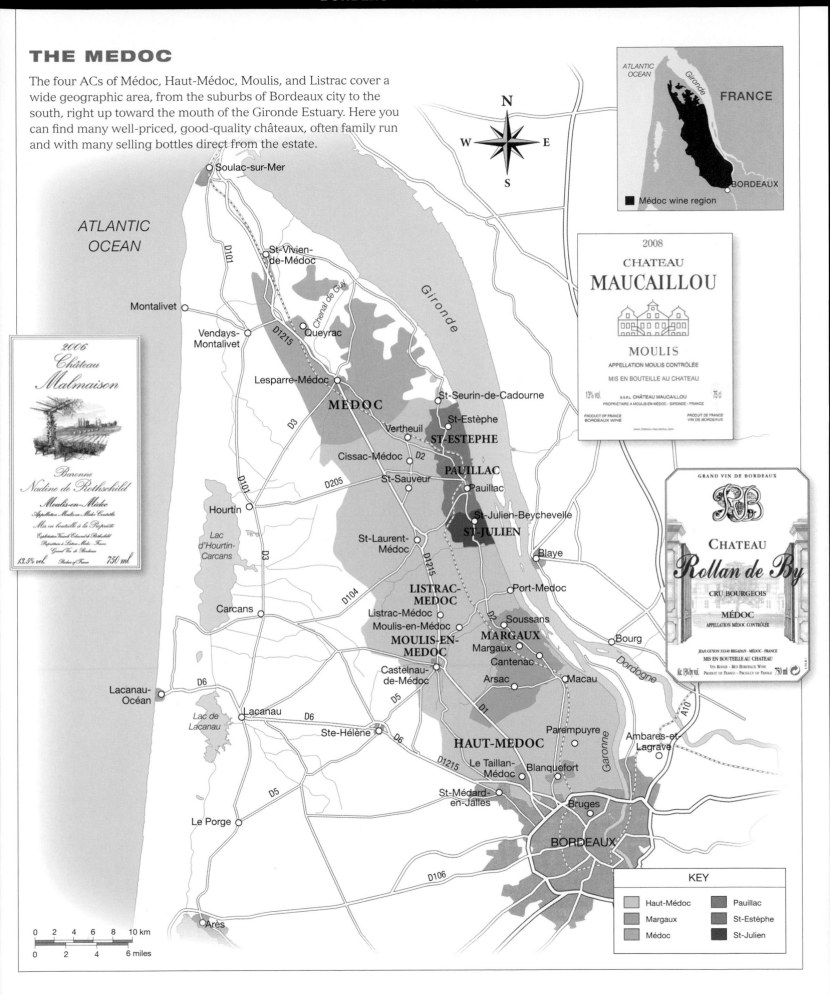

FRANCE

ATLANTIC OCEAN

Gironde

BORDEAUX

■ Médoc wine region

2008
CHATEAU
MAUCAILLOU

MOULIS

APPELLATION MOULIS CONTRÔLÉE

MIS EN BOUTEILLE AU CHATEAU

13% vol.   75 cl

SARL CHÂTEAU MAUCAILLOU
PROPRIÉTAIRE A MOULIS-EN-MÉDOC - GIRONDE - FRANCE

PRODUCT OF FRANCE   PRODUIT DE FRANCE
BORDEAUX WINE   VIN DE BORDEAUX
www.chateau-maucaillou.com

2006
Château
Malmaison

Baronne
Nadine de Rothschild
Moulis-en-Médoc
Appellation Moulis-Médoc Contrôlée
Mis en bouteille à la Propriété

Exploitation Vinicole Edmond de Rothschild
Propriétaire à Listrac-Médoc France
Grand Vin de Bordeaux

13.5% vol.   750 ml

GRAND VIN DE BORDEAUX

CHATEAU
Rollan de By

CRU BOURGEOIS

MÉDOC
APPELLATION MÉDOC CONTRÔLÉE

JEAN GUYON 33340 BEGADAN · MÉDOC · FRANCE
MIS EN BOUTEILLE AU CHATEAU
VIN ROUGE · RED BORDEAUX WINE
PRODUIT DE FRANCE · PRODUCT OF FRANCE   750 ml

ATLANTIC OCEAN

Soulac-sur-Mer

St-Vivien-de-Médoc

Montalivet

Vendays-Montalivet

Queyrac

Lesparre-Médoc

MEDOC

St-Seurin-de-Cadourne

St-Estèphe

ST-ESTEPHE

Vertheuil

Cissac-Médoc

St-Sauveur

PAUILLAC

Pauillac

Hourtin

Lac d'Hourtin-Carcans

St-Laurent-Médoc

St-Julien-Beychevelle

ST-JULIEN

Blaye

Carcans

Port-Medoc

LISTRAC-MEDOC

Listrac-Médoc

Moulis-en-Médoc

MOULIS-EN-MEDOC

Bourg

MARGAUX

Margaux

Castelnau-de-Médoc

Cantenac

Soussans

Lacanau-Océan

Arsac

Macau

Lac de Lacanau

Lacanau

Ste-Hélène

Parempuyre

Ambares-et-Lagrave

HAUT-MEDOC

Le Porge

Le Taillan-Médoc

Blanquefort

St-Médard-en-Jalles

Bruges

BORDEAUX

Ares

Chenal de Guy

Gironde

Dordogne

Garonne

KEY	
Haut-Médoc	Pauillac
Margaux	St-Estèphe
Médoc	St-Julien

Scale:
0 2 4 6 8 10 km
0 2 4 6 miles

Château d'Agassac Cru Bourgeois

D'Agassac is a small but perfectly formed 13th-century château that looks like it has stepped right out of a fairy tale—and the owners make the most of this by running iPod tours for children where they search for a princess hidden in the tower. There is a high proportion of Merlot in this 96 acre (39ha) vineyard, which produces a good quality Médoc that is ready to be cracked open a little earlier than some of its peers. Flavors are often intense and concentrated. The tongue-twisting L'Agassant d'Agassac is a wine produced from just 15 acres (6ha) of 90% Merlot grapes and intended for easy drinking.

15 rue d'Agassac, 33290 Ludon-Médoc
www.agassac.com

Château Anthonic Cru Bourgeois

Owner Jean-Baptiste Cordonnier makes wine from 91 acres (37ha) of clay–limestone and gravel soils, producing 190,000 bottles a year. With more Merlot than Cabernet Sauvignon this is a fleshy wine, with firm but ripe red fruits. Unusually for a Cru Bourgeois, it is sold direct, mainly to independent stores and restaurants. The desire to avoid the usual selling system of Bordeaux and cut out the middleman is brandished on the label—two eagles fighting over a grape, to represent a merchant and an owner fighting over the wine. Fittingly, the second wine is named Les Aigles [Eagles] d'Anthonic.

Malinay Ouest, 33480 Moulis-en-Médoc
05 56 58 34 60

Château d'Aurilhac Cru Bourgeois

There is an international feel here—the château is owned by a Dutch-French couple, and the wine is aged partly in American oak. That oak, together with the rather flashy extraction, means you can expect big, powerful wines that are packed with black fruits. The vineyard itself covers 50 acres (20ha) and is fairly young, due to a recent program of replanting—the vines are around 15 years old on average. A small quantity of Malbec is included in this wine, in addition to the three classic Médoc grape varieties. ★ Rising star

33108 St-Seurin de Cadourne
erik-nieuwaal@wanadoo.fr

Château Belgrave Fifth Growth

Owned and solely distributed by Bordelais négociant house Dourthe, Belgrave has been busy restructuring the 150 acre (61ha) vineyard, adding a new winery with stainless steel vats and banning the use of pumps for moving the grapes around. The work has paid off, as the last few vintages have finally seen this wine get an injection of firm fruit and rounder, riper tannins. It now offers excellent value—at least until everyone else wises up to this—although second wine Diane de Belgrave remains more variable.

No visitor facilities
www.dourthe.com

Château Belle-Vue Cru Bourgeois

Vincent Mulliez worked as a director of JP Morgan bank in London before heading back home to Bordeaux in 2004 and buying two Haut-Médoc properties, Belle-Vue and de Gironville. The vines directly border the Margaux classified growth Château Giscours, but the wine is more

CHATEAU BELGRAVE
A REVIVED CHATEAU NOW PRODUCING EXCELLENT CABERNET-DOMINANT WINES

CHATEAU D'AGASSAC
A TONGUE-TWISTER OF A SECOND WINE FROM CHATEAU D'AGASSAC

peppery than its neighbor, with more than 20% of old vine Petit Verdot. Mulliez, who died suddenly in May 2010, deserves credit for his pricing strategy, as he was one of very few to reduce prices in 2006 and 2007—perhaps his banking friends had given him an early heads-up on the global wobbles.

103 route de Pauillac, 33460 Macau-en-Médoc
www.chateau-belle-vue.fr

Château Brillette Cru Bourgeois

This large estate covers 260 acres (105ha), with 99 acres (40ha) given over to vines, and has been managed by the Flageul family since 1976. The vines have reached an average of 35 years, and are densely planted at up to 4,000 vines per acre (10,000 per hectare). The family has kept the winery up to date, and in 2000 Erwan Flageul introduced a new barrel cellar, a new winery, and new stainless steel vats. Defined by its high proportion of Merlot (up to 55% in some vintages), this has a flattering fruit-forward style. The second wine is called Les Haut de Brillette.

route Peyvigneau, 33480 Moulis-en-Médoc
www.chateau-brillette.fr

Château Cambon la Pelouse
Cru Bourgeois

Nicolas Maestre, son of owner Jean-Pierre, now runs this estate. He looks like he should be hanging out in a New York record store rather than a row of Médoc vines, but he is making fantastic quality wines that are worth the time to search out. The 2007 vintage saw the introduction of a *microcuvée* from the Margaux appellation, 1.2 acres (0.5ha) of vines in between Cantenac Brown and Château Margaux called L'Aura de Cambon. Matured in French oak barrels for at least 12 months, the wine is made up of 50% Cabernet Sauvignon and 50% Merlot.

5 chemin de Canteloup, 33460 Macau-en-Médoc
www.cambon-la-pelouse.com

Château Camensac Fifth Growth

Sandwiched between the area's two other châteaux from the 1855 classification, Belgrave and La Tour Carnet, Camensac was owned until 2005 by the Forner Brothers of Marqués de Cacères in Rioja, Spain. Jean Merlaut is now in charge, assisted by his niece Celine Villars, and Eric Boissenot as consultant. Planted at a density of 4,000 vines per acre (10,000 per hectare), as high as things typically go in Bordeaux, the wine is gentler than its neighbors, with a roughly even split between Merlot and Cabernet Sauvignon. The château also produces a second wine, La Cloiserie de Camensac.

route de St-Julien, 33112 St-Laurent-Médoc
www.chateaucamensac.com

Château Cantemerle Fifth Growth

Cantemerle is one of the oldest estates in the Médoc—there were vines here in 1354, when many of its neighbors were still marshland. Today, it is a reliable workhorse that flies a little too low under the radar but produces accomplished Cabernet Sauvignon-led wines from its 215 acre (87ha) vineyard. You could argue that its modern contribution to the Médoc is as one of the first châteaux to have been bought by an insurance company—the French SMABTP Group purchased it from Bertrand Clauzel in 1981—so starting a trend that is still going strong today. The second label, Les Allées de Cantemerle, comes from the château's younger vines.

1 chemin Guittot, 33460 Macau-en-Médoc
www.cantemerle.com

Château La Cardonne Cru Bourgeois

All 111 acres (45ha) of this estate are certified in sustainable agriculture, and comprise 45% Cabernet Sauvignon, 50% Merlot, and 5% Cabernet Franc vines. This property hasn't always had the best press, but current director Gaëtan Charloux has done a lot to turn things around (helped by a technical director who came from Lynch-Bages). This included upping the density of plantation following a replanting program in the vineyard, and installing an impressive underground cellar. The second wine, Château Cardus, uses younger vines and is aged in stainless steel, with no oak.

33340 Blaignan
www.domaines-cgr.com

Château Caronne-Ste-Gemme
Cru Bourgeois

The 111 acres (45ha) of vines at Caronne-Ste-Gemme are spread around the quiet village of St-Laurent, with an average age of 25 years. Owner François Nony, cousin of the Borie family at Ducru-Beaucaillou, makes a wine in classic Médoc style, evidenced by the majority of Cabernet Sauvignon and one year in oak, and the fact that the UK remains the major market (around 25,000 cases end up there every year). The enologist Olivier Dauga has introduced the concept of green harvesting, which has helped to concentrate flavors and made this a popular and rewarding wine. The second wine is Château Labat.

33112 St-Laurent-Médoc
www.chateau-caronne-ste-gemme.com

Château Castera Cru Bourgeois

Located in the tiny commune of St-Germain d'Esteuil, Castera certainly makes an impression, with a medieval château and 470 acres (190ha) of land, this is one of the biggest estates in the Médoc. Over two-thirds of the estate is forest, parkland, and very attractive gardens, with just 155 acres (63ha) of vineyard, the majority of which (62%) is planted to Merlot. A conscious effort to modernize by the new owners (a group, with Dieter Tondera as director and Jacques Boissenot as enologist) has seen some lovely toasty notes coming through. The second wine is Château Bourbon La Chapelle.

33340 St-Germain d'Esteuil
www.chateau-castera.com

Château Chasse-Spleen
Cru Bourgeois

Non-French speakers miss some of the romanticism of this name, which translates roughly as "chase the blues away". The Villars-Merlaut family are hard at work on the 198 acres (80ha) of vines here. Bernadette Villars, who took over the running in 1976, made vast improvements to the estate and is ably succeeded by her daughter Claire, who continues to improve the wines. A consistently enjoyable, punching-above-its-weight estate, making elegant wines that are high in

Cabernet Sauvignon, but well-worked to ensure accessibility. There are two second wines: L'Ermitage de Chasse-Spleen and L'Oratoire de Chasse-Spleen.

32 chemin de la Raze, 33480 Moulis-en-Médoc
www.chasse-spleen.com

Château Citran Cru Bourgeois

Céline Villars-Merlaut (sister of Claire at Chasse-Spleen) is continuing the long and rather varied history of Citran, which has yo-yoed in size over the course of its existence between 222 acres (90ha), as it is today, and 10 acres (4ha). Proving that the best gardeners often make the best winemakers, Céline is in the process of uprooting acacia trees from high ground on the estate. She realized that these trees would only be thriving on deep, well-drained land such as Médoc gravel—the perfect soil for Cabernet Sauvignon vines. The second label is Moulin de Citran.

chemin de Citran, 33480 Avensan
www.citran.com

Château Clarke Cru Bourgeois

Although its history dates back to the 12th century, the first wine bottled here was in 1978, five years after it was bought by Baron Edmund de Rothschild. Today, it is run by his son Baron Benjamin (who also owns estates in South Africa and Argentina), a cousin of Baron Eric at Château Lafite. Lengthy titles aside, this family knows a thing or two about winemaking: gravity-feeding grapes into large wooden vats, then aging in 100% new oak barrels for 14 to 18 months. The blend has just under 50% Cabernet Sauvignon, but with a good dollop of Cabernet Franc, which gives a lovely aroma to the wine. There is also a very good Rosé de Clarke.

No visitor facilities
www.cver.fr

Château Clément-Pichon Cru Bourgeois

Owner Clément Fayat is also the owner of Château La Dominique in St-Emilion. He fully replanted this 62 acre (25ha) vineyard when he bought the estate in 1976, and ensured 2,630 vines per acre (6,500 per hectare) of 50% Merlot, 40% Cabernet Sauvignon, and 10% Cabernet Franc. Modern winemaking techniques include micro-oxygenation and nicely toasted oak, resulting in a wine that is smooth, rich, and very enjoyable.

30 avenue du Château Pichon, 33290 Parempuyre
No visitors facilities. www.vignobles.fayat.com

Château Fonréaud Cru Bourgeois

Owner Henri de Mauvezin is happy to attest that his vines sit at the highest point of the Médoc, a dizzying 141ft (43m) above sea level (which is why Listrac is rather ambitiously referred to as "the roof of the Médoc"). This is a wine that is often tannic in youth, and needs at least five years to develop in bottle—it is best to head to the second wine, La Tourelle de Château Fonréaud, for anything younger. It is also worth looking out for the white wine, Le Cygne de Château Fonréaud (AC Bordeaux), which comes from just 5 acres (2ha) of Sauvignon Blanc, Sémillon, and Muscadelle vines, aged in 50% new oak.

138 Fonreaud, 33480 Listrac-Médoc
www.chateau-fonreaud.com

WINE LAW

CRU BOURGEOIS

Is it or isn't it? That has been the question ever since 2003, when the new Cru Bourgeois ranking was published and subsequently abandoned. The term dates right back to 1932 and it describes a category of red wine properties (*crus*) below the Cru Classés, or classified growths, that were still of high enough quality to be singled out for distinction. But this new classification was never ratified until, after decades of discussion, an "official" ranking was awarded to 247 châteaux out of the 490 that applied. This rather meager pass rate turned out to be a big mistake, as 77 of the slighted châteaux joined together and successfully had the classification overturned.

Today, you will still see the words Cru Bourgeois on the label, but as of the 2008 vintage, it is an assurance of quality, rather than an actual classification. Châteaux have to apply every year to the Alliance des Crus Bourgeois du Médoc for the right to use the term. Assuming the quality is good enough, and they have followed the strict rules, they can then put the term on their labels. Some of the most prestigious châteaux (in practice this means a former Cru Bourgeois Exceptionnel) may take a wait and see approach as to whether or not to apply.

CHATEAU FOURCAS HOSTEN
INVESTMENT IN THE VINEYARD AND WINERY
HAS BREATHED NEW LIFE INTO THE WINE

CHATEAU FOURCAS DUPRE
FROM A GRAVELLY SITE, THIS IS AN
ELEGANT CABERNET-BASED WINE

Château Fourcas Dupré Cru Bourgeois

Next door to Fourcas Hosten, owner Patrice Pagès makes a more structured wine than his neighbor, largely because a gravel outcrop marks the 114 acres (46ha) of vines on this side of the road. This gravel means a grape mix of 38% Merlot, 50% Cabernet Sauvignon, 10% Cabernet Franc, and 2% Petit Verdot, giving both elegance and structure to the final wine—but it may need a few years to open up. There have been quiet renovations going on over the past few years, including a restored barrel cellar, and the wine is becoming a reliable and enjoyable choice.

Lieu-dit Le Fourcas, 33480 Listrac-Médoc
www.fourcasdupre.com

Château Fourcas Hosten Cru Bourgeois

Peter Sichel, the charming Frenchman who became a key figure of the New York wine scene, sold this family property to Renaud and Laurent Momméja (otherwise known as the Hermès brothers) in 2006. The soils here are split into two very distinct halves, with one full of clay and the other full of gravel, which makes planting an easy split of 45% Merlot, 45% Cabernet Sauvignon, and 10% Cabernet Franc. The wine has not always lived up to its full potential, but the purse strings have been loosened with the new arrivals. The charming second wine, which sees just 25% aged in oak, is Les Cèdres d'Hosten.

2 rue d'Eglise, 33480 Listrac
www.fourcas-hosten.fr

La Goulée

A relative newcomer to the Bordeaux scene, the vines for this wine are found in Port du Goulée at the mouth of the Gironde Estuary, and are the most northerly in the Médoc. Owned by the Reybier family of Cos d'Estournel, Goulée is made by the same team as at Cos, but it is a different vineyard and has different winemaking facilities. According to director Guillaume Prats, the concept was to rival the positioning and consistency of a brand like New Zealand's Cloudy Bay, but from Bordeaux—and this is seriously smooth, silky stuff. The white wine, La Goulée Blanc, is also excellent. ★ **Rising star**

c/o Château Cos d'Estornel, 33180 Saint-Estèphe
www.estournel.com

Château Greysac Cru Bourgeois

Located a long way north of St-Estèphe, in the small town of By, Greysac has a good-sized 235 acre (95ha) vineyard and produces about 540,000 bottles, with about 70% ending up in the aromatic, full-bodied, and decidedly modern first wine, and the remaining 30% going to the second wine, Château de By. Run by the affable Philippe Dambrine (of Cantermerle), Château Greysac also makes a 100% Sauvignon Blanc dry white from 5 acres (2ha) at Bégadan. Both fermentation and aging take place exclusively in barrels (30% of which are new each year), with regular *bâtonnage*, or stirring of the yeast lees.

18 route By 33340 Bégadan
www.greysac.com

Château Jander Cru Bourgeois

Dutch owner Hans Peter Jander keeps things simple with an even 50/50 split between Cabernet Sauvignon (on sandy gravel) and Merlot (on clay–limestone), making around 12,000 bottles a year at this small (17 acre/ 7ha), but dynamic property. The vines are mature at roughly 25 years old. The wine has a pleasant smoky note due to a year-long aging in oak barrels (50% of which are new). Since 1998, Château Jander has also made wine from 4.5 acres (1.8ha) in the Moulis appellation.

41 avenue Soulac, 33480 Listrac-Médoc
05 56 58 01 12

Château La Lagune Third Growth

When you arrive at La Lagune, you know you are out of the murky suburbs of Bordeaux and into the Médoc proper, as its handsome gates mark the start of the attractive Route des Châteaux. There is a long history of female winemakers here, and today, Caroline Frey follows on the tradition. Since the Frey family bought the estate in 2000, the winery has been lined with 72 gravity-fed tanks and produces wine that shows firm, intense fruit with an attractive peppery finish. It comes from the Petit Verdot grape (around 10% in most vintages), blended in with Cabernet Sauvignon and Merlot. Three wines are produced: La Lagune; second label Moulin de La Lagune; and Mademoiselle L, for early drinking.

83 avenue de l'Europe, 33290 Ludon-Médoc
www.chateau-lalagune.com

Château Lestage Cru Bourgeois

A popular wine with the French government, apparently, Jean and Marie-Helene Chanfreau run this 104 acre (42ha) estate where about 250,000 bottles are made from 52% Merlot, 46% Cabernet Sauvignon, and 2% Petit Verdot. It is no wonder they have kept this property in the family for over half a century—the vineyard is surrounded by parkland, and there is a gorgeous Napoleon III château on one of the highest outcrops of the appellation. The second wine is La Dame de Coeur de Château Lestage, but also worth looking for is the tiny Château Caroline in Moulis, owned by the same family.

c/o Château Fonréaud, 33480 Listrac-Médoc
www.chateau-lestage.com

Château Lestruelle Cru Bourgeois

Owned by Patrick Bouey and a Bordeaux négociant firm of the same name, the vines at Lestruelle are 75% Merlot, together with equal proportions of Cabernet Franc and Cabernet Sauvignon. The wine itself is a good-value choice with rich black fruit flavors and firm tannins. Bouey also owns Château Maison Blanche, right next door in St-Yzans-de-Médoc on clay–limestone soils—it is one of the rare 100% Merlots from the Left Bank.

1 rue Loudenne, 33340 St-Yzans-de-Médoc
05 56 09 05 01

Château Malmaison Cru Bourgeois

Unusually for this part of the world, this wine contains up to 80% Merlot grapes in some years (although others are closer to 60%). Run by Nadine de Rothschild, it is located adjacent to Château Clarke, and covers 59 acres (24ha). The wine is a lighter, fruitier expression of Moulis—vinified in stainless steel and followed by aging in a mixture of new and one-year-old barrels.

No visitors facilities
www.cver.fr

Château Maucaillou Cru Bourgeois

This imposing château was built by a former owner as a wedding gift to his lucky wife. The name came from the *mauvais cailloux*, or "bad stones", that were unsuitable for growing grain, but which turned out at a later date to be perfect for vines. The estate is owned by Philippe Dourthe, (who no longer has any connection to the Bordeaux négociant that bears his family name). The modern, clean approach to the wines is reflected in the name of the second label: simply No 2 de Maucaillou.

Quartier de la Gare, 33480 Moulis-en-Médoc
www.chateau-maucaillou.com

Château Mayne Lalande Cru Bourgeois

A cheerful, modern label reflects the light touch that Bernard Lartigue brings to his wines. When he got going, over 30 years ago, he had just 2.5 acres (1ha) of vines going to the local co-operative, and bottled his first vintage in 1982 (not a bad year to start). Today, he has 35 acres (14ha) in Listrac, and a further 12 acres (5ha) in Moulis (Château Myon d'Enclos). The Mayne Lalande Grand Reserve wine is aged for 30 months—very unusual in Bordeaux—and is richer than the first wine.

route du Mayne, 33480 Listrac-Médoc
www.mayne-lalande.com

Château Moulin à Vent Cru Bourgeois

The former president of the Cru Bourgeois Association, Dominique Hessel, owns this low-key but good-quality château. Covering 62 acres (25ha), it produces 120,000 bottles each year, split between Moulin à Vent and the second wine, Château Moulin de St-Vincent. The first wine is 60% Cabernet Sauvignon, lightly filtered, keeping it well-structured, with good, tight fruit.

Bouqueyran, 72 avenue de Médoc, 33480 Moulis-en-Médoc
www.moulin-a-vent.com

Château du Moulin Rouge Cru Artisan

The rather glamorous name is a world away from the reality of this very simple property, owned by the Ribeiro family for more than 200 years. Located in Cussac-Fort-Médoc, just as Haut-Médoc approaches St-Julien, the sometimes gawky tannins evident in the wine have been increasingly tamed in recent years, and, particularly since 2005, this wine has often been excellent quality for the price. The blend is an equal mix of Cabernet Sauvignon and Cabernet Franc, plus 10% Merlot.

18 rue Coste, 33460 Cussac-Fort-Médoc
laurence.ribeiro@free.fr

Château Patache d'Aux Cru Bourgeois

There are a number of estates within the Domaines Lapalu umbrella—Patache d'Aux, Leboscq, Liversan, Lacombe Noaillac, and Lieujean—in the Médoc and Haut-Médoc appellations. All are owned by Jean-Michel Lapalu, a French-Tunisian, and are good bets for reliable quality at reasonable prices. Technical director Olivier Sempé ensures strict traceability at every stage and, increasingly, low-impact, green practices are being brought into the winemaking.

1 rue du 19 mars, 33340 Bégadan
05 56 41 50 18

CHATEAU PREUILLAC
THIS RICH RED IS A BLEND OF 60% MERLOT, 35% CABERNET SAUVIGNON, AND 5% CABERNET FRANC

CHATEAU POUJEAUX
THIS CRU BOURGEOIS SHOULD REACH STELLAR HEIGHTS IN THE NEXT FEW YEARS

Château Peyrat-Fourthon

Château Peyrat-Fourthon covers 49 acres (20ha) on clay–limestone and gravel, with 55% Cabernet Sauvignon, 41% Merlot, and 4% Petit Verdot all planted at 2,670 vines per acre (6,600 per hectare). There are some interesting modern techniques going on at this little-known estate—cold soaking (cooling the crushed grapes prior to ferment), micro-oxygenation, and 100% new oak barrels. The owner, Pierre Narboni, has been here since 2004 (and nearly half of the vineyard has been acquired since he took over). The consultant is Christophe Coupez, director of the Pauillac Oenology Institute. This is one to keep an eye on. ★Rising star

33112 St-Laurent-du-Médoc
www.peyrat-fourthon.com

Château Potensac Cru Bourgeois

Château Potensac is owned by the Délon family of Château Léoville-Las-Cases, making it a very smart buy, particularly in good years when its big brother is going to be asking for serious cash. The estate has 131 acres (53ha), planted to 60% Cabernet Sauvigon, 25% Merlot, and 15% Cabernet Franc at a relatively high 3,240 vines per acre (8,000 per hectare). The first wine is unmistakably a Médoc, because it is firm, structured, and needs time to open up. It is worth noting that the winemaker here is Pierre Rolland, Michel Rolland's brother. The second wine is La Chapelle de Potensac.

33340 Lesparre-Médoc
www.potensac.com

Château Poujeaux Cru Bourgeois

The new owner of Château Poujeaux, Philippe Cuvelier, and a young team led by his son Mathieu, hails from Clos Fourtet over in St-Emilion, marking one of the few occasions that a big Right Bank family has crossed over the Gironde to the Other Side. Consultant Stéphane Derenoncourt works with both properties, and is helping to turn this 128 acre (52ha) estate into a serious prospect—definitely one to watch. Expect big black currant flavors, tempered by savory herbs. ★Rising star

No visitors facilities
www.chateaupoujeaux.com

Château Preuillac Cru Bourgeois

The dynamic Jean-Christophe Mau has been the proprietor of Preuillac since 1998, in partnership with the Dutch liquor company Dirkzwager. Over the last 10 years, they have invested in new drainage channels, higher density planting across the entire 74 acres (30ha), and a new winery with modern equipment, and have also undertaken extensive renovations to the handsome château itself. Stéphane Derenoncourt is consultant both here and at Mau's Pessac-Léognan estate, Château Brown. A good-quality wine, rich and supple, with growing renown.

33340 Lesparre-Médoc
www.chateau-preuillac.com

Château Réal

Next to Tronquoy in St-Seurin-de-Cadourne, Château Réal is owned by the Lemaignan family, but the vines were taken over by Didier Marcellis in 2006. The estate is only 12 acres (5ha), but the intention is to expand it to 17 acres (7ha), enabling it to qualify as a Cru Bourgeois.

CHATEAU SOCIANDO-MALLET
THIS POWERFUL WINE WILL REVEAL ITS
VOLUPTUOUS SIDE AFTER A FEW YEARS

The vineyard is currently planted to 55% Cabernet Sauvignon, 10% Cabernet Franc, and 35% Merlot. With Hubert de Bouärd as consultant, everything in the vineyard is now organic, and worked by hand. They have raised the proportion of Cabernet Franc, increased the surface of the vine canopy to maximize ripening potential, and introduced a policy of no filtration (just egg-white fining) to improve quality. One to watch. ★ **Rising star**

No visitors facilities
www.chateau-serilhan.fr

Château Rollan de By Cru Bourgeois
Jean Guyon would be the first to admit that he had his work cut out for him when he bought this 5 acre (2ha) estate in the far-flung corners of the Médoc back in 1989. But he has worked tirelessly to make this wine better known. Today, Rollan de By covers 205 acres (83ha) and regularly stands equal to the best in blind tastings. The consultant is Alain Reynaud, an equally modern figure, best known for his work on the Right Bank. There is a high degree of new oak, giving an opulence and rich mouth-feel that always makes an impression. It is also worth tracking down Guyon's Château Haut Condissas, made from vines located close by.

3 route du haut Condissas, 33340 Begadan
www.rollandeby.com

Château Saint Paul
A large proportion of this wine ends up in the UK and the US, perhaps a reflection of its full-bodied, crowd-pleasing style with ripe plums and rich black fruits, but with enough acidity to make it a very good food wine. The wine is made up of 60% Merlot, 30% Cabernet Sauvignon, and a 10% mix of Petit Verdot and Cabernet Franc. Owned by Bernard Boucher, the vineyard covers 54 acres (22ha) and comes from parcels from two neighboring châteaux—Le Boscq and Morin, both of which are located in St-Estèphe. Even more reflected glory comes from its position, right next to Sociando-Mallet. The second wine is Terre Brune de Saint Paul.

33180 St-Seurin-de-Cadourne
05 56 59 34 72

Château Sénéjac Cru Bourgeois
Owned by Thierry Rustmann and his wife Lorraine Cordier of Château Talbot, the 18 acres (39ha) of vines at Château Sénéjac are planted to 48% Cabernet Sauvignon, 37% Merlot, 11% Cabernet Franc, and 4% Petit Verdot. Mme Cordier obviously has exquisite taste, as the château is complete with ivy-clad walls, formal gardens, and chic interiors. There have been a number of false starts with this estate—once upon a time a white wine, then a special bottling called Karulos—but today they are concentrating on the increasingly good quality Château Sénéjac itself.

No visitor facilities
www.chateau-senejac.com

Château Sociando-Mallet
This is the estate that every wine geek loves to name-check. Resolutely staying outside of the various classification systems on offer in the Médoc, Sociando-Mallet nevertheless attracts many followers. It is located

CHATEAU SENEJAC
THE SAME CARE TAKEN OVER THE INTERIOR
OF THIS CHATEAU IS APPLIED TO ITS
INCREASINGLY RELIABLE CLARET

on a gravelly outcrop around 1.9 miles (3km) north of St-Estèphe. The success has everything to do with the apparently laid-back Belgian owner, Jean Gautreau, who is in fact obsessive about every detail of his winemaking. He bought a heap of dilapidated buildings and just 12 acres (5ha) of vines back in 1969 and has grown them to 210 acres (85ha). This is not a gentle wine—there are tight tannins and a powerful structure—but it has a voluptuous quality, especially after a few years, that places it way above most of its neighbors.

33180 St-Seurin-de-Cadourne
05 56 73 38 80

Château du Taillan Cru Bourgeois
Another château where women rule the roost, with the five Cruse sisters working closely together from the vineyard through to bottling. This is a beautiful estate, with a wine cellar dating back to the 15th century, and the property itself is a classified historic monument. Wines to try include Château de Taillan, the softer Cuvée des Dames, and their white AC Bordeaux, Château La Dame Blanche.

56 avenue du la Croix, 33320 Le Taillan-Médoc
www.chateaudutaillan.com

Château La Tour Carnet Fourth Growth
Ask a child to draw a picture of a French château and this is probably what he will come up with—towers, moat, battlements, the works. And it is authentic, as the tower here dates back to the 11th century. The vineyard is a substantial 161 acres (65ha) and is planted at just under 4,047 vines per acre (10,000 per hectare), comprising 40% Cabernet Sauvignon, 50% Merlot, 7% Cabernet Franc, and 3% Petit Verdot. La Tour Carnet suffered for a number of years from a cool terroir that led to problems with ripening, but improvements in drainage channels, planting of trees to provide natural shelter, plus serious investments in winemaking from owner Bernard Magrez have seen both the first wine and second label Douves de Carnet begin to make waves. The grapes are put uncrushed into stainless steel vats, and are subject to the usual Magrez care and attention.

33112 St-Laurent-Médoc
www.latour-carnet.com

Château Tour St-Bonnet Cru Bourgeois
This used to be Château La Tour St-Bonnet, until the owners were taken to court by Latour back in 1996, and hastily dropped the "La". Undeterred by the fuss, owner Jacques Merlet-Lafon continues to make one of the best-loved Cru Bourgeois wines from a 99 acre (40ha) site right up in St-Christoly-du-Médoc, where the peninsula starts narrowing as it heads toward the sea. The blend has equal proportions of Merlot and Cabernet Sauvignon, but with a little Malbec thrown in for a rich, spicy edge.

33340 St-Christoly-du-Médoc
www.tour.saint.bonnet.free.fr

ST-ESTEPHE

St-Estèphe is the furthest north of the village appellations of the Médoc. The stony terroir reaches its peak here, but with a clay subsoil that retains more moisture than other parts of the region. There are 3,089 acres (1,250ha) of vines producing wines with a firm style, and there are some excellent, well-regarded properties. The appellation holds five classified growths (led by second growths Châteaux Montrose and Cos d'Estournel, although the overall number is half that of the smaller appellation of St-Julien), and there are also more than 30 Cru Bourgeois, including four of the nine former Cru Bourgeois Exceptionnels: Châteaux Phélan Ségur, de Pez, Les Ormes de Pez, and Haut-Marbuzet.

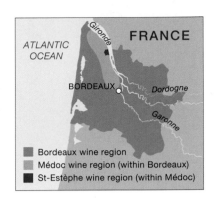

St-Estèphe is the only well-known Médoc appellation where vineyard consolidation and sales of parcels of land have been intense over the past decade, meaning that it is an exciting region to find both new blood and renewed vigor in old names. This is mainly due to the fact that the local co-operative has sold off or rented out large amounts of land following the retirement of some of its members, thus enabling rapid expansion at châteaux such as Montrose, Lilian Ladouys, Tour de Pez, Petit Bocq, and Sérilhan. The movement has injected a sense of dynamism into an appellation that previously had a reputation for making tough, rather rustic wines, and for being much less exciting than its neighbors along the Route des Châteaux to the south. The co-operative cellar itself, one of the oldest in Bordeaux, is feeling the strain of having lost so many members, and there are concerns that the most famous châteaux will continue buying up small plots of land, thereby threatening some of the diversity of the appellation.

In terms of grape varieties, 51% of the plantings are Cabernet Sauvignon (the slightly lower figure than the other three riverside appellations reflects the clay in the soils, as well as the large patches of sand found toward the northern part), along with 40% Merlot, 6.5% Cabernet Franc, 2.3% Petit Verdot, and 0.3% Malbec and Carmenère. This shift away from Cabernet Sauvignon is welcome in this particular appellation, because its rather dour reputation often came from planting the grape on soils that never allowed it to fully ripen. The new

wave of owners—as across much of Bordeaux—has taken far greater notice of geological studies, and planted more suitable grapes accordingly.

Another key advance in the past few decades has been the introduction of first and second wines. Until the 1980s, the majority of estates—even the well-known ones—put their entire production under one label. But as quality concerns became more important, the best producers began separating their various plots and keeping them apart, both during vinification and final blending. This usually means fruit from the older vines ends up in the first, more complex wine, and bears the main château name. This then allows the winemaker to use the younger vines in the second label, producing a fruitier and fresher wine that is usually ready to drink without needing the same length of time in bottle. A few estates have second wines dating back to the 19th century, but the majority only began the practice seriously at the end of the 20th century. Second wines are common now across the entire Bordeaux region, with the biggest concentration being among the classified wines of the Médoc. In St-Estèphe, some of the best examples are La Dame de Montrose, Les Pagodas de Cos, and Franck Phélan.

The results are clear for those who combine this high level of attention to detail with careful vineyard management, and who make the decision to delay picking until grapes are fully ripe. Increasingly, the producers of St-Estèphe are following these techniques, and the appellation is benefiting enormously.

Major grapes
🍇 Reds
Cabernet Sauvignon

Merlot

Vintages

2009
An excellent year—powerful wines with aging potential.

2008
A cool summer caused problems, but September and October were exceptionally dry and sunny, with a long ripening period in which to recover. Good quality for those who waited.

2007
A difficult year with a damp summer meant the clay parts of St-Estèphe struggled to ripen. Good wines, but patchy.

2006
A classic year, with an ideal start to the season but some rain during harvest. Very good wines from the top producers.

2005
Near ideal growing conditions resulted in rich wines that have a long life ahead of them, although St-Estèphe saw no rainfall at all over the summer.

2004
A classic year, with good yields, and the wines offer excellent value for money.

2003
The water-retaining soils of St-Estèphe performed better than most in this hot year.

CHATEAU CALON SEGUR
THE ROMANTIC LABEL REFLECTS THE
AFFECTION IN WHICH THIS WINE IS HELD

CHATEAU COS D'ESTOURNEL
NO EXPENSE IS SPARED IN PRODUCING
THIS WINE AND A SIMILAR APPROACH IS
REQUIRED IN THE BUYING OF IT

Château Beau-Site Cru Bourgeois

Château Beau-Site is a Castéja family wine that is going for the traditional St-Estèphe market. This essentially means tight black fruits and a need to double decant if drinking young. They manage this by keeping the proportion of Cabernet Sauvignon high at 60%, and maturing the wine in oak barrels (50% new) for around 15 months. The 247 acres (100ha) of vines are located right next door to Château Calon Ségur and have an average age of 35 years.

33180 St-Estèphe
05 56 00 00 70

Château Le Boscq Cru Bourgeois

Château Le Boscq is owned by Vignobles Dourthe, the vineyard side of a Bordeaux merchant house that now owns 1,236 acres (500ha) of vines around the region. This estate makes up just 44 acres (18ha) of the total, planted to 60% Merlot, with 26% Cabernet Sauvignon, 10% Petit Verdot, and 4% Cabernet Franc. The high percentage of Merlot gives an unusually smooth and frank expression of St-Estèphe, and this is a definite crowd-pleaser. Some of the key innovations in recent years have been an introduction of sustainable viticulture practices, together with traceability and small vinifications.

No visitor facilities
www.dourthe.com

Château Calon Ségur Third Growth

Proving that the power of marketing helps even classified Bordeaux, the heart on Château Calon Ségur's label is an intimate part of its appeal (recalling a former owner who, although lucky enough to be in possession of Châteaux Lafite and Latour, claimed, "My heart belongs to Calon."). Owned today by the Gasqueton family, this is the most northerly of all Médoc-classified wines, with 183 acres (74ha) of vines planted to 65% Cabernet Sauvignon, 20% Merlot, and 15% Cabernet Franc. Chewy, well-textured wines that pack a punch—and if that's not enough to convince you, the actor Johnny Depp is a fan. The second wine is Marquis de Calon.

2 Château Calon-Ségur, 33180 St-Estèphe
05 56 59 30 08

Château Clauzet Cru Bourgeois

Belgian businessman Maurice Velge has owned Château Clauzet since 1997. His technical director, José Bueno, came from Château Mouton Rothschild, which is an efficient way to inspire confidence in your wine. The vines cover 49 acres (20ha) with a majority of Cabernet Sauvignon and a dash of Petit Verdot giving it a rich, deep color. This is a wine that makes its presence felt, with an imposing structure, and tightly controlled black fruits. The same owner also produces Château de Côme from the same appellation, in a lighter, more fruity style.

Leyssac, 33180 St-Estèphe
www.chateauclauzet.com

Château Cos d'Estournel Second Growth

Ambition is certainly a word that could be associated with Château Cos d'Estournel—from the pricing strategy, to the gleaming new winery, and the precision and professionalism of the wine itself. With 227 acres (92ha) of 60% Cabernet Sauvignon and 40% Merlot, the

Reybier family and director Jean-Guillaume Prats have everything covered. The first wine spends 18 months in new oak (the second wine, Les Pagodes de Cos, gets 12 months) and at the end you get smooth, rich, yet complex bottles. Blanc de Cos d'Estournel is an AC Bordeaux with 80% Sauvignon Blanc and 20% Sémillon, made in the region's most northerly vineyards. It has a purity that is more Loire than Bordeaux, and is just stunning.

33180 St-Estèphe
www.cosestournel.com

Château Cos Labory Fifth Growth

Dense, brooding, difficult in its youth… all of these words are often associated with Château Cos Labory. It is run by Bernard Audoy, a descendant of the Weber family who have been here since the early 20th century. Today, although never reaching the heights of neighbor Château Cos d'Estournel, it has 44 acres (18ha) of old vines planted to 55% Cabernet Sauvignon, 33% Merlot, 10% Cabernet Franc, and 2% Petit Verdot, that are worked by both machine and hand. This is an estate that is sometimes disregarded—and unfairly so, as its firm wines age beautifully.

33180 St-Estèphe
05 56 59 30 22

Château Le Crock Cru Bourgeois

Château Le Crock may not be the most promising of names but that can be forgiven. Owned by the Cuvelier family of Château Léoville Poyferré since 1903, it was not run by a family member until the late 1970s, when Didier Cuvelier took over. The first wine has 79 acres (32ha), with 60% Cabernet Sauvignon, and, as at their other estate, the enologist here is Isabelle Davin, one of the talented group of female winemakers making an impact across the region. Michel Rolland is consultant. The second wine, La Croix St-Estèphe, is fruity and fresh but still has the weight of the appellation.

Marbuzet, 33180 St-Estèphe
05 56 59 08 30

Château Domeyne Cru Bourgeois

Claire Villars and her husband Gonzargue Lurton have owned Château Domeyne since 2006. This small estate is worth keeping an eye on. On a lovely gravelly plateau there are 22 acres (9ha) of vines, planted to 65% Cabernet Sauvignon vines, plumped out by 35% Merlot, and 5% Cabernet Franc. All harvesting is done by hand, and the wine spends between 12–14 months in oak (40% new each year). Domeyne has long enjoyed a quiet reputation for classic and elegant St-Estèphe, but with the combined skills of the new owners is likely to further improve.

rue 3 espace Guyonnaud, 33180 St-Estèphe
05 56 59 72 29

Château Haut-Beauséjour Cru Bourgeois

In 1992, Jean-Claude Rouzaud, enologist and president of Champagne Louis Roederer, bought two Cru Bourgeois vineyards in St-Estèphe. He promptly joined them together, and created what is now the 49 acres (20ha) of Château Haut-Beauséjour. As you would expect at all the Roederer properties, the purchase was followed by some serious investment, from high-tech installations in the winery, to careful vineyard replanting. Director Philippe

ST-ESTEPHE

Situated halfway between Bordeaux city and the Pointe de Grave at the top of the Médoc Peninsula, St-Estèphe is the furthest north of the key communes in this region of Bordeaux. Vines that can be included in AC St-Estèphe wines can be grown in several small villages, including St-Corbian, Pez, Leyssac, and Marbuzet, as well as St-Estèphe itself. The darker shading on the map represents the AC area under vine.

ATLANTIC OCEAN
FRANCE
Gironde
MEDOC
BORDEAUX

Médoc wine region (within Bordeaux)
St-Estèphe wine region (within Médoc)

CHATEAU CLAUZET
SAINT-ESTÈPHE
2007
Baron Velge

ST-SEURIN

Chenal de Calon

St-Corbian

Port de la Chapelle

St-Estèphe

VERTHEUIL

Pez

Aillan

ST-ESTEPHE

Gironde

SECOND GRAND CRU CLASSÉ EN 1855
Château Montrose
2006
Saint-Estèphe
MIS EN BOUTEILLE AU CHATEAU

Laujac

Leyssac

D204

Hanteillan

Marbuzet

Blanquet

CISSAC-MEDOC

Chenal de Lazaret

PRODUCERS

Ch Beau-Site **6**	Ch Haut-Marbuzet **16**	Ch Phélan Ségur **21**
Ch Le Boscq **7**	Ch Lafon-Rochet **12**	Ch Picard **22**
Ch Calon Ségur **24**	Ch Lilian Ladouys **11**	Ch Pomys **10**
Ch Clauzet **8**	Ch Meyney **18**	Ch Ségur de Cabanac **25**
Ch Cos d'Estournel **14**	Ch Montrose **17**	Ch Sérilhan **1**
Ch Cos Labory **13**	Ch Les Ormes de Pez **2**	Ch Tour des Termes **5**
Ch Le Crock **15**	Ch Petit Bocq **4**	Ch Tronquoy-Lalande **19**
Ch Domeyne **23**	Ch La Peyre **9**	
Ch Haut-Beauséjour **20**	Ch de Pez **3**	

KEY

ST-ESTEPHE AC

Rivers, lakes

Roads, tracks

16ft (5m) contours

Commune border

Urban areas

1 Location of one or more producers

0 200 400 600 800 1000 meters
0 400 800 yards

Always check the availability of tasting facilities and the visiting hours at a winery before planning your trip. Some wineries are open by appointment only.

Moureau works both here and at Château de Pez. The wine is firm and controlled, with an appealing fist of blackberry fruits.

rue de la Mairie, 33180 St-Estèphe
05 56 59 30 26

Château Haut-Marbuzet Cru Bourgeois

Henri Dubocsq took over Château Haut-Marbuzet from his father Hervé, and is now helped by his own sons, Bruno and Hughes. The 163 acres (66ha) of vines are planted to 3,642 per acre (9,000 per hectare), taking full advantage of the fact that each vine produces fewer but more concentrated grapes when planted so densely. This is an estate that is quietly getting on with things, and is leading the way in many green practices—preferring ploughing over herbicides, for example. The wine itself is 50% Cabernet Sauvignon/40% Merlot/10% Cabernet Franc and is voluptuous, with notes of chocolate and mocha. The second wine is Château MacCarthy.

33180 St-Estèphe
05 56 59 30 54

Château Lafon-Rochet Fourth Growth

Michel Tesseron is in charge here at Château Lafon-Rochet, aided by his son Basile since 2007. The vineyard covers 111 acres (45ha), planted to 55% Cabernet Sauvignon, 40% Merlot, 3% Cabernet Franc, and 2% Petit Verdot, with an average age of 30 years. High density planting of up to 3,723 vines per acre (9,200 per hectare) helps to deliver big flavors in the wine, with a lovely edge of savory herbs, and it is often recognized as one of the best-value classified wines of Bordeaux. The distinctive label reflects the cheerful yellow color of the château building itself. Pélerins de Lafon-Rochet is the second wine here.

Lieu-dit Blanquet, 33180 St-Estèphe
05 56 59 32 06

Château Lilian Ladouys Cru Bourgeois

Jacky Lorenzetti, the Swiss owner of Château Lilian Ladouys, is a property billionaire and rugby fanatic. He has been installed here since late 2008, although he continues to spend much of his time in Paris. There are 90 plots of vines on 116 acres (47ha), with a majority (58%) of 40-year-old Cabernet Sauvignon. Château de la Devise de Lilian is the second wine, which accounts for 60,000 bottles, with production of the main wine at around 240,000 bottles. The vineyards are very close to those of Château Cos d'Estournel but it is yet to make its way onto the radar, so prices can be good. There has been a lot of activity going on but it does need more investment to fully realize its potential.

Blanquet, 33180 St-Estèphe
www.chateau-lilian-ladouys.com

Château Meyney Cru Bourgeois

Château Meyney offers restrained wine at restrained prices. This is another château owned by the vineyard arm of French bank Crédit Agricole, an organization that has introduced sustainable winemaking practices at all its estates in the past few years. Vines are planted in a single plot of 126 acres (51ha) with 56% Cabernet Sauvignon, 26% Merlot, 9% Petit Verdot, and 9% Cabernet Franc. A fruit-forward wine, which manages to pull a few

CHATEAU LAFON-ROCHET
A DISTINCTIVE AND GREAT-VALUE WINE FROM A CLASSIFIED GROWTH

CHATEAU MEYNEY
THE SITE OF A FORMER CONVENT NOW PRODUCES A FRUIT-FORWARD WINE

surprises at how good it can be for the price. The second wine is Prieur de Meyney, so named because there was a convent at this location in the 17th century.

33180 St-Estèphe
www.meyney.fr

Château Montrose Second Growth

Château Montrose is becoming one of the leading examples of green winemaking in Bordeaux, as owner Martin Bouygues (a construction billionaire) is currently installing solar panels, geothermal energy, and a full waste-recycling system in the sleek new winery. The wine itself is firm, rich, and confident with 65% Cabernet Sauvignon, 25% Merlot, and 10% Cabernet Franc all giving a tannic structure that suggests very long aging potential. You would expect no less from director Jean Delmas, who was lured here after his retirement from Château Haut-Brion. The vineyard is 165 acres (67ha) in a beautiful position, sloping gently down to the Gironde estuary. The second wine is La Dame de Montrose.

33180 St-Estèphe
www.chateau-montrose.com

Château Les Ormes de Pez
Cru Bourgeois

Bright, crisp, and succulent fruit has become increasingly obvious with every recent vintage at Château Les Ormes de Pez. Mirroring this fresh approach is their new label, with a stylized tree that represents the elm (orme) trees that once grew nearby. Owned by the Cazes family of Château Lynch-Bages, the wine itself has 51% Cabernet Sauvignon, 39% Merlot, 8% Cabernet Franc, and 2% Petit Verdot, growing over 82 acres (33ha) of vineyard land that is a mix of sand and gravel (the sand perhaps freeing up the tannins a little compared to the family's Pauillac estates). There is no second wine here.

route des Ormes, 33180 St-Estèphe
www.ormesdepez.com

Château Petit Bocq Cru Bourgeois

Château Petit Bocq sounds like the second wine of Le Bocq, but is in fact its own estate. The owner, Gaëton Lagneaux, quit his job as a doctor to follow his passion of winemaking (there are a few of these doctors-turned-winemakers around Bordeaux), and has turned 5 acres (2ha) of vines into 44 acres (18ha) over the past 10 years. On almost entirely gravel soils, the densely planted vineyards are 65% Merlot with the remaining area given over to Cabernet Sauvignon and a sprinkling of Cabernet Franc. The grapes are picked by hand, the wine is bottled without filtration, and the château offers excellent value. A deep color, with elegance and good acidity, this wine has plum fruits and chocolate flavors that need time to fully open up.

3 route Croix de Pez, 33180 St-Estèphe
www.chateau-petit-bocq.com

Château La Peyre Cru Artisan

The small winery at Château La Peyre, owned by Dany and René Rabiller, started bottling its own wine in 1989, after years of sending it to the local co-operative. There is now a winery on the estate, producing 48,000 bottles a year from 20 acres (8ha) of vines. One-fifth of the yield is AC Haut-Médoc and the rest is St-Estèphe. Winter pruning to reduce potential yields takes precedence over green harvesting here, meaning a naturally limited crop size. Lack of filtering further concentrates the sometimes rustic flavors that are always full of character. Cabernet Sauvignon just slightly dominates over the Merlot in the taste, with plums and damsons, and a lovely gentle toast from the oak.

Le Cendrayre, 33180 St-Estèphe
vignoblesrabiller@wanadoo.fr

Château de Pez Cru Bourgeois

Château de Pez is owned by the champagne house Louis Roederer, along with some other well-known Médoc properties. There are 74 acres (30ha) of vines with 45% Cabernet Sauvignon, 8% Cabernet Franc, 3% Petit Verdot, and 44% Merlot. The wine is unfiltered and aged for 16–18 months in small oak barrels (40% of which are new each year). All of this makes a serious impression, and needs a few years to soften, or at the very least to be decanted a few hours ahead of drinking. The lovely nose of toasted oak gives it an edge of opulence, however, which is appealing right from the start.

No visitor facilities
www.champagne-roederer.com

Château Phélan Ségur Cru Bourgeois

The owner of Château Phélan Ségur, Thierry Gardinier, is also president of the Alliance de Cru Bourgeois. Covering 168 acres (68ha), with 47% Merlot, 22% Cabernet Sauvignon, and the rest Cabernet Franc, the wine is aged in barrels for 14 months (50% new). This gives an attractive smoky nose to the classic black fruit structure. Michel Rolland is consultant here, and together they have developed a special *cuvée* blockbuster called Fée aux Roses from some of their oldest vines, vinified in 100% new oak. There is also a second wine, Frank Phélan, and—a little confusingly—a third label, La Croix Bonnis.

No visitor facilities
www.phelansegur.com

Château Picard

The merchant house Mähler Besse bought Château Picard in 1997, and the grapes are now processed through a gravity-fed system. The vineyard covers 25 acres (10ha) and produces 45,000 bottles per year, with a second wine, Les Ailes de Picard. The wines are deep in color, with evident oak, but there is also balance and elegance to them, and they offer good value in expensive years.

No visitor facilities
www.mahler-besse.com

Château Pomys

There is now a hotel and restaurant at Château Pomys, offering a welcoming place to rejuvenate to those intrepid travelers who have made it this far north. The wine at this 59 acre (24ha) vineyard is 60% Cabernet Sauvignon, 30% Merlot, and 10% Cabernet Franc. The Arnaud family splits the vineyard—one half for Pomys, and the other for Château St-Estèphe. A solid and traditional wine that needs time to open up, this is a good, reliable choice.

Route de Poumeys, Leyssac, 33180 St-Estèphe
www.chateaupomys.com

Château Ségur de Cabanac
Cru Bourgeois

Owned by Guy Dellon of Château Moulin de la Rose in St-Julien, the 17 acre (7ha) estate of Château Ségur de Cabanac is planted with 60% Cabernet Sauvignon and 40% Merlot. It is well-placed on several gravelly outcrops dotted around the appellation. Dellon's son Jean François is the technical director, and he produces around 45,000 bottles each year of an elegant wine of well-crafted red fruits. The grapes are vinified in stainless steel and the resulting wine is aged for 20 months in 30% new oak. There is no second label.

33180 St-Estèphe
www.segur-de-cabanac.com

Château Sérilhan Cru Bourgeois

Didier Marcellis left his high-powered job at Cisco Systems in Paris for the rural charms of Château Sérilhan and St-Estèphe back in 2003. He has since hired technical director Bernard Franc from Château Pontet-Canet, together with wine consultant Hubert de Boüard of Château Angélus in St-Emilion. All of this clearly signals that Marcellis means business, and the wine has certainly gained in depth and intensity in recent years. The wine now has the structure and depth of a St-Estèphe, with the exuberance of a more modern sensibility. Alongside investments in the vineyard and cellar, he has also expanded the vineyard to 57 acres (23ha).

No visitor facilities
www.chateau-serilhan.fr

Château Tour des Termes Cru Bourgeois

There are two plots of vines covering a total of just over 40 acres (16ha) at Château Tour des Termes, producing good quality wines. The château itself is the first one you come to as you enter St-Corbian village, and is owned by the affable Jean Anney, now helped by his son Christophe. Around 100,000 bottles are produced each year, comprising 60% Cabernet Sauvignon and 40% Merlot, but that blend manages to fully bring out the fleshy, feminine Merlot. The second wine is Les Aubaredes de Tour des Termes.

2 rue du Pigeonnier, 33180 St-Estèphe
www.chateautourdestermes.com

Château Tronquoy-Lalande
Cru Bourgeois

It is always a good tip to find the smaller châteaux owned by big names, as you tend to get the winemaking know-how without the price tag. Château Tronquoy-Lalande, which is owned by the brothers Martin and Olivier Bouygues of Château Montrose and run by Jean Delmas, is a fine example of that theory. Since they took over in 2006, the vine-canopy cover has been increased across the 44 acre (18ha) vineyard. The nose on this wine is attractively floral, and the fruit has a delicacy that disguises the punch of tannins. The second wine is Tronquoy de Sainte-Anne.

33180 St-Estèphe
www.tronquoy-lalande.com

THE CELLAR AT COS

Cos d'Estournel's new multi-million-euro winery is haute couture winemaking at its most lavish, and has been the talk of the Médoc since it opened for the *en primeur* season in March 2009. Covering 21,500 sqft (2,000 sqm) of floor space, with 10,750 sqft (1,000 sqm) of passageways, everything in this cellar is gravity-fed, which means that pumps are not used at any stage of the winemaking process and so the grapes are treated more gently. There are 72 stainless steel vats, double-lined for the temperature control, and split into two "floors" for true plot-by-plot vinification. Grapes are chilled down to -40°F (-40°C) so they can be stalked without damaging the skins, and elevators, rather than pumps, move the grapes and juice between floors. Every part of the process has been considered, and the precision that it allows in winemaking, according to director Jean-Guillaume Prats, means Cos d'Estournel can be assured of a greater quantity of the first wine each year.

The 17th-century exterior of Cos d'Estournel is in sharp contrast to its new, multi-million dollar high-tech winery.

PAUILLAC

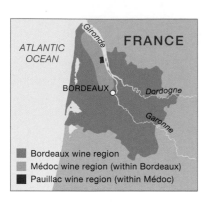

- ■ Bordeaux wine region
- ■ Médoc wine region (within Bordeaux)
- ■ Pauillac wine region (within Médoc)

Three out of the five first growths—Mouton, Lafite, and Latour—are found in this 2,943 acre (1,191ha) appellation, which is seen as the epicenter of classified Bordeaux. In total, there are 18 classed growths, who between them account for 85% of Pauillac's production, and many continue to buy up any available plots of vines. This is possible because the system of ranking on the Left Bank classifies the name of the château rather than the land—unlike St-Emilion, where the vines themselves are classified, and any enlargements have to prove their quality for more than a decade before being allowed to be included in the wine. Here on the Left Bank, they trust that market forces and winemaking expertise will ensure continued excellence.

Major grapes

🍇 Reds

Cabernet Sauvignon

Merlot

Petit Verdot

Vintages

2009
Excellent, with ideal conditions ensuring great potential. Often compared to 1982 and 1947.

2008
A cool summer followed by a dry and sunny fall. The long ripening period ensured good quality, for those who watched and waited.

2007
A difficult year with a damp summer meant uneven ripening. Some good wines, but patchy, and early drinking.

2006
A classic year, but with rain in August that continued into harvest. The best producers made very good wines.

2005
Ideal growing conditions meant rich, long-lived wines.

2004
A classic, with good yields, and the wines now offer excellent value for money.

2003
The extreme heat suited the grapes of Pauillac, but the rich wines are peaking young.

2000
Many fine wines with rich, powerful fruit and firm tannins. Beginning to open up now.

In total, there are 88 producers in Pauillac, but only 34 of them bottle their wines under their own name. The rest send their grapes to the local co-operative cellar, La Rose Pauillac, which is one of the oldest in Bordeaux. In terms of grapes, this is the undisputed land of Cabernet Sauvignon, accounting for 62.5% of plantings. The proportion rises even higher in the first growths, which are built for long aging and almost invariably have more than 90% in the blend. The other varieties are 30.6% Merlot, 5.6% Cabernet Franc, and 1.3% Petit Verdot and Malbec. In total, the area produces 8.2 million bottles of wine each year and many reach some of the highest prices in Bordeaux— selling for hundreds of dollars per bottle *en primeur* (also known as wine futures, where the best-known wines are sold six months after harvest, around 18 months before bottling). They often change hands and sell for many times their initial price over the following years.

Pauillac is ideally situated for making powerful, long-lived wines. Lying between St-Estèphe to the north and St-Julien to the south, its soils are made up of layers of Garonnaise gravel, with important deposits of iron. Only a few of the estates rise particularly high above sea level, but there are numerous elevated outcrops and slopes, making for very effective natural drainage.

All of which explains why, when Bordeaux merchants were asked to make a ranking of the region's best wines in 1855 (based on the price they

had reached on the marketplace over the preceding decades, and in some cases centuries), so many of this area's estates were showcased.

The 1855 classification, put together for the Universal Exhibition in Paris, was the first of its kind in the world (Bordeaux wines had been loosely ranked before this, but not in such an official format). The classification not only established the region as a reliable source of fine wines, but also gave consumers and retailers a simple one-to-five ranking system of the Crus Classés (classed growths) that continues today.

There is no formal system in place to revise the original classification and there have been just two changes since the original assessments in 1855. The first update was the inclusion of Château Cantemerle in Haut-Médoc as a fifth growth a few months after the first list was released. The second, and most recent, was the elevation of Château Mouton Rothschild from a second growth ranking to a first growth in 1973. This promotion was implemented after successful lobbying by Mouton's owner, Baron Philippe de Rothschild, who had described the oversight as a "monstrous injustice." There are regular complaints that the system no longer reflects the true quality of Médoc wines, with second growths said not to deserve their place, and fifth growths regularly outperforming them in both price and quality, but there seems little chance of any serious overhaul taking place.

PAUILLAC

Representing 7% of the Médoc's vineyards, wines bearing the appellation AC Pauillac on their label must come from vines grown in the commune of Pauillac, or certain parts of its neighboring commune, St-Sauveur. Historically, there are also one or two clearly delineated plots of St-Estèphe and St-Julien—appellations that sit directly to the north and south—that allow labeling as AC Pauillac. A port located in the town of Pauillac itself was once the hub of local wine shipments, but today is restricted to fishing boats and pleasure craft.

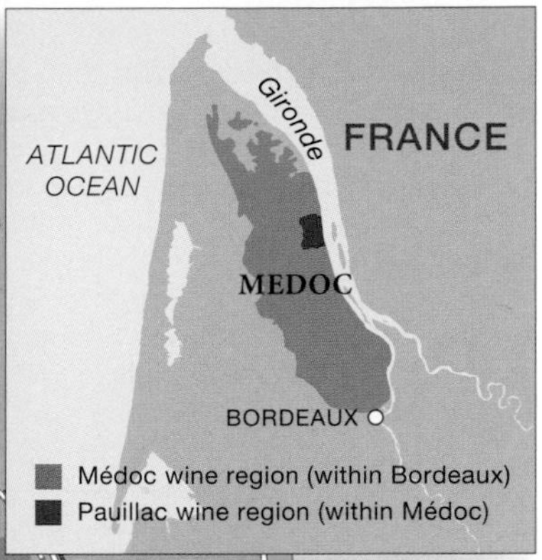

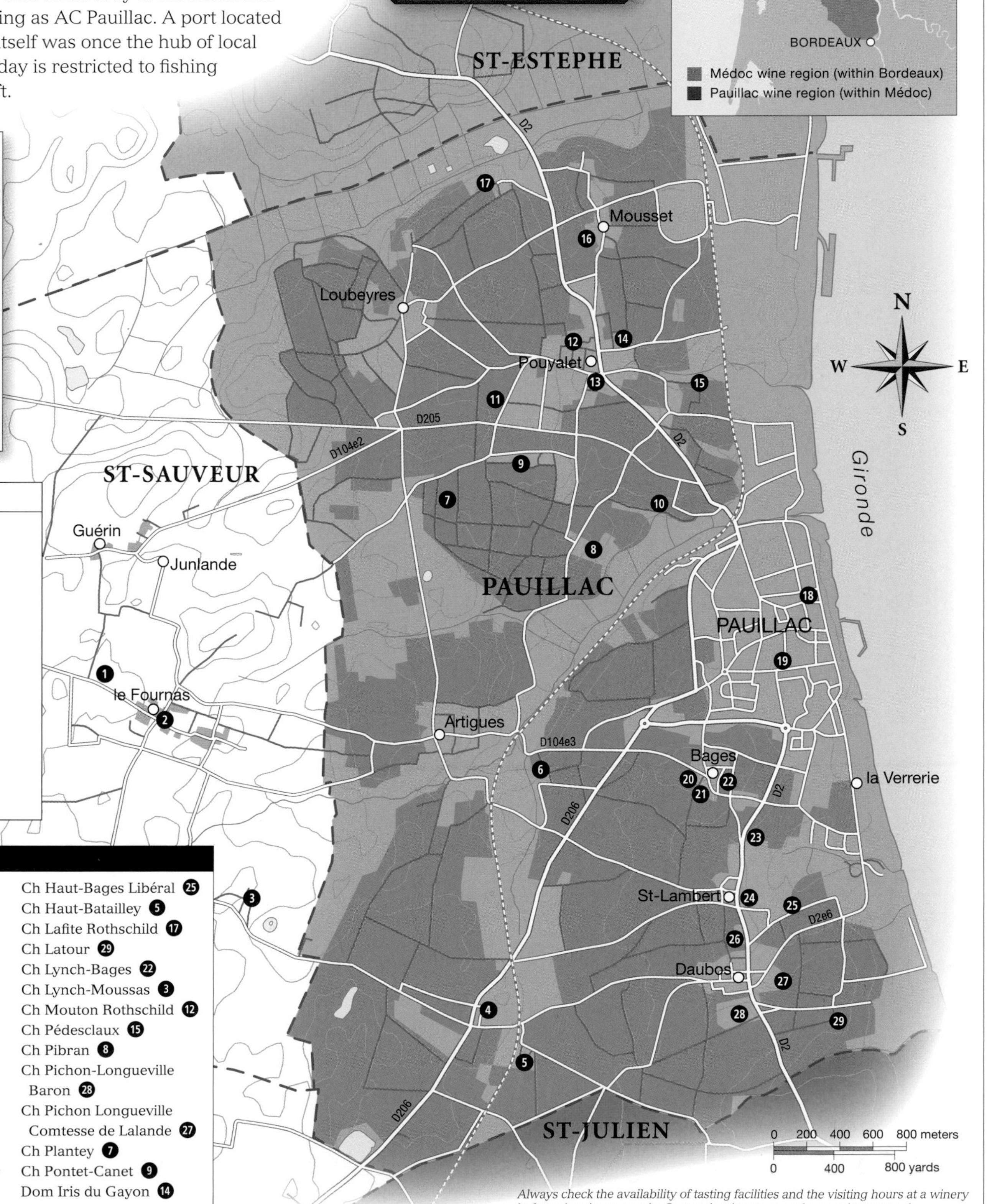

KEY

PAUILLAC	AC
	Rivers, lakes
	Roads, tracks
	16ft (5m) contours
	Commune border
	Urban areas
1	Location of one or more producers

PRODUCERS

Ch d'Armailhac	**11**	Ch Haut-Bages Libéral	**25**
Ch Batailley	**4**	Ch Haut-Batailley	**5**
Ch Béhèré	**13**	Ch Lafite Rothschild	**17**
Ch Bellegrave	**24**	Ch Latour	**29**
Ch La Bécasse	**21**	Ch Lynch-Bages	**22**
Ch Clerc Milon	**16**	Ch Lynch-Moussas	**3**
Ch Colombier-Monpelou	**10**	Ch Mouton Rothschild	**12**
Ch Croizet-Bages	**20**	Ch Pédesclaux	**15**
Ch Duhart-Milon	**19**	Ch Pibran	**8**
Ch La Fleur Peyrabon	**1**	Ch Pichon-Longueville Baron	**28**
Ch Fonbadet	**26**	Ch Pichon Longueville Comtesse de Lalande	**27**
Ch La Fon du Berger	**2**		
Ch Gaudin	**23**	Ch Plantey	**7**
Ch Grand-Puy-Ducasse	**18**	Ch Pontet-Canet	**9**
Ch Grand-Puy-Lacoste	**6**	Dom Iris du Gayon	**14**

Map labels: ST-ESTEPHE, Mousset, Loubeyres, Pouyalet, ST-SAUVEUR, Guérin, Junlande, PAUILLAC, Artigues, le Fournas, Bages, la Verrerie, St-Lambert, Daubos, ST-JULIEN, Gironde, D2, D205, D104e2, D104e3, D206, D2e6

Inset map labels: ATLANTIC OCEAN, FRANCE, Gironde, MEDOC, BORDEAUX

Médoc wine region (within Bordeaux)
Pauillac wine region (within Médoc)

0 200 400 600 800 meters
0 400 800 yards

Always check the availability of tasting facilities and the visiting hours at a winery before planning your trip. Some wineries are open by appointment only.

Château d'Armailhac Fifth Growth

Château d'Armailhac, along with Clerc Milon, is now owned by Mouton Rothschild. One of the first proprietors of this estate promoted the use of Cabernet Sauvignon in the Médoc, so he might be disappointed to learn that today this variety only makes up 54% of the blend. The rest of the vineyard is 31% Merlot, 12% Cabernet Franc, and an even split between Petit Verdot and Carmenère. It is a clever choice though, as this relatively high proportion of Cabernet Franc gives the wine a beautifully perfumed, fleshy touch that has an unmistakable family resemblance to Mouton Rothschild—if you like a sensuous style of claret, this is going to deliver.

33250 Pauillac
www.bpdr.com

Château Batailley Fifth Growth

The wine of Château Batailley appears in the latest James Bond novel by Sebastian Faulks, confirming its status as a smooth, sophisticated yet masculine Pauillac. The estate's owner Philippe Castéja (also owner of Château Beau-Site in St-Estèphe) puts upward of 70% Cabernet Sauvignon in the mix and, by rarely including more than 25% Merlot, the emphasis is kepton cigar-box, pencil lead, and black cherry flavors. The vineyard itself is 143 acres (58ha), and the equipment in the cellars reflects the vineyard exactly. There are 58 vats in the winery, meaning there is effectively one for each individual plot of vines. The wine gains further power and structure by spending 18 months in oak, of which up to 60% is new each year.

Batailley, 33250 Pauillac
05 56 00 00 70

Château Béhèré Cru Artisan

Château Béhèré is classified as a Cru Artisan wine (in a nutshell, this means that it comes from a small estate where one family grows, makes, markets, and sells its own wine), created in 1993 by husband-and-wife team Jean-Gabriel and Anne-Marie Camous. Jean-Gabriel ran his own plumbing business previously but, as with all Médocains, wine had clearly got under his skin and he could not resist when the opportunity presented itself. Today, they have 11.6 acres (4.7ha) of vines that, having previously been sent to the local co-operative, are now vinified in their own tiny winery. The wine is 65% Cabernet Sauvignon, 30% Merlot, and 5% Petit Verdot, aged for 12 months in barrel (of which 25% are new).

13 rue Paul Domer, 33250 Pauillac
05 56 59 11 19

Château Bellegrave

Jean-Paul Meffre ventured into Pauillac from his St-Julien base to acquire this small property, Château Bellegrave, in 1997. Today, his sons Ludovic and Julien are in charge. Covering just 21 acres (8.3ha), the vines are an average age of 22 years. The vineyard consists of 62% Cabernet Sauvignon, 31% Merlot, and 7% Cabernet Franc, all planted on deep gravel, as the name suggests. Bellegrave has long aging potential and firm black fruits. Production of the first wine is 25,000 bottles, along with 12,000 bottles of the second, Les Sieurs de Bellegrave.

22 route des Châteaux, 33250 Pauillac
www.chateau-bellegrave.com

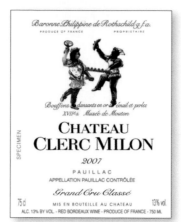

CHATEAU CLERC MILON
PART OF THE ROTHSCHILD STABLE,
THIS ESTATE IS NOW EXPANDING

CHATEAU GRAND-PUY-DUCASSE
THIS FIFTH GROWTH IS SET TO GET EVEN
BETTER IN FUTURE VINTAGES

Château La Bécasse

Good quality, non-classified Pauillac is the holy grail for bargain hunters, and Château La Bécasse is one of the best. The owner, Roland Fonteneau, buys high-quality barrels secondhand, from the five first growth châteaux, in which to age his wine. The resulting bottles are full of finesse, but with the power and structure expected from Pauillac: rich with knitted tannins to back up plenty of black cherry and damson flavors. La Bécasse is a small estate at just 10.4 acres (4.2ha), and the vineyard is divided into 20 tiny plots of vines, painstakingly assembled by Fonteneau's father over a number of years. Everything is carefully worked by hand and the final wine is unfiltered with just a small amount of egg white fining. ★ Rising star

21 rue Edouard de Pontet, 33250 Pauillac
05 56 59 07 14

Château Clerc Milon Fifth Growth

Château Clerc Milon is another Pauillac property owned by Baroness Philippine de Rothschild, bought by her father in 1970. Although slightly more austere when young than its stablemate Château d'Armailhac, this still has the characteristic generosity of Château Mouton Rothschild once it has spent a few years in bottle. The 106 acres (43ha) of vines are found in the northernmost corner of Pauillac, with more than 100 separate plots, and the resulting grapes are vinified in stainless steel followed by aging in oak for 18 months. The vineyard is due to be enlarged over the next few years, as 32 acres (13ha) of vines from Château La Fleur Milon will be incorporated. La Fleur Milon is a Cru Bourgeois property bought in 2004 from the Mirande family and the newly acquired vineyards are dominated by Cabernet Sauvignon. This expansion will allow the property to produce a new second wine to help satisfy the market.

No visitor facilities
www.bpdr.com

Château Colombier-Monpelou

The Jugla family had been making wine at Château Colombier-Monpelou since 1970, before selling in 2007 to Baroness Philippine de Rothschild. The estate has one of the few underground cellars to be found in the Médoc and is well-located close to the vines of Grand-Puy-Ducasse. All grapes from thc 62 acre (25ha) vineyard were harvested by machine prior to the Rothschild era, but this was followed by a thorough sorting by hand in the cellars to ensure only the best-quality fruit was crushed and fermented. The wine is aged in oak barrels (of which 40% are new each year). The wine provides solid Pauillac power, with Cabernet Sauvignon at 65%, plus 25% Merlot, and an equal split of Petit Verdot and Cabernet Franc, and has a loyal following, particularly in France. Those followers may be disappointed to learn that the label is due to disappear, and from the 2009 vintage it will be included in the Rothschild's generic AOC Pauillac.

33250 Pauillac
05 56 59 01 48

Château Croizet-Bages Fifth Growth

There seems to be brighter times ahead at the beleaguered Château Croizet-Bages, as the younger generation of the Quié family takes over, and investment begins in the château itself. Well-located right next to Lynch-Bages and looking out over the pretty village square, the vineyard covers 64 acres (26ha), planted to 65% Cabernet Sauvignon, 30% Merlot, and 5% Cabernet Franc. It has been slightly brought down in size as many under-performing vines have been grubbed up, and are due to be replaced. Other recent quality improvements include raising the trellising in the vineyards to open up the vine canopy; sorting by hand at the vines (before the machine harvesting begins); as well as cold soaking (chilling the crushed grapes prior to fermentation) in the winery. There are new vats to enable the winemaker to carry out plot-by-plot selections and fermentations. Construction of a new winery is due to begin in 2012. Recent vintages have shown plumper fruit and softer tannins, but older years are a gamble.

9 rue du Port de la Verrerie, Bages, 33250 Pauillac
www.domaines-quie.com

Château Duhart-Milon Fourth Growth
Château Duhart-Milon is adjacent to Château Lafite Rothschild and has been owned by the Rothschild family since 1962. The wine has tight black fruits and a spicy vanilla touch from judicious use of new oak. Known as "Lafite's little brother", Duhart-Milon has a vineyard of 180 acres (73ha) split between approximately 70% Cabernet Sauvignon and 30% Merlot, making a total of about 240,000 bottles a year. There is the precision and power of Lafite Rothschild in this wine, but it increasingly deserves to be recognized in its own right, delivering plenty of Pauillac elegance. The second wine is Moulin de Duhart, where the percentage of Merlot rises (in the first wine Cabernet Sauvignon takes at least 80% of the blend, with 50% new oak). A third wine, Baron de Milon, is an equal split of the two grape varieties.

17 rue Castéja, 33250 Pauillac
05 56 59 15 33

Château La Fleur Peyrabon
Cru Bourgeois
Château La Fleur Peyrabon is owned by Patrick Bernard of Millésima wine merchants (a cousin of Olivier Bernard at Domaine du Chevalier) and a lot of money has been lavished on this 17 acre (7ha) property since he bought it in 1998. There is a lot to like about this wine—it has a fine smoky nose, ripe fruits, good structure, and plenty of personality. In most years the blend is made up of 68% Cabernet Sauvignon, 25% Merlot, and 7% Petit Verdot. The secondary malolactic fermentation takes place in barrel and aging lasts for 14 months (50% new barrels). The château also has vines in AC Haut-Médoc, bottled under the name Château Peyrabon.

Vignes des Peyrabon, 33250 St-Sauveur
www.chateaupeyrabon.com

Château Fonbadet Cru Bourgeois
Château Fonbadet is owned by the Peyronie family, and is now run by law graduate Pascale (at one point her father's ancestors were making wine at Château Lafite Rothschild, while her mother's ancestors were doing the same thing at Château Mouton Rothschild). The terroir of the estate is excellent, with gravel outcrops and slopes to help drainage. The 49 acre (20ha) vineyard is planted to 60% Cabernet Sauvignon, 15% Cabernet Franc, 20% Merlot, and 5% Petit Verdot and Malbec, while the average age of the vines is 50 years. The wines are aged for 18 months in a combination of 50% new oak barrels and 50% one-year-old barrels. This is a great label to get to know, offering plenty of Pauillac punch without the price.

45 route des Château, St-Lambert, 33250 Pauillac
www.chateaufonbadet.com

Château La Fon du Berger
Cru Bourgeois
Château La Fon du Berger is a wine that respects the long aging potential of Pauillac, but tries to keep a modern signature. What this means is that the 60% Cabernet Sauvignon, 30% Merlot, 5% Cabernet Franc, and 5% Petit Verdot are all vinified at a low temperature in stainless steel tanks, and the wine then spends a relatively brief 12–14 months in oak (a low proportion—30%—is new oak to promote fruit over toast). The château itself, owned by Gérard Bougès, is located at St-Sauveur, a more rural part of the Médoc to the west of Pauillac (where the shepherd in the name starts to make more sense), and also produces an AC Haut-Médoc bottled under the same château name. The Pauillac wine, La Fon du Berger, was first bottled in 1999.

5 route du Fournas, 33250 St-Sauveur
www.lafonduberger.com

Château Gaudin
Well-located next to the plateau of Bages, Château Gaudin is one of the mystifyingly tiny number of Bordeaux châteaux that offer e-commerce on their websites. The vineyard covers 28.5 acres (11.5ha), and everything is picked by hand. Run by Linette Capdevielle, together with her children, the vineyard is 85% Cabernet Sauvignon, complemented by 10% Merlot and a mix of Carmenère, Malbec, and Petit Verdot. A traditional wine, it is vinified entirely in large vats, without any oak aging, preferring to emphasize just the natural fruit tannins of Cabernet. They also produce a small *cuvée* (1,000 bottles) made from the château's oldest vines (dating back to 1910) that spends 18 months in new oak barrels.

2/8 route des Châteaux, 33250 Pauillac
www.chateau-gaudin.fr

Château Grand-Puy-Ducasse
Fifth Growth
Owned by the French bank Crédit Agricole, Château Grand-Puy-Ducasse is located in the heart of the town of Pauillac, overlooking the river. The vineyards themselves are further afield, in various plots around the appellation. The consultant here is Denis Dubourdieu, a professor of enology at Bordeaux University known for his light touch with wines. Since 2007, the vineyards have been farmed with integrated pest management, a sustainable approach to viticulture that attempts to minimize the use of chemicals rather than discount them entirely. The wine consists of 60% Cabernet Sauvignon and 40% Merlot, resulting in some fresh spice and a good structure, but the château does need time to reap the benefits of recent investments—keep an eye out for future vintages. The second wine is the prettily named Prélude à Grand-Puy-Ducasse.

No visitor facilities
www.grandpuyducasse.fr

CHATEAU LYNCH-BAGES
ONE OF THE MOST TOURIST-FRIENDLY
ESTATES IN PAUILLAC, IT IS WORTH VISITING
FOR THE WINE AND EXPERIENCE

**CHATEAU PICHON-
LONGUEVILLE BARON**
THIS CAREFULLY CRAFTED WINE IS ONE TO
LAY DOWN AND DRINK IN YEARS TO COME

Château Grand-Puy-Lacoste
Fifth Growth
There is exceptional value to be found at the 136 acre (55ha) Château Grand-Puy-Lacoste. The estate has the quality of the big guns, but manages to stay within reach of mere mortals. The wine is another classic Pauillac blend of 75% Cabernet Sauvignon, 20% Merlot, and 5% Cabernet Franc, perfect for the deep, almost pudding-stone gravel that abounds here. The terroir and make-up of the vineyard allows François Xavier Borie to create a confident, muscular, and enormously satisfying wine. The second wine, Lacoste-Borie, is more uneven in quality and should be assessed more carefully.

33250 Pauillac
05 56 73 16 73

Château Haut-Bages Libéral
Fifth Growth
Claire Villars-Lurton, owner of Châteaux Ferrière, Citran, and La Gurgue, has been running the 69 acre (28ha) Château Haut-Bages Libéral since 1992, a decade after her grandfather bought it. A popular "smaller classified", it can be relied upon for offering good-value Cabernet Sauvignon-dominated wine—up to 80% of the blend in most years, the remainder is Merlot—with real depth of fruit and complexity. Around 108,000 bottles are produced each year, with 80,000 of the second wine, La Chapelle de Bages. The softening malolactic fermentation takes place entirely in barrels, and the aging lasts for 16 months in 40% new oak.

33250 Pauillac
www.hautbagesliberal.com

Château Haut-Batailley **Fifth Growth**
Château Haut-Batailley is right next door to Château Batailley and was once part of the same estate. Today, the property is almost half its original size, at 54 acres (22ha). The grape mix in the vineyard is 70% Cabernet Sauvignon, 25% Merlot, and 5% Cabernet Franc, a classic Pauillac blend. The densely planted vines make 108,000 bottles, matured for 18 months in French oak barrels (55% of which are new). Lighter in style than some of its neighboring châteaux, it is run by François Xavier Borie, owner of Château Grand-Puy-Lacoste.

33250 Pauillac
05 56 73 16 73

Château Lafite Rothschild **First Growth**
The Château Lafite Rothschild team, led by Baron Eric de Rothschild, Christophe Salin, and Charles Chevallier, ensures that tiny touches keep this wine at the very top of the game—from the fine gravel that means bone-dry terroir even in rainstorms, to the perfectly manicured vineyard, the on-site barrel maker, and the meticulously designed cellars care of Canadian architect Ricardo Bofill. The château has color-coded uniforms for staff: green for the gardeners; claret for cellar workers; blue for those working in the vines. The most "masculine" of the first growths in terms of style, with well over 90% Cabernet Sauvignon, Lafite Rothschild can sometimes take 15 to 20 years before opening up, but be patient, because once it does you see the purity, elegance, and sumptuous power that has made it so sought after. Since the late 1980s, only one-third of the 255 acre (103ha) vineyard has gone into the first wine (216,000–240,000 bottles annually), while another 50% makes the increasingly celebrated second wine, Carruades de Lafite (300,000–360,000 bottles). The rest is not bottled under the Lafite name, but becomes a generic AC Pauillac.

17 rue Rolland, 33250 Pauillac
www.lafite.com

Château Latour **First Growth**
L'Enclos—the walled 116 acre (47ha) vineyard that forms the core of the legendary Château Latour—is being converted slowly to organic farming. There is a total of 198 acres (80ha), with the balance going to second wine Les Forts de Latour, and third wine AC Pauillac. The drainage system is particularly effective, meaning it can cope admirably even in wet years. Cabernet Sauvignon accounts for 80% of the vines, the remainder is Merlot (18%) and Cabernet Franc and Petit Verdot (2%). The estate is owned by luxury goods billionaire François Pinault, but it is director Frédéric Engerer who is most closely associated with this layered, muscular, and supremely intellectual wine. They have never been afraid of using modern techniques—Château Haut-Brion may have been the first to use stainless steel tanks back in 1961, but Latour swiftly followed in 1964. These are now smaller, to allow plot-by-plot vinification, and all wine is aged for 18 months in 100% new French oak.

Route de Bordeaux, St-Lambert, 33250 Pauillac
www.chateau-latour.com

Château Lynch-Bages **Fifth Growth**
Without the Cazes family, this corner of the Médoc would be a distinctly less welcoming place. Their wine tourism ventures have been enormously successful, and are based on the same philosophy as their wine—that it should be sincere, consistent, and worth talking about. Owner Jean-Michel Cazes has now handed over to his sister Sylvie and son Jean-Charles. They continue to ensure the 237 acre (96ha) vineyard, planted to 75% Cabernet Sauvignon, 17% Merlot, 6% Cabernet Franc, and 2% Petit Verdot, makes a sensuous, rich, and structured wine. The second wine changed its name in 2008 to Eco de Lynch-Bages, and there is also an increasingly lauded Blanc de Lynch-Bages (from 50% Sémillon and 50% Sauvignon Blanc) vinified, with lees-stirring, in individually temperature-controlled oak barrels.

33250 Pauillac
www.lynchbages.com

Château Lynch-Moussas **Fifth Growth**
Château Lynch-Moussas is owned by Philippe Castéja, head of négociant firm Borie-Manoux and president of the Conseils de Grands Crus Classés en 1855. Even with this background, he had his job cut out for him improving the reputation of this under-performing fifth growth. He has opted to keep things simple—70% Cabernet Sauvignon, 30% Merlot, mechanical vineyard work, and stainless steel vats. Consultant Denis Dubourdieu is turning this simple approach into a precise, classic Pauillac. Covering 148 acres (60ha) of vines, the estate has the same again in parkland and forest—this is a great place to go mushroom hunting in autumn.

33250 Pauillac
05 56 00 00 70

Château Mouton Rothschild
First Growth

Château Mouton Rothschild borders Lafite Rothschild, but has a more glamorous feel, with landscaped gardens and perhaps the deepest gravel driveway in Bordeaux. This property has always stood out—it was here that the first wines in Bordeaux were bottled and labelled on the estate rather than by wine merchants, changing centuries of tradition. It was also the first château to install a barrel cellar, in 1926, and then commissioned Parisian stage designer Charles Siclis to provide dramatic lighting within (something no self-respecting château is without today). Baron Philip was also the first to commission different artists to create his wine labels each year, a tradition that is carried on by his daughter Baroness Philippine today. This sense of occasion is carried through into the wine, which is full of rich fruit and powerful tannins, but brought together by a sense of abandon. Covering 188 acres (76ha), the second wine is the charmingly titled Petit Mouton, and the white wine, Aile d'Argent, is made from one-third Sémillon, two-thirds Sauvignon Blanc, with 1–2% Muscadelle.

33250 Pauillac
www.bpdr.com

Château Pédesclaux

Pédesclaux is a delicate-looking château covering 62 acres (25ha) close to the Gironde that has suffered a reputation for austere, unforgiving wines. It is, however, worth reconsidering. Brigitte and Denis Jugla rose to the challenge from the mid-1990s, with new furnishings inside and new practices in the vineyard, and then further changes happened in October 2009, with another new owner Jacky Lorenzetti. He certainly has the means to invest heavily, and this is now definitely one to watch. The second wine is Sens de Pédesclaux, and there is also La Rose de Pédesclaux (AC Haut Médoc). ★ **Rising star**

Route Padarnac, 33250 Pauillac
www.chateau-pedesclaux.com

Château Pibran Cru Bourgeois

Château Pibran has a solid rather than exciting reputation. It is owned by the insurance company AXA Millésimes and run by elegant English director Christian Seely. Recent years have seen it gain in stature, and a new winery means all vinification now takes place on the estate, rather than down the road at its stablemate Château Pichon-Longueville Baron. The wine comes from 42 acres (17ha) of vines, planted with almost exactly 50% Cabernet Sauvignon and 50% Merlot—vines that have been replanted extensively over the last decade. The second wine is La Tour Pibran.

c/o Château Pichon-Longueville Baron, Route des Châteaux, 33250 Pauillac; 05 56 73 17 28

Château Pichon-Longueville Baron
Second Growth

Like Pibran, Château Pichon-Longueville Baron is also owned by AXA Millésimes. At 180 acres (73ha), it is smaller than its former sister property, La Comtesse, but it is undoubtedly bigger in style. The vineyard is planted with 62% Cabernet Sauvignon, but the variety dominates entirely in the style of the first label—it is rich, fleshy, long-lasting, with a meticulous tannic structure. A new underground cellar has just been completed, designed by

CHATEAU PICHON LONGUEVILLE COMTESSE DE LALANDE
RELIABLY ELEGANT WINES THAT COMMAND A HIGH PRICE FROM A DEVOTED FOLLOWING

CHATEAU MOUTON ROTHSCHILD
THE ARTWORK ON EACH NEW LABEL IS AS EAGERLY AWAITED AS THE WINE ITSELF

architect Alain Triaud and built under the famous reflective pond that makes this one of the most recognized and beautiful properties in the Médoc.

Route des Châteaux, 33250 Pauillac
www.pichonlongueville.com

Château Pichon Longueville Comtesse de Lalande Second Growth

The two Pichons are directly opposite each other and were originally the same estate until a family dispute saw one side given to the Countess Virginie Pichon Longueville and the other to her brother, Baron Raoul. La Comtesse, as the estate is invariably known, has 214 acres (87ha) planted to 45% Cabernet Sauvignon and 35% Merlot, with the rest split between Cabernet Franc and Petit Verdot. Owned for years by Dame Eliane de Lencquesaing, today it is in the careful hands of champagne house Louis Roederer and technical director Thomas Dô Chi Nam. They continue to make smooth, supple, and supremely elegant wine with ripe damson fruit and a subtle smoky edge.

Route des Château, 33250 Pauillac
www.pichon-lalande.com

Château Plantey Cru Bourgeois

This single-block, 64 acre (26ha) vineyard, west of Pontet-Canet, is owned by Claude Meffre (the younger brother of Jean Paul at Château Glana in St-Julien) and produces 200,000 bottles a year. The wine is 55% Merlot and 45% Cabernet Sauvignon, making it a slightly atypical Pauillac (Meffre has even upped the percentage in recent years) that is fleshy and enjoyable but not always perfectly balanced.

Artigues, 33250 Pauillac
04 90 62 61 37

Château Pontet-Canet Fifth Growth

If there is one château in the Médoc that has jumped into the public consciousness in recent years, it has got to be Pontet-Canet. Farmed almost entirely biodynamically, this 180 acre (73ha) estate is dominated by Cabernet Sauvignon (67%) with some Merlot (33%). The owners Alfred and Gérard Tesseron play down the farming philosophy, not wanting to seem too "progressive", but the wine has a clean, pure, extremely precise fruit structure that tells you they are doing something right.

125 Pontet-Canet, 33250 Pauillac
www.pontet-canet.com

Domaine Iris du Gayon

A modest house to the north of Pauillac town, together with just 2.5 acres (1ha) of vines, Domaine Iris du Gayon is owned by Pierre and Françoise Siri. Just over 4,000 bottles are produced each year, from two small plots. All work is done by hand and the style of wine stays very much in the traditional vein, with oak being apparent but not dominant, and the grapes being a sturdy 70% Cabernet Sauvignon, 20% Petit Verdot, and 10% Merlot. A good-quality 1995 was the first vintage sold, and today there is plenty to enjoy in the wines here, with rich black currant flavors and classic claret structure.

12 rue Plantier Cornu, 33250 Pauillac
05 56 59 03 82

ST-JULIEN

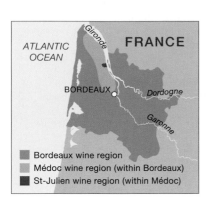

Bordeaux wine region
Médoc wine region (within Bordeaux)
St-Julien wine region (within Médoc)

There are no first growths in St-Julien, but there is a remarkably consistent gravel terroir that reaches a depth of 18ft (5.5m) in places, and makes wines that are, almost without exception, well known, consistent, and excellent quality. This small appellation of 2,249 acres (910ha) accounts for 5.5% of the Médoc vineyard. Of the 24 producers, 11 are classified growths (but who is counting, except, of course, the neighbors?), producing 86.5% of the wine. Finding new names in St-Julien is no easy task—there is no co-operative cellar, and the other growers comprise six Cru Bourgeois, one Cru Artisan, and six families with just a few acres each—but it fully deserves its reputation as a source of distinctive, elegant claret.

Major grapes
🍇 **Reds**
Cabernet Sauvignon
Merlot

Vintages

2009
Excellent, with ideal conditions (likened to 1982 and 1947) ensuring great potential.

2008
A cool summer followed by a dry and sunny fall. The long ripening period ensured good quality, for those who watched and waited.

2007
A difficult year with a damp summer meant uneven ripening. Some good wines, but patchy. Earlier drinking than many St-Julien vintages.

2006
A classic year, but there was some rain during harvest. The best producers made very good wines.

2005
Ideal growing conditions led to rich wines that have a long life ahead of them.

2004
A classic, with good yields, and the wines now offer excellent value for money.

2003
The extreme heat of this summer suited Cabernet Sauvignon better than Merlot, giving the Médoc an advantage—and Petit Verdot performed particularly well.

With an average production of 6.2 million bottles per year, St-Julien is made up of two communes, Beychevelle and St-Julien-Beychevelle, and is bordered by the Ruisseau de Juillac stream to the north, marking the boundary with Pauillac. To the south is a large area of AC Haut-Médoc, before the appellation of Margaux begins. Although there may be no first growth wines here, there are five excellent second growths (more than Pauillac, St-Estèphe, or Margaux), namely Châteaux Ducru-Beaucaillou, Gruaud Larose, Léoville Barton, Léoville Las Cases (whose vines lie right next to Château Latour in Pauillac), and Léoville-Poyferré. Down at fourth growth level, Château St-Pierre is relatively little-known and offers some of the best-value classified wines in the region.

The proportion of Cabernet Sauvignon reaches 63.3% in St-Julien, giving it just slightly more of the grape than Pauillac, and so it can lay claim to being the epicenter of the grape variety that is indelibly associated with fine Bordeaux wine.

It is ironic that over twice as much Merlot is planted across the Bordeaux region as a whole (62% to Cabernet's 25%), and unquestionable that some of its greatest wines are almost entirely Merlot, most notably Pomerol's Le Pin and Pétrus. But in the minds of most wine-lovers, the grape that gives the tannic backbone and decades-long aging potential of classified Bordeaux is Cabernet

Sauvignon. For such an internationally renowned variety, its origins are surprisingly humble. For years it was thought to be a descendant from a Roman vine known as Biturica, until its parentage was finally established in 1997 by DNA fingerprinting as a cross between Cabernet Franc and Sauvignon Blanc. This probably happened naturally in 17th-century Bordeaux, where varieties were routinely planted alongside each other in the same rows. They still were until the 1970s, and even the 1980s in some cases, when it became typical to group them into separate plots to ensure better vineyard control, and the ability to pick each grape variety as it ripened.

Cabernet Sauvignon is a relatively late-ripening variety, and needs a warm climate to fully mature and bring out the elegant, rich black currant flavors that make it so prized. This is one of the reasons that it works so well on the sun-warmed gravel soils of the Médoc, particularly here in the north. Bordeaux wine, however, is above all a blended wine, gaining in complexity from a variety of grapes. Here in St-Julien, the vineyard is also made up of 28.5% Merlot, 3.9% Cabernet Franc, 4.1% Petit Verdot, and 0.2% Malbec.

In style, the wines here tend to be slightly less powerful than those from Pauillac, with a touch more elegance. It is worth remembering that where quality is so uniformly high, the second labels are often worth investigating.

ST-JULIEN

Just to the south of Pauillac, AC St-Julien covers 5% of the vineyard area of the Médoc. Encompassing the two villages of Beychevelle and St-Julien-Beychevelle, the appellation is located on a wide stretch of the River Garonne. Many estates look out over the water and, in past centuries, a few had their own jetties and ports to enable merchant ships to land. Today, just 24 growers make and bottle wine in the appellation of St-Julien, and over 80% of the wine produced is classified.

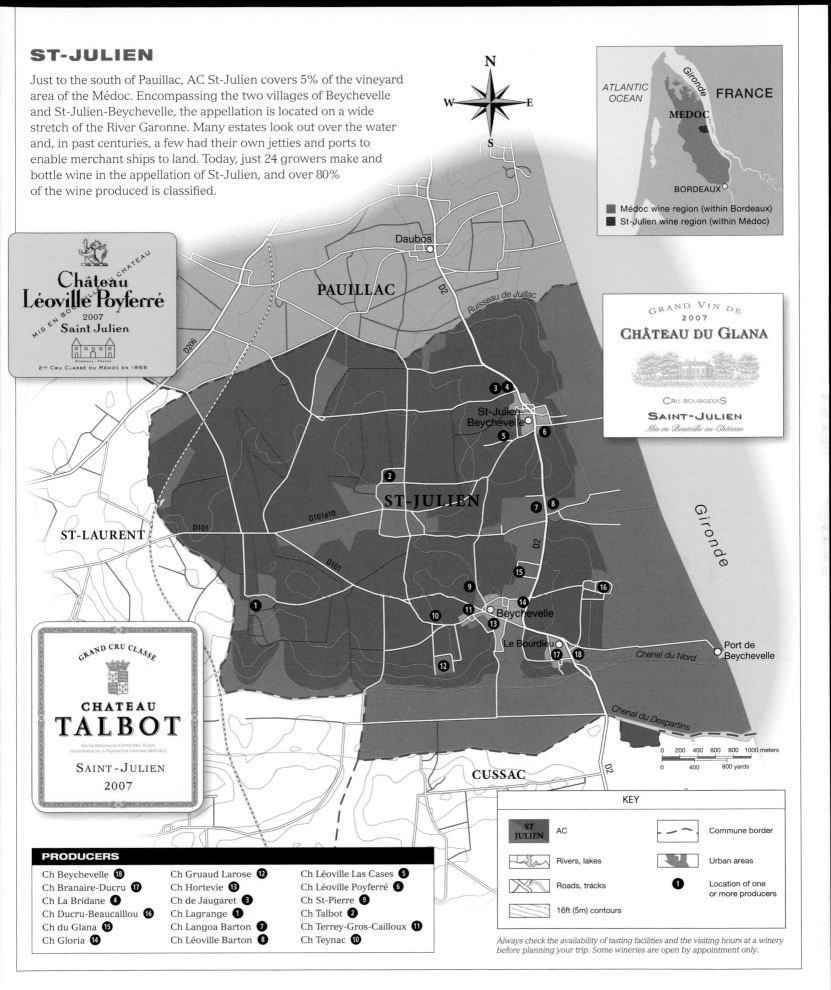

ATLANTIC OCEAN

Gironde

FRANCE

MEDOC

BORDEAUX

■ Médoc wine region (within Bordeaux)
■ St-Julien wine region (within Médoc)

Château Léoville Poyferré
2007
Saint Julien
MIS EN BOUTEILLE AU CHÂTEAU
BORDEAUX - FRANCE
2ᵉ CRU CLASSÉ DU MÉDOC EN 1855

GRAND VIN DE
2007
CHÂTEAU DU GLANA
CRU BOURGEOIS
SAINT-JULIEN
Mis en Bouteille au Château

Daubos

PAUILLAC

D2

Ruisseau de Juillac

ST-Julien-Beychevelle

St-Julien-Beychevelle

ST-JULIEN

D101e10

ST-LAURENT

D101

D101

D2

Gironde

Beychevelle

Le Bourdieu

Chenal du Nord

Port de Beychevelle

Chenal du Despartins

GRAND CRU CLASSÉ
CHÂTEAU TALBOT
ANCIEN DOMAINE DU CONNÉTABLE TALBOT,
GOUVERNEUR DE LA PROVINCE DE GUYENNE 1400-1453
SAINT-JULIEN
2007

CUSSAC

0 200 400 600 800 1000 meters
0   400   800 yards

PRODUCERS

Ch Beychevelle 18	Ch Gruaud Larose 12	Ch Léoville Las Cases 5
Ch Branaire-Ducru 17	Ch Hortevie 13	Ch Léoville Poyferré 6
Ch La Bridane 4	Ch de Jaugaret 3	Ch St-Pierre 9
Ch Ducru-Beaucaillou 16	Ch Lagrange 1	Ch Talbot 2
Ch du Glana 15	Ch Langoa Barton 7	Ch Terrey-Gros-Cailloux 11
Ch Gloria 14	Ch Léoville Barton 8	Ch Teynac 10

KEY

ST JULIEN — AC

Rivers, lakes

Roads, tracks

16ft (5m) contours

- - - Commune border

Urban areas

1 Location of one or more producers

Always check the availability of tasting facilities and the visiting hours at a winery before planning your trip. Some wineries are open by appointment only.

Château Beychevelle Fourth Growth

The low-lying, handsome Château Beychevelle sits at the sweep of the Route des Châteaux as it enters St-Julien, and has underground cellars that open directly onto the river. The 193 acres (78ha) of vines are farmed using sustainable methods, and it has been certified Terra Vitis for its low-impact winemaking. It is now owned by Grands Millésimes de France, a subsidiary of Suntory and insurance groups Ethias and GMF. The Cabernet Sauvignon-dominated wine is filled with tobacco, licorice, and black fruits. The second wine is called Amiral de Beychevelle in keeping with the nautical theme (the château's emblem, a ship with a griffin figurehead and a lowered sail, is sculpted in bronze at the estate).

33250 St-Julien-Beychevelle
www.beychevelle.com

Château Branaire-Ducru Fourth Growth

The owner of Château Branaire-Ducru, Patrick Maroteaux, has for decades been a leading figure in Bordeaux winemaking as president of the Union des Grand Crus, defending the classified growths as the epitome of Bordeaux wines. He has taken an equally thorough and traditional approach with his own château—first restoring the vineyard and winery and, more recently, the beautiful chartreuse building. This is a cellar that uses gravity in winemaking, and has a large number of differently sized vats for precise plot-by-plot vinification. The result is a wine with 70% Cabernet Sauvignon that consciously reflects the best of its appellation: black fruit, good minerality, and a firm grip of tannins. The second wine is Duluc du Branaire-Ducru.

33250 St-Julien-Beychevelle
www.branaire.com

Château La Bridane

Château La Bridane is owned by the Saintout family and covers 37 acres (15ha) of vines, planted to 47% Cabernet Sauvignon, 36% Merlot, 13% Cabernet Franc, and 4% Petit Verdot. The property is situated next door to the classified growth Château Léoville Las Cases and is a great label to look out for if you are hoping for good-value St-Julien. The wine stays traditional to the tight-knit black fruits of the appellation, but retains an edge of rusticity and is unfiltered, keeping it full of character.

33250 St-Julien-Beychevelle
05 56 59 91 70

Château Ducru-Beaucaillou

Second Growth

Bruno Borie has been director at Château Ducru-Beaucaillou since 2003, more than 60 years after his grandfather bought the place in 1941. It is one of the few Médoc classified estates where the owners actually live at the property—not that you can blame them, as the 18th-century house has underground cellars, vast reception rooms, and views over the Gironde estuary. This proximity to the water means very little frost over the entire 185 acre (75ha) estate, which is densely planted with 75% Cabernet Sauvignon and 25% Merlot. The second wine is Croix de Beaucaillou, and a separate label, Lalande-Borie, comes from vines planted in 1970.

No visitor facilities
www.chateau-ducru-beaucaillou.com

CHATEAU LEOVILLE BARTON
THIS BARTON FAMILY WINE IS A CONSISTENTLY GOOD PERFORMER AND WELL PRICED

CHATEAU BEYCHEVELLE
A METICULOUSLY PRESENTED CHATEAU WITH WINES TO MATCH

Château du Glana Cru Bourgeois

Gabriel Meffre, now working with his sons Ludovic and Julien, has seen Château du Glana's vineyards increase from 7.4 acres (3ha) to 106 acres (43ha) over the past 40 years. Denis Dubourdieu is the consultant, and the vineyard and winery have undergone extensive renovations since 1999. This is a modern-style St-Julien that favors the fruit, and offers good value for money, without making any classified growths lose any sleep.

33250 St-Julien-Beychevelle
www.chateau-du-glana.com

Château Gloria Cru Bourgeois

With the same owner as Château St-Pierre, Château Gloria is a similarly fast-rising estate. It was created in the mid-20th century by barrel maker Henri Martin and painstakingly put together from small plots of vines that he charmed from his neighbors. Today, there are 109 acres (44ha) planted with a classic mix of 65% Cabernet Sauvignon, 25% Merlot, and an even split between Cabernet Franc and Petit Verdot. The oldest vines are now reaching 80 years. In style, it is rounder and softer than St-Pierre, with the fruit put firmly center stage. ★Rising star

c/o Domaines Martin, 33250 St-Julien-Beychevelle
www.chateau-gloria.com

Château Gruaud Larose Second Growth

Château Gruaud Larose is not the easiest name to pronounce, but worth the effort. Owned by Jean Merlaut since 1997, the estate's director is David Launay, whose sense of humor might come as a surprise to those expecting the Médoc to be stuffy. Today, the vineyard covers 198 acres (80ha) in one single block, with gravel that reaches up to 18ft (5.5m) deep. In the 1990s, this was one of the first vineyards to ban pesticides, instead controlling pests by introducing pheronomes to cause mating disruption. There is also a water treatment center for recycling the winery water. This well-drained, warm terroir allows the vineyard of 61% Cabernet Sauvignon, 29% Merlot, 5% Cabernet Franc, and 5% Petit Verdot to reach great ripeness, making powerful wines that are deeply colored and long lasting. There are plans to decrease the proportion of Merlot further.

33250 St-Julien-Beychevelle
05 56 73 15 20

Château Hortevie

Château Hortevie is one of the best small estates of this appellation. It produces a refined, elegant wine full of gently smoky oak and rich black fruits. Owners Henri Pradère and Anne Fort (of Terrey-Gros-Cailloux) lavish attention on this tiny 8.6 acre (3.5ha) plot of vines—a blend of 70% Cabernet Sauvignon, 25% Merlot, and 5% Cabernet Franc. Do leave it for a few years though, as the tannins are tight at first, but very much worth the wait.

33250 St-Julien-Beychevelle
05 56 59 06 27

Château de Jaugaret

Château de Jaugaret may be the smallest of the St-Julien properties at 3.2 acres (1.3ha) of vines. The estate has been in the Fillastre family for over 400 years and is today run by the reclusive Jean-François. He makes tiny quantities—perhaps 7,000 bottles a year—of very classic, unfiltered, Cabernet Sauvignon-led wine (80% in most years, plus Petit Verdot and 100-year-old Malbec—no Merlot at all). The concentration in this bottle is unbelievable—get your decanter at the ready and pair it with a good hearty meal. This is a wine that makes you happy there are still some tricks left up St-Julien's sleeve.

33250 St-Julien-Beychevelle
05 56 59 09 71

Château Lagrange Third Growth
The owners at Château Lagrange—the Japanese drinks giant Suntory—are a perfect indication that the Médoc is far from a closed world, and in fact constantly evolves in line with the wider wine world and its changing customer base. The château suffered from a difficult reputation in the 20th century, and went from 692 acres (280ha) to the 289 acres (117ha) it has today. Suntory have invested heavily in restructuring, lessening the percentage of Merlot and planting more Petit Verdot to increase color and structure, and the benefits are beginning to be seen. The excellent white wine, Les Arums de Lagrange, is a blend of Sémillon, Sauvignon, and Muscadelle.

33250 St-Julien-Beychevelle
www.chateau-lagrange.com

Château Langoa Barton Third Growth
Château Langoa Barton is much smaller than its sister next door with 44 acres (18ha) planted to 72% Cabernet Sauvignon, 20% Merlot, and 8% Cabernet Franc. Anthony Barton is continuing two centuries of family tradition, as the Bartons (originally from Ireland) have owned this estate since 1821. The style is remarkably consistent—it takes a few years to open up, then reveals soft gamey notes, black currant and leather, and gentle acidity that gives elegance and a sense of restraint.

33250 St-Julien-Beychevelle
www.leoville-barton.com

Château Léoville Barton Second Growth
If only every Bordeaux château followed Château Léoville Barton's consistent, low-key approach to winemaking and pricing. Covering 124 acres (50ha) with 73% Cabernet Sauvignon, the signature flavors are black truffle, delicate pepper, and rich brambly black fruits. In most years, Léoville Barton is bigger and more tightly knit than Langoa but, as they are vinified and aged in exactly the same way, you have to give a nod to the terroir for this. The second wine is La Réserve de Léoville Barton.

33250 St-Julien-Beychevelle
www.leoville-barton.com

Château Léoville Las Cases
Second Growth
Jean-Hubert Delon is the fifth generation to take charge of the consistently successful Château Léoville Las Cases. The vineyards are right on the border of St-Julien and Pauillac, with Château Latour next door. The price might make your eyes water, but this is a classic, truly wonderful St-Julien. It has structure and power with elegance and style. The second wine is Le Petit Lion.

route Pauillac, 33250 St-Julien-Beychevelle
05 56 73 25 26

Château Léoville Poyferré Second Growth
The Cuvelier family (wine traders from northern France) has owned Château Léoville Poyferré since the 1920s. Today, Didier Cuvelier leads the team, with Isabelle Davin as full-time enologist, and Michel Rolland as consultant (the Cuveliers are also part of Rolland's Argentine adventure, Clos de los Siete). Soil analysis is ongoing and adjustments are made accordingly to pruning, plowing, or canopy cover. The wine itself is modern and fleshy in style. The second wine is Château Moulin Riche, and a "third", Pavillon de Poyferré, is made from young vines.

Le Bourg, 33250 St-Julien-Beychevelle
www.leoville-poyferre.fr

Château St-Pierre Fourth Growth
How long can Château St-Pierre go on being an insider secret? In the past it has suffered from division and sub-division, but since Henri Martin took over in 1982, followed by son-in-law Françoise Triaud, things have been smoother sailing. The vines at this 42 acre (17ha) estate have an average age of 50 years. Cabernet Sauvignon is 75%, with 15% Merlot, and 10% Cabernet Franc. This comes through strongly in the powerful structure and rich tannins. A sexy wine, with swagger.

c/o Domaines Martin, 33250 St-Julien-Beychevelle
05 56 59 08 18

Château Talbot Fourth Growth
Château Talbot is pretty much bang in the center of St-Julien, on one of the highest gravel hills. It is owned by the two Cordier sisters Lorraine and Nancy, and since 2008 Stéphane Derenoncourt has consulted. The modern winery has a variety of wooden and stainless steel vats making wines that are up to 67% Cabernet Sauvignon. The soft and succulent Connétable Talbot is made here. There is also an interesting white wine, Caillou Blanc, made from mainly Sauvignon Blanc, with a touch of Sémillon, aged in burgundy barrels.

33250 St-Julien-Beychevelle
www.chateau-talbot.com

Château Terrey-Gros-Cailloux
Cru Bourgeois
The wines of Château Terrey-Gros-Cailloux are now made by the winemaking team at Ducru-Beaucaillou (located next door). This 35 acre (14ha) estate is owned by the Fort/Pradère family, but the vines are leased out. This is one to watch. ★ **Rising star**

No visitor facilities
05 56 59 06 27

Château Teynac
Everything about Château Teynac is streamlined—the Pairault family keeps to a simple blend of 70% Cabernet Sauvignon and 30% Merlot, planted over 35 acres (14ha). Harvesting is all by hand and grapes are brought in when each vine reaches optimal ripeness—which means it can take several trips into the vines before everything is picked. This translates into well-crafted wines that emphasize purity of fruit and a full-bodied structure. The second wine, Elinor de Teynac, is very good value.

33250 St-Julien-Beychevelle
05 56 59 12 91

ANTHONY BARTON

It is impossible to talk about St-Julien without mentioning the influence of Anthony Barton. Born in Ireland, he came to Bordeaux in 1948 to work with his uncle at Châteaux Léoville and Langoa Barton, and has since been a voice of reason, always taking the view that the Bordelais should be modest and the wines should be the heroes. On Léoville's style, he says, "We have not followed the fashion of late picking. We like to bring the fruit in while it is still alive," and on his sensible pricing strategy, "I want people to buy the wine and to drink it." Just do not expect to find old bottles in his cellar. "We like to enjoy our wines, and when they have gone, they have gone!"

The small, dark blue berries identify these ripe bunches as Cabernet Sauvignon, the grape of choice in Margaux.

MARGAUX

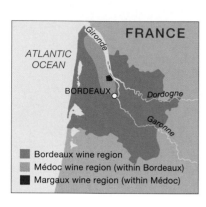

ATLANTIC OCEAN
FRANCE
Gironde
BORDEAUX
Dordogne
Garonne

- Bordeaux wine region
- Médoc wine region (within Bordeaux)
- Margaux wine region (within Médoc)

At 3,484 acres (1,410ha), Margaux is the biggest village appellation in the Médoc (8.5% of the total), covering the five communes of Margaux, Soussans, Arsac, Labarde, and Cantenac. It also packs in the highest number of classified wines, with 21 of the 61 Cru Classé 1855 properties (and manages to have examples at each level, from first growth to fifth growth). With its size, however, comes the inevitable problem of varying quality; as late as the 1980s, there were a number of underperforming Margaux estates, although this has largely been ironed out with the laying of extensive drainage channels across the appellation, and serious investments from leaders such as Châteaux Palmer and Rauzan-Ségla—and, of course, Château Margaux itself.

Major grapes

🍇 Reds

Cabernet Franc

Cabernet Sauvignon

Merlot

Petit Verdot

Vintages

2009

An excellent year—powerful wines with great aging potential. Comparisons with 2005, 1982, even 1947.

2008

A damp summer, but a long, sunny fall, giving quality wines for the best producers.

2007

A difficult year with a damp summer means many wines are light and for early drinking.

2006

A classic vintage despite rain during harvest. The best producers made good wines.

2005

Ideal conditions gave rich wines with a long life. Prices rose across the board but these are wonderful wines.

2004

A classic year, with good yields, and the wines now offer excellent value.

2003

The extreme heat gave the Médoc an advantage. Some wines are evolving quickly.

2000

Great balance and structure; becoming ready to drink.

As with much of the Médoc, vines were dotted around Margaux in Roman times, but it was Dutch engineers in the 17th and 18th centuries who drained the marshes to reveal the famous gravelly terroir. The soil in this appellation is quite different from the rest of the Médoc, with almost all estates having much finer, white gravel compared to the larger stones further north. This change in the soil comes from its geographical setting at the meeting point of the Garonne and Dordogne rivers, where they merge and head up to the Gironde Estuary. The greater force of the water has, over centuries, worn the gravel down into finer fragments, and also ensures great complexity of flavors, as the sediments come from both the Massif Central and the Pyrenees mountains (where the two rivers begin).

As a result, Margaux wines are seen as the most delicate and feminine of the Médoc, with the power and structure of a Pauillac combined with silkier, softer tannins to give a distinctive elegance. With such a large area, however, many styles can be found, and getting to know individual producers remains key.

Even with the region's renowned feminine touch, Cabernet Sauvignon remains the grape of choice for the 74 independent growers of Margaux (plantings of the variety represent 54% of the entire appellation, with Merlot at 37% and the rest a split of Cabernet Franc and Petit Verdot). The appellation fared better than some of its counterparts in the hot 2003 vintage, with the Cabernet Sauvignon better able to withstand the extreme heat—some wines are, nevertheless, evolving more quickly. This is undoubtedly due to the large size of the classified estates as well as the gravelly soils. These estates account for around two-thirds of the total production of the appellation, and are all about making wines that can withstand—and, indeed, encourage—a long period of aging.

Away from the big names, Margaux is also interesting for being the only one of the "big four" Médoc appellations where you can easily find smaller, innovative estates (St-Estèphe is not far behind, but Pauillac and St-Julien have only a handful of small properties). There are several *microcuvées* in Margaux from owners who are working tiny plots of vines, and producing wines that are rich and supple—the result of clever winemaking. Look out for these new producers (some are even owners of bigger estates, wanting to make separate wines on their own terms), as many offer good value for money, and make for an interesting experience.

It is from a combination of these modern and traditional approaches that Margaux produces approximately 9 million bottles each year.

MARGAUX

Vines intended for AC Margaux wines can be grown in the five adjoining villages of Labarde, Cantenac, Margaux, Soussans, and Arsac. The closest to Bordeaux city of the prestigious Médoc appellations, Margaux contains examples of classified wines from first growths through to fifth growths, as well as numerous Cru Bourgeois and Cru Artisan estates.

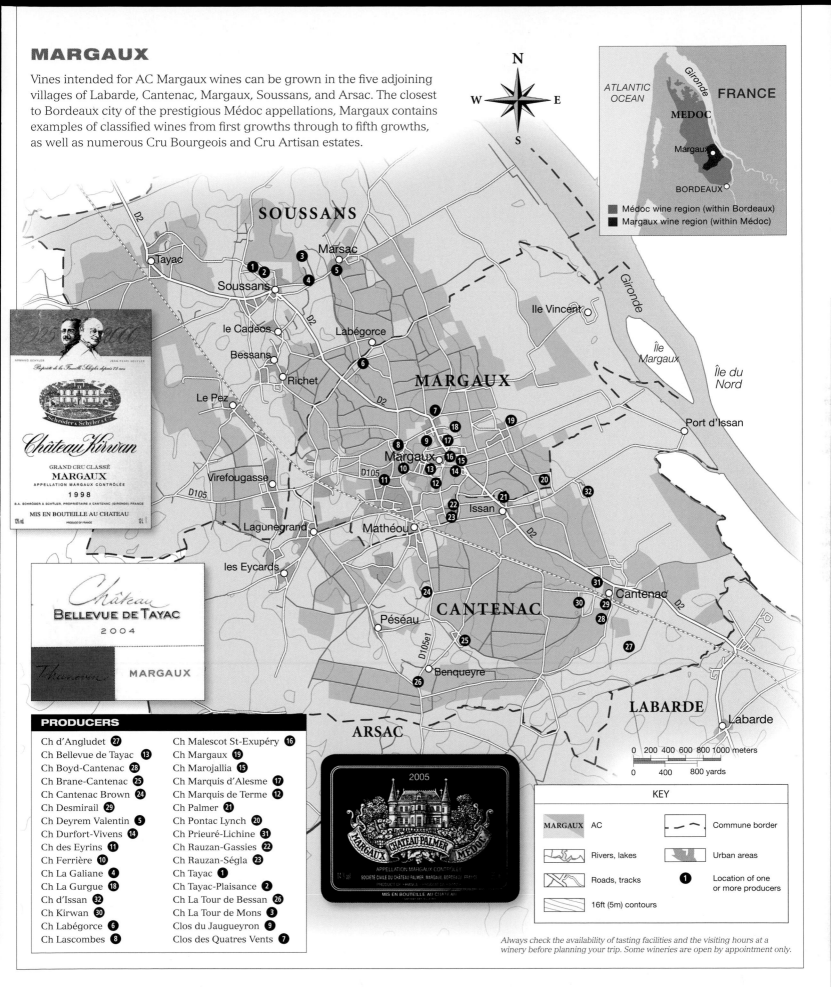

Inset map legend:
- Médoc wine region (within Bordeaux)
- Margaux wine region (within Médoc)

PRODUCERS

Ch d'Angludet 27	Ch Malescot St-Exupéry 16
Ch Bellevue de Tayac 13	Ch Margaux 19
Ch Boyd-Cantenac 28	Ch Marojallia 15
Ch Brane-Cantenac 25	Ch Marquis d'Alesme 17
Ch Cantenac Brown 24	Ch Marquis de Terme 12
Ch Desmirail 29	Ch Palmer 21
Ch Deyrem Valentin 5	Ch Pontac Lynch 20
Ch Durfort-Vivens 14	Ch Prieuré-Lichine 31
Ch des Eyrins 11	Ch Rauzan-Gassies 22
Ch Ferrière 10	Ch Rauzan-Ségla 23
Ch La Galiane 4	Ch Tayac 1
Ch La Gurgue 18	Ch Tayac-Plaisance 2
Ch d'Issan 32	Ch La Tour de Bessan 26
Ch Kirwan 30	Ch La Tour de Mons 3
Ch Labégorce 6	Clos du Jaugueyron 9
Ch Lascombes 8	Clos des Quatres Vents 7

KEY

- MARGAUX — AC
- Rivers, lakes
- Roads, tracks
- 16ft (5m) contours
- Commune border
- Urban areas
- 1 Location of one or more producers

0 200 400 600 800 1000 meters
0 400 800 yards

Always check the availability of tasting facilities and the visiting hours at a winery before planning your trip. Some wineries are open by appointment only.

Château d'Angludet Cru Bourgeois

Of the five Sichel brothers (a Bordeaux wine family for five centuries), Ben Sichel at Château d'Angludet is the one that you would most want making the wine in your glass—he is passionately knowledgeable about vines and winemaking. This passion makes d'Angludet a great wine to discover. The vineyard, covering 79 acres (32ha) just off the main Route des Châteaux, is planted to 55% Cabernet Sauvignon, 35% Merlot, and 10% Petit Verdot and delivers good-value, sensible, and consistent wines that are unfiltered. The second wine is Moulin d'Angludet.

33460 Cantenac
www.chateau-angludet.fr

Château d'Arsac Cru Bourgeois

Château d'Arsac's owner, Philippe Raoux, is a true innovator—his château blends classic lines with startling modern art (if you visit, look out for the huge iron girder that is propped against one side of the building, courtesy of French sculptor Bernar Venet). A few miles down the road, Raoux has also opened a vast steel-and-glass wine cultural center known as La Winery. Back at his own property, he has 133 acres (54ha) of vines in Margaux and 119 acres (48ha) in AC Haut-Médoc vineyards. There is a high proportion of young vines at the moment and this means the wine is elegant, but it will benefit from a few more years to reach its full complexity.

1 Allée Comte, 33460 Arsac-en-Médoc
www.chateau-arsac.com

Château Bellevue de Tayac

Château Bellevue de Tayac is owned by Jean Luc Thunevin, better known for Right Bank wines such as Château de Valandraud. Its 7.5 acres (3ha) of vines saw one-third ripped up and replanted in 2005 and, together with a small parcel that is leased to them, produces around 16,000 bottles a year. The winemaker is Christophe Lardière, who works across all of Thunevin's properties. At 70% Merlot, this is consciously round and smooth, with flattering tannins. It is one to watch.

No visitor facilities
www.thunevin.com

Château Boyd-Cantenac Third Growth

Château Boyd-Cantenac is small for a classified Margaux at 42 acres (17ha). The property is planted to 4,000 vines per acre (10,000 per hectare) with an average age of 44 years. Owner Lucien Guillemet is also the winemaker, with no consultant enologist, and he concentrates on making Cabernet Sauvignon-dominated wines that take a few years to fully open up, with 9% Petit Verdot adding spice. The same family also owns Château Pouget, another little-known, classified Margaux where Cabernet Franc gives a gentler, more aromatic spicy edge. The wines are good value.

33460 Cantenac
www.boyd-cantenac.fr

Château Brane-Cantenac Second Growth

You couldn't hope to meet a more understated, charming château owner than Henri Lurton, who seems happiest among his 210 acres (85ha) of vines at Château Brane-Cantenac. This unshowy style is taken up by his team,

who prefer to let the wines speak for themselves. Round, silky tannins mark the style of the wine, which is made from 55% Cabernet Sauvignon, 40% Merlot, and 5% Cabernet Franc, with black currants on the palate and a nose of violets. The estate manager, Christophe Capdeville, is leading precise experimentation in the use of barrels, looking at grain, origin, and toasting of oak. The second wine, Baron de Brane, offers great value for money.

33460 Cantenac
www.brane-cantenac.com

Château Cantenac Brown Third Growth

The English connections at Château Cantenac Brown go back a long way. Its first owner, John Lewis Brown, built the château in an English country-mansion style, and it is today owned by Simon Halabi, a Syrian-born British businessman. Halabi has invested heavily since his purchase in 2006 and, alongside director José Sanfins, has worked hard at fine-tuning the winemaking. At 119 acres (48ha) they are creating well-made, tightly structured, but exuberant wines from sustainable farming methods. Made up of 65% Cabernet Sauvignon, 30% Merlot, and 5% Cabernet Franc, the wine combines weight of fruit with an effortlessly silky structure. The second wine is BRIO de Cantenac Brown.

33460 Margaux
www.cantenacbrown.com

Château Dauzac Fifth Growth

Over the past few years, Château Dauzac has made serious leaps in quality, thanks to changes such as raising the vine canopy height over its 99 acres (40ha) and changing to gravity-fed winemaking. The people behind these changes are the Lurton family, in this case, the patriarch André Lurton and his daughter Christine. The château is the closest to the Gironde river of all the classified growths, but today there are no vines on the *palus* (the marshy riverbank). This estate is also where Bordeaux Mixture was invented in the 19th century, a treatment that saved most of Europe's vineyard from the vine disease downy mildew. This is an estate worth watching, offering real pleasure at a good price.

Labarde, 33460 Margaux
www.chateaudauzac.com

Château Desmirail Third Growth

Château Desmirail is another Lurton property, this time belonging to Denis, brother of Henri at Brane-Cantenac. Once owned by the nephew of composer Felix Mendelssohn, but broken up in the 1930s, Denis's father Lucien painstakingly pieced it back together to its original 99 acres (40ha). It still has some way to go before his work is fully recognized. The Boissenots consult here and make a subtle, grown-up wine that is 69% Cabernet Sauvignon, 29% Merlot, and 2% Petit Verdot.

28 avenue Vèmw République, 33460 Cantenac
www.desmirail.com

Château Deyrem Valentin Cru Bourgeois

Jean Sorge works with his two daughters, Sylvie and Christelle, at this lovely 35 acre (14ha) estate (along with 5 acres/2ha in AC Haut-Médoc). Meticulous plot-by-plot vinifications are carried out, and the final wine is well-structured, fresh, and full of blackberry and mint. Jean has been known to play around a little with his wines. He has planted 1% Carmenère and, since 2001, has vinified separately a plot of 80-year-old vines (primarily Petit Verdot) that is released under the label of Château Valentin. The second wine is Château Soussans.

1 rue Valentin Deyrem, 33460 Soussans
www.chateau-deyrem-valentin.com

Château Durfort-Vivens Second Growth
The owner of Château Durfort-Vivens, Gonzargue Lurton, is a name to remember in Margaux (and luckily not an easy one to forget). President of the local wine syndicate, he has worked to promote quality across the appellation. He is also a very talented winemaker at his own 136 acre (55ha) property. The gravel here is deep, with white pudding stones from the Garonne river bed. This allows the Cabernet Sauvignon to ripen well, and early, so smoothing out the tannins. Sustainable agriculture, plot-by-plot vinification, and a new cellar create a delicious wine, full of violets and truffles. There are two second wines, Vivens and Relais de Durfort-Vivens.

3 rue du Général de Gaulle, 33460 Margaux
www.durfort-vivens.fr

Château des Eyrins
Château des Eyrins is a new arrival on the Margaux scene, created 25 years ago from 7.4 acres (3ha) of vines belonging to Eric Grangerou, whose father, grandfather, and great-grandfather were all cellar masters at Château Margaux. Today, the enologist is Olivier Dauga, who takes a modern approach of cold soaking, individual plot vinification, and aging in 80% new French oak (a large proportion are burgundy barrels, with only gentle toasting). The wine is 75% Cabernet Sauvignon, 20% Merlot, and 5% Petit Verdot, with no fining and no filtration. In September 2009, Xavier and Julie Gonet Medeville of Château Gilette in Sauternes bought the château, but Eric and Olivier remain as winemakers.

27 cours Pey Berland, 33460 Margaux
05 57 88 95 03

Château Ferrière Third Growth
Château Ferrière is the smallest classified growth in the Médoc, at just 20 acres (8ha), and one of the very few that has remained unchanged in size since 1855. For a number of years, the vines were leased out to other châteaux, but the Villars-Merlaut family took over in 1988 and, since 1992, it has once again been bottled on the estate under its own name. The seemingly tireless Celine Villars has been adding small cement tanks in the winery. It took a while to find its style, but now you can expect to get a rich, tightly structured wine that reflects the 80% Cabernet Sauvignon in the blend.

33 bis, rue de la Trémoille, 33460 Margaux
www.ferriere.com

Château La Galiane Cru Bourgeois
There is a link to the history of Bordeaux here, as the name La Galiane comes from an English general who commanded his troops at a battle during the 15th century, when Bordeaux was still part of the English crown. Today, it is very much French, with Christine Renon working the 12 acres (5ha) and producing 30,000 bottles

per year of 50% Cabernet Sauvignon, 45% Merlot, and 5% Petit Verdot, a classic Margaux mix. The same family produces Château Charmant and Clos Charmant, from 20 acres (8ha) of vines that reach an average age of 65 years, with 50% Merlot, 25% Cabernet Sauvignon, 20% Cabernet Franc, and 5% Petit Verdot.

33460 Soussans
05 57 88 35 27

Château Giscours Third Growth
The handsome gates and sweeping driveway remind you that Château Giscours has always been renowned for its welcome, from polo matches in the 1950s to cricket games today. There are 205 acres (83ha) of 40-year-old vines stretching over four white-gravel hillocks, with a serious investment in replanting in recent years by Dutch owner Eric Albada Jelgersma. The wine is rich and confident, with ripe damsons and a tightly knit tannic structure, made with 55% Cabernet-Sauvignon, 35% Merlot, and a smattering of Petit Verdot and Cabernet Franc. The second wine is Sirène de Giscours, and the same family also owns Château du Tertre.

10 route de Giscours, Labarde, 33460 Margaux
www.chateau-giscours.com

Château La Gurgue Cru Bourgeois
Château La Gurgue produces a gripping, well-fleshed-out wine with luscious black fruits, and is a good example of how many of the most exciting Margaux are outside of the 1855 classification. The estate is owned by the Villars-Merlaut family and covers just 25 acres (10ha) where the Garonne gravel reaches several feet deep through many of the plots. The blend includes up to 70% Cabernet Sauvignon, with the rest Merlot, as the deep gravel means good ripening year after year. The wine is aged in 25% new oak barrels every year.

33 bis, rue de la Trémoille, 33460 Margaux
www.lagurgue.com

Château d'Issan Third Growth
Renaissance gardens, a moat, and turreted walls surround Château d'Issan, one of the oldest estates in the Médoc. It is run by Emmanuel Cruse, who is a serious player in local wine politics. When his family bought the estate in 1945, it had only 5 acres (2ha) of productive vines; today, that has grown to 131 acres (53ha), with an average vine age of 35 years. Emmanuel is working hard at smoothing the tannic structure and coaxing the very best from his Cabernet Sauvignon, which contributes around 70% to the final blend. The second wine, Blason d'Issan, is one of the best examples of its type.

33460 Cantenac
www.chateau-issan.com

Château Kirwan Third Growth
Although the name Kirwan comes from its Irish side, the award-winning rose gardens at this romantic estate are the legacy of a former French owner and botanist, Camille Godard. Today, the estate is owned by the eighth generation of the Schyler family and the general manager is Philippe Delfault (previously at Château Palmer). He has brought the wine back to an elegant and balanced style that will go the distance, with black cherries and an almond dusting. There is 45% Cabernet Sauvignon, 30% Merlot,

ERIC BOISSENOT

This hard-working enologist just happens to be consultant winemaker on four out of the five first growths of Bordeaux—the only one keeping him from a full house is Château Haut-Brion. Eric works with his father Jacques, who in turn trained with and then worked alongside the great Emile Peynaud, known as the godfather of enology. Working as a team for 20 years, father and son have concentrated almost solely on clients in the Médoc (of their 200 clients, 190 of them are in the Médoc with just 10 on the Right Bank. Eric has stepped outside of France to work with Alpha Estate in Greece).

The Boissenots believe in making wines that reflect their terroir, and the philosophy of the people who are behind them. If you seek typicality and non-showy, good-quality bottles, look for their name.

15% Cabernet Franc and 10% Petit Verdot planted over 91 acres (37ha). The second wine is Les Charmes de Kirwan, and there is also an excellent Rosé de Kirwan.

Cantenac, 33460 Margaux
www.chateau-kirwan.com

Château Labégorce

Château Labégorce fully incorporated Labégorce Zédé into the estate as of the 2009 vintage, taking the overall vineyard size to 136 acres (55ha). The woman in charge is 27-year-old Nathalie Perrodo, splitting her time between Bordeaux and London. Technical director Philippe de Laguarigue joined the team from Château Montrose in 2007, and is overseeing the culmination of a 10-year replanting program that is imparting tighter, more fleshed-out fruits. Zédé de Labégorce is the second wine (originally of the second estate), and the second label of Château Labégorce, Château Tour de la Roze, has also been retained.

33460 Margaux
www.chateau-labegorce.fr

Château Lascombes Second Growth

American investment fund Colony Capital bought the 208 acre (84ha) Château Lascombes in 2000. Since 2008, a further 59 acres (24ha) have been leased from Château Martinens and will be included in the second wine, Chevalier de Lascombes. Director Dominique Befve uses Michel Rolland as consultant, and together they have pulled away from a number of disappointing years, with additions such as gravity-flow winemaking and the use of 100% new oak. Although some dissenting voices accuse them of deserting the classic Margaux style, the wine combines lush fruit and violets with fine balance, and is a sumptuous treat, making it hard to stop at one glass.

1 cours de Verdun, 33460 Margaux
www.chateau-lascombes.com

Château Malescot St-Exupéry
Third Growth

Recognized as being a late harvester, Jean Luc Zuger at Château Malescot St-Exupéry favors rich fruit, and has been known to use reverse osmosis when he believes it necessary to concentrate the juice. This is a legal but sometimes controversial technique that can remove the water that dilutes the grapes in a wet vintage. The resulting wine is inky, with some smoky oak, and full of round black fruits. The estate's name comes from a previous owner, who was great-grandfather of *Le Petit Prince* author Antoine de Saint Exupéry. With Michel Rolland as consultant, the property covers 58 acres (23.5ha), as well as 16 acres (6.5ha) of Bordeaux Supérieur (Domaine du Balardin). Whether these winemaking techniques tend toward over-extraction is debated within Bordeaux.

16 rue Georges Mandel, 33460 Margaux
www.malescot.com

Château Margaux First Growth

The gleaming Doric columns were built long before a Greek shipping magnate bought Château Margaux, but his daughter has made it very much her own. Corinne Mentzelopoulos inherited the estate from her father André at the tender age of 27—the same age that director Paul Pontallier was when he joined the team. Several

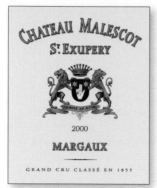

CHATEAU MALESCOT ST-EXUPERY
HARVESTING LATE AND USING HIGH-TECH METHODS LEADS TO RICH WINES

CHATEAU MARGAUX
ONE OF THE FIVE FIRST GROWTHS, CHATEAU MARGAUX IS HIGHLY SOUGHT AFTER

decades later, they produce wine that is sought-after the world over. The 203 acres (82ha) are planted with a majority of Cabernet Sauvignon (up to 87% of the first wine in most years), and make a powerful wine wrapped in rich red fruits with silky elegance and serious finesse. From 2009, a new barrel room allows precise parcel-by-parcel vinification. The second wine, Pavillon Rouge, was one of the first to be produced in the region, and there is also a wonderful white, Pavillon Blanc, made from 100% old Sauvignon Blanc vines.

33460 Margaux
www.chateau-margaux.com

Château Marojallia

Château Marojallia is an unapologetically fruit-forward, smooth and fleshed-out Margaux, with 74% Cabernet Sauvignon and 26% Merlot, making small quantities (6,000 bottles) of a highly polished wine. High walls surround this lovely château, right in the center of the village, with a welcoming central courtyard. There is a meticulous attention to detail in the winemaking, from Jean-Luc Thunevin with Michel Rolland as consultant. Marojallia is the Latin name for Margaux, but the 10 acres (4ha) of vines are all about making use of modern techniques. The second wine is Clos Margalaine.

2 rue du Général de Gaulle, 33460 Margaux
www.marojallia.com

Château Marquis d'Alesme Third Growth

Château Marquis d'Alesme is remarkably little known given its high place in the Cru Classé rankings and its prominent location, right in the center of Margaux village. The estate suffered for years from under-investment, and had another set back in 2006 when it was bought by Hubert Perrodo of Château Labégorce, just a few months before he died suddenly in a skiing accident. Today, both estates are run by his 27-year-old daughter Nathalie. She has dropped the "Becker" from the previous title, and is concentrating on replanting and improving selection across the 37 acres (15ha). A new winery is due to be built in the coming years.

33460 Margaux
www.chateau-marquis-dalesme.fr

Château Marquis de Terme
Fourth Growth

A new director, Ludovic David, has been at Château Marquis de Terme since January 2009, and he is looking to give a modern edge to this classic English-style claret. He is instituting plot-by-plot vinification, pushing maturity in the vineyard and cellar, and is introducing techniques such as a steam-cleaning system of the barrels to ensure the fruit shines through. The densely planted vines cover 94 acres (38ha), unchanged since the classification in 1855. The estate is owned by three brothers, Jean, Philippe, and Pierre-Louis Sénéclauze. Their father was a wine merchant from Marseille before he bought this Médoc estate in the 1930s, and they continue to own two other properties in Bandol and Cassis, down in the South of France. Blackberries and brambly fruits abound, and the 7% Petit Verdot gives the wine an inky depth. ★ Rising star

3 route de Rauzan, 33460 Margaux
www.chateau-marquis-de-terme.com

Château Monbrison

The vineyard here at Château Monbrison was uprooted entirely at the start of World War II, and was left unplanted until 1963. The vines today have reached an average of 30 years and are producing good-quality fruit. The owner, Jean-Luc Vonderheyden, was one of the first in the Médoc to introduce green harvesting (the removal of some bunches to maximize the ripening of the remainder). Innovations are fewer today but this estate can provide good-value Margaux, and there is always a place for that. The second wine is Bouquet de Monbrison.

1 allée de Monbrison, 33460 Arsac
www.chateaumonbrison.com

Château Mongravey Cru Bourgeois

Château Mongravey has been run by Regis and Karin Bernaleau for the past 30 years and the 47 acre (19ha) vineyard covers equal proportions of Margaux and AC Haut-Médoc (bottled under the name Château de Braude). The first vintage was produced in 1981 and, in 1999, a new cellar and barrel room were installed, where 450 barrels from 10 different coopers provide complexity to the bottles. The vines are located close to Château Giscours, and the final wine is full of lean, well-defined fruit with an attractively smoky finish.

8 avenue Jean-Luc Vonderheyden, 33460, Arsac
www.chateau-mongravey.fr

Château Palmer Third Growth

Precise, powerful, gently spiced cassis and fig notes make Château Palmer one of the true stars of the appellation, combining innovation and risk-taking with upholding the traditions of Bordeaux. On paper, the structure seems difficult—it is owned by the négociant families Sichel and Maëhler Besse, with 22 shareholders—but it just keeps delivering. Credit must be given to the director, Thomas Duroux, who oversees the 136 acres (55ha) of gravelly terroir along the edge of the estuary. He has introduced ideas such as recreating a 19th-century wine—a blend of 85% Château Palmer and 15% Hermitage—that goes on very limited sale in certain vintages. The second wine is the much-loved Alter Ego de Palmer, brimming with fruit.

Cantenac, 33600 Margaux
www.chateau-palmer.com

Château Paveil-de-Luze Cru Bourgeois

This wine was being sold in the United States as far back as the 19th century, and continues to have a good market there today. Owned by Baron Frédéric de Luze, who took over from his father Geffrey in 2004, its 79 acres (32ha) of vines have remained unchanged for over 300 years. The 65% Cabernet Sauvignon in the blend gives a classic firm-tannic structure to the wine, but a cold soak and just 12 months in oak barrels ensures the fruit does not get lost.

3 Chemin du Paveil, 33460, Soussans
www.chateaupaveildeluze.com

Château Pontac Lynch Cru Bourgeois

Château Pontac Lynch is an old estate dating back to the 13th century, now run by Marie-Christine Bondon. Sweet, ripe plums dominate on the palate, but the firm tannins need time to open up even in lighter vintages, and it is a wine that will benefit from decanting for a while before drinking. The estate, located close to Château Margaux, appears quaintly old-fashioned in its approach to winemaking and offers lovely, good-value wines.

Issan-Cantenac, 33460 Margaux
www.chateau-pontaclynch.com

Château Prieuré-Lichine Fourth Growth

An actual priory once stood on the site of Château Prieuré-Lichine, and today some of that peaceful atmosphere remains in the ivy-clad inner courtyard. Now owned by the Ballande shipping group from New Caledonia, the estate covers 173 acres (70ha) and is planted to 50% Cabernet Sauvignon, 45% Merlot, and 5% Petit Verdot. It was one of the first Médoc estates to open to wine tourists, and is still one of the very few classified growths open at weekends for visitors wanting to sample the smooth, generous wine. Some micro-oxygenation is used in the vinification to fully round out the tannins. It is also worth trying the Blanc de Prieuré-Lichine.

34 avenue de la 5 République, Cantenac, 33460 Margaux
05 57 88 36 28

Château Rauzan-Gassies Second Growth

Château Rauzan-Gassies is situated right next door to Château Rauzan-Ségla, with the same classification. The estate has endured a bumpy few years in terms of critical attention but the Quié family has kept quietly improving the quality of the wine, turning out successful, long-living Margaux. Expect rich ruby rather than black fruits, with a lovely fresh backbone, in the classic rather than modern style. Recent investments in the property itself have seen the start of a public makeover. The same family own Château Croizet-Bages in Pauillac, and Château Bel-Orme in Haut-Médoc. ★ **Rising star**

rue Alexis Millardet, 33460 Margaux
www.domaines-quie.com

Château Rauzan-Ségla Second Growth

The texture of Château Rauzan-Ségla's wine stands out—the big, rich black fruit flavors are wrapped in silk. This makes it hard to believe that it was seriously under-performing when the Wertheimer brothers (of luxury goods house Chanel) bought this estate in 1993. Today, it is a precise, polished wine from 62% Cabernet Sauvignon and 38% Merlot. This reflects the careful techniques instilled by director John Kolasa (who came from Château Latour). Chanel has added some glamour by bringing in interior designer Peter Marino to design the interior, but it is the new drainage channels, careful vineyard work, high-density plantings, and exacting cellar work that have transformed this 148 acre (60ha) estate. The second wine is called Ségla.

rue Alexis Millardet, 33460 Margaux
www.rauzan-segla.com

Château Siran Cru Bourgeois

You could go a long way to find a more eclectic interior than at Château Siran, with various stuffed animals vying for space with modern art and antique books. Thankfully, the eccentricity stops at the décor—the wine is all about pared down fruits and subtly restrained tannic structure. This is an elegant Bordeaux, and not over-enthusiastically priced. The Mialhe family has been at this property for 150 years, with Edouard at the helm today. There are

CHATEAU RAUZAN-GASSIES
RECENT INVESTMENT HAS SEEN THIS
CHATEAU STEADILY IMPROVING ITS WINES

CHATEAU RAUZAN-SEGLA
THIS SECOND LABEL IS A GOOD-VALUE
OPTION FROM A SECOND GROWTH

62 acres (25ha) planted to 46% Merlot, 41% Cabernet Sauvignon, 11% Petit Verdot, and 2% Cabernet Franc. The second wine is S de Siran.

Labarde, 33460 Margaux, (visitor facilities from 2011)
www.chateausiran.com

Château Tayac Cru Bourgeois
Technical director Guy Portet runs things efficiently at the family-owned Château Tayac, with son Nicolas, wife Nadine, and daughter Nadia helping things along. The blend is made up of 60% Cabernet Sauvignon, 35% Merlot, and 5% Petit Verdot, making around 130,000 bottles each year. The style is firmly traditional rather than modern, with few pretensions. This is still a good-quality wine that remains affordable.

Lieu-dit Tayac, 33460 Soussans
www.chateautayac-margaux.com

Château Tayac-Plaisance Cru Artisan
The wine of Château Tayac-Plaisance displays crisp, well-delineated fruit, creating a modern style of Margaux that offers good value. Owned by Luc Thienpont of Clos des Quatre Vents, with Jacques and Eric Boissenot as consultant winemakers, the estate has just 8.6 acres (3.5ha) of vines producing 21,000 bottles a year. The oldest vines here date right back to 1931, with an average age of 55 years. The wine is a majority of Merlot, at 55%, with the rest being 35% Cabernet Sauvignon and 10% Petit Verdot.

1 imp Valmy Tayac, 33460 Soussans
www.chateau-tayacplaisance.com

Château du Tertre Fifth Growth
Château du Tertre produces seriously classy wine and has been owned by Eric Albada Jelgersma since 1997, under the direction of Alexander Van Beek. Covering 128 acres (52ha), with a carefully balanced planting of 36% Cabernet Sauvignon, 33% Merlot, 26% Cabernet Franc, with 5% Petit Verdot, the wine has suffered from inconsistency in the past, but today it is one of the most elegant, classically restrained Margaux you can find. Fermentation is carried out in oak vats, using gravity to ensure gentle movement around the winery; everything is well thought-out and underplayed.

33460 Arsac
www.chateaudutertre.fr

Château La Tour de Bessan
Cru Bourgeois
The wines at Château La Tour de Bessan have some white pepper and spice apparent in them, which gives a good savory edge to the fruit. Marie-Laure Lurton took over from her father Lucien in 1992, and has made this 47 acre (19ha) estate a leading Cru Bourgeois wine. Marie-Laure applies a mixture of modern techniques, such as increasing the vine canopy in the vineyard, and stainless steel fermentation in the winery, along with traditions such as picking by hand and a long oak-aging. After an extensive replanting program, the vineyard is currently at 40% Cabernet Sauvignon, 24% Cabernet Franc, and 36% Merlot.

route d'Arsac, 33460 Margaux
www.marielaurelurton.com

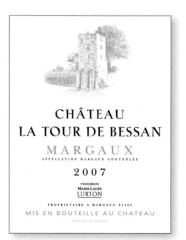

CHATEAU LA TOUR DE BESSAN
A MIX OF MODERN AND TRADITIONAL METHODS IN THE VINEYARD AND WINERY GIVES THIS ESTATE A LEADING EDGE

CHATEAU DU TERTRE
A RESTRAINED BUT TEXTURED WINE THAT COMBINES SUCCULENT AUTUMNAL FRUITS WITH A SAVORY HERBAL OVERTONE

Château La Tour de Mons Cru Bourgeois
Château La Tour de Mons is a reliable, well-made Margaux that is today owned by a French bank (far from unusual, particularly after the most recent financial crisis) and run by talented director Patrice Bandiera. The wine is picked by hand from the 86 acre (35ha) vineyard, vinified traditionally, matured in small oak barrels for 12 months, and bottled without filtering. While it is never over-extracted, the wine still has a firm grip and good fruit from a blend of 45% Cabernet Sauvignon, 45% Merlot, and 10% Cabernet Franc. You will find various "second wines" under different labels from this estate, but the best known is Terre du Mons.

No visitor facilities
05 57 88 33 03

Château Les Vimières Le Tronquéra
Le Tronquéra is a tiny bottling from 2.5 acres (1ha) of vines owned by Jacques Boissenot, the Médoc's understated but ubiquitous consultant enologist. The property covers 6 acres (2.5ha) in total, with the rest making Château Les Vimières under the AC Haut-Médoc. Boissenot bought these vines as a place to experiment on behalf of his other clients but the 3,000 bottles are snapped up while the fruit is still on the vine. It is not on the most fantastic terroir, but nevertheless has wonderful plum and cherry flavors and is rich and chewy, but well-restrained.

47 rue Principale, 33460 Lamarque
05 56 58 91 74

Clos du Jaugueyron
Clos du Jaugueyron is a small property owned by Michel Théron, covering just 12.3 acres (5ha) and making both Margaux and AC Haut-Médoc. Regarded by some as a "garage wine" (the first vintages were genuinely made in Théron's garage), this has an increasingly cult following. A rich, deeply textured wine, with great extraction but not overpowering, it is composed of 60% Cabernet Sauvignon, 30% Merlot, 5% Petit Verdot, and 5% Carbernet Franc. Everything in the vineyard is done carefully by hand, with chemicals kept to a minimum. Even the winery is made out of entirely natural substances, from stone to untreated oak.

4 rue de la Halle, 33460 Arsac
05 56 58 89 43

Clos des Quatres Vents
Clos Des Quatres Vents produces just 7,200 bottles of this wine each year, and while it is not easy to track down, it is worth the effort. The estate is owned by Luc Thienpont, a cousin of Jacques at Le Pin in Pomerol, with Jacques Boissenot as consultant. The wine is a beautiful *microcuvée* made from 65-year-old mainly Cabernet Sauvignon vines. Expect big, bold fruit, with a smoky edge from the 100% toasted new oak. There is a second wine (although strictly speaking it comes from its own separate estate) called Villa Des Quatres Soeurs.

33460 Soussans
www.luc-thienpont.com

GRAVES AND PESSAC-LEOGNAN

Graves is one of the oldest wine-growing regions in Bordeaux, while Pessac-Léognan is one of its most recent. Until 1987, they were one large area, lying south of Bordeaux city to the west of the River Garonne (and so forming the "other" Left Bank). The area received a boost of fame in 1855, when Château Haut-Brion was accorded the same first growth status as Châteaux Latour, Lafite, and Margaux in the Médoc. It was the only one of the 1855 wines to come from this appellation, but in the 1950s, 16 Graves properties were granted their own classified status. This designation is displayed on their labels as Cru Classé de Graves—despite the fact that, today, all are now included in the separate Appellation d'Origine Contrôlée of Pessac-Léognan.

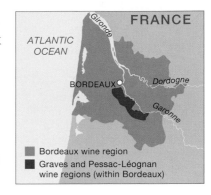

Bordeaux wine region
Graves and Pessac-Léognan wine regions (within Bordeaux)

The Graves ranking system is notable for having classified white wines as well as red wines—the only place in Bordeaux to do so. There are six châteaux that are classified in both colors: Bouscaut, Carbonnieux, Domaine de Chevalier, Latour Martillac, Malartic Lagravière, and Olivier. All of the 16 classified properties are located in the top corner of Graves, toward the urban center of Bordeaux and so, in 1987, this area was given its own separate appellation: AC Pessac-Léognan. The name comes from two of the largest communes in the area, but the appellation in total spans 10 communes: Cadaujac, Canéjan, Gradignan, Léognan, Martillac, Mérignac, Pessac, St-Médard-d'Eyrans, Talence, and Villenave d'Ornon. André Lurton, a renowned local winemaker and property owner, was instrumental in championing this new creation, and he continues to make excellent wine at his numerous estates, including Couhins-Lurton, La Louvière, Coucheroy, de Cruzeau, and Rochemorin.

The vineyard area of the Graves appellation covers 9,390 acres (3,800ha), while Pessac-Léognan has 4,200 acres (1,700ha).

Today, the region has a protected status, but the vineyards, inevitably given that they touch a major city center, have been under threat from urban sprawl for years. Some of the most famous names in this area, including Châteaux Haut-Brion and Pape Clément, are in the middle of busy local neighborhoods. The growth of the Bordeaux suburbs during the 20th century meant that by 1975, the vineyards of Pessac-Léognan were down to 1,236 acres (500ha). However, they have since grown and are now over three times that figure.

Together, these two appellations have some of the most complex terroir in the region. Distinct bands of soils that originated in the Pyrenees mountains were brought down by the River Garonne over several millennia, and the depth of the gravel varies from a shallow covering to up to 9.8ft (3m). To the west, the Landes pine forest acts as an effective windbreak.

There are no co-operative cellars in the whole of Graves or Pessac-Léognan, and most wineries are family-run. Pessac-Léognan, however, has been the site of considerable recent outside investment from families such as the Cathiards at Château Smith Haut Lafitte and the Bonnies at Château Malartic Lagravière. The appellation has an increasingly international, dynamic feel.

The grape varieties here are the same as elsewhere in Bordeaux, but the final blend tends to be a more even mix of Cabernet Sauvignon and Merlot. This differs from the Médoc, where Cabernet Sauvignon is favored, and from the Right Bank, which favors Merlot. For the whites, the permitted varieties are again the same as elsewhere, and the dry whites tend to be a majority of Sauvignon Blanc or Sauvignon Gris, but with a distinctive amount of Sémillon, and occasionally Muscadelle. As previously mentioned, they are also classified within the appellation, alongside the red wines. White wines in the greater Graves region, and particularly in Pessac-Léognan, are most likely to have been aged in oak, and will generally age far better than the white wines from Entre-deux-Mers, gaining in complexity for up to 15 years. Around one-third of the production is white wine, and two-thirds red wine.

Major grapes

🍇 Reds
Cabernet Franc
Cabernet Sauvignon
Merlot

🍇 Whites
Sauvignon Blanc
Sauvignon Gris
Sémillon

Vintages
2009
Excellent. Ideal conditions ensured powerful wines with great potential. Comparisons with 1982, even 1947.

2008
Summer cool, but fall very dry and warm, meaning a long period of ripening—good for those who waited.

2007
A difficult year meant uneven ripening. Some good reds, but a fantastic year for whites.

2006
A classic year, but rain during harvest. Some good wines.

2005
Ideal growing conditions meant rich, long-lived wines.

2004
A classic year, with good yields; the wines now offer excellent value for money.

2003
The extreme heat meant low acidity; although some wines are immediate crowd-pleasers, they are aging fast.

CHATEAU DE FRANCE
RESURRECTED IN THE LATE 20TH CENTURY,
WITH HELP FROM MICHEL ROLLAND

Château Bardins

The Sigoyer-Puel family have been making wine at Château Bardins for four generations. Today, the property is run by siblings Stella, Christol, and Edith. There is limited use of chemicals, with sustainable farming practiced over the 23 acres (9.5ha) of vines, which are approaching 30 years. The wines are steady, and good value, with depth and interest from a touch of Malbec and Petit Verdot in the reds. These two varieties make up 10% of the total, with the rest split three ways between Merlot and Cabernets Franc and Sauvignon. The grape choice is equally generous with the whites, where one-third Muscadelle gives a distinctive floral note.

124 avenue de Toulouse, 33140 Cadaujac
www.chateaubardins.fr.gd

Château Bois-Martin

Château Bois-Martin is owned by Marie-José Perrin (daughter of the Perrin family of Carbonnieux) with her husbane Réné, and is a wine well worth knowing about. The 17 acres (7ha) of red vines are planted to 70% Cabernet Sauvignon and 30% Merlot, producing 40,000 bottles a year. A new winery was built in 1999, where vinification takes place in stainless steel vats. Most vintages see a lovely maturity of tannins in this wine, and an elegant fruit structure. The tiny quantity of succulent white (9,000 bottles) is vinified in bottle.

33850 Léognan
www.carbonnieux.com

Château Le Bonnat

Farmed by Château de Fieuzel until 1997, Vignobles Lesgourgues have now reclaimed Château Le Bonnet. The vineyard is planted with 49 acres (20ha) of red grapes (60% Merlot and 40% Cabernet Sauvignon) and 7.4 acres (3ha) of white grapes (two-thirds Sémillon to one-third Sauvignon Blanc). The reds spend 12–14 months in barrel (one-third new), and the whites get lees-stirring and nine months in barrel. The special *cuvée*, Les Galets, is, unusually, lighter and less tannic than the main wine. The owners also have the excellent Château Haut Selve, here in Graves.

No visitor facilities
www.vignobles-lesgourgues.com

Château Bouscaut

Grand Cru Classé de Graves
Sophie Lurton, with her husband Laurent Cogombles, inherited Château Bouscaut from her father Lucien in 1992. Classified in both red and white, the vineyard covers 116 acres (47ha), planted to 85% red and 15% white vines on gravelly and clay soils. The red wine has a touch of Malbec in the 55% Merlot/40% Cabernet Sauvignon blend, and has highly attractive notes of coffee and mocha. The white is an equal mix of Sémillon (with some vines up to 100 years old) and Sauvignon Blanc, giving it a honeyed roundness in the mouth, and good aging potential. The château was completely destroyed by a fire in the 1960s, but has since been fully restored, and an entirely new cellar is being constructed. The second wine is Les Chenes de Bouscaut and they also own nearby châteaux Lamothe Bouscaut and Valoux.

33140 Cadaujac
www.chateau-bouscaut.com

Château Brown

Château Brown has seen some serious quality drives in recent years, led by director Jean-Christophe Mau with oenologists Stéphane Derenoncourt and Philippe Dulong. Bought in 2004 by the Mau and Dirkzwager families, there are 24ha (59 acres) of 55% Cabernet Sauvignon/40% Merlot/5% Petit Verdot and 4.5ha (11 acres) of 70% Sauvignon Blanc/30% Sémillon. The white is vinified in burgundy casks with lees-stirring, giving modern, exotic fruit flavours, with a clean ripple of acidity. The red is coming into its own, with stainless steel fermentation and barrel ageing (40% new) giving well-defined dark fruit flavours with hints of graphite and meaty tannins. The second wine is Le Colombier de Château Brown.

Allée John Lewis Brown, 33850 Léognan
www.chateau-brown.com

Château Cantelys

Château Cantelys produces slick, modern-style wines and was bought by the Cathiards of Château Smith Haut Lafitte in 1994. There are 24ha (59 acres) of vines at this increasingly impressive estate, located at the top of a gravelly rise. The white is a mix of Sauvignon Blanc and Sauvignon Gris, with a touch of Sémillon for structure, all vinified at low temperatures with lees-stirring in barrel, encouraging toasty, exotic flavours. The excellent red majors on Cabernet Sauvignon, but this is also worked to ensure smooth, fleshy tannins and a certain opulence in style. A Rosé de Cantelys is also produced.

No visitor facilities
www.smith-haut-lafitte.com

Château Carbonnieux

Grand Cru Classé de Graves
Château Carbonnieux is classified in both colours, with a particularly well-regarded white. There are 222 acres (90ha) planted to, unusually, slightly more white vines than red. Located next door to Haut-Bailly, Carbonnieux has been owned by the Perrin family since the early 1950s. For whites, there is skin contact before fermentation, then eight to nine months in barrel, with lees-stirring. The delicate palate shows classic Sauvignon Blanc character, with crisp, fresh citrus and white blossom from a touch of Muscadelle; Sémillon provides the backbone. The reds are 60% Cabernet Sauvignon and 30% Merlot, with a mix of Malbec, Cabernet Franc, and Petit Verdot, giving firm tannins and fleshy fruit.

33850 Léognan
www.carbonnieux.com

Château Les Carmes Haut-Brion

Château Les Carmes Haut-Brion is located next to Château Haut-Brion, and once shared the same owner. Today, it is an entirely separate estate, owned by Didier Furt and family. The wine is vibrant, with fresh fruit and a frank personality, although it lacks the depth and complexity of its neighbour. Covering just 4.7ha (11.6 acres), it is planted to 50% Merlot, 40% Cabernet Franc, and 10% Cabernet Sauvignon in gravelly soils. Its proximity to the city makes it warmer, meaning that ripening here can be both early and even. The second wine is called Le Clos des Carmes.

197 avenue Jean Cordier, 33600 Pessac
www.les-carmes-haut-brion.com

CHATEAU CANTELYS
A MODERN STYLE OF WINEMAKING FROM THE
CATHIARD FAMILY OF SMITH HAUT LAFITTE

Château de Chantegrive

At more than 240 acres (97ha), Château de Chantegrive is one of the largest estates in Graves. It is run by Hélène Lévêque, with winemaking advice from Hubert de Bouärd. The reds are 50% Cabernet Sauvignon, 50% Merlot, with plot-by-plot winemaking. This, and the impressive barrel cellar, help to make it a dynamic estate. For the whites, a special bottling, Cuvée Caroline, is from old vines aged in 50% new oak, while the regular white, which is bottled unoaked, is full of fresh citrus vigor. The red has firm, savory spice and offers superb value. Since the 2007 vintage, a small amount (6,000 bottles) of Cuvée Henri Lévêque has been produced in honor of Hélène's father. The malolactic fermentation happens in barrel, and the wine is bottled unfiltered and unfined.

33720 Podensac
www.chantegrive.com

Château Coucheroy

André Lurton has created a wonderful signature with his white wines in recent years. Château Coucheroy's white is another of his reliable, crisp 100% Sauvignon Blanc pleasers. There is also complexity—the vines are densely planted up to 3,440 vines per acre (8,500 per hectare), and low-temperature vinification is followed by a good stint in barrel. The red is equally split between Cabernet Sauvignon and Merlot, and spends 12 months in barrel. These are both well-priced wines offering real pleasure.

c/o Château La Louvière, 33850 Villenave d'Ornon
05 57 25 58 58

Château Couhins Grand Cru Classé de Graves

An interesting property, Château Couhins is owned by the INRA (a national body for the science of plants), and so is inevitably a center for research and development. Technical director Dominique Forget is currently working with non-aggressive, sustainable agriculture to respect the flora of the soils, and is trialling new technology that uses light and heat sensors to assess vine growth. There are 37 acres (15ha) of red vines (50% Merlot, 40% Cabernet Sauvignon, 9% Cabernet Franc, and 1% Petit Verdot), and 17 acres (7ha) of white (85% Sauvignon Blanc, 15% Sémillon). In the cellars, techniques include cold soaking, fermentation in stainless steel tanks, and barrel aging. The results are good: gooseberry and white peaches, and soft red fruits with non-aggressive tannins. The second wine is Couhins La Gravette.

No visitor facilities
www.chateau-couhins.fr

Château Couhins-Lurton

Grand Cru Classé de Graves

Owned by André Lurton, Château Couhins-Lurton became the first (and so far, the only) classified white Bordeaux to go under screwcap, with the 2003 vintage. The white is also unusual for being 100% Sauvignon Blanc, over 15 acres (6ha), and is a crisp, modern style, full of elegant citrus and a tingle of minerality. The red comes from 42 acres (17ha) of succulent and fruit-forward 77% Merlot and 23% Cabernet Sauvignon. Lurton had rented the vines for a number of years before buying the property in 1992 and fully renovating the whole estate.

c/o Château La Louvière, 33850 Villenave d'Ornon
www.andrelurton.com

Château Ferran

Philippe and Ghislaine Lacoste—descendants of owners stretching back to 1880—have run Château Ferran since 1999. There are 44 acres (18ha) planted with 60% Merlot and 40% Cabernet Sauvignon, and 10 acres (4ha) with 55% Sémillon and 45% Sauvignon Blanc. Careful work in the vineyard includes leaf thinning and green harvesting. The whites are aged in barrel after a cold soak and the lees are regularly stirred, maximizing the rich and structured flavors that make this a white to match with food. The red is also on the soft, gourmet side, majoring in ripe summer fruits. The second wine is called Château de Belloc, and there is an easy-drinking Rosé de Ferran.

33650 Martillac
www.chateauferran.com

Château de Fieuzal

Grand Cru Classé de Graves

Clean, delineated fruit, with well-integrated smoky oak, is the signature of the revitalized Château de Fieuzal, bought by Irish businessman Lochlann Quinn in 2001, with Stephen Carrier as director and Hubert de Bouärd as consultant. Planted to 55% Cabernet Sauvignon, with 25% Merlot, 6% Cabernet Franc, and 4% Petit Verdot, recent years have seen the use of satellite technology to track the ripening of the plots. Another change has been the proportion of Sauvignon Blanc in the white wine moving up to 70%, with 30% Sémillon (the scores rising accordingly). In total, there are 198 acres (80ha) of vines, with 178 acres (72ha) of these red and the balance white. The second wine is Abeille de Fieuzel.

124 avenue de Mont de Marsan, 33850 Léognan
www.fieuzal.com

Château de France

Château de France produces a subtle, Sauvignon Blanc-led white wine and a rich, well-structured red. The Thomassin family, ex-distillers from the Paris region, bought this estate in the early 1970s, making it another local property to be rescued from near-extinction. They first replanted the 96 acre (39ha) vineyard, then restored the winery and surrounding buildings, reintroducing white vines in 1985. Today, Arnaud Thomassin is in charge, with Michel Rolland as consultant winemaker. The second wine is Château Coquillas.

33850 Léognan
www.chateau-de-france.com

Château la Garde

Château la Garde is a top-quality Dourthe property, acquired in 1990, with 133 acres (54ha). Of that, 5 acres (2ha) are planted with a mix of Sauvignon Blanc and Sauvignon Gris, the latter giving aromatic wines with hints of apricot. Careful studies of the terroir have led to precise vineyard plantings, and to plot-led decisions throughout the year. In the cellars, vinification takes place in small stainless steel tanks with barrel aging for up to 18 months. The reds (61% Merlot, with the two Cabernets and Petit Verdot making up the rest) are powerful and supple, with appealing notes of chocolate and rich berries. There are two consultants: Michel Rolland for the reds and Christophe Ollivier for the whites. ★Rising star

No visitor facilities
05 56 35 53 00

RENOVATING AND REBUILDING

A raft of new owners and outside investment have created a sense of dynamism that is reflected in Pessac-Léognan's architecture, from André Lurton's starkly modern Rochemorin, to the clean lines of Luchey-Halde, and the gleaming interior of the winery at Malartic Lagravière. The area is also the location for the new Institut des Sciences de la Vigne et du Vin (ISVV)—Europe's biggest wine research center. Bordeaux architects Nicolas Ragueneau and Jean Marie Mazières designed the modern, eco-friendly building, which is made of stone and glass. It covers 107,639 sqft (10,000 sqm) and has one of the biggest tasting rooms in the world. But it is not just modern design that makes this appellation so visually distinctive—local architects firm Agence de l'Arsenal specialize in restoring 18th and 19th century buildings, and have worked on Haut-Bailly, Smith Haut Lafitte, and Château de la Brède, all stunning examples of revived classicism.

CHATEAU HAUT-BAILLY
AN INSIDER'S TIP FOR QUALITY AND
RARE PRE-PHYLLOXERA VINES

CHATEAU HAUT-BRION
THE ONLY FIRST GROWTH CHATEAU OF
1855 FOUND OUTSIDE THE HAUT-MEDOC

Château Gazin-Rocquencourt

The Bonnie family of Malartic Lagravière bought Château Gazin-Rocquencourt in 2006, and have since completed extensive work, replanting the 54 acres (22ha) of vines, draining the soil, changing the direction of the rows, and increasing the planting density. Completing the picture is a new winery using a gravity-led system with modern stainless steel vats, double-lined to mimic the inert temperature control of cement. Planted to 55% Cabernet Sauvignon and 45% Merlot, the vineyard still needs a few years for the wine to gain in complexity, but it is already full of silky fruits, and is a serious one to watch.

74 avenue de Cestas, 33850 Léognan
05 56 64 77 89

Château Haut-Bacalan

The Michel Gonet champagne family, led by Frédéric and Charles-Henri Gonet, rescued Château Haut-Bacalan in 1998, with the first harvest in 2001. It had gone unplanted for 70 years until they restored the vineyard. Located in Pessac, very close to the city center, there are 15 acres (6ha) of vines planted to 65% Merlot and 35% Cabernet Sauvignon over gravelly soils. Winemaking techniques such as cold soaking and micro-oxygenation ensure a wine with soft fruits and round tannins.

No visitor facilities
www.gonet.fr

Château Haut-Bailly

Grand Cru Classé de Graves
Long the insider's choice, today, Château Haut-Bailly is taking center stage with its elegant interpretation of black fruits and elongated silky tannins. The vineyard sits on a high ridge in Léognan, next door to Carbonnieux, with 74 acres (30ha) of vines. A small percentage of this is a mixture of vines dating from the pre-phylloxera era. The remainder of the estate is planted with 64% Cabernet Sauvignon, 30% Merlot, and 6% Cabernet Franc. Denis Dubourdieu consults, along with, since 2004, Jean Delmas. Owned by the American Wilmers family, the estate is run by Veronique Sanders, whose deft touch helps to sustain this thrilling wine. ★ **Rising star**

avenue de Cadaujac, 33850 Léognan
www.chateau-haut-bailly.com

Château Haut-Bergey

Château Haut-Bergey is an increasingly dynamic estate, owned by Sylviane Garcin-Cathiard (also of Clos l'Eglise in Pomerol) with Alain Reynaud as consultant. The vines cover 94 acres (38ha) of 60% Cabernet Sauvignon and 40% Merlot, vinified in stainless steel and aged in 50% new oak. The resulting wine offers excellent value, with notes of black currant leaf and clean graphite. The 5 acres (2ha) of 80% Sauvignon Blanc and 20% Sémillon give a white with sweet new oak, full of juicy passion fruit and papaya. Modern in style, but it works. ★ **Rising star**

69 cours Gambetta, 33850 Léognan
www.chateau-haut-bergey.com

Château Haut-Brion First Growth

The oldest and the smallest (126 acres/51ha) of the first growths, Château Haut-Brion is owned by the American Dillon family, with Prince Robert of Luxembourg as president and Jean-Philippe Delmas as director. The château was among the first to introduce stainless steel tanks (in 1961). They have their own barrel makers on site, and there is also a large laboratory and a micro-vineyard, established by Jean-Bernard Delmas in 1970, to identify suitable new clones. Over the last 10 years, Haut-Brion has increased the amount of Cabernet Sauvignon, and today it stands at 50%, with 41% Merlot and 9% Cabernet Franc. The result is an enormously layered, textured, and complex wine, with savory touches against the deep-red fruits—effortlessly elegant. The classically structured Château Haut-Brion Blanc (Grand Cru Classé de Graves) is 55% Sémillon and 45% Sauvignon Blanc. The second wine (from 2007) is La Clarence de Haut Brion.

133 avenue Jean Jaurès, 33608 Pessac
www.haut-brion.com

Château Haut Peyrous

Château Haut Peyrous has been owned by Marc Darroze since 2008. With experience in Armagnac, California, and Hungary, he is converting this 30 acre (12ha) estate to organic production (the first organic vintage will be 2012). There are 6 acres (2.5ha) of Sauvignon Blanc and Sémillon. The rest of the vineyard is planted to 55% Merlot, 40% Cabernets Franc and Sauvignon, and the remainder to Malbec and Petit Verdot. Low yields, optimal maturity, and gentle extraction are key, and the wines show Darroze's foodie roots: Retours de Palombière is the top *cuvée*, with long maceration and barrel aging; the second wine is the Merlot-based Pêle-Porc et Cochonailles. For the whites, Pêche au Carrelet is the fleshy, barrel-aged top *cuvée*, and Cueillettes du Bassin is the crisper second wine.

No visitor facilities
www.darroze-armagnacs.com

Château de l'Hospital

Owned by the Lafragettes of Loudenne in Haut-Médoc, Château de l'Hospital is a succulent wine of 90% Merlot and 10% Cabernet Sauvignon. It is good quality for what is often an excellent-value wine, emphasizing flavors of grilled cherry and strawberry fruits, with well-rounded tannins. The second wine is Château Thibaut Ducasse.

Lieu-dit Darrouban, 33640 Portets
www.lafragette.com

Château Larrivet Haut-Brion

Despite the name, Château Larrivet Haut-Brion is a good distance from Haut-Brion. Philippe and Christine Gervoson are the owners, with Bruno Lemoine as winemaker and Michel Rolland consulting. The estate was recently enlarged to 173 acres (70ha) of gravel and sand soils. The red wine is 55% Merlot, 40% Cabernet Sauvignon, and 5% Cabernet Franc, giving notes of black fruit and vanilla from the 50% new oak barrels. The white is 60% Sauvignon Blanc and 40% Sémillon— rich with grilled almonds and peaches. The second wine is Les Demoiselles de Larrivet Haut-Brion.

84 avenue de Cadaujac, 33850 Léognan
www.larrivethautbrion.fr

Château Latour Martillac

Grand Cru Classé de Graves
Château Latour Martillac is a good-quality 104 acre (42ha) estate owned by the Kressman family, and currently under the direction of Tristan, with his brother

Loic as technical director. Classified in both colors, the white is a subtle, citrus-led wine with white blossom highlights, made from 55% Sémillon plus Muscadelle and Sauvignon Blanc. The red makes more of an entrance, with toasty oak and spicy notes coming from 60% Cabernet Sauvignon, 35% Merlot, and 5% Petit Verdot, and it spends up to 18 months in oak (40% new). The second wine is Lagrave Martillac.

chemin de la Tour, 33650 Martillac
www.latour-martillac.com

Château La Louvière
Château La Louvière is an André Lurton estate and an historic monument. Vines have grown here since 1476 and today, the 116 acres (47ha) produce a balanced, elegant red (64% Cabernet Sauvignon), which has a firm structure and needs a few years to bed down before opening. The white is dominated by 85% Sauvignon Blanc and is more instantly accessible, with bright fruits, lively acidity, and a soft smoke from fermentation in oak barrels (30% new). Recent renovations have seen a new winery and cellar. The second wine is L de la Louvière.

33850 Villenave d'Ornon
www.andrelurton.com

Château Luchey-Halde
Château Luchey-Halde was a teaching estate in the late 1990s, and is owned by ENITA, a renowned agricultural-engineering school. There are 54 acres (22ha) of vines, planted to majority red, with 55% Cabernet Sauvignon, 35% Merlot, and an even split between Cabernet Franc and Petit Verdot. Both château and cellars are sleek and modern, and the wines show great maturity of the berries (helped by low yields), with large helpings of new oak. The vines are still young, and do need time to deepen in complexity, but this is an interesting estate. The white is 55% Sauvignon Blanc and 45% Sémillon.

17 avenue du Maréchal Joffre, 33700 Mérignac
www.luchey-halde.com

Château Malartic Lagravière
Grand Cru Classé de Graves
The Bonnie family have built the 131 acre (53ha) Château Malartic Lagravière into one of the most exciting estates of the Pessac-Léognan appellation since they purchased it in 1997. Meticulous, sustainable vineyard work and a technically advanced winery have helped the work started by consultant enologists Michel Rolland and Athanas Fakorellis. Signatures in red and white (classified in both) are star-bright fruit, big, precise flavors, and soft, silky textures. For the 114 acres (46ha) of red, there is a 45/45 split between Merlot/Cabernet Sauvignon, with the balance 8% Cabernet Franc and 2% Petit Verdot. The 17 acres (7ha) of white are 80% Sauvignon Blanc and 20% Sémillon. The second wine is La Réserve de Malartic, and there is also a Rosé de Malartic. ★ **Rising star**

No visitor facilities
www.malartic-lagraviere.com

Château La Mission Haut-Brion
Grand Cru Classé de Graves
La Mission's elegant wrought-iron gates face Château Haut-Brion across an unassuming Bordeaux road. Increasingly, La Mission deserves to be seen as the other

CHATEAU LA MISSION HAUT-BRION
NEXT TO THE FIRST GROWTH HAUT-BRION GEOGRAPHICALLY AND IN TERMS OF QUALITY

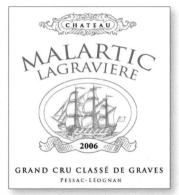

CHATEAU MALARTIC LAGRAVIERE
ATTENTION TO DETAIL AND THE BEST TECHNOLOGY MAKE EXCITING WINES

great estate in Pessac-Léognan. The same team, led by Jean-Philippe Delmas, reveals elegance and richness from the 52 acres (21ha) of 43% Merlot, 51% Cabernet Sauvignon, and 6% Cabernet Franc. On the palate, dark fruits are cut through with tobacco leaf and a delicate smokiness, but the tannins are anything but reticent. The château and winery have been painstakingly renovated in recent years, culminating in a new barrel cellar by architect Guy Troppés in 2007. The celebrated white wine, Château La Haut-Brion Blanc (Grand Cru Classé de Graves; formerly Laville Haut-Brion), is a rich, structured blend of 80% Sémillon and 20% Sauvignon Blanc, and the second wine is La Clarté de Haut-Brion (which also uses vines from the former La Tour Haut-Brion).

33608 Pessac
www.haut-brion.com

Château Montalivet
Owned by Denis Dubourdieu, Château Montalivet is the second wine of Clos Floridène but was originally a separate property. The red is an even split between Cabernet Sauvignon and Merlot, vinified at a low temperature and aged in both stainless steel and barrels to preserve fresh aromas of blueberries and wild herbs. The white is an equally simple 50/50 split, here between Sémillon and Sauvignon Blanc, with fermentation in barrel (25% new) and regular lees-stirring. The result is a toasty, well-rounded wine that has soft citrus flavors.

No visitor facilities
www.denisdubourdieu.fr

Château Olivier Grand Cru Classé de Graves
Financier Jean-Jacques de Bertmann is the owner of Château Olivier, with director Laurent Lebrun and consultant Denis Dubourdieu. Classified in both colors, there are 20 acres (8ha) of white vines, and 99 acres (40ha) of red. The site was first an 11th-century hunting lodge, and remnants of the forests surround the château. Recent advances include a new vat house with truncated stainless steel vats. A soil survey carried out in 2003 by Xavier Chome led to the discovery of an excellent plot of dense gravel that has now been planted with Cabernet Sauvignon. Rich and complex aromas on the white are helped by lees-stirring of the 75% Sauvignon Blanc, 23% Sémillon, and 2% Muscadelle, all harvested by hand into small baskets, then fermented in barrel (30% new oak). The red is an elegant wine majoring in soft red fruits, which spends 12 months aging in 35% new oak.

175 avenue de Bordeaux, 33850 Léognan
www.chateau-olivier.com

Château Pape Clément
Grand Cru Classé de Graves
Bernard Magrez is a modern and uncompromising character, with many estates in Bordeaux and around the world. Château Pape Clément, where the first recorded harvest dates back to 1252, is his most prestigious. Michel Rolland consults on all Magrez properties, and the meticulous attention to detail creates slick wines with a sense of drama. Techniques include hand-stemming and whole-grape vinification in small oak vats. The final wine (50% Cabernet Sauvignon, 45% Merlot, 3% Petit Verdot, and 2% Cabernet Franc) makes an impression, with powerful tannins and a black-fruit core that ages beautifully to reveal the elegance of the appellation. The

CHATEAU RESPIDE-MEDEVILLE
THIS WINE SHOWS LOVELY RED CURRANT
FLAVORS AND SOFT TANNINS

white wine (40% Sauvignon Blanc, 35% Sémillon, 16% Sauvignon Gris, 9% Muscadelle) undergoes integral vinification in small barrels, with regular lees-stirring. The second wine is Le Clémentin de Pape Clément.

216 avenue du Dr Nancel Pénard, 33600 Pessac
www.pape-clement.com

Château Picque-Caillou
Owned by Isabelle and Paulin Calvet, the 54 acre (22ha) Château Picque-Caillou gives over just 2.5 acres (1ha) to its white grapes. With it, they produce a gentle, citrus-focused wine with mouthwatering freshness. The red, vinified in tank with 12 months in barrel (30% new) from 50/50 Cabernet Sauvignon/Merlot, also steers away from blockbusting flavors. The cellar work has become even more precise since Denis Dubourdieu came on board as consultant in 2007 with his protégé Valerie Lavigne.

avenue Pierre Mendès France, 33700 Mérignac
05 57 47 37 98

Château Rahoul
Alain Thiénot, the founder of Champagne Thiénot and owner of Château Rahoul since 1986, took a major step into Bordeaux politics in 2007 when he gained a majority stake in merchant firm CVBG Dourthe Kressman. This gave him access not only to the winemaking expertise and investment of Dourthe, but also wider distribution channels. With sustainable practices in the 104 acre (42ha) vineyard, the white wine has rich stone fruit (up to 78% Sémillon). The red (70% Merlot, 27% Cabernet Sauvignon, with Petit Verdot and Cabernet Franc) undergoes a cold soak and ages in large barrels, giving a non-intrusive smoky finish. The second wines are L'Orangerie de Rahoul and Château La Garance.

No visitor facilities
www.chateau-rahoul.com

Château Respide
This is one of the oldest properties in Graves, owned by the Bonnet family. Château Respide makes a good-quality red wine from 74 acres (30ha) of 65% Merlot and 35% Cabernet Sauvignon. There is also a less well-known white wine made from 37 acres (15ha) of vines that goes for structured stone fruits, with 65% Sémillon livened up by a balance of Sauvignon Blanc.

33210 Roaillan
05 56 63 24 24

Château Respide-Medeville
Xavier and Julie Gonet are increasingly important players in Bordeaux, with properties in Sauternes, Graves, and Margaux (as well as Champagne). Château Respide-Medeville is located on a gravel hill just north of Langon, with 20 acres (8ha) of red planted to 60% Cabernet Sauvignon and 40% Merlot. There are 8.6 acres (3.5ha) of white that are an almost even split between Sauvignon Blanc and Sémillon, with a smattering of Muscadelle to lift the nose. The white is fermented and aged in 100% new oak barrels, with fine lees-stirring. This is a classic Pessac-Léognan foodie wine that offers good value. The second wine is Dame de Respide.

4 rue du Port, 33210 Preignac
www.gonet-medeville.com

Château de Rochemorin
The strikingly modern winery at Château de Rochemorin looks like an Argentine bodega, and the inside is equally impressive. It is a large estate with 260 acres (105ha) of vines, with 44 acres (18ha) of Sauvignon Blanc (lees-stirred to bring out the richness and structure), and the rest planted to 60/40 Cabernet Sauvignon/Merlot. Situated on high ground, the property has been owned by André Lurton since 1973, and has the influential Denis Dubourdieu as consultant. The red wine, bottled unfiltered, is full of smoky red fruits and well-bred tannins.

c/o Château La Louvière, 33850 Villenave d'Ornon
www.andrelurton.com

Château Le Satre
Adjacent to Bois-Martin, and also owned by Marie-José Perrin-Leriche, Château Le Satre is a larger estate, covering 89 acres (36ha). Grapes are hand picked into small crates, and undergo a low-temperature vinification aimed at keeping this wine firmly in the fruit camp (split between the two Cabernets and Merlot). The Sauvignon Blanc-Sémillon whites split their time between stainless steel and oak, and are in a lively, modern style.

No visitor facilities
www.lesartre.com

Château Seguin
Château Seguin's vines were entirely replanted in 1988. Owned by Jean Darriet, together with property group Foncière Loticis, one of the key features here is the low-impact winemaking across the 77 acres (31ha)—very low yields, and often one of the last in the appellation to pick. The 60% Cabernet Sauvignon and 40% Merlot grapes are carefully crafted to deliver maximum impact. This is a confident wine with big flavors of creamy blackberries shot through with savory herbs. ★**Rising star**

33360 Lignan-de-Bordeaux
www.chateau-seguin.fr

Château du Seuil
Château du Seuil produces an award-winning white from its 37 acre (15ha) vineyard, made with 60% Sémillon and 40% Sauvignon Blanc. The owners are Welsh-New Zealanders Nicola and Sean Allison, who impart a sparkle and minerality into the wine. The red is an elegant, structured mix of Merlot and Cabernet Sauvignon, with 5% Cabernet Franc. Since 2009, the conversion of most of the vineyard to organic production has been under way. There are also 25 acres (10ha) in the AC Premières Côtes de Bordeaux bottled under the name Domaine du Seuil, and a few plots in AC Cérons making a sweet wine. In the best vintages, Héritage du Seuil is a special bottling, vinified entirely in large oak barrels (50% new).

1 Au Seuil, 33720 Cerons
www.chateauduseuil.com

Château Smith Haut Lafitte
Grand Cru Classé de Graves
The Cathiard's bought Château Smith Haut Lafitte in 1990, and were in the first wave of dynamic owners who transformed Pessac-Léognan. Today, organic practices over the 166 acres (67ha), extensive replanting, an onsite barrel maker, and a modern winery have all contributed to its renaissance. The exuberant white (90% Sauvignon

CHATEAU SMITH HAUT LAFITTE
THE RENAISSANCE OF THE LATE 20TH
CENTURY CONTINUES AT THIS PROPERTY

Blanc, 5% Sauvignon Gris, 5% Sémillon) takes a modern approach, with fresh apricots and toasted oak. The red is a more classic interpretation at 55% Cabernet Sauvignon, 34% Merlot, 10% Cabernet Franc, and 1% Petit Verdot, with firm fruit, ripe tannins, and a touch of spicy luxury.

4 chemin de Bourran, 33650 Martillac
www.smith-haut-lafitte.com

Château Villa Bel-Air

The Italian-style, 124 acre (50ha) Château Villa Bel-Air has been owned by the Cazes family of Lynch-Bages since 1988. Restructuring of the vineyards and new technical installations have paid dividends in recent vintages, producing wines with the finesse, complexity, and understated balance that the best of the appellation can deliver. Gravelly soil, on a bed of clay–limestone, provides perfect conditions for the Cabernet Sauvignon (40%) in the red. With a balance of Merlot (50%) and Cabernet Franc (10%), this is vinified in stainless steel, then spends 12 months in oak barrels, ending up with wonderfully nuanced red fruits, tinged by smoky notes. The white is a mix of Sauvignon Blanc (65%) and Sémillon, combining freshness and delicacy with lip-smacking juicy citrus.

No visitor facilities
www.villabelair.com

Clos Floridène

Clos Floridène is Bordeaux's white wine *par excellence*, owned by Denis Dubourdieu. The vines cover 77 acres (31ha) on a limestone plateau. Founded in 1982, the name is a play on Denis' name, and that of his wife Florence. The white is 55% Sauvignon Blanc, 44% Sémillion, and 1% Muscadelle, and is full of crisp, mouthwatering fruits. The red is 64% Cabernet Sauvignon, 36% Merlot, and favors elegant, richly perfumed red fruits, with a firm structure. The soils are rich in iron oxide (as in Pomerol), mixed with red clay, leading to intense flavors.

33210 Pujols-sur-Cirons
www.denisdubourdieu.fr

Clos Les Remparts

Clos Les Remparts is a small-production Graves from Sauternes estate Clos Dady. Owners Catherine and Christophe Gachet produce a rich, succulent red from 10 acres (4ha) of 90% Merlot and 10% Cabernet Sauvignon. It delivers concentrated, precise black-fruit flavors and is great value. Plot-by-plot vinification in small vats is followed by no fining and light filtration. The estate also has a dry white from 1.2 acres (0.5ha) of 90% old Sémillon vines and 10% Sauvignon Blanc, vinified in new barrels and aged for four months on the lees.

Château Bastard, 33720 Barsac
www.clos-dady.com

Domaine de Chevalier
Grand Cru Classé de Graves

Domaine de Chevalier is equally successful for its red and white wines, and is justifiably classified for both. The charming Olivier Bernard is in charge of the 106 acres (43ha), and makes a 60% Cabernet Sauvignon, 30% Merlot red, with a dash of Petit Verdot and Cabernet Franc. It has an open, cedar-filled nose, with firm fruit and tannins, and a dusting of mocha. The white is made for aging, with 70% Sauvignon Blanc and 30% Sémillon,

and takes on a beautifully spicy quality. The consultant is Stéphane Derenoncourt, who never picks more than 20–30% of any one plot at any time, thus ensuring optimum ripeness, and does not allow pumping of grapes in the winery. The second wine is L'Esprit de Chevalier.

102 chemin Mignoy, 33850 Léognan
www.domainedechevalier.com

Domaine de la Passion Haut-Brion

For 30 years, the vines of Domaine de la Passion Haut-Brion were used by Château Haut-Brion under a crop-share arrangement. From 2007, they once again formed their own tiny 3.7 acre (1.5ha) estate, owned by 94-year-old Michel Allery, but run by a team headed by consultant Stéphane Derenoncourt. The vines are planted to 60% Cabernet Franc and 40% Cabernet Sauvignon, farmed organically, and fermented in open vats. The first two vintages suffered from low yields due to mildew, but 2009 saw a realization of the full potential, with the personality of the Cabernet Franc giving elegance and gentle spice. A new winery opened in late 2010.

29 rue Edouard Vaillant, 33608 Pessac
www.vigneronsconsultants.com

Domaine de la Solitude

Owned by Olivier Bernard, the romantic name comes from the nuns who used to live on this site. The 74 acre (30ha) property makes red and white wines, but three-quarters of the land is dedicated to red varieties, with 50% Cabernet Sauvignon, 35% Merlot, and 15% Cabernet Franc. The wine is full of rich, red fruits that develop into soft mushroom and leather, with some lovely smoky tones. The aromatic white has around 70% Sauvignon Blanc, and the charming second wine, Le Prieuré de la Solitude, comes from the young vines.

10 route de la Solitude, 33650 Martillac
www.domainedelasolitude.com

La Sérénité

Owned by Bernard Magrez of Pape Clément, the 5 acre (2ha) La Sérénité is part of the 15 acre (6ha) Château Poumey estate. Produced since 2001, it is just over 50% Merlot, with the rest Cabernet Sauvignon. The wine undergoes the same meticulous attention to detail as at all of Magrez's estates—gravity-flow, whole-berry ferments, cold soaking, manual cap-punching, and 18 months aging in new oak. The result is luscious, full of snappy rich fruits, licorice, and dark chocolate.

rue du Professeur Bernard, 33190 Gradignan
05 57 26 38 38

Vieux Château Gaubert

Vieux Château Gaubert is among the best in Graves for red and white despite being unclassified. Owned by Dominique Haverlan, it is divided into 49 acres (20ha) of red and 15 acres (6ha) of white. The white has skin contact and is aged in 60% new oak; the red has cold soaking, is aged in 40% new oak, and spends up to two more years in bottle before release. A special bottling from 5 acres (2ha) of old vines, cropped low, is called Gravéum de Gaubert. This is richer, more tannic, and needs decanting before drinking.

33640 Portets
05 56 67 52 76

DENIS DUBOURDIEU

A scientist, vineyard owner, and winemaker, Denis Dubourdieu was educated as an agro-scientist, and has been Professor of Enology at Bordeaux University since 1987. He has concentrated his research on how to capture varietal aromas in white wines in both the vineyard and cellar. "People rarely talk about white Bordeaux," he says, "so it is paradoxical that the real scientific advances over the past 20 years in Bordeaux have been in whites rather than reds." Dubourdieu owns a number of estates in the region, including Doisy Daëne in Sauternes and Clos Floridène in Graves. He is also a sought-after consultant, and includes Châteaux d'Yquem, Cheval Blanc, and Haut-Bailly among his clients. "A good white is more demanding to make than a red," Dubourdieu says. "Not because of the yields, or even the terroir, but because there is no margin for error."

SAUTERNES

Bordeaux wine region
Sauternes wine region (within Bordeaux)

Good luck asking your bank manager for a loan to make a sweet wine that comes from vines with around one-sixth of the production of a typical vine destined for red or white wine. Not only that, but it has a high chance of failing completely at least twice a decade, and even in the best years, has a patchy market once bottled. That is why, for pretty much everyone in Sauternes, this is a labor of love. About 25 miles (40km) south of Bordeaux, Sauternes covers nearly 5,189 acres (2,100ha) and encompasses the villages of Barsac, Bommes, Fargues, Preignac, and Sauternes. Together, they produce almost 50% of Bordeaux's sweet wine from 250 properties, of which 26 are classified growths from the same 1855 ranking as the Médoc.

Major grapes

 Whites

Muscadelle
Sauvignon Blanc
Sémillon

Vintages

2009
An excellent year. Rich, powerful, and unctuous whites.

2008
Sunshine during harvest favored botrytis, but did not improve the tiny yields.

2007
Difficult for reds, good for dry whites, and exceptional for Sauternes. Great complexity.

2006
A classic year; a good start, but rain during harvest. The best producers made good wines with careful grape selection.

2005
Ideal conditions gave rich, long-lived wines.

2004
A classic year, with good yields but not exceptional wines.

2003
Extreme heat, with a little rain in early September, meant uniform noble rot. One of the easiest harvests on record. Rich wines that lack acidity.

2001
Leading vintage of the decade in Sauternes—combining richness with a perfect finesse and gripping acidity.

These iconic wines are the result of a naturally occuring mold known as *Botrytis cinerea*, or noble rot, which flourishes in this particular spot because of the merging of the River Garonne and its colder tributary, the Ciron. The difference in temperature between the two, along with the topography of undulating hills and valleys, creates a fall microclimate of early morning mists followed by bright sunny days. The botrytis spores love this weather, and begin to bloom across the grape skins, causing an evaporation of the water content and shriveling the skins. Once fully covered in this slightly furry mold, just the sweet syrupy sugar is left behind in the grapes. It is this highly concentrated liquid that is made into wine. The wines almost invariably contain a majority of Sémillon, with varying amounts of Sauvignon Blanc and Muscadelle. Today, about 25% of the AC Sauternes vineyard is planted with Sauvignon Blanc, although it used to be far higher. Until the 17th century, almost all the wines here were dry.

When you look more closely at the numbers, you can see just how tough it is to make money in Sauternes. Classified wines represent 45% of the area under vine, but only 30% of production, and make 70% of the income. The other 200-plus properties are small and often struggling. All vineyard work has to be done by hand, and harvesting can take up to two months. Each bunch of grapes will only be picked when the noble rot has fully developed, necessitating a series of trips through the same plots to pick them individually.

Long may this continue, though, as there is something magical not just about how the wines are made, but also in how they taste, with their forceful contrast of sweet syrup and searing acidity. With powerful, complex, and often haunting fragrances, they easily outclass other wines on the nose, too. Drinking windows are also extended—the best Bordeaux sweet wines have been known to go 20, 50, even 100 years in bottle.

No one is quite sure when noble rot was first discovered, but the first references to it date back to the mid-17th century. Others suggest it was discovered in the 1800s, when the Marquis de Lur-Saluces (a name and family to remember in the region) was late back from a hunting trip, having given instructions not to harvest his vines until his return, by which time the grapes had rotted.

All Bordeaux sweet wines are made through the process of noble rot (although some are mixed with "healthy" grapes and labeled *moelleux*, or semi-sweet). Alongside Sauternes and Barsac, sweet wines can be made in the appellations of Bordeaux Supérieur, Côtes de Bordeaux St-Macaire, Graves Supérieures, Premières Côtes de Bordeaux, Ste-Foy Bordeaux, Cadillac, Cérons, Loupiac, and Ste-Croix-du-Mont.

Château d'Arche Second Growth

Château d'Arche is within walking distance of Sauternes' village church. The attractive estate has 67 acres (27ha) of 90% Sémillon and 10% Sauvignon Blanc for d'Arche, 7.4 acres (3ha) for the powerful *cuvée* Arche Lafaurie, and 25 acres (10ha) for the second wine, Prieuré d'Arche. The first wine is farmed using sustainable agriculture and vinified in oak barrels (30% new); it has caramel top notes with a twist of lime on the finish. For a more contemporary taste, try the second wine from young vines of 70% Sémillon and 30% Sauvignon Blanc. There is also a dry white, A d'Arche.

33210 Sauternes
www.chateaudarche-sauternes.com

Château Broustet Second Growth

Didier Laulan bought the 37 acre (15ha) Château Broustet, which adjoined his 49 acre (20ha) estate St-Marc, in 1994. Since 2008, his nephew Guillaume Fourcade has been ringing the changes. With 70% Sémillon/25% Sauvignon Blanc/5% Muscadelle, all fermented in stainless steel, there is an attractive floral nose and a lightness of touch that is highly appealing. The second wine is Les Charmes de Broustet. Production of Le Blanc Sec du Château Broustet has just been upped to 20,000 bottles (a 50/50 Sémillon/Sauvignon Blanc blend, fermented in 100% new oak with lees-stirring). Another innovation comes with the launch of Sweet Broustet, a non-vintage wine sold in 3.4 fl oz (10cl) glass vials. Gimmicky (Sauternes shooters anyone?), but this appellation needs fresh thinking.

33720 Barsac
www.chateau-broustet.com

Château La Bertrande

Château La Bertrande, owned by the Gillet family, makes a Cadillac and a Loupiac—both little-known appellations on the Right Bank of the Garonne. It is pretty much opposite the villages of Sauternes and Barsac, and has similar conditions (proximity to water, temperature variation, slopes, and mist) that lead to the development of noble rot. The Cuvée Summum (AC Cadillac) is 100% Sémillon and very concentrated; entirely hand harvested, it produces between 1,000 and 6,000 bottles each year. The vineyard is 64 acres (26ha), spread mainly over southwest-facing slopes. The AC Loupiac gives a lighter, fresher expression (although still 100% Sémillon), and is aged in tank rather than barrel. If you are not sure about sweet wines, try this—it is sweet, without being cloying.

33140 Omet
www.chateau-la-bertrande.com

Château Cantegril

Once part of Château Myrat, Cantegril was bought by Denis Dubourdieu's great-grandmother in 1924, and is still in the family's hands. The 54 acre (22ha) estate is located in Haut-Bommes, and is planted to 64% Sémillon, 34% Sauvignon Blanc, and 2% Muscadelle. It is one of the lighter, more delicate wines of the Barsac appellation, with plenty of easy-drinking charm for those who may be a little wary of heavy dessert wines. A red AC Graves called Château Cantegril—a 60% Cabernet Sauvignon/40% Merlot blend—is also produced at the estate.

No visitor facilities
www.denisdubourdieu.fr

CHATEAU CANTEGRIL
A DELICATE, LIGHTER STYLE OF SAUTERNES
FROM THE UBIQUITOUS DENIS DUBOURDIEU

CHATEAU CLIMENS
CAREFUL GRAPE SELECTION DURING HARVEST
PRODUCED THIS CLASSIC BARSAC

Château de Cérons

Jean Perromat's wife Caroline works at Château Haut-Bailly in Graves, and the couple are applying similar attention to detail and careful winemaking techniques at their handsome family estate of Château de Cérons. Jean has recently taken over the 30 acres (12ha) of vines from his parents, and is slowly renovating the winery and château. The wines of Cérons are a touch lighter than those of Sauternes, and this has all the oranges, lemons, cloves, and honey of the more famous neighboring appellation, but with slightly more lift and sour-lemon freshness on the finish.

33720 Cérons
www.chateaudecerons.com

Château Climens First Growth

The lovely Château Climens, owned by Berenice Lurton and located in Barsac, covers 74 acres (30ha) of 100% Sémillon vines. As with Château d'Yquem, Climens is not made in difficult years (in recent memory, this meant no wine was produced in 1984, 1987, 1992, or 1993). When they do produce, however, this is a succulent, honeyed wine, with a rich aromatic structure. The second wine, Cypress de Climens, is lighter and fresher than the Climens, but still with the luscious sweetness of a Barsac. Plenty of honeyed fruit, but beautifully balanced—a seriously enjoyable dessert wine.

2 Climens, 33720 Barsac
www.chateau-climens.fr

Château Clos Haut-Peyraguey
First Growth

There are 42 acres (17ha) in total at this estate, with 30 acres (12ha) in Haut-Peyraguey, and the rest in Haut-Bommes. Martine Langlais-Pauly runs things with a warm and exacting hand, ensuring quality touches such as the use of organic fertilizers and up to seven passes through the vineyard at harvest. Low-temperature fermentation takes place in barrel (50% new oak, 50% one year old), and they do not add cultivated yeast but encourage the development of wild yeast strains with vitamin B1. This is a reliable name worth remembering, which produces wines with enormous depths of sweet fruit.

1 Haut-Peyraguey, 33210 Bommes
www.closhautpeyraguey.com

Château Closiot

Françoise Sirot-Soizeau has been in charge of Château Closiot since 1988. She is helped at her family property in Barsac by her Belgian wine-writer husband Bernard Sirot. This subtly nuanced wine is farmed sustainably, and aged entirely in barrel (25% new each year). A small-production 100% Sémillon *cuvée*, La Passion de Closiot, is aged for 36 months in new oak. Since 2003, a lighter bottling called Les Premières Brumes de Closiot (the name refers poetically to the first mists that form the noble rot) has been produced from 90% Sémillon, with a 10% mix of Sauvignon Gris and Muscadelle. This is the same blend as the first wine of the estate, but from younger vines and aged for a shorter period. There is also a dry white here called Fruit de Closiot.

33720 Barsac
www.closiot.com

CHATEAU GILETTE
FROM A SMALL VINEYARD AND LOW YIELDS, THIS WINE IS HIGHLY SOUGHT-AFTER

CHATEAU DOISY DAENE
DENIS DUBOURDIEU'S OWN ESTATE PRODUCES A CRISP SAUTERNES

Château La Clotte-Cazalis

Bernadette Lacoste and her enologist daughter, Marie-Pierre, have run the 13.6 acre (5.5ha) Château La Clotte-Cazalis as a winery since 2001. It has been in the family for centuries but, until recently, all the vineyards were leased out. The oldest vines have reached 65 years, and careful massal selection (grafting direct from the healthiest vines) is being undertaken to bring the vineyard back up to full quality. With 95% Sémillon and a 5% mix of Sauvignons Blanc and Gris, the wines are well-made and complex. Fermentation takes place in both stainless steel and oak barrels, and blends creamy fruits with a fine, lively squeeze of lime and pink grapefruit. An AC Bordeaux, Château La Clotte-Bassure, is also produced from 10 acres (4ha) of 50% Merlot and 50% Cabernet Sauvignon.

33720 Barsac
www.laclotte-cazalis.com

Château Coutet First Growth

Château Coutet is owned by Philippe and Dominique Baly, and Baroness Philippine de Rothschild has had exclusive distribution rights (and technical direction) since 1994. As you would expect, this has upped the distinction factor a couple of notches. The 96 acres (39ha) are planted to 75% Sémillon, 23% Sauvignon Blanc, and 2% Muscadelle, with the resulting wine matured for 18 months in 100% new oak. The nose has delicate aromas of acacia and honeysuckle, saving the punch of rich, sweet fruit for the palate, and finishing with a mouth-watering dry twist. The second wine is called Chartreuse de Coutet. There is also a Vin Sec de Château Coutet (made from 80% Sauvignon Blanc, 20% Sémillon), and a super-selection named Cuvée Madame. Only released in vintages of exceptional quality (the last was 1995), this is made from the two oldest plots in the vineyard, followed by aging for three years.

33720 Barsac
www.chateaucoutet.com

Château du Cros

Château du Cros is from the little-known sweet wine appellation Loupiac. The area makes good-value wines that often have a lighter, more deft touch than Sauternes. Owned by Vignobles M Boyer, this is one of the best, producing around 30,000 bottles. The wine is 70% Sémillon, 20% Sauvignon Blanc, and 10% Muscadelle; it spends 18 months in oak (one-third of which is new) and is full of peaches and mangoes. The same estate produces Ségur du Cros, which gives a lighter, fresher take on the same flavors.

94 Route de St-Macaire, 33410 Loupiac
www.chateauducros.com

Château Doisy Daëne Second Growth

Professor Denis Dubourdieu, together with his sons Fabrice and Jean-Jacques, puts his extensive research into noble rot to good use at the Barsac estate of Château Doisy Daëne. The 87% Sémillon/ 13% Sauvignon Blanc (with Muscadelle in some years) is rich and sticky, but with a powerful acidity, fresh nose, and a crisp finish to balance the richness. The wine is vinified partly in stainless steel, and partly in oak. The château also produces the appropriately named L'Extravagant (from late-harvest botrytis-affected grapes), and an AC Bordeaux dry white, Grand Vin Sec de Doisy Daëne (100% Sauvignon Blanc). The 40 acre (16ha) estate has been in the Dubourdieu family since 1924.

No visitor facilities
www.denisdubourdieu.fr

Château Doisy-Dubroca Second Growth

Château Doisy-Dubroca is the least known of the Doisy triumvirate, and the smallest at 9.4 acres (3.8ha). Lucien Lurton has owned the property since the 1970s, with first his son Louis and, since 2009, his daughter Berenice (of Climens) in charge. The estate is farmed fully organically, with 100% Sémillon vines. Some unusual practices for Bordeaux include holding the wine back for up to eight years before releasing it onto the market, and low-temperature fermentation. In 2001, this slow ferment took a whole year to complete. Some years have creamy apricot roundness, but others have under-performed. However, the new team may bring in positive changes. The second wine is called Les Demoiselles de Doisy.

No visitor facilities
www.denisdubourdieu.fr

Château Doisy-Védrines Second Growth

Owned by Olivier Castéja of wine merchant Joanne, Château Doisy-Védrines is larger than neighboring Daëne at 77 acres (31ha), having expanded in 2001. And the Castéjas got here first, with a family history at the property dating back two centuries. Today, they continue to lavish care on this well-regarded wine, which is usually 80% Sémillon, 15% Sauvignon Blanc, and 5% Muscadelle. After fermentation in stainless steel, the wine spends 18–20 months in oak (80–100% new, depending on the vintage). In most years, it has a slightly richer, more structured style than Daëne, with plump apricots and honeydew melon. The second wine is La Petite Védrines.

1 Védrines, 33720 Barsac
05 56 68 59 70

Château de Fargues

When the Comte de Lur-Saluces left d'Yquem (once the LVMH regime had taken hold), he went to his other family estate, a dramatic castle set high up on the slopes of a hill with far-reaching views. Strangely, for a family so closely associated with sweet wines, white grapes were only planted here in the 1930s, with the first vintage being 1943. With 37 acres (15ha) of 80% Sémillon and 20% Sauvignon Blanc today, yields are kept very low – less than 1,000 bottles are made per hectare on average. This is an expensive, but seriously impressive wine, with honeyed richness, dripping in caramel but hiding a core of steely freshness. There is no second wine, but a dry white Guilhem de Fargues is produced in some vintages.

Avenue Lur Saluces, 33210 Fargues de Langon
www.chateau-de-fargues.com

Château Filhot Second Growth

The Filhot in the title was guillotined during the French Revolution, but very distant relatives (through a network of marriages) still run the property today, led by Gabriel de Vaucelles. It is a large estate, with 153 acres (62ha) of vines, planted to 60% Sémillon/36% Sauvignon Blanc/ 4% Muscadelle. Vinification takes place in small stainless steel tanks and the wine, which is among the lighter and fresher in the appellation, spends up to 24 months in barrel (30% new). It sometimes lacks concentration, but the former high yields have been severely reduced.

1 Pineau Est, 33210 Sauternes
www.filhot.com

Château Gilette

Château Gilette produces one of those wines that many people have heard about, but few have actually tasted. Husband-and-wife team Julie and Xavier Gonet-Médeville continue a tradition, started in the 1930s, of holding their wine back for at least a decade after harvest before releasing it onto the market. It can often be up to 15, or even 20 years before it is deemed appropriate to release a wine. The 96% Sémillon/4% Sauvignon Blanc blend, sometimes with a touch of Muscadelle, comes from the organically farmed 11 acre (4.5ha) estate. The wine is fermented (slowly, at a low temperature) in stainless steel vats, and then transferred into concrete vats, rather than barrels, for aging. The final result is amazingly youthful—there is very little of the oxygen exchange that happens in barrels, and no added toast; instead, the fruit seems to have deepened, and shows bright grapefruit and candied lemon. There is also a more traditional Sauternes, bottled under the name Les Justices, and the family also produces a wine from Graves, called Respide-Médeville.

Preignac, 33210 Preignac
www.gonet-medeville.com

Château Guiraud First Growth

A close neighbor of d'Yquem, the highly regarded Château Guiraud is jointly owned by the Peugeot family, winemaker Xavier Planty, and Stephan von Neipperg of Canon-La-Gaffelière. Guiraud is a leading estate for sustainable agriculture, with innovations in the vineyard such as pheromone confusion and insect hotels to encourage a healthy ecosystem. Since 2001, the estate has also developed a nursery of high-quality massal selections of Sémillon, to protect the genetic diversity of the vineyard. The wine itself is luxurious, but always with a light touch and a wonderfully fragrant nose that comes from the high proportion of Sauvignon Blanc vines (35% of the 316 acres/128ha). These vines also produce an excellent dry white called G de Guiraud.

33210 Sauternes
www.chateau-guiraud.fr

Château Lafaurie-Peyraguey
First Growth

Château Lafaurie-Peyraguey produces a wine in which you can taste the creamy, rich ripeness of Sémillon. As 90% of the 101 acre (41ha) estate, Sémillon dominates this wine, though it is enlivened by 8% Sauvignon Blanc and 2% Muscadelle. The recently restored cellars ensure a low temperature for vinification at between 64°F (18°C) and 75°F (24°C). This is carried out in barrels (30% new), followed by aging of up to 20 months. The young team—led by Eric Larramona, ex-director of Pape Clément—is working hard. A reliance on cultivated yeasts has been limited, and the lease of 12 acres (5ha) of underperforming vines has ended. The second wine, La Chapelle de Lafaurie-Peyraguey, produces around 24,000 bottles.

Peyraguey, 33210 Bommes
www.lafaurie-peyraguey.com

Château Lamothe-Guignard
Second Growth

Next to Château Lamothe, and once part of the same estate, Lamothe-Guignard has been the more successful of the divided properties—particularly over the last decade. Owned by Phillippe and Jacques Guignard, the wines are fermented partly in tank, partly in barrel, and have a pleasant finesse and elegance, with toasted chestnuts on the nose, and rich stone fruits. Covering 44 acres (18ha), with 90% Sémillon and the rest split between Sauvignon Blanc and Muscadelle, the vines now average 40 years. Red and white Graves, both called Clos de Huz, are also produced here.

2 Lamothe Ouest, 33210 Sauternes
www.chateau-lamothe-guignard.fr

Château Liot

The little-known Château Liot has a lot going for it, not least its charming owners, Jean-Gérard and Elena David. There are 49 acres (20ha) of vines at this Barsac estate, plus a further 19 acres (8ha) in the Graves appellation (bottled under the label Château St-Jean-des-Graves). Planted on red clay and limestone soils, the wines have a full 85% Sémillon in them, freshened up with 10% Sauvignon Blanc and 5% Muscadelle, and are aged in a mix of tanks and barrels. The result is a wine that is full of rich body and structure, yet is silky soft and unassuming. The second wine is Château du Levant.

33720 Barsac
www.chateauliot.com

Château de Malle Second Growth

The Preignac estate of Château de Malle is overseen by Countess de Bournazel and her sons. The 124 acres (50ha) produce Château de Malle, Château de Cardaillan (AC Graves), and the dry white M de Malle. Around half the total area is dedicated to Sauternes, with 40-year-old vines of 69% Sémillon, 28% Sauvignon Blanc, 3% Muscadelle. Fermentation takes place in oak barrels, and aging lasts up to two years. The wines can get a little overshadowed by the fact that this is a classified historic monument and a tourist center for the region. The family have, however, been increasingly following sound winemaking practices, and in the best years this is a luxurious, traditional style of Sauternes. An unoaked white is called Chevalier de Malle.

Preignac, 33210 Preignac
www.chateau-de-malle.fr

Château de Myrat Second Growth

This 54 acre (22ha) property bravely illustrates just how tough it is to produce a Sauternes wine. Château de Myrat is located on a raised plateau in Barsac, and there was a long gap in production after the de Pontac family succumbed to the financial pressures of maintaining the estate during the 1970s. But the vines were replanted in 1988 (by Jacques de Pontac, the next generation of the same family), and bottling began again in 1991, only to be hit by three years of bad harvests and frosts. The first "full" vintage was therefore in 1995, and showed the promise that continues today. With 88% Sémillon, 8% Sauvignon Blanc, and 4% Muscadelle, there are plump, exotic fruits that express themselves well from an early age.

33720 Barsac
05 56 27 09 06

SWEET BORDEAUX

When you have to rely on being the favorite wine of 19th-century Russian tsars, you know its time for a new marketing strategy. That seems to have been the motivation behind the rebranding of "Vins d'Or de Bordeaux" as "Sweet Bordeaux". This new association represents the region's 11 sweet wine appellations—Bordeaux Supérieur, Côtes de Bordeaux St-Macaire, Graves Supérieures, Premières Côtes de Bordeaux, Ste-Foy Bordeaux, Cadillac, Cérons, Loupiac, Ste-Croix-du-Mont, Barsac, and Sauternes—and is trying to appeal to a younger consumer through social media. Measures include "Sweet Hour" cocktail nights, wine tourism, and food-and-music matching events. "These are gourmet wines, often drunk for celebration," says president Philippe Dejean of Château Rabaud-Promis. "Sweet wines can take strong flavors and exciting contrasts, and the idea is to move beyond the traditional matches of foie gras and blue cheese, and to find other moments for enjoyment, from tapas and tapenades to roast chicken or grapefruit sorbet."

CHATEAU SUDUIRAUT
AN ELEGANT WINE FROM THE
AXA MILLESIMES STABLE

Château Nairac First Growth

The proprietor of Château Nairac, Eloise Heeter-Tari, is one of the new generation of Bordeaux owners who take the best traditions of the region, and reinterpret them for the 21st century. She works alongside her parents at this beautiful 40 acre (16ha) estate, with walled gardens full of rose bushes and fruit trees, and vineyards planted to 90% Sémillon, 6% Sauvignon Blanc, and 4% Muscadelle. The first wine is a classic "sticky"; truffle aromas layered with thick-cut orange marmalade and crushed apricots. There is also a fresh, lighter-style label, Esquisse de Nairac, which is consciously appealing to a more contemporary palate.

81 avenue Aristide Briand, 33720 Barsac
www.chateau-nairac.com

Château Rabaud-Promis First Growth

Château Rabaud-Promis is located next to its fellow first growth, Château Sigalas-Ribaud, and was once part of the same estate (and then separate, and then joined again, and then separate… a far from unusual Bordeaux story). It has 82 acres (33ha) of vines producing 60,000 bottles of wine. Although classified as a First Growth of Sauternes, the wine has suffered from quality variation over the years. Today, Philippe Dejean is in charge (he is also president of the new association, Sweet Bordeaux). He has managed to inject new life into the wine by cutting the yields and ensuring very careful selection. A typical year sees 80% Sémillon/18% Sauvignon Blanc/2% Muscadelle, aged for up to 24 months in a mix of cement tanks and new oak barrels. The best years are full of pineapple and grapefruit aromas, veering toward spicy exotic fruits. The second wine (not produced every year) is Domaine de l'Estramade.

33210 Bommes
05 56 76 67 38

Château Raymond-Lafon

The insider's Sauternes, offering exuberant wine at very good prices, Château Raymond-Lafon was bought by Pierre Meslier in 1972. Meslier had spent most of his working life making the wine for neighboring Château d'Yquem. With 40 acres (16ha) of 80% Sémillon and 20% Sauvignon Blanc vines, surrounded by classified names, the yield is always very low, even in relatively abundant years for the appellation, and anything between 20–100% is declassified each year, according to the quality of the vintage. The wine matures in new oak for three years, and more than equals its illustrious neighbors in depth, decadence, and wonderfully contrasting sweet and tart flavors. Today, the château is run by Charles-Henri and Jean-Pierre Meslier.

4 aux Puits, 33210 Sauternes
www.chateau-raymond-lafon.fr

Château de Rayne Vigneau First Growth

Château de Rayne Vigneau was bought by the banking group CA Grands Crus in 2004. There is a schedule of improvements, led by the technical director Anne de Laour, which is taking effect. The consultant enologist is Denis Dubourdieu, and the deft, fresh edge that this château has come to be known for is derived from the 25% Sauvignon Blanc vines and 1% Muscadelle. The two minor varieties inject a fresh seam of lemon and lime blossom into the 74% Sémillon. The vines cover a total area of 198 acres (80ha) and are built on a varied soil structure that contains precious stones, including: agate, onyx, amethyst, and, reportedly, even sapphire.

No visitor facilities
www.raynevigneau.fr

Château Rieussec First Growth

Located in Fargues, close to Château d'Yquem, the 222 acre (90ha) Château Rieussec is owned by Domaines Lafite Rothschild and shares Charles Chevallier as director of winemaking (he began his career with Domaines Baron Lafite here, before moving up to Pauillac). All concentrated elegance, with a powerful structure, this is a wine to sink into, with 90–95% Sémillon and the rest a 50/50 split of Muscadelle/Sauvignon Blanc. The final blend is aged for up to 26 months in oak barrels (50–55% new). As with the best wines of this appellation, levels of production vary hugely depending on vintage, with nothing in 1993, and just 36,000 bottles in 2000. The second wine is Carmes de Rieussec, and there is an excellent dry white, R de Rieussec (an AC Graves of 50% Sauvignon/50% Sémillon).

33210 Fargues
www.lafite.com

Château Romer Second Growth

Château Romer is small for a Sauternes property, with 5 acres (2ha) of vines, and has been run by Anne Farges since 2002. She is delivering increasingly good wines, with caramelized peaches on the nose and palate, roasted hazelnuts and a lime blossom lift from the 5% Muscadelle (to complement the 90% Sémillon and 5% Sauvignon Blanc). Aged in barrels for 18–24 months, the wines have been bottled under the name Romer since Anne took over. There had been a long break when the vines were under lease to another property—there is a lot of work ahead, but this is an interesting small estate to watch.

33210 Fargues de Langon
www.chateau-romer.com

Château Sigalas Rabaud First Growth

Owned by Laure Compeyrot, Château Sigalas Rabaud has been in the same family for over 300 years. It is often a sleeper of the vintage, delivering excellent-quality wine at reasonable prices. The vines cover a single plot of 35 acres (14ha) located on the Sauternes terrace, with gravel and clay on the plateau, and gravel/sand/clay on the slopes. Densely planted at 2,630–3,035 vines per acre (6,500–7,500 per hectare), the ratio is 85% Sémillon, 14% Sauvignon Blanc, and 1% Muscadelle. The vineyard is picked entirely by hand, with up to seven trips through the vines. The enologist here is Georges Poly, and he ensures the grip of acidity provides a thrilling balance to the honeyed marmalade fruits.

33210 Bommes
www.chateau-sigalas-rabaud.fr

Château Suduiraut First Growth

Château Suduiraut is owned by AXA Millésimes, with Christian Seely as managing director, as he is at Châteaux Pichon Baron and Petit-Village. The technical director is Pierre Montegut, looking after 227 acres (92ha) of 90% Sémillon/10% Sauvignon Blanc vines in sandy–clay soil in the commune of Preignac. This is a richly elegant Sauternes, with amber depths even when young, and

CHATEAU SIGALAS RABAUD
2006 WAS A CLASSIC VINTAGE AND THIS WINE
WILL BE AT ITS BEST FROM 2016 ONWARD

an extraordinarily complex nose of undergrowth and stone fruits. Most of the wine is vinified in stainless steel, with up to two years aging in oak. The second wine is Castelnau de Suduiraut and the dry white S de Suduiraut.

33210 Preignac
www.suduiraut.com

Château La Tour Blanche First Growth

Château La Tour Blanche is both a viticulture school and a working vineyard (the two are run as separate concerns), covering 99 acres (40ha) of vines. The winery has recently been renovated, and the wines stepped up a gear. Sémillon (83%) is vinified and aged in 100% new oak barrels, with the 12% Sauvignon Blanc and 5% Muscadelle fermented in stainless steel. There is access to a variety of new techniques here (such as cryoextraction and a cold chamber), due to the educational side of the business, but these are rarely used. The wine is rich and powerful, and has become increasingly renowned. The second wine is called Les Charmilles de Tour Blanche. There is also a dry white, Les Jardins de Thinoy (100% Sauvignon Blanc), and a red AC Bordeaux Cru de Cinquet (90% Merlot and 10% Malbec).

33210 Bommes
www.tour-blanche.com

Château Tour de Mirambeau

Château Tour de Mirambeau is owned by one of Bordeaux's most dynamic winemaking families. The Despagnes have instilled excellence in the less glamorous appellations of the region, and have succeeded again with this Sémillon Noble. From vines overlooking the Dordogne river, in the Bordeaux Supérieur appellation, Thibault Despagne and technical director Joël Elissalde make tiny quantities of this sought-after wine. Tropical fruit flavors from old Sémillon vines give this a luxurious stickiness, with a searingly fresh edge.

No visitor facilities
www.tour-de-mirambeau.com

Château d'Yquem Superior First Growth

The legendary Château d'Yquem retains its reputation for making the greatest sweet wine in the world, despite the vagaries of fashion for Sauternes as a whole. At the highest point of the appellation, it is today owned by luxury goods house LVMH, with Pierre Lurton as director across both Yquem and Cheval Blanc. There are 247 acres (100ha) of 80% Sémillon and 20% Sauvignon Blanc. The standards are famous—140 pickers at harvest time, divided into four groups, going through the vineyard up to 10 times. Fermentation stops naturally, leaving an average of 2oz/pint (125g/l) of residual sugar. Each barrel is racked 15 times to remove the heavy lees. On the palate, it is never the sweetness that strikes first—rather the beautifully sour notes of lemon and lime blossom, and the complex aromas that vary, depending on age and vintage, from marmalade to honey and truffles. There is also a dry wine, Y d'Yquem, made from 50/50 Sémillon/Sauvignon Blanc, picked when the first bloom of botrytis appears. The female enologist Sandrine Garbay has been in charge since 1998, with technical direction by Francis Mayeur, and Denis Dubourdieu as consultant.

No visitor facilities
www.yquem.fr

CHATEAU D'YQUEM
THIS IS THE BEST SWEET WINE
IN THE WORLD, WITHOUT RIVAL

CHATEAU LA TOUR BLANCHE
AS A SCHOOL AND COMMERCIAL VINEYARD,
THIS ESTATE HAS RECENTLY IMPROVED

Clos Dady

The barrels at the dynamic 16 acre (6.5ha) Clos Dady, come from Château d'Yquem, which gives an idea of the meticulous attention to detail followed here. Run by Catherine Gachet and Joseph-Marie Remy, some of the techniques used are a gentle vertical press and only natural yeasts. The luscious wine comes from 90% Sémillon, 9% Sauvignon Blanc, and 1% Muscadelle, vinified and aged in barrel for a minimum of 18 months. There is no chaptilization (the addition of sugar), and cold settling helps to keep the use of sulphur dioxide to a minimum. This also means the wine has crisp, well-defined flavors of exotic fruit and gently toasted oak. The second wine is Mademoiselle de Clos Dady.

33720 Barsac
www.clos-dady.com

Clos Sainte-Anne

Clos Sainte-Anne is run by Sylvie and Marie Courselle, better known for their excellent Château Thieuley in Entre-deux-Mers. They extend the same standards of excellence to this Cadillac property, which covers just 3.7 acres (1.5ha). The vineyard produces 5,000 bottles from 60% Sémillon and 40% Sauvignon Gris. The wine has immediate impact, with rounded apricots and nectarines and a fresh, dry finish. The grapes that go into the wine here are half noble rot, and half *passeurillage* (over-dried grapes that have not been attacked by botrytis), which gives them a lower sugar content and a very different character from most sweet Bordeaux.

c/o Chateau Thieuley, 33670 La Sauve
www.thieuley.com

Cru Barréjats

Cru Barréjats is a relatively new estate, owned by Mirielle Daret and Philippe Andurand, which saw its first harvest in 1990. Both had roots in the area, and their first vintage was made from 2.5 acres (1ha) of vines that had belonged to Mirielle's grandparents. Today, the estate stands at 12 acres (5ha), with some vines reaching up to 80 years in age. The focus is on natural processes—no weedkillers, no chaptilization, low sulphur dioxide. The wine is intense and flavorful with 85% Sémillon, 10% Sauvignon Blanc, and 5% Muscadelle, and fermentation and aging in 100% new barrels.

Clos de Gensac, Mareuil, 33210 Pujols-sur-Ciron
www.cru-barrejats.com

Le Sauternes de Ma Fille

The charmingly named Le Sauternes de Ma Fille, formerly Château Latrézotte, was bought by Bernard Magrez of Pape Clément in 2004. Covering 20 acres (8ha), Magrez has consciously gone for a contemporary-style Sauternes, with a lovely delicacy of touch, majoring on orange peel and lime blossom to give a refreshingly tart edge to the luscious 99% Sémillon wine. Technical director Nicolas Contiero achieves this through the sprinkling of Sauvignons Blanc and Gris, and Muscadelle, but also by gentle pressing, stainless steel fermentation, and a relatively short barrel aging of 10–16 months. A firmer, richer wine called Mon Sauternes is also produced, aged in 100% new oak for up to 22 months.

Chateau Latrezotte, La Pinesse, 33720 Barsac
www.bernard-magrez.com

ST-EMILION

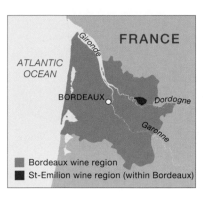

St-Emilion is easily among the most beautiful spots of Bordeaux; the glowing limestone walls of this atmospheric medieval town reflect the terroir that gives its best wines such elegance and finesse. The vineyards cover 13,343 acres (5,400ha) with Merlot the dominant grape, as in Pomerol, accounting for over 60% of the plantings (along with 30% Cabernet Franc and 10% Cabernet Sauvignon). The soils are a mix of limestone, clay, and sand, and give very different styles depending on location. Unusually, there are two separate appellations within the same physical boundary, AC St-Emilion and AC St-Emilion Grand Cru, with 800 winemakers across both. Only the properties within the Grand Cru appellation are able to apply for classification.

Major grapes

 Reds

Cabernet Franc

Cabernet Sauvignon

Merlot

Vintages

2009
An excellent year—powerful wines with great potential.

2008
A damp summer but a long, sunny fall, giving quality wines for the best producers.

2007
A difficult year with a damp summer means many light wines that suit early drinking.

2006
A classic year, with an ideal start, but some rain during harvest. The best producers made very good wines.

2005
Ideal growing conditions gave rich wines that have a long life ahead. Prices rose, but these are wonderful wines.

2004
A classic year and the wines now offer excellent value.

2003
Extreme heat produced wines high in alcohol and often lacking acidity. The term "hedonistic fruitbomb" was thrown around at the time, but many are aging quickly.

1998
A superb year, producing rich, well-structured wines.

The vineyard area of St-Emilion is one of the oldest in Bordeaux, and several remnants of its Roman past survive today, from the remains of a villa in Moncaret to the name of one of its most famous properties, Ausone. Wines were exported from here to Rome as early as the 4th century, but the area also became famous as a religious center, with pilgrims following the path of an 8th-century hermit, Emilion, who arrived here when there was little more than a hill covered in thick forest. The town grew up around the hermit as his fame spread.

Today, St-Emilion is a UNESCO World Heritage Site. When it received the accolade in 1999, it was the first time that vineyard land had been included in a designated "cultural landscape." St-Emilion is celebrated not only for its vines, but also for its 173 acres (70ha) of underground cellars, many of which were former quarries, as well as a monolithic church. The long history of viticulture here explains why estates are often family-owned, and smallholdings are common (over 50% of producers have less than 12 acres/5ha of vines).

As with much of the Right Bank, work in the vineyard tends to be of paramount importance. Many of the techniques that began here, such as severe pruning, green harvesting, and strict grape selection, are now used by big properties across the Bordeaux region. In the cellars, by contrast, a hands-off philosophy means many wines are bottled unfiltered and unfined. The best wines of the region come from the limestone plateau close to the center of the town—11 of the 13 Premiers

Grands Crus Classés are located here. There are two notable exceptions: Château Cheval Blanc and Château Figeac, which are both on clay–gravel soils close to the Pomerol border.

So far, so picturesque. Recent years, however, have seen politics take center stage in this usually peaceful corner of Bordeaux, following emotional disputes over the classification system. Divided into three levels—in ascending order, Grand Cru Classé, Premier Grand Cru Classé (B), and Premier Grand Cru Classé (A)—the system has been in place since the 1950s, and is revised every 10 years. Importantly, the system is closer to that of Burgundy than the Médoc, as the land itself is classified, rather than the property name, meaning that properties change size and shape far less frequently than on the Left Bank.

The assessments are based on tastings of the previous 10 vintages, as well as a variety of other factors such as recent investments and market price. Inevitably with a system where rankings change, there are complaints each time, but in 2006, a small group of demoted properties took the entire system to court, and had the ranking overturned. Years of legal wrangling followed, and as things stand in 2010, the 1996 classification has been reinstated. A second twist to the tale allowed those châteaux who were promoted in 2006 to keep their new status, in addition to the demoted properties getting their positions back. A truce having been reached, life has returned to normal… at least until the next time….

Château Angélus
Premier Grand Cru Classé B

The label of Château Angélus, with its distinctive bell, has graced a number of Hollywood movies (*La Vie en Rose* and *Casino Royale*, to name a few). The owner, Hubert de Bouärd de Laforest, runs Angélus with his cousin, Jean Bernard Grenié. This was one of the first estates in St-Emilion to practice green harvesting, and plot-by-plot vinification. In 2009, they introduced individual hand stemming of the grape bunches across the best plots of the 57 acre (23ha) estate. A high proportion of Cabernet Franc (57%), together with a lovely smoky toast, gives this wine seductive power, packed full of violets and rich black fruits.

1 Mazarat Ouest, 33330 St-Emilion
www.angelus.com

Château L'Arrosée
Grand Cru Classé

Château L'Arrosée was bought in 2002 by self-made aeronautics billionaire Roger Caille. It has been run by his son Jean-Philippe since Roger's death in 2009, and has been slowly working its way back up to full quality after some uneven years. The 25 acres (10ha) of vines are planted to 60% Merlot with 20% each of Cabernet Franc and Cabernet Sauvignon (unusually the latter is planted on clay, but the variety ripens well here because it is on exceptionally well-exposed, south-facing slopes). The wine has good black currant notes, and some interesting violet overtones. The enologist is Gilles Pauquet, who also works at Château Cheval Blanc, among others.

1 rue Larosé, 33330 St-Emilion
www.chateau-larrosee.com

Château Ausone
Premier Grand Cru Classé A

Alain Vauthier is in charge of Château Ausone, one of the oldest estates in the whole of Bordeaux, dating back to Roman times. The estate currently holds the dubious honor of being the region's most expensive wine. The beautiful stone gateposts of the château's entrance, the steeply sloping vineyards, and dry-stone walls dominate the approach to the village of St-Emilion. Underneath the château are vast stretches of stone quarry, the smallest of which, at 19,375 sqft (1,800 sqm), is the wine cellar. The vineyard is just over 17 acres (7ha), planted with 45% Merlot and 55% Cabernet Franc. It is the precision of the winemaking that really separates this wine from the rest—the absolute purity of fruit, and the lilting finish. The second wine is La Chapelle d'Ausone.

No visitors facilities
www.chateau-ausone-saint-emilion.com

Château Balestard La Tonnelle
Grand Cru Classé

Château Balestard La Tonnelle is a big wine and very successful with it. Replete with rich fruit flavors and sweet cedary oak, it will come as no surprise to learn that the consultant here is Michel Rolland. The grapes come from a vineyard of 25 acres (10ha), with 70% Merlot, 25% Cabernet Franc, and 5% Cabernet Sauvignon. Global positioning satellite (GPS) imagery is used to determine the individual plots, and then each of those plots is cultivated according to their position. The same family also owns Château Cap de Mourlin, another classified growth.

33330 St-Emilion
www.vignoblescapdemourlin.com

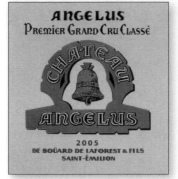

CHATEAU ANGELUS
THIS WINE HAS APPEARED IN SEVERAL FILMS, CONFIRMING ITS ICONIC STATUS

CHATEAU BEAU-SEJOUR BECOT
THE CLASSIFICATION SYSTEM HAS SEEN THIS CHATEAU BOTH DEMOTED AND PROMOTED

Château Barde-Haut

Sylviane Garcin-Cathiard bought Château Barde-Haut in 2000, after selling a chain of supermarkets and sports stores. (She also owns Clos l'Eglise in Pomerol.) This is a wine to watch, with an increasingly long list of admirers. The 42 acres (17ha) of 85% Merlot and 15% Cabernet Sauvignon receive meticulous attention to detail, which follows the grapes into the new winery full of small-scale vats in wood, stainless steel, and cement. The final wine is loaded with fruit, and deep black in color, with 100% new oak that adds a smoky edge. The second wine is Vallon de Barde-Haut.

33330 St-Christophe-des-Bardes
www.bodegapoesia.com

Château Beauséjour
Premier Grand Cru Classé B

Château Beauséjour was once known as Beauséjour Duffau-Lagarrosse; the Duffau-Lagarrosse family sensibly took their name out of the title to make it a bit snappier. They still own the property and, in 2009, installed Nicolas Thienpont (winemaking director at Pavie Macquin) as director, helped by consultants Michel Rolland and Stéphane Derenoncourt. The vineyard covers 12 acres (5ha), planted to 70% Merlot, 20% Cabernet Franc, and 10% Cabernet Sauvignon. Changes in the winery include open-vat fermentation and manual punching down—techniques more common in Burgundy than Bordeaux. The result is more gentle extraction with richer fruit. The second wine is Croix de Beauséjour.

No visitor facilities
05 57 24 71 61

Château Beau-Séjour Bécot
Premier Grand Cru Classé B

Château Beau-Séjour Bécot is a good example of how the local classification system works; it was demoted in 1986 for using non-classified vines, then promoted in 1996, and bumped up to "B" status in the last round. Recent vintages have more than justified the promotion. The 42 acres (17ha) of vineyard, planted to 70% Merlot, 24% Cabernet Franc, and 6% Cabernet Sauvignon, cover the western plateau of the village. During maceration (fermentation on the skins) all punching down is done by hand, and the wine is subsequently run into the barrels without pumps. Expect smoky toast from 90% new oak, and rich structure from being unfiltered and unfined. The second wine is Tournelle de Beau-Séjour Bécot.

33330 St-Emilion No visitors facilities
www.beausejour-becot.com

Château Belair-Monange
Premier Grand Cru Classé B

The "Monange" was added to Château Belair in 2008, after it was purchased by Etablissements JP Moueix. The addition is in honor of Christian Moueix's grandmother, distinguishing it from the many other Bordeaux estates bearing the name "Belair". The vineyard is 80% Merlot and 20% Cabernet Franc, over 32 acres (13ha) and in the final wine, the Cabernet Franc comes through strongly, giving a wonderfully evocative nose. The next few years will see vineyard restructuring and changes in the cellar.

33330 St-Emilion
www.moueix.com

ST-EMILION

The large appellation of St-Emilion covers 13,300 acres (5,400ha) and nine villages. These are St-Emilion itself, plus St-Christophe-des-Bardes, St-Etienne-de-Lisse, St-Hippolyte, St-Laurent-des-Combes, St-Pey-d'Armens, St-Sulpice-de-Faleyrens, Vignonet, and parts of the nearby market town of Libourne. Most of the classified estates are located close to the UNESCO World Heritage village of St-Emilion, where a limestone plateau gives a distinct delicacy to the wines (as well as providing the stone for many of its buildings). Another key grouping of quality châteaux is located closer to the border with AC Pomerol, including Figeac and Cheval Blanc.

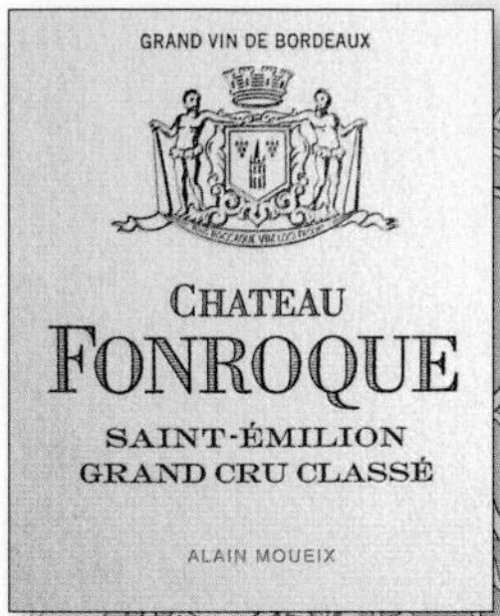

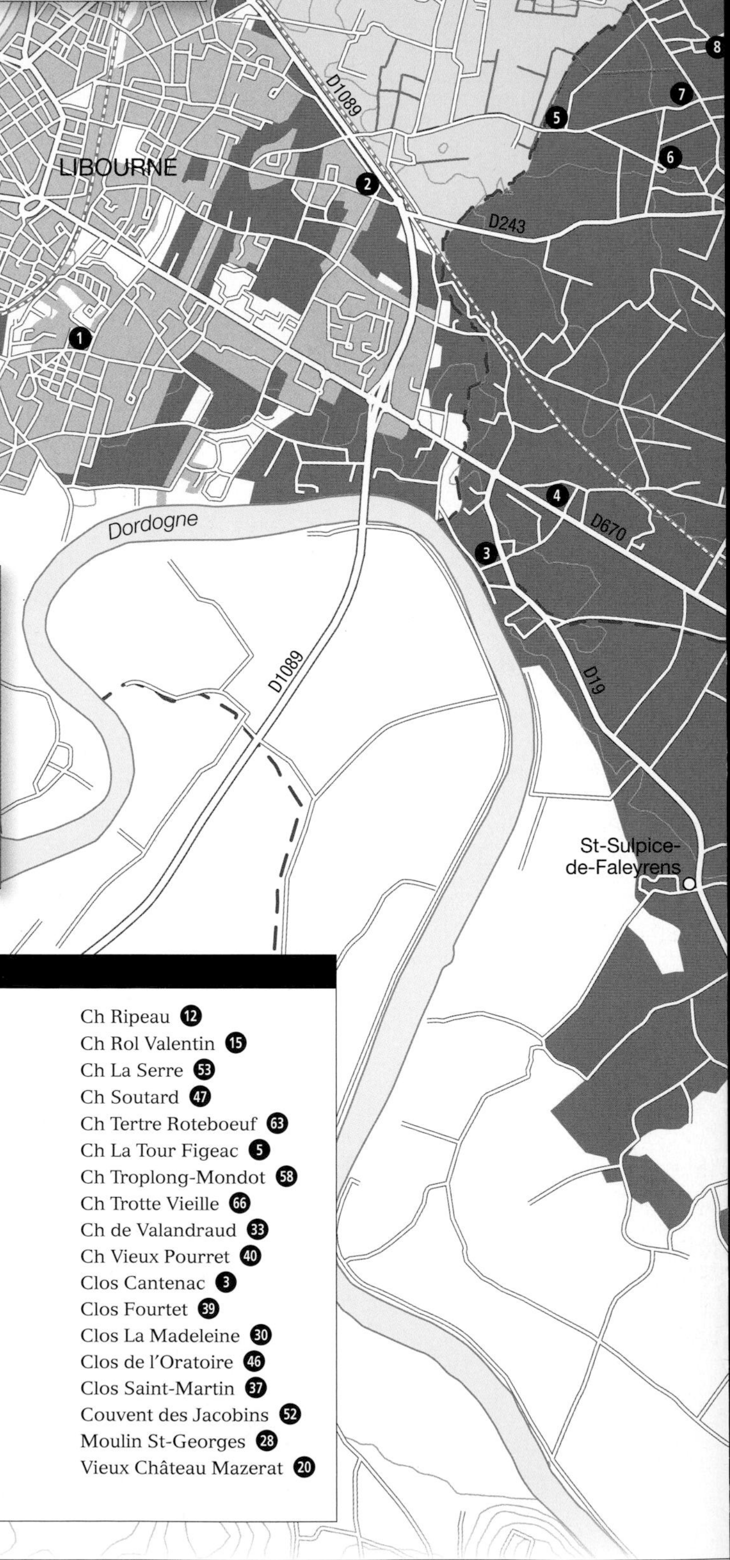

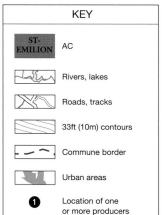

KEY

- ST-EMILION: AC
- Rivers, lakes
- Roads, tracks
- 33ft (10m) contours
- Commune border
- Urban areas
- ❶ Location of one or more producers

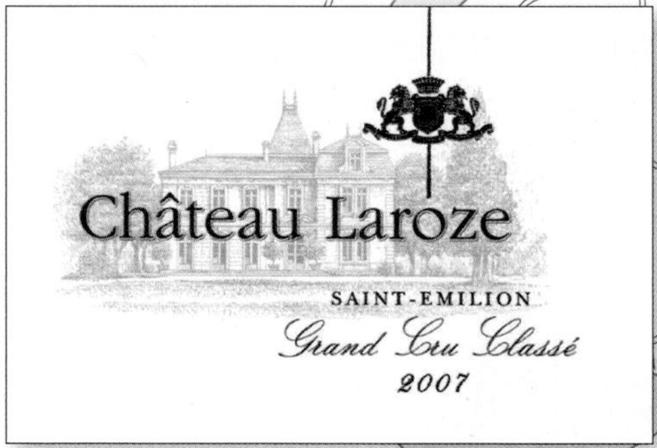

PRODUCERS

Ch Angélus ㉑
Ch L'Arrosée ㉔
Ch Ausone ㉜
Ch Balestard La Tonnelle (67)
Ch Barde-Haut (64)
Ch Beauséjour ㉟
Ch Beau-Séjour Bécot ㊳
Ch Belair-Monange ㉙
Ch Bellefont-Belcier (62)
Ch Bellevue ⑲
Ch Bergat (55)
Ch Berliquet ㉞
Ch Canon ㊱
Ch Canon-La-Gaffelière ㉗
Ch Cantenac ④
Ch Cheval Blanc ⑧
Ch Clos de Sarpe ㊿
Ch La Clotte (54)
Ch La Confession ②
Ch Corbin ⑭
Ch Corbin Michotte ⑩
Ch La Couspaude (51)
Ch Dassault ㊺
Ch Destieux (71)
Ch La Dominique ⑨
Ch Faugères (74)
Ch Faurie de Souchard ㊽
Ch Figeac ⑥
Ch Fleur Cardinale (75)
Ch La Fleur Morange (72)
Ch Fombrauge (70)
Ch Fonplégade ㉕
Ch Fonroque ㊷
Ch Franc Mayne ⑱
Ch La Gaffelière ㉖
Ch Gracia ㉒
Ch Grand Corbin ⑬
Ch Grand Corbin-Despagne ⑪
Ch Grand Mayne ⑰
Ch Gaudet ㊾
Ch Haut-Sarpe (68)
Ch Laniote ㊶
Ch Larcis Ducasse (61)
Ch Larmande ㊹
Ch Laroque (69)
Ch Laroze ⑯
Ch Magdelaine ㉛
Ch Monbousquet ㉓
Ch La Mondotte (56)
Ch Moulin du Cadet ㊸
Ch Pavie (60)
Ch Pavie-Decesse (59)
Ch Pavie Macquin (57)
Ch de Pressac (73)
Ch Le Prieuré (65)
Ch Quinault L'Enclos ①
Ch Riou de Thaillas ⑦
Ch Ripeau ⑫
Ch Rol Valentin ⑮
Ch La Serre (53)
Ch Soutard ㊼
Ch Tertre Roteboeuf (63)
Ch La Tour Figeac ⑤
Ch Troplong-Mondot (58)
Ch Trotte Vieille (66)
Ch de Valandraud ㉝
Ch Vieux Pourret ㊵
Clos Cantenac ③
Clos Fourtet ㊴
Clos La Madeleine ㉚
Clos de l'Oratoire ㊻
Clos Saint-Martin ㊲
Couvent des Jacobins (52)
Moulin St-Georges ㉘
Vieux Château Mazerat ⑳

LALANDE-DE-POMEROL

MONTAGNE-ST-EMILION

Montagne

St-Georges

ST-GEORGES-ST-EMILION

Faure

Balau

ST-EMILION

Musset

PUISSEGUIN-ST-EMILION

Parsac

St-Christophe-des-Bardes

St-Georges

St-Laurent-des-Combes

△107m
(351ft)

101m
(331ft)
△

St-Hippolyte

St-Etienne-de-Lisse

St-Colombe

Les Bigaroux

St-Pey-d'Armens

Vignonet
Dordogne

CHATEAU
CLOS DE SARPE

Saint-Emilion Grand Cru
APPELLATION SAINT-ÉMILION GRAND CRU CONTRÔLÉE

2007
MIS EN BOUTEILLES AU CHATEAU
S.C.A. BEYNEY
PROPRIÉTAIRE À SAINT-CHRISTOPHE-DES-BARDES

Lalande-de-Pomerol

L'Isle

Libourne

DORDOGNE

St-Emilion

Castillon-la-Bataille

Dordogne

St-Jean-de-Blaignac

BORDEAUX

St-Emilion wine region

1ᵉʳ *Grand Cru Classé*
Clos Fourtet
SAINT-ÉMILION
2005
Philippe CUVELIER
PROPRIÉTAIRE

SAINT-EMILION GRAND CRU
Grand Cru Classé
Château Bellevue
Appellation Saint-Emilion Grand Cru Contrôlée
2002
MIS EN BOUTEILLE AU CHATEAU

Château
La Fleur
Morange
Saint-Emilion
Grand Cru
2007

0   0.5   1 km

0   0.25   0.5 miles

Always check the availability of visitor facilities and the visiting hours at a winery before planning your trip. Some wineries are open by appointment only.

CHATEAU BERGAT

THIS IS A GOOD-VALUE WINE FOR
DRINKING RELATIVELY YOUNG

CHATEAU CANON

NEW INVESTMENT BY OWNERS CHANEL
INDICATES IMPROVEMENTS ARE ON THE WAY

Château Bellefont-Belcier
Grand Cru Classé
Château Bellefont-Belcier produces smooth, silky, confident wines. They have good levels of extraction, and new oak barrels (80–100%) coax out licorice and vanilla to top-up the fruit. The château was promoted to a classified growth in 2006 under the direction of three men: Jacques Berrebi, Alain Laguillaumie, and Dominique Hebrard (director at Cheval Blanc until 1999). Gilles Paquet and Michel Rolland are consultants. There are 32 acres (13ha) of vines, planted to 70% Merlot, 20% Cabernet Franc, and 10% Cabernet Sauvignon. Over the past few years the date of picking has been pushed back significantly. The trio also own neighboring Château Trianon.

33330 St-Laurent-des-Combes
www.bellefont-belcier.fr

Château Bellevue   Grand Cru Classé
Château Bellevue was briefly demoted in 2006, but a stay-of-execution saved its Grand Cru Classé status. Better times are ahead, as Hubert de Boüard now has a 50% stake, and consultants Stéphane Derenoncourt and Nicolas Thienpont are on board. The de Lavaux family continues to own the other 50%. The vineyard of 15 acres (6ha) is located right next door to Château Angélus, with 80% Merlot and 20% Cabernet Franc vines, but the final blend often sees more Merlot (98% in 2008).

33330 St-Emilion
www.bellevue-grandcru.com

Château Bergat   Grand Cru Classé
Emile Castéja and the Preben-Hansen family own Château Bergat. It is a very good value St-Emilion that is surprisingly little known outside the region. There is a split of 55% Merlot, 35% Cabernet Franc, and 10% Cabernet Sauvignon over the 10 acre (4ha) vineyard. A gentle touch of new oak means this can be drunk relatively young compared to some classified wines. There is no need to wait more than four or five years to see the tannins round out.

33330 St-Emilion
05 56 00 00 70

Château Berliquet   Grand Cru Classé
Viscount Patrick de Lesquen, a former investment banker (re)turned winemaker, has taken over at Château Berliquet. He is from an old St-Emilion family with ancient links to various local properties, most famously Château Figeac. There are 22 acres (9ha) planted on the limestone plateau, made up of 67% Merlot, 25% Cabernet Franc, and 8% Cabernet Sauvignon. The vines produce a well-defined but delicate wine, bottled unfiltered. The winemaker was Patrick Valette, who now lives full-time in Chile (although he has kept a foothold in Bordeaux via Château Rougerie in AC Bordeaux). Nicolas Thienpont has ably stepped into his shoes. The second wine is Les Ailes de Berliquet.

1 Berliquet, 33330 St-Emilion
www.chateau-berliquet.com

Château Canon   Premier Grand Cru Classé B
Owned by the Wertheimer brothers of Château Rauzan-Ségla (and the fashion house Chanel), Château Canon has been the subject of serious renovations and investments since its purchase in 1996. The most concentrated refurbishment has happened over the past five years. There are 54 acres (22ha) in total, with 49 acres (20ha) in production on the clay–limestone plateau, planted to 75% Merlot and 25% Cabernet Franc. General opinion on the wine has not caught up with the new investments; it is seriously classy, smooth, and richly textured, with some sweet vanilla undertones from the 80% new oak.

1 Saint Martin, 33330 St-Emilion
www.chateau-canon.com

Château Canon-La-Gaffelière
Grand Cru Classé
Stephan von Neipperg, one of the true characters of St-Emilion, has enlisted Stéphane Derenoncourt as winemaker at the 49 acre (20ha) Château Canon-La-Gaffelière. It is pretty much the first estate you come to on the approach to the village. The château is as elegant as its owner, who clearly styles his wines with a similar philosophy in mind. The blend of 55% Merlot, 40% Cabernet Franc, and 5% Cabernet Sauvignon gives great structure and flesh, but always with a delicate nose, and spicy edge.

1 La Gaffelière Ouest, 33330 St-Emilion
05 57 24 71 33

Château Cantenac
Château Cantenac is one of the very few estates for whom the Médoc consultant Jacques Boissenot crosses over the river. It is owned by the charming Roskam-Brunot family, headed up by mother Nicole working alongside her three sons Frédéric, Frans, and Johan (and their three American wives). There are 32 acres (13ha) of vines on the edge of the St-Emilion slopes. The mix is 75% Merlot and 24% Cabernet Franc (the 1% of Cabernet Sauvignon just whispers in a little backbone), and this is traditional-style St-Emilion with red fruits and firm tannins. The best *cuvée* is Climat de Château Cantenac, made with a higher proportion of Cabernet Sauvignon and aged in 50% new oak for 14 months.

2 Cantenac, 33330 St-Emilion
www.chateau-cantenac.fr

Château Cheval Blanc
Premier Grand Cru Classé A
Today, Château Cheval Blanc is owned by luxury goods house LVMH (headed up by Bernard Arnault) and Belgian businessman Albert Frère, along with Château d'Yquem in Sauternes. The real figurehead, however, is elegant director Pierre Lurton. There are 82 acres (33ha) grown in a single block, with a majority of Cabernet Franc (57%). This is complemented by Merlot, Cabernet Sauvignon, and Malbec, all aged in 100% new oak. On the palate, you get lovely creamy violets and blackberries, gorgeous bursts of flavor, with a good acidity that is so subtle you almost do not feel it. One of the best second wines on the market is the Petit Cheval.

No visitors facilities
www.chateau-cheval-blanc.com

Château Clos de Sarpe
Château Clos de Sarpe is highly sought-after—it gets snapped up as soon as it comes on the market. The old vines are lovingly worked, and the tiny yields from the

10 acre (4ha) vineyard are vinified using micro-oxygenation. The blend of 85% Merlot and 15% Cabernet Franc is aged for 16–18 months in new oak barrels. The final wine has wonderfully concentrated flavors of dark damson plums and licorice.

No visitor facilities
www.clos-de-sarpe.com

Château La Clotte Grand Cru Classé
The magic of St-Emilion is captured at Château La Clotte. The château itself is carved out of the limestone rock, five minutes from the main square but almost hidden in its own tiny valley. Many of the underground cellars in the area were once quarries, but this was a troglodyte dwelling. Today, Nelly Moulierac is in charge of the 10 acre (4ha) estate, making wine that is far from flashy, but has hints of licorice and mocha toast, with a quiet sense of confidence from red currant overtones.

Lieu-dit Bergat, 33330 St-Emilion
www.chateaulaclotte.com

Château La Confession
Château La Confession is a Janoueix wine that combines big, juicy blackberry fruit with a small sense of restraint (just), from grilled savory herbs and white pepper spice. There are 6 acres (2.5ha) of vines, with a whopping 45% Cabernet Franc (together with 50% Merlot and 5% Cabernet Sauvignon). Ripening is helped by high-density planting and two sets of crop-thinning to concentrate flavors. The wines are then aged in cigar-shaped barrels, which they claim increases the exchange of oxygen with the wine, and therefore softens the (still fairly meaty) tannins.

183 route de St-Emilion, 33500 Libourne
www.josephjanoueix.com

Château Corbin Grand Cru Classé
Château Corbin is found near to Château Cheval Blanc, as St-Emilion heads over toward Pomerol. Anabelle Cruse-Bardinet is in charge of 32 acres (13ha) of vines on sandy and clay soils, planted to 80% Merlot and 20% Cabernet Franc. Her consultant is Ludwig Vanneron from Laboratoire Rolland, who uses techniques such as cold soaking before fermentation, followed by both malolactic fermentation and aging in 100% new oak barrels. This gives wines that have a lovely freshness of wild strawberries, with a richer contrast of mocha and mint—modern, but successful.

No visitor facilities
www.chateau-corbin.com

Château Corbin Michotte
Grand Cru Classé
There is 30% Cabernet Franc in the mix that goes into Château Corbin Michotte, along with 65% Merlot and 5% Cabernet Sauvignon. Jean-Noël Boidron makes a classic, delicate-style St-Emilion that is big on aromatics but sometimes a little light on fruit. The property produces 38,000 bottles from its 17 acres (7ha) of vines, and a further 5 acres (2ha) of attractive parkland surrounds the château. Boidron also owns Château Cantelauz in Pomerol.

33330 St-Emilion
vignoblesjnboidron@wanadoo.fr

Château La Couspaude Grand Cru Classé
The bronze statues of horses in the paved courtyard of Château La Couspaude tell you that this is an estate with some imagination. Owned by the same family for over a century, today's owner Alain Aubert is helped by his daughter Heloise and niece Vanessa, with Michel Rolland as consultant. Together they make around 55,000 bottles per year of unashamedly modern-style, exuberant St-Emilion from 17 acres (7ha) of vines. The 75% Merlot, 20% Cabernet Franc, and 5% Cabernet Sauvignon plus 100% new oak give notes of mocha and fleshy red fruits.

33330 St-Emilion
05 57 40 15 76

Château Croix de Labrie
Château Croix de Labrie is a tiny *cuvée* owned by Michel and Ghislaine Puzio-Lesage. The estate can be relied upon for flashy wines full of red fruits and soft black truffles. The tannins are worked to within an inch of their lives, and the wine offers plenty of pleasure from an early age—but you will have to look hard to find it, as only 2,400 bottles are made each year.

No visitor facilities
05 57 24 64 60

Château Dassault Grand Cru Classé
This estate was renamed by Marcel Dassault when he bought it in the 1950s (it was previously Château Couperie). The perfectly formed château is today run by Laurent Dassault with director Laurence Brun. Michel Rolland started out here in 1973 (this was one of his first properties as consultant). There are 42 acres (17ha) of vines, planted to a majority of Merlot (85%). This is a good wine, with well-crafted tannins and carefully worked fruit but, more importantly, one that is seriously enjoyable to drink. The Dassaults also own Château La Fleur in St-Emilion.

No visitors facilities
www.chateaudassault.com

Château Destieux Grand Cru Classé
Christian Dauriac, of Pomerol's La Clémence, owns the recently promoted Château Destieux. The wine has an enveloping nose, with good weight of fruit, and gripping tannins. The 20 acres (8ha) of 45-year-old vines are set in a natural amphitheatre, meaning great sun exposure and concentration. Having a double degree in medical biology and enology must help Dauriac when coaxing seductive black currant and fig out of the 66% Merlot and an even split of the two Cabernets. Any questions can be answered by consultant Michel Rolland. Look out also for Dauriac's St-Emilion Grand Cru Château Montlisse.

St-Hippolyte, 33330 St-Emilion
05 57 24 77 44

Château La Dominique Grand Cru Classé
The Fayat family (of Clément Pichon) has owned Château La Dominique since 1969. It is located on the Pomerol border, and this gives a clue to the style—big, deep flavors and a structure you can lean against. The 57 acres (23ha) consist of 86% Merlot/12%/Cabernet Franc/2% Cabernet Sauvignon, aged in oak barrels for 18 months (60% new). Michel Rolland ceased as consultant in 2006, but Jean Philippe Fort from his team has taken over—and further

GERARD PERSE

For anyone who worries that Bordeaux rests too far on its laurels, Gérard Perse represents a breath of fresh air. For a start, he did not inherit his vineyards—Châteaux Pavie, Pavie-Decesse, and Monbusquet—from his winemaking ancestors, but bought them himself with money raised by selling a chain of supermarkets in northern France. He then began to successfully compete with the best of the appellation, introducing extremely low yields, severe green harvesting, lashings of new oak, and no fining or filtration. "Running supermarkets, you have to move very fast, and be constantly reactive. I took that same attitude with me, to Bordeaux, and at first it created confusion—my neighbors were not quite sure what to make of me," says Perse today. "I was entirely focused on making the best wine I could, but have learnt to stop to enjoy it. Here we have discovered genuine tranquility."

CHATEAU FIGEAC
THE "MEDOC OF ST-EMILION"—THE GRAVELLY
SOIL OF THIS ESTATE MAKES IT STAND OUT

CHATEAU FAUGERES
KEEP AN EYE ON THIS CHATEAU AS THE
OWNER HAS SERIOUS AMBITIONS

improvements are expected since the arrival of Yannick Evenou as director in 2009. The Fayats recently bought a neighboring property, Château Vieux Fortin, with the intention of joining it to La Dominique in the future.

33330 St Etienne de Lisse
05 57 51 31 36

Château Faugères
Silvio Denz, Swiss financier and owner of Lalique glass makers, has recently unveiled a new facility at Château Faugères. The winery is built into the earth with a multi-level gravity system, cooling chambers for the grapes, and a laser-optical grape-sorting machine. The intention is to become a serious wine and two heavyweight enologists have come on board—Michel Rolland and Stephan von Neipperg. The top *cuvée*, Peby Faugères, is a luxury, fruit-packed 100% Merlot, while the main wine has a more classic mix of 85% Merlot, 10% Cabernet Franc, and 5% Cabernet Sauvignon. The full range includes Haut Faugères and Cap de Faugères.

33330 St Etienne de Lisse
www.chateau-faugeres.com

Château Faurie de Souchard
Grand Cru Classé
A new generation of the Sciard family is working hard at Château Faurie de Souchard. Aided by consultant Stéphane Derenoncourt, they are making subtle updates to the style of this wine. With 35 acres (14ha) of vines, planted to 75% Merlot, 20% Cabernet Franc, and 5% Cabernet Sauvignon, the winemaking takes place in cement tanks. This is a well-balanced wine, and the fruit is vibrant. The last few vintages have shown plenty of potential. The second wine is Faurie de Souchard.

2 Petit Faurie de Souchard, 33330 St-Emilion
www.fauriedesouchard.com

Château Figeac Premier Grand Cru Classé B
Thierry Manoncourt presides (no other word quite fits) over this unusual St-Emilion wine. Château Figeac contains a full 70% of Cabernet Sauvignon and Cabernet Franc, due to the gravelly terroir. The rest is Merlot, but it is certainly a wine that has more black fruit and tannins than many from the Right Bank, and is often referred to as "the Médoc of St-Emilion". The aging in 100% new oak rounds out the tannins and gives it back some St-Emilion fleshiness.

33330 St-Emilion
www.chateau-figeac.com

Château Fleur Cardinale Grand Cru Classé
Sometimes it takes a marital nudge. Florence Decoster's husband, fresh from his sale of Limoges pottery company Haviland, was convinced by his wife to buy Château Fleur Cardinale in 2001. Together, they have created an exciting, modern, and dynamic estate that covers 44 acres (18ha) and is planted to 70% Merlot, with the rest split between the two Cabernets. Aged in 100% new oak, these are seductive dark-fruit wines that are not afraid to announce their arrival. Other wines include Bois Cardinale and La Secrete de Cardinale.

7 Thibaud, 33330 St-Etienne-de-Lisse
www.chateau-fleurcardinale.com

Château La Fleur Morange
Château La Fleur Morange is an outstanding 5 acre (2ha) estate, farmed biodynamically by Jean François and Veronique Julien. The vines reach over 100 years in age, and produce wines filled with lush black currants and raspberries, and seams of licorice. Both perfectionists by nature (Jean François was once a renowned cabinet maker), there are tiny touches that are eminently sensible yet revolutionary: a balcony in the winery for malolactic fermentation, taking advantage of natural heat rising. The vineyards are 70% Merlot, 15% Cabernet Franc, and 15% Cabernet Sauvignon. Look out also for their other wine Matilde, a 100% Merlot. ★**Rising star**

Ferrachat, 33330 St-Pays-d'Armens
www.lafleurmorange.com

Château Fombrauge
Sit back and sink into the wines at Château Fombrauge—you are in the safe hands of Bernard Magrez. He works hard to ensure his wines get the luxury treatment and that they convey a sense of well-being to their drinkers. A smooth and richly fruity wine, with 70% Merlot backed up by a well-honed core of 30% Cabernet Franc and Sauvignon. The second wine is Cadran de Fombrauge. One of the few St-Emilion estates to make a white wine, Fombrauge Blanc is a successful mix of Sauvignon and Sémillon, with a floral lift of Muscadelle.

1 Fombrauge, 33330 St-Christophe-des-Bardes
www.fombrauge.com

Château Fonplégade Grand Cru Classé
The vineyard of Château Fonplégade directly faces the excellent co-operative cellars in St-Emilion. They might not like the comparison, but both show the bright new face of the appellation even if this is an established classified growth. There are 44 acres (18ha) with 91% Merlot grapes, recently renovated by American banker Stephen Adams to the highest standards. Michel Rolland is on hand for winemaking advice. The wine undergoes five days of cold soaking before fermentation, and is aged for up to 24 months in 100% new oak. The result purrs with luxury—rich summer fruits in a confidently silky structure. The second wine is Fleur de Fonplégade.

1 Fonplégade, 33330 St-Emilion
www.adamsfrenchvineyards.fr.

Château Fonroque Grand Cru Classé
The intellectual, softly spoken Alain Moueix runs the excellent and biodynamic Château Fonroque; the latter being a brave move for a classified wine but one that has paid off. Stately purple in color, the tannins are austere when young, but with purity of fruit beneath, and a crisp seam of minerality pulling the whole thing together. Moueix treats his 42 acres (17ha) of primarily Merlot vines as an ecosystem that needs careful balancing, and further respects the wine it produces by not filtering before bottling.

1 Fonroque, 33330 St-Emilion
www.chateaufonroque.com

Château Franc Mayne Grand Cru Classé
If you are looking for a modern rendition of the St-Emilion tune, Château Franc Mayne is a good option. The wine has vibrant black-cherry flavors, with a

toasted-vanilla frosting of new oak. The Swiss owners, Griet and Hervé Laviale, have extended this modern approach throughout, with an award-winning boutique hotel and a new wine tourism center. These contrast with the centuries-old cellars cut out of the limestone rock beneath. The 17 acre (7ha) vineyard is given over to 90% Merlot and 10% Cabernet Franc. A week-long cold soak sets the tone for a vinification that favors fruit. The second wine, Les Cèdres de Franc Mayne, represents 20% of production.

La Gomerie, 33330 St-Emilion
www.chateau-francmayne.com

Château La Gaffelière
Premier Grand Cru Classé B
The owners of Château La Gaffelière, led by Count Léo de Malet Roquefort, are one of the oldest families in the region. Vines were planted here in Roman times. The château has an underground cellar, built in 1990 by architect Philippe Mazières, which has seen the introduction of techniques such as cold soaking and malolactic fermentation in new oak barrels. A redesigned label in 2009 continued the changes. The 54 acres (22ha) of vines (80% Merlot, 10% Cabernet Sauvignon, and 10% Cabernet Franc) are located in one plot opposite the Ausone hill on the approach into the village.

1 La Gaffelière Ouest, 33330 St-Emilion
www.chateau-la-gaffeliere.com

Château Gracia
Château Gracia is so-named because of its founder, stonemason-turned-winemaker Michel Gracia. Not just any old stonemason, however, as he has crafted some of the most beautiful monuments in the region, and has applied the same kind of precision to his wine. A big, meaty, powerful wine, with 100% new oak and unafraid of a bit of extraction—expect plenty of vibrant black currant, tar, and leather. The vineyard itself covers 10 acres (4ha) and was founded in 1997. The second wine is Les Angelots de Gracia.

St-Christophe-des-Bardes, 33330 St-Emilion
05 57 24 77 98

Château Grand Corbin Grand Cru Classé
The signature of Château Grand Corbin is a good balance of smoky oak, acidity, and fresh fruits. Managed by Philippe Giraud, it is another of the cluster of classified wines on the Corbin plateau. The 37 acres (15ha) are treated without herbicides, and all harvesting is done by hand. New gravity-installations in the cellars have really paid off in recent years, giving a silkiness that has been sometimes lacking. The wine is moved around the winery on a pulley system in mobile tanks, and the final wine is aged for 12–14 months in new oak barrels.

5 Grand Corbin, 33330 St-Emilion
www.grand-corbin.com

Château Grand Corbin-Despagne
Grand Cru Classé
François Despagne is the seventh generation of his family to run the 67 acre (27ha) Château Grand Corbin-Despagne. You can instantly tell he feels part of the land itself. The vineyard is farmed organically—gradually heading toward biodynamic—and all work is done by hand.

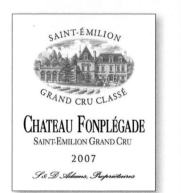

CHATEAU FONPLEGADE
A SMOOTH AND LUXURIOUS WINE, SHOWING THE BENEFITS OF RECENT INVESTMENT

GRAND-CORBIN DESPAGNE
ONE OF ST-EMILION'S SELECT BUNCH OF ORGANIC AND BIODYNAMIC PRODUCERS

Grapes are sorted both at the vine and in the cellar. Among the new experiments is a laser-optic sorting table. The first wine is a blend of Merlot and Cabernet Franc, aged in oak for 14–18 months (40% new). The second label is Petit Corbin-Despagne, of mainly young vines, aged in 50% 2-year-old barrels and 50% vats.

33330 St-Emilion
www.grand-corbin-despagne.com

Château Grand Mayne Grand Cru Classé
The Nony family has owned Château Grand Mayne since the 1930s; they were part of the wave of wine merchants from the Corrèze region who moved to Bordeaux in that decade. There are 47 acres (19ha) with 76% Merlot, 13% Cabernet Franc, and 11% Cabernet Sauvignon. Malolactic fermentation takes place in new oak. This is a complex wine that consistently delivers a good balance of fruit, tannin, and acidity; you will want to decant in most vintages. The second wine, Les Plantes du Mayne, is from 50% non-classified and 50% young vines.

1 Le Grand Mayne, 33330 St-Emilion
www.chateau-grand-mayne.com

Château Gaudet
Grand Cru Classé
Château Gaudet was demoted in the 2006 classification and, although it was reinstated, it is fair to say these wines could do with a boost. From a PR point of view the owner, Guy de Lignis, was made somewhat unfairly the scapegoat for the political fallout. Having Stéphane Derenoncourt as consultant is a good start, as is introducing sustainable agriculture. The château has 14 acres (5.5ha) of vines, enclosed by stone walls at the end of the main street. It is a traditional, well-structured wine that could do with loosening up a little.

4 rue Gaudet, 33330 St-Emilion
05 57 74 40 04

Château Haut-Sarpe Grand Cru Classé
The Joseph Janoueix family own both Château Haut-Sarpe and a Libourne wine merchants. It is a name to remember for the production of interesting bottles across all Bordeaux appellations and price points. This is one of their more established wineries, with 54 acres (22ha) of classified vines on the limestone plateau, making wines that are intense but vibrant. There is sweet tobacco leaf on the nose, with good structure and freshness, and plenty of brambly fruits.

1 Sarpe, St Christophe des Bardes, 33330 St-Emilion
05 57 51 41 86

Château Laniote Grand Cru Classé
This is a true family-run classified growth—Château Laniote has been owned by the Lacoste family for the past two centuries (each time inherited through the female side, so the name over the door has often changed). Today, Arnaud de la Filolie works alongside his wife Florence Ribereau-Gayon (of the famous enologist family) at the 12 acre (5ha) estate. Oak is evident on the nose, but there is also plenty of dark summer fruit, with a perfumed nose from the 20% Cabernet Franc. With good structure and acidity, this is a wine that will age well.

3 La Niotte, 33330 St-Emilion
www.laniote.com

The prized vineyards of the Côtes St-Emilion occupy the slopes around the town of St-Emilion.

CHATEAU DE PRESSAC
THIS WINE INCLUDES A TOUCH OF MALBEC
AND CARMENERE IN THE BLEND

Château Larcis Ducasse Grand Cru Classé

Château Larcis Ducasse has been run by Nicolas Thienpont since 2002, with Stéphane Derenoncourt as consultant. There is great potential for this estate, located on the Pavie slopes overlooking the Dordogne Valley, and owned by the Gratiot Alphandéry family since the 18th century. The vineyard (78% Merlot, 20% Cabernet Franc, and 2% Cabernet Sauvignon) covers 27 acres (11ha), and the wine has a cherry-red color and fresh red currants on the nose. Thienpont has undertaken extensive geological studies to ensure he is matching soil structure with his plantations and viticultural techniques. This is a man who believes passionately in listening to the soil, and it is certainly paying off.

No visitor facilities
www.larcis-ducasse.com

Château Larmande Grand Cru Classé

At 56 acres (23ha), Château Larmande is one of the largest estates in the appellation. It is owned by insurance company La Mondiale—with a further 6 acres (2.5ha) going into Cadet de Larmande, AC St-Emilion Grand Cru. A new vat room was installed in 2003 and there are 16 stainless steel vats with insulated double walls, in differing sizes, that allow extremely precise winemaking. With 65% Merlot, 30% Cabernet Franc, and 5% Cabernet Sauvignon, there is a densely rich mid-palate, with a charred smudge on the nose that is very attractive.

lieu-dit-Larmande, 33330 St-Emilion
www.chateau-larmande.com

Château Laroque Grand Cru Classé

The Louis XV architecture and an almost translucent stone façade give Château Laroque real beauty. The wines reflect this impressive setting more and more, as the Beaumartin family has worked hard and finally saw Laroque elevated to classified status in 1996. There are 143 acres (58ha) of vines with an average age of 35 years, planted to 87% Merlot, 11% Cabernet Franc, and a mere 2% Cabernet Sauvignon on the stony slopes. Only 67 acres (27ha) end up in the first wine, which is aged in oak for 11–13 months (50% new) and results in a modern-style wine with ample red fruits.

33330 St-Emilion
www.chateau-laroque.com

Château Laroze Grand Cru Classé

The 67 acres (27ha) of Château Laroze are largely of clay, and give real power to the 68% of Merlot vines grown here. The density of all new plantings has been upped to further concentrate the flavors. It can be slightly too much in powerful years, but the Meslin family know what they are doing, and err on the right side of extraction. Sweet basil flavors, slightly grilled from the new oak, swirl with red currant fruits. Biodynamics were used here in the 1990s, but today they follow less strict, though still low-impact, practices. The second wine is Lafleur Laroze.

1 Goudichau, 33330 St-Emilion
www.laroze.com

Château Magdelaine
Premier Grand Cru Classé B

Before Jean Claude Berrouet's retirement as winemaker at Château Pétrus, he often said Château Magdelaine was his favorite of the Moueix properties. It is a classic, restrained,

and elegant St-Emilion that has sweet cherry and cedarwood flavors, but an edge of savory herbs that reins in the exuberance. The vineyard is 26 acres (10.5ha) of 90% Merlot/10% Cabernet Franc; a few vines date back to the 1920s. The second wine is Les Sanges de Magdelaine.

33330 St-Emilion
www.chateaupavie.com

Château Monbousquet Grand Cru Classé

The signature Gérard Perse style of big-hitting flavors is evident here at Château Monbousquet, and no-one is going to mistake this for an understatement. What you get are explosive fruits, and a voluptuous texture. This was the first estate that Perse bought in St-Emilion, in 1994, and is still his family home. Promoted in the last classification, it has deep gravel that makes for a hot terroir suited to the 30% of Cabernet Franc and Cabernet Sauvignon, with 70% Merlot. The delicious Monbousquet Blanc—66% Sauvignon Blanc and 34% Sauvignon Gris—is full of peach, apple blossom, and exotic fruits.

33330 St-Emilion
www.chateaupavie.com

Château La Mondotte

Château La Mondotte is one of those small St-Emilion estates that just does luxury so perfectly. Owned by Stephan von Niepperg, the 10 acre (4ha) estate has very low yields of Merlot and Cabernet Franc across limestone terroir. It is located next to Troplong-Mondot, and with Stéphane Derenoncourt as consultant, produces just 11,000 bottles a year. This concentrated elixir, with the 100% new oak fitting perfectly with the blueberry and black chocolate flavors, is set alive with an edge of minerality. This is a wine that lives up to the hype.

33330 St-Emilion
www.neipperg.com

Château Moulin du Cadet
Grand Cru Classé

Château Moulin du Cadet's 12 acres (5ha) of biodynamic vines give a classic, well-structured St-Emilion that veers away from new toasty oak or anything too flashy. Isabelle and Pierre Blois-Moueix converted to organic winemaking in 2002, and went fully biodynamic in 2005. They may have been helped by Isabelle's brother, Alain Moueix (the biodynamic champion at Fonroque), but whatever the reason, the 100% Merlot wine is full of silky red fruit.

Colline du Cadet, 33330 St-Emilion
05 57 25 37 45

Château Pavie Premier Grand Cru Classé B

Château Pavie is often a lightning rod for controversy over old or new styles of St-Emilion, yet it remains a testament to the hard work and vision of owner Gérard Perse. His wine, typically, is 60% Merlot/30% Cabernet Franc/10% Cabernet Sauvignon, with all grapes from the 106 acres (43ha) harvested in small crates to avoid damaging the berries and vinified in 80–100% new oak. The tannins come with hobnailed boots when young, but tasting the rich elegance of older vintages—give it at least eight years—explains why Perse is right to trust his techniques.

33330 St-Emilion
www.chateaupavie.com

CHATEAU PAVIE MACQUIN
AN EXCITING AND MODERN WINE
PRODUCED BIODYNAMICALLY

Château Pavie-Decesse Grand Cru Classé
Château Pavie-Decesse belongs to Gérard Perse of Château Pavie. It is smaller than its famous brother with 22 acres (9ha) of vines (90% Merlot and 10% Cabernet Franc) located on the limestone plateau. As you would expect, the grapes here receive the same Rolls-Royce treatment as at Pavie, with severe green harvesting, hand-picking and sorting, and Michel Rolland overseeing the winemaking. Around 24,000 bottles are made each year, with no second label. The rich, well-defined flavors and gripping tannic structure that Perse coaxes out of his wines is present, with seductive red fruits and a confidence that is hard to resist.

33330 St-Emilion
05 57 55 43 43

Château Pavie Macquin
Premier Grand Cru Classé B
Château Pavie Macquin is one of the classified wines that always create a sense of excitement and occasion when opening. Director Nicolas Thienpont manages, through hard work and techniques based on biodynamic principles, to make excellent wine from 37 acres (15ha) of 80% Merlot grapes. Modern in style (ripe fruit, whole-grape vinification, and micro-oxygenation), it is full of licorice and chocolate, but with an acidity that means it never strays into overkill. There is a history of success here—founder Albert Macquin was responsible for grafting vines onto rootstocks, thereby saving the region from phylloxera. The current owners are his grandchildren.

1 Peygenestau, 33330 St-Emilion
www.pavie-macquin.com

Château de Pressac
Beautifully located on the limestone plateau to the east of St-Emilion, Château de Pressac is at the highest point (262ft/80m) of St-Etienne-de-Lisse, and owned by local wine council president, Jean-François Quenin. One of the most unusual things Quenin did after his purchase in 1997 was cut terraces into the steep hillsides surrounding the château. He also uprooted and replanted vines, and introduced new varieties—today 72% Merlot, 14% Cabernet Franc, 12% Cabernet Sauvignon, and 2% split between Carmenère and Malbec (a former name for this grape being "Pressac"). The wine has well-integrated oak, and is smooth and supple. Also, history buffs, this is where, on July 20, 1453, the English surrendered to the French after the Battle of Castillon. ★ **Rising star**

33330 St-Etienne-de-Lisse
www.chateau-de-pressac.com

Château Le Prieuré Grand Cru Classé
Château Le Prieuré has a freshness that underpins the black-cherry fruit and well-worked tannins. It is a big wine, with good smokiness to the oak, and is altogether highly appealing. The 15 acres (6ha) of vines are looked after by owner Paul Goldschmidt of Domaines Baronne Guichard and enologist Yannick Reyrel. Many of the vines overlook the medieval village itself. With 90% Merlot and 10% Cabernet Franc, the silky tannins make this enjoyable when young, but there is also good aging potential. The second wine, Délice du Prieuré, is 100% Merlot, and is all about immediate gratification.

33330 St-Emilion
05 57 51 64 58

Château Quinault L'Enclos
There is a lot to like about Château Quinault (the L'Enclos was added by previous owner Alain Reynaud to capitalize on the glamour of a walled vineyard), as it manages to be an excitingly modern wine but still with some hints of Old Europe, with sweet new oak balanced by black fruits. It was bought in 2008 by Bernard Arnault and Albert Frère of Cheval Blanc. The success of the wine at this 39 acre (16ha) property has been overshadowed at times by Reynaud's friendship with Robert Parker, and the new team will be looking to redress this. Since Arnault took over, Pierre-Olivier Clouet (who works alongside Pierre Lurton at Cheval Blanc) has been installed as technical director.

30 boulevard de Quinault, 33500 Libourne
www.chateau-quinault.com

Château Reine Blanche
Château Reine Blanche is a small estate worth looking out for, as it is owned by the very talented François Despagne of Château Grand Corbin-Despagne. Here, he produces 36,000 bottles from 15 acres (6ha) of mainly sand and stony soil. A blend of 65% Merlot and 35% Cabernet Franc makes a wine that is powerful but silky smooth, with polished ripe fruits and a chocolate edge.

No visitor facilities
www.grand-corbin-despagne.com

Château Riou de Thaillas
A name to remember, Jean-Yves Dubech owns two vineyards—L'Enclos St-Louis in Canon-Fronsac and this estate, Château Riou de Thaillas. Not only near to the Pomerol border, this 17.5 acre (3ha) property also shares the same iron ore deposits in the clay terroir that bring out powerful violet fruits in the 100% Merlot vines. Both vineyards are farmed biodynamically, helped by enologist Anne Calderoni. While modern, lush flavors are a signature of the wine, the winemaking is rather more old-school. If you ask Jean-Yves when it is the right moment to pick, he will tell you, "When the birds are enjoying the grapes, I know they are ripe enough."

33330 St-Emilion
www.vignoblesdubech.fr

Château Ripeau Grand Cru Classé
As with its neighbors Cheval Blanc and Figeac, Château Ripeau has enough gravel in the terroir to justify a high 35% of Cabernet Franc and Cabernet Sauvignon. The clay-sand of the rest is given over to Merlot, which here takes on some of the power of Pomerol. Classified since the original 1955 ranking, and today run by Barbara Janoueix Coutel and her cousin Louis de Wilde, the vines cover 37 acres (15ha). The new generation use reverse osmosis when necessary, and also cold soaking before fermentation to concentrate flavors and emphasize fruit.

1 Ripeau, 33330 St-Emilion
www.chateauripeau.com

Château Rol Valentin
The flamboyant name of Château Rol Valentin sits perfectly with this hedonistic wine, owned by Nicolas Robin (who bought the estate from Eric Prissette). Around 14,000 bottles are produced from the 11 acres (4.6ha). A majority of Merlot vines (86%) are pushed to their limit through close pruning and green harvesting.

STEPHANE DERENONCOURT

The Right Bank's other big wine consultant, Stéphane Derenoncourt, is known for his natural approach, promoting biodynamic, organic, and sustainable winemaking. He follows Burgundian practices such as plot-by-plot work in the vineyard, whole-berry fermentation, and integral vinification in barrel, looking for "fruit, balance, and pleasure" in wines. Entirely self-taught, he came to Bordeaux in 1982 and worked as grape picker, building up his knowledge slowly, through observation and trial and error. He was the first of "a new generation of consultants, who learned their craft not in the laboratory, but in the vines". Derenoncourt now has his own estate, Domaine de l'A in Côtes de Castillon, along with Les Trois Origines in St-Emilion, and consults for over 70 properties, including Clos Fourtet, Canon-La-Gaffelière, and La Mondotte in St-Emilion; Domaine de Chevalier in Pessac-Léognan; and Prieuré-Lichine in Margaux.

In the cellars, techniques include manual punching down of the cap in small wooden vats and aging in 100% new oak barrels. The consultant is Stéphane Derenoncourt, who seems to throw caution to the wind here, pumping up grilled herbs, toasted oak, and licorice-dipped fruits.

5 Les Cabanes Sud, 33330 St-Emilion
www.rolvalentin.com

Château La Serre Grand Cru Classé

The wine of Château La Serre is delicate and fresh on the nose, but with immense power beneath. This is combined with mint and herb notes and lashings of fresh fruit. A wine that seems to have reached new heights in recent years, La Serre is distributed by Ets JP Moueix, but owned by the d'Arfeuille family (previous owners of La Pointe in Pomerol). The 17 acres (7ha) of predominantly Merlot vines (80%, with 20% Cabernet Franc) are planted on limestone, with just tiny traces of clay, on the St-Emilion plateau. Aged for 16 months in 100% new oak.

33330 St-Emilion
05 57 24 71 38

Château Soutard Grand Cru Classé

A style change in recent years has seen Château Soutard's wine plumped up and rounded out, with notes of mocha and coffee introduced from a higher degree of new oak aging. This has come about through insurance company owners La Mondiale, who bought the 54 acre (22ha) property in 2006. With 70% Merlot/30% Cabernet Franc, and directed by the glamorous Claire Thomas-Chénard, the style change is much more than window-dressing, with intensive vineyard and cellar work, and further restorations planned for the near future. For now, it remains good value, as does the second wine, Jardins de Soutard.

33330 St-Emilion
www.chateausoutard.com

Château Tertre Roteboeuf

François Mitjavile has made Château Tertre Roteboeuf one of the best loved non-classified wines in St-Emilion. There are 14 acres (5.7ha) of 45-year-old vines planted with 85% Merlot and 15% Cabernet Franc, given maximum hang-time and then vinified at unusually high temperatures. Bottled without filtering, the black currant and blackberry flavors are overlaid with smoky vanilla. An opulent and sophisticated wine that can whack you over the head but wake you up with a kiss.

1 le Tertre, 33330 St-Laurent-des-Combes
www.tertre-roteboeuf.com

Château La Tour Figeac Grand Cru Classé

Château La Tour Figeac is one of the few St-Emilion properties located on gravel (Cheval Blanc being the most famous). Owned by the Rettenmaier family, there are 36 acres (14.5ha), and the sandier areas are where you will find the Merlot (60%). The gravelly remainder is given over to Cabernet Franc, and the whole is farmed biodynamically, with consultation by François Bouchet. Taste-wise, you get dense, rich fruit, but with subtle hints of roasted herbs and cedarwood that add complexity. The second wine is L'Esquisse de La Tour Figeac.

33000 St-Emilion
05 57 51 77 62

CHATEAU TERTRE ROTEBOEUF
ALTHOUGH NOT A CLASSIFIED GROWTH, THIS WINE HAS A DEVOTED FOLLOWING

CHATEAU VIEUX POURRET
A BIODYNAMIC ESTATE PIONEERING CROSS-REGIONAL BLENDING

Château La Tour du Pin Grand Cru Classé

Since 2006, Château La Tour du Pin has belonged to Arnault and Frère of Cheval Blanc and is worth knowing about. This is not only because the rather brilliant Pierre Lurton is in charge of winemaking, but also because of improved techniques such as new vineyard management following soil analysis, and plot-by-plot vinification, in small vats. The pure, suave fruit is striking, with engaging fresh raspberries and cherries, and increasingly this wine is not putting a foot wrong. They do have great raw materials, as the terroir is an exceptional mix of gravel, sand, and limestone, planted to 75% Merlot and 25% Cabernet Franc over 27 acres (11ha). ★ **Rising star**

No visitor facilities
www.chateau-cheval-blanc.com

Château Troplong-Mondot
Premier Grand Cru Classé B

Pronounced exactly as it is written, Château Troplong-Mondot is owned by the diminutive but extremely dynamic Christine Valette. Together with her husband Xavier Pariente, she has made enormous strides in the quality of this wine in recent years. At 84 acres (34ha), the vineyard is fairly large for the appellation, with the oldest vines reaching 90 years, planted on a band of thick clay over deep limestone. No weedkillers, chemical fertilizers, or pesticides are used. With 90% Merlot, and the rest an equal split between the two Cabernets, this is a powerful St-Emilion—one to sink into over a good conversation.

33330 St-Emilion
www.chateau-troplong-mondot.com

Château Trotte Vieille
Premier Grand Cru Classé B

Château Trotte Vieille is owned by merchants Borie-Manoux (the Castéja family). The perfumed, elegant wine is almost 50/50 Merlot and Cabernet Franc, with a drizzle of Cabernet Sauvignon to pump up the tannic structure. Aged in 80% new oak barrels for 18 months, it is then bottled unfiltered. Covering 25 acres (10ha) with an average vine age of 50 years, the wine has sometimes underperformed, but seems on an upward trajectory.

1 Trotte-Vieille, 33330 St-Emilion
05 56 00 00 70

Château de Valandraud

Sometimes it is hard to separate the wine from the myth, and Valandraud has courted, and then suffered from, a lot of story-telling since its launch in 1989. Started from just 1.5 acres (0.6ha) by Jean-Luc Thunevin and his wife Murielle Andraud, it became the most high-profile of the garage movement that swept the Right Bank in the 1990s. This sometimes obscured the real achievement of this quality estate now covering 25 acres (10ha): a wine rich with pure fruits, juicy tannins, and delicate balance. The second wine is Virginie de Valandraud, and there is also 3 de Valandraud, and Blanc de Valandraud No 1 and No 2.

33330 Vignonet
05 57 55 09 13

Château Vieux Pourret

Château Vieux Pourret is a biodynamic property of 15 acres (6ha) that has come to light through a joint venture wine, Dixit, between Rhône legend Michel Tardieu and Bordeaux consultant Olivier Dauga. Entirely hand-harvested, with low-temperature vinification done plot-by-plot in small vats, there is a definite touch of elegance here, with lovely finesse on the finish. The main wine from the estate is equally lovely, with owner Sylvie Richert-Boutet and estate manager Jean Philippe Turtaut bringing out aromas of wild berries and wet stones from the 80% Merlot and 20% Cabernet Franc. ★ **Rising star**

Miaille, 33330 St-Emilion
www.chateau-vieux-pourret.fr

Clos Cantenac

Clos Cantenac is a new name in St-Emilion (in fact, the revival of a very old one) from British wine producer Martin Krajewsi (of Château de Sours in Bordeaux and Songlines in Australia) together with New Zealander Marcus Le Grice. This wine has generous damson and red currant flavors, with velvety tannins and a whacking great dose of attitude. A mix of 90% Merlot with 10% Cabernet Franc, its first vintage was 2007 and managed even in that difficult year to deliver the goods. With just 4.2 acres (1.7ha), there are only 7,500 bottles a year.

33330 St-Emilion
www.closcantenac.com

Clos Fourtet

Premier Grand Cru Classé B
Within easy strolling distance of the main St-Emilion church (there are several, even one underground), the beautiful walled Clos Fourtet has been owned by the Cuvelier family since 2001, with Stéphane Derenoncourt as consultant. Its 47 acres (19ha) are dominated by Merlot (85%), with Cabernet Sauvignon and Cabernet Franc making up the balance. Underneath the château, cut out of the limestone bedrock, are extensive underground cellars where the wine is aged for 16–18 months in 80% new oak barrels. This is a wine that ages easily, and offers a great balance between floral notes, crisp minerality, and solid structure. The second wine is Closerie de Fourtet.

1 Le Châtelet Sud, 33330 St-Emilion
www.closfourtet.com

Clos La Madeleine

Hubert de Boüard of Angélus has been consulting at Clos La Madeleine since 2006. At 5.4 acres (2.2ha), it is tiny for St-Emilion. The vineyard is planted to 75% Merlot, 25% Cabernet Franc, with an average age of 32 years. Subtle and elegant, there is a silky quality to the fruit, and the tannins are well managed, with no over-extraction.

SA du Clos La Madeleine, 33330 St-Emilion
www.closlamadeleine.com

Clos de l'Oratoire Grand Cru Classé

A Stephan von Neipperg property since 1991, he has managed in 20 years to make Clos de l'Oratoire a leading wine of the appellation. The vineyard of 25 acres (10ha) is planted primarily to Merlot, and aged in 70% new oak for an average of 18 months. A flamboyant wine with ripe berry fruits and a well-tuned structure, it needs a little longer to smooth out than some Neipperg wines, but this is built to last, and is definitely a wine to indulge in.

33330 St-Emilion
www.neipperg.com

Clos Saint-Martin Grand Cru Classé

Clos Saint-Martin is one of the smallest classified vineyards at just 3.2 acres (1.3ha), and is a wonderful find. Owned by Sophie Fourcade, the consultant is Michel Rolland and the winemaker Benoît Turbet-Delof. With both the malolactic fermentation and aging taking place in 100% new oak, it definitively punches above its weight. The 75% Merlot takes center-stage in the ripe, ruby-fruit tastes. The same family owns another classified wine, Les Grands Murailles.

33330 St-Emilion
www.lesgrandsmurailles.fr

Couvent des Jacobins Grand Cru Classé

There have been quality issues here in recent years, but Couvent des Jacobins deserves a mention as it offers a taste of history. Owned by Rose Noël Borde, the vines cover 26 acres (10.5ha)—the majority Merlot—and the incredible cellars lie under the center of this medieval village. Rose was born right here, in the former convent that was built in the 13th century, and the label declares *"mise en bouteille au couvent"*. Is all of this enough to try the wine? It is certainly well-structured, and can be charming, but sometimes the fruit can get a little lost.

SCEV Joinaud Borde, rue Guadet, 33330 St-Emilion
www.couventdesjacobins.fr

Le Dôme

Le Dôme comes from a 7.4 acre (3ha) vineyard located on well-drained slopes next to Angélus. Owner Jonathan Maltus now has 128 acres (52ha) on the Right Bank, the majority of which are St-Emilion, many from tiny plots bottled as single-estate wines. Up to three runs of green harvesting reduce yields, and the end result has brooding depths of black currant, with some sweetly charred oak and a perfumed nose. You will not find many wines with this amount of Cabernet Franc—73% in most years.

33330 Vignonet
www.teyssier.fr

Moulin St-Georges

This château is known as a "mini Ausone" because the winemaking team is the same. With 17 acres (7ha) of vines, Merlot accounts for 80%, and the rest is Cabernet Franc. The yields are kept low, and everything is done by hand, with vinification in stainless steel. This is a supremely confident wine, full of rich autumn fruits, and with an edge of blueberries and flint. It is bottled unfiltered. Definitely one to track down and hoard. ★ **Rising star**

33330 St-Emilion
05 57 24 70 26

Vieux Château Mazerat

Jonathan Maltus purchased Vieux Château Mazerat in 2008. This completed a transaction begun 10 years earlier with Le Dôme, as it was then a parcel of vines within this estate. Located in two parts, one near Angélus and the other near Canon, it covers 10 acres (4ha) and is planted to 65% Merlot and 35% Cabernet Franc. Some of the vines date back to 1947 and achieve a depth of flavor that is richly satisfying, combining powerful blueberry with sweet woodsmoke. ★ **Rising star**

33330 St-Emilion
www.teyssier.fr

VIEUX CHATEAU MAZERAT
CRAFTED BY JONATHAN MALTUS, THIS
IS A RICH AND SATISFYING WINE

CHATEAU TROTTE VIEILLE
THE BAR HAS BEEN RAISED AND THIS
ELEGANT WINE IS NOW ONE TO SEEK OUT

POMEROL

Bordeaux wine region
Pomerol wine region (within Bordeaux)

Measuring just under 1,977 acres (800ha), the appellation of Pomerol is not only small, but is also divided up into countless individual plots, with the average vineyard holding just 5.4 acres (2.2ha). In the whole appellation of around 155 properties, there are 50 under 5 acres (2ha), and around 30 under 2.5 acres (1ha)—which is why it is described as the Burgundy of Bordeaux. Ownership tends to lie with small growers, rather than huge corporations as in the Médoc. As is true of much of the Right Bank, Merlot is king in Pomerol, but it has a far fruitier, more powerful expression here even than in neighboring St-Emilion. This is due to a component in the soil known as *crasse de fer* (iron oxide), which brings out flavors of truffle and violets in the wines.

Major grapes

🍇 Reds

Cabernet Franc

Merlot

Vintages

2009

An exceptional year, with near ideal conditions, although hail affected yield in parts. Long-living, expressive wines.

2008

A mixed year, with a damp summer and extended sunny harvest. Largely excellent, but exercise some caution.

2007

A difficult year, with varied results. There are some good, lighter-style wines.

2006

A classic year. Pomerol seemed to do better than many others, particularly the early-ripening Merlot.

2005

Ideal conditions gave rich wines that have a long life ahead of them.

2004

Classic, good-value wines. Producers needed to crop closely to avoid dilution from early rains, but harvest took place in sunny conditions.

2000

The millennium year was particularly successful in Pomerol, giving wines with intensity and rich tannins.

For such a famous name, Pomerol is resolutely—almost willfully—understated. The area is a patchwork of small vineyard plots (planted to 70% Merlot, 25% Cabernet Franc, and 5% Cabernet Sauvignon) with most wine made in modest outbuildings; you can count the number of grand châteaux on one hand. Nowhere is this low-key attitude more clearly embodied than in the region's refusal to classify its wines. If you were to go by the label alone, there is nothing to differentiate the famous and hugely expensive Pétrus or Le Pin from any of their neighbors. This has the effect of keeping many of the best wines as "insider secrets" and also means there are fewer constraints in the vineyard and winery. Talented newcomers have a better chance of establishing themselves here than they would in the Médoc or St-Emilion, where classification still reigns.

In the vineyards, Pomerol is where you are most likely to find everything done by hand, and many techniques, such as green harvesting and plot-by-plot selection, were pioneered here before being adopted across Bordeaux. There is a new rule stating that from 2018, all wines labeled as AC Pomerol must be vinified in the appellation. This is intended to safeguard the integrity of the wines, but threatens some smaller producers, who may be forced to sell rather than build expensive wineries within the boundaries. Conversely, the same rule would favor the bigger names, who may buy up these highly sought-after plots. No final decisions have yet been made, but Pomerol is unused to its private issues becoming political, and the subject is an uncomfortable one.

Vines here date back to Roman times, with the area approaching its current shape during the Middle Ages, through plantings by the religious fraternity of the Hospitaliers de Saint Jean de Jérusalem. The vineyards were then devastated during the Hundred Years' War, but replanted in the following centuries, and have steadily gained in reputation ever since, particularly with the influx of winemakers from the rough-and-tumble Corrèze region of central France in the early 20th century.

More recently, two things have had a profound influence on Pomerol—Michel Rolland and the Moueix family. Rolland inherited a family estate here, Château Le Bon Pasteur, and is the closest thing Bordeaux has to a celebrity. The intensely private Moueix family were part of the wave of migration from Corrèze. Both have indelibly marked the area and its winemaking. Rolland still runs the family estate, along with several others, but it has been his increasing influence as a consultant winemaker that has brought international renown to Pomerol, and encouraged powerful fruit flavors from fully ripe grapes. Jean-Pierre Moueix was born in Corrèze in 1913, and moved to St-Emilion with his parents following the 1929 depression. In 1937, he founded a wine merchant business on the Quai du Priourat in Libourne and his son Christian now runs the business, Etablissement JP Moueix, along with several leading estates including Trotanoy and Hosanna. Jean-Pierre's other son, Jean-François, owns Pétrus and a wine merchant house, Duclot. Between them, they distribute or own more than half the properties in Pomerol.

POMEROL

Covering just under 2,000 acres (800ha), this appellation is far smaller than the neighboring St-Emilion. The grapes that can be turned into the renowned and sought-after AC Pomerol wines come primarily from countless small plots surrounding the tiny villages of Pomerol, Catusseau, Le Grand Moulinet, and Pignon. Wine from the neighboring communes of Néac and Lalande-de Pomerol qualify for the AC named after the latter.

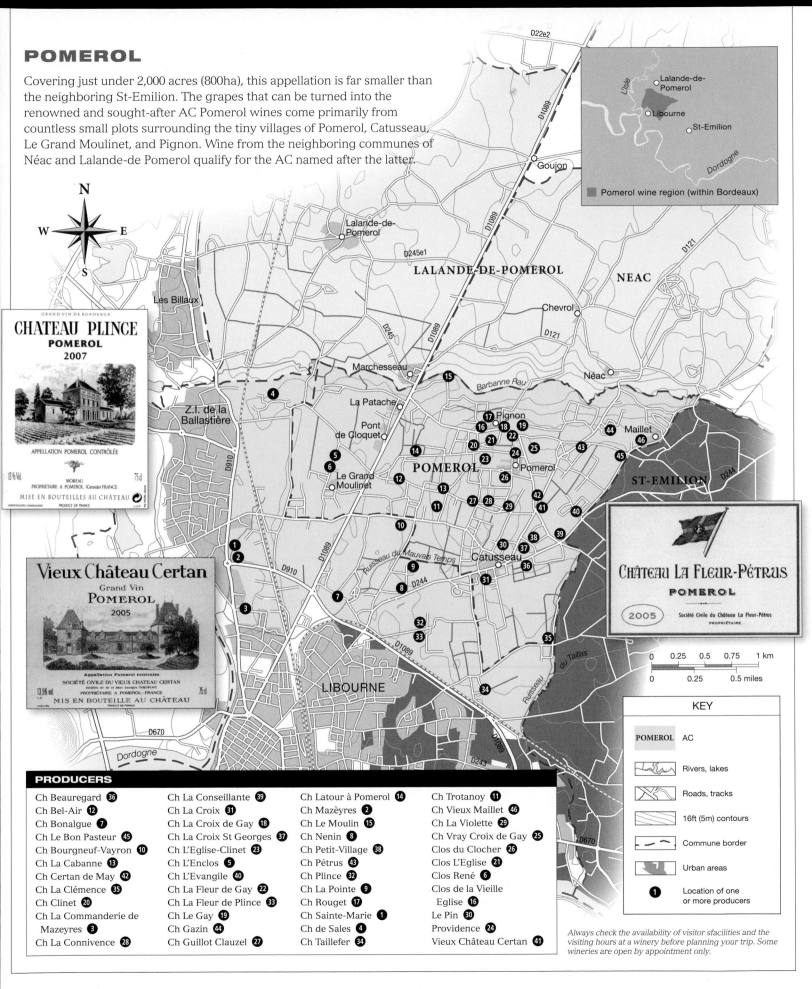

Pomerol wine region (within Bordeaux)

PRODUCERS

Ch Beauregard ㊱	Ch La Conseillante ㊴	Ch Latour à Pomerol ⑭	Ch Trotanoy ⑪
Ch Bel-Air ⑫	Ch La Croix ㉛	Ch Mazèyres ②	Ch Vieux Maillet ㊻
Ch Bonalgue ⑦	Ch La Croix de Gay ⑱	Ch Le Moulin ⑮	Ch La Violette ㉙
Ch Le Bon Pasteur ㊺	Ch La Croix St Georges ㊲	Ch Nenin ⑧	Ch Vray Croix de Gay ㉕
Ch Bourgneuf-Vayron ⑩	Ch L'Eglise-Clinet ㉓	Ch Petit-Village ㊳	Clos du Clocher ㉖
Ch La Cabanne ⑬	Ch L'Enclos ⑤	Ch Pétrus ㊸	Clos L'Eglise ㉑
Ch Certan de May ㊷	Ch L'Evangile ㊵	Ch Plince ㉜	Clos René ⑥
Ch La Clémence ㉟	Ch La Fleur de Gay ㉒	Ch La Pointe ⑨	Clos de la Vieille
Ch Clinet ⑳	Ch La Fleur de Plince ㉝	Ch Rouget ⑰	Eglise ⑯
Ch La Commanderie de	Ch Le Gay ⑲	Ch Sainte-Marie ①	Le Pin ㉚
Mazeyres ③	Ch Gazin ㊹	Ch de Sales ④	Providence ㉔
Ch La Connivence ㉘	Ch Guillot Clauzel ㉗	Ch Taillefer ㉞	Vieux Château Certan ㊶

KEY

POMEROL AC

Rivers, lakes

Roads, tracks

16ft (5m) contours

Commune border

Urban areas

① Location of one or more producers

Always check the availability of visitor sfacilities and the visiting hours at a winery before planning your trip. Some wineries are open by appointment only.

CHATEAU LA CROIX
PATIENCE IS NEEDED BEFORE ENJOYING
THIS DENSE AND MUSCULAR WINE

CHATEAU LA CONSEILLANTE
ONE OF POMEROL'S MOST EXCITING ESTATES,
WHERE INNOVATIVE TECHNIQUES ARE USED

Château Beauregard

The 43 acre (17.5ha) vineyard of Château Beauregard delivers star-bright colors and flavors, with tightly packed fruit (70% Merlot, 30% Cabernet Franc). This has the punch that Pomerol just loves to deliver, with smoothed-out tannins. It is one of the very few "proper" châteaux in the appellation (so attractive that the Guggenheim family commissioned a replica on Long Island). Since the early 1990s, owners Vignobles Foncier have renovated the vineyard, winery, and barrel cellars. The second wine, Benjamin de Beauregard, is lighter in alcohol with a higher percentage of Cabernet Franc.

1 Beauregard, 33500 Pomerol
www.chateau-beauregard.com

Château Bel-Air

The 32 acre (13ha) Château Bel-Air has been owned by the Sudrat-Melet family since 1914. The fresh, plummy wine is 95% Merlot and 5% Cabernet Franc and has improved markedly in recent years. The planting density of vines has been increased and maturity levels have been improved by more specific plot-by-plot harvesting. Particular mention should go to their second wine, Château L'Hermitage de Bel-Air, which is good quality and excellent value. The same family owns Château Beauséjour in Fronsac.

33500 Pomerol
vignsudrat-melet@wanadoo.fr

Château Bonalgue

The Bourotte family of Clos du Clocher has owned Château Bonalgue since the 1920s. The 17 acre (7ha) estate on sandy-clay-gravel soil has the iron-rich seams so typical of the appellation and this is reflected in the 90/10 split of Merlot and Cabernet Franc. Michel Rolland is consultant winemaker, with Jean-Baptiste Bourotte in charge of the daily running of the estate. Steady improvements are further raising the game at this reputable château, with higher density planting, better quality rootstocks, and careful pruning to reduce yield all starting to produce results. Recent vintages have seen a flashy, hedonistic style that is highly appealing.

24 rue de Bonalgue, 33500 Libourne
www.vignoblesbourotte.com

Château Le Bon Pasteur

Château Le Bon Pasteur is Michel Rolland's home estate and, as such, expectations are pretty high. Owned with his wife Dany since 1978, there are just 17 acres (7ha), which are not on the Pomerol plateau. Nevertheless, he gets many of his key philosophies across in this highly pleasurable wine. Made from 90% Merlot and 10% Cabernet Franc, yields are kept very low through winter pruning and green harvesting in the summer, with 40-year-old vines offering complexity and intense flavors. The grapes are, of course, picked as late as possible for optimum ripeness. Stainless steel vats are used for the fermentation, and are open to facilitate the punching down. The wine spends 18 months in oak barrels (80% of which are new). Bottled unfined and unfiltered, undertones of sweet mocha and cassis add real charm to the gripping tannins.

Maillet, 33500 Pomerol
rolland-vignobles@wanadoo.fr

Château Bourgneuf-Vayron

Château Bourgneuf-Vayron produces wine with serious tannins, bedded in for a long life, but with the padding of a smoked meat and licorice core, and plenty of toasty oak. All of this suggests a big wine and this is indeed a little-known Pomerol that is going places. Xavier and Dominique Vayron own this 22 acre (9ha) estate, a single, Merlot-dominated plot right next to Trotanoy. Since 2008, their daughters Frédérique and Marie have taken charge, following a tradition in their family that dates back at this property to 1831. ★ **Rising star**

1 le Bourg Neuf, 33500 Pomerol; visits by appointment only
chateaubourgneufvayron@wanadoo.fr

Château La Cabanne

The owners of Château La Cabanne belong to the community of winemakers in Pomerol who can trace their ancestry back to the Corrèze region, moving here in the early 20th century. The Estager family first founded a wine company and then bought this 22 acre (9ha) estate, producing 50,000 bottles, in 1934. Truffles and spice make this a complex and warming wine, with a delicious savory edge. Merlot features heavily, with just 8% Cabernet Franc. François Estager is in charge, and the family also owns the tiny 5 acre (2ha) Château Plincette, which has up to 30% Cabernet Franc in the mix.

33–41 rue de Montaudon, 33500 Libourne
estager@estager.com

Château Certan de May

The 12 acre (5ha) vineyard of Château Certan de May is right opposite Le Pin. It is owned by Odette Barreau, with her son Jean Luc, and produces 24,000 bottles of wine with a gorgeous floral nose, and crushed violets on the palate. A smoky cedar edge gives it added complexity and, although the tannins are more than evident, there is a freshness to the finish. The vineyard consists of 70% Merlot, 25% Cabernet Franc, and 5% Cabernet Sauvignon—vinified in stainless steel and given 16 months in new oak (40% new).

33500 Pomerol
chateau.certan-de-may@wanadoo.fr

Château Certan Marzelle

The wine of Château Certan Marzelle is deep ruby red in color and, unusually, 100% Merlot. This 5 acre (2ha) estate is right next to Providence and Château Hosanna, and is also owned by Ets JP Moueix. The fairly young vines (25 years old) produce 10,000 bottles with rich red-cherry flavors and a lovely sweet nose, and the 50% new oak adds a smoky complexity that is charming. It is certain to improve as the vines age further.

No visitor facilities
www.moueix.com

Château La Clémence

Château La Clémence is owned by Christian and Anne-Marie Dauriac, who are both doctors when not working in the vineyard. The tiny 7.4 acre (3ha) estate, producing 6,000 bottles, has a glamorous circular cellar constructed from wood, glass, and exposed stone. Winemaking is traditional—and then some—this is one place where you might even see the grapes being trodden by foot during harvest. The vines are split over six plots from rich clay to poor gravel, and the 85%

Merlot and 15% Cabernet Franc vines have an average age of 50 years. Michel Rolland also works his magic here, coaxing out rich, silky textures and a toasty finish to go with the brambly fruits.

Lieu-dit Toutlifaut, 33500 Pomerol
www.vignobles-dauriac.com

Château Clinet

Château Clinet had a bumpy history until the 1980s, but this is now a château to watch, making a polyphenol-rich, exuberant, and powerful wine. Owned by Jean-Louis Laborde, with Michel Rolland as consultant, there has been extensive replanting of the 22 acres (9ha) of 85% Merlot, 10% Cabernet Sauvignon, and 5% Cabernet Franc. (This is significantly less Cabernet Sauvignon than a decade ago.) Sustainable practices have also been introduced in the vineyard. The wine is aged in barrels (60% new) for around 19 months. Laborde also owns Château Pajzos in Hungary.

chemin de Feytit, 33500 Pomerol
www.chateauclinet.fr

Château La Commanderie de Mazeyres

The vineyard at Château La Commanderie de Mazeyres has 45% Cabernet Franc to 55% Merlot, a huge amount for an appellation where Merlot is very definitely king. The 25 acre (10ha) estate has been owned since 2000 by Clément Fayat of La Dominique in St-Emilion. He has invested heavily in renewing the vineyard and the cellars. Jean-Luc Thunevin is the consultant, and all winemaking takes place in small wooden vats, with malolactic fermentation entirely in new barrels. There is fining, but no filtration. You get all the sexy immediacy that you want from a good Pomerol, with a beautiful fragrant nose and gentle spiciness from the Cabernet Franc. The second wine is Château Closerie Mazeyres.

Chemin du Vélodrome, 33500 Pomerol
info@vignobles.fayat-group.com

Château La Connivence

A completely new estate is a rare thing in Pomerol, but the 3.7 acre (1.5ha) Château La Connivence will release its first wine in 2010 (the 2008 had just 2,000 bottles). Four friends are behind the idea: Alexandre de Malet Roquefort (of Château La Gaffelière); local businessman Jean-Luc Deloche; and two footballers from the Bordeaux and French national teams, Matthieu Chalmé and Johan Micoud. So far, so blockbuster. The surprising thing is the elegance that you find here. Perhaps aided by consultant Stéphane Derenoncourt, there is unmistakable power but the final impression is of fresh black currant leaf and pure red fruits. The second wine is La Belle Connivence.

33500 Pomerol
www.chateaulaconnivence.com

Château La Conseillante

The exuberant wine of Château La Conseillante, with juicy black fruits and sweet oak (90% new), is rightly seen as one of the most exciting of the appellation. Owned by the Nicolas-Artefeuille family, with Jean Michel Laporte as director, there are 30 acres (12ha) of vines (86% Merlot/ 14% Cabernet Franc). There are plenty of modern techniques, from cold soaking to micro-oxygenation and co-innoculation (initiating both alcoholic and malolactic fermentation at the same time), with meticulous attention to detail throughout. On the palate, there is firm red fruit, red currants, and black cherries; a textured, confident wine and very successful.

130 rue Catusseau, 33500 Pomerol
www.laconseillante.fr

Château La Croix

Château La Croix is the largest Janoueix property in this appellation at 25 acres (10ha). The complex and varied terroir is reflected in the plantings of a 40% split between Cabernet Franc and Cabernet Sauvignon, together with 60% Merlot. Dense and muscular, with a firm tannic structure and well-defined black currant and cigar box flavors, this is a wine to put away for a few years, allowing the massive structure to soften a little.

Catusseau, 33500 Pomerol
www.j-janoueix-bordeaux.com

Château La Croix de Gay

Dr Alain Reynaud, former owner of Quinault L'Enclos in St-Emilion, has kept hold of his family's Château La Croix de Gay and continues to run it with his sister Chantal Lebreton. There are 23 acres (9.5ha) of mainly Merlot vines, at around 75%, with the rest being Cabernet Franc. A perfumed and silky wine, with crushed raspberries and a gentle waft of percolating coffee. Only 36,000 bottles a year are produced from low-yielding vines, with a cold soak before vinification and careful oaking to give a subtle but warming finish. It is reliable and well priced.

8 route St-Jacques de Compostelle, 33500 Pomerol
contact@chateau-lacroixdegay.com

Château La Croix St Georges

Château la Croix St Georges is a Janoueix wine from 10 acres (4ha) of vines right next to Le Pin. The wine is made from a tub-thumping 95% Merlot on clay–gravel soils rich in *crasse de fer*, which gives the grape a power and generosity that is so unmistakably Pomerol.
The 5% Cabernet Franc lends a gentle elegance to the finish, but this is a blockbuster of a wine that demands to be lingered over. Jean-Philippe Janoueix is in charge at the estate, and has worked intensively at lowering yields and ensuring the vineyard is meticulously cared for. Around 21,000 bottles are produced each year.

Rue de Catusseau, 33500 Pomerol
info@j-janoueix-bordeaux.com

Château L'Eglise-Clinet

Château L'Eglise-Clinet has been owned by the intelligent and forthright Denis Durantou since 1982, with 13.5 acres (5.5ha) of 45-year-old Merlot (85%) and Cabernet Franc (15%) vines. The property itself only came into existence in the 1950s, but has since risen to prominence as one of the best in the appellation, with tightly knit black fruits, rich licorice, and sweet chestnut flavors, all helped by 18 months aging in small oak barrels (70% new). The second wine is La Petite L'Eglise. Durantou also owns a property in Lalande-de-Pomerol, Château Les Cruzelle, as well as a small wine merchants.

10 rue de Catusseau, 33500 Pomerol
www.eglise-clinet.com

MICHEL ROLLAND

Before Michel Rolland, the idea that a visiting winemaker could sprinkle celebrity stardust on a property was unheard of. However, this charismatic man, who was born in Pomerol and still lives in the appellation, has managed to not only establish himself as the world's leading consultant, but also opened the way for others to follow in his footsteps. Today, Rolland consults for over 100 wineries across 12 countries, with star estates such as Masseto in Italy and Harlan in Napa, not to mention a roll-call of big players in Bordeaux, from Pavie to Pape Clément. He also owns (or part owns) several estates himself, including Château Le Bon Pasteur in Pomerol, Bonne Nouvelle in South Africa, and Clos de los Siete in Argentina. His philosophy of winemaking is equally well known—pick grapes only when fully ripe, and ensure the fruit is the real star.

CHATEAU L'ENCLOS
LOW YIELDS AND CLOSE ATTENTION
TO THE WINEMAKING RESULT IN A
DECADENT, LUXURIOUS WINE

CHATEAU GAZIN
A CLASSIC POMEROL WITH A MINTY
CHARACTER AND POWERFUL BODY

Château L'Enclos

A touch of Malbec at Château L'Enclos adds depth and complexity to the Merlot (79%) and Cabernet Franc (19%) vines. Owned by Stephen Adams of Château Fonplégade, the estate covers 25 acres (10ha) on gravel and flinty soils, with some sand. Yields are kept very low, producing around 48,000 bottles—everything is done by hand and the wines undergo cold soaking before vinification, followed by 18 months in barrel (50% new oak). The result is luxurious and a little decadent, with dark chocolate and plump blackberry fruitiness. There are plans to invest in both the vineyard and cellars, and Gilles Paquet has been brought on board as consultant. This already lovely wine is likely to strengthen further over the next few years.

3 rue de Bergerac, 33200 Pineuilh
www.chateaulenclos.fr

Château L'Evangile

Château L'Evangile has been a Lafite Rothschild outreach project on the Right Bank since 1990. The same team—led by Charles Chevallier—ensures that tight tannins and inky concentration keep it in the family. The 40 acre (16ha) vineyard is planted to 80% Merlot and 20% Cabernet Franc over a bed of sand, clay, and gravel. The resulting wine is powerful but restrained, with 18 months spent in 70% new oak barrels. The second wine, Blason de l'Evangile, has a higher proportion of Cabernet Franc, and spends less time in barrel.

33500 Pomerol
www.lafite.com

Château La Fleur de Gay

Château La Fleur de Gay is a small-production wine from 7.4 acres (3ha) of vines belonging to Alain Reynaud of La Croix de Gay. This is produced in a separate winery, and comes from two plots of old vines that have excellent clay–limestone and gravel terroir. First produced in 1983, this is aged in 100% new oak and is a truly gorgeous wine, full of precise flavors of dark fruits, with a licorice and cigar box edge. With real aging potential, this is one of the small-scale stars of Pomerol.

Pignon, 33500 Pomerol
contact@chateau-lafleurdegay.com

Château La Fleur de Plince

At 0.69 acres (0.28ha), Château La Fleur de Plince just might be the smallest estate in Pomerol. The owner Pierre Choukroun lived in Pomerol until he was 14, when he moved away. Coming back in 1998, he bought a few rows of vines and built a tiny winery that makes full use of the term "garage wine". Everything here is farmed organically, and there is a traditional vertical wine press with which he manually presses the grapes. Just 1,600 bottles are produced of this well-textured, concentrated, and powerful wine, from 90% Merlot and 10% Cabernet Franc. He also owns the slightly larger (6 acre/2.5ha) Château La Fleur Haut Brisson in AC Côtes de Castillon.

Chemin de Plince, 33500 Pomerol
05 57 74 15 26

Château Lafleur-Gazin

Lafleur-Gazin is located, as the name suggests, between Château Lafleur and Château Gazin. It is intense without being brooding and has a clean sweetness to the fruit, with cedarwood and barbecue smoke on the nose. Owned by the Delefour-Borderie family, this 21 acre (8.5ha) estate of 80% Merlot and 20% Cabernet Franc is under the management and distribution of Ets JP Moueix.

No visitor facilities
www.moueix.com

Château La Fleur-Pétrus

Château La Fleur-Pétrus' vineyard is 37acres (15ha), right next to Pétrus, but with more gravel in the terroir. It was enlarged with a parcel bought from Château Le Gay in 1994. Owned by the Moueix family, the wine is full of intensity, with a perfumed, spicy nose. Rich fruit and good extraction bring flavors of coffee and licorice, while the 20% Cabernet Franc brings elegance.

No visitor facilities
www.moueix.com

Château Le Gay

Château Le Gay is 15 acres (6ha) of prime Pomerol soil, planted to 65% Merlot and 35% Cabernet Franc, with old vines and tiny yields. Catherine Péré-Vergé bought this estate in 2002, and has worked hard to raise its prestige—not too tough for a château that neighbors Vieux Château Certan. She has Michel Rolland casting an eye over the winemaking, and vinifies in large wooden vats designed by upmarket barrel maker Seguin-Moreau. A heady mix of violet and truffle is immediately apparent in the glass, and it does not disappoint on the palate.

Grand Moulinet, 33500 Pomerol
05 57 51 61 06

Château Gazin

Château Gazin has 57 acres (23ha) under vine (over 3% of the appellation) right on the Pomerol plateau. The vineyard is 90% Merlot, 3% Cabernet Franc, and 7% Cabernet Sauvignon. There is a lovely minty freshness on the finish of this wine, and a powerful core, creating the elegant and classic Pomerol signature that owner Nicolas de Baillencourt looks for. The château building itself is equally impressive, featuring a winery equipped with small concrete vats. There is an excellent second wine, L'Hospitalet de Gazin.

33500 Pomerol
www.chateau-gazin.com

Château La Grave à Pomerol

Château La Grave à Pomerol is at the northeast corner of Pomerol, just next to the Lalande-de-Pomerol border. This is another estate that the Moueix family farmed for years, before purchasing it in 1997. There is a slightly lighter take on the Pomerol theme here, with 85% Merlot and 15% Cabernet Franc vines (averaging 20 years) on 19.5 acres (8ha) of gravelly soils. The aging ensures the fruit stays paramount; the barrels for aging are 25% new, keeping the toast down and minerality up.

No visitor facilities
www.moueix.com

Château Guillot Clauzel

A name to remember, the 4.2 acre (1.7ha) Château Guillot Clauzel is right on the plateau, within nodding distance of Le Pin and Trotanoy. It is run by owner Etienne Clauzel, with commercial advice from Dominique Thienpont, and François Despagne as winemaker since 2002. This is a dream team and, in their hands, the vineyard of 15% Cabernet Franc and 85% Merlot produces a feminine, soft, and voluptuous Pomerol with grilled almond notes from 16 months in barrel (60% new oak). Truffles and leather on the finish make this stand out even further, and the price—for now—remains reasonable. ★ **Rising star**

1 Chemin de Nénin, 33500 Pomerol
05 57 51 14 09

Château Hosanna

Château Hosanna has been fully owned by Christian Moueix since 1999. Full of chewy tannins, with chocolate, mocha, and licorice, but with a softer side that comes in through a perfumed nose and gentle floral finish. With 11 acres (4.5ha) of vines, planted to 70% Merlot and a high 30% Cabernet Franc, this needs a good few years to age before the tannins start to relax. Recent years have seen new drainage channels and increased foliage area.

No visitor facilities
www.moueix.com

Château Lagrange

Gravel-rich soil at Château Lagrange has recently been replanted with 95% Merlot, and just a smattering of Cabernet Franc to add a touch of white pepper. The 21 acres (8.5ha) are well-located next to the Pomerol church, and the wine is fermented in concrete tanks, then aged in oak barrels (30% new) for 18 months. Owned by Ets JP Moueix since the early 1950s, this is a popular, succulent wine that is all about rich red fruits and supple tannins.

No visitor facilities
www.moueix.com

Château Latour à Pomerol

Château Latour à Pomerol is a big, well-extracted wine made and distributed by the Moueix stable, but owned by the Fondation de Foyers de Charité de Châteauneuf de Galaure (a gift from former owner Lily Lacoste before her death in 2002). Picking dates are very precise for such a small property of 20 acres (8ha) and are carried out according to the age of the vines. Quiet power and complexity are the keys here—90% Merlot, 10% Cabernet Franc, aged in 30% new oak, and bottled unfiltered.

No visitor facilities
www.moueix.com

Château Mazèyres

Full of smoky overtones and ripe fruits, the wine of Château Mazèyres is a classic mix of 80% Merlot and 20% Cabernet Franc. An Alain Moueix estate and, while not biodynamic, it is TerraVitis, meaning sustainable practices across the 54 acres (22ha). In the cellar, small vats allow for plot-by-plot vinification, which is essential here as the vineyards are treated to different regimes according to their soil and location. There is good structure to the wine, less exuberant than some Pomerol, but very accomplished. The wine is aged in 50% new oak, with no filtration. The second wine is Seuil de Mazèyres.

56 avenue Georges Pompidou, 33500 Libourne
www.mazeyres.com

CHATEAU PETIT-VILLAGE
THE VISITOR CENTER AND THE GRAVELLY SOIL MAKE THIS ESTATE STAND OUT IN POMEROL

CHATEAU LAGRANGE
A SUCCULENT WINE, WITH 95% MERLOT, WHICH ATTRACTS THE CROWDS

Château Le Moulin

Château Le Moulin is a tiny property of 6 acres (2.5ha) with a modern, flamboyant style, run by Michel Querre. Expect big, confident flavors of fig, chocolate, cassis, and roasted herbs, which have a long life ahead of them. This will need decanting and allowed a few hours to open up when young, but the rewards are impressive. The grape mix is a classic 80% Merlot to 20% Cabernet Franc, but the clay–gravel soil is worked carefully, and yields are kept very low. In the winery, the wooden vats are kept open during punching down in the Burgundian style, and everything is kept in 100% new oak for both malolactic and aging. The second wine is Le Petit Moulin.

Moulin de Lavaud, La Patache, 33500 Pomerol
www.moulin-pomerol.com

Château Nenin

The Delon family of Léoville-Las-Cases took over Château Nenin in 1997, and have been busy restoring and renovating ever since. The vineyard was badly affected by the 1956 frosts, and even the newly replanted vines were neglected. All this has changed, with an extra 10 acres (4ha) from Château Certan-Giraud (no longer in existence) bringing the total to 81 acres (33ha). Extensive replanting has taken place, Cabernet Franc has been raised to 40%, canopy cover has increased, and picking takes place according to the age of the vines. As a result of all this, the big robust flavors that Pomerol does so well are now evident. Jacques Depoizier is director, working with his son Jérome and the consultant Jacques Boissenot. The second wine is Fugue de Nenin.

66 route de Montagne, 33500 Libourne
www.chateau-nenin.com

Château Petit-Village

Gravelly terroir at Château Petit-Village means this is one of the few Pomerol wines with a significant amount of Cabernet Sauvignon—up to 18% of the blend—together with 78% Merlot and 5% Cabernet Franc. This should make the owners—AXA Millésimes of Château Pichon-Baron in Pauillac, with Christian Seely as director and Stéphane Derenoncourt consulting—feel right at home. Serious tannin means it needs a few years to develop in bottle, after which it reveals beautiful, perky black fruits and rich concentration. New cellars and a visitor center designed by architect Alain Triaud have helped make this a real destination for visitors to Pomerol.

33500 Pomerol
www.petit-village.com

Château Pétrus

This is a lush, perfumed wine that manages to transform the Merlot grape into something unforgettable. Château Pétrus is on the highest point of the Pomerol plateau, at around 131ft (40m). The soil is quite different from its neighbors, with a band of iron-rich clay at around 28in (70cm) deep. Together with the 40-year-old vines (planted to 95% Merlot and 5% Cabernet Franc), this gives a rich and complex wine that is famously hedonistic, yet has real delicacy, without any one element being overly insistent. Owned by Jean-Francois Moueix, the enologist is youthful Olivier Berrouet, who took over from his father Jean-Claude in 2008 and has since introduced a few changes. The grapes are still vinified in cement tanks, still aged in 50% new oak, and treated as gently as ever.

CHATEAU VIEUX MAILLET
RECENT RESTORATION IS PRODUCING
A SUBTLE WINE DESTINED FOR
GREATER RECOGNITION

In 2009, Pétrus used a laser optical sorting machine for the first time, and the team is now in-house, rather than working across the Moueix properties.

No visitor facilities
www.moueix.com

Château Plince

Owned by the Moreau family (but managed by Moueix), Château Plince is a good-value wine that offers sweet fruit combined with evident new oak. Planting at this 21 acre (8.6ha) property is 72% Merlot, 23% Cabernet Franc, and 5% Cabernet Sauvignon. Green harvesting has been introduced here recently, and this previous workhorse—one of the very few to use mechanical harvesting—is starting to shine. The second wine is Pavillon Plince.

Chemin de Plince, 33500 Libourne
http://chateauplince.chez-alice.fr

Château La Pointe

Château La Pointe produces a wine that is truly pleasurable to drink, with soft silky tannins and lovely raspberry and plum fruits. Things are changing at this estate since its purchase by Generali France in 2007. Eric Monneret has been installed as director, and the new consultant is Hubert de Boüard. Often maligned for its sandy terroir, a geological survey of the 54 acres (22ha) has revealed far greater complexity, and planting changes have been introduced. The grape varieties are 85% Merlot and 15% Cabernet Franc (the last Cabernet Sauvignon was uprooted in 2008). The winery has also been renovated with smaller vats to fine-tune the blending process. Aging takes place in oak barrels (50% new). ★ **Rising star**

33501 Pomerol
www.chateaulapointe.com

Château Rouget

Proving that France's iconic wine regions can get along, Eduard Labruyère's family owns Domaines Jacques Prieur in Burgundy, and bought the 44 acre (18ha) Château Rouget in 1992. "Burgundians cultivate the vineyards like gardens, with small plots; Pomerol is very much like that, so we felt at home," he says. Not strictly organic, but the viticulture is sustainable, and the vinification has some distinctly Burgundian touches, such as open vats and naturally started malolactic, even if that means waiting until spring. This is a happy marriage of the two cultures, with sour cherry and toasty oak. The second wine is Vieux Château des Templiers. Michel Rolland is consultant.

6 route de St-Jacques de Compostelle, 33500 Pomerol
www.chateau-rouget.com

Château Sainte-Marie

Château Sainte-Marie is an 11 acre (4.5ha) family estate making 30,000 bottles a year. Farmed entirely sustainably, all vineyard work is carried out by hand. The blend of 80% Merlot, 15% Cabernet Sauvignon, and just 5% Cabernet Franc gives this wine a firm structure and tightly knit black fruits. Integral vinification and aging take place in 100% new oak barrels. The wine is not released for sale until it has settled in the bottle for a further nine months (in a style more typical of Rioja than Bordeaux).

41 avenue Georges Pompidou, 33500 Libourne
www.chateau-sainte-jacques-pomerol.com

Château de Sales

Château de Sales is the largest property in Pomerol and is also one of the oldest, having stayed in the same family for over 500 years. It is run today by Bruno de Lambert and the wines are traditional in style (70% Merlot and an even split between the two Cabernets). Firm red fruits and natural fruit tannins are emphasized by spending just six months in barrel, with only 5% new oak. The estate covers 119 acres (48ha) of vines, with the same again of parkland and forest, farmed sustainably. The second label, Château Chantaloulette, is a pleasant early drinker.

11 chemin Sales, 33500 Libourne
www.chateau-de-sales.com

Château Taillefer

Catherine Moueix is in charge at this understated property. There has been a concentration on meticulous practices in the vineyard and winery in recent years. Denis Dubordieu is the consulting enologist; a man known for his light touch, and a good reflection of the philosophy of the estate. In style, expect an elegant rendering of the Pomerol flavor profile, with 25% Cabernet Franc suiting the sandy-gravel soils and coaxing out a fragrant wildflower nose from the wine. On the border with St-Emilion, Château Taillefer covers just under 31 acres (13ha). The winery has been fully renovated with small cement vats. The wine then spends one year in finely grained oak (33% new).

33500 Libourne
www.chateautaillefer.com

Château Trotanoy

Château Trotanoy is a long-standing Moueix estate—less celebrated than Pétrus but not a million miles away in style. Silky-smooth fruits, with a rich tannic structure from the 18 acres (7.3ha) of 90% Merlot, 10% Cabernet Franc. The name (originally *trop ennuie*) comes from the fact that the soil was so difficult to work. It escaped the frost in 1956, so the vines here are particularly old for the appellation. Winter pruning is more important than green harvesting. Vinified in concrete vats, with 50% new oak barrels, this has enormous concentration.

No visitor facilities
www.moueix.com

Château Vieux Maillet

Château Vieux Maillet is an attractive property that has been under new Belgian-French ownership since 2003. Isabelle and Baudoin Motte have had the vat rooms and cellars fully restored. The wine, from 90% Merlot and 10% Cabernet Franc over a tiny 6.4 acres (2.6ha), is aged in 60% new oak. The changes are coming through in the wine, with good acidity, structured tannins, and well balanced ripe fruit. A subtle wine compared to some from the appellation, with good potential.

16 Chemin de Maillet, 33500 Pomerol
www.chateauvieuxmaillet.com

Château La Violette

Catherine Péré-Vergé, assisted by her own excellent team and Michel Rolland, has given Château La Violette a new lease of life. Older vintages are more variable but today, this 8 acre (3.3ha) estate, located by La Croix and Le Pin,

CHATEAU LA POINTE
THIS WINE CAN BE DRUNK NOW BUT WILL
ALSO AGE WELL FOR UP TO 20 YEARS

is producing a low-yield, enormous wine. It is full of licorice, black fruits, and dark chocolate, which are becoming the calling cards of a crowd-pleasing Pomerol.

33570 Montagne
s.dumas@tiscali.fr

Château Vray Croix de Gay

Château Vray Croix de Gay is one of the few properties on the Pomerol plateau that remains affordable. The 9 acres (3.7ha) of vines are divided into three plots, the largest of which adjoins Pétrus, planted to 82% Melot and 18% Cabernet Franc. Owned by Aline and Paul Goldschmidt of Domaines Baronne Guichard, their enologist Yannick Reyrel trained at Pétrus, and the consultant since 2006 is Stéphane Derenoncourt. Double-sorting in the vineyard and plot-by-plot vinification are now standard, and the final wine spends 18 months in oak (40% new). The second wine, L'Enchanteur, comes from younger vines, and is fleshier, with red summer fruits (100% Merlot) replacing the richer, more truffle-filled autumnal ones.

33500 Pomerol
chateausiaurac@aoc.com

Clos du Clocher

Clos du Clocher covers 18 acres (7.3ha), in two parcels, close to the Pomerol church. Owner Jean-Baptiste Bourotte of Audy Négociants in Libourne coaxes well-defined blackberry and loganberry flavors from his 80% Merlot, 20% Cabernet Franc, with an underlying freshness and gently perfumed nose that keeps the meaty tannins well in balance. Michel Rolland is the enologist. A new winery is due to open in 2012, continuing the serious quality strides that have been made in recent years. The family owns several other Right Bank properties.   ★ **Rising star**

57 rue de Catusseau, 33500 Pomerol
www.vignoblesbourotte.com

Clos L'Eglise

Hélène and Patrice Garcin-Levèque own this 12 acre (5ha) Pomerol estate, together with Barde-Haut in St-Emilion, Haut-Bergey in Pessac-Léognan, and Poesia in Argentina. The vineyard is 60% Merlot/40% Cabernet Franc and produces a lovely wine with soft caramel aromas and delicate woodsmoke. With Alain Reynaud as consultant, they pick the grapes earlier than some to ensure full aromatic potential. The new winery is laid out to use gravity to maximum effect, with manual punching down of the cap in the Burgundy fashion.

1 Feytit Clinet, 33500 Pomerol
www.vignoblesgarcin.com

Clos René

Jean-Marie Garde, president of the local wine syndicate, owns the 30 acre (12ha) Clos René. The nearest neighbor of Château L'Enclos, with Michel Rolland as consultant, its wines (72,000 bottles) offer excellent value. An unusual 10% Malbec in this wine gives a deep color and rich spicy undertones. The balance is 70% Merlot and 20% Cabernet Franc. Oak aging is kept to 25% new barrels, balancing sweet woodsmoke and brambly fruits.

Grand Moulinet, 33500 Pomerol
05 57 51 10 41

Clos de la Vieille Eglise

Jean-Louis Trocard is in charge at Clos de la Vieille Eglise. Part of one of the oldest families on the Right Bank he also owns, among others, Clos Debreuil in St-Emilion. This is a small estate, with 3.7 acres (1.5ha) of 70% Merlot and 30% Cabernet Franc on clay–gravel soils, in the center of the appellation. The wine has wonderful blueberry and red currant flavors, dusted with mocha. It is worked gently, with vinification at low temperatures, then both malolactic and aging in 100% new oak (for up to 20 months to fully charge up the toast factor).

2 les Jays-Ouest, 33570 Les-Artigues-de-Lussac
www.trocard.com

Le Pin

Easily the smallest of the Bordeaux Big Guns, Le Pin has 5.4 acres (2ha), but had one plot pulled up for replanting in 2009 so has just 4.8 acres (1.95ha) until 2012. As with Pétrus, its terroir differs from surrounding properties. Here you find 10ft (3m) of deep gravel, planted to 100% Merlot (there is some Cabernet Franc, but this does not make it into the final wine). First produced in 1979, it is owned by Jacques Thienpont and Fiona Morrison, with Alexandre Thienpont as estate manager and co-owner. Around 6,000–7,000 bottles are produced each year, usually sold in cases of six or even three. The vinification takes place in stainless steel with oak barrels for malolactic and aging. Depending on the vintage, the wine stays in barrel for 18–22 months, all new oak, medium toast. It is more profoundly opulent than Pétrus, with layers of silky fruit and a sensuous touch that many compare to the best burgundies.

33500 Pomerol
wine@thienpont-etikhove.be

Providence

Providence was bought by the Moueix family in 2005, and has been completely renovated since. For a start, they dropped the Château from the name, thus cleverly ramping up a sense of drama. Work in the vineyard has been increased, with careful green harvesting and leaf removal. The wine (90% Merlot, 10% Cabernet Franc) is fermented in stainless steel tanks, then aged for 18 months in oak barrels, of which 33% are new. There is a deep, controlled sense of extraction that has been evident in all the Moueix bottlings, and the structure clearly makes it a long player.

7–8 route de Tropchaud, 33500 Pomerol
www.moueix.com

Vieux Château Certan

Vieux Château Certan is the oldest château in Pomerol, with parts of the building dating back to the 12th century. The wine itself is a delight—elegant, refined, and understated, not unlike Alexandre Thienpont himself. Bought in 1924 by his grandfather Georges, its closest neighbor is Pétrus, and they share the iron-ore in the soil, although here there is more gravel with the clay. This difference is reflected in the vineyard; here 60% Merlot, 30% Cabernet Franc, and 10% Cabernet Sauvignon, over 35 acres (14ha). The Cabernet Franc is seen through the aromatic nose, perfumed with violets and summer blossoms, contrasting with the rich black fruits on the palate.

1 route du Lussac, 33500 Pomerol
www.vieux-chateau-certan.com

WINE STYLES

CAN RIGHT BANK WINES AGE AS WELL AS LEFT BANK WINES?

Cabernet Sauvignon is credited as being the long-living grape of Bordeaux. But the majority is on the Left Bank, concentrated in the Médoc, where it dominates the classified growths. The Right Bank, in contrast, is planted to over 60% Merlot, rising to 80% in Pomerol. What does this mean for aging potential? Alain Reynaud, owner of Le Croix de Gay and consultant across both banks, explains, "The fact that the soil structure in Pomerol and St-Emilion makes wines that are accessible when young can be misleading. Aging is traditionally connected to acidity levels in wine, as well as tannic structure, but there are other factors. The real revolution on the Right Bank has been in the vineyard, in terms of low yields, greater concentration, and great phenolic maturity—all contribute to the fact that Pétrus can age just as well as Lafite, and Ausone just as well as Latour."

THE REST OF BORDEAUX

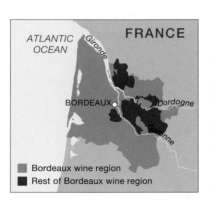

ATLANTIC OCEAN
FRANCE
Gironde
BORDEAUX
Dordogne
Garonne

■ Bordeaux wine region
■ Rest of Bordeaux wine region

It is easy to get lost with the smaller areas in Bordeaux. Across the whole region, there are 54 appellations in total. This is down from 57 following the introduction, from the 2008 vintage, of AC Côtes de Bordeaux, which replaced four of the five former individual Côtes appellations: Blaye, Francs, Castillon, and Premières Côtes de Bordeaux, now going under the village name of Cadillac. Only Côtes de Bourg retained its original name. It is tempting, in the face of such profusion, to stick to tried-and-tested regions that have achieved international recognition. However, that can mean missing out on the many excellent, well-priced properties and producers that have taken lesser-known terroirs and applied stringent winemaking techniques.

Major grapes

🍇 Reds

Cabernet Franc

Cabernet Sauvignon

Malbec

Merlot

Petit Verdot

🍇 Whites

Muscadelle

Sauvignon Blanc

Sauvignon Gris

Sémillon

Vintages

2009

Exceptional; hail affected yields in Entre-deux-Mers and Côtes.

2008

A challenging year, with a damp summer and extended sunny harvest. Excellent wines, but exercise caution.

2007

The cool summer gave mixed results. Some lighter-style red wines, and many wonderful white wines.

2006

A classic year. Merlot on clay soils struggled—this was a Cabernet year, with good weather in the fall.

2005

Ideal conditions gave rich wines that are drinking perfectly now, ahead of classified growths.

2004

Damp weather meant rot was a real risk. Some good results and good value.

More than half of the entire surface area of Bordeaux is vinified in the two generic appellations of AC Bordeaux and AC Bordeaux Supérieur, where 6,300 winemakers are all attempting to make a living. The difference between the two appellations is largely in viticultural methods, permitted yields, and allowed alcohol levels. Together, they farm over 153,202 acres (62,000ha) of vines, and produce over half of Bordeaux's yearly production. The other key smaller appellations are the satellites around St-Emilion and the Libournais appellations around Pomerol—Lussac-St-Emilion, Montagne-St-Emilion, St-Georges-St-Emilion, Puisseguin-St-Emilion, Lalande de Pomerol, and Fronsac. Together, these account for almost 14,826 acres (6,000ha) of vines. Côtes de Bordeaux produces 120 million bottles a year from 32,123 acres (13,000ha). Under the new system, the label on these bottles will either read Côtes de Bordeaux or it will also display the individual region (Francs, Castillon, Blaye, or Cadillac). For the white wines, the biggest appellation (outside of AC Bordeaux Blanc) is AC Entre-deux-Mers.

Stylistically, it is, of course, difficult to generalize when looking at wines from such geographically diverse areas. But, by and large, the smaller appellations from the Right Bank are primarily Merlot-based. This gives the best of them an immediacy and a fruity mouthfeel that can take the most "established" châteaux a few years in bottle to develop. AC Bordeaux and AC Bordeaux Supérieur can come from anywhere in the entire Bordeaux region; however, all of the appellations here are east of the River Garonne, on Bordeaux's Right Bank and on either side of the River Dordogne.

Other stylistic clues include softer tannins and less oak aging. There are exceptions, of course— Girolate by the Despagne family is a pure powerhouse, full of sexy, tight tannins—but

many of these wines offer a pleasurable and more accessible introduction to the wines of Bordeaux. This does mean most red wines from these regions should be enjoyed young, starting at around five rather than ten years old, or even younger. Most whites and rosés are ready for cracking open immediately upon bottling.

In the vines, there is more machine cultivation and harvesting. There is also more direct selling and this, along with the beautiful locations of many properties, makes these areas ideal for wine tourism. Fronsac, in particular, is set on a high ridge overlooking the River Dordogne, while the Côtes are attractively contoured and have plenty of dramatic scenery.

For the winemakers, the difficulty is how to make their wines stand out from the Bordeaux crowd. Increasingly, the best properties are taking risks. This might be through the choice of grape variety, such as the deliciously fragrant 85% Cabernet Franc wine from Château Roques Mauriac, bottled under the name Cuvée Damnation. Or it might be through pushing the vines to their limit in search of greater concentration, as practiced by Jean-Philippe Janoueix at Château Le Conseiller. Or by highlighting the pleasure of a 100% Sauvignon Blanc *cuvée*, as with Divinus de Château Bonnet.

The powers-that-be at the Bordeaux Supérieur wine body are even considering introducing a new appellation—Bordeaux Premier Cru—which would recognize the very best wineries by awarding them a separate, quality-focused AC. Whether this would just add another layer of confusion remains to be seen. What is certain, however, is that there are some wonderful winemakers in Bordeaux who are working outside the classification system, and outside the renowned appellations, but who deserve to be better known.

Château Acappella Montagne St-Emilion

The passion that Béatrice and Christophe Choisy feel for Château Acappella, which they created in 2001, is obvious as soon as you meet them. Their 8.6 acres (3.5ha) of Merlot (60%) and 40-year-old Cabernet Franc (40%) vines are all farmed organically. Consultant Michel Rolland works with ripe fruit but it is the exacting attention of the owners that ensures gravity-led winemaking using only indigenous yeasts to begin fermentation, malolactic in barrels, no filtration, and no fining. This is an indulgent wine, with silky tannins and sweet black fruits that need some time to open up. The second wine, Eugénie d'Acappella (named after their daughter), comes from young vines.

33570 Montagne
www.chateau-acappella.com

Château d'Aiguilhe Côtes de Bordeaux

Château d'Aiguilhe produces a dense, concentrated wine that is aged in 80% new oak and lavished with care; from harvesting in small crates, using gravity-led winemaking, to fermenting whole grapes. Stephan von Neipperg (of Canon-La-Gaffelière) bought the property, with 124 acres (50ha) of 80% Merlot, 20% Cabernet Franc, in 1998. The second wine, Seigneurs d'Aiguilhe, has the fruitiness of a Castillon wine, while the first wine is far more concentrated, and closer in character to a St-Emilion.

33350 St-Philippe d'Aiguilhe
www.neipperg.com

Château Bellevue-Gazin
Côtes de Bordeaux

The owner of Château Bellevue-Gazin, Alain Lancereau, bought this attractive Blaye property in 2003. The family have since invested in new barrels, updated the winery, and renovated the property. The vineyard covers 49 acres (20ha) of clay and gravel soils with 65% Merlot, 20% Malbec, 10% Cabernet Sauvignon, and 5% Petit Verdot (the latter used only in the second wine, Baronnets); all harvesting is done by hand. From the 2005 vintage, they upped the barrel size from 60 gal (225 liters) to 80 gal (300 liters), to reduce the flavor of the oak while keeping the sweetness and complexity that it brings. This is a very accomplished wine, with soft, sweet fruit and lots of personality. They also produce wine from a separate estate, Lers-Loumède, and a Bordeaux Clairet.

33390 Plassac
www.chateau-bellevue-gazin.fr

Château Bertinerie Côtes de Bordeaux

Château Bertinerie uses double-curtain trellising in its organic vineyard. This improves photosynthesis and reduces shade on the grapes, helping maturity. Techniques like this make Daniel Bantegnies a leading winemaker in Blaye, and his 148 acre (60ha) estate makes consistently exciting wines. His special *cuvées* are the best—bottled as Haut Bertinerie, the 100% Sauvignon white is fermented in new oak with lees-stirring, and the red (40% Cabernet Sauvignon, 60% Merlot) matured in 80% new wood with 20% kept back in stainless steel to emphasize fruit and freshness. The second wines, confusingly called Château Bertinerie, are more straightforward in character. The family produces Château Manon La Lagune, also in Blaye.

33620 Cubnezais
www.chateaubertinerie.com

CHATEAU D'AIGUILHE
A CONCENTRATED WINE WITH LOTS OF NEW OAK, SIMILAR TO A ST-EMILION

CHATEAU BONNET
AN EXCELLENT WHITE WINE PRODUCED BY THE LURTON FAMILY AT THIS LARGE ESTATE

Château Bonnet Entre-deux-Mers

Château Bonnet is among the few Bordeaux properties that can claim to have the size and consistency to rival international brands. André Lurton has steadily increased the size of this property to the current 667 acres (270ha), with 420 acres (170ha) for the excellent white wine. The blend is 50% Sauvignon Blanc, 40% Sémillon, and 10% Muscadelle. The vinification temperature is low, to ensure fruit characteristics are bright and sparkling. There is also a 100% Sauvignon Blanc *cuvée*, Divinus de Château Bonnet, which is lees-stirred to round out the citrus flavors, but still held back from any oak, ensuring the fresh fruit stays paramount. The reds—particularly the red Divinus (80% Merlot)—are equally reliable and good value. They do, however, suffer when compared with the best reds of the region, as many AC Bordeaux reds do.

33420 Grézillac
www.andrelurton.com

Château Branda Puisseguin St-Emilion

Château Branda is now 100% owned by Denise Sarna (former co-owner Arnaud Delaire having left in early 2010). She concentrates on well-structured, spicy wine with good extraction that holds back from being overdone. Consultation is from both Michel Rolland and Pascal Chatonnet and there are 89 acres (36ha) of fairly young 70% Merlot vines, with the balance an equal split of the two Cabernets. The wine is aged in oak for 14–16 months, giving a licorice hint to the rich black-cherry core.

No visitor facilities
05 57 74 62 55

Château Calon Montagne St-Emilion

Château Calon is a lovely wine, rich with red fruits and packed with confidence. Owned by Jean-Noël Boidron of Château Corbin-Michotte in St-Emilion, his family have been making wine in this region for more than 150 years. Boidron taught enology at the Bordeaux Wine Institute, and uses modern techniques such as close cropping and green harvesting to ensure low yields, with fruit-focused winemaking in stainless steel. This 94 acre (38ha) estate is a short distance from St-Emilion and shares the same limestone terrain. The Merlot-dominated wines are aged for up to 18 months in new oak, adding a smoky edge.

33570 Montagne St-Emilion
05 57 51 64 88

Château Cap de Faugères
Côtes de Bordeaux

This Castillon property owned by Swiss money-man Silvio Denz of Château Faugères produces 100,000 bottles from 77 acres (31ha) of vines. The wine is 85% Merlot with Cabernet Franc and a touch of Cabernet Sauvignon, and is vinified to maximize fruit and early-drinking ripe tannins, with a cold soak before fermentation in stainless steel. It is aged for 12 months but without any new oak, ensuring the smoky notes are no more than a suggestion.

33330 St-Etienne-de-Lisse
www.chateau-faugeres.com

Château de Carles Fronsac

Château de Carles is an estate to watch, with recent investment in everything from an architect-designed cellar with gravity-flow winemaking to newly landscaped

CHATEAU DE LA DAUPHINE
A MODERN WINERY IN FRONSAC
PRODUCING ELEGANT WINES

gardens. Owners Constance and Stéphane Droulers have been here since the late 1980s. Today, they work with Jean-Luc Thunevin, Alain Renau, and Jean Philippe Fort (of Laboratoire Michel Rolland) for technical advice. Both Haut-Carles and Château de Carles are 90% Merlot and 10% Cabernet Franc/Malbec, the difference comes in plot selection and vinification. Haut-Carles is 100% aged in large oak barrels, and comes from a rigorous selection within the 49 acre (20ha) vineyard. Château de Carles spends 6 months in stainless steel and 12 in barrel. Both demonstrate pure fruit expression, with greater emphasis on power and smoky structure in the first wine. The objective is to increase the density of vines up to 4,047 per acre (10,000 per ha) in the near future. ★ **Rising star**

33141 Saillans
95 57 84 34 03

Château Clos Chaumont
Côtes de Bordeaux
Château Clos Chaumont is just the kind of estate you hope to find in the smaller appellations, with a real sense of dynamism and momentum. The property is owned by Pieter Verbeek, a timber merchant from the Netherlands who had spent years visiting Bordeaux, and finally fell in love with a property (without vines) high on a ridge in the tiny village of Haux. He used the expertise of his friend Kees van Leeuven, enologist at Cheval Blanc and d'Yquem, for soil analysis and plantation of 27 acres (11ha), and now works with Hubert de Boüard. The red is 60% Merlot, with Cabernet Franc from low-yielding old stock. The result is very charming, with fresh minerality and clean red berry fruits. The rich white is full of apricot aromas from the 55% Sémillon and 45% Sauvignon Gris.

8 Chomon, 33550 Haux
05 56 37 23

Château Le Conseiller Bordeaux Supérieur
If you want proof that some winemakers in Bordeaux are taking risks, look to Jean-Philippe Janoueix at Château Le Conseiller, where a 3.7 acre (1.5ha) plot is planted at a density of 8,094 vines per acre (20,000 per ha). To put that in context, Romanée-Conti is at 4,856 per acre (12,000 per ha), Lafite at 4,047 per acre (10,000 per ha). This unusual plot is next to the River Dordogne, on a curve where the wind allows aeration of such closely set vines. First planted in 2000, Janoueix waited until 2005 to bottle his first vintage to allow the vines to gain in complexity. A seriously intense 100% Merlot wine, rich in pencil-lead and black currant essence, is bottled under the name 20 Mille. After fermentation in vats, the wine is transferred into warmed barrels for 18 months, to ensure a gentle extraction and no shock to the young juice. Just 4,000 bottles are produced. If this proves too elusive, the main wine from this estate is also a good bet, with supple red fruits, and still 100% Merlot, from 67 acres (27ha) of vines.

33240 Lugon-et-l'Ile-du-Carnay
www.josephjanoueix.com

Château La Croix Mouton
Bordeaux Supérieur
Consistent, enjoyable, and majoring very definitely on rich autumn fruits, Château La Croix Mouton is an excellent-quality wine (particularly for the price) from Jean-Philippe Janoueix, an increasingly dynamic Right Bank name. A blend of 85% Merlot/15% Cabernet Franc,

CHATEAU GUERRY
A BERNARD MAGREZ ESTATE IN
BOURG TURNING OUT SPICY WINES

the 124 acres (50ha) of vines are located just over the St-Emilion border. The wine has cedary aromas, smoky black currant fruit and firm tannins. You do not need to wait to crack it open, as vinification in stainless steel, malolactic in barrel, then aging for just eight months keeps it all about early drinking.

33240 Lugon-et-l'Ile-du-Carnay
www.josephjanoueix.com

Château de la Dauphine Fronsac
This fast-rising estate makes elegant, fruit-forward wines that are rich in black fruits and demonstrate clearly what Fronsac can be capable of. Château de la Dauphine was formerly owned by Moueix, but has been in the hands of Jean Halley since 2001. Now run by his son Guillaume Halley, with Denis Dubourdieu as consultant winemaker, this 79 acre (32ha) estate has benefited from serious investment over the past decade and has been enlarged with the inclusion of estates in Canon-Fronsac. Today, all its wine is declared AC Fronsac and sold under two labels: La Dauphine, and the second wine, Delphis. The average age of the vines is 33 years, with 80% Merlot and 20% Cabernet Franc, aged for 12 months in oak (33% new). The modern winery has circular vats, gravity-led winemaking, temperature-controlled stainless steel and cement vats, and an underground barrel cellar. ★ **Rising star**

33126 Fronsac
www.chateau-dauphine.com

Château La Fleur de Boüard
Lalande-de-Pomerol
Coralie, daughter of Hubert de Boüard of Angélus, runs Château La Fleur de Boüard. It was bought by her father in 1998, and renamed in her honor. The vineyard covers 48 acres (19.5ha), is planted to 85% Merlot, 10% Cabernet Franc, and 5% Cabernet Sauvignon, and sees careful manual work throughout the growing season. The flavors are big, bold, and confident, with the same sexy, smoky signature of Angélus (created by 18 months aging in 80% new oak barrels) plus ripe black currant fruit. The final wine is bottled unfiltered and unfined.

33500 Pomerol
www.lafleurdebouard.com

Château de Fontenille Entre-deux-Mers
Château de Fontenille is a label to look out for. With vines covering 86 acres (35ha), it is made with great care and attention by Stéphane Defraine. Do not expect great dramatic gestures and pumped-up flavors. There is a simple range: an Entre-deux-Mers white (50% Sauvignons Blanc and Gris, 30% Sémillon, 20% Muscadelle); an AC Bordeaux red (50% Merlot, 30% Cabernet Franc, 20% Cabernet Sauvignon); and a Merlot-led AC Bordeaux Clairet, which is a slightly more full-bodied rosé. You get clean flavors, soft tannins, and exceptional value.

33670 La Sauve Majeure
www.chateau-fontenille.com

Château de Francs Côtes de Bordeaux
Château de Francs is the leading estate in the Francs region of the Côtes de Bordeaux appellation (there are 40 winegrowers here who farm less than 2.5 acres/1ha). It is owned by Dominique Hebrard, the former owner of

Cheval Blanc, and Hubert de Boüard. Wines from this area are typically Merlot-dominated and this is no exception, with 70%, fleshed out with 20% Cabernet Franc and 10% Cabernet Sauvignon. The 99 acres (40ha) are farmed by hand, with plot-by-plot vinification, all aimed at favoring fruit and finesse over power. The wine spends 12 months in oak, just 20% new to ensure it never dominates the flavor. There are also 6 acres (2.5ha) of 50/50 Sémillon/Sauvignon Blanc, making a gourmet-style white, aged in oak (50% new), with lees-stirring.

33570 Francs
www.hebrard.com

Château du Gaby Fronsac
Easily one of the most beautiful estates in Fronsac, Château du Gaby is owned by English investment banker David Curl. It is set high on a ridge overlooking the Dordogne river, with 40 acres (16ha) of vines planted on slopes offering excellent drainage. Enologist Gilles Paquet ferments the 85% Merlot and 15% mix of Cabernets Franc and Sauvignon in epoxy-lined concrete vats, then moves the wine into oak barrels for 12–18 months (40–60% new). This wine should be better known: the 50,000 bottles per year offer fresh, ripe blackberry and loganberry fruits, with good substance and firm structure. The second wine is Les Roches Gaby.

1 Gaby, 33126 Fronsac
www.chateau-dugaby.com

Château Garraud Lalande-de-Pomerol
Château Garraud is a consistently over-performing wine from Jean-Marc Nony, with Michel Rolland as consultant. There is beautiful depth and complexity to the 70% Merlot, 30% Cabernet Franc/Sauvignon, with plenty of Pomerol polish, even if the 79 acres (32ha) of vines lie just over the border in the village of Néac. A large part of the appeal is in the luxurious texture and mouth-feel that come from low-yielding vines and aging in 80% oak barrels. The same family owns the neighboring L'Ancien, which is planted with some of the oldest Merlot vines in Lalande. Their Château Treytins produces small amounts in both the Lalande-de-Pomerol and Montagne St-Emilion appellations.

33500 Néac
www.vln.fr

Château Guerry Côtes de Bourg
One of Bernard Magrez's many Bordeaux estates, Château Guerry is an attractive 52 acre (21ha) property in the Bourg region, overlooking the estuary almost directly opposite Margaux. A lovely, swirling spice comes from 20% Malbec (more prevalent in Bourg and Blaye than other parts of Bordeaux); the balance is a powerful 30% Cabernet Sauvignon, softened by 50% Merlot. Another Magrez wine is Egrégore, a lush, super-charged experience, from a parcel of vines near Blaye.

33710 Bourg sur Gironde
www.bernard-magrez.com

Château Joanin Bécot Côtes de Bordeaux
A younger generation of owners has moved into Castillon, many of them from famous winemaking families in prestigious neighboring appellations. This is one of the best known: Juliette Bécot from Château

Beausejour-Bécot in St-Emilion, working with enologists Sophie Porquet and Jean-Philippe Fort. An excellent-quality wine, with 75% Merlot and 25% Cabernet Franc from 17 acres (7ha) of vines, with ripe damsons and some roasted vanilla from the barrel aging. Alcohol can creep up in the biggest vintages, but there is good structure and tannins to balance it out.

33330 St-Emilion
www.beausejour-becot.com

Château Lucas Lussac St-Emilion
The Vauthier family of Ausone are behind this estate, here led by Frédéric Vauthier. There are just over 128 acres (52ha) of vines with 50% Merlot/50% Cabernet Franc, all farmed sustainably and moving toward certified organic. The vines are split between three wines: a floral Château Lucas aged in 80% stainless steel and 20% oak; Grand de Lucas, hand harvested with low yields and full barrel aging, with mico-oxygentation to smooth the tannins when needed; and Spirit of Lucas, made in exceptional years from old vines, spending 24 months in new oak.

33570 Lussac
www.chateau-lucas.fr

Château de Lussac Lussac St-Emilion
Griet and Hervé Laviale, who also own Franc Mayne in St-Emilion, have turned the 19th-century Château de Lussac into a slightly decadent country manor, complete with dramatic lighting and gold-edged chandeliers. The cellars, in contrast, are all about the winemaking, with a circular layout filled with stainless-steel truncated vats and a grape reception that uses a Tribaie machine to assess sugar levels and ensure the most ripe fruit goes into the wine. This is repaid by lush flavors, with hints of tobacco and chocolate. The estate in total covers 67 acres (27ha), planted to 77% Merlot and 23% Cabernet Franc at 2,226 vines per acre (5,500 per ha). The highly seductive second wine, Le Libertin de Lussac, is from young vines and spends no time in new oak.

15 rue de Lincent, 33570 Lussac
www.chateaudelussac.fr

Château Magdeleine Bouhou Bordeaux
Château Magdeleine Bouhou is a dynamic estate, owned by Muriel Rousseau, which has recently launched two 100% Malbec wines. This grape represented 80% of the Blaye plantings at the beginning of the 20th century, but is now a tiny proportion. There are 12 acres (5ha) of Malbec planted on clay soils here, and all of their red wines have it in some quantity. In 2009, they decided to prepare two *cuvées*, one fresh and uncomplicated table wine called La Petite Madeleine, and one AC Bordeaux called M de Magdeleine (confusingly, a single-varietal Malbec is not allowed in the AC Côtes de Bordeaux) that is aged in oak and has good structure. But they are still a world away from a weightier, richer Cahors Malbec.

Blaye, 33392
05 57 42 19 13

Château Manoir du Gravoux
Côtes de Bordeaux
A rising star in Castillon, Philippe Emile's 47 acre (19ha) medieval estate of Château Manoir du Gravoux is directly opposite one of the more established players in the

LESSER-KNOWN GRAPES

Bordeaux appellation rules allow six red and seven white grape varieties, but only four are widely used—Merlot at 63% of all red plantings, Cabernet Sauvignon at 25%; Sauvignon Blanc at 38% of all white plantings, Sémillon at 53%. Cabernet Franc represents 11% of red plantings, and Muscadelle 6% of white. The other permitted grapes are Ugni Blanc, Merlot Blanc, Mauzac, Odenc, and Colombard (white), and Petit Verdot, Malbec, and Carmenère (red). Recent years have seen a rise in some of these lesser-known grapes. Petit Verdot has increased over 10%, growing from 1,043 acres (422ha) to 1,184 acres (479ha). Malbec is also finding its way into blends in greater quantities, particularly in Bourg and Blaye—mainly due to the recent run of warmer harvests, and a desire to stand out from better-known areas. A few châteaux have released 100% Malbec wines, including Magdeleine Bouhou in Blaye.

PEY LA TOUR RESERVE
THE SECOND WINE OF THIS LARGE ESTATE
IS THE RICHER OF THE TWO

appellation, Stéphane Derenoncourt's Domaine de l'A. He makes use of his neighbor's expertise, and carefully works his low-yielding vines to ensure ripe, rich, and dense berry flavors that are helped by south-facing slopes with good drainage and high trellising to maximize canopy cover. The blend is 88% Merlot with 12% Cabernet Franc. Both alcoholic and malolactic fermentation are in stainless steel to give good extraction but without drying tannins. ★**Rising star**

33350 St-Genes-de-Castillon
www.terraburdigala.com

Château Marjosse Bordeaux

Château Marjosse is the family estate of Pierre Lurton—director of Châteaux d'Yquem and Cheval Blanc—and it is a great wine to know about. Located in Entre-deux-Mers, a somewhat less illustrious setting than his day job, Lurton has just inaugurated a shiny new 25,824 sqft (2,400 sqm) winery designed by architect Guy Tropes, all clean lines and modern installations. This should further help the reputation of an already exciting estate with 198 acres (80ha) of vines. The Merlot-dominated (75%) red is very good value, with smooth tannins and rich firm fruits plus a touch of spice from 3% Malbec—not threatening many classified wines, but easily distinguishing itself from its neighbors. The 52 acres (22ha) of white varieties—59% Sémillon/Muscadelle, 41% Sauvignons Blanc and Gris—make classic Bordeaux; less gooseberry, more cut-grass.

No visitor facilities
05 57 55 57 80

Château Messile-Aubert

Montagne St-Emilion
A great label to look out for, as Heloise Aubert of La Couspaude runs the 25 acre (10ha) Château Messile-Aubert along meticulous lines, with Michel Rolland as consultant. The 60% Merlot, 20% Cabernet Franc, 20% Cabernet Sauvignon is fermented in small wooden vats, with a cold soak and manual punching down, then malolactic in new French oak barrels. After a long aging (for the appellation) of 18–20 months, the wine is sleek and rounded, full of mocha, mint, and summer fruits.

33570 Montagne St Emilion
www.aubert-vignobles.com

Château Mondésir-Gazin

Côtes de Bordeaux
Of all the Gazin properties in Blaye, Château Mondésir-Gazin is one of the best, with 35 acres (14ha) of vines up to 60 years old. Owner Marc Pasquet also has Château Haut-Mondésir (Bourg) and Château Gontey (St-Emilion). He is a meticulous winemaker who was a successful photographer before changing careers in 1990. The wine (24,000 bottles) is fleshy with a touch of spicy exoticism from the Malbec (20%), the balance being 60% Merlot and 20% Cabernet Sauvignon. The rich purple fruits are emphasized by being bottled unfiltered and unfined.

10 Le Sablon, 33390 Plassac
www.mondesirgazin.com

Château Montlau Entre-deux-Mers

Armand and Elisabeth Schuster de Balwill are the owners of Château Montlau, a property that claims evidence of winemaking dating back to the 15th century. Well-located on slopes facing the vineyards of St-Emilion, the vines cover 62 acres (25ha), with two-thirds Merlot to one-third Cabernet Franc. There are also 7.4 acres (3ha) of white grapes, with Sauvignon Blanc, Sémillon, and Muscadelle (up to 55% in some vintages) producing an Entre-deux-Mers and a sparkling Crémant de Bordeaux. These are unfussy, fruity wines, but consistent in quality and with a light touch too often missing from lower-priced Bordeaux.

3 Monleau, 33420 Moulon
www.chateau-montlau.com

Château Mont-Pérat Côtes de Bordeaux

Château Mont-Pérat is another wine that shows how the Despagne family are not content to rest on their laurels in these less well-known appellations of Bordeaux. Led by Thibault Despagne and technical director Joël Elissalde, it is a large estate with 252 acres (102ha) of vines. The red wine is dominated by Merlot and packed full of confident, fleshy red fruits, backed up by a good seam of freshness and a velvety texture. This is a highly reliable wine.

33550 Capian
www.mont-perat.com

Château Penin Bordeaux Supérieur

A name that is worth remembering, Patrick Carteyron has run his 99 acre (40ha) Château Penin since 1982. He makes 270,000 bottles over a range of consistently over-achieving wines, the best of which is his Penin Tradition, made with 90% Merlot and a 10% mix of Cabernets Franc and Sauvignon. It is vinified and aged for 12 months in stainless steel, with no oak and some micro-oxygenation to soften the tannins. Since 2008, he has made an interesting special *cuvée* called Natur, with no added sulphur dioxide to emphasize the soft fruity character of the wine; it tastes good lightly chilled. Blanc de Château Penin has an 85% mix of Sauvignons Blanc and Gris, with the balance Sémillon.

33420 Port Génissac
www.chateau-penin.com

Château Perron Lalande-de-Pomerol

The Massonie family have a long history in Lalande-de-Pomerol, and Michel Massonie (father of current owner Bertrand) was instrumental in the creation of the AC. Château Perron's wine is full-bodied, with smoky, cigar-box flavors and well-structured black currant fruits. The 57 acres (23ha) of vines—20 acres (8ha) having been added in 2008—are planted with 80% Merlot, 10% Cabernet Franc, 10% Cabernet Sauvignon. Bertrand has been in charge since 1999, working with his brother and sister Thibault and Beatrice. Enologist Jean-Philippe Faure uses a little micro-oxygenation when necessary. The second wine is La Fleur; a third is Château Pierrefitte.

33503 Libourne
www.chateauperron.com

Château Pey La Tour Bordeaux Supérieur

Another property that fell foul of Château Latour's fierce identity protection, this Dourthe estate was forced to change its name from Château Clos de La Tour to Château Pey La Tour in the late 1990s. It has settled in well to its new name, and is a reference for consistent, quality winemaking in the smaller appellations. There are 544 acres (220ha) of vines, with some modern techniques such

CHATEAU PENIN
THIS "TRADITION" LABEL IS PREDOMINANTLY
MERLOT, WITH NO OAK AGING

as high-density planting, thermo-vinification for certain vats, and cold soaking or micro-oxygenation for others. Winemaker Guillaume Pouthier says he likes to have a palette of flavors and styles to ensure a complex balance in the final wine. Making only red wine, there are two labels: a toasty, rich Pey La Tour Réserve joins the more easy-drinking first label (82% Merlot, 14% Cabernet Sauvignon, 4% Cabernet Franc and Petit Verdot).

No visitor facilities
www.chateaupeylatour.com

Château Pierrail Bordeaux Supérieur

Château Pierrail is below the radar yet calmly and carefully produces excellent wines. The Demonchaux family are in charge, led by Jacques and Alice with their son Aurélien. The white wine is a blend of Sauvignons Gris and Blanc, from grapes grown on clay–limestone slopes. The 173 acre (70ha) vineyard follows low yields and sustainable farming. The red is 85% Merlot, 15% Cabernets Franc and Sauvignon and has a soft, blue cheese nose, with good chewy tannins and a smoky depth of extraction that is confident but not overdone.

33220 Margueron
www.chateaupierrail.com

Château Plain-Point Fronsac

The south-facing slopes of Château Plain-Point allow easy ripening of the 75% Merlot, 20% Cabernet Sauvignon, 5% Cabernet Franc grapes. Owned by Michel Aroldi, there are 86 acres (35ha) on clay–chalk soils producing a modern-style wine (105,000 bottles) that goes all out for big, rich flavors of red summer fruits, bottled unfiltered and unfined. The second wine, M de Plain-Point, ups this pleasure factor further, with 80% Merlot. Vinification is simple, in concrete vats with natural yeasts and aging in French oak (40% new). An interesting white, Blanc de Plain-Point, is 80% Sauvignon Blanc and 20% Gros Manseng, a variety better known in Southwest France.

33126 St-Aignan
www.chateau-plain-point.com

Château Puygueraud Côtes de Bordeaux

Peppery notes and inky depth of color give this wine its distinctive character; both are attributable to the Malbec grape that makes up 5% of the blend. Nicolas Thienpont ensures the rest of his first wine comes from Merlot and Cabernet Franc, the more typical grape varieties of the appellation, with silky tannins and bright fruits vinified in stainless steel and smoothed out with some micro-oxygenation. Wine was first bottled at this Francs château by Nicolas' father George in 1983, and today there are three wines produced: Château Puygueraud, second label Château Lauriol (from younger vines) and Cuvée George, which is an unusual blend of 35% Malbec, 35% Cabernet Franc, 20% Merlot, and 10% Cabernet Sauvignon.

33570 St-Cibard
www.nicolas-thienpont.com

Château Reynon Bordeaux Blanc

The family estate of white wine guru Denis Dubourdieu offers exceptional value. The insider's tip—the white, of 89% Sauvignon Blanc, 11% old-vine Sémillon from 42 acres (17ha)—gives plenty of cut-grass rather than grapefruit. Dubourdieu stays within the classic Bordeaux

CHATEAU LA RIVALERIE
A CONSISTENT OVER-ACHIEVER, THIS ESTATE IS MAKING WAVES

CHATEAU REYNON
THE HOME OF BORDEAUX'S WHITE WINE GURU PRODUCES THIS REGIONAL CLASSIC

interpretation of the grapes, full of juicy, refreshing fruits, although the percentage of Sauvignon is increasing. The red wine from the estate is reliable; made from 44 acres (18ha) of 82% Merlot, 13% Cabernet Sauvignon, 2% Cabernet Franc, and 3% Petit Verdot. In certain years, an AC Cadillac sweet wine is also made. The second-label wines, Clos de Reynon, are from young vines.

33410 Beguey
www.denisdubourdieu.fr

Château Richelieu Fronsac

When Chinese investment company Hong Kong A & A International bought a majority stake in Château Richelieu in 2008, they were buying a slice of local history—the estate dates back over 1,200 years to the reign of Charlemagne. Today, there are 33 acres (13.5ha) of vines on rich blue clay with fossilized shells, and plans to expand. Planted to 70% Merlot, 28% Cabernet Franc, and 2% Malbec, it is farmed sustainably and only natural yeasts are used during fermentation. Stéphane Toutoundji is the consultant enologist and helps create a wine that mixes savory herbs with gently toasted black fruits.

1 chemin du Tertre, 33126 Fronsac
www.chateau-richelieu.com

Château La Rivalerie Côtes de Bordeaux

Château La Rivalerie is a little-known château that consistently punches above its weight in tastings and competitions. The hard-working young owner, Jérôme Bonaccorsi, recently instigated a redesign that has lifted the property's rather old-fashioned image, reflecting recent investments in the cellar and vineyard. The fruit tannins from the unoaked main red wine are consistently well-worked, with power and dense autumn fruit flavors coming from 50% Cabernet Sauvignon, 40% Merlot, and 10% Cabernet Franc/Malbec. The range also includes a good white that is an even split between Sauvignon Blanc and Sémillon, but vinified to favour a modern, fresh style, and a good-quality Cuvée Majoral from old vines, aged for 12 months in oak barrels.

route de St-Christoly-de-Blaye, 33390 St-Paul-de-Blaye
www.larivalerie.com

Château de la Rivière Fronsac

One of Fronsac's largest properties, the 148 acre (59ha) vineyards of Château de la Rivière consist of 82% Merlot, 13% Cabernet Sauvignon, 4% Cabernet Franc, and 1% Malbec, with additional graceful parkland. The terroir explains how Fronsac wines can offer such good quality—the cellars are cut from the same limestone found in many St-Emilion classified growths. This allows for the same expression of minerality and elegance, with fresh raspberry and blackberry notes. Owned by James Gregoire, the consultant enologist is Claude Gros. The second wine is Les Sources de Château de la Rivière. There is a rosé and a Château du Breuil, also in Fronsac.

33126 La Rivière, Fronsac
www.vignobles-gregoire.com

Château Roc de Cambes
Côtes de Bourg

One of the few Bourg wines with a true international reputation, Roc de Cambes has been owned since 1988 by François Mitjavile of Château Le Tertre-Roteboeuf in

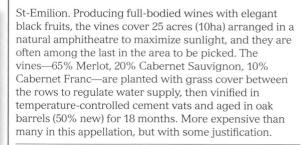

CHATEAU STE-MARIE
DESPITE ITS LOWLY APPELLATION, NO
EXPENSE IS SPARED TO PRODUCE GREAT
WINES AT THIS ESTATE

St-Emilion. Producing full-bodied wines with elegant black fruits, the vines cover 25 acres (10ha) arranged in a natural amphitheatre to maximize sunlight, and they are often among the last in the area to be picked. The vines—65% Merlot, 20% Cabernet Sauvignon, 10% Cabernet Franc—are planted with grass cover between the rows to regulate water supply, then vinified in temperature-controlled cement vats and aged in oak barrels (50% new) for 18 months. More expensive than many in this appellation, but with some justification.

33330 St-Laurent-des-Combes
www.roc-de-cambes.com

Château Roques Mauriac

Vincent and Sophie Levieux of Château Roques Mauriac show how it is done with their Cuvée Damnation, which contains a whopping 85% Cabernet Franc, balanced by 15% Merlot. This gives a beautifully concentrated nose of violets and red currants, with burnt caramel and vanilla on the palate from aging in barrel. A modern-style wine that is round and supple, but fairly powerful. The young vines of the château make an enjoyable summer fruit bottling called L'Avant Gout de Roques Mauriac. The Levieuxes show an absolute belief in Cabernet Franc by keeping it at 50% in their Roques Mauriac Premier Vin.

33540 Mauriac
www.roques-mauriac.com

Château Siaurac Lalande-de-Pomerol

Château Siaurac's owners, Domaines Baronne Guichard, also have Le Prieuré in St-Emilion and Vray Croix de Gay in Pomerol. This 96 acre (39ha) vineyard is just over the border from Pomerol in Lalande. The wine displays the same silky smooth tannins and rich fruit character of its more famous neighbor, but without the hefty price tag. The estate uses plot-by-plot vinification and sustainable agriculture to ensure quality. Enologist Yannick Reyrel trained under Jean-Claude Berrouet of Pétrus. The second wine, Le Plaisir de Siaurac, comes from young vines.

33500 Néac
05 57 51 64 58

Château Ste Barbe Bordeaux

Antoine and Lucy Touton bought Château Ste Barbe in 2000 and have turned it into one of the key performers in AC Bordeaux. The blackberry and roasted herb flavors of the wine come from 70% Merlot and a 30% blend of Cabernets Sauvignon and Franc, fermented in a mix of concrete and stainless steel vats and with up to a year in barrel (30% new, so never intrusive). There is also a 100% Merlot Réserve Privée that is aged for 12 months in entirely new oak, and a second, unoaked, 100% Merlot (Merlot Ste Barbe) emphasizing fruit over the toasted vanilla of the Réserve. A rosé is also unoaked (fermented in stainless steel), giving a raspberry and cherry punch.

33810 Ambès
www.chateausaintebarbe.com

Château Ste-Colombe Côtes de Bordeaux

Another Gérard Perse wine (this time in partnership with Alain Reynaud of Croix de Gay in Pomerol), Château Ste-Colombe comes from a 99 acre (40ha) estate and offers excellent value. A classic mix of Merlot (70%) and Cabernet Franc (30%), vinified to maximize concentration, with rich extracts of black currant, tobacco, and licorice, it is engagingly open and suitable for earlier drinking than his St-Emilion properties. The wine is aged for 12 months in barrels that have come from Pavie, Monbousquet, and Pavie-Decesse, and is bottled unfiltered and unfined. Right next door is another Perse estate, Clos L'Eglise.

No visitor facilities
www.chateaupavie.com

Château St-Georges St-Georges St-Emilion

Set on the highest point of this tiny appellation, surrounded by its own sloping vineyards, Château St-Georges has suffered from a few difficult years. A return to the old direction of Pétrus Desbois signals that they are intent on getting things back on track. The vines cover 124 acres (50ha) and make 250,000 bottles of 60% Merlot, 20% Cabernet Sauvignon, and 20% Cabernet Franc. There is an interesting 100% Merlot *cuvée* called Trilogie du Château St-Georges (because three generations have made wine here). Château Puy St-Georges is the second label.

33570 Montagne
www.chateau-saint-georges.com

Château Ste-Marie Entre-deux-Mers

Château Ste-Marie is pushing back the boundaries of this often overlooked appellation—one of the handful planted to 4,047 vines per acre (10,000 per ha). These grapes go into the Cuvée Madlys (56% Sauvignon Blanc, 22% Sauvignon Gris, 22% Sémillon, with 37,000 bottles), a wine that is worth getting to know for its rich, gourmet flavors and passionfruit and apricot punch. Run by the Dupuch-Mondon family, this 96 acre (39ha) property is converting to organic farming, and uses modern techniques such as closely cropped vines, cold skin-contact, and barrel aging with lees-stirring. Other labels worth investigating are Alios and Château Ste-Marie "Le Moulin".

51 route de Bordeaux, 33760 Targon
www.chateau-sainte-marie.com

Château Tabuteau Lussac St-Emilion

Château Tabuteau is one of three châteaux owned by Sylvie and Bertrand Bessou—Durand-Laplagne in Puisseguin St-Emilion, Cap de Merle in Bordeaux Supérieur, and this 47 acre (19ha) property on iron-rich clay soils in Lussac St-Emilion. The vineyard is planted to 64% Merlot, 16% Cabernet Franc, and 20% Cabernet Sauvignon, with grass between the rows to encourage the roots to grow deeper in competition for water. The wine is aged in concrete and stainless steel vats, and is welcoming, soft, and full of rich cherry flavors.

c/o Ch Durand, 33570 Puisseguin
www.durand-laplagne.com

Château Tayac Côtes de Bourg

A structured, classical-style Bourg wine, with a high proportion of Cabernet Sauvignon (45%), 5% Cabernet Franc, and 50% Merlot. Château Tayac is a leading estate in the appellation, with 74 acres (30ha) of vines on limestone at 177ft (54m), overlooking the Gironde Estuary. Owner Annick Saturny makes a number of wines—the most interesting are Cuvée Reservée and Cuvée Prestige.

St Seuin de Bourg, 33710 Bourg sur Gironde
www.chateau-tayac.fr

CHATEAU ROC DE CAMBES
INTERNATIONALLY RECOGNIZED, WITH A
GOOD PEDIGREE—AND JUSTIFIABLY PRICEY

Château Thieuley Entre-deux-Mers

Run by two sisters, Marie and Sylvie Courselle, Château Thieuley is one of the leading estates in the appellation, covering 148 acres (60ha). The white is the best known, with 74 acres (30ha) of 35% Sauvignon Blanc, 15% Sauvignon Gris, and 50% Sémillon. The red is a classic Right Bank blend of 70% Merlot and 30% Cabernet Sauvignon. A special *cuvée*, named after their father Francis Courselle, ups the Merlot to 80%, with a straight 20% mix of the two Cabernets and 70% new oak. Where this property stands out is with its modern approach to vinification. They use cold soaking, stainless steel, and aging on lees. Their rosé is also excellent, made from grapes picked early to retain their freshness (unlike many Bordeaux rosés, which are essentially juice bled from the main red wine to further concentrate it).

33670 La Sauve
www.thieuley.com

Château Turcaud Entre-deux-Mers

Château Turcaud is a tiny corner of modern, forward-thinking winemaking from the Robert family. There are 124 acres (50ha) of vines, with a range of highly regarded wines. There are several reds (the best of which is Cuvée Majeure), and a fresh, attractive rosé, but it is the whites that stand out. The Entre-deux-Mers is a 60% Sauvignon Blanc, 35% Sémillon, 5% Muscadelle blend, where the grapes are left in contact with the skins then fermented and aged on their lees, giving hints of grapefruit and passionfruit to the fresh citrus. The Bordeaux Blanc is a weightier animal, with 50% Sauvignon Blanc and 50% Sémillon from gravelly soils, fermented and aged in barrels, with lees-stirring.

33670 La Sauve Majeure
www.chateau-turcaud.com

Château de la Vieille Chapelle Bordeaux

There is always something interesting happening at Château de la Vieille Chapelle, located just outside of Fronsac on the banks of the Dordogne river. Owners Frédéric and Fabienne Mallier make wines that reflect the welcome at this 21 acre (8.6ha) estate. They favor easy-to-drink flavors (80% Merlot) and fresh fruit. The tiny production of white is dominated by Sémillon (80%), with just a touch of Sauvignon Blanc to lighten the mood. Low-impact winemaking is followed, with grass growing between the rows, and full traceability through all stages. Their consultant is Olivier Dauga.

4 Chapelle, 33240 Lugon et I'lle du Carney
www.chateau-de-la-vieille-chapelle.com

Clos Les Lunelles Côtes de Bordeaux

A dark ruby-colored, succulent, and indulgent wine from Gérard Perse of Château Pavie, Clos Les Lunelles is a star performer of the Cotes de Bordeaux appellation if you like your wines to make a statement. There are plenty of brambly black fruits, coaxed from closely cropped 80% Merlot, 20% Cabernet Sauvignon (with a touch of Cabernet Franc in most years), aged for 24 months. The first six months are spent in 100% new oak barrels. The vineyard is just 21 acres (8.5ha), and with the low yields, the production is 20,000 bottles.

No visitor facilities
www.chateaupavie.com

Clos Puy Arnaud Côtes de Bordeaux

Clos Puy Arnaud is a biodynamic estate in the Castillon area, owned by Thierry Valette. Stéphane Derenoncourt consulted for the first few years after Valette's purchase in 2000, getting him fully versed in biodynamic principles. The 17 acres (7ha) of vines are planted on limestone bedrock, with just a thin layer of topsoil cover, and have 70% Merlot and 25% Cabernet Franc, with Cabernet Sauvignon and Carmenère. In the cellar, there are open vats for punching down, and vinification is aimed at staying away from over-extraction. There is an enjoyable savory herb note to the wine that lifts the brambly fruits.

33350 Belvès de Castillon
05 57 47 90 33

Domaine de l'A Côtes de Bordeaux

The consultant Stéphane Derenoncourt bought the 20 acre (8ha) Domaine de l'A in 1999 with his wife Christine. They have been instrumental in raising the profile of the entire Castillon appellation. Beautifully located on well-drained slopes, the vineyard is farmed biodynamically, with any composting prepared organically at a nearby farm. As with the home estates of many consultants, experiments are often carried out in the vines and cellars. The 70% Merlot, 30% Cabernets Sauvignon and Franc wine is fermented in small oak vats, and the malolactic always begins naturally. This attention to detail, together with 18 months in barrel, gives a wonderfully balanced and fresh wine that has touches of decadence from mocha and rich dark chocolate.

33350 Ste-Colombe
www.vignerons-consultants.com

D:Vin Bordeaux

D:Vin is a polished bottle of 75% Cabernet Sauvignon and 25% Merlot from Hervé Grandeau of Château Lauduc. First bottled in 1997, from 6 acres (2.5ha) of this 124 acre (50ha) property, all work in the vineyard is done by hand, with careful sorting at harvest time. The wine is made in small stainless steel vats, with a cold soak going right down to 14°F (-10°C) for two to three days, then brought back up to 61°F (16°C) for the fermentation. Only indigenous yeasts from the grape skins are used, and temperatures stay low throughout at below 82°F (28°C), so fruit is always favored over extraction. Malolactic starts in barrel, and helps give the tannins their silky texture. The second wine is D:Vin/2.

No visitor facilities
www.divin.fr

Girolate Bordeaux

Girolate regularly beats many classified wines in blind tastings. This super-charged Despagne family creation comes from 25 acres (10ha) densely planted at 4,047 vines per acre (10,000 per ha), and cropped to around a third of the levels allowed by the appellation. Technical director Joël Elissalde, together with Thibault Despagne, creates rich, smooth, and beautifully polished 100% Merlot wines, showing intense red fruits wrapped in chocolate and mocha. Vinified entirely in barrel, each is rotated at least once a day to ensure the lees move into suspension and the tannins are softened. This is precision winemaking.

No visitor facilities
www.despagne.fr

WINE TOURISM

Since the city of Bordeaux was awarded UNESCO World Heritage status in 2007, joining St-Emilion (which was classified in 1999), tourist numbers have risen to nearly 3 million a year. A significant proportion of these visit the vineyards and recent initiatives, such as Philippe Raoux's La Winery in the Médoc, and architecture-led wine tourism installations like those at Petit-Village in Pomerol and Château Faugères in St-Emilion, are concrete examples of how Bordeaux is opening up. In 2013, they will be joined by a Wine Cultural Center in the city, with 107,640 sqft (10,000 sqm) of space in the Bassins à Flot area, just to the north of the traditional wine merchant district. Inside the building will be permanent and temporary cultural exhibits where visitors can learn about the making, distribution, and enjoyment of wine throughout the world, alongside restaurants, shops, and bars.

BURGUNDY

Sensuous, mercurial, and unpredictable, Burgundy is a demanding yet addictive mistress. This narrow straggle of landlocked vineyards in eastern France has been revered since the Middle Ages, when diligent monk vignerons allegedly tasted the soils in their desire to understand why the wines had such distinctive personalities. Today, Burgundy is renowned as the source of some of the world's finest—and most costly—wines. During the summer, its quaint villages strain with coachloads of wine pilgrims; but these are the converted. This fragmented, complex region can seem impenetrable to the novice, and its wines wilfully disappointing. Burgundy requires attention and an almost intellectual involvement, but it is worth it. At their best, these scented, sinuous reds and intense, refined whites are uniquely memorable.

With vineyards of around 75,000 acres (30,000ha), Burgundy is about one-fifth the size of Bordeaux. The region is a collection of five main areas, each with a localized variation on a continental climate and limestone-rich soils. From top to bottom, Burgundy extends for about 150 miles (240km), but the subregions are scattered and each produces strikingly distinctive wine. Chablis has the feel of an outpost, its vineyards closer to Paris than Dijon. The heart of Burgundy is the Côte d'Or, which comprises the Côte de Nuits and Côte de Beaune; these priceless vineyards stretch for 40 miles (65km) and account for less than 10% of the total area. It is here that the region's most famous wines originate. The Côte Chalonnaise, with pastoral hills, leads south into the rolling expanses of the Mâconnais, the latter producing more good wine from its 25,000 acres (10,000ha) of vineyards.

Burgundy is the antithesis of Bordeaux, the other great French wine region, in every respect. Wines are single varietals, not blends; pure Chardonnay and pure Pinot Noir are responsible for the best whites and reds respectively. Aligoté is behind some simpler whites, and the red Gamay is widely planted in Mâconnais. Smidgeons of Pinot Blanc endure, which may, theoretically at least, be used in some of the basic white burgundies.

Burgundies are defined according to their place of origin, and not (as in Bordeaux) the name of the château. This traceability is reinforced by a four-tier hierarchy that classifies vineyards with increasing specificity and quality potential as either regional, communal, Premier Cru, or Grand Cru.

Burgundy, with its particular topography and soils, lying on the 47th parallel, is the most northerly region in Europe to turn out full-bodied red wines. That it does so is thanks to the deceptively modest-looking ridge that runs through the region, providing sheltered slopes for Pinot Noir to ripen, but not without a fight.

Chardonnay, a late-ripening variety that loves a bit of sun can also struggle here. But the long, slow growing season gives red and white burgundy its paradoxical combination of subtlety and intensity.

The 33 Grand Cru vineyards occupy sites half way up the slope—where exposure, shelter, and drainage deliver optimum quality. Above and below them sit the Premier Crus. There are at least 600 of these, although many of the smaller vineyards are bottled under the name of larger and better-known Premier Crus. The communal vineyards are located on the flatter ground, close to their often eponymous village. The stodgy-soiled regional vineyards stretch away to the east.

The folds of the slopes, however, are further nuanced by geology; fault lines give rise to complex soil profiles that vary from plot to plot. The resulting terroirs are expressed through solo voices of Pinot Noir and Chardonnay in wines of multifaceted nuance. Burgundy makes benchmarks of these two main players. Pinot Noir does not reach these heights anywhere but here. Even Chardonnay, the international traveler, pulls off elegant richness here as nowhere else.

The caveat is that the "best" can be hard to find. In another contrast to Bordeaux, Burgundy's production is fragmented. That prized Grand Cru vineyard can have scores of owners, and their commitment varies as in any other sphere. Many producers have almost identical names, a legacy of inheritances split between siblings and cousins.

This marginal climate exacts a price: a cold, damp summer can afflict both Pinot Noir and Chardonnay. Grapes cannot be blended, as in Bordeaux, where Merlot and Cabernet can help each other out. You need to know your vintages.

Lumped in with Burgundy, but oh-so-different, is Beaujolais. This region majors on Gamay, not Pinot Noir, and its best *crus* represent excellent, albeit unfashionable, value.

Harvesting by hand in Auxey-Duresses in the Côte de Beaune. The AC is a source of very good red wines.

CHABLIS

FRANCE

- Burgundy
- Wine regions of Burgundy
- Chablis wine region

Chablis has an identity quite distinct from the rest of the wine regions of Burgundy. This is Chardonnay country and it is here that this chameleon grape variety takes on its most mineral and vivacious guise. Chardonnay is the perfect conduit for the Chablis terroir. Most wine lovers are familiar with this most ubiquitous restaurant wine, but there is more to Chablis than the generic appellation wine that is most widely available. The varied terroir produces an intriguing variety of form and flavor within the mineral genre. This form of wine appreciation, which is a subtle exercise, makes Chablis among the most fascinating and rewarding wine regions of the world. The best wines repay long cellaring.

Major grapes

🍇 Whites

Chardonnay

Vintages

2009
A good-quality, ripe vintage.

2008
Very good quality. Rich with firm acidity and the capacity for long aging.

2007
A classic vintage. Pure, mineral, and elegant with more body and concentration than 2004.

2006
Straight and powerful, with a richness cloaking a keen mineral core.

2005
Concentrated and generously full-bodied, but with freshness balancing the richness.

2004
A vintage with high acidity. Direct, nervy, and mineral at the best domaines. Dilute at the lesser estates.

Chablis lies 68 miles (110km) to the north of Dijon and historically supplied the Parisian market. It is, however, hazardous to grow vines in such a marginal climate where a spring frost may easily decimate the crop. Traditionally, little fuel burners, or smudge pots, were lit between the vines in the early hours of the morning to ward off frost. More recent methods include aspersion, an expensive technique used in the finest vineyards, where the vines are sprayed with water, which freezes around the bud, forming a protective ice blanket. In 1945, when a particularly vicious frost destroyed the entire harvest, the Chablis vineyards had dwindled to just a few hundred acres.

By the 1960s and 1970s, the region was in the doldrums, with post-war economic migration to the cities and erosion of the Chablis market by southern French wines brought by rail to Paris. However, in the 1980s, some muscular investment brought a change in fortunes. Astute businessmen, including William Fèvre and Joseph Drouhin, bought land cheaply and focused on producing quality. The 1990s and 2000s showed an upward curve, but while developments were largely positive during these years, the vast expansion of the region proved somewhat controversial. Viticulture has improved with better vine material, fewer chemicals, and lower yields. The star growers of the region, Bernard Raveneau and Vincent Dauvissat, have propelled Chablis into the world's top league. This position is supported by a talented younger generation of vignerons that includes Benoît Droin and Stéphane Moreau.

Today, the vineyards cover approximately 12,000 acres (4,800ha) and encompass land around the surrounding villages in which many of the smaller growers are scattered. The hub is the pretty market town of Chablis on the River Serein with its now quiet quayside. Traditionally, this is where the principal producers were based, in smart town houses with capacious cellars, although today many have facilities outside the town.

It may seem strange to include this northerly offshoot within Burgundy, geographically separated as it is from the Côte d'Or. This anomaly is explained by the outcrop of crumbly limestone called Kimmeridge (after the village in Dorset, England) on which the Grand Crus are grown. The slightly different limestone soil known as Portlandian is good, although generally considered inferior to Kimmeridgean.

In such a marginal region, slope and aspect are as crucial as soil. It is no surprise to find the epicenter of Chablis, the Grand Crus, cloaking a southwest-facing hill on the right and more mineral bank of the Serein.

There are seven Grand Crus, of which Les Clos, with its powerful structure, is the best. Vaudésir has intensity, streamlined elegance, and florality, followed by Valmur which has great depth and breadth. A notch below them is the sleek Les Preuses. In the second league are burly Bougros and Grenouilles, and lastly Blanchot, which often has the softest structure and definition.

The block of Grand Crus is fringed by the best Premier Crus: Fourchaume, the steely Montée de Tonnerre, and Mont de Milieu.

Chablis is best unadorned by new oak. However, older oak is widely used at quality domaines. Some, including the excellent Domaine Louis Michel, use only stainless steel *cuve* (tanks). The top wines of Chablis have great aging potential. Do not be deterred by their tight, glassy minerality; they do require—and repay—cellaring.

Domaine Bernard Defaix

Bernard Defaix has 62 acres (25ha) of domaine vineyard and also purchases some fruit. The Grand Cru wines, Bougros and Vaudésir, are labeled Maison Sylvain and Didier Defaix after Bernard's sons, who now run this domaine. The wines are gently appealing, with pretty fruit. Sylvain uses some old oak barrels, but modestly to "keep the typicité of Chablis." Defaix has a staggering 20 acres (8ha) of Côte de Léchet, cloaking the slope behind the house. The 20% oak used for this Premier Cru does not mask the lively minerality, which sings through, but is obvious on the rounded, rich Grand Cru Bougros for which 100% oak is used.

17 rue du Château, Milly, 89800 Chablis
www.bernard-defaix.com

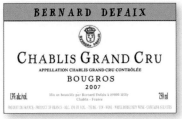

DOMAINE BERNARD DEFAIX
FERMENTED AND AGED IN OAK BARRELS, THIS
WINE HAS A DELICATE FLORAL CHARACTER

Domaine Billaud-Simon

The gruff, chain-smoking Bernard Billaud-Simon makes lucid, transparent Chablis. The glass-fronted winery is state-of-the-art and filled with gleaming stainless steel. The Chablis, and most of his other wines, are made in tanks rather than barrels. However, oak *pièces* (traditional Burgundian 50 gal (228 liter) barrels) are used for three wines, including the Chablis Tête d'Or, in order to balance the minerality in this right bank wine. They have an extensive range showing the precise typicity of terroir, including a floral and exotic Mont de Milieu and a direct and mineral Montée De Tonnerre. There are four excellent Grand Crus here, notably Les Clos and Les Preuses.

1 quai de Reugny, 89800 Chablis
www.billaud-simon.com

Domaine Christian Moreau Père et Fils

Christian Moreau, an affable, larger-than-life Chablis personality, began this venture with his son Fabien in 2002, after claiming back the family vineyards leased to Ets J Moreau. Christian was eager that the limelight should fall on his shy son, who gained experience working at Ngatawara in New Zealand. Fabien was given a free rein and introduced oak, despite Christian's previously staunch no-oak position. The style is full and rich and the quality firmly good. The new oak is most successful on the Grand Cru Valmur, although Les Clos is a more complete and complex wine.

26 avenue d'Oberwesel, 89800 Chablis
www.domainechristianmoreau.com

Domaine Christophe et Fils

Wending your way up through the countryside leads you to Domaine Christophe et Fils, lying high in the middle of nowhere. The family are arable farmers with property that included extensive designated, but unplanted, Chablis land with 62 acres (25ha) of Petit Chablis. In 2000, the son, 24-year-old Sébastien, got planting and also sourced some older vine parcels, including a few in the Premier Cru Fourchaume. He uses only stainless steel in the vinification of his village wine, to maintain what he describes as a pure terroir approach. Sébastien's wines are fresh, clean, and pure and include a lovely Chablis Vieilles Vignes.

Ferme des Carrières Fyé, Chablis 89800
03 86 55 23 10

DOMAINE CHRISTIAN MOREAU
A SMALL PROPORTION OF NEW OAK HAS
BEEN INTRODUCED TO THIS GRAND CRU

Domaine du Colombier

Domaine du Colombier produces charming wines made by the Mothe brothers. Their domaine lies in a picturesque spot in the hamlet of Fontenay-Près-Chablis. They share the work, with Thierry making the wine while Vincent tends the vines. Thierry has a light touch and has refined the style. Their wines have a fragile, tingling minerality. The Premier Cru Fourchaume is slightly nervous and flinty. There is one Grand Cru, Bougros. Made from 60-year-old vines, it has a stony core and well-defined edges. It is currently made in *cuve* (tank), although Thierry is experimenting by fermenting one-third in barriques to give a certain richness.

42 Grande rue, 89800 Fontenay-Près-Chablis
www.chabliscolombier.com

Domaine de la Conciergerie

This Adine family domaine is based in Courgis, a pretty town famous for its starring role in the 18th century novel, *La Vie de Mon Père*. The novel wistfully celebrates old-time moral rectitude, and this upright, firm character is also found in Domaine de la Conciergerie's wines. There is a modern winery, but tasting takes place in the cellar beneath the house. The village Chablis is pure and saline, the Vieilles Vignes from three parcels of 56-year-old vines has a bit more gravelly grunt. The Premier Crus are Côte de Cuissy, an upright Montmains, and Butteaux.

2 allée du Château, 89800 Courgis
03 86 41 40 28

Domaine Corrine and Jean-Pierre Grossot

The pretty estate of Domaine Grossot is on the edge of the village of Fleys and makes traditional wines in a savory, broad, and rounded style. This charming couple are among the best producers in Fleys. They use *bâtonnage* (lees stirring) and some older oak barrels. The village Chablis is made in *cuve* (tank), but the special *cuvée*, La Part des Anges, is made partly in oak *pièces* and is a notch up in intensity. Chablis Fourneaux, a full mineral and savory wine, is aged in 132 gal (600 liter) casks. The wines age attractively, but quite quickly.

4 route de Mont de Milieu, 89800 Fleys
03 86 42 44 64

Domaine Daniel Dampt

Daniel and his two tall sons make glassy, pure fruit Chablis that is crisp and neatly defined. The family, the winery in Milly, and the wine itself have a modern, fresh style. Vincent, with his experience in New Zealand, makes a breezy fruit-driven Chablis, while his father Daniel's version has more depth and minerality, and includes old vines. The Premier Crus are engagingly transparent in reflecting the terroir. Les Lys has white flowers and a fine, chalky line. The Côte de Léchet is tautly focused, linear, and flinty with a touch of gunsmoke; it ages gracefully.

1 rue des Violettes, 89800 Milly-Chablis
www.chablis-dampt.com

Domaine Gérard Duplessis

Gérard Duplessis, who is a man of few words, makes top-quality, austere wines, which he sensibly ages in bottle before release. Even the Fourchaume, typically quite a forthcoming Premier Cru, is battened down and

DOMAINE LOUIS MICHEL ET FILS
OLD VINES, NO OAK, AND WILD YEAST
EXPRESS THE PURE TERROIR OF LES CLOS

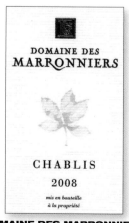

DOMAINE DES MARRONNIERS
PURE AND FRAGRANT VILLAGE CHABLIS
FROM A CHARMING COUPLE IN PREHY

rigid in youth. Given 10 years to open up, the style of these wines is linear and pure with a firm mineral profile. Gérard's son, Lilian, is more forthcoming in his approach. While his father preferred to use neutral oak (older barrels), Lilian is experimenting with new oak barrels on some of his Premier Crus. This includes the Montée De Tonnerre with between 10–20% new oak. *Bâtonnage* is another innovation under the current generation.

5 quai de Reugny, 89800 Chablis
03 86 42 10 35

Domaine Jean-Claude Bessin

Jean-Claude Bessin is a tall and kindly man who makes Chablis in a fine floral style. The wines are matured in older oak barrels in a cellar beneath the church in La Chapelle Vaupelteigne. There are two *cuvées* from the Premier Cru Fourchaume. La Pièce du Comte is a selection of historic parcels that have been in the family since the 19th century, inherited from the viscounts of Maligny four generations ago, via Jean-Claude's wife. Jean-Claude does not make a special label to boast of this connection; it is only evident from the cork. He also makes one Grand Cru, from Valmur.

18 rue de Chitry, 89800 Chablis
03 86 42 46 77

Domaine Jean Collet et Fils

The hale and hearty Gilles Collet quite clearly loves life making Chablis and revels in meeting those who come to his door. He stepped into his role when he was just 19. Though the family have been growers since 1792, Gilles's father, Jean, only began making and bottling the domaine's wines in the 1950s. Gilles runs the domaine with his equally hospitable wife Dominique, who brought more vines with her into their marriage. He uses stainless steel, *pièces,* and *foudres*—gorgeous-looking oval oak casks, which hold 1,760 gallons (8,000 liters). Collet's wines are full and generous, and the range includes a rich and substantial Grand Cru Valmur.

5 avenue de la Liberté, 89800 Chablis
www.domaine-collet.fr

Domaine Jean-Paul & Benoît Droin

Benoît Droin is one of the most talented and innovative winemakers in Chablis; he is certainly not afraid to experiment. He quickly and beneficially changed the domaine style when he took over from his father Jean-Paul, notably pulling back on the oak. The new generation appropriately has a new modern winery in which to introduce the changes. There is no domaine style, as Benoît adapts his winemaking to emphasize the character of each *cuvée*, using more oak to bring out the richness of Grand Cru Grenouilles, with none on the softer Blanchots. Thought-provoking wines come from this domaine, including some fine Grand Cru, Vaudésir, and Les Clos.

14 bis, rue Jean Jaurès, 89800 Chablis
www.jeanpaul-droin.fr

Domaine Joseph Drouhin

The Drouhin family are substantial landowners in both Chablis and the rest of Burgundy. Part of their Chablis property includes a watermill, Moulin de Chichée, now rented out as a gîte. They began purchasing land in 1968 and work their vines organically. The Domaine

de Vaudron, from 2008 labeled Drouhin-Vaudron to celebrate 40 years in Chablis, comes from vines abutting the Premier Cru vineyards of Montée de Tonnerre and Mont de Milieu. These vines may be of lowly village status, but they are farmed biodynamically. The fruit is pressed in Chablis, vinified and aged in Beaune, and Drouhin has recently abandoned the use of new oak. These wines are very accomplished Chablis.

7 rue d'Enfer, 21200 Beaune
www.drouhin.com

Domaine Laurent Tribut

Laurent Tribut is a quiet man with a domaine in Poinchy who makes pure, lithe, nervy Chablis shimmering with terroir. There is an excellent village Chablis, focused and quartzy, which develops lovely saline characters as it ages. The Côte de Léchet is streamlined, with a rapierlike acidity and a cool platinum core. The style is not surprising as Laurent spent a decade making wine with René and Vincent Dauvissat, marrying Vincent's sister, Marie-Clotilde.

89800 Chablis
03 86 42 46 22

Domaine Long-Depaquit

Domaine Long-Depaquit is a grand affair housed in a stately château with a small park in Chablis. The estate, which dates back to 1791, has been owned by the Beaune négociant Albert Bichot since the 1970s. Jean-Didier Basch is in charge and the quality is much improved. There is quite a lot of new oak here, which can detract from the terroir. However, their rendition of Les Clos responds well to a small percentage of new barrels, bringing spicy, glossy, and sensual characters to the fore. Domaine Long-Depaquit's Moutonne, a *monopole* situated within the Grand Cru vineyards, but with its own unique status, is richly perfumed and mineral, and comes from a small amphitheater within Vaudésir.

89800 Chablis
03 86 42 11 13

Domaine Louis Michel et Fils

Top-quality Chablis here from Jean-Loup Michel, whose immaculate cellars are housed beneath his lovely town house in Chablis. Jean-Loup is self-effacing and good humored. He uses no oak whatsoever; everything is in *cuve.* The notable richness comes from the quality of fruit alone and the domaine style shows glossy minerality. The wines are assured, focused, and true to the terroir, from the silky Petit Chablis to the sleek and complex Grand Cru. The Vaudésir is elegant with a core of smooth, polished steel. Les Clos combines power with finesse.

9 boulevard de Ferrières, 89800 Chablis
www.louismicheletfils.com

Domaine des Malandes

Domaine des Malandes produces wines from Petit Chablis to Grand Cru with lovely minerality and terroir character. It was established in the 1980s by the engaging Jean-Bernard and Lyne Marchive. Jean-Bernard has a real feeling for the terroir, reflected in his wine. Lyne now runs the show with their daughter Marion and son-in-law Josh. Guénolé Breteaudeau continues the winemaking in the domaine's pure style. There are two Premier Crus, a quivering, gunflint Côte de Léchet and a quartzy, grippy Montmains. The Grand Cru Vaudésir is poised and Les Clos is sleek and intense. These wines age well.

63 rue Auxerroise, 89800 Chablis
www.domainedesmalandes.com

Domaine des Marronniers

Wine lovers must drive the pretty route up to Préhy to find this domaine, where Bernard and Marie-Claude Legland give a warm welcome. They are a merry couple making pretty wines. The wines are not profound or destined for long aging, but are classic and delightful in the short and medium term. The Petit Chablis wine is blossomy, and for Chablis they have separated the Vieilles Vignes since 2005. The wines are attractive, pure, and fragrant. The domaine also produces an elegant Premier Cru Montmains and a more rounded Côtes de Jouan.

1–3 Grande rue de Chablis, 89800 Préhy
www.domaine-marronniers.com

Domaine Moreau-Naudet

Stéphane Moreau is a talented, impish chap with a young family whose good humor and lively spirit shine through his wines. The range is vibrant, pure, and underpinned by something more serious. The family have grown grapes since the 17th century, but when Stéphane took over in 1991, he began making and bottling his own wines. He has old vines that have been managed organically for the past 20 years and is among the few to pick by hand. The quality of these wines is consistently good. The straight Chablis is racy and floral. A clear favorite is the energetic, steely, and crisp Montée de Tonnerre.

5 rue des Fosses, 89800 Chablis
03 86 42 14 83

Domaine Pinson Frères

Laurent and Christophe Pinson's domaine lies on the Quai Voltaire in Chablis. Laurent likes to use *bâtonnage* for *gras* (body) and older oak, with a tiny proportion of new barrels, for richness. He experiments with modern techniques, such as micro-oxygenation, to make a Chablis which is generous and substantial. Equally, there is no lack of minerality or terroir definition. There is a dense, precise, and stony Montmains; a well-toned Mont de Milieu; and a fine-quality Grand Cru Les Clos. He selects three barrels to become Chablis Les Clos Cuvée Authentic, labeled in honor of his grandfather, which get the "full monty" of a 100% oak fermentation.

5 quai Voltaire, 89800 Chablis
www.domaine-pinson.com

Domaine Raveneau

Bernard Raveneau makes thoroughbred Chablis, sleek, toned, and pure with a steely core. It has a cult following, an international reputation, and prices to match. Bernard, by contrast, is modest. His wines spend two years in oak and have potential for great longevity. Excellent Premier Cru: mineral Montmains, svelte Vaillons, racy Montée de Tonnerre. Grand Cru Valmur has steely muscularity and Les Clos is superbly complex and polished. Stunning wine from one of the great domaines in Burgundy.

89800 Chablis
03 86 42 17 46

DOMAINE WILLIAM FEVRE
A PIONEERING DOMAINE, NO NEW OAK
MASKS THE PRISTINE GRAND CRU WINES

DOMAINE JEAN-PAUL DROIN
FINE GRAND CRU FROM THE NEW
GENERATION OF AN OLD CHABLIS FAMILY

Domaine Servin

The winemaking at Domaine Servin, from François Servin and his amiable American right-hand man Marc Cameron, is intelligent and considered. François' family have been growers in Chablis for 300 years. His great-grandfather was also a cooper. They are market savvy and produce a pretty Petit Chablis and fresh, classic Chablis made purposely for immediate drinking. The Chablis Cuvée Massalle is from older vines and is more concentrated. There are several decent Premier Crus and four good Grand Crus. Of these, the delightful floral and fragrant Blanchots has a racy finish and there is also a powerful, sumptuous, and distinctive Bougros.

89800 Chablis
www.domaine-servin.fr

Domaine/Maison Simmonet-Febvre

Domaine Simmonet-Febvre, founded in 1840, was purchased by Maison Louis Latour in 2003, but is quite distinct from Louis Latour's Côte d'Or-style Chablis. It is made by Jean-Philippe Archambaud in a modern winery outside Chablis. The style is fresh, breezy, and nicely edged. The village wines are under Stelvin screwcaps and only the Grand Crus get any oak treatment. The domaine owns plots in Chapleot, Mont de Millieu, and Preuses, while the rest is made from purchased grapes. It is worth sourcing the Mont de Millieu while it is available. It is dense, intense, and rich and made from old vine, which sadly must soon be grubbed up.

9 avenue d'Oberwesel, 89800 Chablis
www.simonnet-febvre.com

Domaine Vincent Dauvissat

Domaine Vincent Dauvissat makes quintessential Chablis. The wine is capable of taking even the most experienced wine lover's breath away. It is indisputably one of the finest domaines in Chablis, yet Vincent is so discreet and shy. The wines do the talking and eloquently so, from the excellent Petit Chablis to the Grand Crus. They are nervous, racy, saline wines that bring the terroir into sharp focus. Of Dauvissat's Premier Crus, Séchets is tense and chalky while Vaillons is reminiscent of smooth, wet stones. The Grand Crus are outstanding: Les Preuses is elegant and classic and Les Clos is profound.

89800 Chablis
03 86 42 11 58

Domaine William Fèvre

Domaine William Fèvre, today owned by Henriot Champagne, has substantial landholdings, including 30 acres (12ha) of Premier Cru vineyard, making it the largest producer of Premier and Grand Cru wines. The sites are all good quality and the vines are mature, having been purchased and planted by William Fèvre in the late 1950s when interest in Chablis was low. The management of the vineyard is painstaking and requires a team of 24 to work the vines. Didier Séguier is the meticulous winemaker. Key to his approach is very clean juice, letting it settle by gravity before fermentation, and he uses no new oak. The style is cool, classic, and pure. There is a racy, saline Premier Cru Monteée de Tonnerre, as well as pristine Grand Crus from this serious domaine.

21 avenue d'Oberwesel, 89800 Chablis
www.williamfevre.fr

COTE DE NUITS

The Côte de Nuits produces red wine from Pinot Noir that rank among the finest in the world. It forms the northern section of the Côte d'Or, stretching from just south of Dijon. It encompasses the villages of Gevrey-Chambertin, Chambolle-Musigny, and Vosne-Romanée, names that resonate with lovers of fine wine throughout the world. Pinot Noir, possibly the most capricious and challenging red grape variety, thrives in this continental climate. Its history is rooted in the monastic tradition of the Middle Ages. This is, above all, a region of *vignerons*, or farmers, who micro-manage small plots of land to maximize the expression of terroir. Tradition is strong in this region where some top *vignerons* have returned to the horse-drawn plough.

Major grapes

 Reds

Pinot Noir

Whites

Chardonnay

Vintages

2009
This vintage promises to be very good, with rich, dense fruit and ripe tannin.

2008
Streamlined, direct wines with soft tannins, juicy fruit, and notable spicy character.

2007
Very pretty and pure; a lighter vintage with silky tannins, red fruit, and delicious fragrance.

2006
The first of three good middle ranking vintages. Straight and strict. Firm acidity and good terroir distinction.

2005
Splendid fruit. A top-notch vintage. Full, rich, and well balanced.

2004
Atypical. A difficult vintage with firm acidity and tannin. The somewhat herbaceous character is mellowing.

Marsannay, practically in the suburbs of Dijon, was elevated to Appellation Contrôlée Village status in 1989 and produces simple red burgundy as well as pretty rosé and white. The red should be fresh and fruity with lively cherry flavors, and be a notch above Côte de Nuits Village quality. Fixin, the next village to the south, produces somewhat more rustic Village wine and eight Premiers Crus.

At Gevrey-Chambertin, quality catapults from simple to serious. It is a large village sprawling from the Combe de Lavaux, and claims a greedy nine of the 24 Grands Crus of the Côte de Nuits. This includes the architectural Chambertin and the sumptuous, richly scented Chambertin-Clos de Bèze. In simplified terms, Gevrey is known for a masculine, full, and firmly structured style. There are 26 Premiers Crus and the best are found on the southeast-facing slopes flowing from the Combe de Lavaux and include Clos St-Jacques, a wonderful Premier Cru of Grand Cru quality.

The Gevrey-Chambertin Grands Crus form a contiguous block to the south of the village along the Route des Grands Crus. The Gevrey Premier Cru Combottes, nestled in a slight dip that is marginally less well drained, separates Latricières-Chambertin from the plush and seductively exotic Clos de la Roche, one of the Grands Crus of the neighboring village, Morey-St-Denis.

Moving south, the Grand Cru roll call continues with the upright, perfumed Clos St-Denis, Clos des Lambray, the superbly defined Clos de Tart, and a sliver of the toned, lightly muscular Bonnes-Mares. While the Grands Crus have distinctive characters, Premier Cru and Village Morey wines suffer from a somewhat ambiguous identity. They are neither as firmly structured as Gevrey, nor are they as fragrant as neighboring Chambolle, but are luscious, velvet-textured, and fruity. There is a small amount of very good savory white wine.

Chambolle-Musigny is a twisting medieval village sheltering beneath a sinister cliff. The soil is impoverished and pebbly with limestone, and more clay at the appellation edges. It offers the most graceful of Côte de Nuits reds. These are wines of delightful perfume and silky tannins. In the plumper Premiers Crus, the fruit is redolent of strawberry fields on a warm summer day and the tannins are svelte. In Les Cras, shimmering minerality defines the wine, while Les Amoureuses seduces with its silky, fragrant palate. The two Grands Crus are poles apart; the dark, slightly brooding Bonnes-Mares, versus the exquisite, sublimely intense, but ethereal, Le Musigny.

Below Chambolle crouches the heavy stone château of Vougeot, most mysterious when swathed in fog. The Clos de Vougeot Grand Cru dominates this commune and stretches to the deeper soils beside the main road. It is as variable in quality as it is large. On par with the better Clos de Vougeot are Grands-Echézeaux producing dense, black-fruited wines and the slightly lighter Echézeaux. However, it is to Vosne that the wine lover will gravitate. Here lie the great vineyards that set the spine tingling: Romanée Conti—out of this world with a price tag to match—the imposing La Tâche, the exquisite Romanée St-Vivant, and the rich, satin-textured Richebourg.

Vosne is a quiet, rather non-descript village, yet conjures from its fine terroir six Grands Crus and a fine array of Premiers Crus. The Village style combines subtlety with strength.

Across the border lies Nuits-St-Georges, a provincial chest-beating town with a history of négociant houses. Simply put, the style divides into the north with plumper, dark wines and the south with grippy, mineral wines. There are no Grands Crus, but the austere, quartzy, and compact Les St-Georges is one in all but name.

Clos des Lambrays Morey-St-Denis

The rolling Clos des Lambrays, situated slightly higher up the slope than the neighboring Grand Cru, is the focus of this domaine, although it produces some delicious white Premier Cru from Puligny. The 22 acre (9ha) vineyard is virtually a *monopole*. Since 2005, a third of the Clos des Lambrays has been ploughed by horse-drawn plough. The remainder is worked with a lightweight tractor to resemble a horse as closely as possible. The fruit from vines younger than 25 years goes into the Premier Cru. The long-serving manager, Thierry Brouhin, often uses 100% of the stems. He favors a warm temperature peak during fermentation to produce a Grand Cru with rich depth and a velvet-smooth structure.

31 rue Basse, 21220 Morey-St-Denis
www.lambrays.com

Domaine Alain Jeanniard

Morey-St-Denis

Alain Jeanniard is a relatively new domaine, established in 2000, with the small vats squashed higgledy-piggledy outside. The thoughtful Alain was an electrician for 11 years before studying winemaking. He started off with his grandfather's 80-year-old vines in Chenevrey, part of which is Village and part Premier Cru. He makes restrained wine with plenty of energy, lovely clarity of fruit, and not much new oak. He rents vines from his family and has a small négociant on the side. His appellations may be fairly modest to date, but he is certainly talented and one to watch.

4 rue aux Loups, 21220 Morey-St-Denis
www.domainealainjeanniard.fr

Domaine Alain Michelot

Nuits-St-Georges

Elodie, who took over from her father in 2005, is the fourth generation at Domaine Alain Michelot. She describes herself as cautious about change. The Michelot style is fruity, robust, and honest; not at all flashy. The wines have good clarity of fruit and use 30% new oak. Michelot offers the chance to get to grips with different Nuits-St-Georges terroir without spending a fortune. There is a brooding Les Porrets St-Georges, an Aux Chaignots with cool graphite reserve, and a full-bodied Les Vaucrains.

6 rue Camille Rodier, 21700 Nuits-St-Georges
03 80 61 14 46

Domaine Anne Gros Vosne-Romanée

Anne Gros is extremely capable and pragmatic. As a young woman she wanted to do something with her hands and so, when her father fell ill in the late 1980s, she took over his vines and determined to bottle her own wine. At the time, it was sold in bulk and the vines were in poor shape. These days she rates among the best growers in the Vosne and has garnered international acclaim. This is well deserved. All the wines, made by her husband, François Parent, are pristine and streamlined.

11 rue des Communes, 21700 Vosne-Romanée
www.anne-gros.com

Domaine de l'Arlot Nuits-St-Georges

The rather stately Domaine de l'Arlot is in Prémeaux, south of the town of Nuits-St-Georges. The principal two wines from this domaine are from Nuits-St-Georges and

CLOS DES LAMBRAYS
TENDED BY HORSES, THESE VINES PRODUCE
A RICH AND VELVETY GRAND CRU

DOMAINE ARMAND ROUSSEAU
ONLY THE BEST GRAPES MAKE IT OUT OF
THE VINEYARD AND INTO THIS WINE

eloquently express their very different terroir. The Clos de l'Arlot has 60-year-old vines growing in shallow soil and is rather elegant and flowing, while the wine from the deeper soil of Clos des Forêts is rich, full, and firm. There are 5 acres (2ha) of the domaine planted to Chardonnay and the zesty, mineral Clos de L'Arlot Blanc is certainly a curiosity worth trying.

Route Nationale, 21700 Prémeaux-Prissey
03 80 61 01 92

Domaine Armand Rousseau

Gevrey-Chambertin

Armand Rousseau is perhaps the most famous domaine in Gevrey-Chambertin, with a track record of fine wine stretching back 70-odd years to the time of Armand Rousseau. Armand's grandson Eric continues the tradition of making simply brilliant wine. All the selection is done in the vineyard and the bunches are 100% stemmed with just a few of the stalks added back. There are a wealth of Grands Crus here, with unusually little new oak in four of them, rendering the terroir most transparent. There is the ethereal and perfumed Charmes-Chambertin, an assertive, chiseled Mazis-Chambertin, an elegantly racy Ruchottes-Chambertin, and a densely spicy Clos De La Roche. The shimmering Clos St-Jacques has a higher percentage of new oak, and is clearly of Grand Cru quality, regardless of its Premier Cru appellation. Eric is responsible for one of the finest Clos de Bèze, muscular and sumptuously scented, and an outstanding Chambertin.

1 rue de l'Aumônerie, 21220 Gevrey-Chambertin
www.domaine-rousseau.com

Domaine Arnoux-Lachaux

Vosne-Romanée

Pascal Lachaux runs the show here. The landholding is principally in Vosne-Romanée and Nuits-St-Georges. The village wines show excellent typicity and there is an alluring, velvet-textured Les Suchots and some Grands Crus. Pascal places great emphasis on yields, reducing the number of bunches a month before vintage. He also encourages grass between the rows to compete with the vines. He ages some of the wine in 112 gal (500 litre) casks, for the slow oxygenation properties, and combines this with the wines from traditional burgundy barrels.

21670 Vosne-Romanée
03 80 61 09 85

Domaine des Beaumont Morey-St-Denis

Domaine des Beaumont's vineyards straddle the Morey/Gevrey border, and include plots of old vines in the Premiers Crus Morey Les Millandes, Gevrey Combottes, and Cherbaudes, and the Grand Cru Charmes-Chambertin. For many years, the family sold all the wines from these choice holdings to the négociants; Thierry Beaumont ended this practice in the late 1990s. These exuberantly fruity, supple wines are attractively generous and often very approachable, even in youth, characteristics shaped partly by old-vine intensity, and partly by Beaumont's light hand in the winemaking. Cherbaudes, the beautifully sited but relatively unknown Premier Cru, can be really impressive.

9 rue Ribordot, 21220 Morey-St-Denis
www.domaine-des-beaumont.com

COTE DE NUITS

The vineyards of the Côte de Nuits are squeezed into a narrower strip than their Beaune equivalents. Above them, the ridge is a little more severe, the outcrops a little more impressive. A little white wine is made here, but this land is Pinot Noir land. The name of almost every town will resonate with wine lovers. The sweetest spot of all is the horizontal run of Grand Cru vineyards that wriggle, hugging the east-facing shelter of the outcrops above, from the upper west of Gevrey, through the top of Morey-St-Denis, all the way through Chambolle-Musigny, Vougeot, and Vosne-Romanée.

2007

ANNE   RICHEBOURG   GROS

Appellation Richebourg Contrôlée
GRAND CRU

DOMAINE
ANNE GROS

13.5% vol.   750 ml

MISE EN BOUTEILLE AU DOMAINE À 21700 VOSNE-ROMANÉE · PRODUCE OF FRANCE
Propriétaire Viticulteur · www.anne-gros.com

CHAMBOLLE-MUSIGNY

Dom Comte Georges de Vogüé
Dom Georges and Christophe Roumier
Dom Ghislaine Barthod

Dom Jacques-Frédéric Mugnier
Dom Louis Boillot

PREMEAUX-PRISSEY

Dom de l'Arlot
Dom Jean-Jacques Confuron
Dom Michèle et Patrice Rion
Dom Prieuré-Roch
Dom de La Vougeraie

NUITS-ST-GEORGES 1ᴱᴿ CRU

APPELLATION NUITS-ST-GEORGES 1ᴱᴿ CRU CONTRÔLÉE

CLOS DES ARGILLIÈRES

2006

DOMAINE
MICHÈLE & PATRICE RION

KEY

	Chambolle-Musigny
	Fixin
	Gevrey-Chambertin
	Marsannay
	Morey-St-Denis
	Nuits-St-Georges
	Prémeaux-Prissey
	Vosne-Romanée
	Vougeot
	Vineyards
- - -	Commune boundary
——	33ft (10m) contours

NUITS ST-GEORGES

Dom Alain Michelot
Dom Faiveley
Dom Gilles Remoriquet
Dom Henri Gouges

Dom Liogier d'Ardhuy
Dom Robert Chevillon
Maison Jean-Claude Boisset
Maison Nicolas Potel

VOUGEOT

Dom Christian Clerget
Dom Hudelot-Noellat

La Grande Rue
GRAND CRU MONOPOLE
Domaine François Lamarche
Viticulteur à Vosne Romanée (Côte d'Or) France
PRODUCT OF FRANCE
MIS EN BOUTEILLE À LA PROPRIÉTÉ

VOSNE-ROMANEE

Dom Anne Gros
Dom Arnoux Lachaux
Dom Bruno Clavelier
Dom du Comte Liger-Belair
Dom Forey Père et Fils
Dom François Lamarche
Dom Georges Mugneret-Gibourg
Dom Gros Frère et Soeur

Dom Jack Confuron-Cotétidot
Dom Jean Grivot
Dom Leroy
Dom Méo-Camuzet
Dom Michel Gros
Dom de la Romanée-Conti
Dom Sylvain Cathiard
Maison Pascal Lachaux

Map labels: Bois de la Montagne · 399m (1309ft) · 400m (1312ft) · 412m (1352ft) · PREMEAUX-PRISSEY · Prémeaux-Prissey · NUITS-ST-GEORGES · Nuits-St-Georges · Vosne-Romanée · VOSNE-ROMANEE · VOUGEOT · Vougeot · CHAMBOLLE-MUSIGNY · Chambolle-Musigny · Flagey-Echézeaux · Gilly-lès-Cîteaux · N74 · D25 · D8 · D122 · E17-A31

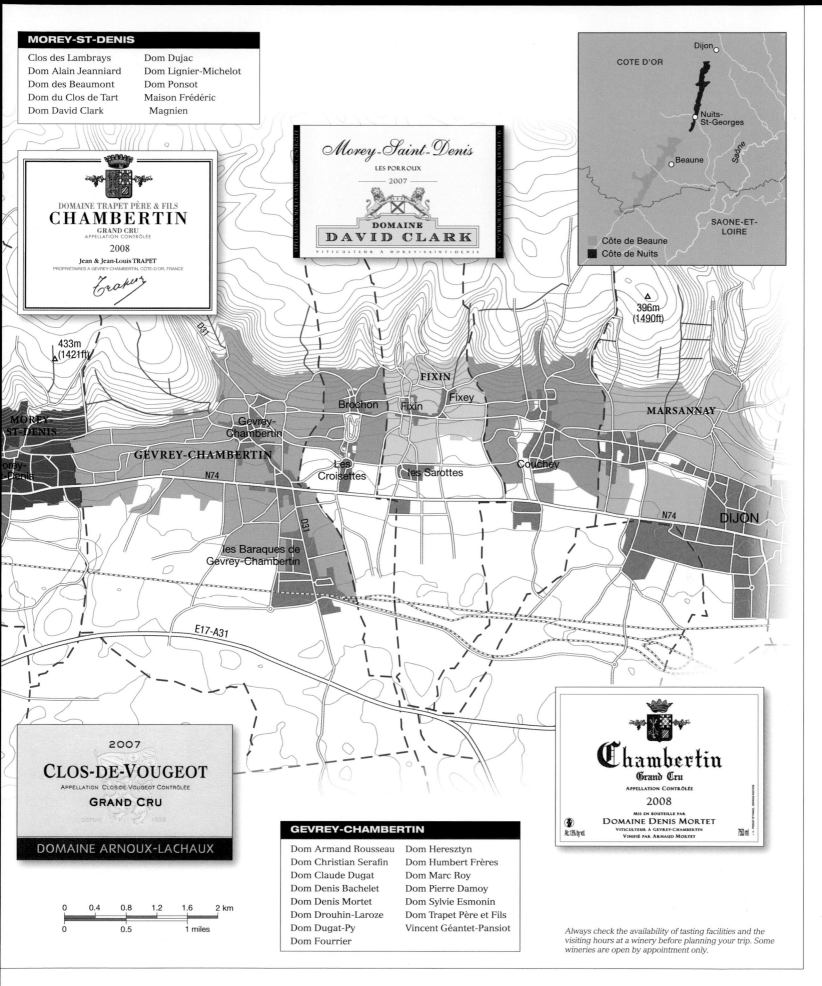

MOREY-ST-DENIS

Clos des Lambrays	Dom Dujac
Dom Alain Jeanniard	Dom Lignier-Michelot
Dom des Beaumont	Dom Ponsot
Dom du Clos de Tart	Maison Frédéric
Dom David Clark	Magnien

Morey-Saint-Denis
LES PORROUX
2007
DOMAINE
DAVID CLARK
VITICULTEUR À MOREY·SAINT·DENIS

DOMAINE TRAPET PÈRE & FILS
CHAMBERTIN
GRAND CRU
APPELLATION CONTRÔLÉE
2008
Jean & Jean-Louis TRAPET
PROPRIÉTAIRES A GEVREY-CHAMBERTIN, CÔTE-D'OR, FRANCE

COTE D'OR
Dijon
Nuits-St-Georges
Beaune

☐ Côte de Beaune
■ Côte de Nuits

SAONE-ET-LOIRE

396m
(1490ft)

433m
(1421ft)

FIXIN

Brochon Fixin Fixey

MOREY-ST-DENIS

Gevrey-Chambertin

MARSANNAY

GÉVREY-CHAMBERTIN

N74

Les Croisettes les Sarottes Couchey

N74 DIJON

les Baraques de
Gevrey-Chambertin

E17-A31

2007
CLOS-DE-VOUGEOT
APPELLATION CLOS-DE-VOUGEOT CONTRÔLÉE
GRAND CRU
DEPUIS 1858
DOMAINE ARNOUX-LACHAUX

Chambertin
Grand Cru
APPELLATION CONTRÔLÉE
2008
MIS EN BOUTEILLE PAR
DOMAINE DENIS MORTET
VITICULTEUR À GEVREY-CHAMBERTIN
VINIFIÉ PAR ARNAUD MORTET
750 ml

0	0.4	0.8	1.2	1.6	2 km
0		0.5			1 miles

GEVREY-CHAMBERTIN

Dom Armand Rousseau	Dom Heresztyn
Dom Christian Serafin	Dom Humbert Frères
Dom Claude Dugat	Dom Marc Roy
Dom Denis Bachelet	Dom Pierre Damoy
Dom Denis Mortet	Dom Sylvie Esmonin
Dom Drouhin-Laroze	Dom Trapet Père et Fils
Dom Dugat-Py	Vincent Géantet-Pansiot
Dom Fourrier	

*Always check the availability of tasting facilities and the
visiting hours at a winery before planning your trip. Some
wineries are open by appointment only.*

**DOMAINE DU COMTE
LIGER-BELAIR**
AN ARISTOCRATIC FAMILY PRODUCE
THIS FLAMBOYANT WINE

Domaine Bruno Clavelier Vosne-Romanée

Bruno Clavelier's domaine is certified organic, and he
also practices biodynamics. In his cellar, he has samples
of the soils from different parcels, explaining these
with a passion that translates to the wines. The wines
show good typicity; for example, from Vosne-Romanée
there is a spicy and mineral Aux Brulées and a rich and
rounded Les Beaumonts. La Combe D'Orveaux, which
lies at the edge of the forest above and to the south of
Musigny, delivers an energetic Chambolle with a tautly
resonant finish. There is also a savory white wine from
80-year-old Aligoté vines.

6 RN 74, 21700 Vosne-Romanée
03 80 61 10 81

Domaine Christian Clerget Vougeot

The pure, refined wines of Christian Clerget can take a
while to get going, but this quality-focused domaine
deserves to be better known. Holdings are scattered
across several Côte de Nuits appellations, and include an
intense Chambolle Charmes Premier Cru and a lively
Echézeaux Grand Cru. Tucked between Chambolle and
the Grand Cru Vougeot is the domaine's Vougeot Premier
Cru Les Petits Vougeot. This relatively unknown
appellation is worth seeking out for its exotic, floral scent
and hedonistic textures. Clerget favors minimal handling
and achieves nuanced, subtle Pinot Noir.

21640 Vougeot
03 80 62 87 37

Domaine Christian Serafin

Gevrey-Chambertin

Christian and next-generation Karine take an organic
approach, respecting the vine, using organic matter for
feeding, and paying great attention to hoeing and turning
the soil. The domaine, which is situated up near the
castle, lies beside the vineyard of Les Cazetiers. The
50-year-old vines make reserved and concentrated wine.
The domaine style is honest, full, and sometimes robust,
but with an expressive perfume to the nose. There is a lot
of new oak; 100% new barrels are used from the excellent
Gevrey-Chambertin Vieilles Vignes upward.

21220 Gevrey-Chambertin
03 80 34 35 40

Domaine Claude Dugat

Gevrey-Chambertin

This is a true family concern, as Claude Dugat, now
in his mid-50s, is assisted by his two daughters and
his son Bertrand. There is a very medieval feel to this
domaine in a former chapter house. The Cellier des
Dîmes lies in the shadow of the church tower and the
sound of the bells resonates to the cellar. Claude Dugat's
wines have an uplifting purity entirely in keeping with
the ecclesiastical setting. He has a fine portfolio, including
three Grands Crus, among which is a taut and dynamic
Griotte-Chambertin, as well as a fine Premier Cru,
Lavaux-St-Jacques. This wine comes from vines
planted in very shallow soil at the top of the vineyard,
which may account for its more mineral note. The
domaine style shows lovely clarity of fruit and a
conservative use of new oak.

1 place de la Cure, 21220 Gevrey-Chambertin
03 80 34 36 18

Domaine du Clos de Tart

Morey-St-Denis

Clos de Tart has cult status. If you are fortunate enough
to be invited through its imposing 19th-century portal,
you will find yourself in a meticulously maintained
medieval complex of buildings. The vines stretch behind
and up the gentle slope. It is a walled and hallowed
sanctuary and the keeper is the infinitely courteous
and studious Sylvain Pitiot. He is responsible for
enabling this Grand Cru to fulfil its potential. The
calcareous soils of the vineyard have been analyzed
and divided into six sections, and each parcel is vinified
separately. It is fascinating to taste them and appreciate
how the blend rises above the individual parts to
something quite sensational.

21220 Morey-St-Denis
03 80 34 30 91

Domaine Comte Georges de Vogüé

Chambolle-Musigny

There are just four wines here at Comte Georges de
Vogüé—but what wines. This top domaine has celebrity
status and a following clamoring for the elegant and
poised wines, which are available and affordable only to
the few. Yet, as you pass under the thick stone arch beside
the church in Chambolle, into the wide courtyard, an
extraordinary sense of stillness and order prevails. The
manager, François Millet, a man of great and quiet
precision, presides over the cellar in a time-honored
ritual where the Chambolle, the Amoureuses, the Bonnes
Mares, and Le Musigny lie sleeping in preparation for
their turn on the international wine stage.

21220 Chambolle-Musigny
03 80 62 86 25

Domaine du Comte Liger-Belair

Vosne-Romanée

The château of this aristocratic family lies in the middle of
Vosne. Louis-Michel, who made the family estate home
for his young family in 2000, is doing a marvelous job in
building the vinous fortunes of the domaine. Increasingly
biodynamic, a horse-drawn plough is used in the vines.
Louis-Michel has brought the parcels, which had been
leased out, back into the fold and now has a serious
portfolio. This includes a flamboyant Aux Reignots and a
gracefully poised Grand Cru, La Romanée. The latter has
been a *monopole* since 1826 and lies above Romanée-
Conti. This domaine goes from strength to strength.

Château de Vosne-Romanée, 21700 Vosne-Romanée
www.liger-belair.fr

Domaine David Clark Morey-St-Denis

Irish engineer David Clark decided during his study
at the Lycée Viticole in Beaune to gain some practical
experience. He took a chance by buying a small
parcel of Grand Ordinaire vines in Morey-St-Denis.
The vineyard, now certified organic, is undeniably
modest, but David is squeezing the best from it. This
is a very promising start from the Irishman, who is
beginning to expand his tiny estate with a Village wine
from Morey-St-Denis. There should be more to come.
He is one to watch. ★**Rising star**

17 Grande rue, 21220 Morey-St-Denis
www.domainedavidclark.com

DOMAINE DU CLOS DE TART
A CULT WINE THAT IS PUT TOGETHER
WITH INFINITE CARE AND ATTENTION

Domaine Denis Bachelet
Gevrey-Chambertin

The entrance to Domaine Denis Bachelet is as discreet as the man, and this quality is reflected in his wines. Denis makes just five classic and thought-provoking wines. If you visit immediately post-vintage, you will find the winery spick and span, and this meticulous attention to detail in cellar and vineyard is reflected in the precision of the entire range of wines from the Bourgogne to the Charmes-Chambertin. Denis stems the grapes to ensure the tannins are silky, and is very gentle with extraction. He uses *remontage* (pumping over of the juice) to create a harmonious blend of the grapes, after which he uses a careful and traditional *pigeage* (punching down of the fermenting grapes). The Gevrey-Chambertin, Les Corbeaux, is textbook, with elegant dark cherry fruit woven with graphite minerality.

25 rue Clos, 21220 St-Philibert
03 80 51 89 09

Domaine Denis Mortet Gevrey-Chambertin

This second-generation Gevrey-Chambertin domaine shot to stardom under its founder, Denis Mortet. Mortet appealed to the modern consumer with showy wines, sleek with new oak. It was not long before the Grands Vins, notably le Chambertin, gained cult status. After Mortet's tragic and untimely death, his son Arnaud, at just 25 years old, took the helm for the 2006 vintage. Arnaud's taste is for a slightly more elegant and restrained style than his father, so he has pulled back a little on the new oak and is working toward finer tannins, while not departing too far from the forward and rich style that has become synonymous with the domaine. In addition to the wine from Gevrey, this domaine also has a lovely Fixin Village.

22 rue de l'Eglise, 21220 Gevrey-Chambertin
www.domaine-denis-mortet.com

Domaine Drouhin-Laroze
Gevrey-Chambertin

Domaine Drouhin-Laroze was established in the mid-19th century and is now run by Philippe Drouhin, a descendant of the founder, Jean-Baptiste. Philippe has transformed its reputation as an underachieving domaine. It has 30 acres (12ha) incorporating a staggering seven Grands Crus, including a muscular, seductive Bonnes-Mares, a smooth, spicy Clos de Bèze, and a silky, perfumed Le Musigny. The structured Clos de Vougeot is clearly from vines well-positioned toward the top of this large, variable vineyard. His wines are approachable, with plenty of fruit.

20 rue du Gaizot, 21220 Gevrey-Chambertin
www.drouhin-laroze.com

Domaine Dugat-Py Gevrey-Chambertin

Tasting at Domaine Dugat-Py takes place in a fine vaulted cellar, a fittingly impressive setting to taste this aromatic, intense, and sophisticated set of wines. Bernard has been making wines for 35 vintages. His three Village wines from Gevrey-Chambertin, Pommard, and Vosne-Romanée show excellent typicity, but this capacity to translate the terroir shines in the Grand Cru and is aided by some very old vines. The Mazoyères-Chambertin is upright and stony, while the Mazis-Chambertin is more generously fruity than the Mazoyères, but not as perfumed as the Charmes. The Chambertin is enrobed in svelte tannins and is majestic. These are lusciously concentrated and fruity wines.

rue de Planteligone, 21220 Gevrey-Chambertin
www.dugat-py.fr

Domaine Dujac Morey-St-Denis

The owner of Domaine Dujac, Jacques Seysses, was a newcomer to Burgundy when he acquired some land more than 30 years ago in Morey-St-Denis. Seysses quickly earned the respect of his neighbors and became known for his use of whole bunches. He married an American, Rosalind, as did his elder son Jeremy. Jeremy, together with his wife Diana, a graduate of UC Davis, and his brother Eric, now runs the show. Morey-St-Denis is where the domaine excels, particularly in the stunning Clos de la Roche. Recently, the family have acquired prestigious Premiers and Grands Crus, ranging from the village of Gevrey to Vosne, including vines in Chambertin and Romanée St-Vivant. There are also two white Morey-St-Denis. These delicious and firmly structured wines are made using the traditional technique of *foulage*, or crushing with feet.

7 rue de la Bussière, 21220 Morey-St-Denis
www.dujac.com

Domaine Faiveley Nuits-St-Georges

This négociant in Nuits-St-Georges has recently been transformed under Ewan Faiveley, who has taken control in his 20s. His youth is balanced by the wisdom of Bernard Hervet, who has joined Faiveley as general manager after many years of experience at Bouchard Père et Fils. The dynamic duo have shaken up this family business, which was established in 1825 by Pierre Faiveley. Gone are the hard tannins and smoky notes of Faiveley reds. The 2007s were a revelation swathed in supple tannin. Bernard estimates that about 50% of the change is due to a switch in barrel maker, or cooper. They now use four coopers and ensure the barrels have just a light toast. Wines from barrels of the old cooper, and those of François Frères, one of the new, taste extraordinarily different. They have also jettisoned some vats in preference for traditional conical-shaped vats in both oak and stainless steel and bought a vertical crusher. "We prefer it. It is going back in terms of technology, but makes cleaner, purer wine with less tannin," remarks Bernard Hervet. This négociant is in the enviable position of owning 297 acres (120ha), including many Grands Crus, allowing the family domaine to supply more than 80% of the necessary grapes. This gives them great control. The portfolio includes an impressive range of Gevrey-Chambertin. The highlight is Clos de Bèze, which is wonderfully scented and has lithe vitality.

21701 Nuits-St-Georges
www.bourgognes-faiveley.com

Domaine Forey Père et Fils
Vosne-Romanée

Régis Forey has moved from the domaine tucked away on rue Derrière-le-Four, almost opposite Domaine de la Romanée-Conti, to more spacious and modern premises on the other side of Vosne's main road. Here, he makes full and structured wines, which nevertheless carry themselves with elegance. He uses a few days of cold maceration (where the grapes, including some stems, soak in the released juice

NICOLE LAMARCHE

Burgundy is a paradox: tradition endures, and female winemakers and viticulturists are in the minority. Yet many of Burgundy's brightest and most influential talents are women, such as Ghislaine Barthod, Lalou Bize-Leroy, Anne Gros, Anne-Claude Leflaive, and the sisters Mugneret.

Nicole Lamarche, and her cousin Natalie, represent the fifth generation to run Domaine Francois Lamarche in Vosne-Romanée. Nicole assumed responsibility for both the vineyards and winemaking in 2006, while still in her 20s. Natalie is taking on sales and marketing. But what makes this domaine so intriguing is the rejuvenation of that most rare and valuable of assets: a Grand Cru vineyard in Vosne-Romanée. The vineyard, La Grande Rue, lies between La Tâche and La Romanée. Its obscurity is the result partly of a failure to register for Grand Cru status in the 1930s, but also of less-than-ideal husbandry. Nicole, diligent and determined, is improving quality with every vintage.

before the fermentation starts) and a relatively long soak after the fermentation. The Grands Crus Echézeaux and Clos de Vougeot, and his Premiers Crus, including Vosne-Romanée Les Gaudichots, are matured in new oak, the lesser wines at a much lower percentage.

2 rue Derrière-le-Four, 21700 Vosne-Romanée
03 80 61 09 68

Domaine Fourrier Gevrey-Chambertin

"The more you are a *vigneron*, the less you need to be an enologist." This was the fundamental lesson Jean-Marie Fourrier learned when working for the inspirational Burgundian, Henri Jayer. He put this into practice at the family domaine when he took over in 1995, after a year of winemaking in Oregon. Jean-Marie is fanatically non-interventionist in the winery. The wine sits undisturbed on the lees (the dead yeast cells), which naturally protect the wine and reduce the quantity of the antioxidant sulphur dioxide needed. (Jean-Marie is particularly sensitive to sulphur dioxide-induced headaches.) He eschews the fashion for new oak and just renews a fifth of his barrels each year. He has a lovely Chambolle-Musigny, but the interest here really lies in the Gevrey wines; three neighboring parcels, found in the top north corner of the village, produce distinctively different wines. The range includes a mineral, direct Les Goulots, an ample, fruity Les Champeaux, and a juicy, vigorous Combe Aux Moines. Jean-Marie makes a fine, ethereal Grand Cru Griotte-Chambertin, but his Clos St-Jacques is the star of the cellar.

7 route de Dijon, 21220 Gevrey-Chambertin
www.domainefourrier.fr

Domaine François Lamarche
Vosne-Romanée

This is a female-run domaine, overseen with an eagle eye by the formidable Madame Marie-Blanche Lamarche. Her daughter Nicole, the mother of baby twins, makes the wine, and cousin Natalie does the paperwork. The two younger women are in their 20s. Together they are revitalizing Lamarche, which has long underperformed considering its landholdings, which include Croix-Rameau (an enclave within Romanée-St-Vivant and potentially a very good terroir) and La Grande Rue, which lies beside Romanée-Conti. Nicole took sole charge in 2007, and is focusing on getting the vineyards into shape with promising results. ★ Rising star

9 rue des Communes, 21700 Vosne-Romanée
www.domaine-lamarche.com

Domaine Georges and Christophe Roumier Chambolle-Musigny

The exceptional wine here shows Christophe Roumier's skill and dedication to quality. His grandfather left him a legacy of wines that are now drinking beautifully and this is what he aims for: wine that can age, but has lightness. He inherited some wonderful terroir and, for the most part, old vines. He uses an organic approach, but not slavishly so. He is probably most famous for his taut, mineral Les Cras, the perfumed, seductive Les Amoureuses, and the gossamer-fine Le Musigny. The quality here is sensational across the board.

21220 Chambolle-Musigny
www.roumier.com

Domaine Georges Mugneret-Gibourg Vosne-Romanée

This domaine is run by Jacqueline Mugneret and her daughters Marie-Christine and Marie-Andrée. The Chagall-inspired label of Saint Vincent, patron saint of *vignerons*, embodies the spirit of the domaine. The style is graceful, lively, and very well defined. They make elegant Vosne and Chambolle. The Nuits-St-Georges Les Chaignots is mineral and stylish. There are three elegant Grands Crus, including Gevrey-Chambertin Ruchottes, which has a steely core cloaked in satin.

5 rue des communes, 21700 Vosne-Romanée
www.mugneret-gibourg.com

Domaine Ghislaine Barthod
Chambolle-Musigny

Barthod offers a range of Chambolle Premier Cru precisely expressing the character of their terroir, from a brooding Beaux Bruns to a streamlined Les Fuées. The delightful Ghislaine Barthod inherited this domaine, but, unlike her parents, believes that Chambolle should not be restricted to feminine elegance and may also have more substance. Accordingly, she does more *pigeage* (punching down) to carefully extract tannins and color during fermentation. Balance, however, is the most important thing for her. Barthod is restrained in her use of new oak, using only using 25–30% to preserve the aromatics. She makes a stunning, racy, and focused Les Cras.

21220 Chambolle-Musigny
03 80 62 80 16

Domaine Gilles Remoriquet
Nuits-St-Georges

Gilles Remoriquet takes his cue from the vineyard, with his objective being to achieve more finesse. He uses only gravity to move wine around—no pumps—and has developed his own machine to stem Pinot Noir, while keeping the grapes whole. The style is bold. There is a pure, tight, sooty Aux Allots with tarry tannins from 60-year-old vines. From an uphill parcel, near the boundary with Vosne Romanée, Remoriquet makes an elegant La Damodes. His Les St-Georges is beefy, but smooth.

25 rue de Charmois, 21700 Nuits-St-Georges
03 80 61 24 84

Domaine Gros Frère et Soeur
Vosne-Romanée

Bernard Gros is Michel's shorter, more gregarious, and burlier brother, but the Frère et Soeur in this case refer to his uncle and aunt. The vines are young, and include three Grands Crus with a massive 5 acres (2ha) of the Echézeaux. Some of the younger-vine Echézeaux is declassified into the Vosne-Romanée Premier Cru. He makes soft, forward, and fruity wines. Everything, except the Hautes-Côtes, goes into 100% new oak. This domaine is run from a vast, gated, and imposing building in the center of the village.

6 rue des Grands Crus, 21700 Vosne-Romanée
03 80 61 12 43

Domaine Henri Gouges
Nuits-St-Georges

Probably the most famous domaine in Nuits-St-Georges, Domaine Henri Gouges has been bottling its own wines since the 1920s. It typically produces serious, tight,

DOMAINE HENRI GOUGES
DENSE, SERIOUS WINE, MADE TO CELLAR FOR A LONG TIME WHILE BELYING ITS AGE

DOMAINE GEORGES MUGNERET-GIBOURG
ELEGANT WINE MADE BY A FEMALE TEAM

densely structured wine for the long term; vintages from the early 1970s still taste fresh. The shy Pierre manages the vines, while his charming brother, Christian, makes the wine in the new, gravity-flow, state-of-the-art winery, which stands shiny and incongruous in the garden (2008 was the inaugural vintage). He is joined by his talented nephew, Grégory, to whom he is handing over. The wines are splendid here, and Les St-Georges is of Grand Cru status in all but appellation.

7 rue du Moulin, 21704 Nuits-St-Georges
www.gouges.com

Domaine Henri Naudin-Ferrand
Hautes-Côte de Nuits

Claire Naudin is a gifted winemaker and an inspiring personality with great strength of character. Not all of Burgundy's greatest talents work with gilt-edged vineyards. Claire's Hautes-Côtes de Nuits Blanc is one of the best-value white burgundies you will ever find. Of the red wines, the Côtes de Nuits Villages Vieilles Vignes shows uncommon refinement and grace for this often clunky appellation. More recently, she has been able to bring her skills to bear on more illustrious appellations, producing small but delicious quantities of the Echézeaux Grand Cru. Her wines have an almost naked, pure quality, perhaps due to the very low levels of sulphur dioxide used in their production. ★ Rising star

rue du Meix Grenot, 21700 Magny les Villers
www.naudin-ferrand.com

Domaine Heresztyn Gevrey-Chambertin

Here, making good wine is very much seen as a matter of a few simple imperatives (namely, attentive viticulture, strict selection, and careful *élevage*—aging of the wine). Heresztyn wines are typically well-colored, with an upright spine. New oak is sensitively handled and not intrusive. The vineyards are in Chambolle, Morey, and Gevrey, and include some superbly sited Premiers Crus, as well as the Clos St-Denis Grand Cru. The range is a great tasting lesson in the classic appellations of the Côte de Nuits. The cellar door is open to the public.

27 rue Richebourg, 21220 Gevrey-Chambertin
03 80 34 13 99

Domaine Hudelot-Noellat Vougeot

Domaine Hudelot-Noellat has three Grands Crus as the stars of their line-up: luscious Clos du Vougeot; intense Romanée-St-Vivant; and brooding, grippy Richebourg. This welcoming domaine also produces very classic, interesting Village Vosne-Romanée and Nuits-St-Georges, as well as Premiers Crus in those appellations, and Vougeot. New oak is used with restraint; these are not glamorous blockbusters, but they are well-made wines that show the distinctive personalities of their appellation. The Village Nuits-St-Georges—intense, but not rustic—is a very good value.

21640 Chambolle-Musigny
03 80 62 85 17

Domaine Humbert Frères
Gevrey-Chambertin

There is something straight and honest about the wines made by the burly Emmanuel Humbert and his brother Frédéric. They are cousins of Claude Dugat

DOMAINE JACQUES-FREDERIC MUGNIER
THIS PREMIER CRU VINEYARD IS NOW BACK UNDER FULL CONTROL OF THE DOMAINE

DOMAINE JEAN GRIVOT
ONE OF THE FINEST GROWERS, PRODUCING STUNNING WINES ACROSS THE BOARD

and Bernard Dugat-Py. This branch of the family has old vines in some good appellations. Although Emmanuel has worked here for 27 vintages, the quality changed in 1998, when he took over the winemaking. They stopped selling to négociants and the yields were lowered. Each year, Emmanuel makes wines that come closer to his ideal of very fresh and round wines to drink. They are more airy and have less tannin, though Emmanuel does like new oak. The domaine has many small parcels, including Petite Chapelle, and it is commendable that they make them under separate labels, as they are not easy to vinify individually. In contrast, they have 2.5 acres (1 hectare) of Les Poissenots, which is fresh, energetic, and spicy.

rue de Planteligone, 21220 Gevrey-Chambertin
03 80 51 80 14

Domaine Jack Confuron-Cotétidot
Vosne-Romanée

Yves Confuron, son of Jacky, has an irrepressible humor and energy. This family can trace its vinous roots in Vosne back to Louis XIV. The Confuron-Cotétidot wines are built to age, yet have plenty of up-front fruit. Yves always emerges from the cellar dusting off old vintages. There is an excellent range of Village wines from across the Côte de Nuits, and the Echézeaux Grand Cru is usually very good. It is easy to spot the domaine in Vosne, as there is a large vegetable garden outside the house, from which Yves's mother conjures wonderful meals.

10 rue de la Fontaine, 21700 Vosne-Romanée
03 80 61 03 39

Domaine Jacques-Frédéric Mugnier
Chambolle-Musigny

The wines at Mugnier are light, in the very best sense of the word. They have an ethereal grace and are hauntingly scented with rose petal. This makes them approachable in youth, yet with the purity and focus to mature beautifully. These are wonderful, intense wines. Frédéric Mugnier does little to vary his approach each vintage and, in his quiet, self-effacing way, would rather the wines told their own story. Since he gave up his job as a pilot in the 1970s, and settled in the family property (an imposing, but slightly sinister house), the vineyards that had been leased out have come back into the domaine. Most recent was La Maréchale, and Frédéric has tamed this Nuits-St-George, with a silken touch.

Château de Chambolle-Musigny, 21220 Chambolle-Musigny
www.mugnier.fr

Domaine Jean Grivot Vosne-Romanée

Etienne Grivot, of Domaine Jean Grivot, is among the very finest growers in Burgundy. He is a quiet man with insight and talent, who makes wine with a special sensitivity. Tasting the previous vintage in his cellar each October, always from older barrels, is a thought-provoking and inspirational exercise. There is a translucency of the terroir and the vintage. The wines combine freshness with great aging potential and are truly delicious. The range peaks with a spine-tingling, complex Richebourg Grand Cru, which never fails to be a highlight of the vintage. This is sensational wine.

6 rue de la Croix Rameau, 21700 Vosne-Romanée
www.domainegrivot.fr

DOMAINE MICHEL GROS
PURE FRUIT EXPRESSION FROM ONE
OF THE LARGE GROS FAMILY

DOMAINE MEO-CAMUZET
AN INNOVATIVE DOMAINE NOT AFRAID
TO TRY NEW TECHNIQUES

Domaine Jean-Jacques Confuron
Nuits-St-Georges

Sophie Confuron had no choice but to take full responsibility for Domaine Jean-Jacques Confuron when she was just 25. After her father passed away, her mother would have sold the domaine. These days, she is helped by her quiet husband, Alan Murnier, who uses organic techniques in the vineyards. She has boundless energy and, when it is not channeled into making wine, she is helping bright, disadvantaged youngsters into the wine trade in South Africa. She makes wines to reflect her personality: generous and open; succulent wines that soak up plenty of smooth, rich oak. Vosne-Romanée Les Beaumont is rich and rounded.

Route Nationale, 21700 Prémeaux Prissey
www.jjconfuron.com

Domaine Leroy Vosne-Romanée

Domaine Leroy has one of the most extraordinary and extensive portfolios in Burgundy. It is the creation of the remarkable octogenarian Lalou Bize, who part-owned and managed Domaine del la Romanée-Conti with Aubert de Villaine until 1993. This formidable woman bought two domaines, Charles Noëllat in 1988 and, subsequently, Philippe Remy. She is firmly in charge and even sleeps on a small day bed at the domaine in Vosne-Romanée during the vintage to oversee proceedings. She rigorously adheres to biodynamic principles to produce complex wines. The prices they achieve are impressive.

15 rue La Fontaine, 21700 Vosne-Romanée
www.domaineleroy.com

Domaine Lignier-Michelot
Morey-St-Denis

Virgile Lignier is a young, talented *vigneron* well on the way to creating a name for this family domaine. He is a serious man, third generation, and clearly determined to make his mark. There are a wealth of small parcels in both Chambolle-Musigny and Morey-St-Denis, allowing him to showcase both villages. Not content with this, he is now buying in grapes from his aunt's vineyards. He is dedicated to low yields and selecting the best grapes. He has invested in not just one, but two, grape-sorting tables to select the best fruit at harvest. The Village wines are very good indeed.

11 rue Haute, 21220 Morey-St-Denis
03 80 34 31 13

Domaine Liogier d'Ardhuy
Nuits-St-Georges

This large domaine of over 100 acres (40ha) has been on a mission to change its image since 2002. Previously, the domaine fruit was sold to the family négociant. Quality has improved considerably since the Dutchman Carel Voohuis took up the challenge. Changes in the vineyard include lower yields, shorter pruning, and higher canopies for greater photosynthesis, and in the winery the old equipment has been replaced to allow for gentler extraction of the tannins. There is a fascinating flight of four Corton Grands Crus, from different terroir around the hill of Corton, and from their Chardonnay vines they produce a stony, powerful Corton-Charlemagne.

Clos des Langres, 21700 Corgoloin
03 80 62 98 73

Domaine Louis Boillot Chambolle-Musigny

Louis Boillot is married to Ghislaine Barthod, and the couple share a cellar on the edge of Chambolle, overlooking the vines. Louis's wines complement Ghislaine's range of Chambolles by offering a surprisingly broad overview. They range from a spicy Fixin in the north, to Beaune, Pommard, and Volnay in the Côte de Beaune. Louis is a reliable source of Pommard. His Pommard Fremiers and Les Croix-Noires show well-managed tannins and plenty of delicious fruit. His Volnay Caillerets is appropriately mineral, yet he can turn his hand to make a more muscular Nuits-St-Georges Pruliers. Many of the vineyards have old vines, and this is clear in the consistent quality across the range.

ruelle St-Etienne, 21190 Volnay
www.domaine-louis-boillot.com

Domaine Marc Roy Gevrey-Chambertin

Marc Roy's daughter, the young and energetic Alexandrine, has put this domaine on the map with her deft hand in the winery, while he looks after the vines. As soon as she has made the wines here, she races across the pond to Oregon for her second job at Phelps Creek winery. This international approach is reflected in an attractive set of Gevrey Village wines, which are generously fruit-driven. The parcel of Clos Prieur in the lower Village section of this vineyard, delivers a sweetly succulent wine. The Cuvée Alexandrine, started in 2005, is produced only in the best vintages from fruit selected for *millerandage* (very small and concentrated berries).

8 avenue de la Gare, 21220 Gevrey-Chambertin
03 80 51 81 13

Domaine Méo-Camuzet Vosne-Romanée

Jean-Nicolas Méo has an inquiring mind and likes to experiment in the winery, trialing techniques that make his traditional neighbors shudder. Méo-Camuzet is a top-flight domaine. There is a nicely defined, mineral Vosne-Romanée aux Brûlées, but the two stars of the domaine are Cros Parentoux and Richebourg. The Cros Parentoux, which is muscular, compact, and a little wacky, needs time to come round, while the Richebourg Grand Cru is classic and polished. Together with his sister, Jean-Nicolas has a small négociant business that offers a sound range, including wines from Marsannay and Fixin.

11 rue des Grands Crus, 21700 Vosne-Romanée
www.meo-camuzet.com

Domaine Michel Gros Vosne-Romanée

Domaine Michel Gros is most famous for the *monopole* Aux Reas, which lies on the southern edge of the village, enclosed within a high stone wall pierced by a picturesque and slightly crumbling gate. When the land belonging to the complicated Gros family was divvied up, the tall, quite shy, but charming Michel (brother of Bernard) received this Premier Cru, which makes elegant, perfumed wine. His parcels also include Vosne-Romanée Suchot and some Clos du Vougeot, which is now coming into its own. Michel makes very pure, lucid, flowing wine. The fruit sings through, from the lively Chambolle to the denser Nuits-St-Georges.

7 rue des Communes, 21700 Vosne-Romanée
www.domaine-michel-gros.com

Domaine Michèle et Patrice Rion
Nuits-St-Georges

Father and son broke away from the family to establish Domaine Rion and négociant in 2000. There is a good selection of wines from Chambolle and Nuits-St-Georges. The domaine's Bourgogne comes from the excellent Bon Batons parcel near Chambolle and has lovely texture and plump fruit. There is a silky Village Chambolle and an intense, mineral Nuits-St-Georges from Clos des Argillières. Maxime, who worked at Dry River in New Zealand, joined his father in 2005.

1 rue de la Maladière, 21700 Prémeaux-Prissey
www.patricerion.com

Domaine Pierre Damoy Gevrey-Chambertin

Pierre Damoy, with his pack of motley dogs, is an eccentric character. When he is not making wine he is experimenting with micro-cider production. Damoy's great-grandfather was the first generation of the family to live and work in Gevrey. The landholding has not changed since then, although Clos Tamisot was used as a garden during World War II. Pierre likes low acidity and is always among the last to harvest in Gevrey, pushing the boundaries of ripeness. He makes deeply juicy, perfumed wine; pure essence of Pinot Noir. From a small mound in the middle of Clos de Bèze, a parcel of vines planted in 1920 delivers that extra dimension, becoming four barrels of deliciously scented Clos de Bèze Vieilles Vignes.

20 rue Mal De Lattre de Tassigny, 21220 Gevrey-Chambertin
03 80 34 30 47

Domaine Ponsot Morey-St-Denis

Laurent Ponsot has a wicked sense of humor. He gasps in horror if asked a technical question about his wine and likes to maintain that the wine makes itself and the winemaker—for which he points out there is no word in French—is just a minor necessity in the chain. He might like to cultivate the image of the traditional *vigneron*, but his penchant for high performance cars and his modern, designer winery reveal the truth. This is a man who likes to be in control of the details. The Ponsot family were at the cutting edge of vine clonal selection in its infancy.

21 rue de la Montagne, 21220 Morey-St-Denis
www.domaine-ponsot.com

Domaine Prieuré-Roch Nuits-St-Georges

Henri-Frédéric Roch gives his wine time to mature, bottling after 22 months. He works on biodynamic lines in his vines, which include the 12 acre (5ha) Clos de Corvées Premier Cru *monopole* in Nuits-St-Georges. He makes three *cuvées* from this parcel, the finest being Nuits-St-Georges Clos de Corvées. As well as some Village wines and Vosne-Romanée Premier Cru Les Souchots, he works an ample 2.5 acre (1ha) slice of the Chambertin Grand Cru, Clos de Bèze. In addition to this, he is co-manager of Domaine de la Romanée-Conti.

Villa Denbee, 6, RN 74, 21700 Prémeaux-Prissey
03 80 62 00 00

Domaine Robert Chevillon
Nuits-St-Georges

This domaine offers the exciting opportunity to taste a broad selection of terroir from Nuits-St-Georges. There are no less than eight Premiers Crus. While they share

the domaine style—sleek and precise—each has the distinctive hallmarks of their specific terroir. Les Cailles is svelte and stylish versus the taut and muscular Les Vaucrains. Les St-Georges is smoothly profound and a very fine Premier Cru indeed. The vines at all three are 75 years old. Robert's sons are now in charge, with the somewhat gruff, tall, dark Bertrand commanding the winery and producing stylish wines.

68, rue Félix-Tisserand, 21700 Nuits-St-Georges
03 80 62 34 88

Domaine de la Romanée-Conti
Vosne-Romanée

Domaine de la Romanée-Conti is the pole star in the Burgundy firmament. This modest-looking domaine, tucked away at the back of Vosne, is possibly the most famous of all time. DRC conjures glitzy images of Sotheby's and Christie's auction houses, where DRC Grands Crus go under the hammer for astronomical sums. It is not just the eponymous Romanée-Conti, so poised and perfumed, but the architectural La Tâche, the exquisitely silky Romanée-St-Vivant, the opulent Richebourg, and the two Echézeaux that command the attention. In Burgundy, however, the action is far less glamorous and is best exemplified by the horse-drawn plough. Run by the cerebral Aubert de Villaine, the wines of DRC truly embody the concept of terroir.

1 rue Derrière-le-Four, 21700 Vosne-Romanée
03 80 62 48 80

Domaine Sylvain Cathiard
Vosne-Romanée

There are beautiful wines at the family-run Domaine Sylvain Cathiard. Sylvain has been joined by his son, Sebastien, who brings his experience of making Pinot Noir at Fromm Winery in New Zealand. There is crystal-clear fruit here from the Bourgogne upward. With a couple of forays into Chambolle and Nuits-St-Georges, this is a Vosne-led domaine and one that reveals the purity and elegance of the terroir. They get to the essence of Pinot Noir and combine this with clarity of structure. The Les Malconsorts has a refined muscularity, while the Romanée-St-Vivant is among the finest examples.

20 rue Goillotte, 21700 Vosne-Romanée
03 80 62 36 01

Domaine Sylvie Esmonin
Gevrey-Chambertin

Sylvie Esmonin, a qualified agronomist and enologist, produces light, elegant, and feminine wines. She makes a charming Côte de Nuits Village from vines south of the village of Brochon, and two Gevrey-Chambertin Village wines that are divided according to vine age. The straight Village vines are a more than respectable 30–40 years old, and the wines show plenty of depth. The Vieilles Vignes are over 60 years old and the wine, which is more substantial, is complemented by a great percentage of new oak. Sylvie is one of five *vignerons* with a parcel of Clos St-Jacques, under which her cellar lies. The division of this *clos* is very unusual, for all five have a vertical cross-section of land. Sylvie's interpretation is smooth, flowing, and mineral.

1 rue Neuve, 21220 Gevrey-Chambertin
03 80 34 36 44

THE SHAPING OF BURGUNDIAN FOOD

In one sense, Burgundy's legendarily rich food is an answer to the call of the sumptuous, intense reds in which the Côte de Nuits specializes. Its most famous recipes—boeuf bourguignon, coq au vin—involve a red-wine sauce to which baby onions, mushrooms, and lardons of bacon are added. These dishes are wonderful with brooding reds from Gevrey and Nuits-St-Georges. Burgundy's red wine also features in the sauce *meurette*, made without mushrooms but with a touch of *marc* (Burgundian Eaux de Vie), and served with eggs, poultry, or fish. Pinot Noir's versatility as a food wine is exemplified by the frequency with which lighter reds, such as Savigny or the Hautes-Côtes, are matched with these dishes. But there is another factor shaping this hugely distinctive and delicious cuisine: nature's bounty. Burgundy is blessed with rich pastures and fine livestock. Charolais cattle, milky white and beautiful, produce some of the world's finest beef.

Burgundy is one of only three regions authorized to rear Bresse chickens, a breed so fine that it is protected by AC law. The rich, creamy dishes (often with tiny, pungent morel mushrooms) featuring these deluxe birds are heavenly with the creamy whites of Meursault. And the cheese… oh, the cheese. Epoisses, a washed rind cheese, is probably the most famous, and pungent. But there are more delicate options: Chevreton de Mâcon is a small goat's cheese that is delicious with the freshly honeyed white wines of this southern Burgundian zone.

MAISON NICOLAS POTEL
DESPITE HAVING NO VINEYARDS OF ITS OWN, THIS NEGOCE PRODUCES VERY FINE WINES

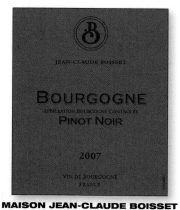

MAISON JEAN-CLAUDE BOISSET
A MORE HANDS-ON APPROACH IN THE VINEYARD ENSURES TOP-QUALITY FRUIT

Domaine Trapet Père et Fils
Gevrey-Chambertin

Jean-Louis Trapet is a thoughtful, conscientious man with a gentle disposition. When he speaks of less intervention in his winemaking, he is not spinning a line. He has been using an organic approach for the past 13 years, and feels it has made him change the way he thinks about everything. He believes that wine needs peace in its creation and those making it need to be respectful and gentle in the vineyard and winery. He has a strong sense of the importance of the viticultural past and attributes the potential of Pinot Noir to reach great finesse to this cultural inheritance dating back to monastic times. His wines are appropriately elegant and uplifting.

53 route de Beaune, 21220 Gevrey-Chambertin
www.domaine-trapet.com

Domaine de la Vougeraie
Nuits-St-Georges

Domaine de la Vougeraie is owned by Boisset Family Estates. Winemaker Pierre Vincent, who came from Jaffelin, is making elegant and restrained wines. The domaine is run organically and Pierre is sure this has an impact on maturity. He experimented with some whole-bunch fermentation in the 2008 vintage with Bonnes-Mares (smoothly muscular) and Charmes-Chambertin (grippy). There is an excellent range, including a pure, lively Vougeot Premier Cru Les Cras, which has saline minerality, and a Les Musigny Grand Cru, which is wafting and perfumed with the scent of rose petal. Amazingly, the fruit is stemmed entirely by hand.

rue de l'Eglise, 21700 Premeaux-Prissey
www.domainedelavougeraie.com

Maison Frédéric Magnien
Morey-St-Denis

In just over 10 years, dynamic Frédéric Magnien has built one of the most successful mini-négociants in the Côte d'Or. One of the fifth generation of Magniens to make wine in Burgundy, Frédéric is the son of Michael Magnien, who is vineyard manager for Maison Louis Latour, as well as the proprietor of an eponymous domaine (whose wines Frédéric also makes). Maison Magnien owns no vineyards; Frédéric sources grapes from across the Côte de Nuits, securing ongoing relationships and an ongoing supply of top-notch raw materials, which he treats with a light hand. The Village Gevrey, Chambolle, and Morey are attractive, unforced, and good value.

26 Route Nationale, 21220 Morey-St-Denis
www.frederic-magnien.com

Maison Jean-Claude Boisset
Côte de Nuits

This family-run merchant is being thoroughly overhauled under the leadership of the innovative Jean-Charles Boisset. It was not so very long ago that Maison Boisset was struggling with the challenges common to many of the Burgundy négociants—adequate, but essentially lackluster, wines. Changes have been made with impressive rapidity: super-talented Gregory Patriat (formerly of Domaine Leroy) has been in charge since 2002. His job title—*viniculteur*—reflects the approach behind the rejuvenated quality of these wines. Today, Boisset wines are made from grapes whose cultivation has been directed by Patriat and his team. It is this ongoing partnership between merchant and grape-grower that is behind the renewed quality here. That, and the support of the now huge empire, Boisset Family Estates. Many of the Jean-Claude Boisset wines are sealed with screwcaps: Jean-Charles is not a man frightened by change. As for the wines, recent vintages of the Bourgogne Pinot Noir have been impressive and represent outstanding value for the price. The Meursault Premier Cru Charmes is a great buy. If you want the absolutely top-notch Burgundian experience, check out Domaine de la Vougeraie. But for well-made and well-priced burgundy, Boisset should be high on your list.

Les Ursulines, 5, quai Dumorey, 21700 Nuits-St-Georges
www.jcboisset.com

Maison Nicolas Potel Nuits-St-Georges

The dark, curly haired Nicolas, who seems always in a hurry, is the son of the legendary Gérard Potel and grew up at Domaine de la Pousse d'Or in Volnay. Having garnered some New World experience at Mount Mary, Mosswood, and Leeuwin Estate, he established his own négociant house in 1997. He specialized in buying grapes, rather than wine, as was more common, particularly in red. He began with Volnay, extending to 40 wines. The style is full and richly textured, yet elegant. Nicolas had no formal training and believes a lack of enology made things much simpler for him. For a start, he also has his own vineyards and leads by example. He believes that the secret to being a good négociant is to go into the vineyard with the growers. He thinks there are many positives to working as a *négoce* versus owning an estate, namely the chance to work with many different grapes. Although Nicolas has recently moved on to another venture, the eponymous Maison is still going strong.

44 rue des Blés, 21700 Nuits-St-Georges
www.nicolas-potel.fr

Maison Pascal Lachaux Vosne-Romanée

In the same cellar as Domaine Arnoux, but in a separate room, slumbers a row of large barrels. They contain some rather select wine. In 2003, Pascal Lachaux established a small and unusual négociant. Small, because there were just 13 barrels in 2005; unusual in the top-notch Premier and Grand Cru it focuses on. Pascal aims to make the best quality and controls every aspect of the viticulture, as well as the winemaking. In 2009, the two businesses combined to form Domaine Arnoux-Lachaux.

21670 Vosne-Romanée
03 80 61 09 85

Vincent Géantet-Pansiot
Gevrey-Chambertin

Some domaines have an atmosphere of serenity, even at busy times; not so Géantet-Pansiot, which seems frenetic, especially during their early bottling (12 months, or so, after vintage). Despite the distractions, the purity of the fruit is riveting. This is an excellent source of Marsannay. The Champ Perdrix has scrumptious sweet cherry fruit. They have "spot on" Village wines, including a luscious old-vine Chambolle-Musigny. From Gevrey-Chambertin there is an intense Premier Cru Poissenot, which has sweetness, chalky minerality, and a fresh, direct finish.

3 route de Beaune, 21220, Gevrey-Chambertin
www.geantet-pansiot.com

A bright green plot of newly planted vines stands out against the sites with older vines in Gevrey-Chambertin.

COTE DE BEAUNE

Burgundy
Wine regions of Burgundy
Côte de Beaune wine region

The Côte de Beaune is renowned for producing the finest and most famous examples of Chardonnay in the world. Villages such as Meursault, Puligny-Montrachet, and Chassagne-Montrachet produce white wines of enthralling paradox, combining richness and freshness. But the Côte de Beaune has more of a dual personality than its northern neighbor; many villages produce their wine in both white and red versions, and the communes of Pommard, Beaune, and Volnay are responsible for some of the finest Pinot Noir of the Côte d'Or. Their bright, often exuberant fruit is less dark, less brooding, than in the wines of the Côte de Nuits. There is a tourist-friendly charm to this Côte; its villages bustle prettily, and Beaune is an entrancing, historic town.

Major grapes

🍇 Reds
Pinot Noir

🍇 Whites
Chardonnay

Vintages

2009
It is early days, but these ripe, juicy, succulent wines show promise. Yields were high.

2008
Fresh, savory whites with bright fruit. Reds are very fresh; the best are nicely supple and nuanced.

2007
Broader and fleshier than 2006; but these are still relatively delicate wines for early drinking.

2006
High acidity makes for linear wines with aromatic clarity. Meursaults are very good.

2005
Rich, ripe, and concentrated. Not to be hurried.

2004
This difficult vintage is yielding some very attractive whites. Reds can be quite green; go for the good producers.

The Côte de Beaune kicks off in style, with the intense Grands Crus—red and white—that girdle the hill of Corton. Corton-Charlemagne is a deep, savory white that can age for decades, and Corton is a sumptuous yet wild Pinot Noir whose prices remain under-hyped. The whites of the little-known appellation Ladoix, and the reds of only slightly more familiar Aloxe-Corton, reflect the character if not the intensity of these Grands Crus, and can be excellent value for money.

The names become more familiar as you move south: Savigny-lès-Beaune and Chorey-lès-Beaune are sources of (relatively) inexpensive, fragrant Pinot Noirs beloved of French sommeliers for their approachability and food-friendliness. The extensive vineyards of Beaune include many decent, and a few superb, Premiers Crus. Quality is improving across the board so expect rounded, glossy, and lightly spicy reds. Pommard has a reputation for producing beefy Pinot Noir, with plenty of brawn and not much finesse. It is partly true as these wines are among the most tannic reds of the Côte de Beaune. Many of today's producers, however, are taking a lighter hand.

Volnay is seen conventionally as the yin to Pommard's yang: silky, delicate Pinot Noir, with an ethereal intensity conferred by its perfume. It is a fair generalization, up to a point. The Premiers Crus, closer to the Pommard side, can be pretty firm and structured and, in contrast to the Pommard producers, many young *vignerons* are employing a firmer touch.

The three pretty villages of Monthelie, Auxey-Duresses, and St-Romain are a little too high and cool to produce great wine. But in warmer vintages they offer fertile bargain hunting.

Meursault is responsible for the broadest, most viscous Chardonnay of the Côte de Beaune. There are no Grand Cru vineyards, but several excellent Premiers Crus, including Perrières. Quality is high and the producers conscientious. A recent trend is to use less new oak and *bâtonnage* (a technique that involves stirring wine in the barrel to add body and weight) and a more refined style is emerging.

Puligny-Montrachet is the home of the world's most sought-after and expensive Chardonnays. The renowned Grand Cru Le Montrachet is shared with the neighboring commune of Chassagne. The white wines of Chassagne are rich, nutty, and impactful; those of Puligny entrancingly delicate, nuanced, and weightlessly intense. Meursault and Chassagne are also made in red versions; they are deliciously vibrant.

High above Puligny is the village of St-Aubin, which produces toned, nervy whites and pure, crunchy reds. These wines are no longer the undiscovered bargains of yore, but remain a smart buy, especially the Premiers Crus.

The vineyards of Santenay and Maranges have more of a south-facing aspect, as the Côte curves gently round to the west. Some appealing whites are made in Santenay, but it is lush, bramble-scented, and eminently drinkable Pinot Noir that is the main attraction in these "lesser" villages.

Benjamin Leroux Beaune

This is an exciting venture and one to watch. Benjamin Leroux is the talented winemaker from Domaine du Comte Armand who has established his own *négoce* based in a spacious warehouse off the ring road in Beaune. Leroux already has an impressive number of appellations that encompass red and white wines, selecting individual vineyards of top quality. A third of the vines he now works with are organically grown. He has been purchasing many of the whites for several years—for example, the lively, mineral Auxey-Duresses—but the contracts with the Pinot Noir growers are newer. When at Comte Armand, Leroux worked with pretty tannic terroir, while this venture gives him the opportunity to explore the finesses of Pinot Noir in lighter appellations. Volnay Clos de la Caves des Ducs is a tiny *monopole* with some 70-year-old vines, over which he has total control. It is gossamer, delicate, and pure.

5 Rue Colbert, 21200 Beaune
03 80 22 71 06

Bonneau du Martray

Pernand-Vergelesses

Jean-Charles Le Bault de la Morinière is every bit the distinguished count and produces an aristocratic Corton-Charlemagne with the perfect balance of steely austerity and intense fruit. This is quintessential Corton-Charlemagne, and as such needs a decade to soften and reveal its true complexity. Jean-Charles is unique for producing only Grand Cru in most years. Naturally, Bonneau du Martray's red is Corton and from the cooler Pernand side. The old Pinot Noir vines lie in the richer soil toward the bottom of the slope beneath the Chardonnay. They make a very decent Corton, but it is the Corton-Charlemagne for which Bonneau du Martray holds its place among the great domaines in Burgundy.

21420 Pernand-Vergelesses
www.bonneaudumartray.com

Bouchard Père et Fils Beaune

This firm was purchased by the Champenois Joseph Henriot in 1995, heralding a change in quality and reputation under the guiding hand of the excellent Bernard Hervet. (Hervet has since moved to Faiveley.) Bouchard has received some muscular investment by Henriot. After surveying some of the best wineries in the world, the company set about building a gravity-flow winery near Savigny, with five reception doors to receive the grapes swiftly at harvest. While not beautiful to look at, it is state-of-the-art inside with a barrel-aging cellar for 4,500 barrels beneath. They use about 250 pickers to give plenty of flexibility to pick the different parcels at the optimum time. Bouchard's style is now much more elegant and the 2008s show a lovely purity. The company has sizeable holdings of 320 acres (130ha), including vines in nine Grands Crus, and a third of their production is estate grown. Traditionally Côte de Beaune focused, they now have land in the Côte de Nuits.

Château de Beaune, 21200 Beaune
www.bouchard-pereetfils.com

Champy Père et Fils Beaune

Champy Père et Fils was the first négocient house to be established in Burgundy in 1720. It was bought, 19 years ago, by Henri and his son Pierre Meurgey, a family of

CHATEAU DE PULIGNY-MONTRACHET
A RISING STAR USING LESS NEW OAK TO ALLOW THE VINEYARD TO SHINE THROUGH

BONNEAU DU MARTRAY
INTENSE, LONG-LIVED, AND ARISTOCRATIC BY OWNERSHIP AND STATUS

wine brokers. "My ambition," says Pierre, "is to produce elegant and pure wine. The terroir has its story to tell." Only the regional wine, Bourgogne Signature, is deliberately marked by oak to make a bridge for those coming from New World wine. Pierre is a passionate believer in organic and biodynamic practices. Champy now has 42 acres (17ha) in the Côte de Beaune that they own or rent. They have noticed greater ripeness and less rot in the biodynamic vineyards versus those that are more traditionally managed. The winemaker Dimitri Bazas has been with the company since 1999. His approach is to make wines that can be enjoyed young, while having the potential to age. The white Corton-Charlemagne is designed to start opening up after four to five years instead of 10. Pernand-Vergelesses is their flagship. They offer neatly made, well-priced wines.

5 rue Grenier à Sel, 21200 Beaune
www.champy.com

Chanson Père et Fils Beaune

When Gilles de Courcel became president of Chanson in 2002, the négociant received a radical shake-up and the wine has greatly improved. Chanson has been owned by Bollinger since 1999, although its origins go back to 1750. The original winery, in the medieval center of Beaune, has now been restored and is used principally for aging wines. The impressive cellars are located in the Bastion de L'Oratoire in the fortified medieval walls. There is a new winery near Savigny where wines from 140 appellations are made. Chanson has an impressive 111 acres (45ha) of domaine land. They need 130 pickers to harvest everything in 10 days. De Courcel has established contracts with many growers, rejecting the policy of buying wine and purchasing mainly in grapes. They also harvest some of the growers' vines using their own pickers. Jean-Pierre Confuron (of the Vosne Confuron-Cotétidot family) took over the winemaking in 2002. He favors whole-bunch fermentation, and by keeping this winemaking technique constant across the appellations, he encourages the wines to reveal their terroir. The technique worked well in the 2008 vintage. There is an impressive range of Premier Cru from Beaune.

Au Bastion de l'Oratoire, rue Paul Chanson, 21200 Beaune
www.vins-chanson.com

Château de Puligny-Montrachet

Puligny-Montrachet

This pretty château is an impressive sight in sleepy, quietly prosperous Puligny. Etienne de Montille (son of the renowned and indomitable Hubert, in Volnay) has been whipping the entire domaine back into shape since he assumed responsibility in 2002. Here is a chap who likes to get things done: the wines (previously easy, obvious, and oaky) are now refined, silky, and juicily elegant. Vineyards are tended biodynamically and yields are reduced. New oak has been slashed. Puligny Folatières is precise and defined; lovers of broad, smoky Meursault should enjoy the Poruzots. ★ **Rising star**

rue de But, 21190 Puligny-Montrachet
www.chateaudepuligny.com

Coche-Dury Meursault

Jean-François Coche has a truly global reputation. His superb wines are sought-after by connoisseurs, who do not flinch at paying the fantastic sums they command.

COTE DE BEAUNE (LOWER)

This lower half of the Côte de Beaune swings away toward the west, its mellower slopes facing almost south, and hinting at the rolling landscapes of the Côte Châlonnaise and Mâconnais to come. Some simply delicious Pinot Noir originates here, but above all this is Chardonnay country. Monthélie, Auxey-Duresses, and St-Romain, above Meursault, are too high and cool for top quality, but are fertile hunting for relative bargains of both colors, especially in the warmer vintages. You can get a satisfying feel for the Côte d'Or's twisted, tortured geology at St-Romain, hemmed in by the looming outcrop of the Combe Bazin. The southeast-facing slopes of Meursault, Puligny-Montrachet, and Chassagne-Montrachet produce the finest Chardonnay in the world.

2006

TÊTE DU CLOS

CHASSAGNE
MONTRACHET

APPELLATION 1ER CRU CONTRÔLÉE

VINCENT DANCER

ST-AUBIN

Dom Hubert et Olivier Lamy
Dom Larue
Marc Colin et Fils

SANTENAY

Dom Roger Belland

Grand Vin   de Bourgogne

CRIOTS BATARD-MONTRACHET
GRAND CRU

Appellation Criots Bâtard-Montrachet Grand Cru Contrôlée

MIS EN BOUTEILLE AU DOMAINE PAR
EARL Roger BELLAND
Viticulteur à Santenay (Côte-d'Or) France
Produit de France - Product of France

14% vol.   750 ml

KEY

- Auxey-Duresses
- Chassagne-Montrachet
- Maranges
- Meursault
- Monthélie
- Puligny-Montrachet
- St-Aubin
- St-Romain
- Santenay
- – – – Commune boundary
- —— 33ft (10m) contours

CHASSAGNE-MONTRACHET

Dom Blain Gagnard	Dom Michel Niellon
Dom Bruno Colin-Deléger	Dom Paul Pillot
Dom Château de la Maltroye	Dom Philippe Colin
Dom Fontaine Gagnard	Dom Ramonet
Dom Guy Amiot	Dom Thomas Morey
Dom Lamy Pillot	Dom Vincent Dancer
Dom Michel Morey-Coffinet	Jean-Nöel Gagnard

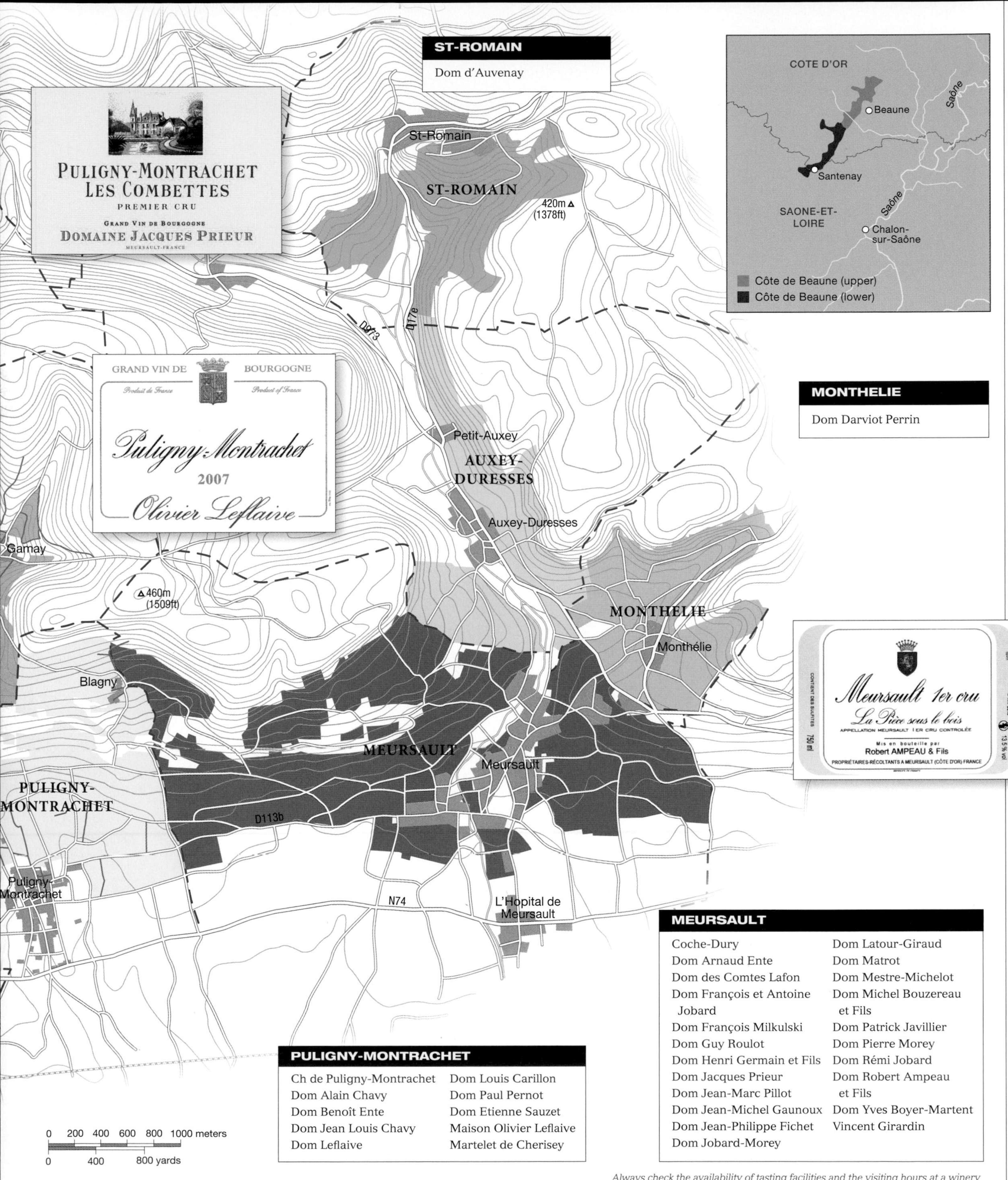

ST-ROMAIN

Dom d'Auvenay

ST-ROMAIN

Dom d'Auvenay

St-Romain

ST-ROMAIN

420m △
(1378ft)

COTE D'OR

○ Beaune

Saône

● Santenay

SAONE-ET-
LOIRE

Saône

○ Chalon-
sur-Saône

■ Côte de Beaune (upper)
■ Côte de Beaune (lower)

MONTHELIE

Dom Darviot Perrin

Petit-Auxey

**AUXEY-
DURESSES**

Auxey-Duresses

△ 460m
(1509ft)

Gamay

MONTHELIE

Monthélie

Blagny

MEURSAULT

Meursault

**PULIGNY-
MONTRACHET**

Puligny-
Montrachet

D113b

N74

L'Hôpital de
Meursault

MEURSAULT

Coche-Dury	Dom Latour-Giraud
Dom Arnaud Ente	Dom Matrot
Dom des Comtes Lafon	Dom Mestre-Michelot
Dom François et Antoine Jobard	Dom Michel Bouzereau et Fils
Dom François Milkulski	Dom Patrick Javillier
Dom Guy Roulot	Dom Pierre Morey
Dom Henri Germain et Fils	Dom Rémi Jobard
Dom Jacques Prieur	Dom Robert Ampeau et Fils
Dom Jean-Marc Pillot	
Dom Jean-Michel Gaunoux	Dom Yves Boyer-Martenot
Dom Jean-Philippe Fichet	Vincent Girardin
Dom Jobard-Morey	

PULIGNY-MONTRACHET

Ch de Puligny-Montrachet	Dom Louis Carillon
Dom Alain Chavy	Dom Paul Pernot
Dom Benoît Ente	Dom Etienne Sauzet
Dom Jean Louis Chavy	Maison Olivier Leflaive
Dom Leflaive	Martelet de Cherisey

0 200 400 600 800 1000 meters

0 400 800 yards

Always check the availability of tasting facilities and the visiting hours at a winery before planning your trip. Some wineries are open by appointment only.

COTE DE BEAUNE (UPPER)

The slopes of the Côte de Beaune are broader and gentler than those of their Nuits counterparts to the north—vines are planted nearly to the top of these steady slopes. This upper section of the Côte de Beaune inherits some of the Nuits legacy for red wine, producing good Pinot Noir from well-known villages such as Volnay, Pommard, and Beaune. It is the (just about) east-facing exposure that is the secret: Pinot Noir needs the morning sun. The protruding, isolated hill of Corton produces a sumptuous, and eponymously named, red Grand Cru (the only one on the Côte de Beaune), as well as, in Corton-Charlemagne, some sensational whites.

FRANÇOIS PARENT
www.parent-pommard.com

MONTHELIE
PREMIER CRU
LES CHAMPS-FULLIOT
APPELLATION MONTHELIE PREMIER CRU CONTRÔLÉE
MISE EN BOUTEILLE PAR
FRANÇOIS PARENT, A BEAUNE, CÔTE-D'OR, FRANCE
13% vol.   PRODUCE OF FRANCE- GRAND VIN DE BOURGOGNE   750 ml

POMMARD

Comte Armand, Le
  Domaine des Epeneaux
Dom de Courcel
Dom François Parent
Dom A F Gros
Dom Jean Marc Boillot

△ 404m
(1325ft)

386m
(1266ft)
△

MONTHELIE

Monthelie

Volnay

Pommard

VOLNAY

POMMARD

BEAUNE

D973

D970

N74

N74

N74

BEAUNE

VOLNAY

Dom Jean-Marc et Thomas
  Bouley
Dom Joseph Voillot
Dom de La Pousse d'Or Dom
Marquis d'Angerville
Dom Michel Lafarge
Dom de Montille
Dom Nicolas Rossignol-
  Jeanniard
Dom Roblet-Monnot

VIEILLES VIGNES

Beaune Les Cras
PREMIER CRU
APPELLATION BEAUNE 1er CRU CONTROLE
— 2005 —
MIS EN BOUTEILLE AU
13.5% alc./vol.   DOMAINE DU CHÂTEAU DE CHOREY   750 mL
WINE   GERMAIN PROPRIÉTAIRE A CHOREY.LES.BEAUNE, COTE.D'OR, FRANCE   VIN

KEY	
	Aloxe-Corton
	Beaune
	Chorey-les-Beaune
	Ladoix-Serrigny
	Monthélie
	Pernand-Vergelesses
	Pommard
	Savigny-les-Beaune
	Volnay
– – –	Commune boundary
——	33ft (10m) contours

0 125 250 375 500 750 meters

0   250   500 yards

BEAUNE

Benjamin Leroux   Joseph Drouhin
Bouchard Père et Fils   Louis Latour
Champy Père et Fils   Maison Alex Gambal
Chanson Père et Fils   Maison Camille Giraud
Dom du Comte Sénard   Maison Louis Jadot
Dom de Croix

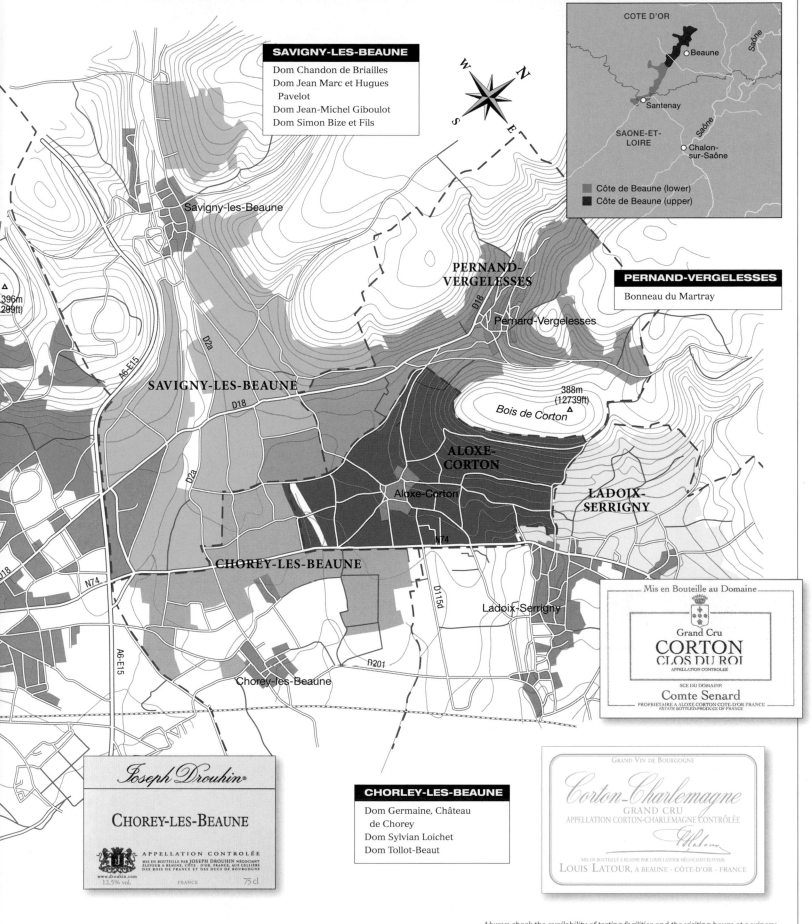

SAVIGNY-LES-BEAUNE

Dom Chandon de Briailles
Dom Jean Marc et Hugues Pavelot
Dom Jean-Michel Giboulot
Dom Simon Bize et Fils

COTE D'OR

Beaune

Saône

Santenay

SAONE-ET-LOIRE

Chalon-sur-Saône

■ Côte de Beaune (lower)
■ Côte de Beaune (upper)

Savigny-les-Beaune

PERNAND-VERGELESSES

Pernard-Vergelesses

PERNAND-VERGELESSES

Bonneau du Martray

396m
(1299ft)

SAVIGNY-LES-BEAUNE

388m
(12739ft)

Bois de Corton

ALOXE-CORTON

Aloxe-Corton

LADOIX-SERRIGNY

Ladoix-Serrigny

CHOREY-LES-BEAUNE

Chorey-les-Beaune

Mis en Bouteille au Domaine

Grand Cru
CORTON
CLOS DU ROI
APPELLATION CONTROLEE

SCE DU DOMAINE
Comte Senard
PROPRIETAIRE A ALOXE CORTON COTE D'OR FRANCE
ESTATE BOTTLED·PRODUCE OF FRANCE

Joseph Drouhin

CHOREY-LES-BEAUNE

APPELLATION CONTROLÉE
MIS EN BOUTEILLE PAR JOSEPH DROUHIN NÉGOCIANT
ÉLEVEUR A BEAUNE, CÔTE-D'OR, FRANCE, AUX CELLIERS
DES ROIS DE FRANCE ET DES DUCS DE BOURGOGNE
www.drouhin.com
12,5% vol.   FRANCE   75 cl

CHORLEY-LES-BEAUNE

Dom Germaine, Château de Chorey
Dom Sylvian Loichet
Dom Tollot-Beaut

GRAND VIN DE BOURGOGNE
Corton-Charlemagne
GRAND CRU
APPELLATION CORTON-CHARLEMAGNE CONTRÔLÉE

MIS EN BOUTEILLE A BEAUNE PAR LOUIS LATOUR NÉGOCIANT-ÉLEVEUR
LOUIS LATOUR, A BEAUNE · CÔTE-D'OR · FRANCE

Always check the availability of tasting facilities and the visiting hours at a winery before planning your trip. Some wineries are open by appointment only.

DOMAINE CHANDON DE BRIAILLES

THIS GRAND CRU IS MADE WITH NO NEW OAK—A RARE DEPARTURE FOR BURGUNDY

These include the Meursault Premiers Crus Perrières and Genevrières as well as several *lieux-dits* from the village. His white Grand Cru is Corton-Charlemagne. The quality and terroir expression result from meticulous attention in the vineyard. The whites are not hurried, but bottled after 20 months. This Burgundian superstar also makes reds, which include Volnay, Clos des Chênes, and Taillepieds.

9 rue Charles Giraud, 21190 Meursault
03 80 21 24 12

Comte Armand, Le Domaine des Epeneaux Pommard

The Pommard Premier Cru, Clos des Epeneaux, is one of Burgundy's iconic wines. Now made by the inspirational and influential Ben Leroux (who himself took over from the renowned Pascal Marchand), Pommard Clos des Epeneaux is a heroic, immortal sort of character. The vineyard itself (a *monopole*, owned exclusively by this domaine) has a rocky, iron-rich limestone soil to which the wine's habitual depth and dense structure is attributed. This, and all the other excellent wines, are produced from grapes grown biodynamically, a method of which Leroux is a passionate and convincing advocate.

7 rue de la Mairie, 21630 Pommard
www.domaine-comte-armand.com

Domaine Alain Chavy Puligny-Montrachet

The former Domaine Gérard Chavy was split between brothers Alain and Jean-Louis. Alain is a charming and careful *vigneron*. He makes precise, toned Pulignys of notable purity and tense freshness. The wines are never obviously oaky, which allows the nuances of different sites to sing out, from floral Pucelles to tautly fleshy Folatières. Les Charmes is a bottling of the best bits of his Village Puligny, and is consistently a very wise buy. ★ Rising star

5 rue des Creux de Chagny, 21190 Puligny-Montrachet
03 80 21 39 27

Domaine Arnaud Ente Meursault

This talented young *vigneron* conjures impressive Village wine from 3.7 acres (1.5ha) of En L'Ormeau, sited on the flat below the village. The best barrels are selected and labeled Les Ambres. Arnaud's style is pure and direct. His Meursault La Seve du Clos is reserved, compact, and mineral, surprising given the site of this modest and low-lying vineyard. Arnaud works hard in the vineyard, reflected in the wines' quality. He also has a Puligny-Montrachet Les Referts, which is well defined and pure.

12 rue de Mazeray, 21190 Meursault
03 80 21 66 12

Domaine d'Auvenay St-Romain

This is Lalou Bize-Leroy's domaine, which is independent of the other Leroy holdings. Her beautiful farm is a collection of medieval buildings on the broad arable plateau above St-Romain. Here, Lalou Bize makes tiny quantities of exceptional red and white wine including four Grands Crus. The whites have verve and intensity, with impressive quality from Auxey-Duresses, and beautifully defined wine from Meursault and Puligny. The Chevalier-Montrachet is splendid, stony, and refined.

Village Bas, 21190 St-Romain
03 80 21 23 27

DOMAINE DES COMTES LAFON

A PREMIER CRU FROM POSSIBLY THE FINEST WHITE WINE MAKER IN THE WORLD

Domaine Benoît Ente Puligny-Montrachet

This young domaine is founded on some old vines: Benoît Ente started commercializing his grandparents' vineyards only in the late 1990s. Benoît has built a fine reputation for direct, vibrant Puligny, with good aging capacity. Yields are extremely low, and use of oak is moderate. The range includes a highly praised Village Puligny. The Premier Cru holdings are in Champ Gain (very mineral), Les Referts (broad and rich), and lesser-spotted En La Richarde (a subsection of La Folatières). ★ Rising star

4 rue de la Mairie, 21190 Puligny-Montrachet
09 64 44 10 32

Domaine Blain Gagnard
Chassagne-Montrachet

The nervy yet elegantly rich wines of Blain Gagnard exemplify the alluring paradox of great white burgundy. Minimal but ultra-attentive is the approach here, from vineyard to cellar. The use of new oak is restrained, and although wines here speak clearly of their origin, there is a clear domaine signature of focused purity and sleek textures. Premier Cru Chassagnes show strikingly defined personalities: Boudriotte, for example, is fresh and linear, and Caillerets richly intense, mineral, and sumptuous. Reds are good and the Grand Crus excellent.

15 route de Santenay, 21190 Chassagne-Montrachet
03 80 21 34 07

Domaine Bruno Colin-Deléger
Chassagne-Montrachet

Domaine Michel Colin-Deléger was one of the most well-respected domaines in Chassagne. In 2003, it was divided between his sons, Bruno and Philippe Colin. Bruno continues in a broadly paternal vein—respectful, low-yielding viticulture, and attentive but sensitive winemaking. There is a lovely range of Premier Cru Chassagne that exemplifies the stylistic range for this commune, from the power of glossy, peachy Chenevottes to the stony refinement of Les Vergers. A carefully crafted St-Aubin Premier Cru Charmois offers Burgundian richness and poise at a (relatively) bargain price.

3 Impasse des Crêts, 21190 Chassagne-Montrachet
03 80 21 93 79

Domaine Chandon de Briailles
Savigny-lès-Beaune

This historic domaine has a distinctively restrained, well-mannered style. The focus is on the vineyards, where biodynamic viticulture yields small quantities of nuanced fruit. To preserve this delicate detail, absolutely no new oak is used. This is a rare decision for a quality-conscious producer in Burgundy, but consistent with their vision for subtle wines. Although in youth their wines (including reds and whites from Savigny, Pernand, and Aloxe-Corton) can taste almost austere, with time they sing out bright, pure, and beautifully defined.

1 rue Soeur Goby, 21420 Savigny-lès-Beaune
www.chandondebriailles.com

Domaine Château de la Maltroye
Chassagne-Montrachet

The gracefully beautiful Château de la Maltroye was built in the 18th century on the burnt-out ruins of a much older property. The house—and original 15th-century cellars

—have been sensitively restored by the current owner, Jean-Pierre Cornut. The domaine produces a nicely extensive range of Chassagne-Montrachet Premiers Crus, in both white and red. The white wines include racy, mineral Dents de Chien, and the broad, spicy Morgeots. The red wines feature Boudriotte and Clos du Château de Maltroye, a vineyard that is also part planted to Chardonnay.

16 rue de la Murée, 21190 Chassagne-Montrachet
03 80 21 32 45

Domaine du Comte Sénard Beaune
The new generation is coming through here at Domaine du Comte Sénard. Lorraine Sénard—daughter of the irresistibly twinkly eyed Philippe—has taken over the winemaking responsibilities from her father. These transitions can be notoriously fraught in Burgundy, but not here. For one thing, Lorraine has real talent, and her father Philippe knows it. At the heart of this domaine is a glorious selection of five red Grands Crus —all in Corton (the only red Grand Cru in the Côte de Beaune). Their white wines, which include a lovely Corton-Charlemagne and a delicious Aloxe-Corton that is full of character, are also very good.

7 rempart St-Jean, 21200 Beaune
www.domainesenard.com

Domaine des Comtes Lafon Meursault
Dominique Lafon is possibly the most famous *vigneron* in Burgundy. The quality at the family's Domaine des Comtes Lafon is of the highest level. From 1982, Dominique reclaimed the family vineyards, which had been previously rented out, and introduced biodynamic methods in tending them. He has matured from talented young buck to a *vigneron* of wisdom and experience, not just in the Côte d'Or, but also further south in the Mâconnais where, together with Les Artisans Vignerons du Sud, he pioneers quality organic, and increasingly biodynamic, wines. In Meursault, the family's château, inhabited by his mother, lies beside his Meursault Village vineyard of Clos de la Barre. The three top Meursault Premiers Crus of the domaine show quintessential terroir expression. Dominique Lafon's Montrachet Grand Cru is indisputably one of the finest white wines in the world.

5 rue Pierre Joigneaux, 21190 Meursault
www.comtes-lafon.fr

Domaine de Courcel Pommard
The wines at Domaine de Courcel are made by the staggeringly hard-working, talented, and self-effacing Yves Confuron (who also makes the wine at his family's domaine Confuron-Cotetidot in Vosne-Romanée—the location of one of the most tempting vegetable gardens to be seen in the region). Across the range, which runs from Bourgogne Rouge to five beautifully nuanced Pommard Premiers Crus, the wines impress with their energy and dense elegance. The Bourgogne Rouge is consistently one of the best-value red wines of Burgundy, and the Pommard Rugiens is unfailingly fine. Since he took over in 1996, Yves has really raised the quality here. ★Rising star

rue Notre Dame, 21630 Pommard
03 80 22 10 64

Domaine de Croix Beaune
The almost preternaturally assured David Croix runs the young boutique Domaine de Croix with great focus. Small but choice parcels of Beaune Premiers Crus are diligently (and organically) cultivated and crafted into sleek red wines of notable poise, precision, and purity. There is a lovely expression of terroir here, from the elegant perfume of Cent Vignes, to the dark and spicy Pertuisots, to the refined energy of Grèves. A satisfyingly lively, savory Corton-Charlemagne points to his gift for making white wines, too. Impressive wines from a hugely talented young *vigneron*. ★Rising star

2 rue Colbert, 21200 Beaune
03 80 22 85 92

Domaine Darviot-Perrin Monthélie
The owners of Domaine Darviot-Perrin, Didier, and Madame Darviot, are a charming and hospitable couple. In 1980, when they married, the Darviot and Perrin vineyards were amalgamated. They work together with just three employees on the terroir they understand best. Their vines are old, between 50–80 years. The cellar is cold and wine spends 12 months in barrel, followed by six months in tank. The domaine style is pure, linear, and racy, and the terroir is immediately apparent. Chassagne-Montrachet Blanchot-Dessus is not a wine one sees often, and their fine example is compact, chalky, and vigorous.

22 Grande rue, 21190 Monthélie
03 80 21 27 45

Domaine Fontaine Gagnard
Chassagne-Montrachet
Richard Fontaine of Domaine Fontaine Gagnard is a heedful *vigneron* of great courtesy and integrity. This 50 acre (20ha) domaine was formed when he married Laurence Gagnard and she took her share of the Gagnard-Delegrange vineyards. (Laurence's sister, Claudine, married Jean-Marc Blain to form the Domaine Blain Gagnard. It is confusing, but this mixing and matching is quite normal in Burgundy.) Richard, now assisted by his daughter Céline, makes beautifully refined, intense, and utterly authentic wines. The heart of the production is represented by white Chassagne-Montrachet, of which the stars are usually La Romanée and Caillerets, but there is excellent quality throughout.

19 route de Santenay, 21190 Chassagne-Montrachet
03 80 21 90 78

Domaine François et Antoine Jobard
Meursault
Domaine François et Antoine Jobard has traditionally produced uncharacteristically austere Meursault: straight and powerful. The quality is very high, but patience is required to appreciate it. This reflects the personality of the civil, but reserved François. His rather more relaxed son, Antoine, however, has now taken over in the winery and has been responsible for vinification since 2008. His changes have been subtle but they have made the wine a little more approachable. François' strict organic approach in the vineyards does, however, remain. These are ploughed to keep weeds down and no herbicides are used. Jobard makes

THE NEW NEGOCIANTS

Ben Leroux is a fine example of Burgundy's present-day evolution. Winemaker at celebrated Pommard producer, Clos des Epeneaux, he began a boutique "négociant" business by making two white wines from purchased grapes. A serendipitous meeting with a wine-loving investor at a winetasting in London has resulted in an expansion. The volumes remain artisanal, but the number of appellations was 20 at the last count, and growing. A passionate and convincing advocate of biodynamics, Leroux pounces on small parcels of high-quality grapes and, increasingly, works with venerable old-timers (for whom he has great respect) to optimize quality in the vineyard.

His wines are structured but unforced, combining reasonable accessibility with authentic character, good aging potential, and very light oak. Now operating from new premises in Beaune (shared with a few up-and-coming mini-négociant friends) he is emerging as an inspirational and influential character to the next generation of Burgundian *vignerons*.

**DOMAINE FRANCOIS ET
ANTOINE JOBARD**
ORGANIC PRINCIPLES IN THE VINEYARD AND
A MODERN APPROACH IN THE WINERY

DOMAINE A F GROS
A MARRIAGE OF WINEMAKERS AND
DOMAINES PRODUCING MUCH-LOVED WINES

one of the best, and powerfully severe, Meursault Porusots, a dense, streamlined Blagny, and a very contained, vigorous Charmes.

2 rue du Leignon, 21190 Meursault
03 80 21 26 44

Domaine François Milkulski Meursault

François Milkulski is of Polish descent paternally, while his mother is of the extensive Burgundian Boillot family, from whom François now rents vines. His cool, laid-back exterior belies the tough time he had building this domaine, as he was not in the direct line to inherit. His winemaking journey took him via California, where he worked at Calera. Today, Milkulski makes good Meursault, including a luscious, concentrated Charmes Vieilles Vignes from vines planted by his grandfather in 1913.

RN 74, 21190 Meursault
03 80 21 25 11

Domaine François Parent Pommard

François Parent represents the 13th generation of his venerable family. Deeply respectful of this history, he is nonetheless a charmingly approachable *vigneron*. Since the late 1990s, when he took his share of the family's Pommard vineyards, he has made wines under the label "François Parent," as well as those from the Côte de Nuits vineyards belonging to his wife, Anne-François Gros. The Beaune Premier Cru, Boucherottes, is a fragrant, supple, and lightly spicy take on this often hearty appellation. The Bourgogne Pinot Noir offers fruity value for money.

5 Grande Rue, 21630 Pommard
www.parent-pommard.com

Domaine Germain, Château de Chorey Chorey-lès-Beaune

This historic domaine has passed parcels of top-notch Beaune terroirs through the generations, but has really moved up a gear under the stewardship of Benoît Germain. His firm, assured hand fashions vibrant Pinot Noir from concentrated yields of impeccably managed vineyards. The Beaune Premier Cru Vignes Franches (from the domaine's oldest vines) is always a gloriously sleek joy, and the juicy, lively Chorey-lès-Beaune is one of the region's best-value buys. The white wines are tautly rich: particularly notable is the hauntingly scented Pernand-Vergelesses, from old vines of a rare clone.

rue Jacques Germain, 21200 Chorey-lès-Beaune
www.chateau-de-chorey-les-beaune.fr

Domaine A F Gros Pommard

This relatively large, and well-run, domaine has prime vineyards in the Côtes de Nuits and Beaune. François and Anne-François (née Gros) Parent brought together his inheritance in Pommard and hers in Vosne-Romanée, and added purchases of their own in Savigny-lès-Beaune and Flagey-Echézeaux. The result is an extensive range of burgundy (made by François) from Bourgogne Rouge to the legendary Grand Cru, Richebourg. There is nice nuance and typicity (the sense of authentic place and character) throughout, as well as a fruity, accessible style that has made these wines internationally popular.

La Garelle, 21630 Pommard
www.af-gros.com

Domaine Guy Amiot Chassagne-Montrachet

Thierry Amiot represents the fourth generation at this well-regarded family-run domaine (his brother, Fabrice, is the commercial director). At its heart are eight Premiers Crus of Chassagne-Montrachet, including six gloriously distinctive white wines (and one, Clos St Jean, both red and white). The domaine also produces a zesty, refined St-Aubin en Remilly; a floral Puligny Demoiselles; and intense, glossy Montrachet. Modern, in the very best sense, with pristine fruit and generous texture, they are both serious and hugely appealing.

13 rue du Grand Puits, 21190 Chassagne-Montrachet
pagesperso-orange.fr/domaine.amiot/accueil.html

Domaine Guy Roulot Meursault

Domaine Guy Roulot produces serious wine with stunningly lucid fruit. The wines show a great finesse and impeccable winemaking from one of the most talented *vignerons* of the Côte de Beaune. Jean-Marc Roulot believes in being very non-interventionist and leaves his wine on the lees (dead yeast cells) for as long as possible. These wines do not conform to the more modern fruit style, but nor are they very austere. They show textbook terroir character and the Meursault Les Perrières is consistently one of the finest.

21190 Meursault
03 80 21 64 36

Domaine Henri Germain et Fils
Meursault

Jean-François Germain took over from his father about 10 years ago and has not radically changed anything. He has about 20 acres (8ha) of vines, some owned and some rented. The style is fruit-driven, forward, sleek, and modern. It accentuates the typically plump Meursault profile and is balanced with freshness and energy. There are five wines from Meursault, including a spicy Village wine. The Chevalières is rich and seductive. The Premier Cru Charmes is generously rounded, creamy, and slightly exotic with notes of orange blossom. There is also a robust Chassagne-Montrachet called Morgeot.

4 rue des Forges, 21190 Meursault
03 80 21 22 04

Domaine Hubert et Olivier Lamy
St-Aubin

Domaine Lamy and the appellation St-Aubin are emerging from the hinterland. Not literally—this high, hilly hamlet above Puligny and Chassagne still feels like a backwater with great views. But the distinctive identity of its terroirs and wines is increasingly recognized. Olivier Lamy—engaging and youthfully enquiring—has adapted techniques since he took over in 1992. New oak aging is now more restrained, to allow the distinctively cool, racy nature of these high and stony terroirs to sing out. Premier Cru En Remilly is a textbook nervy St-Aubin, but the whole range is worthy of attention.

20 rue des Lavières, 21190 St-Aubin
www.domainehubertlamy.com

Domaine Jacques Prieur Meursault

Domaine Jacques Prieur's wines are well-executed and showy, which will appeal to those who like a full-frontal, glossy, concentrated burgundy in a richly oaky style.

Ownership is divided between the Prieur family and the Mercurey négociant Antonin Rodet. The domaine is housed at an elegant château in Meursault. There is a very extensive range of wines, including an extremely good, compact, quartzy Puligny Les Combettes and a fine range of Grands Crus. The Grands Crus include Corton-Charlemagne from a cool east-facing site, which is tight and structural, and a fine Le Montrachet (Chassagne side).

6 rue Santenots, 21190 Meursault
www.prieur.com

Domaine Jean-Louis Chavy
Puligny-Montrachet

The welcoming and genial Jean-Louis has taken his share of the old Domaine Gérard Chavy and now works from spacious, well-designed premises at the edge of the village. These are good wines, their intensity reflecting the low yields and attentive viticulture practiced here. The use of new oak is restrained, allowing the nuance of his four Premier Cru Pulignys to speak clearly. Folatières is often the star, combining the domaine's trademark suave textures with scintillating zest. Here, as at brother Alain's domaine, the Village Puligny Charmes is a delicious over-performer. ★ **Rising star**

27 rue de Bois, 21190 Puligny-Montrachet
09 62 34 94 93

Domaine Jean-Marc Boillot Pommard

The dynamic, energetic Jean-Marc excels at making both red and white wines. In addition to the domaine holdings in Pommard, Volnay, Beaune, Meursault, Puligny, and Chassagne, he also has a négociant, producing wines from grapes purchased in southern Burgundy. Despite this diversity of appellations, there is a definite Boillot signature: his Pinot Noir is vibrant and gutsy, and his Chardonnay (especially the Pulignys) seductive and lusciously scintillating. The Premier Cru Pommard Rugiens can be heroic, whereas his Montagny Premier Cru offers unbeatable bang for the (modest) bucks.

2 route de Beaune, 21630 Pommard
www.jeanmarc-boillot.com

Domaine Jean-Marc et Hugues Pavelot Savigny-lès-Beaune

Jean-Marc—assiduous, grave, and attentive—maintains a steady hand-over to son Hugues. These transitions can be tricky, but the quality of these vital, suavely textured wines endures. Savigny's unofficial re-branding—from little-known source of rustic Pinot Noir, to hot-spot for ageworthy wines of ambition and great value—is now complete, and Pavelot is a top address. Hugues maintains the paternal emphasis on the vineyards, but has adapted winemaking for finer tannin and more expressive fruit. The whole range is excellent, albeit more accessible.

1 chemin des Guettottes, 21420 Savigny-lès-Beaune
www.domainepavelot.com

Domaine Jean-Marc Pillot
Chassagne-Montrachet

Jean-Marc Pillot trained as an enologist at Beaune's famous Lycée, before taking over the family domaine from his father, Jean, in 1991. Since then he has taken the domaine—always well-regarded—into the top league of Chassagne producers, installing a new *cave*, and adapting

DOMAINE JEAN-MARC BOILLOT
A SEDUCTIVE AND LUSCIOUS CHARDONNAY
FROM THIS ENERGETIC PRODUCER

DOMAINE JACQUES PRIEUR
FROM THE CHASSAGNE SIDE OF THE GRAND
CRU VINEYARD—A VERY FINE EXAMPLE

winemaking techniques. Today, the wines, especially the whites, have an international reputation and are praised for their purity, fruit, and precision. Seven white Chassagne Premiers Crus garner the most attention, but reds are also well-made and built for aging.

21190 Meursault
03 80 21 33 35

Domaine Jean-Marc et Thomas Bouley Volnay

Thomas Bouley gained experience in Oregon and New Zealand before taking on full responsibility for winemaking at the family domaine in 2002. He is both an impressive and very likeable young man. The domaine has choice Premier Cru holdings in Pommard and Volnay from which Thomas fashions very pure, intense wines. The tiny Volnay Premier Cru, Carelles, produces what is often the domaine's most striking wine—all perfume and pace. The Bourgogne Rouge is stuffed full of juicy, vibrant Pinot Noir fruit and is excellent value for money. This is one to watch. ★ **Rising star**

12 chemin de la Cave, 21190 Volnay
www.jean-marc-bouley.com

Domaine Jean-Michel Gaunoux
Meursault

This domaine is based in a large and beautifully maintained stone house in the village and the tasting takes place in an impressive hall. There are 15 acres (6ha) in vines in Meursault, Puligny, Pommard, and Volnay. The petite Jean-Michel bottles his wines within 12 months to make way for the next vintage. From Meursault, there is an apricot, honeyed Premier Cru Les Goutte d'Or and a pure and citrussy Les Perrières. With purity and well-handled oak, these wines are accessible relatively early.

1 rue de Leignon, 21190 Meursault
03 80 21 22 02

Domaine Jean-Michel Giboulot
Savigny-lès-Beaune

Updated tradition is the order of the day at this well-run domaine. Restrained yields and very moderate use of new oak produce classic, well-balanced red Savigny from four Premiers Crus, including a very good Gravains. The Village *lieux-dit*, Les Grands Lizards, can be outstanding value. The white wines are also worth a mention, especially the Premier Cru Savigny-lès-Beaune, Les Talmettes. From a tiny parcel producing just 500–700 bottles a year, this interesting white combines generosity with an intriguing perfume and understated, savory fruit. Worth looking out for.

7 rue du Gal-Leclerc, 21420 Savigny-lès-Beaune
03 80 21 52 30

Domaine Jean-Philippe Fichet Meursault

Jean-Philippe produces nervy, mineral Meursault that has energy and precision. He dislikes typical rounded Meursault for being "too rich and fat" and loves precise, firmly acidic wines, which will not appeal to everyone, but will engage those who love a clear expression of terroir. He is undoubtedly a top-flight winemaker, who should probably be making wine in Chablis. There is an excellent straight Village Meursault from five *lieux-dits* (these so-called "named places" are in effect the

DOMAINE LEFLAIVE
CHAMPIONING BIODYNAMICS TO PRODUCE
ONE OF THE BEST PULIGNYS IN THE REGION

second growths of Meursault). His Meursault Tessons is racy. From Puligny, the Premier Cru Les Referts is fine textured, pure, and mineral.

2 Rue de la Gare, 21190 Meursault
09 63 20 79 04

Domaine Jobard-Morey Meursault

The wines here are made by son-in-law Rémy Ehret—a man with a poetic soul, who is quite shy and reserved at first, but eventually opens up. He has a lightness of touch in the winery, uses 15–20% new wood on the Premier Cru, and looks for a delicate toast so as not to "mark" the wine with wood. Each year he likes his two favorite coopers to visit to discuss the oak best suited to each wine. He makes a lovely mineral Bourgogne. The Tillets is reticent and floral and the Charmes, rather charming.

1 rue de la Barre, 21190 Meursault
http://jobard-morey.com

Domaine Joseph Voillot Volnay

Jean-Pierre Charlot is a genial man with refined sensibilities, and a sure but light winemaking touch. Since 1995, he has been making the wines at this, his father-in-law's estate, which has prime Premier Cru plots in three Volnay and four Pommard vineyards, as well as choice bits of Meursault. The wines impress for their striking nuance: for example, Volnays Fremiets is airy and scented, the Champans brooding and dense, and the stony Caillerets all minerality and focus. ★**Rising star**

place de l'Eglise, 21190 Volnay
www.joseph-voillot.com

Domaine Lamy-Pillot Chassagne-Montrachet

This well-regarded family producer is now run by daughter Florence, and her husband, Sébastien. Between them they have impressive qualifications in viticulture and enology, as well as experience gained abroad. The domaine is situated outside of the village, in the hamlet of Morgeot, surrounded by vineyards. With 50 acres (20 ha) of vineyards, this is a sizeable property by Burgundian standards. Prime landholdings in the Côte d'Or include Chassagne Premiers Crus Morgeot and Caillerets, and St-Aubin Premiers Crus Les Castets and Charmois, as well as vineyards in Beaune, Meursault Blagny, and Santenay.

31 route de Santenay, 21190 Chassagne-Montrachet
pagesperso-orange.fr/lamy.pillot/

Domaine de La Pousse d'Or Volnay

This historic and important Volnay estate has been revitalized in recent years by the dedication and investment of Patrick Landanger. It is, by Burgundian standards, a large domaine, with 37 acres (15ha) in the communes of Volnay, Corton, Pommard, and Santenay. These are choice holdings, comprising four Premier Cru Volnays (including the renowned Caillerets), two Grands Crus (sleek Corton Clos du Roi and wild Corton-Bressandes), and Pommard Jarollières. Good Santenay is one of the few remaining Burgundian secrets, and the Premier Cru Clos Tavanne Vieilles Vignes is worth looking out for.

8 rue de la Chapelle, 21190 Volnay
www.lapoussedor.fr

DOMAINE JEAN-PHILIPPE FICHET
A UNIQUE STYLE OF MEURSAULT WITH MORE
ACIDITY AND A NERVY CHARACTER

Domaine Larue St-Aubin

Brothers Didier and Denis, now joined by Denis' son, Bruno, work diligently at this well-respected estate. Of the 11 white wines produced, six are from the backwater of St-Aubin, which is increasingly gaining recognition for the quality potential of its high, stony-soiled vineyards. The wonderfully named St-Aubin Premier Cru Murgers des Dents de Chien (after the "dogs teeth" of bedrock that push up into the soil) is on the Puligny side of St-Aubin, and is notably refined and stony. The Pulignys themselves consistently win plaudits and are good value for the price. The red wines are also good.

32 rue de la Chatenière, 21190 St-Aubin
www.larue-vins.com

Domaine Latour-Giraud Meursault

Jean-Pierre Latour's family have been in Meursault since 1680 on his father's side, while his mother brought vineyards dating back to 1850 to her marriage. This domaine holds a substantial slice of Genevrières and a good range of Meursault Premiers Crus. Latour-Giraud was in the doldrums, but is now back in good form, with Jean-Pierre Latour making rich-style Meursault. He uses a lot of *bâtonnage* (stirring the lees in the barrel) for body, texture, and a rich, nutty taste. The Charmes is silky-smooth and harmonious; the Genevrières has panache.

6 route Départementale 974, 21190 Meursault
www.domaine-latour-giraud.com

Domaine Leflaive Puligny-Montrachet

Anne-Claude Leflaive is a visionary character, as inspiring and potentially formidable as the forces of nature that she champions. This domaine is the most renowned in Puligny, and among the best in Burgundy. An early adopter of biodynamics, Leflaive produces effortlessly intense and balanced wines that combine richness with elegance. As well as 25 acres (10ha) of Premier Cru, the domaine has 12 acres (5ha) of Grand Cru—a fabulously large chunk—comprising Bâtard, Chevalier, and Bienvenues-Bâtard-Montrachet. They are sensational wines at heart-stopping prices. The Bourgogne Blanc, made partly from declassified Puligny, is a relative steal.

place des Marronniers, 21190 Puligny-Montrachet
www.leflaive.fr

Domaine Louis Carillon Puligny-Montrachet

Jacques Carillon—courteous and modest—makes some of the best wines of the Côte de Beaune, never mind Puligny. Vines are tended along green principles, minimizing chemical treatments, and yields are kept low. Red wines are extremely well made, but it is the whites that impress: the danger for Puligny can be that understatement slides into non-statement. But here, all wines, from a staggeringly good Village Puligny, through a range of slinky Premiers Crus, to a super-structured Bienvenues-Bâtard-Montrachet, combine a glossy, sophisticated intensity with striking refinement.

21190 Puligny-Montrachet
www.louis-carillon.com

Domaine Marquis d'Angerville Volnay

This nobly beautiful house at the heart of Volnay is home to one of Burgundy's great wine families. The d'Angervilles have been pioneers and champions of the highest quality since the early 1900s. This is a large domaine, with holdings in eight Volnay Premier Crus, of which the *monopole* Clos des Ducs is the jewel in the crown. Run today by Guillaume d'Angerville and Rénaud de Villette, the domaine practices biodynamic viticulture. These are graceful, yet intense, complex wines of deceptive longevity.

4 rue de Mont, 21190 Volnay
www.domainedangerville.fr

Domaine Matrot Meursault

Thierry is a quirky man with a spontaneous laugh. His pure, streamlined, and mineral wine is awkward in youth and designed to age. Thierry has no desire to compromise and make it more accessible. For Thierry, young wine is about 10 years old, and he likes to drink it with the produce of his vegetable garden, for he is a passionate gardener and an enthusiastic cook, as well as a thoughtful *vigneron*. He makes Meursault, including a racy, finely edged Blagny and a poised, mineral Perrières. From Puligny-Montrachet, Les Combottes is layered and stony.

12 rue de Martray, 21190 Meursault
www.matrot.com

Domaine Mestre-Michelot Meursault

This domaine is run by Jean-François Mestre-Michelot, who makes very accessible wine with plenty of forward fruit and toasty oak. Very sensibly he bottles his fruit-driven Bourgogne Blanc, Domaine de Montmeix, under screwcap. He makes a honeyed Meursault Narvaux from old vines and a softly full-bodied Genevrières.

12 bis rue de Mazeray/19 rue du 11 Novembre,
21190 Meursault; 03 80 21 26 88

Domaine Michel Bouzereau et Fils
Meursault

This domaine is managed by 38-year-old Jean-Baptiste Bouzereau, who is the 10th generation of Bouzereau to have tended vines in Meursault. The fermentation is slow to start here, as the *cave*, which is built into the cliff, is typically very cool. When summer arrives, the doors are opened to raise the temperature and encourage the malolactic fermentation. Excellent Aligoté is produced here, and a floral "come hither" Genevrières. The style is modern, fruity, and forward, but not flashy.

3 rue de la Planche Meunière, 21190 Meursault
03 80 21 20 74

Domaine Michel Lafarge Volnay

Michel Lafarge and his son, Frédéric, craft some of Burgundy's most acclaimed and haunting red wines. The domaine produces some excellent Beaunes and Premier Cru Pommard, but is renowned for its Volnays. As with so many of the world's great winemakers, they see their craft as a matter of a few simple imperatives: respectful, sensitive viticulture; moderate yields; and attentive but light-handed winemaking. From the Village Volnays to the domaine's top bottlings of Volnay Clos du Château des Ducs and Volnay Clos du Chênes, the wines are characterized by a shimmering, twinkle-toed intensity.

15 rue de la Combe, 21190 Volnay
www.domainelafarge.fr

Domaine Michel Morey-Coffinet
Chassagne-Montrachet

This well-established domaine operates from a handsome property at the top of the village, approached by sweeping stone stairs and endowed with large and beautiful vaulted cellars. Thibault Morey joined his father, Michel, in 2000. His sensitive, enquiring approach has prompted a few changes, including a move to ecologically minded viticulture since 2004. The wines are lovely: open, expressive, and elegantly rich, their clean, bright fruit renders them delicious even in youth. Their red Chassagne Premier Cru, Clos St Jean, is a splendid reminder of the historic affinity of this commune for Pinot Noir. ★ Rising star

6 place du Grand Four, 21190 Chassagne-Montrachet
www.domaine-morey-coffinet.com

Domaine Michel Niellon
Chassagne-Montrachet

These beautiful wines are consistently among the very best in Chassagne. Their understated intensity and rich poise are testament to the skill and sensitivity of Michel Niellon. No whistles and bells here: the cellars are spotlessly clean but small and serviceable, and Niellon himself is self-effacing, respectful of his vineyards, and loyal to his devoted customers. The five Chassagne Premiers Crus (all made in tiny quantities) include a sumptuous Les Chaumées, but even his basic Village wine is exemplary stuff and a wise buy. Grands Crus Chevalier and Bâtard-Montrachet are simply outstanding.

1 rue du Nord, 21190 Chassagne-Montrachet
03 80 21 30 95

Domaine de Montille Volnay

Brother and sister Etienne and Alix de Montille run this hugely respected family domaine together. Etienne is responsible for the successful turnaround at Château de Puligny-Montrachet, and they also have a burgeoning négociant business, producing wine from purchased grapes, called "Deux Montille." The heart of the de Montille domaine has, for years, been red burgundy from the Côte de Beaune. Today, the domaine trademarks of purity and longevity endure, but the offering has been considerably expanded, with new vineyards in Corton, Beaune, and in the Côte de Nuits. This is a top-flight address.

rue Pied de la Vallée, 21190 Volnay
www.domainedemontille.com

Domaine Nicolas Rossignol-Jeanniard Volnay

Nicolas Rossignol is a voluble, driven, and hugely likeable man. His passion for his wines, vines, and birthright is particularly close to the surface, even in a region where such passion informs so many. Tasting here is a masterclass in the terroirs and nuance of Volnay and Pommard (since Nicolas took on some vineyards from his uncle, his range of Pommard Premiers Crus alone stands at eight). It is all about the vineyards, as usual, with low yields, sustainable viticulture, and attention to soil health. Nicolas fashions these pristine grapes into memorably vivid, dense Pinot Noir.

rue de Mont, 21190 Volnay
www.nicolas-rossignol.com

THINGS TO DO IN MEURSAULT

Despite the grandeur of their names, and their beautifully preserved medieval charm, many of Burgundy's most famous wine villages are, if not one-horse, one-tabac towns. There is, however, a bit of a buzz about Meursault, especially in summer when children mob the ice-cream man on the Place de L'Hotel de Ville, a classic town square dominated by the gothic church of St Nicolas and the brightly-tiled town hall.

The casual visitor can enjoy tasting wine in Meursault without appointments: Patrick Javillier has a tasting cellar on the Place de Europe, and the wine shop Caves des Vieilles Vignes, offers tastings as well as good wines at fair prices. There are restaurants and hotels to suit a range of budgets, and the full complement of shops, including a good bakery. And behind the church is a bijou beauty spa promising to harness the antioxidant power of grapes.

Château de Corton-André in Aloxe-Corton is one of the most photographed buildings in the Côte de Beaune.

DOMAINE DE MONTILLE
LONGEVITY AND PURITY MARK THIS
DOMAINE'S WINES OUT FROM THE CROWD

DOMAINE PIERRE MOREY
A POWERFUL AND DISTINGUISHED GRAND
CRU FROM ONE OF THE BEST WINEMAKERS

Domaine Patrick Javillier Meursault

It is impossible not to be affected by the enthusiasm of the uber-effusive Patrick Javillier, who, like an eccentric professor, has a chalk diagram scrawled on the wall of the cellar to illustrate how his wines are constructed to mature. Patrick makes typically rich, open, and generous Meursault. His Cuvée Oligocène always over-delivers for a Bourgogne, while the Village *lieux-dits* illustrate the terroir with precision. The Clos du Cromin is full and plump, while Tillets is defined by racy minerality. The Premier Cru Les Charmes is suitably smooth and opulent.

19 place de l'Europe, 21190 Meursault
www.patrickjavillier.com

Domaine Paul Pernot Puligny-Montrachet

Paul Pernot is the type of restrained (almost taciturn) *vigneron* who gives old-school a good name. Tasting here is usually pretty quick; there is no interruption from Paul, who lets you draw your own conclusions. He can afford to: these are good wines. Unshowy and savory in youth (there is very little new oak), with good acidity, they blossom with age and take on an elegantly sinuous texture. Paul continues to sell a large part of his production to Beaune négociants, keeping a small but hand-picked selection to bottle under the domaine name.

21190 Puligny-Montrachet
03 80 21 32 35

Domaine Paul Pillot Chassagne-Montrachet

These bold, generous, and energetic wines express something of the character of their makers (a version, perhaps, of the "dogs looking like their owners" phenomenon). This firmly family-run domaine has prime holdings in Chassagne Premiers Crus, and is increasingly run by siblings Thierry and Chrystelle. Thierry (who gained experience and a refreshingly broad perspective making wine in the New World) practices *bâtonnage* with restraint and favors lees-aging, preserving freshness and emphasizing fruit purity. The Bourgogne Pinot Noir is gorgeously supple and juicy, and the white Chassagne Mazure is excellent Village wine. ★ **Rising star**

3 rue Clos St-Jean, 21190 Chassagne-Montrachet
www.domainepaulpillot.com

Domaine Philippe Colin
Chassagne-Montrachet

Philippe Colin established this domaine in 2004; he had previously worked alongside his father and brother at the family domaine, Michel Colin-Déléger. (His brother, Bruno, founded his own domaine around the same time.) With 27 acres (11ha) of vineyards in and around Chassagne-Montrachet, Philippe produces 28 different wines of both colors (the red wines of Chassagne, in particular, being some of the great underestimated gems of the Côte d'Or). There are nine white Chassagne Premiers Crus, making this a great address for getting to grips with the nuance and terroir of this popular commune.

Haut des Champs, 21190 Chassagne-Montrachet
03 80 21 90 49

Domaine Pierre Morey Meursault

Pierre Morey, who pioneered organic and biodynamic practices in Burgundy, is among the most skillful white winemakers in the region, although you would never

guess, as this self-effacing, gentle man eschews the limelight. Until recently he was also responsible for Domaine Leflaive in Puligny-Montrachet. Together with his daughter, Anne, he now focuses on his domaine and on Morey-Blanc, their excellent négociant. He has a magic touch and coaxes great terroir character from his vines. His Tessons is chalky and tense. The focused and mineral Perrières shows great finesse, and the Bâtard-Montrachet has a powerful and distinguished profile.

9 rue Comte Lafon, 21190 Meursault
www.morey-meursault.fr

Domaine Ramonet Chassagne-Montrachet

This acclaimed domaine is now run by brothers Noel and Jean-Claude. They hold true to the principles of father André: low yields, attentive viticulture, and light-handed winemaking. All pretty timeless stuff, actually. Increased domaine-bottling has only bolstered quality. The Grands Crus are among the most sought-after (and expensive) of white burgundy: Le Montrachet, Bâtard-Montrachet, and a fabulously elegant Bienvenues-Bâtard-Montrachet. Of the white Premier Cru Chassagnes, Morgeot is a textbook example of the refined generosity that characterizes this village. The red Clos St-Jean is juicily lovely.

4 place des Noyers, 21190 Chassagne-Montrachet
03 80 21 35 65

Domaine Rémi Jobard Meursault

The wines here are very well defined, encompassing juicy and seductive fruit in a modern, silky, and accessible style. Rémi combines talented winemaking with a young family, and there is a rabbit hutch in the courtyard. His Meursault Chevalières has lovely depth, richness, and warm perfume, reflecting the mature age of the vines, which were planted in 1940. The Porusots couples glossy fruit and velvet texture with vigor. The typically exotic character of Genevrières is nicely contained. It is rich, but not too overt, and has notes of apricots, almonds, and white flowers.

12 rue Sudot, 21190 Meursault
03 80 21 20 23

Domaine Robert Ampeau et Fils
Meursault

Michel Ampeau is as affable as his wines are reserved. They are *vin de garde*: the grapes picked early to preserve the acidity for aging. After tasting the latest vintage, Michel will disappear to the cellar and return with a collection of older vintages, which he opens in no particular order of vintage or appellation, and his eyes twinkle as you try to place the wine. The 1985 Perrières is still juicy. This pleasurable exercise may perhaps have been less fun with his father, Robert, whose weatherbeaten face observes sternly from a photo on the wall.

6 rue du Cromin, 21190 Meursault
03 80 21 20 35

Domaine Roblet-Monnot Volnay

This quality-obsessed 15 acre (6ha) estate is perhaps too firmly established to be properly termed a rising star. But Pascal Roblet's camera-shy focus on his vines and wines protects his domaine from the most intense media hype. Biodynamically farmed vineyards yield tiny quantities of intensely flavored Pinot Noir, which Pascal fashions into memorably vibrant, vivid wines, which (rather like those of Nicolas Rossignol) challenge the idea of silky, "feminine" Volnay. The Village Volnay St-François is reliably succulent and satisfying. Of the Premiers Crus, Volnay Taillepieds is deeply stony, intense, and heroically long-lived. ★ **Rising star**

rue de la Combe, 21190 Volnay
03 80 21 22 47

Domaine Roger Belland Santenay

This domaine is established as the source of sleek, juicy Santenay. Roger's daughter, Julie, is increasingly responsible for the winemaking, and has reduced the proportion of new oak used in maturation, enhancing the beautifully vibrant and pure fruit of these wines. Santenay (together with near neighbor, Maranges) is now the prime candidate for a source of great-value red burgundy. In addition to one Village and three excellent Premier Cru Santenays (of which Gravières is notably refined), the Bellands produce Premier Cru Chassagne, Volnay, and Pommard, and lovely white wines.

3 rue de la Chapelle, 21590 Santenay
www.domaine-belland-roger.com

Domaine Simon Bize et Fils

Savigny-lès-Beaune

The genial Patrick Bize is gradually sharing more of the winemaking responsibilities with Guillaume Boit. Guillaume, who previously worked at superstar Puligny domaine Etienne Sauzet, joined Bize to make (and improve) the white wines. Increasingly, he is more involved, alongside Patrick, with the reds. Boit is talented and respectful of the reputation and house style built up by Patrick over the decades. Almost all wines are from the Savigny appellation, including four Premiers Crus, and several Village. These days, the white Savigny is delicious, quite refined, and is an outstanding value for the price.

12 rue Chanoine Donin, 21420 Savigny-lès-Beaune
www.domainebize.com

Domaine Sylvain Loichet

Chorey-lès-Beaune

There are plenty of 20-something winemakers in Burgundy, but relatively few who have firmly hit their stride. One such is Sylvain Loichet, from a family of stonemasons in quarry-marked Comblanchien, who has taken back the family vineyards in Côte de Nuits Village, Ladoix, and Clos du Vougeot and is making strikingly vivid wines, full of unforced energy. The appellation of Ladoix is far from a household name, but Sylvain's Village and Premier Cru renderings are alluringly full of character. The Ladoix Premier Cru Les Grechons is exotic, yet serious, and worth seeking out. ★ **Rising star**

2 rue d'Aloxe Corton, 21200 Chorey-lès-Beaune
06 80 75 50 67

Domaine Thomas Morey

Chassagne-Montrachet

The name is new, but this is no start-up. Thomas took his inheritance early, and this domaine is based on half of the old Domaine Bernard Morey. (His father, the ebullient and theoretically retired Bernard, keeps his hand in as a small négociant). Thomas's first solo vintage was 2007, from which he fashioned well-constructed wines with

DOMAINE ROGER BELLAND
ONE OF THE BEST SANTENAY PREMIERS CRUS, OFFERING GREAT VALUE FOR MONEY

good extract and a robust style. The domaine holdings include prime Chassagne Premiers Crus and a Bâtard-Montrachet Grand Cru, but the premier Santenay Premier Cru Grand Clos Rousseau is exuberantly scrummy Pinot Noir, and worth tracking down.

9 rue du Nord, 21190 Chassagne-Montrachet
www.thomasmorey-vins.com

Domaine Tollot-Beaut Chorey-lès-Beaune

This domaine has extensive holdings of Pinot Noir across Aloxe-Corton, Savigny, Beaune, and Chorey. The star of the show is often the Beaune Premier Cru Grèves, which adds scented complexity to the domaine's trademark svelte tannins and textures. For year-on-year consistency and sheer value for money, Tollot-Beaut's Chorey-lès-Beaune is hard to beat: supple, subtle, and irresistibly charming, it has become almost an ambassador for this once obscure appellation, and is hugely popular with smart restaurants for its immediate appeal, and versatility with food.

rue Alexandre Tollot, 21200 Chorey-lès-Beaune
03 80 22 12 61

Domaine Vincent Dancer

Chassagne-Montrachet

Intelligent, dedicated, and diligent, Vincent Dancer has earned a large following for the tiny production of this excellent domaine. With vineyards in Meursault, Chassagne, Beaune, and Pommard, the domaine production is characterized by small quantities of a dozen or so meticulously defined, pure, elegant wines. The outstanding Chassagne Premier Cru Tête du Clos could be labeled "Morgeot." There certainly would be marketing advantages in using the label of this large and well-known vineyard—but retaining the original name sums up the authentic, respectful attitude at this domaine.

23 route de Santenay, 21190 Chassagne-Montrachet
www.vincentdancer.com

Domaine Yves Boyer-Martenot

Meursault

Vincent Boyer-Martenot worked in California and in Australia at Yering Station. He took over from his father in 2002 and, soon after, the family bought a new winery, now fitted with lots of super new equipment. Vincent matures his wine for 11 months in one-quarter new oak for the Village wine and one-third for Premier Cru. There is a sleek Meursault Perrières, and the Puligny Caillerets, which was purchased in 1996, is attractively austere and stony. Over the past few years, the quality has been steadily increasing as Vincent becomes more assured.

17 rue de Mazeray, 21190 Meursault
www.boyer-martenot.com

Etienne Sauzet Puligny-Montrachet

The heart of the production here at Etienne Sauzet is a range of slinky, delicately intense Premier Cru Pulignys, which typically get going around five years of age. Since the early 1990s (when a chunk of the domaine was transferred to his brother-in-law), Gérard Boudot has supplemented the original domaine holdings (which are mostly in the north of the commune) with purchased grapes, and vinified both origins together.

DOMAINE TOLLOT-BEAUT
THE QUALITY AT THIS DOMAINE HAS BECOME AN AMBASSADOR FOR CHOREY-LES-BEAUNE

MAISON LOUIS JADOT
A CONSISTENT AND EXCELLENT NEGOCIANT BRAND, ACROSS THE BOARD

In addition to the Premiers Crus (of which Champ Canet is often the star) there are four excellent Grands Crus. Tip-top quality and prices to match.

11 rue de Poiseul, 21190 Puligny-Montrachet
www.etienne-sauzet.com

Jean-Nöel Gagnard Chassagne-Montrachet

This venerable domaine has been run since the late 1980s by Jean-Nöel's talented and determined daughter, Caroline l'Estimé. The domaine trademark is a balanced combination of richness and elegance, which shines through the varied characters of their nine white and two red Chassagnes. This is a forward-thinking domaine, with a clear commitment to sustainability, and a desire to reach out to consumers. Caroline's investment in vineyards in the Hautes-Côtes has yielded a red and a white wine of outstanding value for the price. Her blog (in perfect English) is lively and informative.

9 place des Noyers, 21190 Chassagne-Montrachet
www.domaine-gagnard.com

Jean-Yves Devevey Demigny

From modest, but always quality orientated, beginnings in the unassuming village of Demigny, Jean-Yves has built up a thriving business and enviable reputation. Since 1992, when he returned to the family domaine to produce basic Bourgogne Blanc, he has shown himself to be a diligent *vigneron*, crafting "lesser" burgundies of uncommon character and distinction. To the original holdings of Bourgogne Blanc and Hautes-Côtes Champs Perdrix he has added more illustrious names by acquiring vineyards and purchasing grapes. Today, the offering covers seven appellations, including the delicious and distinctive Beaune Premier Cru Pertuisots. ★ **Rising star**

rue de Breuil, 71150 Demigny
www.devevey.com

Joseph Drouhin Beaune

Maison Joseph Drouhin has long been a consistent performer in producing top-quality wines and has led the way for the contemporary *négoce* business. Drouhin also has impressive family landholdings (including 10 Grands Crus), some of which have become almost synonymous with Drouhin, including the smoothly textured Beaune Premier Cru Le Clos des Mouches and the taut, mineral Beaune Les Grèves, of which it owns 2.5 acres (1ha). Key to its success is the tall, reserved Philippe Drouhin, who manages the vineyards and oversees the contract land. In the winery, Jéröme Faure-Brac has a light touch. His first solo vintage was 2006 and he skillfully maintains the house style for pure, fruity wines with elegant tannins. Drouhin favors semi-carbonic macerations, where the whole berries are fermented to promote the fruit. It eschews too much extraction and new oak. There is a wide and excellent range of wines, from the crunchy, redcurranty Chorey-lès-Beaune to the graceful, poised Chambolle-Musigny, Les Amoureuses. Les Petits Monts, Véronique Drouhin's parcel in Vosne-Romanée, is always a little wild. The Chambertin, Clos De Bèze, is elegantly rich, spicy, and layered. In Chablis, the Drouhin family is celebrating their 40th anniversary. To mark the occasion, 17 acres (7ha) of estate-owned vineyards, which have been run biodynamically since 1997, have been re-branded as Drouhin Vaudon from the 2008 vintage. Drouhin, which had rather Côte d'Or style Chablis, has

JEAN-NOEL GAGNARD
GREAT-VALUE CHASSAGNE FROM A FORWARD-THINKING DOMAINE

abandoned the use of new wood. It is a pioneer in many respects, as it ventured further afield to Oregon, exporting its Burgundian understanding of Pinot Noir. Philippe's sister, Véronique, is responsible here. This is a talented and dynamic family.

7 rue d'Enfer, 21200 Beaune
www.drouhin.com

Louis Latour Aloxe-Corton

The Latour family have deeply Burgundian roots, making wine from its choice domaine-owned vineyards since at least the 1730s. But it is the négociant arm, established in 1797, that has enabled its international reach and recognition. Today, Latour—still family-owned, and still based in its home town of Aloxe-Corton—produces wines from almost every commune in the Côte d'Or, as well as Chablis, the Mâconnais, and Beaujolais. A juicy chunk of Burgundy's best vineyards is Latour land; the company owns nearly 74 acres (30ha) of precious Grands Crus. Latour is still headquartered at the beautiful Château Corton Grancy, in Aloxe-Corton, one of the oldest *cuveries* in France, and where wines from Latour's own vineyards (labeled Domaine Latour) are made. The white wines, in particular the Grands Crus, are very highly regarded. Latour's Corton-Charlemagne is one of Burgundy's great joys. The reds, which are light and fruity in style, have in the past been rather overshadowed: today, a dedicated new winery in Pommard reflects Latour's efforts to raise the quality and profile of their red wines. Beyond Burgundy, in the South of France, Latour also makes a range of hugely successful Chardonnay in the Ardèche, as well as Pinot Noir in the Côteaux du Verdon.

18 rue des Tonneliers, 21204 Beaune
www.louislatour.com

Maison Alex Gambal Beaune

Alex, a relaxed and jovial American, is a very good source for delicious Pinot Noir, with no pretensions of grandeur. The house style is lucid and captures the fragrance, fruit, and sensual texture of Pinot Noir. These are not wines to keep for a long time, but they are very appealing, particularly Alex's Village wines, where he works with the grapes. The more illustrious wines are bought-in wine. Alex, who has a background in real estate in New York, got itchy feet in the early 1990s. His wanderings led him to Burgundy, where he and his wife decided to stay, and Alex worked for Le Serbet, the American importer, for three years. In his early 40s he studied viticulture and vinification in Burgundy as a mature student, while shuttling back and forth to Cape Cod to sell wine. He had spotted a gap in the market between great wines and the mediocre. His aim is to offer consistency and to make the best Pinot Noir and Chardonnay. He set up his négociant business, working principally with one grower per appellation. Everything is stemmed to avoid super extraction, making transparent and elegant wines.

14 boulevard Jules Ferry, 21200 Beaune
www.alexgambal.com

Maison Camille Giraud Beaune

Maison Camille Giraud was another ailing négociant, nearing bankruptcy, when in 2001, the Giraud brothers sold out to a consortium of Americans. They quickly snaffled David Croix, a talented young winemaker, who had worked an internship in 2000 with Benjamin Leroux at Come Armand, and who had completed his enology degree just 11 days before his appointment with Giraud. Croix quickly threw out the old image along with the outdated equipment, which included burning 700 old barrels. He uses little new oak, generally between 15–20%. Unlike many contemporary négociants, there is negligible domaine land. Croix focuses on sourcing fruit—he has changed almost every contract to ensure that 85–90% is in fruit rather than juice or wine, and where possible, organic. In practice, however, it is difficult to be organic as a négociant, and it represents only about 10%. Whereas this was a Côte de Beaune négoce, towards the end focusing on Village wine, today there is wine from the Côte de Nuits and the portfolio includes a fine range of Grands Crus. The quality is now very good (Croix now also has his own domaine).

3 rue Pierre Joigneaux, 21200 Beaune
www.camillegiroud.com

Maison Louis Jadot Beaune

This is a firmly consistent brand and an excellent source of terroir-focused whites and firm reds. This négociant was established in 1859, and has a gracious maison in rue Eugène Spuller in Beaune, with labyrinthine cellars beneath. Jadot owns and manages a large amount of land, about 380 acres (154ha), split up into five domaines (Louis Jadot; des Heritieres Louis Jadot; Gagey; Duc de Magenta; and Chateau de la Commaraine), as well as the négoce side. Although the portfolio spans the Côte d'Or to the Mâconnais, including a wealth of Grands Crus, many will be familiar with the Beaune Premier Cru Clos des Ursules, owned by the Jadot family prior to becoming négociants. These days, Jadot is no longer family-owned, having been sold in 1985 to the Kobrand Corporation. The real work takes place in a utilitarian-looking building on the periphery of Beaune, which has an impressive circular vat room. Jacques Lardière is an eccentric wizard of a winemaker and has long been a follower of biodynamics. He uses beautiful wooden open-top vats with an automated punching-down system to submerge the cap of fruit that rises to the top of the vat during fermentation. This is supplemented with some manual punching with a long traditional implement called a *pichou*. This is exhausting work in such large vats. Jacques Lardière favors destemming and high fermentation temperatures. Jadot has its own cooperage, Cadus, which allows it to control the whole process, from the selection and maturation of the oak to the toasting and making of the barrels.

2 rue du Mont Batois, 21200 Beaune
www.louisjadot.com

Maison Olivier Leflaive Puligny-Montrachet

This négociant, known for its reliably well-made, accessible white wines, was established in 1984 by Olivier Leflaive, cousin of Anne-Claude of Domaine Leflaive. For the past 22 vintages, Frank Grux has lead a team of two winemakers and an enologist. Grux made wine for his godfather, Guy Roulot, before cousin Jean Marc took over. There are approximately 35 acres (14ha) of domaine land, among them l'Abbaye de Morgeot in Chassagne, which makes a muscular white. They no longer purchase wine here, but now focus on buying grapes; currently 60% grapes and 40% juice. Approximately 70–75,000 cases of wine are turned out from a large utilitarian

building in Puligny. Grux purchases 12% more than needed, so that after the malolactic fermentation he can select the best. The portfolio stretches from Chablis to the Mâconnais and from regional wine to Grand Cru. Meursault, Puligny, and Chassagne are well represented. The svelte, streamlined Puligny-Montrachet Les Folatières is particularly good. They are also a good source of Rully, including the Premiers Crus Rabboucé and Les Clous, and of St-Aubin. Olivier Leflaive has a Table d'Hôte on Place de Monument in Puligny, and has offered this for many years, but the current premises are more modern and rather inviting. Leflaive offer extensive tasting menus, where regional dishes are paired with wine. If this is a bit overwhelming, there are pleasant rooms in which to stay overnight.

place du Monument, 21190 Puligny-Montrachet
www.olivier-leflaive.com

Marc Colin et Fils St-Aubin

The eponymous Marc is semi-retired, but works with his sons to build on an established reputation for quality at this highly-respected domaine. The production includes an elegantly intense Premier Cru Chassagne-Montrachet Caillerets; a juicy, succulent, red Chassagne Vieilles Vignes; and tiny quantities of sought-after and sumptuous Grands Crus Montrachet and Bâtard-Montrachet. But the domaine's most accessible wines, in terms of both price and style, are its fresh, delicately creamy St-Aubins, consistently one of the Côte de Beaune's best-value buys.

1 Rue Châtenière, 21190 St-Aubin
03 80 21 94 44

Martelet de Cherisy Blagny

This domaine is perched in a beautiful spot overlooking Meursault in the miniscule hamlet of Blagny, which produces both Puligny and Meursault. The wines from Blagny have a great expression of minerality, energy, and ripe fruit. Hélèna Martelet, with husband Laurent, works vines from her grandmother, the Comtesse de Montlivault. They are an industrious couple making taut, floral Puligny-Montrachet Hameau De Blagny and rich, polished, stone Meursault-Blagny La Genelotte. Walking around their vineyards as the sun sets across the slopes, the couple exudes passion for true terroir wine. This is certainly a domaine to watch.

Hameau de Blagny, 21190 Puligny-Montrachet
www.vins-martelet-cherisey.com

Vincent Girardin Meursault

Vincent Girardin started out in Santenay-le-Haut with a small plot of inherited land. He expanded to become a négociant and moved to Meursault. He works the vines biodynamically, although they are not yet certified. His portfolio includes the Grands Crus Chevalier-Montrachet, Bâtard-Montrachet, Bienvenues-Bâtard-Montrachet, and Corton-Charlemagne. Girardin makes lovely wines with good terroir definition.

Les Champs Lins, 21190 Meursault
www.vincentgirardin.com

PHILANTHROPY AND VINES

The Hospices de Beaune is, above all else, a hospital. But it is a hospital (or more correctly, a collection of caring institutions) that owns parcels of prime Burgundian vineyards and whose story began in 1443. Founded by Duke Philip "Le Bon," and originally operating from the intricately tiled Hôtel-Dieu in the center of Beaune, this charitable hospital cared for the desperate and destitute at a time of social disorder and hardship. Vineyards (and many artistic treasures) have been donated by the philanthropic through the centuries.

Today, the Hôtel-Dieu is a museum housing those treasures; several of its rooms and buildings are available to rent. Every November, barrels of young wine from the Hospices vineyards are offered at an auction (open to all and available online) held in Beaune's covered market. All proceeds go to fund the continuing works of the (modern) hospital and retirement homes of this venerable charity.

COTE CHALONNAISE

The nearby port of Chalon-sur-Saône gives it name to this 15 mile (24km) long, 4 mile (6.5km) wide region just south of Burgundy's Côte de Beaune. It runs from Chagny in the north down to Cluny and the Mâconnais. While the limestone-based soil is similar, the Côte d'Or's famous golden slope breaks down here into small hills and slopes interspersed with orchards and pastures, forests and meadows. The best vineyards are on the east- and south-facing slopes, which are slightly higher in elevation. The climate is drier and the growing season is slightly cooler, so it is easy to see how these firmer, lighter wines have had trouble emerging from the shadows of their famous neighbors to the north.

Major grapes

 Reds

Gamay

Pinot Noir

 Whites

Aligoté

Chardonnay

Vintages

2009

Very promising vintage with clean, pristine fruit. May well prove better than the exceptional 2005.

2008

An uneven vintage with higher than normal acidity in both whites and reds. Production was low, with the exception of Crémant de Bourgogne.

2007

This may be the vintage of the decade. In the red wines, there is a purity of fruit and excellent expression of terroir.

2006

Cold, wet weather was followed by warm, resulting in good wines. The reds may take longer to open up.

2005

Excellent across the board. Wines are beautifully balanced and will be long-lived.

2004

Cool, wet weather proved challenging; up to a quarter of fruit was discarded because of rot. Overall, the wines are lighter-bodied and slightly less complex than normal.

Two-thirds of the Côte Chalonnaise—also known as the Région de Mercurey (its most important district)—is planted to Pinot Noir, the rest to Gamay, Aligoté, and Chardonnay. Bouzeron, Rully, Givry, Mercurey, and Montagny are the main wine villages, and over 100 Premiers Crus are recognized, although half of these are in Montagny and are granted for reaching a minimum alcohol of 11.5% rather than for superior terroir. Bourgogne Côte Chalonnaise is a relatively recent appellation, and much basic burgundy is made here.

While red, white, and sparkling wines of all quality levels are produced here, négociant wine quality is on the rise—Faiveley's Clos des Myglands is considered one of the best wines of Mercurey. As in Mâconnais, too, a movement toward estate bottling and away from selling fruit to co-operatives is bringing to the fore a group of artisanal producers who look for better fruit concentration from healthier vines. The use of new oak has increased, along with fruit quality, giving richer, more structured, and long-lived wines. As in the Côte d'Or, the best wines are charming, evocative, light- to medium-bodied, and complex. They are also very attractively priced.

Bouzeron is the northernmost appellation and is unique in that it relies exclusively on Aligoté, which ripens beautifully on these sunny slopes. The monks of Cluny began planting here in the Middle Ages and, as early as 1730, wine made from Aligoté was singled out. The most famous producer is undoubtedly Aubert de Villaine of Domaine de la Romanée-Conti.

South of Bouzeron is Rully, a village that was once a center of sparkling wine production. The whites tend to be of more interest, especially the Premiers Crus. The best red is considered to come from the Premier Cru vineyard, Les Cloux.

Mercurey is the largest and most significant wine region, and includes the villages of Bourgneuf-Val d'Or and St-Martin-sous-Montaigu. Mercurey is known for firm, structured, earthy Pinot Noirs. Often lean and tart, they are the most expensive wines of this area, though still a mere fraction of the cost of Pinot Noir from the Côte d'Or. Thirty-two well-sited *climats* (vineyard names) are entitled to Premier Cru status, with Clos des Barraults, Les Champs Martin, Les Croichots, and Clos des Myglands among the best.

Givry is a historic wine village that was recognized by King Henri IV for the high quality of its red wines. The appellation includes the hamlets of Cortiambles, Poncey, and Russilly, as well as the villages of Dracy-le-Fort and Jambles. Like Mercurey, 90% of the production is in Pinot Noir. Twenty-seven *climats* are classified as Premier Cru, and they are worth seeking out. In general, the Givry wines are slightly lighter in style than those of Mercurey.

Montagny is the southernmost village, and is a good source of inexpensive white burgundy. While a handful of artisanal producers are quietly making a name for themselves, the most well-known wine is that of négociant Louis Latour, who purchases wine from the Buxy co-operative.

Antonin Rodet

Founded in 1875, Antonin Rodet is a négociant company that both produces and distributes wines made from sites all over Burgundy. The business operates from its home base in Mercurey. In addition to its own-label wines, the house distributes wines from the ancient fortress Château de Rully, Givry's Domaine de la Ferte, and Château de Chamirey, the latter being a much sought-after Mercurey producer. Chamirey's red Mercurey has notes of raspberry, black turned-earth, leaf litter, and porcini dust. Since the early 1990s, Antonin Rodet has undergone a series of ownership changes. In late 2009, the much bigger négociant house, Boisset, became the new owner.

Grande rue, 71640 Mercurey
www.rodet.com

Caves de Vignerons de Buxy

The Caves de Vignerons de Buxy co-operative produces wines that rival the best of southern Burgundy, thanks in no small part to its network of 120 grape-growing families and their collective 2,500 acres (1,000ha) of vineyards. The wines it produces include a fresh, appley Bourgogne Aligoté; a delicate strawberry, wildflower, and earth-imbued Givry Premier Cru Clos Marceaux from Domaine Laborbe Juillot; and a lovely, honeyed Montagny Premier Cru Les Coeres. Although the production is large, it is of a consistent quality and the prices are an excellent value across the board. The cellars are open daily to the public for complimentary tours and tastings.

Les Vignes de la Croix, 71390 Buxy
www.vigneronsdebuxy.com

Château de Cary-Potet

Château de Carỳ-Potet, in Buxy, has a reputation for elegant, expressive white burgundies. The current generation of the du Besset family is focusing on the individual vineyards rather than regional blends, allowing the personalities of their various plots to shine through. Their Montagny Les Reculerons offers luscious ripe fruit, flinty minerality, and vibrant acidity—it is often compared to the much higher-priced Meursault—while the Montagny Premier Cru Les Burnins shows a bit more smoky oak. Cary-Potet's rendition of Bourgogne Aligoté rivals that of the grape's most famous grower, Aubert de Villaine. ★ **Rising star**

Route de Chenevelles, 71390 Buxy
www.cary-potet.fr

Château de la Saule

The prestigious Château de la Saule is located just outside Montagny-les-Buxy. It is the largest and one of the best domaines in the Montagny appellation. The Roy family purchased this estate in 1805. It is now in the capable hands of Alain Roy, who, since 1972, has been working with healthy, old-vine fruit—much of it from Premier Cru vineyards, and all of it from south-facing sites—to craft stunning, terroir-driven Chardonnays. With the exception of his Montagny Premier Cru Les Burnins, Roy refrains from the use of new oak, so the resulting wines are lean, crisp, and minerally.

71390 Montagny-les-Buxy
03 85 92 11 83

DOMAINE ERKER
GIVRY SITS ABOVE RULLY IN TERMS OF COMPLEXITY, BUT JUST BELOW MERCUREY

CHATEAU DE LA SAULE
A CRISP, CLEAN-TASTING PREMIER CRU FROM ONE OF THE REGION'S BEST SITES

Danjean Berthoux

Quietly gaining a reputation with top sommeliers and wine critics for his high-quality, limited-production wines, Pascal Danjean is the rising star of Givry. He started out with family vineyards in Jambles inherited from his grower parents, has expanded the estate to over 30 acres (12ha), most of it Premier Cru vineyards, and has built a winery, as well. He released his first bottles in 1993, wines that sparked comparisons with Cote d'Or legend Emmanuel Rouget. The hilly hamlet of Jambles has vineyards at a high elevation, perhaps giving Danjean the advantage. ★ **Rising star**

Le Moulin Neuf, 45 route de St-Désert, 71640 Jambles
03 85 44 54 74

Domaine Besson

Xavier and Guillamette Besson hand-craft small lots of red and white Givry as well as white Bourgogne at their domaine, but are best known for their firm, well-structured Givry Premier Cru Les Grands Prétants. The vineyard is not far from their winery, and the vines are an average of 40 years old. The best Besson reds offer sweet cherry, cranberry, and blackberry notes, along with a touch of smoky new French oak (with barrels typically from the Francois Frères cooperage), and generally have firm acidity that softens with age. Annual production tops out at 72,000 bottles, so finding these wines may not be easy.

9 rue des Bois-Chevaux, 71640 Givry
03 85 44 42 44

Domaine Chofflet-Valdenaire

Domaine Chofflet-Valdenaire, a family business for over a century, is now in the hands of Jean Chofflet's son-in-law, Denis Valdenaire. This small producer is located in Russilly, one of Givry's three hamlets. While its white Givry Premier Cru Les Galaffres is lovely, it is the reds that shine. The Givry reds, from entry level up to the wild cherry-imbued Premier Cru Clos de Choue, and the black-fruited, Nuits-St-Georges-like Premier Cru Clos Jus, have a light touch, and are recognized as some of the best-value wines in southern Burgundy.

Russilly, 71640 Givry
03 85 44 34 78

Domaine Emile Juillot

Jean-Claude and Natalie Theulot purchased this estate from Natalie's grandfather Emile Juillot in the 1980s. They have holdings in the Mercurey Premier Cru vineyards of Les Champs Martin, Les Combins, Les Croichots, and Les Saumonts, and their own La Cailloute. Their reds are earthy, while their rich, well-structured white Mercurey Premier Cru La Cailloute is regarded as the best in the appellation. Their white Mercurey Vieilles Vignes is also highly respected. Most of the vineyards are in the prime hillside zones of the region.

4 rue de Mercurey, 71640 Mercurey
03 85 45 13 87

Domaine Erker

Originally from Austria, the Erker family have been in France for several generations. In 1996, Didier Erker took over operations at this 16 acre (6.5ha) Givry estate from his father-in-law, Jean Auguste. He is focusing more

DOMAINE STEPHANE ALADAME
A PREMIER CRU FROM A PREMIER PRODUCER, MADE WITH WILD YEAST AND SOME OAK

on vineyard-designated wines rather than regional appellations. His red Givry Premier Cru Les Boix Chevaux and red Givry Premier Cru Les Grands Prétants, are both made with old-vine fruit, and are more concentrated than most Givrys, offering raspberry, cherry, mocha, and mushroom notes. The property also has a Chambre d'Hôte on site for visitors wishing to stay in the area. ★ **Rising star**

7 Bis Boulevard St-Martin, 71640 Givry
www.domaine-erker.com

Domaine Jaeger-Defaix

Fine white burgundy is the speciality of the family-run Domaine Jaeger-Defaix, though at both ends of the price spectrum. This small domaine in Rully is an outpost of the Chablis producer Domaine Bernard Defaix. Bernard's daughter-in-law, Hélène, and her husband Didier, oversee production. Hélène inherited the vineyards from her great aunt, Henriette Niepce, who, like generations before her, had sold the fruit in bulk. The Rully Mont Palais, Les Cloux, and Rabourcé are fresh and lively with butter, lemon, and vanilla notes, while the reds, Rully Préaux and Clos du Chapitre, are elegant and slightly oaky.

7 rue du Château, 89800 Milly
03 86 42 40 75

Domaine Jean Marechal

The 25 acre (10ha) Domaine Jean Marechal in Mercurey delivers elegant, relatively powerful red burgundy for a fraction of the price of its famous northern neighbors. Like many of their fellow producers, this estate has been handed down through the generations, in this case since 1570. Jean Marechal and his son-in-law, Jean-Marc Bovagne, are known for their reds, including Les Nauges, made from vines with an average age of 70 years. The Premiers Crus Clos L'Eveque and Clos des Barraults offer pretty red and black fruit notes, earth, and a subtle oak spice.

20 Grande rue, 71640 Mercurey
www.jeanmarechal.fr

Domaine Joblot

Domaine Joblot offers yet another example of high-quality, concentrated, flavorful red burgundy at a fraction of the normal price. Jean-Marc and Vincent Joblot produce some of the best Givrys out there, in a user-friendly style that is fairly oaky and complex, with tart berry fruit. The better vintages age well. The top wines to look for are the stellar Givry Premier Cru Clos de la Servoisine and the Givry Premier Cru Clos du Cellier Aux Moines. American wine critics from *Wine Spectator* and Robert Parker of *The Wine Advocate* have taken note of these wines.

4 rue Pasteur, 71640 Givry
03 85 44 30 77

Domaine Laurent Cognard

Like many of his generation, Laurent Cognard transitioned his family's business from grape growing to producing wine. He is also making the transition to organic farming, with his eye on biodynamic certification down the road, and to more natural winemaking. With this new focus, this small estate in Buxy is gaining a

reputation for the fresh, appley Bourgogne Aligoté, the rich, buttery, minerally Montagny Premier Cru Les Bassets, and a lovely, spicy Mercurey Premier Cru Les Ormeaux. The winery is open to visitors, but call first —tastings are by appointment only.

9 rue des Fossés, 71390 Buxy
06 15 52 74 44

Domaine Michel Goubard et Fils

Recognized by the 19th-century abbot and historian Courtepee, and more recently by Robert Parker, the tiny Domaine Michel Goubard et Fils was founded in 1604 in the quaint village of St-Désert. Michel Goubard's sons, Pierre-Francois and Vincent, continue to earn accolades for their wines, including the Côte Chalonnaise Mont Avril from a 48 acre (19ha) hillside vineyard and the red Givry Premier Cru La Grande Berge. Their wines are a light-bodied, classic style of red burgundy—subtle and understated, with notes of cherry, strawberry, and dried leaves.

71390 St-Désert
www.bourgogne-goubard.com

Domaine Michel Juillot

Domaine Michel Juillot was originally a 15 acre (6ha) estate that included Vignes de Maillonge, La Pillotte, and Premier Cru vineyard Clos Tonnere. Michel, in the 1960s, and then his son Laurent in the 1980s, expanded the family's holdings. Today, the estate covers 80 acres (32.5ha), two-thirds of which are in Mercurey. Additional holdings include vineyards in Rully and in Aloxe Corton. Laurent employs natural farming and winemaking techniques. His fresh, minerally white Mercurey is one of the best, as are his red and white Mercurey Premier Cru wines, including the Clos des Barraults and Les Champs Martin. ★ **Rising star**

9 Grande Rue, 71640 Mercurey
www.domaine-michel-juillot.fr

Domaine Michel Sarrazin et Fils

Guy and Jean-Yves Sarrazin have taken the reins from their father Michel, who first began bottling his estate wines after taking over from his parents in 1964. This family property in high-altitude Jambles has origins dating back to the 17th century. The brothers do not fine or filter their wines. The Bourgogne Aligoté is lively and fresh; the white Givry Les Grognots is fuller and oaky; and the Givry red wines, including Champs Lalot and Sous la Roche, are balanced and elegant. Their most serious red wine is the rich and spicy Givry Premier Cru Les Grands Prétants. Frédéric Magnien, Vincent Dureil, and other notable producers in the region have recognized the potential of this up-and-coming domaine. ★ **Rising star**

Charnailles, 71640 Jambles
www.sarrazin-michel-et-fils.fr

Domaine Ragot

Jean-Paul and Marguerite Ragot, and now their son, Nicolas, produce top-notch red and white Givry from their 21 acre (8.5ha) estate, originally established in 1860 by Louis Ragot. In 2003, the family built a new winery, and they work to upgrade the vineyards continually. Their two red Givry Premiers Crus, La Grande Berges

DOMAINE DE SUREMAIN
THIS DELICATE WINE HAS PLEASING AROMAS OF RED CURRANTS AND RASPBERRIES

and La Clos Jus, made from mature vines planted on rocky hillsides, are elegant and understated, with cherry, mushroom, and game notes and fine tannins, while their red Givry Vieilles Vignes from 50-year-old vines is much more ripe and chewy.

4 rue de l'Ecole, 71640 Givry
www.domaine-ragot.com

Domaine Raquillet

Often mentioned as one of the top producers in Mercurey, Domaine Raquillet is definitely a producer to watch. Francois, who took over from his father Jean more than a decade ago, has quietly reduced yields and transitioned toward more natural farming in an effort to increase the concentration and complexity of his wines. The Mercurey Premier Cru Les Naugues is an exquisite expression of Pinot Noir—delicate berry notes, rose petal and mushroom, plus subtle smoky oak notes. His wines show great finesse and are very well priced, if hard to find. ★ **Rising star**

19 rue de Jamproyes, 71640 Mercurey
www.domaine-raquillet.com

Domaine Stéphane Aladame

In 1992, when he was only 18, Stéphane Aladame began producing wine here in Montagny. His organic farming methods and use of indigenous (wild) yeast, along with the atypical use of cement tanks in the aging process, give his wines unique peach and honey notes. His Montagny Premier Cru Les Burnins is made with the intensely aromatic Chardonnay Musque clone, and his sparkling Crémants de Bourgogne are worth seeking out as well. Stéphane Aladame is quite possibly the best producer in Montagny today, an opinion that would be disputed by very few.

rue du Lavoir, 71390 Montagny-les-Buxy
www.aladame.fr

Domaine de Suremain

Yves de Suremain, a cousin of the more high-profile Eric de Suremain of the Côte de Beaune, represents the fifth generation of this winemaking family. In 1870, Charles de Suremain purchased several plots surrounding Mercurey's magnificent Château de Bourgneuf. Today, Yves, his wife Marie-Hélène, and their son Loic, oversee this 20 acre (8ha) estate. They produce traditional, elegant Mercurey red, much of it Premier Cru. The Mercurey Premier Cru Les Crets is light and delicate, while the Mercurey Premier Cru Les Sazenay is richer, riper, and oakier, though often closed in its youth.

Château du Bourgneuf, 71 grande rue, 71640 Mercurey
www.domaine-de-suremain.com

Domaine Thenard

Baron Paul Thenard founded this Givry estate in the village center in 1842, built a dungeon-like cellar, and expanded his holdings by marrying a local landowner. Today, the family's holdings are even more extensive and include Givry Premiers Crus Les Bois Chevaux and Clos St-Pierre, as well as prime sites in the Côte d'Or. For the past several decades, much of what was grown at Domaine Thenard was sold off to the négociant Remoissenet, but that is no longer the case. Thenard's

Givry red wines are understated, softly gamey, well-structured, and long-lived, while the white is round, floral, and very minerally.

rue de l'Hôtel-de-Ville, 71640 Givry
03 85 44 31 36

Domaine A et P de Villaine

Aubert de Villaine established this domaine in 1970, four years before becoming co-director at his family's flagship estate, Domaine de la Romanée Conti. His nephew Pierre de Benoît now oversees operations here in Bouzeron. These organic wines are far more expressive, well-structured, and long-lived than normal. The Bourgogne Aligoté is the varietal's benchmark; it is springtime in a bottle—fresh meadow, hay bale, apple, and honey notes, with a fleshy, tingling palate. Another wine that stands out is the Mercurey Les Montots, from the plot adjacent to Clos des Myglands. It is wild and beautiful, with earth, cherry, tarragon, and black pepper notes.

2 rue de la Fontaine, 71150 Bouzeron
www.de-villaine.com

Domaine Vincent Dureuil-Janthial

In 1994, Vincent Dureil-Janthial started producing his own-label wines, and has since taken over his family estate in Rully. His father, Raymond, had established a reputation for red wines, while Vincent is better known for his top-notch white wines. Vincent's wines are opulent, fleshy, and ripe, with a generous mouthfeel, but always show an intense streak of minerality. He farms naturally, ages wines in oak, and bottles without fining or filtration. The Dureil-Janthials are one of the oldest families in the Côte Chalonnaise, first settling here in the 14th century. ★ **Rising star**

10 rue de la Buisserolle, 71150 Rully
www.dureuiljanthial-vins.com

Maison André Delorme

Jean-Francois and Anne Delorme produce white wines from Bouzeron, Montagny, and Rully, as well as Rully and Mercurey reds. It is their Crémant de Bourgogne, however, that has captured the attention of wine-lovers around the world. The family have roots in Rully going back 100 years, but it was André who began producing this outstanding sparkling wine in 1942. Jean-Francois is president of Crémants de Bourgogne and Crémants de France, and his Cuvée Blanc de Noirs and Cuvée Rose Crémants have won numerous awards. In 2005, Eric Piffaut of Veuve Ambal acquired the domaine.

11 rue des Bordes, 71150 Rully
www.andre-delorme.com

FETE DE BOUZERON

While Chardonnay is the best known white grape of Burgundy, producing wines that rank among the best in the world, the picturesque village of Bouzeron in the Côte Chalonnaise offers something different—a unique white wine made from Aligoté. It is dry, lemony, and honeyed, and has often been overlooked as an inferior grape. A et P de Villaine and a handful of other producers offer Aligoté wines from Bouzeron that are as complex as the best whites of the Côte d'Or. The wine is so delicious with a local speciality—jambon persillé, a cooked ham terrine with garlic, peppercorns, shallots, thyme, tarragon, and parsley—that a special annual festival was created to honor the pairing. Each April, on Palm Sunday, the village streets fill with entertainers, bands, and stands offering this and other local food specialities, as well as local wine and crafts.

MACONNAIS

Burgundy

Wine regions of Burgundy

Mâconnais wine region

Long known for unimpressive Mâcon-Blanc at one end, through simple Gamay-based Mâcon-Rouge, to overpriced Pouilly-Fuissé at the other, this quiet, bucolic area, west of the River Saône in southern Burgundy, is undergoing a quiet transformation. While simple, unoaked Chardonnay is still produced, much of it by co-operatives, there is a subtle shift toward carefully hand-crafted, organic or biodynamically farmed, terroir-driven wines that rival the best offerings of the Côte d'Or. Insiders Jean-Jacques Robert, Jean Thévenet, and Belgian-transplant Jean-Marie Guffens, along with Côte d'Or producers Dominique Lafon and, just recently, Anne-Claude Leflaive, are at the forefront of this paradigm shift.

Major grapes

 Reds

Gamay

Pinot Noir

 Whites

Chardonnay

Vintages

2009
A very clean, promising vintage, though yields were slightly lower than usual.

2008
An uneven vintage, with production down by more than 6% as a result of poor fruit set and some rot and disease problems.

2007
Some producers claim this to be the vintage of the decade. Look for outstanding, long-lasting Chardonnays.

2006
Cold, wet weather before harvest was followed by warmer than normal conditions, resulting in good wines across the board.

2005
Excellent across the board, with fully ripe fruit resulting in naturally rich wines.

2004
Pleasant, lighter-bodied whites and reds after cool, wet growing season and a larger than normal crop.

Nestled between Côte Chalonnaise to the north and Beaujolais to the south, with the River Saône as its western border, the Mâconnais' gently rolling hills and plains are dotted with Charolais cattle, orchards, vineyards, and villages with the ubiquitous Romanesque church. There are 43 villages recognized by the appellation laws as Mâcon-Villages. They are spread throughout the region, but the best of these, La Roche-Vineuse (Olivier Merlin), Verzé (Anne-Claude Leflaive), and Milly-Lamartine (Dominique Lafon) are at the southern end, near the city of Mâcon. Here the landscape changes dramatically.

Two towering limestone escarpments, the Solutré and Vergisson rocks, provide excellent drainage and better sun exposure than any other place in the Mâconnais. It is here that carefully handled Chardonnay has a chance of rivaling the wines of Meursault or Montrachet. Vergisson and Solutré-Pouilly along with Fuissé (an old Roman village), Pouilly, and Chaintré, make up the Pouilly-Fuissé appellation. Vergisson is less dramatic than the prehistoric Solutré rock spur, which was used in the Stone Age for hunting. Satellite appellations include Pouilly-Vinzelles and Pouilly-Loché. Vineyards to the north and south of Pouilly-Fuissé are classified as St-Véran—it was originally intended as a sub-zone of Pouilly-Fuissé. The best St-Vérans come from the village of Davayé.

In the Côte d'Or, *climats*, or vineyard names, guide us to the best wines. Here in the Mâconnais, Grands Crus and Premiers Crus do not exist.

Unclassified vineyards, or *lieux-dits*, such as La Croix or Les Reisses of Domaine Robert-Denogent in Pouilly-Fuissé, are slowly making a name for themselves as unofficial Grands Crus, but in the meantime the wines have broader regional or appellation recognition only. As is the case in the Côte d'Or, quite a bit of mediocre and overpriced wine sells based on a famous name only, without the quality to truly justify it. Fortunately, a new era has begun, and the true potential of the area is beginning to be seen. While the region's reputation is on the way up, prices, especially at the upper end, still represent the kind of value more often associated with southern Burgundy.

Romans, and later the monks from Cluny, gave shape to the early Mâconnais wine industry, and in 1660, Louis XIV had these wines served in his court. Chardonnay is the most widely planted grape, and accounts for two-thirds of the production, though much of it is still underwhelming. The best Chardonnays are lightly oaked and slightly buttery, with soft apple, pear, citrus, floral, green meadow, and often intense mineral notes. Because of their elegance, subtlety, and high natural acidity, they are easy to pair with food, including shellfish, sweetbreads, foie gras, fondue, or perhaps a dish of scallops seared with apple cider. The best of the oak-aged versions tend to be richer, with honeyed, nutty, balsamic, and toasty notes rounding out the fruit, floral, and mineral elements. These can take five years or more to open up fully.

Bret Brothers/La Soufrandière

With Demeter-certified, biodynamically farmed vineyards in Pouilly-Vinzelles, Mâcon-Vinzelles, and Beaujolais-Villages, as well as a wide network of growers for their négociant wines, Jean-Guillaume and Jean-Philippe Bret are earning a reputation for round, seductively fruity wines. Originally from Paris, the brothers shared a developing interest in wine. After a formal wine education, they apprenticed at several French wineries, and then, in 2000, took over Domaine La Soufrandière. Their La Soufrandière Pouilly-Vinzelles Climat "Les Quarts" is one of their finest releases. ★ **Rising star**

71680 Vinzelles
www.bretbrothers.com

Château de Beauregard

Wines from the family-owned Château de Beauregard emphasize the chalky minerality and individuality of unique *climats* within the Mâconnais. Its *lieu-dit* (or single-vineyard) releases include Aux Charmes and La Marechaude from Vergisson, as well as the opulent Vers Pouilly from Fuissé. The Grand Beauregard, made from its best barrels of Pouilly-Fuissé, is comparable to the Grands Crus of the Côte d'Or, the heart of Burgundy. Frédéric Marc Burrier, the fifth generation, oversees the property's 49 acres (20ha) in Pouilly-Fuissé, and 17 acres (7ha) in St-Véran. His style of winemaking is non-interventionist, allowing the terroir to shine through. ★ **Rising star**

71960 Fuissé
www.joseph-burrier.com

Château Fuissé

Father and son Jean-Jacques and Antoine are the current generation of the Vincent family, owners of Château Fuissé since 1864. At the heart of the estate is a parcel of 60-year-old vines, bottled separately as the intense, minerally, and long-lived Château Fuissé Vieilles Vignes. Their Les Brûlés comes from a south-facing slope, and is powerful and concentrated as a result. All the wines are fermented and aged in barrel, so expect some smoky oak notes. The family also releases wines from purchased fruit, under their JJ Vincent label. A Renaissance-era stone porch and 15th-century tower set the tone at this historic château.

71960 Fuissé
www.chateau-fuisse.fr

Domaine de L'Ancestra

Cyril Alonso thinks outside the box—he selects parcels of prime vineyards, oversees the growing, and then makes the wines using an all-natural approach. His unusual Mâcon-Chaintré is made with 60-year-old vines, barrel-fermented with wild yeast, and aged on the lees for 24 months in tank. Remarkably, this nutty, honeyed wine is then aged for five years in bottle before being released! It is no wonder his unusual style of wine is well-received on the export market, especially at the high end; El Bulli restaurant in Spain was a top customer. ★ **Rising star**

route de Graves, 69480 Anse
www.lancestra.fr

Domaine de la Bongran

Jean Thévenet is one of the most influential and perhaps controversial producers in the Mâconnais. Continuing the family tradition that began in the early 1400s—the

BRET BROTHERS
TWO BROTHERS TOOK ON THIS CLIMAT IN 2000 AND THE RESULT IS FINE AND ELEGANT

CHATEAU FUISSE
MADE FROM OLD VINES ON A SUNNY SLOPE. THIS WINE IS INTENSE AND LONG-LIVED

original business was barrel making—Jean and his son Gauthier have earned a reputation for unique ripe to over-ripe Chardonnay. Jean oversees the family's flagship property, Domaine de la Bongran in the Quintaine foothills. He and his son share responsibility at Domaine Emilian Gillet, while Gauthier is at the helm of the third family property, Domaine de Roally. The controversy arises over the use of botrytis (noble rot), and the residual sugar levels of the wines.

71260 Clessé
www.bongran.com

Domaine Cordier Père et Fils

The wines of Domaine Cordier are as rich and oaky as many fine Puligny-Montrachet and Chassagne-Montrachets, and expressive of their origin as well. The biodynamic vineyards are picked selectively over the course of the harvest, giving the visionary winemaker, Christophe Cordier, a headstart. Cordier often picks only half of what the appellation laws allow for and then he gives the wines a long, slow fermentation in oak, including barrels he buys from the cult Côte d'Or producer, Ramonet. The top wines to look for include the St-Véran, Pouilly-Loché, and Pouilly-Fuissé Les Vignes Blanches. ★ **Rising star**

les Molards, 71960 Fuissé
03 85 35 62 89

Domaine de la Croix Senaillet

Close to the historic Solutré rock, the vineyards at Domaine de la Croix Senaillet, in Davayé, surround a cross. It was famously donated by former Mayor Benoît Senaillet to replace one that was lost during the French Revolution. Maurice Martin, and now his sons Richard and Stéphane, produce round, creamy wines from 60 different plots here, where the average vine age is 35 years—vines at this age are in their prime. Two of their wines, St-Véran Les Buis and St-Véran La Grande Bruyère, are particularly notable.

71960 Davayé
www.domainecroixsenaillet.com

Domaine Daniel Barraud

Daniel Barraud's 100% organic wines are often compared to the Côte d'Or's Meursault or Chassagne-Montrachet. They are rich and honeyed, with the silk and minerality that are trademarks of fine white burgundy. Along with his son Julien, he crafts wines including a distinguished Pouilly-Fuissé Alliance Vergisson, sourced from multiple old-vine vineyards in Vergisson, each contributing something different to the blend, and a lemony, tangy Mâcon-Vergisson La Roche. His Pouilly-Fuissé La Verchère Vieilles Vignes demonstrates his deft hand with oak—a bit of toasty oak adds richness and depth to the apple, citrus, and yeasty notes, taking the appellation to new heights. ★ **Rising star**

71960 Fuissé
www.domainebarraud.com

Domaine des Deux Roches

Childhood friends Christian Collovray and Jean-Luc Terrier own this winery in Davayé. Named after the two rocks of Vergisson and Solutré, their St-Vérans, nearly as famous as the landmarks, give Meursault a run for its

money. The highly regarded Les Terres Noirs comes from a vineyard with black soil beneath crumbling limestone, giving a unique mineral character to the wine. Here, and in their Pouilly-Fuissé and Mâcon-Villages, the wines show richness, minerality, and apple and citrus notes.

route de Fuissé, Davayé 71960
03 85 35 86 51

Domaine Drouin

Domaine Drouin's wines often rank among Mâconnais' best in blind tastings by *Decanter* magazine, *Guide Hachette*, and others. This small-production winery, run by Thierry and Corinne Drouin, is one to watch. With full malolactic fermentation, and regularly aged in oak, the wines are rich and creamy, but still retain lovely acidity and a vein of minerality expressive of their terroir. The winery is located near the famous rock of Vergisson.

Le Grand Pré, 71960 Vergisson
www.domaine-drouin.com

Domaine J A Ferret

Domaine J A Ferret was established in 1760 and run, until its recent sale to Maison Louis Jadot, by Colette Ferret. This highly-regarded 37 acre (15ha) domaine in the heart of Fuissé first bottled its own-label wines in 1942, setting the stage for others in the appellation to follow. *Lieu-dit* (single-vineyard) wines include Les Sceles, Les Vernays, Le Clos, and the old-vine plots of Les Menetrieres, Le Tournant de Pouilly, and Les Perrières. Jadot's president, Pierre Henry Gagey, intends to carry on the house style of smoky, ageworthy Chardonnays. The Pouilly-Fuissé is showy, with tropical fruit and sweet oak but has the area's underlying signature of chalky minerality and brisk acidity.

71960 Fuissé
03 85 35 61 56

Domaine Guffens Heynen

Jean-Marie Guffens is to the Mâconnais what Robert Mondavi is to Napa Valley, if a bit more flamboyant—he is a founding father, visionary, and producer of what are considered some of the finest wines of the appellation. His 9 acre (3.6ha) family estate is located in Pouilly-Fuissé, and is known for tightly wound wines such as the electric, Riesling-like Mâcon-Pierreclos Le Chavigne and the fatter, creamier, and nougatlike Mâcon-Pierreclos Tri de Chavigne, from his oldest plot of vines. Like his family estate wines, the wines of his négociant label, Verget, show tremendous minerality and pristine natural acidity.

71960 Vergisson
www.verget-sa.com

Domaine Henri Perrusset

Twenty-five years ago, US wine importer Kermit Lynch shared a bench at a French truckstop with a 21-year-old who, it turned out, was also in the wine business—Henri Perrusset. He was releasing his first wines and, after tasting them, Lynch bought everything he could. The best is the gentle, flowery Mâcon-Farges, made from a vineyard near the village of Chardonnay, though his Mâcon-Villages is also a delight. His wines are fresh and lively with apple and floral notes, and are distinctly oak and butter free.

71700 Farges lès Mâcon
03 85 40 51 88

Domaine Luquet Roger

The Luquet family is in its fifth generation of making wine, a tradition that began with Benoît Luquet in 1847. The winery welcomes visitors year round. At the helm since 1966, Roger and his wife Renée have expanded the domaine's holdings, adding notable vineyards including the Clos de Condemine and Les Mulots, from which they produce fruity, elegant Mâcon-Villages. They, and now their children, also produce classically styled Pouilly-Fuissé Vieilles Vignes and exotically fruity Pouilly-Fuissé Terroir. With a large production, 70% of it exported, you should have no problem tracking down a bottle or two.

rue du Bourg, 71960 Fuissé
www.domaine-luquet.com

Domaine Manciat-Poncet

After selling grapes in bulk for over 20 years, Claude Manciat and Simone Poncet founded this domaine in 1979, combining properties from both families. Now in the hands of their daughter, Marie-Pierre, and her husband Olivier Larochette, the estate continues to turn out their signature oaky, buttery wines, including a Mâcon-Charnay Les Chênes (they also make an unoaked Mâcon-Charnay) and Pouilly-Fuissé Les Crays Vieilles Vignes. Despite their rich, buttery character, the wines are fresh and lively with a backbone of acidity. Their red Mâcon-Bussières is popular, though less complex.

65 chemin des Gérards, 71850 Charnay-lès-Mâcon
03 85 29 22 93

Domaine Michel Cheveau

Founded by André Cheveau in the 1950s, this property is now run by his son Michel and grandson Nicolas. Visitors are welcomed to the family home and winery. The house style is elegant and understated, often with pronounced oak notes of vanilla and toast. Their well-known Mâcon-Chaintré Le Clos is compared by some to Meursault in the Côte d'Or. Their less oaky Mâcon-Fuissé Les Grandes Bruyères and St-Véran Terroir de Davayé are popular, and a Beaujolais-Villages Or Rouge is worth seeking out.

Hameau de Pouilly, 71960 Solutré-Pouilly
www.domaine-cheveau.com

Domaine Michel Delorme

This Pouilly-Fuissé specialist in Vergisson has been in operation since 1820. Michel and his parents oversee the 10 acres (4ha) of vineyards, many of them with 40- to 80-year-old vines. These prime vineyards enjoy south or southeast exposures on the slopes of the Vergisson rock, and the resulting wines are rich and complex. One of these, La Marechaude, produces one of the best single-vineyard Pouilly-Fuissés, while the Vieilles Vignes blends fruit from several old-vine vineyards. The family welcomes visitors to the new cellar they built in 2003.

71960 Vergisson
www.pouillyfuisse-delorme.com

Domaine Olivier Merlin

Merlin Mâcons are regarded as some of the best. Olivier and his wife Corinne first rented, then purchased the holdings of Vieux St-Sorlin in La Roche-Vineuse and Viré-Clessé, carefully restoring them. They then bought the St-Véran Le Grand Bussière vineyard. They also make excellent old-vine Pouilly-Fuissé, though not from their own vineyards. They farm naturally and barrel-ferment the wines with full malolactic fermentation, so the house style is slightly oaky, buttery, and fruit-driven, perhaps as a result of Olivier's early experience in the Napa Valley.

la Roche Vineuse, 71960 Fuissé
www.merlin-vins.com

Domaine de Pouilly
Since 1933, when Petrus Besson transformed from winemaker to owner, Domaine de Pouilly has enjoyed a reputation for fine, if firmly structured, wines. They tend to be rich, but not oaky. Still family-owned, the 37 acre (15ha) property in the middle of Pouilly, with some of the oldest vines in the appellation, is currently run by André and his son Vincent. In 1999, André gave a small parcel to Vincent, who now has his own wine, Domaine Vincent Besson. The cellar is open by appointment.

71960 Solutré-Pouilly
www.domainedepouilly.com

Domaine de Roally
Henri Goyard established this property, situated on a limestone ridge overlooking the River Saône, in what is now the Viré-Clessé AC. Gautier Thévenet, son of the famous Jean Thévenet (Domaine de la Bongran), is the current owner of this 14 acre (5.6ha) parcel of old vines—a mix of several old Chardonnay clones. He farms sustainably, and the wines are fermented slowly in tanks for up to 16 months. They are often released with a bit of residual sugar, something that the AC restricts, so his minerally, petrolly, and yeasty Viré-Clessé and Mâcon-Montbellet are often declassified to Mâcon-Villages.

Quintaine Cidex 654, 71260 Clessé
03 85 36 94 03

Domaine Robert-Denogent
Jean-Jacques Robert produces stunning Pouilly-Fuissé in an appellation that has an unfortunate reputation for mediocrity. His property includes some of the area's best vineyards, two of which are *monopoles* (meaning he alone owns the entire vineyard designation). Robert does not chaptalize (add sugar), use sulfur dioxide, or filter, and uses oak with a deft touch. His savory, honeyed Les Reisses and fleshy, gingery La Croix would certainly be Grands Crus if the appellation allowed such status. Wines from this domaine are bright and intense, often with a gasoline or fennel note—all are long-lived. ★ **Rising star**

Le Plan, 71960 Fuissé
www.robert-denogent.com

Domaine Roger Lassarat
Roger Lassarat has earned a reputation for consistently high-quality St-Véran and Pouilly-Fuissé wines, including the spectacular Pouilly-Fuissé Racines, made from three 100-year-old vine parcels in Solutré and Vergisson. He farms naturally, encourages small yields, uses wild yeast only, and then bottles without fining or filtration. His wines share a trademark vein of intense minerality, along with bright citrus and stone fruit notes, dried herbs, and undertones of oak. Visitors are welcomed, but by appointment only.

Le Martelet, 71960 Vergisson
www.roger-lassarat.com

Domaine Ste-Barbe
Jean-Marie Chaland produces less than 30,000 bottles of outstanding wines, including Mâcon-Villages and Viré-Clessé Vieilles Vignes, so you may have to stay in the hotel at the domaine to enjoy them. If you visit, be sure to ask for the rich, toasty, champagne-like Crémant de Bourgogne Brut Perle de Roche as well as a sweet late-harvest Chardonnay, the Vendange Tardive. The winery is a certified biodynamic producer.

71260 Viré
03 85 33 11 18

Domaine Saumaize-Michelin
Roger Saumaize and his wife Christine Michelin offer warm hospitality at their winery. This biodynamic vineyard, located in Vergisson, has an average vine age of 40 years. Their reputation is for soft, round wines—they barrel-ferment, using up to 25% new oak, with complete malolactic fermentation. The results are silky and fat, with an unctuousness typical of great Chardonnay. The best known are the white wines, Mâcon-Villages Les Sertaux, St-Véran Vieilles Vignes, and Pouilly-Fuissé Pentacrine, and they also produce a Gamay-based Mâcon-Rouge.

Le Martelet, 71960 Vergisson
www.domaine-saumaize-michelin.com

Les Héretiers du Comte Lafon
The wines of Comtes Lafon are regarded as some of the finest in the world. Here in the Mâconnais, Dominique Lafon crafts similarly styled, really quite decadent wines. His magic formula is the use of biodynamic farming, low yields, and green harvesting in the vineyards, followed by malolactic fermentation in the cellar. The single-vineyard wines, including Mâcon-Milly-Lamartine Clos du Four, Mâcon-Uchizy Les Maranches, and Mâcon-Chardonnay Clos de la Crochette (from what is believed to be the world's oldest Chardonnay vineyard), are excellent.

71960 Milly-Lamartine
www.comtes-lafon.fr

Jean Manciat
Jean Manciat's Mâcon-Charnay Franclieu, and to a lesser degree his Mâcon-Villages, are wines of great finesse, showing classic apple, floral, and mineral notes with racy acidity. Mâcon-Charnay Vieilles Vignes, Pouilly-Fuissé, and St-Véran are lightly oaked, giving them a more honeyed, nutty quality, but the style is still understated. Manciat achieves this through low-intervention in the winery, small yields, and natural farming in the vineyards.

557 Chemin des Gérards, 71850 Charnay-lès-Mâcon
03 85 34 35 50

Rijckaert
Jean Rijckaert was in partnership with Jean-Marie Guffens at Domaine Verget, and there is a carry-over in style—keen minerality and refreshing, lively acidity. But Rijckaert, who started his own winery in 1998, whole-bunch-presses to enhance fruitiness, and barrel-ferments with a touch of new oak. The resulting wines have added textural complexity as well as hazelnut notes. Rijckaert also produces wines from the neighboring Jura region.

71570 Leynes
03 85 35 15 09

DEUX ROCHES
Thrusting upward from the rolling plains here are the twin limestone escarpments of Solutré, and the slightly less imposing Vergisson. These Deux Roches, just under 1,640ft (500m) in height, were prehistoric hunting sites, initially for the woolly rhino and later for horses and reindeer, hundreds of which were driven off the bluffs to their deaths. The summits offered early inhabitants protection from the floods of the River Saône, and the cliffs provided shelter. Nomads carved weapons and tools from flint, many of which are now on display at the Solutré Museum of Prehistory. On a clear day, the view from the Solutré summit extends over the vineyards, Saône Valley, and the Bugey Mountains. Climbing, hiking, or cycling up and around the rocks is a good way to spend a morning or afternoon, followed by a tasting of local wines and foods. An easier option is to take in the scenery by hot-air balloon.

BEAUJOLAIS

Despite broad name recognition, Beaujolais remains a misunderstood wine and a misunderstood region. But for those consumers in the know, the best wines are food-friendly, lip-smacking, and affordable, coming from some of France's most talented winemakers. The main confusion revolves around Beaujolais Nouveau. Although this tutti-frutti, proto-wine accounts for only about a third of the region's production, it has come to dominate the region as a whole in the popular consciousness. In the shadows of this annual hoop-la, and sprung from the crumbling granite soil of the north of the region, come the rewarding wines of the 10 Beaujolais *crus*, or smaller appellations.

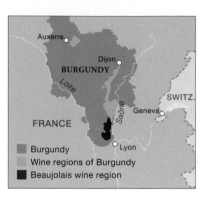

Major grapes

 Reds

Gamay

 Whites

Chardonnay

Vintages

2009
A superb year, according to preliminary reports.

2008
Some hail damage in the north, otherwise very good.

2007
A variable year; good wines from good producers.

2006
Very good throughout the region.

2005
Very warm vintage, resulting in some excellent, if ripe, wines.

2004
A variable year; good wines from good producers.

Millions of gnarly, untrellised Gamay vines dot the charming hillsides of the region. Beaujolais is, for the most part, Gamay, or *gamay noir à jus blanc* in local parlance. Gamay produces wines that mostly aim for a rating of "gulpable." Such were its charms that Philip the Bold, the Duke of Burgundy in the 14th century, banned the cost-effective grape from his region, banishing it to Beaujolais, to protect the premium of Pinot Noir. Thin-skinned and prolific, Gamay ripens early and can produce some inconsequential, knock-em-back sort of wines.

The ultimate wine in this style is Beaujolais Nouveau. Starting in the 1970s, Georges Duboeuf, a négociant in the region, now known as the "king of Beaujolais," turned the arrival of the wine each November into a worldwide celebration. Made from grapes harvested a scant 10 weeks prior, the wines sometimes need a boost in the form of sugar added to the fermentation tank, while commercial yeasts complete the fermentations. Today, Duboeuf is one of the top exporters of French wine.

Against this backdrop, a group of small growers sought a different path. Led ideologically by Jules Chauvet, and practically by Marcel Lapierre, this "Gang of Four" growers favored old vines over younger, slow fermentations over fast, and natural yeasts over commercial. Thus the region became a hotbed of "natural" wines with minimal intervention in the vineyards and the cellars.

Most of these growers work in the 10 subzones of northern Beaujolais, known as the *crus*, or appellations, of Beaujolais. Confusingly for the uninitiated, the name Beaujolais does not often appear on the bottle labels of the *crus* wines, only the name of the smaller appellation.

The pink, sandy, granite soils of Moulin-à-Vent produce some of the most serious, structured, and ageworthy *crus* wines. In the adjacent Fleurie, beautiful perfumes intrigue the nose before the wines delight the tongue. In Morgon, decomposing schist soils lead to some structured wines, especially from the slopes of the Côte du Py. Situated on the flanks of an extinct volcano, Côte de Brouilly produces some rich reds. South of Brouilly, the vineyards of the region mostly produce grapes used for Beaujolais Nouveau.

While the low prices of the land and grapes present a challenge for the growers, they also create an opportunity for Burgundy winemakers seeking good terroirs—some would like to plant Pinot Noir, if it were allowed. In this threat to Gamay lies a compliment to the region—that it has worthwhile growing areas. But even with Gamay, the wines confound perceptions and offer great reward and even improve with age.

Finally, the region produces a small amount of white wines, from the Chardonnay grape, and a tiny amount of rosé wines.

Château du Chatelard

Sylvain and Isabelle Rosier have a relatively rare find in their portfolio: white wine. The Beaujolais Blanc, made from Chardonnay, sees some time in oak while the stony Beaujolais Blanc Vieilles Vignes has impressive verve. The Beaujolais Vieilles Vignes (red) has a delicious balance of fruit and acidity and all these wines offer good value.

69220 Lancié
04 74 04 12 99

Château des Jacques Moulin-à-Vent

Acquired in 1996 by the Burgundy house Louis Jadot, Château des Jacques produces some of the most elegant and long-lived wines of the entire Beaujolais region. Winemaker Jacques Lardière, who also makes the Jadot burgundies, eschews carbonic maceration for the Gamay grapes and makes his Moulin-à-Vents as he does his Pinot Noirs. The 67 acre (27ha) property has five separate *clos*, of which the La Roche and Clos des Rochegrès are particularly enticing. The wines blend the lip-smacking qualities of Gamay with the more serious side of Pinot Noir; they have been known to trip up serious tasters in blind tastings, thinking they are red burgundies.

21 rue Eugène Spuller, 21203 Beaune
www.louisjadot.com

Château Thivin Côte de Brouilly

On the southeastern flanks of the crumbling, anciently volcanic mound that is the Mont Brouilly, Claude Geoffrey tends 20 acres (8ha) of Gamay vines. Some of the vines are not trellised, but cling to the steep slope by their own roots. Fermentation starts with mostly whole clusters of grapes and finishes off in large oak barrels known as foudres, where the wines also age. Founded in 1877, Château Thivin makes a Brouilly and a Côte de Brouilly, including the succulent Cuvée Zaccharie.

69460 Odenas
www.chateau-thivin.com

Christian Ducroux Régnié

Working organically for 25 years, Christian Ducroux now farms 10 acres (4ha) of vineyards in the Régnié appellation. Grass covers the rows between the 60- to 80-year-old vines and Durcroux uses horses to minimize soil compaction. The wines are certified biodynamic with Demeter's seal appearing on the front label. Indigenous yeasts propel the fermentations and then Ducroux performs a semi-carbonic maceration. He bottles a portion of his wines without sulfites, which can benefit from decanting to enhance the ebullient fruit. Try both bottlings for a fun comparison.

Thulon, 69430 Lantignié
04 74 69 20 47

Christophe Pacalet

After starting out in biochemistry, then as a chef, Christophe Pacalet returned to Beaujolais to study winemaking with his uncle, Marcel Lapierre. Pacalet rents vineyards in six of the *crus* and farms them according to sustainable practices. Of the six wines, the Côte de Brouilly has excellent fruit and acidity while the Moulin-à-Vent has more structure and is good value. ★**Rising star**

Sarl Les Marcellins, Les Bruyès, 69220 Cercié
www.christophepacalet.com

CHRISTOPHE PACALET
LIKE OTHER BEAUJOLAIS NOUVEAU WINES, THIS IS RELEASED EVERY NOVEMBER, FOLLOWING A SHORT MACERATION

CHATEAU DES JACQUES
THIS GARNET-RED WINE PROVES THAT LONG-LIVED GAMAY IS NOT AN OXYMORON

Clos de la Roilette Fleurie

Alain Coudert makes the wines at this family estate mostly from vines that his father, Fernand, planted when he purchased the property in 1967. The estate comprises 22 acres (9ha) of vines. The wines tend to be dark and full-bodied for a Fleurie, perhaps because when the line with Moulin-à-Vent was drawn, they ended up just on the Fleurie side. The Cuvée Tardive is a rich wine that ages remarkably well; look for it in a magnum for aging, or for a fantastic gift.

La Roilette, 69820 Fleurie
www.louisdressner.com

Damien Coquelet Chiroubles

Hard as it might be to imagine, Damien Coquelet produced his first vintage (the 2007) at the age of just 20. The step-son of Georges Descombes, Coquelet produced his vintage using some of the 80-year-old vines that are at the heart of the Descombes Chiroubles. Coquelet's wine has bright, intense, and focused fruit and really opens up on the second day of being open. He may be acquiring other prime vineyards, so he is definitely a producer to watch. ★**Rising star**

Vermont, 69910 Villié-Morgon
www.louisdressner.com

Domaine Alain Michaud Côte de Brouilly

This has been a family domaine since its founding by Jean Marie Michaud in 1910. Current owner Alain Michaud took over from his father and uncle in 1973. The 22 acres (9ha) of vines in Brouilly produce most of the Michaud wines. They also have small holdings in the Morgon and in Beaujolais appellations. The vast majority of the vines are more than 50 years old, with some even approaching the century mark. The wines these produce are solid Brouilly offerings.

Beauvoir, 69220 St-Lager
www.alain-michaud.fr

Domaine Diochon Moulin-à-Vent

Bernard Diochon's renown derives from two things: his prodigious moustache and his succulent and sturdy Moulin-à-Vents. While the age of his moustache is not well-known, the vines of the 5 acre (2ha) parcel in Moulin-à-Vent that make up the Vieilles Vignes Cuvée are 80 years old. The estate also produces a straight up Moulin-à-Vent that is dark in color and sturdy with tannic structure. The wines are aged in large vats and are bottled unfiltered.

Le Moulin-à-Vent, 71570 Romaneche-Thorins
03 85 35 52 42

Domaine Dominique Piron

The 14th generation in his family to make wine, Dominique, along with his American wife Kristine Mary, supplements the estate vineyards with some purchased fruit. The Morgon and the Morgon Côte du Py are the most successful and there is a range of other appellations including Beaujolais Nouveau. Piron also collaborates with Jean Marc Lafont from Brouilly to make wine from Chénas, called Quartz.

69910 Villié-Morgon
04 74 69 10 20

GEORGES DUBOEUF
A ROBUST WINE FROM ONE OF FRANCE'S
MOST SUCCESSFUL PRODUCERS

Domaine Louis-Claude Desvignes
Morgon

Owner Louis-Claude Desvignes now works with his daughter Claude-Emmanuel, the eighth generation of winemakers in the family. The 32 acres (13ha) of vines lie in two parts of the Côtes du Py in Morgon. Javernières, the larger of the two vineyards, produces rich and intense reds while the wines from the 12 acre (5ha) Côte du Py bottling have even more structure, dark fruit, and even some minerality. Both can benefit from aging several years after release.

135 rue de la Voûte, 69910 Villié-Morgon
www.louis-claude-desvignes.com

Domaine de la Voûte des Crôzes
Côte de Brouilly

Nicole Chanrion makes her succulent reds on the crumbling schist slopes of Mont Brouilly. She interrupted six generations of the domaine passing from father to son in 1988 to take charge of the estate and its 10 acres (4ha) of 50-year-old vines. She makes the wine with slow fermentations, and the scant 2,500 cases ultimately comes from a blend from five foudres (barrels). The wine has refreshing fruit and acidity with a faint spice.

Les Crozes, 69220 Cercié
04 74 66 80 37

Georges Duboeuf

Georges Duboeuf, the commercially successful négociant known as the "king of Beaujolais," has one of the most successful exported brands in all French wine. He created the Beaujolais Nouveau phenomenon in the 1970s, which stoked demand for a wine made from grapes harvested early, and often aided through fermentation with the addition of sugars and commercial yeasts. Although Nouveau and the Duboeuf flower labels came to define the region for many consumers and producers, for better or for worse, the phenomenon has lost appeal in recent years with increased competition from other low-priced imports. Duboeuf also makes some wines from the *crus*, including Brouilly and Chiroubles, and a Morgon Jean Descombes bottling. The producer has its partisans but also its detractors.

No visitor facilities
www.duboeuf.com

Guy Breton Morgon

When Guy Breton took over this vineyard from his grandfather in 1986, he decided to stop selling the fruit to a négociant and, rather, make his own estate wine. Since then, Breton has pursued natural winemaking, using indigenous yeasts and a fermentation, in barrel, of at least 15 days. The older vines of the small vineyard are bottled separately as Vieilles Vignes, which results in a wine with peppery aromas, surprisingly light in color, but with an enticing blend of red fruits and minerality.

Les Nicouds, 69910 Villié-Morgon
04 74 69 12 67

Jean Foillard Morgon

If you must try only one Beaujolais, a strong case could be made for Foillard. Taking over from his father in the early 1980s, Jean Foillard now tends about 25 acres (10ha) on the estate in Morgon. He farms naturally, although he is neither certified organic nor biodynamic. He does not filter his wines and uses a blend of small barrels—never new—and has two large foudres. The Côte du Puy, a stunning example from a site on this extinct volcano, combines vibrant freshness with a serious, smooth finish. Delicious when young, the wines can benefit from decanting and can also age well. Only about 30% of the production is exported, with the rest being sold in small shops and restaurants in France.

Le Clachet, 69910 Villié-Morgon
04 74 04 24 97

Jean-Marc Burgaud Morgon

Having started in 1989, Jean-Marc Burgaud now farms 47 acres (19ha) of vines in several appellations. Of particular note are the twin Morgon bottlings, the soft and stylish Les Charmes, and the more muscular and structured Côte du Py, which can benefit from cellaring or decanting when young.

La Côte du Py, 69910 Villié-Morgon
www.jean-marc-burgaud.com

Jean-Paul Brun Côte de Brouilly

Iconoclast Jean-Paul Brun makes some of the best wines from the Beaujolais appellation and he does so naturally, using only indigenous yeasts. His family vineyard, located in the town of Charnay, is 40 acres (16ha) and produces his signature Terres Dorées bottling that is a perennial best buy from the region (both the red and the white). With the 2007 vintage, Brun was denied the appellation for half of his Terres Dorées, an event that reflected more on the outdated appellation regulations than it did on the wine's quality. He also makes some *cru* wines from Brouilly and Morgon, as well as a fascinating sparkling wine called FRV 100, a play on the word "effervescent."

69380 Charnay
www.louisdressner.com/Brun

Jean-Paul Thévenet Morgon

One of the so-called "Gang of Four," (see below) Jean-Paul Thévenet makes delicious wines from his 13 acre (5ha) vineyard in the Morgon appellation. The various wines include the Morgon as well as the Vieilles Vignes, both refreshing and satisfying with alluring aromas thanks to the low levels of sulfites. But this also means the wine always needs proper storage, so it can pay to buy a bottle before buying a case. The vineyards are in a transition to biodynamics. Thévenet now works with his son Charly, who also has a vineyard in the neighboring appellation of Régnie.

Le Clachet, 69910 Villié-Morgon
04 74 04 21 43

Marcel Lapierre Morgon

Marcel Lapierre is known for two things: his staunch belief in natural winemaking and his bonhomie. Following the lead of Jules Chauvet, Lapierre and four others (Jean-Paul Thévenet, Jean Foillard, Joseph Chamonard, and Guy Breton) started to bristle against the Nouveau phenomenon and sought to make wines from single vineyards of old vines with as few additions as possible. In Lapierre's case, this means minimal addition of sulfur dioxide, which lets the wine's

PIERRE-MARIE CHERMETTE
THIS PALE-PINK ROSÉ IS RICH AND ROUNDED
—PERFECT FOR SUMMER DRINKING

aromas rise seductively from the glass. Lapierre enjoys drinking his wines, often with local sausage, and has said that the pleasures of the table brought together the "Gang of Four" (Joseph Chamonard died in 1990) as much as their shared philosophy. Marcel's son, Matthieu has an ever-increasing role at the domaine these days and adheres to a similar philosophy of non-interventionist winemaking.

69910 Villié-Morgon
www.marcel-lapierre.com

Michel Chignard Fleurie

Michel Chignard's vineyards lie in Fleurie, and, like those of La Roilette, they abut Moulin-à-Vent. The pièce de résistance of Chignard's 45 acres (20ha) of vines is the 20 acre (8ha) parcel Les Moriers, with its steep, granite slopes. When the conditions are right, Les Moriers can produce wines that are standard-bearers of the appellation, with the aromatic delicacy of Fleurie and the meatiness of Moulin-à-Vent.

Le Point de Jour, 69820 Fleurie
04 74 04 11 87

Michel Tête (Domaine du Clos du Fief) Juliénas

On sloping sites in the Juliénas, Michel Tete's old, untrellised Gamay vines produce succulent wines. The winemaking is natural and the viticulture is organic, although not certified. One of Tête's quality measures includes having his own bottling line. Of the wines, the Cuvée Prestige regularly offers enticing aromas of black cherry and pepper; on the palate, it can be backward in its youth, benefiting from a few years of cellaring. Tête also makes some Beaujolais-Villages and St-Amour.

69840 Juliénas
www.louisdressner.com/Tete

Pascal Granger Juliénas

Born in 1961, Pascal Granger makes the wines at this winery, which has been in his family for 200 years. Housed in a church that has been disused since the 14th century, the winery has both large and small oak barrels as well as stainless steel casks. The regular Juliénas sees time only in the steel tanks, but the Grande Reserve gets a lavish oak treatment with 24 months in small oak barrels. Granger also makes a Moulin-à-Vent, a Chénas, a Beaujolais Blanc, and a rosé.

Les Poupets, 69840 Juliénas
www.cavespascalgranger.fr

Pierre-Marie Chermette (Domaine du Vissoux) Fleurie

Pierre-Marie Chermette makes a delicious, gulpable, and refreshing Beaujolais. He does this by using natural yeasts, low yields, and naturally ripe grapes. He also makes a Beaujolais Nouveau that is relatively solid for the genre. He makes more structured wines from Moulin-à-Vent, such as the Les Deux Roches. This wine has so much structure (which it takes from aging in small oak barrels), that it could pass for a ringer in a line-up of village burgundies.

69620 St-Vérand
www.chermette.fr

Potel-Aviron Morgon

This project, launched with the inaugural vintage in 2000, combines two young winemakers, Nicolas Potel from Burgundy and Stephane Aviron, whose family has roots in Beaujolais. Following a négociant model, they seek out old-vine sites in a variety of the Beaujolais appellations and then apply Burgundian winemaking practices such as maturation in small barrels (about a quarter of which are new). The Chénas Vieilles Vignes includes fruit from vines planted in 1913; the Morgon Côte du Py offers *cru* Beaujolais in a bigger, darker, and denser version. ★ **Rising star**

2093 route des Deschamps, 71570 La-Chapelle-de-Guinchay
03 85 36 76 18

Villa Ponciago Fleurie

Villa Ponciago has had vines planted for centuries. When Pierre-Marie Chermette made the wines, they were among the best of Fleurie. However, in June 2008 Chermette sold the property to the Henriot family of Champagne (and Burgundy). Given the 200 years of winemaking at Henriot and the history of Ponciago, it may seem odd to call this a rising star. But the property, re-christened Villa Ponciago (from Château Poncié), is the first property run by the 35-year-old Thomas Henriot and is certainly one to watch. ★ **Rising star**

69820 Fleurie
04 37 55 34 75

Yvon Métras Fleurie

Despite his tremendous renown as a pioneer in the region, the wines of Yvon Métras remain hard to find, even in France. A hyper-naturalist, Métras makes a Beaujolais as well as several Fleurie wines, including a coveted old vines bottling, and a Moulin-à-Vent. Find them if you can....

La Pierre, 71570 Romanèche-Thorins
03 85 35 59 82

MAKING WINE THE BEAUJOLAIS WAY: CARBONIC MACERATION

Hand harvesting is the norm in Beaujolais. Although it is more costly, the main virtue for Gamay is simple: it delivers whole bunches of grapes to the cellar. These are then put in a fermentation vessel and sealed. The resulting weight of the pile of grapes and stems crushes those on the bottom first and starts a spontaneous fermentation. In the anaerobic environment, carbon dioxide blankets the upper grapes, stimulating fermentation inside those grapes. The resulting wine is often light, juicy, and fruity tasting. Some producers prefer a short (two day) carbonic maceration followed by traditional crushing, stemming, and open-top fermentation.

CHAMPAGNE

The Champagne appellation encompasses 84,000 acres (34,000ha), spread over 319 villages in five different départements. While two-thirds of the vineyard areas lie in the Marne, immediately surrounding the cities of Reims and Epernay, there are also vines in the Aube, Aisne, Haute-Marne, and Seine-et-Marne. To be called "champagne," a wine must be grown within this delimited area and be produced by a specific and traditional method involving a second fermentation in the bottle to create effervescence. This method, combined with Champagne's extremely northern latitude and predominantly chalky soils, results in a sparkling wine of inimitable finesse, character, and complexity that is renowned the world over.

Major grapes

 Reds

Pinot Meunier

Pinot Noir

 Whites

Chardonnay

Vintages

2009
Warm and ripe, yet quality is likely to be variable.

2008
Can be superb, combining ripeness with high acidity.

2007
Firm acidity from cool weather. Chardonnay is probably best.

2006
A warm year that successfully retained balance and finesse, particularly in Chardonnay.

2005
A hot summer created ripe, densely flavored wines, but they can lack balance.

2004
Elegant wines with fresh acidity.

2003
Severe frosts followed by a hot summer created atypical wines.

2002
Outstanding quality: complex, concentrated, and pure.

2000
Fast-maturing, variable wines.

1999
Variable, with ripe fruit and low acidity. Many have aged well.

Champagne is made from three main grape varieties: Pinot Noir and Pinot Meunier are both red grapes, while Chardonnay is white. Despite their color, these red grapes produce white wine, since the skins are not left in the juice. The exception to this is some rosés, but even most rosé champagnes are made from a base of white wine to which a small amount of red wine is added for color.

While most champagnes are a blend of all three main grape varieties, there are some that are more restricted in scope. A champagne that is made exclusively from Chardonnay is known as a Blanc de Blancs, whereas one made entirely from red grapes is called a Blanc de Noirs. Most champagnes are also created by blending wines from various years. This ensures a certain consistency in style, particularly in this northerly region where grapes can sometimes struggle to ripen. If there is a particularly good year, however, a vintage champagne may be produced that contains grapes exclusively from that year.

The majority of champagne is labeled as brut, which means that it is relatively dry, while extra brut is even drier. Ironically, sec (dry) and demi-sec (half-dry) indicate sweeter styles of champagne. The level of sweetness is determined by the addition of dosage—a small amount of sugar that is added to the champagne just before it is corked. The dosage is an important part of the wine, as it balances champagne's unusually high acidity and helps to bring out more complex fruit flavors.

Today, Champagne feels like both a classic, established region and a young, emerging one. Although it makes, arguably, the world's most famous wine and has been making sparkling wines for around 300 years, it is also a region in the midst of significant change, fueled by the vigor of a new generation. There is a greater diversity among the region's wines than ever before. Recent years have seen the rise of small estates that are starting to challenge the hegemony of established houses in the marketplace. Above all, a renewed interest in a more responsible viticulture has become the dominant issue. At this northerly latitude, strictly organic viticulture is often challenging, primarily due to mildew. Yet the interest in organic and biodynamic viticulture is on the rise, and the region as a whole is heavily focused on improving its viticultural practices.

Champagne is often regarded in a singular context, as a wine of celebration or perhaps an apéritif, but there is tremendous, and increasing, diversity of style within the world of champagne. A racy, chalky Blanc de Blancs, for example, bears little resemblance to a muscular, deeply vinous Blanc de Noirs; similarly, the lithe, flowery character of a young champagne is a stark contrast to the multi-dimensional complexity of an example in maturity. Just as with still wine, there is a champagne to suit virtually any occasion, dish, mood, or personal preference, and this diversity of style remains one of champagne's most fascinating qualities.

CHAMPAGNE

The Champagne appellation covers nearly 84,000 acres (34,000ha) of vineyards, largely centered around four regions: the Montagne de Reims, Vallée de la Marne, Côte des Blancs, and Côte des Bar. While the first three are located near the cities of Reims and Epernay, the Côte des Bar, a Pinot Noir-dominated region in the Aube department, lies farther to the south, closer to Chablis than to Reims. Other important wine-growing areas include the Côte de Sézanne and Vitry-le-François in the Marne and Montgueux in the Aube, near Troyes.

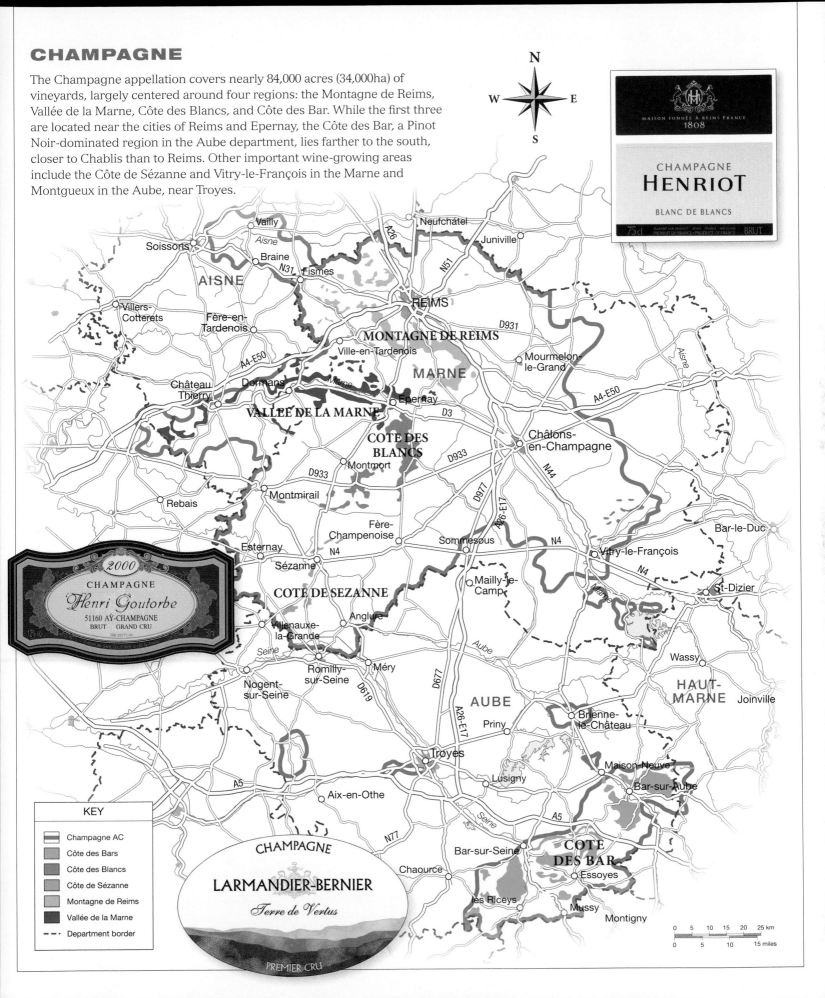

KEY

	Champagne AC
	Côte des Bars
	Côte des Blancs
	Côte de Sézanne
	Montagne de Reims
	Vallée de la Marne
- - -	Department border

HEART OF CHAMPAGNE

The heart of the Champagne region lies around the cities of Reims and Epernay, in the department of the Marne. The vineyards here are divided into three general areas, each with its own character. Pinot Noir thrives in the eastern portion of the Montagne de Reims, both in north-facing sites such as Mailly and Verzenay, and on the south-facing slopes of Bouzy and Ambonnay. The section of the Vallée de la Marne between Tours-sur-Marne and Cumières is also home to some of Champagne's finest Pinot Noir, while to the west of Cumières, Pinot Meunier becomes increasingly more important. South of Epernay, the chalky slopes of the Côte des Blancs yield Chardonnay of exceptional refinement and finesse.

KEY

CÔTE DES BLANC	AC
	Rivers, lakes
	Roads
	65ft (20m) contours
	Department border
	Urban areas
1	Location of one or more producers

VALLEE DE LA MARNE

Alfred Gratien	**13**	Janisson-Baradon	**13**
Ayala	**12**	José Michel	**16**
Bollinger	**12**	Laherte Frères	**17**
De Meric	**12**	Lamiable	**26**
Dehours	**1**	Laurent-Perrier	**26**
Deutz	**12**	Leclaire-Gaspard	**25**
Dom Pérignon	**13**	Leclerc-Briant	**13**
Franck Pascal	**4**	AR Lenoble	**9**
Gaston Chiquet	**11**	Marc Hébrart	**25**
Gatinois	**12**	Michel Loriot	**2**
Georges Laval	**10**	Moët & Chandon	**13**
Gonet-Médeville	**24**	Perrier-Jouët	**13**
Gosset	**12**	Pol Roger	**13**
Gosset-Brabant	**12**	René Geoffroy	**10**
Henri Giraud	**12**	Roger Pouillon et Fils	**25**
Henri Goutorbe	**12**	Tarlant	**3**
Henri Mandois	**14**	Yves Ruffin	**27**
Jacquesson	**11**		

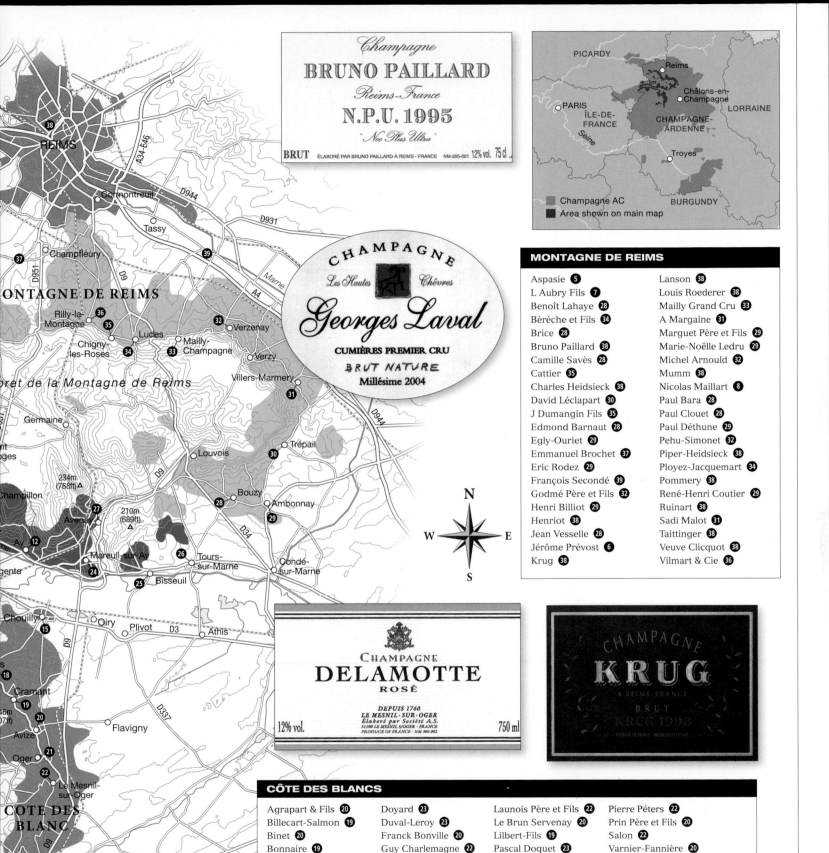

Champagne BRUNO PAILLARD Reims–France N.P.U. 1995 "Nec Plus Ultra" BRUT ÉLABORÉ PAR BRUNO PAILLARD À REIMS – FRANCE NM-265-001 12% vol. 75 cl

CHAMPAGNE Les Hautes Chèvres Georges Laval CUMIÈRES PREMIER CRU BRUT NATURE Millésime 2004

CHAMPAGNE DELAMOTTE ROSÉ DEPUIS 1760 LE MESNIL·SUR·OGER Élaboré par Société A.S. 51190 LE MESNIL S/OGER – FRANCE PRODUCE OF FRANCE · NM 300 002 12% vol. 750 ml

CHAMPAGNE KRUG A REIMS·FRANCE BRUT KRUG 1998

Picardy · Reims · Châlons-en-Champagne · Paris · Île-de-France · Seine · Lorraine · Champagne-Ardenne · Troyes · Burgundy

Champagne AC
Area shown on main map

MONTAGNE DE REIMS

Aspasie	5	Lanson	38
L Aubry Fils	7	Louis Roederer	38
Benoît Lahaye	28	Mailly Grand Cru	33
Bèrèche et Fils	34	A Margaine	31
Brice	28	Marguet Père et Fils	29
Bruno Paillard	38	Marie-Noëlle Ledru	29
Camille Savès	28	Michel Arnould	32
Cattier	35	Mumm	38
Charles Heidsieck	38	Nicolas Maillart	8
David Léclapart	30	Paul Bara	28
J Dumangin Fils	35	Paul Clouet	28
Edmond Barnaut	28	Paul Déthune	29
Egly-Ouriet	29	Pehu-Simonet	32
Emmanuel Brochet	37	Piper-Heidsieck	38
Eric Rodez	29	Ployez-Jacquemart	34
François Secondé	39	Pommery	38
Godmé Père et Fils	32	René-Henri Coutier	29
Henri Billiot	29	Ruinart	38
Henriot	38	Sadi Malot	31
Jean Vesselle	28	Taittinger	38
Jérôme Prévost	6	Veuve Clicquot	38
Krug	38	Vilmart & Cie	36

CÔTE DES BLANCS

Agrapart & Fils	20	Doyard	23	Launois Père et Fils	22	Pierre Péters	22
Billecart-Salmon	19	Duval-Leroy	23	Le Brun Servenay	20	Prin Père et Fils	20
Binet	20	Franck Bonville	20	Lilbert-Fils	19	Salon	22
Bonnaire	19	Guy Charlemagne	22	Pascal Doquet	23	Varnier-Fannière	20
Claude Cazals	22	Guy Larmandier	23	Philippe Gonet	22	JL Vergnon	22
Claude Corbon	20	Jacques Selosse	20	Philipponnat	19	Veuve Fourney &	
De Sousa & Fils	20	Jean Milan	21	Pierre Callot	20	Fils	23
Delamotte	22	José Dhondt	21	Pierre Gimonnet	18	Voirin-Jumel	19
Diebolt-Vallois	19	Larmandier-Bernier	23	Pierre Moncuit	22		

Always check the availability of visitor facilities and the visiting hours at a winery before planning your trip. Some wineries are open by appointment only.

Agrapart & Fils Côte des Blancs

Emphasizing viticulture over vinification, Pascal Agrapart and his brother Fabrice produce naturally grown, terroir-expressive champagnes from their family's estate in Avize. Chalky and racy, these wines contrast mineral intensity with a depth and complexity gained by partial vinification in oak. All of the wines are Blanc de Blancs, except the rosé, which includes a little purchased Pinot Noir, and each offers a different perspective on the Agraparts' various terroirs. Since 2001, the Agraparts have produced an outstanding, single-vineyard champagne called Cuvée Vénus that comes from a parcel of land worked by horse rather than by tractor.

57 avenue Jean Jaures, 51190 Avize
www.champagne-agrapart.com

Alfred Gratien Epernay

This small Epernay house was founded in 1864 by Alfred Gratien. Today, cellarmaster Nicolas Jaeger is the fourth generation of his family to occupy that position, having officially taken over from his father in 2007. Much of the house's practices are staunchly traditional: Gratien's wines are always vinified entirely in secondhand oak barrels, and entirely without malolactic. In addition, their vintage champagnes are fermented on cork rather than capsule. These are ample, generous wines, with a fine balance of complexity and freshness. The vintage *cuvées*, in particular, are superbly ageworthy.

30 rue Maurice Cerveaux, 51201 Epernay
www.alfredgratien.com

Aspasie Montagne de Reims

Previously known as Ariston Fils, this family-owned estate in the village of Brouillet makes round, boldly-flavored champagnes that are distinctly expressive of this far northwestern corner of the Montagne de Reims, where the soils include sand, clay, and alluvial deposits, as well as the typical Champenois chalk. Aspasie wines are made from all three grape varieties and, aside from a barrel-fermented *cuvée* called Brut de Fût, all are vinified in stainless steel tanks.

4 et 8 Grande Rue, 51170 Brouillet
www.champagneaspasie.com

L Aubry Fils Montagne de Reims

Twin brothers Philippe and Pierre Aubry run this highly original estate in the village of Jouy-lès-Reims, making champagnes of distinct personality. They have become renowned for their pursuit of "forgotten" grapes, such as Arbanne, Petit Meslier, and Fromenteau—two of their *cuvées*, Le Nombre d'Or and Sablé Blanc des Blancs, involve these unusual varieties. L Aubry Fils excels with classic grapes as well, as evidenced by the boldly assertive non-vintage brut, dominated by Pinot Meunier, and the richly flavored Aubry de Humbert. But perhaps finest of all is the subtle, exquisitely detailed Sablé Rosé.

4 et 6 Grande Rue, 51390 Jouy-lès-Reims
www.champagne-aubry.com

Ayala Grande Vallée

This is an old house, established in 1860 by Edmond de Ayala, yet its current character dates from 2005, when it was purchased by the Bollinger Group. The idea was to contrast Bollinger, rather than imitate it, and two major factors contribute toward that end: a high proportion of Chardonnay and a low, sometimes zero, dosage. The Zéro Dosage Brut Nature is a fine introduction to the new Ayala style, while the vintage-dated Perle d'Ayala promises to be complex and ageworthy.

2 boulevard du Nord, 51160 Aÿ
www.champagne-ayala.fr

Benoît Lahaye Montagne de Reims

Benoît Lahaye took over his family's property in the village of Bouzy in 1993, and since then he has turned it into one of the finest grower-estates of the Montagne de Reims. Emphasizing organic viticulture, Lahaye makes vinous, terroir-expressive champagnes using a majority of Pinot Noir. A percentage of the wines are vinified in barrel and change according to the vintage: there is no recipe, as Lahaye adapts his vinification to the individual wine. Lahaye's entire range, from the Brut Nature to the Rosé de Macération, is well worth seeking out.

33 rue Jeanne d'Arc, 51150 Bouzy
03 26 57 03 05

Bérèche et Fils Montagne de Reims

This small, family-run estate in the village of Ludes is quietly gaining renown for its dry, complex champagnes. Raphaël Bérèche has been working alongside his father since 2004, increasingly moving toward more natural viticulture. They have also begun to use more cork during lees aging. The Reflet d'Antan, a richly complex champagne made in a solera system, is aged on cork, and future releases of the *non-dosé* (zero dosage) Beaux Regards Blanc de Blancs will be as well. Not to be missed is the non-vintage brut, which shows an uncommon sense of depth and character. ★ Rising star

Le Craon de Ludes, 51500 Ludes
www.champagne-bereche-et-fils.com

Billecart-Salmon Grande Vallée

François and Antoine Roland-Billecart are the seventh generation of their family to manage this famous house since its founding in 1818 by Nicolas François Billecart and Elisabeth Salmon. Billecart-Salmon might be best known for its non-vintage rosé, but the true gems here are the vintage champagnes. The Cuvée Nicolas François combines strength and finesse, while the Grande Cuvée shows additional complexity from longer lees aging. Perhaps best of all is the silky, refined Elisabeth Salmon rosé. The recently unveiled Clos Saint-Hilaire demonstrates another facet of the house's elegant style.

40 rue Carnot, 51160 Mareuil-sur-Aÿ
www.champagne-billecart.fr

Binet Côte des Blancs

Founded in Reims in 1849 by Léon Binet, this house changed hands several times before being purchased in 2000 by Daniel Prin, of Prin Père et Fils in Avize. Prin's own wines are made without malolactic and dominated by Chardonnay, yet with Binet he seeks to maintain this house's full-bodied, creamy style. Binet is still selling some older vintages, but the champagnes made today seem to show more finesse, particularly the vintage-dated *cuvées*.

30 Rempart du Midi, 51190 Avize
www.champagnebinet.com

CATTIER
CLOS DU MOULIN IS PRODUCED IN LIMITED NUMBERS FROM ONE OF THE VERY FEW CLOS IN CHAMPAGNE

AYALA
ZERO DOSAGE IS A HALLMARK OF AYALA'S RECENT MAKEOVER

Bollinger Grande Vallée

Founded in 1829, Bollinger has enjoyed a rich and distinctive history. It is unusual among négociant houses for its high percentage of estate-grown grapes—roughly two-thirds of the house's needs are supplied by its 403 acres (163ha) of vines—and this undoubtedly contributes to the excellence of Bollinger's champagnes. The Bollinger style is one of both richness and finesse, aided in the non-vintage Spécial Cuvée by partial vinification in barrel and an extraordinary collection of reserve wines. La Grande Année, vinified in oak and aged under cork, is capable of tremendous complexity and longevity.

20 boulevard du Maréchal de Lattre de Tassigny, 51160 Aÿ
www.champagne-bollinger.com

Bonnaire Côte des Blancs

One of the most prominent estates in the Côte des Blancs, Bonnaire makes rich, voluptuously creamy champagnes. The finest wines are the vintage Blanc de Blancs, made entirely from the village of Cramant and vinified in stainless steel tanks. These develop extremely well with age, and vintages from the 1980s are still superb today. Bonnaire has been experimenting with oak fermentation in a *cuvée* called Variance, made with Chardonnay from three different Côte des Blancs villages. For his lively, currant-scented rosé, Bonnaire blends Chardonnay with red wine from the Aisne.

120 rue d'Epernay, 51350 Cramant
www.champagne-bonnaire.com

Brice Montagne de Reims

Jean-Paul Brice founded this small house, located in the village of Bouzy, in 1994. While Brice owns 20 acres (8ha) of vines in Bouzy, most of the necessary grapes are purchased from about 20 different villages. The jewels of the Brice portfolio are the four monocru champagnes, intended to show the distinct characters of the four Grand Cru villages of Cramant, Bouzy, Verzenay, and Aÿ. As with all of Brice's champagnes, these are vinified in stainless steel, without malolactic, giving them a lively tension and purity.

22 rue Gambetta, 51150 Bouzy
www.champagne-brice.com

Bruno Paillard Reims

Bruno Paillard founded his négociant house in 1981, when he was just 27 years old. Today, the house has an annual production of about 45,000 cases of champagne. Both barrels and tanks are used for vinification, and barrels are also used to store the house's reserve wines, some of which are up to 20 years old. Paillard's champagnes are light and fresh, emphasizing a fine texture. Since 1990, Paillard has been making a prestige cuvée called NPU, which is vinified entirely in oak and aged for 10 years on the lees.

Avenue de Champagne, 51100 Reims
www.champagnebrunopaillard.com

Camille Savès Montagne de Reims

The Savès family have lived in the heart of Bouzy since 1894 and their 25 acre (10ha) grower-estate has been making estate-bottled champagne since 1910. Aside from the non-vintage Carte Blanche, all of Savès' champagnes are pure Bouzy, demonstrating the plush fruitiness of that village, yet they also maintain a lively freshness, as none

BONNAIRE
BONNAIRE'S BLANC DE BLANCS IS CREAMY
AND RICH, BALANCED BY FRESH ACIDITY

BOLLINGER
THE SPECIAL CUVÉE IS ONE OF
CHAMPAGNE'S MOST RECOGNIZABLE WINES

of the wines go through malolactic. The excellent vintage brut is predominantly Pinot Noir, typical of most of the estate's champagnes, while the Cuvée Prestige contains a majority of Chardonnay, with a quarter of the wine vinified in barrique.

4 rue de Condé, 51150 Bouzy
www.champagne-saves.com

Cattier Montagne de Reims

While the Cattier family have been growing vines since the mid-18th century, they founded their champagne house in 1918. Based in the village of Chigny les Roses, Cattier sources much of its fruit from this sector of the Montagne, giving its wines a rounded, supple feel. The star of the cellar is the excellent Clos du Moulin, a single-vineyard champagne that Cattier has been making since 1952. Blended from three different years, it is made of equal parts Chardonnay and Pinot Noir and demonstrates a distinctive and complex character. Production of this exceptional champagne is limited to 15–20,000 numbered bottles per year.

6/11 rue Dom Pérignon, 51500 Chigny les Roses
www.cattier.com

Cédric Bouchard Aube

Although Cédric Bouchard has only been making champagne since 2000, he has quickly gained a devoted following for his miniscule quantities of carefully handcrafted, terroir-driven champagnes. Bouchard's wines are uncompromisingly original, and even anti-traditional: each of his champagnes is completely unblended, made from a single parcel, a single vintage, and a single grape variety. His estate champagnes are bottled under the Roses de Jeanne label, while the entry level Inflorescence comes from a parcel owned by his father. All share an uncommon finesse and purity of flavor, from the suave Les Ursules Blanc de Noirs to the multi-faceted Rosé de Saignée. ★ **Rising star**

13 rue du vivier, 10110, Celles sur Ource
www.champagne-rosesdejeanne.com

Charles Heidsieck Reims

This Reims house was founded in 1851 by Charles-Camille Heidsieck, a colorful character who was highly successful in the American market, earning him the nickname "Champagne Charlie." Under cellarmaster Daniel Thibault's guidance in the late 20th century, Charles Heidsieck achieved a rich, complex style, characterized by a high proportion of reserve wine and long aging on the lees. Today, Régis Camus continues to make polished and boldly distinctive champagnes: the Réserve is one of the finest non-vintage bruts on the market, and the Blanc de Millénaires is an exceptional prestige cuvée.

4 boulevard Henry Vasnier, 51100 Reims
www.charlesheidsieck.com

Chartogne-Taillet Montagne de Reims

Alexandre Chartogne is taking this highly regarded, 29.5 acre (12ha) grower-estate to even greater heights, making vibrant, vinous champagnes that reflect the sandy and chalky–clay soils of Merfy, in the far north of the Champagne appellation. Look for Chartogne-Taillet's harmonious Cuvée Ste-Anne non-vintage brut or the lively, full-flavored Blanc de Blancs to get an idea of the

DELAMOTTE

DELAMOTTE'S BLANC DE BLANCS IS
DELICATE AND DISCRETE, FOCUSED ON
ELEGANCE RATHER THAN POWER

estate's style. The excellent prestige cuvée is named after Fiacre Taillet, an ancestor of the current owners who grew vines in the area in the early 18th century. ★ **Rising star**

37 Grande Rue, 51220 Merfy
03 26 03 10 17

Christian Etienne Aube

Estate-bottled champagne in the Aube is often thought of as a recent phenomenon, but Christian Etienne has been bottling champagne under his own label since 1978. Etienne makes robust, full-bodied wines, reflecting the generous ripeness typical of this area. His vintage champagnes are aged for an admirably long time on their lees, while his Cuvée Prestige demonstrates that Chardonnay can thrive in this Pinot Noir-dominated region. It's the non-vintage Brut Tradition that is the pick of the cellar, with its silky texture and voluptuous fruit.

12 rue de la Fontaine, 10200 Meurville
03 25 27 46 66

Claude Cazals Côte des Blancs

Based in Le Mesnil-sur-Oger, this grower-estate owns 22 acres (9ha) of vines, all in the southern Côte des Blancs. The top wine of the Cazals cellar is the Clos Cazals, a deeply flavored, chalk-driven champagne from a vineyard of the same name in the village of Oger. Keep an eye out for the Cuvée Vive, a finely balanced extra brut, as well as the vintage-dated Blanc de Blancs, made entirely from Grand Cru Chardonnay and aged for at least six years on the lees.

28 rue du Grand Mont, 51190 Le Mesnil-sur-Oger
www.champagne-claude-cazals.net

Claude Corbon Côte des Blancs

With an annual production of only 1,250 cases, this family-run estate has been producing champagne since 1922 and remains a little-known secret. Corbon's non-vintage Grande Réserve is made with a high proportion of red grapes from the Vallée de la Marne, but the vintage-dated Blanc de Blancs is pure Avize Chardonnay, showing a classic structure and chalky minerality. The unusual Brut d'Autrefois is made in a perpetual *cuvée*, replenished with new wine every year, and it is partially aged in barrel, contributing to its broad, burnished feel.

541 avenue Jean Jaurès, 51190 Avize
www.champagne-corbon.fr

Comte Audoin de Dampierre
Montagne de Reims

The Dampierre family has had an association with the Champagne region for more than 700 years. Audoin de Dampierre currently presides over this small house in Chenay, purchasing grapes largely from Grand Cru villages. The house is renowned for its Cuvée des Ambassadeurs, which is served at many French embassies around the world. The other champagnes in the range show a similar combination of generous fruit and refined elegance. The vintage wines are particularly excellent: the Grand Vintage is roughly two-thirds Pinot Noir; while the two prestige cuvées, the Family Réserve and Cuvée de Prestige, are pure Chardonnay and demonstrate a subtle harmony and grace.

3 place Boisseau, 51140 Chenay
www.dampierre.com

COMTE AUDOIN DE DAMPIERRE

THE CORK OF THE CUVEE DE PRESTIGE IS
HAND-TIED IN THE TRADITIONAL WAY

David Léclapart Montagne de Reims

A passionate advocate of biodynamic viticulture, David Léclapart established his tiny estate in 1998 with 7.5 acres (3ha) of family vines. All of his vineyards are in the village of Trépail, where he produces three Blanc de Blancs champagnes and one rosé, as well as a still wine made from Pinot Noir grapes. The top *cuvées* are vinified in oak barrels, and all the wines come from a single year. At their best, Léclapart's champagnes demonstrate a piercing clarity and mineral expression. As they are released very young, they benefit considerably from additional cellaring. ★ **Rising star**

10 rue de la Mairie, 51380 Trépail
03 26 57 07 01

De Meric Grande Vallée

Founded by Christian Besserat in 1959, Champagne De Meric was bought and owned by American businessman Daniel Ginsburg between 1997 and 2006. Ginsburg made his champagnes entirely from purchased grapes, vinifying a majority of the wines in oak barrels or large casks, without malolactic. Today, De Meric is owned by Reynald Leclaire of Leclaire-Gaspard, who continues to vinify in wood, but with estate-grown grapes. It is anticipated that the quality of the wines should increase under his care.

17 rue Gambetta, 51160 Aÿ
www.champagnedemeric.com

De Sousa & Fils Côte des Blancs

Michelle and Erick De Sousa's champagnes are concentrated and powerful. They are characterized by unusually ripe fruit, pronounced richness from lees aging, and barrel fermentation for the top *cuvées*. Sometimes the richness is too dominant, but when these wines find a harmonious balance, they can be excellent. De Sousa & Fils prestige cuvée, Cuvée des Caudalies, is made from Chardonnay vines that are over 50 years of age. It comes in a vintage-dated version as well as a non-vintage one that is made in a solera system. There is a Cuvée des Caudalies rosé, too, which is blended with Grand Cru Pinot Noir.

12 place Léon Bourgeois, 51190 Avize
www.champagnedesousa.com

Dehours Vallée de la Marne

Jérôme Dehours took over his family's vineyards in 1996, working with natural viticulture and partial vinification in the barrel. He has placed an increasing focus on specific terroirs, releasing a number of single-vineyard champagnes from this sector of the Vallée de la Marne: Les Genevraux, with a harmonious combination of ripeness and vivacity, is a pure Pinot Meunier, the dominant grape variety on the estate, while Brisefer is a Chardonnay of rich breadth and strongly stony minerality. Dehours makes fine blended champagnes as well, particularly the pale, delicately aromatic rosé.

2 rue de la Chapelle, 51700, Cerseuil
www.champagne-dehours.fr

Delamotte Côte des Blancs

This house has focused heavily on Chardonnay ever since its founding in 1760 by François Delamotte. Today, it is owned by the Laurent-Perrier Group, and it is the sister house of Salon, with whom it shares its Le Mesnil-sur-

Oger facilities, nestled in the heart of the Côte des Blancs. The Delamotte house style is one of subtle, discreet refinement, too often overlooked in a world that favors increasingly powerful wines. All of Delamotte's champagnes display different facets of the house's elegant style, from the lithe and citrussy Blanc de Blancs to the silky, quietly pungent rosé.

5-7 rue de la Brèche d'Oger, 51190 Le Mesnil-sur-Oger
www.salondelamotte.com

Deutz Grande Vallée

Deutz has a history going back to its founding in 1838, but its modern story dates from 1993, when it was purchased by Louis Roederer. Today, the house is in top form, creating champagnes that emphasize harmony and finesse. Deutz champagnes are not necessarily light-bodied, but when tasting these wines, finesse always comes before power, as evidenced by the racy, zesty Brut Classic. The vintage wines are excellent, particularly the fine, fragrant rosé, while the house's outstanding prestige cuvée, William Deutz, increases in richness and complexity without ever losing its sense of poise.

16 rue Jeanson, 51160 Aÿ
www.champagne-deutz.com

Diebolt-Vallois Côte des Blancs

One of the finest grower-estates in Champagne, Diebolt-Vallois produces pure, classically racy Blanc de Blancs from 27 acres (11ha) in Cramant and the surrounding villages. The green-labeled non-vintage Blanc de Blancs is one of the best wines of its type on the market, while the vintage champagnes offer even more complexity and longevity. The vintage-dated Fleur de Passion, made from old vines in Cramant and vinified in barrel without malolactic, is an uncompromisingly traditional and superbly expressive champagne that needs many years to show its best.

84 rue Neuve, 51530 Cramant
www.diebolt-vallois.com

Dom Pérignon Epernay

Perhaps the world's most famous champagne, Dom Pérignon was created as a prestige cuvée by Moët & Chandon in 1936, when they launched the inaugural 1921 vintage. Today, it is a separate brand, although it continues to benefit from Moët's vast and unparalleled collection of vineyards. It is a pity that most bottles of Dom Pérignon are drunk far too young, when it is still rather mute, because as it ages, it develops a superb complexity and finesse. The rosé version is, if anything, even more impressive, possessing an ethereal fragrance and impeccably graceful refinement.

18 avenue de Champagne, Epernay
www.domperignon.com

Dosnon & Lepage Aube

Davy Dosnon and Simon-Charles Lepage created their boutique négociant house in 2005, focusing exclusively on fruit in and around the village of Avirey-Lingey in the Aube's Côte des Bar. Their champagnes are warm and generous, amplified by vinification in oak barrels. The duo's passion and attention to detail is evident in the polished, precise character of their wines. Dosnon & Lepage produce four *cuvées*: the Récolte Brute, a full-bodied extra brut;

Récolte Blanche, a lively, stylish Blanc de Blancs; Récolte Noire, a Blanc de Noirs with excellent aging potential; and Récolte Rose, a spicy, sophisticated rosé. ★ **Rising star**

4 bis rue du Bas de Lingey, 10340 Avirey Lingey
www.champagne-dosnon.com

Doyard Côte des Blancs

Yannick Doyard farms 25 acres (10ha) of vines in the Côte des Blancs, but sells half of his grapes to the *négoce*, keeping only the finest lots to make his estate-bottled champagnes. These are sophisticated and finely detailed, partially vinified in barrel and aged for an unusually long time on the lees. Doyard's non-vintage Cuvée endemiaire extra brut, for example, sees a minimum of six years of lees aging. Collection de l'An I is a vintage-dated Blanc de Blancs of superb finesse, while La Libertine is a rare and original *doux* champagne.

39 avenue Général Leclerc, 51130 Vertus
03 26 52 14 74

Drappier Aube

One of the Aube's best-known houses, Drappier makes generous, full-bodied champagnes. Michel Drappier places a high emphasis on sustainable viticulture, vinifying individual parcels separately and working hard to reduce the amount of sulfites in his wines. The non-vintage Carte d'Or is reliable, but even better is Drappier's Brut Nature. Made from pure Pinot Noir, it also comes in a *sans soufre*, (no sulfites), version. At the top of the range is the Grande Sendrée, a vintage-dated, single-vineyard champagne that combines the succulent Drappier fruitiness with chalky finesse.

Rue des Vignes, 10200 Urville
www.champagne-drappier.com

J Dumangin Fils Montagne de Reims

This small house in the village of Chigny Les Roses is now in the hands of Gilles Dumangin, the fifth generation of his family to head it. J Dumangin Fils purchases most of its fruit from villages around Chigny, and its best champagnes combine a forward fruitiness with the broad, earthy character typical of the area. Look for the luscious, full-bodied Premium Blanc de Blancs, as well as the vintage brut, blended from Chardonnay and Pinot Noir. Also worth seeking out are Dumangin's Vinothèques, older vintage champagnes that are unusually dosed so they are extra dry.

3 rue de Rilly, 51500 Chigny Les Roses
www.champagne-dumangin.com

R Dumont & Fils Aube

The "R" in R Dumont & Fils stands for both Raphaël and Robert, two brothers who founded this Aube estate in the 1970s. Today, it is in the hands of their sons, Bernard and Pierre, who make generous, Pinot Noir-driven champagnes. While the non-vintage wines are agreeable, particularly the voluptuously fruity rosé, the vintage champagnes are the ones to seek out here: the vintage brut is boldly fragrant and richly textured, while the Grand Millésime, made only in the best years, is a complex, ageworthy Blanc de Noirs.

10200 Champignol lez Mondeville
www.champagnedumont.fr

THE CRAYERES OF REIMS

Beginning in the Gallo-Roman era, the sedimentary chalk around the city of Reims was quarried in a distinctive fashion, creating hundreds of vast, pyramid-shaped pits that extend up to 164ft (50m) into the ground. In the late 18th century, Claude Ruinart struck upon the idea of using these cool, dry environments as wine cellars, and several other houses soon followed suit. Today, along with Ruinart, the houses of Charles Heidsieck, Henriot, Pommery, Taittinger, and Veuve Clicquot all own *crayères*, or chalk pits, in the southeastern sector of the city. Classified as historic monuments in 1931, these dramatically beautiful *crayères* are ideal for the maturation of champagne, as they maintain a cool and constant temperature, year-round. Some of these *crayères* are closed to the public, but others are open to visitors and are among the highlights of the region.

FRANCK BONVILLE
LES BELLES VOYES IS AGED FOR SEVEN TO EIGHT MONTHS IN OAK BARRELS TO CREATE A SUPPLE SMOOTHNESS

EDMOND BARNAUT
BARNAUT'S BLANC DE NOIRS COMBINES RICHNESS WITH A SILKY FINESSE

Duval-Leroy Côte des Blancs

Founded in 1859, Duval-Leroy remains family-owned, headed today by Carol Duval-Leroy. The house produces a large range of champagnes, from the light and fragrant Fleur de Champagne to the single-vineyard Clos des Bouveries, which was recently, and rather controversially, released in an alternative closure called the Maestro. The prestige cuvée, Femme de Champagne, is made from Duval-Leroy's best parcels and aged for an unusually long time before release. Perhaps best of all, though, are the champagnes in the Authentis series, which are made from organically grown grapes and focus on specific terroirs.

69 avenue de Bammental, 51130 Vertus
www.duval-leroy.com

Edmond Barnaut Montagne de Reims

Edmond Barnaut founded this estate in 1874, in the village of Bouzy. Today, it is in the capable hands of his great-great-grandson, Philippe Secondé. Aside from the Cuvée Edmond, which is blended with grapes from the Vallée de la Marne, all of Barnaut's champagnes are pure Bouzy, reflecting the village's warm, south-facing slopes in their bold ripeness and robust flavors. Edmond Barnaut's Blanc de Noirs consistently demonstrates more finesse than the others in the range.

1 place André Collard, 51190 Bouzy
www.champagne-barnaut.com

Egly-Ouriet Montagne de Reims

Since taking over his family's property in the early 1980s, Francis Egly has turned Egly-Ouriet into one of Champagne's most renowned estates. Egly makes his concentrated, intensely-flavored champagnes predominantly from Pinot Noir and partially vinifies them in barrels from Dominique Laurent in Burgundy. All of the wines see long aging on the lees, giving them a burnished richness—from the non-vintage Brut Tradition up to the VP and Millésime, the wines share a generous depth and complexity. The finest wine from this estate is often the brooding, virile Blanc de Noirs, which is made from-60-year-old vines in the Ambonnay vineyard of Les Crayères.

15 rue de Trépail, 51150 Ambonnay
03 26 57 00 70

Emmanuel Brochet Montagne de Reims

In the village of Villers-aux-Noeuds, Emmanuel Brochet farms a single 6 acre (2.5ha) parcel planted with all three varieties of grape. The vineyard is worked organically, and all of the wines are vinified in barrel. The primary wine of the estate is the non-vintage Le Mont Benoit, which has an exceptional depth and personality. Named for the vineyard, it is earthy, rich, and driven by an intense minerality. Brochet also makes a racy, succulent rosé, and in the future is due to release a Blanc de Blancs, as well as a pure Pinot Meunier. ★ **Rising star**

7 impasse Brochet, 51500 Villers-aux-Noeuds
03 26 06 99 68

Eric Rodez Montagne de Reims

Eric Rodez took over his family's Ambonnay estate in 1984, and today he makes about 4,000 cases of champagne a year from his 16 acres (6.5ha) of vines.

All of Eric Rodez's champagnes are pure Ambonnay, made from biodynamically grown grapes, and largely vinified in oak barrels. His uncommonly sophisticated non-vintage champagnes employ a high percentage of reserve wines, which contribute to their sense of complexity and depth, while the series called Empreinte de Terroir consists of vintage-dated champagnes from Rodez's best parcels vinified entirely in wood.

4 rue de Isse, 51150 Ambonnay
www.champagne-rodez.fr

Franck Bonville Côte des Blancs

Olivier Bonville is at the helm of this Avize estate, making Blanc de Blancs champagnes of increasing finesse. All of Bonville's 44.5 acres (18ha) of vines are classified as Grand Cru and are mostly located in the villages of Avize and Oger, as well as Cramant and Le Mesnil-sur-Oger. While the vintage-dated Blanc de Blancs is the star of the cellar, the non-vintage Prestige is worth seeking out as well. The Cuvée Les Belles Voyes is a single-vineyard champagne from Oger, and the only one of Bonville's champagnes to be vinified in oak.

9 rue Pasteur, 51190 Avize
www.champagne-franck-bonville.com

Franck Pascal Vallée de la Marne

Franck Pascal makes just 2,500 cases of champagne a year, working with 9 acres (3.5ha) of vines in the clay-rich soils on the north bank of the Vallée de la Marne. Pascal took over his family's estate in 1994, and since 2001, the entire estate has been converted to biodynamic viticulture. The Sagesse Brut Nature is energetic and richly vinous, demonstrating the ripeness achieved by natural farming. The Tolérance rosé, which adds a little red wine to the Sagesse blend, shows a spicy complexity and sleek, fragrant length. ★ **Rising star**

1 bis rue V Régnier, 51700 Baslieux-sous-Chatillon
03 26 51 89 80

François Secondé Montagne de Reims

François Secondé is perhaps the only contemporary source of champagnes that are made exclusively from grapes grown in Sillery, a historically renowned Grand Cru village in the northern Montagne de Reims. Secondé's champagnes are ample and lavishly ripe, yet at their best, they retain a firm, harmonious structure and a poignant minerality. The La Loge Blanc de Noirs, made from 50-year-old Pinot Noir vines, consistently shows the most refinement and completeness, while the Cuvée Clavier, a Chardonnay-dominated blend partially aged in barrel, is also worth seeking out.

6 rue des Galipes, 51500 Sillery
03 26 49 16 67

Françoise Bedel Vallée de la Marne

Located in the far west of the Vallée de la Marne, Françoise Bedel and her son Vincent make distinctive, highly individual champagnes from biodynamically farmed vineyards. Pinot Meunier vines thrive in the clay and limestone soils of this sector, and account for four-fifths of Bedel's total vineyard area. Combined with long aging on the lees, this contributes to the particular richness and broad, earthy depth that is found in Bedel's wines. Entre Ciel et Terre is a vivid, spicy champagne that comes from chalky-clay soils, while Dis, Vin Secret, is from limestone, which creates a rounder, more ample wine.

71 Grande Rue, 02310 Crouttes-sur-Marnes
www.champagne-francoise-bedel.fr

Gaston Chiquet Grande Vallée

The champagnes of brothers Antoine and Nicolas Chiquet are fine examples of Champagne's regionality and superbly express the terroir character of this sector of the Grande Vallée. Gaston Chiquet places an emphasis on old vines, and avoids the use of wood in order to preserve a lightness and finesse in the wines from these clay-rich soils. The Spécial Club is the top wine in the cellar, but equally compelling is the Blanc de Blancs d'Aÿ, a rare and intensely soil-driven Chardonnay from this Pinot-dominated village.

912 avenue du Général Leclerc, 51530 Dizy
www.gastonchiquet.com

Gatinois Grande Vallée

Pierre Cheval and his wife Marie-Paule Gatinois run this small, boutique estate in the Grand Cru village of Aÿ, making full-bodied, mouthfilling champagnes. Aÿ is renowned for its Pinot Noir, and this grape accounts for 90% of Gatinois's vineyard area. The non-vintage Tradition is fragrant and sleek, while the more substantial Réserve is the same wine with extra lees aging. The highly sought-after vintage brut sells out quickly and is always worth pursuing. Gatinois also makes excellent red wine, preserving a village tradition that dates back to medieval times.

7 rue de Mailly, 51160 Aÿ
www.champagne-gatinois.com

Georges Laval Grande Vallée

One of the finest grower-estates in Champagne, Georges Laval is virtually unknown even to most champagne connoisseurs, due to the tiny amounts of champagne produced: just 800 cases annually. The Lavals have farmed their vines organically since 1971, and all the champagnes are pure Cumières. George Laval's non-vintage, released in both brut and brut nature versions, is hardly an entry level wine, and in the past, it was essentially the estate's sole *cuvée*. Today, there are also two single-vineyard champagnes, as well as a rosé, all in painfully tiny quantities.

16 ruelle du Carrefour, 51480 Cumières
www.georgeslaval.com

Godmé Père et Fils Montagne de Reims

Hugues Godmé is in charge of this excellent grower-estate in the village of Verzenay, which makes champagnes of a rare vinosity and intensity of expression. The Brut Réserve contains an unusually high percentage of reserve wines, which makes it feel bold, meaty, and dark; while the Blanc de Noirs retains the dark fruit character yet expresses a greater elegance and finesse. The extra brut and vintage wines are both outstanding, showing a deep, resonant complexity and impeccable balance. Godmé has several single-vineyard champagnes in the works, which demonstrate significant promise.

10 rue de Verzy, 51360 Verzenay
www.champagne-godme.fr

GUY CHARLEMAGNE
RACY AND REFINED, THE VINTAGE-DATED MESNILLESIME IS PURE CHARDONNAY FROM LE MESNIL-SUR-OGER

GOSSET
THE GRANDE RESERVE BRUT IS AN ELEGANT BLEND OF ALL THREE GRAPES

Gonet-Médeville Grande Vallée

Xavier Gonet, from a winegrowing family in Le Mesnil, and his wife Julie Médeville, originally from Sauternes, founded this grower-estate in 2000. Half of their 25 acres (10ha) are in the village of Bisseuil, from which they make an excellent Blanc de Noirs. Bisseuil also features prominently in the non-vintage Tradition, and is the source of red wine for Gonet-Médeville's rosé. Most exciting of all is a series of single-vineyard champagnes from Ambonnay and Le Mesnil, which, like all of the estate's wines, demonstrate an expressive intensity and sophisticated poise. ★ **Rising star**

1 chemin de la Cavotte, 51150 Bisseuil
www.gonet-medeville.com

Gosset Epernay

Gosset has been located in Aÿ since the house's founding in 1584, but in 2009 it moved to more spacious cellars in Epernay. While Gosset champagnes have a reputation for being powerful, contemporary releases demonstrate a marvelous finesse, complexity, and balance, which is enlivened by the absence of malolactic. The Grande Réserve is an elegant, upper-tier non-vintage brut, while the vintage-dated Grand Millésime is consistently graceful and refined. The three versions of Gosset's prestige cuvée, Celebris, each highlight a different facet of the house's sophisticated style, and have become even more expressive through their recent conversion to an extra brut dosage.

69 rue Jules Blondeau, 51160 Aÿ
www.champagne-gosset.com

Gosset-Brabant Grande Vallée

Gabriel Gosset left his family's champagne house in the 1930s to found this grower-estate in Aÿ; today it is run by his grandsons, Michel and Christian Gosset. The Gosset-Brabant style is one of rich fruit and concentrated flavor, which is achieved through conscientious viticulture and top holdings in the Grands Crus of Aÿ and Chouilly, among other villages. Aÿ Pinot Noir and Chouilly Chardonnay are blended to create the excellent non-vintage Réserve as well as the estate's prestige cuvée, the vintage-dated Cuvée Gabriel. In contrast, Aÿ Pinot stands majestically alone in the Noirs d'Aÿ.

23 boulevard du Maréchal de Lattre de Tassigny, 51160 Aÿ
03 26 55 17 42

Guy Charlemagne Côte des Blancs

Philippe Charlemagne is at the helm of this prominent grower-estate, located in Le Mesnil-sur-Oger, making brisk, racy champagnes that reflect the chalky soils of the area. While Charlemagne owns vines outside of the Côte des Blancs, his Réserve Blanc de Blancs is made exclusively from the Grands Crus of Le Mesnil and Oger —these villages are also used for the vintage-dated Cuvée Charlemagne. Guy Charlemagne's prestige cuvée, Mesnillésime, is pure Le Mesnil Chardonnay, made from old vines in top parcels and partially vinified in oak barrels.

4 rue de la Brèche d'Oger, 51190 Le Mesnil-sur-Oger
www.champagne-guy-charlemagne.com

Guy Larmandier Côte des Blancs

François Larmandier is in charge of this Vertus estate, farming 22 acres (9ha) of vines in the Côte des Blancs. Aside from a rosé, the estate's champagnes are all Blanc de Blancs, and they are organized according to terroir:

Regimented rows of Chardonnay vines stretch every which way in the Côte des Blancs, south of Epernay.

JOSEPH PERRIER
THE BOTTLE FOR JOSEPH PERRIER'S
PRESTIGE CUVEE IS BASED ON A HAND-
PAINTED, 19TH-CENTURY DESIGN

Vertus vines are used for the non-vintage brut and the rosé, while the Cuvée Perlée is from Chouilly. Larmandier's vines in Cramant are used for both a non-vintage Cramant Blanc de Blancs and a richer, vintage-dated version called the Cuvée Prestige.

30 rue du Général Koenig, 51130 Vertus
www.champagne-larmandier-guy.fr

Henri Billiot Montagne de Reims

This 12 acre (5ha) grower-estate in Ambonnay is one of the village's best, making Pinot-dominated champagnes of unusual elegance and character. All of Billiot's wines are pure Ambonnay and, aside from the oak-aged Cuvée Julie, all are vinified entirely in enameled steel tanks without malolactic. Both the Brut Réserve and non-vintage rosé are exemplary, while the sleekly sculpted vintage champagne is an outstanding expression of Ambonnay terroir. The estate's top wine, Cuvée Laetitia, is made from a perpetual blend, which was started in the mid-1980s and is refreshed with new wine only in the best vintage years.

Place de la Fontaine, 51150 Ambonnay
03 26 57 00 14

Henri Giraud Grande Vallée

Claude Giraud's champagnes are grown exclusively in the village of Aÿ, where his family has been tending vines since the 17th century. The non-vintage Esprit de Giraud shows the rich texture and depth that characterizes Giraud's style, while the Hommage à François Hémart feels even more voluptuous after six months of aging in oak. Henri Giraud vinifies about a third of his wines in oak, which is sourced from the local Argonne forests. The house has achieved renown for its powerful, opulent Cuvée Fût de Chêne, vinified entirely in this local Argonne oak.

71 boulevard Charles de Gaulle, 51160 Aÿ
www.champagne-giraud.com

Henri Goutorbe Grande Vallée

Many Champenois know the Goutorbes for their important vine nursery, located in the village of Aÿ, but the family also makes excellent champagnes from their 62 acres (25ha) of vines. Henri Goutorbe's champagnes are ample and generous in flavor, as demonstrated by the Cuvée Prestige, a non-vintage brut from premier and Grand Cru vineyards, or the Blanc de Blancs, made from Chardonnay vines in Bisseuil. The estate's vintage brut and Spécial Club are both pure Aÿ and they age extremely well, demonstrating perfectly the succulence and finesse of this fabled cru.

9 bis rue Jeanson, 51160 Aÿ
www.champagne-henri-goutorbe.com

Henri Mandois Coteaux Sud d'Epernay

The Mandois family has been making champagne since 1860. Today, Claude Mandois is at the helm of his family's house, which is located in the village of Pierry. Some purchased grapes are used for the non-vintage brut, but all of the rest of Henri Mandois's champagnes are made from the house's own 86.5 acres (35ha) of vines, which are made up of 70% Chardonnay, 15% Pinot Noir, and 15% Pinot Meunier. The brut nature and the vintage-dated Blanc de Blancs show a harmonious balance and

polished texture, while the Cuvée Victor is a prestige cuvée made from 60-year-old Chardonnay vines in Chouilly that are partially fermented in barrel.

51530 Pierry
www.champagne-mandois.com

Henriot Reims

Founded in 1808 by Apolline Henriot, this Reims house makes rich, mouthfilling champagnes that derive a great deal of complexity and finesse from long aging on the lees. The non-vintage Blanc Souverain is the flagship wine of the house, and an excellent introduction to the style. Vintage champagnes are aged for five to eight years on the lees and Henriot typically releases several different vintages at the same time, offering opportunities for comparison and contrast. Henriot's prestige cuvée, Cuvée des Enchanteleurs, is complex and fine and is aged for more than 10 years before release.

81 Rue Coquebert, 51100 Reims
www.champagne-henriot.com

Jacques Lassaigne Aube

The finest producer in the village of Montgueux, this estate has been in the hands of Emmanuel Lassaigne since 1999. Lassaigne supplements his 10 acres (4ha) of vines with some additional purchases from the village, making Chardonnay-based champagnes that showcase Montgueux's luscious, exotic fruit flavors perfectly. Les Vignes de Montgueux is Jacques Lassaigne's non-vintage brut, while Cuvée Le Cotet is a single-vineyard champagne from old vines that shows more depth and detail. Lassaigne's superb vintage brut is vinified entirely in stainless steel, but another *cuvée*, Colline Inspirée, is partially fermented in barrel, and bottled exclusively in magnum. ★ **Rising star**

7 chemin du Coteau, 10300 Montgueux
www.montgueux.com

Jacques Selosse Côte des Blancs

One of Champagne's great personalities, Anselme Selosse creates some of the region's most original wines. Viticulture is at the heart of Selosse's philosophy and this is evident in his wines, which can demonstrate an unparalleled resonance and intensity of character. Vinification is entirely in barrel, with indigenous yeasts, and each wine in the range is exceptionally expressive, from the sophisticated, energetic Initial to the regal and complex Millésime. Substance is an unusual champagne made in a solera system and, while the majority of Selosse's *cuvées* are Blanc de Blancs, Contraste is a pure Pinot Noir from Aÿ and Ambonnay.

22 rue Ernest Vallé, 51190 Avize
03 26 57 53 56

Jacquesson Grande Vallée

This 200-year-old house has been owned by the Chiquet family since 1974, and while they had already gained a devoted following for their richly complex champagnes, vinified in large oak barrels, they have recently chosen to completely renovate the house's portfolio. Today, Jean-Hervé and Laurent Chiquet adhere to traditional methods to create only one blended champagne, which replaces the non-vintage Perfection brut. Rather than aiming for consistency

JACQUESSON
CUVEE NO. 732, FROM THE 700 SERIES, IS AN
ASSEMBLAGE BASED ON THE 2004 HARVEST

from year to year, it's intended to represent the best blend possible. Jacquesson's other four wines are all single-vineyard, vintage-dated champagnes, challenging the notion that great champagne must always be a blended wine.

68 rue du Colonel Fabien, 51530 Dizy
www.champagnejacquesson.com

Janisson-Baradon Epernay

Founded in 1922, this grower-estate is unusual in that most of its vineyards are in Epernay. All of Janisson-Baradon's champagnes are partially fermented in oak, and they often show a round, full-bodied richness. The Sélection is the non-vintage brut, which is made of equal parts Chardonnay and Pinot Noir, while the Grande Réserve is the same blend, aged longer on the lees. Janisson's Spécial Club is a single-vineyard Blanc de Blancs from Les Toulettes in Epernay, which is made only in the best vintages.

2 rue des Vignerons, 51200 Epernay
www.champagne-janisson.com

Jean Milan Côte des Blancs

Founded in 1864, this Oger estate produces flowery, elegant Blanc de Blancs. All of Jean Milan's vines are in the Grand Cru village of Oger, which they supplement with purchases from other growers in the village. Terres de Noël is a single-vineyard Blanc de Blancs from vines up to 65 years old. Symphorine, a selection of top parcels, is also worth seeking out—it feels ripe and rich where the Terres de Noël is chalky and brisk. The Grande Réserve 1864 acquires a full body and breadth from vinification in wood and long lees aging.

6 rue d'Avize, 51190 Oger
www.champagne-milan.com

Jean Moutardier Vallée de la Marne

Englishman Jonathan Saxby runs this house in the village of Le Breuil which was founded in 1960 by his father-in-law, Jean Moutardier. The house's 44.5 acres (18ha) of vines, as well as all its additional purchases, are in Le Breuil and the surrounding villages, giving Jean Moutardier champagnes a particularly broad, fragrant character that is typical of the area. Pinot Meunier is the dominant grape here, and Moutardier's best wines highlight this variety: it is featured alone in the elegantly balanced Pure Meunier, but also accounts for 85% of the non-vintage Carte d'Or.

Route d'Orbais, 51210 Le Breuil
www.champagne-jean-moutardier.fr

Jean Velut Aube

Denis Velut farms 19 acres (7.5ha) in Montgueux, but sells a large portion of his crop to the *négoce*. He bottles roughly 3,000 cases of champagne a year, based largely on Chardonnay. The ripe, fruity, non-vintage brut contains a little Pinot Noir, but the Cuvée Spéciale is pure Chardonnay, elegantly highlighting Montgueux's typically tropical flavors. Since the 1999 vintage, Jean Velut's vintage brut has also been made of pure Chardonnay, giving it a round feeling and a forward aroma.

9 rue du Moulin, 10300 Montgueux
03 25 74 83 31

Jean Vesselle Montagne de Reims

Delphine Vesselle is at the helm of this Bouzy estate, making boldly-flavored, Pinot Noir-driven champagnes. Vesselle owns vines in both Bouzy and Loches, in the Aube, and while most of her wines are a blend of the two villages, the Cuvée Prestige, made in both non-vintage and vintage-dated versions, is pure Bouzy. Look for the harmoniously balanced Extra Brut as well as the Oeil de Perdrix. Le Petit Clos, a single-vineyard champagne made from a tiny vineyard in Bouzy, next to the estate itself, is well worth tracking down.

4 rue Victor Hugo, 51150 Bouzy
www.champagnejeanvesselle.fr

Jérôme Prévost Montagne de Reims

Made from a single vineyard, a single grape variety, and a single year, Jérôme Prévost's champagnes are not typical of the region's traditions. Prévost's first vintage was 1998, and since then he has acquired a cult following for his unusual, complex, soil-expressive wines. He typically only makes one wine each year, a 100% Pinot Meunier from a vineyard called Les Béguines. It is fermented in oak *demi-muid* with indigenous yeasts and released with little to no dosage. These are modern champagnes in the best sense, which reflect a philosophy of natural viticulture and thoughtful winemaking. ★ **Rising star**

2 rue Petite-Montagne, 51390 Gueux
03 26 03 48 60

José Dhondt Côte des Blancs

José Dhondt primarily produces Blanc de Blancs champagnes from his small estate in the Côte des Blancs village of Oger. He owns vines further south in the Sézanne as well, which are used in his entry level Brut Tradition. The Grande Réserve, however, is a crisp, minerally Blanc de Blancs that is made entirely from grapes grown in Oger. At the top of the range is the single-vineyard Mes Vieilles Vignes, made from a parcel of Oger Chardonnay that was planted in 1949.

1 rue de Flavigny, 51190 Oger
03 26 57 96 86

José Michel Coteaux Sud d'Epernay

One of Champagne's great Pinot Meunier specialists, José Michel has been making wine at his Moussy estate since 1952. Michel's champagnes are ample and mouthfilling, reflecting the clay soils of this area, which is south of Epernay. Pinot Meunier figures prominently in Michel's extra brut and non-vintage Carte Blanche, and he has recently introduced an excellent non-vintage brut that is made entirely of Pinot Meunier. Today, Michel's vintage wines are made with a majority of Chardonnay, but in the past, they were 100% Pinot Meunier and he has indicated that he may release a vintage-dated Pinot Meunier again in the future.

14 rue Prélot, 51530 Moussy
www.champagne-jose-michel.com

Joseph Perrier Châlons-en-Champagne

Founded by Joseph Perrier in 1825, this is the only champagne house remaining in the city of Châlons. Ironically, all of the house's vineyards are in the Vallée de la Marne, although they purchase additional grapes

THE INFLUENCE OF ANSELME SELOSSE

Anselme Selosse has undoubtedly been one of the most influential winemakers in the Champagne region in modern times. His philosophies of natural viticulture, his demandingly inquisitive spirit, and his often iconoclastic pursuit of originality have all resonated strongly with a new generation of growers. Often, those growers who have learned from him, such as Alexandre Chartogne, Olivier Collin, Bertrand Gautherot, and Jérôme Prévost, are dubbed "Selosse Disciples." Yet this term implies that there is some sort of dogma, which there definitely is not, and it detracts from the other growers' own individual efforts and original initiatives. Selosse's influence is felt not so much in methodology as in philosophy: these growers all work differently, yet what they have in common are a deep respect for nature, a relentless desire for exploration, and a worldview open to new challenges and possibilities.

KRUG

THE GRANDE CUVEE IS KRUG'S SIGNATURE
CHAMPAGNE AND A FINE EXAMPLE OF
THE ART OF BLENDING

from all over the region. Joseph Perrier's champagnes are full in flavor and finely balanced, feeling forward and accessible. Many of the wines bear the name Cuvée Royale, in reference to the house once supplying the courts of Britain's Queen Victoria and King Edward VII. Cuvée Joséphine, named after Joseph Perrier's daughter, is a refined and elegant prestige cuvée.

69 avenue de Paris, 51016 Châlons-en-Champagne
www.joseph-perrier.com

Krug Reims
This legendary house was founded by Johann Joseph Krug in 1843. The Krug style is one of great complexity, richness, and finesse, achieved through fermentation in wood and a mastery of blending: indeed, many would argue that no house is as skilled at blending as Krug. The Krug philosophy finds its ultimate expression in the Grande Cuvée, a blend of as many as 50 wines from all three grape varieties, 20 to 25 growths, and 6 to 10 different vintages. The vintage brut is more restricted in its scope, yet also demonstrates a marvelous complexity and expression. Ironically, Krug's two most expensive wines, the Clos d'Ambonnay and the Clos du Mesnil, are both single-vineyard champagnes and as such are completely unblended.

5 rue Coquebert, Reims
www.krug.com

Laherte Frères Coteaux Sud d'Epernay
This 25 acre (10ha) estate is making champagnes of increasingly expressive depth and complexity. Characterized by natural viticulture, concentrated fruit, and partial vinification in wood, these are assertive champagnes, full of personality. Look for Les Vignes d'Autrefois, a vintage-dated 100% Pinot Meunier from old vines, or La Pierre de la Justice, a vivid, sleekly-shaped, single-vineyard Blanc de Blancs. Another excellent and unusual single-vineyard champagne, Les Clos, is made of seven grape varieties that are field-blended and vinified together, while Les Beaudiers is an intense, vinous, vintage-dated *saignée* rosé. ★**Rising star**

3 rue des Jardins, 51530 Chavot
www.champagne-laherte.com

Lamiable Montagne de Reims
The Lamiable family farms 15 acres (6ha) in Tours-sur-Marne. Jean-Pierre Lamiable and his daughter Ophélie make ripe, generously fruity wines with a vinous intensity. The harmonious, subtly gripping extra brut is a fine introduction to the estate's style. Les Meslaines is a single-vineyard Blanc de Noirs made from 50-year-old Pinot Noir vines—it is powerful in its fruit, yet also intensely chalky. The Spécial Club contains one-third Chardonnay from the Côte des Blancs, purchased from friends, which is blended with Pinot Noir and Chardonnay from Tours-sur-Marne.

8 rempart Est, 51150 Tours-sur-Marne
www.champagnelamiable.com

Lanson Reims
Jean-Paul Gandon has been in charge of Lanson's cellars for over 30 years, preserving a house style that combines power and freshness. A significant characteristic of Lanson champagnes is the lack of malolactic, which gives

them a lively vivacity to tether their fragrant fruitiness. The Rose Label is a classic example, its fruit kept taut by vibrant acidity, and the newly released Extra Age shows the richness of longer lees aging. The range of Noble Cuvée champagnes focuses on a more discreet finesse, while the vintage-dated Gold Label is capable of great complexity and longevity.

66 rue de Courlancy, 51100 Reims
www.lanson.fr

Larmandier-Bernier Côte des Blancs
Pierre Larmandier makes Blanc de Blancs champagnes of remarkable clarity and purity at his Vertus estate, farmed biodynamically since 2004. Larmandier vinifies partially in wood and always with indigenous yeasts. One of his best-known wines is Terre de Vertus, a racy and intensely chalky brut nature that is grown on the northern side of Vertus, close to Le Mesnil. The outstanding, vintage-dated Vieille Vigne de Cramant is made from two parcels of vines in Cramant that are up to 75 years old, demonstrating the richness and complexity of this Grand Cru terroir.

19 avenue du Général de Gaulle, 51130 Vertus
www.larmandier.com

Launois Père et Fils Côte des Blancs
At 74 acres (30ha), with two-thirds of the vineyards in the Grand Cru villages of Le Mesnil, Oger, Cramant, and Avize, Launois Père et Fils is large for a grower-estate. The champagnes are clean and polished and most of the estate's *cuvées* are Blanc de Blancs, such as the Veuve Clémence, a full-bodied wine made from old vines in Cramant, and the vintage Blanc de Blancs, blended from Le Mesnil and Oger. The Spécial Club is made from two parcels of 50-year-old vines in Oger and Cramant.

2 avenue Eugène Guillaume, 51190 Le Mesnil-sur-Oger
www.champagne-launois.fr

Laurent-Perrier Montagne de Reims
Founded in 1812, this house in the village of Tours-sur-Marne was brought to prominence by Bernard de Nonancourt after the Second World War. Today, Laurent-Perrier is renowned for its Grand Siècle, a prestige cuvée blended from three different years, as well as its non-vintage rosé, made by maceration rather than blending. The *non-dosé* Ultra Brut, made since 1981, is racy and delicate, while the Brut Millésimé combines richness and finesse. Not to be missed is the vintage-dated Alexandra Rosé, an elegantly sophisticated rosé champagne.

51150 Tours-sur-Marne
www.laurent-perrier.fr

Le Brun Servenay Côte des Blancs
Patrick Lebrun heads this 20 acre (8ha) estate in Avize, tending vines not only in the Côte des Blancs, but also in the Coteaux Sud d'Epernay. While the malolactic is avoided, these wines still show a certain richness, derived from ripe fruit. The non-vintage Brut Réserve is fruity and full-bodied, made from all three varieties, while the Brut Sélection is pure Côte des Blancs Chardonnay, showing a chalky minerality and exotic fruit aromas. Le Brun Servenay's rosé is light and crisp, with a zesty freshness.

14 Place Léon Bourgeois, 51190 Avize
www.champagnelebrun.com

LECLERC-BRIANT

THIS 70% PINOT NOIR, 30% MEUNIER IS
PRODUCED WITH BIODYNAMIC METHODS

Leclaire-Gaspard Grande Vallée

Reynald Leclaire and his wife Virginie Thiéfane own this small estate, now based in Mareuil-sur-Aÿ. It was founded in Avize in 1876, by Ernest Alfred Leclaire, and the estate's most important vineyards still lie in that village. Although Leclaire-Gaspard produces fewer than 2,000 cases a year, these complex, finely balanced champagnes are well worth seeking out. The non-vintage Grande Réserve shows a bold, fragrant depth, while the Carte d'Or derives more complexity from longer lees aging. Older vintage wines are occasionally released as well, but in tiny quantities.

26 rue Sadi Carnot, 51160 Mareuil-sur-Aÿ
03 26 52 88 65

Leclerc-Briant Epernay

Leclerc-Briant controls 74 acres (30ha) of vineyards in the Vallée de la Marne, which are increasingly being converted to biodynamic viticulture. The house's champagnes tend to be bold and full-flavored. The best of the range are the single-vineyard champagnes from Cumières: Les Crayères is racy and sleek, driven by chalky minerality, while Les Chèvres Pierreuses is rounder and more ample. Recently, the house has introduced two additional single-vineyard champagnes: La Croisette, a pure Chardonnay from Epernay; and La Ravinne, a Pinot Meunier from Verneuil.

67 rue Chaude Ruelle, 51204 Epernay
www.leclercbriant.com

R & L Legras Côte des Blancs

R & L Legras's champagnes are always pure Chouilly, and are consistently the most sophisticated and refined examples of that village. The house is often associated with fine gastronomy, making the private-label champagnes for restaurants such as La Tour d'Argent and Guy Savoy in Paris. The silky, citrussy non-vintage Blanc de Blancs is a fine introduction to the house style, while the vintage-dated Cuvée Présidence, made from old vines, demonstrates a more intense minerality and depth. The Cuvée St-Vincent is made only in the best vintages, and is capable of terrific complexity and finesse.

10 rue des Partelaines, 51530, Chouilly
www.champagne-legras.fr

A R Lenoble Vallée de la Marne

Armand-Raphaël Graser founded this house in 1920, inventing the name Lenoble to make it sound more French. Today, his descendants Antoine and Anne Malassagne make champagnes of unusually assertive personality, largely from house-owned vines. Over half of A R Lenoble's vineyards are in the Grand Cru village of Chouilly, from which they produce the superb, vintage-dated Gentilhomme Blanc de Blancs and the single-vineyard Les Aventures. It is well worth exploring the rest of the range, particularly if you enjoy vinous, intensely-flavored champagnes.

35-37 rue Paul Douce, 51480, Damery
www.champagne-lenoble.com

Lilbert-Fils Côte des Blancs

This tiny Cramant estate makes exquisite and intricately detailed champagnes from just 9 acres (3.5ha) of Chardonnay vines, all classified Grand Cru. Bertrand

A R LENOBLE
A SINGLE-VINEYARD CHAMPAGNE FROM CHOUILLY, LES AVENTURES IS ELEGANTLY COMPLEX AND INTENSELY CHALKY

LOUIS ROEDERER
LOOK BEYOND CRISTAL TO ROEDERER'S ENTIRE RANGE OF CHAMPAGNES

Lilbert has been in charge of the estate since 1998, and today he makes three wines. The excellent non-vintage brut is blended from Cramant, Chouilly, and Oiry, while the Perle is pure Cramant, made from old vines and bottled at a lower pressure in the style that used to be called *crémant*. Lilbert-Fils's vintage brut is also old-vine Cramant, demonstrating a remarkably complex and refined character.

223 rue du Moutier, 51530, Cramant
www.champagne-lilbert.com

Louis Roederer Reims

One of the finest houses in Champagne, Louis Roederer's roots date back to 1776. Today, the house is widely known for its prestige cuvée, Cristal, which was originally created for Russia's Tsar Alexander II. Cristal is indeed among the best champagnes being made, but don't overlook the rest of the house's range. All of Roederer's vintage wines, including Cristal, are made exclusively from vines owned by the house, and they are uniformly superb, demonstrating the freshness gained by the avoidance of malolactic and the refined complexity and finesse that are the hallmarks of the house's style.

21 boulevard Lundy, 51053, Reims
www.champagne-roederer.com

Mailly Grand Cru Montagne de Reims

No co-operative in Champagne is as impressive as Mailly Grand Cru. Founded in 1929, it is comprised of 80 wine-growers who own 173 acres (70ha) of vines, all in the village of Mailly. Mailly faces north, producing Pinot Noir of finesse and structure. This is clearly demonstrated throughout Mailly Grand Cru's large range of wines, particularly in the expressive non-vintage Blanc de Noirs. The prestige cuvée Les Echansons is intended to show more vinosity and richness, while L'Intemporelle is the reverse, designed to maximize elegance and delicacy.

28 rue de la Libération, 51500 Mailly Champagne
www.champagne-mailly.com

Marc Hébrart Grande Vallée

This grower-estate in Mareuil-sur-Aÿ certainly deserves to be better known. Jean-Paul Hébrart farms 34.5 acres (14ha) of vines in six different villages, making champagnes of mouthfilling depth. The Cuvée de Réserve is a delicious non-vintage brut, while the Sélection is made from old vines and given extra time on the lees. Marc Hébrart's fresh, fragrant rosé is particularly outstanding, as is his Spécial Club, made of Pinot Noir from his oldest vines in Mareuil and blended with Chardonnay from Chouilly and Oiry.

18/20 rue du Pont, 51160 Mareuil-sur-Aÿ
03 26 52 60 75

A Margaine Montagne de Reims

One of the reference points for Chardonnay in the Montagne de Reims, this family-owned estate in Villers-Marmery makes expressive, richly-flavored wines. Each of the estate's three Blanc de Blancs offers a different perspective on this village's distinctive terroir, with the vintage-dated Spécial Club standing out for its complexity and finesse. Proprietor Arnaud Margaine

MARGUET PERE ET FILS
THE RESERVE IS AN UPPER-TIER BLEND OF PINOT NOIR AND CHARDONNAY, PARTIALLY FERMENTED IN BARREL

grows a little Pinot Noir as well, which makes up about 10% of the excellent non-vintage brut and provides red wine for his invitingly silky rosé.

3 avenue de Champagne, 51380 Villers Marmery
www.isasite.net/champagne-margaine

Marguet Père et Fils Montagne de Reims

Benoît Marguet owns no vines, but he has a wide network of grape sources and today makes about 5,000 cases of champagne a year. He has a preference for organically-grown grapes, and his champagnes tend to be deeply-flavored with an unusual intensity of aroma. The non-vintage Tradition is a Blanc de Noirs made of both Pinot Noir and Pinot Meunier, while the Réserve blends Pinot Noir and Chardonnay. Marguet Père et Fil's vintage brut combines Chouilly Chardonnay with Bouzy Pinot Noir, creating a bold and generously fruity champagne. ★ **Rising star**

1 Place Barancourt, 51150 Ambonnay
www.champagne-marguet.fr

Marie-Noëlle Ledru Montagne de Reims

Marie-Noëlle Ledru makes vinous, terroir-driven champagnes at her small Ambonnay estate, bottling just 2,500 cases a year. Both her non-vintage and vintage-dated *cuvées* showcase the sleek, complex character of Ambonnay Pinot Noir, which is balanced with 15% Chardonnay. However, her top wine, Cuvée du Goulté, is pure Pinot Noir and is selected from the best parcels. Ledru's *non-dosé* champagnes are particularly noteworthy—due to their richly ripe fruit, they attain an uncommon harmony and completeness, even in the absence of dosage.

5 place de la Croix, 51150 Ambonnay
03 26 57 09 26

Michel Arnould Montagne de Reims

Verzenay is one of the most famous crus of Champagne —to get an idea of its true character, it is best to taste a pure Verzenay from one of the village's top growers. Patrick Arnould at the Michel Arnould estate crafts fine examples of this fabled terroir. Both his Brut Tradition and Brut Réserve are made entirely from Verzenay fruit, as is the powerful, vintage-dated Memoire de Vignes. Arnould also sources some fruit from Le Mesnil-sur-Oger, combining it with Verzenay Pinot Noir in his boldly complex vintage brut and silky, refined La Grande Cuvée.

28 rue de Mailly, 51360 Verzenay
www.champagne-michel-arnould.com

Michel Loriot Vallée de la Marne

Michel Loriot farms 17 acres (7ha) of vines in and around the Flagot Valley, on the southern banks of the Marne. Pinot Meunier is the dominant variety in these clay soils, so it is no surprise that Loriot's two most distinctive wines are pure Pinot Meunier: his lively, non-vintage Réserve is a surprisingly elegant expression of the grape, while the vintage-dated Pinot Meunier Vieilles Vignes is resonant and complex, with a concentrated character. It is fascinating to compare these with Loriot's vintage brut, where a touch of Chardonnay is added for finesse.

13 rue de Bel Air, 51700 Festigny
www.champagne-michelloriot.com

MICHEL ARNOULD
LA GRAND CUVEE IS TWO-THIRDS PINOT NOIR AND ONE-THIRD CHARDONNAY

Moët & Chandon Epernay

Claude Moët founded this famous house in 1743, and today it is probably one of Champagne's most visible brands. While the house doesn't disclose figures, Moët is the largest landowner in the region, giving cellarmaster Benoît Gouez a vast resource of vineyards to work with. In recent years, Moët & Chandon has streamlined the collection. The light, toasty non-vintage Brut Impérial has counterparts in the Rosé Impérial and Nectar Impérial, while there are two vintage champagnes, the Grand Vintage and Grand Vintage Rosé. Dom Pérignon, once the house's prestige cuvée, is now a separate brand.

18 avenue de Champagne, Epernay
www.moet.com

Moutard Père et Fils Aube

François Moutard produces a wide range of round, full-bodied champagnes that are characteristic of the Aube region. He is best known for his pursuit of unusual grape varieties, although they represent only a small part of his total production. The Cuvée des 6 Cépages Millésime is one of his finest champagnes, blending six different grape varieties; while the Vieilles Millésime Vignes Arbane features the obscure Arbane grape, a variety that has almost disappeared, entirely on its own. Moutard Père et Fil's more usual wines, from Pinot Noir and Chardonnay, are also worth seeking out, particularly the single-vineyard Champ Persin Blanc de Blancs.

Rue des Ponts, 10110 Buxeuil
www.champagne-moutard.fr

Mumm Reims

Founded in 1827, Mumm was one of the region's finest houses up until the end of the 1960s. Its quality plummeted under the ownership of the drinks giant Seagram, but today it is owned by Pernod-Ricard and, under the direction of cellarmaster Didier Mariotti, the house looks to be on its way back up again. The Mumm style is for light, fresh champagnes, such as the Mumm de Cramant that is a particularly delicate interpretation of the cru. However, in comparison, the newly created prestige cuvée, R Lalou, is a serious, complex champagne of depth and character that is sourced exclusively from the house's top vineyards.

29 rue du Champ de Mars, 51100 Reims
www.mumm.com

Nicolas Maillart Montagne de Reims

Nicolas Maillart took over his family's estate in 2003. Since then he has revamped the entire operation, installing a new press, buying thermo-regulated stainless steel tanks, and reworking his viticulture to focus on sustainability. Maillart's non-vintage brut, called Platine, demonstrates the estate's new approach to champagne, showing generous yet lively flavors. The most intriguing wines, however, are the two terroir-specific champagnes from the village of Ecueil: Les Chaillots Gillis is a spicy, deeply toned Chardonnay that is made from 40-year-old vines from two different parcels; and Les Francs de Pied is a rare Pinot Noir from ungrafted vines. ★ **Rising star**

5 rue de Villers aux Noeuds, 51500 Ecueil
www.champagne-maillart.fr

Olivier Horiot Aube

When Olivier Horiot began to make wine in 2000, he didn't even make champagne, choosing to focus instead on tiny quantities of red and rosé wines. Horiot's vines are in Les Riceys, the only village in Champagne that qualifies for three different appellations: sparkling wine, still wine, and the rare Rosé des Riceys. Today, Olivier Horiot bottles a little champagne, but his most exciting wines continue to be his single-vineyard, biodynamically farmed Rosé des Riceys: Barmont is ripely fruity and extroverted, while Valingrain is elegantly detailed, thriving on its chalky finesse. ★ Rising star

25 rue de Bise, 10340 Les Riceys
03 25 29 32 16

Pascal Doquet Côte des Blancs

Pascal Doquet took over his family's Doquet-Jeanmaire estate in 1995. Since then he has slowly phased out the old label in favor of his own, under which he makes organically grown, intensely terroir-driven champagnes. Aside from his rosé, all are Blanc de Blancs. He makes separate *cuvées* from his terroirs in Vitry, Le Mesnil, and the area around Vertus, as well as a vintage-dated Mont-Aimé, from silex soils on the butte south of Vertus. Each one is vivid in its expression, with an unusual intensity, precision, and finesse.

44 Chemin du Moulin de la Cense Bizet, 51130 Vertus
www.champagne-doquet-jeanmaire.com

Paul Bara Montagne de Reims

One of Champagne's legendary figures, Paul Bara began producing champagne after World War II. Today, the estate is in the hands of his daughter, Chantale, who continues to make champagnes of remarkable expression and finesse. All of Paul Bara's wines are pure Bouzy, demonstrating the ample depth and harmonious richness that is typical of the village. The perfumed, fragrant Grand Rosé is particularly compelling, while the Comtesse Marie de France shows the complexity of long lees aging. Bara's Spécial Club is subtle and fine and, as of 2004, it is also produced as a rosé.

4 rue Yvonnet, 51150 Bouzy
www.champagnepaulbara.com

Paul Clouet Montagne de Reims

Marie-Thérèse Clouet created this Bouzy estate in 1992, naming it after her grandfather, Paul. Clouet is married to Jean-Louis Bonnaire, who makes the Clouet champagnes at his estate in Cramant. Clouet wines echo the polished, voluptuous richness found in Bonnaire champagnes, although, given the location of Clouet's vineyards, these rely more on Pinot Noir. The non-vintage Brut Grand Cru is vivid and bold, blended from Bouzy Pinot Noir and Chouilly Chardonnay, while the Brut Grand Cru Prestige is nearly all Pinot Noir, displaying complex, intense flavors.

1 place A Tritant, 51150 Bouzy
www.champagne-paul-clouet.com

Paul Déthune Montagne de Reims

Déthune's champagnes are classic expressions of the Ambonnay terroir, combining depth, complexity, and finesse. Pierre Déthune owns 17 acres (7ha) of vines, all in Ambonnay, and farms his vineyards sustainably, eschewing pesticides and employing exclusively organic manures. His

Blanc de Noirs is outstanding, with a pure, complex depth of fruit. This same Pinot Noir is blended with Chardonnay to create the Cuvée à l'Ancienne, which is aged for longer on the lees. The Princesse des Thunes is vinified in large oak casks, giving it a savory, full-bodied richness.

2 rue du Moulin, 51150 Ambonnay
www.champagne-dethune.com

Pehu-Simonet Montagne de Reims

David Pehu makes a little over 3,000 cases of champagne a year, with grapes exclusively from Grand Cru vineyards. He vinifies a portion of the wines in barrel, and avoids malolactic for all of his champagnes in order to preserve finesse and freshness. Pehu's non-vintage Sélection is both Pinot Noir and Chardonnay from the northern Montagne de Reims, while the ripe, floral Blanc de Blancs is pure Le Mesnil. Finest of all is the vintage brut, which combines Verzenay and Verzy Pinot Noir with Le Mesnil Chardonnay.

7 rue de la gare, 51360 Verzenay
www.champagne-pehu-simonet.com

Perrier-Jouët Epernay

Founded in 1811, this Epernay house is renowned for its Belle Epoque bottle, which was first created in 1902 and is used today for the house's prestige cuvée, which was launched in 1969. The Perrier-Jouët style is one of extreme delicacy, as exemplified by its citrussy, light-bodied non-vintage Grand Brut. The Belle Epoque, called Fleur de Champagne in the US, maintains the same delicate style, while adding more complexity and finesse. Even the house's rosé champagnes are made in an unusually discreet and light-bodied style.

26 avenue de Champagne, Epernay
www.perrier-jouet.com

Philippe Gonet Côte des Blancs

This well known estate is located in Le Mesnil-sur-Oger, but they also have vines in several different sectors of the Champagne appellation. Gonet's three top *cuvées* are all pure Mesnil Blanc de Blancs, while the non-vintage Blanc de Blancs is a blend of Chardonnay from Mesnil and Montgueux, in the Aube. The Réserve Brut is made largely from red grapes. At the top of the range is the vintage-dated Belemnita, a chalky, racy Blanc de Blancs from old vines in Le Mesnil.

1 rue de la Brèche d'Oger, 51190 Le Mesnil-sur-Oger
www.champagne-philippe-gonet.com

Philipponnat Grande Vallée

Since taking over in 1999, Charles Philipponnat has transformed this house, building a new winery in Mareuil-sur-Aÿ, increasing the percentage of barrel-fermented wine, and lowering dosage levels. The Clos des Goisses, Philipponnat's legendary single-vineyard champagne, has always been one of the appellation's finest wines, but the rest of the range has now improved considerably. The Cuvée 1522 is a vintage-dated extra brut of rare personality and expression, and the rosé version is also outstanding. The vintage brut is growing deeper and more confident, while the non-vintage Royale Réserve is finer and more complex than ever before.

13 rue du Pont, 51160 Mareuil-sur-Aÿ
www.philipponnat.com

PIPER-HEIDSIECK
PIPER-HEIDSIECK'S PRESTIGE CUVEE IS A
SUBTLE, DELICATELY COMPLEX CHAMPAGNE
THAT IS AS STRIKING AS ITS PACKAGE

ROGER POUILLON
FLEUR DE MAREUIL IS 50% CHARDONNAY
AND 50% PINOT NOIR, VINIFIED IN BARREL

Pierre Brigandat Aube

Bertrand Brigandat took over from his father Pierre
in 2001 and has slowly been putting a personal stamp
on the wines of this grower-estate, improving the
viticulture and refining the wines. As is typical of this
area in the Aube, most of Brigandat's champagnes
are pure Pinot Noir, such as the round, fruity non-
vintage brut or the boldly fragrant *saignée* rosé.
Their Dentelles & Crinolines blends Pinot Noir from
Brigandat's oldest vines with 30% Chardonnay,
resulting in added finesse and complexity.

25 Grande Rue, 10340 Channes
03 25 29 33 49

Pierre Callot Côte des Blancs

Sixth-generation wine-grower Thierry Callot manages
this Côte des Blancs estate, growing vines in Avize as
well as in the Grand Cru villages of Cramant and
Chouilly. Callot's top wine is the Clos Jacquin, a single-
vineyard champagne from a clay parcel on a hillside in
Avize. The Clos Jacquin is expansive and broad, its
richness amplified by aging in oak barrels. It contrasts
with Pierre Callot's vintage brut, made from old vines in
a chalky parcel in Avize: ripe and forward in fruit, it also
retains a distinct liveliness and finesse.

100 avenue Jean-Jaurès, 51190 Avize
03 26 57 51 57

Pierre Gimonnet Côte des Blancs

Pierre Gimonnet founded this well known Côte des
Blancs estate in 1935 and today it is managed by his
grandsons, Didier and Olivier Gimonnet. All of
Gimonnet's champagnes are Blanc de Blancs, except
for the Paradoxe, which includes Pinot Noir from Aÿ and
Mareuil, and most blend Chardonnay from the villages
of Cuis, Cramant, and Chouilly in varying proportions.
Unusually, Pierre Gimonnet produces no fewer than six
different vintage champagnes, from the fresh, forward
Gastronome to the resonant and complex Spécial Club.
The Oenophile is an excellent *non-dosé* champagne,
which is aged for five years on the lees.

1 rue de la République, 51530 Cuis
www.champagne-gimonnet.com

Pierre Moncuit Côte des Blancs

Nicole Moncuit makes precise, finely delineated
champagnes from 12 acres (5ha) in the Sézanne and
37 acres (15ha) in Le Mesnil-sur-Oger. Unusually,
Moncuit uses no reserve wines, meaning that even
the "non-vintage" champagnes are made from a single
harvest. The Cuvée Hugues de Coulmet comes from the
Sézanne, while the Cuvée Pierre Moncuit-Delos and the
vintage-dated wines are pure Le Mesnil. At the top of
the range is the vibrant, powerful Cuvée Nicole Moncuit,
which is made from 90-year-old vines in Les Chétillons,
one of Le Mesnil's finest vineyards.

11 rue Persault Maheu, 51190 Le Mesnil-sur-Oger
www.pierre-moncuit.fr

Pierre Péters Côte des Blancs

Rodolphe Péters is now at the helm of this renowned
Côte des Blancs estate, making elegant and finely-
tuned champagnes from the Grand Cru villages of
Le Mesnil, Oger, Avize, and Cramant. The Cuvée de
Réserve is a consistently complex and harmonious
non-vintage brut, while the vintage champagne is
richer and more highly structured. A portion of the
vintage blend is released earlier as an extra brut
champagne, which demonstrates excellent balance
and finesse. Finest of all the Pierre Péters wines is
the Cuvée Spéciale, which is made from old vines
in the Chétillons vineyard in Le Mesnil.

26 rue des Lombards, 51190 Le Mesnil-sur-Oger
www.champagne-peters.com

Piper-Heidsieck Reims

Although they make radically different styles of
champagne, Piper-Heidsieck and Charles Heidsieck
are both owned by the same parent company, with
chef de cave Régis Camus overseeing both houses.
The Piper style is almost diametrically opposed to
that of Charles Heidsieck: light, lively, and fresh,
Piper-Heidsieck champagnes emphasize delicacy
and vivacity. While the house is best known for its
non-vintage brut, the vintage-dated champagne is
a significant step up in terms of quality. Best of all
though, is the vintage-dated Rare, which is a complex,
finely balanced prestige cuvée.

12 allée du Vignoble, 51100 Reims
www.piper-heidsieck.com

Ployez-Jacquemart Montagne de Reims

Founded in 1930 by Marcel Ployez and Yvonne
Jacquemart, this small house is now in the hands of
their granddaughter, Laurence Ployez. The Ployez-
Jacquemart style contrasts delicate fruit flavors with
the richness of lees aging, and the elegance of its
champagnes are emphasized by their low dosages.
The style seems to find its full expression in the silky,
fragrant non-vintage rosé, which demonstrates a terrific
balance and finesse. Even more complex is the vintage-
dated Cuvée Liesse d'Harbonville, a beautiful, sleek,
and subtly refined prestige cuvée.

8 rue Astoin, 51500 Ludes
www.ployez-jacquemart.fr

Pol Roger Epernay

One of Champagne's best-known houses, Pol Roger
produces substantial, richly flavored champagnes. The
Brut Réserve is a world-famous non-vintage brut, yet
arguably even better is the Pure, a *non-dosé* champagne
made from a slightly different blend. The Blanc de Blancs
combines the chalky finesse of the Côte des Blanc with
the mouthfilling depth of the Pol Roger style, while the
vintage brut is complex and long-lived. Pol Roger is
famous for being the preferred champagne of Winston
Churchill, and in turn, the house named its prestige
cuvée after him, created in the 1975 vintage.

1 rue Henri Lelarge, 51206 Epernay
www.polroger.com

Pommery Reims

Founded in 1836, this house owes its reputation to Madame
Louise Pommery, who established the current cellars in
Reims and created a strong export market for her wines. By
the time of her death in 1890, it was achieving annual sales
of over 160,000 cases. Thierry Gasco has been *chef de cave*
here since 1992, making champagnes that focus on

freshness and delicacy, rather than power. The Apanage Rosé is a classic example of the house style, while Cuvée Louise Brut shows an elegant and refined complexity.

5 place du Général Gouraud, 51100 Reims
www.pommery.com

Prin Père et Fils Côte des Blancs
Daniel Prin established this small house in 1977 and today it produces about 12,500 cases a year. In addition to the house's own 17 acres (7ha) of vines, Prin Père et Fils also works another 44.5 acres (18ha) that belong to family and friends. The Prin style relies heavily on Chardonnay, and while none of Prin's wines go through malolactic, they are rarely austere, being marked by old, ripe flavors. The Brut Prestige is luscious and rich, while the 6e Sens is a sleekly focused Blanc de Blancs.

28 rue Ernest Vallé, 51190 Avize
www.champagneprin.fr

Raymond Boulard/Francis Boulard & Fille Montagne de Reims
The Raymond Boulard estate comprised 25 acres (10ha) of vines, located across the Marne and Aisne. As of early 2010, Boulard's three children have divided the estate: Francis Boulard, who previously made the Raymond Boulard wines, has set up his own label along with his daughter Delphine. Boulard's winery is in Cauroy-lès-Hermonville, north of Reims, and some of his finest wines come from this sector, such as the old vine Blanc des Blancs and the vividly expressive single-vineyard Les Rachais. From closer to the heart of the Mantagne de Reims, the Grand Cru Mailly is also one of the standouts of the cellar.

Route Nationale 44, 51220 Cauroy les Hermonville
www.champagne-boulard.fr

René Geoffroy Grande Vallée
The Geoffroys are well known for their wines from Cumières, but in 2008, the estate moved to a larger cellar in Aÿ. Despite the move, Jean-Baptiste Geoffroy's champagnes remain as mouthfilling and extroverted as ever, being made with sustainably grown grapes and separate vinification of all parcels. The non-vintage Expression is broad and fragrant, based on Pinto Meunier, and the same wine is also superb as a *non-dosé*, called Pureté. Empreinte is predominantly Pinot Noir, while Volupté is primarily Chardonnay—both are pure Cumières. Geoffroy also makes excellent red wine from Cumières, as well as a deliciously exuberant rosé.

150 rue du Bois des Jots, 51480 Cumières
www.champagne-geoffroy.com

René-Henri Coutier Montagne de Reims
René Coutier makes roughly 4,000 cases a year of boldly flavored champagnes that express the ripe, vigorous character of Ambonnay. Both the non-vintage Brut Tradition and the non-vintage rosé are packed with plenty of red fruit aroma, backed by Ambonnay's chalky minerality. The vintage-dated Cuvée Henri III is made of pure Pinot Noir, half of which is aged in barrique. It is the classic vintage brut, however, that is often the top wine of the cellar, showing a velvety depth and elegant harmony.

7 rue Henri III, 51150 Ambonnay
03 26 57 02 55

SALON
THE BRUT 1997 WAS THE 36TH VINTAGE
CHAMPAGNE TO BE RELEASED BY SALON

POL ROGER
MOST FAMOUSLY, POL ROGER WAS WINSTON
CHURCHILL'S FAVORITE CHAMPAGNE

Roger Pouillon et Fils Grande Vallée
Fabrice and Elodie Pouillon run this 37 acre (15ha) Mareuil estate, vinifying parcels separately and fermenting a portion of their wines in barrel with indigenous yeasts. Pouillon et Fil's champagnes are ripe and rich, with a full-bodied depth. In particular, Fleur de Mareuil is a creamy, opulent champagne that is vinified entirely in barrel, while the boldly-flavored Brut Vigneron is also a pure Mareuil champagne, but made in a solera system. Recently, they have created an unusual *cuvée*, 2Xoz, that has no added sugar—the second fermentation is performed with residual sugar that is obtained from extremely ripe grapes.

3 rue de la Couple, 51160 Mareuil-sur-Aÿ
www.champagne-pouillon.com

Ruinart Reims
Ruinart is the oldest champagne-producing house in the region, having been making sparkling wines here since 1729. Frédéric Panaïotis is in charge of the cellars today, making fresh, lively champagnes. Chardonnay plays a prominent role in the house style, and Ruinart's non-vintage Blanc de Blancs is one of the house's best-known wines. The superb prestige cuvée, Dom Ruinart, is also made of pure Chardonnay, about a third of which, unusually, comes from the Montagne de Reims. The Dom Ruinart rosé is also outstanding.

4 rue des Crayères, Reims
www.ruinart.com

Sadi Malot Montagne de Reims
Franck Malot runs this 25 acre (10ha) estate in Villers-Marmery, a Montagne de Reims village known for its Chardonnay. Sadi Malot's non-vintage Carte Blanche contains some Pinot Noir, and red wine from Pinot Noir is also used to make the rosé, but otherwise Malot's champagnes are all Blanc de Blancs. The Cuvée de Réserve is earthy and broad, while the Vieille Réserve, which is fermented in cement vats, is a finer and more vinous wine. The vintage-dated Cuvée SM is another step up in class, showing a creamy texture and chalky complexity.

35 rue Pasteur, 51380 Villers-Marmery
03 26 97 90 48

Salon Côte des Blancs
Widely regarded as the quintessential Blanc de Blancs, Salon was created in 1911 for the private consumption of Eugène-Aimé Salon, the house's founder. It was commercially released in 1921. The house is unique in Champagne in that it has only ever produced one wine, made exclusively from the village of Le Mesnil-sur-Oger and only in the best vintages. There have been just 36 vintages made prior to the current 1999 release. Salon is a racy and elegantly complex champagne that requires a good deal of aging. It generally shows its best at about 20 years of age.

5–7 rue de la Brèche d'Oger, 51190 Le Mesnil-sur-Oger
www.champagnesalon.com

VOUETTE ET SORBEE
THE VINOUS, INTENSELY-FLAVORED SAIGNEE
DE SORBEE IS ONE OF CHAMPAGNE'S
MOST ORIGINAL WINES

Serge Mathieu Aube

Serge Mathieu began bottling champagne in 1970, and today his daughter, Isabelle, and son-in-law, Michel Jacob, are in charge of this Avirey-Lingey estate. They make champagnes that are are fruity and roundly ripe, typical of the Aube, and Jacob places a particularly high emphasis on sustainable viticulture. Serge Mathieu's non-vintage Brut Tradition is a Blanc de Noirs, while the amply-flavored Brut Prestige contains some Chardonnay. The Brut Select, made mostly from Chardonnay, is finer in tone, but the vintage brut is possibly the best of all and is made entirely from Pinot Noir.

6 rue des Vignes, 10340 Avirey-Lingey
www.champagne-serge-mathieu.fr

Taittinger Reims

With a rich and colorful history that dates back to 1734, Taittinger is one of Champagne's most famous houses, and its traditional chalk mine cellars are renowned as being some of the most beautiful in the region. The Tattinger vines cover 712 acres (288ha) and are distributed over 34 different vineyards. As the Taittinger style emphasizes finesse over richness, it is easy to see why the finest wine in the cellar is a Blanc de Blancs: the Comtes de Champagne is a prestige cuvée of exceptional refinement and harmony that is capable of a detailed complexity with sufficient age. Its rosé counterpart is no less elegant, and will also reward patience if left in the cellar.

9 Place Saint-Nicaise, 51100 Reims
www.taittinger.com

Tarlant Vallée de la Marne

Benoît Tarlant and his father Jean-Mary make distinctive, amply flavored champagnes that strongly express their sector of the Vallée de la Marne. The Brut Zero is a *non-dosé* of uncommon harmony and finesse, while the vintage brut is reliably full of character. Tarlant's top champagnes are highly terroir-specific: La Vigne d'Antan is a vibrantly expressive Blanc de Blancs that is made from an old parcel of ungrafted vines, while La Vigne d'Or is a single-vineyard champagne made from Pinot Meunier vines that were planted in 1947. Cuvée Louis is a richly complex prestige cuvée from the chalky vineyard of Les Crayons.

51480 Oeuilly/Epernay
www.tarlant.com

Thierry Triolet Côte de Sézanne

At the southern end of the Côte de Sézanne, Thierry Triolet farms 27 acres (11ha) that are largely planted with Chardonnay vines. The chalky, south-facing slopes here produce unusually ripe and accessible wines that show well in their youth, such as Thierry Triolet's non-vintage brut, which is a blend of all three grape varieties, or his Grande Réserve, which is made exclusively from Chardonnay vines. The vintage-dated Les Vieilles Vignes comes from Triolet's oldest Chardonnay vines. It shows the same plush character as the Grande Réserve, while adding more depth and complexity to it.

22 rue des Pressoirs, 51260 Bethon
www.champagne-triolet.com

Ulysse Collin Côte de Sézanne

After recently taking over his family's vines, Olivier Collin began making champagne in the 2004 vintage, which was characterized by natural viticulture, indigenous yeast fermentation, and vinification in secondhand barrels. In his first two vintages, Collin made small quantities of only one wine, a Blanc de Blancs from a vineyard called Les Perrières. The 2004 was a particularly impressive debut, showing an uncommon vitality and complexity of character and in 2006, Collin bottled a second single-vineyard champagne, a ripe and powerful Blanc de Noirs. From 2008, another parcel of Chardonnay has also been bottled. ★ **Rising star**

21 rue des Vignerons, 51270 Congy
03 26 52 46 62

Varnier-Fannière Côte des Blancs

Denis Varnier is at the helm of this small grower-estate in Avize. He makes concentrated, energetic champagnes exclusively from Grand Cru vines. Varnier's non-vintage Blanc de Blancs demonstrates an uncommon depth, while the Cuvée Jean Fannière Origine derives extra complexity from older vines and longer lees aging. The Grand Vintage is a prestige cuvée made from Varnier-Fannière's oldest vines, which shows a vibrant structure and depth. It is worth noting, however, that the Cuvée St-Denis Brut, which is made from a single parcel of 70-year-old vines in Avize, is often equally as fine as the Grand Vintage, with a vivid, chalky intensity.

23 Rempart du Midi, 51190 Avize
www.varnier-fanniere.com

Vazart-Coquart Côte des Blancs

Jean-Pierre Vazart's 27 acres (11ha) of vines are all located in the Grand Cru of Chouilly. The round, ripe character of his Chardonnay-based champagnes is typical of this village's terroir. The finest wine of the cellar is the vintage-dated Cuvée Club, which is made from the Vazart-Coquart's best parcels and bottled with cork for its second fermentation. The estate bottles the same blend under capsule and releases it slightly earlier to make the Grand Bouquet. The unusual Spécial Foie Gras is a sec champagne that averages 10 years of age.

6 rue des Partelaines, 51530 Chouilly
www.champagnevazartcoquart.com

JL Vergnon Côte des Blancs

This Le Mesnil estate has been transformed since the arrival of cellarmaster Christophe Constant in 2002. Vergnon's 12 acres (5ha) of vines are all in the southern Côte des Blancs and, despite this area's naturally high acidity, Constant has managed to avoid malolactic and has used low levels of dosage, thanks to harvesting unusually ripe grapes. JL Vergon's racy, chalky non-vintage brut and extra brut are both excellent and the vintage-dated Cuvée Confidence, made from old vines in Le Mesnil, promises to become one of the village's top wines. ★ **Rising star**

1 Grande Rue, 51190 Le Mesnil-sur-Oger
www.champagne-jl-vergnon.com

TAITTINGER
COMTES DE CHAMPAGNE IS A STYLISH
AND COMPLEX PRESTIGE CUVEE

Veuve Clicquot Reims

The widow Clicquot is one of Champagne's most legendary personalities. She played a major part in the introduction of the riddling table—the table that holds the bottles upside down to let the sediment settle at the top so that it can be drawn off, leaving a clear wine. Riddling tables are still used today. Madame Clicquot also achieved worldwide renown for her house in the 19th century, and Veuve Clicquot is equally as prominent today, with its non-vintage Yellow Label currently enjoying immense popularity. The vintage champagnes are a step up in class and finesse, and La Grande Dame is a prestige cuvée with a rich character and complexity. Often the finest of Clicquot's wines are the vintage and La Grande Dame rosés, which demonstrate a marvelous harmony, sophistication, and longevity.

1 place des Droits de l'Homme, 51100 Reims
www.veuve-clicquot.com

Veuve Fourny & Fils Côte des Blancs

Emmanuel Fourny and his brother Charles-Henry run this prominent estate in Vertus, supplementing their 21 acres (8.5ha) of vines with additional purchases from friends and family. All Veuve Fourny champagnes are pure Vertus, although the estate's wines tend to be richer in body than other producers in the village, even the chalky brut nature and the fragrant non-vintage Blanc de Blancs. A portion of the wines are vinified in barrel, and two *cuvées* are made entirely in wood: the ripe, concentrated R de Veuve Fourny and the rare Clos Faubourg Notre Dame, a single-vineyard champagne of intense personality.

Rue du Mesnil, 51130 Vertus
www.champagne-veuve-fourny.com

Vilmart & Cie Montagne de Reims

Laurent Champs has been in charge of this outstanding grower-estate since 1990, making champagnes of highly distinctive personality and exceptional class and introducing the practice of new oak aging for the top *cuvées*. The Vilmart & Cie estate consists of 27 acres (11ha) of vineyards that are planted with 60% Chardonnay, 37% Pinot Noir, and 3% Pinot Meunier. The vineyards are all farmed sustainably and certified organic. The wines are vinified in wood without malolactic: large oak *foudres* are used for the non-vintage Grand Réserve and Grand Cellier, while the vintage-dated Grand Cellier d'Or is made in barriques or 158.5-gallon (600-liter) *demi-muids*. The two prestige cuvées, Cuvée Création and Coeur de Cuvée, are vinified entirely in barrique, and both are wines of great complexity and refinement.

5 rue des Gravières, 51500 Rilly-la-Montagne
www.champagnevilmart.com

Voirin-Jumel Côte des Blancs

This grower-estate in Cramant makes lively, racy champagnes, largely from Grand Cru villages in the Côte des Blancs. While Voirin-Jumel is well known for the Cuvée 555, a Grand Cru Blanc de Blancs fermented entirely in barrique, its other Blancs de Blancs, one from the village of Vertus and the other blended from several Grands Crus, can show more classic finesse and minerality. The Voirins also have some Pinot Noir vines in Aÿ and Mareuil-sur-Aÿ, used in the non-vintage Tradition and the rosé.

555 rue de la Libération, 51530 Cramant
www.champagne-voirin-jumel.com

Vouette et Sorbée Aube

One of Champagne's most passionate advocates of biodynamic viticulture, Bertrand Gautherot has been tending vines at this Aube estate since 1986, but it wasn't until 2001 that he began to actually make champagne. Today, his wines have achieved near-cult status, although with an annual production of only 30,000 bottles, they are not always easy to obtain. The entry level Fidèle is typical of the estate's style, vinified entirely in oak and released without dosage. Blanc d'Argile is a powerfully expressive Blanc de Blancs, while the superb Saignée de Sorbée is one of Champagne's most original rosés. ★ Rising star

8 rue de Vaux, 10110 Buxières-sur-Arce
www.vouette-et-sorbee.com

Yves Ruffin Grande Vallée

Yves Ruffin owns 7.5 acres (3ha) in the villages of Avenay Val d'Or and Tauxières, and has practiced strictly organic viticulture ever since he founded his estate in 1970. All of the wines are fermented in old wood—either large oak *foudres* or secondhand barriques. Unusually, Ruffin's extra brut, which is made predominantly from Chardonnay, is vinified in a *foudre* that is made from acacia wood rather than traditional oak. The vintage-dated Cuvée Précieuse is also largely Chardonnay, while the non-vintage brut is more balanced between Chardonnay and Pinot Noir.

6 boulevard Jules Ferry, 51160 Avenay Val d'Or
www.champagne-yves-ruffin.fr

LOWERING THE DOSAGE

In recent years, there has been a significant growth in the number of extra brut and *non-dosé* champagnes—those that receive little or no dosage of sugar before release. Champagne is typically given a dosage to balance its high acidity, to bring out more complex fruit flavors, and to increase its longevity. Aided by a changing climate and advances in viticulture, however, growers are beginning to harvest riper grapes that allow them to make more forward and more balanced wines for earlier drinking. Unfortunately, not all *non-dosé* champagnes are successful in harmonizing their components, and in the rush to keep up with fashion, some producers are releasing imbalanced and overly acidic wines. The finest examples are capable of remarkable purity and character, particularly those that are driven by conscientious and naturally-oriented viticulture. In essence, these growers are creating an entirely new style of champagne.

SOUTHWEST FRANCE

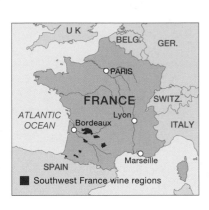

Southwest France wine regions

Covering 18 appellations and 19 Vins de Pays over 12 regional areas, Southwest France is a fascinating, little-known treasure trove for wines. The area stretches from Bergerac, Gascony, and Cahors to Toulouse and neighboring Fronton; and also includes the hillside vines of Irouléguy and Béarn, approaching the Spanish border. The area contains over 20 indigenous grape varieties, the highest number in France. Some, such as Cabernet Franc, have been known internationally for some time, while others have only recently gained world status, such as Malbec (from Cahors, but popular in Argentina) and Tannat (from Madiran, but now known in Uruguay). Still others are seen only on local wine labels—Fer Servadou, la Négrette, Odenc, and Prunelard.

Major grapes

 Reds

Cabernet Franc

Cabernet Sauvignon

Duras

Fer Servadou

Malbec

Négrette

Syrah

Tannat

 Whites

Colombard

Gros Manseng

Loin de l'Oeil

Mauzac

Odenc

Petit Manseng

Sauvignon Blanc

Sémillon

Vintages

2009
Hot weather meant alcohol rose quickly. Some great wines.

2008
Some good wines, but needed careful vineyard management.

2007
A more successful year than much of the rest of France.

2006
Some classic wines, with reds even better than whites.

2005
Not as good as previous years.

2004
Classic wines with some variation. Very good whites.

The total area of vineyards in Southwest France is 113,700 acres (46,000ha), but because less than 20% of the wine is drunk outside of France, most of the regional names in the area are unfamiliar to many international wine drinkers. The appellations of Southwest France are Gaillac, Fronton, Madiran, St-Mont, Jurançon, Coteaux du Quercy, Tursan, Brulhois, Pacherenc du Vic-Bilh, Marcillac, Côtes de Millau, Lavilledieu, Entraygues, Estaing, Floc de Gascogne, Cahors, Irouléguy, and St-Sardos. AC Bergerac is also increasingly included in Southwest France. The most important Vins de Pays include Côtes de Gascogne and Côtes du Tarn.

The size of Southwest France makes it difficult to generalize about wine styles, but there are some rules to follow when trying to make sense of this area. For white wine, the Côtes de Gascogne is France's largest producer of white Vin de Pays. Unusually for this part of France, 80% of Côtes de Gascogne is exported, which indicates how easy it is to find it. The labels usually have the grape variety clearly displayed on them, and they are consumer-friendly, easy-drinking social wines. Richer, more complex whites are found in Jurançon and Pacherenc du Vic-Bilh. The sweet wines of Jurançon are not made through noble rot, like Sauternes, but by *passerillage*, where late-harvested grapes are left to raisin on the vine. Tiny pockets of this sweet wine are increasingly seen in Irouléguy. It is made from the same grapes as Jurançon, but has a delicacy and freshness that the altitude of the area brings.

The red wines of Southwest France have more family characteristics in common. Many have ancient origins, but suffered from near extinction during phylloxera and have experienced a renaissance in the past decade. The most

significant red appellations are Bergerac, Cahors, and Madiran. Of the three, Bergerac is the largest, with 31,630 acres (12,800ha) covering 9% of Southwest France, and producing 8% of its wine. It is the closest in geography, and grape varieties, to Bordeaux, which lies just to the west—Bergerac is increasingly defining itself as part of Southwest France, and not as the little brother of Bordeaux.

Cahors has also re-established its own distinct identity over the past decade. It was once a rival to Bordeaux in terms of fame, but its vineyards were abandoned for many years and only revived in the 1970s and 1980s (it was awarded its AC Cahors in 1971). Today, it is defined by the Malbec grape, which is known here as Côt or Auxerrois, and is becoming an exciting alternative to Argentine Malbecs. In style, it is a drier and more structured wine, with greater natural acidity than the richer, sweeter Argentine examples. The best Cahors Malbecs ensure that the grapes are picked when they are at their full maturity and that the tannins are carefully softened to ensure the overall impression of plump, rather than austere, fruits.

The other red wine regions in Southwest France have also chosen to develop their own styles, rather than following the easier route of famous international styles. Madiran, which is 3,114 acres (1,260ha), has worked hard on softening the Tannat grape, while 5,931 acre (2,400ha) Fronton has done the same with Négrette. Gaillac, which has 6,178 acres (2,500ha) of vines, has Braucol and Duras, and Marcillac (the smallest appellation of the Southwest, with just 420 acres/170ha of vines) has Fer Servadou.

The wines of Southwest France are unpretentious, authentic, and just rustic enough to taste as if they contain the heart and soul of the region.

Chapelle Lenclos Madiran

If it was not for the inspired thinking and hard work of Patrick Ducourneau at this 37 acre (15ha) estate, Madiran wines would have remained almost unapproachably tannic, owing to the burly Tannat grape. He developed the technique of micro-oxygenation—the release of tiny bubbles of oxygen, either during fermentation or afterward—that prevents reduction and also softens tannins and fixes color. The estate itself is called Domaine Mouréou, with Chapelle Lenclos being their most famous wine. Today it is run by Ducourneau's cousins, while he concentrates on consulting and further research. You cannot accuse them of taming the life out of this 100% Tannat—it is still a brawny, swaggering wine, full of smoky black cherries and with a meaty texture—but there is also a softness to the tannins that is highly seductive.

Maumusson-Laguian, Gers
www.famillelaplace.com

Château d'Aydie Madiran

Frédéric Laplace was one of the first winemakers in the appellation to bottle a Madiran wine under his own château name. Today, his grandchildren—Jean-Luc, François, Bernard, and Marie—are in charge, splitting the running of the 86 acre (35ha) estate between the four of them. The excellent Château d'Aydie is 100% Tannat, with well-rounded tannins that are smoother than many in this appellation. This is undoubtedly due to micro-oxygenation—as cousins of the man who instigated the technique, Patrick Ducourneau, they could not help but employ his methods. They also produce a lighter, even less tannic, wine called Cuvée Autour du Fruit, and make a good-quality Pacherenc dry white with 40% Gros Manseng and 60% Petit Manseng.

Vignoble Laplace, 64330 Aydie
www.famillelaplace.com

Château Bellevue La Forêt Fronton

This estate was created in 1974 by the Germain family. Today, it covers 277 acres (112ha) of vines, which makes it the largest vineyard, in one continuous plot, in Southwest France. Since 2008, Irish-born Philip Grant has been the owner, putting his considerable business experience to good use in selling the wines and producing 900,000 bottles a year. Châteaux Bellevue La Forêt makes just red and rosé wines. The 50% Négrette grape in the classic red (along with 35% Cabernet Franc and Cabernet Sauvignon, and 15% Syrah) makes muscular, savory-style red wines that have good levels of spice. Equally interesting is the Imprévu, a 100% Cabernet Franc.

5580 route de Grisolles, 3169 Fronton
www.chateaubellevuelaforet.com

Château du Bloy Bergerac

It has been nearly a decade since business partners Olivier Lambert and Bertrand Lepoittevin-Dubost gave up their jobs in law and IT to buy a 47 acre (19ha) wine estate in Bergerac. All of their vines are farmed sustainably, and they are well on their way toward being certified organic. Their Sirius red (Merlot with Cabernet Franc and Cabernet Sauvignon) has an attractively steady color, backed up by cocoa and damson flavors and a gentle waft of oak. The Lilia Montravel white is

CHATEAU CANTELAUZE
LOW TEMPERATURE WINEMAKING ENSURES
BLACK CHERRY AND RASPBERRY FLAVORS

CHATEAU DU CEDRE
THIS 100% VIOGNIER OFFERS EASY DRINKING
WITH A BITE FROM A TOUCH OF OAK

made in stainless steel, but lees-stirring gives it plenty of body. Cuvée Le Bloy red and white are the prestige wines, fermented in barrel and from the oldest vines.

Le Blois, 24230 Bonneville
05 53 22 47 87

Château Bru-Baché Jurançon

One of the key differences in taste between a Sauternes and a Jurançon sweet wine is that the latter has a touch less stickiness. The nose is often just as rich and full, but on the palate there is excellent acidity and often an almost bone-dry finish. Château Bru-Baché, owned by Claude Loustalot, is a wonderful example of this. The 25 acre (10ha) vineyard is planted to 75% Petit Manseng and 25% Gros Manseng, farmed organically (certified for the 2010 vintage), and is now increasingly involving biodynamics. Try La Quintessance, alongside L'Eminence, to understand what a 100% Petit Manseng can achieve—it is made about every other year. Jurançon Sec is 100% Gros Manseng, with traces of the toffee and hazelnut flavors of a sweet wine, but crisped up to a bracing finish.

Rue Baradat, 64360 Monein
05 59 21 36 34

Château Cantelauze Cahors

Fresh from his own family estate in Champagne, Lauren Nominé took ownership of this 37 acre (15ha) estate in 2001. To steer away from heavy tannins, Nominé picks largely by hand into small crates and keeps the bunches intact. The grapes then undergo a cold soak and the fermentation takes place in stainless steel, with the temperature kept low at 75–82°F (24–28°C). Try Le Cotagé, which is 100% Malbec, and L'Abreuvoir, which is again pure Malbec, but slightly fruitier and more approachable when young.

Route de Vire sur Lot, 46700 Duravel
www.cantelauze.com

Château du Cèdre Cahors

This estate has been the leading light of Cahors for some time, even before the appellation began its edge back into the limelight. It has been run by brothers Pascal and Jean-Marc Verhaeghe since 1988, and they like to describe their winemaking as "a Burgundian philosophy married with a Bordeaux vinification." The Cèdre Blanc is a 100% Viognier, cropped very low and aged partly in oak, with lees-stirring, giving rich apricot flavors. Le Cèdre is a 100% Malbec, aged in 80% new oak, and bottled unfined and unfiltered—a truly delicious wine, but not for the faint-hearted. The property also produces Le Prestige (90% Malbec, 5% Tannat, and 5% Merlot), and GC, another 100% Malbec that turns up the heat even more by using old vines, low cropping, long maceration, and 24 months barrel aging. There is also a good rosé and a Vins du Pays du Lot Merlot.

Bru, 46700 Vire-sur-Lot
www.chateauducedre.com

Château de Chambert Cahors

It is easy to have confidence that Philippe Lejeune, the enthusiastic owner of Château de Chambert, is going to bring about big changes at this Cahors property, which had slipped under the radar until he bought it in 2007.

CHATEAU DE LA JAUBERTIE
THIS QUALITY BERGERAC WINE SHOWS CRISP, WELL-DEFINED, RED FRUIT FLAVORS

Lejeune has enlisted the help of Bordeaux enologist Stéphane Dérénoncourt and invested a large amount of money in restructuring the vineyard (he has taken out all the Tannat grapes), new oak barrels, cellar equipment, and general restoration of the property itself. The estate is now entirely biodynamic and, by uprooting under-performing plots, it has been brought down in size to 148 acres (60ha). As a result of all this effort, the flavor profile of the wine has definitely improved, with an intense spiciness, and an elegance that many Cahors wines lack. The range of wines has also been reduced to the Grand Vin (100% Malbec), Château de Chambert (85% Malbec/15% Merlot), Gourmand Rosé, and an interesting Malbec dessert wine called Rogomme. ★ Rising star

Les Hauts Coteaux, 46700 Floressas
www.chambert.com

Château Clément Termes Gaillac
Among the many interesting wines found in Southwest France is the lightly sparkling Gaillac Blanc Perlé. It uses regional grapes, usually Mauzac, and the wine is bottled under slight pressure to keep in a gentle fizz from the natural carbon dioxide. Château Clément Termes makes a particularly refreshing and elegant version that is relatively light in alcohol and full of gentle fig and walnut flavors. The estate itself dates back to 1860 and is located on a ridge above the pretty town of Lisle-sur-Tarn. Descendants of the founder are still in charge—Olivier David is the director and his sister Caroline heads up sales. In total, the 198 acres (80ha) are planted to Braucol, Duras, Sauvignon Blanc, and Loin de l'Oeil, along with the more international varieties of Cabernet Sauvignon and Merlot.

Les Fortis RD 18, 81310 Lisle-sur-Tarn
www.clement-termes.com

Château La Colline Bergerac
There are a few Englishmen (and women) who have moved into the Bergerac appellation and made wines worthy of note; Charles Martin, at this 44.5 acre (18ha) estate is one of them. He earned his French winemaking spurs at Domaine de la Jaubertie with Hugh Ryman, after picking up a few tips in Napa, New Zealand, and Australia. Martin's winemaking techniques take a mix of Old and New World: the use of inert gas to protect against damaging oxidation after picking, together with high-density plantation and grass growing between the rows to encourage root growth. His sweet wine is the brilliantly named Confit de la Colline, a 100% Sémillon that is like spreading marmalade on your tongue. For the reds he concentrates on Merlot, which is vinified in large open vats and aged in oak barrels. The Carminé has up to 95% Merlot and 5% Cabernet Sauvignon, and is bottled unfiltered.

Les Combes, 24240 Thénac en Dordogne
www.la-colline.com

Château La Colombière Fronton
Philippe and Diane Cauvin have been farming this 42 acre (17ha) estate biodynamically since 2005. They produce the charming Vin Gris, a rosé wine that is a mix of Négrette and Gamay, and the excellent Vinum, a 100% Négrette that is vinified to favor the fruit. The Négrette grape is spicy and licorice in character, but it needs to be handled carefully to avoid the tannins becoming too clunky. The Cauvins clearly know what they are doing with their Cuvée Coste Rouge, which is a 100% unoaked Négrette and made with low-yield viticulture.

190 route de Vacquiers, 31620 Villaudric
www.chateaulacolombiere.com

Château Coutinel Fronton
The Arbeau family have been associated with this estate since the early 20th century. Today, Gérard Arbeau is in charge of what has grown into a large family producer and merchant business. Château Coutinel covers 109 acres (44ha) and is planted to 50% Négrette and a number of other varieties: Cabernet Sauvignon, Cabernet Franc, Gamay, Syrah, Fer Servadou, Malbec, Mérille, and Merlot. The headiest, most crowd-pleasing wine is the Elixir Fût de Chêne, which is full of spicy blackberry aromas with a burnt crumble edge from 12 months of oak aging.

82370 Labastide Saint-Pierre
www.arbau.com

Château Eugénie Cahors
Three members of the Couture family are in charge here: father Claude, son and winemaker Jerôme, and nephew Vincent. Together they work 96 acres (39ha) that are planted to 78% Malbec, 17% Merlot, and 5% Tannat, along with 15 acres (6ha) of Chardonnay and Chenin Blanc that are bottled under Vins de Pays du Lot. Organic and biodynamic practices are slowly, but surely, being adopted. Look out for Cuvée Réservée de l'Aïeul, a robust, traditional-style Cahors mix of Malbec and Tannat. The Haute Collection, an excellent pure Malbec from old vines that are cropped low and softened with fermentation in barrel and a little micro-oxygenation, is also worth seeking out. The first vintage of an attractive sweet white from Chenin Blanc was produced in 2009.

Rivière Haute, 46160 Albas
www.chateaueugenie.com

Château des Eyssards Bergerac
Around 80% of Pascal Cuisset's wine is exported and its international popularity is an indication of how well attuned he is to making palate-pleasing, food-friendly bottles. He is also a particularly friendly person, and his musical prowess (he plays the French horn in a band of local winemakers) is well known. The estate has 110 acres (44.5ha) of vines, with slightly more white grapes than red. The Cuisset family produces an excellent white, made almost entirely from Sauvignon Blanc with a touch of Muscadelle, and also a very good red called L'Adagio des Eyssards, which is largely Merlot blended with Cabernet Franc and Cabernet Sauvignon. Also worth looking out for is the sweet Saussignac, from 80% Sémillon and 20% Chenin Blanc. He also bottles a Chardonnay as a Vin de Pays.

24240 Monestier
05 53 24 36 36

Château de Gaudou Cahors
Fabrice Durou's family have made wine in Cahors for generations, but after phyloxerra they had to practice polyculture to survive—nicely illustrating the fortunes of wine in the region. From the late 1950s, they once

CHATEAU JOLYS
EXPECT TRUFFLES AND MARMALADE FROM THIS LATE-HARVEST, 100% PETIT MANSENG

again concentrated solely on winemaking. The main wine of this 91 acre (37ha) estate, Cuvée Tradition, is a classic example of a meaty, powerful Cahors, made with 80% Malbec, 15% Merlot, and 5% Tannat. Besides the main wine there is also Grande Lignée (85% Malbec, 15% Merlot, and one year in barrel) and two 100% Malbec cuvées—Renaissance spends up to two years in oak and is full of spicy black fruits, and the grapes for the Réserve Caillau are hand-picked, hand crushed, and aged for up to two years in new oak. Both wines reward a few hours decanting.

46700 Vire/Lot
www.chateaudegaudou.com

Château Haut Bernasse Bergerac
Located in Bergerac's AC Monbazillac, many of the 37 acres (15ha) of vines grow on high slopes. Their physical location is reflected in the Coteaux (slopes) des Bernasse: a decadent wine with rich, Christmas pudding flavors and the acidity to carry them off. It gets even more indulgent as you head up the scale: first to their main château wine (80% Sémillon/15% Muscadelle/5% Sauvignon Blanc), with burnt caramel on the palate from integral oak vinification, and then to the heavily concentrated, richly fragrant Cuvée Jules et Marie Villette, which is made only in exceptional years (most recently this includes 2003, 2005, and 2009) and accounts for only around 5% of production).

Le Barouillet, 24240 Pomport
www.haut-bernasse.com

Château de Haute Serre Cahors
The name Vigouroux is legendary in Cahors—Georges Vigouroux was one of the pioneers in the early 1970s to begin replanting the Malbec grape on the higher, less hospitable slopes of the region. Today, Château de Haute Serre is the highest vineyard of the appellation, covering 143 acres (58ha) of vines that are now reaching 30 years of age. Malbec accounts for 80% of the vineyard, with the remainder split between Merlot and Tannat. Bertrand Vigouroux is in charge and has recently launched a soft, new-style, 100% Malbec known as Pigmentum, which is modern and easy drinking, with an emphasis on raspberry, blackcurrant, and blackberry fruits. A barrel-aged Chardonnay and Sauvignon Blanc blend is bottled under the name Albesco.

46230 Cieurac
www.hauteserre.fr

Château de la Jaubertie Bergerac
In the 16th century, the beautiful Château de la Jaubertie was a hunting lodge for Henry IV. Today, Englishman Hugh Ryman is the lucky man who lives in this classified historic monument. The wines from his estate can be relied on to be some of the most consistently enjoyable in Bergerac. The organic vineyard covers almost 124 acres (50ha) and is split evenly between white and red vines. The wines themselves are divided into the low-oak, easy-drinking Tradition range and the higher quality Mirabelle range, from hand-harvested plots of older vines on the best terroir. There is a richly flavored white (50% Sémillon, 50% Sauvignon), a very enjoyable red (35% Merlot, 45% Cabernet Sauvignon, 20% Cabernet Franc), and a sticky Monbazillac (65% Sémillon, 25% Sauvignon Blanc, 10% Muscadelle). In an effort to be environmentally conscious, all the bottles are 85% recycled glass.

24560 Colombier
www.chateau-jaubertie.com

Château Jolys Jurançon
All that is missing from this fairytale castle-style, 16th-century château is a drawbridge and a fairy godmother. At 89 acres (36ha), this is the largest privately owned property in the appellation. Owner Marion Latrille-Henry, with her father Pierre-Yves, excels at producing a particularly well-balanced, quince and truffle-filled sweet wine from an even 50/50 split of Petit Manseng and Gros Manseng. Consistent ripeness is helped by the natural south-facing amphitheaters in which the grapes grow; the exposed location also helps the Foëhn wind to dry out the late-harvest grapes for *passerillage*. On rare occasions, harvests last until January, when a richly intense wine called Epiphanie is produced. Cuvée Jean is 100% Petit Manseng, harvested by hand in November and fermented at below 68°F (20°C), meaning that sulphite levels can be kept low.

330 Route Chapelle de Rousse, 64390 Gan
www.chateau-jolys.com

Château Ladesvignes Bergerac
This estate is a serious player in quality Bergerac winemaking, yet strangely it is often overlooked. Husband-and-wife team Véronique and Michel Monbouché bought Château Ladesvignes in 1989, and at 153 acres (62ha) it is one of the largest of the appellation. It is increasingly following sustainable winemaking and ensuring careful traceability and low-impact processes. Their AC Côtes de Bergerac Rouge Velours is a very good wine—subtle and underplayed, but with a gentle vanilla custard nose over rich black cherries, dusted with chocolate. The Monbazillac Automne (90% Sémillon, 10% Muscadelle, and 24 months in new oak barrel) is also worth a try, retaining a refreshing vigor to the sticky palate. Ma Préference (AC Bergerac Rouge) is a fruity, Merlot-dominant red (85%) with almost zero visible tannins—it is particularly good slightly chilled.

D 17 Ladesvignes, 24240 Pomport
www.ladesvignes.com

Château Lafitte Jurançon
Philippe and Brigitte Arraou have spent the past few decades restoring this 16th-century estate. They have just 15 acres (6ha) of Gros Manseng and Petit Manseng vines, which are cropped low and subject to careful selection, and they produce around 3,000 bottles of wine a year. The grape varieties are kept separate, with the Gros Manseng vinified in stainless steel and producing both a Mouelleux Tradition and a Sec Tradition. In contrast, the Petit Manseng is treated to a more luxurious experience and aged in oak barrels with regular stirring in of the lees for both the dry Cuvée Marine, with toasted almonds over lemons, and the brioche-filled Cuvée Lison.

64360 Monein
www.chateau-lafitte.com

THE FORGOTTEN GRAPES

One of the most appealing things about the wines of Southwest France is their fierce sense of identity, which comes from the countless indigenous grapes that are found here. Two men in particular have been responsible for keeping these varieties alive, and even replanting forgotten ones. André Dubosc of Producteurs Plaimont in Gascony and Robert Plageoles of Domaine Plageoles in Gaillac are both in their 70s. Each has conservatories of vine varieties where they carefully grow young vines ready for wider planting. Plageoles's rescued varieties include Loin de l'Oeil, Mauzac, Odenc, and Prunelard. The favored grapes of Dubosc, whose father and grandfather both worked as ampelographers (identifying and classifying vines), are Arrufiac, Pinanc, and Colombard, which had previously only been used for Armagnac distillation. According to Dubosc, "We do not want to look to international varieties; we want to concentrate on the riches of this small part of the Southwest."

CHATEAU LAGREZETTE
RICH, POWERFUL, AND ALLURING FRUITS
ABOUND IN THIS 100% MALBEC

Château Lagrézette Cahors

A reference estate for Cahors, owned by Alain Dominique Perrin of the Richemont Group (known for luxury names such as Cartier and Chloé). Perrin bought the property in 1980 and has since lavished care and attention on the 15th-century château; its vineyards, planted to 148 acres (60ha) of 77% Malbec, 21% Merlot, and 2% Tannat; and the underground cellar. Lagrézette wine is rich and slightly brooding, full of ripe blackberries and cherries, and layered with gourmet notes of vanilla, mocha, and chocolate. It is carefully crafted and tastes polished, but is no less enjoyable for that. Two other wines are produced at this estate: Le Pigeonnier and the Cuvée Dame Honneur.

46140 Caillac
www.chateau-lagrezette.tm.fr

Château de Mallevieille Bergerac

This low-key family property is led by Philippe Biau, who works with his son-in-law Thierry Bernardinis. There are 74 acres (30ha) of vines, two-thirds of which are red (60% Merlot, 10% Malbec, 10% Cabernet Sauvignon, and 20% Cabernet Franc) and one-third white (50% Sauvignon, 25% Sémillon, and 25% Muscadelle). They produce gentle yet gourmet wines with good weight; particularly the excellent AC Côtes de Bergerac Rouge and Côtes de Bergerac Mouelleux.

Vignobles Biau, 24130 Monfaucon
05 53 24 64 66

Château Montus Madiran

Alain Brumont, who also owns the family vineyard Château Bouscassé, bought Château Montus in 1980. His Montus Prestige was the first wine in the area to contain 100% Tannat and is aged entirely in new oak. His new winery, which opened in 1995 and is now also a luxury hotel, is known as the Cathedral of Tannat. Those who prefer a softer, fleshier style should try Torus (50% Tannat, 30% Cabernet Sauvignon, 20% Cabernet Franc), which undergoes a cold soak and is aged 50/50 in new-oak and one-year-old barrels. Between his two estates, Brumont has 642.5 acres (260ha) of vines in Madiran. He also makes a 100% Petit Corbu and a sweet 100% Petit Manseng.

Vignobles Brumont, 32400 Maumusson Laguian
www.brumont.fr

Château Moulin Caresse Bergerac

Sylvie and Jean-François Deffarge run this estate, with their son Benjamin. Located in Montravel, there is plenty of flint and iron in the soil, which gives the wines an almost severe and highly appealing note. The 67 acre (27ha) estate is increasingly being farmed along organic lines. The wines are bottled under AC Bergerac, Côtes de Bergerac, and Montravel. They are divided into two ranges: the Première Vendanges (First Harvest) and Magie d'Automne (Autumn Magic), which take the ripest grapes from the best plots, cropped low and aged in French oak barrels. Red, white, rosé, semi-sweet, and sweet are all produced.

24230 St-Antoine-de-Breuilh
05 53 27 55 58

CHATEAU DE PELLEHAUT
THIS CHARDONNAY/PETIT MANSENG OFFERS
RICH PEACH AND GRILLED VANILLA FLAVORS

Château de Pellehaut Côtes de Gascogne

Brothers Martin and Mathieu Béraut have built this estate up to 618 acres (250ha)—many of the vines are located on sunny slopes that offer excellent drainage. There is also a large farm that raises cattle and other crops, making this one of the few remaining winemakers to practice polyculture. The farm provides manure for the vines and sustainable viticulture is practiced. The range of wines is extensive: the easy-drinking, unoaked Harmonie range; the more complex Vins Patient from older vines; and the Family Réserve, which is aged in oak. Look out for L'été Gascon, a blend of 50/50 Chardonnay and Gros Manseng that is rich in tropical fruits. The Béraut brothers have recently planted some Pinot Noir in a cool spot, and aim to make a single varietal wine from 2011.

32250 Montréal du Gers
www.pellehaut.com

Château Peyros Madiran

The Lesgourgues family have five châteaux across Southwest France and one in Uruguay. Jean Jacques Lesgourgues bought this 64 acre (26ha) property in Madiran in 1998, and today his son Arnaud is in charge. The vineyards are farmed using sustainable agriculture, including manure from a herd of 200 Brébis ewes that graze around the vineyard from November to March. The richly powerful Vieille Vignes (80% Tannat, 20% Cabernet Franc) and the Greenwich 43N (referring to the 43rd parallel on which the estate is located) are both worth tracking down. Greenwich 43N is made with 95% Tannat and 5% Cabernet Franc, with gentle micro-oxygenation and new oak barrels for 20 months. It is full of roasted coffee beans, bitter chocolate, and rich, baked plums. Most of the wines are unfiltered and will benefit from decanting.

No visitor facilities
www.vignobles-lesgourgues.com

Château Pineraie Cahors

Sisters Anne and Emmanuelle Barc work alongside their parents, Jean-Luc and Arlette, at this 124 acre (50ha) estate, which produces 220,000 bottles a year. It is located at one of the highest points of Cahors, near Puy-L'Evêque. The wines include Pierre Sèche du Château Pineraie (85% Malbec, 15% Merlot), which is from the youngest vines, vinified in stainless steel and bottled with no oak aging. The excellent L'Authentique (100% Malbec) is a successfully textured and complex wine that is aged in 80% new oak for 18 months and ranks among the best in the region.

Leygues, 46700 Puy-L'evèque
www.chateaupineraie.com

Château Plaisance Fronton

Louis Penavayre carefully works his 74 acres (30ha) of vines with his son Marc, making 150,000 bottles of wine a year. The vineyard is planted to Négrette (60%), Syrah (25%), Cabernet Franc (5%), Cabernet Sauvignon (5%), and Gamay (5%). Château Plaisance should be certified organic for the 2010 vintage, which means that no chemical fertilizers or weedkillers are used in the vineyard. The philosophy also extends to the winemaking, so expect natural, wild yeasts and no fining or filtering. Of their impressive range of wines, the 18-month oak aged Tot Co Que Cal is probably the most interesting. It is 80% Négrette and 20% Syrah from plots of low-yielding old vines at the highest point of the vineyard (656ft /200m). A gentler version is the Grain de Folie (70% Négrette, 30% Gamay).

Place de la Mairie, 31340 Vacquiers
www.chateau-plaisance.fr

Château Le Raz Bergerac

Patrick Barde installed a two-level cellar at his 148 acre (60ha) estate in the Bergerac region long before it became fashionable. He was also one of the first producers in the region to use micro-oxygenation. In a similar pioneering spirit, Barde has released, from the 2008 vintage, a 100% Cabernet Sauvignon sparkler called Le Raz Perlant, which is made traditionally with the second fermentation in bottle. For his principal wines, he splits his grapes evenly between white and red, leading with Sauvignon Blanc (at least 70%) for the white, and Merlot, blended with Cabernet Franc, Cabernet Sauvignon, and Malbec, for the reds. In the vineyard, the work is entrusted to an all-female team because he believes women to be meticulous in their approach to trimming, bunch thinning, and crop selection. He has called his top Montravel Rouge cuvée Les Filles in their honor.

24610 Saint Méard de Gurçon
www.le-raz.com

Château de Saurs Gaillac

When the Gaillac appellation was established in 1936, Château de Saurs was one of the first to put the AC on its label. Today, it has 104 acres (42ha) of vines growing on steep slopes that run down to the River Tarn. The majority, around 80%, are red varieties (Duras, Fer Servadou, Syrah, Merlot, and Gamay) and the rest are white (Mauzac, Loin de l'Oeil, and Sauvignon Blanc). The top wine is the Réserve Eliézer, which is barrel aged for nine months and is an interesting blend of Merlot, Duras, Syrah, and Fer Servadou. The Cuvée Tradition uses the same grapes, but it is bottled unoaked. Do not miss the Gaillac Doux, a 100% Loin de l'Oeil that is tarte tartin in a glass.

81310 Lisle sur Tarn
www.chateau-de-saurs.com

Château St-Didier-Parnac Cahors

The 185 acre (75ha) estate of St-Didier-Parnac is owned by Rigal, one of the largest wine producers in Cahors and part of the Jean Jean group that is most closely associated with the Languedoc. Three wines are produced at Château St-Didier-Parnac—Tradition, Prestige, and Apogée. Each is a blend of Malbec and Merlot, using vines of different ages and plot locations and a varying percentage of new oak. If you are looking for a fleshy, highly toasted, and modern Cahors, Apogée is a great example, being full of spicy vanilla notes. On the entry level side, Rigal also produces The Original Malbec, a well-rounded and easy-drinking wine.

46140 Parnac
www.chateau-st-didier-cahors.com

Château Thénac Bergerac

Thénac is the rustic dream of many Francophiles, with 205 acres (83ha) of vines nestled among parkland, plum orchards, and fishing lakes. The Russian owner (and one-time oil magnate), Eugene Shvidler, has invested a significant sum since he bought the estate in 2001. He has more than doubled the size of the vineyard, entirely renovated the château and cellars, and brought in ex-Michel Rolland colleague Ludwig Vanneron as director. The flagship wines are bottled simply under Château Thénac (AC Côtes de Bergerac). They are confident and extremely accomplished, coming in red, white, and sweet styles, with evident oak aging and plump fruits. The estate also makes Fleur du Périgord in an unoaked, fruitier style. ★ Rising star

Le Bourg, 24240 Thénac
www.chateau-thenac.com

Château Tirecul La Gravière Bergerac

This renowned Monbazillac estate focuses on luxury. With just 16 acres (6.5ha), and careful selection keeping the yields tiny, only a small amount of wine is made here. The vineyard is an even 50/50 split of Muscadelle and Sémillon. Owners Bruno and Claudie Bilancini are currently converting to organic farming, with the official certificate due in 2011. All the vines face north and east, which means the grapes take their time to ripen and develop complexity and intensity. Three sweet Monbazillacs are produced: the main Tirecul La Gravière, Cuvée Madame, and Les Pins. The latter two are aged in 100% new oak and only made in exceptional years, which is becoming increasingly frequent as the vines get older and more complex. Two dry whites complete the range and are both from chalky limestone plots: the Blanc Sec de Tirecul La Gravière Mademoiselle, which is 100% Muscadelle with a delicately fragrant nose, and the more structured, oak-aged Andréa.

24240 Monbazillac
05 53 57 44 75l

Château de Tiregand Bergerac

An imposing estate in the Pécharmant region of Bergerac, the property extends over a hefty 1,137 acres (460ha). Just 106 acres (43ha) of this is vines, however, while the rest is made up of woods, parkland, and even a riding school. François-Xavier de Saint-Exupéry runs the château and concentrates mainly on good-quality reds, which are planted to 54% Merlot, 23% Cabernet Sauvignon, 18% Cabernet Franc, and 5% Malbec. There are also 3 acres (1.2ha) of white grapes, although these have recently been replanted and will not be bottled under the Château de Tiregand Blanc label until 2011. Of the reds, the Cuvée Grand Millésime is a succulent Merlot-led blend that is aged for 18 months in barrel. For a lighter style, try the Clos Montalbanie from younger vines.

Creysse 24100 Bergerac
www.chateau-de-tiregand.com

Château Tour des Gendres Bergerac

The de Conti family, perhaps most notably Luc de Conti, is well known in the appellation of Bergerac. Perhaps it is their Italian roots—they moved here in 1925—but they manage to maintain a close family and respect for the good life. This extends to how they treat their vines, as all 128.5 acres (52ha) are farmed organically and biodiversity is encouraged with orchids, birds, butterflies, and even truffles. Among the many excellent wines is La Gloire de Mon Père (50% Merlot, 25% Cabernet Sauvignon, 15% Malbec, 10% Cabernet Franc), which has a lovely, bright burst of fruit, and the 100% Sauvignon Blanc Anthologia, which is fermented and aged in barrel. There is also a very interesting 100% Muscadelle à Petit Grains, which is a traditional grape variety in Bergerac.

Famille de Conti, Les Gendres, 24240 Ribagnac
www.chateautourdesgendres.com

CHATEAU PLAISANCE
FRESH RASPBERRY FRUITS SHINE IN THIS
UNFILTERED AND UNFINED ORGANIC WINE

CHATEAU PEYROS
THIS MODERN TAKE ON THE TANNAT GRAPE
GIVES ROAST COFFEE AND RICH PLUM FRUITS

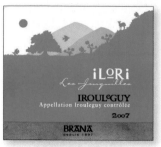

DOMAINE BRANA

THIS LILTING WINE HAS A SUBTLE FLORAL NOSE, WILD HERBS, AND A FRESH FINISH

CHATEAU VIELLA

THE TANNIC STRUCTURE MEANS THIS WINE HAS LONG AGING POTENTIAL

Château Viella Madiran

Alain Bortolussi is the owner of this 62 acre (25ha) estate, with a main building that dates back to the 13th century—the vaulted cellars beneath the château are quite beautiful. The range of wines is split, which is typical in this area, into reds bottled under AC Madiran and whites bottled under AC Pacherenc de Vic Bilh. The Viella Madiran Expression is 80% Tannat and 20% Cabernet Sauvignon, with 12 months barrel aging. The property also produces a 100% Tannat, the Cuvée Prestige, which also spends a year in barrel, but this time it is entirely new oak. It has a firm, but well worked, tannic structure and some delicious deep red berry fruits. The dry Pacherenc comes from 2.5 acres (1ha) of vines, and is a blend of 20% Arrufiac, 20% Petit Manseng, and 60% Gros Manseng.

Route de Maumusson, 32400 Viella
www.chateauviella.com

Clos La Coutale Cahors

The Grand Coutale is the wine to really look out for at this 148 acre (60ha) estate, owned by Valmy and Philippe Bernède. It is a succulent, richly textured wine that offers the brushed leather tannins of Cahors, but with the ripe, rich fruit of an Argentine Malbec. Yield is kept low, all the grapes are hand-picked, and aging takes place in large oak vats, with skins kept in regular contact with the juice by manual punching down. Unusually for a special *cuvée*, it mixes some Merlot and Tannat (depending on vintage) with the Malbec. The regular Clos La Coutale keeps the blend to just Malbec and Merlot, and is a softer, more subtle wine that is richly perfumed and great with food. The innovative Philippe also makes his own Coutale Sommelier corkscrews.

46700 Vire sur Lot
www.closlacoutale.com

Clos de Gamot Cahors

Yves and Martine Jouffreau-Hermann are owners of the 30 acre (12ha) Clos de Gamot, which is entirely Malbec and where they produce some wonderful wines. These include the deeply colored and richly spiced Cahors Cuvée Centenières, from a small parcel of pre-phylloxera vines. For the past decade they have also produced wines bottled under the label Clos St-Jean, from 10 acres (4ha) of vines replanted along slopes that had been abandoned for years. These are also entirely Malbec and have only recently been commercialized.

46220 Prayssac
05 65 21 40 81

Clos Triguedina Cahors

Jean-Luc Baldès is the latest generation of this established Cahors family to take over the estate. Set in an attractive corner of the Lot near the village of Puy l'Evêque, the 148 acres (60ha) of vines are put to good use over a wide range of wines, including the New Black Wine. This 100% old-vine Malbec *cuvée* spends 18 months in oak and is vinified in the manner traditional to the area during the 13th century. This involves a short burst of 60°F (15.5°C) heat to fix the color and super-charge the tannins. Another single-varietal Malbec, called Probus, aims to be slightly more approachable when young, but do not expect it to be too delicate. A better bet for younger drinking is possibly the classic Clos Triguedina

(80% Malbec, 15% Merlot, 5% Tannat) or Le Petit Clos, which has far less oak. The attractive Vin de Lune is a sweet Chenin Blanc.

46700 Vire sur Lot
www.jlbaldes.com

Clos Uroulat Jurançon

Charles Hours has owned Clos Uroulat since 1983. He makes just two wines—one sweet, one dry—both of which are a revelation. There are 40 acres (16ha) of vines at the estate, planted to Gros Manseng and Petit Manseng with a small plot of Petit Courbu. No chemical fertilizers or weedkillers are used, and the vines are trained high, up to 8.2ft (2.5m), to optimize photosynthesis and help with the raisining process during fall. Since 2006, Hours has been joined by his daughter, Marie. Besides giving her name to the liltingly dry Cuvée Marie (almost entirely Gros Manseng), she has also introduced two wines to the range that are known simply as Happy Hours Cool (100% Gros Manseng), which is dry, and Happy Hours Fruity (100% Petit Manseng), which is gently sweet.

Quartier Trouilh, 64360 Monein
www.uroulat.com

Domaine Abotia Irouléguy

This charming estate has been in the Errecart family for generations. It is set close to the Citadel, above the attractive town of St-Jean-Pied-de-Port, and is part wine estate and part working farm, rearing pigs for farmhouse sausages and hams. The grapes are farmed in terraces or on steep slopes almost entirely by hand. The red wine is a sturdy reflection of their no-nonsense approach, with 65% Tannat, 25% Cabernet Sauvignon, and 10% Cabernet Franc. The rosé wine keeps the blend to just Cabernet Franc and Tannat, but is still deep in color and structure—a great summer wine to crack open with a barbecue.

64220 Ispoure
www.irouleguy-abotia.fr

Domaine de l'Ancienne Cure Bergerac

One of the most famous estates in Bergerac, it was created by the Roche family and first bottled in 1968. Today, Christian Roche is in charge, working alongside his brother and sister, Christine and Michèl. For an idea of what Bergerac can produce at the top end, try their Extase Monbazillac, a special *cuvée* of sweet wine, made with 90% Sémillon, 10% Muscadelle, and 24 months in new barrels. The 109 acre (44ha) estate also produces three good dry whites, the most food-friendly of which is the Cuvée Abbée, which uses up to 50% Muscadelle, depending on the vintage, with 20% Sauvignon and 30% Sémillon. For the red wines, the Extase uses low-yielding, old vines and is full of ripe, silky tannins.

Vigneron, 24560 Colombier
www.domaine-anciennecure.fr

Domaine Arretxea Irouléguy

The Pyrenees Mountains that surround the appellation of Irouléguy dictate the form of this 21 acre (8.5ha) vineyard, half of which is cut into terraces in the steeply banked slopes, while almost all the rest lies at a 40° gradient. Thérèse and Michel Riouspeyrous farm organically, and have been fully certified since 1996—they also work biodynamically, but have not yet been certified. Whites form just 5 acres (2ha), which are planted to Gros Manseng, Petit Manseng, and Petit Corbu. These are vinified partly in wooden vats and partly in stainless steel, all on fine lees. For the reds, Tannat, Cabernet Franc, and Cabernet Sauvignon are split into two wines: Rouge Tradition, an unoaked, unfiltered wine that is aged in cement vats and has a soft sweep of tannins; and Haitza, which means "oak" in Basque and gives a strong clue as to its style. This top *cuvée* is far more concentrated, but the barrels ensure a soft smoke and gentle structure that is not intrusive.

64220 Irouléguy
05 59 37 33 67

Domaine Bellegarde Jurançon
Particularly recognized for its dry whites, the grapes from here were sold to the local co-operative until 1986. With 40 acres (16ha) of vines, planted to 60% Petit Manseng and 40% Gros Manseng, Pascal Labasse follows sustainable agriculture. He keeps his dry white principally in stainless steel, with some lees-stirring for a fuller weight in the mouth that gives a lemon curd, sweet yet tart effect. Another interesting dry white is Cuvée La Pierre Blanche, where 20% old-vine Gros Manseng is blended with 80% young Petit Manseng and fermented and aged in oak barrels—the rich effect makes it a great wine to kick off a meal, particularly against a salty paté or foie gras. Labasse does not totally neglect the sweet side of Jurançon; his Cuvée Thibault is a 100% Petit Manseng that drips with honey and melted toffee.

Quartier Coos, 64360 Monein
www.domainebellegarde-jurancon.com

Domaine La Bérangeraie Cahors
Figs, plums, and plenty of earthy undertones make this a lovely Cahors. You will never fully lose the rusticity of this appellation, which is part of its charm, and the Berenger family (originally from Provence) do a good job of proving this point. The wines from their 74 acre (30ha) estate are all named after family members. Cuvée Juline (90% Malbec and 10% Merlot) is aged solely in concrete, with no oak, and has softly textured tannins that let the fruit speak. Cuvée Maurin (100% Malbec) changes up a gear—still no oak, but bottled unfiltered with licorice hints and plenty of rich black fruits. For an unrestrained oak experience with plenty of chocolate, coffee, and grilled meats, try the La Gorgée de Mathis Bacchus, which spends 20 months in 100% new oak barrels.

Coteaux de Courneau, 46700 Grezels
05 65 31 94 59

Domaine Berthoumieu Pacherenc du Vic Bilh
Didier Barré's family have made wine here since 1850, on an estate of 62 acres (25ha) with vines that are up to 100 years old. He grows all the classic Pacherenc grapes—Petit Corbu, Gros Manseng, and Petit Manseng —and makes both a sweet and dry version. His Madiran is a full-blown expression of Tannat: rich, meaty, and in need of a decanter. The Pacherenc has an exciting Doux (semi-sweet), and a dry that has the signature sour lime twist of the appellation—a really interesting bottle as an alternative to the more usual Sauvignons or Chardonnays. For the really adventurous, try Tanatis, a 100% Tannat dessert wine that is sticky, rich, and best served slightly chilled.

32400 Gers
www.domaine-berthoumieu.com

Domaine Brana Irouléguy
Irouléguy has a powerful co-operative cellar that makes wine for over 90% of the 50 winemakers in the area. Jean Brana is a notable exception and was the first to begin bottling under his own name in 1988. He was also the first to re-introduce white wine to the area, a practice that had died out decades earlier. His white comprises 60% Petit Courbu, 35% Gros Manseng, and 5% Petit Manseng. The red grapes on the 57 acre (23ha), steeply sloped estate include Cabernet Sauvignon and Tannat, but it is the Cabernet Franc (60% of the total plantings) that makes the wines truly stand out, with some vines being over 100 years old. A 100% Cabernet Franc wine is bottled under the name Axeria. Jean's sister Martine runs the family distillery business, making some seriously good fruit liqueurs.

64220 St-Jean-Pied-de-Port
www.brana.fr

Domaine des Cailloutis Gaillac
A good-quality, organically farmed vineyard from Bernard Fabre, who spent the best part of a decade teaching enology in Burgundy before moving to Gaillac in 1998. He works closely with his wife, Patricia, focusing on the traditional grapes varieties of the region. The most crowd-pleasing of the wines is the Cuvée Prestige, which has rich cherry and plum and is given structure by some oak aging. A less obvious choice, not made every year, is the 100% Loin de l'Oeil sweet white, which has that has an attractive spicy edge with layers of subtle cinnamon and dried apricots. Single-varietals are also made in some years from Mauzac and Odenc.

81140 Andillac
05 63 33 97 63

Domaine des Cassagnoles
Côtes de Gascogne
Janine and Gilles Baumann were among the first, back in the early 1980s, to list the grape variety on the label, so starting a trend that has been widely followed across Côtes de Gascogne. Their approach to winemaking is similarly unorthodox—they are unembarrassed to say that grape typicity is as important as soil typicity, not something you often hear in France—and ensures that everything favors crisp, fresh aromas and flavors. In the cellar, it is all about keeping the temperature low, and the oxygen out. There is a large range of wines—five single varietals of Colombard, Gros Manseng, Chardonnay, Sauvignon, and Ugni Blanc. They also have a number of blends, including an excellent Colombard-Sauvignon. The estate covers a total of 198 acres (80ha).

32330 Gondrin
www.domainedescassagnoles.com

Domaine Cauhapé Jurançon
This 99 acre (40ha) estate is meticulously farmed by owner Henri Ramonteu. The wines are made from Gros Manseng and Petit Manseng and sing out of the glass. What you get

LOCAL FOOD, LOCAL WINE

The traditional food of Southwest France seems to have grown hand-in-hand with the classically structured, rich red wines of Cahors and Madiran. Menus are filled with duck dishes—foie gras, confit de canard (preserved duck), and magret de canard (duck breast)—all of which are usually accompanied by chips cooked in duck fat. But there is a new generation of young chefs, such as Philippe Combet, Eric Sampietro, and Pierre Landet, that are pairing their food with the more food-friendly wine styles that come from micro-oxygenation, new oak, and riper grapes. The many rivers of the region, not to mention the Atlantic coast, also produce fish for the fragrant whites of Irouléguy and Gascony. As Alain Brumont, one of Madiran's leading wine producers, points out, "We have one of France's most modern chefs, Michel Guérard, living and working near Madiran. The food here has evolved along with the wine. We still work with the same basic ingredients, but the most famous product of the region today is the black pork of Baigorry, a lighter meat than duck. The traditional Gascon ingredients are all around us, but we can interpret them differently, just as we can our wines."

DOMAINE DU CROS
JUST RUSTIC ENOUGH TO BE AUTHENTIC AND
PACKED FULL OF PERSONALITY

DOMAINE LAPEYRE
AN UNUSUAL BLEND OF 70% PETIT MANSENG
WITH COURBU AND CAMARALET

each year, however, depends entirely on the weather conditions. Quintessence du Petit Manseng, for example, is picked just before Christmas, and in the last decade was made in 2000, 2001, 2005, 2006, and 2009—expect dried fruit and roasted nut flavors. Even rarer is Folie de Janvier, where the grapes are picked in the frosts of January and have a wonderful mix of tartness and syrup; the only example from the past decade is 2000. The dry whites are also worth trying, particularly a highly aromatic example from Petit Manseng, which is usually reserved for the sweet wines, called La Canopée.

64360 Monein
www.cauhape.com

Domaine Chiroulet Côtes de Gascogne
The vines here sit at one of Gascony's highest points, at around 591ft (180m) above sea level. There are 111 acres (45ha) of vines on the estate, which is owned by Philippe Fezas. Try the delicious late-harvest white wine (100% Gros Manseng) called Soleil d'automne, which is harvested in November and vinified half in vat and half in barrel. It is a low sulphite wine and not exactly sweet, but it has a rich, honeyed flavor that makes it a great accompaniment to a rich goose liver paté. A more classic Côtes de Gascogne is the Terres Blanches dry white, which is made from 50% Gros Manseng, 25% Sauvignon Blanc, and 25% Ugni Blanc old vines, and matured for 10 months with regular stirring in of the fine lees.

32100 Larroque sur L'Osse, Gers
www.chiroulet.com

Domaine Cosse Maisonneuve Cahors
Former rugby player Matthieu Cosse, with his partner Catherine Maisonneuve, has been garnering increasing praise in recent years for making exciting wines that rewrite accepted expectations of Cahors. The range, from their 43 acre (17.5ha) biodynamic vineyard, includes three 100% Malbec wines: La Fage, Le Combal, and their top wine Les Laquets. Made from 40-year-old Malbec vines and aged for 20 months in barrels (mainly new oak, but with some one-year oak), Les Laquets has rich damson fruits and a savory toasted almond note. Le Petit Sid comes from younger vines. There are also three Vins de Pays des Coteaux du Quercy—look out for the 100% Cabernet Franc and 100% Gamay. ★ **Rising star**

46800 Fargues
05 65 24 22 37

Domaine du Cros Marcillac
Philippe Teulier's estate is tucked away among steeply banked hills of ruby-red soil, known as *rougier*, that reflect its rich iron content. Teulier makes wine from 64 acres (26ha) of vineyards, most of which are owned and some are rented, planted with Fer Servadou, known locally as Mansois. Just like everywhere else in the southwest, there is little reliance on oak, partly because the grapes are high in natural fruit tannins, and also because of the desire to let the taste of the grape and the soil through in the wines. This means vinification takes place in stainless steel, although the older vines (Cuvée Vieilles Vignes) are aged in oak and have a rich licorice finish. The younger vines (Cuvée Lo Sang del Païs) have fruitier, raspberry flavors.

12390 Goutrens
www.domaine-du-cros.com

Domaine Eliane da Ros
Côtes de Marmandais
The fact that Eliane da Ros makes such well-respected wines in such a lowly appellation speaks volumes about his approach and determination. Da Ros took over the family estate in 1997, and the following year he left the local co-operative and built his own winemaking facilities. Today, he has almost 54 acres (22ha) of vines, growing Bordeaux varietals—Merlot and Cabernet Sauvignon (with some Syrah and Malbec) and Sémillon and Sauvignon—that he mixes with his own particular approach. He farms biodynamically, having previously worked with Zind Humbrecht in Alsace, who is a famous proponent of the philosophy. There is no filtering or fining, and the resulting wines are very precise. Try the textured Clos Baquey, or the more intense and complex Chante Coucou.

Laclotte, 47250 Cocumont
05 53 20 75 22

Domaine d'Escausses Gaillac
Roselyn and Jean-Marc Balaran are in charge of this 86 acre (35ha) property. The vines are planted fairly high, on a ridge around 820ft (250m) above sea level, and are set into limestone bedrock. This helps to instil a sense of purity and minerality in both the red and white wines. This is particularly evident in La Croix Petite (45% Fer Servadou, 45% Syrah, and 10% Cabernet Sauvignon), which undergoes a cold soak and gentle micro-oxygenation. It is also worth looking out for their daughter Aurelie's nearby estate, Château L'Enclos des Roses, which has 37 acres (15ha) of old vines that are increasingly farmed organically. The d'Escausses is more contemporary in style, while L'Enclos concentrates more closely on traditional regional grapes.

81150 Ste-Croix
www.domainedescausses.com

Domaine Ilarria Irouléguy
This 25 acre (10ha) estate is owned by the energetic Peio Espil, who worked at La Tour Blanche in Sauternes and Domaine Cauhapé in Jurançon before returning to Southwest France in 1988. Espil has been certified organic since 1999, and follows a highly rigorous "natural farming" philosophy that includes no ploughing and abundant ground cover between rows. Wines include Domaine Ilarria Rouge that always has a high degree of Cabernet Franc, giving some redcurrant lift to the richness of the Tannat. The white wines are made from Petit Corbu and Petit Manseng. Cuvée Bixintxo—the Basque name for Saint Vincent, the patron saint of winemakers—is only made in exceptionally sunny years, which more recently includes 2001, 2003, 2004, and 2009. It has a high degree of Tannat, mixed with Cabernet Sauvignon and a touch of Cabernet Franc, with a smokier finish and licorice hints.

64200 Irouléguy
05 59 37 23 38

Domaine Jean Luc Matha Marcillac
Owner Jean-Luc Matha has a touch of the philosopher about him, perhaps because he once trained to be a priest. He farms, almost entirely organically, 38 acres (16ha) of Fer Servadou vines and keeps things simple with just two red *cuvées*. The younger vines

go into Laïris, which is a bright, easy-drinking bottle that is vinified in stainless steel and combines redcurrant flavors with crushed raspberry leaves. The more complex Peirafi comes from old vines and spends 20 months in large-sized oak casks made from old wood that is intended to soften the structure rather than impart any oak flavor. Alongside the two red *cuvées* there is also a heavily colored and robust Cuvée Vignou rosé and an unusual white wine that is blended from Muscat Petit Grain, Muscadelle, Chenin Blanc, and Odenc. This estate is sometimes referred to as Domaine du Vieux Porche.

12330 Bruéjouls
www.matha-vigneron.fr

Domaine de Joÿ Côtes de Gascogne

The enticing name is backed up by fresh and fragrant Côtes de Gascogne wines. Descendants of a Swiss family who moved to the region at the turn of the 20th century, Véronique and André Gessler and their sons, Olivier and Roland, are in charge. They grow almost entirely white grapes over 272 acres (110ha), and produce Bas-Armagnac and Floc de Gascogne apéritifs alongside the wines. As with the best dry whites of the region, vinification is aimed at keeping oxygen out and fruit flavors in. This means gentle pressing and settling with low temperature fermentation. L'Etoile is the signature wine, made with 50% Colombard, 25% Ugni Blanc, and 25% Gros Manseng. At the other end of the scale, Grain de Joy is made with late-harvested 100% Petit Manseng and is full of lychée and toffee.

32110 Panjas
www.domaine-joy.com

Domaine Laffont Madiran

Owned by Belgian Pierre Speyer since 1993, this estate covers 10 acres (4ha); he also buys in another 7 acres (3ha) of grapes. It has been farmed organically since 2005, with an increasing lean toward biodynamics. The range of wines is small and focused. Erigone (80% Tannat, 20% Cabernet Franc) is from old vines that are cropped low and cold soaked to extract fruit flavors. Winemaking is done by gravity, and the wine is aged in barrel, with no new oak, and bottled unfiltered and unfined. New oak makes its appearance with the top *cuvée*, Hécate, which is 100% Tannat and spends 20 months in barrel—expect full-throttle licorice and damson plums. To round out the selection, a 100% Petit Manseng provides a sweet Pacherenc du Vic Bilh, labeled simply Laffont.

32400 Maumusson
05 62 69 75 23

Domaine Lapeyre Jurançon

Jean-Bernard Larrieu has taken over full time from his father, Marcel, and turns out confident, deftly made wines from an attractive vineyard, built into terraces. The 42 acres (17ha) of vines are farmed organically, and traceability is taken seriously throughout the growing season and right up to bottling. The varieties that are planted are Petit Manseng (60% of the vineyard), Gros Manseng, Petit Courbu, Courbu, and Camaralet. Perhaps the most succulent wine of the property is La Magendia, a late-harvested Petit Manseng that is full of dried apricots and bittersweet candied lemon.

In certain years, the estate also produces the hard to find, dry Mantoulan, a 70% Petit Manseng, Courbu, and Camaralet that is aged in oak.

La Chapelle de Rousse, 64110 Jurancon
www.jurancon-lapeyre.fr

Domaine de Laulan Côtes de Duras

The Geoffrey family clearly relishs a challenge. They bought this property in 1974, in the little-loved appellation of Duras, and set about replanting and extending the vineyard to its current 86 acres (35ha). They then built a modern winery with stainless steel tanks and a new barrel cellar. These are serious investments in such a small appellation, but they have paid off. Their Domaine de Laulan Sauvignon is a lovely, crisp wine, full of varietal aromas of citrus fruit and wet grass. The other wine worth looking out for is M de Laulan, a 100% Merlot, aged in oak, that puts full emphasis on gourmet red berries.

Petit ste Foy, 47120 Duras
www.domainelaulan.com

Domaine de Lauroux Côtes de Gascogne

British couple Nicolas and Karen Kitchener left their jobs in IT and sales to buy this attractive 40 acre (16ha) estate in 2004. It has become a model of sustainable agriculture: recycling rainwater, using their own forest wood and vine cuttings for all-winter heating, biodynamically approved vine treatments, and natural yeasts. The finished wines are all low sulphite and suitable for vegans and vegetarians. Leaving all this aside, the taste of their Blanc Sec is equally attractive. They use local varietals—Colombard, Ugni Blanc, and Gros Manseng—to produce a clean and immediately appealing glass, with juicy citrus fruit from low temperature (70°F/ 21°C) fermentation. Red Côtes de Gascognes are rarely as interesting as the whites, but their Lauroux Confiance is a succulent blend of Merlot, Cabernet Sauvignon, and Cabernet Franc.

32379 Manciet, Gascony
www.lauroux.com

Domaine du Merchien VDQS Coteaux de Quercy

Coteaux de Quercy is one of the least known southwest regions. This did not deter English couple David and Sarah Meakin from moving here in 1994 and setting about making good-quality, well-regarded wines, and also a range of bottle-conditioned ales. Look out for Chien Bleu, a blend of 10% Gamay, 10% Merlot, 60% Cabernet Franc, 10% Malbec, and 10% Tannat. It has low sulphites, is vinified in concrete tanks, and is bottled without any oak. This well-priced, refreshing wine shows gentle autumnal fruits.

Penchenier, 46230 Belfort du Quercy
www.merchien.com

Domaine Plageoles Gaillac

Robert Plageoles has passed the day-to-day running of the estate onto his son, Bernard, but he is still an important influence. Their collection of wines include many of the forgotten local grapes that Robert Plageoles rescued over the course of his career, such as Loin de L'Oeil, Mauzac, Odenc (all white), and Prunelard (red). Try the Vin de Voile, a 100% Mauzac in similar style to a Vin Jaune from the Jura, or the lovely Vin d'Autan, a sweet 100% Odenc made

DOMAINE DE LAULAN
A CRISP AND ZINGY WHITE FROM THE LITTLE-KNOWN DURAS AC

DOMAINE DE JOY
THE DRY WHITE OF THIS ESTATE IS JUST AS LIGHT AND FRESH AS THE NAME SUGGESTS

DOMAINE ROTIER
CAREFUL MICRO-OXYGENATION HAS
SOFTENED THE TANNINS IN THIS WINE

from grapes that are naturally dried and concentrated by the Autan wind. The estate brings together two family properties: Domaine des Très Cantous and Domaine de Roucou-Cantemerle. It covers 49 acres (20ha), two-thirds of which are white and one-third red. It is farmed organically and natural yeasts, low sulphites, and minimal filtering or fining are used in the winemaking process. Recently, another new grape variety has been introduced: the white Verdanel, of which just 1,000 bottles are made.

Très Cantous, 81140 Cahuzac Sur Vere
www.vins-plageoles.com

Domaine Le Roc Fronton

The local grape variety in Fronton is the Négrette, and Château Le Roc makes one of the best-known and most successful versions of it. The property is run by Frederic Ribes, a straight-talking *vigneron* who takes a poetic approach to his wines—the labels, and even the tanks, are covered with floral motifs. An enologist by training, his winemaking is meticulous, with a low yield in the vines to emphasize the typical violets, spice, and licorice aromas of the grape. According to Ribes, "La Négrette has low acidity and can be prone to reduction, but if it is well made there is a purity of fruit that makes it the Pinot Noir of the southwest". Try La Folle Noir d'Ambat (100% Négrette) and the meaty, rather wonderful Domaine Le Roc Don Quichotte (60% Négrette/40% Syrah).

31620 Fronton
www.leroc-fronton.com

Domaine Rotier Gaillac

Expect good-quality, careful winemaking from this estate, run by brothers-in-law Alain Rotier and Francis Marre. They farm sustainably and have not used chemical fertilizers for over 25 years—oats and barley are grown between the rows to encourage microbiological activity instead. Red grapes dominate, with 62 acres (25ha), and are planted to Syrah (over 80%), Braucol, Duras, Gamay, and Cabernet Sauvignon. Whites make up 25 acres (10ha) and concentrate on Loin de l'Oeil and Sauvignon Blanc. The wines bottled under the Renaissance label best illustrate the philosophy of this estate—low yields, a touch of micro-oxygenation to soften the tannins, and careful oak aging. The Initiales range, from younger vines and fermented at a lower temperature, is fresher and lighter.

Petit Nareye 81600, Cadalen
www.domaine-rotier.com

Domaine des Savarines Cahors

Domaine des Savarines is a fully certified organic and biodynamic 10 acre (4ha) estate that makes attractive, food-friendly Cahors. This is not much of a surprise, as it is owned by Eric Treuille of Notting Hill's foodie destination, Books for Cooks. The blend softens the 80% Malbec with 20% Merlot, giving it an elegant edge, and Sulphite levels are kept low to help emphasize the fruit. Treuille holds the wines back from the market until they are ready to drink, usually at around five years after bottling. Their green winemaking philosophy extends to the new building, which uses natural materials where possible, such as sheep wool for insulation. ★Rising star

Trespoux, 46090 Cahors
www.domainedessavarines.com

DOMAINE DES SAVARINES
THIS WINE IS RELEASED ONTO THE MARKET
ONLY WHEN IT IS READY TO DRINK

Domaines Grassa Côtes de Gascogne

The name Yves Grassa is most commonly associated with one wine in particular: Château du Tariquet. The estate looms over Côtes de Gascognes, with over 2,471 acres (1,000ha) of vines and a wide range of consistent, approachable, and good-quality bottles. Grassa's studies at UC Davis in California had a profound influence—when he returned home he was the first to use skin contact for white wines, to vinify at low temperatures, and also to believe in highlighting the grape variety on the label. Domaines Grassa proves that big production does not always have to come at the cost of quality—do not expect fireworks, but the Tariquet Classic (70% Ugni Blanc, 30% Colombard) is an unpretentious, frank, and appealing wine. There is also a 100% Sauvignon Blanc, and a 100% Chardonnay —for a smokier version, try the Tête du Cuve, which has been aged in oak, or the Côté Tariquet, a blend of 50% Chardonnay and 50% Sauvignon.

32800 Eauze, Gers
www.tariquet.com

Herri Mina Irouléguy

This small estate in Irouléguy is owned by Jean-Claude Berrouet, who, for a long time, was winemaker at the iconic Moueix estate Pétrus, in Bordeaux's Pomerol. Berrouet's father came from the Basque town of Itxassou, and his introduction to winemaking took place in Gaillac. Returning to these roots, he purchased 4.5 acres (1.8ha) of vineyards in the commune of Ispoure in 1997. His initial focus was Herri Mina Blanc, a fresh, star-bright wine comprising of Manseng and Courbu grapes. Since 2003, he has also produced a Herri Mina Rouge from Cabernet Franc. Although there are plans to build a winery, the wines are currently vinified at Domaine Brana, and are all about expressing their terroir. For Irouléguy this means no maceration before fermentation, no wood, high-quality hand harvesting, and indigenous grape varieties. Just grapes, pressing, fermenting, and bottling.

No visitor facilities
05 59 37 00 44

Producteurs Plaimont Côtes de St-Mont

There are not many co-operative wine cellars that manage to make it onto the lists of the best wines of France, but Plaimont is no ordinary place. It is run by the indefatigable André Dubosc, who makes sure all his winemakers are fully committed, not only to producing great grapes, but also to holding tastings and wine tourism events. He is also a great defender of southwest indigenous grapes. The range of wines is extremely large, as would be expected from a producer with 13,100 acres (5,300ha) of vines, and includes many of the local appellations, from Madiran and St-Mont to Côtes de Gascogne and Pacherenc du Vic-Bilh. It is the attention to detail and unashamedly food-friendly, consumer-focused flavors that make these wines worth getting to know. It is hard to single out just one, but the Vignes Retrouvée from St-Mont, which is available in all three colors and is particularly enjoyable as an Arrufiac, Petit Courbu, and Gros Manseng white, shows how unfussy and pleasurable wine from this part of France can be.

32400 St-Mont
www.plaimont.com

LOIRE VALLEY

If value, diversity, food-friendliness, and ageability are what you look for in wine, then the Loire is your region for one-stop-shopping. From minerally Muscadet to stony Sancerre, the largest French wine region spans 400 miles (600km) along the River Loire running from east to west. As one of the most northerly of wine regions, vintages matter in the Loire, since vineyards planted on stony soil face the sun to soak up the rays. Although climate change has contributed to more frequent warm growing seasons, the wines remain typically lower in alcohol and with more refreshing acidity than many warm regions today. The Loire is also home to a great diversity of wine production that encompasses many kinds of red, white, rosé, and bubbly.

The vast area is home to many grapes. The most magisterial is clearly the aromatic and expressive Chenin Blanc, which comes in various guises including dry, off-dry, sweet, and sparkling. Sauvignon Blanc from the Loire's subregions, notably Sancerre, tends to have a more minerally expression than it does when it is produced in other parts of the world.

In the west of the region, toward the Atlantic coast, the little-known Melon de Bourgogne grape provides the raw material for Muscadets. At their best, these whites can have a crackling, vaguely saline quality that makes them the perfect accompaniment to fresh seafood. Beyond these white grapes, there are an assortment of others that drop under the radar but are nonetheless worthwhile, such as Menu Pineau, Grolleau, and even Romorantin from Cour-Cheverny.

The reds are equally deserving of attention and tend to be centered on the Cabernet Franc grape. A blending grape in Bordeaux—and a majority at that in Cheval Blanc—this Cabernet plays a starring role in the Loire, mostly singing solo. The best expressions come from the subregions of Chinon, Saumur-Champigny, Bourgeuil, and St-Nicholas de Bourgeuil. In the glass, the young wines often have a lovely herbal quality, a meaty note, good acidity, and tannins that can be fine. Other reds cultivated in the area include Gamay, Malbec (aka Côt), Pinot Noir, and Pineau d'Aunis, an intriguing heirloom grape that is making a comeback.

The Loire has also become a hotbed of so-called "natural" winemaking, one of the wine world's most important developments in the past couple of decades. Generally speaking, this includes not using synthetic fertilizers or pesticides in the vineyard, hand harvesting, and eschewing commercial yeasts for fermentation in favor of those that naturally occur on the grape or in the winery. Nicolas Joly, in Savennières, was a pioneer of biodynamics, which goes beyond organic to blend in a celestial timetable, and many growers in the region have assumed this practice in whole or in part.

Generally, the Loire offers tremendous value. Estate wines made by some of the best winemakers in the world from such spectacular sites would fetch several times the price in better-known regions of the wine world. Loire wines remain something of an insider's secret.

Despite being undervalued, some of the wines make for superb aging. Given the recent problems with premature oxidation in white wines from Burgundy, the top whites from Savennières, Vouvray, and Montlouis, made from the magical Chenin Blanc, could experience increased interest from collectors. Heck, even Muscadet from the best sites and producers can easily tack on a decade of age and still be rewarding. Ageworthy wine for an everyday price? In the Loire, it does happen. If you can resist opening them while they are young, that is.

Major grapes

Reds
Cabernet Franc

Côt (Malbec)

Gamay

Pineau d'Aunis

Pinot Noir

Whites
Chenin Blanc

Grolleau

Melon de Bourgogne

Menu Pineau

Romorantin

Sauvignon Blanc

Vintages
2009
Producers say there is excellent ripeness and acidity.

2008
A solid vintage despite inconsistent weather.

2007
The weather in the Central Loire was inconsistent. Sancerre and Muscadet were generally good.

2006
Sancerre and Muscadet were largely spared the difficulties experienced elsewhere.

2005
The reds have excellent concentration and acidity; the whites are mixed.

2004
A classic vintage with Sancerre and Pouilly-Fumé having the best ageability.

LOIRE VALLEY

The Loire wine region, home to 63 appellations, spans 400 miles (600km), from the gneiss soils of Muscadet, in the Pays Nantais, near the Atlantic coast, to the kimmeridgean marl of Sancerre in the Upper Loire. The Pays Nantais is the largest white wine region in France. Anjou is Chenin Blanc territory, from dry to sweet, as well as home to the well-known rosé. In Touraine, caves are often carved out bluffs, while castles and aristocratic hunting lodges intersperse the countryside's vineyards. Its wines are varied, and include sparkling as well as still whites, and reds that come mainly from Cabernet Franc and a handful of other heirloom varieties. The Upper Loire is a home to Sauvignon Blanc and Pinot Noir.

ANJOU-SAUMUR

Agnès and René Mosse ⑥	Dom de la Cotellaraie ㉑
Caves des Vignerons de Saumur ⑮	Dom FL ⑬
	Dom Filiatreau ⑱
Ch du Hureau ⑰	Dom Frédéric Mabileau ㉑
Ch Pierre-Bise ⑦	Dom La Grange aux Belles ⑫
Ch de Villeneuve ⑯	Dom de Juchepie ⑧
Clos Rougeard ⑰	Dom de Montgilet ⑲
Coulée de Serrant ⑪	Dom Ogereau ⑥
Damien Laureau ⑪	Dom Philippe Delesvaux ⑤
Dom de Bablut ⑭	Dom Roches Neuves ⑱
Dom des Baumard ⑩	Eric Morgat ⑪
Dom le Briseau ⑳	Ferme de la Sansonnière ⑨
Dom de la Butte ㉔	Langlois Chateau ⑱
Dom du Closel/Ch des Vaults ⑪	Pithon-Paillé ⑥
	Serge Dagueneau & Filles ⑯
Dom du Collier ⑰	Yannick Amirault ㉔

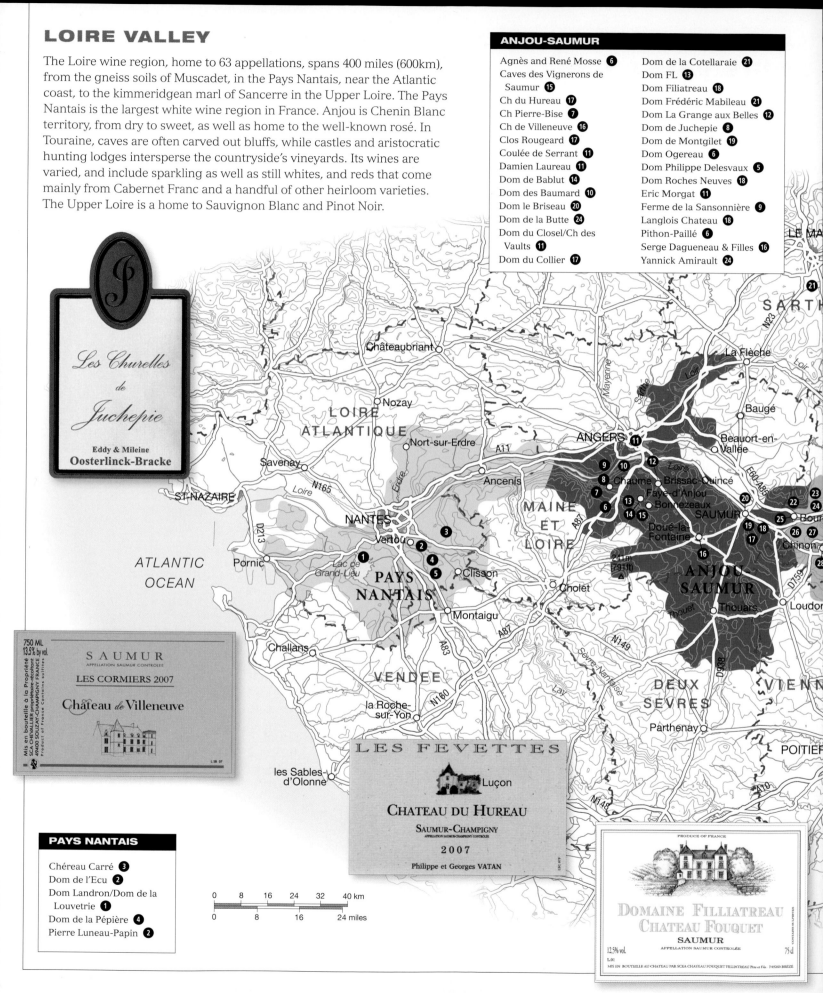

Les Churelles de Juchepie
Eddy & Mileine
Oosterlinck-Bracke

750 ML 13.5% by vol.
SAUMUR
APPELLATION SAUMUR CONTROLEE
LES CORMIERS 2007
Château de Villeneuve
Mis en bouteille à la Propriété SCA CHEVALLIER propriétaire-récoltant 49400 SOUZAY-CHAMPIGNY FRANCE Product of France Contains sulfites
L SB 07

LES FEVETTES
Luçon
CHATEAU DU HUREAU
SAUMUR-CHAMPIGNY
APPELLATION SAUMUR-CHAMPIGNY CONTROLEE
2007
Philippe et Georges VATAN

PRODUCE OF FRANCE
DOMAINE FILLIATREAU
CHATEAU FOUQUET
SAUMUR
12.5% vol. APPELLATION SAUMUR CONTROLEE 75 cl
L.01
MIS EN BOUTEILLE AU CHATEAU PAR SCEA CHATEAU FOUQUET FILLIATREAU Père et Fils. F49260 BREZE

PAYS NANTAIS

Chéreau Carré	③
Dom de l'Ecu	②
Dom Landron/Dom de la Louvetrie	①
Dom de la Pépière	④
Pierre Luneau-Papin	②

Scale:
0 8 16 24 32 40 km
0 8 16 24 miles

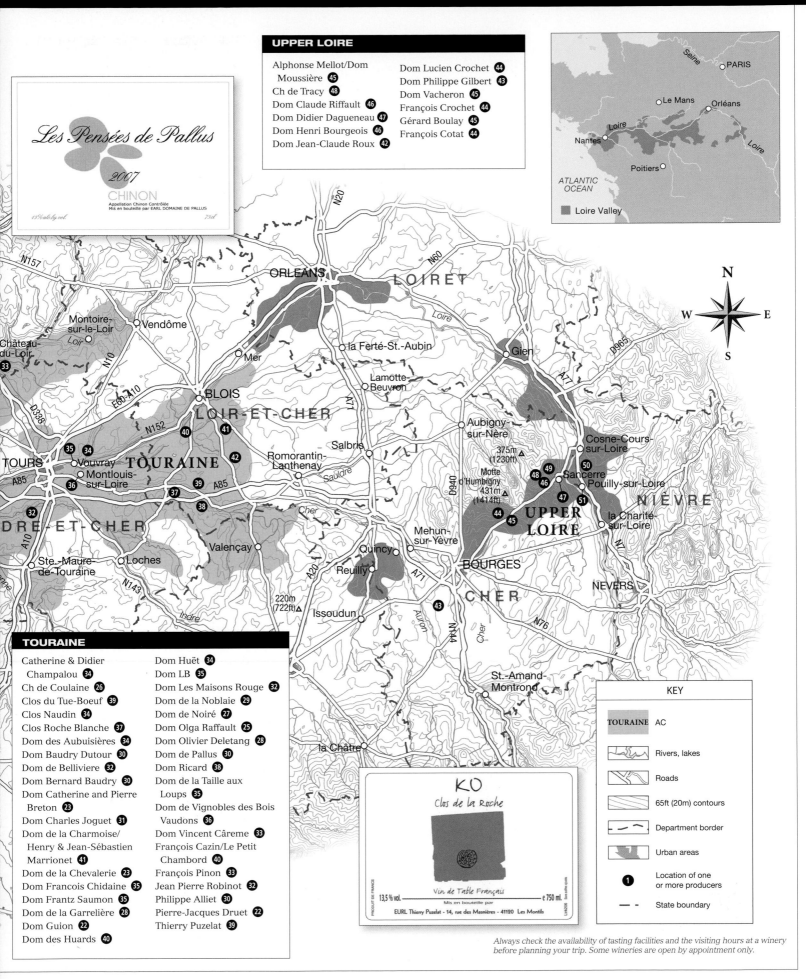

UPPER LOIRE

Alphonse Mellot/Dom Moussière **45**
Ch de Tracy **48**
Dom Claude Riffault **46**
Dom Didier Dagueneau **47**
Dom Henri Bourgeois **46**
Dom Jean-Claude Roux **42**

Dom Lucien Crochet **44**
Dom Philippe Gilbert **43**
Dom Vacheron **45**
François Crochet **44**
Gérard Boulay **45**
François Cotat **44**

TOURAINE

Catherine & Didier Champalou **34**
Ch de Coulaine **26**
Clos du Tue-Boeuf **39**
Clos Naudin **34**
Clos Roche Blanche **37**
Dom des Aubuisières **34**
Dom Baudry Dutour **30**
Dom de Belliviere **32**
Dom Bernard Baudry **30**
Dom Catherine and Pierre Breton **23**
Dom Charles Joguet **31**
Dom de la Charmoise/ Henry & Jean-Sébastien Marrionet **41**
Dom de la Chevalerie **23**
Dom Francois Chidaine **35**
Dom Frantz Saumon **35**
Dom de la Garrelière **28**
Dom Guion **22**
Dom des Huards **40**

Dom Huët **34**
Dom LB **35**
Dom Les Maisons Rouge **32**
Dom de la Noblaie **29**
Dom de Noiré **27**
Dom Olga Raffault **25**
Dom Olivier Deletang **28**
Dom de Pallus **30**
Dom Ricard **38**
Dom de la Taille aux Loups **35**
Dom de Vignobles des Bois Vaudons **36**
Dom Vincent Câreme **33**
François Cazin/Le Petit Chambord **40**
François Pinon **33**
Jean Pierre Robinot **32**
Philippe Alliet **30**
Pierre-Jacques Druet **22**
Thierry Puzelat **39**

KEY

TOURAINE AC

Rivers, lakes

Roads

65ft (20m) contours

Department border

Urban areas

1 Location of one or more producers

State boundary

Always check the availability of tasting facilities and the visiting hours at a winery before planning your trip. Some wineries are open by appointment only.

ALPHONSE MELLOT
GENERATION XIX IS A RICH, PROFOUND
SAUVIGNON BLANC

Agnès and René Mosse Anjou

Agnès and René Mosse came to love natural wines the best way: by drinking them. As proprietors of a wine bar in Tours in the 1990s, they met many local winemakers such as Jo Pithon and Francois Chidaine. In 1999, they purchased a 32 acre (13ha) vineyard (and house and cellar) in the Coteaux-du-Layon part of Anjou. They have farmed organically since the beginning, and have also added some biodynamics. They make a range of exciting wines, including a red, dry whites, rosé, and sweet wines, when the weather permits.

4 rue de la Chauvière, 49750 St-Lambert-du-Lattay
www.domaine-mosse.com

Alphonse Mellot/Domaine Moussière
Sancerre

As the 19th generation of winemakers here, one could be forgiven for thinking Alphonse Mellot has Sancerre rouge coursing through his veins. In the 1980s, the house decided to focus on estate wines, which now come from the 125 acres (47ha) of organically farmed, hand-harvested vines. The serious La Moussière wines come from hand-sorted grapes, and both red and white see time in vat and new oak casks. At the top of the line, the Génération XIX white comes from almost 100-year-old vines and is aged in 198-gallon (900-litre) vats.

Domaine de la Moussière, 18300, Sancerre
www.mellot.com

Catherine & Didier Champalou Vouvray

Catherine and Didier Champalou farm their 50 acres (20ha) sustainably to produce still and sparkling Vouvray. The Vouvray ferments in stainless steel and ages in old oak vats known as *demi-muids*; the Cuvée des Fondraux, which has more concentration, ages in old oak casks. The sparkling wine is dependable.

7 rue du Grand Ormeau, 37210 Vouvray
www.champalou.com

Caves des Vignerons de Saumur
Saumur, Saumur-Champigny

With 200 member-growers working 4,450 acres (1,800ha), this co-operative produces many wines, sparkling and still, dry and sweet. The basic, fruit-driven Réserve des Vignerons range of dry Chenin Blanc and Cabernet Franc is an excellent value for the money, but the overarching aim is to make terroir-driven wines. To that end, the vineyards are split into 3,700 parcels, so viticulture and winemaking can be adapted to site. Burgundian winemaker Eric Laurent adeptly captures Cabernet Franc's Pinot Noir-like perfumed, fresh, and silky qualities. The single-vineyard Saumur-Champigny Les Poyeux is a great ambassador for site and variety.

Route Saumoussay, 49260 St-Cyr-en-Bourg
www.cavedesaumur.com

Château de Coulaine Chinon

Château de Coulaine is a family-owned estate, located on prime clay–limestone and gravel soils, and boasting a viticultural tradition dating back to the 14th century. Run by Pascale and Etienne de Bonnaventure since 1988, quality has increased dramatically. The vineyard, now cultivated organically, has expanded to 30 acres (12ha). Younger vines are channeled into a round and raspberry-

CHEREAU CARRE
LE CLOS DU CHÂTEAU L'OISELINIÈRE IS
A TERROIR-DRIVEN MUSCADET

fruited entry level unoaked red. Ageworthy oaked *cuvées* Clos de Turpenay and La Diablesse derive from 40- to 80-year-old vines. Supple and sensual, they develop savory notes with age, which make them a perfect complement to game dishes. ★**Rising star**

37420 Beaumont en Véron
02 47 98 44 51

Château du Hureau Saumur-Champigny

Saumur-Champigny's soft tufa limestone produces the Loire's most perfumed, silk- or velvet-textured Cabernet Francs. These elegant traits, and sheer fruit purity, are pronounced in Philippe Vatan's Château du Hureau reds because he prefers micro-oxygenation over barrel-aging to soften tannins. Just 5% of his top wines, Les Fevettes and Lisgathe, see oak. Their powerful structure derives from tufa with a deeper clay topsoil. Cultivated organically, the 46 acre (18.5ha) estate is divided into 21 plots that also yield two unoaked reds and a small quantity of generally dry, but sometimes sweet, Chenin Blanc (depending on the occurrence of botrytis).

49400 Dampierre-sur-Loire
www.domaine-hureau.fr

Château Pierre-Bise Anjou

Claude Papin is intellectually curious. That is clearly on display in the dizzying array of wines that he makes in sites that straddle the Loire and encompass reds, rosés, and whites, dry and sweet. That he only assumed the duties at Pierre-Bise, his wife's family estate, in 1990 makes it more impressive. The Quarts de Chaume sweet whites are impressive; he also makes several sweet Layons, a dry Savennières in Roche aux Moines, as well as Cabernet Franc, Gamay, and even an off-dry rosé d'Anjou. These diverse efforts have received lavish praise and, as a result, the wines can be frustratingly difficult to find.

49750 Beaulieu-sur-Layon
02 41 78 31 44

Château de Tracy Pouilly-Fumé

Vines have been planted at Château de Tracy for more than six centuries. When Jacqueline de Tracy married Count Alain d'Estutt d'Astay in the 1950s, the couple renovated the 69 acre (28ha) vineyard and forged a reputation for classy, long-lived Pouilly-Fumé. The next generation's legacy is two extreme wines. Haute Densité, made since 2004, hails from young vines planted at high density (6,900 vines/acre or 17,000/ha). Limestone soils yield a weighty but subtle wine, of which 15% is oaked. From 2008, it is joined by 101 Rangs, a powerfully mineral, oak-aged Sauvignon Blanc from 101 rows of 55-year-old vines planted on flint soils.

Tracy-sur-Loire, 58150, Pouilly-sur-Loire
www.chateau-de-tracy.com

Château de Villeneuve
Saumur-Champigny, Saumur Blanc

Jean-Pierre Chevallier studied enology in Bordeaux and took over the family estate in 1982. His accomplished range combines the best of tradition with modern technology. Dry reds and whites show amply concentrated ripe fruit, but not at the expense of poise and finesse. Flagships Le Grand Clos (Cabernet Franc) and Les Cormiers (Chenin Blanc) are powerfully structured, ageworthy wines, with fabulous underlying minerality. A sweet Coteaux de Saumur Chenin Blanc is made in warmer years.

49400 Souzay-Champigny
www.chateau-de-villeneuve.com

Chéreau Carré Muscadet Sèvre et Maine
Chéreau Carré makes consistently fine Muscadet Sèvre et Maine from four prime estates: Château l'Oiselinière de la Ramée, Château de Chasseloir, Château de la Chesnaie, and Domaine du Bois Bruley. Each produces subtly different wines. La Griffe Bernard Chéreau is a young-vine blend from all four estates. Le Clos du Château l'Oiselinière hails from a precocious south-facing *cru* communal site with schist and ortho-gneiss soils. Aged at least 17 months on the lees, it is broad-shouldered, yet mineral.

44690 Saint Fiacre sur Maine
www.chereau-carre.fr

Clos Naudin Clos Naudin
Acquired in 1924 by the Foreau family, the Clos Naudin vineyard produces some of the best wines of Vouvray. Philippe is the third generation to make the wines, which express the full range of Chenin Blanc, from sec to moelleux to a contemplative brut. The vines, with their feet in flinty clay soil, are kept to a low yield and harvested by hand in several passes. The pure, elegant, minerally wines have a lively acidity and are tremendously ageworthy, but also delectable while young.

14 rue de la Croix Buisée, 37210 Vouvray
02 47 52 71 46

Clos Roche Blanche Touraine
Catherine Roussel and Didier Barrouillet craft wines that are friendly to both wallets and palates from the 44 acre (18ha) Clos Roche Blanche family estate. They practice non-interventionist winemaking as well as organic grape growing. The Sauvignon Blanc is refreshing and pure, the Pineau d'Aunis peppery, the Gamay lip-smacking, and the Cabernet (a blend of Franc and Sauvignon) more intense. But the top wine is clearly the Côt (Malbec), which includes vines that range from 25 to 115 years old.

19 route de Montrichard, 41110, Mareuil-sur-Cher
02 54 75 17 03

Clos Rougeard Clos Rougeard
If many Loire Cabernet Francs are as serviceable as a Honda, and the better ones add the zip of a Saab, then Clos Rougeard is a Ferrari. A benchmark estate for the Loire, the Foucault brothers Charlie and Nadi run this 25-acre (10-ha) property, which has been in their family for generations. Of the wines, the Clos is profound but sees little new oak; the Poyeux and the Bourg have greater raw material, but also see more new oak.

15 rue de l'Eglise, 49400 Chacé
02 41 52 92 65

Clos du Tue-Boeuf Clos du Tue-Boeuf
When Jean-Marie and Thierry Puzelat took over their father's 40 acre (16ha) estate in the 1990s, they made two difficult decisions: to not uproot the vast assortment of heirloom grape varieties planted and to redouble the efforts on organic viticulture. Inspired by Marcel Lapierre and other natural winemakers, they also decided to make the wines as naturally as possible. This has meant leaving the appellation (sacrilege to most *vignerons*) and selling wines such as the La Guerrerie, a red blend, as Vin de Table. Lively, quirky, and often downright delicious, the wines can also be hard to find.

6 route de Seur, Les Montils, 41120
02 54 44 05 06

Coulée de Serrant Savennières
Coulée de Serrant is a magnificent site. It includes an amphitheater of Chenin Blanc looking down onto the River Loire, and is one of the top sites of the Loire Valley, first planted by monks in 1130. Today, that site is one of two in France to have its own appellation. The estate has 32 acres (13ha) with two wines coming from adjacent appellations. Nicolas Joly practices biodynamics and makes the wines, but his daughter, Virginie, is taking on a larger role. The wines are different from others, and often polarizing. The younger wines benefit from decanting: if you stop by the Coulée, the wines for tasting will have been decanted for 24 to 48 hours.

Château de la Roche aux Moines, 49170, Savennières
www.coulee-de-serrant.com

Damien Laureau Savennières
Aged 39 and a father of six, Damien Laureau is a busy man. From a family of cereal farmers near Versailles, he is largely self-taught in wine. Starting out in 1999 with a vineyard near Anjou, he now has long-term leases on two vineyards in Savennières. Over the past five years, he has transitioned the vineyards from conventional to organic. The stony Savennières wines are excellent examples of dry Chenin Blanc. The impressive Les Genets is aged mostly in vat for 18 months; the rich Le Bel Ouvrage is aged mostly in barrel for almost two years. ★ **Rising star**

Chemin du Grand Hamé, Epiré, 49170, Savennières
www.damien-laureau.fr

Domaine des Aubuisières Vouvray
Bernard Fouquet farms 57 acres (23ha) of Chenin Blanc to make every expression of the grape: dry, off-dry, sweet, and sparkling. The grapes are almost all hand harvested, often in several passes through the vineyard. The slightly sweet Cuvée de Silex has minerally precision with a slight honeyed quality; the sparkling brut is a delicious apéritif.

Vallée de Nouy, 37210, Vouvray
www.vouvrayfouquet.com

Domaine de Bablut
Anjou-Villages Brissac, Coteaux de L'Aubance
Domaine de Bablut's Christophe Daviau makes powerful reds with ripe but present tannins. With Rocca Nigra, a 100% Cabernet Sauvignon, he skillfully avoids the unforgiving tannins that often result from Anjou's schist soils. His finely honed top Cabernet Franc, Petra Alba, is grown on easier-going limestone soils. Daviau also makes accomplished Chenin Blancs—a toothsome range of sweet Coteaux de L'Aubance (Grandpierre is a great buy) and the ageworthy, dry, oaked Ordovicien.

49320 Brissac-Quincé
www.vignobles-daviau.fr

CHENIN BLANC

Sauvignon Blanc is known as a member of wine's club of so-called "noble" grapes. But the multifaceted expressions of Chenin Blanc may be gearing up for a defenestration of its regional rival. At its best in the middle Loire, Chenin Blanc comes dry, off-dry, sweet, and sparkling. From the tiny Savennières, the wines, once favored in the royal court, are always dry yet have a multi-layered texture. In Vouvray, the wines run the gamut, reflecting the beautiful balance between acidity and sweetness. In Coteaux du Layon and Quarts de Chaume, the grapes are harvested late and covered in the nobly-rotten mold known as botrytis. The best examples of each category are phenomenally ageworthy. They also happen to be phenomenally undervalued.

WINE STYLES

DOMAINE BAUDRY-DUTOUR
CHATEAU DE LA GRILLE IS ONE OF THIS
DOMAINE'S MANY IMPRESSIVE CHINONS

DOMAINE DE BELLIVIERE
VIEILLES VIGNES EPARSES IS CLASSIC 100%
CHENIN BLANC FROM COTEAUX DU LOIR

Domaine Baudry-Dutour Chinon

In 2003, the merger of Domaine de la Perrière and Domaine du Roncée combined the talents of Christophe Baudry and Jean-Martin Dutour. Baudry, a third-generation *vigneron*, brought his detailed understanding of Chinon. Dutour, Roncée's young winemaker, trained at Montpellier's prestigious wine school. The dynamic duo have since built a state-of-the-art, gravity-fed winery and acquired new vineyards, notably Château de la Grille, making Baudry-Dutour Chinon's biggest domaine with some 300 acres (120ha) under vine. Their limited-production, old-vine *cuvées* are impressive. But the investment in quality is equally apparent in Baudry-Dutour's smooth and fruity entry level reds, and in Cuvée Marie-Justine, a pretty, off-dry rosé. ★ Rising star

12 Coteau de Sonnay, 37500 Cravant les Coteaux
www.baudry-dutour.com

Domaine des Baumard Anjou (including Quarts–de-Chaume and Savennières)

Florent Baumard makes a stunning array of wines. It runs from red to rosé as well as—and more importantly—all gradations of Chenin Blanc, including sparkling. Straddling both sides of the Loire, the family domaine was established in 1634. The dry Savennières from the Clos du Papillion vineyard is a perennial classic (and the Trie Speciale in select years). From the Rochefort side of the river, the more unctuous Coteaux du Layon and Quarts de Chaume are excellent, enticing examples. Baumard's viticultural curiosity is such that he also maintains a small amount of old Verdelho.

8 rue de l'Abbaye, 49190, Rochefort-sur-Loire
www.baumard.fr

Domaine de Belliviere

Jasnières, Coteaux du Loir
Thirty miles (50km) north of Tours, along the banks of the Loir River (which feeds into the larger Loire), lie the almost forgotten vineyards of Jasnières and Coteaux du Loir. Eric and Christine Nicolas purchased some of the older vines and quickly started to put these appellations on the map. They reduced yields and planted one vineyard with an astounding 16,200 vines/acre (40,000/ha). The Chenin Blanc is their calling card, and of the many bottlings Les Rosiers comes from younger vines, the concentrated Calligrame from 50-year-old vines. The Nicolases are also fans of the red grape Pineau d'Aunis and have two bottlings.

72340 Lhomme
www.belliviere.com

Domaine Bernard Baudry Chinon

Over the past 30 years, Domaine Bernard Baudry has quietly moved into the vanguard of the Loire's red wine producers. Bernard Baudry was trained in Beaune and now has 75 acres (30ha), including some choice vineyard parcels. Les Granges, by the Vienne River, has the youngest vines; the Domaine has older vines and some hillside plots; Les Grézaux has old vines on limestone and clay; the Clos Guillot includes some ungrafted vines. The rosé is an annual delight. After studying in France, and traveling to Tasmania and California, Bernard's son, Matthieu, now works alongside him at the estate.

9 Coteau de Sonnay, 37500 Cravant-les-Côteaux
www.chinon.com/vignoble/Bernard-Baudry

Domaine Le Briseau

Jasnières, Coteaux du Loir
Once under the radar, Jasnières and Coteaux du Loir have become magnets for idiosyncratic winemakers like Christian and Nathalie Chaussard, who arrived at Domaine Le Briseau in 2002. Patapon, a Pineau d'Aunis and Côt red blend is as fun and exuberant as its name and label suggest. Les Mortiers, 100% old-vine Pineau d'Aunis, is paler, delicately structured, and intense. The common thread for the Chenin Blancs (which are dry or sweet depending on the vintage), is character. A hands-off approach produces vital, edgy wines with pronounced minerality. The estate is certified organic and has been converting to biodynamic since 2006. ★ Rising star

Les Nérons, Marçon carte, Sarthe
02 43 44 58 53

Le Domaine de la Butte Bourgueil

In 2002, Montlouis-sur-Loire maestro Jacky Blot acquired a stunning 37 acre (15ha) vineyard in Bourgueil. Most vineyards are flat, but Blot had greater ambition for his Cabernet Franc. La Butte's steep, sunny, south-facing slope naturally produces low yields of ripe, concentrated fruit, making for sensual but structured wines. A terroir-driven approach accounts for subtle differences between Le Haut (the highest point and flintiest soils), Mi-Pente (mid-slope with limestone soils), La Pied (at the bottom, with richer clay–limestone soils), and Les Perrières (a stony, limestone parcel). ★ Rising star

La Butte, 37140, Bourgueil
www.jackyblot.fr

Domaine Catherine and Pierre Breton Bourgueil

Pierre and Catherine Breton have become leaders of the natural wine movement, celebrated in hipster wine bars in Paris and beyond. Pierre started the vineyard in 1982 and shortly after Catherine joined in 1989, they adopted organic practices and later converted some of their vineyards to biodynamics. The line-up includes the gulpable Trinch (the sound of two glasses clinking); the lip-smacking Les Nuits d'Ivresse (drunken nights) is bottled without sulphites. Of the many single-vineyard bottlings, two stand out: Clos Sénéchal, a top vineyard site, is aged in vats and finished in barrel; Les Perrières, another top terroir, receives some new oak. Both of these wines will probably age tremendously.

Les Galichets 8 rue du Peu Muleau, 37140 Restigné
www.domainebreton.net

Domaine Charles Joguet Chinon

Under the direction of Charles Joguet, this estate was arguably the finest in Chinon. However, Joguet retired in 1997. Jacques Genet then bought the property, and he added his 59 acres (24ha) of new vineyards, bringing the estate's total to 89 acres (36ha). The estate, now on its third winemaker post-Joguet, bottles the various wines, often quite dark in color, by vineyard plot. The top wines are the Clos de la Dioterie, which comes from old vines and the Clos du Chêne Vert. Despite the changes over the past decade, the estate still has passionate supporters.

La Dioterie, 37220 Sazilly
www.charlesjoguet.com

Domaine de la Charmoise/Henry & Jean-Sébastien Marrionet Touraine

Unstinting in his commitment to quality and innovation, Henry Marrionet is one of Touraine's leading lights. Between 1967 and 1978 he completely replanted his 148 acre (60ha) domaine. Marrionet specializes in ripe, exuberantly fruity Gamay and Sauvignon Blanc. The real lure for wine enthusiasts are the idiosyncratic Vinifera range (from young ungrafted vines), Provignage (a Romorantin sourced from ungrafted, pre-phylloxera vines planted in 1850, among France's oldest), and Les Cépages Oubliés (named after the near-extinct red-fleshed Gamay de Bouze). Complex, structured, and mineral, these are serious wines.

La Charmoise, 41230 Soings-en-Sologne
02 54 98 70 73

Domaine de Châtenoy Menetou-Salon

Although the Clément family is now on the 15th generation of vineyard owners in Menetou-Salon, the Domaine de Châtenoy winery is modern. Pierre Clément is the big fish in the small pond of Menetou, both as past president of the appellation and as the AC's largest producer, having grown the family estate from 30 acres (12ha) in the 1980s to 150 acres (60ha) today. The entry-level white offers pleasant, minerally refreshment at a reasonable price. The estate also makes a Pinot Noir from hand-harvested grapes, fermented and matured in one-third new oak casks.

18510, Menetou-Salon
www.clement-chatenoy.com

Domaine de la Chevalerie Bourgueil

Fourteen generations of the Caslot family have made wine at Domaine de la Chevalerie, founded in 1640. Cultivated biodynamically, the 82 acre (33ha) domaine runs the gamut of Bourgueil's soil types. Silky and perfumed, the entry level Peu Muleau comes from sandy soils, while clay and limestone produce more structured, powerful wines, especially old-vine Chevalerie and Busardières. Irrespective of which *cuvée* is being made, the fruit is hand-picked, sorted, stemmed, and gently extracted, which accounts for Chevalerie's signature seductively textured, sweetly spiced wines.

7-14 rue du Peu Muleau, 37149 Restigné
www.domainedelachevalerie.fr

Domaine Claude Riffault Sancerre

Claude Riffault won renown for his sophisticated, but good value, fruity wines. His son, Stéphane, looks set to take the domaine to fresh heights, focusing even more intently on vineyard expression. He makes five Sauvignon Blancs and two Pinot Noirs from 33 acres (13.5ha) of vines that are divided into 33 parcels across four villages. From silex soils, flinty, tight Sauvignon Les Chailloux starkly contrasts with full-bodied new *cuvée* Les Denisottes, which is sourced from deep limestone and clay soils. The use of two presses for the quick processing of grapes means that excellent fruit expression remains a strength, especially for the Pinot Noirs, which are among the region's most approachable. ★ Rising star

Maison Salle, 18300 Sury-en-Vaux
02 48 79 38 22

DOMAINE BERNARD BAUDRY
LE CLOS GUILLOT IS A HIGH-QUALITY WINE
FROM RELATIVELY YOUNG VINES

DOMAINE DE LA CHEVALERIE
CAREFUL WINEMAKING DRAWS OUT THE
TERROIR IN THE CHEVALERIE CUVEE

Domaine du Closel/Château des Vaults Savennières

A long line of women have ruled Domaine du Closel/Château des Vaults. Michèle de Jessey took it over from her aunt, Madame du Closel. Today, Evelyne de Jessey oversees the estate, and under her there has been a transition to biodynamics. The château lies on handsome grounds (with a sculpture garden), but the vineyards are located a short walk uphill and look down onto the Loire. The best wines of the estate are from the 10 acres (4ha) in the Clos du Papillon vineyard.

49170 Savennières
02 41 72 81 00

Domaine du Collier Saumur

The co-founder of Domaine du Collier, Antoine Foucault, is the son of Charlie Foucault of Clos Rougeard fame. Father and son worked together for a time before Antoine established Domaine du Collier with Caroline Boireau in 1999. Although Foucault *père* is best known for reds, Domaine du Collier's 14 acres (5.5ha) are mostly planted to Chenin Blanc, and whites are the strong suit. La Charpentrie, a barrel-fermented and aged Chenin from 95-year-old vines is sumptuous and layered, with Burgundian balance and minerality. ★ Rising star

62 place du Collier, 49400 Chace
www.domaineducollier.free.fr

Domaine de la Cotellaraie
St-Nicolas-de-Bourgueil

Since becoming winemaker in 1997, Gérald Vallée has propelled his family's 62 acre (25ha) Domaine de la Cotellaraie into the Loire's top tier of Cabernet Franc producers. The vineyards, which include around 10% Cabernet Sauvignon, are meticulously worked by hand and Vallée achieves a deft balance of ripe but succulent black cherry and currant with modest alcohol. Sensitive winemaking allows the fruit and his vineyard's gravelly minerality to shine. Only flagship L'Envolée, sourced from 60-year-old vines, sees new oak. Le Vau Jaumier and Les Perruches are single parcel wines from clay–limestone and flint–clay soils respectively. ★ Rising star

2, La Cotelleraie, 37140 St-Nicolas-de-Bourgueil
02 47 97 75 53

Domaine Didier Dagueneau Pouilly-Fumé

Didier Dagueneau was an iconoclast who took Sauvignon Blanc to arguably its highest expression. A motorcycle racer in his youth, he started off with a small parcel of vines in 1982, and by the 1990s had downshifted to a horse-powered plough in the vineyard. His quest for quality ruffled feathers in his stuffy appellation. His old-vine, barrel-fermented Pur Sang ("thoroughbred") and Silex are known for richness and minerally precision—and are priced accordingly. Tragically, this rebel winemaker died in September 2008, aged 52, when his small plane crashed. His son Benjamin has taken over the estate.

1–7 rue Ernesto Ché Guevara, 58150, St-Andelain
03 86 39 15 62

Domaine de l'Ecu Muscadet de Sevre et Maine

The delicious wines of Guy Bossard's Domaine de l'Ecu remain touchstones for quality in the region—both Muscadet and the Loire. Bossard, an exceptional

LE DOMAINE DE LA GARRELIERE
GAMAY SANS TRA-LA-LA: CHARMING LABEL, CHARMING FRUIT, CHARMING WINE

winemaker, converted his estate to organic viticulture in the 1970s and was certified biodynamic in 1986 (his wines sport the certification in a neck label). Touchstone is apt since each *cuvée* reflects the rocks: the Expression de Gneiss has tangy refreshment; the Expression de Orthogneiss has greater breadth and length; the Expression de Granite shimmers with elegance and minerality. As with all top Muscadets, try these with age.

La Bretonniére, 44430 Le Landreau
02 40 06 40 91

Domaine FL

Savennières, Savennières La Roches-aux-Moines, Anjou, Coteaux du Layon, Quarts de Chaume
Philippe Fournier, a telecommunications tycoon, acquired the prestigious vineyards of Domaine Jo Pithon and Château de Chamboreau, complete with winemaking teams, in 2005 and 2006. Since Pithon left, in 2008, wines from both estates have been sold under the snappy new name Domaine FL and are made by Hugues Daubercies (ex-Chamboreau) with Bordeaux guru Stéphane Derenoncourt. While Pithon's dry Anjou and sweet Coteaux du Layon Chenin Blancs were justly renowned, Chamboreau's Savennières was in the doldrums. Quality has leapt under the new regime, which is crafting a subtly modern, dry, oak-buffed Savennières of great purity, poise, and minerality. La Roches-aux-Moines particularly impresses. ★ Rising star

1 place François Mitterrand, 49100 Angers
www.domainefl.com

Domaine Filiatreau Saumur-Champigny

Downriver from Chinon lies the all-red appellation of Saumur-Champigny. Here, in a dramatic site, lies La Grande Vignolle, where a plateau of vines meets a formidable limestone bluff. This is one of the old-vine vineyard sites of Domaine Filliatreau, which encompasses 100 acres (40ha) to make it the largest domaine in the appellation. Carved out of the bluff are the chai (wine shed) and cellars where Paul and his son Frédrik make their various *cuvées*, including the serious examples of Cabernet Franc, the Chateau Fouquet, and the more structured Les Grandes Vignolles.

Chaintres, 49400 Saumur
www.filliatreau.fr

Domaine François Chidaine

Montlouis, Vouvray
Is there a hipper appellation in the Loire than Montlouis? Across the river from the better-known Vouvray, Montlouis has developed a reputation for its trendy art galleries. The leader (unofficially and officially, as the president of the appellation) of Montlouis is François Chidaine. From his early days two decades ago, Chidaine farmed his plots organically, transitioning to biodynamics in 1999. Now he has 74 acres (30ha), including 25 acres (10ha) in Vouvray proper, the Clos Baudin. The low-yielding grapes are hand-harvested. In Montlouis, his excellent range includes the dry Clos du Breuil, the off-dry Tuffeaux and Clos Habert, and a sweet moelleux. All are ageworthy, enticing examples of Chenin Blanc in all its guises. ★ Rising star

5 Grande Rue, Husseau, 37270 Montlouis-sur-Loire
www.francois-chidaine.com

Domaine Frantz Saumon

Montlouis
Ex-forester Frantz Saumon purchased 12 acres (5ha) in 2001 and has swiftly made his mark in Montlouis-sur-Loire. His barrel-fermented and aged Chenin Blancs show an innate understanding of wood. As the name of his demi-sec, Minerale+, suggests, oak is used judiciously, not at the expense of terroir, to enhance structure and complexity. Le P'tit Caporal and Clos de Chêne are precise, dry, well-focused wines with persistent bright pear fruit. The latter, made from vines nearing a century in age, shows great depth and concentration. Vineyards are worked organically. ★ Rising star

15 B Che des Cours, 37270 Montlouis-sur-Loire
06 16 83 47 90

Domaine Frédéric Mabileau

St-Nicolas-de-Bourgueil, Bourgueil, Anjou, Saumur
Rather than join the family domaine, Frédéric Mabileau established his own label in 1991. He has steadily accumulated 67 acres (27ha), certified organic since 2009. Naturally, Cabernet Franc dominates, but, in 2007, Mabileau made a powerful, oaked Saumur Blanc and, in 2009, another dry Chenin Blanc from his Anjou vineyard (which also produces a Cabernet Sauvignon). As for Cabernet Franc, selection tables and gravity-fed winemaking have increased standards still higher. Premium *cuvées* Les Racines (Bourgueil), Les Coutures, and flagship Eclipse show lustrous fruit and supple tannins, gently buttressed by oak. Fresh and aromatic with lively, gravel-edged red cherry and berry fruit, Les Rouilléres is for earlier drinking. ★ Rising star

6 rue du Pressoir, 37140 St-Nicolas-de-Bourgueil
www.fredericmabileau.com

Le Domaine de la Garrelière Touraine

Since 1985, François Plouzeau has focused his energies in Touraine rather than in the more reputable Chinon, home to his father's domaine. Certified biodynamic, Plouzeau's low-yielding, south-facing 50 acre (20ha) vineyard on prime clay, limestone, and flint slopes accounts for his Sauvignon Blanc's structure, ripe citrus, and minerality. Rich but lithe, the more complex Cendrillon is part barrel-fermented Sauvignon Blanc with Chardonnay and Chenin Blanc. Gamay Sans Tra-la-la's exuberant bramble fruit is guaranteed to charm, as are Plouzeau's artist-designed labels. ★ Rising star

37120 Razines
www.garreliere.com

Domaine La Grange aux Belles Anjou

Former geologist Marc Houtin is the man behind Domaine La Grange aux Belles, founded in 2004. After an internship at Château d'Yquem, Houtin first tried his hand at sweet wine. Today he focuses on great-value dry wines. Since being joined by ex-Mongilet viticulturist Julien Bresteau in 2006, the vines have been cultivated naturally and are revealing their full potential. Le Vin du Jardin reds (Grolleau and Gamay) show fresh, vivid fruit. Beautifully balanced Anjou Princé Cabernet Franc and Anjou Fragile Chenin Blanc offer a seamless synthesis of fruit and minerals. ★ Rising star

Quartier artisanal de l'églantier, 49610 Murs-Erigne
02 41 80 05 72

DOMAINE FREDERIC MABILEAU
INDEPENDENT-MINDED FREDERIC MABILEAU APPLIES HIS TALENTS IN MANY APPELLATIONS

Domaine Guion Bourgeuil

Certified organic since 1965: these words on the label say quite a bit about Stephane Guion's philosophy. Two generations of organic farming, hand harvesting, and native yeasts produce two 100% Cabernet Franc wines, the domaine (unoaked) and the *cuvée* prestige (gentle oak), from 35- to 80-year-old vines. These fantastic-value wines are lip-smacking and delicious, with pure fruit and tannic structure. they are ready to be the house wine at discriminating restaurants around the world. The best secret about them? They can age, too.

3 route de Saint Gilles, 37140 Benais
www.domaineguion.com

Domaine Les Hautes Noëlles

Muscadet-Cotes de Grandlieu, Muscadet

The Hautes Noëlles domaine produces reliable, affordable Muscadet. Serge Batard owns and runs this family estate, which has been around since the 1930s (he previously owned a wine shop and is a Burgundy fan). The estate eschews chemical treatments in the vineyards, harvests by hand, has long fermentations, and ages the wine *sur lie*. The Muscadet Côtes de Grandlieu has a citrussy, almost saline, tongue-tingling refreshment. Batard also makes some other wines including a Gamay/Grolleau blend as Vin de Pays.

La Haute Galerie, 44710 St-Léger-les-Vignes
www.vigneron-serge-batard.com

Domaine Henri Bourgeois

Sancerre, Pouilly-Fumé

Domaine Henri Bourgeois is based in Chavignol where, 60 years ago, the estate consisted of 5 acres (2ha).The 10th-generation family house now has 165 acres (65ha), which provide grapes for about half the wines made. The family also has a property in New Zealand's Marlborough region and are even bottling some of their tasty Sancerres in screwcap. The top wines from Sancerre and Pouilly-Fumé see time in oak barrels.

Chavignol, 18300 Sancerre
www.henribourgeois.com

Domaine des Huards

Cheverny, Cour-Cheverny

Michel Gendrier makes high-toned, minerally whites and reds from two appellations using organic farming. Reds and whites come from Cheverny, where he makes Gamay and Pinot Noir, as well as Sauvignon Blanc and some Chardonnay. But in Cour-Cheverny, Huard makes the white Romorantin, the only grape permitted in the appellation. These wines, which do well in France but are difficult to find abroad, not only drink well upon release, but are ageworthy, picking up an intriguing waxy note.

41700 Cour-Cheverny
02 54 79 97 90

Domaine Huët Vouvray

Any doubters of the greatness of Vouvray (or Chenin Blanc) need to try the superb wines of Huët. Founded in 1928 by Victor Huët and his son Gaston, the winery has been run for more than two decades by Gaston's son-in-law, Noël Pinguet (although the American Anthony Hwang now owns the estate). In the 1990s, Pinguet transitioned to biodynamic farming. The wines are stunning examples of the full expressions of Vouvray: single-vineyard dry, off-dry, and sweet wines, with the sweetest wines having separate bottlings from each pass through the vineyard. The sparkling wine is also a benchmark. Visiting the modest tasting room at the winery yields tastes of older vintages; it is hard to resist purchasing more from the cool cellar.

11 rue de la Croix Buisée, 37210 Vouvray
www.huet-echansonne.com

Domaine Jean-Claude Roux Quincy

Roux is one of a band of cereal farmers encouraged by government subsidies to grow grapes. He made his first medal-winning wine in 1995, since when the domaine has grown from 4 acres (1.5ha) to 16 acres (6.5ha) to cope with demand. He makes just one wine—a ripe, stone-fruited Sauvignon Blanc whose finesse derives from its racy, citrus acidity and mineral complexity. Since 2009, it has been made at Maison Blanche, a state-of-the-art winery built in collaboration with 17 other *vignerons*.

18340 Arçay
www.domaine-roux-vin-quincy.com

Domaine de Juchepie Coteaux de Layon

South of the Loire, along the Layon tributary, lie the vineyards of Eddy and Marie-Madeleine Oosterlinck, who make their concentrated wines at Domaine de Juchepie. Organic since 1994, and now incorporating biodynamics, the Oosterlinks are demanding viticulturalists: instead of a green harvest, they prune early in the season, allowing only six to 10 bunches per vine, a riskier but perhaps more rewarding practice. Harvested late, the grapes are fermented and aged in oak.

Les Quarts, 49380 Faye D'anjou
www.juchepie.com

Domaines Landron/Domaine de la Louvetrie Muscadet

Jo Landron is one of the bright stars of Muscadet. Sporting a bushy moustache, he looks every bit the French *vigneron*. And the wines are similarly classic, refreshing examples of Muscadet. Taking over the family estate of approximately 89 acres (36ha) in 1990, Landron shifted to organic viticulture, attaining certification in 1999, and is now transitioning to biodynamics. The Melon de Bourgogne vines produce mainly three wines: the zippy Ampholite Nature; the vivacious Hermine d'Or; and the substantial and ageworthy Le Fief du Breil.

route de Bellevue, 44690, La Haye-Fouassiere
02 40 54 83 27

Domaine LB Montlouis-sur-Loire

Husband-and-wife team Lise and Bertrand Jousset are the dynamic duo behind the sizeable 54 acre (22ha) Domaine LB, which was created in 2004. They have swiftly forged a reputation for meticulous attention to detail in both the vineyard and the winery. Precise and persistent dry wines, Premier Rendez-vou, and the tight-knit, old-vine Singulier, show pear and citrus fruit, while demi-sec Trait d'Union and moelleux Sur le fil lead with honeyed stone fruits. ★Rising star

36 rue des Bouvineries, 37270, Montlouis-sur-Loire
02 47 50 70 33

NICOLAS JOLY

Nicolas Joly speaks with the zeal of the convert. The symbolic leader of biodynamics for wine originally went to Columbia University and started a career in finance. But he quit and returned to his mother's vineyard, Coulée de Serrant in Savennières, in 1978. He adopted conventional viticulture with chemical treatments in the vineyard. After two years, he noticed that the soil and vine health had declined. He happened upon Rudolf Steiner's *On Agriculture* and applied its biodynamic teachings to grape growing (Christine Saahs at Nikolaihof in Austria started a few years before Joly). The vine health returned and Joly began to talk up the practice around the world, not as a winemaker but as "nature's assistant" (as his business card reads). Today, many of the world's top vineyards use biodynamics, and Joly has spearheaded an annual tasting of more than 100 of the wine estates for consumers worldwide.

Looking like something from a fairytale, the beautiful Château de Saumur dates back to the 10th century.

DOMAINE DE LA NOBLAIE
THE CHINON ROSE ESCHEWS SWEETNESS IN
FAVOR OF CONCENTRATED FRUIT

DOMAINE LES MAISONS ROUGES
ALIZARI IS ONE OF THE BEST EXAMPLES OF
THE RARE GRAPE PINEAU D'ANUIS

Domaine Lucien Crochet Sancerre

Gilles Crochet, son of Lucien, makes the wines at this modern winery located in Bué. Grapes are harvested by hand from the domaine's 96 acres (38ha) and sorted before fermentation; the estate also makes a line from purchased fruit. Most of the vineyards are planted to Sauvignon Blanc but 23 acres (9ha) is given to Pinot Noir for reds and rosé. The entry level Sancerre white has a surprising intensity; the La Croix du Roy whites and reds both have enticing aroma and zippy acidity.

place de l'église, 18300, Bué
www.lucien-crochet.fr

Domaine Les Maisons Rouges

Jasnières, Coteaux du Loir

Benoît and Elisabeth Jardin are not from the Loire. But since establishing Domaine Les Maisons Rouges in 1994, they have acquired some magnificent old vines, up to 100 years old. These inform the intense concentration and mineral charge of the flagship *cuvées*, Clos des Jasnières (Chenin Blanc, typically bone-dry) and Coteaux du Loir Alizari (Pinuea d'Aunis). To maximize vineyard expression, cultivation is biodynamic and winemaking natural, with minimal sulphites. Long, natural ferments and maturation in used oak enhances complexity without detracting from the pure house style. ★ **Rising star**

26 route des Hautes Touches, 72340, Ruillé sur Loir
www.maisonsrouges.com

Domaine de Montgilet

Coteaux de l'Aubance, Anjou Brissac

Three generations of Lebretons have grown grapes on Juigné-sur-Loire's blue schist soils. Domaine de Montgilet pioneered fermenting and aging its famously concentrated sweet Coteaux de L'Aubance in barrique. During the 1990s, brothers Victor and Vincent Lebreton planted new vineyards in neighboring communes, Clos Prieur (purple schist) and Clos des Huttiéres (grey schist), expanding the estate to 91 acres (37ha). The ripest fruit, preferably botrytised, is harvested in successive waves for Montgilet's most unctuous sweet wines, each of which is named after the vineyard. Le Tertereaux hails from blue schist soils, while Les Trois Schistes comes from all three parcels.

49610 Juigné-sur-Loire
www.montgilet.com

Domaine de la Noblaie Chinon

For Jérôme Billard, the difference between good and great wine is detail. Billard's influences include his father, a professor of enology, and the world-famous producers Château Pétrus (in Bordeaux) and Dominus Estate (California's Napa Valley), where he has worked vintages. Since taking over the family estate in 2003, better canopy management, organic practices, hand selection, and vinification by parcel have led to the creation of three lithe, premium Cabernet Franc *cuvées*. Les Chiens Chiens and Les Blancs Manteaux are differentiated by soil and vine age. Pierre de Tuf is fermented in a 600-year-old rock vat, hollowed out of the cellar. A dry rosé, direct-pressed and bottled under screwcap, it flatters with fruit not sugar. ★ **Rising star**

21 rue des Hautes Cours, Le Vau Breton, 37500 Ligre
www.lanoblaie.fr

Domaine de Noiré Chinon

Jean-Max Manceau and his wife Odile run the 20 acre (8ha) Domaine de Noiré in Chinon planted to Cabernet Franc. Manceau also made the wine at the larger Château de la Grille in Chinon, and has served as the president of the Chinon appellation. Their hillside vineyards abut the Clos de Noiré vineyard site with its chalky, gravelly soils. They make a tank-fermented rosé as well as reds, notably entry level Elegance and Caractère made from old vines.

160 rue Olive, 37500, Chinon
02 47 98 44 13

Domaine Ogereau

Coteaux du Layon, Anjou, Savennières

Vincent Ogereau is the fourth generation of his family to work this 50 acre (20ha) domaine in the commune of Ste-Lambert. Table wines are good, but honeyed Coteaux du Layon dessert wines are the forte and among the Loire's best. Successive harvests ("*tries*") guarantee that only over-ripe, *passerillé* (shriveled), or botrytised grapes make the cut. Pure, with fresh pear and camomile, the basic Coteaux du Layon is unoaked. Cuvée Prestige and Clos des Bonnes Blanches are aged in 88-gallon (400-litre) barrels. Though sumptuous, especially the latter (a vinous nectar with saffron-edged apricots, ripe and dried), they retain a remarkable balancing freshness and minerality.

44 rue de la Belle Angevine, 49750 St-Lambert-du-Lattay;
www.domaineogereau.com

Domaine Olga Raffault Chinon

This old-school producer has 65 acres (24ha) close to the Vienne River. Olga Raffault has passed the torch to her granddaughter, Sylvie, who maintains the traditional winemaking in large, neutral vats. The most ageworthy wine is Les Picasses made from hand-harvested grapes from old vines on limestone and clay soil. The rosé from Cabernet Franc is also worth seeking out.

1 rue des Caillis, "Roguinet", 37420 Savigny-en-Véron
www.olga-raffault.com

Domaine Olivier Deletang Montlouis

The fourth generation of winemakers in his family, Olivier Deletang tends 42 acres (17ha) of mostly Chenin Blanc on the south bank of the Loire. The wines are dry, off-dry, and sweet. Les Petits Boulay comes from younger vines in gravelly limestone and clay soils and often has as much as 1¾oz (50g) of residual sugar. Les Batisses, from older vines in flint–clay soil, is richer still.

7270 Montlouis-sur-Loire
www.domaine-deletang.com

Domaine de Pallus Chinon

Bertrand Sourdais was still in his 20s when he returned to his father's estate, Domaine de Pallus, in 2003. But he had already worked for some of the world's best producers (Mouton Rothschild, Léoville Las Cases, and Alvaro Palacios) before making his name at Dominio de Atauta in Spain's Ribero del Duero. Now he is forging a reputation for Pensées de Pallus and Pallus. With their super-fine tannins and mineral finish, they are among Chinon's most seductive, elegant reds. ★ **Rising star**

37500 Cravant les Coteaux
www.lespenseesdepallus.info

Domaine de la Pépière Muscadet

Wine enthusiasts looking for superb, crackling, tingly whites rush to the Muscadets of Domaine de la Pépière from Marc Ollivier. The vineyards are hand harvested, unusual for the region, and fermentation occurs with native (not added) yeasts. All the wines are matured *sur lie* (on the lees or spent yeast cells), to provide additional richness. The entry level wine is a refreshing bargain match for shellfish; Clos de Briords comes from older vines and provides more depth, complexity, and aging ability. Find it in magnum for party and gift-giving needs.

44690 Maison-sur-Sèvre
02 40 03 81 19

Domaine Philippe Delesvaux

Anjou, Coteaux du Layon

Philippe Delesvaux established his 25 acre (10ha) domaine, now certified biodynamic, in 1983. He won swift recognition for super-concentrated, lush, sweet wines, which helped redeem Coteaux du Layon's flagging reputation. Almost 30 years later, it is a case of mission accomplished; his intense not dense wines have certainly achieved a more sophisticated balance. Whether it is the dry Anjou Blanc *cuvées* Authentique (made from ungrafted vines planted in 2000) and Feuille d'Or, or the botrytised Sélection de Grains Nobles Chenin Blanc, a backbone of rapier-like acidity makes for tightly structured, mineral wines that benefit from time in the cellar.

Les Essards, La Haie Longue 49190 St-Aubin-de-Luigné
02 41 78 18 71

Domaine Philippe Gilbert Menetou-Salon

Following his father's retirement in 1998, playwright Philippe Gilbert returned to the domaine to continue a family tradition of grape growing dating back to 1768. Like his father, he studied in Burgundy and, atypically, the 67 acre (27ha) domaine grows more Pinot Noir than Sauvignon Blanc. Gilbert tends the vineyard biodynamically, while winemaker Jean Philippe-Louis' light touch maximizes terroir expression. The pair have elevated the domaine into Menetou-Salon's first division. The unoaked domaine white and red are fruity, fresh, and mineral. Ageworthy old-vine, single-vineyard Les Renardières white and red are oak-aged wines of great precision and intensity. ★ **Rising star**

Les Faucards, 18510, Menetou-Salon
www.domainephilippegilbert.fr

Domaine Ricard Touraine

Until Vincent Ricard established this 42 acre (17ha) domaine in 1998, his forebears sold their grapes to the local co-operative. Having worked with Philippe Alliet in Chinon and François Chidaine in Vouvray and Montlouis, Ricard set his sights higher. Made from 70-year-old vines, "?", his rich and creamy flagship Sauvignon Blanc, spends 15 months in barrel. Les Trois Chênes, made from 45-year-old vines, also sees oak. Younger 20- to 30-year-old vines account for the juicy, gooseberry-loaded Le Petiot (unoaked). Ricard makes reds too, but these insouciantly labeled, concentrated, and exuberant Sauvignon Blancs are his calling card. ★ **Rising star**

19 rue de la Bougonnetière, 41140, Thesee La Romaine
www.domainericard.com

DOMAINE ROCHES NEUVES
MEATY WINES FROM A BIODYNAMICALLY
FARMED ESTATE

DOMAINE LB
SINGULIER IS A POWERFUL, DRY CHENIN
BLANC OF GREAT PURITY

Domaine Roches Neuves

Saumur-Champigny

Thierry Germain of Domaine Roches Neuves is jocular; talk with him for a few minutes and it feels as if you have known him for a decade. From Bordeaux, where his family owns a château, Germain is more interested in his compost pile in the Loire than he is in his native region. He fanatically farms the 50 acre (20ha) estate biodynamically and keeps the yields low. Of the wines, the Terres Chaude shows the bloody meatiness of Cabernet Franc, unadorned by wood; the Marginale, from 80-year-old vines, has more overt wood influence.

56 boulevard St-Vincent, 49400 Varrains
www.rochesneuves.com

Le Domaine de la Taille aux Loups

Montlouis, Vouvray

Until 1989, when Jacky Blot started making wine in Montlouis-sur-Loire, its reputation was humdrum compared with Vouvray over the river. In appellations, dry wines were often made by default, the product of a poor vintage. Through painstaking grape selection, for dry and sweet wines alike, Blot has put bright apples, pears, and quince to the fore at Le Domaine de la Taille aux Loups, and enhanced structure and complexity with subtle oak. Regal top *cuvées* Remus (dry) and Romulus (sweet) show immense concentration and finesse and, in exceptional years, are suffixed "Plus."

8 rue des Aîtres, Husseau 37270 Montlouis-sur-Loire
www.jackyblot.fr

Domaine Thomas-Labaille Chavignol

Jean-Paul Labaille now makes the racy wines at this estate, formerly belonging to his father-in-law, Claude Thomas. On the steep slopes of kimmeridgian (chalky) soil of the Monts Damnés in Chavignol, the vines are hand harvested and naturally made. The basic Sancerre has a fine, stony quality; the higher-end Cuvée Buster (with a small dog on the label) has crackling intensity.

Chavignol 18300
02 48 54 06 95

Domaine Vacheron Sancerre

Two cousins in their 30s, Jean-Dominique and Jean-Laurent Vacheron have now taken over this 100 acre (40ha) family estate from their fathers, and are raising the wines to an even higher level. Certified organic in 2003, then switching to biodynamics, the vineyards on flinty clay over limestone remain entirely hand-harvested. The house style is very minerally: Les Romains is a single-vineyard Sauvignon Blanc aged in oak vats; the Belle Dame is a serious, single-vineyard, old-vine Pinot Noir.

18300 Sancerre
02 48 54 09 93

Domaine de Vignobles des Bois Vaudons Touraine

Jean-François Meriaux's prolific range of interesting, handcrafted wines show no little ambition, and punches above its weight price-wise. He restructured the 79 acre (32ha) Domaine de Vignobles des Bois Vaudons family estate when he took it over in 2000, and modernized the winery in 2002. In organic conversion, its location on south-southeast facing slopes ensures good ripeness

PITHON-PAILLE
COTEAU DES TREILLES HAILS FROM
A 17 ACRE (7HA) VINEYARD IN
BEAULIEU-SUR-LAYON

levels. Wines differentiated by parcel include four Sauvignon Blancs: the round and subtly vegetal lees-aged L'Arpent des Vaudons; two rich and toasty oaked *cuvées*, Coeur de Roche and Tu le Boa; and a sweet wine, Le Siècle Georgina. The reds are among the region's best, especially the aromatic Gamays (Boa le Rouge and Le Bois Jacou), and the supple, fleshy Côts (Cent Visages and Gueule du Boa). ★ **Rising star**

30 route de la vallée, 41400, St-Julien-de-Chédon
www.merieau.com

Domaine Vincent Câreme Vouvray
Vincent Câreme, one of Vouvray's modernizers, has an unusually colorful background for a *vigneron* in this conservative appellation. He has worked four vintages in South Africa, lectures in wine, and consults for a Thai Chenin Blanc producer. Since 1999, Câreme has accumulated 35 acres (14ha) of vineyard cultivated naturally, using organic and biodynamic practices. Long and linear, drier Chenin Blancs show mouthwatering citrus fruit. The honeyed sweet wines are rich in texture, with juicy, rich, round orchard and stone fruits, and even tropical fruits in warmer years. ★ **Rising star**

1 rue du Haut Clos, 37210 Vernou sur Brenne
02 47 52 71 28

Eric Morgat Savennières
Originally from Coteaux du Layon, Eric Morgat has been making Savennières since 1995. In the vanguard of a shift toward a more forward, contemporary style of this famously austere appellation, his Chenin Blanc may be dry, but it has flesh on its bones. The first to admit it has been a learning curve, Morgat no longer uses botrytised grapes and malolactic fermentation. Less work in the cellar and a greater focus on his rising portfolio of vineyards have paid dividends. With ripe fruit around a mineral core, his single *cuvée*, L'Enclos, embodies the best of modern and traditional winemaking. ★ **Rising star**

Clos Ferrand, 49170 Savennières
www.ericmorgat.com

Ferme de la Sansonnière
Coteaux de l'Aubance, Anjou Brissac
In the vanguard of the Loire's natural wine movement since he started out in 1990, former stonemason and environmentalist Mark Angeli is an ideologue. He has experimented with ungrafted and unsulphured wines. He works biodynamically and, because self-sufficiency is a key tenet, grows crops to feed the horses that plough the 25 acre (10ha) vineyard, and the cows whose manure feeds the vines. It explains why Sansonnière is described as a "ferme" (farm), not a domaine. Angeli's powerful, dry Chenin Blancs are among the Loire's most textured and full of character. Rosé d'un Jour, an unchaptalized (no added sugar), medium-dry rosé is a playful riposte to the region's bulk-produced Cabernet d'Anjou.

49380 Thouarcé
02 41 54 80 80

François Cazin/Le Petit Chambord
Cheverny, Cour-Cheverny
Not far out of cannon range of Blois and its castle, François Cazin makes a tapestry of wines reflective of the Loire. In the Cheverny appellation, he makes reds based

LANGLOIS CHATEAU
LANGLOIS CHATEAU IS ONE OF THE LOIRE'S
VERY BEST SPARKLING WINE PRODUCERS

on Gamay and Pinot Noir and whites based on Sauvignon Blanc, but blended with some Chardonnay. All of the grapes are hand-harvested. In the miniscule Cour-Cheverny, blending stops to make way for the rare Romorantin grape with its delicious aromas of waxy honey. The off-dry Cuvée Renaissance, released with a few years of age on it, is particularly worth seeking out.

41700 Cheverny
02 54 79 93 75

François Cotat Sancerre
The 23 acre (9ha) Cotat vineyard sites on the chalky slopes of Les Monts Damnés have been prized for decades. However, brothers Francis and Paul, who had made the wines, retired in the 1990s leaving the sites to their sons, Pascal and François, who now make the wines in separate estates. François farms organically, harvests by hand (often late, which can add body and, sometimes, residual sugar in the wines) from the outrageously steep slopes, and vinifies in Chavignol. His wines are known for their intensity and age-worthiness. The Monts Damnés, La Grande Cote, and Les Culs de Beaujeu are reference points for Sancerre.

Bourg de Chavignol, 18300 Chavignol
02 48 54 21 27

François Crochet Sancerre
François Crochet took over his father's 26 acre (10.5ha) estate in 1998. A new, well-equipped cellar reflects the needs of today's generation of qualified, well-traveled winemakers, but Crochet's clean, precise style is the perfect canvass for terroir. Single-vineyard Sauvignon Blancs range from the flinty, tight Exils (silex soils) to the powerful, expressive Le Chêne Marchand (stony limestone) and Les Amoreuses (chalky clay). Pinot Noirs are fruity but refined, especially Réserve de Marcigoué from a chalk–clay vineyard. ★ **Rising star**

Marcigoué, 18300, Bué
02 48 54 21 77

François Pinon Vouvray
François Pinon, a former child psychologist, is a conscientious, disciplined grower and winemaker producing some excellent, and excellent-value, wines—from Vouvray. The estate is certified organic, the harvests done by hand, and Pinon uses only natural yeasts in the fermentation. The sparkling brut, the Cuvée Tradition, and the Silex Noir all show a great range of Chenin Blanc.

55 rue Jean Jaurès, Vallée de Cousse, 37210, Vernou-sur-Brenne; 02 47 52 16 59

Gérard Boulay Chavignol
Gérard Boulay is on a roll, and given the steepness of the Monts Damnés, it is no surprise he has gathered speed so quickly. He has the same kimmeridigian soil as his neighbors, the Cotat cousins, and the wines share an intensity. The wines are made naturally and the youngest vines were planted in 1972. The Chavignol is pure, minerally, well-priced Sancerre blanc. The Monts Damnés has more depth and the Clos de Beaujeu even more intensity. This is benchmark Sancerre.

Chavignol—18300 Sancerre
02 48 54 36 37

Jean-Pierre Robinot
Jasnières, Coteaux du Loir

Since 2001, ex-Paris wine bar owner Jean-Pierre Robinot has invested his considerable energy and talent into an ever-expanding range of wines. L'Ange Vin wines come from his organically tended vineyards (15 acres/6ha); the Opera du Vin label is made from locally sourced grapes. In both cases, Robinot's typically bone-dry Chenin Blanc (fermented for up to three years) and Pineau d'Aunis reds are as interesting and intense as their maker. Unsulphured, unfined, and unfiltered they will not appeal to everyone, but they are an experience. ★ Rising star

Le Présidial, 72340 Chahaignes
02 43 44 92 20

Langlois Château
Crémant de Loire, Saumur Blanc, Saumur-Champigny

Part of the Bollinger group since 1973, Langlois Château's forte is Crémant de Loire—traditional method fizz. The house owns 180 acres (73ha) of vineyards across six communes and, uniquely, exerts control over 100% of its handpicked grapes. The dry Cabernet Franc Rosé Brut has a delicate leafy, spicy edge to its red berry and cherry fruit. Chenin Blanc brings a honeyed note to white Crémants, while Chardonnay brings elegant fruit. Aged on its lees for at least four years, the flagship vintage *cuvée*, Quadrille, is complex and sophisticated.

rue Léopold Palustre, St-Hilaire-St-Florent 49400, Saumur;
www.langlois-chateau.fr

Philippe Alliet Chinon

Philippe Alliet travels to Bordeaux several times a year, in part to buy barrels, but also because he likes the wines. The wines he makes in Chinon are Bordeaux-like in many ways: he is not shy about new oak, he stems the fruit and practices *pigeage*. Of the three wines, the Coteau de Noiré comes from a sun-drenched, limestone vineyard with a 40% slope, while the Vieilles Vignes hails from gravelly soils and sees less new wood. The regular estate bottling is solid, but can benefit from some bottle age.

37500 Cravant les Coteaux
02 47 93 17 62

Pierre Luneau-Papin Muscadet

A qualitative leader in the Muscadet region, Pierre Luneau-Papin makes an enticing range of wines from his 75 acre (30ha) estate. The grapes are harvested by hand and kept on the lees for added depth and richness. The calling card is the Clos des Allées, which enlivens seafood with its acidity and minerality. The L d'Or, from old vines, is more intense and lingering—it also effortlessly ages in the cellar, becoming more golden and the nose more honeyed. Finally, the limited-production Excelsior sees a staggering 30 months' aging on lees and is exceptional.

44430 Le Landreau
02 40 06 45 27

Pierre-Jacques Druet Bourgueil, Chinon

Pierre-Jacques Druet studied at Bordeaux University under the famous enologist Emile Peynaud. He started making wine in Bourgueil in 1980 and, influenced by his mentor, fastidious vineyard selection and vinification by parcel typify his approach. In poorer vintages, high temperature ferments in bespoke conical fermentors with auto-plungers maximize fruit expression, while minimizing tannin extraction. His wines are deep-fruited, spicy, and mineral. The top *cuvées* Grand Mont and Vaumoreau reward keeping, the best for 20 years plus. A complex, off-dry rosé is slowly fermented in open casks.

Le Pied Fourrier, 37140 Benais
02 47 97 37 34

Pithon-Paillé Anjou, Savennières

During the 1990s, Jo Pithon led the move to flamboyantly sweet and complex, dry Chenin Blancs from vineyards traditionally dedicated to sweet Coteaux du Layon. Apart from 12 acres (5ha), his eponymous domaine, re-named Domaine FL, was purchased by Philippe Fournier in 2005. After splitting with Fournier in 2008, Pithon joined forces with his stepson, Joseph Paillé. Exciting, mineral domaine wines from Les Treilles and La Fresnaye (Anjou Blanc and Rouge) and Savennières are now fresher in style. Grapes and juice from across the Loire are purchased for their négociant label, with priority given to organic growers whose vineyards they supervise. ★ Rising star

19 rue St-Vincent, 49750 St-Lambert-du-Lattay
www.pithon-paille.com

Serge Dagueneau & Filles
Pouilly-Fumé

Serge Dagueneau—the uncle of Didier—and his daughter Valérie run this 42 acre (17ha) estate. The house style is richer than many Pouilly-Fumés, despite stainless steel fermentation, whether in the straight Pouilly-Fumé or (especially) in the Les Filles bottling, which can be quite ripe. Valérie's winemaking sister, Florence (the other "Fille" in the domaine's name), died of cancer in 2010.

58150 Pouilly-sur-Loire
www.s-dagueneau-filles.fr

Thierry Puzelat Touraine

Thierry Puzelat makes wines sought by hipsters around the world. He has a separate winemaking facility from Clos du Tue-Boeuf for this, his négociant project. He delights in sourcing grapes from retro-chic varieties and vinifying them as naturally as possible and often without sulphites. His "In KO we trust" riffs off the local name (Côt) for Malbec; decant it to soften youthful tannins balanced with acidity. The Pineau d'Aunis has a delicious grind of cracked pepper. The PN (Pinot Noir) has a delectable snap. ★ Rising star

14 rue des Masnières, 41120 Les Montils
www.puzelat.com

Yannick Amirault
Bourgueil, St-Nicolas de Bourgueil

Yannick Amirault is widely hailed as a top producer in Bourgueil. He has made many changes at the family estate since taking over 9 acres (3.5ha) of scattered vineyards in 1977. The estate (now organic) has 47 acres (19ha), mostly in Bourgueil but also in St-Nicolas-de-Bourgueil. Wines include easy-drinking La Coudraye from gravelly soils and the ageworthy les Quartiers, which impressed critic John Gliman so much he wondered if it was the Cheval Blanc of Bourgueil.

5 Pavillon du Grand Clos, 37140 Bourgueil
www.yannickamirault.fr

THE PUZELAT BROTHERS

In 1993, on the fringes of the Solonges forest that aristocrats had used for hunting, the growing area Cheverny became an appellation. This formal recognition is often seen as a positive for an area. But in Cheverny, it had the effect of narrowing the permitted range of grapes that wines could be made from. That meant that Thierry and Jean-Marie Puzelat, who were just taking over their father's vineyard, had to make a decision whether to uproot the diverse varieties planted in the 1960s and replant with authorized varieties. They took the high-risk step of embracing Pineau d'Aunis, Menu Pineau, Grolleau, and others to make the wines as Vin de Table, a category so lowly that wines cannot state the grape nor vintage on the label. The brothers have now set up a non-profit organization to administer 17 acres (7ha) of such heirloom vineyards. They are rebels with a cause—to save the past.

ALSACE

The wines are first-class, yet there are issues with Alsace. There are 51 Grand Crus—a vast number—and yet no second or third tier. Are all these vineyards stretching along the region's 105 mile (170km) wine route from Than in the south to Marlenheim in the north really all equal, especially when planted with all the permissible varieties? These prime vineyard sites produce some of the world's best gastronomic wines—the sublime Pinot Gris (all smoky apple and pear with a weighty palate), the minerally, tight, and long-lived Rieslings (usually dry, unlike those from neighboring Germany), the aromatic apéritif par excellence, Muscat, and the heady, exotic fruit-and-ginger-spiced Gewurztraminer—yet these specific terroirs are often ignored by producers.

Major grapes

 Reds

Pinot Noir

Whites

Gewurztraminer

Muscat

Pinot Gris

Riesling

Vintages

2009

An excellent harvest across all varieties.

2008

Good for Riesling, Pinot Gris, and Gewurztraminer, less so for Muscat.

2007

Hail had a severe impact on many vineyards, but the wines produced are good.

2006

A very patchy vintage, select with care.

2005

A little uneven, but generally reliable and correct.

2004

A superb vintage with wines showing great purity and elegance.

While the likes of Albert Boxler and Marc Kreydenweiss bottle tight, lime-dominated, citrus and mineral drenched Rieslings from their tiny Grand Cru vineyards, offering the epitome of terroir-led wines, firms such as Trimbach have chosen to ignore these designations. Their bottles do not even mention the Grand Cru sites from which the grapes are sourced; instead they feel that their tiny corner of the Grand Cru represents even greater quality, picking up the subtleties and expressing the terroir even better than the Grand Cru as a whole. So they label their wines with proprietar names or use the word clos (self-contained vineyards) to designate specific bottlings. This is fine for consumers that understand the specific designations and respect the producers' ideas and motives, but it is an added complication for the less knowledgeable.

While the Rieslings may be dry, and the Pinot Gris weighty and perhaps slightly off-dry, these descriptions are subjective and the consumer may again be left a little confused. Delving into the producers' websites throws up all the technical details— ½oz (16g) of residual sugar in this wine, just ⅙oz (5g) in another, linked to this amount of acidity, and so on. But what does this mean? Are they dry or dryish? Domaine Zind Humbrecht labels its wines with a proprietary sweetness scale with the Selection de Grains Nobels (the very sweetest styles, usually made from grapes affected by noble rot) at one end, and the steely dry Rieslings at the other. It is not a universally adopted scale, and with age, the apparent sweetness of a wine can change, making such a scale unreliable (especially as many Alsace wines benefit from some aging). However, it remains a very useful gauge in judging a wine's sweetness.

What is indisputable is that the wines of Alsace are world class. Trimbach's Clos Ste-Hune Riesling is a benchmark by which others are judged. Even the humble, flinty tinged Sylvaner grape is lifted to almost sublime perfection in certain vineyard sites. Throughout the region, which is one of the prettiest to explore, the link between the local wines and the world-class cuisine available is paramount. Which wine-and-food-lover can fail to be delighted by the pairing of Gewurztraminer and Munster cheese, Pinot Blanc with quiche and other egg-based dishes, Pinot Gris with foie gras, Sylvaner with Alsace Onion Tart or garlic-rich snails, Riesling with all manner of fish, or Crémant d'Alsace, the local sparkling wine, with caviar and canapés? The only blots on the region are the rather lackluster Pinot Noirs, the only red wine produced in Alsace and one that every producer insists on making, and the slightly one-dimensional aspect to some of the sparkling wines (although there are some notable exceptions).

Albert Boxler

A family affair for over 300 years, Boxler has a miniscule acreage of vines, but produces some of the small gems that entice the wine-lover with a grand expression of terroir and varietal character. From the pristine, basic Rieslings to the exciting and complex Sommerberg Rieslings, the wines can be a little austere in their youth and, like many, benefit from some aging.

78 rue des Trois-Epis, 68230 Niedermorschwihr
03 89 27 11 32

Albert Mann

In Alsace terms, 47 acres (19ha) of vines is a large estate. Since taking command in 1984, brothers Jacky and Maurice Barthelme have built a fine reputation for the Albert Mann estate. The Gewurztraminers especially have garnered excellent press and an eager following, while the Pinot Gris wines, with their rich, floral aromas, are distinctive and full of finesse. The textural Pinot Blanc has proved itself to be very versatile when matched with food—summery fare in particular.

13 rue du Chateau, 68920 Wettolsheim
www.albertmann.com

André Kientzler

Located in the delightfully attractive town of Ribeauville, overlooked by hilltop castles, this five-generation family firm produces wonderfully expressive wines across its range, from the Chasselas up to the Grand Cru Rieslings. The latter benefit hugely from cellaring. This is a small but very fine producer, with passionate enthusiasm that makes the wines shine. ★ **Rising star**

50 route de Bergheim, 68150 Ribeauville
03 89 73 67 10

André Ostertag

This estate comprises 31 acres (12.5ha), all farmed biodynamically but spread over an impressive 120 different plots. From these, an extensive range (typical of Alsace) of 17 wines is made, divided into three groups: the Vin de Fruits for multi-vineyard blends, Vin des Pierres for terroir-expressive wines, and Vin de Temps for sweet wines. André Ostertag has a maverick reputation, perhaps because of its sometimes untraditional approach (for example, aging wines in oak barrels), but offers stunning wines.

67680 Epfig
03 88 85 51 34

André Pfister

In 2006, husband-and-wife team André and Marie-Anne Pfister were joined at their estate by their daughter Mélanie, the eighth generation of the family to be involved. The Pfisters have just under 25 acres (10ha) of vines, divided into 40 different plots around the family home. Riesling dominates their affections, representing more than 25% of vines, although the Les 3 Demoiselles Muscat, the Pinot Gris Selection, and the Gewurztraminer Silberberg receive equal love and attention both in the vineyard and the winery. "Authenticity, distinction, and elegance" is their creed across the range.

53 rue Principale, 67310 Dahlenheim
www.domaine-pfister.com

DOMAINE BOTT-GEYL
A COMPLEX AND INTENSE WINE, WITH NOTES OF POMELO, PINEAPPLE, AND FLOWERS

ALBERT MANN
THIS WINE HAS RIPE PEAR AND MELON AROMAS AND A CREAMY, SPICY FINISH

Cave de Pfaffenheim

It is not just the small estates that can produce interesting wines. This co-operative's 620 acres (250ha) of vines, including five Grand Cru sites, offer a range of wines with individuality and often a delightfully rustic edge. Look out for the Black Tie blend of Pinot Gris and Riesling for something a little different. ★ **Rising star**

5 rue du Chai, 68250 Pfaffenheim
www.pfaffenheim.com

Cave de Ribeauville

This is another top co-operative offering a large range of wines. Dry wines are preferred, with the winemakers seeking purity and varietal expression with the aim of a "harmonious marriage" with food. Some smaller bottlings of Riesling from Grand Cru sites of Altenberg de Bergheim and Osterberg are particularly expressive. The Vin de l'A Terroir of Bergheim is a blend of Riesling, Pinot Gris, and Gewurztraminer, all vinified together.

68150 Ribeauville
www.vins-ribeauville.com

Domaine Bernhard-Reibel

This producer was born as a result of the merger of the Bernhards of Châtenois and the Reibels of Scherwiller. It used to sell its grapes to the local co-operative, but since 2002 it has produced its own wine, and recently became organic. Rieslings are Bernhard-Reibel's strong point but the range is well worth exploring. Its Pinot Noir is one of just a few from Alsace worth getting excited about, while the quality of the Pinot Blanc Caprice is excellent. In 2009, Cécile Bernhard-Reibel, the matriarch of the family, became the first female Grand Maître of the Confrérie St-Etienne, Alsace's august wine body. ★ **Rising star**

Rue de Lorraine, 67730 Châtenois
www.domaine-bernhard-reibel.fr

Domaine Bott-Geyl

Increasingly catching the attention of critics, the wines of Bott-Geyl—small in number, but large in range—offer purity, concentration, and layers of texture. The limestone soils of the Furstentum Grand Cru site produce some pithy, elegant Rieslings and wonderfully defined, heady Gewurztraminers. ★ **Rising star**

Rue du Petit-Chateau, 68980 Beblenheim
www.bott-geyl.com

Domaine Marcel Deiss

Current owner Jean-Michel Deiss is descended from a family of wine-growers who first settled Bergheim in 1744, and is the grandson of Marcel Deiss, who founded the winery in 1947. Hot on terroir and biodynamics, he has crafted a superb range of wines that one critic described as "one of the most stimulating in the region." While the whole range is worth exploring, the Grand Vin de l'Altenberg de Bergheim explodes any preconceptions about Alsatian wines. A blend of all 13 of the region's grape varieties, it needs at least an hour to breathe before its gorgeous crystallized lemon, ginger, honey, creamy exotic fruits, and vanilla complexity reaches its zenith, and its rich texture and extreme elegance come through.

68750 Bergheim
www.marceldeiss.com

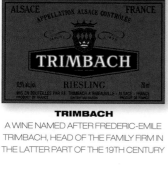

TRIMBACH

A WINE NAMED AFTER FREDERIC-EMILE TRIMBACH, HEAD OF THE FAMILY FIRM IN THE LATTER PART OF THE 19TH CENTURY

MAISON PAUL ZINCK

POWERFUL, OPULENT, RICH, AND INTENSE, THIS IS A FINE WINE WITH A LONG FINISH

Domaine Paul Blanck

This domaine has gained an enviable reputation since its creation in the 16th century, building a company firmly focused on offering a range of expressive, modern wines that are generous, balanced, and very food-friendly. The Grand Cru offerings, in particular, express the limestone and clay soils perfectly, especially if given a few years of aging. Even the more basic wines are highly appealing.

32 Grand-rue, 68240 Kientzheim
www.blanck-alsace.com

Domaine Rémy Gresser

Another exponent of the biodynamic method of wine production, Rémy Gresser produces three Grands Crus —Wiebelsberg, Moenchberg, and Kastelberg—that typify their terroirs. Wiebelsberg, with its sandstone, is very floral; Moenchberg, on limestone, produces succulent wines; and Kastelberg, a unique terroir on Steige schist, produces wines loaded with minerality. Even the designated vineyards offer distinctive flavors from the different soils. Overall, Rémy Gresser produces exciting wines of great purity and expression. ★**Rising star**

2 rue de l'Ecole, 67140 Andlau
www.gresser.fr

Domaine Schoffit

The greatest wines from this domaine undoubtedly emanate from Clos St-Théobald in Rangen. Their Chasselas is often cited as the best wine this grape can produce, its quality hailing from the 70-year-old vines —hence the Vieilles Vignes (old vines) designation. While the carefully constructed, varietally pure St-Théobald Riesling is a marvel, Schoffit also coaxes the best from the flat vineyards around Colmar. The Pinot Blanc sourced from here is particularly worth trying.

Par Rue des Aubepines, 68000 Colmar
03 89 24 41 14

Domaine Weinbach

Domaine Weinbach is located at the foot of the majestic Schlossberg hill. It is named after the "wine brook," a stream that meanders through the estate. The impressive family house and cellars are matched by equally impressive and expressive wines. The range is large and the naming sometimes confusing. Stunning Grand Cru bottlings jostle with impressive single-vineyard wines, while Réserve and Réserve Personelle wines sit alongside special *cuvées* such as Cuvée Ste-Catherine (often harvested on St. Catherine's Day, November 25th) and Cuvée Laurence (from grapes harvested even later). Perhaps the Weinbach's take on Riesling encapsulates the estate in a single bottle and word—elegance.

Clos des Capucins, 68240 Kaysersberg
www.domaineweinbach.com

Domaine Zind-Humbrecht

Consistently one of the top producers in the whole of France, Zind-Humbrecht was formed following the marriage of Leonard Humbrecht and Geneviève Zind in 1959. Their son, Olivier Humbrecht, the first French Master of Wine, has installed policies of low yields, natural wine-making techniques, and non-interventionism in the domaine, with the result that his wines are perfect expressions of the terroir. The wide range is made of grapes from four different Grand Cru vineyards, three single-vineyard plots, and three walled vineyards (clos). The most famous of the latter is Clos Widsbuhl, the source of their greatest wines.

4 route de Colmar, 68230 Turckheim
03 89 27 02 05

Domaines Schlumberger

This is the largest estate in Alsace with 358 acres (145ha) of vines, some on incredibly steep and impressive slopes. You need to look above the basic wines for the real delights, especially those wines from Spiegel, Kitterlé, and Kessler. The Vendanges Tardive Gewurztraminer is a joy, with its deep, powerful, and spicy intensity, and is cherished by those who make it. Today, the estate is run by two generations working together—Alain Beydon-Schlumberger (sixth generation) and Séverine Schlumberger (seventh generation).

100 rue Theodore Deck, 68501 Guebwiller
www.domaines-schlumberger.com

Frederic Mochel

A family-owned estate, Frederic Mochel dates back to 1669. Father-and-son team Frederic and Guillaume take great pride in their 25 acres (10ha) of vines with 12.5 acres (5ha) of Grand Cru vineyards. The wines offer a fine expression of the way the grapes reflect distinctive terroirs and vintages. For example, compare the subtleties in various years of their Riesling Grand Cru Cuvée Henriette, or marvel at the dry, honeysuckle edge of the delightful Muscats.

56 rue principale, 67310 Traenheim
www.mochel.net

Hugel et Fils

An Alsace stalwart and proven ambassador for the region, Hugel et Fils produces clean-cut wines, perfectly expressing their grape varieties. It is one of the region's largest land owners, but rejects the Grand Cru system, instead labeling wines as Varietals for the basic quality level, Tradition for the mid-range, and Jubilee for the finest. The latter benefit from some aging, with most displaying a dry, precise core. The historic Hugel cellars house a barrel that is certified by the Guinness Book of Records as the oldest in continuous use—it was first used in 1715. This family-run estate covers 160 acres (65ha) planted only with the noble varieties Gewurztraminer, Riesling, Pinot Gris, and Pinot Noir, and some vines are up to 70 years old.

68340 Riquewihr
www.hugel.com

Josmeyer

Biodynamics and food-focused wines are the core aims of Josmeyer. At the basic level, the wines have been criticized as being a little dull and restrained, but the top level reveals polished, deep, and incisive wines of the best Alsace can produce. Generally the wines are dry, hence the food-focus, but the excellent Vendange Tardive and Selection des Grains Nobles have that all-important sweetness and still express the house style.

68920 Wintzenheim
www.josmeyer.com

Kuentz-Bas

Two centuries of winemaking have more recently seen the venerable Kuentz-Bas suffering from lack of investment and some family squabbles. Thankfully these seem to have been resolved and the estate has returned to producing quality wines. The special *cuvées* Cuvée Caroline and Cuvée Jeremy (a Selection de Grains Nobles) are worth sampling, as is the Pinot Gris.

14 route des Vins, 68420 Husseren-Les-Chateaux
www.kuentz-bas.fr

Leon Beyer

The Beyer family has been growing wine in Eguisheim since 1580. This is a stunning, historic town designed in concentric circles around three lines of ramparts. Today, around 75% of Beyer's extensive production is exported. The wines are of a clean-cut, varietally correct style, generally dry, poised, balanced, and highly drinkable.

Rue de la 1ère Armée, 68420 Eguisheim
www.leonbeyer.fr

Maison Paul Zinck

Founded in 1964, this estate is a youngster among the estates of Alsace. Father-and-son team Paul and Philippe Zinck have invested hugely in modern technology to produce a clean-cut, expressive range. There are three grades of wines: the Portrait collection, with the focus on balance and varietal traits, are from vines planted at the base of the foothills; the Terroir set, gourmet wines that are complex and well constructed, are sourced from a higher altitude; and the Grand Cru wines have a fine delicacy and a harmonious intensity. ★ Rising star

18 rue des Trios Chateaux, 68420 Eguisheim
www.zinck.fr

Marc Kreydenweiss

Kreydenweiss uses a different artist each year to produce its wine labels. This creates a new feel with each vintage, although the wines remain true to the family style. The family vineyard holdings have expanded beyond their Alsace homeland, with estates in Germany (Pfalz) and the Rhone (Costières de Nîmes). The wines from Alsace have a distinctive house style—edgy, with a clean-cut acidity and a stony backbone. The Gewurztraminers are delicate and more subtle than many. As the younger generation imparts its stamp on the biodynamic vineyards, this will be an estate to watch develop. ★ Rising star

12 rue Deharbe, 67140 Andlau
www.kreydenweiss.com

Michel Fonné

One of the best producers of Alsace sparkling wine—Crémant d'Alsace—Michel Fonné places as much care and attention on the bubbly as on his other wines. The wines are labeled with the name of Michel's uncle, Rene Barth, who handed the estate over in 1989. ★ Rising star

24 rue du Général Charles de Gaulle, 68630 Bennwihr
www.michelfonne.com

René Muré

The major strand of René Muré's endeavors is the 37 acre (15ha), fully organic Clos St-Landelin, forming the major, and some suggest the best, section of Grand Cru Vorbourg. For one of the finest expressions of Pinot Noirs you need look no further than René Muré's beautifully intense, deeply colored, and perfectly structured example. The lively Riesling and the richly powerful Gewurztraminer are also worth trying.

68250 Rouffach
www.mure.com

Rolly Gassmann

Carrying a distinguished reputation nearly as old as Alsace winemaking itself, this inspiring company maintains quality right across its range. The wines are famed for their richness and their velvety sweetness (which usually come from higher residual sugar levels than is the norm in Alsace), but this is tempered by a streak of fine acidity to form wines with a seductive quality. Grapes are sourced from vines over a large area (82 acres/33ha), which allows the company to offer a varied range of wines.

1–2 rue de l'Eglise, 68590 Rorschwihr
03 89 73 63 28

Seppi Landmann

With only a small holding of vineyards, it is amazing that Seppi Landmann's range of 30 different wines is not only produced, but offered with pure deliciousness across the board. Especially worth trying are the expressive Crément d'Alsace sparkling and the wines from their holdings in the Grand Cru Zinnkoepflé.

68570 Soultzmatt
www.seppi-landmann.fr

Trimbach

This classic brand is recognized the world over by its distinctive yellow and black labels. As the family states in its publicity material, the aim of the house is to produce "dry wines, very strictly structured, long-living and fruity, elegant and balanced." The best description is one of reserved elegance, aristocratic perhaps, but never overtly flashy or over-the-top. The basic wines offer a run of simplicity with clean-cut flavors and an austere core. Another producer ignoring the Grand Cru designations, Trimbach uses Réserve and Réserve Personelle, and named *cuvées* for its bottles. The top wines may see about five years' estate aging before being released, while even the basic wines are kept for a year. The Trimbach Clos Ste-Hune Riesling (from the Grand Cru Rosacker) is the wine by which all others are judged.

68150 Ribeauville
www.maison-trimbach.com

Valentin Zusslin

Brother and sister Jean-Paul and Marie Zusslin are the latest holders of this estate, which has been in their family since 1691. Jean-Paul is the winemaker, although both his father and grandfather keep their hands in. Operated along biodynamic lines since 1997, the estate is gradually gaining the attention of the world's wine commentators as the output produces stunning wines such as the Riesling Grand Cru Pfinstberg and the Grand Cru Bollenberg Gewurztraminer. ★ Rising star

57 Grand Rue, 68500 Orschwihr
www.zusslin.com

THE ALSACE WINE ROUTE

Situated at the foot of the Rangen Grand Cru slope in Thann, the Witches Tower, built in 1360, marks the start of the 105 mile (170km) Alsace Wine Route. With the tree-covered Massif Vosgien to the west, the route threads its way north through Guebwiller, which hosts an annual wine fair in May, and on through often fortified villages and countless vineyards to Colmar, the wine capital of Alsace. From Colmar and its historic center, the route continues through Ribeauvillé (dominated by its three castles), and yet more historic and delightful villages before ending its gentle twists and diversions in Marlenheim.

The route is punctuated by signposted vineyard walks with those leading up the hill terraces offering wonderful views across to the German border and, in the far north, Strasbourg. Wine Route maps, which are freely available in the tourist information centers, give details of the historic sites to see, in addition to the wine highlights.

NORTHERN RHONE

Southern Rhône wine region
Northern Rhône wine region

The Northern Rhône Valley produces only about one-tenth as much wine as the Southern Rhône. However, the relatively little wine that is produced in the north is usually extraordinary and almost never dull. Long overshadowed by Bordeaux and Burgundy, the Northern Rhône has risen to a stature comparable with these two great French regions during just the past two decades. This is certainly true when measured in terms of the prices commanded by top wines from Côte-Rôtie and Hermitage. Top bottlings from Cornas, St-Joseph, and Condrieu are also climbing to rarified price levels, and the region as a whole is rapidly earning global renown commensurate with the remarkable quality of its wines.

Major grapes

 Reds

Syrah

 Whites

Marsanne

Roussanne

Viognier

Vintages

2009
A great vintage for Syrah across the region, and nearly as good for whites.

2008
A very wet year resulted in relatively light wines.

2007
A vintage of uneven quality due to the poor August weather, but some excellent wines were made.

2006
An outstanding vintage for white wines and a very good one for Syrah.

2005
An excellent vintage of long-living wines, both whites and reds.

2004
A vintage of beautifully balanced whites and very good reds.

The excellence of these scarce wines is still not fully recognized around the world, but that is probably all that keeps prices below truly stratospheric levels. To place the scarcity issue into perspective, a single vineyard like the famous To Kalon in California's Napa Valley is much larger than the entire appellation of Hermitage and almost identical to the whole of Côte-Rôtie. St-Joseph and Crozes-Hermitage are significantly larger, but all of the Northern Rhône appellations combined are smaller in area than the Côte de Beaune portion of Burgundy's Côte d'Or.

Consequently, the importance of the wines from this narrow valley has nothing to do with quantity but everything to do with character and complexity, which are perhaps their most outstanding attributes. The red wines—made exclusively from Syrah—are not quite the world's ripest or most weighty renditions of this great grape, as that distinction belongs to Australia. However, few would dispute the proposition that they are the most exotically perfumed and character-filled, and recent trends toward late harvesting and increased use of new oak have placed a lot of additional power beneath all that perfume.

The reds of Hermitage and Cornas are the biggest of the breed, with Cornas featuring a robust, rustic intensity in comparison with Hermitage's more aristocratic finesse. Although Hermitage can seem quite tight and restrained in its youth, the reds from this famous hill above the River Rhône develop into one of the world's most riveting wines when afforded sufficient time to age

and unwind. The fact that they were shipped off to fortify Bordeaux in earlier centuries should serve to explain the cliché that casts them as the masculine counterpart to the more feminine style of Côte-Rôtie.

That cliché is becoming ever more dubious as far as Côte-Rôtie is concerned, since higher selling prices have enabled vintners to reduce yields and use newer barrels to make more concentrated, ageworthy wines that do true justice to this formidable growing site. A southeast-facing slope that deserves its adjective (*rôtie* means "roasted") on account of perfect sun exposure on gradients as steep as 60%, Côte-Rôtie producers are allowed to "feminize" their wines by adding up to 20% of the white Viognier grape, though this practice is ever rarer these days.

However, Viognier is allowed to display its marvelously aromatic and rich nature immediately to the south of Côte-Rôtie in Condrieu and Château-Grillet, a single-producer appellation within the boundaries of Condrieu. The other whites of the region are made from the lush Marsanne and the nervier Roussanne, sometimes in sparkling form in St-Péray, or as still wines there and in Hermitage, Crozes-Hermitage, and St-Joseph. Whites from these last two can be every bit as good as the reds, though the very best sites in Crozes and St-Joseph are capable of producing noble Syrahs that recall—if not quite rival—Hermitage and Côte-Rôtie for much less money.

The most affordable wines of the area are labeled as Côtes du Rhône or Vin de Pays des Collines Rhodaniennes.

NORTHERN RHONE

The vineyards are set close to the river, along a stretch of about 43 miles (70km) from Vienne down to Valence. At the northern end, the major appellations are all situated on the west bank, starting with Côte-Rôtie and extending down to Condrieu and Château-Grillet. St-Joseph continues down the west bank, flanked by Crozes-Hermitage on the east. Hermitage and its famous hill are set below the town of Tain l'Hermitage on the river's east, with Cornas and St-Péray to the west across from Valence.

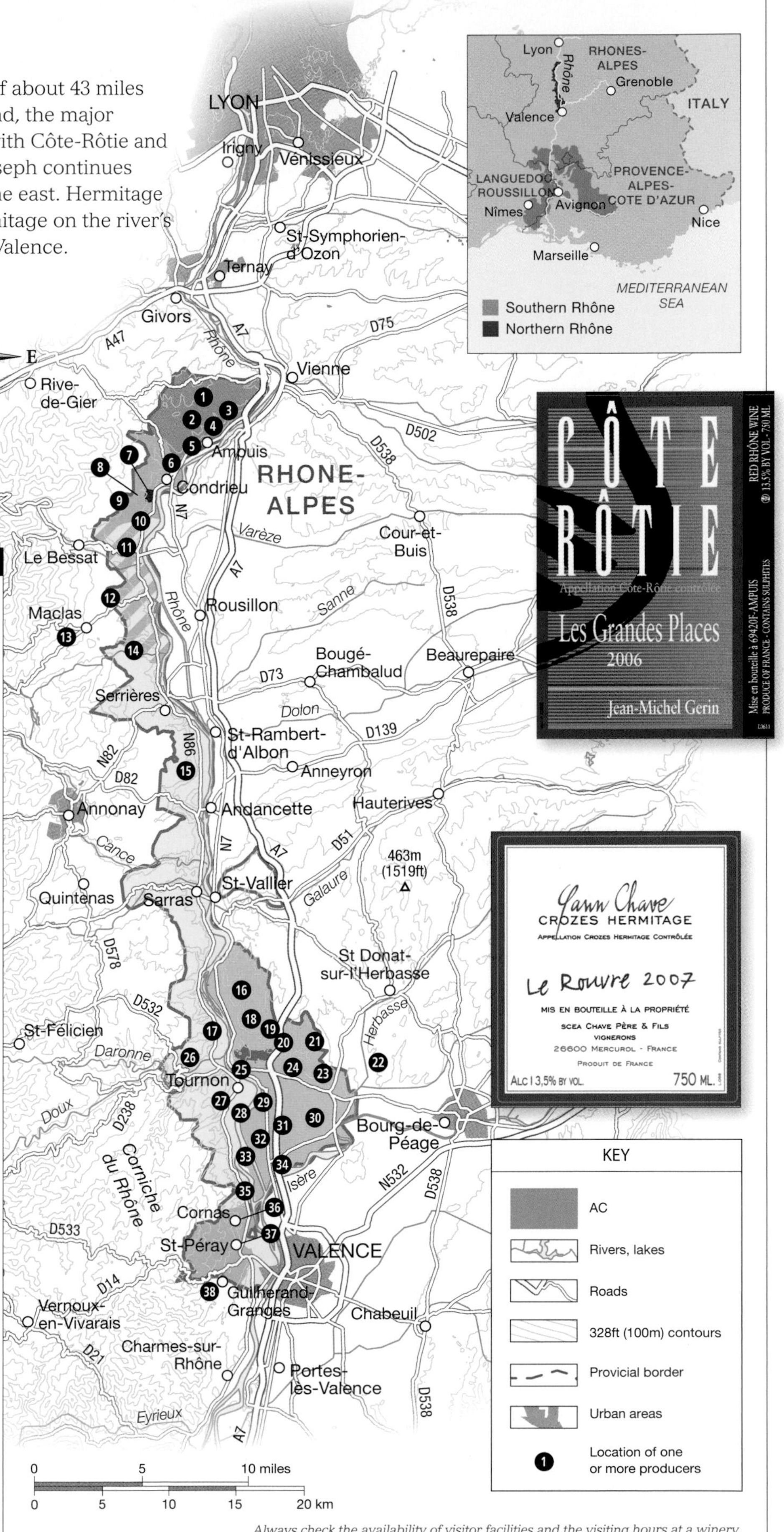
N
S
W
E
LYON
Irigny
Vénissieux
St-Symphorien-d'Ozon
Ternay
Givors
Vienne
Rive-de-Gier
Ampuis
Condrieu
RHONE-ALPES
Le Bessat
Cour-et-Buis
Maclas
Rousillon
Serrières
Bougé-Chambalud
Beaurepaire
St-Rambert-d'Albon
Anneyron
Annonay
Andancette
Hauterives
Quintenas
Sarras
St-Vallier
463m (1519ft)
St Donat-sur-l'Herbasse
St-Félicien
Tournon
Bourg-de-Péage
Cornas
St-Péray
VALENCE
Guilherand-Granges
Chabeuil
Vernoux-en-Vivarais
Charmes-sur-Rhône
Portes-lès-Valence
Corniche du Rhône
Rhône
Varèze
Sanne
Dolon
Cance
Galaure
Herbasse
Daronne
Doux
Isère
Eyrieux
A47
A7
N7
N86
N82
D82
D75
D502
D538
D73
D139
D51
D578
D532
D238
D533
D14
D21
N532
Lyon
RHONES-ALPES
Rhône
Grenoble
ITALY
Valence
LANGUEDOC-ROUSSILLON
PROVENCE-ALPES-COTE D'AZUR
Nîmes
Avignon
Nice
Marseille
MEDITERRANEAN SEA
Southern Rhône
Northern Rhône
CÔTE RÔTIE
Appellation Côte-Rôtie contrôlée
Les Grandes Places
2006
Jean-Michel Gerin
RED RHÔNE WINE
13.5% BY VOL · 750 ML
Mise en bouteille à 69420F-AMPUIS
PRODUCE OF FRANCE · CONTAINS SULPHITES
Yann Chave
CROZES HERMITAGE
APPELLATION CROZES HERMITAGE CONTRÔLÉE
Le Rouvre 2007
MIS EN BOUTEILLE À LA PROPRIÉTÉ
SCEA CHAVE PÈRE & FILS
VIGNERONS
26600 MERCUROL - FRANCE
PRODUIT DE FRANCE
ALC 13,5% BY VOL
750 ML.
KEY
AC
Rivers, lakes
Roads
328ft (100m) contours
Provicial border
Urban areas
Location of one or more producers
0 5 10 miles
0 5 10 15 20 km

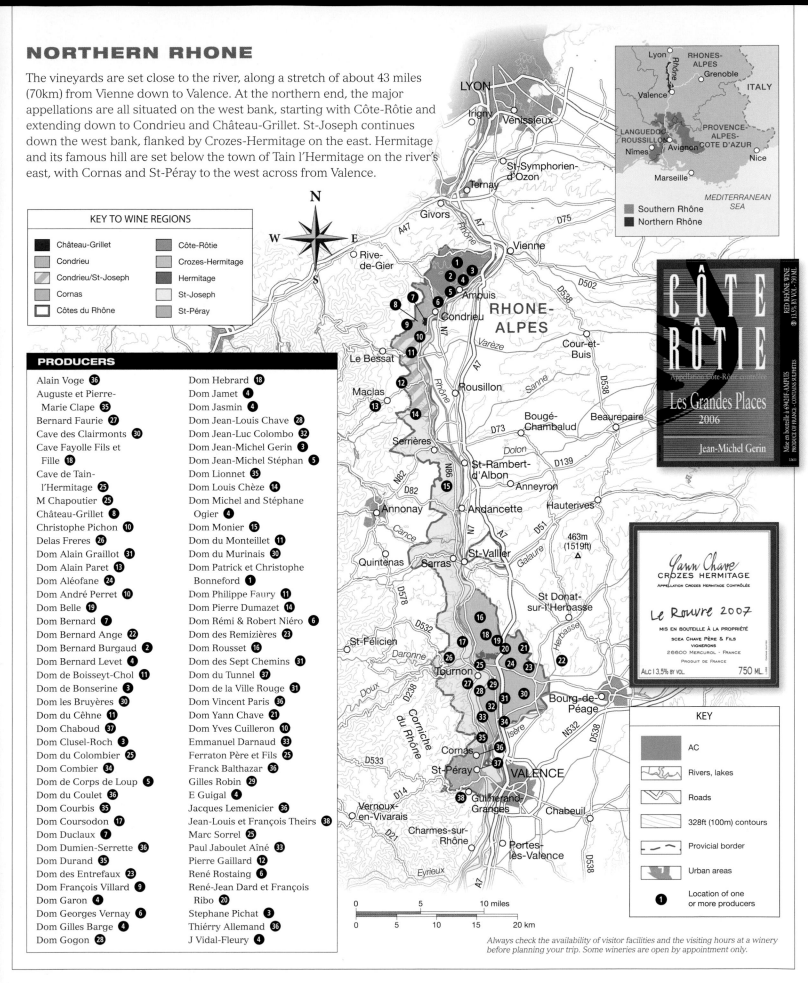

KEY TO WINE REGIONS

- Château-Grillet
- Condrieu
- Condrieu/St-Joseph
- Cornas
- Côtes du Rhône
- Côte-Rôtie
- Crozes-Hermitage
- Hermitage
- St-Joseph
- St-Péray

PRODUCERS

Alain Voge 36
Auguste et Pierre-Marie Clape 35
Bernard Faurie 27
Cave des Clairmonts 30
Cave Fayolle Fils et Fille 18
Cave de Tain-l'Hermitage 25
M Chapoutier 25
Château-Grillet 8
Christophe Pichon 10
Delas Freres 26
Dom Alain Graillot 31
Dom Alain Paret 13
Dom Aléofane 24
Dom André Perret 10
Dom Belle 19
Dom Bernard 7
Dom Bernard Ange 22
Dom Bernard Burgaud 2
Dom Bernard Levet 4
Dom de Boisseyt-Chol 11
Dom de Bonserine 3
Dom les Bruyères 30
Dom du Cêhne 11
Dom Chaboud 37
Dom Clusel-Roch 3
Dom du Colombier 25
Dom Combier 34
Dom de Corps de Loup 5
Dom du Coulet 36
Dom Courbis 35
Dom Coursodon 17
Dom Duclaux 7
Dom Dumien-Serrette 36
Dom Durand 35
Dom des Entrefaux 23
Dom François Villard 9
Dom Garon 4
Dom Georges Vernay 6
Dom Gilles Barge 4
Dom Gogon 28
Dom Hebrard 18
Dom Jamet 4
Dom Jasmin 4
Dom Jean-Louis Chave 28
Dom Jean-Luc Colombo 32
Dom Jean-Michel Gerin 3
Dom Jean-Michel Stéphan 5
Dom Lionnet 35
Dom Louis Chèze 14
Dom Michel and Stéphane Ogier 4
Dom Monier 15
Dom du Monteillet 11
Dom du Murinais 30
Dom Patrick et Christophe Bonneford 1
Dom Philippe Faury 11
Dom Pierre Dumazet 14
Dom Rémi & Robert Niéro 6
Dom des Remizières 23
Dom Rousset 16
Dom des Sept Chemins 31
Dom du Tunnel 37
Dom de la Ville Rouge 31
Dom Vincent Paris 36
Dom Yann Chave 21
Dom Yves Cuilleron 10
Emmanuel Darnaud 33
Ferraton Père et Fils 25
Franck Balthazar 36
Gilles Robin 29
E Guigal 4
Jacques Lemenicier 36
Jean-Louis et François Theirs 38
Marc Sorrel 25
Paul Jaboulet Aîné 33
Pierre Gaillard 12
René Rostaing 6
René-Jean Dard et François Ribo 20
Stephane Pichat 3
Thiérry Allemand 36
J Vidal-Fleury 4

Always check the availability of visitor facilities and the visiting hours at a winery before planning your trip. Some wineries are open by appointment only.

ALAIN VOGE

LES VIEILLES FONTAINES IS A POWERFUL
WINE BASED ON 80-YEAR-OLD VINES

CHATEAU-GRILLET

CHATEAU-GRILLET IS PROBABLY THE
WORLD'S MOST FAMOUS VIOGNIER

Alain Voge

Now in his early 70s, Alain Voge produces outstanding Cornas and St-Péray, though most of the winemaking work is now being performed by the enologist Albéric Mazoyer, Voge's partner and manager of the domaine. In addition to an entry-level Cornas, there are two special *cuvées* made from older vines, a Vieilles Vignes wine and an exceptional Les Vieilles Fontaines. Voge is an important presence in St-Péray, with 12 acres (5ha) of vines from which he produces a little sparkling and two excellent still wines, Terres Boisses and Fleur de Crussol.

4 impasse de l'Equerre, 07130 Cornas
www.alain-voge.com

Auguste et Pierre-Marie Clape

A long-time mayor of Cornas, and by general consensus its most respected resident, Auguste Clape has now turned over the winemaking reins to his capable son, Pierre-Marie, whose son Olivier is now on board as well. The Cornas wines are sourced from more than 12 acres (5ha) of vines, most of which are owned by the family. In terms of cellar techniques, Clape is among the most traditional producers in Cornas, and though the cellar itself reflects this, the wines are pure and complex rather than rustic, though they are firmly tannic. Along with the straight Cornas, there is a Renaissance *cuvée*, a little white and red Cotes du Rhône, and a red Vin de Pays.

146 route Nationale 86, 07130 Cornas
04 75 40 33 64

Bernard Faurie

Bernard Faurie produces small quantities of high-quality Hermitage and St-Joseph in a painstaking, traditional manner. Vines and wines are both subjected to minimal manipulation, with a horse used in the vineyard and whole cluster fermentations performed with native yeasts in the small cellar. Three excellent wines from St-Joseph are made from 5 acres (2ha) of vines, a red and a white as well as a Vieilles Vignes bottling. Faurie is best known for Hermitage, where plots in the *lieux-dits* Les Greffeux and Le Méal are the base for two bottlings as well as straight Hermitage red and white.

27 ave Hélène de Tournon, 07300 Tournon
04 75-08 55 09

Cave des Clairmonts

Small by co-operative standards but nevertheless the second-largest producer of Crozes-Hermitage, Cave des Clairmonts is an interesting, increasingly important enterprise. Started in 1972 by three families, it is now based on the endeavors of seven, all of whom work their vineyards biodynamically. Their combined holdings add up to an impressive 335 acres (135ha). Much of the wine is sold off in bulk, but the bottled wines are quite good, headed by a red and a white Cuvée des Pionniers.

Quartier Vignes Vieilles, 26600 Beaumont-Monteaux
www.cavedesclairmonts.com

Cave Fayolle Fils et Fille

Laurent and Céline Fayolle are earning high marks for their work at this domaine after losing their father in 2008. Céline runs the commercial side of the operation and Laurent concentrates on the vineyards and cellar. The foundation is 18.5 acres (7.5ha) of vines in Crozes-Hermitage and another 1.2 acres (0.5ha) in Hermitage. The Hermitage plot yields a red and a white bearing the vineyard's *lieu-dit*, Dionnières, and the same naming practice is followed for the whites and reds from Crozes: Les Pontaix, Les Cornirets, and Les Voussères.

9 rue de Ruisseau, 26600 Gervans
www.fayolle-filsetfille.fr

Cave de Tain l'Hermitage

The Tain l'Hermitage co-operative is very large and very important for the viability of small growers in the Northern Rhône. At its best, it is also capable of producing very good wines. It vinifies roughly 70% of all the wine made in Crozes-Hermitage, producing nearly 2 million bottles in some vintages from fruit provided by more than 200 growers. It would be an error, however, to assume that the co-operative is limited to the region's less glamorous appellations, as demonstrated by the fact that it owns or directly rents more than 50 supremely prized acres (20 hectares) on the hill at Hermitage and produces roughly a quarter of the appellation's total output. It is also an important producer of Cornas, Côte-Rôtie, and St-Péray, as well as of regional Vin de Pays wines.

22 route de Larnage, 26600 Tain l'Hermitage
www.cavedetain.fr

M Chapoutier

Now more than two centuries old, the Chapoutier house has recently risen to the very top echelon of producers in the Rhône, especially in the north where it is based. However, thanks to the vision and drive of Michel Chapoutier during the past two decades, Chapoutier is now a global leader in the biodynamic viticulture movement and a winemaking presence not only in the Rhône but also in the Ardèche, Roussillon, Portugal, and Australia. The house was founded in 1808 by Polydor Chapoutier, and leadership has passed within the family for seven successive generations—a record for longevity among Rhône producers. Michel has headed the firm since 1990, shifting emphases at several different points along the way, first in pursuit of greater concentration and intensity in the wines, then seeking greater finesse and more precise expression of particular terroirs. All of the Chapoutier vineyards in France have been cultivated biodynamically since 1995, and the house now holds more biodynamically farmed vineyard land than any wine producer in the world. Chapoutier makes a range of wines from the southern Rhône, including the excellent Châteauneuf-du-Pape Croix de Bois and Barbe Rac, but the house's center of gravity is definitely in the north and in Hermitage in particular. Holdings there include 64 acres (26ha), nearly 50 acres (20ha) of which are planted to Syrah in famous *lieux-dits* such as L'Hermite, Greffieux, Méal, and Bessards. There are four single-vineyard Hermitage reds and three whites made entirely from Marsanne. Enjoyable while very young, but capable of improving for decades, these are remarkable—if expensive—wines. Top wines from other Northern Rhône appellations are also among the very best in each region, including Condrieu Invitare, Côte-Rôtie La Mordorée, Crozes-Hermitage Les Varonnieres, St-Joseph Les Granits, and St-Péray Les Tanneurs.

18 ave Dr Paul Durand, 26600 Tain l'Hermitage
www.chapoutier.com

Château-Grillet Château-Grillet

Château-Grillet is among the most singular wines produced in France. It is made from a single grape—Viognier—from a single vineyard with a single owner who happens to be the sole producer in one of the smallest appellations in the entire country. The vineyard is a bit smaller than 10 acres (4ha) in size, arrayed in a natural amphitheater facing the south and southeast and perched on the hillside in a series of narrow terraces. Owned since 1840 by the Neyret-Gachet family, the wine is very rare and usually about twice as costly as its counterparts from Condrieu.

42410 Vérin
04 74-59 51 56

Christophe Pichon

Christophe Pichon makes a little Côte-Rôtie and more than a little St-Joseph, but it is his Condrieu that is really making his name stand out. He makes an occasional late-harvest Condrieu to accompany his complex and admirably consistent regular AOC release, which is fermented entirely with native yeasts. His two Côte-Rôtie bottlings, Le Champon and La Comtesse, are made from small, rented parcels of roughly 1.2 acres (0.5ha) each. He also has 4.2 acres (1.7ha) in St-Joseph, from which he makes a firm, intense red. ★ **Rising star**

Le Grand Val Verlieu, 42410 Chavanay
04 74-87 06 78

Delas Frères

In 1996, following decades of mediocrity, the Delas Frères négociant house, founded in 1835, began an impressive renaissance. Managing director Fabrice Rosset deserves great credit for piloting the turn-around, which involved important improvements in vineyards and winemaking facilities, as well as the hiring of enologist Jacques Grange, vineyard manager Vincent Girardini, and winemaker Jean-François Farinet. Delas is now making excellent wines from both the Southern and Northern Rhône, though the center of gravity remains in the north. Delas operates as a *négociant-éleveur* in the south, buying base wines and finishing them from 14 appellations, including prestigious ones such as Châteauneuf-du-Pape and Vacqueyras. In the north, the house produces some wines from grapes grown in partnership with growers, whereas others are made from estate vineyards managed solely by Delas. Some 35 acres (14ha) of the estate's vineyards are in the appellations of Hermitage, St-Joseph, and Crozes-Hermitage, including very important parcels atop the steep granite slopes of Hermitage, with 20 acres (8ha) in the Les Bessards *lieu-dit* and 5 acres (2ha) in l'Ermite. The top Delas wines include Hermitage Rouge Les Bessards and the red and white Hermitage Marquise de la Tourette, along with Condrieu Clos Boucher, Côte-Rôtie La Landonne, and St-Joseph Rouge Ste-Épine.

07300 St-Jean de Muzols
www.delas.com

Domaine Alain Graillot

Alain Graillot gravitated into wine from a job as an engineer in the agrochemical industry, bringing with him a dynamism and a commitment to quality that has raised the profile of the entire appellation of Crozes-Hermitage. Along with his son, Maxime, he tends 52 acres (21ha) of

vines in Crozes, with 7 acres (3ha) devoted to white grapes. These produce a little Crozes-Hermitage Blanc, a very good red, and a downright exemplary La Guiraude red that combines intensity with elegance. The St-Joseph red from Graillot is worth a search.

Les Chênes Verts, 26600 Pont-de-l'Isère
04 75-84 67 52

Domaine Alain Paret

Alain Paret and his son Anthony travel in fast company, working vineyard parcels in several different areas, some of which are co-owned with Marcel Guigal and actor Gérard Depardieu. Paret, a skilful grower and winemaker, is attaining some fame in his own right thanks to two fine red St-Joseph wines (as well as some white), a Cotes du Rhône, and two bottlings of Condrieu: Les Ceps du Nébadon and Lys de Volan. On top of all this, Paret also runs a domaine in the Languedoc.

place de l'Eglise, 42520 St-Pierre-de-Boeuf
www.maison-alain-paret.fr

Domaine Aléofane

Natacha Chave purchased a vineyard of 3.2 acres (1.3ha) in St-Joseph in 2004 and made her first wine at Domaine Aléofane in 2006. A young woman with an advanced degree in philosophy, she has thrown herself energetically into wine-growing, working her steep site without the aid of machines in a very natural manner. She uses novel non-chemical treatments against mildew and oidium, and utilizes only wild yeasts for fermentation. Chave's St-Joseph Aléofane is racked minimally to minimize the need for sulfites, and is bottled without fining or filtration. With a new site in Crozes-Hermitage coming on line, this is a producer to watch. ★ **Rising star**

La Burge, 26600 Mercurol
04 75 08 00 82

Domaine André Perret

André Perret divides his efforts between Condrieu and St-Joseph, but his Condrieu plots and resulting wines are so outstanding that he is much more widely known as a conjurer of excellent Condrieu. He holds nearly 12 acres (5ha) there, with 7 acres (3ha) of those in a superb portion of the Coteau du Chéry. In addition to a straight Condrieu, he makes a Clos Chanson and a Coteau du Chéry *cuvée*, along with sweet wines in some vintages. From St-Joseph there is a red and a white, as well as a red Les Grisières made from older Syrah vines.

17 Route Nationale 86 Verlieu, 42410 Chavanay
04 74 87 24 74

Domaine Belle

The medium-sized Domaine Belle is most closely associated with Crozes-Hermitage, where most of its 50 acres (20ha) are planted. However, it also makes very fine red and white Hermitage. The reds are produced in a traditional manner with whole clusters and extended maceration. The whites (a blend of Marsanne and Roussanne) are fermented in stainless steel. There is a white Crozes wine and three highly-regarded reds: Louis Belle, Les Pierrelles, and Roche-Pierre.

Les Marsuriaux, 26600 Larnage
04 75 08 24 58

MATCHING FOOD WITH SYRAH

Syrah-based wines from Australia or California have their charms and their defenders, but many observers regard Rhône renditions of the grape as peerless for gastronomic purposes. Rich, powerful Rhône Syrahs from warm years in Cornas, Hermitage, and St-Joseph are superb partners for robust stews or full-flavored preparations of beef or lamb. They also pair very well with game dishes based on venison or wild boar, as do fuller wines from Côte-Rôtie or Crozes-Hermitage. Top wines from each of these appellations can attain remarkable versatility as they age. As their aromatic complexity grows, and they soften in structure, they provide great pleasure with hearty meats without threatening to overwhelm less assertive foods such as duck, goose, or game birds. Syrahs from the Northern Rhône can also accompany many cheeses successfully, and are among the very best reds with blue-veined or goat cheeses.

DOMAINE BERNARD BURGAUD
WINEMAKER BERNARD BURGAUD IS A
PASSIONATE BELIEVER IN TERROIR, AS IS
REVEALED IN HIS COTE-ROTIE

DOMAINE COMBIER
COMBIER'S CROZES-HERMITAGE IS
WELL-STRUCTURED WITH SOFT TANNINS

Domaine Bernard

Young brothers Frédéric and Stéphane Bernard make a little Condrieu at Domaine Bernard, but they are best known for two 100% Syrah Côte-Rôtie bottlings. Fourth-generation winemakers, they have 11 acres (4.5ha) of vineyard in several different locations, some of which have old vines dating as far back as the 1920s. The regular release of Côte-Rôtie and the special old-vine Vieilles Vignes releases are both characterized by soft texture with deep, persistent flavors and pure fruit notes. Frédéric and Stéphane are poised for decades of excellence in the future. ★ **Rising star**

route nationale 86, 69420 Tupin et Semons
04 74 59 54 04

Domaine Bernard Ange Crozes-Hermitage

Bernard Ange established this domaine in 1998, tending 18.5 acres (7.5ha) in Crozes-Hermitage. The majority is planted to Syrah— 2.5 acres (1ha) divided between Roussanne and Marsanne. Over the years, Ange has turned toward a more natural process for working his vines, and there is no doubting the traditional character of his cellar, which affords 20ft (6m) of headroom and was cut out of rock roughly 600 years ago. In addition to making standard red and white Crozes-Hermitage, Ange also releases a red *cuvée*, Rève d'Ange, in most years.

pont de l'Herbasse, 26260 Clérieux
04 75 71 62 42

Domaine Bernard Burgaud Côte-Rôtie

Bernard Burgaud produces a rich, intense Côte-Rôtie from 10 acres (4ha) of vines. His scattered vineyard plots have differing exposures, each producing distinctive fruit, and Burgaud plays upon their particular properties to fashion a finished wine marked by complexity and balance. Some sites are situated on the appellation's plateau, but the majority are set on Côte-Rôtie's famous slope. Comprised entirely of Syrah, the wine is aged exclusively in small oak barrels, with roughly 20% new barrels rotated into the cellar each year. Production averages around 13,000 bottles annually.

Le Champin, 69420 Ampuis
coterotieburgaud.monsite.wanadoo.fr

Domaine Bernard et Fabrice Gripa

Bernard and Fabrice Gripa are leading forces in both St-Joseph and St-Péray, crafting admirably consistent wines at a very high level, and selling them at admirably fair prices. From St-Joseph, there are two bottlings each of white and red, including an upper-tier called Le Berceau, which uses fruit (100% Marsanne for the white, Syrah for the red) from the domaine's oldest vines. Both are exemplars of ageworthiness in their appellation, as are the two still wines from St-Péray—an entry-level bottling and the firmly but judiciously oaked Les Figuiers.

5 ave Ozier, 07300 Mauves
04 75 08 14 96

Domaine Bernard Levet Côte-Rôtie

This traditional Côte-Rôtie domaine is run by Bernard and his wife Nicole, along with their daughter, Agnès. The cellar is located smack in the middle of Ampuis, and

the wines are based on 9 acres (3.5ha) of vines divided between six parcels. Fruit from one of these parcels, in the *lieu-dit* Chavaroche, is vinified and sold separately. There is also a Côte-Rôtie Les Journaries, and both these wines are made in a manner that is a throwback to an earlier time, with fermentation performed in concrete tanks and minimal use of new oak.

26 boulevard des Allées, 69420 Ampuis
04 74 56 15 39

Domaine de Boisseyt-Chol

Boisseyt-Chol's proprietor, Didier Chol, turns out very tasty wines in a rather traditional style from three appellations. Chol's Côte-Rôtie is sourced from a small parcel of vines on the Côte Blonde, and it contains an unusually high percentage of Viognier—up to 15%. There is also a little Condrieu, but the lion's share of the domaine's production is divided between four St-Joseph wines: a white, a classic red, and two *lieux-dits*: Les Garipolées and the serious and sturdy Les Rivoires.

Route Nationale 86, 42410 Chavanay
www.deboisseyt-chol.com

Domaine de Bonserine

Bonserine has 25 acres (10ha) within the Côte-Rôtie appellation, but it also produces a Condrieu and a St-Joseph red from purchased fruit. The vineyard holdings in Côte-Rôtie, predominantly located in the northern portion of the region, are particularly enviable. Top sites include nearly 2.5 acres (1ha) on the Côte Brune as well as a very desirable plot in La Garde atop the Côte Blonde. The basic Côte-Rôtie is labeled La Serrasine, and the single-site wines are La Garde and La Viallière, sourced from the Côte Brune.

2 chemin de Viallière Verenay, 69420 Ampuis
04 74 56 14 27

Domaine Les Bruyères

Domaine Les Bruyères has been in David Reynauld's family for four generations, yet he is taking it in a novel direction by vinifying the fruit rather than sending it to the Cave de Tain l'Hermitage co-operative. Centered on Crozes-Hermitage, the vineyards consist of 32 acres (13ha) of Syrah with a bit of Marsanne and Roussanne, as well as a little Syrah and Viognier outside the Crozes appellation and designated as Vin de Pays des Collines Rhodaniennes. Reynauld makes a red and a white Crozes, as well as the Les Croix Rouge *cuvée*. ★ **Rising star**

Les Bruyères, 26600 Beaumont-Monteaux
04 75 84 74 14

Domaine du Cêhne

Marc and Dominique Rouvière started Domaine du Cêhne from scratch, without family predecessors or inherited vineyards. Marc took an early interest in wine, enrolling in the Mâcon wine school at 16. The Rouvières purchased a rather run-down property in Chavanay in the mid-1980s that they have since resolutely improved. They now have vineyards in St-Joseph and Condrieu, plus a little Syrah in the Vin de Pays zone. The top red is St-Joseph Anaïs, and the Condrieus are very good.

Le Pêcher, 42410 Chavanay
04 74 87 27 34

Domaine Chaboud

Stéphan Chaboud produces a wide variety of wines, including some St-Joseph and two bottlings each of Cornas and Côtes du Rhône, but it is with St-Péray that he is particularly closely identified. Indeed, Chaboud is by general consensus the leading figure in the appellation —especially with regard to sparkling wines—and he and his father have long been the principal advocates for St-Péray as a quality wine region. Chaboud tends what others might consider a daunting number of vineyard plots (eight each in Cornas and St-Péray) and likewise crafts an astonishing range of wines, including as many as five *cuvées* of sparkling St-Péray. Perhaps it is fitting in light of all these efforts that the world comes to Chaboud rather than vice-versa, as he sells most of his wine directly to customers.

21 rue Ferdinand Malet, 07130 St-Péray
04 75 40 31 63

Domaine Clusel-Roch

Clusel-Roch is led by Gilbert Clusel and Joséphine Roch, with Clusel working principally in the vineyards and Roch in the cellar. Since assuming control from Clusel's father, René, they have replanted some plots and added some vineyards and the domaine now consists of 11 acres (4.5ha) in Côte-Rôtie and another 1.2 acres (0.5ha) in Condrieu. There are three Côte-Rôties: La Petite Feuille (a young-vine *cuvée*), Classique, and the single-site Grandes Places, plus a Condrieu called Verchery.

15 route du Lacat Verenay, 69420 Ampuis
04 74 56 15 95

Domaine du Colombier

An attractive property run by Florent Viale, Colombier has moved from selling most of its wine in bulk to bottling nearly all of it. The cellars are located on the left bank of the Rhône, and the vineyards are comprised of 32 acres (13ha) of Syrah and 5 acres (2ha) of Marsanne for Crozes-Hermitage, along with a small prized holding in Hermitage, distributed across three plots. Wines include straight bottlings in red and white from both appellations, plus a young-vine Primavera and an old-vine Cuvée Gaby Crozes-Hermitage Rouge.

2 route de Chantemerle, 26600 Tain l'Hermitage
www.domaineducolombier.fr

Domaine Combier

Like his father, Maurice, Laurent Combier is a committed organic farmer and a very successful one, now working 54 acres (22ha) of Syrah in Crozes-Hermitage and another 5 acres (2ha) of Marsanne and Roussanne, along with a little Syrah in St-Joseph. Maurice was an organic pioneer, taking the domaine into virtually uncharted territory in 1970. The St-Joseph and the straight red and white Crozes-Hermitage are very good, but the real highlights here are the elegantly fruity, finely wrought Crozes-Hermitage Clos des Grives red and white.

2 route de Chantemerle, 26600 Tain l'Hermitage
www.domaine-combier.com

Domaine de Corps de Loup

Corps de Loup is sited on 23 acres (9.5ha) of land, 7 acres (3ha) of which have been gradually planted or replanted since brothers Bruno and Martin Daubrée bought the estate in 1992. Bruno was killed in a tragic cellar accident in 1995, but Martin then devoted himself full-time to the estate, becoming very skilled in the cellar as well as the vineyard. A new cellar was finished in 2007 and now issues a Condrieu and three Côte-Rôtie *cuvées*: Corps de Loup, Paradis, and Marions-Les.

69420 Tupin et Semons
www.corpsdeloup.com

Domaine du Coulet

Mathieu Barret is a trailblazer in Cornas, where he became the first to work his vineyards biodynamically, back in 2001. He now farms a little more than 32 acres (13ha) of vines at Domaine du Coulet, some of which are owned and others leased. Fully 25 acres (10ha) are in Cornas, with another 7 acres (3ha) split between red and white Côtes du Rhône plantings of Syrah, Roussanne, and Viognier. He makes three *cuvées* of Cornas: Les Terrasses du Serre and the small-production, low-yield Billes Noires and Brise Cailloux. ★ **Rising star**

41/43/45 rue de Ruisseau, 07130 Cornas
04 75 80 08 25

Domaine Courbis

Dominique and Laurent Courbis have taken over leadership of this 50 acre (20ha) estate from their father, Maurice. The vineyard holdings are rather lavish by Northern Rhône standards—they include 42 acres (17ha) in St-Joseph (mostly red) and 7 acres (3ha) in Cornas. The Vin de Pays de l'Ardeche Syrah is very good, as are the red and white St-Joseph, but the real stars here are four single-vineyard reds named after their *lieux-dits*: Les Royes from St-Joseph and Champelrose, La Sabarotte, and Les Eygats from Cornas. ★ **Rising star**

route de St-Romain, 07130 Châteaubourg
04 75 81 81 60

Domaine Coursodon St-Joseph

Young Jérome Coursodon, now in his mid-30s, produces admirably concentrated, juicy St-Joseph from more than 37 acres (15ha) of vineyards. Many of the vines are quite old, thanks in large part to the efforts of Jérome's grandfather, Gustave, who was a force of nature at the domaine—and in the wider appellation—for decades. The two white wines, St-Joseph Silice and Le Paradis St-Pierre, are filled with mineral-laden flavors; the reds bearing these same names (as well as the l'Olivale) are notably but judiciously oaked.

place du Marché, 07300 Mauves
04 75 08 18 29

Domaine Duclaux Côte-Rôtie

David and Benjamin Duclaux took over the family domaine in 2003 from their father, Edmond, and it has steadily moved toward the top rank of producers in the southern part of Côte-Rôtie. Their two most important plots (each of them 5 acres/2ha) are in the Côte-Rôtie *lieux-dits* of Maison Rouge and Coteau de Tupin. Along with roughly 20,000 bottles of Côte-Rôtie La Germine, the brothers produce a 100% Syrah bottling from the steep, terraced Maison Rouge vineyard. ★ **Rising star**

34 route de Lyon, 69420 Tupin et Semons
www.coterotie-duclaux.com

DOMAINE DE CORPS DE LOUP
THE PARADIS COTE-ROTIE DRAWS ON FRUIT FROM A PRIME SITE IN THE COTE BRUNE

DOMAINE COURBIS
COMING FROM OLD VINES ON GRANITE AND LIMESTONE SOILS, THE CHAMPELROSE RED IS PACKED WITH DENSE FRUIT FLAVORS

DOMAINE FRANCOIS VILLARD
RICH, HEADY, AND LUXURIOUS, FRANCOIS VILLARD CONDRIEU IS A FINE EXAMPLE OF NORTHERN RHONE VIOGNIER

DOMAINE GILLES BARGE
TRADITIONAL METHODS ARE USED FOR THE BROODING GILLES BARGE COTE BRUNE

Domaine Dumien-Serrette Cornas

The small Domaine Dumien-Serrette consists of 5 acres (2ha) of vines in Cornas, located mostly in the *lieu-dit* of Patou and divided equally between the upper and lower portion of the slope. Although Gilbert Serrette experimented with modernist winemaking methods inspired by Jean-Luc Colombo in the 1980s, he has since reverted to traditional methods such as crushing of whole grape clusters by foot and pressing with a wooden basket press. His wife, Danielle Dumien, does the labeling for the domaine's sole wine, Cornas Patou.

18 rue de Ruisseau, 07130 Cornas
www.serrette.com

Domaine Durand

Energetic brothers Joël and Eric Durand are rapidly gaining renown on the strength of an impressive set of red wines sourced from family vineyard holdings in Cornas and St-Joseph. Joël takes the lead in the vineyards, working 17 acres (7ha) in St-Joseph and another 12 acres (5ha) in Cornas. Eric's influence in the cellar produces wines that show interesting stylistic elements that are both modern and traditional, with pure fruit notes accented with smoky, gamey complexities. Three very good Cornas wines are released, along with three St-Josephs that are leaders in the appellation.

2 impasse de la Fontaine, 07130 Châteaubourg
04 75 40 46 78

Domaine des Entrefaux Crozes-Hermitage

Brothers-in-law Charles Tardy and Bernard Ange established this domaine in 1979 and worked together for a decade before Ange broke away to work on his own. Charles's energetic son, François, now works alongside his father in farming 86 acres (25ha) in Crozes-Hermitage that are divided between 52 acres (21ha) of Syrah and 10 acres (4ha) of Marsanne. Grapes are harvested by hand and the clusters are entirely stemmed. A range of different red and white *cuvées* are crafted, headed by the excellent Crozes-Hermitage Les Machonnières Rouge.

Quartier de la Beaume, 26600 Chanos-Curson
04 75 07 33 38

Domaine François Villard

The supremely energetic François Villard is a dynamic force in each of the three appellations in which he works: Condrieu, Côte-Rôtie, and St-Joseph. Patching together a variety of owned and rented vineyard parcels, this former chef makes ripe, flamboyantly flavorful, botrytis-tinged whites from Condrieu and St-Joseph, including a couple of sweet wines and a Vin de Pays from young vines in Condrieu. On the red side, there are two bottlings of St-Joseph and two Vin de Pays and two fine bottlings of Côte-Rôtie. ★ Rising star

Montjoux, 42410 St-Michel-sur-Rhône
04 74 56 83 60

Domaine Garon Côte-Rôtie

Jean-François and Carmen Garon run this up-and-coming domaine along with their two sons, Kévin and Fabien. They work 11 acres (4.5ha) in Côte-Rôtie that have been cleared and planted during the past quarter of a century after having been abandoned for many decades by earlier generations of the family. In addition to a basic

Côte-Rôtie, there is now a Côte-Rôtie Les Rochains as well as a Les Triotes made from 100% Syrah from parcels on the Côte Blonde. The wines are quite complex and are rapidly gaining an international following. ★ Rising star

58 Le Goutay, 69420 Ampuis
04 74 56 14 11

Domaine Georges Vernay

The heart of this enterprise is a little more than 17 acres (7ha) of vineyard in Condrieu, including a superb plot of 4.2 acres (1.7ha) that is the source for the flagship wine of the house and arguably of the entire appellation: Condrieu Coteau de Vernon. Georges Vernay was a champion for Condrieu when the appellation was whittled down to only 20 acres (8ha) under vine in the 1960s. Today, his daughter Christine runs the house along with her husband Paul and her brother Luc, making three bottlings of Condrieu, Vin de Pays Viognier, and Syrah, a St-Joseph, and two bottlings of Côte-Rôtie.

1 route nationale, 69420 Condrieu
www.georges-vernay.fr

Domaine Gilles Barge

Wines from this family were first bottled in 1929. Gilles Barge, currently president of the Union of Côte-Rôtie Vignerons, assumed leadership of the domaine in 1994, but has been making the family's wines since the late 1970s. The vineyards total 16 acres (6.5ha), including a parcel on the Côte Brune that produces an excellent wine of the same name. Other releases include a basic Côte-Rôtie bearing the proprietary name Du Plessy, as well as a Condrieu La Solarie and a St-Joseph Rouge Clos des Martinets.

8 blvrd des Allées, 69420 Ampuis
www.domainebarge.com

Domaine Gogon St-Joseph

Gogon is an outstanding source for both white and red St-Joseph. Brothers Pierre and Jean Gogon took the reins from their father in the late 1980s. They inaugurated a new cellar in 2002 that handles the fruit from 19 acres (7.5ha), 5 acres (2ha) of which are devoted to enviably old Marsanne and Roussanne vines. The Syrah vines are mostly quite mature as well, and Pierre and Jean take care to let their high-quality fruit stand at center stage in wines that are never marked by overt oak. Despite the new cellar, winemaking here remains quite traditional.

34 ave Ozier, 07300 Mauves
04 75 08 45 27

Domaine Hebrard

Hebrard is a rising domaine based on 37 acres (15ha) of vines, mostly in Crozes-Hermitage but also in Hermitage and St-Joseph. Marcel Hebrard and his sons, Emmanuel and Laurent, will soon achieve organic certification for their vineyards. The tiny Hermitage plot of old Marsanne vines produces an excellent barrel-fermented white. The St-Joseph debuted in 2006 and is off to a good start, but Crozes-Hermitage is definitely the center of gravity for this domaine, with single white and red bottlings that offer excellent consistency and value.

7 route des Blancs, 26600, Gervans
www.domainehabrard.com

Domaine Jamet Côte-Rôtie

Brothers Jean-Luc and Jean-Paul Jamet produce two excellent bottlings of Côte-Rôtie from an array of vineyard plots that are among the most impressive of any establishment in the appellation. Their holdings include 25 separate plots that are widely dispersed among 17 different *lieux-dit* locations. Variations in soil, exposure, and altitude enable Jean-Luc and Jean-Paul to grow grapes with a range of different properties that can then be blended in varying proportions to make their classic Côte-Rôtie and the high-end Côte Brune bottling among the most consistently fine reds of the Northern Rhône.

Le Vallin, 69420 Ampuis
04 74 56 12 57

Domaine Jasmin Côte-Rôtie

Patrick Jasmin and his wife, Arlette, currently preside over this celebrated Côte-Rôtie domaine with cellars in Ampuis. Patrick is a fourth-generation proprietor who found himself in the role suddenly after his father, the well-known and much-loved Robert, died in an accident in 1999. The domaine is based on around 12 acres (5ha) of vineyards in 11 parcels scattered up and down the region. Robert was famously traditional as a winemaker, and while Patrick is hardly a modernist in method, he has updated the estate's single wine, a Côte-Rôtie, with techniques such as stemming and *saignée* (tank bleeding).

14 rue des Maraîchers, 69420 Ampuis
04 74 56 16 04

Domaine Jean-Louis Chave

Having been the gold standard for Hermitage wines for a generation, this domaine remains one of the handful of France's most admired estates. Jean-Louis Chave has assumed leadership from his modest but nevertheless famous father, Gérard, who remains involved with the wines despite nominal retirement. Vineyard holdings in Hermitage include a relatively lavish 22 acres (9ha) of Syrah as well as nearly 12 acres (5ha) of Marsanne and Roussanne. The seven Syrah parcels are vinified and aged separately prior to blending, and the blend differs for the regular *cuvée* of Hermitage Rouge and the Cuvée Cathelin, which is not made in every vintage. Marsanne is utilized more than Roussanne for the Hermitage Blanc, and the Chaves also make a bit of late-picked *vin de paille* in selected years. There is also an excellent St-Joseph Rouge, and a growing négociant business under the name Jean-Louis Chave Séléction.

37 ave St-Joseph, 07300, Mauves
04 75 08 24 63

Domaine Jean-Luc Colombo

Now, having reached his early 50s, Jean-Luc Colombo is no longer quite the polarizing figure that he was in the early 1980s when he arrived from the south and established himself as a winemaking consultant. Nevertheless, he remains the person most closely associated with modernism in Rhône winemaking, having successfully popularized the practices of green harvesting, stemming grape clusters, and using smaller, newer oak barrels. In addition to his ongoing consulting work, the ultra-dynamic Colombo makes a wide range of his own domaine and négociant wines

from Châteauneuf-du-Pape and Tavel in the south, as well as white and red Cotes du Rhône, St-Joseph, St-Péray, Crozes-Hermitage, Hermitage, Condrieu, and four highly-esteemed *cuvées* from Cornas.

La Croix des Marais, 26600 La Roche-de-Glun
04 75 84 17 10

Domaine Jean-Michel Gerin

Jean-Michel Gerin produces Vin de Pays Syrah and Viognier, a red from St-Joseph, and a highly regarded Condrieu La Loye sourced from a 4.5 acre (1.8ha) plot. However, he is most widely known for his *cuvées* from Côte-Rôtie. Of the 20 acres (8ha) of vines he works in the appellation, 15 acres (6ha) provide the foundation for his Cuvée Champin Le Seigneur, with the balance shared between Les Grandes Places and La Landonne. The Côte-Rôtie wines are aged for two years in barrels; the Condrieu is 60% fermented in barrels and 40% in vats.

19 rue Montmain Verenay, 69420 Ampuis
www.domaine-gerin.fr

Domaine Jean-Michel Stéphan

Still in his 30s, Jean-Michel Stéphan is one of the youngest—and most innovative—winemakers in Côte Rôtie. He owns a little more than 7 acres (3ha) of vines in seven parcels in the southern part of the appellation. He crafts four different bottlings of Côte Rôtie, each of which is made to express the purity and freshness of the fruit. The entry-level wine is a Côte Rôtie Classic, and at the upper end are Côte Rôtie Côteaux de Tupin, Côteaux de Bassenon (incorporating roughly 10% Viognier), and Vieille Vigne en Côteaux. ★ Rising star

69420 Tupin et Semons
04 74 56 62 66

Domaine Lionnet Cornas

Corinne Lionnet and her husband, Ludovic, have been in charge at this defiantly traditional family domaine since the retirement of Pierre Lionnet in 2003. Their methods offer an insight into how Cornas was made a generation ago—or perhaps two. The organically farmed vineyard is worked with a horse. Whole clusters are fermented, with crushing and punch-downs performed by foot. The fruit comes from 5 acres (2ha) located in four parts of the Cornas appellation, and all of it is devoted to a single, high-quality wine: Cornas Terre Brûlée.

160 route Nationale, 07130 Cornas
domainelionnet.fr

Domaine Louis Chèze

Louis Chèze took up the reins of the family farm in 1978 and effected something of a transformation, breaking with the practice of selling off the grapes and planting many more vines. Having started with just 2.5 acres (1ha), he now holds 74 acres (30ha), with major Syrah holdings in St-Joseph, a significant parcel in Condrieu, and Vin de Pays vineyards planted to Marsanne, Viognier, and Syrah. The three St-Joseph Rouges—Anges, Caroline, and Ro-Rée—are consistently successful, with notable oak but also pure fruit and complex aromas.

Pangon, 07340 Limony
www.domainecheze.com

JEAN-LUC COLOMBO: ARCH MODERNIZER

To a remarkable degree, the distinction in the Northern Rhône between "traditional" and "modern" wines boils down to a single factor: were they crafted under the influence of Jean-Luc Colombo? Colombo's impact has been greatest with reds and with Cornas in particular, but he has directly or indirectly influenced the way producers work on every grape and in every appellation in the region. His prominence is especially unlikely since he arrived in this relatively insular area as an outsider from Marseilles, originally trained as a pharmacist. However, based on his own estate-grown wines, his négociant business, and his sway with hundreds of consulting clients, he has gradually turned a host of innovations into standard practices. These include aggressive crop-thinning, late harvesting, complete de-stalking of grape clusters, extended maceration, extractive fermentations, and extended aging in newer oak barrels. Some detractors remain, but today it is they rather than Colombo who are in the minority.

Domaine Michel & Stéphane Ogier

Ogier is a relatively new domaine, and certainly a fast-rising one. Michel Ogier, the father, broke with past family practice of selling the Côte-Rôtie wine to négociants and began to bottle on his own. Stéphane, son of Michel and Hélène, has introduced a host of winemaking innovations. In recent years, the family enterprise has expanded into Condrieu and into production of Syrah-based Vin de Pays des Collines Rhodaniennes wines from sites to the north of Côte-Rôtie. The straight Côte-Rôtie and the single-site *cuvées*, Belle Hélène and Lancement Terroir de Blonde, are consistently excellent. ★ Rising star

3 chemin du Bac, 69420 Ampuis
04 74 56 10 75

Domaine Monier

This biodynamically farmed domaine is headed by Jean-Pierre Monier, who began working in wine in 1977 and left his membership of the co-operative at St-Désirat to begin bottling his own wines in 2001. A little more than 12 acres (5ha) of vineyards are meticulously farmed, yielding a fine St-Joseph Blanc and three reds, including an entry-level Tradition bottling and two excellent *cuvées* called Les Terres Blanches and Les Serves. Monier also bottles a Vin de Pays des Collines Rhodaniennes that is made entirely from Viognier.

route des Vignobles Brunieux, 07340 St-Désirat
04 7 34 20 64

Domaine du Monteillet

Monteillet is a family estate run at top speed by the young Stéphane Montez. Montez works around 15 acres (6ha) of Syrah in St-Joseph and makes four reds from them, alongside two bottlings of St-Joseph Blanc. From Côte-Rôtie he makes three wines, La Pèlerine, Fortis, and Les Grandes Places, which is the domaine's flagship wine from this appellation, sourced from a site atop the *lieu-dit* of this same name. From 6 acres (2.5ha) of vines in Condrieu, Montez makes a basic *cuvée* tagged with the domaine's name as well as the superb oak-aged Les Grandes Chaillées. ★ Rising star

Le Montelier, 42410 Chavanay
04 74 87 24 57

Domaine du Murinais   Crozes-Hermitage

Luc and Catherine Tardy are a young couple in charge of a very old property at Domaine du Murinais, with a house owned by the family since 1683. Luc was trained in enology at Montpellier, and the estate is based on 32 acres (13ha) of vines in Crozes-Hermitage. There is a little Marsanne and Roussanne, but the primary emphasis here is on the two red wines, a Vieilles Vignes bottling and the Crozes-Hermitage Caprice de Valentin, assembled from the best barrels and given an additional period of aging.

Quartier Champ Bernard, 26600, Beaumont-Monteux
04 75 07 34 76

Domaine Patrick et Christophe Bonnefond

The Bonnefond family, headed by Charles and his two sons, Patrick and Christophe, produces a range of exemplary wines. It includes three bottlings of

DOMAINE PHILIPPE FAURY
THE LA BERNE IS AN AROMATIC OFFERING
WITH FLORAL AND MINERAL NOTES

DOMAINE REMI & ROBERT NIERO
THE CELEBRATED CHERY VINEYARD
PRODUCES FRESH BUT AROMATIC VIOGNIER

Côte-Rôtie, a Syrah-based Vin de Pays des Collines Rhodaniennes, and an exceptional Condrieu that is predominantly fermented in new oak barrels. The Côte-Rôtie bottlings include a standard release, a more limited offering from the *lieu-dit* Côte Rozier, and the flagship wine, Côte-Rôtie Les Rochains. All three are impressively complex and consistent, and all of the domaine's releases reflect the conscientiousness of this energetic, hard-working family.

Mornas, 69420 Ampuis
04 74 56 12 30

Domaine Philippe Faury

Philippe Faury's domaine is located in the little hamlet of La Ribaudy on the slope in the Condrieu appellation, and although he also produces Côte-Rôtie and several bottlings of St-Joseph, he is known most widely for his stylish wines from Condrieu. The Côte-Rôtie is sourced from two plots totaling 3.7 acres (1.5ha) and includes about 15% Viognier. From his 7 acres (3ha) in Condrieu, Faury makes two dry wines—a straight AOC Condrieu and a *cuvée* called La Berne—as well as a late-harvest Condrieu known as Brumaire.

La Ribaudy, 42410 Chavanay
04 74 87 26 00

Domaine Pierre Dumazet

Pierre Dumazet makes a range of wines from fruit that he vinifies in partnership with single growers, including a Côte-Rôtie sourced from the Côte Brune, a fine St-Joseph Rouge called La Muzolaise, and a Cornas Cuvée Charlemagne. He also makes some Vin de Pays and a Côtes du Rhône Viognier from plots of his own, but by far his most renowned wines are two bottlings of rich, deeply flavored Condrieu made from his vineyard sites on the *lieux-dits* Coteau de Côte Fournet and Rouelle-Midi. A late-harvest Condrieu called La Myriade is also worth a look.

07340 Limony
04 75 34 03 01

Domaine Rémi & Robert Niéro

Robert Niéro grows and makes a bit of Côte-Rôtie, but is most notable for his bottlings of Condrieu, where he served a stint as president of the Growers Union in the late 1990s. He holds 7 acres (3ha) of Condrieu vineyards set in five different portions of the appellation, including one in the *lieu-dit* of Chéry that provides the fruit for his top wine, Cuvée de Chéry. He also makes a bottling called Les Ravines, and both wines are made partly in wood and partly in stainless steel.

20 rue Cuvillière, 69420 Condrieu
www.vins-niero.com

Domaine des Remizières

In recent years, Domaine des Remizières has grown from just 10 acres (4ha) to 74 acres (30ha). Fortunately, the quality has risen markedly, too, with Philippe Desmeures and his daughter Emilie turning out modern-style wines with impressive concentration and lots of flashy oak. The largest vineyard holdings are in Crozes-Hermitage, with 60 acres (24ha) producing fruit for multiple white and red *cuvées* led by the Autrement bottling selected from the best barrels. The duo also makes a fine St-Joseph and excellent wines from Hermitage, including a white and a red Cuvée Emilie and the estate's flagship wine, the Hermitage Autrement. ★ Rising star

route de Romans, 26600 Mercurol
www.domaineremizieres.com

Domaine Rousset

One of Crozes-Hermitage's leading lights for a number of years, Robert Rousset is a sturdy man making very sturdy wines along with his son, Stéphane. The two men tend a little under 25 acres (10ha) of vines in Crozes-Hermitage, and many of those vines are quite old, lending admirable concentration to the wines. The prime plot is Picaudières, a steep site with decomposed granite soil that provides fruit for a special bottling of the same name that is Rousset's calling-card wine. Very good Crozes-Hermitage Blanc and Rouge are also produced, as well as a St-Joseph Rouge made from a small plot owned by a cousin.

route de Gervans, 26600 Erôme
04 75 03 30 38

Domaine des Sept Chemins

Crozes-Hermitage
Named after a nearby junction where seven roads meet, the 52 acre (21ha) Domaine des Sept Chemins is worked by Jean-Louis Buffière and his sons, Jérome and Rémy. Roughly 12 acres (5ha) of the vineyard were replanted in the wake of phylloxera in the 1930s, so there are some very old vines from which to draw more concentrated fruit. The wines are vinified in a relatively traditional manner, but in a relatively new cellar, which is perhaps a combination of the best of both worlds. The top wine is Crozes-Hermitage Cuvée des 7 Chemins Rouge, based on hand-harvested, old-vine Syrah.

Les 7 Chemins, 26600 Pont-de-l'Isère
04 75 84 75 55

Domaine du Tunnel

Stéphane Robert established Domaine du Tunnel—a domaine now very much on the rise—in 1994, at the tender age of 24. He began by sourcing fruit from leased vineyards and then steadily acquired some land of his own. He now tends nearly 9 acres (3.5ha) in Cornas, 6 acres (2.5ha) in St-Joseph and 5 acres (2ha) in St-Péray, most of which he owns. From these he fashions a fine Cornas as well as an aptly named high-end cuvée called Vin Noir. Robert's St-Joseph Rouge is polished and pure, and the bottlings of St-Péray, where the domaine is located, are among the appellation's best wines. ★ Rising star

20 rue de la République, 07130 St-Péray
04 75 80 04 66

Domaine de la Ville Rouge

Sébastien Girard is making striking wines for his family at the relatively new estate of Domaine de la Ville Rouge, which is centered on Crozes-Hermitage. After serving a stint in St-Joseph with the Courbis brothers, he determined that the family's grapes should not be sold off as in the past, but vinified and bottled on the estate. Holdings include 37 acres (15ha) of Crozes-Hermitage red and 1.2 acres (0.5ha) each of Crozes-Hermitage white and St-Joseph red and white. The top wines are

DOMAINE YVES CUILLERON
CUILLERON SAINT-JOSEPH LYSERAS
IS A FRESH AND FRUITY WHITE

DOMAINE VINCENT PARIS
FROM 60-YEAR-OLD VINES, THIS WINE IS DEEP, INTENSE, AND AGEWORTHY

Crozes-Hermitage Rouge Terre d'Eclat and Inspiration, both marked by deeply concentrated fruit.

Les Chassis, 26600, Mercurol
domainedelavillerouge.fr

Domaine Vincent Paris

A rising star in Cornas who also makes a fine St-Joseph Rouge, Vincent Paris is the nephew of Robert Michel, who was one of the most important winemakers in Cornas until his retirement in 2006. Michel then sold a portion of his holdings to Paris, who now owns or rents 20 acres (8ha) in the small Cornas appellation. He releases three bottlings of Cornas: La Geynale, Granit 30, and Granit 60 Vieilles Vignes. Future releases will include a rare white made from Viognier and Roussanne vines he planted in Cornas, though it will be labeled as Cotes du Rhône since there is no Appellation Contrôlée status for white wines in Cornas. ★ Rising star

chemin des Peyrouses, 07130 Cornas
04 75 40 13 04

Domaine Yann Chave

Only now entering his 40s, Yann Chave already has more than a dozen vintages under his belt. Economics and banking did not quite suit his taste, so he studied winemaking and joined his father, Bernard, who still works the vines. The domaine has developed since then, and now consists of more than 37 acres (15ha) of Crozes-Hermitage (mostly Syrah) and a little more than 2.4 acres (1ha) of Hermitage. The line-up includes two levels of Crozes-Hermitage in both red and white, headed by Le Rouvre bottlings, as well as about 7,000 bottles of complex, convincing Hermitage.

26600 Mercurol
04 75 07 42 11

Domaine Yves Cuilleron

Yves Cuilleron is one of the most dynamic wine producers in the Northern Rhône. He began by purchasing a mere 9 acres (3.5ha) from his uncle in 1986, but now holds 100 acres (52ha) spread, in descending order of size, between St-Joseph, Vin de Pays, Condrieu, Côte-Rôtie, Saint-Péray, and Cornas. The reds are vinified in open vats prior to aging in barrels, whereas the whites are both fermented and aged in barrels. Cuilleron remains very much a man on the move. ★ Rising star

58 route Nationale 86 Verlieu, 42410 Chavanay
www.cuilleron.com

Emmanuel Darnaud Crozes-Hermitage

Young Emmanuel Darnaud is off to a flying start in his first decade as a wine producer. Darnaud's estate has grown rapidly in that time, and as a result, he now works 37 acres (15ha) of vines in the southern portion of Crozes-Hermitage. His father was a grower and his uncle a winemaker, and Bernard Faurie—for whom Emmanuel worked for four years in Hermitage—provided another formative influence. Gentle but meticulous work in the vineyard and cellar pays dividends in the detailed, balanced wines, led by Crozes-Hermitage Les Trois Chênes Rouge. ★ Rising star

21 rue du Stade, 26600 La Roche-de-Glun
04 75 84 81 64

E GUIGAL
THE CONDRIEU IS ONE OF MANY WINES
THAT HAVE ESTABLISHED E GUIGAL AS
ONE OF FRANCE'S GREAT PRODUCERS

PIERRE GAILLARD
PIERRE GAILLARD SAINT-JOSEPH LES PIERRES
IS AGED FOR UP TO 20 MONTHS IN NEW OAK

Ferraton Père et Fils

Ferraton produces both estate and négociant wines under the direction of Michel Chapoutier, who has recently pushed for serious improvements in quality much as Marcel Guigal has ramped up Vidal-Fleury. The vineyards have now been tended biodynamically for a decade, and estate-owned plots provide the fruit for the house's top wines from Hermitage, Les Dionnières Rouge and Le Meal Rouge. Other standard-bearers for Ferraton include white Hermitage bottlings Le Miaux and Le Reverdy, as well as Crozes-Hermitage Le Grand Courtil and St-Joseph La Source Blanc and Rouge. The négociant wines have shown marked improvement in recent years, and the whole enterprise is clearly on the rise.

13 rue de la Sizeranne, 26600 Tain l'Hermitage
www.ferraton.fr

Franck Balthazar Cornas

Franck Balthazar assumed the reins of this very small and traditional domaine from his father, René, in 2002. At that point, there were just 3.7 acres (1.5ha) of vines, though in 2004 Balthazar added another 1.2 acres (0.5ha) thanks to the retirement of his uncle, Joël Verset. Traditional practices extend from plowing behind a horse in the vineyards, to fermenting with whole clusters, and aging in large, older *demi-muid* barrels. The sole wine released is a floral, fruity Cornas that recalls the very best wines produced in the appellation in decades past.

1 impasse des Basses Rues, 07130 Cornas
04 75 80 01 72

Gilles Robin

Born in 1971, Gilles Robin has rapidly earned a top reputation among producers in Crozes-Hermitage. Robin's family had long sent their grapes to the Cave de Tain l'Hermitage co-operative, but he now puts the estate's 37 acres (15ha) of vines to very good use as sources for his five highly regarded wines. Three of these are reds from Crozes-Hermitage: Cuvée Papillon, and two *cuvées* that use fruit from older vines, Albéric Bouvet and 1920. The Crozes-Hermitage Blanc Les Marelles is a blend of 60% Roussanne and 40% Marsanne, and the new St-Joseph Cuvée André Péléat is off to a great start. ★ **Rising star**

Les Chassis Sud, 26600 Mercurol
gillesrobin.com

E Guigal

Headed by Marcel Guigal, E Guigal is the most important producer and négociant in the Northern Rhône and also a principal source for Southern Rhône wines such as Châteauneuf-du-Pape, Gigondas, and Côtes du Rhône Blanc and Rouge, making Guigal the pivotal producer for the entire Rhône Valley. Guigal's significance is highlighted by the fact that the house vinifies more than 40% of all the wine produced in the appellations of Condrieu and Côte-Rôtie, but even more impressive is Marcel Guigal's ability to make the very best (and most expensive) wines from appellations such as these. The house was established by Marcel's father, Etienne, who struck out on his own in 1946 after 15 years of rising through the ranks at Vidal-Fleury. Etienne lived long enough to see the Guigal family

acquire Vidal-Fleury in 1984, in a remarkable reversal that is of enduring importance due to the 17 acres (7ha) of superb vineyards that were included in the acquisition. This purchase signaled the ascent of the Guigal family into the global aristocracy of wine, and if there were still any doubts about this, they were dispelled in 1995 when Marcel purchased the Château d'Ampuis, a 12th-century fort that was developed into a Renaissance château in the 16th century. Guigal's company headquarters, as well as its own cooperage, are now housed in the château, which is set on the Rhône amid the lowest vines. In 2000, Marcel set his sights on additional vineyards, purchasing the St-Joseph estate of Jean-Louis Grippat as well as the Domaine de Vallouit's parcels in Côte-Rôtie, Hermitage, St-Joseph, and Crozes-Hermitage. E Guigal's vineyard holdings now total more than 110 acres (45ha), with sites in each of the appellations of the Northern Rhône. These include the flagship sites of La Mouline, La Landonne, and La Turque in Côte-Rôtie, which provide fruit for single-vineyard bottlings that are among the world's most prized wines. With Marcel's son, Philippe, now fully engaged in the family firm, Guigal's place at the pinnacle of French winemaking looks to be assured for years to come. ★ **Rising star**

Château d'Ampuis, 69420 Ampuis
www.guigal.com

Jacques Lemenicier

Jacques Lemenicier is known for making a stylishly fruity Cornas that is quite consistent and rather traditional in character. More recently, he has begun to bottle a high-end *cuvée* sourced from his older vines in the Cornas *lieu-dit* of Pigeonnier. Lemenicier also makes two wines from St-Péray, the Cuvée De l'Elegance and the Cuvée Boisée, but his growing reputation for quality is firmly based on the finely crafted wines from Cornas, which are produced with minimal oak influence.

Quartier des Grays, 07130 Cornas
04 75 81 00 57

Jean-Louis et Françoise Theirs

Jean-Louis Theirs makes consistently good wines from both St-Péray and Cornas, as well as a little Vin de Pays Syrah. The Cornas is sourced from just under 2.5 acres (1ha) of vines located in the southern portion of the appellation, and tends to be relatively soft and inviting in structure but complex and interesting in aroma and flavor. Most of the St-Péray is made as sparkling wine, with malolactic fermentation blocked in order to keep the finished wine crisp and refreshing. The still St-Péray often shows an interesting interplay between ripe richness and mineral accents.

Le Biguet, 07130 Toulaud
04 75 40 42 44

Marc Sorrel

Marc Sorrel is a rare small producer holding significant parcels of prime land on the hill in Hermitage. These include almost 5 acres (2ha) planted to Syrah and just under 2.5 acres (1ha) for white varieties, mostly Marsanne with a bit of Roussanne. During the past two decades, the vines have been treated ever more naturally, and cellar work is likewise quite traditional. In addition to straight

Hermitage Blanc and Rouge, there are high-end bottlings of white and red called Le Gréal, as well as very good renditions of Crozes-Hermitage in both colors.

128 ave Jean Jaurès, 26600 Tain l'Hermitage
04 75 07 10 07

Paul Jaboulet Aîné

Founded in 1834, Paul Jaboulet Aîné was long the leading producer of wines from the Northern Rhône, as well as an extremely important négociant firm that promoted Rhône wines around the world with greater fame and success than any other business. One could argue that the most important Rhône wine of the 20th century was either Jaboulet's Côtes du Rhône Parallèle 45, which probably passed more lips than any other quality wine from the region, or the 1961 Hermitage La Chapelle, which is perhaps the single greatest Rhône wine ever made. Sadly, however, the house's performance slipped quite notably after the sudden death of Gérard Jaboulet in 1997, and only recently have prospects seemed to brighten with the purchase of the house by the Frey family, who have enjoyed great success at Bordeaux's La Lagune and Champagne's Billcart-Salmon. The négociant side of the business is now being de-emphasized in favor of the estate-grown wines. That leaves a lot with which to work, since Jaboulet owns 13.5 acres (5.5ha) in the Southern Rhône and an impressive 119 acres (48ha) in the Northern Rhône, including more than 50 acres (20ha) on the hill in Hermitage. Current releases are arrayed on four tiers, ascending from négociant wines in the Les Grands Classiques range up to a Les Grands Terroirs and then to estate wines at the Les Domaines level. At the top are Les Icônes, Hermitage La Chapelle Blanc and Rouge.

Les Jalets RN7, 26600 La Roche-de-Glun
www.jaboulet.com

Pierre Gaillard

Since starting from scratch in the mid-1980s, Pierre Gaillard has built holdings of more than 7 acres (3ha) in Côte-Rôtie, 6 acres (2.5ha) in Condrieu, and 25 acres (10ha) in St-Joseph. In addition to basic St-Joseph Blanc and Rouge, he makes two red *cuvées* labeled Les Pierres and Clos de Cuminaille. From Condrieu, there is a dry wine, a sweet, late-harvest Fleurs d'Automne, and a *vin de paille*, Jeanne-Elise, that is technically a Vin de Table. Gaillard makes a very good straight Côte-Rôtie as well as a Rose Pourpre *cuvée* from the Côte Brune.

Chez Favier, 42520, Malleval
www.domainespierregaillard.com

René Rostaing

René Rostaing makes a very fine, steel-fermented Condrieu as well as a Syrah-based Vin de Pays, but is by far best known for his bottlings of Côte-Rôtie. The latter are based upon some of the most enviable vineyard sites in the appellation. He inherited 8.6 acres (3.5ha) of prime land in 1990 from his father-in-law, Albert Dervieux-Thaize, and then another 3 acres (1.2ha) in 1993 from his uncle, Marius Gentaz-Dervieux. Rostaing produces three classic and complex, but restrained, Côte-Rôties: Classique, Côte Blonde, and a La Landonne.

petite rue du Port, 69420, Ampuis
www.domainerostaing.com

René-Jean Dard et François Ribo

François Ribo and René-Jean Dard, who met in wine school in Beaune in their late teens, forged an alliance in 1984. Starting with 2.5 acres (1ha) of vines from the Dard family, they leased other plots and gradually scratched together a total of 18.5 acres (7.5ha). Most of those vines are located in Crozes-Hermitage, along with a little St-Joseph and a tiny (1.2 acre/0.5ha) patch of Hermitage. The wines are consistently pure, quick to open and soften, and easy to enjoy.

Blanche-Laine, 26600 Mercurol
04 75 07 40 00

Stephane Pichat

Young Stephane Pichat holds 6 acres (2.5ha) of vines, from which he makes two very highly-regarded bottlings of Côte-Rôtie. The first, Le Champon, is aged for two years in barriques; the other, Les Grandes Places, is aged in barriques for as long as 36 months. Both wines are made in small quantities with a prominent signature of new oak. Pichat has also started producing a Condrieu La Caille as well as white and red Vin de Pays wines based on Viognier and Syrah. Born in 1978, Stephane has already established a fine reputation, and looks set to rise up the Northern Rhône ranks. ★ **Rising star**

6 chemin de la Viallière, 69420 Ampuis
www.domainepichat.com

Thiérry Allemand

The tenacious Thiérry Allemand has scratched and clawed his way up from next to nothing in terms of vineyard holdings to a point where he now holds more than 10 acres (4ha) of precious vines in Cornas. Conspicuously independent and driven in character, Allemand works in the vineyards and in his cellar in ways that interweave innovation with respect for the most traditional of techniques. Although Allemand emphasizes purity of fruit and a roundness of texture in his two Cornas wines, Reynard and Chaillot, they develop slowly and age very well.

22 impasse des Granges, 07130 Cornas
04 75 81 06 50

J Vidal-Fleury

J Vidal-Fleury has a long history—this venerable négociant house dates from 1781. Today, however, it is owned by the celebrated Guigal family, and the ownership has undoubtedly helped transform its reputation. All the same, Vidal-Fleury's wines are not simply Guigal wines in all but name. Marcel Guigal has elected to let the company operate separately under distinct management, and has invested in a new winemaking facility that is set beneath the vineyards of the Côte Blonde in Côte-Rôtie. In addition to two well-known bottlings of Côte-Rôtie, Brune et Blonde and La Chatillhonne, wines are also made in the Northern Rhône appellations of Condrieu, Cornas, Crozes-Hermitage, Hermitage, and St-Joseph. The portfolio also includes a Côtes du Rhône, a Châteauneuf-du-Pape, and a Côtes-du-Ventoux.

19 route de la Roche, 69420, Ampuis
www.vidal-fleury.com

GROWING CHALLENGES

Centuries of cultivation in the Northern Rhône have provided producers with an intimate knowledge of the particular tendencies of the region's four leading grape varieties. And yet the wines remain much easier to enjoy than the vines are to tend. Syrah can reach its loftiest expressions here due to a long growing season at the climatic margin of the vine's ability to reliably ripen its fruit. However, being this far north in the Northern Hemisphere requires a near-perfect exposure to the sun for optimal ripening, which in turn limits the very best sites to the ultra-steep slopes of Côte-Rôtie, Hermitage, and Cornas. Merely setting foot in these vineyards is enough to place a winemaker in peril, and the vines must often be staked onto the slopes and trained up individual poles. Adjacent vines are often intertwined with one another to protect them from breakage in the winds that buffet the hillsides—they spend much of the growing season clinging to one another as if holding hands for dear life. This practice is also used for Viognier in Condrieu and Château-Grillet, but Viognier poses problems of its own. It ripens at a rapid rate in an unpredictable manner, requiring vigilance to pick the fruit after it has attained its famous perfume but before it turns formless and fat from over-ripening. Marsanne is nearly as difficult to ripen perfectly. All three of these varieties, along with Roussanne, share a susceptibility to oidium and problems of flowering and fruit set.

The *galets* (pebbles) of Châteauneuf-du-Pape absorb heat by day and release it at night, aiding the ripening process.

SOUTHERN RHONE

Planted with vines by the Romans, promoted by medieval popes, and significant enough to become the birthplace of the country's Appellation Contrôlée regulations, the Southern Rhône is perhaps the most historic of France's wine regions. Bathed in sunshine for most of the year and covering a vast area dotted with ancient stone villages, orchards, and olive groves, it is also among the warmest, largest, and prettiest. The sloping mass of Mont Ventoux and the cool, jagged peaks of the Dentelles de Montmirail, visible from everywhere, temper the heat. So does the chilly *mistral* wind that blasts down from the north, helping to keep the vines disease- and pest-free.

Châteauneuf-du-Pape has been the jewel in this grand old region's crown since the 14th century. It is almost as famous for its *galets*—the large, round stones that carpet many vineyards—as for the perfumed, opulent red wine that helped it to maintain a strong identity when many other parts of the Southern Rhône had little or none. Only relatively recently have international consumers become familiar with the names of other villages where superb wines come in distinctive styles: Gigondas meaty; Vacqueyras redolent of red fruits; Rasteau warmingly rich; Cairanne more restrained.

Many more are becoming better known as the current generation chooses to make worthwhile wine rather than sell their grapes to the nearest co-operative. Lirac, Vinsobres, Beaumes-de-Venise, Séguret, Sablet… these are just some of the villages about which we will soon hear more. With new energy driving so many growers (there are more than 6,000), the infinitely bigger appellations of Côtes du Rhône-Villages and Côtes du Rhône, further down the hierarchy, are also improving in quality—as are promising satellites like the Ventoux, Luberon, and Costières de Nîmes.

The celebrated *galets*, deposited millennia ago by glaciers and polished smooth by the Rhône, are strewn across the region. Their capacity to soak up the sun and reflect its warmth back to the vines at night particularly suits heat-loving Grenache, the most important red grape variety. But there are many other terroirs—sand, gravel, limestone, sandstone, marl, clay. Even in a small area, there may be several, each contributing different nuances to the finished wine.

The tradition of combining different grapes also enhances complexity. Heady Grenache is the prima donna, highly prized for its ability to perform brilliantly in old age. (The gnarled stumps of 60- to 100-year-old vines are shown off by every producer lucky enough to have any). But in supporting roles, Syrah and Mourvèdre are important for structure and spicy depth. Some producers also favor old-vine Carignan and Cinsault, and the latest trend is to reinstate some of the more obscure among Châteauneuf-du-Pape's 13 permitted varieties—grapes like Counoise and Vaccarèse.

Although red wines dominate overwhelmingly, whites and rosés (currently contributing about 5% each to total output) are gaining ground—the whites usually built around Grenache Blanc and Clairette with help from Bourboulenc, Marsanne, Roussanne, and Viognier while Grenache and Cinsault underpin the rosés.

In a region not short of sunshine (and the resulting high alcohol levels), climate change poses particular difficulties. The response is to focus increasingly on cooler vineyard sites in the hills; on varieties associated with freshness; on organic or biodynamic methods which seem to produce fruit with better natural balance. The new quest for finesse rather than turbo-power also affects decisions about maturation—so the small barrels that supplanted traditional giant casks (*foudres*) a decade or two ago are being partially replaced by 131-gallon (600-liter) *demi-muids*. While these are viewed by many as the perfect compromise, some terrific wines see no wood at all.

Major grapes
🍇 Reds
Grenache

Mourvèdre

Syrah
🍇 Whites
Bourboulenc

Clairette

Grenache Blanc

Marsanne

Roussanne

Viognier

Vintages
2009
A small crop, but the quality is good, especially in Châteauneuf-du-Pape.

2008
A difficult year with hail and rain, so the wines lack depth.

2007
The vintage of the decade, with seductive fruit and fine tannins.

2006
A very good year of elegant wines with staying power.

2005
A vintage of concentrated, structured wines.

2004
A lack of extreme conditions resulted in a classic vintage.

2003
A heatwave year of jammy blockbusters.

SOUTHERN RHONE

Whereas the vineyards farther north lie in a slim strip along the river, those in the Southern Rhône fan out across a vast area. More than 188,000 acres (76,000ha) and 6,000 producers make this France's second-largest wine region after Bordeaux. At its heart lies the celebrated Châteauneuf-du-Pape and the other best-known *crus*. Fine wines would be difficult to make in the sun-drenched Southern Rhône were it not for the mistral wind, which blasts down the valley from the north, and the mountain masses of the Dentelles de Montmirail, Mont Ventoux, and the Montagne du Luberon, which act as giant coolers.

KEY

Châteauneuf-du-Pape	Côtes du Ventoux	Beaumes-de-Venise
Costières de Nîmes	Côtes du Vivarais	Rasteau
Côtes du Luberon	Gigondas	Tavel
Coteaux du Tricastin	Lirac	Vacqueyras
Côtes du Rhône-Villages	Muscat de Beaumes-de-Venise	Vinsobres

SOUTHERN RHONE

Ch d'Aquéria **5**
Ch La Canorgue **48**
Ch de Fonsalette **22**
Ch Mas Neuf **1**
Ch Mourgues du Grès **4**
Ch d'Or et de Gueules **2**
Ch Pesquié **44**
Ch St-Roch **9**
Le Clos de Caveau **38**
Dom Alary **25**
Dom de l'Amauve **32**
Dom de l'Ameillaud **25**
Dom des Amouriers **37**
Dom des Anges **45**
Dom Les Aphillanthes **24**
Dom Brusset **25**
Dom de Cassan **41**
Dom Chaume-Arnaud **26**
Dom de la Citadelle **47**
Dom du Coriançon **28**
Dom des Coteaux des Travers **30**
Dom Cros de la Mûre **21**
Dom Delubac **25**
Dom de Durban **42**
Dom Duseigneur **8**
Dom des Escaravailles **29**
Dom des Espiers **38**
Dom de Fenouillet **40**

Dom de Fondrèche **43**
Dom la Fourmone **38**
Dom Jaume **27**
Dom Lafond Roc-Epine **6**
Dom Maby **6**
Dom Marc Kreydenweiss **3**
Dom Marcel Richaud **25**
Dom de la Monardière **37**
Dom de Montvac **38**
Dom de la Mordorée **6**
Dom du Moulin **26**
Dom de Mourchon **33**
Domaine Oratoire St-Martin **25**
Dom Pelaquié **7**
Dom de Piaugier **31**
Dom de la Pigeade **42**
Dom La Réméjeanne **19**
Dom de la Renjarde **23**
Dom Le Sang des Cailloux **39**
Dom La Soumade **30**
Dom de la Verrière **34**
Dom Vindémio **46**
Gourt de Mautens **30**
Mas de Libian **20**
Montirius **39**
Perrin & Fils **18**
Tardieu-Laurent **49**

2008

LA FONTAINE AUX ENFANTS
PINOT BLANC

MARC KREYDENWEISS

DOMAINE DUSEIGNEUR

Antarès

2·0
0·7

CHATEAU MOURGUES DU GRES

Terre d'Argence

COSTIERES DE NIMES
APPELLATION COSTIERES DE NIMES CONTRÔLÉE

Mis en Bouteille au Château

FRANÇOIS COLLARD, PROPRIÉTAIRE-RÉCOLTANT, BEAUCAIRE 30300 FRANCE

GIGONDAS

Ch de St-Cosme 36	Dom La Roubine 36
Dom des Bosquet 36	Dom St-Damien 36
Dom La Bouïssière 36	Dom St-Gayan 36
Dom Grand Romane 35	Dom Santa Duc 36
Dom du Grapillon d'Or 36	Moulin de la Gardette 36
Dom Les Pallières 35	

DOMAINE DU
GRAPILLON D'OR
Propriété famille Chauvet - Fondée en 1806
1806
2006
GIGONDAS
APPELLATION GIGONDAS CONTRÔLÉE
mis en bouteille au domaine

LE CLOS
DE
CAVEAU
FRUIT SAUVAGE 2007
VACQUEYRAS
Appellation Vacqueyras Contrôlée
Cru des Côtes du Rhône
750 ml   ALC 14.2% BY VOL

Domaine de
CRISTIA
2007
Châteauneuf-du-Pape
appellation châteauneuf-du-pape contrôlée
Mis en Bouteille au Domaine

DOMAINE
DE LA
JANASSE
Chaupin
CHÂTEAUNEUF DU PAPE
2007

KEY

	AC
	Rivers, lakes
	Roads
	328ft (100m) contours
	Provincial border
	Urban areas
1	Location of one or more producers

MILLÉSIME 2006
CHÂTEAUNEUF
DU-PAPE
PRESTIGE
ROGER SABON
PROPRIÉTAIRE RÉCOLTANT À CHÂTEAUNEUF-DU-PAPE
PRODUCT OF FRANCE

CHATEAUNEUF-DU-PAPE

Ch de Beaucastel 15	Dom de Cristia 17
Ch de la Gardine 10	Dom de la Janasse 17
Ch La Nerthe 12	Dom de Marcoux 16
Ch Rayas 15	Dom de Pégaü 14
Le Clos du Caillou 15	Dom Pierre Usseglio 14
Clos des Papes 14	Dom Roger Sabon 14
Clos St-Jean 14	Dom de la Roquète 11
Dom de Beaurenard 14	Dom St-Préfert 11
Dom Bosquet des Papes 14	Dom de la Vieille Julienne 16
Dom Les Cailloux 14	Dom Le Vieux Donjon 14
Dom Chante-Cigale 14	Dom du Vieux Télégraphe 13

Always check the availability of visitor facilities and the visiting hours at a winery before planning your trip. Some wineries are open by appointment only.

CHATEAU DE BEAUCASTEL
HOMMAGE A JACQUES PERRIN IS 60%
MOURVEDRE FROM OLD VINES

Château d'Aquéria Tavel

There is a modest grandeur about Château d'Aquéria, a charming neoclassical mansion surrounded by vineyards stretching back in history to 1595. Allied to this is the sense of quiet integrity that brothers Vincent and Bruno de Bez bring to the management of their 160 acre (66ha) estate. These qualities shine through in the wines, which are unflashy, fairly priced, and consistently reliable. While three-quarters of the output is finely balanced Tavel rosé, the Lirac that makes up the balance is even more alluring, the complex, silky red outshining the simpler white.

route de Roquemaure, 30126 Tavel
www.aqueria.com

Château de Beaucastel
Châteauneuf-du-Pape

The Perrin family has steered Beaucastel into Châteauneuf's uppermost echelon over the past century, and the fifth generation seems set to keep it there. Its 170 acres (70ha) include all 13 permitted grape varieties. Unusually, Mourvèdre has equal billing with Grenache, contributing leather and spice notes and backbone, while significant amounts of Cinsault, Counoise, and other old grapes build wines of immense complexity. Hommage à Jacques Perrin (60% old-vine Mourvèdre) is a stirring special *cuvée* and Roussanne Vieilles Vignes a honeyed gem, but Beaucastel's cast-iron reputation rests on the classic, long-living red and white. The Coudoulet de Beaucastel wines are top-drawer Côtes du Rhône.

chemin de Beaucastel, 84350 Courthézon
www.beaucastel.com

Château La Canorgue Luberon

Jean-Pierre Margan and his daughter Nathalie recognize that some visitors to their 300-year-old property are film buffs. The exquisitely faded château and its vineyards were the setting for *A Good Year* (2006). But many, including the film's director Ridley Scott, soon become customers—won over by the purity and verve of the wines. A distant cousin of Australian winemaker Andrew Margan, Jean-Pierre likes the notion that his wines are multi-faceted: "Just like me—as comfortable with jeans as with a dinner jacket."

route du Pont Julien, 84480 Bonnieux
04 90 75 81 01

Château de Fonsalette Massif d'Uchaux

The Reynaud family of Châteauneuf-du-Pape's renowned Château Rayas bought this large property with woods, olive trees, and 30 acres (12ha) of vines in 1945. The grapes are vinified at Rayas and the style shows some of the same delicacy, particularly in the red Côtes du Rhône with (in youth) pretty raspberry fruit, clean bite, and paper-fine tannins. (Cinsault makes up 35% of the blend for freshness). Fonsalette Syrah marries pure berry fruit with great acidity and firmness. Like their Châteauneuf cousins, these wines age extremely well—and cost a lot.

84290 Lagarde-Paréol
www.chateaurayas.fr

Château de la Gardine
Châteauneuf-du-Pape

Pioneering Gaston Brunel bought this old property in 1946; then it had 20 acres (8ha) compared with today's 128 acres (52ha) in one vast plot. His sons Patrick and Maxime eventually took over and now Maxime's son Philippe is involved. The aim, Philippe says, is to avoid over-ripeness and create dry wines to suit food and cellaring. The wines are nevertheless quite plump and modern (barriques have replaced large *foudres*), with the super-concentrated old-vine Cuvée des Générations and fabulously rich L'Immortelle leaving the Cuvée Tradition in the shade.

route de Roquemaure, 84230 Châteauneuf-du-Pape
www.gardine.com

Château Mas Neuf Costières de Nîmes

It seems unlikely that the wines of Mas Neuf would have shot to prominence in less than a decade without the energy and ambition of Luc Baudet. Besides putting together the consortium that bought this sizeable estate in 2001, he has steered viticulture and winemaking uncompromisingly toward quality at a reasonable price. While the top *cuvées*, sometimes experimental, are worth sampling (look out for the voluptuous Avec des Si, made from old-vine Syrah), the mid-range Compostelle white and red are reliably superb with the entry level Paradox wines only a step behind. ★ **Rising star**

30600 Gallician
www.chateau-mas-neuf.com

Château Mourgues du Grès
Costières de Nîmes

The motto *sine sole nihil* (without the sun, nothing) was carved on the front of Mourgues du Grès centuries ago when it was a convent farm. For François and Anne Collard, who have made their large estate the most widely acclaimed in the Costières de Nîmes, it still applies. Across a wide portfolio, their wines unleash the exuberant flavors of perfect, sun-ripened grapes underscored by the minerality of great terroir. Peachy whites, vibrant rosés, finely structured reds… everything is juicily appealing. Grenache-rich Terre de Feu ages well for up to a decade.

route de Bellegarde, 30300 Beaucaire
www.mourguesdugres.com

Château La Nerthe Châteauneuf-du-Pape

In a region not noted for imposing châteaux, neoclassical La Nerthe stands out for its architectural splendor. But the second-largest estate in Châteauneuf-du-Pape (200 acres/82ha), and one of the most historic, is also making an impact with its modern wines, thanks to investment by the coffee-importing Richard family since 1985. Whites are important (15% of the total—three times the average); the Réserve Beauvenir is built to live for years. The reds also age majestically—both the classic *cuvée* and the powerful old-vine Cuvée des Cadettes.

BP43 route de Sorgues, 84232 Châteauneuf-du-Pape
www.chateaulanerthe.fr

Château d'Or et de Gueules
Costières de Nîmes

Diane de Puymorin is Action Woman—and just as well. Formerly an international marketing executive, she turned her vineyard-owning dream to reality the tough way, training as an enologist and entirely overhauling 160 acres (65ha) when she bought this old estate in 1998. She makes rich, ageworthy reds that reflect skilful taming of the tannins in Carignan and Mourvèdre. While La Bolida, almost 100% very-old-vine Mourvèdre, delivers immense

CHATEAU PESQUIE
QUINTESSENCE HAS HELPED TO ESTABLISH
PESQUIE'S FINE REPUTATION

power with refinement, Trassegum (50% Syrah, 25% old-vine Carignan, 25% old-vine Mourvèdre) offers spicy vigor at less than half the price.

route de Générac, 30800 St-Gilles
www.chateau-or-et-gueules.com

Château Pesquié Ventoux

In the up-and-coming Ventoux, Château Pesquié has a settled, confident air that makes it seem long-established. In fact it was only in the 1980s that Edith and Paul Chaudière left other careers to study viticulture. Now with a substantial 205 acres (83ha) and preparing for organic certification, perfectionist Pesquié is the estate against which others are measured. The wines reach hedonistic heights in exotic white, Quintessence (mainly barrel-fermented Roussanne) and velvety Artemia (from 80-year-old Grenache and 50-year-old Syrah).

route de Flassan, 84570 Mormoiron
www.chateaupesquie.com

Château Rayas Châteauneuf-du-Pape

No amount of hearsay is preparation enough for the peculiarities of Rayas, the most revered and eccentric of the Châteauneuf estates. In charge since 1997, Emmanuel Reynaud shares some of the characteristics of his late uncle Jacques, keeping the cellar in what looks like dilapidated chaos and holding visitors at bay. A pity, since the vineyards—25 acres (10ha) on poor, sandy soil—are a little paradise lost among cool woods. The honeyed white is richly satisfying; the almost Burgundian red (100% Grenache) offers mesmerising delicacy, minerality, and remarkable staying power. A rare (but costly) treat.

84230 Châteauneuf-du-Pape
www.chateaurayas.fr

Château de St-Cosme Gigondas

One of the movers and shakers of Gigondas, Louis Barruol has a mix of impatience, drive, and intellectual rigor that produces impressive wines. Since taking over St-Cosme, which has been in his family since 1490 (14 generations), he has created exciting new *cuvées* while giving traditional blends an overhaul. Modern and sophisticated, all his wines combine depth of flavor with refinement, with old-Grenache *cuvées* Valbelle and Le Claux reaching hedonistic peaks. Barruol favors fermentation in oak and aging in new barrels, believing large old casks can create dry tannins and a rustic taste.

La Fouille et les Florets, 84190 Gigondas
www.saintcosme.com

Château St-Roch Lirac

Eve Brunel trained as an enologist and married into the family that owns Château de la Gardine in Châteauneuf-du-Pape. Château St-Roch was bought in 1998 when she was ready for a new project. Where better than here, given her supreme faith in Lirac's Châteauneuf-like terroir? In a bid for quality, she has doubled vine density and her carefully crafted wines (both white and red) are among the classiest in the appellation. Do not miss the succulent *cuvée* Confidentielle—Grenache, Syrah, and Mourvèdre from older vines, in equal parts. ★ **Rising star**

chemin de Lirac, 30150 Roqemaure
www.chateau-saint-roch.com

CLOS DES PAPES
FEW WINES IN THE RHONE CAN MATCH
THOSE OF THE AVRIL FAMILY

CHATEAU LA NERTHE
CHATEAU LA NERTHE IS ON AN UPWARD PATH
THANKS TO THE RICHARD FAMILY

Le Clos du Caillou Châteauneuf-du-Pape

Near famous Château Rayas, Le Clos du Caillou, a walled estate around an old hunting lodge, is one of Châteauneuf's most visitor-friendly domaines thanks to enthusiastic owner Sylvie Vacheron and an ancient cellar hollowed out of sandy rock. Twenty-two acres (9ha) within Châteauneuf-du-Pape on two terroirs determine the styles of the main reds—Les Safres (sand) is almost daintily elegant, Les Quartz (*galets*) spicily robust. The estate owns 106 acres (43ha) just outside the Châteauneuf appellation (some across the road from Beaucastel), making it a source of serious Côtes du Rhône.

Pouizin-Vacheron, 84350 Courthézon
www.closducaillou.com

Le Clos de Caveau Vacqueyras

So many things are fascinating at Le Clos de Caveau. The vineyard—a single plot, surrounded by trees like a secret hideaway high up in the Dentelles de Montmirail. The owner—clinical psychologist and psychoanalyst Henri Bungener, who arrived from London in 2005 to take over from his father Gérard, a Swiss parfumier. And, not least, the wines—organic, usually unoaked, deliciously fresh (Bungener harvests earlier than many), and often gloriously hedonistic. For quality at a modest price, juicy Fruits Sauvages leads the field.

route de Montmirail, 84190 Vacqueyras
www.closdecaveau.com

Clos des Papes Châteauneuf-du-Pape

Prominent in the history of Châteauneuf-du-Pape for centuries as consuls and mayors, the Avrils are quasi-aristocratic—yet extraordinarily approachable. The wines produced by Vincent Avril, who has overseen this 86 acre (35ha) estate since 1987, display similar qualities. Both the white and the red (just one of each—super-*cuvées* are frowned upon) are consistently among the appellation's very best. Mainly Grenache and Mourvèdre, with small proportions of Syrah, Muscardin, Vaccarèse, and Counoise, the red is a wine of breathtaking finesse—supple and multi-faceted. The white (unoaked) is simply sublime. Both age magnificently.

13 avenue Pierre de Luxembourg, 84230
Châteauneuf-du-Pape; www.clos-des-papes.fr

Clos St-Jean Châteauneuf-du-Pape

Although Pascal and Vincent Saurel have been involved at Clos St-Jean since the 1980s, their wines have improved dramatically in recent years. Sweeping changes were initiated in 2002 following the appointment of Châteauneuf's most prominent consultant enologist, Philippe Cambie. Now, with a brand new cellar, the brothers are realizing the fine potential of their 100 acres (40ha), half of which are on the famous plateau of La Crau. The wines, sumptuous and sleek, show some new oak influence—luxury *cuvées* La Combe des Fous and Deus-ex-Marchina especially. ★ **Rising star**

chemin du Bois de la Ville, 84230 Châteauneuf-du-Pape
04 90 83 58 00

Domaine Alary Cairanne

A cousin of the Oratoire St-Martin brothers, Denis Alary shares the same sense of inheritance and respect for terroir —here spread over three sites with less in the hills.

DOMANE DE LA CITADELLE

LE CHATAIGNIER IS AN ACCESSIBLE, EASY-DRINKING RED BLEND

Articulate and open, Alary says he has changed tack since 2006 to make slightly more supple wines—but his fondness for a dash of Carignan (picked ultra-ripe) remains steadfast. Two whites and four reds showcase Cairanne at its elegant best. Look out especially for the opulent Font d'Estevenas white and smokily succulent La Brunote red—but every wine from this organic estate is rewarding.

route de Rasteau, 84290 Cairanne
04 90 30 82 32

Domaine de l'Amauve Séguret

Gentlemanly Christian Voeux appears to be quiet, almost sedate. Impossible. Besides zooming around to supervise production at Chateau La Nerthe, Domaine de la Renjarde, and a third Richard-owned property in Tavel, Voeux has launched his own estate, Domaine de l'Amauve. At least he had time to plan, for his father (who sold to the co-op) only retired in 2005 at the age of 81. Drawn from 17 acres (7ha) of low-yielding vines on varied terroirs, Voeux's Séguret white and two reds are very finely judged. ★ **Rising star**

chemin du Jas, 84110 Séguret
www.domainedelamauve.fr

Domaine de l'Ameillaud Cairanne

When Nick Thompson left the British steel industry to manage Domaine de l'Ameillaud in 1983, it was a bulk wine facility owned by a group of investors and twice its current size. "I had come from an agricultural background and studied a bit in Burgundy," he shrugs, making it sound easy. Now sole owner, Thompson admits his 125 acre (50ha) plot of flattish land does not represent Cairanne's best terroir. Nevertheless, by reducing yields and limiting chemical treatments, Thompson makes round, attractive wines. Pure fruit flavors dominate: oak has no place here.

route de Rasteau 84290, Cairanne
www.domaine-ameillaud.com

Domaine des Amouriers Vacqueyras

Young Igor Chudzikiewicz owes his surname to an immigrant Polish great-grandfather. Vines came into the family a generation later and Igor's father Jocelyn created Domaine des Amouriers in 1984. Headquartered in a former silk worm farm, it has recently almost doubled in size—to 35 acres (14ha) with a high quotient of old vines. As a result, Chudzikiewicz, an enology graduate who took over in 2008, is able to make more Genestes—a mid-range *cuvée* that offers terrific Vacqueyras red-fruit-and-spice oomph without rusticity. ★ **Rising star**

Les Garrigues, 84260 Sarrians
04 90 65 83 22

Domaine des Anges Ventoux

At the top of the Colline des Anges (the angels' hill), Domaine des Anges's situation is heavenly. It is also good for wine, with slopes facing north/northwest for red grapes and east for whites. White wine is important at this Irish-owned organic estate run by winemaker Ciaran Rooney. Altitude, evening breezes, and limestone soil give the wines a backbone of rippling minerality—this is particularly apparent in the white Archange. The red Archange can be impressive too, after a period of aging.

84570 Mormoiron
www.domainedesanges.com

Domaine Les Aphillanthes
Côtes du Rhône-Villages

Daniel Boulle sold his grapes to local co-ops until, in 1999, the sheer quality of his fruit persuaded him to start Domaine Les Aphillanthes. He has since adopted biodynamic methods on his 90 acres (37ha) extending across the Plan de Dieu toward Rasteau and into Cairanne. Boulle believes in meticulous effort in the vineyard and minimal intervention in the cellar. The result is an outstanding line-up of Côtes du Rhône-Villages wines. Stars include the hedonistic Cuvée des Galets, the vibrant Vieilles Vignes, and the power-packed pure Syrah Cuvée du Cros. ★ **Rising star**

Quartier St-Jean, 84850 Travaillan
04 90 37 25 99

Domaine de Beaurenard
Châteauneuf-du-Pape

With records stretching back to 1695 and wine in the blood through seven generations, Beaurenard is deeply entrenched in Châteauneuf history. But Daniel and Frédéric Coulon are among the most forward-thinking of winemakers. Their estate (consisting of 80 acres/32ha here, 60 acres/25ha in Rasteau) is fully biodynamic, with new oak fermenters in an impressive cellar and splendid visitor facilities. The wines are wonderfully engaging—the classic *cuvée* is enjoyable while young, but is well capable of aging, while the oakier Boisrenard Réserve needs time. The Rasteau wines are great buys too—the richly satisfying Argiles Bleues especially.

10, ave Pierre de Luxembourg, 84231 Châteauneuf-du-Pape; www.beaurenard.fr

Domaine Bosquet des Papes
Châteauneuf-du-Pape

Nicolas Boiron is quick to point out that, although Bosquet des Papes was not founded until 1976, his family has grown grapes for 150 years. Drawing on 40 parcels of vines, he makes a classic white and red and (in good enough years) three special *cuvées*—silkily elegant A La Gloire de Mon Père, more structured Chantemerle, and blockbuster-ish La Folie. However, 30% of the prized fruit on which these are based goes into the red Tradition. Pure, mineral-edged and fleshy, it is extremely likeable—not least for its reasonable price.

route d'Orange 18, 84232 Châteauneuf-du-Pape
04 90 83 72 33

Domaine des Bosquets
Gigondas

Like many young winemakers, Julien Bréchet has explored ways of achieving more finesse and less tannic thrust in his Gigondas. At Domaine des Bosquets, an estate whose history can be traced back to 1644, this is especially important because some vines are planted on the famous blue clay that, though highly prized, delivers powerful, muscular wines. His efforts have paid off handsomely. Recent vintages have seen wines that are plump, velvety, and moreish. Quality shines through everywhere, from the gleaming winery to the Syrah vineyard planted with cuttings from posh Château Rayas-owned estate Fonsalette. ★ **Rising star**

84190 Gigondas
www.famillebrechet.fr

DOMAINE DES BOSQUETS

TALENTED YOUNG WINEMAKER JULIEN BRECHET SEEKS ELEGANCE IN HIS GIGONDAS

Domaine La Bouïssière Gigondas

With minimal fanfare and careful attention to detail, quietly spoken Thierry Faravel and his brother Gilles have made La Bouïssière one of the most consistently reliable estates in Gigondas. From vineyards high up above the village, they make complex wines whose layers of flavor unfurl slowly, revealing a firm core of minerality. Their Gigondas outshines their Vacqueyras for spicy depth; the brooding Font de Tonnerre, aged partly in new oak, is particularly striking. But for everyday drinking, Les Amis de la Bouïssière, a Merlot/Syrah/Grenache blend, is a gem.

rue du Portail, 84190 Gigondas
04 90 65 87 91

Domaine Brusset Cairanne

Laurent Brusset is lucky to have had a grandfather with a talent for winemaking. And a father with the canny knack of buying up plots of superb land—often at bargain basement prices because the owners found the steep slopes he coveted high above Cairanne and Gigondas difficult to work. Brusset wines bear the stamp of their stony, mineral-rich terroir. The silkily refined old-vine Cairanne Les Chabriles and rich, spicy Gigondas Les Hauts de Montmirail explain the stylistic differences between these two appellations with lipsmacking ease.

84290 Cairanne
www.domainebrusset.fr

Domaine Les Cailloux Châteauneuf-du-Pape

So low-profile is Les Cailloux's André Brunel that he can be hard to find—but this quiet man makes some of the most exquisitely refined wines in Châteauneuf-du-Pape. While most of his 50 acres (20ha) are on *galets*, varied subsoils impart subtly different characteristics. Brunel is eager for Mourvèdre to counteract the lavishness of Grenache. His heady Cuvée Centenaire (from 100-year-old vines) is justly renowned, but for precision, vitality, and sheer delight, not to mention value, his classic *cuvées* are extremely difficult to beat.

84230 Châteauneuf-du-Pape
04 90 83 73 20

Domaine de Cassan Beaumes-de-Venise

In a fold of the craggy Dentelles de Montmirail, with vineyards rising up almost vertically on all sides, the Domaine de Cassan sits at the heart of a hikers' paradise. Gérard Paillet, who took over the estate from his father-in-law, loves this lofty situation that brings freshness to his wines. With 42 acres (17ha) in Beaumes-de-Venise and another 17 acres (7ha) in Gigondas, he makes only reds—the Beaumes-de-Venise oozing juicy, spicy elegance while the Gigondas (with less oak and less extraction in recent vintages) combines depth of flavor with finesse.

84190 Lafare
04 90 62 96 12

Domaine Chante-Cigale
Châteauneuf-du-Pape

Alexandre Favier looks young to run the 100 acre (40ha) estate handed down mainly from his mother's family, but he already has a decade of experience. A third of the vines (in 30 parcels) are 70 years old—a valuable resource, though none of their fruit goes into the classic *cuvée*. The wines are attractive and well made. The citrussy,

fennel-edged white, barely oaked, is a delightful apéritif; the red Tradition a finely judged middleweight. Top *cuvée* Extrait, oozing kirsch and oak, is the only attention-seeker.

avenue Louis Pasteur, 84230 Châteauneuf-du-Pape
www.chantei-cigale.com

Domaine Chaume-Arnaud Vinsobres

Very few women ran estates in the Southern Rhône back in 1987 when cheerfully determined Valerie Arnaud assumed control of her parents' vineyards to launch her own wines. With husband Philippe Chaume, Arnaud has built Chaume-Arnaud into one of the most highly regarded estates in Vinsobres. Organic since 1997, it was certified biodynamic in 2009 in a bid to bring higher natural acidity and minerality to wines made heavier through climate change. Unoaked and oozing authenticity, both the delicate white Côtes-du-Rhône-Villages and the poised, brambly Vinsobres are a delight.

Les Paluds, 26110 Vinsobres
04 75 27 66 85

Domaine de la Citadelle Luberon

Below the pretty hilltop village of Ménerbes, retired film producer Yves Rousset-Rouard established Domaine de la Citadelle in 1989. North-facing limestone slopes help to fashion the elegant wines that have made it the preeminent estate in the Southern Rhône's most southerly appellation. Now run by Yves's son, Alexis, la Citadelle is noted for suave reds with a high proportion of cool-toned Syrah (especially the long-living *cuvée* Gouverneur), but the whites are also outstanding. With visitor facilities including an intriguing corkscrew museum, it should be on the itinerary of any wine-lover loose in the Luberon.

route de Cavaillon, 84560 Ménerbes
www.domaine-citadelle.com

Domaine du Coriançon Vinsobres

Bottling under the Domaine du Coriançon estate name since 1982, Francois Vallot has followed the old-fashioned principle of mixing varieties within parcels—so the grapes ripen together, facilitating co-fermentation. In 2003 he also adopted biodynamics. With their floral and red fruit notes, fine tannins, and marked minerality, his wines are fine examples of Vinsobres, an appellation where Syrah on cool sites creates an identity halfway between Southern and Northern Rhône. The barrique-matured *cuvée* L'Exception is mainly Syrah.

Hautesrives, 26110 Vinsobres
www.domainevallot.com

Domaine des Coteaux des Travers
Rasteau

Robert Charavin belongs to a family whose wine roots stretch back to the French Revolution. Established by his father in 1955, the small Domaine des Coteaux des Travers is on the south side of Rasteau (with a few acres in Cairanne). When Charavin started work in 1983, he made the first white wine in the appellation—and very tasty it is too, its richness lifted by a salty aftertaste. But his triumph is the sumptuous red Cuvée Prestige from 90-year-old vines grown on high terraces.

84110 Rasteau
www.coteaux-des-travers.com

TRUFFLE MANIA

To show off its wines in the best possible light, the Southern Rhône has a secret weapon. Truffles, glorious truffles. The Vaucluse département (responsible for 70% of French truffle production) has two famous weekly winter markets—one in Carpentras, the other in Richerenches. The heady scent of the *Tuber melanosporum* fills the air as dealers somewhat surreptitiously exchange their precious booty for wads of cash. Prices currently run to around $600 per pound (€1,000 per kg). Even so, truffle and wine tastings are offered increasingly by wine producers (go-ahead co-operatives included). So intensely flavored is the prized tuber that simple dishes work best. Medium- to full-bodied white wines are delicious with truffles on toast, truffle omelet, or pasta in a cream and truffle sauce. Older red wines flatter richer fare—beef fillet with truffled foie gras, perhaps. Although less revered (and vastly cheaper), the summer truffle, *tuber aestivum*, does not taste bad either—especially with champagne.

DOMAINE GRAND ROMANE
GRAND ROMANE GIGONDAS IS
BIG, BROAD, AND POWERFUL

Domaine de Cristia Châteauneuf-du-Pape
Like many others, the Grangeon family at Domaine de Cristia sold their wine in bulk until the late 1990s. Young Baptiste took over from his father in 2002 and has been regarded as one of Châteauneuf's rising stars ever since. He adopted organic viticulture on the estate's 52 acres (21ha), on four terroirs, and replaced all the large old *foudres* with small oak barriques. Used for Syrah and Mourvèdre, these contribute toasty muscularity to the finished wines. The Cristia style is full-on, reaching a peak of intensity in the flamboyant old-vine *cuvée* Renaissance. ★ **Rising star**

33 Faubourg St-Georges, 84350 Courthézon
www.cristia.com

Domaine Cros de la Mûre Massif d'Uchaux
Up in the wilds of the Massif d'Uchaux, Eric Michel has little truck with passing wine fashions—or indeed passing wine writers. He does his own thing, painstakingly regenerating the ancient soils on his 40 acres (16ha) to make serious terroir wines. "Traditional, artisan wines with the aromas and flavors of the past," he stresses. Did any old-time wines taste as good as his deep-toned, light-footed, earthily alluring beauties? Based on scarily low yields and matured extra-long in tank before release (oak features only in his limited Châteauneuf-du-Pape and Gigondas), they are thrilling.

84430 Mondragon
04 90 30 12 40

Domaine Delubac Cairanne
Vincent and Bruno Delubac feel indebted to their grandfather, not just for his vineyards and wise advice when they were beginners 20 years ago, but also for his open-mindedness. "Do not imagine you are brilliant—so are plenty of others," they were told by this relentless entrepreneur who ran grocery stores in Avignon and Paris before returning home to reclaim his vines. As a result, the Delubacs keep re-assessing their approach. Their white Cairanne is admirably fresh; the main red, Les Bruneau, smooth but earthy, and the richly enveloping L'Authentique subtler than before.

route de Carpentras, 84290 Cairanne
04 90 30 82 40

Domaine de Durban Beaumes-de-Venise
In a region steeped in wine for generations, few estates can rival the Domaine de Durban for history (records go back to 1159)—or for scenery. In the hands of the Leydier family for the past 60 years, this sizeable hilltop estate, with its steeply sloping vineyards, has giddy views down over the village of Beaumes-de-Venise. Although the production includes a good deal of Vin de Pays, some red Beaumes-de-Venise, and a little Gigondas, Durban's fine reputation rests on its delicate sweet wine—a masterpiece of pear and apricot refinement.

84190 Beaumes-de-Venise
www.domainedurban.com

Domaine Duseigneur Lirac
Courage must run in the Duseigneur genes. In 2004, brothers Bernard and Frédéric decided to convert entirely to biodynamics an estate that their father had largely cleared of woodland in order to plant vines

DOMAINE DE DURBAN
DURBAN MUSCAT DE BEAUMES-DE-VENISE IS
ONE OF THE BEST IN THE APPELLATION

40 years before. Motivated by the hope of creating wines with more personality ("we were a bit like poker players," admits Frédéric), they have been amply rewarded. The Duseigneur Liracs (especially the red Antarès) and the high-end Laudun, made in association with influential French restaurateur Philippe Faure-Brac, are juicy, vibrant, multi-layered beauties with no flab.

rue Nostradamus, 30126 St-Laurent-des-Arbres
www.domaineduseigneur.com

Domaine des Escaravailles Rasteau
Take your hiking boots if you plan to visit Escaravailles. The name is Occitan for beetles—a term applied to the black-hooded, penitent monks who used to trek up here on impossibly steep, stony ground. Planted in the 1950s and now totaling 160 acres (65ha), some in Cairanne and Roaix, Escaravailles is run by Gilles Ferrand with help from his friend, the prominent enologist Philippe Cambie. In a decade they have developed a wide range of very smart wines. Standouts? Rasteau La Ponce, enhanced by the freshness of altitude, and juicy, velvet-smooth Cairanne Le Ventrabren. ★ **Rising star**

84110 Rasteau
www.domaine-escaravailles.com

Domaine des Espiers Vacqueyras
Philippe Cartoux makes no Vacqueyras (yet), even though he is headquartered there at his wife's winery, Domaine de Montvac. A self-taught vigneron, he abandoned his career as an electrical technician soon after buying 5 acres (2ha) of vines in Gigondas in 1989. Not all autodidacts are as insightful. Now with additional vineyards in Gigondas, the Côtes du Rhône, and Sablet (his "laboratory"), Cartoux is constantly refining his approach—these days favoring aromas and freshness over structure. The wines are all thoroughbreds, the beautifully layered Gigondas half a head in front.

route de Vaison La Romaine, 84190 Vacqueyras
04 90 65 81 16

Domaine de Fenouillet Beaumes-de-Venise
With vineyards on many different sites, brothers Patrick and Vincent Soard have built up a wide portfolio of wines in their two decades of running Fenouillet, established by their great-grandfather. The output is roughly one-third sweet Muscat, one-third red Beaumes-de-Venise, and one-third Ventoux white, red, and rosé. With black fruit flavors and smoky minerality, the Beaumes-de-Venise reds stand out. Especially noteworthy is the densely packed Cuvée Yvon Soard with a high proportion of Syrah, which the brothers favor. "The wind of the Dentelles keeps Syrah fresh," they claim.

allée St-Roch, 84190 Beaumes-de-Venise
www.domaine-fenouillet.fr

Domaine de Fondrèche Ventoux
How many enology students have parents who buy them a wine estate with great terroir and glorious views? Fondrèche's Sebastien Vincenti was that lucky. But he was also committed, from the start, to renewing the vineyards fastidiously, going organic, and aiming high with the wines. As a result, Fondrèche has been a Ventoux trailblazer for over a decade. The star in a strong line-up is mouthfilling white Persia—made with mainly

Roussanne, barrel-fermented but tank-matured for freshness. And the lively, zero-sulfur Nature Rouge will find a fan base far beyond asthma sufferers. ★ **Rising star**

84380 Mazan
www.fondreche.com

Domaine La Fourmone Vacqueyras

Taking its name from *fromentum*, the Latin word for wheat, La Fourmone was a mixed farm with grain crops, olives, and silk worms as well as vines when first established in the 1760s. Today, it is run by artist and fourth-generation winemaker Marie-Thérèse Combe, who applies the principles of sustainable viticulture to 50 acres (20ha) in Vacqueyras and 25 acres (10ha) in Gigondas. The opulent old-vine Vacqueyras Ceps d'Or (golden vines) and intense Gigondas Cuvée Fauquet show off the Fourmone approach—round and generous with fine tannins.

route de Bollène, 84190 Vacqueyras
www.domaine-la-fourmone.com

Domaine Grand Romane Gigondas

Among the vast Gigondas holdings of the Amadieu family, Grand Romane—the highest vineyard of them all —is the jewel in the crown. Planted in the 1950s at 1,300ft (400m), its old vines produce a brooding, tightly packed wine with a powerful tannic frame—amplified by aging in new barriques for one-third of the blend. It is a style that may not appeal to everyone—unless it is given time to settle down, or a steak to match its macho personality.

Quartier Petit Chemin, 84190 Gigondas
www.pierre-amadieu.com

Domaine du Grapillon d'Or Gigondas

Since Céline Chauvet loves to cook, a tasting at Grapillon d'Or (the family estate for five generations) inevitably turns into a chat about dishes to match the wines. (Mushroom and potato gratin with the savory 2001 Gigondas? Yum.) With 35 acres (14ha) in Gigondas, mainly in the hills, and 7 acres (3ha) in Vacqueyras, Chauvet makes round, ripe wines with staying power in a traditional cellar where her father Bernard is still active in the background.

84190 Gigondas
www.domainedugrapillondor.com

Domaine de la Janasse
Châteauneuf-du-Pape

Christophe Sabon was just 19 when, in 1990, he took over the Janasse estate created by his father. "Dad gave him the cellar keys and said: do whatever you like," says sister Isabelle, an enologist who joined in 2002. Now vastly expanded, Janasse takes in large Côtes-du-Rhône and Villages holdings as well as 37 acres (15ha) on several terroirs in Châteauneuf-du-Pape. The Sabons make ripe, modern, extrovert wines. Old vines underpin lavish Chaupin (pure Grenache) and Vieilles Vignes. The rich, marzipan-toned white Prestige is also a charmer.

27 chemin du Moulin, 84350 Courthézon
www.lajanasse.com

Domaine Jaume Vinsobres

With 200 acres (80ha) of vines on two terroirs, fourth-generation growers Pascal and Richard Jaume are among the most significant producers in Vinsobres. Close to

DOMAINE MABY
THE NESSUN DORMA CUVEE IS A SPICY, CELLAR-WORTHY RED

DOMAINE JAUME
DOMAINE JAUME VINSOBRES REFERENCE HAS A RICH AND ASSERTIVE STYLE

organic in approach, they have also been among the first here to combat pests with sexual confusion techniques, keep yields low, fertilize with sheep manure, green-harvest when appropriate, and use wild yeasts where possible. The benefits shine through in a competent portfolio—from the easygoing Altitude 420 to the deeply ambitious Le Clos des Echalas, made from 80-year-old vines (in the best years) and treated to new oak.

24 rue Reynarde, 26110 Vinsobres
www.domainejaume.com

Domaine Lafond Roc-Epine Tavel

When Pascal Lafond began to work with his father three decades ago, the family estate was entirely in Tavel, with vineyards on the three terroirs that together generate rosés of legendary power and depth. Now half of Lafrond Roce-Epine's 200 acres (80ha) is in Lirac and Côtes du Rhône with a tiny foothold in Châteauneuf-du-Pape. Although not built to age as long as some, the wines are attractive—modern yet not entirely divorced from their Provençal roots. Given Lafond's earnest approach and imminent organic status, they may soon be even better.

route des Vignobles, 30126 Tavel
04 66 50 24 59

Domaine Maby Tavel

Richard Maby left his Paris stock exchange job in 2004 to take over from his father. Energetic and hands-on, he has lifted quality dramatically at this family estate, which has 57 acres (23ha) in Tavel and another 74 acres (30ha) in Lirac. Maby's finely textured wines are pure in flavor and generous in style—the whites perhaps even more striking than the amply proportioned rosés and the spicy, mineral-edged reds. The mouthfilling Lirac Cuvée Prestige, a 50/50 Grenache Blanc/Viognier blend aged in oak, is especially rewarding; terrific with foie gras, Maby says. ★ **Rising star**

rue St-Vincent, 30126 Tavel
www.domainemaby.fr

Domaine Marc Kreydenweiss
Costières de Nîmes

The world is just beginning to discover this estate run by well-known Alsace producer Marc Kreydenweiss since 1999. Curious to make red wines after long immersion in whites, Kreydenweiss was attracted by the terroir—*galets* and soils of broken schist, quartz, and sandstone "exactly like Alsace." He and winemaker wife Emmanuelle follow biodynamics and pick early in the hot Costières to achieve fresh wines with mineral complexity—her perfumed, fruity Grimaudes contrasting with his rich, layered Perrières. Their latest venture: 5 acres (2ha) of old vines in Châteauneuf-du-Pape. ★ **Rising star**

701 chemin des Perrières, 30129 Manduel
www.kreydenweiss.com

Domaine Marcel Richaud Cairanne

With his long, gray hair and modish spectacles, Marcel Richaud has an assured, slightly raffish air that seems to match his wines. A fifth-generation grower, he has been bottling under his own name since 1974. Since then, helped by his wife Marie, he has expanded his largely organic estate to 125 acres (50ha) in 30 varied parcels. Old-vine fruit from the best terroirs fashions concentrated, almost Châteauneuf-like L'Ebrescade,

DOMAINE LA MONARDIERE
LA MONARDIERE VIELLES VIGNES IS AGED FOR
18 MONTHS IN LARGE OAK CASKS

but less ambitious wines are also stylish—from an exotic, mango-toned white Cairanne down to a lovely, easy-going red Côtes du Rhône.

route de Rasteau, 84290 Cairanne
04 90 30 85 25

Domaine de Marcoux Châteauneuf-du-Pape

From a family whose vine roots stretch back to the 1300s, Philippe Armenier created Châteauneuf's first biodynamic estate at Marcoux in 1990 before moving abroad. Although slightly less extreme in approach, his sisters have followed the same path: Catherine tending 42 acres (17ha), many with old vines, and Sophie vinifying. Their wines, sometimes described as feminine ("whatever that means!" says Catherine) are perfumed, hedonistic, exceptionally pure, and fine-boned. The sumptuous Vieilles Vignes takes just half of the old-vine fruit, the regular *cuvée* benefiting from the rest.

84230 Châteauneuf-du-Pape
04 90 34 67 43

Domaine de la Monardière Vacqueyras

Armed with an agriculture degree and work experience in California and Burgundy, Damien Vache is typical of the younger generation of Rhône winemakers—well educated, articulate, open-minded. Focused on organic viticulture, he believes in the importance of biodiversity —a natural feature of the Monardière vineyards, which are mainly in the hills. Although white and rosé wines account for only 5% of the appellation, they make up 20% of the output here. Look out for the unctuous white Galéjade—though the red Les 2 Monardes is lipsmacking Vacqueyras at a very decent price. ★ **Rising star**

84190 Vacqueyras
www.monardiere.fr

Domaine de Montvac Vacqueyras

Before she took over Montvac, which has been passed from mother to daughter through four generations, Cécile Dusserre wanted to be a ballet dancer. So maybe it is no surprise that her wines—Gigondas as well as Vacqueyras —are remarkably poised and graceful. Although full-bodied and richly textured, they dance across the palate in a light-footed way. "I am incapable of making a wine which I myself do not like," she says. The barrel-fermented white Vacqueyras and the vibrant old-vine red Cuvée Vincila share top honors in a strong line-up.

84190 Vacqueyras
www.domaine-de-montvac.com

Domaine de la Mordorée Tavel

Brothers Christophe and Fabrice Delorme produce sophisticated Tavel, Lirac, and Côtes du Rhône at Domaine de la Mordorée. The Mordorée style is hedonistic, combining satin texture with depth of flavor and admirable balance. Anybody who is interested in discovering traditional, full-bodied, cellar-worthy Tavel should sample the *cuvée* Reine des Bois, which ages gracefully for up to ten years. Other highlights include the suave red Liracs and—latest addition—a small amount of sumptuous Châteauneuf-du-Pape.

chemin des Oliviers, 30126 Tavel
www.domaine-mordoree.com

DOMAINE LES PALLIERES
LES PALLIERES GIGONDAS IS FINELY
STRUCTURED AND CELLAR-WORTHY

Domaine du Moulin Vinsobres

Denis Vinson, his wife Frédérique, and their son Charles run Moulin, which they claim is the smallest and oldest private winery in Vinsobres. Not far from Nyons, famous for black olives, it was mainly an olive estate until the devastating frost of 1956 killed many of the trees. Vines, seen as a safer bet, replaced them (although fortunately enough trees remain to produce superb estate olive oil). The two best wines are the finely wrought old-vine Cuvée Jean Vinson and the oakier, more Syrah-driven Cuvée Charles Joseph—both juicily alluring.

26110 Vinsobres
04 75 27 65 59

Domaine de Mourchon Séguret

Two things are remarkable about the estate set up by Walter and Ronnie McKinlay as a retirement project in 1998. One is the location, teetering high above the village of Séguret. The second, equally breathtaking, is the youthful energy they have summoned to develop a bare 42 acres (17ha) of vines into a dynamic enterprise. The wines go from strength to strength with subtler oak now in the ageworthy Grande Réserve and the appearance, in top years, of two impressive old-vine Family Réserves. The unoaked Tradition is also a safe bet. ★ **Rising star**

La Grande Montagne, 84110 Séguret
www.domainedemourchon.com

Domaine Oratoire St-Martin
Cairanne

From a family steeped in Cairanne for more than 300 years, Francois and Frédéric Alary make some of the Southern Rhône's best wines at L'Oratoire St-Martin. Their quiet confidence reflects ten generations of wisdom, yet they are forward-looking—adopting biodynamic methods on their 64 acre (26ha) estate (organic since 1993) and removing heat-absorbing stones from the vineyards to slow down ripening and promote freshness. The wines are exemplary—the Haut-Coustias white (Marsanne, Roussanne, and Viognier) is rich, with a salty tang; the Mourvèdre-dominated Haut-Coustias red is a smooth amalgam of peppery fruit and rippling minerality.

route de St-Roman, 84290 Cairanne
www.oratoiresaintmartin.fr

Domaine Les Pallières Gigondas

The Bruniers, owners of Châteauneuf-du-Pape estate Le Vieux Télégraphe, searched all over the Côtes du Rhône for an estate whose wines would combine a distinctive personality with drinking pleasure. Finally, in 1998, in partnership with their American importer Kermit Lynch, they bought Les Pallières—neglected but magnificently sited on high, wooded ground with a treasury of old vines. Rigorous in their methods, they allow their two *cuvées* a full year in vat and a further year in cask before bottling. The result? Gigondas at its most stylish—finely textured, strikingly harmonious, and ageworthy, too. ★ **Rising star**

route d'Encieu, 84190 Gigondas
www.vignoblesbrunier.fr

Domaine du Pégaü Châteauneuf-du-Pape

Laurence Féraud and her wines at Domaine du Pégaü have charmed critics so effectively for so long that the feisty young woman who used to argue with her dad in the cellar ("I will do it my way!") is now part of the establishment. The domaine, created around old family vineyards in 1987, has 50 acres (20ha) in 17 diverse parcels—some still planted with Châteauneuf's 13 varieties. Traditionally made, the wines are firm, with smoky, meaty concentration and mineral thrust. Confusingly, Cuvée Réservée is the main red. Powerful Cuvée da Capo is the result of a parcel selection in top years.

avenue Impériale, 84230 Châteauneuf-du-Pape
www.pegau.com

Domaine Pelaquié Laudun

Luc Pelaquié is the most significant individual producer in Laudun, with 160 acres (65ha) of vines stretching as far as the eye can see around his fine old house. White wines account for 25% of his output—the highest proportion, he maintains, in the entire Southern Rhône. In a wide range, which embraces Côtes du Rhône, Tavel, and Lirac alongside Laudun, the whites are the undisputed stars—the unoaked but ample Laudun especially. The rosés and reds may be a tad too lush to suit all tastes.

7 rue Vernet, 30290 St-Victor la Coste
www.domaine-pelaquie.com

Domaine de Piaugier Sablet

With 50 acres (20ha) of vines in countless small parcels around Sablet, fourth-generation grower Jean-Marc Autran and his wife Sophie launched Domaine de Piaugier in 1985. Unsurprisingly their focus was on red wines—and their classic Sablet red is textbook proof of this appellation's potential for juicy elegance. But they were among the first here to vinify white wines in barrique and their poised Sablet blanc has inspired others to follow their example. Also intriguing is the lively red Sablet Ténébi, made almost entirely from the old grape variety Counoise.

route de Gigondas, 84110 Sablet
www.domainedepiaugier.com

Domaine Pierre Usseglio

Châteauneuf-du-Pape

Since the early 1990s, brothers Thierry and Jean-Pierre Usseglio have been running this estate founded by their grandfather—an energetic vineyard worker from Piedmont, driven to Châteauneuf in the hungry 1930s. Since 1998, they have honored his memory with the rich Cuvée de Mon Aïeul, based on 95-year-old Grenache; 20,000 bottles are produced annually. But the traditional *cuvée*, toward which the meticulous Usseglios direct equal attention, delivers impressive quality at around half the price. Their style, restrained rather than super-opulent, also finds expression in a fresh, light-footed white.

route d'Orange, 84230 Châteauneuf-du-Pape
04 90 83 72 98

Domaine de la Pigeade

Beaumes-de-Venise

Marina and Thierry Voute are energetic ambassadors for Muscat de Beaumes-de-Venise, feeling they have a mission to promote one of the leading sweet wine appellations in France. Three-quarters of the 104 acre (42ha) Pigeade estate are planted with Muscat à Petits Grains (the remainder produces very respectable Vacqueyras and Ventoux). Trained as winemakers in California, they make a light-footed Muscat with lychee and tangerine notes and cleansing acidity. They say it cellars well for up to 20 years—certainly long enough to win over sweet wine sceptics.

route de Caromb, 84190 Beaumes-de-Venise
www.lapigeade.fr

Domaine La Réméjeanne

Côtes du Rhône-Villages

Over the past 20 years, Rémy Klein has propelled La Réméjeanne, his 94 acre (38ha) northern Gard estate, to the front ranks of Côtes du Rhône-Villages. Two things stand out. First the landscape, wilder and windier up here than in sun-baked Provence—bringing freshness to the wines. Next, Klein's love of untamed nature, showing through in *cuvées* named after arbutus, honeysuckle, juniper, dog-rose. And then there are the wines, which are consistently good across an ambitious range. Rich, savory Les Genévriers is particularly impressive.

Cadignac, 30200 Sabran
www.laremejeanne.com

Domaine de la Renjarde Massif d'Uchaux

On the site of a Roman villa, the vineyards of La Renjarde sit in one vast plot with sweeping vistas in front and woods behind. After many years as part-owners, the Richard family of Château La Nerthe bought the property in 2000, appointing Christian Voeux to manage production in 2008. Improvements are under way—from conversion to organic viticulture and 100% hand-picking to vineyard renewal and the introduction of white grapes. But the tradition of producing plump reds with a modern feel had already been well established.

route d'Uchaux, 84830 Sérignan-du-Comtat
www.renjarde.fr

Domaine Roger Sabon

Châteauneuf-du-Pape

There is a family feel to the estate set up by Roger Sabon in 1952; his sons are still around and current winemaker Didier Négron is married to his granddaughter, Séverine. The wines—open, frank, and unpretentious—behave like a family too, avoiding extremes of ripeness, extraction, or oak across a strong range. Does blending before aging rather than afterward enhance their harmony? Perhaps. The classic *cuvée* (Les Olivets) is juicily enticing, the meatier Réserve suave, and the intense Prestige ageworthy without costing silly money.

avenue Impériale, 84230 Châteauneuf-du-Pape
www.roger-sabon.com

Domaine de la Roquète

Châteauneuf-du-Pape

Although the Bruniers of Vieux Télégraphe bought the 74 acre (30ha) Domaine de la Roquète in 1986, they say it took well over a decade to get to grips with its terroir. Near famous Chateau Rayas, it has some of the same sandy soil that delivers freshness, but less of the power associated with *galets*. The wines have taken a major step forward since 2003. Like Vieux Télégraphe, red Roquète benefits from two years of aging before release. Smooth, ripe, and yummy, it is best drunk within a decade.

2 avenue Louis Pasteur, 84230 Châteauneuf-du-Pape
www.brunier.fr

SPECIAL CUVEES —GOOD OR BAD?

Twenty years ago, only a tiny handful of estates in Châteauneuf-du-Pape produced a special *cuvée*—a top wine made in limited quantities in outstanding years, usually from the fruit of a vineyard parcel valued for old vines and outstanding terroir. Today, the opposite is true: only a few estates do not make a special *cuvée* (Clos des Papes, Vieux Télégraphe, and Vieux Donjon being prominent naysayers). Many produce several, based on a selection of the best lots in the cellar rather than a particular plot. Often super-concentrated and super-expensive, are these luxury wines a good thing? Arguments rage. They tend to attract rave reviews, which means they carry obvious marketing benefits, both for their creators and for Châteauneuf-du-Pape in general. But if a significant amount of an estate's best output is diverted into one or more *cuvées spéciales*, the main red wine (upon which its reputation should principally rest) may be impoverished. You have been warned.

Domaine La Roubine Gigondas

Eric Ughetto left his job as a Paris fireman to return to Gigondas, lured by the sun and the chance to take over the small holding of vines that his father had managed on weekends. Fastidious in approach, he gave himself 10 years to master his new *métier* and expand La Roubine (now 37 acres/15ha divided between Gigondas, Vacqueyras, and Sablet). Since the first vintage in 2000, his reputation has soared. With low yields, organic methods, and, where possible, the co-fermentation of Grenache and Syrah, he fashions seamless, succulent wines. ★ **Rising star**

84190 Gigondas
04 90 65 81 55

Domaine St-Damien Gigondas

If you want carefully crafted, classically styled Gigondas at a reasonable price, remember the name St-Damien, and be grateful that fifth-generation grape-grower Joël Saurel decided in 1995 to stop supplying négociants in bulk, abandon chemicals and herbicides, and start producing serious wines the old-fashioned way. His three *cuvées* reflect a high proportion of old vines on three terroirs, the scented, almost feminine La Louisiane from vineyards on the garrigue contrasting dramatically with the chunkier, clay-derived Les Souteyrades. Release at least three years after vintage delivers extra harmony.

Hameau de la Beaumette, 84190 Gigondas
04 90 70 96 72

Domaine St-Gayan Gigondas

Although the Southern Rhône is steeped in tradition, few producers can boast an estate that has been in the family for nearly 400 years, as is the case at St-Gayan. Not that Jean-Pierre and Martine Meffre would boast. The self-effacing pair seem almost unaware that their wines are considered benchmark examples of Gigondas (and no disgrace to Rasteau). Traditional in style, the powerful Gigondas can take time to open up, but ages superbly. Even the basic Côtes du Rhône offers meaty depth.

Le Trignon, 84190 Gigondas
www.saintgayan.com

Domaine St-Préfert
Châteauneuf-du-Pape

Isabel Ferrando was a teetotal banker until a sudden wine epiphany a decade ago—triggered by a dinner-party glass of Coche-Dury Meursault. She promptly bought a 40 acre (16ha) plot of vines and trained as a winemaker to start Domaine St-Préfert. "New converts are the most extreme perfectionists," she says—a point borne out by her immaculate cellar and precise, poised wines. Unusually, the superb old-vine Réserve Auguste Favier is made in greater quantities than her basic *cuvée*. Refined 100% Grenache Colombis from a recently purchased parcel is sold as Domaine Isabel Ferrando. ★ **Rising star**

Quartier des Serres, 84230 Châteauneuf-du-Pape
www.st-prefert.fr

Domaine Le Sang des Cailloux
Vacqueyras

"The blood of the stones" (Le Sang des Cailloux) is an apt name for the vivid red winery of Serge Férigoule, a driven man who has sweated blood to make the domaine a success since he took over in 1990. His 44 acre (18ha)

biodynamic estate on the Sarrians side of Vacqueyras yields individualistic wines that are strongly stamped by the vintage—sometimes juicily seductive, sometimes austere, but always with a firm mineral undertow. With orange and honey tones, the white is mesmerizing.

Route de Vacqueyras, 84260 Sarrians
www.sangdescailloux.com

Domaine Santa Duc Gigondas

The French use the word *gras* (fat) to describe smooth, full-bodied wines with a plump cushion of ripe fruit. Yves Gras, fourth-generation owner of Santa Duc, fashions wines that are true to his name. With roughly half of his vineyards in Gigondas (and the rest in Rasteau, Vacqueyras, Cairanne, Sablet, and Roaix), he favors very ripe grapes for his reds and does not stem them: tannin from the stems counterbalances the luscious fruit. The exuberant white wines are also worth seeking out.

Les Hautes Garrigues, 84190 Gigondas
www.santaduc.fr

Domaine La Soumade Rasteau

Although André Romero and his son Frédéric produce some Châteauneuf-du-Pape and Gigondas, La Soumade is strongly bound to Rasteau, where the family has grown grapes and peaches for generations. On their 69 acre (28ha) estate, younger vines on sandy soil generate a lusciously approachable Cuvée Tradition. Older vines on heavier clays promote denser, more structured wines —yet these too have a sumptuous side that is typical of Soumade. In ascending steps of spicy intensity, Prestige, Confiance, and limited-quantity Fleur de Confiance all repay some cellaring. The sweet red is also superb.

84110 Rasteau
04 90 46 11 26

Domaine de la Verrière Ventoux

Refurbished by Xavier Rolet, current French boss of the London stock exchange, over a 15-year period, La Verrière makes jaws drop half a dozen times. On the crest of a hill with 74 acres (30ha) of vines, it looks magnificent —like an entire village encompassing a luxury hotel, a restaurant, and a wine school, as well as a super-swish winery. No surprise, then, that the Chêne Bleu wines launched in 2006 are expensive—but quality is high, with the Syrah-dominated Héloïse providing a silky foil to the denser Grenache-based Abelard. ★ **Rising star**

Chemin de la Verrière, 84110 Crestet
www.laverriere.com

Domaine de la Vieille Julienne
Châteauneuf-du-Pape

On north-facing terraces, the main part of Vieille Julienne's 25 acres (10 ha) produces grapes with high natural acidity. The reflective, rigorous owner Jean-Paul Daumen retains this freshness by including a dash of Cinsault and by not picking too late. Underscoring it is a tangy minerality, which conversion to biodynamics has amplified. Since 2003, all of the old-vine fruit goes into the estate's impressively complex main wine. The top terraces yield a pricey Cuvée Réservée in outstanding years.

Le Grès, 84100 Orange
www.vieillejulienne.com

Domaine Le Vieux Donjon
Châteauneuf-du-Pape
In some ways, Le Vieux Donjon is a very traditional estate. It makes just one wine, on the grounds that special *cuvées* might impoverish the classic *cuvée*. This is fermented in cement tanks and aged in large casks in the time-honored way. But the winemaker is now young Claire Michel (fourth generation), an enology graduate who worked at Napa's Harlan Estate. Could anything be more modern? Three terroirs, including *galets* with 100-year-old Grenache, distinguish Vieux Donjon. Silky elegance, vibrancy, fine tannins, depth… it has them all.

9 Avenue St-Joseph, 84230 Châteauneuf-du-Pape
04 90 83 70 03

Domaine du Vieux Télégraphe
Châteauneuf-du-Pape
Standing on the plateau of La Crau, where the vineyards are thickly carpeted with stones, you see why the Brunier family was able to extend a modest vineyard planted in 1898 into today's 170 acre (70ha) panorama. "Nobody else wanted it—too hard to work," says Daniel Brunier. He and his brother Frédéric have seen Vieux Télégraphe rank consistently among the appellation's frontrunners for its complex, classy wines. The gloriously savory red, incorporating Counoise, Cinsault, and Clairette for freshness, is superb at around ten years. The white is a model of peachy elegance.

3 Route de Châteauneuf-du-Pape, 84370 Bédarrides
www.brunier.fr

Domaine Vindémio Ventoux
Jean Marot was hailed as a rising star at Domaine de Murmurium before his decade there ended in a dissolved business partnership and financial disaster. Now, having managed to retain 32 acres (13ha) of vines, he is up and running again at Vindémio, with son Guillaume. Marot makes well-priced, delightful wines—pure, fresh, refined —without a whisper of oak. His vineyards, organic for years, are now biodynamic "for extra vibrancy in the wines." The red Imagine is especially good. ★ **Rising star**

Avenue Jean Jaurès, 84570 Villes sur Auzon
www.vindemio.com

Gourt de Mautens Rasteau
If Jérome Bressy's wines are ambitiously priced, they reflect his singular determination to make "*un grand vin*" at Gourt de Mautens. With 32 acres (13ha) on seven terroirs incorporating a treasury of old vines, he abandoned the co-op to set up his estate in 1996. Organic since 1989, the vineyards are now farmed biodynamically. Yields are kept drastically low, Carignan is preferred to Mourvèdre, old varieties like Counoise are favored, and 160-gallon (600-liter) casks have replaced small barrels. The end result? Sensually polished yet soulful wines in limited quantities: one white, one red, no special *cuvées*.

Route de Cairanne, 84110 Rasteau
www.gourtdemautens.com

Mas de Libian Côtes du Rhône-Villages
Hélène Thibon looks too glamorous to haul hoses around a cellar—and too young to have been hailed as a rising star for a decade. But since she became the driving force behind Mas de Libian, an old Ardèche hunting estate where wild boar still eat the grapes, quality has kept on rising. Blessed by terroir carpeted by large *galets*, Thibon follows biodynamic methods on her 42 horse-plowed acres (17ha). She makes elegantly seductive wines— luscious red Khayyam is the best known; Mourvèdre-rich La Calade is the most distinctive. ★ **Rising star**

Quart Libian, 07700 St-Marcel d'Ardèche
06 61 41 45 32

Montirius Vacqueyras
Serious is the word that best sums up Montirius, a well-sited estate with 100 acres (40ha) in Vacqueyras and 50 acres (20ha) in Gigondas. Committed to biodynamics, owners Eric and Christine Saurel are dauntingly passionate. Fermentations proceed in cement tanks at their own pace and oak is eschewed on the basis that ripe grape pips have enough woody character. Although the wines may not always quite live up to expectations, they are distinguished by a mineral-edged vigor.

Le Devès, 84260 Sarrians
www.montirius.com

Moulin de la Gardette Gigondas
With just 22 acres (9ha), fifth-generation vigneron Jean-Baptiste Meunier's Moulin de la Gardette may be one of the smaller estates in Gigondas, but its growing reputation defies its compact size. The vines—in 23 small parcels around the village—are now cultivated organically and the wines are made with wild yeasts. Alongside Grenache, Syrah, and Mourvèdre, Cinsault accounts for 10% of each of the estate's two wines, adding elegance and keeping alcohol down. The opulent Cuvée Ventabren is the one to seek out. ★ **Rising star**

Place de la Mairie, 84190 Gigondas
www.moulindelagardette.com

Perrin & Fils
Côtes du Rhône-Villages & Côtes du Rhône
What the Guigal dynasty is to the Northern Rhône, the Perrins of Château de Beaucastel are to the south. Besides acting as wine négociants, they own or lease vineyards on enviable terroirs in many prominent villages, their empire expanding year by year. Sustainable viticulture is practiced as in Châteauneuf. The result: a wide range of wines that capture the typicity of their origins with remarkable consistency—from the everyday Vieille Ferme white and red up through appellations like Rasteau, Vacqueyras, Gigondas, Cairanne, and Vinsobres.

84100 Orange
www.perrin-et-fils.com

Tardieu-Laurent Luberon
Most négociant houses are sizeable, but Tardieu-Laurent is boutique in scale. It dates from 1989, when wine-obsessed civil servant Michel Tardieu persuaded Burgundy micro-négociant Dominique Laurent to form a partnership focused on the Rhône. Good relationships with leading estates enable Tardieu-Laurent to obtain small quantities of top *cuvées*, which they blend and age in barrique to make powerfully concentrated wines. Even the Côtes du Rhône is a densely packed blockbuster.

Route de Cucuron, 84160 Lourmarin
www.tardieu-laurent.com

HELENE THIBON
Except, perhaps, for her extreme elegance (few vignerons sport chiffon tops among the vines), Hélène Thibon of Mas de Libian typifies the young growers who are revitalizing the Southern Rhône. With her parents in the background, husband Alain at her side, sister Catherine in the vineyard, and teenage son Aurélien helping out, she may be just as family-minded as previous generations—but today the approach is vastly different. With wines of optimal quality the aim, vine health is the main focus of attention—so, besides progressing from organic to biodynamic methods (like many others), Thibon has acquired Nestor the plow-horse to work her stony vineyards. He plows with more precision (and fewer carbon emissions) than a tractor, causing less damage to the roots of precious old vines. Deeper roots, stronger vines, better resistance to disease and drought… "Our great-grandparents knew more than we realized," runs today's retro refrain.

Beaumes-de-Venise produces a pale gold, perfumed, sweet Vin Doux Naturel from the Muscat grape.

LANGUEDOC

Languedoc wine region

The Languedoc is a vast region stretching in an arc through southern France from west to east, across the departments of the Aude, Hérault, and the Gard. It is less sophisticated (and less glitzy) than Provence, with which it vies (along with Southern Rhône) to be the oldest French viticultural region dating back to Roman or even Greek times. The Languedoc is certainly the largest and most important area in terms of volume of production in France (10% of the country's total production). It would be an injustice, however, to suppose that the region is only responsible for cheap, mass-produced plonk. Rather, the Languedoc is currently one of the most exciting and evolving regions in Europe, attracting keen and passionate individuals with its potential.

Major grapes

 Reds

Carignan

Cinsault

Grenache

Mourvèdre

Syrah

 Whites

Bourboulenc

Clairette

Maccabéo

Picpoul

Vintages

2009
The aromatic whites have low acidity, but the reds have deep color and structured tannins.

2008
The yields were quite low due to water stress, leading to concentrated wines. The best will continue to improve.

2007
Very similar in terms of both style and vintage conditions to 2006.

2006
A year of good quality. The wines are less concentrated than those from 2005; most are ready to drink.

2005
A vintage full of wines of similar quality to 2004, which are ready to drink.

2004
The reds are of good quality and ready to drink.

Generally speaking, the Languedoc's climate is warm, with summer temperatures often in excess of 86°F (30°C) during the day, more than 2,500 hours of sunshine a year, and low annual rainfall of 16in (400mm). This reduces the risk of vine diseases, such as downy and powdery mildew, but drought can be a problem. Red wine production dominates the region, with wines high in alcohol and low in acidity produced by a high number of co-operatives. Within this generalization, however, there can be huge variations in site-specific microclimates.

To the north of the region runs the Cevennes mountain range, part of the Massif Central, which runs northeast from the Montagne Noire north of Carcassone all the way up to the Monts du Vivarais in Ardèche. There are two strong winds that affect the climate in the Languedoc. The mistral, the strong cold north wind that funnels down through the Rhône Valley, affects the northeast of Languedoc; and the tramontane blows from the north-northwest between the Pyrenees and the Massif Central. Geologically, the Languedoc is an array of soil types resulting from volcanic activity, ice ages, and mountains and seas, that have come and gone.

While most vineyards are planted on the vast, flat, low-lying alluvial plain, where large quantities of lower quality wines are produced, there are opportunities afforded by the foothills of the mountains or outcrops. It is the varying combination of factors—sun, temperature, shelter, altitude, wind, and proximity to the sea—that enables the region to produce a panoply of wine styles.

There is no doubt that red wine dominates production, but quality white, rosé, sparkling, and sweet wines are also produced. The best wines are often produced on the higher altitude sites, with areas such as Pic St-Loup and St-Chinian up to 2,000ft (600m). La Clape, which in Roman times was an island, is now attached to the mainland. Essentially a coastal mountain nature reserve, it makes quality white wines from Bourboulenc. The Picpoul de Pinet appellation makes fresh citrus-flavored white wine from the Picpoul grape.

As one moves westward, the region tends to become more rugged around Corbières and Minervois. Limoux, at the southwestern extremity of the Languedoc, higher and further from the Mediterranean than any appellation, makes quality sparkling wines. North of here, Cabardès and Malepère have both Atlantic and Mediterranean influences in terms of the climate, and, therefore, the choice of grape varieties cultivated. And at Frontignan, the most famous of Languedoc's sweet wines are produced.

This is a land rich in history. Narbonne, established in 118BCE, was the first Roman colony in Gaul, and a prosperous port. The medieval fortified Cité de Carcassone (which was also the site of an important Roman trading area in the 6th century) was classified as a UNESCO World Heritage site in 1997. The 150 mile (240km) Canal du Midi completed in 1681, connects the Atlantic to the Mediterranean coast and is also a UNESCO site.

The Languedoc has survived through good times and bad, and continues to be a land of vinous opportunities.

Antech Limoux

Antech is a family-owned operation run by Françoise Antech. Its main focus is on producing sparkling wines —AC Crémant de Limoux, AC Blanquette de Limoux, and AC Blanquette Méthode Ancestrale—although some still wines are also made. The traditional method of production—the same as that employed in the Champagne region—is used, and it is claimed that sparkling wines fermented in bottle were developed here at the Abbey of Saint Hilaire in 1531, long before they appeared in Champagne. However, the grape varieties are different—Mauzac, Chenin Blanc, and Chardonnay— and Antech sources from growers around the region, as well as its own 150 acre (60ha) vineyard. The proportion used depends on the appellation—Blanquette de Limoux must have at least 90% of the traditional Mauzac varietal.

Domaine de Flassian, 11500 Limoux
www.antech-limoux.fr

Borie la Vitarèle Languedoc

The small Borie la Vitarèle estate, created in 1990, lies at the end of a dirt track close to Causses et Veyran. Cathy Planes and Jean-Francois Izarn cultivate 40 acres (16ha) of vines organically on gravel schist, clay, and limestone soils planted with typical grapes of the region, as well as Merlot, Cabernet Sauvignon, and Lledoner Pelut. Four *cuvées* are produced according to their terroir—Terres Blanches, La Combe, Les Schistes, and Les Crés—and are all aged for a year in barrel. There is also a *ferme-auberge* on the estate where you can enjoy traditional local cuisine while tasting the wines. ★**Rising star**

La Combe, 34490 St-Nazaire-de-Laderez
www.borielavitarele.fr

Cave de Mont Tauch Fitou

Cave de Mont Tauch is one of the oldest co-operatives in the Languedoc (it dates back to 1913), situated in the oldest appellation in the Languedoc. The Fitou appellation, established in 1948, sits on the Languedoc-Roussillon boundary and Mont Tauch is responsible for 50% of its production. Overlooking the village of Tuchan, the co-operative has 250 growers spread around the villages of Paziols, Tuchan, Durban, and Villeneuve. It continues to evolve, and winemaker Michel Marty makes consistently good-value Fitou, Corbiéres, and sweet wines (Fitou is the only area outside of Roussillon permitted to produce Rivesaltes and Maury).

Les Vignerons Du Mont Tauch, 11350 Tuchan
www.mont-tauch.com

Château de l'Anglès La Clape

Attracted to Château de l'Anglès in the La Clape natural conservation area in 2001, Eric Fabre was previously technical director at Bordeaux's Château Lafite-Rothschild. The estate comprises 100 acres (40ha) of vines surrounded by 100 acres (40ha) of garrigue and 7 acres (3ha) of Aleppo pine forest, and includes a three-bedroom gîte. Elegant white wines are produced, based on Bourboulenc blended with some Marsanne, Roussanne, and White Grenache. Mourvèdre, Syrah, Grenache, and Carignan produce spicy reds with flavors reminiscent of the surrounding garrigue, as well as a rosé.

11560 St-Pierre la Mer
www.chateaudangles.com

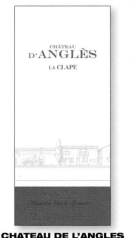

CHATEAU DE L'ANGLES
THE CLASSIQUE CUVEE IS A BEAUTIFULLY MADE REFLECTION OF THE LOCAL TERROIR

ANTECH
EMOTION CREMANT DE LIMOUX IS ONE OF THE REGION'S BEST SPARKLING WINES

Château d'Aussières Corbières

Purchased by Domaines Barons de Rothschild (Lafite) of Bordeaux fame in 1999, Château d'Aussières has been completely renovated. A state-of-the-art winery has been built and 420 acres (170ha) of vineyard replanted with the traditional regional varieties Syrah, Grenache, Mourvèdre, and Carignan. These are used to make rich and fine AOC Corbières, which are aged in oak barrels produced at Lafite in Pauillac, producing ripe, peppery flavors and good length. The Bordeaux varieties Cabernet Sauvignon and Merlot and even a few acres of Chardonnay were also planted and used to produce Vin de Pays d'Oc.

Départementale 613, Route de l'Abbaye de Fontfroide, 11100 Narbonne; www.lafite.com

Château de Camplazens La Clape

Château de Camplazens was bought by English couple Peter and Susan Close in 2000. It has approximately 100 acres (40ha) of vines located on the site of an ancient Roman camp in the center of the La Clape massif facing the sea. It is predominantly planted with red grape varieties, including the newcomer Marselan (a cross between Grenache and Cabernet Sauvignon bred in 1961). As well as producing appellation wines, a 100% Syrah Vin de Pays is dense, richly concentrated, and spicy. A small quantity of barrel-fermented Viognier, aged for six months in oak, is also produced. ★**Rising star**

Château de Camplazens, 11110 Armissan
www.camplazens.com

Château Capion Languedoc

Dating back to the 16th century, Château Capion, nestled in the Gassac Valley between the villages of Gignac and Aniane, was bought by the Buhrer family from Switzerland in 1996. It has subsequently been completely restored, the vineyard replanted, and the cellar facilities upgraded. The domaine covers 185 acres (75ha), of which 110 acres (45ha) are planted with traditional red varieties, as well as Chardonnay, Roussanne, and Viognier. A range of wines are produced by Alsatian winemaker Frederic Kast and can be tasted in the Vintners House while looking out over the Gassac Valley.

SCA de Château Capion, 34150 Gignac
www.chateaucapion.com

Château de Caraguilhes Corbières

Near St-Laurent de la Cabrerisse within the Corbières-Boutenac region, Château de Caraguilhes was one of the first vineyards in the region to use organic techniques, pioneered in the 1950s by the then owner Lionel Faivre, a French-Algerian. Currently owned by Pierre Gabison, the property has a vinous history dating back to the 12th century, developed by Cistercian monks. The château is surrounded by 320 acres (130ha) of vineyard, which continue to be organically managed. A range of white, rosé, and red wines are produced. Whites include the Solus Corbières Blanc (100% barrel-fermented Grenache Blanc) and the Classique (65% Marsanne, 35% Grenache Blanc, with a small part aged in oak). Of the reds, Solus, an oak-aged blend of Carignan, Grenache, Syrah, and Mourvèdre, has peppery notes and fine tannins.

11220 St-Laurent de la Cabrerisse
www.caraguilhes.fr

CHATEAU DES ERLES
CHATEAU DES ERLES IS AN ATTRACTIVE FITOU
FROM BORDEAUX'S FRANCOIS LURTON

CHATEAU DE LASCAUX
LES NOBLES PIERRES IS A DELIGHTFULLY
JUICY RED BLEND

Château Cazal Viel St-Chinian

Situated near Cessanon-sur-Orb at the foot of the Caroux Mountains, Château Cazal Viel has been in the Miquel family since the French Revolution in 1789, and is currently run by Laurent Miquel. Vines were first planted here by Roman warriors and ruins of their villas and well still stand on the estate. With more than 335 acres (135ha) of vines, this is the largest private producer in St-Chinian. Laurent also has long-term agreements with growers in the vicinity. The estate produces AC and Vin de Pays wines including a white Sauvignon Blanc; a rosé from Syrah, Grenache, and Cinsault; the traditional Vieilles Vignes aged in oak for 12 months; and an unoaked blend of Syrah and Viognier—Cuvée des Fées. The estate also has a gîte available for hire.

Hameau Cazal Viel, 34460 Cessenon-sur-Orb
www.laurent-miquel.com

Château de Cazeneuve Pic St-Loup

André Leenhardt purchased Château de Cazeneuve in the early 1990s and re-built the winery in 1991. Leenhardt manages 90 acres (35ha) made up of 80% red varietals (Syrah, Grenache, Cinsault, and Carignan) and 20% white (Roussanne, Viognier, Marsanne, with a little Rolle, Muscat, and Petit Manseng) arranged in 30 parcels with south-southwest exposure between 490–1,300ft (150–400m) altitude and protected from the winds and frost. The vineyards are managed organically with yields restricted, producing savory, herbal wines.

34270 Lauret
www.cazeneuve.net

Château de Combebelle St-Chinian

Located at Villepassans, at 870ft to 985ft (265m to 300m) above sea level, Château de Combebelle has the highest vineyard in St-Chinian. The drive behind this 42 acre (17ha) estate is English woman Catherine Wallace, who has had a passion for wine since she was a child. When Catherine and her husband Patrick purchased the domaine in 2005, the estate had already started to develop a reputation for quality wines, which they have continued to develop. They make a fruity rosé, Cerisiers, with strawberry aromas, and a powerful red Syrah/Grenache, which is fermented in open tanks and aged in oak for 12 months, and has smoky aromas and licorice flavor.

34360 Villepassans
www.combebelle.com

Château Coupe Roses Minervois

Based in the small (250 inhabitants), pretty, medieval village of La Caunette, nestled below the Minervois, Château Coupe Roses has been owned by the Calvez family since 1614. It has been run by Françoise de Calvez and her husband Pascal Frissant since 1987. Vineyard plots totaling 75 acres (30ha) are dotted around hillsides in the La Causse region between 820ft–1,300ft (250–400m), altitude, producing good-value wines.

Rue de la Poterie, 34210 La Caunette
www.coupe-roses.com

Château des Erles Fitou

With a serious wine family background, brothers Jacques and François Lurton from Bordeaux set up their own business in 1988 with a view to developing wines in quality areas outside their home terrain. Languedoc was just one of the areas that attracted them, alongside Argentina, Chile, and Spain. In 2001, the brothers took over Château des Erles at Villeneuve-les-Corbières. Now with approximately 220 acres (90ha) of vineyard, the company is run solely by François. The Château des Erles is an attractive blend of Syrah, Grenache, and Carignan.

Villeneuve-les-Corbières 11360
www.francoislurton.com

Château des Estanilles Faugéres

Michel Louison and his wife purchased Château des Estanilles in 1976. Their daughter, Sophie, joined the team in 1999 after completing her studies in viticulture and enology. The domaine comprises 86 acres (35ha) planted with Syrah, Mourvèdre, and Grenache with a little Cinsault and Carignan. A full range of white, rosé, and red wines are produced, including a dry white wine from Marsanne, Roussanne, and Viognier, with delicate white fruit aromas and a rich mineral palate. It was partly due to Michel's campaigning and tenacity that white wines were officially recognized in the Faugères appellation.

34480 Lentheric-Cabrerolles
www.chateaudesestanilles.fr

Château Flaugergues La Mejanelle

Situated on the outskirts of Montpellier in the La Mejanelle subregion, Château Flaugergues was named after an advisor to the court in Montpellier—Etienne de Flaugergues—who purchased the estate in 1696. The château was further extended by him and formal gardens laid out around it. It is worth a visit, as much for the rare tapestries and furniture as for the wines. Seventy-five acres (30ha) of Grenache, Syrah, Mourvèdre, Carignan, and Cinsault are used in a range of quality wines.

1744 Ave Albert Einstein, 34000 Montpellier
www.flaugergues.com

Château de Gourgazaud
Minervois-La-Livinière

Château de Gourgazaud's Roger Piquet was the first person to plant Syrah and Mourvèdre grapes in the Minervois-La-Livinière, and was instrumental in pushing for the area to be given Cru status. The Château de Gourgazaud, which dates back to the 17th century, was purchased by Piquet in 1973. After Roger passed away in 2005, the estate, which now covers 240 acres (100ha), was taken over by his daughters, Chantale Piquet and Annick Tiburce. A range of wines are produced, including Cabernet Sauvignon, Viogner, Chardonnay, and Sauvignon Blanc.

34210 La Livinière; 04 68 78 10 02
www.gourgazaud.com

Château Haut Gléon Corbières

Situated in the Durban area (which is due to be classified as a Cru), Château Haut Gléon was purchased by the Duhamel family in the early 1990s. It dates back to the 13th century, and the domaine consists of 100 acres (40ha) of various varieties. An elegant aromatic white, Vallee du Paradis, is produced, as well as a rosé and red *cuvées* including Pinot Noir La Chapelle de Haut Gléon.

11360 Durban
www.hautgleon.com

Château L'Hospitalet La Clape

Château L'Hospitalet is the base for the operations of ex-international rugby player, Gérard Bertrand. The considerable Bertrand wine empire extends over 800 acres (325ha) of vineyards, and also takes in partnerships with growers and co-operatives in different areas of the Languedoc. The L'Hospitalet estate, farmed by monks as far back as 1561, was completely renovated by the Ribourel family, who sold to Bertrand in 2002. It has 2,470 acres (1,000ha) of land, including 200 acres (82ha) of vines, as well as a 22-bedroom hotel and "H" restaurant, offering gastronomic cuisine based on natural and local products. The range of wines includes the Reserve. Produced from traditional varieties and aged 12 months in oak, it is full of black fruits, spice, and smoky flavors, with firm but elegant tannins.

11100 Narbonne
www.gerard-bertrand.com

Château de Lascaux Pic St-Loup

Château de Lascaux is a family estate at Vacquières on the eastern edge of the Pic St-Loup appellation 16 miles (25km) from Montpellier. It dates back to 1750, and has been in the Cavalier family for 13 generations. Since Jean-Benoît Cavalier took the reins in 1984, the estate has grown, and a winery was established in the early 1990s. It now has 210 acres (85ha) at 390ft (120m) surrounded by 740 acres (300ha) of garrigue with oak and pine trees. Planted principally with Syrah and Grenache, with some Mourvèdre and Cinsault, Lascaux makes whites, rosés, and reds including Les Noble Pierres, an 80/20 Syrah/Grenache blend with crunchy, cherry fruit.

34270 Vacquieres
www.chateau-lascaux.com

Château La Liquière Faugères

Château La Liquière has been in the Vidal family for generations, and in the late 1960s, Bernard and Claudie Vidal bottled their first wine. The estate covers 150 acres (60ha), producing a range of 10 wines from Grenache, Syrah, Carignan, Mourvèdre, and Cinsault. The Cuvée les Amandiers red has sour cherry flavors, with slightly dry but subtle tannins on the finish. A white made from Grenache Blanc is full-bodied and rich.

34480 Cabrerolles
www.chateaulaliquiere.com

Château Mansenoble Corbières

Château Mansenoble was purchased by Guido and Marie-Annick Janseger-De Witte, a Belgian couple, in 1992. In the northern part of the Corbières appellation near Moux, at the foot of Mont Alaric, it consists of 50 acres (20ha). The couple have made improvements in the vineyard and wine cellar, restored the 19th-century house, and built gîtes. They make AOC red wines based on traditional varieties grown on the region's cooler, north-facing slopes, and some Vin de Pays from Merlot and Cabernet Sauvignon. The *cuvée* Marie-Annick, a blend of Syrah, Grenache, Mourvèdre, and Carignan, is only produced in good years, with a large proportion aged in oak. The Reserve is a slightly different blend of the same grapes, with a smaller proportion aged in oak.

11700 Moux
www.mansenoble.com

Château Maris Minervois

Robert Eden, the great-nephew of former UK prime minister Anthony Eden, adopted the Minervois as his home in the late 1990s, having lived and worked around the world. Eden is passionate about the environment and biodynamics. The only treatments used on the vines are homemade infusions using natural herbs and flowers, such as nettles and chamomile, prepared and applied according to the lunar calendar. A new wine cellar was built with the same respect for the environment and the aim of being carbon neutral in time for the 2010 harvest. The walls are made of hemp, solar panels on the roof are the source of electricity, and egg-shaped tanks are used to age the wines . ★ Rising star

Chemin de Parignole, 34420 La Livinière
www.mariswine.com

Château Moulin de Ciffre

Located in the upper valley of the Taurou River, 1 mile (1.5km) west of Autignac, the Moulin de Ciffre estate was bought by Bordeaux's Lesineau family in 1998. It has more than 75 acres (30ha) of vines in three appellations—Faugères, St-Chinian, and Coteaux du Languedoc. Traditional varieties are complemented by Cabernet Sauvignon and Viognier in a range of well-priced wines.

34480 Autignac
www.moulindeciffre.com

Château de la Negly La Clape

Located at Fleury, on prime chalky terroir in La Clape, Château de la Negly has been in the Rosset family for generations. However, it is only in the last 10 years or so that it has started to produce world-class wines under the stewardship of Jean-Paul Rosset. Previously, all the grapes were sent to the local co-operative and quantity, not quality, was the aim. All that has changed—working with winemaker Cyril Chamontin and Narbonne-based consultant Claude Gros, yields are kept to an absolute minimum and a range of premium red *cuvées* and the white La Brise Marine are produced. ★ Rising star

11560 Fleury d'Aude
04 68 32 36 28

Château Pech-Latt Corbières

The 300 acre (120ha) Château Pech-Latt at the foot of Mont Alaric has been certified organic since 1991 and owned by Burgundian négociant Louis Max since 1999. It produces attractive white, rosé, and red AC Corbières, as well as some good, Grenache-based sweet wine.

11220 Lagrasse
04 68 58 11 40

Château Pech Redon La Clape

Château Pech Redon was owned by one of La Clape's innovators, Jean Demolombe, until his death in 1988. Demolombe was the first to plant Mourvèdre and Viognier in the region, and one of the first to experiment with barriques. Current owner Jean-Claude Bousquet's range of organic whites and reds includes Les Genets, a barrel-fermented Chardonnay/Viognier blend, and the oak-aged red *cuvées*, L'Epervier and La Centaurée.

11100 Narbonne
04 68 90 41 22

ORGANIC AND BIODYNAMIC VITICULTURE

More and more grape growers in France are moving to organic farming, and the warm sunshine, low rainfall, and regular breezes in southern France are a distinct advantage. By 2008, France had more than 69,000 acres (28,000ha) cultivated in this way (of which 44% were in conversion), an increase of 21%. Languedoc-Roussillon is the largest area, with 542 organic producers and 30% of the total French organic acreage planted. Organic grape growing means that no man-made chemical fertilizers, herbicides, or pesticides are used. Instead, there is generally more manual laboring of the vineyards with composting and sowing of cover crops. A number of different bodies certify organic practices and there is a conversion period of three years before this can be attained. Biodynamic viticulture takes organics a step further and is also increasing in France. Developed by the Austrian Rudolf Steiner at the start of the 20th century, it is a holistic approach to nurturing the soil and the life within it. The phases of the moon and planetary constellations are taken into account to create the biodynamic calendar, which determines when work is carried out in the vineyard (and also which are the best days to taste wines—according to whether it is a fruit, root, or leaf day).

LES CLOS PERDUS
AN ANGLO-AUSTRALIAN DUO MAKES THE
OUTSTANDING PRIOUNDO IN TINY AMOUNTS

CHATEAU STE-EULALIE
THE MAGNIFICENT LA CANTILENE IS CHATEAU
STE-EULALIE'S TOP CUVEE

Château Pennautier Cabardès

Inspired by the Palace of Versailles, Château Pennautier was built in the 17th century for Bernard Pennautier, and in 1622 it received King Louis XIII. The 75 acre (30ha) formal gardens were laid out by landscaper Le Notre. The château was fully refurbished in 2008 by current owners Nicolas and Miren de Lorgeril, 10th-generation descendants of the family, who own a number of other estates in Languedoc and Roussillon. Standout wines include a rosé from Cinsault, Syrah, Côt, Grenache, and Cabernet Sauvignon with simple red fruit flavors, while the red wines have ripe damson fruit with chocolate flavors and are well-priced for the quality of wine.

11610 Pennautier
www.lorgeril.com

Château Puech Haut Gres de Montpellier

Château Peuch Haut is a large domaine built up from scratch by ex-industrialist Gérard Bru. Located close to the village of St-Drézéry, 9 miles (15km) northeast of Montpellier, it all started with an initial parcel of 75 acres (30ha), but no buildings, no winery, and not a vine in sight. Peuch Haut is now more than 420 acres (170ha) in total, with 285 acres (115ha) of vines, and even includes an 18th-century building, formerly Montpellier's town hall, that has been transported in its entirety and re-built on the site. Bru also built a winery and employed the Bordeaux consultant, Michel Rolland. The estate now produces a range of good-quality wines, as well as olive oil and truffles, and has an unusual collection of barrels decorated by artists and other celebrities.

2250 Route de Teyran, 34160 St-Drézéry
www.chateau-puech-haut.com

Château La Roque Pic Saint Loup

Originally an 8th-century posting house, vines were planted at Château La Roque in the 13th century by Jean and Guillaume de La Roque, and the tasting room is housed in a fine old vaulted cellar. Currently owned by Jacques Fiquette, and using the expertise of consultant Claude Cros, the estate has 79 acres (32ha) of vines on south-southeast-facing terraces with clay and limestone scree soils. White, rosé, and red wines are produced, including the premium Cupa Numismae, a blend of 60% Syrah and 40% Mourvèdre with concentrated spicy herbal flavors, and a fine, old-vine Mourvèdre.

84210 La Roque Sur Pernes Vaucluse
www.chateau-laroque.fr

Château St-Jacques d'Albas Minervois

At the western end of the Minervois region, Château St-Jacques d'Albas is rich in history. It was purchased by Englishman Graham Nutter and his wife Beatrice in 2001. Before that, all grapes were taken to the local co-operative. Improvements in the vineyard have been made working with consultant Jean-Pierre Cousine and adopting a holistic approach. Primarily red wines are produced, based on traditional grape varieties with the top *cuvée* La Chapelle, a 100% Syrah. There is also a Syrah rosé and a new white wine made from Vermentino, with some Viognier and Roussanne.

11800 Laure Minervois
www.chateaustjacques.com

Château St-Martin de la Garrigue
Picpoul de Pinet

The history of Château St-Martin de la Garrigue dates back to before the 9th century. The Roman chapel is referred to in documents dated August 11th, 847AD, but relics believed to be from the Iron Age were uncovered during excavations in the 1970s. The château itself has been modified many times, and possesses features typical of the 16th century. Having been virtually abandoned in the 1970s, and after a series of owners, the estate was purchased by a group of investors in 1992. Since that time, a new winery has been built, vineyards replanted with 19 different grape varieties, and a range of wines made, including a very good Picpoul de Pinet.

34530 Montagnac
04 67 24 00 40

Château Ste-Eulalie Minervois

Founded in 1996 by Isabelle and Laurent Coustal, and situated above the Roman village in La Livinière, Château Ste-Eulalie has 84 acres (34ha) of vineyard in the surrounding area. A range of Minervois wines—reds from Carignan, Grenache, and Syrah, with the top *cuvée* Cantilene aged in oak; rosé with a Cinsault base; and a Sauvignon Blanc Vin de Pays from grapes grown in Limoux—are all made by Isabelle, who is also the head of the local growers' association. Gîtes are available among the vines if you are looking for a hideaway.

34210 La Livinière France
www.chateausainteeulalie.com

Château de Sérame Languedoc

A large and very old property with a great château and lots of history, Château de Sérame is sited on what was a Roman camp at the northern border of the Corbières appellation. In 2001, the estate attracted the Bordeaux négociant Dourthe, which took over the management of the vineyard and winemaking. Dourthe has replanted more than 284 acres (115ha) of vines, and works closely with top consultant Denis Dubourdieu to make good-value AC and Vin de Pays wines.

11200 Lézignan-Corbières
www.chateaudeserame.com

Château de Valflaunès Languedoc

Winemaker Fabien Reboul made wine around the world before returning to his home village, Valflaunès, and his family's eponymous château to the north of Montpellier. Reboul's first vintage was 1998, and since then he has developed a cult following. The vineyard has 32 acres (13ha) of mostly young vines (five years), with some 30-year-old Carignan and 40-year-old Grenache. They are used to make some great wines, starting with the Cuvée Esperance, which is 80% Carignan with 10% each of Syrah and Grenache. Top wines—the T'em T'em from Syrah, and Grenache and Un Peu de Toi, a Syrah/Carignan blend—are only made in tiny quantities.

34270 Valflaunès
www.chateaudevalflaunes.com

Château La Voulte-Gasparets Boutenac

Based in the recently classified sub-appellation of Boutenac, La Voulte-Gasparets' 136 acre (55ha) vineyard stands at an average altitude of 260ft (80m) and is protected by the Boutenac hills behind it. Patrick Reverdy is a craftsman whose philosophy is to "listen to nature, live in harmony with it, respect it, and pay attention to it." His wines reflect this philosophy. The star is the Cuvée Romain Paul made from very old (45 to 115-year-old) vines with low yields. A blend of Carignan (50%) with Grenache, Mourvèdre, and Syrah aged 12 months in oak, it is dense, rich, and full of black fruits. ★Rising star

11200 Boutenac
www.lavoultegasparets.com

Clos de l'Anhel Corbières
In 2000, a young and passionate couple, Sophie Guiraudon and Philippe Mathias, purchased some very old vines near Lagrasse overlooking the Orbieu Valley at 720ft (220m) altitude. Originally less than 17 acres (7ha) of vines (including some 60-year-old Carignan, plus some Grenache and a little Cinsault and Syrah), Clos de l'Anhel has increased in size with new plantings of Syrah and Mourvèdre. All chemicals are banned here, and much of the work in the vineyard could not be carried out without the help of friends and family. ★Rising star

11220 Lagrasse
www.anhel.fr

Clos Bagatelle St-Chinian
Clos Bagatelle is situated just outside St-Chinian. It has 96 acres (39 ha) divided between Grenache, Syrah, Carignan, Mourvèdre, and Cinsault vines up to 80 years old. The estate, which has been in the Simon family since 1963, is now run by brother and sister Luc and Christine. The soil is primarily schist, producing fruit-driven wines with a dense, rich texture. The *cuvée* Veillée d'Automne is a 40/30/30 blend of Syrah/Grenache/Mourvèdre aged in Vosges and Allier oak barrels. A Muscat de Saint Jean de Minervois is also produced.

34360 St-Chinian, Hérault
www.closbagatelle.com

Clos Centeilles Minervois
Patricia Boyer and her husband, Daniel Domergue, have been at Clos Centeilles since 1990. The domaine, which is 1.6 miles (2.5km) north of the village of Siran in the heart of Minervois-La-Liviniere, was attractive for two reasons. First, despite the low rainfall in the region, they were told that the vines did not suffer from water stress. Second, the previous owner harvested Cinsault at a very high yield of 1070gal/acre (120hl/ha) without any rot. A range of reds are produced, including 100% Carignan and blends based on Cinsault. Visitor facilities include accommodation.

Campagne de Centeilles, 34210, Siran
www.closcenteilles.com

Les Clos Perdus Corbières
The name of Les Clos Perdus refers to small plots of old vines, which had been all but abandoned on forgotten, remote hillsides. The plots were re-discoverd by the duo of Paul Old, an Australian ex-dancer, and Hugo Stewart, formerly a farmer in the UK, who between them started the winery of the same name in Peyriac de Mer. Today, all grapes are grown according to biodynamic principles relating to the phases of the moon, and the estate is part of Loire Valley producer Nicolas Joly's Renaissance des Appellations group. The team now farm a total of 27 acres

(11ha) with yields as low as 90gal/acre (10hl/ha) in some parcels, which means that total annual production runs to a rather tiny 1,500–2,000 cases. ★Rising star

17 rue du Marche, 11440, Peyriac de Mer
www.lesclosperdus.com

Domaine Alain Chabanon Languedoc
Alain Chabanon bought his first plot of land in the 1980s. He says his ambition is simple: "to make superb wines," and he has achieved it. He now has 50 acres (20ha) of vines scattered around the villages of St-Saturnin, Montpeyroux, Jonquières, and the hamlet of Lagamas where the wines are made. The vineyards on stony clay and limestone soil are all farmed organically. Varieties traditional to the region are planted alongside less obvious choices such as Chenin Blanc from the Loire, which is blended with Vermentino and matured in oak or dried to produce a *vin passerillé* known as Le Villard.

Chemin de St-Etienne, 34150, Lagamas
www.domainechabanon.com

Domaine de l'Aigle Languedoc
Part of the Gérard Bertrand stable, Domaine de l'Aigle is one of the highest estates in the Languedoc at 1,475ft (450m), with views over the village of Roquetaillade in the Limoux region in the foothills of the Pyrenees. It was the former owner, Jean-Louis Denois, who proved good-quality Pinot Noir could be made here. But Denois had to be bailed out financially, selling up to Burgundy house Antonin Rodet, who in turn sold to Bertrand. Rich, ripe, oak-aged Pinot Noirs remain the focus, although Chardonnay and Chenin Blanc are also planted.

11300 Roquetaillade
04 68 31 39 12

Domaine de l'Aiguelière Languedoc
Set up in 1983, Domaine de l'Aiguelière has 60 acres (25ha) of vineyards split between 19 different parcels around Montpeyroux. Owner Aimé Commeyras specializes in old-vine Grenache and Syrah to produce complex, rich wines made to last. The top *cuvées*, Côte Rousse and Côte Dorée, are both produced from 60-year-old Syrah vines on two different soils, and aged in new oak from Nievre and Allier respectively, to give wines with great length. A delicate white wine, Sarments, with aromas of white peach and blossom is also produced from Sauvignon Blanc and Viognier, along with a 100% Grenache, Grenat, and the red blends Tradition and Tradition Boisé.

2 Place du Square, 34150 Montpeyroux
04 67 96 61 43

Domaine des Aires Hautes Languedoc
The 86 acre (35ha) Domaine des Aires Hautes at Siran in the Minervois-La-Livinière is owned by Gilles Chabert. In a wide range of wines, both AC and Vin de Pays, the top *cuvée* is the Clos de l'Escandil, which is named after the small walled vineyard in La Livinière where it is produced. Here, low-yielding, 50-year-old Grenache is grown with Syrah and Mourvèdre to give a classy, elegant wine with ripe coffee aromas. Le Combelles Minervois and the Malbec Vin de Pays are worth a look.

34210 Siran
04 68 91 54 40

CLOS CENTEILLES
THIS 2005 MINERVOIS IS A GREAT EXAMPLE OF HOW MUCH THIS APPELLATION HAS IMPROVED

CLOS BAGATELLE
VEILLEE D'AUTOMME IS A RICH, POWERFUL BLAST OF THE NEW LANGUEDOC

DOMAINE COMBE BLANCHE
THE MINERVOIS IS A CONVENTIONAL WINE
IN AN EXPERIMENTAL PORTFOLIO

Domaine de l'Arjolle Languedoc

Established by two brothers in 1974, and subsequently joined by the next generation, Domaine de l'Arjolle is a family affair that continues to innovate. Initially, plantings were with international varieties Cabernet Sauvignon, Merlot, and Sauvignon Blanc. But more quirky varieties have been introduced, including, after a trip to the United States, Zinfandel (which is used to make "z" the only 100% Zinfandel in France), Carmenère, Viognier, and Muscat à Petits Grains. Equinoxe is a deliciously delicate, aromatic, dry, barrel-fermented blend of Sauvignon Blanc, Viognier, and Muscat à Petits Grains. All the wines are sold as Vin de Pays Côtes de Thongue, with most aged in barrel.

7 bis rue Fournier, 34480 Pouzolles
www.arjolle.com

Domaine d'Aupilhac Montpeyroux

Although Sylvain Fadat comes from a long line of *viticulteurs*, Domaine d'Aupilhac, in the heart of Montpeyroux village, was only established in 1989 and a winery built in 1992. Since then, Fadat has built a reputation for high quality with particular focus on Cinsault and old-vine Carignan. The vineyards (all organic) are in two areas: 33 acres (13.5ha) on southwest-facing terraces at 330ft (100m) planted with traditional red grape varieties; and 20 acres (8ha) on cooler north-northwest-facing slopes at 1,150ft (350m), where Syrah predominates with some Mourvèdre, Grenache, and white varieties. The wines show intense fresh fruit characters.

8 rue du Plô, 34150 Montpeyroux
www.aupilhac.com

Domaine Begude Limoux

The 60 acre (25ha) Domaine Begude estate bought by British couple Catherine and James Kinglake in 2003, has wine history dating back to the 16th century. Previously owned and managed by Robert Eden, it has been farmed organically for the last 25 years, and a modern winery was built in 1993. Using Australian consultant winemaker Richard Osborne, this hilltop vineyard (at 1,300ft/400m) produces a range of wines including a Sauvignon Blanc Vin de Pays with fresh varietal flavors and zesty finish. The Limoux Chardonnay is barrel-fermented (as is the requirement for the appellation) with honeyed aromas and creamy texture on the palate.

11300 Cepie
www.domainebegude.com

Domaine Bertrand-Bergé Fitou

Based in the village of Paziols, Jerome Bertrand is a sixth-generation *vigneron*. In 1993, he withdrew from the local co-operative and created Domaine Bertrand-Bergé —now one of the leading quality producers in the region. The Fitou appellation is split into two enclaves within Corbières—one area is on the coast; the second, which includes Domaine Bertrand-Bergé, sits in the mountainous schist inland. Eighty-two acres (33ha) of low-yielding old vines (on average 60 years old) produce intensely concentrated red Fitou, Vin de Pays, and sweet wines. Cuvée Ancestrale is a blend of Carignan, Syrah, and Grenache with spicy, savory flavors.

Avenue de Roussillon, 11350 Paziols
www.bertrand-berge.com

DOMAINE DE L'ARJOLLE
EQUINOXE IS ONE OF MANY INNOVATIVE
WINES MADE AT DOMAINE DE L'ARJOLLE

Domaine Borie de Maurel La Livinière

Domaine Borie de Maurel's owner, Michel Escande, was the first president of the then newly created La Livinière appellation in 1999. Michel and his wife, Sylvie, started with 12 acres (5ha) in 1989, and have subsequently built Borie de Maurel up to more than 86 acres (35ha) today. The innovative wines are always high quality and include the flagship Cuvée Sylla made from Syrah; a 100% Mourvèdre wine, Maxime; and a sparkling Grenache Belle de Nuit. The whites are based on Marsanne blended with other varieties, such as Roussanne or Muscat.

Rue de la Sallèle, 34210 Félines-Minervois
www.boriedemaurel.fr

Domaine de Cabrol Cabardès

Domaine de Cabrol has 52 acres (21ha) of vines near Mazamet in the center of the Cabardès appellation. The owner, Claude Carayol, bought the estate in 1989 and planted Syrah, Cabernet Sauvignon, Grenache, and Cabernet Franc from 1990. Apart from a handful of old Carignan and Aramon plants, few old vines remain. The focus is very much on red wines, although a white Vin de Table from Viognier, Grenache Blanc, and Sémillon is produced. Of the reds, Vent de L'Est is a Syrah-based blend, Vent de l'Ouest is Cabernet Sauvignon, and the red blend La Dérive is aged in oak for two years.

11600 Aragon
www.domainedecabrol.fr

Domaine du Clovallon Languedoc

Domaine du Clovallon's Catherine Roque works with grape varieties not traditionally found in this region. One such is Pinot Noir, which Roque blends with 80% Syrah to make her *cuvée*, Palagret. Her choice of varieties and blends means most of the wines are produced in the more flexible Vin de Pays designation. An architect by training, Roque bought the domaine in 1989 and now has more than 30 acres (12ha). The vineyards (all organic) are north-facing at 660ft to 1,310ft (250m to 400m)—a cool climate suitable for Pinot Noir. Roque also produces Viognier of rich peach and pear flavors, and a sweet white from Muscat, Clairette, and Chardonnay.

Route Col du Buis, 34600 Bedarieux
www.clovallon.fr

Domaine Combe Blanche Minervois

Belgian Guy Vanlacker came to the Minervois region in 1981, initially tending to his vines in his spare time while working for other estates and "borrowing" their facilities to make his wine. The Combe Blanche vineyards north of La Livinière in the hamlet of Calmaic are at 660ft to 880ft (200m to 300m). Here, Vanlacker chose to go against local tradition and plant Tempranillo (at that time little known outside of Spain) and later, Pinot Noir. In 1997, he teamed up with Dominic Hanoulle from Luxembourg and built a small winery, and finally in 2000 devoted himself full-time to the development of Domaine Combe Blanche wines.

34210 La Livinière
www.lacombeblanche.com

Domaine Félines Jourdan Picpoul de Pinet

Purchased by the Jourdan family in 1983, the Domaine Félines Jourdan estate on the banks of the Thau lagoon is best known for its Picpoul de Pinet. However, it has more than 270 acres (110ha) of vines planted with 10 different grape varieties, and the majority of its production is classified as Vin de Pays. The Picpoul grape is cultivated on three different soil types, each bringing a different character to the wine—Félines gives citrus notes, La Coulette aniseed and fennel aromas, and Les Cadastres exotic fruit. Each of these elements is fermented separately, aged on the lees to give extra richness, and then blended to give a finished wine with pineapple, herbal dill aromas, and a mineral finish.

34140 Mèze
www.felines-jourdan.com

Domaine de la Granges des Pères
Languedoc
Located in Aniane, next door to the original pioneer of the region, Mas de Daumas Gassac, Laurent Vaillé chooses to spend his time and energy tending to the 27 acre (11ha) Domaine de la Granges des Pères and does not receive visitors. Following his first vintage in 1992, a certain mystique and cult following has built up around his wines, which are now considered to be among the best (and most expensive) in the region. Vines are planted on steep slopes and the greatest attention to detail applied in the vineyard. Wines are classified as Vin de Pays due to the presence of Counnoise in the blend, combined with Syrah, Cabernet Sauvignon, and Mourvèdre to give herbal, savory wines. An opulent white wine is also produced from Chardonnay and Roussanne. ★ **Rising star**

34150 Aniane
04 67 57 70 55

Domaine du Grand Crès Corbières
Hervé Lefferer was a manager at the world-famous Domaine de la Romanée-Conti in Burgundy before he bought the 12 acre (5ha) Domaine du Grand Crès in the Corbières, east of Lagrasse, near Ferrals-les-Corbières in 1989. Since then, 24 acres (10ha) of vines have been planted on land cleared of the garrigue typical of this area. The high altitude, low yields, and remoteness of these vineyards lead to little disease pressure. Using Burgundian winemaking techniques, Lefferer produces silky textured, elegant wines from this traditionally rustic region. Try the delicious white Roussanne/Viognier or Grenache-based Cressaia (classified as table wine).

40 Ave de la Mer, 11200 Ferrals-les-Corbières
www.domainedugrandcres.fr

Domaine de l'Hortus/Clos du Prieur
Languedoc
Jean Orliac and his wife, Marie-Therese, planted vineyards in this rugged land dominated by the peaks of Pic St-Loup and the Montagne de l'Hortus in the late 1970s at Combe de Fambétou. In 1995, the odd-looking wooden winery was built. Perched up on hillsides, the vineyards now cover 136 acres (55ha) and produce white, rosé, and red wines. The Cuvée Classique has lots of juicy fruit; the Grande Cuvée (Syrah/Mourvèdre/Grenache) has fresh fruit, oak, and an elegant finish. Bergerie de l'Hortus wines are sourced from neighbors, and the family owns a walled vineyard, Le Clos, at St-Jean de Buèges, where a stone winery makes Clos du Prieur.

34270 Valflaunès
www.vignobles-orliac.com

Domaine des Jougla St-Chinian
Domaine des Jougla is a family affair, located right in the middle of the appellation at Prades-sur-Vernazobre, northeast of St-Chinian village. The wine-growing history of the family goes back to 1595. Wines produced include a dry Viognier; a sweet Viognier Passerillé made from dried grapes, with aromas of white peach, apricot, and almonds; a light rosé Initiale from Syrah, Grenache, and Mourvèdre grown on schist; and a number of reds.

Prades sur Vernazobres, 34360 St-Chinian
www.domainedesjougla.com

Domaine Leon Barral Faugères
Based in the hamlet of Lenthéric, close to Cabrerolles, with 60 acres (25ha) of vines, Didier Barral is an environmentalist obsessed with soil and manure. Biodynamic principles are applied; all chemicals and weed-killers are banned. Cows are used to fertilize the soil, which is ploughed every way in order to fully "mix" the ground. Life in any shape or form is encouraged—spiders, beetles, birds, weeds—to create real biodiversity. As one would imagine, winemaking is also a natural affair. The red Cuvée Jadis blend of Syrah, Grenache, and Carignan is quite rustic in style. A white Vin de Pays blends 90-year-old vines of old Languedoc varieties such as Terret Gris and Terret Blanc with Roussanne and Viognier to give a tight, mineral style.

Lentheric Faugères, 34480 Cabrerolles
www.domaineleonbarral.com

Domaine Maria Fita Fitou
Fitou is the oldest appellation in Languedoc, established in 1948 with two enclaves at the border with southern Corbieres appellation. Marie-Claude and Jean-Michel Schmitt established Domaine Maria Fita at Cascatel-des-Corbières close to Villeneuve-les-Corbières in 2001, and have 25 acres (10ha) of vineyards in the inland area of Fitou. The couple lived for over 33 years in the Luberon where Jean-Michel set up and ran a number of restaurants, giving him the taste for producing his own wine. They now have built their reputation as one of the leading producers.

12 rue du pont-neuf, 11360 Villeneuve-les-Corbières
04 68 45 81 21

Domaine St-Antonin Faugères
After experience in other winemaking regions in France, Frédéric Albaret chose to settle in Faugères, and had his first vintage at Domaine St-Antonin in 1995. Initially 30 acres (12ha), now 50 acres (20ha), St-Antonin has a range of varieties and an average vine age of 40 years. Albaret makes three *cuvées*, aiming to produce wines that are elegant, concentrated, and for keeping. The top *cuvée*, Magnoux, has flavors of damsons and cherries, with great potential to age. The traditional Domaine St-Antonin *cuvée* offers great value for money.

34600 Faugères
04 67 90 13 24

Domaine Thierry Navarre St-Chinian
Thierry Navarre is a third-generation winegrower at Roquebrun in the north of the St-Chinian appellation. He has 30 acres (12ha) planted on brown schist terraces, with a range of grape varieties including the almost forgotten Ribeyrenc—a very old Languedoc variety that Navarre has propagated and replanted. Wines include Le Laouzil, with

THE RENAISSANCE OF CARIGNAN

At one stage, the Carignan grape variety dominated the Languedoc vineyards. However, this was not for any reason other than its high yield—up to 1780gal/acre (200hl/ha). The wines produced were high in acidity, low in alcohol, with firm, astringent, rough tannins. It is not an easy variety to grow: it buds late, is susceptible to the two main diseases of powdery and downy mildew, is prone to rot, and on top of all that, rarely ripens! For years, growers were incentivized to uproot it and to plant more "noble" quality grape varieties. However, it remained the most widely planted variety in the Languedoc until it was overtaken by Merlot in the late 1990s. Recently, however, Carignan has started to develop something of a quality following. Old gnarled bush vines, some up to 100 years old, planted on hillsides in places such as St-Chinian and Montpeyroux have come into their own. The change in fortunes is thanks to growers such as Sylvain Fadat of Domaine d'Aupilhac, (who looks for freshness, acidity, and minerality) and Jean Marie Rimbault, who believes that Carignan is a true expression of his terroir, with smoky, black fruit flavors.

its notes of tobacco and leather; La Cuvée Olivier, from very old-vine Carignan, Grenache, and Syrah, with meaty, spicy, peppery notes; and two sweet Vin Doux Naturel made from Grenache and Muscat.

Roquebrun 34460
www.thierrynavarre.com

Domaine de Villemajou Languedoc

Purchased by the father of Languedoc wine bigwig Gérard Bertrand in 1970, Domaine de Villemajou is where Bertrand first acquired his interest in wine. The estate claims to be the oldest viticultural domaine in Corbières, and in the Middle Ages it belonged to the abbey of Villemajac. It now has 345 acres (140ha) of vines, including some very old Carignan, and is at the forefront of driving the Corbières-Boutenac appellation forward.

11200 St-André-de-Roquelongue
04 68 45 36 00

La Grange de Quatre Sous St-Chinian

Of Swiss origin, Hildegard Horat came to the region in the 1990s. All her vineyards at La Grange de Quatre Sous are in the AC St-Chinian area, but Hildegard chose to plant non-permitted varieties such as Petite Arvine from her home-land, Cabernets Franc and Sauvignon, and Malbec, as well as traditional varieties from the region. The wines produced all have a distinctive character combining minerality and richness in unusual blends. All are sold as Vins de Pays.

34360 Assignan
04 67 38 06 41

Hegarty Chamans Minervois

Sitting in the foothills of the Montagne Noire near Trausse, Hegarty Chamans is owned by Sir John Hegarty, chairman, creative director, and founding partner of leading advertising agency, BBH. A black sheep is used as the logo for BBH along with the strapline "when the world zigs—zag." A black sheep also appears on Hegarty's wine labels, although it is facing the other way (which may or may not be significant!). Since Hegarty bought his 50 acre (20ha) estate in 2002, substantial investments have been made in the winery, which is a state-of-the-art, no-expense-spared affair. His partner, Philippa Crane, and Burgundian winemaker, Samuel Berger, manage the estate biodynamically.

1160 Trausse-Minervois
www.hegartychamans.com

Mas Belles Eaux Languedoc

The Mas Belles Eaux estate, part of the AXA Millésimes portfolio since 2002, consists of 220 acres (90ha) at Caux in the Pézenas subregion. It takes its name from the large number of natural springs around the property that flow into the River Peyne and the Mas (farmhouse) with its vaulted cellar, which dates back to the 17th century. A new winery was built in 2008, and improvements in the vineyard have been made by the AXA team headed up by Englishman Christian Seely. The top *cuvée*, Sainte Hélène, uses grapes from the highest hillside and is a blend of Syrah, Grenache, and Carignan, aged in French oak barrels for 15 months. It is rich, concentrated, and spicy.

34720 Caux
www.mas-belleseaux.com

DOMAINE THIERRY NAVARRE
TASTY CUVEE OLIVIER HAS A LARGE AMOUNT OF OLD-VINE CARIGNAN IN ITS BLEND

MAS DE DAUMAS GASSAC
AIME GUIBERT'S ESTATE HAS ASSUMED LEGENDARY STATUS IN THE LANGUEDOC

Mas Brugière Pic Saint Loup

The Brugière family has been farming at Valflaunès since the 13th century. Today, the family estate is run by Guilhem, his wife Isabelle, and their son Xavier. Having returned to the area in 1973, Guilhem set about planting quality varieties and in 1986 he produced his first estate wine. With 30 acres (12 ha) of vines, 80% of the production is red, producing five different *cuvées* including la Grenadière (Syrah, Grenache, and Mourvèdre aged in oak for 12 months) with its spicy peppery flavors, a rosé from Grenache and Syrah; and a white Cuvée Les Muriers, which is 80% Roussanne, 20% Marsanne, with honeyed notes and a dry finish.

34270 Valflaunès
www.mas-bruguiere.com

Mas Cal Demoura Languedoc

It was his son's passion and example that inspired lifelong *vigneron* Jean-Pierre Jullien to withdraw from the local co-operative and start making his own wine. Taking a quality focus in the vineyard, he sold off a number of parcels, only retaining the best. And so the wines of Mas Cal Demoura were born in 1993. Jean-Pierre retired in 2004, and the 27 acre (11ha) domaine is now owned and run by Isabelle and Vincent Goumard. The couple applies the same quality approach. The range of wines includes the elegant, dry white L'Etincelle from Grenache Blanc, Roussanne, Muscat, Viognier, and Chenin Blanc, and the fine, velvety red Les Combariolles from Syrah, Grenache, and Mourvèdre.

3A Route de St-André , 34725, Jonquières
www.caldemoura.com

Mas Champart St-Chinian

Matthieu and Isabelle Champart moved to the Languedoc in 1976 from Normandy and Paris respectively. The original Mas Champart estate, south of St-Chinian village, consisted of a run-down farmhouse surrounded by 20 acres (8ha) of vines. The house has since been refurbished, the vineyard expanded to 40 acres (16ha), and a winery built. The first vintage arrived in 1988, followed, in 1996, by a white wine. The Côte d'Arbo from Grenache, Carignan, and Mourvèdre is an intense red with aromas of cherry and licorice and a hint of animal.

34360 St-Chinian
04 67 38 20 09

Mas de Daumas Gassac Languedoc

In 1970, Aimé Guibert, a glove-maker from Paris, and his wife, Véronique, were searching for a family home in the Hérault. They came across an old abandoned farmhouse. The following year, their friend Henri Enjalbert, a professor of geology, told them the soil on the property would be suitable to produce "Grand Cru" wines, but that it would take 200 years for them to be accepted as such. Still, this was enough to whet the couple's appetite. Planting of Cabernet Sauvignon started the following year, using cuttings from the Médoc in Bordeaux, and by 1978 they had a winery and were visited by the famous Bordeaux consultant, Emile Peynaud. The estate, now one of the most celebrated in the Languedoc, has 86 acres (35ha) producing complex, tarry, textured wines.

Haute Vallée de Gassac, 34150 Aniane
www.daumas-gassac.com

Mas Foulaquier Pic St-Loup

Near the village of Claret, the small (20 acre/8ha) Mas Foulaquier estate was purchased, with the help of his associates, by Swiss architect Pierre Jequier in 1998. In 2003, Jequier was joined by Blandine Chauchat, bringing a further 7 acres (3ha). The team use biodynamic principles in the vineyard and only natural products in winemaking. They have extended the cellar using stones reclaimed from the vineyard and installed an automatic system to regulate the temperature. A range of wines are produced, including the premium Le Rollier *cuvée*, a blend of 40% Syrah and 60% Grenache aged 18 months in concrete tanks, and Les Calades, 60% Syrah, 40% Grenache aged for 24 months, partly in oak. ★ **Rising star**

Route des Embruscalles, 34270 Claret
www.masfoulaquier.com

Mas Jullien Languedoc

Olivier Jullien is a pioneer and a perfectionist. He established Mas Jullien in 1985 at a time when there was little understanding or belief in the quality of Languedoc wines. Although he has been a prime mover in changing those attitudes, he is always searching for ways to improve his wines. Currently he has about 37 acres (15ha) of vines around the village of Jonquières that are all farmed biodynamically but which vary dramatically according to altitude, exposure, and varietal. Under the Mas Jullien label is the serious red Syrah/Carignan/Mourvèdre blend for the long term, and a white wine from Carignan and Grenache Blanc. He also makes the approachable, earlier drinking Les Etats d'Ame wines.

Route St-André, 34725 Jonquières
04 67 96 60 04

Mas du Soleilla Languedoc

In the La Clape subregion, Mas du Soleilla was bought by the Swiss, Peter Wildbolz in 2002. It comprises 47 acres (19ha) planted with 25-year-old vines including Syrah, Grenache Noir, Mourvèdre, Merlot, Cabernet Sauvignon, Bourboulenc, and Roussanne. Among its wines are Les Bartelles, based on Syrah with some Grenache, which has flavors of black fruits, herbs, and spice, while Les Chailles is a Grenache/Syrah blend with lots of blackberry fruit. There is also a reserve white (Roussanne with Bourboulenc) and an oak-aged Vin de Pays Cabernet Sauvignon, called Jason. ★ **Rising star**

Route de Narbonne Plage, 11100, Narbonne
www.mas-du-soleilla.com

Prieuré St-Jean de Bébian Languedoc

Prieuré St-Jean de Bébian was revolutionized in the 1970s by Alain Roux, whose grandfather Maurice had purchased it in 1954. It has 79 acres (32ha) near Pézenas, planted to Rhône varieties grown from cuttings sourced at leading estates, such as Grenache from Château Rayas in Châteauneuf-du-Pape and Mourvèdre from Domain Tempier in Bandol, alongside the original Cinsault and Carignan vines. The domaine has been owned since 1994 by Chantal Lecouty and her husband, Jean-Claude Le Brun (previous owners of leading French wine magazine, *La Revue des Vins de France*), who continue to make quality wines with elegance and finesse.

Route de Nizas, 34120, Pézenas
www.bebian.com

HEGARTY CHAMANS
AD-MAN JOHN HEGARTY'S CUVEE NO1
IS LUSH BUT BEAUTIFULLY BALANCED

MAS DU SOLEILLA
LES BARTELLES IS A CHARACTERISTICALLY
SPICY, HERBY LANGUEDOC RED BLEND

La Sauvageonne Terrasses du Larzac

Owned by Englishman Fred Brown since 2001, La Sauvageonne is perched on a hill above St-Jean-de-la-Blaquière. It consists of 80 acres (32ha) at an altitude of 490ft to 1,310ft (150m–400m) in the northwest of the Terrasses du Larzac zone. There are three distinct soil types—ruffes, schist, and gres. A dry white from Sauvignon Blanc and Muscat is produced, as well as a rosé and four red wines. The *cuvée* Puech de Glen uses Syrah grown on the highest schist vineyards with low yields. Aged in oak for 14 to 18 months, it has delicious dark cherry and licorice flavors, and a lingering finish.

Route de St-Privat, 34700 St-Jean-de-la-Blaquiere
www.lasauvageonne.net

Sieur d'Arques Languedoc

Sieur d'Arques is a co-operative responsible for the production of 80% of Limoux wine. A large part of the production is sparkling wine with well-known brands, such as Aimery. However, Sieur d'Arques has also been instrumental in the development of still, barrel-fermented Chardonnay and in promoting these wines through organizing an annual auction for charity Toques et Clochers. The Quatre Clochers Chardonnay has real cool-climate elegance, with minerality and toasty oak.

Ave du Mauzac 11300 Limoux
www.sieurdarques.com

Yannick Pelletier St-Chinian

Yannick Pelletier only started his eponymous estate in the northern part of the St-Chinian appellation in 2004, but he has already developed a strong reputation. He has 24 acres (10ha) spread across different parcels and soil types, including schist, clay, limestone, and *galets*. The main grape varieties are Syrah, Grenache, Carignan, Cinsault, and Mourvèdre planted 15 to 75 years ago. A 1.2 acre (0.5ha) parcel of 50-year-old Terret Blanc was also recently purchased. Most of the work in the vineyard and in the winery is done manually, and the vineyards are in the process of conversion to organic. Three reds are made: l'Oiselet, L'Engoulevent (predominantly Grenache and Carignan, with a little Syrah and Cinsault), and the top *cuvée*, Les Coccigrues, from old vines, a blend of 70% Carignan with 15% of both Syrah and Grenache aged in oak for 18 months.

52400 Coiffy le Haut
03 25 90 21 12

Vignobles Alain Maurel Cabardès

This 215 acre (87ha) estate at Ventenac has been owned by Alain Maurel since 1973. It sits in the Cabardès appellation, where the climatic influences from the Mediterranean and the Atlantic meet. Maurel has grape varieties from both these areas (the appellation rules dictate there must be a minimum of 40% of each type in the final blends), planted at a high density of 2400 vines/acre (6,000 vines/ha) to concentrate flavors in the grapes. Three levels of wine are made using the skills of consultants Stéphane Yerles and Claude Gros: Vins de Pays Domaines Ventenac; AC Cabardès Château Ventenac; and the prestigious Mas Ventenac, an oak-aged Cabernet Franc, Merlot, and Syrah blend, with complex animal and leather notes.

1 place du Château, 11610 Ventenac-Cabardès
04 68 24 93 42

ROUSSILLON

Roussillon wine region

At the far west end of France's Mediterranean coast, in a bottom corner on the border with Spain, Roussillon can sometimes feel like a forgotten land. This natural amphitheater sits within the boundaries of the Pyrénées-Orientales department with the Corbières hills to the north, the Canigou massif to the west, and the Massif des Albères, the start of the Pyrenees, to the south. And yet, as with Languedoc, the neighbor to the east with which it is so often associated, Roussillon has much to offer the modern-day wine drinker. Quality in the region has been transformed in the past few decades, and it has become one of Europe's most progressive and dynamic winemaking regions.

Major grapes

 Reds

Cabernet Sauvignon

Carignan

Grenache

Mourvèdre

Syrah

 Whites

Bourboulenc

Clairette

Grenache Blanc

Maccabéo

Marsanne

Roussanne

Vermentino

Vintages

2009
Concentrated, rich wines, though more variable than 2005 or 2007.

2008
Concentrated wines. Some vines suffered water stress in this year.

2007
A good year produced perfumed wines with elegant fruit and concentration.

2006
An average vintage.

2005
A warm year resulted in ripe fruit and wines with good tannic structure.

2004
An average vintage.

Roussillon is split by three main rivers running west to east—the Tech, the Tet, and the Agly—and there exists a wide variety of landscapes, from small, picturesque valleys to dramatically rocky amphitheaters, creeks, and arid slopes covered in wild scrub. The diversity of the landscape is matched by the wide range of soils found within them. Roussillon terroir features quartz and gneiss interspersed between black schist, limestone, and clay.

Climatically speaking, Roussillon is characterized by 300 days of sunshine a year, which makes it second only to Corsica in France. The summer weather is dry and hot, with just 20–24in (500–600mm) of rainfall.

Make no mistake, this is a wild land. But it is one where man has been present for millennia. At Tautavel, the prehistoric remains found in the Arago Cave are among the oldest human remains ever found in Europe, dating back 690,000 years. And the landscape is dotted with evocative Cathar castles from the 11th and 12th centuries.

So much for the history. Today, Roussillon is in the grip of a vinous revolution. The area produces more than 90% of France's sweet Vin Doux Naturel (literally "natural sweet wine") wines. More recently, however, efforts have been made to produce intensely concentrated dry red and white wines. This move has been helped by the fact that Roussillon has the highest proportion of old vines planted in France. Parcels of old bush vines of

Carignan that had hitherto been almost completely abandoned, have been rediscovered. And the wines produced from those vines have helped transform Carignan's reputation. So much so that, after years during which the INAO (Insitut National de l'Origine et de la Qualité), the body that controls the rules of France's appellation system, had advised its eradication, Carignan is now becoming a star grape variety.

Of all of Roussillon's many subregions, the upper Agly Valley is arguably the most intriguing. Its distinctive soil around the village of Maury produces fine dessert wines. But it is the work of the hugely respected, pioneering winemaker Gérard Gauby that has attracted the most attention. Gauby has inspired a generation of young winemakers eager to make serious, powerful wines, while respecting nature and the environment. Indeed, a small fraternity of like-minded producers has developed around Gauby in the last 10 years. Many of those winemakers are employing biodynamic principles and the climate is certainly conducive to this method of production.

Banyuls—France's most powerful and complex Vin Doux Naturel—is produced around the ports of Banyuls-sur-Mer and Collioure from grapes grown on vertiginous terraced slopes close to the Mediterranean sea. The same area is used to make rich, powerful reds from Mourvèdre, Syrah, and Grenache, with wines named Collioure after the pretty, historic seaside port.

Cave de l'Abbé Rous

Cave de l'Abbé Rous is a co-operative in Banyuls-sur-Mer with 750 growers and 2,840 acres (1,150ha) of vineyard specializing in good-value Banyuls and Collioure wines. One of the top Banyuls Grand Crus, the Cuvée Christian Reynal, is aged for 11 years prior to bottling and has spicy fruit, orange peel aromas, and a rich palate. The red AOC Collioure Cornet & Cie is a blend of 60% Grenache Noir, 20% Syrah, 10% Carignan, and 10% Mourvèdre with intense, concentrated, rich fruits, and fine silky tannins. The white version is 80% Grenache Gris, 10% Grenache Blanc, 4% Roussanne, 3% Marsanne, and 3% Vermentino and is fermented in oak to give rich, buttery flavors.

56 avenue du Général de Gaulle, 66650 Banyuls-sur-Mer
www.abberous.com

Château La Casenove

Etienne Montès gave up his paparazzi lifestyle to return to run the family estate at La Casenove in 1994. This 125 acre (50ha) estate, about 7 miles (12km) from Perpignan, outside the village of Trouillas in the Aspres region, is a single plot with clay soils and *galets* (large pebbles). A number of varieties is planted and used to make a range of white, rosé, and red still wines and Vins Doux Naturels under the guidance of consultant Jean Luc Colombo. Red wines include La Garrigue, which has the dark fruits and touch of animal typical of Carignan, Grenache, and Syrah. Cuvée du Commandant François Jaubert, a pure Syrah, is also made.

66300 Trouillas
04 68 21 66 33

Château de Jau

The Château de Jau at Cases de Pène looks down over the Agly valley. It was purchased in 1974 by the Dauré family, who also owns properties in Collioure and Chile. The estate, first established by Cistercian monks in the 12th century, was completely renovated. Managed today by brother and sister Simon and Estelle, it represents 330 acres (134ha) of vines on a patchwork of terroirs. The wines are pretty good value for money with the red Château de Jau (52% Syrah, 30% Mourvèdre, 10% Carignan, and 8% Grenache) having abundant dark fruits and black olive flavors. The estate also has a restaurant and a contemporary art exhibition.

66000 Cases de Pène
www.chateau-de-jau.com

Clos des Fées

Clos des Fées was set up in 1999 by former sommelier, restaurateur, and wine journalist Hervé Bizeul. Over the years, Bizeul has built up the estate from the original 18.5 acres (7.5ha), buying parcel after parcel to arrive at nearly 74 acres (30ha). The vines divide into 26 plots in a number of areas—Vingrau, Tautavel, Maury, Bélésta, and Calce —up to 19 miles (30km) apart. The wines are rich and generous in style, if a little expensive, and include Grenache- and Carignan-based Les Sorcières; oak-aged Vieilles Vignes; barrel-fermented and aged Le Clos des Fées; and the rare Petite Sibérie—a tiny selection from an ancient parcel of Grenache vines at high altitude, so called because of the strong, cold winter winds there.

69 rue Maréchal Joffre, 66600 Vingrau
www.closdesfees.com

CLOS DE FEES
LE CLOS DE FEES MAKES WELL REGARDED
WINES FROM ITS SCATTERED VINEYARDS

CAVE DE L'ABBE ROUS
THE CORNET & CIE BLANC IS AN EXOTIC
BLEND OF FIVE GRAPE VARIETIES

Clos Matassa

Clos Matassa is a Franco-Kiwi collaboration. Specifically, it is the project of three people: Tom Lubbe (a New Zealander with experience in South Africa who spent two years making wine with Roussillon star winemaker Gérard Gauby), Lubbe's wife, Nathalie Gauby (Gérard's sister), and Sam Harrop MW (another New Zealander who lived and worked in London, sourcing wines for retailer Marks & Spencer). In 2002, the trio bought the Clos Matassa vineyard near the village of Le Vivier at 1,640–1,970ft (500–600m) altitude. More vines have since been acquired in the Coteaux des Fenouillèdes and around the village of Calce to give a total of 35 acres (14ha), all farmed biodynamically. Star of the range is the lifted, spicy, finely textured, and long Cuvée Romanissa, a blend of 70% Grenache, 15% Carignan, 10% Mourvèdre, and 5% Cabernet Sauvignon.

10 route d'Estagel, 66600 Calce
www.matassawine.com

Domaine de Cazes

Close to Rivesaltes, Domaine de Cazes has more than 490 acres (200ha) of vineyards on mid-slope terraces looking over the Agly valley. That makes it the largest organic and biodynamic estate in France. Originally started by Michel Cazes in 1895 with several acres, Emmanuel Cazes now produces no fewer than 90,000 bottles divided between 15 different wines each year. The spectrum runs from dry to sweet, and pale to dark amber, with the top wines being matured in oak vats for up to 20 years. The Vin Doux Naturel Muscat de Rivesaltes has elegant citrus notes, a sweet palate, and 15% alcohol, but still has a fresh, clean finish.

4 rue Francisco Ferrer BP 61, 66602 Rivesaltes
www.cazes-rivesaltes.com

Domaine des Chênes

Owned by the Razungles family for more than 100 years, Domaine des Chênes is currently managed by Gilbert and Simone and their son, Alain (who also happens to be a professor at the Institute of Oenology in Montpellier). Located at the north of the appellation near Vingrau in the foothills of the Corbières mountain range, 74 acres (30ha) of vineyard are cultivated at 984ft (300m) altitude. There is a range of dry and sweet wines, including the rich and powerful red Le Mascarou, a blend of 50% Syrah, 40% Grenache, and 10% Mourvèdre.

7 rue du Maréchal-Joffre, 66600 Vingrau
04 68 29 40 21

Domaine Força Réal

Seven miles (20km) west of Perpignan, near the village of Millas, clay stony terraces and limestone slopes between 330–1,480ft (100–450m) make up the 100 acres (40ha) of vineyards at Domaine Força Réal. There are amazing views of the Canigou peak and out toward the Mediterranean. Previously known as Mas de la Garrigues, the name was changed when Jean-Paul Henriques purchased the estate in 1989 and began a program of investments. A number of reds (sweet and dry) are made, with the spicy, herbal Les Hauts de Força Réal, a Syrah/Mourvèdre blend aged in oak for 24 months, a standout.

Mas de la Garrigue, 66170 Millas
www.forcareal.com

DOMAINE DE LA RECTORIE
THE DELICIOUS CÔTE MER IS TESTAMENT
TO THE ESTATE'S RIGOROUS APPROACH

Domaine des Foulards Rouges

Having previously worked at the Estézargues co-operative in the Southern Rhône, Jean-François Nicq took over the Domaine des Foulards Rouges at Montésquieu des Albères (6.2 miles/10km from the sea west of Collioure) in 2002. Originally 25 acres (10ha), Nicq planted a further 5 acres (2ha) on schist and gneiss slopes. Using the same techniques as at Estézargues, wines are made naturally without the use of sulfites. Frida, a 50/50 blend of 80-year-old Carignan and Grenache, is medium-bodied, with some nice chewy fruit.

10 Chemin du Roi, 66740 Montésquieu des Albères
04 68 81 53 02

Domaine Gauby

Owned by the Gauby family for many years, it was only when Gérard Gauby inherited the 27 acre (11ha) estate in 1985 that its full potential was unleashed. Gérard is now heralded as Roussillon's superstar, and he continues to inspire younger generations of winemakers. The estate, which is situated 12 miles (20km) northwest of Perpignan in the village of Calce, has expanded over the years. It now has in excess of 110 acres (45has) of vines up to 120 years old and, since 2001, it has been completely biodynamic. White wines are all classified as Vin de Pays, the reds are Côtes du Roussillon-Villages. The flagship wine, Muntada, is a blend of 45% 40-year-old Grenache Noir, 45% 120-year-old Carignan, 5% Mourvèdre, and 5% Syrah aged for 30 months in oak with the aim of producing a wine of finesse.

La Muntada, 66600 Calce
www.domainegauby.fr

Domaine Lafage

The family of Jean-Marc Lafage have been cultivating vines on Catalan soil for six generations. However, Jean-Marc himself had much broader horizons. With various qualifications in viticulture, enology, and the marketing of wine, he and his wife—also an enologist—worked in Australia, South Africa, and Chile but always knew that one day they would return. In 1996 they bought an estate, in 2001 they took over Jean-Marc's father's vineyards, and now they have a total of 340 acres (138ha) of vines in Roussillon. They make a range of good-value Vin de Pays, Roussillon-Villages, and Vins Doux Naturels, including the rich, dense Cuvée Authentique blend of Syrah, Grenache Noir, and Carignan.

Route de Canet, 66000 Perpignan
www.domaine-lafage.com

Domaine du Mas Blanc

Domaine du Mas Blanc is one of the leading estates in Banyuls. It is a family property, currently run by Jean-Michel Parcé, whose father, Dr. André Parcé, was a leader and innovator in this area, reintroducing noble varieties, helping to push through the Collioure appellation, and developing the term *rimage* in Banyuls—equivalent to Vintage Port. Some 52 acres (21ha) of old vines are cultivated on steep terraces to make three Collioure *cuvées*—Cosprons Levants, Le Clos du Moulin, and Le Junquets—as well as an exceptional range of Banyuls.

66650 Banyuls-sur-Mer
www.domainedumasblanc.com

Domaine Mas Cremat

Domaine Mas Cremat was bought by Jean-Marc Jeannin from Burgundy and his wife Catherine in 1990. Following his untimely death, the estate at Espira-de-l'Agly is now run by Catherine and son and daughter Julien and Christine, who are both following the enological trail blazed by their parents. The 86 acres (35ha) are entirely located on black schist soils. The most interesting wines are the Côtes de Roussillon blended from Grenache, Syrah, and Mourvèdre, the unoaked Cuvée l'Envie with its fresh fruit aromas, and the Cuvée Bastion aged in oak for a year giving a well-structured and balanced wine. Muscat, Rivesaltes, and Vin de Pays are also produced.

66600 Espira-de-l'Agly
www.mascremat.com

Domaine Olivier Pithon

Originally from Coteaux du Layon in the Loire Valley, and with a passion for wine from an early age, Olivier Pithon gained experience in other areas in France before falling in love with the village of Calce. After meeting Gérard Gauby, he chose to settle here. Starting in 2001 with 21 acres (8.5ha) of old-vine Carignan on schist, he has built the vineyard up to 37 acres (15ha). All are cultivated biodynamically and everything is done by hand. White and red wines are produced with original names such as Cuvée Lais (after a cow), la D18 (the name of his road), and Le Pilou (made from 60- and 100-year-old Carignan grown on chalk and shale respectively).

19 route d'Estagel, 66600 Calce
www.domaineolivierpithon.com

Domaine Piquemal

Based in Espira-de-l'Agly, Domaine Piquemal has 119 acres (48ha) in the Agly valley, run by Frank and Marie Pierre Piquemal. Their father, Pierre, was instrumental in restructuring the domaine in the 1970s and the vines have an average age of 35 years. A project is underway to build a winery on the outskirts of the village. As is the norm, Vin de Pays, AC, and sweet wines are produced. The Cuvée Pygmalion, from 70% Syrah, 25% Grenache Noir, and 5% Carignan, has black summer fruits with a touch of toasty oak and fine tannins.

1 rue pierra Lefranc, 66600 Espira-de-l'Agly
www.domaine-piquemal.com

Domaine de la Rectorie

An old family estate, Domaine de la Rectorie was inherited by brothers Marc and Thierry Parcé in the early 1980s. Since their first bottling in 1984, the pair have developed a strong reputation. Approximately 67 acres (27ha) are divided into 27 small plots at a variety of altitudes from sea level up to 1,310ft (400m) and with different exposures to the sun. Each of those plots is harvested and vinified separately. The majority of the production is red Collioure with wines from different sites such as L'Oriental (Grenache-based), Côté Mer (Grenache with Carignan and Syrah; more savory spice), and Côté Montagne (Grenache, Carignan, Mourvèdre, Counoise, Syrah; concentrated). However, white, rosé, and Banyuls (the chocolately, dense, concentrated Cuvée Léon Parcé) are also produced.

65 rue de Puig del Mas, 66650 Banyuls-sur-Mer
www.la-rectorie.com

MAS AMIEL
THIS WELL-KNOWN ESTATE HAS ENJOYED
A REVIVAL OVER THE PAST DECADE

Domaine Le Roc des Anges

Domaine Le Roc des Anges was created by Majorie Gallet in 2001. Gallet started with 25 acres (10ha) of vines near the village of Montner, including some Carignan planted in 1903. Through acquisitions, the vineyard has been extended to 62 acres (25ha). Schist soils are planted with Carignan Noir, Grenache Noir, Grenache Gris, Maccabeu, and Carignan Blanc and produce low yields. Winemaking takes place in a newly restored cellar in the village with many of the wines aged in concrete tanks to retain their fruit and allow the flavor of the terroir to shine through. The Vieilles Vignes is a rich, powerful, elegant blend of Carignan, Grenache, and Syrah. Cuvée 1903 is from the old Carignan and the white has fine, complex character.

2 Place de l'Aire, 66720 Montner
www.rocdesanges.com

Domaine Sarda-Malet

Jérôme Malet has run Sarda-Malet, which was founded by his father, since 1992. Malet works 4 113 acres (6ha) of vineyards south of Perpignan. Over the last 25 years, he has increased the proportion of Syrah and Mourvèdre while retaining old-vine Carignan and Grenache. The white Terroir Mailloles has honeyed notes and an elegant palate. The Muscat de Rivesaltes has exotic fruit and floral flavors, a sweet mid-palate, and balanced acidity.

Chemin de Ste-Barbe, 66000 Perpignan
www.sarda-malet.com

Domaine Singla

From a family of vignerons, Laurent Singla made his first wine in 2001 at the tender age of 21. He now manages 170 acres (70ha) in two domaines: Mas d'En Alby and Mas Passe Temps. The best 62 acres (25ha) are now cultivated biodynamically and go into the domaine wines. The balance is sent to the co-operative in Rivesaltes. La Pinède, with its plum fruit and medium body is produced using grapes from some of the oldest Grenache, Carignan, and Syrah vines.

4 rue de Rivoli, 66250 St-Laurent-de-la-Salanque
www.domainesingla.com

Domaine le Soula

Set up by star winemaker Gérard Gauby in the late 1990s, le Soula is based at high altitude in St-Martin-des-Fenouillèdes. The white, from Grenache Blanc, Sauvignon Blanc, Maccabeu, Roussanne, Vermentino, and Chenin Blanc, has layers of complexity and a tight mineral style. The reds, based on Grenache, Carignan, and Syrah, are complex and meaty with soft tannins.

66220 St-Martin-de-Fenouillet
04 68 64 35 19

Domaine Thunevin-Calvet

A partnership between Bordeaux *garagiste* and owner of St-Emilion's Château Valandraud, Jean-Luc Thunevin, and Jean-Roger Calvet, a young wine-grower from Maury, Thunevin-Calvet started with a handful of acres vinified in a garage. It now has 150 acres (60ha) producing wines such as Cuvée Constance, a 50/50 blend of Grenache and Syrah with ripe fruit and tobacco notes.

13 rue Pierre Curie, 66460 Maury
www.thunevin-calvet.fr

Domaine La Tour Vieille

The 30 acre (12ha) Domaine La Tour Vieille is, rather neatly, made up of 12 separate parcels around Collioure and Banyuls. Owned by Vincent Cantié and his wife Christine, the vineyards are perched on terraced hillsides falling into the Mediterranean. They have fairly homogenous schist soils, but differences in altitude and degree of influence of the wind create different characters and flavors. The couple has a strong reputation for Collioure and fortified wines using the traditional solera system as well as more modern vintage styles. The top *cuvée*, Puig Oriole, has intense blackberry aromas with a rich, concentrated palate.

12 Route de Madeloc, 66190 Collioure
04 68 82 44 82

Jean-Louis Tribouley

Another disciple of Gérard Gauby, Jean-Louis Tribouley created this 26 acre (10.5ha) estate in 2002 in the village of Latour-de-France. Stony vineyards with schist and gneiss mixed with veins of granite are all farmed organically with the use of a mule. Orchis, a Grenache-based blend, takes its name from the wild flowers that grow in the vineyards. It is rich and concentrated with blueberry flavors and muscular tannins. Other wines include the Côtes de Roussillon-Villages blends Alba and Les Copines, and a straight Carignan, Elepolypossum.

9 Place Marcel Vie, 66720 Latour-de-France
04 68 29 03 86

Mas Amiel

In 1999 Mas Amiel was sold to the then managing director of the Picard frozen food store chain, Olivier Decelle. Despite its stellar reputation, at that time the vineyard was in a poor state and sweet wines were not selling. Since his arrival, Decelle has done much to revive the 385 acre (155ha) estate in Maury, and he has now left corporate life behind to concentrate fully on Mas Amiel. Among other things, Decelle replanted 125 acres (50ha) of vines, hired a new permanent team, and recruited outside consultants such as the Bordeaux-based Stéphane Derenoncourt. Today, Mas Amiel makes a vast range of sweet Maury and dry still wines and it is recognized as the leading producer in this region.

66460 Maury
www.masamiel.fr

La Preceptorie de Centernach

La Preceptorie de Centernach is a collaboration between the Parcé family from Banyuls and growers in Maury. At St-Arnac, its cellar stands at the top of a hill overlooking the Maury valley. The rather grand name comes from the Knights Templar, who used the word *preceptorie* (preceptory) to refer to a small foundation, while Centernach is an ancient name for St-Arnac. The vineyards are scattered around the Maury appellation, and a variety of AC and Vin de Pays wines are made. Maury Cuvée Aurélie, which is named after one of the growers, is an oak-aged blend of Grenache (90%) with Carignan (10%) and has black fruit, vanilla, spicy aromas, and dense concentration.

1 Moulin de St-Arnac, 66220 St-Arnac
www.la-preceptorie.com

VIN DOUX NATUREL

The literal translation of Vin Doux Naturel is "natural sweet wine." However, this can be misleading. These sweet wines also have higher alcohol levels than dry table wines. Many table wines are fermented through to "dryness," which means the natural sugars in the grape juice are transformed by yeast into alcohol, at the same time producing all the aromatic compounds that make up the wine's aroma. For the Vins Doux Naturels, this process is arrested through the addition of alcohol which kills off the yeast, creating the combination of high sugar and high alcohol content.

Roussillon accounts for 90% of the production of France's Vins Doux Naturels. Depending on whether they are produced from Muscat or Grenache grapes and on how they are aged, these wines can have very different characters and colors. The most widely produced—Rivesaltes and Muscat de Rivesaltes—are produced throughout the region. Rivesaltes can range in style from Grenat (young and relatively fruity) to Ambre and Tuilé (aged for at least two years in oak). The areas of Maury and Banyuls produce the finest examples.

PROVENCE AND CORSICA

Provence and Corsica wine regions

Immortalized in the art of Cézanne and Van Gogh, Provence is one of France's most popular regions for tourists. They are attracted by the stunning scenery and warm climate, the history, and the local cuisine. In wine terms, this southeastern region stretches from the River Rhône in the west to the border with Italy in the east, taking in the administrative departments of the Bouches-du-Rhône, Var, Vaucluse, and the Alpes Maritimes, and a series of mountain ranges. In many respects, Provence has much in common with the Mediterranean island of Corsica (which is geographically closer to Italy). Both enjoy lots of sunshine (Corsica has the most sunshine hours of anywhere in France) as well as long, hot, dry summers, low rainfall, and mild winters.

Major grapes

 Reds

Carignan

Cinsault

Grenache

Mourvèdre

Nielluccio

Syrah

Tibouren

Whites

Clairette

Marsanne

Muscat à Petit Grains

Ugni Blanc

Vermentino (Rolle)

Vintages

2009
Although a little early to judge, this appears to be a relatively successful vintage.

2008
A vintage showing great promise across all styles

2007
Average to good vintage.

2006
A notch below 2005, with wines generally less concentrated.

2005
An average to good vintage, warm, dry conditions resulting in ripe tannins. The best red wines will continue to improve.

2004
An average vintage; the best wines can be kept.

In terms of terrain, Provence and Corsica are quite similar, ranging from coastal zones and rocky cliffs to hills and mountain peaks. They also both have a long history of being invaded and conquered, with all the influences on culture that has left behind. Traditional landscapes are the *garrigue* of Provence or *maquis* in Corsica—wild scrub with highly aromatic smells of juniper, lavender, sage, wild thyme, and rosemary.

Long before these lands became popular with vacationers, they had the habit of attracting outsiders. Marseille, France's largest commercial port and second most populous city, was founded by Phocaean Greeks in 600BCE, making it France's oldest city. And the cultivation of vines in Corsica is believed to date back to the Phoenician settlement in 570BCE, at Aleria on the east coast of the island.

The majority of Provence's vineyards are in Var, and about 80% of wine production is devoted to light-colored, dry rosé wines. However, vines are present at both extremities—from Les Baux de Provence at the western end to the appellation of Bellet north of Nice—and more serious red and white wines are also produced.

The spectacular hilltop village of Les Baux de Provence sits by the rugged Alpilles mountain range with the omnipresent mistral wind blowing. The eponymous appellation was the first to stipulate that all its wines be produced from grapes grown organically or biodynamically. The region includes the village of St-Rèmy-de-Provence, birthplace of Nostradamus in the 16th century and sometime home to Vincent Van Gogh. Just east of Aix is the small appellation of Palette. Here, no less than 35 grape varieties are permitted, and it is best known for the famous Château Simone estate.

Running eastward from Marseille is a rugged coastline interspersed with fjords known as the Calanques. This leads to the ancient fishing port of Cassis, which is protected from the mistral by the Cap Canaille, the highest sea cliff in France. Here fine, dry, white, herbal wines are made, mainly from Clairette and Marsanne. Further along the coast, the region of Bandol makes deep-flavored, Mourvèdre-based reds—some of Provence's finest.

The largest appellation is Côtes de Provence, which covers a large part of Var as well as a few other discrete areas. Around 80% of production here is rosé, and the most widely planted grape varieties are Grenache, Carignan, Syrah, and Cinsault. The appellation has a total of 13 permitted grape varieties, however, including Mourvèdre, Tibouren, Rolle, Sémillion, and Clairette, and it is often these that are used to produce the more distinguished reds and whites.

While Corsica also attracts its fair share of tourists, its landscape is wilder and less developed. About 110 miles (180km) long and 50 miles (80km) wide, the island is a series of mountains (average altitude 1,940ft /590m) around which runs a series of capes, gulfs, and sandy beaches. The first appellation was created in 1968 at Patrimonio in the north of the island, where there are chalk and clay soils particularly suited to the indigenous Nielluccio (similar to Italy's Sangiovese) and Vermentino (aka Rolle). The beautiful, wild Cap Corse, with its schist soils, produces fine dry white wines at Clos Nicrosi, as well as a delicate, citrus-flavored Vin Doux Naturel from Muscat à Petit Grains. On the west side, granite soils close to Ajaccio work well with the Sciacarello variety, which is unique to Corsica.

Château Barbeyrolles Côtes de Provence

Château Barbeyrolles, with its 30 acres (12ha) of vineyards, is owned by Régine Sumeire. Schist soils date to the Palaeozoic era and the vines are in conversion to organic viticulture. A pale rosé wine is produced from Grenache, Cinsault, Mourvèdre, and Cabernet Sauvignon; a red wine aged 18 months in oak from Grenache and Syrah. The wines are good, if a little pricey.

83580 Gassin
04 94 56 33 58

Château Crémade Palette

Located close to the small pretty village of Le Tholonet (Cézanne used to paint around here), Château Crémade is a small estate with only 22 acres (9ha) of vines. But there are no less than 25 different varieties planted here. Vines are 50 to 60 years old. The estate was purchased in 1997 by the Baud family from Burgundy and daughter Sophie, a qualified enologist, makes the white, rosé, and red wines. The rosé has no less than six principal grape varieties—Grenache, Cinsault, Syrah, Mourvèdre, Muscat, and Cabernet Sauvignon—with 10% of the blend made up of a mix of others, giving a complex nose of redcurrants, cherries, apricots, and a hint of rose petal.

route de Langesse, 13100 Le Tholonet
www.chateaucremade.com

Château de Crémat Bellet

The tiny (119 acre /48ha) Bellet AC is tucked away in the hills above Nice with vineyards overlooking the city and the Mediterranean. Château de Crémat has a history that sounds like an F. Scott Fitzgerald novel. Built at the beginning of the 20th century, it was renowned for its wild parties entertaining rich aristocrats and the likes of Coco Chanel. The estate has 27 acres (11ha) producing reds and rosés from Grenache and Cinsault aged in oak barrels. But it is particularly reputed for its white wine made from 80% Rolle and 20% Chardonnay, barrel-aged for four months to give delicious fresh, toasty vanilla notes.

442 Chemin de Crémat, 06000 Nice
04 92 15 12 15

Château d'Esclans Côtes de Provence

Château d'Esclans is an impressive, large (660 acre/267ha) property located at La Motte, southeast of the town of Draguignan. Bought in 2006 by Sacha Lichine (son of Alexis Lichine of Château Prieuré-Lichine in Margaux), it has 109 acres (44 ha) of vines planted with different grape varieties, and an average age of 80 years. The advice and expertise of both Patrick Léon (ex-Château Mouton Rothschild) and international consultant Michel Rolland are used to produce a range of no less than five types of rosé and a red wine. The entry-level Whispering Angel has fresh strawberry fruit and a supple palate. The flagship wine, Garrus, is from selected plots of some of the oldest vines, and is fermented and aged in large oak barrels to give extra richness.

4005 route de Callas, 83920 La Motte en Provence
www.châteaudesclans.com

Château du Galoupet Côtes de Provence

Situated close to the sea at La Londe les Maures, 178 acres (72ha) of the 408 acre (165ha) estate is planted with vines. From here one can see out to the so-called Iles d'Or of Pourquerolles, Port-Cros, and Ile du Levant. Old maps and documents suggest that the château dates back to the 17th century and the reign of Louis XIV, and one can still see the vaulted cellar today. Whites, rosés, and reds are made at different quality levels under different labels. The red Château du Galoupet, with its nice concentration and soft tannins, is usually a pretty safe bet.

Quartier St-Nicolas, 83250 Le Londes Les Maures
www.galoupet.com

Château Minuty Côtes de Provence

On the St-Tropez peninsula, Château Minuty's 185 acre (75ha) vineyards look out over the bay and the villages of Gassin and Ramatuelle. It was Etienne Farnet, the grandfather of current incumbents Jean-Etienne and François Matton, who set himself up here in 1936. Prior to his role managing the vineyard, François qualified as an enologist and gained experience at Château Margaux in Bordeaux and Champagne Taittinger. Jean-Etienne is responsible for marketing. Together they are focused on producing high-quality rosés (mainly Grenache-based with some Tibouren) and they have restructured the vineyard, replacing Carignan and Ugni Blanc with Grenache and Rolle.

Golfe de St-Tropez, 83580 Gassin
www.minuty.fr

Château de Pibarnon Bandol

When Henri and Catherine de Saint Victor bought Château de Pibarnon in 1978, it had a mere 9 acres (3.5ha) of vines. Some 30 years later, it comprises 125 acres (50ha). Much of that is planted on terraces in the shape of an amphitheater (now known as the Théâtre d'Epidaure), created with the aid of bulldozers and a lot of hard graft. A small amount of white wine is made from 40% Clairette, 40% Bourboulenc, and 20% others grown on the few north-facing slopes. Red wines are produced with 90–95% Mourvèdre with dark fruits, cassis, and soft, supple, ripe tannins. A fresh rosé is also made.

Comte de St-Victor, 83740 La Cadière d'Azur
www.pibarnon.fr

Château Pradeaux Bandol

Château Pradeaux is an estate at St-Cyr-sur-Mer that has been in the Portalis family since 1752. It has been through some tough times: it was devastated during the French Revolution in 1789; in the 19th century, phylloxera destroyed part of the vineyard; and it suffered again during Nazi occupation in World War II. It was resurrected by Suzanne and Arlette Portalis, and today it is run by Arlette's son Cyrille, aided in turn by his son, Edouard. Fifty acres (20ha) are planted with vines of an average age of 35 years. The red wines are robust and concentrated with 95% Mourvèdre and 5% Grenache. A 55% Mourvèdre/45% Cinsault rosé is also produced.

676 Chemin des Pradeaux, 83270 St-Cyr-sur-Mer
www.chateau-pradeaux.com

Château Romassan Bandol

Château Romassan was acquired in 1956 by the Ott family, who were originally from Alsace. The family also owned Château de Selle and Clos Mireille in the administrative department of Var. All three estates were sold to Champagne Louis Roederer in 2004. However,

CHÂTEAU PRADEAUX
POWERFUL BUT BALANCED WINES ARE PRODUCED AT THIS HISTORIC BANDOL ESTATE

CHÂTEAU D'ESCLANS
GARRUS IS ONE OF THE WORLD'S MOST EXPENSIVE ROSÉS

CLOS STE-MAGDELEINE
THE WHITE BLEND FROM THE CASSIS AC HAS
DELICATE WHITE FLOWER AROMAS

Jean-François Ott remains as the technical director and the same quality approach is followed. The domaine dates from the 18th century and is located in the village of Castellet with 183 acres (74ha) of vines planted to Mourvèdre, Grenache, Cinsault, and Sauvignon Blanc. A number of different rosé wines are produced for early drinking or keeping, with some aged in oak. The red, with a high proportion of Mourvèdre, merits keeping and improves with age.

83330 Le Castellet
04 94 98 71 91

Château Ste-Roseline
Côtes de Provence
Château Ste-Roseline was a 12th-century abbey. It takes its name from Roseline, the daughter of the Marquis de Villeneuve, who was born in 1263 and devoted her life to helping the poor before being declared a saint. Her body lies in a glass case in the Roman chapel, which is a destination for pilgrims and also contains works of art including a mosaic created by Marc Chagall in 1975. The vineyards are planted with 11 different grape varieties to produce white (Rolle, Sémillon), rosé (Syrah, Mourvèdre, Cinsault, Tibouren), and red (Syrah, Mourvèdre, Cabernet Sauvignon) wines. The pale salmon-pink rosé is delicate with notable oak character.

83460 Les Arcs-sur-Argens
www.sainte-roseline.com

Château de Selle—Domaines Ott
Côtes de Provence
Château de Selle was the first estate purchased by Alsatian agronomist Marcel Ott in 1912 at Taradeau, close to Draguignan. The 18th-century house is surrounded by 272 acres (110ha) of land, of which 150 acres (60ha) are planted to vines including Cabernet Sauvignon, Grenache, Syrah, and Cinsault. The majority of the production is rosé and, unusually for the region, this is aged in large oak casks for six to nine months to give extra weight and complexity. A small quantity of white is produced, predominantly from Sémillon, and two Cabernet Sauvignon-based red wines. The estate was sold to Champagne's Louis Roederer in 2004, but is still run by Jean-François Ott.

route Départementale 73, 83460 Taradeau
www.domaines-ott.com

Château Simone Palette
One cannot consider the tiny appellation of Palette without immediately thinking of Château Simone—with just 42 acres (17ha), it accounts for about half of the total appellation. It sits just east of Aix-en-Provence at Meyreuil, on the north-facing banks of the River Arc at the foot of the Montagne Sainte-Victoire. The château dates back to the 16th century, as the underground cellars bear witness, and has been the property of the Rogier family since 1850. Instrumental in the creation of the appellation in 1948, Simone produces white, rosé, and red wines from a plethora of varieties. However, its stellar reputation was really established for the high-quality red wines produced using traditional winemaking and extended aging in oak.

13590 Meyreuil
www.chateau-simone.fr

**CHATEAU DE SELLE—
DOMAINES OTT**
CHATEAU DE SELLE ROSE IS A SUBTLE BLEND
OF FOUR GRAPE VARIETIES

Château Vannières Bandol
Situated between the villages of Cadière d'Azur and St-Cyr-sur-Mer, Château Vannières is an historic domain dating back to the 16th century. Its 86 acres (35ha) of vineyards with south/southeast exposure are protected by the Massif Ste-Baume to the north. Vines with an average age of 40 years are planted with a high density of 2,000 plants per acre (5,000 per hectare). Varieties include Mourvèdre and Grenache for the red, Grenache and Cinsault for the rosé, with Clairette and Rolle for the white. Bandol and Côtes de Provence wines are produced.

83740 La Cadière d'Azur
www.chateauvannieres.com

Château Vignelaure
Côteaux d'Aix en Provence
Château Vignelaure feels like it is in the middle of nowhere. But vines have been cultivated here for 1,000 years and archaeologists have recently unearthed a Roman winery dating back to the first century. However, it was under the stewardship of Georges Brunet, who, during the 1960s, was the first to plant Cabernet Sauvignon in Provence, that the estate became what it is today. One hundred forty-eight acres (60ha) of Cabernet Sauvignon, Syrah, Grenache, and Merlot are planted on limestone clay at 1,150–1,575ft (350–480m). The wines are concentrated and are aged in oak barrels to add extra complexity and depth. There is also a modern art collection with works by César, Miro, Hartung, and others. The estate was owned by Irish couple David and Catherine O'Brian until 2007, when it was sold to Swedish-Danish couple, Mette and Bengt Sundström.

route de Jouques, 83560 Rians
www.vignelaure.com

Clos de Bernardi Patrimonio
Were it not for the persistence and drive of Pierre de Bernardi, the appellation of Patrimonio may not have been established in 1968 (it was the first region in Corsica to gain such recognition). It was Bernardi's father, a teacher in Patrimonio, who created the estate in 1880 with 25 acres (10ha) just 660ft (200m) from the Mediterranean sea—an incredible terroir with its own microclimate. Today, the estate is run by two of Bernardi's sons, Jean-Laurent and Jean-Paul, and the wine is made in the original small winery in the center of Patrimonio village. Of particular note is the rich and concentrated Clos de Bernardi red, made from 100% Nielluccio.

Lieu-dit Santa Maria, 20253 Patrimonio
04 95 37 01 09

Clos Mireille Côtes de Provence
The second domaine to come into the Domaines Ott fold, Clos Mireille was purchased by Alsatian Marcel Ott in 1936. Close to the sea at La Londe, near Hyères, it has 116 acres (47ha) of Sémillon, Ugni Blanc, and Rolle, and specializes in whites. Two *cuvées* are made. The Blanc des Blancs uses the three varieties, slowly fermented, aged in oak casks, and bottled eight months to a year prior to release. A small quantity of the white Blanc L'Insolent is made from Sémillon and Ugni Blanc from the oldest plots, fermented and aged in large oak barrels for eight months.

2 bis bd des Hortensias, 83120 St-Maxime
04 94 49 39 86

Clos Nicrosi Cap Corse

At Rogliano, at the top of the beautiful and rugged Cap Corse, Clos Nicrosi is the most northern vineyard in Corsica and produces some of the finest white wines on the island. It was established in 1959 by Toussaint Luigi and his brother, Paul. When the local co-operative went bust at the end of the 1960s, the brothers decided to make their own wines—a dry white 100% Vermentino and the sweet Muscat du Cap Corse. In 1993, Jean-Noël Luigi took over the running of the expanded 50 acre (20ha) estate from his uncle. He continues to do so with his son, Sebastien, and they now also make rosé and red wines.

Lieu-dit Pian Delle Borre, 20247 Rogliano
04 95 35 41 17

Clos Ste-Magdeleine Cassis

Clos Ste-Magdeleine is a beautiful domaine with 50 acres (20ha) of terraced vineyards leading right down to the sea. It is flanked to the east by the Cap du Canaille, the highest sea-cliff in France at more than 1,300ft (400m), which protects it from the ravages of the mistral wind. The domaine has been owned by the Zafiropulo family since 1920, and is currently run by descendants Georgina and François Sack with their children, Grégoire and Jonathan, who have transformed it over the past 35 years. The majority of the production is good, aromatic, floral white wines with 85% Marsanne, plus Clairette, Ugni Blanc, and Sauvignon Blanc. There is also a good rosé.

avenue du Revestel, 13260 Cassis
www.clossaintemagdeleine.fr

La Commanderie de Peyrassol
Côtes de Provence

La Commanderie de Peyrassol has a long and varied history. It can trace its origins back to the 13th century and the Knights Templar, who founded the Commanderie near Flassans-sur-Issole. Since then, its owners have included the Maltese Order, the French state, and the Rigord family, who bought the estate in 1790 and held on to it until 2001, when it was sold to French businessman Philippe Austruy. Under Austruy, the estate has been entirely renovated and a new winery built. Two quality levels of white, rosé, and red wines are produced—Commanderie de Peyrassol and Château Peyrassol (aged in oak). The white Château Peyrassol, produced from 45-year-old Rolle (70%) and Sémillon (30%) fermented in oak, is ripe and honeyed with an elegant, fresh palate.

83340 Flassans/Issole
www.peyrassol.com

Domaine de la Bastide Blanche Bandol

Domaine de la Bastide Blanche is owned and run by the Bronzo brothers, Louis and Michel. The original estate has grown from just 25 acres (10ha) of vineyards in 1972 to more than 28ha (11 acres) of vines today, all of it farmed organically. More than 60% is dedicated to the cultivation of Mourvèdre, with Grenache, Cinsault, Clairette, Ugni Blanc, Sauvignon Blanc, and Bourboulenc making up the balance. Cuveé Estagnol is 85% Mourvèdre/15% Grenache grown on clay–limestone and gravel. It has the meaty, savory nose typical of the grape variety, with hints of leather and firm concentration.

367 route des Oratoires, 83330 St-Anne-du-Castellet
www.lastide-blanche.fr

Domaine de la Bégude Bandol

Domaine de la Bégude was purchased by the Tari family (of Château Giscours in Margaux) in 1996 and is run by Guillaume Tari. The property itself is 1,240 acres (500ha), but only 42 acres (17ha) are planted with vines. At 1,310ft (400m) altitude they are the highest, as well as the northernmost, in the Bandol appellation with magnificent views over the bay of La Ciotat. Seven different grape varieties are planted to produce whites, rosés, and reds. The top *cuvée*, La Brulade, dominated by Mourvèdre, has intense blackberry fruits and a very long finish.

route des Garrigues, 83330 La Camp du Castellet
www.domainedelabegude.fr

Domaines Bunan–Moulin des Costes
Bandol

Purchased in 1961 by brothers Pierre and Paul Bunan from Algeria, Moulin des Costes has 40 acres (16ha) of vines at La Cadière d'Azur. The brothers went on to purchase Château de la Rouvière in 1969. Here, the 18th-century château sits on a steep, terraced hillside with 9 acres (3.5ha) of 50-year-old vines. The wines from both properties are made at Moulin des Costes. The Bunans' children now play an integral role in developing the business, bringing new ideas including the introduction of a Domaines Bunan label for wines blended from different properties and terroirs. All the wines are relatively well-priced for Bandol AC. If you happen to be passing through Nice, the family also own a wine shop with a good selection of wines in the old town.

83740 La Cadière d'Azur
www.bunan.com

Domaine Comte Peraldi Ajaccio

Ajaccio is probably better known as the birthplace of Napoleon Bonaparte in August 1769 than for its wines. However, vines have been grown at Domaine Comte Peraldi since the 16th century. It was restructured in 1965 by the father of current owner Guy De Poix. There are 125 acres (50ha) of vines nestled on hillsides in Mezzaviat, 3 miles (5km) from the town and the gulf of Ajaccio. The speciality of the appellation and the domaine is the Sciaccarellu grape variety, which grows on the granitic soils of this area, producing fine, light, elegant reds and rosés. The Domaine Comte Peraldi red is very much the benchmark for Sciaccarellu.

Chemin du Stiletto, 20167 Mezzavia
www.domaineperaldi.com

Domaine de la Courtade
Côtes de Provence

On the small island of Porquerolles, Domaine de la Courtade was established by Richard Auther in 1983. Today, there are 74 acres (30ha) of vines that have been farmed organically since 1999 and an olive grove with trees up to 100 years old. The estate makes white, rosé, and red wines. The La Courtade red is rich, dense, and elegant, produced from 97% Mourvèdre from selected plots, plus 3% Syrah with an average age of 12 years. It is aged in oak for 12–18 months. The white La Courtade is 100% Rolle, fermented and aged in oak barrels for 11 months, giving rich, honeyed fruit flavors.

Ile de Porquerolles, 83400 Hyères
www.lacourtade.com

PROVENCE ROSES

Provence is associated very strongly with rosé wines. This is not surprising, since more than 80% of production here is of light, dry examples of the style. Rosé wine gets its color from black grapes—more specifically from the skin of black grapes, since in the vast majority of black grapes, the fruit pulp and juice are not colored. Essentially, there are two methods of production—maceration (also known as *saignée* or skin contact) and direct pressing. In the former, grapes are picked, usually stemmed, and lightly crushed, after which the skins are left to soak in the juice for a number of hours, so that the color leaches into the juice. This is then separated from the skins and fermented. For direct pressing, as the name suggests, the grapes are put directly into a wine-press where the juice is extracted and run off directly. This method tends to give lighter-colored juices, which are then fermented in the same way. For Côtes de Provence rosé, regulations stipulate that at least 20% of the wine must be produced by the *saignée* method, and this is even higher in Coteaux d'Aix-en-Provence and Les Baux de Provence, at 30% and 50% respectively. Some producers, such as Domaines Ott, also use oak in their rosés to give extra richness and complexity.

DOMAINE RABIEGA
THE SWEDISH-OWNED RABIEGA PRODUCES
RICH, POWERFUL, GUTSY REDS

DOMAINE DES TERRES BLANCHES
AN ESTATE OF BEAUTIFUL ORGANIC WINES

Domaine de la Ferme Blanche Cassis
An old estate with 74 acres (30ha) of vines, Domaine de la Ferme Blanche was established in 1714 by the Comte François de Garnier. It has since been in the Imbert family for generations and is currently run by François Paret. The white Cuvée Excellence is a 50/50 blend of Marsanne and Clairette, while the standard white includes Ugni Blanc, Bourboulenc, and Sauvignon Blanc. A rosé with raspberry red fruit aromas is produced from Grenache Noir, Cinsault, and Mourvèdre.

route de Marseille, 13260 Cassis
04 42 01 00 74

Domaine Gavoty Côtes de Provence
At Cabasse, and close to the 12th-century Cistercian Abbey of Thoronet, Domaine Gavoty is an historic estate from the 16th century. Owned by the Gavoty family since 1806, it is currently managed by Roselyne Gavoty and her husband, Pierre. The 18th-century cellar still houses the original wooden vats. It has 110 acres (45ha) devoted to whites, rosés, and reds. The Cuvée Tradition rosé is a fruity, dry, refreshing Cinsault/Grenache blend; the Clarendon white has received much critical acclaim.

83340 Cabasse
www.gavoty.com

Domaine Hauvette Les Baux-de-Provence
Just outside the town of St-Rémy-de-Provence on the northern side of the Alpilles mountain range, Domaine Hauvette was established by Dominique Hauvette in 1982. Starting with just 5 acres (2ha), it has grown to 37 acres (15ha) today. Vines are cultivated biodynamically on clay–limestone soils rich in sea shells and fossils. The red is typically a 40/30/30 blend of Grenache, Cabernet Sauvignon, and Syrah. It is intensely concentrated, with a slightly animal character and fine tannins on the finish.

chemin Trou-des-Boeufs, La Haute Galine, 13210 St-Rémy-de-Provence; 04 90 92 03 90

Domaine Orenga de Gaffory Patrimonio
Started by Pierre Orenga in the 1960s, Domaine Orenga de Gaffory now covers 150 acres (60ha) with more than 50 acres (20ha) of 50-year-old vines. Run by Pierre's son, Henri, the vineyards are located in four sites around St-Florent, Patrimonio, Barbaggio, and Poggio d'Oletta, with traditional varieties selected according to the site's soil and microclimate, including Nielluccio, Vermentino (Rolle), and Muscat. Three ranges of wine are produced and the winery has regular contemporary art exhibitions.

Lieu-dit-Morta-Majo, 20253 Patrimonio
www.orengadegaffory.com

Domaine Pieretti Cap Corse
Lina Venturi-Pieretti took over running the family estate from her father Jean in 1989. He was a well-known character who initiated the annual Corsican wine fair in Luri every first weekend of June. Since then, the estate has grown from 7 acres (3ha) to 25 acres (10ha) of vineyards. These are planted at 330ft (100m) altitude in Santa Severa, within spitting distance of the coast near the port of Luri in Cap Corse. Among the varieties planted on rocky clay/schist soils are Nielluccio, Grenache, Vermentino, and Muscat. The winery itself, constructed in 1994, is even closer to the sea. Lina now produces a range of white, rosé, red and Muscat wines including a special *cuvée*, A Murteta, which is 100% Alicante, a variety traditionally grown in Cap Corse.

Santa Severa, 20228 Luri
www.vinpieretti.com

Domaine Rabièga Côtes de Provence
The 25 acre (10ha) Domaine Rabièga is owned by Swedish entrepreneur Anders Akesson. A vineyard has been present on the site since the 15th century, and since Akesson took over, it has been farmed organically. The best wines are the top tier, Clos Dière.

Clos Dière, 83300 Draguignan
www.rabiega.com

Domaine Richeaume Côtes de Provence
Domaine Richeaume is a respected estate at Puyloubier in the foothills of the Montagne Ste-Victoire. The German owner, Hennig Hoesch, an organic pioneer in the region, started with just 5 acres (2ha) of vines in 1972. He now has 62 acres (25ha) of Grenache, Cabernet Sauvignon (a variety he was one of the first to plant), and Syrah. Hoesch's son, Sylvain, now manages the estate, having studied enology in California and Australia. The wines are powerful and full-bodied with the top wines, such as Cuvée Columelle, aged in oak.

13114 Puyloubier
04 42 66 31 27

Domaine St-André de Figuière
Côtes de Provence
After 22 years of association with Michel Laroche in Chablis, Alain Combard decided to return to Provence and go it alone. In 1992, he bought Domaine St-André de Figuière (then 42 acres/17ha at La Londe-les-Maures). The property now has 110 acres (45ha), planted with 10 grape varieties, and is farmed organically. Combard has since been joined by all three of his children to run the estate. The rosé *cuvée* Magali (named after one of Combard's daughters) is complex, with herbal notes and spicy red fruit. A white Vieilles Vignes is produced from Rolle and Sémillon and is rich and round on the palate.

83250 La Londe-Les-Maures
www.figuiere-provence.com

Domaine Tempier Bandol
Domaine Tempier is quite simply one of the leading and most important historical estates in Bandol. It was established and put on the map in its current form by Lucien Peyraud in the period from 1940 through to his death in 1998. It was Peyraud who saw the potential of the Mourvèdre grape and pushed for this to form an important part of the appellation's regulations in 1941. Still owned by his heirs, Tempier has been run by Daniel Ravier since 2000, and he continues to make benchmark wines. The winery is close to Plan du Castellet, with the 74 acres (30ha) of vineyards in three separate areas (Le Castellet, Le Beausset, and La Cadière), each with different terroirs. The majority of the production is red wine (to classify as AC, these must be aged 18 months in oak vats) with some rosé and a small amount of white wine.

1802 chemin des Fanges, 83330 Le Plan du Castellet
www.domainetempier.com

Domaine de Terrebrune Bandol

On the edge of Ollioules village at the eastern boundary of the Bandol appellation, Domaine de Terrebrune was created by George Delille in 1963. After taking 10 years to restore the vineyards, a winery was built in 1975 and the first bottles were released in 1980. The estate, which makes reds, whites, and rosés, is now run by Delille's son, Reynald. The 67 acres (27ha) of vineyards are farmed organically on terraces on the limestone massif Gros Cerveau. The sub-soils from the Triassic age (some 200 million years ago) have a peculiar brown clay at the surface, which inspired the name of the estate.

724 chemin de la Tourelle, 83190 Ollioules
www.terrebrune.fr

Domaine des Terres Blanches

Les Baux-de-Provence

Domaine des Terres Blanches founder Noel Michelin was one of France's original converts to organics in the early 1970s. He sold up to Badouin Parmentier in 2007, but the focus remains. Ninety acres (37ha) are planted with 12 varieties. The Cuvée Aurelia Syrah/Grenache leads a portfolio of reds, whites, and rosés. Visitors can take a 45-minute walking tour around the estate.

route de Cavaillon RD-99, 13210 St-Rémy-de-Provence
www.terresblanches.com

Domaine de Torraccia Porto-Vecchio

Christian Imbert came to Corsica in 1964 and was immediately taken with the wild beauty of the island. He purchased land near Lecci some 8 miles (13km) from Porto-Vecchio and spent the next seven years clearing scrub land and planting vines. The 106 acre (43ha) Domaine de Torraccia estate is now run organically by Imbert's son, Marc. In a full range, the flagship wine is Cuvée Oriu, an 80/20 Nielluccio/Sciaccarellu blend with peppery, clove notes, medium weight and soft tannins.

Torraccia, 20137 Lecci
04 95 71 43 50

Domaine de la Tour du Bon Bandol

Located in the village of Castellet in the northeast of the Bandol appellation, Domaine de la Tour du Bon is named after a lookout tower originally used to protect the village. It is run by Agnès Henry-Hocquard, who took over from her parents at the age of 27 in 1990. She works 35 acres (14ha) of vines planted at 590ft (180m) with a 360° panoramic view of the Mediterranean and the Ste-Baume mountain. The standout wine is the Cuvée Saint Ferréol, which contains up to 90% Mourvèdre.

714 chemin de l'Olivette, 83330 Le Brûlat du Castellet
www.tourdubon.com

Domaine de Trévallon

Les Baux-de-Provence

At St-Etienne-du-Grès on the northern slopes of the Alpilles range, the 42 acre (17ha) Domaine de Trévallon was established by Eloi Durrbach in 1973. The majority of the production is evenly split between Cabernet Sauvignon and Syrah. At the time it was most unusual to plant these varieties, but the family had links with Georges Brunet, who had already proven their potential in Provence at Château Vignelaure. Despite the high quality of the wines produced, Trévallon was forced out of the AC in 1993 when new rules came in limiting the quantity permitted of Cabernet Sauvignon and Syrah. To date, all the wines produced are classified as Vin de Pays des Bouches de Rhône. Characterized by blackcurrants and tobacco, they are rich and elegant.

13103 St-Etienne-du-Grès
www.domainedetrevallon.com

Domaine de Triennes Côteaux Varois

Domaine de Triennes is a partnership between two Burgundian superstars—Jacques Seyss of Domaine Dujac and Aubert de Villaine from Domaine Romanée Conti—and Michel Macaux. The trio were originally attracted to the estate (previously called Domaine du Logis-de-Nans) for its potential: high altitude (1,480ft /450m); gentle south-facing slopes; and clay–limestone soils. The vineyard was converted to Chardonnay, Viognier, Syrah, Merlot, and Cabernet Sauvignon, and a new winery was built. A range of good varietal and AC wines are made.

route Nacional 560, 83860 Nans-Les-Pins
www.triennes.com

Mas de Cadenet Provence

Guy Négrel is the sixth generation at Mas de Cadenet at the foot of the Montagne Ste-Victoire, facing south at an altitude of 820ft (250m). Some 110 acres (45ha) of vines are cultivated in the Ste-Victoire and Côtes de Provence ACs. Several quality tiers are produced. The Prestige rosé made from Grenache, Syrah, and Cinsault is oak-aged for weight and longevity; red wines are based on blends of Grenache, Syrah, and Cabernet Sauvignon; and Rolle is used for whites—fermented in oak for Prestige; fresh and fruity for Tradition.

Chemin départemental 57, 13530 Trets
www.masdecadenet.fr

Mas de la Dame Côtes de Provence

Close to the hilltop, touristy village of Les Baux, Mas de la Dame is a beautiful property (painted by Van Gogh in 1889) lying on the southern flanks of the Alpilles range. It has 140 acres (57ha), making it the largest estate in the appellation. The property in its current form was established by Auguste Faye, a wine merchant from Burgundy, in 1903. Faye's great-granddaughters, Caroline Missoffe and Anne Poniatowski, have run it since 1993. Wine quality has been improved with the advice of consultant Jean-Luc Colombo. The Cuvée Gourmand Syrah/Grenache has dark fruit flavors.

Chemin départemental 5, 13520 Les Baux de Provence
www.masdeladame.com

Rimauresq Côtes de Provence

Rimauresq is an old estate, bought in 1988 by the Wemyss family from Scotland. The family have invested in restructuring the vineyard and in building a winery and tasting area. They have 89 acres (36ha) of vines at Pignans on the north side of the Massif des Maures. Nine grape varieties are planted on crystalline rock with sand and gravel. White, rosé, and red wines are made by chief winemaker Pierre Duffort. The R of Rimauresq rosé is pale, with notes of apricot and citrus.

Route Notre Dame des Agnes, 83790 Pignans
www.rimauresq.fr

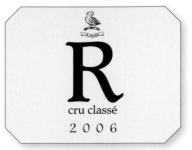

RIMAURESQ
THE RUMARESQ R RED IS FULL OF THE
GARRIGUE FLAVORS OF PROVENCE

MAS DE CADENET
MAS NEGREL CADENET BLENDS SYRAH,
GRENACHE, AND CABERNET SAUVIGNON

Bush-training vines makes them sturdy and more able to withstand the mistral wind that blows through Provence.

JURA AND SAVOIE

Jura and Savoie wine regions

The two smallest wine regions in France, Jura and Savoie are situated in the foothills of the mountains in eastern France. Jura is famous for its esoteric *vins jaunes*, including those from Château-Chalon; the rest of its highly individual range is also gaining a small cult following. Savoie's very different, light white and red wines are made from rare, local grape varieties and have, until recently, been mainly enjoyed in the ski resorts above the vineyards. With a warming climate and greater dedication to quality from a new generation of growers, including several organic producers, these food-friendly wines are gaining wider recognition. Wines from the nearby Bugey region, made with both Jura and Savoie grapes, are also improving.

Major grapes

 Reds

Gamay (Savoie)

Mondeuse (Savoie)

Pinot Noir

Poulsard (Jura)

Trousseau (Jura)

 Whites

Altesse (Savoie)

Chardonnay

Chasselas (Savoie)

Jacquère (Savoie)

Roussanne/Bergeron (Savoie)

Savagnin (Jura)

Vintages

2009
Jura: excellent for all varieties. Savoie: record ripeness levels; richer wines than normal.

2008
Jura: difficult for reds; good for whites. Savoie: decent Mondeuse and Jacquère.

2007
Jura: Savagnin and Trousseau did best. Savoie: saved by a good fall; nice Mondeuse.

2006
Jura: whites are good and reds are light. Savoie: a difficult, relatively lightweight year.

2005
Jura: a classic year. Savoie: excellent Roussanne, Altesse, and Mondeuse.

2004
Jura: Savagnin and Trousseau are best. Savoie: variable.

On the western foothills of the Jura mountains, 50 miles (80km) east of Burgundy, the hilly Jura vineyards lie on fossil-rich, clay–limestone soils, with outcrops of blue and grey marl. This distinctive soil, coupled with a northern continental climate, is ideal for Chardonnay and, in parts, for Pinot Noir, but it is the exciting Savagnin, Trousseau, and Poulsard grape varieties that give Jura wines their individuality. The tradition of making *vin jaune* by maturing Savagnin wine in old, unfilled barrels, allowing a film of yeast (similar to sherry flor) to form, and leaving it for six years before bottling, also influences other white wine styles in the area.

The two main apellation contrôlées (AC), Arbois and Côtes du Jura, are used for all styles of wines. The small AC Etoile is for whites, *vin jaune,* and *vin de paille* only, and AC Château-Chalon is used exclusively for *vin jaune.* A *vin de paille*, or "straw wine" is a luscious, long-lived wine made from grapes that were traditionally dried on straw mats to concentrate the sugars. Today, the grapes are mostly dried in well-ventilated lofts, either in boxes or hung from the rafters. Sparkling AC Crémant du Jura and *vin de liqueur* AC Macvin du Jura are made across the entire region. A *vin de liqueur* is sweet fortified wine made by adding grape spirit (marc) to the grape juice before fermentation.

The excellent-value sparkling Crémant du Jura, which is mostly 100% Chardonnay, is deservedly popular. The good producers keep better Chardonnay grapes for exciting, mineral-laden, still white wines that have a characteristic streak of acidity and rival those of Burgundy. While the best Savagnin is used for the long-lived, nutty, and spicy *vins jaunes*, and for younger oxidative whites, growers are also starting to experiment with the fresh, lemony styles of Savagnin. Jura reds,

meanwhile, are improving year after year. They are usually single-varietal wines, with earthy Trousseau being particularly exciting. Both red and white grapes are dried to make the rare, oak aged, medium to sweet *vin de paille*.

The AC Savoie covers vineyard areas scattered from the southern shores of Lac Léman near Geneva, to just south of Chambéry. Certain villages are known as a *cru*, such as Apremont and Abymes, where white Jacquère grapes are grown, Arbin for red Mondeuse grapes, and Chignin for both red and white. Crépy and Ripaille are known for their Chasselas wines. Roussette de Savoie is a separate appellation that exclusively grows white Altesse, with Frangy and Marestel being the best of the *crus*.

The climate in Savoie is influenced by the proximity of the Alps, the Isère and Rhône rivers, and several large mountain lakes. The best vineyards are located on steep slopes with poor, rocky soils that are often glacial in origin. Two-thirds of the wines are white and mainly light, dry, and floral in style, especially the ones made from Jacquère or Chasselas. Some more long-lived and intense whites are made and occasionally oaked, such as Altesse, or the rich, apricotty Roussanne, called Bergeron, that is only produced in Chignin. Light red Gamay and Pinot Noir are also produced, but it is the Mondeuse grape that gives the most interesting, savory, raspberry reds—the more serious, structured versions are often oak matured.

Bugey, a new AC to the west of Savoie, makes similar wines with Chardonnay, Gamay, Altesse, and Mondeuse grapes. The Bugey *cru* Cerdon is reserved for a delicate, semi-sweet, sparkling rosé wine from Gamay and Poulsard grapes, using the Méthode Ancestrale.

Denis and Didier Berthollier Savoie

One of Savoie's up-and-coming estates, the Berthollier brothers, Denis and Didier, are focused firmly on producing quality rather than quantity. Although their reds are improving, it is their whites that already shine. Along with very decent Chignin from Jaquère and an excellent Roussette de Savoie, they produce two Chignin-Bergerons from Roussanne grown on steep, stony slopes. The best is the complex St-Anthelme, which is aged in barrique for a few months and inspired by Denis' time working at Château de Beaucastel. ★ **Rising star**

Le Viviers, 73800 Chignin
www.chignin.com

Domaine André and Michel Quenard
Savoie

This is one of several Chignin domaines with the name Quenard. Today, it is run by Michel and his son, Guillaume, who has recently joined him after extensive wine studies. Both Michel Quenard and his wines are excellent ambassadors for Savoie. From well-exposed, steep vineyard sites, he successfully brings out the character of each grape variety and he is not afraid to experiment with oak, preferring *foudres* to barriques. Star of the reds is the deep colored, brooding Mondeuse. Among the whites, the rich, honeyed, apricotty Chignin Bergeron Les Terrasses stands out.

Torméry, 73800 Chignin
04 79 28 12 75

Domaine André et Mireille Tissot Jura

The son of André and Mireille, hard-working Stéphane Tissot has taken this Arbois estate to great heights. He farms the 99 acre (40ha) vineyard biodynamically and experiments constantly in the winery, challenging traditional Jura techniques. Most notable are five single-vineyard Chardonnays, with La Tour de Curon from a replanted, steep vineyard selling at a higher price than *vin jaune*. Stéphane's reds, aged in different sizes of oak barrel, are among Jura's best. He also makes a range of unctuous sweet wines that are sold as *vin de table*, as they do not fit the *vin de paille* criteria.

Place de la Liberté, 39600 Arbois
www.stephane-tissot.com

Domaine Dupasquier Savoie

Noël Dupasquier and son David farm seriously steep vineyards, which they harvest later than their neighbors in Jongieux. After aging both red and white wines in *foudres*, they release them a year later than other producers, at very modest prices. Understated Pinot Noir and Mondeuse reds shine in fruit, but pride of place is given to the Altesse grape for a bone-dry Roussette de Savoie and a nervy, mineral, and rich Marestel that can age for decades.

Aimavigne, 73170 Jongieux
04 79 44 02 23

Domaine Ganevat Jura

Irrepressible Jean-François Ganevat took over running his family's domaine, which is located in a sleepy village in the southern part of the region, in 1998, after 10 years' experience in Burgundy. While it remains small, he has grown the vineyard holding to 21 acres (8.5ha)—30% of

DENIS AND DIDIER BERTHOLLIER
THE 2004 VINTAGE CHIGNIN-BERGERON
SHOWS FINESSE AND ELEGANCE

DOMAINE PIGNIER
AN EXCELLENT VIN JAUNE IN THE TRADITIONAL
JURA CLAVELIN BOTTLE

which are red varieties—and converted it first to organic and then to biodynamic growing. He is best known for an exemplary Pinot Noir and an extraordinary range of 23 different *cuvées* of Chardonnay, all barrel fermented and, since 2008, mostly made without the addition of sulphites.

La Combe, 39190 Rotalier
03 84 25 02 69

Domaine Jacques Puffeney Jura

Jaques Puffeney grows all five Jura grape varieties in his vineyards in Montigny-les-Arsures, one of the largest Arbois wine villages. He transforms these grapes into some of Jura's best traditional wines. Aged in large *foudres*, his Trousseau and Poulsard reds are outstanding, with a distinctive mineral streak and delicate fruit. The Pinot Noir, also aged in barrel, is not far behind. Puffeney's whites can be fine, too, but it is his Arbois Vin Jaune, the result of rigorous barrel selection, which excels.

Quartier Saint Laurent, 39600 Montigny-les-Arsures
03 84 66 10 89

Domaine Macle Jura

Jean Macle is a living legend in the Jura. He has worked tirelessly to maintain the good name of Château-Chalon as one of France's legendary appellations. Today, his son Laurent Macle continues to consistently make the finest Château-Chalon of the appellation. Jean Macle maintains that Château-Chalon should not be drunk before 10 years after bottling (16 years after harvest). Some great vintages coming up include 1983, 1985, 1986, and 1989.

Rue de la Roche, 39210 Château-Chalon
03 84 85 21 85

Domaine Pignier Jura

Based in a 13th-century vaulted cellar and located above Jura's department capital, Lons-le-Saunier, Domaine Pignier is run by brothers and sister, Antoine, Jean-Etienne, and Marie-Florence Pignier. The wines have improved dramatically since the early 2000s, when Antoine persuaded his siblings to allow him to convert to biodynamic methods and to introduce non-traditional wines into the range. Excellent *vin jaune* and *vin de paille* are joined by a superbly elegant and steely, non-oxidative Chardonnay à la Percenette and increasingly interesting red wines, especially Trousseau. ★ **Rising star**

Cellier des Chartreux, 39570 Montaigu
www.domaine-pignier.com

Domaine du Prieuré St-Christophe
Savoie

Michel Grisard is focused on producing high-quality wines from two grape varieties: Mondeuse for reds and Altesse for Roussette de Savoie whites. He was the first grower in Savoie to convert to biodynamics and to age his wines regularly in barrique. His wines are particularly notable for their longevity; the elegant Mondeuse Tradition lasts more than 15 years and the more powerful Mondeuse Prestige, made only in some years and often reminiscent of fine Syrah, lasts even longer. Tiny quantities of superb, complex, oak-fermented Roussette de Savoie are made, which show the true potential of the Altesse variety.

73250 Fréterive
04 79 28 62 10

VINS DE PAYS

The Vin de Pays classification was created in the 1970s to provide what might be called a "third way" in French wine. Before its existence, wines were either classified as basic Vin de Table or as Appellation d'Origine Contrôlée (AC for short). The problem with this binary classification was that many wines did not quite fit into either category. Such wines were usually of a much higher standard than average Vins de Table, but the location of their vineyards and/or the manner of their production meant they did not fit into the strict AC rules. The AC system is strongly based on the notion of terroir—the idea that the soil and climate of a given place lead to wines that are unique to that place—and on the maintenance of traditional practices.

Major grapes

 Reds

Cabernet Sauvignon

Carignan

Grenache

Merlot

Mourvèdre

Syrah

 Whites

Chardonnay

Chenin Blanc

Colombard

Sauvignon Blanc

Ugni Blanc

Vintages

The various Vin de Pays appellations cover such a vast area that it is impossible to make generalizations about vintages. A great year for Vin de Pays d'Oc in the South of France, for example, could be a terrible year in the Loire. However, in the case of the best producers making wines for keeping, it is certainly worth looking out for the 2005 vintage, which was unanimously good across France. 2009 was a year of very concentrated reds in the Vin de Pays d'Oc region.

The Vin de Pays system, by contrast, is designed to be much more flexible. Which is not to say that anything goes. For example, although many Vin de Pays cover large geographical areas, they do have a broad sense of place based on the general climatic conditions that determine wine styles. Similarly, permitted yields for Vin de Pays may be higher than AC, but they are not unlimited. Finally, while a huge number of grape varieties are permitted (32 in the Vin de Pays d'Oc alone), and while the guiding principle is to allow the planting of varieties not traditionally cultivated in a given region, it is not true that Vin de Pays allows grape growers to grow any variety they like, anywhere they like.

The Vin de Pays legislation was reformed in 2009, in theory to simplify the system and to bring France into line with the rest of Europe. Vins de Pays will become Indications Géographiques Protégées (IGP), that is Protected Geographical Indications, and there is a transition period to complete this by 2011.

There are four levels of Vin de Pays, based on geographical areas that become smaller and more specific, creating a pyramid structure. At the base of the pyramid, the current Vin de Pays des Vignobles de France will become Varietal Wines of France (if they fall within the varietal labeling laws, otherwise they will become Vins de France with the other Vins de Table). Essentially, these wines can be blended across vast areas of France between the six regional Vin de Pays. A wine with a varietal on the front label must be at least 75% of that varietal, a dual-varietal must be blended 100% from the two stated varieties.

Most of still wine-producing France falls within one of these six regional IGP: Vin de Pays du Val du Loire in the north (previously Vin de Pays du Jardin de la France); Vin de Pays de l'Atlantique on the west side around Bordeaux; Vin de Pays du Comté Tolosan running further south to the Spanish border; Vin de Pays des Comtés Rhodaniens; Vin

de Pays de Méditerranée (previously Vin de Pays des Portes de la Méditerranée), and Vin de Pays d'Oc. The latter is by far the largest producer, accoung for two-thirds of total Vin de Pays wine.

At the next level in the pyramid are the departmental Vin de Pays (France is divided into 100 administrative departments) such as Vin de Pays de l'Hérault or Vin de Pays de Gard. Both in the Languedoc, these represent the largest producing departments; Hérault alone represents around 30% of total Vins de Pays production.

At the pinnacle of the pyramid are the most specific areas: zonal Vin de Pays, of which there are around 100, 54 of them within Vin de Pays d'Oc, and examples being Vin de Pays des Côtes de Thau within the Hérault department.

There are a number of reasons why a producer may decide to produce a Vin de Pays rather than an AC wine, and one certainly cannot assume that all Vins de Pays are lesser quality. Indeed, over the years a number of leading producers have chosen to go against both tradition and the AC regulations to plant non-permitted grape varieties. Their decision is based on the belief that such varieties are best suited to their particular vineyard site. In other instances, new vineyards have been established in areas that do not fall within AC boundaries. Two celebrated examples are Mas de Daumas Gassac in the Languedoc and Domaine de Trévallon in Provence. These producers have pioneered new, high-quality styles of wine and they command high prices.

In the South of France, home to the vast majority of Vin de Pays, many producers make both AC and Vin de Pays. The Vin de Pays framework allows producers to compete with countries such as Australia by making modern, varietal wine, from internationl varieties, sourcing the best value each vintage, and achieving consistency through blending. Many of the best-value Vins de Pays are made by market-orientated large companies and the better co-operatives.

Ampelidae Vin de Pays de la Vienne

Ampelidae is based in Marigny-Brizay, near Poitiers in the Vienne department, within the Vin de Pays du Val de la Loire. It was set up by the biochemist and psychologist Frédéric Brochet in 1995. Brochet, who also has a doctorate from Bordeaux University under the tutelage of celebrated winemaking consultant Denis Dourbourdieu, on the perception of wine, had been inspired to create something new in France after trips to Australia. Starting with only a few acres of land, Ampelidae now covers more than 125 acres (50ha), with vines a minimum of 30 years old and the oldest more than 100 years old. A range of modern wines are made, all aged in oak barrels and beautifully packaged in heavyweight bottles. Wines in the top range are denoted by a single letter such as K, a blend of Cabernet Sauvignon and Cabernet Franc.

Manor de Lavauguyot, 86380 Marigny-Brizay
www.ampelidae.com

Badet, Clément & Co Vin de Pays d'Oc

The young Burgundian winemakers Catherine and Laurent Delaunay started Badet, Clément & Co in 1995. With a winery base in Minervois and a team of winemakers, the duo are passionate about producing quality varietal Vin de Pays d'Oc based on their experience of the New World. The Delaunay's Les Jamelles brand is made in partnership with growers in the region and includes Chardonnay, Sauvignon Blanc, Muscat, a rosé from Cinsault, and red varieties such as Merlot, Syrah, and Mourvèdre.

39 rue de Beaune, 21220 L'Etang-Vergy
www.badet-clement.com

Clos du Gravillas Vin de Pays Côtes de Brian

In the space of just over 10 years, Nicole Bojanowski and her wines at Clos du Gravillas have come a long way. Initially, Bojanowski's plan was to plant new vineyards with Syrah, Cabernet Sauvignon, and Mourvèdre. However, in 1999 she managed to get her hands on 6 acres (2.5ha) of Carignan planted in 1911 and destined to be uprooted. She also found a parcel of very old Grenache Gris. With a total now of 15 acres (6ha) planted with 13 different grape varieties (all farmed organically), she produces no less than seven different wines. Lo Vièlh, a dense 100% Carignan Vin de Pays des Côtes de Brian, and the white Grenache Inattendu, are the best known.

34360 St-Jean-de-Minervois
www.closdugravillas.com

Domaine d'Embidoure

Vin de Pays Côtes de Gascogne

The family-owned Domaine d'Embidoure is located at Réjaumont in the northeast of the Gers department. It has been run by two sisters, Nathalie and Sandrine Ménégazzo, since 2006, and they produce a range of Vin de Pays Côtes de Gascogne including dry and sweet whites, rosés, and reds. Sixty acres (25ha) of vines are planted with 80% black grapes (Merlot, Cabernet Sauvignon, Cabernet Franc, Egiodola, Gamay, Tannat, and Syrah) plus Colombard, Chardonnay, Sauvignon Blanc, Gros Manseng, and Petit Manseng. The sisters' sweet *moelleux* wines are particularly highly regarded.

2390 Réjaumont
www.domaine-embidoure.com

CLOS DU GRAVILLAS
NICOLE BOJANOWSKI'S LO VIELH SHOWS THE POTENTIAL OF OLD-VINE CARIGNAN

DOMAINE GAYDA
CHEMIN DE MOSCOU IS A SMOOTH BUT POWERFUL SYRAH-DOMINATED BLEND

Domaine Gayda

Situated southeast of Carcassone at Brugairolles, Domaine Gayda possesses 27 acres (11ha) of vineyard here, with a further 20 acres (8ha) in Minervois and a network of suppliers in other parts of the Languedoc. Gayda's young French winemaker, Vincent Chansault, met co-owners Tim Ford (an Englishman) and Anthony Record (a South African) while he was working at Boekenhoutskloof in Franschoek, South Africa. The Gayda Chemin de Moscou is a rich, savory Syrah/Grenache blend with a touch of Cinsault.

11300 Brugairolles
www.gaydavineyards.com

Domaines Paul Mas

The Mas family have a long history of vineyards in the Hérault department but it is Jean-Claude Mas who has developed the business into what it is today. Bringing a New World approach to the region, the company owns 420 acres (170ha) with estates in Pézanas, Montagnac, and Limoux, as well as partnerships for a further 1,730 acres (700ha). His range of quality Vins de Pays d'Oc varietal brands includes La Forge Estate and Arrogant Frog.

route de Villeveyrac, 34530 Montagnac
www.paulmas.com

Domaine de Ravanès

Vin de Pays des Coteaux de Murviel

Marc Benin has a passion for Bordeaux. So when he took over the 133 acre (54ha) Domaine de Ravanès in Thézan-les-Béziers in the Aude from his father, it was no surprise that he planted classic Bordeaux varieties Merlot, Cabernet Sauvignon, and Petit Verdot. Benin leaves grape skins in contact with the juice for up to four weeks for maximum extraction, producing concentrated wines for keeping. Diogène is a 70/20/10 blend of Merlot, Petit Verdot, and Cabernet Sauvignon with ripe black fruits, licorice aromas, and fine tannic structure. Ugni Blanc is used to make a botrytised, noble-rot, late-harvest wine.

34490 Thézan-les-Béziers
www.domaine-de-ravanes.com

Domaine Tariquet

Vin de Pays Côtes de Gascogne

Tariquet's Yves Grassa was the first to plant Chardonnay, Sauvignon Blanc, and Chenin Blanc in the heart of the Armagnac region 25 years ago. It caused a stir in the region at the time, as did his decision to blend Chardonnay and Sauvignon Blanc. The Chardonnay Tête de Cuvée, aged in new oak for 12 months, is elegant with ripe fruit and vanilla. Les 4 Réserve is a blend of Gros Manseng, Chardonnay, Sauvignon Blanc, and Sémillon.

32800 Eauze
www.tariquet.com

François Lurton

François Lurton and his brother Jacques have been making fresh, modern varietal wines across the world for many years. Now on his own, François makes a number of good Vin de Pays brands: Les Bateaux, Les Salices, Les Fumes Blanches, and the organic Terra Sana range.

Domaine de Poumeyrade, 33870 Vayres
www.francoislurton.com

LES VIGNOBLES FONCALIEU
LE VERSANT IS A TYPICALLY ZESTY
SAUVIGNON BLANC FROM FONCALIEU

LAURENT MIQUEL
LAURENT MIQUEL'S REFINED SYRAHS HAVE
MADE HIM A STAR OF THE VIN DE PAYS D'OC

Gérard Bertrand

As well as owning five properties in different areas of the Languedoc, ex-rugby player Gérard Betrand has also developed partnerships with 40 growers and 10 co-operatives. Despite the size of the operation (it sells 12 million bottles worldwide each year), Bertrand remains dedicated to producing quality wines. His estate in La Clape, Château Hospitalet is also a hotel, restaurant, and *caveau*, where the full range of wines can be tasted.

route de Narbonne plage, 11104 Narbonne
www.gerard-bertrand.com

Jean Jean

A family company based in the heart of the Languedoc, Jean Jean has expanded into Roussillon, Provence, Bordeaux, and Châteauneuf-du-Pape. However, it remains most closely associated with the Languedoc, where it makes traditional AC wines as well as more innovative, fun wines for everyday drinking. An example of the latter is the Jean Jean varietal range of major grape varieties, which come in an odd-shaped bottle meant to convey "nature's turns and twists of the vines."

34725 St-Felix-de-Lodez
www.jeanjean.fr

Laurent Miquel Vin de Pays d'Oc

Laurent Miquel is a qualified mechanical engineer by trade. But, inspired by his father's passion for wine, he studied enology and, after gaining experience with a local merchant, he started his eponymous winery in 1996. Based at the family estate, Cazal Viel in St-Chinian, Laurent has established relationships with like-minded growers and produces a range of Vins de Pays d'Oc. His specialities are Viognier and Syrah. The Verité Viognier is produced from low-yielding plots and fermented in oak to give peachy, honeyed aromas and a generous palate.

Hameau Cazal Viel, 34460, Cessenon-sur-Orb
www.laurent-miquel.com

Maison Virginie

Maison (formerly Domaines) Virginie was one of the first estates in the region to use an Australian winemaker. Originally owned by the Belgian Pierre de Groot, it has been a part of the Castel group since 1999. Winemaker Cédric Jenin works with 100 partner-growers and has a reputation for good-value wines.

No visitor facilities
www.maisonvirginie.org

Producteurs Plaimont

Based in the heart of the rural and isolated Armagnac region, the members of the Plaimont co-op used to be major suppliers of grapes for distillation. As sales of Armagnac declined, however, they switched their attention to making aromatic, crisp, herbal Vin de Pays Côtes de Gascogne and Comté Tolosan wines. The driving force behind this switch was André Dubosc, who, along with a group of wine-growers, created Plaimont in 1979. From the beginning, Dubosc's focus was on producing fresh wines that express the varietal characters of Colombard and Sauvignon Blanc.

32400 St-Mont
www.plaimont.com

Skalli

Robert Skalli was one of the pioneers of varietal wines in the South of France. He comes from a strong wine background: his family made wine in Algeria in the 1920s, and his father returned to France in 1961 to set up a business importing Algerian wines, as well as planting vines in Corsica. In 1974, Skalli developed a cellar in the town of Sète, and over the next 10 years he encouraged growers in the Languedoc to improve wine quality through planting "improving" varieties such as Chardonnay, Sauvignon Blanc, Syrah, Merlot, and Cabernet Sauvignon. Skalli was the first to produce these varietal wines in the 1980s; his company is still vital.

No visitor facilities
www.robertskalli.com

Val d'Orbieu

Val d'Orbieu was founded in 1967 by a handful of producers wanting to "share their passion and skills." By the 1980s, the group had grown to more than 100 producers. Each member winery makes its own wine, while Val d'Orbieu looks after the distribution. A variety of AC and Vin de Pays wines are produced. The flagship brand is the Cuvée Mythique: the reserve red is a blend of the best barrels of Syrah, Mourvèdre, Grenache, and old Carignan; the white, a blend of Roussanne, Viognier, Marsanne, and Grenache Blanc.

12 rue du Rec de Veyret, 11104 Narbonne
www.valorbieu.com

Les Vignobles Foncalieu

Foncalieu is a group of more than 1,600 growers, with 22,000 acres (9,000ha) of vines and 19 wineries in Languedoc, Provence, the Southern Rhône Valley, and Gascony. The majority of the wines produced are Vin de Pays, although the group does also make AC wines. Winemaking is led by Nathalie Estribeau, who works closely with the growers to determine picking times. Her aim is to stagger the harvest in order to produce an array of different aromas and flavors in the grapes. This is perhaps best exemplified by the Sauvignon Blanc, which has mineral, herbal, and nettle notes as well as riper tropical fruit. The wines are clean, fresh, and good value.

Domaine de Corneille, 11290 Arzens
www.foncalieuvignobles.com

Les Vins de Vienne

Les Vins de Vienne is the work of three leading producers from the Northern Rhône—Pierre Gaillard, Yves Cuilleron, and François Villard. It was set up with a view to re-establishing vineyards at Seyssuel above Vienne after the trio came across 17th-century references to vineyards in the area. The first vineyards were planted in 1996, on south-facing schist slopes on the east of the Rhône river, in a protected spot. The company makes three Syrahs: Sotanum, Heluicum (from more recent plantings), and Taburnum (a parcel selection). The whites, produced from Viognier, include Taburnum Blanc, which has 18 months in 80% new oak to give delicate floral and vanilla aromas, a rich palate, and a long finish. These wines are Vin de Pays since they fall outside any appellation. However, the company also acts as a négociant for AC Rhône wines.

42410 Chavanay
www.vinsdevienne.com

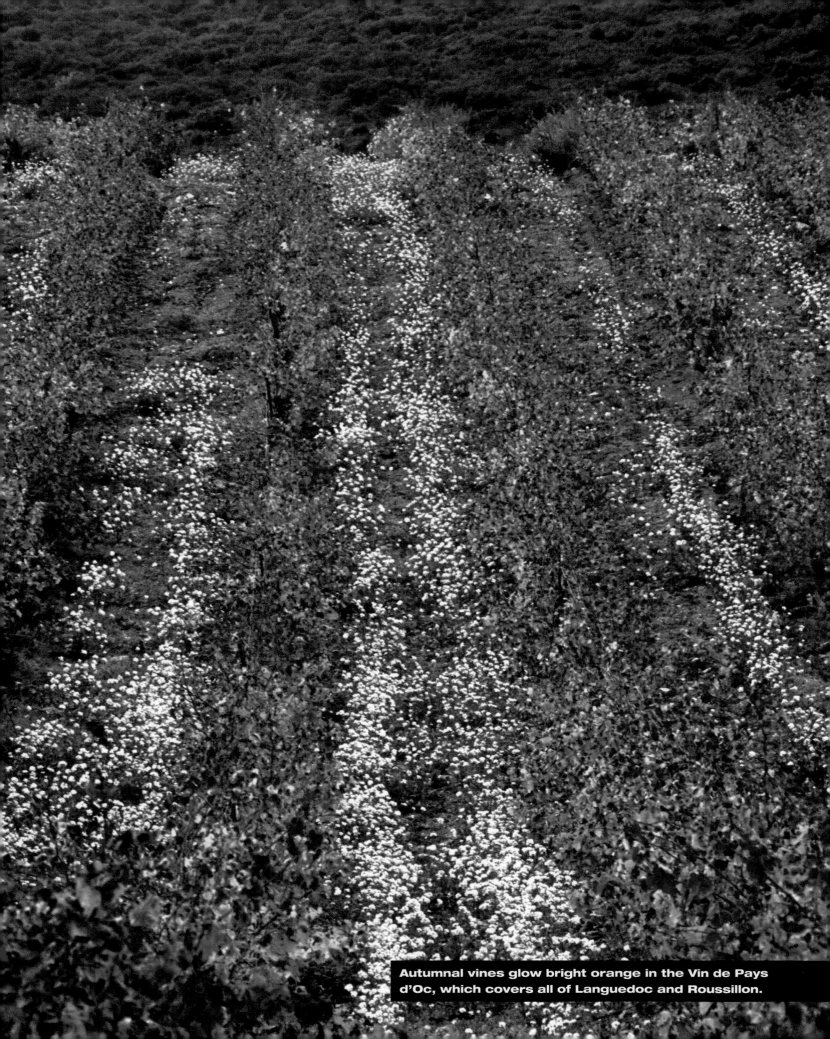

Autumnal vines glow bright orange in the Vin de Pays d'Oc, which covers all of Languedoc and Roussillon.

There has never been a better time than now to enjoy Italian wine, although you could say that this moment has been a long time coming. Wine production has been part of Italian history for millennia: the ancient Greeks, in building their city-state colonies in Southern Italy and Sicily, called their new land "enotria," the land of the vine. To the north, the Etruscans introduced cultivation practices that can still be seen today. Later, the Roman Empire's thirst for wine led to the spread of the vine throughout Europe.

Despite that long history, however, the Italian wine industry as we recognize it is largely a modern construct. Somewhere in the centuries between the fall of Rome and the first release of Sassicaia, wine mostly assumed an everyday, almost earthy role. The average Italian peasant grew grapes in addition to other crops; whatever was not used for the homebrew was sold in bulk to a nearby co-operative and consumed in the local market. That could have been the end of the story, but during the 1960s and 70s, a few producers began to look beyond their home regions for inspiration. In fact, were it not for the efforts of producers such as Angelo Gaja in Piemonte, the Antinori and Frescobaldi families in Tuscany, and Mastroberardino in Campania, to name a few, it is possible that an entire generation of young Italians might never have decided to give up city life and resurrect the small vineyards originally planted by their grandparents.

These vineyards drive today's dynamic industry, and have wine professionals from every corner of the globe looking for Italy's next new thing. It is hard to imagine another wine-producing country

ITALY

NORTHWEST ITALY

Northwest Italy is one of the most diverse fine wine regions in the world, with an impressive variety of indigenous grapes grown in distinctive terroirs that range from mountain terraces and Alpine valleys to sun-baked hills just a few miles from the coast. Amazingly, this diversity is preserved, and, in fact, relished by a high proportion of small grower estates making relatively low quantities of wine. Large wine companies are rare in this region, and yet even they tend to reflect the artisanal attitudes of their neighbors. The Northwest is arguably Italy's most significant and vibrant wine region, boasting a gastronomic heritage that is second to none, and a proud, passionate people eager to share this bounty with visitors.

Major grapes

 Reds

Barbera

Dolcetto

Nebbiolo

 Whites

Arneis

Cortese

Petite Arvine

Vintages

2009

A very hot summer led to ripe wines. In general, a good, potentially very good, vintage for all of Northwest Italy.

2008

Cooler temperatures, with rain in the summer. Earlier-ripening varieties fared worse than later-ripening ones. Potentially very good for Nebbiolo.

2007

A ripe, warm year, but with a cooler late summer and fall; should be a very good vintage across the region.

2006

Uneven conditions, though there are good Dolcettos and Barberas to be had; in Liguria, it was a good year for Pigato.

2005

Generally a warm year, with ripe, balanced wines across the region.

2004

Cool throughout the summer, with a dry, even harvest period; approaching classic levels for Barolo and Barbaresco.

Few wine regions in the world inspire the kind of passion, excitement, and outright lust that one finds among those devoted to the wines of Northwest Italy. The region centers on Piemonte (Piedmont), one of Italy's most renowned and important cultural centers, and framed almost entirely by mountains. Spiraling outward from Piemonte, Northwest Italy includes the provinces of Valle d'Aosta to the north, Lombardy to the east, and Liguria to the south. In terms of area, the region is, like much of Italy, relatively compact. But given the terrain—undulating hills, towering mountains, large rivers—Northwest Italy can often feel much bigger than it actually is.

If Piemonte is the heart of Northwest Italy, then the heart of Piemonte—and the soul, too—is the finicky, noble Nebbiolo grape. And while Barolo and Barbaresco—the medieval towns that lend their names to two of Italy's most magnificent wines—represent the apex of Nebbiolo, you will find Nebbiolo-based wines off the beaten track, in zones like the Roero, Gattinara, and Valtellina in Lombardy.

Spend some time tasting through various takes on the Nebbiolo grape and you will come to understand why lovers of Barolo are at least twice as obsessed as burgundy aficionados. Giacomo Conterno's Monfortino versus La Tàche from Domaine de la Romanée-Conti? Game on.

Piemonte's other major red grapes, such as Dolcetto and Barbera, tend to get overshadowed by loftier Nebbiolo bottlings. In truth, these are the wines that most often grace the dinner table in Piemonte. Dolcetto's dark, inky charms make it a go-to red during the colder months, while the naturally high levels of acidity found in Barbera speak of that grape's impressive versatility. And, with a few exceptions—like Vietti's Barbera Scarrone—these wines tend to be modestly priced, affording casual drinkers a chance to sample the diverse terroir and winemaking styles found in Piemonte. Move from Barbera and Dolcetto to Grignolino, Pelaverga, Ruchè, and Freisa and you enter pretty serious enthusiast territory.

White wines from Northwest Italy have lagged behind the reds, at least in perception. However, in recent years, growers of Arneis in the Roero, Cortese in Gavi, or Petite Arvine in the Valle d'Aosta have taken these grapes to new levels. And for some of the most compelling white wine in Italy, venture across the Maritime Alps to the coastal strip of Liguria. Here you can find everything from simple, refreshing whites to sip while lounging on the Italian Riviera- to complex, minerally wines made from Pigato and Vermentino.

When it comes to sparkling wine, Franciacorta and Oltrepò Pavese, both traditional method wines from Lombardy, rank among Italy's most complex. And while in Oltrepò Pavese, keep an eye out for distinctive still reds made from Pinot Nero.

Northwest Italy offers a wealth of choice for nearly every level of wine drinker. Be warned, though: it is a road that once taken, often proves irresistible. Real passion is contagious.

NORTHWEST ITALY

Mountains define the wine regions of Northwest Italy, even those found in coastal Liguria. As such, the inland areas of Piemonte, Valle d'Aosta, and Lombardia (Lombardy) all boast a cooler continental climate that belies the proximity of the sunny Mediterranean. These conditions make for some of Italy's most complex wines. Nebbiolo, the region's most important grape, is an early budding and late-ripening variety that reaches its zenith in the terroirs of Piemonte, and in the signature wines of Barolo and Barbaresco.

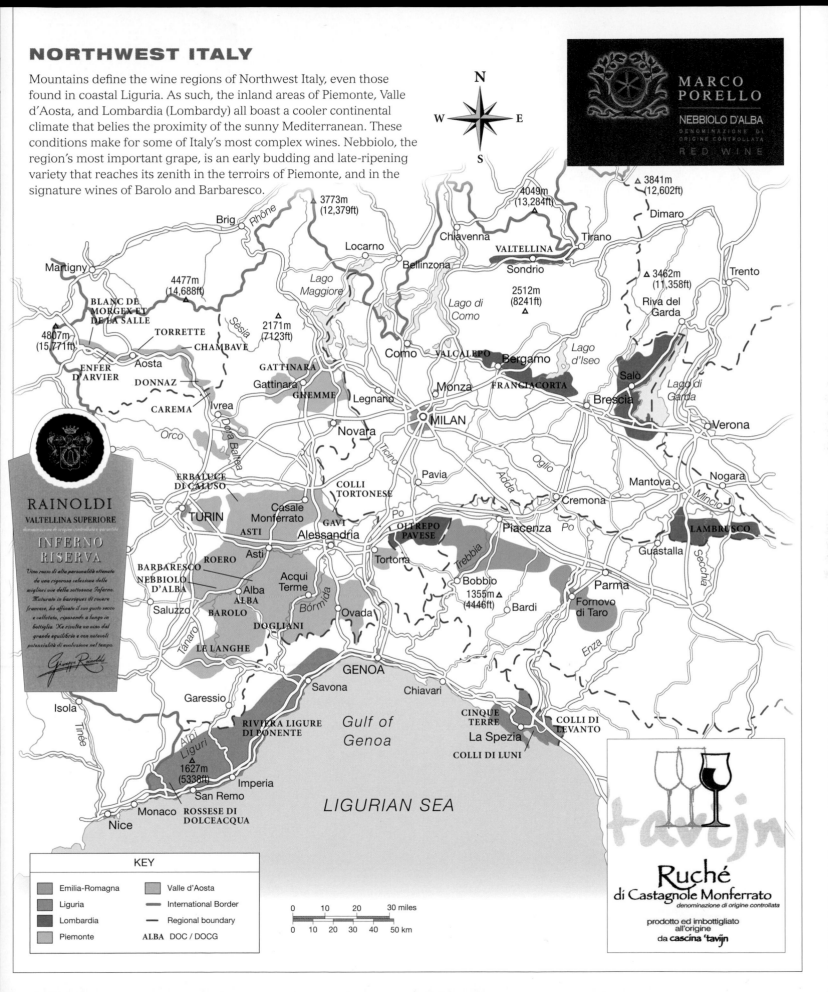

MARCO PORELLO
NEBBIOLO D'ALBA
DENOMINAZIONE DI
ORIGINE CONTROLLATA
RED WINE

RAINOLDI
VALTELLINA SUPERIORE
denominazione di origine controllata e garantita
INFERNO
RISERVA
Vino rosso di alta personalità ottenuto
da una rigorosa selezione delle
migliori uve della sottozona Inferno.
Maturato in barriques di rovere
francese, ha affinato il suo gusto secco
e vellutato, riposando a lungo in
bottiglia. Ne risulta un vino dal
grande equilibrio e con notevoli
potenzialità di evoluzione nel tempo.
Giuseppe Rainoldi

Ruché
di Castagnole Monferrato
denominazione di origine controllata

prodotto ed imbottigliato
all'origine
da cascina 'tavijn

KEY

Emilia-Romagna	Valle d'Aosta
Liguria	—— International Border
Lombardia	— Regional boundary
Piemonte	**ALBA** DOC / DOCG

0   10   20   30 miles
0 10 20 30 40 50 km

ARPEPE

THIS SINGLE-VINEYARD WINE SHOWS
REMARKABLE CLARITY AND FRESHNESS
ON THE PALATE

Ada Nada Barbaresco

Carlo Nada first planted vines in the Barbaresco hills near Treiso in 1919. This small estate includes almost 2.5 acres (1ha) in the prestigious Valeirano *cru*, and is run today by Carlo's great-granddaughters, Anna Lisa and Sara Nada. The stylish Barbaresco Valeirano is Ada Nada's top wine, combining gentle, gripping tannins and brisk acidity informed by the relatively high altitude of the site. Be sure to try the Barbaresco Elisa, a selection made from the Valeirano *cru*. Gentle and pretty, with fine-grained tannins, it is Nebbiolo at its most charming.

Via Ausario 12, 12050 Treiso
www.adanada.it

Agostino Pavia e Figli Asti

This 17 acre (7ha) estate bottles three top expressions of Barbera: Bricco Blina, Moliss, and La Marescialla. Bricco Blina is fermented in stainless steel and represents a typical unoaked expression of Barbera that accentuates the variety's vivid fruit. La Marescialla comes from the other extreme; aged in small barriques, it combines concentration and soft tannins. Moliss occupies the middle ground; aged in larger barrels and casks, it shows the earthy, savory side of Barbera, yet finds structure in acidity rather than oak. The result is an understated, elegant, food-friendly wine.

Regione Bologna 33, 14041 Agliano Terme
www.agostinopavia.it

Alario Claudio Diano d'Alba

Claudio Alario's family have grown grapes in Diano d'Alba for over a century, but the winery itself dates from 1988. Dolcetto is the heart of Alario's production, from old vines planted in crumbly tufa soils. Costa Fiore, Alario's most pure expression of Dolcetto, is filled with bright fruit framed by gentle tannins that give the wine a mineral edge. Montagrillo balances dry tannins with extracted sour cherry flavors, perfect for pairing with roasted game. As a side note to the Dolcetto, Alario's first Barolo was released in the mid-1990s. ★ **Rising star**

Via S Croce 23, Diano d'Alba
0173 231808

Albino Rocca Barbaresco

This 44 acre (18ha) estate is spread between the communes of Barbaresco, Nieve, and San Rocco Seno d'Elvio—the heartland of the Barbaresco zone. Run today by Angelo Rocca, Albino Rocca is responsible for two noteworthy Barbarescos. Vigneto Brich Ronchi is a stylish Nebbiolo that feels supple and generous; Vigneto Loreto is a more traditionally styled wine aged in large oak casks, and built for the long haul. Albino Rocca also makes one of the better Chardonnays in the Langhe: Da Bertu is a bright, zesty expression of the region's soils.

18 Strada Ronchi, 12050 Barbaresco
www.roccaalbino.com

Aldo Marenco Dogliani

This small estate is located in the Dolcetto-covered hills of Dogliani. Dolcetto and Barbera grapes are organically farmed (Marenco has been certified for over a decade), and tend toward a more rustic style—the kind of robust red wines you would casually drink with a weekday dinner at home. The bright, juicy flavors of Surì, made from vines grown at Pironi, a village near Dolgiani, are a fine introduction to the pleasures of unoaked Dolcetto. Marenco's best Barbera is Pirona, a hearty red that belongs on the dinner table.

Frazione Pamparato, Borgata Pironi 25, 12063 Dogliani
www.marencoaldo.it

Aldo Rainoldi Valtellina

Aldo Rainoldi, the son of a prominent local merchant, started this winery in 1925, and his family continues to run it today. Located in the middle of Valtellina in Chiuro, Rainoldi claims top Nebbiolo terraces in the region's subzones of Sassella, Grumello, Inferno, Maroggia, and Valgella. Look for its "classic" wines from these names—aged in large casks, they show the finesse and elegance possible with Nebbiolo in this region. The Sfursat—similar to Amarone in being made from air-dried grapes—is powerfully concentrated and intense. Try it with a pungent cheese, such as Taleggio.

Via Stelvio, 23030 Chiuro
www.rainoldi.com

Angelo Gaja Barbaresco

The Gaja family history in Piedmont stretches back nearly three centuries, but it was Angelo Gaja who thrust the family name into the limelight beginning in the 1960s. He was at the forefront of his generation's embracing of temperature-controlled fermentations, small barriques, and the use of French grapes. That he did so in then staunchly traditional Barbaresco only added to his notoriety. Later, Gaja began blending his single-vineyard Nebbiolos with Barbera; both Sorì Tildin and Sorì San Lorenzo carry the Langhe Rosso designation. Collectors may swoon over these wines, but Gaja's straight-up, traditionally-styled Barbaresco is consistently among the most complex expressions of Nebbiolo in the region.

Via Torino 36, 12050 Barbaresco
0173 635255

Anna Maria Abbona Dogliani

Anna Maria Abbona's family history is a common story among growers in the Langhe hills. Her grandfather, Giuseppe, first planted vines in the 1930s; his son later ran the estate while working in industry, and sold grapes to the local co-operative. In 1989, after hearing of her father's decision to tear out the vines, Anna Maria and her husband abandoned their urban careers to rebuild the family winery. In the years since, Abbona has helped elevate Dolcetto to new heights in Dogliani. Her vines, especially Maioli, a vineyard planted by her grandfather, yield concentrated and powerful expressions of this indigenous variety. ★ **Rising star**

Frazione Moncucco 21, 12060 Farigliano
www.amabbona.com

Antichi Vigneti di Catalupo Ghemme

The Arlunno family have farmed vines in Alto Piemonte for generations. In 1969, after the Ghemme DOC was created, Carlo Arlunno took over the family vineyard; in 1977, the Arlunno vineyard became Antichi Vigneti di Catalupo. Today, the winery produces a range of Nebbiolo-based wines (here called Spanna), including two ageworthy, single-vineyard bottlings called Carellae and Breclemae. Catalupo's straight Ghemme is

ANTICHI VIGNETI DI CATALUPO

A WINE WITH VELVETY TANNINS, VIOLET
FLAVORS, AND A CLASSIC, RUSTIC ACIDITY

traditionally made, and is a good window into this particular zone. For casual drinking, there is Il Mimo, a young, delightful Nebbiolo wine that is all about pleasure.

Via M Buonarroti 5, 28074 Ghemme
www.cantalupo.net

ArPePe Valtellina

Arturo Pelizzatti Perego re-founded his family's historic winery (dating from the 1860s) in 1984 after regaining ownership from a corporation. He renamed the estate ArPePe and set about crafting elegant, bracing wines from Nebbiolo. Pelizzatti Perego died in 2004, leaving his son Emanuele and daughter Isabella to run the estate. Located in the middle of Valtellina, at the base of the Grumello subzone, ArPePe makes a range of individualistic wines that show how profound Nebbiolo from this pre-Alpine region can be. Start with the ethereal, unforgettable Sassella Vigna Regina. ★ **Rising star**

Via Buon Consiglio 4, 23100 Sondrio
www.arpepe.com

Azelia Barolo

Established in 1920 by the grandfather of current proprietor Luigi Scavino, Azelia is a notable producer of Barolo from the Bricco Fiasco *cru*. The family owns about 6 acres (2.5ha) of vines that are up to 40 years old. The intensity typical of the site is matched in the cellar with a light, modernist touch, and as a result Azelia's Barolo Bricco Fiasco boasts a plush, generous texture to balance the wine's taut acidity. Do not miss the Dolcetto Bricco dell'Oriolo, a sexy take on the region's classic table wine.

Via Alba-Barolo 53, 12060 Castiglione Falletto
www.azelia.it

Azienda Agricola Antoniolo Gattinara

One of the leading estates in Gattinara, Antoniolo was established in 1948 by Mario Antoniolo. His daughter Rosanna, along with her son and daughter, run the estate today. Of the three single-vineyard wines at the estate, look for the earthy, savory-edged Gattinara Osso San Grato as an affordable and earlier drinking alternative to the pricier Barbaresco or Barolo. And do not miss the Coste delle Sesia, a grippy, young Nebbiolo fermented in tanks, meant for drinking at the dinner table with pasta dishes like ravioli with brown butter and sage.

Piemonte corso Valsesia 277, Gattinara
0163 833612

Azienda Agricola Conterno Fantino
Barolo

Conterno Fantino is contemporary by Langhe standards, both in terms of style and history. Established in 1982 by Guido Fantino and Claudio Conterno—both from families with long winemaking traditions—Conterno Fantino makes a style of Barolo that favors elegance and seamlessness. Barolo Sorì Ginestra, the estate's top wine, comes from the Ginestra *cru* in Monforte. It feels soft and plush thanks to careful tannin management, with big flavors that will appeal to drinkers of bold New World reds. The chewy Dolcetto Bricco Bastia is also worth seeking out.

Via Ginestra 1, Monforte d'Alba
www.conternofantino.it

Bartolo Mascarello Barolo

Bartolo Mascarello was heralded for many years as the guardian of tradition in the Langhe. When many of his neighbors switched to small barrels and short fermentations, Mascarello would move in the opposite direction, producing old-school Barolo fermented for weeks without temperature control and aged in large casks, and always as a blend rather than a single-vineyard. Mascarello died in 2005, leaving his daughter Maria-Teresa in charge of the estate, including vines in the *crus* of Cannubi, San Lorenzo, and Rué. Also not to be missed are the winery's Dolcetto and Barbera, both lovely examples of each variety.

Via Roma 15, 12060 Barolo
0173 56125

Bellavista Franciacorta

Vittorio Moretti established Bellavista in 1977, when he acquired the vineyards that would make up the grand estate found today. Bellavista spans almost 470 acres (190ha) in the heart of the Franciacorta zone between Brescia and Bergamo. For an introduction to Italy's noble *metodo classico* sparkling wine, look for Bellavista's elegant and precise entry level Cuvée Brut. The Gran Cuvée contains a larger percentage of reserve wine, and is accordingly richer and more complex. Also of note is the Gran Cuvée Satèn, made completely from Chardonnay from a single vintage.

Via Bellavista 5, 25030 Erbusco
www.bellavistawine.com

Bisson Liguria

Pierluigi Lugano started Bisson in Chiavari, on the Ligurian coastline, in 1978, first as a wine shop and then, as he began to purchase bulk wine and later grapes, a full winery. Bisson specializes in traditional white varieties like Vermentino, Pigato, and Bianchetta Genovese, all cultivated in steeply terraced vineyards that practically rise from the sea. Look for the Vermentino Vignaerta, a saline-tinged, mineral-driven expression of this classic Mediterranean grape. Not to be missed is Ü Pastine, Bisson's elegantly structured selection of Bianchetta Genovese. Both wines naturally pair with seafood.

Corso Gianelli 28, 16043 Chiavari
www.bissonvini.com

Boroli Barolo

First established in the 1990s by Silavano and Elena Boroli, and run since 2000 by their son, Achille, Boroli makes polished, elegant wines from Nebbiolo, Dolcetto, and Barbera. These latter varieties, in the form of the Dolcetto Madonna di Como and the Barbera Quattro Fratelli, offer exceptional value—they are two wines that over-deliver in terms of flavor and complexity. Boroli also controls sections of the *crus* Cerequio and Villero; the Barolo *normale* is a nuanced, expressive red, while the Barolo Villero is built for the cellar.

Frazione Madonna di Como 34, 12051 Alba
www.boroli.it

Braida di Giacomo Bologna Asti

Few individuals in Piedmont have done more for their grape variety of choice than what Giacomo Bologna has accomplished with Barbera. Long considered a rustic,

BARBERA: THE PEOPLE'S WINE

When it comes to Piedmont's great wines, Nebbiolo tends to hog the limelight. But if Barolo is the wine of kings, then the humble, affordable Barbera is the people's wine. Grown almost everywhere in Piedmont, Barbera is prized by growers for its dark color, moderate tannins, and high acidity—precisely the qualities that make it such a food-friendly wine.

Barbera also presents an opportunity to appreciate the different winemaking styles on display in Piedmont, from light and fruity to extracted and rich. Some producers, like Vietti in Castiglione Falletto, make serious, ageworthy Barbera. Scarrone is their single-vineyard Barbera, a concentrated, powerful wine buffed out in French oak. Venture to the Asti and Monferrato regions and Barbera takes center stage. Producers like La Casaccia, with their elegant Calichè, or Cascina 'Tavijn, with their deliciously quaffable, traditionally made Barbera d'Asti, are helping to put this under-appreciated grape on the map.

BRUNO ROCCA

THIS ELEGANT WINE MAY REWARD
CELLARING FOR UP TO 20 YEARS

acidic red of passing interest, Bologna treated the Barbera from his Braida estate in the manner of a Nebbiolo grower in Treiso or La Morra. Bologna's wines, both in terms of concentration and use of oak, show a modern touch, yet the wines themselves feel classic. The *cru* Bricco dell'Uccellone, aged in barriques for a year, balances energetic acidity and firm tannins; it will age beautifully.

Via Roma 94, 14030 Rocchetta Tanaro
www.braida.it

Broglia Gavi

Established by Piero Broglia, who rented his father's 180 acre (73ha) farm and vineyard, La Meirana, in 1972, Broglia today produces a modern, clean style of Gavi with the help of consulting enologist Donato Lanati. The basic Gavi di Gavi La Meirana is the best bet, with crisp flavors and a generous texture that make it a perfect match for grilled fish. Gavi Bruno Broglia is a single-vineyard selection from older vines, planted in the 1950s. It is highly concentrated for Gavi, with the mineral depth and richness to handle roast chicken.

Località Lomellina 22, 15066 Gavi
www.broglia.eu

Bruna Liguria

Riccardo Bruna started this winery in 1970 with the intention of becoming a specialist in Pigato, a local Ligurian variety related to Vermentino. His daughters run the estate today, and they have largely succeeded in realizing that vision. From vineyards located close to the French border in western Liguria, Bruna makes two striking Pigatos from different soils. Villa Torrachetta is from grapes grown in fossil-laden clay, while Le Russeghine is grown in reddish, iron-heavy soils. U Baccan, made from a selection from old vines planted in both soils, is one of Italy's top whites.

Via Umberto 81, 18020 Ranzo
www.brunapigato.it

Bruno Giacosa Barbaresco

Bruno Giacosa transcends the notion of traditionalists versus modernists in the Barolo and Barbaresco zones. Indeed, Giacosa's wines are among the best produced in Italy, vehicles that clearly represent the country's diversity of soil, climate, and winemaker passion. Powerful, bold, and austere in their youth, Giacosa's wines are meant to evolve in the cellar. With time, the Barolo becomes a refined expression of Nebbiolo, while the Barbaresco is utterly mesmerizing in its beauty. In exceptional vintages, such as 2001 or 2004, look for Giacosa's epic red label, single-vineyard wines like Barbaresco Asili or Barolo Le Rocche del Falletto.

Via XX Settembre 52, Neive
www.brunogiacosa.it

Bruno Rocca Barbaresco

Few modernist Barbaresco producers achieve the combination of textural elegance and intensity with Nebbiolo that Bruno Rocca does at his small estate. First established by his father in 1958, Rocca took over the estate in 1978, the same year that he made his first vintage of Barbaresco. That his wines handle the oak so well is a testament to Rocca's land. In addition to plots in Treiso and Neive, Rocca farms 12 acres (5ha) of the famous Rabajà *cru*. His cellar-worthy Barbaresco Rabajà typically shows elegance and firm structure.

Cascina Rabaja 29, 12050 Barbaresco
www.brunorocca.it

Bruno Verdi Oltrepò Pavese

Bruno Verdi began bottling wines from his family's vineyards shortly after the end of World War II. His son, Paolo, runs the winery today, having modernized vinification and viticulture practices in the estate's vineyards. From the Cavariola site comes Verdi's ageworthy Oltrepò Pavese Rosso Riserva, a blend of Croatina, Uva Rara, Ughetto, and Barbera. Buttafuoco is a Croatina/Barbera blend that is lighter in style, with a forward juiciness that calls out for food. Also of note is the zippy, bright Riesling Renano.

Via Vergomberra 5, 27044 Canneto Pavese
www.verdibruno.it

G B Burlotto Barolo

Giovan Battista Burlotto established this historic estate in the august commune of Verduno in the late 19th century. Burlotto was one of the few regional wineries of that era to establish a name outside of Italy, and its wines regularly won awards at European exhibitions during the 1880s. The estate is centered on the Monvigliero *cru*, from which Burlotto offers an elegant, profoundly aromatic take on Nebbiolo that hints at Verduno's potential to take its place alongside the zone's more famous communes. Do not miss the feisty Pelaverga, an indigenous grape that the winery rescued from extinction.

Via Vittorio Emanuele 28, 12060 Verduno
www.burlotto.com

Cà Viola Dogliani

Giuseppe ("Beppe") Caviola started the Cà Viola winery in 1991, around the same time that his role as a winemaking consultant began to take off (he has consulted for Villa Sparina, Sella and Mosca, and Damilano). Caviola does not shy from aging his Dolcetto and Barbera in French barriques, although the wines, on the whole, feel superbly balanced. Look for Bric du Luv, a seamless blend of Dolcetto and Barbera that is all about finesse. Made without oak is Barturot, a potent, concentrated Dolcetto that harmonizes brightness and structure. ★ **Rising star**

Borgata San Luigi 11, 12063 Dogliani
www.caviola.com

Ca' del Bosco Franciacorta

When Maurizio Zanella established his winery at his parents' Ca' del Bosco estate in the early 1970s, he was determined to make quality wines in the model of great French regions like Champagne and Burgundy. Ca' del Bosco has certainly come close with sparkling wine, especially with releases like the Cuvée Prestige, a precise, vibrant expression of Franciacorta. Echoing current trends in Champagne, Ca' del Bosco has also released a no-dosage sparkler called Dosage Zéro Millesimato. The estate makes serious still wines as well, including top-flight Chardonnay and Pinot Noir.

Via Albano Zanella 13, Erbusco
www.cadelbosco.com

BROGLIA

A CRISP WINE WITH GENEROUS TEXTURE—
A GREAT ACCOMPANIMENT TO SEAFOOD

Ca' Rome' di Romano Marengo
Barbaresco

Romano Marengo established this 12 acre (5ha) estate in 1980, after logging nearly 30 years as an enologist. His son, Giuseppe, joined as winemaker in 1993, and together they craft a style of Barbaresco that straddles the line between modern flash and old-school earthiness. The Marengos employ both small barriques and large oak casks in the aging of their Nebbiolo, a middle ground that translates to a light touch in the cellar. Look for the Söri Rio Sordo, an elegant, complex expression from one of Barbaresco's top sites. ★ Rising star

Via Rabaja 36, 12050 Barbaresco
www.carome.com

G Camerano e Figli Barolo

Camerano is a small, traditionalist producer of estate wines located in the commune of Barolo. Established in 1875, the winery is run today by Francesca and Vittorio Camerano. The family owns land in both the Terlo and Cannubi-San Lorenzo vineyards, two excellent sites for Nebbiolo. Camerano's Barolo Cannubi-San Lorenzo is aromatically powerful, with an elegant, vibrant structure. The Barolo Gold Label, sourced from the Terlo vineyard, feels more masculine, with earthy tannins and strong minerality. Dolcetto and Barbera grow alongside the Nebbiolo at the estate, and both are worth seeking out.

Via Roma 10, 12060 Barolo
www.cameranoBarolo.net

Cantina del Pino Barbaresco

Renato Vacca runs this small winery situated in the heart of Barbaresco. Vacca's family have lived in the region for generations, yet Cantina del Pino is a relatively new-wave producer here. With vineyards concentrated in and around the famed Ovello *cru*, the estate also happens to make incredibly good Barbaresco. The *normale* bottling typically represents Nebbiolo at its most charming, with bright floral scents to lift the earthy fruit. Ovello, on the other hand, is powerful and firm, and its earthy flavors are matched by fine red fruit. Give it time in the cellar. ★ Rising star

Via Ovello 31, 12050 Barbaresco
www.cantinadelpino.com

Cantine Giacomo Ascheri Barolo

Matteo Ascheri directs the efforts of this family of long-time grape-growers and merchants based in Bra. Ascheri is composed of three estates: Sorano in Serralunga, Rivalta between La Morra and Verduno, and Montalupa in the Roero. Sorano's vineyards were planted in the mid-1990s and yield two Barolos, the eponymous Sorano and the Barolo Sorano Coste & Bricco. The latter wine sees a bit more new oak, and is softer in texture. Barolo Vigna dei Pola, from Rivalta, is an early-drinking Barolo with lifted aromas and gentle tannins.

Via G Piumati 23, 12042 Bra
www.ascherivini.it

Cascina Morassino Barbaresco

Roberto Bianco is a talented young winemaker working with one of Barbaresco's most noteworthy *crus*, Ovello. Cascina Morassino has just over 9 acres (3.5ha) of vines within the *cru*, which Bianco and his father Mauro tend

BRUNO GIACOSA
THIS IS A POWERFUL AND BOLD SINGLE-VINEYARD WINE MADE FOR THE CELLAR

CASTELLO DI VERDUNO
THIS TRADITIONALLY STYLED BAROLO IS DELICIOUS WHEN YOUNG, BUT AGES WELL

themselves by hand. There are two Barbarescos: one is labeled as Ovello, a powerful, potent expression of Nebbiolo that needs time in the cellar to tame its hard tannin; the other wine is from the Morassino vineyard, which is located within the Ovello *cru*. Lighter and more perfumed in style, the latter displays the feminine expression of Nebbiolo. ★ Rising star

Strada Da Bernino 10, 12050 Barbaresco
0173 635149

Cascina 'Tavijn Asti

Nadia Varrua runs the cellar at this small, traditionally minded estate near Asti. The Varrua family have worked these vineyards since 1908; today, the work is split between Nadia Varrua in the cellar and her father, Ottavio, in the vineyard. Vines are cultivated with organic methods, while only spontaneous fermentations and large oak casks are used in the winery. The Barbera d'Asti is refreshing and lean, with nervy acidity and focused flavors of earth and berries. Likewise, the Ruché di Castagnole Monferrato feels vibrant under its inky, dark flavors. Try it with Taleggio, a local cheese. ★ Rising star

Frazione Monterovere 10, 14030 Scurzolengo
www.cascinatavijn.it

Cascina degli Ulivi Gavi

Stefano Bellotti took over his family's farm in 1977, when he was 18 years old. Belloti worked the land organically and, starting in 1984, he eventually transitioned to biodynamic practices. Today, Cascina degli Ulivi is a vibrant farm that supports approximately 54 acres (22ha) of vineyards, as well as several extra acres of wheat, fruit trees, and vegetables, in addition to livestock. The estate's Gavi is lively and rich, with pronounced mineral character. Filagnotti is a more radical take on Cortese—fermented in wooden vats, it is an intensely structured Gavi that can age. ★ Rising star

Strada della Mazzola, 15067 Novi Ligure
www.cascinadegliulivi.it

Cascina Val del Prete Roero

Mario Roagna of Cascina Val del Prete is one of the Roero's top winemakers, in part because of the excellent amphitheater-shaped vineyard land his parents bought in 1977. Bartolomeo and Carolina had been sharecroppers on this farm, and Val del Prete remains a working farm beyond viticulture. Mario Roagna mixes organic and biodynamic practices in his farming, and the resulting wines feel lively and expressive. Luet, a single-vineyard Arneis, is bracing and vibrant. And do not miss Roagna's two Barberas, the forward Serra dei Gatti and the complex, oak-aged Carolina. ★ Rising star

Strada Santuario 2, 12040 Priocca
www.valdelprete.com

Castello di Verduno Barolo

Castello di Verduno has belonged to the Burlotto family since the early 1900s, although it is the work of the current proprietors, Gabriella Burlotto and Franco Bianco, along with enologist Mario Andrion, that makes this winery one to watch. Castello di Verduno makes clean, traditionally styled Barolo from two *crus*, Massara and Monvigliero, and Barbaresco from Faset and Rabajà. These elegant, aromatic wines are delicious when young,

FAMIGLIA ANSELMA
A SAVORY, POWERFUL WINE THAT
HAS BEEN AGED IN OAK CASKS AFTER
A LONG FERMENTATION

but age beautifully in strong vintages. The winery also specializes in Verduno's native Pelaverga, a variety that yields a zesty, bright, and savory red. ★**Rising star**

Via Umberto 9, 12060 Verduno
www.castellodiverduno.com

Ceretto Barolo

The best Barolo tends to come from artisan producers making a small amount of wine. Yet there are large companies like Ceretto who not only produce quality wine at several price levels, but also rank among the region's leading wineries. Established in the early 20th century, Ceretto is today one of the larger landowners in Piedmont, with approximately 300 acres (120ha) of vineyards spread between Barolo, Barbaresco, and the Roero. Beyond the excellent single-vineyard Barolos—Bricco Rocche is a standout—Ceretto's Blangè Arneis helped put this local variety on the map.

Località San Cassiano 34, 12051 Alba
www.ceretto.com

Chionetti Dogliani

Quinto Chionetti is one of the leading producers in Dogliani. Established in 1912 by Quinto's grandfather, Giuseppe, the estate today includes vineyards in two of the zone's best *crus*, San Luigi and Briccolero. The Dolcetto from these sites shows remarkable concentration and structure, thanks to impressive fruit tannins. These deeply textured wines are not for the faint of heart, yet there is also a lightness to them thanks to bright acidity. Briccolero grows more elegant after a few years in the cellar and forms a strong argument for aged Dolcetto.

Frazione San Luigi 44, 12063 Dogliani
www.chionettiquinto.com

Ciabot Breton Barolo

Luigi Oberto established this 29 acre (12ha) estate in 1960, and for decades he sold much of his production to larger wineries. Oberto was joined in 1990 by his daughter Paola and son Marco, and together they tend vineyards that include sections of four *crus* located between La Morra and Verduno. Ciabot Breton's Barolo *normale* is blended from three sites: Bricco San Biagio, Roggeri, and Rive. It is a traditionally styled wine with lifted floral notes and strong acidity. The Barolo Roggeri is firm and structured for time in the cellar.

Frazione S Maria I, 12064 La Morra
www.ciabotbreton.altervista.org

Cigliuti Barbaresco

Renato Cigliuti took over this 16 acre (6.5ha) estate at the top of the Serraboella hill in 1964. His work over the last several decades helped establish the west-facing vineyards on this hill as one of the most important Barbaresco subzones in the Neive area, and Cigliuti's Barbaresco Serraboella remains the iconic expression of the site. The use of both small barriques and large casks for the aging of the wine helps it to maintain a balance between a soft, generous mouthfeel on the one hand, and a firm, powerful structure on the other.

Via Serraboella 17, 12057 Neive
www.cigliuti.it

ELIO GRASSO
AN AGEWORTHY BARBERA FROM ONE OF
THE TOP PRODUCERS IN BAROLO

Claudio Vio Liguria

Ettore and Natalina Vio established this small estate in the 1970s. Their son, Claudio, tends the vines today, producing a small amount of Pigato and Vermentino, as well as a blended red table wine. The Pigato is a subtle expression of minerality and tart, snappy fruit, while Vio's Vermentino tends toward greater richness, with lasting flavors of bitter almond and lime. Both wines share an energy and tension that places them firmly among the wave of exciting new Italian white wines. ★**Rising star**

Frazione Crosa 16, 17032 Vendone
018 276338

Contadi Castaldi Franciacorta

This leading Franciacorta estate was established in the early 1990s by Vittorio Moretti of nearby Bellavista. Notable for wines that capture the region's potential for ripeness, yet maintain a clear flavor and energy, Contadi Castaldi produces a range of sparkling and still wines from more than 300 acres (120ha) of vineyards. Look for the Franciacorta Brut, a toasty, elegantly formed sparkling wine that shows real complexity. Not to be missed, too, is the rosé, a nervy sparkler that feels savory and firm, with a razor-like acidity. ★**Rising star**

Via Colzano 32, 25030 Adro
www.contadicastaldi.it

Conti Sertoli Salis Valtellina

This ancient noble family started bottling wines in 1869, although wine production at the Salis palazzo in Tirano dates back much further; the underground 16th-century cellars remain in use today. One of the most striking wines produced here is the white Chiavennasca (the local name for Nebbiolo). The juice is immediately separated from the skins, and the result is a refreshing blast of tart cherries. Among the reds, look for the elegantly defined Grumello or the brawny Inferno, which shows the earthen side Nebbiolo can achieve in Valtellina.

Via Stelvio 18, 23037 Tirano
www.sertolisalis.com

Coppo Canelli

Established in the town of Canelli as a producer of sweet, sparkling Moscato in the 1900s (there is an impressive network of tunnels in the cellar under the house), Coppo is today responsible for a wide range of wines including Barbera, Grignolino, and Freisa, along with international varieties like Cabernet Sauvignon and Chardonnay. Look for L'Avvocata, a juicy Barbera with mouthwatering acidity that is aged in large casks. Mondaccione is a barrique-aged Freisa that balances fruit and spice, while Moncalvina is the family's floral Moscato, marked by gentle, sweet fruit.

Via Alba 68, 14053 Canelli
www.coppo.it

Damilano Barolo

The Damilano family has been involved in winemaking for a few generations, but the winery's history really began in 1998 when cousins Paolo and Guido Damilano took over the operation. Recently, the winery expanded its holding in Cannubi, making it a leading player in the region. Beyond Cannubi, Damilano draws from top sites like Liste, Fossati, and Brunate. Consulting enologist

Beppe Caviola helps craft structured wines with a modern sensibility. Barolo Lecinquevigne, the basic bottling, is an outstanding value. Barolo Liste is compelling and elegant, and meant for the cellar. ★ **Rising star**

Via Roma 31, 12060 Barolo
www.cantinedamilano.it

DeForville di Anfosso Barbaresco

The DeForville family arrived in Barbaresco from Belgium in 1860, and soon planted vineyards. A DeForville daughter married Paolo Anfosso in 1907, which increased the family land holdings to nearly 25 acres (10ha) divided between Barbaresco, including sections of the *crus* Rabajà and Loreto, and Castagnole Lanze. Brothers Paolo and Valter Anfosso run the estate today, and they hold a traditional line in the cellar with long maceration periods for Nebbiolo, and aging wine in large oak casks. DeForville's powerful Barbera from the Ca'Grossa *cru* is also worth seeking out.

Via Torino 44, 12050 Barbaresco
0173 635140

Destefanis Alba

Giuseppe Destefanis first planted vines at his small estate in Montelupo Albese in the 1960s. His grandson, Marco, took over in 1985, renovating the cellar and replanting vineyards with grapes like Dolcetto, Barbera, and Nebbiolo. Destefanis's renditions of Barbera and Nebbiolo are good, but it is the estate's Dolcettos that are worth seeking out. Bricco Galluccio is a modern-styled Dolcetto, lush with flavors of blueberries and peppery spice. Vigna Monia Bassa is made from a selection of older vines and will benefit from a few years in the cellar.

Via Mortizzo 8, 12050 Montelupo Albese
www.marcodestefanis.it

Elio Altare Barolo

Giuseppe Altare first established this estate in La Morra in 1948, and like many small farms in the region, the Altare family grew crops like pears, wheat, and hazelnuts in addition to grapes. Elio Altare, Giuseppe's grandson, took things in a radical direction after a trip to Burgundy in the mid-1970s. He introduced small barriques to the cellar, and began experimenting with shorter fermentations for Nebbiolo. The results, as shown with wines like the Barolo Brunate, yielded wines of finesse and beauty that can be enjoyed in their youth.

Frazione Annunziata 51, 12064 La Morra
www.elioaltare.com

Elio Grasso Barolo

With holdings in two of Monforte's best vineyards, Gavarini and Ginestra, the Grasso family have long been among the top growers in the Barolo zone. Today, the estate is run by Elio Grasso who, along with his son Gianluca, crafts an elegant, powerful style of Barolo that strikes a balance between the modern and traditional schools of thought. Nebbiolo is given lengthy, unhurried fermentations, and is then aged in a mix of large Slavonian oak casks and, for the Barolo Rüncot, smaller barriques. Do not miss the ageworthy Barbera, Vigna Martina.

Località Ginestra 40, 12065 Monforte d'Alba
www.eliograsso.it

Elvio Cogno Barolo

Wineries like Elvio Cogno launched the communes in the periphery of the Barolo zone into the same league as well-known areas like Serralunga and La Morra. Based in Novello, the Elvio Cogno winery is built at the top of the relatively high-altitude Ravera *cru*. Its best Barolos come from this site; look for either Ravera or Vigna Elena, a single-parcel selection from within the Ravera *cru*. These powerful expressions of Nebbiolo are notable for their balance and elegance. ★ **Rising star**

Località Ravera 2, 12060 Novello
www.elviocogno.com

Ermes Pavese Valle d'Aosta

Ermes Pavese established this small winery in 1999 near Morgex in Valle d'Aosta. Pavese works exclusively with Prié Blanc, which is planted on its own roots at up to nearly 3,900ft (1,200m)—among the highest altitudes for viticulture in Europe. Pavese makes three wines, and the lean, dry Blanc de Morgex et de la Salle is the ideal introduction to the minerally whites from this fascinating growing region. Nathan, named for Pavese's young son, is aged in barrique for structure, while Ninive, named for his daughter, is a luscious Passito. ★ **Rising star**

Strada Pineta 26, 11017 Morgex
0165 800053

Famiglia Anselma Barolo

Anselma is a new producer that has firmly embraced the traditional side of Barolo, including long fermentations, aging in large oak casks, and refusing to bottle a single-vineyard wine. The family owns more than 190 acres (77ha) in the communes of Barolo, Monforte, and Serralunga. Anselma's first vintage was in 1993, and its style has changed little in the years since: both the regular Barolo and the Riserva Adasi remain savory, powerful wines capable of aging. ★ **Rising star**

Località Castello della Volta, 12060 Barolo
www.anselma.it

Filippo Gallino Roero

Filippo Gallino was the first member of his family to bottle wine at their small farm near Canale in the heart of the Roero zone. Today, the Gallino operation includes a solid line-up of Barbera, Nebbiolo, and Arneis, all fine examples of their type as grown in the sandy soils of this small region. The Barbera d'Alba in particular is generous and bright, with a vibrancy that begs for rich, wintery stews. Not to be missed is Gallino's Birbét, a lightly sweet, fizzy wine made from Brachetto.

Valle del Pozzo 63, 12043 Canale
www.filippogallino.com

Francesco Boschis Dogliani

Francesco Boschis began as a private grower selling most of his grapes to larger producers. In 1968, Boschis and his son, Mario, began to bottle their own wines. Today, the estate of Francesco Boschis makes some of the best examples of Dolcetto di Dogliani around. Do not miss the spicy freshness of the Sorì San Martino, sourced from old vines in the *cru* of the same name.

Frazione San Martino di Pianezzo 57, 12063 Dogliani
www.boschisfrancesco.it

A MODERN RETURN TO TRADITION?

Until the 1960s and 1970s, Barolo and Barbaresco were made using techniques that had been in place for at least a century. Nebbiolo grapes were given long fermentations, with little to no temperature control, and then aged in large old casks.

Then, winemakers like Angelo Gaja introduced techniques from France and other regions, such as temperature control and small barrels made from French oak. Others, like Elio Altare, began experimenting with shorter fermentations. The end result was softer, more concentrated Barolo and Barbaresco that earned immediate praise— entirely different from the wines made by staunch traditionalists like Bartolo Mascarello, Giovanni Conterno at Giacomo Conterno, and Bruno Giacosa.

However, a few decades later, the pendulum seems to be swinging back. Producers like Walter Fissore at Elvio Cogno are increasingly striking a balance between both extremes, using barrels of various sizes, temperature control, and medium-length fermentations to make elegant, graceful Nebbiolo.

FRATELLI ALESSANDRIA
THIS LIGHT, ELEGANT WINE IS MADE FROM
THE LITTLE-KNOWN PELAVERGA VARIETY

GIOVANNI ALMONDO
A BRACING, FRESH WINE FROM GRAPES
GROWN AT RELATIVELY HIGH ALTITUDE

Francesco Rinaldi e Figli Barolo

This estate traces its roots back to 1870, when Francesco Rinaldi inherited vineyard land in Barolo. Run today by Luciano Rinaldi and his niece, Paola, Francesco Rinaldi continues to craft wines in the old style. The Barolos are sourced from holdings that include the *crus* of Cannubi and Brunate and typically take up to a decade to be ready to drink. The Barbaresco tends to mature sooner, offering lifted aromas and firm tannins. Not be missed is the Grignolino d'Asti, a refreshing, light red made from the local Grignolino variety.

Via U Sacco 4, 12051 Alba
www.rinaldifrancesco.it

Franco Noussan Valle d'Aosta

Franco Noussan began making wine in the Valle d'Aosta as a hobby when he was not teaching at the local university. Through his wife's family, Noussan acquired some old vineyards planted with varieties like Petit Rouge, Mayolet, Fumin, and Pinot Gris. In 2003, he leased additional vineyards, bringing the total to about 13 acres (5ha). Noussan started his own label in 2005, releasing gentle, aromatic wines that emphasize finesse and freshness over power. Look for the Torette, a compelling blend of Petite Rouge, Mayolet, and Cornalin. This is a red that goes with anything. ★ **Rising star**

Frazione Maillod 2, 11020 Saint Christophe
0165 541297

Fratelli Alessandria Barolo

This Verduno-based producer traces its roots back to the 19th century, when the commune might have enjoyed greater prestige for its wines than in the modern day. Not that the Barolos of Verduno nor Fratelli Alessandria are second-rate. Gian Battista Alessandria and his son Vittorio source from notable *crus* of Monvigliero and San Lorenzo to make aromatic Barolo that is notable for its finesse rather than its power. Elegant wines like these are building Verduno's reputation. Worth seeking out is the Verduno Pelaverga, a feisty, light local red that happily accompanies most kinds of food.

Via Beato Valfre 59, 12060 Verduno
www.fratellialessandria.it

Fratelli Brovia Barolo

Originally established in 1863 by Giacinto Brovia, and then re-founded in 1953 by his grandchildren Giacinto, Raffaele, and Marina, Brovia is recognized as a member of Barolo's old guard. The estate produces traditionally styled wines from notable vineyards like Rocche, Villero, and Garbelet Sué in Castiglione Falletto; Ca' Mia (Brea) in Serralunga; and Rio Sordo in Barbaresco. Barolo Rocche best shows the elegant, earthy expression common to Brovia's wines, though it needs time in the cellar to fully develop. Meanwhile, Vignavillej shows that finesse rather than intensity yields delicious Dolcetto.

Via Alba Barolo 54, 12060 Castiglione Falletto
www.brovia.net

Fratelli Cavallotto Barolo

Cavallotto was established in 1929 in Castiglione Falletto, where the family owns Bricco Boschis, one of the commune's top Barolo *crus*. Because of the site's large area—approximately 57 acres (23ha)—Cavallotto calls its single-vineyard riserva wine Vigna San Giuseppe, while the winery's basic bottling carries the name of the cru. Barolo Bricco Boschis is by no means a lesser wine, though it will likely require less time in the cellar than the San Giuseppe. Cavallotto also bottles a formidable, ageworthy Riserva Barolo from the Vignolo cru. Think 30 or more years.

Via Alba-Monforte, Bricco Boschis, 12060 Castiglione Falletto
www.cavallotto.com

Frères Grosjean Valle d'Aosta

Though the Grosjean family can trace its roots in the Valle d'Aosta back for several generations, the winery's history began in 1969, when its wines were bottled for a regional wine exhibition. Grosjean has farmed organically since 1975, and grows local varieties like Petite Rouge, Petite Arvine, Fumin, Cornalin, Prëmetta, and Vuillermin, in addition to more familiar names like Gamay and Pinot Noir. The charming Gamay is a refreshing red that can last through an entire meal. The minerally Petite Arvine offers a clear look at the region's complex soils.

Frazione Ollignan 1, 11020 Quart
www.grosjean.vievini.it

Germano Ettore Barolo

When Ettore Germano and his father, Alberto, started this small estate near Serralunga, production was for the most part sold to larger wineries, although Ettore did begin to bottle a small amount of wine in the 1970s. The big step into serious winemaking came in 1993 when Ettore's son, Sergio, took over the estate full time. Germano's Barolos are balanced, powerful wines with focus and depth. Look to the *cru* wines, Prapò, Ceretta, and Lazzarito, for a glimpse at Serralunga's diverse terroir. The recently released Hérzu is a vibrant, minerally Riesling from the estate's vineyard in Ciglié. ★ **Rising star**

Borgata Cerretta 1, 12050 Serralunga d'Alba
www.germanoettore.com

Giacomo Borgogno e Figli Barolo

This historic estate—owned since 2009 by businessman Oscar Farinetti—controls nearly 49 acres (20ha) of vineyard land between the communes of Barolo and La Morra, including sections of renowned *crus* such as Cannubi, Fossati, and Liste. Established in 1761, the Borgogno style for many years reflected the most traditional approach to Barolo; indeed, wines from the 1950s and 1960s still taste fresh and alive today. The estate has gradually modernized in recent years, the result being wines that are relatively easy to approach when young, though still lovely examples of their type.

Via Gioberti 1, 12060 Barolo
www.borgogno-wine.com

Giacomo Conterno Barolo

In the eyes of Barolo lovers worldwide, there is often only one wine: Giacomo Conterno's Monfortino. This historic estate, born in the early decades of the 20th century, arguably forms the pillar of traditional Barolo. Giovanni Conterno (Giacomo Conterno's son and Aldo Conterno's older brother) ran the estate from 1959 until his death in 2003; his son Roberto is now the winemaker. In 1974, the estate acquired 39 acres (16ha) in the Francia *cru* in Serralunga; both Barolo Cascina Francia and

Monfortino now come from this site. Both wines are powerfully structured and built to live for many decades after release.

Via Bussia Sottana 62, 12065 Monforte d'Alba
0173 78221

Giacomo Grimaldi Barolo
The Grimaldi family have farmed this estate since the 1930s, but have only been releasing wine under their own name since 1996. Managed by Ferruccio Grimaldi and his father, Giacomo, the estate totals almost 19 acres (7.5ha) in Novello, Barolo, and the Roero. Barolo Le Coste, Grimaldi's first and most important wine, comes from the south-facing *cru* of the same name in the commune of Barolo. Made in a modern style, it combines aromas of rose and cherry with a rich texture. The Roero-grown Nebbiolo d'Alba is also worth trying.

Via L Einaudi 8, 12060 Barolo
0173 560536

Giovanni Almondo Roero
This 29 acre (12ha) estate is arguably the leading producer of Arneis in the Roero. Giovanni Almondo cultivates the variety at the relatively high altitude of 1,240ft (380m), so that in addition to the chalky minerality commonly found in Arneis, there is an unusually high level of acidity. Bricco degli Cigliegie, named for the cherry trees planted around these hillside vines, is bracing and fine, with lasting, fresh flavors and subtle grip. Almondo's single-vineyard Arneis, Vigna Sparse, is more complex, offering significant concentration and mineral expression. It will age longer than most Arneis.

Via S Rocco 26, 12046 Monta' d'Alba
www.giovannialmondo.com

Giulia Accornero e Figli Monferrato
The Accornero family organically farms 49 acres (20ha) of vineyards in the Monferrato region, including some rather excellent Barbera plantings. Look for Giulin, a delicious, earthy Barbera aged in a mix of large barrels and steel tanks. Bricco Battista is Accornero's more ambitious Barbera—aged for up to 18 months in barriques, it is a densely structured, ageworthy wine that combines concentration and bright acidity. Look also for Bricco de Bosco, a light, unoaked red made from the delightful Grignolino grape. An ideal picnic wine.

Cascina Ca'cima, Vignale Monferrato
www.accornerovini.it

Giuseppe Mascarello e Figlio Barolo
Another legendary producer named Mascarello, this winery has been in operation since its establishment by Giuseppe Mascarello in 1881. In 1904, Giuseppe's son, Maurizio, bought a parcel in the Monprivato *cru* in Castiglione Falletto. The winery is run today by Mauro Mascarello and his son, Giuseppe. If the Monprivato site is the heart of the enterprise, then coming a close second is the old Mascarello winery, where the large oak casks purchased in the 1950s are still in use. The Barolo Monprivato is one of the region's greatest treasures, and from a good vintage it can go for decades.

Via Borgonuovo 108, 12060 Monchiero
www.mascarello1881.com

GIUSEPPE MASCARELLO E FIGLIO
THIS PRESTIGIOUS AND SOUGHT-AFTER BAROLO CAN BE CELLARED FOR DECADES

GERMANO ETTORE
MADE FROM RIESLING, THIS VIBRANT, MINERALLY WINE IS A RECENT RELEASE

Giuseppe Rinaldi Barolo
Part of a large family with historical roots in Barolo, Giuseppe Rinaldi started his winery in the 1920s. His son, Battista, took over the estate in 1947, which included sections of Cannubi San Lorenzo, Le Coste, Brunate, and Ravera. These four sites were typically blended together for the basic Barolo, while a selection of Brunate was bottled as a riserva. When Battista's son Giuseppe ("Beppe") took over as winemaker, he changed this formula. Today, Rinaldi makes two classic, long-aging Barolos: Le Coste, labeled Brunate, and Canubbi San Lorenzo, labeled Ravera.

Via Monforte 3, 12060 Barolo
0173 56156

Hilberg-Pasquero Roero
Although vine-growing at this estate dates back to 1915, its modern history began more recently under the direction of Michele Pasquero and Annette Hilberg. The couple practise ecologically sensitive farming and gentle, hands-on winemaking. The resulting wines feel modern and stylish, combining a sense of complexity and fun. A case in point is Vareij, a blend of the floral notes of Brachetto with the earthy juiciness of Barbera that feels easy and refreshing to drink. The Barbera d'Alba is a lightly oaked, structured red that calls out for braised beef. ★ **Rising star**

Via Bricco Gatti 16, 12040 Priocca
www.hilberg-pasquero.com

La Casaccia Monferrato
Elena and Giovanni Rava's family have been making quality wine in the Monferrato region for generations. Today they run an organic estate, where they cultivate Barbera, Freisa, and Grignolino (some from very old vines planted in tufa-based soils), in addition to a small amount of Chardonnay. Look for Monfiorenza, a delightful take on Freisa that relishes the grape's bright character. Do not miss the Barbera d'Asti, a savory red that backs its fruit flavor with a firm, minerally structure. Charnò is La Casaccia's unpretentious Chardonnay; lean and fresh, it recalls the French Macôn.

Via Dante Barbano 10, 15034 Cella Monte
www.lacasaccia.biz

La Morandina Asti
Giulio and Paolo Morando took over their family's estate in Castiglione Tinella in 1988. Moscato dominates this area, and La Morandina's version is one of the best efforts around—an energetic combination of fresh floral notes and bright fruit that is as delicious as it is refreshing. The Morando brothers also make noteworthy Barbera from pre-phylloxera vines in Asti. Look for Zucchetto, a powerful expression of Barbera that seems to pull its structure straight from the soil. La Morandina's Barbaresco Bricco Spessa, from a vineyard near Neive, is also worth seeking out.

Località Morandini 11, 12053 Castglione Tinella
www.lamorandina.com

La Spinetta Asti
Giuseppe and Lidia Rivetti established La Spinetta in Castagnole Lanze in 1977, and the following year released two single-vineyard Moscatos: Bricco Quaglia and

LA SPINETTA

THIS FRESH AND COMPLEX WHITE WINE
IS MADE FROM MUSCAT GRAPES

Biancospino. Both of these wines show incredible complexity for Moscato, with ravishing notes of citrus and mint, and a freshness that can be attributed to the high altitude of both sites. During the 1980s, La Spinetta expanded its production to include red wines, making Barbera and Nebbiolo in a primarily modern style under the direction of Giorgio Rivetti. Look for the Barbaresco Valeirano, a wine that marries potent tannins with a plush texture. ★ **Rising star**

Via Annunziata 17, 14054 Castagnole Lanze
www.la-spinetta.com

Laura Aschero Liguria

Laura Aschero was one of the few women working at her level in the world of Ligurian wine. Coming from a family of growers and winemakers, Aschero started her own winery in the 1980s, working with Ligurian staples like Vermentino, Pigato, and Rossese, all planted on steep hillsides. She died in 2006, leaving the winery in the control of her son, Marco. The Laura Aschero Pigato remains one of the most compelling examples of this Ligurian speciality. It combines refreshing flavor with complex minerality and lasting notes of bitter almond.

Piazza V Emanuele 7, 18027 Pontedassio
0183 293515

Les Crêtes Valle d'Aosta

Costantino Charrère started Les Crêtes in 1989 near the town of Aymavilles in the Valle d'Aosta. Mount Blanc towers over the vineyards at Les Crêtes, and on a visit to these rolling slopes and Alpine terraces of vines, you could be forgiven for thinking that you had left Italy entirely. Look for the Petite Arvine, which balances austere minerality with a mouthwatering character that begs for food. Also of note is Coteau La Tour, a spicy, cool-climate Syrah that is one of the best made in Italy. ★ **Rising star**

Località Villetos 50, 11010 Aymavilles
www.lescretes.it

Luca Ferraris Monferrato

Luca Ferraris's family have been tending vines in Castagnole Monferrato for generations. This region specializes in one of Piedmont's more distinctive indigenous varieties, Ruché. Luca Ferraris makes a version that matches the grape's dark purple color with an equally intense flavor. Beyond Ruché, Ferraris makes lip-smacking Grignolino (Vigna del Casot) and a compelling single-vineyard Barbera, called Vigna del Martin. More unusual for Piedmont is Ferraris's Syrah vineyard, which he planted on a hillside in 2000. It is blended with Ruché for the stylish Il Re, a powerful, cellar-worthy red.

Via al Castello, 14030 Castagnole Monferrato
www.lucaferraris.it

Luciano Sandrone Barolo

Luciano Sandrone occupies a rare space. While his wines embrace the modern, there is, nevertheless, something classic and timeless about the man and his Barolo. Sandrone started his winery in 1978, after working as a cellarhand for many years. His estate is based around a parcel of the famed Cannubi *cru* that he purchased in the 1970s; it now includes vineyards in Monforte, Barolo,

MAJOLINI

A FULL-BODIED SPARKLING WINE WITH
AROMAS OF YEAST AND BREAD CRUSTS

and the Roero. There are two Barolos: Le Vigne and Cannubi Boschis. Both wines combine elegance and power in a way that feels breathtaking. ★ **Rising star**

Via Pugnane 4, 12060 Barolo
www.sandroneluciano.com

Luigi Baudana Barolo

Luigi and Fiorina Baudana have tended this 11 acre (4.5ha) estate near Serralunga since 1975. The Baudana holdings include sections of the Baudana and Cerretta *crus*, from which grapes were sold off to other producers until 1996. Baudana makes good-quality Dolcetto and Barbera, two food-friendly reds with enough grip to handle substantial meat dishes. The Barolo Cerretta is made in an approachable style, though it has the structure to age for up to a decade. It makes for an easy introduction to the often powerful wines of Serralunga.

Frazione Baudana 43, 12050 Serralunga d'Alba
www.baudanaluigi.com

Luigi Ferrando Carema

The Ferrando family have been making wine in mountainous northern Piedmont since the early 1900s. Luigi Ferrando, along with his sons Roberto and Andrea, grow Nebbiolo and some Barbera on steep terraces in the Carema DOC. Look for the white label Carema, an elegant, almost ethereal red that feels firm and composed. Ferrando also makes a black label Carema in outstanding vintages. From the estate's vineyards closer to Caluso comes the versatile Erbaluce, a white grape used for distinctive still and sparkling wines.

Via Torino 599, 10015 Ivrea
www.ferrandovini.it

Luigi Pira Barolo

This Serralunga-based estate consists of just over 19 acres (7.5ha), with holdings in three of Barolo's most highly regarded *crus*: Marenco, Margheria, and Vigna Rionda. Luigi Pira originally established the estate in the 1950s, although the first wines were not released until 1993. The wines skirt toward the modern spectrum of Barolo, combining short- to moderate-length fermentations with the use of French barriques to produce a style of Nebbiolo that feels aromatically forward, yet retains the tannic structure common to Serralunga. The Dolcetto d'Alba is also worth trying.

Via XX Settembre 9, 12050 Serralunga d'Alba
0173 613106

Majolini Franciacorta

In the early 1980s, brothers Gianfranco, Piergiorgio, Stefano, and Ezio Majolini re-founded the family wine business that their father Valentino had launched in the 1960s. Based on the eastern edge of the Franciacorta zone, in the village of Ome, Majolini produces elegant, ageworthy sparkling wines. The basic brut feels racier than typical Franciacorta, and offers a lean, refreshing blast of crisp, apple flavor. At the other end of the spectrum is the complex Riserva Valentino Majolini, a selection made in top vintages and then aged for several years at the winery.

Via Manzoni 3, 25050 Ome
www.majolini.it

Malvirà Roero

Massimo and Roberto Damonte have turned Malvirà, the estate that their father Giuseppe started in the 1950s, into one of the Roero's leading private wineries. And like Giovanni Almondo, the Damonte brothers have largely built their reputation with the region's local variety, Arneis. Malvirà makes three single-vineyard Arneis wines: Renesio and Trinità, which are both fermented in steel tanks, and Saglietto, which sees partial barrel fermentation. (A blend of all three is used for its basic bottling.) Renesio is the most classic, offering a chalky texture and rich fruit, while the Saglietto is an ambitiously structured white.

Via Case Sparse 144, 12043 Canale d'Alba
www.malvira.com

Marcarini Barolo

Luisa and Manuel Marchetti run this estate located in La Morra, which was first established by Luisa's family in the mid-19th century. Marcarini owns a prime section of the Brunate vineyard, a site that the winery has indicated on the label for its Barolo since 1958. Marcarini's traditionally made Barolo Brunate is powerful and closed when young, but in strong vintages, it can easily last for decades in the cellar. Also worth trying is Boschi di Berri, made from century-old Dolcetto vines planted on their own roots in sandy soils.

Piazza Martiri 2, La Morra
www.marcarini.it

Marchesi di Barolo Barolo

This historic estate was once the seat of the Falletti family, who controlled much of the land around Alba. The first dry Nebbiolo wine to be called Barolo was made here under the auspices of Giulia Falletti. Today, under the ownership of the Abbona family, the winery maintains an extensive cellar of very old vintages. These ancient cellars are worth a visit, as they offer a unique window into the region. The line-up of current Barolos is impressive, too, including bottles from Cannubi, Brunate, and Sarmassa.

Via Alba 12, 12060 Barolo
www.marchesiBarolo.com

Marchesi di Grésy Barbaresco

Although it has owned land in the Barbaresco region for generations, Marchesi di Grésy's modern history began in 1973, when Alberto di Grésy started bottling wine from the family vineyards. The property spans the Langhe and Monferrato regions, though the heart of the estate is the Martinenga *cru*, long recognized as one of Barbaresco's top sites. Three Barbarescos come from here, including Martinenga and two sub-sections, Gaiun and Camp Gros. These powerful wines see plenty of wood, yet they remain poised and firm. To appreciate the site unadorned, try the un-oaked Nebbiolo Martinenga.

Via Rabaja Barbaresco 43, 12050 Barbaresco
www.marchesidigresy.com

Marco Porello Roero

Marco Porello is a rising star of the Roero. The young, affable Porello took over his family's vineyards in 1994; he lowered yields and modernized the wine cellar in Canale, the Roero's principal town. Not far from the winery is Porello's Camestrì vineyard, a steep hillside of Arneis on sandy soils. The wine is firm and vivid, with refreshing acidity, and is a terrific value. Porello's Favorita, a white variety indigenous to Piedmont, is more straightforward and light. The delightful Nebbiolo d'Alba is less tannic than Barolo or Barbaresco. ★ **Rising star**

Via Roero 3, 12050 Guarene
www.porellovini.it

Marenco Asti

Giuseppe Marenco began bottling wines from his family vineyards in the 1950s. Based in the region of Strevi, Marenco is known for two sparkling dessert wines: Pineto, a vivid, juicy-sweet Brachetto d'Acqui, and Scrapona, a zesty Moscato d'Asti. While both wines are easy to understand and enjoy, there is enough complexity in them to not only pair them with savory desserts and cheeses, but to enjoy them as an off-dry apéritif.

Piazza V Emanuele 10, 15010 Strevi
www.marencovini.com

Massolino Barolo

Franco Massolino is the latest generation to helm this producer of traditional-leaning Barolo. Following his father and uncle in an enterprise that began in 1896, Massolino's first order of business is tending the family's vineyards, including an enviable array of top sites in Serralunga, such as Vigna Rionda, Parafada, and Margheria. These single-vineyard wines need cellar time to reach their full potential. Meanwhile, do not miss the Nebbiolo d'Alba. Made from declassified Barolo and a selection of younger vines, it represents an affordable way into some of the region's best vineyards.

Piazza Cappellano 8, 12050 Serralunga d'Alba
www.massolino.it

Matteo Correggia Roero

A visit to the Correggia winery can be both delightful and disconcerting. The wines produced here are compelling arguments for the Roero's potential, showing elegance and mineral expression with both Nebbiolo and Barbera. The disconcerting part comes from tragedy. The talented Matteo Correggia inherited his vineyards and winery following the premature death of his father, Giovanni, in 1985; Matteo Correggia himself was killed in an accident in 2001. His wife and two children, along with a dedicated cellar team, have carried on his legacy with wines like Roero Ròche d'Ampsej, a powerful Nebbiolo.

Case Sparse Garbinetto 124, 12043 Canale d'Alba
www.matteocorreggia.com

Mauro Veglio Barolo

As with many small estates in this region, Mauro Veglio took over the reins at the family farm and, beginning in 1992, modernized practices in the vineyard and cellar. With guidance from Elio Altare, Veglio developed an approachable style of Barolo that favors concentration of flavor over tannic strength. Veglio tends vineyards in both La Morra and Monforte, two areas known for powerful reds. Look for that power in the Barolo Castelletto, a wine that embraces its structure, yet feels soft and warm on the palate.

115 Regione Annunziata, 12064 La Morra
www.mauroveglio.com

DEFYING GRAVITY IN VALTELLINA

Valtellina is arguably the only wine region to achieve a truly noble expression of Nebbiolo outside of Barolo and Barbaresco. This narrow mountain valley, located deep in the Alps along the Swiss border, is in many ways its own world. Nebbiolo here even has its own name—Chiavennasca.

However, more unique to the region is the improbable terracing that rises vertically from the valley floor. The origins of these ancient terraces—essentially walls built with rocks and then filled in with soil from the valley floor—are somewhat mysterious, but the result is effective. Imagine a giant vineyard rotated 90° on its side, so that it faces south to fully capture the intense mountain sun. Valtellina is divided into five subzones: Grumello, Valgella, Maroggia, Sassella, and Inferno. This last is an indication of how well the terracing works in terms of ripening grapes. Nebbiolo, it seems, loves a challenge.

WINE INNOVATIONS

MICHELE CHIARLO
A TOP OF THE RANGE BAROLO FROM ONE OF
THE LARGEST PRODUCERS IN PIEDMONT

PECCHENINO
A DARK AND RICH SINGLE-VINEYARD WINE
MADE FROM DOLCETTO GRAPES

Michele Chiarlo Barolo

Established in 1956 by Michele Chiarlo as a grower of Barbera, and shortly thereafter, Nebbiolo from the Barolo and Barbaresco zones, today the firm is one of the largest growers in Piedmont, producing wine from nearly every major appellation in the region. Michele Chiarlo remains a go-to winery for quality Barbera; look for Le Orme, an easy-drinking, flavorful Barbera d'Asti. At the top of the range are the *cru* Barolos, including Cerequio and Cannubi. Rather than chase a particular style, they tend to reflect elegance and balance most of all.

Strada Nizza, Canelli, 14042 Calamandrana
www.chiarlo.it

Mirabella Franciacorta

Mirabella is effectively a private co-operative, established by a group of eight businessmen from nearby Brescia, all of whom owned vineyards in the Franciacorta zone. The winery shows an affinity for Pinot Bianco, which features prominently in the blends for its sparkling wines. The basic Franciacorta Brut is typically half Chardonnay and half Pinot Bianco. The result is a satisfyingly rich, yet lifted wine. Be sure to try the Dosaggio Zero, an austere, bone-dry blend of Chardonnay, Pinot Bianco, and Pinot Nero, made without added sugar.

Via Cantarane 2, 25050 Rodengo Saiano
www.mirabellavini.it

Nino Negri Valtellina

Nino Negri and his son Carlo established this winery in 1897. It is owned today by Gruppo Italiano Vini, and has been under the direction of enologist Casimiro Maule for decades. The winery owns more than 90 acres (36ha) in the four subzones of Valtellina, from which they produce specific wines, including the well-structured Inferno. Vigneto Fracia is a *cru* owned by Nino Negri; picked late in the season and aged in small barrels, it is often concentrated and rich. Also of note is 5 Stelle, a Sfursat, or air-dried style of Nebbiolo.

Via Ghibellini 3, 23030 Chiuro
www.ninonegri.it

Orsolani Caluso

This producer is situated in the Canavese area of Piedmont, to the north of Turin and into the mountain passes that become the Valle d'Aosta. Established as an inn and farm at the end of the 19th century, Orsolani is one of the premier producers of Erbaluce, an indigenous white grape that is found as both a still and sparkling wine, as well as a *passito* (from dried grapes). La Rustia is Orsolani's basic dry Erbaluce di Caluso. It is a refreshing partner with foods, from cheese to seafood.

Via Michele Chiesa 12, 10090 San Giorgio Canavese
www.orsolani.it

Paolo Saracco Asti

If anyone were to be called the godfather of Moscato d'Asti, it would be Paolo Saracco. The Saracco family has been growing grapes in Castiglione Tinella since the early 20th century, and when Paolo Saracco took over the estate he modernized and expanded the vineyards and winery. Saracco's Moscato d'Asti is consistently brisk and fresh, with energy and concentration to spare. In more recent years, Saracco has expanded into still wines, specifically Chardonnay and Pinot Nero, two varieties that appreciate the cooler Monferatto climate and the estate's limestone soils.

Via Circonvallazione 6, 12053 Castiglione Tinella
www.paolosaracco.it

Paolo Scavino Barolo

Paolo Scavino established his estate in 1921, and the winery is run today by his son, Enrico Scavino. Scavino is a thoroughly modern producer, with advanced cellar technology and exacting techniques in the vineyard. Yet, rather than make wines that are simply approachable, Scavino's techniques emphasize the sexy side of Nebbiolo. The winery sources from great vineyards, including Cannubi and Rocche di Castiglione, but it is the Barolo Bric del Fiasc that best captures the Scavino spirit. Elegant and refined, it grows more charming over time.

Via Alba Barolo 59, 12060 Castiglione Falletto
www.paoloscavino.com

Parusso Barolo

The brother and sister team of Marco and Tiziana Parusso manage this estate located between Monforte and Castiglione Falletto. Thanks to the use of small barrels for aging Nebbiolo, Parusso's Barolos feel contemporary and stylish, yet match these attractive qualities with gripping tannins and lively acidity. Wines like Barolo Bussia or the basic blended Barolo feel elegant and refined. Parusso also makes one of the better Sauvignon Blancs in the region; both the basic Langhe Bianco and the single-vineyard Bricco Rovella combine bright flavors and chalky mineral notes.

Località Bussia 55, 12065 Monforte d'Alba
www.parussovini.com

Pecchenino Dogliani

In 1987, when Orlando and Attilo Pecchenino took over the estate in Dogliani that their grandfather had started in the early 20th century, Dolcetto barely registered in the Italian wine world. Today, the Pecchenino brothers produce wine that has in many ways become the signature of Dogliani. These are dark wines filled with deep fruit flavors and an almost crunchy minerality. Do not miss Pecchenino's *cru* wines, Sirì d'Jermu and San Luigi, two delicious wines that make a strong case for ageworthy Dolcetto.

Borgata Valdiberti 59, 12063 Dogliani
0173 70686

Pertinace Barbaresco

Pertinace is the "other" wine co-operative in Barbaresco, the most famous being Produttori del Barbaresco. The winery was established near Treiso in 1973 by Mario Barbero and a group of 12 growers. Today, its network of 15 member-growers spans nearly 173 acres (70ha), and draws from the *crus* of Castellizzano, Nervo, and Marcarini. The wines tend to be honest expressions of their site, with Marcarini the most powerful of the lot. An excellent example of Pertinace's classical house style can be found in the *normale* Barbaresco, an earthy, traditionally vinified, food-friendly red.

Loc. Pertinace 2, 12050 Treiso
www.pertinace.com

Pio Cesare Barolo

Cesare Pio started this winery in the city of Alba in 1881. The estate covers nearly 130 acres (53ha), including prime sites in Barolo, like Ornato, Roncaglie, and Ravera, and Il Bricco in Barbaresco. Pio Cesare also purchases fruit from contracted growers. Pio's great-grandson, Pio Boffa, manages the winery today, and the wines have modernized somewhat under his direction, employing moderately long fermentations and a mix of barriques and large casks in the cellar. Look for the basic Barolo and Barbaresco, two wines that feel classic in their scope.

Via Cesare Balbo 6, 12051 Alba
www.piocesare.it

E Pira e Figli Barolo

First established as a wine producer at the end of the 19th century, this estate is today run by Chiara Boschis, whose family bought the winery after the untimely death of Luigi Pira. Boschis modernized the estate with an eye toward showing off the vineyards, which include Cannubi, Cannubi San Lorenzo, and Via Nuova, in addition to about 10 acres (4ha) purchased in Monforte in 2009. Barolo Cannubi represents the Pira signature—a powerful wine that moves elegantly across the palate.

Via Vittorio Veneto 1, 12060 Barolo
www.pira-chiaraboschis.com

Poderi Aldo Conterno Barolo

Along with his brother Giovanni, Aldo Conterno is considered one of Barolo's most legendary figures. He has inspired and challenged his fellow winemakers and Nebbiolo lovers worldwide. Though the Conterno family's roots in Monforte d'Alba stretch back several generations, Aldo Conterno's history began with his split from his brother at the family estate and the establishment of his own winery in 1969. Conterno's traditionally styled Barolos, like the Riserva Granbussia, are powerful beasts. A blend of three vineyards, and aged for six years at the winery before release, it will live for decades more.

Località Bussia 48, 12065 Monforte d'Alba
www.poderialdoconterno.com

Poderi e Cantine Oddero Barolo

The Oddero family have run this estate near La Morra since 1878. Over the years they have amassed a vineyard roster that includes notable *crus* like Vigna Rionda, Villero, Rocche di Castiglione, and Bussia Soprana. Check out the Barolo Villero; given a long maceration period and a mix of aging in large cask and smaller barrels, it is often an elegant balance of earthy flavors and firm structure. Not to be missed is the basic Barolo blend that offers a real sense of terroir at a fair price.

Frazione S Maria 28, 12064 La Morra
www.oddero.it

Poderi Colla Barolo

Ernesto "Tino" Colla and his niece, Federica (daughter of Beppe Colla, formerly of Prunotto), established this winery in 1993. A collection of three properties—Cascina Drago and Tenuta Dardi Le Rose, both in Barolo, and Tenuta Roncaglia in Barbaresco—Poderi Colla is making impressive, traditional-leaning wines. Look for the Barolo Bussia, a firm, powerful expression of Nebbiolo. Barbaresco Roncaglie shows more finesse and elegance,

E PIRA E FIGLI
A POWERFUL WINE WITH SWEET-SCENTED NOTES OF RIPE FRUIT, MINT, AND EUCALYPTUS

PODERI COLLA
AN INTENSE, RUBY-RED WINE CHARACTERISTIC OF THE NEBBIOLO GRAPE

with lifted floral notes and lasting fruit. From the same vineyard comes the Barbera d'Alba, a firm, meaty red that will match any slow-cooked food. ★ **Rising star**

San Rocco Seno d'Elvio 82, 12051 Alba
www.podericolla.it

Poderi Luigi Einaudi Dogliani

Luigi Einaudi is one of the giants of 20th century Italian history, serving as president of the Italian Republic from 1948–55. He was also a passionate agriculturalist who first bought land near Dogliani in 1897. His descendants run the winery today, where they produce a range of striking Dolcettos from the estate. In the late 1990s, Poderi Luigi Einaudi expanded into Barolo with the purchase of 5 acres (2ha) of the renowned Cannubi *cru*. Stylish and powerful, it is one of the best Barolos made from this site.

Borgata Gombe 31, 12063 Dogliani
www.poderieinaudi.com

Principiano Barolo

Americo Principiano established this small estate in the 1950s, selling most of his grapes to other producers. In 1993, his son Ferdinando began to bottle Barolo and Barbera. Like many of his contemporaries, he explored modern vinification techniques, significantly lowering yields and using small barriques. However, beginning in 2000, and fully implemented by 2004, Principiano reverted to more traditional methods, eliminating new oak, temperature control, and punch-downs for his Barolo, and aging the wines in *botti* (large Slovenian oak barrels). The Barolo Boscareto favors elegance over power, and will gain complexity in the cellar. ★ **Rising star**

Via Alba 19, 12065 Monforte d'Alba
www.ferdinandoprincipiano.it

Produttori del Barbaresco Barbaresco

Easily one of the top co-operative wineries in Italy, Produttori del Barbaresco is also a benchmark producer of Barbaresco. It was first established in 1894, and then re-founded in 1958. The wines of this co-op are made from classic vineyards including Rio Sordo, Ovello, Asili, and Rabajà. Under the direction of Aldo Vacca, Produttori del Barbaresco employs a neutral approach in the cellar, making each of the winery's nine *cru* bottlings an accurate reflection of its origins. And relative to other private wineries in Barbaresco, the wines from this co-op remain the region's best bargains.

Via Torino 54, 12050 Barbaresco
www.produttoridelbarbaresco.com

Prunotto Barolo

This historic winery began life in the early 20th century as a co-operative, and, in the 1920s, was taken over by winemaker Alfredo Prunotto, who continued to buy grapes on long-term contract from growers. Prunotto retired in 1956 and sold his business to Beppe Colla, who ran the winery until 1994, after it was bought by Antinori in 1989. Colla made significant contributions to the region in general, such as indicating vineyard names for wines like Barolo Bussia in the 1960s. Bussia remains one of Prunotto's best wines.

Località San Cassiano, 12051 Alba
www.prunotto.it

TENIMENTI FONTANAFREDDA
A SUMPTUOUS WINE THAT WILL PROBABLY
REACH ITS PEAK 12–15 YEARS AFTER HARVEST

Renato Ratti Barolo

Renato Ratti set up his winery in 1965 after working for Cinzano in Brazil. His nephew, Massimo Martinelli, joined the winery a few years later and together the two began to develop modern, elegantly styled wines based around the *crus* Rocche dell'Annunziata and Conca near La Morra. Ratti also developed the Carta del Barolo during the 1980s, an attempt to identify the great vineyards and subzones of the region, and it remains a valuable tool for understanding Barolo. Ratti died in 1988, leaving his son Pietro in charge of the winery.

Frazione Annunziata 7, 12064 La Morra
www.renatoratti.com

Roagna Barbaresco

This family of long-time growers in Barbaresco—the Roagnas have been here since the 1800s—is responsible for intense, powerful wines that last for decades. Austere and tough in their youth, wines like the Barbaresco Pajé or Barolo La Rocca e La Pira, become elegant vehicles for the complexities that can make Nebbiolo so great. The estate is today run by the father and son team of Alfredo and Luca Roagna, and in addition to their embrace of traditional techniques in the cellar, the Roagnas are firm believers in organic viticulture.

Località Paglieri 9, 12050 Barbaresco
www.roagna.com

Robert Voerzio Barolo

Roberto Voerzio is regarded by many as one of Barolo's bright lights. Voerzio started his winery in 1987 and almost immediately pursued a course of rigorous vineyard management. Yields in his vineyards are incredibly low, and this—combined with medium-length fermentations and barrique-ageing—results in wines that show astonishing concentration of flavor. Barolo Brunate is one of the best, an elegantly modern take on this classic site. Beginning with the 2003 vintage, Voerzio introduced a riserva-level wine to be aged at the winery for 10 years.

Località Cerreto 1, 12064 La Morra
0173 509196

Sandro Fay Valtellina

Sandro Fay established his winery from family-owned vineyards in 1973. The winery's outlook, on the surface at least, is more contemporary and stylish than many of its neighbors. However, the wines favor a lighter, elegant style that seems to complement mountain-grown Nebbiolo. Fay controls just over 34 acres (14ha) in the Valgella subzone of Valtellina. The winery makes two single-vineyard wines from this area: Cà Moréi and Carterìa, both of which are aged in barrique. The traditional-leaning Nebbiolo Terrazze Retiche di Sondrio, blended from both Sassella and Valgella vineyards, is aged in cask. ★ **Rising star**

Via Pila Caselli 1, San Giacomo di Teglio
www.vinifay.it

Scarzello Barolo

This small estate, run by a family of established growers in Barolo, first started bottling its wines in the late 1970s. The family's vineyards include holdings in the *crus* Terlo and Sarmassa, the latter being the source for Scarzello's

RENATO RATTI
THIS WINE GIVES OFF DELICATE AROMAS OF
STRAWBERRIES AND RASPBERRIES

profound Barolo Vigna Merenda, a powerful single-vineyard Nebbiolo with great potential for long aging. Federico Scarzello, who took over from his father Giuseppe in 1998, follows mostly a traditional line in the cellar, relying on long fermentations and large vessels in which to age the wines. The *normale* Barolo remains a great-value wine.

Via Alba 29, 12060 Barolo
www.scarzello.eu

Sella Lessona

The Sella family have been producing wine in Lessona since the 17th century. Today, the estate consists of about 49 acres (20ha) of vineyards in Lessona (Sella owns most of the Lessona DOC) and nearby Bramaterra. The primary grape variety is Nebbiolo, along with lesser amounts of Barbera, Vespolina, Croatina, and Cabernet Franc. Sella's Lessona, blended from 80% Nebbiolo and 20% Vespolina, is the benchmark wine of the appellation, showing all the fragrance and tension of Nebbiolo along with a ferrous minerality. The Bramaterra is the richer wine that is delicious when young.

Via IV Novembre 130, 13853 Lessona
015 99455

Sottimano Barbaresco

Established in 1974, Sottimano is run by Rino Sottimano and his son Andrea. Known for elegant, expressive Barbaresco from prime vineyards like Cottà, Currà, Fausoni, and Pajoré, Sottimano has quickly gained a place among the region's top producers. Also worth tracking down is the Langhe Nebbiolo, sourced from younger vines at the Basarin *cru*. Combining bright fruit and powerful tannins, it can easily pass for a "baby" Barbaresco, yet it comes at an affordable price. Also, be sure not to miss Bric del Salto, a feisty unoaked Dolcetto marked by vibrant fruit.

Via Cottà 21, 12057 Neive
www.sottimano.it

Tenimenti Fontanafredda Barolo

This historic producer was established in 1878 by Count Emanuele Alberto Guerrieri di Mirafiori, the illegitimate son of Italy's King Vittorio Emmanuele II, on the grounds of his father's hunting estate. His family later sold the estate to a bank, then, in 2008, Oscar Farinetti, who also owns Borgogno, acquired a majority stake in Fontanafredda. The best change at the winery was the arrival of Danilo Drocco, who took charge of the cellar in 1999. Tenimenti Fontanafredda's *cru* Barolos, especially the Lazzarito, are powerful and deep, while the basic Barolo is a great value.

Via Alba 15, 12050 Serralunga d'Alba
www.tenimentifontanafredda.it

Teobaldo Cappellano Barolo

The Cappellano family history in Barolo reaches back to the 19th century. In the 1890s and early 1900s, Giuseppe Cappellano, a trained pharmacist, experimented at his family's winery with herb infusions and grape must to create Barolo Chinato. Along with staunchly traditional Barolo and Barbera d'Alba, his descendants continue to produce the benchmark Barolo Chinato. Teobaldo Cappellano, proudly one of Barolo's old guard, died in 2009; his son Augusto now runs the winery. Their wines are highly personal, an elegant and emotional response to Nebbiolo and the Barolo terroir.

Via Alba 13, Frazione Bruni, 12050 Serralunga d'Alba
0173 613103

Travaglini Gattinara

This winery—with its distinctive curved bottlenecks—is one of the larger private producers in Gattinara. Founded in the 1920s, the estate is run today by Cinzia Travaglini and husband Massimo Collauto. The Nebbiolo vineyards (locally called Spanna) are planted in iron-laden soils containing magnesium and calcium, and the resulting wines can feel bracing and firm. The basic Gattinara is aged in a mix of barriques and large casks, and is an excellent introduction to this region's take on Nebbiolo. Tre Vigne, a vineyard blend, is Travaglini's top *cuvée*.

Strada delle Vigne, 13045 Gattinara
www.travaglinigattinara.it

Triacca Valtellina

With vineyards in Valtellina and Tuscany, Triacca is a Swiss-run winery and much of its production is sold in Switzerland. The family's origins lie across the border from Valtellina in the Poschiavo area of Switzerland, though they have been engaged in viticulture on the Italian side since 1897, when Domenico and Pietro Triacca bought a vineyard in Valgella. Their descendants purchased the La Gatta estate in 1969, and it is these vineyards that yield the refined Valtellina Riserva La Gatta. Aged for several years in large casks, this is profound Nebbiolo.

Via Nazionale 121, 23030 Villa di Tirano
www.triacca.com

GD Vajra Barolo

Aldo Vajra, with increasing help from his energetic son, Giuseppe, runs this small estate that his grandfather established in the early part of the 20th century. Located up in the hills above the village of Barolo, Vajra's wines tend to run high in the acidity department. The top Barolo, the traditionally made Bricco delle Viole, feels brisk and wound, its powerful structure belied by notes of violets and roses. Bracing acidity informs all of the Vajra wines, including Kyè, made from the local Freisa grape, and the estate's energetic Riesling.

Via delle Viole 25, 12060 Barolo
www.gdvajra.it

Vietti Barolo

Growers since the 19th century, the Vietti family started bottling wine in 1919. In the subsequent decades, Vietti has emerged as one of the great names in Piedmont winemaking. The wines—whether Nebbiolo grown in Barolo or Barbaresco, Barbera from the famous Scarrone vineyard, or the floral Arneis from the neighboring Roero zone—manage to feel stylish and modern, yet for the most part remain classic expressions of Piedmont's indigenous varieties. Also worth tracking down is the feisty Perbacco, an approachable Nebbiolo that could easily pass for a "baby" Barolo.

Piazza Vittorio Veneto 5, 12060 Castiglione Falletto
www.vietti.com

Vigneti Massa Colli Tortonesi

Walter Massa has spent the last couple of decades in the Colli Tortonesi, in southeast Piedmont, honing a natural, unhurried approach with native varieties like Barbera, Croatina, and the white Timorasso. Massa is often cited as the man responsible for saving Timorasso from extinction. His Derthona Timorasso combines a rich palate feel with racy acidity and mineral notes. It is a complex take on this native grape that has excited serious Italophiles. Massa's earthy Barbera is worth trying, too, whether the unoaked Sentieri or the barrique-aged Monleale, a potent, ageworthy red. ★ **Rising star**

Piazza Capsoni 19, 15059 Monleale
013 180302

Villa Sparina Gavi

Gavi is generally pretty simple stuff, a light, quaffable white made from the local Cortese grape. Rarely does it try to be much more—that is, until one encounters Villa Sparina. Founded in the 1980s by Mario Moccagatta, the estate has been run by his children Stefano, Massimo, and Tiziana since 1997. The younger Moccagattas modernized the cellar and vineyards, and hired Beppe Caviola as consulting winemaker. The resulting wines range from the fresh, lime-inflected Gavi di Gavi to the refined and ambitious Burgundian-leaning Monterotondo *cru*. ★ **Rising star**

Frazione Monterotondo 56, 15066 Gavi
www.villasparina.it

Vittorio Bera e Figli Asti

This estate dates to the 18th century, and is today run by brother and sister Gianluigi and Alessandra Bera. The Beras pursue a style that lands them among the loose-knit group of Italian natural winemakers—meaning organic practices in the vineyard that encourage the development of native yeasts, and minimal intervention in the cellar. Bera's Moscato d'Asti feels different than most, not just lively but life-full, and energetic. Beyond Moscato, the estate makes uncomplicated Dolcetto and mouthwatering Barbera. Most interesting is the sparkling Arcese, a blend of the white grapes Arneis, Favorita, and Cortese.

Regione Serra Masio 21, 14053 Canelli
0141 831157

OFF THE BEATEN TRACK: LIGURIA'S WILD WEST

Liguria is known for a stunning coastline that brings crowds of tourists to enjoy the towns of the Riviera and Cinque Terre. But few visitors ever venture inland past the A12 autostrada that connects Genoa and Nice. For those that do cross the highway line, however, there exists an unspoiled region of thyme-covered hills, vineyards, and farms that has quietly developed an impressive food and wine scene. In fact, traveling here is the best way to sample regional wines like Pigato and Rossese, since many vineyard estates tend to be too small to attract much attention on the export market. Head to Ranzo, a small town in the Imperia province that makes an excellent base for exploring the area. The restaurant and enoteca Il Gallo della Checca serves excellent regional cuisine and boasts a deep collection of vintages from local wineries like Bruna and Laura Aschero.

NORTHEAST ITALY

In terms of wine production, Northeast Italy is a study in incongruity. On the one hand, the region boasts some of the largest wine companies in Italy, responsible for a staggering amount of the country's overall production. On the other, the region is a hotbed of experimental techniques and the kind of endless tinkering that has given birth to some of Italian wine's most colorful iconoclasts. In between the two extremes can be found a compelling range of styles that merit serious exploration. Stretching from the hilly region north of Tuscany to the borders of Austria and Slovenia, the Northeast is one of Italy's most important and richly endowed cultural regions.

Major grapes

 Reds

Cabernet Franc

Lagrein

Merlot

Pinot Nero

Refosco

 Whites

Gargenega

Gewürztraminer

Pinot Bianco

Pinot Grigio

Ribolla Gialla

Vintages

2009
Abundant sunshine in late summer led to a long harvest; generally a very good year.

2008
Great for high-acid whites like Pinot Bianco from Alto Adige; wines tend to fit a lean, more classic profile.

2007
An early harvest across the region, with abundant sunshine, produced ripe reds.

2006
Uneven throughout the region, but strong for Friuli whites.

2005
Generally lower yields than 2004, good for Pinot Nero in Alto Adige.

2004
Much cooler than 2003, with some producers reporting a classic vintage, with high yields; generally good to high quality.

Northeast Italy packs an astonishing amount of diversity into a relatively compact area. It is possible, for instance, to enjoy a breakfast of muesli, dried fruit, and local honey in the Germanic Alpine village of Termeno (also known as Tramin), the home of Gewürztraminer, and then hop in your car for a breakneck drive on the autostrada to catch dinner in Udine. In this graceful city, in the eastern province of Friuli-Venezia Giulia, names and grape varieties nod as much toward nearby Slovenia and Croatia as they do to the Italian peninsula.

Along the way, you will pass through the Teroldego-growing mountain valleys of Trentino-Alto Adige (also known as Südtirol), and then turn east through the Veneto's famous regions of Soave and Valpolicella. As you cut across the Venetian heartland, the craggy peaks of the Alps frame the view to the north, their foothills home to the charmingly effervescent Prosecco. And be sure to keep an eye out for the lion of Saint Mark, the symbol of the ancient Republic of Venice.

To the south stretches the flat plain of the Po Valley, across which the Apennines form the border between Tuscany and Emilia-Romagna. The Sangiovese grown here has recently begun to challenge its cousins from Chianti Classico and Montalcino, yet it remains a relative bargain. Likewise, the once disparaged Lambrusco is seeing a resurgence as artisan growers like Lini and Cà de Noci prove that Emilia-Romagna's famous fizzy red deserves the respect of wine lovers everywhere.

The provinces of Northeast Italy represent different things to different people, and at first glance, it seems like a rather incongruous region. The principal language in Trentino-Alto Adige is German, and the region's wines share a racy precision with the Germanic versions grown and made on the other side of the Alps.

In the Veneto, a visitor encounters at first hand Italy's great postwar miracle of rapid industrialization and vibrant economic centers. Here, alongside some of the country's largest wine producers, you will find artisans dedicated to the exacting process of air-drying grapes for Amarone, one of Italy's most renowned reds.

The eastern borderlands of Friuli-Venezia Giulia are where things become exotic, and where the status quo seems to mean restless experimentation rather than continuity. In addition to the region's technically precise and powerful "super whites" —a sort of response to the famous red blends of Tuscany—you can find winemakers like Josko Gravner and Stanislao Radikon, for whom the latest cellar technology and practices more closely resemble those used by the ancient Romans.

This juxtaposition is, in fact, what makes the wines of Northeast Italy so endlessly fascinating. In a country that thrives on the discovery of something new, or the rediscovery of wines made according to long-standing traditions, the wines of Northeast Italy stand out as some of the most unique and authentic available.

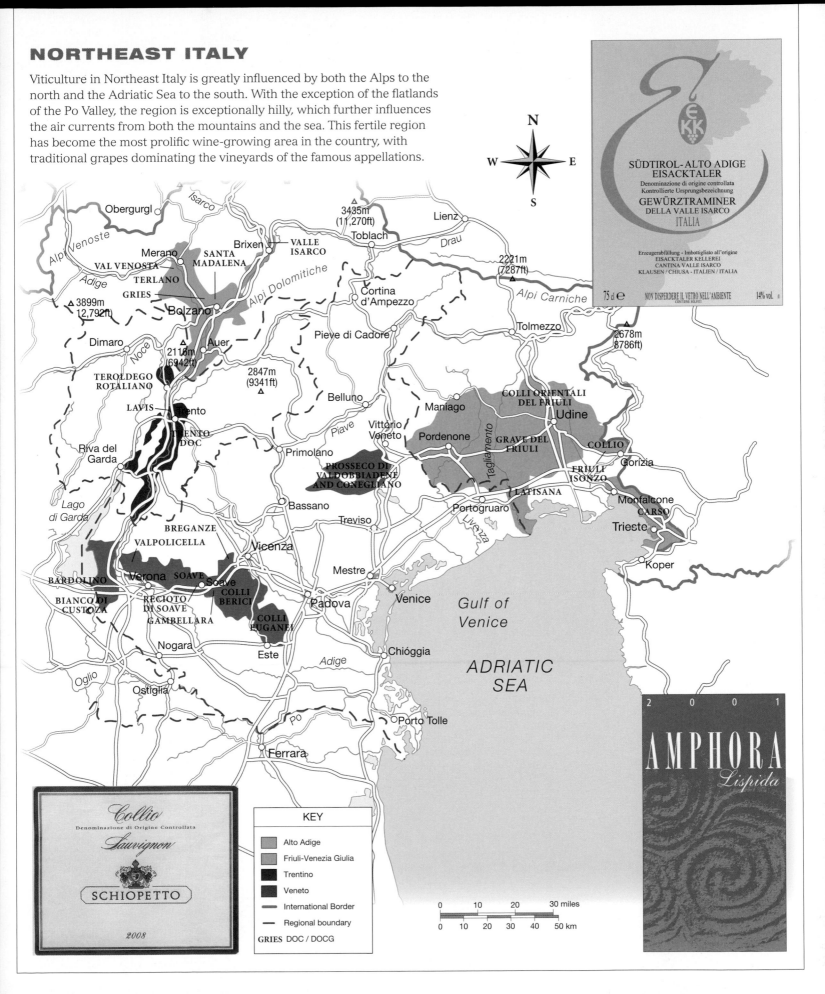

NORTHEAST ITALY

Viticulture in Northeast Italy is greatly influenced by both the Alps to the north and the Adriatic Sea to the south. With the exception of the flatlands of the Po Valley, the region is exceptionally hilly, which further influences the air currents from both the mountains and the sea. This fertile region has become the most prolific wine-growing area in the country, with traditional grapes dominating the vineyards of the famous appellations.

SÜDTIROL-ALTO ADIGE
EISACKTALER
Denominazione di origine controllata
Kontrollierte Ursprungsbezeichnung
GEWÜRZTRAMINER
DELLA VALLE ISARCO
ITALIA

Erzeugerabfüllung - Imbottigliato all'origine
EISACKTALER KELLEREI
CANTINA VALLE ISARCO
KLAUSEN / CHIUSA - ITALIEN / ITALIA

75 cl ℮   NON DISPERDERE IL VETRO NELL'AMBIENTE   14% vol.

KEY

	Alto Adige
	Friuli-Venezia Giulia
	Trentino
	Veneto
	International Border
	Regional boundary

GRIES DOC / DOCG

Collio
Denominazione di Origine Controllata
Sauvignon
SCHIOPETTO
2008

2 0 0 1
AMPHORA
Lispida

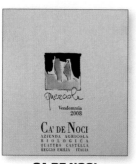

CA DE NOCI

THIS WINE'S BUBBLES ARE CREATED DURING
A NATURAL FERMENTATION IN THE BOTTLE

Abbazia di Novacella
Südtirol/Alto Adige/Eisacktaler

Abbazia di Novacella is both a working monastery (dating from 1142) and a winery (with evidence of winemaking activity dating to the same era). A series of medieval and Renaissance buildings tucked against a low spur of the northern Italian Alps, Abbazia di Novacella is one of the most visually arresting wineries in Europe. It also represents the extreme northern edge of Italian viticulture, specializing in aromatic white varieties such as Gewürztraminer, Sylvaner, and Kerner.

Via Abbazia 1, 39100 Varna
www.kloster-neustift.it

Accordini
Valpolicella/Amarone

The Accordini family have grown the classic grapes of Valpolicella in the foothills outside Verona for several generations. In 1980, Guido Accordini took over the family estate, in the process expanding the vineyards and modernizing the cantina. The heart of Accordini remains the Bessole *cru*, which provides the fruit for Accordini's two best wines, the basic Valpolicella bottling and the Superiore, which, like the brooding Amarone, is made with a percentage of air-dried grapes. The house style balances intense flavor with mouthwatering acidity. These are wines for the table.

Via A Bolla 9, Fraz. Pedemonte, 37020 S Pietro in Cariano
045 770 1733

Adriano Adami
Valdobbiadene

Because its second fermentation happens in a tank rather than the bottle, Prosecco's production often recalls a more industrial approach to the making of sparkling wines. Yet wineries like Adriano Adami seek to prove otherwise. The heart of the Adami estate is an amphitheater-shaped vineyard called Vigneto Giardino. Fermented dry, Adami's Vigneto Giardino is a singular expression of Prosecco that is vibrant and complex, yet perfectly refreshing. This approach informs the house style, as Adami's wines show bright fruit and fresh, crisp acidity. They are nimble, delicious, and ready for anything.

Via Rovede 27, 31020 Colbertaldo di Vidor
www.adamispumanti.it

Alois Lageder
Alto Adige

Alois Lageder's winery sits in a suntrap at the southern end of the wide Adige Valley, ideally situated to take advantage of the warm conditions here—although it is only one of the many microclimates Lageder works with. Lageder's strong commitment to the local environment is apparent in his low-impact winery, and both organic and biodynamic viticulture. Look for the Beta-Delta, a thrilling blend of Chardonnay and Pinot Grigio, and one of Lageder's new wines made from Demeter-certified biodynamic grapes.

Vicolo dei Conti 9, 39040 Magrè
www.aloislageder.eu

Anselmi
Soave

Roberto Anselmi took over his family's winery in Soave in 1980, and aggressively modernized the vineyard and winemaking practices, most notably through a reduction of yields in the estate vineyards. The resulting wines are intensely aromatic, with a much greater flavor concentration. More recently, in 2000, Anselmi abandoned the Soave appellation in favor of labeling his wines with the broader designation Veneto IGT (Indicazione Geografica Tipica). One of Anselmi's best efforts is the lively, unoaked San Vicenzo, which blends a percentage of Chardonnay and Trebbiano with the steely Garganega.

Via S Carlo 46, 37032 Monteforte d'Alpone
www.anselmi.eu

Barbolini
Castelvetro

Established in 1889 by Egidio Barbolini, and run today by his descendants, Barbolini specializes in quality Lambrusco. An old private estate, it is an oddity in terms of Lambrusco production, as massive co-operatives churn out the bulk of these wines. Barbolini's Lambruscos maintain a sense of fun, especially Lancillotto, made from the Grasparossa variety of Lambrusco. Dry and full-bodied, with lasting notes of violets, this will win sceptics over to the idea of sparkling red wines. Bellerofonte, made from the Sorbara variety of Lambrusco, is dense and savory, and ready for wild mushroom pizza.

Via Adriano Fiori, 41043 Formigine
www.barbolinicantina.it

Baron Widmann
Alto Adige

Based in the small mountainside village of Cortaccia, Baron Widmann specializes in the kind of wines that epitomize the Alto Adige region. They are pure, precise expressions of their variety—a nod to the area's Austro-Germanic heritage—yet lusty and flavorful, and, like many regional varieties, are meant to be enjoyed at a warm table in good company. Limited production means that Baron Widmann wines can be difficult to track down. If you do find them, look for the powerfully aromatic and strong Gewürztraminer, or the delicate and spicy red, Vernatsch (Schiava in Italian).

Endergasse 3, 39040 Cortaccia
www.baron-widmann.it

Bastianich
Colli Orientali

Established in 1998 by the American restaurateurs Lidia and Joseph Bastianich, this winery is an effort to reconnect with the family's roots in northeastern Italy and Croatia. And while the wines can be unconventional and challenging, notably with regards to texture—a small percentage of botrytis is added to the Tocai Plus for richness, while the Pinot Grigio is fermented on its skins like a red wine—they remain true to their variety and place. Beyond the whites, look for Calabrone, a seamless blend of Pignolo and Refosco with Cabernet Franc and Merlot. ★ **Rising star**

Via Darnazzacco 44/2, 33043 Gagliano
www.bastianich.com

Battistotti
Trentino

Situated in the Vallagarina subzone of Trentino, Battistotti is one of the region's leading producers of indigenous varieties. Grapes like the medium-bodied red Marzemino and the white, aromatic Nosiola—both born of the thin, fresh mountain air—take the primary position, while the international Cabernet Sauvignon and Chardonnay have a secondary role here. That is not to say that those varieties are not distinctive (the wines boast brisk, bright

BISOL

THIS SINGLE-VINEYARD WINE YIELDS AROMAS
OF FLOWERS, APPLES, PEARS, AND PEACHES

flavors), but who can deny the feisty charm and vibrancy of Battistotti's engaging Marzemino, especially with wild mushroom risotto?

Via 3 Novembre 21, 38060 Nomi
www.battistotti.com

La Berta Brisighella
This striking farm and vineyard is perched on a ridge near the medieval town of Brisighella in the Apennine Mountains. Sangiovese, Cabernet Sauvignon, Trebbiano, and Malvasia are grown at La Berta at around 700ft (200m) above sea level, and although the wines take a fairly modern approach—notably the liberal use of barriques—they have bright acidity thanks to their elevation. Look for the stylish Solano, La Berta's Sangiovese di Romagna. Fruity and forward, it represents a different take on Tuscany's classic variety.

Via Berta 13, 48013 Brisighella
www.laberta.it

La Biancara di Angiolino Maule
Gambellara
Angiolino Maule is one of the leading proponents of natural winemaking in Italy. He came to wine through the kitchen (he had been a pizza chef), and for nearly 20 years at his small estate in Gambellara he has employed biodynamic and organic practices in his vineyards, while following a rigorous philosophy of minimal intervention in the cellar. Maule works primarily with the Garganega grape (the main component of Soave), which seems to gain intensity when grown in the volcanic soils of his estate. Check out Sassaia (blended with a little Trebbiano) for a taste of Maule's mineral-driven style. ★ **Rising star**

Contrà Biancara 14 , Gambellara
www.biancaravini.it

Bisol Valdobbiadene/Conegliano
The Bisol family have been associated with the Cartizze hill in the Valdobbiadene region since the 16th century. Eliseo Bisol was the first in the family to bottle and sell wine, and his descendants still run the estate today. Bisol can claim some of the region's best vineyards as part of its patrimony, including several acres in the limited Cartizze *cru*. From these vines comes a complex and powerful Prosecco. Crede, the name of another *cru*, is a lively blend of Prosecco, Pinot Bianco, and the racy Verdiso.

31040 Fol di Valdobbiadene
www.bisol.it

Bolognani Trentino
Unexpected thrills are one of the great joys of exploring wine. Bolognani, a family winery established near the Valle di Cembra in the early 1950s, makes a Moscato Giallo that challenges preconceptions about the aromatic yet rather lackluster Muscat family. It smells of wild mountain flowers and feels charged by intense acidity. Bone-dry, you could pair it with almost anything. Also worth seeking out is Bolognani's Armilo, a satisfying, hearty red made from the local Teroldego variety. It sees little time in oak, so the flavors feel fresh and pure.

Via Stazione 19, 38015 Lavis
www.bolognani.com

Bortoluzzi Gorizia
Established in 1982 by enologist Giovanni Bortoluzzi, this winery is known for its modern, forward style. Merlot grows well in the estate's gravelly soils, resulting in a savory wine marked by soft, generous tannins. But Bortoluzzi is at its best when it comes to white wines like the steely Pinot Grigio or mineral-driven Sauvignon. Then there is Gemina, a luscious, acacia-scented blend of Friulano, Pinot Grigio, Sauvignon, and Chardonnay.

Via Roma 43, 34072 Gradisca d'Isonzo
www.bortoluzziwines.com

Cà de Noci Reggio Emilia
Giovanni and Alberto Masini started this small estate in 1993 with the intention of focusing strictly on Emilia's indigenous varieties, including Lambrusco Grasparossa, Lambrusco Maestri, Malbo Gentile, and Spergola. All 12 acres (5ha) of Cà de Noci are farmed organically; the vineyards may be young, but they have taken to the estate's rocky soils. The wines are hardly conventional, but they are quite compelling. Check out the Sottobosco, a lightly sparkling dry red with gripping tannins, thanks to extended skin contact during fermentation. And do not miss Querciole, made from the racy Spergola variety— great with prosciutto. ★ **Rising star**

Via Fratelli Bandiera 1/2, Località Vendina
www.cadenoci.it

Caldaro Alto Adige
Named for the small shallow lake in the lower ridges of the Adige Valley, Caldaro (Kellerei Kaltern in German) is a co-operative winery founded in 1906 with 450 member-growers. Today, the co-operative acts as an umbrella organization, with a line of Classic wines produced under the Caldaro name, a series of Selections (mostly riserva-level wines and vineyard-designates), and lastly, the Estates. Into this latter category come the wines of Castel Giovanelli, a small, organically farmed vineyard near Caldaro. Look for the Sauvignon Blanc, a mineral-driven and powerful Alpine white.

Via cantine 12, 39052 Caldaro
www.kellerei-kaltern.com

Camillo Donati Parma
Camillo Donati is one of the leading (and few) winemakers in Emilia Romagna committed to organic and biodynamic farming, and a philosophy of minimal intervention in the cellar. Donati's Lambrusco is not for everyone, but then again, it is the kind of wine that can redefine a category. The Lambrusco dell'Emilia, made from the Maestri variety of Lambrusco, coils dark fruit flavors around a core of gripping, savory tannins, a tension soothed by light effervescence. Do not miss Donati's Malvasia Frizzante; fermented on the skins like a red wine, it is a beguiling, complex statement in sparkling wine.

Localita Arola 32, 43010 Parma
www.camillodonati.it

Canella Valdobbiadene/Conegliano
Established by Luciano Canella in 1947, Canella is today a large-scale producer of sparkling wines and pre-made, wine-based cocktails, like the Bellini, based on the classic Prosecco and peach drink popular in Venice. However, the heart of the company remains the Prosecco di

WINEMAKING AT THE FRINGE: JOSKO GRAVNER
Josko Gravner's remarkable winemaking innovations place him near the top of Italy's long list of wine iconoclasts. In the early 1980s, he introduced temperature-controlled, stainless-steel fermentations in his cellar, which put him in the vanguard of the new style of clean, crisp Italian whites. Later, he began to use small barriques for a soft, richer style.

Gravner significantly altered his approach after tasting a wine in California that to him felt over-made by technology. He stopped using pesticides in his vineyards, while in the cellar he employed longer fermentations and extended skin contact—a move that has influenced several of Gravner's neighbors. The most radical changes came in 1997, when Gravner started to ferment his wines in clay amphorae, an ancient practice used by the Greeks and Romans. He stripped his winery of tanks and barrels to accommodate the amphorae, which now yield some of Italy's most singular and challenging wines.

Conegliano, grown in the hills at the eastern end of the main Prosecco appellation. Prosecco from Conegliano tends to give a fleshier wine, and Canella's version features strong pear and apple notes, and gentle acidity. It makes a lovely apéritif, with or without the peach nectar.

Via Fiume, 7, 30027 San Donà di Piave
www.canellaspa.it

Cantina Rotaliana di Mezzolombardo
Trentino

Another of this region's quality-focused co-operative wineries, Cantina Rotaliana hangs its hat (and those of its 300 or so member-growers) on the regional Teroldego variety. Rotaliana makes four levels of Teroldego, each worth trying. The Novello is made using carbonic maceration (like Beaujolais Nouveau) and is released the year of harvest; the Red Label is produced from vines surrounding the winery; a Riserva is aged for two years in large casks and small barriques; and Clesurae, made with fruit from a selection of older vines, is aged in French oak.

Via Trento 65B, 38017 Mezzolombardo
www.cantinarotaliana.it

Cantina Terlano Alto Adige

Cantina Terlano is a model for how a quality-oriented co-operative winery should run. Established in 1893 on the lower slopes of the Alps, Cantina Terlano today boasts a network of more than 100 member-growers. While the winery produces a complete range of regional whites and reds, it is the bracing, vivid expressions of varieties like Gewürztraminer, Pinot Bianco, and Sauvignon Blanc that most impress. Vineyard designates like Winkl Sauvignon Blanc and Vorberg Pinot Bianco are worth cellaring.

Via Silberleiten 7, 39018 Terlano
www.kellerei-terlan.com

Cantina Tramin Alto Adige

Cantina Tramin is one of the most highly regarded co-operative wineries in Alto Adige. Established in 1898, the winery today is composed of 290 member-growers with vines planted in Tramin, Neumarkt, Montan, and Auer. While Tramin has long been associated with Gewürztraminer, the variety has been taken to new heights by Willi Stürz, who has been with Cantina Tramin since 1992. To get a sense of the winery's style, check out the Nussbaumer Gewürztraminer, an intensely spicy and aromatic white with remarkable concentration.

Strada del Vino 144, 39040 Termeno
www.tramin-wine.it

Cantina Valle Isarco Alto Adige

Compared to the other co-operatives in the region, Cantina Valle Isarco is rather young. First organized in 1961, the winery today occupies a modern facility near Chiusa. The co-operative is known for the aromatic whites that thrive in this northerly region, such as Gewürztraminer, Müller-Thurgau, Grüner Veltliner, and Kerner. Grown on dramatically steep terraces, these varieties typically show bright acidity and pronounced mineral notes. Also worth trying is Valle Isarco's Zweigelt, a fruity red that is a rarity in Italy.

Località Coste 50, 39043 Chiusa
www.eisacktalerkellerei.it

La Cappuccina Soave

Established in the 1890s by the Tessari family, La Cappuccina is today run by Sisto, Pietro, and Elena Tessari. La Cappuccina's 66 acres (27ha) of vines have been farmed organically since 1985. Accordingly, this attention to detail in the vineyard favors a clean, bright style of Soave, as reliable as it is contemporary. The Classico balances lime and floral notes with an almond-like nuttiness. Meanwhile, the oak-fermented Cru San Brizio is more substantial, and makes a good introduction to Soave for those used to richer New World whites.

Via San Brizio 125, 37030 Costalunga di Monteforte d'Alpone
www.lacappuccina.it

Castello di Lispida Padova

The present buildings at the grand Castello di Lispida date from the 18th century, although the property had been a monastery in the Middle Ages. Winemaking at the estate also dates from the late 1700s, as evidenced by the network of old tunnels and use of terracotta bricks. Today, under the direction of Alessandro Sgaravatti, Lispida edges the extremes of natural wine, including the use of amphorae and biodynamically inspired farming. The Amphora Bianco, a 100% Tocai (Friulano), holds its own with similar efforts from Friuli.

Via IV Novembre, 35043 Monselice
www.lispida.com

Castello di Luzzano Colli Piacentini

This medieval fortress and estate straddles the hilly border between Emilia Romagna and Lombardy, as well as the dividing line between two DOCs: the Colli Piacentini and the Oltrepò Pavese. This crossroads has long informed Luzzano's history, and ruins of a Roman villa have been discovered on the property. Run by Giovannella Fugazza, who inherited the estate from her father, Castello di Luzzano specializes in racy Barbera and Bonarda. Look for Carolino, an Oltrepò Pavese Bonarda, a gentle, unoaked red. From the Colli Piacenti, try Romeo, a cask-aged riserva-level blend of Barbera and Bonarda.

27040 Rovescala
www.castelloluzzano.it

Castello di Rubbia Carso

Castello di Rubbia is a 16th-century castle in the Carso zone of eastern Friuli, near the Slovenian border. The estate's wine history is more recent—it was bought in 1998 by the Černic family, and is being renovated as a tourist destination. For now, the wines are the main attraction. Castello di Rubbia specializes in the Carso's regional varieties, Vitovska and Malvasia—two formidably structured whites—and Terrano, an earthy, chewy red. Leonard, the estate's leading white, is an impressive, powerful Malvasia, with the ability to age several years. ★ Rising star

Gornji Vrh 54, Savogna d'Isonzo, 31470 Gorizia
www.castellodirubbia.it

Castello di Spessa Carso

Part of Pali Wines, a regional wine group and resort operator, Castello di Spessa is a historic estate known for richly textured white wines and forward, internationally styled reds. Look for the Ribolla Gialla, a fresh, bright rendition of this classic grape. Likewise, the Friulano

CANTINA TERLANO
LIGHT YELLOW-GREEN, WITH A FRUITY BOUQUET, THIS IS A GENTLE WINE WITH WELL-BALANCED ACIDITY

CORTE SANT'ALDA
SUNNY VINES PRODUCE WELL-RIPENED GRAPES FOR THIS IMPRESSIVE VALPOLICELLA

shows bright flavors under a weighty texture, making it a lovely partner for thinly sliced prosciutto. Torriani, the estate's Merlot, melds ripe, berry flavors with soft, chewy tannins and the plushness of new oak.

Via Spessa 1, 34070 Capriva del Friuli
www.paliwines.com

La Castellada Collio

Originally established in the late 1950s as a vineyard to supply wine for the Bensa family's inn, La Castellada is today among the top wineries in the Collio. Giorgio and Nicolò Bensa, who took over the estate in the 1970s from their father, farm their vineyards organically and use old-style techniques in the cellar, such as spontaneous fermentation in open vats using indigenous yeasts and a long period of skin contact for white grapes. Try the Ribolla Gialla; typically aged for two years in oak casks, it feels charged with a saline minerality.

Fraz. Oslavia 1, 34170 Gorizia
048 133 670

Coffele Soave

Alberto and Chiara Coffele trace their roots to the Visco family, an old name in Soave. The modern Coffele estate began in 1971, when their parents Giovanna Visco and Giuseppe Coffele resurrected the estate. Coffele makes concentrated Soave with vividly bright flavors, sourced from vineyards planted in the Soave Classico zone. Coffele's basic Soave Classico is lean and bright, with lasting lemon flavors. Also worth looking for is the ambitious Ca'Visco, a field selection that shows remarkable depth and concentration.

Via Roma 5, 37038 Soave, Verona
www.coffele.it

Col Vetoraz Valdobbiadene/Conegliano

Built along the spine of a ridge that abuts the famed Cartizze hill, with sweeping views over Valdobbiadene, Col Vetoraz is one of the most striking wineries in the region. Established in 1993 by enologist Loris dall'Acqua, along with Paolo De Bortoli and Francesco Miotto, Col Vetoraz has quickly become a top player in quality Prosecco. This is not surprising, given the estate's enviable vineyard holdings. Look no further than the basic Prosecco di Valdobbiadene for the house style: deep, vibrant flavors that last for minutes. ★ Rising star

Strada delle Treziese 1, 31040 S Stefano di Valdobbiadene
www.colvetoraz.it

Corte Sant'Alda Valpolicella/Amarone

Marinella Camerani has been continuously reinvigorating her family estate since the mid-1980s. Corte Sant'Alda today has nearly 47 acres (19ha), all farmed organically; biodynamic practices have also been introduced recently. Fermentation takes place without temperature control, in wooden vats, using only the yeasts present on the grapes or in the winery. The Valpolicella Ca'Fiui is one of Corte Sant'Alda's top wines, with vivid fruit expression and a lively, juicy mouthfeel. Or, for a wine with greater complexity, try the Amarone, which coils its luscious fruit in electrifying acidity. ★ Rising star

Via Capovilla 28, 37030 Mezzane di Sotto
www.cortesantalda.it

DREI DONA
PRUNO RISERVA AGES 18 MONTHS IN OAK CASKS AND IS BOTTLED UNFILTERED

CANTINA TRAMIN
THIS VINEYARD'S MOST FAMOUS WINE IS SPICY AND INTENSELY AROMATIC

Dal Forno Romano Valpolicella/Amarone

Romano Dal Forno took over his family's estate in the early 1980s, radically modernizing the vineyards and cellar. Dal Forno dropped yields and, in 1990, introduced French oak and other modern techniques. The result is a supremely elegant and sleek Valpolicella—one that is notably made outside of the Classico zone. Dal Forno's Valpolicella Superiore has been made using 100% dried grapes (in the manner of Amarone) since 2002, creating a massive and extracted wine that demands cellaring. The Amarone is likewise cloaked when young, only hinting at the power lurking beneath.

37039 Cellore di Illasi
www.dalfornoromano.it

Damijan Podversic Collio

Damijan Podversic could be considered the star pupil of iconoclastic winemaker Josko Gravner. From a patchwork of vineyards in the subregion of Monte Calvario, he makes some of the most striking wines in the region. Following Gravner's lead and encouragement, Podversic began to experiment with longer skin contact during fermentation, resulting in red and white wines of intense structure. The wines are fermented in wooden, open vats using ambient yeasts. While the Rosso Prelit is all savory power, the star wine is the Bianco Kaplja, a beguiling, complex blend of Chardonnay, Friulano, and Malvasia Istriana. ★ Rising star

Via Brigata Pavia 61, 34170 Gorizia
www.damijanpodversic.com

Dario Princic Collio

Dario Princic is an original member of the Italian natural wine movement. His estate is known for mineral-driven, idiosyncratic wines produced from vineyards farmed according to a combination of biodynamic and organic methods. Some of Princic's wines, like his orange-tinted Pinot Grigio, are downright unusual, yet entirely captivating. Complex and charged, the wine takes its copper color from long maceration on the grape skins, which also gives it a substantial weight on the palate.

Via Ossario 15/a, 34170 Oslavia
www.darioprincic.com

Drei Donà Forlì

Over two decades, Count Claudio Drei Donà and, more recently, his son Enrico have revitalized the 57 acres (23ha) of vineyards at their family estate, identifying and propagating a clone of Sangiovese unique to the property. La Palazza is fashioned after a French château, only the wines are named after the family's prize-winning horses. Pruno, the top wine, is selected from the best lots of Sangiovese and aged in both oak casks and small barrels. Massively structured, it needs cellar time. Notturno, a second selection, is more forward and approachable.

Via del Tesoro 23, Massa di Vecchiazzano 47100, Forlì
www.dreidona.it

Drusian Valdobbiadene/Conegliano

Sometimes you just need that "go-to" wine, and Drusian's Extra Dry Prosecco di Valdobbiadene seems to hit all the right notes. Crisp and refreshing, it hints at full fruit flavors like pear and peach without ever feeling heavy. The Drusian family have been growing grapes in the Valdobbiadene region for three generations, although

INAMA

THIS INTENSE YELLOW WINE IS LARGE
AND ROUND ON THE PALATE WITH A FINISH
OF SWEET ALMONDS

they only started making their own sparkling wine in the late 1980s. Beyond the Extra Dry Prosecco, look for the Cartizze: lightly sweet, elegant, and refreshing.

Strada Anche 1, 31030 Bigolino di Valdobbiadene
www.drusian.it

Le Due Terre Colli Orientali del Friuli

Established by Silvana Forte and Falvio Basilicata in 1984, Le Due Terre is a small, bucolic estate in the hills near Prepotto. Basilicata, who was a consulting winemaker in the region in the 1970s, mixes traditionalist methods, like spontaneous yeast fermentation, with more modern techniques, like temperature-control and the use of French barriques. His best effort is Sacrisassi Bianco, a barrel-fermented blend of Friulano and Ribolla Gialla that combines powerful structure with intense flavors of ripe lemon and sage. Sacrisassi Rosso is a rustic, hearty blend of Refosco and Schiopettino.

Via Roma 68B, Prepotto, 33040 Udine
043 271 3189

Elena Walch Alto Adige

Elena Walch's winemaking career began in 1985, after she had married into one of Tramin's most established wine families. She renovated the Walch's two estates, Castel Ringberg and Kastelaz, both of which are now among the best vineyards in the region. Kastelaz, in particular, is an exciting site: steep and broad, on a south-facing slope that creates opulent and powerful Gewürztraminer. Pinot Grigio—often dull and forgettable —is a different beast in Walch's hands. Balancing a rich texture with racy acidity, it is a wine rich with character.

Andreas Hoferstrasse 1, 39040 Tramin
www.elenawalch.com

Elisabetta Foradori Trentino

Elisabetta Foradori took over her family's 100-year-old estate in Mezzolombardo in 1984, with the goal of revitalizing Trentino's native Teroldego. She lowered yields and propagated selections from some of the estate's 80-year-old vines. Teroldego, which bears some similarity to Lagrein and Syrah, can often seem rustic and coarse. In Foradori's hands, it becomes elegant and refined, with profound aromatics and a potent earthiness. The Teroldego Rotaliano is fresh with violet scents, while Granato is more concentrated and full, perhaps the most significant Teroldego made in these hills. ★ **Rising star**

Via Damiano Chiesa 1, 38017 Mezzolombardo
www.elisabettaforadori.com

Eugenio Collavini Colli Orientali

This historic estate, named for its founder, is known mostly for a sparkling Ribolla Gialla. First developed in the 1970s, the Ribolla Gialla Brut is a curious wine that crosses the secondary tank fermentation technique common to Prosecco with the bottle fermentation and riddling of traditional champagne production. The result is a vibrant, richly textured sparkling wine marked by lemon-bright acidity. Remarkably versatile, the wine makes a compelling argument in favor of enjoying a sparkling wine throughout the course of an entire meal.

Via della Ribolla Gialla 2, 33040 Corno Rosazzo
www.collavini.it

JOSEF WEGER

A DRY, MELLOW, VELVETY WINE, WITH MILD
TANNINS AND ACIDITY AND FIRM STRUCTURE

Fantinel Collio

Established in 1969 by Mario Fantinel, active in both the restaurant and hotel industries, this is a multi-faceted wine company anchored in Friuli. Fantinel's lean Prosecco is one of the better efforts produced outside of Valdobbiadene. A lovely apéritif, it is an ideal partner for cured meats like prosciutto or bresaola. For reds, do not miss the Vigneti Sant'Helena Refosco, a powerful, mineral-driven single-vineyard selection from Fantinel's estate in Grave del Friuli.

Via Tesis 8, 33097 Tauriano di Spilimbergo
www.fantinel.com

Franz Haas Alto Adige

In 1986, Franz Haas took over the winery established by his family in the 1880s. He began modernizing the estate vineyards, introducing higher density planting and lowering yields. Of particular note is the engaging Moscato Rosa, an attractively floral wine grown at relatively low altitudes. The Franz Haas Lagrein is an appealing, stylish take on the grape, more forward and smooth than others. Also worth seeking out is Manna, an unusual and expressive blend of Riesling, Chardonnay, and Sauvignon Blanc with late-harvest Gewürztraminer, which makes for a richly textured wine.

Via Villa 6, 39040 Montagna
www.franz-haas.com

Gini Soave

Sandro and Claudio Gini manage this 74 acre (30ha) estate in Monforte d'Alpone, where they produce a clean, modern style of Soave from an enviable collection of old vines. The basic level Soave Classico is their freshest: here, the floral Garganega achieves bright, lifted flavors with notable mineral depth. La Froscà is the name of Gini's 55-year-old vineyard, and the wine from here sees some time in barrel, adding roundness to the concentrated flavor intensity. Salvarenza, a *cru* dating from 1925, produces a potent Soave fermented entirely in oak.

Via Matteotti 42, 37032 Montefort
www.ginivini.com

Giuseppe Quintarelli Valpollicella/Amarone

Every Italian region has its lion of tradition, and in the Veneto that title is owned by Giuseppe Quintarelli. Quintarelli took over his family's estate in the mid-1950s and it is fair to say that little has changed since. Highly sought-after by collectors around the world, Quintarelli's Amarone and Recioto della Valpolicella are statements in contemporary Italian wine. For those new to this style and tradition, check out Primofiore, Quintarelli's evocative and richly flavored entry-level wine.

Via Ceré 1, 37024 Negrar
045 750 0016

Gottardi Alto Adige

The area around Mazzon in lower Alto Adige is a small microclimate renowned for Pinot Noir. The Gottardi family—wine merchants based in Innsbruck, Austria, but with roots in the region around Mazzon—bought 16 acres (6.5ha) of land here in 1986. Pinot Noir grows at high altitudes (900–1,200ft /275–365m) on west-facing slopes here, so acidity levels remain bracingly high, while the afternoon sun allows the wine to develop generous flavors. Beyond these characteristics, Gottardi's Blauburgunder Mazzon shows pronounced minerality and firm tannins. Another wine worth seeking out is the spicy Gewürztraminer.

Weingut Gottardi Mazzon, 39040 Neumarkt Mazzon
www.gottardi-mazzon.com

J Hofstätter Alto Adige
The cellars of J Hofstätter are located just off the main square of the Alpine village of Tramin, the possible birthplace of the aromatic variety Gewürztraminer. Hofstätter's Kolbenhof Gewürztraminer—from a vineyard of the same name—is an iconic example, balancing lush aromatics with a firm, bracing acidity. Likewise, the Barthenau Vigna Sant'Urbano, a single-vineyard Pinot Nero from old vines planted on the opposite side of the Adige Valley from Tramin, is a study in balance, and easily one of Italy's best Pinots.

Piazza Municipio 7, 39040 Tramin-Termeno
www.hofstatter.com

I Clivi di Ferdinando Zanusso Collio/Colli
Ferdinando Zanusso bought and rehabilitated two dilapidated, old vineyards in the mid-1990s with a firm belief that older vines, in this case between 40- and 80-years old, make truly profound wines. Zanusso is committed to organic practices in I Clivi's vineyards and he takes a minimal interventionist approach in the cellar. Two wines come from the Galea vineyard: a blend of indigenous white varieties, including Friulano and Verduzzo, and a Merlot that shows powerful minerality. From the ancient vines at Brazen, I Clivi makes a complex blend of Friulano and Malvasia Istriana. ★**Rising star**

Località Gramogliano 20, 33040 Corno di Rosazzo
www.clivi.it

Inama Soave
Established in the 1950s by Giusseppe Inama, this 74 acre (30ha) estate has been managed since 1992 by his son, Stefano. Inama is an innovative estate: along with a range of excellent Soaves, the winery has achieved notable success with Sauvignon Blanc (especially the sweet Vulcaia Après) as well as Carmenère, which is planted at Inama's vineyard in Colli Berici. Among the Soaves, look for Vigneti di Foscarino, a graceful expression of Garganega aged in neutral barrels. This complex wine gives many white burgundies a run for their money.

Località Biacche, 50, 37047 San Bonifacio
www.inamaaziendaagricola.it

Jermann Collio
Jermann is a historic estate established in 1881 in the hilly region around Gorizia. Run since the 1970s by Silvio Jermann, the estate is one of the pioneers of Friulian "super whites." Look for the iconic Vintage Tunina, a complex blend of Sauvignon, Chardonnay, Ribolla Gialla, Malvasia Istriana, and Picolit that is structured and built for the long haul. To experience Jermann's take on a fresher, more immediate style, do not miss the crisp mineral notes of the Afix Riesling, or the bright, spicy flavors of the Sauvignon Blanc.

Via Monte Fortino 21, 34070 Villanova di Farra
www.jermann.it

Josef Weger Alto Adige
The Weger family have been involved in viticulture since the 1820s, when Josef Weger established his estate in Cornaiano. Like nearby Caldaro, this area has a relatively warm climate. A wine like Josef Weger's assertive Gewürztraminer shows the ripe, floral side of the grape, yet is often lower in alcohol than some of the heady wines from Tramin. Also worth tracking down is Josef Weger's traditional-styled Vernatsch (Schiava in Italian). Aged in large oak casks, this is a medium-bodied red with lasting flavors of wild berries.

Jesuheimstrasse 17, 39057 Girlan
www.wegerhof.it

Kuenhof Alto Adige
Peter Pliger and his wife Brigitte are the proprietors of the astonishing Kuenhof estate in the northern Valle Isarco. Kuenhof dates from the 9th century and, until 1989, supplied the nearby Abbazia di Novacella with grapes. Pliger released his first vintage in 1990 and set about restoring the terraced vineyards at Kuenhof; in recent years, he has purchased old terraces and planted Müller-Thurgau vines. Pliger employs a mix of organic and biodynamic practices in the vineyard, and minimal intervention in the cellar. Kuenhof's Kaiton Riesling and Sylvaner are especially thrilling. ★**Rising star**

Località Mara 110, 39042 Bressanone
047 285 0546

Lini Correggio
Alicia Lini, along with her father, Fabio, makes artisan Lambrusco that will change the way you think about sparkling red wine. However, one of Lini's best sparkling wines happens to be white. Made from Lambrusco Salamino, and Ancellotta, both separated from the skins during fermentation to keep the juice free from color, the Lambrusca Bianco is amazingly zesty and fresh. Lini has been around for nearly a century, but this small producer's wines are now picking up momentum in export markets. ★**Rising star**

Via Vecchia Canolo 7, 42015 Correggio
www.lini910.it

Lis Neris Collio
Led by Alvaro Pecorari, whose family has farmed in the region since 1879, Lis Neris has emerged as one of the most dynamic estates in Friuli. Most of its vineyards are planted in San Lorenzo, with smaller plots in the communes of Corona and Romans. San Lorenzo is the coolest of the three areas, imparting brisk acidity to its white grapes. Look for Gris, a complex, weighty expression of Pinot Grigio that nevertheless feels vibrant and focused. This is Pinot Grigio that will make you think.

Via Gavinana 5, 34070 San Lorenzo
www.lisneris.it

Livio Felluga Colli Orientali
Livio Felluga is one of the pioneers of modern winemaking in Friuli. His eponymous winery, which today is run by his children, helped lead the regional push for crisp, bright whites. Livio Felluga is also well established in international markets, meaning that wines like the vibrant and chalky Pinot Grigio are a likely introduction for many to the beauty and complexity

WINE CO-OPS THAT ROCK

Italy has a long history of co-operative winemaking, and nowhere is that tradition more prevalent and vibrant than the neighboring Alpine provinces of Trentino and Alto Adige. What is perhaps most surprising to outsiders, and is indeed unusual within Italy, is that several of these co-operatives are responsible for some of the two regions' best wines. Vineyards in both Trentino and Alto Adige tend to occupy steep terraces rather than large tracts of valley floor, and by nature they are often quite small. For most growers, it can be easier and more efficient to belong to a local co-operative than to start a private winery. Some co-operatives here, like Mezzacorona, specialize in honest, everyday wines that represent good value. Others, like Cantina Tramin and Cantina Terlano, make iconic wines that are among the best of their types in Italy—such as Tramin's Nussbaumer Gewürztraminer or Terlano's Vorberg Pinot Bianco.

MEDICI ERMETE
THIS AWARD-WINNING SPARKLING
DRY RED WINE IS PRODUCED USING
A NATURAL FERMENTATION

LIVIO FELLUGA
THIS WINE HAS THE COPPERY HIGHLIGHTS
THAT ARE PINOT GRIGIO'S HALLMARK

of Friuli's wines. Keep an eye out for the estate's reds, too. Sossó, a blend of Refosco, Merlot, and Pignolo, shows the generous flavors of the region's local varieties.

Via Risorgimento 1, 34071 Brazzano-Cormons
www.liviofelluga.it

Manni Nössing Alto Adige

The gregarious Manni Nössing took over his family's vineyards in 2000; before then, the Nössings sold their grapes to the neighboring Abbazia di Novacella. As is increasingly common in this tiny northern valley on the Austrian border, growers' children are not only taking over their family vineyards, but are starting new wineries. Nössing worked briefly with Peter Pliger at Kuenhof before starting out on his own. Look for Nössing's zesty and complex Kerner, or his racy Veltliner—a rare example of the variety in Italy. ★ **Rising star**

Weinbergstrasse 66, Via dei Vigneti, 39042 Brixen
www.manni-noessing.com

Marco Felluga Collio

Marco Felluga is the younger brother of Livo Felluga. He established his own estate in the 1950s in Gradisca d'Isonzo. Roberto Felluga, son of Marco, is in charge of the estate today, and the family controls more than 250 acres (100ha) of vineyards. Marco Felluga is primarily known for robustly flavored, elegant whites (although the Carantan, from Merlot, Cabernet Franc, and Cabernet Sauvignon, is a sophisticated red blend). Look for Mongris, a steely, firm Pinot Grigio, or Molamatta, a luscious blend of Friulano, Pinot Bianco, and Ribolla Gialla that feels elegant and complex.

Via Gorizia 121, 34072 Gradisca d'Isonzo
www.marcofelluga.it

Masi Valpolicella

In addition to being a leader in Amarone production, Masi is also a research center. The Masi Technical Group, spearheaded by the winery's owner Sandro Boscaini, conducts ongoing research into the complicated techniques used to produce Amarone—*appassimento* (air-drying of grapes) and double fermentation. Results are then shared with other producers in the Veneto. Masi makes several wines, but perhaps not surprisingly, its best efforts remain its Amarones. Richly styled and aromatically seductive, they are balanced with piercing acidity and firm structure, giving them the potential to age for decades.

Via Monteleone 26, 37015 Gargagnago di Valpolicella
www.masi.it

Maso Poli Trentino

In 1979, Luigi Togn bought and renovated an old estate with vines overlooking the broad Adige Valley near Lavis. Maso Poli is notable for its two blended wines, Sorni and Marmoram. Sorni, a blend of Chardonnay, Nosiola, and Müller-Thurgau, is forward and rich, mixing Alpine aromatics with generous texture. Marmoram is representative of the modern style that has emerged from Trentino and Alto Adige. Blended from two local varieties, Teroldego and Lagrein, its texture is made smooth and rich by the use of small barriques.

Pressano di Lavis, Strada del Vino 33, 38015 Lavis
www.masopoli.com

Medici Ermete Reggiano

Established over a century ago by Remigio Medici, and then run by his son, Ermete, Medici Ermete is today one of the leading producers of the Lambrusco renaissance. Concerto, a feisty, dark, concentrated sparkling wine from the family's La Rampata estate, is the firm's best-known brand. It won the Tre Bicchieri award from Gambero Rosso for the 2010 edition of Italian wine guide *Vini d'Italia*—the first Lambrusco Reggiano to receive this recognition. There are better Lambruscos out there, but Concerto is a solid introduction to this unique category in Italian wine.

Via Isacco Newton 13/a, 42100 Reggio nell'Emilia
www.medici.it

Mezzacorona Trentino

This massive co-operative sits on the border between Trentino and Alto Adige. Boasting an enormous member network of more than 1,500 growers, as well as one of the most sleek and modern wineries in Italy, Mezzacorona produces an astonishing amount of wine. Yet that size can be deceiving, for these are among the most consistently good and reliable everyday wines available. The Pinot Grigio is a clean, fresh, and easy-drinking white. For a more serious effort, check out NOS, Mezzacorona's stylish take on the local hero, Teroldego.

Via del Teroldego 1, 38016 Mezzocorona
www.mezzacorona.it

Mionetto Valdobbiadene

Established in the late 1880s, Mionetto is now one of the leading, and largest, makers of quality Prosecco in Valdobbiadene. Because of the company's long history in the region, it has built a strong network of small growers who vinify the still wines that Mionetto later makes into sparkling Prosecco. One of the best is the MO Prosecco di Valdobbiadene, a bright, crisp sparkler sourced from near the base of the Cartizze *cru*. For everyday refreshment, do not miss the basic level Prosecco di Valdobbiadene.

Via Colderove 2, 31049 Valdobbiadene
www.mionetto.com

Muri-Gries Alto Adige

Muri-Gries is a Benedictine monastery that just happens to own some of the best Lagrein vineyards around Bolzano. Wine production has long been a part of the monastery's history. Muri-Gries was built as a fortress at the end of the 11th century, and it has been church property since 1407. The monks still do much of the work in the vineyards and cellar, though the estate also employs an enologist. Muri-Gries makes several wines, including Müller-Thurgau and Pinot Grigio, but it is the velvety, spicy Lagrein that is not to be missed.

Grieser Platz 21, 39100 Bolzano
www.muri-gries.com

Muzic Collio

Giovanni Muzic's family tended vineyards and orchards in San Floriano for generations before buying their own land in the 1960s. Today, the Muzic estate totals 32 acres (13ha) in the Collio and just under 5 acres (2ha) in Isonzo. Muzic's flagship white is the Bianco Bric, a potent blend of Friulano, Malvasia Istriana, and Ribolla Gialla. In general, Muzic follows a clean, precise style that yields crisp wines like the Ribolla Gialla and Pinot Grigio. Also worth a try is the Cabernet Franc. Powerfully aromatic, it combines ripe fruit with darkly savory tannins.

Località Bivio 4, 34070 San Floriano del Collio
www.cantinamuzic.it

Nino Franco Valdobbiadene/Conegliano
Nino Franco is one of the oldest wineries in Valdobbiadene; established in 1919 by Antonio Franco, it is run today by his grandson, Primo. Primo Franco travels widely, actively promoting his wines in markets around the world. The perspective gained on his travels has clearly influenced the style of the wines at Nino Franco. Modern and robust, these are serious Proseccos. The creamy, rich flavors of the Rustico, the estate's best-known *cuvée*, are made light by brisk acidity. That bracing character also informs the Rive di San Floriano, a graceful expression of Prosecco from a single vineyard.

Via Garibaldi 147, 31049 Valdobbiadene
www.ninofranco.it

Novaia Valpolicella/Amarone
This 15 acre (6ha) estate is located in the high foothills of Alta Valpolicella. Run today by brothers Gianpaolo and Cesare Vaona, Novaia produces a vibrant style of Amarone, one that captures the relatively high altitude of these vineyards and translates it to a vivid tension that lifts the often heavy flavors of Amarone. Look for Novaia's single-vineyard Amarone, Le Balze; it balances savory notes like tobacco and earth with potent fruit flavor and mouthwatering acidity. Novaia cultivates a rare indigenous variety called Oseleta, popular with traditionalist producers in the Veneto.

37020 Marano Di Valpolicella
www.novaia.it

Nusserhof Alto Adige
Nusserhof is an old estate that has been walled in by the growth of Bolzano, the region's main city. Elda and Heinrich Nusser tend the 6 acre (2.5ha) plot as their family has done since the 18th century. Lagrein is Nusserhof's principal red; here, it is made in a traditional fashion, with aging done in large casks. The result is vibrant and fresh, with vivid wild berry flavors and firm tannins. You would never think that it grows within the city limits of Alto Adige's provincial capital.

Josef-Mayr Nusserweg 72, 39100 Bolzano
047 197 8388

Peter Sölva and Söhne Alto Adige
This historic estate is so old-school that they claim to have only been bottling their wines since 1960. Prior to that, the estate's wines were sold in small casks directly to merchants and restaurants. Peter Sölva and Söhne has gradually modernized since, and today produces a range of wines, including Amistar and De Silva. The De Silva wines are typically selected from the estate's older vines. The Lagrein, in particular, shows impressive concentration and varietal character. Amistar consists of red and white blends like the complex and sophisticated Rosso.

Via dell'Oro 33, 39052 Caldaro
www.soelva.com

PIEROPAN
A SOAVE WITH DELICATE AROMAS OF ALMOND BLOSSOM AND MARZIPAN

PRA
A WINE WITH INTENSE AND PERSISTENT AROMAS OF ALPINE GRASSES

Pieropan Soave
Leonildo "Nino" Pieropan is one of the benchmark producers of Soave. He and his wife, Teresita, together with their sons, run this staunchly traditional winery based inside the medieval city of Soave. Blessed with incomparable vineyards like La Rocca and Calvarino, Pieropan produces complex whites that defy Soave's cheap supermarket reputation, and also age beautifully. Start with the Classico, a wine that frames its bright fruit with nervy acidity. La Rocca, fermented in large oak tonneaux, is deep with firm, mineral flavor and lasting tension. It can be glorious in a good vintage.

Via Camuzzoni 3, 37038 Soave
www.pieropan.it

Plozner Grave del Friuli
Plozner was started by Lisio Plozner in 1967. His granddaughter, Sabina Maffei, took over the company in 2002. Maffei has updated things, injecting a little youthful vitality into a brand that has a reputation for simple, everyday wines. Winery equipment has been upgraded, new wines created, and new labels designed to showcase the changes. Two new wines, Moscabianca and Malpelo, show great promise. Moscabianca is an evocative, fresh Friulano, while Malpelo is a Pinot Grigio that spends additional time on its skins, producing a pale orange tint.

Via delle Prese 19, Fraz. Barbeano, 33097 Spilimbergo
042 729 02

Prà Soave
Graziano Prà, along with his brothers Sergio and Flavio, launched this winery from his family's modest holdings in the Soave Classico zone. Today, Prà controls nearly 50 acres (20ha) of vineyards in the region's best sites, including Montegrande, Foscarino, Froscà, Monte Croce, Sant'Antonio, and Ponsara. The wines skew toward the traditional, showcasing Gargenega's characteristic notes of pear and almond, although barrique fermentation is used for the Soave Colle Sant'Antonio. The result is a compelling statement in Soave—of the place, yet bold and ambitious.

Via della Fontana 31, 37032 Monteforte d'Alpone
www.vinipra.it

Radikon Oslavia
Stanislao Radikon took over his family's 27 acres (11ha) near Oslavia in 1980. Like his neighbors, Radikon navigated the enological trends that swept Friuli. In the 1980s, he began fermenting wines in temperature-controlled, stainless-steel tanks; he later abandoned that method and introduced small barriques. In 1995, he did an about-face and returned, as he puts it, to the way his grandfather made wine in the 1930s, using large open-topped wooden vats, long maceration periods, minimal sulphur dioxide, and no cultured yeasts or added enzymes. Wines like the golden-hued Ribolla Gialla are thrillingly charged with flavor and tension. ★ Rising star

Località Tre Buchi 4, 34170 Gorizia
www.radikon.it

La Roncaia Colli Orientali del Friuli
La Roncaia is the name of the Fantinel family's estate in the Colli Orientali subzone of Friuli. Generally, the focus here is on native varieties like Refosco, Picolit, Verduzzo,

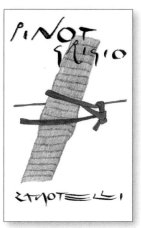

ZANOTELLI
A WINE BEST ENJOYED YOUNG, WHEN ITS DELICATE AROMAS ARE SUPPORTED BY THE BALANCE OF ITS STRUCTURE

SCARBOLO
ON THE PALATE, THIS WINE HAS A STRONG PERSONALITY AND ROBUST STRUCTURE

and Schiopettino, although grapes like Cabernet Franc, Sauvignon Blanc, and Pinot Grigio make their way into the blends. Eclisse, for instance, is a brisk, mineral-tinged white that combines the spiciness of Sauvignon Blanc with the rich, silky texture of Picolit. However, Refosco stars at La Roncaia. It straddles the line between massive and nimble, balancing ripe fruit with savory tannins.

Via Verdi 26, 33045 Nimis-Udine
www.fantinel.com

Roncús Collio
Run by Marco Perco, this small estate makes compelling, stylish white wines. Perco's 29 acres (12ha) of vineyards include old plantings of Malvasia Istriana, Friulano, and Ribolla Gialla, all of which are in the Bianco Vecchie Vigne. After fermentation in large Slavonian oak casks, the wine is racked to stainless steel tanks, where it is aged on the lees for two more years. The result is an elegant, mineral-tinged wine with a compelling purity and finesse.

Via Mazzini 26, 34070 Capriva del Friuli
www.roncus.it

Ruggeri Valdobbiadene/Conegliano
Established in 1950 by Giustino Bisol, Ruggeri is probably best known for its Giall'Oro Prosecco di Valdobbiadene, a lightly sweet and satisfying sparkling wine. Ruggeri also produces a vintage-dated Prosecco called Giustino B. More complex than Ruggeri's other wines, with concentrated flavor and depth, this is the thinking man's Prosecco. And while there is some debate as to the ability of Prosecco to age, vintage-dated Prosecco—unlike champagne—should be enjoyed almost immediately.

Via del Pra' Fontana, Valdobbiadene
www.ruggeri.it

Russiz Superiore Collio
While Russiz Superiore's history dates back to the Middle Ages, this ancient estate's modern chapter began in 1967 when it was bought by Marco Felluga. The vines here grow on steep hillsides composed of sandstone, with limestone and clay soils. The resulting wines, both white and red, seem to be framed by a firm, almost stony structure. Russiz Superiore's most ambitious wine is Col Disôre, a barrel-fermented and aged blend of Pinot Bianco, Friulano, Sauvignon, and Ribolla Gialla. Powerful and massive, Col Disôre will reward patient cellaring.

Via Russiz 7, 34070 Capriva del Friuli
www.russizsuperiore.it

San Patrignano Rimini
San Patrignano is unique among Italian wineries. It is part of the San Patrignano Foundation, which helps recovering drug addicts regain control of their lives through career training. Winery activities have been a part of the program since the beginning. Today, San Patrignano cultivates some 200 acres (80ha) of vineyards. Under the guidance of the consultant Riccardo Cotarella, it produces Sangiovese and Sangiovese-based blends that show the coastal influence of the nearby Adriatic Sea. Look for Avi, a warm, satisfyingly dense, yet lively, expression of Sangiovese. ★ **Rising star**

Via San Patrignano 53, 47852 Ospedaletto di Rimini
www.sanpatrignano.org

Scarbolo Pavia di Udine
Between his small estate winery and renowned restaurant, La Frasca, Valter Scarbolo embodies the passion and energy driving the food and wine scene in Friuli. Scarbolo's wines feel modern and precise, yet remain true expressions of variety and technique. The Ramato XL Pinot Grigio, for instance, is partially fermented on its skins in a nod to Friulian tradition. Other wines, like the elegantly structured Refosco, follow standard artisan techniques, like frequent punchdowns during fermentation and aging in French oak. Also good is Campo del Viotto, an impressive single-vineyard Merlot. ★ **Rising star**

Viale Grado 4, 33050 Pavia di Udine
www.scarbolo.com

Schiopetto Collio
Mario Schiopetto, an innkeeper's son from Udine, started making wine in the 1960s after traveling through France and Germany. Schiopetto was inspired by modern German practices for white wine fermentation, such as temperature control and the use of stainless steel tanks. He brought these techniques back to the Collio region of Friuli, and in the process helped to revolutionize Italian white wine. His three children have continued his efforts, positioning the Schiopetto winery at the forefront of Italian wine. Look for Schiopetto's Sauvignon, a seamless blend of nervy tension with powerful expression.

Via Palazzo Arcivescoville, 34070 Capriva del Friuli
www.schiopetto.it

Sorelle Bronca Valdobbiadene/Conegliano
Antonella and Ersiliana Bronca, along with their young enologist Federico Giotto, are among the few Prosecco producers to employ a single fermentation to make their sparkling wine (normally yeast and sugar are added to a finished base wine in a pressurized tank). At Sorelle Bronca, the must from freshly pressed, organically grown grapes is chilled and then put into a tank where both fermentation and carbonation occur, thanks to the already present grape sugars. The result is a splendidly fresh and natural-feeling Prosecco, with just enough complexity to make you think. ★ **Rising star**

Via Martiri 20, 31020 Colbertaldo di Vidor
www.sorellebronca.it

St-Michael-Eppan Alto Adige
Founded in 1907, St-Michael-Eppan is one of Alto Adige's leading co-operative wineries. It boasts a network of 355 member-growers, with vineyards planted around the picturesque village of Eppan (Appiano in Italian). Part of that network includes four of this subregion's renowned *crus*: Sanct Valentin, Schulthaus, Gleif, and Montiggl. St-Michael-Eppan considers the wines produced from Sanct Valentin as its top tier, so for the most part it functions as its own brand. Look for the spicy brightness of the Gewürztraminer, or the gamy, powerfully structured Sanct Valentin Lagrein.

Umfahrungsstrasse 17/19, 39057 Appiano
www.stmichael.it

La Stoppa Colli Piacentini
Elena Pantaleoni manages this old estate that her family acquired in 1973. Planted to mostly French varieties at the end of the 19th century, the Pantaleonis revitalized the old

vineyards to determine which varieties worked best. Today, La Stoppa is planted mostly to Barbera, Bonarda, Malvasia, Cabernet Sauvignon, and Merlot. Stoppa, the estate's red blend, takes advantage of the old plantings of Bordeaux grapes; it is a concentrated, structured beast. La Stoppa's most striking wine, though, is Ageno, an orange-tinted blend of Malvasia and other grapes fermented for up to 30 days on their skins.

29029 Rivergaro
www.lastoppa.it

Suavia Soave

Giovanni Tessari started Suavia in 1982, and today runs this small estate in the hamlet of Fittà with his four daughters. Suavia's immaculate vineyards are planted at a relatively high altitude, so the wines feel correspondingly crisp and energetic. The Soave Classico is a clean, honest expression of Garganega, while the family's two old-vine *crus*, Le Rive and Monte Carbonare, show greater complexity. Monte Carbonare is arguably the more elegant, displaying a fine-grained minerality that makes for a bracing wine.

Frazione Fittà, Via Centro 14, Soave
www.suavia.it

Tenuta San Leonardo Trentino

Italy's Alpine valleys are not exactly at the top of the list of places to produce ambitious Bordeaux-style blends of Cabernet Sauvignon, Merlot, and Cabernet Franc. Yet Tenuta San Leonardo, an estate established in the 18th century by the aristocratic Guerrieri Gonzaga family, makes a strong case that such wines are possible here. San Leonardo, the flagship red, is defined as much by the region's mountainous soils as anything else. Intense and herbal, it is a far cry from warmer climate Cabernet-based wines. Time reveals the elegance and complexity of this singular wine.

S Leonardo, 38060 Borghetto
www.sanleonardo.it

Tenuta Sant'Antonio Valpolicella

This young estate, established in 1995 by four brothers whose father had previously supplied grapes to the local co-operative, has come a long way in a short time. The heart of the estate is Monti Garbi, a series of vineyards planted in the chalky, calcareous soils near Mezzane. In addition to Valpolicella's traditional varieties, Tenuta Sant'Antonio grows Cabernet Sauvignon for the smooth Bordeaux-like Torre Melotti. However, the real star is the estate's powerful Amarone, especially the Selezione Antonio Castagnedi. Massive, yet entirely seductive, it makes for a satisfying drink. ★ **Rising star**

Via Ceriani 10, 37030 Colognola Ai Colli
www.tenutasantantonio.it

Thurnhof Alto Adige

Thurnhof is a small estate located on the warm slopes just outside Bolzano. Owned by the Berger-Mumelter family since 1850, Thurnhof is today run by the young, dynamic Andreas Berger. He approaches local varieties like Goldmuskateller (Moscato Giallo) and Lagrein with an eye toward traditional production methods, such as the use of large casks, yet the wines feel attractively modern and stylish. They reflect a common direction taken by the younger generation at the smaller independent estates in Alto Adige. Look for Merlau, Thurnhof's energetic and savory, single-vineyard Lagrein. ★ **Rising star**

Küepachweg 7, 39100 Bozen
www.thurnhof.com

Vodopivec Carso

Paolo and Valter Vodopivec farm about 11 acres (4.5ha) of vines in the Carso region near the Italian border city of Trieste. Vodopivec is part of the Italian natural wine movement (and members of the Vini Veri coalition), and as such the brothers farm organically and practice a philosophy of minimal intervention in the cellar. And like Josko Gravner, they have begun using terracotta amphorae for some of their fermentations. The Carso's little-known Vitovska is Vodopivec's speciality; their first vintage was 1997. Dense and powerful, yet remarkably light and energetic, it is thrilling stuff. ★ **Rising star**

Località Colludrozza 4, 34010 Sgonico
www.vodopivec.it

Weingut Niklas Alto Adige

Dieter Sölva is the affable young winemaker in charge of Weingut Niklas, a small winery and agriturismo perched on the steep mountain slopes above the town of Kaltern. While this region has one of Alto Adige's warmer microclimates, Niklas's vineyards are planted at high enough altitudes that the wines are subsequently marked by vivid acidity. The Niklas Sauvignon Blanc thrillingly combines rich tropical flavors with a firm mineral crunch. Be sure not to miss the estate's juicy Lagrein. Fresh and bright, it shows a versatility that is perfect for the table. ★ **Rising star**

Brunnenweg 31, 39052 Kaltern
www.niklaserhof.it

Zanotelli Alto Adige

Located in the Valle di Cembra subzone of Trentino, Zanotelli produces a range of stylish, crisp wines that reflect their high-altitude origins. Zanotelli's Müller-Thurgau, grown on steep slopes, feels fiercely charged with acidity, an aspect that energizes the wine's characteristic floral aromas and ripe pear flavors. Likewise, Zanotelli's Pinot Grigio is a far cry from more pedestrian versions of the grape. Here, it feels angular and firm, with ripe notes of apple and pear focused by distinctive minerality.

Via IV Novembre 52, 38034 Cembra
www.zanotelliwines.com

Zidarich Carso

Benjamin Zidarich started his winery in 1988 on land that his father and grandfather had farmed before him. He has since expanded to just over 14 acres (5.5ha) in the wild, windy hills of the Carso region, where he grows Vitovska, Malvasia, Sauvignon, and Terrano. Like those of Vodopivec, these are unusual wines that require some effort on the part of the drinker. Be patient: Zidarich's Vitovska may seem challenging at first, but it is rewarding and full of character. Also worth seeking out is the Terrano, with vivid scents of wild berries and fresh herbs.

Località Prepotto 23, Duino Aurisina
www.zidarich.it

VARIETIES TO WATCH: VITOVSKA AND REFOSCO

Italy's great strength lies in its viticultural diversity. Friuli is no exception, as the province is host to a range of indigenous grapes that co-exist alongside internationals like Chardonnay and Merlot. Two varieties to look for, Vitovska and Refosco, have names that are as fun to say as they are to drink. Vitovska is a white variety whose mixed Italian and Slovenian origins reflect the shifting boundaries of this part of Europe. Grown primarily in the Carso region, not far from Trieste, Vitovska can yield a beguiling, richly textured, and layered wine. Zidarich and Vodopivec make two of the best. Refosco, an indigenous red variety that is often found blended with Merlot, is increasingly in demand outside of Friuli. It can range from simple, juicy plum flavors to a more structured, hearty red gripped by savory tannins. La Roncaia, Il Roncal, and Marco Felluga are among the best producers.

CENTRAL ITALY

Central Italy is arguably the most beautiful part of a deeply alluring country. The Apennines reach their zenith in the Abruzzo, Lazio holds the key to the Eternal City, and the Marche's natural splendor is without equal. The region's viticulture is equally impressive and there is much more to Central Italy than oceans of cheap Frascati and Orvieto. The combination of lofty peaks and sun-drenched coasts generates an infinite variety of climatic permutations. For the reds, Sangiovese remains firmly in command, although its leadership is being challenged not only by the local Montepulciano, but increasingly from dynamic Bordeaux blends. The whites lead with Verdicchio, but Malvasia, Grechetto, and even Trebbiano are beginning to earn their keep.

Major grapes

Reds
Cabernet Sauvignon
Merlot
Montepulciano
Sangiovese

Whites
Grechetto
Malvasia
Trebbiano
Verdicchio

Vintages

2009
A slightly irregular and precocious vintage providing delicious drinking in the short to medium term.

2008
A flawless vintage with the long, regular growing season that native grape varieties adore. Both reds and whites are for the long haul.

2007
Excessive heat robbed this vintage of classic status.

2006
Another textbook vintage across central Italy with aromatic whites and ageworthy reds aplenty.

2005
A thorn between two roses, 2005 was cool and suffered from rain during the harvest.

2004
Perfect in every way, the reds from 2004 deserve a home in every serious cellar.

Central Italy acts as a buffer between the well-oiled, industrial north and the slower, soulful south. The factories and the juggernauts that characterize Italy's manufacturing heartland are here replaced with swathes of equally diligent agriculture. Neat farmhouses surrounded by pasture dominate the valley floors, while olive groves and vineyards race up the steep hills. It is a land that time and, to some extent, tourists appear to have forgotten.

The horizontal is difficult to find around Italy's axis, and mountains define not only what is arable, but also what is habitable. The Apennines, which here soar to more than 10,000ft (3,000m), demarcate the four key regions and have for centuries encouraged trade and transportation along clearly defined routes that are signposted by vineyards as often as they are by monasteries.

Umbria has an abundance of both, although for centuries many would have argued that the churches merited more attention. Latterly, however, Umbria has silenced its critics with a raft of impressive wines including the flagship DOCG of Sagrantino di Montefalco, a rejuvenated Orvieto, and clever blends of Sangiovese, Montepulciano, Cabernet, and Merlot.

Next door, and perennially under-appreciated, despite its natural beauty and the quality of its wines, the Marche handsomely rewards a little exploration. It is best known as the home of Verdicchio, Central Italy's finest white wine. The jagged Monti Sibillini form a dramatic backdrop for the vineyards of Verdicchio di Matelica DOC—this superb variety's finest moment is far removed from the villainous swill in amphora-shaped bottles. The DOCG of Cónero is Montepulciano's northern outpost and fashions inky reds that give most versions from the Abruzzo a run for their money. Standing guard on the Marche's southern border is Rosso Piceno, the only DOC on the Adriatic coast, where Sangiovese continues to play a leading role.

Although the Abruzzo has some way to go before it can rival the Marche for viticultural diversity, there are signs that its two stalwarts, Trebbiano and Montepulciano, are beginning to up their game. The former is one of Europe's most ubiquitous varieties, a grape of easy virtue that reliably ripens a mammoth crop load with minimum fuss. With restricted yields, however, it produces affordable, characterful whites that are a dab hand at matching the Abruzzo's abundant marine harvest. Montepulciano, on the other hand, is held in the highest regard both in the Abruzzo and further afield. Its heady mix of alcohol, acidity, and tannins places it firmly in the top division, and serious examples are no longer the exception to the rule.

Dwarfed by its northern neighbor, Molise's party trick is the ancient red variety, Tintilia. Lazio may host the nation's capital, but its wines have never flown the Tre Colore with anything approximating national pride. The occasional Frascati demonstrates the undeniable potential of Malvasia, but Lazio's strongest efforts come from international varietals grown in the north, near the border with Tuscany.

CENTRAL ITALY

Italy's rugged and mountainous "thigh" is the most densely planted area of the peninsula. Vineyards creep up the foothills of the Apennines from both the Adriatic and Tyrrhenian coasts, and pockets of viticulture dot the interior. The moderating influence of the sea diminishes as one heads inland, and vineyards in Umbria and central Tuscany experience colder nights and hotter days than those near the coast. Many of Italy's most famous wines, including Chianti Classico, Orvieto, and Frascati, hail from land-locked hideaways in Central Italy.

MIRUM
MIRUM
VERDICCHIO DI MATELICA
Denominazione di Origine Controllata
RISERVA
2007
75 cl. e   la Monacesca   14%vol

25
2006
SAGRANTINO DI MONTEFALCO
DENOMINAZIONE DI ORIGINE CONTROLLATA E GARANTITA
ARNALDO·CAPRAI

Lamborghini

TRESCONE

UMBRIA
INDICAZIONE
GEOGRAFICA
TIPICA

FRUTTI D'OLTRAGGI PURI
E D'OGNI VIZIO INTATTI
OFFRIVANO AL MORSO
LISCE POLPE E
COMPATTE.

LIGURIAN
SEA

TYRRHENIAN
SEA

ADRIATIC
SEA

N
W   E
S

Cremona
Mantova
Monselice
Piacenza
Ostiglia
Rovigo
Chioggia
Oglio
Po
Po
Fidenza
Parma
Carpi
Ferrara
Codigoro
Reggio nell'Emilia
Modena
Commachio
2017m
(6617ft)
Bologna
COLLI DI
IMOLA
Ravenna
SANGIOVESE
DI ROMAGNA
1945m
(6381ft)
COLLI DI
FAENZA
Faenza
COLLI DI
RIMINI
La Spezia
Massa
TREBBIANO DI
ROMAGNA
Cesena
Rimini
Lucca
Prato
ALBANA DI
ROMAGNA
SAN
MARINO
Pesaro
CARMIGNANO
Florence
Pisa
Arno
Bagno di
Romagna
Urbino
VERDICCHIO
DEI CASTELLI
DI JESI
Ancona
Pontedera
Empoli
VERNACCIA
DI SAN
GIMIGNANO
Arezzo
1702m
(5584ft)
Jesi
ROSSO
CONERO
Livorno
CHIANTI
CLASSICO
CHIANTI
Siena
VERDICCHIO
DI MATELICA
Ceciana
Cecina
VINO NOBILE DI
MONTEPULCIANO
Tevere
TORGIANO
Macerata
LACRIMA DI
MORRO D'ALBA
BOLGHERI
SASSICAIA
Montepulciano
Perugia
Fermo
Piombino
BRUNELLO DI
MONTEPULCIANO
Lago
Trasimeno
ROSSO
PICENO
1738m
(5702ft)
ORVIETO
Orvieto
MONTEFALCO
Foligno
1575m
(5167ft)
Ascoli
Piceno
San Benedetto
del Tronto
Grosseto
Elba
434m
(1424ft)
Lago di
Bolsena
Terni
CONTROGUERRA
Teramo
Orbetello
EST! EST!!
EST!!!
Viterbo
2623m
(8606ft)
L'Aquila
MONTEPULCIANO
D'ABRUZZO
Pescara
Chieti
Lago
di Bracciano
2487m
(8159ft)
TREBBIANO
D'ABRUZZO
Vasto
Civitavecchia
Tivoli
2241m
(7352ft)
Avezzano
Sulmona
Sinello
Termoli
ROME
Fiumicino
Albano
Frosinone
Sora
Campobasso
FRASCATI
Biferno
Anzio
1090m
(3576ft)

KEY

- Abruzzo
- Emilia-Romagna
- Lazio
- Marche
- Tuscany
- Umbria
- International Border
- Regional boundary

CHIANTI DOC / DOCG

0   20   40   60 miles
0   20   40   60   80   100 km

BINOMIO
A MUCH SOUGHT-AFTER WINE THAT
REWARDS CELLARING FOR UP TO 20 YEARS

CASALE CENTO CORVI
THIS WINE IS MADE FROM LATE-HARVESTED
GRAPES OF A LOCAL, ANCIENT VARIETY

Adanti Umbria
Wine-lovers looking to discover the soul of Sagrantino, a uniquely Umbrian variety, could do worse than start their trip here, at Adanti, a stalwart of the DOCG Sagrantino di Montefalco since the 1960s. Alvaro Palini's Sagrantino is sourced from two vineyards of the estate's 79 acres (32ha) in the commune of Arquata. Unconvinced of the merits of barriques, Palini continues to age his Sagrantino in large, old oak. It is a variety that takes kindly to lengthy maturation, and his interpretation shows Sagrantino's telltale tannins, offset by sweet black fruit and complex, spicy aromas.

Vocabolo Arquata, Bevagna 06031
www.cantineadanti.com

Antonelli San Marco Umbria
Filippo Antonelli's roots in the rolling hills of Montefalco stretch back five generations to 1881, when Francesco Antonelli purchased this 395 acre (160ha) estate in the heart of the current DOCG. Sagrantino is, therefore, at the heart of the operation, but it would be a mistake to miss its superb Grechetto. A simple white from the grape that put Orvieto on the map, this has citrus notes and punches well above its weight in the value-for-money arena. The Sagrantino Chiusa di Pannone is a particularly elegant iteration, with just a trace of wood.

Località San Marco 60, 06036 Montefalco
www.antonellisanmarco.it

Arnaldo Caprai Umbria
This estate is synonymous with Sagrantino. No one has spent more money, or more time, perfecting this variety than Marco Caprai, the son of the estate's founder, Arnaldo. A long association with the University of Milan has yielded crucial insights into the variety's predilections for soil types, training systems, and rootstocks, and this research has guided the estate's hand at every turn. The wine that typifies this estate's relentless search for quality is Marco's peerless Sagrantino 25 Anni, an inky-black, brooding red that needs at least a decade in bottle.

Località Torre, 06036 Montefalco
www.arnaldocaprai.it

Binomio Abruzzo
This cult Montepulciano d'Abruzzo DOC is not made every year, but when it is, collectors and critics alike tend to take notice. Binomio translates loosely as "two names," a reference to the owners, Stefano Inama and Sabatino de Properzio, whose families have, between them, more than two centuries of winemaking experience. The grapes are grown in an immaculately trained 11 acre (4.5ha) plot of old-clone Montepulciano. Impenetrable purple when young, it ages at a glacial pace for up to 20 years, adding layers of spice (from 15 months in French oak), cherries, prune, and cocoa. ★ **Rising star**

Via Torretta 52, 65010 Spoltore
www.lavalentina.it

Boccadigabbia Marche
This part of the Marche has associations with France stretching back more than two centuries. Napoleon annexed the area surrounding Civitanova in 1808 and, bizarrely, it remained in his family's hands until after the World War II. In fact, the Alessandri family bought the 25 acre (10ha) Boccadigabbia estate in 1956 directly from Prince Luigi Napoleone Bonaparte. They have preserved the tradition of cultivating French varieties and have made a name for themselves with a particularly toothsome Cabernet Sauvignon called Akronte that would have brought a tear to the old emperor's eye.

Contrada Castelletta 56, 62012 Civitanova Marche
www.boccadigabbia.com

Cantine Giorgio Lungarotti Umbria
There cannot be many estates in Italy that can boast their very own DOCG. Torgiano Rosso Riserva DOCG now has two producers, but it will be forever linked to Lugnarotti, a massive firm with more than 750 acres (300ha) of vineyard and an annual production approaching 3 million bottles. Its Vigna Monticchio does much more than just set the standard for the DOCG—it is a compelling blend of Sangiovese and Canaiolo that throws down the gauntlet to the neighboring Tuscan DOCGs.

Via Mario Angeloni 16, 06089 Torgiano
www.lungarotti.it

Casale Cento Corvi Lazio
This part of the Tyrrhenian coast may technically be part of Lazio, but it has more in common with Bolgheri than it does with Frascati. The maritime influence is keenly felt, and the vineyards amble from the coast into the languorous volcanic hills that characterize this part of the world. The "House of 100 Crows" continues a viticultural tradition, dating back to the Etruscans, with a merry range of native and international varietals. The late-harvested Giacchè Rosso, from an ancient grape of the same name, is the succulent, cherry-scented pick of the bunch.

Via Aurelia Km 45+500, 00052 Cerveteri
www.casalecentocorvi.it

Casale Del Giglio Lazio
Purists may wag their finger disapprovingly at Antonio Santarelli's 20-year research into the potential of international varieties in Lazio, but, given what was here before—a swamp—most wine drinkers are pretty happy he decided to persevere. The estate is best known for an incredibly seductive and affordable Shiraz, but all its wines show the attention to detail that winemaker Paolo Tiefenthaler brings to this project. The Antinoo, a Chardonnay/Viognier blend, is creamy and rich, and the Cabernet Sauvignon sports a fine, oaky cloak around the traditional notes of blackcurrant and mint.

Strada Cisterna-Nettuno Km 13, 04100 Le Ferriere
www.casaledelgiglio.it

Castel de Paolis Lazio
Castel de Paolis is to Frascati what Ferrari is to the car. The vineyards had been in his family since the 1960s, but it was not until Giulio Santarelli met professor Attilio Scienza that the renovation of every aspect of this estate began. Now with 32 acres (13ha) of high-density vineyards, this estate is absolutely at the top of its game. Its Frascati Vigna Adriana is a revelation, given the standard of this clichéd DOC. A dash of both Viognier and Sauvignon Blanc add zest to Malvasia's solemn, herbal demeanor.

Via Val De Paolis, 00046 Grottaferrata
www.casteldepaolis.it

Castello delle Regine Umbria

Umbria has always been the crossroads of Italy, and its viticulture reflects a curious mix of north and south, east and west. Nowhere is this more evident than at Castello delle Regine, where Paolo Nodari, with a little help from consultant winemaker Franco Bernabei, produces wines from an eclectic band including Merlot, Sangiovese, Montepulciano, Syrah, Trebbiano, Grechetto, Malvasia, Chardonnay, Sauvignon, Pinot Grigio, and Riesling. The Merlot and the Sangiovese are currently neck and neck in terms of the awards they have garnered; both perform extremely well in the sandy clay soils of this southern corner of Umbria.

Via di Castelluccio Amerino, Località Le Regine, 05022 Amelia
www.castellodelleregine.com

Castello della Sala Umbria

No less than 26 generations of the Antinori family have produced wines in Tuscany. However, their Orvieto estate dates only to 1940, when Niccolò Antinori purchased the 1,250 acre (500ha) Castello della Sala estate and set about restoring both the castle and its vineyards. Today it boasts 395 acres (160ha) planted with equal parts local and international varieties. It is the latter that have caused such a stir, and in particular the Chardonnay Cervaro della Sala, now considered one of Italy's finest exponents of this Burgundian variety. Its swirling notes of new oak and tropical fruit are unmistakable.

Località La Sala, 05016 Ficulle
www.antinori.it

Cataldi Madonna Abruzzo

Montepulciano needs heat, and here, on either side of the River Tirino in what is known as the oven of the Abruzzo, temperatures regularly hit 104°F (40°C). This estate has 62 acres (25ha) of traditional varieties, including Montepulciano, Trebbiano, and Pecorino, a local white in which it places great store. The latter is exemplary, with a delicate floral character, while the rosé Montepulciano, Cerasuolo Piè delle Vigne, is as big and dangerous as any you would care to know. Tonì, a hefty, barrel-aged Montepulciano d'Abruzzo, completes the range.

Località Piano, 67025 Ofena
0862 954252

Colonnara Marche

Not many co-operatives find their way into the guide books, but Colonnara is most deserving of its place in the canon of eminent Marche producers. Founded in 1959, it now boasts 200 members who, together, farm 618 acres (250ha) of vineyards in the hills surrounding Cupramontana. Vines here benefit from a perfect marriage of maritime and alpine influence, and the origins of the unique Marche variety, Verdicchio, can be traced to Cupramontana. Like most co-ops, Colonnara produces a vast range of wines, but their Verdicchio Cuprese represents the best value.

Via Mandriole 6, 60034 Cupramontana
www.colonnara.it

Decugnano dei Barbi Umbria

In the race to taste the next 100-pointer, it is all too easy to overlook estates that consistently produce a useful range of affordable classics. Decugnano dei Barbi may

CASALE DEL GIGLIO
MADE FROM LOW-YIELD VINES, THIS WINE IS AGED IN OAK CASKS FOR UP TO 20 MONTHS

DECUGNANO DEI BARBI
A FRUITY BLEND OF GRECHETTO, VERMENTINO, AND CHARDONNAY

not be the most fashionable name in Umbria, but its wines are as tasty as ever. Leading the charge is a reliable Orvieto Classico Superiore that delivers a healthy dollop of candied fruit and prescient acidity, allowing the wine to develop for a decade or more. The unctuous Pourriture Noble, made from botrytis-affected Grechetto and Sauvignon Blanc, also merits a place in the cellar.

Località Fossatello 50, 05019 Orvieto
www.decugnanodeibarbi.com

Dino Illuminati Abruzzo

Five generations of the Illuminati family have produced wines in this remote northern outpost of the Abruzzo, where international varieties such as Cabernet Sauvignon and Chardonnay join the local working party of Montepulciano and Trebbiano. This is reflected in the legislation here which, uniquely, permits three overlapping DOCs. The Illuminati family makes the most of this anomaly. The white Daniele and red Lumen are both skilful blends of local and international varieties under the Controguerra DOC. These are joined by a cheerful Montepulciano and Trebbiano d'Abruzzo DOC, and the epic Zanna Montepulciano d'Abruzzo Colline Termane DOCG.

64010 Controguerra
www.illuminativini.com

Emidio Pepe Abruzzo

In the cellars of Emidio Pepe, time really does stand still. Run biodynamically by sisters Daniela and Sofia, the white grapes are still crushed by foot, and the reds are still stalked by hand. The cellars contain more than 200,000 bottles stretching back some 30 years, and Rosa Pepe, the matriarch of this 37 acre (15ha) estate, still decants and re-bottles each one by hand before applying labels and shipping. Examples with 10–20 years' bottle age are still relatively easy to find, and showcase a bygone era of winemaking.

Via Chiesi 10, 64010 Torano Nuovo
www.emidiopepe.com

Falesco Umbria

The wine that marked Italy's rebirth as a nation that did actually pay heed to what the rest of the world was drinking was Falesco's affordable, gluggable Montiano. Made from 100% Merlot, it took the world by storm when it first appeared in 1993, and proved that not all Italian reds are either ludicrously expensive or inexcusably tannic. Along the way, it established winemaker Riccardo Cotarella as a household name and put this part of Italy firmly on the map. Falesco—and the Cotarella brothers who own it—never looked back.

Località San Pietro, 05020 Montecchio
www.falesco.it

Fattoria Coroncino Marche

The Canestrari family began production as recently as 1985, but their estate is already one of the Marche's top producers. With 23 acres (9.5ha) of vineyards in the legendary Staffolo commune, it is no surprise that owner Lucio Canestrari's focus has been solely on Verdicchio. Production is small—fewer than 4,000 cases a year—but the quality is superb. The Gaiospino Cru is a Marche legend. Made from late-harvest Verdicchio, it is a

LAMBORGHINI
AN UNUSUAL BLEND OF CABERNET
SAUVIGNON, SANGIOVESE, AND
MONTEPULCIANO GRAPES

MASCIARELLI
A BRIGHT AND BRILLIANT TREBBIANO THAT
GOES WELL WITH FISH AND WHITE MEAT

sensuous example of this grape that shrugs off the staggering alcohol and assaults the senses with notes of lychee, peach, and oriental spice.

Contrada Coroncino 7, 60039 Staffolo
0731 779494

Fattoria Le Terrazze Marche

Antonio and Georgina Terni work 50 acres (20ha) of vineyards at the foot of Monte Cónero. This striking peak rises vertically from the Adriatic and vines first raced up its steep slopes well before Pliny eulogized its wines. Cónero is the Marche's only red DOCG and Le Terrazze provides a fine interpretation. The regulations specify at least 85% Montepulciano, but all three iterations from this estate are pure varietals. Of these, the cherry-scented Sassi Neri, aged in new and second-fill barriques, provides the optimal balance between fruit and oak.

Via Musone 4, 60026 Numana
www.fattorialeterrazze.it

Fattoria Nicodemi Abruzzo

The Nicodemi estate was founded in the early 20th century by Elena Nicodemi's grandfather, Carlo. Bruno, her father, assumed the reins in the early 1960s and when he passed away unexpectedly, in 1998, Elena turned her back on a promising career as an architect and returned to the homestead with great clarity of purpose. Ably assisted by Federico Curtaz and Paolo Caciorgna, her wines are shining examples of the unparalleled value found in the Abruzzo. The Trebbiano shows lovely stone fruit character and mouth-watering acidity, while the Montepulciano is marvelous with roast meats and game.

Contrada Ventriglio, 64024 Notaresco
www.nicodemi.com

Gioacchino Garofoli Marche

The Garofoli family remain at the forefront of the Marche's transformation from viticultural backwater into one of Italy's most dynamic regions. Resolutely family-owned, this company is a leviathan of the Ancona province, with annual production of more than 2 million bottles. Its range includes all the Marchigiani classics, such as Verdicchio, Rosso Piceno, Cónero, and Lacrima, of which Verdicchio enjoys the lion's share. The estate pioneered barrel aging, but aging Verdicchio in wood is a case of gilding the lily. Its late-harvest Podium, aged in stainless steel, is the current favorite.

Piazzale G. Garofoli 1, 60022 Castelfidardo
www.garofolivini.it

La Carraia Umbria

Founded in 1988, La Carraia is a joint venture between Odoardo Gialetti and Riccardo Cotarella. Their pioneering work with the humble DOC of Orvieto helped polish its tarnished reputation. Their affordable Orvieto is a delight, with citrus-fruit notes and more than enough stuffing to see off a plate of linguine. The Poggio Calvelli, thickened with a quarter Chardonnay, is similarly moreish. In 1995, La Carraia released Fobiano, a Bordeaux blend aged in new French oak. Its come-hither nose of ripe black fruit and creamy oak proved an immediate hit.

Località Tordimonte 56, 05018 Orvieto
www.lacarraia.it

Lamborghini La Fiorita Umbria

Yes, *that* Lamborghini. The same Ferruccio Lamborghini that brought us snarling bulls and 12 cylinder engines now brings us a range of equally desirable reds. To be fair, wine is not a recently acquired affectation—he purchased the estate in 1971. It is only recently, however, that his reputation as a winemaker has begun to overshadow that of carmaker. Trescone is a lithe and youthful red, Campoleone is the estate's biggest seller, and, like the sports car, it is hardly for every day, but its sensuous curves have the broadest appeal.

Località Soderi 1, 06064 Panicale
www.lamborghinionline.it

La Monacesca Marche

Part *bon viveur* and part farmer, the cigar-smoking, Porsche-driving Aldo Cifola is responsible for single-handedly raising the reputation of this achingly beautiful DOC. High in the Apennines, the north–south valley of Matelica enjoys some of the most dramatic swings in temperature anywhere in the wine world. Scorching days and freezing nights reduce yields and delay ripening—a situation that is disastrous for yields, but perfect for increasing concentration. In his Verdicchio di Matelica Riserva Mirum, Aldo has created one of Italy's greatest whites. Like Sophia Loren, it ages gracefully for decades.

Contrada Monacesca, 62024 Matelica
www.monacesca.it

La Palazzola Umbria

Umbria's evergreen consultant, Riccardo Cotarella, has helped shape the iconoclastic wines of La Palazzola since the early 1990s. It is a surprising appointment, given the estate's fiercely independent owner, Stefano Grilli. Winemaker and philosopher in equal measure, Grilli produces red sweet and sparkling wines (not a still white in sight) from a ragtag band of grapes, including Riesling, Muscat, Syrah, Pinot Noir, and Merlot. There is much to recommend, including his silky Cabernet Rubino, but the traditional method sparkling Sangiovese and red Vin Santo are among Stefano's more idiosyncratic creations.

Via Di Vittorio 69, 05100 Terni
www.lapalazzola.it

La Valentina Abruzzo

Sabatino de Properzio (see also Binomio) is the dynamo behind this thoroughly modern estate founded in 1990. La Valentina controls 111 acres (111 acres) of vineyards and produces consistently excellent wines vinified in modern facilities a few miles from the Adriatic. The classic range comprises exemplary Montepulciano, Trebbiano, and Cerasuolo, but it is the Bellovedere that sets pulses racing. Produced from a 5 acre (2ha) vineyard, a maximum of just 6,000 bottles are produced each year. Full-bodied, inky black, and erupting with super-ripe fruit, this is a most hedonistic expression of Montepulciano.

Via Torretta 52, 65010 Spoltore
www.lavalentina.it

Masciarelli Abruzzo

The late Gianni Masciarelli, who passed away in 2008 aged just 53, was a giant of the Abruzzo. His influence, both in terms of the size of his estate— 680 acres (275ha) and 3 million bottles a year—and in terms of raising the region's profile, cannot be overstated. Gianni worked tirelessly to improve both his vineyards and cellar through the sensitive introduction of new grape varieties and modern technology. Wines such as his elegant Montepulciano Villa Gemma and his hedonistic Chardonnay, Marina Cvetic, are a fitting tribute to one of the wine world's few originals.

Via Gamberale 1, 66010 San Martino sulla Marrucina
www.masciarelli.it

Moroder Marche
The Moroder family traces their roots in this beautiful corner of the world back to the 700s, long before it became part of the Monte Cónero National Park. You would be right in expecting them to know what they are doing, and they do not disappoint. Most of the estate's 79 acres (32ha) are planted with Montepulciano in this, the variety's most northerly outpost. Franco Bernabei is the consultant enologist, and he has cast his spell over a characterful rosé and a brace of Rosso Cóneri, of which the Riserva Dorico is this DOCG's finest example.

Via Montacuto 112, 60129 Ancona
www.moroder-vini.it

Oasi degli Angeli Marche
Marco Casolanetti and his long-term partner, Eleonora Rossi, have been extracting something truly unique from Oasi delgi Angeli's vineyards. Kurni is a cult wine in Italy, and Marco enjoys basking in the fame that has accompanied his meteoric rise to stardom. His philosophy is extreme, in the sense that all aspects of viticulture (ridiculously low yields) and vinification (50 days on the skins and placed in 100% new oak) are designed to push boundaries. The result is, predictably, a more-of-everything assault on the senses that, like a bodybuilder, flirts with the boundaries of what most would consider attractive. ★**Rising star**

Contrada Sant'Egidio 50, 63012 Cupra Marittima
www.kurni.it

Palazzone Umbria
A string of adjectives including breathtaking, beautiful, and brilliant would fail to capture the backdrop for the Dubini's 86 acre (35ha) property. Occupying an exquisite promontory on the old pilgrim's route to Rome, this spot's outstanding beauty was first recognized in the 13th century. If Palazzone's natural charms do not melt the heart, then there is always the Orvieto Classico Campo del Guardiano, the DOC's finest example, made exclusively from local varieties. Tight and unforgiving when young, with time it develops silky floral notes and complex citrus fruit that instantly silence critics of this unfashionable DOC.

Località Rocca Ripesena, 05019 Orvieto
www.palazzone.com

Piero Costantini Villa Simone Lazio
The name Piero Costantini is unalterably linked to wine —his Enoteca Costantini in central Rome boasts more than 4,000 bins. Villa Simone is Costantini's estate in Monteporzio Catone in the very heart of the Frascati DOC, some 12.5 miles (20km) southeast of Rome. Annual production only just exceeds 300,000 bottles a year from

SERGIO MOTTURA
THIS GOLDEN-YELLOW, SINGLE-VINEYARD WINE IS MADE FROM 100% GRECHETTO

SARTARELLI
THIS COMPLEX, AROMATIC WINE IS HIGH IN ALCOHOL BUT SOFT AND ELEGANT

a total of 67 acres (27ha) of vineyards. The Frascati Superiore Vigneto di Filonardi DOC is a superb example of the potential of Malvasia, with a fine mineral backbone and notes of candied fruit, apple, and banana.

Via Frascati-Colonna 29, 00040 Monteporzio Catone
www.pierocostantini.it

Saladini Pilastri Marche
The Count Saladini Pilastri traces his roots here in the southern Marche back more than 1,000 years. The estate has been producing wine for 300 of them, and with 790 acres (320ha) of vineyards, organically cultivated since 1995, Saladini Pilastri ranks as one of the first adherents to organic cultivation in the Italian peninsula. Its immense vineyard holdings mean that it can afford to be fussy about what goes into a bottle (half its production is sold in bulk), and the result is a range that would be an odds-on favorite in the Italian best-value stakes.

Via Saladini 5, 63030 Spinetoli
www.saladinipilastri.it

Sartarelli Marche
With 163 acres (66ha) of Verdicchio under vine, Donatella Sartarelli and Patrizio Chiacchiarini are a leading family producer in the Marche. In the 1970s, they breathed life back into the family estate and set their sights on producing white wines that would rival the very best. They have succeeded admirably. Sartarelli's Verdicchio dei Castelli di Jesi is a juicy, scented white, while the Tralivio is a selection from low-yield vineyards. The epic Balciana, which is harvested in mid-November, tips the scales at 15% alcohol, and offers an explosion of apple, honey, and sweet spices.

Via Coste del Molino 24, 60030 Poggio San Marcello
www.sartarelli.it

Sergio Mottura Lazio
Orvieto is one of those curious Italian DOCs that straddles a regional boundary—in this case Umbria and Lazio. The Mottura estate, however, is firmly in Lazio where it comprises 91 acres (37ha) of certified organic vineyards. Porcupines—part of the estate long before Sergio's grandfather arrived in 1933—feature on every label, and are considered part of the family. The white Latour a Civitella is an epic Grechetto IGT that fully deserves its many gongs, but the Orvieto, at half the price, is a savvy choice for those in the know.

Località Poggio della Costa, 01020 Civitella d'Agliano
www.motturasergio.it

Stefano Mancinelli Marche
The warm and welcoming Stefano Mancinelli is an ideal ambassador for Lacrima di Morro d'Alba, a forgotten variety in a neglected DOC. Production remains tiny, but it has tripled in the last decade, largely due to Stefano's efforts to popularize it. He makes two versions. The more expensive and traditionally fermented Lacrima delivers a healthy dose of the floral perfume for which the grape is famous. The Sensazione di Frutto, however, redefines the word "fruity" with an explosive, fragrant bouquet of rose, violet, and blueberry that positively leaps from the glass.

Via Roma 62, 60030 Morro d'Alba
www.mancinelli-wine.com

VELENOSI
THIS FRESH AND FRAGRANT CHARDONNAY IS
BEST ENJOYED IN ITS SECOND YEAR OF LIFE

VILLA BUCCI
THIS MEDIUM-BODIED RESERVE WINE IS MADE
FROM 100% VERDICCHIO

Tenuta Còlpetrone Umbria

Saiagricola is the agricultural investment arm of the SAI Insurance Company, the Italian equivalent of AXA Millésimes in France. Like its French counterpart, Saiagricola controls a thoroughbred stable of leading estates. One of these is Tenuta Còlpetrone, located in Montefalco, in the Umbrian province of Perugia. Measured investment in the cellar and in its 156 acres (63ha) of vineyards is now bearing fruit, and Tenuta Còlpetrone's Sagrantino Gòld is as impressive as any Sagrantino. However, as fine as it is, this wine is pipped to the post by the aromatic and unctuous Sagrantino Passito, whose fine acidity and layers of mulberry fruit are without peer.

Via Ponte La Mandria 8/1, Frazione Marcellano, 06035 Gualdo Cattaneo; www.saiagricola.it

Trappolini Lazio

The Trappolini estate is another of the Orvieto clan that decided to go walkabout and found itself in Lazio. Roberto Trappolini now manages both the winery and 59 acres (24ha) of vineyards established by his grandfather in the 1960s. Roberto has dragged the estate firmly into the 21st century, but both tradition and Orvieto remain equally important here. Orvieto remains the mainstay of the Trappolini estate, but since 1989, Roberto has also made 40,000 bottles of a varietal Sangiovese called Paterno. Its remarkable ability to age surprised everyone, including the owner, but firmly established the estate's reputation.

Via del Rivellino 65, 01024 Castiglione in Teverina www.trappolini.com

Umani Ronchi Marche

This Marche giant produces 4 million bottles a year and controls 500 acres (200ha) of vineyards in an empire that stretches from Cónero DOCG in the north to Colline Teramane DOCG in the Abruzzo. It may be tempting to throw stones at this Goliath, but Umani Ronchi walks the quality/quantity tightrope with apparent ease. Michele Bernetti keeps an eye on every wine, from the serviceable Verdicchio and Montepulciano to the multi-award winning Cúmaro and Pelago. Pride of place, however, must go to the Plenio, the only Verdicchio that happily marries oak with fruit.

Via Adriatica 12, 60027 Osimo www.umanironchi.com

Valentini Abruzzo

More spiritual leader than winemaker, Edoardo Valentini was a giant of Italian viticulture whose fastidious attention to detail crafted some of the world's greatest wines. Tastings with Francesco, his son, continue to be prefaced with the same, immortal introduction: "you can ask me anything except how I grow my grapes and how I make my wine." Fortunately, the wines speak for themselves. Trebbiano, that perennial underdog, is transformed into a Cinderella white that develops effortlessly for 30 years. Valentini's Montepulciano, which is made only in the finest vintages, can hold its own against anything from Bordeaux or Burgundy.

Via del Baio 2, 65014 Loreto Aprutino 085 8291138

Velenosi Marche

The rather fetching Angela Velenosi is the head of this young company whose headquarters are in the heart of the Rosso Piceno DOC. With 259 acres (105ha) under her control, and annual production nudging a million bottles, this newcomer has now come of age. Production is reassuringly consistent, with an entry level white Falerio and Rosso Piceno as keenly priced, and as delightful to drink, as any in the Marche, while the Villa Angela Chardonnay shows fine oak integration. Velenosi also makes a traditional Visciole, the sweet, medieval wine flavored with sour cherries. ★ **Rising star**

Via dei Biancospini 11, 63100 Ascoli Piceno www.velenosivini.com

Villa Bucci Marche

Villa Bucci is a vast, rambling estate comprising more than 1,000 acres (400ha) in the heart of the Verdicchio dei Castelli di Jesi DOC. In among the wheat, sugar beets, and sunflowers, lie 52 acres (21ha) of organic, manicured vineyards from which the Bucci family produces two archetypal versions of this Marche white. The Bucci Verdicchio is a sound performer, but the Villa Bucci is one of the DOC's foremost ambassadors. The low-yielding, 40-year-old vines give an intense minerality that is enhanced by 18 months' aging in large, old oak casks.

Via Cona 30, 60010 Ostra Vetere www.villabucci.com

TUSCANY

For many wine lovers, Tuscany is synonymous with Italy, and for good reason. Beyond the region's long history of fine wine production—Grand Duke Cosimo III granted official designation to the wines of Carmignano, Chianti, Pomino, and Valdarno in 1716—Tuscany is today the most accessible gateway into the world of Italian wine. Accessibility, of course, is relative, and for every individual who discovered Italian wine through the aristocratic Brunello di Montalcino, there is at least one person who got there through the wicker-covered "fiasco" of a Chianti bottle. But times have changed, perhaps no more so than in Tuscany, a region that for more than two centuries has helped set the pace for Italian wine.

Sangiovese is the noble dark horse of Tuscany. At its best, the grape is capable of the subtlety and nuance often associated with Pinot Noir in Burgundy or, to put it in an Italian context, Nebbiolo in Piemonte. Yet for much of the modern era, Sangiovese was either overcropped and turned into thin, blandly rustic, industrial reds, or thought of as awkward and uncontrollable, a grape to be blended away or bolstered with more potent varieties.

That Sangiovese can be difficult was recognized by Baron Bettino Ricasoli, who, in the 19th century, first proposed the blend of grapes for Chianti, which was later adopted for the DOC. The arrival of the first so-called Super Tuscans, in the 1970s, reconsidered those challenges by adding Cabernet Sauvignon or Merlot, or dispensing with Sangiovese altogether, and created an entirely new group of wines. It can be argued that some of these new wines lack true Tuscan character, but this would be to ignore their generally high quality and their potential to be wines of their own class, with their own typicity. Some, such as Sassicaia, Ornellaia, and Tignanello, have become legends.

However, for lovers of Tuscan wine, the pendulum always swings back to Sangiovese. While the grape grows everywhere in Italy, it is in Tuscany that Sangiovese achieves its finest expression.

The journey in Sangiovese, as it were, begins to the north and east of Florence with the bracing wines of Chianti Rùfina; sweeping around the city you will find the broader district of Chianti as well as the more specific Chianti Colli Fiorentini, both destinations for good value. South from Florence stretches the historic Chianti Classico zone, with its distinct microclimates. Thanks to long-term research projects, as well as the determination of purists like Montevertine, the star of Sangiovese has never shown brighter in Chianti Classico. Going forward, this region may even challenge Montalcino for primacy in Sangiovese production.

Of course, the town of Montalcino has held the world's attention for years with its Brunello. Here, Sangiovese (made with Sangiovese Grosso) walks a fine line between power and elegance. In nearby Montepulciano, the Vino Nobile presents another take on structured, ageworthy wines.

Head west to the Maremma, and Sangiovese becomes a component of blends: the rustic Morellino di Scansano, the refined Bordeaux-inspired wines or, increasingly, Mediterranean wines that bring grapes like Grenache and Carignan into the Tuscan fold.

And that is just scratching the surface. Tuscany is a world unto itself, always with something to draw you back.

Major grapes

Reds
Cabernet Sauvignon
Canaiolo
Merlot
Sangiovese

Whites
Chardonnay
Trebbiano
Vernaccia

Vintages

2009
Very warm to hot conditions yielded ripe wines with higher than average alcohol levels.

2008
A good to very good year. Some problems with drought in the summer, but late-ripening varieties fared well.

2007
A good, possibly excellent vintage. A dry summer, followed by rain and then a warm and dry harvest meant ripe, strong wines.

2006
A very good year, with high quantity in addition to quality. Chianti Classico is a standout.

2005
Uneven weather meant that some areas struggled to get their grapes ripe. An earlier-drinking vintage.

2004
An excellent year, with near-classic conditions; particularly good Brunello di Montalcino.

CHIANTI

In recent years, the designations of Chianti have become more refined, resulting in a group of regions beyond Chianti Classico. Probably the best-known is Chianti Rufina, to the east of Florence, which has a relatively cool climate and produces more elegant wines. The distinctions between the wines from the different zones are testament to Sangiovese's remarkable ability to showcase different growing regions and microclimates.

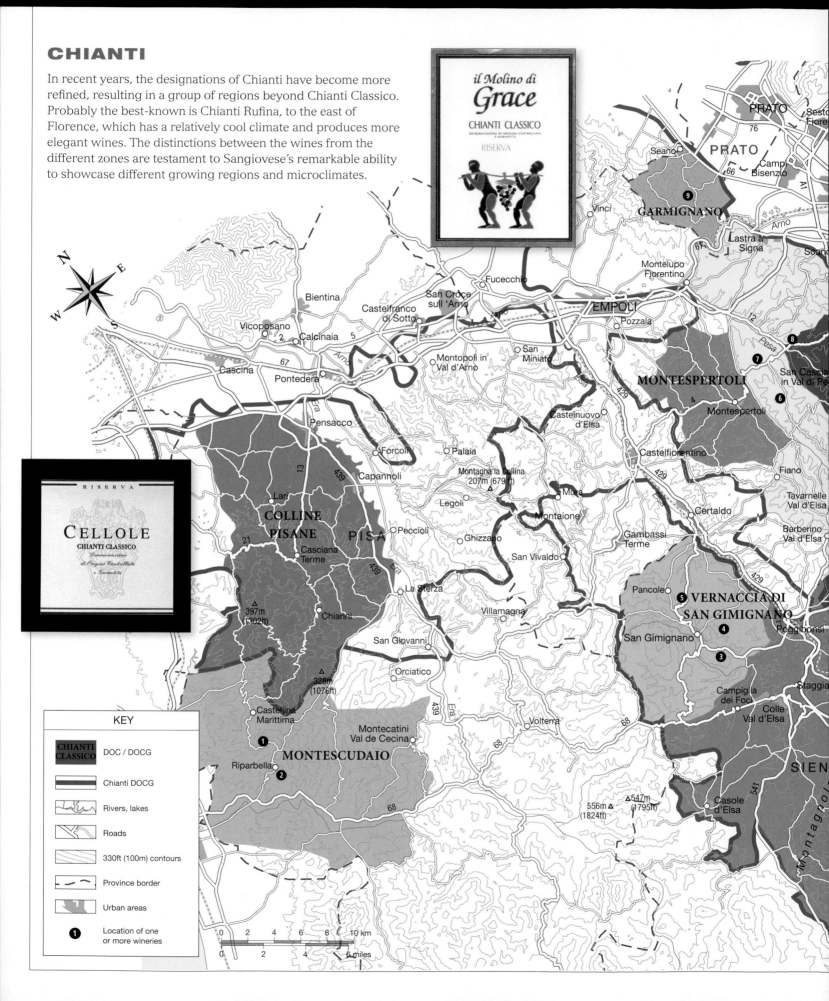

KEY

CHIANTI CLASSICO	DOC / DOCG
	Chianti DOCG
	Rivers, lakes
	Roads
	330ft (100m) contours
	Province border
	Urban areas
❶	Location of one or more wineries

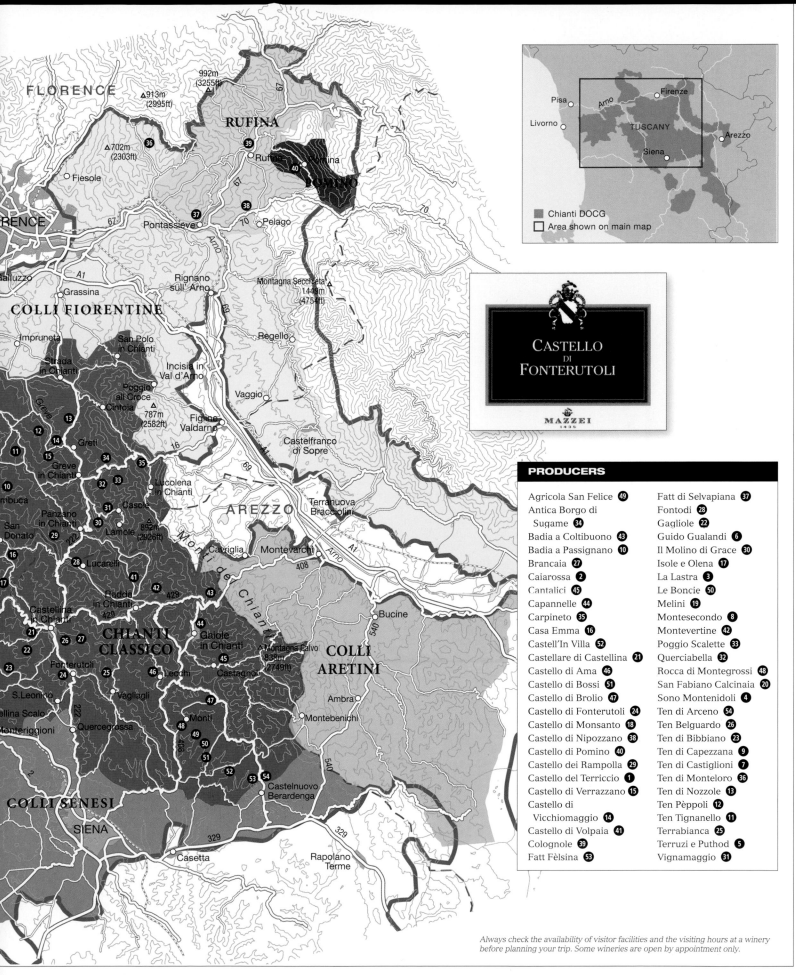

CASTELLO
DI
FONTERUTOLI

MAZZEI
1435

PRODUCERS

Agricola San Felice **49**	Fatt di Selvapiana **37**
Antica Borgo di	Fontodi **28**
Sugame **34**	Gagliole **22**
Badia a Coltibuono **43**	Guido Gualandi **6**
Badia a Passignano **10**	Il Molino di Grace **30**
Brancaia **27**	Isole e Olena **17**
Caiarossa **2**	La Lastra **3**
Cantalici **45**	Le Boncie **50**
Capannelle **44**	Melini **19**
Carpineto **35**	Montesecondo **8**
Casa Emma **16**	Montevertine **42**
Castell'In Villa **52**	Poggio Scalette **33**
Castellare di Castellina **21**	Querciabella **32**
Castello di Ama **46**	Rocca di Montegrossi **48**
Castello di Bossi **51**	San Fabiano Calcinaia **20**
Castello di Brolio **47**	Sono Montenidoli **4**
Castello di Fonterutoli **24**	Ten di Arceno **54**
Castello di Monsanto **18**	Ten Belguardo **26**
Castello di Nipozzano **38**	Ten di Bibbiano **23**
Castello di Pomino **40**	Ten di Capezzana **9**
Castello dei Rampolla **29**	Ten di Castiglioni **7**
Castello del Terriccio **1**	Ten di Monteloro **36**
Castello di Verrazzano **15**	Ten di Nozzole **13**
Castello di	Ten Pèppoli **12**
Vicchiomaggio **14**	Ten Tignanello **11**
Castello di Volpaia **41**	Terrabianca **25**
Colognole **39**	Terruzi e Puthod **5**
Fatt Fèlsina **53**	Vignamaggio **31**

Always check the availability of visitor facilities and the visiting hours at a winery before planning your trip. Some wineries are open by appointment only.

ALTESINO

THIS SINGLE-VINEYARD BRUNELLO HAS
GREAT COMPLEXITY AND ELEGANCE

Agricola San Felice Chianti Classico

This large estate near Castelnuovo Berardenga is owned by the financial group Allianz, although the grape-growing and winemaking affairs of San Felice are left to Carlo Salvinelli and Leonardo Bellacini, the estate's long-serving viticulturalist and enologist, respectively. San Felice follows a classical line with Chianti Classico, blending traditional grapes and aging them in large oak *botti*. The result is a terroir-driven red relaxed enough for the table. Poggio Rosso is San Felice's powerfully old-school, single-vineyard *riserva* that feels thoroughly Tuscan.

Località San Felice, 53019 Castelnuovo Berardenga
www.agricolasanfelice.com

Altesino Montalcino

Altesino has long been considered one of the more forward thinking and internationally minded producers in Montalcino, planting varieties like Cabernet Sauvignon and Merlot at an early stage, as well as aging Sangiovese in small barriques rather than the traditional large casks. The estate has been owned since 2002 by Elisabetta Gnudi Angelini, who, with the help of consulting enologists Pietro Rivella and Paolo Caciorgna, has maintained a forward yet refined style. The basic Brunello is earthy and full, with gripping tannin. Alte d'Altesi, a blend, is elegant and soft.

Località Altesino 54, 53024 Montalcino
www.altesino.it

Ampelaia Maremma

Ampelaia is an ambitious young estate that was established in southern Tuscany near Grosseto in 2002 by Elisabetta Foradori, Giovanni Podini, and Thomas Widmann. Rather than produce Bordeaux-inspired blends, Ampelaia looks to the Mediterranean basin, so the estate's wines are as likely to feature Mourvèdre and Alicante as they are Sangiovese. Look for its eponymously named *cuvée* of Cabernet Franc, Sangiovese, and other varieties including spicy Carignan and minty-cool Grenache. Kepos is a fragrant, vibrant blend of Grenache, Mourvèdre, Carignan, Alicante, and Marselan. Both wines mark a departure from Tuscany's traditional super blends. ★ **Rising star**

Località Meleta, 58036 Roccastrada
www.ampeleia.it

Antico Borgo di Sugame Chianti Classico

Sugame is perched on a hilltop overlooking the Val di Greve and the Val d'Arno in the heart of Chianti Classico. Lorenzo and Catrina Miceli bought the estate in 2000, and immediately began to refurbish the cellars and buildings, installing stainless steel tanks in the winery, and converting some of the buildings into a tranquil agriturismo. They also introduced organic farming practices, and planted new vines alongside existing 28-year-old blocks. Such meticulous care is apparent in the estate's firm, elegantly structured Chianti Classico. ★ **Rising star**

Via Convertoie, 50022 Greve in Chianti
www.borgo-di-sugame.com

Argiano Montalcino

The roots of this estate stretch back to the 16th century. However, the outlook here is much more modern than that history would suggest. Owned since 1992 by Noemi

AVIGNONESI

A RARE, SWEET WINE, AGED IN BARRELS
FOR 10 YEARS BEFORE BOTTLING

Marone Cinzano, Argiano produces a ripe, approachable, and forward style of Brunello, thanks to a combination of barrique and cask aging. The Rosso, made from a winery selection, is aromatic and fresh, and generally good value. Solengo is Argiano's smooth, seamless blend of Cabernet Sauvignon, Merlot, and Syrah that emphasizes textural richness and drinkability over austerity and restraint.

S Angelo in Colle, 53024 Montalcino
www.argiano.net

Avignonesi Montepulciano

One of Montepulciano's best-known producers, Avignonesi is an old estate that received a new lease of life in 1974 when Alberto and Ettore Falvo assumed control. They modernized the estate, planted new international varieties, experimented with different planting systems, and generally updated the winery. They were joined in the early 1990s by enologist Paolo Trappolini; more recently, Virginie Saverys bought a majority share in Avignonesi. The estate's Vino Nobile, an elegant, structured red, is the top wine. Also look out for the rare, angelic Vin Santo.

53045 Valiano di Montepulciano
www.avignonesi.it

Badia a Coltibuono Chianti Classico

Housed in the grounds of an 11th-century abbey, the Coltibuono winery (the name literally means "good crops") has been one of the leading Chianti Classico estates since the 1950s when Pietro Stucchi Prinetti began to focus on *riserva* level wines, and commercializing the winery's production. His children, led by daughter Emanuela, run Coltibuono today; they have introduced organic farming at the estate vineyards and built a state-of-the-art gravity-flow winery. Look for the elegant estate bottled Chianti Classico, or the more structured Riserva. Both wines are nuanced expressions of Sangiovese.

Località Badia a Coltibuono, 53013 Gaiole in Chianti
www.coltibuono.com

Badia a Passignano Chianti Classico

The vineyards surrounding this stunning monastery complex—an amalgamation of medieval and High Renaissance buildings—have been owned by the Antinori family since 1987. Approximately 123 acres (50ha) have been planted with Sangiovese clonal material taken from the Tignanello estate. Here, those vines yield an elegantly formed Chianti Classico Riserva. Made from 100% Sangiovese aged in small- and medium-sized barrels, it is delicately perfumed and soft around the edges, yet feels energized by bright acidity. While it will benefit from some age, it can be enjoyed young.

No visitor facilities
www.antinori.it

Biondi-Santi/Tenuta Greppo Montalcino

Franco Biondi Santi has run this legendary estate since 1969. Credited as the birthplace of modern Brunello, after Franco's ancestor Ferruccio Biondi Santi bottled a wine from the Sangiovese grosso clone grown here in the 19th century, Tenuta Greppo has since ranked as one of Italy's most iconic wineries. The wines are, it almost goes without saying, resolutely traditional in style, and the

Brunellos from here—both the Riserva, only produced in outstanding years, and the *normale*, only made in good enough years—are capable of living for decades.

Villa Greppo 183, 53024 Montalcino
www.biondisanti.it

Brancaia Chianti Classico

Brancaia is made up of two estates, Poppi in Radda and Brancaia in Castellina. Brigitte and Bruno Widmer have owned both since 1981; their daughter and son-in-law run the operation today. With help from consultant Carlo Ferrini in the cellar, Brancaia produces stylish wines made from Sangiovese and international varieties like Merlot and Cabernet Sauvignon. The Chianti Classico, which combines Sangiovese and Merlot, is rich and full, with a plush texture. Il Blu ups the Merlot and Cabernet in the blend, and shows a soft yet firm structure.

Località Poppi, 53017 Radda in Chianti
www.brancaia.com

Ca'Marcanda Maremma

Angelo Gaja established this Maremma outpost of his empire in 1996. Unlike Gaja's other Tuscan project, Pieve Santa Restituta in Montalcino, Ca'Marcanda is thoroughly international in its chosen grape varieties: Cabernet Sauvignon, Merlot, Cabernet Franc, and Syrah, with only some Sangiovese. Magari, Ca'Marcanda's supple and delicious Merlot-based wine, makes a fine supporting argument for the proliferation of French grapes on the Tuscan coast. Promis, which sees both Syrah and Sangiovese blended with Merlot, is firm and savory, ready for food. ★ **Rising star**

Località Santa Teresa 272, Bolgheri
0173 635255

Caiarossa Maremma

This pristine estate in northern Maremma was first established in 1998 and has been owned since 2004 by Dutch businessman Eric Jelgersma, who also owns both Château Giscours and Château du Tertre in Bordeaux. Caiarossa's vineyards are farmed biodynamically; since 2004, winemaking has been under the eye of Dominque Génot. The blend for the top wine, also called Caiarossa, varies depending on the vintage, with either Merlot or Sangiovese jostling for the main spot. It feels seamless and fine, an elegant red from the Tuscan coast. Pergolaia, the second wine, is earthy and robust. ★ **Rising star**

Località Serra all'Olio 59, 56046 Riparbella
www.caiarossa.com

Cantalici Chianti Classico

Carlo and Daniele Cantalici started as viticulture and farming consultants in the mid-1990s and set up their own winery in Castagnoli in 1999. Cantalici controls about 50 acres (20ha) between estate and contracted vineyards, and makes a modern-styled Chianti Classico that combines Merlot and Cabernet Sauvignon with around 85% Sangiovese, as well as the vineyard selection Messer Ridolfo. The latter feels rich from barrique aging yet retains bright, mouthwatering acidity thanks to the relatively high altitude (1,350ft/410m) of the site.

Via Della Croce 17/19, Località Castagnoli, 53013 Gaiole in Chianti; www.cantalici.it

BADIA A COLTIBUONO
A WELL-BALANCED CHIANTI CLASSICO WITH SUPPLE TANNINS AND A FRESH ACIDITY

CARPINETO
A FRUITY, AROMATIC BLEND OF CHARDONNAY, GRECHETTO, AND SAUVIGNON BLANC

Capanna Montalcino

The Cencioni family has owned this estate at the northern end of the Montalcino zone since 1957. Their wines tend to be honest expressions of Sangiovese grown in Montalcino. The basic Rosso is aged for a short period in large casks; it shows the gentle, aromatic, and lifted side of Sangiovese. More substantial is the potent Brunello, a savory, gripping red that demands a few years in the cellar. The Riserva is a similarly powerful red with generally more depth and complexity.

Podere Capana 101, Località Santa Restituta, 53024 Montalcino; www.fattoi.it

Capannelle Chianti Classico

This old estate was reinvigorated as a fine wine producer by Raffaele Rossetti in 1974. Capannelle has been owned since 1997 by American businessman James Sherwood, and, under enologist Simone Monciatti, it remains one of the most modern and stylish producers in Chianti Classico. 50-50, a sleek blend of Capannelle's earthy Sangiovese and Merlot from Avignonesi in Montepulciano, best embodies the spirit of the winery—a luxurious expression of Tuscan soil. The estate's Chianti Classico Riserva, blended from Sangiovese, Canaiolo, and Colorino, combines savory tannins and lively acidity.

Località Capannelle 13, 53013 Gaiole in Chianti
www.capannelle.com

Caprili Montalcino

Caprili has about 38 acres (15ha) of vineyards planted in the southwestern end of the Montalcino appellation. Established in 1965 by Alfo Bartolommei, whose family had long farmed in the region under the *mezzadria* (sharecropping) system, Caprili's first vintage was in 1978. Through careful farming (only copper and sulfur are used in the vineyards) and traditional vinification and aging methods (indigenous yeasts and large casks), this estate produces a gentle style of Brunello as notable for its typicity and elegance as it is for its consistency.

Podere Caprili 268, 53024 Montalcino
www.caprili.it

Carpineto Chianti Classico

Giovanni Sacchet and Antonio Zaccheo established Carpineto—makers of the well-known, good-value red Dogajolo—in 1967 as a négociant business, buying in grapes to produce a range of Tuscan wines from Chianti Classico to Vino Nobile. Carpineto became a landowner in its own right over the decades, and now has vineyards in Greve, Gaville, Chianciano, Montepulciano, and toward the coast in Gavorrano. The Chianti Classico Riserva, blended from Sangiovese and Colorino and aged in barrels of various size, combines rusticity and elegance. Also look for the silky Vino Nobile.

Località Dudda 17/B, 50022 Greve in Chianti
www.carpineto.com

Casa Emma Chianti Classico

The Emma of this serene 50 acre (20ha) estate near Castellina is Emma Bizzarri, a Florentine noblewoman who sold Casa Emma to the Bucalossi family in the early 1970s. With guidance from enologist Carlo Ferrini, Casa Emma approaches Chianti with a mix of modern and traditionalist approaches—the Chianti Classico *normale*

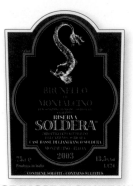

**CASE BASSE DI GIANFRANCO
SOLDERA**

A GRACEFUL, TRADITIONALLY STYLED WINE
THAT MAY BE CELLARED FOR MANY YEARS

CASTELLO DI BROLIO

A FRESH, GREAT-VALUE CHIANTI CLASSICO
MADE FOR EARLY DRINKING

and Riserva are both blended from traditional grapes like Sangiovese, Canaiolo, and Malvasia Nera, yet both see time in French barrique. The result is an earthy, gripping wine marked by elegant tannins and bright flavors. Soloìo is Casa Emma's sleek Merlot.

SP di Castellina in Chianti 3, San Donato in Poggio, 50021 Barberino Val d'Elsa; www.casaemma.com

Casanova di Neri Montalcino

This estate dates from 1971, when Giovanni Neri began acquiring land in Montalcino. Today, his son, Giacomo, manages vineyards in four areas of Montalcino: Cerretalto and Fiesole in the north, Pietradonice and Cetine at the southern end. Casanova di Neri favors a polished style that is reflected across the estate's line-up of Brunellos. The smart, sophisticated Brunello di Montalcino combines ripeness and tannic strength with a silky texture. Brunello Cerretalto is a powerful single-vineyard wine defined by muscular tannins and structure.

Località Fiesole, 530245 Montalcino www.casanovadineri.com

Case Basse di GianFranco Soldera Montalcino

GianFranco Soldera takes an uncompromising position when it comes to his philosophy of Brunello di Montalcino. He bought the Case Basse estate, which was uncultivated, in the early 1970s. Along with his wife Graziella, he has transformed it into a vibrant garden and vineyard where careful attention is paid to natural cycles and only organic methods are used. Soldera, with help from the legendary Giulio Gambelli, crafts an uber-traditional Brunello; aged for an extended period in large casks, this is a graceful, electrifying wine that can live for decades.

Località Case Basse, 53024 Montalcino www.casebasse.it

Castel Giocondo Montalcino

The Frescobaldi family has owned this massive estate (230 acres/93ha) since 1989. Located in the south of the Montalcino zone, Castel Giocondo is notable for a relatively classic style of Brunello—forward and aromatic in its youth, yet with the gripping tannin and strong backbone of acidity, that means the wine will age well. Campo ai Sassi is the estate's Rosso di Montalcino, which is generally ready to drink on release. Also notable is Lamaione, a 100% Merlot that feels polished and elegant.

Marchesi de' Frescobaldi, Via S Spirito 11, 50125 Firenze www.castelgiocondo.it

Castell'In Villa Chianti Classico

This magnificent estate, located in Castelnuovo Berardenga, is owned and managed by Coralia Pignatelli della Leonessa. Castell'In Villa has more than 130 acres (53ha) of vineyards and is notable for long-lived wines. Even the basic Chianti Classico, a concentrated, savory red made entirely from Sangiovese, typically needs time in the cellar to uncoil from its tension. The Riserva is likewise built for the long haul, its dense core of fruit wrapped in savory, dark tannins. Santacroce is an elegant blend of Cabernet Sauvignon and Sangiovese.

Località Castell'in Villa, 53019 Castelnuovo Berardenga www.castellinvilla.com

Castellare di Castellina Chianti Classico

This estate claims more than 80 acres (32ha) of vineyards planted in a natural amphitheater just outside the town of Castellina. Originally a series of neighboring farms that were consolidated in 1968, Castellare has been owned since 1979 by Paolo Panerai. The estate has been modernized significantly since, and has an updated cellar and meticulously farmed vineyards. Castellare's wines are typically refined and elegant, rather than international in outlook. The top wine, I Sodi di San Niccolò, is always Sangiovese and Malvasia Nera. Like the Chianti Classico, it is firm and vibrant.

Località Castellare, 53011 Castellina in Chianti www.castellare.it

Castello di Ama Chianti Classico

This large estate is located in the hill country around Gaiole. Thanks to the high altitude of the site (1,600ft/490m), the wines from here tend to feel brisk in character, with naturally high acidity. Owned since 1977 by a group of Roman families, the estate is today managed by Lorenza Sebasti, a daughter of one of the owners, and Marco Pallanti, the enologist. The Vigneto Bellavista *cru*, a single-vineyard Chianti Classico, is a potent, powerful wine that sets a high standard.

Località Ama, 53013 Gaiole in Chianti www.castellodiama.com

Castello Banfi Montalcino

This American-owned estate is in many ways responsible for Brunello di Montalcino's stature in international markets, and the subsequent boom of newcomers in the region. Established by John and Harry Mariani in 1978, Castello Banfi today has more than 7,000 acres (2,800ha) that feature an elaborate visitors complex in addition to vineyards and a winery. It is not all show; since the early days, Banfi has funded extensive research into Sangiovese clonal material and shared the results. To get a sense of the entire venture, start with the basic Brunello.

Castello di Poggio alle Mura, Località Sant' Angelo Scalo 53024; www.castellobanfi.com

Castello di Bossi Chianti Classico

The Bacci family acquired this ancient estate in the early 1980s as a rural retreat. Gradually, Marco Bacci became more involved in the business, overseeing improvements in the cellar as well as a massive replanting program. The wines are modern and elegant, yet feel entirely Tuscan in their warm fruit and often gripping tannins. Corbaia, blended from Sangiovese and Cabernet Sauvignon, balances sweet fruit with iron-clad tannins and mouthwatering acidity. Look for the Chianti Classico, an earthy expression of Sangiovese.

Località Bossi in Chianti, 53019 Castelnuovo Berardenga www.castellodibossi.it

Castello di Brolio Chianti Classico

The family seat of the barons Ricasoli, this large estate is in many senses the birthplace of modern Chianti. It was here that Bettino Ricasoli developed the blend of Sangiovese and Canaiolo, along with white grapes originally used for the Chianti DOC. Today, under the direction of Francesco Ricasoli, that blend allows international varieties like Cabernet Sauvignon and

Merlot, both of which find their way into the savory, elegant Castello di Brolio Chianti Classico. Ricasoli makes another Chianti Classico meant for early drinking, simply called Brolio; this fresh wine offers great value.

Cantine del Castello di Brolio, 53013 Gaiole in Chianti www.ricasoli.it

Castello di Fonterutoli Chianti Classico

The Mazzei family has owned Fonterutoli since 1435, and the enterprise is today run by Lapo Mazzei and his sons, Francesco and Filippo. Since the 1970s, the estate has undergone many changes, including higher-density plantings, the addition of Bordeaux varieties, and a gradual replanting scheme. A new winery with modern equipment was also completed recently. To taste this long history and dedicated winemaking, look for the Chianti Classico, which combines ripe flavors with savory power.

Via Ottone III di Sassonia 5, Località Fonterutoli, 53011 Castellina in Chianti; www.mazzei.it

Castello di Monsanto Chianti Classico

Fabrizio Bianchi began to modernize the Il Poggio vineyard at Castello di Monsanto in 1968, removing the white grapes that had been interplanted with Sangiovese, Canaiolo, and Colorino. The wine from this site, Chianti Classico Riserva Il Poggio, remains Monsanto's most compelling wine, and ranks among the top single-vineyard wines of Tuscany. It has the structure and balance for long aging. The estate's basic Chianti Classico is a good introduction to Monsanto's leaner, more austere style. Nemo is a sleek, potent Cabernet Sauvignon from the estate's Il Mulino vineyard.

Via Monsanto 8, 50021 Barberino Val D'Elsa www.castellodimonsanto.it

Castello di Montepò Maremma

In the mid-1990s, Jacopo Biondi Santi, son of the legendary Franco Biondi Santi of Montalcino, set out to carve his own path in Italian wine. After working with contracted vineyards, Biondi Santi bought the Montepò estate in Scansano. The vineyards have been expanded to about 123 acres (50ha), and from here, Biondi Santi produces a range of stylish wines that feel contemporary yet reflect real Tuscan character. Look for Sassoalloro, a 100% Sangiovese that balances lifted aromas with high acidity and smooth tannins. ★Rising star

Castello di Montepò, 58050 Scansano www.biondisantimontepo.com

Castello di Nipozzano Chianti Rùfina

This imposing 11th-century fortress is arguably the best among the Frescobaldi family's many estates. Nipozzano's vineyards rise to elevations of 1,300ft (400m) in the Chianti Rùfina zone to the northeast of Florence. Besides Sangiovese, the estate grows Cabernet Sauvignon and Merlot, along with other Bordeaux varieties, which are used for the regal and stylish Mormoreto. Perhaps more Tuscan in character is the Chianti Rùfina Riserva, a savory, firm red with minerally tannins. Montesodi, a single-vineyard Sangiovese, is a more powerful, concentrated expression of Rùfina suitable for the cellar.

No visitor facilities www.frescobaldi.it

Castello di Pomino Pomino

One of the Frescobaldi wine estates, Castello di Pomino is the premier producer in this high-altitude zone. Mountains and forests define this region, rather than the rolling hills and cypress trees common to lower areas of Tuscany, and the wines tend to show a greater degree of cool-climate tension. The Pomino Bianco, a brisk, minerally blend of Chardonnay and Pinot Bianco, is one of the most engaging Tuscan whites. Also of note is the Pomino Rosso, a savory blend of Sangiovese and Pinot Nero.

No visitor facilities www.frescobaldi.it

Castello di Potentino Maremma

After selling the Montepò estate to Jacopo Biondi Santi, the Greene family bought and began to restore this 11th-century castle near Grosseto in 2000. Along with the restoration of the castle, they have set about making wine from approximately 10 acres (4ha) of Sangiovese, Alicante, and Pinot Nero. Sacromonte is Potentino's wine from the Montecucco DOC, made entirely from Sangiovese. Bright and aromatic, it has a vibrancy and energy that makes it appealing on many levels. Piropo blends Pinot Nero and Alicante with Sangiovese in a manner that feels harmonious and firm. ★Rising star

Castello di Potentino, Provincia di Grosseto, 58038 Seggiano www.potentino.com

Castello dei Rampolla Chianti Classico

The di Napoli Rampolla family has owned this estate near Panzano since the 18th century. In the mid-1960s, Alceo di Napoli Rampolla began planting vineyards, and was bottling wine at the estate 10 years later. With guidance from Giacomo Tachis, di Napoli Rampolla began to experiment with blending Bordeaux grapes and Sangiovese. The result was Sammarco, a formidable, mineral-edged blend of Cabernet Sauvignon with 5% Sangiovese. Today, the estate is run by di Napoli Rampolla's children, Luca and Maurizia, who have introduced biodynamic practices in the vineyards.

Via Case Spase 22, 50020 Panzano in Chianti 0558 52001

Castello del Terriccio Maremma

Gian Annibale Rossi di Medelana Serafini Ferri's family has owned this sprawling coastal estate since 1921. A vineyard had always been present on the estate, however viticulture did not become the main focus at Terriccio until a replanting and expansion program commenced in the mid-1980s. Thanks to input from consulting enologist Carolo Ferrini, Terriccio's wines feel polished and international in style. The primary red is Lupicaia, a sleek blend of Cabernet Sauvignon, Merlot, and Petit Verdot that is richly fruited with supple, slightly savory tannins.

Località Terriccio, 56040 Castellina Marittima www.terriccio.it

Castello di Verrazzano Chianti Classico

This ancient estate, once the property of the Verrazzano family (Giovanni da Verrazzano explored the North American Atlantic coast in the 1520s), is owned today by Luigi and Silvia Cappellini. The estate has been modernized by the Cappellini family in recent decades. The entry level Chianti Classico displays the fruit intensity

CHIANTI CLASSICO 2000: THE RESULTS

Chianti has been trying for decades to finally ditch the bad old days of the wicker basket bottle. While a few old-school Italian restaurants still display these bottles—often covered in 30 years' worth of dripped candle wax—Chianti has for the most part completely reinvented itself. In addition to changing the specific blends mentioned for DOC rules, one of the most influential factors in Chianti's dramatic swing upmarket is the Chianti Classico 2000 Project.

Conceived by the regional growers' consortium in 1987, the project was a 16-year study that considered clonal material for traditional red grapes like Sangiovese and Colorino, rootstock characteristics, planting density, vine training methods, and soil treatments. The study resulted in the adoption of new Sangiovese and Colorino clones to the national grape registry, and it also provided an important template for growers in the region looking to modernize their vineyards.

CASTELLO DI VOLPAIA
THIS SINGLE-VINEYARD CHIANTI CLASSICO
IS MADE FOR AGING IN THE CELLAR

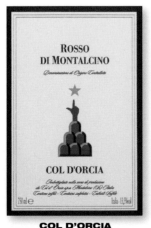

COL D'ORCIA
A FULL AND STRUCTURED WINE WITH
SUPPLE AND WRAPPING TANNINS

common to wines from the Greve zone, while the Riserva feels more firm and structured. Sassello is Verrazzano's single-vineyard Sangiovese; its texture is softened by barrique aging.

Via San Martino in Valle 12, Greti, 50022 Greve in Chianti
www.verrazzano.com

Castello di Vicchiomaggio Chianti Classico

This Renaissance manor estate has been owned by the Matta family since the mid-1960s. John Matta runs it today, making reliable Chianti Classico that edges toward a modern style. San Jacopo is the freshest and most approachable of the line up. Aged in larger barrels, it is lighter in body and marked by vibrant acidity. Riserva La Prima is all Sangiovese, selected from the estate's oldest vineyards and aged in barriques. It sheds some of the oak with time, and its fruit flavors are focused by bright acidity.

Via Vicchiomaggio 4, 50022 Greve in Chianti
www.vicchiomaggio.com

Castello di Volpaia Chianti Classico

Volpaia is a picturesque hilltop village that just happens to hide one of the Chianti region's top wineries within its walls. Perched above an organically farmed vineyard that runs from 1,470–2,100ft (450–640m) on southeast and southwest facing slopes, Castello di Volpaia, under the supervision of the Mascheroni Stianti family, consistently produces an elegant and brisk Chianti Classico. Look for the Riserva bottling, which packs vibrancy and tension onto its meaty frame. Also impressive is Coltassala, the estate's single-vineyard Chianti Classico. In good years it rivals wines of twice its price. ★**Rising star**

Di Giovanna Stianti, Località Volpaia, 5317 Radda in Chianti
www.volpaia.it

Cerbaiona Montalcino

Diego Molinari, a former airline pilot, started this small estate in the late 1970s. At Cerbaiona, Molinari follows a path of minimal intervention, preferring organic methods in the vineyard and traditional vinification practices such as the use of native yeast fermentation and large oak casks for aging. As such, his Brunello seems lighter and more feminine than those produced by some of his neighbors. But make no mistake, hiding beneath the floral aromas and gentle fruit flavors are firm, sinewy tannins and strong acidity. These elegant wines age beautifully.

Località Cerbaiona, 53024 Montalcino
0577 848660

Ciacci Piccolomini d'Aragona
Montalcino

Giuseppe Bianchini, the former general manager of this old aristocratic estate, inherited it in 1985 from the last of the Ciacci-Piccolominis, who was without an heir. Bianchini himself passed away in 2004 and today his children, Paolo and Lucia, run the estate. The house style tends toward the modern, with richly textured and generously flavored wines. On the lighter side, however, is the attractive and straightforward Rosso di Montalcino. The single-vineyard Brunello Pianrosso is worth tracking down for its balance of elegant aromas and earthy power.

Località Molinello, Frazione Castelnuovo D'Aragona, 53024
Montalcino; www.ciaccipiccolomini.com

Cima Colli Apuani

The Cima family has farmed the steep foothills of western Tuscany since the early 1800s. In recent years, led by Aurelio Cima, the estate has expanded and modernized, and hired enologist Donato Lanati. Vermentino thrives in this part of Tuscany, and Vigneto Candia Alto is Cima's mineral-driven, single-vineyard rendition of the variety. Be sure to look for the Massaretta, a variety native to coastal Tuscany that yields a fragrant, refreshing red. The grape takes a more serious tone when blended with Sangiovese for the potent Romalbo. ★**Rising star**

Via del Fagiano 1, Frazione Romagnano, 54100 Massa
www.aziendagricolacima.it

Col d'Orcia Montalcino

The affable Count Francesco Marone Cinzano has run this historic Montalcino estate since 1992, after taking over from his father who had purchased the property in 1973. Col d'Orcia was a well-established producer by 1933 when the estate, then known as Fattoria di Sant'Angelo in Colle, entered several wines at the Italian wine exhibition held that year in Siena. Col d'Orcia is today one of the most active Montalcino estates in terms of research. Fine wines are, of course, part of it too. The basic Brunello is top notch.

S Angelo in Colle, 53020 Montalcino
www.coldorcia.it

Colle Santa Mustiola Tuscany

This small estate near Chiusi in southern Tuscany was established in 1992 by Fabio Cenni. It produces just one wine, Poggio ai Chiari. It is a luxurious expression of Sangiovese, blended with a small amount of Colorino, both grown in alluvial soils. While the wine is certainly polished, it nevertheless wraps its core of bright cherry fruit in firm, savory tannins. With a strength that comes from the earth, rather than oak barrel aging, Poggio ai Chiari is a wine set for graceful aging. ★**Rising star**

Via delle Torri 86/A, 53043 Chiusi
www.poggioaichiari.it

Collemattoni Montalcino

Marcello Bucci took over this small estate near Sant'Angelo in Colle in 1995, and he has since turned it into one of the most promising and more humble-minded wineries in the region. Bucci, whose father Aldo had originally launched the winery in 1988 after he had inherited the vineyard from his uncle, has introduced organic practices and sticks to an essentially traditionalist line in the cellar, employing long maceration times and large Slavonian oak casks. Look for the basic Brunello, an elegant, earthy red with an underlying vibrancy that charges the wine. ★**Rising star**

Località Podere Collemattoni 100, 53020 Sant'Angelo in
Colle; www.collemattoni.it

Colognole Chianti Rùfina

The Spallettti family has been in the wine business since the late 19th century. Colognole has about 67 acres (27ha) of vineyards near the Sieve River in the Chianti Rùfina subzone. The estate's wines veer toward the traditional end of the spectrum, and combine Sangiovese and Colorino grapes with various vinification techniques that include fermentation in both stainless steel and concrete, and aging in large casks and smaller barrels. Look for the expressive Chianti Rùfina, a gentle, fresh red. Riserva del Don is more concentrated and built for the cellar.

Via del Palagio 15, Località Colognole, 50068 Rùfina
www.colognole.it

Conti Costanti Montalcino

The Costanti family has been part of Montalcino history since the middle of the 16th century. Somewhat more recently, the family was among the region's pioneering wineries when Tito Costanti made his first vintage of Brunello in 1865. Today, the family business is run by Andrea Costanti, who took over in 1983, shortly after finishing college. Costanti follows a middle road between the traditional and modern as he prefers a mix of large casks and small barriques for the aging of Brunello. The result tends toward elegance and finesse, rather than blunt power.

Località Colle al Matrichese, 53024 Montalcino
www.costanti.it

Contucci Montepulciano

It does not get much more old-school than Contucci. The family has been producing wine in Montepulciano for centuries. Their cellars are still located within the walls of the medieval town of Montepulciano beneath the family palazzo (Contucci is one of the last local wineries to continue this custom). Only indigenous grapes such as Prugnolo (Sangiovese), Canaiolo, and Colorino are used, and aging takes place in large casks, giving the wines a gentle, elegant structure. The aromatic Vino Nobile emphasizes the finesse and charm of Sangiovese, rather than power.

Via del Teatro 1, 53045 Montepulciano
www.contucci.it

Dei Montepulciano

Alibrando Dei, the grandfather of current proprietor Maria Catarina, bought an old estate near Montepulciano as a vacation home in 1964. Soon after, he planted the Bossona vineyard, and the family sold the grapes that were not used for home production. The family vinified their first commercial wine in 1985 and has since become known for elegant, stylish wines like the ageworthy Vino Nobile Riserva Bossona, made from the estate's oldest vines. The regular Vino Nobile feels rich and full, its generous fruit matched by gripping, savory tannins.

Villa Martiena, 53045 Montepulciano
www.cantinedei.com

Enrico Santini Bolgheri

Generally, it has been outsiders who have come to Bolgheri to make a splash in the wine world. Enrico Santini, however, is a native of the region. Santini, whose first vintage was in 1999, produces a handful of wines from 32 acres (13ha) of vines that include French grapes like Cabernet Sauvignon and Syrah, as well Italian varieties like Vermentino and Sangiovese. Montepergoli, with its dark, layered intensity, represents Santini's style. Poggio al Moro is marked by ripe fruit and chewy tannins. These bold, forward wines are eager to please. ★Rising star

Località Campo alla Casa 74, 57022 Castagneto Carducci
www.enricosantini.it

FATTORIA FELSINA
MADE FROM 100% SANGIOVESE, THIS COMPLEX WINE HAS SMOOTH TANNINS

COLOGNOLE
THIS GENTLE, FRESH CHIANTI RUFINA IS AN EXPRESSIVE WINE

Fattoria del Cerro Montepulciano

With nearly 420 acres (170ha) of vineyards planted, Fattoria del Cerro is one of the largest estates in Montepulciano. The estate is owned by Saiagricola, the agricultural investment division of the Fondiaria-SAI insurance company. Fortunately, the corporate owners have kept Lorenzo Landi on as winemaker for years, ensuring an appealing, consistent style. Look for the estate's Vino Nobile; soft around the edges, yet zippy from vibrant acidity, it is a fine example of approachable Sangiovese. The Riserva adds a layer of texture, and is a deep, powerful wine capable of aging.

Via Grazianella 5, 53040 Acquaviva di Montepulciano
www.saiagricola.it

Fattoria Fèlsina Chianti Classico

Giuseppe Mazzoclin oversees this Sangiovese-obsessed estate in the southern end of the Chianti Classico zone. During the 1980s and '90s, he updated and replanted Fèlsina's vineyards, increasing vine density and paying careful attention to the estate's diverse soils. The leading wines, Rància and Fontalloro, are complex expressions of Sangiovese, with Rància being perhaps the more mineral-driven of the two. Look for the estate's powerful Chianti Classico, the white-label Berardenga, which holds an elegant line under its potency. The Riserva, meanwhile, is a prime candidate for the cellar.

Via del Chianti 101, 53019 Castelnuovo Berardenga
www.felsina.it

Fattoria La Peschiera Scansano

This 17 acre (7ha) vineyard and farm was established in 1980, not far from the hot springs and wild badlands of Saturnia and Pitgliano in southern Tuscany. From Sangiovese, Ciliegiolo, Merlot, and Alicante comes a charming, rustically styled Morellino di Scansano, fermented and aged in stainless steel. It feels dense with fruit, yet remains mouthwatering and fresh across the palate. Antiglio is Peschiera's take on Pitgliano Bianco, a floral, refreshing Trebbiano and Vermentino blend.

Località La Peschiera, 58050 Saturnia
www.fattorialapeschiera.it

Fattoria La Torre Lucca

This small estate in Montecarlo near Lucca in western Tuscany has just under 7 acres (3ha) of vines. Owned by sister and brother Elena and Mauro Celli, who employ biodynamic practices, Fattoria La Torre produces warm, Mediterranean wines from grapes like Syrah and Vermentino. Look for the Montecarlo, a zesty blend of Trebbiano, Vermentino, Pinot Grigio, and Roussanne that would feel as much at home by the seaside as it would at the dinner table. Esse is La Torre's peppery Syrah. It is atypical in a Tuscan sense perhaps, but certainly delicious.

Via Provinciale di Montecarlo 7, 55015 Montecarlo
www.fattorialatorre.it

Fattoria Le Pupille Scansano

Elisabetta Geppetti took over her family's estate near Scansano in 1985. She proceeded not only to raise the profile of Le Pupille, with the introduction of wines like Saffredi and Poggio Argentato aimed at the international market, but also helped to organize the growers' consortium for Morellino di Scansano. In fact, the basic

FONTODI
MADE FROM 100% SANGIOVESE, FARMED
ORGANICALLY, THIS IS AN ELEGANT WINE

Morellino di Scansano is the place to start exploring Le Pupille's wines. Bright and fresh, it is a vivid expression of Sangiovese. Poggio Valente is the estate's single-vineyard Morellino; richly textured and firm, it will age well.

Piagge del Maiano 92/A, Località Istia d'Ombrone, 58100 Grosseto; www.elisabettageppetti.com

Fattoria di Selvapiana Chianti Rùfina

This traditionally minded estate was purchased by Michele Giuntini Selvapiana in 1827, and for years was run by his descendant Francesco Giuntini Antinori. In more recent times, the management of the estate has been in the hands of Federico Giuntini Masetti and his sister Silva; Franco Bernabei has been the consulting enologist at Selvapiana since 1979. Known for regal, aromatic Sangiovese that can verge on austere, Selvapiana is responsible for some of the most compelling wine in the Rùfina subzone. Look for Bucerchiale, a single-vineyard selection of Sangiovese from older vines.

Località Selvapiana, 50068 Rùfina
www.selvapiana.it

Fontodi Chianti Classico

Fontodi is one of the leading estates in Chianti Classico, blessed with an incredible, relatively high-altitude vineyard in the heart of the Panzano region. Giovanni Manetti, whose family has owned Fontodi since 1968, follows organic practices in the vineyards and olive groves (the oil is exceptional), and exacting winemaking in the cellar. The resulting wines, like Flaccianello, a 100% Sangiovese, balance earthy power with vibrant, zinging acidity. Do not miss Fontodi's regular Chianti Classico, a firm, elegant red made using only Sangiovese.

Via San Leolino 89, Frazione Greve in Chianti, 50020 Panzano in Chianti; www.fontodi.com

Fornacelle Bolgheri

Stefano Billi began planting vines at Fornacelle in 1998, after he inherited the estate from his grandfather. Today there are nearly 37 acres (15ha) of mostly international varieties with a smattering of Italian grapes such as Vermentino and Fiano, all planted quite near the coast. Billi has also discovered a sweet spot for Cabernet Franc, and along with a handful of producers in this part of Tuscany, Fornacelle is making distinctive reds based on this grape. Foglio 38 is a polished, elegant Cabernet Franc framed by firm, savory tannins. ★ **Rising star**

Località Fornacelle 232/A, 57022 Castagneto Carducci
www.fornacelle.it

Fuligni Montalcino

The Fuligni family has run this estate on the eastern side of Montalcino—claimed by many to be the classical growing area for Brunello—since 1923. Run today by Maria Flora Fuligni and her nephew, Robert Guerrini, the estate is one of the more traditionally minded in Montalcino. The Brunello Riserva, sourced from the oldest vines at the estate and only made in the best years, is a classic expression of the somewhat picky Sangiovese. Aromatic and fine, with firm tannins and strong acidity, it is built for the cellar.

Via S Saloni 32, 53024 Montalcino
www.fuligni.it

Gagliole Chianti Classico

This small estate in Castellina is owned by husband and wife Thomas and Monika Bär. Their consulting enologist is Stefano Chioccioli, and with his guidance, Gagliole is producing distinctive Sangiovese-based wines. The estate's flagship is Pecchia, a blend of Sangiovese with a small amount of Merlot. It feels rich and full, with a plush texture that finds depth thanks to mineral-edged tannin. The Gagliole IGT blends Cabernet with Sangiovese and as a result, shows darker fruit and concentration, if less elegance. Rubiolo is the highly drinkable Chianti Classico.

Località Gagliole 42, 53011 Castellina in Chianti
www.gagliole.com

Guido Gualandi Chianti Colli Fiorentini

Guido Gualandi is something of a perfectionist, and he does nearly everything by hand at his farm in Montespertoli. He farms organically and practices a philosophy of minimal intervention in the cellar, as well as relying on native yeast fermentations. Additionally, Gualandi is working with some of Tuscany's more obscure indigenous grapes, such as Pugnitello and Foglia Tonda. Along with a local clone of Sangiovese, those varieties make up Gualandus, a bright, perfumed red with gripping tannins aged in large chestnut casks. Also look out for the earthy, firm Chianti Colli Fiorentini. ★ **Rising star**

Via delle Ripe 19, Poppiano, 50025 Montespertoli
www.guidogualandi.com

Il Molino di Grace Chianti Classico

American-owned Il Molino di Grace is hardly the typical expatriate winemaking project. Frank Grace bought the property in 1995, and with the help of his winemaker, German-born Gerhard Hirmer, and the consultant Franco Bernabei, he quickly created one of the top estates in Panzano. With their stylish, rich flavors, the wines veer toward international tastes, yet those aspects are balanced by firm, old-school Sangiovese tannin. While some of the wines are softened with Merlot, it is the estate's Chianti Classico Riserva that boasts the power and structure to age several years. ★ **Rising star**

Località Il Volano Lucarelli, 50022 Panzano in Chianti
www.ilmolinodigrace.com

Il Palazzone Montalcino

This small estate owned by American businessman Richard Parsons has just over 7 acres (3ha) of vineyards planted in separate areas of the region, including two plots of older vines near Castelnuovo dell'Abate. Consulting enologist Paolo Vagaggini maintains a gentle touch in the cellar. The regular Brunello feels firm and ripe, framed by fruit tannin and acidity, rather than oak influence. Likewise, the Riserva is judiciously balanced and ready to age. In the short term, look for the Rosso del Palazzone, a declassified multi-vintage blend that offers great value.

Località Le Due Porte 245, 53024 Montalcino
www.ilpalazzone.com

Il Poggione Montalcino

This large estate owned by Leopoldo Franceschi is widely considered a Montalcino benchmark. The house style, shaped by the father and son winemaking team of

ISOLE E OLENA
THIS BRIGHT AND FRESH CHIANTI CLASSICO
IS MADE FOR THE TABLE

Fabrizio and Alessandro Bindocci, is one that favors balance and typicity over the more oak and extract-dominated style popular with many producers here. To appreciate this, track down a bottle of the regular Brunello. Powered by delicate aromatics and firm acidity, this wine shows the subtle nature of carefully matured Sangiovese. For all its intensity, the single-vineyard I Paganelli Brunello Riserva remains a wine of great finesse.

Frazione Sant'Angelo in Colle, Località Monteano, 53020 Montalcino; www.tenutailpoggione.it

I Poderi di San Gallo Montepulciano
Olimpia Roberti manages this traditionally minded estate. Consisting of two vineyards called Le Bertille and Casella, San Gallo has about 19 acres (7.5ha) of vines planted, and a similar area soon to come on stream. Roberti favors a long maceration during fermentation, and the resulting wines pick up a deep ruby color and firm, gripping fruit tannin. Even the Rosso di Montepulciano, blended from Prugnolo (Sangiovese), Ciliegiolo, Colorino, and Mammolo, is a well-structured red. Look for the Vino Nobile, which explores the herbal aromatics and savory fruit of Sangiovese. ★ Rising star

Via delle Colombelle 7, 53045 Montepulciano www.ipoderidisangallo.com

Isole e Olena Chianti Classico
Paolo de Marchi's family has owned Isole e Olena since the mid-1950s. The estate is located at the northern end of the Chianti Classico region and has long been dedicated to using Sangiovese on its own. The top wine, Cepparello, has been 100% Sangiovese since its first vintage in 1980. It has also remained outside of the DOC system since that time (it could, in fact, be labeled Chianti Classico under today's regulations). Isole e Olena's regular Chianti Classico is delightfully bright and fresh, and made to enjoy at the table.

Località Isole 1, 50021 Barberino Val d'Elsa 0558 072763

La Cerbaiola di Giulio Salvioni Montalcino
Giulio Salvioni, with the help of enologist Attilio Pagli, makes a refined, elegant, and sought-after Brunello at this small estate. Salvioni and Pagli follow a traditional line in the cellar, using long macerations and large casks. The Brunello finds its power in the fine balance between acidity and strong tannin—two elements that will become more seamless and integrated over time. Meanwhile, the Rosso di Montalcino, made in the same manner though aged for less time in cask, is every bit as serious as its big brother.

Piazza Cavour 19, 53024 Montalcino 0577 848499

La Gerla Montalcino
Sergio Rossi, a former European advertising executive, bought this tranquil estate in 1976 and began a fairly extensive remodeling program, both in the cellar and the vineyards. From just over 28 acres (11ha), Rossi produces the typical range of Brunello and Rosso di Montalcino wines with the help of consulting enologist Vittorio Fiore. The house style has shifted toward a riper, more modern feel in recent years (though large

botti are still used for aging Sangiovese). Look for the basic, flavorful Brunello, which can often be found at a very fair price.

Località Canalicchio, Podere Colombaio, 53024 Montalcino www.lagerlamontalcino.com

La Lastra San Gimignano
Renato Spanu, Nadia Betti, and Enrico Paternoster launched this estate near San Gimignano in 1994. La Lastra has about 14 acres (5.5ha) of vineyards planted with Vernaccia, Sangiovese, Canaiolo, and other varieties that form the basis for the estate's white and red wines. Look for La Lastra's basic Vernaccia di San Gimignano, which shows a high degree of minerality and focus for this traditional white. The Chianti Colli Senesi is a serious red, while perhaps the most enjoyable is the Rosso—pure Sangiovese fermented in cement vats and aged in large casks. ★ Rising star

Via R de Grada 9, 53037 San Gimignano www.lalastra.it

La Mozza Scansano
La Mozza is owned by American restaurateur Joseph Bastianich and his mother, Lidia Bastianich. On roughly 90 acres (35ha), they grow Sangiovese, Syrah, and Alicante, varieties that they feel perform best in the region's arid climate, a sensibility that seems apparent in the hearty reds the estate's winemaker Maurizio Castelli makes here. Aragone is a blend of the aforementioned grapes plus Carignan; where there is power and presence in the blend, there is also cut and verve. I Perazzi is a Morellino di Scansano that is at home on the dinner table. ★ Rising star

Monte Civali, Magliano in Toscana, 68061 Grosseto www.bastianich.com

La Torre Montalcino
Luigi Anania established this 13 acre (5ha) estate in 1977; his first vintage was in 1982. The wines from this small domain strike a traditional tone with their combination of elegance and structure. Look for the basic Brunello, an earthy, savory red that feels lifted and light thanks to bright acidity and high-toned fruit. It has the structure to age for several years. The Rosso di Montalcino is meant for earlier drinking; the bright Sangiovese character makes this a wine for the table.

Frazione Sesta, Località La Torre, 53024 Montalcino 0577 844073

Le Boncie Chianti Classico
Giovanna Morganti owns this small property situated at a relatively high altitude (approximately 1,300ft/400m) in Castelnuovo Berardenga. From here, she produces just one wine: a tense, nervy Chianti Classico called Le Trame. Showing the elegant, more finessed side of Sangiovese, Le Trame opts for freshness over power, and thanks to its vivid acidity, the wine feels balanced enough for aging. Morganti's attentive farming and reliance on native yeast fermentations has earned her a place among Italy's natural winemakers—and hopefully a (slightly) larger audience. ★ Rising star

Strada delle Boncie 5, Località San Felice, 53019 Castelnuovo Berardenga; www.leboncie.it

SUPER MED REDS

The term Super Tuscan has long been used to describe powerful reds blended from varying percentages of Sangiovese and Bordeaux grapes, such as Cabernet Sauvignon, Merlot, or Cabernet Franc. As these wines have proliferated throughout Tuscany, a few producers in the coastal Maremma zone have begun to look closer to their backyards for inspiration.

That this is happening in the home territory of original super-blends like Sassicaia and Ornellaia seems to give the idea more credibility. Wineries like Ampelaia, Valgiano, Belguardo, and La Mozza all prominently feature grapes such as Grenache, Mourvèdre, Carignan, and Alicante in their blends. What these wines all have in common is a more relaxed sensibility. Rather than exist only as a trophy to be hidden away in a dark cellar, this new generation of Tuscan blends revel in their table-ready, food-friendly qualities. They will not depose Sassicaia, but then they do not really need to.

Complete with vines and rows of cypress trees, the rolling hills of Greve in Chianti encapsulate the Tuscan idyll.

ORNELLAIA

A POWERFUL WINE MADE FROM A BLEND OF
CABERNET SAUVIGNON, MERLOT, CABERNET
FRANC, AND PETIT VERDOT

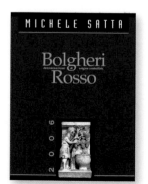

MICHELE SATTA

AN ACCESSIBLE, FRESH AND FRUITY WINE
WITH A SOLID BACKBONE OF TANNIN

Le Macchiole Bolgheri

This dynamic estate is one of Bolgheri's leading lights. Established in 1975 by Eugenio Campolmi, Le Macchiole has made a name for itself with its single-varietal expressions of Cabernet Franc (Paleo), Merlot (Messorio), and Syrah (Scrio). Campolmi, who died prematurely in 2002, had an affinity for Cabernet Franc, and he was convinced that Bolgheri's clay soils were the perfect home for the grape. His widow, Cinzia Merli, and the estate's longtime winemaker, Luca d'Attoma, have continued that dedication. Paleo is one of the world's great expressions of Cabernet Franc.

Via Bolgherese 189, 57020 Bolgheri
www.lemacchiole.it

Le Potazzine Montalcino

Giuseppe Gorelli is a young winemaker in Montalcino who, in the years since starting this small estate, has managed to gain considerable notice for his classically made wines. The Brunello combines intensity of flavor and expression with supple tannins. It is a wine that will benefit from medium-term aging, although it is enjoyable at an earlier age than might be expected, especially with a hearty stew. The Rosso, which sees some time in barriques, is forward and soft, and also a wine that is meant to accompany food. ★ **Rising star**

Località Le Prata 262, 53024 Montalcino
www.lepotazzine.it

Le Presi Montalcino

Bruno Fabbri started this small estate in 1970. His son Gianni took over in 1998, continuing his father's work, including organic farming and a traditional approach in the cellar. Fabbri likes to champion the estate's respect for Sangiovese. Each year, the annual VinItaly trade show sees a new T-shirt proclaiming Le Presi's devotion to Sangiovese. Look for the Brunello, a powerful wine of great intensity and focus, made for aging. Le Presi's Rosso, with its gentle aspect, is more accessible when young.

Via Costa della Porta, Frazione Castelnuovo Abate, 53020 Montalcino; 0577 835541

Lisini Montalcino

The Lisini family is one of the storied names of Montalcino, with roots in the commune reaching back to the 1700s. Its estate has more than 44 acres (18ha) of vineyards, the result of substantial renovations carried out by Elina Lisini in the early 1970s. Management remains in the hands of the Lisini family, with winemaking help from Giulio Gambelli. As might be expected from the combination of Gambelli with an old Montalcino family name, Lisini's Brunello is proudly traditional—an elegant wine that pries delicacy and finesse.

Località Sant'Angelo in Colle, 53020 Montalcino
www.lisini.com

MaremmAlta Montalcino

This project was established by Stefano Rizzi in the early 2000s in the southern Maremma not far from Grosseto. MaremmAlta is notable for affordable, unpretentious wines like Lestra, a bright, refreshing Vermentino that makes for easy summertime drinking. Poggiomaestro, an unoaked red made entirely from Sangiovese, is deliciously bright and fresh. Micante adds Cabernet Sauvignon to the Sangiovese and as a result is a darker, more concentrated red. Meant for immediate consumption, these wines represent great value from the Tuscan coast.

Località Casteani, 58023 Gavorrano
www.maremmalta.it

Massa Vecchia Maremma

Massa Vecchia is one of the founders of the Italian natural wine movement, having started Vini Veri along with producers including Paolo Bea, Stanislao Radikon, and Angiolino Maule. Established in 1985 by Fabrizio Niccolaini and Patrizia Bartolini, the estate has been run by Bartolini's daughter, Francesca Sfondrini, since 2009. Farming and winemaking are both done as naturally as possible, meaning a chemical-free and holistic approach in the vineyard, and non-interventionist methods in the cellar. These are authentic, vibrant wines of great individuality. ★ **Rising star**

Via Le Coste 21B, 58024 Massa Marittima
0566 904144

Melini Chianti Classico

This large producer, established in 1705 and today owned by Gruppo Italiano Vini, was among the first to use the infamous wicker bottles for Chianti sold on the export market. The winery has modernized considerably since those days, although the house style tends toward the traditional. Given Melini's size and traditional bent, these wines, especially the basic Chianti bottling of Sangiovese and Canaiolo, represent exceptional value. At the higher end, try the Vigneti La Selvanella, a well-structured Chianti Classico Riserva from Melini's vineyard in Radda.

Località Gaggiano, 53036 Poggibonsi
www.gruppoitalianovini.com/melini

Michele Satta Bolgheri

Michele Satta moved to Bolgheri as an agronomy student in 1974. He worked on a fruit and vegetable farm at first, before being bitten by the vineyard bug. Satta started making his own wine in the early 1980s, and by 1988, he had built a winery and begun to plant his own vineyards, slowly building the estate. Satta's wines resemble others in Bolgheri in terms of elegance, yet they feel neither hurried nor pushed. Look for the Bolgheri Rosso, which blends the customary Cabernet, Sangiovese, and Merlot with Syrah and Teroldego. ★ **Rising star**

Località Casone Ugolino 23, 57022 Castagneto Carducci
www.michelesatta.com

Montesecondo Chianti Classico

In the mid-1990s, Silvio and Catalina Messana moved their family from New York to a farm outside of Florence that Silvo's parents owned. His father had planted a vineyard in the 1970s, which the Messanas began to work themselves using first organic and later biodynamic methods. Such natural farming methods allow Silvio Messana to rely on healthy native yeasts for fermentations; he also has a light touch with oak, preferring larger *tonneaux* to small barriques. Look for the Chianti Classico, a vivid, hearty blend of Sangiovese, Canaiolo, and Colorino. ★ **Rising star**

Via per Cerbaia 18, Località Cerbaia, 53017 San Casciano Val di Pesa; www.montesecondo.com

Montevertine Chianti Classico

The Montevertine story began in 1967, when the late Sergio Manetti bought an old farm in Radda, and then, with the help of the legendary Giulio Gambelli, planted the Le Pergole Torte vineyard a year later. Manetti had an infamous falling-out with the Chianti Classico Consorzio over the classification of his wines, and the result is that all of Montevertine's wines are labeled as IGT rather than DOC. His son Martino follows the same principles today, including long fermentations in cement tanks and an aging philosophy that values finesse over power in each of the estate's wines.

Località Montevertine, 53017 Radda in Chianti
www.montevertine.it

Moris Farms Maremma

The Moris family has been involved in the agriculture business of the southern Maremma for generations. In more recent years, the family's two estates—one located in the Scansano region, the other in Massa Marittima—have been fully developed with an eye toward quality wine production. From the Scansano property comes a bright, fruity expression of Morellino that is easy on the palate. More substantial and complex is Avvoltore, a Sangiovese, Cabernet Sauvignon, and Syrah blend. Also look for the herb-tinged and focused Vermentino, grown near Grosseto.

Fattoria Poggetti, Località Cura Nuova, 58024 Massa Marittima; www.morisfarms.it

Ornellaia Bolgheri

This benchmark of modern Tuscan wine was established in the early 1980s by Ludovico Antinori and his winemaker Tibor Gál. The estate quickly achieved prominence with elegant reds fashioned from Bordeaux grapes, in particular the single-vineyard Merlot called Masseto. Ornellaia went through a tumultuous period of ownership in the early 2000s, having been bought first by the Mondavi family of California. It was then part of a joint venture with the Frescobaldi family; after acquiring Mondavi, Constellation Brands sold its shares to the Frescobaldis, who now own the estate outright.

Via Bolgherese 191 Bolgheri, 57022 Castagneto Carducci
www.ornellaia.com

Palazzina Le Macioche Montalcino

Matilde Zecca and Achille Mazzocchi bought and renovated this tiny estate, beginning in 1985. From a little over 7 acres (2.8ha) that they farm with organic methods, they produce—with help from consulting enologist Maurizio Castelli—delicate, classically structured wines. Le Macioche's Brunello di Montalcino combines floral aromas and gentle red fruit with firm, sinewy tannins. The Riserva comes from a selection at harvest, and like the basic Brunello, sees a long maceration time. This wine shows greater intensity and power, with both elements balanced by subtle aromatics, and will reward patience.

S P di Sant'Antimo Km 4.85, 53024 Montalcino
0577 849168

Pian dell'Orino Montalcino

This estate spins the concept of modern and contemporary on its head, embracing as it does more currently en vogue (and therefore modern) ideas

PIAN DELL'ORINO
THIS POWERFUL AND INTENSE BRUNELLO IS MATURED IN BARREL FOR TWO TO THREE YEARS

like organics and natural winemaking than intensive handling and barrique aging. Established in 1997 by Caroline Pobitzer and her husband Jan Erbach, Pian dell'Orino has 15 acres (6ha) of vineyards adjacent to Biondi Santi's Tenuta Greppo, from which they produce elegant and engaging wines. Look for the Rosso di Montalcino, made in an appealing and forward style. The Brunello, thanks to long maceration, is powerful and intense. ★ **Rising star**

Località Piandellorino 189, 53024 Montalcino
www.piandellorino.com

Piandibugnano Montecucco

Giorgio Bucelli, Paolo Trappolini, and Carlo Filippeschi started this small winery in 2002 in the Montecucco zone of southern Tuscany. The vineyard has just over 7 acres (3ha) planted on the slopes near Mount Amiata at relatively high elevations (1,300–1,650ft/400–500m), meaning that acidity levels tend to stay rather high in the final wines. Look for Cuccaia, a blend of Sangiovese and Merlot that feels energetic and lifted. L'Erpico is Piandibugnano's 100% Sangiovese, an exotic wine that combines feminine aromatics with strong, masculine tannins. ★ **Rising star**

Località Piandibugnano, 58038 Seggiano Grosseto
www.piandibugnano.com

Pieve Santa Restituta Montalcino

Originally established by Roberto Bellini in 1974, this estate has been controlled by Angelo Gaja since 1994. Here, with customary intensity, Gaja is intent on making wines of purpose. To that end, he has updated and expanded the vineyards, and rebuilt the winery. Pieve Santa Restituta focuses primarily on two Brunellos that see both barrique and cask aging. Reninna is a selection from multiple sites; charming and gracious, it is the more forward of the two wines. Sugarille is a single-vineyard Brunello framed by strong mineral tannins and firm acidity.

Località Santa Restituta, 53024 Montalcino
www.gaja.com

Poderi Boscarelli Montepulciano

Paola de Ferrari Corradi's father bought the Boscarelli estate in the early 1960s; Paola and her husband Ippolito de Ferrari ran it together until Ippolito tragically died in an accident in 1983. Paola hired Maurizio Castelli shortly after, and he helped to shape the current style of Boscarelli. Paola's son, Luca de Ferrari Corradi, is now involved in the cellar. The wines flirt cautiously with modern styling in that they are typically less austere than others from Montepulciano. Try the savory, refined Vino Nobile before checking out the powerful Riserva.

Via di Montenero 28, 53040 Cervognano di Montepulciano
www.poderiboscarelli.com

Poggio Antico Montalcino

Thanks to its relatively high altitude— 1,475ft (450m) —Poggio Antico makes wines that feel bright and fresh, even in extremely hot vintages like 2003. Originally purchased in 1984 by Giancarlo Gloder, Poggio Antico has been managed by his daughter Paolo Gloder since 1987 (and her husband Alberto Montefiori since 1998). Look for the basic Brunello bottling, rendered here as

PIANDIBUGNANO
AN EXOTIC WINE, WITH FEMININE AROMATICS, BUT STRONG TANNINS

POGGIO VERRANO
A FRUITY BLEND OF ALICANTE, CABERNET
SAUVIGNON, AND MERLOT, PART-AGED IN OAK

POGGIO ARGENTIERA
THIS BLEND OF ALICANTE AND SYRAH IS
COMPLEX, LAYERED, AND SAVORY

a wine that can be drunk at a younger age than other wines from the region. The Riserva is more compact and sturdy—a wine built to age.

Località Poggio Antico, 53024 Montalcino
www.poggioantico.com

Poggio Argentiera Maremma
Established in 1997 by Gianpaolo Paglia and his wife Justine, Poggio Argentiera is one of the new-wave wineries helping to put Morellino di Scansano on the map with precise, focused wines. Bellamarsilia is the estate's unoaked Morellino, blended from the traditional grapes of the region—Sangiovese, Ciliegiolo, and Alicante. This wine is full of juicy, cherry-scented fruit, and is made for the table. For Mediterranean complexity, look for Finisterre, a layered, savory blend of Alicante and Syrah.

Località Banditella 2, Alberese, 58100 Grosseto
www.poggioargentiera.com

Poggio Scalette Chianti Classico
Vittorio Fiore and his wife Adriana purchased this abandoned property in the hills high above Greve in 1991. They produce one wine, Il Carbonaione, from the more than 80-year-old Sangiovese vines that had come with the land. Fiore is one of Italy's most highly regarded consulting enologists; at Poggio Scalette, his son Jurij joined him in winemaking duties in 1993. The estate was expanded in 1996 when a neighboring property became available. In its youth, Il Carbonaione can show the influence of oak. It will gain elegance with patient cellaring. ★ Rising star

Via Barbiano 7, Località Ruffoli, 50022 Greve in Chianti
www.poggioscalette.it

Poggio di Sotto Montalcino
Poggio di Sotto sits high on a ridge outside Castelnuovo dell'Abate with a view that looks south and west across a wide valley. That vast expanse exerts some effect on the vines grown here by Piero Palmucci, whether that is focused acidity or simply stress. Palmucci purchased the estate in 1989 after a long search to find the right place to make the most traditional Brunello. With the help of the legendary Giulio Gambelli, Palmucci makes classic, elegant wines that are among the most thrilling produced in Montalcino today. ★ Rising star

Castelnuovo dell'Abate, 53024 Montalcino
www.poggiodisotto.com

Poggio Verrano Maremma
This estate marks Francesco Bolla's entry into the viticultural hotbed of western Tuscany. Bolla, the former managing director of the large wine company founded by his great-grandfather Abele, is approaching the business from the ground up at Poggio Verrano, which he established in 2000. The new estate consists of 67 acres (27ha) of Sangiovese, Alicante, Cabernet Sauvignon, Merlot, and Cabernet Franc. The flagship red, Dròmos, is a seamless, focused blend of each of those varieties. Brighter, if less complex, is Dròmos L'Altro, a pure Sangiovese that boasts a rich texture. ★ Rising star

S da Provinciale 9, Km 4, 58051 Magliano
www.poggioverrano.it

Poliziano Montepulciano
Federico Carletti's father, Dino, purchased the first 54 acres (22ha) of the estate that would become Poliziano in 1961. Federico himself joined the winery sometime later, after completing an agricultural degree. Today, Poliziano is thoroughly modern, employing exacting methods and techniques in the vineyards and relying on new technology in the winery. Look for the estate's finely crafted, perfumed Vino Nobile—an irresistible wine with a smooth texture and generous flavor. Also worth trying is the juicy, food-friendly Rosso.

Via Fontago 1, 53040 Montepulciano
www.carlettipoliziano.com

Querciabella Chianti Classico
Querciabella's story began in the 1970s when the late Giuseppe Castiglioni began buying land around Greve and Radda. But it has been under his son Sebastiano's lead that Querciabella has jumped to the forefront of the Chianti Classico scene, beginning at the end of the 1980s with the application of environmentally sensitive farming practices. By 2000, the estate had transitioned entirely to biodynamic agriculture. The best introduction is the estate's elegantly formed Chianti Classico. Also of note is Batàr, a Chardonnay/Pinot Bianco blend that is one of Tuscany's top whites. ★ Rising star

Via di Barbiano 17, 50022 Greve in Chianti
www.querciabella.com

Renieri Montalcino
Marco Bacci, the man behind Castello di Bossi in Chianti Classico, purchased this 316 acre (128ha) estate in 1998. The old vineyards have been replaced with more modern, higher-density plantings, mostly to Sangiovese, but also to Cabernet Sauvignon, Merlot, and Syrah. The result, as shown by the Brunello, is stylish and modern, and textural richness and pleasure is emphasized over austere firmness. Re di Renieri is an intense, concentrated blend of the estate's Bordeaux grapes. Mouthwatering acidity keeps it feeling fresh. ★ Rising star

Località Renieri, 53024 Montalcino
www.renierimontalcino.com

Rocca di Montegrossi Chianti Classico
Marco Ricasoli-Firidolfi, a descendant of the father of Chianti, Bettino Ricasoli, started Rocca di Montegrossi in the late 1990s at Vigneto San Marcellino, a family property. He completed the winery building in 2000 and has since gradually expanded the vineyard itself to about 45 acres (18ha), planted to traditional grapes like Sangiovese and Canaiolo, as well as Malvasia—used for the estate's beguiling and hypnotic Vin Santo. The Sangiovese at Rocca di Montegrossi feels refined and aromatic; both the vibrant Chianti Classico and the ageworthy Riserva San Marcellino are elegant reds. ★ Rising star

Località Monti in Chianti, San Marcellino, 53010 Gaiole in Chianti; www.roccadimontegrossi.it

Salcheto Montepulciano
This estate was started as a farm in 1984; the first vineyards were planted later that decade, and the first wines were launched with the help of consulting winemaker Paolo Vagaggini and manager Michele Manelli. Salcheto makes a bold style of Vino Nobile, with ripe fruit flavors framed

by austere tannins and cooling acidity. There is also a mouthwatering character in Salcheto's wines, especially as captured by the frisky Rosso di Montepulciano, which is blended from Sangiovese, Canaiolo, and Merlot, and aged entirely in steel tanks. **★ Rising star**

Via di Villa Bianca 15, 53045 Montepulciano
www.salcheto.it

Salicutti Montalcino

A chemist by training, Francesco Leanza got into wine-growing late in life after buying a 27 acre (11ha) site in the south of the Montalcino appellation in 1990. During the following decade, Leanza rehabilitated the estate, planted vines, and built a small winery. He introduced organic practices and decided to follow a non-interventionist path in the cellar. Look for the bright Brunello Piaggione, a vivid expression of Sangiovese that has the energy and staying power to age well. **★ Rising star**

Località Podere Salicutti 174, 53024 Montalcino
www.poderesalicutti.it

San Fabiano Calcinaia Chianti Classico

Guido and Isa Serio bought and began to renovate San Fabiano Calcinaia in 1983. It produces concentrated, stylish wines that should charm lovers of more forward New World reds. Look for Cellole, a single-vineyard Riserva that combines Sangiovese with 5% Merlot. The basic Chianti Classico, made from entirely Sangiovese, is similarly rich, with a texture made plush from barrique aging. Both wines feel finely balanced and have the concentration and power to age for several years.

Località Cellole, 53011 Castellina in Chianti
www.sanfabianocalcinaia.com

Sassotondo Maremma

Ciliegiolo, one of Tuscany's "other" red grapes, has in recent years become the center of attention for some rather intrepid producers, among them Sassotondo in the southern Maremma. Established in 1990 by Edoardo Ventimiglia and Carla Benini, Sassotondo released its first vintage in 1997. For a primer, look for the Ciliegiolo (blended with 10% Alicante), an unoaked expression of this distinctive red. Also of note is San Lorenzo, a powerful, ageworthy single-vineyard selection of Ciliegiolo from old vines. Save the refreshing Bianco di Pitigliano for a hot summer's day. **★ Rising star**

Pian di Conati 52, 58010 Sovana
www.sassotondo.it

Schiaccionaia Montecucco

Marcella Turziani and Dagoberto Rolla established this winery and farm in 2000. They grow their 14 acres (5.5ha) of vines according to organic methods. Marcella and her son Riccardo run the cellar with guidance from enologist Luca D'Attoma, and together they make distinctive wines from Sangiovese and Syrah. Start with Schiaccionaia's Vela Ventis, a bright rosato that feels as serious as it is refreshing. Trasubie is a potent blend that combines the mouthwatering acidity of Sangiovese with Syrah's peppery, savory tannins. Impressively structured, it should develop well in the cellar.

Via Della Fontanella Bagnoli 3, 58031 Arcidosso
www.domenicoselections.com

Silvio Nardi Montalcino

Silvio Nardi bought the Casale del Bosco estate in 1950. Eight years later, he released his first bottle of Brunello and then expanded the estate with the purchase of Tenuta di Manachiara in 1962. His daughter Emilia runs the estate today, and it was she who introduced the winery's single-vineyard Brunello in 1995. Vigneto Manachiara is a firm, elegant red sourced from the oldest vineyards at the Manachiara estate. The regular Brunello is finely balanced and often approachable when young.

Casale del Bosco, 53024 Montalcino
www.tenutenardi.com

Sono Montendioli San Gimignano

Elisabetta Fagiuoli has been tending the vines and olive trees at Sono Montendioli since 1965. Farming at this small estate is organic in practice, and Fagiuoli has imparted that energy and careful attention to detail to her wines, especially the vivid whites made from Vernaccia. There are three iterations of Vernaccia di San Gimignano at this estate: Tradizionale, which receives a long period of skin contact during fermentation; Fiore, which is made from the free-run grape juice; and Carato, an oak-aged white capable of a surprisingly long life.

Località Cortennano, 53037 San Gimigano
www.montenidoli.com

Talenti Montalcino

This well-regarded estate was established in 1980 by winemaker Pierluigi Talenti. Run today by his grandson Riccardo, Talenti remains a source for traditionally styled, classic Brunello. Subtle and perfumed, with elegant, earthy tannins, it is a wine that can be enjoyed after only a few years in bottle, although there is plenty of bright acidity to prolong its life. The Riserva is the sturdier wine, with firm tannins that frame its bright core of fruit. Also look for Talenti's appealing Rosso di Montalcino, an elegant, food friendly expression of Sangiovese.

Pian di Conte, S Angelo in Colle, 53020 Montalcino
www.talentimontalcino.it

Tenuta di Arceno Chianti Classico

This 220 acre (90ha) estate has been owned by American Jess Jackson (of Kendall-Jackson fame) since 1994. Although the estate is situated in the Chianti Classico zone, its focus tilts toward blends of French grapes like Cabernet Sauvignon, Merlot, and Syrah in a trio of stylish wines called Arcanum I, II, and III. Arcanum I combines Cabernet Sauvignon and Merlot in a seamless blend edged by powerful, earthy tannin. Arceno's sleek, balanced Chianti Classico blends Sangiovese with Merlot and Cabernet Sauvignon. **★ Rising star**

Località Arceno, San Gusme, Castelnuovo Berardenga 53010; www.tenutadiarceno.com

Tenuta Belguardo Maremma

The Mazzei family, of Fonterutoli fame, purchased this estate in the 1990s to expand their holdings into the Maremma. Naturally, there is a notable Cabernet Sauvignon-based blend called Tenuta Belguardo that combines the dusty, earthy character common to this region with a polished sheen. The real star of the estate, however, is Serrata, a graceful blend of Sangiovese and Alicante. Firm and rich, yet with bright, mouthwatering

SASSICAIA
THIS RENOWNED AND SOUGHT-AFTER WINE
HAS BECOME AN ITALIAN CLASSIC

TENUTA BELGUARDO
A CABERNET SAUVIGNON-BASED WINE
WITH AN EARTHY CHARACTER

acidity, it represents an exciting future for the Maremma, one that looks as much to the Mediterranean as to Bordeaux for inspiration. ★ **Rising star**

Località Montebottigli, VIII° Zona, 58100 Grosseto
www.mazzei.it

Tenuta di Bibbiano Chianti Classico
Tommaso and Federico Marrocchesi Marzi run this old estate in Castellina. There is a traditional feel to Bibbiano's wines, thanks in part to the legendary Giulio Gambelli, who was the estate's consulting winemaker from 1943 until 2000, when Stefano Porcinai took over. The Chianti Classico is the best place to start; it is a firm, vibrant wine made from Sangiovese, Colorino, and Canaiolo fermented in cement tanks and aged in Slavonian oak casks. The elegant Montornello adds a small percentage of Merlot.

Via Bibbiano 76, 53011 Castellina In Chianti
www.tenutadibibbiano.com

Tenuta di Capezzana Carmignano
This historic estate has been owned by the Contini Bonacossi family since the mid-1920s. Benedetta Contini Bonacossi runs Capezzana's cellars, along with consulting enologist Stefano Chioccioli. The estate's top wine, and the wine that laid the foundation for the Carmignano DOC is Villa di Capezzana. A blend of Sangiovese (80%) and Cabernet Sauvignon (20%), it feels firm and structured, yet shows deep, earthy character. Meanwhile, the Barco Reale is one of Tuscany's most accomplished and widely recognized high-quality table wines.

Via Capezzana 100, 59015 Carmignano
www.capezzana.it

Tenuta di Castiglioni Chianti Colli Fiorentini
This ancient estate, belonging to the Frescobaldi family, focuses on IGT wines made primarily of Bordeaux varieties. The signature wine, Tenuta di Castiglione, is a darkly colored wine of mostly Cabernet Sauvignon and Merlot that picks up a red-cherry brightness from a small amount of Sangiovese added to the blend. Giramonte, the estate's plush Merlot and Sangiovese blend, is stylish and rich—a steakhouse wine.

No visitor facilities
www.frescobaldi.it

Tenuta Guado al Tasso Bolgheri
Once part of the massive Maremma holdings of the Della Gherardesca family, this estate is owned today by the Antinori family. The estate has a long history of producing quality rosato, today called Scalabrone, but the main focus is on the proprietary blend of Cabernet Sauvignon, Merlot, and Syrah named for the estate. Guado al Tasso is polished and refined, with an elegant structure that speaks of its pedigree.

No visitor facilities
www.antinori.it

Tenuta Monteloro Fiesole
One of the many estates surrounding the greater Florence region owned by Antinori, Monteloro has more than 130 acres (53ha) of vineyards planted primarily to white varieties. Thanks in part to the altitude—about 1,600ft (490m)—and the large daily temperature change,

grapes like Pinot Bianco, Riesling, and Pinot Grigio fare reasonably well here. Those three varieties make up Mezzo Braccio, Antinori's Monteloro wine. Aromatic and fresh, it maintains a racy cut across the palate that makes it ideal for seafood.

No visitor facilities
www.antinori.it

Tenuta di Nozzole Chianti Classico
Located near Greve, Nozzole is an old estate that has belonged to the Folonari family since 1971. Today, Nozzole is part of Amborgio and Giovanni Folonari's small empire of wine estates, and it is from here that they produce Il Pareto, one of Tuscany's top varietal Cabernet Sauvignons. Concentrated and rich, with a bright core of brambly fruit, Il Pareto is an elegant, internationally styled wine that is built for the cellar. The most classic wine is the Villa Nozzole Chianti Classico, made from the property's oldest Sangiovese vines.

Via di Nozzole 12, Località Passo dei Pecorai, 50020 Greve in Chianti; www.tenutefolonari.com

Tenuta Oliveto Montalcino
Aldemaro and Monica Machetti bought and renovated this abandoned estate in 1994. Between 1994 and 1998, approximately 29 acres (12ha) of vineyards were planted at varying exposures and at relatively high density. The house style, as arrived at by enologist Roberto Cipresso, veers toward the modern in aspect, with ripeness and generous texture apparent in the wines. The Brunello combines dark fruit and savory herbal notes with soft tannins. Enjoyable in its youth, it is a good introduction to Brunello for fans of rich, New World reds.

Località Oliveto, Frazione Castelnuovo dell'Abate, 53020 Montalcino; www.tenutaoliveto.it

Tenuta Pèppoli Chianti Classico
Another Antinori property, the 245 acre (100ha) Pèppoli estate is located a short distance from the Tignanello vineyard. From this estate comes Antinori's approachable Pèppoli Chianti Classico. Made from 90% Sangiovese, with varying amounts of Merlot and Syrah, it is an internationally styled, fruit-forward wine that is meant for early drinking. The estate's stony soils seem to lend the wine depth; it is never a profound wine, but it does have enough character to make you think. The place for it, of course, is at the table with hearty rustic fare.

No visitor facilities
www.antinori.it

Tenuta Pian delle Vigne Montalcino
Antinori purchased this 459 acre (186ha) estate in 1995 as a foothold in the booming premium wine region of Montalcino. Following the purchase, the firm planted 76 acres (31ha) of Sangiovese; an additional 81 acres (33ha) were planted more recently, partly using clonal material developed from Antinori's own research. The Brunello produced at this estate is polished and refined, with an aristocratic bearing that belies its ripe, modern style. It gains complexity with a few years in bottle, so this one should spend some time in the cellar.

Tenuta Pian delle Vigne, 53024 Montalcino
www.antinori.it

Tenuta San Guido (Sassicaia) Bolgheri

Sassicaia, the Bordeaux-inspired blend of Cabernet Sauvignon and Cabernet Franc, needs no introduction in the context of Tuscan, or Italian wine. Considered the pioneering wine of its type when it was released in 1968, Sassicaia is today a classic Italian wine, and a member of the old guard. Aside from the introduction of two additional wines, Guidalberto and Le Difese, little has changed at the estate of Tenuta San Guido over the years. Since the late 1990s, Sassicaia is its own DOC, a unique feat among Italian wines.

Località Le Capanne 27, 57022 Bolgheri
www.sassicaia.com

Tenuta Tignanello Chianti Classico

This estate, owned by the Antinori family since the middle of the 19th century, needs little introduction. Beginning with the 1970 vintage, Tignanello first appeared as a barrique-aged, single-vineyard Chianti Classico Riserva. In 1971 it became Vino da Tavola; by the early 1980s, the current blend of 85% Sangiovese, 10% Cabernet Sauvignon, and 5% Cabernet Franc was firmly in place. Tignanello remains a powerful, age-worthy wine. From the same estate comes Solaia, another Cabernet/Sangiovese blend that feels sleek and elegant.

No visitor facilities
www.antinori.it

Tenuta di Valgiano Colline Lucchesi

From its position in the hills above Lucca, Valgiano clearly looks to the Mediterranean for inspiration. This young estate's 39 acres (16ha) of biodynamically farmed vineyards yield wines made from Syrah and Vermentino in addition to Sangiovese. Giallo dei Muri is an aromatic and ample white blended from Malvasia, Trebbiano, and Vermentino. For a juicy, refreshing red wine, look for Palistorti, a vibrant blend of Sangiovese, Syrah, and Merlot that has more character than its stylish bearing might first suggest. Scasso dei Cesari is all Sangiovese from Vagiano's oldest vines. ★ **Rising star**

Via di Valgiano 7, 55010 Valgiano Lucca
www.valgiano.it

Terrabianca Chianti Classico

Swiss-born Roberto Guldener, with guidance from Vittorio Fiore, purchased this estate in the late 1980s. In 1989 he began to replant and modernize the existing vineyards, and plant new ones. Today, Terrabianca is comprised of nearly 126 acres (51ha) of Sangiovese, Cabernet Sauvignon, Merlot, and Canaiolo. From these vines comes a series of carefully crafted, stylish wines. Look for the Chianti Classico Scassino, a concentrated single-vineyard wine that boasts a formidable structure. Perhaps the most emblematic wine is Campaccio, an elegant, barrique-aged Sangiovese and Cabernet blend.

Località San Fedele a Paterno 17, 53017 Radda in Chianti
www.terrabianca.com

Teruzzi e Puthod San Gimignano

Tuscany is better known for reds than whites, yet Italy's first DOC in 1967 was, perhaps controversially, Vernaccia di San Gimignano. In 1974, Enrico Teruzzi and Carmen Puthod started their forward-thinking winery, Teruzzi e Puthod (now owned by Cinzano). The couple embraced

VALDIPIATTA
A WINE THAT COMPLEMENTS RICH SAUCES, RED AND GAME MEATS, AND AGED CHEESES

UCCELLIERA
A GENEROUS AND FULL BRUNELLO WITH RICH FRUIT AND BALANCING ACIDITY

technology in the cellar (and clean, striking labels for their bottles), creating a refined, brightly flavored style of wine with international appeal. The traditional Vernaccia di San Gimignano, Ronodlino, is the top wine. Simple and refreshing, it tastes best on a hot day.

Località Casale 19, 53037 San Gimignano
0577 940143

Tua Rita Maremma

Rita Tua and Virgilio Bisti planted the first sections of Tua Rita in 1984. The couple later expanded the vineyards and released their first commercial vintage in 1992. Tua Rita achieved success with both critics and the market when the winery released a 100% Merlot called Redigaffi. A powerful wine of deep extraction and concentration, Redigaffi remains highly sought-after. Perlato del Bosco Rosso, a blend of Sangiovese and Cabernet Sauvignon, shows a similarly concentrated palate yet feels more lifted and higher-toned thanks to bright acidity.

Località Notri 81, 57028 Suvereto
www.tuarita.it

Uccelliera Montalcino

Andrea Cortonesi purchased this estate in 1986. Today, Uccelliera is a fairly typical artisan producer, farming just under 15 acres (6ha) of vineyards using organic methods. The warmer climate of the Castelnuovo dell'Abate subzone shows in the ripeness levels of the estate's wines. The Brunello, for instance, is generous and full, with plenty of sweet fruit, yet there is generally enough acidity to keep those flavors feeling fresh rather than cooked. Rapace is the estate's richly flavored blend of Sangiovese, Merlot, and Cabernet Sauvignon.

Podere Uccelliera 45, Frazione Castelnuovo Abate, 53020 Montalcino; www.uccelliera-montalcino.it

Valdipiatta Montepulciano

Miriam Caporali runs this modern estate, which her father Giulio bought in the late 1980s. Valdipiatta has nearly 75 acres (30ha) of Sangiovese, Canaiolo, and Mammolo planted at about 1,200ft (365m), in addition to international grapes like Cabernet Sauvignon, Merlot, and Pinot Noir. Look for Vigna d'Alfiero, a single-vineyard Vino Nobile Riserva that shows the firmness and strength Sangiovese can achieve in this region. Softer and more approachable is the regular Vino Nobile. The estate also makes a Chianti Colli Senesi called Tosca that is worth tracking down.

Via della Ciarliana 25/A, 53040 Montepulciano
www.valdipiatta.it

Vignamaggio Chianti Classico

This historic villa and estate—famously the home of Mona Lisa—is a popular tourist destination in the Chianti Classico region. Located near Greve, the estate was bought and restored by Gianni Nunziante in 1988. The wines, particularly the Chianti Classico *normale* and Riserva, are made in a forward, international style, yet feel balanced by savory, earthy tannins. They would appeal to fans of ripe New World reds. Also worth trying is the estate's 100% Cabernet Franc. Made from older vines, it feels elegant and cool.

Via di Petriolo 5, 50022 Greve in Chianti
www.vignamaggio.com

SOUTHERN ITALY AND THE ISLANDS

SWITZERLAND   AUSTRIA
FRANCE   SLOVENIA
Milan
Venice
Florence
ITALY
ROME
SARDINIA
Cagliari   Naples
Palermo
■ Southern Italy,
Sardinia and Sicily   SICILY

Italy's long leg stretches deep into the Mediterranean, and the feeling of isolation from the rest of Europe increases as one heads toward the south. An area that was once the hub of the known world is now more known for government corruption and organized crime—a result of the shift in the world's agricultural axis away from Italy in the early 20th century. Italy's deep south has been on its uppers ever since. However, of late it has begun to recover some of that ancient brio, largely through European Union grants that have proved crucial in transforming its rural economy. New vineyards and cellars are springing up like mushrooms, and the wines are finally beginning to reflect the potential first recognized 3,000 years ago.

Major grapes

 Reds

Aglianico

Cannonau (Grenache)

Malvasia Nera

Negoramaro

Nero d'Avola

Primitivo

Whites

Fiano

Greco

Vermentino

Zibibbo (Moscato)

Vintages

2009
Vineyards suffered from reduced yields due to the previous year's drought. Particularly difficult in Sicily— especially for late varieties and at higher altitudes—due to heavy rains in September.

2008
A drought vintage for Southern Italy, but very good in Sicily.

2007
Excellent across the board.

2006
Lovely vintage, with very little disease, making classic wines. Reds coming along nicely.

2005
A cooler than usual growing season. A firm hand in the vineyard yielded wines of elegance and perfume.

Despite Southern Italy's economic frailty and political uncertainty, the pride of its people has never been broken. On the contrary, it appears that the heat of the *Mezzogiorno* has distilled a fierce spirit of independence that poverty has done nothing to expunge. South of Rome, emotions run high, and although the north of Italy may be wealthy, the south is unspeakably beautiful. Rarely has such an abundance of the flora and fauna necessary for human habitation been found in such a small area. For the lucky inhabitants, the living is easy.

Introduced by the Greeks when they first landed in Puglia in 750BCE, the vine has been part of proceedings ever since. The early settlers of Magna Graecia, as these colonies became known, were astonished by the vine's propensity for its new home. For *Vitis vinifera* (the common grapevine) and the arid climate of Italy's deep south, it was love at first sight. Today's grapes Aglianico (from "Hellenic") and Greco (from "Graeci") are direct descendants of this happy union.

Like successive waves of invaders, the vine initially flooded the Italian peninsula, but what remains after three millennia are isolated pools of viticulture where the natural adaptation was greatest. Puglia demonstrates this complex patchwork admirably. It boasts a clutch of native grapes, including Primitivo, Negroamaro, and Malvasia Nera, but the vast majority of its colossal production is destined for discreet blending elsewhere. In fact, less than 4% is designated quality wine and yet there are more than 25 DOCs, each faithfully holding a candle for a proud tradition of winemaking, and each seemingly oblivious to the paucity of disciples.

Next door, in Basilicata and Abruzzo, the situation could not be more different. Between them they have just six DOCs, most of which are varietal and look to the same trio of southern stalwarts: Montepulciano, Trebbiano, and Aglianico.

Campania is decidedly hilly. The altitude makes for cool summers, late ripening, and the south's finest wines. It is home to no fewer than three DOCGs—more than any other region south of Tuscany—and one of these is Taurasi, the south's greatest red. Taurasi may be 31 miles (50km) inland from Lacryma Christi and Mount Vesuvius, but the soils here share similarly high levels of the trace elements and minerals that impart such complexity to the grapes of Taurasi, Greco, Fiano, and Falanghina—a quartet of impeccable provenance.

Mount Etna, another volcano, welcomes visitors from the viticultural backwater of Calabria to Sicily, Italy's most sensuous island. From giant co-operatives to one-man bands, from Chardonnay and Shiraz to Inzolia and Nero d'Avola, Sicilian wine is without peer in terms of scale and variety. Sardinia, Italy's second island, has always taken its cues from Spain rather than from the mainland. The island's only DOCG is for the itinerant Vermentino and there are considerable plantings of both Grenache and Carignano.

Abbazia Santa Anastasia Sicily

This abbey, with its 150 acres (60ha) of vineyards, occupies a painfully beautiful site high in the Madonne mountains, overlooking the Mediterranean. Founded in 1100, the Abbazia eventually fell into disrepair and, in 1980, was purchased by Francesco Lena. He painstakingly restored both its buildings and its biodynamic vineyards to their former glory. Riccardo Cotarella keeps an eye on the cellar and together they make an excellent team. Litra is a polished 100% Cabernet Sauvignon with ripe black fruit and a fine track record for aging.

Contrada Santa Anastasia, 90013 Castelbuono
www.abbaziasantanastasia.it

Accademia dei Racemi Puglia

Gregory Perrucci is the businessman behind this estate whose stated aim is to "research, vinify, and sell native Puglian varieties." He controls nearly 500 acres (200ha) of vineyards and produces more than a million bottles a year under a host of labels including Felline, Pervini, Sinfarosa, and Masseria Pepe. Chardonnay has crept in among the native varieties, but there are also significant new plantings of Sussumaniello and Ottavianello that have helped revive the fortunes of these forgotten heroes. The Primitivo is also well received.

Via Santo Stasi I – ZI, 74024 Manduria
www.accademiadeiracemi.it

Agricola Punica Sardinia

Agricola Punica is a joint venture between Sebastiano Rosa, winemaker at Sassicaia, and Cantina di Santadi. Therefore it is no surprise that the wines are exceptional, despite the fact that their maiden vintage was as recent as 2002. Punica makes just two wines, Montessu and Barrua. Both look to old-vine Carignano for inspiration, but the Montessu is lighter and has 40% international varieties. Barrua is the real star: 85% Carignano provides authority and a touch of new oak adds balance. ★ **Rising star**

Località Barrua, 09010 Santadi
www.agripunica.it

Agricole Vallone Puglia

Founded in 1934, this remains a family-run business. Sisters Vittoria and Maria Teresa oversee 420 acres (170ha) and an annual production of more than 600,000 bottles. In an area where winemaking disappointments greatly outnumber triumphs, Vallone remains a beacon of consistency. Its reputation is unquestionably built on Graticciaia, a Negroamaro made from carefully selected grapes left to dry on mats in the *passito* style. It is a wine of epic proportions with a huge nose of dried fruit and spice that introduces a palate of equal proportions.

Via XXV Luglio 5, 73100 Lecce
www.agricolevallone.it

Alberto Longo Puglia

Alberto Longo has followed the well-worn path of businessman-turned-winemaker and it shows at every turn. No expense has been spared on the 86 acres (35ha) of high-density vineyards, the shiny new winery, or the clever packaging that looks so incongruous against a backdrop of Puglian labels. Alberto's first wine was a Cacc'e Mmitte di Lucera DOC (a tongue-twister even for Italians), and this almost charitable act toward a virtually

ATTILIO CONTINI
THIS DESSERT WINE IS ALSO EXCELLENT
SERVED CHILLED AS AN APÉRITIF

ACCADEMIA DEI RACEMI
A DARK, RUBY-RED WINE WITH FRUIT AND
SPICES ON THE NOSE AND FIRM TANNINS

derelict DOC won him much political capital at home. More wines followed, including the polished Calcara Vecchia, made from Bordeaux varieties.

SP Pietramontecorvino Km 4, Contrada Padulecchia, 71036 Lucera; www.albertolongo.it

Antonio Caggiano Campania

Antonio Caggiano's life has been dedicated to Aglianico in general, and to Taurasi in particular. He established his winery in 1990 and was in the vanguard of the new wave of Campanian producers who have subsequently rebuilt the region's reputation. Antonio produces other wines, but his Taurasi Vigna Macchia dei Goti DOCG steals the show. Made from Aglianico grown at altitude on the volcanic slopes that surround the town of Taurasi, it is a textbook example with complex black fruit flavors and a hint of oak from its 18 months in barrel.

Contrada Sala, 83030 Taurasi
www.cantinecaggiano.it

Apollonio Puglia

There is much to like about this estate's excellent wines and the charming Apollonio brothers, Massimiliano and Marcello. The family can trace its history in Lecce back four generations when Noah Apollonio first produced wines for local consumption. They started bottling in 1975 and have gradually increased their holdings. Wines bottled under the Apollonio label are sourced from their own vineyards and include a wonderfully bitter pair of Salentine classics: Copertino DOC and Squinzano DOC. The Rocca dei Mori line offers exceptional value and is vinified from grapes grown to their specification.

Via San Pietro in Lama 7, 730470 Monteroni di Lecce
www.apolloniovini.it

Argiolas Sardinia

Antonio Argiolas has had the pleasure of watching his children, and then his grandchildren, build his childhood dream into one of Sardinia's largest and most successful wineries. Through careful acquisition, the Argiolas family now own more than 618 acres (250ha) of vineyards planted exclusively to local varieties. Most are at altitudes above 1,150ft (350m) and these wines are characterized by a lively freshness that belies their hot-climate origins. From their gluggable Nuragus di Cagliari DOC, through the exemplary Cannonau di Sardegna DOC, to their flagship Turriga IGT, this estate does not put a foot wrong.

Via Roma 56, 09040 Serdiana
www.argiolas.it

Attilio Contini Sardinia

Vernanccia di Oristano DOC has been, and always will be, linked to the Contini family. For more than a century, their winery has kept alive a tradition that reflects Sardinia's historical links with both Spain and Italy. Oristano has, since the 11th century, grown Vernaccia, a grape usually associated with San Gimignano in Tuscany. Even more curious, however, is the practice of aging the wine under a layer of flor (a film of yeast), a tradition enduringly linked with Jerez. The result, immortalized in their Antico Gregori, is a memorable synthesis of two Mediterranean cultures.

Via Genova 48, 09072 Cabras
www.vinicontini.it

SOUTHERN ITALY AND THE ISLANDS

Italy's southern extremities wriggle deep into the azure waters of the Mediterranean and create a wealth of sites ideally suited to the vine. From the volcanoes of Vesuvius and Vulture to the plains of Puglia, southern Italy offers an unparalleled breadth of geographical features. The south's natural aptitude for the vine is reflected in scores of obscure DOCs and grape varieties that, even today, remain largely undiscovered.

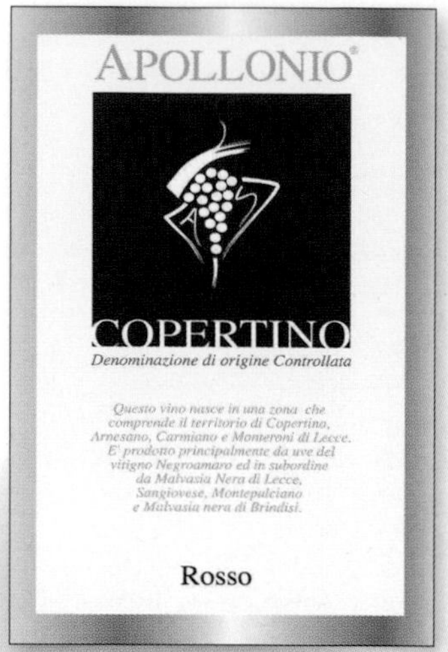

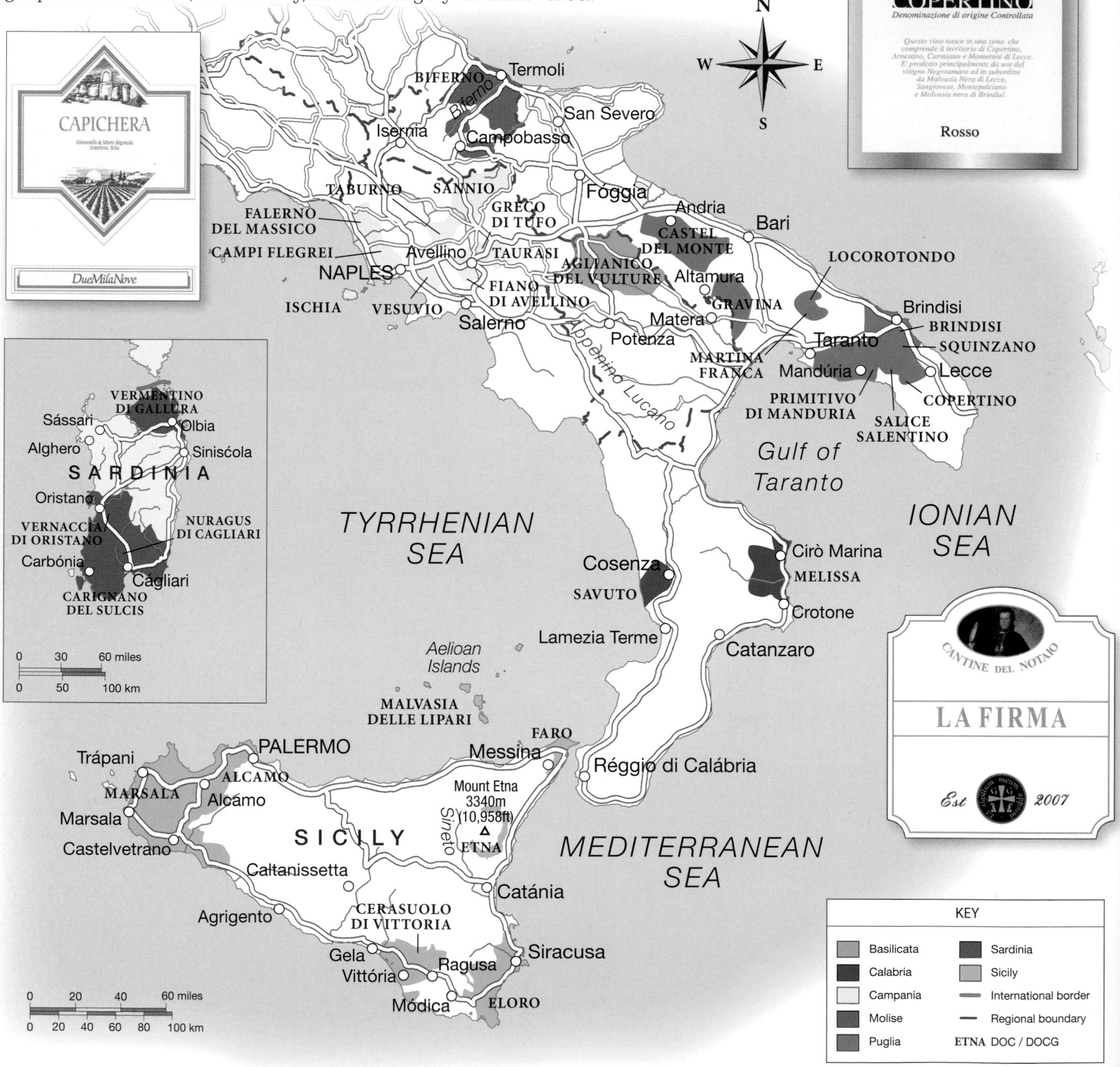

APOLLONIO

COPERTINO
Denominazione di origine Controllata

Questo vino nasce in una zona che comprende il territorio di Copertino, Arnesano, Carmiano e Monteroni di Lecce. È prodotto principalmente da uve del vitigno Negroamaro ed in subordine da Malvasia Nera di Lecce, Sangiovese, Montepulciano e Malvasia nera di Brindisi.

Rosso

CAPICHERA
Gallura & Sibero Regnola
Arzachena, Italia

DueMilaNove

N W E S

BIFERNO · Termoli
Biferno
Isernia · San Severo
Campobasso

TABURNO · SANNIO · Fóggia
FALERNO · GRECO · Andria · Bari
DEL MASSICO · DI TUFO · CASTEL
CAMPI FLEGREI · Avellino · TAURASI · DEL MONTE · LOCOROTONDO
NAPLES · AGLIANICO · Altamura
· FIANO · DEL VULTURE · Brindisi
ISCHIA · DI AVELLINO · GRAVINA · BRINDISI
VESUVIO · Salerno · Matera · SQUINZANO
Potenza · Taranto · Lecce
MARTINA · Manduria · COPERTINO
FRANCA
PRIMITIVO · SALICE
DI MANDURIA · SALENTINO

VERMENTINO
DI GALLURA
Sássari · Olbia
Alghero · Siniscola
S A R D I N I A
Oristano
VERNACCIA · NURAGUS
DI ORISTANO · DI CAGLIARI
Carbónia · Cágliari
CARIGNANO
DEL SULCIS

0   30   60 miles
0   50   100 km

Gulf of Taranto

TYRRHENIAN SEA

IONIAN SEA

Cirò Marina
Cosenza · MELISSA
SAVUTO · Crotone
Lamezia Terme
Aelioan Islands · Catanzaro

CANTINE DEL NOTAIO

LA FIRMA

Est 2007

MALVASIA
DELLE LIPARI
FARO
PALERMO · Messina
Trápani · Réggio di Calábria
MARSALA · ALCAMO
Marsala · Alcámo
Castelvetrano · Mount Etna
3340m
(10,958ft)
MEDITERRANEAN SEA
S I C I L Y · ETNA
Caltanissetta · Catánia
Agrigento
CERASUOLO
DI VITTORIA · Siracusa
Gela · Ragusa
Vittória
Módica · ELORO

0   20   40   60 miles
0   20   40   60   80   100 km

KEY

▮ Basilicata	▮ Sardinia	
▮ Calabria	▮ Sicily	
▮ Campania	— International border	
▮ Molise	— Regional boundary	
▮ Puglia	**ETNA** DOC / DOCG	

SICILY

A continent as much as an island, Sicily boasts an astonishing variety of climates and grape varieties. This diversity is due in part to a winemaking legacy that stretches back three millennia, and in part to the island's unique topography. Although Sicily is undeniably hot—summer temperatures can top 104°F (40°C)—the surrounding Mediterranean brings cooling breezes and Mount Etna casts a shadow over the island's northeastern corner. Native varieties thrive in these arid conditions, and recent technological improvements have heralded a new age in Sicilian winemaking.

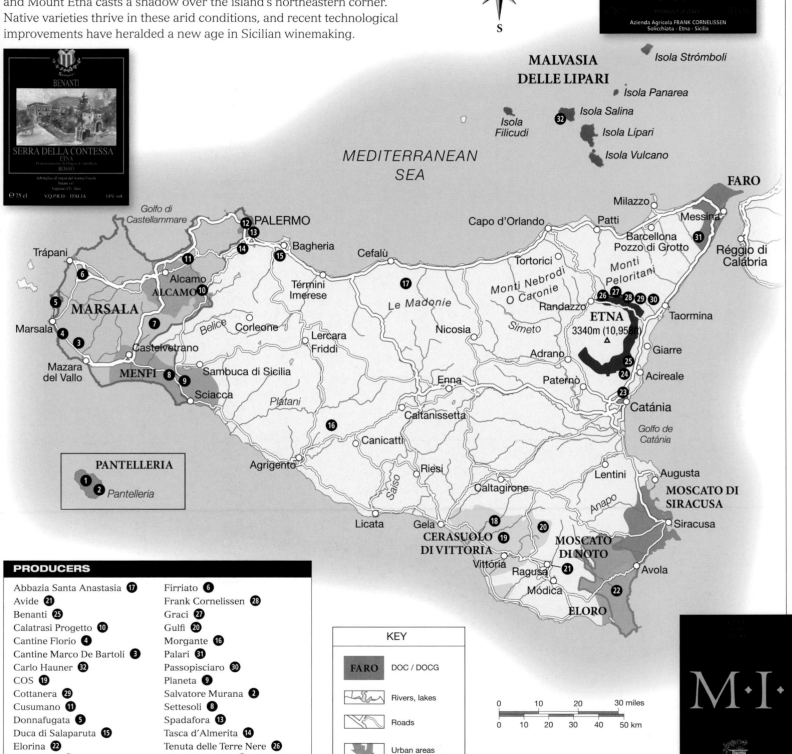

PRODUCERS

Abbazia Santa Anastasia ⑰	Firriato ⑥
Avide ㉑	Frank Cornelissen ㉘
Benanti ㉕	Graci ㉗
Calatrasi Progetto ⑩	Gulfi ⑳
Cantine Florio ④	Morgante ⑯
Cantine Marco De Bartoli ③	Palari ㉛
Carlo Hauner ㉜	Passopisciaro ㉚
COS ⑲	Planeta ⑨
Cottanera ㉙	Salvatore Murana ②
Cusumano ⑪	Settesoli ⑧
Donnafugata ⑤	Spadafora ⑬
Duca di Salaparuta ⑮	Tasca d'Almerita ⑭
Elorina ㉒	Tenuta delle Terre Nere ㉖
Ferrandes ①	Valle dell'Acate ⑱
Ferreri ⑦	Vini Biondi ㉔
Feudo Montoni ⑫	Zenner ㉓

KEY

FARO	DOC / DOCG
	Rivers, lakes
	Roads
	Urban areas
①	Location of one or more producers

0   10   20   30 miles
0   10   20   30   40   50 km

Always check the availability of visitor facilities and the visiting hours at a winery before planning your trip. Some wineries are open by appointment only.

CANTINE DE FALCO
A WARM, TANNIC WINE THAT GOES
PERFECTLY WITH ROAST MEATS AND CHEESE

Avide Sicily
Avide's gentle introduction to winemaking began in the mid-19th century when the Demonstene family, one of Sicily's legal dynasties, began to produce their own wine. They tended a few vines, harvested the fruit, and made wine each year. Gradually, the quality improved and, several generations later, Avide finds itself as one of the largest producers of Cerasuolo di Vittorio DOCG. Its vibrant, pomegranate-scented Black Label flies the flag for Avide, but has now been joined by a more serious, barrique-aged version called Barocco. The Herea range of varietals offers particularly good value.

Corso Italia 131, 97100 Ragusa
www.avide.it

Basilisco Basilicata
Basilisco is another estate dedicated to the enormous potential of Basilicata's Aglianico del Vulture DOC. With 15th century cellars and 25 acres (10ha) of vineyards in the heart of the action, it is no surprise that Michele Cutolo has already made a lasting impression on critics in both Italy and the US. He produces just two wines with the help of Lorenzo Landi, one of the region's top Aglianico specialists. Made from a strict selection of Aglianico, the Teodosio is tightly knit, but extremely impressive. Ten months in French oak adds drama to the already impressive plum and black cherry notes. ★ **Rising star**

Via Piave 35, 85022 Barile
ww.basiliscovini.it

Benanti Sicily
Mount Etna functions as Sicily's very own air-conditioner, and the mountain's vineyards benefit from a microclimate that is more Alpine than Mediterranean. The Benanti vineyards make the most of this unique terroir and have more than three centuries of experience in the cultivation of local grape varieties. Although Nerello Mascalese may be all the rage, this estate specializes in Carricante, a white variety found nowhere else in the world. Their *cuvée* Pietramarina is a distinguished white that really needs a decade before the herbal notes and mineral character are fully integrated. ★ **Rising star**

Via Garibaldi 475, 95029 Viagrande
www.vinicolabenanti.it

Benito Ferrara Campania
This winery was built in the early 1970s by Benito Ferrara, father of Gabriella, who now makes the wines along with her husband and consultant winemaker, Paolo Caciorgna. With only 20 acres (8ha) of vineyards, their production is limited, but they produce a complete range of classic DOC wines from Greco, Fiano, and Aglianico. Of these, the Greco di Tufo Vigna Cicogna DOCG is their strongest suit. Planted at altitude, the vineyards produce wines with fine natural acidity and a delicate character reminiscent of grapefruit and candied peel.

Frazione San Paolo 14a, 83010 Tufo
www.benitoferrara.it

Bisceglia Basilicata
The Bisceglia estate was founded in 2001 by Mario Bisceglia who, like so many successful industrialists, has decided to get closer to his roots. About 86 acres (35ha) of immaculate vineyards are farmed within the DOC of

Aglianico del Vulture, although Mario decided to augment his traditional production of Aglianico with Chardonnay, Merlot, and Syrah. The Terre di Vulcano range offers excellent value, and comprises six varietals sourced from vineyards in Puglia, Basilicata, and Campania. A dramatic new winery, complete with wine bar, rounds out one of the south's most impressive new starts.

Contrada Finocchiaro, 85024 Lavello
www.agricolabisceglia.com

Calatrasi Progetto Sicily
In 1750, the Miccichè family moved to San Cipirello in central Sicily. Just over two centuries later, brothers Giuseppe and Maurizio built a state-of-the-art winery that is now at the heart of this international concern. With both vineyards and wineries in Puglia, Sicily, and Tunisia the Calatrasi group produces more than 5 million bottles of friendly, reliable wines at tempting prices each year. They are best known for their Terre di Ginestra range, which comprises a huge number of both local and international varietals including Nero d'Avola, Catarratto, and Cabernet Sauvignon.

Contrada Piano Piraino, 90040 San Cipirello
www.calatrasi.it

Candido Puglia
Anywhere but in Southern Italy Alessandro and Giacomo Candido's 346 acres (140ha) of vineyards and 2 million-bottle production would seem prodigious. However, their reputation has been built on quality rather than quantity, and the solid, sweet-and-sour Salice Salentino has served as the DOC's standard-bearer for decades. Negroamaro gets top billing here, although it is artfully blended with Cabernet Sauvignon in the modern Immensum and with Montepulciano in their oaky, flagship wine, Duca d'Aragona. Small quantities of Chardonnay and Sauvignon are also produced, along with an exquisite example of the rare Aleatico, Puglia's answer to the Veneto's Recioto.

Via Armando Diaz 46, 72025 San Donaci
www.candidowines.it

Cantina Gallura Sardinia
In 1956, this co-op opened its doors to 160 members who cultivate more than 800 acres (325ha) high above the sea on Sardinia's northern coast. Home to Sardinia's only DOCG, Vermentino di Gallura, it is no surprise that this co-op produces no fewer than five iterations, each showcasing subtle differences in the predominantly granitic soil. Of these, the Canayli is the most noteworthy, with an ambitious nose and fine natural acidity. Curiously, the co-op also specializes in Nebbiolo, a grape that arrived here in the 1700s direct from its native Piemonte.

Via Val di Cossu 9, 07029 Tempio Pausania
www.cantinagallura.com

Cantina del Locorotondo Puglia
Founded in 1930, this co-op eventually lobbied successfully for the creation of its own DOC, Locorotondo, for the local white variety, Verdeca. This thriving winery now controls more than 2,500 acres (1,000ha) of vineyards, and produces 3.5 million bottles a year under a bewildering array of more than 30 labels. However, Locorotondo remains the star attraction and all three versions are just

CALATRASI PROGETTO
THIS INTENSE, GOLDEN-YELLOW
CHARDONNAY IS AGED IN FRENCH BARRIQUES

as cheerful as they are affordable. The Vigneto di Talinajo is the pick of the bunch, with a lively citrus nose, attractive mineral notes, and good persistence.

Via Madonna della Catena 99, 70010 Locorotondo
www.locorotondodoc.com

Cantina di Santadi Sardinia

This co-operative was established in 1960, but it was not until the arrival of Giacamo Tachis that its reputation began to spread beyond Sardinia's southwest corner. The region's considerable reserves of ungrafted bush-vine Carignano provided superb raw material for Tachis, a man who originally cut his teeth at Sassicaia. In the early 1980s, the characterful and affordable Rocca Rubia and Terre Brune were released to huge international acclaim. These wines were proof of Sardinia's enormous potential, and they paved the way for a new generation determined to raise the island's game.

Via Cagliari 78, 09010 Santadi
www.cantinadisantadi.it

Cantina del Vermentino Sardinia

Although 1956 was a disastrous vintage in Bordeaux, it was a banner year for co-ops in Sardinia. Both this and the Cantina Gallura were founded in the same year. Of the two, the Cantina del Vermentino is larger, with 350 members and more than 1,250 acres (500ha) under vine. The Vermentino grape remains in pole position; there is a barrel-fermented version, Arakena, but the winery is most famous for a stainless steel iteration, Funtanaliras. The traditional Sardinian reds are joined by both Cabernet Sauvignon and Sangiovese.

Via San Paolo 2, 07020 Monti
www.vermentinomonti.it

Cantine de Falco Puglia

Founded in 1960, this stalwart of the Salento continues to produce a thoroughly honest range of Puglian must-haves. Salvatore de Falco manages its 62 acres (25ha) of vineyards and a winery located a stone's throw from the Puglian jewel of Baroque architecture, Lecce. Production averages 200,000 bottles per year. The range includes fine interpretations of Squinzano DOC and Primitivo, but their strongest effort is the Salice Salentino Riserva Falco Nero. It is produced from 80% Negroamaro and 20% Malvasia Nera, and aged for 12 months in 100% new oak barriques.

Via Milano 25, 73051 Novoli
www.cantinedefalco.it

Cantine Florio Sicily

Born in the middle of the 19th century, when Marsala was in vogue, the Florio family established an empire that comprised not only wine but also fisheries, textiles, and even an automobile rally, the Targa Florio. Today, along with Duca di Salaparuta, it is part of the Illva Saronno group and specializes in sweet and fortified wines. Although Florio produces wines from the islands of Pantelleria and Lipari, Marsala is still Florio's strongest suit. The unfortunately named, but excellent, Terre Arse is bone dry and aged for almost a decade in cask.

Via Vincenzo Florio 1, 91025 Marsala
www.cantineflorio.it

Cantine Gran Furor Divina Costiera di Marisa Cuomo Campania

Seeing is believing, and no one would imagine that grapes could be produced on the almost inaccessible cliff face that Maria Cuomo cultivates with her husband, Andrea Ferraioli. Their vineyards are planted on narrow terraces that cling to rocks 1,600ft (600m) above the beaches of the Amalfi coast. Yields are disastrous, the grapes largely unknown (the whites include Fenile, Ginestra, and Ripoli), and the labor is backbreaking. The Italian government officially recognized the couple's contribution to the nation's viticultural patrimony when it granted DOC status to the Costa d'Amalfi. Scant reward, some might say, for a lifetime's work.

Via GB Lama 16/18, 84010 Furore
www.granfuror.it

Cantine Marco De Bartoli Sicily

In the wine world, Marsala is about as fashionable as a swizzle stick and, therefore, it takes a particular character to persevere in its production. A race car driver of international repute and general bon viveur, Marco de Bartoli took charge of his family's 62 acre (25 ha) farm in the 1970s. The first consignments were delivered via a sports car with Marco himself behind the wheel. His obsession for automobiles eventually turned into a passion for Marsala and today, this estate produces three exquisite examples and a rare, unfortified version called Vecchio Samperi.

Contrada Fornara Samperi 292, 91015 Marsala
www.marcodebartoli.com

Cantine del Notaio Basilicata

At the age of seven, Gerardo Giuratrabocchetti was told by his grandfather that, one day, he would inherit the family vineyards. Although his father became a notary, Gerardo continued in what he clearly saw as his destiny, and now controls 64 acres (26ha) of vineyards. His flagship wine, Aglianico del Vulture La Firma DOC, is made from a selection of Aglianico aged in new French oak. It is as impressive as Gerardo himself, and reflects a similar dedication to this region with layers of sweet vanilla oak, cocoa, and liquorice on the nose.

Via Roma 159, 85028 Rionero in Vulture
www.cantinedelnotaio.com

Cantine Viola Calabria

One could be forgiven for thinking that a retired primary school teacher would make an unlikely viticultural hero, but Luigi Viola, with his pension firmly in hand, has devoted his retirement to safeguarding the future of Moscato di Saraceno, an ancient dessert wine crafted from shriveled Moscatello grapes added to a base wine made from Malvasia and Guarnaccia. Viola's ingenuity and enterprise have preserved one of the world's most compelling sweet wines; it has an amber hue and captivating nose. Annual production is just 4,500 bottles.

Via Roma 18, 87010 Saracena
www.cantineviola.it

Capichera Sardinia

The Capichera story began three generations ago with 25 acres (10ha) of vineyards and a fervent belief in the potential of two local grapes, Vermentino and Carignano.

MOUNT ETNA: WINEMAKING ON THE EDGE

Mount Etna is Europe's largest and most active volcano. Snow-capped for much of the year (there is a small ski resort at the top) and inevitably puffing both smoke and ash, it is difficult to imagine that anything could grow in the lunar landscape that characterizes Etna's upper reaches. The vine, however, goes where others fear to tread, and high above the orchards, olive groves, and greenhouses are some of Europe's last surviving pre-phylloxera vineyards.

An ancient duo, Nerello Mascalese (red) and Carricante (white), are planted more or less in equal measure. Scratching a living from the naked lava, the vines are gnarled, frequently more than a century old, and yield tiny quantities of extraordinary grapes. Nerello is a delicate grape with an exotic and vegetal nose reminiscent of mature burgundy, even when young. Carricante is just the opposite, a forthright, strapping white with ferocious acidity and a seemingly endless appetite for aging.

COS

A BIODYNAMIC WINE MADE FROM NERO D'AVOLA AND THE LOCAL FRAPPATO GRAPE

CASA D'AMBRA

THIS SINGLE-VINEYARD WINE, MADE FROM BIANCOLELLA, MAY IMPROVE WITH AGE

Today, Capichera produces more than 300,000 bottles of consistently brilliant (and expensive) single varietals, grown in their vineyards on Sardinia's windswept northeastern extremity. Brothers Fabrizio and Mario Ragnedda are justifiably proud of their achievements, but their decision to bottle their wines as IGT (they now have one Vermentino di Gallura DOCG) left many locals wondering if the family has forgotten its roots.

Località Capichera, 07021 Arzachena
www.capichera.it

Carlo Hauner Sicily

The island of Lipari owes much to Carlo Hauner, a painter who settled on this impossibly beautiful ancient volcano off Sicily's northeastern corner in the 1960s. The tradition of cultivating and drying grapes here dates back to biblical times, when the island's sweet wine was known as "the nectar of the gods." Malvasia probably arrived in the 16th century, some 400 years before Carlo Hauner decided to craft his own particular example. Deep gold, and languid in the glass, its intense nose of dried fruits and herbs captures the timeless spirit of the Mediterranean.

Via Umberto 1, Località Lingua, 98050 Marina Salina
www.hauner.it

Casa D'Ambra Campania

Casa D'Ambra is situated on the beautiful volcanic island of Ischia, just off the coast of Naples. Founded in 1888 by Francesco D'Ambra, it is now run by the fourth generation of his family. Ischia is a viticultural Jurassic Park with varieties planted there that are not seen anywhere else in the world. Casa D'Ambra makes the most of this natural advantage and fashions a range of endless intrigue. The Frasitelli vineyard is the jewel in the family crown: terraced Biancolella grown at 1,640ft (500m) produces a steely and ageworthy white.

Via Mario d'Ambra 16, 80075 Forio d'Ischia
081 907210

Cianfagna Molise

Vincenzo Cianfagna has single handedly secured the future of Tintilia, a rare grape of which there are fewer than 250 acres (100ha) in cultivation. Vincenzo's deep agrarian roots and profound understanding of this bleak yet strangely beautiful countryside instilled in him a determination to bring Tintilia to a wider audience. He had no trouble acquiring 25 acres (10ha) of derelict vineyards and patiently set about restoring them. His Tintilia del Molise Sartor DOC was worth the wait. Exuberantly fruity, with plum, black cherry, prune, and vegetal notes, it fully justifies Vincenzo's belief in the potential of Tintilia. ★ **Rising star**

Contrada Bosco Pampini, 86030 Acquaviva Collecroce
www.cianfagna.com

Contrade di Taurasi Campania

On their estate founded in 1998, the Lonardo family cultivate just 12 acres (5ha) of vineyards inside the DOCG of Taurasi. Although barely a decade old, they show a quiet determination to produce wines that will, before long, rival the best in the area. Strong links to the University of Palermo provide the estate with an army of consultant agronomists and enologists who ensure that the estate

continues to refine its wines. Fortunately, this significant investment has yet to impact on prices, and their Taurasi Riserva DOCG remains one of Campania's best-value reds.

Via Municipio 39, 83030 Taurasi
www.contradeditaurasi.it

COS Sicily

In 1980, three school friends bought a farm together. They named it COS, the first letter of each of their surnames, and although only Giusto Occhipinti and Titta Cilía remain in the business, this has not stopped this dynamic (and biodynamic) duo from acquiring a very respectable 62 acres (25ha) of vineyards. They specialize in Cerasuolo di Vittoria, Sicily's first DOCG, made from a minimum of 40% Frappato, a local grape of considerable ability. Their entry level Cerasuolo is a fine and fruity wine more than a little reminiscent of *cru* Beaujolais.

SP 3 Acate-Chiaramonte, 97019 Vittoria
www.cosvittoria.it

Cosimo Taurino Puglia

The passage of time and fashion both appear to have neatly sidestepped the Taurino winery, which has produced wines since the early 18th century. Its 210 acres (85ha) are planted with traditional grapes such as Negroamaro and Malvasia Nera, although sightings of international varieties have been reported. Nevertheless, the focus is very much on tradition, and the reds can be aged in old wood for up to five years. Curiously, the estate's best-loved wines are both IGT—Patriglione and Notarpanaro. Each undergoes lengthy aging and both showcase the savory complexity of Negroamaro.

SS 605, 73010 Guagnano
www.taurinovini.it

Cottanera Sicily

Mariangela and Francesco Cambria are the third generation in charge of this dynamic Etna winery. Although founded in the 1960s, Cottanera was re-launched in the 1990s with a refurbished cellar and a new direction. Convinced of the enormous potential of the Etna terroir, the Cambria family made the unusual decision to introduce international varieties alongside the red Etna classic, Nerello Mascalese. The wisdom of this decision can be seen in their structured, aromatic Cabernet Nume, and in the refined, spicy Merlot, Grammonte.

Strada Provinciale 89, Contrada Iannazzo, 95030 Castiglione di Sicily; www.cottanera.it

Cusumano Sicily

The irrepressible Diego Cusumano is the man behind this winery's meteoric rise. Since 2001, ambitious expansion and significant investment have seen production soar to 2.5 million bottles a year, and a string of awards arrive on the mantelpiece. Diego's pride in his beloved homeland means that local varieties occupy center stage, and the lead is taken by the estate's gloriously fat, unoaked Cubía, made from 100% Inzolia. Sàgana is a fulsome, spicy, and vanilla-scented interpretation of Nero d'Avola, while Benuara and Noá see this Sicilian native blended with Cabernet Sauvignon and Syrah respectively.

Contrada San Carlo SS113, 90047 Partinico
www.cusumano.it

D'Angelo Basilicata

Separating the D'Angelo family from Aglianico would be inconceivable. They have been here for more than a century and flew the flag for this historic DOC during Italy's darkest days. Brothers Donato and Lucio now run the business and continue to bottle one of the region's standard bearers. Vigne Caselle is an ultra-traditional rendering of Aglianico that spends two years in large oak casks. Their Canneto is also Aglianico del Vulture DOC, but it spends 18 months in barrique, which renders it marginally more polished and just that bit less seductive.

Via Provinciale 8, 85028 Rionero in Vulture
www.dangelowine.com

Di Majo Norante Molise

It cannot be easy to make wine in Molise, Italy's smallest and youngest region, and yet the di Majo family have been doing exactly that for more than 200 years. Far from the more fashionable appellations of Piemonte, Tuscany, or even Campania, this estate has nonetheless made its mark with an impressive range of indigenous varieties and clever blends. Their Don Luigi is a great example. Made from 80% Montepulciano and 20% Tintilia, it matures in new French oak and is the first wine from Molise to win Italy's top wine award, the Tre Bicchiere.

Contrada Ramitelli 4, 86042 Campomarino
www.dimajonorante.com

Donnafugata Sicily

In 1983, when the writing was on the wall for Marsala, Giacomo Rallo made the bold decision to turn his back on his family's 150-year-old link with Sicily's most famous wine. From now on, his family's wines would be made without the addition of alcohol. His gamble paid handsome dividends and Donnafugata now controls 750 acres (300ha) of vineyards. Its wines include a toothsome Mille e Una Notte Nero d'Avola that takes some beating for sheer sophistication, and the haunting Vigna di Gabri with its nose of summer fruits, yellow plums, and acacia.

Via San Lipari 18, 81015 Marsala
www.donnafugata.it

Duca di Salaparuta Sicily

Giuseppe Alliata, the Duke of Salaparuta, established this estate in 1824 to produce fine wine for his guests. In the late 19th century, Giuseppe's son, Edward, turned the winery into Italy's most successful exporter and cleverly employed a French winemaker to ensure they used only the latest technology. Duca di Salaparuta never looked back, and today produces more than 10 million bottles as part of the Illva Saronno group of wineries. Its Corvo range is the company's bread-and-butter, but it also makes a Nero d'Avola of note, called Duca Enrico.

Via Nazionale SS113, 90014 Casteldaccia
www.duca.it

Elena Fucci Basilicata

Born in 1981, Elena Fucci is the young, and undeniably talented, winemaker behind this rising star. Working with her father and grandfather, the estate's first vintage was in 2000, and by 2002 Elena was already hailed as a leading producer with a string of awards behind her. Production is tiny—she has just 15 acres (6ha) of vineyards situated at an altitude of 2,130ft (650m) on an ancient lava flow

DONNAFUGATA
THIS SOPHISTICATED WINE IS A GREAT ACCOMPANIMENT TO COMPLEX MEAT DISHES AND SAUCES

DUCA DI SALAPARUTA
A DRY, INTENSE, AND FULL-BODIED RED WITH A SCENT OF MORELLO CHERRIES

known as Titolo. The estate produces just one wine, the Aglianico del Vulture Titolo, whose intense minerality reflects its volcanic origins. ★**Rising star**

Contrada Solagna del Titolo, 85022 Barile
www.elenafuccivini.com

Elorina Sicily

Elorina is a tiny co-op with just 50 members, 86 acres (35ha) of vineyards, and a production of fewer than 200,000 bottles. However, two things distinguish it from its rivals. The first is that 90% of its production is DOC, and the second is that it is dedicated to preserving one of Italy's oldest wines, the sweet Moscato di Noto DOC. Established in 1978, Elorina gives growers in this remote part of Sicily an opportunity to remain commercially viable, while maintaining a tradition that dates to 200BCE.

C.da Belliscala SP Rosolini-Pachino Km 7, 96017 Noto
www.elorina.it

Ferrandes Sicily

The tiny island of Pantelleria lies some 31 miles (50km) south of Sicily. For many years it was the crossroads of the known world, and it boasts not only an extraordinary archaeological heritage, but also an unrivaled range of climatic phenomena that makes it particularly suited to the cultivation of the sun-worshipper, Moscato (here known as Zibibbo). The super-ripe grapes are harvested by hand and dried in the vineyard. Ferrandes's Passito di Pantelleria, the finest expression of this ancient dessert wine, artfully preserves sufficient acidity to balance the substantial residual sugar. ★**Rising star**

Via del Fante 28, Contrada Tracino Kamma, 91017 Pantelleria; 0923 915475

Ferreri Sicily

Founded in 1932 by three men who recognized the potential of western Sicily, Ferreri now produces wine from 124 acres (50ha) of vineyards planted at 820–1,640ft (250–500m). The vineyards are deliberately planted in diverse orientations to match each variety to the ideal exposure. As in so many Sicilian estates, both local and international varieties are planted, but what makes Ferreri different is its use of chestnut casks to age wines bottled under the Brasi label. Both a Nero d'Avola and a Catarratto are treated to the process, which confers a pleasant tarry complexity.

Contrada Salinella, 91029 Santa Ninfa
www.ferrerivini.it

Feudi di San Gregorio Campania

At the forefront of Campanian winemaking for more than 20 years, the consultant enologist Riccardo Cotarella continues to produce an exemplary range at Feudi. Tradition and modernity coexist peacefully with the usual suspects (Greco, Fiano, Falanghina, and Aglianico) treated to the very latest technology. There are a number of star performers, including the white Campanaro, a blend of Greco and Fiano that adroitly blends tropical fruit with barrel maturation notes. There cannot be much Merlot planted in Campania, but the monumental Patrimo suggests that there ought to be more.

località Cerza Grossa, 83050 Sorbo Serpico
www.feudi.it

GULFI
THIS AWARD-WINNING, SINGLE-VINEYARD
RED WILL REWARD CELLARING

MASTROBERARDINO
THIS WINE HAS A COMPLEX BOUQUET AND IS
ELEGANT AND PERSISTENT ON THE PALATE

Feudi Di San Marzano Puglia
It is all too easy to miss huge wineries such as Feudi Di San Marzano in the rush to find the next small, family-run concern. However, without the vision of Valentino Sciotti (from the Abruzzo giant, Farnese), the failing co-op at San Marzano would have been forced to declare bankruptcy. Sciotti—no stranger to economies of scale—quickly saw the winery's potential and launched a range of well-made, intelligently priced Puglian varieties with huge international appeal. Of these, the Sessantanni Primitivo di Manduria DOC is proof that big can still be beautiful.

Via Regina Margherita 149, 74022 San Marzano di SG
www.feudisanmarzano.it

Feudo Montoni Sicily
Deeds dating back to 1595 attest to the quality of the red wines produced on the Fuedo Montoni estate. Recent research suggests that the vineyards here may have been the first in Sicily to cultivate Nero d'Avola on a commercial scale. Be that as it may, more than 400 years later, a very fine example of this grape is still produced, called Selezione Vrucara. Today, however, Feudo Montoni's 180 acres (73ha) of vineyards also include Catarratto and Grillo, which produce crisp whites that are light on their feet and keenly priced.

Contrada Montoni Vecchi, 92022 Cammarata
www.feudomontoni.it

Firriato Sicily
This relative newcomer to the Sicilian wine scene has had a considerable impact. Although Firriato's first vintage was as recent as 1994, husband-and-wife team Salvatore Di Gaetano and Vinzia Novara have already established Firriato as one of the island's leaders, not only in terms of quantity (5 million bottles per year), but also for the quality of their extensive range. The careful use of Antipodean winemakers has brought much-needed international appeal, and Firriato's accessible style has drawn praise from critics in both Italy and abroad.

Via Trapani 4, 91027 Paceco
www.firriato.it

Fontanavecchia Campania
The word "old" is perhaps insufficient to describe the sense of tradition that courses through this estate's veins. In the last decade, however, the candles and the old vats have gradually been replaced by the glint of stainless steel and the familiar shapes of barriques. Libero Rillo, and his father Orazio, are determined to ring the changes in Torrecuso. Fontanavecchia's flagship Aglianico Grave Mora has benefited from the new regime, and its concentrated black-cherry character indicates that Taburno DOC deserves much wider recognition.

Via Fontanavecchia, 82030 Torrecuso
www.fontanavecchia.info

Frank Cornelissen Sicily
Frank Cornelissen challenges every conception of how wine should look, taste, and be made. A Belgian by birth, Frank left the world of wine retailing in the late 1990s to try his hand at making it, and in so doing, he has rewritten the rule book. His 21 acres (8.5ha) of incredibly old, ungrafted Nerello Mascalese are planted exclusively at altitudes above 328ft (1,000m) on Mount Etna's northern slopes. Yields are extremely small, fermentation occurs in clay amphorae, and the maceration can last for a year. ★ Rising star

Via Nazionale 281/299, 95012 Solicchiata
www.frankcornelissen.it

Galardi Campania
The four cousins who own this estate can trace their roots here back to the 9th century, when this part of Campania was known as Terra di Lavoro or "the land of work." Today that work involves producing just one wine, a field blend of 80% Aglianico and 20% Piedirosso. It is big and bold; new French oak adds a glossy layer of spice to the plump black fruit of Aglianico. Terra di Lavoro is one of the south's most sought-after reds and, with just 1,000 cases produced each year, you will need to be quick.

SP Sessa Mignano, 81030 Sessa Aurunca
www.terradilavoro.com

Giovanni Battista Columbu Sardinia
Every day since 1972, Battista Columbu has lovingly tended his 9.5 acre (3.8ha) plot of Malvasia perched high on the vertiginous slopes above the village of Bosa. Usually he is alone, one of the last producers keeping the candle burning for a wine that, over a century ago, was drunk in every court in Europe. It is not difficult to see why this is a near-derelict appellation. The ruinous yields, the two years' aging in chestnut casks, and the backbreaking labor ensure that few want to pick up the reins. Malvasia di Bosa DOC, a wine of rare concentration, is officially an endangered species.

Via Marconi 1, 08013 Bosa
www.vinibosa.com

Giovanni Cherchi Sardinia
The Cherchi winery was founded in 1970 with a modest inheritance of just 5 acres (2ha) of Vermentino. Since then, it has grown to 75 acres (30ha) divided equally between Vermentino and two red grapes, Cannonau and Cagnulari. The latter is perhaps Sardinia's least-known variety; with its thin skin and low yields, it had few supporters and in the 1980s was on the brink of extinction. Intrigued by its shocking violet hue and fragrant blackberry nose, Giovanni Cherchi restored his old vineyards and produced the island's first bottling of pure Cagnulari.

Via Ossi 20/22, 07049 Usini
www.vinicolacherchi.it

Graci Sicily
Alberto Graci attended the Frank Cornelissen school of weirdness, but mercifully has stopped short of complete viticultural anarchy. Graci's 62 acres (25ha) of ancient Nerello Mascalese are both un-grafted and organically cultivated. Fermentation is exclusively in open-topped wooden fermentors and the wines are unfiltered. Graci's Quota 600 is only released when climatic conditions on the shoulder of Europe's largest active volcano permit. When they do, Graci fashions a red of rare finesse that deftly weaves improbable amounts of alcohol, acidity, and tannins with an equally impressive quantity of complex, red fruit aromas. ★ Rising star

Contrada Arcuria, Passapisciaro, 95012 Castiglione di Sicilia
www.graci.eu

Guido Marsella Campania

Guido Marsella is known affectionately as Signore Fiano, a reflection of his dedication to this most noble of Campanian varieties. His 10 acres (4ha) of vineyards produce a scant 20,000 bottles of mesmeric Fiano di Avellino DOCG. Grapes picked at optimal maturity are pressed, then fermented and aged in stainless steel for at least two years before release. Never less than 14% alcohol, it combines the power of the New World with the subtlety of the Mediterranean. Opulent, with notes of hazelnut, broom, and crème patissière, it unquestionably deserves wider appreciation. ★ Rising star

Via Marone 1, 83010 Summonte
www.guidomarsella.com

Gulfi Sicily

Vito Catania, a successful businessman from the automotive industry, has gone back to his native Sicily to lead this impressive venture on the island's southeastern extremity. This is Nero d'Avola country—Catania's favorite grape—and he now cultivates more than 173 acres (70ha) organically near Chiaramonte Gulfi. There are three single-vineyard *cuvées* made from old-vine parcels that he refused to replant, including the award-winning Neromaccarj, which even 18 months in oak can barely soften. It is a structured, aromatic, and extremely ageworthy red made in the tradition of great Bordeaux.

Contrada Partia, 97010 Chiaramonte Gulfi
www.gulfi.it

L'Astore Masseria Puglia

L'Astore is owned by the Benegiamo family, who have been farming the land since the 1930s. In the early 1990s, they embarked on an ambitious program of renovation, which included a complete overhaul of the *masseria* (farmhouse) itself. The vineyards were also replanted and a host of international varieties introduced, including Chardonnay and Cabernet Sauvignon. The ubiquitous Riccardo Cotarella is winemaker-in-chief. The range includes six impressive wines, all humming a modern tune. L'Astore is a fleshy blend of Aglianico and Petit Verdot, while Krita is a similarly proportioned duo of Chardonnay and Malvasia.

Via G Di Vittorio 1, 73020 Cutrofiano
www.lastoremasseria.it

Leone de Castris Puglia

The site of the current Leone de Castris cellars is in precisely the same location that Duke Oronzo founded the company in 1665. Almost 300 years later, in 1943, their fleshy and exuberant Five Roses was sold in the US, the first Italian rosé to be bottled and exported. In 2005, their Salice Salentino Riserva DOC celebrated its 50th vintage. Leone de Castris may produce 28 different wines, and more than 2.5 million bottles each year, but its range remains as dynamic and relevant today as it ever was.

Via Senatore De Castris 50, 73015 Salice Salentino
www.leonedecastris.com

Librandi Calabria

The proudly family-owned Librandi winery is now in its fourth generation, and is big by anyone's standards. With more than 625 acres (250ha) of vineyards and a dozen labels, the Librandi estate dominates viticulture in Calabria and leads the field in resuscitating ancient varieties. In total, eight different grape varieties are grown, including both local heroes and international stars such as Sauvignon Blanc and Chardonnay. Librandi originally made the headlines with Gravello, a toothsome blend of Gaglioppo and Cabernet, but these days its Magno Megonio (100% Magliocco) receives the rave reviews.

SS 106, Contrada San Gennaro, 88811 Cirò Marina
www.librandi.it

Macarico Basilicata

Just two wines are produced from Rino Botte's 12.5 acres (5ha) of vineyards, which nestle under the shadow of Mount Vulture. The combination of extremely late harvests (the first week of November) and high-density plantings (3,840 vines per acre/9,600 vines per ha) result in one of the DOCs finest wines, Aglianico del Vulture Macarico DOC. The name of the estate—and Rino's best vineyard—derives from the Greek meaning "he who is blessed" and there is no doubting the good fortune of anyone who acquires a bottle of this profound red.

Piazza Caracciolo 7, 85022 Barile
www.macaricovini.it

Macchialupa Campania

Straddling the border between Benevento and Avellino, at nearly 1,640ft (500m) altitude, Macchialupa is ideally situated to produce Campanian classics of the very highest quality. The estate is a joint venture between Angelo Valentino, an enologist, and Giuseppe Ferrara, an agronomist, and between them they craft six different wines from the 20 acres (8ha) of vineyards, which Giuseppe inherited from his father. Their Taurasi is a particularly subtle rendering of the south's most famous red, with Aglianico's classic violet notes overlaid with tobacco, cinnamon, and vanilla. ★ Rising star

Via Fontana, Frazione San Pietro Irpino, 83010 Chianche
www.macchialupa.it

Mastroberardino Campania

Think of Taurasi and one inevitably thinks of Mastroberardino, a winery that, since 1878, has produced Taurasi Riserva Radici DOCG. For decades, Radici was the sole source of inspiration in the particularly bleak viticultural panorama of Italy's deep south. Made from low-yielding Aglianico and aged for three years in wood, Radici shows astonishing durability, and vintages from the 1950s and '60s are still impressive. Today, the winery produces dozens of sound wines from the usual Campanian appellations, but it will forever be associated with Radici, a wine whose quality was never compromised.

Via Manfredi 75/81, 83042 Altripalda
www.mastroberardino.com

Montevetrano Campania

In the late 1980s, Silvia Imparato, one of Italy's leading photographers, decided to experiment with Bordeaux varieties in her family's vineyards just outside Salerno. She enlisted the help of consultant winemaker Riccardo Cotarella, and together they produced the first vintage of Montevetrano, in 1991. The rave reviews for this graceful and ageworthy red produced from 60% Cabernet Sauvignon, 30% Merlot, and 10% Aglianico quickly attracted the attention of the world's collectors. Nobody

WINE CO-OP INNOVATION

Sicily is not the first place that springs to mind when one mentions groundbreaking research, world-leading initiatives in traceability and sustainability, and devoted teams eager to embrace international varieties.

Producer Settesoli's roots may have plunged deep into the Sicilian soil for half a century, but its colossal production of more than 27 million bottles could not be more progressive. Since 1973, the man behind the astonishing transformation of Settesoli from sleepy co-op to international trendsetter is Diego Planeta. Proud of his native Sicily, and profoundly aware of its enormous potential, Diego managed to convince all 2,300 members to turn their backs on bulk sales and focus exclusively on quality. The results are nothing short of miraculous. The top 10% of all wines are destined for Mandrarossa, the winery's multi-award-winning premium brand. The all-conquering Inycon range is attacking foreign markets with an unbeatable range of varietal crowd pleasers.

MONTEVETRANO
THIS CELEBRATED WINE IS MADE OF
CABERNET SAUVIGNON AND MERLOT, WITH
A SMALL AMOUNT OF NATIVE AGLIANICO

MORGANTE
MADE FROM OLD-VINE GRAPES, THIS WINE
HAS A PERSISTENT, BALANCED TASTE

was more surprised than Silvia herself, whose 12.5 acre (5ha) experiment vaulted her onto the world's winemaking stage.

Via Montevetrano 3, 84099 Cipriano Picentino
www.montevetrano.it

Morella Puglia
An Australian by birth, and a Roseworthy graduate, work originally took Lisa Gilbee to Puglia, but it was love that made her stay. Lisa and her husband, Gaetano, now dry farm 17 acres (7ha) of 75-year-old, unirrigated, bush-trained Primitivo. The age of the vines, the iron-rich soils, and the cooling sea breezes all temper the sweltering Puglian summer, and the Old Vine Primitivo di Manduria is unquestionably this DOC's finest effort. Tipping the scales at more than 15% alcohol, it shows an intense nose of prune and blackcurrant, and outstanding complexity.

Via per Uggiano 147, 74024 Manduria
www.morellavini.com

Morgante Sicily
Carmelo Morgante is the latest of many generations of his family to grow grapes on Sicily's southern highlands. Morgante's first bottling was in 1998, and Riccardo Cotarella subsequently added a certain polish to the superb raw material coming from its 75 acres (30ha) of vineyards. The Morgante estate specializes in Nero d'Avola and produces three iterations. First released in 2008, Scinthily spends just two days on the skins; the straight Nero d'Avola spends three months in oak; while the Don Antonio old-vine *cuvée* spends a year in new barriques.

Contrada Racalmare, 92020 Grotte
www.morgantevini.it

Odoardi Calabria
The Odoardi family can trace their history in this remote Calabrian town back to the 13th century. The latest generation, brothers Gianbattista and Gregorio, continue to embrace tradition by using local varieties, including Gaglioppo and Magliocco grown on an alberello system. The family have also continued to use both historic DOCs and this has given a much-needed fillip to Savuto and Scavigna DOC. Vigna Garrone, their top bottling, is a monumental wine in which 80% Gaglioppo is married with a dollop of Cabernet Sauvignon and softened in barrique for 18 months. ★ Rising star

Contrada Campodorato, 88047 Nocera Terinese
www.cantineodoardi.com

Palari Sicily
In 1990, the noted Italian wine journalist Luigi Veronelli approached Salvatore Giraci, an architect from Messina, with an ambitious undertaking. He asked Giraci to save the DOC of Faro from extinction. Giraci's family owned 10 acres (4ha) of terraced vineyards, but had always sold the wine locally in demijohns. Fortunately, Giraci took up the challenge, releasing his first wine in 1995 and scooping a host of awards along the way. Crafted from low-yielding Nerello Mascalese and Nerello Cappuccio, Palari's Faro is an elegant composition of new oak and sweet berry fruit.

Contrada Barna, 98137 Stefano Briga
www.palari.it

Passopisciaro Sicily
The dynamic Andrea Franchetti, who owns this small estate perched on Etna's northern shoulder, is a tireless publicist for the world-class potential of his ancient vineyards, which include not only Nerello Mascalese, but also Chardonnay and Petit Verdot, and praise for all three is effusive. Both his Pinot-like Nerello and the unoaked Chardonnay walk a dignified line of purity and elegance. The heftier Petit Verdot is crafted from some of the highest vineyards in Europe, which do not mature their meager crop until the end of October.

Via Santo Spirito, 95030 Castiglione di Sicily
www.passopisciaro.com

Pietracupa Campania
Sabino Loffredo produces Greco, Fiano, and Aglianico according to biodynamic principles on his 8.5 acre (3.5ha) farm in the hamlet of Montefredane, not far from Macchialupa and Vadiaperti. Given the small scale (just 25,000 bottles a year) and superb quality, the modest prices that Sabino asks for his wines come as a most welcome surprise. The Taurasi is excellent, but he is best known for his two white superstars: Cupo, a herculean Fiano d'Avellino DOCG, and G, a Greco di Tufo DOCG of similarly titanic proportions with concentrated aromas of quince and pear. ★ Rising star

Via Vadiaperti 17, 83030 Montefredane
0825 607418

Pietratorcia Campania
Located on the western side of Ischia is Pietratorcia, a newcomer in this most decidedly ancient of islands. Established in 2000 by a group of three young and completely insane entrepreneurs dedicated to preserving the island's agrarian heritage, it now cultivates 15 acres (6ha) planted with such viticultural exotica as Biancolella, Forastera, and Uva Rilla Guernaccia. Their Vigne di Chignole blends these three white varieties with confidence. Mid-gold color, with a nose of ripe peach, liquorice, and spice, this is a thoroughly modern expression of island viticulture that dates back 3,000 years. ★ Rising star

Via Provinciale Panza 267, 80075 Forio d'Ischia
www.pietratorcia.it

Planeta Sicily
Year after year, cousins Alessio, Francesca, and Santi Planeta deliver more than 2 million bottles of wine that continue to set Sicily's standards. Although the obvious, international charms of their Chardonnay and Cabernet Sauvignon initially won the awards, the family is most proud of its achievements with Italian varieties. Cometa, a 100% white Fiano, delivers a virtuoso performance with an intense palate of dried fruit and spice; Santa Cecilia is a fleshy, muscular Nero d'Avola; while their Cerasuolo di Vittorio is a fine, willowy summer red.

Contrada Dispensa, 92013 Menfi
www.planeta.it

Rivera Puglia
In the early 1990s, Giuseppe de Corato established the vast Rivera estate. It fell to his son, Sebastiano, and his grandson, Carlo, however, to realize the potential of their vineyards in the heart of the Castel Del Monte DOC.

There is little doubt that Rivera is in the vanguard of Puglian winemaking and its range offers value at every price point. At the top of the pyramid is a range from its own vineyards and Il Falcone, a sumptuous red that is unquestionably the finest wine of the DOC.

SP 231 Km 60,500, Andria 70031
www.rivera.it

Salvatore Murana Sicily

Salvatore Murana, the unofficial Prince of Pantelleria, is one of Sicily's foremost exponents of its eponymous dessert wine made from sun-dried Moscato d'Alessandria grapes. Although Salvatore also produces a dry wine called E Serre, he is much more famous for his Passito di Pantelleria. The Martingana is a single-vineyard creation made from grapes dried for no fewer than 20 days. It reveals Moscato's signature orange blossom and sultana aromas, allied to a velvety peach and honey finish. It is sufficiently decadent and hedonistic to render most desserts superfluous.

Contrada Khamma 276, 91017 Pantelleria
www.salvatoremurana.com

Sella e Mosca Sardinia

Although owned by Gruppo Campari, Sella e Mosca —all 1,600 acres (650ha) of it—is run independently and produces more than 20 wines to suit every palate and budget. Propping up the company's fortunes is a sound range of indigenous varieties including the little-known Torbato, a toothsome Vermentino, and the trusty duo of Carignano and Cannonau. An international midfield includes Sauvignon Blanc and Cabernet Sauvignon, but the estate's leading player is, in fact, a dessert wine. The exotic Anghelu Ruju, made from late-harvest Cannonau, is a port-style red aged for five years in cask.

Località I Piani, 07041 Alghero
www.sellaemosca.com

Settesoli Sicily

Settesoli's success in revolutionizing the co-operative mentality in Italy is well documented. What is perhaps less well known is the innovative work done by winemakers Owen Bird and Domenico di Gregorio in pioneering new varieties. Experiments with Chenin Blanc, Sauvignon Blanc, and Viognier are now literally bearing fruit and an increasing number are varietally labeled under the Mandrarossa banner. The Sauvignon Blanc is particularly successful, given Sicily's withering climate, and shows a ripe, stone fruit palate with a stylish, grassy note. The honeyed Chenin Blanc and peachy Viognier are also impressive.

SS115, 92013 Menfi
www.cantinesettesoli.it

Spadafora Sicily

It is difficult to find anyone more profoundly Sicilian than Francesco Spadafora, scion of I Principe di Spadafora, a family whose lineage can be traced to the 13th century. Spadafora's 250 acres (100ha) of vineyards are planted at 1,312ft (400m) above sea level, near Palermo, and enjoy an ideal climate for both local and international varieties. The latter were introduced by Francesco's father in the 1980s, and Spadafora is Sicily's leading producer of Syrah, a grape well-matched to the island's arid

RIVERA
ONE OF THE REGION'S TOP WINES, IT WILL CELLAR WELL FOR MORE THAN 20 YEARS

TENUTE DETTORI
PRODUCED FROM THE ANCIENT CANNONAU GRAPE, THIS WINE IS VERY HIGH IN ALCOHOL

conditions. Both the Sole dei Padri and the Schietto are excellent, with an impenetrable ruby hue, complex black fruit, and finely judged oak.

Via Ausonia 90, 90144 Palermo
www.spadafora.com

Tasca d'Almerita Sicily

Tasca d'Almerita is an estate redolent of both history and success, and its importance in maintaining a tradition of fine-wine production in Sicily is profound. Founded in 1830, and still under family control, it has upheld tradition and championed innovation in equal measure. The 1,000 acre (400ha) Tenuta Regaleali, in the central highlands, is one of five estates under its control, and total production tops 3 million bottles. Tasca d'Almerita produces an exemplary range, including a rare white Grillo from the island of Mozia and a sweet Malvasia from Salina.

Contrada Regaleali, 90020 Sciafani Bagni
www.tascadalmerita.it

Tenuta Le Querce Basilicata

In 1995, the Pietrafesa family bought the Sasso winery and with it 173 acres (70ha) planted exclusively to Aglianico at a density of 2,400 vines per acre (6,000 vines per ha). This estate—a giant by Basilicata standards— produces five versions of Aglianico, two of which are bottled under the Cantine Sasso label. These wines offer unparalleled value. The finest grapes, as one might expect, go into the Le Querce brand. The Vigna della Corona is the most accomplished *cuvée*, with notes of rhubarb and graphite reminiscent of Tuscany's Sangiovese.

Via Appia 123, 85100 Potenza
www.tenutalequerce.it

Tenuta delle Terre Nere Sicily

Marc de Grazia is a leading exporter of fine Italian wines, and he knows the country like few others. His decision to purchase a small property on the northern slopes of Etna therefore came as a surprise to many, but worked wonders for the reputation of the DOC. He produces just under 100,000 bottles from 52 acres (21ha) of vineyards planted with local varieties including Nerello Mascalese and the white Carricante. Different vineyards are each vinified separately, including an historic, pre-phylloxera parcel that yields tiny quantities of a sublime Etna Rosso.

Contrada Calderara, 95036 Randazzo
095 924002

Tenute Dettori Sardinia

Despite his immaculate suits and perfect English, Alessandro Dettori is an ardent supporter of the old-fashioned ways. Farming 74 acres (30ha) of gobelet-trained Vermentino, Cannonau, and Moscato, Alessandro's anthology of Sardinian classics is unrivaled. For example, take his Dettori Rosso. The scorching sun and distressing yields (less than 10.5oz/300g per plant) coax an unbelievable 17.5% natural alcohol from a patch of unirrigated, pre-phylloxera Cannonau. Fermented and aged in nothing but cement, its clarity and balance challenge the belief that great wine can only be made in wineries bristling with technology. ★Rising star

Località Badde Nigolosu, 07036 Sennori
www.tenutedettori.it

TERREDORA
AN IDEAL ACCOMPANIMENT TO HORS
D'OEUVRES AND FISH DISHES, THIS IS A WINE
THAT IMPROVES WITH AGE

VINI BIONDI
A POWERFUL RED WINE WITH COMPLEX
AROMAS OF FRUIT AND SPICES

Tenute Rubino Puglia

The young and ambitious Luigi Rubino has taken this estate from bench warmer to star player in a very short time indeed. Tenute Rubino controls more than 500 acres (200ha) of vineyards planted largely to local Puglian varieties, which are vinified in a sparkling new winery where consultant winemaker Riccardo Cotarella works his magic. The range comprises 11 wines including the acclaimed Torre Testa IGT Salento made from the near-extinct Susumaniello variety. Never released without a few years under its belt, it has a garnet rim and a complex nose of blackcurrant, chocolate, and nutmeg.

Via E Fermi 50, 72100 Brindisi
www.tenuterubino.it

Terredora Campania

Terredora is the other Campanian estate owned by a Mastroberardino—this time Lucio. This branch of the family controls more than 308 acres (125ha) of prime vineyards located at the confluence of the south's leading DOCGs: Fiano d'Avellino, Greco di Tufo, and Taurasi. Terredora remains strictly an Azienda Agricola, which is to say that it would never consider producing any wine from grapes that it did not grow. For an estate of this size, the uniformly high quality is no mean feat. Watch out for the impressively nuanced Greco di Tufo DOCG and the "best buy" Falanghina.

Via Serra, 83030 Montefusco
www.terredora.com

Vadiaperti Campania

The Troisi family has been in the wine business for three generations, but it was Antonio II, a history teacher with a passion for wine and an interest in local traditions, who produced and bottled their first Fiano di Avellino DOCG, in 1984. Antonio's son, Raffaele, now controls the estate and continues a tradition of excellence in white wine-making. These days, good Greco and Fiano are easy to find, but Vadiaperti's Coda di Volpe remains without peer. Its delicate aromas of iris and honeysuckle echo the estate's clean mountain air.

Contrada Vadiaperti, 83030 Montefredane
www.vadiaperti.it

Valle dell'Acate Sicily

The Acate River snakes through Sicily's southeastern tip, and in so doing leaves a number of alluvial terraces that are ideal for viticulture. The Jacono family has been growing grapes here for centuries, but it was Gaetana Jacono who brought a pharmacist's eye for detail to the business in the mid-1990s. Today, the delicate red fruit and unexpectedly fresh acidity of her Cerasuolo di Vittoria make it the pick of this new DOCG. Her vibrant red Frappato is equally beguiling, and the animated Il Moro Nero d'Avola rounds off a faultless range.

Contrada Bidini, 97011 Acate
www.valledellacate.it

Vigne e Vini Puglia

The Greeks stepped ashore here in the 8th century BCE and immediately recognized the potential of the gentle hills south of Taranto. Cosimo Varvaglione and his wife Maria Tessa make the most of the land's natural affinity for the vine, and produce no fewer than 17 Puglian

classics labeled largely under the permissive IGT regulations. Their Moi Verdeca is a delightful version of this classic Puglian white, and the Papale Primitivo di Manduria DOC offers a rich, brambly nose that astutely captures the scorching Puglian summers.

Via Amendola 36, 74020 Leporano
www.vigneevini.it

Villa Matilde Campania

Some 2,000 years ago, it was decided that the only wine worthy of slaking an emperor's thirst was Falernian, and it was soon both glorified by poets and forged by publicans throughout the land. In 1970, Francesco Avallone decided it was high time someone recreated the most famous drink of the ancient world. His high-density vineyards of Aglianico, Piedirosso, and Falanghina have brought to life Falerno del Massico DOC, a rich, smoky red and Eleusi, a sweet white IGT redolent of apricots and vanilla. Toga parties will never be the same again.

SS Domitiana 18, 81030 Cellole
www.villamatilde.it

Vini Biondi Sicily

The fortunes of the Biondi family may have waxed and waned over the centuries, but they were one of the first to grow grapes in this deeply fashionable DOC. Today, they are at the top of their game and credit for the estate's revival goes to Ciro Biondi. His Etna Rosso Monte Ilice is sourced from a vertiginous vineyard clinging to an extinct volcanic cone almost 3,300 feet (1km) above sea level. With power to spare, and a complex nose of red fruit and spice, it is one of the DOC's flagship wines.

Corso Sicily 20, 95039 Trecastagni
www.vinibiondi.it

Vitivinicola Alberto Loi Sardinia

Three generations of the Loi family have worked their 124 acres (50ha) of vineyards in the hills of Ogliastra, Italy's least populous province. In this remote region, traditions run deep. The Loi winery specializes in Cannonau, and it produces no fewer than nine different versions, of which three are from single vineyards. Of these, the Cannonau di Sardegna Riserva Alberto Loi is the most impressive, with integrated oak spiciness and layers of both red and black fruit. There is also a rare white Cannonau made from a hypochromatic clone.

SS 125 km 124+200, 08040 Cardedu
www.cantina.it

Zenner Sicily

Nina and Hans Zenner were in the vanguard of the wave of foreigners who fell in love with Sicily when they moved there permanently in 1970. The estate produces just one wine, a biodynamic Nero d'Avola, from its 15 acres (6ha) of vineyards. It is a textbook example that showcases Nero d'Avola's affinity for the scorching conditions found on the island's south coast. The naturally high acidity provides a counterpoint to the alcohol, and the fruit character is surprisingly refined, with notes of mulberry, plum, and spice, and a delicate, mineral edge.

Via Pietro Mascagni 72, 95100 Catania
095 6170728

Vines begin to spring to life in a coastal vineyard near Palermo. The area is noted for its Marsala production.

Germany's "Riesling Renaissance" has become as well-known around the world as the aromatic and expressive white wines behind it have become well-loved and successful. During the past decade, the quality of Germany's best Rieslings has taken a great leap forward, and the quantity of good German wines of all kinds has increased dramatically. As the wines have improved, so Germany's international reputation as a fine wine producer has been restored to the position it enjoyed in the 19th and 20th centuries, when its wines commanded prices comparable to those of Bordeaux and Burgundy.

Behind the snappy catchphrase, there are a number of factors contributing to the revival: renewed German national pride, a new generation of winemakers, and climate change. To quantify the last of these, Germany's vineyards have warmed up by, on average, 1.8°F (1°C) during the last 25 years. There is now enough summer heat to produce good reds, and the proportion of red grapes planted has risen from 12% to 37% in a generation. Even in the "cool-climate" Mosel and Rheingau, winemakers are seeking out high-altitude vineyards to keep making the crisp Kabinett style of Riesling.

Of equal importance have been the Jungwinzer, or young winemakers, who swept away the mistrust endemic to their parents' generation, replacing it with the free exchange of ideas and mutual support. Their wine tastings are more like parties, where pop music and their wines fuse in a new pop-wine culture. They are well-educated, having attended wine schools such as the famous Geisenheim, and many have worked for top winemakers around the world. This has resulted not only in better quality Riesling and other, often dry wines, but has also led to a mind-blowing stylistic diversity. A generation ago you could make a generalized description of German wines in a few words. Today, this is completely impossible.

GERMANY

MOSEL

Mosel wine region

For wine-lovers around the world, the steep-sided, vine-clothed valley of the Mosel, extending from the point where Germany borders both France and Luxembourg to the river's confluence with the Rhine at Koblenz, is the defining image of German wine-growing. And the Rieslings from here are the defining wines of Germany—from San Francisco to Singapore, consumers expect the Rieslings from the wine-growing region formerly known as Mosel-Saar-Ruwer to contain only 7–9% alcohol, generous natural grape sweetness, intense fruity and floral aromas, and a pronounced refreshing acidity. Often they refer to these wines as "classic" style Mosel wines and will tell you that they taste this way because of the very cool climate and the slate soil.

Major grapes
 Reds

Spätburgunder (Pinot Noir)

Whites

Elbling

Grauburgunder (Pinot Gris)
Müller-Thurgau

Riesling

Weissburgunder (Pinot Blanc)

Vintages
2009
Excellent—ripe, balanced sweet and dry Rieslings. Yields were low, however.

2008
There are some sleek, racy, sweet wines, but some of the dry wines are a little tart.

2007
A first-class vintage. Rich, ripe dry and sweet Rieslings with healthy acidity.

2006
The most extreme vintage of modern times. The sweet wines are either monumental or completely overblown; dry wines mostly the latter.

2005
The greatest vintage for sweet Rieslings since 1949 and some excellent dry wines, with sensational concentration.

2004
The wines are similar to the racy, "classic" 2001s, if not quite as elegant.

In fact, what we think of as classic Mosel is only one side of the story. The diversity of the region's wines has dramatically increased in recent years as Weissburgunder (Pinot Blanc), Grauburgunder (Pinot Gris), and Spätburgunder (Pinot Noir) grapes for dry wines have become important specialties. There are even a few good Sauvignon Blancs. On the Obermosel (the upper reaches of the German Mosel), and around Bremm on the Terrassenmosel (close to the river's confluence with the Rhine at Koblenz), 1,800 acres (730ha) of the ancient Elbling grape are grown for its light, crisp, dry whites.

With 60% of the region's 22,000 acres (9,000ha) of vineyards, Riesling is still the dominant variety planted, however, and generally it grows on stony gray slate. Because winemaking approaches vary greatly from producer to producer, and because there are so many geographic variables in the vineyards—such as the depth of the soil (which ranges from 1.5ft/50cm to 20ft/6m), the gradient of the slopes, the amont of exposure to the sun, and the level of protection from the wind—the wines have great stylistic diversity. They can be bone dry or unctuously sweet, light or powerful, and textural.

As its name suggests, the Terrassenmosel's vineyards tend to be terraced, with extremely stony soils, and the wines are unusually full and supple for the region. The vineyards of the Saar are generally further from the river and more exposed to wind, resulting in sleeker wines with more pronounced acidity. In the tiny Ruwer Valley, close to the ancient city of Trier, the high diurnal temperature fluctuation (the difference between the maximum and minimum daily temperature) leads to highly aromatic, vibrant wines. More succulent, but rarely opulent or weighty, the wines from the Mittelmosel (Middle Mosel) lie between these extremes.

Contemporary Mosel Rieslings can roughly be divided into two schools: those that fit the earlier description of "classic" Mosel, and those that are drier, fuller in body, richer, and spicier. This "new" style is as varied as the classic style, and tends to be what younger German consumers associate with the region. Paradoxically, half a century ago, Mosel wines were closer to the new style than to the style now thought of as classic.

As with all German wines, it is important to grasp the rather complex system of labeling under which they are sold. The better classic-style Mosel wines, such as those described in the following pages, are classified as Prädikatswein (formerly Qualitätswein mit Prädikat or QmP). Rather than the finished wines being classified though, they are categorized according to the amount of sugar in the must (unfermented grape juice) at harvest, moving up in degree of sugar content through Kabinett, Spätlese, Auslese, Beerenauslese (BA), Trockenbeerenauslese (TBA), and Eiswein, the last of those being a wine made from grapes frozen on the vine. Top wines may also be labeled as Grosses Gewächs, or "Great Growth," meaning the wine comes from a distinguished vineyard site. Other terms include trocken (dry), halbtrocken (half-dry), and feinherb (another term for off-dry or half-dry; this term is gradually replacing halbtrocken).

It is likewise impossible to understand the Mosel without grasping the fiercely independent mentality of its wine-growers, each of whom has a distinctive take on the region. This characteristic, coupled with the hand-crafted nature of the best wines, is as much responsible for the vinous variety as the complexities of the terroir. And it is a characteristic that has only been strengthened by an influx of outsiders who, with minimal capital, have founded micro-wineries whose wines can, on occasion, match those of Mosel's top producers.

A J Adam Mittelmosel

Andreas Adam founded one of the first Mosel micro-wineries in 2000; since then he has expanded to more than 5 acres (2ha). More importantly, he has developed a range of first-class Rieslings from the Hofberg site of Dhron. It is hard to choose between the concentrated, minerally, dry Spätlese feinherb or the dazzlingly racy, succulently sweet Spätlese and Auslese. ★ **Rising star**

Brückenstrasse 51, 54347 Neumagen-Dhron
www.aj-adam.com

Ansgar Clüsserath Mittelmosel

Eva Clüsserath is one of the most talented young winemakers in the Mosel. Since her first vintage in 2001, her dry and sweet Rieslings have gained enormously in depth and sophistication. The substantial, crisp Vom Schiefer, "from slate," is the basic dry Riesling, followed by the elegant, polished Steinreich, "rich in stone," and the complex Trittenheimer Apotheke. The sweet Rieslings from the Apotheke taste every bit as much of ripe grapes, slate, hard work, and excellent vinification. ★ **Rising star**

Spielesstrasse 4, 54349 Trittenheim
06507 2290

Carl Loewen Mittelmosel

With the dry Varidor and off-dry Quant—both of them aromatic and racy—modest owner Karl Josef Loewen has two of the best regular-quality wines in the region. But the real fireworks come from his sweet Spätlese and Auslese with great minerality from Thörnicher Ritch and Leiwener Laurentiuslay. In 2008, Loewen added wines named after the year a parcel of vines was planted in the Longuicher Maximiner Herrenberg site: 1896. ★ **Rising star**

Matthiasstrasse 30, 54340 Leiwen
www.weingut-loewen.de

Clemens Busch Terrassenmosel

Anyone who says Mosel wines cannot be powerful and richly textured has not tasted the organic monster Rieslings from Clemens and Rita Busch and their son Florian. The Buschs made their name with dry wines and their dry Grosse Gewächse from the Pündericher Marienburg site are enormously mineral and spicy, like their off-dry Spätlese bottled under the names of a handful of single parcels of vines in this site which together form the top of their regular range. The Auslese, BA, and TBA dessert wines are likewise of titanic concentration, crammed with dried fruit and spice aromas.

Kirchstrasse 37, 56862 Pünderich
www.clemens-busch.de

Clüsserath-Weiler Mittelmosel

Despite having only 15 acres (6ha) of vines, father-and-daughter team Helmut and Verena Clüsserath make a range of excellent Rieslings, spanning the white wine spectrum from the light, dry HC up to the concentrated, off-dry Färhfels from a parcel of 100-year-old vines in the Trittenheimer Apotheke site, to Eisweins and botrytis wines of stunning richness. The wines from Trittenheim tend toward cool elegance, while those from Mehring show more muscle and opulence. ★ **Rising star**

Brückenstrasse 9, 54349 Trittenheim
www.cluesserath-weiler.de

DR. LOOSEN
ERNST LOOSEN'S GREATEST WINES ARE
FROM THE ERDENER PRALAT

CLEMENS BUSCH
THE BUSCH FAMILY CREATES SOME OF THE
MOST POWERFUL WINES IN THE MOSEL

Daniel Vollenweider Mittelmosel

In 2000, Daniel Vollenweider, a sharp, young Swiss unknown in wine circles, borrowed some money to buy 4 acres (1.6ha) of super-steep vineyards in the forgotten Wolfer Goldgrübe site. Within five years, his estate was in the Mosel's premier league. His sweet Riesling Spätlese and Auslese from the Goldgrübe are some of the region's raciest and most elegant. The wines from old vines in the Shimbock site are a complete contrast: powerful and enormously spicy. A star is born. ★ **Rising star**

Wolfer Weg 53, 56841 Traben-Trarbach
www.weingut-vollenweider.de

Dr. Loosen Mittelmosel

Ernst Loosen planned to be an archaeologist rather than a winemaker, but in the past 20 years, he has done more to improve the image of German wine than anyone else. Aside from a handful of impressive, minerally, dry Rieslings his range is composed entirely of beautifully balanced, distinctive sweet Kabinett, Spätlese, and Auslese from top sites such as Bernkasteler Lay, Graacher Himmelreich, Wehlener Sonnenuhr, and Erdener Treppchen. From the Erdener Prälat he produces only the luscious, exotic Auslese that are his greatest wines. The Dr. L wines from bought-in grapes are lighter, but similar in style. Loosen also works in the Pfalz and the state of Washington.

St Johannishof, 54470 Bernkastel
www.drloosen.com

Dr. Siemens Saar

Dr. Jochen Siemens abandoned a successful career as a newspaper editor to turn the former Bert Simon estate around, and since 2007 he has succeeded. As good as the light and juicy dry Pinot Blanc and Pinot Gris are, it is the minerally dry and off-dry Rieslings from the monopole Herrenberg and Würtzberg sites that shine the brightest. These are great vineyards whose potential Siemens is only just beginning to explore. ★ **Rising star**

Römerstrasse 63, 54455 Serrig
www.dr-siemens.de

Dr. H. Thanisch—Erben Thanisch Mittelmosel

In the past decade, the sweet Riesling Kabinett and Spätlese from the famous Thanisch estate have gained in concentration without losing their hallmark elegance. The range divides into two: the slightly drier, lighter wines from the Bernkasteler Badstube and the more opulent, complex wines from the legendary Bernkasteler Doctor. Prices are not as high as the reputation would suggest.

Saarallee 31, 54470 Bernkastel-Kues
www.thanisch.com

Dr. Wagner Saar

Heinz Wagner has remained true to a sleek, steely style of Saar Riesling at Dr. Wagner since the early 1970s and his daughter Christiane has no intention of changing it. The sweet wines have the same vibrant acidity that gives the dry wines their crystalline clarity. Depending on your taste, the top site is either the Saarburger Rausch (earthy and racy) or the Ockfener Bockstein (more floral).

Bahnhofstrasse 3, 54439 Saarburg
www.weingutdrwagner.de

MOSEL

Aside from Obermosel (Upper Mosel), all of this region has slate soils. In most of the steep vineyards the soils are covered with stones—although there is always soil underneath—and even on gentle slopes there is a lot of slate in the soil. Many of the older buildings, including the famous wine estates and some of the rising stars, were constructed from this slate. Wherever you turn, there is the one rock type again and again. This has led many people to assume that Mosel wines are all the same: light, flowery in aroma, and fruity. However, anyone who spends some time tasting and drinking the wines will soon find out that the wines of some vineyards, such as Wehlener Sonnenuhr, invariably produce rich wines, while others, such as Scharzhofberg, invariably yield sleeker ones. The typical aromas also vary greatly—for example, black currant is typical for Piesport and Graach—in this multidimensional region.

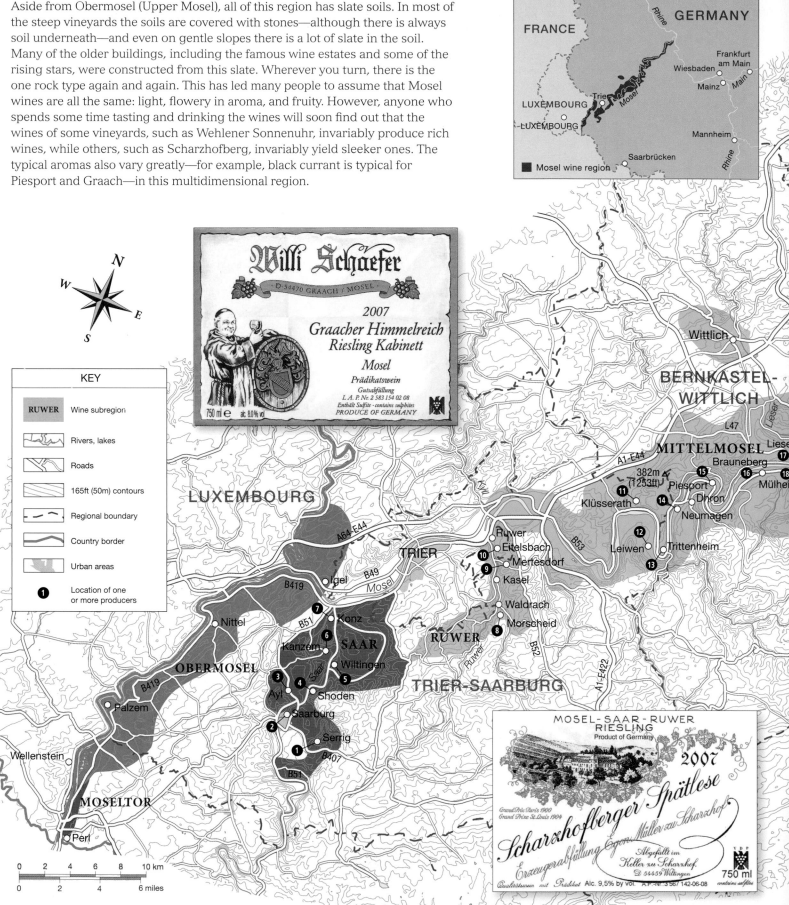

KEY

RUWER — Wine subregion

Rivers, lakes

Roads

165ft (50m) contours

Regional boundary

Country border

Urban areas

1 — Location of one or more producers

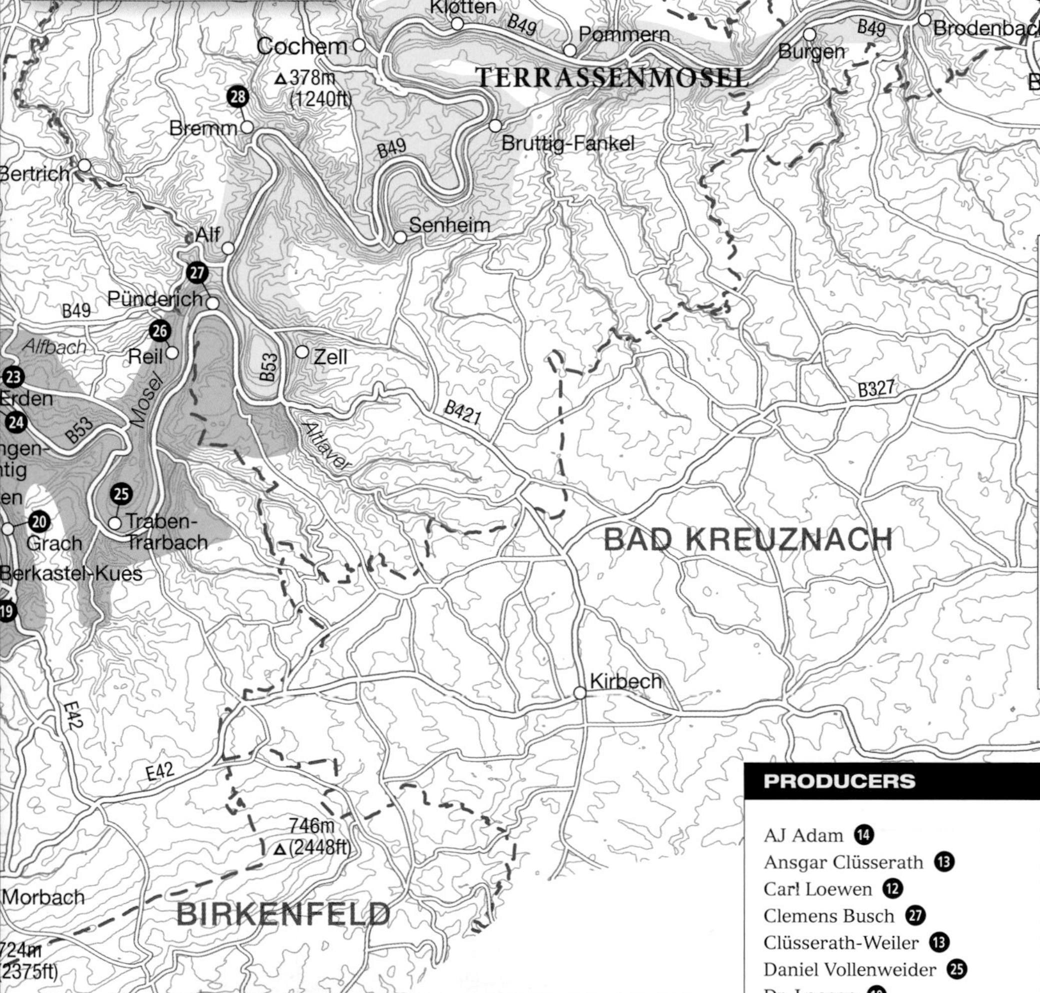

KERPEN
2007
RIESLING

Bertrich
Bremm
△378m
(1240ft)
Cochem
Klotten
B49
Pommern
Burgen
TERRASSENMOSEL
Bruttig-Fankel
Senheim
Alf
Bertrich
B49
Pünderich
Reil
Zell
B53
B421
Altlaver
Traben-Trarbach
Grach
Berkastel-Kues
Morbach
BIRKENFELD
746m
△(2448ft)
724m
2375ft)

MAYEN-KOBLENZ
A1-E44
A1-E44
Kobern
Winningen
KOBLENZ
L82
Niederfell
B49
B416
Münster-Maifield
Mosel
E31
B49
Brodenbach
Braubach
Boppard
RHEIN-LAHN
COCHEM-ZELL
B327

BAD KREUZNACH
Kirbech

KARL ERBES
Weingut
ÜRZIGER WÜRZGARTEN
RIESLING BEERENAUSLESE
2009
Prädikatswein
Gutsabfüllung · A.P.Nr. 2 602 138 14 10 · D-54539 Ürzig
PRODUCE OF GERMANY · ENTHÄLT SULFITE
ALC. 6.5% BY VOL
MOSEL
375 ml

Weingut Max Ferd. Richter
D-54486 MÜLHEIM/MOSEL
Familienbesitz seit 1680
2007
Graacher Himmelreich
Riesling Kabinett
alc. 8.5% vol
Prädikatswein · A.P.Nr. 2 593 049 07 08
750 ml
MOSEL-SAAR-RUWER

PRODUCERS

AJ Adam ⑭	Heymann-Löwenstein ㉚	SA Prüm ㉑
Ansgar Clüsserath ⑬	Joh. Jos. Prüm ㉑	Rebenhof/Johannes
Carl Loewen ⑫	Karl Erbes ㉓	Schmitz ㉓
Clemens Busch ㉗	Karlsmühle ⑨	Reichsgraf von
Clüsserath-Weiler ⑬	Karthäuserhof/Tyrell ⑩	Kesselstatt ⑧
Daniel Vollenweider ㉕	Kees-Kieren ⑳	Reinhold Franzen ㉘
Dr. Loosen ⑲	Kerpen ⑲	Reinhold Haart ⑮
Dr. Siemens ❶	Kirsten ⑪	Schloss Lieser ⑰
Dr. H. Thanisch—Erben	Knebel ㉚	Schloss Saarstein ❶
Thanisch ⑲	Loch ❹	Schmitges ㉔
Dr. Wagner ❷	Lubentiushof ㉙	Selbach-Oster ㉒
Egon Müller-Scharzhof/Le	Markus Molitor ⑲	St. Urbans-Hof ⑫
Gallais ❺	Max Ferd. Richter ⑱	van Volxem ❺
Erben von Beulwitz ⑨	Maximin Grünhaus/von	von Hövel ❼
Forstmeister	Schubert ⑨	von Othegraven ❻
Gelt-Zilliken ❷	Melsheimer ㉖	Weiser-Künstler ㉕
Fritz Haag ⑯	Müllen ㉕	Willems-Willems ❼
Grans-Fassian ⑫	Peter Lauer ❸	Willi Schaefer ⑲

Always check the availability of visitor facilities and the visiting hours at a winery before planning your trip. Some wineries are open by appointment only.

JOH. JOS. PRUM

THE BERNKASTELER BADSTUBE SPATLESE
FEINHERB IS "JJ" PRUM'S BEST DRY WINE

EGON MULLER

OUTSTANDING AUSLESE RIESLING FROM THE
LEGENDARY SCHARZHOFBERG SITE

Egon Müller-Scharzhof/Le Gallais
Saar

Tradition is the vital force behind the great twin estate of Egon Müller-Scharzhof/Le Gallais, where the wines are models of refinement even at the highest levels of honeyed concentration. Egon Müller IV makes no dry wines, but his regular Scharzhof Riesling is almost dry and full of white fruit aromas. The other Müller-Scharzhof wines all come from the legendary Scharzhofberg site; the Le Gallais wines from the monopole Wiltinger Braune Kupp in the Ruwer. Riesling Kabinetts combine lightness with character and depth, while the Spätlese are rich and complex, but never exaggeratedly sweet. In Germany, Müller commands the highest prices for Saar wines in these categories, but in an international context, they still seem reasonable. The great Auslese and the sensational BA, TBA, and Eiswein, are formidably expensive, however.

Scharzhof, 54459 Wiltingen
www.scharzhof.de

Erben von Beulwitz Ruwer

Always light and bright with lively apple, white peach, and berry aromas, Herbert Weis's wines at Erben von Beulwitz are model Ruwer Rieslings. Good as the drier style wines are, it is the Spätlese and Auslese Alte Reben from old vines that stand out here. Suprisingly, on paper, it is not the wine estate but the Hotel Weis, Restaurant Vinum, and Weinstube von Beulwitz (all recommended, all at the address below) that are this charming polymath's main business. ★ **Rising star**

Eitelsbacher Strasse 4, 54318 Mertesdorf
06519 5610

Forstmeister Gelt-Zilliken Saar

Hanno Zilliken has produced classic Saar Rieslings at Forstmeister Gelt-Zilliken since the 1970s, but it is only during the last decade that he has made his greatest wines: Spätlese and Auslese from the Saarburger Rausch site that define the word racy. With the 2002 vintage, Zilliken introduced a new off-dry estate Riesling called Butterfly whose name caused some head-shaking in this conservative region, but which today accounts for 50% of production from his 27 acres (11ha). A new winery extending the existing deep barrel cellars has recently been constructed and Zilliken's daughter Dorothee is now part of the team.

Heckingstrasse 20, 54439 Saarburg
www.zilliken-vdp.de

Fritz Haag Mittelmosel

Few producers manage to maintain the quality and stylistic consistency that Wilhelm Haag and his son Oliver have for almost 50 years at Fritz Haag. It is a measure of the continuity here that nobody noticed when Oliver took over the cellar with the 2005 vintage; the wines had the same diamondlike brilliance and clarity, and aromatic subtlety, as ever. Although a small number of dry wines are produced, this 30 acre (12ha) estate focuses on its famed Spätlese and Auslese with natural grape sweetness. The BA and TBA are amazingly elegant, but you pay handsomely for the name.

Dusemonder Strasse 44, 54472 Brauneberg
www.weingut-fritz-haag.de

Grans-Fassian Mittelmosel

The mercurial Gerhard Grans of Grans-Fassian is somewhat hit-and-miss: either he hits the bull's-eye with his Riesling Spätlese and Auslese or the balance of piercing acidity, grape sweetness, and explosive freshness is just too extreme for optimum harmony. Although his name is closely associated with the great Trittenheimer Apotheke site, Grans has long made some dramatic dry Rieslings from old vines in the Leiwener Laurentiuslay and he has recently added an impressively rich, dry Grosses Gewächs from the Dhron-Hofberger. ★ **Rising star**

Römerstrasse 28, 54340 Leiwen
www.grans-fassian.de

Heymann-Löwenstein Terrassenmosel

Since founding Heymann-Löwenstein with his wife Cornelia Heymann in 1980, Reinhard Löwenstein has revolutionized the Mosel. Almost single-handedly, Löwenstein created the new style of richly textured and spicy, but dry (or almost dry) Rieslings. Simultaneously, he did more to raise awareness of the region's terroir than anyone else, not least by bottling three strikingly dry Rieslings from different sections of the Uhlen site of Winningen from 2001: Roth Lay, Laubach, and Blaufüsser Lay. In spite of intense competition, he remains the master of this style.

Bahnhofstrasse 10, 56333 Winningen
www.heymann-loewenstein.de

Joh. Jos. Prüm Mittelmosel

Katharina Prüm is the third generation to direct the Joh. Jos. Prüm estate since "JJ" became synonymous with great Mosel Riesling during the 1920s, and her wines are the product of an ongoing process of refinement of the wine style established by her grandfather Sebastian Prüm. Though a few dry wines are made (best is the Bernkasteler Badstube Spätlese feinherb), the Riesling Spätlese and Auslese from Wehlener Sonnenuhr and Graacher Himmelreich with natural grape sweetness form the majority of production. These slow-developing and extremely long-living wines often start life with a pronounced yeasty aroma, but also with a cornucopia of fruit and floral aromas and dazzling freshness.

Uferallee 19, 54470 Wehlen
www.jjpruem.com

Karl Erbes Mittelmosel

Stefan Erbes, the son of Karl Erbes who founded his eponymous estate in 1967, is an unashamed promoter of the "classic" style of Mosel Riesling with generous natural grape sweetness, lavish fruit aromas, and fresh acidity. Most of his super-succulent Spätlese, Auslese, BA, and TBA come from vineyards high above the red cliffs of Urzig, which act like chimneys, funneling heat from the riverside up to the vines. ★ **Rising star**

Würzgartenstrasse 25, 54539 Urzig
www.weingut-karlerbes.com

Karlsmühle Ruwer

With a talent for improvisation and an instinctive feeling for Riesling, Peter Geiben has steadily built up Karlsmühle into a producer of powerful, original Ruwer wines. The wines are not subtle, but if the aromatic equivalent of free jazz sounds good, then Geiben's expressive, dry and sweet wines from his Lorenzhöfer monopole, and his sweet wines from Kaseler Nies'chen, are sure to excite. The wines below Auslese level offer great value. ★ **Rising star**

Im Mühlengrund 1, 54318 Mertesdorf
www.weingut-karlsmuehle.de

Karthäuserhof/Tyrell Ruwer
The entire production of Karthäuserhof/Tyrell comes from its 47 acre (19ha) monopole Karthäuserhofberg, at the foot of which nestles an idyllic complex of historic buildings. The trademark of dynamic duo Christoph Tyrell and long-time winemaker Ludwig Breiling is aromatic, racy brilliance, the interplay of fruit and acidity either subtly underlined by natural grape sweetness or by a modest amount of alcohol. The long-living wines display intense berry and fresh herb aromas.

Karthäuserhof, 54292 Trier-Eitelsbach
06515 121

Kees-Kieren Mittelmosel
For more than 20 years, brothers Ernst-Josef and Werner Kees have made the small Kees-Kieren estate one of the most consistent in the Mittelmosel. Fruit-driven, but not superficial, fresh, but not too acidic, the wines are easy to like, yet with a style entirely their own. Top of the range are usually the dry Riesling Grosses Gewächs and the sweet Spätlese and Auslese from the excellent Graacher Domprobst site. ★ **Rising star**

Hauptstrasse 22, 54470 Graach
www.kees-kieren.de

Kerpen Mittelmosel
When it comes to naturally sweet Riesling Spätlese and Auslese, Martin Kerpen is a traditionalist. He vinifies all his wines in neutral oak, yet they are bright, aromatic, and juicy. However, his dry Rieslings have undergone a considerable transformation since the 2003 vintage, when alcohol levels jumped to 13%, but the wines tasted rounder as a result rather than alcoholic. Today, Kerpen welcomes these alcohol levels, regarding them as positive for dry Mosel Riesling. ★ **Rising star**

Uferallee 6, 54470 Bernkastel-Wehlen
www.weingut-kerpen.de

Kirsten Mittelmosel
Bernhard Kirsten and Inge von Geldern's airy steel-and-glass winery is unique on the Mittelmosel and their wines are too. Rich, dry Rieslings are the almost exclusive focus, and in spite of their concentration and ripeness, they have a wonderful smoothness and harmony. The most powerful is the Alte Reben from old vines in the excellent Brüderschaft site, which contrasts with the more elegant and lively Herzstück from the heart of the same site. The unusually ripe and supple Riesling and rosé sparkling wines are no less innovative. ★ **Rising star**

Krainstrasse 5, 54340 Klüsserath
www.weingut-kirsten.de

Knebel Terrassenmosel
Beate Knebel is the specialist for botrytis Riesling on the Terrassenmosel, her best wines bursting with dried fruit aromas, honey sweetness, and bright acidity. At less exalted prices, the Alte Reben dry and sweet Spätlese from Röttgen (exotic, luscious) and Uhlen (firm, intensely mineral) are substantial and expressive. ★ **Rising star**

August-Horch-Strasse 24, 56333 Winningen
www.weingut-knebel.de

Loch Saar
With a little more than 7 acres (3ha), Loch is the smallest top-class estate on the Saar, but also the most original. Claudia and Manfred Loch built it from scratch, beginning in 1992 and learning as they went. Very low yields, organic hand cultivation, and minimalist winemaking result in atypically concentrated, rich wines for the Saar, which are vinified dry when there is little noble rot and sweet when there is plenty of botrytis. The off-dry, super-succulent QuaSaar is the best value in the range. ★ **Rising star**

Hauptstrasse 80–82, 54441 Schoden
www.lochriesling.de

Lubentiushof Terrassenmosel
Andreas Barth's day job is directing the famous von Othegraven estate on the Saar, but his own Lubentiushof estate on the Terrassenmosel is his first love. Almost all of Barth's top dry and sweet Rieslings come from the little-known but first-class Gondorfer Gäns site, from which he conjures creamy, golden wines. ★ **Rising star**

Kehrstrasse 16, 56332 Niederfell
www.lubentiushof.de

Markus Molitor Mittelmosel
Markus Molitor is continually pushing the envelope to see how much power he can pack into a Mosel wine, particularly those from the Zeltinger Sonnenuhr site. Even his sweet Spätlese are bold wines, rippling with fruit and spice, and the Auslese are often huge. The mandarin aroma in many of his Rieslings is a result of extremely long fermentation; the creamy texture from late picking and long lees contact. Molitor also makes excellent, almost dry feinherb wines and the region's most powerful Spätburgunder. ★ **Rising star**

Haus Klosterberg, 54470 Bernkastel-Wehlen
www.markusmolitor.com

Max Ferd. Richter Mittelmosel
Max Ferd. Richter is a 37 acre (15ha) bastion of tradition producing few dry wines, its main focus being sweet Kabinett, Spätlese, and Auslese from top sites reaching from the Brauneberger Juffer-Sonnenuhr to the Wehlener Sonnenuhr. Since the late 1980s, owner Dr. Dirk Richter has achieved remarkable consistency given the range and number of wines. Almost every wine spends time in neutral oak and they age very well.

Hauptstrasse 37/85, 54486 Mülheim
www.maxferdrichter.com

Maximin Grünhaus/von Schubert
Ruwer
Director Dr. Carl von Schubert and winemaker Stefan Kraml have put the 77 acre (31ha) Maximin Grünhaus/von Schubert estate back on course after a difficult patch. New features include excellent feinherb wines, of which the Superior is a near-perfect example of great mineral depth. Each of the three monopole sites has its own unique notes:

THE STARS AND THE HOBBITS

Between 2000 and 2010, the vineyard area of the Mosel shrank by more than a quarter, yet leading Mosel winemakers such as Ernst Loosen and Egon Müller of the eponymous estates, or Katharina Prüm of JJ Prüm, are still the biggest German stars in the wine universe. This seeming paradox is explained by the existence of an older generation of small growers whose children do not want to follow in their footsteps up those brutally steep slate slopes. Nearly all the stars have expanded their vineyards to the limits of their cellars' capacities, so the region's best hopes now lie with the "hobbits." This is the local nickname for undercapitalized outsiders who leap in the deep end of Mosel Riesling, or locals who start out as amateur winemakers, then turn professional. Places such as Traben-Trarbach, with no famous vineyards and cheap land, offer an ideal habitat for "hobbits." It is easy to rent a disused cellar and there is plenty of secondhand winemaking equipment available. Selling the wine is the only challenge for these "no-names."

REINHOLD HAART
THEO HAART'S RIESLINGS FROM PIESPORTER
GOLDTROPFCHEN ARE INTENSELY RICH

REICHSGRAF VON KESSELSTATT
THE JOSEPHSHOFER SPATLESE IS ONE
OF THIS PRODUCER'S BEST WINES OF 2008

S A PRUM
PRUM BLUE RIESLING KABINETT IS AN
AFFORDABLE ENTRY-POINT TO THE BROAD
PORTFOLIO OF THE HISTORIC SA PRUM

the Bruderberg smelling of blackberry, the Herrenberg of berries and herbs, the Abtsberg of peach. Good dry wines and great sweet Kabinett and Spätlese are also made.

Hauptstrasse 1, 54318 Mertesdorf
www.vonschubert.com

Melsheimer Mittelmosel
With its easterly exposure, the little-known Reiler Mullay-Hofberg site has gained greatly through global warming, but that would not have been enough to create great wines without ex-volleyball player Thorsten Melsheimer to interpret it. Low yields and organic viticulture, plus a healthy dose of ambition, have sent this 27 acre (11ha) estate shooting to the top. The distinctive lemon aroma and super-charged racy style of the wines (dry and sweet) make them unique on the Mosel.

Dorfstrasse 21, 56861 Reil
www.melsheimer-riesling.de

Müllen Mittelmosel
Martin Müllen is one of the great unsung heroes of Mosel Riesling. From humble beginnings in 1991, the fanatical yet modest winemaker has created a small estate focused exclusively on top quality. All the grapes go into a basket press and everything ferments in neutral wooden casks with separate cellars for dry and sweet wines. Müllen's Rieslings are always concentrated, super-ripe, and highly expressive, but the pungently floral, brilliantly racy wines from Trabener Hühnerberg stand out. ★Rising star

Alte Marktstrasse 2, 56841 Traben-Trarbach
www.weingut-muellen.de

Peter Lauer Saar
Peter Lauer was one of the best winemakers on the Saar, but his estate has only improved since his son Florian joined in 2006. The Lauers have an excellent restaurant, so dry and almost-dry wines are the specialty here. They are moderate in alcohol, but rich in texture, with minerally acidity and complexity. The best are sold under the names of individual parcels in the Ayler Kupp site. The equally limited-production dry Riesling from the Saarfeilser site has a unique silkiness for a Saar Riesling. ★Rising star

Trierstrasse 49, 54441 Ayl
www.lauer-ayl.de

S A Prüm Mittelmosel
The historic S A Prüm has significantly expanded in recent years, adding parcels in the Urziger Würzgarten and Erdener Treppchen to long-standing holdings in the famous Wehlener Sonnenuhr and Graacher Himmelreich. In the past few years, the father-and-daughter team of Raimund and Saskia Prüm has produced a wide range of impressive, classic sweet Rieslings from these sites, and improving dry wines made from Pinots Blanc and Gris, Chardonnay, and Riesling.

Uferallee 25-26, 54470 Wehlen
www.sapruem.com

Rebenhof/Johannes Schmitz Mittelmosel
In the conservative context of Urzig, where sweet Spätlese dominate, Johannes Schmitz is a revolutionary with his dry and off-dry Rieslings. The wines combine finely nuanced aromas (pineapple and strawberry) with the

distinctive spiciness of the great Würzgarten site, the most concentrated being the Alte Reben bottlings from ancient, ungrafted vines. Auslese, BA, and TBA are also brilliant and never too sweet. The new winery being built promises even better things in the future. ★Rising star

Hüwel 2–3, 54539 Urzig
www.rebenhof.de

Reichsgraf von Kesselstatt Ruwer
Although Reichsgraf von Kesselstatt's 86 acres (35ha) of vineyards on the Mittelmosel, Saar, and Ruwer have benefited from consistent direction under Annegret Reh-Gartner for two decades, the change of winemaker in 2005 (Wolfgang Mertes is now responsible for the cellar) seems to have made its wines much less consistent. Many wines from the 2006 and 2008 vintages lack harmony when compared with those of the "odd" years, 2005 and 2007. That said, the powerful, dry Grosses Gewächs from the Josephshöfer site and the rich and complex sweet Spätlese from the same site are both well worth looking out for.

Schlossgut Marienlay, 54317 Morscheid
www.kesselstatt.com

Reinhold Franzen Terrassenmosel
Extremists abound among Mosel winegrowers, but it would be hard to find one to top Ulrich Franzen. He has lived like a mountaineer for years in order to replant some of the best vineyards on the slate cliff faces of Bremer Calmont, arguably the steepest in the entire world. Franzen's dry and just off-dry Rieslings (the top wines are marked with a gold capsule) are also some of the most extreme wines in the region with full to massive body, great ripeness, and mineral spice. ★Rising star

Gartenstrasse 14, 56814 Bremm
www.weingut-franzen.de

Reinhold Haart Mittelmosel
Theo Haart does not make lavish claims for his Rieslings from the famous Piesporter Goldtröpfchen site, but they certainly are lavish and some of the region's greatest. His Kabinett, Spätlese, and Auslese have full natural grape sweetness, balanced by supple acidity, a concentrated blackcurrant aroma (Piesport's hallmark), and intense mineral spice. In contrast, his wines from the Wintricher Ohligsberg site are more steely. Even the basic dry Riesling, Heart to Haart, is a generous, ripe wine in the Mosel context.

Ausoniusufer 18, 54498 Piesport
www.haart.de

Schloss Lieser Mittelmosel
In 1992, Thomas Haag (son of Wilhelm) picked up the pieces of this once great and famous estate and began putting them back together again. In just three years, he achieved his goal of putting it in the top league for Riesling Kabinett, Spätlese, and Auslese with natural grape sweetness. The wines from the slopes of the Lieserer Niederberg-Helden are a touch more powerful and robust than the super-elegant wines from the Brauneberger Juffer-Sonnenuhr. ★Rising star

Am Markt 1-5, 54470 Lieser
www.weingut-schloss-lieser.de

Schloss Saarstein Saar

Since Dieter Ebert purchased the 25 acre (10ha) Schloss Saarstein in 1956, it has been one of the most consistent producers on the Saar. Today, Dieter's son Christian makes a small range of dry and sweet Rieslings that are fresh and bright with a pronounced blackcurrant note. With its pear and hazelnut aromas, the good dry Pinot Blanc is a rarity on the Saar.

Schloss Saarstein, 54455 Serrig
www.saarstein.de

Schmitges Bernkastel

Since the 1980s, Andreas Schmitges has slowly expanded his estate to 35 acres (14ha) and steadily refined his wines from the top vineyard sites of Erden, Treppchen, and Prälat. His twin focuses are substantial dry Rieslings (the best are often the feinherb wines), which combine juiciness with a delicate spiciness, and rich and succulently sweet Spätlese and Auslese. ★ **Rising star**

Im Unterdorf 12, 54492 Erden
www.schmitges-weine.de

Selbach-Oster Mittelmosel

Johannes Selbach is a tireless promoter of the Mosel and German Riesling and you are more likely to meet him in New York or Stockholm than at home. Selbach's sweet Kabinett and Spätlese wines are much less sweet than at most top estates in the region and as mineral as anywhere on the Mittelmosel. The finest wines are the concentrated, refined Zeltinger Sonnenuhr Auslese from the single parcels Schmitt and Rothlay, but the small range of dry wines is impressive, as are great BA, TBA, and Eiswein. A well-made range of wines with strong regional character is also sold under the Selbach name.

Uferallee 23, 54492 Zeltingen
www.selbach-oster.de

St Urbans-Hof Mittelmosel

The hundreds of thousands of bottles of modestly priced, excellent-quality estate Riesling that St Urbans-Hof's Nik Weis produces every year are one of his greatest achievements. The other side of this 80 acre (32ha) estate is the wealth of excellent vineyard-designated sweet Riesling Kabinett, Spätlese, and Auslese from Ockfener Bockstein on the Saar and Piesporter Goldtröpfchen and Leiwener Laurentiuslay on the Mosel. All of these wines are juicy, super-fresh, and full of fruit. ★ **Rising star**

Urbanusstrasse 16, 54340 Leiwen
www.urbans-hof.de

van Volxem Saar

Since 2000, Roman Niewodniczanski has transformed his van Volxem property from a run-down, second-class Saar estate into one of the most important producers of wines in the new, rich and spicy, dry style. Tiny yields, very late harvesting, and long fermentation are the norm here, and even the regular quality Saar Riesling is a substantial wine. The single-vineyard bottlings, most notably the Braunfels Volz, Gottesfuss Alte Reben, and Kanzemer Altenberg, are all enormous wines in the context of the wines generally produced in the Mosel. ★ **Rising star**

Dehenstrasse 2, 54459 Wiltingen
www.vanvolxem.com

SELBACH-OSTER
THE ZELTINGER SONNENUHR RIESLING
AUSLESE IS IMPRESSIVELY CONCENTRATED

ST URBANS-HOF
NIK WEIS'S LEIWENER LAURENTIUSLAY
RIESLING IS JUICY, FRESH, AND FRUIT-DRIVEN

von Hövel Saar

The jovial Eberhard von Kunow may have a modest profile compared to some of the other star winemakers on the Saar, but his naturally sweet Riesling Spätlese and Auslese often belong in the first rank. Most of these come from his monopole Oberemmeler Hütte site, but he also has holdings in the Scharzhofberg and another monopole site in the tiny Kanzemer Hörecker. Aside from the latter, all of these wines offer excellent value for money.

Agritiusstrasse 5–6, 54329 Konz-Oberemmel
www.weingut-vonhoevel.de

von Othegraven Saar

After a long period in the doldrums, then a hard struggle to overcome all manner of problems, Dr. Heidi Kegel and her winemaker, Andreas Barth, have revived the famous von Othegraven estate. Whether dry or sweet, these are sophisticated Saar Rieslings of great aromatic subtlety, neither overly acidic nor a jot too rich. The estate is best known for its wines from the great Kanzemer Altenberg site, but those from the Wiltinger Kupp and Ockfener Bockstein are often every bit as good.

Weinstrasse 1, 54441 Kanzem
www.von-othegraven.de

Weiser-Künstler Mittelmosel

Konstantin Weiser was a banker and his wife Alexandra Künstler a senior social worker when they started the Weiser-Künstler micro-winery in 2005. Remarkably, they have not made a disappointing wine since, producing off-dry and sweet Riesling Kabinett, Spätlese, and Auslese from the Enkirch Ellergrub with aromatic richness, great succulence, and perfect balance. ★ **Rising star**

Wilhelmstrasse 11, 56841 Traben-Trarbach
www.weiser-kuenstler.de

Willems-Willems Saar

Carolin Hofmann had not finished her winemaking studies when she made her first wines for Willems-Willems back in 2001. Now Hofmann is one of the rising stars of the region thanks to a wide range of dry, off-dry, and sweet Saar Rieslings which combine ripeness and elegance. Top of the dry range are the concentrated and complex single-vineyard Altenberg and Herrenberg bottlings, but all her wines offer excellent value for money. There's also a Spätburgunder red of astonishing quality for the ultimate cool-climate region. ★ **Rising star**

Mühlenstrasse 13, 54329 Konz-Oberemmel
www.weingut-willems.de

Willi Schaefer Mittelmosel

Father-and-son team Willi and Christoph Schaefer make some of the most vibrant, racy, and individual Rieslings on the Mosel. Most of their wines have a generous amount of unfermented grape sweetness, but nowhere in the region is this as discreetly packed into a sleek frame. The wines are hard to come by, however. After years of expansion, the Schafers still have only 10 acres (4ha) in the great sites of Graacher Himmelreich (juicier wines) and Domprobst (the ultimate in minerally brilliance) and there are customers literally lining up for every bottle.

Hauptstrasse 130, 54470 Bernkastel-Graach
06531 8041

The sinuous River Mosel has its sharpest bend at Bremm, between Cochem and Zell, in the Terrassenmosel.

RHEINGAU

Rheingau wine region

No wine region in Germany is so richly endowed with historical monuments as the Rheingau. Castles and monasteries dating back to the 12th century stud the landscape of the nation's most famous wine-producing area. In their cellars lie dusty bottles of historic vintages going back to the 19th century. However, for many years, this sense of history, and the aura of aristocracy, hobbled the region's development. Although the Rheingau is only bordered by the waters of the Rhine on two sides—its long southerly flank and its short western side—it seemed as if it were an island whose inhabitants lived in glorious isolation as wine-growers in "humble" Rheinhessen on the opposite bank of the Rhine passed them on the inside lane.

Major grapes
🍇 **Reds**
Spätburgunder (Pinot Noir)
🍇 **Whites**
Riesling

Vintages
2009
An excellent vintage—wines with ripeness and healthy acidity, although problems with downy mildew and drought stress affected yields.

2008
Rüdesheim was the star of an unexpectedly great vintage of super-minerally Rieslings.

2007
The late-picked wines are racy and "classic," if seldom mind-blowing. The Spätburgunder reds are the best to date.

2006
Many of the dry Rieslings are overblown, but some sweet Rieslings are spectacular.

2005
A vintage in which richness and harmony are often perfectly balanced—the best wines recall the great 1949s.

2004
The Rieslings are sleek but substantial; some of the Spätburgunders are even better than that.

The times they are finally a-changin' in the 7,650 acre (3,100ha) Rheingau due to a group of radical independent winemakers and the dynamic new directors at several of the historic estates. The prime focus of their interest remains Riesling, which accounts for almost 80% of the region's vineyards, but red wine made from Spätburgunder (Pinot Noir) has become a new obsession. A handful of winemakers are now pulling out all the stops—from very low yields to two years in barrique—to make deeply colored, richly textured, and concentrated reds.

During the 1980s, many of the region's leading producers gathered under the banner of Charta, an association formed to proclaim the gospel of dry Riesling. For a while, this worthy attempt to reanimate the region's prime wine tradition seemed to be working. Then, during the 1990s, the campaign came unstuck and the region's wines drifted into a plump and kitschy mode.

This spell of ill-focus was brought to an end by the creativity of the leading independent winemakers, who proved that dry Rheingau Rieslings could be harmonious, full of character, and moderate in alcoholic content. A broader reorientation of the region followed and continues to this day. Its fundamental principle is the re-establishment of a regional wine profile that reflects the special situation of this strip of gently undulating vineyards sandwiched between the Rhine and the Taunus Mountains.

Rheingau Rieslings are generally less aromatic and playfully fruity than their cousins from the Mosel, tending instead toward a certain earthy robustness lifted by an animating acidity. Today, the majority of them are dry or just off-dry, the better wines often sold under the Erstes Gewächs designation, which translates as "First Growth" and which is equivalent to the Grosses Gewächs, or "Great Growth," designation for wines from classified vineyards used elsewhere in Germany. It is in these styles that the region shines brightest. The best examples are dramatic and refined wines in which strength of expression and elegant harmony are beautifully matched. Their full aging potential is as yet unproven, but dry Rheingau wines going back to the end of the 19th century can still impress. Here, history has almost turned full circle.

The remaining problem for the Rheingau is the stream of potential customers who drive into the region from the Rhine-Main conurbation at weekends and on vacations. There are some very pleasant rustic wine restaurants catering to this market, but in such establishments it is also possible to find cheap, poor quality wine that does the region's good name no favors. The problem is that these lesser wines sell, making it possible for producers in a significant part of the Rheingau to ignore the Riesling renaissance happening around them.

The picturesque wine region of Hessische Bergstrasse to the southeast of the Rheingau is Germany's smallest with just 1,077 acres (435ha) of vineyards. Most of the production here is consumed by tourists to a region renowned for being the place where spring blossoms first in Germany.

August Kesseler

For 20 years, August Kesseler and his winemaker Matthias Himstedt have worked to grow world-class Spätburgunder on the slate soil of Assmannshausen's steep Höllenberg site, and since 2003 they have repeatedly succeeded. Old vines, low yields, long macerations, and two years' aging before release result in high-priced wines with an intense blackcurrant and violet perfume, and a breathtaking balance of richness and tannic power. The sleek, racy Rieslings from Lorch and Rüdesheim are thankfully less expensive.

Lorcher Strasse 16, 65385 Assmannshausen
www.august-kesseler.de

J B Becker

Hajo Becker makes traditional dry Rieslings that spend a full year in large wooden casks before bottling. Becker and his sister Maria are anything but old-fashioned though, being the first producers in Germany to use glass closures in place of cork. Their concentrated, but seldom heavy, wines are released late as they need a long time to reach optimum harmony. Substantial stocks of older vintages show just how well these "real" Rieslings can age. Becker also makes elegant unoaked Spätburgunders.

Rheinstrasse 6, 65396 Walluf
06123 72523

Chat Sauvage

Since 2000, Hamburg businessman Günter Schulz and winemaker Michael Städter have created a unique Rheingau winery in Chat Sauvage. Almost totally focused on Spätburgunder, the team produce some of the best red wines in the Rheingau. Most impressive are the two Erste Gewächse: the plush, velvety Assmannshausen Höllenberg and the intensely fragrant, racy Lorcher Kapellenberg. A good dry Pinot Noir rosé and a barrel-fermented Chardonnay also impress. ★ **Rising star**

Grund 65, 65366 Johannisberg
www.chat-sauvage.de

Eva Fricke

With the 2006 vintage, Eva Fricke from Bremen in the north of Germany launched her miniature winery specializing in "Bladerunner" Rieslings from ancient vines in Lorch. It is hard to imagine how Riesling could get more minerally than her dry wine from the Krone site with its diamondlike brilliance, but even her regular Lorcher Riesling is super-racy. ★ **Rising star**

Suttonstrasse 14, D 65399 Kiedrich
www.evafricke.com

Flick

The energetic Reiner Flick built up his 36 acre (15ha) estate in the least-known corner of the Rheingau from scratch, concentrating on excellent, fruit-driven dry Rieslings, powerful Spätburgunders, and the region's best Sauvignon Blanc. Some of his most striking wines, such as the racy and juicy F. Vini et Vita, are absurdly low in price. However, at the top end—the single-vineyard Erste Gewächse Rieslings from the Mönchsgewann and Nonnberg sites—there are no bargains. ★ **Rising star**

Strassenmühle, 65439 Flörsheim-Wicker
www.flick-wein.de

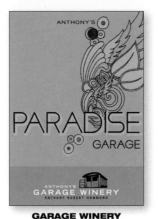

GARAGE WINERY
A HEAVENLY HALF-DRY SCHEUREBE WITH
AN UNCONVENTIONAL LABEL

GEORG BREUER
A SLEEK, ELEGANT, LONG-LIVING RIESLING
FROM RÜDESHEIM

Franz Künstler

A tour of California in 1988 inspired Gunter Künstler to crank up the ripeness of his grapes to create a uniquely sleek, yet powerful, style of dry Riesling, packed with fruit and minerals. His wines, particularly those from the top sites of Hochheim, the Domdechaney (broad and earthy), Kirchenstück (elegant and subtle), and the Hölle (an apricot note, power, and extraordinary freshness, even after 20 years), are unmatched anywhere on the Rhine. The Spätburgunders are also powerful, with a firm tannic core that means they need time in the bottle to shine.

Geheimrat-Hummel-Platz 1a, 65239 Hochheim am Main
www.weingut-kuenstler.de

Friedrich Altenkirch

Since the Japanese winemaker Tomoko Kuriyama took over with the 2007 vintage, Friedrich Altenkirch, a little-known producer in one of the Rheingau's least-known communes, has rapidly risen in importance. Kuriyama matches the steely acidity typical of Lorch with enough ripe citrusy aromas, minerals, and body to create dry and feinherb wines that are dramatic and elegant. The most complex are those from old vines in the Bodenthal-Steinberg site. ★ **Rising star**

Binger Weg 2, 65391 Lorch
www.weingut-altenkirch.de

Fürst Löwenstein

Although the grapes of the 50 acre (20ha) Fürst Löwenstein estate are trucked to the owner's estate in Kreuzwertheim/Franken to be pressed and vinified, the results have been consistently impressive since the beginning of the 21st century. The focus is racy, dry, and off-dry Rieslings. Late harvesting is used to balance the acidity typical of (high-altitude) Hallgarten and sometimes results in 13% alcohol or more. The rich and fragrant Frühburgunder and Spätburgunder red wines are the best in the central area of the region.

Niedertwaldstrasse 8, 65375 Hallgarten
www.loewenstein.de

Garage Winery

With his ponytail and off-the-wall manner, American Anthony Hammond is one of the least conventional wine-growers in Germany, and critics have snubbed him as a result. Following improvements in the improvised cellars in 2008, the whole range impresses, from the dry Auxerrois, with its honey nose and silky texture, to the dry Rieslings, to Wild Thing (semi-dry, funky, complex), and Sugar Babe (succulently sweet). Indications are that Hammond has plenty more up his sleeve. ★ **Rising star**

Friedensplatz 12, D 65375 Oestrich
www.garagewinery.de

Georg Breuer

Following the sudden death of regional quality leader Bernhard Breuer in May 2004, Breuer's daughter, Theresa, a hip young woman light years removed from the stuffy Rheingau norm, successfully leapt into the saddle at the 80 acre (32ha) Georg Breuer estate. With the help of long-time winemaker Hermann Schmoranz, Theresa has maintained the once-revolutionary, now classic, sleek, minerally style her father pioneered. But she has also given the wines more polish and grace. Top

KLOSTER EBERBACH
A TYPICALLY FRUIT-DRIVEN DRY RIESLING
FROM THE STEINBERG SITE

of the single-vineyard hierarchy are the super-elegant and extremely long-living Berg Schlossberg from Rüdesheim, and the more extrovert, citrusy, and juicy Nonnenberg from Rauenthal. The commune-designated wines from these villages are also impressive.

Grabenstrasse 8, 65385 Rüdesheim
www.georg-breuer.com

Graf von Kanitz

Since the arrival of Kurt Gabelmann in 2004, Graf von Kanitz has been back on form. Its hitherto rather light, steely Rieslings have put on a lot of flesh, gaining considerably in alcohol content and exotic fruit aromas without losing their brightness or freshness. The top wines are the dry Erste Gewächse from Pfaffenwies and Kapellenberg. Very solid quality and value for money can be found at the bottom of the range too. **★ Rising star**

Rheinstrasse 49, 65391 Lorch
www.weingut-graf-von-kanitz.de

Hans Lang

Dry wine specialist Hans Lang is no Riesling mono-tasker, having also long made a rare oak-aged Weissburgunder in the Rheingau. There is nothing spectacular about his wines, their strength lying in harmony and consistency. Top of the range is the elegant, dry Erstes Gewächs from Hattenheimer Wisselbrunnen with its delicately spicy finish. **★ Rising star**

Rheinallee 6, 65347 Eltville-Hattenheim
www.weingut-hans-lang.de

Jakob Jung

After graduating from the Geisenheim wine school, Alexander Johannes Jung fell straight into making wines for Jakob Jung in the 2006 "harvest from hell." Jung not only came through this baptism of fire unscathed, but garnered ample praise for his first wines. Since then, he has done much to improve consistency at this 25 acre (10ha) estate, whose best dry and off-dry wines were always ripe, fleshy, and generous. The powerful and moderately tannic Alexander Johannes Spätburgunder red is also impressive. **★ Rising star**

Eberbacher Strasse 22 65346, Erbach
www.weingut-jakob-jung.de

Johannishof

At the 44 acre (18ha) Johannishof estate, Johannes Eser makes a wide range of dry, off dry, and nobly sweet Riesling from the top vineyards of the Rüdesheimer Berg (full and supple) and Johannisberg (sleek and racy), all of which share the same vibrancy, clarity, and aromatic charm. Aside from a few minor modernizations, such as the introduction of several dry, single-vineyard Erste Gewächse, Eser carries on the work of his father, Hans Hermann. The sweet Spätlese and the higher Prädikat dessert wines can live for decades.

Grund 63, 65366 Johannisberg
www.weingut-johannishof.de

Josef Leitz

In a decade, the Leitz estate grew from a small family operation to a 80 acre (32ha) property that also buys in a significant amount of grapes. The astonishing thing is

ROBERT WEIL
LUSCIOUS RIESLING FROM THE RHEINGAU'S
LEADING DESSERT WINE PRODUCER

that the quality of almost all the wines seemed to grow with the scale of production. The Riesling wines divide into two families: the dry (even the feinherb wines are distinctly dry) and the forthrightly sweet. The enormous minerality and perfect balance of both "families" from the top sites of the Rüdesheimer Berg place them among the most sophisticated wines on the Rhine. The dry Magic Mountain offers something close for half the price.

Theodor-Heuss-Strasse 5, 65385 Rüdesheim
www.leitz-wein.de

Kloster Eberbach

The gigantic (in the German context), state-owned Kloster Eberbach winery recently moved its cellars to a largely subterranean high-tech facility next to its monopole Steinberg vineyard site, but is still based in the medieval monastery of Kloster Eberbach made famous by the film *The Name of the Rose*. The change has greatly improved the wines. Since 2008, they have been much livelier, more fruit-driven, and consistent. The estate has many top sites including majority ownership in the famous Rauenthaler Baiken, as well as large holdings in Assmannshausen planted exclusively with Spätburgunder. The impressive top reds are vinified separately in Assmannshausen.

Kloster Eberbach, 56346 Eltville
www.weingut-kloster-eberbach.de

Langwerth von Simmern

From the 1950s until the 1980s, Langwerth von Simmern was one of the great aristocratic estates of the Rheingau, but like so many others it faltered thereafter. In recent years, thanks to Georg-Reinhard Freiherr Langwerth von Simmern and his dynamic wife, Andrea, great strides have been made in getting the 75 acre (30ha) estate back on track. The dry and sweet Kabinett and Spätlese wines may never win top prizes for power and concentration, but their delicacy and refinement are noteworthy and befit the history of this estate. The most impressive wine is arguably the super-elegant, subtly spicy dry Riesling Erstes Gewächs from the Hattenheimer Mannberg site.

Kirchgasse 6, 65343 Eltville
www.langwerth-von-simmern.de

Peter Jakob Kühn

Peter Jakob Kühn's biodynamic dry Rieslings are the most extreme and controversial wines in the Rheingau. Even the simplest, Jacobus, has a tannin content (from long skin contact) that is shocking at first, even though it is married with ripe pear and citrus aromas. The name of the Quarzit dry Riesling accurately reflects its minerally, steely style; a wine with enormous character. The single-vineyard Rieslings from the Mittelheimer St Nikolaus and Oestircher Doosberg sites ferment on the skins for several weeks like red wines. The generous tannin and power do not obscure the opulence of the former and the elegance of the latter. **★ Rising star**

Mühlstrasse 70, 65375 Oestrich
www.weingutpjkuehn.de

Prinz

After long stints with Georg Breuer and the Rheingau's State Domaine, Fred Prinz dramatically expanded his tiny family winery in order to go solo. Given the weak reputation of Hallgarten this was a brave thing to do, but Prinz quickly proved this commune can produce Rheingau Rieslings of the highest quality. The high natural acidity (due to the high altitude) gives the dry and sweet wines alike a racy brilliance that is quite breathtaking. In 2008, Prinz introduced a dramatic, intensely mineral dry Riesling from Hendelberg that matches his more supple and fleshy Erstes Gewächs from the Schönhell site. Look out for the super-concentrated sweet Riesling Spältese Gold Cap. ★ **Rising star**

Im Flachsgarten 5, 65375 Hallgarten
06723 999847

Prinz von Hessen

The 80 acre (32ha) Prinz von Hessen estate was a sleeping dinosaur until director and winemaker Dr. Clemens Kiefer arrived. He still has some way to go, but his modernizations have so far resulted in more fruit-driven, harmonious wines. He has, however, retained the small range of very good Riesling dessert wines from the previous regime.

Johannisberg im Rheingau, Grund 1, 65366 Johannisberg
www.prinz-von-hessen.de

Querbach

Peter Querbach is no glory hunter, preferring to concentrate on making the best possible wine. During a period when his contemporaries were experimenting wildly, he stuck to a conservative style of dry Riesling with moderate alcohol, fresh, but not dominant, acidity, and discrete fruit aromas. Unspectacular in their youth, his wines develop beautifully in the bottle. ★ **Rising star**

Lenchenstrasse 19, 65375 Oestrich-Winkel
www.querbach.com

Robert Weil

No producer more perfectly embodies the modern Rheingau than the 180 acre (73ha) Robert Weil estate owned by Suntory and Wilhelm Weil. The expensive Auslese, BA, and TBA wines are renowned as the ultimate in Rheingau dessert wine extravagance. In recent years, enormous effort has gone into the single-vineyard dry Rieslings from Kiedrich: the wines from the Gräfenberg site are exotically perfumed, those from the Turmberg and Klosterberg sites come in a sleeker, racier style resulting from their high altitude. Several hundred thousand bottles of the regular dry Riesling are also produced. Ripe and fresh as it is, you pay for the name.

Mühlberg 5, 65399 Kiedrich
www.weingut-robert-weil.com

Schloss Johannisberg

Founded around AD 1100 as a Benedictine monastery, Schloss Johannisberg can claim to be the birthplace of modern German Riesling, with vines planted in 1720. The wines lacked excitement for a couple of recent decades, but since 2006, director Christian Witte has made wines of elegance and individuality. Today, the dry Rieslings are as good as the traditional sweet ones (whose history here goes back to the first German Spätlese in 1775). Witte also directs the much bigger, if not quite so exciting, G H von Mumm estate, with Riesling planted close to the schloss plus Spätburgunder grown in Assmannshausen.

Schloss Johannisberg, 65366 Johannisberg
www.schloss-johannisberg.de

Schloss Schönborn

The rich, concentrated, dry Riesling Erstes Gewächs or sweet Riesling Spätlese from Schloss Schönborn's top sites (most importantly Erbacher Marcobrunn and its monopole Hattenheimer Pfaffenberg) are among the best in the Rheingau. In the lower realms of the Schönborn range, however, quality is something of a lottery.

Hautpstrasse 53, 65347 Hattenheim
www.schoenborn.de

Schloss Vollrads

Under the direction of Rowald Hepp, the famous Schloss Vollrads has become one of the most consistent of the larger Rheingau producers. That it manages to produce and sell 500,000 bottles of good-to-excellent quality Riesling each year is an achievement some competitors could learn from. The dry wines have always been sleek, with pronounced acidity, but in recent years, they have become juicier and more aromatic. Top of the range are the dry Erstes Gewächs (more restrained and refreshing than many) and the vibrant, honey-sweet Auslese.

Vollradser Allee, 65375 Winkel
www.schlossvollrads.de

Schön

If Klaus Schön was not located so far off the beaten track, high in the hills above Rüdesheim, he would be far better known. His mid-weight, elegant dry Rieslings are all of high quality and his Spätburgunders from the Rüdesheimer Berg Schlossberg site are arguably the richest and most opulent in the region. The estate's wine bar is rustic, but often full of people attracted to this source of fine value in an expensive region. ★ **Rising star**

Hauptstrasse 80, D 65385 Aulhausen
www.weingut-schoen.de

Spreitzer

The Spreitzer brothers, Bernd and Andreas, are two of the most talented young winemakers in the Rheingau. When much of the region was trying to imitate the opulent dry wines from further south, they reinvented the traditional crisp, lighter style of dry and off-dry Rheingau wine, adding a bright citrus touch while keeping the alcohol content to 11.5%. The brothers also make complex, concentrated dry Riesling Erstes Gewächs from Oestricher Lenchen and Hattenheimer Wisselbrunnen, plus spectacularly juicy sweet Riesling Spätlese. Prices are moderate for the Rheingau. ★ **Rising star**

Rheingaustrasse 86, 65375 Oestrich
www.weingut-spreitzer.de

Wegeler

Wegeler, once known as Wegeler-Deinhard, has been transformed in the past decade by the ambitious Dr. Tom Drieseberg, with the dry and sweet Rieslings becoming more polished and fragrant. Of the dry wines, the racy, juicy *cuvée* Geheimrat J is joined by the more powerful Erstes Gewächs from the Rüdesheimer Berg Schlossberg and Winkeler Jesuitengarten sites. Eiswein remains a specialty; Spätburgunder reds have been added through part-ownership of the Krone estate in Assmannshausen.

Friedensplatz 9-11, 65375 Oestrich
www.wegeler.com

WINE HISTORY

THE REVIVAL OF SCHLOSS JOHANNISBERG

Schloss Johannisberg claims to have planted the first Riesling monoculture back in 1720, and although this is contested, the estate undeniably produced the first documented botrytis wines in Germany in 1775. From Goethe's time up to the 1971 vintage, Schloss Johannisberg was not only a German wine legend, but also one of the world's greatest producers of sweet white wine. However, changes to the way the estate was run hit the quality and character of the wines; suddenly it looked like an historic monument, quietly gathering dust. Then the dashing Christian Witte was made director, and since 2006 the wines have been back on top form. Better than that, Witte has also put the estate on the map as one of Germany's best dry Riesling producers. Whether these new wines can match those of the region's most dynamic new producers, such as Flick, Leitz, Spreitze, or Eva Fricke, is a question that only time can answer.

Some of the Nahe's greatest vineyards—Hermannsberg, Brücke, and Kupfergrube—lie on this stretch of the river.

NAHE

Traditionally, the wines from the valley of the River Nahe, an important tributary of the Rhine, were described as being between those of the Mosel and the Rheingau in type. That characterization could be taken as recognition of the fact that this dramatic and beautiful region long lacked a distinct identity of its own. And it has to be said that there is some truth in it—although wine has been grown in the Nahe since Roman times, the borders of the wine-growing region were only finally delineated in 1971. Recent years, however, have seen a dramatic rise in the region's renown due to the excellent quality of its best white wines, which today enjoy demand that far exceeds their limited production.

The international excitement generated by the region's top dry and naturally sweet Rieslings is the main reason for the region's changed image. Try one of these intensely mineral wines and you might well feel that you can literally taste the dramatic contours of massive red volcanic cliffs and precipitous vineyards. However, that is only one side of this 10,200 acre (4,100ha) region, where the wide range of wines reflects a handful of major grape varieties, as well as considerable geological complexity.

Far more than on the Mosel, the upturn in the Nahe has been accompanied by a dramatic shift in the ownership of the most famous vineyards. Here, Jungwinzer (young winemakers) have often had the chance to show what they can do very early in their careers and invariably they have eagerly grasped it. Like their colleagues in Rheinhessen to the east, they have also worked hard to realize the full potential of good vineyard sites that had been forgotten. Today, high quality wines are being produced in every part of the region, including the valleys of the Alsenz, Glan, and Guldenbach.

Another important aspect of the recent positive development was a communal drive to lift the quality of the dry whites made from the Weissburgunder (Pinot Blanc) and Grauburgunder (Pinot Gris) grapes up to the same level as the best dry Rieslings. A variety of styles from the Burgundy-inspired use of new oak to sleek, aromatic, unoaked wines, can be found even within a single wine-growing village. Although this is still a work-in-progress, already some of the best German wines from these grapes grow on the Nahe. They combine restrained power with bright fruit aromas and a refreshing but moderate acidity.

At the same time, there has also been a good deal of experimentation in the vinification of dry Riesling wines, most notably through long skin-contact before pressing and long lees contact after fermentation. The goal of these methods was to muscle up the wines so they could better stand comparison with dry wines from further south. However, global warming has already given the wines significantly more alcohol and weight, and some of these experiments went too far. Thankfully, the obsession with living up to the wines of other regions is becoming a thing of the past. In a comparable way, the days of Riesling Spätlese and Auslese wines with excessive sweetness, retained in order to garner high scores from the critics, are also passing. In short, the region is maturing.

That this development has come rather late is one reason why the Nahe is not more widely known, the other is that it has been short of charismatic winemakers who are compelling ambassadors for their region and fluent in English. But that too is changing fast. The beauty of many of the Nahe's landscapes has always been under-appreciated and even today, tourists are inexplicably few and far between.

Major grapes

Reds
Dornfelder
Spätburgunder (Pinot Noir)

Whites
Grauburgunder (Pinot Gris)
Müller-Thurgau
Riesling
Weissburgunder (Pinot Blanc)

Vintages

2009
An excellent vintage with high ripeness and acidity levels below those of 2008.

2008
The best dry and sweet wines combined staggering aromatic intensity with racy brilliance.

2007
A very good vintage of beautifully balanced wines. The best dry Weissburgunders sometimes match the top dry Rieslings.

2006
This was a much less problematic vintage here than in most German regions, with some sensational Rieslings.

2005
Another excellent vintage with ripeness and elegance across the board.

2004
High acidity levels sometimes make the wines a little one-sided, but the best are sleek and minerally.

VON RACKNITZ
RICHLY TEXTURED AND INTENSELY
SPICY RIESLINGS

DONNHOFF
EXTREME ELEGANCE IS COMPLEMENTED
BY AN UNDERPLAYED STRENGTH

Bürgermeister Willi Schweinhardt

When he inherited his family's 80 acre (32ha) wine estate, Axel Schweinhardt also inherited a succulent style of dry, off-dry, and sweet Rieslings. In recent years, Schweinhardt has successfully refined this further, adding some impressive dry Weissburgunders. The top dry Riesling takes its name from the "Terrasse" of the Langenlonsheimer Rothenberg site.

Heddesheimer Strasse 1, 55450 Langenlonsheim
www.schweinhardt.de

Crusius

For some years, this famous estate struggled to live up to its reputation, but since the turn of the century, Dr. Peter Crusius has put it back on top. All the wines have a wonderful crystalline clarity, with a delicate interplay of fruit and minerally acidity, the finest of them being from the Schlossböckelheimer Felsenberg and Traiser Rotenfels sites. Roman numerals indicate the sweetness (in grams per liter) on the labels of some wines. At Crusius, as much as "XV" still tastes dry.

Hauptstrasse 2, 55595 Traisen
www.weingut-crusius.de

Dönnhoff

Helmut Dönnhoff has been the quality leader on the Nahe for the past 20 years, but as the man himself would point out, his achievement lies far more in the production of Rieslings in which extreme elegance is married with an underplayed strength. This style finds its fullest expression in Dönnhoff's dry Grosses Gewächs and sweet Spätlese from the great Niederhäuser Hermannshöhle and Norheimer Dellchen sites. However, even the smallest wine here possesses all the Dönnhoff virtues to a significant degree: these are unique wines.

Bahnhofstrasse 11, 55585 Oberhausen
www.doennhoff.com

Emrich-Schönleber

The father-and-son team of Werner and Frank Schönleber at Emrich-Shönleber make some of the most concentrated, minerally, dry, and sweet Rieslings in all of Germany. Indeed, the question is whether there are any other white wines in the world that could claim to be more minerally than the Schönlebers'. Only the top dry wines (most importantly the sensational Grosse Gewächse) along with the brilliant sweet Spätlese and Auslese, are marketed under the names of the top vineyards of Monzingen, Frühlingsplätzchen, and Halenberg.

Soonwaldstrasse 10a, 55569 Monzingen
www.emrich-schoenleber.de

Gebrüder Kauer

Brothers Christoph and Markus Kauer, who run Gebrüder Kauer, make some of the most vibrant and minerally dry Weissburgunder and Grauburgunder on the Nahe. These, and the Krauers' impressive dry Rieslings, are slow-developing wines that benefit greatly from at least some months of aging as they can sometimes be very closed in both taste and aroma immediately after bottling. ★ **Rising star**

Bürgermeister-Dielhenn-Strasse 1, 55452 Windesheim
www.kauerwein.de

Gutsverwaltung Niederhausen-Schlossböckelheim Nahe

A second change of ownership after the privatization of this once famous state-owned winery has put it in the hands of the businessman Jens Reidel, with young star winemaker Karsten Peter in charge of the cellar. After years of solid and well-made, but not exactly exciting, wines, the new situation seems to finally offer the chance of a return to top form from the 2009 vintage.

Ehemalige Weinbaudomäne, 55585 Niederhausen
www.riesling-domaene.de

Hahnmühle

The Alsenz Valley might have been entirely forgotten were it not for Peter and Martina Linxweiler of Hahnmühle. The wines from their small biodynamic estate have only improved over the past few years, but the Linxweilers have remained true to the sleek and crystalline style they pioneered from the beginning. Aside from the excellent dry Rieslings, also look for the unusually racy dry Silvaner and a virtually unique blend of Riesling and Traminer. ★ **Rising star**

Alsenzstrasse 25, 67822 Mannweiler-Cölln
www.weingut-hahnmuehle.de

Hexamer

Harald Hexamer's only problem is differentiating between the rather large number of different wines he produces from the Meddesheimer Rheingrafenberg site. This means several of his most impressive wines—for example the imposing, but vibrant dry XXL and the succulent off-dry Quarzit—bear unusual names. Here, sweet means full grape sweetness, but the wines have the acidity needed to carry it off. ★ **Rising star**

Sobernheimer Strasse 3, 55566 Meddersheim
www.weingut-hexamer.de

Jakob Schneider

Jakob Schneider has long been the best-known estate in Niederhausen, but for many years, quality was erratic. That changed when Jakob Schneider Jr. completed his studies at the famous Geisenheim wine school, but the improvement in quality has yet to be reflected in the prices. His excellent-value spicy and racy Rieslings, both dry and sweet, come from the top sites of Niederhausen. ★ **Rising star**

Winzerstrasse 15, 55585 Niederhausen
www.schneider-wein.com

Joh. Bapt. Schäfer

Since the turn of the century, Sebastian Schäfer has firmly put the small Joh. Bapt. Schäfer estate firmly on the map with dry and sweet Rieslings that combine raciness with juiciness and almost perfect balance. The vom Kieselstein and vom Schiefergestein dry Rieslings offer excellent value for money. ★ **Rising star**

Burg Layen 8, 55452 Burg Layen
www.jbs-wein.de

Klostermühle

Of the four Berlin lawyers who own the Klostermühle estate in the Glan Valley, Christian Held effectively runs the show. Although good dry Rieslings from the Kloster Disibodenberg site are also produced, the most exciting wines are often the sleek, dry Weissburgunder, Grauburgunder, and Chardonnay, particularly those from the monopole Monfort site. The sparkling versions of each of these wines are also good. ★ **Rising star**

Am Disibodenberg, 55571 Odernheim
www.claretum.de

Korrell/Johanneshof

Martin Korrell of Korrell/Johanneshof is one of the most talented young winemakers along the Rhine and its tributaries. Arguably his most exciting wines are the complex and elegant dry Weissburgunder and Grauburgunder from the excellent but almost unknown Paradies site, which are marketed under the Johannes K name. However, the dry Riesling Goldkapsel bottlings from the In den Felsen and Königsfels sites of Schlossböckelheim also belong in the front rank of Nahe wines. Korrell makes some impressive off-dry and sweet Rieslings too. ★ **Rising star**

Parkstrasse 4, 55545 Bosenheim
www.korrell.com

Kruger-Rumpf

For more than 20 years, Stefan Rumpf has consistently produced dry and sweet Rieslings at Kruger-Rumpf that combine the Nahe virtues of raciness and aromatic richness. Those qualities are particularly evident in the wines from the top sites of Münster, the Dautenpflänzer (more powerful, weighty wines), and Pittersberg (sleek and more piquant wines). Since he joined the business, Rumpf's son Georg has been giving a lot of attention to the rapidly improving Spätburgunder reds.

Rheinstrasse 47, 55424 Münster-Sarmsheim
www.kruger-rumpf.com

Lindenhof/Martin Reimann

Martin Reimann has almost as much Weissburgunder planted in his 25 acres (10ha) of vineyards as he has Riesling, and when you taste his wines, it is not hard to understand why. The cool, windy climate that gives Windesheim its name is ideally suited to those vines. Reimann's talent lies in the way he is able to balance the acidity and freshness of his wines with sufficient ripeness and body to give them an appealing harmony. The dry Rieslings lag slightly behind the Weissburgunder, but the sparkling wines are excellent.

Lindenhof, 55452 Windesheim
www.weingutlindenhof.de

Rudolf Sinss

Since Johannes Sinss began making the wines at Rudolf Sinss along with his father Rudolf in 1997, the quality at this small estate has taken a jump upward. The dry Rieslings from the Sonnenmorgen (more juicy and substantial) and Römerberg (more aromatic and racy), and the dry Weissburgunder and Grauburgunder from the Rosenberg have all improved, and the best bottlings are indicated with an "S." Rudolf Sinss also produces some impressive Spätburgunder reds, and the estate is very much a star in the making. ★ **Rising star**

Hauptstrasse 18, 55452 Windesheim
www.weingut-sinss.de

Schäfer-Fröhlich

Since taking over the winemaking at the Schäfer-Fröhlich estate in 1995, Tim Fröhlich has shown himself to be not only one of the most talented young winemakers in Germany, but also a fanatic for the precise vineyard work that is required to achieve the very best quality. His dry and sweet Rieslings combine considerable power with racy brilliance. Everything with a single-vineyard designation on the label needs some time in bottle, and the wines can age for at least a decade, often more, but Fröhlich's most important vineyard is Bockenauer Felseneck, which was an unknown site until Fröhlich emerged on the scene. ★ **Rising star**

Schulstrasse 6, 55595 Bockenau
www.weingut-schaefer-froehlich.de

Schlossgut Diel

Though the Diel estate continues to be associated with the larger-than-life wine journalist Armin Diel, today it is Armin's daughter, Caroline, who makes the wines. Since taking over, Caroline has given the impressive dry Rieslings, Weissburgunder, and Grauburgunder a new lease of life and elegance. Now those wines frequently match the already well-regarded, succulent, and racy sweet Rieslings from the top sites of Dorsheim, Burgberg, Goldloch, and Pittermännchen. In the German context the Diel wines might appear expensive, within an international context, however, the prices do not seem high in the least.

Burg Layen 16-17, 55452 Burg Layen
www.schlossgut-diel.com

Tesch

Martin Tesch is not just a winemaker, he is a phenomenon, someone who effortlessly bridges the gap (before his appearance on the scene it was a chasm) between rock music and wine. Tesch's bone-dry Riesling, Unplugged, with its whiplash aftertaste, is as much a new classic of German wine as Ramstein is classic Krautrock. His top wines are the color-coded series of dry Rieslings from the Krone (lemon yellow) and Karthäuser (rust red) sites of Laubenheim, and the Königsschild (powder blue), Löhrer Berg (sap green) and St Remigiusberg (orange-red) sites of Langenlonsheim. The taste of each wine is as strikingly different as its looks, but all are uncompromisingly dry. The supple and limpid Deep Blue is a pale, but rich rosé for those seeking something a shade softer. ★ **Rising star**

Naheweinstrasse 99, 55450 Langenlonsheim
www.weingut-tesch.de

Von Racknitz

Since 2003, former financial wizard Matthias Adams von Racknitz and his wife Luise have turned this once-slumbering estate around. Richly textured and intensely spicy Rieslings are the focus of production, but a dry Silvaner in the same vein is also planned. At the top of the von Racknitz internal hierarchy are the single-vineyard bottlings from the Schlossböckelheimer Königsfels, Traiser Rotenfels, and Disibodenberg, all of which are already playing at the top of the premier league of Nahe wines. ★ **Rising star**

Disibodenbergerhof 3, 55571 Odernheim
www.von-racknitz.com

MARTIN TESCH

Plenty of young German winemakers try to bring pop music and wine together, but none has succeeded in the way Martin Tesch has. Tesch's connections—from German punk band Die Toten Hosen to the guitar company Gibson—certainly helped, but these alone would not have been enough to cross the divide between wine and pop culture. Tesch's book, *Riesling People Volume One*, tells the story of how he did it in 200 pages of black and white photos and just two words with a double meaning: "cool climate." His wines are certainly definitive cool climate dry Rieslings, with a pronounced acidity and subtle fruit, herb, and mineral aromas, but he has also made them cool thanks to his use of pop-poetry, pop-imagery, and pop events such as his "Rolling Riesling Show" tour of Germany, which featured Tesch wines and performances by up-and-coming young musicians. He has a great sense of humor, too, as the name of his latest dry Riesling—Kraut Wine—proves. The wine was a big hit with German hip hop and funk singer Jan Delay, and it doesn't get any cooler than that.

AHR AND MITTELRHEIN

Ahr & Mittelrhein wine region

The wines of these two distinct regions could not be more different. The Ahr majors in rich Spätburgunder (Pinot Noir) reds and the Mittelrhein in sleek Riesling whites. All the same, these close neighbors have much in common. Their size, for one thing: the Ahr has only 1,360 acres (550ha) of vineyards, and the Mittelrhein just 1,130 acres (460ha). But they share far more than a position among Germany's smallest wine regions. The common threads linking the two include the slate they share as the dominant soil type; the fact that they are both located in narrow, steep-sided valleys (of the Ahr and Rhine rivers); and the fact that they both lie north of 50° North latitude (as a comparison, most of the Mosel lies south of that line).

Major grapes

 Reds

Frühburgunder

Spätburgunder (Pinot Noir)

Whites

Riesling

Vintages

2009
An excellent vintage for Ahr reds and Mittelrhein Rieslings.

2008
Sleek wines. The Rieslings are sometimes a shade tart, but the best are impressive.

2007
Another excellent vintage, with powerful, balanced Ahr reds and dry and sweet Rieslings in the Mittelrhein.

2006
The great Ahr reds are plush, fragrant, and beautifully balanced. In the Mittelrhein, the sweet Rieslings are often spectacular, but the heavy dry wines seldom impress.

2005
A very good vintage in both regions, in which richness and freshness are well matched.

2004
Lighter wines than the following vintages, but not without charm or elegance.

It would be hard to imagine a more picturesque region than the Ahr, the scenery resembling the Mosel, but on a more intimate scale. The wine industry here is intimate too, which may be construed as a disadvantage, since small wine regions can easily find themselves lost in cosmopolitan wine markets such as Germany's. In fact, the Ahr is almost too successful. This is partly explained by its proximity to the Cologne-Bonn conurbation, whose inhabitants constitute an enthusiastic local market. But the dramatic improvement in red wine vinification that began in the late 1980s has been just as significant. Today, 13–14% natural alcoholic content, generous tannins, and vanilla and toast aromas from maturation in new wood are normal for the region's reds. Thanks to an exceptional climatic situation and some ambitious winemakers, the best of these, despite the northerly location, are every bit as concentrated as those from further south, but more aromatic. Most are Spätburgunder (Pinot Noir), but an important regional specialty, with close to 100 acres (40ha), is Frühburgunder, an early-ripening mutation of Spätburgunder with exotic aromas, full body, and velvety tannins.

The Mittelrhein is the romantic Rhine of the Lorelei, Heinrich Heine, and J M W Turner, with dramatic castles, cliffs, and precipitous vineyards. The region's wine industry came badly unstuck during the 1990s, however, when too many of the wine-growers focused on producing bulk wines for cheap sparkling wine. The region's steep slopes made the economics of this shaky at the best of times, then the sparkling wine industry switched to cheaper sources, leaving the Mittelrhein high and dry. The vineyard area then shrank rapidly.

Thankfully, at this time several independent-minded winemakers demonstrated that the combination of slate with Riesling—a comparative newcomer here, having been virtually unknown just a century ago—can be as magical in the Mittelrhein as in the Mosel. The conferring of UNESCO World Heritage status in 2002 gave the region a new impetus, underlining the reorientation to quality. Because the Mittelrhein lacks the reputation of its neighbors, prices remain modest and the best wines look like a steal. One could not say the same about the Ahr reds, however, as the intense local demand pushes the prices high.

The one question mark that hangs over the future of these regions is the increased drought-stress that global warming is expected to bring to the vineyards with the stoniest soils. This would promote tannin production by the vines, a development that could benefit red wines, but would have an undesirable effect on white wines, particularly Riesling. With 67% Riesling, the Mittelrhein in particular looks at risk, and large-scale irrigation will surely become necessary there. The Rhine might seem to offer a ready source of water, but there may be obstacles preventing its use in this way, namely its purity and the question of having the rights to the water.

J J Adenauer Ahr

The Spätburgunder red wines from brothers Frank and Marc Adenauer often weigh in with 14% natural alcohol or more and see plenty of new oak during their maturation. But somehow they always remain elegant and fine, with a wonderful purity of fruit aroma. Top of the range is the Grosses Gewächs from the monopole Walporzheimer Gärkammer site from 70-year-old vines. The regular bottlings are also impressive.

Max-Planck-Strasse 8, 53474 Ahrweiler
www.adeneuer.de

Deutzerhof/Cossmann-Hehle Ahr

Wolfgang Hehle has never been afraid to give the red wines of Deutzerhof/Cossmann-Hehle plenty of oak aroma and tannin, and as they have gained in stature, so has their ability to carry the oak successfully. Hehle's wines may have slightly ridiculous names, such as Grand Duc (a Spätburgunder) and Alpha & Omega (a Frühburgunder), but that does not alter the fact that they are among the best on the Ahr. The portfolio also includes one of the best reds made from the German crossing Dornfelder.

Deutzerwiese 2, 53508 Mayschoss
www.deutzerhof.de

Dr. Randolf Kauer Mittelrhein

This tiny estate is one of the pioneers of organic viticulture in Germany, a subject that Randolf Kauer also teaches at the famous Geisenheim wine school. The emphasis here is firmly on dry and off-dry Rieslings, which are invariably sleek and mineral with a crystalline purity and excellent aging potential.

Mainzer Strasse 21, 55422 Bacharach
www.weingut-dr-kauer.de

Jean Stodden Ahr

While many of his peers are obsessed by the pursuit of silkiness and delicacy in their Spätburgunders, Gerhard Stodden of Jean Stodden has a completely different vision. In recent years, along with son Alexander, he has developed an uncompromising style of concentrated, tannic, and slow-developing Pinot Noir that is unique in the region. All this means high prices even within the expensive Ahr context.

Rotweinstrasse 7–9, 53506 Rech
www.stodden.de

Matthias Müller Mittelrhein

The 30 acre (12ha) Matthias Müller estate is currently the shooting star of the Mittelrhein thanks to its wide range of dry, off-dry, and sweet Rieslings from the top sites of the Bopparder Ham, an amphitheater of steep slopes just south of Koblenz. Müller's wines combine juiciness, minerality, and racy brilliance, and are great value.

Mainzer Strasse 45, 56322 Spay
www.weingut-matthiasmueller.de

Meyer-Näkel Ahr

Nobody on the Ahr has been making top class Spätburgunder reds longer than Meyer-Näkel, but even this estate only began in the early 1990s. Since 2005, Werner Näkel has been assisted in the cellar by his daughter Meike, which has further improved consistency.

MEYER-NAKEL
A CONSISTENTLY COMPLEX, YET REFINED
SPATBURGUNDER FROM A TOP PRODUCER

JEAN STODDEN
THIS SLOW-DEVELOPING PINOT NOIR STANDS
APART FROM THE REST OF THE AHR

Yields as low as at the top producers in Burgundy and minimalistic winemaking are the secrets behind the four Grosse Gewächse (three Spätburgunders and a Frühburgunder), which are arguably the most refined and complex wines produced in the region. An excellent Spätburgunder Blanc de Noirs, Illusion, is also produced.

Friedenstrasse 15, 53507 Dernau
www.meyer-naekel.de

Nelles Ahr

Do not be deceived by the name "B 52" on the label of Thomas Nelles' top Spätburgunder red wine; this is not a reference to the American bomber. However, Nelles' wines certainly pack a considerable punch, never being short of fruit, tannin, or oak aromas. ★Rising star

Göppinger Strasse 13a, 53474 Heimersheim
www.weingut-nelles.de

Ratzenberger Mittelrhein

For decades, the 35 acre (14ha) Ratzenberger estate has remained true to a sleek and racy style of Riesling, spanning the spectrum from bone dry to lusciously sweet. However, Jochen Ratzenberger, Jr. has also added a number of new wines to the range, most importantly the stunning dry Riesling Grosses Gewächs from the Bacharacher Wolfshöhle and Steeger St Jost sites. Ratzenberger also produces some good sparkling wines.

Blücherstrasse 167, 55422 Bacharach
www.weingut-ratzenberger.de

Selt Mittelrhein

Leutesdorf, in the far north of the Mittelrhein, used to be known only to locals, but Horst Peter Selt's intensely mineral, dry and off-dry Rieslings prove the village is more than a backwater. Recently, Selt has abandoned the use of vineyard site names in favor of labels that reflect the soil type, for example Goldschieder, or "golden slate."

Zehnthofstrasse 22, 56599 Leutesdorf
www.weingutselt.de

Toni Jost Mittelrhein

Toni and Linde Jost have produced the most consistently impressive dry and sweet Rieslings in the Mittelrhein for more than 20 years. The wines from the great Hahn site are usually the most impressive, with a lush peach bouquet and exceptional ripeness, but the dry Riesling Devon S is very good value, as are the impressive Rieslings from the Josts' vineyards in Walluf/Rheingau.

Oberstrasse 14, 55422 Bacharach
www.tonijost.de

Weingart Mittelrhein

During the last decade, Florian Weingart has done more than anyone else to breathe new life into the Mittelrhein and its wines. In many ways, his most impressive wine is the regular dry Riesling, a wine packed with fruit and freshness and sensational value for money. However, you could say the same for his excellent Kabinett and Spätlese or the BAs and TBAs. Indeed, every Weingart wine displays exemplary ripeness, clarity, and harmony.

Mainzer Strasse 32, 56322 Spay
www.weingut-weingart.de

RHEINHESSEN

How can a wine region of more than 65,000 acres (26,000ha) make a 180-degree turn in just a few years? That is exactly what Germany's largest wine-growing region, Rheinhessen, did. If you do not live in Germany, then it is quite possible that you have never read this region's name before, but domestically it is the new star of German wine. The success is based almost entirely upon dry wines (white, red, and rosé) and many of them are exciting and innovative. Yet only 20 years ago, Rheinhessen was the largest source of Liebfraumilch, the cheap and sweet blended white sold only in export markets, often under brand names, and with packaging that emphasized the product's inherently nostalgic personality.

Major grapes

🍇 Reds
Dornfelder

Frühburgunder

Portugieser

Spätburgunder (Pinot Noir)

St Laurent

🍇 Whites
Grauburgunder (Pinot Gris)

Huxelrebe

Riesling

Scheurebe

Silvaner

Weissburgunder (Pinot Blanc)

Vintages

2009
A very successful vintage of ripe but fresh wines.

2008
The wines are not as opulent as in previous years.

2007
The late-picked top wines are rich but lively and the reds are excellent.

2006
The dry wines tend to be pretty massive. Only the best of them will age gracefully.

2005
The dry wines are creamy, the sweet Rieslings succulent, all with great aging potential.

2004
A vintage of balanced, crisp, lively, medium-bodied wines.

Back in the early 1990s, things were going so badly wrong for Rheinhessen that the producers of Riesling wines on the region's eastern border—where the steep vineyards of Nierstein, Nackenheim, and Oppenheim lie directly on the banks of the Rhine—found it extremely difficult to sell their wines, however good they were, simply because the region's name was on the label. Experts looked down their noses at the vineyards in the Hügelland (hill country), which makes up most of the region, since that was where the base wines for Liebfraumilch were grown.

Recent years, however, have seen the Rheinhessische Jungwinzer (Young Winemakers of Rheinhessen) prove those experts wrong by uncovering the enormous forgotten potential of the Hügelland for quality wine production. This process only began in earnest at the end of the 1990s, but the geological diversity of the Rheinhessen—which includes loess, limestone, sandstone, porphyry, and quartzite—was rapidly rediscovered while the standard of wine-growing took a quantum leap upward.

The Rheinhessen's Liebfraumlich generation were actually wine farmers, since they usually sold everything off in bulk as soon as possible after the harvest. They had little interest in their region's history, but their children now scour old vineyard maps and wine books for information about past wine glories with the goal of reviving them. As a result, communes and vineyard sites famous a century ago, such as Siefersheim in the far west

and the Morstein site of Westhofen in the southeast, are becoming well known again.

Within a couple of miles of one another it is possible to find ideal terroirs for Riesling, Weissburgunder (Pinot Blanc), Grauburgunder (Pinot Gris), and Spätburgunder (Pinot Noir), along with the regional specialty Silvaner (planted on 6,150 acres/2,500ha), and the aromatic Scheurebe and Huxelrebe. Rheinhessen has become a region of boutique wineries, each offering a range of highly individual products.

The quality competition is both more intense and friendlier here than anywhere else in Germany due to the extreme openness of the Jungwinzer. This has enabled the emergence of new wine types such as the dry white Scheurebe, with its aromatic spectrum reminiscent of Sauvignon Blanc (indeed, it is widely referred to in the Rheinhessen as "our Sauvignon Blanc"). Progress with Spätburgunder reds has also been dramatic, despite the grape having almost no tradition here (in contrast to the red Portugieser, Frühburgunder, and St Laurent varieties that are currently enjoying a renaissance).

Impressive as these achievements are, however, there is still a way to go. If you divide the number of really good Rheinhessen producers by the total vineyard area and then compare that figure with, for example, the Mosel, you will find that the density of exciting winemakers is still low. If Rheinhessen is to become cool beyond Germany's borders, then the process of reinvention must continue for many more years to come.

Battenfeld-Spanier

In astonishingly few years, Hans Oliver Spanier has built his 60 acre (24ha) Battenfeld-Spanier biodynamic estate into a producer of some of the most strikingly original wines in Rheinhessen. The young innovator's powerful, concentrated, spicy dry Rieslings hail from vineyard sites such as the Kirchenstück of Hohen-Sülzen and the Frauenberg of Nieder-Flörsheim that were forgotten until he began to realize their potential. The top wines are fermented and matured in neutral oak. ★ **Rising star**

67591 Hohen-Sülzen
www.battenfeld-spanier.de

Becker-Landgraf

Julia and Johannes Landgraf have only been making wine together since 2005, but their wines at Becker-Landgraf include arguably the finest Spätburgunder in Rheinhessen. The emphasis is on silkiness of texture, fine fruit aromas, and discreet oak. The dry Riesling and Weissburgunder do not quite match this elegance, but have plenty of fruit and substance. ★ **Rising star**

Im Felsenkeller 1, 55239 Gau-Odernheim
www.weingut-beckerlandgraf.de

Brüder Dr. Becker

On paper, the top wines of Brüder Dr. Becker (which has been organic since the early 1970s) are Lotte Pfeffer's dry Riesling Grosse Gewächse from the Falkenberg and Tafelstein sites of Ludwigshöhe. But the much cheaper dry Silvaner is one of the finest in the region, while the elegant dry Weissburgunder and the juicy sweet Scheurebe are both important specialties.

Mainzer Strasse 3–7, 55278 Ludwiogshöhe
www.brueder-dr-becker.de

Dreissigacker

Bechtheim, where Dreissigacker is located, was a famous, successful commune a century ago, but lost its way during the second half of the 20th century. Nobody has done more to put it back on the map than young Jochen Dreissigacker. Even his regular dry estate Riesling is silky, succulent, and packed with apricot aroma. The dry Riesling from the Geyersberg site is the biggest, most opulent wine of its type in the region. ★ **Rising star**

Untere Klinggasse 4–6, 67595 Bechtheim
www.dreissigacker-wein.de

Fleischer/Stadt Mainz

Siblings Michael and Sabine Fleischer have turned the 50 acre (20ha) Fleischer/Stadt Mainz estate into one of the most important red wine specialists in Rheinhessen. Their varietal Cabernet Sauvignon and Syrah, and their Cabernet/Merlot/Spätburgunder blend Moguntiacum are all impressive. However, the dark, concentrated, tannic Syrah Edition Michael Fleischer is certainly the star. ★ **Rising star**

Rheinhessenstrasse 103, 55129 Mainz-Hechtsheim
www.weingut-fleischer.de

Fritz Ekkehard Huff

Since Christine Huff took over the winemaking at Fritz Ekkehard Huff in 2006, this small estate has been one of the rising stars in the Nierstein area. Dry Rieslings are

BECKER-LANDGRAF
A FINE SPATBURGUNDER FROM
AN EXCELLENT YEAR

BRUDER DR. BECKER
A GOOD-VALUE DRY RIESLING
WITH MINERAL FRESHNESS

her prime focus and they all display the sleek, pristine, and intensely mineral personality of the little-known, but excellent, Schloss Schwabsburg site. Huff also makes an elegant dry Grauburgunder from old vines and rapidly improving Spätburgunders. ★ **Rising star**

Hauptstrasse 90, 55283 Nierstein-Schwabsburg
www.weingut-huff.de

Geil

Year in, year out, Johannes Geil's rich and succulent dry Silvaner "S" is a reference point for this underrated grape variety in Rheinhessen. Geil's dry Weissburgunders and dry and sweet Rieslings are similarly appealing, and the reds, made from a handful of different grapes, are equally well made. Everything is good value. ★ **Rising star**

Kuhpfortenstrasse 11, 67595 Bechtheim
www.weingut-geil.de

Georg Gustav Huff

Daniel Huff of Georg Gustav Huff is in the lucky position of having sizeable holdings in the Schloss Schwabsburg site of his home village and in the far more famous Hipping and Pettenthal sites of Nierstein. He produces a wide range of dry Rieslings that combine racy mineral freshness with power and ripeness. ★ **Rising star**

Woogstrasse 1, 55283 Nierstein-Schwabsburg
www.weingut-huff.com

Göhring

Arno Göhring does not blow his own trumpet, although the quality of his wines gives him reason enough to do so. Unusually for a young winemaker in the Rheinhessen, Göhring is best known for his dry Scheurebe "S," an elegant alternative to top-class, unoaked Sauvignon Blanc. But his powerful, dry Rieslings from the Bürgel, Frauenberg, and Goldberg sites of his home town offer great value for money, and his reds from the unfashionable Portugieser and Schwarzriesling grapes are very impressive, too. ★ **Rising star**

Alzeyer Strasse 60, 67592 Flörsheim-Dalsheim
www.weingut-goehring.de

Groebe

The small Groebe estate's vineyards are situated around the town of Westhofen on the opposite bank of the Rhine from its HQ in Biebesheim. Friedrich Groebe crafts some of the most original, ageworthy Rieslings in the region. The complex, slow-developing dry Grosse Gewächse from the Aulerde (opulent, creamy) and the Kirchspiel (super-ripe, elegant, minerally) are Groebe's finest wines, but the dry Westhofener Riesling and off-dry Westhofener Spätlese are also full of character. ★ **Rising star**

Bahnhofstrasse 68–70, 64584 Biebesheim am Rhein
www.weingut-k-f-groebe.de

Gunderloch

Fritz and Agnes Hasselbach's hat-trick of 100-point scores from the American magazine *Wine Spectator*, for their enormously concentrated Riesling TBAs, resulted in the nickname "Mr. and Mrs. 100 points." But their remarkable botrytis wines are only one side of their production. In Germany, Gunderloch is far better known for the racy, off-dry Riesling Kabinett Jean-Baptiste and

KELLER

THE HUBACKER RIESLING HAILS FROM ONE
OF THE BEST SITES IN THE RHEINHESSEN

for its dry Rieslings, most importantly the imposing yet refined Grosses Gewächs from the great Rothenberg site of Nackenheim.

Carl-Gunderloch-Platz 1, 55299 Nackenheim
www.gunderloch.de

Gutzler

Father-and-son team Gerhard and Michael Gutzler have built their reputation on powerful, tannic, oaky reds, most importantly the Spätburgunder Grosses Gewächs from the Morstein site of Westhofen. However, in 2008 their dry whites took a leap forward with the introduction of the highly unconventional Burgundian-style Silvaner, Dorn Dürkheimer, from 70-year-old vines. The top dry Riesling is the Grosses Gewächs from the Wormser Liebfrauenstift-Kirchenstück site. ★ **Rising star**

Rossgasse 19, 67599 Gundheim
www.gutzler.de

Gysler

When Alex Gysler took over the family estate in 1999, he developed a sleek and subtly aromatic white wine style light years removed from the generous and fleshy Rheinhessen norm. This is most striking in his dry Weissburgunders and Grauburgunders, which have not an ounce of unnecessary fat on the bone. His dry Silvaners and Rieslings are even more minerally, while the sweet Rieslings taste as if they came from the Mosel. Gysler has been biodynamic since 2007. ★ **Rising star**

Grosser Spitzenberg 8, 55232 Alzey-Weinheim
www.weingut-gysler.de

Hedesheimer Hof

Michael Beck's Hedesheimer Hof is best known for fresh, dry Riesling, Grauburgunder, and Weissburgunder, even the most powerful of which have a lightness of touch. But Beck also produces a number of highly distinctive wines that shoot in different directions, such as the super-juicy sweet Riesling Late Night; the honey-and-butter flavored, barrel-fermented Auxerrois; and opulent reds from Spätburgunder and Portugieser. ★ **Rising star**

Schildweg 2, 55271 Stadecken-Elsheim
www.hedesheimer-hof.de

Heyl zu Herrnsheim/St Antony

With 150 acres (60ha) of vineyards, the double estate Heyl zu Herrnsheim/St Antony is the largest producer of Riesling from the top sites of the Roter Hang (red slope) between Nierstein and Nackenheim. However, most of the wines are marketed without vineyard designations, for example the impressive dry Rotschiefer (red slate) bottlings from both estates. Although all the wines are made in a single cellar, the St Antony wines are vibrant and fruity, the Heyl zu Herrnsheim reserved and subtle.

Wilhelmstrasse 4, 55283 Nierstein
www.heyl-zu-herrnsheim.de; www.st-antony.de

Hofmann

Jürgen Hofmann is one of the great new winemaking talents of Rheinhessen and it is hard to decide which of his dry whites is his greatest achievement. His Rieslings from the limestone of the Hundertgulden site are among the most concentrated and minerally wines from the region's

WITTMANN

THE AULERDE RIESLING IS ONE OF YOUNG
STAR PHILIPP WITTMANN'S TOP WINES

under-appreciated north (even the second grade marketed as vom Muschelkalk is stunning). Hofmann's dry Silvaners are also full of life and character, particularly the oak-matured "S." The largest bottling is the Sauvignon Blanc, one of the finest in Germany. ★ **Rising star**

Obergasse 20, 55437 Appenheim
www.weingut-hofmann.de

Johanninger

The Johanninger estate is a union of three estates blessed with vineyards in Rheinhessen, the Nahe, and the Rheingau. Jens Heinemeier—who owns the Rheingau vineyards, from which the elegant Spätburgunders come—is winemaker and he has developed a style of dry white wine far removed from the modern Rheinhessen norm, with the emphasis on clarity and silky texture. The top Riesling, Berg, and the Weissburgunder/Chardonnay blend, Kessler, gain extra richness from extended lees aging. ★ **Rising star**

Hauptstrasse 4-6, 55546 Biebelsheim
www.johanninger.de

Keller

Klaus-Peter Keller built on the achievements of his father who lifted this modest-sized estate in the then unknown town of Flörsheim-Dalsheim into the top rank of German wine producers. Today, the focus is firmly on dry whites, with the opulent, beautifully balanced "S" bottlings of Grauburgunder, Weissburgunder, and Silvaner among the best from these grapes in the region. The dry Riesling Grosse Gewächse from the Kirchspiel and Morstein sites of Westhofen and the Hubacker of Dalsheim are a shade sleeker, but also rich, concentrated wines. The effusively aromatic, brilliantly racy Riesling Auslese, BA, and TBA are stunning. Good as the rather oaky Spätburgunder reds are, they cannot quite match the whites for finesse or harmony.

Bahnhofstrasse 1, 67592 Flörsheim-Dalsheim
www.keller-wein.de

Kühling-Gillot

Carolin Gillot has turned her family estate Kühling-Gillot upside-down in the past 10 years, switching to organic viticulture, building a startlingly modern vinotech, and rebuilding the range of wines. The fruit-driven dry Riesling, Scheurebe, and Grauburgunder marketed under the Qvinterra brand are model examples of modern Rheinhessen whites. With every vintage, the Spätburgunders get more refined, and they never lack tannic power. ★ **Rising star**

Ölmühlstrasse 25, 55294 Bodenheim
www.kuehling-gillot.de

Milch

Karl Hermann produces Germany's most original Chardonnays at Milch, ignoring the Burgundian examples a couple of hours' drive away in favor of developing his own fruit-driven, but by no means superficial, style. Do not be put off by the name of the top bottling: Blauarsch or "blue ass." Milch also makes solid dry Rieslings and moderately oaky reds. ★ **Rising star**

Rüstermühle, 67590 Monsheim
www.weingut-milch.de

Riffel

In less than five years, the publicity-shy Erik and Carolin Riffel have pushed the hitherto unknown Riffel estate into the Rheinhessen's first rank. The top bottlings of dry Riesling and Silvaner from the steep quarzitic slopes of the great Binger Scharlachberg site appear under the Turm label, which refers to the tower crowning the estate's new cellars. They marry minerality with crystalline clarity and great finesse, but even the regular dry Riesling and Silvaner are full of fruit and freshness. ★ Rising star

Mühlweg 14a, 55411 Bingen-Büdesheim
www.weingut-riffel.de

Sander

The 60 acre (24ha) Sander estate has been biodynamic since Stefan Sander's grandfather rejected the introduction of modern chemistry in the 1950s. This unswerving policy, and modest yields, results in wines of character, substance, and vigor. The dry Silvaner, Alte Reben, from old vines, the dry Rieslings from the Mettenheimer Schlossberg, and the dry Weissburgunder from the Mettenheimer Michelsberg vie for top honors.

In den Weingärten 11, 67582 Mettenheim
www.weingut-sander.de

Seehof/Fauth

The Seehof/Fauth estate's history may go back 1,200 years, but it is the winemaking talent of energetic young Florian Fauth that now impresses. The quality Fauth achieves in the mid-range vom Kalkstein dry Riesling, Scheurebe, Weissburgunder, and Grauburgunder, which all grow on limestone marl soils, is arguably his greatest achievement. However, the more concentrated, but extremely clean, dry Rieslings from the Morstein (elegant and minerally) and Steingrube (more powerful and slower to develop) are also impressive. ★ Rising star

Seegasse 20, 67593 Westhofen
www.weingut-seehof.de

Sekthaus Raumland

Founded by Volker and Heide-Rose Raumland in 1990, Sekthaus Raumland is now Germany's most renowned sparkling wine producer. With its toast and brioche notes, creamy full body, and elegant acidity, the Triumvirat Grand Cuvée could easily be mistaken for a top-class vintage champagne. The modestly priced Riesling Brut is lighter, crisper, and more Germanic in style. Between them in price and style lie impressive sparkling Silvaner, Weissburgunder, and Spätburgunder. ★ Rising star

Alzeyer Strasse 134, 67592 Flörsheim-Dalsheim
www.raumland.de

Spiess

The Spiess family is not the only producer of ripe, powerful, dry Rieslings from the top sites of Bechtheim, but theirs are certainly the most succulently fruity and lively—and young winemaker Johannes Spiess has only just completed his studies. Of the big, bold, and oaky reds, the varietal Cabernet Sauvignon and Merlot are the stars, closely followed by the Cuvée CM, which is a blend of the two varieties. ★ Rising star

Gaustrasse 2, 67595 Bechtheim
www.spiess-wein.de

Steitz

It is difficult to say whether Christian Steitz's dramatic and minerally dry Rieslings from the (famous) Niersteiner Hipping and (little-known) Neu-Bamberger Heerkretz sites are his best wines, or the opulent, creamy dry Silvaner and Grauburgunder from the Goldenes Horn. Even his simplest wines are full of character. ★ Rising star

Mörsfelder Strasse 3, 55599 Stein-Bockenheim
www.weingut-steitz.de

Teschke

Nobody in Rheinhessen takes Sylvaner as seriously as wild wine man Michael Teschke, who not only makes an entire range of uniquely expressive wines from the grape, but also insists on the old spelling ("y" instead of "i"). However, since 2006 the red wines from the equally underrated Portugieser grape have also been extremely impressive. Every Teschke wine is marked by strength, concentration, character, and individuality. ★ Rising star.

Laurenziberg 14, 55435 Gau-Algesheim
www.weingut-teschke.de

Wagner-Stempel

Daniel Wagner's dry whites at Wagner-Stempel are about as far from the stereotype of Rheinhessen wines as being full and round as it is possible to get. Their sleekness and aromatic effusiveness is explained by the high-altitude location of Wagner's vineyards in the hilly extreme west of the region. The racy, concentrated, dry Riesling Grosse Gewächse from the Heerkretz and Höllberg also reflect the porphyry soil of these sites, whose greatness Wagner rediscovered. His brilliant, sweet Riesling Spätlese from these sites are hardly less vibrant or minerally and could be mistaken for Nahe or Mosel wines. Wagner is a great winemaker coming to the peak of his talent. ★ Rising star

Wöllsteiner Strasse 10, 55599 Siefersheim
www.wagner-stempel.de

Winter

Nobody had heard of Dittelsheim-Hessloch until young winemaker Stefan Winter's Leckerberg (literally "delicious hill") dry Riesling from the 2003 vintage caused a sensation. Since then, Winter has built a range of powerful, richly textural, beautifully balanced dry whites from Riesling, Silvaner, Weissburgunder, Grauburgunder, Chardonnay, and Scheurebe grapes. Excellent value for money across the entire range. ★ Rising star

Hauptstrasse 17, 67596 Dittelsheim-Hessloch
www.weingut-winter.de

Wittmann

Wittmann's 62 acre (26ha) vineyard has been organic since 1990, but it is the quality of the wine made by Philipp Wittmann since 1998 that has catapulted it from the middle ranks to international fame and acclaim. Four complex and imposing, but never opulent or thunderous, dry Riesling Grosse Gewächse—Aulerde, Kirchspiel, Brünnenhäuschen, and Morstein—form the top of the range. But every wine is impressive, each having the balance and elegance that make Wittmann synonymous with all that is good about the new Rheinhessen.

Mainzer Strasse 19, 67593 Westhofen
www.wittmannweingut.com

STEFAN WINTER

Stefan Winter's parents were typical of their generation of Rheinhessen winemakers. Until the profit margins began to dry up, they were happy to make easy money producing large quantities of simple bulk wine to help fill the millions of bottles of Liebfraumilch exported in that distant "golden October" of German wine in the 1970s and early 1980s. But Stefan Winter ignored all this. He began making bold, dramatic, dry whites while he was still studying winemaking, and he was just 24 years old when his 2003 Leckerberg became an overnight sensation. That kind of success seemed outrageous in Rheinhessen at the time, but has since become normal; a measure of how fast and radically things have changed. Winter is now a role model for winemaking students, who see him as proof that coming from somewhere nobody has heard of need not prevent you from making world-class wines—or from being acclaimed for them. Thanks to thirtysomethings like Winter, it sometimes seems anything is possible in the dream factory of dry wine this region has become.

PFALZ

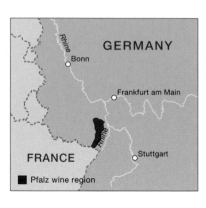

At the beginning of the 1990s, an article in the respected German gastronomic magazine *Der Feinschmecker* (The Gourmet) described the Pfalz region as Germany's answer to Tuscany. Given that most of the Pfalz's terrain is either flat or gently sloping, and that steep hills like those found in the Chianti region are hard to find, it was a daring comparison. However, when, almost 20 years later, a young winemaker made the quip on German television that Tuscany was now "the Pfalz of Italy," he was only half-joking, and few would have found reason to laugh. Indeed, his words were simply a reflection of the quantum leap the region has made in both self-confidence and wine quality in the past couple of decades.

Like the Mosel, the Pfalz has been on a roll since the late 1980s, but while the Mosel's winemakers divided their attention between dry and sweet wines, their colleagues in the Pfalz focused solely on dry wines. Recently, the Pfalz has gained the domestic reputation of being first among equals of Germany's wine regions for dry wines.

In fact, dry wines have deep roots here. The most important reason for this is the region's comparatively warm, dry climate, which gives a Mediterranean feel to its towns and villages in summer. This is the result of the region's position in the rain shadow of the forested Haardt mountains, a situation comparable to Alsace in France, immediately to the south. The other reason is cultural. The Pfälzer love their food and their regional dishes have long been substantial in quantity and flavor. Dry wines with plenty of substance have also long been in strong demand. The development of a sophisticated gastronomic scene came simultaneously with the upturn in wine quality, each stimulating the other's development.

The history of quality wine production in the Pfalz goes back to the early years of the 19th century. During the next 150 years, production was centered on the Mittelhaardt area around the small town of Deidesheim, and many older wine books portray this as the consequence of a uniquely advantageous terroir within the 58,000 acre (23,000ha) region. In reality, it was rather the result of social factors; in Deidesheim and its environs there were large estates in the hands of wealthy owners who could afford the high labor costs that quality wine production required before the advent of tractors.

During the immediate post-World War II years, a small group of independent winemakers in the Southern Pfalz began matching their neighbors to the north and in recent years, the number of talented young winemakers in this part of the Pfalz has increased rapidly to overtake the Mittelhaardt. While nearly all the famous vineyards of the Mittelhaardt are gentle slopes at best, further south the scenery is more dramatic, with significant areas of vineyards on the foothills of the Haardt mountains. There is a greater geological diversity here, so while Riesling (of which there is more than 12,000 acres/5,000ha in the region) thrives, in the Southern Pfalz many other grape varieties produce good and exciting wines. Some of the best dry whites in the world made from Weissburgunder (Pinot Blanc) and Grauburgunder (Pinot Gris) come from here—lushly concentrated yet bone-dry.

Arguably, the Pfalz has made more progress in improving red winemaking than any other German region. For at least half a century, the Pfälzer missed this opportunity their climate and soils gave them, but now 40% of the Pfalz is planted with red varieties. Along with the ubiquitous Spätburgunder (Pinot Noir), the traditional regional specialties of Portugieser and St Laurent, as well as the modern crossing Dornfelder (of which there is 8,000 acres/3,000ha), give deeply colored wines that pack a rustic punch.

Acham-Magin

Anna-Barbara Acham has focused on properly dry wines since the 1980s, but in recent years, her wines have only gotten better. Top of her wide range are the concentrated Riesling Grosse Gewächse from the Ruppertsberger Reiterpfad, Forster Pechstein, and Forster Kirchstück sites, but even the simplest wines here are full of ripe fruit aromas and minerally acidity. ★ **Rising star**

Weinstrassse 67, 67147 Forst
www.acham-magin.de

Bergdolt

In contrast to the recent trend for lush, opulent wines in the Pfalz, father-and-daughter team Rainer and Carolin Bergdolt are committed to a sleek and elegant style of dry Riesling and Weissburgunder. They might not leap out of the glass at you, but they are subtle and full of character with great aging potential. Top of the range are the superb Riesling Grosses Gewächs from the Ruppertsberger Reiterpfad and the Weissburgunder Grosses Gewächs from the Kirrweiler Mandelberg. The latter is one of the finest examples of this internationally underrated grape you'll find anywhere on Planet Wine.

Klostergut Sankt Lamprecht, 67435 Duttweiler
www.weingut-bergdolt.de

Bernhart

During the 1990s, Gerd Bernhart leapt from nowhere into the first rank of Pfalz red wine producers. His Spätburgunder Grosses Gewächs from the Rädling site (just over the French border in Alsace) is rich, complex, and velvety. Even the simpler reds, from the regional specialty St Laurent, have substance and wonderful harmony, and Bernhart produces good, if not stunning, dry whites, too. ★ **Rising star**

Hauptstrasse 8, 76889 Schweigen
www.weingut-bernhart.de

A Christmann

Steffen Christmann is best known as president of the VDP association of Germany's leading winegrowers. However, at his own estate, he makes some of the most sophisticated and individual dry whites and reds in the Pfalz. In particular, the powerful and richly textural dry Riesling Grosse Gewächse from the Idig site of Königsbach have done much to shape this entire new category of German wine. The recent conversion of the estate to biodynamics has lowered alcohol levels slightly, making all the wines more elegant and the standard quality dry Riesling more minerally. The Spätburgunder reds are concentrated and beautifully balanced with discreet oak, and the red Grosses Gewächs from the Idig has as long an aging potential as the white version. ★ **Rising star**

Peter-Koch-Strasse 43, 67435 Gimmeldingen
www.weingut-christmann.de

Dr. Bürklin-Wolf

With more than 80ha (200 acres) of vineyards, the most famous estate in the Pfalz is the region's, and possibly Germany's, largest biodynamic producer. This method of cultivation, coupled with low yields, means that the prices for the top single-vineyard (Hohenmorgen and Kalkofen in Deidesheim, Jesuitengartend, Kirchenstück, Pechstein, and Ungeheuer in Forst) dry Rieslings are among the

A CHRISTMANN
THE BIODYNAMIC ESTATE MAKES SOME OF
THE BEST WINES IN THE PFALZ

GIES-DUPPEL
VOLKER GIES MAKES VIVID, HIGHLY
INDIVIDUALISTIC RIESLINGS

highest in Germany. However, they are also some of the most imposing and complex wines of this type produced anywhere in the country. A long tradition for nobly sweet Riesling Auslese, BA, and TBA is very much alive and these wines also belong among the best of the region.

Weinstrasse 65, 67157 Wachenheim
www.buerklin-wolf.de

Dr. von Bassermann-Jordan

This 50ha (120 acre) estate is one of a quartet owned by local entrepreneur Achim Niederberger. The experienced duo of director Gunther Hauk and winemaker Ulrich Mell steer a clear stylistic course—you will not find more fruit-driven Pfalz wines than these. Quality is extremely dependable and prices fair. Although Riesling accounts for 85% of production, the aromatic Traminer, Muskatteler, Goldmuskateller, and Sauvignon Blanc are all important and highly successful specialties.

Kirchgasse 10, 67146 Deidesheim
www.bassermann-jordan.de

Dr. Wehrheim Pfalz

It is hard to think of a dry German wine that is internationally more undervalued than Karl-Heinz Wehrheim's enormously concentrated and multi-dimensional dry Weissburgunder Grosses Gewächs from the Mandelberg site. However, it has tough internal competition from Wehrheim's two dry Riesling Grosse Gewächse, the Kastanienbusch (from a part of the site with red slate soil) and Kastanienbusch Köppel (from the part with sandstone soil). Both are titans without being a jot overdone. Then there is the opulent and spicy red Spätburgunder Grosses Gewächs from the Kastanienbusch and a myriad of other supple wines bursting with character. The fact that all are bone dry, and that Wehrheim prefers hunting to PR and sales trips, explains his comparative lack of fame.

Weinstrasse 8, 76831 Birkweiler
www.weingut-wehrheim.de

Friedrich Becker Pfalz

Fritz Becker Sr. put Friedrich Becker, in the extreme south of the Pfalz, on the map more than 20 years ago with some of the first completely convincing German Pinot Noirs. Many of the single-vineyard bottlings actually grow just across the French border in Alsace, but although the inspiration of Burgundy is clearly perceptible in the most concentrated examples, these are not slavish copies (the acidity is softer, for example). Since 2007, Fritz Becker Jr. has greatly improved the previously somewhat rustic dry whites, which look cheap compared with the pricey reds. The Riesling Grosses Gewächs from the Schweigerer Sonnenberg site is an imposing wine.

Hauptstrasse 29, 76889 Schweigen
www.friedrichbecker.de

Gies-Düppel

Volker Gies' greatest achievement at Gies-Düppel is arguably his series of dry Rieslings named after soil types: Buntsandstein (sandstone), Muschelkalk (limestone), and Rotliegendes (red slate), each of which combines succulence with clarity in its own distinct manner. Along with his regular Spätburgunder red wine, they offer excellent value for money. To see what this star

MUNZBERG
MUNZBERG'S WEISSBURGUNDERS ARE
RICH BUT NEVER OVERWHELMING

KRANZ
WINEMAKER BORIS KRANZ LIKES TO
EXPERIMENT, BUT HIS WINES ARE DELICIOUS

in the making can really do, however, one should taste the imposing and spicy dry Riesling and Weissburgunder from the Kastanienbusch site. ★ **Rising star**

Am Rosenberg 5, 76831 Birkweiler
www.gies-dueppel.de

Hensel

The 50 acre (20ha) Hensel estate was a vine nursery until Thomas Hensel made his first wines in the early 1990s. Ten years later, his Ikarus was one of the first completely successful new-style German reds (today it is 100% Cabernet Cubin) in a rich, tannic style closer to Californian Cult Cabernet than anything else. Even his simplest red, Aufwind, an eccentric *cuvée* of Cabernet Sauvignon and St Laurent, is a big, bold wine with excellent balance. Between these lie the rich, plush Höhenflug bottlings of Spätburgunder, Merlot, and a red *cuvée*. Hensel's generous, succulent dry whites are all about spontaneous drinking pleasure, the Riesling Höhenflug being the star. The coolest of the shooting stars in the Pfalz. ★ **Rising star**

In den Almen 13, 67098 Bad Dürkheim
www.henselwein.de

Herbert Messmer

It might seem absurd to call Gregor Messmer a rising star when his talent was already apparent 20 years ago, but realizing the full potential of Riesling, Weissburgunder, Grauburgunder, and Chardonnay for dry whites along with Spätburgunder and St Laurent for reds in this unknown corner of the Southern Pfalz took some doing. The most remarkable of Messmer's many impressive wines is the dry Riesling Grosses Gewächs from the Schäwer site of Burrweiler, the only Pfalz vineyard with a slate soil. With its combination of richness and brilliance, it could easily be mistaken for a great dry Riesling from the Wachau in Austria. ★ **Rising star**

Gaisbergstrasse 5, 76835 Burrweiler
www.weingut-messmer.de

Josef Biffar

Biffar is best known to many Germans as the country's leading producer of candied fruits, but it is also an important wine estate with 30 acres (12ha) of holdings in the top sites of Deidesheim, Wachenheim, and Ruppertsberg. Since Lilli Biffar-Hirschbil took over the direction, several changes of winemaker have led to inconsistent quality, but the top dry Rieslings (Spätlese trocken and Grosses Gewächs) continue to impress.

Niederkirchener Strasse 13, 67146 Deidesheim
www.josef-biffar.de

Jürgen Leiner

Sven Leiner is the most daring of the new generation of winemakers in the Southern Pfalz. His wines are not only biodynamic, but highly idiosyncratic—even the regular Handwerk (Handmade) series of standard quality dry varietal wines is full of character at modest alcoholic levels for today, and the single-vineyard wines are full of spice and minerals. The reds include a successful Tempranillo and the rich, earthy Kruiosum, arguably Germany's most impressive Dornfelder. ★ **Rising star**

Arzheimer Strasse 14, 76831 Ilbesheim
www.weingut-leiner.de

Knipser

Nobody has done more to revolutionize the red wines of the Pfalz than the Knipser brothers, Werner and Volker. Spätburgunder is their traditional strength, and their Grosse Gewächse from the hitherto unknown Kirschgarten and Burgweg sites regularly impress with their power and depth. But it is with new varieties such as Syrah (proof that this grape has a future in Germany), Cabernet Sauvignon, Cabernet Franc, and Merlot (the latter trio in the imposing Cuvée X) that they make the most noise. Though the Knipsers only produced their first dry Riesling Grosse Gewächs in 2001, those wines immediately established them as producers of rich and complex Riesling, a style they have since refined. Their featherlight dry Sauvignon Blanc lies at the other end of the taste spectrum, but is also a cult wine. You have to wonder if there is anything that these multi-talented winemaking brothers cannot do. ★ **Rising star**

Hauptstrasse 47-49, 67229 Laumersheim
weingut-knipser.de

Koehler-Ruprecht

Long before dry Riesling was a well-established part of the Pfalz winemaking portfolio, Bernd Philippi was making world-class dry Rieslings at Koehler-Ruprecht from the chalky slopes of the Saumagen site of Kallstadt. They could challenge the best from Alsace or Austria—indeed, they still can—and they aged magnificently. For more than four decades, Philippi has remained true to the winemaking style of his grandfather, Ernst Koehler, for the Koehler-Ruprecht wines. But Philippi has not stopped there, having also built up a broad range of innovative wines (generally barrique-fermented and/or matured) under the Philippi label, among which the rich, mellow, and complex Spätburgunder reds stand out. The best of these, and also the best of the Saumagen dry Rieslings, are marketed as mature wines with an "R" or "RR" (meaning "Reserve" and "Double-Reserve") and do not appear on the main price list.

Weinstrasse 84, 67169 Kallstadt
06322 1829

Kranz

The energetic and creative Boris Kranz is one of the new stars of the Southern Pfalz. However, aside from his single-vineyard bottlings of dry Riesling, Weissburgunder, and Spätburgunder, his prices remain very friendly. The dry Kranz wines are never short on aroma, fruit, or charm, none more so than the Riesling Terrassen from the Kalmit site. Sylvaner is another specialty and the bottling from the Hagedorn site is both juicy and complex. ★ **Rising star**

Mörzheimer Strasse 2, 76831 Ilbesheim
www.weingut-kranz.de

Lucashof/Pfarrweingut

Lucashof/Pfarrweingut is a low-key winery, in spite of producing impressive Rieslings year in, year out from almost 60 acres (24ha) of vineyards. Top of the range are the dry Rieslings from the Pechstein and Ungeheuer sites of Forst. Perhaps it is because Klaus Lucas's wife Christine comes from the Mosel that he also makes some excellent nobly sweet Riesling Auslese. ★ **Rising star**

Wiesenweg 1a, 67147 Forst
www.lucashof.de

Matthias Gaul

Matthias Gaul is another young Pfalz winegrower who has turned his family estate upside down in only a few years. Even his basic dry Riesling is strongly marked by the chalky soils that give it its name, t' c, from terrain calcaire. Its big brother, Auf dem Berg, is more corpulent and powerful, but also has a cool freshness that makes it easy to drink. The reds are all full, generous wines but made with a light touch that makes them appealing in their youth. ★ **Rising star**

Weinstrasse 10, 67269 Grünstadt-Asselheim
www.gaul-weine.de

Mosbacher

If you are looking for the generous fruit and succulence typical of Pfalz dry Riesling, but want the ultimate in elegance too, then the wines from Sabine Mosbacher-Düringer and Jürgen Düringer are for you. Their dry Riesling Grosse Gewächse from the Kieselberg site of Deidesheim, the Freundstück, Pechstein, and Ungeheuer of Forst combine these virtues with a pronounced, but subtle, mineral character and have great aging potential (not always the case in this category where too much power can make wines become clumsy as they mature).

Weinstrasse 27, 67147 Forst
www.georg-mosbacher.de

Müller-Catoir

Owner Heinrich Catoir and estate manager Hans-Günther Schwarz were like night and day, but together they built Müller-Catoir's fame from the 1970s to the 1990s with dry and sweet whites of spectacular brilliance. Today, under Philipp Catoir and estate manager Martin Franzen, history is repeating itself and the wines are once again breathtaking. The bone-dry Muskateller is the most expressive example of this grape in Germany and the super-succulent sweet Scheurebe is also one of the best of its type. The gleaming pinnacle among the dry whites is the intensely mineral Riesling Grosses Gewächs Breumel in den Mauern, while the Rieslaner Auslese, BA, and TBA are a fireworks display of nobly sweet Pfalz wines. Only the oaky, new dry Weissburgunder and Grauburgunder fail to live up to the estate's nickname "MC^2."

Mandelring 25, 67433 Haardt
www.mueller-catoir.de

Münzberg

Brothers Gunter and Rainer Kessler make rich, muscular dry Weissburgunders (30% of the 37 acres/15ha) and Grauburgunders that are still under-appreciated, even in the domestic market where this is a sought-after style. Top of the range is the dry Weissburgunder Grosses Gewächs from the Schlangenpfiff site. The Kesslers also make serious Spätburgunder reds. ★ **Rising star**

Hofgut, 76829 Godramstein
www.weingut-muenzberg.de

Odinstal

A number of Odinstal's dry white wines feature "350 NN" on the label. This enigmatic code refers to the fact that, at 1,000ft (350m) above sea level, this is the highest-altitude vineyard in the Pfalz, which results in atypically sleek and racy low alcohol wines for the region. Andreas Schumann's biodynamic viticulture and extremely cautious winemaking capture the mountain freshness of this site in wines that are never loud and often profound. Although the Riesling Basalt is the estate's most remarkable and concentrated wine, the Auxerrois, Weissburgunder, and Silvaner under the 350 NN label are also very special. ★ **Rising star**

Odinstalweg, 67157 Wachenheim
www.odinstal.de

Okonomierat Rebholz

Though widely acknowledged as the region's top winemaker, Hans-Jörg Rebholz's dry whites are far removed from the rich and weighty style currently in vogue in the Pfalz. Rebholz's preference is instead for bone-dry wines with more character than weight or volume, a style based on family tradition dating back to his grandfather and the immediate post-war years. Which is the greatest of his wines today? Is it the intensely herbal and mineral Riesling Grosses Gewächs from the high altitude Kastanienbusch (Chestnut Bush) vineyard? Or the creamy and honeyed Weissburgunder Grosses Gewächs from the Im Sonnenschein (In the Sunshine)? Or could it be the Burgundian-style, barrel-fermented Chardonnay? Maybe the regular dry Rieslings and Weissburgunders deserve more praise for their strength of personality and value for money? Then there is the lush and complex sweet Gewürztraminer from ancient vines in the Latt site and the concentrated, tannic Spätburgunder Grosses Gewächs Im Sonnenschein, which scales the same heights in red.

Weinstrasse 54, 76833 Siebeldingen
www.oekonomierat-rebholz.de

Pfeffingen/Fuhrmann-Eymael

Pfeffingen/Fuhrmann-Eymael sits on the site of the residence of Pfeffo, the Roman who first settled this area. It made its reputation under Karl Fuhrmann during the 1950s and 1960s, but under Fuhrmann's grandson, Jan Eymael, this Pfalz institution has been thoroughly modernized and it now produces some of the region's most striking wines. The sweet Auslese, BA, and TBA wines have a sensational tropical succulence, but remain modestly priced. Jan's successful innovations include the Sauvignon Blanc-like dry Scheurebe and the powerful and brilliant dry Riesling Grosse Gewächse from the Weilberg and Herrenberg sites of Ungstein.

Pfeffingen 2, 67098 Bad Dürkheim
www.pfeffingen.de

Philipp Kuhn

Back in 1988, at the age of just 16, Philipp Kuhn planted his first vineyard. Since then, he has earned a reputation as one of the most talented new winemakers in the Northern Pfalz and has expanded the estate to 50 acres (20ha). Even Kuhn's simplest dry Riesling is rich and juicy, while his dry Riesling Grosse Gewächse are bold and dramatic, the Kirschgarten being the most opulent and the Steinbuckel the most austere. The Spätburgunder Grosse Gewächse reds from these sites follow the same pattern. Luitmar is Kuhn's crazy *cuvée* of Lemberger, Cabernet Sauvignon, St Laurent, and Sangiovese, a wine with deep chocolatey richness and expansive body, but also firm tannins and fresh acidity; a masterpiece of originality. ★ **Rising star**

Grosskarlbacher Strasse 20, 67229 Laumersheim
www.weingut-philipp-kuhn.de

THE FUTURE IS DRY

During the last generation, global warming has raised temperatures in Germany's winegrowing regions by an average of about 1.8°F (1°C). That means more sugar in the grapes, of course, and it translates into an extra degree of alcohol in the finished wines when that extra sugar is allowed to ferment out. In the dry and sunny Pfalz, alcohol levels have often risen as much as 1.5% since the 1980s, pushing many dry Rieslings toward 14% and some dry Weissburgunders and Grauburgunders to 15%. The hot 2003 vintage was a rude awakening to these realities for many winegrowers, and even stars such as Hansjörg Rebholz added acidity to their wines (successfully in Rebholz's case). One scientific assessment says that by the middle of the 21st century, when 3.6°F (2°C) more of warming is expected, the optimum varieties for the lesser Pfalz vineyards on the Rhine Plain will be Chardonnay and Merlot. It is likely the first victims will be the early-ripening grape varieties that were once the region's backbone. Already, viticultural practices are being adapted to bring down alcohol levels for Riesling. Quo vadis Weissburgunder and Grauburgunder?

REICHSRAT VON BUHL
THE UNGEHEUER FORST RIESLING IS
COMPLEX, SPICY, AND RICH

SCHNEIDER
THE POWERFUL STEINSATZ SHOWS HOW
GOOD NEW-WAVE PFALZ REDS CAN BE

Reichsrat von Buhl

The 150 acre (60ha) Reichsrat von Buhl estate has gone from strength to strength under the ownership of local entrepreneur Achim Niederberger and the trio of director Stefan Weber, winegrower Werner Sebastian, and winemaker Michael Leibrecht. Except for the simplest qualities offered, the dry Rieslings are all full-bodied, ripe, and succulent with considerable individuality.

Weinstrasse 16, 67146 Deidesheim
www.reichsrat-von-buhl.de

Rolf & Tina Pfaffmann

Many of young Tina Pfaffmann's best dry varietal whites are sold under the Exklusiv designation. But, instead of eating a hole in your wallet, these juicy and substantial Pfalz beauties represent excellent value for money, with the Silvaner arguably the most distinctive. The dry Riesling Steingut is an eccentric wine fermented in large ceramic jars; the powerful Cuvée T a blend of Riesling with Weissburgunder and Silvaner. ★ **Rising star**

Am Stahlbühl, 76833 Frankenweiler
www.wein-pfaffmann.de

Scheu

Klaus Scheu may have a ponytail and be highly unconventional for a Pfalz wine-grower, but he makes excellent dry whites. Even his cheapest Riesling, Weissburgunder, and Grauburgunder are generous wines. Top of the range are the complex dry Weissburgunders from the Rädling and Strohlenberg sites, which always pack a big flavor punch without being heavy. ★ **Rising star**

Hauptstrasse 33, 76889 Schweigen-Rechtenbach
www.weinhof-scheu.de

Schneider

It must have seemed quite an achievement back in 1994 when, aged 18 years old, Markus Schneider made his first wine. But since then, he has taken ever-bigger leaps to become a 125 acre (50ha) estate producing 400,000 bottles a year, none of which are sold cheaply. Packing all this winemaking into one cellar required the construction of a hyper-modern winery that looks like a spaceship that has landed just outside the small, sleepy town of Ellerstadt. Bold and expressive dry Rieslings, Weissburgunders, and Grauburgunders are Schneider's main whites, but it was the deep-colored, powerful, but supple reds that put him on the map. Finest of these are the tannic Tailor and Steinsatz—both with a pronounced blackcurrant note from Cabernets Franc and Cubin—and the rich, sauve Einzelstück from ancient Portugieser vines. ★ **Rising star**

Am Hohen Weg 1, 67158 Ellerstadt
www.black-print.net

Siegrist

Unusually for Germany, Thomas Siegrist markets all his Spätburgunder as Pinot Noir. These are also his most ambitious wines, at once substantial, tannic, and oaky. In recent years, Siegrist has made considerable progress with his dry Rieslings, which have gained in fruit and charm. Barrique-vinified Chardonnay is an important and successful specialty. ★ **Rising star**

Am Hasensprung 4, 76829 Leinsweiler
www.weingutsiener.de

Siener

Peter Siener's dry Rieslings and Weissburgunders—no less than the Spätburgunder reds with which he first attracted attention—are all big, bold statements that are strong on intensity and harmony, but sometimes a little short on subtlety. The top bottlings are all named after the soil type of the sites where they grew: Schiefer (slate) for Riesling, Kalkgestein (limestone) for the Weissburgunder, and Buntsandstein (red sandstone) for the Spätburgunder. ★ **Rising star**

Weinstrasse 31, 76831 Birkweiler
www.weingutsiener.de

Stiftsweingut Frank Meyer

With their long-term commitment to bone-dry whites with modest alcoholic content, Frank Meyer and Manuela Cambeis-Meyer seem positively eccentric in the contemporary Pfalz context. But their wines never taste as if they had to diet to be like Kate Moss. Maturation of the dry Rieslings in neutral wood is used to smooth out any rough edges, while the Weissburgunder and Grauburgunder are bottled with full youthful freshness. Of the reds, the "S" Portugieser is impressive, as is the 100% Cabernet Cubin Cuvée No. 37. ★ **Rising star**

Weinstrasse 37, 76889 Klingenmünster
www.stiftsweingut-meyer.de

Theo Minges

Juicy and elegant dry Rieslings make up the larger part of Theo Minges's production. But the nobly sweet Spätlese and Auslese, and the sensational dry and off-dry aromatic whites he makes from Gewürztraminer, are among the best examples of these styles in the entire region. A new addition to the range is the off-dry Riesling Spätlese Froschkönig (Frog King), which spends 18 months on the lees before bottling. ★ **Rising star**

Bachstrasse 11, 76835 Flemlingen
www.weingut-minges.com

Weegmüller

Larger-than-life powerfrau Stefie Weegmüller has been running the family estate for 20 years, and during this time her dry and sweet whites have only gotten more elegant. Aromatic and vibrantly fresh, they offer excellent value for money. The stars of the range are the dry Riesling Spätlese from the Herrenletten site and the nobly sweet Scheurebe and Rieslaner. ★ **Rising star**

Mandelring 23, 67433 Haardt
www.weegmueller-weine.de

J L Wolf

The J L Wolf estate, housed in a breathtaking complex dating back to 1843, was the first exercise in multi-tasking by Ernst Loosen of Weingut Dr. Loosen in Bernkastel in the Mosel. Changes of personnel have robbed it of a decisive breakthrough several times, but the dry and off-dry Rieslings have maintained a distinctive style since 1996 and they continue to eschew the tendency to high alcohol and heaviness common in the region. Top of the range are the single-vineyard bottlings from the Jesuitengarten, Pechstein, and Ungeheuer sites of Forst.

Weinstrasse 1, 67157 Wachenheim
www.jlwolf.de

FRANKEN

Franken, or Franconia as English speakers often call it, has long been different from Germany's other wine-growing regions, not least because it wanted to be different. During the 1970s and 1980s, when most of the nation's wine-growers were fixated upon cheap and sweet wines, Franken based its claim to uniqueness on bone-dry, earthy whites that Bavarians in particular seemed to enjoy. This image became so firmly entrenched that it seemed inevitable that Franken should produce such wines. However, the sad truth is that the palates of an entire generation of Bavarians became accustomed to dry whites that were lacking in ripe fruit aromas, with coarse tannins and green acidity.

The state of affairs three decades ago suited the winemakers of Franken, since it meant they could continue to get away with making wine from unripe or half-ripe grapes and did not need to pay attention to detail in the vineyard or cellar. Things have moved on remarkably, however. Indeed, the contrast between those dull and meager wines and the best contemporary Franken wines is as dramatic as the contrast between some of the region's remote wine-growing villages and the great baroque Residenz palace in its capital, Würzburg. A top-class dry white from Würzburg's famous Stein vineyard, a steep south-facing hillside with limestone soil overlooking the historic city and the River Main, is powerful and elegant with citrus, pear, and honey aromas.

One reason why these wines are still so little known is that many of the best are made from the Silvaner grape, a regional specialty accounting for 21% of the vineyards (3,155 acres/1,277ha). Silvaner may have just celebrated the 350th anniversary of its introduction to Germany, but it is hardly known outside the German-speaking world.

This is a shame, for in Franken, Silvaner gives good wines in four styles. There are mid-weight dry whites with 11.5–12.5% alcohol in which apple and citrus tend to be the dominant notes. Then there are full-bodied dry whites with 13% to almost 15% alcohol, often marked with ripe plum and exotic fruit aromas (sometimes with "GG" for Grosses Gewächs or "Great Growth" on the label, which refers to a quality designation based on distinguished vineyard sites). Next are similar wines in which fruit and/or wood tannins are perceptible but not dominant. Finally, there are the dessert wines

made from botrytized or frozen grapes, which are lusher than comparable Rieslings.

Two of the most important reasons for this diversity are that Silvaner responds positively both to yield reduction and to differing soil types and vineyard exposures. Wines from grapes grown on the gypsum marl of the Steigerwald subregion, for example, are muscular with vegetal and smoky notes, while the red sandstone of the Kurfranken subregion on the lower reaches of the Main makes for sleeker Silvaners with herbal and berry aromas.

These qualities are shared by the region's dry wines from the Riesling and Weissburgunder (Pinot Blanc) grapes, which can be considered Franken classics even if they are not as widely planted as Silvaner. The humble Müller-Thurgau (the most widely planted variety at 30% of the total vineyard area) generally gives light, fresh, apple- and lemon-flavored dry whites often marketed under the communal Frank & Frei brand.

Kurfranken has a deserved reputation for red wines from Spätburgunder (Pinot Noir) while the striking reds of the remote Tauber Valley come from Spätburgunder and Tauberschwarz, an indigenous variety that was recently rescued from the brink of extinction.

Franken has profited considerably from global warming, serious frost damage to the vines now being a rarity. Indeed, in recent years some leading winemakers have begun working in the vineyard to try to moderate alcohol levels. The new generation of Franken winemakers is far more open-minded than their parents and a great deal of experimentation is taking place in the vineyards and cellars. Today, this is arguably Germany's most dynamic wine-growing region.

Major grapes

Reds
Spätburgunder (Pinot Noir)

Tauberschwarz

Whites
Bacchus

Müller-Thurgau

Riesling

Silvaner

Weissburgunder (Pinot Blanc)

Vintages

2009
A great year for dry Silvaner; very good for everything else.

2008
Good dry whites in this high-acidity vintage.

2007
An excellent vintage of balanced, ageworthy wines. The reds are superb.

2006
Many wines big and bold but with enough freshness. Poorer examples, however, are heavy and tiring.

2005
Where producers mastered botrytis, the dry whites are complex and concentrated.

2004
A very good vintage of medium-bodied, fresh dry whites.

HORST SAUER
HORST SAUER'S FRUIT-DRIVEN WINES HAVE
PLAYED A KEY ROLE IN THE FRANKEN REVIVAL

BURGERSPITAL
THE WURZBURGER STEIN SILVANER
IS PERFECTLY POISED

Bickel-Stumpf

Matthias Stumpf is one of the wild young winemakers of Franken, but his wines are remarkably polished and well-balanced. The range divides in two: one part is based on the vineyards with limestone soil in Frickenhausen (bigger, rounder wines with a touch of exotic fruits at the top level). The other uses vineyards with sandstone soil in Thüngersheim (sleeker, more racy wines with herbal and berry notes). Along with the excellent dry Silvaner and Riesling, there are also some impressive dry Scheurebe and Traminer. ★Rising star

Kirchgasse 5, 97252 Frickenhausen
www.bickel-stumpf.de

Brügel

Modest Harald Brügel has rapidly matured into one of Franken's young shooting stars. His wines all share a pristine clarity and very good balance, even when alcohol levels top 14%. The super-ripe Spätburgunder Blanc de Noir is as remarkable a wine as the succulent dry Silvaner "Pur" or the excellent nobly sweet wines. They are as good as anything that the established quality leaders in the Steigerwald area of Franken have to offer. ★Rising star

Hauptstrasase 49, 97355 Greuth
www.weingut-bruegel.de

Bürgerspital

Robert Haller (previously at Fürst Löwenstein) has given the 270 acre (110ha) Bürgerspitel estate a much needed new impulse. Here, the focus is firmly on dry Riesling and Silvaner from the famous Stein vineyard of Würzburg, and already the wines marketed as Kabinett trocken are full of character and elegance. Top of the range are the dry Grosse Gewächse, with the Riesling from the "Hagemann" section of the Stein one of the most subtle and filigree dry Rieslings in the entire region.

Theaterstrasse 19, 97070 Würzburg
www.buergerstpital.de

Castell Franken

With 173 acres (70ha) of vineyards, this estate, whose full name is Fürstlich Castell'sches Domänenamt, is the largest privately owned estate in Franken. However, until Napoleon turned Germany upside-down, it was part of the independent fiefdom of Castell. From the regular dry wine under the Schloss Castell label, up to the multi-dimensional dry Grosses Gewächs from the Casteller Schlossberg, the Silvaner are among the finest in the region—which makes sense when you consider that it was one of Earl Ferdinand Castell's ancestors who planted the first vines of this variety in Germany in 1659. The dry Rieslings are almost equally impressive, and the nobly sweet Auslese, BA, and TBA are invariably good, most of all the brilliant Rieslaner.

Schlossplatz 5, 97355 Castell
www.castell.de

Fürst Löwenstein

A radical restructuring initiated by the late prince Carl F zu Löwenstein has taken this estate out of its historic quarters and replaced most of the team who kept it at the pinnacle of the region during the decade to 2007. Wines from this part of Franken, where sandstone soils predominate, can be lean and edgy if everything is not done just right in the vineyard—and that is how the regular quality wines from the last vintages tasted. The dry Silvaner and dry Riesling Grosse Gewächse from the remarkable amphitheater of terraced vineyards that is the Homburger Kallmuth site, continue to impress with their intensely herbal-mineral character.

Schlosspark 5, 63924 Kleinheubach
www.loewenstein.de

Graf von Schönborn

How can a historic estate like Graf von Schönborn be a rising star? Only after removing a serious microbial infection from the cellar did director Georg Hühnerkopf realize how much the estate's wines had been marred by it before. These are powerful, harmonious wines, most strikingly the three-star bottling (an informal ranking) of dry Silvaner, one of the most original new wines from this grape in this very dynamic region. ★Rising star

Schloss Hallburg, 97332 Volkach
www.schoenborn.de

Hans Wirsching

With 185 acres (75ha), the famous Hans Wirsching estate is one of Franken's largest. Given the scale of production, the consistency of quality both from year to year and within the large range is impressive. However, the competition in Franken has seriously heated up since the estate's reputation was made by Dr. Heinrich Wirsching during the 1970s and 1980s. The wines are strongest at the top end of the range (the pairs of dry Riesling and Silvaner Grosse Gewächse from the Kronsberg and Julius-Echter-Berg sites) and most likely to disappoint at the bottom end.

Ludwigstrasse 16, 97346 Iphofen
www.wirsching.de

Hofmann

Young Jürgen Hofmann has done more than anyone else to focus attention on the often ignored Tauber Valley (which is part in Franken, part in Baden and part in Württemberg due to an accident of history). Although his sleek and racy dry Silvaner and dry Riesling are remarkably expressive for their low alcoholic content, it is his perfumed and concentrated reds from Spätburgunder and the indigenous Tauberschwarz (with only 37 acres/15ha, a great rarity) that have made his name. ★Rising star

Strüther Strasse 7, 97285 Röttlingen
www.weinguthofmann.de

Horst Sauer

The meteoric rise to fame of Horst Sauer during the late 1990s was proof to Franken's winemakers that they were not stuck in a winemaking backwater. Though detractors sometimes dismiss Sauer's wines as only fruit-driven, they combine breathtaking fruit aromas with exceptional elegance and a distinct mineral character. Top of the range are the dry Riesling and Silvaner Grosse Gewächse from the Lump site, but it is the dry Kabinett and Spätlese below these that offer great value for money. Also excellent are the dry Müller-Thurgau and the best sweet wines in Franken. Sauer's daughter, Sandra, now does much of the winemaking, but is cautious about change.

Bocksbeutelstrasse 14, 97332 Escherndorf
www.weingut-horst-sauer.de

Johann Ruck

It does not concern Johann Ruck if his wines prove too eccentric for some tastes. While never thin or mean, sometimes they can be pretty funky for such a conservative wine region. The massive and intensely spicy-earthy dry Silvaner and Riesling Grosse Gewächse from the great Julius-Echter-Berg site share the limelight with the barrique-fermented Scheurebe "Estheria" and great dry Grauburgunder from old vines.

Marktplatz 19, 97346 Iphofen
www.ruckwein.de

Juliusspital

The 420 acre (170ha) Juliusspital estate is arguably the largest single wine estate in Germany. It is also one of Franken's finest, producing a wide range of aromatic, succulent dry Silvaner and dry Riesling. The dry Weissburgunder Grosses Gewächs is a match for the Silvaner and Riesling Grosse Gewächse. And the rich yet elegant Würzburger Stein, the opulent wines from the Randersackerer, Pfülben, and Escherndorfer Lump (all three with limestone soils), and the muscular, slower developing wines from the Iphofer Julius-Echter-Berg (gypsum marl), offer a great introduction to Franken.

Klinikstrasse 1, 97070 Würzburg
www.juliusspital.de

Luckert/Zehnthof

Brothers Ulrich and Wolfgang Luckert's Unter der Mauer (a Silvaner/Riesling blend) is one of Franken's greatest and most original dry wines. Like all the Luckert wines, which include dry Silvaner, Riesling, and Weissburgunder, it puts strength before mere alcohol. Even their "simple" dry Müller-Thurgau is full of character, and there are great red wines, though the quantities are sadly tiny. ★ **Rising star**

Kettengasse 3–5, 97320 Sulzfeld;
www.weingut-luckert.de

Michael Fröhlich

Michael Fröhlich is the most modest of the top winemakers in this small town and his wines are sometimes unjustly overlooked for this reason. His wines may be less dramatic than others, but they are models of balance and harmony. The complex and unusually spicy dry Silvaners are the stars, offering excellent value. ★ **Rising star**

Bocksbeutelstrasse 41, 97332 Escherndorf
www.weingut-michael-froehlich.de

Rainer Sauer

Until his son Daniel returned from wine school and began to experiment with dry Silvaner, Rainer Sauer seemed happy to play second fiddle to his neighbor (and distant relative) Horst Sauer. Now, the long-established Silvaner "L" is one of the world's top dry wines from this grape, while the expressive, vital Freiraum completely reinterprets what dry Silvaner can be. ★ **Rising star**

Bocksbeutelstrasse 15, 97332 Escherndorf
www.weingut-rainer-sauer.de

Rudolf Fürst Franken

Father-and-son team Paul and Sebastian Fürst produce one of the most mind-bogglingly diverse ranges of top wines in Germany, perhaps even the world. The dry

HOFMANN
JURGEN HOFMANN'S WINES ARE LIGHT BUT
BEAUTIFULLY CONCENTRATED

JULIUSSPITAL
THE SILVANER TROCKEN IS ALIVE WITH
GOOSEBERRY AND KIWI FRUIT FLAVORS

Rieslings vinified in neutral oak (by Paul) are concentrated, slow-developing wines whose aromas blossom with at least two years in the bottle, but show great crystalline mineral clarity from day one. The Burgundian-style barrique-fermented and matured dry Weissburgunder (made by Sebastian) is Germany's finest example of this style. However, it is the complex and tannic Spätburgunders (made by Sebastian) that are widely regarded as the estate's greatest wines, despite competition from the richer, very sexy reds from the Frühburgunder grape (a mutation of Pinot Noir).

Hohenlindenweg 46, 63927 Bürgstadt
www.weingut-rudolf-fuerst.de

Schmitt's Kinder Franken

It took a few years for Martin Schmitt to find his own distinctive style after taking over from his father, Karl Martin Schmitt. But since 2007, this estate's wines belong in the Franken premier league. They are now distinctly lighter in body, more lively and elegant, but without sacrificing intensity. The dry Silvaner and Riesling from the unclassified Marbserg site often come very close to matching the (somewhat more spicy) Grosse Gewächse from these grapes from the famous Pfülben site.

Am Sonnenstuhl 45, 97236 Randersacker
www.schmitts-kinder.de

J Störrlein & Krenig Franken

Armin Störrlein and his son-in-law Martin Krenig have a distinctive wine style that is often (inadequately) described as "old-fashioned." Their wines are bottled later than is the norm in the region and most spend many months in neutral wood, but they are full of life and aroma. This is most apparent in the imposing, creamy dry Weissburgunder Grosses Gewächs from Sonnenstuhl, which is one of the top wines from this grape in Franken. There are impressive dry Rieslings and Silvaners, too.

Schulstrasse 14, 97236 Randersacker
www.stoerrlein.de

Weltner Franken

Paul Weltner makes the most charmingly fruity dry wines in the Steigerwald area of Franken, whose gypsum marl soils tend to push the wines in a massive, but sometimes charmless, direction. Dry Scheurebe is an important specialty next to the dry Silavners, Rieslings, and Müller-Thurgaus. ★ **Rising star**

Wiesenbronner Strasse 17, 97348 Rödelsee
www.weltnerwein.de

Winzerhof Stahl Franken

Christian and Simone Stahl have created a brand new style of super-racy, explosively vibrant, dry Franken wine that gives the region's rustic side a strikingly modern feel. The lightest wines, sold as Feder Stahl (Feather Steel), are full of character. The mid-range Damaszener Stahl are bold and expressive, particularly the mineral Müller-Thurgau from Hasennet in the Tauber Valley. The concentrated, dangerously drinkable Best of Silvaner is final proof that Christian Stahl is the Quentin Tarantino of German dry white wine. ★ **Rising star**

Lange Dorfstrasse 21, 97215 Auernhofen
www.winzerhof-stahl.de

BADEN AND WURTTEMBERG

Baden and Württemburg wine regions

Both Baden and Württemberg are substantial wine regions. Baden has 40,000 acres (16,000ha) of vineyards along the western side of the Rhine Valley, and Württemberg has 28,000 acres (11,000ha) close to the River Neckar, a tributary of the Rhine. Despite their scale, few people outside Germany know these names. And the feeling is mutual, for when wine-growers in Baden and Württemberg talk about "exports" they usually mean places such as Berlin or Cologne. The reason for this parochial attitude is simple. In contrast to most of the rest of Germany, wine in Baden and Württemberg has always been part of the regional diet, and, no matter what their social position, people in these regions have always enjoyed consuming it.

Major grapes

🍇 Reds
Lemberger
Spätburgunder
Trollinger (Württemberg only)
Weinsberg Cabernets

🍇 Whites
Grauburgunder (Pinot Gris)
Riesling

Vintages

2009
An excellent vintage across the board, with rich-to-opulent wines of all colors.

2008
A vintage of atypically crisp, fresh dry whites and quite sleek, impressively concentrated reds.

2007
The best vintage for reds to date, and some very good rich dry whites.

2006
Botrytis marred many of the dry whites and slashed yields too, but there were some good reds.

2005
Not as spectacular as further north, but some very good dry whites and some even better reds.

2004
A back-to-normal vintage of mid-weight dry wines with attractive, fresh aromas.

Much of Baden's generally warm and generous dry wine is consumed by locals and tourists with the often excellent local cooking. The majority of the southern section of the region lies on the western foothills of the Schwarzwald and the dramatic vineyard scenery is a major tourist attraction. In Württemberg, the consumption of traditional light dry wines in quarter-liter glasses known as Viertele along with a "Vesper" (platter of cold cuts) is an essential part of everyday life. Climatic differences from one subregion to the next enable both Baden and Württemberg to produce an enormous diversity of wines.

Baden's image in Germany has been positive since its cooks started collecting Michelin stars and after its signature white wine was reinvented. In 1979, the Pinot Gris grape, previously known as Ruländer—a name associated in popular consciousness with heavy, sweet wines incompatible with fine cuisine—was renamed Grauburgunder. A simultaneous change in winemaking slimmed down, freshened up, and dried out the wines, making them modern Germany's first fashionable indigenous food wines. With Alsace Pinot Gris now frequently off-dry or sweet, Baden's top Grauburgunders are arguably the most impressive dry wines from this grape.

More recently, the area has become red wine country. A flurry of planting has given Baden more than 14,500 acres (5,900ha) of Pinot Noir, here called Spätburgunder. The best of these wines can stand comparison with top-quality Pinots from Burgundy or anywhere else on Planet Wine. The only problem is that the top wines are far outnumbered by more ordinary wines, and a great deal of Baden's Spätburgunder is full, supple, and harmless.

In Württemberg, 71% of the vineyards are planted with red wine varieties, but almost a third of this is taken up by the humble Trollinger, which gives pale, light wines. All too often the variety is over-cropped, resulting in thin, tart wine, which is the reason why Württemberg earned the nickname, "The Trollinger Republic." The problem with Trollinger is that it needs the warmest vineyard sites to ripen properly, so it covers a large proportion of the sites well suited to the production of high-quality red wine from other varieties. It is possible to turn Trollinger into a real red wine through drastic yield reduction, and many Jungwintzer are now following this course.

Serious Württemberg reds are either spicy, sleek Lembergers (the variety is also known as Blaufränkisch in Austria and Kékfrankos in Hungary) or more powerful and bolder *cuvées*, often including the new Weinsberg Cabernets. These crossings of Cabernet Sauvignon and local varieties, bred at the famous wine school of Weinsberg close to Heilbronn, are much better suited to the local climatic conditions than Cabernet Sauvignon. However, this dynamic category is as unknown outside Germany as the rich and aromatic new Sauvignon Blancs from the Remstal area; cult wines in Germany.

Both regions are dominated by co-operative wineries, many of them quite small and of a high general standard. In Baden the co-operative of Durbach stands out, while in Württemberg, Collegium Wirtemberg and Weinmanufaktur Untertürkheim are the leaders. These three co-ops are among the most important producers pioneering the dry Riesling renaissance in the two regions. Baden has 2,500 acres (1,000ha) of this variety, Württemberg 5,000 acres (2,000ha).

BADEN AND WURTTEMBERG

On this map, the 100 miles (160km) over which the regions of Baden and Württemberg stretch do not look like much. However, the regions' size means that their wines are difficult to describe in a few words. The wide range of grape varieties cultivated in both regions has a lot to do with their enormous climatic and geological diversity. Wines from the warmest pockets regularly tip the scales at more than 14% alcohol and taste correspondingly opulent, yet across the regions there are high-altitude areas that produce wines that are sleek, pristine, and delicate.

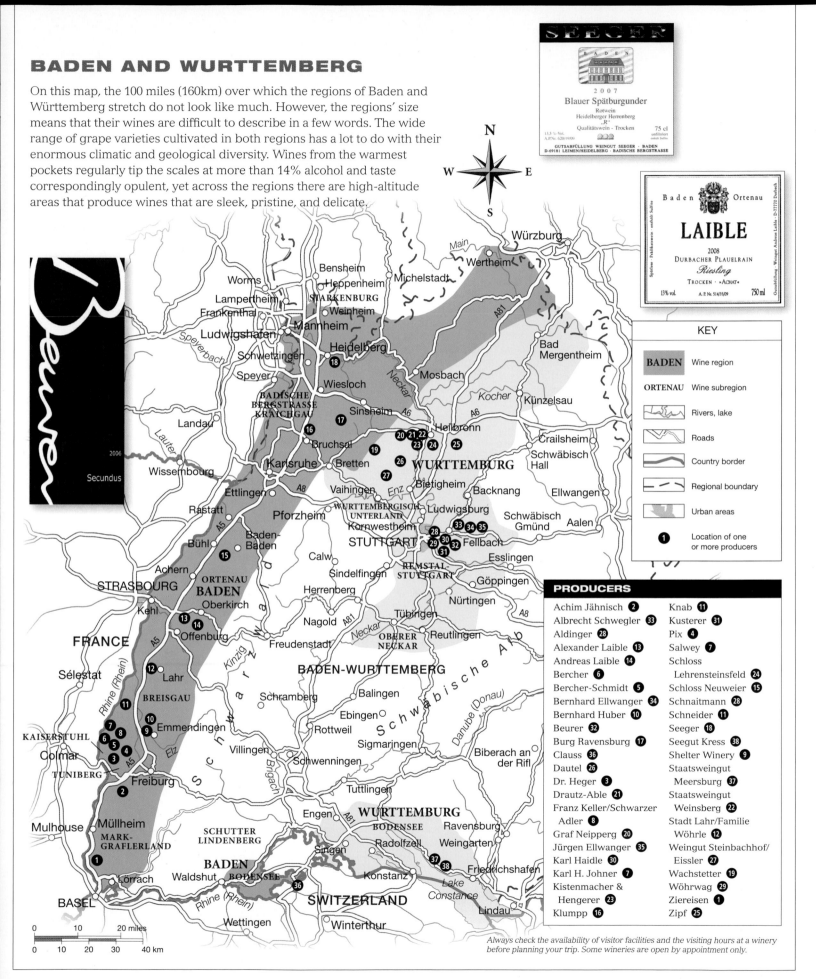

KEY

BADEN	Wine region
ORTENAU	Wine subregion
	Rivers, lake
	Roads
	Country border
	Regional boundary
	Urban areas
1	Location of one or more producers

PRODUCERS

Achim Jähnisch	**2**	Knab	**11**
Albrecht Schwegler	**33**	Kusterer	**31**
Aldinger	**28**	Pix	**4**
Alexander Laible	**13**	Salwey	**7**
Andreas Laible	**14**	Schloss	
Bercher	**6**	Lehrensteinsfeld	**24**
Bercher-Schmidt	**5**	Schloss Neuweier	**15**
Bernhard Ellwanger	**34**	Schnaitmann	**28**
Bernhard Huber	**10**	Schneider	**11**
Beurer	**32**	Seeger	**18**
Burg Ravensburg	**17**	Seegut Kress	**38**
Clauss	**36**	Shelter Winery	**9**
Dautel	**26**	Staatsweingut	
Dr. Heger	**3**	Meersburg	**37**
Drautz-Able	**21**	Staatsweingut	
Franz Keller/Schwarzer		Weinsberg	**22**
Adler	**8**	Stadt Lahr/Familie	
Graf Neipperg	**20**	Wöhrle	**12**
Jürgen Ellwanger	**35**	Weingut Steinbachhof/	
Karl Haidle	**30**	Eissler	**27**
Karl H. Johner	**7**	Wachstetter	**19**
Kistenmacher &		Wöhrwag	**29**
Hengerer	**23**	Ziereisen	**1**
Klumpp	**16**	Zipf	**25**

Always check the availability of visitor facilities and the visiting hours at a winery before planning your trip. Some wineries are open by appointment only.

ALEXANDER LAIBLE
ALEXANDER LAIBLE'S CHARA RIESLING IS
PRECISE AND RICHLY CONCENTRATED

BERCHER
THE POWERFUL BERCHER REDS NEED TIME
IN THE CELLAR TO SHOW THEIR BEST

Achim Jähnisch Baden

Geisenheim wine school graduate Achim Jähnisch founded his tiny estate back in 1999 and rapidly became one of the leading producers of dry whites in Southern Baden. Many of these are vinified in used barriques and the oak influence is discreet or imperceptible, the intensely mineral Rieslings and Grauburgunder having great aging potential. The refined and slow-developing Chardonnay is the only white to show some obvious oak, while the characterful, crisp Gutedel is sensational value for money. The Spätburgunder reds are austerely tannic, but also impressive. ★ **Rising star**

Hofmattenweg 19, 79238 Kirchhofen
www.weingut-jaehnisch.de

Albrecht Schwegler Württemberg

In 1990, with no capital and a tiny area of vines, Albrecht and Andrea Schwegler set out to revolutionize Württemberg red wines. With the first vintage of their *cuvée* Granat, they hit the bullseye. Based on Merlot and Zweigelt, sometimes with a dash of Syrah or Cabernet Franc, this remains the region's most consistently impressive "big red" and is capable of long bottle-aging as few of its competitors are. Saphir is a slightly less concentrated and tannic cuvée, but also one of Württemberg's top reds, and Beryll is a more forthrightly fruity wine for drinking younger. All spend two full years in barrique. ★ **Rising star**

Steinstrasse 35, 71404 Korb/Württemberg
www.albrecht-schwegler.de

Aldinger Württemberg

Three generations of the Aldinger family stand behind a wide range of excellent wines. The range extends from the generous, fruit-driven dry white and red Bentz up to the complex, non-grassy Sauvignon Blanc "S," the muscular red "C" from various Cabernets, and the plush "M" Merlot. It is debatable whether the red Grosse Gewächse from the Untertürkheimer Gips (Spätburgunder) and Fellbacher Lämmler (Lemberger) benefit from the strong toast and vanilla aromas from new oak. Thankfully, the generous, ripe, dry Riesling Grosses Gewächs from the Lämmler site is no longer given any oak. The nobly sweet Auslese and Eiswein are also excellent.

Schmerstrasse 25, 70734 Fellbach/Würrtemberg
www.weingut-aldinger.de

Alexander Laible Baden

The new estate of Alexander Laible is based in a former bakery. That it has Riesling vineyards 25 miles (40km) to the north, and Weissburgunder, Grauburgunder, and Chardonnay growing 25 miles to the south, is an example of how Baden is reinventing itself. Although the first vintage was 2007, the dry whites are richly aromatic with explosive freshness and look to have great aging potential. The top Rieslings are the Chara and Dios bottlings; with the other grapes, look for "SL" on the label. ★ **Rising star**

Unterwewiler 48, 77770 Durbach/Baden
www.weingut-alexanderlaible.de

Andreas Laible Baden

From just 18 acres (7ha) of precipitously steep, weathered granite hillside, Andreas Laible, the leading winemaker of the Ortenau subregion of Baden, conjures a wide variety of fragrant and filigree dry Rieslings unique in this part of Germany. Top of the range are the Grosses Gewächs and the Achat in which the balance of multi-faceted fruit aromas and mineral freshness is near perfect. The nobly sweet Auslese from the Scheurebe and Traminer grapes are often spectacularly succulent, yet delicate and clean. No wonder Laible has won just about every winemaking prize on offer in Germany!

Am Bühl 6, 77770 Durbach/Baden
www.andreas-laible.com

Bercher Baden

No Bercher wine ever disappointed, but there is no question that the arrival of the new generation here—Martin Bercher is in charge of the vineyards and his brother Arne is winemaker—has given the estate a new impulse. The dry Kabinett wines continue to dominate production and they impress both with their clarity and effusive fruit. In contrast, the dry Grosse Gewächse—Grauburgunder from Schlossgarten and Feuerberg, Weissburgunder from the latter site—are powerful and succulent with intense mineral character. The reds remain as imposing as ever, but a shade more lively.

Mittelstadt 13, 79235 Burkheim/Baden
www.weingutbercher.de

Bercher-Schmidt

Franz Wilhelm Schmidt's dry Weissburgunders and Grauburgunders are the unsung heroes among Kaiserstuhl white wines. They combine the body and ripeness typical of this subregion of Baden with a rare elegance and excellent aging potential. The stars are the Weissburgunder from the Rosenkranz site and the Grauburgunder from the Steinbuck. The dry Silvaner is excellent, too. ★ **Rising star**

Herrenstrasse 28, 79235 Oberrotweil/Baden
www.bercher-schmidt.de

Bernhard Ellwanger Württemberg

Taste mercurial Sven Ellwanger's Sauvignon Blanc Junges Schwaben (or "Young Swabia," the group of young Württemberg winemakers he belongs to) with its honeydew melon and snow pea aromas, and you will understand why this was once the main white grape in the Remstal Valley. However, Ellwanger's juicy and vibrant dry Rieslings and the wide range of reds impress no less. Among the best of these is the modestly priced Kreation Nero, a fruit-driven, gently tannic Lemberger/Spätburgunder/Dornfelder/Merlot blend. A producer that is fast going places. ★ **Rising star**

Rebenstrasse 9, 71384 Grossheppach/Württemberg
www.weingut-ellwanger.com

Bernhard Huber Baden

Bernhard and Barbara Huber's garage winery, started in 1987, was one of Germany's first. Since then, it has become Baden's leading producer of Spätburgunder reds. A high-tech winery enabled Bernhard to perfect a style that is inspired by Burgundy, but which, since the 2000 vintage, has been absolutely his own. Extremely concentrated, plush and generously tannic, but never a jot too big, hard, or oaky, his four single-vineyard bottlings—the Grosse Gewächse from the Bienenberg, Sommerhalde, and Schlossberg sites, and the Wildenstein—are world-class

Pinot Noirs. However, even the Spätburgunder Junge Reben from young vines is full of fruit and charm. Barrique-matured dry Weissburgunder, Grauburgunder, and Chardonnay (from rare old vines) are all imposing wines with excellent balance, and the similarly styled Malterer (a *cuvée* of Weissburgunder and the forgotten Freisamer grape) is a startlingly textural dry white.

Heimbacher Weg 19, 79364 Malterdingen/Baden
www.weingut-huber.de

Beurer Württemberg

In 1997, the Beurers left the local co-operative winery and started turning their grapes into wine in their garage. Since then, ex-European BMX champion Jochen Beurer has become Württemberg's most radical dry Riesling producer, marketing his wines strictly by vineyard soil type. Packed full of mineral character and spice, powerful, but never heavy or broad (a frequent problem for Riesling in this region), they taste like nothing else in Germany. The finest of them is the bottling from Kiselsandstein (gravel-sandstone). The muscular dry Grauburgunder and off-dry Gewürztraminer are produced in a similar mode and are equally impressive, while the reds are rapidly improving, too. ★ Rising star

Lange Strasse 67, 71394 Kernen-Stetten/Württemberg
www.weingut-beurer.de

Burg Ravensburg Baden

Burg Ravensburg produces some of the most impressive white and red wines in Baden's underrated north. Though never short of full, ripe fruit aromas, the dry whites—most importantly Riesling, but also Weissburgunder and Grauburgunder—always retain a cool mineral freshness. Of these, the Riesling Grosses Gewächs from the Husarenkappe site is the finest. The estate also makes big, tannic reds that never taste too fat.

Am Mühlberg 3, 76684 Östringen-Tiefenbach
www.burg-ravensburg.de

Clauss Baden

From vineyards often only yards from the border with Switzerland, Susanne and Berthold Clauss make some of the sleekest and raciest dry whites in Baden. These include the region's finest Müller-Thurgau—one of the great Baden bargains. Top of the range are the fragrant, elegant Weissburgunder and Grauburgunder from Nack, and the Spätburgunder Blanc de Noirs Belemnit (a rare, fossil-rich rock type), one of Baden's most original dry whites. The reds are also rapidly improving. ★ Rising star

Obere Dorfstrasse 39, 79807 Nack/Baden
www.nackerwein.de

Dautel

Ernst Dautel worked tirelessly through the 1990s and the first years of this century to improve the quality of Württemberg's red wines, so much so that the impressive dry whites were overshadowed. Nobody in the region makes better Weissburgunder (the three-star bottling without oak, the four-star with toasty oak) and the robust and crisp dry Rieslings are also first rate. These wines age well too, taking a decade in the bottle in their stride. Most of the top reds are sold under the "S" designation, with the firm and concentrated Lemberger the star. Those who like plenty of dry tannin might prefer the powerful red

JURGEN ELLWANGER
JURGEN ELLWANGER CREATES SOME OF WURTTEMBERG'S BEST REDS

DR. HEGER
MIMUS IS A RICH, POWERFUL, BUT CAREFULLY OAKED SPATBURGUNDER

Kreation, a Cabernet/Merlot/Lemberger blend. Dautel's son, Christian, has joined the winemaking team, and is just beginning to bring in new ideas. ★ Rising star

Lauerweg 55, 74357 Bönnigheim/Württemberg
www.weingut-dautel.de

Dr. Heger Baden

During the 1980s, Joachim Heger was one of the pioneers of the new-style dry Pinot Gris, or Grauburgunder, in Baden. During the 1990s, he was at the forefront of the development of the new-style barrique-matured Pinot Noir, or Spätburgunder. Today, the wide range of dry whites from the Ihringer Winklerberg, and Achkarrer Schlossberg sites (the greatest in the Kaiserstuhl sub-area of Baden) are of uniformly high quality and the tendency to over-oak some wines has been overcome. Even the wines from the often-overlooked Silvaner grape show the elegance and delicate spice of the Winklerberg. The Spätburgunder reds are big, warm, and bold.

Bachenstrasse 19, 79241 Ihringen/Baden
www.heger-weine.de

Drautz-Able Württemberg

Markus Drautz had a hard act to follow when he succeeded his charismatic father, Richard, whose contribution is marked by "RD" on a range of Drautz-Able's well established and successful reds. However, Markus quickly shook up the dry whites, giving them more freshness and aroma. The dry Riesling, Weissburgunder, Grauburgunder, and a *cuvée* (the two "Burgunders" plus a healthy dose of Silvaner) under the Drei Tauben (Three Doves) label all impress. The new reds are more supple and elegant with the varietal Merlot and Lemberger under the Hades label impressing as much as the Cabernet/Merlot/Lemberger red blend, Jodokus.

Faissstrasse 23, 74076 Heilbronn
www.drautz-able.de

Franz Keller/Schwarzer Adler Baden

Schwarzer Adler is the self-confidently conservative restaurant that won Germany's first Michelin star and successfully defends it each year. The bone-dry, slow-developing gastronomic style of Fritz Keller's dry whites is shaped by this dining room. It is difficult to know whether to prefer the pristine clarity of the unoaked dry Weissburgunder and Grauburgunder or the suave refinement of the gently oaked Selection and more powerful Selection A versions of these grapes. Since the beginning of the 21st century, the Spätburgunder reds have taken a leap upward in quality, and have become even more Burgundian in style. ★ Rising star

Badbergstrasse 23, 79235 Oberbergen/Baden
www.franz-keller.de

Graf Neipperg Württemberg

The Graf Neipperg estate dates back at least to 1248, but it is by far the most dynamic of the region's larger estates thanks to the tireless Karl Eugen Erbgraf zu Neipperg and the radical replanting program he instigated. The dry Rieslings from the Neipperger Schlossberg site have a wonderful perfume and elegance, which only the off-dry Muskatteler tops. Like the nobly sweet Traminer, this is the best example of its type in the region. The expressive dry Trollinger is also a candidate for the best wine from

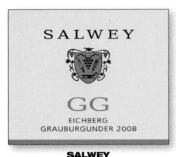

SALWEY

SALWEY'S EICHBERG GRAUBURGUNDER
IS ONE OF THE BEST IN THE REGION

this grape in Württemberg. Legend has it that the Neippergs brought the Lemberger grape here from Austria (where it is called Blaufränkisch) in the 17th century, so it is appropriate that their Lemberger Grosses Gewächs from the Schlossberg is a many-layered and elegant wine. In terms of power, the remarkable new Merlot SE tops it though. ★ **Rising star**

*Schlossstrasse 12, 74193 Schwaigern/Württemberg
www.graf-neipperg.de*

Jürgen Ellwanger Württemberg

Jürgen Ellwanger's modesty, and the fact that this estate is tucked away in the narrow section of the Remstal Valley, perhaps explains why its profile is not as high as the quality deserves. The rich and tannic Nicodemus, a Merlot/Lemberger/Cabernet Cubin blend, is one of the region's finest reds. But it faces tough internal competition from the bold, plummy Hades Zweigelt and the sauve, concentrated Spätburgunder Grosses Gewächs from the Lichtenberg site. This is another Württemberg producer whose dry Rieslings—which are in this case racy and mineral in flavor—are lost in the shadow of its reds.

*Bachstrasse 21, 73650 Winterbach/Württemberg
www.weingut-ellwanger.de*

Karl Haidle Württemberg

Hans Haidle made his name with bone-dry Rieslings during the 1980s. Today, though, he is famous for some of the most powerful and tannic reds in Württemberg, none more so than the Lemberger-based *cuvée* Ypsilon with its opulent blackberry fruit, toast, and balsamic vinegar notes. No less concentrated or alcoholic (14%), but more discreet, is the Spätburgunder Grosses Gewächs from the Schnaiter Burghalde site. In recent years, the dry Rieslings have gained enormously in peachy aroma, juiciness, and power, and they are now model examples of modern Württemberg winemaking.

*Hindenburgstrasse 21, 71394 Kernen-Stetten/Württemberg
www.weingut-karl-haidle.de*

Karl H Johner Baden

Back in 1985, when he founded his eponymous estate in his garage, Karl Heinz Johner had a day job as winemaker at Lamberhurst in England and was a long-distance commuter. Then as now, everything is matured in barrique, even the dry Rivaner (aka Müller-Thurgau). Karl Heinz Johner's description of this wine—"thank goodness it does not taste like a typical Müller-Thurgau!"—sums up the dare-to-be-different ethos that reigns here to this day under Johner's son, Patrick. The dry Weissburgunder/Chardonnay blend continues to be one of Germany's most successful barrique-matured whites, while the New Zealand-inspired Sauvignon Blanc is also excellent. The Spätburgunder reds are powerful and beautifully balanced. "SJ" designates the reserve wines.

*Gartenstrasse 20, 79235 Bischoffingen/Baden
www.johner.de*

Kistenmacher & Hengerer
Württemberg

Anyone who doubts the Trollinger grape (the Vernatsch of Alto Adige in Italy) can give real red wines must try Hans Hengerer's Alte Reben bottling. It tastes like a

smaller brother of his muscular, tannic Spätburgunder Junges Schwaben, the best Pinot Noir in northern Württemberg. Altogether, his reds are big and bold with masses of character. Hengerer makes full-bodied, succulent dry Rieslings, too. ★ **Rising star**

*Eugen-Nägele-Strasse 23-25, 74074 Heilbronn/
Württemberg; www.kistenmacher-hengerer.de*

Klumpp Baden

Ulrich and Marietta Klumpp started the leading estate of the Kraichgau area of northern Baden back in 1983. They kept their day jobs until 1990 in order to build the estate (currently almost 60 acres/24ha in extent). Today, their ambitious son, Markus, is pulling out all the stops to take Klumpp into the first rank of Baden producers. Every drop of ripe, fragrant, but firm Spätburgunder red produced is barrique-matured. St Laurent and Lemberger (rare grapes in Baden) are just as rich and have even more tannic power. The barrique-matured top bottlings of Chardonnay and Grauburgunder are not a jot over-oaked, but rather models of harmony. ★ **Rising star**

*Heidelberger Strasse 100, 76646 Bruchsal/Baden
www.weingut-klumpp.com*

Knab Baden

Since Thomas and Regina Rinker took over the Knab estate in 1994, they have pushed quality ever higher. Ripe, succulent, but beautifully balanced, their Weissburgunders and Grauburgunders are among the best dry whites made in the Kaiserstuhl and are excellent value for money. Though the Spätburgunder reds are not quite as elegant, they are full and ripe, developing nutty and caramel aromas as they mature. Regina Rinker is also a talented artist whose works decorate the very stylish and modern tasting room. ★ **Rising star**

*Hennengärtle 1a, 79346 Endingen/Baden
www.knabweingut.de*

Kusterer Württemberg

Esslingen, where the Kusterer estate is based, was once famous for its steep terraced vineyards. But those vineyards were forgotten until Hans and Monika Kusterer started to show what they are capable of back in 1983. The couple are now sole owners of the Neckarhalde site, where they produce one of the most imposing Spätburgunder reds in Württemberg. It is a tough call to choose whether to praise their peppery Blauer Zweigelt more than their spicy Lemberger. Both, however, are topped by the rich and powerful Mélac, a Merlot/Zweigelt *cuvée*. As well as these great reds, the Kusterers make strikingly original dry Riesling and Grauburgunder.

*Untere Beutau 44, 73728 Esslingen/Württemberg
www.weingut-kusterer.de*

Pix Baden

This small organic (since 1984) producer has long produced some of the best-value dry Silvaner, Riesling, Weissburgunder, and Grauburgunder in the Kaiserstuhl subregion of Baden, as well as good Spätburgunder. Thanks to Geisenheim wine school-trained son, Hannes, quality is improving further. ★ **Rising star**

*Eisenbahnstrasse 19, 79241 Ihringen/Baden
www.weingut-pix.de*

KLUMPP

THE SK IS A SPÄTBURGUNDER THAT CAN
COMPETE WITH BURGUNDY'S PINOT NOIR

Salwey Baden

Since Konrad Salwey took over from his father, Wolf-Dietrich, there has been a marked change of style for the 100 acre (40ha) estate's top dry whites. The Weissburgunder Grosses Gewächs from the Kirchberg site, and the Grauburgunder Grosses Gewächs from the Eichberg, are rich, concentrated, and creamy wines with a subtle kiss of oak. However, the quality of the much lighter and crisper regular bottlings is, if anything, more impressive. In recent years, a big leap forward has been made with the racy dry Riesling from the granitic slopes of the Glottertal where the Salweys have long produced one of the most elegant Spätburgunder rosés in all of Germany. The big Spätburgunder reds have plenty of fruit and tannin, but lack the elegance of the whites.

Hauptsstrasse 2, 79235 Oberrotweil/Baden
www.salwey.de

Schloss Lehrensteinsfeld Württemberg

Christoph Ruck of Schloss Lehrensteinsfeld is one of the great new winemaking talents in Württemberg, but often gets underrated because he is an outsider. His sleek dry and off-dry Rieslings have an explosive vibrancy and complexity rare in this region and they unquestionably deserve their local nickname, "LSD." However, it is his elegant and refined Spätburgunder reds—which are more than a little reminiscent of fine burgundy—that are the estate's most impressive wines. ★ **Rising star**

Schlossstrasse 18, 74251 Lehrensteinsfeld/Württemberg
www.schloss-lehrensteinsfeld.de

Schloss Neuweier Baden

Since 1992, when the architect Gisela Joos bought it and appointed Alexander Spinner as winemaker, the historic Schloss Neuweier estate has maintained a high standard with its dry Rieslings from the steep Mauerberg and Schlossberg sites. The combination of poor granite and porphyry soils and hands-off winemaking results in wines with a sleek elegance that invariably taste lighter than they actually are. Top of the range is the super-ripe, but racy, dry Riesling Grosses Gewächs from the terraced Goldenes Loch parcel of the Mauerberg. The regular quality wines are impressive, too. ★ **Rising star**

Mauerbergstrasse 21, 76534 Neuweier/Baden
www.weingut-schloss-neuweier.de

Schnaitmann Württemberg

In 1997, the young Rainer Schnaitmann turned his back on the local co-operative winery to go solo and become the shooting star winemaker of Württemberg. More than anyone else, he has (re-) established the reputation of Sauvignon in the Remstal Valley with opulent, multi-dimensional wines that have no parallel anywhere on Planet Wine. Then he went on to do the same for Spätburgunder and Frühburgunder reds, proving that the area can produce world-class Pinot Noir in a concentrated, lusciously fruity, contemporary mode without imitating Burgundy. Since 2007, the dry Rieslings belong in the same league, at once rich and subtle. Genius has its price, but by international standards, these are not expensive wines for the quality. ★ **Rising star**

Untertürkheimer Strasse 4, 70734 Fellbach/Württemberg
www.weingut-schnaitmann.de

Schneider Baden

The small, family-owned-and-run Schneider estate produces some of the most individual dry white and red wines in the Kaiserstuhl area of Baden, even though Endingen lacks famous vineyard sites. Instead of writing the vineyard site names on the label, the Schneiders designate their top wines with "A" if they grew on loam, "C" if the vineyard soil was loess, and "R" if it was volcanic. Their richly fruity Spätburgunder reds are their best known wines, but the dry white Weissburgunder and Ruländer (here preferred to the modern name Grauburgunder) are equally impressive. ★ **Rising star**

Königschaffhausener Strasse 2, 79346 Endingen/Kaiserstuhl
www.weingutschneider.com

Seeger Baden

Though situated in the far north of Baden, immediately south of Heidelberg, Thomas Seeger makes some of the most powerfully tannic and concentrated Spätburgunder in the entire region. The very low yields and perfectionism have their price though. The more modestly priced Weissburgunder and Grauburgunder are rich, highly textural dry whites in a no less distinctive style than that of the reds. ★ **Rising star**

Rohrbacher Strasse 101, 69181 Leimen/Baden
www.seegerweingut.de

Seegut Kress Baden

Kristin and Thomas Kress are the leading white winemakers on the northern shore of Lake Constance. Their wines combine the bright, racy freshness of this subregion of Baden with intense fruit aromas and a whiplash freshness. The vibrant dry Müller-Thurgau could be mistaken for Riesling, while the succulent but uplifting Grauburgunder is worlds away from some of the weighty and ponderous examples of this grape from the Kaiserstuhl. The Spätburgunder rosé is one of Germany's best pink Pinot Noirs. ★ **Rising star**

Hauptstrasse 2, 88709 Hagnau/Baden
www.seegut-kress.de

Shelter Winery Baden

North Germans Hans-Bert Espe (from Osterode) and Silke Wolf (from Paderborn) met while studying in Geisenheim and founded their tiny winery in Offenburg/Baden in 2003. The eccentric name they gave their winery derives from the fact that initially the cellar was a shelter—that is, a bunker for jet fighters—on the former Canadian air base in Lahr. They have since moved to Kenzingen in the Breisgau subregion of Baden, close to their 10 acres (4ha) of vineyards, and have a custom-built winery. Their powerful, tannic, and complex Pinot Noir is one of the region's top reds; its smaller brother, the Spätburgunder, is lighter and quite austere. Shelter also makes champagne-like Sekt and Blanc de Noirs, both 100% Pinot Noir. ★ **Rising star**

Mühlenstrasse 17, 79341 Kenzingen/Baden
www.shelterwinery.de

Staatsweingut Meersburg Baden

Under the direction of Dr. Jürgen Dietrich, this state-owned winery has turned into the dynamo of the upturn in the Lake Constance (Bodensee) subregion of Baden. Here, Spätburgunder is grown for rosé—look out for the great dry rosé from the Bengel site—as much as for reds.

SPATBURGUNDER

Spätburgunder is German for Pinot Noir and the world is just waking up to the fact that the alternative name is no fundamental impediment to producing great Pinot Noir red wine. Since the mid-1980s, winemakers throughout Germany have been planting new clones, slashing yields, and turning cultivation methods and cellar practices upside-down to reach the premier league with this grape. Now they have succeeded, and German winemakers are beginning to realize the potential of their 30,000 acres (12,000ha) of Pinot Noir. People like Bernhard Huber, in previously unknown Malterdingen in Baden, who founded his winery only in 1990 and now easily sells out his sensational Pinot Noirs for high prices, show what is possible. The idea that Germany is too cool to produce top-quality reds was finally disproven in 2003 when the problem with wines from this grape variety was definitely too much alcohol and power, rather than too little.

STAATSWEINGUT MEERSBERG
THE WEISSBURGUNDER MARRIES POWER
WITH DELIGHTFUL FRESHNESS

Of the reds, the most powerful and complex is the Spätburgunder from the Ritterhalde site of Gaillingen, where the soil resembles that in Châteauneuf-du-Pape. The dry Müller-Thurgau from Germany's highest-altitude vineyard site, the volcanic Hohentwieler Olgaberg, is remarkably mineral and racy for this grape. ★**Rising star**

Seminarstrassse 6, 88709 Meersburg/Baden
www.staatsweingut-meersburg.de

Staatsweingut Weinsberg
Württemberg
The commercial arm of the Weinsberg wine school makes a wide range of wines from 100 acres (40ha). Thanks to winemaker Dr. Dieter Blankenhorn, great strides have been made with dry Riesling in recent years. The fruit-driven "S" bottling gives the slower-developing, intensely mineral Grosses Gewächs from the high-altitude Burg Wildeck site serious competition. The plush, but tannic *cuvée* Traum, from the new Cabernet varieties bred at the school, is one of Germany's most important new "big reds." The Spätburgunder Grosses Gewächs from the Himmelreich site is a rich and spicy-oaky Pinot Noir with several prizes under its belt.

Traubenplatz 5, 74189 Weinsberg/Württemberg
www.staatsweingut-weinsberg.de

Stadt Lahr/Familie Wöhrle Baden
The Stadt Lahr/Familie Wöhrle estate has been organic since 1990 and always made good dry whites in a fruit-driven, very clean style. Since Markus Wöhrle finished studying at the Geisenheim wine school and returned from working at Müller-Catoir in the Pfalz in 2003, quality took another step up and today these are clearly the best wines from the northern end of the underrated Breisgau subregion of Baden. The entire range of Weissburgunder and Grauburgunder is of impeccable purity and great elegance, and even the concentrated Grosse Gewächse are good value for money given the great quality. ★**Rising star**

Weinbergstrasse 3, 77933 Lahr/Baden
www.weingut-stadt-lahr.de

Weingut Steinbachhof/Eissler
Württemberg
If you are looking for deeply colored, oaky blockbuster reds, then Weingut Steinbachhof/Eissler is the wrong place to go. However, if it is finesse and silky textures in red wines that turn you on, then Ulrich and Nanna Eissler's small estate will most certainly meet with your approval. The only question is whether their Lembergers or their Schwarzrieslings (Pinot Meunier) are the more subtle, complex, and seductive. From the 2008 vintage, the dry Rieslings took a leap forward and are beginning to match the elegance of the reds. ★**Rising star**

Hofgut Steinbachhof 1, 71665 Enz-Gündelbach/
Württemberg; www.weingut-steinbachhof.de

Wachstetter Württemberg
Confident, yet thoughtful Rainer Wachstetter has the reputation of being the new Mr. Lemberger, and it is true that this variety flourishes in this high-altitude part of the Zaber Valley. Then again, so do Spätburgunder, Merlot, and many other red grapes. The Ernst Combé series of barrique-matured reds is the official top of the range, but

ZIEREISEN
THE ZIEREISENS ARE PROVING IT IS POSSIBLE
TO MAKE GREAT SYRAH IN GERMANY

wines such as the juicy, yet substantial Lemberger Felix and more elegant Spätburgunder Louis are almost as impressive and are great value for money. The same can be said of the talented young winemaker's underrated dry whites, particularly the rapidly improving Rieslings, which combine generous fruit with freshness. There is excellent sparkling Sekt, too. ★**Rising star**

Michelbacher Strasse 8, 74397 Pfaffenhofen/Württemberg
www.wachstetter.de

Wöhrwag Württemberg
In 1994, the dry Riesling "Goldkapsel" (Gold Cap) from Hans-Peter and Christin Wöhrwag revolutionized the wines of this grape in Wurttemberg, proving that it could make aromatic Rieslings with crispness and vitality like those of Christin's native Rheingau. In the same vintage, they also began production of nobly sweet Riesling Auslese and Eiswein, which remain the pinnacle for this style in the region, thanks to their combination of great concentration and sensational brilliance. Recent vintages of Lemberger and Spätburgunder reds have also impressed with rich fruit and elegantly dry tannins. Be warned: all the wines sell out fast upon release. ★**Rising star**

Grunbacher Strasse 5, 70327 Untertürkheim/Württemberg;
www.woehrwag.de

Ziereisen Baden
Husband-and-wife team Hans-Peter and Edeltraud Ziereisen embody the new spirit of Baden's far south. It is a spirit that combines half-forgotten local tradition with innovative winemaking and an atypically German ability to improvise. The latter is particularly essential given the five cellars the Ziereisens have in town. Here, the humble Gutedel (aka Chasselas) grape variety gives wines with bright citrusy fruit and a surprising amount of substance. The regular dry Grauburgunder and Weissburgunder are ripe and effusive, the barrique-matured versions of these wines having the depth and complexity of top white burgundy. The high points, however, are the Ziereisen's super-elegant, slow-developing Spätburgunders, of which the Jaspis is the richest and most spicy, the Rhini the most brilliant and concentrated. These—not to mention Germany's finest Syrah—are all sold as "Deutsche Tafelwein." ★**Rising star**

Markgrafenstrasse 17, 79588 Efringen-Kirchen
www.ziereisen.de

Zipf Württemberg
In recent years, young husband-and-wife team Jürgen and Tanya Zipf have turned this small family-owned estate into one of the region's most dynamic producers. The high-altitude location and a climate influenced by the forests that surround the small town, make possible some highly elegant Rieslings with racy acidity and pronounced mineral character—the couple are pushing the envelope with this style. Next to an unusally floral, ripe Trollinger red, the new Lembergers are the most impressive reds, being packed with berry aromas and spice, but moderate oak and a near-perfect balance of fruit and tannin. There is excellent value for money to be found right through the range. ★**Rising star**

Vorhofer Strasse 4, 74245 Löwenstein/Württemberg
www.zipf.com

The steeply terraced vineyards of the Kaiserstuhl and nearby Tuniberg produce around a third of Baden's wine.

SAALE-UNSTRUT, SACHSEN, AND THE NEW FAR NORTH

Even in Germany, many consumers remain sceptical about the wines of the two wine-growing regions situated in the former East Germany. And it is true that they almost all lie significantly further north (at least 51° North) than the regions further to the west. The widespread assumption that this geographic position means their wines must be thin and acidic is wrong, however. It has certainly not been the case since the arrival of modern winemaking technology and modern vine clones after the fall of the Berlin Wall. During the same period, the effects of global warming have also made themselves felt, and the wines have improved immeasurably.

■ Saale-Unstrut and Sachsen wine region

Major grapes

Reds
Portugieser
Spätburgunder
Zweigelt

Whites
Gewürztraminer
Grauburgunder
Müller-Thurgau
Riesling
Silvaner
Traminer
Weissburgunder

Vintages

2009
A very good, possibly even great, vintage right across the varietal spectrum.

2008
Aromatic and racy wines that seldom showed any of the greenness initially feared.

2007
Rich, well-balanced dry whites and some impressive reds.

2006
A vintage of full-bodied and ripe-to-very-ripe dry wines.

2005
Excellent: near-perfect balance in the dry whites, and some great dessert wines.

2004
A good, rather typical vintage of medium-bodied dry whites with not too much acidity.

These are, and have always been, beautiful regions, with terraced vineyards clinging to the steep terraced sides of the valleys of the Saale and Unstrut (after which one region is named) and the Elbe. The replanting of almost all the vineyards and the renovation of a wealth of historic buildings during the past couple of decades has only accentuated the beauty.

The way in which the area is thriving can largely be attributed to another element in the vinous "Aufbau Ost," or upturn in the East: the enthusiasm of the locals for cultivating their vineyards and a regional chauvinism that keeps wine prices high compared with the wine-growing regions of the former West Germany.

Significant political decisions have also played their part in shaping the region's modern-day character and dimensions, however. Shortly after German reunification, the two established wine-growing regions of the former East Germany were permitted by the European Union (where there has been a ban on increasing the vineyard area since the early 1980s due to over-production) to expand their vineyard areas to a total of around 2,500 acres (1,000ha). This opportunity was grasped much more fervently by the winegrowers of Saale-Unstrut, where the vineyard area has expanded from 1,070 acres (430ha) in 1994 to 1,600 acres

(650ha) today. Sachsen, by contrast, grew from 790 acres (320ha) in 1992 to 1,090 acres (440ha) today.

The other direction of growth has been northward. At around 51°30′N to the west of the industrial city of Halle, 45 minutes drive north of the main body of the Saale-Unstrut vineyards, there are now 210 acres (85ha) of vines. At 52°23′N in Werder, to the west of Berlin, are 16 acres (6ha) and at 53°30′N in Rattey, a good hour's drive north of Berlin, almost 9 acres (3.5ha) of vines have been planted. All of these places are historic vineyard land that fell out of cultivation when the railroads arrived in the mid-19th century, bringing with them cheaper wines from further south.

The whites from this New Far North of German wine tend to be light and crisp. In contrast, the predominantly dry whites of the leading producers from the heartlands of Sachsen and Saale-Unstrut often boast astonishingly high natural alcoholic contents, 12% being normal for Riesling and Silvaner, Weissburgunder, Grauburgunder, and Traminer (a historic specialty in both regions) all regularly tipping the scales at 13% or more. In the past few years, some deep-colored, substantial reds have also been produced.

These wines are very difficult to find outside Germany, but that is certainly no reason to underestimate their quality.

Harzer Weingut Kirmann
Saale-Unstrut

Situated far outside and to the north of the main body of this region, the Kirmann's estate lies on the rocky lower slope of the Harz Mountains. Hard as it might be to believe, the perfumed and silky Spätburgunder reds are some of the best in Saale-Unstrut. The dry Riesling and Traminer also impress. A rising star still testing the potential of this extreme terroir.

Gartenstrasse 532, 06484 Westerhausen, Saale-Unstrut
www.harzer-weingut.de

Karl Friedrich Aust   Sachsen

Friedrich Aust's small estate is historic in more than one sense. It features a beautiful house, part of which dates back to the Renaissance, and, in the past decade, Aust has replanted many historic vineyard terraces. His are some of the most original dry whites in Sachsen, with the intensely mineral dry Riesling one of the region's finest wines. The wines from the "inferior" Bacchus and Kerner grapes and, since 2007, the Spätburgunder are also impressive.

Weinbergstrasse 10, 01445 Radebeul, Sachsen
www.weingut-aust.de

Klaus Böhme Saale-Unstrut

Klaus Böhme's best wines are his dry and off-dry whites, particularly the Rieslings and Weissburgunders, which have some extremely appealing fruit aromas, pleasingly moderate alcoholic content, and a real lightness of touch. In a rather expensive region they represent very good value for money, too.

Lindenstrasse 43, 06636 Kirchscheidungen, Saale-Unstrut
www.weingut-klaus-boehme.de

Klaus Zimmerling Sachsen

Mechanical engineer Klaus Zimmerling founded his estate in 1992 after learning winemaking at Weingut Nikolaihof in the Wachau/Lower Austria area. Since then, he has transformed it from an improvised micro-winery into Sachsen's top producer. His new cellars look like they were beamed down from Bordeaux, except for the astonishing bronze sculptures by his Polish wife, Malgorzata Chodakowska, decorating the roof. His organically cultivated terraced vineyards resemble a Mayan pyramid. After experimenting with red wines during the 1990s, Zimmerling now concentrates entirely on dry and off-dry whites. They are always brimming with ripe fruit, perfectly balanced, and intensely mineral. Here, the rich Grauburgunder, Gewürztraminer, and Traminer are every bit as exciting as the Riesling. All the best wines are bottled in 500ml or 375ml bottles.

Bergweg 27, 01326 Pillnitz, Sachsen
www.weingut-zimmerling.de

Lützkendorf Saale-Unstrut

After 50 years of enforced membership in the regional co-operative, the Lützkendorf family finally got back full control of their vineyards in 1991. Since then, the wines Uwe Lützkendorf has made from them have only gotten better. It is hard to imagine how white wine could be more mineral than his sleek, firm, dry Riesling Grosses Gewächs from the Hohe Gräte site of Karsdorf with its quarzitic soil (unique in the region). But you could say the same thing about his more savory dry Silvaner and richer dry Weissburgunder Grosses Gewächs from this site. There are also excellent, if equally uncompromising, regular quality whites from these grapes. The new Hohe Gräte vineyards in an abandoned quarry look like a cross between the moon and Southern France, but seem to be an ideal location for growing powerful reds.

Saalberge 31, 06628 Bad Kösen, Saale-Unstrut
www.weingut-luetzkendorf.de

Pawis Saale-Unstrut

There can be few more beautiful settings for a wine estate than Pawis's home in the ancient abbey of Zsheiplitz. It has spectacular views over the Unstrut Valley and the terraced vineyards of Freyburg where Bernard and Kerstin Pawis's rich and imposing dry Riesling and Weissburgunder Grosses Gewächs grow. However, the Pawises' greatest achievement is arguably the large number of moderately priced, impeccably balanced dry whites they make from Riesling and Weissburgunder, and also Grauburgunder, Traminer, and Müller-Thurgau —wines that are simply bursting with life and fruit. They also make some excellent nobly sweet BA and Eiswein.

Auf dem Gut 2, 06632 Zscheiplitz, Saale-Unstrut
www.weingut-pawis.de

WINZERHOF GUSSEK
HIGH-QUALITY RIESLINGS PROVE ANDRE GUSSEK IS MORE THAN A RED STAR

KLAUS ZIMMERLING
KLAUS ZIMMERLING MAKES SUPERB WHITES FROM LOW-YIELDING ORGANIC VINES

Sächsische Staatsweingut Schloss Wackerbarth Sachsen

Sächsische Staatsweingut Schloss Wackerbarth is Sachsen's largest estate. It marries hi-tech modernity reminiscent of California with one of the most beautiful complexes of Baroque buildings in a region rich in monuments from this period. Good as the wines are, some of the supposed "top" bottlings from the Goldener Wagen site do not have that much more depth than the regular wines. The focus is firmly on dry whites and on the sparkling wines, which are all good.

Wackerbarthstrasse 1, 01445 Radebeul, Sachsen
www.schloss-wackerbarth.de

Schloss Proschwitz Sachsen

In 1991, Dr. Georg Prinz zur Lippe bought back Schloss Proschwitz, which the Russian occupying forces confiscated from his family in 1945. It did not take him long to transform it into one of the best German producers on this scale (165 acres/66ha). So uniformly impressive are the vibrant and elegant dry whites, that it is difficult to say whether the effusively aromatic Scheurebe, the supple and discreetly creamy Grauburgunder, or the sleek, racy Rieslings are the best. The sparkling Sekts are certainly the best in the region, and the powerful and deeply-colored reds astonishing for the northerly location. Prinz zur Lippe is establishing a second estate close to Weimar in the Saale-Unstrut region.

Dorfanger 19, 01665 Zadel, Sachsen
www.schloss-proschwitz.de

Winzer Martin Schwarz Sachsen

What is a wine estate doing in the coolest street in the hip Neustadt district of Dresden? This is the home of Martin Schwarz, winemaker at Schloss Proschwitz, and HQ for the best of Sachsen's many micro-wineries. Aside from his racy, elegant, dry Riesling from the Kapitelberg site, Schwarz matures all his dry whites and reds in barrique. Already, his Müller-Thurgau is a substantial wine and the Riesling/Traminer a uniquely aromatic blend, while the Weissburgunder/Grauburgunder is a creamy and richly textural *cuvée*. His simultaneously tannic and silky Spätburgunder/Portugieser blend is one of Sachsen's most powerful reds.

Alaunstrasse 70, 01099 Dresden, Sachsen
barriquewein@aol.com

Winzerhof Gussek Sachsen

Since 2002, when he retired as winemaker for the regional co-operative, André Gussek has concentrated on making a confusingly wide range of excellent dry and off-dry whites, plus the region's finest reds. His vineyards are divided between Naumburg—where his best Rieslings come from old vines in the Steinmeister site—and the terraced Kaatschener Dachsberg just over the border in the state of Thüringen (a growing subregion of Saale-Unstrut). Rich and spicy, but never heavy, his whites are often ignored because attention gets focused on his powerful, tannic, and often imposing reds.

Kösener Strasse 66, 06618 Naumburg, Saale-Unstrut
www.winzerhof-gussek.de

So successfully has Austria reinvented itself as a specialist in high-quality, aromatic dry whites that it is hard to believe that its dynamism grew out of an ugly (but ultimately harmless) scandal. Thankfully, the 1985 antifreeze furore, when some Austrian wine brokers were found to have adulterated cheap sweet wines with diethylene glycol, is now but a distant memory. Today, Austria is positively "Groovy," that being the American way of rewriting the name of the indigenous Austrian Grüner Veltliner grape (young Austrians prefer "Grü-ve"). Even regular-quality Grüner Veltliner has distinctive aromas of green apple, white pepper, and herbs, and is typically medium-bodied with great freshness. At higher ripeness levels, aromas from plum to mango, floral honey, and tobacco leaf develop. These wines can be spectacularly opulent and concentrated, yet they retain great balance. Bottle aging makes them take on an uncanny resemblance to white burgundy, though Grüner Veltliner is not fermented or matured in new oak. No wonder the world is excited!

At their best, Austria's other premium dry whites (Weissburgunder, Chardonnay/Morillon, Sauvignon Blanc, and Riesling) can all match the top Grüner Veltliners, but they all face very strong international competition. By contrast, the dessert wines of Burgenland, most notably Ruster Ausbruch and the TBAs from the Neusiedlersee, are unique wines quite unlike the German and French classics.

Until the 1990s, the nation's red wines lagged behind the whites. But the global red wine boom coincided with the emergence of a new generation of winemakers in Burgenland, resulting in a wave of exciting, rich new reds. Typically blends of Austrian and French varieties, for a while there was a dangerous "the-bigger-the-better" syndrome. But recently there has been a swing back toward fresher, more elegant reds, particularly from Blaufränkisch.

AUSTRIA

LOWER AUSTRIA

Lower Austria wine region

With its spectacular setting in the dramatic, rocky section of the Danube between the monastery of Melk and the city of Krems, the Wachau is unquestionably Austria's most famous wine-growing region. Its fame owes nothing to its size, since there are only a shade more than 3,600 acres (1,460ha) of vineyards here. Neither is it the only worthwhile wine-growing region in Niederösterreich (Lower Austria). Indeed, many experts lump the wines from the neighboring regions of Kremstal and Kamptal, sometimes also the Traisental and Wagram, together with those of the Wachau, and not without good reason. The eastern border of the Wachau was the product of political expediency, and these regions have a lot in common.

 Major grapes

Reds

Blauburgunder (Pinot Noir)

Cabernet Sauvignon

Merlot

Zweigelt

Whites

Chardonnay

Grüner Veltliner

Riesling

Vintages

2009
A year of ripe, aromatic wines with considerable power.

2008
A difficult vintage. Acidity was quite high even for patient producers who picked late.

2007
Another rich vintage of opulent and creamy wines.

2006
A stunning vintage of rich, concentrated whites with excellent balance, and superb reds, too.

2005
A great, classic year of big, ripe, succulent whites.

2004
A vintage of relatively sleek wines now at their best.

1999
The last great vintage before global warming significantly raised alcohol levels, with Riesling and Grüner Veltliner of great elegance.

The common ground begins, appropriately enough, in the loess soil to be found in parts of all of these regions. This fertile, water-retentive, and often deep soil is as ideally suited to the Grüner Veltliner vine as is the combination of warm days and cool nights. Niederösterreich is the homeland of Grüner Veltliner, with 50% of the vineyards in many of the regions given over to it. In comparison, Riesling is a specialty. Even the Wachau devotes just 18% of its vineyards to this variety, despite all the terraced hillsides with primary rock soils that might look like paradise for this variety.

In the past, extreme drought stress in vineyards of this type resulted in two or three poor vintages per decade for the Wachau and other places such as the great Heiligenstein vineyard of the Kamptal region. One of the most important changes here (far more fundamental than the widespread switch from fermentation and maturation in neutral oak to stainless steel) was the construction of the irrigation systems that began at the end of the 1970s. These have almost completely solved the drought problem, although strict limits on the amount of watering allowed were imposed and climate change has made warm summers far more common than they were a generation ago.

These days, the dry whites in Lower Austria's top category (known as Smaragd in the Wachau) are full, aromatic, and fresh year in, year out. They are often also lush and richly textural, with a complex and subtle spiciness. In contrast, the regular-quality wines (known in the Wachau as Federspiel) tend to be medium-bodied with more lively fruit aromas and refreshing acidity. Several of the co-operative wineries, most notably of the Wachau and Winzer Krems, are consistent producers of wines in this style.

Until recently, these wine-growing regions were very conservative. Young winemakers almost invariably orientated themselves to the achievements of the previous generation and experimentation with unfamiliar grape varieties or new wine styles was rare. However, in the past decade, modernity has begun to creep in. Some wineries have changed hands and a few new enterprises have been founded by outsiders.

The region that has taken perhaps the biggest leap forward (though this has attracted scant attention) is the Thermenregion, known to many Viennese as the Südbahn, because it is easily reached by the local railroad running south from the city. Here, the traditional sweet wines sold as Gumpoldskirchener (though these often came from neighboring communes) are increasingly being replaced by reds that sometimes bear an uncanny resemblance to Pinot Noir from Burgundy. Viennese wine-growers also experimented with this direction (not without success) before finding their traditional Gemischter Satz multi-variety plantings gave more original and exciting wines.

On paper, these regions always qualified as cool climate. But the best wines of Lower Austria were never low in alcohol and a combination of global warming and winemaker ambition has pushed alcohol levels up so that levels of 14% are not unusual. One wonders what will happen if predictions of future temperature rises prove right.

LOWER AUSTRIA

The outstanding feature of the Lower Austrian landscape is undoubtedly the Danube, as the important vineyards lie in its valley and those of its tributaries. Impressive a sight as the river often is, particularly if seen from a vantage point such as high up in the vineyards of Hollenburg in Kremstal, the climatic influence of the river is small. In fact, the taste of the wines is far more influenced by what is under your feet—the soil. Lower Austria has two dominant soil types: loess and gneis. The former is fertile and water-retentive yielding generous and fruity wines, the latter is infertile and much more arid, leading to sleeker, more racy wines.

WEINGUT
JOHANN
DONABAUM

OFFENBERG
SPITZ·RIESLING
SMARAGD
2008

WACHAU
12,5 % vol   0,75 l

N
W E
S

CZECH REPUBLIC

Litobratice

Drösendorf
Znojmo
Mikulov
Breclav

Waidhofen
an der Thaya
Göpfritz
Retz
Falkenstein
Poysdorf
Senica

Thaya
Dyje
Laa an der
Thaya
Kúty

Pulkau
Mailberg
Horn
Enzersdorf

Rastenfeld
Hollabrunn
Mistelbach
an der Zaya
SLOVAKIA

KAMPTAL
536m
(1758ft)
Ziersdorf
WIENVIERTEL
Zaya

Zöbing
Langenlois
Strass
Feuersbrunn
Malacky

KREMSTAL
Fels am Wagram
March

Dürnstein
Krems
Stockerau
Krems

Loiben
Spitz
Kirchberg
Korneuburg
Gänserndorf

WACHAU
Tulln
Donau
8

TRAISENTAL
WAGRAM
Klosterneuburg

Mitterndorf
VIENNA
(WIEN)
Russbach
BRATISLAVA

St. Pölten
A1
VIENNA
(WIEN)
Hainburg

WINZER KREMS
SANDGRUBE 13
Mödling
CARNUNTUM
9

Traisen
Wienerwald
Göttlesbrunn
Leitha

18
Gumpoldskirchen
10

GRÜNER
VELTLINER
Altenmarkt
Baden
Traiskirchen
Bruck an der Leitha

2009
1341m
(4399ft)
Bad Vöslau
Leithagebirge
50

AUSTRIA
Ebreichsdorf
Mönchhof

THERMENREGION
Donnerskirchen
Piesting
Eisenstadt
Neusiedler
See

Pernitz
2075m
(6807ft)
Wiener
neustadt
Rust

Mariazell
Leitha
BURGENLAND
16

Neunkirchen
ST. LAURENT

Gloggnitz
Sopron

Neckenmarkt
R
RESERVE

Aspang
Markt
Frauenfeld

Horitschon

Johanneshof
REINISCH

KEY

Carnuntum	Wachau
Wagram	Wien
Kamptal	Wienviertel
Kremstal	International border
Thermenregion	Regional boundary
Traisental	

0   10   20 miles

0   10   20   30   40 km

BRUNDLMAYER
THE 2006 KAFERBERG GRUNER VELTLINER
IS A HEADY COCKTAIL OF HONEY AND
A RANGE OF EXOTIC FRUITS

DOMANE WACHAU
RIESLING SMARAGD KELLERBERG IS MADE
IN AN ELEGANT, MINERAL STYLE

Alzinger Wachau

Leo Alzinger and his son (also Leo) focus entirely upon dry Riesling and Grüner Veltliner. The wines have an entirely distinctive, sleek, racy style and they need several years of bottle age before they give their best. Steinertal is the top site for the Riesling Smaragd, giving intensely herbal-mineral wines that are cool even when they have fully 13.5% alcohol. The top Grüner Veltliner is the Reserve, a multi-vineyard blend of exceptional opulence in this context. The Federspiel from Riesling and Grüner Veltliner are appealingly light and crisp, but ripe and elegant.

Unterloiben 11, 3601, Dürnstein
www.alzinger.at

Bernhard Ott Wagram

Bernhard Ott is a larger-than-life character, and that's the way his wines taste. Like their maker though, those wines never seem heavy, rather dangerously light-footed. With 90% of his vineyards devoted to the grape, Ott is Mr. Grüner Veltliner, making a range that extends from the staggeringly refreshing Am Berg up to the breathtaking, golden Tausend Rosen ("thousand roses"). In the middle is Der Ott, arguably Austria's best-value top-flight Grüner Veltliner. On the side, Ott makes the country's finest sweet Riesling, named Rheinriesling in homage to his ideal. ★ Rising star

Neufang 36, 3483, Feuersbrunn
www.ott.at

Birgit Eichinger Kamptal

Step by step, Birgit Eichinger's dry whites have gained in quality and individuality. Compared with many of her colleagues, she is cautious about high alcoholic contents and is non-fanatical about dry meaning bone-dry. Her most important wines are the Riesling, Grüner Veltliner, and Chardonnay (all fermented only in stainless steel) from the Gaisberg site of Strass, which all have a distinctive smoky-spicy note. ★ Rising star

Langenloiserstrasse 365, 3491, Strass im Strassertale
www.weingut-eichinger.at

Bründlmayer Kamptal

Willi Bründlmayer's achievement lies not so much in the excellence of his top wines, though excellent is certainly what they are. Rather, it is in the high quality he has maintained throughout his annual production of 350,000 bottles for more than 20 years. Wines such as the modestly priced, racy-spicy Grüner Veltliner from the Berg Vogelsang site are every bit as well made and attractive as his extremely concentrated and complex Riesling Alte Reben from the great Heiligenstein vineyard or the enormously powerful but impeccably balanced Grüner Veltliner from the Lamm site. The estate's elegant, perfumed Blauburgunder (Pinot Noir) Cecile and the great champagne-like Brundlmayer Brut (not to mention its impressive new rosé sister), are often forgotten though they belong to Austria's finest in these fields.

Zwettlerstrasse 23, 3550, Langenlois
www.bruendlmayer.at

Christ Wien

Rainer Christ is one of Vienna's most talented young winemakers. His dry whites divide into fresh and vibrant varietal dry Grüner Veltliner and Riesling on the one hand and the more textural, spicy, and complex Wiener Gemischter Satz from old mixed-variety plantings in the Bisamberg site in the northwest of Vienna.

Amtsstrasse 10–14, 1210, Wien-Jedlersdorf
www.weingut-christ.at

Christian Fischer Thermenregion

Though located a short drive from the white wine region of Vienna, the Thermenregion today majors in big rich reds thanks to its warm, dry climate. Nobody makes richer, plusher wines here than Christian Fischer, whose Gradenthal Premium blend of Zweigelt with Cabernet Sauvignon and Merlot is a modernist blockbuster without being over-oaked or overly alcoholic. A high standard is maintained right through the red-dominated range.

Hauptstrasse 33, 2500, Sooss
www.weingut-fischer.at

Domäne Wachau Wachau

With slightly more than 1,000 acres (400ha), this co-operative is the largest producer in the region. Under the direction of Roman Horvath and winemaker Heinz Frischengruber, the wines have become bolder, weightier, and more modern. On paper, the top wines are the Riesling and Grüner Veltliner Smaragd from Achleiten, Kellerberg, Loibenberg, and Singerriedel, but sometimes the lighter, bone-dry Federspiel can be just as good.

Domäne Wachau, 3601, Dürnstein
www.domaene-wachau.at

Edlmoser Wien

The rich, but vibrantly fresh dry whites from Michael Edlmoser are as hard to pigeon-hole as his rich, but perfumed reds. As with the city's other top winemakers, the most interesting wine is unquestionably the Gemischter Satz from old mixed plantings, a wine that needs some bottle age to reveal its full complexity.

Maurer-Lange-Gasse 123, 1230, Wien
www.edlmoser.com

Emmerich Knoll Wachau

Emmerich Knoll combines fanaticism for quality with pragmatism in a way that has enabled him to cope with the changing climatic situation during the last two decades. His Vinothekfüllung, or cellar reserve, from Grüner Veltliner and Riesling are opulent, super-rich wines. They are made from nobly-rotten and over-ripe grapes separated from those used for the dry Smaragd to ensure the latter are neither too big nor too obviously marked by botrytis. The perfumed Riesling Selection from the Pfaffenberg site just over the border in Kremstal is every bit as exciting as the more discreet Riesling Smaragd from the Schütt and Loibenberg sites. The light, crisp, herbal Grüner Veltliner Federspiel is arguably the best wine of its type. Great Auslese, BA, and TBA dessert wines are made in vintages with ample noble rot.

Unterloiben 7, 3601, Dürnstein
www.loibnerhof.at

F X Pichler Wachau

Beginning in the early 1980s, Franz Xaver Pichler began pushing to see where the limits of possibility in the Wachau lie. His adventures involved the cellar, naturally, but even more it took him into the vineyards. Occasionally, Pichler pushed one notch too far, but the great majority of his dry Riesling and Grüner Veltliner Smaragd were spectacularly concentrated and aromatically complex wines that continue to define the contemporary Wachau. Pichler's son, Lucas, now runs the estate, maintaining the same high standards, though his wines are more consistently elegant than those of his father. He has worked hard to improve the lighter Federspiel wines, adding a zesty Riesling with great mineral freshness that is now the finest example of this style in the region. He also makes very fine Sauvignon Blanc, indeed the wines are world-class across the board.

Oberloiben 27, 3601, Dürnstein
www.fx-pichler.at

Forstreiter Kremstal

Meinhard Forstreiter is not a superstar winemaker, and may never be one. But in recent years, he has consistently made impressive dry Grüner Veltliners and Rieslings that combine fruit and character with excellent harmony. They also offer excellent value for money, particularly the Riesling and Grüner Veltliner under the DAC Reserve Schiefer label. ★ **Rising star**

Hollenburger Kirchengasse 7, 3506, Krems-Hollenburg
www.forstreiter.at

Franz Hirtzberger Wachau

Nobody has pushed late and selective harvesting in the Wachau to the limits that Franz Hirtzberger and son Franzi have, sometimes picking into December. Likewise, nobody has taken more trouble to revive historic terraced vineyards that had fallen out of cultivation due to the high cost of working them. These two factors have enabled the Hitzbergers to produce some of the most exotic and concentrated dry Rieslings and Grüner Veltliners the world has ever seen. The only problem with their monumental Smaragd wines from the Singerriedel and Honivogl sites is that they need several years' bottle age to reach their ideal harmony. The rich, creamy Grauburgunder and Neuburger Smaragd are the best examples of these grapes in the region. At the other end of the scale, the Riesling and Grüner Veltliner Federspiel wines are sleek and racy.

Kremserstrasse 8, 3620, Spitz
www.hirtzberger.com

Gerhard Markowitsch Carnuntum

Gerhard Markowitsch is the man who put this small region on the Austrian wine map with rich, oaky, tannic reds. His most imposing wines (such as M1) blend the Zweigelt with Merlot. They are unashamedly modernistic, but the young Markowitsch has a great feeling for harmony and they never seem over-done. His success has resulted in plenty of local imitators. Indeed, Carnuntum lacks stylistic diversity, so much has this one winemaker (unintentionally) dominated its public face!

Pfarrgasse 6, 2464, Göttlesbrunn
www.markowitsch.at

Geyerhof Kremstal

Ilse Meyer has cultivated the Geyerhof vineyards organically since 1988. It took some time to get right, but recent vintages have seen a quantum leap in the quality

EMMERICH KNOLL
KNOLL'S RIESLINGS ARE THE PRODUCT OF
OBSESSIVE ATTENTION TO DETAIL

HIRSCH
THE HIRSCH WINES HAVE GAINED IN
DEFINITION SINCE GOING BIODYNAMIC

of her dry whites such as the sleek, taut, minerally Grüner Veltliner Steinleithn and Riesling Sprinzenberg from the high-altitude home vineyards; and rich, opulent Riesling from Goldberg in Hollenburg. ★ **Rising star**

Oberfucha 1, 3511, Furth bei Göttweig
www.geyerhof.at

Hiedler Kamptal

Ludwig Hiedler's top dry Riesling, Grüner Veltliner, and Weissburgunder are all marketed under the Maximum brand, which gives a good idea of his wine style. They are indeed rich and bold wines with plenty of power, but are never over-blown or too heavy. At the other end of the scale, Hiedler's simplest wines, like his light-footed, bone-dry Grüner Veltliner Löss are model examples of the Austrian tradition for easy-drinking dry whites with real character. ★ **Rising star**

Am Rosenhügel 13, 3550, Langenlois
www.hiedler.at

Hirsch Kamptal

Since Johannes Hirsch turned biodynamic, his dry whites have been transformed from classic examples of Lower Austrian winemaking tradition into highly individual wines with complex smoky, spicy, and mineral character. The top Rieslings are from the great Heiligenstein and the less-famous Gaisberg sites, the former being more elegant, the latter more spicy and powerful. The contrast between the Grüner Veltliners from the Heiligenstein and Lamm sites follows a similar pattern. Hirsch also makes an expressive, herbal lightweight Grüner Veltliner, Trinkvergnügen ("drinking-pleasure"). ★ **Rising star**

Hauptstrasse 76, 3493, Kammern
www.weingut-hirsch.at

Johann Donabaum Wachau

Johann Donabaum is certainly not lacking in ambition, but the young winemaker is anything but pushy or egotistical. His great talent is marrying richness and effusive aroma with clarity and elegance, which is what, historically, the Wachau is all about. Which are better, his Rieslings from the Offenburg and Setzberg sites or his Grüner Veltliner from Spitzer Point? It's really hard to say, because during the last decade he's maintained an extraordinary consistency. ★ **Rising star**

Laaben 15, 3620, Spitz
www.weingut-donabaum.at

Johanneshof Reinisch Thermenregion

Johannes Reinisch is one of the leading red winemakers in Austria. His wines completely demolish the myths outside the German-speaking world that Austrian reds are either thin and weedy or just alcohol and oak. Here, the rich and complex Grand Reserve Pinot Noir and St-Laurent are a dynamic duo of top-class reds, both of which completely avoid the common tendency to copy French or New World role models. The lighter standard bottlings are no less individual, though. Somewhat lost in the long shadows of the red Grand Reserves are the excellent dry whites made from the indigenous Rotgipfler grape, with their distinctive aromas of pear and hazelnut.

Im Weingarten 1, 2523, Tattendorf
www.j-r.at

THE WACHAU QUARTETS

The Wachau always specialized in elegant dry whites. But, in the 1940s, there was a brief period of experimentation with chaptalization (the addition of sugar to the unfermented must) to try to raise the wines' alcoholic content. During the early 1960s, opposition to this method, and to exploitation of the region's name by its neighbors, united the first "Wachau Quartet" of leading wine-growers: Josef Jamek, Franz Prager, Wilhelm Schwengler (director of the region's co-operative), and Franz Hirtzberger Sr. Through dedication and political savvy, they achieved those goals. Since the founding of the regional wine-growers association Vinea Wachau in 1983, leadership has been in the hands of another "Wachau Quartet:" Emmerich Knoll, Franz Hirtzberger, Franz Xaver Pichler, and Toni Bodenstein (of the Prager estate). They introduced the Wachau Categories—in ascending order of body: Steinfeder, Federspiel, and Smaragd—and opposed the use of must concentration to increase the alcoholic content of wines as chaptalization had done before. The question now is what balance the Wachau will strike between these traditions and innovation.

Josef Högl Wachau

From his house almost 1,000ft (300m) above sea level in the Spitze Graben, a side valley of the Danube, Sepp Högl's vines climb the steep slope of the Schön site another 500ft (150m) in 57 narrow terraces. This is where Högl's finest Grüner Veltliner Smaragd grows. His equally rich and complex, yet clean and uplifting, Riesling Smaragd Brück hails from a similarly extreme site nearby. Högl is an extremist in the best sense, making excellent-quality wines at fair prices right across the range. ★ **Rising star**

Viessling 31, 3620, Spitz
www.wein-plus.de

Josef Jamek Wachau

Hans Altmann and his wife Jutta run the historic Josef Jamek estate, which is also one of the nation's most famous restaurants. The Riesling from the precipitously steep, terraced Ried Klaus—here the traditional Austrian word for a vineyard, "ried," is still very much alive—is legendary, but also the region's most exquisitely elegant dry Riesling. These are gastronomic wines that eschew the race for journalists' points in favor of achieving perfect harmony with food. The delicately honeyed, nutty Weissburgunder Smaragd from old vines in the Hochrain site is the finest example of this grape in the region.

Joching 45, 3610, Weissenkirchen
www.weingut-jamek.at

Jurtschitsch Kamptal

Everything changed at the famous family-owned Jurtschitsch estate back in 2006. The family switched their more than 180 acres (72ha) to organic viticulture and wild-yeast fermentation. The transformation is still somewhat a work-in-progress. Some of the dry whites are brilliantly expressive and intensely mineral. Others are suffering from a slight lack of freshness or broadness (which is perhaps due to over-long fermentations). There is no denying the ambition of the new generation here though, most importantly of young Alwin. Jurtschitsch remains best known in Austria for the impeccable Grüve, a dry white nouveau from Grüner Veltliner. The solid reds lag behind the whites. ★ **Rising star**

Rudolfstrasse 39, 3550, Langenlois
www.jurtschitsch.com

Kurt Angerer Kamptal

Precise work in the vineyard, keep-it-simple cellarwork, and no unnecessary frills. These are the principles that enabled Kurt Angerer to become one of Lower Austria's leading producers of dry Grüner Veltliner in the space of a decade. These are big, bold, and expressive wines of which the Loam is the most succulent, Kies the lightest and most straightforwardly fruit-driven, and Spies the most mineral and austere. The Riesling Ametzberg belongs in the same league and is likewise capable of long aging. ★ **Rising star**

Schickenberggasse 4, 3552, Lengenfeld
www.kurt-angerer.at

Lagler Wachau

Karl Lagler has been making consistently fine dry Riesling and Grüner Veltliner for decades and is now assisted by his son, Karl Jr. The wines are full and ripe

with good balance particularly the Riesling Smaragd from the Tuasendeimerberg and the Grüner Veltliner Smaragd from the Steinborz. Attached to the estate is the four star Hotel Garni Weinberghof.

Rote Torgasse 10, 3620, Spitz
www.weingut-lagler.at

Laurenz V Kamptal

Though based in downtown Vienna, this innovative winery founded by Laurenz Moser V in April 2005 works exclusively with grapes from the Kamptal region. The most important product is the mid-weight, fruit-driven Charming Grüner Veltliner, though the recently introduced Silver Bullet in 17fl oz (500ml) bottles is the top wine. The ambitious goal is a global Grüner Veltliner brand that does for this grape what New Zealand's Cloudy Bay did for Sauvignon Blanc. ★ **Rising star**

Mariahilfer Strasse 32, 1070, Wien
www.laurenzfive.com

Leth Fels

Franz Leth makes bold and succulent dry whites that are hard not to enjoy. His consistency of style and quality with Grüner Veltliner, Roter Veltliner, Riesling, and Sauvignon Blanc is impressive. More recently, his surprisingly powerful Zweigelt Gigama has attracted a lot of attention, since this is not a region with a great red wine tradition. ★ **Rising star**

Kirchengasse 6, 3481, Fels
www.weingut-leth.at

Loimer Kamptal

In recent years, Fred Loimer's wines have been transformed—from high-quality mainstream to daring individuality with no concessions made to the popular demand for fruit-driven charmers. The finest of the dry whites are the intensely spicy-mineral Grüner Veltliner from almost 50-year-old vines in the Spiegel site, and the ripe, yet cool Riesling from the high-altitude Steinmasssel site. The black-box-modernism of the new winery is equally uncompromising. In 2005, Loimer took over the well-known Schellmann estate in Gumpoldskirchen/ Thermenregion whose top wines—the complex and textural Chardonnay Gumpold and the sophisticated Pinot Noir Anning—belong to the nation's best examples of these grapes. ★ **Rising star**

Haindorfer Vögerlweg 23, 3550, Langenlois
www.loimer.at

Ludwig Ehn Kamptal

The Ehns are a complex phenomenon. It may be a slight simplification, but the extrovert Michaela is the public face of this small estate, while her brother Ludwig is the introvert winemaker. With a few exceptions (the monster Grüner Veltliner Titan and Chardonnay/Grüner Veltliner blend Incredible), these are extremely elegant wines designed for the dining table. The Gemischter Satz is a rare example of a site of mixed plantings whose grapes are fermented together. But the Riesling from the Heiligenstein, with its floral and mineral character, is the star.

Bahnstrasse 3, 3550, Langenlois
www.ehnwein.at

Machherndl Wachau

No doubt about it, Erich Machherndl is the bad boy of the Wachau and he gets a rough ride from the arch-conservative Austrian wine media. One of the problems is that he makes amazingly rich yet vibrant Pinot Blanc. He also produced the first convincingly peppery Syrah in the region. The other problem is that his critical observations about the Wachau are spot on, frequently hitting sensitive nerves among his colleagues. What his opponents ignore is the fact that he makes a lot of dry Riesling and Grüner Veltliner wines that are appealing, rather than overbearing, and which taste charming in their youth but can also age very well. The Mitz & Mutz Riesling is a perfect example.

Hauptstrasse 1, 3610, Wösendorf
www.machherndl.com

Malat Kremstal

Michael Malat was lucky to inherit an estate whose wines were already of high quality across the board, and were known for being so. He has successfully mastered the balancing act between retaining what his father Gerald achieved and putting his own mark on the estate. The range is dominated by half a dozen Grüner Veltliners and a handful of Rieslings, plus Chardonnay, Pinot Gris, Pinot Blanc, and Sauvignon Blanc. Das Beste vom… ("the best of"), produced both from Riesling and Grüner Veltliner, are the opulent, often exotic top of the range. But recent vintages of the aromatic, supple Pinot Noir Reserve have also impressed. The sparkling wines are good, too.

Weinkeller Hafnerstrasse, 3511, Palt-Krems
www.malat.at

Manfred Jäger Wachau

Manfred Jäger runs this small, quietly ambitious estate whose HQ is one of the most idyllically situated historic houses in the entire region. Here, as much work goes into the lighter, bone-dry Riesling and Grüner Veltliner Federspiel as into the more powerful and expensive Smaragd. Even the richest of them is moderate in alcohol with a wonderful freshness and vitality. Quality seems to improve with every vintage. ★**Rising star**

Kremser Strasse 1, 3610, Weissenkirchen
weingut.jaeger@utanet.at

Mantlerhof Kremstal

Mantlerhof is too often underrated and taken for granted in Austria, precisely because it has been making good wines for decades and because Sepp Mantler does not do any sexy marketing. The wonderfully juicy, subtly spicy Grüner Veltliner stands in the foreground, the DAC Reserve from the Spiegel generally being the top bottling, though the Roter Veltliner from the Reisenthal, with its honey and orange peel bouquet and rich, creamy body, gives it tough internal competition. Right across the range, there is excellent quality and value for money.

Brunn im Felde, Hauptstrass 50, 3494, Gedersdorf
www.mantlerhof.com

Mayer am Pfarrplatz & Rotes Haus
Wien

The wines of Mayer am Pfarrplatz and Rotes Haus (two estates in one cellar) have been dramatically modernized by winemaker Barbara Wimmer in recent years, though the emphasis remains firmly on dry Riesling and Grüner Veltliner with a lightness of touch. Look out for the aromatic dry white Asia Cuvée from Mayer am Pfarrplatz and the rich, exotic Gemischter Satz Reserve from old mixed plantings from Rotes Haus. There is great dry Traminer, too. ★**Rising star**

Pfarrplatz 2, 1190, Wien
www.pfarrplatz.at; www.weingut.rotes-haus.at

Muhr-van der Niepoort Carnuntum

This mini-winery specializing in Blaufränkisch reds from the great, but forgotten, Spitzerberg site was founded by PR powerfrau Dorli Muhr and her then husband, the Dutch-Portuguese star winemaker Dirk van der Niepoort. Since their split and the 2006 vintage, she has made the wines alone and they are a radically sleek, racy and pungent expression of Blaufränkisch unlike anything else in the region. ★**Rising star**

Alte Bundesstrasse 1, 2463, Stixneusiedl
www.weingutmuhr.com

Neumayer Traisental

Ludwig Neumayer is a white wine genius, but not a great self-publicist. His Der Wein vom Stein (or "the wine from stone") bottlings of dry Riesling, Grüner Veltliner, Weissburgunder, and Sauvignon Blanc are exactly what the name says and rich, concentrated wines that are also sleeker and more elegant than comparable wines from the Wachau. They remain underrated by the wine media. His intensely herbal and beautifully balanced Grüner Veltliner from the Zwirch site is a top example of this grape for a very friendly price. ★**Rising star**

22, 3130 Inzersdorf ob der Traisen
www.weinvomstein.at

Nigl Kremstal

Martin Nigl surprised himself even more than he did the Austrian wine scene when the then unknown winemaker's 1988 dry Riesling from the equally unknown Hochäcker site scored a great success in an international Riesling tasting the next year. Beautiful as this narrow and rocky section of the Krems Valley is, it has a fickle climate and vintage variation is greater than in the Wachau. In the good and top vintages, Nigl's peachy and racy Riesling from the Hochäcker and the even more concentrated Privat, along with the spicy, elegant Grüner Veltliner Privat, clearly belong in the first rank of Austrian dry whites. Lower down the range, the Riesling from the Dornleiten and the Grüner Veltliner Piri are sleek wines packed full of character and aroma that offer great value year in, year out. ★**Rising star**

Kirchenberg 1, 3541, Senftenberg
www.weingutnigl.at

Nikolaihof Wachau

The historic Nikolaihof estate was biodynamic before anyone else in the wine and food scene even knew what the word meant. The wines always had a uniquely unspectacular style, slowly unfolding like the buds of old-fashioned roses. No wine more aptly embodies the Saahs family's alternative conception of the Wachau than the dry Grüner Veltliner Vinotheque. It spends fully 15 years in neutral wood, yet manages to be at once mellow, deep, and lively. The estate Riesling Federspiel and Smaragd, with the enormously mineral Riesling Reserve

NIGL
NIGL PRIVAT RIESLING IS A MODEL OF
CONSISTENCY IN KREMSTAL

NIKOLAIHOF
NIKOLAIHOF'S WINES ARE DISTINGUISHED BY
LONG AGING BEFORE RELEASE

PICHLER-KRUTZLER
THE EARLY RELEASES OF THIS
NEW PRODUCER HAVE BEEN
PRECOCIOUSLY IMPRESSIVE

SALOMON UNDHOF
THE KÖGL RIESLING IS ONE OF SALOMON
UNDHOF'S MOST GRACEFUL WINES

from the Steiner Hund site (in Kremstal), do the same, though they are released rather sooner. Nikolaus Saahs is in his early 30s, but does not consider any of this extreme or old-fashioned, the most common criticisms in Austria.

Nikolaigasse 3, 3512, Wachau
www.nikolaihof.at

R & A Pfaffl Weinviertel

Roman Pfaffl Sr. and Jr. run this 140 acre (60ha) estate. It is best known for its characterful, excellent-value dry Grüner Veltliners and the red *cuvée* Excellent in which local Zweigelt makes a convincing partner for Cabernet Sauvignon and Merlot. Less well known are the Pfaffls' ambitious Chardonnays made in an international barrel-fermented style that does not mask their Austrian freshness. Likewise the Rieslings, of which the Terrassen Sonnleiten is the archetype of a sleek dry wine with white peach aroma, medium body, and minerally acidity.

Schulgasse 21, 2100, Stetten
www.pfaffl.at

Pichler-Krutzler Wachau

2008 was the first full vintage for this start-up founded by the daughter of Wachau superstar winemaker F X Pichler, Elisabeth, and Erich Krutzler, previously of Weingut Krutzler in Deutsch Schützen/Burgenland. Their rich, ripe, fruit-driven dry Wachau Rieslings, Grüner Veltliners, and Pinot Blanc have put them on the map. ★ **Rising star**

3601 Wachau
www.pichler-krutzler.at

Prager Wachau

This estate is one of the quartet of producers that put the Wachau back on the map during the decades following the end of the post-World War II Russian occupation. It remains one of the region's most dynamic producers. The first vintage for the Riesling Wachstum Bodenstein, named after winemaker-director Toni Bodenstein, was 1999. The fruit for this wine comes from vines grown at an altitude of 1,400–1,500ft (425–460m), where it was previously assumed grapes would never ripen. Grüner Veltliner Stockkultur, from a 75-year-old vineyard with each vine trained on its own pole in the old style, debuted in 2005. In both cases, the result is an aromatic supernova. Bodenstein also makes dry Riesling and Grüner Veltliner Smaragd of great clarity and concentration from more conventional vineyards in Weissenkirchen and Dürnstein. ★ **Rising star**

Wachaustrasse 48, 3610, Weissenkirchen
www.weingutprager.at

Proidl Kremstal

The mercurial Franz Proidl's dry whites are either a little bit too much of a good thing (high alcohol and sometimes unintended sweetness) or land plum in the middle of the target and combine richness with great balance. His top site is the Ehrenfels, a steep terraced slope immediately below the ruined castle of Senftenberg from where the late-picked Riesling and Grüner Veltliner Reserves push concentration to the limit. New is the exotic and succulent sweet Riesling Proidl Spricht Deutsch. ★ **Rising star**

Oberer Markt 19, 3541, Senftenberg
www.proidl.at

Rainer Wess Wachau

In 2003, the tiny Rainer Wess estate became the first new producer in the Wachau founded in 476 years. Wess has 7 acres (3ha) of his own and buys grapes from a handful of local growers. His wines are full of ripe fruit and spicy character, but are models of balance and harmony, full of character. Even the top Rieslings (from Achleiten and Pfaffenberg) and the richest Grüner Veltliner (Achleiten, Loibenberg, and Pfaffenberg) can be drunk young with great pleasure, yet will age beautifully. ★ **Rising star**

Kellergasse, 3601, Unterloiben
www.weingut-wess.at

Rudi Pichler Wachau

Rudi Pichler does things differently. Whereas the established stars of the Wachau accept, or seek, a certain amount of noble rot in the grapes for their top Riesling and Grüner Veltliner Smaragd wines, he rejects this completely, insisting that he can only do extended skin-contact in his hyper-modern winery if the fruit is completely clean. This strategy results in utterly different wines with a very strong mineral personality, a firm tannic backbone, and an aroma spectrum that extends far beyond the peachy note typical for Wachau Rieslings and the white pepper of average Grüner Veltliners. In contrast to the more charming but hardly less characterful Federspiel, they really need some years of bottle aging to give their best. These are wines that will either electrify you, or leave you cold. ★ **Rising star**

Marienfeldweg 122, 3610, Wösendorf
www.rudipichler.at

Salomon Undhof Kremstal

Sal'mon Groovy and the Riesling Sal'mon are the internationally successful, fruit-driven, off-dry basic wines from Bertold Salomon. They stand in stark contrast to the estate's other Rieslings and Grüner Veltliners, however, which are elegant, dry, and balanced rather than big, opulent, or sweet. The most famous of these is the refined Riesling from the Kögl site, which has great citrus-mineral freshness. The architecture has a freshness about it too, with strident modernism meeting lovingly restored history.

Undstrasse 10, 3504, Krems-Stein
www.salomonwines.com

Schloss Gobelsburg Kamptal

The Schloss Gobelsburg label proudly declares that the estate's wine history goes back to 1171. But the modern era here dates back to February 1996, when Michael Moosbrugger, from a well-known hotelier family in Austria's far west, took over the run-down estate. Moosbrugger put all the barrels of local oak (only the simplest wines are made in stainless steel) on wheels, and his wonderfully textural and subtly spicy Tradition bottlings of Grüner Veltliner and Riesling spend 18 months in them. The other dry Rieslings and Grüner Veltliners are fruitier (due to shorter barrel-aging), but are also concentrated, aromatically complex, and individual. In recent years, Moosbrugger's Pinot Noir and St-Laurent reds took a big leap forward, now combining tannic power with freshness and elegance. ★ **Rising star**

Schlossstrasse 16, 3550, Gobelsburg
www.gobelsburg.at

Schlossweingut Graf Hardegg
Weinviertel

Graf Hardegg is best known as the maker of Austria's finest Viognier, a rich peachy wine called simply V for legal reasons. But this aristocratic estate is actually more important as the producer of the consistent, fruit- and pepper-driven Grüner Veltliner Veltlinsky brand. The top dry Riesling and Grüner Veltliner marketed under the vom Schloss name are fresh, citrussy, and very clean—the best-known face of Weinviertel modernism.

Grosskadolz 1, 2062, Seefeld-Kadolz
www.grafhardegg.at

Schmelz Wachau

Johann and Monika, and their sons Thomas and Florian, are consistent producers of ripe, succulent, and expressive dry Grüner Veltliner and Riesling in the Wachau with vineyard holdings extending from Joching downstream to Loiben. Here, the Federspiel wines are extremely charming and attractive, making those of some famous producers look a bit plain and tart.

Weinbergstrasse 14, 3610, Joching/Wachau
www.schmelzweine.at

Sepp Moser Kremstal

Nikolaus Moser took over this estate from his father Sepp in 2000 and quickly converted it to biodynamic cultivation and wild yeast fermentation. The result is bone-dry wines bursting with fruit, character, and acidity. The Gebling site proves that Riesling can give top-class wines when grown on supposedly second-rate loess soil. Banfalu is the most striking of the small range of reds from the family's vineyards in Apetlon/Neusiedlersee. ★ **Rising star**

Untere Wienerstrasse 1, 3495, Rohrendorf bei Krems
www.sepp-moser.at

Stadlmann Thermenregion

Johann Stadlmann makes a wide range of whites and reds, but the focus of his life's work has been the indigenous Zierfandler grape. Unlike most Lower Austrian dry whites, Zierfandler does not have big, fresh fruit aromas. Instead, it offers notes of dried apple, pear, and herbs with mild acidity; sleek rather than broad. The Grosse Reserve bottling is massive, concentrated, and often slightly sweet; the single-vineyard bottling from the Madel-Höh site more human in scale.

Wiener Strasse 41, 2514, Traiskirchen
www.stadlmann-wein.at

Stadt Krems & Weingut Stift Göttweig Kremstal

For the first three years after Fritz Miesbauer and Leopold Figl took over at Stadt Krems in the summer of 2003, they turned it upside-down. They replanted half the 75 acres (30ha) of vineyards, re-equipped the cellar, and pushed it back into the front ranks of Lower Austria's dry white producers. The style is modern, but not one-sidedly so, as the spicy Grüner Veltliner DAC Reserve from the Wachtberg proves. The same team runs the estate of Stift Göttweig, with more than 120 acres (50ha) of vineyards.

Stadtgraben 11, 3500, Krems; www.weingutstadtkrems.at;
Göttweig 1, 3511 Furth; www.weingutstiftgoettweig.at

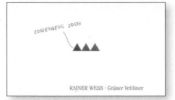

RAINER WEISS
RAINER WEISS MAY BE A NEWCOMER TO THE WACHAU, BUT HIS WINES ARE OUTSTANDING

SCHLOSS GOBELSBURG
SCHLOSS GOBELSBURG'S RIESLINGS ARE COMPLEX AND MULTI-LAYERED

Weinrieder Weinviertel

Friedrich Weinrieder is Austria's "Mr. Icewine" making serious quantities of Riesling and Grüner Veltliner Icewines that are often among the nation's best examples of this style. His dry Grüner Veltliners are good, too: full of green fruit and pepper character.

Unstere Ortrasse 44, Weinviertel
www.wewinreider.at

Wieninger Wien

In 1999, Fritz Wieninger changed the face of Viennese wine by co-fermenting the grapes from an old mixed-variety planting in the Nussberg site. The result was a multi-dimensional dry white unlike anything else tasted in living memory. Previously, Wieninger had been obsessed with making international-style Pinot Noir and Chardonnay, so this meant a gigantic shift of emphasis (though those Pinots and Chardonnays are still impressive, if expensive). Today, he is the prophet of Gemischter Satz and has invested great energy into improving the estate's varietal dry Grüner Veltliner and Riesling, which are increasingly rich and imposing.

Stammersdorfer Strasse 80, 1210, Wien
www.wieninger.at

Winzer Krems Kremstal

With almost 2,500 acres (1,000ha) of vineyards, this is a big co-operative winery, but the wines under the "Kellermeister Privat" label are impressive, fruit-driven, but never superficial. There are plenty of simpler, but well-made wines further down the range, too.

Sandgrube 13, 3500, Krems
www.winzerkrems.at

Winzerhof Ewald Walzer Krems

There's nothing pretentious about Ingrid Walzer or her generous, spicy, and authentic dry Grüner Veltliners from the terraced vineyards of Krems, where the fertile and water-retentive loess soil, warm days, and cool nights provide ideal conditions for the ripening of this grape.

Geixendorfer Hauptstrasse 16, 3500, Krems
www.winzerhof-walzer.at

Zahel Wien

Richard Zahel makes some of the most impressive and mineral dry Rieslings in Vienna. But that is not all. Zahel's Gemischter Satz (particularly the Reserve bottling) from mixed plantings are some of the most complex and textural whites in the region.

Maurer Hauptplatz 9, 1230, Wien
www.zahel.at

Zull Weinviertel

Father-and-son team Werner and Phillip Zull are specialists for dry Riesling and Grüner Veltliner. Their wines show what the underrated Weinviertel region is capable of when quality is taken seriously, and they do the precise vineyard work necessary to achieve this. Their wines are cool and elegant even at high levels of ripeness, with great aromatics.

Schrattenthal 9, 2073, Schrattenthal
www.zull.at

BURGENLAND

Austria
Burgenland wine region

There are two preconceptions surrounding the wine-growing region of Burgenland —that its terrain is rather flat and that its wines are all full-bodied and rich. Both ideas are quite understandable. Many of the vineyards around the Neusiedlersee Lake (which, at just 6ft/2m at its deepest point, is in fact a gigantic puddle) are indeed super-flat, and you can certainly find those kinds of wine here. However, the story of this region's recent development is all about something else: the rediscovery of the potential of the higher-altitude vineyards for elegant and aromatic wines. And this discrepancy makes clear how the wine-growing regions of this Austrian state are far more diverse and complex than appears to be the case at first glance.

Major grapes

🍇 Reds
Blauer Zweigelt
Blaufränkisch
Cabernet Sauvignon
Merlot
Pinot Noir
St-Laurent

🍇 Whites
Chardonnay
Grauburgunder
Grüner Veltliner
Neuburger
Welschriesling

Vintages

2009
Excellent ripeness and balance that bodes well for the future.

2008
The reds are lighter, the whites good, but not great.

2007
Great sweet wines and perfumed, elegant reds.

2006
The greatest vintage for reds in many decades with excellent sweet wines.

2005
An excellent sweet wine vintage, and full-bodied reds.

2004
A good, but not great vintage across the board.

2000
A superb vintage for the reds, but almost no sweet wine.

Take, for example, the town of Rust on the western bank of the Neusiedlersee. It has a recorded history of systematic dessert wine production dating back to the early 17th century. It was exports of these to Russia and Poland that paid for the town's abundant Baroque architecture. But you will not find any trace of that in Ilmitz on the opposite bank of the lake. This rustic area was described by the recently deceased star winemaker Alois Kracher as "the California of Austria," meaning that in terms of wine, almost everything there was new.

The renaissance of opulent, but beautifully balanced, dessert wines (such as Kracher's masterpieces or the legendary Ruster Ausbruch) was one of two factors that helped propel Burgenland back to domestic and international acclaim after decades of slumber. The other was big reds. With its warm-to-hot, dry summers and a clutch of dynamic winemakers, Burgenland became the center of Austria's red wine boom during the 1990s. The combination of new vine varieties (most notably Cabernet Sauvignon) and new winemaking technology (must concentrators and new barriques), plus a serious dose of ambition, led to some overblown wines. However, they prompted some good, perception-changing headlines, and recently a mood of caution has spread among winemakers.

The biggest change in Burgenland's red wine vineyards in recent years has been the widespread grubbing up of Cabernet Sauvignon and a shift back to the long-established Blaufränkisch (known as Kékfrankos in Hungary and Lemberger in Germany) and indigenous Blauer Zweigelt. The only problem for the latter was that it was not taken seriously and therefore tended to be over-cropped, leading to wishy-washy wines. Blaufränkisch, meanwhile, tended to be over-oaked, obscuring its vibrant fruit and spice aromas. Thankfully, all this is changing fast as the true potential of these grapes is becoming realized.

These regions remain somewhat polarized when it comes to dry whites. A few outstanding barrel-fermented Chardonnays prove that it is possible to reach for the stars in this direction. However, the majority of dry whites are rather broad and round, lacking the freshness and expressive aromas that are the strength of Lower Austrian wines of this kind. Even in Austria, most people imagine that Burgenland produces rather little dry white, when it actually has almost 4,500 acres (1,800ha) of Grüner Veltliner alone.

One of the places where potential is finally being realized—with Grüner Veltliner and Chardonnay in white and Blaufränkisch in red— is in the Leithaberg hills, where wines that break the Burgenland mold have been grown on limestone and slate since 2004. These wines have already created quite a buzz in Austria and have encouraged winemakers in Mittelburgenland to pursue a similar direction.

No doubt some of the high-alcohol, heavily oaked blockbuster reds from Burgenland are here to stay. But there is equally no question that the stylistic diversity of these regions is only going to increase in the years to come.

Claus Preisinger

The Preisinger labels' minimalistic white paper purity is only marred by what looks like a pencil inscription in the middle: "Claus." This dangerously talented young winemaker was never afraid to shock or to awe, most importantly with the striking taste of his daring reds. Big and bold, yet sweet and polished, they have a freshness and aromatic complexity more reminiscent of the best wines from cool corners of California than this warm corner of Austria. Preisinger's powerful, yet silky Pinot Noir is his most sought-after wine, but his new Buehl Blaufränkisch is even more dramatic.

Obere Hauptstrasse 33, 7122, Gols
www.clauspreisinger.at

Ernst Triebaumer

In 1986, Ernst Triebaumer's Blaufränkisch from the Mariental site proved that Austria could produce world-class reds. Since then, he has been best known in Austria as "E.T.," and that is what is printed largest on his label. This dense, yet vibrant red with its chocolate and liquorice aromas has an impressive smaller brother in the form of the great-value Blaufränkisch Gemärk. He also makes some very good Sauvignon Blanc, plus some excellent modern Ausbruch dessert wines.

Raiffeisenstrasse 9, 7071, Rust
www.triebaumer.com

Feiler-Artinger

By the 1980s, Rust's 300-year-old tradition of making Ausbruch dessert wines had gathered a thick layer of dust. More than anyone else, Kurt Feiler of Feiler-Artinger was responsible for its radical rejuvenation. Since 1993, the estate's Ruster Ausbruch Pinot Cuvée, a blend of the white Pinots, Chardonnay, and indigenous Neuburger, has defined modern Ausbruch. It has intense tropical fruit aromas and fine vanilla oak from barrique, with more acidity and less alcohol than old-style Ausbruch or Sauternes, but less sweetness than TBA. The powerful, elegantly tannic reds Solitaire (Blaufränkisch with Cabernet Sauvignon and Merlot) and 1000 (Cabernet Franc and Merlot) are among Austria's finest.

Hauptstrasse 3, 7071, Rust; 02685 237
www.feiler-artinger.at

Gernot and Heike Heinrich

"International-style winemaking" is all too often an insult, but this is what Gernot and Heike Heinrich do in the most positive sense of those words. Their most important reds are the Pannobile, a *cuvée* of indigenous Zweigelt, Blaufränkisch, and St-Laurent, and Gabrainza from the same trio plus a generous splash of Merlot. Both successfully combine considerable blackberry richness and spice with plush tannins and fine vanilla oak, with production quantities large for this quality in the Austrian context. The more expensive, small-production Salzberg is considerably more chocolatey, opulent, and sexy.

Baumgarten 60, 7122, Gols
www.heinrich.at

Gesellmann

Albert Gesellmann was already building a reputation for powerful tannic reds during the early 1990s and his Bela Rex Cabernet Sauvignon/Merlot blend remains one of the

FEILER-ARTINGER
THE RUSTER AUSBRUCH IS A SIMPLY DELICIOUS DESSERT WINE

JUDITH BECK
THE WELL-TRAVELED JUDITH BECK HAS DEVELOPED HER OWN UNIQUE STYLE

archetypal Austrian reds in this style. Similar winemaking lies behind his Opus Eximum *cuvée* of indigenous Blaufränkisch, Zweigelt, and St-Laurent, which is somewhat less oaky and more spicy.

Lange Gasse 65, 7301, Deutschkreutz
www.gesellmann.at

Haider

Gerhard Haider did not become a winemaker in order to grab the limelight. And considering the excellence of the TBA dessert wines from his 30 acres (12ha) of vineyards around Illmitz, he keeps a remarkably low media profile. These wines combine textural richness and concentrated exotic aromas with great harmony and delicacy. They all see zero oak and are marketed with zero pretension.

Seegasse 16, 7142, Illmitz
www.weinguthaider.at

Hans and Anita Nittnaus

When Hans "John" Nittnaus took over the family estate back in 1985, he wanted to match Bordeaux's finest reds. But he only started making really interesting wines when he abandoned this goal. Today, Nittnaus makes two contrasting top reds: the powerful but beautifully balanced barrique-matured Comondor, in which indigenous Zweigelt and Blaufränkisch are blended with Merlot, and the sleek, minerally Blaufränkisch Leithaberg. There is also a Kalk & Schiefer Blaufränkisch from high-altitude vineyards with slate and limestone soils. The latter, along with the lighter reds, matures in puncheons (barrels with double the capacity of barriques) in order to avoid over-oaking.

Untere Hauptstrasse 49, 7122, Gols
www.nittnaus.at

Heidi Schröck

Heidi Schröck has been running her small family winery since 1983. Her wines were always good, but they have leapt up in quality in the past decade or so, particularly the Ruster Ausbruch dessert wines. The finest of these is the Thurner, a varietal Furmint, but the blended Auf den Flügeln der Morgenröte is not far behind. These are neither modernist nor traditional, instead having their own style, which marries aromatic and textural complexity with great freshness and vitality. Schröck also makes impressive reds with the emphasis firmly on fruit aromas and elegance, rather than flashy oak, chunky tannins, or high alcohol.

Rathausplatz 8, 7071, Rust
www.heidi-schroeck.com

Judith Beck

It is difficult to know which of the wines made by the intelligent and creative Judith Beck deserves more praise. Is it her rich, plush top red Judith (a blend of indigenous Blaufränkisch and St-Laurent with Merlot)? Or her impressive regular reds, such as the varietal Zweigelt? The latter always have great harmony and pure ripe fruit aromas un-obscured by oak. Although Beck has worked in Bordeaux, Piedmont, and Chile, her winemaking never strays in the direction of imitation. ★**Rising star**

In den Reben 1, 7122, Gols
www.weingut-beck.at

JURIS/STIEGELMAR

THE ST-LAURENT FEATURES THE TRADEMARK
STIEGELMAR RICHNESS AND ELEGANCE

Juris/Stiegelmar

Axel Stiegelmar was one of only a handful of Austrian winemakers making world-class reds 15 years ago. Today, although the wines have become richer, the tannins are as well-judged as they were back then. The reserve wines —varietal St-Laurent and the Ina'mera, St-Georg, and Wolfsjäger *cuvées*—are given bottle age before release, further accentuating their harmony. He also makes good, discreetly oaked Chardonnay and fresh Sauvignon Blanc.

Marktgasse 12–18, 7122, Gols
www.juris.at

Kloster am Spitz

Thomas Schwarz describes his winery as his "treehouse, commando HQ, and favorite retreat," which gives an idea of what makes this free-thinker tick. He produces the most uncompromising wines from the Leithaberg hills and his radically elegant, spicy, and minerally reds are met with incomprehension by the conservative wing of the Austrian wine scene. The trio of Blaufränkisch reds —Leithaberg, Eisner, and Rohrwolf—are some of the most striking and original wines from this indigenous grape, but one can say the same of his dry white Leithaberg, arguably Burgenland's best Grüner Veltliner.

Waldsiedlung 2, 7083, Purbach; 0676 9608875
www.klosteramspitz.at

Kollwentz

The Kollwentz family were the first in Austria to master Cabernet Sauvignon during the 1980s. Impressive as their varietal Cabernet is, it faces serious competition from the more recently introduced Blaufränkisch Point and their very Burgundian Pinot Noir Dürr. The three barrique-matured Chardonnays—Gloria (very elegant and refined), Tatschler (bolder and more powerful), and vom Leithagebirge (less oaky with floral and herbal aromas)— are very sophisticated and likewise could be mistaken for top-class wines from the grape's Burgundian homeland.

Hauptstrasse 120, 7051, Grosshöflein
www.kollwentz.at

Kracher

With some help from his grandfather, Gerhard Kracher has been running Austria's most famous dessert wine producer since the death of his father Alois in the fall of 2007. Gerhard has retained the two styles of TBA that his father developed: Nouvelle Vague for wines that are vinified in barriques and the Zwischen den Seen, or "between the lakes," which only see steel. They are numbered from No.1 (already a big succulent wine) upward, with No.15 the sweetest and most opulent so far. Unlike many of the world's great dessert wines, Kracher's drink beautifully from release, yet also age impeccably. Grand Cuvée tends to be the largest bottling and the most widely distributed. A joint venture with Heidi Schöck, producing wines from the Rust has also yielded impressive results since the first vintage in 2006.

Apetlonerstrasse 37, 7142, Illmitz
www.kracher.at

Krutzler

In the cool, hilly south of Burgenland, Reinhold Krutzler has been the established number one since launching Perwolff, a concentrated, elegantly tannic red *cuvée* of Blaufränkisch with a dash of Cabernet Sauvignon. The less oaky and tannic Blaufränkisch Reserve is almost as impressive and long-living; the regular Blaufränkisch lively and fruit-driven with ripe acidity.

Hauptstrasse 84, 7474, Deutsch-Schützen
www.krutzler.at

Meinklang/Michlits

Werner Michlits is the most original biodynamic producer in Austria. Top of the eccentric range is the St-Laurent Konrket, a big, velvety red vinified in concrete eggs with an amazingly intense, ripe-cherry aroma and wonderful freshness for such a big wine. The delicately exotic, rich, and mellow barrique-vinified Grauburgunder Graupert is arguably the best wine currently produced from a zero-pruning vineyard. Across the board, the reds are immediately attractive and the Grüner Veltliners supple and dry, even under the second label of Michlits. The wines have none of the extraneous funkiness often found in biodynamic wines.

Hauptstrasse 86, 7152, Pamhagen
www.meinklang.at

Moric

Ex-casino croupier and wine philosopher Roland Velich only founded Moric in 2001. But he has already succeeded in creating both a new style of Blaufränkisch and fresh excitement for this grape variety around the world. Even his top bottling, the Neckenmarkt Alte Reben from ancient vines, never smells oaky. Instead, the Moric style emphasizes the fruit, floral, and spice aromas of the grape and terroir. The wines from the heavier soils of Lutzmannsburg are richer and more fleshy than the Neckenmarkt wines, which grow primarily on slate. Thanks to the high-altitude location, low yields, and hands-off winemaking, the reds are sophisticated and elegant, from the basic Blaufränkisch up and, by global standards, the prices are moderate for the quality.

Kirchengasse 3, 7051, Grosshöflein
www.moric.at

Paul Achs

Paul Achs is Austria's most highly regarded producer of Pinot Noir on the domestic market. He produces equally impressive Blaufränkisch, which share the same ripe and fragrant berry fruit aromas, fine vanilla oak, and polished, elegant style. Neither alcohol nor tannin levels are excessive—common failings in big Burgenland reds. Nor does Achs have even a whisker of the arrogance that sometimes accompanies winemaking success in Austria.

Neubaugasse 13, 7122, Gols
www.paul-achs.at

Prieler

Dr. Silvia Prieler is an enologist and microbiologist who makes some of the most imposing reds in this region, with Blaufränkisch an important specialty. Among the best are the highly extracted, dense, and oaky Goldberg and the fresher, more filigree Leithaberg. The dry white Leithaberg, a Weissburgunder matured in large oak barrels, marries liveliness with tropical fruit and herbs.

Hauptstrasse 181, 7081, Schützen am Gebirge
www.prieler.at

KRACHER

THE 2006 SCHEUREBE TBA NO.11
IS THRILLINGLY PURE AND RICH

Rosi Schuster

Since Hannes Schuster took over the winemaking here in 2005, the wines have become sleeker, more subtle, and less oaky. This is particularly apparent in the cool, herbal reds from the indigenous St-Laurent and Blaufränkisch grapes from the heavy chalky soils of Zagersdorf. The Blaufränkisch Rusterberg from the sandy soil of St Margarethen is a fresh charmer in comparison. The wines are individual and distinctive across the range.

Prangergasse 2, 7062, St-Margarethen
www.rosischuster.at

Schloss Halbturn

This large aristocratic estate underwent a radical transformation under Markus Graf zu Koenigsegg from 2001. The cellars were completely renovated in the style (pastiche?) of a Bordeaux château and the range was revamped along similar lines. The new top wine is the massive, opulent, tannic red Jungenberg, a Merlot/Cabernet Sauvignon that has been described by local critics as a kind of Austrian Château Pavie. The other wines are all good examples of modern winemaking, with prices as ambitious as the rest of the operation.

Parkstrasse 4, 7131, Halbturn
www.schlossweine.com

Weingut Schönberger

Former rock musician Günther Schönberger successfully reinvented himself as a wine-grower in the early 1990s. His opulent and concentrated reds do not conform to Austrian conventions, even though he uses plenty of new oak. Spicy and mineral notes are generally more intense than the fruity aromas, perhaps due to the low yields and organic viticulture. His finest wine, the powerful, subtle Schönberger red, is one of Austria's great unique wines.

Setzgasse 9, 7072, Mörbisch am See
www.schoenberger.eu

Tinhof

Erwin Tinhof is best known for his rich, yet elegant reds, most notably the smoky-spicy Blaufränkisch Gloriette and the sleeker Leithaberg (a Blaufränkisch/St-Laurent blend). Dry whites from Neuburger are no less a specialty —even the regular bottling offers plenty of ripe apple-pear fruit and substance for a friendly price. The Leithaberg blends Neuburger with Weissburgunder for one of Austria's most original medium-bodied dry whites.

Gartengasse 3, 7000, Eisenstadt
www.tinhof.at

Tschida/Angerhof

Hans Tschida's imposing TBA, BA and Schilfwein (*vin de paille*) dessert wines are opulent and super-succulent, with masses of sweetness, dried fruits, and honey aromas, but never broad, fat, or cloying. The most extravagant is usually the Sämling (Scheurebe).

Angergasse 5, 7142, Illmitz
www.angerhof-tschida.at

Umathum

Josef Umathum is best known in Austria for his massive, tannic, oaky Zweigelt from the Hallebühl site, with its deep chocolate and balsamic vinegar aromas. But his most extraordinary red is Pinot Noir Unter den Terrassen from the Joiser Berg site at the northern end of the Neusiedlersee—Austria's most concentrated, complex, and long-living wine from this grape. Even Umathum's regular varietal bottlings of Blaufränkisch, St-Laurent, and Zweigelt have impressive substance and excellent harmony. He makes distinctive dry whites (particularly Traminer) and excellent dessert wines, too.

St-Andräer Strasse 7, 7132, Frauenkirchen
www.umathum.at

Uwe Schiefer

Ex-sommelier Uwe Schiefer began producing some of the most striking and original red wines in southern Burgenland from Blaufränkisch back in 1995. They combine tannic power and ripeness with the freshness typical of this hilly, high-altitude corner of the region. The top bottlings, Reihburg and Szápary, stand out from the basic but generous and fleshy Eisenberg as much through greater elegance as through greater concentration. All have excellent aging potential.

Welgersdorf 3, 7503, Welgersdorf
www.weinbau-schiefer.at

Velich

The Velich family were the first producers to break the big reds and sweet wine mold in eastern Burgenland with their dry white 1991 Tiglat Chardonnay. It was the first barrique-matured wine of this style from Austria to gain international recognition, and its fresh banana and citrus aromas, subtle oak, intensity, and elegance make it unique. The Darscho Chardonnay is less oaky with more charm, and the family also makes small quantities of TBA from Welschriesling that are among the most noble in Austria. OT is an excellent-value blend of Chardonnay, Sauvignon Blanc, and Welschriesling with a hint of oak.

Seeufergasse 12, 7143, Apetlon
www.velich.at

Weninger

The smoky, fleshy Blaufränkisch, St-Laurent, and blended CMB (Cabernet Sauvignon/Merlot/Blaufränkisch) reds from Franz Weninger Sr. in Horitschon are only one side of this estate's production. Franz Weninger Jr. makes impressive reds and dry whites just over the border in Sópron, Hungary, where Blaufränkisch is known as Kékfrankos and the wines are softer and spicier.

Florianigasse 11, 7312, Horitschon
www.weninger.com

Wenzel

The Rust-based Wenzel estate is best known for its traditional Ruster Ausbruch. Among them are Saz (a deliberately old-fashioned blend of Furmint and Gelber Muskateller) and am Fusse des Berges (Sauvignon Blanc, Grauburgunder, and Welschriesling). But the reds are arguably even more interesting. The Pinot Noir has rich red fruit aromas and a mellow style thanks to the warm, dry climate of the hills above Rust and a cautious hand with oak. This is an underrated producer making distinctive wines of great harmony and aging potential.

Hauptstrasse 29, 7071, Rust
02685 287

ALOIS KRACHER

Seldom has the modern history of a wine-growing region been so decisively influenced by a single individual as Burgenland's was during the last 15 years in the life of Alois Kracher (1959 – 2007). Kracher's road to fame began in London in 1994 when his 1981 Welschriesling TBA beat 1983 Château d'Yquem in a blind tasting. Just half a year later, Kracher was declared White Winemaker of the Year at the International Wine Challenge. From then on his prime focus shifted to the United States where he untiringly worked to establish not only his TBAs in the nation's top restaurants and wine retailers, but also his homeland as one of the world's quality wine producers. He also found time to make sweet wines in California with Manfred Krankl of Sine Qua Non under the Mr. K label. He completely remodeled the family winery, introduced a range of food products based on botrytis wine, and became a domestic media personality who redefined in the Austrian public consciousness what it means to be a winemaker in Austria. His death from cancer came before his joint-venture wines with Heidi Schröck could be released.

STYRIA

Styria wine region

At first glance, the wine country of the Steiermark, or Styria, close to the border between Austria and Slovenia, looks like an intensely green version of the hill country of Chianti in Tuscany. This beautiful region lies at the point where the Central European and Mediterranean climatic systems meet, and it is a land of high-altitude viticulture. Vineyards need to be planted at an altitude of at least 980ft (300m) above sea level in order to avoid the worst effects of fog on the vines. On a summer evening, from the vantage point of one of Styria's delightful hilltop wineries or restaurants, you can watch the fog forming in the valley bottoms. But then you might need to dash indoors quite quickly to get out of the cold.

Major grapes

 Reds

Blauburgunder (Pinot Noir)

Blauer Wildbacher

Zweigelt

Whites

Gewürztraminer

Grauburgunder (Pinot Gris)

Morillon (Chardonnay)

Muskateller

Sauvignon Blanc

Welschriesling

Vintages

2009
An almost ideal vintage for the Steiermark dry whites.

2008
Less summer rain than further north and a perfect October led to another excellent vintage, but the wines have quite some acidity.

2007
Not as extremely aromatic as 2008, but somewhat more body and moderate acidity.

2006
A very typical vintage for the region in which ripe aromas are matched by fresh, but not aggressive, acidity.

2005
Another very good vintage of harmonious wines; the top wines are now at their peak.

2004
A rather average vintage and many of the dry whites are now showing a few gray hairs.

Styria's unique climate is responsible for some sleek, highly aromatic wines that have an acidity ranging from pronounced to piercing. The best of them have enough fruit and substance to master this searing character, but if high-acidity wines are not your thing, be prepared for a jolt. This applies particularly to the regular-quality, bone-dry whites from the Welschriesling grape (Riesling Italico by another name) and to the bone-dry Schilcher rosés (from the Blauer Wildbacher grape) from the wild west of the region. Warm summer days are needed for their consumption unless you were initiated into these specialties long ago.

The best known area of Styria is the Südsteiermark, where many of the best vineyards lie within a few yards of the Slovenian border. Thankfully, that has not presented any serious problems since the fall of the Iron Curtain, and it has been even less of an issue since Slovenia joined the European Union.

In the Südsteiermark you find some of the most complex Sauvignon Blancs on Planet Wine. Sadly, there are also some over-oaked and over-priced examples. The oak is thankfully less often problematic in the region's Chardonnays, here called Morillon since the variety's arrival around the end of the 19th century. In recent years, traditional varieties such as Muskateller (Muscat á Petite Grains), Gewürztraminer, and Grauburgunder (Pinot Gris) have enjoyed something of a renaissance and the argument could be made that they are every bit as exciting here as fashionable Sauvignon Blanc and Morillon/Chardonnay.

During the past few years, Austria has experienced a boom of new winery construction and nowhere was this more dramatic, nor the results more breathtaking (in the positive and the negative senses), than in Styria. One winery looks like an art museum, the next you encounter is more like an airport terminal, then suddenly you think a UFO has landed. Thankfully, other winemakers were more cautious and there are plenty of wineries that blend well into the landscape. Much less obvious to the untrained eye is the way the vineyard area here has increased by 45% during the past quarter century. Styria has been on a roll since the late 1980s.

Because so much (99%) of Austria's wine production takes place in the east of the country, the Austrian wine and gastronomic media tend to completely ignore the fact that, at the other end of the country, close to the border with Switzerland, is some historic wine country. A number of viticultural experiments are under way in these mountainous landscapes. The prospect of continued global warming considerably increases their chances of success.

Erich & Walter Polz/Schloss Seggau

The Polz brothers' finest wines are concentrated, slow developers that need a couple of years aging to give their best. Sometimes one or other of the wines gets pushed too far by Erich and Walter's ambition and ends up on the massive side. But when the Sauvignon Blanc Theresa is on form, it is one of the raciest and most complex wines in the region. They also make very good Traminer that avoids the excessive oak sometimes thrown at this grape in Styria. Be prepared for a pronounced acidity in the bone-dry regular-quality Steirische Klassik wines. Since 2007, the brothers have run the vineyards of Schloss Seggau, further extending an already wide range.

Grassnitzberg 54a, 8471, Spielfeld
www.polz.co.at

Franz Nachbaur

The vineyards in Austria's extreme west are often ignored, because the area they cover is so small. This might be justified, but for the excellent biodynamic wines Franz Nachbaur makes from high-altitude vineyards in the Austrian section of the Rhine Valley. The finest of the dry whites are the racy, intensely mineral Riesling and the full-bodied, floral-honeyed Grauburgunder (one of Austria's best). The Blauburgunder proves that Pinot Noir can give exciting reds that are fragrant and silky.

Zehentstrasse 4, 6832, Röthis
www.weingut-nachbaur.at

Gross

Johannes Gross is one of Styria's most consistent winemakers, with a wide range of crisp, aromatic dry wines under the Steirische Klassik designation and a large handful of single-vineyard bottlings, of which the dry Sauvignon Blanc, Morillon (Chardonnay), and sweet Gewürztraminer from the Ratscher Nussberg are the most sought-after. These are big wines that regularly top 14% alcohol, but they are also richly textural and brimming with fruit. Almost as good is the concentrated, but cooler, intensely citrussy Sauvignon Blanc from Sulz.

Nr. 26, 8461, Ratsch an der Weinstrasse
www.gross.at

Hannes Sabathi

The daring young Hannes Sabathi makes some highly original dry whites that are powerful, spicy, and mineral. Top of the range are the reserve bottlings, most notably of Sauvignon Blanc, which have great aging potential. But everything has its own highly individual personality.

Kranachberg 51, 8462, Gamlitz
www.sabathi-weine.at

Lackner-Tinnacher

The media-shy Fritz Tinnacher and Wilma Lackner shun the limelight to concentrate on the job of making great dry whites. Even their most concentrated wines taste weightless, with near-perfect balance and aromatic subtlety. Dry Gelber Muskateller and Grauburgunder are important specialties. For the critics, the Sauvignon Blancs from Welles, with their pronounced paprika and blackcurrant aromas, are the most "serious" wines.

Steinbach 12, 8462, Gamlitz
www.tinnacher.at

TEMENT
THE SLOPING ZIEREGG VINEYARD PRODUCES
RENOWNED SAUVIGNON BLANC

HANNES SABATHI
HANNES SABATHI IS CHALLENGING RECEIVED
WISDOM ABOUT STYRIAN WINES

Neumeister

With its explosive fruit, herbal, and spice aromas, Albert Neumeister's Sauvignon Blanc from the Klausen site is one of the most extrovert and vibrant dry whites in Styria. It is typical of the full-throttle style of a large (250,000 bottles a year), modernistic estate that has helped put this once-neglected region back on the Austrian wine map. From mid-April to the end of December, the wines can be drunk in the estate's own gourmet restaurant, Schlafgut Saziani.

Straden 42, 8345, Straden
www.neumeister.cc

Sattlerhof

Willi Sattler is unquestionably one of the finest dry white wine producers in Styria. Even the simplest wines here have the substance to balance their acidity without any trouble, but this means they also tend to be significantly more alcoholic than Styria's light image would have one expect. Top of the range is the rich and exotic Sauvignon Blanc from the great Kranachberg site.

Sernau 2, 8462, Gamlitz
www.sattlerhof.at

Strohmeier

Franz Strohmeier is a star of Schilcher, the bone-dry and acidic rosé from the Blauer Wildbacher grape. Of his large range, the sparkling version is probably the most accessible for novices. He also makes a striking, sleek and fruity red called Zweigelt aus Trauben, Liebe und Zeit, or "Zweigelt made from grapes, love and time."

Lestein 148, 8511, St-Stefan ob Stainz
www.strohmeier.at

Tement

Manfred Tement's is the biggest and most dramatic-looking of the many new wineries in Styria. It looks like a new airport terminal at the top of the steep Zieregg site where Tement's most famous Sauvignon Blanc grows. Tement has reduced the new oak in his top wines in recent years, replacing barriques with large new oak casks, particularly for Sauvignon Blanc. Often, Tement's Sauvignon Blanc from Sernau, with its intense herbal aromas and salty mineral finish, is as good as the more muscular Zieregg. The great dry Muskateller and Gewürztraminer are often unjustly ignored. The wines of tennis star Thomas Muster are vinified by Tement and sold under his label with the designation "TOMS."

Weingut Zieregg 13, 8461, Berghausen
www.tement.at

Winkler-Hermaden/Domäne Stürgkh

George Winkler-Hermaden is best known for producing one of the best dry Grauburgunders in Styria—the rich, spicy, faintly oaked Reserve. With its herbal-floral notes, his Sauvignon Blanc from Kirchleiten is also one of the most elegant, minerally wines in the region. The same could be said of Olivin Zweigelt red. Since 2004, Winkler-Hermaden has also revived the sweet Kellerbraut Gewürztraminer at the Domäne Stürgkh estate.

Kapfenstein 105, 8353, Kapfenstein
www.winkler-hermaden.at

If it is true that a vine must struggle in order to create truly great wine, then the northern reaches of Europe, with their short growing season, certainly provide the necessary challenge. Wine-growers in Switzerland, the Low Countries, England, and Wales have responded and, aided in recent years by climate change, are now showing surprisingly good results, even hints of greatness.

Mountainous Switzerland's three languages—French, Italian, and German—are reflected in the diversity of its wines. The Swiss are hardly newcomers to winemaking, but they have found new success with unusual varieties such as Humagne Rouge, Amigne, and Arvine, along with more familiar types including Syrah and Merlot.

Wine-growing in Britain dates to Roman rule, but a quality wine scheme akin to the appellation rules of Continental Europe has been in place only since 1992. Non-classic grape types are giving way to traditional vinifera vines thanks to improved growing practices, and more than 120 wineries are now producing over two million bottles per year. Even chilly Scotland has its vineyards.

Climate change has pushed wine-growing further north in Europe than anyone had imagined. Southern Sweden is home to a project consulted upon by winemaker José Luis Perez of Priorat in Spain, while Denmark's nascent wine production—it was only allowed by the EU in 1999—is based in the Jutland and Lolland regions.

Homegrown wine tourism underwrites much of the Low Countries' wine production, while clever vine management coaxes aromatic whites to give what they can. Luxembourg's many small wineries and its one dominant co-operative have begun making wines with grapes sourced from its neighbors in a new initiative, and the banks of the River Moselle are a fine place to relax over a bottle of sparkling Crémant.

REST OF NORTHERN EUROPE

SWITZERLAND

The biggest problem with Switzerland as a wine producer is its obsession with its domestic market. It is an inward-looking tendency that has its origins in protectionist government legislation, which for many years made it very expensive for Swiss wine-drinkers to buy imported wines. That legislation has now been abolished, and it is quite easy to find foreign wines in today's Switzerland. It is rather more difficult to buy good Swiss wines in neighboring Germany, however, never mind in America, Japan, or Scandinavia. The historical background to all this is the dramatic decline in vineyard area from just over 80,000 acres (30,000ha) in 1877 to only 30,000 acres (12,000ha) in 1957; for some decades, supplies were limited. Today, that can only be said of the nation's best wines, most of which are produced in small to tiny quantities.

Major grapes

 Reds

Gamay

Merlot

Pinot Noir (Blauburgunder)

Whites

Chasselas

Müller-Thurgau

Vintages

It is not possible to generalize about specific vintages in Switzerland because of the huge diversity in climatic conditions across the country, from the Germany-like climate in the north to the more Mediterranean type of climate found close to the border with Italy. The varying altitudes of the vineyards also plays a part. But, overall, quality has been good to very good in recent years.

That not enough good Swiss wine is produced to make exporting worthwhile is very much the loss of those of us who do not live in Switzerland. And this has led to a widespread ignorance of the qualitative virtues and stylistic originality of Swiss wines. Only slowly is this sad situation beginning to change significantly. The contrast with neighboring Austria's dynamic expansion of exports and its positioning as a sophisticated supplier of good and top-quality wine is striking. Is Switzerland capable of following this example? Only time will tell.

It is extremely difficult to come up with a general description of Swiss wine, since all 23 cantons, or administrative districts, produce it. There is an enormous range of grape varieties, too, growing under greatly divergent climatic conditions and at altitudes up to more than 3,300ft (1,000m) above sea level (Europe's highest-altitude vines are at Vispertermin in Wallis). On top of this, there is the cultural diversity of the nation's wine-growers, who come from all the main communities. Like their fellow citizens, the nation's wine-growers are therefore French-, German-, or Italian-speakers who feel united by pride in being Swiss. However, until recently, there were three wine-making communities divided by language. Even now, few are willing to openly admit influences from members of the other communities making up their nation.

On the other hand, 45% of the present 37,000 acres (15,000ha) of vineyards are planted with the ancient Chasselas vine, which yields so generously that it accounts for 60% of Swiss wine. Traditionally, it has been vinified as a light, bone-dry white whose acidity has been softened by full malolactic fermentation. Increasingly, the latter practice has been questioned and a previously unknown stylistic diversity is emerging. The other major Swiss speciality, in quantity terms, is the red Dôle, an equally light and soft blend of Gamay and Pinot Noir, and here, too, there has been progress.

There is no doubt, though, that the finest Swiss wines are far removed from these two classics. They fall into two groups, of which the larger comprises wines made from French grape varieties such as Pinot Noir (in Switzerland for many centuries), Merlot, or Chardonnay (recent arrivals). Seldom do they fall into familiar international pigeon-holes, however.

The other, potentially more fascinating, group consists of wines made from indigenous grape varieties such as Petite Arvine, Heida (both white), or Cornalin (red). These almost invariably taste completely distinctive and often match the wines from more familiar grape varieties. However, the majority of Swiss wine-growers would be happier working with the better-known grape varieties. Here, too, Switzerland stands at a crossroads.

Adriano Kaufmann Sottoceneri

Pio della Rocca, a 75% Merlot/25% Cabernet Sauvignon blend, is the most daringly tannic of the Italian-speaking Ticino canton's new top reds. As such, it fits the extrovert personality of its maker, Adriano Kaufmann. Kaufmann also makes good dry Sauvignon Blanc and a Sémillon dessert wine called Vino da Meditatzione in a region where these grapes are rarities. Since 2004, Kaufmann's 12 acres (5ha) of vineyards have been cultivated using biodynamic methods.

6931 Beride
adokauf.vini@bluewin.ch

Andreas Davaz Graubünden

The most difficult issue to get to grips with when it comes to Andreas Davaz's Blauburgunder (Pinot Noir) red wines is deciding which one is the best. Is it Davaz's muscular, tannic, barrique-matured Uris? Or is it the regular bottling with its almost supernaturally intense cherry and berry aromas, which was "only" matured in stainless steel? Davaz, a young winemaker with time on his side, is still trying to work this out for himself. Consequently, changes, some of them no doubt surprising, are very much to be expected over the next few years at this very exciting Graubünden estate.

Porta Raetia, 7306 Fläsch
www.davaz-wein.ch

Baumann Weingut Schaffhausen

The German-speaking Schaffhausen canton has a uniquely perfumed and gentle style of Pinot Noir. And husband-and-wife team Beatrice and Ruedi Baumann have been perfecting their take on it since 1995. The Baumann's R *cuvée*—which stands for the vineyard site Röti, not reserve—is an unusually firm and oaky wine for the region. The even firmer Zwaa is an unusual joint-venture wine made with Weingut Bad Osterfingen in neighboring Osterfingen.

Dorfstrasse 23, 8216 Oberhallau
www.baumannweingut.ch

Christian Zündel Sottoceneri

Christian Zündel founded his 10 acre (4ha) estate in 1982, and since then he has been working toward perfecting an entirely distinctive style of Ticino red wine. His quest has progressively taken him away from his initial goal, which was focused on tannic power. Instead, today Zündel's wines are increasingly marked by fragrance, silkiness, and elegance. Recent vintages of the Orizzonte, a blend of Merlot with a dash of Cabernet Sauvignon, have fully realized those finer qualities, thanks to reductions in extraction and in the use of new oak. Zündel has been biodynamic since 2004.

6980 Beride
christian.zuendel@bluemail.ch

Daniel Huber Ticino

In 1980, Dani Huber left Zürich for Ticino with the goal of revolutionizing the often thin and green Merlot-based reds of the region. Despite having studied forestry and not winemaking, his wines stood out from the very earliest vintages, due to their unusual ripeness and power. Today, Huber has just short of 17 acres (7ha) of vines at his estate in a set of 17th-century buildings in

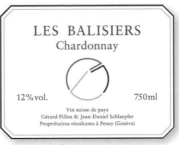

DOMAINE DES BALISIERS
LES BALISIERS CHARDONNAY IS AN EXCEPTIONALLY WELL-MADE WHITE

DOMAINE JEAN-RENE GERMANIER
JEAN-RENE GERMANIER FENDANT IS A FRESH, COOL EXAMPLE OF THE CHASSELAS GRAPE

Monteggio, where he also lives with his wife and children. His top wine, Montagna Magica, is a blend of Merlot with just a dash of Cabernet Franc, and is one of the region's most elegant and sophisticated reds, with excellent aging potential.

Termine, 6998 Monteggio
www.hubervini.ch

Domaine Anne-Catherine and Denis Mercier Valais

The red Cornalin grape is a true Alpine original. It has its roots in the Aosta Valley in northwestern Italy—although, confusingly, the wine made there by the name of Carnalin d'Aosta is actually made from the grape that Swiss wine-growers call Humagne Rouge. Still, confusing or not, the husband-and-wife team of Anne-Catherine and Denis Mercier make the most exciting wine from this capricious vine. The intense cherry aromas literally leap from the glass, while the powerful tannins support the full body and give it excellent aging potential.

Crêt-Goubing 44, 3960 Sierre
027 455 47 10

Domaine des Balisiers Le Mandement

Gérard Pillon and Jean-Daniel Schlaepfer make the most impressive reds at their operation, Domaine des Balisiers, in the often underrated vineyards of Geneva. Their top wine, Comte de Peney, is two-thirds Cabernet Sauvignon and one-third Cabernet Franc, part of which is matured in amphora and part in used barriques. These unusual winemaking methods result in balanced wines very much reminiscent of a traditional-style wine from Médoc in Bordeaux, but with more gentle tannins. Their attention to detail is not confined to the cellar, either. The vineyards are no less meticulously managed, and the estate has been biodynamic since 2004.

12 Route de Peney-Dessus, 1242 Satigny
www.balisiers.ch

Domaine Jean-René Germanier Valais

With the first vintage of Syrah Cayas in 1995, Jean-René Germanier and his nephew, winemaker Giles Besse, changed the face of their region. They did it by proving that the Swiss Rhône Valley could produce great red wines from the most important grape of the French Rhône. The wine has a perfumed and elegant style, with only the most discreet of peppery notes and none of the leathery aromas that often mark Syrahs from the French Rhône. It is completely distinctive. The team also makes excellent aromatic and lively Fendant (from the Chasselas grape), with the Balavaud Grand Cru bottling being particularly good.

1963 Vétroz
www.jrgermanier.ch

Domaine Louis Bovard Lavaux

Considering his advanced age, Louis-Philippe Bovard is outrageously active and innovative. His most important wine is the supple, dry, and intensely minerally Chasselas "Médinette." It comes from the 10 acres (4ha) Bovard owns in the Grand Cru site of Dézaley, the precipitously steep, terraced slope that rises straight up from the northern bank of Lake Geneva. Bovard has many other interesting wines, too, however. He makes a fascinating

KELLEREI CHANTON

GWASS IS ONE OF SEVERAL INDIGENOUS
VARIETIES USED AT CHANTON

PROVINS

MAITRE DE CHAIS VIEILLES VIGNES IS
RICH AND HONEYED, BUT DRY

experimental Sauvignon Blanc that he has christened Buxus, and a very good Chenin Blanc that goes by the name of Salix.

Place d'Armes 2, 1096 Cully
www.domainebovard.com

Domaine du Mont d'Or Valais

The 50 acres (20ha) of terraced vineyards of the famous Valais producer Domaine du Mont d'Or lie at more than 1,500ft (450m) altitude close to the town of Sierre. Johannisberg, or Silvaner as it is known elsewhere, has been the main grape variety here since the estate's founder imported it from the Rheingau in 1870. Today, director Simon Lambiel's top wine is the late-harvested Johannisberg du Valais Saint-Martin. This is a unique dessert wine that combines great richness with a pronounced minerality. The estate also produces a rare Swiss Riesling called Amphitryon. And it offers visitor attractions such as guided walks through the precipitous vineyards, as well as the usual wine tastings.

Pont-de-la-Morge, 1964 Conthey
www.montdor.ch

Donatsch Graubünden

The Donatsch estate was one of the first to experiment with barrique-maturation of Pinot Noir in Graubünden more than 20 years ago. Today, apart from his light, fruity Tradition bottling, all of Martin Donatsch's Pinot Noirs mature in barrique. Top of his range is the Unique Pinot Noir, which has plenty of tannin, alcohol, and oak, and needs several years of bottle-maturation to reach its best harmony. No less striking are the rich and powerful Unique Chardonnay and the austerely racy, late-picked Completer, based on the ancient Swiss variety of that name. The Zum Ochsen restaurant's regional cuisine is also recommended.

Zum Ochsen, 7208 Malans
www.donatsch-malans.ch

Fromm Graubünden

Georg Fromm is best known for founding the La Strada winery in Marlborough, New Zealand, where since 1994, he has produced many top-class Pinot Noirs. That has also been Fromm's goal since he returned to full-time winemaking in his home town. Fromm's are now the most elegant Pinot Noirs Switzerland has to offer, full of a trademark mountain freshness and finesse. Just as in New Zealand, Fromm has a broad range of other varieties to play with. He makes an impressive dry Riesling-Silvaner (Müller-Thurgau), an elegant Chardonnay, a spicy Gewürztraminer with moderate acidity, and a good mid-weight Merlot in the warmest years.

Oberdorfgasse 11, 7208 Malans
www.fromm-weine.ch

Gantenbein Graubünden

Daniel Gantenbein trained as a mechanic rather than as a winemaker. And so it was a brave decision when, back in 1982, Gantenbein and his energetic wife Martha took over some 10 acres (4ha) of vines from Martha's family. Brave, but, as it turned out, far from foolhardy. Progress has been significant, and today the couple produces the most concentrated, rich, and ageworthy Pinot Noir in Switzerland in a stunningly original modern winery.

No less striking is their unashamedly Mosel-style Rheinriesling, which marries fine citrussy aromas with racy acidity and natural fruit sweetness.

Im Feld, 7306 Fläsch
081 302 47 88

Gialdi Vini Sottoceneri

Feliciano Gialdi's powerful and tannic Sassi Grossi is arguably the best varietal Merlot produced in Switzerland. The mineral note in the finish comes from the sandy granite-gneis soils in Gialdi's vineyards in Biasca and Giornico. Gialdi is also a pioneer of Merlot Bianco, an eccentric speciality of the Ticino region, which makes a fresh white wine for early drinking from the red grape variety Merlot. Other lines in the Gialdi portfolio include the sweet Müller-Thurgau/Muscat dessert wine, Mino, and a range of grappas.

Via Vignoo 3, 6850 Mendrisio
www.gialdi.ch

Grillette Domaine de Cressier
Three Lakes

Hans-Peter Mürset of Grillette Domaine de Cressier was one of the first Swiss wine-growers to plant Chardonnay (back in 1964), Sauvignon Blanc, and Viognier. A combination of the limestone soil of his vineyards (which are located between Lake Biel and Lake Neuchâtel) with cautiously modern vinification, gives racy whites with a pronounced minerality. Mürset has not stopped innovating as he has grown older. His latest projects include a remarkably substantial and supple Cabernet Franc, a Merlot/Malbec blend, and a varietal Merlot for this cool-climate location.

Rue Molondin 2, 2088 Cressier
www.grillette.ch

Hermann Schwarzenbach Zürichsee

Hermann Schwarzenbach is by far the most dynamic wine-grower in the Zürich region. He grows 12 grape varieties in 10 different vineyards, and produces a huge variety of wines. From that broad range, his fresh and discreetly aromatic dry white from the indigenous Räuschling vine from the Seehalden site is probably his most famous wine. One could argue that his Mosel-style Riesling-Silvaner (Müller-Thurgau) and his light, aromatic Pinot Noir and Lemberger reds are every bit as interesting, however.

Seestrasse 867, 8706 Meilen
www.reblaube.ch

Irene Grünenfelder Graubünden

Irene Grünenfelder was still a journalist when she planted her vineyards in 1992 to 1993. But by the time Grünenfelder had harvested her first Pinot Noir grapes in 1995, she had already taught herself the fundamentals of vinification. Ten years later, her elegant, dry regular bottling of Pinot Noir (which is aged in large neutral wood) and her even more tannic and powerful barrique-matured Pinot Noir Eichholz wines are without doubt among the best in Graubünden. Grünenfelder makes some very good Sauvignon Blanc, too.

7307 Jenins
www.weinguteichholz.ch

Kellerei Chanton Valais

From 1964, "Chosy" (Josef-Marie) Chanton worked untiringly on his mission to save indigenous grape varieties from extinction. The most original of those, Heida, from which the "glacier wine" is traditionally made, topped the list, but Chanton also wanted to preserve the more exotic varieties, such as Lafnetscha (with its banana and curry leaf aromas) and the steely Gwäss (also known as Heunisch and Gouais Blanc). Today, Chanton's son, Mario, continues his father's conservation work. But he is also responsible for some of Switzerland's finest Rieslings, which he makes both in a medium-bodied dry style and as a superb Beerenauslese-type dessert wine.

Kantonsstrasse 70, 3930 Visp
www.chanton.ch

Marie-Thérèse Chappaz Valais

For more than 20 years, Marie-Thérèse Chappaz has been one of the great innovators of Swiss wine. Among her many and varied achievements is Grain Noble, which is undoubtedly Switzerland's finest dessert wine. Produced from the indigenous Petite Arvine grape, it is packed full of enormously rich, dried-fruit aromas, with complex notes of honey and spice from botrytis. No less fascinating is her dry Petite Arvine Grain Blanc which, in spite of also being vinified in barrique, is absolutely straight and pure, shot through with austere originality.

La Liaudisaz, 1926 Fully
www.chappaz.ch

Michael Broger Thurgau

Michael Broger worked for his now-deceased neighbor, the highly esteemed Hans-Ulrich Kesselring, for eight years at the start of his career. But his adventures as a winemaker really began when he purchased just under 7 acres (3ha) of vineyards (and a house) just 100m (110 yards) from Kesselring's Schlossgut Bachtobel in 2003. It was then that Broger decided to take the plunge and go solo, setting up his own estate. Broger is best known for his elegant, mid-weight Blauburgunders (Pinot Noirs), although he also produces one of the richest and most sophisticated dry Müller-Thurgaus in Switzerland, and a quite wonderfully refreshing dry Weissherbst rosé.

Schnellberg 1, 8561 Ottoberg
www.broger-weinbau.ch

Obrecht Graubünden

Christian Obrecht is one of Switzerland's best producers of Blauburgunder (Pinot Noir). The top wines he makes from the grape, Torcla Nera and Monolith, stand out for their vibrant raspberry aroma. They are simultaneously intense and elegant, with an entirely distinct personality and more freshness than is usually found in the great majority of Graubünden Blauburgunders. Though Blauburgunder is clearly the main focus at this estate, Obrecht's talents stretch to many other grapes, too. He makes a very substantial dry Riesling Silvaner and an impressive Chardonnay, which is partly fermented on the skins, as is the practice in red wine vinification.

Malanserstrasse 2, 7307 Jenins
www.obrecht.ch

Provins Valais

The dynamic Madeleine Gay has done a huge amount to improve quality at Valais's co-operative winery—which is very much a good thing, since Provins's importance to the region's wine industry is enormous. With 2,700 acres (1,100ha) of vineyards, it is responsible for fully a quarter of the region's wine production. The Vieilles Vignes Maître de Chais dry white, a unique blend of Marsanne and Pinot Blanc with the indigenous Amigne and Heida grapes, is Gay's best known wine. But the wines are all well made and modern right across the range. And crucially, they never taste as if they have been forced into a stylistic mold.

Rue de l'Industrie 22, 1951 Sion
www.provins.ch

Schlossgut Bachtobel Thurgau

From 1967 until his death in 2008, Hans-Ulrich Kesselring pursued a policy of natural, instinctive winemaking that placed him at the front rank of producers in Switzerland. Or, as Kesselring put it: "the laboratory does not stand in the way of drinking pleasure," at his 15 acre (6ha) estate. His last vintages of Pinot Noir "No. 3" were without doubt some of the finest Swiss wines ever made from this grape. But then, the same could also be said for Kesselring's dry Müller-Thurgau, Riesling, and Sauvignon Blanc. His nephew, Johannes Meier, continues his work with great dedication to Kesselring's first principle, with the same varieties, as well as wines such as the Clairet Bordeaux blend, a Weisser Riesling, and a Pinot Gris.

Bachtobelstrasse 76, 8570 Weinfelden
www.bachtobel.ch

Simon Maye Valais

It would be very easy to mistake the powerful and robust Chamoson Syrah from Simon Maye for a top-class wine from a Northern Rhône appellation like St-Joseph or Crozes-Hermitage. Thirty-year-old vines growing over 1,300ft (400m) above sea level and long maceration of the ripe grapes, followed by a year in barrique, are the secrets of this imposing wine, which is produced by brothers Jean-Francois (vineyards) and Axel Maye (cellar). The Mayes make a great number of other wines, however, including several from more obscure white varieties such as Fauconnier, Trémazières, and Moette.

Collombey 3, 1956 St-Pierre-de-Clages
www.simonmaye.ch

Urs Pircher Schaffhausen

Urs Pircher began cultivating 15 acres (6ha) of steep vineyards in the Stadtberg of Eglisau directly above the Rhine in 1979 after the sudden death of his father. Pircher grows one of the most fragrant and refined Swiss Blauburgunders (Pinot Noirs) around. He puts the emphasis very much on the wine's fruit character, rather than attempting to impress with heavy oak and big tannins. As well as the Pinot Noir, Pircher is also responsible for one of the crispest and most refreshing dry Riesling-Silvaners (Müller-Thurgaus) currently being made in Switzerland. Gewürztraminer, Pinot Gris, Räuschling, and Regent complete the range.

Stadtbergstrasse 368, 8193 Eglisau
www.weingut-pircher.ch

MEMOIRE DU VINS SUISSE

In 2002, the wine journalists Stefan Keller, Andreas Keller (no relation), Susanne Scholl, and Martin Kilchmann founded a unique organization of Swiss wine-growers. Mémoire du Vins Suisse (MDVS) focused on the ability of the nation's finest wines to mature in the bottle. They settled on a minimum time frame of a full decade's aging, and a similar period of consistent production was also required. From its hesitant beginnings as a club largely concerned with internal matters, it rapidly matured into an association that actively promotes what one might call "serious" Swiss wine —in contrast to the light and simple white Fendant and red Dôle that still dominate the Alpine republic's production. Each member also donates several cases of his or her top wine every year to the association's cellar, which will be used to test and demonstrate their aging ability. Since the first wines put in the cellar were from the 1999 vintage, the day of reckoning has come for the first members—and for the others it is fast approaching.

ENGLAND AND WALES

Traditionally, the British Isles are not widely renowned for producing international quality wine. If you have heard of, let alone tasted, English or Welsh wine, you may have dismissed it as a novelty. However, while production levels are certainly inconsequential compared to those of most other regions, the quality of the UK's sparkling wines has begun to rival those of Champagne. Growing grapes at their northern extreme means only the truly dedicated growers succeed. There are many factors that conspire against them, including rain (plenty of it, and invariably at the most inopportune times), a high risk of disease, frosts, and unpredictable yields.

Major grapes

Reds
Pinot Meunier

Pinot Noir

Rondo

Whites
Bacchus

Chardonnay

Müller-Thurgau

Reichensteiner

Seyval Blanc

Vintages

2009
Great weather at flowering, followed by a perfect growing season and a dry Indian summer, produced great yields as well as fantastic quality. Better in the southeast than the southwest.

2008
Wet and stormy conditions at all the wrong times led to tiny yields and generally under-ripe grapes throughout.

2007
A poor year in terms of both yield and quality.

2006
A high-quality harvest with some wonderfully rich sparkling wines that are still showing well.

Winemaking in the UK in the latter half of the 20th century was heavily influenced by German varieties and techniques, with the belief that the climate there was directly comparable to that of the UK. More recently, the similarities with Champagne are reflected in the new vineyards of Chardonnay, Pinot Noir, and Pinot Meunier. The deep chalk deposits running through the South Downs, visible as the White Cliffs of Dover, are a continuation of those around Epernay.

The prohibitive cost of land in the most suitable counties—namely those bordering London—may prove to be the most restrictive factor. There are around 400 vineyards planted in England and Wales (Scotland does not yet have a commercial industry to speak of), some of which are tiny, amateur ventures. The bulk of production is concentrated in the southern half of the UK.

The revival in the industry's fortunes in recent years has continued a long tradition. England has had vineyards for centuries, dating from the Roman occupation in the 1st century CE. Since then, the vineyards have been grubbed up, abandoned, destroyed by Henry VIII's dissolution of the monasteries in the 16th century, and subsequently replanted. In the 1950s, Hambledon Vineyard in Hampshire, planted by Major-General Sir Guy Salisbury-Jones, was the pioneer of the current generation. The site has had vines planted on it ever since but, having changed hands several times, its fortunes have peaked and dipped. It is, as yet, unclear which direction the current owner will take this historically important site. He could do worse than listen to Bill Carcary, Sir Guy's original vineyard manager, who still lives on the property, and has decades of knowledge about growing vines in the challenging northern climate.

In recognition of the difficulty in ripening grapes to decent sugar levels, the UK industry has had to adapt. The hundreds of acres of vines planted in England and Wales over the last decade differ from previous generations with the concentration of the three classic champagne varieties. To make quality sparkling wine, you need to start with grapes that are not as ripe as those used in still wines, and that have a reasonably high acidity. This was first attempted by Stuart and Sandy Moss at Nyetimber in Sussex. In 1998, the Mosses achieved their ambition of producing world-class sparkling wine when their 1993 Classic Cuvée won the Yarden Trophy for Best Worldwide Sparkling Wine. Different vintages of the same wine have won the award on two subsequent occasions. Nyetimber's former winemaker, Dermot Sugrue, has moved a few miles to Wiston Estate, where he is responsible for realizing the dream of the Goring family. Not only does he make the Estate wine (not yet released) at the state-of-the-art winery, but he also undertakes contract winemaking for several clients in southeast England.

By competing directly with champagne, English sparkling wine is also competing for the top-end of the market. To capitalize on the growth that English wine is undoubtedly enjoying, there needs to be something uniquely English about it, rather than it being a copy of a product (champagne) that is itself already suffering from over-supply.

However, some producers are gamely continuing with their existing plantings of varieties such as Seyval Blanc for sparkling, Bacchus for still whites, and Rondo for still reds, and they should be applauded for their passion and dedication to the English cause. Bookers Vineyard, Breaky Bottom, and Camel Valley spring to mind.

A'Beckett's Vineyard Wiltshire

A'Beckett's nearly 5 acres (2ha) of vines is small, even by English standards, but the wines produced by owners Paul and Lynn Langham have made their presence felt on the UK market. Their wines are available from stockists across the British Isles. The vineyard was established in the early 2000s and has been trellised in a way that enables the vines to take full advantage of any sunshine. It is worth looking out for the sparkling white wine made from Seyval Blanc and Auxerrois, as well as the Estate Rosé made from Reichensteiner and Pinot Noir. Tours and tastings are available at their Wiltshire vineyard. The wines are made at Wickham Vineyards in Hampshire.

A'Beckett's Farmhouse, High Street, Littleton Panell, Devizes, Wiltshire SN10 4EN; www.abecketts.co.uk

Biddenden Vineyard Kent

Established in 1969, Biddenden Vineyard is the oldest commercial vineyard in Kent. Julian Barnes has grown up there, and the years of experience show in the unrivaled knowledge he has of his vines. They cover more than 22 acres (9ha) and represent 10 different grapes, mainly German varieties. Biddenden produces a full range of rosé, sparkling, red, and white, but it is the Ortega Dry and Gribble Bridge Sparkling that stand out. The Ortega has a pleasingly English hedgerow character while the sparkling marries citrus fruit with yeasty lees-age in a very attractive combination.

Gribble Bridge Lane, Biddenden, Kent TN27 8DF www.biddendenvineyards.com

Bookers Vineyard West Sussex

Having started in 1972 with 3 acres (1.2ha) of vines, the Bolney Wine Estate, home of Bookers Vineyard, now covers 22 acres (9ha). Its winemaker, Samantha Linter, is a second-generation winemaker, and one of England's most respected and experienced. The estate produces a wide range of still and sparkling wines. The Pinot Gris is a wonderfully crisp, yet subtly sophisticated example of this Italian variety. Dark Harvest, a red mainly made of Rondo, is a deep-colored but medium-bodied wine that showcases Sam's skills in using barrel fermentations. In 2009, a really promising Pinot Noir was produced and, although it is still in tank, it proves what can be achieved with a commitment to quality and dedicated winemaking.

Bolney Wine Estate, Foxhole Lane, Bolney, West Sussex RH17 5NB; www.bookersvineyard.co.uk

Breaky Bottom Vineyard East Sussex

The impossibly picturesque setting of Breaky Bottom Vineyard is not the only reward for those who venture this deep into the heart of the South Downs. The wines crafted by Peter Hall since he first planted vines in 1974 are worth the potential damage to your car as you descend the rutted track into this hidden valley. Peter has stuck with Seyval Blanc, proving year after year that this variety can produce world-class sparkling wine with a very English twist. He also produces Chardonnay and Pinot Noir, but it is his Seyval that stands out. Mixed with a drop of his homegrown cassis, it produces a uniquely English kir with a fine soft-rose color and a delicate hint of blackcurrant.

Rodmell, Lewes, East Sussex BN7 3EX www.breakybottom.co.uk

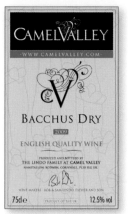

CAMEL VALLEY
THE BACCHUS DRY 2009 IS AN AROMATIC WINE WITH A STEELY FINISH

BOOKERS VINEYARD
FLAVORS OF RED BERRIES AND CEDAR-WOOD CHARACTERIZE THIS WINE

Brightwell Vineyard Oxfordshire

Brightwell has a significant 14 acre (5.7ha) planting, where the owners Carol and Bob Nielsen tend their vines with great attention to detail. The winemaking is contracted out to the very capable Vince Gower at Stanlake Park, allowing them to concentrate on producing quality fruit. The Brightwell Oxford Flint is a wonderfully fresh still white wine, made from Huxelrebe and Chardonnay. As the name suggests, it has a steely, mineral character. They also make a Bacchus, a rosé, a dry red blended from Dornfelder grapes, and a sparkling white wine from Chardonnay.

Rush Court, Shillingford Road, Wallington, Oxon OX10 8LJ www.brightwellvineyard.com

Camel Valley Cornwall

One of the pioneers of the late-20th-century resurgence, proprietor Bob Lindo has raised the profile of Camel Valley, with production now outstripping the actual size of the vineyard. A big purchaser of grapes from contract growers, Camel Valley, more recently under the stewardship of Bob's son, Sam, has gone from strength to strength. Relentless promotion, the winning of competitions, and the heavy tourist traffic to its sun-drenched slopes on the famous Camel River in Cornwall help to sell all they can make. Of the sparkling wines, the White Pinot (a blanc de noirs) is the best, and the Bacchus Dry stands out among the still wines.

Nanstallon, Bodmin, Cornwall PL30 5LG www.camelvalley.com

Chapel Down—English Wines Group Kent

Owen Elias, the man behind Chapel Down's reputation, was at the winemaking helm until recently, but he has now left to set up a new venture. Andrew Parley currently has responsibility for the hands-on winemaking. Chapel Down has its own estate vineyards, long-term contract growers, and contract winemaking clients. One of the biggest winemaking operations in England, it is now a publicly traded company. The sparkling wine is slightly cheaper than its rivals, and is less complex. The still wines, now making up a smaller proportion of the whole, are good value. The Bacchus is floral, aromatic, and refined, while the Flint Dry is a simpler offering but with an attractively steely character.

Tenterden Vineyard, Small Hythe, Tenterden, Kent TN30 7NG; www.englishwinesgroup.co.uk

Chilford Hall Cambridgeshire

Chilford Hall is a long-established vineyard and winery, part of a bigger estate that houses one of eastern England's largest conference centers as well as other visitor attractions. With a lot of the production sold directly to the captive audience, quality has not always been the over-riding factor. However, in recent years, Mark Barnes, a graduate of Plumpton College, has upped the game in the vineyard and winery, producing some very attractive, well-made wines. The sparkling wine is unusual in being made entirely of Müller-Thurgau, while the single varietal Schönberger is a light but wonderfully aromatic still wine.

Balsham Road, Linton, Cambridgeshire CB21 4LE www.chilfordhall.co.uk

PEBBLEBED VINEYARD

THEIR FIRST SPARKLING VINTAGE IS DRY WITH
GOOD UP-FRONT FRUIT AND A LONG FINISH

Davenport Vineyards Sussex

A serious commitment to organic viticulture marks out
Will Davenport and his approach to winemaking. The
extra pressure that this puts on a vine-grower working
with the vagaries of the English climate is extraordinary.
That he produces such excellent wines is testament to his
capabilities. The Limney Estate sparkling wine has an
earthy character, but keep an eye out for the limited
edition Diamond Fields Pinot Noir, made only in
exceptional years. Will is also responsible for Prince
Charles's Duchy of Cornwall sparkling wine.

Limney Farm, Castle Hill, Rotherfield, East Sussex TN6 3RR
www.davenportvineyards.co.uk

Denbies Wine Estate Surrey

No longer the UK's largest vineyard, Denbies does retain
the title of the largest contiguous vineyard planting. It is
an impressive tourist attraction, more like its New World
counterparts than any other English vineyard. The tour
involves a train ride through the winery, and a panoramic
film complete with a light shower to demonstrate
opening a bottle of bubbles. The winery has 300,000
visitors a year and the range of wines caters to their
demands. The many different styles, from semi-sweet
through to dry, can be bland, but try the single varietals
of Schönberger, Ortega, and Bacchus for more interest.

London Road, Dorking, Surrey RH5 6AA
www.denbiesvineyard.co.uk

Halfpenny Green Staffordshire

This 30 acre (12ha) estate is considerably further north
than the major vineyard plantings of southern England.
Halfpenny Green shows how site selection makes all the
difference in this marginal climate. A full range of wines,
from still to sparkling, have found national recognition,
even being served to visiting world leaders at state
dinners. A new winemaking facility was built in 2005,
with the emphasis on quality. Available locally.

Tom Lane, Halfpenny Green, Staffordshire DY7 5EP
www.halfpenny-green-vineyards.co.uk

Hush Heath Estate Kent

Balfour Brut Rosé, the sole label produced here, burst
onto the scene a few years ago, garnering many wine
press inches for the fact that it won a major award on
release, with a price tag to rival Bollinger. The most
expensive wine produced in the UK to date, this sparkling
rosé will be closely watched by the industry to see where
and how it progresses. The wine is made at Chapel Down
for Hush Heath owner, Richard Balfour-Lynn.

Hush Heath Manor, Cranbrook, Kent TN17 2NG
www.hushheath.com

Kenton Vineyard Devon

Matthew Bernstein stands apart in the single-minded
way he went about setting up Kenton Vineyard. He
studied at Plumpton College, while he scoured the Devon
countryside for the right site on which to plant. His
dedication has paid off, with some interesting reds in the
making, along with a promising traditional method
sparkling wine, Vanessa. ★Rising star

Helwell Barton, Kenton, Devon EX6 8NW
www.kentonvineyard.co.uk

Leventhorpe Yorkshire

Although Leventhorpe is no longer the only vineyard
planted at this latitude (between 53° and 54° north), it is
possibly the most persistent. A small vineyard, at only 5
acres (2ha), it is located within the city limits of Leeds,
one of the major conurbations in the north of England.
Vine variety is limited by the geography. The sparkling
wine is made from Seyval Blanc, while some very
attractive still wines are made from Madeleine
Angevine. Triomphe d'Alsace provides the color for a
rosé and a red, but it is the cool-fermented whites, with
their aromatics and steely acidity, that reward some
patience, needing a few years to soften.

Bullerthorpe Lane, Woodlesford, Leeds, West Yorkshire
LS26 8AF; 01132 889088

New Hall Essex

At 166 acres (67ha), this is East Anglia's largest vineyard
and one of the biggest suppliers to Chapel Down in Kent.
The grapes that remain on site are made into crowd-
pleasing varietal wines with rather old-fashioned labels.
New Hall plays host to a wine festival each September,
where visitors can try and buy the wines and other local
produce. It is a popular tourist attraction all year round,
especially with its proximity to London. Try the Signature
white, often made as a single varietal Siegerrebe, an
early-ripening grape that bursts with English character.

Chelmsford Road, Purleigh, Chelmsford, Essex CM3 6PN
www.newhallwines.co.uk

Nyetimber Sussex

Nyetimber continues to lead the way with high-quality,
traditional method sparkling wine. The estate was bought
by Eric Heerema in 2006, when a massive expansion
in both planting and winery capacity was initiated,
and Cherie Spriggs was recruited to take over the
winemaking. Wine from the new plantings has yet to
hit the shelves. The 2003 Classic Cuvée has the autolytic
character one would expect from six years on lees,
while retaining a fresh, aperitif style. The 2001 Blanc
de Blancs really shows the extra aging on lees and
post-disgorging, with a depth and complexity that
would partner well with seafood.

No visitor facilities
www.nyetimber.com

Pebblebed Vineyard Devon

Situated on the foreshore at Topsham, within spitting
distance of the quay, there is a cellar and tasting room at
Pebblebed where Geoff Bowen will offer you a tasting of
his wines and feed you with some simple but excellent
local food. In a setting reminiscent of an Italian enoteca,
it is hard for Geoff's enthusiasm not to rub off on you. His
wines, from three vineyard sites he has planted locally,
are beautifully presented and include a delicate sparkling
rosé, a slightly sweet still rosé, and a floral Madeleine
Angevine with a hint of aniseed. ★Rising star

46a Fore Street, Topsham, Exeter, Devon EX3 0HY
www.pebblebed.co.uk

Plumpton Estate East Sussex

Part of Plumpton College, the wines grown and made by
the students are sold as a popular and lucrative sideline.
The wide variety of vines grown, on numerous trellising

NYETIMBER

THE HOT SUMMER OF 2003 PRODUCED ONE
OF THE FRUITIEST WINES FROM NYETIMBER

systems, gives the students a great insight into the way vines are grown around the world, but provides a headache for the winemaker, Peter Morgan, who has to vinify many tiny batches before producing commercial quality blends each vintage. The rosé is reliably good. Also worth trying are the two very different sparkling wines, one from Pinot Noir and Chardonnay and another from Seyval Blanc.

Plumpton College, Ditchling Road, Plumpton, East Sussex BN7 3AE; www.plumpton.ac.uk

Polgoon Cornwall

Although two tough vintages have depleted the stocks of Polgoon, the healthier 2009 harvest should replenish the supply of John and Kim Coulson's so far excellent wines. One of the most westerly commercial vineyards in the British Isles, Polgoon has produced world-class rosé wines, both sparkling and still. The 2009 rosé, tasted from tank, is bursting with fruit. They also make a bottle-fermented apple cider called Aval that has been very successful. ★Rising star

Rosehill, Penzance, Cornwall TR20 8TE www.polgoon.co.uk

Ridgeview Wine Estate Sussex

The Roberts family concentrates purely on sparkling wine using the latest equipment, including a Coquard champagne press. There is a wide range of styles and prices. The Bloomsbury, a classic mix of the three champagne varieties, is consistently one of the best English sparkling wines. The Fitzrovia rosé is a lovely pale salmon pink with delicate fruit character, and the premier *cuvée* Knightsbridge is a wonderfully complex blanc de noirs. Simon Roberts runs the winemaking operation while his father Mike works tirelessly to promote both Ridgeview and the UK industry as a whole.

Fragbarrow Lane, Ditchling Common, East Sussex BN6 8TP; www.ridgeview.co.uk

Sharpham Vineyard Devon

This vineyard is wonderfully situated on the River Dart. The man currently in charge of Sharpham, Mark Sharman, has raised the profile and the production of the operation by both improving the viticultural practices and buying in grapes from other vineyards. The Estate Selection white made from Madeleine Angevine is crisp, refreshing, and light, while the Dart Valley Reserve is made for a sweeter palate. The really interesting wine here is the Beenleigh Red, made on Mark's own site on which he grows Merlot and Cabernet Sauvignon in polytunnels. It is intense, rich, and complex, but despite the protective growing conditions, it has a typically cool-climate vegetal note.

Sharpham Estate, Totnes, South Devon TQ9 7UT www.sharpham.com

Stanlake Park Berkshire

Formerly known as Valley Vineyards, this 25 acre (10ha) estate was bought by Annette and Peter Dart in 2005. Under the careful husbandry of winemaker Vince Gower, the range of wines is wide and features sparkling rosé and white wines, in addition to a full spectrum of still wines. Very important in terms of contract winemaking for the local industry, the winery has had much

investment from the current owners, which shows in the improved quality. Look out for the single varietals such as Gewürztraminer, Ortega, and Bacchus—they benefit from the long, cool fermentations now possible.

Twyford, Berkshire RG10 0BN www.stanlakepark.com

Three Choirs Gloucestershire

Three Choirs is a large operation, with 75 acres (30ha) planted. The winery is also an important regional center for contract winemaking with riddling and disgorging facilities for local sparkling wine producers. Martin Fowke, who has been in charge of the winemaking since the 1980s, is widely respected within the industry and won the UKVA Winemaker of the Year Trophy in 2008. There is an extensive range of still wines as well as some serious lees-aged sparkling wines. Bacchus, a notoriously fickle variety, here produces a delicate, aromatic white that showcases English still wine at its best.

Newent, Gloucestershire GL18 1LS www.three-choirs-vineyards.co.uk

Wickham Vineyard Hampshire

Under the supervision of William Biddulph, a New Zealand trained viticulturist and winemaker, the winery and vineyard at Wickham are undergoing expansion. The focus is on early release still wines, although there is a sparkling rosé and white. The on-site restaurant, Vatika, is run by Michelin-starred chef Atul Kochhar, where locally produced organic produce is married with the finest Indian influences. The Fumé Special Release 2009, a blend of Bacchus and Reichensteiner, is subtly oaked and worth seeking out.

Botley Road, Shedfield, Hampshire SO32 2HL www.wickhamvineyard.com

WINE PRODUCERS —THE NEW WAVE

The UK has seen a huge explosion in the quality sparkling wine industry. The following names have invested heavily and early signs show great promise:

Bride Valley, Dorset
If Stephen Spurrier, the famed wine writer and organizer of the 1976 Judgement of Paris Tasting, thinks it is worth planting in the UK, who are we to argue?

Furleigh Estate, Dorset
An ambitious project focusing on quality production.

Gusbourne Estate, Kent
2006 planting, with the wine being made at Ridgeview.

Hambledon Vineyard, Hampshire
Potential to revive England's first commercial winery— if followed through.

Hattingley Valley Vineyard, Hampshire
Significant new planting with quality aspirations.

Henners Vineyard, East Sussex
A fantastic microclimate at Pevensey Bay.

Leckford Estate (Waitrose), Hampshire
The leading retailer of English wine gets in on the act with their own extensive vineyard.

Wiston Estate, Sussex
Estate wines and contract winemaking by former Nyetimber winemaker.

Established as a wine estate in 1984, Denbies in Surrey, England, now entertains around 300,000 visitors a year.

BELGIUM, THE NETHERLANDS, AND LUXEMBOURG

In the world of wine, small often means better. In the case of the Benelux countries, it not only means better, but also undiscovered, both in terms of export volumes and global exposure. The Grand Duchy of Luxembourg meets France and Germany in the historic treaty town of Schengen, at the southern tip of the Moselle River wine district. Its wine production has been estimable and unbroken for centuries. By contrast, Luxembourg's northern neighbors, Belgium and the Netherlands, have only recently started to produce wines of note and are slowly developing their wine industries.

Luxembourg's sole wine region is geologically divided into dolomitic limestone to the north, and marl subsoils to the south. To take full advantage of the limited northern light, nearly all vineyards face south or southeast. The personality of Luxembourg's wines reflect that of its people—discreet and reticent. The ancient and neutral Elbling, once the staple grape of Germany's long-ago booming Sekt industry (to which Luxembourg helped give rise), and Rivaner (also known as Müller-Thurgau), are Luxembourg's most prolific grapes, but both are in slow decline. Most others are reminiscent of those popular in Alsace or the Pfalz, both of which share with Luxembourg a common geology. Climate change has seen an increase in both quality and quantity of Pinot Noir, while recent small-scale plantings of Sauvignon Blanc and St Laurent show promise.

Crémant de Luxembourg, an appellation wine comparable to those in France, is one of the world's best-value sparkling wines. Typically comprised of varying amounts of Riesling, Pinots Blanc and Noir, and Auxerrois, its style is soft and minerally, falling somewhere within brut and extra dry levels of sweetness, and drinking well in the early- to mid-term.

Luxembourg's wine governing body, the Institut Viti-Vinicole (IVV), oversees matters concerning the three wine-producing sectors—co-operatives, merchants, and independents. Domaines de Vinsmoselle, a federation of six co-operatives established in 1966, dominates Luxembourg,

representing 60% of total wine production. In 1988, a group of seven wineries founded Domaine et Tradition, an association that was designed to respond to a paucity of quality standards. As a testament to their success, Domaine et Tradition's primacy has since been challenged by others outside their group. Some, such as Schengen native Henri Ruppert, are making their names by pursuing wine's Holy Grail—great Pinot Noir.

With the new millennium, Belgium and the Netherlands have joined the ranks of wine-producing countries. Both lay claim to wine production dating from the 9th century, though little of note happened until the latter half of the 20th century. Most vineyards are planted upon land once given to fruit orchards and potato fields.

The 130 or so growers in the Netherlands divide their parcels on approximately 420 acres (170ha) spread across several unorganized areas. Whites, both straight aromatic and German-style crosses, dominate plantings and production.

Belgium's five demarcated appellations—Hageland, Haspengouw, Heuvelland, Côtes de Sambre et Meuse, and Flemish Quality Sparkling Wine—are coupled with the two Vin de Pays of Vlaamse Landwijn and Des Jardins de Wallonie. As in the Netherlands, aromatic and crossed whites dominate its vineyards. Attention from important corners of the international wine press has been focused upon those bold enough to forge ahead with the Burgundian varieties of Chardonnay, Pinot Noir, and Pinot Meunier.

Major grapes
 Reds
Pinot Noir
 Whites
Auxerrois
Chardonnay
Elbling
Pinot Blanc
Pinot Gris
Riesling
Rivaner

Vintages
2009
Stunning Rieslings and Crémants with yields down. Good white and red Pinots.

2008
Healthy wines. Relatively normal yields, improved on years of short crops.

2007
Nearly ideal weather provided optimal sugar and ripeness. Great Rieslings and white Pinots; good Pinot Noir.

2006
Widely variable quality, due to summer humidity and fall rains. Low yields.

2005
Terrific whites of all types—the best will age for years. Solid Pinot Noirs; many great Icewines. Huge yield decline.

2004
Most whites healthy, though high in acid, and aging well. Excellent Gewürztraminer.

CLOS DES ROCHERS
THIS MINERALLY, BONE-DRY RIESLING IS
SUITABLE FOR MID-TERM CELLARING

Alice Hartmann Luxembourg

This producer's namesake is no more, but Trittenheim native Hans-Jörg Befort makes some of Luxembourg's most complex Rieslings in her name from the country's most identified vineyard, the Wormeldange Koeppchen. Some of the best, and most expensive, Pinot Noirs and Chardonnays—oaky but with the fruit to handle it—are also made here. Dosage for the Crémant is of Riesling Icewine, making it Luxembourg's richest wine in both senses. Side projects have included St-Aubin Blanc and Trittenheimer Apotheke Riesling. French former sommelier André Klein sees to the company's daily business activities in a decidedly clever manner.

rue Principale 72–74, L-5480 Wormeldange
www.alice-hartmann.lu

Apostelhoeve Netherlands

Apostelhoeve's Hulst family wisely concentrates on Riesling, the noblest of whites, along with Auxerrois, Müller-Thurgau, Pinot Gris, and Pinot Blanc. Once primarily a fruit farm, in 1970 the family embarked on a small project with support from colleagues in France, Germany, and Luxembourg. The Apostelhoeve estate—the finest in the Netherlands—is the result. Sandy marl and flint soils predominate on the 15 acre (6ha) estate, which is partly protected by the Louw hills. A few examples of its Riesling and Pinot Gris have been shown to stand the test of time. Expect even better things to come.

Susserweg 201, 6213 NE Maastricht
www.apostelhoeve.nl

Caves Gales SA Luxembourg

Négociant Marc Gales produces much of Luxembourg's most consistently affordable and drinkable Crémant and Vins Mousseux out of a new, state-of-the-art facility. Astute business acumen has led to the acquisition of the venerable Krier Frères and its prized Remich Primerberg vineyards, adding to an already impressive line-up of affordable, minerally dry, and sweet whites. An onsite restaurant on the northern reaches of Remich complements the cellars built deep into the chalky *fels* (cliffs) looking on to the River Mosel. The three lines of wines are all great value for money, with Marc Gales's namesake brand offering some of Luxembourg's best-value Riesling and Pinot Gris.

6, rue de la Gare, L-5690 Ellange
www.gales.lu

Cep d'Or Luxembourg

After years spent traveling the world selling wine, Jean-Marie "Johnny" Vesque eventually decided to settle in his native Luxembourg. His landmark winery, perched over the Mosel River and looking across to Germany, was the first here to use contemporary design as a means to drive modern wine tourism. With his nephew assisting him in the winery, newcomer Vesque has been open to experimentation, and this has gained him a steady stream of followers. The wide array of wines include a very good Pinot Blanc and Pinot Gris, and a "Hommage" Elbling aged several years on the lees. As is to be expected from a former salesman, exports are a strong focus and are growing in volume.

15, route du Vin, L-5429 Hëttermillen
www.cepdor.lu

Charles Decker Luxembourg

Once known for his bucking of the system in the face of financial oblivion, Decker now has a loyal following for his unctuous and riveting dessert wines, well-aged sparkling wines, and more straightforward Riesling, Auxerrois, and Pinot Gris. Although his introduction of Muscat Ottonel set tongues wagging years ago, now many emulate his innovations. A tireless experimenter of varieties and styles in the southern Moselle, Decker's wines are slowly gaining recognition outside Luxembourg.

7 Mounereferstrooss, L-5441 Remerschen
23 60 95 10

Château Pauqué Luxembourg

Content to keep his personal project in the shadow of his mother's Aly Duhr estate, Abi Duhr, Luxembourg's premier winemaker and its greatest proponent on the international stage, launched his Château Pauqué label in 2008. Stunning Rieslings (dry through to medium sweet) and Chardonnays from the Grevenmacher Fels are the centerpieces of his portfolio, though he is not averse to placing Auxerrois and Elbling in barrels for extended periods and charging high prices for them. The guiding light of the wine association Domaine et Tradition, Abi Duhr not only finds time to be a member of wine's European Grand Jury, as well as an importer of fine wines, but also teaches at a local hospitality school. ★Rising star

73 route de Trèves, L-6793 Grevenmacher
52 75 84 17

Clos Mon Vieux Moulin Duhr Frères Luxembourg

The creator of Luxembourg's first red Pinot Noir, this producer now excels with its wide range of long-lived Rieslings, Auxerrois, and Pinot Gris, along with some of the Duchy's best sweet wines from both dried and frozen grapes. Extended family members Jean, Frank, and Luc Duhr's winery and vineyards are centered in sleepy Ahn, one of Luxembourg's iconic wine villages. During a tour of the Moselle in 2007, several European wine writers tasted a bottle of its 1959 Riesling Palmberg. This exquisite wine disproved naysayers about the ageworthiness of dry Rieslings and Luxembourg's wines.

25, rue de Niederdonven, L-5401 Ahn
www.duhrfreres.lu

Clos d'Opleeuw Belgium

Clos d'Opleeuw's owner, Peter Colemont, an enology instructor and importer of Burgundy wines, is blessed with a south-facing 2.5 acre (1ha) walled vineyard for some of his Chardonnay and Pinot Noir vines. Very low yields are the norm, as is extended aging in French and even Belgian barriques; the wines are unfiltered and unfined, and sold at reasonable prices. Although early examples showed an overemphasis on oak, this estate's more recent wines are well-balanced and exhibit true fruit characters.

Martinusstraat 20, 3840 Gors-Opleeuw
www.clos-d-opleeuw.be

Clos des Rochers Luxembourg

Clos des Rochers is one of two high-quality still wine labels within the great Bernard-Massard négociant umbrella. It covers the north, while Thill Frères is its

CEP D'OR
A WELL-BALANCED PINOT BLANC WITH
A FRESH AND CRISP PALATE

southerly sister. Proprietor Hubert Clasen, owner of France's Monmousseau, oversees the day-to-day business, leaving winemaking duties to Freddy Sinner. He crafts sleek, long-lived Rieslings, Pinot Gris, and what are regularly some of the country's finest Gewürztraminers. Bernard-Massard's sparkling wines are exported, and are relatively popular worldwide, while its still wines attract little notice outside Luxembourg and its neighbors. This is a pity, as Clos des Rochers's wines are among the most amazingly fine, minerally expressions Luxembourg offers, with the best examples suitable for mid-term aging.

8, rue du Pont, L-6773 Grevenmacher
www.bernard-massard.lu

A Gloden et Fils Luxembourg

Located behind the large Vinsmoselle facility in Wellenstein, Claude and Jules Gloden's estate fashions delicious traditional Pinot Gris, Pinot Noir, and Riesling, along with Crémants aged *sur lie* longer than any other in the country. Glodens has been making wine for more than 250 years and has begun to brand its better wines as Tradition du Domaine. Some of these hit the mark, some nearly do, but all show true spirit, with the Riesling perhaps being the best of all.

12, Albaach, L-5471 Wellenstein
www.gloden.net

Mathis Bastian Luxembourg

Along with daughter Anouk and vineyard manager Hermann Tapp, Mathis Bastian delights wine lovers with his decidedly feminine-style wines. Intriguing Pinot Gris and Pinot Blanc, delicate Auxerrois and Gewürztraminer, and spirited Rieslings—all at fair prices—are always made with attention to detail and to a high standard. This small-production family estate is delightfully situated, overlooking the vineyards above Remich and the town below. Its fine-boned wines nearly sell out before the next vintage is released.

29, route de Luxembourg, L-5551 Remich
23 69 82 95

Mme Aly Duhr et Fils Luxembourg

Nelly Duhr could easily have retired long ago to leave her fully capable son Abi to run the estate without her, but then what fun would life be? A founding member of Domaine et Tradition, this 1ha (9ha) estate is located in Ahn with choice parcels of the prized Palmberg and Nussbaum vineyards for Riesling, the nearby Machtum Ongkâf for terrific Pinot Gris, and a section of the Wormeldange Koeppchen dedicated to Auxerrois. Maker of Luxembourg's best Pinot Noir (from the 2003 vintage), this producer also offers consistent good value.

9, rue Aly Duhr, L-5401 Ahn
www.alyduhr.lu

Schumacher-Knepper Luxembourg

This 22 acre (9ha) family enterprise, passed in recent years to siblings Frank and Martine Schumacher, has surprised many with its fine-boned, minerally Rieslings, which account for a third of its output, and Pinot Gris grown solely on the Wintrange Felsberg. Dry wines predominate, although it makes some good late-harvest wines. The assignation Constant Knepper is reserved

WIJNKASTEEL GENOELS-ELDEREN
AN ELEGANT, FRUITY, AND FRESH DRY WHITE WINE WITH AROMAS OF HONEY, FRESH PINEAPPLE, AND APPLES

A GLODEN ET FILS
A TRADITIONAL RED PINOT NOIR FROM ONE OF THE OLDEST PRODUCERS IN LUXEMBOURG

for the best wines. The new generation of owners has brought this family domaine its newfound fame in Luxembourg and in Germany. ★ **Rising star**

28, route du Vin, L-5495 Wintrange
www.schumacher-knepper.lu

Sunnen-Hoffmann Luxembourg

Siblings Yves Sunnen and Corinne Kox-Sunnen are Luxembourg's only 100% organic wine-growers. Based in the southern village of Remerschen, they grow Riesling, Pinot Noir, Pinot Blanc, Chardonnay, and Auxerrois (from which they sometimes make a straw wine), along with a little Muscat. Recent vineyard expansion has quickly led to some experimentation with biodynamics and to an overall improvement in the wines. An ongoing, hands-on, government-approved program allowing schoolchildren to learn to work with natural methods has been in place for several years. Sunnen-Hoffmann is doing admirably in the face of its neighbors in abutting vineyards who use chemical sprays.

6, rue des Prés, L-5441 Remerschen
www.caves-sunnen.lu

Wijnhoeve De Kleine Schorre
Netherlands

This producer's director, Johan van de Velde, is an alumnus of Luxembourg's Cep d'Or estate, with whom he shares ownership of this 15 acre (6ha) enterprise. In 2001, he and his father abandoned their vegetable farming business to produce wine for domestic clients, including KLM. Other shareholders in the business take part in the building of facilities and grape harvesting, which lends a communal spirit to this unique Zealand operation. Van de Velde boasts that at 6 miles (10km) from the North Sea, his vines receive 200 more hours of sun than most parts of the Netherlands, all the while growing upon chalky soils once submerged by the North Sea.

Zuiddijk 4, 4315 PA Dreischor
www.zeeuwsewijn.nl

Wijnkasteel Genoels-Elderen Belgium

Château de Genoels-Elderen, Belgium's oldest and largest vineyard, was established in 1991 over 50 acres (20ha). It focuses on Pinot Noir and Chardonnay to produce both still and sparkling wines. The former noble estate's claim to high quality is based upon its topsoil of clay and marl subsoils reminiscent of France's Burgundy region. High technical expertise, Burgundian vinification applications, and extended lees aging characterize these wines, which are destined primarily for the higher-level domestic and northwestern European restaurant markets. A heavy hand with oak can mar these wines; the best choice is the sparklers.

Kasteelstraat 9, 3770 Riemst
www.wijnkasteel.com

From the young Czech Republic to the divided island of Cyprus, the lesser known wine-producing countries of Europe's southeastern reaches are making some amazing-value wines, even if the overall quality remains somewhat variable. Great progress has been made in many former Eastern Bloc countries, where there was little focus on quality winemaking for so long under Soviet rule, but where the best producers are now making wines that suggest a bright future.

Hungary, one of the more established wine-producing countries in this part of the world, is perhaps best known for its sweet wines from Tokaj, but some of Europe's most exciting dry wines are also being made here, many pairing magnificently with the Magyar kitchen. However, Hungary has also had an unstable economy to contend with and has yet to promote itself properly as a top wine nation. Greece is a similar case in many ways, struggling to cast off its stereotype as a repository of cheap wines, with and without the addition of pine resin. In fact, clever winemakers are creating memorable wines throughout the country, many using exciting native varieties of grape. Greece's neighbor to the east, Cyprus, is also receiving attention for its many indigenous varieties.

Slovenia, with its geographical proximity to Northeast Italy, is a land of boutique wineries, a high proportion following natural and extra-natural methods of production. Its wines should be enjoyed alongside the similarly elegant and experimental Slovenian cuisine. But do not make the mistake of confusing Slovenia with the similarly named Slovakia—there, as in the neighboring Czech Republic, only the best wines are really worth seeking out, but these, nonetheless, provide hope for the future. Rumblings of excellent whites and sparkling wines in Croatia are a further source of encouragement in what is potentially the world's most diverse region for quality wines.

CENTRAL AND SOUTH EASTERN EUROPE

CZECH REPUBLIC AND SLOVAKIA

Very little of the wine produced in the Czech Republic or Slovakia is exported. Much is quite ordinary, but both countries have up-and-coming producers that are determined to show what their terroirs can do. Most of the vines in the Czech Republic are in Moravia in the south, with just 5% in Bohemia. White wines predominate in styles similar to neighboring Austria—sweet Icewines and straw wines can be glorious. Slovakia's vineyards also focus on whites and are divided into six regions in the south. Eastern Slovakia also claims a small corner of the world-famous Tokaj region in Hungary.

Major grapes

🍇 Reds

Frankovka (Blaufränkisch/ Lemberger)

Rulandské Modré (Pinot Noir)

Svätovavřinecké (St Laurent)

Zweigeltrebe

🍇 Whites

Müller-Thurgau

Rulandské Bílé (Pinot Blanc)

Ryzlink Rýnský (Riesling)

Ryzlink Vlašský (Welschriesling)

Sauvignon Blanc

Veltlínské Zelené (Grüner Veltliner)

Vintages

2009
Small crops, but very good for reds, and nicely balanced whites. Sweet wines are very concentrated.

2008
Good, fruity wines that are already drinkable.

2007
A warm year with excellent results for reds, dry whites, and sweet wines. Good keeping potential.

2006
High-quality, well-balanced whites. Very good reds.

2005
Low yields, but aromatic and ripe whites. Average reds.

2004
A late and cool vintage – best for fresh whites.

Château Béla Sturovo
World-renowned Mosel winemaker Egon Müller works in partnership with the Ullmann family. The family owns the historic Château Béla, which fell into disrepair under communism, but has since been totally renovated. They make a stunning dry Riesling that is elegant and expressive with great mineral intensity and finesse. A new, unreleased icewine is one to watch. ★ Rising star

Béla č 1, SK-943 53 Béla, Slovakia
www.chateau-bela.com

J&J Ostrožovič Tokajska
Husband and wife Jaro and Jarka Ostrožovič started out in 1990 with five barrels and a lot of enthusiasm. Since then, they have gradually built up a cellar and vineyard. Their classic Tokaj wines range from three to six putňový (puttonyos), in a more traditional style than the current trend in Hungary, with rich toffee and dried apricot notes. Try the sweeter 5 and 6 putňový wines, as well as the Selected Muscat and luscious Tokaj straw wines.

Nižná 233 076 82 Veľká Tŕňa, Slovakia
www.ostrozovic.sk

Martin Pomfy-Mavín Vinosady
Martin Pomfy began making wine as a hobby in 2001. His passion gradually took over, and by 2007, he had invested in modern equipment and started bottling his own wine. Medals have quickly followed and with them a reputation as one of Slovakia's rising stars. His whites are beautifully crafted, with intense fruit and vibrant fresh acids. Highlights include delicious local Devín, and stylish Pinot Gris, Riesling, and Grüner Veltliner. ★ Rising star

Pezinská 7, 902 01 Vinosady, Slovakia
0908 777 066

Nové Vinařství Mikulov
The "New Winery" launched its first wines in 2005, after huge investment. Nové Vinařství is committed to high quality through diligent work and low yields. It focuses on white wines and blends, such as the dry, elegant Cuvée Cygnus and fine sweet Cuvée Lange´Warte, Cuvée To'No', and Cuvée Gabriel. The winery pioneered both glass stoppers and screwcaps to ensure the aromatic freshness of its wines. ★ Rising star

Výsluní 613, 691 83 Drnholec, Czech Republic
www.novevinarstvi.cz

Patria Kobylí Velkopavlovická
Patria Kobylí was founded in 1999, with 376 acres (152ha) of vineyards. Grapes are grown using integrated production to protect the environment, as well as focusing on high quality. Reds and whites are consistent and well-handled, with two impressive flagship wines called Patria Cuvée. The white is an unusual, but successful, blend of Traminer and Chardonnay, while the red is a harmonious melding of André, St Laurent, and Pinot Noir.

Augusta Sebestové 716 691 10 Kobylí, Czech Republic
www.vinozkobyli.cz

Stapleton & Springer South Moravia
Former US ambassador Craig Stapleton fell in love with Jaroslav Springer's Pinot Noir in 2001. After retiring in 2004, he and his lawyer brother started a winery in Moravia, putting Jaroslav at the helm. Using organic techniques, the winery only produces reds. While Rouči is an elegant yet complex blend of Pinot Noir and St Laurent, Jane's Jungle St Laurent is bright and fruity. ★ Rising star

Bořetice 476691 08, Czech Republic
www.stapleton-springer.cz

Vinařství Sonberk Sonberk
The area of Sonberk has a historic reputation that dates back to 1520. It is here that a dramatic new winery was built in 2003, surrounded by 99 acres (40ha) of vines. Hand-harvesting, low yields, and minimal intervention are the philosophy. The result is complex and nicely balanced whites, though the winery's highlights are the delicious sweet wines from grapes such as Pinot Gris, local Palava, and even Sauvignon Blanc. ★ Rising star

Sonberk 1, 691 27 Popice, Czech Republic
www.sonberk.cz

Znovín Znojmo Znojmo
Znovín Znojmo is one of the Czech Republic's larger wineries. It worked hard researching terroirs in the stunning Znojmo region, and has selected its own yeast for its top wines. The winery produces a wide range of wine styles from dry to sweet, but the best are the gorgeous, sweet straw wines made from Riesling, and the luscious Icewines.

Znovín Znojmo, Satov 404, 671, 22, Czech Republic
www.znovin.cz

SLOVENIA

Slovenia has rapidly developed since breaking off from the former Yugoslavia in 1991. While new development is apparent throughout this small country at the northern end of the Balkans, one of the most exciting and noticeable areas of change is the country's wine industry. As in neighboring Italy, wine has been an intrinsic part of Slovenian culture for centuries, and in the past two decades, that culture has been enthusiastically reborn. Led, in part, by established wineries like Movia in Goriska Brda, and helped by the influence of nearby wine regions in Italy (notably Friuli) for western Slovenia and Austria for eastern Slovenia, these distinctive wines are steadily making inroads into international markets.

Guerila Vipava

This young upstart winery was established in 2006 by Zmago Petric, whose family owns approximately 9 acres (4ha) of vineyards, and Uros Bolcina, who is in charge of the cellar. The vineyards contain a host of varieties, including Merlot, Rebula (Ribolla), and indigenous grapes such as Zelen and Pinela. The house style tends toward clean and modern, coaxing fine aromatics and brisk acidity from the wines. The Zelen is dry and firm with a herbaceous character, while the Pinela offers a richer palate and more floral aromas. ★ Rising star

Planina 111, 5270 Ajdovščina
www.guerila.si

Kogl Podravje

This regal estate in eastern Slovenia dates back to the 17th century, although in its current incarnation, its history dates to the early 1980s, when the Cvetko family bought it. The Sämling, a crisp, distinctive, unoaked white wine made from a variety of the same name, is worth seeking out. Kogl also makes compelling Riesling, both as a stand-alone wine and in a complex and engaging blend with Muscat and Auxerrois called Magna Dominica Albus.

Velika Nedelija 23, 2274 Velika Nedelija
www.kogl.net

Movia Goriska Brda

The charismatic Ales Kristancic is the latest generation to run this old estate, located on the border between Italy and Slovenia. Established in 1820, Kristancic insists that little has changed since the days of his grandfathers, which is another way of saying that Movia practices natural winemaking and viticulture. The estate's wines are singular and full of character, and Lunar, a barrel-fermented Ribolla Gialla made with extended maceration, is a revelatory experience. Also worth trying is Veliko Bianco, a substantial, elegant blend of Ribolla, Chardonnay, and Sauvignon Blanc.

Ceglo 18, 5212 Dobrovo y Brdih, Pisarma
www.movia.si

Santomas Primorje

The Glavina family can trace its roots back to the Middle Ages—this branch of the family has tended vines and made wine at their estate since the 1850s. Today, the Santomas estate consists of approximately 47 acres (19ha) of vineyards, which are managed by Ludvik Nazarij Glavina.

His daughter Tamara manages the cellar. The wine most worth seeking out is Malvazija, a refined Malvazija Istriana that boasts vibrant acidity and firm structure. This is a benchmark version of the Istrian white from the Santomas estate.

Ludvik Nazarij Glavina, Šmarje 10, 6274 Šmarje
www.santomas.si

Simcic Goriska Brda

Marijan Simcic took over this estate in 1988, modernizing the winery and vineyards that had been in his family since 1860. From approximately 45 acres (18ha) of vineyards—some of which are nearly 60 years old—Simcic produces stylish, elegant wines. Look for the mineral-inflected Pinot Grigio, which is a balanced, floral, and surprisingly complex take on this popular variety. The Teodor Reserve is a blend of Merlot and Cabernet Sauvignon that balances richness of flavor with a firm texture.

Ceglo 3b, 5212 Dobrovo
www.simcic.si

Tilia Vipava

Melita and Matjaž Lemut launched their small winery in 1994 in the southern Vipava Valley. Their wines feel modern and light, with a fresh, vibrant character that marks both the reds and whites. Look for the Sauvignon Blanc, a bright, refreshing wine marked by lasting citrus notes. The Pinot Gris aims for similarly strong flavors, but offers a richer, more plump texture. Tilia also makes one of the region's better Pinot Noirs: the Modri Pinot is a gripping red with ripe, lasting flavors. ★ Rising star

Potoče 41, 5263 Dobravlje
386 5 364 66 84

Vinakoper Koper

This large co-operative winery was established in 1947 in the Adriatic town of Koper, which is located on the Istrian Peninsula south of Trieste. Look for the elegantly formed Malvazija, with scents of Mediterranean herbs and an underlying saline quality. The Plemenito Belo is a more complex and structured white, with substantial mouthfeel and depth of flavor—if you are used to richer New World whites, this is a wine to check out. The Refosk (Refosco) is a savory, wintery red.

Smarska cesta 1, 6000, Koper
www.vinakoper.si

Major grapes

🍇 Reds

Blaufränkisch
Cabernet Franc
Cabernet Sauvignon
Merlot
Pinot Noir
Refosk (Refosco)

🍇 Whites

Malvazija Istriana
Pinela
Pinot Grigio
Rebula (Ribolla Gialla)
Riesling
Sämling
Sauvignon Blanc
Zelen

Vintages

Recent vintages (2006–2009) have been generally good for Slovenia. As the country's wineries modernize, vintage variation is becoming less of an issue as quality levels tend to be quite good. Since Slovenian wines are relatively new arrivals on the export market, however, it is more useful to track individual producers, rather than rely on specific vintages.

HUNGARY

Landlocked Hungary, Central Europe's quality wine leader, has a rich history of cuisine and wines. Its diversity of soils, varieties, and extremes of temperature have it poised to become Europe's greatest new discovery. With the demise of the Soviet Union, and the huge volumes of simple wine that was produced for it, investment has come from France (AXA at Disznókő), Spain (Vega Sicilia at Oremus), Italy (Antinori at Bátaapáti), Austria (Weninger's partnership with Gere), and Britain (Hugh Johnson at Royal Tokaji). Despite this investment, however, erratic marketing, economic tumult, and an international market indifferent to saving the once-legendary sweet wines of Tokaj mean that Hungary's wines remain comparatively obscure.

Major grapes

🍇 Reds
Cabernet Franc
Kadarka
Kékfrankos
Pinot Noir
Portugieser
Zweigelt

🍇 Whites
Furmint
Hárslevelű
Irsai Olivér
Királyleányka
Olaszrizling
Szürkebarát (Pinot Gris)

Vintages

2009
Good conditions, though little botrytis for Tokaj's Aszú wines.

2008
A rainy vintage ruined hopes for most growers. Better whites than reds.

2007
A long, even summer and little rain in the fall. Excellent wines of all types.

2006
A perfect year provided an excellent overall vintage.

2005
A disappointing summer, but a good fall. Good whites and sturdy reds.

2004
A late, cool season with plenty of rain and/or humidity gave high-acid, fruity wines.

The 14th-largest wine producer in the world, Hungary punches above its weight in overall production, with whites outnumbering reds 3:2. Vintage variation is common, as summers are often very warm with cool nights and extended vegetative seasons, while the winters are often numbingly cold.

In 2006, with an eye to impending EU entry, the Hungarian government consolidated the wine-growing areas into six wine regions: Balaton, Dél-Pannónia (South Pannonia), Duna (Danube), Észak Dunántúl (North Trans-Danubia), Észak-Magyarország (North Hungary), and Tokaj-Hegyalja. Full-bodied, intensely mineral-dry whites are found in Badacsony, Somló, and more recently in the sweet wine heaven of Tokaj, while the warmer, southerly Villány district provides Hungary's finest reds—all of which are grown on volcanic soils. A majority of blending wines come from the flat Pannonian Plain (Alföld), but good reds can also be found in its Csongrád district.

South-facing slopes of clay, loess, and rocky ash over volcanic bedrock are the foundation for Tokaj's famous sweet wines. They are based on white grapes, primarily Furmint with some Hárslevelű—other, lesser, grape varieties include Zéta, Kabar, Sárgamuskotály (Yellow Muscat), and Kövérszőlő. The area supports ideal conditions to encourage the growth of *Botrytis cinerea* (noble rot). Such is the particularity of these wines that naturally occurring yeasts can ferment to 18% alcohol, some doing so over the course of a year, even when they are outside in winter temperatures below 32°F (0°C). The minimum legal standards for sweet Tokaj Aszú wines are two years maturation in barrel and one in bottle, before it can be sold.

Eger is known for its most famous blended red wine, Egri Bikavér. It is based on Kadarka grapes and best known by the brand name "Bull's Blood" —the late winemaker Tibor Gál produced some of the finest examples of Bull's Blood, along with some great Pinot Noir, at the GIA Winery in Eger.

Native white wines, with spicy characteristics that suit native Hungarian dishes, include Furmint, Hárslevelű, Sárgamuskotály, Irsai Olivér, Juhfark, Kéknyelű, Szürkebarát (Pinot Gris), Olaszrizling (Riesling Italico), Riesling, and Leányka. Indigenous Hungarian reds include Kadarka, Kékfrankos (Lemberger or Blaufränkisch), and Portugieser (formerly Kékoportó), all of which make wines of varying intensity and ageworthiness. International interlopers, Chardonnay, Sauvignon Blanc, Cabernet Sauvignon, Cabernet Franc, Merlot, and Pinot Noir, are more recent introductions, but they have performed well in Hungary and received much acclaim.

Disznókő Tokaj
Like many of Tokaj's great estates, foreign investment followed the fall of communism when, in 1992, the French insurance company AXA purchased the 247 acre (100ha) estate. Disznókő sources 90% of its 1,000 barrels from local coopers. It uses wood from the nearby Zemplén forest, a practice that has gathered steam after years of using French barrels. The winery buildings are a mix of classic and contemporary styles, and create a striking image for first-time visitors. Winemaking, overseen by László Mészáros, is extremely good and in a broad, international style.

H-3910 Tokaj, Pf 10
www.disznoko.hu

Dobogó Tokaj
Izabella Zwack, scion of Hungary's notable distilling family, and her winemaker Attila Domokos grow and produce their wines as biodynamically as possible, adding only bentonite and a minimum of sulfur dioxide in the winemaking process, and no casein, gelatin, or enzymes. They cultivate four vineyards that total 12 acres (5ha); 7 acres (3ha) of which is located in the "Grand Cru" of Mad and 2.5 acres (1ha) is near their Tokaj-based facility, which dates to around 1869. Their vines include Portugieser, Pinot Noir, Malbec, Cabernet Sauvignon, Petit Verdot, and Blaufränkisch. ★ Rising star

H-3910 Tokaj, Dózsa Gy út 1
www.dobogo.hu

Attila Gere Villány

Attila Gere re-established his family's Villány winery in 1991. He prefers to work the 148 acres (60ha) by hand and his efforts were recognized in 2004 when his 2000 vintage Solus Merlot beat Bordeaux's Chateau Pétrus in a blind tasting in Austria. Gere also produces 100% varietal Cabernet Franc and Cabernet Sauvignon along with his Cuvée Kopar, and has recently taken to working with the native Portugieser in blends with another native, Kékfrankos, and also as a mono-varietal wine. By the end of 2010, all of the Gere family vineyards will be organically or biodynamically farmed.

Florianigasse 11, H-7312, Horitschon (A)
www.gere.hu

István Szepsy Tokaj

Hungary's most formidable winemaker, István Szepsy, has an impressive family background in winemaking that dates back to the 16th century. Having first proved himself as winemaker at Királyudvar, in 2000 he set about forming his own 156 acre (63ha) winery. His sweet wines are already legendary and, since 2002, he has been pushing boundaries with his dry Furmint. This has been followed more recently by a dry Hárslevelű.

H-3909, 59 Mád, Batthyány út
www.szepsy.hu

Királyudvar Tokaj

Anthony Hwang, also the owner of the Huët estate in the Loire, acquired Királyudvar in 1997. With its former winemaker, István Szepsy, he set about restoring the estate's 193 acres (78ha) of vineyards and cellars in the town of Tarcal. As with all Tokaj estates, sweet wines are Királyudvar's calling card, but a dry, Furmint-dominated blend has also been produced since 2005. Hungarian oak is used and the wines tend toward the pristine and clear side of Tokaji, expressing fruit and minerality with common purpose.

H-3915 Tarcal, Fő út 92
www.kiralyudvar.com

Malatinszky Villány

Csaba Malatinszky resurrected his family's winemaking tradition in 1997, following his time as a sommelier, a wine shop owner, and a stint working at some top Bordeaux estates. His 74 acre (30ha) estate is dedicated to Cabernet Franc and Cabernet Sauvignon, and his flagship wine, Kúria, is based on Cabernet Franc. Malatinszky has also made a name with an unusual blend of Pinot Noir and Kékfrankos, which is called Pinot Bleu. By sourcing barrels exclusively from Hungarian wood, Malatinszky ensures a maximum of terroir is achieved. Kadarka, Merlot, and Chardonnay are also produced, but without the regular elegance of the other bottlings. ★ **Rising star**

H-7773 Villány 12th, Batthyany L. u.27
www.malatinszky.hu

Oremus Tokaj

In 1993, after the fall of communism, the Alvarez family, of Spain's venerable Vega Sicilia, embarked on a project to launch a modern Tokaj winery. Oremus currently has 284 acres (115ha) of vineyards in Mandulás and Kútpatka, of which 148 acres (60ha), spread over four villages, are planted to 70% Furmint and 30% Hárslevelű. Oremus

OREMUS
ONE OF TOKAJ'S LARGEST EXPORTERS, THESE WINES ARE EASY TO FIND OUTSIDE HUNGARY

PENDITS WINERY
LATE-HARVEST SZELLO IS PART OF A NEW GENERATION OF FINE WINES FROM TOKAJ

also has its own cooperage which provides some of its barrels. Their excellent dry white wine, called Mandulás, is also well worth seeking out.

H-3934 Tolcsva Bajcsy – Zs út 45
www.tokajoremus.com

Patricius Tokaj

This winery was purchased in 2002 by Hungary's retired ambassador to France, Dezső Kékessy, whose ancestors began wine-growing in the 18th century. Along with his daughter and co-owner Katinka, they gradually acquired properties in five villages along the Bodrog River, perfect locations for fashioning Aszú wines. The current winemaker, Péter Molnár, utilizes all six permitted Tokaji grape varieties, along with an experimental vineyard of 16 other grape varieties. The winery has a four-level, gravity-designed cellar and, in addition to the plethora of small, used barrels, Molnár employs state-of-the-art machines for extracting some of the region's purest wines. ★ **Rising star**

H-3910 Tokaj, Kossuth Tér 1
www.patricius.hu

Pendits Winery Tokaj

Taking the name of their winery from one of their top vineyard sites, Marta Wille-Baumkauff and her son Stefan established this 25 acre (10ha) estate, which is divided among three villages, at the end of communism in 1991. Their first wines were produced in 1995 and in 2005, and they have since achieved organic certification and begun to experiment with biodynamic viticulture. Yields are purposely low and added yeasts are avoided. ★ **Rising star**

H-3881 Abaújszántó, Béke út 111
www.pendits.de

Szeremley Badacsony

In 1992, Huba Szeremley began the process of renewing his family's 284 acre (115ha) vineyards, which are nestled between Mount Badacsony and the shores of Lake Balaton in the Balaton Uplands National Park. The volcanic soil is best appreciated through the native white wines they produce: Kéknyelű, Budai Zöld, Zeus, and Riesling Italico (made in single-variety form in a late-harvest style). Szürkebarát (Pinot Gris), Muscat Ottonel, and a blend of Riesling called Selection are also grown. Reds are aged in locally made barrels and include Pinot Noir, Kékfrankos, Cabernet Sauvignon, Syrah, and the rare Bakator.

H-8258 Badacsonytomaj, Fő út 51-53
www.szeremley.com

Weninger & Gere Sopron

The Weninger family own vinyards and a winery in their native land of Austria. In 1997, they partnered up with Attila Gere, who had re-established himself in the Hungarian wine industry in 1991, to work on a joint Hungarian venture. Blaufränkisch and Kékfrankos make up the majority of the 54 acres (22ha) of vines with Gamay, Syrah, Merlot, and Pinot Noir comprising the remainder. All the vines are grown biodynamically. ★ **Rising star**

H-9494 Balf, Sopron Fő u.23
www.weninger.com

Fall mist rises from the Bodrog river promoting the botrytis that enables the creation of Tokaji Aszú.

CROATIA

With an equal number of whites and reds, Croatia's narrow Dalmatian and Istrian coast has a climate that is distinct from its continental neighbors, Slavonia and Podunavlje. Between them, they have 12 subregions and 300 defined wine-producing areas. Whites, dominated by the native Graševina (Riesling Italico) and followed by Malvasia, outnumber reds 2:1, with the iconic red grape Plavac Mali (an ancestor of Zinfandel) reaching its zenith in the Postup and Dingač districts of Dalmatia. Familiar varieties, such as Muscat, Riesling, Chardonnay, Sauvignon Blanc, Pinot Noir, Merlot, and Cabernet Sauvignon, can be found among intriguing natives, such as Pošip, Refošk, Vranac, Grk, and Žlahtina.

Major grapes

🍇 Reds

Cabernet Franc
Cabernet Sauvignon
Merlot
Pinot Noir
Plavac Mali
Refošk
Vranac

🍇 Whites

Chardonnay
Gewürztraminer
Graševina
Malvasia
Pinot Gris
Pošip
Riesling

Vintages

2009
An excellent harvest, but best in Dalmatia and Istria.

2008
An excellent harvest, many ageworthy wines.

2007
Good to great wines of all types; best along the coast.

2006
Dilute wines of varying quality.

2005
A bad harvest, but some good light reds.

2004
Good quantities of average to good wines.

Arman Istria
The Armans have been making wine here since the 19th century and were among the first to adapt to modern standards when the opportunity arose in the 1990s. South- and southwest-facing slopes assure even ripening, with the nearby Mirna River providing a moderating element to climatic extremes. Marijan Arman's winemaking style accentuates texture as well as aroma. All the whites, except the Chardonnay, are aged in stainless steel. The Chardonnay is a terrific example, with rich varietal character. The Teran is also very good.

Narduci 3, 52447 Vizinada
www.arman.hr

Dubrovački Dalmatia
Just south of the ancient city of Dubrovnik lies the Konavle Valley, which is separated from the balmy Adriatic Sea by a 164ft (50m) high ridge. The valley enjoys an unusual, semi-continental winter and since 1877, 173 acres (70ha) of Plavac Mali, Cabernet Sauvignon, Merlot, and other grape varieties have grown here on alluvial clay soils. A new line of unfiltered wines, emphasizing earth and structure, has recently emerged from this winery. One to watch. ★ Rising star

Gruda bb, 20215 Gruda
www.dubrovacki-podrumi.hr

Grgić Dalmatia
Expat Miljenko "Mike" Grgich, of Napa Valley's Grgich Hills estate, became famous for making a wine at Chateau Montelena that upset judges at the 1976 Paris showdown. Along with his American-born daughter, Violet, he makes dynamic, powerful Korčula-grown Pošips, which have set the standard for Croatia's finest native white grape, and Plavac Malis with real elegance and length.

Trstenik bb, 20245 Trstenik
385 (0)20 748 090

Korta Katarina Dalmatia
Texan Jeff Reed and his Croatian wife Ankica have applied modern technology to their wines, grown on the scenic Pelješac Peninsula, to produce vigorously minerally Pošips and complexly flavored, if muscular, Plavac Malis. ★ Rising star

Bana Jelačića 3, 20250 Orebić
www.kortakatarinawinery.com

Krauthaker Slavonia
This family-owned winery covers 141 acres (57ha) in the rich soils of the Kutjevo Valley. It sets a high standard for whites, including two good Graševinas and a Pinot Sivi (Gris). It also produces a great Chardonnay and a concentrated, floral and honey-scented Sauvignon Blanc, 40% of which is barrel-fermented. ★ Rising star

Ivana Jambrovića 6, 34340 Kutjevo
www.krauthaker.hr

Korak Dalmatia
Velimir Korak's winery is located just 19 miles (30km) west of Zagreb. He grows 12 acres (5ha) of his own grapes and buys in as much again for his wines. His minerally, off-dry Rieslings possess good concentration and a varietally correct lees-fermented Chardonnay is judiciously influenced by oak.

Plešivica 34, 10450 Jastrebarsko
www.vino-korak.hr

Pjenušci Peršurić Istria
Under the brand name "Misal," Katarina Peršurić Bernobić, with assistance from her husband and fellow winemaker Marko Bernobić, crafts the finest sparkling wines in Croatia. They adhere to traditional methods for their 40,000-bottle production, and styles range from extra brut to a surprisingly good off-dry red. Aging for a minimum of 30 months before release is the norm here, which is reflected in the numerous medals they have won in competitions worldwide. ★ Rising star

Peršurići 5, 52463 Višnjan
www.misal.hr

Zlatan Otok Dalmatia
This small, highly professional company is located on the south end of Hvar. They are known for their white wine, known as Bure (meaning strong northern wind), which is an indigenous blend redolent of almonds and lemons. They also produce a range of award-winning, sturdy Plavac Malis, along with a good, off-dry Crljenak—an antecedent of Zinfandel, which they refer to solely as Zinfandel. Organic certification is expected in 2011.

Sveta Nedjelja, 21465 Jelsa
www.zlatanotok.hr

UKRAINE

Most people's knowledge of Ukrainian wine does not extend beyond the Imperial Massandra collection, yet the country also offers a range of dry and sweet, sparkling, and fortified wines. The picturesque Crimean Peninsula maintains a century-old tradition of producing sparkling and sweet fortified wines; the latter are usually made in port or Madeira-like styles. Winemaking, originally practiced by the ancient Greeks, was brought to an industrial scale in the Soviet era. Vineyards thrive in the south, where the continental climate is tempered by the influence of the Black Sea, but they also grow in the far west, beyond the Carpathian Mountains. The Odessa region, in the southeast, has the largest vineyard area, with a total of 247,000 acres (100,000ha).

Guliev Wines Odessa

This father-and-son operation has been producing modern, high-quality wines from their estate vineyards since 2005. Ruben and Robert Guliev make two ranges. Value-oriented Chardonnay, Riesling, Merlot, and Cabernet Sauvignon are sold under the Select label, while Chardonnay and Cabernet Sauvignon from the Reserve range are aged in new barrels and display good depth.

10 Frantsuzsky Blvd, Odessa 65044
www.gulievwine.com

Inkerman Crimea

Inkerman is one of the largest Ukrainian producers and part of a wine holding that includes 20 estates, all of which supply grapes to this winery. They have taken advantage of tunnels, originally excavated to provide stone for the rebuilding of Sevastopol city after World War II, to store and age their wines. The range is large and focused on dry white and red wines. Sauvignon Blanc and Cabernet Sauvignon are of particular merit.

20 Malinovsky St, Sevastopol 99703
www.inkerman.ua

Koktebel Crimea

Koktebel's winery is located in a picturesque part of the Crimea, next to a seaside resort, and the vineyards are planted on the slopes of a former volcano. It continues the tradition of producing fortified wines, but its signature wine is the dessert Muscat Koktebel. The wine collection of half a million bottles contains some fascinating, if sometimes strange, examples of Soviet winemaking.

27 Lenin St, Tschebetovka, Feodosia, Crimea 98187
www.koktebel.ua

Massandra Crimea

Built on the orders of the last Russian tsar, this landmark property is now state owned. Massandra prides itself on having a unique collection (around one million bottles) of its own and other European wines, which it has been gathering since the late 19th century. Massandra wines are made at this and other facilities using grapes from 9,884 acres (4,000ha) of coastal vineyards. Sweet fortified styles dominate the range—Muscat Bely Krasnogo Kamnya being one of the best examples.

9 Vinodel Egorov St, Massandra, Yalta, Crimea 98650
www.massandra-wine.com

Novy Svet Crimea

Count Golitsyn, the father of Russian winemaking, owned this estate over a century ago, making remarkable sparkling wines. Today, Novy Svet is known exclusively as a producer of traditional method bubbly. Chardonnay and Pinot Noir are used, along with unorthodox Riesling and Aligoté for their flagship brut. The Rosé Pinot Noir has a refined, creamy bouquet.

1 Shalyapin St, Novy Svet, Sudak, Crimea 98032
www.nsvet.com.ua

Odessavinprom Odessa

The Frantsuzsky Bulvar (French Boulevard) brand is synonymous with this producer, the oldest in Ukraine. International grapes are grown on the estate, along with local Rkatsiteli, Fetyaska, Bastardo Magarachsky (a cross of Iberian Bastardo and Georgian Saperavi), and others, which are used for an array of white, red, and sparkling wines. The Special Edition range is more expensive and features, among others, a sparkling red brut.

10 Frantsuzsky Blvd, Odessa 65044
www.fbulvar.com.ua

Shabo Odessa

The Wine Culture Center is this winery's main attraction, so much so that you might be forgiven for forgetting the primary purpose of the place. Reserve Chardonnay and Cabernet Sauvignon stand out, and a sherry-style fortified wine, made with Aligoté, Rkatsiteli, and Sauvignon Blanc, is unconventional but worth trying.

10 Dzerzhinsky St, Shabo, Belgorod-Dnestrovsky District, Odessa 67770; www.shabo.ua

Veles Odessa

The famous Bordeaux consultant Olivier Dauga is in charge of winemaking here. Distinctively fresh and flavorful wines are sold under the Kolonist label. Original offerings include an exotic-fruit white, based on the Sukholimansky grape (a cross between Chardonnay and rare Plavay), and an unrestrained red from Odessky Chiorny (a Black Odessa grape originating from Cabernet Sauvignon and Alicante Bouschet).

4 Bolgradskaya St, Krynichnoe, Bolgradsky District, Odessa 68742; www.kolonist.com.ua

Major grapes

Reds
Bastardo Magarachsky
Cabernet Sauvignon
Merlot
Odessky Chiorny
Pinot Noir

Whites
Aligoté
Chardonnay
Fetyaska
Muscat
Riesling
Rkatsiteli
Sauvignon Blanc
Sukholimansky

Vintages

2009
A great year; balanced whites and reds.

2008
Red wines fared better than the white wines.

2007
Warm weather was particularly favorable for reds.

2006
Small, but good-quality crop, especially for sparkling wines.

2005
Rich and expressive wines.

2004
Average quality.

MOLDOVA

Sandwiched between Romania and Ukraine, Moldova is perhaps the least well known Eastern European wine country. This makes exploring its classic whites and reds, sparkling wines, and original local blends even more exciting. More than 247,000 acres (100,000ha) of vineyards are concentrated in four winemaking zones: Northern, Central, Southeastern, and Southern. White varieties fare better in the cool north, while reds are more suited to the warmer south. Today, winemaking is the country's principal agricultural activity, and the main source of income for many Moldovans. State-owned companies, such as Mileştii Mici, may produce the largest volumes, but private wineries provide more exciting ranges and styles.

Major grapes

Reds

Cabernet Sauvignon

Malbec

Merlot

Pinot Noir

Rara Neagră

Saperavi

Whites

Aligoté

Chardonnay

Feteasckă Albă

Muscat

Pinot Blanc

Pinot Gris

Riesling

Rkatsiteli

Sauvignon Blanc

Traminer

Vintages

2009
Best vintage of the decade.

2008
Very hot summer; rich Merlot and Cabernet Sauvignon.

2007
Hot, dry weather created concentrated wines.

2006
Frosts, so better for whites.

2005
Reds fared better, especially Pinot Noir.

2004
A difficult year. Merlot, Pinot Gris, and Traminer are best.

Acorex Wine Holding Southern (Chişinău)

In just two decades, Acorex went from being a wine exporter to one of the largest and most innovative producers of high-quality wines in Moldova. While its headquarters are in Chişinău, all the vineyards and vinification facilities are in Cahul, in the south. From the beginning, the company relied on international expertise to help it craft clean, modern styles in attractive packaging. All 7,410 acres (3,000ha) of its vineyards are organically certified. The distinctive Amaro de la Valea Perjei, in the Private Reserve range, is made with partially dried grapes, which imitates the production techniques used for Italian Amarone.

45 G. Banulescu-Bodoni St, MD-2012 Chişinău
www.acorex.net

Château Vartely Central, Southern (Orhei)

A long-forgotten tradition of making wine from frozen grapes is being rediscovered by several Moldovan producers, including Château Vartely. Its Riesling, Muscat Ottonel, and Traminer are vinified into wonderfully balanced and mineral Icewines. Indigenous white Fetească Albă is another curiosity, presented in a light, refreshing style. Château Vartely offers vineyard and winery tours, as well as local sightseeing trips. Guests can stay in a cozy hotel complex and sample Moldovan food in the winery restaurant.

170/B Eliberarii St, MD-3501 Orhei
www.vartely.md

Cricova Central (Cricova)

When the Moldovan president wants to impress his guests, he takes them to the Cricova cellars—75 miles (120km) of tunnels, deep underground. This former limestone quarry houses one of the world's largest wine collections, with 1.3 million bottles. The conditions are also ideal for aging the current production, from traditional-method sparkling to the Cellar Collection range. In terms of value for money, mature red and dessert wines from the Cellar Collection are excellent bargains.

1 Ungureanu St, MD-2084 Cricova
www.cricova.md

DK-Intertrade Southern, Central (Chişinău)

Firebird Legend is a Moldovan brand that more adventurous wine drinkers may already be familiar with. Created with help from British consultant Angela Muir, the range features fashionable varieties, such as Pinot Grigio and Cabernet Sauvignon, and offers characterful, yet restrained, fruit with instant appeal. The wines come from the south, where the vineyards benefit from limestone soils and a temperate climate. DK-Intertrade has another facility in Central Moldova that specializes in the production of tank-method sparkling wines.

202 Stefan cel Mare St, MD-2004 Chişinău
www.dionis.md

Lion-Gri Central, Southern, Southeastern (Chişinău)

This company's vineyards, which total 2,470 acres (1,000ha), are scattered across the country. This gives its winemakers the opportunity to showcase the best of Moldova's diverse terroirs. Sauvignon Blanc from Vulcaneşti in the south has a distinct acacia blossom note, while the oak-flavored Cabernet Sauvignon from Talmaza in the east needs time in the bottle to develop its complex character. The traditional-method sparkling wines are aged over 30 months in the cellar.

801 Muncesti St, MD-2029 Chişinău
www.lion-gri.com

Vinăria Bostavan Central, Southern (Chişinău)

The success of this relatively new company, founded in 2002, is built on offering good-value quality wines. The most recent additions are the reliable Chardonnay, Cabernet Sauvignon, Merlot, and sweet Kagor under the Daos label. Most vineyards are located in the south, where the warmer climate is well suited to red grapes.

17 Calea Iesilor St, MD-2069 Chişinău
www.bostavan.md

Vinăria Purcari Southeastern (Dniester)

This winery is original in many aspects, from the French-German founders who established it in 1827, to the ingenious and historic Roşu and Negru de Purcari wines it produces. The Roşu is a robust blend of Cabernet Sauvignon, Merlot, and Malbec, while Negru de Purcari is made with Cabernet Sauvignon, Rara Neagră, and Saperavi grapes in a dense and full-bodied style. The property has received a complete makeover since its acquisition by Bostavan in 2003 and is now a leading wine producer as well as a top tourist destination.

Stefan Voda dis., MD-4229 Purcari
www.purcari.md

ROMANIA

Romania possesses a wealth of indigenous grapes, along with a variety of climates and cultural influences. Whites predominate, but Romania is best known for its reds. Tămâioasă Românească, Fetească Alba, and Fetească Regală are all exciting whites, with Fetească Neagră being the signature red grape. The influence of the Germans, who settled in Transylvania in the 13th century, along with Austrians and Hungarians, is still felt, while winemakers trained in Australia, France, Spain, and South Africa are commonplace today. Wide variations in temperature and precipitation plague growers seeking consistency and some of the industry remains stifled by lack of investment and poor vineyard maintenance, while others have taken advantage of generous EU subsidies.

Casa Davino Dealu Mare

Established in 1992 by Dan Balaban, Davino was quickly hailed as one of the country's best, and most expensive, labels. Balaban focuses on single variety wines from Romania's native Fetească, although the signature wine, Domaine Ceptura, is a remarkably balanced and ageworthy blend of Cabernet Sauvignon, Merlot, and Fetească Neagră. Davino's latest release is Revelatio, a dry white blend of Sauvignon Blanc and Fetească Alba.

Ceptura de Jos 59, Prahova District
0244 445 371

Halewood Dealu Mare, Murfatlar-Cernavodă, Sebeş-Apold

Shortly after purchasing the former Prahova Company from the government in 1998, Sir John Halewood became the largest exporter of Romanian wines. Four winemakers, each with their own areas of expertise, supervise a total of 988 acres (400ha) of vineyards. 2009 saw the launch of Halewood's joint venture, Metamorfosis, with Piero Antinori—a 13,000-bottle run of the 2007 Cantus Primus, a 100% Cabernet Sauvignon from the Dealu Mare. A large hotel and restaurant attract tour groups at their sparkling wine facility in the skiing village of Azuga.

Tohani Village, Gura Vadului, Prahova District
www.halewood.com.ro

Domeniul Coroanei Sergecea

The Crown Domaine was purchased in 2002 by Mihai and Cornelia Anghel, owners of a former state cereal processing facility. After touring the French wine regions for inspiration, they set about reorganizing this historic, south-facing 791 acre (320ha) vineyard. Once the property of Carol I, Romania's last king, the vines are quite tightly spaced and planted on limestone subsoils, interlaced with clay and silex. The temperature-controlled winery has four levels, and uses gravity for some of its processing. The winery is set to become fully organic by 2013, and the Anghels expect to open a new tourist facility in 2011. ★ Rising star

Str. Dealul Viilor nr.108, Sergecea, Dolj
www.domeniulcoroanei.com

Recaş Banat

The co-owner and commercial director of Recaş, Philip Cox, bought the existing state-owned winery and vineyard in 2000, with his two silent partners.

Conveniently located 17 miles (27km) east of Romania's second city, Timişoara, the 1,730 acres (700ha) of well-tended vineyards boast 17 grape varieties: five are local and the remainder are international, including relative oddities Grenache, Nero d'Avola, and Sangiovese.

Complex de Vinifcatie CP1, Recas 307340, Jud. Timis
www.recaswine.ro

SERVE Dealu Mare, Babadag

Founded in 1994 by Count Guy Tyrel de Poix, a Corsican wine producer, SERVE and its Terra Romana brand was the first foreign investment in Romania's wine industry. Eight varieties of grape are grown on 237 acres (96ha)—Sauvignon Blanc, Riesling, Riesling Italico, Fetească Alba, Merlot, Pinot Noir, Cabernet Sauvignon, and Fetească Neagră—with an additional 49 acres (20ha) maturing in the near future. The mix of new to two-year-old-oak barrels are primarily sourced from Romania.

Ceptura 125C, 107126 Romania
www.serve.ro

Stirbey Drăgăşani

Jakob and Ileana Kripp run one of the few family wineries in Romania—it has been in Ileana's family for more than 300 years. Their 62 acres (25ha) lie on a ridge of hills with deep loam–clay–sand soils. The cellar was renovated in 2003 and equipped with steel tanks and wood casks from both France and Romania. German winemaker Oliver Bauer joined in 2003 to oversee the production of single varietal wines, which have a minimum of technical intervention. ★ Rising star

Str. Al. Donici 36, ap.8, 020479 Bucureşti
wwww.stirbey.com

Vinarte Dealu Mare, Sâmbureşti, Vanju Mare

Fabio Albiseti, an Italian wine producer from the Chianti district, established this winery in 1998, with assistance from manager Rodica Fronescu. Its 717 acres (290ha) of alluvial, limestone vineyards are spread throughout four areas and planted to Pinot Noir, Cabernet Sauvignon, Merlot, Fetească Neagră, Sauvignon Blanc, Muscat Ottonel, Riesling Italico, and Riesling. Teganeanu, planted with Merlot, is its top site.

Str. Plantelor nr.50, Sector 2, Bucureşti
www.vinarte.com

Major grapes

🍇 Reds

Cabernet Sauvignon

Fetească Neagră

Merlot

Pinot Noir

Zweigelt

🍇 Whites

Fetească Alba

Fetească Regală

Pinot Gris

Sauvignon Blanc

Tămâioasă Românească

Vintages

2009
Plenty of grapes, due to new vineyards. Quality is average to good.

2008
Good quality overall, best for whites.

2007
Reds are good and whites are average to good.

2006
Good overall vintage, best reds in many years.

2005
High yields, but quality is just adequate.

2004
Average to good, better for whites, but almost all should have been drunk by now.

BULGARIA

Wine has been important to Bulgaria for centuries—in ancient times Bulgaria was part of Thrace and claimed to be the birthplace of Dionysius, the god of wine. The last few decades have seen considerable changes in the Bulgarian wine industry. The communist era saw a higher volume of production from collective vineyards, which resulted in cheerful, inexpensive, varietal wines that became popular in the West in the 1980s. Once the Iron Curtain came down, the complex process of privatization and the return of land to its former owners brought a lack of focus on grape quality. More recently, however, EU membership, along with substantial subsidies for investing in wine and vineyards, have been a powerful force for progress.

Major grapes

🍇 Reds
Cabernet Sauvignon

Gamza

Mavrud

Merlot

Pamid

Shiroka Melnishka Loza (Broad-Leaved Melnik)

🍇 Whites
Dimiat

Muscat Ottonel

Red Misket

Rkatsitelli

Vintages

2009
Early tastings show fresh varietal whites and expressive, ripe reds.

2008
A very good year, with better balance than 2007.

2007
A hot, dry year, which has made weighty, structured reds and serious Chardonnays.

2006
An excellent year, possibly the best of the decade.

2005
Frost damage and heavy rain meant another difficult year.

2004
A difficult year, with widespread flooding and disease.

Officially, Bulgaria has around 333,600 acres (135,000ha) of vineyards, but in reality it is almost certainly less. The country is divided into two regional wine zones—the Danube Plain and the Thracian Lowlands—with 47 specific Denominations of Origin. The last few years have seen huge investments in the vineyards and a new focus on controlling grape quality. At the same time a number of new boutique and estate producers have appeared, determined to show what Bulgaria has to offer. This has not been an easy task, however, with wineries frequently having to wrangle with hundreds of small owners in order to put together decent-sized plots. Substantial foreign investment and the arrival of Michel Rolland as consultant to Telish have all added credibility to Bulgaria's new focus on quality.

Reds dominate production, except in the maritime areas of the Black Sea coast. Cabernet Sauvignon is the grape that made Bulgaria's name and it is still, after the lowly Pamid, the second-most important grape, closely followed by Merlot. Bulgarian producers are increasingly trying out other international grape varieties, such as Cabernet Franc, Syrah, Viognier, Pinot Noir, and even Tempranillo, to learn what really suits Bulgaria's soils.

Of the local grapes, Mavrud is traditionally grown around Plovdiv in the south, as it needs a long ripening season. It is capable of serious, dense, and tannic wines with the potential to age, though perhaps its most exciting role is in blends, where it can add a real sense of Bulgarian identity. Rubin can also make velvety, fleshy, and characterful wines, though they do not age well. The Struma Valley, in the southwest, is dominated by the Broad-Leaved Melnik vine, which is late-ripening and Nebbiolo-like in style, while its daughter, Early Melnik, makes more mellow, dark, plummy wines. Gamza (called Kadarka in Hungary) is another local grape that is grown in the north. It makes light reds that are, at best, bright and fruity.

Bulgaria's wine industry is still a toddler in its current incarnation, but it has undoubtedly taken its first steps on the road to a modern and exciting future in wine.

Bessa Valley Thracian Lowlands
Founded in 2001, Bessa Valley was one of the first true estates in Bulgaria, backed by Count Stephan von Niepperg (of Château La Mondotte) and Dr Karl Hauptmann. It has 346 acres (140ha) of vines that were planted on abandoned vineyard land in the foothills of the Rhodope Mountains. The winery focuses just on red grapes, under the guidance of French winemaker Marc Dworkin. Enira, Enira Reserva, and Syrah all impress in their categories, while the star is the flagship BV by Enira, which is a wonderfully rich and beautifully balanced wine. ★ Rising star

Zad Baira, Pazardjik, 4417 Ognianovo
www.bessavalley.com

Château de Val Danube Plain
Val Markov of Château de Val escaped the repressive communist regime on foot, and started a new life in America in high-tech engineering. A few years ago, he returned to his family's former vineyards in Bulgaria to change his lifestyle. Markov grows organically, with minimal intervention in the winery, and makes a rich, complex Chardonnay and juicy Merlot. His most exciting wines are the blends: Grand Claret, which includes 12 varieties, and the velvety Reserve, which includes old-vine Saperavi and previously forgotten varieties such as Storgozia and Buket. ★ Rising star

201 Parva St, Gradetz, Vidin
www.chateaudeval.com

Domaine Boyar Thracian Lowlands
Domaine Boyar is one of Bulgaria's largest and most important commercial producers. It makes most of its wine at the modern Blueridge winery at Sliven, but it also has a smaller winery at Korten where it makes boutique wines. It is here that the flagship Solitaire wines are produced—the Elenovo Merlot has reached cult status for its generous, velvety style. Recent

additions to the range are a promising Pinot Noir, a harmonious Cabernet Franc, and the selected barrel Vin de Garage wines.

10 Arch J Milanov St, 1164 Sofia
www.domaineboyar.com

Edoardo Miroglio Thracian Lowlands

Edoardo Miroglio is an Italian textile producer who also owns a winery in Piemonte. In 2002, he discovered the perfect combination of soils and microclimate around the village of Elenovo and has since invested around $33 million in it. Over 494 acres (200ha) of vines have been planted and an immaculate winery has been built. Pinot Nero is a feature here in all its forms, including an attractive Blanc de Noir (a delicate rosé) and reds that have more finesse than most. The bottle-fermented sparkling wines (especially the Rosé Brut) are also delicious.

Elenovo, 8943 Nova Zagora
www.emiroglio-wine.com

Katarzyna Estate Thracian Lowlands

Katarzyna is leading the way among the new crop of estate producers in Bulgaria. It has 902 acres (365ha) of vines that are planted in the red soils of the "no man's land" border zone in the warm south. The state-of-the-art winery is decorated with images of the Thracian wine god Dionysius. The wines produced reflect their sunny origin, being ripe and silky in style. Highlights include Viognier/Chardonnay, Encore Syrah, Mezzek Mavrud, Seven Grapes, Question Mark, and the excellent Katarzyna Reserve—a blend of weighty Cabernet Sauvignon and velvety Merlot. ★ **Rising star**

Svilengrad, Haskovo
www.katarzyna.bg

Logodaj Thracian Lowlands

Logodaj is located in the beautiful Struma River valley, Bulgaria's warmest and sunniest region. The team here has set out to combine local traditions with modern, innovative technology, making wines that are "warm like the sun," according to the winemaker, Stoycho Stoev. Local grape varieties such as Melnik and Rubin under the Nobile label are an important feature and are some of Bulgaria's best examples. Hypnose Reserve Merlot is also excellent, being serious, rich, and concentrated. ★ **Rising star**

41 Todor Alexandrov St, Blagoevgrad
www.logodajwinery.com

Maxxima Northwest Bulgaria and Thracian Lowlands

Owner Adriana Srebinova was the first to launch a premium wine in Bulgaria, with the 2000 Maxxima Reserve, at a time when the industry was still pursuing quantity over quality. Her philosophy has always been to seek out parcels of the best grapes from the best sites across the country, but she has recently planted some vines of her own, too. Expressive varietal character is typical of Srebinova's wines, which feature Cabernet Sauvignon, Mavrud, Gamza, and Chardonnay, while her top wine, the rich and weighty Maxxima Private Reserve blend, continues to impress. ★ **Rising star**

6 Danail Yurukov St, 4002 Plovdiv
32 649493

CASTRA RUBRA
THE FIRST RELEASE FROM THIS EXCITING
PROJECT IN SOUTHERN BULGARIA

BESSA VALLEY
AN INTENSE BLEND OF MERLOT, SYRAH,
CABERNET SAUVIGNON, AND PETIT VERDOT

Rumelia Thracian Lowlands

A new winery, but already promising, Rumelia was founded in 2006 on a site where vines had already been grown in the 19th century. The vineyards are planted with Merlot, Mavrud, Cabernet Sauvignon, and Syrah, and wines are made with utmost attention to detail in the pursuit of quality. The best wines so far are the very pure Merul Reserve Merlot and the ripe, characterful Merul Reserve Mavrud. ★ **Rising star**

4 Bratia Deikovi St, 4500 Panagyurishte
www.rumelia.net

Santa Sarah Danube Plain and Thracian Lowlands

Santa Sarah's team travel the country with three caravans and some winemaking equipment. Owner Ivo Genowski aims to seek out individual parcels, to work closely with the growers, and to handcraft each wine. Black C is always reliable as an entry point to the range, but high spots are the elegant Bin 41 Merlot and the wonderful Bin 42 Rubin, while the superb Privat (Mavrud and Cabernet Sauvignon) is one of Bulgaria's stars. ★ **Rising star**

1 Hadji Dimitar Asenov St, 6000 Stara Zagora
www.santa-sarah.com

Telish and Castra Rubra Danube Plain and Thracian Lowlands

Telish in Pleven is already well established as a reliable producer of good-value, well-made reds. In 2005, owner Jair Agopian persuaded Michel Rolland to be the consultant on his new Castra Rubra project, planning the vineyards, which are managed organically, and the stone-built winery in the southern Sakar Mountains. The wines bode well for the future: the first release of Castra Rubra is ripe, rich, and serious. ★ **Rising star**

Kolarovo, 6460 Haskovo
www.telish.bg

Terra Tangra Thracian Lowlands

Terra Tangra is Bulgaria's only certified organic vineyard. Owner Emil Raychev was previously a vegetable grower, he now has 741 acres (300ha) on the slopes of the famous Sakar Mountains. The wines are well made and show the winery's hallmark rich, ripe softness. Juicy Mavrud, supple Rubin, the Organic blend, and the fine Syrah are all worth seeking out. Best of all is the Single Barrel selection, a rich and very concentrated blend of five grapes including local Mavrud and Rubin. ★ **Rising star**

35 Nikola Petkov St, 6450 Harmanli
www.terratangra.com

Valley Vintners Danube Plain

Owner Ognyan Tzvetanov is a bit of an industry maverick. He worked in America at a time when few people traveled outside of Bulgaria, adding valuable experience to his academic background. Tzvetanov is passionate about the terroirs of northwest Bulgaria, where the hillside vineyards enjoy long hours of sunshine without baking heat. Tzvetanov pioneered Bulgaria's first real terroir wine, called Sensum, and in 2009 he released his flagship, Dux, which is aged for five years in barrel and is remarkably classy and elegant. ★ **Rising star**

Borovitza Winery, Vidin
887 806222

RUSSIA

A quiet revolution is taking place in southern Russia, where wineries are gradually abandoning their Soviet legacy and learning to produce quality wines. Winemaking was introduced to this area by the Ancient Greeks, and later flourished in imperial Russia. A vast area between the Black Sea and the Caspian Sea, walled off by the Caucasus Mountains in the south, offers diverse landscapes and microclimates. Most of the 148,300 acres (60,000ha) of vineyards are planted close to the coast of the Black Sea, making them accessible to the nearby popular seaside resorts. International and local grapes are used for varietal or blended bottlings, with the most exciting results coming from Cabernet Sauvignon, Tsimliansky, Sauvignon Blanc, and Aligoté.

Major grapes

 Reds

Cabernet Sauvignon

Krasnostop

Merlot

Pinot Noir

Tsimliansky

Whites

Aligoté

Chardonnay

Muscat

Riesling

Sauvignon Blanc

Sibirkovy

Vintages

2009
Good to excellent quality across the board.

2008
Rich whites and rounded reds.

2007
A very warm year, so wines have lower than usual acidity.

2006
Winter frosts damaged many vineyards, leading to average quality wines.

2005
A superb vintage that is balanced in both quality and quantity.

2004
Fresh whites and light reds.

Abrau-Durso Krasnodar

After a period of neglect, this once-renowned historic producer of sparkling wines is back on the path to glory. SVL Group, a major shareholder since 2006, initiated a large-scale investment program to upgrade the vineyards and winery. As a result, and also thanks to the contribution from Champagne winemaker Hervé Jestin, the quality of wines has improved. The Abrau-Durso range includes both Charmat and traditional method sparkling wines. The latter are crowned by the opulent Imperial Collection Vintage Brut, which is cellared for at least seven years prior to release. Imperial Cuvée Art Nouveau Brut is younger and offers an expressive floral style. An original winery building from the 19th century was recently restored and converted into a museum, with adjacent tasting areas and a shop.

19, Promyshlennaya St, Abrau-Durso, Novorossiysk, Krasnodar Region, 353995; www.abraudurso.ru

Château Le Grand Vostock Krasnodar

This company was the first in Russia to start premium-quality production. It was set up with Russian money, but its French-sounding name was not just chosen for effect. French architect Philippe Mazieres designed the stylish winery, modeled on a Bordeaux château, and a resident French team has been in charge of the wine since the first vintage. The vineyards are located in the foothills of the Caucasus Mountains. White Cadet Karsov and Cuvée Karsov are blends of Chardonnay and Sauvignon Blanc made in a clean style. Midweight, fruity reds Cuvée Karsov and Le Chêne Royal are crafted with Merlot, Cabernet, and some indigenous Krasnostop for additional structure and coffee nuances. The late-harvested Fagotine Pinot Gris is a curious novelty.

7, 60 let Oktyabrya St, Sadovy, Krymsky District, Krasnodar Region, 353358; www.grandvostok.ru

Fanagoria Krasnodar

The buildings of this massive 22 acre (9ha) winery complex may still be Soviet in appearance—after all, they were built during the Khrushchev era and until quite recently were equipped to produce natural varietal juices—but the company itself is at the forefront of the quality movement in Russia and is also the largest producer of estate-bottled wines. With Australian consultant John Worontschak at the helm, Fanagoria makes good to excellent wines in the Cru Lermont and NR (Numbered Reserve) ranges. Aligoté from old vines displays bright fruit, while Sauvignon Blanc gravitates toward white currants and yellow fruit expression. Cabernet Sauvignon is the signature red grape, although the delicate varietal character of the Pinot Noir is also satisfying.

49, Mira St, Sennoy, Temriuksky District, Krasnodar Region, 353540; www.fanagoria.ru

Myskhako Krasnodar

Unusually, this winery operates within city limits, being located in Novorossiysk, a port on the Black Sea. Founded as a Soviet agricultural enterprise, today Myskhako is a private company that owns over 2,100 acres (850ha) of vineyards. It is also official supplier to the Kremlin. Consultant John Worontschak oversees production of a large range of wines that are made with international varieties, from Sauvignon Blanc and Muscat Ottonel to Merlot and Pinot Noir. Floral Chardonnay and fruity Cabernet are Myskhako favorites, though one may be more impressed with the intriguing apricot and honey flavors of the Riesling Icewine.

1, Tsentralnaya St, Myskhako, Novorossiysk, Krasnodar Region, 353993; www.myskhako.ru

Vina Vedernikoff Rostov

Protecting vines against winter frosts is just one of the challenges that wine-growers have to deal with in the extreme local climate of Konstantinovsky District. The plants are painstakingly laid horizontally and blanketed with soil in the fall, before being resurrected in the spring. Vina Vedernikoff grows around 30 local and international varieties on the right bank of the mighty River Don. Its main focus is on indigenous grapes, whose cultivation in the area can be traced back to at least the 17th century. A varietal bottling of white Sibirkovy shows fine aromas that are reminiscent of the dry steppe herbs that proliferate in the area. Inky-red Krasnostop may be an acquired taste, but its wild combination of fruit, liquorice, herbal, and bitter elements is certainly distinctive. Other offerings include eclectic white and red blends that are made with local and European grapes.

7, Tsentralnaya St, Vedernikov, Konstantinovsky District, Rostov Region, 347267; www.vinnkvart.ru

GEORGIA

Justifiably proud of its heritage and contemporary wine culture, Georgia boasts 500 indigenous grapes. It is also famous for the ancient *kvevri*, a narrow clay jar in which some of its most distinctive wines are made. Sheltered by the Caucasus and Gombori mountains, the Kakheti is Georgia's oldest, most unique, and important region and home to three-quarters of Georgia's 118,600 acres (48,000ha) of vines. The remaining areas of western Georgia mostly make medium-sweet wines, especially reds. Other appellations are scattered throughout the country—Racha is notable as the place where Georgia's first Icewine was made. Climate-wise, spring weather is variable, summer nights are warm, and early fall can vary considerably in temperature.

Chandrebi Estate Kakheti

Giorgi Sulkhanishvili and Georgian/Australian winemaker Lado Uzunashvili released their first wines from their 99 acre (40ha) estate in 2006, under the Orovela brand. They produce two reds, a Saperavi and a Saperavi/Cabernet Sauvignon blend, and a white, a Mtsvane/Rkatsiteli blend. Unlike most Georgian vineyards, harvesting is done by machine. ★Rising star

34 Rustaveli Ave, Tbilisi 0108
www.orovela.com

Kakhuri Winery Kakheti

Zurab Goletiani and Davit Dolmazashvili left Pernod Ricard's GWS operation in 2004 to launch this Telavi-based winery, housed in a former silk factory. Nearly half of their 124 acres (50ha) of vineyards are planted to Saperavi, with the remainder being Rkatsiteli and Chardonnay. All bottlings are monovarietal. The indigenous whites, Mtsvane and Kisi, are currently under consideration as additions to their small, but promising, portfolio.

1 Tibilisi Rd, Telavi 2200
www.kakhuri.com

Kindzmarauli Marani Kakheti

Kindzmarauli Marani was founded in 2001 and it is owned by three Georgian partners, one of whom is, unusually for this country, a woman. They immediately set about planting what now amounts to nearly 1,000 acres (400ha) of vineyards and the first vintage, in 2005, was released in an incredible 24 separate bottlings. Kindzmarauli Marani formerly only exported semi-sweet reds to Russia, but it is slowly realizing its potential for great dry red wines.

55 Chavchavadze St, Kvareli 383320
www.kmwine.eu

Metekhi Kartli

David Maisuradze, formerly of the Telavi group, consults to this and nine other wineries, while overseeing his own domaine. The winemaker is Merab Mikashavidze, who focuses on indigenous varieties. The portfolio includes a 50:50 blend of the white grapes Chinuri and Mtsvane, which is accented with delicious mandarin and floral notes. ★Rising star

No visitor facilities
www.cgw.ge

Schuchmann Wines Kakheti

In 2002, third-generation winemaker Gogi Dakishvili, along with star consultant David Maisuradze, became the first to make new-style *kvevri* (clay jar) wines, and instituted previously unknown microbiological controls for wines fermented with their skins and seeds. Red *kvevri* wines undergo 20 days of maceration and the whites for as long as six months, with no added yeasts. Their more standard offerings do include added yeast and are produced in large steel tanks and French oak barrels. These are big-boned, strong wines that are rich in tannins and flavor. ★Rising star

37 Rustaveli St, Telavi 2200
www.schuchmann-wines.com

Tbilvino Tbilisi

This winery, designed to classic Soviet specifications, has been making wines on the outskirts of the capital, Tbilisi, since 1962. In 1998, brothers Zura and Giorgi Margvelashvili restructured the company, instituting a program to buy in higher quality, indigenous grapes from over 300 farmers. Plans are now in place to develop their own vineyards. French oak barrels are used for the top-level wines, but the vast majority are made in epoxy-lined steel tanks. Tbilvino produces 1.3 million bottles a year, making it the second-largest producer in Georgia.

2 Sarajishvili Ave, Tbilisi
www.tbilvino.com.ge

Telavi Wine Cellar Kakheti

Georgia's largest winery, Telavi covers 1,112 acres (450ha) in three districts of Kakheti. It also buys in grapes from growers in Kakheti and the outlying western wine regions. Young winemaker Beka Sozashvili, helped by Frenchman Raphael Jenot, adds a little Malbec to Saperavi to attenuate the native grape's natural astringency. Marani is the main brand name, with Satrapezo, a top Saperavi, having one month's maceration in *kvevri* before moving to oak barrels for three rackings and finally being transferred into steel.

Kurdgelauri, Telavi 2200
www.tewincel.com

Major grapes

 Reds
Cabernet Sauvignon
Saperavi

 Whites
Chardonnay
Chinuri
Mtsvane
Rkatsiteli
Tsolikauri

Vintages
2009
Whites vary in quality and the reds are still an unknown quantity.

2008
Good to great, with many wines suitable for cellaring.

2007
Very good overall; many wines have great aging potential.

2006
A mediocre vintage with many underripe wines.

2005
Good overall; best for reds.

2004
Very good whites and reds, but a few reds have peaked.

GREECE

With more than 300 indigenous grape varieties and a climatic and geographical diversity that ranges from sun-baked Mediterranean islands to cool, fog-shrouded mountains, when it comes to wine, Greece rivals Italy for variety. The country has made wine for millennia, perhaps beginning on Crete, where evidence points to wine production as early as 2BCE. Occupation by the Ottoman Turks in the 15th century took a toll on the Greek wine industry, and the combination of the vine disease phylloxera, the Balkan War, two world wars, and a civil war left the industry in a shambles by the mid-20th century. However, it has since staged a comeback that has returned it to the league of the world's great wine regions.

Major grapes

 Reds

Agiorgitiko

Xinomavro

 Whites

Assyrtiko

Malagousia

Moschofilero

Muscat

Robola

Roditis

Savatiano

Vilana

Vintages

2009

Challenging due to cool temperatures and rain; whites fared best, as did southern appellations.

2008

Exceptional in Santorini; Naoussa challenged by drought and high heat; other areas good.

2007

Very good in the north; wildfires badly hurt Nemean production.

2006

Particularly good for Northern Greece, Santorini, and Crete. Challenging in Nemea.

2005

Excellent nearly everywhere.

2004

Excellent whites; good reds.

2003

Very good in Nemea and Santorini; mixed in the north.

The beginning of the modern-day, post-retsina wine industry in Greece can be traced to the 1970s, when the country began readying itself to join the EU. Appellations based on the French model were drawn up, and large companies such as Boutari started ramping up the focus on quality, setting their sights on an international marketplace. Small boutique wineries such as Parparoussis in the Peloponnese began to appear, and winemakers increasingly began to travel overseas, studying and working, and tasting a wider range of wines than their forebears were exposed to. The establishment of a high-caliber enology program in Athens further helped to speed the industry's maturation.

By the 1990s, the revolution was in full swing, and it has showed no signs of slowing down. Today, there are hundreds of wineries spread among eight OPEs (Controlled Appellation of Origins, applied solely to sweet wines), 20 OPAPs (Appellation of Superior Quality), and more than 75 Topikos Oinos (TOs), or regional wines.

The Peloponnese is arguably the country's most important wine region, with several appellations. Just 90 minutes southwest of Athens, over the Corinth Canal, Nemea produces some of the country's best reds, based on Agiorgitiko (ah-gheeor-GHEE-tee-ko). An extremely versatile grape, its wines range from refreshing rosés to dark reds brimming with spiced cherry flavor. The peninsula also turns out top whites, most notably from Mantinia, with its floral, spicy Moschofilero grape, as well as from Patras on the northern coast, where Roditis rules.

Another important region is Macedonia, at the very north of the country. Naoussa, its most famous appellation, is the Piedmont of Greece, its cool, damp mountain slopes turning out tannic, truffle-scented reds based on Xinomavro. Further west, Amyndeon has been gaining attention for its even cooler continental climate, led by the success of wineries such as Alpha Estate with both Xinomavro and imported grape varieties.

International grapes hold sway south and east of Thessaloniki, although Evangelos Gerovassiliou, whose estate is just south of the city in Epanomi, has made Malagousia the grape of the moment, with his satin-textured, peach-scented example. Meanwhile, his Avaton red blend is drawing attention to the indigenous Limnio and Mavrotragano.

In Epirus, along Greece's western edge, Zitsa is known for its sparkling wines from the local Debina grape, while the rugged slopes around Metsovo turn out Cabernet Sauvignon, a legacy of the Katogi estate. Even the flat lands of Attica, not far from Athens airport, produce quality wines, particularly broad, almond-toned whites from Savatiano.

And then there are the 3,000 islands. Of these, Santorini shines with the Assyrtiko grape; its best wines can echo Grand Cru Chablis in their minerality and their ability to age. Rhodes specializes in delicate whites from the Athiri grape, while Crete excels in reds, made mainly from Kotsifali and Mandilaria. Limnos and Samos specialize in sweet Muscats, some of the best value in dessert wines anywhere.

Given today's quality, Greece has enough to keep any wine-lover busy, and quite happy, for a lifetime.

Achaia Clauss Patras

Achaia Clauss put Mavrodaphne of Patras on the map. In fact, the vineyards around Patras had mostly been converted to currants by the time Gustav Clauss erected his fairytale castle and winery there in 1861. But Clauss thought that the vines could make a good port-style wine. Achaia Clauss is now a multi-million-case winery with dozens of wines, yet its Mavrodaphne of Patras remains central. The spicy and sweet Imperial is an excellent value, while the Grand Reserve, made of wines up to 100 years old, is unchallenged for complexity.

98–100 Riga Ferraiou, Patras, Peloponnese 26221
2610 368 100

Alpha Estate Amyndeon

Angelos Iatrides made a name for Amyndeon when he started Alpha Estate in the late 1990s. Given that the Bordeaux-trained enologist had made wine all over the world, the fact he invested in 160 acres (65ha) on a cool, high plateau west of Naoussa made quite a splash. Now he is putting out some of the most intense, modern wines in Greece, from a satin-textured Sauvignon Blanc to a smoky Syrah, and the gargantuan, flagship Estate red, a blend of Xinomavro, Merlot, and Syrah.

2nd km Amyndeon, Ag. Panteleimon, Amyndeon 53200
www.alpha-estate.com

Argyros Estate Santorini

When most Santorini vineyards were being replaced by tourist attractions, Yiannis Argyros was stealthily saving what he could, building on the estate his family started in 1903. He began bottling wines in 1987 and now, working alongside his son, Mattheos, he relies on 65 acres (26ha) of vines, many of them ancient, to supply the fruit for his Santorini wines. The dry whites are terrific, but the particular draw is the Vinsanto, a complex, mahogany-hued, sweet wine made from sun-dried grapes.

Santorini, Mesa Gonia Episkopis, Santorini 84700
www.estate-argyros.com

Biblia Chora Estate Macedonia

Head east from Thessaloniki, then climb up the slopes of Mount Pangeon, and you will find Biblia Chora, one of the most exciting wineries in northeastern Greece. Owner Vassilis Tsaktsarlis worked with star winemaker Evangelos Gerovassiliou in the late 1980s at Porto Carras, then Greece's most ambitious winery; Gerovassiliou also helped him establish this winery in 1999. The reds are good but the whites are excellent in this cool clime, especially the crisp Sauvignon Blanc and the rich, creamy Ovilos, a blend of Sauvignon and Assyrtiko grapes.

Kokkinochori, Moustheni 64008
www.bibliachora.gr

Boutari Naoussa

Boutari is arguably the most important wine company in Greece. Founded in 1879 in Naoussa, in the misty, cool hills west of Thessaloniki, the company has long put out the definitive Xinomavro, the tannic, truffle-scented Grande Reserve Naoussa. Yet with six wineries around the country and the guidance of chief enologist Yiannis Voyatzis, the company has inspired winemaking renaissances everywhere. Look especially for the clean, fresh Santorini wines; the fruity Moschofileros from

DOMAINE GEROVASSILIOU
A SILKEN, PEACH-SCENTED BEAUTY FROM THE INDIGENOUS MALAGOUSIA

DOMAINE SKOURAS
A JUICY, FRESH AGIORGITIKO WITH A DASH OF CABERNET SAUVIGNON TO ADD STRUCTURE

Mantinia; the silken Malagousia from Matsa Estate in Attica; and Skalani, a plummy Syrah/Kotsifali blend from its Fantaxometocho estate in Crete.

Stenimachos, Naoussa, 59200
www.boutari.gr

Domaine Gerovassiliou Macedonia

Bordeaux-trained Evangelos Gerovassiliou is widely considered Greece's best winemaker. On 111 acres (45ha) sloping down toward the sea in Epanomi, a suburb of Thessaloniki, he produces a range of wines that show his French leanings: a leesy Sauvignon Blanc, a toasty, barrel-fermented Chardonnay, and a lusciously plummy Syrah. However, his most exciting wines are from grape varieties he has saved from near-extinction: Malagousia, from which he makes a satiny, peach-laden white, and Limnio, Mavroudi, and Mavrotragano, a trio that makes up Avaton, a wild and deeply purple red.

Epanomi, Thessaloniki 57500
www.gerovassiliou.gr

Domaine Sigalas Santorini

On a quiet stretch of low hills on the northern end of Santorini, Paris Sigalas farms 47 acres (19ha) of vines. He started making wine in 1991, inspired by the Burgundies he fell in love with as a student in Paris. His wines show that influence, having a breadth and minerality that recall Grand Cru Chablis. He also produces a spicy Mavrotragano, which has rekindled interest in this near-forgotten red grape, and showcases the local Mandilaria in Apiliotis, a fascinating red version of Vinsanto, sweet and tannic at once.

Baxes, Oia, Santorini 84702
www.sigalas-wine.com

Domaine Skouras Nemea

George Skouras studied in Dijon before coming home to Nemea to establish a winery in 1986. He believed strongly in the local Agiorgitiko grape, but hedged his bets with some Cabernet Sauvignon and Merlot; that Cabernet now forms a portion of his flagship Megas Oenos, a firm, smoky blend with Agiorgitiko that ages terrifically. Skouras also makes an outstanding Burgundy-style Chardonnay, Dum Vinum Sperum, and an exotic Viognier called Eclectique. Yet it is hard to beat his Nemea Grande Cuvée—pure Agiorgitiko, spicy and cherry-filled, powerful yet elegant.

10th km Argos-Sternas, Malandreni, Argos,
Peloponnese 21200; www.skouras.gr

Domaine Spiropoulos Mantinia

Spiropoulos is synonymous with Mantinia, an appellation given over solely to Moschofilero, a dark pinkish-grey grape with a spicy, floral scent. With 148 acres (60ha) of organically grown vines, the estate produces an array of wines that show the variety at its best. This includes an easy-drinking, entry-level white; a pale pink, rose-scented vin gris; the nervy, reserve-level Astála; and Odé Panos, an elegant sparkling version. Spiropoulos also built a winery in nearby Nemea in 2007; look for the Estate Nemea.

15th km Tripoli-Artemisio Road, Anc. Mantinia,
Peloponnese 22100; www.domainspiropoulos.gr

MERCOURI ESTATE
AN ELEGANT RED FROM ONE OF GREECE'S
MOST BEAUTIFUL ESTATES

GAIA WINES
A BRIGHT, FRESH BLEND OF MOSCHOFILERO
AND RODITIS, PRICED FOR EVERYDAY DRINKING

Domaine Tselepos Mantinia

Bring a jacket to visit Tselepos. It may be in the heart of the Peloponnese, but the wind can really whip across the high plain of Mantinia. Yiannis Tselepos located his winery at the edge of the appellation, climbing up the slope of Mount Parnon, for extra chill factor. That chill—and his Burgundy training—is evident in the delicacy of his ethereal, restrainedly floral Moschofilero. It also gave him access to a vertiginous slope of sheer slate upon which he planted Gewürztraminer, which makes gorgeous wine—spicy and elegant.

14th km Tripolis-Kastri, Rizes, Arcadia, Peloponnese 21200
www.tselepos.gr

Emery Winery Rhodes

On what is claimed to be the sunniest isle in Europe, Emery has made wines since 1966. The winery, right in the middle of the island in Embona, on the slopes of Mount Atavyros, focuses on indigenous grapes, particularly Athiri, which makes up the delicately floral, sparkling Grand Prix Brut and a crisp, wonderfully affordable still wine. Do not miss Efreni, a dessert Muscat that captures the sun in its pure, honeyed sweetness.

28 Afstralias Street, Embona, Rhodes 85100
www.emery.gr

Gaia Wines Santorini/Nemea

In the 1980s, Yiannis Paraskevopoulos spent years studying Santorini's vineyards for Boutari. His findings inspired him to start his own company. In partnership with agronomist Leo Karatsalos, Paraskevopoulos started Gaia (pronounced yay-ah) in 1994, quickly gaining a reputation for austerely elegant Santorini whites. Soon after, the duo acquired a vineyard on a mountaintop in Nemea, in the Peloponnese, to concentrate on the local Agiorgitiko. Here they produce a full range of wines, from an everyday red and white under the Nótios label, to the structured Estate, a red made for the cellar.

No visitor facilities
www.gaia-wines.gr

Gentilini Kefalonia

Across the street from Gentilini is a blindingly white wall of chalk. It is one of the reasons why Spiros Cosmetatos believed he could make fine wine here when he founded the winery in 1978. The chalk soils, along with abundant sun and cooling sea breezes, make possible wines like Gentilini Robola, a limey, refreshing example of this popular local grape, as well as the thirst-quenching white blend Aspro Classico. Now run by daughter Marianna with husband Petros Markantonatos and winemaker Gabrielle Beamish, Gentilini is gaining a name for Syrah, here given a Greek accent with a dash of Mavrodaphne.

76 Papanastassiou Street, Paleo Psychiko, Kefalonia 15452
www.gentilini.gr

Hatzidakis Santorini

Hatzidakis Winery is not much more than a roof over a hole in the ground, jam-packed with tanks and barrels, but it is definitely worth seeking out. Haridimos Hatzidakis was the head enologist at Boutari's Santorini winery before starting this winery in 1997. He culls grapes mostly from the organically farmed vineyards that his wife's family farmed in the 1950s, producing whites that stand out for their broad texture and minerality, as well as a wild-fruited, tannic red from Mavrotragano and an exceptional, caramel-hued Vinsanto.

Pyrgos Kallistis, Santorini, 84701
www.hatzidakiswines.gr

Katogi and Strofilia Epirus

Established in 1989, Katogi Averoff was one of the first serious wineries in Metsovo in western Greece. Strofilia is based in Annavysos, just down the coast from Athens. The two joined forces in 2001, together producing more than 20 wines from four regions. Look particularly for the juicy, easy-going Fresco wines—a Roditis-based white and a red Agiorgitiko, priced for everyday drinking—and the earthy Averoff Estate, made primarily from Cabernet Sauvignon planted in Metsovo in the 1950s.

Metsovo, Epirus 44200
www.katogi-strofilia.gr

Kir-Yianni Naoussa

"Kir-Yianni" (Mr. John) is Yiannis Boutari, a godfather-like figure in Greek wine, known for his immense knowledge, kindness, and endless support of the Greek winemaking industry. He ran the Boutari winery with his brother Constantinos until the mid-1990s, when he left to focus on a vineyard he had set up in Yianakohori, Naoussa's highest point. Here he pioneered the combination of Merlot and Xinomavro, exemplified by the plummy yet structured Kir-Yianni Estate, and established Ramnista, an intense Xinomavro built for cellaring. Whites are made in Amyndeon, as is Akakies, a wonderfully thirst-quenching Xinomavro rosé.

Yianakohori, Naoussa, 59200
www.kiryianni.gr

Ktima Driopi Nemea

Ktima ("Domaine") Driopi came out of nowhere in 2003, when Yiannis Tselepos, a prominent winemaker from Mantinia, joined with winemaker Paris Sigalas, from Santorini, and investor Alexander Avataggelos to buy a plot of old-vine Agiorgitiko in Koutsí—essentially the Grand Cru area of Nemea. The quality of the grapes was such that the trio made wine that very year—a deep, dark, plum-filled Nemea. Now run solely by Tselepos, Driopi remains one of the very top wineries in Nemea, producing textbook Agiorgitiko built to age. ★ **Rising star**

65 Vasilis Sofias Street, Ampelokipi, Peloponnese 11528
2107 2957134

Ktima Voyatzis Velventós

Yiannis Voyatzis is the chief enologist of Boutari. After work, he drives southwest for two hours to Velventós, a region of sparkling lakes framed by sharp mountain peaks, to the vineyard he began planting in the early 1990s. There he's supplemented Xinomavro, the area's prime grape, with Chardonnay, Cabernet, and Merlot, among other experimental plantings. The core of his portfolio is composed of a juicy Xinomavro blend, a bright, crisp rosé, and a delicate, floral white showcasing Malvasia, but don't miss the black-fruited, lightly herbal Tsapournakos, a grape discovered to be Cabernet Franc.

Velventós, Kozani, 5040
2246 4032283

Lyrarakis Dafnes

Sotiris Lyrarakis has done more for Cretan wine than any other individual. On his 20 acre (8ha) estate, he concentrates almost exclusively on indigenous grapes, some of which were long forgotten before he got to them. The mouthwatering, herbal Dafni is a particular standout (dafni means bay leaf in Greek); the bright Vilana makes a case for a grape more usually found in bulk blends. However, his greatest accomplishment may be in taming the native Kotsifali and Mandilaria to produce polished reds: The Last Supper is a favorite.

Heraklion, Crete 71305
www.lyrarakis.gr

Mercouri Estate Ilias

Arguably Greece's most stunning winery, Mercouri sits at the far western edge of the Peloponnese, a sprawling estate of overgrown gardens, preening peacocks, and bay laurels overlooking the sea. It dates back to the 1870s but began its present incarnation in the mid-1980s, when Hristo and Vassilis Kanellakopoulos took over. The Foloi white is a crisp blend of Roditis and Viognier that is perfect to sip while taking in summer concerts on the lawn. The forest-scented Estate Red, made from old-vine Refosco and Mavrodaphne, is a long-lived, elegant wine that deserves a place in any cellar.

Korakohori, Ilias, Peloponnese 27100
www.mercouri.gr

Oenoforos Patras

Built into a hillside overlooking the sea, high above the bustle of the busy port of Patras, Oenoforos was founded by Bordeaux-trained enologist Aggelos Rouvalis in 1990. Now run in partnership with Greek Wine Cellars, Oenoforos excels particularly with local varieties. The citrussy and fresh Asprolithi Roditis remains the benchmark for the variety, while limey, melon-scented Mikros Vorias Lagorthi resurrected interest in a near-extinct variety.

Selinous, Aigio, Peloponnese 25100
www.oenoforos.gr

Papagiannakos Winery Attica

Located not far from Athens airport, Papagiannakos is one of Greece's most beautiful modern wineries. The low-slung building is suffused with light, giving a feeling much like its best wine, the sunny, sleek Savatiano. This is the variety that is often mixed with pine resin to make Retsina. Vassilis Papagiannakos, however, prefers to keep yields low in his 100 acres (40ha) of vineyards to produce Savatiano that is juicy with pear-like flavors. Of course, good Savatiano also makes for better Retsina, and Papagiannakos makes one of the best.

Markopoulo, Mesogaia, Attica 19003
www.papagiannakos.gr

Papaioannou Estate Nemea

Thanasis Papaioannou started assembling prime vineyards in Nemea far before it was fashionable to do so. Since he established his winery in 1984, it has grown to 141 acres (57ha) of vines. Now the most respected vine-grower in the region, he and his son, George, turn out a mind-boggling array of wines. The best are the plummy Agiorgitikos, particularly the straightforward,

KIR-YIANNI ESTATE
VIN DE PAYS D' IMATHIA/DRY RED WINE

2004

KIR-YIANNI

NET. CONT. 750 ML   ALC. 14% BY VOL
PRODUCED AND BOTTLED AT KIR-YIANNI ESTATE NAOUSSA.GR
P R O D U C T   O F   G R E E C E

KIR-YIANNI
A POWERFUL, YET ELEGANT, BLEND
OF XINOMAVRO AND MERLOT

KATOGI AND STROFILIA
A GAMY, SMOOTH RED FROM SOME OF
GREECE'S OLDEST CABERNET VINES

traditional Peloponnese bottling. The creamy, ripe Chardonnay and the cherry-scented Pinot Noir are also worth a taste.

Ancient Nemea/Corinthia, Peloponnese 20500
www.papaioannou.gr

Parparoussis Winery Patras

Patras, the port city on the north coast of the Peloponnese, is famous for its sweet Muscats, but if there is a single exemplary version, it is the satin-smooth, melon-filled Muscat de Rio Patras from Parparoussis. Founded in 1973 by Burgundy-trained Athanassios Parparoussis, the winery was one of the first artisan wineries in Greece. It was also one of the first to accent local varieties such as Sideritis, a rare grape that makes up the dry, cucumber-crisp Gift of Dionysos, and Mavrodaphne, which Parparoussis crafts into a tart, tannic, dry red called Taos.

1 Achilleos Street, Proastio Patron, Peloponnese 36442
www.parparoussis.com

Samos Union of Vinicultural Co-operatives Samos

Samos makes things easy. This northern Aegean island has only one grape, Muscat, and one winery, the Union of Vinicultural Co-operatives. Created in 1934 to ease relations between growers and traders, the winery takes in the production of more than 4,000 grape growers across the island, crafting everything from light, dry Muscats to altar wine. The honeyed, golden Samos Vin Doux is the winery's calling card, but it is worth splurging on the more delicate Grand Cru or the Nectar, an aged version made from sun-dried grapes that is rich and nutty.

Malagari, Samos 83100
www.samoswine.gr

Thimiopoulos Vineyards Naoussa

There is not much of a winery to speak of at Thimiopoulos, but its single wine, Ghi Ke Uranos, has gained a cult following since the first vintage in 2004. It is the work of Apostolos Thimiopoulos, who returned to his father's vineyards after studying enology in Athens. These are in Naoussa's lower elevations, where rich soils and warm temperatures, combined with Thimiopoulos's modern methods (the "40" on the label refers to the number of days the grapes macerate with their skins), make for one of the richest, darkest Xinomavros around. ★ **Rising star**

Trilofos, 59100, Naoussa
2310 346586

Vatistas Winery Laconia

Three hours south of Athens, at the Peloponnese's southeastern tip, is the wild, herb-scented Laconian peninsula. Winemaking is a family affair at all but a few wineries here; Yiannis Vatistas was among the first to go commercial, establishing his winery in 1990. Now working with consulting enologist Yiannis Flerianos, he farms some 75 acres (30ha) of vines, with particular attention given to varieties found nowhere else in Greece. The Petroulianos is a standout, with a limey flavor and sea salt tang. The Kidonitsa, juicy with "kidoni" (quince) flavors, reveals a variety that deserves more attention.

Lahi Lakonias, 23053
www.vatistas-wines.gr

CYPRUS

Since joining the European Union in 2004, Cyprus has been in a big hurry to join the ranks of the best wine-producing regions in the world—exactly where it was centuries ago, when its most famous wine, Commandaria, was being poured for the court of Richard the Lionheart. Four wineries—ETKO, KEO, Loel, and SODAP—produce more than three-quarters of the island's exported wines, but dozens of smaller wineries have also joined the scene, making the best of the phylloxera-free soils and cool mountain slopes towards the island's western end. Sweet Commandaria remains the island's most famous wine, but there are now many exciting dry wines from grapes that are not found anywhere else, particularly the white Xynisteri and red Maratheftiko.

Major grapes

 Reds

Maratheftiko

 Whites

Xynisteri

Vintages

2009
Good, but better for whites than reds.

2008
Very good year, especially for whites.

2007
Heat and continued drought made for low yields and intense reds.

2006
Good for Xynisteri, but tannic, tough reds were produced.

2005
Overall, a good year.

2004
Good, fresh reds and whites.

ETKO   Limassol Wine Villages

Picking a favorite when it comes to the Big Four (ETKO, KEO, Loel, and SODAP) is hard, as they all are working diligently to make better wines. When it comes to Cyprus's famous Commandaria, however, ETKO's Centurion excels. Produced like a sherry, in which multiple vintages of wine are mellowed together in oak barrels, this wine brims with all the caramel, raisin, and spicecake flavors that Commandaria is known for, only with more depth and succulence. Founded in 1844 near the port of Limassol, the winery is Cyprus's oldest. Recently, it has been renovating its dry wine portfolio, planting new vineyards, and building the Olympus Winery, a state-of-the-art facility 26 miles (42km) northwest of Limassol in the ancient mountainside town of Omodos. Olympus Maratheftiko also stands out, being light and fresh with dusky cherry notes.

3602 Limassol
www.etkowines.com

Ezousa Winery   Paphos

The wineries nestled on the south slopes of the Troodos Mountains tend to get the most attention, but it is worth driving further west, through the orange, olive, and eucalyptus-covered hillsides of the Paphos region, to visit the wine scene there. Ezousa, a winery named for the nearby river, is a good place to start. It is run by Michael Constantinides, a 30-something winemaker who gave up a comfortable civil service position to study enology in Athens and then set up a winery in Kannaviou in 2003. He focuses on local varieties, turning out a crisp, clean Xynisteri called Ayios Chrysostomos, which gains a little richness from time on the lees. His Maratheftiko wines are exemplary, from the fresh, red-berried Eros rosé to the dark, earthy Metharme. ★ **Rising star**

8746 Kannaviou
357 70 008 844

Tsiakkas Winery   Pitsilia

Stay at Anassa, the five-star hotel in Polis on the western tip of the island, and you will be poured Tsiakkas if you ask for the house red. This wine is the work of Costas Tsiakkas, an energetic man who traded a lucrative banking career for a life of wine in the late 1980s. His tile-roofed winery sits more than 3,281ft (1,000m) up the south side of the Troodos Mountains, above the town of Pelendri. He puts out a wide range of wines, most notably a fresh, lemony Xynisteri, a Grenache rosé that is perfectly pitched to beachside dining, and a juicy, vanilla-tinged Maratheftiko, which he labels under the grape's local name—Vamvakada. More vineyards are currently maturing and Tsiakkas's son, Orestes, is studying enology in Adelaide, suggesting that this winery is set up for long-term success.

4878 Pelendri
www.swaypage.com/tsiakkas

Vlassides   Limassol Wine Villages

Sophocles Vlassides is one of the island's most respected winemakers. He began consulting for local wineries, such as Tsiakkas and Vasa, after returning from the University of California at Davis in 1998. He also set up his own winery right in the middle of Kilani, a beautiful village of narrow streets and old, traditional limestone houses about 22 miles (36km) northwest of Limassol. He makes around 4,000 bottles of wine a year, in a building that used to be his grandfather's grocery store. Most notable is a startlingly supple, rich Shiraz, although the mouth-staining Cabernet Sauvignon/Grenache/Lefkada blend is also well worth a try. With about one-third of his 37 acres (15ha) newly planted and plans to build a new winery in 2010, Vlassides is one to watch. ★ **Rising star**

4776 Kilani
357 99 441 574

Zambartas Winery   Limassol Wine Villages

Akis Zambartas could be considered the savior of Cyprus's indigenous vines. During his 33-year tenure at KEO he worked at saving forgotten vines, while most of the country embarked on a love affair with international varieties. Now working at the winery he established in 2006 with his son Marcos, he is crafting wines under the motto "New World Wines on Old Soil." Here, they focus on local grapes and combine them with modern techniques and imported varieties to give the finished wines a sleeker and more modern feel. A perfect example of this is the Shiraz/Lefkada, a brawny yet classy red with plenty of plummy fruit to counteract Lefkada's tannins. Zambartas Xynisteri is another good example, getting extra depth from a dollop of satiny Sémillon. Production is currently only about 2,300 bottles a year, but there are plans to nearly double this, making more room for rarities, such as a varietal Yannoudi. ★ **Rising star**

Gr. Afxentiou 39, 4710 Agios Amyrosios
www.zambartaswineries.com

TURKEY

Despite having the world's fourth-largest area under vine, barely 3% of Turkey's grapes are destined for fermentation. Wine was produced in Anatolia as early as 4000BCE, but came to a halt under the Ottoman Empire. After centuries of prohibition, Atatürk founded the first modern winery in 1925. Although technically a secular state, current government policy in terms of alcohol is still restrictive, imposing harsh taxes on both domestic and imported wines. With increasing expertise, improvements in equipment, and a wealth of indigenous varieties (600–1,200 indigenous varieties have survived, thanks to their use as table grapes), there is tremendous potential for Turkey to become an exciting, world-class producer, if the current obstacles can be overcome.

Büyülübag Winery and Vineyards
Island of Avşa
Founded in 2003, Büyülübag is a boutique winery located on the island of Avşa in the Sea of Marmara. It also sources grapes from around Izmir. The first and only gravity-flow winery in the country, it works mainly with international varieties. The reds tend to be of more interest than the whites, with very good results from Cabernet Sauvignon and Merlot in a Bordeaux style. ★ **Rising star**

Değirmenyolu Mevkii, No: 11/416 Yiğitler Köyü, Avşa, Balıkesir; www.buyulubag.com

Corvus Vineyards *Island of Bozcaada*
Corvus has been creating a serious buzz. Founded by a Turkish-born architect, it is producing quality wines from local and international varieties on the island of Bozcaada. With a solid portfolio, it is hard to pick favorites, but the top performers include the bright and fruity Rarem, made with indigenous grapes, the Cabernet Sauvignon/Merlot/Syrah Corpus, and the stylish and structured Corvus Blends Nos 1, 2, and 3. ★ **Rising star**

Bozcaada
www.corvus.com.tr

Doluca Wines *Thrace and Marmara*
A giant of the Turkish wine industry, Doluca was responsible for introducing European varieties to Turkey. It began production in the late 1920s, making wine from local varieties under a different name: it was not until international grapes were added into the mix that it re-branded itself as Doluca. With more than 35 products, it continues to work with both traditional and international varieties, often blending the two.

Yali Caddesi No: 17 Murefte, Tekirdag
www.doluca.com

Gülor Winery *Thrace and Marmara*
A very interesting small producer located in the Thrace region, with a focus on international varieties. In addition to the more popular Cabernet Sauvignon, Merlot, and Shiraz, they have also thrown less conventional grapes, such as Sangiovese and Cinsault, into the mix.

Oto Sanayi Sitesi, Çamlik Caddesi No: 2, 4 Levent 80660 Istanbul; www.gulorwine.com

Kavaklidere Winery *Central Anatolia*
Kavaklidere is one of the largest producers in Turkey. Most of their production is straightforward, early-drinking table wines. Egeo is considered by many to be their best wine, using only international varieties. The Vin-Art Series and Ancyra labels are good value and use indigenous and international grapes. Their Altin Köpuk Brut is one of the best Turkish sparkling wines.

Çankırı yolu 6.km, 06750, Akyurt/Ankara
www.kavaklidere.com

Kayra Wines *Anatolia*
Kayra has two wineries, one located in Elazig and the other in Sarköy. American consultant-winemaker Daniel O'Donnell oversees both operations and has been instrumental in improving the quality of the wines produced. They work with over 20 grape varieties and have a wide range of labels, many of which are easy-drinking, everyday wines. Of particular interest are the Kayra Vintage and Kayra Imperial labels which have reasonable concentration and structure.

Abide-i Hurriyet Cad. No: 285, Bolkan Center B Blok, 34381 Sisli/Istanbul; www.kayrasaraplari.com

Melen Winery *Hoşköy*
This boutique operation uses fruit from its estate vineyards to produce regionally specific wines. Located on the northern shore of the Sea of Marmara, the Çetintaş family has been making wine for three generations. Their wines, made from local and indigenous grapes, are organized into three tiers: the Ganohora label, Melen Manastir (Monastery), and the more structured Reserve series.

Sahil Yolu No: 6 Hoşköy-Şarköy, Tekirdağ
www.melenwinery.com

Sevilen Group *Aegean Coast*
Sevilen has two Bordeaux-based consultants overseeing the producton of its modern, terroir-driven wines. Its grapes come from two very different sites: the warmer area around Izmir and a cooler, high-altitude location close to Denizli. It focuses on international grapes, cultivating Sauvignon Blanc, Chardonnay, Sémillon, Cabernet Sauvignon, Cabernet Franc, Merlot, and Syrah.

Akçay caddesi No: 239 Gaziemir – İzmir 35410
www.sevilengroup.com

Major grapes
Reds
Bogăzkere
Cabernet Sauvignon
Kalecik Karasi
Karalahna
Kuntra
Malencik
Merlot
Oküzgözü
Shiraz
Syrah

Whites
Chardonnay
Dökülgen
Emir
Kabarcik
Muscat
Narince
Sauvignon Blanc
Sultaniye

Vintages
2009
Consistent weather meant a long, balanced harvest. Good concentration in the reds.

2008
Very hot, thin vintage. Ripe flavors in the West and Mountains. Eastern wines are very ripe and raisiny. Drink now.

2007
Warm spring and a long, warm summer. Great results in Western, Southwestern, and Mountain regions. Long-lived.

The Koran's proscription against wine limits its spread within the Muslim world, but heroic efforts may be found in all corners. With few appellation statutes in place, quality is generally producer-led and often driven by foreign visitors. Political and social instability, whether real or imagined, keep North Africa and the Near and Middle East from maximizing their potential.

Lebanon is the region's most sophisticated wine country, with the finest Arabic food and, in cosmopolitan Beirut, the liveliest nightlife. The urbane Serge Hochar of Château Musar has been the leading light here, but wines from other producers—including those of Syrian transplants the Saade family, with their twin facilities in Lebanon and their native land—may be found here and abroad.

Turkey is home to numerous indigenous grapes (many with names baffling to English speakers) and varied growing areas from seaside to mountain plains. Leading wine archeologist Professor Patrick McGovern has declared Turkey's remote Eastern Anatolia region as the birthplace of wine, supplanting Georgia. A group of pioneering wineries are now leading the way into a new era for Turkish wine.

In a move away from the medium-sweet wines of the past, Israeli wineries are fashioning a wide range of modern wines made from mostly French grapes. Jordan has entered the game with Ribero del Duero's Gabriel Rivero, a side project to his Lebanese activities. Without a wine culture to support it, producers are casting their nets wide as Egypt shifts from processing Europe's concentrates for tourists to pushing the limits of growing along the Nile.

Once the engine pulling along French bulk wine production, western North Africa makes some great reds and rosés, including those associated with actor-cum-vigneron Gérard Depardieu, though whites trail some way behind.

NORTH AFRICA AND THE MIDDLE EAST

NORTH AFRICA

The three North African countries of Algeria, Morocco, and Tunisia are grouped together because they share many similarities. The important one in terms of winemaking is the Atlas Mountains and their effect on the region's climate. If the countries did not have these often snow-capped peaks, they would largely consist of sand, save for the cooler coastal strips. The Atlas range lends the region the potential to make good wine, but, as vineyard development and wine promotion are not actively encouraged by the countries' Muslim governing bodies, quantities are limited. The wine industry of this region dates back more than 2,500 years to Phoenician times and in its heyday, during the early 1900s under French governance, was responsible for more than 60% of internationally traded wine.

Major grapes

🍇 Reds

Alicante Bouschet

Cabernet Sauvignon

Carignan

Cinsault

Grenache Noir

Merlot

Mourvèdre

Syrah

🍇 Whites

Chardonnay

Vintages

Given the wide geographical area spanned by this region, and the variety of growing conditions that are consequently found therein, it is not possible to provide an accurate summary of any given vintage.

The makeup of the vineyards across the three countries is still a hangover from colonial times. They largely contain low-yielding bush vines of the varieties planted by the French (Carignan, Cinsault, Grenache, and Alicante Bouschet), though more recent plantings have been of international varieties (Cabernet Sauvignon, Syrah, Merlot, Mourvèdre, and Chardonnay). These now account for around 20% of the vineyard area.

New plantings are largely in Guyot style (trellised) to make picking easier and to increase the volume of the crop. Almost all grapes are still hand-picked due to the plentiful availability of cheap labor. The better producers are now employing hot-climate practices within the vineyards (instead of slavishly copying French methods) and using better temperature control throughout the winemaking process.

Much of the wine is still made in *caves* (two-story buildings with banks of cement fermentors above similar cement storage vessels), but the use of stainless steel is increasing in Tunisia and Morocco. Oak aging is also on the rise, for quality producers looking to export.

Throughout the region, there are designated areas that are considered to be higher quality. These are known as AG (Appellation d'Origine Garantie) and AC (Appellation d'Origine Contrôlée), but these delineations are broad and the producer is the more reliable barometer of quality in all cases.

While the three countries certainly have much in common, there are some significant differences between them, such as size, stage of development, and political climate.

Algeria, by far the largest of the three countries (and once the world's fifth-largest producer of wine), lags behind in terms of development, partly due to political unrest. The Algerian Civil War (1994–2002) saw the closure of most of the remaining 300 wineries when Islamic militants issued vineyard owners with death threats. The government stepped in and its winemaking arm (ONCV) is now largely responsible for the country's output, which is once again on the rise. There has been heavy investment in new plantings, and there are plans for widespread improvements in the wineries. For the time being, however, the wines remain generally rustic in style.

Until the early 2000s, the state of Tunisia's wine industry was broadly similar to that of Algeria's, with a de facto state monopoly dominating. Since then, an aggressive drive for exports has led to a number of promising private partnerships between local producers and foreign companies.

Morocco, in terms of its volume of quality wine, now leads North Africa. The number of overseas partnerships is similar to that in Tunisia, though most are longer established and larger.

Only time will tell whether Algeria, Morocco, and Tunisia can reach their true potential, since the political conditions are still unfavorable.

Castel Morocco

The Castel property is centered on an old colonial stud farm outside Meknès. The operation comprises five large estates, covering the high-altitude Guerrouane and Beni M'Tir appellations. Wines are bottled under different labels for different markets, but include: Domaine de Sahari, Domaine Larroque, Domaine Mayole, Excellence de Bonnassia, and Halana. All are well made and the styles are modern and fresh.

No visitor facilities
www.halana-wines.com

Ceptunes Tunisia

Ceptunes is a Tunisian-Swiss partnership in the hills north of Grombalia in Cap Bon. It is responsible for a number of the country's more prominent labels such as the easy-drinking Jour et Nuit brand and the more premium Didona range. The wines are solid and dependable, and aimed at the home market. Grapes are sourced from a variety of appellations from contract growers. The Didona Reserve red is the winery's standard bearer, a juicy Syrah-based wine that bears a little aging.

El Karmla, 8030, Grombalia
www.ceptunes.com.tn

Château Roslane—Les Celliers de Meknès Morocco

Les Celliers de Meknès is Morocco's largest producer, creating wines at all price points. With more than 50 years of winemaking experience, Rene Zniber, the owner, is widely regarded as the founder of the renaissance of Moroccan wine. His passion is nowhere more apparent than at Château Roslane, the company's flagship estate in Morocco's only AC region, Coteaux d'Atlas. A range of brands is also made at Château Roslane alongside the Château Roslane Premier Cru White and Red.

11 Rue Ibn Khaldoune, 50,000 Meknès
www.lescelliersdemeknes.net

Domaine Atlas Tunisia

The charming 250 acre (100ha) Domaine Atlas was formed in 2001 in the hills between Grombalia and Hammamet to capitalize on existing old-vine Carignan and Syrah vineyards. The Tunisian-Austrian proprietors have planted Chardonnay, Muscat, and Vermentino to complement the reds. The estate has several modern, well-made brands including Ifrica and Punique. The Grand Patron, a silky red from 50-year-old Carignan vines, is an excellent value.

Route de Sousse, 8040, Bou Argoub
www.domaineatlas.com

Domaine des Ouled Thaleb/Thalvin
Morocco

Established in 1927, Domaine des Ouled Thaleb is the oldest winery still in use in the country, and has been in partnership with French firm Thalvin since 1968. It uses coastal vines around Ben Slimane and two other vineyards inland to make more than 20 bottlings. The estate's wines top most of the country's wine lists, and new garage wines from old vines are planned.

Ben Slimane, 24190, Fath
www.thalvin.com

UCCV
THE POWERFUL MAGON HAS BENEFITED
FROM UCCV'S MODERNIZING PROJECT

CHATEAU ROSLANE
THE PREMIER CRU RED IS A BLEND OF
MERLOT, SYRAH, AND CABERNET SAUVIGNON

Domaine Neferis Tunisia

Nestled in a mountainous amphitheater in Cap Bon, Domaine Neferis is one of the most progressive of Tunisia's modern partnerships. The 545 acre (220ha) estate produces some of the country's most expressive wines: from an unusual dry Pedro Ximénez, under the Château Defleur label, to an old-vine Carignan, Selian Reserve, which is arguably Tunisia's best wine. Methods are modern and barrique aging is employed for reds. The estate is progressive in other areas, too: the wines are made by Tunisia's only female winemaker, and the winery is experimenting with solar power for its needs.

No visitor facilities
www.calatrasi.it

Kurubis Tunisia

A joint venture between Rhône winemaker Didier Cornillon and a local agribusiness, Kurubis began in 2000 with the planting of 52 acres (21ha) on the outskirts of Korba in Cap Bon. Kurubis is modern in its thinking, has a well-equipped winery, and uses organic practices wherever possible in the vineyards. The vines are young, but the first bottlings of Syrah-based reds show promise, as does a surprisingly crisp, sparkling Chardonnay.

4 Ave du 7 Novembre, 8070, Korba
www.kurubis.com

Les Deux Domaines Morocco

A Franco-Moroccan partnership involving Bordeaux kingpin Bernard Magrez, Les Deux Domaines was established in the early 1990s. In the relative cool of the hills south of Meknès, the 158 acre (64ha) estate creates a delicious barrel-aged Syrah/Grenache called Kahina, and a similar blend for Gérard Depardieu's Lumière label, both of which show great potential.

Visits by appointment only, c/o Château Pape-Clément,
75002 Paris, France; www.bernard-magrez.com

UCCV—Les Vignerons de Carthage
Tunisia

Established in 1948, before Independence, the UCCV co-op is Tunisia's largest and most important wine producer. Since the early 1990s, it has invested large sums in modernizing its operation, giving the wines an international style in taste and presentation. It produces some of Tunisia's best wines, including the locally renowned Vieux Magon, a surprisingly youthful, oak-aged blend of 60-year-old Carignan and Syrah.

Route de Mornag, 1009, Jebel Jelloud
www.uccv.com.tn

Volubilia—Domaine de la Zouina
Morocco

An exciting project from Bordeaux's Gérard Gribelin (formerly of Château Fieuzal) and Philippe Gervoson (Larrivet Haut-Brion), Volubilia—Domaine de la Zouina's first vintage was 2005. The 156 acre (63ha) estate is still developing, but the wines have already won praise. Thanks to warm-climate viticultural practices, the whites and rosés are as exciting as the reds. Of particular note is the Gris, a savory and serious rosé in the Tavel mold.

51000 Aït Bourzouine, El Hajeb
domaine_zouina@menara.ma

ISRAEL

Israel has one of the oldest wine cultures in the world—the numerous, ancient wine presses that dot the land are evidence of this—yet it is also the newest of all the Mediterranean wine-producing countries. Whatever grapes were being grown in King David's time have long since disappeared, destroyed along with the area's rich winemaking industry by the Muslim conquest in the 7th century. French varieties, such as Carignan and Grenache, were brought to Jewish settlements in the late 1800s, and more recently, in the 1970s, international varieties, such as Cabernet Sauvignon, have come to dominate. This, along with the fruit-forward style the country favors, makes Israel one of the most accessible wine-producing countries of the Mediterranean.

Major grapes

 Reds

Cabernet Franc

Cabernet Sauvignon

Carignan

Merlot

Petit Verdot

Shiraz

 Whites

Chardonnay

Sauvignon Blanc

Vintage

2009
Overall a good year, but not high yields; best in the northern reaches.

2008
Excellent year for both reds and whites.

2007
Fair, with the best quality in higher altitudes.

2006
A challenging, wet vintage in all locations.

2005
Widely considered to be one of best vintages of the decade.

2004
Very good; cool temperatures gave fresh whites and structured reds.

The most important recent-day change in the Israeli wine industry is probably its geographical shift from plains to mountain slopes. For much of the 20th century, grape growing was concentrated on the coastal lowlands, where sunny warmth enabled grapes to reach prodigious levels of ripeness, which is well suited to sacramental wine. But the Golan Heights Winery, founded in the early 1980s in an area that is high and cool enough for snow to fall in winter, proved that it is also possible to grow Bordeaux and Burgundy varieties in Israel.

The success of this winery inspired many followers, who began to head for the hills, trading in their Carignan, Grenache, and Argaman (a cross of the Portuguese Sousão and Carignan) for more marketable grapes, and elegant wines. Today, Galilee and its four subregions—Upper and Lower Galilee, Tabor, and the Golan Heights—form the country's most prestigious wine-growing region.

After this, the hills around Jerusalem, often referred to as the Judean Hills on wine labels, is the next most important area, with more than two dozen boutique wineries. The Shomron region, located between Galilee and the Judean Hills, produces the highest volume of wine grapes in the country, from its low-lying coastal areas. Together with Shimshon, the humid area that slopes west from Jerusalem to the sea, it contributes primarily to the production of affordable quaffs and sacramental wines. Recent attention has also turned to the Negev, a desert region in southern

Israel, where the well-known winery Carmel has planted some vineyards. This is perhaps not so surprising, given that Israel has been a leader in irrigation technology for some time. Quality wine production has traditionally been focused in Ramat Arad, where altitudes reach 2,300ft (700m) above sea level and nights can be invigoratingly cool.

Perhaps the greatest challenge Israel faces is the misconception that kosher precludes quality. In fact, kosher certification has absolutely no bearing on the quality of the wine, it is simply an assurance to the religiously observant that the wine was made in keeping with certain religious tenets—the vineyards must be at least four years old, the wine must be made by Sabbath-observant Jews in a kosher-certified facility, and it may not contain non-kosher ingredients. It is important to realize that not all Israeli wines are kosher. At one time, kosher certification was essential, as most wineries depended on the country's kosher supermarkets for distribution and certification also gave them a unique hook in foreign markets. Today, however, quality is such that many Israeli wines do not need to be kosher to encourage people to buy them.

Mevushal certification is what has given kosher wines a bad name, however, as it requires the wine to be heated. These days, even this no longer affects wines as much as it used to, as the wines are flash-pasteurized and not boiled. Examples of Mevushal wine are rare.

Carmel Shomron

Carmel is Israel's largest and most illustrious winery, having been bankrolled by Baron Edmond de Rothschild in 1882. At one point it controlled more than 90% of the country's production, but the last decade has seen huge changes under CEO Israel Izvan, significantly slimming down production in order to focus on high-quality wines. The work has paid off with wines such as the Single Vineyard Kayoumi Cabernet Sauvignon, with black fruit and green peppercorn notes, and the Bordeaux-style Limited Edition. The Appellation series offers solid value with wines such as a stunning old-vine Carignan, which is chewy with cherry fruit. Carmel also owns Yatir, an impressive, forward-looking winery in the Negev.

Winery St, Zichron Ya'acov 30900
www.carmelwines.co.il

Clos de Gat Judean Hills

Just north of the Ayalon Valley, Eyal Rotem runs Clos de Gat, the winery he founded with Kibbutz Har'el in 1998 after finishing his winemaking studies in Australia. An ancient wine press ("gat" in Hebrew) sits on the property, around which he has planted 35 acres (14ha) of French varieties. In a departure from Israeli norms, Rotem avoids using irrigation and commercial yeasts in order to draw out the terroir expression of his wines. The results number less than 6,000 cases a year, but his wines are well worth seeking out. Of particular note are the Chanson, a flirty, light white blend; the creamy Chardonnay; and a restrained, chocolatey Merlot. Sycra is the label they use to showcase the best grapes from the best years: the Sycra Syrah, with its deep, purple plum flavors and velvet texture, shows great promise for this variety in Israel.

Harel Vineyards, Kibbutz Harel, Ayalon Valley 99740
www.closdegat.com

Ella Valley Vineyards Shomron

In a pastoral Judean valley of olive trees and grapevines, where David fought Goliath, young, Burgundy-trained winemaker Doron Rav Hon has been making wines since 2002. He has the enviable advantage of 800 acres (324ha) of vineyards, all of which are located near the winery in Kibbutz Netiv Halamed Hey—only a fraction of the grapes are needed for the winery's 200,000-bottle production. Doron insists on manual night harvests to keep the fruit fresh, a practice that pays off in wines such as the crisp, limey Sauvignon Blanc and bright, unoaked Chardonnay. Vineyard's Choice showcases the best fruit produced in a particular vintage: a recent Syrah showed excellent balance, being dense, but not heavy, with a plummy flavor.

Kibbutz Netiv Halamed He 99855
www.ellavalley.com

Golan Heights Winery Golan Heights

Golan Heights Winery transformed the Israeli wine scene almost overnight when it began producing wines in Katzrin, high up in the Golan Heights, in 1984. The vineyards had been planted in 1976 and the crisp, clearly defined wines they produced inspired a rush for similar cool, high-altitude land across the country. Under the direction of winemaker Victor Schoenfeld, Golan Heights puts out about 380,000 cases of wine a year, which is divided among three labels: Golan, for easy-drinking wines; Gamla, for more intense varietals; and Yarden,

YATIR
A DARK, HERBAL CABERNET THAT IS GROWN
ON THE NORTHERN EDGE OF THE NEGEV

CLOS DE GAT
A RICH BORDEAUX BLEND FROM ONE OF
ISRAEL'S BEST BOUTIQUE WINERIES

for premium wines such as the crisp, finely sparkling Blanc de Blancs and the single-vineyard, organic Odem Chardonnay. In 2010, the winery also introduced Yarden Rom, a "Super-Israeli" red, made in collaboration with the renowned consultant Zelma Long. Four years in the making, the first vintage (2006) is a blend of Syrah, Cabernet Sauvignon, and Merlot, all grown in the Golem Heights and Upper Galilee and aged for 21 months in barrels. Also look out for the sleek Galil Mountain wines that come from a separate winery run with Kibbutz Yiron.

Katzrin 12900
www.golanwines.co.il

Margalit Shomron

Former chemistry professor Yair Margalit is widely regarded as a catalyst for the boutique winery boom in Israel, not only for the winery he established in 1989, but also for his textbooks that guide the small winery owner—a rarity in Israel until recently. Side-by-side with his son, Asaf, in a winery outside of Tel Aviv, he puts out around 1,600 cases a year. The Cabernet Franc he makes from vineyards near Binyamina in Shomron is varietally spot-on, with mouthwatering black fruit and green herb notes. The Special Reserve Cabernet Sauvignon would fit proudly into any cellar, with cassis flavors that are guarded with tight tannins. Enigma is the top of the range and is a blend of Cabernets Franc and Sauvignon with some Merlot.

No visitor facilities
www.margalit-winery.com

Recanati Galilee

Lewis Pasco was a chef before becoming a winemaker for Recanati, a winery established in 2000 by banking mogul Lenny Recanati. His preference is for wines for the table, unburdened by wild ambitions of extract or oak. Pasco returned to California in 2008 and was replaced by another UC Davis graduate, Gil Schatzberg, formerly of boutique winery Amphorae. So far, Schatzberg seems to be holding to this clean, restrained style, with delicious results. Yasmin is the Mevushal line and the Diamond Series presents vibrant varietal wines, such as a simple, bright Chardonnay. The Reserve line stars some unusual wines, such as a minty Cabernet Franc and a deeply purple Petite Sirah/Zinfandel. Special Reserve is the flagship, an intense, cherry-scented, Cabernet-based wine from high-altitude vineyards.

Industrial zone Emek Hefer 38895
www.recanati-winery.com

Yatir Negev

In an echo of David Ben-Gurion's dream of making "the desert bloom," in 2000 the Carmel Winery founded Yatir in the desert region of Negev. It was originally an equal partnership with local vine growers, but today Carmel owns all of it. The winery itself is independently run and led by Australian-trained winemaker Eran Goldwasser. The vineyards are not actually in the heart of the desert, but 10 minutes north of the winery, 2,950ft (900m) up in the Judean Hills and surrounded by the cool greenness of the Yatir forest. The wines show it in cool, herbal flavors and graceful balance. Yatir forest is the reserve level Bordeaux blend; in the varietal series, look for the rich, firm Shiraz and the peach-laden Viognier.

Tel Arad, Arad 89100
www.yatir.net

LEBANON

In the Ancient World, the Phoenicians were skilled winemakers, shipping their wines to the far reaches of the Mediterranean. More than five millennia later, Lebanon's wineries continue this legacy, producing around 6.5 million bottles a year. With many Lebanese returning from studies abroad, a wealth of homegrown talent has injected the wine industry with a newfound vitality. Through the adoption of modern vineyard practices, international grape varieties, and improved production techniques, this new generation of formally trained winemakers has taken the industry forward. Wineries in Lebanon have traditionally placed significant importance on the development of export markets, but more recently, local demand has been increasing.

Major grapes

 Reds

Cabernet Franc

Cabernet Sauvignon

Carignan

Cinsault

Grenache

Merlot

Mourvèdre

Syrah

 Whites

Chardonnay

Merwah

Muscat

Obeideh

Sauvignon Blanc

Viognier

Vintages

2009

Good for whites, exceptional for reds. A great vintage.

2008

A heat wave meant high sugar and low maturity. Good for whites, not as good for reds.

2007

Good-quality whites and reds.

2006

A great year for whites and reds. Cooler weather, so good acidity levels and complexity.

2005

Very humid and a cool summer. Best for whites.

2004

Good for Cabernet Sauvignon.

The story of modern winemaking in Lebanon began with the establishment of Château Ksara by Jesuit monks in 1857. They were responsible for the introduction of French varieties, as well as French-Algerian winemaking techniques. After the First World War, the Lebanese wine industry thrived under the French Mandate, with French occupation proving a ready market and helping to promote wine culture.

In 1979, during the Lebanese civil war, the world's attention was turned to Lebanon's wine. The charismatic eldest son of the founder of Château Musar, Serge Hochar, was attending the Bristol Wine Fair in England, looking for an export market, when the then head of Christie's, Michael Broadbent, tasted Hochar's wines and declared them to be the discovery of the fair.

In the minds of many wine lovers, Lebanese wine has become synonymous with Château Musar, but there is far more to this country than that. In fact, Musar's idiosyncratic style is the exception rather than the rule, and their extreme minimalist approach to winemaking stands in stark contrast to the more New World practices of many other producers.

Situated between Mount Lebanon and the Anti-Lebanon mountain range, the Bekaa Valley is the primary wine-growing region in Lebanon. At 3,280ft (1,000m) above sea level, the soils are predominantly argilo-calcaire and extremely rocky. Viticulture is concentrated in the western part of the valley, around the town of Zahlé; however, experimentation is also taking place in Bhamdoun, Kfifane, Richmaya, Jezzine, and the Eastern Bekaa.

Vines have traditionally been trained in the goblet style (bush vines), but these days more than half of all vines are wire trained, either as double guyot or cordon. Techniques such as green harvesting and canopy management are now common practice and many producers work organically, although few are officially certified.

Southern French varieties have traditionally dominated plantings, but since the 1990s, savvy producers have been planting international varieties. Cabernet Sauvignon is now the most widely planted wine grape in the country, and Merlot, Cabernet Franc, and Syrah are all important, particularly for higher-end wines. More traditional grapes, such as Carignan, Cinsault, Grenache, and Mourvèdre, remain commonplace. Taking a back seat to the reds, popular white varieties include Chardonnay, Sauvignon Blanc, Viognier, and Muscat.

Even with all the new developments that have occurred, Lebanon proudly retains aspects of its wine heritage and has preserved several indigenous grape varieties. Obeideh, an ancient white variety, is often compared to Chardonnay, and its sister grape, Merwah, is likened to Sémillon. Perhaps one of the reasons for the survival of these local grapes has been their role in the traditional Lebanese drink, arak. Similar to other anise-based spirits produced in the Mediterranean basin, arak is made by triple distilling wine with anise. Arak is commonly mixed with water and is consumed with nearly every meal in Lebanon, so most producers continue to make arak in addition to wine.

Château Belle-Vue Mount Lebanon

Château Belle-Vue is a small, family-run winery founded by Naji and Jill Boutros. After living abroad, they dreamed of returning to Lebanon and initiating a project to help revive the disheartened community of the small mountain village of Bhamdoun, where Naji had grown up. They planted their first vines on the terraced mountainside in the spring of 2000 and now produce around 2,000 cases from 54 acres (22ha) of organically farmed vines. The results have been very impressive: seriously structured reds that show great depth and complexity. ★Rising star

Amin Abdelnour St, Bhamdoun Mhatta
www.chateaubelle-vue.com

Château Kefraya Bekaa Valley

Château Kefraya is the second-largest winery in Lebanon, producing around 2 million bottles a year. Founded in 1979 in the village of Kefraya, it has 299 acres (121ha) of vines that supply all the grapes for its wine. The premium wine, Comte de M 1996, a serious Cabernet Sauvignon/Syrah blend, brought Kefraya well-deserved international recognition.

Village of Kefraya, Zahle, Bekaa Valley
www.chateaukefraya.com

Château Khoury Bekaa Valley

Château Khoury was founded in 2004 by Raymond and Brigitte El Khoury. Since 2005, the wines have been made by their son, Jean-Paul. Château Khoury is the first and only producer to plant Alsace varieties (Pinot Gris, Pinot Noir, Gewürztraminer, and Riesling) in Lebanon—a move inspired by Madame Khoury's Alsace heritage. They currently produce 50,000 bottles a year of crisp, clean whites and elegantly layered reds. An environmentally conscious producer, they have their own water purification system on the property.

Zahle, Bekaa Valley
www.chateaukhoury.com

Château Ksara Bekaa Valley

With more than 150 years of uninterrupted winemaking history, Ksara is the largest producer in Lebanon. With an output of 2.7 million bottles annually, it accounts for 38% of the country's total wine production. As a leader in the industry, Ksara had the foresight to begin wire training vines and planted Cabernet Sauvignon and Syrah in the early 1990s. French winemaker James Palgé oversees the production of a large portfolio of wines, including their flagship Château de Ksara label—a meaty and structured, ageworthy red. The Cuvée du Troisième Millenaire is also a highlight.

Zahle, Bekaa Valley
www.ksara.com.lb

Château Musar Bekaa Valley

Ask any wine buff about Lebanese wines and they are certain to mention the legendary Château Musar. It produces 700,000 bottles a year, 80% of which are exported. Known for its distinctive and somewhat controversial style, often described as oxidized and high in volatile acidity, Musar is a favorite of connoisseurs, but is not always to the taste of the average consumer. Château Musar is their flagship label, known for its

CHATEAU MUSAR
WITH A DISTINCTIVE STYLE, THESE ARE THE
AMBASSADORS OF LEBANESE WINES

complexity and long-term aging potential. The Hochar Père et Fils label is made in the same vein as the Château wines, but is more youthful and approachable in style. The Cuvée Musar wines are softer and more playful—well suited to everyday drinking and very food-friendly.

Dlebta Rd, Ghazir, Mount Lebanon
www.chateaumusar.com.lb

Clos St Thomas Bekaa Valley

The Touma family have been producing arak since 1888, but switched to wine production when they established the Clos St Thomas winery in 1997. From their 161 acres (65ha), they produce around 400,000 bottles, over half of which are exported. Their portfolio includes several different labels, culminating in the flagship Château St Thomas red that displays bright red fruit and spice aromas and is suitable for mid-term aging. The entry level Les Gourmets range is well suited to everyday drinking, while the Les Emirs mid-range label is an impressive Cabernet Sauvignon/Syrah/Grenache blend.

Kab Elias, Main Rd, Bekaa Valley
www.closstthomas.com

Domaine de Baal Bekaa Valley

Domaine de Baal is an exciting new venture, established in 2006 by Sebastien Khoury. A premium boutique winery with 12 acres (5ha), it currently produces 1,000 cases. By 2012, another 7acres (3ha) will reach maturity, boosting production to 1,800 cases. De Baal produces only two wines: a white blend of Chardonnay and Sauvignon Blanc, and a red blend of Cabernet Sauvignon, Merlot, and Syrah. Emphasis is placed on respect for the environment here; the vineyards are organic and the winery was designed to be energy efficient. ★Rising star

Zahle, Bekaa Valley
www.domainedebaal.com

Domaine Wardy Bekaa Valley

Since its first vintage in 1998, Domaine Wardy has been one of the few producers to successfully concentrate on varietal wines. It has 161 acres (65ha) of estate vineyards and another 178 acres (80ha) on long-term lease. In 2003, it released its small-production, premium bottlings of Wardy Private Selection—a red blend of Cabernet Sauvignon and Syrah and an unusual white blend of Viognier and Muscat.

Industrial City, Zahle, Bekaa Valley
www.domaine-wardy.com

Massaya Bekaa Valley

Massaya is the result of an alliance between the Ghosn brothers and their notable French partners, Dominique Hébrard (formerly of Château Cheval Blanc), and the Brunier family of Châteauneuf-du-Pape's Domaine du Vieux Télégraphe. Trendy and well marketed, the winery was established in 1998 and produces 250,000 bottles of wine annually. It exports 90% of its production and has been very successful abroad, particularly in France. Five wines are produced: a white, a rosé, and three reds—the unoaked Classic Red, the Rhône-style Silver Selection, and the Bordeaux-style Gold Reserve.

Tanail Property, Bekaa Valley
www.massaya.com

MASSAYA
WITH SUCCESS ON THE EXPORT MARKET, THE
GOLD REVERVE IS MASSAYA'S FLAGSHIP WINE

South Africa provokes diverse emotions. This is certainly true of the country's controversial past, from which it has only recently emerged. It is true, too, of its dramatically varied scenery which, from arid bush to lush vineyard, is incapable of eliciting a tepid response. But it is also true of its wines—a marriage of the Old and New Worlds where classic Chenin Blancs and Bordeaux blends are as much at home as rustic Pinotage and Shiraz.

Winemaking in South Africa is no new endeavor. Farms were established in the 17th century by Dutch and English settlers in the Cape winelands regions of Constantia and Stellenbosch. Early winemakers recognized the agricultural bounty of the country, with its dizzying array of microclimates and soil types. Home to nearly 9,600 plant species, the Cape winelands region also offers some of the planet's oldest viticultural soil. In this soil, more than 25,000 plants have been found within a single 10ft^2 (3m^2) patch of earth. Since the 17th century, but especially in the last 10 years, winemakers have striven to harness this power—no small feat.

Today, the wine industry is succeeding in the catch-up game that the isolation and trade sanctions during the apartheid era created. The country produces more than 6,000 wines yearly, making its mark in Europe and America with world-class, yet affordable Cabernet Sauvignon, Sauvignon Blanc, Chenin Blanc, and more. Pinotage, the love-it-or-hate-it local variety, is gaining a foothold in elegant red blends that capture the unique terroir of the country in an approachable style. A mix of well-traveled young winemakers and winery empowerment programs for the vineyard workers who were so long oppressed is infusing new life into traditional mindsets. Already the eighth-largest wine-producing country in the world, South Africa is on the cusp of an explosion of exposure and influence.

SOUTH
AFRICA

SOUTH AFRICA

Winemakers in South Africa are passionate about their terroir, and it is easy to understand why. The country is home to a multitude of soil types, terrains, and microclimates which together represent an extreme challenge, but also offer delightful potential for the experimental and creative viticulturist. From the lively minerality of seaside vineyards to the deep granite, slate, and limestone of verdant valley floors surrounded by ancient peaks, the country is a playground for winemakers with a sense of adventure and vision. Although curious, innovative producers are constantly unearthing new subregions in the South African Cape, several established regions stand out as winemaking leaders.

Major grapes

 Reds

Cabernet Sauvignon

Merlot

Pinotage

Pinot Noir

Shiraz

Whites

Chardonnay

Chenin Blanc

Muscat

Sauvignon Blanc

Semillon

Viognier

Vintages

2009
A difficult, but impressive vintage for reds and whites.

2008
A cool, wet season yielded delicate red and white.

2007
A good year for classic styles, from crisp Sauvignon Blancs to lush, concentrated reds.

2006
A spectacular year for whites, particularly Chenin Blanc.

2005
A truncated growing season and erratic weather made for unbalanced reds and only average-quality whites.

2004
Cool conditions meant lower alcohol levels and a more restrained, classic style of whites and reds.

The venerable, historic winelands of Constantia and Stellenbosch are at the top of the list of leading regions. Constantia, one of the most expensive regions in South Africa to farm, is the home of the legendary Vin de Constance, a wine beloved of both English novelist Jane Austen and French Emperor Napoleon. Its cool sea breezes and ancient, granite-rich soils create a perfect nursery for sophisticated whites from varieties such as Sauvignon Blanc, Muscat, and Semillon. With their elegant, minerally crispness, and lush, tropical fruit flavors, the wines are studied and exotic. The reds, such as Merlot and Cabernet Sauvignon, are also rising in prestige.

In Stellenbosch—a region that lives and breathes wine—the mountainous terrain, with lush, varied, and well-drained soils, produces world-class Cabernet Sauvignon, Pinotage, Chenin Blanc, and Chardonnay. South Africa's only viticulture and enology program is offered at Stellenbosch University, annually churning out the young talent that is bringing new life into this sophisticated, Old World-oriented region. This is not to say that Stellenbosch mimics the styles and approaches of France, Italy, and Spain, however; the same go-to, experimental spirit driving the country as a whole is alive and well here and producers are proud of the unique terroir and heritage of the region. But Stellenbosch strives to tackle the classic wines of the world head-on, and is serious about putting its best bottles on the wine collector's map alongside the likes of Bordeaux, Burgundy, or Brunello. This conviction extends to the Pinotage grape variety, a South African crossing of Pinot Noir and Cinsaut which thrives here. Producers are fired up about the grape's potential in the global market, and their creation of a South African flagship red blend (known as a "Cape blend" and containing varying amounts of Pinotage alongside other red varieties such as Cabernet Sauvignon and Merlot) has brought on fierce but friendly debate in the domestic wine world and beyond.

There is greatness elsewhere in the country, though. Paarl, with its lush, inland vineyards located beneath a massive granite outcrop, is a paradise for grape varieties that can thrive in its hot climate, such as Shiraz, Cabernet Sauvignon, Pinotage, and Chardonnay. In style, the elegant, distinctive Paarl Cabernet Sauvignons and red blends range from bold to classic, while whites such as Viognier and Sauvignon Blanc offer top-quality, terroir-driven character thanks to the region's rich patchwork of soils. Shiraz, meanwhile, works best in the sunny climes at the foot of Paarl Mountain, and varies from big and muscular to taut and restrained.

Other regions to watch include Elgin, the coastal region whose cool-climate sea breezes produce exquisite, aromatic Sauvignon Blanc, Gewürztraminer, and Pinot Noir; Swartland, a wild, rustic region producing collectable Cabernet Sauvignon, Shiraz, and Pinotage; Franschhoek, the Huguenot settlement now producing delicious Cap Classique sparkling wines, Sauvignon Blanc, and reds; and Walker Bay, a breezy, seaside region where Pinot Noirs, Chardonnays, and more are being made with distinction. All these regions exemplify an exuberant experimentation balanced by a love of elegant, Old World styles.

Avondale Paarl

Care for the environment is very important at Avondale, and general manager and winemaker Jonathan Grieve does not go halfway with the sustainable effort. Biological, organic, and biodynamic farming approaches, including restoring the fungi that naturally lived in the soil, all add to the health of the vines. The rustic approach pays off: Avondale's leathery but refined reds and refreshing whites exhibit purity of fruit, finesse, and style. In the Avondale Reserve range, pay special attention to the MCC Brut and ageworthy Camissa Syrah. Many wineries profess an interest in sustainable farming, but Avondale is the real deal. ★ Rising star

Klein Drakenstein, Suider Paarl 7624
www.avondalewine.co.za

Backsberg Estate Cellars Paarl

Founded in 1916 by C L Back and passed down through several generations of the Back family, Backsberg offers a range of easy-drinking, stylish wines that are both structured and food friendly. The family is dedicated to the environment, and uses LED lighting and skylights, a bio-digester for methane extraction, and trees for renewable energy. The winery was the first in the country to be declared carbon neutral. Owner Michael Back and winemaker Guillame Nell are staying true to the Backsberg creative character with wines in several ranges: check out the Klein Babylonstoren Cabernet/Merlot, with its savory violet and blackcurrant folds, and the Premium Range Chardonnay, a combination of crisp minerality and nutty richness.

Suider Paarl 7624
www.backsberg.co.za

Badenhorst Family Wines Swartland

In 2008, Adi Badenhorst, one of South Africa's most promising winemakers, struck out with his cousin, Hein Badenhorst, to form Badenhorst Family Wines at a derelict winery in the Pederburg area. Adi, a surfing, parrot-breeding, laid-back rebel, proved his mettle at Rustenberg Wines and continues to impress with Secateurs Chenin Blanc, Badenhorst Red blend, and a white that beautifully marries Roussanne, Grenache Blanc, Viognier, Chenin Blanc, and Sauvignon Blanc. ★ Rising star

Stellenbosch 7599
adi@iafrica.com

Boekenhoutskloof Winery Franschhoek

Boekenhoutskloof's energetic winemaker and partner Marc Kent is a fixture on the Franschhoek wine scene, but do not expect him to stay in one place for long. His pioneering spirit has helped put the once-hidden region on the country's list of top winemaking sites, but his sourcing from other areas such as Somerset West shows that his brand is about diversity as well as quality. Boekenhoutskloof is a Syrah leader, its bottlings exhibiting a dense, dark character, but it also excels in classic Cabernets and red blends for the cellar. The Chocolate Block, a muscular but stylish blend of Syrah, Grenache, Cabernet Sauvignon, Cinsaut, and Viognier, is a crowd favorite, as is the Wolftrap, a fun red with plucky South African character.

Excelsior Road, Franschhoek 7690
www.boekenhoutskloof.co.za

BOUCHARD FINLAYSON
BOUCHARD FINLAYSON'S SAUVIGNON BLANC IS DISTINCTIVELY LINEAR AND MINERAL

BOEKENHOUTSKLOOF
A CABERNET IN THE CLASSIC STYLE FROM MARC KENT WHO ALSO PRODUCES AGEWORTHY RED BLENDS

Bouchard Finlayson Walker Bay

Poised, Old World-style Pinot Noir is the main name of the game for Peter Finlayson, whose sixth decade in winemaking continues to yield great results. Situated amid the cool maritime breezes of Walker Bay, the 12,000-case winery makes minerally, restrained Pinots, elegant red blends such as Hannibal (a blend of Pinot Noir and Shiraz with Italian varieties Sangiovese, Nebbiolo, and Barbera), and crisp, flinty Chardonnays, while the Sauvignon Blanc shows the linear, mineral character distinctive of the region. Green-grape harvesting takes place at veraison, emphasizing the Burgundian bent here. Stewardship of the fynbos-covered mountain land on the property is also a focus. ★ Rising star

Klein Hemel en Aarde Farm, Hemel en Aarde Vall,
Hermanus 7200; www.bouchardfinlayson.co.za

Buitenverwachting Constantia

Complex, aromatic wines are the hallmark of this stylish wine farm with the impossible name. Internationally acclaimed for classic-style reds that exhibit poised cassis, spice, and mineral notes, the farm produces 90,000 cases a year from the deep, granite soils of Constantia. Established reds, such as the Christine Bordeaux blend, have put the winery on the map, but the whites are elegant, too: the Chardonnay offers nutty fig and butterscotch flavors, while the Sauvignon Blanc exhibits distinctive Constantia minerality and snap. Owner Lars Maack is ambitious, and has invested in new cellar technology and in combating the spread of the leaf-roll virus with new plantings in 2008.

Klein Constantia Road, Constantia, Cape Town 7550
www.buitenverwachting.co.za

Cabrière Franschhoek

A 17th-century wine farm originally granted to French Huguenot farmer Pierre Jourdan, today, Cabrière is a Franschhoek luxury farm acclaimed for its *méthode champenoise* wines and gourmet restaurant, Haute Cabrière. Its owner, the artist and writer Archim von Arnim, adheres to the winery's poetic philosophy—"Wine is bigger than one, it is the combination of four: Sun, Soil, Vine, Man"—and crafts wines that capture the champagne style: golden, honeyed mousse, apple-citrus palate and all. The still wines—Chardonnay, Pinot Noir, rosé—are also geared toward the gourmand, but maintain the zippy South African character.

Pass Road, Franschhoek 7690
www.cabriere.co.za

Capaia Philadelphia

Capaia's mission statement—"to produce one of the best wines of South Africa"—may sound overly ambitious, but a few sips of the boutique winery's flagship Capaia red blend is proof that it means business. Founded in 1997 by Ingrid Baroness and Alexander Baron von Essen, the winery is a gleaming, state-of-the-art facility dedicated to quality. The collectable, ageworthy Capaia offers elegant waves of black fruit, leather, and spice; the Blue Hill Grove Sauvignon Blanc and Merlot/Cabernet are excellent, affordable alternatives that are great for everyday enjoyment.

Botterberg Road, Philadelphia 7304
www.capaia.de

WESTERN CAPE

The winemaking industry of South Africa is primarily situated in the lush Western Cape area, in the southwestern region of the country. Although new areas are continually being explored for grape-growing, most of the wine production in the country takes place near the cities and towns of Cape Town, Stellenbosch, and Paarl. South Africa is divided into 60 appellations within the Wine of Origin (WO) system, established in 1973. Mainly used for wine labeling, this system categorizes the different winemaking areas by size. From largest to smallest, these are: regions (for example, the Coastal Region), districts (Tygerberg), and wards (Durbanville). The latter are areas with distinctive climates and soil types.

SOUTH AFRICA

- Western Cape
- Wine regions, districts, and wards of the Western Cape

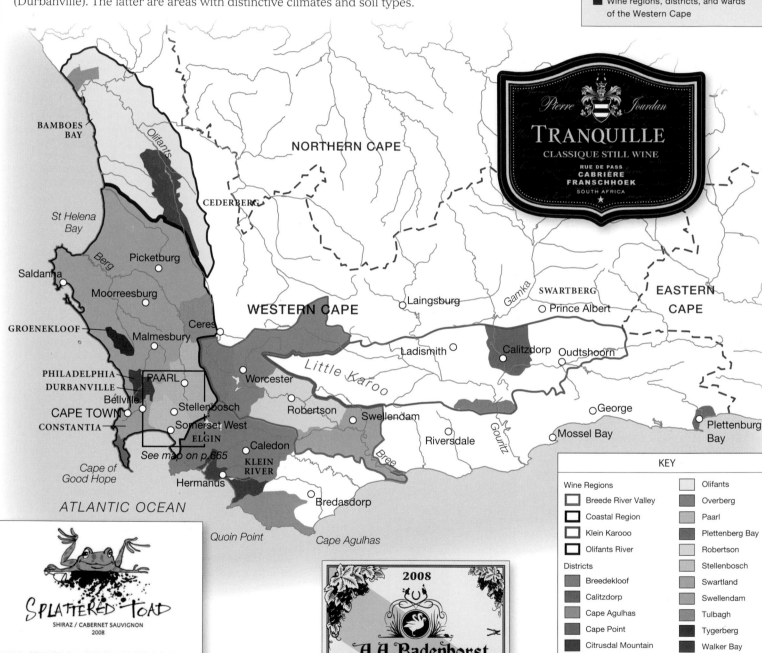

See map on p.665

TRANQUILLE

Pierre Jourdan
TRANQUILLE
CLASSIQUE STILL WINE
RUE DE PASS
CABRIÈRE
FRANSCHHOEK
SOUTH AFRICA

SPLATTERED TOAD
SHIRAZ / CABERNET SAUVIGNON
2008

2008
A.A. Badenhorst
FAMILY WINES
CHENIN BLANC
ROUSSANNE
GRENACHE BLANC
VIOGNIER
VERDEHLO
CHARDONNAY
14.5% vol   75cl
Wine of
South Africa   Wine of Origin
Coastal Region
P.O.Box 1177, Malmesbury, 7299, Kalmoesfontein, Paardeberg.

KEY	
Wine Regions	Olifants
Breede River Valley	Overberg
Coastal Region	Paarl
Klein Karooo	Plettenberg Bay
Olifants River	Robertson
Districts	Stellenbosch
Breedekloof	Swartland
Calitzdorp	Swellendam
Cape Agulhas	Tulbagh
Cape Point	Tygerberg
Citrusdal Mountain	Walker Bay
Citrusdal Valley	Worcester
Darling	**KLEIN RIVER** Ward
Langeberg-Garcia	– · – Regional boundary
Lutzville Valley	

Scale: 0   20   40   60 miles
0   20   40   60   80   100 km

STELLENBOSCH AND PAARL

The Cape Winelands district of Stellenbosch is situated 30 miles (50km) east of Cape Town. It includes a city of the same name that is also home to South Africa's only viticulture and enology program, at Stellenbosch University. Generally considered the heart of the South African wine industry, the district enjoys a Mediterranean climate and is celebrated for its ageable Cabernet Sauvignons and elegant Chenin Blancs. The bustling town is a haven for food and wine lovers. The Paarl district, and its eponymous town, enjoys a thriving winemaking culture—Shiraz and Cabernet especially—as well as an active outdoor community, thanks to Paarl Rock, a haven for hikers and climbers.

PRODUCERS

Avondale **26**	Miles Mossop Wines **12**
Backsberg Estate Cellars **25**	Mischa Estate **28**
Boekenhoutskloof Winery **32**	Morgenhof **14**
Cabrière **31**	Mulderbosch **16**
Cape Chamonix Wine Farm **30**	Neil Ellis **10**
Coleraine **24**	Quoin Rock **15**
De Trafford Wines **9**	Rustenberg Wines **13**
Ernie Els Wines **7**	Rust en Vrede **8**
Fairview **23**	Scali **27**
Glen Carlou **20**	Simonsig **17**
Hartenberg **1**	Solms-Delta **21**
Jordan **2**	Thelema Mountain **11**
Kanonkop **18**	Tokara **12**
Kanu **3**	Vergelegen **6**
Ken Forrester Wines **5**	Vilafonté **22**
La Motte **29**	Warwick Estate **19**
Meerlust Estate **4**	

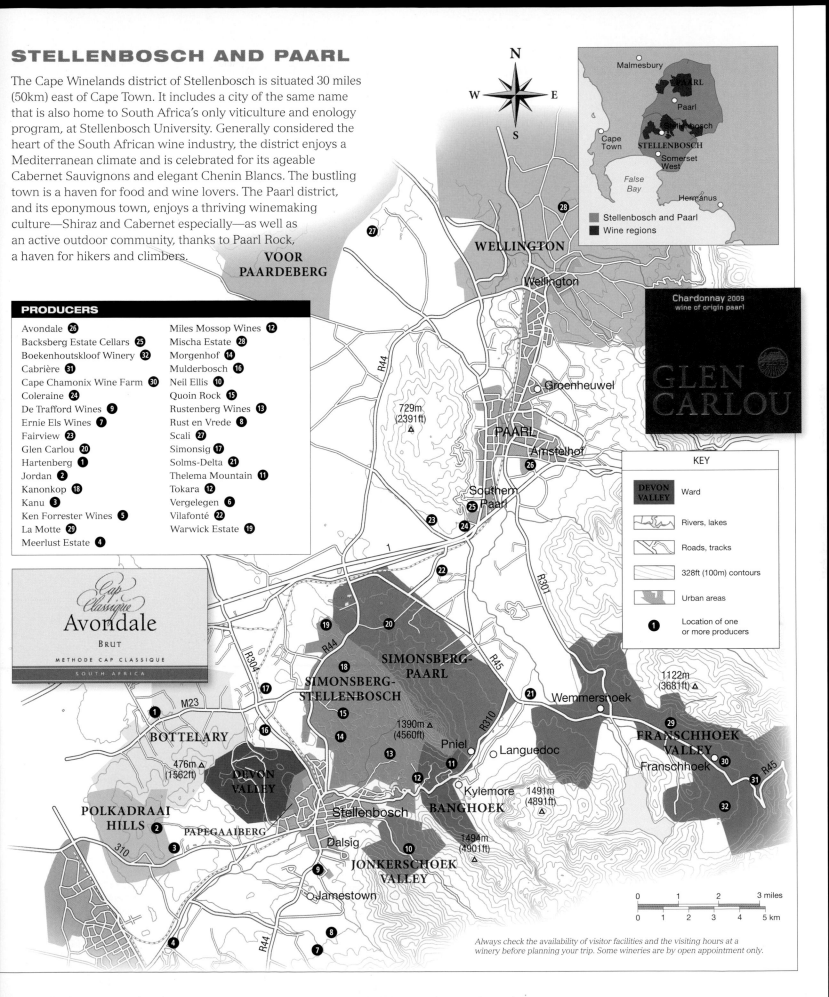

KEY

DEVON VALLEY	Ward
	Rivers, lakes
	Roads, tracks
	328ft (100m) contours
	Urban areas
1	Location of one or more producers

Always check the availability of visitor facilities and the visiting hours at a winery before planning your trip. Some wineries are by open appointment only.

Cape Chamonix Wine Farm Franschhoek

Innovative, energetic winemaker Gottfried Mocke joined Chamonix believing that Franschhoek could be a world contender in serious, food-oriented wines. The awards and critical acclaim the region has attracted in recent years have proved him right. Mocke's dedication to refined wines with unique character and experimental wood treatments have resulted in Pinot Noirs, Chardonnays, Sauvignon Blancs, and more that strike a delicious balance between fruit and wood—perky but poised, and always with a deft touch. Visitors to the farm can taste the wines at Cape Chamonix's Mon Plaisir restaurant with dishes that feel very much South African but have international panache—a perfect pairing. ★ **Rising star**

Franschhoek 7690
www.chamonix.co.za

Cape Point Vineyards Cape Point

Cape Point might well top a list of the world's most beautiful winery locations, with its perfectly manicured vineyards rolling toward the sea in Cape Town's Noordhoek neighborhood. But the view is secondary to the stunning wines made here. Winemaker Duncan Savage oversees an exquisite, small-production portfolio of Sauvignon Blanc, Semillon, Chardonnay, and white blends, as well as a Cabernet/Shiraz red blend. The whites dance between flinty minerality, citrus notes, and exotic fruits in a style that is both food-friendly and ethereal, while the red offers a more grounded punch of spice, leather, and tobacco. ★ **Rising star**

Noordhoek 7985
www.capepointvineyards.co.za

Catherine Marshall Wines Elgin

Catherine Marshall's new winery in Elgin reflects her passion, Pinot Noir, but the energetic winemaker is also a master of minerally, Rhône-style Syrah from Paarl. Intelligent, engaging, and full of charm, Marshall is all about meticulous detail, and her boutique, handcrafted wines reflect her expertise. Syrahs are fresh, dry, and finely constructed with a spin of subtle pepper; the Pinots earthy and expressive, with lively acidity. Marshall is also making a Sauvignon Blanc and a Pinot/Merlot blend, both exhibiting her trademark restrained elegance. Her experience making wine with some of the best in the business—Martin Meinert and Ken Forrester among them—attests to her pedigree; the wines, ageworthy and world-class, speak for themselves.

Mowbray 7705
www.cmwines.co.za

Cederberg Cederberg

Fifth-generation winemaker David Nieuwoudt has the highest-lying vineyard in South Africa (3,280ft/1,000m above sea level in the Cederberg Mountains), with snow in the winter and intense sun in the summer. Grown in a multitude of soil types, from shale/slate to clay, the Cederberg portfolio ranges from creamy Chenins to refined, peppery Shiraz. Nieuwoudt is fiercely terroir-driven, hoping that his wines will evoke their stunning origins. Walks, hikes, and mountain biking on the property add to its environmentally-oriented appeal.

Clanwilliam 8135
www.cederbergwine.com

ERNIE ELS WINES
THE GOLFER'S PROJECT HAS APPEAL
BEYOND THE CELEBRITY ASSOCIATION

CAPE CHAMONIX
FOR THOSE WHO CAN WAIT, THIS SAUVIGNON
BLANC WILL BE AT ITS BEST IN 2013

Coleraine Paarl

This small, under-the-radar producer in Paarl makes 4,000 bottles of layered, mouthfilling Merlot and Syrah, as well as Cabernets, red blends, and alluring whites like the peachy, exotic Viognier. Planted on granite shale on Paarl Mountain, the deep, well-drained soil and cool evening breezes add to the intensity of the fruit. Vines are harvested and tended by hand, and winemaker Clive Kerr has a hands-off approach in the cellar, preferring to let the vines speak for themselves. The result? Good and improving wines at an estate that is well worth watching. ★ **Rising star**

Pieter Hugo Street, Suider Paarl 7624
www.coleraine.co.za

Constantia Uitsig Constantia

Winemaker André Rousseau is shifting this 12,000-case winery's focus from reds and whites to primarily whites, harnessing the graceful elegance typical of Constantia. The wines already shine: dense but lively Semillon, the complex but minerally Constantia White, and a beautifully balanced Sauvignon Blanc attest to the winery's worth. For visitors, the stunning estate includes a hotel/spa, café, and two restaurants, and is located in the shadow of Table Mountain. Everything smacks of class and a meticulous sensibility. An impressive full package, with more to come. ★ **Rising star**

Spaanschemat River Road, Constantia, Cape Town
www.constantia-uitsig.com

De Grendel Durbanville

Established in 1720 but now truly coming into its own, De Grendel's expanding, 20,000-case operation focuses on Sauvignon Blanc, white blends, and reds including Pinot Noir and Merlot. The wines are layered and lush, with expressive, exotic fruit balanced by the minerality of the cool-climate Durbanville conditions. Winemaker Elzette du Preez and cellarmaster Charles Hopkins are effectively growing the brand while at the same time maintaining its classy, distinctive personality.

Panorama 7506
www.degrendel.co.za

De Trafford Wines Stellenbosch

Owner and winemaker David Trafford's humility and humor belie the excellence of the terroir-driven wines produced at his estate, founded in 1992. Cabernet, Merlot, and Shiraz all offer deep complexity, ageability, and balance. Chenin Blanc and the unique straw wine (made using air-dried grapes) have classic restraint and lingering flavors. The winery is situated on a scenic mountain farm in Stellenbosch, its high-altitude slopes a great match for the winery's red varieties. The wines are limited in production (3,500 cases), which Trafford says "means we can pay every attention to detail."

Mont Fleur Farm, Blaauwklippen Road, Stellenbosch 7599
www.detrafford.co.za

De Wetshof Estate Robertson

If South Africa has a Chardonnay peerage, it surely must include Danie de Wet. Descended from 17th-century pioneers who cultivated wine from their arrival in South Africa, De Wet's focus is noble white varieties. The estate's multi-decade dedication to Chardonnay is reflected in the award-winning versions of the grape: yeasty, complex, and full of lingering, lemony accents, the varied bottlings reflect the diversity of the Robertson region. Sauvignon Blanc and balanced red blends are also standouts here, as is the pure fruit freshness of the winery's dessert wines. An annual Chardonnay festival in the grounds further promotes the elegant focus of the winery.

Robertson 6705
www.dewetshof.com

Diemersdal Durbanville

Bone-dry, cool-climate Sauvignon Blanc keeps winemaker Thys Lous busy at this expanding Durbanville estate, which is also distinguishing itself for its exquisite Bordeaux blends and high-minded Chardonnay. A balance of Old and New World styles, the portfolio's concentrated flavors are a result of diverse soils and cooling sea breezes from the Atlantic Ocean. Traditional open fermenters combined with state-of-the-art equipment show that Lous means business, and the wines are succeeding in putting this sixth-generation winemaker, his wines, and the emerging region in which they are made, on the map. ★ **Rising star**

Adderley Road, Cape Town 7550
www.diemersdal.co.za

Durbanville Hills Durbanville

The elegant, balanced, and food-friendly wines of cellarmaster Martin Moore are a direct result of the cool maritime breezes found in Tygerberg, where the 140,000-case Durbanville Hills winery is situated. The region's diverse soils and microclimates are reflected in the winery's portfolio, which ranges from lush Merlots to flinty Sauvignon Blancs. A food focus is played out at the winery's popular restaurant, and a worker's trust, offering shares in the property, is on the horizon. The winery is also making laudable progress with sustainability.

Durbanville 7551
www.durbanvillehills.co.za

Ernie Els Wines Stellenbosch

Golfing legend Ernie Els's focused prowess on the links extends to his eponymous winery, which produces confident and muscular reds that go the long haul in the cellar. Along with partner Jean Engelbrecht—a respected name in South African winemaking—and the studied determination of winemaker Louis Strydom, Els produces wines that age well and are internationally acclaimed as an exotic alternative for serious collectors of Napa Cabernets and Bordeaux. Big fruit, savory spice, and a consistently showy but sophisticated style give the wines legitimate appeal far beyond the celebrity association.

Annandale Road, Stellenbosch 7599
www.ernieelswines.com

Fairview Paarl

Visitors—and there are many—to Fairview's Paarl winery are greeted by a tower inhabited by goats, a telling reflection of the playful edge of this serious producer. Owner Charles Back and winemaker Anthony de Jager are using grapes from across the Cape in their ongoing experimental search for the next great South African wine, and the wines speak of that rich diversity. Shiraz is king here—smoky, savory, and in the Rhône style for their classic bottling—but other reds, such as Pinotage and

Petite Sirah, are also noteworthy. The winery's onsite store sells local food products (the cheese selection is excellent) and the restaurant is very popular.

Suid Agter Paarl Road, Suider-Paarl 7646
www.fairview.co.za

Glen Carlou Paarl

Everything about Glen Carlou evokes drama and power, from the incomparable, sweeping Paarl views from the winery's patio, to the stunning modern art in its Hess Art Collection gallery, and the rich, structured wines. Glen Carlou excels in Cabernet Sauvignon, Syrah, and its Grand Classique Bordeaux blend, these ageworthy wines exhibiting classic cedar, dark chocolate, and black fruit. Chardonnay is another strength. The winery produces 65,000 cases annually, exporting to 40 countries. Owned by the Swiss Hess Group, visitors can taste wines from Hess properties in Australia, Argentina, and California.

Simondium Road, Klapmuts 7625
www.glencarlou.co.za

Graham Beck Wines Robertson

Pioneering winemaker Graham Beck founded his eponymous winery in 1983, and the Robertson estate is entering its third generation as a family-run endeavor. Beck's goal to establish a world-class winery in the Robertson region has been fully realized and has also extended to estates in Stellenbosch and Franschhoek. Beyond his efforts in staff empowerment, conservation, and biodiversity, Beck makes serious wine in four ranges: Ultra Premium (with focus on the dense Cabernet and elegant Syrah), Super Premium (the Viognier and Sauvignon Blanc shine), Premium, and Methode Cap Classique (the Brut Blanc de Blancs is a must-try).

Robertson 6705
www.grahambeckwines.com

Groot Constantia Constantia

History abounds at Groot Constantia, founded in 1685 and a tourist draw for its beautiful Cape Dutch architecture and lush grounds. The oldest operating winery in South Africa, Groot Constantia is lauded for its classic, elegant whites—Sauvignon Blanc, Semillon, Chardonnay, and the dessert wine Grand Constance—but also produces solid reds, Shiraz being its most successful in that category. Winemakers Boela Gerber and Michelle Rhodes produce 450,000 bottles yearly, including some port-style wines and a Cap Classique, among other diverse selections.

Constantia 7848
www.grootconstantia.co.za

Groote Post Darling

Venturing into the rural region of Darling is worth the effort when Groote Post is at the end of the trail. Charming owners Peter and Nicholas Pentz are doing a fine job promoting this emerging area via food-friendly wines with class such as the lively Merlot, indulgent Noble Late Harvest, and the smoky, spicy Shiraz. The 18th-century winery is a step back in time, and makes for a delightful day trip to the country. Onsite restaurant Hilda's Kitchen focuses on homegrown Darling fare. ★ **Rising star**

Darling 7345
www.grootepost.com

KEN FORRESTER

Gregarious, gentlemanly, and focused, the Stellenbosch winemaker and restauranteur Ken Forrester is synonymous with South African Chenin Blanc. Although Chenin (also known as "Steen" in South Africa) now accounts for nearly one-fifth of all domestic vineyard plantings, it has not always been so highly regarded. Forrester, known as "Mr. Chenin Blanc," has made it his mission to establish South African Chenin as an elegant, complex, world-class wine with infinite food-pairing potential. His mission began with the purchase of a rundown farm in the 1990s, from where he produced Sauvignon Blanc for his first vintage in 1994. Against the wishes of some viticultural consultants, Forrester planted Chenin Blanc and has continued to produce a variety he has described as "shy" and "misunderstood." His collaboration with Martin Meinert of Meinert Wines has proved successful: the Icon and Ken Forrester range Chenins are top scorers and exhibit drupe (stone fruit), honey, and almond buoyed by a crisp, lime minerality.

The Worcester district in the Breede River Valley
produces more wine than any other region in the Cape

KANONKOP
THE FAMED KANONKOP ESTATE HAS BEEN
MAKING WORLD-CLASS WINES FOR MORE
THAN A CENTURY

IONA
A CLASSIC, PEPPERY SYRAH WITH RED BERRY
FLAVORS AND RIPE TANNINS

HAMILTON RUSSELL
JUST ONE SIP OF THIS CHARDONNAY WILL
TRANSPORT THE DRINKER TO SOUTH AFRICA

Hamilton Russell Vineyards Walker Bay

A few minutes with Anthony Hamilton Russell and you will understand why this lauded winery's Pinot Noirs and Chardonnays are considered among South Africa's most prestigious. Poised and serious, Hamilton Russell has put considerable time, money, and passion into producing classic, world-class wines. The Pinot, a refined red with cedary spice and black fruit character, and the Chardonnay, complex and expressive, are Old World in style and a perfect reflection of Hamilton Russell's philosophy: discover what you do best, and perfect it. The wines prove that South Africa can compete alongside the best traditional wines in the world, but they are also a beautiful expression of the uniquely South African Walker Bay terroir.

Hemel-En-Aarde, Hermanus 7200
www.hamiltonrussellvineyards.co.za

Hartenberg Stellenbosch

Hartenberg's popularity with consumers and critics alike gives it extra power in the international market. The wines at this 42,000-case winery are approachable, consistent, and stylish—pay special attention to the Cabernets, Shirazes, and Merlots at the top end, and the poised and pretty The Eleanor Chardonnay, named after the former owner Eleanor Finlayson. The winery has a heart too, making serious efforts to empower its staff with adult literacy courses, sponsored after-school childcare, and more.

Bottelary Road, Stellenbosch 7605
www.hartenbergestate.com

Iona Elgin

Iona's owner Andrew Gunn is on a mission to harness the elegant exuberance of Elgin grapes, and his 13,000 cases of stylish wine prove he is getting it right. Fine-minded, minerally Chardonnay, flinty Sauvignon Blanc, and stony, crisp Syrah are the trademarks, reflecting the core characteristics of Elgin's crops. The apple trees that once grew on the farm have been replaced by vines, but the property still exhibits a natural bent that feels close to the land. Gunn is organically minded, protecting local plants and animals in his winemaking endeavors. ★ Rising star

Grabouw 7160
www.iona.co.za

Jardin Stellenbosch

Food-friendly wines from food-loving owners is one of the key characteristics of Jordan (known as Jardin in the US), established in 1982 and run by Gary and Kathy Jordan. The 65,000-case winery is pretty much equal parts red and white, with three tiers of bottling. As a start, you could do worse than the blackcurrant elegance of the Cabernets, the creamy oaked Chardonnays, and the bright, lively Sauvignon Blancs. The husband-and-wife winemaking team are ambitious and constantly seeking new projects, including the Jordan Restaurant at the winery—a Mediterranean eatery that showcases the wines well.

Stellenbosch 7600
www.jordanwines.com

Kanonkop Simonsberg-Stellenbosch

This famed red wine estate, founded in 1910, and owned today by Johann and Paul Krige, is still producing world-class wines in the top tier. The Cabernet, Pinotage, and Paul Sauer Merlot/Cabernet blend are award winners with deep cedar, spice, and black fruit flavors. Ageworthy, classic, but full of South African character, Kanonkop reds attract serious collectors and fans of big, distinctive wines. The winery, located on the lower slopes of Simonsberg Mountain, is branching out into art, with a new gallery in the grounds furthering its tourist draw.

R44, Stellenbosch 7600
www.kanonkop.co.za

Kanu Stellenbosch

Although this 38,000-case winery excels in reds (the Shiraz and Keystone Cabernet blend are exotic and sexy, with savory and spicy characters), the real gem here is the KCB Chenin Blanc. Winemaker Richard Kershaw is renowned for his way with South Africa's most widely planted grape variety, and Kanu's interpretation is gaining popularity fast. The food-friendly Chenin is full of luscious, curvy fruit backed by clean acidity, but just as good is the mouthwatering Kia-Ora Noble Late Harvest: its nutty, honeyed layers are a testament to Kershaw's immense skill and deft touch. ★ Rising star

Goedgeloof Farm, Polkadraai Road, Stellenbosch 7600
www.kanu.co.za

Ken Forrester Wines Stellenbosch

The wine world gained a star when restauranteur Ken Forrester decided to move beyond the kitchen and found his Stellenbosch winery in 1994. Forrester began by making high-end Sauvignon Blanc, but soon saw potential for boutique Chenin Blanc in the region. Today, he is a vocal proponent of world-class Chenin from South Africa, producing intense, silky wines that are fast gaining momentum worldwide. His reds are of high quality too—check out the exotic black fruit and tobacco of the Gypsy blend or the elegant, savory notes of his Merlots. His Stellenbosch restaurant, 96 Winery Road, is a must for its eclectic regional cuisine and thoughtful wine list.

Stellenbosch 7599
www.kenforresterwines.com

Klein Constantia Constantia

Incomparable, lush setting aside, Klein Constantia is renowned for its Vin de Constance dessert wine, an interpretation of the 18th-century unfortified dessert wine from the Constantia region lauded by enophiles such as Napoleon and Charles Dickens. Made from Muscat de Frontignan, it is packed with nutty peach and spice flavors—a layered but delicate wine with versatile food-pairing ability. Owner Lowell Jooste and winemaker Stiaan Cloete also produce top-notch Sauvignon Blanc, as well as sparkling wine, Riesling (both dry and botrytized late harvest), and a red blend.

Constantia 7848
www.kleinconstantia.com

La Motte Franschhoek

Elegant inside and out, the regal La Motte produces Shiraz, Bordeaux blends, and Sauvignon Blanc. The 46,000-case winery's classical bent goes beyond wine, however. Part-owner Hanneli Rupert-Koegelenberg is a classical singer and concerts are held monthly in the grounds. Winemaker Edmund Terblanche's bottlings range from the showy mocha and black fruit of the

Shiraz/Viognier to the grassy freshness of the Sauvignon Blanc. Food-friendly and balanced, the wines are award winners and please myriad palates. As well as wine, La Motte cultivates flowers for essential oils such as rose, geranium, and Cape snow bush.

R45 Main Road, Franschhoek 7690
www.la-motte.com

Meerlust Estate Stellenbosch
Founded in the 17th century, Meerlust has long been recognized as one of the premier wine producers in South Africa. But the winery does not rest on its laurels —consistently excellent reds such as the intense, vibrant, Cabernet, classic Pinot Noir, and cellar-worthy, balanced Rubicon blend continue to gain new followers. The Chardonnay impresses too: complex, creamy, and full of tropical fruit, it is a serious drinker's white. Winemaker Chris Williams takes terroir and vintage variation seriously, effectively maintaining the tradition of Meerlust while pushing it forward.

Stellenbosch 7599
www.meerlust.com

Miles Mossop Wines Stellenbosch
Young winemaker Miles Mossop cut his teeth at Tokara (where he remains the winemaker), before establishing his own label in 2004. So far, the results have been more than promising from this 900-case winery. The Max, named after Mossop's son, is a Bordeaux blend and the Saskia, a nod to his daughter, a marriage of Chenin Blanc with Viognier. Both wines exhibit a fine balance of exuberant fruit and elegant tautness—an expression of both Old and New World styles that stems from Mossop's belief in "guiding" the grapes, rather than directing them, "through the natural process of winemaking." ★ **Rising star**

Helshoogte Pass, Stellenbosch 7600
www.milesmossopwines.com

Mischa Estate Wellington
Mischa Estate's winemaker Andrew Barnes is an earnest, deeply serious man with a nascent interest in Bordeaux blends. The Barnes family's story is romantic—upon returning from active military service in North Africa and Italy after World War II, Andrew's grandfather, "Kelpie" Barnes, and his wife, ballet dancer Yvonne Blake, abandoned sophisticated urban life for the farm, eventually establishing an important grapevine nursery in the 1960s. Since 1996, Andrew has crafted acclaimed Cabernets and Shirazes at this 4,000-case winery. His reds exhibit spicy, blueberry notes, while the whites are altogether more fresh and bracing. The aromatic Viognier is a real hit. ★ **Rising star**

Oakdene Road, Wellington 7655
www.mischaestate.com

Morgenhof Simonsberg-Stellenbosch
Though the internationally popular, 350-year-old Morgenhof estate is best known for its flagship, complex, full-bodied Bordeaux blend, it also offers solid quality in its approachable Sauvignon Blanc, Pinotage, and Cabernet. Chenin and Chardonnay are alluring stars here, too. At the winery, an impressive underground barrel maturation cellar—open for viewing—can hold up to 20,000 French oak barrels, showing that Morgenhof is

KLEIN CONSTANTIA
RELEASED WHEN READY TO DRINK, 5 YEARS AFTER BOTTLING, VIN DE CONSTANCE WILL TASTE JUST AS GOOD INTO THE NEXT DECADE

PAUL CLUVER
PAUL CLUVER'S NOBLE LATE HARVEST RIESLING IS A SOPHISTICATED DESSERT WINE

serious about creating collectable, elegant wines. The winery's focus on female wine consumers and their palates is an interesting change of tack for South Africa.

Stellenbosch 7599
www.morgenhof.com

Mulderbosch Stellenbosch
Poet, farmer, and philosopher extraordinaire Mike Dubrovic is also a lauded winemaker and visionary, and his efforts over the past 19 years have brought his winery, and South African wines, to the forefront. Wildly popular among international enophiles and critics, Mulderbosch wines are truly terroir-driven, and consistently good. The distinctive Faithful Hound, a Bordeaux blend with a soft, earthy touch, and the Sauvignon Blanc, steely and crisp, are of exceptional quality, but the curvy Chenin Blanc is also a winner. Dubrovic's newsletter—humorous missives from the farm including reports on his chickens—attest to his eco-friendly approach.

R304, Stellenbosch 7599
www.mulderbosch.co.za

Neil Ellis Stellenbosch
The Neil Ellis partnership brings together trailblazing négociant Neil Ellis and innovative businessman Hans-Peter Schroder. Ellis has sought out the best grapes in South Africa's winelands since 1986, whether it is Stellenbosch for its dense power, Darling for its maritime crispness, or Elgin for its delicate reserve. The wines are evidently terroir-driven and they offer a lovely expression of South African varietal character. The Sauvignon Blanc provides waves of typical gooseberry, the Cabernet is savory, rich, and full of plum, and the Chardonnay round, with a minerally edge. "Expressive" is the description the winery uses to characterize these wines, and the voice is loud and clear.

Oude Nektar Farm, Stellenbosch 7600
www.neilellis.com

Nitida Cellars Durbanville
Established in 1992, the 8,000-case Nitida Cellars, owned by engineer Bernhard Veller, has been on a roll since the very start. Savory red blends, serious, stony Sauvignon Blanc, and plush Pinotage grown in clay-based soils, are among the best here, and the winery is committed to the environment, practicing under IPW (Integrated Practice of Wine) standards. The Cassia restaurant focuses on seasonal, rustic fare reflecting the bounty of the region, with a changing, organically-minded menu styled to pair with Nitida's food-friendly pours. ★ **Rising star**

Durbanville Hills 7552
www.nitida.co.za

Paul Cluver Estate Wines Elgin
Paul Cluver has played an important part in putting the emerging, cool-climate region of Elgin on the map for crisp, sophisticated whites, dessert wines, and reds. Under the direction of the Cluver family, winemaker (and son-in-law of estate founder, Paul Cluver) Andries Burger's focus is the elegant expression of Elgin's coastal terroir—which he achieves most successfully in the award-winning Gewurztraminer, Pinot Noir, Riesling, and Sauvignon Blanc. The Chardonnay is also making a play

on the international market; with its balance of flinty minerals and creamy toast, it is an intriguing expression of Old and New World styles.

Grabouw 7160
www.cluver.com

Quoin Rock Simonsberg-Stellenbosch

Carl van der Merwe, the winemaker at the 5,000-case-and-growing Quoin Rock, has an inventive, eco-minded energy about him. To take just one example, van der Merwe, in the spirit of making lemonade when life gives you lemons, is clearing foreign plants and using them to make compost in order to re-establish the fynbos (the Cape's unique indigenous species of flora). On the winemaking front, his wines are making a splash with their stylish, trendsetting appeal. The zippy Sauvignon Blanc and mesquite-laden Syrah are the stars here, but the vine-dried Sauvignon Blanc is a unique bottling worth savoring. Keep posted for van der Merwe's next brainwave—it is sure to surprise you. ★ Rising star

Stellenbosch 7599
www.quoinrock.com

Raka Walker Bay

The sea might have been owner and ex-fisherman Piet Dreyer's passion—Raka is named after his black fishing vessel—but today, vineyards in Kleinrivier are his focus. The 15,000-case winery is making waves with its Quinary Bordeaux blend, ripe with black fruit and spice, its swanky, plush Merlot, and juicy Pinotage. With his lively wit and pet parrot Kulula, Dreyer has an eccentric bent, but the wines are studied, serious, and collectable. The winery is still evolving, but consumers and critics have taken notice already. ★ Rising star

Caledon 7230
www.rakawine.co.za

Rudera Wines Stellenbosch

Established in 1999, Rudera has a track record for excellence, especially with Chenin Blanc. Winemaker Eleonor Visser, late of Spier Wines fame, drives the terroir-focused boutique line of stunning Chenins, as well as bright, distinctive Cabernets and elegant Syrahs. At 3,400 cases, the winery focuses on the kind of premium bottlings preferred by owners Johan and Elbie van Vuuren and Jasper Raats. The terroirs of Elgin, Stellenbosch, and Walker Bay speak through wines that are, according to Raats, left to develop "naturally," reflecting the winery's purist leanings and love of "age-old [viticultural] traditions."

No visitor facilities
www.rudera.co.za

Rustenberg Wines Stellenbosch

Wines grown on the rich red slopes of the Simonsberg and Helderburg mountains exhibit power and masculine grace—a trademark of the lauded Rustenberg and its second label, Brampton. The efforts here are collaborative, with owner Simon Barlow, viticulturist Nico Walters, and cellar head Randolph Christians offering an experienced meeting of minds. Classically oriented and serious wines such as the John X Merriman (a Cabernet blend with grippy tannins and dense fruit) and the Peter Barlow (Rustenberg's beefy Cabernet) are favorites among red

SOLMS DELTA
THE ACCESSIBLE ASTOR RANGE WAS
INSPIRED BY TRADITIONAL LOCAL MUSIC

SADIE FAMILY WINES
CLASSY WINES LIKE COLUMELLA HAVE
ATTRACTED ATTENTION TO SWARTLAND

wine buffs all over the world. But the Brampton whites have staying power too, especially the unoaked Chardonnay and Sauvignon Blanc.

Schoongezicht Street, Stellenbosch 7600
www.rustenberg.co.za

Rust en Vrede Stellenbosch

The Rust en Vrede pedigree is formidable. The farm is more than 300 years old and its wine was selected for President Nelson Mandela's Nobel Peace Prize banquet. The first South African estate to specialize in red wine alone, Rust en Vrede has garnered numerous awards in the more than three decades it has been making premium wine. Shiraz, Cabernet, and the flagship Estate red blend are the draws here, with supple, elegant black fruit, smoke, and savory layers. The Rust en Vrede restaurant is also recognized as world-class, while game drives, nature hikes, and guest cottages give the estate tourist appeal.

Stellenbosch 7599
www.rustenvrede.com

Sadie Family Wines Swartland

Before visionaries like Eben Sadie dug their heels into the rugged Swartland, the region was better known for its black shrub than its impressive vineyards. Today, rising rocket Sadie—an unassuming yet worldy winemaker who still waxes lyrical about this remote land—is turning out terroir-focused collectables such as the Columella, a Shiraz/Mourvèdre blend with velvety, multi-layered richness, and the red and white bottlings under the Palladius name—expressive, exuberant yet classy. Sadie continues to impress, and his successes are attracting more serious investment in the region.

Aprilskloof Road, Paardeberg Malmesbury 7299
www.thesadiefamily.com

Scali Voor Paardeberg/Paarl

Scali's boutique production of 1,400 cases of Pinotage, Syrah, and white blend wines is all about handcrafted details. Owners Willie and Tania de Waal produce refined, expressive wines in their Voor Paardeberg vineyards that are food-friendly and grown to organic standards. "We work closely with nature and we do this with a whole-hearted passion," claim the kindly couple, whose rustic but refined lodgings evoke a more genteel age. Willie's winemaking tradition was passed down the generations—his great-great grandfather bought vineyard land in 1877 with a diamond he found at Kimberley in the Northern Cape. ★ Rising star

Paarl 7623
www.scali.co.za

Simonsig Stellenbosch

The famed Simonsig estate was established in 1953 and is at the forefront of classic Pinotage production today. Cellar master Johann Malan is a tastemaker and respected voice in the industry, and he produces wines of power and grace. The integrated, layered Frans Malan Cape blend is one of the most elegant expressions of Pinotage in South Africa. The whites, such as the "superquaffer" Chenin and luscious Gewürztraminer, are equally impressive.

De Hoop Krommerhee Road, Stellenbosch 7605
www.simonsig.co.za

Solms-Delta Franschhoek

And now for something completely different. Neurosurgeon-turned-vineyard owner Dr. Marc Solms has resurrected an ancient Roman method of grape cultivation called desiccation, in which grapes are vine-dried for intense concentration. The result is a Shiraz and a white blend with dramatic, power-packed flavors. A relative newcomer, Solms is still climbing fast with meticulously crafted bottlings of everything from Pinotage and Grenache to Viognier and Muscat d'Alexandria, but his groundbreaking efforts in black empowerment and founding the Wijn de Caab Trust prove he is there to make an impact that goes beyond the glass. ★ Rising star

1460-4 Franschhoek Road, Paarl 7680
www.solms-delta.co.za

Steenberg Constantia

Backed by the prestigious Graham Beck since 2005, and producing lauded reds such as Merlot and Nebbiolo, the 50,000-case Steenberg is already a force to be reckoned with in Constantia and beyond. The wines to watch here are the whites and white blends. The Sauvignon Blanc Reserve is a standout, produced from old vines and full of grace and a dry, poised minerality, and the Magna Carta, a new blend of Sauvignon Blanc and Semillon, is both refreshing and complex. The winery's cutting-edge facilities, restaurant, and scenic location add to the appeal.

Steenberg 7947
www.steenberg-vineyards.co.za

Stormhoek Wellington

Stormhoek is a Wellington winery that is as much about advancing Internet 2.0 trends as it is about producing food-friendly, affordable wines. Founded by the creative Graham Knox in 1993, the winery is located on the steep slopes of a hidden valley up the Bains Kloof Pass. It makes elegant but approachable Pinotage, Chenin Blanc, Shiraz, and more, but Stormhoek really began to catch on after Knox and his partners started writing an online diary that attracted the attention of the blogosphere, and gained the wines a loyal international following. "A case study for successful online marketing," says the website, which is still notable for its blog and videos. But once you have tasted the exuberant fruit of these wines, you will know that the Stormhoek story is about so much more than digital finesse. ★ Rising star

No visitor facilities
www.stormhoek.co.za

Thelema Mountain Stellenbosch

Thelema Mountain is perched on the top of Stellenbosch's Helshoogte Pass, making it one of the region's highest and coolest vineyards. Formerly a fruit farm, the 40,000-case winery was founded by the Webb family in 1983, and it specializes in classic cool-climate reds and fine, flinty whites (some of which are produced from grapes sourced from Elgin). The high altitude and microclimate of the mountain give Thelema's wines a distinctive edge, marrying the rich fruit of Stellenbosch with the crisp restraint of cooler climes. Discerning winemaker Gyles Webb (with Rudi Schultz) is dedicated to exacting canopy management standards, and the resulting wines prove his skill.

Helshoogte Pass, Stellenbosch 7600
www.thelema.co.za

Tokara Stellenbosch

With artistic Miles Mossop at the winemaking helm, Tokara is emerging as one of South Africa's most promising wineries. The wine farm produces 50,000 cases a year, and standouts include the Walker Bay and Elgin Sauvignon Blancs—minerally, and wafting elements of the sea—and the Tokara Red, a traditional Cabernet, Merlot, and Petit Verdot blend with a refined character. Tokara also has a reputation for its creamy, complex, artisanal olive oils. ★ Rising star

Helshoogte Pass, Stellenbosch 7600
www.tokara.co.za

Vergelegen Stellenbosch

At more than 300 years old, Vergelegen has achieved "grande dame" status, not just in South Africa, but worldwide. Age aside, it is still undoubtedly one of the top producers of world-class wine in South Africa. Winemaker Andre Van Rensburg maintains the refined, Old World touch for which the winery is famous with deep, layered Bordeaux blends in the Flagship range; stylish favorites such as Chardonnay, Semillon, and Cabernet in the Reserve range; and beautifully balanced Chardonnay and Sauvignon Blanc in the Premium range. At the winery, the "Interpretive Center," impressive Cape Dutch architecture, and tour of the old homestead have great appeal to history buffs.

Lourensford Road, Somerset West 7130
www.vergelegen.co.za

Vilafonté Paarl-Simonsberg

The first American/South African winemaking joint venture, Vilafonté was established in 1996 by an impressive quartet: trailblazing Californian winemakers Zelma Long and Phil Freese, Mike Ratcliffe of South Africa's Warwick Estate, and Bartholomew Broadbent (wine merchant son of celebrated auctioneer and wine writer, Michael Broadbent). The powerful Series C and Series M red blends offer distinctive, site-specific black fruit, cedar, and savory spice. These are serious wines for collectors, and the 2,500-case winery makes no excuses for its luxury positioning, boasting an "obsession with quality" and a state-of-the-art winemaking facility "intimately designed by Zelma Long."

7C Lower Dorp Street, Bosman's Crossing,
Stellenbosch 7600; www.vilafonte.com

Warwick Estate Simonsberg-Stellenbosch

Does Warwick Estate managing director Mike Ratcliffe ever stand still? At the forefront of Pinotage pioneers and an active, traveling ambassador for South African wine, Ratcliffe runs a 23,000-case winery that is a fixture in Simonsberg-Stellenbosch and beyond. Ambitious expansion has not taken the focus from the supple, ageable wines for which the estate is known. Take note of the lush Three Cape Ladies, a Cabernet Sauvignon, Pinotage, Merlot, and Shiraz blend that is making a serious case for Pinotage worldwide, and the Trilogy, the Cabernet blend flagship bottling with spicy black fruit and muscular tannins. A thriving worldwide wine club attests to the popularity of Warwick Estate wines among myriad palates.

Elsenburg 7607
www.warwickwine.com

VIN DE CONSTANCE

Napoleon collected it, Dickens praised it, and Jane Austen recommended its "healing powers on a disappointed heart" in her 1811 novel *Sense and Sensibility*. The late-harvest dessert wine Vin de Constance, originally made from Muscat de Frontignan, Pontac, red and white Muscadel, and Chenin Blanc in Constantia, was—and remains—one of South Africa's most prized and historic wines. The unctuous elixir, with its honeyed tones of tropical fruit and spice, was but a memory after phylloxera devastated vines in the 1880s. Inspired by records of the wine's greatness, Duggie Joost of Klein Constantia revived production of a new Vin de Constance, made from Muscat de Frontignan, in the 1990s. In addition, Groot Constantia has produced its Grand Constance, made from white and red Frontignac grapes, since 2003. Vin de Constance is akin to a Sauternes or Trockenbeerenauslese. Though perhaps not quite as ageable as those wines, its price is certainly comparable.

Those people who describe Asia as the "New Wine Continent" are both right and wrong. While wine-growing may be new in countries such as Thailand and India, elsewhere in Asia the newcomer tag could justifiably be dismissed by locals as Eurocentric. For example, the vine arrived in China in 126BCE, 1,600 years before it reached the Americas. Moreover, it came from what is now Uzbekistan, where wine-growing was already well-established.

Anyone still inclined to dismiss Asian wine should consider the fact that the OIV (International Organisation for the Vine and Wine) lists China as the world's sixth-largest wine producer. In the rapidly developing economies of many Asian nations, wine has become a cool status product for yuppies, with consumption concentrated in major urban conurbations. Assuming the rapid economic growth continues, it seems likely that the current increases in consumption of 10–30% a year (depending on the nation) will continue. One would also expect consumer sophistication to develop at a comparable pace. Indeed, Japan has already shown what is possible given such development for a long enough period. Not only does the Land of the Rising Sun produce refined Chardonnay and Merlot, it also makes remarkable wines from indigenous varieties such as Koshu (white) and the table grape Muscat Bailey A (red).

Many of Asia's vineyards lie within the tropics and/or have monsoon climates, but cultivation methods capable of overcoming the problems of these zones were developed in the 1990s. New rootstocks better suited to these conditions appear to have opened up the possibility of another leap forward during the next few years. Already, in blind-tastings, experts frequently identify the better Asian wines as European. World-class Vietnamese Cabernet Sauvignon? Maybe that will one day be possible.

ASIA

INDIA

Wine is not new to India. Alcohol, for that matter, is not new to India. However, compared to Scotch whisky, which arrived in the subcontinent in the earlier part of the 20th century, not to mention the considerably older traditional local brews, wine is a relative newcomer. Early French collaborations helped pave the way: wine grapes replaced local seedless varieties, and winemaking know-how and equipment followed. Progress has been constant, if a little slow. Still, no great epic was ever completed overnight; certainly not without the concerted efforts and experiments of many an enthusiast. From awful table grape wines to very drinkable wines in a little over two decades, the saga of Indian wines is one such story.

Major grapes

🍇 Reds
Cabernet Sauvignon

Merlot

Shiraz

Zinfandel

🍇 Whites
Chenin Blanc

Sauvignon Blanc

Viognier

Vintages

The concept of vintage is neither prevalent nor relevant in India yet. Most production is focused on wines for immediate consumption. Wineries have only recently started marking vintages on their bottles, replacing the rather unromantic, legally mandatory, "date of manufacture." Currently, there are no published or recognized vintage charts.

One big obstacle in the way of progress for Indian wine comes in the shape of prohibitive taxes, which make wine inaccessible to many. Controlled sales channels and advertising restrictions further add to the problems. Despite all this, foreign wines abound and home-grown Indian wines are even more commonplace, dominating the market. Winemaking is becoming increasingly popular and the reasons are easy to sum up: a high-yielding, high-in-demand cash crop, providing employment and boosting tourism.

From whisky-soaked parties to elegant wine soirées, wine is becoming a visible and much-discussed social phenomenon. A steady rise in the national GDP is swelling disposable incomes, allowing more people to aspire to the good life. And wine's supposed health benefits further its popularity, with doctors advising the switch from whisky to wine.

Perhaps the biggest achievement so far is that wine is (gradually) being enjoyed with local cuisines. After politics and baseball, the back-and-forth apropos, "Are Indian dishes wine-friendly?" has become a heated discussion at many social gatherings. The general trend and response weighs in favor of this gastronomic union.

Nasik, about 125 miles (200km) from Mumbai, is the first quasi-organized wine-producing region in the state of Maharashtra. The initial grapes of choice were Chenin Blanc for whites and Zinfandel for rosés and reds, but the current favorites—and the varieties likely to comprise the next generation of Nasik wines—are Sauvignon Blanc, Cabernet Sauvignon, and Shiraz.

The competition for Nasik is a handful of producers toiling on the Nandi hillsides, not too far from the city of Bangalore, in the neighboring state of Karnataka. The state of Himachal Pradesh in the north is also gearing up for a serious vinous attack. Located in the foothills of the Himalayas, they possess excellent potential terroir. The eastern and northeastern states of West Bengal and Assam (both famous for their tea), Sikkim, and the Seven Sisters are also considering grape cultivation.

From July to September, the monsoon season is important in India. It is the reason why India is a Northern Hemisphere country following the vine-planting cycle of the Southern Hemisphere. Unlike France, Italy, or California, where harvesting usually starts in September, an Indian harvest takes place around March. The rains are strong and can cause many problems—from a watered-down crop to reduced yields and problems with bacteria and fungus.

Sunshine, however, is not a problem, so crop-maturity is guaranteed. Initial harvests were often mistakenly gauged by sugar levels as opposed to phenolic maturation, resulting in wines that were hot and heady with little aroma and a thin mouthfeel. But things are improving and upcoming brands are making the qualitative leap.

Winemaking in India is still a nascent story, but it is a dramatic and action-packed one, with plenty of surprises. It is similar, in fact, to that much bigger industry—Bollywood. And presumably, as is the case with most Indian epic films, this story, too, will be thoroughly entertaining and have the predictably heart-warming ending.

Chateau de Banyan Karnataka

Although Chateau de Banyan has its own vineyards planted in the state of Karnataka, the first harvest was contract-sourced from Nasik, and then bottled in Goa. Thus, it is a bit of a trans-national winery. In the hands of the present Italian winemaker, Lucio Matricardi, Banyan is making some pretty good wine with satisfying varietal character under the label of Big Banyan. Although the reds have consistently improved, the whites remain the showcase, especially the Chenin Blanc. There is also a limited-production late-harvest white, which is comfortably among the best on the market. ★ Rising star

John Distillery Limited, M-21 Cuncolim Industrial Estate, Cuncolim, Goa 403703; www.bigbanyanwines.com

Château d'Ori Maharashtra

Château d'Ori started with everything right. It had a passionate owner with a cultured taste for fine wines, a renowned international (Greek) winemaker, well-spent marketing money, and great reviews all around, including from some big names across the globe. Yet, in spite of it all, save for some artistic label design, they have little else to show for it today. The wines are good, the whites more than the reds, but the proposed promise of eating into the share of the other more popular château remains just that: a distant promise.

Gate No 529, Dindori – Shivar, Maharashtra www.chateaudori.com

Deccan Plateau Maharashtra

The pictures of spices with Indo-Western fonts on Deccan Plateau's labels may not make for the catchiest of labels but they are definitely recognizably Indian. The Sauvignon Blanc shows a great nose, even if it is a bit thin on the palate. In the reds, the Zinfandel and the Shiraz are good but fade next to the Trivalli blend (Cabernet Sauvignon/Merlot/Shiraz) and the pure Cabernet Sauvignon, which are stunningly good. They are strong and well formed with plenty of tannic muscle that the wines are not shy of flexing. ★ Rising star

Gate No 235, Burkegaon, Pimpri Sandas, Haveli, Pune, Maharashtra 412216; www.deccanplateauwines.com

Four Seasons Maharashtra

The formidable formal backing of some of the biggest and most experienced names in the Indian drinks industry ensures Four Seasons has a strong reputation before you even take a sip. The five wines are simple yet structured, and although they are still only a few vintages old, they have already attracted attention in the form of awards and accolades. The Viognier and Shiraz deserve special mention. ★ Rising star

Four Seasons Wines Ltd, Village Roti, Taluk Daund, Pune, Maharashtra 412219; www.fourseasonsvineyards.com

Grover Vineyards Karnataka

Grover founder, Kanwar Grover, was a pioneer for the Indian wine industry, having started a vinous endeavor way before its time had come; almost three decades earlier in fact. Bordeaux's Michel Rolland provides consultancy and the Cabernet/Shiraz reds show his signature palate profile. These are good, award-winning wines, and before the competition heated up, they were the undisputed

MANDALA VALLEY
THIS SHIRAZ IS A FULL-BODIED WINE WITH BLACKBERRY FLAVORS

GROVER VINEYARDS
A LIGHT, FRUITY WINE THAT GOES WELL WITH FISH, SEAFOOD, AND ASIAN CUISINE

Indian wine of choice. Cool-climate Karnataka generally seems to score over Nasik, but few winemakers have ventured here, preferring to stick with the more proactive state across the border.

Raghunathapura, Devanahalli, Doddaballapur Road, Doddaballapur, Bangalore 561203; www.groverwines.com

Indage Vintners Maharashtra

The brainchild of Ranjit Chowgule and the first of the Indian wineries, Indage has done it all over the last few decades—winery, bars, and shops—but with little lasting success anywhere. From the award-winning Omar Khayyam sparkling wine to the fairly average Chantilli and Riviera range, followed by poor-quality wine in plastic PET bottles, Indage has finally realized the folly of its ways and has recently relaunched all its labels, with much better wine. The Tiger Hill label is also commendable, but many remain sceptical about whether the future of this house is promising.

Narayangaon, Nashik Pune Highway, Taluka Junnar www.indagevintners.com

Indus Wines Maharashtra

(Mumbai) Dreamz, Indus Wines' entry-level offering is a decent effort, clean and fruit-forward. If books were to be appraised by their covers then these have among the most attractive and Indian-yet-Western contemporary labels: think Nouveau India. Indus's more recent wines have shown improvement, especially the whites. Among the reds, the Cabernet Sauvignon is a good bet—fruit-laden and ripe and without trying too hard to impress. The heavy-bottled, Syrah-based Moksha, is big and bold but will need time (and some work) before it raises eyebrows for the right reasons.

Gate No 1062, Village Murambi, Off. Wadhiware, Taluka Igatpuri, District Nasik 422403; www.induswine.com

Mandala Valley Karnataka

Situated in the hills around the Silicon Valley of India, Bangalore, Mandala Valley has been around for a while now and manages some pretty whistle-wetting-worthy stuff. The Reserve Shiraz is a good show of Mandala's winemaking prowess. For the rest, quality has not entirely been consistent, but given the resolute vision of the proprietor, Ramesh Rao, a wine lover and active participant in the winemaking process, great expectations should be realized soon.

2984, 2nd Floor, 12th Main, Indira Nagar, Bangalore 560008 www.mandalavalley.com

Mercury Maharashtra

Mercury's wines are mostly sold under the Aryaa brand, whose bright and pretty labels are bound to catch the consumer's attention. That said, the wines themselves would be reason enough to buy: they exhibit gentle extraction, soft fruit, and a light, lingering finish. Mercury's good range comprises easy whites, which tease with some residual sugar, and reds, which manage to be fruity and ripe. The Cabernet Sauvignon is peppery, and the Shiraz has nice powdery tannins and a gradual fade. ★ Rising star

10 Mile Ozar Mig, Nashik 422206 22 280 79287

ZAMPA/VALLEE DE VIN
ZAMPAGNE HAS BEEN RENAMED ZAMPA
SOIREE BUT IS STILL MADE USING
THE CHAMPAGNE METHOD

Nine Hills Maharashtra

When drinks giant Diageo pulled out of the local wine market in India, withdrawing their maiden venture Nilaya, all waited to see what direction the Pernod Ricard owned and managed Nine Hills would take. The wines have always lagged behind the competition, but somehow Nine Hills has managed to stand the test of taste and time and survive. Given the strong marketing support from the French multinational, and the strength of international winemaking know-how, this producer will surely be able to turn tables around and find itself more widely sold.

Pernod Ricard India Pvt Ltd, 126-127, Valkhed, Dindori, Nashik 422202; 98 500 76135

Renaissance Maharashtra

Shivaji Aher is a wine enthusiast, and it is this very personal interest that has formed the skeleton for his offerings at Renaissance. The Chenin Blanc is nice and floral-fruity and outshines the Sauvignon Blanc, the Zinfandel rosé, and the Merlot. However, it is the Cabernet Sauvignon that represents the best of the Renaissance house style and philosophy: made in regular and Classique versions, the emphasis is on well-ripened, mature fruits, sometimes a touch jammy. A bit austere perhaps, for some, but still enjoyable.

Gate No 2317, Mumbai-Agra Highway, Ozar (Mig), Nashik 422206; www.renaissancewineryindia.com

Reveillo Maharashtra

One of the currently most raved about wine houses on the Indian scene, Reveillo has quite an admirable and enviable range. All the wines show promise, the Reserve range more so, but then it comes at a price. The Late Harvest is made in tiny quantities, but is worth fighting over. The residual sugar can appear a bit daunting, but it helps enhance the wine's fruitiness, something that a burgeoning Indian palate immensely appreciates. The wines show technical aptitude, but most importantly, they give us a taste of true Indian terroir.

Gate No 71, Gitakunj (Kundewadi), Niphad, Nashik 422303 22 263 70134

Sula Vineyards Maharashtra

Sula Vineyards—the house that single-handedly introduced wine to the Indian masses—is still going strong. Initially lauded for its whites, today Sula has managed to create a balanced and diverse portfolio. The Sula wines—including the original Chenin Blanc, the off-dry white Dindori Reserve Viognier, the mineral-lined Riesling, the plum-laden Cabernet Sauvignon, the spicy rich Dindori Reserve Shiraz, and the Late Harvest Chenin Blanc—are all well-made, structured wines with a sense of Indian terroir. They are a safe reference point for quality Indian wines.

Survey 36/2, Govardhan, Off Gangapur-Savargaon Road, Nashik 422222, Maharashtra; www.sulawines.com

The Good Earth Winery Maharashtra

"Decant before drinking" is the standing instruction from The Good Earth Winery for its range of three: one white (Sauvignon Blanc) and two reds (Shiraz and Cabernet Sauvignon). The wines are serious and strong, with flavor aplenty and pronounced aromatic profiles, all of which show good varietal character. But they take time to express themselves, and the tannins, too, may need some taming. Winter wines for the fireplace could be one description—and so what if India happens to be mostly tropical? After all, the quality of each of the wines in the porftfolio is highly commendable. ★ **Rising star**

C1, Ground Floor, Chaitraban Residency, Aundh, Pune 411007; www.goodearthwinery.com

Vallonné Maharashtra

In spite of a slightly confusing name, Vallonné is poised to become a people's favorite. Shailender Pai, the man behind Vallonné, started out with another successful winery before setting out to make wine "holistically and with a greater vision." The whites are modest, but expressive. In the reds, the Merlot is stunning—a silky wine with a great sense of balance. The other wines are rich with plenty of muscle, and will need some time to evolve and soften. ★ **Rising star**

Gate No 504, Kavnai Slopes, Near Sanjegaon, Igatpuri, Nashik 422402; www.vallonnevineyards.com

Vinsura (Sankalp Winery) Maharashtra

Vinsura is one of the oldest of entrants into the Indian wine business, and, like many others, it started off by supplying quality fruit to the top producers of the region before going solo. Since then, its rise has been slow and a tad sporadic. The wines have shown improvement, but a lot of work remains, some to be done, and some, undone. From the entire range, the sparkling wine stands out, with a nice toasty nose and a persistent effervescence.

CU-31, Vinchur Wine Park, Vinchur , Niphad , Nashik 422305; www.vinsura.com

York Winery Maharashtra

York Winery is a new house, but it could quite easily be one of the best and most prolific houses to make its mark on the market in a long time. Currently, the team here do not make whites. The rosé is good but it is the range of reds that are the show-stoppers: the Reserve versions of both Cabernet Sauvignon and Shiraz are highly commendable. On the whole, this is an excellent effort for the initial vintages. ★ **Rising star**

Gate No 15/2, Gangavarhe Village, Gangapur-Savargaon Road, Nashik 422222, Maharashtra; www.yorkwinery.com

Zampa/Vallée de Vin Maharashtra

For a relatively new set-up, Vallée de Vin has had quite a bit of shuffling and internal movement among its staff. Still, perhaps that is for the best, since the wines—labelled Zampa—have improved incredibly since their first commercial outing. Among the stars are a much-liked pink sparkler called Soirée (its former name of Zampagne flirted dangerously close to you-know-what for the liking of French bureaucrats) and a lovely, fruit-laden Sauvignon Blanc that shows typicity minus all the aggression. On the whole, this is a good portfolio of very approachable wines.

Gate No 967 & 1026, At Post Sanjegaon, Igatpuri, Nashik www.vallee-de-vin.com

SULA VINEYARDS
SULA SAUVIGNON BLANC IS PART OF A RANGE
THAT HAS PROVED POPULAR IN INDIA

CHINA

Just as in so many other respects, when it comes to wine, China is a rapidly growing giant. Like the nation's economy as a whole, China's vineyard area has been growing at a rate of roughly 10% per annum in recent years. According to the OIV, it reached 1.2 million acres (500,000ha) in 2010, though the same body's estimate of wine production at more than 300 million gallons (12 million hectolitres) suggests that less than a fifth of this area was being used for wine production (by comparison, almost a third of Californian grapes are used for raisins). The Chinese wine market has been growing even faster, doubling every five years since the mid-1990s. Domestic production accounts for 95% of Chinese wine consumption, but China is also the second-biggest wine importer in Asia.

In order to understand wine in and from China properly it is essential to become familiar with the Mandarin vocabulary. *Jiu* is the word for alcoholic beverages, while *putao jiu* is the word for grape wine, as opposed to *huang jiu* or rice wine, *pi jiu* or beer, and *bai jiu* or distilled grain spirit. Western readers please note that Chinese writing is based on signs, and *putao jiu* is composed of two signs, the right hand one for *jiu* and the left hand one for *putao,* or grapes.

This explanation may seem unnecessarily detailed, but *putao* derives from *budawaa/badaawa,* the ancient Persian for grapes. This is significant, for the vine was brought to China from the Ferghana Valley in contemporary Uzbekistan and Tajikistan, not far north of Persia, by Zhang Qian, an imperial ambassador, around 126BCE. China's tradition of wine poetry dates back to the 3rd century CE and reaches its high point in the work of Li Bai (701–762). Under Kublai Khan (c.1216–1294), grape wine was used to worship ancestors and wine cellars were constructed under an imperial palace in 1291. This wine culture went into decline during the Ming Dynasty (1368–1644) after the previously preferential taxation of grape wine was abandoned. This was also the time tea established itself as the pre-eminent Chinese drink.

A new beginning came when the dynamic entrepreneur Chang Bishi founded the Changyu Wine Co. in Yantai on the Shandong Peninsula in 1892, his wines winning four gold medals at the Panama-Pacific Exposition in San Francisco in 1915 (for a red wine, a Riesling, a vermouth, and a grape brandy). Changyu remains China's most important winery, which together with Great Wall and Dynasty accounts for more than 50% of national production. Apart from Great Wall, which is entirely Chinese owned, all the nation's major players have significant minority foreign investors. But that foreign influence does not mean modern Chinese wine should be understood as some kind of *jiade,* that is, an inferior copy of a noble original.

Having said that, it *is* an easy mistake for Western tourists to make when confronted with one of China's many wine châteaux and cellars. Even in poor weather the most perfect of these are clearly 1:1 replicas of the "original," but in the right light they look like hyper-real creations that outshine the "real thing." The same applies to packaging, which sometimes slavishly imitates Bordeaux for the same reason as winery architecture; from the Chinese perspective, they are the red wines with the highest reputation. Wine-growing is a different matter, though, since the chemical composition (sugars, acidities, aromas, tannins, etc) of grapes is determined by genetics and by ripening conditions. The bitterly cold winters and humid summers with limited sunshine in many of the 26 Chinese provinces where the vine is cultivated for winemaking lead to grapes with a very different composition to the place that the architecture and packaging imitate.

China's most successful wines are those produced by winemakers who do not slavishly imitate. No doubt they will do even better during the coming years as new economic structures and practices develop. Until recently, all grapes were grown by farmers who leased tiny plots from the state (which owns all land in China). Many of the new vineyards have been planted on land leased by wineries from dozens of farmers. Better control over growing methods will undoubtedly reduce quantitative and qualitative losses due to fungal disease, and opens the door for cultivation focused on optimizing ripeness and balance. For the most dynamic producers, such as Grace Vineyards in Shanxi Province, this makes the production of wines as good as any in the world a real possibility.

At present more energy, ambition, and investment is being poured into red wine production than white, not only because higher prices can be realized, but also because in Chinese culture the color red stands for power and strength. Thanks to their experience with tea

Major grapes

 Reds

Cabernet Franc

Cabernet Gernischt

Cabernet Sauvignon

Merlot

Shiraz

Whites

Chardonnay

Mare's Teat

Vidal

Vintages

We would never imagine a vintage in Southern Italy to have the same characteristics of Bordeaux or the Mosel Valley. Likewise, one cannot generalize about vintages in a country as large and diverse as China. Across the country's 26 provinces there is a gigantic range of geographical and climatic differences, and it is not in the remit of this book to deal with those different provinces one by one.

(on which many of them spend an extraordinary percentage of their income) the Chinese are also familiar with the dominant dry tannins typical in red wines. This preference could well change with time, though, since white wines generally taste better with Chinese food.

It is important to remember that Chinese wine producers are still in the early stages of exploring which grape varieties grow best where—this process only having begun around 1993 when the young Huadong winery in Shandong won its first international awards (its Chardonnay was then as good as many Australian Chardonnays, and very similar in style). The range of conditions, from the semi-alpine vineyards of Yunnan Province, home to Shangri-La winery, to the semi-desert of Xinjiang, where Suntime has large plantings, should provide a wider variety of wines than is currently the case.

How long will it be before climatic profiling identifies ideal locations in China for Riesling, Nebbiolo, Mourvèdre, or the indigenous Mare's Teat? With investors as diverse as the Tsing Tao brewer in Qing Dao/Shandong and Gernot Langes-Swarowski of the Swarowski crystal company having entered the game, it cannot be long before the picture becomes far more complex.

An example of stylistic diversity matching ambition and perfectionism is Gold Ice Wine Valley, northeast of Beijing. In some parts of Europe, the valley's more than 1,000 acres (400ha) of Vidal vines might count as an entire appellation. And, true to this idea, it only markets one type of wine: Icewine made from naturally frozen grapes in the German and Canadian tradition. The top Gold Label is one of the world's best Icewines. But, thanks to the Chinese fixation with red wines, it has failed to receive the domestic acclaim it deserves.

GRACE VINEYARD
GRACE VINEYARD IS ARGUABLY CHINA'S MOST CONSISTENTLY HIGH-QUALITY WINE PRODUCER

Bodega Langes Hebei Province
Gernot Langes-Swarowski, owner of the Swarowski crystal company, invested $30 million US dollars in the 500 acre (200ha) Bodega Langes in Hebei Province. A sizeable chunk of that cash went into the construction of an Italianate palazzo. Sometimes the vineyards ring with the sound of Viennese waltzes, and the Cabernet Sauvignon, Cabernet Franc, and Merlot blend is another attempt to imitate Bordeaux in China. It would be hard to get more multicultural than this.

Changli, Hebei Province
www.bodega-langes.com

Changyu Winery Shandong Province
Founded in Yantai in 1892 by Chang Bashi, Changyu Winery is not only China's oldest modern winery, it is also the major force in the modernization of the nation's wine industry and its push for a piece of the action in all major wine markets. The elegant, supple, spicy Cabernet Gernischt (a variety of obscure origins with aromas reminiscent of Cabernet Sauvignon, but more spicy), from the joint venture Château Changyu Castel just outside Yantai, is currently the top red wine. However, the top bottling of Icewine (Gold Label) from the 940 acre (380ha) Golden Ice Wine Valley estate is even more impressive. Since 2005, a third of the company's stock has been held by the Italian Illva Saronno Group (owners of Cinzano) and 10% by the International Finance Corp.

Yantai, Shandong Province
www.changyu.com.cn

Château Changyu AFIP Global
Beijing Hebei Province
The most ambitious of Changyu Winery's joint ventures, Château Changyu AFIP Global Beijing resides in a 1:1 replica of a Bordeaux château one-and-a-half hours' drive down a brand new highway northeast of Beijing. This perfect embodiment of the current Chinese wine zeitgeist is named after the nationalities of the foreign investors: America, France, Italy, and Portugal. The first vines were

planted in 2005, so chief winemaker Gérard Fagnoni's first bottlings under this label are from Yantai-sourced grapes. Top of the small range is the imposing and tannic Cabernet Sauvignon Master's Choice. A five-star hotel and golf course are part of the complex.

Mi Yun, Beijing
www.changyu.com.cn

Dragon Seal Beijing
Founded in central Beijing by a French missionary in 1910, the sizeable Dragon Seal winery was relaunched in its present form in 1987 with Pernod Ricard as partner. The company has since sold its holding, but the chief winemaker it appointed, Jérôme Sabaté, remains. Sabaté makes no bones that his home country is Dragon Seal's role model for the Hualai Reserve Cabernet Sauvignon and Reserve Chardonnay. The regular bottlings are much less special than these well-made clones of French originals.

Haidian District, Beijing
www.dragonseal.com

Dynasty Hebei Province
A French-Chinese joint venture established in 1980, Dynasty's founding partner, Rémy Cointreau, still holds 33% of the stock, but the rest of the shares change hands frequently thanks to the winery's listing on the Hong Kong stock exchange. The simple quality bottlings sold in Asian stores and Chinese restaurants around the globe are just that, simple. More emphasis on freshness would do them a lot of good.

Tianjin, Hebei Province
www.dynasty-wines.com

Grace Vineyard Shanxi Province
Grace Vineyard is now directed by Judy Leisner, the dynamic daughter of the supermarket magnate who founded the winery in 1997. Since Leisner appointed Australian Ken Murchison (of Portree Vineyard in Victoria) before the 2006 vintage, Grace has clearly

CHATEAU CHANGYU AFIP GLOBAL
THE MASTER'S CHOICE IS AN IMPOSING WINE WITH AN EQUALLY IMPOSING PRICE TAG

been China's quality leader if you compare entire ranges rather than just limited-edition bottlings. However, Grace also boasts some excellent top wines, most notably Deep Blue—a rich, plush blend of Merlot with Cabernets Sauvignon and Franc. New plantings designed for precision viticulture with varieties such as Riesling and Shiraz promise another leap in quality.

Dongjia, Taigu County, Shanxi Province
www.grace-vineyard.com

Great Wall Hebei Province
Unlike its major competitors, the huge Great Wall winery is still 100% Chinese-owned. It boasts the largest winery building in Asia and a barrique cellar that looks like an exact copy of Château Lafite Rothschild. The regular Cabernet Sauvignon sold in Asian stores around the world is fresh and fruity, tasting rather like a regular wine of this grape from Chile. The top bottlings are far more powerful, tannic, and austere, so if you enjoy drinking lean, traditional-style red Bordeaux, they might impress.

Tianjin, Hebei Province
www.huaxia-greatwall.com.cn

Huadong Winery Shandong Province
Founded by the late Hong Kong-based entrepreneur Michael Parry in 1985, Huadong was the first Chinese winery to attract international praise following the adoption of China's Reform and Opening policies.

The Australian-style wines made by Australian flying winemakers have been replaced by wines that more closely conform to the French-inspired Chinese norm under chief winemaker, Gloria Xia.

Qingdao, Shandong Province
www.huadongwinery.com

Shangri-La Wine
In the unlikely setting of the mountainous Yunnan Province, Shangri-La makes some of the best Bordeaux-style reds in China and, unusually for China, they also age very well. The beautiful Italian designer-style packaging makes an odd contrast to the taste of the wines.

Shangri-La Economic Development Zone, Diqing, Yuannan;
www.shangeri-la.com

Vini Suntime
Although its first vintage was 1998, the huge Vini Suntime winery in the remote Xinjiang Uyghur Autonomous Region in China's far west already processes the grapes from 25,000 acres (10,000ha) of vineyards. Wine-growing in this desert environment is made possible by irrigation waters from Tian Shan Mountains, and the result is robust red wines with more body and ripeness than is usual in modern China.

51 Wuyi Road, Manas County, Xinjiang
994 663 3638

GREAT WALL
GREAT WALL HAS HAD SOME INTERNATIONAL SUCCESS WITH ITS BORDEAUX-STYLE WINES

Not Bordeaux but Beijing—Château Changyu AFIP Global Beijing rises above the vines in Hebei Province.

JAPAN

Japan's role as a leading consumer of fine wines is well known internationally. But its achievements as a quality producer are almost completely unknown. The grape vine came to Japan from China along with the Kanji writing system, Buddhism, and much else from the 6th century onward, but the modern wine industry dates back to the late 19th century in Katsunuma in Yamanashi prefecture. Today, wine is grown in 23 prefectures, but Yamanashi, two hours' drive northwest of Tokyo, remains the center, with roughly a fifth of the 57,000 acres (23,000ha) under vine and almost half of the 200 or so wineries. Japan might well have more vineyards were it not for the scarcity of land in a country where mountains occupy more than two-thirds of the land mass.

Major grapes

 Reds

Cabernet Sauvignon

Dornfelder

Merlot

Muscat Bailey A

Zweigelt

 Whites

Chardonnay

Gewürztraminer

Kerner

Koshu

Vintages

Japan's extreme weather conditions and humid climate mean that a producer's throughness in protecting their grapes and combating fungal disease can be more important than vintage. However, 2009's dry and sunny August and September made for near ideal ripening conditions, and fungal disease was not a problem, resulting in one of the best vintages in years. Although 2008 did not quite reach the same heights, a moderate summer and harvest rains made for a considerably better vintage than 2007.

The monsoon climate, humid summer, and frequent fall typhoons pose Japanese wine-growers considerable problems, particularly in combating fungal disease, which regularly threatens both quality and crop levels. However, Japanese perfectionism and a good deal of experimentation during recent years has made the nation Asia's most successful wine producer.

To understand Japanese wine it is necessary to recognize how wine entered the modern Japanese consciousness. European wine first made an impact in Japan around 1870 during the early years of the Meiji period. At that time, the country was opening up to the outside world after more than two centuries of isolation, and was rapidly adopting Western science and industry in order to avoid being colonized. Wine was a product that symbolized *bunmai kaika* (modern civilization) with its standards and progress. Another part of this process was the official ending of the prohibition of meat eating. Abruptly the Japanese people were actively encouraged to change their traditional diet and customs. These changes were no less fundamental—and much more sudden—than those during the period 1,000 years before when Chinese customs, ideas, and methods were imported.

A second period of extremely rapid economic growth followed Japan's disastrous experiment with imperialism. European wine returned during the run up to the 1964 Tokyo Olympics, during which the market was opened for imported alcoholic beverages. Since then, wine has been an important high-status, luxury product and gift, particularly for business men, although the latter tend to view Japanese wines as inherently inferior to the "real thing" from France or Italy.

Japan's climate not only causes its wine producers problems, it also makes wine consumption highly seasonal. The established "wine season" is the last three months of the year, and in recent years a shorter secondary season has developed in the spring. The enormous

consumption of beer during the Japanese summer is also a result of a combination of climatic and cultural factors. Interestingly, wineries owned by major breweries account for almost half of all Japanese wine sales.

Another change in recent years has been the growing number of young women who frequently consume wine. The purchasing decisions of male consumers tend to be strongly influenced by the major international critics and the opinions of local top sommeliers, therefore favoring powerful, tannic reds. Young women, by contrast, are most likely to seek information on the internet and look for wines with lightness, subtlety, and a cool image. A major shift in the nature of wine consumption in Japan seems to be under way. The fact that a wine *manga* (graphic novel) with the improbable name of *Les Gouttes de Dieu* (The Droplets of God) has a significant influence upon new wine consumers looks like a sure sign of this.

The fixation with France in older consumers has had a huge effect upon the development of Japanese winemaking. For decades, the major French grape varieties, particularly Cabernet Sauvignon, Merlot, and Chardonnay, offered easily the best chance of success for local winemakers, though there are rather few locations where they grow and ripen well. The identification of those locations, plus a great deal of fine tuning to vineyard cultivation techniques, and the increasing recognition that trying to slavishly imitate France is not a good idea, has enabled some impressive wines to be made from these grapes. They sell out for high prices on the domestic market.

In recent years the varieties that are best adapted to the Japanese climate—the indigenous white Koshu and red Muscat Bailey A (originally bred as a table grape)—have finally received more attention from talented winemakers, leading to the development of a dizzying range of new styles. Nowhere are Japan's winemaking achievements on better display than in the new Koshus. The best

Koshu wines used to be dessert wines made by selecting berries with noble rot and imitating Sauternes. Today many producers large and small make *"sur lie"* wines. These are aged on the yeast lees accentuating the Koshu grape's delicate fruit character and pronounced minerally character.

In many regions the possibilities offered by the wealth of indigenous grape varieties, such as those known collectively as *amabudo* (mountain grapes), remain largely unexplored. However, winemakers on the cool-climate northern island of Hokkaido are experimenting with a wide range of grape varieties from Northern Europe such as Zweigelt, Dornfelder, Kerner, and Gewürztraminer. No doubt this process of experimentation will go much further as Japanese winemakers recognize that the obsession with French role models has not helped the development of their industry.

Japanese wine's share of the domestic market has now risen to almost 40%. That growth is thanks, at least in part, to the introduction of an integrity of origin policy by some of the larger wineries. For decades before that, Japanese wine was often made from imported grapes or blends of domestic and imported wine. As respect for its production grows, Japan's wine industry seems destined for moderate quantitive growth, but a further quantum leap in quality and diversity.

GRACE WINERY
FEW JAPANESE WINERIES CAN COMPETE
WITH GRACE'S MASTERY OF KOSHU

Château Mercian

Château Mercian is a large, extremely professional winery. It makes a huge range of good, interesting wines from the Koshu grape, including the dry Sur Lie, Barrel Fermented; Kiiroka, the sweet Toriibira Vineyard bottling; the sparkling Katsunuma no Awa; and the semi-rosé Gris de Gris. Under director Katsuhisa Fujino and chief winemaker Kousai Ajimura, Château Mercian's rich and silky Signature Merlot from the Kikyogahara Vineyard has become arguably Asia's greatest red wine. The elegant Private Reserve Chardonnay from the Hokushin Vineyard (also in Nagano Prefecture) is one of the continent's finest dry whites.

1425-1 Shimoiwasakai, Katsanuma, Yamanashi Prefecture 409-1313; www.mercian.co.jp

Diamond Winery/Chanter

"Nous sommes une grande domaine garagiste!" is how Burgundy-trained Yoshio Anemiya describes his small family-owned winery. He boldly calls his elegant, medium-bodied *sur lie* vinified "Chanter YA" Koshu, though his remarkably powerful and subtle barrique-fermented Hishiyama Vineyard Koshu is the more extraordinary wine. Thanks to low yields and Burgundy-inspired winemaking his "Chanter YA" Muscat Bailey "AYcube" red wine shows what the Muscat Bailey can do when quality is pursued uncompromisingly. It combines the silkiness of Pinot with a spiciness reminiscent of Zinfandel.

880 Shimoiwasaki, Katsunuma, Yamanashi Prefecture 409-1313; www.wine.or.jp

Grace Winery

Grace Winery's owner, Shigekazu Misawa, believes in the indigenous Koshu grape with almost religious fervor. From the lively, off-dry Gris de Koshu to the concentrated, racy, bone dry Cuvée Misawa from Toriibira Vineyard, Misawa's wines define modern Japanese Koshu. New wines from the high-altitude Akeno Vineyards—the pristine, steely Kayagatake, and the more supple Kurajirushi—are impressive examples of cool-climate Koshu further extending this dynamic producer's range. The red Cuvée Misawa is a sleek, dry blend of Cabernet Sauvignon and Merlot, with better harmony and significantly riper aromas than is the norm for such blends in Japan.

173 Todoroki, Katsunuma, Yamanashi Prefecture 409-1315 www.grace-wine.jp

Ikeda Winery

Toshikazu Ikeda's small winery makes a small range of impeccable dry white and red wines, which are full of fruit and beautifully balanced. The new Yama Sauvignon, is a rich, spicy red made from a cross of the Japanese *Vitis coignetiae* with Cabernet Sauvignon.

266-4 Osade, Katsunuma, Yamanashi Prefecture 409-1303 ikedawinery@katsunuma.ne.jp

Katsunuma Winery/Aruga Branca

Katsunuma's Yuji Aruga and his winemaker Shigeyuki Hirayama are best known for their joint venture, Magrez-Aruga, a Koshu from the Isehara Vineyard made with Bordeaux producer, Bernard Magrez. It is a good introduction to modern Koshu, but you pay for the Magrez name. At least as interesting are the winery's own Koshu wines marketed under the Aruga Branca label.

371 Shimoiwasakai, Katsunuma, Yamanashi Prefecture 409-1313; www.kastsunuma-winery.com

Marifuji Winery/Rubaiyat

"Maison fondée en 1890" stands proudly on the wall of Marifuji, an excellent small winery idyllically situated in the vineyards of Katsunuma. Haruo Omura's *sur lie* Koshu is the most consistent of the top-quality wines from this indigenous grape made in Yamanashi Prefecture. It invariably combines concentration and supple elegance with a pronounced mineral character. It is primarily vinified in 2,377 gallon (9,000 litre) enameled steel tanks made for the saké industry. Omura also makes interesting red wines from a wide variety of grapes.

780 Fuji, Katsunuma, Yamanashi Prefecture 409-1314 www.rubaiyat.jp

Suntory

The Suntory drinks giant has interests ranging from health food to beer and whisky (many of good or excellent quality). It also owns wineries in Nagano, Okayama, Yamagata, and Yamanashi Prefectures, and produces a wide range of well-made modern wines from local and imported grapes. Although the Special Reserve from the Tomi Vineyard is a serious attempt to make a world-class Bordeaux blend, in terms of media profile, it has been overtaken by top wines from competitors.

No visitor facilities www.suntory.com

CHATEAU MERCIAN
KIKYOGAHARA MERLOT IS SOFTER AND
LIGHTER THAN A TYPICAL BORDEAUX MERLOT

This huge country has a diverse range of wine regions and a fully fledged fine wine dimension. Despite this, however, it has primarily been known overseas as a source of fruity, tasty, inexpensive branded wines—"bottled sunshine" that has been devoured hungrily.

Wine-growing in Australia dates back to the mid-19th century, when early European settlers planted vineyards. Australia's historically important wine regions are therefore located close to the major cities in the southeast—the area where Europeans first settled.

The modern fine wine scene owes a great deal to the success of dry wines from three legendary winemakers—Colin Preece, Max Schubert, and Maurice O'Shea. Over the last 40 years, Australian fine wine has continued to grow into a diverse and healthy industry, with hundreds of high-achieving winegrowers and some promising new wine regions propelling it forward.

Established regions, such as the Barossa Valley, McLaren Vale, Hunter Valley, and Clare Valley, were joined by newcomers, such as Margaret River and the reborn Yarra, in the early 1970s. These were followed by the Mornington Peninsula, Heathcote, Tasmania, and Canberra District, to name just a few, and Australia now boasts over 60 GIs (geographical indicators—the official term for wine regions).

Australia's strengths include a diverse range of Shiraz and Chardonnay, dry Riesling, Hunter Valley Semillon, and Cabernet Sauvignon from Margaret River and Coonawarra. There are also some fantastic fortified wines, increasingly promising sparkling wines, and even some very stylish Pinot Noirs from the cooler areas.

Issues such as drought, bush fires, a wine surplus, and global warming are a continuing challenge to Australian winegrowers, but they have proven remarkably resourceful in the past, so there is no reason why they should not continue to thrive in years to come.

AUSTRALIA

NEW SOUTH WALES

New South Wales

Australia's most densely populated state, New South Wales, is where the Australian wine story began back in the early 19th century. The Great Dividing Range and the Southern Alps create a broad range of climatic zones that are capable of supporting many different wine styles. The hot, wet Hunter Valley is the best-known region in the state, famous for its ageworthy, unoaked Semillons and Shiraz. Crossing over the Dividing Range, Mudgee and Orange are cooler regions, where a variety of distinctive red and white wines are produced. Finally, the Southern New South Wales Zone is home to the highly promising Canberra District, Hilltops, and Tumbarumba, which are emerging as increasingly important cooler-climate regions.

Major grapes

 Reds

Cabernet Sauvignon

Semillon

Shiraz

 Whites

Chardonnay

Riesling

Sauvignon Blanc

Vintages

2009
Early days yet, but looking promising for most regions, especially Hunter Semillon and early-picked Mudgee and Orange reds.

2008
A terrible year. The Hunter and Mudgee had the worst vintage in memory, with a cool summer followed by lots of rain.

2007
Like much of Australia, this area struggled with the heat, but good vintages came from the Central Ranges regions.

2006
Superb vintage in the Hunter, and pretty good elsewhere.

2005
Very promising vintage in the Hunter for both whites and reds. A good year for the rest of the state, too.

2004
A difficult vintage in the Hunter, with summer heatwaves and harvest rain. A better year in the other NSW regions.

Australia's first vines were planted in New South Wales by European settlers, way back in 1788. Unfortunately, this first attempt failed and it wasn't until the early 1800s that John MacArthur established Australia's first commercial vineyard on his Camden Park property, a short distance southwest of Sydney. Despite this early start, however, New South Wales has since lagged behind South Australia and Victoria in the development of its wine industry.

The most famous wine region in the state is the Hunter Valley, where the first vines were planted in 1830. It is an anomaly of a region—the hot, wet climate would seem to be entirely unsuited to quality wine production—but the Hunter is responsible for two of Australia's most distinctive fine wine styles. The first is Hunter Semillon, which ripens with low potential alcohol and high acid, making a lean, bracing wine that matures beautifully into toasty richness. The second is Hunter Shiraz, a medium-bodied interpretation of this variety that has the potential to age into a complex, gamey, yet elegant, maturity. With its proximity to Sydney, the Hunter is also a focus for wine tourism, but despite the touristy feel of the region, some serious wines are being made here.

Just over the Dividing Range from the Hunter Valley lie three regions that together form the Central Ranges Zone: Mudgee, Orange, and Cowra. Here, the climate is moderated by altitude.

Mudgee, the largest of the three, is capable of making superb red wines, mainly from Shiraz and Cabernet Sauvignon, and has a tradition of wine-growing stretching back to the 1840s. Orange is the coolest of the three. It is not well known as a region in its own right and it has relatively few wineries, but it is an important source of cool-climate fruit: even varieties such as Sauvignon Blanc do well here. Cowra is the warmest of the Central Ranges regions, due to its lower altitude, and Chardonnay is the specialty here.

Moving south and west, the large Southern New South Wales Zone includes three particularly exciting regions. Canberra District, just north of Canberra, was pioneered by star winery Clonakilla in the 1970s. It is a relatively new region and has an interesting range of mostly cool micro-climates, with Shiraz and Riesling being the most promising varieties. It is now home to a number of high-achieving boutique wineries. Hilltops, a short distance northwest, is a growing region with a moderately cool continental climate. Just 30 acres (12ha) were planted in 1989 and now there are more than 988 acres (400ha), specializing in Shiraz, Cabernet Sauvignon, and Chardonnay. The third district, Tumbarumba, is a particularly cool, alpine climate that has proved to be a great source of sparkling base wines and elegant Chardonnays. It is also showing potential for Pinot Noir. The hot, irrigated district of Riverina is a mass-producing area that borders with Victoria.

Allandale Hunter Valley

A small boutique winery in the Hunter Valley, Allandale has developed quite a reputation for its complex, full-flavored Chardonnays since its establishment in 1978. This reputation has achieved continuity through winemaker Bill Sneddon, who has been at Allandale since 1986. As is often the case with many wineries in this area, fruit from the estate's 17 acres (7ha) of vineyards is supplemented with grapes purchased from growers in the Hunter, Mudgee, and other areas.

132 Lovedale Rd, Lovedale, NSW 2320
www.allandalewinery.com.au

Audrey Wilkinson Hunter Valley

Audrey Wilkinson, a Hunter Valley pioneer from the 19th century, established this beautifully situated Hunter Valley winery, in the foothills of the Brokenback mountain range. It was originally part of the Pepper Tree group, but since 2004, it has been under the ownership of Brian Agnew. The wines, all made from estate fruit, come in two ranges: the Audrey Series, and the Reserve Range. Pick of the bunch are the Semillons, made in traditional Hunter style. The Lake Shiraz, with spicy, earthy depth, is also impressive.

DeBeyers Rd, Pokolbin, NSW 2320
www.audreywilkinson.com.au

Barwang Hilltops

Now owned by McWilliam's, Barwang was originally planted by Peter Robertson. He was the first to plant in the Young region of New South Wales, which lies along the southwest slopes of the Great Dividing Range. Under McWilliam's, the vineyard area has expanded from 32 acres (13ha) to over 247 acres (100ha), but wine quality has not been compromised. Wines are made from both Hilltops and Tumbarumba fruit: look out for the spicy, peppery Hilltops Shiraz and the elegantly balanced Tumbarumba Chardonnay.

Barwang Rd, Young, NSW 2594
www.mcwilliams.com.au

Bimbadgen Hunter Valley

This striking Hunter Valley winery, with its imposing bell tower and faux-Tuscan architecture, has been through a number of name changes and ownership shifts in its time. The vineyards, planted in the 1960s and originally a source of grapes for other wineries, are very good and now form the basis of the Bimbadgen wine range. A typical, Hunter-style Shiraz and a light but ageworthy Semillon are the highlights.

790 McDonalds Rd, Pokolbin, NSW 2320;
www.bimbadgen.com.au

Botobolar Mudgee

Botobolar's claim to fame is that it is Australia's first organic vineyard. The estate's 54 acres (22ha) of vines, in the Mudgee region, have been cultivated organically since they were planted in 1971. As well as making a conventional range of red and whites, Botobolar also makes a preservative-free red, with no added sulfur dioxide.

89 Botobolar Rd, Mudgee, NSW 2850
www.botobolar.com

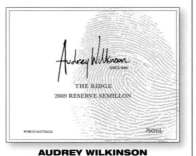

AUDREY WILKINSON
THIS CLASSIC HUNTER SEMILLON CAN BE CELLARED FOR AT LEAST 10 YEARS

CASELLA
THIS EASY DRINKING RED HAS PROVED POPULAR IN MANY COUNTRIES

Brindabella Hills Canberra District

Founder Dr. Roger Harris has a PhD in chemistry, as well as a winemaking degree. He initially tried growing grapes here, 15.5 miles (25km) north of Canberra, as a kind of experiment in the late 1980s. More than 20 years later, it is fair to say that the results have been positive: the 12 acre (5ha) vineyard, on granitic soils, produces successful Shiraz, Sangiovese, Riesling, Sauvignon Blanc, and Pinot Gris, as well as a Chardonnay/Viognier blend called Aureus. The reds, meanwhile, are carefully aged in French and American oak for 1–2 years.

156 Woodgrove Rd, via Hall, NSW 2618
www.brindabellahills.com.au

Brokenwood Hunter Valley

Brokenwood was founded in 1970 by a consortium of three wine-loving lawyers, which included the famed wine writer James Halliday (who sold his shares in 1983). The distinctive winery was built in 1975, and in 1978 the famous Graveyard Vineyard was purchased. Since then, this has been the source of one of Australia's iconic wines: the elegant, ageworthy Graveyard Shiraz, which is known for its restraint, concentration, and complexity. Iain Riggs, the current custodian, joined as winemaker in 1982. Since then, Brokenwood has expanded its production to include wines from other premium regions. Still, it is the Graveyard Shiraz and ILR Reserve Semillon, fresh and pure when young and complex and toasty when aged, that are the stars of the show here.

401-427 McDonalds Rd, Pokolbin, NSW 2320
www.brokenwood.com.au

Capercaillie Hunter Valley

Originally from Scotland, Alasdair Sutherland had already accumulated 30 years of experience in the wine industry when he founded Capercaillie in 1995. Since then, the 12 acres (5ha) of estate fruit (from a vineyard planted in Lovedale in 1970) have supplied about one-third of the winery's needs, with the remainder being sourced from vineyards around New South Wales and South Australia. Sutherland's Scottish heritage is reflected in the estate's name and the distinctly Gaelic-sounding names given to the wines. The star wine, from a broad, eclectic range, is the 100% Hunter Ghillie Shiraz, but the less expensive Ceilidh Shiraz also impresses.

4 Londons Rd, Lovedale, NSW 2325
www.capercailliewine.com.au

Casella Riverina

The Casella story is a remarkable one. Filippo and Maria Casella came to Australia from Sicily in the late 1950s, and their family eventually became grape growers in the Riverina region. But it was the launch of the [yellow tail] brand, with its famous kangaroo label, and the explosive growth that it enjoyed in the US, that made Casella the behemoth it is today—it now crushes just shy of one-tenth of Australia's total grape output each vintage. The range has expanded to take in a number of varieties, but it is the signature Shiraz, with its sweet, smooth, moreish berry fruit profile and significant residual sugar, that has the most fans.

Wakley Rd, Yenda, NSW 2681
www.casellawines.com

NEW SOUTH WALES

The largest region in New South Wales is the irrigated Riverland, in the center of the state. This a hot area producing large volumes of inexpensive wine, much of which ends up in the big brands. More interesting is the string of regions running along the Great Dividing Range, where altitude helps to moderate the temperature and makes fine wine production possible. Running almost in a line are Tumbarumba, Canberra District, Hilltops, Cowra, Orange, and Mudgee. The anomaly here is the Hunter Valley, which has a damp, warm, subtropical climate and yet still makes some of Australia's most interesting wines. With its proximity to Sydney, this historically important region is also a key wine-tourism destination.

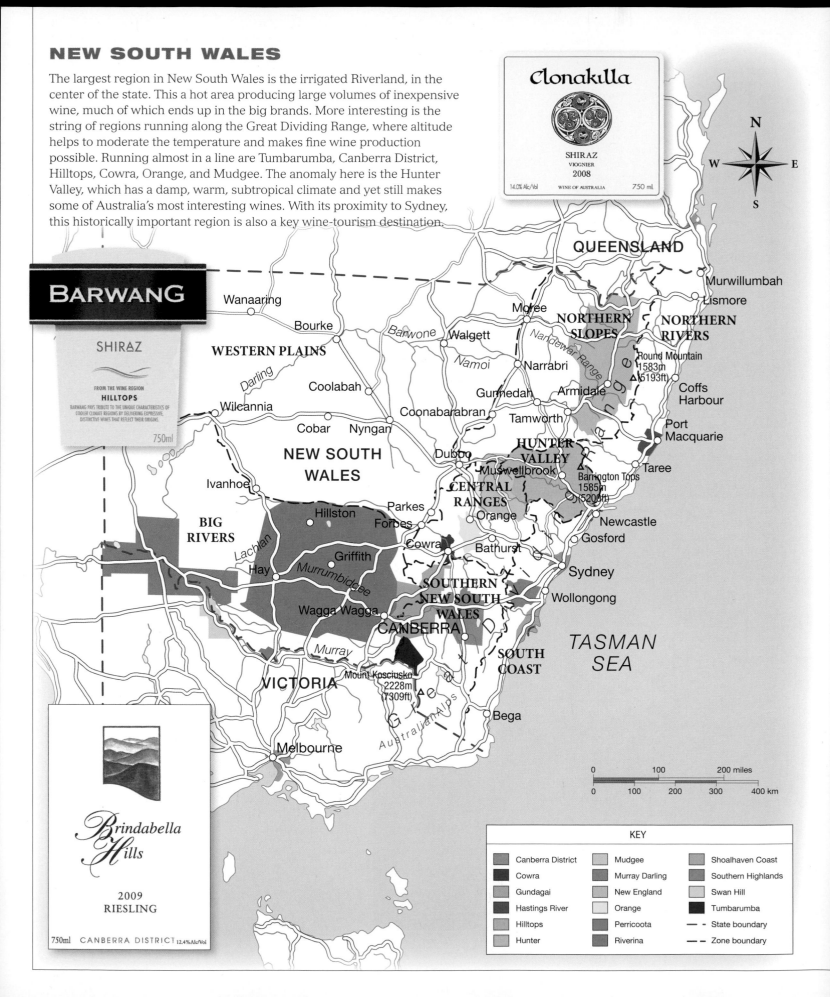

KEY

Canberra District	Mudgee	Shoalhaven Coast
Cowra	Murray Darling	Southern Highlands
Gundagai	New England	Swan Hill
Hastings River	Orange	Tumbarumba
Hilltops	Perricoota	- - - State boundary
Hunter	Riverina	— — Zone boundary

Clonakilla
SHIRAZ
VIOGNIER
2008
14.0% Alc/Vol   WINE OF AUSTRALIA   750 mL

BARWANG
SHIRAZ
FROM THE WINE REGION
HILLTOPS
BARWANG PAYS TRIBUTE TO THE UNIQUE CHARACTERISTICS OF COOLER CLIMATE REGIONS BY DELIVERING EXPRESSIVE, DISTINCTIVE WINES THAT REFLECT THEIR ORIGINS.
750ml

Brindabella Hills
2009
RIESLING
750ml   CANBERRA DISTRICT 12.4% Alc/Vol

HUNTER VALLEY

The best-known wine region in New South Wales, Hunter Valley consists of two separate regions, the Upper Hunter and the Lower Hunter. The latter is the most important, and is home to most of the wineries. The vineyards and wineries are almost all located in a pretty much contiguous block northwest of the town of Cessnock. This area is far from ideal for viticulture, with a subtropical climate, and most of the year's rainfall occurring close to harvesttime. Although this can lead to some uneven vintages, the Hunter Valley produces some excellent wines.

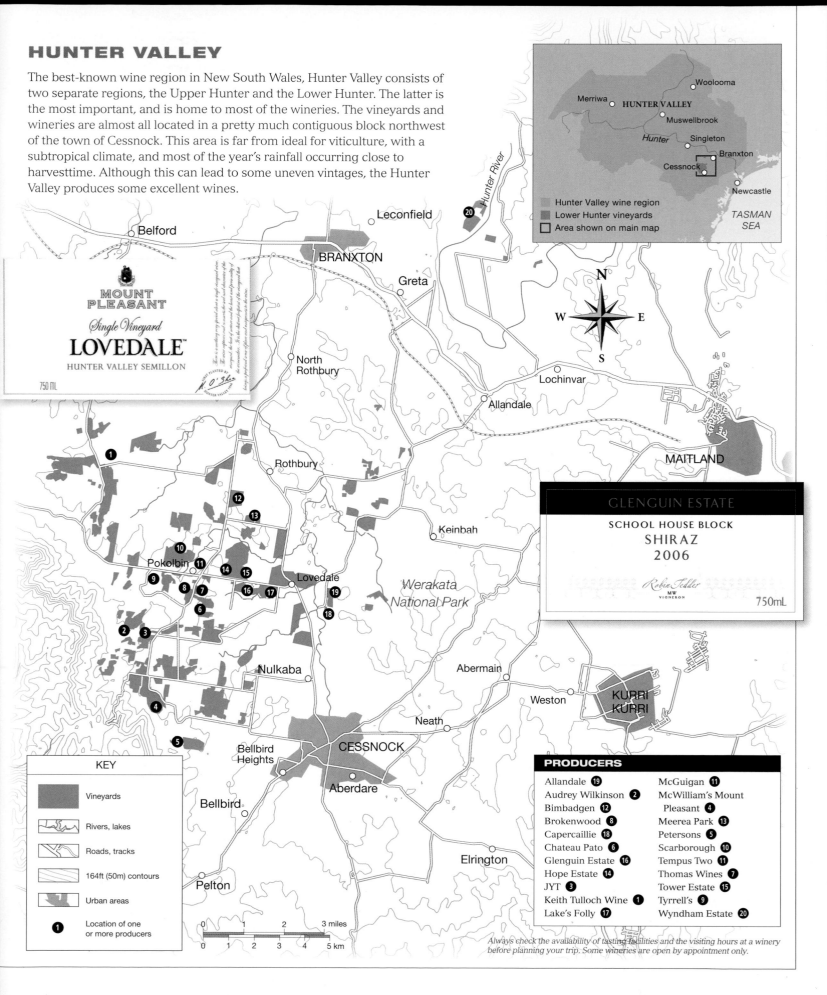

HUNTER VALLEY

- Hunter Valley wine region
- Lower Hunter vineyards
- Area shown on main map

Places: Woolooma, Merriwa, Muswellbrook, Hunter, Singleton, Branxton, Cessnock, Newcastle, TASMAN SEA

MOUNT PLEASANT
Single Vineyard
LOVEDALE™
HUNTER VALLEY SEMILLON
750 ML

GLENGUIN ESTATE
SCHOOL HOUSE BLOCK
SHIRAZ
2006
Robin Tedder
MW
VIGNERON
750mL

KEY

- Vineyards
- Rivers, lakes
- Roads, tracks
- 164ft (50m) contours
- Urban areas
- ❶ Location of one or more producers

Map labels: Belford, Leconfield, BRANXTON, Greta, North Rothbury, Lochinvar, Allandale, Rothbury, Keinbah, MAITLAND, Pokolbin, Lovedale, Werakata National Park, Nulkaba, Abermain, Weston, KURRI KURRI, Neath, Bellbird Heights, CESSNOCK, Aberdare, Bellbird, Elrington, Pelton, Hunter River

PRODUCERS

Allandale	❶⑲	McGuigan	⑪
Audrey Wilkinson	❷	McWilliam's Mount	
Bimbadgen	⑫	Pleasant	❹
Brokenwood	❽	Meerea Park	⑬
Capercaillie	⑱	Petersons	❺
Chateau Pato	❻	Scarborough	⑩
Glenguin Estate	⑯	Tempus Two	⑪
Hope Estate	⑭	Thomas Wines	❼
JYT	❸	Tower Estate	⑮
Keith Tulloch Wine	❶	Tyrrell's	❾
Lake's Folly	⑰	Wyndham Estate	⑳

0 1 2 3 miles
0 1 2 3 4 5 km

Always check the availability of tasting facilities and the visiting hours at a winery before planning your trip. Some wineries are open by appointment only.

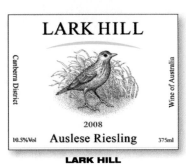

LARK HILL

THIS LUSCIOUS DESSERT WINE IS GERMANIC
IN BOTH NAME AND NATURE

Chalkers Crossing Hilltops

French-born and Bordeaux-trained winemaker Celine
Rousseau is establishing quite a reputation for the
Chalkers Crossing wines. The winery is based in the cool
Hilltops region of New South Wales, roughly halfway
between Sydney and Canberra, but grapes are also
sourced from another cool-climate region, Tumbarumba,
which produces excellent Chardonnay, Pinot Noir, and
Sauvignon Blanc grapes. The first wines were made here
in 2000, and in a relatively short space of time, the winery
has won a devoted following. ★ **Rising star**

285 Henry Lawson Way, Young, NSW 2594
www.chalkerscrossing.com.au

Chateau Pato Hunter Valley

A small, high-quality boutique operation based in the heart
of the Hunter, with just 10 acres (4ha) under vine. The
winery was founded in 1980 by the late David Paterson,
and winemaking is now in the hands of his son, Nicholas,
who has also worked at Brokenwood and Tyrrells, as well
as consulting elsewhere. Most of the grapes are sold, but
a small amount of ageworthy, high-end Shiraz is made
each year from 20-year-old, dry-grown vines. It is well
worth the effort required to seek it out.

Thompson's Rd, Pokolbin, NSW 2321
02 4998 7634

Clonakilla Canberra District

Almost 40 years ago, research scientist David Kirk
decided that Murrumbateman, a cool area 25 miles (40km)
north of Canberra, would be a good place to grow wine
grapes, and he was right. He planted Cabernet Sauvignon
and Riesling in 1971 and the first commercial vintage was
in 1976. Today, the winemaking is in the hands of David's
theologically trained son, Tim, and Clonakilla is rightly
regarded as one of Australia's top wineries. The star wine
here is the ageworthy, elegant Shiraz Viognier (since
1992), which has more than a hint of northern Rhône
focus to it. More recent additions to the range, including
a well-defined, intensely peachy Viognier and the O'Riada
Shiraz, are also top notch. The more affordable Hilltops
Shiraz is an excellent introduction to the Clonakilla
style, offering lovely, focused, subtly meaty dark fruits.
Production is small, but these wines are worth sourcing.

3 Crisps Lane, Murrumbateman, NSW 2582
www.clonakilla.com.au

Cumulus Orange

Cumulus was born in 2004 when the insurance company
Assetinsure bought what was previously Reynolds wines
—then in liquidation—and appointed ex-Rosemount
winemaker Philip Shaw to head up the business. The
majority shareholder is now Jo Berardo, who also owns
several wine businesses in Portugal. Cumulus is based
in Orange, the high-altitude, cool-climate region in the
New South Wales highlands, and has just over 1,236 acres
(500ha) of vineyards. The wines, with their quirky,
intriguing labels, are precise and fresh, with a focus on
prime fruit. Two ranges are available: Climbing, higher-
end wines from Orange vineyards over 1,969ft (600m),
and Rolling, from slightly lower vineyards that are
labeled as Central Ranges.

2416 Davys Plains Rd, Cudal via Orange, NSW 2864
www.cumuluswines.com.au

DE BORTOLI

ONE OF AUSTRALIA'S MOST FAMOUS
DESSERT WINES AND DESERVEDLY SO

De Bortoli Riverina

There are two faces to De Bortoli. First, there is the huge
winery in the Riverina that produces around 4.5 million
cases a year, and second there is the more fine wine-
focused Yarra operation. As well as inexpensive branded
wines, the Riverina winery is also responsible for Noble
One, which, since its first vintage in 1982, has been one of
Australia's most revered sweet wines. A rich, botrytized
Semillon of great complexity, Noble One has the potential
to develop in bottle. Also of note is the Black Noble, a
delicious solera-style sweet wine, which is also based on
Semillon, and the port-style Old Boys 21 years.

De Bortoli Rd, Bilbul, NSW 2680
www.debortoli.com.au

Glenguin Estate Hunter Valley

Robin Tedder is an Australian winemaker with a Scottish
heritage. He inherited the title Baron of Glenguin from his
grandfather, Air Chief Marshall Arthur Tedder, who was
awarded the title for his service during World War II.
Robin's winery, Glenguin, makes some of the Hunter
Valley's best Shiraz, from his estate's own vineyards and
also from a 50-year-old, dry-grown block in Pokolbin.
The star wine is the Aristea Shiraz, from the old vines,
but the Schoolhouse Block Shiraz is also excellent. An
oddity here is a varietal Ironbark Tannat, which is made
from 2.5 acres (1ha) of vines. The wines share lovely
definition and have some Old World elegance.

Cessnock, NSW 2325
www.glenguinestate.com.au

Grove Estate Hilltops

Grove Estate began life in 1989, when three partners
(the Flanders, Mullany, and Kirkwood families) bought a
property in the Hilltops region near the town of Young.
Their goal was to grow premium, cool-climate grapes,
so they planted over 124 acres (50ha) with an eclectic
list of varieties, including Cabernet Sauvignon, Shiraz,
Merlot, Zinfandel, Barbera, Sangiovese, Petit Verdot,
Nebbiolo, Chardonnay, and Semillon. In 1997, they
decided to retain some grapes and make their own wine.
Since 2003, the wines have been made by Tim Kirk at
Clonakilla and Richard Parker at Long Rail Gully, under
Tim Kirk's supervision. Look out for the focused,
textured Cellar Block Reserve Shiraz Viognier and
the cherry-ish, chewy Sommita Nebbiolo.

4100 Murringo Rd, Young, NSW 2594
www.groveestate.com.au

Hope Estate Hunter Valley

Michael Hope made his money from a chain of
pharmacies in New South Wales, then decided to follow
his passion and make wine in the Hunter Valley. His first
winery home was at Broke, on the site of the former
Saxonvale winery, but when a mining company made
him an offer he couldn't refuse, he purchased the 593
acre (240ha) Rothbury Estate in 2006 and this became
Hope Estate's new home. As well as 247 acres (100ha) in
the Hunter, Hope also owns 99 acres (40ha) in Victoria
and 72 acres (29ha) in Western Australia. This makes for
a broad range of wines, all of which are bottled under the
Hope label, with the exception of Virgin Hills from Victoria.

2213 Broke Rd, Pokolbin, NSW 2320
www.hopeestate.com.au

Huntington Estate Mudgee

Widely regarded as the leading wine producer in the Mudgee region, and equally famous for its annual music festival, Huntington Estate is also one of the oldest wineries. It was founded back in 1969 by Sydney lawyer Bob Roberts, who worked hard to realize his dream of producing great wine at affordable prices. Bob Roberts retired in 2006 and his neighbor and friend Tim Stevens, who owns the next door vineyard, Abercorn, took over the running of the estate. The focus at Huntington Estate is on solid red wines that are traditionally made and capable of developing in bottle. Cabernet Sauvignon and Shiraz are the main grape varieties, and overall the estate has 99 acres (40ha) of vines separated into 24 blocks. Most of the vines are now approaching 40 years of age. The dense, slightly chunky, ageworthy wines enjoy a loyal following and are rarely seen outside Australia.

Cassilis Rd, Mudgee, NSW 2850
www.huntingtonestate.com.au

JYT Hunter Valley

In 1996, Jay Tulloch left the then Southcorp-owned Tulloch winery and established a small 7 acre (3ha) vineyard in the Hunter Valley. He began making wines from his new winery in 1997, under the JYT label. He now produces a wide range of varietal wines, including a lemony fresh Verdelho and a bright Semillon. Jay managed to buy back the Tulloch family winery in 2001, so JYT is now being run alongside the larger Tulloch operation.

DeBeyers Rd, Pokolbin, NSW 2320
02 4998 7528

Keith Tulloch Wine Hunter Valley

Part of the famous Tulloch wine family, Keith Tulloch is a fourth generation Hunter Valley winemaker. Using this experience, he began his own company in 1997, focusing on the classic Hunter Valley varieties: Chardonnay, Semillon, Merlot, Shiraz, and Cabernet Sauvignon. These handmade wines are only produced in small quantities, with just 600 bottles each of the top wines, under the Field of Mars label, being available. The total estate production is 12,000 cases annually.

Hunter Ridge, Hermitage Rd, Pokolbin, NSW 2321
www.keithtullochwine.com.au

Lake's Folly Hunter Valley

Lake's Folly was the original Hunter Valley boutique winery and the first new vineyard to be planted in the Hunter Valley in the 20th century. It was established by the Sydney-based surgeon Max Lake in 1963, but since 2000 it has been owned and run by Peter Fogarty and his family, with local winemaker Rod Kempe. Despite all the changes, Lake's Folly is still regarded as one of the Hunter's top wineries. Just two wines are made from the estate's 30 acres (12ha) of vines: a Chardonnay and a Cabernet Sauvignon-based red blend, which is unusual for this region. Their total production of just 4,500 cases means that few people are lucky enough to try these wines, which are very highly regarded and sell mostly through a mail order list.

Broke Rd, Pokolbin, NSW 2320
www.lakesfolly.com.au

Lark Hill Canberra District

Established in 1978, with the first vintage the same year, this biodynamic producer is located in the Canberra District. Lark Hill has some of Australia's highest vineyards, at 2,822ft (860m), that grow on an escarpment overlooking Lake George. The cool, dry environment here results in low cropping and concentrated, intensely flavored fruit. A number of varieties are grown, including a new plantation of 2.5 acres (1ha) of Grüner Veltliner (Australia's very first Grüner Veltliner was produced by Lark Hill in 2009). Stars of the show are the limey, mineral Riesling and the sweet Auslese Riesling. A delicate, elegant Pinot Noir is also made.

521 Bungendore Rd, Bungendore, NSW 2621
www.larkhillwine.com.au

Logan Mudgee

This mid-sized, family-owned winery produces around 42,000 cases of wine from both Mudgee, where it is based, and Orange. After starting in pharmaceuticals, Peter Logan made a career change and began his own company in 1997, while he was still in his 20s. His aim was to marry the fresh fruit flavors of Australian wine with European structure and finesse. The wines labeled Logan are all from the high-altitude vineyards of Orange, while the Weemala and Apple Tree Flat ranges contain some Mudgee grapes. Logan wines represent great value for money.

Castlereagh Hwy, Apple Tree Flat, Mudgee, NSW 2850
www.loganwines.com.au

Margan Hunter Valley

This top-quality Hunter Valley operation is headed by experienced winemaker Andrew Margan. Since starting out in 1997, Margan has accumulated 320 acres (130ha) of vineyards, all in the Broke Fordwich region of the lower Hunter Valley. Andrew's emphasis is on making wines with a sense of place, and he aims to let the old vine vineyards in his care express themselves. Small quantities of the Hunter classics, Semillon and Shiraz, are kept back from good vintage years and released as White Label Aged Release wines. As well as fantastic Shiraz and Semillon, Margan also makes good Cabernet Sauvignon and Barbera.

1238 Milbrodale Rd, Broke, NSW 2330
www.margan.com.au

McGuigan Hunter Valley

A 1.4 million-case giant, McGuigan Simeon was recently renamed Australian Vintage Limited, but McGuigan, based in the old Hungerford Hill Winery, is still a presence in the Hunter Valley. Brian McGuigan had established Wyndham Estate in the 1960s, but sold it to Orlando, before starting McGuigan with his brother Neil. McGuigan now crushes 200,000 tons (181,400 tonnes) of grapes, 3,000 tons (2,700 tonnes) of which go through the Hunter winery under the eye of winemaker Peter Hall. The bold, limey Bin 9000 Semillon is consistently good, inexpensive, and ages nicely. More ambitious, the 2000 Pokolbin Shiraz is super-elegant with density and focus, and is aging well.

Rosebery, NSW 1445
www.mcguiganwines.com.au

WINE STYLES

HUNTER VALLEY SEMILLON

One of Australia's unique fine wine styles, Hunter Semillon is a paradox. The hot, damp climate of the Hunter Valley produces Semillon grapes that reach physiological ripeness with low potential alcohol and high acidity. No one knows why, but it could partly be because of the humidity and cloud cover that is present during the growing season. The unoaked wines that result are fresh, lemony, and unremarkable in their youth, but with age, they undergo a metamorphosis, turning complex, broad, and toasty with bottle age. This is also a style of wine that has benefited greatly from the widespread move to screwcaps, which should ensure that the wines show far less bottle variation than they have done aging under cork. While Hunter Valley Semillons are often cellared and enjoyed by connoisseurs, they don't get the widespread recognition they deserve.

TYRRELL'S
THIS EXCELLENT CHARDONNAY IS EXPORTED
TO MORE THAN 30 COUNTRIES

PETERSONS
THE BACK BLOCK SHIRAZ IS HARVESTED
FROM VINES PLANTED IN 1972

McWilliam's Mount Pleasant
Hunter Valley

Mount Pleasant was established in 1921 by the now legendary winemaker Maurice O'Shea. The McWilliam family purchased a half share in the property, and in 1941, they also acquired Maurice's share. They retained Maurice and gave him the financial backing he needed to acquire and plant the Lovedale and Rosehill properties in 1946. The wines that O'Shea went on to make still, to this very day, inspire winemakers across Australia. Mount Pleasant's wines, now made by winemaker Phil Ryan, are classic Hunter in style. Lovedale Semillon is one of the greats, with pure, fresh citrus flavors in its youth, gaining toasty complexity with a decade or more in bottle. The more affordable Elizabeth Semillon is a bargain, and is also available as a museum release. Mount Pleasant's Shiraz, made in the classic Hunter style, is also excellent.

401 Marrowbone Rd, Pokolbin, NSW 2320
www.mcwilliams.com.au

Meerea Park Hunter Valley

Meerea Park was established in 1991 and is owned by Rhys and Garth Eather, descendants from an old wine-producing family. It is a small boutique winery that produces 10,000 cases a year. Rhys Eather is in charge of winemaking and produces some of the Hunter Valley's best wines from purchased grapes. The stars in the portfolio are the Alexander Munro Shiraz and the Alexander Munro Semillon, but the Hell Hole Shiraz and Hell Hole Semillon are also good contenders, as are most of the other wines made at Meerea Park.

188 Palmers Lane, Pokolbin, NSW 2320
www.meereapark.com.au

Miramar Mudgee

Ian MacRae has been an important part of Mudgee ever since he arrived as a consultant to the Montrose winery in 1975. He quickly saw the potential of the area and began to plant his own vines, producing his first vintage under the Miramar name in 1977. The majority of the grapes from his 104 acres (42ha) are sold, but he keeps enough to make 6,000 cases of his own wines, with a focus on whites. A grassy Sauvignon Blanc and a toasty Chardonnay are the pick of the crop.

Henry Lawson Drive, Mudgee, NSW 2850
www.miramarwines.com.au

Nugan Estate Riverina

The Nugan family originally made their money from other aspects of horticulture, before turning to wine in 2001. The drive of Michelle Nugan and her son, Matthew, and daughter, Tiffany, has led to Nugan Estate developing into one of Australia's leading wine exporters. Nugan produces a massive 400,000 cases a year. It is based in the Riverina, has vineyards in McLaren Vale and King Valley, and sources grapes from Coonawarra. The wines are consistently good, with the balanced, blackcurranty Coonawarra Alcira Vineyard Cabernet Sauvignon and the peachy King Valley Franca's Lane Chardonnay stealing the show.

Kidman Way, Willbriggie, NSW 2680
www.nuganestate.com.au

Petersons Hunter Valley

The Peterson family began growing grapes in the Hunter Valley in 1971. After expanding their vineyard holdings to 40 acres (16ha), and planting them with a range of varieties, they decided to make their own wines, with their first vintage in 1981. Today, the Petersons' Hunter Valley holdings have been joined by 100 acres (40ha) in Mudgee and a further 18 acres (7ha) in the cool climate of Armidale. With their charmingly old-fashioned labels, these are solid wines with plenty of flavor: the reds in particular offer dense, structured fruit.

552 Mount View Rd, Cessnock, NSW 2325
www.petersonswines.com.au

Philip Shaw Orange

Philip Shaw initially achieved fame as the winemaker at Rosemount Estate, but he is now making wines under his own name in the cool-climate region of Orange. He purchased the 116 acre (47ha) Koomooloo vineyard site in 1988 and planted it over the next two years. Peaking at 2,953ft (900m), it is one of the highest vineyards in Australia, and consequently one of the coldest. From it, Shaw makes a range of wines, including Sauvignon Blanc, Pinot Noir, Chardonnay, Cabernet Sauvignon, and Shiraz. The top tier are labeled by number; the second tier are labeled by character. As you'd expect from such a cool site, these wines have a pure, fresh fruit focus. ★ **Rising star**

Caldwell Lane, Orange, NSW 2800
www.philipshaw.com.au

Robert Oatley Vineyards Mudgee

What was previously known as Poet's Corner (a cellar door that was the public face of three Mudgee brands: Craigmoor, Montrose, and Poet's Corner) was purchased by the Oatley family in 2006. Run by Bob Oatley, the man behind the highly successful Rosemount Estate, it was renamed Robert Oatley Vineyards in 2009. When he sold Rosemount Estate, he retained seven vineyard sites in the Mudgee region, totaling 1,236 acres (500ha). Along with the Poet's Corner purchase, the ex-Rosemount plots have been used to create two new brands: Wild Oats and Robert Oatley. Montrose, a historical Mudgee label, has also been retained. The US market has been a particular export focus for Oatley's wines. ★ **Rising star**

Craigmoor Rd, Mudgee, NSW 2850
www.robertoatley.com

Rosemount Estate Hunter Valley

During the 1990s, Upper Hunter producer Rosemount, with winemaker Philip Shaw at the helm, went through a period of explosive growth. It became well known for its high-quality, affordable branded wines, as well as high-end bottles. However, things went awry after a merger with Southcorp in 2001, and the brand entered a period of decline. Rosemount, along with the other Southcorp brands, was acquired in 2005 by Fosters, who have streamlined the range and attempted to revive it. Wines to look out for include the intensely flavored Roxburgh Chardonnay and the blockbuster-style Balmoral Syrah and Mountain Blue Shiraz Cabernet, as well as the five well-made Show Reserve wines.

McDonalds Rd, Pokolbin, NSW 2320
www.rosemountestate.com

Scarborough Hunter Valley

Ian Scarborough has now been joined by his son, Jerome, with whom he shares winemaking duties at this small, family-owned Hunter Valley winery. The 30 acre (12ha) estate vineyard has terra rossa soils, with friable red loam over limestone, which makes Chardonnay the house specialty. Three styles are made with varying degrees of richness and oak: Blue Label (restrained), Yellow Label (full flavored), and White Label (powerful). In 1998, Scarborough purchased a further 100 acres (40ha), formerly part of the famous Lindemans Sunshine Vineyard, adding Semillon to the portfolio. Scarborough also have a reputation for their Pinot Noir.

179 Gillards Rd, Pokolbin, NSW 2320
www.scarboroughwine.com.au

Tempus Two Hunter Valley

Tempus Two is the wine brand developed by Lisa McGuigan, who is part of the famous McGuigan wine family. Tempus Two began in a corner of the McGuigan winery in 1998 and was originally established as Hermitage Road, but the name was changed when the French appellation body took issue with the use of the word "Hermitage." The new name, Tempus Two, means "second time" in Latin. Since the renaming, growth has been dramatic. Now based in a futuristic-looking winery in the middle of the Hunter Valley, the wines are made from grapes sourced across the southeast of Australia. Three ranges are made: Varietal, Pewter, and Copper, with the last two having distinctive metal labels and novel bottle shapes.

Cnr Broke and McDonalds Rd, Pokolbin, NSW 2320
www.tempustwo.com.au

Thistle Hill Mudgee

A pioneering organic winery in Mudgee, Thistle Hill was founded in 1975 by David and Lesley Robertson. The first commercial vintage was in 1984, and they have developed quite a reputation for gutsy, full-flavored red wines that are traditionally made and basket pressed. In 2009, Thistle Hill was purchased by Rob and Mary Loughan, who own the neighboring Erudgere winery: the plan is to turn Erudgere organic, too. Winemaker Michael Slater, former senior winemaker at McGuigan, is in charge of both sites.

74 McDonalds Rd, Mudgee, NSW 2850
www.thistlehill.com.au

Thomas Wines Hunter Valley

After 13 years with Tyrrell's, Andrew and Jo Thomas produced their own Hunter Valley vintage in 1997. Thomas Wines specializes in the classic Hunter varieties of Semillon and Shiraz. The wines have met with critical acclaim, and Andrew was voted Hunter Valley winemaker of the year in 2008. The Braemore Semillon, with its tight, minerally, citrussy core is a brilliant platform for future development, and is one of the Hunter's best. Total production is 4,000 cases annually. ★ Rising star

McDonalds Rd, Polkolbin, NSW 2320
www.thomaswines.com.au

Tulloch Hunter Valley

A historic name in the Australian wine scene, J Y Tulloch built up a sizeable winery in the Hunter Valley in the first two decades of the 20th century. The company continued

MEEREA PARK
COOL CONDITIONS MADE 2004 A GOOD YEAR FOR SEMILLON IN THE HUNTER VALLEY

WYNDHAM ESTATE
WYNDHAM HAS VINEYARDS IN VICTORIA, SOUTH AUSTRALIA, AND THE HUNTER VALLEY

to thrive until it was sold outside the family in 1969 to Reed Consolidated Publishing. During subsequent decades, numerous changes of ownership left the Tulloch brand in a state of disarray. Eventually, it was brought back into the family by Jay Tulloch, who purchased it from Southcorp in 2001. The focus is now on making high quality, reasonably priced wines from Hunter fruit. The range spans a broad varietal base, including some new, emerging varieties. The re-released Pokolbin Dry Red Shiraz is the pick of the pack, but the Verdelho also impresses.

Cnr McDonalds and DeBeyers Rd, Pokolbin, NSW 2320
www.tulloch.com.au

Tower Estate Hunter Valley

The late Len Evans was one of the partners in this high-end Hunter Valley winery, which was established in 1999. The model is an interesting one: wines are made from the best fruit grown across Australia's premium wine regions. For example, Shiraz comes from the Barossa, Pinot Noir from Tasmania, Riesling from Clare Valley, and Cabernet Sauvignon from Coonawarra. Tower Estate also produces some iconic Hunter Valley wines: Semillon, Verdelho, and Shiraz. Another focus at this estate is hospitality, with the Tower Lodge a much-lauded five-star hotel.

Cnr Halls and Broke Rd, Pokolbin, NSW 2320
www.towerestatewines.com.au

Tyrrell's Hunter Valley

This family-owned winery in the Hunter Valley dates back to 1858, when English immigrant Edward Tyrrell established his winery in the lee of the Brokenback mountain range. The current success of Tyrrell's owes much to the drive of Murray Tyrrell and his son Bruce, the current managing director. Tyrrell's grew rapidly during the 1980s and 1990s, but recently sold their successful, but non-Hunter-based brand Long Flat in order to focus more on premium wines. This estate is currently very much on form and their range contains some of Australia's best wines. Vat 1 Semillon is a Hunter classic, and has been joined by three single-vineyard Semillons of equal interest. Vat 47 Chardonnay is one of Australia's best, made in a rich, opulent, but ultimately balanced style, and Vat 9 Shiraz is a brilliant example of the Hunter style, with great concentration and depth to the taut, focused dark fruits.

1838 Broke Rd, Pokolbin, NSW 2320
www.tyrrells.com.au

Wyndham Estate Hunter Valley

This historic Hunter Valley producer is now part of the Pernod Ricard group and the Hunter winery is now simply a cellar door, as the Hunter wines are made elsewhere. The approach is now a multi-regional one and, although some Hunter wines are still made under this label, you are more likely to encounter the well-distributed brands. The entry-level bin numbered brands, such as the chunky Bin 555 Shiraz and dense Bin 444 Cabernet Sauvignon, over-deliver in terms of flavor, but the new George Wyndham wines offer a step up in quality for only a small increase in price.

700 Dalwood Rd, Dalwood, NSW 2335
www.wyndhamestate.com

VICTORIA AND TASMANIA

INDONESIA | PAPUA NEW GUINEA
Darwin
PACIFIC OCEAN
AUSTRALIA
Brisbane
Perth
CANBERRA   Sydney
INDIAN OCEAN
TASMANIA
■ Victoria and Tasmania

Victoria has more fine wine regions and wineries than any other Australian state, and many now consider it the country's leading producer of fine wine. Shiraz is Victoria's star performer, expressing itself very differently in regions such as the Yarra Valley, Beechworth, the Grampians, and Heathcote. Pinot Noir from Mornington Peninsula and Geelong is often exciting, and several regions are achieving great things with Chardonnay. Meanwhile, the unique fortified wines of the Rutherglen have earned a place among Australia's greatest vinous treasures, and across the Bass Strait, Tasmania is starting to realize its cool-climate potential with exciting Chardonnay, Riesling, and Pinot Noir.

Major grapes

 Reds

Cabernet Sauvignon

Pinot Noir

Shiraz

 Whites

Chardonnay

Muscat

Riesling

Topaque (Tokay)

Vintages

2009
A challenging year: two weeks of very high temperatures in January and February, while bush fires also hit some areas.

2008
South Australia struggled in the heat. Victoria fared better, with an early, but high-quality vintage in most regions.

2007
A problematic year, with most regions suffering drought, and some bush fires. Many good wines were made, though.

2006
A good and sometimes very good vintage for all regions, including Tasmania.

2005
A great vintage, combining high yields with good quality.

2004
A generally good, but cool, vintage, resulting in some great wines, but Tasmania struggled this year.

While South Australia has always been the heart of Australia's wine industry, Victoria can justifiably lay claim to being the country's most exciting state for fine wine. It boasts a broad array of interesting wine regions, each with a quota of high-achieving boutique wineries, and takes in a range of climates from the positively cold Macedon Ranges to the hot Rutherglen region in the northeast of the state.

The Yarra Valley, east of Melbourne, is Victoria's most significant region. A combination of changing tastes—in favor of beer and fortified wines—and post-war depression meant that the Yarra vineyards all but disappeared for almost 50 years, until a small band of pioneers began working the area again in the 1970s. Since then, the region has flourished, and now boasts a wide array of high-end producers making exciting Chardonnay, Pinot Noir, Shiraz, and even Cabernet Sauvignon blends. It is the variety of microclimates found in the Yarra that has enabled this versatility.

Also close to Melbourne are three other regions that are capable of greatness: the Mornington Peninsula, Geelong (on either side of Port Phillip Bay), and the Macedon Ranges to the north of the city. Chardonnay, Pinot Noir, and cool-climate Shiraz are the wines that are creating a buzz here, with a significant number of small, high-quality wineries leading the way.

Moving west, Central Victoria has five significant regions, mostly known for their dense, focused, primarily Shiraz-based red wines: Bendigo, Heathcote, Goulbourn Valley, Upper Goulburn, and the Strathbogie Ranges. Of these, Heathcote is creating the most excitement for its aromatic and beautifully defined Shiraz. Part of the North East Victoria Zone, Beechworth is another exciting and lively region. It is still small, but, in the hands of a talented group of high-end producers, some of Australia's most thrilling Chardonnay and Shiraz wines are currently being made, as well as some interesting aromatic varieties.

The fortified wines—Muscats and Tokays (now officially known as Topaques, but also sometimes referred to as Muscadelles)—that come from the Rutherglen region are perhaps some of Australia's most unique and thrilling contributions to the world of fine wine. With age, the best of these are among the most complex and exciting wines to come from Australia.

Moving further west, three high-quality regions form the Western Victoria Zone. The Grampians (also known by some as Great Western) is a relatively cool-climate region that is responsible for some very exciting Shiraz, as well as some acclaimed sparkling reds. The Pyrenees has a small band of boutique wineries making fine Shiraz and Cabernet Sauvignon, and Henty has a cool, almost marginal climate suited to exciting Riesling and Pinot Noir, when the grapes can be persuaded to ripen.

And what of Tasmania? Although vines were first planted here in the 1820s, it is only relatively recently that the state's cool-climate promise has started to be realized. It now produces exciting wines, including sparkling wines, from Pinot Noir, Chardonnay, Riesling, and aromatic varieties, with real potential for great things to come.

VICTORIA AND TASMANIA

It can be argued that Victoria and Tasmania are the most interesting wine regions in Australia. A great diversity of climates and terroirs across the region produces a wide array of interesting wine styles. It is hard to pick out the most significant subregion, but the Yarra Valley and Mornington Peninsula have a concentration of wineries operating at the top of their game. Tasmania has a growing number of serious producers making both still and sparkling wines.

CRAWFORD RIVER
ESTABLISHED
1975

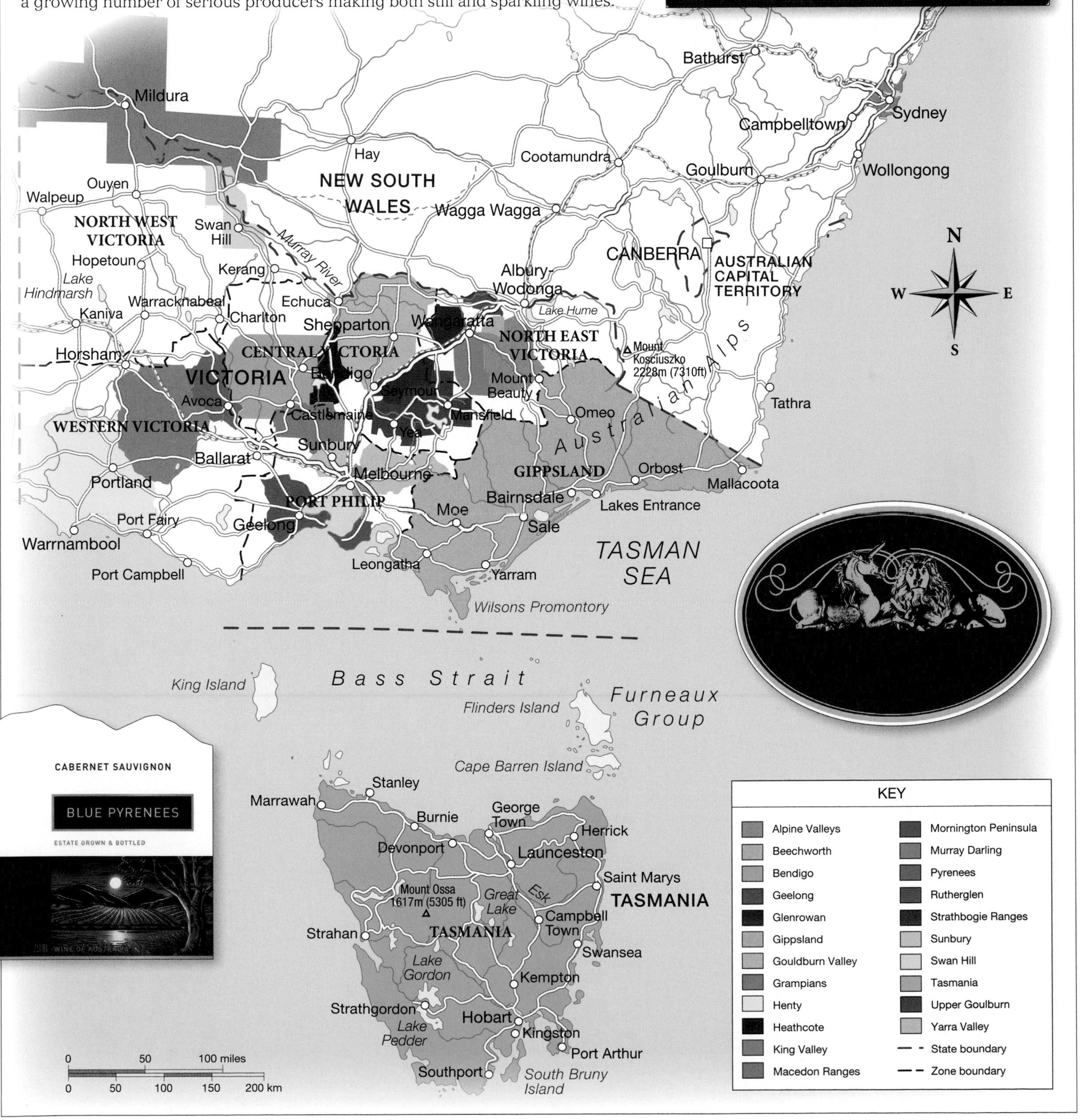

Bathurst
Mildura
Sydney
Campbelltown
Wollongong
Hay
NEW SOUTH WALES
Cootamundra
Goulburn
Ouyen
Walpeup
NORTH WEST VICTORIA
Swan Hill
Wagga Wagga
Hopetoun
Lake Hindmarsh
Kerang
Murray River
Albury-Wodonga
CANBERRA
AUSTRALIAN CAPITAL TERRITORY
N
Warracknabeal
Echuca
Lake Hume
Kaniva
Charlton
Shepparton
Wangaratta
W E
Horsham
CENTRAL VICTORIA
NORTH EAST VICTORIA
Mount Kosciuszko 2228m (7310ft)
S
VICTORIA
Bendigo
Seymour
Mount Beauty
Tathra
Avoca
Castlemaine
Mansfield
Omeo
Australian Alps
WESTERN VICTORIA
Sunbury
Yea
Portland
Ballarat
Melbourne
GIPPSLAND
Orbost
Port Fairy
Geelong
PORT PHILIP
Moe
Bairnsdale
Lakes Entrance
Mallacoota
Warrnambool
Sale
TASMAN SEA
Port Campbell
Leongatha
Yarram
Wilsons Promontory

CABERNET SAUVIGNON
BLUE PYRENEES
ESTATE GROWN & BOTTLED
WINE OF AUSTRALIA

King Island
B a s s   S t r a i t
Flinders Island
F u r n e a u x   G r o u p
Cape Barren Island
Stanley
George Town
Marrawah
Burnie
Herrick
Devonport
Launceston
Saint Marys
Mount Ossa 1617m (5305 ft)
Great Lake
Esk
TASMANIA
Strahan
Campbell Town
TASMANIA
Swansea
Lake Gordon
Kempton
Strathgordon
Hobart
Lake Pedder
Kingston
Port Arthur
Southport
South Bruny Island

0   50   100 miles
0   50   100   150   200 km

KEY

▮	Alpine Valleys	▮	Mornington Peninsula
▮	Beechworth	▮	Murray Darling
▮	Bendigo	▮	Pyrenees
▮	Geelong	▮	Rutherglen
▮	Glenrowan	▮	Strathbogie Ranges
▮	Gippsland	▮	Sunbury
▮	Gouldburn Valley	▮	Swan Hill
▮	Grampians	▮	Tasmania
▮	Henty	▮	Upper Goulburn
▮	Heathcote	▮	Yarra Valley
▮	King Valley	— · —	State boundary
▮	Macedon Ranges	— — —	Zone boundary

BANNOCKBURN

SERRE IS GROWN IN CONDITIONS THAT
EMULATE FRENCH GRAND CRU BURGUNDY

CASTAGNA

THIS WINERY IS LOCATED HIGH IN THE
FOOTHILLS OF THE AUSTRALIAN ALPS

All Saints Estate Rutherglen

Established in the mid-19th century, this historic
Rutherglen winery specializes in Tokays and Muscats.
Stocks of wine dating back 80 years help add
complexity to the wines, which come in Classic (entry-
level), Rare (more refined), and Grand (richer and more
complex) styles. Peter Brown bought this winery from
his family (Brown Brothers) in 1999. He died in 2005
and the fourth generation of Browns, Eliza, Angela,
and Nicolas, have now taken over. As well as excellent
sweet wines, All Saints also makes full-flavored, old
vine Shiraz and Durif.

All Saints Rd, Wahgunyah, VIC 3687
www.prbwines.com.au

Armstrong Vineyards Grampians

Based in the Grampians region of Victoria, this tiny,
800-case, vineyard is owned by Tony Royal. Its 12 acres
(5ha) are devoted to Shiraz, a variety that does well in
this area, and Tony makes just two wines, a Shiraz and
a Shiraz Viognier. They are concentrated and expressive,
with ripe fruit that meshes well with the new oak.

Lot 1 Military Rd, Armstrong, VIC 3381
08 8277 6073

Baileys of Glenrowan Glenrowan

A relatively small, historic winery in Glenrowan, northern
Victoria, Baileys has for some years been rather lost in
the Fosters portfolio. It was put up for sale in April 2009
and its future is currently uncertain. A solidly good pair
of Shiraz wines, made from vines planted in 1904
and 1920, are made here, as well as some rich, sweet
Muscats and Tokays in the Founders (more affordable)
and Winemaker's Selection series. The wines are all made
from fruit grown on the company's own 353 acres (143ha).

Glenrowan, VIC 3675
www.baileysofglenrowan.com.au

Balgownie Bendigo

One of the first wineries established in the Bendigo "Gold
Fields" region of central Victoria in 1969. After a period
in the doldrums, the property was bought by brothers
Des and Rod Forrester in 1999. The pair expanded the
vineyard to 82 acres (33ha), and in 2002 planted a further
17 acres (7ha) of Chardonnay and Pinot Noir in the Yarra
Valley. The Bendigo vineyard is planted with a range of
grape varieties—Cabernet Sauvignon and Shiraz are the
focus. With this amount of investment, the hope is
that the wines will recapture their former glories.

Hermitage Rd, Maiden Gully, VIC 3551
www.balgownieestate.com.au

Bannockburn Vineyards Geelong

This Geelong winery was established in 1974. As a
pioneer of the region, it went on to develop a stellar
reputation for its wines and also for the Geelong region
itself. All the wines are made from estate-grown fruit,
taken from 67 acres (27ha) of vines spread across three
sites. From its inception until 2005, the wines were made
by celebrated Pinot Noir expert Garry Farr, who spent
12 vintages working at Domaine Dujac in Burgundy,
as well as stints at Cristom in Oregon and Calera in
California. The winemaking is now in the hands of Michael
Glover. The elegant, complex, Old-World-style Serre Pinot

Noir is the standout wine, but the Chardonnay and Shiraz
are also excellent. The Cabernet Merlot is regularly
criticized, however, for having a green leafy edge.

Kelly Lane, Bannockburn, VIC 3331
www.bannockburnvineyards.com

Bass Phillip Gippsland

Phillip Jones' Bass Phillip is one of Australia's iconic small
producers, fashioning Pinot Noir that, when it is good,
is without parallel in Australia and can compete with
the world's best. Unfortunately, it isn't always that good,
having a reputation for variability. In part, this is because
of the very cool Gippsland climate, where the close-
planted, biodynamically farmed vines struggle in difficult
vintages. When they are on form, these wines are pure,
complex, and super-elegant, with relatively low alcohol
levels. A range of Pinots are made that vary in price, but
all are good. The 2001 reserve is thrilling, with complex
dark cherry, plum, and spice notes. A little Chardonnay
and Gamay are also made, but the 1,500-case production
and cult status keep prices high.

Toschs Rd, Leongatha, VIC 3953
www.bassphillip.com.au

Bay of Fires Tasmania

This is the brand used by Hardys for their Tasmanian
wines. The winery here, which also makes the excellent
House of Arras sparkling wines, produces an array of
still and sparkling wines from around the island. The
non-vintage Pinot Noir Chardonnay is the benchmark
sparkling wine, and the fresh, limey Riesling and focused,
cherryish Pinot Noir also impress. One to watch.

40 Baxters Rd, Pipers River, TAS 7252
www.bayoffireswines.com.au

Best's Grampians

By Australian standards, Best's is prehistoric. Founded
in 1866 by the Best family, the only other owner has been
the Thomson family, who purchased it in 1920. The stars
of the show here are the Thomson Family Shiraz, made
from a small block of centenarian vines, and the ageworthy
Bin 0 Shiraz. The 1996 Thomson Family shows striking
liqueurlike cherry and plum fruit, with some leathery
savoriness. As well as making Pinot Noir, which is
unusual for the region, an oddity here is a varietal Pinot
Meunier red. Since 2006, a sparkling Shiraz, a specialty
of the region, has also been added to the range.

111 Best's Rd, Great Western, VIC 3374
www.bestswines.com

Bindi Macedon Ranges

Nestled in the Macedon Ranges of Victoria, Michael
Dillon makes two of Australia's most sought-after Pinot
Noirs: the Bindi Block 5 and Original Vineyard. His
Chardonnays are also excellent and well worth seeking
out. The vines were first planted on the family property
in 1988 by Michael's father, and fortunately for Michael,
who is now working with biodynamics, the terroir
proved to be very good. The 2007 Block 5 Pinot shows
rich, yet restrained berry fruit with complex spicy,
medicinal, soy notes. ★Rising star

343 Melton Rd, Gisborne, VIC 3437
www.bindiwines.com.au

Blue Pyrenees Estate Pyrenees

Originally established in 1963 as Chateau Remy by Remy Martin, this large 420 acre (170ha) Pyrenees estate is now owned by a consortium of Australian businessmen. The climate here is quite cool by Australian standards, and the vineyards were planted with the intention of making base wines for brandy and sparkling wine. While good-quality sparkling wine is still made, the main focus is now on table wines, with winemaker Andrew Koerner turning out well-regarded Shiraz and Cabernet Sauvignon, as well as a full range of other varieties.

Vinoca Rd, Avoca, VIC 3467
www.bluepyrenees.com.au

Brown Brothers King Valley

This sizeable, million-case winery is well known for its broad range of affordable varietal wines, including oddities like its Beaujolais-style, cherry fresh Tarrango and a stylish sparkling wine made from Prosecco. The estate's 1,853 acres (750ha) of vineyards, spread across Victoria, supply most of Brown Brothers' needs. Some of the more unusual varieties grown include Crouchen, Mondeuse, Graciano, Dolcetto, Barbera, and Sangiovese. The quality is pretty consistent, but the best wines are the Patricia series (launched in 2003) and the Limited Releases.

239 Milawa Bobinawarrah Rd, Milawa, VIC 3678
www.brownbrothers.com.au

Buller Rutherglen

Buller is a small, 4,000-case, Rutherglen producer specializing in the classic fortified wines of the region. They also have another vineyard, Beverford, near Swan Hill that has a separate winery and cellar door. While the table wines from both sites are good, it is the fortified wines that steal the show. Buller's old Tokays and Muscats are sweet, complex, and intense; they are also good value.

Three Chain Rd, Rutherglen, VIC 3685
www.buller.com.au

By Farr Geelong

A small vineyard of 12 acres (4.8ha) in Bannockburn, Geelong, is the new home of legendary Australian winemaker Gary Farr. From 1978 until 2005, he was winemaker at Bannockburn, which, under his tutelage, established a reputation for its terroir-driven wines. Now he is working with his son, Nick, in this new venture. Nick has completed harvests in Burgundy (Dujac) and Oregon (Christom) and he has his own label, Farr Rising. In 2009, By Farr released three single-vineyard designated Pinots for the first time. In addition to Pinot, Viognier, Chardonnay, and a little Shiraz are also grown. The wines here are world class. ★**Rising star**

Bannockburn, VIC 3331
www.byfarr.com.au

Campbells Rutherglen

The hot Rutherglen region is home to one of Australia's unique contributions to the world of fine wine—sweet, fortified Muscat and Tokay wines that are commonly referred to as "stickies." Campbells is one of the best producers and, while they also make solid table wines (the Barkly Durif and Bobbie Burns Shiraz are highlights), their fortified wines are truly world class. The Isabella Rare Topaque is spellbindingly complex and rich with warm British Christmas cake, tea, malt, and citrus flavors. The Campbell brothers, Colin and Malcolm, have been working here for over 30 years, giving continuity to the business.

Murray Valley Hwy, Rutherglen, VIC 3685
www.campbellswines.com.au

Castagna Beechworth

The charismatic Julian Castagna left his career in the film industry and reinvented himself as a wine-grower in the Beechworth area of Victoria. One of Australia's small but growing band of biodynamic growers, his wines are already among the region's best. The Genesis Syrah, with a splash of Viognier, comes from young vines and has lovely savory elegance. La Chiave is a varietal Sangiovese and one of the best examples of this grape in Australia, with minerally dark fruits and robust tannic structure. The highlight of the range is Un Segreto, a blend of Syrah and Sangiovese with a wonderful, meaty dimension to the minerally, savory, spicy fruit. ★**Rising star**

88 Reesom Lane, Beechworth, VIC 3747
www.castagna.com.au

Chambers Rosewood Rutherglen

One of the historic Rutherglen wineries famous for making top quality, complex, fortified Rutherglen Muscat and Tokays. Established in 1858, Chambers is still in family ownership with the sixth generation now working in the company. The wines here are all great and possibly the best of their style, in particular, the Rare Muscadelle (a Tokay) is thrilling, with mind-blowing complexity and an eternal finish. The secret is the stocks of very old wines that Chambers hold as blending components.

Barkly St, Rutherglen, VIC, 3685
02 6032 8641

Chateau Leamon Bendigo

This small producer was one of the pioneers of the Bendigo region when it started out in 1973. It consists of just 20 acres (8ha) of vineyards, producing Shiraz, Cabernet Merlot, and Semillon. A small amount of Riesling is also made with grapes from the Strathbogie Ranges.

487 Bendigo, VIC 3552
www.chateauleamon.com.au

Cobaw Ridge Macedon Ranges

This small, high-end, biodynamically farmed vineyard was first planted by Nelly and Alan Cooper in 1985. The 15 acres (6ha) of vineyards are at an elevation of 2,000ft (610m), and the philosophy is that the wine is made in the vineyard and not in the cellar. The Syrah and Shiraz/ Viognier are beautifully focused, aromatic wines, but the headlines are usually reserved for the Lagrein, an Italian mountain variety that shows fresh, peppery fruit. Pinot Noir and Chardonnay are also made here.

31 Perc Boyers Lane, East Pastoria, VIC 3444
www.cobawridge.com.au

Coldstream Hills Yarra Valley

When celebrated Australian wine critic James Halliday moved to Melbourne in the mid-1980s, he sold his shares in Brokenwood and began a new venture—Coldstream Hills. Halliday sold to Southcorp (now Fosters) in 1996, but is still involved as a consultant and lives on the

JAMES HALLIDAY

For over 30 years, James Halliday has been Australia's most important wine writer. It is through his knowledgeable but clear writing style that many have been introduced to Australian wine. But Halliday is unusual, as well as being an influential author and journalist, he has also been a winemaker, first with Brokenwood in the Hunter Valley, and then with Coldstream Hills in the Yarra Valley, where he now lives. He trained as a lawyer, becoming a partner at Clayton-Utz in 1966, around the same time he met his mentor, the legendary Len Evans, and developed a taste for fine wine. This was also the time when Australian wine was entering a period of growth. Much of Halliday's writing work was done while he was still a lawyer, but shortly after moving to the Yarra he decided to focus solely on making wine and writing about it.

DELATITE

THIS ESTATE IS CURRENTLY APPLYING FOR
ORGANIC CERTIFICATION

CRITTENDEN ESTATE

THE PINOT NOIR IS A FLAGSHIP WINE, MADE
FROM 100% MORNINGTON PENINSULA FRUIT

vineyard, which sits in a beautiful natural amphitheater. Chardonnay and Pinot Noir were the focus at the outset, and have been joined by the likes of Shiraz, Cabernet Sauvignon, Sauvignon Blanc, and Merlot. The Reserve Pinot is the best, and has a track record for aging well.

31 Maddens Lane, Coldstream, VIC 3770
www.coldstreamhills.com.au

Craiglee Sunbury
Pat Carmody first planted vines in Sunbury in 1976. The first commercial release was the 1980 Shiraz in 1982. Carmody is still at the helm, assisted by his family, and makes elegant, structured, cool-climate wines with the ability to age. The 1990 Shiraz is harmonious and elegant, with spicy minerality. As well as Shiraz, Chardonnay is also made, along with small amounts of Pinot Noir, Cabernet Sauvignon, and Sauvignon Blanc.

Sunbury Rd, Sunbury, VIC 3429
www.craiglee.com.au

Craigow Tasmania
One of Tasmania's leading producers, Craigow has 25 acres (10ha) of Pinot Noir, Riesling, Chardonnay, and Gewürztraminer vines. Established by Dr. Barry Edwards in 1989, with a first vintage in 1993, Craigow was one of the pioneers of the Coal River Valley, which is currently attracting a lot of attention. The top wine here is the intense, pungent, citrussy Riesling.

528 Richmond Rd, Cambridge, TAS 7170
www.craigow.com.au

Crawford River Henty
Henty, a cool maritime region in southwest Victoria, is quite marginal for grape growing, so when John Thompson planted his 28.5 acre (11.5ha) vineyard here in 1975 it must have been quite an act of faith. Over the last 30 years, however, Crawford River has established itself as one of Australia's leading Riesling producers. Limey and minerally in its youth, the 1996 shows that these wines can age. Young Vine Riesling is also delicious. As well as Riesling, Cabernet Sauvignon and a small amount of Sauvignon Blanc/Semillon is made.

741 Upper Hotspur Rd, Condah, VIC 3303
www.crawfordriverwines.com

Crittenden Estate Mornington Peninsula
Gary Crittenden achieved fame with his Dromana Estate, which was one of the earliest wineries in the Mornington Peninsula and the one responsible for putting it on the map. He began his own family operation in 2003, when he left Dromana, and son Rollo joined him in 2007. As well as making excellent Pinot Noir and Chardonnay, the Crittendens also make a stylish Los Hermanos Albariño, which is taut, fresh, minerally, and structured.

25 Harrisons Rd, Dromana, VIC 3936
www.crittendenwines.com.au

Curly Flat Macedon Ranges
Philip Moraghan studied in Switzerland in the 1980s and became besotted with European wines, in particular Pinot Noir. When his passion led him and his wife Jeni to start their own vineyard, they naturally chose the buzzy, cool-climate Victorian region of the Macedon Ranges. They

planted Pinot Noir, Chardonnay, and a dribble of Pinot Gris in the early 1990s, and built a gravity-flow winery in 2002. The focus here is on terroir. The supple, velvety Pinot and balanced, fruity Chardonnay are excellent; second label Williams Crossing is also very good. Only 5,000 cases are produced, so prepare to get in line. ★ **Rising star**

263 Collivers Rd, Lancefield, VIC 3435
www.curlyflat.com

Dal Zotto King Valley
Otto Dal Zotto moved to Victoria's King Valley from his family's vineyard near the town of Valdobbiadene, Italy in 1967. They were tobacco share croppers for 20 years until they turned to wine grapes, acting as suppliers to other wineries and making a bit of their own wine on the side. In the mid-1990s, they decided to plant Italian varieties—Barbera, Sangiovese, Pinot Grigio, Prosecco, and Arneis—and the Dal Zotto estate wines became their main focus. The wines are good quality, with the pick of the bunch being the laser-sharp, minerally Arneis.

Main Rd, Whitfield, King Valley, VIC 3733
www.dalzotto.com.au

Dalwhinnie Pyrenees
One of the best wineries in Victoria's Pyrenees region, Dalwhinnie has 44.5 acres (18ha) of mature vineyards at an altitude of almost 1,969ft (600m). Family-owned since its inception in 1976, Dalwhinnie makes excellent, intense Chardonnay, Shiraz, and Cabernet Sauvignon, producing around 5,000 cases annually. All the wines benefit from some bottle age and are potentially long lived. A new 20 acre (8ha) vineyard called Forest Hut was planted in 1999, which provides more Shiraz, some Viognier, and a bit of Sangiovese for blending options.

448 Taltarni Rd, Moonambel, VIC 3478
www.dalwhinnie.com.au

De Bortoli Yarra Valley
De Bortoli's Yarra outpost is establishing a reputation for making some of the best wines in the valley. Steve Webber, who married into the De Bortoli family, is the European-influenced genius at the helm here. In recent years, he has steered the wines in a more elegant and complex direction. The Reserve Chardonnay is stylish and restrained, the Reserve Syrah peppery and profound, and the Reserve Pinot Noir is made in a distinctly savory, restrained, and elegant style. The Shiraz/Viognier is also elegantly fine. Bargain hunters should look out for the inexpensive, but delicious, Windy Peak Pinot Noir.

Pinnacle Lane, Dixons Creek, VIC 3775
www.debortoli.com.au

Delatite Goulburn
Since 2001, Delatite have been converting their vineyards to biodynamics. They are located in the Upper Goulburn, a fairly cool region in the northeast of Victoria, and specialize in aromatic whites including a distinctive, plump, yet minerally Pinot Gris, an off-dry Sylvia Riesling, and a dense, varietally true Dead Man's Hill Gewürztraminer, which is the pick of the bunch. Look out for a new wine: the textured, off-dry Catherine Gewürztraminer.

Stoney's Road, Mansfield, VIC 3722
www.delatitewinery.com.au

Diamond Valley Yarra Valley

This small, 7,000-case Yarra producer, whose first wines were released in 1982, helped to put Yarra Pinot on the map. Two lines are made: White Label (estate wines) and Blue Label (from purchased fruit). The estate Cabernet Merlot (in warm years), Pinot Noir, and Chardonnay are the wines to watch.

Croydon Hills, VIC 3136
www.diamondvalley.com.au

Domaine A Tasmania

This is possibly Tasmania's best producer. Peter Althaus' Domaine A, an 28.5 acre (11.5ha) vineyard in the Coal River Valley, is making immensely seductive Pinot Noir and super-elegant Cabernet Sauvignon, as well as a Bordeaux-style Sauvignon Blanc. The 2000 Cabernet Sauvignon is thrilling, with a gravely edge to pure, well-defined blackcurrant fruit. The densely planted vines are tended by hand and, with the cool climate, this European approach results in European-style wines.

Tea Tree Rd, Campania, TAS 7026
www.domaine-a.com.au

Domaine Chandon/Green Point
Yarra Valley

Established in 1980 by Moët et Chandon, Domaine Chandon (known as Green Point in some markets) has gained a reputation for making some of Australia's best sparkling wines, from a range of cool-climate vineyard sites. It also makes very impressive Pinot Noir, Shiraz, and Chardonnay. The talented and experienced Tony Jordan has officially retired, but has been retained as a consultant. Chandon sparkling wines have a purity and precision of fruit to them that is very much Jordan's signature. With a 120,000-case per year production and an impressive cellar door, this is one of the most important Yarra wineries.

727 Maroondah Hwy, Coldstream, VIC 3770
www.domainechandon.com.au

Dromana Estate Mornington Peninsula

Garry Crittenden was a pioneer in the Mornington Peninsula when he planted his first vines in 1982. Although vines had already been grown here for a century, he was largely responsible for the renaissance of the region. He established a reputation for making top-quality Chardonnay and Pinot Noir from 54 acres (22ha) of estate vines. He also built a portfolio of successful Italian varietals from vineyards around Victoria, under the i Garry Crittenden label (now known as just i). Crittenden left when Dromana was publicly listed in 2002 and his son Rollo took over the helm. In 2007, Rollo left to join his father at Crittenden Estate.

555 Old Moorooduc Rd, Tuerong, VIC 3933
www.dromanaestate.com.au

Giaconda Beechworth

Former mechanical engineer Rick Kinzbrunner first planted vines here in 1982, adding to them gradually over the following years. Recent plantings have taken the total up to 15 acres (6ha), but demand still far outstrips supply for these sought-after wines. The Pinot Noir has received critical acclaim, but is perhaps eclipsed by the stunning Chardonnay; with its rich texture, lively aromatics, and

GREENSTONE VINEYARD
MADE FROM YOUNG 2–4 YEAR-OLD
VINES, THIS WINE CAN ONLY GET
BETTER AS IT MATURES

GIANT STEPS
GIANT STEPS IS NAMED AFTER JAZZ MUSICIAN
JOHN COLTRANE'S FIRST SOLO ALBUM

concentration it is one of Australia's best. The Aeolia Roussanne is also stunning, with a rich texture and a complex pear fruit character. The excellent Warner Shiraz is also worth looking out for.

30 McClay Rd, Everton Upper, VIC 3678
www.giaconda.com.au

Giant Steps/Innocent Bystander
Yarra Valley

Entrepreneur Phil Sexton had already developed and sold a wine company (Devil's Lair) and a beer brand (Little Creatures) before setting his sights on the Yarra. In 2006, the innovative Giant Steps winery and cellar door, in downtown Healesville, was completed. Here, as well as tasting the wines, customers can also buy artisanal pizza, bread, and cheese—there is even a state-of-the-art coffee bean roaster. Giant Steps wines are excellent, with Chardonnay in particular excelling. A second brand, Innocent Bystander, is also very good and a bit more affordable. ★ **Rising star**

336 Maroondah Hwy, Healesville, VIC 3777
www.innocentbystander.com.au

Greenstone Vineyard Heathcote

A collaboration between Brown Brothers viticulturalist Mark Walpole, UK-based merchant David Gleave, and celebrated Italian wine consultant Alberto Antonini, Greenstone is based on 52 acres (21ha) of well-situated vineyards in Heathcote. Shiraz is the main focus here, but there are also 2.5 acres (1ha) each of Mourvèdre, Tempranillo, and Sangiovese. The 2007 Greenstone Sangiovese, with its savory, cherry, and plum character and warm spiciness, is worth looking out for. The vines, planted between 2003 and 2005, are still young, so keep an eye on this producer. ★ **Rising star**

319 Whorouly South Rd, Whorouly South, VIC 3735
www.greenstoneofheathcote.com

Hanging Rock Macedon Ranges

This is the largest winery in the ultra coolclimate Macedon Ranges. Hanging Rock was established by John and Ann Ellis in the early 1980s, with a view to producing Australia's finest sparkling wine. As well as their Macedon vineyard, they also have vines in Heathcote and source from elsewhere in Victoria. Look out for the numbered Macedon Late Disgorged NV, a striking, rich, toasty sparkling wine with a base wine that is produced in a kind of oak solera system. The Macedon LD, Heathcote Shiraz, and Jim Jim Sauvignon Blanc are also highly regarded.

88 Jim Rd, Newham, VIC 3442
www.hangingrock.com.au

Heathcote Winery Heathcote

One of the first commercial wineries in the Victorian region of Heathcote, which has proved to be an excellent place to grow Shiraz. Since 1997, the winery has been under the ownership of a consortium of wine lovers led by Stephen Wilkins. The flagship wine is the intense, concentrated Curagee Shiraz. Aside from this, Mail Coach is premium range, while Cravens Place is more entry level.

183–185 High St, Heathcote, VIC 3523
www.heathcotewinery.com.au

KOOYONG

THE 2007 CHARDONNAY HAS GREAT
POTENTIAL FOR AGING

Hoddles Creek Estate Yarra Valley

This boutique winery was founded in 1997 by the D'Anna family, on a property they have owned since 1960. There are now 62 acres (25ha) of hand-tended vines and a new winery that was completed in 2003. The young Franco D'Anna is in charge and he has established a reputation for his wines, all of which are single-vineyard estate bottlings. The Chardonnay, in particular, is among the best in the valley. Prices are very reasonable, too.

505 Gembrook Rd, Hoddles Creek, VIC 3139
www.hoddlescreekestate.com.au

Holly's Garden King Valley

Neil Prentice established his 5 acre (2ha) Pinot Noir Moondarra Vineyard in Gippsland in 1991, but then shifted his focus to Whitlands in the King Valley. At altitudes of 2,461–2,789ft (750–850m), he planted 15 acres (6ha) of Pinot Gris and 10 acres (4ha) of Pinot Noir in a vineyard called Holly's Garden, which is farmed using some biodynamic principles. Holly's Garden Pinot Gris is one of Australia's best examples of this variety: the 2008 is rich, quite sweet, and pure with a rounded texture. ★ Rising star

Browns Rd, Moondarra, VIC 3825
www.hollysgarden.com.au

House of Arras Tasmania

This high-quality sparkling wine operation is owned by Hardys. Here, talented winemaker Ed Carr makes some of Australia's best sparkling wine from Chardonnay and Pinot Noir, with his distinctive "house" style. The 2003 Grand Vintage is bold, complex, and mouthfilling, with rich fruit in almost a still-wine style. These are world-class wines and worth seeking out. ★ Rising star

40 Baxters Rd, Pipers River, TAS 7252
www.houseofarras.com.au

Jansz Tasmania

Owned by the Hill Smith family of Yalumba, Jansz is a premium sparkling wine producer from northern Tasmania. It was originally established in the 1970s as Heemskerk and briefly collaborated with Roederer in the mid-1980s. The wines are consistently good, with the star of the show being the vintage Late Disgorged: the 2001 is taut and focused with complex, savory, herby fruit characters, and fresh acidity.

1216B Pipers Brook Rd, Pipers Brook, TAS 7254
www.jansz.com.au

Jasper Hill Heathcote

Perhaps the best known of the Heathcote producers, Ron Laughton's Jasper Hill wines are among the most sought-after bottles in Australia. One of the country's biodynamic pioneers, Laughton takes a hands-off approach in order to let his special terroirs speak for themselves—no artificial chemicals have been applied to the vineyard since its inception in 1975. The results are a compelling and powerful yet elegant pair of Shiraz wines (Emily's and Georgia's Paddock), as well as a lighter Grenache, a structured Riesling, and tiny quantities of Nebbiolo and Semillon.

Drummond's Lane, Heathcote, VIC 3523
www.jasperhill.com

HOUSE OF ARRAS

HOUSE OF ARRAS MAKES SOME OF
AUSTRALIA'S BEST SPARKLING WINE

Josef Chromy Wines Tasmania

Tasmanian wine pioneer Josef Chromy is in his 70s, but this has not stopped him from starting another venture. After fleeing Czechoslovakia in the 1950s, he began a new life in Tasmania. In 1994, he bought Heemskerk, Janz, and Rochecombe, selling them a few years later and starting again with Tamar Ridge. This was sold in 2003, and with the proceeds he bought a 148 acre (60ha) vineyard near Launceston. The wine range is in two tiers, with a full range of whites and Pinot Noir being the sole red. Joseph Chromy is the main label, while the Pepik range is more entry level. Look out for the great-value Pepik Pinot Noir and the complex, pure Botrytis Riesling.

370 Relbia Rd, Relbia, TAS 7258
www.josefchromy.com.au

Kooyong Mornington Peninsula

Mornington Peninsula producer Kooyong only made first vintage in 2001, but already they have climbed to the top of Australia's quality tree. With 84 acres (34ha) of vines, winemaker Sandro Mosele is making a fantastic range of single-vineyard Chardonnays and Pinot Noirs that show richness and intensity, allied to complexity and elegance. Kooyong is owned by the Gjergja family, who also own Port Phillip Estate, where the wines are made. The 2006 Ferrous Pinot Noir is dense, rich, structured, and ripe, but it shows elegance, too. In fact, everything Kooyong makes seems to be great. ★ Rising star

263 Red Hill Rd, Red Hill South, VIC 3937
www.kooyong.com

Lethbridge Geelong

This small, 3,000-case, Geelong winery is dedicated to producing what the owners describe as "European-accented" wines. The winery is made from straw bales, which insulate the building to ensure that no heating or cooling of the facility is needed. Vineyard management is organic, with biodynamic influences. Because different blocks are kept separate, a large number of wines are made here from a range of varieties. Chardonnay is particularly successful, but the 2008 Kabinett Riesling is also lively, racy, minerally, and intense, with nicely poised sweetness and acidity. ★ Rising star

74 Burrows Rd, Lethbridge, VIC 3332
www.lethbridgewines.com.au

Luke Lambert Wines Yarra Valley

Syrah and Nebbiolo are the sole focus for young winemaker Luke Lambert. He leases just under 7 acres (3ha) in the Yarra and makes wines in a hands-off way, using wild yeast and no fining or filtration. The relatively low alcohol Syrah has a lovely savory character and the Nebbiolo, with its sappy, cherry fruit and sweetness, represents the friendly side of this tricky variety—it is one of Australia's few world-class examples. ★ Rising star

Healesville, VIC 3777
www.lukelambertwines.com.au

Mac Forbes Yarra Valley

Mac Forbes is becoming one of Australia's wine superstars. He learned his trade at the iconic Yarra producer Mount Mary before starting his own small, 2,000-case business, focusing on single-vineyard Pinot

Noir, Chardonnay, and Riesling. The Rieslings, from the Strathbogie Ranges, have the residual sugar level indicated in the name: the 2008 rs9 and rs37 are both stunningly precise wines. All the Pinot Noirs are good, with Coldstream, Woori Yallock, Gruyere, and EBL standing out. The peppery Gruyere Syrah is also impressive. ★ **Rising star**

770 Healesville Koo Wee Rup Rd, Healesville, VIC 3777
www.macforbes.com

Main Ridge Mornington Peninsula
Nat White was one of the Mornington Peninsula pioneers when he established Main Ridge in 1975. Since then, it has stayed small and quality focused, producing just three wines: a Chardonnay and two Pinot Noirs (Half Acre and The Acre). The Half Acre Pinot Noir is more structured and long lived: the 2004 is concentrated, sappy, and shows vibrant cherry fruit. The small, 1,200-case production makes these wines hard to find.

80 William Rd, Red Hill, VIC 3937
www.mre.com.au

Mitchelton Nagambie Lakes
Now part of the Lion Nathan group, Mitchelton is based in the Nagambie Lakes region in central Victoria, and has a sizeable production (220,000 cases annually). Back in 1967, Colin Preece was commissioned by Melbourne businessman Ross Shelmerdine to prospect for a great place to make wine. Preece identified a grazing estate in Nagambie because of its combination of soil, climate, and access to water, and this became Mitchelton. Since 2007, talented young winemaker Ben Haines has been in charge here, and makes a solid range of wines focusing on Shiraz, Marsanne, Viognier, and Riesling, which all seem to do pretty well here. The wines are reasonably priced and show nice freshness and fruit definition. Pick of the bunch is the Crescent Grenache/Shiraz/Mourvèdre, which is bright and berryish.

Mitchellstown Rd, Nagambie, VIC 3608
www.mitchelton.com.au

Morris Wines Rutherglen
One of the top producers of "stickies:" fortified Muscats and Tokays (aka "Muscadelle" or "Topaque") from the Rutherglen region in Victoria. There's history here, because Morris was established in 1859 and is still run by the same family, Morris, although ownership is now in the hands of Pernod Ricard. Although some respectable red wines are made here (including a well-regarded Durif and a varietal Cinsault), it is the fortifieds that win the accolades. They are simply incredible, with amazing complexity and concentration. Three levels (Liqueur, Cellar Reserve, and Old Premium) are produced. The Old Premium Liqueur Tokay recently tried showed brilliant spicy complexity and smooth, lush sweetness; the 1928 Morris Liqueur Muscat tried alongside it was one of the most breathtaking wine experiences imaginable.

Mia Mia Rd, Rutherglen, VIC 3685
www.morriswines.com

Mount Avoca Pyrenees
The Pyrenees region in Victoria is home to a number of highly regarded wineries, including Mount Avoca. Its 59 acres (24ha) of vineyards, tended organically and currently undergoing organic certification, produce around 16,000 cases each year. Matthew Barry, the young owner, is working hard to improve the quality of the wines, which were previously a little off pace.

Avoca, VIC 3467
mountavoca.com.au

Mount Langi Ghiran Grampians
Part of the Rathbone group, Mount Langi is famous for its beautifully well-defined, slightly peppery Shiraz—one of Australia's best. The 2004 shows focused, precise, dark fruits with a lovely black pepper edge. This wine is made exclusively from estate fruit, while a second Shiraz, Cliff Edge, is made from younger vines and bought-in fruit. There is also an inexpensive, deliciously forward Billi Billi Shiraz that represents great value. Riesling and Pinot Gris are made here, as well as a Cabernet Sauvignon from Limestone Coast fruit, but the Shiraz steals the show.

80 Vine Rd, Bayindeen, VIC 3375
www.langi.com.au

Mount Mary Yarra Valley
John Middleton, who died in 2006 aged 82, pioneered the rebirth of the Yarra Valley when he established Mount Mary in 1971. The 25 acres (10ha) of vineyards produced wines that established a cult following, selling out quickly each year. A range of varieties are grown aside from Shiraz, which Middleton hated. The grapes are picked early by Australian standards, as Middleton aimed to get them in before 13.5% potential alcohol. The resulting wines are brilliant, lean, and restrained in their youth, but with the ability to age gracefully over a couple of decades. Triolet is a white blend of Sauvignon, Semillon, and a touch of Muscadelle; the Chardonnay is elegant and minerally; the Pinot is intense and cherryish; and the Quintet is a Bordeaux blend with gravely depth and potential for development. The winery is run by John's son, David.

Coldstream West Rd, Lilydale, VIC 3140
www.mountmary.com.au

Nicholson River Gippsland
Ken and Juliet Eckersley decided to plant a vineyard in the Gippsland region of Victoria, 186 miles (300km) east of Melbourne, in 1978. They now have 20 acres (8ha) of vines that are planted with a range of grape varieties, but with intense Chardonnay being the focus. The majority of sales are by mail order and cellar door.

Liddells Rd, Nicholson, VIC 3882
www.nicholsonriverwinery.com.au

Oakridge Yarra Valley
Oakridge had a difficult time while it was under the ownership of Evans & Tate from 2001 until 2008, but its recent return to private ownership has given this high-end producer a boost. The top range of wines are labeled 864, the core range is Oakridge, and there is a separate label called Over the Shoulder, which has a more contemporary feel and fresh fruit focus. Winemaker David Bicknell is getting rave reviews for his Chardonnays, with the complex, minerally 864 Chardonnay being the star turn. ★ **Rising star**

864 Maroondah Hwy Coldstream, Yarra Valley, VIC 3770
www.oakridgeestate.com.au

PINOT NOIR

It was not so long ago that Australian Pinot Noir was considered a bit of a joke. A fussy variety, it was planted in the wrong places and the resulting wines were dark and jammy. In recent years, however, Australia has been making small quantities of world-class Pinot Noir with vineyard sites in Victoria and Tasmania at the heart of this movement. The Yarra Valley, Mornington Peninsula, Geelong, Gippsland, the Macedon Ranges, and Tasmania are all yielding special examples of Pinot Noir, capturing its elegance, finesse, balance, and focus, while imparting their own unique site-specific characters to the resulting wines. It may be early days yet, but wines from the likes of Bass Phillip, Bannockburn, Kooyong, Stoney Rise, Stefano Lubiana, and Mac Forbes are amply demonstrating the potential for Australian Pinot Noir when it is properly matched to a vineyard site.

Delatite's vineyards in Upper Goulburn lie at altitude and benefit from a cooler climate than some parts of Victoria.

PIPERS BROOK
2009 WAS A GOOD YEAR FOR THE RIESLING, WITH A BALANCED RIPENING SEASON

Paringa Estate Mornington Peninsula

Lindsay McCall established this Mornington Peninsula winery in the mid-1980s, keeping his day job as a teacher until 1996, when the home vineyard was fully planted. Recent years have seen growth, with more than 200 tons (203 tonnes) of grapes crushed each year from a mixture of estate and leased vineyards, and 16,000 cases produced anually. The chief focus is on Pinot Noir and Shiraz, with the single-vineyard reserves at the top of the range only being released in good years. The Reserve Pinot is the pick of the bunch: the 2003 shows intense, lush, dark cherry fruit with some mellow oak influence.

44 Paringa Rd, Red Hill South, VIC 3937
www.paringaestate.com.au

Pipers Brook Tasmania

Perhaps the best known Tasmanian winery, Pipers Brook was founded by Dr. Andrew Pirie in 1974. It is now part of the Kreglinger group of wine estates, with Kreglinger also being a brand of high-end sparkling wine within the Pipers Brook portfolio. The vineyards are scattered around the Tamar River inlet, on the north coast of Tasmania, and holdings now total more than 494 acres (200ha), which is huge by Tasmanian standards. The wines cover a range of varieties and quality can vary a bit, with the chief problem being lack of ripeness in some vintages. But when they are good, these are elegantly fine wines.

1216 Pipers Brook Rd, Pipers Brook, TAS 7254
www.kreglingerwineestates.com

Pirie Tasmania Tasmania

Dr. Andrew Pirie is famous for putting Tasmania on the viticultural map and for founding Pipers Brook in the mid-1970s. In 2002, he left to pursue other projects, one of which was his own wine venture—Pirie Tasmania. The wines are produced in four ranges: South (fresh, fruit-focused, and affordable), Pirie Estate (more serious and elegant), Pirie Reserve (high-end special releases), and Pirie Sparkling. The cherryish, supple, Estate Pinot Noir is the one to look out for.

1A Waldhord Drive, Rosevears, TAS 7277
www.pirietasmania.com.au

Pondalowie Bendigo

Dominic Morris has for some years been responsible for the wine at Quinta do Crasto in Portugal's Douro. Along with his wife Krystina (also a winemaker), he is now making his own wines at Pondalowie in Bendigo with 25 acres (10ha) of vines spread over two vineyards. One of the vineyards is a 10 acre (4ha) property owned by Dominic's parents and planted in 1996 with Shiraz, Cabernet Sauvignon, and Malbec. The other vineyard is the Morris' own property, which is planted with Shiraz, Tempranillo, Cabernet Sauvignon, and Viognier. The wines are made in an unashamedly forward style that emphasizes fruit quality and, with the more ambitious bottlings, are bolstered by generous oak. Quality is quite high across the board.

6 Main St, Bridgewater-on-Loddon, VIC 3516
www.pondalowie.com.au

Port Phillip Estate Mornington Peninsula

Sharing the same ownership (Gjergja family) and winemaker (Sandro Mosele) as the wonderful Kooyong, this Mornington Peninsula estate has an excellent reputation for its wines. As well as a focused, structured Pinot Noir, Port Phillip also makes a powerful Chardonnay, a barrel-fermented Sauvignon Blanc and a fresh, spicy Shiraz. Accompanying the regular range is another label, Quartier, which includes Arneis and Barbera that are both made from bought-in grapes. ★ **Rising star**

261 Red Hill Rd, Red Hill South, VIC 3937
www.portphillipestate.com.au

Redbank King Valley

Redbank was a brand established in 1973 by Neill and Sally Robb, who made Sally's Paddock under this label. In 2005, the name was purchased by the Hill Smith family (of Yalumba) who now use it as a brand for wines that are made from fruit bought-in from various Victorian regions. The Robbs still use the name Redbank Winery, however, which can cause confusion. Wines from a wide range of varieties are produced by Redbank under the labels The Anvil, The Long Paddock, and Emily (sparkling wines). The Anvil Beechworth Shiraz is the wine to look out for here.

1 Sally's Lane, Redbank, VIC 3478
www.sallyspaddock.com.au

Redesdale Estate Heathcote

This small Heathcote producer makes just 800 cases a year from 10 acres (4ha) of middle-aged vines. When the current owners, the Williams, purchased this property in 1988, it was run down and for some years, they sold their grapes. In 1999, they decided to bottle their own wine, which was made by Tobias Ansted at Balgownie. Today they make two wines, a Shiraz and a Cabernet Sauvignon blend, which are both made from hand-picked estate fruit.

North Redesdale Rd, Redesdale, VIC 3444
www.redesdale.com

Red Hill Estate Mornington Peninsula

By Mornington Peninsula standards, Red Hill is a big player, drawing on 174 acres (70ha) of vineyards that are spread over five sites. In 2006, it joined forces with the Hunter Valley winery, Arrowfield, to form the InWine Group Australia. At the top of the quality tree sit a Reserve Chardonnay and Pinot Noir. These are joined by a Shiraz, Sauvignon Blanc, and Pinot Gris in the Estate range, which also includes two sparkling wines. There is also a separate label, Bimãris, which is more affordable and user friendly.

53 Shoreham Rd, Red Hill South, VIC 3937
www.redhillestate.com.au

Sally's Paddock Pyrenees

There is great potential for confusion here. Neill and Sally Robb established the Redbank Winery in the Pyrenees region of Victoria in the early 1970s. In 2005, the Hill Smith family acquired the Redbank brand, but the Robb's still use the name Redbank Winery. They own four vineyards: Sally's Paddock, Sally's Hill, Rocky Ridge, and The Westerner. Sally's Paddock is the most famous of their wines, a cool-climate Bordeaux blend, with added Shiraz, that has the potential to age.

1 Sally's Lane, Redbank, VIC 3478
www.sallyspaddock.com.au

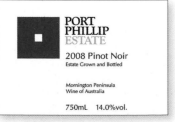

PORT PHILLIP ESTATE
SITUATED IN A NATURAL AMPHITHEATER, PORT PHILLIP HAS AN IDEAL COOL CLIMATE

Savaterre Beechworth

Owner Keppell Smith takes a decidedly Old World approach to his wines—his Beechworth vineyard is close planted and managed organically. Just Chardonnay and Pinot Noir are grown, and both are fantastic. The 2006 Chardonnay is made in a strikingly intense style, with concentrated spicy, toasty character. The intense and powerfully flavored Pinot Noir needs a bit of bottle age to show its best. ★ Rising star

Beechworth, VIC 3747
www.savaterre.com

Scotchmans Hill Geelong

A major vineyard in the Geelong region, family owned and operated Scotchmans Hill has a reputation for good-quality wines that offer value for money. They are located on the Bellarine Peninsula, where they have their main vineyard, but grapes are also sourced from 170 acres (69ha) of growers' vineyards that are spread throughout Geelong and the peninsula itself. As well as five separate wine ranges from Geelong, Scotchmans Hill also produces wines from Mornington Peninsula, Western Australia, and Marlborough in New Zealand.

190 Scotchmans Rd, Drysdale, VIC 3222
www.scotchmans.com.au

Seppelt Great Western Grampians

Now part of the Fosters group, this is one of the historic names in Australian wine and producer of the country's best-known sparkling wines. Seppelt also used to own the Seppeltsfield winery in the Barossa, which specialized in fortified wines, but this has now been sold to Kilkanoon. It is their series of table wines, from regions such as Heathcote, Bendigo, Henty, and Grampians, that are winning all the accolades now. The 2002 St Peters Great Western Shiraz is massive, with concentrated, rich, oak-bolstered fruit. The Mount Ida Vineyard Shiraz from Heathcote is equally compelling, with dense, focused fruit. Drumborg Riesling is also top quality—tight in its youth, but aging superbly.

Moyston Rd, Great Western, VIC 3377
www.seppelt.com.au

Seville Estate Yarra Valley

Seville Estate is one of the small band of wineries responsible for the second coming of the Yarra Valley in the early 1970s. It was run by its founder, Dr. Peter McMahon, until he retired in 1997. For eight years, it was under the ownership of Hunter Valley's Brokenwood, before being sold to Graham and Margaret Van der Meulen in 2005. Peter's grandson, Dylan MacMahon, is the winemaker. The vineyards are located on a volcanic ridge in a cool spot in the Upper Yarra, and the wines reflect this with focused, bright fruit flavors. The Chardonnay, Pinot Noir, and Cabernet Sauvignon are very good, but it is the Shiraz that gets the most praise. A second wine range, the Barber, uses bought-in grapes and includes a Beechworth Pinot Gris.

65 Linwood Rd, Seville, VIC 3139
www.sevilleestate.com.au

Shadowfax Port Phillip

Established in 2000, Shadowfax is an exciting and fairly new venture based at Port Phillip in Victoria. New Zealander Matt Harrop is the winemaker, with previous

SAVATERRE
THE 2006 CHARDONNAY IS ONE OF
SAVATERRE'S FINEST VINTAGES TO DATE

STANTON & KILLEEN
THERE HAVE BEEN SIX GENERATIONS OF
STANTON & KILLEEN WINEMAKERS

experience at Brokenwood. As well as buying in grapes, Shadowfax also owns their own vineyards in key Victorian sites. Three are located in Heathcote, including the oldest in the region (planted in 1968); one is in Weribee, also home to the winery, which was planted in 1998; another is in Geelong, where new clones of Pinot Noir were planted in 2002; and one is in Tallarook, which was planted in 1999. From their large and consistently good range, look out for the Pink Cliffs Heathcote Shiraz and the One Eye Heathcote Shiraz. ★ Rising star

K Rd, Werribee, VIC 3030
www.shadowfax.com.au

Spear Gully Yarra Valley

Dr. Tony Jordan is famous for his work, initially as a wine consultant and latterly in running LVMH's wine portfolio. With his wife Michele, he has established a small 6.2 acre (2.5 ha) vineyard near their home in Hoddles Creek, in the Upper Yarra. He also buys in grapes from other regions for the Spear Gully wines. The Chardonnay, from the home vineyard, is really impressive, with taut, precise flavors and the potential to develop.

455 Lusatia Park Rd, Hoddles Creek, VIC 3139
04 1733 1599

Stanton & Killeen Rutherglen

Stanton & Killeen is one of the small band of top Rutherglen producers specializing in the unique fortified liqueur Muscats and Tokays that are an Australian national treasure. They also make a well-regarded Vintage Fortified (until recently labeled as "Port") from Shiraz, a characterful and intense Durif red table wine, and a bevy of Portuguese varieties.

Jacks Rd, Murray Valley Hwy, Rutherglen, VIC 3685
www.stantonandkilleenwines.com.au

Stefano Lubiana Tasmania

Steve Lubiana is one of Tasmania's top producers. He has 44.5 acres (18ha) of close-planted vines that overlook the tidal estuary of the Derwent River, just north of Hobart. Pinot Noir and Chardonnay are the main focus, but he also grows Nebbiolo, Pinot Gris, Merlot, and Sauvignon Blanc. The Pinot Noir is fantastic here: the 2006 Estate Pinot is a rich, ripe style, but shows amazing elegance, while the 2005 Sasso Pinot Noir takes the concentration up a notch, but still shows spellbinding elegance. World class. ★ Rising star

60 Rowbottoms Rd, Granton, TAS 7073
www.slw.com.au

Stoney Rise Tasmania

A rising star on the Tasmanian wine scene, Stoney Rise began life in 2000, but really came to life in 2004 when Joe and Lou Holyman purchased the former Rotherhythe vineyard. They set to work restoring it, and are now making some of Australia's best Pinot Noir, as well as some smart Chardonnay. The 2007 Holyman Pinot Noir is beautifully focused and aromatic, with brilliantly balanced cherry fruit and a spicy structure. Holyman is the label used for the top wines and Stoney Rise for the more approachable, young wines. ★ Rising star

96 Hendersons Lane, Gravelly Beach, TAS 7276
www.stoneyrise.com

TAMAR RIDGE
ONLY GRAPES GROWN AT THE KAYENA
VINEYARD ARE IN THE SAUVIGNON BLANC 2008

YERING STATION
ORIGINALLY PLANTED IN 1838, YERING STATION
IS VICTORIA'S OLDEST VINEYARD

Stonier Mornington Peninsula

Now part of the Lion Nathan group, Stonier was one of the first wineries established on the Mornington Peninsula. It remains one of the best, making beautifully textured and elegant Pinot Noir and Chardonnay. Both the Reserve Chardonnay and Reserve Pinot Noir are fantastic, and a notch above the already excellent regular bottlings. There are also single-vineyard selections of each variety: the KBS Vineyard Chardonnay being complex and toasty, with fresh citrus fruit and powerful oak flavors that mesh well. Long-term winemaker Geraldine McFaul left in 2008 and it is hoped that these wines will maintain their style and elegance.

2 Thompsons Lane, Merricks, VIC 3916
www.stoniers.com.au

Summerfield Pyrenees

A boutique producer from the Pyrenees region of Victoria, Summerfield was established by its current owner, Ian Summerfield, in 1979 on his own property. Ian's son, Mark, now makes the wines, focusing on powerful and intense Shiraz and Cabernet Sauvignon, with the potential to age.

5967 Stawell-Avoca Rd, Moonambel, VIC 3478
www.summerfieldwines.com

Sutton Grange Bendigo

This Bendigo producer is making waves with its boldly flavored wines. For many years, Sutton Grange was a thoroughbred horse-racing facility, and vines were first planted here by Peter Sidwell, the current owner, in 1998. The first wines were made by Giles Lapalus, who hails from Burgundy, where he trained and were released in 2003. There are two wine ranges: Fairbank is the earlier drinking wines and Sutton Grange is the top wines. The surprises here include the Sangiovese-based Giove and the unusual, but wonderful, Ratafianovese, a Fiano/Sangiovese blend. ★ **Rising star**

Carnochan's Lane, Sutton Grange, VIC 3448
www.suttongrangewines.com

Tahbilk Nagambie Lakes

Tahbilk is a winery steeped in tradition and probably best known for its ageworthy and affordable Marsanne. The estate is based near the Nagambie Lakes in central Victoria. The 494 acres (200ha) of vines include some of the country's, if not the world's, oldest Shiraz vines, which date back to 1860. Tiny quantities of the 1860 Shiraz are made—a complex, ageworthy, and expensive wine. Production of their other wines is sizeable at 100,000 cases a year. The Marsanne shows focused lemony, peachy fruit in its youth, developing with a decade's bottle age to show notes of toast, beeswax, and honey. Also worth looking out for are the Cabernet and Shiraz that are made under the Eric Stevens Purbrick label.

Goulburn Valley Hwy, Nagambie, VIC 3608
www.tahbilk.com.au

Taltarni Pyrenees

Owned by a French family (the Goelets), who established this pioneering Pyrenees vineyard in 1969, Taltarni has always had quite a European feel to it. The wines have also been largely fashioned by French winemakers, initially Dominique Portet, and now Loïc de Calvez, and the reds have often shown levels of structure that demand some bottle age. As well as wines from the Pyrenees, Taltarni also owns vineyards in Tasmania, which are used for sparkling wine production, and sources Shiraz from Heathcote.

339 Taltarni Rd, Moonambel, VIC 3478
www.taltarni.com.au

Tamar Ridge Tasmania

Although the vines were only planted in 1994, and the first wines were released as recently as 1999, Tamar Ridge is already emerging as one of Tasmania's leading lights. It is a large venture, with around 741 acres (300ha) of vines located in three different sites. All the vineyards are overseen by the well-known viticultural consultant Richard Smart. Another famous name here is that of CEO and chief winemaker Andrew Pirie, who is well-known for establishing the Tasmanian superstar winery Pipers Brook. Tamar Ridge produces impressive cool-climate wines, especially the Pinot Noir and Sauvignon Blanc. There are three wine ranges: Kayena Vineyard (high end), Research Series (experimental wines), and Devil's Corner (more approachable). ★ **Rising star**

653 Auburn Rd, Kayena, TAS 7270
www.tamarridge.com.au

Tarrawarra Yarra Valley

Winemaker Clare Halloran is making some of the Yarra Valley's best Pinot Noir and Chardonnay at Tarrawarra. In the 10 years of her tenure here, she has made the wines more elegant and given them good aging potential. The high-end MDB Chardonnay is a good example of this, with fine aromatics and a rounded and restrained, yet concentrated, palate that shows almost perfect balance. Also worth seeking out is the Estate MRV (Marsanne/Roussanne/Viognier). The Tin Cows range features some bought-in fruit. ★ **Rising star**

311 Healesville-Yarra Glen Rd, VIC 3775
www.tarrawarra.com.au

Ten Minutes by Tractor
Mornington Peninsula

The unusual name of this winery refers to the distance between the three vineyards that supply it—McCutcheon, Wallis, and Judd. All of these vineyards are within the Main Ridge subregion, which is the highest and coolest part of the Mornington Peninsula. Chardonnay and Pinot Noir are the focus here, and they are made in a complex, expressive style with lovely fruit purity. ★ **Rising star**

1333 Mornington Flinders Rd, Main Ridge, VIC 3928
www.tenminutesbytractor.com.au

Virgin Hills Macedon Ranges

From a marginal climate in the Macedon Ranges, Virgin Hills makes just one wine: an ageworthy Bordeaux blend that, in good vintages, is one of Australia's best. This wine was the vision of Hungarian-born sculptor and restaurateur Tom Lazar, who bought 741 acres (300ha) of bushland in 1968. His intention was to grow cherries, but when the cherries did badly, he turned the property into a vineyard and grew grapes instead. Virgin Hills is now owned by Michael Hope, who owns Hope Estate in the Hunter Valley, and the vineyard is now tended organically, with a traditional, low intervention approach in the winery.

Salisbury Rd, Lauriston West via Kyneton, VIC 3444
www.virginhills.com.au

Wild Duck Creek Heathcote

Wild Duck Creek, in the Heathcote region, is famous for the controversially alcoholic Shiraz Duck Muck. David Anderson only makes around 200 cases of this annually and this, combined with rave reviews in the US, has led to it becoming one of Australia's cult wines. It is a thick, viscous, intense, and sweetly fruited wine: the 2004 weighed in at a hefty 16.5%, but it is delicious and quite balanced in this supercharged style—a guilty pleasure.

762 Spring Flat Rd, Heathcote, VIC 3523
www.wildduckcreekestate.com

William Downie Yarra Valley

A rising star on the Australian wine scene, William Downie established his own label in 2003. He specializes exclusively in Pinot Noir, and sources grapes from the Yarra Valley, Gippsland, and the Mornington Peninsula. His own property in the Yarra was planted in 2008, and is not yet producing. The 2006 Yarra Valley Pinot Noir is richly aromatic, with a concentrated and spicy, yet still elegant, palate. One to watch. ★ **Rising star**

121 Yarragon Sth Rd, Yarragon, VIC 3823;
www.williamdownie.com.au

Yabby Lake Mornington Peninsula

The arrival of Tom Carson, one of Australia's most celebrated young winemakers, from Yering Station has certainly raised the profile of Yabby Lake. This is one of four properties owned by the Kirby family, which are all brought together under the Yabby Lake banner. Four wine ranges are made at Yabby Lake in the Mornington Peninsula: Yabby Lake, Red Claw, Heathcote Estate, and Cooralook.

112 Tuerong Rd, Tuerong, VIC 3933
www.yabbylake.com

Yarra Yarra Yarra Valley

Ian Maclean caught the wine bug in the mid-1970s and purchased a 42 acre (17ha) site in the warmer, northern end of the Yarra Valley in 1977, with a view to starting a vineyard. He began planting two years later and the first wines appeared in 1983. Since then, he has been the only winemaker at Yarra Yarra, and his wines have received wide critical acclaim. Just over 22 acres (9ha) are planted. Initially the focus was on Bordeaux varieties, which do well in this warmer spot, but more recently 2.5 acres (1ha) of Syrah has also been planted.

239 Hunts Lane, Steels Creek, VIC 3775;
www.yarrayarravineyard.com.au

Yarra Yering Yarra Valley

One of Australia's vinous treasures, Yarra Yering was set up by the eccentric Dr. Bailey Carrodus, who died in 2008. In 1973 Carrodus produced the first commercial vintage from the Yarra since 1922. From dry grown vineyards, and using primitive winery equipment, he managed to fashion some fabulously elegant, long lived reds. Carrodus did everything in the winery himself, and the distinctive hand-drawn labels were the work of his partner. A number of wines were made, but the best are the Dry Red No 1 (based on Cabernet Sauvignon) and the Dry Red No 2 (based on Shiraz). While the wines can be a little inconsistent, when they perform they are excellent—at a recent tasting, the 1980 No 2 and 1989 No 1 were on superb form, showing beautiful purity and superb elegance. The winery was bought by Kaesler wines in 2009, but they intend to keep Yarra Yering the way it was, in the spirit of Carrodus.

4 Briarty Rd, Gruyere, VIC 3770
www.yarrayering.com

Yering Station Yarra Valley

Yering Station was established in 1837, but in the 1860s, the original Yarra Valley property was split into three properties: Yering Station, Yeringberg, and St Huberts. Yering Station is now part of the Rathbone group and, under the guidance of young winemaker Tom Carson, has established a stellar reputation for its wines. These include a complex, well-defined Shiraz Viognier and a rich, but fresh, Chardonnay. Carson left in 2008, and the winemaking is now in the hands of Willy Lunn. Yering Station also make some stylish sparkling wines, in partnership with Champagne Devaux and under the brand name Yarrabank.

38 Melba Hwy, Yarra Glen, VIC 3775
www.yering.com

Yeringberg Yarra Valley

Third-generation wine-grower Guill de Pury was responsible for resurrecting Yeringberg as a wine estate in the 1970s. This heralded the start of the Yarra renaissance, after a 50-year period when wine-growing disappeared from the valley. De Pury's Yeringberg winery is a piece of living history, dating back to the 19th century. His grandfather, Frederic Guillame de Pury, was a Swiss baron who bought part of the original 43,000 acre (1,740ha) Yering Station in 1863. To this day, Yeringberg is predominantly a 1,200 acre (486ha) sheep and cattle farm, but it now also has 50 acres (20ha) of vines, from which five wines are made in a very simple, hands-on fashion. The pick of the bunch is the estate wine, Yeringberg, which is an elegant Bordeaux blend.

Maroondah Hwy, Coldstream, VIC 3770
www.yeringberg.com

AUSTRALIA'S GREAT FORTIFIED WINES

In the northeastern corner of South Australia lies the hot Rutherglen region. It is famous for its great fortified sweet wines: the Liqueur Muscats and Tokays, now officially called "Topaques," which are made from the Muscadelle grape variety. In the early part of the last century, fortified wines constituted 80% of Australia's wine production. Today, Rutherglen continues that tradition. Made by blending wines of different ages in a sherrylike solera system, the resulting wines can gain incredible complexity and concentration with age, which is the key to their character. Although they may be unfashionable and easily overlooked, they are one of Australia's greatest contributions to the world of fine wine.

SOUTH AUSTRALIA

South Australia

The traditional heart of the Australian wine scene, South Australia encompasses historical regions such as the Barossa Valley, McLaren Vale, and the Clare Valley, as well as the newer fine wine regions of Adelaide Hills and Coonawarra. Because South Australia has remained free of the vine pest phylloxera, it still has many old vineyards with ancient vines that are planted on their own roots. A wide range of wines are made in this state, from the big, warm reds of the Barossa, to the lean, citrus Rieslings of the Clare and Eden valleys. South Australia is also renowned for its long-lived Cabernet Sauvignons from Coonawarra and some of the country's most refined Chardonnays, which are produced in the Adelaide Hills.

Major grapes

 Reds

Cabernet Sauvignon

Grenache

Mataro (Mourvèdre)

Pinot Noir

Shiraz

 Whites

Chardonnay

Pinot Gris

Riesling

Sauvignon Blanc

Viognier

Vintages

2009
Late heatwave reduced yields. Adelaide Hills had a great vintage. Barossa and Coonawarra were very good; McLaren Vale was mixed.

2008
Heatwave late in the growing season: early harvested fruit made great wines, but some vineyards suffered.

2007
The year of the drought.

2006
Adelaide Hills had spring frosts, but good quality and harvest across most regions.

2005
Ideal conditions yielded a large crop of good quality.

2004
A large vintage with irregular quality. Ideal weather in Adelaide Hills and Coonawarra.

South Australia has always been at the heart of the Australian wine industry. The first vineyards were planted in the Barossa Valley by immigrants in the 1840s. The state has remained phylloxera free, so the Barossa retains a treasure trove of ancient, ungrafted vineyards. The area specializes in richly flavored red wines made primarily from Shiraz, but Grenache and Mataro (the local name for Mourvèdre) also do well—one of the region's classic styles is GSM, a blend of all three varieties.

Considered part of the Barossa, neighboring Eden Valley to the east is a cooler, higher area that is known for producing some of Australia's best dry Rieslings. Unfortunately, the Barossa went out of fashion as a warm-climate region in the 1980s and many vines were pulled up. Thanks to the efforts of producers such as Peter Lehmann, Charles Melton, and Rocky O'Callaghan, however, it was revived and now some of Australia's most treasured red wines are made here.

A short drive northwest of the Barossa lies the Clare Valley—which is in fact a series of narrow valleys—where the climate is moderated by altitude. The Clare is unusual in that its best wines —fine, mineralic dry Rieslings and reds from Cabernet Sauvignon and Shiraz—do not seem to naturally fit together, but all three varieties do extremely well in this area.

The McLaren Vale is another warm-climate region that is best known for its big red wines. It is also where the first vines in South Australia were planted, in 1838. Here, unlike the Barossa, Cabernet Sauvignon performs well, although the

star performer is the richly flavored Shiraz. Part of the Fleurieu Peninsula, McLaren Vale is neighbored by the Langhorne Creek. This is a far less visible region, but nonetheless an important one in terms of production, making rich, soft Cabernet Sauvignon and Shiraz.

One of South Australia's most exciting regions is the Adelaide Hills, an old region where grape growing had disappeared until it was pioneered again in the late 1970s by Brian Croser. Elevation is the key here, as it results in a cooler climate that is ideal for producing fine Sauvignon Blanc, refined Chardonnay, stylish Shiraz, and even Pinot Noir. In recent years, aromatic varieties, such as Viognier and Pinot Gris, have also started to achieve success here.

Moving further south and east, toward the border with Victoria, Coonawarra is an isolated region that has turned into a special place for growing Cabernet Sauvignon. The most important factor here is the soil: a shallow, red top soil over a free-draining limestone base, which, coupled with the relatively cool climate, is perfect for red Bordeaux varieties. While other grapes, including Shiraz and Chardonnay, can perform respectably here, Cabernet Sauvignon is Coonawarra's specialty, and one of Australia's top wine styles.

Also falling within the Limestone Coast Zone are four other relatively unknown, but promising, regions. Wrattonbully (just north of Coonawarra), Padthaway (even further north, with limestone soils), and Mount Benson and Robe (both cool limestone-dominated regions on the coast).

Annie's Lane Clare Valley

Fosters now own this well regarded Clare Valley winery, which used to be known as Quelltaller. It sources its grapes from across the valley and the wine is made at the Wolf Blass facility in the Barossa. A wide variety of wines are made in two ranges: Copper Trail (high end) and the Core Range. The wines have a reputation for over-delivering in terms of quality, reinforcing the fact that the Clare really is a great place to grow grapes.

Quelltaler Rd, Watervale, SA 5452
www.annieslane.com.au

Arrivo Adelaide Hills

Arrivo is an exciting new winery based in the Adelaide Hills that focuses solely on the tricky Nebbiolo grape variety. Peter Godden, of the Australian Wine Research Institute, is the man behind Arrivo, and he released his first wines in 2006. The 2006 Lunga Macerazione Nebbiolo is thrilling, with 72 days of skin contact that has resulted in a wine with a wonderful tannic structure supporting cherryish, spicy fruit. As well as two reds, a Rosato (rosé) is also made. ★Rising star

Aldgate, SA 5154
www.arrivo.com.au

Ashton Hills Adelaide Hills

One of the most highly regarded of the wineries in the Adelaide Hills, Stephen George's Ashton Hills is a small boutique operation of 7 acres (3ha) that specializes in Pinot Noir, but also produces excellent Riesling and sparkling wine. Fifteen clones of Pinot are grown here, in vineyards established back in 1982. The 2003 Estate Pinot Noir, tasted in 2009, showed lovely complexity, sweet cherry fruit and a touch of herbiness. George also makes the wines for Wendouree in the Clare Valley, one of Australia's most iconic wineries.

Tregarthen Rd, Ashton, SA 5137
08 8390 1243

Balnaves of Coonawarra Coonawarra

Balnaves is currently one of the stars of Coonawarra. After 17 years with Hungerford Hill, Doug Balnaves left to form his own consulting company in the late 1980s. He established his own vineyard in 1990, and in 1996 built a new winery. The current winemaker at Balnaves of Coonawarra is Pete Bissell, who joined from neighboring Wynns in 1995. Its top wine, The Tally, is one of Coonawarra's best Cabernet Sauvignons. It shows sweet, ripe, brooding blackberry and blackcurrant fruit with great definition and depth, in a ripe style—both the 2004 and 2006 are fantastic. The regular Cabernet Sauvignon is also excellent, and The Blend offers great quality at an affordable price.

Main Rd, Coonawarra, SA 5263
www.balnaves.com.au

Balthazar of the Barossa Barossa

Balthazar is owned and run by Anita Bowen, who is also a sex therapist in another life. Anita has 75 acres (30ha) of vines, which she planted in 1998 on the site of an original 19th century vineyard. She sourced her Shiraz vines from one of the oldest-known vineyards in the Barossa Valley, which dates back to 1847. The main focus here is on the Balthazar Shiraz, which is rich

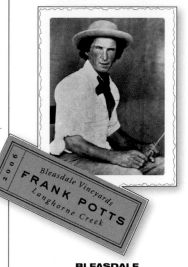

BLEASDALE
THE 2006 FRANK POTTS IS A BLEND OF
CABERNET SAUVIGNON AND MALBEC

BATTLE OF BOSWORTH
WHITE BOAR SHIRAZ USES GRAPES THAT ARE
DRIED ON THE VINE FOR ABOUT TWO WEEKS

and complex, with plenty of impact. Anita Bowen also makes a range of varietal wines called Ishtar, with fruit sourced from vineyards around South Australia.

Stonewell Rd, Marananga, SA 5353
www.balthazarbarossa.com

Barossa Valley Estate Barossa

Unusually for Australia, this operation is a co-operative. It was formed in the mid-1980s, involving around 80 growers, but it has now become a joint venture with Constellation Wines (Hardys). Stuart Bourne is the winemaker here, and with access to some great vineyards he is creating impressive wines. Top of the range is the fabulously dense and concentrated E&E Black Pepper Shiraz, which is among the best examples of this variety from this region. The Ebenezer range is also superb and includes good Shiraz, Cabernet, and Chardonnay.

Seppeltsfield Rd, Marananga, Barossa Valley, SA 5355
www.bve.com.au

Battle of Bosworth McLaren Vale

The Edgehill Vineyard, from which Battle of Bosworth wines are made, was established in 1970 by Peter and Anthea Bosworth. When their son Joch took over in 1995, he decided to switch to organic cultivation and begin producing wines under the Battle of Bosworth label. A broad range of attractively packaged wines are made here that share bright fruit flavors and high acidity. Pick of the bunch is the powerful White Boar Shiraz.

McLaren Vale, SA 5171
www.edgehill-vineyards.com.au

Bleasdale Langhorne Creek

The second-oldest family-owned winery in Australia, Bleasdale is steeped in history. Frank Potts planted his first vines in the Langhorne Creek in 1858; the winery still has the 140-year-old red gum wine press that he built, which is still in working order. The wines, made by fifth-generation Potts, are certainly not lacking in flavor. The two top wines here are the Frank Potts, a blend of Cabernet and Malbec, and the Generations Shiraz.

Wellington Rd, Langhorne Creek, SA 5255
www.bleasdale.com.au

Bowen Coonawarra

One of the famous names of Coonawarra, Bowen was established in 1972 by Doug Bowen, who now has 81 acres (33ha) of the renowned terra rossa soil. Doug still runs things here, but he is now assisted by his daughter Emma. Unusually for Coonawarra, the vineyards are pruned by hand and an arched cane trellis system is used. Just three wines are made: a Chardonnay, a Shiraz (aged in American oak), and a Cabernet (aged in French and Russian oak). The surprise here is the Shiraz, which is every bit as good as the Cabernet, even though this is very much a Cabernet region.

Riddoch Hwy, Coonawarra, SA 5263
www.bowenestate.com.au

Bremerton Langhorne Creek

Probably Langhorne Creek's best producer, Bremerton is run by sisters Lucy and Rebecca Willson, and Rebecca is the winemaker. The family owns 272 acres (110ha) of

SOUTH AUSTRALIA

Looks can be deceptive. Many of the larger regions indicated on this map are not significant producers of interesting wines. The heart of the South Australian wine region is actually a cluster of regions surrounding Adelaide, of which the most famous is the Barossa Valley. The neighboring Eden Valley is also included under the umbrella of Barossa, and together the two form the historic center of South Australian wine production. Also significant are the Adelaide Hills, a relatively cool climate region northeast of the city, and the McLaren Vale to the south. The Clare Valley, a couple of hours northwest of the Barossa, is another important region. The outliers here are the regions of the Limestone Coast, which are situated further south and are cooler. These include Coonawarra, which produces some of Australia's best Cabernet Sauvignon.

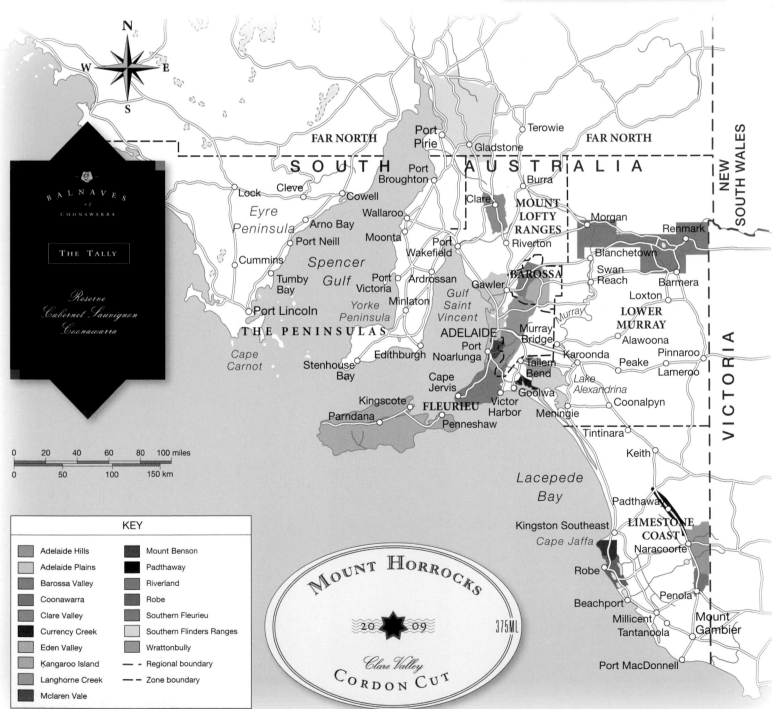

KEY

Adelaide Hills	Mount Benson
Adelaide Plains	Padthaway
Barossa Valley	Riverland
Coonawarra	Robe
Clare Valley	Southern Fleurieu
Currency Creek	Southern Flinders Ranges
Eden Valley	Wrattonbully
Kangaroo Island	– – Regional boundary
Langhorne Creek	– – – Zone boundary
Mclaren Vale	

BAROSSA VALLEY

Australia's largest quality wine region, the Barossa Valley, is an area of back-to-back vineyards, just a couple of hours' drive from Adelaide. The vineyards are planted largely on the flat valley floor, following the North Para River from Lyndoch through Tanunda, and past Nuriootpa. Phylloxera has never reached the Barossa, and so the region still boasts some fabulous ungrafted old-vine vineyards. Many of the Barossa vineyards are owned by long-time grape-growing families, creating a real sense of community,

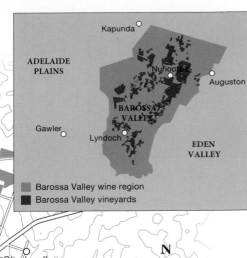

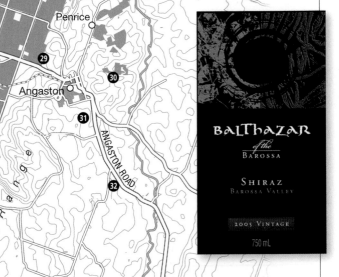

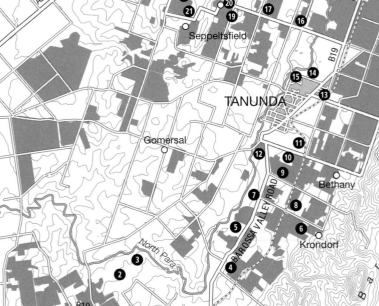

KEY

▨	Vineyards
	Rivers, lakes
	Roads, tracks
	65ft (20m) contours
	Urban areas
1	Location of one or more producers

0   2   4 miles
0   2   4   6   8 km

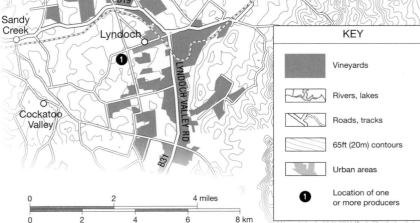

PRODUCERS

Balthazar of the Barossa **17**	Kalleske **23**	Spinifex **10**
Barossa Valley Estate **20**	Langmeil **15**	St Hallett **7**
Charles Melton **6**	Magpie Estate **16**	Standish Wine Co **3**
Colonial Estate **25**	Massena **2**	Teusner Wines **26**
Dutschke Wines **1**	Penfolds **28**	Thorn Clarke **30**
Elderton **27**	Peter Lehmann **14**	Torbreck **18**
Glaetzer **12**	Rockford **8**	Turkey Flat **11**
Grant Burge **5**	Rolf Binder Wines **16**	Two Hands **19**
Greenock Creek **22**	Rusden **13**	Wolf Blass **24**
Hobbs **32**	Saltram **29**	Yalumba **31**
Jacob's Creek **4**	Schwarz Wine Company **9**	
	Seppeltsfield **21**	

Always check the availability of visitor facilities and the visiting hours at a winery before planning your trip. Some wineries are open by appointment only.

FOX CREEK
THIS SPARKLING SHIRAZ/CABERNET FRANC
IS RICH, POWERFUL, AND OPULENT

vineyards and are joint owners/managers of a further 445 acres (180ha). From this, they select the best grapes for their own wines and sell the rest. Their top wines are the fantastic Old Adam Shiraz, which is aged in American oak, and the barrel selected Best of Vintage (BOV) Shiraz Cabernet. The house style is for lush, intense wines with prominent, but well-integrated, oak.

Strathalbyn Rd, Langhorne Creek, SA 5255
www.bremerton.com.au

Cascabel McLaren Vale

This boutique McLaren Vale winery was established by Susana Fernandez and Duncan Ferguson in 1997. Cascabel differs from other McLaren Vale producers in that it focuses largely on Spanish varieties, such as Tempranillo, Graciano, and Monastrell. Great care is taken in both the vineyard and winery: they harvest all the fruit by hand; use small, open fermenters for their reds, with no yeast inoculations; and age the wine in 132-gallon (500-liter) barrels. In addition to what they produce from their own 12 acres (5ha), they also buy in some Shiraz from the Fleurieu Peninsula and Riesling from Eden Valley. The wines are consistently good and range from a vibrant, early-release Tempranillo, to a monster, ageworthy Monastrell and a delicious Roussanne/Viognier.

Rogers Rd, Willunga, SA 5172
www.cascabelwinery.com.au

Chain of Ponds Adelaide Hills

An ambitious Adelaide Hills producer which, until a recent sale, was one of the largest vineyard holders in this well regarded, cool-climate region. It now sources grapes from around the Adelaide Hills, making a wide range of wines, with Italian varieties the specialty. The best wines are the Cachet Cabernet Sauvignon/ Shiraz/Merlot, the Amadeus Cabernet Sauvignon, and the Ledge Shiraz.

Adelaide Rd, Gumeracha, SA 5233
www.chainofponds.com.au

Chapel Hill McLaren Vale

One of the stars of the McLaren Vale region, Chapel Hill first made its name under the ownership of the Sellick and Gerrard families in the 1980s and 1990s, when Pam Dunsford was the winemaker. It was sold in 2000 to the Schmidheiny family, who owns Cuvaison in California's Napa Valley. Chapel Hill's viticulturalist, Rachel Steer, works sustainably using biodynamic principles to reduce chemical input in the vineyards. Winemaker Michael Fragos joined in 2004 and has been credited with a clear improvement in the already good wines. The best wines here are the Vicar, a powerful, dense, spicy Shiraz, and the Cabernet Sauvignon, which demonstrates just how good McLaren Vale Cabernet can be.

Corner Chapel Hill and Chaffey's Rd, McLaren Vale,
SA 5171; www.chapelhillwine.com.au

Charles Melton Barossa

Charlie Melton is a bit of a Barossa legend. He began making his own wines in 1984, at a time when the old-vine heritage of the Barossa was seriously undervalued. He made his name with a top-quality Shiraz and the wonderfully named Nine Popes, which is a blend of Grenache and Shiraz. The wines are made from old,

D'ARENBERG
COPPERMINE ROAD BECOMES MORE
HARMONIOUS WITH BOTTLE AGE

dry-grown vineyards and traditional techniques that include a mix of French and American oak barrels. It is worth looking out for the Sotto di Ferro, an oddity in this area, which is a sweet wine made principally from Pedro Ximénez grapes that have been laid out to dry after picking. Melton has recently purchased 73 acres (29.5ha) of land in the Eden Valley, with a view to planting Shiraz, Grenache, and other Rhône varieties.

Krondorf Rd, Tanunda, SA 5352
www.charlesmeltonwines.com.au

Chris Ringland Barossa

Chris Ringland's iconic Shiraz is made from the centenarian vineyard near his home in the Barossa Ranges, and spends more than three years in new French oak before bottling. Very little is made—around 100 cases a year—and because of the demand created by prodigious critic scores in the US, including 100 Parker Points for the 1996, 1998, and 2001, it sells for crazy prices.

No visitor facilities
www.ringlandvinters.com

Clarendon Hills McLaren Vale

Roman Bratasuik's Clarendon Hills became one of Australia's cult wineries during the 1990s. It is famous for dense, ripe, extracted red wines that have immense concentration, but while this is a style that has won over many people, it has also courted controversy. Astralis, a Shiraz, is the best wine here. The 2004 is sweet, jammy, and perhaps a little overdone, but the 2006, while also very sweetly fruited and concentrated, has an attractive, meaty dimension that works brilliantly. The 1996 shows that this wine can age, with a rich, complex, animally depth. The wine range consists of 19 single-vineyard, single-varietal wines. They are undoubtedly world class, but whether or not they suit you depends on your appreciation of this distinctive, super-ripe style.

Brookmans Rd, Blewitt Springs, SA 5171
www.clarendonhills.com.au

Colonial Estate Barossa

Colonial Estate is owned by Jonathan Maltus, the man behind Château Teyssier in St-Emilion in France, and the cult wine Le Dôme. He began acquiring small parcels of old Barossa vineyards in 2002 and takes a very French approach to winemaking, importing all his equipment from St-Emilion. There are currently 12 wines in the range and all are handmade, with great attention to detail. The top wines are the Exile, made with old-vine Shiraz and some Mourvèdre and Muscadelle, and Emigré, which is a multi-varietal blend. Initial releases were a bit too rich and porty, but the wines are improving and are now among the valley's best. ★ **Rising star**

Lot 264, Kalimna Rd, Light Pass, SA 5355
www.maltus.com

Coriole McLaren Vale

This mid-sized McLaren Vale producer is well known for being an early adopter of Italian varieties, having planted Sangiovese in 1985. Shiraz is still its strongest variety, accounting for 65% of plantings, followed by Sangiovese. In addition to this, Cariole also grows Chenin Blanc, Cabernet Sauvignon, Fiano, Grenache, Barbera, Montepulciano, Merlot, and Semillon. Lloyd

Reserve Shiraz is the top wine, but the regular Shiraz and The Soloist Shiraz are also superb. Of the Italian varieties, the Fiano is an interesting, mineralic white, and both the Sangiovese and Nebbiolo are worth tasting. The reds share a sense of balance and a lovely savory dimension.

Chaffeys Rd, McLaren Vale, SA 5171
www.coriole.com

Crabtree Clare Valley

Based in Watervale in the Clare Valley, Crabtree is a boutique winery with 32 acres (13ha) of vineyards. The winery was purchased in 2007 by Richard Woods and Rasa Fabian. Their high ambitions were quickly signaled by the hiring of Riesling expert Kerri Thompson as winemaker. While Riesling is the main focus here, Shiraz and Cabernet Sauvignon are also grown. This is definitely one to watch. ★ Rising star

North Terrace, Watervale, SA 5452
www.crabtreewines.com.au

D'Arenberg McLaren Vale

The exuberant Chester Osborn has transformed this traditional McLaren Vale winery, founded in 1912, into one of Australia's most dynamic and visible producers. The range of imaginatively labeled wines has widened over recent years, and production is now up to 250,000 cases. The top wines are largely deserving of the considerable hype and are made from old, low-yielding vines using traditional techniques that catch amazing levels of fruit and intensity. Best known of all the wines is the concentrated, ageworthy Dead Arm Shiraz, but perhaps even better is the Coppermine Road Cabernet Sauvignon, which is one of Australia's best. The Grenache-dominated Ironstone Pressings is also extremely good; in fact, quality across the entire range is impressive at this level of production.

Osborn Rd, McLaren Vale, SA 5171
www.darenberg.com.au

Dutschke Wines Barossa

Dutschke's wines come from an old vineyard in the southern end of the Barossa Valley, at Lyndoch. The company is a collaboration between experienced winemaker Wayne Dutschke and his uncle, grower Ken Semmler. In 1990, instead of selling all their grapes, they decided to keep some for themselves to produce wine under the Willowbend label. Volumes increased significantly in the late 1990s, when these wines became a hit in the US, and the name Dutschke Wines was adopted. St Jakobi is a rich, ripe, American oak-aged Shiraz; the French oak-aged Oscar Semmler Shiraz is similarly rich, but a little more profound; while the Single Barrel Barossa Shiraz possibly pushes ripeness a little too far. A number of fortified wines are also made.

Gods Hill Rd, Lyndoch, SA 5351
www.dutschkewines.com

Elderton Barossa

The secret of this family-owned winery's success is a 72 acre (29ha) vineyard on the Barossa Valley floor that contains a couple of blocks of ancient vines. Owned by the Ashmead family since the late 1970s, the first wines were made in 1982. Since then, their full-throttled,

sometimes oak-influenced style has won many fans. The top wines are the Ashmead Cabernet Sauvignon and the Command Shiraz, from centenarian vines. Both age well.

3–5 Tanunda Rd, Nuriootpa, SA 5355
www.eldertonwines.com.au

First Drop Barossa

A young, ambitious "virtual winery" (it does not own vineyards or a winery), First Drop is a collaboration between St Hallett winemaker Matt Gant and John Retsas of Schild Estate. The grapes are sourced from the Barossa, Adelaide Hills, and McLaren Vale, and a wide range of wines are produced, including oddities such as Barbera, Arneis, Nebbiolo, and Montepulciano, and a number of different Barossa Shirazes. The Minchia Montepulciano is an interesting wine, showing bold, spicy, brambly fruit, while the Bellia Coppia Arneis is fresh and mineralic. The Two Percent Barossa Shiraz demonstrates that First Drop can also do the classics well, showing a lovely focus and freshness to the sweet, dense fruit. ★ Rising star

No visitor facilities
www.firstdropwine.com

Fox Creek McLaren Vale

The Fox Creek story is a recent one. Although the project began in 1984, when Jim and Helen Watts bought this 79 acre (32ha) McLaren Vale property, the first wine, a Shiraz, was not released until 1994. This wine instantly put them on the map and gained a cult following, especially in the US. Part of the reason for this success was the winemaking talent of Sparky and Sarah Marquis (Sarah is the daughter of Jim and Helen Watts). Sparky and Sarah have since left to work on their own projects, but the quality has been maintained under the guidance of a new winemaking team, Dan Hills and Tony Walker, and more recently, Chris Dix and Scott Zrna. The top wine here is the dense Reserve Shiraz, but the Vixen Sparkling Shiraz/Cabernet Franc is also excellent.

McLaren Vale, SA 5171
www.foxcreekwines.com.au

Geoff Merrill McLaren Vale

Previously a winemaker for Hardys, Geoff Merrill left to run his own Mount Hurtle winery in the McLaren Vale in 1988. He also owns a vineyard in Coonawarra. Merrill's wines can be a little unsubtle and obvious, with evident oak, and are often released a bit later than most. The top wine is the dense, rich Henley Shiraz.

291 Pimpala Rd, Woodcroft, SA 5162
www.geoffmerrillwines.com

Geoff Weaver Adelaide Hills

Adelaide Hills wine-grower Geoff Weaver used to be the chief winemaker at Hardys. He began making wines from his own vineyard in 1985, and finally left the corporate world in 1992 to focus solely on his 30 acre (12ha) vineyard at Lenswood, high in the Adelaide Hills. Powerful, full-flavored Sauvignon Blanc is the focus, with Ferus being a separate bottling of this variety that is wild yeast fermented and oak aged. Chardonnay is strong, Pinot Noir is elegant, and a fresh Cabernet/Merlot is also made.

2 Gilpin Lane, Mitcham, SA 5062
www.geoffweaver.com.au

ANCIENT VINES

South Australia is one of the few vineyard areas not to have been affected by the root-munching aphid phylloxera, which devastated many of the world's wine regions in the late 19th century and led to replanted vines being grafted onto disease-resistant, American vine rootstocks. Some of the world's oldest vines now grow in South Australia, in particular the Barossa Valley and McLaren Vale, where there are many centenarian vineyards. The vines that grow here, some of which date back to 1840, are remarkable-looking, thick-trunked, gnarled specimens that produce low yields and, typically, make superb wines. No one knows exactly why old vines make exceptional wine, although after such a long time in the ground, the extensive root systems and naturally low yields of grapes may mean that the vines have reached a natural state of balance. The vineyards that are allowed to get so old are also likely to be those that perform the best.

GROSSET
THE POLISH HILL RIESLING IS BRIGHT, WITH A
YOUTHFUL TANG AND A TAUT STRUCTURE

GLAETZER
AMON-RA IS MADE FROM VINES THAT ARE
BETWEEN 50 AND 120 YEARS OLD

Glaetzer Barossa

Brilliant young winemaker Ben Glaetzer has revitalized the family label since he took over in 2002. The style change has been marked—Ben's hallmark is purity of fruit and his wines are ripe, but still very much alive. He uses oak from 16 different coopers, most of which is American and seasoned in France, mainly to add structure and texture rather than flavor. The grapes are sourced from old vineyards around the Barossa area. Some Glaetzer wines have achieved cult status, particularly in the US. Among the most popular is the rich, pure Amon-Ra Shiraz, with the Anaperenna (a Shiraz/Cabernet Sauvignon blend that used to be called Godolphin) close behind. The Wallace (Shiraz/Grenache) and Bishop (Shiraz) are also excellent, and a little more affordable. ★ **Rising star**

34 Barossa Valley Way, Tanunda, SA 5352
www.glaetzer.com

Grant Burge Barossa

Barossa legend Grant Burge bought the run down Krondorf winery in 1978, improved its wines dramatically, then sold it to Mildara in 1986. He began his own operation a couple of years later, steadily acquiring vineyards and buying back Krondorf in 1999. With 1,087 acres (440ha) spread across the valley, Grant Burge is now one of the largest private vineyard owners in the area. The wines are made in a richly flavored, generously oaked style. The pinnacle of the extensive range is a trio of biblically named wines: Meshach (Shiraz), Shadrach (Cabernet Sauvignon), and Abednego (Grenache/Shiraz/Mourvèdre). Sitting just below these, but also very good, are the Holy Trinity, Filsell Shiraz, and Balthasar Shiraz/Viognier.

Barossa Valley Way, Tanunda, SA 5352
www.grantburgewines.com.au

Greenock Creek Barossa

Owned by Michael and Annabel Waugh, Greenock Creek is a tiny boutique Barossa winery with a production level of only 2,500 cases per year. The wines are fashioned from old, late-picked, low-yielding vineyards by consultant winemaker Chris Ringland. They are rich, concentrated, and extracted in style and have accumulated quite a reputation. This is one of the Barossa wineries that has achieved cult status in the US on the back of glowing critical reviews from Robert Parker, but some have also criticized the wines for being a little too rich and sweet.

Radford Rd, Seppeltsfield, SA 5355
gckwines@dove.net.au

Grosset Clare Valley

The talented and studiously intense Jeffrey Grosset is Australia's most prominent Riesling expert. He has been making exceptional Riesling in the Clare Valley since 1981, first from Polish Hill and more recently from Watervale. Both age well: the 1984 Polish Hill, for example, has developed beautifully and shows lovely precision and complexity. Grosset does not just produce Riesling, though. His Gaia red, from an elevated single vineyard in the Clare, is thrilling, fresh, and ageworthy, while his Chardonnay and Pinot Noir, both from Adelaide Hills fruit, are also top class.

King St, Auburn, Clare Valley, SA 5451
www.grosset.com.au

Hardys McLaren Vale

One of the most famous names in Australian wine, Hardys is now part of the giant Constellation drinks company. Most of the wines in its large portfolio are of little interest to wine connoisseurs, but there is no disputing the quality of their two top wines, the Eileen Hardy Shiraz and Eileen Hardy Chardonnay, which are both multi-regional blends. The 1999 Eileen Hardy Shiraz is aging beautifully and is already a modern classic. Also worth noting are Hardys' sparkling wines, including the vintage-dated Sir James.

Reynell Rd, Reynella, SA 5161
www.hardys.com.au

Heartland Langhorne Creek

This is a collaborative venture that includes vineyards in Limestone Coast and Langhorne Creek. Heartland has five owners, including major shareholder Ben Glaetzer, and owns 1,000 acres (405ha) of vineyard—450 acres (164ha) in Limestone Coast and 550 acres (223ha) in Langhorne Creek. As well as using their grapes for the Heartland wines, some are also sold. What is impressive about Heartland is the quality of their wines; considering their cost, and the quantities in which they are made, they outclass many wines twice the price. Particularly noteworthy are the richly flavored Dolcetto/Lagrein blend and the rich, smooth Director's Cut Shiraz.

34 Barossa Valley Way, Tanunda, SA 5352
www.heartlandwines.com.au

Henschke Eden Valley

One of Australia's most celebrated producers, Henschke is a fifth-generation, family-owned winery based in Eden Valley. The first family vines were planted in 1861 in Keyneton by Johann Christian Henschke, an immigrant from Silesia in Poland. It is currently run by dynamic winemakers and viticulturalists Stephen and Prue Henschke, who are also husband and wife. After trialing organics, they decided to go fully organic and have also adopted some biodynamic practices. Hill of Grace, which is made from an ancient 20 acre (8ha) vineyard, is second only to Penfolds Grange in iconic status. As well as Hill of Grace, Henschke has another old-vine vineyard, Mount Edelstone, which also makes excellent wine. The Henschke house style is for reds with rich fruit, a softness of structure, and a subtle influence of American oak. Along with their Eden Valley vineyards, they also have a 32 acre (13ha) property in the Adelaide Hills, which produces Sauvignon Blanc, Pinot Noir, and Riesling.

Henschke Rd, Keyneton, SA 5353
www.henschke.com.au

Hewitson Barossa

Dean Hewitson set up his own label in 1998. His wines are made from long-term contracted vineyards that use traditional winemaking practices and are located across the South Australian regions of Barossa, McLaren Vale, Adelaide Hills, and the Fleurieu Peninsula. The Old Garden Mourvèdre is made from what is thought to be the world's oldest Mourvèdre vines, which were planted at Rowland Flat in 1853. Also look out for the French oak-aged Mad Hatter McLaren Vale Shiraz.

No visitor facilities
www.hewitson.com.au

Hobbs Barossa

This small boutique producer in the Barossa Ranges has just 15 acres (7ha) of vines. Greg Hobbs came to wine late in life, after previously working as a policeman in an anti-terrorist unit in Adelaide and then as a fireman. He bought the property next door to Chris Ringland in 1996 and his first wines were made in 1998 from just half a ton (0.5 tonne) of Shiraz. In 1999, he made the same quantity and sold it all to the American importer Dan Phillips. In 2003, Hobbs finally stopped selling his grapes to other people and decided to use them all himself. The concentrated, rich, old-vine Shiraz is his best wine, but he also produces an impressive range of sweet white wines, from grapes that are dried on racks in the Italian way, and a sumptuous Gregor Shiraz. The wines are made by the talented Pete Schell of Spinifex, with consultancy from neighbor Chris Ringland.

Cnr Flaxman's Valley Rd/Randalls Rd, Angaston, SA 5353
www.hobbsvintners.com.au

Hollick Coonawarra

This mid-sized Coonawarra winery has 198 acres (80ha) of vines planted on the famous terra rossa over limestone soil and also at nearby Wrattonbully, which has similar soil. The focus at Hollick is on the regional specialty of Cabernet Sauvignon, with some Shiraz, Merlot, and small parcels of alternative varieties (Tempranillo, Barbera, Nebbiolo, and Sangiovese). The top wine is Ravenswood Cabernet, which is only produced in the best years. Varietally and regionally true, Ravenswood has a track record for aging well.

Coonawarra, SA 5263
www.hollick.com

Jacob's Creek Barossa

Pernod Ricard, the wine company behind mega-brand Jacob's Creek, has recently brought high-end Orlando Wines under the banner of Jacob's Creek. This means that the fabulous Steingarten Riesling from the Eden Valley, the dense and ageworthy St Hugo Cabernet Sauvignon from Coonawarra, and the Johann Shiraz Cabernet are now Jacob's Creek wines. Other top wines in the Jacob's Creek portfolio include the Centenary Hill Shiraz, which is made from old Barossa vineyards, and Reeves Point Chardonnay.

Barossa Valley Way, Rowland Flat, SA 5351
www.jacobscreek.com

Jim Barry Wines Clare Valley

Clare Valley legend Jim Barry died in 2004, but his work is being continued by his son Peter. Jim was the 17th winemaker to graduate from Adelaide's Roseworthy College back in 1946. He went to work for the Clarevale Co-operative and became the first qualified winemaker to operate in the Clare. He followed this with a spell at Taylor's, also in the Clare, before purchasing his own property in 1959, followed by another in 1964. He began by selling grapes from his vineyards to other winemakers, but in 1974 he set up his own operation. Today, Jim Barry Wines has more than 494 acres (200ha) of vines in 10 different sites around the Clare; there is also a 37 acre (15ha) vineyard in Coonawarra. Two red wines stand out: the Armagh Shiraz, a dense, complex, and ageworthy wine; and the Benbournie Cabernet Sauvignon, new to the portfolio.

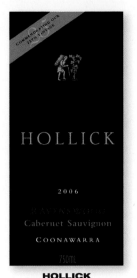

HOLLICK
A LUSCIOUS TEXTURE AND SILKY TANNINS
ACCOMPANY THE DARK FRUIT FLAVORS

JACOB'S CREEK
A CONTEMPORARY-STYLE CHARDONNAY,
THIS IS PART OF THE HERITAGE COLLECTION

In addition, the McRae Wood and Lodge Hill are excellent examples of Clare Valley Shiraz, and the Florita Riesling is also a superb wine.

Craigs Hill Rd, Clare, SA 5453
www.jimbarry.com

John Duval Wines Barossa

John Duval spent 29 years at Penfolds, where, from 1986 to 2002, he was Penfolds' chief winemaker and the custodian of Grange. In 2003, when he started his own label, people expected a big, Grange-like creation, but instead he produced the relatively elegant Plexus, which is a Grenache/Shiraz/Mourvèdre blend. In 2004, he added the Entity Shiraz to the range, and in 2005, the reserve-style Eligo Shiraz. These wines strive for Barossa-style balance and elegance, and to a large extent, they succeed. ★ **Rising star**

No visitor facilities
www.johnduvalwines.com

Kalleske Barossa

Kalleske is currently one of the best vineyards in the Barossa. In the last 150 years, the Kalleske farm has grown from 60 acres (24ha) to its 500 acres (202ha), 120 acres (48.5ha) of which is planted with vines. The farm is located in Greenock, east of the heart of the Barossa, at 1,148ft (350m) altitude, which helps to moderate temperatures during the growing season. It is run by Troy Kalleske, who is the sixth generation of his family to live and work in Barossa. Troy first made wines under his own label in 2002. The vineyards are certified organic and consist of Shiraz and Grenache, with a bit of Cabernet Sauvignon and a smidgeon of Chenin Blanc. The wines are simply brilliant, with the best being the Johann Georg Shiraz, which is concentrated, structured, and superbly balanced. The Old Vines Grenache and Greenock Shiraz are also fantastic. ★ **Rising star**

Vinegrove Rd, Greenock, SA 5360
www.kalleske.com

Katnook Estate Coonawarra

Katnook is one of Coonawarra's largest properties, with just under 494 acres (200ha) of vines. Winemaker Wayne Stehbens has been at the helm since 1980, when the first wines were made under the Katnook label, despite several changes of ownership along the way—in 2008, Katnook was sold to Freixenet. As you would expect for Coonawarra, Cabernet Sauvignon is king here and accounts for half the vineyard area. The wines are consistently good, and also great value. They are made in a rich, very ripe, and sometimes rather oaky style, but they tend to settle down with bottle age. The top wine is the super-concentrated, immense Odyssey Cabernet Sauvignon.

Riddoch Hwy, Coonawarra, SA 5263
www.katnookestate.com.au

Kay Brothers McLaren Vale

Tradition is important at this McLaren Vale winery, as the fabulously retro labels suggest. Founded in 1890, Kay Brothers is currently in the hands of third-generation winemaker Colin Kay. The focus here is on Shiraz, much of which comes from very old vines and is aged in American oak. The flagship wine is the dense, spicy,

MOLLYDOOKER
TWO LEFT FEET IS BIG AND SPICY, AND ONE
OF MOLLYDOOKER'S TOP-RATED WINES

rich Block 6 Shiraz, which is made from centenarian vines in small quantities (400–1,000 cases). Perhaps just as good is the Hillside Shiraz, which is complex, spicy, and tarry, with some mint and menthol notes from the oak. Easier to obtain, and almost as impressive, is the regular Shiraz.

Kays Rd, McLaren Vale, SA 5171
www.kaybrothersamerywines.com

Kilikanoon Clare Valley
The first Kilikanoon wines were made in 1997 by winemaker/owner Kevin Mitchell. Initially, the wines were made at Torbreck, in the Barossa Valley, but since 2005, Mitchell has had his own winery. Collaboration with a number of investing partners has led to expansion and the acquisition of new vineyards in other South Australian regions—they now own or control more than 1,236 acres (500ha) of vines, and make 40,000 cases a year. Their Clare Valley wines are impressive. Mort's Reserve Riesling is a tight, mineralic example of how the Clare excels with this variety. The Cabernet Sauvignons (Blocks Road and Reserve) are excellent, and the Oracle Shiraz and the cult Attunga 1865 Shiraz, which is made from just 900 vines, are even better. R (Barossa) and M (McLaren Vale) Reserve Shirazes are also highly rated and made in a very rich, full style.

Penna Lane, Penwortham, SA 5453
www.kilikanoon.com.au

KT and the Falcon Clare Valley
KT is Kerri Thompson, a talented winemaker with a passion for Riesling; the Falcon is viticulturalist Stephen Farrugia. The vineyards here are managed along organic lines with some biodynamic preparations. In addition to the 20 acre (8ha) home farm, which is located between Watervale and Leasingham, grapes are also sourced from the Peglidis and Churinga vineyards in Watervale. Riesling is the main focus, but some Shiraz is also made. The 2008 Peglidis Riesling shows crisp, spicy, limey fruit, with lovely precision and complexity. ★ Rising star

Watervale, SA 5452
www.ktandthefalcon.com.au

Langmeil Barossa
Langmeil is a Barossa winery with a sense of history. Its Freedom vineyard was planted in 1843, and many of the venerable old vines survive to this day. More recently, however, Langmeil has undergone a rebirth, which, despite its history, has put its wines firmly into "new Barossa" territory. The winery used to operate under the Paradale label, which began life in the 1930s. In 1996, Richard Lindner, Carl Lindner, and Chris Bitter purchased and renovated the then disused winery and renamed it Langmeil. They began making wine again, and acquired some new vineyards and grower contracts. The 1843 Freedom Shiraz, from the old vineyard, and the Fifth Wave Grenache are the star turns here.

Cnr Langmeil and Para Roads, Tanunda, SA 5352
www.langmeilwinery.com.au

Mad Dog Barossa
A small operation, Mad Dog is the label of fourth-generation Barossa grower Matthew Munzberg. He sells most of the grapes from his 86 acres (35ha) of vines, but he makes 400 cases of wine a year from what he keeps.

The bulk of Mad Dog wine is Shiraz, which is aged in French oak, but since 2006 a small amount of Sangiovese has also been made. The Shiraz is archetypal Barossa: richly fruited, but with good definition, framed by high-quality oak.

No visitor facilities
www.maddogwines.com

Magpie Estate Barossa
This is a joint venture between the exuberant, and irreverent British wine merchant Noel Young and Barossa winemaker Rolf Binder. Some of the grapes come from Rolf's own vineyards, while the rest are bought-in. Magpie Estate's wines are full-throttle, with new oak and a sense of wildness. They include the Malcolm Shiraz, the Black Sock Mourvèdre, the Gomersal Grenache, and the Schnell Shiraz. None of these wines will cheat you for flavor.

Tanunda, SA 5352
www.veritaswinery.com

Majella Coonawarra
One of Coonawarra's top producers, Majella was primarily a grower, but it is increasingly using its 148 acres (60ha) of vineyards to make its own wines. The Lynn family planted the first grapes on their land in the late 1960s, and in 1980 they began supplying Wynns. They made their first wine, a Shiraz, in 1991. This was followed by Cabernet Sauvignon in 1994, and by their top wine, The Malleea, in 1996. Interestingly for Coonawarra, The Malleea is a 55% Cabernet Sauvignon/45% Shiraz blend. It shows lovely, intense, lush blackcurrant fruit with beautiful purity and focus. Also very impressive, and great value for money, is another Cabernet/Shiraz blend called The Musician. The straight Cabernet Sauvignon is superb, with real intensity and focus, showing a gravelly, spicy depth to the vivid blackcurrant fruit.

Lynn Rd, Coonawarra, SA 5263
www.majellawines.com.au

Massena Barossa
Massena is an impressive collaboration between Barossa winemakers Dan Standish and Jaysen Collins that saw its first vintage in 2000. They source grapes from various old vineyards and borrow winery space to come up with a range of fairly serious wines. Current production now runs at around 5,000 cases. The rich, sweetly fruited Moonlight Run is predominantly Grenache and Shiraz, while 11th Hour Shiraz is a little more structured and defined. Howling Dog Durif is a structured beast, and the Surly Muse is an impressive Viognier. ★ Rising star

Tanunda, SA 5352
www.massena.com.au

Mitchell Clare Valley
Andrew and Jane Mitchell's mid-sized Clare winery is sometimes overlooked, but their Rieslings are among the Clare's very best. Andrew comes from a family of Clare growers and studied economics at Adelaide University, followed by a course in Wine Science at Wagga in New South Wales. Andrew's first wines were made in 1975 from his family's vineyards. Mitchell now produces 30,000 cases a year, entirely from their own 185 acres (75ha) of vineyards. Watervale Riesling ages beautifully, and the

MITOLO
THE SAVITAR SHIRAZ IS A DARK, RICH,
LAYERED, AND FULL BODIED WINE

new McNichol Riesling is perhaps even better. Sevenhill Vineyard Cabernet Sauvignon is the other standout wine here, with lovely focused fruit. Also keep an eye out for the McNichol Shiraz.

Hughes Park Rd, Sevenhill, SA 5453
www.mitchellwines.com

Mitolo McLaren Vale

Mitolo is a relatively new label and a collaborative venture between top Barossa winemaker Ben Glaetzer and Frank Mitolo. Frank supplies the capital, while Ben provides winemaking know-how and facilities. The majority of the grapes come from a grower in Woolunga, at the southern end of the McLaren Vale. Mitolo's entry level wines, which offer lovely fruit purity, are called Jester. The higher-end reds are fantastic, and include the Amarone-method Serpico Cabernet Sauvignon, and the GAM and Savitar Shirazes. ★ **Rising star**

Angel Vale Rd, Angel Vale, Virginia, SA 5120
www.mitolowines.com.au

Mollydooker Wines McLaren Vale

The controversial, but lively, Mollydooker label was established in 2005 by Sarah and Sparky Marquis of Fox Creek fame. The wines, with their crazy and imaginative labels, are extreme, with alcohol levels commonly exceeding 16%. They are hugely successful in the US, where they have received stratospheric critic scores—the Velvet Glove, Carnival of Love, and Blue Eyed Boy (all Shiraz) have been given scores in the high-90s from magazine *The Wine Advocate*. More affordable are the Boxer Shiraz and Two Left Feet, which is a red blend. Mollydooker has enjoyed explosive growth and now has more than 100 acres (40.5ha) of vineyards. It also buys in grapes from other growers, with 1,000 tons (1,016 tonnes) passing through the winery every year.

8/938 South Rd, Edwardstown SA 5039
www.mollydookerwines.com.au

Mount Horrocks Clare Valley

Stephanie Toole is married to Clare legend Jeffrey Grossett, but she has her own boutique winery in Mount Horrocks, which is among the best of the valley. With 25 acres (10ha) of vines spread over three sites, Stephanie makes top-class Riesling, Cabernet Sauvignon, Shiraz, and Semillon. Her specialty is the Cordon Cut Riesling, a sweet wine with added concentration that comes from allowing the grapes to dry for a while on the vine after the cordon is cut.

The Old Railway Station, Curling St, Auburn, SA 5451
www.mounthorrocks.com

Mountadam Eden Valley

Established in 1972 by David Wynn, Eden Valley winery Mountadam became well known for its Chardonnay and Pinot Noir. It lost its way for a time, during a period of ownership by the French company LVMH (2002–2006), but it is now back on form and in private hands with ex-Petaluma winemaker Con Moshos at the helm. Look out for the rich, fresh Pinot Gris and the precise Riesling.

High Eden Rd, Eden Valley, SA 5235
www.mountadam.com.au

Ngeringa Adelaide Hills

Ngeringa is an exciting new biodynamic producer in the Adelaide Hills. Erinn and Janet Klein planted 12 acres (5ha) of vines in 2001 and manage them as part of an integrated farm system—livestock are used for weed and pest control as well as manure creation. The wines really thrill here, the Ngeringa Syrah is beautifully elegant, with sleek, dark-cherry fruit and smooth minerality. The Viognier is distinctive, with pear, cinnamon, nut, and peach flavors. Chardonnay and Pinot Noir are also made, as well as the Vin Santo-style Altus—a delicious oddity that is made from a pink-skinned clone of Semillon from the McLaren Vale. ★ **Rising star**

91 Williams Rd, Mount Barker, SA 5251
www.ngeringa.com

O'Leary Walker Clare Valley

In 2001, David O'Leary and Nick Walker achieved their long-standing ambition and began making wines together. Based in the Clare Valley, their most celebrated wines are Clare Rieslings from Polish Hill and Watervale. They also source grapes from Adelaide Hills, Coonawarra, McLaren Vale, and Barossa. Production is currently just under 20,000 cases annually. ★ **Rising star**

Main Rd, Leasingham, SA 5452
www.olearywalkerwines.com

Parker Coonawarra Estate Coonawarra

Since its beginning in 1985, the Parker Coonawarra Estate has consistently produced top-quality wines. Their range is wonderfully straightforward. The flagship wine, the provocatively named Terra Rossa First Growth, has intense, brooding, concentrated, gravelly blackcurrant fruit and is only made in the finest seasons. There is also the Terra Rossa Cabernet Sauvignon, the Merlot, and three wines that come under the Favourite Son label. The grapes for these wines come from 99 acres (40ha) of estate vineyards, situated at the cooler southern end of Coonawarra.

Riddoch Hwy, Coonawarra, SA 5263
www.parkercoonawarraestate.com.au

Penfolds Barossa

Possibly the most famous name in Australian wine, Penfolds' top wine, Grange, enjoys legendary status all over the world. Made since 1951, it is a wine with a wonderful story, and an ability to age gracefully over many decades—the most recent release, 2004, is spellbindingly good. The Penfolds portfolio also contains other ageworthy reds. RWT Shiraz is a different style from Grange and aged in French oak rather than American, but it is almost as compelling as its iconic stablemate. Bin 707 Cabernet Sauvignon and Bin 389 Cabernet Shiraz are serious, ageworthy wines; the latter being the best bargain in the Penfolds range. St Henri is the estate's oddity in that it sees no new oak, but regardless of this, it still has a good track record for aging very well. Bin 28 and 128 are more commercial, but still deliver. Of the whites, Yattarna is a world-class Chardonnay, with the potential for development and known unofficially as the White Grange, while newcomer Bin 311 Chardonnay is a serious cool-climate effort.

Tanunda Rd, Nuriootpa, SA 5355
www.penfolds.com.au

MAX SCHUBERT AND GRANGE

Australia's most famous wine has to be Penfolds Grange, the brainchild of legendary Penfolds winemaker Max Schubert. Working at a time when the Australian wine industry was focused on fortified wines, Schubert had a hard job trying to persuade the Penfolds hierarchy to take his dry Grange Hermitage seriously. In 1951, the debut vintage year, Schubert discovered that the marriage of Shiraz with new American oak was a happy one and made five barrels. More was made in 1952, and in 1953, a little Cabernet Sauvignon was included in the blend. Penfolds's top brass tasted the first five vintages in 1956, but no one liked it and Schubert was told to stop production. Undeterred, he carried on in secret, entering the 1955 vintage Grange in the 1962 Sydney show—it blew people away, and Grange has done so ever since.

PIKES
THE FISH LOGO HAS BEEN USED SINCE PIKES
WAS A BREWING COMPANY IN THE LATE 1800s

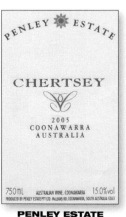

PENLEY ESTATE
CHERTSEY IS A BLEND OF CABERNET
SAUVIGNON, CABERNET FRANC, AND MERLOT

Penley Estate Coonawarra

Kym Tolley can trace his ancestry back to Penfolds founder Christopher Rawson Penfold. Tolley worked for Penfolds for 25 years, before setting up his mid-sized Coonawarra estate in 1988. He has 274 acres (111ha) of Coonawarra's precious terra rossa over limestone terroir. He makes a range of wines, top of which are a trio of reds: the Chertsey (a Bordeaux blend), Reserve Cabernet Sauvignon, and Special Select Shiraz.

McLeans Rd, Coonawarra, SA 5263
www.penley.com.au

Petaluma Adelaide Hills

Brian Croser is no longer involved with the label that he founded in 1976, although he has bought back the winery. Petaluma is now owned by Lion Nathan, but they have continued the Croser style (Croser acted as a consultant for some years), which is a pure, lean, and unadorned expression of the various regions the grapes are sourced from. Focused, ageworthy Riesling comes from the Clare Valley, while Coonawarra is responsible for an elegant, long-lived red and a fresh Merlot. Adelaide Hills yields a minerally, fresh Chardonnay, which may be the best of them all, and there is also a tight, focused, vintage-dated sparkling wine of some merit.

Spring Gully Rd, Piccadilly, SA 5151
www.petaluma.com.au

Peter Lehmann Barossa

Although Peter Lehmann's wine company was sold to the Hess group in 2003, the wines have not suffered at all. During the dark ages for the Barossa in the late 1970s, when many growers were facing ruin, Lehmann found some investors and founded his own winery, making wine from purchased grapes. The company now makes 750,000 cases a year from bought-in grapes from 180 Barossa growers. The entry level wines are good value for money, especially the bright Semillon and a juicy Grenache, but the higher-end wines really excel. Margaret Semillon is one of Australia's best, on a par with top wines from the Hunter Valley. Wigan Riesling is a superb example of what the Eden Valley does best, while Stonewell Shiraz is powerful—a bit oaky when young, but it ages beautifully. Eight Songs Shiraz is a new Barossa classic, and the Cabernet-based Mentor is also worth looking out for.

Para Rd, Tanunda, SA 5352
www.peterlehmannwines.com.au

Pewsey Vale Eden Valley

This famous old vineyard in the Eden Valley was revived by the then owner in collaboration with Yalumba in the 1960s. Riesling vines were planted with distinctive contoured rows, at altitudes of 1,591–1,640ft (485–500m). Since then, this vineyard has been the source of some serious Riesling, particularly since 1996, when Yalumba winemaker Louisa Rose became responsible for the wines. Regular Pewsey Vale Riesling is taut and lemony in its youth, but ages gracefully with a decade or more in bottle. The Contours is a museum release of the finest Riesling, and new additions to the range include a Gewurztraminer and the Prima Riesling, which is picked early, has lower alcohol, and some residual sugar.

Browns Rd, Eden Valley, SA 5353
www.pewseyvale.com

Pikes Clare Valley

Pikes is a reliable, mid-sized Clare Valley producer that makes consistently good wines from its 136 acres (55ha) of estate vineyards. Brothers Andrew (the viticulturalist), and Neil (the winemaker), established Pikes in 1984, in the cool Polish Hill River subregion of Clare. Riesling is their specialty, but they also work with a wide range of other varieties, including Sangiovese, and a highly rated Shiraz.

Polish Hill River Rd, Sevenhill, SA 5453
www.pikeswines.com.au

Pirramimma McLaren Vale

Owned and operated by the Johnston family since 1892, Pirramimma is a mid-sized McLaren Vale winery that offers a range of boldly flavored and well-priced wines. They have sizeable vineyard holdings, recently expanding them to 445 acres (180ha). Reds are the main focus, with the intense, inky Petit Verdot, the pick of the range, although the Cabernet Sauvignon is also superb.

Johnston Rd, McLaren Vale, SA 5171
www.pirramimma.com.au

Primo Estate Adelaide Hills

Joe Grilli's Primo Estate is the leading producer in the warm Adelaide Plains region. It is famous for one wine in particular: the Moda (previously labeled Moda Amarone), which is made from Cabernet Sauvignon and Merlot grapes that are dried in racks. As well as the original Adelaide Plains vineyard, Primo Estate also has two more vineyards in the McLaren Vale, which supply grapes for most of the flagship reds. The top wines here come under the Joseph label and, as well as the Moda, include Nebbiolo, Angel Gully Shiraz, and one of Australia's best sparkling reds.

McMurtie Rd, McLaren Vale, SA 5171
www.primoestate.com.au

Ralph Fowler Mount Benson

Ralph Fowler was previously head winemaker at Tyrrell's in the Hunter Valley. He subsequently worked in a number of other wineries, before starting up his own business in the emerging coastal region of Mount Benson (Limestone Coast) in the late 1990s. Shiraz, Merlot, and Viognier are the main focus here, with lyre trellising and partial root drying irrigation being some of the vineyard technologies employed to help produce top-quality wines. Some grapes are also sourced from the nearby regions of Mount Gambier and Coonawarra.

101 Limestone Coast Rd, Mount Benson, 5275
www.ralphfowlerwines.com.au

Rockbare Barossa

Ex-Southcorp winemaker Tim Burvill struck out on his own in 2001, with a view to making premium wines from South Australian wine regions. He is based in the McLaren Vale, from where he sources his fresh, tight Chardonnay, which is picked earlier than most, and his gutsy, old-vine Shiraz. The adventurously packaged Barossa Babe Shiraz is another, rich old-vine red. Mojo is Rockbare's range of more affordable, varietal wines: a Barossa Shiraz and an Adelaide Hills Sauvignon Blanc.

No visitor facilities
www.rockbare.com.au

Rockford Barossa

One of the classic Barossa wineries, Rockford has a real sense of history. The owner, Robert O'Callaghan, is one of the people credited with the Barossa revival in the 1980s. His wines hold their own with the best of the valley, with Basket Press Shiraz as the flagship wine. It is made from the fruit of 30-year-old vines and is a Barossa classic that benefits from bottle age. Rod and Spur, a Cabernet/Shiraz blend, and Moppa Springs, a Grenache/Shiraz/Mataro, are delicious and also traditionally Barossa in style. Also look out for the sparkling Black Shiraz. A loyal following means that mail order and cellar door sales are sufficient to sell everything that Rockford produces, so these wines can be hard to find.

Krondorf Rd, Tanunda, SA 5352
08 8563 2720

Rolf Binder Wines Barossa

Rolf Binder had been making wines at his family-owned Veritas winery, which was established by his parents in 1955, for some time when a legal challenge necessitated a change in name. The wines are now labeled Rolf Binder, although the winery is still known as The Veritas Winery. Rolf has access to some excellent vineyards and makes a solidly good range of wines. The Bulls Blood Shiraz Mataro Pressings, renamed the Hubris for some export markets, is a beautifully dense, vibrant, affordable red. More serious are the single-vineyard Heysen Shiraz and the Henrich Shiraz Grenache Mourvèdre. The star here though is the dense, focused Hanisch Shiraz. Binder is also involved in a joint venture called Magpie Estate, whose wines are made at the Veritas Winery.

Cnr Seppeltsfield Rd and Stelzer Rd, Tanunda, SA 5352
www.veritaswinery.com

Rusden Barossa

Rusden is a Barossa success story. In 1979, Dennis and Christine Canute purchased 40 acres (16ha) of run-down vines. Dennis continued his day job as a teacher in order to give Christine, a fifth-generation grape grower, the opportunity to start rejuvenating the vines. This was a tough time in the Barossa and grape prices were absurdly low. Coupled with this, they were fed up with being told that grapes grown on the sandy Vine Vale soils were no good, so they decided to make their own wines. In 1992, Dennis and his friend Russell made a barrel of Cabernet Sauvignon for their own consumption, which they labeled Rusden (for Russell and Dennis). Things grew from there, and in 1997 Dennis's son Christian, who was then working at Rockford, became involved; he now makes all the wines. Today, half the Canute's grapes are sold and half are used for Rusden. The wines initially tend to show as very forward and sweet, but they are not overwhelming. The top wine here is the much sought-after Black Guts Shiraz, but the Boundaries Cabernet Sauvignon, the Christine Grenache, and the Christian Chenin Blanc are also worth checking out.

Magnolia Rd, Tanunda, SA 5352
www.rusdenwines.com.au

Saltram Barossa

Saltram is a famous old name from the Barossa—the No 1 Shiraz was first made in 1862. It lost its way in the 1980s, but has recently undergone a revival under winemaker Nigel Dolan, who worked here from 1992 to 2007. Saltram

RALPH FOWLER
THIS MERLOT DEVELOPS RICH TRUFFLE AND ANTIQUE LEATHER CHARACTER OVER TIME

ROCKFORD
BASKET PRESS SHIRAZ
BENEFITS FROM 10 YEARS OF CELLARING

has 111 acres (45ha) of its own vineyards, but also draws heavily on local growers to supply its needs. The top wines here are the dense, rich No 1 Shiraz from the Barossa and the Metala Original Plantings Shiraz Cabernet from the Langhorne Creek.

Nuriootpa Rd, Angaston, SA 5355
www.saltramwines.com.au

SC Pannell McLaren Vale

Stephen Pannell is one of the most respected red winemakers in Australia, but it was not until 2004 that he quit his job as chief winemaker for Hardys and set out on his own. Although he does not own vineyards or a winery, he is rapidly developing the reputation of his label, SC Pannell, which focuses on red wines from McLaren Vale and Adelaide Hills. His 2006 McLaren Vale Shiraz Grenache is elegantly structured and sweetly fruited. A straight Grenache, one of Pannell's specialties, and Shiraz are also made from McLaren Vale fruit. Worth looking out for is an acclaimed Adelaide Hills Nebbiolo. Definitely one to watch. ★ Rising star

14 Davenport Terrace, Wayville, SA 5034
08 8299 9256

Schwarz Wine Company Barossa

Jason Schwarz started small. His father is a grower with more than 100 acres (41ha) of vineyards in the Barossa. In 2001, Jason persuaded his father to let him play with 1 ton (1 tonne) of fruit from the Nitschke Block vineyard, a Shiraz vineyard, planted in 1967, over the road from Turkey Flat. The results were impressive and Jason added Thiele Road Grenache to his range. Recently, Schwarz Wine Company has produced the Dust Kicker pair: Hunt and Gather and Shiraz Mataro. These are quite big, ripe, balanced wines with incredible fruit quality. ★ Rising star

Biscay Rd, Bethany, Barossa Valley, SA 5352
www.schwarzwineco.com.au

Seppeltsfield Barossa

This famous old winery specializes in fortified wines and has a treasure trove of old wines. When fortified wines became unfashionable, however, its owners (first Southcorp and then Fosters) did not know what to do with it. To the great relief of those who cared about Australian wine heritage, Fosters sold it to Kilikanoon in 2007, and with specialist winemaker James Godfrey at the helm, it is turning out some stunning fortified wines. Sherry style is a specialty: Seppeltsfield Museum Oloroso DP104 shows incredible concentration, complexity, and length. DP90 Tawny is thrillingly fine and elegant, and the 2005 Vintage is a fresh, fruity, approachable take on vintage port. Paramount Rare Topaque is super-concentrated and thrillingly complex, and the 1909 100-year-old Para is one of the most incredibly intense and exciting wines available.

1 Seppeltsfield Rd, Seppeltsfield via Nuriootpa, SA 5355
www.seppelt.com.au

Shaw + Smith Adelaide Hills

Cousins Michael Hill Smith and Martin Shaw established Shaw + Smith in 1989. Initially, they became known for their Adelaide Hills Sauvignon Blanc, which still remains an important wine for them and is one of Australia's best. This was joined by an excellent, single-vineyard

STANDISH WINE COMPANY
THE RELIC IS MADE FROM 90-YEAR-OLD
SHIRAZ VINES (93%) AND VIOGNER (7%)

Chardonnay from the M3 vineyard, planted in 1994, which shows precision, balance, and elegance. Equally exciting are their two reds. The Shiraz, from warmer sites in the Adelaide Hills, shows wonderful focus and elegance, while the Pinot Noir, first made in 2005, is thrilling. A top performer in the Adelaide Hills, Shaw + Smith is currently cementing its position as one of Australia's top wineries.

Jones Rd, Balhannah, SA 5242
www.shawandsmith.com

Shirvington McLaren Vale
A small premium producer from McLaren Vale, Shirvington began life in 1996 when the Shirvington family purchased 40 acres (16ha) of prime vineyard land. They have since added two more vineyards to their holding, and from their 74 acres (30ha) of vines make just two wines, a Cabernet Sauvignon and a Shiraz, both of which are lush and ripe in style. Initially, Sarah and Sparky Marquis of Mollydooker were involved in the winemaking, but it is now in the hands of Kim Jackson. These wines have a particular following in the US, where they are highly acclaimed.

McLaren Vale, SA 5171
www.shirvington.com

Skillogalee Clare Valley
This medium-sized Clare Valley producer was established in the early 1970s and released its first wines in 1976. It is now owned by David and Diana Palmer, who make all the Skillogalee wines from the 124 acres (50ha) of estate vineyards. A range of varietal wines are made, but the Riesling, Cabernet Sauvignon, and Shiraz are the best. The stunningly precise 2008 Trevarrick Riesling is one of the finest Australian examples of this variety.

Trevarrick Rd, Sevenhill via Clare, SA 5453
www.skillogalee.com.au

Spinifex Barossa
Spinifex is one of the most exciting new wineries in the Barossa—husband-and-wife team Pete Schell and Magali Gely have been strongly influenced by the South of France in deciding its direction. Magali's family were vignerons in the Languedoc, and Pete has done a number of vintages in France, so it is unsurprising that their focus is on southern French varieties. Pete began making Spinifex wines back in 2001, while he was still working elsewhere, but he now devotes all his energies to these brilliant wines. The Shiraz/Viognier is sweetly fruited, but well defined, while Indigene, a Shiraz/Mataro/Grenache blend, is lush, with lovely structure. Esprit is an aromatic blend, DRS Vineyard Durif is dense and spicy, and Taureau is an unusual blend that is dominated by Carignan and Tempranillo. Lola, a blend of southern French white varieties, is also worth looking for. ★ **Rising star**

Biscay Rd, Bethany, SA 5352
www.spinifexwines.com.au

St Hallett Barossa
Along with the likes of Rockford and Charles Melton, St Hallett was one of the wineries at the forefront of the Barossa revival in the 1980s. It became famous for its Old Block Shiraz, a dense and structured, yet lushly fruited, Barossa classic with a track record for aging.

TAPANAPPA
THIS WARM VINTAGE CHARDONNAY SHOWS
RIPE PEACH WITH SUBTLE MARZIPAN

A merger with Tatachilla, followed by purchase by the Lion Nathan group, has seen St Hallett take a slightly more commercial direction, which has lost it some of its geek appeal. Old Block is still a very good wine though, and Blackwell Shiraz is also impressive. At the other end of the scale, the Gamekeeper's Reserve and Poacher's Blend white offer fun flavors and great value for money.

St Hallett Rd, Tanunda, SA 5352
www.sthallett.com.au

Standish Wine Company Barossa
Dan Standish, winemaker with Torbreck, makes small quantities of exceptional Shiraz under his own label. A sixth-generation Barossa Valley vigneron, Dan first made wine from his parents' old-vine Shiraz in 1999. Standish Wine Company now makes two wines: The Standish, a straight Shiraz, and The Relic, a Shiraz/Viognier blend. The wines are made using indigenous yeasts in open top fermenters, and show lush, intense, ripe fruit characters backed up by a smooth yet firm structure. They are really good, but unfortunately also rather expensive. ★ **Rising star**

100 Barritt Rd, Lyndoch, SA 5351
www.standishwineco.com

Tapanappa Adelaide Hills
Brian Croser is a revered figure on the Australian wine scene. As well as running a successful consultancy business, he also formed his own winery, Petaluma, in 1976. Croser was largely responsible for the rebirth of the Adelaide Hills in the 1980s, but lost control of Petaluma when it was bought by the Lion Nathan wine group in 2001. He stayed on in a consultancy role until 2005, but soon needed a new project of his own. Tapanappa began as the result of a collaboration between Croser, Champagne Bollinger, and Jean-Michel Cazes of Bordeaux. Whalebone Vineyard is a supple, smoothly textured Cabernet/Merlot blend from a vineyard in Wrattonbully. Etages Tiers Vineyard Chardonnay is elegant and understated, and comes from the vineyard next to Croser's home in the Adelaide Hills. The newest wine is a precise, well-balanced Pinot Noir from the Foggy Hill vineyard in the Fleurieu Peninsula. ★ **Rising star**

Crafers, SA 5152
www.tapanappawines.com.au

Taylors/Wakefield Clare Valley
A large, 500,000-case winery in the Clare Valley, Taylors produces excellent wines in decent volumes. Adam Eggins has been chief winemaker here since 2000, and he is doing really good work. Basic Cabernet Sauvignon is generally the Clare Valley's most popular wine, but Chardonnay is the focus here. The top wines are released under the St Andrews label: the Cabernet Sauvignon, Chardonnay, and Riesling are particularly good. For legal reasons, Taylors is known as Wakefield in export markets.

Taylors Rd, Auburn, SA 5451
www.taylorswines.com.au

Teusner Wines Barossa
Kym Teusner is a young winemaker who is establishing quite a reputation as one of the new Barossans. Teusner Wines is a collaborative venture with his brother-in-law, Michael Page. In 2002, some old bush vine Grenache in

the Ebenezer district was about to be bulldozed. At the time, a large wine company was paying Aus$900 per ton for the fruit, so Kym and Michael offered Aus$2,500 and the Teusner label was born. Their range has grown over the years and now includes the Joshua (a juicy, focused, unoaked Grenache/Shiraz/Mataro), Avatar (the same blend, but oak aged), Albert (a dense, ageworthy Shiraz), and two new super-high-end wines released as the Astral Series. ★ **Rising star**

Cnr Research Rd & Railway Terrace, Nurioopta, SA 5355
www.teusner.com.au

The Lane Adelaide Hills
John Edwards is the man behind Adelaide Hills winery The Lane. For seven years, until 2005, he also made Starvedog Lane wines in partnership with the Hardys Wine Company. The Lane wines come from John's own 128.5 acres (52ha) of vines, which are located high up, above 1,476ft (450m), near Hahndorf. Nine grape varieties are grown and Chardonnay, Pinot Gris, and Shiraz all do well. The wines are made under two labels: Ravenswood Lane and The Lane.

Ravenswood Lane, Hahndorf, SA 5245
www.thelane.com.au

Thorn Clarke Barossa
David Clarke, a geologist by training, formed Thorne Clarke, one of the largest family-owned Barossa wineries, with his wife Cheryl in the late 1980s. The estate has more than 618 acres (250ha) of Barossa vineyards—two sites in the Barossa Valley and two in the Eden Valley. They produce around 80,000 cases of wine a year, under a number of different labels. Reds are the main focus, and are made in a rich style that represents good value for money. The flagship wine is the William Randell Shiraz, which is dense and concentrated, with some oak influence. The Shotfire range, the next level down, includes an alluring Shiraz that is worth looking out for.

Gawler Park Rd, Angaston, SA 5353
www.thornclarkewines.com.au

Tim Adams Clare Valley
One of the most consistent of the Clare Valley wineries, Tim Adams began in partnership with a local cooper, Bill Wray, in 1985. Bill died shortly after, and Adams & Wray became Tim Adams Wines in 1987. Since then, Tim's broad portfolio of Clare wines has established a great reputation for quality and value. The wines are sourced from 11 vineyards from across the valley, of which Tim owns four. After recent expansion, he is now crushing 1,000 tons (1,016 tonnes) annually. The best wines here are the limey, intense Riesling and the powerful, taut, ageworthy Semillon. Of the reds, The Fergus is a midweight blend with American oak to the fore, and The Aberfeldy is a dense, rich, powerful Shiraz with plenty of staying power. An impressive Pinot Gris and a stylish Tempranillo are new to the portfolio.

Clare, SA 5453
www.timadamswines.com.au

Tin Shed Barossa
Originally a collaboration between restaurateur Peter Clarke and viticulturalist Andrew Wardlaw, Tin Shed began life in 1997 when the first wines were made in a rustic, tin-roofed building in the Eden Valley. Since then, the range has grown slowly, but steadily, and now five wines are made each year. Andrew left to pursue other ventures in 2006, and Peter has since been joined by Nathan Norman, who now makes the wines. Wild Bunch Riesling is in a classic Eden Valley style and is very good. The reds, sourced from Eden Valley and Barossa Valley, are made in a fresh, pure style. The flagship wine here is the focused, aromatic Single Wire Eden Valley Shiraz.

No visitor facilities
www.tinshedwines.com

Torbreck Barossa
Dave Powell's Torbreck is currently one of the Barossa's "hot" wineries. Since its debut in 1994 (the first wines were released in 1997), it has built up a substantial following, particularly in the US, which has led to higher prices than many of its neighbors can achieve. The house style is for big, rich, aromatic reds that are never over-ripe and always manage to retain some definition, despite their size. Everything here is good, from the wonderfully expressive, meaty, unoaked Juveniles, to The Steading, The Struie, The Factor, Descendant, and their flagship, Runrig. Descendant and Runrig are blends of Shiraz and Viognier with exotic, almost over-the-top aromatics. Torbreck also makes Les Amis, a high-end 100% Grenache. The wines made here are so alluring when they are young that it is hard to say if bottle aging will give you anything extra, but the 1999 Runrig is currently showing very well.

Roennfeldt Rd, Marananga, SA 5355
www.torbreck.com

Torzi Matthews Eden Valley
Domenic Torzi's family were originally olive oil producers in the Adelaide Plains, but he decided to break away and make wine. With his wife, Tracy, he bought a block of land on Mount McKenzie in the Eden Valley and planted vines, even though he knew it was a frost-prone site. His first wine was the smooth, elegantly ripe 2002 Frost Dodger Shiraz, made from partially dried grapes. In 2005, he added the minerally Frost Dodger Eden Valley Riesling, with wild yeast ferment. More recently, he has produced a Shiraz and a Riesling, under the Schist Rock label, and the first of a series of Italian varietals, a Barossa Sangiovese. ★ **Rising star**

Angaston, SA 5353
www.torzimatthews.com.au

Turkey Flat Barossa
The Schulz family have owned the Turkey Flat property since 1865. The family ran a butchery business and, latterly, a dairy farm alongside grape growing until the early 1990s, when fourth generation Peter Schulz decided to start making wines, along with his wife Christie. The results have been impressive. Their French-oak aged Shiraz shows just what the Barossa can do with this variety. Butcher's Block red and white, both Rhône-style blends, offer lots of flavor and personality. Particularly successful is the full-flavored rosé, which accounts for around 40% of production here.

Bethany Rd, Tanunda, SA 5352
www.turkeyflat.com.au

THE AWRI: HOW SCIENCE HAS HELPED AUSTRALIAN WINE

The Australian Wine Research Institute (AWRI) is located on the fringes of the city of Adelaide and is one of the finest wine science research establishments in the world. Funded by a grape grower/winemaker levy, which is added to by the federal government, the AWRI carries out research, develops tools for the industry, provides an extension service, and runs a commercial service carrying out analysis of 100,000 wine samples a year. Because of this practical focus, the Australian wine industry has benefited greatly from the AWRI's work. Research on the spoilage yeast Brettanomyces, and its implementation across the industry, for example, has resulted in measurable improvements in wine hygiene. The extensive AWRI closure trial, which began in 1999, also empowered winemakers to make the switch to screwcaps. In addition to this, the AWACs (advanced wine assessment courses) that the AWRI runs have helped train and identify talented wine show judges.

TWO HANDS
MADE FROM FRONTIGNAC GRAPES, THIS IS
A LOW-ALCOHOL, SLIGHTLY SPRITZY WINE

TURKEY FLAT
A LEADER IN THE ROSÉ REVIVAL, THIS IS AN
EXTREMELY POPULAR WINE

Two Hands Barossa

A collaboration between Michael Twelftree and Richard Mintz, Two Hands is a Barossa négociant/winery that has stormed the US market with its enormous, boldly flavored, ripe, and sometimes quite alcoholic, reds. The wines are well made and brilliantly packaged, but, stylistically, they risk achieving concentration and ripeness at the cost of definition. This comes down to personal preference, however, so if you like full-flavored wines that pack a real punch, then these will appeal. The broad range at Two Hands draws on several premium regions, including McLaren Vale, Padthaway, and Heathcote, in addition to Barossa. The delicious and affordable Brilliant Disguise Moscato is well worth looking out for.

Neldner Rd, Marananga, SA 5355
www.twohandswines.com

Wendouree Clare Valley

One of Australia's national wine treasures, iconic Clare Valley producer Wendouree makes profound, ageworthy red wines from fabulous old-vine vineyards. AP Birks Wendouree Cellars (to use the full name) is one of Clare Valley's historic properties, with vines that were first planted here in 1892. The current owner, Tony Brady, bought the property in 1974 and makes no concessions to modernity. Altogether, Wendouree has 28 acres (11ha) of vines that are all dry grown and yield around 50 tons (50.8 tonnes) per vintage. The grapes are not picked super ripe, but at around 13.5% alcohol. The resulting wines are taut, focused, and profound, but demand long aging and can be challenging in their youth. All the wines share a similar house style, but Shiraz is the most sought-after; 1985, 1990, 1991 all need more time to peak. The Shiraz Malbec, Shiraz Mataro, and Cabernet Malbec are also fabulous. The wines are only sold through a mailing list, which is now closed, so if you want some, you will have to hunt for bottles on the secondary market.

Wendouree Rd, Clare, SA 5453
08 8842 2896

Wirra Wirra McLaren Vale

The recent history of this historic McLaren Vale winery began in 1969 when cousins Gregg and Roger Trott rebuilt it from ruins and began making wine again. Over the years, production has grown to its current level of around 100,000 cases annually. The portfolio includes a broad range of well-made wines, most of which come from the McLaren Vale. Flagship wines are the rich, bold, chocolatey RSW Shiraz, the Angelus Cabernet Sauvignon, which shows that McLaren Vale Cabernet is somewhat underrated, and the Chook Bloc, which is only released in top vintages. In 2007, Wirra Wirra acquired the 49.5 acre (20ha) Rayner Vineyard, which previously supplied Brokenwood with grapes for its Rayner Vineyard Shiraz.

McMurtrie Rd, McLaren Vale, SA 5171
www.wirrawirra.com

Wolf Blass Barossa

One of the key brands in the Fosters portfolio, Wolf Blass offers admirable quality at a range of price levels—no mean achievement considering that this is a 4 million-case brand. The range is tiered by label color. The wines start to get interesting with the Yellow Label and gradually get more complex as they go up the tiers —President's Selection, Gold Label, Grey Label, Black Label, and Platinum Label. The top wines are impressive, but they are also quite expensive.

97 Sturt Hwy, Nuriootpa, SA 5355
www.wolfblass.com.au

Wynns Coonawarra Estate Coonawarra

Legendary Coonawarra winery Wynns is responsible for some of Australia's best Cabernet Sauvignon. With around 2,224 acres (900ha) of vines, it is a dominating presence in Coonawarra, but despite its size, Wynns does a great job under the leadership of winemaker Sue Hodder. Riesling and Chardonnay are good, but it is the reds that really steal the show. The Shiraz is balanced and expressive, and the high-end Michael Shiraz is one of Australia's very best, if a little oak-dominated in its youth. The black label Cabernet Sauvignon is a serious effort that ages well, but it is the John Riddoch that gets most of the attention, being a concentrated, intense, characterful expression of Cabernet Sauvignon with lovely definition and purity of fruit. The 1982 is beautifully elegant and expressive, showing just how well this wine can age.

Memorial Drive, Coonawarra, SA 5263
www.wynns.com.au

Yalumba Barossa

Proud to be Australia's oldest family-owned winery, Yalumba is an example of how it is possible to be big —producing almost a million cases annually—and also very good. Oxford Landing is one of its better big brands and the Y Series varietals offer fantastic value for money, especially the bright Viognier. Things get progressively better as you work through the extensive range, culminating in the Cabernet Sauvignon-dominated Reserve, which ages beautifully. High-end Virgilius Viognier is one of Australia's best, and the Signature Cabernet Shiraz is also a fantastic wine. Octavius old-vine Shiraz is wonderfully concentrated, but can be a little oaky.

Eden Valley Rd, Angaston, SA 5353
www.yalumba.com

Zema Estate Coonawarra

This family-owned wine estate has grown progressively since its origins in 1982 to its current 151 acres (61ha), which are split between three sites. Cabernet Sauvignon is dominant here, but there is quite a bit of Shiraz and just a little Merlot, Malbec, Cabernet Franc, and Sauvignon Blanc making up the balance. The top wines are the Family Selection Cabernet Sauvignon and Family Selection Shiraz. Both are big and dense, but with very good fruit expression. The regular varietal wines offer fantastic value for money.

Riddoch Way, Coonawarra, SA 5263
www.zema.com.au

Nets are draped over individual rows of vines in Adelaide Hills to keep birds away from the ripe grapes.

WESTERN AUSTRALIA

Western Australia may only be small in terms of the amount of wine it produces, but it more than makes up for this in terms of quality. Although the geographically isolated fine wine areas of Margaret River and Great Southern were first planted as recently as the mid-1960s, they are now producing, arguably, Australia's top Cabernet Sauvignons and some of the country's best Chardonnays. Riesling and cool-climate Shiraz are also showing great promise, especially from the coolest spots in Great Southern. As other parts of Australia struggle with rising temperatures and drought, it is likely that the cool-climate regions of Western Australia will become an increasingly important part of Australia's fine wine dimension.

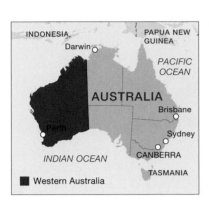

Major grapes

 Reds

Cabernet Sauvignon

Malbec

Pinot Noir

Shiraz

 Whites

Chardonnay

Riesling

Sauvignon Blanc

Semillon

Vintages

2009
Looking like a promising vintage with a steady, mild, even growing season. Margaret River did very well.

2008
A really good vintage with a warm, late summer, creating ideal harvest conditions.

2007
A superb vintage with good quality across the board. Reds are particularly promising.

2006
A difficult, cold, late vintage, resulting in some tight, lean wines. Whites are better.

2005
A mild summer and low yields led to a good-quality vintage.

2004
Cool early conditions, a warm summer, and a January heat wave resulted in a very good vintage, with Cabernet Sauvignon excelling.

While grapes have been grown in Western Australia since the mid-19th century (the first vineyards in the Swan Valley, near Perth, were planted in the 1830s), it is only relatively recently that the state has become a serious player on the Australian wine scene.

Western Australia's most important wine region is the Margaret River area, about a three-hour drive south of Perth. It was first planted in the late 1960s, after a survey by government scientist Dr. John Gladstones identified it as a promising location. But Gladstones was not the only scientist to have spotted Western Australia's potential. A decade earlier, in 1956, Californian Professor Harold Olmo identified the Mount Barker and Frankland areas in the Great Southern as being particularly promising. This led to the first plantings, by Forest Hill, in Mount Barker in 1965.

It was Margaret River that gained momentum first, however, and the quality of the wines it has since produced has proved Gladstones right. Led by the four pioneering wineries of Moss Wood, Cape Mentelle, Vasse Felix, and Cullen, Margaret River has now established itself as one of Australia's top regions for fine wine, making some of the country's best Cabernet Sauvignon, as well as impressive Chardonnay and stylishly fresh Sauvignon Blanc/Semillon blends. Only Coonawarra comes close to producing Bordeaux-style blends with as much definition as Margaret River. As well as these staples, Margaret River also produces some nice Shiraz wines, fresh Rieslings, and deeply impressive Malbecs—a grape that looks to have a bright future here.

Great Southern encompasses some rather marginal, extremely cool wine-growing regions. Despite producing some of Western Australia's most exciting wines, it may be these conditions, along with the geographical isolation of this part of Western Australia, that has held this area back. Frankland River is the largest of the subregions, producing good Riesling and Sauvignon Blanc, and even doing quite well with Cabernet Sauvignon. Mount Barker, the coolest and oldest of the subregions, excels with cool-climate Shiraz and Riesling. Neighboring Denmark and Albany are both fairly cool, wet regions that do quite well with Pinot Noir and Chardonnay. Finally, Porongurup, another cool region, has yet to make its mark, but it shows promise. These cooler-climate regions are already making some of Western Australia's most exciting wines, and they are likely to become even more important as global warming increases.

Elsewhere in the state, there are some widely dispersed vineyards of real merit. Between Margaret River on the coast and Great Southern are the subregions of Pemberton, Manjimup, Blackwood Valley, and Geographe. Further north is Peel, then Perth, sandwiched between the Swan District to the north and the Perth Hills. Close to Perth, the climate is too warm for fine wine production, although there are some interesting examples of dessert wines that stand out among the more commercial offerings.

WESTERN AUSTRALIA

From looking at this map, you would be left with the impression that large areas of the state of Western Australia are under vine. Actually, the vineyards are pretty spread out. The oldest vines are in the least interesting areas, close to Perth. It was only in the 1960s that planting began in the much cooler regions of Margaret River and Mount Barker, and such has been the success here that other cool regions, including the decidedly chilly Denmark and Albany regions, have been pioneered.

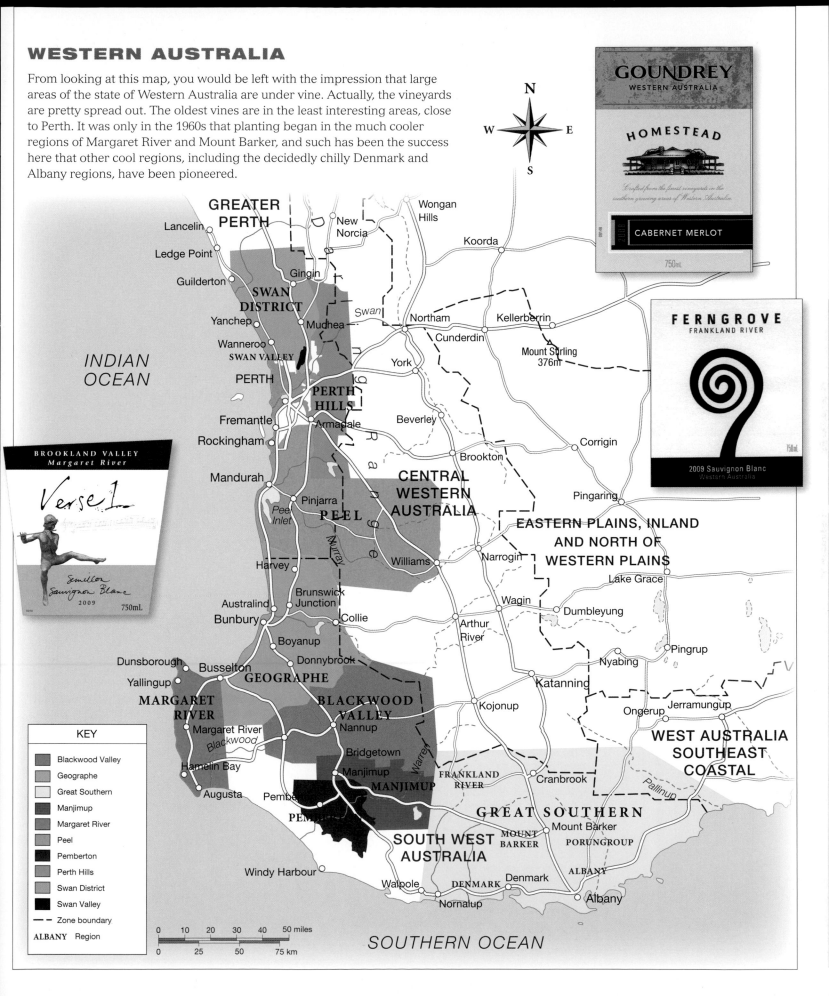

GOUNDREY
WESTERN AUSTRALIA

HOMESTEAD

Crafted from the finest vineyards in the southern growing areas of Western Australia.

CABERNET MERLOT

750mL

FERNGROVE
FRANKLAND RIVER

2009 Sauvignon Blanc
Western Australia

BROOKLAND VALLEY
Margaret River

Verse 1

Semillon
Sauvignon Blanc
2009   750mL

KEY

■	Blackwood Valley
■	Geographe
□	Great Southern
■	Manjimup
■	Margaret River
■	Peel
■	Pemberton
■	Perth Hills
■	Swan District
■	Swan Valley
- - -	Zone boundary

ALBANY Region

0   10   20   30   40   50 miles
0   25   50   75 km

INDIAN
OCEAN

SOUTHERN OCEAN

GREATER PERTH
Lancelin
Ledge Point
Guilderton
SWAN DISTRICT
Yanchep
Wanneroo
SWAN VALLEY
PERTH
Fremantle
Rockingham
Mandurah
Gingin
Mudhea
Swan
PERTH HILLS
Armadale
Peel Inlet
Pinjarra
PEEL
Murray
Harvey
Brunswick Junction
Australind
Bunbury
Boyanup
Donnybrook
Collie
Dunsborough
Busselton
Yallingup
GEOGRAPHE
MARGARET RIVER
Margaret River
Blackwood
Hamelin Bay
Augusta
BLACKWOOD VALLEY
Nannup
Bridgetown
Manjimup
MANJIMUP
Warren
Pember
PEMBERTON
Windy Harbour
New Norcia
Wongan Hills
Koorda
Northam
Cunderdin
York
Mount Surling 376m
Kellerberrin
Beverley
Brookton
CENTRAL WESTERN AUSTRALIA
Williams
Corrigin
Pingaring
EASTERN PLAINS, INLAND AND NORTH OF WESTERN PLAINS
Narrogin
Lake Grace
Wagin
Dumbleyung
Arthur River
Pingrup
Nyabing
Katanning
Kojonup
Ongerup
Jerramungup
WEST AUSTRALIA SOUTHEAST COASTAL
Pallinup
FRANKLAND RIVER
Cranbrook
GREAT SOUTHERN
SOUTH WEST AUSTRALIA
MOUNT BARKER
Mount Barker
PORUNGROUP
ALBANY
DENMARK
Denmark
Walpole
Nornalup
Albany

CAPE MENTELLE
A CLASSIC EXAMPLE OF THE SEMILLON/
SAUVIGNON BLANC BLEND THAT IS A
MARGARET RIVER SPECIALITY

Alkoomi Frankland River

The Frankland River region is one of the most remote
wine regions in Australia, and Alkoomi, with just over 247
acres (100ha), is one of the largest vineyards in the
region. Still owned by the Lange family, who established
vines here in the early 1970s, it is ancient by this region's
standards. Alkoomi makes wines that range from solidly
good to superb in quality. Particularly good are the
aromatic Shiraz Viognier, the Blackbutt (a high-end
Bordeaux blend), and Jarrah, their top Shiraz, which
demands some cellaring.

1141 Wingebellup Rd, Frankland River, WA 6396
www.alkoomiwines.com.au

Brookland Valley Margaret River

Established in the mid-1980s, with the aid of super-
consultants Croser and Jordan, Brookland Valley is now
owned by Hardys (Constellation). Despite the reasonably
high production of 130,000 cases annually, quality is not
overlooked and the wines are really good. The reserve
range includes Cabernet, Chardonnay, and Semillon that
are among the best from the region. The Semillon/
Sauvignon Blanc 2008 is a Margaret River classic, with
green herb and pepper character to the fore.

Caves Rd, Wilyabrup, WA 6280
www.brooklandvalley.com.au

Cape Mentelle Margaret River

David Hohnen planted the first Cape Mentelle vineyard
in 1970, which makes him one of the Margaret River
pioneers. In 1990, Veuve Clicquot acquired 50% of the
business; then, in 2000, they took 100% ownership. In
2002, LVMH bought Veuve Clicquot and with it, Cape
Mentelle. Hohnen chose the location, just 3 miles (5km)
from the ocean, because of its gravelly soils. As well as
the 1970 Cabernet vineyard, Cape Mentelle also has three
other vineyards and sources fruit from a dozen growers.
Bold, structured Cabernet is the star here, but Shiraz and
Zinfandel (a popular oddity) are also good. The Sauvignon
Blanc/Semillon is a benchmark for this Margaret River
staple. Look out for the Wallcliffe Semillon/Sauvignon
Blanc, with its added barrel-ferment complexity.

331 Wallcliffe Rd, Margaret River, WA 6285
www.capementelle.com.au

Capel Vale Geographe

From its mid-1970s origins in the Geographe subregion,
Capel Vale has expanded significantly. It now has
sizeable holdings in each of the Margaret River,
Pemberton, Mount Barker, and Geographe regions
that total 544 acres (220ha). The Regional Series wines
are varietals that excel in each of these four regions.
The top wines, not made every vintage, are the
single-vineyard bottlings, with Whispering Hill Mount
Barker Riesling and Scholar Margaret River Cabernet
Sauvignon particularly worth seeking out.

Lot 5 Stirling Estate, Mallokup Rd, Capel, WA 6271
www.capelvale.com

Cullen Margaret River

Cullen is one of the pioneering wineries in Margaret
River and, arguably, the best. It was the work of Dr. John
Gladstones in the 1960s that first led the Cullens to plant
a trial 0.25 acres (0.1ha) of vines in this previously

CULLEN
THE DIANA MADELINE IS STRUCTURED,
DENSE, AND AGEWORTHY

unplanted area. Encouraged by their success, and that of
others such as Dr. Tom Cullity of Vasse Felix, in 1971 the
Cullens planted 19 acres (7.7ha) of Cabernet Sauvignon
and Riesling on what is now the Cullen Vineyard. They
added other varieties in 1976, and Sauvignon Blanc in
1988. Cullen has two vineyards, Mangan and Cullen, and
produces a total of 15,000 cases of wine a year. Recently,
the focus at Cullen has been on improving the viticulture
to make it more sustainable, so biodynamics has been
implemented. The top wine is the Cabernet-based Diana
Madeline, one of Australia's very best. Also impressive
is the Mangan, a red Malbec-containing blend, which is
dense, structured, and satisfying. The Chardonnay is
superb, too.

Caves Rd, Cowaramup, WA 6284
www.cullenwines.com.au

Devil's Lair Margaret River

Founded by Phil Sexton in 1981, Devil's Lair thrived
in part because of its lively, fun packaging and clever
marketing. Sexton, who now makes wine in the Yarra
Valley, sold to Southcorp in 1996, so the winery is now
part of the Fosters portfolio. It produces a sizeable
220,000 cases a year, but the quality is uniformly good.
You are most likely to come across the simple, but tasty,
Fifth Leg wines, but the estate bottlings can be quite smart.

Rocky Road, Forest Grove, WA 6286
www.devils-lair.com

Evans & Tate Margaret River

Even when they were experiencing a period of financial
turmoil in the early years of the 21st century, Evans &
Tate continued to produce fantastic wines in considerable
quantities. They are now part of the McWilliam's Wine
Group. Their top wines are Redbrook Chardonnay and
Cabernet Sauvignon, which are among the best from the
region. Less expensive wines labeled Classic are a good
bet for those on a budget.

Corner of Metricup Rd/Caves Rd, Wilyabrup, WA 6280
www.evansandtate.com.au

Fermoy Margaret River

This mid-sized winery, producing 30,000 cases, is a solid
performer, making some nice Cabernet Sauvignon and
a deliciously structured Nebbiolo. It also makes a varietal
Semillon, a restrained wild-ferment Chardonnay, and
a Verdelho that sells out fast, even though it is far from
the best wine.

Cowaramup, WA 6284
www.fermoy.com.au

Ferngrove Frankland River

Based in the cool Frankland River region, which is part
of Great Southern, Ferngrove is a premium producer
founded in 1998 by Murray Burton. Shiraz, Cabernet
Sauvignon, and Malbec all do well here, and Sauvignon
Blanc, Chardonnay, and Riesling lead the way among the
whites. Ferngrove has two vineyards that total around
556 acres (225ha), and sells grapes as well as making
estate wines. Its flagship red wine is The Stirlings, a
Cabernet/Shiraz blend.

276 Ferngrove Rd, Frankland River, WA 6396
www.ferngrove.com.au

Flame Tree Margaret River

Newcomer Flame Tree hit the ground running when it won the Jimmy Watson trophy for its first release Cabernet Merlot in 2007, as well as taking a host of other medals and trophies. The winery is based in the Margaret River, but grapes are sourced from elsewhere, too. The wines were initially made by Jeremy Gordon, but he left in 2009 and has been replaced by the talented Cliff Royale. The Frankland River Shiraz is a wine to look out for, as is the straight Cabernet Sauvignon. ★ Rising star

Corner of Caves Rd/Chain Ave, Dunsborough, WA 6281
www.flametreewines.com

Fonty's Pool Pemberton

Hailing from the cool subregion of Pemberton, the oddly named Fonty's Pool winery makes a broad array of wines that range from Viognier to Pinot Noir. The highlight, however, is the Shiraz, with its focused, cool-climate, peppery fruit. Since it was established in 1989, Fonty's Pool has expanded regularly and it now covers 272 acres (110ha). The grapes not used in its own wines are sold to other Western Australian wineries.

Seven Day Rd, Manjimup, WA 6258
www.fontyspoolwines.com.au

Forest Hill Mount Barker

Being the oldest cool-climate winery in the state, Mount Barker winery Forest Hill has a special place in Western Australian viticulture. The first vines, Riesling and Cabernet, were planted in 1965, before Margaret River was even a recognized wine region. Initially, the wines were made at Houghton in the Swan Valley, but later the winery was purchased by the Holmes à Court family, who owned Vasse Felix. The current owners, the Lyons family, bought Forest Hill in 1996. The wines have a distinctive, cool-climate character—the Riesling, Chardonnay, Cabernet Sauvignon, and Shiraz all excel.

South Coast Hwy, Denmark, WA 6333
www.foresthillwines.com.au

Frankland Estate Frankland River

Organically certified from the 2009 vintage, Frankland Estate is one of the top wineries in the cool Frankland River region of the Great Southern. Riesling is a particular speciality—the Isolation Ridge Riesling is precise, intense, and limey, with a lovely transparency. Frankland Estate also makes superb cool-climate Shiraz, and a flagship Bordeaux blend called Olmo's Reward. It was in 1988 that Barrie Smith and Judy Cullam decided to begin a new career as wine-growers on the wool-growing property they had owned since the mid-1970s. It has proved to be a wise choice. The Isolation Ridge vineyard is located on their estate, while their other single-vineyard wines are made with fruit sourced from local growers.

Frankland Rd, Frankland, WA 6396
www.franklandestate.com.au

Fraser Gallop Margaret River

Fraser Gallop's first vintage was in 2002 and its winery was constructed in 2008; this makes it a relative newcomer to the Margaret River scene. The focus is on single-vineyard wines, primarily Cabernet-based Bordeaux blends and Chardonnay. Clive Otto, who used to work for Vasse Felix, is the winemaker.

547 Metricup Rd, Wilyabrup, WA 6280
www.frasergallopestate.com.au

Goundrey Mount Barker

With 593 acres (240ha) of vineyards, Goundrey is a significant presence in Mount Barker. It was purchased by the Constellation group in 2006, and then sold in 2009 to West Cape Howe. The Goundrey name is still owned by Constellation and some of the fruit from the original vineyards is sold back to Constellation to make the wines. The G range and the Goundrey Reserve wines can be very good indeed.

Muirs Hwy, Mount Barker, WA 6324
www.goundreywines.com.au

Houghton Swan Valley

Now part of drinks giant Constellation, Houghton has quite a history. Based in the Swan Valley, near Perth, it is Western Australia's largest producer. Despite this, the wines are very good, ranging from fresh, entry-level bottles such as the deliciously crisp HWB (which used to be known as Houghton's White Burgundy) to the more serious Jack Mann Cabernet Sauvignon. Houghton has 124 acres (50ha) of estate vineyards, but most of the grapes are sourced from around the state's premium grape-growing regions. Look out for a new wine, the vibrant and affordable Bandit Tempranillo Shiraz.

Dale Rd, Middle Swan, WA 6065
www.houghton-wines.com.au

Howard Park Margaret River

With its impressive new Margaret River winery and cellar door, Howard Park is one of the star attractions of the region. It started out in 1986 in the Great Southern region, where it was a pioneering presence. Jeff and Amy Burch, the current owners, established the Margaret River vineyards in 1996, followed by the winery in 2000, and wines are now made at both locations. The current winemaker, Tony Davis, is continuing the excellent work of Michael Kerrigan with a pure and focused house style. Steely Rieslings, taut Sauvignons, and restrained, ageworthy Cabernet Sauvignons are all first rate. Howard Park also makes the deliciously fresh and thankfully affordable Madfish wines.

Miamup Rd, Cowaramup, WA 6284
www.howardparkwines.com.au

Kalgan River Great Southern

In 2000, John Ciprian left the jewelry industry to become a wine-grower. He planted vines in Western Australia's Great Southern region, and Kalgan River's first vintage followed in 2005. Andrew Hoadley is the winemaker here, and he is fashioning some beautiful, cool-climate wines, including a fantastic Shiraz Viognier that is savory and peppery, and can quite happily compete with the best from Western Australia. The Riesling is also very good. Kalgan River currently has 49.5 acres (20ha) planted. ★ Rising star

Albany, WA 6332
www.kalganriverwines.com.au

DR. JOHN GLADSTONES

Dr. John Gladstones was a lupin researcher working for the Western Australian Department of Agriculture when he became friendly with legendary Houghton winemaker, Jack Mann, in the 1950s. Gladstones began to think about regions in Western Australia that might be suitable for viticulture, compiling a report in 1965 entitled "The Climate and Soils of Southern WA in relation to Vine Growing," in which he identified the Margaret River area as having a very similar climate to Bordeaux and ideal soils for quality grape-growing. Gladstones' work inspired a band of pioneers to plant grapes here. The first, in 1967, was Dr. Thomas Cullity from Vasse Felix. He was closely followed by the Hohnens (Cape Mentelle), the Cullens (Cullen), and the Pannells (Moss Wood). History has proved Gladstones right, and Margaret River now arguably makes Australia's best Cabernet Sauvignon-based wines.

SANDALFORD
A MEDIUM- TO FULL-BODIED WINE WITH
BERRY FLAVORS AND A SWEET FRUIT FINISH

LEEUWIN ESTATE
BRIGHT IN COLOR, THIS WINE HAS A CLEAN,
RICH, CITRUS PALATE AND BALANCED ACIDITY

Larry Cherubino Wines　Frankland River

Larry Cherubino is an experienced flying winemaker, who, in 2005, started his own wine company making wines from leading regions in Western Australia. Cherubino is the top label, followed by The Yard and Ad Hoc. The Yard 2006 Frankland River Acacia Vineyard Shiraz is stunningly aromatic with a nice, meaty dimension—one of Western Australia's best. The Yard Frankland River Riversdale Vineyard Cabernet 2007 shows thrilling, concentrated, rich fruit that is countered by freshness and fine-grained tannins, and the Cherubino Margaret River Cabernet 2007 is just brilliant. Seek out his wines with some urgency. ★**Rising star**

15 York St, Subiaco, Perth WA 6008
www.larrycherubino.com.au

Leeuwin Estate　Margaret River

Celebrated for producing one of Australia's very best Chardonnays (the red wines are a little underrated, but can also be fantastic), Leeuwin is also famous for its series of music concerts. The estate came about somewhat by accident. Denis Horgan bought the property in 1969 because it was attached to a plumbing business he wanted to acquire, but he soon fell in love with the region. In 1973, Denis got a call from a Seattle attorney asking whether he was interested in selling the property. He found out that the potential buyer was none other than Robert Mondavi, which alerted Denis to the potential of his property for making world-class wine. In 1975, he started to plant a vineyard, and over the next five years 200 acres (81ha) of vines were established.

Stevens Rd, Margaret River, WA 6285
www.leeuwinestate.com.au

McHenry Hohnen　Margaret River

David Hohnen, founder of Cape Mentelle and Cloudy Bay, left the role of corporate CEO with LVMH in 2003 to strike out on his own. His chief interest now is farming sheep and a few pigs, but wine is hard to get out of the system, so, with his brother-in-law Murray McHenry, he started a new winery based around the four Margaret River vineyards that were already in the family. David's daughter, Freya, is in charge of winemaking duties. McHenry Hohnen wines are interesting, and made in an elegant, more European style than many from Margaret River. Particularly interesting is the use of varieties not normally associated with the region, such as Tempranillo, Barbera, Petit Verdot, and Grenache. ★**Rising star**

Margaret River, WA 6285
www.mchv.com.au

Moss Wood　Margaret River

Moss Wood is one of the most celebrated Margaret River wineries. In the late 1960s, when John Gladstones first identified the promise of this region, Bill and Sandra Pannell spent six months searching for ideal land. In 1969, they found a site at Wilyabrup, which became one of the four Margaret River pioneer sites, along with Cape Mentelle, Vasse Felix, and Cullen. In 1978, Roseworthy graduate Keith Mugford was hired as winemaker, and eight years later he and his wife, Clare, purchased Moss Wood from the Pannells. Today, they produce 15,000 cases a year from the 49.5 acres (20ha) of vines. No irrigation is used and the vines are all cane pruned. The Old Block Cabernet vineyard, which produces the best fruit, was the second vineyard planted in Margaret River, making it almost 30 years old. In 2000, Moss Wood purchased the neighboring Ribbonvale vineyard. The Chardonnay here is good; the exceptional Cabernets, though, are among Australia's very best. Seek out the 2004, which is perhaps the best recent vintage.

Metricup Rd, Wilyabrup, WA 6284
www.mosswood.com.au

Peel Estate　Peel

Peel Estate is a small winery with 39.5 acres (16ha) of vines in the Peel region, south and inland of Perth and north of Margaret River. Established by Bill Nairn in 1973, several varieties are made here, including Chenin Blanc, Verdelho, and Zinfandel, as well as the more usual Cabernet, Shiraz, and Chardonnay. The powerful, berry-fruited, peppery Shiraz is the top wine here.

290 Fletcher Rd, Karnup, WA 6171
www.peelwine.com.au

Picardy　Pemberton

Bill and Sandra Pannell were Margaret River pioneers, establishing Moss Wood in 1969. They now own this small, 5,000-case winery in Pemberton and make a range of restrained, relatively elegant wines, with Pinot Noir and Chardonnay the key focus. The peppery Shiraz is also pretty good. The top wine is the Tête de Cuvée Pinot Noir, which, rather than being a barrel selection, is made by an even more rigorous approach in the vineyard.

Cnr Vasse Hwy and Eastbrook Road, Pemberton, WA 6260
www.picardy.com.au

Pierro　Margaret River

Boutique winery Pierro was established by medical doctor Michael Peterkin in 1979, who followed his medical degree with one in enology. As well as making one of Australia's most highly rated Chardonnays, he also makes some stylish red wines.

Caves Rd, Wilyabrup, Busselton, WA 6280
www.pierro.com.au

Plantagenet　Mount Barker

With its first release in 1974, Plantagenet was the first winery to be established in the Mount Barker region, and it is still one of the best. Tony Smith bought the property in 1968 and gradually built its reputation and the vineyard area, before selling it in 2000 to Lionel Samson & Son. Tony stayed on as chairman, and in 2007 the well-known winemaker John Durham, who had spent 21 years at Cape Mentelle, was hired. The current portfolio includes a focused, peppery Shiraz; a refined, delicate Riesling; a structured Cabernet; and a fairly serious Chardonnay.

Lot 45, Albany Hwy, Mount Barker, WA 6324
www.plantagenetwines.com

Salitage　Pemberton

John Horgan, the man behind Salitage, was also the co-founder (with his brother Denis) of Leeuwin Estate. Salitage was established in 1988, making it one of the pioneers of the Pemberton region, along with Picardy. Pemberton has since grown considerably as a wine region, and Salitage remains one of the top wineries in the area, specializing in Pinot Noir and Chardonnay from their 62 acres (25ha) of vines. A Bordeaux blend, simply labeled Pemberton, is also quite respectable.

Vasse Hwy, Pemberton, WA 6260
www.salitage.com.au

Sandalford Swan Valley

Sandalford is a historic winery that can trace its origins back to 1840—ancient history by Australia's standards. Having started in the Swan Valley, a hot region whose key attribute is its proximity to Perth, it now has a significant presence in Margaret River. The Swan Valley operation remains important for wine tourism, but the best fruit comes from the 296.5 acres (120ha) of vines in Margaret River, and hence, so do the best of Sandalford's well-priced and flavorful wines. The top tier is the Prendeville Reserve, which includes a Cabernet Sauvignon and a Shiraz. The 2005 Prendeville Reserve Cabernet Sauvignon is focused and elegant, with bright berry fruits.

3210 West Swan Rd, Caversham, WA 6055
www.sandalford.com

Smithbrook Pemberton

Originally established in the 1980s by Bill Pannell, this Pemberton winery was purchased by Petaluma and became part of the Lion Nathan stable of wineries. With 148 acres (60ha) of vines, it is a relatively large winery in the region, specializing in Merlot and Sauvignon Blanc. In June 2009, Lion Nathan sold the vineyard and winery to the Fogarty Wine Group, but retained the brand name. It is likely that Fogarty's future involvement will be good for wine quality.

Smithbrook Rd, Pemberton, WA 6260
www.smithbrook.com.au

Stella Bella Margaret River

With their lively, imaginative labels, Stella Bella wines deliver fresh, vibrant, delicious flavors. They have been extremely commercially successful, but the wines have not suffered for this and are pretty smartly made. The more serious wines come under the Suckfizzle label, and include an aromatic and beautifully expressive Cabernet Sauvignon.

205 Rosabrook Rd, Margaret River, WA 6285
www.stellabella.com.au

Vasse Felix Margaret River

Dr. Tom Cullity was the first to plant grapes in the Margaret River region in 1967, in the Wilyabrup subregion. His inaugural vintage, 1971, was mostly ruined by rot and bird damage, but in 1972 he made a respectable Riesling. These days, Vasse Felix is owned by the Holmes à Court family and is one of the top wineries in the region. With the exception of a rather green Semillon, the wines are simply superb, with the jewel in the crown being the Cabernet-dominated Heytesbury red, and the intense, rich, concentrated Heytesbury Chardonnay. The regular Cabernet Sauvignon, Cabernet Merlot, and Shiraz are all superb, too. There is a lot of wine made at Vasse Felix, which makes their level of quality all the more impressive.

Cnr Caves Rd/Harmans Rd South, Cowaramup, WA 6284;
www.vassefelix.com.au

VASSE FELIX
A DENSE BUT ELEGANT BLEND OF MALBEC, CABERNET SAUVIGNON, AND PETIT VERDOT

PIERRO
A SUPERB CHARDONNAY WITH SWEET, LUSH FRUIT AND WELL-INTEGRATED OAK

Voyager Estate Margaret River

Acquired in 1991 by mining magnate Michael Wright, significant investment has been made in this Margaret River winery—its mock Cape Dutch architecture is certainly a tourist draw. In the past, the wines have been more correct than exciting, but this seems to be changing. Look out for the excellent Chardonnay, which is one of the region's best, and the Cabernet Sauvignon/Merlot blend.

Lot 1 Stevens Rd, Margaret River, WA 6285
www.voyagerestate.com.au

West Cape Howe Great Southern

A prominent Great Southern winery, named after the most southerly point in Western Australia, West Cape Howe is a serious operator—it recently purchased 586 acres (237ha) of Goundrey vineyards and the winery from Constellation. Most of the grapes will continue to be sold to Constellation, who retained the Goundrey brand. As well as owning its own vineyards, West Cape Howe also sources fruit from other subregions in Great Southern. Its top wines are the Great Southern range, which includes highly rated Chardonnay and Shiraz.

678 South Coast Hwy, Denmark, WA 6333
www.westcapehowewines.com.au

Woodlands Margaret River

Woodlands is a boutique Margaret River winery with a long history—the first vines were planted in 1973. More recently, it has developed a reputation as one of the region's best wine producers. Since 2008, its small vineyard in Wilyabrup has been supplemented with fruit from another vineyard. Perhaps their best wine is the Colin Cabernet Sauvignon Woodlands, which has a lovely mineral complexity and creamy blackcurrant fruit. Also of interest is the Reserve Cabernet Franc, which shows a varietally distinct leafy, green edge to the abundant dark fruit.

3948 Caves Rd, Wilyabrup, WA 6284
www.woodlandswines.com

Xanadu Margaret River

This winery has been on a bit of a roller coaster ride in recent years. It was founded in 1977 by Irishman Dr. John Lagan. He named his new vineyard Xanadu, after the poem *Kubla Khan* by Coleridge. Lagan's ownership came to an end in 2001, when the winery was publicly listed on the Australian stock market. In the space of just three years it went on a massive growth spurt, from crushing 450 tons (457 tonnes) annually to a massive 2,300 tons (2,337 tonnes). The company was then purchased by the Rathbone family, owners of Yering Station and Mount Langhi Ghiran, and operations were refocused—the first year of Rathbone ownership saw a crush of 650 tons (660 tonnes). The wines are now steadily improving, having lost their way for a time. They are well judged and are a fairly good value; the Cabernet Sauvignon and the Shiraz are both reasonably serious efforts.

Boodjidup Rd, Margaret River, WA 6285
www.xanaduwines.com

QUEENSLAND

It may be surprising to some that there is a thriving wine industry in Queensland. The climate should be just too warm and damp for successful viticulture, with rainfall concentrated in the growing season rather than in the winter. But in the Granite Belt region, a couple of hours' drive southwest of Brisbane, altitude moderates the heat and makes the production of high-quality wines possible. There are currently around 50 wineries in the Granite Belt region—some are supported largely by tourism, but others are making genuinely high-quality wines. Queensland is also home to another significant wine region, called South Burnett, as well as some unofficial wine-growing zones that are scattered across the southeast corner of the state.

Major grapes

 Reds

Cabernet Sauvignon

Shiraz

 Whites

Chardonnay

Semillon

Vintages

2009
Early days yet, with some rain in the growing season, but it is looking very good for whites and good for reds.

2008
A tricky, cool vintage with too much rain in January and February.

2007
Late frosts were a problem for some, but it was a dry growing season. Overall, a good-quality vintage.

2006
Mainly a good vintage, but plenty of rain in the growing season caused challenges.

2005
An excellent year with a warm growing season.

2004
A hot spring was followed by a hot, rainy growing season, which created difficult conditions.

Wine production in Queensland is largely, but not entirely, concentrated in just one region—the Granite Belt. This area is the northern extension of the New England Tableland: a granite protrusion, 1,969–3,281ft (600–1,000m) above sea level. Given its northerly latitude, this region would normally be too hot for growing quality wine grapes, but because of its altitude, the climate is just about tolerable, although far from ideal, for viticulture.

The late harvest dates in the Granite Belt might suggest that this is a cool-climate region, but there is sufficient warmth to ripen Shiraz and Cabernet Sauvignon reliably. Unusually for a continental climate, much of the rainfall occurs during the growing season. Although this has the benefit of eliminating the need for irrigation, it creates problems for growers by increasing the risk of fungal diseases, which are one of the main viticultural hazards here, alongside spring frosts.

There are around 50 wineries in this region, the best of which are producing top-quality wines largely from Shiraz, Cabernet Sauvignon, Semillon, and Chardonnay. Were it not for the support of wine tourism from relatively nearby Brisbane, it is possible that the Granite Belt wineries would struggle to survive, but as it is, they are doing reasonably well and the area under vine has increased in recent years.

The other significant viticultural region in Queensland is South Burnett, northwest of Brisbane, which has over a dozen wineries and almost matches the Granite Belt for vineyard area, although the wines do not always reach the same heights. This exciting area is relatively new, since it was first planted as recently as 1995. The altitude here is lower, at 984–1,969ft (300–600m), so it is far warmer, with a subtropical climate and rain throughout the year, including a fair amount during the growing season. South Burnett's vineyards, which are interspersed with other types of farmland, are spread over a wide area, but with a concentration around the town of Kingaroy. Shiraz and Chardonnay grapes perform best here, but the climate seems to limit the quality that can be achieved.

In addition to the Granite Belt and South Burnett, there are also a number of unofficial regions that each have a handful of wineries. Some of these—such as Gold Coast and Hinterland, Brisbane and Scenic Rim—are driven more by tourism than by their suitability for wine-growing. However, the Darling Downs, a small region located inland from Brisbane, and the most significant of the unofficial regions, does boast good conditions for viticulture, even if the number of wineries here remains small.

Bald Mountain Granite Belt

This Granite Belt winery was established by Denis and Jackie Parsons in 1985. They sold the winery in 2009 to Steve and Lisa Messiter, but have stayed on in a managing capacity for the time being. The 16 acres (6.5ha) of vines are planted at relatively high altitude (2,723–2,953ft/830–900m) on free-draining, decomposed granite. Chardonnay, Sauvignon Blanc, Shiraz, and Cabernet Sauvignon are grown. Their wines include a Sauvignon Blanc/Verdelho blend called Dancing Brolga and two sparkling wines—a Shiraz and a non-vintage Chardonnay/Pinot Noir.

41 Hickling Lane, Wallangarra, QLD 4383
www.baldmountainwines.com.au

Ballandean Estate Granite Belt

Proud to be Queensland's oldest and largest family-owned-and-operated winery, Ballandean can trace its winemaking history back to 1930. Its commercial history began in 1968 when Angelo and Mary Puglisi took over the farm from Angelo's parents. They initially operated under the name Sundown Valley Vineyards, before changing the winery's name to Ballandean in 1988. A large range of wines are made from 74 acres (30ha), including a Viognier, a Chardonnay, a Semillon/Sauvignon Blanc, and a specialty late-harvest Sylvaner, while the reds encompass Shiraz, Merlot, and Cabernet Sauvignon. The cellar door first opened in 1970 and is still a very important part of the business.

354 Sundown Rd, Ballandean, QLD 4382
www.ballandeanestate.com

Boireann Granite Belt

Arguably the top producer in the Granite Belt region, this small winery is making world-class wines, albeit in tiny quantities, in what is sometimes a poorly regarded region. Winemaker Peter Stark focuses solely on red wines using Grenache, Barbera, Tannat, Mourvèdre, Shiraz, Merlot, and Petit Verdot grapes. The vines are planted at an altitude of 2,871ft (875m) and experience cool nights during the growing season, which delays ripening and results in deep, intense flavors. The wine is made traditionally, using open fermenters, basket pressing, and barrel aging. The 2005 Tannat is beautifully defined, with good structure and forward blackberry and raspberry fruit. ★Rising star

26 Donnellys Castle Rd, The Summit, QLD 4377
www.boireannwinery.com.au

Clovely Estate South Burnett

By Queensland standards, Clovely is a huge winery, owning or managing 432 acres (175ha) of vines in the South Burnett region. This is a relatively new region that was first planted in 1995. It has a similar climate to the Hunter Valley in New South Wales, and now boasts more than 13 cellar doors. Clovely was established in 1997, and today makes a wide of range of wines, all from estate-grown fruit, in six different tiers. The top wine is the rich, dark Double Pruned Shiraz, made from vines that are pruned for a second time after they have flowered. This is followed by the Estate Reserve series, which includes Cabernet Sauvignon, Shiraz, Chardonnay, and Verdelho.

Macalister St, Murgon, QLD 4605
www.clovely.com.au

BOIREANN
WITH A GAMEY NOSE AND SOFT TANNINS, THIS WINE SHOULD BE DRUNK YOUNG

CLOVELY ESTATE
THE 2007 ESTATE RESERVE IS AGED FOR 18 MONTHS IN FRENCH AND AMERICAN OAK

Heritage Estate Granite Belt

Established in 1992 by husband-and-wife team Bryce and Paddy Kassulke, this family-owned-and-operated Granite Belt winery has two cellar doors: one at Stanthorpe and one at Tamborine Mountain. The latter—as an extra tourist attraction—is located in a restored church. Bryce and Paddy's son, John Handy, is the winemaker; he works with both estate-grown grapes and grapes that are purchased from other growers. While some of the wines are clearly designed to appeal to cellar door visitors, the Reserve Chardonnay and the Cabernet Sauvignon are highly regarded. The Verdelho has also done well at some of the wine shows.

747 Granite Belt Drive, Cottonvale, QLD 4375
www.heritagewines.com.au

Robert Channon Granite Belt

Located close to Stanthorpe, in the Granite Belt region, Robert Channon Wines is particularly well known for its prize-winning Verdelho. Since the first vintage in 2001, the winery has been instrumental in establishing Verdelho as a suitable and successful variety for the cool-climate Granite Belt. As well as the famous Verdelho, Robert Channon also makes very attractive Chardonnay, Pinot Gris, Cabernet Sauvignon, and Merlot. The 20 acre (8ha) estate vineyards produce around 3,000 cases of wine each year. A distinctive feature of the vineyard is its permanent bird netting, which also acts as important hail protection for the vines.

50 Amiens Rd, Stanthorpe, QLD 4380
www.robertchannonwines.com

Sirromet Granite Belt

One of the largest Queensland wineries, 395 acre (160ha) Sirromet has expanded its vineyard holdings over recent years and now encompasses one-quarter of the Granite Belt. The sprawling range consists of eight tiers. At the top of the range are the Private Bin LM Pinot Noir and TM Viognier; these are followed by the St Jude's Reserve Cabernet. The Seven Scenes wines comprise the core of the range—the Seven Scenes Chardonnay and Seven Scenes Cabernet Sauvignon are the pick of the bunch.

850–938 Mount Cotton Rd, Mount Cotton, QLD 4165
www.sirromet.com

Summit Estate Granite Belt

Founded in 1997 by a collaborative group of wine-loving families, Summit Estate is a 20 acre (8ha) Granite Belt property that has gradually been planted with a range of varieties. These include relative oddities such as Marsanne, Tempranillo, Monastrell, and Petit Verdot, as well as such standard varieties as Verdelho, Shiraz, Viognier, Pinot Noir, and Chardonnay. The goal is to produce wines with a distinct European accent—these are made at their 50-ton (50,800-kg) capacity winery, built in 2005.

291 Granite Belt Drive, Thulimbah, QLD 4377
www.summitestate.com.au

Of all New World wine countries, New Zealand is probably the biggest success story. In a relatively short amount of time, a tiny wine industry, which did not get so much as an index entry in the 1971 edition of Hugh Johnson's influential *World Atlas of Wine*, metamorphosed into one of the world's most dynamic. Much of the growth is quite recent. In 1995, New Zealand had 204 wineries and 15,200 acres (6,110ha) of vines; by 2009, there were 643 wineries and 72,400 acres (29,300ha) of vines. Perhaps most significantly, in 1995, 2.1 million gallons (7.8 million litres) of wine were exported; by 2009, this had risen to 30 million gallons (113 million litres).

New Zealand's largest and best-known region is Marlborough. The first vines were planted in this remarkable region as recently as 1973. Marlborough Sauvignon Blanc is its most famous export, accounting for 57% of the country's total harvest in 2009. Although Marlborough excels with Sauvignon Blanc, it also produces attractive Pinot Noir, Pinot Gris, Chardonnay, and Riesling.

Hawkes Bay, the second-largest region, is less than a third of the size of Marlborough, but is able to make a wide range of wines, including fabulous Syrah and Bordeaux-style blends from the famed Gimblett Gravels subdistrict. Hawkes Bay Chardonnay can also be very good. Central Otago has recently emerged as a star region, particularly for Pinot Noir. Wairarapa, which includes the district of Martinborough, is another Pinot Noir-dominated region, and Waipara on South Island is known for the same variety. Other significant regions include Gisborne, Nelson, and Auckland.

New Zealand's wine industry is commendably green and sustainable. Wine-growing New Zealand (NZWZ) has been a great success, resulting in a 72% reduction in insecticides and a 62% reduction of fungicides in vineyards between 1999 and 2007.

NEW ZEALAND

NORTH ISLAND

Historically, the North Island has been the heart of New Zealand's wine industry, but since the 1980s it has been overtaken by developments in the South Island. Hawkes Bay is the most important of the North Island's wine regions, with a growing reputation for making serious red wines from Bordeaux varieties and more recently Syrah, in addition to good Chardonnay. Wairarapa, the region near Wellington, includes Martinborough, which is famous for its Pinot Noir. Gisborne, the most easterly region, focuses on white varieties, with Chardonnay the star. Further north, there are several small regions close to Auckland, of which Waiheke Island is the most high-profile, making smart Bordeaux blends, Syrah, and Chardonnay.

Major grapes

Reds

Pinot Noir

Syrah

Whites

Chardonnay

Chenin Blanc

Gewurztraminer

Pinot Gris

Riesling

Sauvignon Blanc

Viognier

Vintages

2009
Looks promising. Excellent conditions in Wairarapa.

2008
Frost and rain caused problems in Hawkes Bay. Expect light, simple Pinot Noirs from Martinborough.

2007
Great vintage in Hawkes Bay and Gisborne. Low quantities in Martinborough, but excellent quality.

2006
Early-harvested whites did well; reds are more variable.

2005
Generally good quality. Auckland and the northern regions had a brilliant, dry vintage.

2004
A cool vintage with some rain in February. Quality was reasonable; some nice reds from Hawkes Bay in particular.

The North Island is where New Zealand wine began. Until the 1980s, Auckland and Hawkes Bay dominated the New Zealand wine scene, but since the emergence of Marlborough, and more recently Central Otago, there has been a power shift in the industry toward South Island.

Hawkes Bay is New Zealand's second-largest region, although it is now just a third of the size of Marlborough. With a long history of wine-growing, Hawkes Bay is particularly well known for its excellent red wines—New Zealand's best Bordeaux blends come from Hawkes Bay, largely because of the special terroir of the Gimblett Gravels subdistrict. Increasingly, however, attention is focusing on Syrah: while relatively small amounts are planted, Hawkes Bay now makes superb cool-climate expressions of this fashionable variety. Chardonnay is also a strength in this region.

Gisborne, on the east coast, is a significant grape-growing area—New Zealand's third-largest—but it has relatively few wineries. Although the climate is warm and quite humid, Gisborne produces excellent-quality grapes with an almost exclusive focus on white varieties. Chardonnay is its strong point, but Gewurztraminer, Viognier, Chenin Blanc, and Pinot Gris also thrive. Many of the grapes that are grown in this area are vinified elsewhere by large companies.

Wairarapa is a small, but important, region northeast of Wellington at the bottom of North Island. It includes Martinborough and is well known for its excellent Pinot Noir, as well as good Sauvignon Blanc, Riesling, and Chardonnay. The other two, newer subregions are Gladstone and Masterton, which share similar soils and climate to Martinborough and also focus on Pinot Noir. There is considerable vintage variation in Wairarapa, largely because it is exposed to strong winds, which can cause problems with flowering, as well as early season frosts.

New Zealand's largest city, Auckland, has a number of flourishing wine-growing regions within easy striking distance, all of which are quite small. The warm, humid, subtropical climate here is not ideal for grape growing, but the heat is moderated by high levels of cloud cover. Auckland itself has the Kumeu, Huapai, and Henderson subdistricts to the west, and the Matakana region about an hour's drive north, where full-flavored, intense Chardonnay is the speciality. The increasingly important wine region of Waiheke Island is also close to Auckland. It is fast establishing a reputation for its fabulous Syrah and Bordeaux blends, and supports a growing number of wineries. Pinot Gris and Chardonnay also do well in Waiheke Island.

Alana Estate Martinborough

Founded in 1993, with their first vintage four years later, Alana Estate has 42 acres (17ha) of vineyards on the Martinborough Terrace. Since their first vintage, they have developed a reputation for producing some serious Pinot Noir, which is made in the on-site, gravity-flow winery. The 2007 Pinot Noir is a thrilling effort: intense dark cherry and raspberry fruit with a spicy structure underpinning the fruit. The 2008, as befits the vintage, is lighter and more simple.

Puruatanga Rd, Martinborough, South Wairarapa
www.alana.co.nz

Alpha Domus Hawkes Bay

The Ham family were nursery owners when they decided to diversify into wine, planting their first vineyard block in Hawkes Bay in 1991. They now have 49 acres (20ha) of vines in the Heretaunga Plains, west of Hastings, that are planted on a thin silt loam over river gravels. Three ranges are made, all from estate grapes. The AD range is the top tier and includes a deliciously rich, complex Chardonnay and a richly fruited Bordeaux blend called the Aviator. The next tier is the Alpha Domus wines, of which the rich, dense Navigator Bordeaux blend and the opulent Wingwalker Viognier are the stars. The third tier is the fruit-focused Pilot range.

1829 Maraekakaho Rd, Hastings, Hawkes Bay
www.alphadomus.co.nz

Ata Rangi Martinborough

This is one of the stars of Martinborough, and is known for making one of New Zealand's most consistently fine Pinot Noirs. For a long time, Ata Rangi was run on a shoestring budget by founder Clive Paton, who was one of the pioneers of this area when he planted his first vineyard block in 1980. The fruit comes from 74 acres (30ha) of vines, from which winemaker Helen Masters is fashioning some seriously good wines. Lismore Pinot Gris is beautifully textured with nice mineral flavors offsetting the richness. The Sauvignon Blanc is restrained and minerally, while Craighall Chardonnay is one of New Zealand's best, with bold fig, peach, and pear flavors. Crimson Pinot Noir is a lighter, brighter stablemate to the show-stealer, the Ata Rangi Pinot Noir, which has focused, floral, dark cherry fruit and a hint of savory meatiness. Also delicious is the Célèbre, a blend of Merlot, Syrah, and Cabernet Sauvignon, which shows lovely, gravelly, dark fruits.

Puruatanga Rd, Martinborough, South Wairarapa
www.atarangi.co.nz

Babich Wines Auckland

One of New Zealand's larger, family-owned wine companies, Babich Wines is based in Auckland, but also has vineyards in Hawkes Bay and Marlborough, as well as contract growers in Gisborne. Their home vineyard in Henderson is now surrounded by west Auckland urban sprawl, and they are partners in a contract winemaking facility, Rapaura Vintners, in Marlborough. A wide range of wines are made, but the most impressive are the peppery, brightly fruited Syrahs from the Gimblett Gravels in Hawkes Bay.

Babich Rd, Henderson, Auckland
www.babichwines.co.nz

ALPHA DOMUS
STAR OF THE WINERY, THIS VIOGNIER SHOWS DELICATE AND COMPLEX AROMAS

BILANCIA
THE RICHLY FRUITED, PEPPERY, BUT ELEGANT LA COLLINA IS A SOUGHT-AFTER NZ SYRAH

Bilancia Hawkes Bay

Warren Gibson (of Trinity Hill) and his wife Lorraine Leheny are the people behind Hawkes Bay super-premium producer Bilancia. Syrah is the key focus of this boutique operation, which began in 1997. La Collina, which is made from grapes grown on a terraced hillside vineyard, is one of New Zealand's best Syrahs. There is obvious Italian influence here. Bilancia is the Italian name for the zodiac sign Libra, which is shared by Warren and Lorraine. It also means "balance" or "harmony," which is something they strive for, and achieve, in their wines. Pinot Grigio, both regular and reserve, is brilliant here, and the Viognier and Syrah/Viognier are also worth seeking out. ★**Rising star**

Stortford Lodge, Hawkes Bay
www.bilancia.co.nz

Cable Bay Vineyards Waiheke Island

As with many Waiheke Island wineries, Cable Bay also makes wines with grapes from other regions; in this case, Marlborough. The winery is relatively new and was started by ex-Babich winemaker Neil Culley in 1996, with the first wines released as recently as 2002. Several grape varieties are grown on their five Waiheke-based sites—Chardonnay, Viognier, Pinot Gris, Merlot, Cabernet Sauvignon, Cabernet Franc, Malbec, and Syrah—while Sauvignon Blanc, Pinot Gris, Gewurztraminer, Riesling, and Pinot Noir are contract-grown in Marlborough. The focus is on producing small lots of high-quality wines. Taut, fresh, powerful Waiheke Chardonnay is particularly promising, as is the silky, textured Marlborough Pinot Noir. ★**Rising star**

12 Nick Johnstone Drive, Oneroa, Waiheke Island
www.cablebayvineyards.co.nz

Cambridge Road Vineyard Martinborough

A small 5.4 acre (2.2ha) estate on the Martinborough Terrace, Cambridge Road Vineyard is managed biodynamically, with the wine-growing in the hands of Lance Redgwell. The vineyard was planted in 1986 and is three-quarters Pinot Noir, a quarter Syrah. The wines are very impressive, particularly the Syrah, which is beautifully expressive with a subtle peppery edge to the lush, but well defined, blackberry and dark cherry fruit, and amply demonstrates the potential for this wine in Martinborough. Noblestone Pinot Noir is ripe, with real intensity to the meaty, dark cherry fruit, and an oddity, a blend of Pinot Noir with Syrah, works really well, with lovely vibrant berry and cherry fruit and an attractive spiciness. ★**Rising star**

32 Cambridge Rd, Martinborough
www.cambridgeroad.co.nz

C J Pask Winery Hawkes Bay

One of Chris Pask's claims to fame is that, in 1981, he was the first to plant vines in the important Gimblett Gravels district of Hawkes Bay. Today, of 222 acres (90ha) of vines, 148 acres (60ha) are planted on the Gravels. Managing director and chief winemaker Kate Radburnd joined C J Pask in 1991 and is now fashioning a stylish range of wines, with Merlot the most planted variety. The Gimblett Road wines are consistently good, with an aromatic floral Syrah; a supple, blackcurranty Merlot; and an aromatic, spicy Cabernet/Merlot/Malbec, which is particularly noteworthy. The reserve-level Declaration range is a step

NORTH ISLAND

This is the historical heart of New Zealand wine. While the map may indicate contiguous vineyards through much of the North Island, most of them are concentrated in a few small areas. Most significant is the Hawkes Bay region, centered around the twin towns of Napier and Hastings. This is not the most scenic of regions, and the vineyards are quite spread out, but some of the wines being made here are quite serious. The Wairarapa region, close to the capital city of Wellington, has the Martinborough subdistrict at its center. This is a small but significant region making some of New Zealand's best Pinot Noir. Gisborne, the most easterly of all the country's regions, has fewer wineries but is an important grape-growing area. The Auckland area's most significant wines are now being made on Waiheke Island.

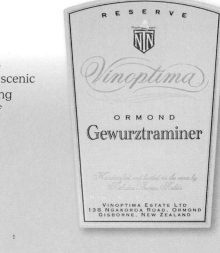

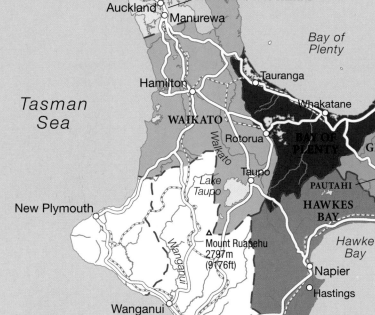

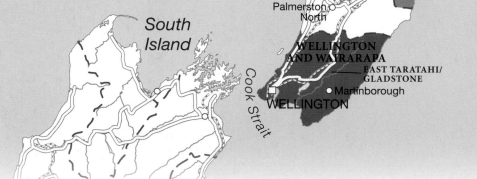

KEY

- Auckland and Northland
- Bay of Plenty
- Gisborne
- Hawkes Bay
- Waikato
- Wellington and Wairarapa
- - - Regional boundary
- MATAKANE Wine subregion

HAWKES BAY

As a first-time visitor, it is quite hard to get a handle on Hawkes Bay, historically New Zealand's most important wine region. The hub of the region consists of two towns, Napier and Hastings, in quite close proximity, but the scattered vineyards reflect the very different soil types found in the area. Since the 1990s, the Gimblett Gravels subdistrict has been the center of attention for its fantastic red wines from Syrah and Bordeaux varieties.

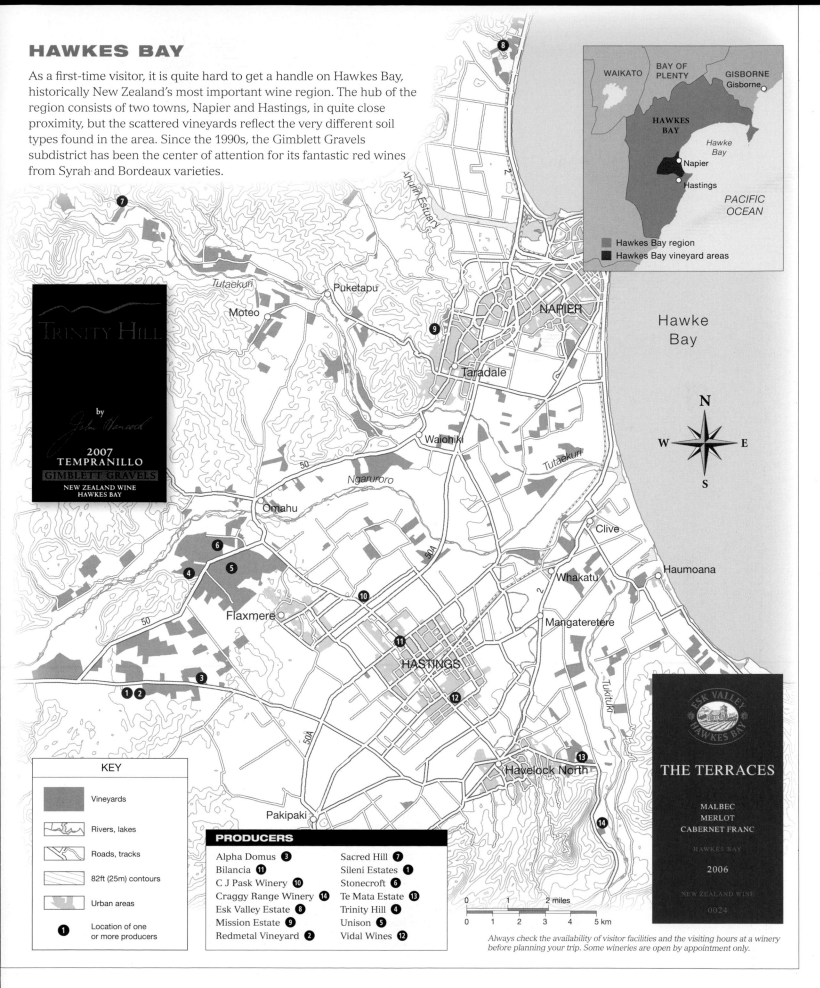

WAIKATO

BAY OF PLENTY

GISBORNE
Gisborne

HAWKES
BAY

Hawke
Bay

Napier

Hastings

PACIFIC
OCEAN

Hawkes Bay region
Hawkes Bay vineyard areas

TRINITY HILL

by
John Hancock

2007
TEMPRANILLO
GIMBLETT GRAVELS
NEW ZEALAND WINE
HAWKES BAY

Tutaekuri

Moteo

Puketapu

NAPIER

Hawke
Bay

Taradale

Waiohiki

N

W   E

S

Tutaekuri

Ngaruroro

Omahu

Clive

Haumoana

Whakatu

Flaxmere

Mangateretere

HASTINGS

Havelock North

THE TERRACES

MALBEC
MERLOT
CABERNET FRANC

HAWKES BAY

2006

NEW ZEALAND WINE

0024

Pakipaki

KEY

	Vineyards
	Rivers, lakes
	Roads, tracks
	82ft (25m) contours
	Urban areas
1	Location of one or more producers

PRODUCERS

Alpha Domus	**3**	Sacred Hill	**7**
Bilancia	**11**	Sileni Estates	**1**
C J Pask Winery	**10**	Stonecroft	**6**
Craggy Range Winery	**14**	Te Mata Estate	**13**
Esk Valley Estate	**8**	Trinity Hill	**4**
Mission Estate	**9**	Unison	**5**
Redmetal Vineyard	**2**	Vidal Wines	**12**

0   1   2 miles

0   1   2   3   4   5 km

Always check the availability of visitor facilities and the visiting hours at a winery before planning your trip. Some wineries are open by appointment only.

THE MILLTON VINEYARD
RICH YET SUBTLE, THIS IS A COMPLEX WINE
FROM A SPECIAL HILLSIDE VINEYARD

KUMEU RIVER WINES
THE 2007 IS ONE OF THE BEST EXPRESSIONS
TO COME FROM THE MATE'S VINEYARD

up with an astonishingly intense, aromatic Chardonnay, concentrated yet fine Merlot, and a vibrant, gravelly, dark-fruited Cabernet/Merlot/Malbec.

1133 Omahu Rd, Hastings, Hawkes Bay
www.cjpaskwinery.co.nz

Craggy Range Winery Hawkes Bay
Craggy Range's talented team, headed up by Steve Smith, fashions a range of high-end, mostly single-vineyard wines from across the country. Based in Hawkes Bay, but with vineyards in most of the significant regions, their wines are all excellent, with the red wines being of particular merit. Two Central Otago Pinots stand out (Calvert and Bannockburn Sluicings), with the Te Muna Road Pinot from Martinborough also showing sleek elegance. From the famed Gimblett Gravels district of Hawkes Bay, the Quarry Bordeaux blend is fantastic, with Le Sol and Block 14 Syrahs among New Zealand's best. Block 14 is particularly good value, with its exuberant peppery notes.

253 Waimarama Rd, Havelock North, Hawkes Bay
www.craggyrange.com

Dry River Martinborough
One of New Zealand's iconic producers, Neil McCallum's Dry River makes a superb range of wines from its Martinborough vineyards. Its viticulture is precise: a split canopy system is employed, with reflective white sheeting under the vines, and full fruit-zone leaf plucking to ensure proper physiological ripening of the grapes. Everything in the range is superb. A linear, bold, ageworthy Pinot Noir is matched by intense, meaty, aromatic Lovat Vineyard Syrah. The Pinot Gris is complex and mouthfilling, while the Gewurztraminer and Viognier are restrained and beautiful examples of their type. Finally, the minerally, taut Riesling is a thrilling, intellectual wine.

Martinborough, South Wairarapa
www.dryriver.co.nz

Escarpment Martinborough
Being the man behind the establishment of Martinborough Vineyards, Larry McKenna is a very well-known figure in Martinborough. He is now responsible for his own project, Escarpment, which he established in 1999 in partnership with his wife Sue and Robert and Mem Kirby. The winery is based on a vineyard that is planted on terraces of the River Te Muna, just east of Martinborough town. The main focus is Pinot Noir, which accounts for 70% of plantings, but there is also Chardonnay and a small amount of Pinot Gris, Riesling, and Pinot Blanc. Other vineyards are leased to supply more grapes. The Chardonnay is pretty serious, but it is the Pinot Noirs that steal the show, in particular a new series of single-vineyard Martinborough Insight wines: Kupe, Kiwa, Te Rehua, and Pahi.

Te Muna Rd, Martinborough, South Wairarapa
www.escarpment.co.nz

Esk Valley Estate Hawkes Bay
Established in the 1930s as Glenvale, the speciality at this winery used to be fortified wine. The brand Esk Valley was created in the 1970s and Glenvale went into receivership in the 1980s, when it was purchased by George Fistonich,

owner of Villa Maria. Despite this, Esk Valley has remained an autonomous operation with its own facilities and winemaking team, which has been headed, since 1993, by Gordon Russell. Esk Valley sources from 28 different vineyards that are spread throughout the region, crushing around 750 tons (762 tonnes) each vintage. Gordon Russell takes a hands-off, terroir-driven approach to winemaking, and tries to allow the different sites to express their characters. The wines are pretty good—the range is broad and includes some unexpected examples, such as Verdelho and Chenin Blanc, as well as some serious reds. Top of the line is The Terraces, a concentrated red blend made from the terraced vineyards that surround the winery, and only in the best years.

Main Rd, Bay View, Napier, Hawkes Bay
www.eskvalley.co.nz

Gladstone Vineyard Wairarapa
Christine and David Kernohan's Gladstone Vineyard is located in the Gladstone subregion of the Wairarapa. Originally from Scotland, the couple moved to New Zealand in the 1970s and David worked as a professor at the faculty of architecture in Wellington University. In 1996 they purchased Gladstone Vineyard, which had been established a decade earlier. Since then, they have expanded the vineyard area and added a restaurant and a winery. While they are not fully organic, they are using cover-cropping to encourage beneficial insects, and have a light touch in the vineyard. The Pinot Noir is fresh and elegant with some depth to the dark cherry fruit. Sophie's Choice is a rich, textured, nutty oaked Sauvignon Blanc, and the Pinot Gris shows rounded, herby, pear fruit with a nice texture. Finally, the Auld Alliance is an impressively bright, minerally, dark-fruited Bordeaux blend.

Gladstone Rd, RD2, Carterton, Wairarapa
www.gladstone.co.nz

Goldwater Estate Waiheke Island
One of the pioneers of Waiheke, Goldwater Estate was established in 1978 by Kym Goldwater. It recently joined forces with Marlborough producer Vavasour under the banner of the New Zealand Wine Fund, which bought both estates in 2006. Goldwater Estate has 35 acres (14ha) of vineyards planted to red Bordeaux varieties, Syrah, and Chardonnay. They also source Sauvignon Blanc and Pinot Noir from Marlborough, which now form the bulk of their production. Highlights of the range are the intense Cabernet Sauvignon/Merlot (now called The Goldie) from Waiheke and the expressive Wairau Valley Sauvignon Blanc, which is sourced from Marlborough.

18 Causeway Rd, Putiki Bay, Waiheke Island
www.goldwaterwine.com

Kumeu River Wines Auckland
The Brajkovich brothers, Michael, Milan, and Paul, look after the winemaking, viticulture, and marketing of their family winery, which is based in Kumeu, north west of the city of Auckland. Their range covers three tiers, with entry-level Village wines, Estate wines, and the top tier series of single-vineyard wines. The vineyards are trellised in a lyre arrangement and all the fruit is hand harvested. Chardonnay works best here, and Kumeu River can justifiably claim to make some of New Zealand's best expressions of this variety. Its boldly flavored, complex Estate Chardonnay is serious,

and three single-vineyard wines (Maté's, Coddington, and Hunting Hill) are a step above. Although the Pinot Noir is supple and fresh, it is not in the same league as the Chardonnay.

550 State Hwy 16, Kumeu
www.kumeuriver.co.nz

Kusuda Martinborough

Hiroyuki Kusuda emigrated with his family from Japan to New Zealand in 2001, with a view to making great Pinot Noir in the Martinborough region. With some help from German viticulturalist Kai Schubert, but without any vineyards or a winery, he started Kusuda in October 2001 and is now making some of the region's best Pinot Noir and Syrah from leased vineyards. Hiroyuki's winemaking is meticulous: the grapes are hand-picked into small trays and then hand-sorted back at the winery. Both the 2006 and 2007 Pinot Noirs are thrilling, with elegance, purity, and freshness to the cherry and berry fruits. The 2006 Syrah is peppery, elegant, and fresh, with real precision—it can justifiably claim to be one of New Zealand's best. Although most of Kusada's small production is exported to Japan, these wines are well worth seeking out if you can. ★ **Rising star**

5 Hawkins Drive, Martinborough
www.kusudawines.com

Man O' War Waiheke Island

In 1993, the Spencer family decided to plant a vineyard on their ruggedly beautiful 4,500 acre (1,821ha) block of land at the far northeastern end of Waiheke Island. Initially, the wines were sold under the label Stoney Batter, after fortifications that are on the property, but they were later renamed Man O' War. In total, 150 acres (61ha) of vineyards are planted in almost 90 small blocks, from which two ranges of wine are made. White Label wines are more fruit and varietal driven, but still quite serious, while the Black Label wines (Gravestone Sauvignon/Semillon, Valhalla Chardonnay, Dreadnought Syrah, and Ironclad Bordeaux Blend) are brilliant expressions of their terroir. The Dreadnought Syrah is particularly thrilling, with wonderful dark, peppery, meaty, and complex flavors—a beautiful expression of cool-climate Syrah at its best. ★ **Rising star**

Man O' War Bay Rd, Man O' War Bay, Waiheke Island
www.manowarvineyards.co.nz

Martinborough Vineyard Martinborough

In 1978, Dr. Derek Milne was commissioned to write a report on the areas of New Zealand that he considered to be best suited to quality wine-growing. He picked Martinborough as New Zealand's potential Burgundy equivalent, and was so convinced by its potential that he became one of the investors in the Martinborough Vineyard, which was first planted in 1980. The first vintage was in 1984, and in 1986 they hired Larry McKenna as winemaker. Larry left in 1999, and his work has been continued by Claire Mulholland, who is now at Amisfield, and more recently by Paul Mason. Everything Martinborough Vineyard does is worthwhile but their Pinot Noir and Riesling really stand out. Te Tera Pinot Noir, a second label, is pretty serious in its own right. Regular Pinot Noir comes from the oldest vineyards and is a step up, with smooth, elegant texture and raspberry and cherry fruit. Look out for the 2007

vintage, which was a ripe, short year with great concentration. Three Rieslings are made in differing styles, with the gently dry Manu Riesling and the Spätlese-style Late Harvest being the most impressive. Also worth tracking down is the thrilling Syrah/Viognier, which is sadly only made in tiny quantities.

Princess St, Martinborough, South Wairarapa
www.martinborough-vineyard.com

Matakana Estate Matakana

Matakana is the name of a small wine region north of Auckland. It is home to a handful of wineries that are spread across two peninsulas and share a similar climate to that of Waiheke Island. Matakana Estate is a boutique winery making impressive wines from both the Matakana region and elsewhere in New Zealand. The quality is high, with bold-flavored Chardonnay and Pinot Gris from Matakana; impressive, lively Sauvignon Blanc and elegant Pinot Noir from Marlborough; and a serious, medium-bodied, but complex, Merlot/Cabernet Franc from Hawkes Bay.

568 Matakana Rd, Matakana
www.matakanaestate.co.nz

The Millton Vineyard Gisborne

James Millton is a well-known pioneer of biodynamic wine-growing in the New World. Remarkably, he is located in Gisborne, which, with its warm and rather damp conditions, is far from the easiest of New Zealand's wine regions in which to work organically. He started the Millton Vineyard in 1984, when he was 28. His wife Annie's father had developed vineyards on his Opou estate in Gisborne, so it seemed an obvious place to start. Today, the estate consists of four different vineyards in the Gisborne region: Opou, 19 acres (7.7ha); Te Arai, 7 acres (2.8ha); Riverpoint, 17 acres (6.8ha) of Chardonnay and Viognier; and the spectacular Naboth's Vineyard, a hillside vineyard that first produced in 1993, with five parcels making up Clos de Ste-Anne estate. The wines are extremely good, with Chenin Blanc being the star, a mineralic and focused Clos Ste-Anne Pinot Noir, and a surprisingly excellent, peppery Syrah.

119 Papatu Rd, CMB 66, Manutuke, Gisborne
www.millton.co.nz

Mission Estate Hawkes Bay

Founded in 1851 by Catholic missionaries who needed wines for communion, this is New Zealand's oldest, and now Hawkes Bay's largest, winery. It makes exclusively Hawkes Bay wines in four ranges: Estate, Vineyard Selection, Mission Reserve, and Jewelstone. Highlights of the range are the Estate, Reserve, and Jewelstone Syrahs, all of which demonstrate the fresh, peppery, vividly fruited Hawkes Bay style in ascending levels of concentration and complexity. Also worth looking for is the Jewelstone Chardonnay, which shows superb balance and style.

198 Church Rd, Napier, Hawkes Bay
www.missionestate.co.nz

Murdoch James Winery Martinborough

Roger and Jill Fraser began in 1986 with a 12 acre (5ha) vineyard on the Martinborough Terrace. They have since expanded, buying the 50 acre (20ha) Blue Rock

THE GIMBLETT GRAVELS

The Gimblett Gravels is a distinctive terroir in the Hawkes Bay region that consists of around 1,977 acres (800ha), almost all of which is now planted with vines. Thirty years ago, however, this now valuable land was little regarded. In 1988, 371 acres (150ha) of the Gravels were bought by a concrete company, who wanted to extract the gravel to make roads. Against the odds, a campaign against the planning application by a coalition of growers succeeded and now the Gravels is producing some of New Zealand's finest red wines. Free-draining, with low fertility and temperatures a couple of degrees higher than the surrounding areas, it is the perfect site for the Bordeaux varieties: Merlot, Cabernet Sauvignon, Malbec, and Cabernet Franc. Syrah is also producing some great results, even though not much is grown.

TE MATA ESTATE
THE INTENSE FLAVORS WILL DEVELOP IN
BOTTLE FOR 10 YEARS FROM HARVEST

vineyard in 1998. They also lease two other Martinborough vineyards. Pinot Noir is the main focus, with Blue Rock and Fraser, the top two bottlings, showing generous, fleshy, ripe fruit. A promising, fresh, peppery Saleyards Syrah is also worth looking out for.

Dry River Rd, Martinborough, South Wairarapa
www.murdochjames.co.nz

Palliser Estate Martinborough
Palliser Estate was one of the pioneers of the Martinborough region when it planted its first vines in 1984. Today, with over 198 acres (80ha) of vineyards, it is one of the largest wineries in the region. The managing director, Richard Riddiford, was one of the founding shareholders and is also one of the great characters of the New Zealand wine scene. The wines, made by chief winemaker/viticulturalist Alan Johnson, who has been here since 1991, are consistently good, with the standouts being the aromatic, linear Sauvignon Blanc; a rich yet balanced Chardonnay; and a full-flavored Pinot Noir.

Kitchener St, Martinborough, South Wairarapa
www.palliser.co.nz

Redmetal Vineyard Hawkes Bay
This boutique winery is named after the soils on which the vineyards are planted. The free-draining, river-deposited gravels, known as redmetals, led Grant Edmonds (of Sileni) to plant this small 18 acre (7ha) vineyard here in 1991. The focus is on Cabernet Franc and Merlot, although Chardonnay and some Cabernet Sauvignon are also grown. Regular Merlot/Cabernet Franc is mid-bodied with fresh, ripe berry fruits. Basket Press Merlot/Cabernet Franc is a little more intense, with perfumed dark cherry and spice notes and the potential to age.

2006 Maraekakaho Rd, RD1, Hastings, Hawkes Bay
www.redmetalvineyards.co.nz

Sacred Hill Hawkes Bay
Tony Bish is the man behind Sacred Hill, which is especially well known for making some serious Chardonnay. After setting up this winery in 1985, Bish left for a sojourn in Central Otago, before returning in 1994. Sacred Hill now produces around 300,000 cases a year, of which around 40% are exported. Rifleman's Chardonnay is a New Zealand icon, with powerful nutty, toasty richness and mandarin freshness. Barrel Ferment Chardonnay is cheaper, yet still superb. Also worth looking for are the dark-fruited Helmsman Cabernet Sauvignon and the taut, focused, spicy Deerstalkers Syrah.

1033 Dartmoor Rd, Puketapu, Napier
www.sacredhill.com

Schubert Wines Martinborough
Geisenheim-trained Kai Schubert relocated with his partner, Marion Deimling, from Germany to the Martinborough region with a dream of making great Pinot Noir. In 1998 they bought a small 3.5 acre (1.4ha) vineyard in Martinborough and 99 acres (40ha) of unplanted land in East Taratahi, on a terrace next to the Ruamahanga River, where they planted 30 acres (12ha) of vines from 1999 onward. The estate Pinot Noir they now

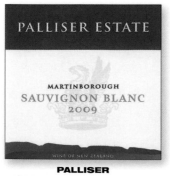

PALLISER
MARTINBOROUGH IS NOT KNOWN FOR ITS
SAUVIGNONS, BUT THIS WINE IS EXCELLENT

make (known as Block B) is superb, with sweet, elegant, quite rich cherry fruit, and one of the best of the region. The fresh, peppery, spicy Syrah, which is made in small quantities, is also impressive. ★ **Rising star**

57 Cambridge Rd, Martinborough
www.schubert.co.nz

Sileni Estates Hawkes Bay
This winery is the result of a collaboration between medical publisher Graeme Avery, financial director Chris Cowper, and winemaker Grant Edmonds. Since its beginnings in 1997, Sileni has grown—as well as making wine from its own 262 acres (106ha) of estate vineyards in Hawkes Bay, it also produces wine from Marlborough fruit. There are four tiers to the range, of which the top two are the Estate Selection and Exceptional Vintage. Both of the top two tiers are worth looking out for, but some of the Cellar Selection wines can also impress.

2016 Maraekakaho Rd, RD1, Hastings, Hawkes Bay
www.sileni.co.nz

Stonecroft Hawkes Bay
Alan Limmer is a chemist by training, and widely recognized for his role in establishing the Gimblett Gravels as a special place to make red wine. He began working here in 1982, released the first Stonecroft wine in 1987, and in 1989 produced New Zealand's first Syrah of the current era. From 1989–1992 Limmer was involved in a legal fight to protect the Gravels from quarrying, and won a spectacular victory—without this fight, one of New Zealand's top wine regions would have been lost. The Stonecroft wines are all good, but the standouts are the three Syrahs: Crofters is a deliciously fresh, peppery wine made from young fruit; the regular Syrah is more structured and ageworthy, but still has beautiful peppery precision; and Serine is a high-end bottling that is beautifully expressive and focused.

Mere Rd, RD5, Hastings, Hawkes Bay
www.stonecroft.co.nz

Stonyridge Vineyard Waiheke Island
Dr. Stephen White returned to New Zealand in 1981, after spending three years skippering yachts around the world, and decided to turn his hand to wine-growing. His 15 acre (6ha) vineyard in Waiheke Island produced its first wines in 1985, and in 1987 it produced the first famed Larose, a wine that has helped to establish a reputation for Stonyridge Vineyard as one of New Zealand's top producers of Bordeaux-style reds. As well as Bordeaux varieties, Grenache, Syrah, and Mourvèdre are also grown here. In addition to the famed Bordeaux blend Larose, Luna Negra (Malbec), Pilgrim (GSM blend), and Airfield (second label Bordeaux blend) are also made.

80 Onetangi Rd, Ostend, Waiheke Island
www.stonyridge.co.nz

Te Hera Martinborough
Boutique winery Te Hera's claim to fame is that it was the first commercial vineyard in the now hugely successful Te Muna Road subdistrict of Martinborough. Steady planting from 1996–2002 has resulted in 12 acres (5ha) of Pinot Noir and 1 acre (0.4ha) of Riesling. The winery was

built in time for the 2003 vintage. Te Hera's Pinot Noir is a benchmark for the region, with smooth, pure, ripe cherry and berry fruit, with some mineral undertones.

Martinborough, South Wairarapa
www.tehera.co.nz

Te Kairanga Wines Martinborough

Now the largest producer in the Martinborough region, Te Kairanga has six vineyards here, including four on the famous Martinborough Terrace. TK, as it is commonly known, dates back to 1983, when founder Paul Draper purchased a small plot of vines that had been planted a few years previously. Early releases were of patchy quality, but improved through the 1990s, although quality has not reached that of the top Martinborough producers. Despite this, the John Martin Reserve Pinot Noir and the Casarina Reserve Chardonnay are both impressive wines.

Martins Rd, Martinborough, South Wairarapa
www.tekairanga.co.nz

Te Mata Estate Hawkes Bay

This historic winery, based in Havelock North, was purchased by current owner John Buck in 1978. Since then, it has become one of New Zealand's leading producers, making 35,000 cases annually, of which just over half is red. The estate vineyards total 296.5 acres (120ha), and are spread across three sites in the Hawkes Bay region. The most famous Te Mata Estate wine is the Coleraine, an ageworthy Bordeaux blend that was first made in 1982. The other three standout wines are the fresh, slightly leafy, berryish Cabernet/Merlot Awatea, the Bullnose Syrah, and the bold yet focused Elston Chardonnay, which is one of New Zealand's best.

349 Te Mata Rd, Havelock North, Hawkes Bay
www.temata.co.nz

Trinity Hill Hawkes Bay

Trinity Hill is a three-way partnership between John Hancock, Robert and Robyn Wilson, and Trevor and Hanne James. They bought their first vineyard— 49.5 acres (20ha) of the wonderful Gimblett Gravels—in 1993, and the first wines were made in 1996. An impressive, angular winery was built in 1997 and a further 49.5 acres (20ha) of the Gravels were purchased in 2000. Currently, 600 tons (610 tonnes) of grapes are crushed and 35,000 cases of wine are produced each year. The top wine is one of New Zealand's best reds, the Homage Syrah, but it is also worth looking out for the Gimblett, a Bordeaux blend, and the regular Gimblett Gravels Syrah.

2396 State Hwy 50, RD5, Hastings, Hawkes Bay
www.trinityhill.co.nz

Unison Hawkes Bay

Respected red wine producer Unison is now owned by an English couple, Philip and Terry Horn. They recently purchased the estate from the founders, Anna-Barbara and Bruce Helliwell, who started here in 1993. The vineyard is a 39.5 acre (6ha) block in the Gimblett Gravels district of Hawkes Bay, and is planted almost entirely with red varieties. All the wines are impressive. Unison (known from 2007 as Classic Blend) is a blend of Merlot, Cabernet, and a splash of Syrah. Unison Selection is the top red, which blends together the same varieties and

STONECROFT
MADE FROM THE OLDEST PRODUCING SYRAH VINES IN NEW ZEALAND, THE GIMBLETT GRAVELS SYRAH IS PEPPERY AND LIVELY

UNISON
WITH NATURAL CONCENTRATION, THIS WINE IS DENSELY STRUCTURED AND AGEWORTHY

shows beautifully elegant, smooth blackcurrant fruit, with some gravelly structure. The Syrah is a stylish, sophisticated, and ageworthy expression of this variety, with some peppery notes and grippy, gravelly tannins. Since 2006 they have also made one white, a Pinot Gris.

2163 State Hwy 50, RD5, Hastings, Hawkes Bay
www.unisonvineyard.co.nz

Urlar Wairarapa

Angus Thomson sold his family farm in Scotland to move to New Zealand and grow wine. He chose the Wairarapa, where he established the biodynamic estate Urlar (Gaelic for "earth") in 2004. The 77 acres (31ha) of vines will, when in full production, eventually produce 15,000 cases a year, with the first proper vintage, 2008, yielding just 3,500 cases. Winemaking is in the hands of Guy McMaster, who used to work with Larry McKenna at Escarpment. The first signs are promising: the Riesling is complex and minerally; the Pinot Gris is rich, creamy, and nutty with lovely texture; and the Sauvignon Blanc is precise and intense with some barrel ferment component. ★Rising star

No visitor facilities
www.urlar.co.nz

Vidal Wines Hawkes Bay

Vidal is a historic Hawkes Bay producer that dates back to 1905. It now makes a full range of wines that draw on a number of premium wine regions, although with a strong Hawkes Bay focus. Since 1976, when it was purchased by George Fistonich, Vidal has been part of the Villa Maria group along with fellow Hawkes Bay winery Esk Valley, although it is run separately. Syrah is the most impressive of a consistent line-up, with both the regular and reserve bottlings offering lots of vibrant, cool-climate Syrah personality.

913 St Aubyn St East, Hastings, Hawkes Bay
www.vidal.co.nz

Vinoptima Gisborne

Nick Nobilo's choice of specialist grape variety is, perhaps, a surprising one, but his Gewurztraminers, made from vineyards in Ormond, Gisborne, are some of New Zealand's very best white wines. Nick was one of the pioneers of the modern New Zealand wine industry and started Vinoptima in 2000, after selling the family company to Constellation. He has just under 25 acres (10ha) of vineyards, which are planted with five clones of Gewurztraminer. His first vintage was 2003, and he has not looked back. These wines are truly spectacular: as well as the regular wine, look out for the thrilling Noble Late Harvest, made in 2004 and 2007. ★Rising star

138 Ngakoroa Rd, Ormond, RD1, Gisborne
www.vinoptima.co.nz

Sunrise over the Richmond Ranges, which form the
northern boundary of Marlborough's Wairau Valley

SOUTH ISLAND

AUSTRALIA PACIFIC OCEAN
○Sydney
Tasman Sea
Auckland○
WELLINGTON○
TASMANIA Christchurch○
NEW ZEALAND

▪ North Island
▪ South Island

New Zealand's South Island boasts the country's most important wine region: Marlborough. No vines were planted here until 1973, but it now has by far the largest vineyard area in the country, and its incredible Sauvignon Blancs have driven the success of New Zealand wine. South Island has two other important regions that are both well known for making great Pinot Noir. Central Otago's vineyards, stretching north from Queenstown, enjoy a continental climate and are making world-class Pinot Noir. The Canterbury region, including Waipara, is also known for its Pinot Noir, as well as impressive Chardonnay and Riesling. Another, smaller, region is Nelson, west of Marlborough, which is turning out stylish Chardonnay, Riesling, and Pinot Noir.

Major grapes

🍇 Reds

Pinot Noir

🍇 Whites

Chardonnay

Pinot Gris

Riesling

Sauvignon Blanc

Vintages

2009
A combination of good quantity with good quality throughout South Island. Some very promising wines.

2008
Good conditions during flowering led to a bumper crop, but average quality.

2007
Low quantity, but good quality vintage in Central Otago. Poor flowering in Waipara reduced crops. Marlborough had an excellent vintage.

2006
A really good vintage, with good ripening conditions and a dry fall.

2005
Low crop levels, but a good growing season and harvest in Marlborough. Reduced yields in Waipara and a difficult year in Central Otago.

2004
A cool vintage with some harvest rain in Marlborough.

Marlborough dominates the New Zealand wine scene, with a vineyard area that stands at 39,540 acres (16,000ha), out of New Zealand's total of 71,660 acres (29,000ha). It is therefore hard to believe that just 25 years ago there were hardly any vines in this area, and before 1973 there were none at all. It is the success of Sauvignon Blanc from this region that has driven the growth of the entire New Zealand wine industry, which has enjoyed steady expansion since the 1980s and has become five times larger since 1995.

Marlborough manages to make Sauvignon that combines passion fruit ripeness with zingy grapefruit and gooseberry freshness—a style that has taken the world by storm. Other grape varieties also do well in Marlborough, particularly when yields are lower, most notably fresh, cherryish Pinot Noir; full flavored Chardonnay; zippy, intense Riesling, and textured, pure Pinot Gris. At the heart of the region is the flat Wairau Valley, with Rapuara, Brancott, and the Waihopai Valley as distinct subregions. To the south lies the Awatere Valley, which is noticeably cooler and makes Sauvignon Blanc with a distinct, crisp character and frequently a touch of tomato leaf aroma.

West of Marlborough, at the tip of South Island, lies the small region of Nelson, where it is quite cool, but sunny, and the mountains to the west provide a rain shadow. The scattered vineyards, some on the hillsides and some on the alluvial loams of the Waimea Plains, produce some highly regarded Pinot Noir, Riesling, Chardonnay, and Sauvignon Blanc.

As a wine region, Central Otago is just a tenth of the size of Marlborough, but over the last couple of decades it has established itself as a single-variety region concentrating on Pinot Noir. With their continental climate, the subregions of Gibbston, Alexandra, the Cromwell Basin (Bannockburn, Pisa, Lowburn, Bendigo), and Wanaka have all proved to be great locations for making top-quality Pinot Noir that has vibrant, rich fruit, and a degree of elegance. Riesling also thrives here, but has proved to be a tough sell. A new region to watch is Waikari in North Otago, which is quite marginal, but is making some interesting Pinot Noir.

Canterbury is also the focus of a number of high-quality wine regions, the most significant of which is Waipara, a short distance north of Christchurch. While wind can be a problem, causing low yields due to poor flowering, Waipara makes some of New Zealand's best Pinot Noir, as well as interesting Riesling and Chardonnay. One of the keys to Waipara's success is its soils, including alluvial gravels and even some limestone. New vineyard developments in the limestone outcrops of the north Canterbury hills are showing particular promise with both Chardonnay and Pinot Noir.

Allan Scott Wines Marlborough

Allan Scott was a contract grower when he planted his first vineyards in 1975. In a story that has now become familiar in Marlborough, the Scott family decided that, rather than just grow grapes, they would make their own wines—Allan Scott Wines is now an important presence in Marlborough. As well as sourcing grapes from their own four vineyards, they also buy from growers. The Estate wines are made from the usual collection of Marlborough varieties, while a high-end selection of single-vineyard wines, the Prestige range, includes Pinot Noir, Riesling, Chardonnay, and Sauvignon Blanc. In addition to the Marlborough wines, a Scott Base Pinot Noir and Pinot Gris are made from Central Otago fruit.

Jackson's Rd, Blenheim RD3, Marlborough
www.allanscott.com

Amisfield Wine Company Central Otago

A significant presence on the Central Otago wine scene, Amisfield began planting its 148 acres (60ha) of vines on the shores of Lake Dunstan, in the Pisa district, in 1999. Unusually, it chose to focus on Sauvignon Blanc, as well as the more usual Pinot Gris, Riesling, and Pinot Noir. With an attractive cellar door and restaurant just out of Queenstown, which is separate from the impressive new 600 ton (610 tonne) winery in Lowburn, Amisfield attracts plenty of tourists. Jeff Sinnott, the original winemaker, was recently succeeded by Claire Mulholland, previously of Martinborough Vineyards. Crisp, minerally Sauvignon Blanc and textured Pinot Gris both impress. Lowburn Terrace Riesling, made in a low alcohol, off-dry style is pure and limey. Pinot Noir has been made here since 2002, and is ripe and elegant, with the high-end *cuvée* Rocky Knoll particularly impressive.

10 Lake Hayes Rd, RD1, Queenstown, Central Otago
www.amisfield.co.nz

Ara Marlborough

This impressive operation is headed up by Dr. Damian Martin, a New Zealander who trained in Bordeaux before returning to his native country. Ara is a river terrace at the meeting point of the Waihopai and Wairau rivers in the Marlborough region. It consists of around 3,954 acres (1,600ha), of which Ara has so far planted around 988 acres (400ha) to Sauvignon Blanc and Pinot Noir. The project is still in its early stages: the idea is to create an entirely new appellation, with others making wines on the same site. So far the wines have been very good, but not great, with a savory, plummy Composite Pinot Noir and a leanish Composite Sauvignon as the core of the range. Top of the range is an attractive, terroir-driven Resolute Pinot Noir from a special block.

Renwick, Marlborough
www.winegrowersofara.co.nz

Astrolabe Wines Marlborough

Established in 1996 by a group of friends, Astrolabe is a boutique winery located in the Marlborough region. The focus is on Sauvignon Blanc, which accounts for 80% of production, and rates among the region's best. Winemaker Simon Waghorn makes a wide range of wines, including the Discovery series, and focuses on wines from specific subregions of Marlborough. Look

AMISFIELD
LEATHER, SPICE, AND DARK FRUITS
CHARACTERIZE THIS CLASSIC PINOT NOIR

ARA
ARA'S PATHWAY SAUVIGNON BLANC IS
MADE IN A MORE FORWARD, OPEN STYLE

out for the Kekerengu Coast Sauvignon Blanc, which is made from the far southern outposts of the Marlborough region. ★ **Rising star**

Blenheim, Marlborough
www.astrolabewines.co.nz

Bald Hills Central Otago

In 1997, Blair and Estelle Hunt bought a 27 acre (11ha) subdivision of a sheep ranch in Bannockburn, Central Otago. They began to plant vines, and now have 18.5 acres (7.5ha) of Pinot Noir, Pinot Gris, and Riesling. Winemaking is in the hands of Grant Taylor. As well as the single-vineyard Pinot Noir, he also makes an earlier-drinking style Pinot Noir called Three Acres. The other Bald Hills wines are Pinot Gris and Riesling, both of which are made in a dry style.

Cromwell, Central Otago
www.baldhills.co.nz

Bell Hill Vineyard North Canterbury

Located in Waikari, in the hills that are set inland from the Waipara region and close to Christchurch, Bell Hill is an exciting Burgundy-inspired domaine based on a remarkable vineyard site. The chalky slopes are planted, tight-spaced, with 15 acres (6ha) of Pinot Noir and Chardonnay. From these vines, Marcel Giesen and Sherwyn Veldhuizen, the husband-and-wife team behind Bell Hill, are making some of New Zealand's most thrilling expressions of these varieties. Although planting started in 1997, they only finished putting vines in the ground in December 2009, and the first commercial release was in 2003. Both the 2006 and 2007 Pinots are thrilling wines with elegance and power. The Chardonnay develops beautifully in bottle, and the 2004 is a profound experience. ★ **Rising star**

Waikari, North Canterbury
www.bellhill.co.nz

Black Ridge Vineyard Central Otago

Black Ridge is one of the Central Otago pioneers. They began planting vines as early as 1981, and as well as being the world's most southerly winery and vineyard, they can also claim to be Central Otago's first commercial vineyard. Verdun Burgess and Sue Edwards, the owners of this rather wild, 21 acre (8.6ha) rocky site with its schist outcrops in the Alexandra subdistrict, had to use gelignite to blast holes for the vine posts. They attempted to make wine in 1985, 1986, and 1987, but failed. In 1988, their first commercial vintage was made under contract at Rippon. As well as Pinot Noir they also make well-regarded old-vine Gewürztraminer and Riesling from vines that are now over 25 years old—ancient by Central Otago standards.

Conroys Rd, Alexandra, Central Otago
www.blackridge.co.nz

Blind River Awatere

The boutique Blind River winery began life as a retirement project for Barry and Diane Feickert, but it has grown in stature (if not in size) and is now run by their three daughters: Debbie (a Roseworthy-trained winemaker with experience in Australia and California), Suzie, and Wendy. Just two wines are made from the 28 acres (11.25ha) of river terrace flats: a Sauvignon Blanc

SOUTH ISLAND

New Zealand's South Island has now eclipsed the North Island in terms of the volume of wine it produces, which is remarkable considering that until the mid-1970s, almost no wine was made there at all. Marlborough is New Zealand's most productive region, with a particular emphasis on Sauvignon Blanc. In the South, Central Otago has emerged, since the late 1980s, almost as a single variety region, with Pinot Noir being the star. This is also the world's most southerly fine-wine outpost. In between, Canterbury and Waipara are represented by a small area of vineyards mostly concentrated just north of Christchurch. Again, Pinot Noir is a key grape variety, but other varieties also do well. Adjoining Marlborough, at the top of the island, is the rather underrated Nelson region.

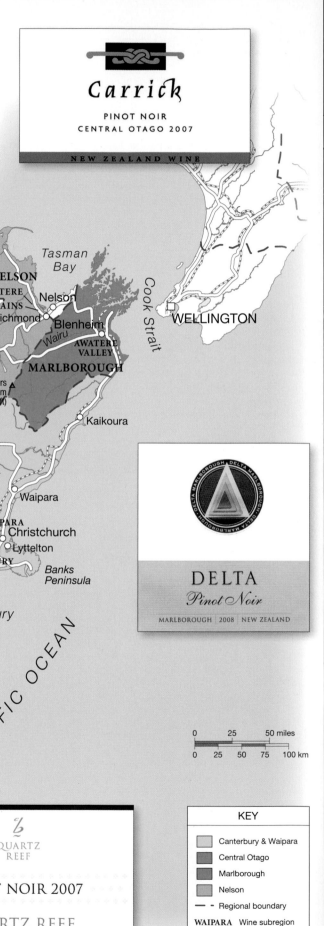

KEY

	Canterbury & Waipara
	Central Otago
	Marlborough
	Nelson
- - -	Regional boundary
WAIPARA	Wine subregion

MARLBOROUGH

New Zealand's largest wine region has seen considerable expansion in recent years. At the heart of Marlborough is the Wairau Valley, a long, broad plain heading west from the town of Blenheim, away from the coast. This is pretty much back-to-back vineyards. Framing the valley to the north are the Richmond Ranges, and to the south are the Wither Hills. The Awatere Valley is a second growing region, south of the Wairau, over the Wither Hills. This also has a subregion, called Seaview, which is closer to the coast. Awatere has a maritime influence and its grapes benefit from a longer ripening season.

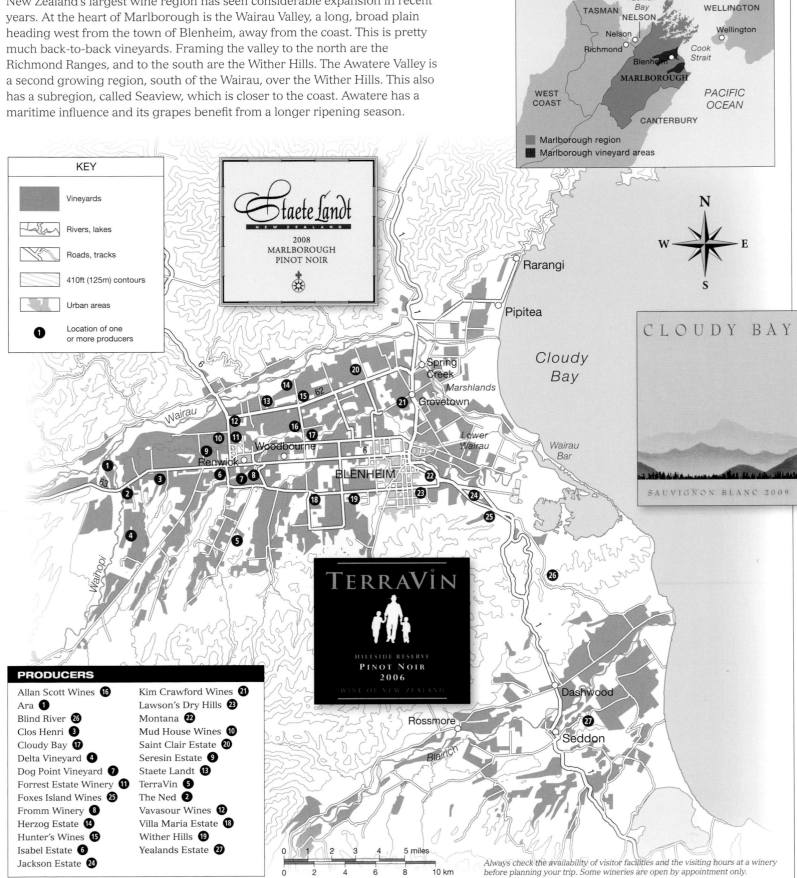

KEY

Vineyards

Rivers, lakes

Roads, tracks

410ft (125m) contours

Urban areas

1 Location of one or more producers

PRODUCERS

Allan Scott Wines	**16**	Kim Crawford Wines	**21**
Ara	**1**	Lawson's Dry Hills	**23**
Blind River	**26**	Montana	**22**
Clos Henri	**3**	Mud House Wines	**10**
Cloudy Bay	**17**	Saint Clair Estate	**20**
Delta Vineyard	**4**	Seresin Estate	**9**
Dog Point Vineyard	**7**	Staete Landt	**13**
Forrest Estate Winery	**11**	TerraVin	**5**
Foxes Island Wines	**25**	The Ned	**2**
Fromm Winery	**8**	Vavasour Wines	**12**
Herzog Estate	**14**	Villa Maria Estate	**18**
Hunter's Wines	**15**	Wither Hills	**19**
Isabel Estate	**6**	Yealands Estate	**27**
Jackson Estate	**24**		

Always check the availability of visitor facilities and the visiting hours at a winery before planning your trip. Some wineries are open by appointment only.

FELTON ROAD
BLOCK 5 COMBINES STRUCTURE AND
FINESSE; ONE OF NEW ZEALAND'S BEST PINOTS

and a Pinot Noir. Both are thrilling, showing precision, focus, and great balance. The Pinot Noir is silky and spicy, while the Sauvignon Blanc obtains extra depth from old French oak aging. ★ **Rising star**

Redwood Pass, Awatere Valley, RD4, Blenheim,
Marlborough; www.blindriver.co.nz

Carrick Wines Central Otago
Steve Green used to work in local government, but now has a much more appealing occupation: running one of Central Otago's top wineries. He founded Carrick Wines with his wife Barbara in 1994. It is located in the prime Bannockburn district and ex-Villa Maria viticulturalist Blair Deaker has been moving the estate in the direction of organics. Jane Docherty, who previously worked at Felton Road, has been winemaker here since 2008. A new and welcome addition to the range has been the super-*cuvée* Excelsior Pinot Noir, which was first made in 2005. The 2007, not yet released, is the best so far, and well worth waiting for. The regular Pinot Noir is also excellent, but it was not made in 2008; instead a new second wine, Southern Cross, was made. Off-dry Josephine Riesling is also excellent.

247 Cairnmuir Rd, Bannockburn, RD2, Central Otago
www.carrick.co.nz

Chard Farm Central Otago
One of the small band of Central Otago pioneers, brothers Greg and Rob Hay established Chard Farm in 1987 and had their first vintage in 1990. It is located close to Queenstown in the Gibbston subdistrict. As well as sourcing fruit from their beautifully situated, 49 acre (20ha) vineyard, they also, like many others in the unreliable but exciting Gibbston area, make use of vineyards in the Cromwell basin. Finla Mor Pinot Noir is made in a supple, fresh, elegant style: the 2005 is drinking well. Moving up in price, The Tiger is made in smaller quantities and is supple, spicy, and focused, aiming at elegance rather than power.

RD1, Queenstown
www.chardfarm.co.nz

Clos Henri Marlborough
This is the New Zealand outpost of Domaine Henri Bourgeois (Sancerre). Clos Henri began life in 2000, when Jean Marie Bourgeois bought an unplanted 230 acre (93ha) block in the Wairau Valley. Since 2001, 15 acres (6ha) have been planted each year. It is renowned for its stylish Sauvignon Blanc, which, as you might expect, is a more European interpretation of the terroir than most of its peers. All recent vintages have been worth seeking out, and may well benefit from a couple of years in bottle. The Pinot Noir is also quite serious: the 2007 is taut, dense, a bit reduced, and in need of time to settle down. ★ **Rising star**

639 State Hwy 63, West Coast Rd, RD1 Blenheim,
Marlborough; www.clos-henri.com

Cloudy Bay Marlborough
Perhaps the most famous New Zealand winery on export markets, Cloudy Bay's iconic Marlborough Sauvignon Blanc put New Zealand on the map for many people, with its wild, exotic, aromatic assault and bold flavors. Established by Australian David Hohnen in

HUNTER'S WINES
THIS CLASSIC MARLBOROUGH SAUVIGNON
BLANC HAS A CRISP, LINGERING PALATE

1985, it was the 1986 vintage that found its way to the UK and created huge interest. As well as the famous Sauvignon, a focused and quite serious Pinot Noir and a flavor-packed Chardonnay are also made. Their sparkling wine, Pelorus, is still one of New Zealand's best, and there is also Te Koko, a rather different oak-aged, wild ferment interpretation of Sauvignon Blanc. Volumes of their regular Sauvignon have gone up, and the quality may not be exactly what it was a decade ago, but Cloudy Bay Sauvignon Blanc still has a special place in the affections of many wine lovers.

Jacksons Rd, Blenheim, Marlborough
www.cloudybay.co.nz

Delta Vineyard Marlborough
Delta is a collaboration between winemaker Matt Thomson and London-based merchant David Gleave, who have worked together a lot in Italy. In 2000, Matt found a site at the mouth of the Waihopai Valley in Marlborough that he thought was particularly well suited to Pinot Noir. Along with two other investors, Gleave and Thomson bought the site and began planting in 2001 and 2002. The low vigor, clay-rich soils yield an aromatic, expressive Pinot Noir, as well as a high-end bottling called Hatter's Hill that comes from the slopes. Both wines are worth seeking out and offer really good value for the price. A Sauvignon Blanc is also made under this label from a separate vineyard. ★ **Rising star**

2A Opawa St, Blenheim, Marlborough
www.deltawines.co.nz

Dog Point Vineyard Marlborough
One of the most exciting Marlborough producers, Dog Point brings together the talents of James Healy and Ivan Sutherland, previously winemaker and viticulturalist at Cloudy Bay. They make Pinot Noir, Chardonnay, and Sauvignon Blanc. The regular Sauvignon Blanc is a beautifully pure example of Marlborough at its best. Block 94 Sauvignon Blanc is a step up, made in a distinctive, powerful, mineralic style with real appeal. The Pinot Noir is one of the region's best, being textured and elegant with a lovely, savory spiciness: the 2006 and 2007 are both excellent. ★ **Rising star**

Dog Point Rd, Renwick, Marlborough
www.dogpoint.co.nz

Felton Road Central Otago
Felton Road is Central Otago's leading producer—it makes a thrilling range of wines, all of which are fantastic. Nigel Greening purchased the 21 acre (8.6ha) Cornish Point Vineyard in 1998. In 2000, he added the 36 acre (14.6ha) Elms Vineyard, which has become the home vineyard for Felton Road—the entire estate is now run biodynamically. The heart of the range consists of a series of five, world-class Pinot Noirs: Cornish Point, Block 3, Block 5, the regular Pinot Noir, and Calvert from a leased 25 acre (10ha) neighboring vineyard, whose fruit is shared with Craggy Range and Pyramid Valley. All the wines are worth seeking out and show their subtle differences well. In addition, three superb Rieslings and a couple of solid Chardonnays make up this exciting range.

Felton Rd, RD2, Bannockburn, Central Otago
www.feltonroad.com

Forrest Estate Winery Marlborough

John and Brigid Forrest have been making wine in Marlborough since 1988, which is early history by this region's standards. They now own seven vineyards and manage a further two in the prime Wairau Valley, which total 321 acres (130ha)—a sizeable operation. The wines are textbook examples of their style, with Riesling being a strong point, along with the super-premium Collection whites: a low-cropped Sauvignon Blanc and a premium blend. They also make a Pinot Noir from Central Otago, called Tatty Bogler.

Blicks Rd, Renwick, Marlborough
www.forrest.co.nz

Foxes Island Wines Marlborough

John Belsham is the man behind this well-regarded Marlborough producer. He first got into wine while he was living and traveling overseas as a young man, when he ended up at Château de Saturnin in Bordeaux in 1977. He stayed there for five years, and on returning to New Zealand worked at Matua Valley and Hunter's before setting up Vintec, a contract winemaking facility. In 1988, he planted his own Pinot Noir and Chardonnay on an 11 acre (4.5ha) vineyard in the Rapaura Road area. To complement this, he purchased a further 49 acres (20ha) in the Awatere in 2000, and also draws on grapes from two other vineyards. Belsham makes Pinot Noir, Chardonnay, Sauvignon Blanc, and Riesling, with Pinot Noir and Chardonnay being his main focus, and the most successful.

8 Cloudy Bay Drive, Cloudy Bay Business Park, RD4, Blenheim, Marlborough; www.foxes-island.co.nz

Fromm Winery Marlborough

Founded in 1992 by fourth-generation Swiss winemaker Georg Fromm, this leading Marlborough producer may have changed hands, but the Swiss connection remains as it is now owned by Pol Lenzinger and his business partner, Georg Walliser. Winemaking is in the hands of Hätsch Kalberer, who has been with the winery from the start, and William Hoare. There are four estate vineyards (Clayvin, Fromm, William Thomas, and Quarters), and two ranges of wines—Fromm wines, which are more terroir-based, and La Strada wines, which are more style-based. Pinot Noir is the focus here: both Clayvin Vineyard Pinot Noir and Fromm Vineyard Pinot Noir show seriousness, lovely texture, and Old World elegance. The 2000 La Strada Pinot Noir shows that these wines can also age excellently. A wide range of other varietal wines are also made, including Syrah and Malbec—both rare in Marlborough—as well as the more usual Chardonnay, Riesling, Sauvignon Blanc, and Gewurztraminer.

Godfrey Rd, RD2, Blenheim, Marlborough
www.frommwinery.co.nz

Gibbston Valley Wines Central Otago

This pioneer Central Otago producer began life in 1983, when Alan Brady planted vines on what was previously a merino sheep farm. The first vintage was in 1987, and further vineyards were planted in Alexandra and Bendigo, which is now the most significant source of fruit for these wines. Bendigo is warmer and more reliable, while the home block at Gibbston is perilously cool, but in good years can produce brilliant Pinot Noir.

Gibbston Valley has four different plots making quite distinct wines. Talented young winemaker Christopher Keys has been in charge since 2006. He aims at, and achieves, elegance and finesse in his wines. Highlights from the range include the superb Le Fou Riesling, an astonishingly refined Reserve Pinot Noir, superbly elegant Le Mineur d'Orient Pinot Noir, and the bright, aromatic Le Maître Pinot Noir from the home block.

Gibbston RD1, State Hwy 6, Queenstown, Central Otago
www.gvwines.co.nz

Herzog Estate Marlborough

Known, for legal reasons, as Hans Family Estate in export markets, Hans Herzog, a Swiss expat who trained at Wädenswil, makes a fantastically original range of wines that are at odds with those of most of his Marlborough peers. Most striking is the Montepulciano, with its dense, fresh cherry and berry fruit. Also excellent are the pure, elegant Pinot Noir and the beautifully textured, varietally true Viognier. The wines come from a 27 acre (11ha) vineyard that Herzog planted in 1994—the first vintage was 1998. An acclaimed restaurant was established at the winery in 2000.

81 Jeffries Rd, RD3, Blenheim, Marlborough
www.herzog.co.nz

Hunter's Wines Marlborough

This well-known Marlborough winery was founded by Ernie and Jane Hunter in 1983, and has been run by Jane since 1987. It has grown considerably since it was established—the range is consistently strong and great value for money. Miru Miru sparkling wine is aromatic and toasty, and one of New Zealand's best. The Sauvignon Blanc is a strength, balancing passion fruit richness and crisp herbiness, while the Chardonnay is expressive, fresh, and toasty, and the dense, limey Riesling is superb. Stars of the show are the beautifully perfumed Gewurztraminer and the expressive, elegant, cherry fruited Pinot Noir.

Rapaura Rd, Blenheim, Marlborough
www.hunters.co.nz

Isabel Estate Marlborough

Isabel Estate was established in 1982, but owner Michael Tiller, a pilot, and his wife Robyn, initially operated as growers supplying the grapes for some of Marlborough's leading wineries. In 1994 they decided to start bottling their own wines, and they now operate entirely on an estate basis, making wines produced only from their own vineyards. The estate is located on the Omaka Terrace, just south of Renwick in Marlborough's Wairau Valley. Vines are planted at a relatively high density, and the deep, free-draining gravels are underlain with a narrow layer of calcium-rich clay that retains moisture and reduces the need for irrigation. Both the Sauvignon Blanc and Chardonnay are very good, and the Pinot Noir is possibly even better.

70–72 Hawkesbury Rd, Renwick, Marlborough
www.isabelestate.com

Jackson Estate Marlborough

One of Marlborough's leading producers, Jackson Estate was established by John Stichbury in 1987, with the first wines released in 1991. Drawing on fruit from five

DAVID HOHNEN AND CLOUDY BAY

It is perhaps ironic that one of the main figures behind the success of Marlborough Sauvignon Blanc, David Hohnen, is an Australian. In the early 1970s, Hohnen's Cape Mentelle winery was one of the pioneers of the Margaret River region in Western Australia. In 1983, some New Zealanders attending a technical conference in Western Australia left some bottles of Marlborough Sauvignon Blanc. Hohnen was so amazed by the wine that he went to New Zealand, determined to establish his own Marlborough winery. He raised finance, and in 1985 made the first Cloudy Bay Sauvignon, with winemaker Kevin Judd, from 40 tons (41 tonnes) of purchased grapes. In 1986, Judd built a winery and they signed up for 120 tons (122 tonnes) of grapes a year from Corbans. This second release found its way to the UK, where it was rapturously received. Cloudy Bay quickly became an iconic wine, establishing Marlborough Sauvignon Blanc as a unique style.

PEGASUS BAY

AN ELEGANT WINE, DEMONSTRATING WHY
WAIPARA PINOT IS SO WELL REGARDED

vineyards, the portfolio of wines is uniformly impressive. Stich Sauvignon Blanc is precise and focused; Grey Ghost Sauvignon Blanc, fermented in old oak, is textured and minerally; Shelter Belt Chardonnay is understated and elegant; and a pair of textured, focused Pinot Noirs—Vintage Widow and Gum Emperor—are probably the pick of the range. Chief winemaker Mike Paterson is evidently on top of his game.

22 Liverpool Street, Renwick, Marlborough
www.jacksonestate.co.nz

Kawarau Estate Central Otago
Located under the Pisa range in the heart of Central Otago's Cromwell basin, Kawarau Estate is a small boutique producer with 37 acres (15ha) of organically farmed vines that were first planted in 1992. Winemaking is by Dean Shaw at the Central Otago Wine Company—Chardonnay, Pinot Gris, Sauvignon Blanc, and Pinot Noir are made. The regular Pinot Noir is from younger vines, sees no new oak, and is bright and supple; Reserve Pinot is from the original 1992 plantings and shows focused, cherry fruit.

927 Wanaka Rd, Cromwell, Central Otago
www.kawarauestate.co.nz

Kim Crawford Wines Marlborough
This négociant operation was started by Kim Crawford in 1996. She sold to Vincor in 2003, and it is now part of the Constellation wine portfolio. A wide range of wines are made, drawing on grapes from across New Zealand's premium regions. Quality is consistently good, with some very impressive wines in the Reserve series, including the Spitfire Marlborough Sauvignon Blanc and the Mistress Waipara Riesling.

SH1, Grovetown, Blenheim, Marlborough
www.kimcrawfordwines.co.nz

Lawson's Dry Hills Marlborough
Ross and Barbara Lawson were originally Marlborough growers, but they decided to go it alone in 1992. Lawson's Dry Hills has grown considerably since then and is now considered a major player in Marlborough. It sources grapes from 12 vineyards, spread across the region, and is also a member of the Family of Twelve coalition of prestigious family-owned New Zealand estates. A full range of wines is made, including the usual spread of Marlborough varieties, but Gewurztraminer is their particular strength. Quality is consistently good across the entire range.

Alabama Rd, Blenheim, Marlborough
www.lawsonsdryhills.co.nz

Montana Marlborough
Montana, part of the Pernod Ricard portfolio, is an extremely important producer for New Zealand. It has been around for some time, by New Zealand standards —2008 marked its 30th vintage. Its basic Sauvignon Blanc is a great introduction to the Marlborough style, and is consistently good, inexpensive, and available all over the world. Montana crushes around 20,000 tons (20,320 tonnes) of Sauvignon Blanc each year. It is also one of the world's leading Pinot Noir producers, crushing 3,000 tons (3,048 tonnes) annually. Much of its Pinot Noir is destined for its sparkling wines –

Deutz and Lindauer—which are another important part of the business. Worth looking out for is the new-ish high-end Terroir series of Sauvignon Blancs and Pinot Noirs.

State Hwy 1, Riverlands, Blenheim, Marlborough
www.montana.co.nz

Mount Difficulty Central Otago
One of Central Otago's largest producers, Mount Difficulty began as a collaborative project with five separate vineyard-owning partners. The first wines were released in 1998. Since then, the ownership has been reorganized with the formation of a single company and the construction of a new winery on the Felton Road. The range of wines consists of the more commercial, and very successful, Roaring Meg range, alongside the Mount Difficulty wines. Pinot Noir is the main focus, with an attractive, fairly serious estate wine and one or more single-vineyard wines, depending on vintage conditions. Three of the vineyards are potentially capable of producing single-vineyard wines—Target Gully, Long Gully, and Pipeclay Terrace. The three Rieslings are also excellent: the minerally, precise Dry Riesling, the off-dry, lower alcohol Target Gully Riesling, and the Long Gully Late Harvest Riesling.

Cromwell, Bannockburn, Central Otago
www.mtdifficulty.co.nz

Mount Edward Central Otago
Established in 1997 by Central Otago pioneer Alan Brady (who also founded Gibbston Valley), Mount Edward sources grapes from six small vineyards, taking in the Gibbston, Bannockburn, Pisa, and Lowburn subdistricts. Winemaker Duncan Forsyth is currently making some very smart wines. The regular Pinot Noir is beautifully aromatic and pure; Morrison Vineyard Pinot Noir is fresh and has a lovely mineral elegance; and Muirkirk Vineyard Pinot Noir is ripe, smoothly textured, and elegant. Riesling is also a strength here— look out for the off-dry Drumlin Riesling, sadly only made in small quantities.

34 Coalpit Rd, Gibbston Hwy, RD1, Queenstown,
Central Otago; www.mountedward.com

Mountford Estate Waipara
Perfectionist winemaker C P Lin is fashioning some of New Zealand's most elegant Pinot Noirs at this boutique Waipara winery. Lin, who lost his sight at the age of two, was famously rude about previous owner Mike Eaton's wines and was consequently hired to see if he could do a better job, which he most certainly has. Mountford was purchased by Dutch couple Kathryn Ryan and Kees Zeestraten in 2007, and since then, further Pinot Noir, Chardonnay, and Riesling have been planted, taking the vineyard area up to 25 acres (10ha). In addition, some fruit from contract growers is used to make the Village and Liason Pinot Noirs. Estate Pinot Noir shows silky texture and purity of fruit, while the Gradient Pinot Noir, which has so far only been made in 2006 and 2008, is from a single block and is tight wound, structured, and super-elegant. Mountford Estate also makes Chardonnay, Pinot Gris, and Riesling.

434 Omihi Rd, State Hwy 1, Waipara, RD3, Amberley,
North Canterbury; www.mountfordvineyard.co.nz

OSTLER

THE FLAGSHIP PINOT GRIS IS A COMPLEX
WINE—SPICY, YET CREAMY

Mud House Wines Waipara

With vineyards in Marlborough, Waipara, and Central Otago, Mud House makes a large range of well-priced wines, offering real regional personality. John and Jennifer Joslin founded Mud House in the late 1990s. After making money from business in the UK and Belgium, they had spent six years touring the world in their yacht before starting this Marlborough winery. They sold it in 2006 and Mud House is now part of the MH Wine Group, which also owns Waipara Hills and a couple of other brands. Both the Marlborough Sauvignon Blanc and Marlborough Pinot Noir are benchmark examples; there is also a high-end reserve label, called Swan, for occasional special releases.

780 Glasnevin Rd, State Hwy 1, Waipara
www.mudhouse.co.nz

Neudorf Vineyards Nelson

Tim and Judy Finn founded Neudorf in 1978, which is ancient history by New Zealand standards. Since then, they have cemented their reputation as one of New Zealand's leading boutique wineries. Their vineyards are spread over two sites: the home block at Moutere, and also at Brightwater, south of Nelson. While the elegantly lean Pinot Noir is highly regarded, the star wine is the powerful, yet elegant, Moutere Chardonnay. This is closely followed by the bold, spicy Nelson Chardonnay and a superb Pinot Gris. Brightwater Riesling is also beautifully precise.

138 Neudorf Rd, RD2 Upper Moutere, Nelson
www.neudorf.co.nz

Olssens Central Otago

John Olssen and Heather McPherson were early pioneers in the now important Cromwell Basin area of Central Otago, when they planted their Bannockburn vineyard in 1989. The 25 acre (10ha) vineyard is mostly planted to Pinot Noir, with some Chardonnay and Riesling, and Gewurztraminer and Sauvignon making up the balance. Somewhat bizarrely, there are also tiny amounts of Pinotage, Cabernet Sauvignon, and Syrah that are used to make Robert The Bruce, a "folly" wine. The Riesling is off-dry in a focused, mineral style, but the top wines are a trio of Pinots: Slapjack Creek, Nipple Hill, and Jackson Barry.

306 Felton Rd, Bannockburn, RD2, Cromwell,
Central Otago; www.olssens.co.nz

Ostler Waitaki Valley

Ostler is a pioneering winery in the Waitaki Valley region of South Island, where the vines are planted on limestone-rich soils. It is located inland, along the river valley from Oamaru and a short distance north of Dunedin in north Otago. The cool, maritime climate means that the harvest is late, being in April or sometimes even May. It is a partnership between Jim Jerram and his brother-in-law and winemaker Jeff Sinnott, who was previously with Amisfield and Isabel Estate. The first vines were planted in 2002 and the first wine, a Pinot Noir, was made in 2004. In addition to Pinot Noir, there are also Pinot Gris and Riesling vines on the estate. ★Rising star

4626 Kurow-Duntroon Rd, Waitaki Valley
www.ostlerwine.co.nz

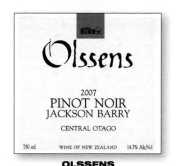

OLSSENS
THE 2007 PINOT NOIR SHOWS FOCUS AND
FRESHNESS TO THE SWEET BERRY FRUIT

PYRAMID VALLEY
HILLE SEMILLON COMES FROM A VINEYARD
AT THE TOP OF THE BRANCOTT VALLEY

Pegasus Bay Waipara

One of the top Waipara wineries, Pegasus Bay is owned by the Donaldson family, with winemaking in the hands of husband-and-wife team Matthew Donaldson and Lynette Hudson. The top-performing varieties, from 99 acres (40ha) of estate vineyards, are Riesling and Pinot Noir. Watch out for the focused, off dry Riesling; the complex, sweet Auslese-style Aria Riesling; and both the regular and Prima Donna Pinot Noirs. Chardonnay and a Merlot/Cabernet Bordeaux blend red are also very good. Second label Main Divide uses fruit from South Island contract growers.

Stockgrove Rd, Waipara, RD2 ,Amberley,
North Canterbury; www.pegasusbay.com

Peregrine Wines Central Otago

Based in the Gibbston region of Central Otago, Peregrine began life as a "virtual" winery in 1998, but has grown significantly and now boasts an impressive, architectural-award-winning winery and cellar door, which was opened at the end of 2003. A wide range of consistently good wines are made, but the Pinot Noirs really stand out. Both the regular and Karearea Pinot Noir, which are made in small quantities, are beautifully fresh and elegant with the potential to develop in bottle. For those who like lighter-style Pinot Noirs, the pale-colored 2008 is beautifully elegant and the second label Saddleback Pinot is also very appealing in a light, leafy style. Also worth looking out for is the Karearea Pinot Gris.

Kawarau Gorge Rd, RD1, Gibbston, Queenstown,
Central Otago; www.peregrinewines.co.nz

Pisa Range Estate Central Otago

Warwick and Jenny Hawker spent their life traveling abroad as part of the diplomatic corps, before deciding to settle down. It was while they were still posted in Beijing in 1995, however, that they founded their Pisa Range Estate in the Pisa district of Central Otago and had their vineyard planted. The late Mike Wolter helped them in the early stages, and subsequently winemaking has been in the hands of Rudi Bauer of Quartz Reef. They have 10 acres (4ha) of Pinot Noir and 1.2 acres (0.5ha) of Riesling, which is yet to produce grapes. Their first vintage was in 1998, but it was not until 2000 that they bottled their own wine. A single Pinot Noir is made each year—it is a wine that shows focused, elegant, spicy dark cherry character, and is consistently superb.

SH6 Cromwell/Wanaka Hwy, Cromwell, Central Otago
www.pisarangeestate.co.nz

Pyramid Valley North Canterbury

Mike and Claudia Weersing's Pyramid Valley is one of New Zealand's most exciting projects. The home vineyard, near Waikari in the North Canterbury Hills, has Pinot Noir and Chardonnay planted according to Burgundian principles (close-planted and trellised low to the ground), with biodynamic management. The first vintage from these vineyards was in 2006 and the two Pinot Noirs it produced—Earthsmoke and Angel Fire—are breathtakingly elegant and complex. The series of wines launched as the Growers Collection, from special vineyard sites across New Zealand, is also superb. It includes Riesling, Semillon, Pinot Blanc, and Cabernet

THE NED

A FABULOUS VINTAGE WITH SUBTLE
MINERALITY AND A SOFT, DRY FINISH

TWO PADDOCKS

THIS COOL-CLIMATE PINOT NOIR COMES
FROM THE GIBBSTON SUBDISTRICT

Franc, as well as Pinot Noirs from Marlborough and
Central Otago. Everything with Pyramid's name on
it is worth seeking out. ★ **Rising star**

548 Pyramid Valley Rd, RD Waikari, North Canterbury
www.pyramidvalley.co.nz

Quartz Reef Bendigo

Austrian Rudi Bauer is one of the most talented and
respected winemakers in Central Otago. He founded
Quartz Reef in 1996 in partnership with Clotilde Chauvet
(of Marc Chauvet Champagne), John and Heather
Perriam, and Trevor Scott. They initially used contracted
vineyards, but the wines are now based on 74 acres
(30ha) of vines in the Bendigo subdistrict. One
of the vineyards is a 37 acre (15ha), north-facing slope
with clay, fine gravel, and quartz soils that is largely
planted with Pinot Noir, but also with Chardonnay,
Pinot Gris, and more recently, some Grüner Veltliner.
The other, adjacent, vineyard is 37 acres (15ha) of sandy
loam soils that is planted with Pinot Noir, Chardonnay,
and Pinot Gris. As well as making a stylish, structured
Pinot Noir that is among the region's best, Quartz Reef
is also a sparkling wine specialist.

8 Hughes Crescent, Cromwell, Bendigo, Central Otago
www.quartzreef.co.nz

Rippon Vineyard Wanaka

Beautifully situated on the banks of Lake Wanaka, Rippon
Vineyard is one of the pioneers of Central Otago. In 1982,
inspired by discovering that his property had similar
schistous soils to Portugal's Douro Valley, Rolfe Mills
decided to plant vines on a commercial scale. The hunch
was a good one, and after much experimentation Rippon
now has 37 acres (15ha) of vines, with Pinot Noir and
Riesling the key varieties. In 2002, Rolfe's son, Nick,
returned from a four-year stint in Burgundy to take
the helm. He has moved vineyard management to
biodynamics and taken the wines a step further in terms
of quality. Until 2008, just two Pinot Noirs were made:
Jeunesse and the Rippon Pinot Noir. From the
2008 vintage, two of the oldest blocks, Tinker's Field
and Emma's Block, will be bottled separately; they are
stunningly expressive wines. The 1990 Pinot Noir is
beautiful, showing that this site produces wines that
can age well. The Riesling is also impressive.

246 Mt Aspiring Rd, Wanaka
www.rippon.co.nz

Saint Clair Estate Marlborough

With winemaking in the very capable hands of
Matt Thomson, Saint Clair is turning out some of
Marlborough's most distinctive expressions of Sauvignon
Blanc, and also some very tidy Pinot Noir. Neal and Judy
Ibbotson had been growing grapes in Marlborough since
1978, but it was not until 1994 that they released their
first wines. Grapes are now sourced from five different
vineyard sites, spanning a range of microclimates. The
Sauvignon Blancs are all good and made in a thiol-rich
style, with Pioneer Blocks 18 and 3 being the pick of the
bunch. Look out for the intense, bold Omaka Reserve
Chardonnay and the ripe, focused Block 14 and Omaka
Reserve Pinot Noirs.

13 Selmes Rd, RD3, Rapaura, Belheim, Marlborough
www.saintclair.co.nz

Seresin Estate Marlborough

Film maker Michael Seresin owns one of the star wineries
in Marlborough. From biodynamically run, organically
certified vineyards, Seresin Estate is now turning out
some fantastic wines. The vineyard holdings are extensive,
with the 111 acre (45ha) Home and 37 acre (15ha) Tatou
vineyards in the Wairau Valley and the 126 acre (51ha)
Raupo Creek vineyard in the Omaka Valley. Since 2006, the
winemaking has been in the hands of Clive Dougall, and
quality is first-rate. The range of six different Pinot Noirs
is stunning, with all showing real complexity, depth, and
balance. Sauvignon Blanc is beautifully focused and
supplemented with a dribble of Semillon. Richly textured
Marama Sauvignon Blanc is remarkable, a true icon. The
Chardonnay Reserve is also worth seeking out.

85 Bedford Rd, Renwick, Marlborough
www.seresin.co.nz

Staete Landt Rapaura

Dutch couple Ruud Maasdam and Dorien Vermaas
purchased a 52 acre (20ha) block of land in the Rapaura
area of Marlborough in 1997. On the basis of extensive soil
surveys, they divided their prospective vineyard into 24
blocks, before planting and managing each one differently.
Most of the focus is on Sauvignon Blanc, Chardonnay,
Pinot Gris, and Pinot Noir, but Riesling (in both dry and
Auslese forms), Syrah, and Viognier are also made. All
the wines show lovely focus and elegance, with Pinot
Noir particularly standing out, displaying mineral elegance
through to sweet, perfumed cherry fruit.

48 Jeffries Rd, Blenheim, Marlborough
www.staetelandt.co.nz

TerraVin Marlborough

Mike and Jo Eaton purchased their current vineyard in
1998. It was originally a 30 acre (12ha) property, but they
recently sold some and now have just 10 acres (4ha) of
vines, which they supplement by buying fruit from other
growers. They established the Clayvin vineyard in 1981,
from which they sold the fruit. In 1998, they sold the
Clayvin vineyard to Fromm, but are now leasing back
part of it. The star turn here is Pinot Noir, with a superb
standard Pinot Noir and also a thrilling Hillside Reserve
bottling, which is beautifully focused, with elegance and
freshness. Look out for a stunning 2009 TerraVin Vineyard
bottling, which, if the barrel samples are any kind of
indication, will be very exciting. Also look for Bordeaux
blend "J," which is unusual for this region.

367 Brookby Rd, RD2, Blenheim, Marlborough
www.terravin.co.nz

The Ned Marlborough

Brent Marris is the man behind The Ned. He built Wither
Hills into one of Marlborough's leading brands before
selling it to Lion Nathan in 2002. He finally left Wither
Hills to strike out alone in 2007. The Ned is based on a 662
acre (268ha) vineyard in the Waihopai River region
of Marlborough, which Brent purchased in 2003. From
here, he makes commercially astute, flavorful wines
from Sauvignon Blanc, Pinot Gris, and Pinot Noir, as
well as a noble Sauvignon Blanc dessert wine, 85% of
which are exported. A new winery is under construction.

26 Arney Crescent, Remuera, Marlborough
www.thened.co.nz

Tinpot Hut Marlborough

Tinpot Hut is a collaboration between New Zealand winemakers Matt Thomson (of Saint Clair) and Fiona Turner, and UK wine merchant David Gleave (from Liberty Wines). Four wines are made from their Marlborough base: Sauvignon Blanc, Pinot Gris, and Pinot Noir from Marlborough, and a Hawkes Bay Syrah. The Marlborough wines are of real interest, with beautiful floral aromatics and lovely fresh berry fruits. As you would expect from such a team, all the wines are extremely worthwhile.

2A Opawa St, Blenheim, Marlborough
www.tinpothut.co.nz

Two Paddocks Central Otago

Two Paddocks is the actor Sam Neill's foray into the world of wine. It began life in 1993, when 5 acres (2ha) of Pinot Noir were planted in the Gibbston subdistrict of Central Otago. This small vineyard was expanded to 12 acres (5ha) and augmented with two other sites in the Alexandra subdistrict: the 7 acre (3ha) Alex Paddocks, and a larger 148 acre (60ha) property called Redbank Paddocks, which is now the home vineyard for Two Paddocks, and has had another 15 acres (6ha) of vines added to it. Winemaking is in the hands of Dean Shaw at the Central Otago Wine Company, and the wines are impressive. As well as the regular Two Paddocks Pinot Noir, two single-vineyard bottlings are also made, but not every year. First Paddock comes from the Gibbston vineyard, and shows stylishly focused, dark cherry fruit with fresh acidity. Last Chance is from Alexandra, and combines pure fruit and good structure.

Alexandra, Central Otago
www.twopaddocks.com

Valli Central Otago

Well-traveled winemaker Grant Taylor had had some Burgundian experience, at the famous Dujac, and was winemaker with Gibbston Valley when he started his own project, Valli, in 1998. In 2006 he left Gibbston Valley to concentrate solely on Valli, and now has vineyards in Gibbston and Bannockburn in Central Otago. More recently, he has also acquired a vineyard in Waitaki in North Otago, which is an exciting new region with limestone-rich soils. Separate Pinot Noirs are made from each vineyard, as well as a Riesling that is produced from Alexandra fruit.

Wakatipu, Central Otago
www.valliwine.com

Vavasour Wines Marlborough

Vavasour were pioneers of the Awatere Valley in Marlborough—they took the plunge in 1985 and planted 30 acres (12ha) of vines. The area is drier, with less fertile soils and a cooler climate than the Wairau Valley. They struck lucky and the wines that resulted were good enough to convince others of the merits of this now important subregion. Winemaker Glenn Thomas has been at Vavasour Wines since 1988. The wines exhibit freshness and poise; the elegantly expressive Sauvignon Blanc is the pick of the wines.

26 Rapaura Rd, Blenheim, Marlborough
www.vavasour.com

Villa Maria Estate Marlborough

One of New Zealand's most important wine companies, Villa Maria has grown large, while still producing high-quality wines. Founded in 1961 by George Fistonich, Villa Maria now has vineyards in Auckland, Gisborne, Hawkes Bay, and Marlborough, as well as two wineries in Auckland and Marlborough. The wines range from solidly commercial to fine and are tiered in four levels: Private Bin, Cellar Selection, Reserve, and Single Vineyard. At every level they punch above their weight and offer great value for money. Particularly noteworthy are the Reserve and Cellar Selection Hawkes Bay Syrahs, the richly fruited Single Vineyard Pinot Noirs, and the Reserve and Single Vineyard Bordeaux Blends, but everything is pretty serious once you get to the Reserve level. Villa Maria also owns Esk Valley and Vidal wineries.

Cnr Paynters Rd and New Renwick Rd, Fairhall, Blenheim, Marlborough; www.villamaria.co.nz

Wither Hills Marlborough

Brent Marris built Wither Hills into one of the Marlborough region's leading wineries before selling it to the Lion Nathan wine group in 2002. Brent stayed on as senior winemaker until 2007, when he handed over to his deputy, Ben Glover, who is now in charge. Quality has not suffered at all as a result of this, and Wither Hills is still making some of Marlborough's most attractive and best-value Sauvignon Blanc, combining passion fruit richness with fresh grassiness to good effect. Pinot Noir is also a strength at Wither Hills—it is made in a ripe and accessible style, but with more than a hint of seriousness. With over 741 acres (300ha) of vineyards, Wither Hills has significant land holdings.

211 New Renwick Rd, RD2, Blenheim, Marlborough
www.witherhills.co.nz

Yealands Estate Marlborough

This is an ambitious project based on extensive new vineyard plantings in both the Awatere (Seaview and Flaxbourne) and the Wairau (Grovetown, a reclaimed marsh, and Riverlands). Peter Yealands is an entrepreneur who established the first greenshell mussel farms and then, in the 1980s, turned to deer farming. Yealands's approach to wine has a strong focus on sustainability and respect for the environment—the new winery is carboNZero certified. Winemaking is in the hands of Tamra Washington, previously senior winemaker at Calatrasi in Italy. The first vintage was in 2008 and, although it is still early days, the wines look very promising.

Cnr Seaview Rd and Reserve Rd, Seddon, Blenheim, Marlborough; www.yealands.com

VALLI
MADE FROM SOME OF THE SOUTH ISLAND'S OLDEST VINES, PRODUCTION IS VERY LIMITED

SERESIN
THIS WINERY IS NOW MAKING, ARGUABLY, MARLBOROUGH'S FINEST PINOT NOIRS

GLOSSARY

Use this glossary to find the definitions of more than 600 wine words, many of which appear elsewhere in *Opus Vino*. Grape varieties, wine tasting terms, grape growing and winemaking techniques, and much of the terminology commonly found on wine bottle labels are all covered here. For more on the thousands of official wine regions (appellations of origin) of the world and the specific wine types made in them, please go to the maps and the written entries organized under the pertinent country.

LABEL TERMINOLOGY

Concise explanations of the most common terms found on wine labels in Europe and the New World are given on the following four pages. More detailed explanations of some of these terms, for example, Premier Cru, are given in the general glossary.

EUROPE

FRANCE

Geography

Appellation d'Origine Contrôlée (AOC or AC) A named and clearly defined region or locality. If this appears on a label, the wine legally must be from the designated place and made according to the local rules.

AOP Appellation d'Origine Protégée (PDO Protected Designation of Origin); IGP Indication Géographique Protégée (PGI Protected Geographical Indication) A new EU-wide labeling system to guarantee the origin of wine and other products.

VDQS A quality designation now being phased out. Current labels will either be promoted to AC or downgraded to IGP (which replaces Vins de Pays).

Vins de Pays A regional quality designation now being phased out and replaced by IGP.

Vin de Table Still found on labels, indicating the lowest quality level, these wines can now feature grape variety and vintage.

Other label terms

Château Not necessarily a castle, but the estate at which the vineyard is planted.

Contains albumin On any wine that may contain traces of egg or milk-derived products (from fining operations).

Côtes de/Côteaux de Hills or hillside.

Cru "Growth." Indicating a specific plot of land or vineyard.

Cru Classé Classification of a single vineyard to indicate a higher quality level.

Domaine More common in Burgundy, this indicates the wine is made and bottled by the vine-grower, rather than a négociant.

Grand Cru Highest-level vineyard designation in Burgundy, but of no particular significance in Bordeaux.

Mis en bouteille au Château/Domaine The wine was made and bottled at the château or domaine. This can be an indication of quality.

Premier Cru "First growth." In Bordeaux, Premier Grand Cru Classé designates the five first growths; in Burgundy, Premier Cru is one designation below Grand Cru.

Propriétaire-Récoltant Owner, vine-grower, and winemaker.

Récoltant Winemaker or vine-grower.

Récolte Vintage

Réserve A term that has no legal meaning on a French label though a producer may use it to indicate a longer aging time.

Supérieur Suggests a wine usually from lower yields and with slightly higher alcohol levels.

Vieilles Vignes Old vines, meaning the wine may be from low-yielding vines and have more complexity, but this is not a legal definition.

Vigneron Vine-grower

Villages Usually attached to a commune or parish name and indicates origin of the grapes.

Viticulteur Vine-grower

CHAMPAGNE

Blanc de Blancs White wine from white grapes, that is, Chardonnay.

Blanc de Noirs White wine from black grapes, that is, Pinot Noir and/or Pinot Meunier.

Cuvée The finest juice from each pressing at harvest, on a label it means the final blend.

NV Non-vintage Wine that is blended across several vintages to maintain a consistent house style.

Vintage The grapes will have come from a single and usually exceptional year.

Style

Brut Nature With no dosage or added sugar—a searingly dry champagne.

Extra Brut Very dry

Brut Dry

Sec Medium

Demi-sec Semisweet

Doux Sweet

Producer information

Récoltant-manipulant (RM) Vine-grower making his own wine.

Négociant-manipulant (NM) A winemaker who makes champagne from bought-in grapes.

Co-opérative-manipulant (CM) A co-operative making wine for its clients.

Récoltant-co-opérateur (RC) A vine-grower selling wines made in a co-operative.

Marque d'acheteur (MA) The own-label brand of a buyer.

SPAIN

Geography

Denominación de Origen Calificada (DOCa) The highest classification in Spain. Only awarded to the few top wine regions such as Rioja and Priorat.

Denominación de Origen (DO) Controlled and guaranteed place of origin. Very similar to the AC system in France.

Denominación de Origen Pago (DO Pago) A very specific classification awarded to individual estates.

Vino de Calidad con Indicación Geografica (VCIG) A stepping stone classification for wines on their way to DO status.

Vino de la Tierra (VdT) A regional classification similar to France's Vin de Pays or Italy's IGT.

Vino de Mesa (VdM) The basic classification for table wine.

Other label terms

Año Year

Bodega Winery

Cava Sparkling wine from northeast Spain, made in the traditional bottle-fermented style.

Cosecha Vintage

Crianza Wines with this label must have been aged for at least two years, with 6–12 months of that time in oak, depending on the region.

Dulce Sweet

Embotellado de origen Made and bottled on the same estate.

Espumoso Sparkling

Vendimia Vintage

Gran Reserva Wines with this label must have been aged for at least five years, with 18 months of that time in oak.

Joven Young wine, made, bottled, and sold within a year of harvest.

Reserva Wines with this label must have been aged for at least three years, with 12 months of that time in oak and 12 months in bottle.

Rosado Rosé

Seco Dry

PORTUGAL

Geography

Denominção de Origem Controlada (DOC) The highest classification in Portugal; very similar to the AC system in France.

Indicação de Proveniencia Regulamentada (IPR) The stepping stone to DOC status.

Vinho Regional (VR) Regionally identified wines that are generally made from non-indigenous grape varieties.

Vinho de Mesa The basic classification for table wine.

Other label terms

Adega Cellar

Amarzém Cellar

Colheita Vintage

Doce Sweet

Garrafado na origem Made and bottled on the same estate.

Garrafeira A reserve wine from a merchant.

Maduro Mature

Quinta Estate

Rosado Rosé

Séco Dry

Verde Young wine (green wine).

Port styles

Colheita A wood-aged port from a single year, rather than a blend, can be drunk immediately on bottling.

LBV (late bottled vintage) Aged in barrel for at least four years before bottling, this port is usually ready to drink on release.

Ruby A blend of cheaper ports, aged in wood for some time before bottling. The blending allows the port shipper to get a consistent product.

Tawny A blended and wood-aged port that can be very fine. Usually either 10 or 20 years old, (though they can be older) these tawny ports have a paler color from the wood-aging and are often very smooth.

Vintage Only made in exceptional years, all the grapes are from that single harvest. It is bottled after two years and then aged indefinitely.

ITALY

Geography

Denominazione di Origine Controllata (DOC) Designates wines from a specific growing region. Usually a sign of wine quality but politics often interfere.

Denominazione di Origine Controllata e Garantita (DOCG) Controlled and guaranteed place of origin. This is the highest quality designation in Italy.

Indicazione Geografica Tipica (IGT) Classification similar to the French Vins de Pays/IGP system, used by some producers to circumvent the clumsy DOCG system.

Vino da Tavola Table wine, sometimes found on incredibly expensive wines that do not adhere to the above rules.

Other label terms

Amabile Semisweet

Annata Year or vintage.

Azienda Agricola A wine estate producing its own grapes.

Cantina Winery

Chiaretto Very pale red color.

Classico For example, Chianti Classico. From the original demarcated zone, rather than from the extended area.

Consorzio An association of growers.

Dolce Sweet

Fattoria Farm

Frizzante Slightly sparkling

Imbottigliato all'originie Made and bottled on the same estate.

Liquoroso Fortified or very strong wine.

Metodo classico Traditional bottle-fermented sparkling wine.

Passito Sweet wine often made from dried grapes.

Recioto A portion of the grapes will have been dried to concentrate the flavors.

Riserva A wine that has been aged for longer.

Rosato Rosé

Secco Dry

Spumante Sparkling

Superiore Often more complex, has more age and higher alcohol.

Tenuta Estate or small farm.

Vendemmia Vintage or harvest.

Vendemmis tardiva Late harvest

Viticoltore Vine-grower

GERMANY

Geography

Qualitätswein bestimmter Anbaugebiete (QbA) Wine from a named and protected region. There are currently 13 of these regions. It is no guarantee of quality, purely one of origin.

Grosses Gewächs or Erstes Gewächs Great or First Growth. This classification applies to wines of Spätlese quality (or better) from a designated vineyard site. There are two lower tiers "Classified" and "Gutswein" or "Ortswein" to indicate wider geographical boundaries.

Landwein A rough equivalent to Vins de Pays, but not widely used.

Deutscher Tafelwein Table wine, a very basic classification for light wines

Quality Designations

Qualitätswein mis Prädikat (QmP) or Prädikatswein This classification system refers to the ripeness of the grapes rather than the geographic origins. Only those grapes that have naturally achieved ascending levels of ripeness (no chaptalization allowed) are rated within the Prädikat.

Kabinett Fully ripe grapes harvested to give a light, refreshing style of wine.

Spätlese Harvested later and with more sugar, this style can be fermented to be fully dry or semisweet. The wines are more full-bodied.

Auslese Selected for later harvest from the best vineyards. The term indicates the level of sugar at harvest, rather than in the resulting wine. These can be dry or sweet wines.

Beerenauslese (BA) Made from grapes affected by botrytis (*beeren*), thus concentrating the sugar, to make rare and sweet wines.

Eiswein Icewine. The sugars are concentrated and the acidity preserved by the grapes being frozen on the vine.

Trockenbeerenauslese (TBA) Incredibly rare and very sweet and only found in exceptional years when the conditions are right. The berries are picked when they are very ripe and have been dried out (*trocken*) by botrytis.

Other quality terms

Abfüllung Bottled by...

Erzeugerabfüllung Bottled by the producer, whether a co-operative or single estate.

Gutsabfüllung Made and bottled on the same estate.

Amtliche Prüfnummer (AP Nr) This number appears on all QmP wines to indicate exactly where the wine is from, who made it and exactly when it was bottled.

Bereich A generic term encompassing large regions, usually best avoided.

Classic Dry wines with no more than 15g/l of residual sugar from one grape variety.

Grosslage A defined region, which has no bearing on quality, and can be misleading.

Halbtrocken Medium-dry, with between 9 and 18g/l residual sugar.

Selection dry Wines with no more than 12g/l of residual sugar from one grape variety.

Weingut A wine estate that produces all of its own grapes.

Weinkellerei A wine producer that buys in grapes to make wine.

NEW WORLD

Geography

New World producers have far fewer restrictions on their vine-growing and winemaking, although, as some areas and regions become known for their particular qualities, the idea of protecting their identities has become more popular. You will still find dubious labeling in some of these countries, for example, "Mountain Chablis" or "Almond Champagne" in the United States and "Tawny Ports" in Australia. These wines are usually (but not always) relying on the famous name to sell their goods rather than the actual quality of the wine inside the bottle.

UNITED STATES

Geography

American Viticultural Area (AVA) A defined geographical area, approved by the US government, which can be as specific as a single vineyard or as wide-ranging as Central Valley, for example, covering a vast inland area. No guarantee of quality, it merely confirms the origin of the grapes.

Estate-bottled The wine must have been made and bottled on the same estate.

Single vineyard Where a single vineyard is named, 100% of the grapes must have come from that vineyard.

Quality Terms

Bottled by Must appear with the name and address of the bottler.

Produced and bottled by Can be used if 75% of the wine was made by the named winery.

Made and bottled by May be used if 10% of the wine was made by the named winery.

Cellared, vinted, or prepared by Can be used if the named winery subjected the final wine to any treatment, such as fining or filtration.

Vintage May only appear on the label if 95% of the wine comes from that year.

Variety Where a single grape variety is mentioned on the label, the wine must contain no less than 75% of that variety.

AUSTRALIA AND NEW ZEALAND

Geography

Geographic Indication (GI) Similar to AVA in the US, a GI can cover an entire state (or three as in the case of South Eastern Australia) or much smaller, higher-quality areas such as Marlborough in New Zealand.

Estate-bottled The wine must have been made and bottled on the same estate.

Single vineyard Where a single vineyard is named, 100% of the grapes must have come from that vineyard.

Quality Terms

Variety Where a single variety is mentioned on the label, the wine must contain no less than 85% of that variety. Where two or more varieties are blended, the dominant grape must be listed first with the others following.

Vintage Where a vintage year is indicated, at least 85% of the grapes must have come from that year.

Bottle-fermented For sparkling wine this indicates the wine was fermented in bottle then disgorged to a tank under pressure before being re-bottled—a slightly less labor-intensive sparkling wine method.

Traditional method For sparkling wine, this indicates the wine was made in the style normally associated with champagne: fermented, riddled, and disgorged in the same bottle.

SOUTH AFRICA

Geography

Wine of Origin A program to recognize and protect wines from distinct geographical places.

Estate The wine must have been grown, made, and bottled on the same contiguous estate vineyard and winery.

Ward A very clearly demarcated geographical area that has been identified as having distinctive influencing factors such as soil type and climate. For example, Constantia.

District Similar to a ward but with a wider definition marked out by geographical features; it may have a more diverse range of soils and climates within the area. For example, Robertson.

Region Usually tied to an existing named region covering a much wider area, such as the Breede River Valley.

Quality Terms

Variety Where a single variety is mentioned on the label, the wine must contain no less than 85% of that variety. Where two or more varieties are blended, the dominant grape must be listed first with the others following.

Vintage Where a vintage year is indicated, at least 85% of the grapes must have come from that year.

Cap Classique A name reserved for sparkling wines from the Cape made in the traditional (Champagne) method.

Vin de Constance A naturally high-alcohol sweet wine from the Muscat de Frontignan (Muscat à Petits Grains). It is from the ward of Constantia and is made from grapes that have dried on the vine, rather than having been affected by botrytis

NEW EUROPEAN LABELING LAWS

Since August 1, 2009, new European Union wine-labeling laws have been in place. In practice, little will change in terms of what you will see on the shelf, but there are a few important things to know. The reforms are intended to standardize labeling practices across an increasingly large and diverse European Union, where each country has been taking its own very particular approach to wine labels. The reforms state that wine quality will be based on origin, with Protected Designations of Origin (PDO) and Indications Géographiques Protégées (IGP), in English, Protected Geographical Indications (PGI), clearly indicated on the label.

This does not mean that you will start seeing these acronyms on labels. All of the well-established traditional national labeling programs (such as AOC for Appellation Contrôllée in France, DO for Denominación de Origen in Spain,or DOC for Denominazione di Origine Controllata in Italy) will be kept and protected. Also, certain traditional terms and bottle shapes will continue to be protected. The big difference is that the ability to write the vintage and the grape variety on the label has now been extended to all wines—even those without PDO/IGP status, more commonly known as "table wines".

Country-specific amendments
Specific amendments have been made to take into account existing countries' anomalies. For example, the Prädikat system in Germany, where wines are labeled according to sugar level, rather than origin, will continue to be used for the wines, but alongside new regional protected designations of origin.

Above all of these traditional terms, a new protection has been introduced at European level applying to a wide range of consumable products, such as Parmesan cheese or Iberian ham, known as Appellation d'Origin Protegée (AOP). It does not replace the current country-level systems, but sits above them, and reforms some of the barriers formerly imposed. The AOP also establishes procedures for protecting, objecting to, canceling, or modifying any country-level systems.

What will be on the label
For the wine consumer, many of these changes will be invisible. You may see a few changes on wine labels, but not many. For example, from January 2011, you will begin to see "Contains albumin" if the wine contains any derivatives of egg or milk products. And you may see the term "European Community Wine" if the wine is made from a blend of grapes of several different EU countries. You will also see the term IGP replacing the old Vins de Pays system. This is because the EU wants to standardize protection of all local products, not just wine, and the term IGP will apply to various other food and drinks also.

Finally, do bear in mind that increasingly across Europe, the front label contains the bare minimum of information, to keep the design clean and simple, and most of these changes will be found on the back label.

Abfüllung German for bottled. On a label it indicates where the wine was bottled and can give hints about its potential quality. *See* Erzeugerabfüllung.

Acid, acidity Good acidity brings crispness or tanginess to a wine. The acidity comes mostly from the grape as tartaric and malic acids, but can include lactic acid, too, created by the natural malolactic conversion that most red wines and some whites undergo. Acidity is an essential element of a well-balanced wine, and gives it freshness as well as helping it to age well in some cases.

Aftertaste The taste sensation that lingers in the mouth and nose after swallowing a sip of wine. Also known as the "finish" and, in France, the *caudalies*, referring to the length of time in seconds that the aftertaste lingers. In general a long aftertaste, if pleasant, is a very positive sign of wine quality.

Aging A wine ages In barrels or tanks at the winery, and in bottles after it is ready to release. Some winemakers like to say that wine is alive, meaning that it changes with aging as a myriad of minute natural chemical reactions take place. Many wines, considered the best in the world, like fine Bordeaux, vintage port, and great white burgundies, improve with time in the bottle, as their fresh fruit and fermentation characters mellow and evolve, producing unique aromas and softer textures.

Airén White wine grape planted very widely in Spain, particularly in the hot central regions. Usually not known for making distinctive wines on its own, winemakers use Airén with other white and even red varieties. Some newer style white Airen wines can be fresh and nicely fruity.

Albana di Romagna White wine from Italy's Emilia-Romagna region that carries DOCG status, though few consider it a great wine. More famous for its smooth texture than for distinctive flavors.

Albariño Bracing, refreshing, and fragrant white grape variety from the Galicia region of Spain, known as Alvarinho in Portugal where it is one of the grape varieties used in Vinho Verde (green wine). Rarely made elsehwere in the world, Albariño is a classic, traditional white wine of Spain that has plenty of contemporary appeal.

Albariza An unusual white soil type found in the Jerez region of Spain. Made up of calcareous mineral components and sea fossils it is highly prized for growing the sherry varieties, as attested by the classification of vineyards containing Albariza as Jerez Superior.

Alcohol The intoxicating component of wine. Scientifically, ethyl alcohol or ethanol is a natural byproduct of fermentation as yeast convert the sugar in grape juice into alcohol and benign carbon dioxide. Physiologically, alcohol is the main reason that wine has inspired poets and lovers for thousands of years. The level of alcohol in wine derives directly from the amount of sugar in the grape juice, so the ripest grapes give the most alcoholic wines. Levels range from roughly 9% in a light German Riesling to 16% in a full-bore Australian Shiraz. Typical table wines contain about 13–14%. Alcohol gives wine its body, and much of its texture.

Alcoholic When used to describe a wine, it means the wine has too much alcohol to be well-balanced against its other constituents, including fruit flavor, acidity, and, in red wines, tannin.

Alicante Bouschet A supporting player in French and Californian wines, this grape variety is known for its intense red color and large crops. In most black grapes the juice is white or clear, but this variety gives red juice and, combined with the extra color extracted from the grape skins during fermentation, it is excellent at adding color to lighter-tinted reds.

Aligoté Most associated with the Côte Chalonnaise region in Burgundy, this white grape variety is also planted widely in eastern Europe. Aligoté in Burgundy makes dry wines with subdued flavors and a straightforward character.

Alvarinho Portuguese for Albariño. *See also* Vinho Verde.

Amabile Italian term that on a wine label means sweet.

Amarone New member of the elite DOCG club in Italy, Amarone della Valpolicella is a full-bodied, dry red wine made from the Corvina, Rondinella, and Molinara grape varieties, a portion of them being dried before fermentation to concentrate the sugar content.

Amelioration Process of making a wine better by intervention after harvesting the grapes. The winemaker may add acid, sugar, or water to correct an imbalance that existed in the grapes, subject to laws that vary by country and wine region. In many parts of Europe, for example, it is illegal to add water to a wine, but sugar may be added to make up for a short growing season or too little sunshine. In California, by contrast, water is often added to bring down the alcohol strength of many wines, while sugar addition (*See* chaptalization) is outlawed.

American Viticultural Area *See* AVA.

Amontillado Well-aged sherry that starts as a fino, but if during its aging in casks the protective layer of flor yeast floating on the top dies and sinks into the wine, then the cellar master fortifies it with neutral brandy to raise the alcohol high enough to preserve it for more extended aging. The result is a rich-textured, oxidized, nutty flavored, amber-colored wine with the strength of a port. A cask of this sherry was the subject of an eerie short story by Edgar Allen Poe.

Anbaugebiet Term for a quality wine-growing region in Germany, representing the A in QbA. There are 13 anbaugebiete.

Añejo Spanish term for an aged or mature wine; the term is loosely defined.

AOC Abbreviation for the French legal term that designates geographical origins for wine and other agricultural products—Appellation d'Origine Contrôlée—and often shortened further to AC. Most wine regions of France have AC status.

Apéritif Among wine drinkers the word for a pre-dinner drink normally indicates a dry, tangy, appetizing white wine or fortified wine that is thought to stimulate the appetite. Apéritif wines can be dry sherry, champagne, Cava, Prosecco, or other sparkling wine, crisp Sauvignon Blanc, or whatever one prefers—in Bordeaux the traditional apéritif was a sweet Sauternes.

Appellation In wine usage appellation refers to the name of the place where the grapes were grown. Appellations in most wine-growing countries are regulated by law to reassure the wine trade and wine consumers that they will get what they pay for. Only appellations approved by law are permitted on wine labels.

Appellation d'Origine Contrôlée *See* AOC

Aramon Black grape variety that was once among the most popular in France, grown particuarly in the Languedoc-Roussillon area of the south. Now declining.

Arena In wine parlance it refers to sandy soil in Spanish vineyards.

Arneis White grape variety from Piemonte, Italy, which can make excellent, dry, peach-scented wines with vivid acidity, when harvested at the right moment, and a pleasant tang on the finish. Common in Roero and Langhe districts.

Aroma The fragrance of a wine. The term is used to differentiate between smells detected by the nose and flavors tasted by the mouth or palate. It most often refers to the primary aromas coming from the grapes, the fermentation process, and the barrels in which the wine may have been stored. The term "bouquet" traditionally indicates the smells that develop later in the bottle as a wine ages.

Assemblage The assembly or putting together of a wine from component batches from different vineyards, grape varieties, barrels, and tanks. A classic example of assemblage takes place in Bordeaux when, several months after the harvest, the cellar master combines the young wines from different varieties such as Cabernet Sauvignon, Merlot, and Cabernet Franc to create a blend that will then be aged further before bottling.

Asti Spumante Produced near the town of Asti in northern Italy, this is a sweet, sparkling, rather low alcohol wine made from the flagrantly fragrant Moscato Bianco grape. Fine to drink with dessert, when many dry sparkling wines fall flat against sweet confections.

Astringency Mouth-drying sensation that is mainly caused by tannins in wine. A little astringency is good, as it cleans the palate after a bite of food and makes one anticipate the next bite, but too much creates a harsh, unpleasant feeling in the mouth particularly after swallowing. Many high-quality red wines, especially those intended to improve with age, have considerable astringency when they are young, but become softer over time.

Aszú Tokaji Aszú wines are sweet, late harvest Hungarian wines made from botrytis-affected grapes. *See also* Tokaji.

Aurora Versatile if undistinguished French-American hybrid grape variety planted mostly in the eastern US.

Ausbruch Style of wine made in Austria that resembles Hungary's famous Tokaji.

Auslese Literally "select harvest" in German, it indicates a wine made from fully ripened grapes and traditionally meant a sweet wine. Today, Auslesen (plural) wines can be dry or sweet, because the term officially describes the sweetness of the grapes at harvest time, not the style of the resulting wine. Modern German Auslesen are comparable in body and food pairing potential with many good-quality dry table wines of the world.

Autolysis What happens when a wine is left to age on the lees, or dead yeast cells, remaining in a barrel, tank, or bottle after the fermentation. Long a factor in enhancing the flavor of sparkling wine, autolysis is frequently used today in white wines (and even red ones such as Pinot Noir) intended to be complex in flavor. Autolysis adds richness to the wine's texture and give aromas of bread dough and toast. It is a natural step in barrel fermentation of Chardonnay and other grapes. Winemakers can amp up the process by regular stirring of the lees (*see bâtonnage*) to distribute them throughout the barrel.

Auxerrois Grape variety name that is used for very different varieties. In the Cahors region of France growers call their Malbec or Côt grapes Auxerrois. In Alsace it refers to a white variety.

AVA Wine-growing area (or appellation) recognized by the US government, and often shown on wine labels to verify that a certain percentage of grapes used to make that wine were grown in that area. An AVA does not indicate wine quality nor regulate vineyard and winery practices, as appellations often do in Europe. An AVA only guarantees the origin of the grapes.

Bacchus Ancient Roman god of wine and intoxication, known as Dionysus to the Greeks. Also, a modern white wine grape variety developed in Germany

from Müller-Thurgau and a cross of Sylvaner and Riesling. This *Vitis vinifera* variety is grown in Franken, England, and elsewhere.

Baco Noir Black grape variety popular among wine-growers in the eastern United States that generally makes medium-bodied local wines. As a French-American hybrid, it survives the cold winters and humid summers.

Balance, balanced A much-discussed quality of wine that is difficult to explain, but enjoyable to taste. A wine is balanced when its component attributes of fruit flavor, acidity, tannins, body, and so on enhance rather than overshadow each other. A Châteauneuf-du-Pape may have extra rich fruit flavors, relatively high alcohol, and rather thick tannins, but if they achieve balance then the wine remains harmonious. Conversely a Riesling from the Saar Valley of Germany balances lean, spicy fruit flavors with fresh acidity, minimal tannin, and low alcohol.

Balling A scale for measuring the percentage of sugar in fermenting grape juice. *See also* Brix.

Balthazar Poetic name for a giant 3.2 gal (12 liter) wine bottle rarely seen outside Champagne cellars and glamour-striving restaurants.

Banyuls This French sweet wine is a gem of the wine world, made from late-harvested Grenache grapes around the village of Banyuls near the Mediterranean coast. Concentrated, chocolate-like flavors, a luxurious texture, fulll body, and lingering finish make it memorable.

Barbera Italian black grape variety known mostly for deep-colored, nicely acidic, dry red wines. It can rise above the normal in a few places, such as the Piemonte region of Northwest Italy, where it carries its own appellations of Barbera d'Alba and Barbera d'Asti. Careful cultivation and barrel aging can tranform it into a world-class beverage that commands rather high prices and can age well for several years.

Barrel Traditional, portable wooden container for holding wine, almost always made of oak. The typical size holds about 60 gals (225 liters). Barrels were first used for storing and transporting wine, as they were for many other goods from pickles to gunpowder. The semioval shape makes them easy to roll and steer. Winemakers eventually discovered that barrels of different sizes, shapes, ages, and wood origins diversely affected the flavor of the wines they held. Today barrels are used mostly for their ability to enhance the texture, color, and flavor of wine. Made from French, eastern European, and American oak, they are often a winemaker's biggest yearly investment. A new barrel gives flavor for about three years after which it is a "neutral" barrel that may still

be useful for storing and softening a wine witout imparting oak flavors

Barrel aging After fermentation, most traditional style red wines, as well as some white wines, undergo a period of maturation in oak barrels before bottling. Contact with the wood lends additional wide-ranging flavors to the wine, described in such terms as vanilla, spice, smoke, even coconut and chocolate. During a period ranging from a few months to several years, small amounts of oxygen enter the wine, aiding the many subtle chemical changes that naturally occur in the young wine.

Barrel fermented While many wines are aged in barrels, some are also fermented in the barrel. Chardonnay, in particular, has long been fermented in barrels in its traditional home of Burgundy. Barrel fermentation can deepen the texture of a Chardonnay, Viognier, or other white wine partly due to the oak contact and partly due to the presence of the yeast cells and later the dead yeast cells, or lees, which contribute to the wine's texture and complexity. A few winemakers today are also fermenting their red wines in small barrels to increase their quality.

Barrique French term for an oak barrel made in the standard small size, holding about 60 gals (225 liters).

Basket press Traditional type of wine press in which the grapes are held in a cylindrical basket made of wood slats or a metal mesh, and force is applied from the top down to press out the juice. Considered a gentle press that does not squeeze the grape skins and seeds so hard that harsh flavors are released into the wine.

Bâtonnage Stirring the lees from the bottom of a barrel or tank with a "bâton" or similar tool to improve a wine's texture and flavor by increased contact with the dead yeast cells and bits of grape skin that make up this sediment.

Baumé Term for specific gravity (sugar reading), used in France, Australia, and New Zealand.

Bereich Designation for a wine district in Germany that is smaller than a region but larger than one vineyard site.

Bianco Italian for white, or white wine.

Big Not the literal size of a wine, but its imagined magnitude. A big wine is not always a good wine. The term often refers to a high level of alcohol, a rough or thickly tannic texture, and robust ripe flavors.

Biodynamic A method of growing grapes and other crops related to organics, and which is increasingly popular among ambitious wine-growers internationally, who seek to maximize the quality of their grapes and draw extra attention to their brands. Biodynamics limits chemical fertilizers and pesticides, and requires attention to natural cycles including the phases of the moon, and the preparation of natural composts and "teas" with which to spray the vines and enhance the soil. The method evolved from the teachings of Rudolf Steiner.

Black rot Fungal disease that attacks common varieties of wine grapes and can destroy crops if not prevented with fungicides and careful farming practices. So-called because of the dark color that affected plants acquire.

Blanc de Blancs A white wine, often a sparkling wine, made from white grape varieties. Literally "white of whites."

Blanc de Noirs White wine made from black grapes, most often applied to sparkling wines. In Champagne it refers to the lightly colored wine produced from Pinot Noir and Pinot Meunier—black grapes that give red wine when fermented in the table wine style. For Blanc de Noirs, winemakers press the grapes immediately after picking to separate the clear juice from the dark skins before the juice starts to darken from contact with the skins. After fermentation and aging the resulting wine is light gold or at the most lightly pink.

Blaufränkisch Black grape variety. *See* Lemberger.

Blending Essential winemaking practice that combines separate lots of wine into one that will be bottled and sold. Blending can involve wines from different grape varieties that have been fermented separately, diverse lots of the same variety, wines bought from other sources, etc. The winemaker can soften, stiffen, add color and texture, hide defects, highlight attributes or simply stretch a given lot of wine to create more quantity by blending. *See also* Assemblage.

Blush Wine American term for a form of rosé: light-colored, usually sweet, and simple wines that are pink in color, such as white Zinfandel.

Bocksbeutel German word for an unusual shape of wine bottle—a flattened oval—used in Franken and occasionally elsewhere in Europe.

Bodega On wine labels this Spanish term means winery or wine cellar.

Body Perceived weight of a wine, determined largely by alcohol content. Light-bodied wines are usually under 12% alcohol, medium-bodied, roughly 12–13.5%, and full-bodied above that. Body gives a good hint about food-matching suitability, in that light-bodied wines often pair with more delicate foods and heavier wines with richer dishes.

Bonarda Name used promiscuously for at least three different black grape varieties in Italy and one in Argentina, where it is one of the most widely planted.

Bordeaux Mixture Fungicide used widely in European vineyards to control mildew damage to vines.

Bordeaux varieties Five grape varieties are considered to be classics for red wine in the Bordeaux region and for winemakers around the world emulating Bordeaux: Cabernet Franc, Cabernet Sauvignon, Malbec, Merlot, and Petit Verdot. Merlot is the most widely grown in the region, but the tradition is to blend two to five varieties to achieve complexity in the wine and to outwit the whims of nature by using a blend of early ripening and later ripening grapes, so that if a downpour during flowering or an early fall rain damages one or two varieties, the others may save the vintage.

Botrytis In its malignant form this fungus, also known as gray rot, can spoil a grape crop. But when it affects ripe bunches of certain grapes destined for dessert wines, it earns the name noble rot. Full name *Botrytis cinerea*, it is the catalyst for the great sweet wines of Sauternes in Bordeaux made largely from Sémillon, and the trockenbeerenauslese wines of Germany made largely from Riesling, and others. The fungus grows readily in humid, warm weather, and does its best work by weakening the skins of the berries, letting moisture out while concentrating the sugar and flavor components. In almost all table wine vineyards, the grower sprays sulphur or other fungicides on the vines to prevent this gray rot from forming.

Bottle The glass bottle remains the most common packaging for wine, despite the increasing popularity of wine distributed in boxes, cartons, pouches, and cans. The weight of bottles used is an environmental issue, with most manufacturers now offering lighter versions. The standard international bottle size is 750ml, holding the equivalent of five generous glasses.

Bottle aging Many wines are aged at the winery in tanks or barrels before bottling, but a wine's flavor evolution continues in the bottle. Perhaps 95% of the world's wines only go downhill in quality after a few months in the bottle, but a few of the classic types such as classified-growth Bordeaux, Barolo, vintage port, and champagne, late harvest Riesling and the top California Cabernet Sauvignons improve in the bottle for 5–10 years. Very rare examples continue to transform favourably for many decades. Storage in a cool, dark place with a consistent temperature and horizontal placement of the bottles to keep the corks wet are the ideal conditions for bottle aging.

Bouchonné French term for "corked" in the sense of a bad cork that has spoiled the wine via contamination with TCA (trichloroanisole) the common cause of cork taint. *See also* Corked.

Bouquet A flowery term that refers generally to a wine's aroma. When used as "bottle bouquet" it is more specific and descriptive of the aromatic evolution that

occurs in some wines over time. In those few classic wines that improve with age, straightforward smells of the grapes, the fermentation, and the oak barrels in which the wine aged, transform into more complex and unusual aromas that vary from type to type.

Brachetto Black grape variety that has its own appellation in the Piemonte region of Northwest Italy, Bracchetto d'Acqui. The resulting wine is a very fruity, light, slightly carbonated rendition.

Breathing What a wine does when the bottle is opened, and the wine is poured into glasses, or even better, into a decanter or pitcher. This movement aerates the wine, mixing oxygen into it and encouraging the wine's aromas and flavors to open and expand. The process is most helpful for young red wines, because it semisimulates the process of aging, and can enhance the drinking experience. Note that simply removing the cork or cap for a few minutes allows practically no breathing to take place.

Brix Scale that winemakers use to measure the proportion of sugar in grape juice before and at harvest. During fermentation the reducing measurement becomes known as Balling. Technically it measures the dissolved solids in the juice, and reflects a percentage of sugar. So a wine with 25 degrees Brix has 25% sugar content, which in a dry wine will convert to alcohol at about 0.55 times the Brix number, or 13.75% alcohol.

Brunello di Montalcino Great red wine of Italy, made from Sangiovese Grosso grapes grown around the hill town of Montalcino in southern Tuscany and holding DOCG status. Brunellos are typically dark, tannic, extremely complex in flavor and needing several years to mature before they reach their peak of enjoyment. The grape variety is a type of Sangiovese, but making wines bigger and bolder than the Sangioveses of Chianti Classico a short distance away.

Brut Dry-tasting style of sparkling wine that is essentially the standard in most Western countries. While not totally dry in technical terms (meaning zero residual sugar in the wine) a brut wine must have less than 1.5% sugar. When balanced against the assertive acidity of champagne or other well-made sparkling wine, this level is perceived as pleasantly dry.

Brut Nature An extremely dry and rare style of Champagne, made without any sugar added at the *dosage* stage.

Bush vine A method of growing vines without trellising, usually in older vineyards in warmer regions. Sometimes referred to on wine labels. Known as *gobelet* in the French region of Beaujolais.

Butt A wooden cask or large barrel used primarily in the Sherry region of Spain and holding about three times as much wine, 172 gal (650 liter), as the standard small barrel.

Cabernet Franc Parent grape of Cabernet Sauvignon, along with Sauvignon Blanc. It is grown widely in the Loire Valley of France, in Bordeaux (particularly in St-Emilion) and almost anywhere that Bordeaux-style blended wines are made. It is one of the five classic black Bordeaux grape varieties. When vinified alone it gives frankly fruity, floral, and herbal aromas, medium-rich flavors, moderate tannins, and often a light finish. Loire versions tend to be lighter. The great red wines of Château Cheval Blanc in St-Emilion consist of a majority of Cabernet Franc, and may represent this grape's greatest expression.

Cabernet Sauvignon One of the great red wine grape varieties of the world, it originated in Bordeaux, France, as an accidental cross between the white grape variety Sauvignon Blanc and the black variety Cabernet Franc. When grown in the right places Cabernet Sauvignon makes complex, flavorful, long-lasting red wines that can improve in the bottle for decades. The wines are known for their deep cherry and black currant aromas and flavors, sometimes shaded by accents of herb, cedar, and other interesting elements. Among Cabernet Sauvignon-based wines are the five first growths of Bordeaux's Médoc and Graves districts: Château Latour, Château Lafite Rothschild, Château Mouton Rothschild, Château Margaux, and Château Haut-Brion. Napa Valley in the United States owes much of its fame to Cabernet Sauvignon wines from older wineries such as Beaulieu Vineyard as well as the more recent "cult Cabernet" producers such as Harlan Estate and Screaming Eagle. Australia, Chile, Washington State, Tuscany, and many other parts of the world have found that Cabernet Sauvignon makes excellent wine under their conditions, too. The variety is known for its small berries and thick skin, the combination of which increases the proportion of flavor compounds to juice when the wine ferments, and can result in extraordinary concentration in the wines.

Canaiolo Italian red wine grape planted widely in Tuscany and other parts of Italy such as the Marches and Sardinia, that has been declining in popularity but still covers a large area. It is blended with Sangiovese in some Chianti wines, is a component in Vino Nobile di Montepulciano, and is approved for blending in many other appellation wines.

Cannonau Name used on the Italian island of Sardinia for the Grenache black grape variety, also the stalwart of Châteauneuf-du-Pape. It makes a full-bodied dry wine in Sardinia.

Canopy management What vineyard owners and viticulturists do to the canopy, the upper parts of the grapevine where the green growth and fruit appear each year, to improve quality, resist pests, and disease, and adjust yield. This starts with the design of the trellis, and the annual pruning, but focuses on a particular year's growth, including such measures as removing unwanted shoots, pulling leaves, positioning shoots, green harvesting or thinning the grape clusters, hedging of canes, and other viticultural practices.

Cap The layer of grape skins that rises to the top of a container of grape must during fermentation, due to the carbon dioxide given off as a by-product of the yeast's action. This layer can become dry and stiff like a thick crust on top of the juice. It must be punched down, pumped over, or stirred back into the fermenting juice frequently in order to make high-quality wine, since it is the skins that contain most of the color and flavor components. How, and how often, a winemaker immerses the cap is an important variable in red winemaking.

Capsule Sleeve or cap that covers the cork and neck of a wine bottle, usually made of tin, plastic, or aluminum.

Carbonic maceration Process used in fermentation of certain black grape varieties, especially Gamay in the Beaujolais region of France. Sometimes Pinot Noir is vinified like this in various regions to gain extra freshness and overt fruitiness in the wine. It involves fermenting whole grape berries, that have not been crushed or pressed to release the juice. Essentially the fermentation takes place inside the berries. The grapes soak or macerate under a blanket of carbon dioxide released by the fermentation.

Carignan A black grape variety widely planted in Spain and southern France, but not distinguished as a source of high-quality wines and often blended with other varieties as way to fill or stretch the quantity of a wine. Its plantings have been reduced drastically in the last 20 years in the Languedoc-Roussillon region of France. Small plantings exist in California and other regions, too. Spelled Cariñena in Spain, Carignano in Italy, and Carignane in California.

Carmenère A late-ripening black grape variety seen most often on Chilean labels, but known to come from France. Chilean wineries brought Carmenère into the spotlight as their mystery grape in the 1990s when they discovered that large plantings of what they thought was Merlot was really Carmenère. It can and does make excellent, dark-colored wines that bear a family resemblance to Merlot and Cabernet Sauvignon, also Bordeaux varieties. Once a major grape variety in Bordeaux and possibly more important than Cabernet Sauvignon, the vines came to Chile in the 19th century. It is rarely seen in Bordeaux today.

Case production The annual output of a particular wine or winery expressed as 12 bottle cases of 750ml bottles, or the equivalent—2.4 gals (9 liters).

Cask wine Container, almost always wooden and usually larger than the common 60 gal (225 liter) barrel. In Australia the term can also refer to a box of wine.

Catawba North American pink grape variety with native *Vitis labrusca* parentage that was a workhorse of old-school winemaking in New York, Ohio, and other eastern regions. It is still used for sweet, sparkling, and dry wines, and imparts a strong, jelly-like labrusca flavor.

Caudalie French term for the length of the aftertaste or finish that lingers in one's mouth after swallowing a sip of wine, measured in seconds.

Cava Clever coinage for sparkling wines made in Spain and bottle-fermented in the style of true champagne from France. Meaning "cave" or "cellar" it aptly represents the use of cool storage conditions for the sparkling wine as it undergoes its second fermentation. This occurs in individual bottles, giving the characteristic carbonation and subtle bread dough flavors as the wine ages on its yeast. Made mostly in the Penedès region and from the grapes Parellada, Macabeo, and Xarel-lo, Cava is one of the world's best bargains in carefully made sparkling wine.

Cave Some wine storage cellars are literally caves in the English sense of the word, as in Bordeaux's Château Ausone. But in French, the word *cave* is a broad term that means wine cellar and or winery. Caves represent the best natural conditions for storing wine, as deep ones usually maintain a constant temperature, rather high humidty, and darkness.

Cayuga White White grape variety of North America, developed by New York's Cornell University, which can make flavorful dry wines and sparkling wines.

Cellar Has multiple meanings in wine parlance, but always means a place suitable for storing wine. Cellar is a synonym for winery in many English speaking regions, and is equivalent to the French *cave* in that sense. Cellar can also refer to a wine storage room in or under a restaurant or private home. As a verb, "to cellar" means to hold a wine in barrel, tank, or bottle until it reaches a suitable maturity.

Cement tanks What is old is new again in cellars around the world as a minority of quality-oriented winemakers use tanks of various shapes and sizes made of cement in which to ferment wine. Winemakers praise the dense material for its insulating properties, which tend to keep fermenting grape musts from varying quickly in temperature, and giving more control to the winemaker.

Cépage French term for grape variety.

Chai A storage place for wine on the premises where it is fermented or bottled, typically for wine aging in barrels. Most common in Bordeaux, where many traditional châteaus use one *chai* for wines of the most recent vintage and another for the previous vintage until it is bottled. Usually more of an underground room or hall than a cave or tunnel.

Chambourcin French-American grape variety that makes good-quality wines in eastern North America and in France.

Chancellor Seen on labels of red wine mostly in eastern North America, this black grape variety is a French-American cross used mostly for red and rosé table wines.

Chaptalization The addition of sugar to grape juice in order to aid fermentation and add extra alcoholic strength to a wine. Since yeast converts sugar to alcohol and carbon dioxide during fermentation, adding sugar means adding potential alcohol. Traditional way to improve a wine grown in climatic or weather conditions—as in Northern Europe—that prevent full sugar ripeness in the grapes as the growing season ends. Chaptalization is legal in many such areas, and illegal in others, mostly where a sunny climate and long growing season make it unnecessary.

Character Can mean simply the overall taste impression of a wine, but sometimes refers to an agreeable personality in a wine that reflects its unique combination of aromas, flavors, body, texture, and finish.

Chardonnay One of the most popular wines and most widely planted grape varieties in the world. Chardonnay wines tend to have flavors of apple, lemon, and even butter, and to a richness, viscosity, and full body that sets them apart from more lean, tart varietals. While not having the most overt or memorable flavor characteristics, Chardonnay wines tend to express their growing environment or terroir very well. In the Burgundy region of France where the great white burgundies of Montrachet, Meursault, and Chablis are all made from this variety, they show perceptibly different personalities. Chardonnay is also the principal white variety in champagne and the signature white wine of California and Australia.

Charmat A method of producing sparkling wine in bulk that is less expensive and time consuming than the bottle-fermented process which is traditional in Champagne and has spread to other quality sparkling wine regions around the world. Wines made by the Charmat process tend to be inexpensive, and can be enjoyable, but do not present the same flavor complexity and delicate effervescence of bottle-fermented wines.

Charta An association of wine producers in Germany's Rheingau region who regulate their own wines to assure high quality standards. Members' wines are bottled in distinctive tall brown bottles with the Charta symbol of double arches in relief on the glass. Founded in 1983, the association requires that all wines labeled Charta be made from Riesling grapes, and that the wines meet strict standards of low sweetness and high acidity for balance. Members organize tasting panels to blind-taste each Charta wine three times before approving it, and require extended months of bottle aging before release. The Charta merged with the Verband Deutscher Prädikatsweingüter in 1999.

Chasselas Grape variety for white wines most closely identified with Switzerland, but also planted in parts of France, Germany, Italy, and other regions. Chasselas goes by other names in some parts of Switzerland, including Fendant in the Valais, and Weisser Gutedel in Germany. The resulting wine is generally soft in texture without a strong, specific flavor profile.

Château "Castle" or "grand house" are good English synonyms for the word itself, while in wine usage château can mean more. The term is most often used for Bordeaux wines that are grown on one property, traditionally represented by an image of the estate's château on the label.

Château-bottled Has a specific meaning implying, but not guaranteeing, high quality in a wine. Château-bottled wines are grown, fermented, aged, and bottled on the same property. It means that grapes or wines from other properties and other regions have not been blended into the wine.

Chef de cave French for "cellar master," or chief winemaker, the person directly in charge of winemaking at a given facility.

Chenin Blanc Classic white grape variety from France that produces a wide range of wine styles from fresh, crisp, and dry, to sparkling, and sweet. Best known in the Loire Valley, Chenin Blanc is planted in many other countries including South Africa (where it is used mostly for dry table wines called Steen) and the United States, where it makes mostly inexpensive and bland table wine in California. Grown in cool regions, and with yields kept relatively low, it has a characteristic fruity, aromatic character reminiscent of Anjou pears or crisp apples, with floral accents.

Cinsault Also spelled Cinsaut (in South Africa), it is a red wine grape variety widely planted in southern France, particularly the Languedoc, and is one of the 18 varieties approved for the wines of Châteauneuf-du-Pape in the Southern Rhône, and appearing in some Côtes du Rhône blended wines. Often compared to Grenache, Cinsault can make full-bodied but not particularly tannic dry red wines, and is also popular for rosé. In South Africa, it was called Hermitage, and when crossed with Pinot Noir created South Africa's unique variety of Pinotage. Cinsault has been an important variety in Lebanon, North Africa, and Corsica.

Clairette For white, red, rosé, and sparkling wines, this is a term used across France's southern wine regions, and it is very confusing. The grape variety Clairette Blanche has the best claim to the term, probably. It has grown in the Mediterranean districts of France for centuries, particularly the Rhône, Provence, and Languedoc, and tends to produce a deep yellow-colored, sometimes oxidized style of white wine. Clairet is a semirosé wine made in Bordeaux from black grapes. Clairette de Die is a traditonal sparkling wine of southern France, and the list goes on.

Claret Traditional English term for dry red wines from Bordeux. Still used in some circles as a synonym for Bordeaux wine, or wines blended from traditional Bordeaux varieties, it stems from a time when Bordeaux was prized as a light, "clear" red wine.

Clarify *See* Fining.

Classico Means what it sounds like: an Italian wine of a classic origin, from a wine region or small district known for producing the best wines of a type. So, Chianti Classico is a geographic area and a higher quality subset of Chianti. Soave Classico is at least theoretically a step above Soave, and so on. The term is codified in the DOC regulations of the country.

Classification of 1855 Quality ranking of Bordeaux estate wines that named the best château properties as Premier Crus, or first growths, and established four other tiers of quality classification. The hierarchy is still followed in large measure today.
The 1855 classification was based on the market value of wines at the time, in preparation for the Exposition Universelle de Paris. It classified only the red wines of the Médoc district, the exception being the first growth Château Haut-Brion in Graves. The sweet wines of Sauternes and Barsac were also classified at that time.

Classified growth *See* Cru Classé.

Clean Descriptive term that indicates a fresh, well-made wine with no defects, but not necessarily with much personality.

Climat Vine-growers in Burgundy use this term to designate specific vineyard sites and for subsections of vineyards.
It means the piece of land referred to is a site well-suited for wine-growing and the characteristics of soil, exposure, and microclimate that come with that land. Very similar to "terroir."

Clonal selection The practice of carrying forward favorable genetic material from an existing grapevine to new vines or a whole new vineyard grown from cuttings of that vine. Vines are planted by cuttings, not by seeds, so when the vineyard owner selects an especially well-performing grapevine from which to cut one-year canes, each bud on which can grow a whole new vine, he is selecting from a particular clone of the grape variety. Individual vineyard owners and grapevine nurseries may propagate thousands of new plants this way over time.

Clone Wine grapes are differentiated by species, then by varieties, then by clones. Multiple clones are created by mutations of individual vines, giving slightly different traits to the wines made from them, such as thicker skins on the grapes that add more concentrated flavors and deeper colors, looser grape clusters that might discourage mildew, and so on. The traits are preserved via clonal selection, when a grape grower takes buds from those vines and propagates new vines directly from them. Pinot Noir is particularly famous for its clonal variety. While many Bordeaux-style wines result from the blending of compatible grape varieties, such as Merlot, Cabernet Franc, and Cabernet Sauvignon, producers of red burgundy and other Pinot Noir wines often use a variety of clones to add layers of flavor to the wine.

Clos French for enclosure. Often refers to a walled or fenced vineyard.

Cloudy Murky appearance in a wine, almost never a good sign.

Cloying Overly sweet. Wines can be very sweet but not cloying if they are balanced by equally strong acidity.

Coarse Describes a wine that lacks finesse. It is likely to have a rough mouthfeel from the presence of tannin and/or acidity that is not sufficiently balanced by viscosity and flavor.

Cold soaking Allowing harvested grapes or crushed must for red wine to rest at a cool temperature for a period of hours or a few days before starting fermentation. This maceration increases the amount of color and flavor extracted into the juice before the alcoholic fermentation.

Cold stabilization Technique in the winery to eliminate the possibility of natural potassium tartrate crystals forming later in wine bottles. The wine is typically cooled in refrigerated stainless steel tanks to force the crystals to form and precipitate out before filtration and bottling.

Colheita "Vintage" or "crop" in Portuguese. Also describes a port or madeira made from one vintage and aged for several years in casks before bottling. Not the same as vintage port, however.

Colombard Neutral white grape used for base wines for the French brandies of Southwest France, Cognac, and Armagnac. Colombard lacks a strong varietal character, which is preferred for a wine that will be distilled into brandy, and can produce large crops. It is approved for white Bordeaux wines and for Gascony table wines. Called French Colombard in California, this variety has been grown for decades to make inexpensive, almost generic white jug wine. It is also grown in South Africa and Australia.

Color Most wines are classified as either white, rosé, or red in color. Within those color categories lie many nuances, however, and winemakers and wine writers use all of them. White wines range from a very pale green or yellow to bright gold and amber, especially after extended aging. Rosés can be light pink, salmon, and even bright red. Red wines are normally deep red-purple or almost black with a red ring visible at the rim of the glass. Wine types all have characteristic colors, and the variations give clues to the wine's potential quality and age. Red wines lighten in color with age, and white wines darken.

Commune Describes a village and the surrounding area in French wine regions. Similar to township or parish in English.

Concord The common grape-jelly grape, native to eastern North America. This big-berried, dark-skinned black grape can be and is used for wine, but its strong flavors are so different from the traditional European wines that Concord wines are difficult for consumers to appreciate.

Consorzio A consortium or association of wine producers in Italy that often is formed to regulate and promote the quality of a district's wines.

Cooperage Means either a company that crafts wooden wine barrels and casks, or a collection of these vessels, as in an individual winery.

Co-operative An association of wine-grape growers that operates winery facilities to process their grapes, then ferment, age, and sometimes market the resulting wines. Such member-owned wineries enable grape growers to share equipment and expertise that they might not be able to afford on their own.

Cork In wine, a bottle stopper made from the bark of the cork oak tree. Today, natural corks remain very popular, but are just one bottle closure option among many including screwcaps, synthetic cork-like stoppers, glass stoppers, and others.

Corkage The fee a restaurant charges to allow customers to bring a bottle of wine from home to consume at the restaurant.

Corked, corky Omnipresent misnomer for a wine spoiled by the moldy odor of trichloroanisole. Also known as TCA, this taint can develop in corks, in wood barrels, in cardboard within a winery and readily spreads to the wine, spoiling or at least dampening its aromas and flavors. It is always appropriate to return a corked bottle to the wine waiter or wine merchant who sold it, for a refund.

Corkscrew A device for removing wine bottle corks. It normally includes a spiral "worm" to pierce and grab the cork while it is levered out.

Cortese This white wine grape variety is perhaps best known for making the elegant white wines of Gavi in Northeast Italy. It is used in many DOC and DOCG wines from Piemonte and Lombardy.

Corvina Italian black grape variety that gives Valpolicella and Bardolino wines their nervy structures and cherry-like flavozscvrs. While these two are often light reds, Corvina can make concentrated, full-bodied Amarone wines when the grape bunches are partially dried before crushing and fermenting, and also as a stand-alone rich red wine when carefully grown and aged in small barrels. Also known as Corvina Veronese.

Cosecha Spanish for vintage year.

Côt, Cot See Malbec.

Côte Means hillside or slope in French, which in general has proven to be the ideal terrain on which to grow wine grapes. Often seen on wine labels to indicate a broad area of vineyards, such as Côtes du Rhône in the Rhône Valley and Côte d'Or in Burgundy.

Cotnari Traditional sweet white wine from Romanian Moldavia that is made from botrytis-affected grapes, and also the name of the district where it is grown.

Coulure The imperfect flowering of the immature grape clusters, resulting in fewer berries per cluster, which lowers the yield for that season. Conversely, it often can improve wine quality because the yield is lower and the vines can ripen the grapes more fully, and because the clusters are looser, air can circulate through and the risk of mildew is decreased.

Courtier A wine broker in France, especially one in Bordeaux, who brokers deals between wine producers and the négociants who may buy their wine.

Crasse de ferre A clay subsoil rich in iron that is famous for enouraging excellent wines in parts of Pomerol, Bordeaux, including the property of Château Pétrus.

Cream sherry A sweet sherry that blends dry sherry such as oloroso with a very sweet one such as one made from Pedro Ximénez grapes.

Crémant French term for a sparkling wine that is not from the Champagne region. While many are simple and soft, others can be of excellent quality. Various wine-growing districts apply strict rules for crémant, dictating maximum yields, methods of harvesting, and approved grape varieties. Crémant du Loire, Crémant du Bourgogne, and Crémant du Limoux from the South of France are good examples.

Crianza Spanish term used to indicate a wine aged for a minimum period. For Rioja red wines it is at least two years, including six months in barrel, before it can be sold.

Crisp Attractively acidic and appetizing, a

trait particularly of good white wines.

Cross Genetic combination of two grapevine varieties that yields a new variety with different traits. Accidental crosses have occurred many times in the history of wine-growing, producing for instance, Cabernet Sauvignon as a cross of Sauvignon Blanc and Cabernet Franc. Many crosses are still produced today by nurseries, in the pursuit of vines that resist disease, pests, and/or adapt to difficult climates and soil conditions.

Cru French for "growth" but it more accurately indicates an individual vineyard property or plot, rather than the growth of the vines.

Cru Bourgeois Bordeaux wine estates of the Médoc originally classified in 1932 for their relatively high quality, but set under the Cru Classés. Some have earned prices equal to or greater than some of the original classified growths, and rival or surpass them in quality. Others are nice wines at reasonable prices. The Cru Bourgeois list was revised most recently in 2003. When 247 of the 490 applications were turned down, including 77 from the original list, a can of worms was opened. That revision was annulled in court, in 2007, amidst much controversy and infighting. The term is no longer a classification, merely an indication that the wine has reached a certain level of quality and châteaux are obliged to apply each year for the right to use the name.

Cru Classé A classed or classified vineyard in France. It has been officially singled out for the quality of its wine over time. In Bordeaux, Cru Classé properties range from first growth (Premier Cru) at the top end to fifth growth.

Crush To crush grapes is to squeeze or break open the berries just after harvesting to release the juice from the skins before fermentation. Generally red wine grapes are removed from the stems and crushed, then the mixture of juice, skins, and seeds (called the must) ferments together. White wine grapes are usually pressed first to squeeze out the juice, which is then fermented without the skins. "Crush" is also a reference to the harvest season, especially in California.

Crusted port A full-bodied port blended from multiple vintages that, like vintage port, develops sediment, or a crust, in the bottle over time and needs decanting before drinking.

Cryoextraction A way to make Icewine without naturally freezing temperatures in the vineyard. Grapes are harvested, then chilled with refrigeration equipment to below freezing before being pressed to release their juice. This binds up much of the water content of the juice and so increases the concentration of sugar and flavor in the remaining liquid.

Cultivar Alternate term for grape variety.

Custom crush A winery or facility that offers contract winemaking services to grape-growers and winemakers without their own equipment. It can be a specialist facility or an existing winery with spare capacity. Common term in North America.

Cuvaison The period of time that a young wine remains in a cask or tank (cuve in French) during and after fermentation, in contact with the grape skins and seeds. This contact is what gives a red wine most of its color, flavor, and tannin, since these traits come largely from the skins, and the juice absorbs them during this period. "Maceration" is a good synonym. Also the name of a Napa Valley winery.

Cuvée In French a tank or vat is a cuve. The wine in that tank is a cuvée. The term has a special meaning for sparkling wine, where it describes the best of the base wine that will undergo a second fermentation to create the carbonation and unique texture of the bubbly end product.

Débourbage French term for setting, meaning to let grape must settle so solids drop to the bottom. This is done with most white wines before fermentation.

Decant To draw the clear wine off its lees or sediment. This is done in the winery by siphon or pump for clarification of a young wine, and called "racking". In a restaurant or at home, decanting an older wine accomplishes the same goal, since a fine sediment often accrues in bottles of good wine after several years. Decanting before drinking also aerates young wines to soften their texture and amplify their aromas. Young wines should be decanted assertively to splash and aerate the wine as much as possible. An old wine with sediment should be stood upright a day before decanting, to allow the sediment to drop to the bottom. Then it must be uncorked without shaking or turning the bottle. Gently pour the wine into a decanter in one slow steady motion. Positioning a candle or small light behind the neck of the bottle while pouring enables one to see the sediment and know when to stop pouring.

Decanter Container into which a wine is decanted before serving. This can be as simple as a ceramic pitcher, or as elaborate as an expensive lead crystal decanter with glass stopper and silver trim. It is also the name of a long-running wine magazine from the UK.

DeChaunac French-American black grape variety widely planted in Ontario and the northeastern US.

Declassify Set aside a portion of wine in the winery as lesser quality. See also "Selection". It is a fundamental step in improving wine quality, separating the lesser quality lots from the better ones before blending and bottling. The winemaker may then use the declassified wine for a less-expensive bottling or perhaps sell it in bulk to another winery.

Deficit irrigation Practice in irrigated vineyards of giving the grapevines less than the maximum amount of water that they could use. This intentional stressing of the vines became popular in many New World vineyards in the past decade, as growers realized that vines with full water uptake were not ripening their grapes in the best way possible for quality wines.

Degorging See Disgorging.

Degree days Calculation used by grape growers to match grape varieties to regions with the optimum climate in which to grow them. Degree days represent the number of days during a growing season when the temperature is above 50°F (10°C) multiplied by the number of degrees over that limit on those days. First developed by Albert Winkler at the University of California, Davis, the degree days formula helped map potential vineyard sites as climatic regions 1 through 5, or coolest through hottest. For example, cool-climate varieties such as Riesling, Chardonnay, and Pinot Noir are best planted in Regions 1 or 2 sites, while Zinfandel, Grenache, and port varieties are suitable for Region 3 or 4.

Delicate An attribute of lightness in a wine, usually applied to white wines with lower alcohol and subtle flavors.

Demi-muid The term implies a medium-size barrel (based on old terminology), but at about 160 gals (600 liters) these are more than twice the size of the internationally utilized barrique, or small barrel.

Demi-Sec Means "half-dry" in French. In effect it means rather sweet, especially in sparkling wines including Champagne.

Denominación de Origen See DO

Denominazione di Origine Controllata See DOC.

Denominazione di Origine Controllata e Garantita See DOCG.

Dessert wine Sweet wines, sometimes also fortified to a higher alchol content than table wines. This covers a whole gamut of interesting wines, underappreciated by many wine drinkers today, and are delicious with dessert or as dessert themselves, after a meal. The group includes Sauternes from Bordeaux, late harvest Riesling from Germany, ports of many types, sweet forms of sherry and madeira, Banyuls from the south of France, Tokaji from Hungary, Icewine from Canada, and many more.

Dionysus The Ancient Greek god of wine, also known as Bacchus to the Ancient Romans. He personified the pursuit of pleasure and abandon.

Disgorging An important step in preparing bottle-fermented sparkling wine for the market. The process removes the dead yeast cells (lees) from the bottle, where a second fermentation has occured, so that the remaining wine is clean and clear of sediment. The longer a wine spends "on lees" before disgorging usually means a higher quality, more complex, and intricate wine. In fine champagne, some vintages age for years on their yeast and are only disgorged a few months before their release. The letters RD are sometimes used on a label to indicate recently disgorged.

DO Spanish appellation system, Denominación de Origen, which seeks to guarantee that a wine's origin is accurately portrayed on its label. Equivalent to the French AC system.

DOC Italy's category for wines that come from a specific growing region. This Denominazione di Origine Controllata is usually a good sign of wine quality, and wines with this designation are just one step under the most tightly controlled wines of origin, DOCG.

DOCG Stands for Denominazione di Origine Controllata e Garantita, and means controlled and guaranteed place of origin. DOCG indicates a wine whose provenance is as strictly controlled as any in Italy.

Dolcetto Most wine references refer to this red wine grape as making light and easy everyday wines. Dolcetto can be easy but it is rarely light; a deep ruby color, full aromas of fresh berries, and reasonably high alcohol add up to a substantial but not too tannic red wine. Identified mostly with the Piemonte region of Northwest Italy.

Domaine Term for a vineyard holding owned by one family or company, particularly in the Burgundy region of France, where it is common for a wine producer to own small vineyard plots in many different appellations.

Dornfelder Black grape variety that was developed in Germany. Now grown there and in other countries including the UK for its ability to produce red wines with deep color in cooler growing areas where traditional varieties might not succeed.

Dosage Process of adding a shot of sweetness and flavoring to a bottle-fermented sparkling wine just after disgorging and before corking and final packaging. Up to this point most quality bubblies have been aging in a bone-dry state, with no sugar left in the wine, and with high acidity. The dosage is often a sweetened reserve wine that adds complexity along with a touch of sugar.

Double Magnum Bottle containing 3 liters or the equivalent of 4 standard bottles. Most often found in Champagne, where the larger format enables the wines to age for longer.

Doux Sweet; used for still and sparkling wines.

Dry Lacking sweetness. Dry wines have fermented fully, to the point where virtually all the grape sugar has been converted to alcohol by yeast. Most table wines are dry, but

depending on the type of wine and local regulations and customs a wine described as dry might contain up to 1% residual sugar.

Dry farmed, dry grown In areas where irrigation of vines is common because of the dry summers typical of mediterranean climates such as California, Australia, and Israel, the term refers to those exceptional vineyards where vines grow without added water. In many traditional wine regions of Europe, however, dry farming has long been the norm because nature provides the irrigation through periodic rainfall throughout the growing season.

Dutchess North American white grape variety created from a cross of *Vitis vinifera* and *Vitis labrusca*. Rarely seen on good bottles of table wine.

Earthy A tasting term signifying an aroma of damp soil—a positive attribute in some complex red wines if other good qualities are present, and a negative one with regard to most other wines.

Edelfäule German term for *Botrytis cinerea*, the noble rot that shrivels and concentrates the flavors in ripe grapes when it appears under the right conditions near harvest time.

Edelzwicker Term used mostly in Alsace for a white wine blended from various grape varieties.

Egri Bikavér The traditional red wine of Hungary, with a name meaning "bulls blood of Eger". It has been blended from various grapes over the years, but focuses on Kadarka. It can be a decent red wine, but cannot shake its bloody image in western markets.

Eiswein Not difficult to translate as "Icewine." Orginally a German invention but now popular in Canada and elsewhere, Eiswein takes the late harvest dessert wine concept to the extreme. To make Icewine a grape grower leaves a section of his Riesling or Vidal Blanc vineyard unharvested until well into the winter, when the temperature drops far below freezing for an extended period, and the grapes partially freeze. Workers painstakingly harvest the grapes, the winemaker presses the semifrozen harvest and extracts mostly the sweet, extremely flavorful components of the berry leaving the watery component behind as ice in the press. It is nature's way of concentrating the grapes' flavor. The result is usually an extremely sweet but well-balanced wine that presents a quite different, more pristine taste experience than those of the botrytis-affected wines of Germany, Tokaji, or Sauternes.

Elbling Minor but very traditional white grape variety grown in Germany and Luxembourg that produces tart, usually low-alcohol wines.

Elegant Hard-to-define but very positive characterization of a wine. Means well-balanced, lighter rather than heavier, silky

rather than coarse, and long rather than short on the finish.

Eleveur In French, one who raises a wine to a higher level of quality. The meaning is similar to one who trains horses. Often seen hyphenated to négociant. A *négociant-éleveur* is one who buys already fermented wines from various growers or wineries, and then elevates them to a better state of quality through aging in barrels, blending with other wines, fining, and so on.

Enology The science of wine. Sometimes synonymous with winemaking, but usually indicating more knowledge of wine biochemistry. Oenology in UK.

Enologist Wine scientist, or qualified winemaker. Comes from the Greek word Oenos for wine. Oenologist in UK.

Enoteca Often translated as "wine library", this Italian term means a repository of wine. In Italy an enoteca is often a wine shop that may offer tasting and sales.

Enzymes Some winemakers add commercially produced fruit enzymes to their grape must before fermentation to enable easier extraction of color and flavor from the skins. Enzymes can also be added to aid settling of juice, for aroma extraction, and to expedite lees-aging.

Erben Seen in the names of many German wineries, it means "heirs".

Erstes Gewächs Term used for the highest level of quality wines from specific sites in the Rheingau region of Germany. Literally, "first growth" as in the Premier Cru designation of Bordeaux.

Erzeugerabfüllung Means bottled by the producer in German. It is a good if not foolproof indication of quality when seen on the wine label.

Essencia The highest classification of Tokaji Aszú sweet wines from Hungary. Essencia wines are very rare, made from an extreme form of "free run" juice that flows naturally out of the harvested botrytis-affected grapes before pressing.

Estate-bottled Used for American wines that are bottled by the owner of the vineyard where the grapes grew. It is a reassuring confirmation of the wine's authenticity, and often indicates higher quality than non estate-bottled wines. Many wineries buy grapes grown by other individuals or companies, and many also buy bulk wine made by others, then finish the wine and bottle it. An estate-bottled wine is essentially grown, fermented, aged, and bottled on the same property. However, this also applies to separate plots of land in the same American Viticultural Area, owned or leased by the same producer. Equivalent to château-bottled in France.

Estufa Hot storage area used in the making of madeira wines to achieve the desired level of oxidation and premature aging for which this wine type is famous. An *estufa* is designed to mimic the conditions in a ship's hold, sailing through warm seas, which originally created the unique flavor profile.

Extra brut A very dry champagne or other sparkling wine, made with just a drop of sweetness in the dosage. Drier than normal brut wines, but almost imperceptibly sweeter than the extremely rare Brut Nature wines.

Extra Dry Confusing term for champagne and other sparkling wines that are noticeably sweet. It arose from the evolution of champagne from very sweet to less sweet over several hundred years. When extra dry wines were first promoted they were drier than the prevailing demi-sec wines, which in turn had been drier than the previous style of champagne.

Extract Not a flavoring added to wine, as in many foods and beverages. Extract refers to the flavor, color, and texture components of a wine, derived from the grape skins, and are extracted during the winemaking process. Wines described as extracted tend to be bold, dark-colored (if red), viscous, and often high in astringent tannins.

Fat A wine is "fat" if its sweetness and/or body (alcoholic strength) overwhelms the acidity and tannins which otherwise would keep it in balance. It is a negative description in most table wines, but can be a positive in a sweet dessert wine or in an intentionally extreme red wine.

Fattoria Italian word related to factory, or production facility. It often functions as a synonym for winery.

Fermentation The natural process that makes all alcoholic beverages possible. It is conducted by yeast, the cells of which consume the sugar in grape juice and produce alcohol and carbon dioxide gas as by-products. Fermentation occurs readily in ripe grapes, as early humans must have discovered when they gathered grapes, stored them in a warm place in a gourd or clay jug and returned a week or two later to find that they had invented wine. Grapes will begin fermentation without human help, thanks to native yeast that exist in the environment, but that does not necessarily yield drinkable wine. Some winemakers still rely on wild yeast to make their wines, but most add cultured yeast to the crushed or pressed grapes to conduct a controlled fermentation that may last from one week to several, depending largely on the fermentation temperature and the style of wine desired. Fermentation is the most critical procedure of the winemaking year. Guiding it correctly ensures that good grapes are transformed into good wine. Lack of knowledge or care at this stage, however, can ruin the fruits of the harvest.

Fiasco In wine parlance it means, not a disaster, but a traditional straw-wrapped bottle of wine from Italy.

Filtering A great majority of the world's wines are filtered before bottling, to remove spoilage microorganisms and to clarify. Filtering can be light, merely to remove tiny bits of solids such as remnants of dead yeast or grape skins, or heavier to sterilize. The most common method involves pumping wine under pressure through a filtration medium such as fiber pads. Reverse osmosis and crossflow-filtration are newer methods that can remove alcohol and unwanted flavors. Some winemakers avoid filtration altogether to produce more natural wines, especially for expensive, ambitious wines from outstanding vineyard areas.

Finesse Fine-ness. Term used by winemakers, sommeliers, and wine writers usually to describe an otherwise indescribable combination of quality factors in a wine that makes it elegant or memorable.

Fining Process for clarifying wine, in which a fining agent such as gelatin, bentonite clay, milk or cream derivatives, or sometimes egg whites, is added to a wine in tanks or barrels. A winemaker stirs in the agent, waits for the agent to bond with proteins, tannins, or other unwanted substances in the wine, and then it precipitates out. The clear wine is then removed from the sediment. This can be done lightly as is the tradition in Burgundy, barrel by barrel with egg whites, or more heavily in large tanks with strong agents that can clean a wine quickly to prepare it for bottling.

Finish Aftertaste. Most high-quality wines leave a lingering pleasant taste in the mouth because of the concentration of flavor and textural elements. Winemakers and connoisseurs generally agree that the longer the finish, the better the wine.

Fino Perhaps the most appetizing style of sherry, dry and relatively light in body but dramatically flavorful and long on the finish due to its aging under a layer of flor yeast. A fino sherry makes a wonderful apéritif with cured olives, roasted almonds, and other tapas-type foods.

First growth A vineyard or winery of first rank, the English translation of the French Premier Cru. Five leading châteaux of Bordeaux carry this classification: in the Médoc region, Château Lafite Rothschild, Châeau Margaux, Château Latour, and Château Mouton Rothschild; in the Graves region, Château Haut-Brion. All but Mouton Rothschild were first ranked as such in the 1855 Classification, with Mouton being elevated in 1973, after decades of wine improvements and lobbying by owner Baron Philippe de Rothschild. There are three estates on the Right Bank of Bordeaux which are classified within their districts and often considered first growths as well: Château Pétrus in Pomerol, and Châteaux Cheval Blanc and Ausone in St-Emilion.

Fleshy Ample texture and body in a wine, as if it had flesh on its bones.

Flinty The smell of steel struck against flint to produce a spark. It shows up subtly in certain white wines and is considered an attractive trait, and a sign of authenticity. For example in Chablis (Chardonnay) or Sancerre (Sauvignon Blanc).

Flor A layer of yeast that forms on the surface of sherry when the barrels are left slightly under-filled to allow air space. The flor or "flower" yeast seals in the wine, preventing too much oxygen or other microorganisms from spoiling it, despite the head space in the barrel.

Flowering Grapevines do not produce obvious flowers like fruit trees, but they do go through a flowering phase, usually in May or June in the northern hemisphere, establishing the grape clusters for that growing season. The flowering period, or bloom, is critical for the development of the vintage; adverse weather, especially heavy rain or hail, can damage a portion of the tiny blossoms so they do not pollinate, thus reducing the number of grape berries that form, and ultimately the crop size. This can sometimes be good for wine quality, however, because fewer berries can mean better ripeness in each, and better ventilation through the grape bunch to discourage mildew.

Flûte A tall, narrow glass for sparkling wine, which shows the bubbles to great effect as they rise slowly (in a high-quality bubbly like champagne) from the bottom to the top. Interestingly, though flutes are elegant for apéritif sparkling wines, such as non-vintage brut, a broader glass with a shorter bowl, like a white wine glass, is best to get full enjoyment out of a special bottle, such as a vintage-dated brut or prestige *cuvée*.

Flying winemaker Term that came into vogue in the 1990s for a skilled winemaker who consults in different countries and especially on different continents. With clients in both northern and southern hemispheres, these winemakers have the opportunity to gain twice the harvest experience each year.

Folle Blanche Grape variety once popular in France for making brandy, but now declining.

Fortified wine A class of wine to which distilled spirits have been added to raise the alcohol percentage. This is often done during the fermentation to stop the yeast from completing its job, and thus retaining natural grape sugar in the wine. Port, sherry, madeira, and vermouth are traditional examples. These typically contain about 17–18% alcohol compared to 13–14% for table wine. Most are traditionally consumed before or after meal.

Foudre Much like the German word *fuder*, this French term represents a large oak barrel or cask.

Foxy Odd but accepted term used in

North America to describe the intense and characteristic aroma and flavor of wines made from the native *Vitis labrusca* species of grapes. Difficult to put into words, but easy to recognize this aggressive musky note in some old-school wines from eastern Canada and the midwestern and eastern US.

Frascati White wine made in and around the Italian town of Frascati. It is a blend of Trebbiano and Malavasia.

Free run The juice that flows freely out of the grapes at harvest time when they are stemmed and/or crushed, but before they are pressed.

Freisa Black grape variety from northwest Italy's Piemonte region that makes light red wines.

French-American hybrids These were orignally a solution to the phylloxera epidemic that devasted European and Calfornian vineyards planted with the European grape species of *Vitis vinifera* in the late 19th century. Since the native American grape species such as *Vitis labrusca* are resistant to the root louse phylloxera, grape breeders crossed labrusca varieties with vinifera varieties and created new rootstocks that resisted the root louse and, in some cases, powdery mildew, too. New hybrids have been added continously over the past 130 years, and are widely used in eastern North America as well as parts of Europe. *See also* Rootstock.

Frizzante A lightly sparkling wine from Italy, that has about half the pressure of a champagne. These can be red, as in Lambrusco, or white, as in Prosecco. You will not see a champagne-style cork and wire cage on many of these wines.

Frost The new shoots of grapevines are sensitive to frost in the first few weeks after bud-burst in the spring. A light frost, just at 32°F (0°C) rarely does damage, but at 28°F (-2°C) for a few hours, a real freeze can wreak havoc on the the new growth. The result is that affected shoots die off, and the vine pushes out new ones. But the new ones get a late start on the growing season, and rarely produce fruit that ripens properly or in enough quantity to please the grape grower before the fall rains and cold temperatures arrive. To prevent frost damage, vineyard owners use wind machines or helicopters to keep the cold air moving, burners in the vineyard, and water sprinklers to coat the shoots with a protective layer of ice which does not get as cold as the air might be.

Frühburgunder German grape variety; a mutation of Pinot Noir. Also known as Pinot Précoce or Early Pinot because it ripens earlier and is popular in cooler climates.

Fruity A positive description of most wines. What is the point in drinking a wine made from the fruit of the vine if one cannot taste the fruit flavor? Fruity aromas and flavors are much to be desired over earthy, woody, vegetative, or dirty notes in most table wines. However, a fine wine should go beyond mere fruitiness and add layers of other flavors to make it complete.

Fuder Large oak wine cask in Germany that holds about four times the wine that a typical wine barrel does. *See also* Foudre.

Full-bodied A wine that tastes full and strong. Body refers to the heft, texture, and viscosity of the wine in the mouth, and is directly related to the alcohol content. Full-bodied wines tend to be have 13.5% alcohol or higher.

Fumé Blanc The term was coined by the Robert Mondavi Winery in the 1960s to differentiate its oak-aged Sauvignon Blanc wines from the typically tank-fermented and tank-aged white wines of California at that time. The name means smoky white and recalled the Pouilly-Fumé wines of France's Loire Valley, also made with Sauvignon Blanc grapes. Many other California wineries took up the term for a time, but its use has now waned. The oak influence on a New World Sauvignon Blanc is hard to gauge based on the label.

Furmint A white wine grape associated most with Hungary, where it is important in the making of sweet Tokaji wines, which display generous honey and nut flavors. Furmint also grows in Austria and Slovenia.

Fût A French word for barrel that is used in Burgundy. Describes any wooden vessel of any capacity having bent sides and flat ends. It is synonymous with cask and barrique (Bordeaux).

Galestro Name for a light white wine produced in Tuscany and also the mineral-laden soil in many prized Chianti Classico district vineyards. The soil is mostly schist, rock composed of elongated slices, and easy draining, which is usually desired for quality wine.

Gallo Nero Means "black rooster" in Italian and is the symbol for the Chianti Classico Wine Consortium.

Gamay The grape variety of red Beaujolais wines, produced just south of the more celebrated Burgundy vineyards, and yielding a wide range of wines based on the vineyard location and winemaking methods. Simple Beaujolais is a light to medium red wine that once dominated Parisian cafes. Beaujolais Nouveau is a very fresh and juicy, weeks-old wine released in November each year. At the top are the the the higher-quality Beaujolais-Villages and the 10 Beaujolais *cru* from villages such as Morgon, Juliénas, and Moulin-à-Vent make excellent and sometimes ageworthy estate-bottled wines that rival fine burgundies.

Garagiste/garage wines Excellent wines made in recent years, primarily in Bordeaux, without the accoutrements of a château or official classification. Some are literally fermented in garages rather than traditional cellars.

Garganega Main white grape variety used in the Soave wines of the Veneto region of Italy. It does not have a strong personality, but the wines, especially Soave Classico, can be elegant and distinctive when grown in prime locations and carefully made.

Garnacha Usually refers to Garnacha Tinta, one of the great grapes of Spain. It is instrumental in forming the red wines of Rioja, Navarra, Priorat, Penedès, and elsewhere. Garnacha Blanca is the white version. Garnacha is the most widely grown black grape in Spain. It can make very flavorful but not overly tannic red wines, and tends toward full body. Known in France and elsewhere as Grenache.

Garrafeira Portuguese wine label term similar to Reserve.

Gewürztraminer White grape variety with distinctive pink skin that has few rivals for making wines with an instantly recognizable aroma, full body, and exotic floral flavors. The name incorporates gewürz (spicy) with Tramin (a town in Northern Italy). Alsace is home to most of the world's best Gewurztraminer wines (where it has no umlaut on the "u"), though vintners in Germany, Australia, New Zealand, California and other countries make it, too. The aroma is like roses, or some say lychees, and the fruit flavors are a bowl full of Comice pears and Fuji apples drizzled with honey.

Glasses Wine does taste better when sipped from a good glass, as Austrian glassmaker Georg Riedel and others have demonstrated many times. In general, it is better to have thin glass or crystal, a large, wide bowl and a rim that tapers in to concentrate the aromas that evaporate from the wine into the bowl's air space. Most white and sparkling wines are best sipped from a somewhat smaller-capacity glass with a more vertical shape than those used for red (*see* flûte). Smaller glasses are usually appropriate for apéritifs like sherry, and for sweet wines. A wine glass should be poured no more than one-third full to leave room to swirl the wine and for the aromas to gather in the bowl.

Glycerol Viscous liquid that forms in small quantities in wine during fermentation, and adds a sensation of sweetness and even richness of texture if present in high enough concentrations. Same as glycerine.

Goût "Taste" in French. Often used in the phrase "*goût de terroir*," which refers to the particular taste properties that a wine gets from the terroir (*see also* terroir) where the grapes were grown.

Governo Process used especially in the Chianti region to add extra body and sometimes sweetness to a wine, and to speed the completion of the malolactic conversion so the wine can be sold sooner. The cellar master sets aside a portion of the grapes to dehydrate for several weeks, thus boosting the proportion of sugar. He crushes or presses the grapes then adds the sweet juice to wine that has finished or nearly finished fermentation, to restart the yeast and warm the new wine, aiding the malolactic fermentation. It also gives a slightly fizzy texture to the wine from the new carbon dioxide created. Not practiced much today since the style of Chianti has becomer drier and more quality oriented.

Grafting Grapevines, like fruit trees and roses, adapt readily to the grafting of a fruiting variety onto a rootstock of a different species or variety. This is a necessity for vineyards using the traditional European *Vitis vinifera* in areas where the phylloxera louse is present in the soil because ungrafted vinifera vines can wither and die in a few years from phylloxera eating the roots. Phylloxera is ubiquitous across most vineyard areas of Europe, California, and eastern North America, but not all of the New World.

Gran Reserva Term used by Spanish wineries to indicate a red wine that has been aged for at least five years before it is sold (with a minimum of 18 months of that time in oak), and a white or rosé aged for at least four years. *Reserva* and *crianza* wines are aged for less time.

Grand Cru Literally "great growth" in French, meaning great vineyard. The terms denotes the top-rated vineyards in Burgundy (where there are 33 such) including Montrachet for white burgundy and Echézeaux for red burgundy, and in Alsace. The term is used in a different manner in St-Emilion (Bordeaux) and Champagne. The Grand Cru designation indicates the potentially outstanding quality of the wines made from these vineyards. Burgundy and Alsace hold the term Grand Cru above Premier Cru. In St-Emilion 53 properties are classified as Grand Crus, while 13 more are Premier Grand Crus (or "first great growths). *See* Premier Cru.

Grand Cru Classé Usage specific to wines from St-Emilion. *See* Grand Cru.

Grand Vin "Great wine" in French, used to indicate the top-quality wine of an estate where, frequently, more than one level of quality is bottled.

Grandes Marques Immodest French term used by an association of Champagne producers to distinguish their "great brands." Nearly all do make great top-end champagnes, along with often much larger quantities of basic wines.

Grape A small, naturally manufactured package of winemaking ingredients that contains juice, seeds, pulp, skin, and yeast. The grape is considered by many

to be the only source of true wine, and it is certainly the best suited, containing just enough sugar to transform itself with the help of yeast into a beverage whose alcohol level is high enough to kill any microorganisms harmfull to humans, but low enough to allow its regular consumption at mealtime.

Grauburgunder Pinot Gris in German.

Gravity flow Moving wine in the winery without using a pump. In the days before electric pumps, most wineries were designed to use gravity flow in transferring wine from fermenting tank to barrels and from barrels to bottling when the time came. Today, many vintners who can afford it also construct their facilities in vertical levels to take advantage of siphoning. An inexpensive way to achieve the same gentle transfer as gravity flow is to elevate small tanks and barrels with a motorized fork lift and then use gravity.

Gray rot Common name for botrytis bunch rot, especially when it is not wanted in a vineyard. *See* Botrytis.

Grechetto White wine grape of Italy used notably in Orvieto wines in the Umbria region, along with other grapes including Trebbiano, Malvasia, and Verdello, as well as in the Torgiano district. Its rich character also makes it suitable for the distinctive, sweet Vin Santo wines.

Green Characterization of a wine that usually indicates unripe aromas or flavors, and possibly an overly tart balance. Not always a bad thing, however, because wines like Sauvignon Blanc from New Zealand and Albariño from Spain make a virtue out of this lean, fresh attribute.

Green harvest The practice of removing a portion of a grape crop early in the growing season, usually when the grapes are still green, to reduce the yield and concentrate the vines' energy on the remaining grapes, which should improve their ripeness and overall quality.

Grenache In France and the New World this prolific black grape is known as a Rhône variety because of its use in the Rhône Valley wines labeled Châteauneuf-du-Pape, Gigondas, Côtes du Rhône, and others. In these areas, Grenache delivers generous, ripe fruit flavors, rather high alcoholic strength and only moderate tannic astringency compared to many other full-bodied reds. Grenache can also be used for lighter reds and roses. *See* Garnacha as a synonym in Spain.

Grignolino Popular grape variety in Italy's Piemonte region, where it makes a light, tart and often tannic red wine.

Grip Refers to the texture of a wine in one's mouth, and signifies a desired level of tannins, acid, and alcohol. Often used for port and full-bodied red table wines.

Grolleau Also known as Groslot, a black grape variety of the Loire Valley of France,

which makes everyday quality wines.

Groppello Or Groppello Gentile, is a black grape variety grown in the Lombardia region of Italy.

Gros Plant Tart, straightforward white wine made from Folle Blanche grapes near Nantes in the Loire Valley of France.

Grosses Gewächs First growth wine of at least Spätlese quality from a single vineyard or estate in Germany. *See* Erstes Gewächs for reference to Rheingau wines.

Grosslage "Large vineyard' in German. Usually refers to a collection of small neighboring vineyards.

Grüner Veltliner Now internationally recognized as a white grape variety that makes distinctive wines, Grüner Veltliner labored long as a local favorite in Austria, where it is the country's most widely planted variety. Its wines range from lean and light, to rich and spicy depending on the vineyard site and winemaking techniques used.

Gyropalette Equipment used to rotate and tilt many bottles of sparkling wine at once, during the riddling process that prepares bottle-fermented bubbly for disgorging and corking. An automated method of doing automatically what used to be accomplished by hand. *See* Riddling.

Hail Ice particles or balls that fall from the sky during warm weather thunderstorms, posing a threat to vineyards. Hail can shred leaves, reducing a vine's ability to continue ripening, and damage the grapes themselves, opening them up to insects and disease which can also spoil the crop. In especially hail-prone wine districts, some grape growers cover their vines with fine netting to protect them.

Halbtrocken "Half-dry" in German, indicating a wine with relatively low sugar content and enough balancing acidity that the wine tastes dry.

Harmonious Similar to "balanced", it refers to a wine in which all the parts blend well for a pleasurable drinking experience.

Haut "High" in French, referring either to the physical position of vineyards or to quality level.

Heavy High in alcohol or sweetness and without sufficient balance from acidity.

Hectare Abbreviated to ha. Unit for land measurement in the metric system equal to 100m by 100m, or 10,000 sq m. One hectare equals 2.47 acres in the English/American system.

Hectoliter Abbreviated to hl, and equal to 100 liters, or 26 US gallons, and 22 Imperial gallons. Countries using the metric system measure their grape harvests in volume of hectoliters, rather than in weight of tons, as in the US. When expressing the yield of a vineyard, 80 hl/ha is roughly equivalent to six tons per acre (an average size yield in many areas).

Herbaceous Taste descriptor for a wine

that is herb-like. Certain grape varieties produce more naturally herbaceous aromas and flavors (Sauvignon Blanc and Cabernet Sauvignon are good examples), especially when less than fully ripe. It can be a negative trait in a wine whose typical style is riper. Grape-growers can minimize herbaceous qualities by winter pruning to reduce yields and trimming or training the vines in summer to let more sunshine touch the grape clusters.

High-density planting Fashionable but not necessarily scientifically proven practice of planting vines extremely close together to increase quality by limiting yields in the individual vines. The theory is that the vines compete for moisture and nutrients in the soil and thus mutually reduce each others productivity, which in turn is expected to increase the concentration of flavors in the grapes that do form. The effect of high-density planting is very much dependent on the climate and region in which the vines are grown.

Hochgewächs "High growth" or high-quality Riesling wine from Germany which is made from riper grapes than the minimum for QbA status.

Horizontal tasting Not the tasters, but the wines are arranged "horizontally" in this educational type of comparative wine tasting. Wines from the same vintage and/or region and/or grape varieties but from different wine producers are poured and sampled in the same session to compare and contrast their flavors.

Hospices de Beaune A nearly 600-year-old hospital for the needy in Burgundy's walled city of Beaune. The building is called the Hôtel-Dieu, and is the site of an annual charity wine auction in which wine merchants bid on young wines from the surrounding vineyards, which they later bottle. One often sees "Hospices de Beaune" printed on the labels of such wines.

Huxelrebe A white wine grape developed in Germany in the early 20th century and now also planted in England. It ripens well in northern climates and has assertive fruit flavors.

Hybrid In the realm of wine, a hybrid (or interspecies cross) is a vine type resulting from the crossing of grapevines from two different species. French-American hybrids are perhaps the most common. They were bred from native American vine species crossed with traditional French ones to outsmart vine pests, and diseases and to give better resistance to extreme winter cold while approximating the winemaking qualities of the French parent. A true cross is a vine type created from two parent vines of the same species. Wines resulting from hybrid varieties are subject to strict labeling laws in Europe.

Hydrogen Sulphide Disagreeable sulphur compound in wine that gives off a rotten egg smell. It can develop especially during fermentation when the grape must has low levels of nitrogen. Not the same thing as sulphites which are added to wine as a preservative. *See* Sulphites.

Icewine *See* Eiswein.

IGP Indication Geographique Protegée. The French interpretation of new EU labeling laws that will see the Vins de Pays and VDQS quality designations phased out in the coming years. *See also* PDO and PGI.

Imbottigliato Italian for "bottled". On a wine label it gives a partial indication of a wine's origin.

Imperial Wine bottle that holds 6 liters, equivalent to 8 normal bottles.

Indication Geographique Protegée *See* IGP, PDO, PGI.

Integral vinification Another way to say barrel fermented and aged.

Jeroboam Indicates a 3 liter bottle in Bordeaux, and a 4.5 liter bottle in Champagne and Burgundy.

Johannisberg Riesling Term sometimes seen in California to distinguish the Riesling grape of Germany from the once-popular Gray Riesling.

Kabinett German term that indicates a level of ripeness just below Spätlese. Kabinett wines are made from what the Germans call fully ripened grapes from the normal harvest period (not late harvest) which yield rather light wines in either a sightly sweet, half-dry, or dry style.

Keller "Cellar" in German, often indicating a winery.

Kerner Useful white grape variety planted mostly in Germany's Pfalz and Rheinhessen regions. It is a recent cross of Riesling with the black grape variety Trollinger, and it has unusually good flavors, higher sugar and acidity, and better frost resistance than many other crosses planted in Germany.

Kir Drink made by adding white or sparkling wine to black currant liqueur.

Kosher wine Wine made in a way that satisfies the Jewish dietary guidelines. Kosher wines today include examples of many styles from many grape varieties, and vary from château-bottled Bordeaux and fine Israeli Chardonnay down to simple sweet wines made from native American grape varieties in New York State.

Labrusca *Vitis labrusca* grapevines are native to the northern and eastern sections of North America. They have been used for wine since colonial times, but there is no evidence that American Indians fermented them. Labrusca wines tend to be extremely grapey and musky in character.

Lactic acid The soft, buttery acid found also in dairy products, that is converted from the harsher malic acid in wine during the malolactic fermentation.

Lagar A large trough or low-sided vat in Portugal in which wine ferments. It is traditional for workers and guests to tread the *lagar* with their bare feet to extract maximum color and flavor from the grape skins during fermentation.

Lagrein Italian black grape variety grown in limited quantities in the Alto Adige region. It can make good red and rosé table wine on its own, and is also blended with other varieties.

Lambrusco Red varietal sparkling wine from Italy that can be dry or sweet. Much of it is mass produced in Emilia, but flavorful, high-quality versions also exist. there are several sub-varieties of Lambrusco.

Landwein In Austria and Germany, a classification for common table wines made from different varieties that are dry or nearly dry, and offering a bit more body than the simplest table wines.

Late Bottled Vintage A port wine made from grapes all harvested in the same vintage, aged in casks and sold between four and six years after the vintage. Abbreviated as LBV, it is similar to vintage port but designed to be ready to drink on release, while vintage port is bottled younger but needs further aging in the bottle to mature.

Late harvest When wine grapes are picked later in the season than is required for normal dry table wine. Late-harvested grapes have hung on the vine until the growing season is essentially over, and no more juice is being added to the grapes by the vine. Instead, a process of dehydration takes over, removing water from the juice and increasing the relative proportion of sugar. Late-harvested grapes make wine either higher in alcohol than table wine or sweeter, when the fermentation is stopped before consuming all the sugar.

Leaf thinning Also "leaf pulling," the practice of removing by hand or machine a portion of grapevine leaves to improve ripening and air flow through the vine to prevent disease. The leaves shading the grape clusters are partially or fully removed to let sunlight reach the grapes.

Leaf-roll virus Leaf-roll disease caused by a group of viruses is a resurgent problem for grapevines in California, New York, and other parts of the world. The beautiful red and purple color of vine leaves in fall (and occasionally a curling effect) can signal an infection in red varieties. White grape varieties show less obvious signs. Leaf-roll impedes ripening and lowers yields. The viruses live in grapevine tissue and spread when vines are propagated by cuttings that use infected tissue, and by rootstock plants grown from virus-infected stock. This was long thought to be the only way to spread leaf-roll, but it has been confirmed that it also can spread from vine to vine via insects such as mealybugs. Using only clean plant material to plant vineyards is the primary preventive measure.

Lees The dregs that fall to the bottom of a barrel or tank in a winery. Composed of bits of grape skin and dead yeast cells. The lees have antioxidative properties which some winemakers use to their advantage by stirring them periodically during the wine's aging process in the winery. They also impart flavor as the wine ages, a key element to the quality sparkling winemaking process, as the wines age in bottle in close contact with their secondary fermentation lees.

Lees stirring Known as *bâtonnage* in French, this practice keeps the dead yeast cells (lees) in a barrel or tank in contact with the wine as it ages, helping prevent oxidation, adding subtle bread-like nuances to the wine's flavor, and enriching the wine's texture. Often used with barrel-fermented Chardonnay. Can be done by hand with a thin baton inserted in a barrel, or by various other means.

Legs Rivulets that run down the inside of a glass that has been wetted with wine. Alcohol forms them.

Lemberger An exciting grape variety in Germany today for making well-colored, medium- to full-bodied spicy red wines, especially in Württemberg. Lemberger is usually made dry, and resembles the Rhône varieties in some respects. Also known as Blaufränkisch, (in Austria) and Kékfrankos, (in Hungary).

Liebfraumilch An overwrought name meaning "mother's milk" for sweet, low-priced wines exported from Germany, often made from Müller-Thurgau.

Lieu-dit "Place name" used in Burgundy, Alsace, and other French wine regions for traditional, named vineyard sites that do not have official appellation status. *Climat* is a synonym in Burgundy.

Limousin A French forest region in the south-central part of the country that supplies oak staves for wine barrels.

Liqueur A sweetened, flavored, and fortified beverage often based on wine.

Liquoreux French for sweet-style or after-dinner wines.

Liquoroso Italian term for a fortified wine, to which alcohol has been added to make it more full-bodied than a table wine. Often sweet, too.

Liter Metric unit of measure, consisting of 1,000mls. One litre equals 33.8 fl oz.

Lodge English term for a winery in the Oporto region of Portugal where port wines are blended, aged, and bottled.

Macabeo White vine variety with a modest varietal flavor that is planted in Spain, especially in Rioja, and the Penedès region where it is blended with Xarel-lo and Parellada to make the base wine for Cava, and to a lesser extent in southern France. Also known as Viura and Macabeu, Macabeo can be the main ingredient in white Rioja and is sometimes blended into white wines, too.

Maceration The practice of soaking grape skins in the juice or wine before, during, or after fermentation, to allow more color and flavor compounds to move from the skins into the juice, and ultimately the wine. Classified-growth Bordeaux wines are famous for their extended macerations, extending the *cuvaison* period from the week or 10 days of fermentation to three weeks or more.

Maderized Having become like madeira, but not usually in such an elegant way. Refers to premature oxidation that can be easily detected in aromas and flavors.

Magnum Bottle size containing 1.5 liters or the equivalent of 2 standard bottles.

Malbec Black grape variety traditional in Bordeaux, and now the hot varietal wine of Argentina. Has a family resemblance to the other traditional Bordeaux varieties. Also known as Côt and Auxerrois.

Malic acid A fruit acid that is strong in apples and also in wine grapes. The malolactic conversion which most red wines and many white wines undergo converts much of this crisp, tangy acid into the softer, more buttery lactic acid.

Malmsey The ripest type of wine from Madeira, with the most residual sugar. Made from Malvasia grapes.

Malolactic fermentation Not really a fermentation, but a conversion of malic acid to lactic acid which winemakers allow to happen naturally, or induce in certain types of wine, to lower overall acidity and create a smoother texture and longer finish. Many, many red wines around the world go through malolactic, and some whites, notably Chardonnay. The process is part of the traditional Burgundian regimen along with barrel fermentation and lees stirring. Malolactic is subtle compared to the primary fermentation, and winemakers need to watch it closely, to achieve the style of wine they want and to ensure that it does not occur later in the bottle, where it can create unwanted carbonation and off odors.

Malvasia Mediterranean family of white grape varieties known for millennia to produce perfumed wines with full body, often significant sweetness and luscious textures. Many sub-varieties of the original, probably from Greece, exist in several European countries.

Malvoisie Apparently not related to Malvasia, this term is used in France for various wines usually white, sweet and aromatic, in some ways like Malvasia.

Manzanilla Relatively light style of sherry that is usually dry, tangy, and excellent as an apéritif. Similar to fino sherry in that it ages in barrels with a layer of flor yeast resting on its surface. Made in the oceanside town of Sanlúcar de Barrameda, it can also be released in sweeter versions: manzanilla oloroso and manzanilla pasada.

Marc French term for the brandy (like grappa, in Italian) distilled from the grape skins and seeds left over after fermentation. It is also the name for the mass of skins and seeds left after pressing a wine after fermentation.

Maréchal Foch A French general from World War I and a vinifera-labrusca hybrid grape variety that bears his name. Still common in eastern North America because of its cold-hardiness and mildew resistance, it can make good quality, fresh, and fruity red wines, but in many places is being replaced by vinifera varieties.

Marque French term for "brand." *See also* Grandes Marques.

Marsala An Italian wine bottled at several degrees of sweetness, and aged for varying periods. Often seen recommended in cooking, it is best known as a dessert wine, but can be produced as Marsala Vergine which is dry.

Marsanne Rhône white wine grape variety, often spoken of in the same sentence with Roussanne, another popular white grape of the Rhône Valley region and other parts of the wine world that emulate it, including California and Australia. Marsanne tends to make full-bodied, rich and assertive, dry wines.

Massal selection One technique for selecting the grapevine cuttings to be used in growing new vines. In massal or mass selection the viticulturist cuts one-year canes from numerous vines that appear to have good growing traits, and either roots them to grow on their own, or cuts out the buds and grafts them on to rootstock vines. Since individual vines usually vary in small ways, massal selection carries that variablility forward to the new vineyard helping to add complexity to the resulting wine, but possibly passing on undesired traits as well. *See also* the alternate method of clonal selection.

Master of Wine/MW Title awarded to people who have studied and passed the rigorous series of exams from the UK-based Institute of Masters of Wine. The extensive syllabus covers grape and wine production, tasting expertise, wine trade regulations, and more. The MW has been awarded to at least 280 people in 23 countries.

Mataró Synonym for the black grape variety Mourvèdre, mainly used in Portugal and the New World.

Mavrodaphne Greek black grape variety usually made into a sweet, high-alcohol after-dinner wine called Mavrodaphne of Patras. The literal translation is "black laurel."

Melon White grape variety originally identified in Burgundy, and fittingly known today as Melon de Bourgogne. Used mostly in making the crisp, straightforward wines of Muscadet. Can still be found in parts of Burgundy, and has been identified as the same grape that in California was once called Pinot Blanc.

Mercaptans Chemical compounds that can cause putrid off odors and flavors in wine. They sometimes develop during fermentation through an interaction of yeast and sulphur (which may have been sprayed on the grapes during the growing season to prevent mildew). Mercaptans can be dispersed by aerating the young wine or by the addition of a copper compound. In minute quantities mercaptans can add favorable flavor characteristics, too.

Merlot Black grape variety and wine type formerly associated mostly with Bordeaux that has been one of the fastest growing in the world over 20 years. California, Australia, Chile, Italy, the South of France, even New York State claim Merlot as an important variety. It is the most widely planted variety in the greater Bordeaux region, and is the dominant grape in the typical red Bordeaux blend of all but a few districts. In terms of price and prestige Château Pétrus, in Pomerol, may be the ultimate Merlot wine. American consumers in particular developed a taste for its plum and red cherry flavors and softer-than-Cabernet texture, to the point that Merlot's popularity endangered its quality. Merlot ripens earlier than Cabernet Sauvignon, but being thinner-skinned is more prone to damage from weather and pests.

Méthode Cap Classique Legally defined term for sparkling wines from the Cape region of South Africa, made in the traditional method similar to that of Champagne in France.

Méthode Champenoise Method developed in the Champagne region of France over several hundred years for producing high-quality sparkling wines by conducting in the individual bottles the second fermentation that produces the characteristic carbonation. Champagne wines must age on the lees from this process for at least 15 months, before disgorging and bottling. Sparkling wine producers in other parts of the world have used the term to indicate their wines were made in a very similar manner to those of Champagne, but the Champenois have lobbied to restrict its use only to their region. Other terms include Méthode Traditionnelle and Méthode Classique in French, Metodo Classico and Metodo Tradizionale in Italian.

Micro-oxygenation Winemaking technique developed in the early 1990s that exposes fermenting must or new wine in tanks to oxygen with minute doses bubbled through from multiple emitters. The goals include encouraging healthy yeast during fermentation, mimicking the aging process

that would otherwise occur in oak barrels, smoothing the wine's texture by a complex process that softens the often harsh tannins in certain grape varieties, and curing overly herbaceous flavors in red wines. The first known use was in Madiran, France, to tame the notoriously tough wines made there from Tannat grapes.

Microclimate Describes the very individual climatic conditions of a vineyard or sub-block of a vineyard. Microclimate recognizes that climate varies not just region by region but between vineyard sites, depending on the slope of the land, its orientation toward the sun, surrounding geographic features, prevailing winds, common fog patterns, and so on. Understanding microclimates helps wine-growers choose the proper grape varieties and clones, most appropriate trellis set-up and vine-training pattern, proper irrigation, and more.

Mildew Common disease of grapevines that growers spend lots of money and time to prevent from forming. Powdery and downy mildew are the most common types that affect the popular *Vitis vinifera* vines of Eurasian origin. Mildew thrives in humid, warm summer growing conditions, but not in sunny, well aerated spots. It affects shoots, leaves, canes, and grape bunches and can damage or destroy a crop if not controlled, usually with sprays of a copper mixture, powdered sulphur, and other fungicides.

Millésime "Vintage" year in French.

Minerality, mineral taste Term that winemakers and writers use to give special praise to wines that go beyond simply fruity in flavor, and those which are made from old vines and low yields. Its existence has not been scientifically proven, and wine chemists say it does not stem from actual mineral compounds entering the grapes through the roots and so on. Yet, mineral water tastes different from rainwater, so perhaps an explanation of this ethereal quality will yet come forth.

Mise en bouteille au château "Bottled at the château." Usually indicates that the grower and the bottler were the same entity, which is often a good sign of wine quality.

Mission The first grape variety to be widely planted in Mexico and the west coasts of North and South America, by Roman Catholic missionaries during Spanish occupation of the region. The dark grapes were used primarily for communion wine in church services, and their cultivation and production of the wine was considered God's work.

Moelleux A French term to describe wine that is mellow, rather sweet, and with a soft texture.

Monastrell Synonym for the black grape variety Mourvèdre, found mainly on Spanish wine labels

Mondeuse Black grape variety in Savoie,

France, that produces a robust wine with deep color and spicy flavors when grown on good sites. Mondeuse Blanche is a white wine variety of the same region, probably more famous as a parent variety of Syrah than for its wine quality.

Monocru Term used mostly in the Champagne region to refer to a wine made solely from grapes harvested on one *cru* or property. Similar to single vineyard designations on New World wines.

Monopole Literally a "monopoly," indicating a French wine district where all the vineyard property is owned by one proprietor. For example, the Domaine de la Romanée-Conti in Burgundy has *monopoles* with the top vineyard sites of Romanée-Conti and La Tâche.

Moscato The same as Muscat in French and English, Moscato is a white wine variety of Italy that makes spicy, floral, often sweet, and sometimes sparkling wines in many parts of the country. Moscato Bianco and Moscato di Canelli are more complete names.

Moscato d'Asti One of the best known Italian wines made from Moscato (Muscat) grapes in the northern Italian town of Asti in Piemonte, where Asti Spumante is made, too, in a fully sparkling form. Moscato d'Asti is a low-pressure sparkling wine, usually slightly sweet, low in alcohol, and charming for its floral and fresh fruit flavors.

Mourvèdre Black grape variety best-known in the Rhône Valley of France, and one of the common constituents of Châteauneuf-du-Pape wines, which are famously blended from as many as 13 different varieties. Mourvèdre provides deep color, firm tannins, and a fruit flavor that edges into earthy, gamey attributes. Mourvèdre wines are also made in California, Australia, and elsewhere, sometimes as a single varietal wine. Mataró and Monastrell are synonyms.

Mousse The foam or head on top of a glass of sparkling wine.

Mousseux Sparkling, or made in a sparkling style.

Müller-Thurgau Former workhorse grape variety of Germany, now declining, producing large yields in less than ideal growing conditions and making mostly nondescript white wines with a bit of the peachy flavor of one of its parent varieties, Riesling.

Muscadelle In Bordeaux and Bergerac, a white grape variety used in sweet wines and dry table wines, often blended with the more distinctive Sémillon and Sauvignon Blanc varieties. Especially important in Entre-deux-Mers and sweet wine appellations such as Monbazillac and Cadillac.

Muscadine A family of native North American grape species. A common form is Scuppernong, still grown in the southern US, where it yields large berries and makes grapey wines that are an acquired taste.

Muscat French name for a grand family of *Vitis vinifera* grapevines that has spread around the world, producing a vast variety of aromatic, exuberantly floral and fruity, and usually sweet wines of all colors, with an unforgettable flavor profile that ties them together. Perhaps the most famous variation planted in France is Muscat Blanc à Petits Grains, which makes white-or amber-colored wines, and a lighter sibling: Muscat Ottonel. A dark-skinned version is Muscat Hamburg. Known as Moscatel in Spain and Portugal and Moscato in Italy, Muscat is enjoying a revival in the United States.

Must The liquid grape mixture after red wine grapes have been stemmed and crushed, but before the liquid has finished fermentation. Red wine must includes the grape skins, pulp, and seeds, so it is a thick, lumpy mixture. It also refers to the freshly pressed white grape juice before it is racked off for fermentation.

Nebbiolo Superb Italian black grape variety that makes the classic and ageworthy Barolo and Barbaresco wines of the Piemonte region, as well as less-expensive types including Nebbiolo d'Alba. Nebbiolo has a rare and almost exclusive relationship with the steep hills of the Langhe Valley, where this grape is planted on the most coveted hillsides, while Barbera and Dolcetto fill in elsewhere. Nebbiolo makes intense, tannic wines that are notoriously tight when young, but can mature into gloriously perfumed and complex taste experiences.

Négociant Wine firm that does not grow grapes and ferment wine, but one that buys wine already fermented and sometimes already cellared for some months or years, then bottles and markets it under its own brand.

Négociant-éleveur Wine bottler who buys pre-made wine in bulk, then elevates or "raises" it to a higher quality level by aging in barrels, blending with other bulk wines, perhaps fining and filtering it, before bottling and selling it under his own brand.

Neutral Wine taste descriptor that indicates an aroma or flavor that is neither attractive nor off-putting.

Neutral oak Refers to a barrel or other wooden cask in a winery that has been used for at least three years, and has given as much oak flavor as it can to wine stored in it. Neutral oak can be fine for the other purposes of oak aging, such as the slow, positive oxidation through the wood, and other processes such as lees stirring.

New oak Any form of oak cooperage being used for the first time, when the oak staves provide the most potent flavor contribution of their useful lives. New barrels or oak tanks give a variety of desirable taste characteristics to wine, including vanillin, coconut, smoke, pepper, almond, cedar, cinnamon, and others. An important consideration, especially for red wines, is what percentage of new oak should be used, versus oak that has held wine previously for a year or more. The uusual formula is the stronger the flavors of the young wine, the more new oak it can benefit from.

Niagara North American white wine grape used for jam, juice, and wine.

Noble rot *See* Botrytis.

Noble varieties An old term in the wine business that is of little use today. The "noble" grape varieties established of yore were all French. Among them were Chardonnay, Riesling, Cabernet Sauvignon, Merlot, Pinot Noir, and Syrah. The term neglects the great Italian varieties such as Nebbiolo and Sangiovese, and Spanish ones such as Tempranillo and Garnacha and therefore has less relevance today.

Nose Affected term to describe the smell of a wine.

Nouveau "New" in French. The most popular wines of the world described as *nouveau* are the Beaujolais Nouveau of France, fresh and grapey tasting wines bottled and shipped to market within a few weeks of harvest.

Oak The type of wood preferred by winemakers around the world in which to age wine to improve its flavors and textures. Three types of oak trees are widely used as sources: in Europe, the *Quercus sessille* and *Quercus robur* (also known as *Quercus pedunculata*), and in North America the *Quercus alba* or white oak. Oak has proven itself over several hundred years to have the qualities of flavor, protection from over-oxidation, and strength needed to contain large, heavy quantities of wine. Oak is often used as a short way to say oak barrel, but increasingly it may refer to barrel adjuncts such as oak chips.

Oak adjuncts Products made of cooperage grade oak to flavor wine while it matures in tanks and/or barrels. The formats include oak chips, powder, stave inserts, nuggets, and blocks of various shapes and sizes.

Oaky Descriptor for a wine that shows strong aroma and/or flavor influences from the oak barrels or barrel adjunct products that were used to store and/or flavor it.

Oechsle Scale used mostly in Germany to indicate the ripeness of grape juice at harvest time and to follow the progress of fermentation. Hydrometry is used to measure sugar content as a function of density. Other countries use the Brix or Baumé scales.

Oenology *See* Enology.

Oidium French for powdery mildew, a grapevine disease. *See* Mildew.

Old vines Known as "*vieilles vignes*" in French, the term on a label indicates that a wine was made from grapes grown on fully mature vines. It generally means a wine of higher quality, because old vines have settled into consistent growth and ripening cycles, and their usually deep roots insulate them from extreme temperatures and drought. The minimum age for old is the subject of debate. In Burgundy, it might indicate 30 years or more, in California an old-vine Zinfandel could be 40 to 100 years old.

Oloroso Legally defined term for a richer, nuttier, more full-bodied style of sherry, made in a distinctly different way to the lighter "fino". Naturally dry, the term "oloroso" is often misappropirated to indicate a level of added sweetnesss in various dark sherry-like wines.

Optima German white grape variety, crossed in recent times and with 25% Riesling parentage, which ripens early even in northern climes and provides high sugar and thus alcohol levels for wine.

Ordinaire "Ordinary" in French. A "*vin ordinaire*" is an everyday wine as opposed to a special occasion wine.

Organic Indicates agricultural produce grown without the use of synthetic herbicides, pesticides, and fertilizers, to encourage healthy soil and provide a safe and healthy product for the consumer. An organic wine is one for which strict procedures are extended into the winery and only approved non-synthetic materials may be used to process the wine. A significant difference exists in the rules for organic wine in the EU and other parts of the world, where the use of sulphur dioxide or metabisulphites are permitted in the winemaking process. The wines can only be described as "wine made from organically grown grapes" versus the United States where only wines procesed without added sulphur dioxide may be called "organic." Since the sulphur dioxide is considered essential to preserve wine and has been used for centuries for virtually all commerciall wines, organic wines in the United States often have a quite different flavor profile to that which consumers are accustomed.

Organically grown On a wine label, particularly, in the United States, this term means the grapes have been grown using strict organic practices. It does not indicate that the wine has been processed organically. *See* Organic.

Overcropped A vineyard that produces too many grapes per vine so that the sugar content and flavor constituents are not concentrated sufficiently to make the desired quality of wine. The vineyard owner or manager has many ways to prevent overcropping, such as pruning aggressively during the winter to reduce the number of buds (and thus the number of grape bunches), thinning clusters during the growing season, and avoiding over-irrigation and over-fertilization.

Own-rooted *See* Ungrafted.

Oxidation Chemical process by which oxygen interacts with wine and changes its composition. Over-oxidation can spoil a wine, which is why protecting wine from air is a vital part of the winemaking process from the time the grapes are crushed or pressed until and even after the wine is bottled. Leaving a half-empty wine bottle at room temperature for two days and then tasting it gives you an idea of what an excess of oxygen can do to a wine. The wine turns stale and will eventually become brown, beginning a process that will lead to vinegar. But slow, controlled oxidation during the time a wine ages in a winery or private cellar enables it to develop valued nuances of flavor.

Oxidized Characterization of a stale or spoiled wine suffering from too much exposure to oxygen.

Paille "Straw" in French. A "*vin de paille*" is a wine for which the grapes were traditionally dried on straw mats to become raisins, and only then fermented for wine. The drying reduces the water in the grapes and increases the relative sugar content while also affecting the flavors in a positive way. Many other ways to dry the grapes are used today, but they all give a similar effect of a riper, sweeter, more full-bodied dessert wine with rich and unusual flavors.

Palo cortado A small and unusual category of sherry which can create some of the best wines from Jerez. Palo cortado wines are selected as among the finest lots early in their aging process, but do not go on to develop the natural layer of flor yeast which would turn them into amontillado. They technically become the more oxidized oloroso sherries, but are prized as more elegant.

Palomino A white grape variety famous in Spain for making sherry, and which also can be used for table wines or table grapes. It is naturally low in acid and sweetness, and with a neutral flavor profile that lends itself to the sherry-making techniques that add their own flavors.

Paris Tasting of 1976 Also known as the Judgement of Paris. A blind tasting of French and California wines organized by the English wine merchant and writer Stephen Spurrier during the United States' bicentennial year, in which French wine professionals awarded higher marks to a Cabernet Sauvignon and a Chardonnay from Napa Valley than they did to first growth red Bordeaux and Grand Cru white burgundy. At the time France was viewed almost universally as the source of the world's best wines. The tasting became a milestone in the acceptance of California wines in America as well as internationally.

Partial root drying A form of deficit irrigation which improves wine-grape quality by alternately depriving a portion of the vine's roots of irrigation water. This has the effect of making the entire vine react as if it were water-starved and modify its growth by ripening the grapes more quickly rather than growing more leaves.

Passerillage Grape-drying process used in France to concentrate the sweetness and flavors before fermentation.

Passetoutgrains Bourgogne Passtoutgrains is a red wine popular in the Burgundy region. It is a blend of Pinot Noir and Gamay for a basic level table wine.

Passito An Italian term for wine made from dried grapes.

Paulée A feast for wine-growers in France, the most famous of which is probably the annual wine-swapping party in Burgundy's commune of Meursault, where the revelry starts at lunchtime and continues into the evening.

Pays "Country" or "countryside" in French.

PDO Protected Designation of Origin. A new EU-wide labeling system to guarantee the origin of wines and other products.

Pedro Ximénez Grape grown mostly in Spain for white and dessert wines which can make some of the world's most viscous and rich bottlings. Sherry makers use it, but most of the plantings are in southern Spain's Montilla-Moriles region often shortened to PX.

Peduncle Stem of a bunch of grapes.

Perfume Ambitious word for a wine's aroma or smell.

Periquita Portuguese term for parakeet. It is the name of a black grape variety that can make value-oriented medium-bodied reds, as well as a brand name.

Perpetual cuvée A store of reserve wine that is blended from many vintages, and used to augment new vintages. It is replenished with newer wine when reserve wine is drawn off, so a portion of the reserve wine can be very old, adding unusual and desirable flavor notes.

Persistence Means nearly the same as "finish" and indicates a wine whose taste lingers long on the palate after one has swallowed the wine.

Pétillant Slightly sparkling.

Petit Small or little.

Petit Verdot One of the five classic black grape varieties of Bordeaux, known for its extremely deep color and rich tannins. Little celebrated until the 1990s, this late-ripening grape has become a darling of producers of Bordeaux-style blends around the world, though still planted sparsely compared to its brethren: Cabernet Sauvignon, Merlot, Cabernet Franc, and Malbec. Occasionally bottled as a single varietal in the New World, the grapes often command higher prices than Cabernet Sauvignon from California winemakers who covet Petit Verdot's potency and spicy flavor profile.

Petite Sirah A black grape variety with forebears in the Rhône Valley that is most closely linked to California. There is nothing petite about its color, body, or tannin content. It shows adequate but restrained flavors of blackberry and sometimes black pepper, and has the structure to age for 10 to 20 years. Petite Sirah was interplanted with more popular Zinfandel and other varieties in the common field blends of the 19th century. Even today, it is often blended at up to 25% to strengthen the typically lighter colored and less tannic Zinfandel.

PGI Protected Geographical Indication. A new EU-wide labeling system to guarantee the origin of wines and other products.

pH Scale for expressing the acid-base balance of solutions. Winemakers like to know the pH of their soil, of the grapes before harvest, and monitor the pH as their wines go through fermentation and maturation, as the pH affects many factors of vine health and wine quality. Most wines measure between 2.7 and 4.3 in terms of pH. Neutral water has a pH of 7. A lower number means a wine feels more acidic or tart in one's mouth, and a higher number means a wine feels less acidic, softer and, at the extreme, fat. Grapes that hang longer on the vine to ripen more fully tend to lose acidity while they gain sugar and fruit flavor intensity, and their pH goes up. In chemistry terms, pH is the negative logarithm of the molar concentration of dissolved hydrogen ions.

Phylloxera A tiny louse with a taste for grapevine roots so strong that it wiped out most of the European and Californian vineyards in the late 19th century and forced changes in grape growing that persist today. The louse was native to eastern North American soils, where the native grape varieties resisted it. But when it spread to Europe, probably in a shipment of vines with roots and soil attached, it found a new universe of *Vitis vinifera* roots on which to dine and which it had never tasted before. With no innate resistance, the vines died quickly as the lice spread from vineyard to vineyard across the continent, and then spread back to America to destroy vinifera vines planted in California and elsewhere. European vine breeders soon determined that they could plant phylloxera-resistant vineyards by either using native American grape varieties, which unfortunately had little flavor resemblance to the traditional European grapes, or by grafting vinifera scion wood to American rootstock, similar to the way many nut and fruit trees were grown. The latter plan was most successful and became the norm that has persisted until today. Phylloxera made a big comeback in California in the late 1980s when growers there had become complacent and relied on a rootstock called AxR1, which was known to have limited phylloxera resistance but which produced high-quality grapes with relatively high yields. As it weakened or killed vines up and down the state, vineyard owners bulldozed their vines and started from scratch, with new plants grafted on different rootstock, with many new clones of fruiting stock and using more modern and effective trellis and irrigation systems.

Picolit Generally made into a wine via drying of the grapes before pressing and fermenting, this lightly sweet, peach-tinged white wine of the Friuli region of Northeast Italy is so-called because the grape clusters are small, or *piccolo*.

Picpoul This grape variety of France's Languedoc region comes in three forms: blanc, gris, and noir. The crisp white version is most often seen.

Pierce's Disease A malady of grapevines that is native to the North American South and endemic in growing regions such as Texas and southern California, where it wiped out swathes of vines at the beginning of the 20th century. Pierce's disease is feared by vineyard owners because of its ability to infect and kill plants within a year or two of exposure. This disease of the plant's vascular system can spread quickly by insect vectors, particularly the glassywinged sharpshooter, which broadcast it through the vineyards of the Temecula region in the 1990s and wiped out a large portion of the vineyards there. Grape growers farther north on the West Coast are constantly on guard for it, and have encountered limited infestations. Some American native grapevines are not affected by the disease, and vine breeders have made many attempts to develop resistant varieties crossed with *Vitis vinifera* for better flavors, but with no great success so far.

Pigato An Italian white wine variety in Liguria that is better known as Vermentino and in Piemonte is called Favorita.

Pigeage *See* Punching down.

Pineau de la Loire *See* Chenin Blanc.

Pinot Bianco Same grape variety as Pinot Blanc, which originated in France, but more widely grown in Italy, especially in the Northeast, where it is the star white wine of Alto Adige.

Pinot Blanc The whitest variation in the grape family that also includes Pinot Noir and Pinot Gris. Associated with Burgundy and Alsace, but grown in various places in Central and Eastern Europe as well as the New World. Wines from this grape are not as aromatic as Pinot Gris, and more soft and full-bodied. known as Pinot Bianco in Italy and Weissburgunder in Germany.

Pinot Grigio The Italian name for Pinot Gris. Wines labeled as Pinot Grigio are often quite simple, fresh and light-bodied, while French and Oregon wines labeled Pinot Gris, for example, are often richer, fruity and fuller-bodied. In California, winemakers use both terms.

Pinot Gris A classic grape variety of France and Italy, also known as Pinot Grigio. It is grown widely in Germany, North America, and other parts of the world. In the same family as Pinot Noir and Pinot Blanc, Pinot Gris is so-called because the grapes turn semi-dark or gris (like gray) in color. It has plentiful fruit flavors, very lively acidity and sometimes a tinge of pink color. In Alsace especially, Pinot Gris can be rich, full-bodied, and dry. Formerly known there as Tokay d'Alsace, it can be crafted as a late harvest sweet wine, too.

Pinot Meunier The other black grape variety of Champagne besides Pinot Noir and in fact the most widely planted variety in the region (Chardonnay is the key white grape). Not often cited as a major component of the top-line Champagnes, Pinot Meunier is a reliable variety that ripens earlier and has bigger yields than Pinot Noir, of which it is a mutation. Rarely made as a wine on its own, though Domaine Chandon in California and The Eyrie Vineyard in Oregon are two wineries that have done so. Also grown in Germany, where it is known as Müllerrebe.

Pinot Noir Several books have been devoted solely to this intriguing grape variety that comes from Burgundy in France. Pinot Noir makes a medium-bodied, smooth-textured red wine, in a world where most reds are full-bodied and tannic. Its wide and enticing array of flavors ranges from strawberry and herbs in light versions to dark cherry, mushroom, and forest floor in more exotic incarnations. Maturing in new oak barrels, where one third new is enough, brings out cinnamon nuances. With age in the bottle, a well-made red burgundy from a favoured vineyard site develops an almost ethereal bottle bouquet yet holds enough acidity and grip to make the most of roast duck or grilled squab. Pinot Noir has been famous since the Middle Ages for expressing terroir (or the flavor of a specific vineyard) better than many other varieties. Monks in Champagne (where it is one of the three grapes used) and Burgundy determined hundreds of years ago that sloping, well-drained vineyards with mostly southern or eastern exposures brought out the best in Pinot Noir. The vines bud out early in the spring, making them susceptible to cold weather damage, and the grapes have thin skins, making them prone to mildew and rot, and the yields need to be kept low for high-quality wine, so the variety has a rather poor reputation among vineyard owners. This also explains why the best examples are expensive and rare, whether from Burgundy or other Pinot-producing areas such as Germany, Oregon, California, and New Zealand.

Pinotage Black grape variety identified with South Africa, where it is grown widely. As a cross between Pinot Noir and Cinsault, Pinotage leans more toward the latter in flavor and heft, making Rhône-style reds with dark fruit flavors and earthy, spicy accents.

Formerly an acquired taste for non-South Africans, Pinotage wines today are more mainstream and inviting due to modern techniques in the vineyard and winery.

Pipe Originally, a large wine barrel as used in Portugal. Now it is employed in the wine trade to indicate a volume of wine that varies, but is usually about 160 gals (600 liters).

Plonk Dismissive term for wines of average to poor quality.

Pomace The grape skins, seeds, and other bits of grape detritus that remain after a wine is pressed. Pomace can be composted and later added to the vineyard to aid soil nutrition.

Port Fortified wine made in Portugal, the grapes for which are grown in the Douro Valley, while the wines are aged in cellars in and around the city of Porto. Port wines come in several styles, even in white, all full-bodied, high in alcohol, and at least slightly sweet. The lightest style is ruby port, while tawny port is aged the longest, and multiple variations on vintage port exist. Basic port is inexpensive and simple, the best vintage ports are classic wines on the quality level of great Bordeaux, and are known for aging for many decades. Grape varieties commonly used in port are Touriga Nacional, Touriga Franca, Tinto Cão, Tinto Roriz, and Tinta Barroca. After the grape must has fermented for two or three days, but while it is still sweet, the winemaker adds distilled spirits to kill the yeast, stopping the fermentation and raising the alcohol content to about 19%.

Porto *See* Port.

Portugieser Austria and Germany are home to the misleadingly named Portugieser grape variety, but it also grows in other places in Central and Eastern Europe. Also called Blauer Portugieser, it makes a fairly nondescript, inexpensive red in the most northern regions, but can be interesting and full of flavor in Hungary and Romania.

Prädikat "Distinction." Used in Germany to identify wines of various quality levels based on ripeness of the grapes. *See* Qualitätswein mit Prädikat.

Prädikatswein Under the new German wine regulations this is the top classification level, encompassing distinctive wines from Kabinett wines with low sugar ripeness to the late harvest wines with maximum sweetness.

Premier Cru *See* First Growth.

Press Machine used in wineries to squeeze the juice or wine out of the grape skins. To press is the act of using a press. The equipment, procedure, and pressure applied can have a huge effect on the style and quality of the wine made. Many wines today are less harsh and tannic than in the past due to modern wine presses that extract the liquid more slowly and gently. By contrast there has been a return to the centuries-old basket press design, which had all but disappeared except for amateur-scale winemaking and in the Champagne region of France, where juice quality is all important. Winemakers press most white wines before fermentation because they want to use only the juice, and not the skins and seeds. It is the opposite for nearly all reds, which the winemaker ferments in contact with the skins and seeds and then presses when the fermentation is nearly or completely done.

Press wine The portion of wine that flows from the wine press only after pressure is applied. This is routinely kept separate from the free-run wine, because it has different flavor and texture characteristics. It is typically higher in tannin and astringency because the pressing action forces liquid and solids out of the grape skins and seeds (pomace), where many of the more astringent compounds in wine reside. The winemaker keeps the press wine in barrels or tanks separate from the free run, and later conducts taste trials to determine how much, if any, of the press wine should be blended back into the final product before bottling.

Primeur French for a young wine sold a few months after the harvest. Beaujolais Nouveau is a prime example. "*En primeur*" is the practice in Bordeaux of selling young wines as futures, while they are still aging in barrels, at least a year before bottling.

Primitivo Black grape variety grown in Italy that is similar to the Zinfandel of California, and sharing the same ancestor in Croatia: Crljenak Kastelanski. Primitivo is especially popular in Puglia. While able to produce light-to medium-bodied wines, Primitivo can also ripen to an extreme level and create full-bodied wines that drink almost like port without the sweetness. Interestingly, some growers in California now plant Primitivo vines from imported Italian stock, as regulation allows them to label the wine as either Zinfandel or Primitivo.

Prohibition Period in United States and Canadian history when the commercial sale of most beverages containing alcohol was prohibited due to over-zealous health and moral concerns. Enacted in 1918 and not lifted entirely until 1933 in the US, Prohibition did not wipe out winemaking totally, but changed its face dramatically. Many wineries had to close their doors, while others survived making communion wine for the Catholic Church, or by marketing grapes and grape juice. Private citizens were permitted to make and consume their own wine, however, so a temporary grape-growing boom occurred in California to supply them. Grapes were packed in cartons sent by rail to thirsty people on the Eastern seaboard, many of whom were immigrants from winemaking countries and knew what to do with them. Eventually, the loss of taxes on alcohol production had as

much to with the repeal of Prohibition as a desire to let the citizens again buy intoxicating beverages. North American winemakers found themselves in the middle of the Great Depression, with vineyards now planted to thick-skinned grape varieties that shipped well, not to fine wine varieties. That situation was not fully corrected until the 1970s.

Prosecco White grape variety from the Veneto of Italy, best known for its lightly sparkling, lightly sweet, lightly alcoholic wine at around 9%, making it a suitable lunch or brunch drink when a serious wine is not needed. Dry and merely *frizzante* versions are made in smaller quantities.

Protected Designation of Origin *See* PDO.

Protected Geographical Indication *See* PGI.

Pruning The essential task of taming the otherwise wildly growing grapevine. Done during the winter dormant period, pruning resets the vine for the desired quantity and quality of fruit production. Each year vineyard crews remove with shears most of the previous summer's growth, precisely choosing which canes (one-year-old branches) or spurs (small sections of one-year-old growth) will be spared to produce the fruiting growth for the next growing season. The number of buds on these canes or spurs largely determines how many grape bunches that will grow. Cut off too many and the vine may try to compensate with too much shoot and leaf growth, which can create green flavors in the grapes and/or require extra leaf and shoot removal during the summer. Cut off too few canes and buds and a too-large crop will set, usually leading to high yields with low flavor and sugar development.

Pulp The gelatinous or fleshy part of the grape that holds juice and seeds.

Pumping over The act of pumping the clear juice from the bottom of a fermenting tank of red wine and spraying it over the cap of grape skins at the top, to keep it from drying out and to prevent spoilage organisms forming. *Remontage* in French.

Punching down English term for the task of mixing the cap of grape skins back into the wine as it ferments. *Pigeage* in French. During red wine fermentation, the heat and carbon dioxide that result from yeast fermentation, push the skins to the top of the slurry of juice and skins, called must. Since the skins hold most of the color and flavor compounds, they must be thrust back down into the juice perhaps two to four times each 24 hours to allow for the compounds to be extracted. The mixing also releases excess heat from the fermentation. Small-scale punching down is done by hand with a long-handled tool. Larger tanks sometimes have mechanized or hydraulic punch down devices that work automatically.

Punt The indentation in the bottom of a wine bottle. A punt adds structural strength to the glass, particularly important in bottles for sparkling wine.

Pupitre A rack with many holes in it, in which sparkling wine bottles may be placed during the riddling process which prepares them for final corking and labeling. The pupitre has been replaced by automated riddling racks, sometimes called gyropalettes, in most large sparkling wine operations.

Puttonyos Measure of sweetness used in Hungarian Tokaji dessert wines. Three puttonyos equals 60g/l (definitely sweeter than a table wine) and the scale then runs up to six puttonyos at 150g/l, which is extremely sweet. The next step sweeter makes the ultimate Tokaji, Aszú Eszencia.

QbA This is the broadest category for quality wine in Germany indicating that the grapes come from one of the 13 designated quality regions. *See also* Anbaugebiet.

QmP German for a quality wine with distinction. The *prädikat* rules include six levels of sugar ripeness in the must, and other rules about the growing and harvesting, but do not necessarily indicate the sweetness or dryness in the finished wine. The levels rise from the lightest, Kabinett, through Spätlese, Auslese, Beerenauslese, Trockenbeerenauslese, and Eiswein.

Qualitätswein German term for quality wine on a very broad level.

Qualitätswein bestimmter Anbaugebiete *See* QbA.

Qualitätswein mit Prädikat *See* QmP.

Quinta Name used in Portugal for a farm, or vineyard estate. A single-quinta wine uses only grapes grown on that property.

Raboso Black grape variety of Italy's Veneto region generally producing stiff, coarse wines with high levels of tannin and acid.

Racking Ancient technique of transferring wine from one vessel to another to leave behind the lees and thus clarify it, and to keep barrels and tanks full to preclude oxygen from spoiling the wine. Can be done by using gravity to siphon through a hose or by pumping.

Racy Positive term often applied to German Rieslings to note their vivid acidity.

Rancio Term used in a generally positive manner to describe wines and spirits that have matured for a long time, and that usually have been exposed to heat or oxidation as part of that maturing. It comes from the word rancid, but has a more gentle meaning of buttery, cheesy, or nutty.

Ratafia Old-school wine made in the French countryside by using dried grapes and adding water before fermentation. Or by mixing distilled spirits into fermenting grape must, as in port, but aiming for a very different-tasting product.

Recioto Type of wine, red or white, made from dried grapes in the Veneto area of Italy. Recioto della Valpolicella is a sweet, full-bodied red wine made largely from Corvina and Rondinella grapes. The dry version of this is full-bodied Amarone. A white wine, Recioto di Soave, made from Gargenega grapes, is much more rare.

Récoltant One who harvests, in French. In other words, a grape grower. When abbreviated on a champagne label as RM for *récoltant-manipulant*, it indicates a grower who makes his own wine rather than selling the grapes. Usually a good sign of individuality and authenticity, because a large majority of champagne is produced by the Grandes Marques from purchased grapes and/or wine that they then finish and bottle.

Récolte Word for "harvest" in French. The related term "récoltant" means one who harvests, or a vineyard owner.

Red wine Wine made from black grapes even if the color is rarely a true red, except along the rim of the glass. Red wine usually indicates a dry table wine from medium to full-bodied, with a wide variety of aromas and flavors. Red wine is made by crushing the grapes and fermenting the juice, pulp, skins, and seeds together, allowing the color and flavor stored largely in the skins to seep into the new wine.

Reduction, reductive In a wine context, this refers to the opposite of oxidation or the chemical status of a wine that is cut off from oxygen during its processing time in a winery. Technically it means a decrease in the oxidative state of an ion, atom, or molecule. Many white wines and some reds are given reductive handling by the winemaker to preserve their freshness, while certain very structured red wines and a number of dessert or fortified wines are handled oxidatively to soften tannins, bring out desired flavors, and so on. Pinot Noir and Syrah, for example, are often made reductively, with very little racking or other aeration until bottling time.

Refosco Name for a family of black grape varieties in Slovenia, Northeast Italy, and Croatia. They can make good, hearty wine, especially in Fruili.

Rehoboam Large bottle size holding 4.5 liters of wine, used sometimes in Burgundy and Champagne.

Reichsgraf Term for a nobleman in Germany that is used in several winery estate names.

Remontage *See* Pumping over.

Repeal The legal action that ended the Prohibition on most alcoholic beverage sales in the United States in the early 20th century. Its final effects were in 1933.

Reserve Can mean a wine that has been aged for longer, but the term has no legally binding meaning.

Reserva Spanish term for wine that has been aged for at least three years (with one in oak) before selling, and thus should be more smooth and ready to drink.

Retsina Traditional, in fact, Ancient Greek wine flavored with pine resin that comes in white or rosé styles.

Ribolla, Ribolla Gialla White grape variety grown in Northeast Italy, Slovenia, and Greece, sometimes under other names. It makes an aromatic, rather deeply colored white wine.

Riddling Process of moving sparkling wine bottles a little at a time over a period of weeks to tilt them upside down and allow the spent yeast cells inside to fall into the bottle neck where they can be removed by disgorging. Traditionally done by hand, but now more commonly tackled with automated riddling cages. *Remuage* in French.

Riesling The premier grape variety of Germany, which creates a fascinating array of white wines from light and crisp to elegant and delicious, to rich, honeyed, and ageworthy, depending on vineyard and vintage locations. Germany has long grown other grape varieties, but its producers have always put forward Riesling as the pinnacle of the country's winemaking prowess. Riesling is an aromatic grape, yielding abundant apple, peach, and lemon nuances among other characteristics. Whether grown in the Rheingau or Mosel valleys of Germany, or in New York State, the Clare Valley of Australia, or other cooler climate locations, Riesling tends to provide more flavorful, distinctive wines than competing varieties, and is famous for its compelling crispness when young and mellow, nutty richness when 10 or 20 years old.

Ripasso Technique used for a type of Valpolicella in Italy's Veneto region (and occasionally for other wines around the world) in which partially dried grape skins are saved from fermentation tanks and "re-passed" into other vats of newly fermenting wine to add more flavor and color.

Riserva Italian term, indicating a wine that has been aged longer than normal.

Rkatsiteli Ancient white grape variety from the country of Georgia that is also grown in several other Eastern European countries. Makes aromatic, crisp, and flavorful white wines.

Rondo Black grape variety common in the United Kingdom and grown in other Northern European countries, too, for its winter resistance and disease resistance. Tends to make light, fruity wines.

Rootstock The base vine onto which the preferred wine-grape variety is grafted. In Europe and some other parts of the world grapevines are commonly grafted, to thwart pests living in the soil that would destroy the more susceptible *Vitis vinifera* varieties used for European-style wine. The phylloxera vine root louse is the main culprit. The rootstock, if chosen carefully, can add other useful characteristics to the grafted vine, such as high or low vine-growing vigor, drought resistance, and higher or lower yields.

Rosato Rosé or pink wine, in Italian.

Rosé Wine typically made from black grapes using white wine methods to create a light red, pink, or amber hue, and flavors that fall between those of white and red wines. Rosé wines are especially appropriate for spring and summer meals, and can span a wide variety of foods, from grilled or sautéed seafood to spicy Latin or Asian cuisine and on to richer meat and fowl. Rosé can be sweet or dry, still or sparkling. In traditional rosé winemaking, the black grapes are pressed instead of crushed, leaving the skins and most of their pigment behind before fermentation.

Rossese Liguria, Italy, is home to this black grape variety which ferments into an easy, fresh wine for drinking soon after bottling.

Rosso Italian for red.

Rotundifolia *Vitis rotundifolia* is a grape species native to North America that is well suited to the hot, humid growing conditions in the southern and central United States. It is not so well suited to winemaking for wine drinkers accustomed to European wine styles. Used for table grapes, too.

Rouge French for red.

Round Term to describe the texture of a wine that is rounded, or smooth, rather than overly tart, tannic or, on the other hand, too fat or flat.

Roussanne Rhône Valley white grape variety that is used in the white wines of Hermitage, Crozes-Hermitage and St-Joseph, as well as in white Châteauneuf-du-Pape. When harvested ripe, Roussane adds distinctive fruit aromas, a honey flavor, and a rich texture to blends that often include Marsanne. Winemakers in Italy, Australia and California also use Roussane, sometimes labeled as a varietal wine, but often also in Rhône-style blends.

Ruby port The basic, least expensive level of port wine from Portugal. It is sweet, fortified to an alcohol content of about 19%, and aged for two to three years before bottling and sale. While ruby port is sipped as an apéritif in some countries, it is usually more of a dessert wine or after-dinner drink in others.

Rupestris *Vitis rupestris* is one of many native American grape species. It has been used to breed many hybrid grape varieties and useful rootstock varieties over the last two centuries, due largely to its genetic resistance to many common vine pests and diseases.

Saint Laurent Burgundy is apparently the home of this black grape variety, related to Pinot Noir, which is now grown in Alsace, Austria, the Czech Republic Germany, and other regions. It gives spicy cherry-like flavors akin to Pinot Noir but can be easier to grow in northern climates because of an earlier harvest date.

Salmanazar Giant bottle of wine holding 9 liters.

Sangiovese One of the great red wine grapes of the world, and the stalwart variety of Tuscany. Chianti, Brunello di Montalcino, and many Super Tuscan wines get some or all of their character from Sangiovese. This variety can make light, simply fruity wine for quaffing as in Sandioese or medium-to-full-bodied fine wines that can also age well. Sangiovese wines often have a spicy, earthy, or violet aroma and an appetizing austerity in texture that help them stand apart from the popular French and New World wine styles. Sangiovese is like Pinot Noir in that the variety must be planted in just the right sites to excel, and then it expresses the terroir of those sights with remarkably individual taste nuances. In Chianti and Chianti Classico other varieties can be blended in. Brunello di Montalcino uses a clone of Sangiovese called Brunello or Sangiovese Grosso to make very distinctive, full-bodied wines that almost always need bottle aging of 10 or more years to reach a good level of maturity. Sangiovese is one of the few varieties that has rarely, if at all, succeeded in making noteworthy wines when planted outside its home turf.

Sangria Cold wine punch, orginally from Spain, that incorporates red wine, fruit and fruit juice, carbonated water or soda, and sometimes a liqueur such as triple sec or spirit such as brandy.

Saône River in eastern France that flows through a number of vineyard districts, such as the Mâconnais and Chalonnaise parts of Burgundy, on its way to join the River Rhône in Lyon.

Sauvignon Blanc Versatile white wine grape variety originating in France and still grown widely there, especially in the Loire region, where it makes crisp white Sancerre, Pouilly-Fumé, among other wines. In Bordeaux, along with Sémillon, it is grown for substantial dry table wines as well as the famous sweet wines of Sauternes and Barsac. Sauvignon Blanc is an aromatic grape variety, well-known for its vibrant acidity, with diverse fruit and herbal flavors, depending on where and how it is grown. From the cooler parts of New Zealand it gives pungent, gooseberry-like wines, from slightly warmer areas in California and Chile it can be simply grassy, or more complex and ripe with fruit nuances.

Sauvignon Gris A white wine variety related to Sauvignon Blanc, but which shows a semi-dark or pink color on the grape skins and produces wines generally of less flavor intensity. Also known as Sauvignon Rose.

Sauvignon Vert Also known as Sauvignonasse, this aromatic white wine grape grown largely in France is apparently not closely related to Sauvignon Blanc, though enough flavor similarities exist that the two are often confused. In Italy, the same grape is known as Friuliano. Growers in California have a variety they call Sauvignon Vert, but it is not the same, rather it is the Muscadelle grape from Bordeaux.

Savagnin The Jura region of France grows this white grape variety to make the local specialty of *vin jaune*, which is prematurely oxidized, somewhat like sherry. It is thought to be a very old variety, and grows small berries, yielding very light crops. It is identical to the Traminer variety, and is called Fränkisch in Austria and Kleyner in Alsace.

Scheurebe Grape variety developed in Germany by crossing Sylvaner and Riesling and rather widely planted in the Rhine regions and Franken. While less crisp in balance than Riesling, it does have attractive fruit flavors and lends itself to full ripening and even late-harvesting for botrytis-affected dessert wines.

Schiava Grown mostly in northern Italy and southern Germany this is a family of black grape varieties, the most widely planted of which is Schiava Grossa. The version grown in Germany, particularly Württemberg, is known as Trollinger or Frankenthaler. Schiava makes light-to medium-bodied, rather simple-flavored red wines.

Schloss German for castle, used in wine estate names in the same manner as the French use château.

Screwcap Increasingly popular alternative to the cork for a wine bottle stopper. A screwcap solves the problem of "corked" wines that are ruined by the musty scent of TCA that comes from wood corks and as a bonus it makes the wine bottle easier to open. A screwcap affects the wine inside the bottle in different ways than a natural cork, however, and a debate continues to simmer among winemakers about their contrasting benefits. Wines that age well in the bottle do so largely because of a slow controlled oxidation process that has long been regulated by their corks. Corks allow a fairly consistent but minute ingress of air into the bottle. Screwcaps generally allow much less ingress (*see* Reduction), so winemakers who want their aging wines to taste the same as they used to under cork need to make some adjustments in their winemaking practices to adapt.

Scuppernong A native North American grape variety that is used for an aggressively aromatic wine in the southern United States.

Sec, Seco, Secco Means "dry" in French, Spanish, and Italian. For wine, the opposite of sweet.

Sediment Minute particles in wine that slowly settle out of the solution over time, and form a murky layer in the bottom of the bottle. Common in red wines more than 10 years old, espeically those that have been filtered minimally or not at all. Larger crystal particles are usually something else: potassium tartrate crystals. Both forms of sediment are harmless, but avoid pouring them into the wine glass. Better to decant the wine slowly into a decanter or pitcher and leave the sediment behind in the bottle.

Sekt Sparkling wine in Germany. It is not particularly well known outside Germany, but can be of very high quality when made with better grape varieties using the classic method of champagne.

Selection Simple concept for improving quality in wine: identify the poorer quality lots of wine in the cellar and exclude them from the bottling. Since most wines are assembled from numerous tanks or barrels before bottling, the selection method involves the cellar master tasting carefully from each container, noting the inferior lots, and setting them aside to blend into a less expensive wine or perhaps to sell to another winery in bulk. Selection was a key element in the great improvement of château-bottled Bordeaux wines in the 1980s and 1990s. It can also refer to selection in the vineyard, when harvesting grapes. Pickers can be trained to select only the ripest, disease-free bunches.

Sélection de Grains Nobles Abbreviated to SGN. Used mostly in Alsace, France, for wines made from grapes affected by the "noble rot," *Botrytis cinerea*, which shrivels the grapes and concentrates the sugars when it occurs under the right conditions near harvest. SGN wines are sweet, appropriate for dessert, and can improve with bottle age.

Sémillon A white grape variety from Bordeaux that provides the foundation for many of the region's dry table wines as well as the fabled sweet wines of Sauternes and Barsac. Sémillon is blended with Sauvignon Blanc and other varieties, adding the alto notes of richness and depth to the soprano acidity and herbaceousness of Sauvignon. Varietal Semillons (note the accent disappears) in Australia, especially from the Hunter Valley, can be quite expressive and ageworthy.

Sercial Refers to a white grape variety in Portugal, also spelled as Cerceal, and also to a relatively light, dry style of madeira wine traditionally made from this variety on the Portuguese island of Madeira.

Seyval Blanc French-American hybrid white grape variety that still pleasantly surprises critics with its crisp vinifera-like flavors even though it has been successfully made in eastern North America for decades. Resembles a more subdued Sauvignon Blanc, with good acidity and freshness when well made. It is also widely planted in England where its resistance to disease makes it an attractive option for the wet, cool climate. Often used as a base wine for sparkling.

Sherry A many-splendored, multi-styled wine made in and around the city of Jerez, Spain, which is under-appreciated in many parts of the world. A fortified, thus high alcohol, white wine, it comes in dry and sweet, aged, and fresh, purposely oxidized and non-oxidized versions that run the gamut from refreshing apéritif (dry fino) to rich, nutty digestif (oloroso).

Shiraz Australian synonym for the black grape variety Syrah from the Rhône Valley, and which makes typically full-bodied, full-flavored red wines over a range of prices and quality. Shiraz is the grape that brought Australian wine to the international stage in the late 20th century, and which continues to inspire probably the greatest winemaking efforts in that country. Australian Shiraz is usually made in a different style than French Syrah, with riper fruit flavors, a thicker texture, and a greater impression of sweetness. At lower price levels Shiraz can be plump, pleasantly viscous, with grapey, jammy flavors, and a slightly sweet finish. Higher quality Shiraz will be more complex in flavor, often with blueberry and violet aromas, a touch of anise in the fruit flavors, a mouth-filling texture, and richness, yet backed by a firming astringency. Aussie winemakers and connoisseurs like to age these wines for 10 to 20 years, during which time they evolve a fantastic set of new aromas and more subtle flavors.

Skin contact When the grape juice stays mixed with the grape skins after crushing. This contact is essential to all red wines because it allows the color and flavor compounds, which rest largely in the skins, to transfer into the juice. Skin contact happens during fermentation for virtually all red wines. Many winemakers also promote skin contact before fermentation begins, by cooling the crushed must and/or adding sulphur dioxide to suppress native yeast acitivity, then waiting a day or four before letting the must warm up enough for the cultured or wild yeasts to begin their activity. For some wine types, especially Bordeaux varieties, the winemaker extends the period of skin contact after fermentation has converted all the sugar to alcohol, to continue extracting elements from the skins, now in an alcohol solution instead of a simple water-based solution.

Solera System of blending and aging used especially for sherry and other fortified wines. The key practice is that whenever wine is drawn out of one tank or barrel after a period of cellar aging, the cellar master retains some of that wine as the basis for the next batch. When new wine is added, the average maturity of the batch is older, and more interesting and mature flavors are retained.

Traditionally this involved a system of barrels arranged vertically on three or more racks. When the bottom barrel was mostly drawn off for bottling, the cellar master topped it up via siphon from a barrel one level above. Then that second barrel was topped from a barrel on the third tier, and so on. It means that in every batch bottled, at least a small portion of that wine has been aged much longer than the newest portion. Solera-aged wines are not vintage dated. Some solera systems in Jerez have been continuously refreshed for decades.

Sommelier Chief wine waiter or wine steward, in French. When titled "sommelier" this individual usually has had formal wine education or an unofficial apprenticeship and has acquired a level of expertise in wine origins, winemaking, the wine trade, and especially wine service. He or she often buys the restaurant's wine, writes the wine list, and directly serves diners. A good sommelier is well versed in wine-food pairings and can be a great help to customers in making their menu selections.

Sorí Italian word sometimes used on vineyard names in the Piemonte region. It indicates a vineyard site on a slope, facing south, enabling it to catch the most hours and intensity of sunshine possible, which helps the grapes ripen fully.

Spanna Synonym for Nebbiolo, the king of black grapes in Italy's Piemonte region.

Spätburgunder German word for Pinot Noir. It is a grape variety that has grown steadily in popularity and quality in Germany in the last decade. New techniques in the vineyard and winery, and climate change are given as reasons by German winemakers.

Spätlese "Late harvest" in German, it refers to wines of medium body. In the Qualitätswein mit Prädikat regulations it indicates a level of sugar ripeness (or must weight) in the grapes beyond that of the lighter Kabinett wines and just short of Auslese, where the rich, often sweet wines begin. Spätlese wines today can be either dry or slightly sweet, and they compare in body to many normal white table wines from other countries.

Spraying Virtually all grape-growers around the world spray their green, growing vines during spring and summer to prevent common fungi such as powdery and downy mildew. *Vitis vinifera* grapevines, which make most of the world's wines, are sensitive to pests and disease. In dry mediterranean climates they often spray powdered sulphur. In other regions a spray containing copper, such as Bordeaux Mixture, is common. Some growers spray their vines with foliar nutrients, compounds that the vines take in through their leaves to encourage better growth or fruit ripening. Growers often spray insecticides also, either as a matter of course or when the pests appear. Some growers also spray

weeds with herbicides, especially those in the under-vine row. This can be done very early in the growing year. Spraying by organic and Biodynamic grape growers is highly regulated and they may not apply synthetic sprays, but instead use approved naturally derived treatments and cultural methods.

Spritz A slight carbonation that is normal and pleasant in certain wines, especially very fresh, recently released white wines. When it occurs in dry red table wines it can be a sign of poor quality, possibly occuring from a rogue malolactic fermentation in bottle or the completion of a primary fermentation accidentally taking place in the bottle. Either indicates a lack of care in winemaking. A third reason could be over-zealous use of carbon dioxide in the bottling process in an attempt to reduce the risk of oxidation.

Spumante The equivalent of "sparkling wine" in Italian, used specifically for those fully sparkling versions that have greater pressure than merely *frizzante* wines.

Steen South Africa's synonym for the Chenin Blanc grape variety of French origin. It is a very popular white wine grape there, having been naturalized over at least 150 years of planting.

Stemmer Vital machine used at harvest time to remove the grapes from the bunch stems before fermentation. Sometimes also called a destemmer. Typically the stemming function is combined with a crushing function, so that what emerges from the the operation is a pulpy mixture of crushed grapes, juice, pulp, skins, and seeds. *See* Must.

Stemming Removing the grape berries from the stems to prepare for fermentation. This happens in conjunction with crushing for most red wines, and with pressing for most whites. A few wines are fermented in whole-cluster form, with the stems included, to enable carbonic maceration, or simply to allow the tannins and other elements in the stems to add their influences to the juice while it transforms into wine.

Stemmy Negative taste descriptor. If you have ever chewed the stems from a bunch of grapes you know the stemmy taste. It is an astringent, unripe, acidic sensation that is normally undesirable in a finished wine.

Still For wine, it means lacking effervescence. The opposite of sparkling.

Stuck wine A wine where fermentation has stopped before the winemaker wanted it to. In other words the yeasts have stopped converting the sugar to alcohol, possibly because the fermentation became too hot, or because the must was not properly balanced (lacking in nutrients) to encourage the yeasts.

Sulphites Word used on some wine labels to indicate the presence of sulphites, bisulphites, and free and total sulphur dioxide in wine. Applied to the grape must or wine as either sulphur dioxide gas (in liquified form) or in powdered form as a metabisulphite. Sulphites are used in small quantities as a preservative, to prevent oxidation, prevent the growth of unwanted microorganisms that can spoil the wine, and sometimes to delay the beginning of fermentation. All but a few winemakers in the world add sulphites during regular winemaking procedures, and have done so for generations, because it is extremely difficult to make clean, unspoiled wine without them. Wines sold in the United States must be labeled as containing sulphites (sulfites in US) if their level is 10 parts per million (10mg/liter) or higher. Many countries do not require such labeling, so the same wine that carries this declaration in the US may appear in another country with no such notation on the bottle. European Union regulations allow more than 100ppm for red wines, more than 200ppm for white wines, and even higher levels for sweet wines, where the high concentration of sugar may require extra suppression of an accidental fermentation. Wines without any added sulphites may still contain a few ppm of sulphites, because they are produced as a by-product during fermentation.

Sulphur Sulphur is an element that exists in pure form in the ground. It is widely used in vineyards, either in pure dust form, or powdered and then mixed with water and sprayed onto the vine leaves and branches to control fungicides. Traditionally, winemakers have burned small sticks of sulphur in empty barrels to purify them, as the smoke kills bacteria.

Super Tuscan Popular term that evolved for ambitious and innovative wines, made from nontraditional grape varieties in Italy's Tuscany region, which do not meet the DOC rules for the districts in which they were made. Often they used French grape varieties blended with the native Sangiovese. Officially they were considered merely basic *Vino da Tavola*, but the wine trade and consumers recognized the high quality of many of them, and their demand and prices rose. Wine brands Sassicaia, Tignanello, Luce, and Summus are a few examples.

Superiore Used to indicate Italian wines that have attained a higher level of potential quality due to riper grapes and higher alcohol content.

Supple Indicates a soft but not weak texture in a wine.

Sur Lie "On the lees" in French. Refers to a wine which stayed in contact with the dead yeast cells and other particles that remain after fermentation. Often used in barrel-fermented wines. These lees have an oxygen-scavenging effect which helps to keep wines fresh, while lending them an attractive aroma of fresh bread or toast.

Süssreserve A "sweet reserve" of grape juice that has been prevented from fermenting and kept in reserve to sweeten another wine.

Sylvaner Grown mainly in Germany and in Alsace, but also in other parts of Europe and even California in small quantities, this white wine grape is very productive and makes rather generic tasting wines with floral flavors.

Symphony Grape variety for aromatic white wines developed in California by crossing Grenache Gris and Muscat of Alexandria. Makes a floral, seemingly sweet wine with plenty of perfume. Rarely bottled as a single variety, but used to liven up other wines when blended into them.

Syrah The signature black grape variety of the Northern Rhône Valley in France, responsible for the distinguished and long-lived wines of Côte-Rôtie and Hermitage, among others. It grows in less abundance in the Southern Rhône and can be part of the famous Châteauneuf-du-Pape blend or in basic Côtes du Rhône wines. Syrah, more so than most grape varieties, develops different flavor characteristics based on the vineyard site, showing more peppery, herbal notes in cooler spots and more rich, plummy, anise flavors in warmer areas. It is sometimes praised for a hard-to-describe gamey quality as in wild venison, or with an earthy personality, all of which adds to its allure. Known in Australia as Shiraz, which normally is made in a richer style than in the Rhône. Syrah is planted widely in other parts of France, in California, in South Africa, in parts of Italy, and elsewhere around the globe.

Szamorodni A type of Tokaji wine from Hungary made from grapes happily affected by *Botrytis cinerea* to concentrate their flavors. It is fermented dry.

Szürkebarát Grape variety in Hungary. Same as Pinot Gris in France.

T-budding Method used in vineyards to quickly change vines from one fruiting variety to another. The vineyardist cuts the vine trunk, makes a grafting slit, selects a bud that already has been cut from a different variety and secures it in that slit. The bud grows in the following year to begin a new vine, and by the second growing season it can bear a small crop. This beats the normal three to four years for most newly planted vines to bear a good amount of fruit.

Table wine Can mean simply a still dry wine styled for consumption with meals, as opposed to sparkling, sweet or fortified wines. It is also a basic level of wine quality in areas, including the European Union, where quality levels are intricately layered and regulated by government agencies.

Tafelwein "Table wine" in German. A basic quality of wine. Better wines are labeled QbA or QmP.

Tannin Class of compounds found in wine, in black tea, and other foods and beverages that creates a drying, astringent, puckering effect in one's mouth. White wines have little tannin, but most reds have a reasonable amount, and many of the world's top red wines and ports have very high tannin levels, especially when they are newly fermented. Tannins help preserve wine and provide a positive textural element when balanced with enough body and flavor. The proper amount of tannin helps make a wine appealing and refreshing especially when consumed with high-protein or fatty foods.

Tastevin Traditional small tasting cup, often made of silver, worn by a sommelier on a neck chain. Largely symbolic and decorative today, but formerly used by cellar masters when evaluating their wine's progress.

Tasting The evaluation of a wine's quality and appeal by using one's senses. Not the same as drinking, although in the ideal situation tasting leads to enjoyable drinking. A careful wine taster looks closely at the wine to see its color and level of clarity, smells the wine to sense its various characteristics from the grapes and the winemaking process, then takes a small sip and holds it in the mouth for further evaluation. Are the flavors the same as the aromas? Does it feel full and rich, or lean and light? Finally the taster spits the sample into a spittoon and observes how long and how enjoyable the aftertaste (finish) may be. Wine professionals and serious amateurs write a few notes to help them remember the wine.

Tauberschwarz Little-grown black grape variety planted in the Tauber Valley of Germany's Württemberg wine region.

Tawny port Style of port that ages in wood casks for as much as 40 years, losing its dark red color and turning a tawny brown while transforming in flavor from powerful and fruity, to something more like a wonderful aged brandy. Tawny port is labeled without vintage, but those that do declare an age on the bottle (10 years, 20 years, and sometimes 40 years) are usually the highest quality. They represent blends of port from various casks that have an average age stated in round numbers.

TBA Abbreviation of either Trockenbeerenauslese, the highly concentrated German sweet wine, or for a chemical compound similar to cork taint that spoils wine: 2,4,6-tribromoanisole.

TCA The culprit for the notorious "corked" or "corky" bottles of wine that smell musty, spoiling their enjoyment. The acronym stands for 2,4,6-trichloroanisole. People can smell concentrations as small as a few parts per billion, and it is not just the disagreeable smell of TCA that is a problem, but also its effect of flattening or scalping the other desirable aromas and flavors in a wine. TCA forms in cork, wooden boards, oak barrels, and cardboard, amongst other things, through an interaction of phenolic compounds from the grapes and chlorine. Cork producers and wineries have gone a long way toward controlling TCA by eliminating chlorine from their cleaning processes, even using non-chlorinated water in some cases, and by minimizing the use of cellulose materials in their processing facilities. Many very modern wineries are almost all steel, glass, and concrete, with no wood, because TCA can form in the cellar, not just in the cork.

Temperature One's enjoyment of wine can be enhanced by serving the wine at the proper temperature. Sparkling wines and fresh, light whites such as Riesling or Sauvignon Blanc should be served well chilled at 45°F (7°C). Richer whites such as Chardonnay, fresh young reds such as Beajolais Nouveau or Lambrusco, and most sweet and fortified wines are best at a very cold cellar temperature, 55°F (12°C). Most red wines for dinner are ideal at a coolish 65°F (18°C). Temperature is also important when storing wine in the bottles. A constant temperature of 50-55°F (10-12°C) and rather high relative humidity are best for long-term aging of prized Bordeaux, vintage port, California Cabernet, and so on. The consistency of temperature avoids the wine from expanding with warmth, and then contracting when re-cooled, which tends to cause more air to pass between the perimeter of the cork and the interior surface of the bottle neck, encouraging premature aging from oxidation.

Tempranillo Spain's signature black grape variety is the main component in the wines of Rioja and Ribera del Duero, and can make everything from young and fruity wines to deep, rich, and long-aging estate-bottled reds for special occasions. It is Spain's most widely planted variety. It tends to give medium-to-full-bodied wines with similar fruit flavors to the Bordeaux varieties of Cabernet Sauvignon and Merlot, but with more dusky, herbal, and earthy notes that marry beautifully with the effect of oak barrels during aging. Tempranillo vines produce clusters of small berries with thick skins, which ripen rather early. It provides plenty of good tannins to its blends with Garnacha, Mazuelo, and other varieties in Rioja or on its own. Tempranillo is known as Tinta Roriz in the Douro Valley of Portugal (same river as the Duero in Spain), where it is used in port and red table wines. Tempranillo has spread to other parts of the world, including Argentina and the United States, where a few fine examples are being made in Oregon and California.

Tenuta "Estate" in Italian, meaning a property devoted to wine-growing.

Terra rossa "Red soil" that is prized in some regions for vineyards, including Italy, Spain, Australia, and California. The rusty brown color often indicates a high iron content, and is associated with limestone strata that offer good drainage for grapevines.

Terroir Vine-growing conditions that give a taste of place to a wine. Wine producers and astute drinkers have known for millennia that wines taste different when the same grape varieties are grown in different locations, in different types of soil, under the care of different owners, and so on. This diversity of terroir (a combination of soil, climate, and an indefinable sense of place) is highly prized among wine producers and especially by collectors of rare, expensive wines.

Tête de Cuvée French word for the top-quality or highest-priced wine in a champagne producer's portfolio.

Texture The feel of a wine in one's mouth, varying from light and lean, to crisp and tangy, to rich and tannic, to thick and viscous.

Thermo-vinification Heating grape must to a much higher temperature than a normal fermentation, to speed the extraction of color and, to a lesser extent, flavor compounds from the grape skins into the juice. A winemaking short cut.

Thief A kind of large pipette about half a meter long, made of glass or plastic and used by a winemaker to draw a sample of wine through the small bunghole of a barrel for tasting.

Thompson Seedless Versatile white grape variety, grown extensively in California and also in other countries. It can be used for fresh grapes, raisins, grape juice, and even wine, though it makes a very bland drink unless blended with more flavorful varieties. Called Sultana in some countries, including Australia where it contributes to fortified wines.

Tinta, Tinto Spanish for red. Often used as part of a grape variety's name. Tinto is the masculine form.

Tirage The process of adding a yeast and sugar culture to a base wine for sparkling wine when it is bottled for the second fermentation. *En tirage* is the time period in which a wine, particularly a sparkling wine, rests in the winery cellar before release. For sparkling wine, the spent yeast cells remain in the bottles following the secondary fermentation, and the *en tirage* period helps the wine to deepen its flavors via continued contact with these lees.

Toasted, toasty A smell or taste similar to that of toasted bread, or of newly made oak barrels that are toasted with flame as part of their construction process. The toasty aroma in a wine can indeed come from the barrels but is also drawn from aging on lees.

Tocai Friuliano Italian name for the white grape variety Sauvignon Vert.

Tokaji, Tokay The Hungarian and Anglicized terms for Hungary's most famous and respected wines, which are made largely from Furmint grapes, with Harslevelu as a secondary variety, and others. Tokaji comes in several styles. The driest is Tokaji Furmint, next in sweetness is Tokaji Szamorodni and finally comes the treasured Tokaji Aszú, itself broken into five sweetness levels, labeled as three to six puttonyos, then in its purest form as Tokaji Essencia. The Aszú level must use grapes affected by *Botrytis cinerea*, which concentrates the sweetness and flavor of the juice.

Tokay d'Alsace Name used in Alsace, France, for many years for the grape variety known elsewhere in France as Pinot Gris, and in Italy as Pinot Grigio.

Topping A never-ending chore in wineries that protects wine in tanks and barrels from oxidation. The simple solution is to keep each container filled to the top to allow little or no room for air to remain inside. Since wine evaporates slowly through barrel staves, around bungs, even through the seals of stainless steel tanks, a winemaker has be vigilant about the process.

Torbato Grape variety for white wines, grown mostly in Sardinia, but known in the Roussillon region of France as Tourbat.

Torrontés A family of grape varieties best known in Argentina, which produce very aromatic and often full-bodied, rich white wines. The most popular in terms of planting and often considered the best quality is Torrontés Riojana, while two others are Torrontés Sanjuanino and Torrontés Mendocino. Long consumed mostly in Argentina, these wines are now popular export items.

Touriga Franca More widely planted in the Douro Valley than Touriga Nacional, this black grape variety is the most dominant in the blends that contribute to port, and is also grown for dry table wines. It adds fragrance and fruitiness.

Touriga Nacional Highly reputed grape variety for making port in Portugal's Douro Valley and for dry table wines in the Dão region and elsewhere. Known for small berries and low yields, it is prized by winemakers because it gives deep color, very concentrated flavors, and desirable tannins.

Traminer This white grape variety preceded Gewürztraminer, which is its offspring and is more widely known and grown today. Traminer has a green-white skin compared to Gewürztraminer's pink or gris color and makes more subtle but still floral and fragrant wines.

Traditional method *See* Champagne method.

Transfer method A method of making sparkling wine that, in terms of the important second fermentation, falls in between the classic bottle-fermented method of Champagne and the tank-fermented Charmat method. The wines are expected to have more sophisticated aromas and flavors than Charmat, but may not have the finesse of the traditonal champagne method. In the transfer method, the wine undergoes its second fermentation in individual bottles to provide the bubbles and desirable flavor characteristics from the yeast used. But instead of being directly disgorged, corked, and finished, bottles are all emptied into a tank under pressure and become mixed before bottling.

Treading Also known as *pigeage* in French, treading is the practice of crushing grapes by foot. It was a traditional practice before crushers and stemmers were invented, but has seen a resurgence among small, iconoclastic wine producers around the world. Some port makers never abandoned treading, and make an annual party of it.

Trebbiano White wine variety famous for big yields and mostly non-descript, crisp white wines. It is Italy's most-planted white wine variety, and under its French name of Ugni Blanc it is also France's most-planted white wine variety, where it makes the base wine for Cognac. Central Italy is its base. Tuscany used to allow it to be mixed into Chianti Classico, and winemakers over most of the country use it alone or blended. The variety goes by several regional names, including Trebbiano d'Abruzzo, Trebbiano Giallo, Trebbiano Romagnolo, and perhaps the most popular, Trebbiano Toscana.

Triage Term for sorting grapes prior to fermentation, usually on a *table de tri,* a conveyor that carries the grapes past workers who pick off the poor quality grapes and unwanted MOG (Material Other than Grapes) such as leaves, stems, and insects before the grapes go into a fermentation tank. Increasingly, this function is automated, with conveyors that vibrate, use air blasts, and other means to pick out the debris and leave sound individual grapes behind.

Tribaie machine Grape-sorting machine used after stemming and before fermentation to remove poor quality grapes. It sorts them, floating in juice, by relative weight, to eliminate the underripe individual grapes.

Trie French word for a "pass" through the vineyard to harvest just the grapes that have reached optimum ripeness that day. In rare dessert wines affected by *Botrytis cinerea* such as Sauternes (and in Germany, Riesling) it is a necessity, but the method is also used by picky vine-growers elsewhere to maximize wine quality.

Trocken Means "dry" in German, to indicate wines of a normal table wine style, rather than sweet wines which were the norm in Germany a generation ago. Trocken and halbtrocken (half-dry) wines can be produced from various levels of sweetness in the grapes.

Trockenbeerenauslese A German wine produced from grapes shrivelled by *Botrytis*

cinerea, and late-harvested berry by berry to make a very sweet, very concentrated, very rare wine that can age for decades. Usually made from Riesling and packaged in small 375ml (37.5cl). bottles, this is Germany's ultimate achievement in sweet wine production. Abbreviated to TBA.

Trollinger Southern Germany produces medium-bodied red wines with this variety that has been planted in Baden-Württemberg for hundreds of years. Also known as Frankenthaler and in northern Italy, from whence it came, as Schiava.

Ugni Blanc *See* Trebbiano.

Ullage Head space or air space inside a wine bottle. It grows larger over the years as a wine gains bottle age, and is an important concern when buying mature wines. Too little ullage in a supposedly old wine might indicate a counterfeit, too much probably indicates a defective cork or poor storage conditions, and thus a spoiled wine. Slow, gradual expansion of the ullage is normal as minute quantities of wine evaporate around the cork and a similar quantity of outside air seeps in to replace it. A perfectly stored 1961 Bordeaux today might have ullage down into the shoulder of the bottle. But any noticeable ullage in a young wine of less than 10 years would be concerning.

Unfiltered Most wines of the world are pumped through filters during their period of maturation and/or just before bottling to remove tiny bits of sediment and make the wine very clear in appearance. Many, in fact, are sterile-filtered through very tight filter media to remove any microorganisms that might affect their quality. Some wine producers, however, choose not to filter their wines, to present a more natural, complete taste experience and what they perceive as higher quality wine. These are more likely to develop a harmless sediment in the bottle after several months or years, and in this case need decanting before drinking.

Unfined A wine for which the winemakers has omitted the fining process, which is quite normal in red wines, to present a more natural, often darker, and more tannic wine. *See also* Fining.

Ungrafted vines Since most grapevines in Europe and North America are grafted—a rooting variety supports a different fruiting variety above it—ungrafted vines may seem exotic to those growers. But in regions where the vine-killing root louse phylloxera is not endemic in the soil vineyards often plant own-rooted vines in the millennia-old tradition, from vine cuttings that have been allowed to grow roots under nursery conditions, and are later planted out in the field. Winemakers and connoisseurs argue whether ungrafted vines make better wines, but one thing is for sure: they save the grower money when planting.

Unoaked So many of the world's wines

now show an obvious oak flavor from being aged in barrels or flavored with other oak products that a marketing niche has emerged for wines that boast about not being oaked. Oak treatments add flavors of vanilla, coconut, various spices, smoke, while unoaking can leave the wine more lean, fresh, and uncomplicated.

Varietal A varietal wine, or simply varietal, is a wine made from just one, or predominantly, one grape variety. In the proper usage, "variety" equals the type of grapevine, while "varietal" equals the wine made from it. Designating wines primarily as varietals is the norm for most New World wineries, while many European producers still stress the appellation or place name first.

Variety In wine parlance, a specific sub-species of grapevine that has horticultural and flavor characteristics that distinguish it. For example, most fine wines of the world are made from a single vine species, *Vitis vinifera,* but thousands of varieties of *Vitis vinifera* exist, from Airén to Zinfandel, giving us wine-drinking pleasure in seemingly infinite forms.

Vat Large wine container of various sizes often made of stainless steel or oak, and sometimes from concrete or plastic. Almost synoymous with "tank".

VDP The association of self-selected top German wine producers, Verband Deutscher Prädikatsweinguter, numbers about 200 members but accounts for only about 4% of the country's vineyard land. The VDP's stylized eagle with a grape cluster is printed on the foil capsules of their bottles. Not an official designation of quality, but a good sign of it.

VDQS Vins Délimités de Qualité Supérieure. A quality level for French wine, now being phased out. Wines with this classification can apply to be upgraded to Appellation d'Origine Contrôleé or start to use the new IGP designation.

Vendange French for harvest.

Vendange Tardive French for late harvest. Term seen frequently on sweet wines from Alsace and a few other regions that are made from grapes left to hang on the vines until late in the growing season, during which time they lose water through dehydration and gain more concentrated flavors and a higher sugar percentage.

Vendimia Spanish term for "harvest."

Veraison Stage in the growth cycle of grapes when they begin ripening and take on their harvest color. All grapes start their growth green. In midsummer white grapes gain a more yellow or gold color, in-between varieties turn pink or dusky red, and red-wine varieties darken dramatically to purple or almost black.

Verbesco Light-colored, dry, sparkling wine from Italy's Piemonte region made from dark Barbera grapes by pressing the juice out of the skins just after harvest.

Verdelho, Verdello Two names for what are probably identical white grape varieties grown in Portugal, Madeira, and Australia as Verdelho and in Spain's Galicia as Verdello or Godello.

Verdicchio Traditional grape variety that makes large quantities of tangy, lemony white wine in Central Italy and elsewhere. Sometimes abused by too-high yields, Verdicchio still makes wines of personality from many regions.

Verduzzo Friuli and other parts of Northeastern Italy have grown this white grape variety for many centuries. It is used for both firmly tannic dry wines and lush semi-sweet wines.

Verjus "Green juice" in French. Fresh, tart grape juice squeezed from white wine grapes before normal wine ripeness is reached. Cooks in vine-growing areas use it as a condiment, in marinades, and for other culinary purposes.

Vermentino Pigato and Favorita are other names for this floral, flavorful Italian white variety which makes very good wines in Liguria and Sardinia, and is also grown in France's southern Languedoc region and Corsica.

Vermouth A fortified and herb-flavored wine known mostly as a mixer for cocktails including the famous gin martini with a splash of dry white vermouth, and the bourbon-based Manhattan, with a splash of sweet red vermouth and dash of bitters. But it can be and is consumed straight or on ice.

Vertical press A form of wine press that uses motion along a vertical axis to squeeze the juice and pulp out of white wine grapes and red wine must. The classic basket press is a prime example of this generally gentle form of press. Gentle because it may extract fewer of the harsh tannin compounds from skins and seed than other press formats.

Vertical tasting Vintage years are arranged "vertically" in this type of analytical tasting exercise that examines how a wine's aromas and flavors evolve over time. In a classic vertical tasting, several examples of the same wine from the same producer and vineyard but from different vintages are tasted and compared in the same session.

Vidal Blanc Considered one of the most successful hybrid grape varieties produced from European and native American parents. It is popular in the northeast United States and nearby Canadian vineyards, partly because of its high resistance to winter freeze damage and its propensity for making delicious Icewines.

Vieilles vignes See Old vines, for which this is the French term.

Vieux French word for "old" often seen in the names of wine producers.

Vigne French for vine.

Vigneron French for vine-grower.

Commonly used for small-scale wine producers who ferment mostly their own grapes, or who are growers only and may sell their crop to a nearby winery.

Vignoble French for vineyard.

Villard Blanc, Villard Noir The white and black versions of a French-American hybrid vine that was once very popular with growers in France for its disease resistance and high yields, but is now disappearing.

Vin French for wine.

Vin Blanc French for white wine.

Vin de Garde A wine to keep. Describes a substantial wine that may taste rough when young but, with the proper balance and body to improve, will age for many years.

Vin de Paille Wine made from dried grapes. See Paille.

Vin de Pays Now being phased out and replaced with IGP. It was the official designation for "country wine," which usually indicates a simple, inexpensive wine but with a specific regional appellation of origin making it more authentic than the more basic Vin de Table designation. It will still appear on wine labels for a few years. See IGP.

Vin de Table The basic level of inexpensive, low-quality wine recognized by the French government.

Vin Doux Naturel French for a naturally sweet wine. A wine made by the same method employed for port, madeira, and other strong, sweet wines. A great assortment are made in the Languedoc-Roussillon region of southern France. Muscat de Beaumes-de-Venise is a famous example. The winemaker unnaturally stops the fermentation of the wine mid-way by adding distilled spirits. This kills the yeast, stops the fermentation and leaves a sweet wine with at least 14% alcohol and a high natural sugar.

Vin Gris Another French expression for a rosé wine. It helps to understand that "gris" in French is not simply "gray", but describes a tone in between dark and light.

Vin Jaune Unusual "yellow wine" made in the Jura region of France with Savagnin grapes handled in the manner of sherry. Vin jaune undergoes a controlled oxidation over many years of barrel aging which helps develop its vivid color and unforgettable flavors.

Vin Rosé See Rosé.

Vin Santo Rare wine resembling sherry or madeira but made in Tuscany from extremely sweet, dried grapes using an unusual method. Growers harvest Trebbiano and Malvasia grapes late in the year then spread them out in warm storage areas to dry for a few weeks or months before pressing the juice. The winemaker fills small barrels with the juice, seals them tight, stores them in a place that heats considerably in summer and simply

waits—for between four and 10 years—to see what happens. This foregoes the usual racking, tasting, addition of sulphur dioxide, temperature control, and so on. When finally opened, the winemaker discovers either a dry, semisweet, or sweet wine that seems miraculous (or holy) when it comes out beautifully, which is often enough to keep the winemaker trying.

Vinho Verde Bracingly crisp white Portuguese wine made from Alvarinho grapes, and called "green wine" presumably for its freshness and acidity.

Viniculture Cultivation of grapevines and growing of grapes. See Viticulture, the more common modern term in North America.

Vinifera Vitis vinifera is the traditional Middle Eastern and later European species of grapevine that has been used for winemaking for several millennia. A great majority of the world's most popular wines are made with vinifera varieties, and there are thousands of them, including Chardonnay, Riesling, Merlot, Sangiovese, Syrah, Pinot Noir, Cabernet Sauvignon, Tempranillo, Grenache, to mention but a few of those known best internationally.

Vinification Winemaking, especially the steps taken in the winery to ferment, mature, and ready a wine for the market.

Vino da Tavola Italian for table wine. Usually refers to inexpensive, undistinguished wines, but there are exceptions (see Super Tuscan) when producers make excellent wines that do not meet all the requirements to be officially labeled with a more specific appellation of orgin.

Vino de Mesa Spanish for "table wine."

Vintage Both the year in which a particular wine's grapes were harvested, and the time of year when the grape harvest and frenzied winemaking activity takes place.

Vintage port See also Port. The style of fortified wine made in Portugal that is most prized by wine collectors of all the variations made. Vintage port is made from the best vineyards in the Douro Valley, bottled while still young, rich, tannic, and almost fiery to taste, and needs many more years of bottle-aging before it reaches its intended level of enjoyment. Connoisseurs may be cautiously sampling their 1994s now while drinking other vintages 10 or even 30 years older.

Viognier Aromatic and exotic white grape variety, long grown in the Condrieu area of the Rhône Valley of France which has spread to many other regions and countries. The characteristics of Viognier vary greatly depending on location and ripeness of the grapes, from light and lean with flowery aromas when less ripe, to full-bodied, honeyed, and rich when more ripe. Growers find it more difficult to handle than other popular white varieties, so fine examples can be somewhat rare.

Viticulture The science or labor of

grapevine growing. At ground level, viticulture is the collection of tasks and techniques used by vineyard owners and their crews to plant, maintain, and harvest grapes for wine, raisins, or as fresh produce. At the highest level, it is an advanced agricultural science that takes in genetics, vine breeding, vine disease and pest research, and a host of related topics. A common saying in the wine business is that "wine is made in the vineyard," indicating the degree of importance that viticulture has on the final fermented and bottled product.

Vitis Term for the genus of grapevines, in scientific parlance. *Vitis vinifera* is the most common wine grape species.

Viura *See* Macabeo.

Volatile acidity Abbreviated to VA and refers to acids naturally occuring in wine due to the interaction of alcohol and oxygen, primarily acetic acid, which is the vinegar acid. When VA grows to a level detectable as the smell of vinegar or nail polish, then it has gone too far and the wine is flawed.

VQPRD Vin de Qualité Produit dans une Region Determinée. A now defunct quality designation in the European Union. *See* IGP, PDO, PGI.

Wein German for wine.

Weinbaugebiete One of five German wine regions assigned to produce basic German table wine (Deutscher Tafelwein).

Weingut German for wine estate, where wine is made from grapes grown on the same property.

Weinkellerei German for wine cellar and usually indicating a wine production facility that buys rather than grows grapes.

Weissburgunder Literally "white Burgundian," this grape variety grown in Germany and Austria is the same as Pinot Blanc of Burgundy. Makes rather full-bodied, rich-textured white wines with subltle flavor qualities.

Welschriesling White grape variety common in Northern and Eastern Europe, especially Austria, which is not related to the true Riesling of Germany. Still, it does have somewhat similar aromatics, possesses lively acidity, and can be made into distinctive botrytis-affected sweet wines like Riesling.

White Riesling A name used in some countries to distinguish the classic German Riesling grape variety from other locally planted varieties. *See* Riesling.

White Zinfandel Not a grape variety, but a style of light, slightly sweet rosé wine made from dark Zinfandel grapes in California, in the manner of a Blanc de Noirs. Its popularity has waned in recent years, but this blush wine remains a big seller in North America.

Whole-berry ferments See Carbonic Maceration.

Wild yeast Also native yeast or indigenous yeast. A yeast type that pre-exists in a vineyard or winery environment and will go to work on grape must without the winemaker's help. The decision to let the wild yeast take over is that of the winemaker, who can prevent it with a sulphur dioxide addition to the must to kill the wild yeast and then add a cultured commercial yeast strain to start the fermentation. Most cultured yeasts (*Saccharomyces cerevisaie*) will have a killer strain to overpower wild yeasts. Proponents of wild yeast say it makes a more natural wine, perhaps with added flavor complexity. The jury is still out, however, because often even when wild yeast starts a fermentation, often a normally tamed *Saccharomyces cerevisaie* version arrives unbidden to complete it.

Wine Intoxicating, healthful, inspiring, ancient alcoholic beverage made from the fermented juice of fresh grapes.

Winemaker Person whose job is to help grapes and grape juice become wine. "Enologist" is a near synonym. In the New World the term "winemaker" usually refers to the person supervising or actually performing the many and varied tasks of winemaking, not necessarily the winery owner. The equivalent in France is cellar master or enologist.

Winery The physical premises where wine is made, or sometimes the legal entity that is responsible for producing wine and documenting it for legal and tax purposes.

Woody Usually negative taste descriptor for aromas, flavor, and textures in wines that suggest it was fermented, stored and/or aged in wooden containers or with wooden flavoring products added. The convention is that "woody" tends to be bad, but "oaky" is good.

Yeasts Microscopic single-celled organisms that convert the sugar in grape juice into ethyl alcohol and release carbon dioxide in the process. Yeast fermentation also releases various by-products called congeners that help to flavor the wine. Wine, beer, and other alcoholic beverages would not exist without yeast to perform the essential transformation. Yeasts are nearly ubiquitous in the environment, so the accidental conversion of grape sugar to alcohol in grapes or spilled juice occurred for many millennia before humans noticed the effect and began to take advantage of the fermentation. *Saccharomyces cerevisaie* is the favored, cultured yeast added to most commercial wines and gives the winemaker an element of control over the fermentation.

Yeasty Aroma or flavor that resembles that of rising bread dough, sometimes detected in wine.

Yield Proportional measure of the productivity of grapevines in a particular vineyard. Often given in tons per acre (US) or hectoliters per hectare (metric system). It does not account for planting density.

Zinfandel Black grape variety that has been growing in California for 150 years, making it the most traditional European variety in western North America. Zinfandel grapes are versatile for winemakers, able to produce light, fresh fruity versions if harvested early or grown in cool regions, or more balanced and medium-bodied wines in warm regions, but they can also produce wines topping 15% alcohol in sunny, hot areas with long growing seasons. Zinfandel wines tend to polarize consumers. Those who grew up with more lean and subdued European varieties may not appreciate its bold blackberry and raspberry flavors and high alcohol, but devotees prize its concentration, exuberance, and overt ripeness. The grape variety is similar to the Primitivo of Italy and shares the parent Crljenak Kastelansk variety of Croatia.

INDEX

Page numbers appearing in bold type indicate a main entry. Italics indicate a photograph or other image. See also the glossary (pages 754–783) for more than 600 wine terms with explanations.

ACKNOWLEDGMENTS

Our first thank you goes to Norman Brown for helping us to develop the concept of the book.

Special thanks go to Jim Gordon for his fantastic work as Editor-in-Chief.

We would also like to thank the following for their assistance:

AUSTRALIA
Lisa McGovern (Wine Australia)

BRAZIL
Andreia Gentilini Milan (Wines from Brazil)

BULGARIA
Margarita Levieva (National Vine and Wine Chamber)

CHILE
Gabrielle Cole (Wines of Chile)

CROATIA
Zelijka Kolak

CYPRUS
Georgios Hadjistylianou

FRANCE
Chris Skyrme (Sopexa)

Bordeaux
Astrid Deysine (Conseil des Vins de Saint-Emilion)
Valerie Descudet (Conseil Interprofessionnel des Vins de Bordeaux)
Frédérique Dutheillet de Lamothe (Alliance des Crus Bourgeois)

Burgundy
Cecile Mathiaud (Bureau Interprofessionnel des Vins de Bourgogne)

Rhône
Aurélie Mauchand, Charlotte Révillon (InterRhône)
Michel Blanc (Fédération des Syndicats de Producteurs de Châteauneuf-du-Pape)

Southwest France
Paul Fabre (Interprofession des Vins du SudOuest)
Xavier de la Verrie (Comité Interprofessionnel des Vins de la Région de Bergerac)

GEORGIA
Tina Kezeli (Vine & Wine)

GREECE
Konstantinos Lazarakis MW
Sofia Perpera

ISRAEL
Gary Landsman

LUXEMBOURG
Nathalie Reckinger (Commission de Promotion des Vins and Crémants)

MOLDOVA AND UKRAINE
Levgeniia Rodionova

NEW ZEALAND
Sarah Land (New Zealand Winegrowers)

USA

California
Terry Hall (Napa Valley Vintners)
Betsy Rogers (Mendocino Winegrape & Wine Commission)

Mid-Atlantic and the South
Fred Frank (Dr. Konstantin Frank Vinifera Cellars)
Dick Reno (Chateau LaFayette Reneau)
Tony K. Wolf (Director and Professor of Viticulture AHS Jr Agricultural Research and Extension Center Virginia Tech)

New York and New England
Susan Spence (Vice President New York Wine & Grape Foundation)

Washington
Gary Werner (Washington Wine Commission)

PORTUGAL
Ana Sofia de Oliveira (ViniPortugal)

SPAIN
Alison Dillon (Dillon Morrall/Wines of Spain)
Anna Noble (Wines from Rioja/Phipps PR)

Special thanks to the Wine Society for supplying bottles of wine for photography:
The Wine Society Ltd
Gunnels Wood Road
Stevenage, Hertfordshire
SG1 2BG
www.thewinesociety.com

PHOTO CREDITS